Contemporary American Composers

a biographical dictionary

Contemporary American Composers

a biographical dictionary

Second Edition

Compiled by

E. RUTH ANDERSON

G. K. HALL & CO., 70 LINCOLN ST., BOSTON, MASS. 1982

Library of Congress Cataloging in Publication Data

Anderson, Ruth.
    Contemporary American composers.

    1. Composers—United States—Biography. I. Title.
ML390.A54 1982   780'.92'2 [B]   81-7047
ISBN 0-8161-8223-X   AACR2

Contents

Preface

The format of this second edition remains much the same as that of the first edition with certain exceptions. The addendum has been incorporated into the text, the women's list has been omitted, and the criteria for inclusion are somewhat altered. Birth date no earlier than 1870 and American citizenship or extended residence in the United States are still prerequisites. However, because of the great number of contemporary American composers, those who have written only one or two compositions and those who have not responded to questionnaires have been dropped. As before, composers who write teaching pieces only, jazz only (with a few exceptions), popular music only, and rock or folk music only are omitted. Also as before, information given on questionnaires was accepted as presented with a minimum of verification.

Again, thanks are due to all composers who supplied names and addresses of colleagues. Thanks also to Samuel Sprince of Quincy, Mass., for furnishing many otherwise unobtainable dates; to Vera and William Filby for their help on composers in the Baltimore-Washington area; and to the American Music Center for valuable assistance with composer lists and biographical data.

It seemed not unreasonable to expect that as the number of American composers increased, the number of performances of their music would increase proportionally. In Europe, American composers have fared well. For example, the orchestra of the Swiss-Italian Radio presented an all-American season in 1980-81. But in their own country, contemporary American composers, until recently, have remained under the cloud of a centuries-old cultural inferiority complex and could only trust in Emily Dickinson's "Hope is the thing with feathers that perches in the soul, and sings the tune without the words, and never stops at all."

However, the 1980s seem to be bringing greatly improved performance prospects for the American composer. Through the efforts of many people: Ralph Shapey in Chicago, Arthur Weisberg in New York, Gunther Schuller in New York and Boston, The American Society of University Composers, the Cal Arts Contemporary Music Group, the Houston Opera Company (for Carlisle Floyd's Willie Stark), the Portland (Ore.) Opera Company (for Herrmann's Wuthering Heights in 1982), Charlotte Opera (for Robert Ward's Abelard and Heloise, 1982); commissions from several major orchestras (four of six commissions by the Boston Symphony went to Americans), commissions from several of the more affluent chamber groups; and increased recordings of American composers by American companies, including Composers Recordings, Inc., Opus One, 1750 Arch, Eastman-Rochester Archives, and others.

Of course, if a composer has the grace to die, all the recording companies become interested and practically his whole output will be recorded.

Preface to the First Edition

In the early 1940s when Deems Taylor was inter-mission commentator for the New York Philharmonic Radio Broadcasts, he received letters from two listeners on opposite sides of the continent, both putting forth the theory that music thrives and composers abound in a country that is unhappy in its government. Perhaps the present proliferation of composers can be attributed not to the state of our government (or the world, for we are not alone in this musical abundance), but to the development and practice of the Schillinger System of Musical Composition combined with a more relaxed definition of music, and also to the tremendous increase in government and private foundation grants. The large number of twentieth-century composers listed in this director is testimony to all of these factors and more.

When in 1970 I began listing contemporary American composers found in some old Schwann catalogs, I had no idea that I was getting involved in a major project that would dominate my life for five years. By the time I had recorded over 700 names, I thought the task was almost completed. In fact, the number of composers identified reached over 6,000 with the addition of names from the College Music Society's list of composers; the American Society of University Composers; the Southeastern Composers' League; the National Association of American Composers and Conductors; the American Society of Composers, Authors and Publishers; Bakers's Biographical Dictionary of Musicians; The Directory of American Women Composers; Bull's Index to Biographies of Contemporary Composers; Central Opera Service Bulletin; publisher's lists; recording company lists; concert announcements in the New York Times and elsewhere; Schwann catalogs; and the many names supplied by composers to whom I sent questionnaires. Of the 6,000 names gathered, approximately a third either did not meet the criteria established for inclusion in this volume or were unlocatable.

The criteria for inclusion were: birth date no earlier than 1870; American citizenship or extended residence in the United States; and at least one original composition published, commerically recorded, performed in an urban area, or selected for an award in composition. Because of sheer numbers, composers who wrote teaching pieces only, jazz only (with a few exceptions), popular only, rock, or folk were not included. Those who received two questionnaires and did not reply were omitted unless they also appeared in publishers' sources such as lists and concert announcements.

Concentrating on twentieth-century American composers allowed the listing of lesser-known, unknown, and minor composers of this period. Information given in returned questionnaires was accepted as presented with a minimum of verification. An asterisk preceding an entry indicates that the information included is not based upon a completed questionnaire, but gathered from other sources such as concert announcements, publishers' lists, and recordings. It is possible that some of the names included in this category are in fact Canadians or other nationalities, or pen names, which have eluded identification. Because of the increased interest in women composers a separate list appears on page 511.

* * *

Thanks are due to all composers who suggested names of colleagues, and special thanks to those who provided more than twenty-five names: Donald Aird, J. Ross Albert, Sy Brandon, David Cope, Festival of Northwest Composers, Eusebia Hunkins, Virginia Kendrick, H. Owen Reed, Halsey Stevens, Nancy Van de Vate, and Walter R. Watson. I am grateful for the cooperation of the American Conference of Cantors; the American Society of Composers, Authors and Publishers; the MacDowell Colony; the Yaddo Colony; and many publishing and recording companies. I should like to acknowledge the help of John Watts of Composers' Theatre and Nicholas Slonimsky, who graciously sanctioned my using Baker's Biographical Dictionary as a source and in addition supplied several dates that he had received too late for inclusion in his 1971 supplement. Vera and William Filby also helped enormously with just about every composer who ever set foot in Maryland. I am particularly grateful for the cooperation of all the composers who graciously completed and returned questionnaires.

Biographical Dictionary

ABBINANTI, FRANK
b. Chicago, Ill., 24 Nov. 1949. He is self-taught in music. He was codirector of the Modern Music Workshop, 1969-71, and from 1971, of the Mixed Media Workshop, both in Chicago.
WORKS: <u>Konzert for</u>, any instrument, 1970; <u>Rebus</u>, percussion solo, 1971; <u>Oracle</u>, any pitched instrument, 1971; <u>Derbies, black and white</u>, any instrument, 1972; <u>Piano piece</u>, 1972; <u>Liberation song</u>, mixed media, 1972.

ABEL, PAUL LOUIS
b. Clarksdale, Miss., 23 Nov. 1926. Studied with John LaMontaine and A. I. McHose at Eastman School of Music. He was on the faculty, Univ. of Montana, 1950-54; from 1954, assistant to full professor, Louisiana State Univ.
WORKS: ORCHESTRA: <u>Vignette</u>, 1962, received the Edward Benjamin award; <u>In memorium astro-nautarium</u>; <u>Fantasia on Gregorian themes</u>; BAND: <u>Cyrano de Bergerac</u>, symphonic poem, 1954; <u>Symphony for five winds</u>, 1970; <u>Vanquished</u>; CHORUS: <u>Mass in honor of St. Louis, king of France</u>, with organ, 1959; <u>Gloria, sing praise to God</u>, a cappella, 1973; <u>Dies sanctificatus</u>, motet.
389 Kay Dr., Baton Rouge, LA 70815

ABRAMOWITZ, DAVID G.
b. Brooklyn, N.Y., 18 Nov. 1950. Studied with Malcolm Williamson at Westminster Choir Coll., B.M.E. 1972; with Paul E. Karvonen, Mankato State Univ., M.M. 1975. He was choral director, Maxson School, Plainfield, N.J., 1973-74; from 1975, at Fieldstone School.
WORKS: ORCHESTRA: <u>Fantasy in d</u>, for strings; CHAMBER MUSIC: trio for viola, flute, trombone; <u>Fanfare and melody</u>, 4 euphoniums; <u>Four character pieces</u>, piano; <u>Lower East Side scherzo</u>, piano; <u>Prelude and fugue</u>, saxophone quartet; CHORUS: <u>Shma Yisroael</u>; <u>Variations on Merrial</u>.
1015 Avenue N, Brooklyn, NY 11230

ABRAMS, DANIEL
b. Cleveland, Ohio, 18 Jan. 1931. He studied with Gardner Read and Marcel Dick, Cleveland Institute of Music; with Felix Salzer, Mannes College of Music; with Darius Milhaud, Aspen Festival; and with Howard Ferguson and Lenox Berkeley, Royal Academy of Music, London, on a Fulbright award in piano and composition. He joined the faculty at Goucher College in 1962.
WORKS: ORCHESTRA: piano concerto; flute concerto; trumpet concerto; CHAMBER MUSIC: string quartet; quartet for flute and strings; quartet for 4 flutes; woodwind quartet; sonata for two flutes and piano; flute sonatina; several jazz works for flute and piano; piano pieces.
Music Dept., Goucher College, Towson, MD 21204

ABRAMSON, ROBERT M.
b. Philadelphia, Pa., 23 Aug. 1928. Studied at Manhattan School of Music, B.M. 1965, M.M. 1966; had advanced study in composition with Peggy Glanville-Hicks, Max Wald, Donald Lybbert, David Diamond; harpsichord and baroque music with Edith Weiss-Mann; conducting with Pierre Monteux. His awards include the National Film Board award and Edinburgh Festival award, both for <u>The ages of time</u>, 1962; a Rockefeller grant; MacDowell and Fulbright fellowships; and in 1973 Outstanding Educator of America award. In the U.S. Army, 1952-54, he was director and conductor of the orchestra, band, and chorus at Ft. Sam Houston, Tex. Faculty positions have included Westminster Choir Coll., 1962-64; Hartford Cons. of Music, 1964-69; Herbert H. Lehman Coll., 1968-69; and Manhattan School of Music, 1969-, chairman of theory, 1974-. In the summers of 1965-67, he was consultant to the U.S. Govt. Title III Project Acorn for Children (K-3). He has given many lecture demonstrations and seminars on eurhythmic techniques in music education.
WORKS: OPERA: <u>Dr. Faustus lights the lights</u>, 1956; <u>Rapunzel</u>, 1956; <u>The gloating geezel</u>, 1958; <u>The donkey's tale</u>, 1958; <u>The return of Agamemnon</u>, 1967; BALLET: <u>Night piece No. 1</u>, 1952; <u>In the evening</u>, 1958; <u>Touch and go</u>, 1969; OTHER STAGE WORKS: <u>Countess Kathleen</u>, on W. B. Yeats, 1957; <u>The cat and the moon</u>, also on Yeats, 1960; many film and television scores. ORCHESTRA: <u>Dance variations</u>, piano and orch., 1965; CHAMBER MUSIC: <u>Landscapes</u>, string quartet, 1950; <u>Night piece No. 2</u>, flute and percussion, 1956; <u>Two nocturnes</u>, cello and piano, 1960; piano trio, 1968; woodwind quintet, 1968; string quartet, 1968; piano sonata; piano pieces; many songs.
250 W. 94 St., New York, NY 10025

ACHRON, ISIDOR
b. Warsaw, Poland, 24 Nov. 1892; U.S. citizen 1928; d. New York, N.Y., 12 May 1948. Brother of Joseph Achron, he studied at the St. Petersburg Cons. with Liadov; was accompanist for Jascha

ACHRON, JOSEPH

Heifetz for about 10 years, then resumed his
career as a concert pianist.
    WORKS: ORCHESTRA: piano concerto, premiere
at New York with the composer as soloist, 9 Dec.
1937; Suite grotesque, St. Louis, 30 Jan. 1942;
piano pieces.

ACHRON, JOSEPH
    b. near Suwalki, Poland, 13 May 1886; U.S.
citizen 1930; d. Hollywood, Calif., 29 Apr. 1943.
Brother of Isidor Achron, he studied violin with
Leopold Auer and theory with Liadov at St.
Petersburg Cons. After years as a soloist with
European orchestras, he came to the U.S. and
eventually settled in Hollywood as violinist and
composer in film studios.
    WORKS: ORCHESTRA: Hazan, cello and orch.,
1912; 3 violin concertos, no. 1, premiered in
Boston, 24 Jan. 1927, no. 2 in Los Angeles, 19
Dec. 1936, and no. 3, Los Angeles, 31 Mar. 1939,
all with the composer as soloist; Golem, suite
for chamber orch. in which the last section was
an exact retrograde rendition of the first section, 1932; piano concerto, 1941; CHAMBER MUSIC:
4 Tableaux fantastiques, violin and piano, 1907;
Chromatic string quartet, 1907; 2 violin sonatas,
1910, 1918; 2 Hebrew pieces, violin and piano,
1912; Suite bizarre, violin and piano, 1916;
Scher, violin and piano, 1916; Elegy, string
quartet, 1927; sextet for winds, 1938; VOICE:
songs, choral pieces, and liturgical works.

ADAIR, JAMES
    b. Quincy, Ill., 21 Sept. 1909. Studied violin
with Jacques Gordon in Chicago and Hugo Kortschak
in New York; composition with Leo Sowerby, Howard
Hanson, Paul Hindemith, and Darius Milhaud. His
career as a violinist began with the Denver Symphony on his 14th birthday; he has played with
the St. Louis Symphony, Chicago Little Symphony,
and the Rochester Philharmonic. He was on the
faculty of Stephens Coll., Columbia, Mo., to
1947, then joined the staff at California State
Coll., Sacramento. He has appeared in concerts
of his own works in the U.S. and abroad. His
composition style is described as contrapuntal,
melodic, with conservative 20th-century dissonn-
ance.
    WORKS: 3 operas, 2 symphonies, 5 violin
concertos, sonatas for all the standard orchestral instruments, 3 string quartets, numerous
woodwind compositions, songs, and incidental
works.
    82 Sandburg Dr., Sacramento, CA 95819

ADAM, CLAUS
    b. Sumatra, 5 Nov. 1917; to U.S. 1931. He
studied at the Salzburg Mozarteum; cello with
Emanual Feuerman in New York; after serving with
the U.S. Air Force in World War II, studied
composition with Stefan Wolpe. His awards include grants from the National Endowment for
the Arts and the Guggenheim Found., 1975. He
was cellist with the New Music Quartet, 1948-55,
with the Julliard Quartet, 1955-74. He is on
the faculty at Juilliard and at Mannes Coll. of
Music, and is music administrator of the National
Orchestral Assoc., New York.

    WORKS: ORCHESTRA: cello concerto,
Cincinnati, 26 Oct. 1973; Concerto variations,
cello and orch., 1976, New York, 5 Apr. 1977;
CHAMBER MUSIC: piano sonata, Saltzburg Festival,
1952; string trio, 1967; Herbstgesänge, soprano
and piano, 1969; 2 string quartets, #2 written
in 1975, won 3rd prize in the Friedheim composition contest at the Kennedy Center, Washington,
D.C., 16 Sept. 1979.
    33 W. 12 St., New York, NY 10011

ADAMS, ERNEST HARRY
    b. Waltham, Mass., 16 July 1886; d. Newton,
Mass., 25 Dec. 1959. Studied piano with his
mother, harmony with Benjamin Cutter, organ with
Henry Dunham at the New England Cons. His published works, chiefly for piano or voice, included a piano suite, In the flower garden, published at age 18. His many unpublished works
included a piano concerto, a piano concertino,
5 sonatas, and a string quartet.

ADAMS, GEORGE (GEZA LENGYEL)
    b. Budapest, Hungary, 12 June 1904; U.S. citizen;
d. 1959. Composed a piano sonata, 1959, and
songs.

ADAMS, JOHN
    b. Worcester, Mass., 15 Feb. 1947. He studied
composition at Harvard Univ. with Leon Kirchner,
Earl Kim, and Roger Sessions, B.A. (magna cum
laude) 1969, M.A. 1971; studied conducting with
Mario di Beneventura. He was awarded the Julius
Stratton prize by the Friends of Switzerland,
1969; in 1970 was composer-in-residence at the
Marlboro Festival. In 1972 he joined the faculty
of the San Francisco Cons. of Music and also
became director of the New Music Ensemble, in
which capacity he has commissioned works by
American and English composers.
    WORKS: INSTRUMENTAL: Electric wake, 1968;
piano quintet, 1970; American standard, 1973;
Mary Lou--a routine, 1973; Ktaadn, with chorus,
1973; Phrygian verses, piano, San Francisco, 21
Jan. 1978; Shaker loops, 7 string players, 1979;
ELECTRONIC: Heavy metal, 1971; Hockey seen,
tape, slides, dancers, 1972; Etudes and a continuum, tape and clarinet; Globose floccose,
ensemble and tape, 1976; Onyx, Grounding, Sermon,
Strident bands, Wavemakers, 1978.
    San Francisco Conservatory of Music,
    1201 Ortega St., San Francisco, CA 94122

ADAMS, JOHN
    b. Attleboro, Mass., 28 Nov. 1947. He studied
composition at Boston Cons. of Music, B.M. 1969,
M.M. 1971. He received a BMI student composer
award in 1971, and was appointed to the faculty
at Boston Cons. in the same year.
    WORKS: CHAMBER MUSIC: Study, violin and
piano, 1966; 7 canons, clarinet and bass clarinet,
1967; For tomorrow, chamber orch., 1971; string
quartet, 1971-72; VOICE: Genesis, cantata,
chorus and orch., 1968-70; Kyrie and sanctus,
chorus, 1969; Lord's prayer, chorus; Job's final
answer, song, 1971; 5 songs, soprano and piano,
1972; piano pieces.
    Boston Conservatory of Music, 8 The Fenway,
    Boston, MA 02215

ADAMS, JOHN LUTHER
   b. Meridian, Miss., 23 Jan. 1953. Studied with
Fred Coulter at Wesleyan Coll. and Mercer Univ.,
1969-70; with James Tenney and Leonard Stein,
California Institute of the Arts, B.F.A. 1973;
graduate study with Charles Knox, Georgia State
Univ., 1973-74. His honors include the Young
Musicians Found. composers award, 1972; American
Guild of Organists composer award, San Jose,
1973; National Endowment for the Arts grant,
1974; composer-in-residence, Ossabaw Island
Project, 1975, Hambidge Center, 1976 and 1977;
shared in the Atlanta Circle of Drama Critics
music award, 1977; National Fed. of Music Clubs
prize, 1978.
   WORKS: CHAMBER MUSIC: Always very soft,
string bass and percussion, 1973; Floating
petals, flute violin, harp, piano, vibes, 1974;
Green corn dance, percussion ensemble, 1974;
The sound goes round and round, organ and percussion, 1975; Songbirdsongs, piccolo and percussion, 1975-76; Wind garden, flute and percussion, 1975-77; Three on Hira, flute, koto,
and percussion, 1977-78; Celestial silence, 2
choruses, harp, percussion, 1977.
   Rte. 2, Culdesac, ID 83524

ADAMS, LESLIE
   b. Cleveland, Ohio, 30 Dec. 1932. He studied at
Oberlin Cons., Manhattan School of Music,
Juilliard School, Calif. State Univ. at Long
Beach, and Ohio State Univ.; with teachers
Herbert Elwell, Joseph Wood, Vittorio Giannini,
Robert Starer, and Marshall Barnes. His works
were twice selected for performance at the
Kansas Univ. Symposium of Contemporary American
Music; a program of his works was presented by
the Ira Aldridge Society of New York. Other
honors include a composition award from the Nat.
Assoc. of Negro Musicians and a grant from the
Nat. Endowment for the Arts, 1978. He joined
the faculty of the Univ. of Kansas at Lawrence
in 1970; in 1978 he began a one- to three-year
leave for the purpose of composition and research.
   WORKS: BALLET: A kiss in Xanadu, in 3 acts,
performed in concert version, Clevelan, Feb.
1978; ORCHESTRA: piano concerto; symphony no. 1,
1978; Ode to life, commissioned and performed by
Cleveland Civic Orch. 13 May 1979; CHAMBER MUSIC:
violin sonata; cello sonata; horn sonata; Pastorale, violin; trombone quartet, 1977; CHORUS:
Psalm 121, a cappella; Madrigal; Hosanna to the
son of David; Tall tales; Harlem love song;
Vocalize for voices; Under the greenwood tree;
SONGS: Prayer; Drums of tragedy; Since you went
away; Night song; Creole girl; For you there is
no song, Millay text, 1978; PIANO: 3 preludes.
   9409 Kempton Ave., Cleveland, OH 44108

ADDISS, STEPHEN
   b. New York, N.Y., 2 Apr. 1935. He studied with
Walter Piston, 1956-57; with Lester Trimble,
1957-58; and with John Cage, 1958-60.
   WORKS: OPERA: A tree, a rock, a cloud,
chamber opera, 1960; ORCHESTRA: Passacaglia,
1958; CHAMBER MUSIC: duets, flute and clarinet,
1958; fugue, string quartet; Piano fantasy,
1959; 2 cello sonatas; VOICE: Songs from Thomas

Campion, 1959; Songs from Yeats plays, 1961;
other song cycles for voice and chamber ensembles.
   704 Indiana St., Lawrence, KS 66044

ADELBERG-RUDOW, VIVIAN. See RUDOW, VIVIAN ADELBERG.

ADLER, CLARENCE
   b. Cincinnati, Ohio, 10 Mar. 1886; d. New York,
24 Dec. 1969. Concert pianist; published piano
pieces.

ADLER, JAMES
   b. Chicago, Ill., 19 Nov. 1950. He studied at
Curtis Inst. of Music, B.M. in piano 1973, M.M.
in composition 1976.
   WORKS: ORCHESTRA: Classic ragtime suite,
on Joplin themes, 1974; March grotesque; suite
for strings, 1974; PIANO: Passacaglia, 1975.
   2201 Penn. Ave., Philadelphia, PA 19130

ADLER, SAMUEL
   b. Mannheim, Germany, 4 Mar. 1928; U.S. citizen
1942. He studied at Boston Univ., B.M. 1948;
Harvard Univ., M.A. 1950; received an honorary
doctorate in music from Southern Methodist Univ.,
1969. Composition teachers were Walter Piston,
Randall Thompson, Paul Hindemith, Aaron Copeland,
and Herbert Fromm. His many awards include the
Dallas Symphony prize from Univ. of Texas, 1953;
6 first prizes of the Texas Composers Guild,
1955-63; first Lazare Saminsky Memorial award,
1959; a Rockefeller grant; a Ford grant; and
many commissions. In 1950 he joined the U.S.
Army and was sent to Germany, where he organized
the 7th Army Symph. Orchestra and toured Germany
with a repertoire of more than 100 works. For
this he received the Medal of Honor for benefit
to cultural relations. Returning to the U.S., he
was director of music for Temple Emanu-El, Dallas,
1953-66; professor of composition, North Texas
State Univ., 1958-66; organized and conducted
the Dallas Chorale, 1954-56; conducted Dallas
Lyric Theater, 1955-57. In 1966 he was appointed
to the faculty at Eastman School of Music and
has been chairman of composition from 1973. He
was eastern regional director of the contemporary
music project sponsored by MENC and the Ford
Found., 1967-69.
   WORKS: THEATER: The outcasts of Poker Flat,
1-act opera, 1959; The wrestler, 1-act opera,
1971; The lodge of shadows, music drama, sponsored by the Nat. Endowment for the Arts, 1973;
The disappointment, a reconstruction of an early
(1767) American ballad opera, 1974; ORCHESTRA:
5 symphonies, 1953, 1957, 1960, 1967, 1975;
Toccata, 1954; Summer stock, 1955; The feast of
lights, 1955; Jubilee, 1958; Rhapsody, violin
and orch., 1961; Requiescat in pace, in memory
of J. F. Kennedy, 1963; Song and dance, viola
and orch., 1965; City by the lake, 1968; Lament,
baritone and chamber orch., 1968; organ concerto,
1970; Sinfonietta, 1970; Concerto for orchestra,
1971; flute concerto, 1977; WIND ENSEMBLE:
Concert piece, 1946; Praeludium, 1947; Divertimento, 1948; Southwestern sketches, 1961; Festive
prelude, 1965; concerto for winds, brass, percussion, 1968; 5 vignettes, trombone choir, 1968;
Brass fragments, 1970; Histrionics, brass and

ADOLPHUS, MILTON

percussion, 1971; A little night and day music, 1976; CHAMBER MUSIC: horn sonata, 1948; Miscellany, mezzo-soprano, English horn, string quartet, 1956; 2 violin sonatas, 1956, 1965; 4 string quartets, 1963-1975; piano trio, 1964; 5 movements, brass quintet, 1963; 4 studies for woodwinds, 1965; Harobed, flute or clarinet solo; unaccompanied cello sonata, 1966; 7 epigrams, woodwind sextet, 1966; Songs with winds, soprano and woodwind quintet, 1967; Capriccio, harp solo; Intrada, woodwind quintet, 1967; Cantos I-IX, varying instruments, 1968-76; L'olam Vaed, 1975; many works for piano and organ; CHORUS: B'shaaray Tefilah, baritone, choir, organ or orch., 1963; The binding, an oratorio, 1967; A whole bunch of fun, secular cantata, 1969; We believe, an ecumenical mass for chorus and 8 instruments, 1974; A falling of saints, tenor, baritone, chorus and orch., 1977; many other choral works, numerous songs; many children's songs and choruses.

   54 Railroad Mills Rd., Pittsford, NY 14534

ADOLPHUS, MILTON
   b. New York, N.Y., 27 Jan. 1913. He settled in Philadelphia in 1935 and studied composition with Rosario Scalero at the Curtis Inst. of Music. He was for a while head of the Philadelphia Music Center. From 1938 until he retired in 1974, he held an administrative position in the Dept. of Labor and Industry, Commonwealth of Pennsylvania, Harrisburg. Although not engaged in music professionally, he has been an exceedingly industrious composer, producing 13 symphonies, 1931-54; 28 string quartets, 1935-73; and opus numbers up to 140 that include orchestral and chamber music and songs. String quartet #28, written in April 1973, won honorable mention in a competition sponsored by the Catgut Acoustical Society for a composition for mezzo, alto, tenor, and baritone stringed instruments which were developed by the society. His most recent major works are Oratorio of faith, opus 123, 1976, and Concerto for orchestra, opus 136, 1978.
   3920 Chambers Hill Rd., Harrisburg, PA 17111

AGAY, DENES
   b. Budapest, Hungary, 10 June 1911. He studied piano and composition at the Liszt Acad. of Music and received the Ph.D. from the Univ. of Budapest. In the U.S. since 1939 (citizen 1943), he has held positions with several music publishing firms as composer, editor, and educational consultant, and was active as piano teacher in New York until retirement. In addition to a long list of compositions for the piano, he has written works for orchestra, band, chorus, and solo voice.
   1052 Pine St., Norton, VA 24273

AHLSTROM, DAVID
   b. Lancaster, N.Y., 22 Feb. 1927. He studied at the Cincinnati Cons. of Music and Eastman School of Music with Alan Hovhaness, Henry Cowell, and Bernard Rogers. In 1965 he was awarded a Danforth Found. grant for composition and to study electronic music. He held faculty positions at Northwestern Univ., 1961-62, Southern

Methodist Univ., 1962-67, and Eastern Illinois Univ., 1967-75.
   WORKS: OPERA: Three sisters who are not sisters, melodrama in 3 acts, libretto by Gertrude Stein, 1953, rev. 1962; INSTRUMENTAL: Scherzo, trumpet, winds, and percussion, 1959; Toccatas and passacaglias, percussion, piano-celesta, string bass, speaking voices, 1961; piano sonata no. 2, 1961-62; Sonata no. 4 in 8 scenes, clarinet and piano, 1963; Sonata no. 8, bass solo, 4 dancers, electronic tape, and electronic manipulation, 1966, performed on CBS-TV, 17 Aug. 1969.
   62 Oakwood St., #4, San Francisco, CA 94110

AHNELL, EMIL
   b. Erie, Pa., 6 Apr. 1925. Studied at New England Cons., Northwestern Univ., and Univ. of Illinois with David Barnett, Anthony Donato, Wallingford Riegger, and Burrill Phillips. In 1965 he received the Centennial Choral Composition award from the Univ. of Kentucky. His faculty positions have been Houghton Coll., 1951-52; Univ. of Illinois, 1952-57; Toledo Museum of Art, 1957-58; and Kentucky Wesleyan Coll., 1958-.
   WORKS: CHAMBER MUSIC: flute sonata; Antigone, brass instruments; piano trio; 3 pieces, cello; 5 sketches, flute, violin, cello; and a number of unpublished orchestral, choral, and small chamber works.
   Kentucky Wesleyan College, Owensboro, KY 42301

AHRENDT, KARL
   b. Toledo, Ohio, 7 Mar. 1904. Studied composition with Carl Grimm, Cincinnati Cons., in Paris with Jean Rivier, and at Eastman School of Music with Bernard Rogers and Howard Hanson. His honors include the Philadelphia Arts Alliance choral award, 1954; first prize, Ohio Music Teachers Assoc. 1972 composition contest; and first prize, 1972 Roth Competition. He was faculty member, Florida State Univ., 1937-44; director, School of Music, Augustana Coll., Rock Island, Ill., 1946-50; from 1950, faculty member, Ohio Univ., becoming Distinguished Professor Emeritus in 1974.
   WORKS: ORCHESTRA: Johnny Appleseed, 1950; Dance overture; Montage, 1972; Concert piece, violin and orch., 1978; concerto for oboe and strings; WIND ENSEMBLE: Affirmations; CHAMBER MUSIC: 3 movements for string quartet, 1963; piano trio; Integrations, piano, 1973; 5 by 7, woodwind trio, piano, percussion, 1978; VOICE: The Lord Sun, cantata for chorus, soloists, orch., narrator, 1970; 67th Psalm, women's voice and piano, 1954; Poems from a calendar, a song cycle, 1972.
   5 Old Peach Ridge Rd., Athens, OH 45701

AHROLD, FRANK
   b. Long Beach, Calif., 12 Dec. 1931. Studied with John Vincent and Lukas Foss, Univ. of California, Los Angeles. He has had commissions from the Oakland Symphony Orchestra, Oakland Ballet, Amer. Guild of Organists, Vocal Arts Ensemble, and others. His positions have included conductor, Long Beach Civic Chorus,

1961–65, and Camerata de Musici, 1964–68; assistant musical director, Long Beach Civic Light Opera, 1965–68; pianist, Oakland Symph. Orch., 1973–78.

WORKS: OPERA: The view, 1 act; BALLET: The spider and the fly; ORCHESTRA: piano concerto; concerto for strings; Song without words, 1971; Second coming, tenor and orch.; suite for cello and orch.; CHAMBER MUSIC: 3 poems of Sylvia Plath, soprano and chamber orch.; flute sonata; 3 piano sonatas; CHORUS: Behold the joy; The canticle of Judith.

3163 Mission St., San Francisco, CA 95110

AIKEN, KENNETH
b. Deerfield, Mich., 21 June 1885; d. Detroit, Mich., 24 July 1970. Studied at Boston Univ. and with Ernest Hutcheson at the New England Cons. of Music. He was on the faculty of the Detroit Inst. of Musical Art and a private teacher until retirement in 1968. He also was author of two pedagogical books: Modern technique for the student of piano and The child and his study of the piano. His compositions were chiefly choral works, the best known being the anthem, For Christ is born.

AIRD, DONALD BRUCE
b. Provo, Utah, 24 May 1924. Studied at Univ. of California, Berkeley, with Charles Cushing, Edward Lawton, Roger Sessions; and at Univ. of Southern California with Ingolf Dahl. He received the 1960 Helen S. Armstead award in composition. He has held faculty positions at Stanford Univ., Univ. of Minnesota, Univ. of California, and California State Univ., San Francisco. He is director of the Berkeley Chamber Singers.

WORKS: Psalm 31, full orchestra and double chorus; Psalm 150, chamber orch. and 6-part chorus; chamber concerto; Symphonia concertante, violin, viola, chamber orch.; Songs for Carol, mezzo-soprano, chamber ensemble; oboe quartet; Songs for Ian Partridge; Movements and interludes, for one piano with 1, 2, or 3 players.

252 Stanford Ave., Kensington, CA 94708

AITKEN, HUGH
b. New York, N.Y., 7 Sept. 1924. Studied with Vincent Persichetti, Bernard Wagner, and Robert Ward, Juilliard School, B.M. 1950. His awards include commissions from E. S. Coolidge Found. and the Naumburg Found., and a Nat. Endowment for the Arts grant. He was faculty member at Juilliard until 1970, then professor, William Patterson Coll., Wayne, N.J.

WORKS: THEATRE: The Moirai, ballet, 1961; Fables, chamber opera after La Fontaine, for 4 singers, 9 instrumentalists, 1975; ORCHESTRA: piano concerto; CHAMBER MUSIC: oboe quintet; 8 pieces for wind quintet; quintet for clarinet and strings; Montages, solo bassoon; suite for solo cello; suite for solo clarinet; 4 partitas for various groups; Trumpet!, solo trumpet, 1974; quintet for oboe and strings, 1975; Tromba, quintet for trumpet and string quartet, 1976; CHORUS: sacred choruses; 5 cantats; songs and piano pieces including Piano fantasy, 1966.

58 Ramapo Hills Blvd., Oakland, NJ 07436

ALBAM, MANNY
b. Dominican Republic, 24 June 1922; U.S. citizen 1945. He studied composition privately with Tibor Serly. He is codirector of the Arrangers' Laboratory Workshop, Eastman School of Music; project specialist at Glassboro State Coll.; music director for Solid State Records; arranger-composer for other record companies.

WORKS: FILM SCORES: 4 clowns; Dancers in May; The black pearl; CHAMBER MUSIC: brass quintets, woodwind quintets, string quintets; CHORUS: The horns and voices of a dilemma, choir, jazz ensemble, wind ensemble; Sisterhood is powerful, women's chorus and jazz band. He has also composed for the TV series: "Glory trail," "Artists USA," "Legacy."

850 Seventh Ave., New York, NY 10019

ALBERS, BRADLEY GENE
b. Houston, Tex., 26 Aug. 1952. Studied at Sam Houston State Univ., B.M. summa cum laude 1975; with Thomas Frederickson, Salvatore Martirano, John Melby, Paul Zonn, Univ. of Illinois, M.M. 1976, D.M.A. 1978. He held full scholarships at Sam Houston State Univ., 1973–75, and for his doctoral work at Univ. of Illinois, 1976–78; and unlimited computer time grant for research at Univ. of South Florida, where he is faculty member and director of the Systems Complex for the Studio and Performing Arts.

WORKS: BAND: Aggregate; CHAMBER MUSIC: Martial cadenza, on poems by Wallace Stevens, male voice, bassoon, vibraphones, bells, computer; Exegeses, clarinet and computer; 2 verses of the Rubaiyat of Omar Khayyam, soprano, flute, violin, string bass; Omphaloskepsis, string quartet.

Sycom, Univ. of South Florida, Tampa, FL 33620

ALBERT, J. ROSS
b. Lebanon, Pa., 1 Sept. 1922. Studied at Lebanon Valley Coll., Pa., Converse Coll., S.C., and Univ. of North Carolina, Greensboro, with composition teachers Eddie Bass, Jack Jarrett, Roger McDuffie, and E. P. Rutledge. He taught for a while in the Lebanon public schools and then moved to Atlantic Christian Coll., Wilson, N.C.

WORKS: ORCHESTRA: prelude and fugue, strings; WIND ENSEMBLE: 4 Marys, band; 2 madrigals, brass ensemble; Shards and marbles, brass ensemble; Contradictions, trio sonata for trumpet, horn, and tuba; CHAMBER MUSIC: flute sonata; piano sonata; VOICE: Palm Sunday motet, choir and organ; The beginning, Christmas cantata; 3 song cycles: The choice songs, The lonely songs, 5 songs of the dark; many anthems and children's anthems.

ALBERT, STEPHEN
b. New York, N.Y., 6 Feb. 1941. Studied privately with Elie Siegmeister, 1956–58; with Bernard Rogers, Eastman School of Music, 1958–60; with Joseph Castaldo, Philadelphia Musical Acad., B.A. 1962; and with George Rochberg, Univ. of Pennsylvania. He received first prize, B.M.I. Hemispheric Competition, 1961; Columbia Univ. Nearns prize, 1962; 3 MacDowell fellowships; Huntington

ALBERT, THOMAS RUSSELL

Hartford fellowship; 2 Rome prizes; Ford grant,
1967-68; 3 Rockefeller grants; 2 Guggenheim
grants; ASCAP award; Fromm Found. commission,
1975; Nat. Endowment for the Arts grant for a
piano concerto, 1977-78. He taught at Philadelphia Musical Acad., 1968-70; at Stanford
Univ., 1970-71; and at Smith Coll., 1974-76.
WORKS: ORCHESTRA: Illuminations, brass,
2 pianos, harps, percussion, 1962; Winter songs,
tenor and orch., 1965; Bacchae, narrator, chorus,
and orch.; Orchestrabook; Cathedral music, with
electric organ and piano, 2 grand pianos, and
amplification; Voices within, with concertino
ensemble, 1975; concerto for 4 quartets;
CHAMBER MUSIC: Supernatural songs, soprano and
chamber orch., 1964; 2 toccatas for piano;
Imitations, string quartet, 1964; Wedding songs,
soprano and piano; Wolf time, soprano and chamber
orch.; To wake the dead, soprano and chamber
ensemble, 1977.
Sherry Rd., Harvard, MA 01451

ALBERT, THOMAS RUSSELL
b. Lebanon, Pa., 14 Dec. 1948. Studied with
William Duckworth at Atlantic Christian Coll.;
with Paul Zonn, Morgan Powell, and Ben Johnston,
Univ. of Illinois. He won first prize in the
Atlantic Christian Coll. Arts Festival composi-
tion contest, 1969, 1970; Nat. Endowment for the
Arts composer grant, 1976. He was lecturer,
Univ. of Illinois, 1970-74; instructor of guitar,
Parkland Coll., 1971-74; faculty member,
Shenandoah Coll. and Cons. of Music, 1974-.
WORKS: OPERA: Lizbeth, 1 act, premiere,
Winchester, Va., 1976; BAND: B-flat piece;
CHAMBER MUSIC: Permutations, horn and piano;
Sound frames, oboe, saxophone, trombone, vibra-
phone, in 3 movements, 1969; Five for 2 tubas;
An octet, indeterminate ensemble; Winter monarch,
soprano, flute, piano, text by his father, 1973;
Changing of the lights, baritone and piano,
Washington, D.C., 2 Nov. 1975; CHORUS: Communion
hymn cluster, for 3 small choirs, a simultaneous
setting of 3 hymns, 1970.
405 Green St., Winchester, VA 22601

ALBERTI, SOLON
b. Mt. Clemens, Mich., 6 Dec. 1889. Studied at
Chicago Musical Coll., B.A., and also in Paris,
Milan, and in Berlin. He taught at Chicago
Musical Coll., 1904-14, and at Kansas City Cons.,
1914-19, where he founded the Kansas City Little
Symphony and conducted the Kansas City Grand
Opera Society. In 1919 he settled in New York,
achieving great success as pianist, conductor,
coach, and accompanist to many top operatic
singers. He was also organist and music director
at Park Avenue Christian Church in New York for
35 years.
WORKS: PIANO: White swan of Samarkand; The
gypsy; Four sketches from the Far East; SONGS:
Trees; The hour; Oriental serenade; other songs
and anthems.
Hotel Ansonia, Broadway at 73 St., New York,
NY 10023

ALBRECHT, MOONYEEN
b. Chicago, Ill., 31 Mar. 1936. Studied with

Anthony Donato at Northwestern Univ. In 1963 he
composed the score for the documentary film,
Kahli Nihta, Socrates, which won first prize in
the Venice International Film Festival and the
Jesse Laske award in Hollywood. Since 1963 he
has been faculty member at Central Michigan Univ.
WORKS: ORCHESTRA: symphony; 3 movements
for chamber orch.; CHORUS: Vespers of the
Blessed Virgin Mary, with soloists and orch.;
Salve Regina; Madrigals; ORGAN: Concert piece.
108 W. Orchard Ave., Shepherd, MI 48883

ALBRIGHT, WILLIAM
b. Gary, Ind., 20 Oct. 1944. Studied with Rose
Lee Finney, Leslie Bassett, Univ. of Michigan,
B.M., M.M., D.M.A.; with George Rochberg at
Tanglewood; with Max Deutsch and Olivier
Messiaen in Paris. His honors include 2
Koussevitzky composition awards, annual ASCAP
awards from 1967; Fulbright fellowship, 1968;
Niagara Univ., symphonic composition award, 1968;
Amer. Acad. of Arts and Letters award, 1970;
Rackham Research Grant, 1972. Since 1970 he has
been on the faculty, Univ. of Michigan, and
associate director of the Electronic Music
Studio. He is also music director, First
Unitarian Church, Ann Arbor; in 1979, was composer-in-residence, American Academy in Rome.
WORKS: THEATRE: Tic, 2 groups of performers,
tape, soloist, films, 1967; Beulahland rag, jazz
quartet, improvisation ensemble, tape, film,
narrator, slides, 1967-69; Cross of gold, actors,
choir, instruments, 1975; ORCHESTRA: Alliance,
1967-70; Night procession, 1972; Gothic suite,
organ concerto, 1973; BAND: Foils, 1963;
Introduction, passacaglia and rondo capriccioso,
solo track piano and winds, 1974; Heater, solo
saxophone and band, 1977; CHAMBER MUSIC:
Frescos, woodwind quartet, 1964; Salvos, mixed
ensemble, 1964; 2 pieces for 9 instruments, 1965-
66; Caroms, 9 players, 1966; Amerithon, indeterminate ensemble, 1967; Marginal worlds, 12
players, 1969; Danse macabre, 5 players, 1971;
Take that, 4 drummers, 1972; 7 deadly sins, 7
players and narrator, 1974; Doo-dah, 3 saxophones,
1975; Peace pipe, 2 bassoons, 1976; Saints
preserve us, solo clarinet, 1976; Shadows, solo
guitar, 1977; CHORUS: An alleluia super-round,
1973; hymn setting, for choir or congregation,
1973; mass in D, 1974; Chichester mass, 1974;
The birth of Jesus/Alleluia, treble voices, 1979;
ORGAN: chorale-partita, 1963; Juba, 1965;
Pneuma, 1966; Organbook I, 1967; Organbook II,
1971; Stipendium peccati, with piano and percussion, 1973; Dream and dance, 1974; Sweet
sixteenths, 1976; Jericho, battle music for
trumpet and organ, 1976; Organbook III, 1978;
Halo, 1978; King of instruments, with narrator,
1978; many works for piano; songs.
School of Music, Univ. of Michigan, Ann
Arbor, MI 48109

ALETTE, CARL
b. Philadelphia, Pa., 31 May 1922. Studied with
Wayne Barlow, A. I. McHose, and Bernard Rogers,
Eastman School of Music. His honors include an
award from the Louisville Symphony, 1955, and
many commissions. He has held faculty positions

at Univ. of Tennessee, 1951-54; State Univ. of New York, Brockport, 1954-57; Univ. of Mississippi, 1957-68; from 1968, at Univ. of Southern Alabama. In 1964-65 he was visiting professor at Univ. of California, Los Angeles.

WORKS: ORCHESTRA: Resurgence; symphony for chamber orch.; CHAMBER MUSIC: trombone sonata; suite for clarinet choir; Scherzo, brass quintet; 4 songs.

4584 Hawthorne Pl., Mobile, AL 36608

ALEXANDER, JEFF
b. Seattle, Wash., 2 July 1910. Studied at Becker Cons. and with Joseph Schillinger.

WORKS: ORCHESTRA: Yellow and brown; CHAMBER MUSIC: suite for flute and strings; Divertimento, viola and piano; FILM SCORES: The tender trap; The mating game; The gazebo; and others; also scores for television.

ALEXANDER, JOSEF
b. Boston, Mass., 15 May 1907. Studied piano at the New England Cons.; orchestration with Edward B. Hill and composition with Walter Piston at Harvard Univ., B.A. 1938, M.A. 1941; also at Tanglewood and in Paris. Awards include yearly ASCAP awards, 1960-78; John Knowles Paine, Walter Naumberg, and Fulbright fellowships; Bernard Ravitch Found. award; Internat. Humanities award; 2 Harvey Gaul awards; and a Nat. Endowment for the Arts grant. He was faculty member, Brooklyn Coll., City Univ. of New York, from 1945 to retirement.

WORKS: ORCHESTRA: piano concerto, 1938; Epitaphs, 1947; concertino, trumpet and strings, 1950; 4 symphonies, 1951, 1954, 1961, 1968; Celebrations, 1960; Quiet music for strings, 1966; 3 symphonic odes, men's chorus and orch., 1974; Duo contertante, trombone, strings, percussion; Salute to the whole world, narrator and orch., premiere, Symphony of the New World, Oct. 1977; BAND: Processional; Campus suite; CHAMBER MUSIC: Clockwork for strings; string quartet, 1940; piano quintet, 1942; piano trio, 1944; wind quintet, 1949; piano quartet, 1952; clarinet sonata, 1957; 4 movements for brass, 1958; trombone sonata, 1959; Nocturne and scherzo, violin and piano, 1963; Requiem and coda, trombone; 2 essays, 3 trombones; 3 pieces for 8 instruments, 1965; Burlesque and fugue, trumpet and piano; CHORUS: 3 American episodes; Dialogue spirituel, soprano, chorus, orch.; VOICE: Songs for Eve, cycle for soprano, harp, violin, cello, English horn; Gitanjali, text from Tagore, for soprano, harpsichord, percussion, New York, 14 Nov. 1975; many piano pieces and other instrumental and vocal works.

229 W. 78 St., New York, NY 10024

ALEXANDER, PHILIP
b. Lompoc, Calif., 8 Nov. 1927. Studied at Univ. of California, Santa Barbara, B.M. 1949; George Peabody Coll., M.M. 1951, D.M. 1957.

WORKS: CHAMBER MUSIC: 3 string quartets, 1951, 1977, 1978; 3 sketches, oboe and piano, 1959; suite for woodwind quartet and piano, 1976.

ALEXANDER, PHILIP R.
b. Tex., 11 Mar. 1944. Studied music at Curtis Inst. with de Lancie, Colucci, and Kincaid, then became an M.D. He was music instructor at Texas Technological Univ., Lubbock, 1966-67; assistant instructor in internal medicine, Baylor, Coll. of Medicine, Houston, from 1972.

WORKS: ORCHESTRA: oboe concerto; CHAMBER MUSIC: Voluntary in D, trumpet and piano; Concert etude, trumpet and piano; Symphonic corral, 2 oboes and English horn; CHORUS: Chorale fantasy; Chorale prelude on Old 100th; PIANO: Serenade; Theme and variations; Rhapsody; ORGAN: Toccata; 5 preludes; Chaconne; 3 preludes.

ALEXIUS, CARL JOHN
b. New Orleans, La., 30 Apr. 1928. Studied with Helen Gunderson, Louisiana State Univ.; with Hermann Reutter in Stuttgart, Germany; with Leslie Bassett and Ross Lee Finney, Univ. of Michigan. His awards include 3 awards of the Louisiana Fed. of Music Clubs, a Fulbright fellowship, Southern Fellowships Found. grant, Horace H. Rackham grant, and the first Sigvald Thompson composition award. He served on the faculty of Louisiana State Univ., 1954-55; Univ. of North Carolina at Greensboro, 1955-62; from 1962, at Univ. of Michigan.

WORKS: THEATRE MUSIC: incidental music for 3 television plays by Michael Casey: The story of Momotaro, The story of Esther, Ol' Fried Dragoman; Arnold Colbath's A crow in the heart; Bertholt Brecht's Good Woman of Setzuan; ORCHESTRA: Theme and variations; Diptych for orchestra; CHAMBER MUSIC: duets, violin and viola; trumpet sonatina; 2 string quartets, 2 piano sonatas; cello sonata; CHORUS: Christmas cantata, women's choir and small orch.; SONGS: 8 Jewish folk songs; many other choral works, songs, organ pieces, and jazz arrangements.

1229 Traver Rd., Ann Arbor, MI 48105

ALLANBROOK, DOUGLAS PHILLIPS
b. Melrose, Mass., 1 Apr. 1921. Studied with Nadia Boulanger at the Longy School, 1939-40; then earned his B.A. at Harvard Univ. under Walter Piston; studied again with Boulanger in Paris, 1948-50. His awards include the John Knowles Paine fellowship of Harvard, 1948-50 and a Fulbright fellowship in Italy, 1950-52. He was faculty member, Peabody Cons., 1956-57, and has been a tutor at St. John's Coll., Annapolis, from 1952.

WORKS: OPERA: Ethan Frome, a lyric tragedy; Nightmare abbey, comic opera; ORCHESTRA: 6 symphonies (some of which are subtitled, #2 Elegy, #3 4 orchestral landscapes, #5 for brass quintet and orch was first performed in Annapolis on 20 Feb. 1977, #6 5 heroic attitudes); violin concerto; harpsichord concerto; CHAMBER MUSIC: Fantasy, violin and piano; A set of passions, violin and harpsichord; A game for two, piano and percussion; 4 string quartets; CHORUS: The seven last words, with soprano, baritone and orch.; Psalms 100 and 131, with organ; An American miscellany, a cappella; PIANO: 40 changes; 12 preludes for all seasons; Bagatelles; HARPSICHORD: 2 little sonatas; Fantasy; 5 studies in black

ALLEN, CREIGHTON

and white.
6 Revell St., Annapolis, MD 21401

ALLEN, CREIGHTON
b. Macon, Miss., 26 Mar. 1900; d. New York, 18 July, 1969. Studied with Ernest Hutcheson, Harold Bauer, and Rubin Goldmark at Juilliard School. He made his New York debut as pianist in 1927; settled in New York as teacher, pianist, and composer.
WORKS: ORCHESTRA: piano concerto; violin concerto; many songs and piano pieces.

ALLEN, JUDITH SHATIN. See SHATIN, JUDITH

ALLEN, PAUL HASTINGS
b. Hyde Park, Mass., 28 Nov. 1883; d. Boston, Mass., 28 Sept. 1952. Studied at Harvard Univ., B.A. 1903; and in Italy. He received the Paderewski prize for his Pilgrim symphony in 1910. During World War I, he served in the U.S. diplomatic corps in Italy, returning to Boston in 1920.
WORKS: OPERA: 12 operas, including O munasterio, 1911; Il filtro, 1912; Milda, 1913; The last of the Mohicans, 1916; Cleopatra, 1921; La piccola Figaro, 1931; all performed in Italy; ORCHESTRA: 2 symphonics; Serenade, 1928; Ex hocte, 1930; CHAMBER MUSIC: suite for chamber orch., 1928; Dans le nuit, 1928; 3 pieces, 1928; 4 string quartets; quartet for 2 clarinets, basset horn, bass clarinet; woodwind trio; also choral works, songs, several piano sonatas, many piano pieces.

ALLEN, ROBERT E.
b. Minneapolis, Minn., 1 Feb. 1920.
WORKS: CHAMBER MUSIC: string quartet; violin sonata; Partita, piano; Introduction, cello and piano; many choral works.
37 Charles St., New York, NY 10011

ALLGOOD, WILLIAM THOMAS
b. Raleigh, N.C., 28 Dec. 1939. Studied with Martin Mailman at East Carolina Univ.; with Ben Johnston at Univ. of Illinois; and with Emerson Myers at Catholic Univ. He has held faculty positions at Univ. of Illinois, 1965-66; Univ. of Maryland, 1966-69; from 1969, Western Michigan Univ.
WORKS: CHAMBER MUSIC: 2 woodwind quintets, 1964, 1965; brass quintet, 1964; trio for trumpet, bassoon, cello, 1964; MULTIMEDIA: Pentacycle, bassoon and tape, 1969; Vectors, tuba and electronic sounds, 1970; Music da camera, Repetitions, oboe, trumpet, string bass, percussion, tape, slides, film, 1971; anthem for choir and tape.
Western Michigan University, Kalamazoo, MI 49008

ALLISON, HOWARD K., II
b. Pittsburg, Kans., 19 Dec. 1948. Studied at Kansas State Coll., Illinois Wesleyan Univ., and Indiana Univ. From 1970 he has been music director and teacher, Bradford, Ill., Unit School District, and from 1972, director of the Curriculum Research Div., Music Materials Development Center.

WORKS: OPERA: an improvisational opera; ORCHESTRA: 3 symphonies; CHAMBER MUSIC: suite for solo clarinet; Evolution, bass trombone; works for strings, woodwinds, brasses, percussion; also choral works, songs, and piano pieces.

ALLISON, IRL
b. Warren, Tex., 8 Apr. 1896; d. Austin, Tex., 6 Sept. 1979. Studied at Baylor Univ., B.A., M.A.; Columbia Univ.; Univ. of Texas; Chicago Musical Coll.; and holds honorary doctorates from Hardin-Simmons Univ., Southwestern Cons. (Dallas), and Houston Cons. He served on the faculty of Rusk Coll., Montezuma Coll., and Hardin-Simmons Univ.; was president and founder of the Nat. Guild of Piano Teachers and the American Coll. of Musicians, 1929-70, and chief council of the Piano Guild USA, 1970-73. He wrote many songs and piano pieces, the latter chiefly educational.

ALLURED, DONALD E.
b. Lansing, Mich., 14 Sept. 1922. Studied at Alma Coll.; with Harold Friedell and Frederick Schlieder at the School of Sacred Music, Union Theological Seminary. His Fantasia for handbells won the Area II contest of the American Guild of English Handbell Ringers. He was organist-choirmaster in churches in Springfield, Ill., Fort Wayne, Ind., Lansing, Mich., Lake Charles, La., 1947-76; since then, has been full-time specialist in handbells as composer, conductor, and workshop leader.
WORKS: HANDBELLS: Listen to the bells; Rhapsody for bells; Bells ring the classics; Masterworks for bells; Concertante for bells and organ; Jubilate for bells, double choir; The celebration; Introduction and allegro; Don't let us be strangers, Lord, an anthem for choir and handbells; also Joyfully ring, a methods book.
P.O. Box 3091, Lake Charles, LA 70602

ALMAND, CLAUDE
b. Winnsboro, La., 1915; d. 1957. He was faculty member, Univ. of Louisiana, then dean, School of Music, Stetson Univ., Deland, Fla., to 1957. His compositions include The waste land, a symphony, 1940; piano concerto, 1949; John Gilbert: a steamboat overture, performed by the Louisville, Ky., Philharmonic Orch., 1949.

ALTER, MARTHA
b. New Bloomfield, Pa., 1904; d. Newport, Pa. Studied at Vassar Coll.; with Seth Bingham, Columbia Univ.; Bernard Rogers, Eastman School of Music; and with Rubin Goldmark. Awards include several fellowships and a Vassar publication grant. She taught at Vassar and at Connecticut Coll.
WORKS: OPERA: Groceries and notions, 3-act operetta; BALLET: Anthony Comstock; ORCHESTRA: Bric-a-brac suite; Rhythmic dance; also chamber music and choral works.

AMATO, BRUNO
b. Hartford, Conn., 21 Oct. 1936. Studied at Univ. of Hartford, B.M. 1958; Manhattan School of Music, MM. 1963; Acad. Naz. di Santa Cecilia,

dipl. 1967; Princeton Univ., M.F.A. 1969, Ph.D. 1973. His teachers were Arnold Franchetti, Goffredo Petrassi, Milton Babbitt, Edward Cone, Peter Westergaard, Gunther Schuller, Luciano Berio. His awards include the Premio d'Atri; Koussevitzky award, 1969; Sinfonia Found. awards, 1969, 1970; Fulbright grant; Tanglewood, MacDowell, Princeton, and NDEA fellowships; and commissions. He was faculty member, Ball State Univ., 1970-71; Indiana Univ., 1971-78; then at California State Univ., Fullerton.

WORKS: THEATER: incidental meusic to It should happen to a dog, Wolf Mankowitz, 1967; ORCHESTRA: Andante and scherzo, 1960; Compound, 1965; Bells and buttercups, with soprano solo, 1967; Aria, strings, 1969; Tiny Tin, children's story with narrator, 1969; Tiny suite, children's orch., 1970; Canticle, with narrator, 1972; Canticle variations, 1972; Larghetto, strings, 1973; Psalmody, antiphonal orchestras, 1976; CHAMBER MUSIC: 2 string quartets, 1958, 1966; 4 love songs, soprano and string trio, 1960; woodwind quartet, 1960; string quintet, 1961; piano sonata, 1964; 3 canzoni, brass quintet, 1965; Divertimento, 3 flutes, 1966; Study, chamber orch., 1966; Frequencies, flute, clarinet, piano trio, 1968; Soliloquy I, violin, 1968; Chinese love lyrics, tenor, chamber ensemble, 1969; Basses and brass, 1969; Soliloquy II, viola, 1969-72; 2 together, soprano and tuba, 1971; Alleluia, 6 horns, 1972; Music for Emily, soprano and brass quintet, 1972; Soliloquy III, cello, 1973; 5 bagatelles, tenor saxophone and piano, 1973; Hommage, organ, 1973; Pezzetto, 3 tubas, 1973; saxophone quartet, 1973; many choral works and songs.

  California State University, Fullerton, CA 92634

AMES, ROGER
  b. Cooperstown, N.Y., 2 Dec. 1944. Studied at Crane School of Music, Potsdam, N.Y.; Hartt Coll. of Music; American Univ.; composition teachers were Samuel Barber, Carlisle Floyd, Robert Washburn, Lloyd Ultan, and Ezra Laderman. His awards have included 2 grants from Nat. Endowment for the Arts; an Exxon workshop grant; American Univ. fellowship; New York State Regents graduate fellowship; various college scholarships. He was music director in 2 New York State school systems, 1967-72; composer-in-residence, West-moreland Church, Washington, D.C., 1972-78; artistic director, Masterworks Chorus, 1975-78, and Washington Madrigal Singers, 1975-76; music director, Street 70 Theater Ensemble, 1974-78.

WORKS: THEATRE: Magical touch, musical play, 1976; Amistad, opera in 2 acts, 1978; VOICE: Thanksgiving mass, chorus, 1974; 5 American folk songs, 1976; 4 songs on Edna St. Vincent Millay texts, 1976; Mass for all saints, oratorio, 1978; various smaller choral works and vocal chamber music.

  Kierbergerstrasse 15, 5 Köln 51, West Germany

AMES, WILLIAM T.
  b. Cambridge, Mass., 20 Mar. 1901. Studied at Harvard Univ., A.B. 1924; with Nadia Boulanger in Paris. He was appointed instructor at

Eastman School of Music in 1938.
  WORKS: ORCHESTRA: Rhapsody; 2 symphonies; CHAMBER MUSIC: violin sonata; cello sonata; 2 string quartets; piano quintet; clarinet quintet; piano sonata; also choral music, songs, many piano pieces.

  147 Tinker St., Woodstock, NY 12498

AMFITHEATROF, DANIELE
  b. St. Petersburg, Russia, 29 Oct. 1901; U.S. citizen 1944. Studied with Joseph Wihtol in St. Petersburg; with Jaroslav Krichka in Prague; and with Ottorino Respighi in Rome. He was assistant conductor, Augusteo Symphony, Rome, 1924-29; music director, Italian Broadcasting Corp., 1929-37; assistant conductor, Minneapolis Symphony, 1938-41; then settled in Hollywood as a film composer.

WORKS: ORCHESTRA: Poeme del mare, 1925; Miracolo delle rose, 1927; American panorama, 1934; FILM SCORES: Lassie come home; Letters from an unknown woman; Another part of the forest; O.S.S.; The fan; Major Dundee; also chamber music and songs.

  75 via Valle della Muletta, Casale S. Nicola, La Storta, 00123 Rome, Italy

AMIRKHANIAN, CHARLES BENJAMIN
  b. Fresno, Calif., 19 Jan. 1945. Is autodidact as a composer. He was commissioned by the Swedish Radio and Fylkingen Society in 1972 to produce text-sound pieces in Stockholm, and commissioned in 1973 by the Connimicut Found. for text-sound peices in Berkeley, Calif. In 1968-69 he was music director of Dancers Workshop Company, San Francisco; from 1969, music director of KPFA-FM, Pacific Radio, Berkeley. With 2 visual artists and a poet, he organized in 1975 a group called Mugicians Union; and in 1977, was named to the faculty of the Interdisciplinary Creative Arts Dept., San Francisco State Univ.

WORKS: Compositions no. 1, 2, 3, 4, & 5, for solo amplified rachets, 1965-67; Symphony 1 for viola, 3 trumpets, trombone, clarinet, piano, and 4 percussionists playing over 200 noninstruments, mobile stage, and electronics, 1965; Mooga Pook, 1968, and Bake and Eeet, 1969, are visual transduction scores for performance in any medium or combination of media; Words, 1-hour text-sound work; Data, for 2 voices, 1979; other text-sound pieces, all composed on tape: Spoffy nene, 1970; Oratora Konkurso rezulto: Autoro de la jaro (an Esperanto portrait of Lou Harrison), 1970; If in is, 1971; Sound nutrition, 1972; Dzarin Bess Ga Khorim, 1972; Heavy aspirations (portrait of Nicolas Slonimsky), 1973; Seatbelt seatbelt, 1973; MUGIC, 1973; Muchrooms, 1974; Beemsterboer, 1975; Mahogany ballpark, 1976; Dutiful ducks, 1977.

  1639 Curtis St., Berkeley, CA 94702

AMOS, THOMAS EARL
  b. Orange, Calif., 28 July 1948. Studied at Chapman Coll.; with Alan Chaplin at Calif. Inst. of the Arts; Lloyd Rodgers and Nicolas Slonimsky at California State Univ. at Fullerton, M.A. 1978. He was teaching assistant at C.S.U., Fullerton, 1976-78, then studied with Boguslaw

AMRAM, DAVID

Schaeffer in Krakow, Poland.
WORKS: ORCHESTRA: Cleopatre, 1978; WIND
ENSEMBLE: Ohio hunt, 6 tenor trombones, 2 bass
trombones, 1977; CHAMBER MUSIC: Ennui flaire,
string trio, 1975; Collette d'Espagna, 4 players
on winds, keyboards and percussion, 1977; Nash's
zoo, 14 poems by Ogden Nash set for mezzo-
soprano, tenor, piano, 1976.

AMRAM, DAVID
b. Philadelphia, Pa., 17 Nov. 1930. Learned
piano, trumpet, and horn at an early age; then,
while an undergraduate at George Washington
Univ., served as extra horn with the National
Symphony. On graduation he entered the U.S.
Army and was assigned to play horn with the 7th
Army Symph. Orch. in Germany. On return to the
U.S., he studied with Vittorio Giannini at
Manhattan School of Music, 1955-56. He was
musical director of the New York Shakespeare
Festival, 1956-68; and in 1967, was composer-in-
residence with the New York Philharmonic and
also made his New York debut as a conductor.
His appointments as composer-in-residence have
been many, and in 1976 he received the Composer's
award of the Lancaster Symph. Orch.
WORKS: OPERA: The final ingredient, 1 act,
premiere on ABC-TV network, 11 April 1965;
Twelfth night, text adapted from Shakespeare by
Joseph Papp, Lake George Opera Festival, 1 Aug.
1968; INCIDENTAL MUSIC: The rivalry, 1959;
Kataki, 1959; After the fall, play by Arthur
Miller; Far Rockaway, play by Frank D. Gilroy;
Heracles and J.D., plays by Archibald MacLeish;
and some 30 Shakespearean plays; ORCHESTRA:
King Lear variations, wind symphony, 1967; The
American bell, with narrator; Autobiography for
strings; Elegy, violin and orch.; bassoon concerto; horn concerto; Shakespearean concerto,
oboe, 2 horns, strings; triple concerto, woodwind
quintet, brass quintet, jazz quintet, and orch.,
New York, 10 Jan. 1971; The trail of beauty,
mezzo-soprano, oboe, orch., Philadelphia, 3 Mar.
1977; En memoriam de Chano Pozo, Davenport,
Iowa, 7 May 1978; violin concerto, St. Louis,
2 May 1981; CHAMBER MUSIC: Dirge and
variations, piano trio; Discussions, flute, cello,
percussion, piano; Overture and allegro, flute
solo; Zohar, alto recorder and flute; The wind
and the rain, viola and piano; 3 songs for
Marlboro, horn and cello; 3 songs for America,
bass voice with piano or string quintet and 4
woodwinds; Fanfare and processional, brass quintet; piano sonata; solo violin sonata; violin
sonata; string quartet; trio for saxophone, horn,
bassoon; wind quintet; Portraits, piano and
string trio, New York, 18 Jan. 1976; Native
American portraits, violin, piano, percussion,
on Indian themes, Washington, 7 May 1977;
CHORUS: A year in our land, cantata, New York,
13 May 1965; By the rivers of Babylon, women's
voices; Let us remember, with soli and orch.;
Shir L'Erev Shabat, with solo tenor and organ;
The passion of Joseph D. by Paddy Chayefsky,
soli, chorus a cappella; FILM SCORES: Splendor
in the grass; The Manchurian candidate; Pull my
daisy; The arrangement; also many jazz scores.
His autobiography, Vibrations: The adventures
and musical times of David Amram was published

in New York in 1968.
c/o Ostertag, 501 5th Ave., New York, NY
10017

ANDERSEN, ARTHUR OLAF
b. Newport, R.I., 30 Jan. 1880; d. Tucson, Ariz.,
11 Jan. 1958. Studied at American Cons.,
honorary D.M.; with Vincent d'Indy and Alexandre
Guilmant in Paris; with Durra in Berlin; and
with Sgambati in Rome. His faculty posts included American Cons., 1908-33; dean, Coll. of
Fine Arts and head, composition department, Univ.
of Arizona, 1934-50. He was author of books on
harmony, counterpoint, and orchestration, and a
contributor to music journals.
WORKS: THEATRE: Arizona hi-ho, 3-act
operetta; music for The jade bracelet; ORCHESTRA:
symphony; suite for strings; BAND: 4 marches;
WIND ENSEMBLE: Arizona sketches 1 and 2, brass
ensemble; CHAMBER MUSIC: 3 string quartets; 3
string trios; piano trio; 2 woodwind quintets;
quartet for flute and strings; numerous pieces
for violin and piano, etc., songs and vocal duets.

ANDERSEN, MICHAEL
b. Los Angeles, Calif., 26 Jan. 1938. Studied
with Ingolf Dahl, Halsey Stevens, and Miklos
Rozsa, Univ. of Southern California. He held
the Alchin fellowship at the university.
WORKS: ORCHESTRA: trumpet concerto; concert overture; 7 songs for voice and orch.; WIND
ENSEMBLE: Music for brass; CHAMBER MUSIC:
Variations on a Gregorian theme, violin and piano;
viola sonata; suite for solo viola; Serenade, 2
flutes; string quartet; 3 piano sonatinas; FILM
SCORES: The Tower of London; Wings of chance;
12 to the moon; The runaway.
17631 Kittridge, Van Nuys, CA 91406

ANDERSON, ADRIAN DAVID
b. Palo Alto, Calif., 27 Dec. 1952. Studied with
Richard Feliciano, San Francisco Cons.; with
David Del Tredici, Boston Univ.; and with
Gottfried Koenig, Inst. for Sonology, Holland.
His awards include an ASCAP grant, 1980; finalist, Politist Internat. Comp., 1980; finalist,
Mass. Arts Council fellowship program, 1980,
1981; MacDowell Colony residence, 1981.
WORKS: CHAMBER MUSIC: Embryon, chamber
orch. and 6 voices, 1980; Ki Arcana, chamber
orch.; string quartet, Boston, 17 Feb. 1981.
22 Ortalon Ave., Santa Cruz, CA 95060

ANDERSON, BETH
b. Lexington, Ky., 3 Jan. 1950. Studied at Univ.
of Kentucky, 1966-68; Univ. of California at
Davis, B.A. 1971; Mills Coll., M.F.A. in piano
1973, M.A. in composition 1974; New York Univ.,
Ph.D. candidate 1977-78. Her composition
teachers have included John Barnes Chance, Helen
Lipscomb, Kenneth Wright, Richard Swift, John
Cage, Larry Austin, and Terry Riley. Awards
include Elizabeth Mills Crothers awards, 1972,
1974; Nat. Endowment for the Arts grant, 1975;
Meet the Composer grants, 1976, 1977; Nat. Fed.
of Music Clubs award, 1977; and several commissions. She taught in the Mills Coll. preparatory program, 1971-73, and was at the time co-

editor and copublisher of EAR magazine; then moved to New York, established an East Coast publication of EAR, and has held various positions as teacher and accompanist.

WORKS: OPERA: Queen Christina, Mills Coll., 1 Dec. 1973; ORATORIO: Joan, Cabrillo Festival, 22 Aug. 1974; VARIOUS ENSEMBLES: Music for Charlemagne Palestine, 1973, string quartet; I am uh am I, string quartet, 1973; Tower of power, organ and tape, 1973; Recital piece, piano and tape, 1973; Good-bye Bridget Bardot or Hello Charlotte Moorman, cello and tape, 1974; Peachy Keen-o, 4 instrumentalists, voices, dancers, lights, tape, 1973; Tulip clause, tape, organ, 7 instruments, 1973; They did it, piano and tape, 1975-76; and many text-sound pieces and songs.

26 2nd Ave., #2B, New York, NY 10003

ANDERSON, DENNIS
b. Duluth, Minn., 2 Aug. 1951. Studied with Donal Michalsky and Lloyd Rodgers, California State Univ., Fullerton; with George Cacioppo, Curtis Curtis-Smith, George Wilson, and William Albright, Univ. of Michigan. In 1978 he received a Fulbright-Hays grant and a Polish govt. grant for study in Krakow, Poland.

WORKS: Chiefly percussion, alone or with other instruments, voices, or other media: Voices in the chromium sunrise, tape, human voice sounds, dance; Shadow fantasy, harp and percussion; Aurora borealis, 4 marimbas; A.M. negative, saxophone, percussion, tape; Heroes and martyrs/lament on the death of Arabella, percussion and slides; also improvisational pieces.

2152 Tremmel, Ann Arbor, MI 48105

ANDERSON, GARLAND
b. Union City, Ohio, 10 June 1933. Studied with Hans Gal at Univ. of Edinburgh; with Roy Harris at Indiana Univ.; piano with Joseph Battista and Michel Bourgeot. His awards include several commissions and a grant from the Nat. Endowment for the Arts. He is active as a pianist and also contributes articles and music criticism to music journals.

WORKS: OPERA: Soyazhe, 1 act, set in a Navajo village, libretto by Jamie Lee Cooper, 1977, premiere, Central City (Colo.) Opera Festival, 28 July 1979; ORCHESTRA: piano concerto, Richmond, Ind., 28 Apr. 1968; piano concertino, Richmond, Ind., 9 Feb. 1969, composer at the piano; piano concertino, commissioned by the Richmond Symph. Orch. as a contest piece for children under 12; Symphony for saxophones; We, the dreamers, oratorio, chorus, tenor solo, orch., 1975; CHAMBER MUSIC: 2 sonatas for alto saxophone, 1967, 1978; violin sonata, 1964; Elegy, violin, 1965; Sarabande, tenor saxophone and piano, 1967; saxophone quartet; sonata for baritone saxophone, 1973; also piano pieces, choral works, and songs.

316 N. Mulberry St., #305, Muncie, IN 47305

ANDERSON, JAY
b. New Haven, Conn., 9 Sept. 1920. Studied at Longy School of Music. Her compositions are chiefly vocal works: Softly, softly fell the

snow, women's voices; Echo below, medium solo voice and piano; Song in the mist, etc.

389 Kailua Rd., #201, Kailua, HI 96734

ANDERSON, LAURIE
b. Chicago, Ill., 5 June 1947. Studied at Barnard Coll., B.A.; at Columbia Univ., M.F.A. in sculpture 1972. Her awards include CAPS grants, 1974, 1977; ZBS Media Residency, 1975; Nat. Endowment for the Arts grants 1975, 1977. She has been lecturer in New York colleges and an art reviewer.

WORKS: LIVE/TAPE: For instants part 10, performed in Houston, 1978; For instants part 11, performed Los Angeles; For instants part 12, in Berlin, Basel, and Geneva; Like a stream, St. Paul Chamber Orchestra, 1978; Time to go for guitar, violin, and organ, is the exhortation of a museum guard to visitors to leave at closing time; New York social is a satire for voice and tamboura; in It's not the bullet that kills you--(It's the hole), the singer is required to shoot himself in the arm. Ms. Anderson uses audio tapes and tape heads in individualistic ways. The bridge on one violin is replaced with a tape head and the bow hair with a tape on which words and phrases have been recorded. A speaker mounted in the violin body reproduces the words as the bow is drawn across the tape head (forward and backward).

530 Canal St., New York, NY 10013

ANDERSON, LEROY
b. Cambridge, Mass., 29 June 1908; d. Woodbury, Conn., 18 May 1975. Studied at New England Cons. and Harvard Univ., B.A. magna cum laude 1929, M.A. 1930, with teachers Spalding, Ballantine, Heilman, Hill, Enesco, and Piston. He was a tutor in music at Radcliffe Coll., 1930-32; director of the Harvard Univ. Band, 1931-35; organist and choir director in Milton, Mass., 1929-35. From 1931 he was also frequently guest conductor of the Boston Pops and other orchestras. Almost all his sophisticated, witty, and expertly orchestrated works have been arranged for band, symphonic band, solo instruments, and small ensembles.

WORKS: Alma mater, Arietta, Balladette, Belle of the ball, Blue bells of Scotland, Blue tango, Bugler's holiday, The captains and the kings, Chicken reel, China doll, Christmas day, A Christmas festival, Clarinet candy, Fiddle-faddle, The first day of spring, Forgotten dreams, The girl I left behind me, The girl in satin, Goldilocks (musical comedy, New York, 11 Oct. 1958), The golden years, Home stretch, Horse and buggy, Irish suite, Irish washerwoman, Jazz legato, Jazz pizzicato, The minstrel boy, Penny whistle song, The phantom regiment, Plink, plank, plunk!, Promenade, The rakes of Mallow, Sandpaper ballet, Sarabande, Serenata, Sleigh ride, Song of Jupiter, Song of the bells, Suite of carols, Summer skies, The syncopated clock, Ticonderoga march, A trumpeter's lullaby, Turn you to me, The typewriter, The waltzing cat.

ANDERSON, RUTH
b. Kalispell, Mont., 21 Mar. 1928. Studied at

ANDERSON, THOMAS JEFFERSON, JR.

Univ. of Washington, B.A. magna cum laude 1949, M.A. 1951; Manhattan School of Music, 1952; Mannes Coll. of Music., 1953-55; Princeton Univ. Graduate School (first woman admitted) 1962-63; Columbia Univ. Electronic Music Studio, 1965, 1966, 1969; New York Univ. Computer Synthesis of Music, 1967; private study with Darius Milhaud and Nadia Boulanger; flute with John Wummer and Jean-Pierre Rampal. Awards include Huntington Hartford composers grant, 1951; American Composers Alliance grant, 1956; Rockefeller grant, 1957; 2 Fulbright awards, 1958-60; MacDowell Colony fellowships, 1957-73; Ingraham-Merrill grants, 1963-64; Yaddo fellowship, 1969; Research Found. of CUNY grant, 1974. She was flutist with Totenberg Instrumental Ensemble, 1951-58, and with Boston Pops Orch., 1958; orchestrator, under name of Robert Russell Bennett, NBC-TV, 1960-66, at Lincoln Center, 1966; faculty member at Hunter Coll. from 1966; and director of the Electronic Music Studio from 1969.
    WORKS: CHAMBER MUSIC: Fugue for piano; 2 pieces for strings; 2 movements for strings; The merchant's song, contralto and piano; TAPE AND MIXED MEDIA: Dump, tape collage; SUM (State of the Union message) tape collage of TV commercials; Ma Belle, tape; Veils, piano and tape; Christmas oratorio, (Auden), chorus, small orch., actors, dancers, 4 portable audio speakers; LL (Bogan), tape; EF, tape; Sappho (Lardos), tape; Points, multichannel electronic sound built entirely on sine waves, 1974; The pregnant dream (Swenson), tape; Silent sound, 1978; Sound portraits I-II; Centering through sound; Sound environment, a sound installation, 1975.
    Baron de Hirsch Rd., Crompond, NY 10517

ANDERSON, THOMAS JEFFERSON, JR.
    b. Coatesville, Pa., 17 Aug. 1928. Studied at West Virginia State Coll., B.M. 1950; Pennsylvania State Univ., M.Ed. 1951; Univ. of Iowa, Ph.D. 1958; also composition with Scott Huston, 1954, Philip Bezanson and Darius Milhaud, 1964. His honors include 4 MacDowell fellowships; Copley Found. award; 2 Fromm Found. awards; 2 Yaddo fellowships; chairman of honorary advisory committe, Black Music Center, Indiana Univ., 1970-71; Nat. Endowment for the Arts grant, 1974; lecturer for U.S. State Dept. in Brazilian universities, 1976; and many commissions. Before becoming chairman of the music dept., Tufts Univ., he held faculty positions at Morehouse Coll., Tennessee State Univ., Langston Univ., West Virginia State Univ., and was composer-in-residence, Atlanta Symphony Orchestra, 1970-72. He was codirector with Wendell Whalum of the Afro-American Music Workshop, Morehouse Coll., which presented the premiere of Scott Joplin's opera, Treemonisha, in Jan. 1972. The opera was orchestrated by Anderson and coedited by Anderson and William Bolcom.
    WORKS: OPERETTA: The shell fairy, 1976; ORCHESTRA: New dances, 1960; Trio concertante, 1960; Classical symphony, 1961; 6 pieces for clarinet and chamber orch., 1962; symphony in 3 movements, in memory of J. F. K., 1964; Squares, 1965; Chamber symphony, 1969; In memoriam Zack Walker, 1969; Intervals, 1971;

Horizons '76, soprano and orch., 1976; CHAMBER MUSIC: Connections, string quintet, 1968; Transitions, chamber ensemble, 1971; Minstrel man, bass trombone; Block songs, soprano and children's toys, 1972, premiere, Cambridge, 13 Apr. 1976; Variations on a theme by M. B. Tolson, soprano and chamber ensemble, 1972; Swing set, clarinet and piano, 1972; Beyond silence, chamber ensemble, 1973; 5 easy pieces, violin, piano, Jew's harp, 1974; CHORUS: Personals, cantata for chorus, narrator, and brass ensemble; PIANO: 5 bagatelles, 1963; 5 portraitures of 2 people, piano 4 hands, 1965; Watermelon, 1971.
    34 Grove St., Winchester, MA 01890

ANDREW, DAVID S.
    b. Detroit, Mich., 13 July 1943. Studied at Univ. of Michigan with Ross Lee Finney, Leslie Bassett, and George Cacioppo; was Ph.D. candidate, Washington Univ., 1973. He received the Founders' award of the Society of Architectural Historians in 1973. In 1968-71 he was instructor, dept. of fine arts, Univ. of Detroit.
    WORKS: CHAMBER MUSIC: Sins, piano 4 hands, 1966; DMZ, 3 pianists and winds, 1966; String music no. 1, 12 strings, 1969; ELECTRONIC: Revival meeting, tape and film, 1965; Flying saucers have landed, film, tape, and actors, 1966; Cross country, film, tape, and actors, 1971.

ANDREWS, BRUCE
    b. Chicago, Ill., 1 Apr. 1948. Studied at Johns Hopkins Univ., B.A., M.A.; and at Harvard Univ. He has published poetry in books and magazines; in addition, writes vocal and performance scores going a step beyond Gertrude Stein in stress on nonreferential characteristics and ordering of language, e.g., foregrounding the musical elements of discrete language units as sound for live performance or tape. Rather than setting poetry to music in the traditional sense, he selects words according to sound and object-like qualities, and then further underplays the referents by specification of pitch, tempi, duration, volume, etc., use of indeterminacy, multiple voices, accompaniment, movement, theatre, tape installations.
    WORKS: MULTIMEDIA: Love songs No. 1-174.
    41 W. 96th St., Apt. 100, New York, NY 10025

ANDREWS, CARROLL THOMAS
    b. Milwaukee, Wis., 27 Oct. 1918. Attended Albertus Magnus Coll., Racine, Wis., B.M. magna cum laude 1946; Univ. of Montreal, licentiate in music summa cum laude 1947. He was church music director in Toledo, 1964-65, and also guest teacher at Gregorian Inst. of America. In 1965 he became music director for the Diocese of St. Augustine, Fla., and later of St. Petersburg, Fla. His compositons include numerous masses with Latin texts and English texts; many anthems and other choral works; works for organ; piano pieces; 35 pieces for tower chimes.
    2151 Norfolk St. N., St. Petersburg, FL 33710

ANDREWS, GEORGE
b. Winnipeg, Manitoba, 24 Jan. 1927; U.S. citizen
1957. After attending Tufts Univ. and Berklee
Coll. of Music, Boston, he studied in California
with Nelson Keyes, Halsey Stevens, and Donal
Michalsky, taking his degrees (B.A. 1966, M.A.
1967) at California State Univ., Fullerton. A
free-lance composer and arranger from 1952, he
was also a school music director, 1966-73, and
conductor, South Bay Chamber Players, 1973-.
    WORKS: ORCHESTRA: Symphonic variations,
1972; BRASS CHOIR: brass sextet, 1966; music
for 3 brass quintets, 1973; CHAMBER MUSIC: duet
for clarinet and cello, 1966; 3 songs for chamber
chorus, 1967; piano trio, 1969; string quartet,
1971; suite for unaccompanied cello, 1972.
    3810 Shad Pl., San Pedro, CA 90732

ANDREWS, MARK
b. Gainesborough, Lincolnshire, England, 21 Mar.
1875; to U.S. 1905; d. Montclair, N.J., 10 Dec.
1939. Studied with John Thomas Ruch at Westminster Abbey, London. On coming to the U.S., he
was church organist and choirmaster in Montclair,
N.J., and was a member of the examining committee
of the American Guild of Organists.
    WORKS: CHAMBER MUSIC: string quartet; 2
organ sonatas; CHORUS: Galilee, cantata; The
highwayman, cantata; also sacred and secular
songs.

ANDRIX, GEORGE
b. Chicago, Ill., 15 June 1932. Studied at Univ.
of Illinois with Burrill Phillips and Robert
Palmer; at Trinity Coll. of Music, London, with
Richard Arnell and Matyas Seiber. He was on the
faculty of Ithaca Coll., N.Y., 1960-67, Morehead
State Univ., Ky., 1967-68; and is violinist and
conductor.
    WORKS: 5 pieces for orchestra; CHAMBER
MUSIC: sonata for percussion, 2 players; 5
perspectives, percussion, 6 players; Free forms,
bass trombone and strings; Miniatures, solo
trumpet; 5 pieces, violin and percussion; 14
duets, violin and viola; brass quintet; other
owrks for brass and mixed ensembles and for solo
instruments.
    The Fourth Estate, Dayton, MT 59914

ANDRUS, DONALD GEORGE
b. Seattle, Wash., 13 Sept. 1935. Studied at
Western Washington State Coll., B.A. 1957; with
John Verrall, Univ. of Washington, M.A. 1960;
with Gordon Binkerd, Kenneth Gaburo, and Lejaren
Hiller, Univ. of Illinois, D.M.A. 1968. His
awards include Univ. of Washington composition
award, 1960, and a Fulbright grant for study in
Utrecht, 1963-64. He was faculty member, Univ.
of Illinois, 1966-68; from 1968, at California
State Univ., Long Beach.
    WORKS: Orchestra piece #1; CHAMBER MUSIC:
piano quintet, 1959; Imbrications for 4 performers; VOICE: 6 songs, soprano, viola, piano;
ELECTRONIC: sound tape for Shakespeare's Macbeth,
1964; Psssh, tape, 1964; Deciduata, 4 choruses
and electronics, 1974; The aardvark shuffle,
string bass and electronics, 1974, rev. 1979;
Space dust with bird?, 4-channel tape, 1977;

Undersøkelser (Researches), bass flute and electronics, 1977, 1978.
    21516 Encina Rd., Topanga, CA 90290

ANGELINI, LOUIS A.
b. Utica, N.Y., 13 June 1935. Studied with
Warren Benson, Ithaca Coll.; with Bernard
Rogers and Howard Hanson, Eastman School of
Music; with Witold Lutoslawski and Lucas Foss at
Berkshire Music Center; with Luigi Nono and
Franco Evangelisti in Italy. His awards include
the Koussevitzky prize at Berkshire Music Center;
a Fulbright scholarship for Italy; Contemporary
Music Project fellowship, 1967-69; Utica Coll.
faculty grants for composition. He taught at
East Texas State Univ., 1966-67; from 1969, at
Utica Coll. of Syracuse Univ.
    WORKS: ORCHESTRA: Festive music; Poems and
dances, with narrator; 2 graphs, for strings;
Composition plan for orch.; Baroque adagio and
allegro for strings; BAND: Evocation, winds and
percussion; Composition plan for band; CHAMBER
MUSIC: Adagio and rondo, violin and piano;
Fantasy, flute and piano; woodwind sextet;
Ostinato improvisation, ensemble; The blue
winged sun ghost, ensemble; The songs between us,
piano, trumpet, bass, percussion; A way of
happening, small ensemble; 4 pieces, violin;
Silver fountain, flute; CHORUS: Buffalo Bill's,
double chorus, e. e. cummings text; Hosanna,
double chorus; A gift of peace and joy; Do not go
gentle into that good night; Festive mass;
SONGS: Scenes, soprano, guitar, percussion;
Time kaleidoscopes, voices and instruments;
Dairy of a teenage rock star; Songs of Nod,
voice and flute; mixed media pieces.
    Snowden Hill Rd., New Hartford, NY 13413

ANGELL, WARREN M.
b. Brooklyn, N.Y., 13 May 1907. Studied at
Syracuse Univ., B.M., M.M.; Columbia Univ.,
Ed.D.; Eastman School of Music; piano in Vienna.
His honors include 3 ASCAP awards, and in 1956,
the college of which he is dean was named
Warren M. Angell Coll. of Fine Arts; in 1973
Governor Bond of Missouri proclaimed 29 March as
Dr. Warren M. Angell Day. After 2 years as head
of the piano dept. at Murray State Coll., Ky.,
1934-36, he went to Oklahoma Baptist Univ. as
dean. He has published 5 books on vocal and
choral techniques and has more than 53 published
compositions in the choral field, 4 published
piano pieces, many choral arrangements, and unpublished vocal and instrumental works.
    1920 N. Bell, Shawnee, OK 74801

ANTHEIL, GEORGE
b. Trenton, N.J., 8 July 1900; d. New York, N.Y.,
12 Feb. 1959. Studied with Constantine von
Sternberg, Ernest Bloch, and Clark Smith in
Philadelphia. From 1920 to 1936 he played concerts of his piano works and presented his
ballets and orchestral works in Europe and New
York; then settled in Hollywood.
    WORKS: OPERA: Transatlantic, 1929; Helen
retires, 1933; Volpone, 1952; The brothers,
1953; The wish, 1954; BALLET: Ballet mechanique,
1924, required 8 pianos, an airplane propeller,

ANTONINI, ALFREDO

sirens, and other unorthodox instruments, was
performed in New York, 1927; <u>The capitol of the
world</u>, 1953; ORCHESTRA: <u>Zingareska</u>, 1921;
6 symphonies, 1926, 1937, 1942, 1943, 1947, 1948;
violin concerto, 1946; CHAMBER MUSIC: 3 string
quartets; 4 violin sonatas; 4 piano sonatas;
concerto for flute, bassoon, and piano; chamber
concerto for 8 instruments; violin sonatina;
<u>Serenade for strings</u>; <u>Crucifixion</u>, strings;
CHORUS: <u>Cabeza de vaca</u>, cantata, CBS television,
10 June 1962; FILM SCORES: <u>Once in a blue moon</u>;
<u>Angels over Broadway</u>; <u>The plainsman</u>; <u>We were
strangers</u>; <u>In a lonely place</u>; <u>The buccaneer</u>;
<u>Spectre of the rose</u>. He wrote an autobiography:
<u>Bad boy of music</u>, New York, 1945.

ANTONINI, ALFREDO
b. Italy, 31 May 1901; U.S. citizen 1938.
Studied at the Royal Cons., Milan, where he
earned degrees in composition, organ, and choral
work. He was accompanist, conductor, WOR, New
York; music director, CBS Television; chairman,
music dept., St. John's Univ., Brooklyn; guest
conductor of many orchestras in U.S., Canada,
and Europe; from 1957, music director, Tampa
Philharmonic.
    WORKS: ORCHESTRA: <u>Sicilian rhapsody</u>; suite
for cello and orch.; <u>La vida</u>; <u>Mexican sketches</u>;
<u>American sketches</u>; suite for strings; also film
scores.

ANTONIOU, THEODORE
b. Athens, Greece, 10 Feb. 1938. Studied violin,
voice, and composition at the Nat. Cons., 1947-
58; at Hellenic Cons., 1958-41; Hochschule fur
Musik, Munich, and Siemens Studio for Electronic
Music with J. A. Riedle, 1961-65; attended
Internat. Courses for New Music, Darmstadt,
1963-66. His awards include composition prizes
from Hellenic Cons., 1961; Athens Tech. Inst.,
1962; City of Munich, 1964; City of Stuttgart,
1966; Greek Ministry of Education, 1967; Premio
Ondas, 1970; Koussevitzky prize, 1972; 2 Nat.
Endowment for the Arts grants, 1975, 1977;
Guggenheim fellowship, 1979. While still a
student, he edited the works of his compatriot,
Nikos Skalkottas, 1959-61. In 1967 he was
director of the Athens Symph. Orch. and of the
Hellenic Group for Contemporary Music. After a
year in Berlin by invitation of the city, he
came to the U.S. and was composer-in-residence
and visiting professor of composition at
Stanford Univ., where he also founded the
Stanford new music ensemble, Alea II. At
Tanglewood in 1969, he received a commission
from the Boston Symphony and the Fromm Found.
for his work <u>Events II</u>. He spent 1970 as composer-in-residence at the Univ. of Utah, then
became professor at Philadelphia Coll. of the
Performing Arts until 1979, when he joined the
faculty at Boston Univ. From 1974 he has also
been assistant director of contemporary activities
at Tanglewood.
    WORKS: ORCHESTRA: concertino, piano,
strings, percussion, 1961; <u>Melos</u>, medium voice
and orch., 1962; <u>Antitheses</u>, 1962; concertino,
piano winds, percussion, 1963; <u>Jeux</u>, cello and

strings, 1963; <u>Micrographs</u>, 1964; violin concerto, 1965; <u>Kinesis ABCD</u>, 2 groups of strings,
1966; <u>Op overture</u>, with tape, 1966; <u>Events I</u>,
violin, piano and orch., 1967-68; <u>Climate of
absence</u>, voice and orch., 1968; <u>Chorochronos II</u>,
1973; <u>Fluxus I</u>, 1974-75; <u>Circle of accusation</u>,
1975; percussion concerto, 1977; CHAMBER MUSIC:
<u>Epilogue</u>, mezzo-soprano, narrator, chamber
ensemble, 1963; <u>Quartetto giocoso</u>, oboe, violin,
cello, piano, 1965; <u>6 likes</u>, solo tuba, 1967;
<u>Lyrics</u>, violin and piano, 1967; <u>5 likes</u>, solo
oboe, 1969; <u>4 likes</u>, solo violin, 1972; <u>3 likes</u>,
solo clarinet, 1973; <u>Fluxus II</u>, piano and
chamber orch., 1975; <u>Stichomythia</u>, flute and
guitar, 1976; <u>2 likes</u>, solo contrabass, 1976;
<u>Stichomythia II</u>, solo guitar, 1977; <u>The do quin-
tet</u>, brass, 1978; CHORUS: <u>Kontakion</u>, soloists,
choir, strings, 1965; <u>Nenikikamen</u>, cantata composed on the marathon runners' victory shout,
1971; <u>Verlein Uns Frieden</u>, 3 choirs a cappella,
1972; <u>Die Weisse Rose</u>, boys' choir, chorus,
narrators, baritone, orch., 1975; <u>Circle of
Thanatos and Genesis</u>, tenor, narrator, chorus,
orch., 1978; SONGS: <u>Moirologhia for Jani
Christou</u>, voice and piano, 1970; <u>Parodies</u>,
voice, actor, piano, 1970; MIXED MEDIA:
<u>Clytemnestra</u>, sound-action for actress, dancers,
orch., tape, 1967; <u>Katharsis</u>, flute, orch.,
tape, projections, 1968; <u>Events III</u>, orch.,
tape, slides, 1969; <u>Cassandra</u>, choir, orch.,
dancers, actors, tape, lights, and projections,
1969; <u>Protest II</u>, 13 instruments, actors, tapes,
lights, 1971; <u>Synthesis</u>, 4 players, 4 synthesizers, 1971; <u>Chorochronous I</u>, baritone, narrator, instruments, tape, film, slides, lights,
1973; and others.
    School of Music, Boston University,
    855 Commonwealth Ave., Boston, MA 02215

APONTE-LEDEE, RAFAEL
b. Guayama, P.R., 15 Oct. 1938. Studied composition with Cristobal Halffter at Madrid Cons.,
1957-64; with Ginastera in Buenos Aires, 1965-
66. In San Juan in 1967, he cofounded with
Francis Schwartz the "Fluxus" group for the
promotion of new music. He taught at the Univ.
of Puerto Rico, 1968-74.
    WORKS: ORCHESTRA: <u>Elvira en sombras</u>, piano
and orch., 1973; <u>El palacio en sombras</u>, orch.
without violins and cellos, 1977; CHAMBER MUSIC:
<u>Tema y seis differencias</u>, piano, 1963; <u>Dia-
logantes</u>, flute and violin, 1965; <u>Elejia</u>, 13
strings, 1965; <u>Epithasis</u>, winds and percussion,
1967; <u>Dialogantes 2</u>, 3 flutes, 3 trombones, 3
clarinets, 1968; <u>La ventana abierta</u>, 3 mezzo-
sopranos, 12 instrumentalists, 1968 (version for
large ensemble, 1969); <u>Streptomycine</u>, soprano,
flute, clarinet, trumpet, piano, 1970; <u>SSSSSS</u>^{2},
solo doublebass, 3 flutes, trumpet, percussion,
1971; <u>Volumenes</u>, piano, 1971; ELECTRONIC:
<u>Presagio de pájaros muertos</u>, narrator and tape,
1966; <u>Estravagario, in memoriam Salvador Allende</u>,
orch. and tape, 1974; <u>Cuidese de los angeles que
caen</u>, musique concrète, 1974; <u>Los huevos de
pandora</u>, clarinet and tape, 1974.

APPERT, DONALD L.
b. Moses Lake, Wash., 2 Jan. 1953. Studied at

the New England Cons., B.M., M.M. in trombone.
He is principal trombonist, Virginia Philharmonic,
Virginia Opera; and faculty member, Hampton
Inst., from 1978.
WORKS: CHAMBER MUSIC: Elegy for unaccom-
panied cello; Query, unaccompanied trombone; 3
songs of praise, soprano, horn, trombone; 3
pieces for piano; JAZZ ENSEMBLE: This man Jesus;
Come bless the Lord; and others.
213 Cynthia Dr., Hampton, VA 23666

APPLEBAUM, EDWARD
b. Los Angeles, Calif., 28 Sept. 1937. Studied
with Henri Lazarof and Lukas Foss, Univ. of
California, Los Angeles; and with Ingvar Lidholm
in Stockholm. His awards include grants from
the American-Scandinavian Found.; Rockefeller
Found.; Nat. Endowment for the Arts; Creative
Arts Inst., Univ. of California; ASCAP awards;
Stanford Univ. fellowship. He was faculty
member, California State Univ., Long Beach,
1968-71; then at Univ. of California, Santa
Barbara.
WORKS: OPERA: The frieze of life, 1 act;
ORCHESTRA: Variations for orchestra, 1966;
viola concerto, 1967; symphony no. 1, 1970; When
dreams do show thee me, clarinet, cello, piano,
chamber chorus and orch., 1972; Times three,
flute choir and percussion; CHAMBER MUSIC:
piano sonata, 1965; string trio, 1966; Montages,
clarinet, cello, piano, 1969; Shantih, cello
and piano, 1969; Foci, viola and piano, 1971;
piano trio, 1972; Face in the cameo, clarinet
and piano; Stemmen, soprano, cello, piano; To
remember, clarinet, cello, piano; piano sonata,
no. 2.
226 Selrose Lane, Santa Barbara, CA 93109

APPLEBAUM, STANLEY
b. Newark, N.J., 1 Mar. 1922. Studied with
Stefan Wolpe, Wallingford Riegger, and Leon
Barzin. He has been arranger for dance orchestras, records, and musicals; was on staff of
Warner Bros., 1962-63; established his own publishing company.
WORKS: ORCHESTRA: piano concerto, 1951;
BAND: Spring magic; Marrakech bazaar, suite,
1973; Voices from Kaluga; Hometown hoedown;
Cimmaron; Irish suite; CHAMBER MUSIC: brass
quintet, 1948; 2 string quartets, 1951; PIANO:
scherzo and toccata, 1955; Frenzy, toccata,
Double play, 4 hands, 1975; many educational
works and arrangements for band, instrumental
ensembles, piano, and chorus; numerous under-
scores for commercials, many of which have won
international awards (e.g., Pan Am makes the
going great won a Clio).
330 W. 58th St., New York, NY 10019

APPLETON, JON HOWARD
b. Los Angeles, Calif., 4 Jan. 1939. Studied at
Reed Coll., B.A.; with Andrew Imbrie at Univ. of
California, Berkeley; with Henri Lazarof and
Homer Keller, Univ. of Oregon, M.A.; with
Vladimir Ussachevsky and Mario Davidovsky,
Columbia-Princeton Electronic Music Center. His
awards include Guggenheim and Fulbright fellow-
ships; Bourges prize for electronic music, 1973;

Nat. Endowment for the Arts grant, 1976; Internat. Society for Contemporary Music prize,
1977. He had held faculty posts at Univ. of
Oregon, 1963-65; Columbia Univ., 1965-66;
Oakland Univ. 1966-67; professor and director,
Bregman Electronic Music Studio, Dartmouth Univ.,
1967-76, 1977-; director, Swedish Nat. Center
for Electronic Music, 1976-77.
WORKS: THEATRE: The ghost sonata, 1969;
several dance scores, 1971-77; ORCHESTRA: After
"Nude descending a staircase," 1965; The American
songs, tenor and orch., 1966; CHAMBER MUSIC:
4 explorations, violin and piano, 1964; 4 inventions, 2 flutes, 1965; 2 movements, wind quintet,
1963; 6 movements, wind quintet, 1964; Winesburg,
Ohio, flute, clarinet, violin, cello, piano,
1972; string quartet, 1976; CHORUS: The green
wave, 1964; Ballad of the soldier, men's voices,
1974; This is America, 1976; SONGS: 2 songs,
1964; The dying Christian to his soul, 1965;
PIANO: 3 lyrics, 1963; piano sonata no. 2 for
Gabriel Chodos, 1968; FILM SCORES: Nobody knows
everything, 1965; Anuszkiewicz, 1968; Scene
unobserved, 1969; Computer graphics at 110 Baud,
1969; Charlie item and double X, 1970; Glory,
glory!, 1971; MIXED MEDIA: Scene unobserved,
winds, strings, percussion, piano, film, tape,
1969; The Bremen town musicians, concerto for
toy piano and 12 toy instruments, commissioned
by Martha Baird Rockefeller Found. for Richard
Bunger, 1971; Double structure (with Christian
Wolff), 1971; also many electronic compositions.
P.O. Box 187, Norwich, VT 05055

ARBATSKY, YURY
b. Moscow, 15 Apr. 1911; to U.S. 1949; d. New
Hartford, N.Y., 3 Sept. 1963. Studied with
Grabner at Leipzig Cons.; later received a
doctorate in music in Belgrade, where he was a
choral conductor and cathedral organist. After
coming to the U.S., he was church organist in
Chicago, 1950-53, and a consultant with the
Newberry Library. He composed 8 symphonies and
numerous chamber and choral works.

ARCHIBALD, BRUCE
b. White Plains, N.Y., 2 May 1933. Studied with
Robert Palmer, Hunter Johnson, and Karel Husa,
Cornell Univ., 1951-57; with Aaron Copland at
Tanglewood, 1958; with Walter Piston and Leon
Kirchner at Harvard Univ., Ph.D. 1962. His
awards include a B.M.I. prize, 1954; Friends of
Music award, 1956; Fels Found. grant, 1962-63.
He was faculty member at Amherst Coll., 1962-63;
and from 1967, at Temple Univ.
WORKS: CHAMBER MUSIC: 4 songs on poems of
e. e. cummings, soprano, string quartet, piano,
1954; string quartet, variations, 1957; VOICE:
God's grandeur, male chorus and piano, 4 hands,
1961; What the thunder said, cantata for solo
baritone and 8 instruments; ORGAN: Chemquasa-
bamticook, variations, 1971; other works for
orchestra, small ensembles, chorus, piano.
421 Wyndon Rd., Ambler, PA 19002

AREL, BÜLENT
b. Istanbul, Turkey, 23 Apr. 1919; U.S. citizen
1973. Graduated from Ankara State Cons., 1947;

ARGENT, JAMES

studied composition with Edward Zuckmayer and
Necil Kazim Akses; sound engineering with Joze
Bernard and Willfried Garret, both of Radio
Diffusion Francaise. His awards include a
Rockefeller grant for research at the Columbia-
Princeton Electronic Music Center, 1959; 2 Nat.
Endowment for the Arts grants; New York Research
Found. grant; and several commissions for both
instrumental and electronic music. He taught in
Ankara, 1945-51; was musical director, Radio
Ankara, 1951-59, 1963-65; faculty member, Yale
Univ., 1961-62, 1965-70; from 1971, professor
and music director, Electronic Music Studio,
State Univ. of New York, Stony Brook.
    WORKS: INSTRUMENTAL: Music for unaccompanied
viola, 1962; Music for unaccompanied violin,
1962; For violin and piano, 1966; Interrupted
preludes, 1967; Short piece for orchestra, 1967;
ELECTRONIC: Music for string quartet and tape,
1957; Electronic music no. 1, 1960; Fragment,
1960; Scapegoat suite, after Kafka's "The Trial,"
1960; Stereo electronic music no. 1, 1961; Music
for a sacred service: prelude and postlude,
1961; Wall Street impressions, 1961; Mimiana I:
Flux, 1968; Mimiana II: Frieze, 1969; Capriccio
for T.V., 1969; Stereo electronic music no. 2,
1970; Out of into, film score, 1972; Mimiana III:
6 and 7, 1973; Fantasy and dance for 5 viols and
tape, 1974.
    P.O. Box 457, East Setauket, NY 11733

ARGENT, JAMES
    b. Thayer, W.Va., 15 July 1927. Studied at
Wilberforce Univ. and Chicago Cons. Coll. From
1971 he has been chairman of music, Wilberforce
Univ.
    WORKS: PIANO: Travel suite; Suite fan-
tastique; 6 etudes.
    483 E. Market St., Kenia, OH 45385

ARGENTO, DOMINICK
    b. York, Pa., 27 Oct. 1927. Studied with
Nicolas Nabakov, Vittorio Rietti, Henry Cowell,
Peabody Cons., B.M. 1951, M.M. 1954; with Bernard
Rogers, Howard Hanson, and Alan Hovhannes,
Eastman School of Music, Ph.D. 1957. Awards in-
clude the Gustav Klemm composition prize, 1951,
1954; teaching fellowship, Eastman School;
Fulbright fellowship for study in Italy, 1951;
2 Guggenheim fellowships, 1957, 1964; ASCAP
award, 1973; Pulitzer prize for the song cycle,
From the diary of Virginia Woolf, 1975; 3 Nat.
Endowment for the Arts grants, 1974, 1975, 1976.
Elected to American Acad. and Inst. of Arts and
Letters, 1980. He was faculty member, Hampton
Inst., 1952-55; professor, Univ. of Minnesota,
from 1958.
    WORKS: OPERA: Sicilian lives, 1954; The
boor, 1957; Masque of angels, 1963; Christopher
Sly, based on "The taming of the shrew," 1963;
Postcard from Morocco, Minneapolis, 14 Oct.
1971; Jonah and the whale, Minneapolis, 9 Mar.
1974; Krapp's last tape, 1 act, 1974 NEA grant
for American Bicentennial; A water bird talk,
1-act monodrama based freely on Chekhov's "The
harmful effects of tobacco" and "The birds of
America" by J. J. Audubon, 1975 NEA grant; The
voyage of Edgar Allan Poe, Minneapolis, 24 Apr.

1976; Miss Havisham's fire, 2-act monodrama,
1976 NEA grant, New York City Opera, 22 Mar.
1979; ORCHESTRA: The resurrection of Don Juan,
ballet suite, 1956; Ode to the west wind,
soprano and orch., 1957; Variations: the mask
of night, 1965; Royal invitation or Homage to
the Queen of Tonga, small orch., 1964; A ring of
time: In praise of music, 7 songs for orchestra,
22 Sept. 1977; CHAMBER MUSIC: Divertimento,
piano and strings, 1954; Divertimento, piano,
4 hands; 6 Elizabethan songs, 1958; Letters from
composers, high voice and guitar, 1968; To be
sung upon the water, high voice, clarinet, piano,
1972; CHORUS: The revelation of St. John the
Divine, men's voices, brass, percussion, harp,
piano, 1966; A nation of cowslips, 1968; Trio
Carmina Paschalia, women's voices, guitar, and
harp, 1970.
    Dept. of Music, University of Minnesota,
Minneapolis, MN 55455

ARLEN, HAROLD
    b. Buffalo, N.Y., 15 Feb. 1905. Studied with
his father, a cantor; went to New York at an
early age as pianist and singer. He wrote songs
for Broadway musicals, then stage scores, and in
Hollywood, 1943-55, film scores. His musicals
included Bloomergirl, 1944; St. Louis woman,
1946; House of flowers, 1954; Jamaica, 1957;
most popular songs were Stormy weather, 1932,
and Over the rainbow from The wizard of Oz,
1939. Other successful film scores were Let's
fall in love; Rio Rita; Gold diggers of 1937;
Star spangled rhythm; Cabin in the sky; and many
others.

ARMSTRONG, LOUIS
    b. New Orleans, La., 4 July 1900; d. New York,
6 July 1971. Black jazz trumpeter and composer.
See his autobiography, Satchmo, My life in New
Orleans, New York, 1954; and Horn of plenty, The
story of Louis Armstrong by R. Goffin, New York,
1947.

ARNATT, RONALD
    b. London, England, 16 Jan. 1930; U.S. citizen
1953. Attended Trent Coll., Derbyshire, Trinity
Coll. of Music, London, and Durham Univ., B.M.
1954. He was named a fellow of Trinity Coll.,
1951, and of the American Guild of Organists,
1952; in 1970 was awarded an honorary D.M. by
Westminster Choir Coll. He was faculty member,
American Univ., 1951-54; organist and choirmaster, St. Louis, 1954-58; then joined the
faculty of Univ. of Missouri. His compositions
include many anthems, sacred solos, and organ
works.
    412 S. Gore Ave., St. Louis, MO 63119

ARNOLD, BYRON
    b. Vancouver, Wash., 15 Aug. 1901; d. Los
Angeles, Calif. Studied at Willamette Univ.,
B.A. 1924; with Bernard Rogers and Howard Hanson,
Eastman School of Music. He taught at Univ. of
Alabama, 1938-48; was professor, California State
Univ., Los Angeles, 1948-71.
    WORKS: ORCHESTRA: 5 incapacitated preludes,
1937; 3 fantasticisms; also songs and piano
works.

ARNOLD, CORLISS RICHARD
  b. Monticello, Ark., 7 Nov. 1926. Studied at
Hendrix Coll., Ark., B.M. 1947; Univ. of Michigan,
M.M. 1948; Union Theological Seminary, S.M.D.
1954; composition teachers included Normand
Lockwood, Seth Bingham, Leo Sowerby, Nadia
Boulanger, Jean Langlais. He was awarded a
Fulbright grant in 1956 for study in France; is
a fellow, American Guild of Organists. He has
served colleges and churches in Arkansas, New
Jersey, New York, Illinois, and Michigan. Since
1959 he has been professor, Michigan State Univ.
  WORKS: ORGAN: Fantasy chorale and toccata
on "Veni Emmanuel"; sonata in D, trumpet and
organ; CHORUS: Magnificat; A child this day is
born, with soprano or tenor solo.
    114 Sunset Lane, East Lansing, MI 48823

ARNOLD, HUBERT EUGENE
  b. New Orleans, La., 2 Mar. 1945. Studied with
H. Owen Reed, Michigan State Univ., B.M. 1966,
M.M. 1970; with Hall Overton at Juilliard
School, 1971. He was staff arranger, U.S.
Military Acad. Band, West Point, 1969-71, then
free-lance arranger and composer.
  WORKS: INSTRUMENTAL: Sonata for 2 trumpets
and piano, 1969; Dithyramb, saxophone quartet,
1970; Fantasy, clarinet and piano; Anamnesis,
tenor saxophone and piano; Tale of an electric
eel, jazz ensemble, 1975.
    330 E. 85th St., #2A, New York, NY 10028

ARTHUR, JAN
  b. Rochester, Minn., 1 Jan. 1939. Studied at
Univ. of Chicago, Sherwood School, and North
Park Coll., Chicago, B.M.E. Since 1965 he has
been church organist and music director; associated with Schmitt Music Centers from 1971. He
has published anthems.

ASCHAFFENBURG, WALTER
  b. Essen, Germany, 20 May 1927; U.S. citizen
1944. Studied at Hartford School of Music;
with Herbert Elwell, Oberlin Coll., B.A. 1951;
with Bernard Rogers, Eastman School, M.A. 1952;
and with Dallapiccolo in Florence, 1956. His
awards have included Fromm Found grant, 1953;
Guggenheim grants, 1955, 1973; and Nat. Inst.
of Arts and Letters citation and award, 1966.
He has been on the faculty of Oberlin Coll. from
1952.
  WORKS: OPERA: Bartleby, Oberlin, 12 Nov.
1964; ORCHESTRA: Ozymandias, symphonic reflections, Rochester, N.Y., 22 Apr. 1952; Oedipus
Rex, overture, 1952; 3 dances; CHAMBER MUSIC:
piano trio, 1951; Divertimento, trumpet, horn,
trombone, 1951; cello sonata, 1954; sonata for
solo violin, 1954; string quartet, 1955; woodwind quintet, 1967; Proem, brass and percussion;
duo for violin and cello; CHORUS: 23rd Psalm.
    49 Shipherd Circle, Oberlin, OH 44074

ASH, RODNEY
  b. Reading, Pa., 2 Jan. 1931. Studied with
Louis Mennini, Eastman School of Music; with
Bernhard Heiden, Indiana Univ.; and with John
Cowell, Univ. of Arkansas. He was faculty mem-
ber, Oklahoma State Univ., 1958-60; professor of

music, Western State Coll., Gunnison, Colo.,
1960-.
  WORKS: CHAMBER MUSIC: Okanagan in tempera,
piano suite; Songs of experience, song cycle on
poems of Blake; piano sonata.
    Rt. 1, Castle Mt., Gunnison, CO 81230

ASHFORTH, ALDEN
  b. 1933. He is a faculty member at Univ. of
California, Los Angeles.
  WORKS: VOICE: The unquiet heart, soprano
and chamber ensemble, 1968; Aspects of love,
song cycle, 1977; ORGAN: Byzantia--2 journeys
after Yeats, with tape, 1970-73.
    4211 Saugus Ave., Sherman Oaks, CA 91403

ASHLEY, ROBERT
  b. Ann Arbor, Mich., 28 Mar. 1930. Studied at
Univ. of Michigan, M.B. 1952; Manhattan School of
Music, composition with Wallingford Riegger,
M.M. 1954; psychoacoustics with Roberto Gerhard,
Univ. of Michigan, 1961. He was cofounder of
the ONCE Festival of Contemporary Music and the
Cooperative Studio of Electronic Music, both at
Ann Arbor; also founder and director of the ONCE
Group, 1963-70, a touring multimedia ensemble.
With Gordon Mumma, David Behrman, Alvin Lucier,
he is a member of the Sonic Arts Union, which
toured the U.S. and Europe, 1966-73. He is
faculty member, Mills Coll., and director of its
Center for Contemporary Music.
  WORKS: OPERA: In memoriam Kit Carson,
1963; ORCHESTRA: In memoriam Crazy Horse, symphony, 1963; In memoriam John Smith, concerto,
1963; CHAMBER MUSIC: In memoriam Estoban Gomez,
quartet, 1963; Quartet for any number of instruments, 1965; Trios (White on white), various
instruments, 1965; CHORUS: She was a visitor,
1967; In Sara, Mencken, Christ, and Beethoven,
there were men and women, text-sound piece,
1976; PIANO: sonata, 1959; Maneuvers for small
hands, 1961; Details for 2 pianists, 1 piano,
1962; ELECTRONIC: The 4th of July, 1960; Something, clarinet, piano, tape, 1961; Complete with
heat, 1962; Boxing, 1963; The wolfman, 1964;
Kitty Hawk, an antigravity piece, 1964; Combination wedding and funeral, 1964; Joy road interchange, 1964; Orange dessert, 1965; Untitled
mixes, 1965; Unmarked interchange, 1965; Night
train, 1966; Purposeful lady, slow afternoon,
1968; Illusion models, for hypothetical computer,
1970; FILM SCORES: The image in time, 1957;
The bottleman, 1960; Jenny and the poet, 1964;
My May, 1965; Overdrive, 1968; Portraits, self-
portraits and still life, 1969; Battery Davis,
1970.
    Center for Contemporary Music, Mills College,
    Oakland, CA 94613

ASHTON, JOHN H.
  b. Pittsburgh, Pa., 11 July 1938. Studied with
Nikolai Lopatnikoff and Roland Leich, Carnegie-
Mellon Univ., B.F.A. 1960, M.F.A. 1961; with
Thomas Canning, West Virginia Univ. He received
composition awards from West Virginia Univ.,
1961, and from Nat. Assoc. of Coll. Wind and Percussion Instructors, 1963. He has played trumpet
in several symphony orchestras; was faculty

ASIA, DANIEL ISAAC

member, Univ. of Nebraska, 1969; from 1970, at
Fairmont State Coll.
   WORKS: ORCHESTRA: Symphonic movement,
1961; For the love of Phoebe, chamber orch.,
1961; Music for a community orchestra, 1977;
BAND: Rhapsody, 1964; Variations and epilogue,
1977; CHAMBER MUSIC: clarinet quintet, 1960;
trumpet sonata, 1963; trio for clarinet, bassoon
and piano (an alternate version of the clarinet
quintet), 1972; A tonal trio, woodwinds, 1972;
Lyric piece, brass quintet, 1973; Dialogues,
discourses on the motet: Pucelete-Je languis-
Domino, saxophone quartet, 1974; VOICE: Dulce
et decorum est, baritone and 11 brass instruments, 1972; Songs from the unknown Eros, baritone, small chorus, 1973; The request for sick
leave, baritone, 1975; Evening star, soprano,
4 instruments, 1976; Gloria, soprano, flute,
horn, chorus, 1976; Psalm 26, speaker, chorus,
1977.
   1109 Alexander Pl., Fairmont, WV 26554

ASIA, DANIEL ISAAC
   b. Seattle, Wash., 27 June 1953. Studied with
Randall McClellan, Hampshire Coll.; with Ronald
Perera and Stephen Albert, Smith Coll.; with
Jacob Druckman, K. Penderecki, Robert Morris,
and Bruce MacCombie, Yale School of Music. He
received the John Jay Jackson prize at Yale for
his string quartet, 1977; Nat. Endowment for the
Arts composer grant, 1978-79; ASCAP grant, 1979.
   WORKS: INSTRUMENTAL: Piano set 1, 1976;
Dream sequence, amplified trombone, 1976; string
quartet, 1976-77; Sand 1, flute, horn, double
bass, 1977; Piano set 11, 1977; Plum-DS 11,
flutes, 1977; Sand 11, chamber ensemble, 1978;
Live images, 4 woodwinds, 1978; ELECTRONIC TAPE:
Miles mix, 1976; Shtay, 1976.
   771 West End Ave., #5A, New York, NY 10025

ASPER, FRANK W.
   b. Logan, Utah, 9 Feb. 1892. Studied at New
England Cons.; Boston Univ.; Univ. of Utah;
honorary D.M., Bates Coll. He taught at the
New England Cons., then at McCune School of Music
and Art; was organist at Salt Lake City Tabernacle and conducted the choir for broadcasts;
gave concerts in U.S., Canada, Mexico, and
Europe. His works include many sacred and
secular pieces for organ and voice.

ATHERTON, PERCY LEE
   b. Roxbury, Mass., 25 Sept. 1871; d. Atlantic
City, N.J., 8 Mar. 1944. Studied with John
Knowles Paine at Harvard Univ., B.A. 1893; with
Rheinberger in Munich; Sgambati in Rome; and
with Widor in Paris.
   WORKS: OPERA: The heir apparent; The
maharajah; ORCHESTRA: Noon in the forest, symphonic poem; many songs.

ATOR, JAMES DONALD
   b. Kansas City, Mo., 15 Oct. 1938. Studied at
Drake Univ., B.M.E. 1960; Wichita State Univ.,
M.M. 1964; and North Texas State Univ., D.M.A.
1971; composition teachers were Samuel Adler,
Merrill Ellis, and William Latham. He has held
faculty positions at North Texas State Univ.,

1969-71; Millikin Univ., 1971-73; then at
Indiana Univ. at Fort Wayne.
   WORKS: ORCHESTRA: Adagio, 1969; Piece for
orchestra and prepared tape, 1971; CHAMBER MUSIC:
woodwind quartet, 1971; Enuffispluntee, saxophone, piano, percussion, 1972; VOICE: 4 haiku,
mezzo-soprano and piano, 1972.
   1925 Coronet, Fort Wayne, IN 46805

AUSLENDER, LEONARD STANLEY
   b. Los Angeles, Calif., 24 Oct. 1936. Studied
at Univ. of California, Los Angeles, B.A. 1963;
and California State Univ., Los Angeles, M.A.
1974. His teachers included Leonard Stein, Roy
Harris, Henri Lazarof, Boris Kremenliev,
Byong-Kon Kim, Dudley Foster, and Tak Shindo.
In 1969 he became president of Bright Star Music
Pub.
   WORKS: CHAMBER MUSIC: 4 miniatures, violin
and cello; Scherzo in C, woodwind quartet;
Visions in crystal, rainbows in stone, mixed
chamber ensemble.
   911 N. Formosa Ave., W. Hollywood, CA 90046

AUSTIN, LARRY
   b. Duncan, Okla., 12 Sept. 1930. Studied at
North Texas State Univ., B.M. 1951, M.M. 1952;
composition with Milhaud at Mills Coll., 1955,
and at Univ. of California, Berkeley, 1955-58;
course in computer-generated music systems at
Stanford Univ., 1969. His awards include 2
MacDowell fellowships; 2 Univ. of Calif. Inst.
for Creative Arts grants, 10 grants from the
Committee for Research; B.M.I. awards; Univ. of
South Florida grant, 1974; Distinguished Composer award, Music Teachers Nat. Assoc., 1974;
first prize in composition, Florida Festival of
New Music, Fine Arts Council of Florida, 1976;
and many commissions. He has held posts at
Univ. of Calif., Berkeley, 1956-58, at Davis,
1958-72; chairman and professor, Univ. of South
Florida, 1972-78, director of the Systems Complex
for Studio and Performing Arts, 1973-78; editor
of SOURCE magazine, 1967-70; from 1978, professor,
North Texas State Univ. With colleagues at
Davis in 1963, Austin evolved a technique of
group improvisations which he terms "open style"
and applies in composition.
   WORKS: ORCHESTRA: Prosody, 1953; Improvisations, orchestra and jazz soloists, 1961; Open
style, orch. with piano solo, 1967; BAND:
fanfare and procession, 1953; Music galore:
Outdoor suite, 1958; Suite for massed bands,
1961; In memoriam J. F. Kennedy, 1964; JAZZ
ENSEMBLES: Fantasy on a theme by Berg, 1960;
Homecoming, alto saxophone and jazz quintet,
1973; CHAMBER MUSIC: woodwind quartet, 1948;
woodwind quintet, 1949; brass quintet, 1949;
violin sonata, 1950; 3 violin duets, 1951;
string trio, 1951; concertino, flute, trumpet,
strings, 1962; 2 string quartets, 1954, 1955;
Collage for a variety of instruments, 1963;
Continuum, 2 to 7 instruments, 1964; A broken
consort, 7 instruments, 1964; Current, clarinet
and piano, 1968; CHORUS: mass, with orch., 1959;
Triptych, with string quartet, 1961; PIANO:
Variations, 1964; Piano set in open style, 1968;
Charly's cornet, cornet and piano, 1975;

ELECTRONIC AND MIXED MEDIA: Roma, theatre piece, 1965; Duet Amphitryon, 1967; Bass, in open style, 1967; Changes, trombone and tape, 1967; Catharsis, in open style, 2 ensembles, tapes, conductor, 1967; Accidents, prepared piano, tape, mirrors, actions, projections, 1967; The magicians, 1968; 3 film scores, Black/white study, Color study, Transmission one, all 1969; Agape, a celebration for priests, musicians, actors, poets, 1970; Plastic surgery, electric piano, percussion, tape, film, 1970; Quadrants: Event/Complex nos. 1-9, 1971-74; Phantasmagoria, 3 fantasies for various ensembles and tape, based on integrated fragments of Ives's Universe symphony, 1974-77.

School of Music, North Texas State Univ., Denton, TX 76203

AVERITT, WILLIAM EARL
b. Paducah, Ky., 14 Nov. 1948. Studied with James Woodward at Murray State Univ., B.M. 1970; with John Boda, Florida State Univ., M.M. 1972, D.M. 1973; and with Betsy Jolas at Tanglewood, 1976. His awards include Florida State Univ. fellowships, 1970-73; Ellen Battell Stoeckel Trust grant, 1972; Nat. Endowment for the Arts grant, 1977. Since 1973 he has been faculty member at the Shenandoah Cons. of Music.

WORKS: ORCHESTRA: Elegy, solo flute, strings, percussion, 1977; CHAMBER MUSIC: sonata, woodwind quintet, 1969; sonata, brass choir, 1970; trio, woodwinds, 1970; Permutation, flute and harpsichord, 1971; quartet, flute, clarinet, bass, piano, 1971; Chamber variations for 9 performers, 1972; Chamber symphony, 1973; Chamber music, soprano, flute, piano, 1975; November music for 9 instruments, 1976; CHORUS: mass, soprano, chorus, organ, 1969; Libera me, double chorus and solo quartet, 1970; 2 songs of William Blake, male chorus, 1970; O vos omnes, 1973; 3 poems of James Joyce, 1974; SONGS: 2 songs of Poe, baritone and percussion, 1967; Nazi songs (Brock), soprano and 5 instruments, 1972; PIANO: Introduction and allegro, 1970; 2 motets for 2 pianos, 1972.

Rt. 2, Box F71A, Stephens City, VA 22655

AVERRE, RICHARD
b. Trenton, N.J., 19 Jan. 1921. Studied at Juilliard School; Cincinnati Coll. Cons.; Westminster Choir Coll., B.M.; Trenton State Coll., M.M.Ed. He was music director of the Lambertville (N.J.) Music Circus, 1962-66, and of the Trenton Theatre-in-the-Park, 1967. Since 1968 he has been on the faculty at Bucks County Community Coll., Pa. He has published many sacred and secular choral compositions.

Box 81, Washington Crossing, PA 18977

AVSHALOMOV, AARON
b. Nikolayevsk, Siberia, 11 Nov. 1894; to U.S. 1947; d. New York, 26 Apr. 1965. Studied at Zurich Cons. In 1914 he was sent to China to avoid the draft. There he composed on Chinese themes, attempting to fuse Chinese thematic and rhythmic elements with the Western style of composition. His first opera, Kuan Yin, had its premiere in Peking in 1925; was performed in Portland, Ore., in 1926, and in New York, 1927. His second opera, The great wall, was presented in Shanghai in 1945. His second, third, and fourth symphonies were composed in the U.S. (1949, 1950, 1951).

AVSHALOMOV, JACOB
b. Tsingtao, China, 28 Mar. 1919; U.S. citizen 1944. Studied with his father, Aaron Avshalomov; with Ernst Toch in Los Angeles, 1938; with Bernard Rogers, Eastman School of Music, B.M. 1942, M.A. 1943; Columbia Univ., 1946. His awards include Ditson fellowship, 1946; Ernest Bloch award, 1948; Guggenheim fellowship, 1951; New York Music Critics' Circle award, 1953; Naumburg award, 1956; Ditson conductor's award, 1965; honorary doctorates, Univ. of Portland, 1966, Reed Coll., 1974; appointment to Nat. Council for Humanities, 1968-74; MacDowell fellowship, 1977. After serving as translator during World War II, he taught at Columbia Univ., 1946-54; became conductor of the Portland Junior Symphony, 1954. He has also been visiting professor at Tanglewood and Aspen and at several universities, and guest conductor in the northwest. He was appointed to the planning section, Nat. Endowment for the Arts, 1974.

WORKS: THEATRE: The little clay cart, incidental music; ORCHESTRA: The taking of T'ung Kuan, 1943, rev. 1947, 1953; Slow dance, Wash., D.C., 13 Aug. 1945; Sinfonietta, 1946, rev. 1952; Evocations, clarinet and chamber orch., 1947; How long, O Lord, cantata for alto solo, chorus, orch., 1949; Suite from the plywood age, with unison chorus, 1955; Inscriptions at the City of Brass, chorus, female narrator and orch., 1956; Phases of the Great Land, 1958; The Oregon, a symphony, Portland, 19 Mar. 1962; City upon a hill, chorus, narrator, orch., and liberty bell, 1965; CHAMBER MUSIC: 2 bagatelles, clarinet and piano; Disconsolate muse, flute and piano; Evocations, clarinet or viola and piano, 1947; sonatine, viola and piano, 1947; Quod libet montagna, brass sextet, 1975; sonatine, cello and piano, Wash., D.C., 17 June 1975; CHORUS: Prophecy, with tenor solo, 1948; Proverbs of hell, men's voices; Tom O'Bedlam, with oboe, tabor, and jingles, New York, 15 Dec. 1953; Whimsies, text from The New Yorker; Wonders, Blake text; I saw a stranger yestere'en, with violin solo; Psalm 100, with winds or organ and percussion, 1957; Of man's mortalitie; Praises from the corners of the earth, 1965; also songs and piano pieces.

2741 Southwest Fairview Blvd., Portland, OR 97201

AXT, WILLIAM
b. New York, N.Y., 19 Apr. 1888; d. Ukiah, Calif., 12 Feb. 1959. Studied privately in Berlin. He was assistant conductor, Hammerstein Grand Opera Company, N.Y.; music director, Capitol Theatre, N.Y., 1919; head of MGM music department. He wrote film scores including: Grand Hotel; Parnell; The garden murder case; Reunion in Vienna; The thin man; Rendezvous; and others.

AYOOB, JOSEPH N.

AYOOB, JOSEPH N.
    b. Waterville, Maine, 14 Feb. 1938. Studied with
Amram David, Boston Cons.; with Hugo Norden,
Boston Univ.; with Morton Subotnick, California
Inst. of the Arts. From 1978 he has been
director, Electronic Music Studio, School of
Contemporary Music, Boston.
    WORKS: ELECTRONIC: Rhythming; Ice Palace;
3 poems of love; Form no. 1--1978; Form no. 2--
1978, with voice.
        1 Lee St., Walpole, MA 02081

AYRES, FREDERIC
    b. Binghamton, N.Y., 17 Mar. 1876; d. Colorado
Springs, Colo., 23 Nov. 1926. Studied with
Edgar Stillman Kelley and Arthur Foote.
    WORKS: ORCHESTRA: From the plains, over-
ture; CHAMBER MUSIC: 2 string quartets; 2 piano
trios; 2 violin sonatas; cello sonata; many
songs.

BABBITT, MILTON
    b. Philadelphia, Pa., 10 May 1916. Studied with
Marion Bauer, New York Univ., B.A. 1935; at
Princeton Univ., M.A. 1942; privately with
Roger Sessions. His awards include New York
Music Critics' citation, 1949, 1964; Guggenheim
fellowship, 1961; election to Nat. Inst. of Arts
and Letters, 1965; his 60th birthday was honored
by several concerts of his music. He is a member of the music faculty, Princeton Univ., and a
director of the Columbia-Princeton Electronic
Music Center from 1959.
    WORKS: THEATRE: The fabulous voyage,
musical, 1946; ORCHESTRA: Relata I and II,
1965 and 1968; Occasional variations, 1969;
JAZZ ENSEMBLE: All set, 1957; CHAMBER MUSIC:
3 compositions for piano, 1947; Composition for
4 instruments, 1948; Composition for 12 instruments, 1948; The widow's lament in springtime,
voice and piano, 1950; Du, song cycle, 1951;
woodwind quartet, 1953; 4 string quartets, 1948,
1954, 1970, 1971; 2 sonnets, voice and 3 instruments, 1955; Semi-simple variations, piano,
1956; Sounds and words, voice and piano, 1958;
Composition for voice and 6 instruments, 1960;
Phonemena, soprano and piano, 1970; Aria da capo,
chamber ensemble, New York, 25 Apr. 1974; A solo
requiem, soprano and 2 pianos, New York, 10 Feb.
1979; ELECTRONIC: Vision and prayer, soprano
and tape, 1961; Composition for synthesizer,
1961; Philomel, soprano and tape, 1964; Reflections, piano and tape, 1974; Phonemena, voice
and tape, a 1974 version of the earlier work for
voice and piano; both versions premiered at
Manhattan School of Music, 3 Nov. 1975 (Phonemena
uses as text Babbitt's organization of phonemes,
the basic speech sounds in various languages of
the world); Concerti for violin, orch., and
tape, New York, 13 Mar. 1976; More phonemena for
mixed chorus, 1977.
        Music Dept., Princeton Univ., Princeton, NJ
    08540

BABCOCK, MICHAEL
    b. Centralia, Wash., 12 June 1940. Studied with
Iannis Xenakis, Juan Orrego-Salas, Roque Cordero,
and John Eaton, Indiana Univ., M.M. 1971. He

was research fellow, Center for Mathematical and
Automated Music, Indiana Univ., 1969-71;
director, Studio for Electronic and Experimental
Music, Chicago Musical Coll., Roosevelt Univ.,
1972-76; then on faculty, Univ. of Wisconsin.
    WORKS: CHAMBER MUSIC: Minutia, 2 movements
for cello and piano; Inflexaleus, 5 percussionists, Chicago, Dec. 1971.
        University of Wisconsin, P.O.B. 413,
    Milwaukee, WI 53201

BABER, JOSEPH
    b. Richmond, Va., 11 Sept. 1937. Studied with
H. Owen Reed and Mario Castelnuovo-Tedesco,
Michigan State Univ.; with John LaMontaine and
Howard Hanson, Eastman School of Music. His
awards include the Louis Lane prize, 1965; ASCAP
award, 1972; American Recorder Society prize;
Eastman School Alumni award. He was faculty
member, Southern Illinois Univ., 1967-70; from
1971, at Univ. of Kentucky.
    WORKS: OPERA: Frankenstein, 4 acts;
Rumpelstiltskin, 2 acts, Philadelphia, Dec. 1978,
called a satire on practically everything;
ORCHESTRA: Rhapsody, 1965; viola concerto,
Tokyo Philh., 1967; Divertimento, string orch.;
Rhapsody for cello and orch., Omaha Symph. 1978;
CHAMBER MUSIC: trio for oboe, viola, piano;
string quartet; violin sonata; sonata for unaccompanied cello (received Calif. Cello Club
prize); CHORUS: Missa brevis, women's voices
and organ; also songs.
        108 Arcadia Park, Lexington, KY 40503

BABIN, STANLEY
    b. Latvia, 10 Oct. 1932; U.S. citizen. Studied
at Curtis Inst. of Music.
    WORKS: ORCHESTRA: piano concerto; CHAMBER
MUSIC: string quartet; woodwind quintet; PIANO:
4 piano studies; 3 piano pieces; 2 sonatinas.

BABIN, VICTOR
    b. Moscow, 12 Dec. 1908; to U.S. 1937; d.
Cleveland, Ohio, 1 Mar. 1972. Studied at the
Riga Cons.; with Artur Schnabel in Berlin;
honorary doctorate from Univ. of New Nexico,
1961. In 1933 the 2-piano team of Vronsky and
Babin began concert tours in Europe, making a
New York debut in 1937. After service in the
U.S. Army in World War II, the 2-piano concerts
were resumed. He was director, Cleveland Inst.
of Music, 1961-72.
    WORKS: ORCHESTRA: 2 concerti for 2 pianos
and orch.; Concert piece, violin and orch.;
Capriccio; CHAMBER MUSIC: string quartet;
Variations on a theme by Purcell, cello and
piano; Sonata-fantasia, cello and piano; piano
trio; PIANO: 6 etudes for 2 pianos; Hillandale
waltzes; 3 fantasias on old themes; and a song
cycle, Beloved stranger.

BABITS, LINDA (PATRICK)
    b. New York, N.Y., 28 July 1940. Studied at
Manhattan School of Music, B.M.; with Roger
Sessions, Oberlin Cons.
    WORKS: ORCHESTRA: Western star, a piano
concerto; Clinton Corner Delancey; ELECTRONIC:
Vocalize, voice and tape, 1964.

BACH, JAN MORRIS
b. Forrest, Ill., 11 Dec. 1937. Studied with
Robert Kelly, Kenneth Gaburo, Burrill Phillips,
Univ. of Illinois, M.M. 1962; with Donald
Martino, Yale Univ. 1960; with Aaron Copland and
Roberto Gerhard at Tanglewood, 1961; and with
Thea Musgrave, London and Aldeburgh, 1974. His
awards include Koussevitzky award, 1961; City of
Birmingham composition prize, 1966; Harvey Gaul
prize and Mannes Opera prize, 1973; Sigma Alpha
Iota award, 1974; Inst. for Adv. Musical Studies
(Switz.) award for Laudes, 1974; Nat. Endowment
for the Arts grant, 1975; Northern Ill. Univ.
research grants, 1975-78; T.U.B.A. commission,
1977. He was faculty member, Univ. of Tampa,
1965-66; from then, assoc. prof., Northern
Illinois Univ.
WORKS: OPERA: The system, 1 act, New York,
7 Mar. 1974; The student from Salamanca, 1-act
opera, libretto by composer, New York, 9 Oct.
1980; ORCHESTRA: Toccata, 1959; Burgundy Variations, 1968; piano concerto, 1975; BAND:
Dionysia--Dirge and dithyrambic dances, 1964;
The eve of St. Agnes, antiphonal wind ensemble,
1976; Praetorius suite, 1977; CHAMBER MUSIC:
Divertimento, oboe and bassoon, 1956; string
quartet, 1957; clarinet sonata, 1957; Partita,
flute, cello, harpsichord, 1958; quintet for
oboe and strings, 1958; Dance, horn and piano,
1959; Mountain, desert, soil, and sea, 11 instruments, 1960; Rondelle, violin, flute, horn,
piano, 1964; 4 two-bit contraptions, flute and
horn, 1964; movements for viola and winds, 1966;
Turkish music, solo percussion, 1967; Skizzen,
woodwind quintet, 1967; Woodwork, 4 percussionists, 1970; Laudes, brass quintet, 1971;
Eisteddfod, flute, harp, viola, 1972; My very
first solo, saxophone and electric piano, 1974;
Canon and caccia, 5 horns, 1977; Concert variations, euphonium and piano, 1977; The happy
prince, narrator and chamber orch., 1978;
CHORUS: 3 Shakespearean songs, 1960; 3 choral
dances, women's voices, 1969; Dirge for a
minstrel, 1969; Spectra, with soloists, orch.,
tape, 1970; My wilderness, a cappella cycle,
1974; The Oregon Trail, with soloists and orch.,
1975; Hair today, a cappella antiphonal choir,
1977; and songs.
9 Moraine Terrace, DeKalb, IL 60115

BACHARACH, BURT F.
b. Kansas City, Mo., 12 May 1928. Studied with
Henry Cowell and Darius Milhaud, New School for
Social Research; Mannes Coll. of Music; and with
Bohuslav Martinu. He has been composer, arranger,
accompanist, and conductor in New York since
1952.
WORKS: THEATRE: Promises, promises,
musical, 1968; FILM TITLE SONGS: Wives and
lovers; A house is not a home; Send me no
flowers; What's new pussycat?; Promise her anything; Alfie; Butch Cassidy and the Sundance
Kid; and many other highly successful songs;
FILM SCORE: What's new pussycat?

BACON, ERNST
b. Chicago, Ill., 26 May 1898. Studied with
Arne Oldberg at Northwestern Univ.; with

Thorwald Otterstroem at Chicago Univ.; with Karl
Weigl in Vienna; and with Ernest Bloch in San
Francisco and at Univ. of California, Berkeley,
M.A. His awards include a Pulitzer prize, 1932;
3 Guggenheim fellowships; MacDowell and Hartford
fellowships; Bispham award; Nat. Inst. of Arts
and Letters award; Nat. Endowment for the Arts
grant, 1978. He was director, WPA-San Francisco,
1936-37; dean, School of Music, Converse Coll.,
1938-45; director, School of Music, Syracuse
Univ., 1945-62; visiting professor at various
universities; author of books and articles.
WORKS: THEATRE: A tree on the plains,
musical play, 1940, rev. 1962; A drumlin legend,
folk opera, 1949; Jehovah and the ark, ballet,
1968-70; The parliament of fowls, ballet, 1975;
Dr. Franklin, music play for the Bicentennial,
1976; ORCHESTRA: 4 symphonies (no. 1 with
piano), 1932, 1937, (no. 3, Great River, with
narrator), 1956, 1963; Ford's Theatre, 1943;
Enchanted island, 1954; Riolama, piano and orch.,
1964; piano concerto, 1978; CHAMBER MUSIC:
piano quintet, 1946; cello sonata, 1946; string
quartet, 1951; CHORUS: John Hardy, Colorado
Trail, Shouting pilgrim, choral songs; From
Emily's diary, soloists, women's chorus, orch.,
1945; By blue Ontario, oratorio on Walt Whitman
text, 1958; The last invocation, a requiem on
texts by Whitman, Dickinson, and others, 1968-
71; Saws, a suite of canons, chorus and piano,
1971; SONGS: Billy in the Darbies, bass and
piano, text from Melville; Songs of eternity,
1932; Black and white songs, baritone and orch.,
1932; Twilights, 3 songs for voice and orch.,
1932; Midnight special, 4 songs, voice and orch.,
1932; 2 published books of songs; Tributaries,
30 songs, and Dragon's teeth, 50 songs.
57 Claremont Ave., Orinda, CA 94563

BAHMANN, MARIANNE E.
b. Schuykill Co., Pa., 1 Dec. 1933. Studied at
Drake Univ., with Francis J. Pyle. She received
the Des Moines Symph. Young Artists award in
composition, 1957, and won the 1961 Capital
Univ. competition for an anthem. She taught at
Drake Univ., prep. dept.; at Chicago Evangelistic
Inst., Iowa; was accompanist and singer in New
York, 1957-58; from 1959, a free-lance performer
and composer.
WORKS: VOICE: Magnificat, solo voice and
orch.; The altar of God, choir and organ; A
setting of the Lutheran Liturgy based on
spirituals, for congregation, cantor, and organ;
ORGAN: pastorale on 'Greensleeves'; Voluntary
on a theme of Tschaikowsky; Meditation for
chimes.
522 Georgia Ave., Palo Alto, CA 94306

BAIL, GRACE SHATTUCK
b. Cherry Creek, N.Y., 17 Jan. 1898. Graduated
from Dana School of Music, Warren, Ohio, 1919;
also studied violin with Michael Banner and
composition with John Christopher at Meadville
Coll. of Music. She has received many awards
for violin solos, string trios, piano, and
choral works. Her compositions include symphonic
works, string quartets, string trios, choral
works, and pieces for violin, piano, and organ.
451 E. 8th St., Beaumont, CA 92223

BAILEY, PARKER

BAILEY, PARKER
b. Kansas City, Mo., 1 Mar. 1902. Studied with David Stanley Smith, Yale Univ.; piano with Beryl Rubinstein and composition with Ernest Bloch in Cleveland; law at Cornell Univ.; L.L.B. 1934. He has practiced law in New York from 1943; was on board of directors of the MacDowell Assoc., 1954-62. His published works include a flute sonata, 1929; Variations symphonique for orch., 1930; and Toccata, ricercata, finale for organ. He is a nephew of Horatio Parker.

BAKALEINIKOV, VLADIMIR ROMANOVITCH
b. Moscow, 12 Oct. 1885; to U.S. 1927; d. Pittsburgh, Pa., 5 Nov. 1953. Graduated from the Moscow Cons., 1907, and taught there, 1920-24. He was violist and conductor in Cincinnati and then Pittsburgh. His compositions included a viola concerto, 1937; 2 oriental dances for orchestra.

BAKER, CLAUDE
b. Lenoir, N.C., 12 Apr. 1948. Studied with Samuel Adler, Wayne Barlow, Warren Benson, Eastman School of Music. His awards include MacDowell and Yaddo fellowships; ASCAP awards; a grant from New York State Council of the Arts. He was faculty member, Univ. of Georgia, 1974-76; Univ. of Louisville, 1976-.
WORKS: ORCHESTRA: Rest, heart of the world, with soprano solo, (BMI award, 1973); 4 songs on poems of Kenneth Patchen, with soprano solo; BAND: Capriccio; CHAMBER MUSIC: Speculum musicae, string quartet, woodwind quartet, brass trio, percussion, piano; Banchetto musicale, clarinet, violin, piano, percussion, 1978, won 2nd prize in the Friedheim composition contest, Kennedy Center, Wash., D.C., 16 Sept. 1979.
P.O. Box 7112, Louisville, KY 40207

BAKER, DAVID A.
b. Hamitlon, Ohio, 27 Mar. 1949. Studied with John Barnes Chance, Univ. of Kentucky, B.A. 1971; with Carlisle Floyd and John Boda, M.M., D.Mus. 1974. He taught at Florida State Univ., 1971-74; from 1976, at Univ. of Wisconsin, Eau Claire.
WORKS: ORCHESTRA: Concerto for piano, strings, percussion; CHAMBER MUSIC: Sonata concertante, saxophone and piano; Fantasy, serenade, and fugue, flute, guitar, bassoon; Prelude and dance, trombone and piano; 5 pieces, for piano.
2809 Richard Dr., Eau Claire, WI 54701

BAKER, DAVID N.
b. Indianapolis, Ind., 21 Dec. 1931. Attended Indiana Univ., B.M.Ed., M.M.Ed.; studied composition with George Russell, William Russo, John Lewis, Thomas Beversdorf, Bernhard Heiden, Gunther Schuller, Norman Merrifield, and Juan Orrego-Salas. He also studied tuba, trombone, cello, and bass, and holds a Lenox School of Jazz diploma. His awards include the Indiana Philharmonic gold award, 1954; Down Beat Hall of Fame scholarship, 1959, and New Star award, 1962; 2 Notre Dame Collegiate Jazz Festival awards, 1959, 1964; Nat. Assoc. of Negro

Musicians award; many commission, appointments to boards, etc. He has been faculty member and chairman of jazz studies, Indiana Univ., 1966-; and at Tanglewood, 1968-.
WORKS: ORCHESTRA: A song of faith, with jazz band, chorus, soloists, narrators; Levels, solo bass viol, jazz band, flute quartet, horn quartet, string quartet, 1973; Le chat qui peche, with soprano and jazz quartet; JAZZ BAND: flute concerto; violin concerto; trombone concerto; bass viol concerto; Soul of '76, national television, 20 June 1976; CHAMBER MUSIC: many pieces for string orch.; trio for alto saxophone, horn, cello; The dude, cello and piano; 2 string quartets; Romanza and march, 3 trombones; sonata for piano and string quintet; Hymn and deviation, brass quartet; Dirge and dance, brass quartet; viola sonata; Modality, tonality, and freedom, saxophone and chamber ensemble; violin sonata; sonatina for tuba and string quartet, 1971; cello sonata, New York, 16 Feb. 1974; 3 woodwind quintets; sonata for violin and cello; The new Americans, brass choir; Contrasts, piano trio, Laramie, Wyo., 22 June 1976; Roots, piano trio, 1976, Wash., D.C., 27 Feb. 1977; CHORUS: Bratitudes, with dancers, narrator, and orch.; Black America, a cantata in memory of Martin Luther King, Jr.; But I am a worm, with jazz ensemble, orch.; Catholic mass for peace and Lutheran mass, both with jazz ensemble; Lutheran mass, high voice and piano; jazz mass, with jazz septet; I am poured out like water, men's voices and string orch.; I will tell of thy name, with dancers, jazz ensemble, strings; My God, my God, with jazz ensemble, strings; Psalm 22, oratorio; Psalm 23; 5 songs to the survival of black children, a cappella chorus; SONGS: cycle for tenor; cycle for soprano; FILM SCORES: Black frontier, The trial of Captain Henry Flipper, NET series; and numerous pieces for jazz ensemble. He is author of many books and articles on the contemporary music scene.
3151 Arrow Ave., Bloomington, IN 47401

BAKER, LARRY
b. Ft. Smith, Ark., 7 Sept. 1948. Studied with Woodrow James and Spencer Norton, Oklahoma Univ.; with Donald Erb, Cleveland Inst. of Music. Awards include the Okla. Fed. of Music Clubs composition award, 1970, 1971; member, Vermont Composers' Conf., 1972, 1973; Nat. Endowment for the Arts grant, 1976; and commissions. From 1973 he has been faculty member, Cleveland Inst. of Music.
WORKS: ORCHESTRA: A game of shadows; From the worlds of the Imperium; Echo image, 1975; Homage, piano and orch., 1977; CHAMBER MUSIC: Trimophony; Night ancestor I; Before assemblages III, chamber orch.; Masterpiece and Masterpiece II, percussion; Quiet, chamber orch., 1977; Childness, 1978.
2496 Derbyshire #11, Cleveland Heights, OH 44106

BAKER, ROBERT A.
b. Leavenworth, Kans., 6 Nov. 1933. In 1973, was on the faculty at Washington Univ., St. Louis, Mo. He has published choral works.

BALDWIN, RALPH LYMAN

Music Dept., Boise State Univ., Boise, ID
83725

BALDWIN, RALPH LYMAN
b. Easthampton, Mass., 27 Mar. 1872; d. Canaan,
N.H., 30 Sept. 1943. Was organist, choir
director, composer, and music supervisor in
Northampton, Mass., and Hartford, Conn.; after
1900, was faculty member, Inst. of Music Pedagogy, Northampton. Rollins Coll., Winter Park,
Fla., confers an award in his name.

BALDWIN, RUSSELL (T. R.)
b. Chicago, Ill., 9 Jan. 1913. Studied with Leo
Sowerby, American Cons.; with Ingolf Dahl, Univ.
of Southern Calif.; and with Peter Korn in
Munich. From 1947 he was on the faculty, San
Bernardino Valley Coll.
WORKS: ORCHESTRA: Symphonic interlude;
CHAMBER MUSIC: trio for horn, clarinet, piano;
4 piano pieces; CHORUS: Missa brevis; Francis-
can prayers.
1390 Pacific St., Redlands, CA 92373

ALENT, ANDREW
b. Washington, Pa., 13 July 1934. Attended
Univ. of Michigan, B.M. 1956, M.M. 1960; and had
private study with William Russo in Chicago.
Since 1956 he has taught instrumental music and
directed bands in Michigan, from 1962, in
Warren, Mich. He has published many compositions
r school concert bands.
17585 Oak Dr., Detroit, MI 48221

CHARD
xandria, Va., 3 Feb. 1915. Attended
School of Music, M.B. 1936; studied con-
on a fellowship at Juilliard School,
and with Koussevitzky at Tanglewood,
s honors include many awards and cita-
conducting; first prize from the
Arts Club for composition; and
missions. Since 1943 he has been
or, Nat. Gallery of Art, and con-
Gallery Orchestra.
RCHESTRA: 4 National Gallery
for strings; Primavera; 3 songs
a; Episodes from a Lincoln
sions from an animated cartoon;
e for strings; The great Amer-
try, music for a series of 4
produced by the U.S. Dept. of
et of jade, song cycle for
ch.; In memory of Leopold
, 25 Sept. 1977; CHORUS:
Union, The Republic, 3
oists, speaker, and orch.;
away, Death; God's
ir; many songs and piano

estra, National Gallery
20565

1878; d. Santa Ana,
at Cleveland Cons.;
for Witmark
res for musicals,
of Paddy Whack;

and many extremely popular songs, such as Will
you love me in December as you do in May?,
Mother Machree, When Irish eyes are smiling,
Dear little boy of mine.

BALLANTINE, EDWARD
b. Oberlin, Ohio, 6 Aug. 1886; d. Martha's
Vineyard, Mass., 2 July 1971. Studied with
Walter Spalding and Frederick Converse, Harvard
Univ., 1903-7, highest honors in music; with
Artur Schnabel and Rudolf Ganz in Berlin, 1907-9.
He was faculty member at Harvard, 1912-37,
retiring as associate professor emeritus.
WORKS: THEATRE: The lotus eaters, musical
play, 1907; ORCHESTRA: Prelude to The delect-
able forest; From the garden of Hellas; The eve
of St. Agnes; By a lake in Russia; CHAMBER
MUSIC: violin sonata; songs; Mary had a little
lamb, a set of piano variations in the styles
of 10 eminent composers, 1924; a second set
brought the variations up to date with the
styles of Stravinsky, Gershwin, and others, 1943.

BALLARD, GREGORY
b. Battle Creek, Mich., 18 July 1954. Studied
with Ross Lee Finney, Leslie Bassett, George
Balch Wilson, and William Bolcom, Univ. of
Michigan. He was winner of the ISCM piano com-
position contest, 1976, and received the Nat.
Inst. of Arts and Letters Charles Ives award in
1977. He is free-lance composer and pianist in
New York.
WORKS: ORCHESTRA: Fantasy, piano and orch.;
CHAMBER MUSIC: Piano music 2, 1975; Plastic
dream music, mixed ensemble of 10 players;
Mercury, oboe and piano.
256 E. 10th St., New York, NY 10009

BALLARD, LOUIS W.
b. Quapaw, Okla., 8 July 1931. Attended Univ.
of Oklahoma, B.A., B.M.Ed. 1954; Univ. of Tulsa,
M.M. 1962; studied composition with Bela Rozsa,
Darius Milhaud, Castelnuovo-Tedesco, and Carlos
Surinach. His honors include annual ASCAP
awards; the first Marion Nevins MacDowell award
for American chamber music; Ford Found. grant;
Nat. Endowment for the Arts, commission and 2
grants; Distinguished Alumnus award of Tulsa
Univ.; Nat. Indian Achievement award, 1972;
honorary D.M., Santa Fe Coll., 1973, etc. He
has been chairman of music and drama, Inst. of
American Indian Arts, Santa Fe, 1967-; music
curriculum specialist, Bureau of Indian Affairs,
1969-; consultant and arranger for music textbook publishers, author and lecturer on Indian
music.
WORKS: BALLET: Ji-Jo-Gweh (The witch water
gull), 1962; Koshare, Barcelona, Spain, 16 May
1966; The four moons, Tulsa, 28 Oct. 1967;
ORCHESTRA: Scenes from Indian life, 1966; Why
the duck has a short tail, Phoenix, 8 May 1969;
Devil's promenade, Tulsa, 20 May 1973; The
trail of tears, ballerina and orch., Washington,
1 Oct. 1976, Bicentennial program; CHAMBER
MUSIC: Ritmo Indio, woodwind quintet and Sioux
flute; Desert trilogy, mixed octet, Lubbock,
Tex., 28 Oct. 1971; Kateri Tekakwitha, double
quintet and vocalists, 1973; Kacina dances,
cello and piano; string trio; Rhapsody, 4

BAKER, ROBERT S.
    b. Ill., 7 July 1916. Studied at Illinois
Wesleyan Univ.; with Clarence Dickinson, Union
Theological Seminary; with Seth Bingham, Columbia
Univ.; with T. Tertius Noble and R. Huntington
Woodman in New York. He has been church organist
1945-; on faculty, Union Theological Seminary,
1961-73; Yale Univ., 1973-. He has published
anthems.
        School of Music, Yale Univ., New Haven, CT
        06510

BAKSA, ROBERT FRANK
    b. New York, N.Y., 7 Feb. 1938. Studied with
Henry Johnson and Robert McBridge, Univ. of
Arizona; with Lukas Foss at Tanglewood; but is
primarily self-taught. He is a free-lance
music copyist.
        WORKS: OPERA: Aria da capo, 1 act, text
by Millay, 1968; Red carnations, 1 act, text by
Hughes; ORCHESTRA: Meditation, 1955; Chamber
concerto, wind quartet and strings; Serenade,
string orch.; CHAMBER MUSIC: Canzonas, brass
quintet; trio for clarinet, cello, piano; piano
trio; woodwind octet; nonet for winds and strings; CHORUS: Herrick songs; 7
anthems for Holy Week; Shakespearean madrigals,
a cappella; The last days of Christ; many songs
on texts by Housman, Bierce, Dickinson; and film
scores.
        625 West End Ave., New York, NY 10024

BALADA, LEONARDO
    b. Barcelona, Spain, 22 Sept. 1933; to U.S.
1956. Attended Barcelona Cons., 1953-54;
Juilliard School, 1960; Mannes Coll. of Music,
1961-62; studied composition with Aaron Copland,
Alexander Tansman, Vincent Persichetti, conducting with Igor Markevitch. His awards include the Martinu prize, Mannes Coll., 1962;
ASCAP awards; Ciudad de Zaragoza internat. music
prize, 1974; Barcelona prize, 1976; Nat. Endowment for the Arts grant, 1977; many commissions.
He was faculty member, United Nations Internat.
School, 1963-70, then at Carnegie-Mellon Univ.,
professor from 1975.
        WORKS: ORCHESTRA: Musicila tranquila,
string orch., 1960; piano concerto, 1964;
concerto, 1965; Guernica, New Orleans, A
1967; Sinfonia en negro, homage to Mar
King, Jr., Madrid, June 1969, New Or
1970; Maria Sabina, narrator, chor
New York, April 1970; bandoneon c
Persistencias, guitar and orch.
1972; Transparencias, 1973; P
narrator and orch., New Orl
Requiem, with chorus and r
homages, Pablo Casals, P
burgh, 7 May 1976; BAN
phony, 1971; concerto t
band, New York, April 197
Musica en 4 teimpos, piano,
1960; concerto for cello and 5
1962, premiere, Pittsburgh, 18 M
Geometrias for 7 instruments, 1966,
no. 2, string quartet, 1967; Cuatris,
ments, 1969; End and beginning, rock an
temporary music ensembles, 1970; Mosaico,

quintet, Aspen, July 1970; Tresis, guitar, flute,
cello, New York, 22 May 1973; Sketches, guitar
quartet, 1974; Geometrias no. 3, bandoneon,
1977; 3 anecdotes, percussion and chamber orch.,
Pittsburgh, 8 Nov. 1978; CHORUS: Las moradas,
with 7 instruments, 1970; Voces no. 1, a
cappella, 1971; many songs and instrumental
solos.
        Music Dept., Carnegie-Mellon Univ.,
        Pittsburgh, PA 15213

BALAZS, FREDERIC
    b. Budapest, 12 Dec. 1920; U.S. citizen 1956.
Studied violin in Budapest, winning the Remer
prize at age 16. Other awards include thos
from the Internat. Society for Contempora
Music, Texas Composers competition, Ali
Ditson fund, honorary membership in th
Twain Literary Society for his "outs
contribution to American music."
conducting posts with several or
faculty positions in several c
became director and conducto
for Orchestra and Ensemble.
Honolulu Symph. Orch. He
violinist and lecturer.
        WORKS: BALLET: F
narrator, orch., per
dances after David
a plain-chant fr
after Walt Whi
faith; cello
Kennedy; Ke
string or
Los Ang
tions
Symr
4

BALES, R
    b. Al
Eastma
ducting
1939-41
1940. H
tions for
Washington
several con
music direc
ductor, Nat.
        WORKS: O
suites: Music
of early Ameri
ballet; 2 impres
Stony brook, suic
ican fishing indu
documentary films
Commerce, 1976; A
mezzo-soprano and o
Stokowski, Washington
The Confederacy, The
suites for chorus, so
Gate of the year; Come
presence, a cappella ch
pieces, a cappella ch
        National Gallery Orch
        of Art, Washington, D

BALL, ERNEST R.
    b. Cleveland, Ohio, 22 July
Calif., 3 May 1927. Studied
was staff composer and pianist
Company, 1907-27. He wrote sc
including Macushla and The hea

bassoons; Cacega Ayuwipi, percussion ensemble; Incident at Wounded Knee, chamber orch., 1974; CHORUS: The gods will hear, cantata, text based on poem of Indian poet, Lloyd H. New, Liberty, Mo., 8 Mar. 1966; Thus spake Abraham; Espiritu de Santiago, lyrics in English and Spanish; Portrait of Will Rogers, cantata for soloists, chorus, narrator, dancers, Oklahoma City, 8 Feb. 1976; also vocal and instrumental teaching pieces.

P.O. Box 4552, Santa Fe, NM 87501

BALLASEYUS, VIRGINIA
b. Hollins, Va., 14 Mar. 1892; d. Calif., 27 Mar. 1969. Studied with Darius Milhaud. She wrote music for California Centenary productions and for television.

BALLOU, ESTHER WILLIAMSON
b. Elmira, N.Y., 17 July 1915; d. Washington, D.C., 12 Mar. 1973. Studied at Bennington Coll.; Mills Coll.; with Bernard Wagenaar, Juilliard School, M.A.; privately with Otto Luening and Wallingford Riegger. Her awards included a MacDowell fellowship; an honorary doctorate, Hood Coll.; ASCAP award, 1969. She taught at Juilliard and at Catholic Univ.; was associate professor, American Univ., 1959-73.
WORKS: ORCHESTRA: concertino for oboe and strings, 1953; Prelude and allegro, 1955; Early American portrait, soprano and chamber orch., 1961; CHAMBER MUSIC: 2 sonatas for 2 pianos, 1943, 1959; Beguine, 2 pianos, 1951; piano trio, 1956; Suite for winds, 1957; sextet, brass and piano, 1961; Capriccio, violin and piano, 1963; Lament, cello and piano; and choral works.

BALOGH, ERNO
b. Budapest, 4 Apr. 1897; U.S. citizen 1929. Entered the Royal Acad. of Music at age 7; received diploma at the Royal Cons., 1915; studied piano with Bela Bartok and composition with Zoltan Kodaly; later studied in New York with Josef Lhevine. His awards include a citation from the Nat. Assoc. of American Composers and Conductors for performing the most contemporary American music in 1947. He was associate conductor, Royal Opera, Budapest, 1915-18; conductor of the Chamber Opera, 1918-19; on the faculty, Peabody Cons., Baltimore, 1947-60; concert pianist and accompanist to such artists as Fritz Kreisler and Lotte Lehmann.
WORKS: ORCHESTRA: Divertimento; Portrait of a city, a suite; PIANO: Dirge of the North; Caprice antique and Arabesque (both transcribed for violin and played by Fritz Kreisler); Pastorale at dawn, 1947; Dance infernale, 1949; La cigale joyeuse, 1951; Nothing but problems, 1966; Peasant dance, 1966; Debate, 1968; Restless, 1968; Complaining, 1969; A short jet flight, 1970; and many songs. He is author of magazine articles and one play, $25 an hour, produced on Broadway, and many years later, made into the movie One night of love.

3900 Watson Pl., N.W., Washington, DC 20016

BAMBACH, PAUL ANTON
b. Bay Village, Ohio, 14 Apr. 1950. Studied with Brian Dykstra, Wooster Coll.; with T. Scott Huston and Ellsworth Milburn, Cincinnati Coll. Cons. He has received commissions. He teaches clarinet and winds privately.
WORKS: CHAMBER MUSIC: fugue, string quartet, 1971; 3 dances for piano, 1971; 3 pieces for viola solo, 1974; trio for clarinet, viola, piano, 1974; Short piece, koto and percussion.

25585 Hilliard Blvd., Westlake, OH 44145

BAMERT, MATTHIAS
b. Ersigen, Switz., 5 July 1942; to U.S. 1969. Studied composition with Sandor Veress, Bern Cons., 1957-59; with Jean Rivier, Paris Cons., 1959-64; with Pierre Boulez at Darmstadt; conducting with Louis Forrestier in Paris, and George Szell in Cleveland. His awards include the Jeunesses Musicales award, Geneva, 1968; George Szell Memorial award for conducting, 1971; Cleveland Arts prize for Music, 1974; and several commissions. He was conducting fellow, Cleveland Orch., 1969-70; assistant conductor, American Symphony, 1970-71; assistant conductor, Cleveland Orchestra, 1971-76; resident conductor, 1976-78; became music director, Swiss Radio Orchestra, in 1977.
WORKS: ORCHESTRA: concertino, strings, English horn, piano, 1966; Rheology, strings, Lucerne, Dec. 1971; Septuria lunaris, Lucerne, Aug. 1970; Mantrajana, New York, 12 Dec. 1971; Circus parade, for young audience and orch., 1974; Once upon an orchestra, with narrator and 12 dancers, 1975; BAND: Inkblot, New York, July 1971; CHAMBER MUSIC: woodwind quintet, 1967; Introduction and tarantella, flute, percussion, piano, New York, Jan. 1973; Incon-Sequenza, tuba solo, Cleveland, May 1973; +Ations, theater piece for 3 cellists, 1975; 01-Okun, 1976; brass quintet, 1976.

2653 N. Moreland Blvd., Cleveland, OH 44120

BAMPTON, RUTH
b. Boston, Mass., 7 Mar. 1902. Attended New England Cons., diploma with advanced honors 1927, M.B. 1931; Boston Univ.; Eastman School of Music; Union Theological Seminary, M.S.M. 1933; studied in Paris with Nadia Boulanger and Marcel Dupre. She is a member of the American Guild of Organists. She taught at Vermont Coll., 1928-30; at Beaver Coll., Pa., 1935-43; was director of music, Pasadena Polytechnic School, 1945-64; organist and choir director, 1928-67. She has published numerous choral works, piano pieces, piano ensembles, and songs.

900 E. Harrison Ave., #D68, Pomona, CA 91767

BANAITIS, KAZIMIERAS VIKTORAS
b. Lithuania, 1 Jan. 1896; to U.S. 1949; d. New York, 1963. Studied in Prague, 1921, and at the Leipzig Cons., 1922-28. He was instructor, Kaunas State Music School, 1928-37; director, Lithuanian Cons., 1937-40; private teacher, Brooklyn, N.Y., 1949-63.
WORKS: OPERA: Jurate and Kastytis; SONGS: 100 Lithuanian folk songs for solo voice or male chorus and piano.

BANCHZ, WILLIAM

BANCHZ, WILLIAM
b. Caracas, Venezuela, 8 Oct. 1948; to U.S. 1963.
Studied piano with Margaret Chaloff, composition
with Avram David in Boston; with Earl Kim at
Harvard Univ., where he was teaching fellow,
1972-73.
WORKS: ORCHESTRA: El deseo sagrado, 1974;
CHAMBER MUSIC: string quartet; septet; clarinet
sonata, unaccompanied; clarinet sonata in 9 movements; The Lord's prayer, soprano, clarinet,
cello; Psalm of joy, 1973; Omega, paino, clarinet,
violin, 1973.

BANCROFT, B. RICHARD
b. White Plains, N.Y., 17 Mar. 1936. Studied at
Fredonia State Univ. Coll., B.S.; with Robert
Crane, Univ. of Wisconsin, M.S.; with Robert
Marvel, New York Univ., Ed.D; also with Percy
Grainger and Rudolph Kolisch. He received 2
prizes in a Wisconsin state composition contest
and a New York State Education Dept. grant. He
taught in New York and Wisconsin schools, 1958-
62; at Minot State Coll., N. Dak., 1962-64; and
at Westminster Coll., Pa., associate professor,
1971-78.
WORKS: ORCHESTRA: 3 songs, soprano and
orch.; BAND: Epithets; CHAMBER MUSIC: Soliloquy,
solo trumpet; brass sextet; woodwind trio;
string quartet; Sketches for piano; Diversion,
woodwind trio; Days, voice and piano.
R.D. #3, Randall Drive, New Castle, PA
16105

BARAB, SEYMOUR
b. Chicago, Ill., 9 Jan. 1921. Has been cellist
with several major orchestras; also played viola
da gamba with New York Pro Musica Antiqua.
WORKS: OPERA: Chanticleer, comic opera,
1954; The rajah's ruby, farce, 1954; Game of
chance, comic opera, 1956; Philip Marshall,
libretto based on Dostoevski's The idiot;
Little Red Riding Hood, children's opera;
ORCHESTRA: Tales of rhyme and reason, narrator,
dance pantomine and orch.; CHAMBER MUSIC: woodwind quintet; sextet for piano and woodwinds;
Little suite, 3 flutes; 6 pieces, recorder trio,
1957; CHORUS: The silver swan, a cappella,
1956; An angel chorus, a cappella, 1956; First
person feminine, women's voices; SONGS: A
child's garden of verses; Songs of perfect
propriety; The rivals, song cycle.

BARATI, GEORGE
b. Gyor, Hungary, 3 Apr. 1913; U.S. citizen
1944. Studied at Franz Liszt Cons., Budapest,
and with Roger Sessions at Princeton. His
honors include a Naumburg award; Guggenheim
fellowship; Ditson award; and honorary doctorates
from the Univ. of Hawaii and the Music and Arts
Inst., San Francisco. He was first cellist,
Budapest Symph. Orch., 1936-38; taught at
Princeton Univ., 1939-43; bandmaster, U.S. Army,
1944-46; cellist, San Francisco Symph., 1946-50;
conductor, Honolulu Symph. and Opera, 1950-68;
conductor, Santa Cruz County Symph., 1971-,
music director from 1968.
WORKS: OPERA: The feather cloak, 1970;
Noelani, 1971; BALLET: The love of Don

Perlimplin, 1947; The dragon and the phoenix,
1960; ORCHESTRA: Scherzo, 1946; Configuration,
1947; cello concerto, 1957; piano concerto;
chamber concerto; symphony, 1964; Polarization,
1965; South Sea suite, guitar and orch., 1971;
Cities of the interior, soprano and orch.,
Santa Cruz, 15 May 1976; guitar concerto, Santa
Cruz, 16 Apr. 1977; CHAMBER MUSIC: 2 string
quartets, 1944, 1962; violin sonata; harpsichord
quartet, 1964; octet for harpsichord, flute,
oboe, string quintet, 1966; Hawaiian bird-
catching song, clarinet and piano, Santa Cruz,
10 Oct. 1976; duo, flute and viola, 1978;
CHORUS: The waters of Kane, festival ode for
chorus and orch., 1966; piano pieces.
Villa Montalvo, P.O. Box 158, Saratoga, CA
95070

BARBER, GAIL G.
b. New Iberia, La., 23 Feb. 1939. Studied harp
at Eastman School of Music. She has received
citations from the American Harp Society.
Faculty, Texas Tech. Univ. Her works for harp
include Windmill sketches, a suite for solo
harp; Improvisation on a familiar melody; duets
for harp; and transcriptions.
P.O. Box 64189, Lubbock, TX 79464

BARBER, SAMUEL
b. West Chester, Pa., 9 Mar. 1910; d. New York,
23 Jan. 1981. Studied with Scalerio, Curtis
Inst. of Music, honorary D.M. His other awards
include an honorary doctorate, Harvard Univ.,
1959; Prix de Rome, 1935; Pulitzer traveling
fellowships, 1935-36; New York Music Critics
awards, 1946, 1964; Guggenheim fellowship, 1947;
Pulitzer prize, 1958, 1963; membership in the
Nat. Inst. of Arts and Letters and Amer. Acad.
of Arts and Letters; Edward MacDowell prize,
1980; numerous commissions. He served in the
U.S. Army Air Force, 1942-45, then settled near
New York.
WORKS: OPERA: Vanessa, 1956, performed by
Metropolitan Opera, New York, 15 Jan. 1958; A
hand of bridge, 1 act, 1958, Spoleto, Italy, 17
June 1959; Antony and Cleopatra, commissioned by
the Metropolitan Opera for the opening of Lincoln
Center on 16 Sept. 1966, rev. and performed at
Juilliard, 6 Feb. 1975; BALLET: Cave of the
heart, 1945-47; ORCHESTRA: Overture to the
school for scandal, 1933; Music for a scene from
Shelley, 1935; A stopwatch and an ordnance map,
male chorus and orch., 1940; symphony in one
movement, 1936; violin concerto, Philadelphia,
7 Feb. 1941; Essays no. 1 and 2, 1942; Capricorn
concerto, flute, oboe, trumpet, strings, New
York, 8 Oct. 1944; symphony no 2, Boston, 3 Mar.
1944, rev. and performed Philadelphia, 21 Jan.
1948; Media suite, Philadelphia, 5 Dec. 1947;
Knoxville, summer of 1915, soprano and chamber
orch., 1948; Prayers of Kierkegaard, soprano,
chorus, orch., 1954; Die natali, Boston, 22 Dec.
1960; Toccata festiva, organ and orch., 1961;
Andromache's farewell, soprano and orch., 1962;
piano concerto, New York, 24 Sept. 1962; The
lovers, baritone, chorus, and orch., 1970;
Fadograph from a yestern scene, Pittsburgh, 10
Sept. 1971; 3rd essay for orchestra, New York,
15 Sept. 1-78; oboe concerto, New York, 15 Feb.

1979; BAND: Commando march, 1943; CHAMBER MUSIC: Serenade for string quartet, 1929; Dover beach, voice and string quartet, 1931; cello sonata, 1932; string quartet, 1936; piano sonata, 1949; Summer music, woodwind quintet, 1956; string quartet, op. 45, New York, 29 Jan. 1973; SONGS: Nuvoletta, 1947; Hermit songs, 1953; Despite and still, song cycle, 1969; Sure on this shining night, baritone and piano; also choral works, piano pieces.

BARBOUR, J. MURRAY
b. Chambersburg, Pa., 31 Mar. 1897; d. Homestead, Pa., 4 Jan. 1970. He was chiefly a musicologist but composed Childe Rowland, symphonic poem; a Requiem; and chamber works.

BARCLAY, ROBERT L.
b. Penticton, B.C., Canada, 2 Feb. 1918; U.S. citizen 1951; d. Ft. Lauderdale, Fla., 11 Mar. 1980. Studied at Juilliard School, holding a fellowship, 1944-45, scholarships, 1945-47, received diploma, 1947. In the 1950s he was music critic with Music and Musicians and Records and Recordings; in 1976, was artist-in-residence, Indiana State Univ.; then partner in the publishing firm, Barger and Barclay.
WORKS: ORCHESTRA: Legend, 1940; Scherzo, chamber orch., 1942, rev. 1976; overture, 1949; concerto for piano and strings, 1950; symphony in 1 movement, 1950; Variations, 1975; CHAMBER MUSIC: quartet for clarinet and string trio, 1945, rev. 1976; piano sonatine, 1947; duo for violin and piano, 1954; Night episode #2, solo flute, 1976; other shorter chamber pieces.

BARKER, WARREN E.
b. Oakland, Calif., 16 Apr. 1923. Studied at Univ. of California, Los Angeles; privately with Henri Pensis in Iowa and Castelnuovo-Tedesco in Los Angeles. He was staff music director, Warner Bros. Records, 1948-60, and a free-lance composer for television and motion pictures, 1960-70.
WORKS: Scores for the following television series: Bewitched, Daktari, The flying nun, The ghost and Mrs. Muir, Here come the brides, The iron horse, Lawbreaker, Ripcord, That girl, Follow the sun, Valentines day, The man and the challenge, Bracken's world, My world and welcome to it, Nanny and the professor, Room 222; and the motion picture, Zebra in the kitchen.
Rte. 3, Box 3503, Red Bluff, CA 96080

BARKIN, ELAINE
b. New York, 15 Dec. 1932. Studied at Queens Coll. with Karol Rathaus; Brandeis Univ. with Irving Fine, Harold Shapiro, Arthur Berger; and at Berlin Hochschule für Musik with Boris Blacher. Her awards include a Fulbright grant, 1956; Princeton Univ., Council of Humanities junior fellowship; New York State Council on the Arts commission; ISCM commission, 1974; 2 grants, Nat. Endowment for the Arts, 1976, 1978. She has held faculty positions at Queens Coll., Sarah Lawrence Coll., Univ. of Michigan, Princeton Univ. (visiting fellow, spring 1974); from 1974, at Univ. of California, Los Angeles,

professor from 1978.
WORKS: CHAMBER MUSIC: Refrains, 6 players, 1967; string quartet, 1969; 6 compositions for piano, 1969; Prim cycles for 4, 1972; Plus ca change, strings and percussion, 1971-72; Sound play, violin, 1973; Mixed modes, clarinet, string trio, piano, 1974; Inward and outward bound, large ensemble, 1975; string trio, 1976; Plein chant, flute, 1977; Ebb tide, 2 vibraphones, 1977; CHORUS: Dickinson choruses, 1976.
12533 Killion St., N. Hollywood, CA 91607

BARLOW, HOWARD
b. Plain City, Ohio, 1 May 1892; d. Bethel, Conn., 31 Jan. 1972. Studied at Reed Coll., B.A., L.L.D.; on scholarship with Frank E. Ward and Cornelius Rybner at Columbia Univ. He was conductor, CBS Symphony, 1927-43; Baltimore Symphony, 1939-42; Firestone program, 1943-59; guest conductor, New York Philharmonic. He composed the songs: Lament; Garden; Mother, I cannot mind my wheel; Margaret.

BARLOW, SAMUEL L. M.
b. New York, N.Y., 1 June 1892. Studied at Harvard Univ., B.A. 1914; with Ottorino Respighi in Rome. His honors include the French Legion of Honor; Bonn Government Cross of Merit; election to membership, Internat. Acad. of Arts and Letters. He is author of The astonished muse, 1961.
WORKS: OPERA: Mon ami Pierrot, 1 act, Paris, 1935; Amanda, 1936; Eugenie; ORCHESTRA: Cortege from Ballo Sardo, 1928; piano concerto, 1930; Biedermeier waltzes, 1935; Babar, symphonic concerto uses magic lantern slides, 1935; Circus overture, 1960; choral works and songs.

BARLOW, WAYNE
b. Elyria, Ohio, 6 Sept. 1912. Studied with Bernard Rogers, Howard Hanson, and Schoenberg, Eastman School of Music, B.M. 1934, M.M. 1935, Ph.D. 1937; electronic music with Myron Schaeffer, Univ. of Toronto, 1963-64. He received 2 Fulbright grants and many commissions. On the faculty at Eastman since 1937, he is also associate dean for graduate research studies and director of the Electronic Music Studio. He has been a frequent guest lecturer, conductor, and visiting composer.
WORKS: BALLET: 3 moods for dancing, 1940; The black madonna, 1941; ORCHESTRA: Songs from the silence of Amor, 1939; Nocturne, chamber orch., 1946; Rondo-overture, 1947; Sinfonietta in C, 1950; Lento and allegro, 1955; Night song, 1957; Poems for music, soprano and orch., 1958; Images, harp and orch., 1961; Vistas, 1963; Intrada, fugue, and postlude, brass ensemble, 1959; Sinfonia da camera, 1962; saxophone concerto, 1970; CHAMBER MUSIC: The winter's passed, oboe and strings, 1938; Lyrical piece, clarinet and strings, 1943; Prelude, air, and variations, bassoon and string quartet, 1949; piano quintet, 1951; Triptych, string quartet, 1954; Rota, chamber orch., 1959; trio, oboe, viola, piano, 1964; Elegy, viola and piano, 1967; piano sonata, 1947; Dynamisms, 2 pianos, 1967; 2 inventions for piano, 1968; Vocalize and canon, tuba and

BARNARD, WILLIAM

piano, Rochester, N.Y., 11 Oct. 1976; CHORUS: Zion in exile, cantata, with soloists and orch., 1937; Madrigal for a bright morning, 1942; The 23rd Psalm, with orch., 1944; Mass in G, with orch., 1951; Missa sancti tomae, 1959; Diversify the abyss, men's glee club, 1964; We all believe in one true God, 1965; Wait for the promise of the Father, cantata, 1968; Voices of faith, with narrator and orch., Augusta, Ga., 28 Feb. 1976; Out of the cradle endlessly rocking, with tenor solo, clarinet, viola, piano, tape, Rochester, N.Y., 4 Apr. 1978; ELECTRONIC: Dialogues, harp and tape, 1969; Soundscapes, orch. and tape, 1972; Voices of darkness, percussion, piano, reader, tape, 1976.
    Eastman School of Music, Rochester, NY 14604

BARNARD, WILLIAM
b. N.C., 19 May 1918. Studied at Univ. of Michigan; with Harold Friedell, Union Theological Seminary, New York. He has been organist and choirmaster in New Jersey and Houston, Tex. His published choral works include Benedictus in C.
    1925 Albans, Houston, TX 77005

BARNEA, URI
b. Petah-Tikvah, Israel, 29 May 1943; to U.S. 1971. Studied at Rubin Acad. of Music, Jerusalem, B.M. 1971; composition with Domenick Argento, Paul Fetler, Eric Stokes, Univ. of Minnesota, M.A. 1974, Ph.D. 1977; also studied conducting. He was winner, Aspen composition contest, 1976, and Oberhoffer contest, 1976; Diploma of Distinction, Viotti Internat. competition, 1975. He has been orchestra and choral conductor in Minneapolis from 1973; in 1977, founded the Univ. of Minnesota Summer Symphony.
  WORKS: ORCHESTRA: Passacaglia, 1972; Ruth, a ballet for orch., 1974; Fantasy, organ and orch., 1976; Variations on a theme by Stravinsky, 1976; CHAMBER MUSIC: A picture of Chagall, mezzo-soprano, tenor, chamber ensemble, his own text, 1969; Mini-suite for piano, 1972; Piece for brass quintet, 1973; flute sonata, 1975; string quartet, 1976; CHORUS: Fortune favors fools, children's musical, 1972; America, cantata, with tenor solo, brass, percussion, organ, 1975.
    606 Jefferson St. N.E., Minneapolis, MN 55413

BARNES, EDWARD SHIPPEN
b. Seabright, N.J., 14 Sept. 1887; d. Idyllwild, Calif., 14 Feb. 1958. Studied with David Stanley Smith and Horatio Parker, Yale Univ.; organ with Louis Vierne in Paris. He was church organist in New York, New Jersey, Philadelphia, and Santa Monica, Calif. His compositions included 2 organ symphonies; cantatas and other choral works; sacred songs.

BARNES, JAMES CHARLES
b. Hobart, Okla., 9 Sept. 1949. Studied with John Pozdro, Edward Mattila, Charles Hoag, and Allen I. McHose, Univ. of Kansas. He was 1978 winner of the ABA-Ostwald Band composition contest for symphony, op. 35. He is assistant to the band director and staff arranger, Univ. of Kansas.
  WORKS: ORCHESTRA: Silhouettes; Trilogy, a suite; Today, jazz-rock overture; BAND: Rhapsodic essay; Colours, winds and tape; Commencement festival overture; Hunter Park, tone poem; 2 preludes; Rapscallion, overture-scherzo; Golden brass, concert march; symphony, op. 35; CHAMBER MUSIC: Study for 7, brass; duo, clarinet and bassoon; string quartet.
    214 Murphy Hall, Univ. of Kansas, Lawrence, KS 66045

BARNES, LARRY JOHN
b. Cleveland, Ohio, 17 July 1950. Studied with Donald Erb, Cleveland Inst. of Music, B.M. 1972, M.M. 1973; with Mario Davidovsky, Bennington Composers' Conf., 1970-71; with Samuel Adler, Warren Benson, Joseph Schwantner, Eastman School of Music, D.M.A. 1979. His awards include the Cleveland Orchestra student award, 1973; Gund Found. grant, 1976; Sernoffsky prize, 1978; Nat. Endowment for the Arts grant, 1977-78; Howard Hanson Orchestral prize, 1970. He has held teaching posts at Heidelberg Coll., 1973-77; Eastman School, 1977-79; from 1979, at Univ. of Texas at San Antonio.
  WORKS: ORCHESTRA: Solar winds, 1972; piano concerto, 1979; CHAMBER MUSIC: The 800th lifetime, piano; The devil tree, brass quintet.
    Div. of Music, University of Texas, San Antonio, TX 78285

BARNES, MARSHALL
b. Fairfield, Iowa, 2 Oct. 1921. Studied with Philip Clapp and Addison Alspach, Univ. of Iowa; with James Friskin, Katherine Mann, and Bernard Wagenaar at Juilliard School. He has had awards from Iowa Fed. of Music Clubs, Juilliard School, and Ohio Music Educators Assoc. His faculty positions have included Univ. of Iowa; Parsons Coll., Iowa; Trinity Univ., Tex.; and Ohio State Univ. from 1957.
  WORKS: A dirge of 4 cities, chorus and orch.; Salt water ballads, chorus and orch.; Old Worthington suite, flute, clarinet, piano, narrator; songs, choral works, piano pieces.
    33 Wilson Dr., Worthington, OH 43085

BARNETT, ALICE
b. Lewiston, Ill., 26 May 1888; d. San Diego, Calif., 25 Aug. 1975. Studied piano with her father, then at Chicago Musical Coll. with Rudolph Ganz and Heniot Levy, composition with Felix Borowski; then at American Cons., Chicago, and in Berlin with Hugo Kaun. In 1917 she settled in San Diego as a teacher, helped found the San Diego Civic Symphony, Opera Guild, etc. She published more than 60 songs, including a cycle of 8 songs on Robert Browning's In a Gondola; Serenade, on a text of Clinton Scollard; Chanson of the bells of Oseney, poem of Cale Young Rice; Music when soft voices, by Shelley; and others.

BARNETT, CAROL
b. Dubuque, Iowa, 23 May 1949. Studied with Paul Fetler and Dominick Argento, Univ. of Minnesota.
  WORKS: ORCHESTRA: Adon Olam, 1976, com-

missioned and performed by the First Unitarian Soc. Orchestra, Minneapolis; BAND: <u>Arabesques</u>, 1976; <u>Allusions</u>, 1978; CHAMBER MUSIC: <u>Memoriam</u>, viola and piano; horn sonata.

3120 Fremont Ave. S., Minneapolis, MN 55408

BARNETT, DAVID
b. New York, N.Y., 1 Dec. 1907. Studied at Columbia Univ., B.A.; with Howard Brockway, Mannes Coll. of Music; with Rubin Goldmark, Juilliard School; with Rosario Scalero, Curtis Inst.; and earned a diploma, Ecole Normale de Musique, Paris. His awards include a commission from the Harvard Musical Assoc. He has held faculty posts at Wellesley Coll., New England Cons., Harvard Coll., Columbia Univ. in summer sessions, and from 1968, has been professor, Univ. of Bridgeport.
WORKS: OPERA: <u>Inner voices</u>, 1 act; CHAMBER MUSIC: <u>Ballade</u>, viola and piano; <u>Fantasie</u>, clarinet and piano; piano trio; <u>Ballad</u>, trombone, 3 saxophones, contrabass, piano; oboe sonatina; <u>Gallery</u>, piano; also vocal works. He is author of the book, <u>The performance of music</u>, New York, 1972.
Box 1304, Weston, CT 06880

BARON, MAURICE
b. Lille, France, 1 Jan. 1889; d. Oyster Bay, N.Y., 5 Sept. 1964. He was arranger and staff composer at Radio City Music Hall in New York, 1933-43; composed hundreds of works in all forms including film scores. His <u>Ode to democracy</u>, for narrator, chorus, and orch., was performed in New York, 23 Jan. 1949.

BAROVICK, FRED
b. New York, N.Y., 28 June. Studied at Curtis Inst.; Univ. of Pennsylvania, Ph.D. He was arranger for many dance and jazz bands, and for Broadway shows, television, records, and educational films.
WORKS: ORCHESTRA: symphony for strings; trombone quartet with orch.; trombone solo with brass choir; <u>The lost horizons</u>; and popular songs.

BARR, JOHN GLADDEN
b. Myrtle Point, Oreg., 24 July 1938. Studied with R. Gary Deavel, Manchester Coll., Ind.; with Joseph Goodman, Union Theological Seminary, S.M.M., S.M.D.; with Bruce Benward, Univ. of Wisconsin at Madison; also studied organ and piano. He taught at Hillcrest School for Missionary Children in Nigeria, 1962-65; was organist-choir director, Madison, Wis., 1965-68; then joined the faculty at Bridgewater Coll., Va.
WORKS: CHORUS: <u>Magnificat and nunc dimittis</u>, unison voices and organ, 1961; <u>Pastorale and song of the angels</u>, cantata for mixed chorus and chamber orch.; ORGAN: <u>How brightly shines the morning star</u>, chorale prelude on a melody of Phillip Nicolai, 1971; other works for voice, organ, piano, band, strings.
308 E. College St., Bridgewater, VA 22812

BARRETT, ROGER L.
b. Skidmore, Mo., 12 May 1924. Studied with

Francis J. Pyle at Drake Univ. He won first place in an Iowa Young Composers contest and a Music Educators Nat. Conf. commission, 1956. At St. Cloud State Coll. he was band director, 1949-66; department chairman, 1965-70; then professor of theory and composition.
WORKS: ORCHESTRA: <u>Suite: it's a boy</u>; <u>MENC golden anniversary march</u>; <u>In the beginning</u>, wind ensemble; CHAMBER MUSIC: <u>Nocturne</u>, clarinet, horn, string trio.
State College, St. Cloud, MN 56301

BARRETT-THOMAS, NANCY
b. 21 May 1948. Studied with Gardner Read and Hugo Norden, Boston Univ.; with Michael Hennagin, Univ. of Oklahoma. She received first prize in the Mu Phi Epsilon composition contest 1969 and 1975. She was resident accompanist and theory teacher, National Center for Afro-American Artists, 1972-75; from 1977, has been executive board member, League of Women Composers, and business administrator, Kodály Musical Training Inst.; from 1978, business manager, New England Women's Symphony.
WORKS: CHAMBER MUSIC: <u>Perpetuum mobile</u>, flute, violin, viola, bassoon, 1969; <u>Reflected</u>, song cycle for soprano and piano; <u>Songs of singing</u>, contralto, cello, piano, 1970; <u>Gregarious chants</u>, viola and clarinet, 1975; viola sonata, 1976; CHORUS: <u>Songs to a handsome woman</u>, with jazz piano; <u>From the land of the carib</u>, with wind ensemble.
P.O. Box 508, Allston, MA 02134

BARROW, ROBERT GEORGE
b. Washington, D.C., 9 July 1911. In his early years, studied privately in England with Ralph Vaughan Williams and Paul Hindemith; later with Richard Donovan at Yale Univ., B.A., M.A., M.M.; also piano with Bruce Simonds and organ with Harry Jepson. He received 2 Ditson fellowships. He was organist at National Cathedral, 1935-39; on faculty at Williams Coll. from 1940; professor and department chairman, 1949-71.
WORKS: ORCHESTRA: suite for strings; <u>Suite concertante</u>, organ and strings; <u>Divertimento</u>; <u>Partita</u>; <u>Sinfonia concertante</u>, English horn, trumpet, double bass, orch.; CHAMBER MUSIC: 3 string quartets; 2 woodwind quintets; CHORUS: <u>The risen Christ</u> and <u>Emanuel</u>, cantats with organ; <u>3 Psalms</u>, men's voices and string orch.; ORGAN: <u>Christus natus est: 3 chorale preludes</u>.

BARROWS, JOHN
b. Glendale, Calif., 12 Feb. 1913; d. Madison, Wis., 11 Jan. 1974. Studied horn at Eastman School of Music, 1930-32; theory at San Diego State Teachers Coll., 1933-34; composition with Richard Donovan and David Stanley Smith at Yale Univ., 1934-38. He played horn in the Minneapolis Symphony, 1938-42; with the New York City Opera, 1946-49; City Ballet Orch., 1952-55; Casala Festival Orch., 1958-61; was member of the New York Woodwind Quintet, 1952-61; taught horn at Yale Univ. and New York Univ., then at Univ. of Wisconsin, 1961-74. His compositions included 2 string quintets, a string trio, pieces for woodwind quintet.

BARRUS, LAMAR

BARRUS, LAMAR
    b. Sugar City, Idaho, 22 July 1935. Studied
with Leroy Robertson, Ned Rorem, and Alexi
Haieff, Univ. of Utah, Ph.D. 1968. He won
first place in a Utah State composition contest.
He was violinist in the Utah Symph. Orch. inter-
mittently, 1959-65; conductor, Idaho Falls
Symph., 1965-70; faculty member, Ricks Coll.,
from 1960, and chairman of the music department
from 1972.
    WORKS: ORCHESTRA: Ode to libertad, a
choral symphony; CHAMBER MUSIC: trio for 2
violins and viola; Elegy, viola and piano;
Soliloquy and Berceuse for organ; Whispers of
heavenly death, song cycle for soprano, viola,
and piano.
    260 S. 3rd East, Rexburg, ID 83440

BARRYMORE, LIONEL
    b. Philadelphia, Pa., 28 Apr. 1878; d. Van Nuys,
Calif., 15 Nov. 1954. Noted actor, director,
artist, also composed Farewell symphony, 1-act
opera; orchestral works; piano pieces.

BARTH, HANS
    b. Leipzig, Germany, 25 June 1897; U.S. citizen
1912; d. Jacksonville, Fla., 8 Dec. 1956.
Studied at Leipzig Cons. on a scholarship; gave
piano recitals in New York at age 12. He made
a special study of tonal and octave divisions
and invented a portable quarter-tone piano
(1928) on which he played in Carnegie Hall on
3 Feb. 1930 and for which he wrote extensively.
He gave concerts in Europe and America, playing
harpsichord, piano, and the quarter-tone piano.
His concerto for the quarter-tone piano and
quarter-tone strings was played by the Philadelphia, Cincinnati, and Havana orchestras with the
composer as pianist. He was director, Yonkers
Inst. of Musical Art and of the Nat. School for
Musical Culture, New York, and taught piano at
Mannes School of Music.
    WORKS: THEATRE: Miragia, operetta, 1938;
incidental music for Save me the waltz;
ORCHESTRA: piano concerto, 1928; concerto for
quarter-tone piano, quarter-tone strings, 1930;
Drama symphony, 1940; Peace symphony, 10 etudes
for piano and orch., 1943; CHAMBER MUSIC: quintet for quarter-tone strings and piano, 1930;
PIANO: 2 sonatas, 1929, 1932; and songs.

BARTHELSON, JOYCE HOLLOWAY
    b. Yakima, Wash., 18 May 1908. Studied composi-
tion with Julius Gold, Otto Cesana, Roy Harris;
piano with Elizabeth Quaile, Helene Barere;
conducting with Antonia Brico. In 1967 she
received first prize of ASCAP and the Nat. Fed.
of Music Clubs for an opera. She was vocal and
ensemble coach at NBC in San Francisco, 1930-33;
assistant conductor, N.Y. Women's Symph., 1935-
40; composer-in-residence, Western Maryland
Coll., 1942-44; director of many choruses in the
N.Y. area; cofounder and codirector of a music
school in Scarsdale, N.Y., from 1944.
    WORKS: OPERA: Feathertop, opera buffa;
Chanticleer, comic fantasy; Greenwich village,
1910; The king's breakfast, Atlantic City, April
1973; Lysistrata, 1 act, New York, 27 Mar. 1981;
ORCHESTRA: overture in a; Of time and the

river, a suite; The Forty-niners, with soloists
and chorus; Spin, spin, with soloists; concerto
for 2 pianos; oboe concerto with chamber orch.;
Savannah, overture; The tin soldier; Weather
report, suite in 6 movements; many choral works
including The first Palm Sunday, a cantata; and
piano pieces.
    45 Popham Rd., Scarsdale, NY 10583

BARTHOLOMEW, MARSHALL MOORE
    b. Belleville, Ill., 3 Mar. 1885; d. Guilford,
Conn., 16 Apr. 1978. Studied with Horatio
Parker and David Stanley Smith, Yale Univ., B.A.
1907; later in Berlin. He founded the Yale Glee
Club in 1921. He was chiefly a choral conductor
and arranger, but wrote many songs.

BARTLES, ALFRED H.
    b. Nashville, Tenn., 10 Nov. 1930. Studied at
Univ. of Mississippi, B.A.; cello with Claus
Adam; composition with Karl Ahrendt, Ohio Univ.,
M.F.A. He received 2 Waldorf Educ. Found.
grants for residence and composing in Germany,
1969-71. He was free-lance cellist, composer,
and teacher in New York, 1954-69; on faculty,
Schiller Coll., Heidelberg, Germany, 1970-73;
then joined the faculty at Tennessee Tech. Univ.
    WORKS: ORCHESTRA: Theme in three, 1954;
Music for symphony orchestra and jazz ensemble,
1966; Ballad, cello and chamber orch., 1968;
Engadine overture, 1970; Excalibur, 1972; BAND:
Music City, USA, 1964; Appalachian portrait,
1965; scherzo, with tuba solo, 1969; CHAMBER
MUSIC: trio, clarinet, cello, piano, 1954;
quartet for piano, viola, clarinet, cello, 1967;
Ceremonial music, trumpet and organ, 1968;
Elegy, bass trombone and piano, 1969; Lament,
variations, and metamorphoses, woodwind quintet,
1969; trumpet sonatina, 1972; CHORUS: Child
Jesus, 1967; JAZZ: Louisiana jazz suite, 1961;
Ballad, for trumpet and jazz ensemble, 1962.

BARTON, LOUIS
    b. New York, N.Y., 24 Aug. 1949. Studied with
Jonathan Kramer at Yale Univ.; with Ran Blake
at the New England Cons. He is organist at St.
John Vianney Church, Sedona, Ariz. He has composed many church works for organ and voice, and
secular works for piano, voice, and small
orchestra.
    P.O. Box 415, Flagstaff, AZ 86002

BARTOW, NEVETT
    b. New York, N.Y., 7 Nov. 1939; d. Blairstown,
N.J., 21 Nov. 1973. Studied with Vittorio
Giannini and Ludmila Ulehla at Manhattan School
of Music; in Rome with Ildebrando Pizzeti; and
in Vienna with Karl Schiske. He received the
Nat. Arts Club young artists' award, 1959;
nominated for Princeton Univ. Distinguished
Teachers award for New Jersey, 1972; Outstanding
Secondary Educator of America, 1973. He was
chairman of the music department, Blair Academy,
1962-73.
    WORKS: ORCHESTRA: Summer shadow, elegy for
orch.; 3 symphonic dances, Norwalk, Conn., Dec.
1973; CHAMBER MUSIC: flute sonata, 1970;
Divertimento , woodwind quintet; 3 organ sonatas;

clarinet sonata; <u>Soliloquy</u>, cello and piano; <u>Variations and fugue</u>, piano; toccata, piano; CHORUS: <u>The tower of Babel</u>, cantata; <u>Christmas cantata</u>; <u>A Thanksgiving exultation</u>.

BASART, ROBERT
b. S. Dak., 17 Nov. 1926. Studied with Andrew Imbrie, Univ. of California, Berkeley; with Darius Milhaud at Mills Coll. He received a Hertz traveling fellowship. He was lecturer, California State Univ., San Francisco, 1966-68; then named to faculty, California State Univ. at Hayward.
WORKS: CHAMBER MUSIC: <u>Fantasy</u>, flute and piano, 1963; <u>Serenade</u>, soprano, flute, clarinet, piano, and tape, 1966; <u>Kansas City dump</u>, clarinet, violin, cello, piano, tape, 1968; variations, cello and piano, 1973; <u>Stem, leaf, leaves, small flower</u>, piano trio, 1977.
2419 Oregon St., Berkeley, CA 94705

BASKERVILLE, DAVID
b. Freehold, N.J., 18 Aug. 1919. Studied at Univ. of California, Los Angeles, M.A., Ph.D. His faculty posts have included Westlake Coll. of Music, 1947-48; Univ. of California, 1951-56; later at Univ. of Colorado.
WORKS: BAND: <u>Grand entry swing march</u>; <u>Ventura overture</u>; <u>Moonride</u>; <u>Hollywood swing march</u>.
Univ. of Colorado, 1100 14th St., Denver, CO 80202

BASNEY, ELDON E.
Studied with Gustav Strube, Peabody Cons. His awards include a MacDowell fellowship and performances at Lincoln Center, Nat. Assoc. of American Composers and Conductors, and Eastman Festival, 1968. He has published <u>Serenade</u> for string trio.
Music Dept., Houghton College, Houghton, NY 14744

BASS, CLAUDE L.
b. Gainesville, Tex., 31 Oct. 1935. Studied with Violet Archer, Univ. of Oklahoma; with Samuel Adler, North Texas State Univ. He won 2 awards in the Broadman anthem competition, 1959, 1962. Since 1965 he has been faculty member, Oklahoma Baptist Univ. He composes primarily choral works and has published anthems such as <u>Thy boundless love</u> and <u>Jesus, Thou joy of loving hearts</u>.
Oklahoma Baptist Univ., Shawnee, OK 74801

BASSETT, KAROLYN WELLS
b. Derby, Conn., 2 Aug. 1892; d. Conn., 2 June 1931. She composed songs and choral works.

BASSETT, LESLIE
b. Hanford, Calif., 22 Jan. 1923. Studied at Fresno State Coll., B.A. 1947; with Ross Lee Finney, Univ. of Michigan, M.M. 1949, D.M. 1956; with Arthur Honneger, Ecole Normale de Musique, Paris; Nadia Boulanger, Paris; Roberto Gerhard, U.S.; electronic music with Mario Davidovsky. His many honors include the Pulitzer prize, 1966; Prix de Rome; grant and citation, Nat. Inst. of Arts and Letters; Koussevitzky Found.

award; 2 Guggenheim fellowships; Naumburg award; UNESCO award; Nat. Council on the Humanities and Arts grant; Univ. of Michigan Regents citation; Distinguished Alumnus award, Calif. State Univ. at Fresno, 1978. He has been faculty member, Univ. of Michigan, School of Music, since 1952.
WORKS: ORCHESTRA: <u>5 movements for orchestra</u>, Rome, 5 July 1962; <u>Variations for orchestra</u>, Rome, 6 July 1963; <u>Colloquy</u>, 1969; <u>Forces</u>, 1972; <u>Echoes from an invisible world</u>, Philadelphia, 27 Feb. 1976; concerto for 2 pianos, Midland, Mich.; 30 Apr. 1977; BAND: <u>Designs, images and textures</u>, 1964; <u>Sound drums and trumpets</u>, 1974; <u>Sounds, shapes and symbols</u>, 1977; BRASS: trombone quartet, 1949; horn sonata, 1952; brass trio, 1953; trombone sonata, 1954; suite for unaccomp. trombone, 1957; <u>Easter triptych</u>, tenor voice and brass, 1958; <u>Chamber music for horns</u>, 1974; 12 duos for 2 or 4 trombones, 1974; CHAMBER MUSIC: trio, viola, clarinet, piano, 1953; string quintet, 1954; clarinet duets, 1955; viola sonata, 1956; <u>5 pieces for string quartet</u>, 1957; woodwind quintet, 1958; violin sonata, 1959; cello duets, 1959; piano quintet, 1962; string quartet (3rd), 1962; <u>Music for cello and piano</u>, 1966; nonet, winds and piano, 1967; <u>Music for saxophone and piano</u>, 1968; piano sextet, 1971; <u>Sounds remembered</u>, violin and piano, 1972; <u>Wind music</u>, 1975; <u>Soliloquies</u>, clarinet solo, 1976; CHORUS: <u>The lamb</u>, Blake text, 1952; <u>Out of the depths</u>, 1957; <u>For city, nation, world</u>, cantata, 1959; <u>Moonrise</u>, Lawrence text, 1960; <u>Remembrance</u>, Rupert text, 1960; <u>Prayers for divine service</u>, men's voices, 1965; <u>Hear my prayer, O Lord</u>, children's choir, 1965; <u>Notes in the silence</u>, Hammarskjöld text, 1966; <u>Moon canticle</u>, 1969; <u>Celebration, in praise of earth</u>, with instrumental ensemble, 1970; <u>Of wind and earth</u>, 1973; ELECTRONIC: <u>3 studies in electronic sound</u>, 1965; <u>Triform</u>, 1966; <u>Collect</u>, chorus and tape; also songs and piano and organ pieces.
1618 Harbal Dr., Ann Arbor, MI 48105

BATEMAN, FLORENCE GOLSON. See GOLSON, FLORENCE

BATES, AUGUSTA CECCONI. See CECCONI-BATES, AUGUSTA

BATSTONE, PHILIP NORMAN
b. Boston, Mass., 4 Jan. 1933. Studied at Boston Univ.; with Boris Blacher, Hochschule für Musik, Berlin; with Roger Sessions and Milton Babbitt, Princeton Univ. He has received many commissions. He was on the faculty, City Coll. of New York, 1963-65; Univ. of Colorado, 1965-71; Univ. of Illinois, 1971-73.
WORKS: <u>Parvum</u>, a music theatre piece comprised of <u>A Mother Goose primer</u>, <u>Fun and games</u>, and <u>The phoenix and the turtle</u>; <u>John Street</u>, piano solo; many other compositions in all genres.

BAUER, MARION EUGENIE
b. Walla Walla, Wash., 15 Aug. 1887; d. South Hadley, Mass., 9 Aug. 1955. Studied with Nadia Boulanger and Louis Campbell-Tipton in Paris; with Paul Ertel in Berlin; and with Henry Holden Huss in New York. She received an honorary M.A. from Whitman Coll., Walla Walla, in 1932. She

BAUMAN, JON WARD

held teaching posts at Mills Coll; Carnegie
Inst. of Tech.; annually at Chautauqua Inst.;
New York Univ.; Juilliard School; and from 1940,
at the Inst. of Musical Art.
WORKS: ORCHESTRA: American youth concerto,
piano and orch., 1943; China, chorus and orch.,
Worcester, 12 Oct. 1945; Sun splendor, a 1926
piano piece orchestrated by Stokowski and performed with the New York Philharmonic, 25 Oct.
1947; CHAMBER MUSIC: string quartet, 1928;
Fantasia quasi una sonata, violin and piano,
1928; suite for oboe and clarinet, 1932; viola
sonata, 1936; Pan, choreographic sketch for
7 instruments and piano, 1937; concertino for
oboe, clarinet, and string quartet, 1940; oboe
sonatina, 1940; trio sonata, flute, cello, piano;
also many piano pieces and choral works.

BAUMAN, JON WARD
b. Big Rapids, Mich., 7 June 1939. Studied with
Cecil Effinger, Univ. of Colorado, B.A. 1961;
with Robert Kelly and Salvatore Martirano, Univ.
of Illinois, M.M. 1963, D.M.A. 1972; with
Bernd-Alois Zimmermann in Cologne, Germany. His
awards include a Fulbright grant and private
commissions. From 1970 he has been faculty member at Frostburg State Coll.
WORKS: ORCHESTRA: variations for orchestra,
1963; Aubade, 1966; Contrasts, jazz quintet and
chamber orch., 1971; concerto for oboe d'amore,
1975; Little symphony, 1977; CHAMBER MUSIC:
string quartet, 1962; piano quintet, 1963; 7
songs of the city: Chicago, 2 pianos, 2 percussionists, narrator, 1964; Chamber music, 10
performers, 1965; Incidents, solo oboe, 1966;
Aphorisms, 4 percussionists, 1968; brass quartet,
1977; MULTIMEDIA: The pineapple story, 1969;
Dissertation, chamber choir, chamber orch., tape,
1972; Mobiles, saxophone quartet and tape, 1972.
12 Beall St., Frostburg, MD 21532

BAUMGARTNER, H(OPE) LEROY
b. Rochester, Ind., 1891; d. 18 Sept. 1969. He
published The city, choral suite, and The vision
for organ.

BAUR, JOHN WILLIAM
b. St. Louis, Mo., 27 Feb. 1947. Studied with
Jeno Takacs and Paul Cooper, Univ. of Cincinnati,
Coll.-Cons.; with Thea Musgrave and Richard
Rodney Bennett in London, 1971-72. His awards
include a Fulbright grant and 2 grants from the
Nat. Endowment for the Arts, 1974, 1978. He
taught at Shenandoah Cons., 1973-74; then joined
faculty at Tulane Univ.
WORKS: ORCHESTRA: Anastrophe; Alaomai I;
Canti II: Prisms, chorus and orch., 1974;
Shadow rites, ballet, chorus and orch., 1978;
BAND: Symphonics; Sinfonia I; Phonics II, 1974;
symphony no. 1, 1976; CHAMBER MUSIC: string
quartet; chamber concerto I, 6 singers and ensemble; chamber concerto 2; Songs of livingdying, mezzo-soprano and percussion, 1975;
Impressions I, violin and piano, 1975; Phonics
III, chamber orch., 1976; string quintet no. 2
(guitar/quartet), 1977; The moon and the yew
tree, soprano, flute, cello, piano, 1977; Songs
of livingdying II, soprano, chamber ensemble,

1978; Patterns of love, tenor and tape, 1978;
Impressions II, clarinet and tape, 1978; CHORUS:
Acquainted with the night; Praise the Lord.
1320 Audubon St., New Orleans, LA 70118

BAVICCHI, JOHN
b. Boston, Mass., 25 Apr. 1922. Studied engi-
neering until service in U.S. Navy in World
War II; then studied wtih Francis Judd Cooke and
Carl McKinley, New England Cons., B.M. 1952;
with Walter Piston and A. T. Davison, Harvard
Univ., 1952-55. He has received grants from the
Nat. Inst. of Arts and Letters, 1959, Amer.
Symph. Orch. League, 1961, and many commissions.
Since 1952 he has taught in many schools in the
Boston area and conducted numerous choruses and
orchestras; in 1964, joined the faculty at
Berklee Coll. of Music.
WORKS: ORCHESTRA: Tobal, 1952; 4 songs,
contralto and orch., Cambridge, 17 Dec. 1952;
clarinet concerto, Boston, 14 May 1958; suite
no. 1, Cambridge, 16 Apr. 1961; Farewell and
hail, poem by Farber, soprano, trumpet, strings,
1957; Concertante, 1961; 3 Psalms, with chorus
and soloists, Boston, 23 Apr. 1963; Fantasia on
Korean folk tunes, Brookline, 10 June 1969;
Caroline's dance, 1975; BAND: Festival symphony,
1965; J.D.C. march, 1967; Spring festival overture, 1968; suite no. 3, 1969; symphony no. 2,
1975; concerto no. 2, 1975; CHAMBER MUSIC: 7
trios for various instruments; 3 string quartets,
1950, 1952, 1960; 12 sonatas; 2 woodwind quintets; 2 saxophone quartets; 3 preludes, trombone
solo; A duet dozen, piano, 4 hands, 1975; 4
miniatures, wind quintet, 1976; many vocal works.
Box 182, Astor Station, Boston, MA 02123

BAXTER, LINCOLN
b. Winchester, Mass., 6 July 1951. Studied with
Charles Stackford, Connecticut Coll.; with
Clifford Taylor and Robert Morgan, Temple Univ.
He held a fellowship at Temple Univ., 1976-77.
In 1978 he became an instructor, Temple Univ.,
Coll. of Music.
WORKS: ORCHESTRA: movement for string
orchestra, selected for performance at the 1977
Penn. Composers Project; CHAMBER MUSIC: string
quartet; piano trio; Land blowing out to sea,
baritone voice and chamber ensemble; 3 pieces
for unaccompanied cello; 3 canonic movements for
organ.
1517 S. Corlies St., Philadelphia, PA 19146

BAYLOR, HUGH MURRAY
b. What Cheer, Iowa, 8 Apr. 1913. Studied with
Philip Greeley Clapp, Univ. of Iowa; with Nadia
Boulanger and Robert Casadesus in France. He
has been faculty member at Knox Coll. since 1942.
His compositions include songs, chamber music,
and a comic opera, By Gemini.
Knox College, Galesburg, IL 61401

BAZELON, IRWIN ALLEN
b. Evanston, Ill., 4 June 1922. Studied with
Leon Stein, De Paul Univ., B.A. 1945, M.A. 1946;
with Paul Hindemith, Yale Univ.; with Darius
Milhaud at Mills Coll.; and with Ernest Bloch,
Univ. of California. His honors include Fed. of

Women's Clubs prize for a string quartet, 1947; first prize, of the Cleveland Symph., 1970; Nat. Endowment for the Arts grant, 1976; was first composer-in-residence at Wolf Trap Farm Park. He taught a course on music for motion pictures at the School for Visual Arts, New York, 1968-73, but is primarily a full-time composer.

WORKS: THEATRE: incidental music to The merry wives of Windsor and The taming of the shrew; ORCHESTRA: Ballet Centauri 17, concert ballet, 1960; Concert overture, 1952, revised 1960; 6 symphonies: no. 1, 1960, Kansas City, 29 Nov. 1963; no. 2, Short symphony, Testament to a big city, Washington, 4 Dec. 1962; no. 3, for brass, percussion, piano, and sextet, 1963; no. 4, 1965; no. 5, Indianapolis, 1966; no. 6, Kansas City, Dec. 1970; Excursion for orchestra, Kansas City, 5 Mar. 1966; symphony concertante, clarinet, trumpet, marimba, and orch., 1969; Dramatic fanfare for 1970, Cleveland, 1970; De-tonations, brass quintet and orch., 1976; A quiet piece for a violent time, 1977; CHAMBER MUSIC: 2 string quartets; suite for clarinet, cello, piano, 1947; Ballet suite, for small ensemble, 1949; Movimento da camera, flute, bassoon, horn, harpsichord, 1955; chamber symphony, 7 instruments, 1957; brass quintet, 1963; string quartet with amplified contrabass, 1967; Early American suite, harpsichord and woodwind quintet; duo, viola and piano, 1963; Churchill Downs, chamber concerto for 14 players, New York, 16 May 1971; 3 piano sonatas; Propulsions, percussion, 1974; Concatenations, percussion and viola, Boston, 1 May 1977; Triple play, 2 trombones and solo percussion; Sound dreams, chamber ensemble; Cross-currents, brass quintet and percussion; woodwind quintet; Imprints . . . on ivory and strings, piano, New York, 10 Feb. 1979; also music for industrial, documentary, and art films. He is author of Knowing the score: notes on art films, New York, 1975.

142 E. 71st St., New York, NY 10021

BEACH, BENNIE
b. Miss., 1925. Studied at Delta State Coll., B.A. 1948; at George Peabody Coll., M.A., M.Ed. 1951-52. In 1976 he was named Kentucky Composer of the Year by the Kentucky Music Teachers Assoc., and commissioned jointly by the Kentucky group and the Nat. Assoc. In the same year he was named Distinguished Music Alumnus of Delta State Univ., and a concert of his works was presented. He is professor at Western Kentucky State Univ.; plays trumpet in the Nashville Symphony Orch.

WORKS: BAND: Petite suite, Louisville, 6 Feb. 1976; wind ensemble: fanfare and chorale, brass choir; brass quintet; Triangles, squares, circles, and things, clarinet ensemble, Chicago, 14 Apr. 1978; CHAMBER MUSIC: Soliloquy, chamber orch.; Lamento, tuba solo; suite for trombone; Peace, song for soprano to Teasdale text; Divertissement, tuba solo; Dance suite, tuba and triangle, New York, 15 Feb. 1976; CHORUS: Remember me; Kyrie; Aestiva missa, Lexington, Ky., 31 Oct. 1976.

1670 Normal Dr., Bowling Green, KY 42101

BEACH, BRUCE C.
b. Philadelphia, Pa., 19 July 1903; d. Pa., 30 June 1973. Studied at Girard Coll.; Univ. of Pennsylvania, B.M.; Philadelphia Cons., M.M., Ph.D. He was on the faculty at the Philadelphia Cons., Philadelphia Musical Acad., and Eastern Baptist Coll.

WORKS: ORCHESTRA: Plaza, ballet-symphony, received a Univ. of Pennsylvania award; Ode to American Youth, chorus and orch.; BAND: Festive processional; Beowulf, symphonic poem; CHAMBER MUSIC: 5 miniatures, bassoon and piano; scherzo; woodwind quintet; CHORUS: A maiden's like unto a rose.

BEACH, JOHN PARSONS
b. Gloversville, N.Y., 11 Oct. 1877; d. Pasadena, Calif., 6 Nov. 1953. Studied piano at the New England Cons. and in Europe; on returning to Boston, studied with Charles Martin Loeffler.

WORKS: OPERA: Pippa's holiday, Paris, 1915; BALLET: The phantom satyr, Italy, 1925; Mardi gras, New Orleans, 1926; ORCHESTRA: New Orleans street cries, Philadelphia, 1927; Asolani, 1926; CHAMBER MUSIC: Naive landscapes, piano and woodwind trio, 1917; Poem, string quartet, 1929; Angelo's letter, tenor and chamber orch., 1929.

BEACH, PERRY W.
b. Lincoln, Nebr., 24 Oct. 1917. Studied at Univ. of Nebraska; with Bernard Rogers, Howard Hanson, and Herbert Elwell, Eastman School of Music, Ph.D. 1953. He has held faculty positions from 1940, and since 1957, has been professor, Loma Linda Univ., La Sierra Campus.

WORKS: ORCHESTRA: piano concerto, 1952; symphony movement, 1953; CHORUS: Christmas spiritual; Song of Zion, a cappella; Rejoice in the Lord, double chorus with brass; Kyrie eleison, double chorus with brass; Ode to a fallen president, with alto solo, organ, percussion; Clap your hands; Then said Isaiah, cantata with solo voice and orch.; O Thou Remember, with string ensemble; also songs and piano pieces.

5208 Peacock Lane, Riverside, CA 92505

BEADELL, ROBERT MORTON
b. Chicago, Ill., 18 June 1925. Studied with Anthony Donato at Northwestern Univ., B.M. 1949, M.M. 1950; with Leo Sowerby at Chicago Musical Coll.; and with Darius Milhaud at Mills Coll. His awards include a Thor Johnson award, 1950; Woods fellowship, 1962-63; grants from the Ford Found., Univ. of Nebraska, Nat. Endowment for the Arts; and many commissions. His faculty positions have been at Central Coll., Fayette, Mo., and from 1954, professor, Univ. of Nebraska.

WORKS: OPERA: The kingdom of Caraway, operetta, 1957; The Sweetwater affair, 1960; The number of fools, 1966 (rev. 1976); Napoleon, 1973; Out to the wind, music drama, 1975-78; ORCHESTRA: Trilogy, 1950; Canzona, 1952; New frontier overture, 1961; symphony no. 1, 1963; Children's zoo fantasy, 1969; Mayflower, children's ballet, 1972; Prairie trilogy, with chorus, 1974; Sunpath, with chorus, 1974;

BEALE, DAVID BROOKS

Improvisation and dance, with jazz ensemble, 1974; Variations, jazz trio, flügel horn, strings, 1976; concerto grosso, jazz quintet and jazz ensemble, 1977; adagio, 1978; BAND: Introduction and allegro, 1950; Song of Normandy, 1955; Contours, with solo trombone, 1955; Gemini, 1956; adagio, 1961; Dialogue, 1964; The mercenaries, 1968; 3 sketches, tuba ensemble, 1971; Chicago dance no. 1, jazz ensemble, 1973; Elegy for the Duke, 1975; CHAMBER MUSIC: cello sonata, 1949; piano trio, 1949; woodwind quintet, 1949; Eclogue, chamber orch., 1949; theme and variations, clarinet, cello, piano, 1959; Lyric piece, oboe and piano, 1963; 3 sketches, clarinet quartet, 1963; Soul thoughts, soprano and small ensemble, 1970; and many choral works, including Elegy for a dead soldier, the U.S. entry for the 1958 Italia prize.
7541 Old Post Rd., Lincoln, NB 68508

BEALE, DAVID BROOKS
b. Martin, Tenn., 15 Jan. 1945. Studied at Duke Univ., 1963-67; with Roger Hannay, Univ. of North Carolina, 1967-68; with Karel Husa, Cornell Univ., 1970-73. He received a scholarship to Composers Conference, 1972, and a performance award, Delius Composition Contest, 1974. As a Peace Corps volunteer, he was municipal band director at Abrego, Colombia, 1968-70.
WORKS: CHAMBER MUSIC: Prelude and allegro for strings, 1968; Spirit of St. Louis, brass quintet, 1970; Pattern studies, woodwind quartet, 1972; Martir doloroso, low brass and saxophone, 1972; Asamadaki, trombone sextet, 1973; CHORUS: Ecclesiastes, a cappella, 1971.
Box 82, R.D. 1, Richford, NY 13835

BEALE, FREDERIC FLEMING
b. Troy, Kans., 13 July 1876; d. Caldwell, Idaho, 16 Feb. 1948. He was church organist in Chicago; from 1939, director of music, Coll. of Idaho at Caldwell.
WORKS: OPERETTA: The magic wheel; Fatima; Poor Richard; ORCHESTRA: Dance caprice; and many songs.

BEALE, JAMES
b. Wellesley Hills, Mass., 20 Jan. 1924. Studied with Irving Fine, Walter Piston, Aaron Copland, Harvard Univ., A.B. 1945; with Richard Donovan, Yale Univ., B.M. 1946, M.M. 1947. He received the Woods-Chandler prize; Guggenheim grant, 1958-59. He was faculty member, Univ. of Louisville, 1947-48; visiting professor, Carnegie-Mellon Univ., 1969-70; from 1948, professor, Univ. of Washington.
WORKS: ORCHESTRA: symphony for chamber orch.; Cressay symphony; Music for soprano and orchestra; BAND: Sinfonietta; chamber music; 2 string quartets; piano trio; 8 piano sonatas; Pisces ascending, percussion and piano; SONGS: How beautiful are the dwellings of peace; Proverbs, baritone voice.
4552 51st N.E., Seattle, WA 98105

BEALL, JOHN
b. Belton, Tex., 12 June 1942. Studied with Charles Eakin and Richard Willis, Baylor Univ.,

B.M., M.M. 1966; with Sanuel Adler and Wayne Barlow, Eastman School of Music, 1971-73. His honors include the Dallas Symphony Composers/ Performers award, 1965-66; Louis Lane prize, 1972; Howard Hanson prize, 1973; Nat. Endowment for the Arts grant, 1978. He was faculty member, Southwest Texas State Univ., 1973-76; Eastern Illinois Univ., 1976-78; then named associate professor and composer-in-residence, West Virginia Univ.
WORKS: ORCHESTRA: Essay for orchestra, 1965; Songs of autumn, tenor and orch., 1966; Lament for those lost in the war, 1972; concerto for piano and wind orch., 1973; concerto for brass quintet and winds, 1978; CHAMBER MUSIC: partita for piano, 1967; 2 violin sonatas; string quartet; saxophone sonata, 1974; sextet, piano, and woodwind quintet, 1976; also choral works, songs, piano pieces.
Creative Arts Center, West Virginia Univ., Morgantown, WV 26506

BEASLEY, RULE
b. Texarkana, Ark., 12 Aug. 1931. Studied with Jack Kilpatrick, Southern Methodist Univ.; with Robert Ward at Juilliard School; and with Thomas Frederickson, Univ. of Illinois. He won first place in a Southern Composers League contest in 1963. He was director, School of Music, Centenary Coll. of Louisiana, 1963-66; associate professor, North Texas State Univ., 1966-73; on music faculty, Santa Monica Coll., from 1973.
WORKS: Lyric prelude for orch.; concerto for tuba and band; Dialogue, bassoon and 11 instruments; Music for brass, 1972; 3 studies for bassoon and piano.
2837 Dunleer Pl., Los Angeles, CA 90064

BEATON, ISABELLA
b. Grinnell, Iowa, 20 May 1870; d. Mt. Pleasant, Iowa, 19 Jan. 1929. Studied with Moszkowski in Berlin, 1894-99; at Western Reserve Univ., M.A. 1902. She was private teacher and recitalist in Cleveland, 1910-19.
WORKS: OPERA: Anacoana; ORCHESTRA: symphony; scherzo; many piano pieces.

BEATY, DANIEL JOSEPH
b. Sapulpa, Okla., 25 Apr. 1937. Studied with Bela Rozsa, Univ. of Oklahoma; with Samuel Adler, North Texas State Univ. He was faculty member, Bishop Coll., Dallas, 1960-64; from 1964, Stephen F. Austin State Univ.
WORKS: ORCHESTRA: piano concerto; CHORUS: 5 Irish canons; ELECTRONIC: A ballet for Jasper Johns; many piano pieces and songs.
Music Dept., Stephen F. Austin State Univ., Nacogdoches, TX 75961

BEAULIEU, JOHN
b. Indianapolis, Ind., 8 Feb. 1948. Studied at Purdue Univ., B.A. in recreation therapy 1970; composition with Franz Kamin, Iannis Xenakis, and John Eaton, Indiana Unib. He was president of FIASCO, Bloomington, Ind., 1972-73, then a board member; from 1973, supervisor of music therapy, Bellevue Hospital, New York.
WORKS: PIANO: Spots, Barcarolle, At the

ballet, Gymnastique no. 1, 2, 3, Variations on
Claire de lune, all 1973; MIXED MEDIA: many
works such as The enlightenment of Morris, 3
dancers, tuba, flute, piccolo, percussion, 2
mini-dirty sine-wave generators, soprano and
bass narrators, weight lifter, timer, 3 slide
projectionists, piano, and cat house, 1972.
    19 Leonard St., New York, NY 10013

BEAVER, PAUL H., JR.
    b. Salem, Ohio, 14 Aug. 1925. Studied with
Henry Leland Clarke, Paul Glass, Garth Edmundson,
Franklyn Marks, and Marion MacArtor. His film
scores have won 2 awards, 1969 and 1973, at the
Atlanta Film Festival. He has been composer-
producer and executive of Parasound, Inc., San
Francisco, since 1967.
    WORKS: FILM SCORES: Breakthrough, Legend
days are over, The Baggs (educational films);
Close but free (television); Come to your
senses, The final programme (theatrical films);
Ragnarock, In a wild sanctuary, Gandharva, All
good men (extended works for the record media).
He published Nonesuch guide to electronic music
a syllabus, textbook, with recorded examples,
1967.
    2825 Hyans St., Los Angeles, CA 90026

BECK, JOHN H.
    b. Lewisburg, Pa., 16 Feb. 1933. Studied per-
cussion at Eastman School of Music. In 1976
he received the Mu Phi Epsilon Musician of the
Year award. He was percussionist, U.S. Marine
Band, 1955-59; has been timpanist, Rochester
Philharmonic Orch., and faculty member, Eastman
School, from 1962.
    WORKS: PERCUSSION: Rhapsody for percussion
and band; Jazz variants, percussion ensemble;
timpani sonata; overture for percussion ensemble;
Colonial drummer; Colonial capers; Episode for
solo percussion; Episode for percussion trio;
concerto for drum set and percussion ensemble,
commissioned by the Univ. of Oklahoma percussion
ensemble and performed there on 10 Feb. 1978.
    Eastman School, 26 Gibbs St., Rochester, NY
14604

BECK, JOHN NESS
    b. Warren, Ohio, 11 Nov. 1930. Studied composi-
tion at Ohio State Univ., B.Mus. and M.A. He
taught at Ohio State for a while, then resigned
to head a retail sheet music store in Columbus.
In 1975 his interest in music publishing had
increased so that he devotes full time to it and
composing.
    WORKS: Reflection, concert band; flute
sonata; 5 carol fantasies for piano; more than
30 sacred choral works including Hymn for our
time; Litany of Thanksgiving; Upon this rock;
also many vocal solos.
    3841 N. High St., Columbus, OH 43214

BECK, MARTHA (Mrs. G. Howard Carragan)
    b. Sodaville, Oreg., 19 Jan. 1902. Studied with
George Whitfield Andrews at Oberlin Coll., B.M.
1924; with Adolf Weidig, American Cons., M.M.
1927; with Silvio Scionti, Juilliard School,
1927-29; and with Hugo Leichtentritt in Berlin.

She received 2 Mu Phi Epsilon prizes and the
Adolf Weidig Gold Medal. She taught at both
American Cons. and North Central Coll., Naper-
ville, 1924-29; at Emma Willard School, Troy,
N.Y., 1932-48; then privately in Troy.
    WORKS: ORCHESTRA: Prelude for orchestra,
commissioned by the Albany Symphony and performed
under Julius Hegyi in Albany, Troy, and New York
in May 1977; CHAMBER MUSIC: suite in 5 movements for piano; suite for violin and piano;
piano quintet; American pageant, 2 pianos,
Schenectady, Apr. 1976; CHORUS: Psalm 122, with
organ, brass quintet, and percussion, performed
by Festival Chorus of 500 voices, Saratoga, N.Y.,
June 1976; many other commissioned choral works.
    Box 261, R.D. 3, Troy, N.Y. 12180

BECK, THEODORE
    b. Oak Park, Ill., 17 Apr. 1929. Studied with
Anthony Donato and Ewald Nolte, Northwestern
Univ. From 1953 he has been professor, Concordia
Coll., Seward, Nebr.; was organist and choir
director in Lincoln, Nebr., 1954-56.
    WORKS: CHORUS: The Christmas story; Little
Christmas concert; 8 anthems for treble voices
and instruments; INSTRUMENTAL: Christmas songs
for handbells; 47 hymn intonations for organ.
    Concordia College, Seward, NB 68434

BECKER, JOHN J.
    b. Henderson, Ky., 22 Jan. 1886; d. Wilmette,
Ill., 21 Jan. 1961. Studied at Wisconsin Cons.
in Milwaukee. He then taught at Notre Dame
Univ., 1918-28; Coll. of St. Thomas in St. Paul,
1928-33; was Minnesota state director for the
Fed. Music Project, 1935-41; professor, Barat
Coll. of the Sacred Heart, Lake Forest, Ill.,
1943-57; was associate editor of New Music
Quarterly, 1936-40. See Don Gillespie, "John
Becker, Musical Crusader from St. Paul," Musical
Quarterly, April 1976; and Baker's Biographical
Dictionary of Musicians, 6th ed.
    WORKS: THEATRE: 13 stage works, including
A marriage with space, a drama in color, light
and sound, with solo and mass recitation, solo
and group dancers, and large orch., 1935;
ORCHESTRA: 7 symphonies; 2 piano concertos;
horn concerto; viola concerto; violin concerto;
CHAMBER MUSIC: 8 soundpieces for various instru-
ments including a violin sonata, piano sonata,
3 string quartets; many choral works and songs.

BECKER, RICHARD
    b. White Plains, N.Y., 27 Sept. 1943. Studied
with Samuel Adler, Eastman School of Music; with
Gardner Read and Alan Schindler, Boston Univ.
His awards include a composition grant from the
Univ. of Richmond. He has held piano teaching
posts at Univ. of Texas, 1967-71; Boston Univ.,
1971-75; from 1975, at Univ. of Richmond.
    WORKS: CHAMBER MUSIC: string quartet, 1966;
VOICE: The cat and the moon, vocal quartet,
trumpet, horn, oboe, trombone, 1979; PIANO:
Karyokinesis, sonata, 1974; sonata for 2 pianos,
1975; Mavromata, 1979.
    4301 Wythe Ave., Richmond, VA 23221

BECKETT, WHEELER M. A.

BECKETT, WHEELER M. A.
    b. San Francisco, Calif., 7 Mar. 1898. Studied piano in Paris with Camille Decreuse; composition with Daniel Gregory Mason at Columbia Univ.; conducting with Feliz Weingartner in Basel, Switz. He has been guest conductor of the Berlin Philh.; Vienna Philh.; Straram Orch., Paris; Water Gate Concerts, D.C.; Boston Pops; and others. He was organist-choirmaster, Grace Cathedral, San Francisco, 1922-27; conductor of Young People's Concerts in San Francisco, Boston, Richmond, Va., and New York; was appointed by the State Dept. to found and conduct orchestras in the Far East, 1959-62.
    WORKS: OPERA: The queen's mirror; INCIDENTAL MUSIC: Asses ears; Rajvara; ORCHESTRA: symphony in c; The mystic trumpeter; The sea at Point Lobos; Open road; Dedication to Indonesia, chorus, orch., and soprano vocalise; and songs. He was conductor and commentator for two record albums widely used in music appreciation classes: Essential musical knowledge and The complete orchestra.
    277 Walnut St., Englewood, NJ 07631

BECKHELM, PAUL
    b. Kankakee, Ill., 3 July 1906; d. Mt. Vernon, Iowa, 6 Nov. 1966. Studied at Northwestern Univ., B.M.; Eastman School of Music, M.M., Ph.D. 1949; and with Nadia Boulanger. He taught at Kansas State Coll., Ft. Hays; Hood Coll.; and at Cornell Coll. His works include Tragic march for brass choir, a violin sonatina, and piano teaching pieces.

BECKLER, S. R.
    b. Escondido, Calif., 26 Dec. 1923. Studied with J. Russell, Univ. of the Pacific, M.A. 1951; with Wayne Barlow, Eastman School of Music; with George Perle, Univ. of Southern California. His awards include Pi Kappa Lambda prize, 1960, and commissions. From 1970 he has been professor, Univ. of the Pacific.
    WORKS: CHAMBER OPERAS: Faust, 1945; The outcasts of Poker Flat, 1960; The catbird seat, 1973; INCIDENTAL MUSIC: Othello, 1957; Oedipus, the king, 1966; Hamlet, 1966; ORCHESTRA: 5 symphonies, 1946, 1951, 1953, 1956, 1977; Festival overture, 1957; Etude on an old French tune, 1963; Dirge, 1966; The battle symphony, 1970; The 7 ages of man, 1972; BAND: Capriccio, with baritone horn, 1955; 7 bagatelles, brass and percussion, 1975; CHAMBER MUSIC: 4 piano sonatas, 1945, 1948, 1955, 1976; Rhapsody, violin and piano, 1957; 4 woodwind quintets, 1957-68; 7 little wind sonatas, 1958-61; 2 string quartets, 1961, 1964; Firewater music, mixed octet, 1967; Quotations from Mr. Agnew, oboe, viola, piano, 1969; violin sonata, 1970; cello sonata, 1973; Percussion sonata, with oboe, horn, violin, cello, piano, 1973; The Stars and Stripes forawhile, violin and percussion, 1973; little suite for contrabass quartet, 1976; viola sonata, 1977; Briefs, flute, contrabass, and percussion, 1978; CHORUS: The resurrection, oratorio, 1955; Man and divers bestiall companyons, 1969; also songs and piano pieces.
    Conservatory Annex, Univ. of the Pacific, Stockton, CA 95204

BECKON, LETTIE MARIE
    b. Detroit, Mich., 13 Apr. 1953. Studied with James Hartway, Wayne State Univ.; held a scholarship in 1976.
    WORKS: ORCHESTRA: Symphonic essay, strings and percussion; Piece, small orch.; Integrated concerto, piano and orch.; CHAMBER MUSIC: 3 implied jesters, solo clarinet; Pulsations, solo violin; Head-a-woe, 2 violins and cello; Moods for piano; Effigy, oboe, piano, percussion; Composition I: for 12 tones, clarinet ensemble; Visions, marimba and piano; CHORUS: Help, women's voices and quartet.
    1934 Glendale, Detroit, MI 48238

BECKSTEAD, JOSEPH R.
    b. Pocatello, Idaho, 3 May 1907. Studied at Univ. of Wyoming, Univ. of Utah, Columbia Univ.; composition with Ingolf Dahl, Univ. of Southern California, D.M.A. 1968. From 1951 he was professor at California State Univ., Los Angeles. His works are chiefly hymns, choral compositions, and arrangements for strings.
    1908 Orange Grove Ave., Alhambra, CA 91802

BEDELL, ROBERT LEECH
    b. Jersey City, N.J., 13 Feb. 1909. Studied at Southwestern Coll., D.M.; and at Findlay Coll., Litt.D. He has been organist and choirmaster in Brooklyn and at Passeonest Monastery. His works include Fantasia in C, for orch.; Legende, for organ; Methinks I hear, chorus.

BEECHER, CARL MILTON
    b. Lafayette, Ind., 22 Oct. 1883; d. Portland, Oreg., 21 Nov. 1968. Studied at Northwestern Univ., graduating in 1908; then studied piano with Josef Lhevinne in Berlin. He was faculty member at Northwestern Univ. 1913-35; then, after 11 years in Tahiti, returned to teach at Portland School of Music. His compositions are chiefly for piano: 5 aquatints; 9 musical profiles; Remembrances of times past.

BEELER, C. ALAN
    b. St. Louis, Mo., 10 Feb. 1939. Studied with Will Ogdon, Illinois Wesleyan Univ.; with Harold Blumenfeld, Robert Wykes, and Robert Baker, Washington Univ., Ph.D. 1973. He was faculty member, Wisconsin State Univ., Stevens Point, 1967-70; and from 1970, at Eastern Kentucky Univ.
    WORKS: ORCHESTRA: Quintessence I, 1964, received a Rockefeller grant for rehearsal by the St. Louis Symph.; Quintessence II, 1966; CHAMBER MUSIC: oboe sonata, 1960; Piece for piano after Roger Sessions, 1960; 3 pieces for piano, 1962; Chamber piece for flute, clarinet, viola, piano, 1965; Electronic mobile for rocks and metal, 1965; Serial sonata, for woodwind quartet, 1975-76.
    65 Brooklyn, R. 7, Richmond, KY 40475

BEERMAN, BURTON
    b. Atlanta, Ga., 12 June 1943. Studied with John Boda and Harold Schiffman, Florida State Univ. , B.M. 1966; with Ross Lee Finney, Leslie Bassett, George B. Wilson, George Cacioppo, and Eugene Kurtz, Univ. of Michigan, M.M. 1968, D.M.A.

1971. He won first prize in the Pittsburgh Flute Club composition contest, 1970, and was finalist in the 1968 Gaudeamus Internat. Festival, Netherlands. He has been faculty member, Bowling Green State Univ., from 1970, and is also director of the Electronic Music Studios; he was visiting lecturer, Univ. of Utah, 1975-76.

WORKS: BAND: Ensemble II, with solo clarinet; CHAMBER MUSIC: Frame, 6 flutes, 1970; Impressions of birth, 16 solo voices, percussion, 2 pianos; 4 in 6, string quartet, 1976; Moments 1978, alto saxophone and piano; MIXED MEDIA: Mixtures, chorus, instruments, tape; Sensations, clarinet and tape; Improvisations, dancers, actors, instruments, 1970; mass for tenor voice, flute, harp, tape, 1968; Misogamy, string quartet and tape; Polygraph II, piano, live electronics, visuals; "C", organ, dancer, percussion, electronics, visuals; Polygraph VI, amplified flute, harp, and tape.

1628 Juniper Dr., #92, Bowling Green, OH 43402

BEESON, JACK
b. Muncie, Ind., 15 July 1921. Studied with Burrill Phillips, Bernard Rogers, and Howard Hanson, Eastman School of Music, B.M. and M.M. 1943; privately with Bela Bartok, 1944-45; conducting and musicology, Columbia Univ., 1945-47; American Acad. in Rome, 1948-50. His honors include the Lillian Fairchild award; the Rome prize; Fulbright and Guggenheim grants; composer-in-residence at the American Acad. in Rome, 1965-66; Marc Blitzstein award; election to Nat. Inst. of Arts and Letters, 1968; Gold Medal for Music, Nat. Arts Club, 1976; and ASCAP awards. In addition to being on the faculty at Columbia Univ. from 1945, and MacDowell professor of music from 1967, he was on the conducting staffs of Columbia Opera Workshop, 1945-50, and Columbia Theatre Associates, 1945-52; and lecturer at Juilliard School, 1961-63.

WORKS: OPERA: Jonah, 1950; Hello out there, N.Y., 27 May 1954; The sweet bye and bye, N.Y., 21 Nov. 1957; Lizzie Borden, N.Y., 25 Mar. 1965; My heart's in the Highlands, NET, 17 Mar. 1970; Captain Jinks of the Horse Marines, Kansas City, Mo., 20 Sept. 1975; Dr. Heidegger's Fountain of Youth, N.Y., 17 Nov. 1978; ORCHESTRA: Transformations, 1959; a symphony, 1959; BAND: Fanfare, 1963; Commemoration, with chorus, 1960; CHAMBER MUSIC: 5 piano sonatas; Song, flute and piano, 1945; Interlude, violin and piano, 1945; viola sonata, 1953; The Hoosier balks, 10 instruments, 1967; The Hawkesley blues, 10 instruments; piano and organ pieces; many vocal solos and choral works including The bear hunt, text by Abraham Lincoln, set for tenor, baritone, and bass, N.Y. 21 Apr. 1961. He is author of music reviews and magazine articles and has adapted the texts of some of his operas and vocal works.

404 Riverside Dr., New York, NY 10025

BEGLARIAN, GRANT
b. Tiflis, Georgian S.S.R., 1 Dec. 1927; U.S. citizen 1954. Studied with Ross Lee Finney, Univ. of Michigan, D.M.A. 1957; and with Aaron Copland at Tanglewood. He received the Gershwin

Memorial award, 1957, and the Ford Found. Young Composers award, 1960. He taught at the U.S. Army Music School in Munich, 1952-54, and played viola in the 8th Army Symph. Orch. In 1961-68 he was director of the Ford Found. Contemporary Music Project. In 1969 he was named dean, School of Performing Arts, Univ. of Southern California.

WORKS: ORCHESTRA: symphony in 2 movements, 1950; Divertimento, 1957; Sinfonia, 1965; Diversion, with solo viola and cello, 1972; BAND: A hymn for our time, for 3 bands, 1967; CHAMBER MUSIC: string quartet, 1948; cello sonata, 1951; 2 violin sonatas, 1949, 1955; woodwind quintet, 1966; Of foibles, fables and fancies for cello, N.Y., 31 Oct. 1971; CHORUS: And all the hills echoed, cantata, 1968; many smaller works for instrumental ensembles and chorus.

333 S. Windsor Blvd., Los Angeles, CA 90020

BEHREND, JEANNE
b. Philadelphia, Pa., 11 May 1911. Studied composition with Rosario Scalero, Abram Chasins, Reginald Owen Morris, piano with Josef Hofmann, Curtis Inst. of Music, graduating in 1934. She received the Columbia Univ. Bearns prize in 1936. She has held faculty positions at Curtis Inst.; Western Coll. for Women, Oxford, Ohio; Juilliard School; Philadelphia Cons.; Temple Univ.; and since 1969, at the New School of Music, Philadelphia.

WORKS: ORCHESTRA: From dawn to dusk, 1944; Fanfare, a prelude to The Star Spangled Banner; CHAMBER MUSIC: Quiet piece and Dance into space, flute; string quartet; VOCAL: song cycle on poems of Sara Teasdale, 1936; Song of the United Nations, soprano solo, soprano chorus, 2 pianos, 1945; Easter hymn, soprano, soprano chorus, harp, organ; other songs, chamber works, piano pieces.

2401 Pennsylvania Ave., Apt. 4A1, Philadelphia, PA 19130

BEHRENS, JACK
b. Lancaster, Pa., 25 Mar. 1935. Studied with William Bergsma, Vincent Persichetti, Peter Mennin at Juilliard School, B.S. 1958; M.S. 1959; with Darius Milhaud at Aspen, Colo., 1962; with Stefan Wolpe, 1964, and John Cage, 1965, at Emma Lake, Sask.; with Leon Kirchner and Roger Sessions, Harvard Univ., Ph.D. 1973. He received 3 Juilliard scholarships; Edward Benjamin award, 1956; Copley Found. award, 1962; Canada Council Scandinavian Research grant, 1965; Simon Fraser Univ. grant, 1969; Calif. State Coll., grant, 1971; Carnegie grants, 1972-73; and commissions. He taught at private schools, 1959-62; Univ. of Saskatchewan, 1962-66; Simon Fraser Univ., 1966-70; California State Coll., 1970-76; from 1976, chairman and professor, Univ. of Western Ontario.

WORKS: THEATRE: The lay of Thrym, opera, Regina, Sask., 13 Apr. 1968, composer conducting; Transfigured season, ballet, 1960; Encounters, ballet, 1963; Midsummer night's dream, incidental music, 1964; ORCHESTRA: Declaration, 1964; The sound of Milo, with narrator, New Orleans, 4 Mar.

BEHRMAN, DAVID

1970, won prize in New Orleans Philh. Symph. contest; triple concerto for clarinet, violin, piano, 1971; Fantasia on my days have been so wondrous free, tune by Francis Hopkinsin, Fresno, Calif., 20 Mar. 1976; CHAMBER MUSIC: Introspection, strings, 1956; Quarter-tone quartet, 1960; concertino, trombone and 8 instruments, 1961; Pentad, vibraphone and piano, 1965; violin sonata, Vancouver, B.C., 3 Feb. 1970; PIANO: Passacaglia, 1963; A pocket size sonata, 1964; Feast of life, 1975; FILM SCORE: The old order Amish, 1959.

>Music Dept., Univ. of Western Ontario, London, Ontario, Canada

BEHRMAN, DAVID

b. Salzburg, Austria, of American parents, 16 Aug. 1937. Studied privately with Wallingford Riegger; then with Walter Piston at Harvard Univ., B.A., magna cum laude, 1959; with Karlheinz Stockhausen in Darmstadt; with Henri Pousseur in Brussels, 1960; at Columbia Univ., M.A. 1963; also studied the IBM system/360-assembler language programming at The New School, New York, 1971. He received the Knight prize, 1957-58; Bohemians prize, 1958-59; and the John Knowles Paine fellowship, 1959-60. He worked in New York and in Cologne as translator and copyist for Stockhausen; with Columbia Records in New York, 1965-70; was guest lecturer and director, Electronic Music Studio, Ohio State Univ., 1972; on faculty, New Music in New Hampshire, Chocorua, N.H., 1973; and in 1966, cofounder of the Sonic Arts Union, a group comprised of Robert Ashley, Behrman, Alvin Lucier, and Gordon Mumma, that presents programs of individual and collaborative music using simple or sophisticated electronics, photography, film, and theater. The group has performed widely in the U.S. In 1976 Behrman joined the faculty at Mills Coll.

WORKS: INSTRUMENTAL: Canons, piano and percussion, 1959; Signals, 10 instruments and percussion, 1960; Ricercar, piano, 1961; Whistling six, 6 players, 1962; From place to place, 2 pianos, 1963; Northwest, chamber chorus, 5 instruments, 2 conductors, 1963; Parallel tracks, orch. with 2 conductors; MIXED MEDIA OR ELECTRONIC: Milwaukee combination, 4 wind players, 1964; Track, 6 winds and 6 tapes, 1965; Players with circuits, 2 performers play pianos, zithers, or guitars, 2 operate electronic gear, 1966; Wave train, 2-4 players, 1966; Runthrough, 4 performers with electronic devices, 1967; For nearly an hour, 3 performers with 6 channels of tape, commissioned by Merce Cunningham for the dance Walkaround, 1968; Questions from the floor, 2 speaking performers, with tape and sound system wired into audience area, based on political events in the U.S. in 1968; A new team takes over, a later version of Questions from the floor, 1969; Sinescreen, 1970; Net for catching big sounds, 4 instruments and electronics, 1974; On the other ocean, flute, bassoon, cello, and electronics, 1978; Touch-tones, synthesizer-generated dance using such acoustic sources as a hair dryer and a power drill, 1979.

>Music Dept., Mills College, P.O. Box 9970, Oakland, CA 94613

BELL, CLARA HUSTON

b. Mont., 11 May 1944. Studied at Univ. of Montana and Columbia Univ., M.A., M.Ed., Ed.D. She held a fellowship at Columbia and has received ASCAP awards. She has taught at Dalton School and Trinity School, both in New York.

WORKS: CHORUS: Love is the color, 1974; Suite for a Greek Festival, 1976; Ode to Martin Luther King, 1977; SONGS: Let the rain fall on me; Reflection; In anticipation.

>501 W. 121st St., #65, New York, NY 10027

BELL, LUCILLE ANDERSON

b. St. Louis, Mo., 27 Nov. 19[?]. Studied at Chicago Musical Coll. with Alexander Raab; with Paul Creston in New York. She has received ASCAP awards and has been a pianist on radio in Chicago and New York.

WORKS: 3 moods, flute and piano; Lead us on, Thomas Paine, march for piano; Runaway slave, a song cycle.

>117 W. Scribner Ave., Du Bois, PA 15801

BELL, RANDY M.

b. Fort Smith, Ark., 23 May 1945. Attended Univ. of Arkansas and Berklee Coll. of Music, Boston, where he is on the faculty.

WORKS: ML-Moods of life, woodwind quartet; Phantasy, flute and piano; woodwind quintet, commissioned by the Denver Symph.

>c/o Berklee College of Music, 1140 Boylston St., Boston, MA 02215

BELLAMY, MARIAN MEREDITH

b. Woodbury, N.J., 17 Mar. 1927. Attended Western Maryland Coll., B.A. 1948, and Drexel Univ.; studied composition with Matthew Colucci, Orlando Otey, John Davison, Harold Boatrite, and Romeo Cascarino; piano with Temple Painter and Stafford Newhall.

WORKS: Serenade, string quartet, 1968; 4 preludes, piano, 1967-68; Pisces suite, oboe and piano, 1970; Capricorn suite, harp and cello, 1971; Asia, piano sonata, 1972; 3 offices, brass quintet, Philadelphia, 14 Oct. 1973.

>127 Kenilworth Rd., Merion, PA 19066

BELLEROSE, SR. CECILIA, C.S.C.

b. Suncook, N.H., 8 Nov. 1897. Studied at Laval Univ. and Montreal Univ., D.M. She was chairman of the music department, Notre Dame Coll., Manchester, N.H., 1950-73, also composer-in-residence at Notre Dame and director of music in New England schools.

WORKS: VOCAL: Concert d'oiseaux, cantata; Dieu nous voit; Gradations; Sayez bini; La fontaine; Lux; The burning babe; Notre Dame Coll. song; many sacred motets and piano pieces.

>2321 Elm St., Manchester, NH 03104

BELLOW, ALEXANDER

b. Moscow, 22 Mar. 1912; d. Conn., 12 Mar. 1976. Taught classical guitar in New York for many years. His works for guitar include a sonata; 5 diversions; Prelude and rondo; Suite miniature.

BELLSON, LOUIS

b. Rock Falls, Ill., 6 July 1924. Studied drums

with his father, and with Roy Knapp, Bert Winans, and Murray Spivack. He has received Downbeat, Metronome, Esquire, Playboy, and Columbia awards; has played with Benny Goodman, Tommy Dorsey, Harry James, Duke Ellington, Count Basie, and his own band.
WORKS: PERCUSSION: Jazz ballet, performed at Las Vegas Jazz Festival, 1962; 4 stories, 4 complete drum sets; Percussion suite no. 1, 5 players.
8433 Melvin Ave., Northridge, CA 91324

BELMONT, JEAN FORD
b. Redlands, Calif., 25 Dec. 1939. Studied with Wayne Bohrnstedt, Univ. of Redlands, B.M.; with Philip Slates and Gilbert Trythall, George Peabody Coll., M.M. Her honors include a Sigma Alpha Iota scholarship, 1961; NDEA scholarship, 1961-63; Missouri Fed. of Music Clubs composer award, 1976. She has held faculty posts at Univ. of Alabama, 1965-67; St. Margaret's School, Waterbury, Conn., 1968-70.
WORKS: CHAMBER MUSIC: Courtship cycle, soprano, baritone, and string quartet; clarinet sonata; Commedia dell' arte sketches for 4 winds; cello sonata; 5 songs, soprano and piano; piano sonata; CHORUS: Cartoons, women's voices and percussion.
2112 W. 61st Terrace, Shawnee Mission, KS 66208

BELTON, PAUL D.
b. Memphis, Tenn., 21 Aug. 1942. Studied with Helen Gunderson and Kenneth Klaus, Louisiana State Univ., and with Nadia Boulanger in Paris on a grant from L'Alliance Francaise de New York, 1964-65. He has held faculty posts at Nicholls State Univ., La., 1967-70; Louisiana State Univ., 1970-71; and Washington State Univ., 1972-75.
WORKS: ORCHESTRA: symphony, 1967; CHAMBER MUSIC: horn sonata, 1964; string quartet, 1973; Variations, clarinet and piano, 1973; VOCAL: 3 songs, for soprano, 1964.
N.W. 1530 Turner Drive, Pullman, WA 99163

BENARY, BARBARA
b. Bay Shore, N.Y., 7 Apr. 1946. Studied at Sarah Lawrence Coll., B.A., and Wesleyan Univ., M.A., Ph.D. She held a Woodrow Wilson dissertation fellowship, 1972-73. Since 1973 she has been on the faculty at Livingston Coll. (Rutgers Univ.).
WORKS: THEATRE (incidental music): 3 sisters who are not sisters, Gertrude Stein text, 1967; The only jealously of Emer, Yeats text, 1971; Interior castle, John Braswell text, 1973; The gauntlet, or the moon's on fire, Braswell text, 1976; Sanguine, Braswell text, 1976; also chamber music for traditional instruments, Japanese gamelan, and mixed improvisational groups.
Call Hollow Road, Stony Point, NY 10980

BENCRISCUTTO, FRANK
b. Racine, Wisc., 21 Sept. 1928. Studied at Univ. of Wisconsin, B.M. 1951, M.M. 1975; with Howard Hanson and Bernard Rogers, Eastman School

of Music, D.M.A. 1960. He won an award for best percussion ensemble, 1959; and first prize ($6000) in the Neil A. Kjos 1977 Internat. Composition Contest for the "most significant contribution to band literature." Since 1960 he has been director of bands and professor of music, Univ. of Minnesota.
WORKS: BAND: Serenade with solo saxophone; concertino, tuba and band; Lyric dance, The president's trio, 3 trumpets and band; concerto grosso, saxophone quartet and band; Lamp of liberty, with optional narrator; Symphonic jazz suite, with jazz solo or duo and jazz rock combo; Sing a new song (Psalm 96) with chorus, 1977.
3071 Churchill St., St. Paul, MN 55113

BENDER, JAN
b. Haarlem, Netherlands, 3 Feb. 1909; to U.S. 1960. Studied with Karl Straube in Leipzig, 1930-33; with Sem Dresden in Amsterdam, 1933-34; and with Hugo Distler in Luebeck, 1934-35. His honors include the Canticum Novum Award, 1974, and an honorary doctorate, 1974. He was director of church music in Germany, 1934-60; then joined the faculty at Concordia Teachers Coll., Seward, Nebr.; was professor at Wittenberg Univ., Springfield, Ohio, 1965-76.
WORKS: He has written numerous works for the Lutheran church service, including St. Louis cantata, 1964, and instrumental works, such as a cello sonata, concerto for brass and timpani, woodwind quartet, and organ pieces.
164 W. College Ave., Springfield, OH 45504

BENEDICT, DAVID
b. Philadelphia, Pa., 24 Feb. 1923. Studied piano, voice, and opera coaching at Juilliard School. After 4 years in the Army during World War II, he resumed vocal studies and began singing in opera, oratorios, and concerts. In 1953 he was appointed cantor at Temple Israel, N.Y., and 1960, music director. He has been on the faculty at Adelphi Univ. since 1958, and at Dowling Coll. since 1966. He is accompanist and coach to many opera singers.
WORKS: CHORUS: Dance service for Friday evening; Psalms 121, 137, 29, 150; May the words; Matovu; Service for Saturday morning; Adon Olam; Service in classic style, et al.
Pound Hollow Rd., Old Brookville, Glen Head, NY 11545

BENJAMIN, THOMAS
b. Bennington, Vt., 17 Feb. 1940. Studied with Carlos Surinach at Bard Coll.; with Robert Moevs at Harvard Univ.; with Arthur Berger and Ernst Krenek, Brandeis Univ.; and with Bernard Rogers and Wayne Barlow at Eastman School of Music. He has had 2 grants from Univ. of Houston; Louis Lane prize, 1967; MacDowell fellowship, 1975; awards in the Delius and Meeker contests; ASCAP awards, 1975-78; several commissions. He has been faculty member, Univ. of Houston from 1968; and at the Nat. Music Camp, 1969-71, 1977-.
WORKS: OPERA: The rehearsal; Hammer in his hand, operetta; ORCHESTRA: violin concerto, 1967; piano concerto, 1968; a symphony; CHORUS: 3 Psalm fragments, 1961; Pooh cycle, 1965; 3

BENJAMIN, WILLIAM E.

songs after Frost, 1966; Adoremus Te, 1969; 3 motets, 1970; Sabbath music, 1971; The righteous nation; The fruit of love; Festival Te Deum; Celebration; many chamber works and song cycles.
2629 Cason St., Houston, TX 77005

BENJAMIN, WILLIAM E.
b. Montreal, 7 Dec. 1944; to U.S. 1966. Studied at McGill Univ., M.B. 1965; with Milton Babbitt, Edward T. Cone, James K. Randall, and Peter Westergaard at Princeton Univ., M.F.A. 1968. He received a B.M.I. award, 1966, and a Tanglewood fellowship, 1967. He was faculty member at Wellesley Coll., 1970-72; Univ. of Michigan, 1972-77; and from 1978, Univ. of British Columbia, Vancouver.
WORKS: ORCHESTRA: piano concerto, 1970-73; CHAMBER MUSIC: Variations for 4 players, 1967; At sixes and sevens, sextet, 1968; string trio, 1972; CHORUS: Mah Tovu, a cappella, 1966.
Music Dept., Univ. of British Columbia, Vancouver, B.C., Canada V6T 1W5

BENNARD, GEORGE
b. Youngstown, Ohio, 4 Feb. 1873; d. Reed City, Mich., 10 Oct. 1958. He was a hymn writer.

BENNETT, DAVID
b. Chicago, Ill., 3 Sept. 1897. He has published a saxophone concerto; pieces for various small wind ensembles; The spirit of music, chorus and piano; etc.
Rte. 2, Box 149, St. Charles, IL 60174

BENNETT, ROBERT CHARLES
b. Houston, Tex., 10 Nov. 1933. Attended Univ. of Houston, B.S., M.Ed. He has been organist-choirmaster in Houston since 1954, and is organ instructor at St. Thomas Univ. He has published choral compositions.
6004 Buffalo Speedway, Houston, TX 77005

BENNETT, ROBERT RUSSELL
b. Kansas City, Mo., 15 June 1894; d. New York, N.Y., 19 Aug. 1981. Studies with Carl Busch in Kansas City and with Nadia Boulanger in Paris. His many honors include 2 Guggenheim fellowships; Musical America prize, 1927; RCA Victor prize, 1929; an Oscar, an Emmy, many medals, citations, and commissions; an honorary L.H.D. from Franklin and Marshall Coll.; and the Kappa Kappa Psi Distinguished Service to Music Medal, 1976. He was composer-arranger-conductor and one of the most noted orchestrators in New York theaters from 1919, Hollywood films from 1930, radio networks from 1940, and television networks from 1951. In 1975, he published a book on orchestration, Instrumentally speaking.
WORKS: OPERA: An hour of delusion, 1 act; Maria Malibran, N.Y., 8 Apr. 1935; The enchanted kiss, N.Y., 30 Dec. 1945; Endymion, operetta, 1927; ORCHESTRA: Sights and sounds, 1926, Abraham Lincoln, 1926 (these 2 works won 2 of the 5 prizes in the 1929 RCA Victor contest); Charleston rhapsody, 1926; Paysage, 1928; March, 2 pianos and orch., 1930; Early American ballade, 1932; concerto grosso, dance band and orch., 1932; Adagio eroico, 1935; Hollywood

scherzo, 1936; 8 etudes for orch., 1938; 3 symphonies, 1941, 1946, 1963; violin concerto, 1941; The 4 freedoms, 1943; Classic serenade, 1945; Overture to an imaginary drama, 1946; concerto grosso for woodwind quintet, 1958; concerto for violin, piano and orch., Portland, Ore., 18 Mar. 1963; BAND: Symphonic songs, 1958; Track meet, suite, 1960; Suite of old American dances; Down to the sea in ships; Kentucky; Ohio River suite; 3 humoresques; West Virginia epic; That war in Korea, 1965; CHAMBER MUSIC: violin sonata, 1927; Toy symphony, 5 woodwinds, 1928; organ sonata, 1929; Water music, string quartet, 1937; Hexapoda, violin and piano, 1940; 2 piano sonatinas, 1941, 1944; suite for violin and piano, 1945; 5 improvisations, trio, 1946; Sonatine, soprano and harp; 6 souvenirs, 2 flutes and piano, 1958; Rose variations, trumpet and piano, 1955; CHORUS: Epithalamium, text of John Milton, with orch.; Verses 1, 2, 3, text by composer; Nietzsche variations; He is risen; and songs.
65 W. 54th St., New York, NY 10019

BENNETT, WILHELMINE
b. Carmi, Ill., 14 June 1933. Studied with Anthony Donato at Northwestern Univ., M.M., D.Mus.; with Wolfgang Fortner in Germany; and Chou Wen-Chung at Columbia Univ. She has received a William T. Farley award for creative writing; a Fulbright fellowship, 1964; and a grant from the Nat. Council on the Arts, 1966. In 1971 she was lecturer at the Univ. of California, Santa Cruz Extension.
WORKS: ORCHESTRA: Thumbelisa; 2 symphonies; Enola Gay; CHAMBER MUSIC: woodwind quintet; Hyperbolex; La suite absurdite; 5 quick visions of the apocalypse.
Box 512, West Branch, IA 52358

BENSON, BRUCE
b. Port Chester, N.Y., 4 June 1951. Studied with Frederick Piket, Hebrew Union Coll.-Jewish Inst. of Religion, School of Sacred Music. He has been cantor at Temple B'nai Israel, Elmont, N.Y., from 1972. He has published Ma'agal chozer--a circle without end, a folk-rock service for Shabbat eve.
2200 Central Rd., #7-M, Fort Lee, NJ 07024

BENSON, WARREN
b. Detroit, Mich., 26 Jan. 1924. Is self-taught in composition. His awards include 2 Fulbright teaching grants to Greece, 1950-51; Phi Mu Alpha, Sinfonia, 1970; Lillian Fairchild award, 1971. He was timpanist, Detroit Symph. Orch. and Ford Orch., 1946; on faculty, Anatolia Coll., Salonica, Greece, 1950-52; band and orchestra director, Mars Hill Coll., N.C., 1952-53; professor and composer-in-residence, Ithaca Coll., 1953-67; from 1967, professor, Eastman School of Music.
WORKS: ORCHESTRA: horn concerto; BAND: The leaves are falling, 1963-64; Remembrance; Night song; symphony for drums and wind orch.; Aeolian songs, saxophone and band; WIND ENSEMBLE: concertina, saxophone and winds; Transylvania fanfare, 1953; Recuerdo, oboe, English horn, and

winds; <u>Star edge</u>, saxophone and winds; <u>Helix</u>, tuba and winds, 1966; <u>The solitary dancer</u>, 1966; <u>Shadow wood</u>, soprano and winds; CHAMBER MUSIC: <u>Nara</u>, saxophone, flute, piano, percussion; <u>Capriccio</u>, violin, viola, cello, piano, 1971; <u>The dream net</u>, saxophone and string quartet; <u>Prologue</u>, trumpet; <u>Soliloquy</u>, horn; <u>Aubade</u>, trombone; <u>Arioso</u>, tuba; <u>Marche</u>, wind quintet; <u>Largo tah</u>, bass trombone, marimba; <u>Embers</u>, trumpet, trombone, percussion; <u>Wind rose</u>, 4 saxophones; CHORUS: <u>Love is</u>; <u>An Englishman with an atlas</u>; <u>Sweet hallelujah</u>, piano and antiphonal choruses; SONGS: <u>5 lyrics of Louise Bogan</u>, mezzo-soprano and flute.

    10 Reitz Parkway, Pittsford, NY 14534

BENTER, CHARLES
    b. New York, N.Y., 29 Apr. 1887; d. New York, 2 Dec. 1964. He was apprentice boy musician, U.S. Navy 1905; received an honorary D.M. from Columbia Univ. He organized the Navy Band in Washington in 1919 and was its leader up to retirement in 1942; was first to attain officer rank in the music branch of the Navy and was commissioned Lt. by act of Congress in 1923; was founder and officer in charge of the Navy School of Music. After his naval career, he conducted the Metropolitan Police Dept. Band in Washington to 1962. His many works for band include the marches: <u>Irresistible</u>; <u>Lure of Alaska</u>; <u>Major Denby</u>; <u>Washington Times</u>; <u>Light cruisers</u>; <u>All hands</u>; et al.

BENTLEY, BERENICE BENSON
    b. Oskaloosa, Iowa, 2 Jan. 1887; d. Claremont, Calif., 2 Apr. 1971. Studied at Grinnell Coll., Iowa, and with Mary Wood Chase in Chicago. She taught at the Mary Wood Chase School and was associated with Guy Maier in summer workshops. Her compositions for piano included <u>4 northern sketches</u>, sonatina, and several albums.

BENTZ, CECIL
    b. 1916. His works include a 1-act opera, <u>Window games</u>, performed in New York, 18 Nov. 1967; choral settings of 2 poems by Robert Frost, <u>Nothing gold can stay</u> and <u>Waspish</u>.

BERBERIAN, HAMPARTZOUM
    b. Adana, Turkey, 25 May 1905; U.S. citizen 1968. Left Turkey after the Armenian massacre in 1915; by 1922 he had reached Greece and there attended the Athens Cons. on full scholarship, graduating in 1929; his teachers included Dmitri Mitropoulos on conducting. He studied composition in Paris. He was music director of various schools and colleges in the Middle East until coming to the U.S.
    WORKS: OPERA: <u>Areknagan</u>; <u>Teeter</u>; <u>Mer Okhda</u>; ORCHESTRA: violin concerto, 1950; cello concerto; <u>Requiem aeternam</u>, chorus and orch., 1972; other choral works.
    14 Irma Ave., Watertown, MA 02172

BERCKMAN, EVELYN
    b. Philadelphia, Pa., 1900. Has written 2 ballets, <u>From the Odyssey</u> and <u>County fair</u>; many works for orchestra and chamber groups; also

songs including <u>Die Nebelstadt</u> and <u>Sturm</u>, 1924, both for high voice.

BEREZOWSKY, NICOLAI
    b. St. Petersburg, Russia, 17 May 1900; to U.S. 1921; d. New York, 27 Aug. 1953. In New York he was first a theater violinist, then in the New York Phil., 1923-29; was a member of the Elizabeth Sprague Coolidge String Quartet, 1935-40. He received a Guggenheim fellowship in 1948.
    WORKS: OPERA: <u>Prince Batrak</u>; <u>Babar, the elephant</u>, a children's opera; ORCHESTRA: 4 symphonies, 1931, 1934, 1936, 1943; violin concerto, 1930; viola concerto, 1941; harp concerto, 1944; <u>Concerto lirico</u>, cello and orch., 1934; Christmas festival overture, 1943; CHAMBER MUSIC: 2 string quartets; 2 woodwind quintets; string sextet; suite for brass; <u>Fantasy</u> for 2 pianos, 1930.

BERG, CHRISTOPHER
    b. Detroit, Mich., 30 June 1949. Studied with Robert Helps, Manhattan School of Music; with Jeanne Stark, Centre Musical Font'neuve. His awards include a Martha Baird Rockefeller recording grant; Yaddo fellowships; and commissions. From 1977 he has been musical director of various Santa Fe theatre companies; was founder-director, New Music/New Mexico, 1977-78; was acting dean of faculty, New Mexico Music Festival at Taos, 1979.
    WORKS: BALLET: <u>Nocturnae</u>, harp, bassoon, celesta, Santa Fe, 10 Mar. 1979; ORCHESTRA: <u>Outmoded forms</u>, 5 sketches, 1977-78; Latin mass, mezzo-soprano, chorus, orch., Taos, N.M., 15 Aug. 1979; CHAMBER MUSIC: <u>3 short piano pieces</u>, 1970-78; <u>Not waving, but drowning</u>, mezzo-soprano and chamber orch., Albuquerque, 18 Jan. 1980; and other songs.
    16551 Winston Ave., Detroit, MI 48219

BERG, SIDNEY
    b. Superior, Wis., 25 July 1918. Attended Univ. of Michigan. He has been music director in public schools from 1944 and in 1971 was named assistant conductor of the Tidewater Youth Symphony. He has published a timpani method and solos for percussion instruments including <u>Holliday</u>, <u>Rolling rhythms</u>, <u>South American capers</u>, <u>The visitor</u>, <u>Rambling along</u>, etc.
    4043 N. Witchduck Rd., Virginia Beach, VA 23455

BERGAMO, JOHN J.
    b. Englewood, N.J., 28 May 1940. Studied with Michael Colgrass in New York, 1963-64, and with Gunther Schuller at Tanglewood, 1965. Since 1970 he has taught percussion at California Inst. of the Arts.
    WORKS: <u>Interactions</u>, vibraphone and 6 percussionists, 1963; <u>4 pieces</u> for timpani, 1963; <u>Haiku</u>, young voices and percussion, 1964; <u>Tanka</u>, solo percussion, 1964; <u>Style studies</u>, etudes for keyboard percussion.
    California Institute of the Arts, 24700 McBean Parkway, Valencia, CA 91355

BERGENFIELD, NATHAN J.
    b. New York, N.Y., 8 Mar. 1935. Studied with

BERGER, ARTHUR V.

Vittorio Giannini, Nicholas Flagello, and Ludmila
Ulehla, Manhattan School of Music, B.M. 1960,
M.M. 1961; musicology with Jan LaRue, New York
Univ., Ph.D. 1978. He taught in public schools,
1964-70, and at Brooklyn Coll., 1971.
WORKS: Concerto barocco, 3 trumpets; Canzona,
3 horns; Diversions, 3 trombones; and a piano
method.
2725 E. 22nd St., Brooklyn, NY 11235

BERGER, ARTHUR V.
b. New York, N.Y., 15 May 1912. Studied with
Walter Piston at Harvard Univ., M.A. 1936; with
Nadia Boulanger and Darius Milhaud in Paris.
His awards include the John Knowles Paine
fellowship, 1937-39; membership in the Nat. Inst.
of Arts and Letters, 1972; a concert of his
works given at Carnegie Hall, New York, 1 Apr.
1973, honoring his 60th birthday. He was music
critic in New York, 1943-53; held faculty posts
at Mills Coll., Brooklyn Coll., Juilliard School;
from 1953, at Brandeis Univ., professor from
1972.
WORKS: BALLET: Entertainment piece, 1940;
ORCHESTRA: 3 pieces for string orch., 1945;
Serenade concertante, violin, woodwind quartet,
small orch., 1945, rev. 1951; Ideas of order,
1953; Polyphony, 1956; CHAMBER MUSIC: 2 episodes
for piano, 1933; woodwind quartet, 1941; 2 duos,
violin and piano, 1948, 1950; duo for cello and
piano, 1951; duo, oboe and clarinet, 1952;
Chamber music for 13 players, 1956; duo for
clarinet and piano, 1957; string quartet, 1958;
3 pieces for pianos, 1961; woodwind trio; septet
for woodwind trio, string trio, piano, 1966;
5 pieces for piano, 1969; trio for guitar, violin,
piano, 1972.
9 Sparks St., Cambridge, MA 02138

BERGER, DAVID
b. New York, N.Y., 30 Mar. 1949. Studied with
Karel Husa, Ithaca Coll., B.M. 1971; with
Rayburn Wright and Manny Albam, Eastman School
of Music; and at Berklee Coll. of Music, Boston.
His awards have included a Downbeat scholarship,
1966; Duke Ellington award, 1967; and a grant
from the Nat. Endowment for the Arts, 1973.
WORKS: JAZZ ENSEMBLE: Idiom '73, concerto
for Clark Terry; Influence: within and without.

BERGER, JEAN
b. Hamm, Germany, 27 Sept. 1909; U.S. citizen
1943. Studied at Heidelberg Univ., Ph.D. 1931;
with Louis Aubert in Paris. He held a MacDowell
fellowship, 1973. He served in the U.S. Army in
World War II; was faculty member, Middlebury
Coll., 1948-49; Univ. of Illinois, 1959-61;
Univ. of Colorado, 1961-68.
WORKS: ORCHESTRA: Caribbean concerto,
harmonica and orch., 1942; Creole overture, 1949;
CHAMBER MUSIC: 4 sonnets, voice and string
quartet, 1941; Intrada, brass quartet; Elegy for
strings; 5 pieces, woodwind quintet; CHORUS:
Brazilian psalm, 1941; Vision of peace, 1949;
No man is an island; How lovely are thy taber-
nacles; A diversion, chorus and dancers; The
fiery furnace, dramatic cantata, 1962; The pied
piper, with orch., 1968; Stone soup, a parable

for out time, Chapel Hill, N.C., 9 Sept. 1976;
The exiles, with 2 soloists, 2 pianos, and percussion; Of life, with soloists and instruments,
1977.
1107 Cedar Ave., Boulder, CO 80302

BERGH, ARTHUR
b. St. Paul, Minn., 24 Mar. 1882; d. on shipboard
en route to Honolulu, 11 Feb. 1962. He played
violin in the Metropolitan Opera Orch., 1903-8;
was free-lance conductor in New York; from 1941,
was librarian for motion picture companies in
Hollywood.
WORKS: THEATRE: Niorada, an opera; The
pied piper of Hamelin and The raven, melodramas
with orch.; In Arcady and The goblin fair,
operettas; choral works; more than 100 songs;
violin pieces.

BERGSMA, WILLIAM
b. Oakland, Calif., 1 Apr. 1921. Studied at
Stanford Univ.; with Howard Hanson and Bernard
Rogers at Eastman School of Music, B.A., M.A.
His awards include an Amer. Acad. of Arts and
Letters grant; 2 Guggenheim fellowships; many
commissions. He was on the faculty at Juilliard
School, 1946-63; from 1963, director, School of
Music, Univ. of Washington.
WORKS: OPERA: The wife of Martin Guerre,
1956; The murder Comrade Sharik, 1973; BALLET:
Paul Bunyan, 1938; Senor commandante, 1941;
ORCHESTRA: Music on a quiet theme, 1943; The
fortunate islands, string orch., 1947; a symphony, 1949; Dance from a New England album,
small orch.; Documentary 1: portrait of a city;
Carol on 12th night, with chorus, 1954; March
with trumpets, 1957; concerto for wind quintet,
1958; Chameleon variations, 1960; In celebration:
toccata for the 6th day, 1962; violin concerto,
1966; Sweet was the song the virgin sung and
Tristan revisited, variation and fantasy, both
for viola and orch. and both premiered in
Seattle, 10 Apr. 1978; CHAMBER MUSIC: 4 string
quartets; suite for brass quartet, 1940; Fantastic variations on a theme from Tristan, viola
and piano, 1961; Serenade, to await the moon,
chamber orch., 1965; Illegible canons, clarinet
and piano, 1969; Clandestine dialogues, cello
and percussion, 1972; Changes for 7, woodwind
quintet, piano, percussion, 1975; In space,
soprano and instruments, 1975; CHORUS: On the
beach at night, 1945; In a glass of water, 1946;
Wishes, wonders, portents, charms; Confrontation
from the Book of Job, chorus and 22 instruments,
1963; The sun, the soaring eagle, the turquoise
prince, the god, New York premiere, 12 Feb. 1971.
School of Music, Univ. of Washington,
Seattle, WA 98105

BERK, MAYNARD
b. Bucyrus, Ohio, 27 July 1913. Studied at Univ.
of Redlands, B.M.; Union Theological Seminary,
N.Y., S.M.M.; with Philip James and Edwin
Stringham, New York Univ., Ph.D.; with Ernest
Kanitz and Halsey Stevens, Univ. of Southern
California; and with Henk Badings in the Nether-
lands. He has been faculty member at Sioux Falls
Coll. from 1949.

WORKS: CHORUS: <u>Kyrie eleison</u>; <u>Sanctus</u>; <u>Vocalise</u>, unison choir, instruments, organ; many organ, piano, and vocal pieces.
    Dept. of Music, Sioux Falls College, Sioux Falls, SD 57101

BERKOWITZ, LEONARD
    <u>Divertimento</u> for winds; <u>Toccata, theme and varia-tions</u> for winds; <u>4 songs</u>, on poems of Emily Dickinson; <u>Chamber music</u>, women's chorus, on text by Robert Frost.
    Music Dept., California State Univ., Northridge, CA 91324

BERKOWITZ, RALPH
    b. New York, N.Y., 5 Sept. 1910. Studied at Curtis Inst. and taught there, 1933-42; taught summers at the Berkshire Music Center, where in 1947 he was named dean and executive assistant to Koussevitzky. He was manager of the Albu-querque Symph. Orch., 1958-69. He is also con-cert pianist, accompanist, lecturer, painter, and author of magazine articles and the book, <u>What every accompanist knows.</u>
    WORKS: <u>A telephone call</u>, voice and orchestra, with text by Dorothy Parker, premiere in Rio de Janeiro, 1957; <u>Syncopations</u> for piano, 1956; transcriptions and orchestrations of Bach, Purcell, Haydn, etc.
    620 Rio Grande Blvd., N.W., Albuquerque, NM 87104

BERKOWITZ, SOL
    b. Warren, Ohio, 27 Apr. 1922. Studied at Queens Coll., CUNY, with Karol Rathaus and Otto Luening, Columbia Univ., M.A. He received a Ford Found. grant in 1956. He was professor at Queens Coll., 1946-61, and from 1972.
    WORKS: OPERA: <u>Fat Tuesday</u>, a jazz opera, 1956; ORCHESTRA: <u>Diversion</u>; BAND: <u>Paradigm</u>, a jazz adventure in sonata form; <u>Game of dance</u>; CHAMBER MUSIC: <u>9 pieces for 9 winds</u>; <u>Scherzo, blues and dance</u>, viola and piano; <u>Serenade</u>, wind quintet; <u>Suite for winds</u>, woodwind quintet; <u>4 blues for lefty</u>, piano; CHORUS: <u>Without words</u>, vocalize for women's voices.
    Music Dept., Queens College, CUNY, New York, NY 11367

BERLIN, DAVID
    b. Pittsburgh, Pa., 23 Jan. 1943. Studied with Leonardo Balada, Nicolai Lopatnikoff, James Beale, Roland Leich, and Philip Catelinet, Carnegie-Mellon Univ. He has received awards in 4 composition contests. From 1965 he has been a teacher in the North Allegheny School District, Pittsburgh.
    WORKS: ORCHESTRA: <u>Variants</u>, 1972; piano concerto; BAND: <u>Divertimento</u>; <u>Music for brass and percussion</u>; <u>Caricature for wind band</u>, 1976; CHAMBER MUSIC: octet, 1971; <u>Quadraphonics</u>, brass quintet, 1974; <u>Fragments</u>, percussion, 1974; quintet, bassoon and strings, 1975; <u>Structures</u>, chamber orch., 1975; <u>Patterns</u>, saxophone quartet, 1975; <u>Fluctuations</u>, flute choir, 1976; <u>Synergism no. 1</u>, variable ensemble, 1976; trio for flute, oboe, guitar, 1977; trio for flute, oboe, clar-inet, 1977; woodwind quintet, 1977; CHORUS:

<u>Exclamations</u>, 1974; MIXED MEDIA: <u>3 mixtures</u>, 4 bassoons and tape, 1973; <u>Articulations</u>, soprano and tape, 1973; <u>Synchronization</u>, band and tape; <u>Interactions</u>, flute and tape, 1973; <u>Essences</u>, viola and tape.
    4809 Baptist Rd., Pittsburgh, PA 15227

BERLIN, IRVING
    b. Temun, Russia, 11 May 1888; to U.S. 1893. He never learned to read music, but nevertheless wrote words and music for enormously successful songs for nearly four decades. His first big hit, <u>Alexander's ragtime band</u>, 1911, was followed by innumerable exceedingly popular songs, musi-cals, and film scores. He was one of the first ten inductees into the Entertainment Hall of Fame on 23 Apr. 1974.

BERLINSKI, HERMAN
    b. Leipzig, Germany, 18 Aug. 1910; to U.S. after World War II. He was instructor, Hebrew Union Coll., then became organist and music director, Washington Hebrew Congregation, D.C.
    WORKS: ORCHESTRA: <u>Symphonic visions</u>, 1949; <u>Merrymount</u>; CHAMBER MUSIC: 3- or 4-part canons for winds; flute sonata, 1941; violin sonata, 1944; CHORUS: <u>Kaddish</u>, 1953; <u>Avodat Shabbat</u>, 1957; <u>Kiddush, Ha-Shem</u>, 1958; <u>It hath been told thee</u>, <u>O man</u>; <u>Job</u>, oratorio, excerpts performed in New York, 11 June 1973; ORGAN: <u>The burning bush</u>, 1956; <u>Sinfonia #3 (Sounds and motions)</u>; <u>Sinfonia #9, The glass bead game--Magister Ludi</u> was premiered in Carnegie Hall, New York, in Feb. 1975.
    4000 Tunlaw Rd., N.W., Washington, DC 20007

BERLINSKI, JACQUES
    b. Radon, Poland, 13 Dec. 1913; U.S. citizen 1973. Studied in Paris with Nadia Boulanger and Jean Roger-Ducasse; then fought in the French Army in World War II. In 1948 he won first prize in a New York composition contest for his first symphony, which was later dedicated to the memory of Winston Churchill and subtitled <u>Sym-phony of glory</u>, 1965. His <u>America 1976</u> for narrator, chorus, and orchestra was premiered in San Diego on 6 May 1976.

BERNAT, ROBERT
    b. Johnstown, Pa., 3 July 1931. Taught for several years at Indiana Univ. of Pennsylvania. His <u>Passacaglia, in memorium: John F. Kennedy</u>, had its premiere in Pittsburgh on 25 Nov. 1966 and was recorded by the Louisville Orch.

BERNHARDT, STEPHEN
    b. Glendale, Calif., 20 Nov. 1947. Studied with Donal Michalsky and Robert Stewart at California State Univ., Fullerton.
    WORKS: ORCHESTRA: <u>Symphonic metamorphoses #2</u>, small orch.; CHAMBER MUSIC: piano variations, 1972; concerto for 5 instruments, 1974; <u>Symphonic metamorphoses #1</u>, 8 woodwinds, 1977; variations on Stravinsky's double canon for string quartet, 1978.
    2401 Foxdale Ave., La Habra, CA 90631

BERNSTEIN, DAVID STEPHEN

BERNSTEIN, DAVID STEPHEN
b. Boston, Mass., 6 Jan. 1942. Studied with
Carlisle Floyd and John Boda, Florida State
Univ.; with Juan Orrego-Salas at Indiana Univ.
He taught at Indiana Univ., 1969-71; joined the
faculty at Univ. of Akron in 1972.
WORKS: ORCHESTRA: Dialogue, double orch.
and percussion; CHAMBER MUSIC: sonata for chamber orch.; quartet for clarinet, trumpet, cello,
harpsichord; 4 songs, tenor and 14 instruments;
Ziz, 6 percussionists; Sette, piano.
3327 Overlook Dr., Akron, OH 44312

BERNSTEIN, ELMER
b. New York, N.Y., 4 Apr. 1922. Held scholarships for study of piano at Juilliard School,
1934-49, and composition with Israel Citkowitz,
Roger Sessions, Ivan Langstroth, and Stefan
Wolpe; attended New York Univ., 1939-42. Except
for service in the Army in World War II, he was
concert pianist, 1939-50, then turned to composing film scores for which he has won an
Academy Award, 9 Academy Award nominations, an
Emmy, 2 Golden Globe awards, Western Heritage
award, and a Downbeat award.
WORKS: The award-winning film scores are:
The man with the golden arm, 1955; The magnificent 7, 1960; Summer and smoke, 1961; Walk on
the wild side, 1961; To kill a mockingbird, 1962;
The making of a president--1960, 1963; Hallelujah
trail, 1965; Hawaii, 1966; Return of the 7, 1966;
Thoroughly modern Millie, 1967; and the stage
musical score: How now Dow Jones, 1967. Some
other scores are: Drango, 1956; Toccata for toy
trains, 1957; God's little acre, 1958; Love with
the proper stranger, 1962; The scalphunters,
1968; True grit, 1969; A cannon for Cordoba,
1970.
Winter River Ranch, Malibu, CA 90265

BERNSTEIN, LEONARD
b. Lawrence, Mass., 25 Aug. 1918. Studied at
Harvard Univ., A.B. 1939; Curtis Inst. of Music,
grad. 1941; conducting with Fritz Reiner and
Serge Koussevitzky; composition with Walter
Piston and Edward Burlingame Hill; piano with
Helen Coates, Heinrich Gebhard, and Isabelle
Vengerova; holds a number of honorary degrees.
His numerous other honors include an Emmy for
the TV Young People's Concerts, Grammy award,
Sonning Prize of Denmark, election to the Nat.
Inst. of Arts and Letters, N.Y. Music Critics
Circle award, N.Y. Drama Critics award; and a
concert honoring his 60th birthday broadcast by
PBS on 26 Aug. 1978 with the Nat. Symph. Orch.
featuring his music. He was assistant conductor,
N.Y. Philharmonic, 1943-44; conductor, N.Y. City
Center Orch., 1945-48; music adviser, Israel
Philharmonic, 1948-49; on faculty, Brandeis
Univ., 1951-56; music director and conductor,
N.Y. Philharmonic, 1958-59, then appointed
laureate conductor for life; named institute
lecturer, M.I.T., 1974. He has conducted all
major orchestras of the U.S. and Europe, the
Metropolitan Opera, N.Y., Vienna State Opera,
and was the first American to conduct at La
Scala, Milan, 1953.

WORKS: OPERA: Trouble in Tahiti, 1 act, to
his own libretto, 1952; BALLET: Fancy free,
1944; Facsimile, 1946; THEATRE: On the town,
1944; incidental music to Peter Pan, 1950, and
The lark, 1957; Wonderful town, 1952; On the
waterfront (film), 1954; Candide, 1956, rev.,
Brooklyn, 19 Dec. 1973, New York, 5 Mar. 1974;
West side story, Washington, 19 Aug. 1957; Mass,
a theater piece written for the opening of the
John F. Kennedy Center for the Performing Arts,
Washington, 7 Sept. 1971; Dybbuk, New York City
Ballet, 16 May 1974; 1600 Pennsylvania Avenue,
musical, New York, 4 May 1976; ORCHESTRA:
Jeremiah symphony, 1944; The age of anxiety,
symphony #2, Boston, 8 Apr. 1949; Kaddish, symphony #3, with narrator and chorus, Tel Aviv,
9 Dec. 1963; Prelude, fugue, and riffs, jazz
combo and orch., 1950; Serenade, solo violin,
strings, percussion, 1954; Chichester psalms,
with chorus, New York, 14 July 1965; Slava (A
political overture), Meditations (with solo
cello), Songfest (a cycle of American poems set
for 6 singers and orch.), all premiered at
Washington, 14 Oct. 1976; CHAMBER MUSIC: clarinet
sonata, 1942; 7 anniversaries, piano, 1942; 4
anniversaries, piano, 1964; SONGS: I hate music,
a cycle, 1943; La bonne cuisine, a cycle on
texts of cookbook recipes, 1949; 2 love songs,
1949; Afterthought, 1951; Silhouette, 1951. He
is author of The joy of music, 1959; Young
People's Concerts for reading and listening,
1962, rev. 1970; The infinite variety of music,
1966.
205 W. 57th St., New York, NY 10019

BERNSTEIN, SEYMOUR
b. Newark, N.J., 24 Apr. 1927. Studied with
Felix Salzer, Mannes Coll. of Music; at Juilliard
School; with Nadia Boulanger, Fontainebleau,
France; composition with Ben Weber. His awards
include a Beebe Found. grant; 2 Rockefeller
grants; 4 State Dept. grants; Premiere Prix and
Prix Jacques Durand at Fontainebleau; Nat. Fed.
of Music Clubs award for furthering American
music abroad. He has held faculty posts at
Chatham Square Music School; Hoff-Barthelson
Music School; and New York State Univ. Coll.,
Purchase, N.Y.
WORKS: PIANO: Interrupted waltz; Korean
bluebird; Toccata francaise; Birds, books 1 and
2; Concerto for our time; Insects; and a series
of educational works for piano.
10 W. 76th St., New York, NY 10023

BERRY, DAVID BRUCE
b. San Diego, Calif., 29 Apr. 1947. Studied at
Univ. of California, Berkeley, B.A., majoring
in visual communications; with Robert Ashley and
Terry Riley at Mills Coll., M.F.A. He received
the Elizabeth C. Mills award for composition in
1973. He was instructor at Mills Coll., 1972-
74; staff member, KPFA-FM, Berkeley, 1974-77;
then head, Multi Media Works, Inc.
WORKS: ELECTRONIC: Use speakophone or fiber
needles only, Buckla, 1970; Vietnam hamburger,
Moog, voice, weaponry, 1973; Up-down fire music,
1973; Elegia squalus, flute, piano, saxophone,
tape, Moog, 1973; A substratum of uncertainty,

1973; several other electronic works written with collaborators.
415 Moraga Ave., Piedmont, CA 94611

BERRY, WALLACE
b. La Crosse, Wis., 10 Jan. 1928. Studied with Halsey Stevens, Univ. of Southern California, Ph.D. 1956; with Nadia Boulanger in Paris. His awards include a Fulbright grant, 1953-54; Univ. of Michigan, Distinguished Faculty award, 1963, and election to Society of Fellows, 1975; Univ. of So. Calif. Outstanding Music Alumnus, 1973; first prize, Nat. Flute Club competition, 1970; American Academy-Inst. of Arts and Letters composer award, 1978. He was faculty member, Univ. of Michigan, Ann Arbor, 1957-77; from 1978, professor and head of music dept., Univ. of British Columbia, Vancouver.
WORKS: ORCHESTRA: 5 pieces for small orch.; piano concerto; CHAMBER MUSIC: duo for violin and piano; 2 canons for 2 clarinets; 8 20th century miniatures for piano; 2 string quartets; Divertimento, 5 winds, piano, percussion; Threnody, violin alone; Canto lirico, viola and piano; Fantasy in 5 statements, clarinet and piano; duo, flute and piano; piano trio; Anachronisms, violin and piano; piano sonata, 1975-76; CHORUS: No man is an island; ORGAN: Fantasy on Von Himmel Hoch; Variations on a martyr's tune.
Music Dept., Univ. of British Columbia, Vancouver, B.C., Canada V6T 1W5

BERTCHUME, GARY
b. St. Louis, Mo., 29 Dec. 1949. Studied with Robert Wykes, Roland Jordan, and John Perkins, Washington Univ.; with Jack Beeson, Mario Davidovsky, Vladimir Ussachevsky, Chou Wen-Chung, Columbia Univ. He has received the Antoinette Dame award and the St. Louis Forum for Composers award.
WORKS: CHAMBER MUSIC: Phases, chamber orch., St. Louis, 1 Mar. 1973; Lateral planations, clarinet, cello, piano, percussion, 1974; trio, clarinet, piano, percussion, 1975; sonata for vibraphone, cello, perc., 1977; Dance music, clarinet, cello, piano, perc., 1978; septet, 3 winds, cello, piano, perc., 1978.
322 W. 77th St., New York, NY 10024

BERTHELOT, JOHN
b. New Orleans, La., 8 Oct. 1942. Studied with John Butler and Patrick McCarty, Loyola Univ., New Orleans; with Kenneth Klaus, Louisiana State Univ.; with Rayburn Wright, Eastman School of Music; and with Barry Vercoe, Mass. Inst. of Technology. His awards include the Sam Houston State Univ. jazz composition award, 1967; Louisiana Fed. of Music Clubs award, 1968. He has been music teacher in New Orleans public schools from 1970.
WORKS: ORCHESTRA: Essay for orchestra; WIND ENSEMBLE: rondo for winds; Serenade to spring, soprano and winds; JAZZ: Cityscape for jazz ensemble; chamber jazz suite; The roach; The streetcar; Blues for computer.
P.O. Box 13977, New Orleans, LA 70185

BEST, HAROLD M.
b. Jamestown, N.Y., 1 Oct. 1931. Studied with Karl Kohn in Claremont, Calif.; with Searle Wright and Seth Bingham at Union Theological Seminary. He was faculty member at Nyack Coll., 1956-70; since then, director of the Coll. Cons., Wheaton Coll.
WORKS: ORCHESTRA: piano concertino; VOCAL: Psalm II, chorus; A call to service, chorus; Song of the divine presence; KEYBOARD: toccata for 2 pianos; scherzo for organ; 7 voluntaries on early American hymn tunes, organ; several original hymn tunes.
151 Travers, Wheaton, IL 60187

BESTOR, CHARLES
b. New York, N.Y., 21 Dec. 1924. Studied with Paul Hindemith at Yale Univ.; at Swarthmore Coll., B.A. 1948; with Vincent Persichetti and Peter Mennin, Juilliard School, B.S. 1951; with Burrill Phillips, Univ. of Illinois, M.M. 1952; and with Charles Eakin, Univ. of Colorado, D.M.A. 1973. He has held faculty and administrative positions at Juilliard School, 1951-59; Univ. of Colorado, 1959-64; Willamette Univ., 1964-71; Univ. of Alabama, 1971-74; Univ. of Utah, 1974-77; then named head of the music and dance department, Univ. of Massachusetts.
WORKS: BALLET: Undine, 1951; THEATRE: Incidental music to J.B., MacLeish, 1961, and Measure for measure, Shakespeare, 1963; ORCHESTRA: concerto grosso for percussion and orch., 1968; Music for the mountain, 1972; Until a time, 1977; BAND: suite for winds and trumpet, 1962; concertino, trumpet and band, 1973; CHAMBER MUSIC: piano sonata, 1963; A wind in the willows, solo flute, 1964; 12 short movements for string quartet, 1976; CHORUS: My love and I, 1966; In memoriam, to texts from The autobiography of Malcolm X, 1972; several a capella choruses; MIXED MEDIA: improvisation I and II, for instruments and tape, 1971; Poem, choir, soprano soloist, electronic synthesizer, 1972; Variations, violin and piano with synthesizer, 1973; Day of the lake, flute and tape, 1976; Second moon of Venus, 1976.
19 Birchcroff Lane, Amherst, MA 01002

BETJEMAN, PAUL
b. London, England, 26 Nov. 1937; permanent U.S. resident 1962. Studied at Berklee Coll. of Music and at Harvard Grad. School of Education; composition with Stefan Wolpe; electronic music with Mario Davidovsky, Vladimir Ussachevsky, and Charles Dodge at Columbia Univ. He has held a Nat. Endowment for the Arts grant, MacDowell fellowship, and has been a guest at Yaddo. He is consultant in computer music at Columbia Univ.
WORKS: THEATRE: Pueblo, incidental music; Forbidden, electronic ballet score; ORCHESTRA: Hawthorn; CHAMBER MUSIC: string quartet; Hawthorn 2, 2 pianists and 2 percussionists, 1975; Hawthorn 3, piano and string quartet, 1975; Slow burn, clarinet, string quartet, bass viol; CHORUS: St. Mark XV 17-21; ORGAN: Paces, with trumpet; ELECTRONIC: 3 songs on scriptural texts, soprano and tape; 6 breaths, soprano and electronic sound; Rattler.
Riverdale Country School, Bronx, NY 10471

BEVERIDGE, THOMAS G.

BEVERIDGE, THOMAS G.
b. New York, N.Y., 6 Apr. 1938; d. 1981. Studied with Walter Piston and Randall Thompson,
Harvard Coll., A.B. 1959; with Nadia Boulanger
at Fontainebleau, 1958-60. His awards include
a Ford grant and commissions.
WORKS: He has composer chamber music, choral
works, and songs including 4 song cycles:
Odysseus, Prometheus, 3 serious songs, Leaves of
grass, all for bass voice and piano; Once: in
memoriam Martin Luther King, Jr., a cantata;
Serenade for baritone and string quartet, on
text of Walt Whitman, 1977; a total of more than
300 works.
3511 Turner Lane, Chevy Chase, MD 20015

BEVERSDORF, (SAMUEL) THOMAS
b. Yoakum, Tex., 8 Aug. 1924. Studied with Kent
Kennan, Arthur Kreutz, Eric DeLamarter, Univ. of
Texas, B.M.; with Bernard Rogers and Howard
Hanson, Eastman School of Music, M.M., D.M.A.;
and with Aaron Copland, Arthur Honneger, and
Serge Koussevitzky at Tanglewood. He has re-
ceived many commissions and composition awards.
He was first trombonist in the Houston Symph.,
1946-48, Pittsburgh Symph., 1948-49; instructor,
Univ. of Houston, 1946-48; from 1951, professor,
Indiana Univ.; composer-in-residence, Bucknell
Univ., 1970-71.
WORKS: OPERA: The hooligan, 1 act, on
Chekhov's The boor, 1964-69; ORCHESTRA: Essay
on mass production, 1946; 4 symphonies, 1946,
1950, 1954, 1960; Reflections, 1947; Mexican
portrait, 1947; concerto grosso, oboe and chamber
orch., 1948; concerto for 2 pianos, 1951; Ode,
1952; New frontiers, 1955; Serenade, 1956; violin
concerto (Danforth), 1959; Variations, 1965;
Generation with the torch, an overture for youth,
1965; Divertimento concertante, 1970; concerto
for tuba and orchestra winds, 1975; Murals,
tapestries, and icons, orchestra winds, electric
bass and piano, 1975; BAND: Cathedral music,
brass choir, 1950; 3 epitaphs in memory of Eric
DeLamarter, brass quartet, 1955; Serenade, winds
and percussion, 1957; CHAMBER MUSIC: sonatas for
piano, 1944, horn, 1945, tuba, 1956, trumpet,
1962, violin, 1964, flute, 1966, cello, 1969;
2 suites on baroque themes, 1947, 1949; prelude
and fugue, woodwind quintet, 1950; 2 string
quartets, 1952, 1955; Divertimento da camera,
flute, oboe, doublebass, harpsichord, 1968;
Walruses, cheesecake, and Morse code, tuba and
piano, 1972; La petite exposition, solo violin
or clarinet and 11 strings, 1976; sonata for
violin and harp, 1977; also choral works, songs,
and piano pieces. He has written a libretto for
Metamorphosis, a 3-act opera freely adapted from
Kafka.
4950 E. Cedar Crest, Bloomington, IN 47401

BEYER, FREDERICK H.
b. Chicago, Ill., 3 Dec. 1926. Studied with
Otto Luening and Jack Beeson at Columbia Univ.;
with John Boda at Florida State Univ. He received the Ostwald Band Composition award in
1965. From 1966 he has been faculty member at
Greensboro Coll.
WORKS: ORCHESTRA: Visions of time and the
river (3rd symphony) premiered at the Eastern
Music Festival, 1978; BAND: overture, 1965;
CHAMBER MUSIC: Conversations, brass trio; Man
with the blue guitar, chorus and piano; several
compositions using tape and live performers.
5006 Forest Oaks Dr., Greensboro, NC 27406

BEYER, HOWARD
b. Chicago, Ill., 25 Mar. 1929. Studied with
Leo Sowerby at American Cons., B.A., M.A. His
honors include a Thor Johnson award, U.S. Army
march composition award in Europe, and an ASCAP
award. From 1957 he has been staff musician at
radio station WCFL; from 1970, pianist with the
Norm Ladd Orch.
WORKS: Suite for brass instruments; trumpet
concerto; organ prelude; and popular compositions.
3824 Grand Ave., Western Springs, IL 60558

BEZANSON, PHILIP
b. Athol, Mass., 6 Jan. 1916; d. Hadley, Mass.,
11 Mar. 1975. Studied with David Stanley Smith
and Richard Donovan, Yale Univ.; with Philip
Greeley Clapp at Univ. of Iowa. His awards included a Fromm Found. grant, 2 publication
grants, and a Guggenheim grant. He was professor, Univ. of Iowa, 1954-64, then professor and
head of music department, Univ. of Massachusetts,
Amherst.
WORKS: OPERA: Golden child, NBC-TV, Hall-
mark Hall of Fame, 1960; ORCHESTRA: piano concerto, New York, 1953; Rondo-prelude, 1954;
sinfonia concertante, Iowa City, 1972; CHAMBER
MUSIC: string quartet, 1965; Prelude and dance,
brass sextet; diversion for brass trio, 1964;
other solo, chamber, vocal and orchestral works.

BIALOSKY, MARSHALL H.
b. Cleveland, Ohio, 30 Oct. 1923. Studied with
Lionel Nowak and Ernst Bacon, Syracuse Univ.,
B.M. 1949; with Robert Delaney at Northwestern
Univ., M.M. 1950; and with Luigi Dallapiccola
in Italy on a Fulbright fellowship, 1954-56.
His other honors include Wisconsin State com-
posers' award, 1954; Wechsler Commission at
Tanglewood, 1958; Piano Quarterly citation, 1968.
He has held faculty positions at Milton Coll.,
Wis., 1950-54; Univ. of Chicago, 1956-61; State
Univ. of New York, Stony Brook, 1961-64; from
1964, has been professor and chairman, fine arts
dept., California State Coll., Dominguez Hills.
WORKS: CHAMBER MUSIC: 2 movements, brass
trio; suite for flute, oboe, clarinet; oboe
sonatina; Fantasy scherzo, saxophone and piano;
2 voices in a meadow, voice and viola; 2 movements, string quartet and piano; sonata for solo
violin; Fantasy, solo cello; Starting over, solo
flute; 2 songs for soprano voice and bass trombone; 3 songs for soprano and clarinet; Pastoral
(with dark edges), solo viola; Guitarondo, solo
guitar; CHORUS: There is a wisdom that is woe;
A song of degrees; Of music and musicians; Be
music, night; Little ghost things; 5 nonsense
songs about animals; An old picture; many other
choral works; piano pieces.
88 Cresta Verde, Rolling Hills Estates, CA
90274

BIDDELMAN, MARK J.
b. Newark, N.J., 7 June 1943. Studied at Hebrew Union Coll.-Jewish Inst. of Religion, School of Sacred Music and at Carnegie Inst. of Technology. He has been a cantor since 1962 and at Temple Emanuel, Westwood, N.J., from 1967.
WORKS: Shiru Ladonai Shir Chadash (Let us sing a new song unto the Lord), a folk-rock service for the Sabbath eve.
568 Hillsdale Ave., Hillsdale, NJ 07642

BIELAWA, HERBERT
b. Chicago, Ill., 3 Feb. 1930. Studied with Gordon Binkerd, Burrill Phillips, Robert Kelly, Univ. of Illinois, B.M. 1954, M.M. 1958; with Ingolf Dahl, Halsey Stevens, Ellis Kohs, Univ. of Southern California, D.M.A. 1969; with Darius Milhaud at Aspen. His awards include Univ. of Illinois fellowship; Aspen composition prize; BMI fellowship; MENC and Ford Found. grants, 1964-66; Music Teachers Nat. Assoc. commission; Burke Found. grant; Bay Area Synthesizer Ensemble commission. He was instructor at Bethany Coll., 1958-60; from 1966, professor at San Francisco State Univ.
WORKS: THEATRE: A bird in the bush, chamber opera, 1962; What do you care? It's beyond repair!, satirical review, 1968; ORCHESTRA: Concert piece, 1954; Abstractions, string orch., 1965; Divergents, 1968; BAND: Concert fanfare, 1964; toccata, 1964; Chorale, 1965; Spectrum, with tape, 1966; CHAMBER MUSIC: trumpet duo, 1960; clarinet sonatina, 1962; Movements and moments, woodwind trio, 1974-78; Warp, piano and flute, 1976; Nocturne, 2 pianos, 1978; guitar quartet, 1978; Sidebands, 7 winds, 3 strings, 1979; MIXED MEDIA: Quodlibet SF 42569, organ and electronic sounds, 1969; Discoveries, 1970; Laps, gaps, and overlaps, tape only, 1973; A Dickinson album, choir, tape, and instruments, 1973; many choral works, vocal solos, piano and organ pieces.
81 Denslowe Dr., San Francisco, CA 94132

BIGGS, JOHN
b. Los Angeles, Calif., 18 Oct. 1932. Studied with Leonard Stein at Los Angeles City Coll.; with Lukas Foss, Roy Harris, John Vincent, Univ. of California, Los Angeles; with Halsey Stevens and Ingolf Dahl, Univ. of Southern California; and with Flor Peters, Royal Cons., Antwerp. He has had awards from Phi Mu Alpha, Atwater-Kent, Ohio State Univ., Celia Buck, ASCAP, a Fulbright grant, and many commissions. He has held faculty positions at Univ. of Calif., Los Angeles, 1961-63; Los Angeles City Coll., 1965-67; Kansas State Teachers Coll., 1967-70; then director, John Biggs Consort.
WORKS: ORCHESTRA: symphony, 1964; concerto for viola, woodwinds, percussion, 1965; Symphonic ode, 1971; Foreground music, 35 winds and percussion, 1971; variations on a theme of Shostakovich, with piano solo, Santa Barbara, 19 Mar. 1978; CHAMBER MUSIC: Tre canzoni, 3 clarinets, 1964; aria and toccata, organ, 1965; Invention, piano and tape, 1970; Invention, viola and tape, 1972; Invention, organ and tape; CHORUS: Invention, voices and tape, 1971;

Train, speaking chorus and tape; Nuages, chorus and string quartet.
1717 N. State College, Fullerton, CA 92631

BILCHICK, RUTH COLEMAN
b. New York, N.Y., 16 May 1904. Graduated from Barnard Coll., 1926; studied composition with Seth Bingham, Columbia Univ.; with Howard Brockway at Juilliard School; held a fellowship for study with Ernst Toch, 1934-35. She taught at Haaren High School, N.Y., 1931-37; then to 1954, at New York High School of Music and Art, where she originated teaching music composition at the secondary school level and concerts of the students' original work. Her own and others' articles on her teaching have appeared in Educational Music Magazine and The New York Times.
WORKS: THEATRE: Reality and fantasy, operetta with music, libretto, lyrics, and choreography by composer; Dreaming, flute, incidental music to An evening with the Brontes, New York, 15 Mar. 1973; ORCHESTRA: Fifth Avenue, symphonic suite, Forest Park, N.Y., 23 Aug. 1934, a reduced score was premiered by the Georges Barrere Little Symphony in N.Y., 4 Dec. 1932. BAND: Moods for symphonic band, premiere, 1945, Aberdeen Proving Grounds, Md., at the Officer Candidate School graduation, many other performances, including Carnegie Hall, N.Y., 22 May 1978; American holiday, Roslyn, N.Y., 1975; CHAMBER MUSIC: Little trio, violin, cello, piano; CHORUS: Shepherds were watching, treble voices on an old Bohemian carol with English text written by Sigmund Spaeth; also songs and piano pieces.
166 E. 63rd St., New York, NY 10021

BILIK, JERRY H.
b. New Rochelle, N.Y., 7 Oct. 1933. Studied with Ross Lee Finney, Leslie Bassett, and Tibor Serly, Univ. of Michigan, B.M., M.M. His honors include an American Legion award, Stanley Medal, Pi Kappa Lambda award, Standard Oil Faculty award, ASCAP awards. He was faculty member at Univ. of Michigan, 1962-68, then adjunct professor there and at Wayne State Univ.
WORKS: THEATRE: Brass and grass forever, musical play, for which he also wrote the book and lyrics; ORCHESTRA: Aspects of man, 4 essays; BAND: symphony for band; They walked in darkness; American Civil War fantasy; concertino for alto saxophone and band.
2635 W. Delhi Rd., Ann Arbor, MI 48103

BILLINGSLEY, WILLIAM A.
b. Glasgow, Mont., 28 June 1922. Studied principally with Francis J. Pyle at Drake Univ. He has had commissions from the Boise Tuesday Muscicale and the Spokane Symphony. He played trumpet in the Des Moines Symphony, 1951 and 1953, and at radio station WHO, Des Moines; with the Spokane Symphony, 1960-61. From 1954 he has been faculty member at Univ. of Idaho.
WORKS: ORCHESTRA: work for soprano and orch., premiere, Spokane Expo '74; Requiem, ballet and orch., Moscow, Idaho, 14 Sept. 1976; WIND ENSEMBLE: symphony for winds and percussion, Moscow, 15 Feb. 1977; The starry night, 1978;

BILOTTI, ANTON

CHAMBER MUSIC: chamber ballet, string quartet and 2 dancers, 1968; Images of a village celebration, solo trumpet, Moscow, 9 Dec. 1976; flute sonata, Moscow, 25 Jan. 1977; VOICE: Mr. Nobody, women's voices; James Joyce songs, tenor and piano.

School of Music, Univ. of Idaho, Moscow, ID 83843

BILOTTI, ANTON

b. New York, N.Y., 17 Jan. 1906; d. New York, 10 Nov. 1963. His compositions include 2 piano concertos; violin concerto; saxophone concerto; chamber music.

BILYEU, LANDON

b. Lufkin, Tex., 30 Dec. 1939. Studied at Centenary Coll., La.; with Bela Rozsa, Univ. of Tulsa; and with Ulysses Kay, Boston Univ. He was faculty member, Midwestern Univ., 1964-71; Univ. of Idaho, 1971-77; then at Virginia Commonwealth Univ.

WORKS: BALLET: The debutante's ball, violin, winds, percussion; CHAMBER MUSIC: Prelude, flute and small orch.; Invention and 2 fugues, winds; Andante and allegro, flute and piano; flute sonatina; piano sonata, 4 12-tone piano pieces.

Virginia Commonwealth Univ., Richmond, VA 23284

BIMBONI, ALBERTO

b. Florence, Italy, 24 Aug. 1882; d. New York, 18 June 1960. Came to the U.S. in 1912 as an opera conductor. In 1930 he joined the faculty at Curtis Inst., and from 1933, taught opera classes at Juilliard School. He was accompanist for Eugene Ysaye, John McCormack, and others.

WORKS: OPERA: Winona, Portland, Oreg., 11 Nov. 1926; Karina, 1928; Il cancelleto d'oro, New York, 11 Mar. 1936; In the name of culture, Rochester, N.Y., 9 May 1949. He also wrote piano and organ pieces and many songs.

BINDER, ABRAHAM WOLFE

b. New York, N.Y., 13 Jan 1895; d. New York, 10 Oct. 1966. Studied at Columbia Univ., B.M. 1926; taught at Jewish Inst. of Religion.

WORKS: OPERA: A goat in Chelm, New York, 20 Mar. 1960; ORCHESTRA: Ha-Chalutzim (The pioneers), 1931; Holy land impressions, 1932; The Valley of Dry Bones, 1935; Dybbuk suite for chamber ensemble, 1956; VOICE: The legend of the Ari, oratorio; Israel reborn, oratorio; Palestinian song suite.

BINGHAM, SETH

b. Bloomfield, N.J., 16 Apr. 1882; d. New York, 21 June 1972. Studied with Horatio Parker at Yale Univ., B.A. 1904, B.M. 1908; organ and composition in Paris, 1906, 1907. He received an honorary doctorate from Ohio Wesleyan Univ., 1952. He was instructor, Yale Univ., 1908-20; associate professor, Columbia Univ., 1920-54; continued to lecture at Union Theological Seminary to 1965; was organist and music director, Madison Ave. Presbyterian Church for 35 years.

WORKS: OPERA: La Charelzenn, 1977;

ORCHESTRA: Wall Street fantasy, 1912, performed in New York, 6 Feb. 1916; Tame animal tunes, 18 instruments, 1918; Memories of France, 1920; Wilderness stone, narrator, soloists, chorus, orch., 1933; organ concerto, Rochester, 24 Oct. 1946; Connecticut suite, organ and strings, 1954; concerto fro brass, snare drum, and organ, 1954; ORGAN: suite, 1926; Pioneer America, 1928; Harmonies of Florence, 1929; Carillon de Chateau Thierry, 1936; Pastoral psalms, 1938; 12 hymn preludes, 1942; Variation studies, 1950; 36 hymn and carol canons, 1952.

BINKERD, GORDON

b. Lynch, Nebr., 22 May 1916. Studied with Bernard Rogers, Eastman School of Music; with Walter Piston, Harvard Univ.; with Gail Kubik and Russell Danburg at Wesleyan Univ. His awards include a Nat. Inst. of Arts and Letters award, Guggenheim grant, and many commissions. He served in the U.S. Navy, 1942-46; has held faculty posts at Garden City Jr. Coll., Kans., 1937-38; Franklin Coll., Ind., 1938-40; Univ. of Illinois, 1949-71.

WORKS: ORCHESTRA: 3 symphonies, 1955, 1957, 1961; movement for orchestra, 1963; A part of heaven, 2 romances for violin and orch., 1972; WIND ENSEMBLE: Canzonas, brass choir; The battle, brass and percussion; Noble numbers; CHAMBER MUSIC: cello sonata, 1952; flute sonatina; trio for clarinet, viola, cello, 1955; 2 string quartets, 1956, 1961; violin sonata, commissioned by the McKim Fund, Library of Congress, and performed there, 2 May 1974; song cycle, mezzo-soprano and string quartet; song cycle, mezzo-soprano and string duo; piano sonata; string trio, Urbana, 8 Feb. 1976; many choral works; solo songs; piano and organ works.

R.R. #2, Urbana, IL 61801

BIRD, BERNARD

A musical theory on the interpretative powers of the human mind, 1966, won the Kodaly prize in 1971; concert duet, violin and piano, 1972; Quartology, a study of 4 instruments, 1972; Agnus Dei, double chorus, 3 violins, 3 cellos, 1972; piano pieces.

515 S. Council, Muncie, IN 47302

BIRD, HUBERT C.

b. Joplin, Mo., 12 Oct. 1939. Studied with Merrill Ellis in Joplin; with Markwood Holmes, Pittsburg (Kan.) State Univ.; with Charles Eakin, Cecil Effinger, and Richard Toensing, Univ. of Colorado. His awards include first prize, D.C. chapter, American Guild of Organists contest, 1973; Bicentennial award, 1975; commission by N.H. Music Teachers Assoc., 1978. From 1967 he has been on the faculty, Keene State Coll.

WORKS: BRASS ENSEMBLE: Fanfare for an uncommon child, Christmas work, 3 horns, 4 trumpets, organ, 1966; CHAMBER MUSIC: Dialogues, flute, clarinet, piano, 1973; piano sonata, 1979; CHORUS: The cricket sang, 1965; Magnificat, with soloists, 4 trumpets, organ, 1966; A hope for peace, cantata, with orch., 1970; Have you not known?, National Cathedral, Washington, 1973; Blessed is the nation whose God is the Lord, with

baritone solo, brass quartet, organ, 1975; SONGS: 5 songs on poems of Robert Graves, 1965; Songs of a singing people, texts by Langston Hughes.
    68 Blossom St., Keene, NH 03431

BIRKBY, ARTHUR ALFRED
    b. Collingsworth, N.J., 15 Dec. 1924. Studied with Robert Elmore and H. Alexander Matthews, Philadelphia; and at Temple Univ. and Trinity Coll. of London. Two of his compositions were selected for performance at the Wyoming program in the Bicentennial Parade of American Music in Washington, D.C., 1976; and he was chosen Commissioned Composer of the Year for Wyoming by the Music Teachers Nat. Assoc. He held faculty posts at Westminster Coll., 1952-56; Western Michigan Univ., 1956-61; then named professor, Univ. of Wyoming, Laramie.
    WORKS: ORGAN: Chaconne on 12 notes; Fantasy on an old English tune; trio on 2 carols and finale; choral fantasy on Cwm Rhondda, with chorus; PIANO: Rhapsody, chorale, and polonaise.
    Music Dept., Univ. of Wyoming, Laramie, WY 82071

BIRNBAUM, MARK J.
    b. Geneva, Switz., of American parents, 11 Feb. 1952. Studied with Noah Creshevsky, Jacob Druckman, and Stephen Dankner at Brooklyn Coll.
    WORKS: ORCHESTRA: Metamorphoses; CHAMBER MUSIC: piano sonata; Coffee, flute, violin, piano, 1972; Survey of literature, clarinet, tenor, piano; Rhinoceros, flute, bass clarinet, cello, piano, percussion, 1973; string quartet, 1973.

BISCARDI, CHESTER
    b. Kenosha, Wis., 19 Oct. 1948. Studied with Leslie Thimmig, Univ. of Wisconsin, B.A. 1970, M.A. 1972; M.M. in composition 1974; with Robert Morris, Krystof Penderecki, Toru Takemitsu, and Yehudi Wyner, Yale Univ., M.M.A. 1976; also studied in Bologna, Italy, 1969-70. His awards include 2 Ford Found. grants, 1970-72; 2 fellowships, Composers' Conf., Johnson, Vt., 1974, 1975; NIAL Ives scholarship, 1975-76; 2 grants from Nat. Endowment for the Arts, 1976, 1977-78; Rome prize, American Acad. in Rome, 1976-77. He has held various teaching posts; from 1977, has been on the music faculty, Sarah Lawrence Coll.
    WORKS: ORCHESTRA: At the still point; CHAMBER MUSIC: Tartini, violin and piano, 1972; Turning, violin, soprano, string trio, 1973; Chartres, solo piano and chamber ensemble, 1973; orpha, string quartet, marimba, vibraphone, 1974; they had ceased to talk, violin and viola, horn, piano, 1975; trusting lightness, soprano and piano, 1975; Tenzone, 2 flutes and piano, 1975; Music for the Duchess of Malfi, 9 instrumentalists and voices, 1975; piano trio, 1976; CHORUS: Indovinello, 12 voices, 1974; Heabakes: 5 Sapphic lyrics, chorus, soloists, and percussion, 1974.
    12 Meadow Ave. West, Bronxville, NY 10708

BISCHOFF, KURT
    b. San Francisco, Calif., 24 Sept. 1949. Studied with Larry Austin, Richard Swift, and Arthur Woodbury, Univ. of California at Davis; privately with Stanley Lunetta and Robert Fylling. He is a percussion instructor.
    WORKS: Mick Martin's orthopedic blues band, theatre piece for blues band electronic preachers, 1968; War piece, projectionists, navigator, artillery crew, 1969; AMRA/ARMA's repetition piece, variation no. 3007 for electronics wizard, cybernaut bassist, 2 droube percussionists, and a bird, 1973; Wedding song, for pseudo cosmic calypso group, 1972.
    6005 Wardell Way, Sacramento, CA 95823

BITGOOD, ROBERTA (Mrs. J. G. Wiersma)
    b. New London, Conn., 15 Jan. 1908. Studied with J. Lawrence Erb, Connecticut Coll. for Women; at Guilmant Organ School, N.Y.; with Edwin Stringham and David McKay Williams, Columbia Univ., M.A.; with Clarence Dickinson, Union Theological Seminary, M.S.M., S.M.D.; with Wayne Bohrnstedt, Univ. of Redlands. Her honors include the Conn. Coll. College Medal, 1974 (the first alumnae award ever given in music); election as president of the American Guild of Organists, 1975, re-elected 1977 (the first non-New Yorker and first woman to hold the post). She has been organist and choirmaster since 1932, at First Congregational Church, Battle Creek, Mich., 1969-76; St. Mark's Episcopal Church, Mystic, Conn., from 1977.
    WORKS: Her many choral compositions include: 3 cantatas, Job, Joseph, Let there be light; many commissioned anthems and organ works.
    13 Best View Rd., Quaker Hill, CT 06375

BITTER, JOHN
    b. New York, N.Y., 8 Apr. 1909. Studied at Curtis Inst. of Music. He was conductor, Jacksonville Symphony, 1934-36; Florida Symphony, 1936-40; was faculty member, Univ. of Miami, 1940-42, dean, School of Music, 1951-59. His works include a suite and 3 tone poems for orchestra, a string quartet, songs, instrumental solos, etc.
    5671 S.W. 98 Terrace, South Miami, FL 33143

BITZEL, CHARLES RAYMOND
    b. Baltimore, Md., 10 May 1946. Studied with Howard Thatcher at Peabody Cons., B.M. 1968. He won an international composition contest sponsored by the American Accordion Musicological Soc. He taught in public schools, 1968-70; became a member of the Maryland Symphonette in 1973.
    WORKS: 2 symphonies; 3 atonal pieces and 2 caricatures for accordion.
    1918 Englewood Ave., Baltimore, MD 21207

BLACK, CHARLES
    b. Augusta, Maine, 24 Nov. 1903. Studied at Eastman School of Music, B.M.; and Union Theological Seminary, M.S.M. He has published choral works.

BLACK, FRANK J.
    b. Philadelphia, Pa., 28 Nov. 1896; d. Atlanta, Ga., 29 Jan. 1968. Attended Missouri Valley Coll., honorary D.M.; studied piano with Rafael

BLACKWOOD, EASLEY

Joseffy in New York. He made his debut as concert pianist at age 10; became theatre conductor in Philadelphia and New York; then conductor on radio; was general music director, NBC, 1932-48.
WORKS: ORCHESTRA: Bells at eventide; A sea tale; FILM SCORES: White cliffs of Dover; Murder of Lidice.

BLACKWOOD, EASLEY
b. Indianapolis, Ind., 21 Apr. 1933. Studied with Olivier Messiaen at Tanglewood, 1949; with Paul Hindemith at Yale Univ.; with Bernhard Heiden, Indiana Univ.; and with Nadia Boulanger in Paris, 1954-56. His awards include a Fulbright grant; Koussevitzky Found. award, 1958; and several commissions. Since 1958 he has been on the faculty at Univ. of Chicago; spent a sabbatical 1978-79 at Webster Coll., St. Louis, studying nontraditional tuning systems and new musical systems.
WORKS: ORCHESTRA: 4 symphonies, #1, 1955, Boston, 18 Apr. 1958, #2, 1960; #3, 1964, #4, 1972-76, Chicago, 22 Nov. 1978; clarinet concerto, 1964; Symphonic fantasy, 1965; concerto for oboe and strings, 1966; violin concerto, 1967; concerto for flute and strings, 1968; piano concerto, 1970, Cleveland, 7 June 1972; CHAMBER MUSIC: viola sonata, 1953; chamber symphony for 14 winds, 1955; 2 string quartets, 1957, 1960; concertino for 5 instruments, 1959; 2 violin sonatas, 1960, 1975; Fantasy, cello and piano, 1960; Pastorale and variations, wind quintet, 1961; Fantasy, flute, clarinet, cello, piano, 1965; Un voyage à Cythère, soprano and 10 instruments, 1966; piano trio, 1968; KEYBOARD: 3 short fantasies, piano, 1965; Symphonic movement, organ, 1966.
Music Dept., Univ. of Chicago, Chicago, IL 60637

BLAKE, DOROTHY GAYNOR
b. St. Joseph, Mo., 21 Nov. 1893; d. Webster Groves, Mo. Composed songs and piano pieces.

BLAKE, JAMES HUBERT (Eubie)
b. Baltimore, Md., 7 Feb. 1883. Studied in Baltimore with Margaret Marshall and Llewelyn Wilson; the Schillinger system with Rudolf Schramm at New York Univ. He has received honorary doctorates from Brooklyn Coll., 1973, Rutgers Univ., Dartmouth Coll., and New England Cons., 1974, Univ. of Maryland, 1978. His 95th birthday in 1978 was a national event. He was pianist and organist in cafes, vaudeville, theatre; then in 1915, joined with Noble Sissle, lyricist, in the vaudeville team of Sissle and Blake. During World War I they toured in a musical show organized from musicians in the U.S. 369th Infantry by James Europe. Blake toured 5 years with the USO in World War II. But the greatest successes of the team came with the musical shows and songs they wrote.
WORKS: MUSICALS: Shuffle along, 1921; Chocolate dandies, 1924; Elsie, 1924; Blackbirds, 1930; and over 300 songs, including I'm just wild about Harry and Memories of you. See Reminiscing with Sissle and Blake, Kimball and Bolcom, 1973.
284 A, Stuyvesant Ave., Brooklyn, NY 11221

BLAKE, RAN
b. Springfield, Mass., 20 Apr. 1935. Attended Bard Coll., B.A.; Columbia Univ.; School of Jazz, Lenox, Mass.; and studied privately with Gunther Schuller, Mal Waldron, Mary Lou Williams, Bill Russo, Margaret Chaloff, Ray Cassarino, Willis L. James, Oscar Peterson. He organized the Bard Jazz Festivals in 1957, 1958, 1959, and helped in organizing other jazz festivals. In 1965 he won first prize in Germany for outstanding pop-jazz of the year. He was music critic in New York, 1958-60, and has held administrative and faculty positions at the New England Cons. from 1968; has been arts columnist, Bay State Banner, from 1974.
WORKS: The mariage of oppression in 3rd-stream realizations, pianist and 3 narrators, Boston, 12 Apr. 1971; The newest sound around, vocalist and piano; Blue potato; Breakthru; Take one, take two; and other piano solos.
New England Cons., 290 Huntington Ave., Boston, MA 02115

BLANCHARD, WILLIAM G.
b. Greencastle, Ind., 5 Sept. 1905. Studied at De Pauw Univ., B.M.; Univ. of Michigan, M.M.; also with Seth Bingham and Hugh Porter. He was church organist in Greencastle, 1919-27; school music supervisor, 1930-36; then on faculty at Pomona Coll. His works include church anthems and organ pieces.

BLAND, WILLIAM KEITH
b. Shepherdstown, W.Va., 11 Nov. 1947. Studied with Benjamin Lees, Ernst Krenek, Richard Rodney Bennett, and Earle Brown at Peabody Cons., M.M. 1970, D.M.A. 1972. He taught at Peabody Cons., 1970-72, then joined the faculty at Brooklyn Coll., CUNY. As an author, he has contributed articles to the new edition of Grove's Dictionary of Musicians.
WORKS: ORCHESTRA: Between moments II and III, with solo marimba; CHAMBER MUSIC: Speed, organ, 1969; Sonic nocturne, horn and piano, 1969; Like a mad animal, 5 instruments and solo contrabass, 1971; Between moments I, guitar; 5 subtitled pieces, various instruments; Cantilena and varient I (Cocaine says), solo violin; 4 songs for guitar and soprano, 1973; Years after morality, theater piece for guitar, bariton, percussion; Beverly, poet, piano, baritone, percussion; CHORUS: Songs of morality, 8-part chorus playing percussion, 1973.
Shepherdstown, WV 25443

BLANK, ALLAN
b. Bronx, N.Y., 27 Dec. 1925. Studied privately with Dante Fiorillo, 1942-44; with Bernard Wagenaar, Juilliard School, 1945-47; New York Univ., B.A. 1948; Univ. of Minnesota, M.A. 1950; Columbia Univ., 1955-57, 1965-66; Univ. of Iowa, 1966-67. His awards include a conducting fellowship at Juilliard; Award of Merit, Nat. Fed. of Music Clubs, 1973; CUNY faculty award, 1974; first prize for 4 dream poems, Phi Mu Alpha, 1977; and many commissions. He was violinist with the Pittsburgh Symph., 1950-52; faculty member, Western Illinois Univ., 1966-68;

Paterson State Coll., 1968-70; Lehman Coll., CUNY, 1970-77; from 1978, at Virginia Commonwealth Univ., Richmond.

WORKS: THEATRE: Aria da capo, chamber opera; Excitement at the circus, children's musical; ORCHESTRA: Music for orchestra, 1968; Meditation; BAND: Concert piece; CHAMBER MUSIC: 13 ways of looking at a blackbird, soprano and 6 instruments, 1964, London, 6 June 1973; 2 parables by Franz Kafka, soprano and chamber ensemble, 1964; 2 simple canons, 2 flutes; woodwind quintet, 1970; A song of ascents, solo viola; Variations, clarinet and viola; Music for violin, 1961; Music for solo trumpet; 4 bagatelles, oboe and clarinet; 3 novelties, alto saxophone; Knock on wood, percussion; 2 studies, brass quintet; Composition for 11 players, 1966; Esther's monologue, cantata for soprano, oboe, viola, cello, 1970; many other chamber pieces and works for chorus.
 Barnes St., Ossining, NY 10562

BLANKENSHIP, LYLE MARK
 b. Chicago, Ill., 11 May 1943. Studied with Warren Angell at Oklahoma Baptist Univ.; with Alexander von Kreisler at Univ. of Texas, where he received the Ford composition award. In 1973 he was named minister of music at the North Phoenix Baptist Church. All of his published works are religious choral compositions.
 Baptist Church, 6225 Central Ave. N., Phoenix, AZ 85012

BLATTER, ALFRED
 b. Litchfield, Ill., 24 Dec. 1937. Studied with Kenneth Gaburo, Ben Johnston, and Robert Kelly, Univ. of Illinois, B.M. 1961, M.M. 1965, D.M.A. 1974. He was an arranger and played horn in the U.S. Army Band, Fort Myer, Va., 1962-65; faculty member, Marshall Univ., 1966-69; then became professor, Univ. of Illinois.
 WORKS: Fusions, solo percussion and orchestra, 1969; suite for brass; A study in time and space, string quartet; 5 sketches, trombone and piano; A dream within a dream, tenor, piano, and piano interior; Fanfare for 12 trumpets.
 310 Pond Ridge Lane, Urbana, IL 61801

BLEDSOE, JULES
 b. Waco, Tex., 29 Dec. 1898; d. Hollywood, Calif., 14 July 1943. Studied at Chicago Musical Coll., B.A. 1919; then studied voice in Paris and Rome. He made his debut in Aeolian Hall, New York, in 1924; sang the central role in Show boat in 1927; then went into grand opera, singing the title role in Gruenberg's Emperor Jones in 1933. His compositions included African suite for orchestra and songs in the style of Negro spirituals.

BLEWETT, QUENTIN H.
 b. Galena, Ill., 11 Apr. 1927. Studied with Leo Sowerby, American Cons., B.M. 1951; with Nicolas Flagello and Wallingford Riegger, Manhattan School of Music, M.M. 1955.
 WORKS: ORCHESTRA: symphony #1, 1955, received a performance award at Manhattan School; Ballad for orchestra, 1957; Dramatic overture,

1960; Revolutionary suite, 1976, was commissioned for the Bicentennial; CHAMBER MUSIC: piano sonata, 1951; Prelude and poem, piano, 1953; string quartet #2, 1969; cello sonata, 1971; 3 songs for soprano and piano, performed at N.E. Composers Conf., Johnson Coll., Vt., 1972.
 38 Tallman Pl., Nyack, NY 10960

BLEY, CARLA BORG
 b. Oakland, Calif., 1938. Studied piano from an early age with her father, performed at recitals and church services. As soon as it was legal, she dropped out of school and began to support herself as pianist and arranger, eventually settling in New York. Her awards include a Guggenheim fellowship, Ford Found. grant, many recording awards in the U.S. and abroad, and numerous commissions. She was a cofounder of the Jazz Composers' Orchestra Assoc., and has performed and recorded with many of the top jazz artists.
 WORKS: A genuine Tong funeral, jazz quartet and orchestra; Elevator over the hill, a multimedia opera, which won great critical acclaim and for its composer, grants from the Creative Artists Service Program and the Nat. Endowment for the Arts; 3/4 for piano and 15 players, New York, 17 Mar. 1974.
 c/o Jazz Composers of America, 6 W. 95th St., New York, NY 10025

BLICKHAN, CHARLES TIMOTHY
 b. Quincy, Ill., 9 June 1945. Studied with Leon Karel and Tom V. Ritchie, Northeast Missouri State Univ., 1963-67; with Paul Zonn and Ben Johnston, Univ. of Illinois, 1973-76. He received a Nat. Fed. of Music Clubs award for composition and arranging with the U.S. CONARC Band, Ft. Monroe, Va., 1972. From 1976 he has been faculty member at Northern Illinois Univ.
 WORKS: ORCHESTRA: Dialectics for orchestra, 1975; Night music, song cycle for soprano, harp, percussion, strings, 1978; CHAMBER MUSIC: Niche of time, indeterminate ensemble, 1973; Hymn, 4 or more winds, 1974; Speak softly, song cycle for soprano, flute, vibraphone, 1974; Nonet 3, percussion, 1974; Variations/permutations, winds, percussion, piano, 1974; quintet for flute, viola, trombone, percussion, piano, 1975; Bon mot finesse, solo trombone, 1975; State of the art, solo alto saxophone, 1977; CHORUS: Polymorphous canon.
 Music Dept., Northern Illinois Univ., DeKalb, IL 60115

BLISS, MARILYN S.
 b. Cedar Rapids, Iowa, 30 Sept. 1954. Studied with Jerry Owen at Coe Coll., B.M. 1976; with George Rochberg, George Crumb, Richard Wernick, Univ. of Pennsylvania, M.A. 1978; privately with Harvey Sollberger. Her awards include Nat. Merit scholarship; Nitzche award in composition; Paul Rochberg and M. H. Cross fellowships; and the American Acad. and Inst. of Arts and Letters Charles Ives scholarship, 1979.
 WORKS: WIND ENSEMBLE: Chamber symphony, 1975-76; CHAMBER MUSIC: 3 songs, soprano and piano, 1973; Piece, oboe and piano, 1974;

BLISS, MILTON CLAY

Encounter, solo flute, 1975; 3 short pieces, solo trombone, 1976; Tapestry, string quartet, 1976; Shadowflowers, soprano, tenor, chamber ensemble, 1977-78; Fantasies, piano solo, 1977.
4206 Walnut St., Philadelphia, PA 19104

BLISS, MILTON CLAY
b. Charlotte, N.C., 19 Apr. 1927. Studied with Glen Haydon, Univ. of North Carolina, Chapel Hill. He is on the faculty at North Carolina State Univ. and at Page High School in Greensboro.
· WORKS: THEATRE: incidental music to The gathering, Medea, and The Trojan women; ORCHESTRA: Lamentation and dance; BAND: Pastoral and march; CHORUS: Tower of Babel; Sing unto the Lord a new song; The raven days; There came a wind like a bugle.
2726 Van Dyke Ave., Raleigh, NC 27607

BLISS, P. PAUL
b. Chicago, Ill., 25 Nov. 1872; d. Oswego, N.Y., 2 Feb. 1933. Wrote 3 operettas, a piano suite, songs, and choruses.

BLITZSTEIN, MARC
b. Philadelphia, Pa., 2 Mar. 1905; d. Martinique, W.I., 22 Jan. 1964. Studied at Univ. of Pennsylvania; with Rosario Scalero, Curtis Inst. of Music; with Nadia Boulanger in Paris and Arnold Schoenberg in Berlin. His awards include 2 Guggenheim fellowships; American Acad. of Arts and Letters grant; Ford Found. grant; American Aeronautical Inst. award; and commissions. He served in the U.S. Army in World War II.
WORKS: THEATRE: Triple sec, opera farce, 1924; Parabola and circula, 1-act opera, 1929; Cain, ballet, 1930; The harpies, musical satire, 1931, rev. Composers' Showcase, New York, 5 Dec. 1973; The cradle will rock, 1-act opera, 1937; I've got the time, musical play, 1937; No for an answer, short opera, 1941; Regina, full-length opera based on Lillian Hellman's The little foxes, Boston, 11 Oct. 1949; (was commissioned by the Ford Found. to write an opera on Sacco and Vanzetti for production at the Metropolitan Opera, but the work was never finished); ORCHESTRA: Jig-saw, ballet suite, 1927; Romantic piece, 1930; piano concerto, 1931; Freedom morning, 1943; The airborne symphony, 1945, performed by the Tulsa Philharmonic under Skitch Henderson with the Metropolitan Opera's general manager, Schuyler Chapin as narrator, 26 Nov. 1973; CHAMBER MUSIC: string quartet; Percussion music for piano, 1929.

BLOCH, ALEXANDER
b. Selma, Ala., 11 July 1881. Attended Columbia Univ.; studied with Eduard Herrmann in New York, Ottakar Sevcik in Vienna, and Leopold Auer in Petrograd. He was concertmaster and soloist with the symphony orchestra in Tiflis, Russia, in the early 1900s, made his New York debut in 1913. He was teaching assistant to Leopold Auer during his residence in the U.S. and taught at Washington Coll. of Music and Rollins Coll. Cons.; conducted Central Florida Symph. Orch., 1936-43, Florida West Coast Symph., 1950-62; was guest conductor of the NBC Symph. and the Nat. Symph. Orch.; gave many recitals in the U.S.
WORKS: Roeliff's dream, children's operetta, libretto by Mrs. Bloch; The lone tree, Christmas play with music; art songs on poems by Shelley, Edna St. Millay, and Arthur Davison Ficke. He has published various technical works for violin and magazine articles.
(summer) Springhill Farm, Hillsdale, NY 12529; (winter) 126 Garden Lane, Sarasota, FL 33581

BLOCH, ERNEST
b. Geneva, Switz., 24 July 1880; U.S. citizen 1924; d. Portland, Oreg., 15 July 1959. Studied in Geneva, Brussels, Frankfurt, and Munich. He received the Coolidge prize, 1919; first prize, Musical America contest, 1927; New York Music Critics Circle award, 1947. He was on the faculty, Mannes School of Music, 1917-19; director, Cleveland Inst. of Music, 1920-25; director, San Francisco Cons., 1925-30; resided in Europe, 1930-39; then returned to the U.S. and settled in Oregon, devoting most of his time to composition; also taught summer courses at Univ. of California, Berkeley, to 1952.
WORKS: OPERA: Macbeth, Paris, 1910; ORCHESTRA: symphony, 1910; Israel symphony, 1912-16; Schelomo, cello and orch., 1917; concerto grosso #1, strings and piano, 1925; America, 1926; Voice in the wilderness, with cello obligato, 1936; violin concerto, 1938; Suite symphonique, 1944; concerto grosso #2, strings, 1950; Suite Hebraique, viola and orch., 1953; Sinfonia breve, 1953; Proclamation, trumpet and orch., 1953; symphony for trombone and orch., 1954; Suite modale, flute and strings, 1957; CHAMBER MUSIC: 5 string quartets, 1916, 1946, 1951, 1953, 1956; suite for viola and piano, 1919; 2 violin sonatas, 1920, 1924; Baal Shem, violin and piano, 1923; 2 piano quintets, 1923, 1956; Meditation Hebraique, cello and piano, 1925; 4 episodes, chamber orch., 1926; piano sonata, 1935; 3 suites for solo cello, 1956; 2 suites for solo violin, 1958; suite for solo viola, 1958; 2 last poems, flute and chamber orch., 1958; many other instrumental works and works for voice.

BLOCK, ROBERT PAUL
b. Cincinnati, Ohio, 17 Aug. 1942. Studied with Karel Jirak, Robert Lombardo, Robert Muczynski, Chicago Musical Coll., with Richard Hervig, Univ. of Iowa.
WORKS: ORCHESTRA: Music for orchestra and timpani, 1968; concerto for recorder and strings, 1968; CHAMBER MUSIC: Prelude and toccata, clarinet quartet, 1968; Incantation and canzone, 3 trombones, 1971; Ein dekadenter Walzer, 4 violas or 4 cellos, 1971; 4 fantasies for solo instruments; violin, viola, cello, double bass, all 1973; Sonatine enigmatique, solo treble recorder, 1978.
629 N. Linn, Iowa City, IA 52240

BLOOD, ESTA
b. New York, N.Y., 25 Mar. 1933. Studied at Manhattan School of Music. Her awards include 2 grants from Meet the Composer, 1977, 1978; an

award from S.I.M.S., 1978. She has taught piano privately from 1950.
WORKS: CHAMBER MUSIC: Nocturne, violin and piano; Jack and the beanstalk, 4 instruments and narrator; Bulgarian trio, flute, violin, piano; Variations on an Armenian theme, string quartet, 1976; Sculpture dance, solo harp, 1977; VOCAL: A psalm of David, cantor, 4-part choir, keyboard accompanist; Starsong, poem of Tagore, soprano; Fall, poem by Carl J. George, soprano; Improvisations on Shaker tunes, soprano, flute, violin, viola, 1976; 5 Armenian folksongs, soprano, flute, guitar, 1978.
1218 Regent St., Schenectady, NY 12309

BLUMENFELD, HAROLD
b. Seattle, Wash., 15 Oct. 1923. Studied at Eastman School of Music, 1941-43; with Paul Hindemith, Yale Univ., B.M. 1949, M.M. 1950; Zurich Univ. and Cons., 1948; with Leonard Bernstein, Robert Shaw, and Boris Goldovsky at Tanglewood. His awards include $2000 in a national composition contest, 1955; a MacDowell fellowship; 2 Yaddo fellowships; American Acad. and Nat. Inst. of Arts and Letters $3,000 composition award, 1977. He has been professor at Washington Univ. from 1950; was director, St. Louis Opera Theatre, 1964-70; visiting professor, Queens Coll., CUNY, 1971-72.
WORKS: OPERA: Gentle boy, adapted from Hawthorne text for television, 1968; Amphitryon 4, after Moliere, 1952-56; The road to Salem, opera for television, 1973; ORCHESTRA: Elegy for the nightingale, baritone, chorus, orch., 1954; Contrasts, 1955; Miniature overture, 1958; Songs of innocence, text by Blake, 2 soli, 2 choruses, orch., 1973; CHAMBER MUSIC: Transformations, piano, 1963; Expansions, woodwind quintet, 1964; Movements for brass, septet, 1966; Night music, guitar, 1973; CHORUS: 3 Scottish poems, a cappella, 1949; 4 tranquil poems, D. H. Lawrence texts, a cappella, 1950; Songs of war, texts of Siegfried Sassoon, 1970; SONGS: Eroscapes, texts by Isabella Gardner, soprano and 8 instruments, 1970; Rilke for voice and guitar, 1975; Starfires, mezzo-soprano, tenor, strings, percussion, brass, 1975; Circle of the eye, 11 songs on texts of Tom McKeown, medium voice and piano, 1975, New York, 2 Apr. 1979; La vie anterieure, spatial cantata on texts of Baudelaire for 2 groups, 1976; Essences, 11 songs on poems of Osip Mandelstam, 1978; Voyages, cantata on poems by Hart Crane, for baritone, viola, guitar, percussion, New York, 18 Nov. 1977.
34 Washington Terrace, St. Louis, MO 63112

BOARDMAN, HERBERT
b. Somerville, Mass., 4 Apr. 1892. Graduated from the New England Cons. in 1916. He composed chamber music and songs.

BOATWRIGHT, HOWARD
b. Newport News, Va., 16 Mar. 1918. Had early training in violin and piano and gave a full-length violin recital at age 14. Studied with Paul Hindemith at Yale Univ., B.M. 1947, M.M. 1948. At Yale he held Bradley-Keeler and Horatio Parker fellowships; was Fulbright lec-

turer in India, 1959-60; received a Rockefeller grant to study the kritis of Tyagaraja and South India violin playing; Soc. for Pub. of American Music award, 1962; Yale alumni award, 1970; Fulbright grant to Romania, 1971-72. He has made many concert tours in the U.S., Mexico, and Europe, sometimes with his wife, Helen Boatwright, noted soprano. He was faculty member, Univ. of Texas, 1943; Yale Univ., 1948-64; concertmaster, New Haven Symph., 1950-62; from 1964, professor, School of Music, Syracuse Univ.
WORKS: ORCHESTRA: A song for St. Cecilia's day, string orch.; Variations, small orch.; Sinner man, Appalachian folk hymn, baritone and orch., 1961; The false knight upon the road, baritone and orch., 1961; Canticle of the sun, chorus, soprano, orch., 1963; Movement for orchestra, 1971; Larghetto espressivo, trio scherzando, 1972; symphony, Syracuse, 12 Jan. 1979; CHAMBER MUSIC: string quartet, 1947; trio for 2 violins and viola, 1948; Serenade, 2 strings, 2 winds, 1952; Canon, 2 violins and piano, 1953; quartet for clarinet and strings, 1958; Variations, piano, 1966; 3 inventions, keyboard, 1971; suite for clarinet alone, 1973; 12 pieces, violin alone, performed by composer, Syracuse Univ., 5 Feb. 1978; VOICE: many works for chorus including The passion according to St. Matthew, 1962; many songs for solo voices. He is author of Introduction to the theory of music (N.Y., 1956), A handbook for staff notation for Indian music (Bombay, 1960), and Indian classical music and the western listener (Bombay, 1960).
School of Music, Syracuse Univ., Syracuse, NY 13210

BOCK, FRED
b. New York, N.Y., 30 Mar. 1939. Studied with Warren Benson, Ithaca Coll., B.S. 1960; with Halsey Stevens and Robert Linn, Univ. of Southern California, M.M. 1962. He has been organist and choir director, Bel Air Presbyterian Church, Los Angeles, from 1964.
WORKS: He has composed for piano, organ, and chorus, including a cantata, Song of triumph, and a musical, One solitary life (with Paul Johnson).
5404 Topeka Dr., Tarzana, CA 91356

BODA, JOHN
b. Boyceville, Wis., 2 Aug. 1922. Studied at Eastman School of Music. He has been on the faculty at Florida State Univ. from 1946.
WORKS: ORCHESTRA: Sinfonia, 1960; CHAMBER MUSIC: 2 piano sonatas; Prelude, scherzo, postlude, brass quartet, 1964; trombone sonatina; 4 Byzantine etudes, guitar; cornet sonatina; clarinet sonatina; Introduction and dance, guitar.
Florida State Univ., Tallahassee, FL 32306

BOEHLE, WILLIAM RANDALL
b. Waxahachie, Tex., 1 July 1919. Studied with Helen Gunderson, Louisiana State Univ., with Philip Greeley Clapp, Univ. of Iowa. He was faculty member, Chadron State Coll., Nebr., 1952-60; from 1960, professor, Univ. of North Dakota.

BOEHNLEIN, FRANK

WORKS: ORCHESTRA: piano concertino; trumpet concerto; CHAMBER MUSIC: brass suite; woodwind quintet; sonatine for 2 pianos; Sonnet, voice and piano; Passacaglia and fugue for piano; CHORUS: The aviary, on 7 Ogden Nash poems.
406 22nd Ave. South, Grand Forks, ND 58201

BOEHNLEIN, FRANK
b. Bedford, Ohio, 2 Feb. 1945. Studied with John Carter at Rollins Coll.; with Donald Erb and Marcel Dick, Cleveland Inst. of Music, D.M.A. 1972. His awards include Presser Found. scholarships, 1964-66; Ralph Lyman Baldwin award, 1967; Ford Found. grant, 1971; Composers' Conference, 1970, 1973; Nat. Endowment for the Arts, 1973-74; Univ. of Portland (Oreg.); Ohio Composers' Symposium; Texas Mss. Archives. He was faculty member, St. Mary of the Plains Coll., 1971-73; and at Texas Woman's Univ., 1973-78.
WORKS: CHAMBER MUSIC: Canto, string quartet, 1972-73; CHORUS: Missa l'homme armé, 12-part a cappella choir, 1971, command performance at Sistine Chapel, 1972; Anthology of praises, women's choir; Psalm sonnet, women's choir; PIANO: sonata, 1970; Old songs; New songs; A moon child's piano book; MIXED MEDIA: The death of the ball turret gunner, chorus, instruments, theatre media, 1967; Karma dreams, orch., soprano, tape; Gog, magog, and other passions, 4 dancers, instruments, tape, theatre media, 1973; The last best hope of Earth; Aftermath; FILM SCORE: To teach yourself.
P.O. Box 962, Denton, TX 76201

BOERINGER, JAMES LESLIE
b. Pittsburgh, Pa., 4 Mar. 1930. Studied at Coll. of Wooster, B.A. 1952; with Seth Bingham and Douglas Moore, Columbia Univ., M.A. 1954; at Union Theological Seminary, D.S.M.; and at New York Univ. His awards include associate of American Guild of Organists, 1953; Lutheran Church grant, 1967; Distinguished Visitor, Haverford Coll., 1970; research grant and sabbatical year from Susquehanna Univ., 1972, 1974. He has held faculty positions in public schools and at Univ. of South Dakota, 1959-62; Oklahoma Baptist Univ., 1962-64; then at Susquehanna Univ., professor from 1977.
WORKS: He has composed chiefly for chorus and organ; is the author of many articles and reviews in music journals.
Susquehanna Univ., Selinsgrove, PA 17870

BOHRNSTEDT, WAYNE R.
b. Onalaska, Wis., 19 Jan. 1923. Studied with Albert Noelte and Robert Delaney at Northwestern Univ.; with Herbert Elwell and Howard Hanson, Eastman School of Music. He won first prize, Oppenheimer Contest for Ohio composers, 1951, and from the Nat. Fed. of Music Clubs, 1951. His faculty positions include Northwestern Univ., 1946-47; Bowling Green State Univ., 1947-53; then professor, Univ. of Redlands, where he is also director, School of Music, and dean, Div. of Fine and Performing Arts.
WORKS: OPERA: The necklace, chamber opera; ORCHESTRA: Romantic overture, 1951; trumpet concerto; symphony #1; concertino for timpani, xylophone and orch.; concertino for trombone and strings; CHORUS: Mass for the people.
School of Music, Univ. of Redlands, Redlands, CA 92373

BOLCOM, WILLIAM
b. Seattle, Wash., 26 May 1938. Studied composition with George Frederick McKay and John Verrall, Univ. of Washington, School of Music (which he entered at age 11); with Darius Milhaud, Mills Coll., 1958; later with Milhaud, Jean Rivier, and Olivier Messiaen, Paris Cons.; with Leland Smith, Stanford Univ., D.M.A. His awards include a Copley grant, 1960; Kurt Weill Found. grant, 1961; 2 Guggenheim grants, 1964, 1968; Marc Blitzstein award, 1965; Rockefeller grants, 1963, 1965, 1969-71; Creative Arts Public Service grant, 1971; Koussevitzky Found. grant, 1974; Nat. Endowment for the Arts grant, 1974; Henry Russel award, Univ. of Michigan, 1977. His faculty posts have included Univ. of Washington, 1965-66; Queens Coll., CUNY, 1966-68; Yale Drama School, 1968-69; New York Univ., School of Arts, 1969-70; Brooklyn Coll., CUNY, 1973; from 1973, Univ. of Michigan.
WORKS: OPERA: Dynamite tonight, New York, 21 Dec. 1963; ORCHESTRA: 2 symphonies, 1957, 1965; Oracles, Seattle, 2 May 1965; Songs of innocence and experience, on poems of William Blake, soloists, chorus, and orch., St. Paul, 18 Oct. 1975; piano concerto, Seattle, 8 Mar. 1976; CHAMBER MUSIC: Concerto-serenade, violin and strings, 1964; Sessions I-IV, for various chamber groups, 1965-73; Commedia, chamber orch., 1971; 9 string quartets, #9, New York, 21 May 1973; Open house, song cycle on Roethke poems, tenor and chamber ensemble, 1975; Seasons, guitar, New York premiere, 9 Jan. 1976; 2 violin sonatas, #2 commissioned by the Library of Congress McKim Fund and given its premiere at Coolidge Auditorium, 12 Jan. 1979; KEYBOARD: Frescoes, 2 players, 1971; War in the heavens, 2 performers; 12 etudes, 1959-66; Hydraulics, organ, 1973; Whisper moon, Bowdoin Coll., 10 Apr. 1973; Morning and evening poems, 1973; numerous rags for piano; Revelation studies for carillon, 1976; MIXED MEDIA: Black host, percussion, organ, tape, 1967.
3080 Whitmore Lake Rd., Ann Arbor, MI 48103

BOLIN, NICOLAI P.
b. Ukraine, 6 Oct. 1908. Studied at Univ. of Califronia, B.S. He has won the Hollywood Bowl Gershwin Memorial award.
WORKS: ORCHESTRA: Symphonic sketches, a suite; Symphonie tsigane; Los Angeles concerto, piano and orch.

BOLLE, JAMES
b. Evanston, Ill., 26 July 1931. Attended Harvard Univ., 1949-52; studied composition with Charles and Darius Milhaud, 1950-52. His awards include a Ford Found. recording grant. He was on the faculty, Univ. of Saskatchewan, 1953-59; since 1966, has been director of the Monadnock Music Center, Jaffrey, N.H.
WORKS: OPERA: Oleum canis, text after Ambroise Bierce, 1972; CHAMBER MUSIC: 4 capriccii

for various small ensembles; Children's pieces, soprano and instruments, 1978; Elizabethan sequence, soprano and piano trio, 1978; CHORUS: Cantata 1, 1959; La catafalque des dieux, 1966; cantata with texts of Christopher Smart, 1970; God forbid that those who have sucked Bostonian breasts, Boston, 23 Apr. 1979; PIANO: 4 capriccii.

Box 133, Francestown, NH 03043

BOLZ, HARRIETT (Mrs. Harold A.)
b. Cleveland, Ohio. Attended Case Western Reserve Univ., B.A. 1933; Ohio State Univ., M.A. 1958; studied privately with Leo Sowerby and Paul Creston. Her many awards include those from Nat. Fed. of Music Clubs, 1965; Phi Beta Fraternity, 1968; Nat. League of Pen Women, 1970, 1972, 1976, 1978; and a grant from New York Arts Council, Meet the Composer, 1978. She has been a private teacher of piano and composition and lecturer and author on contemporary music.
WORKS: CHAMBER MUSIC: Duo scherzando, trumpet and piano, 1968; Sonata for string and woodwind septet; Vis-a-vis, woodwind trio; Invocation, soprano and string quartet; Polychrome patterns, clarinet, New York, 12 Apr. 1971; cello sonata; Pageant, woodwind quintet, 1972; CHORUS: Star over star, with baritone and orch.; Not by words alone, 1970; Teach us Thy peace, 1972; 4 Christmas songs; Carol of the flowers; That I may sing; KEYBOARD: Floret, piano; Break forth into joy, organ; Andante con moto, allegro and fugue, organ; numerous other choral works, songs, and keyboard pieces.
3097 Herrick Rd., Columbus, OH 43221

BOND, VICTORIA
b. Los Angeles, Calif., 6 May 1945. Studied with Ingolf Dahl and Ellis Kohs, Univ. of Southern California, B.M. 1973; with Roger Sessions and Vincent Persichetti, Juilliard School, M.M. 1975, D.M.A. 1977. Her awards include Juilliard scholarships and a conducting fellowship, 1973-77; Victor conducting award, 1975; ASCAP award, 1977. She was assistant conductor, Juilliard Contemporary Music Ensemble, 1973-77, Juilliard orch., 1975-77; conductor, New Amsterdam Symphony, 1977-78; then was named assistant conductor of the Pittsburgh Symphony.
WORKS: BALLET: Equinox, suite, was performed at Evergreen, Colo., 16 Aug. 1978; ORCHESTRA: 4 fragments, 1972; Sonata for orchestra, 1972; C-A-G-E-D, strings, 1974; CHAMBER MUSIC: duet, flute and viola, 1969; brass trio, 1969; woodwind quintet, 1970; Can(n)ons, clarinet and violin, 1970; cello sonata, 1971; Conversation piece, viola and vibraphone, 1975; CHORUS: Tarot, with percussion, Fairmont Coll., W.Va., 17 Apr. 1978; SONGS: Mirror, mirror, flute, viola, soprano, 1969; Cornography, soprano and instruments, 1970; Suite aux troubadours, soprano and instruments, 1970; Aria, soprano and strings, 1973; From an antique land, song cycle, New York, 10 Dec. 1976; Peter Quince at the clavier, voice and piano, New York, 16 Apr. 1978; FILM SCORE: Mirror of nature, 2 cellos and chorus, 1971.
349 W. 71st St., New York, NY 10023

BONDE, ALLEN
b. Newton, Wis., 22 Nov. 1936. Studied with James Ming at Lawrence Univ., with George Thaddeus Jones and Robert Hall Lewis at Catholic Univ. His awards include a Rockefeller Found. grant, 1968, and Mount Holyoke Coll. faculty grant, 1972. He has held faculty positions at Hood Coll., 1963-71; then at Mount Holyoke Coll.
WORKS: ORCHESTRA: Fantasia, piano and orch.; symphony; CHAMBER MUSIC: Romance, viola and piano, 1961; Contrasts, violin and piano, 1961; Romance, violin and piano, 1965; string quartet, 1967; 5 preludes, guitar, 1972; CHORUS: 3 masses; Magnificat, women's voices, oboe, harpsichord, marimba; PIANO: suite, 1965; 5 preludes, 1972; Sonus I, Sonus II, 2 pianos, 1973; Umore, 1971; MIXED MEDIA: Kaleidoscope II, oboe, percussion, marimba, harpsichord, metronome, dances, 1972.
Mount Holyoke College, South Hadley, MA 01075

BONDS, MARGARET
b. Chicago, Ill., 3 Mar. 1913; d. Los Angeles, 26 Apr. 1972. Studied at Northwestern Univ., B.M., M.M.; with Robert Starer at Juilliard School; privately with Roy Harris. Her awards include scholarships from Nat. Assoc. of Negro Musicians, Alpha Kappa Alpha, Julius Rosenwald, and Roy Harris; and the Rodman Wanamaker award. She was a concert pianist; taught at the American Theatre Wing; was music director, East Side Settlement House and the White Barn Theatre.
WORKS: THEATRE: music for Shakespeare in Harlem and U.S.A.; Migration, a ballet; CHORUS: The negro speaks of rivers; Ballad of the brown king; mass in d; SONGS: 3 dream portraits, texts by Langston Hughes; Didn't it rain?; PIANO: Spiritual suite.

BONFIGLIO, ROBERT
b. Ft. Lewis, Wash., 6 Sept. 1946. Studied with Charles Jones and David Tcimpidis, Mannes Coll. of Music, B.S.; with Charles Wuorinen, Manhattan School of Music, M.M.; also attended master classes with John Cage and Aaron Copland. His awards include a Milhaud scholarship to the Aspen Music Festival and an Eleanor Stanley White scholarship. He was musical director, Bernson-Mullis Dance Company, 1973-77; from 1973, on faculty, Turtle Bay Music School.
WORKS: THEATRE: incidental music to Olyesha's Conspiracy of feelings; modern dance works; ORCHESTRA: guitar concerto; Piece for string orch.; CHAMBER MUSIC: Variations, flute, marimba, violin, cello, 2 blues harmonicas; Piece to be played before the radio news, woodwind quintet; string quartet; trio for harmonica, cello, clarinet.
97 St. Paul's Ave., Staten Island, NY 10301

BONNEAU, GILLES YVES
b. St. Jean, P.Q., Canada, 26 July 1941; U.S. citizen 1949. Studied at the New England Conservatory, extension div., 1967-71. His works are chiefly for small chamber ensembles, including a trio for guitar, flute, bassoon; a woodwind quintet; organ preludes, and songs.
10 Stevens St., Winooski, VT 05404

BONNER, EUGENE MAC DONALD

BONNER, EUGENE MacDONALD
b. Washington, N.C., 1889. Studied at Peabody
Cons. and in London. After service in the U.S.
Army in World War I, he remained in Paris for
study until 1927. On return to the U.S., he
settled in New York and for a time was music
critic for the Brooklyn Daily Eagle.
WORKS: OPERA: Barbara Fritchee, 1921;
Celui qui épousa un femme muette, 1923; The
Venetian glass nephew, 1927; The gods of the
mountain, 1936; ORCHESTRA: Whispers of heavenly
death, with chorus on texts of Walt Whitman,
1922; White nights, prelude, 1925; CHAMBER MUSIC:
Flutes, voice and 4 instruments, 1923; piano
quintet, 1925; Suite Sicilienne, violin and
piano, 1926. In 1945 he was commissioned to
write a score for Frankie and Johnny for presentation by the New Opera Company in New York.

BOONE, CHARLES
b. Cleveland, Ohio, 21 June 1939. Studied with
Karl Schiske, Acad. of Music, Vienna, 1960-61;
Univ. of Southern California, B.M. 1963; San
Francisco State Coll., M.A. 1968; privately with
Ernst Krenek and Adolf Weiss. His awards include
a Nat. Endowment for the Arts grant and commissions. He was chairman of the San Francisco
Composers' Forum, 1964-66; coordinator, Mills
Coll. Tape Music Center and Performing Group,
1966-68; active as concert organizer and music
critic.
WORKS: ORCHESTRA: 2 landscapes; The yellow
bird, 1967; The edge of the land, 1968; Shadow,
with solo oboe, 1968; Chinese texts, with solo
soprano, 1970; San Zeno/Verona, small orch., Los
Angeles, 11 Oct. 1976; String piece, San Francisco, 15 Dec. 1978; CHAMBER MUSIC: Icarus,
flute solo, 1964; Song of suchness, soprano and
ensemble, 1964; Parallels, violin and piano,
1964; Oblique formation, flute and piano, 1965;
Vocalize, soprano solo; Cool glow of radiation,
flute and tape; Not now, clarinet solo, 1969;
Vermilion, oboe solo; quartet for clarinet and
piano trio, 1970; Zephyrus, oboe and piano, 1970;
Raspberries, 3 drummers, 1974; Linea meridiana,
8 instruments, 1975; Shunt, 3 drummers, 1978;
Streaming, solo flute, San Francisco, 11 Feb.
1979.
2340 Pacific Ave., Apt. 204, San Francisco,
CA 94115

BOONE, CLARA LYLE (Lyle de Bohun, pseudonym)
b. Stanton, Ky., 6 Sept. 1927. Studied at Centre
Coll. of Kentucky; Cincinnati Coll. of Music;
with Walter Piston, Harvard Univ.; with Darius
Milhaud, Aspen School of Music. She was school
music teacher from 1951, in Washington, D.C.,
1962-77; in 1974, founded the Arsis Press for
publication of music composed by women.
WORKS: ORCHESTRA: Annunciation of spring;
CHAMBER MUSIC: Songs of estrangement, soprano
and string quartet; The Americas, flute, clarinet, bassoon; also songs, choruses, piano pieces.
1719 Bay St., S.E., Washington, DC 20003

BOOZER, PATRICIA P.
b. Atlanta, Ga., 14 Mar. 1947. Studied with
Newton Strandberg, James Jenson, Bob Burroughs,

and Philip Landgrave at Samford Univ. She
taught at Trusswood School of Music, Birmingham,
1969-71; Samford Univ., preparatory dept., 1971-
73; then at Southern Baptist Theological Seminary,
Louisville. Her published works are for church
choral groups.

BORDEN, DAVID
b. Boston, Mass., 25 Dec. 1938. Studied with
Klaus George Roy, Boston Univ.; with Louis
Mennini, Bernard Rogers, Howard Hanson, Eastman
School of Music, B.M. 1961, M.M. 1962; with
Boris Blacher, Hochschule für Musik, Berlin,
1965; with Wolfgan Fortner and Gunther Schuller
at Tanglewood, 1966; Harvard Univ., 1963-67 M.A.;
privately with Jimmy Giuffre, Jaki Byard, and
Robert Moog. His awards include a Fulbright
scholarship; 2 Ford Found. grants; ASCAP fellowship; 3 Meet the Composer grants; 3 Cornell
Council for the Performing Arts grants; and
commissions. In 1969 he founded Mother Mallard's
Portable Masterpiece Co., a performance group
specializing in live electronic music; and in
1974, started the record label Earthquack and
the Lameduck Publishing Co.
WORKS: ORCHESTRA: concertino for piano and
orch., 1960; The force, with soprano solo, 1962;
Trudymusic, with piano solo, 1967; BAND: all-
American, 1967; Variations, 1968; CHAMBER MUSIC:
Counterpoint, harp, cello, flute, 1978; ELEC-
TRONIC: many pieces for Mother Mallard's
Portable Masterpiece Co., which consists of 5
synthesizers and an electric piano with 3 players,
1969-78.
P.O. Box 842, Ithaca, NY 14850

BORETZ, BENJAMIN A.
b. New York, N.Y., 3 Oct. 1934. Studied with
Irving Fine and Arthur Berger, Brandeis Univ.;
with Darius Milhaud at Aspen; with Milton
Babbitt and Roger Sessions, Princeton Univ. His
awards include the Fromm composition prize, 1956;
Ingram Merrill grant, 1966; American Music Center
grant, 1967; Fulbright-Hays senior fellowship,
1970-71; and Princeton Univ. Council of the
Humanities fellowship, 1971-72. He was music
critic for The Nation, 1962-69; and has served
as editor of Perspectives of New Music from
1961, and as consultant, Fromm Music Found.,
1960-70. He has held faculty positions at
Brandeis Univ., 1962-63; New York Univ., 1964-
65; Columbia Univ., 1969-72; Princeton Univ.,
1967-68, 1970-71, 1972-74; and from 1973, at
Bard Coll.
WORKS: ORCHESTRA: concerto grosso for
strings, 1954; violin concerto, 1956; Group
variations for small orch., 1964-67; CHAMBER
MUSIC: Partita for piano, 1955; Divertimento,
chamber ensemble, 1955; string quartet, 1957;
Donne songs, 1955-61; brass quintet, 1961-62;
Group variations for computer, 1968-72, Boston,
29 Oct. 1976; Compositions 3, 4, 5, 1973-74;
My chart shines high, piano, New York, 18 Apr.
1979.
Bard College, Annandale-on-Hudson, NY 12504

BORISHANSKY, ELLIOT
b. New York, N.Y., 17 Mar. 1930. Studied with

Karol Rathaus, Queens Coll.; with Vittorio Giannini, Juilliard School of Music; Jack Beeson and Otto Luening, Columbia Univ.; Philipp Jarnach, Hamburg Cons., Germany; Ross Lee Finney and Niccolo Castiglioni, Univ. of Michigan. His awards include Gershwin Memorial award, 1958; 2 Fulbright grants; Europa Kolleg scholarship; Denison Univ. Research Fund grant; Ford Humanities grant. He has held faculty posts at Rhode Island Coll.; Bucknell Univ., 1965-66; Univ. of Wisconsin, 1967; and from 1968, at Denison Univ.

WORKS: ORCHESTRA: Music for orchestra, 1958; That time of year, with speaker; CHAMBER MUSIC: Aus dem West--Ostlichen Divan, 4 Goethe settings for soprano and piano; 2 pieces, solo clarinet; Constellations, piano; 3 mosquitos for trumpet trio; Silent movie, clarinet theatre piece; 3 pieces, piano solo; Less and less human, O savage spirit, baritone, speaker, and chamber ensemble.

Music Dept., Denison University, Granville, OH 43023

BORLING, THOMAS
b. Cleveland, Ohio, 27 June 1942. Studied with Bernhard Heiden at Indiana Univ.; with Burton Weaver, Univ. of Dayton. He was percussionist with the St. Joseph Symph., 1966-70; instructor, Mt. St. Scholastica Coll., Kan., 1966-70; then on faculty, Univ. of St. Thomas.

WORKS: ORCHESTRA: The lure, a ballet; CHAMBER MUSIC: Duet for 3 moons, brass quartet; timpani sonata; trombone sonata; Why not now?, solo flute; What's happening?, variable ensemble, theatre piece; Swiatovid, wind ensemble.

6425 Mobud Dr., Houston, TX 77036

BORNSCHEIN, FRANZ CARL
b. Baltimore, Md., 10 Feb. 1879; d. Baltimore, 8 June 1948. Studied at the Peabody Cons. and joined the faculty in 1906.

WORKS: OPERETTA: The willow plate, 1932; ORCHESTRA: The phantom canoe, 1916; The sea god's daughter, symphonic poem, 1924; Old Louisiana, 1930; Leif Ericson, 1936; Southern nights, 1936; Moon over Taos, 1939, New York, 9 Oct. 1944; Ode to the brave, Washington, D.C., 7 Nov. 1944; The earth sings, Baltimore, 21 Nov. 1944; CHORUS: Onowa, cantata, 1916; The vision of Sir Launfal; Arethusa; Tuscan cypress; Joy; The conqueror worm.

BOROS, DAVID JOHN
b. New York, N.Y., 17 May 1944; d. Nov. 1975. Studied at Univ. of California at Berkeley and Los Angeles, 1962-66; with Seymour Shifrin, Martin Boykan, and Arthur Berger, Brandeis Univ., 1966-70. His awards include the Weisner Award for Creative Arts, Univ. of California, Berkeley, 1966; and a Fulbright-Hays grant for study with Goffredo Petrassi in Rome. He was lecturer at Brandeis Univ., 1973-74.

WORKS: CHAMBER MUSIC: 3 fables, tenor, harp, clarinet, bassoon; piano trio; Yet once again, solo flute; Wedding music and waltz, piano; The anecdotes of the jar, chamber chorus; The pleasure of merely circulating, piano.

BOROWSKI, FELIX
b. Burton, England, 10 Mar. 1872; to U.S. 1897; d. Chicago, 6 Sept. 1956. He taught at Chicago Musical Coll., 1897-1916, was president, 1916-25; professor, Northwestern Univ., 1932-42.

WORKS: OPERA: Fernando del Nonsensico, a satire, 1935; ORCHESTRA: 4 symphonic poems, 1920, 1924, 1925, 1954; piano concerto, 1914; 3 symphonies, 1933, 1936, 1939; 2 ballets; many other works for orch.; also 3 string quartets and many pieces for solo instruments, including the very successful Adoration for violin and piano.

BORROFF, EDITH
b. New York, N.Y., 2 Aug. 1925. Studied with Irwin Fischer, American Univ., B.M. 1946, M.M. 1948; with Ross Lee Finney, Univ. of Michigan, Ph.D. 1958. Her awards include an Andrew Mellon postdoctoral award, 1960-61; Univ. of Wisconsin grant, 1964. She has held faculty posts at Milwaukee-Downer Coll., 1950-54; Univ. of Michigan, 1955-57; Hillsdale Coll., 1958-62; Univ. of Wisconsin, 1962-66; Eastern Michigan Univ., 1968-73; visiting professor, Univ. of N. Car., 1972-73; from 1973, professor, State Univ. of New York at Binghamton.

WORKS: THEATRE: Spring over Brooklyn, a musical to her own text, 1952; incidental music for Shaw's Pygmalion, 1955, and for Giraudoux's La Folle de Chaillot, 1962; The sun and the wind, 1-act opera, to her own text, 1977; ORCHESTRA: Idyll, violin and orch.; Abelard's monologue, baritone and orch.; The dreamer, overture; Poem, violin and orch.; CHAMBER MUSIC: Variations, oboe and piano; 3 string quartets; woodwind quintet; clarinet quintet; sonatas for violin, viola, cello, horn; canons, flute and viola; VOICE: mass, solo voice or unison choir; PIANO: suite; sonata on English folk tunes, piano, 4 hands.

900 Lehigh Ave., Binghamton, NY 13903

BOTTJE, WILL GAY
b. Grand Rapids, Mich., 30 June 1925. Studied with Vittorio Giannini at Juilliard School; with Howard Hanson and Bernard Rogers, Eastman School, D.M.A. 1955; with Henk Badings in Holland and Nadia Boulanger in Paris, 1952-53; electronic music at Univ. of Utrecht, 1962-63, and in Stockholm, 1973. His awards include the Thor Johnson brass composition contest award; Composers Press publication award, 1952; Fulbright grant, 1952-53; 4 Southern Illinois Univ. Creative Research awards, 1959-72; and several commissions. He taught at Univ. of Mississippi, 1955-57, and has since 1957 been professor, Southern Illinois Univ.

WORKS: THEATRE: Altgeld, 3-act opera, 1968; Root, comic chamber opera, 1972; incidental music to Gorelik's play, Andrus, 1978; ORCHESTRA: The ballad singer, 1951; 7 symphonies (#4 and #6 are for wind ensemble), 1951-70; flute concerto, 1955; concertino for piccolo, 1956; piano concerto, 1961; Rhapsodic variations, viola, piano, strings, 1962; Chiaroscuros, 1975; tuba concerto, 1977; Mutations, small orch.; WIND ENSEMBLE: concerto for trumpet, trombone, and

BOWDER, JERRY L.

winds, 1959; Sinfonietta, 1960; Sinfonia concertante, 1961; Duo-sonatina, 2 euphoniums and
14 winds, 1969; concerto for cello and winds;
Metaphors, with tape, 1971; Facets, piano and
winds, 1973; CHAMBER MUSIC: 3 string quartets,
1950, 1959, 1962; Fantasy sonata, viola and
piano, 1954; quintet for flute and strings,
1954; Diversions, Thurber text, wind quintet,
piano, narrator, 1954; woodwind quintet, 1957;
trumpet sonata, 1959; cello sonata, 1959;
Serenade, nonet for winds and strings, 1961;
saxophone quartet, 1963; Fluctuations, 5 clarinets, 1966; Interplays, horn piano, harpsichord,
tape, 1970; Modalities I, saxophone quartet and
tape, 1970; Modalities II, clarinet and tape,
1971; Reflections, flute, harp, tape, 1971;
Incognitos, 4 tubas, 1972; Symbiosis, 2 flutes,
clarinet, cello, tape, 1974; Cycles, oboe and
piano, 1975; Chaconne, 5 guitars, 1975; Modules
II, double bass and piano, 1976; Dances: real
and imagined, guitar and string quartet, 1976;
Soundings, oboe and harpsichord, 1977; Ban-
dyings, guitar and bassoon, 1977; CHORUS: What
is a man, Whitman text, with winds, brass, 2
pianos, narrator, 1959; Wayward pilgrim,
Dickinson text, with soprano solo and chamber
orch., 1961; Diptych, Rilke text, double chorus
and piano; Solo voice: In a word, Daniel
Berrigan text, soprano, oboe, horn, piano, tape;
In praise of music, Elizabethan songs, soprano;
Patterns, Amy Lowell text, alto and piano;
Quests of Odysseus, text by Kazantzakis trans-
lated by Friar, tenor and piano; MIXED MEDIA:
From the winds and the farthest spaces, texts of
Loren Eiseley, wind quintet, narrator, tapes,
dancers, visuals; many works for tape alone.
    914 Taylor Dr., Carbondale, IL 62901

BOWDER, JERRY L.
    b. Portland, Oreg., 7 July 1928. Studied with
George F. McKay and John Verrall, Univ. of
Washington; with Robert Stoltze, Lewis and
Clarke Coll.; with Bernard Rogers, Alan
Hovhaness, and Howard Hanson, Eastman School of
Music, D.M.A. 1960. His awards include scholarships for doctoral work at Eastman; selection of
his second symphony to represent Eastman in a
1960 symposium; a commission from Music in Maine,
1966. From 1960 he has been professor at Univ.
of Maine, Portland-Gorham.
    WORKS: ORCHESTRA: 3 symphonies; BAND:
Variation on a plainsong; BRASS ENSEMBLE: Folk
suite; suite for brass, 1968; CHAMBER MUSIC:
string quartet; woodwind quintet; VOCAL: 3
songs for baritone; Brigg Fair, chorus, continuo,
flute.
    Osborne Rd., Gorham, ME 04038

BOWEN, EUGENE EVERETT
    b. Biloxi, Miss., 30 July 1950. Studied with
Harold Budd, William Douglas, Mel Powell,
Leonard Stein, Morton Subotnick, James Tenney,
California Inst. of the Arts. From 1973 he has
been faculty member at Moorpark Coll., Calif.
    WORKS: CHAMBER MUSIC: Now, oh friends,
piano and female voice, 1972; Chamomile, piano,
1972; Longbow angels, 5 basses, 1973; MIXED
MEDIA: Casida del llanto, tape or live improvi-

sation and 2 readers, 1971; Drift, tape and instruments, 1973; also works for tape alone.
    280 S. Maine, Fillmore, CA 93015

BOWERS, ROBERT HOOD
    b. Chambersburg, Pa., 24 May 1877; d. New York,
N.Y., 29 Dec. 1941. He was recording director
of the Columbia Phonograph Co. for 16 years.
His compositions include The anniversary, a
1-act opera, and 4 operettas: The red rose,
1911; Old English, 1924; Oh, Ernest, 1927;
Listen in, 1929.

BOWERS, STACEY ALAN
    b. Eau Claire, Wis., 7 Nov. 1952. Studied with
Paul Steg and Russell Peck, Northern Illinois
Univ., B.M., M.M. He has been a member of the
Blackearth Percussion Group from 1975; in 1977,
was named to the percussion faculty at Univ. of
Cincinnati.
    WORKS: PERCUSSION: Limit exceeded, 1975;
Pattern study #2, 1976; Studies for prepared
marimba, 1976-78.
    1358 Grace Ave., Cincinnati, OH 45208

BOWLES, PAUL
    b. New York, N.Y., 30 Dec. 1910. Attended Univ.
of Virginia; studied composition with Aaron
Copland in New York and Berlin, 1930-32; with
Nadia Boulanger and Virgil Thomson in Paris,
1933-34. He received a Guggenheim fellowship,
1941, and a Rockefeller grant, 1959. He was
music critic on the New York Herald Tribune,
then traveled and lived in Spain, North Africa,
the Antilles, South and Central America, studying and collecting folk music. He eventually
settled in Morocco.
    WORKS: OPERA: Denmark Vesey, 1937; The
wind remains, 1943; Yerma, 1958; BALLET: Yankee
clipper, 1937; The ballroom guide, 1937; Sentimental colloquy, 1944; Pastorale, 1947; INCI-
DENTAL MUSIC: Dr. Faustus; My heart's in the
highlands; Love's old sweet song; Twelfth night;
Watch on the Rhine; Liberty Jones; The glass
menagerie; Jacobowsky and the colonel; continues
to write scores for theatrical productions of
the American School of Tangier; ORCHESTRA:
suite, 1933; Danza Mexicana, 1941; concerto for
2 pianos, winds, percussion, 1947; CHAMBER MUSIC:
Scenes d'Anabase, voice, oboe, piano, 1932;
trio, 1936; Melodia, 9 instruments, 1937; Music
for a farce, 1938; Prelude and dance, winds,
bass, percussion, piano, 1947; Picnic cantata,
4 women's voices, 2 pianos, percussion, 1954;
sonata for 2 pianos; Preludes for piano; FILM
SCORES: Roots in the soil; Congo. As an author
he has published a novel, The sheltering sky,
1949; The delicate prey and other stories, 1950.
    2117 Tanger Socco, Tangier, Morocco

BOWLES, RICHARD WILLIAM
    b. Rogers, Ark., 30 June 1918. Studied with
Robert Sanders, Indiana Univ.; with Cecil
Burleigh, Univ. of Wisconsin. He was band
director in the air force and in public schools
to 1958, when he joined the faculty at Univ. of
Florida.
    WORKS: Many concert marches and arrangements

for band, works for orchestra, small ensembles, and solo instruments. His march, Burst of flame is listed in a compilation of the world's 100 most popular band marches.

827 N.W. 15th Ave., Gainesville, FL 32601

BOWMAN, CARL
b. Philomath, Oreg., 14 Dec. 1913. Studied at Willamette Univ., B.M.; with George F. McKay, Univ. of Washington, M.A.; with Vittorio Giannini, Juilliard School; with Normand Lockwood, Columbia Univ.; and at New York Univ., Ph.D. He has held faculty posts at New Jersey Musical Coll., Brooklyn Music School, King's Coll., Shelton Coll., City Univ. of New York, and from 1975, at Manhattan Community Coll.

WORKS: ORCHESTRA: Triptych symphony; Ballad, horn and orch.; Fantasy on a carol tune, a festival piece for orchestra, or band, or brass ensemble, or chorus, or organ; BRASS EN-SEMBLE: Toccacciata; Nocturne; CHAMBER MUSIC: trio for trombone, viola, cello; CHORUS: Festi-val of praise, chorus and brass or organ; Magni-ficat, mezzo-soprano, chorus, brass, or organ.

140 W. 69th St., New York, NY 10023

BOYADJIAN, HAYG
b. Paris, France, 15 May 1938; U.S. citizen, 1964. Studied at the Liszt Cons. in Buenos Aires and at Brandeis Univ., but is largely self-taught in composition.

WORKS: CHAMBER MUSIC: 2 duos for flute and piano; Canticles of a memory, cello and piano; Movements, #1-5, piano; Capriccioso, #1-2, piano; Fusion, string quartet, optional brass, slide projection; Nocturne, cello solo; Contours, clarinet and piano; Discourses, clarinet and cello; Mobile, flute, harp, cello, 1978; song cycle on poems of William Blake, voice and 7 instruments, 1978.

43 Fern St., Lexington, MA 02173

BOYD, JACK
b. Indianapolis, Ind., 9 Feb. 1932. Studied with Cecil Effinger, Univ. of Colorado; at Abilene Christian Univ., B.S.; with Samuel Adler, North Texas State Univ., M.M.; at Univ. of Iowa, Ph.D. He taught at Univ. of Dubuque, 1964-67; in 1968, joined the faculty at Abilene Christian Univ.

WORKS: BAND: Jackson's purchase; CHAMBER MUSIC: 3 pieces, flute and piano; CHORUS: 3 lyrics, with string orch.; Thus saith the preacher, a cappella; Jefferson: American, with brass; The death of Socrates, double chorus; Kubla Khan, with narrator and chamber ensemble.

541 College Dr., Abilene, TX 79601

BOYD, JEANNE
b. Mt. Carroll, Ill., 25 Feb. 1890; d. Jones-boro, Ark., 8 Aug. 1968. Graduated from Shimer Acad., 1909; had informal studies with Leo Sowerby, 1914-22; held a MacDowell fellowship, 1922. She was on the faculty at Shimer Acad., 1909-14; Lyceum Arts Cons., 1914-25; Bush Cons., 1925-32; American Cons., 1932-65; then retired and accepted a position teaching a few piano

students at Holy Angels Convent, Jonesboro, Ark. Her orchestral works were performed by the Eastman-Rochester Symphony; in 1960 a retrospec-tive recital of her works was given in Chicago in honor of her 70th birthday.

WORKS: ORCHESTRA: Andante lamentabile, 1922; Song against ease, 1940; Eleventurous dances, piano and chamber orch., 1943 (also for full orch. and piano, 1951); Introduction and fugue, 1949; CHORUS: Mist of the night, 1915; The hunting of the snark, cantata with orch., 1918, rev. 1929; Flag of my land, 1932; Lead on, O king eternal, 1942; Winter, 1955; also piano works and some 40 songs.

BOYD, WYNN LEO
b. Gaithersburg, Md., 28 July 1902. Piano teacher and tuner; organized a piano rebuilding firm. His works include choral pieces and songs on texts of Paul Laurence Dunbar.

BOYKAN, MARTIN
b. New York, N.Y., 12 Apr. 1931. Studied with Walter Piston at Harvard Univ.; with Paul Hindemith at Univ. of Zurich and at Yale Univ.; with Aaron Copland at Berkshire Music Center. His awards include the Jeunesses Musicales award, 1967; Martha Baird Rockefeller grant; Fromm Found. commissions. He has been faculty member at Brandeis Univ. from 1956; on editorial board, Perspectives of New Music, from 1973.

WORKS: CHAMBER MUSIC: 2 string quartets, 1949, 1967; flute sonata, 1950; duo for violin and piano, 1951; quintet for flute, piano, strings, 1953; Concerto for 13 players, Boston, 12 Nov. 1972; piano trio; CHORUS: Psalm, a cappella.

155 Summer St., Newton Centre, MA 02159

BOYKIN, HELEN
b. River Falls, Ala., 5 Nov. 1904. Was an honor graduate of Alabama Coll., B.M. 1927; studied in Munich, 1930-33; and at Yale summer school, 1952-53. Her awards include the Nat. Fed. of Music Clubs award of merit, 1971. She taught at Alabama Coll., 1927-30; privately in Atlanta, Ga., 1933-65; from 1965, in Montgomery.

WORKS: PIANO: concerto in F; Geechee dance; En bateau; Seafoam; Carnival scenes; etc., and many teaching pieces.

3220 Montesuma Rd., Montgomery, AL 36106

BOYLE, GEORGE F.
b. Sydney, Australia, 29 June 1886; to U.S. 1910; d. Philadelphia, Pa., 20 June 1948. Studied piano with Busoni, then toured as con-cert pianist and conductor in Australia, Germany, Holland, Great Britain. He then taught at Peabody Cons., Curtis Inst., and Juilliard School.

WORKS: OPERETTA: The black rose, ORCHESTRA: piano concerto, 1911; piano concertino; cello concerto, 1918; Symphonic fantasie; Holiday over-ture; CHAMBER MUSIC: 3 piano trios; violin sonata; cello sonata; piano sonata; Ballade elegiaque, piano trio; CHORUS: Pied Piper of Hamelin; many piano pieces and songs.

BOYLE, HARRISON ROBERT

BOYLE, HARRISON ROBERT
b. Philadelphia, Pa., 9 Jan. 1953. Studied with Paul Epstein, Robert P. Morgan, and Clifford Taylor, Temple Univ., 1970-74; at Britten-Pears School of Advanced Musical Training, 1978. From 1976 he has been a tenor with Pennsylvania Pro Musica.
    WORKS: ORCHESTRA: harpsichord concerto; Triptych, with chorus; CHAMBER MUSIC: The losing straw, voice and string quartet; Chamber serenade; piano sonata; Sinfonia Caesia, brass and organ; VOCAL: Equinoxes, chorus; Imaginary songs; 3 songs for baritone; Songs of religion, baritone and piano duet.
    2217 Bainbridge St., Philadelphia, PA 19146

BRACALI, GIAMPAOLO
b. Rome, Italy, 24 May 1941; to U.S. 1968. Studied with Virgilio Mortari in Rome; with Nadia Boulanger in Paris; with Lennox Berkeley in London. His awards include scholarships from the French government, the British Council; a Fulbright fellowship; Bonaventura Somma prize, 1965; F. M. Napolitano, 1966; Lili Boulanger prize, 1967; second place, Prix de Composition Prince Pierre de Monaco, 1968. From 1968 he has been faculty member, Manhattan School of Music.
    WORKS: BALLET: Cyrano de Bergerac; ORCHESTRA: organ concerto; piano concerto; 3 psalms, with chorus; WIND ENSEMBLE: Musica, winds and percussion; Sextour, 3 trumpets, 3 trombones; CHAMBER MUSIC: Openings, strings, quintet, guitar and strings; duo for harp and flute; Viajes, solo guitar.
    601 Kappock St., Riverdale, NY 10463

BRADLEY, RUTH
b. New Jersey; d.
    WORKS: VOICE: Prince Toto II, women's chorus, mezzo or baritone solo; Rain, women's chorus; Abraham Lincoln walks at midnight, cantata for solo voice; Bleecker Street market, for medium voice.

BRADSHAW, MERRILL
b. Lyman, Wyo., 18 June 1929. Studied with Leon Dallin, Brigham Young Univ., A.B. 1954, M.A. 1955; with Gordon Binkerd, Robert Kelly, Robert Palmer, and Burrill Phillips, Univ. of Illinois, M.M. 1956, D.M.A. 1962. His awards include the Karl G. Maeser Creative Arts award, 1967, and several Brigham Young Univ. grants. He has been on the faculty at Brigham Young Univ. from 1957; was lecturer with the Contemporary Music Project, 1972-75.
    WORKS: THEATRE: incidental music for Midsummer night's Dream, 1964 and 1974; music for the Oedipus cycle, 1968; The title of liberty, musical, 1975; ORCHESTRA: piano concerto, 1955; 5 symphonies, 1957, 1962, 1967, 1968, 1978; Facets, 1965; Feathers, 1968; Piece for strings, 1967; Peace memorial, 1972; 4 mountain sketches, 1974; Centennial fantasy, 1975; Nocturnes and revels, 1974; Lovers and liars, 1976; Homages, viola and orch., 7th Internat. Viola Congress, Provo, Utah, 14 July 1979; BAND: Divertimento, 1964; Fanfares and solemnities, 1967; Elegy, improvisation, and romp, 1971; Festivities,

1974; CHAMBER MUSIC: 2 string quartets, 1957, 1969; violin sonata, 1957; 3 pieces for viola, 1963; suite for viola alone, 1956; flute sonatina, 1966; suite for oboe and piano, 1966; Dialogue, flute and horn, 1966; brass quintet, 1969; Nocturne, 2 horns and strings, 1977; many vocal works, including an oratorio, The restoration; numerous piano pieces.
    248 E. 3140 North St., Provo, UT 84601

BRADSHAW, SAMUEL L. JR.
b. Columbus, Ohio, 30 Jan. 1937. Studied with Ernest Kanitz, Univ. of Southern California; with Burrill Phillips, Univ. of Illinois. His awards include scholarships and a Woodrow Wilson fellowship. He is employed at the Topeka V.A. Hospital.
    WORKS: ORCHESTRA: Festival overture; 5 movements for orchestra; symphony; Music for strings; CHAMBER MUSIC: string quartet; piano trio; trio for piano, violin, clarinet; clarinet sonata; 5 pieces, cello and piano; also songs and choir pieces.
    2205 High Ave., Topeka, KS 66611

BRAGGIOTTI, MARIO
b. Florence, Italy, 29 Nov. 1909; to U.S. at an early age. Studied with Frederick Converse, New England Cons.; with Nadia Boulanger and Alfred Cortot in Paris. He played in a duo-piano team with Jacques Fray; toured in concert programs; was radio program director with U.S. Army of Occupation in Africa and Italy, World War II; piano soloist with orchestras.
    WORKS: BALLET: The princess; ORCHESTRA: Variations on Yankee Doodle; VOICE: Lincoln's Gettysburg address, cantata for chorus.

BRAINE, ROBERT
b. Springfield, Ohio, 27 May 1896; d. New York, N.Y., 26 Aug. 1940. Studied at Cincinnati Coll. of Music. He was a radio conductor in New York.
    WORKS: OPERA: The eternal light, 1924; Virginia, 1926; Diana, 1929; ORCHESTRA: S.O.S., 1927; The raven, baritone and orch., 1928; The song of Hiawatha, 1930; Concerto in jazz, string quartet, 1935; Barbaric sonata, piano; also songs and piano pieces.

BRAND, MAX
b. Lwow, Poland, 26 Apr. 1896; U.S. citizen 1945. His works in the U.S. included Stormy interlude, 1-act opera to his own libretto; ORCHESTRA: The wonderful one-hoss shay, after Oliver Wendell Holmes, Philadelphia, 20 Jan. 1950; Night on the bayous of Louisiana, tone poem, 1953; CHORUS: The gate, oratorio with narrator, 1944.

BRANDON, GEORGE
b. Stockton, Calif., 4 Feb. 1924. Attended Union Theological Seminary, School of Sacred Music, M.S.M. 1952. He was organist-choirmaster 1941-67, and a faculty member at Midwest colleges 1957-62. His published works include some 200 choral octavos, 55 organ pieces, many hymn tunes and choir responses, piano pieces.
    P.O. Box P, Davis, CA 95616

BRANDON, SY
b. New York, N.Y., 24 June 1945. Studied with
Warren Benson, Ithaca Coll.; with Elie
Seigmeister, Hofstra Univ.; with Robert McBride,
Univ. of Arizona. His awards include first
prize in the Kappa Gamma Psi composition contest,
1962; honorable mention in several competitions,
1969-78; and commissions. He was composer-in-
residence, Boise State Univ., 1973-74; from
1976, faculty member, Millersville State Coll.,
Pa.
    WORKS: ORCHESTRA: Amendment I; BAND:
Symphonic set; Bachburg concerto, tenor saxophone and band; Expression for band; CHAMBER
MUSIC: Introduction and dance, alto sax and
piano; brass trio; Concert overture, saxophone
quartet; Renditions, trombone quartet; Micro-
pieces, saxophone; Designs and patterns, tuba
and piano; Random 7, trombone and percussion;
Conversations, alto sax and piano.
    120 Maple St., Wrightville, PA 17368

BRANDT, DOROTHEA
b. Frewsburg, N.Y., 1 May 1896. Studied composition with Henry P. Eames and Carl Parrish in
Claremont, Calif. She has been a piano teacher
in Yakima and Seattle, Wash., and Pomona, Calif.
Her published works for piano include Wagon
train, 1954; Japanese print, 1955; Zapateado,
1960; Dancing Japanese marionettes, 1963; Chinese
woodcutter, 1964; Arietta, 1968; Calico mountain
trail; also many anthems.
    2934 N. Towne Ave., Claremont, CA 91711

BRANDT, WILLIAM EDWARD
b. Butte, Mont., 14 Jan. 1920. Studied with
Russell Danburg, Washington State Univ.; with
Howard Hanson and Bernard Rogers, Eastman School
of Music. His awards include performances at
Eastman's American Music Festival, 1949; Washington State Univ. grant, 1962; a prize in a
Chicago Diocese anthem contest, 1973. He taught
at Univ. of Rochester, 1948-50; privately in
Seattle, 1950-56; then became professor, Washington State Univ.
    WORKS: CHAMBER OPERA: No neutral ground,
after Beaumarchais; ORCHESTRA: Sinfonietta #2,
1948; King Lear suite, 1948; symphony, 1950;
suite for small orch., 1960; Music for the Decalogue, narrator and orch., 1967; piano concerto,
1972; CHAMBER MUSIC: string quartet, 1949;
flute sonata, 1953; 2 clarinet sonatas, 1960,
1973; Divertimento, woodwind trio, 1960; Lyric
movement, piano, 1973; The meditation of Mary
and Rachel's lamentation, contralto and chamber
ensemble; various songs.
    N.E. 1115 Indiana St., Pullman, WA 99163

BRANNING, GRACE
b. Washington, D.C., 10 Oct. 1912. Earned a
B.M. at Univ. of Pittsburgh; studied composition
with Nicolai Lopatnikoff and Mildred Gardner.
She received 3 composition awards from the
Pittsburgh Piano Teachers Assoc. She has taught
piano privately since 1937, at Pittsburgh Musical Inst., 1937-60, and at Fillion Studios from
1960.
    WORKS: OPERA: Scene for Icelandic saga,

soprano, tenor, and chorus; CHAMBER MUSIC:
Allegro risoluto, violin; Aria and dance, flute
solo; VOCAL: God's world, women's voices; Songs
of Foo, a cycle to own words; Gethsemane; Night
song; Sea-love; PIANO: Caprice in c; Ballade;
Miniature suite; Capriccio, duet; Cardinals,
duet.
    160 Montclair Ave., Pittsburgh, PA 15237

BRANSCOMBE, GENA
b. Picton, Ont., 4 Nov. 1881; U.S. citizen 1910;
d. New York, N.Y., 26 July 1977. Graduated from
Chicago Musical Coll., where she was Gold Medal-
ist in composition for two successive years.
She studied piano with Rudolph Ganz and Hans von
Schiller; composition with Felix Borowski and
Engelbert Humperdinck; conducting with Frank
Damrosch, Walter Rothwell, Clifton Chalmers,
and Albert Stoessel. Her many awards and cita-
tions included an honorary M.A. from Whitman
Coll., 1932; selection to conduct the Golden
Jubilee massed chorus of 1000 voices for the
50th anniversary of the General Fed. of Women's
Clubs, 1941, and as guest conductor of her own
choral and orchestral works in concert and
broadcast performances throughout the U.S. and
Canada. She taught piano at Chicago Musical
Coll., 1902-7; was head of the piano department,
Whitman Coll., 1907-9; conductor of the MacDowell
Chorus, Mountain Lakes, N.J., 1931-43; conductor,
Branscombe Choral, New York, 1933-54; etc. She
composed in all forms, published more than 150
songs and 60 choral works as well as orchestral
and chamber works.
    WORKS: Pilgrims of destiny, a choral drama
for soli, chorus, and orch., 1920, Plymouth,
Mass., Quebec suite, prelude, balladine, procession, tenor and orch., 1927; Youth of the
world, cycle for women's voices and orch., 1933;
Coventry's choir, women's voices and orch., New
York, 1944; Prayer for song, women's voices,
1952; 91st psalm, chorus, piano, organ, percussion, horn, 1955; Pacific suite, horn and piano,
1957; Arms that have sheltered us, chorus and
band, written for the Canadian Royal Navy and
sung at a special celebration by massed bands
and choruses, Halifax, 1962; Bridesmaid's song,
women's voices, Boston Pops, 1965; A joyful
litany, chorus, 1967; Introit, prayer response,
and amen, written for the choir of Riverside
Church, New York, 1973; many songs and song
cycles.

BRANT, HENRY DREYFUS
b. Montreal, Canada, 15 Sept. 1913; U.S. citizen.
Studied with Leopold Mannes, Inst. of Musical
Art; with Rubin Goldmark, Juilliard School;
privately with Wallingford Riegger, Aaron Copland,
and George Antheil. His awards include the
Premio Radio Television Italiana, 1955; Guggenheim fellowships, 1946, 1955; Nat. Inst. of Arts
and Letters grant, 1955; Dollard grant; Coolidge,
Loeb, and Seligman prizes at Juilliard; Nat.
Endowment for the Arts grant, 1978; and commissions. He has taught at Columbia Univ., Juilliard School, Peabody Cons., and from 1957, at
Bennington Coll.
    WORKS: THEATRE: The great American goof,

BRATT, C. GRIFFITH

ballet, 1940; December, dramatic oratorio, text
by Patricia Brant, 1955; The grand universal
circus, opera, 1956; Everybody, Inc., operatic
spectacle, 1978; ORCHESTRA: 4 symphonies,
1931, 1942, 1945, 1947 (#4 is named The promised
land); Angels and devils, flute solo and flute
ensemble, New York, 6 Feb. 1932; double bass
concerto, 1932; Coquette overture, 1935; clarinet
concerto, 1938; violin concerto, 1940; saxophone
concerto, 1941; Downtown suite, 1942; jazz clarinet concerto, 1946; Music for an imaginary
ballet, 1947; Origins, percussion, 1952; Stresses,
2 synchronized orch., 1953; Signs and alarms,
percussion ensemble, 1953; Antiphony I, 5 synchronized orch., 1953; Labyrinth, 2 orch., 1955;
Encephalograms, 1955; On the nature of things,
1956; Heiroglyphics, 1957; Conversations in an
unknown tongue, flute and string orch., 1958;
Atlantis, antiphonal symphony with chorus and
narrator, 1960; violin concerto with lights,
1961; Voyage 4, voices and orch., 1963; Odyssey--
Why not, flutes and orch., 1965; Kingdom come,
voices, 2 orch., spaced instruments, 1969; An
American requiem, soprano and orch., New York
premiere, 17 Dec. 1975; Homage to Ives, baritone
and orch., Denver, 21 Feb. 1975; American
weather, chorus and orch., 1976; Spatial concerto ("Questions from Genesis"), piano, women's
chorus, orch., and instruments spaced in bal-
conies and around the hall, 1976, Cambridge,
Mass., 17 Apr. 1979; CHAMBER MUSIC: sonata for
2 pianos, 1931; oboe sonata, 1932; viola sonata,
1937; Chico, Groucho and Harpo, tin whistle and
chamber orch., 1938; Galaxy II, chamber orch.,
1954; Ice age, clarinet, xylophone, piano;
Mobiles, solo flute; Quombex, viola d'amore,
music boxes, and organ, 1960; Heiroglyphics 3,
viola, mezzo-soprano, chamber group; Millenium
4, brass quintet, 1963; Heiroglyphics 4, violin,
harp, celeste, organ, offstage soprano, 1966;
Dialogues in the form of secret portraits,
harpsichord; Music 1970; Windjammer, woodwind
quintet, 1968; Crossroads, 4 violins, 1971;
Divinity, harpsichord and brass quintet, 1973;
From Bach's menagerie, saxophone quartet, 1974;
Prevailing winds, woodwind quintet, 1974; piano
sextet,1976; CHORUS: Underground cantata, 1946;
Fire in cities, with winds and percussion, 1961;
Vita de Sancto Hieronymo, chorus and instruments,
1973; Solomon's gardens, New York, 23 Mar. 1974.
Orbits, a symphony for 80 trombones and organ
had its premiere in San Francisco early in 1979.
    Music Dept., Bennington College, Bennington,
VT 05201

BRATT, C. GRIFFITH
    b. Baltimore, Md., 21 Nov. 1914. Studied with
Gustav Strube, Howard Thatcher, and Katharine
Lucke at Peabody Cons.; with Leroy Robertson,
Univ. of Utah. His awards include the Idaho
Governor's award for excellence in the arts;
Distinguished Alumnus award, Peabody Cons.;
several citations from Nat. Fed. of Music Clubs;
Idaho Arts Council award of merit. He was
organist-choirmaster in Baltimore and Washington
to 1946, then at St. Michael's Cathedral, Boise,
Idaho; and was faculty member and composer-in-
residence, Boise State Univ., 1946-76.

WORKS: OPERA: Rachel; A season for sorrow;
Year of the one reed; ORCHESTRA: 2 symphonies;
CHAMBER MUSIC: 2 string quartets; clarinet
quintet; KEYBOARD: a complete cycle of organ
voluntaries for the church year; many choral
works, songs, and piano pieces, making a total
of over 375 compositions.
    1020 N. 17th, Boise, ID 83702

BRAUER, JAMES LEONARD
    b. Julesburg, Colo., 29 Sept. 1938. Studied
with Jan Bender, Concordia Seminary, St. Louis,
and with Joseph Goodman at Union Theological
Seminary, New York. From 1965 he has been
faculty member, Concordia Coll., Bronxville,
N.Y., and organist-choirmaster, St. Mark's
Lutheran Church, Yonkers.
    WORKS: He has composed for brass, strings,
woodwinds, piano, and chorus, including Magnificat for soprano and chorus, and Nunc dimittis,
tenor and chorus.
    228 Midland Ave., Tuckahoe, NY 10707

BRAUNLICH, HELMUT
    b. Brünn, Czechoslovakia, 19 May 1929; U.S.
citizen 1954. Studied with Kornauth and Keller
at the Salzburg Mozarteum; with George Thaddeus
Jones at Catholic Univ.; and with Leon Kirchner
at Tanglewood. From 1961 he has been faculty
member at Catholic Univ.
    WORKS: ORCHESTRA: concerto for oboe,
strings, and brass; concerto for 10 instruments;
CHAMBER MUSIC: wind quintet; quartet for flute,
viola, bassoon, piano; 3 songs with string quartet; viola sonatina; duo for violin and trombone,
Washington, 19 Dec. 1977; Barbro variations 1978
(V), piano, Washington, 18 Dec. 1978.
    School of Music, Catholic University, Wash-
ington, DC 20064

BREHM, ALVIN
    b. New York, N.Y., 8 Feb. 1925. Attended
Juilliard School and Columbia Univ.; studied
composition with Wallingford Riegger. His
awards include grants from the Ford Found. and
New York State Council on the Arts; many commissions. He was faculty member, Manhattan
School of Music, 1968-76; State Univ. of New
York at Stony Brook, 1969-76; and from 1972, at
State Univ. Coll. at Purchase.
    WORKS: ORCHESTRA: Hephaestus, an overture,
1966; concertino for violin and string orch.;
CHAMBER MUSIC: Dialogues, bassoon and percussion, 1963; brass quintet, 1967; cycle of 6
songs for voice and 10 instruments; Dialogues
and consort, flute and 4 instruments, New York,
27 Apr. 1974; piano variations, 1965; cello
variations; brass trio; Metamorphosis, piano,
New York, 26 Feb. 1979.
    302 W. 86th St., New York, NY 10024

BREIL, JOSEPH CARL
    b. Pittsburgh, Pa., 29 June 1870; d. Los Angeles,
Calif., 23 Jan. 1926. He wrote 2 operas: The
legend, 1919, and Asra, 1925; 3 comic operas:
Love laughs at locksmiths, 1910, Prof. Tattle,
1913, The seventh chord, 1913; and one of the
earliest motion picture scores, Queen Elizabeth,
Chicago, 1912.

BRENNER, WALTER

b. Wynberg, Union of South Africa, 21 Jan. 1906; became U.S. citizen; d. Calif., 19 Dec. 1969. Studied music in Europe and with Dominico Brescia.

WORKS: ORCHESTRA: piano concerto; Home they brought her warrior dead, symphonic poem; The birth of Venus; Adoration; Prophecy; Capriccio; Valse symphonique; CHAMBER MUSIC: quintet for flute and strings; string sextet; Impromptu, Ole torero, Wanderlust, all accordion; CHORUS: Psalm 121; Memorial prayer; Hashkivenu; God is love; Kol nidre; ORGAN: Glory to God; Sabbath joy; Contemplation hassidique.

BRESNICK, MARTIN

b. New York, N.Y., 13 Nov. 1946. Studied with Arnold Franchetti, Univ. of Hartford, B.A. 1967; with Leland Smith, John Chowning, Gyorgy Ligeti, Theodore Antoniou, Stanford Univ., M.A. 1968, D.M.A. 1972; with Gottfried von Einem and Friedrich Gerna at Vienna Akad., 1969-70. His awards include a Fulbright fellowship, 1969-70; National Endowment for the Arts grant, 1975; Rome prize fellowship, 1975-76. His faculty posts have been at San Francisco Cons., 1971-72; Stanford Univ., 1972-74; and from 1976, at Yale Univ.

WORKS: ORCHESTRA: Ocean of storms, 1970; Wir weben, wir weben, string orch.; CHAMBER MUSIC: piano sonata, 1963; Theme and variations, oboe, solo, 1964; 3 two-part pieces for piano, 1964; trio for 2 trumpets and percussion, 1966; Tammuz, string quartet, 1968; Introit, wind ensemble, 1969; 3 intermezzi, solo cello, 1971; B.'s garlands, 8 celli; COMPUTER AND MIXED MEDIA: PCOMP, 1969; 3 fables of the ant, violin, lecturer, computer, dancers, etc.; Fragment, 1971; Musica, 9 instruments and computer, 1972; FILM SCORES: Man machine meets machine man, woodwind quartet, 1968; Pour, computer collage, 1969; television spots for Operation sentinel, guitar, flutes, computer.

Music Dept., Yale University, New Haven, CT 06520

BREWER, RICHARD H.

b. San Diego, Calif., 12 Aug. 1921. Studied with Warren Martin, Westminster Choir Coll.; with Robert Nelson and Robert Stevenson, Univ. of California, Los Angeles; and with Halsey Stevens, Univ. of Southern California. He has held faculty posts at Minot State Coll., 1949-51; Omaha Univ., 1952-55; and from 1962, at Pfeiffer Coll., where he was named Mame Boren Spence Professor of Music in 1976.

WORKS: CHORUS: My sheep hear my voice; Sing to the Lord of harvest; Rejoice and be merry; One prayer; Peace; This cup of blessing; et al.

Pfeiffer College, Misenheimer, NC 28109

BRICCETTI, THOMAS

b. Mt. Kisco, N.Y., 14 Jan. 1936. Studied at Columbia Univ.; with Bernard Rogers, Eastman School of Music; and with Samuel Barber, Peter Mennin, and Alan Hovhaness. His awards include Prix de Rome, 1959; Ford Found. grants, 1960,

1961; Yaddo fellowship, 1963; Nat. Endowment for the Arts grant, 1967. He has held conducting posts with St. Petersburg Symph. Orch., 1963-67; Indianapolis Symph., 1967-72; Fort Wayne Philharmonic Orch., from 1970; Univ. Circle Orch., Cleveland Inst. of Music, from 1972; and from 1976, has been faculty member, Nebraska Univ. at Omaha.

WORKS: ORCHESTRA: Fountain of youth, overture, 1972; violin concerto; Song of Solomon, cello and orch.; BAND: Turkey Creek march; CHAMBER MUSIC: Eclogue No. 2, trombone and strings; Eclogue No. 4, tuba and winds; flute sonata; trio from Roman sketches, violin, viola, cello; CHORUS: Psalm 150; Milaydy's madrigals.

Music Dept., Nebraska Univ., 60 St. and Dodge, Omaha, NB 68162

BRICKEN, CARL ERNEST

b. Shelbyville, Ky., 28 Dec. 1898; d. Sweet Briar, Va., 25 Jan. 1971. Studied at Yale Univ., B.A. 1922; with Rosario Scalero, Mannes School of Music; with Alfred Cortot in Paris and Hans Weisse in Vienna. He received the Pulitzer award, 1929; Guggenheim fellowship, 1930. He held teaching posts at Mannes School, Univ. of Chicago, Univ. of Wisconsin; was conductor of the Seattle Symphony Orch., 1944-48.

WORKS: ORCHESTRA: 3 symphonies; Daniel Boone, legend for orch.; The prairie years; also chamber music, choral works, songs. His violin sonata, 1944, was performed for the Bicentennial Parade of American Music, Washington, 19 Jan. 1976.

BRICKMAN, JOEL I.

b. New York, N.Y., 6 Feb. 1946. Studied at Montclair State Coll.; with David Diamond at Juilliard School; with Nicolas Flagello and Ludmila Ulehla, Manhattan School of Music, B.M., M.M. He was winner in a Manhattan School composition contest 1970; and an accordion work was chosen as the 1973 Coupe Mondiale world contest solo. He has held faculty posts at Manhattan School from 1971, and Marymount Coll., from 1972.

WORKS: ORCHESTRA: symphony, 1968; Prelude and dithyramb, concert overture, 1969; Thousands of days, piano concerto with solo soprano, 1970; 3 songs for voice and orch., 1977; CHAMBER MUSIC: saxophone sonata; Dialogue, oboe and wind ensemble, 1972; woodwind trio; woodwind quintet; Prelude and caprice, accordion, 1973; CHORUS: Of wonder, a cappella.

90-H Edison Ct., Monsey, NY 10952

BRIECE, JACK

b. San Francisco, Calif., 28 Jan. 1945. Reports continuous and discontinuous studies in various localities in the U.S., Mexico, Central and South America, and Europe. His principal teachers have been William Wendlandt, John Cage, Yoko Ono, and the Book of Changes. From 1965 to 1972, he composed for acoustic and electric instruments, e.g.: Wonderful music for everybody, music for nonmusicians; Movies for your ears, various instruments and ensembles; Infinity crescendos, flutes; m.a.p., piano music for children. Since 1972 he has been engaged in

BRIEF, TODD
> situational composition: <u>Tortoise</u>, for perfor-
> mance at sunrise and sunset by people playing
> stones, bamboo windchimes, and Indian nose
> flutes; <u>Situation--ta yu</u>, for television receiv-
> ers, stones, and primitive flute; <u>Situation kô</u>,
> for Chinese temple bells and stones.
>> 69 Central Ave., San Francisco, CA 94117

BRIEF, TODD
> b. New York, N.Y., 25 Feb. 1953. Studied with
> Donald Martino, Gunther Schuller, William Thomas
> McKinley, New England Cons., B.M. 1976, M.M.
> 1978; with Leon Kirchner and Earl Kim, Harvard
> Univ., A.M. 1981; also with Ralph Shapey, Univ.
> of Chicago; privately with Bulent Arel. His
> awards include the Bearns prize, 1976; Sprague
> prize; first prizes, East & West Artists Contest,
> NFMC-ASCAP contest, ASUC contest, 1978; ASCAP
> Found. grant, 1979; ASCAP Tanglewood fellowship;
> MacDowell Colony fellowship, 1980; Paul Found.
> award; Meet the Composer grant; Rome prize,
> 1981-82; and commissions.
> WORKS: ORCHESTRA: <u>Prelude</u>; <u>Cantares</u>, with
> soprano solo, 1978; CHAMBER MUSIC: <u>Mobile</u>,
> mezzo-soprano and vibraphone; <u>Idol</u>, soprano and
> 10 instruments; <u>Canto</u>, solo cello; <u>Fantasy</u>,
> violin and piano, New York, 19 Mar. 1978;
> <u>Moments</u>, harp; <u>Concert etude</u>, piano, Cambridge,
> Mass., 25 Apr. 1981; <u>Arabesques</u>, flute; duo for
> cello and piano.
>> 31-A Anderson St., Boston, MA 02114

BRIGGS, G. WRIGHT
> b. Taunton, Mass., 17 Oct. 1916. Studied with
> Walter Piston, Harvard Coll., B.A., M.A.; with
> Carl McKinley, New England Cons.; and at Harvard
> Business School. Since 1955 he has been director
> of radio and television for Batten, Barton,
> Durstine, and Osborn, Inc., Boston. His composi-
> tions include <u>Commemoration march</u>, <u>Concord and
> Lexington march</u>, <u>Boston's on the move again</u>;
> <u>Andante</u> for piano trio; <u>20th century gavotte</u>.
>> 2000 Prudential Center, Boston, MA 02199

BRIGGS, RALPH
> b. Bettendorf, Iowa, 4 Aug. 1901. Studied with
> George Leighton and Karol Liszniewski at Cincin-
> nati Cons., B.M. 1928, M.M. 1935; and with Mme.
> Henri Dumesnil in Paris. He received the national
> publication award of Composers Press, Inc. in
> 1954. His faculty positions included Murray
> State Coll., Ky.; Southwestern Coll., Winfield,
> Kan.; Ohio Wesleyan Univ.; Univ. of Oregon; West
> Virginia Univ.; Univ. of Texas, El Paso, 1950-71.
> WORKS: ORCHESTRA: <u>Burlesque</u>, 1958; <u>Poem</u>;
> <u>Prelude, fugue, and aria</u>, 1960; PIANO: <u>Moods</u>;
> <u>Facetious</u>, 1955; scherzo for 2 pianos.
>> 368 Shadow Mountain Dr., El Paso, TX 79912

BRIGHT, HOUSTON
> b. Midland, Tex., 21 Jan. 1916; d. Canyon, Tex.,
> 8 Dec. 1970. Studied with Halsey Stevens and
> Ernest Kanitz, Univ. of Southern California,
> Ph.D. He was professor and composer-in-residence
> at West Texas State Univ.
> WORKS: BAND: concerto grosso; <u>Passacaglia</u>;
> <u>Prelude and fugue</u>; <u>Marche de concert</u>; <u>Legend and
> canon</u>, brass ensemble; CHAMBER MUSIC: <u>3 short
> dances</u>, wind quintet; <u>4 for piano</u>; CHORUS:

> <u>Vision of Isaiah</u>, with orch.; <u>Premonition</u>; <u>Sea-
> weed</u>; <u>Softly flow</u>; <u>Soliloquy</u>; <u>The tale untold</u>;
> <u>When the spring is in the air</u>; <u>Jabberwocky</u>, with
> brass, percussion, contrabass, piano; many of
> the choruses are set to his own texts.

BRINDEL, BERNARD
> b. Chicago, Ill., 23 Apr. 1912. Studied with
> Max Wald, Chicago Musical Coll., graduated magna
> cum laude; studied privately with Paul and Isaac
> Levine. He received an American Fed. of Music
> Clubs award, 1973, William Byrd Artists competi-
> tion award in 1976. He taught at Chicago Musical
> Coll., 1944-53; from 1953, at Morton Coll.,
> Cicero, Ill.; has been choir director at various
> churches and temples.
> WORKS: ORCHESTRA: 4 symphonies; 2 cello
> concertinos; CHAMBER MUSIC: violin sonata; 3
> string quartets; suite for saxophone and piano;
> <u>Autumnal meditation</u>, saxophone; many sacred and
> secular choral works and songs.
>> 2740 Lincoln Lane, Wilmette, IL 60091

BRINGS, ALLEN
> b. Brooklyn, N.Y., 24 Feb. 1934. Studied at
> Queens Coll., B.A. 1955; with Otto Leuning,
> Columbia Univ., M.A. 1957; with Roger Sessions,
> Princeton Univ.; with Gardner Read, Boston Univ.,
> D.M.A. 1964. His awards include fellowships at
> Columbia and Princeton; BMI student composer
> radio award, 1956; ASCAP awards. He has held
> teaching posts at Bard Coll.; Boston Univ.; and
> from 1963, at Queens Coll., CUNY.
> WORKS: ORCHESTRA: symphony; concerto for
> orch.; <u>Capriccio</u>; <u>Nocturne</u>; BAND: <u>Variations</u>;
> <u>Essay</u>; <u>Canzone</u>, double brass quartet; CHAMBER
> MUSIC: <u>Divertimento</u>, flute, viola, harpsichord;
> <u>Burlette</u>, flute, clarinet, trombone; sonatas for
> piano, violin alone, viola or clarinet and piano;
> 3 chamber concertos, #1 piano and small orch.,
> #2 violin and percussion, #3 flute and strings,
> #2 had its premiere in Boston, 19 Dec. 1976;
> CHORUS: <u>Altaforte</u>, with piano; <u>Shall I die for
> Mannis sake?</u>, women's voices; <u>The apparition</u>;
> ORGAN: <u>Passacaglia, interlude, and fugue</u>.
>> 199 Mountain Rd., Wilton, CT 06897

BRINGUER, ESTELA
> b. Argentina, 3 June 1931; to U.S. 1952. Studied
> in Argentina with Manuel de Falla, Jaime Pahissa,
> and Clemens Krauss. Her awards include first
> municipal prize of the City of Buenos Aires;
> award of the Inst. of Contemporar Arts, Washing-
> ton; Woman of the Year award, 1971, Buenos Aires.
> She has been guest conductor American Symph.
> Orch.; Colon Opera House Orch., Buenos Aires;
> Philharmonic Orch., Buenos Aires; and others.
> In 1975 she was to tour the U.S. and Canada
> conducting the Colon Opera House Orch.
> WORKS: ORCHESTRA: 2 symphonies; piano con-
> certo; <u>Carnival in Humahuaca;</u> <u>Elegy</u>; <u>Cold spring</u>;
> <u>Song of my valley</u>; <u>Echo of Tupac</u>.

BRISMAN, HESKEL
> b. New York, N.Y., 12 May 1923. Studied at
> Juilliard School and Columbia Univ.; with Richard
> Donovan, Quincy Porter, and Paul Hindemith, Yale
> Univ.; privately with Ernst Toch and Luigi

Dallapiccola. His awards include a Tanglewood fellowship; Harvey Gaul award; Berlin prize for film scoring; Nat. Endowment for the Arts grant; New Jersey Arts Council grant. In 1959-62 he was composer for the Sermi Film Co., Rome; then director, Joseph Achron Cons., Israel, 1964-67; on editorial staff, Carl Fischer, Inc., 1967-69.

WORKS: OPERA: The 3 strangers, 1 act; Whirligig, 1 act; ORCHESTRA: concerto for piano and strings; Sinfonia breve; CHAMBER MUSIC: string quartet, 1952; woodwind quintet, Dialogue, flute and percussion; Concerted music for piano and percussion; CHORUS: Psalms; Cantata '78, Englewood, N.J., May 1978.

961 E. Lawn Dr., Teaneck, NJ 07666

BRISTOL, LEE HASTINGS, JR.
b. Brooklyn, N.Y., 9 Apr. 1923. Studied at Hamitlon Coll., A.B. 1947; Trinity Coll. of Music, London, Licentiate in Organ, 1947. His numerous awards include 11 doctorates and many memberships in honorary societies. He was organist-choirmaster, All Saints Church, Bay Head, N.J., 1941-77; president, Westminster Choir Coll., 1962-69, named president emeritus in 1976. He has composed extensively for chorus and organ. His anthem, When in our music, was given its premiere in Princeton, N.J., 31 May 1976, and also sung by a 650-voice choir at a choral festival at the New York Cathedral of St. John the Divine on 6 June 1976.

210 Mercer St., Princeton, NJ 08540

BRITAIN, RADIE
b. Silverton (near Amarillo), Tex., 17 Mar. 1903. Studied at American Cons., B.M. 1924; with Albert Noelte, Leopold Godowsky, and Henoit Levy in Munich; organ with Pietro Yon and Marcel Dupre in Paris. On returning to the U.S., she spent two seasons at the MacDowell Colony. Her awards include more than 50 national or international awards for compositions; Juilliard publication award, 1945; honorary doctorate, Musical Arts Cons., Amarillo; Nat. League of American Penwomen award of merit; and others. She is a private teacher in Hollywood.

WORKS: STAGE WORKS: Happyland, operetta, 1946; Carillon, opera, 1952; The spider and the butterfly, children's operetta, 1953; Kuthara, chamber opera, 1961; Lady in the dark, 1962; Western testament, 1964; Wheel of life, ballet, 1933; Kambu, ballet, 1963; ORCHESTRA: Heroic poem, 1929; Rhapsodic fantasy, piano and orch., 1933; Southern symphony, 1935; Light, 1935; suite for strings, 1940; Drouth, 1939; Ontonagon sketches, 1939; Phantasy, oboe and orch., 1942; Cowboy rhapsody, 1956; Cosmic mist symphony, 1962; Les femeux douze, 12 instruments, 1966; CHAMBER MUSIC: Epic poem, string quartet, 1927; string quartet, 1934; Chipmunks, woodwind orch., 1940; Barcarola, 8 celli and soprano, 1958; In the beginning, 4 horns, 1962; Phantasy, flute and piano, 1962; Awake to life, brass quintet, 1968; CHORUS: Drums of Africa, a cappella, 1935; Noontide, 1935; Prayer (Quarry), 1935; Immortality, a cappella, 1937; Nisan, women's voices, strings, piano, 1963; Harvest heritage, 1963; Brothers of the clouds, with orch., 1964;

The flute song, women's voices, flute, piano, 1965; also many songs including Translunar cycle, dedicated to NASA, 1969.

1945 N. Curson Ave., Hollywood, CA 90046

BROCK, BLANCHE KERR
b. Greenfork, Ind., 3 Feb. 1888; d. Winona Lake, Ind., 3 Jan. 1958. Studied at Indianapolis Cons. and American Cons.; published songs.

BROCKMAN, JANE E.
b. Schenectady, N.Y., 17 Mar. 1949. Studied at Univ. of California, Santa Barbara; with George B. Wilson, Eugene Kurtz, and Leslie Bassett, Univ. of Michigan, B.M., M.M., D.M.A. 1977; with Max Deutsch in Paris. Her awards include the Sigvald Thompson award, 1973; Fulbright-Hays fellowship, 1975-76; Horace H. Rackham predoctoral fellowship, 1976-77; commissions. She was on the faculty, Univ. of Rhode Island, 1977-78; then at Univ. of Connecticut.

WORKS: ORCHESTRA: Eventail, 1973; Ballinkeele music, 1977; CHAMBER MUSIC: Finger prints, piano, 1971; August thaw, piano, 1971; horn sonata, 1972; 2 vignettes, chamber ensemble, 1972; Labyrinths, chamber ensemble, 1974; string trio, 1974; CHORUS: A day of summer, 1975; CARILLON: Tower music, performed at World Congress of Carilloneurs, Douai, France, Sept. 1974; MIXED MEDIA: Metamorphosis, lighting, dancer, tape, 1978.

R.D. #1 Luchon Rd., W. Willington, CT 06279

BROCKWAY, HOWARD A.
b. Brooklyn, N.Y., 22 Nov. 1870; d. New York, N.Y., 20 Feb. 1951. Studied in Berlin. He taught privately in New York and at the Peabody Cons. in Baltimore. His compositions include a symphony, 1895; Sylvan suite, for orch., 1901; choral works; piano pieces.

BRODY, JOSHUA
b. New York, N.Y., 15 Sept. 1916. Studied with Philip James and Marion Bauer, New York Univ.; privately with Wallingford Riegger in New York and Robert McBride in Tucson. He has been accompanist for the Kadiman Dancers from 1962; on faculty, dance dept., Univ. of Arizona, from 1972.

WORKS: THEATRE WORKS: incidental music for plays by Sholem Alechem, 1956; Tragi-comedy of Don Christobita and Donna Rosita, opera after Garcia Lorca, 1963; ORCHESTRA: Ballad, 1960; Requiem for 2 veterans, with narrator, 1962; CHAMBER MUSIC: 2 string quartets, 1940, 1953; violin sonata, 1942; woodwind quintet, 1960; Dialogue, violin and piano, 1966; piano sonata, 1968; Wedding music, 1970; numerous pieces for woodwinds, piano, and songs.

1226 Swan Rd., Tucson, AZ 85712

BROEGE, TIMOTHY
b. Neptune, N.J., 6 Nov. 1947. Studied with Alan Stout, M. William Karlins, Anthony Donato, Northwestern Univ. His awards include numerous commissions. He has been music director, First Presbyterian Church, Manasquan, N.J., from 1972.

WORKS: ORCHESTRA: Sinfonia I, orch. and

BROEKMAN, DAVID

jazz-rock ensemble; Songs without words, marimba and 10 players; Songs without words, clarinet and 15 players; WIND ENSEMBLE: Sinfonias III, V, VII, IX; 3 pieces for American band; CHAMBER MUSIC: 4 partitas, #I baroque ensemble, #II harpsichord, #III brass quintet, #IV saxophone quintet; Songs without words, chamber ensemble; suite for harpsichord; VOICE: Alleluia, choir, trumpets, organ; Songs from the gold key, voice and 3 players; PIANO: Hartford dances; 5 bagatelles; 3 piano rags; Chicago songs.
612 Rankin Rd., Brielle, NJ 08730

BROEKMAN, DAVID
b. Leyden, Netherlands, 13 May 1902; to U.S. 1924; d. New York, N.Y., 1 Jan. 1958. He was a music editor in New York, then film composer in Hollywood; returning to New York, he was conductor of ultramodern music. His compositions include 2 symphonies and scores for the films All quiet on the western front and The phantom of the opera.

BROGUE, ROSLYN (Roslyn B. Henning)
b. Chicago, Ill., 16 Feb. 1919. Attended Drake Univ.; Univ. of Chicago; Radcliffe Coll., A.M. 1943, Ph.D. 1947; studied with Walter Piston. She plays harpsichord, piano, organ, violin, and viola, and is soprano soloist, artist, and poet as well as composer. She was on the faculty at Boston Univ., 1959-60; and at Tufts Univ., 1962-77.
WORKS: ORCHESTRA: suite for small orch., Boston, 29 Apr. 1948; Andante and variations, harpsichord and orch., 1954-56; CHAMBER MUSIC: woodwind trio, 1946; Allegretto, flute and piano, 1948; suite for recorders, 1950; quartet for piano and strings, 1949; string quartet, 1951; Duo lirico, violin and harpsichord, 1952; trio for violin, clarinet, piano, 1953; Quodlibet, flute, cello, harpsichord, 1953; Arabesque, cello and piano, 1955; sonatina, flute, clarinet, harpsichord, 1957; Juggler, 1962; woodwind quintet, Tufts Univ., 9 May 1972; Equipoise, alto saxophone, harpsichord, piano, Tufts Univ., 6 May 1972; many works for varying instrumental ensembles and songs for soprano voice.

BROMLEY, RICHARD H.
b. Charleston, Ill., 18 July 1938. Studied with James Ming, Lawrence Coll., B.M. 1960; with Leo Sowerby and Stella Roberts, American Cons., M.M. 1967; with Philip Batstone, Charles Eakin, and David Diamond, Univ. of Colorado, D.M.A. 1974. His awards include a Nat. Endowment for the Arts grant, 1971. He has been faculty member at Eastern Kentucky Univ. from 1974.
WORKS: ORCHESTRA: Tensegrity, 1967; Synergia No. 4, 1971; Texture of time, 1973.
Music Dept., Eastern Kentucky Univ., Richmond, KY 40475

BROOKS, JOHN BENSON
b. Houlton, Maine, 23 Feb. 1917. Studied at the New England Cons. and with Joseph Schillinger and John Cage in New York. He has been pianist, arranger, and composer in New York City since

1937.
WORKS: ORCHESTRA: Alabama concerto; The twelves; and many popular songs.
c/o ASCAP, 1 Lincoln Plaza, New York 10023

BROOKS, RICHARD JAMES
b. Syracuse, N.Y., 26 Dec. 1942. Studied at Crane School of Music, B.S. 1966; with Karl Korte and William Klenz, State Univ. of New York, Binghamton, M.A. 1971; with Ursula Mamlok, Michael Czajkowski, New York Univ. His awards include a MENC first prize in composition, 1973; Composers' Conf. scholarship, Johnson, Vt., 1973; SUNY Research Found. grant, 1977. He was faculty member, Brooklyn Coll., 1971-72; staff member, Music Div., New York Public Library, 1973-75; then on faculty, Nassau Community Coll., Garden City, N.Y.
WORKS: THEATRE: Rapunzel, 1-act opera, 1969; The wishing tree, operetta, 1977; ORCHESTRA: Rondo capriccioso, with piano obligato, 1965; Ecossaise, string orch., 1967; Bacchanale, 1969; symphony, 1977-78; CHAMBER MUSIC: piano sonata, 1962; Piece for brass quartet, 1965; Movements, string quartet, 1966; Variations, piano, 1967; trio for viola, oboe, piano, 1970; Prelude and lament, woodwind quintet, 1970; string quartet, 1971; violin sonata, 1973; suite for percussion, 1975; Last night I was the wind, baritone and woodwind quintet, 1976; Cassation, 2 celli, 1976; Chorale variations, 2 horns, 1978; Sonic gestures, piano, 1978; many choral works.
107 W. 86th St., New York, NY 10024

BROOKS, WILLIAM
b. New York, N.Y., 17 Dec. 1943. Studied with Richard Winslow, Wesleyan Univ.; with Kenneth Gaburo, Benjamin Johnston, Herbert Brün, and Edwin London, Univ. of Illinois, B.A. cum laude. His awards include Woodrow Wilson and Danforth fellowships; Fulbright-Hays professorship, 1977-78. He was instructor, Univ. of Illinois, 1969-73, with a year out to be research assistant in the Biological Computer Lab.; on faculty, Univ. of California, Santa Cruz, 1973-75; U.C., San Diego, 1975-77; professor, Univ. of Keele, England, 1977-78.
WORKS: CHAMBER MUSIC: Poempiece I: white-gold blue, solo flute, 1967; Poempiece II: How I fooled the armies, solo bass trombone; Many returns, voice and piano, 1977; Madrigals, 4 virtuoso vocalists, performed by the Extended Vocal Techniques Ensemble, Valencia, Calif., 1979; THEATRE PIECES: Untitled, 8 solo singers, 2 actors, 1972; That it was built, 10 dancers, 10 percussionists, 1973; Ensemble, collaboration with 12 performers, 1974; Shopwork, collaboration with 10 performers, 1974; duets, voice and live electronics, 1978; Bryant's Ridge disco phase no. 1, singers, rock group, 1978.
c/o Howard Brooks, 714 Ridge Rd., Orange, CT 06477

BROSCH, BARRY A.
b. Cleveland, Ohio, 5 July 1942. Studied with Hugh Glauser, Kent State Univ., B.M. 1968; with Ben Johnston, Edwin London, and Salvatore

Martirano, Univ. of Illinois, M.M. 1969. He has held faculty posts at Univ. of West Florida, 1967-68; Univ. of Illinois, 1969-73; Univ. of Miami from 1975.

WORKS: ORCHESTRA: Beware! The vipersnap, children's piece for orch., narrator, tape, and dance; CHAMBER MUSIC: Prolations, solo cello; Divergencies, piano; Allegatoons; Gifts; many other concert and dance pieces, mostly electronic.

Univ. of Miami, P.O. Box 248165, Coral Gables, FL 33124

BROSH, THOMAS DENTON
b. Montrose, Colo., 25 Aug. 1946. Studied with Cecil Effinger and Philip Batstone, Univ. of Colorado, B.M. 1969; with Normand Lockwood, Univ. of Denver, M.A. 1972. He taught at Univ. of Denver, 1970-72; Univ. of North Carolina, 1972-80; then at Community Coll. of Denver, Aurora Campus.

WORKS: THEATRE: incidental music to Alfred Jarry's Ubu roi, 1972; to Arthur Kopit's Indians, 1973; CHAMBER MUSIC: Spectrum, mezzo-soprano, flute, oboe, 1968; Pastel, alto saxo-phone, wind ensemble, percussion, 1972; Dialogue, treble instruments, 1973; Innerchange I, viola and electronic piano, 1974; Series 2, solo clar-inet, 1976; Plaza polka, woodwind quartet, 1978.

4774 Peoria St., Denver, CO 80239

BROUK, JOANNA
b. St. Louis, Mo., 20 Feb. 1949. Studied at Univ. of California, Berkeley, B.A. 1972, and at Mills Coll. Electronic Music Studio. She has been radio announcer for KPFA, Berkeley from 1972. She composes chiefly electronic music using Moog and Buchla synthesizers; also works for piano, gong, and flute; sound poetry pieces; and music emphasizing a sense of serenity and relating to states of meditation.

2420 Fulton, Berkeley, CA 94704

BROWN, CHARLES SAMUEL
b. Marianna, Ark., 26 Sept. 1940. Studied privately in Detroit; theory and voice at More-house Coll., Atlanta, 1963-66; composition with Leslie Bassett and William Bolcom, Univ. of Michigan, 1975-76. He is primarily a singer; was bass soloist, Mariner's Episcopal Church, Detroit, 1970-77; then joined the music faculty at Lincoln Univ., Jefferson City, Mo. His com-positions are mostly for voice, e.g., The lamb, mixed chorus; many songs; chamber pieces and piano pieces.

821-R Southwest Blvd., Jefferson City, MO 65101

BROWN, DAVID AULDON
b. Birmingham, Ala., 6 Feb. 1943. Studied with Myron Fink at Curtis Inst. He won first prize, Composers Guild contest, Salt Lake City, 1972. He has been on the faculty, Wilmington Music School, Del., from 1967, and Univ. of Delaware, from 1972.

WORKS: CHAMBER MUSIC: suite for flute and piano; flute sonata; woodwind quintet; Varia-tions, string orch.; piano trio, Washington, D.C., 7 May 1975; PIANO: Toccata, 1971; sona-

tina, 1972; 4 piano sonatas; Rondo fantasy.
2220 Marsh Rd., Wilmington, DE 19810

BROWN, EARLE
b. Lunenburg, Mass., 26 Dec. 1926. Studied engineering at Boston Univ.; composition at the Schillinger School in Denver. His awards in-clude a Guggenheim fellowship, 1965; a grant of $3000 from American Acad. of Arts and Letters, 1972; and many commissions. He taught at the Denver Schillinger School, 1950-52; at Peabody Cons., 1968-70; was composer-in-residence, Rotterdam, Neth., 1973-74, and at California Inst. of the Arts in 1978.

WORKS: ORCHESTRA: Folio and 4 systems, piano and orch., 1952; Available forms I, for 18 instruments, 1961; Available forms II, 98 players, 2 conductors, 1963; From here, chorus and orch., Chicago, 22 Jan. 1970; Syntagm III, 1970, an open-form composition in which one group can be played against another in varying ways; Modules I and II, American premiere, Baltimore, 3 Mar. 1971; Time spans, Kiel, Germany, 2 Sept. 1972; New pieces--loops, Venice, 16 Sept. 1972; Cross sections and color fields, Denver, 1975; New piece, 4 groups of instruments in the 4 corners of the hall, Oberlin, 28 Feb. 1976; Sign sounds, an open-form piece for about 20 players, 1972; CHAMBER MUSIC: piano trio, 1952; In 25 pages, for from 1 to 25 pianos, 1953 (the pages can be played upside down at will); music for cello and piano, 1955; clarinet sonata; prelude and fughetta, bass clarinet; Pentathis, 9 instruments, 1958; Hodograph I, flute, piano, percussion, 1959; Indices, 12 players, 1960; string quartet, 1965; Corroborree, 2 or 3 pianos, 1964; Centering, solo violin and 10 instruments, 1973; New piece, chamber ensemble, San Francisco, 14 Oct. 1976; ELECTRONIC: 2 octets for 8 mag-netic tapes, 1953, 1954; Light music, electric lights, electronic equipment, and a varying number of players, 1961; Times five, 5 players and magnetic tape, 1963.

BROWN, ELIZABETH BOULDIN (Mrs. J. Stanley Brown)
b. Halifax, Va., 11 Jan. 1901. Studied with Edgar Stillman Kelley, Cincinnati Cons., grad-uated 1921. Her awards include first prize, Penn. Fed. of Music Clubs, 1965; 2 awards from Nat. League of American Pen Women, 1967, 1968; and commissions. She has published many anthems and hymns, and has also composed for strings, flute, piano, etc.

762 Lebanon Ave., Mt. Lebanon, Pittsburgh, PA 15228

BROWN, ELIZABETH VAN NESS
b. Topeka, Kans., 12 June 1902. Studied at Kansas State Coll., Manhattan, B.M. 1925; Univ. of Kansas, Lawrence, M.Ed. 1945; and at Washburn Univ., Topeka. She was public school music supervisor for 30 years; violinist, Topeka Symph., 10 years; organist and choir director in several churches. She composed anthems and pieces for violin, piano, etc.

BROWN, J. E.
b. Huntington, N.Y., 27 Dec. 1937. Studied with

BROWN, J. HAROLD

George Andrix and Warren Benson at Ithaca Coll.;
privately with Robert Palmer; and with Arthur
Berger at Brandeis Univ. His awards include a
Bennington Composers Conf. scholarship, a Brandeis fellowship, and the Lies Memorial award.
He was coordinator, Information Service, N.Y.
State Dept. of Arts and Humanities, 1971-72;
joined the faculty at Lehigh Univ. in 1973.
    WORKS: CHAMBER MUSIC: Impromptu, trombone
and tape; Theme and variations, brass quintet;
Fragments, small orch.; trio for flute, clarinet,
cello; Cut up, tape; Foreplay, piano; Number one,
brass quintet; Dry wood, clarinet and tape, 1977;
quartet for clarinet, trombone, piano, percussion,
1977.
    R.D. 5, Creek Rd., Bethlehem, PA 18015

BROWN, J. HAROLD
    b. Shellman, Ga., 28 Sept. 1909. Studied at
Fisk Univ., B.M., and at Indiana Univ., M.M.
His honors include 6 Wanamaker awards. He was
director of music, Florida A&M, then at Southern
Univ., Baton Rouge; in the 1950s, was director
at Karamu House and Huntington Playhouse,
Cleveland. His compositions are chiefly for
voice and include Job, an oratorio; The saga of
Rip Van Winkle, for chorus; and The African
chief, a cantata.

BROWN, JONATHAN BRUCE
    b. Highland, Ill., 18 June 1952. Studied with
Robert Hays, Central Michigan Univ.; with Neil
McKay, Univ. of Hawaii. In 1976 he joined the
faculty at Pikeville Coll., Ky.
    WORKS: ORCHESTRA: Warmth of distant suns,
3 pieces; Galaxy visions, 6 pieces; Lyric variations, tuba and string orch., CHAMBER MUSIC:
Laminations brass, brass quintet; Strata, tuba
and percussion quintet.
    4385 Eastport Dr., Bridgeport, MI 48722

BROWN, KEITH CROSBY
    b. Port Maitland, Nova Scotia, 1 Sept. 1885; to
U.S. 1886; d. Newton Centre, Mass., 8 Sept.
1948. Studied at the New England Cons., Harvard
Univ., and in Rome. He was chairman of the
music department, Mt. Ida Junior Coll.
    WORKS: OPERETTA: Who discovered America?;
ORCHESTRA: On the Esplanade; Bostonia suite;
Latin American suite; and songs.

BROWN, MERTON LUTHER
    b. Berlin, Vt., 5 May 1913. Studied with
Wallingford Riegger in New York, 1944-48; with
Carl Ruggles in Vermont, 1948-50; then spent
some years in Rome, returning to the U.S. in
1967. He received a commission from M.I.T. for
a band piece.
    WORKS: THEATRE: La infanta, full-length
ballet; ORCHESTRA: chorale for strings, 1948;
concerto breve per archi, 1959; concertino for
string orch., 1974; double concerto for woodwinds; BAND: concerto grosso; CHAMBER MUSIC:
Consort for 4 voices, 2 pianos, 1947; piano
sonata, 1948; duo for violin and piano, 1956;
Metamorfosi, piano, 1965; Dialogo, cello and
piano, 1970; Divertimento, piano, 4 hands, 1975;
5 pieces, clarinet and piano; Fantasia, piano;

VOICE: Psalm 13, 1976.
    48 Washington St., Charlestown, MA 02129

BROWN, NEWEL KAY
    b. Salt Lake City, Utah, 29 Feb. 1932. Studied
with Leroy J. Robertson, Univ. of Utah; with
Bernard Rogers, Howard Hanson, and Wayne Barlow,
Eastman School of Music, Ph.D. He was on the
faculty, Centenary Coll. for Women, 1961-67;
Henderson State Coll., 1967-70; from 1970, North
Texas State Univ.
    WORKS: ORCHESTRA: On the third summer day,
soprano and orch.; Eulogy, cello and orch.;
Music for trumpet and orchestra; CHAMBER MUSIC:
woodwind quintet; brass quintet; Pastorale and
dance, 5 winds; saxophone sonata; trombone
sonata; Postures, bass trombone and piano; 4
duets, flute and clarinet; Lyric, flute and
harp; Silhouettes, trumpet and tuba; Poetics,
trumpet and piano, 1970; suite for trumpet;
Anagrams, trumpet and marimba, 1977, New York
premiere, 19 Sept. 1978; CHORUS: Born today is
Christ our king; Sing noel, ring noel; The Earth
is the Lord's.
    North Texas State University, Denton, TX
76203

BROWN, RAYNER
    b. Des Moines, Iowa, 23 Feb. 1912. Studied at
Univ. of Southern California, M.M. 1946. His
awards include Ford Found. recording grants and
ASCAP awards. He was professor of music, Biola
Coll., 1948-77; and organist, Wilshire Presbyterian Church, Los Angeles, 1941-77.
    WORKS: ORCHESTRA: 3 symphonies, 1952, 1957,
1958; Variations on a hymn, 1957; 3 organ concertos, 1959, 1966, 1967; BAND: Sinfonietta,
1963; prelude and fugue, brass and percussion,
1963; concerto for harp, brass, percussion,
1964; concerto grosso, brass and percussion,
1965; Fantasy-fugue, brass and percussion, 1965;
piano concertino, 1966; symphony for clarinet
choir, 1968; concerto for 2 pianos, brass, percussion, 1971; sinfonietta, trombone choir,
1976; prelude and quadruple fugue, piano and
clarinet choir, 1976; CHAMBER MUSIC: 2 flute
sonatas, 1944, 1959; piano quartet, 1947; 3
fugues for 5 flutes, 1952; string quartet, 1953;
Triptych, violin, viola, piano, 1954; prelude
and scherzo, 7 flutes, 1956; 2 brass quintets,
1957, 1960; trio for flute clarinet, viola,
1958; flute sonatina, 1961; concerto for harp
and brass quintet, 1962; prelude and fughetta,
bass clarinet and piano, 1965; harp sonata,
1967; sonata breve, baritone, saxophone and piano,
1969; 6 fugues, horn, trombone, tuba, 1969;
double fugue, clarinet and piano, 1970; Symbols,
2 clarinets, 1970; fugue for 3 saxophones, 1970;
variations, piano and brass quintet, 1972; Kolb
versets, 3 clarinets, 1972; scherzi, 4 trombones,
1973; Phoenix avatara, oboe, English horn,
bassoon, piano, 1976; violin sonata, 1977;
ORGAN: 35 sonatinas; 19 chorale preludes;
sonatas with organ for viola, 1956, cello, 1961,
oboe, 1962, clarinet, 1965, flute, 1969, bassoon,
1972, oboe d'amore, 1975, 4 trumpets, 1976; quintet, 4 saxophones and organ, 1969; partita, 2
trumpets, 2 trombones, organ, 1970; Chaconne,

violin and organ, 1973; also choral music and
piano works.
2423 Panorama Terrace, Los Angeles, CA
90039

BROWN, RICHARD E.
b. Gloversville, N.Y., 21 Feb. 1947. Studied
with Robert J. Rittenhouse, Central Coll., Pella,
Iowa, B.A. magna cum laude; with Charles Carter,
Carlisle Floyd, John Boda, Florida State Univ.,
M.M., D.M. 1974. He was school band director in
Wellsburg, Iowa, 1969-71.
WORKS: ORCHESTRA: clarinet concerto; Tor-
ment of Medea, monodrama for soprano and orch.;
BAND: Divertimento for winds; CHAMBER MUSIC:
2 brass quartets; Delineations, brass; Serenata,
violin and cello; Suite pastorale, piano; Sex-
tuplets, piano; CHORUS: Kyrie eleison.

BROWN, STEPHEN
b. New York, N.Y., 28 Apr. 1945. Studied at
Harvard Univ. and privately with Harold Zabrach
in St. Louis. His awards include a scholarship
at Harvard and four first prizes in composition
contests. He has been on the staff at Southern
Illinois Univ. from 1967.
WORKS: CHAMBER MUSIC: song cycle on poems
of James Joyce, soprano and guitar; Memoirs of a
survivor, cello and piano; Cinq phrases d'une
histoire, flute and harp; A Larkin cycle, baritone and piano; Sister Sonji, flute and piano;
also incidental music to Merry wives of Windsor
and As you like it.
212 W. Washington St., O'Fallon, IL 62269

BROWN, THOMAS A.
b. Schnectady, N.Y., 24 June 1932. Studied at
Hartwick Coll., B.S.; State Univ. Coll., Potsdam,
N.Y., M.A. He was music director in public
schools, 1957-74; on faculty Coll. of St. Rose,
Albany, N.Y., 1972-74; percussion instructor at
music camps and conferences.
WORKS: PERCUSSION: Percussionata, with
band accompaniment; Rock velvet, jazz-rock ensemble; Mallets in mind; Tropicussion; Percussion particles; etc.
10 St. Stephens Lane, Scotia, NY 12302

BROWNE, DONALD KURTZ, JR.
b. Columbus, Ohio, 23 Nov. 1946. Studied with
Donald McGinnis at Ohio State Univ., B.S. 1968;
was music director in public schools, 1968-72;
Florida Symphony Orch., 1970-73. He has composed
for percussion: 3 by 3; 5 by 5; Peace for all
children, with flute, 1980.
6980 S.W. 83rd Court, Miami, FL 33143

BROWNE, PHILIP
b. Norman, Okla., 27 July 1933. Studied at
Arizona State Univ., B.A.; with Bernard Rogers
and Wayne Barlow, Eastman School of Music, M.M.;
with Darius Milhaud and Roy Harris, Univ. of
California, Los Angeles. His awards include
selection as Outstanding Educator of America,
1972; and the Max Winkler $1,000 award for a
band composition, 1973. From 1963 he has been
faculty member and band director, California
State Polytechnic Univ.
WORKS: ORCHESTRA: concerto for strings;

Serenade; Inaugural procession; BAND: Windroc
overture; Ballad for trumpet; suite no. 2;
Sonoro and brioso, for winds.
California State Polytechnic University,
3801 W. Temple Ave., Pomona, CA 91768

BROWNE, RICHMOND
b. Flint, Mich., 8 Aug. 1934. Studied with
H. Owen Reed, Michigan State Univ.; with Richard
Donovan at Yale Univ. His awards include BMI
student awards, 1957, 1958; Fulbright grant for
Austria, 1958; Yale Morse grant, 1964. He was
on the Yale faculty, 1960-68; from 1968, has
been faculty member, Univ. of Michigan.
WORKS: ORCHESTRA: Translations, 1964-73;
CHAMBER MUSIC: Trio for solo viola, 1965; 2 In-
troductions, 3 cadenzas, and 6 maps, sextet,
1964; CHORUS: Chortos I, speech chorus, 1967;
Chortos II, speech chorus, 1970; ORGAN:
Klasmata, 1964.
School of Music, University of Michigan,
Ann Arbor, MI 48105

BROWNING, MORTIMER
b. Baltimore, Md., 16 Nov. 1891; d. Milford,
Del., 24 June 1953. Studied at Peabody Cons.;
with Percy Grainger, Chicago Musical Coll.; with
Hans Weisse, Mannes School of Music. He taught
at Greensboro Coll.; Juilliard School; Westchester Cons.; Greenwich Music School and Chapin
School in New York; was organist and choirmaster
in Baltimore and New York.
WORKS: ORCHESTRA: Scherzo rondo, violin
and orch.; concerto for theremin, New York, 27
Mar. 1944; CHAMBER MUSIC: piano trio; piano
suite; Caprice burlesque, violin and piano; also
documentary film scores.

BROZEN, MICHAEL
b. New York, N.Y., 5 Aug. 1934. Studied with
Paul Nordoff at Bard Coll; with Lukas Foss at
Tanglewood; with Vincent Persichetti at Juil-
liard School. His awards include a Howard
Hanson commission; ASCAP awards; Nat. Inst.-
American Acad. of Arts and Letters grant; Ingram
Merrill and Guggenheim fellowships; special
citation of the Koussevitzky Internat. Recording
award. He was musical adviser, modern dance
dept., Brooklyn Coll., 1959-60; assistant editor,
Musical America, 1961-64.
WORKS: ORCHESTRA: Canto; Dark night, gentle
night, with soprano and tenor soloists; In memoriam, soprano and string orch.; CHAMBER MUSIC:
The bugle moon, baritone and 9 instruments; The
ways of water, baritone and piano; Fantasy,
piano.
86 Horatio St., New York, NY 10014

BRUBECK, DAVID WARREN
b. Concord, Calif., 6 Dec. 1920. Studied at
Univ. of the Pacific, B.M. 1942; at Mills Coll.;
and privately with Darius Milhaud. He holds
honorary doctorates from Univ. of the Pacific
and Fairfield Univ. After military service in
World War II, he formed the Dave Brubeck Trio
and then the Dave Brubeck Quartet, which soon
became known throughout the jazz world. In the
1970s his three musician sons were drafted into

BRUBECK, HOWARD

the New Brubeck Quartet.
WORKS: ORCHESTRA: Elements; Happy anniversary, a fugal fanfare; Glances, ballet score; CHORUS: The light in the wilderness, oratorio; Gates of justice, cantata; Truth is fallen, cantata, commissioned by the Midland, Mich., Symphony for the opening of the Midland Center for the Arts on 1 May 1971; La fiesta de la posada, Christmas choral pageant; Beloved son, oratorio, premiere, Minneapolis, Aug. 1978; hundreds of jazz tunes recorded and published.
221 Millstone Rd., Wilton, CT 06897

BRUBECK, HOWARD
b. Concord, Calif., 11 July 1916. Brother of David Brubeck, also studied with Darius Milhaud. He was chairman of the music department, Palomar Coll., La Mesa, Calif.
WORKS: ORCHESTRA: Elizabethan suite, women;s voices and chamber orch., 1944; The devil's disciple, overture, 1954; 4 dialogues for jazz combo and orch., 1956; The gardens of Versailles, a suite, 1960; also chamber music and choral works.

BRUCE, FRANK NEELY
b. Memphis, Tenn., 21 Jan. 1944. Studied with Thomas Canning, J. F. Goossen, David Cohen, Univ. of Alabama, B.M. 1965; with Ben Johnston and Hubert Kessler, Univ. of Illinois, M.M. 1966, D.M.A. 1971. His awards include Martha Baird Rockefeller grant, 1976; Nat. Endowment for the Humanities grant, 1977. He was faculty member, Univ. of Illinois, 1968-74; then professor, Wesleyan Univ.
WORKS: THEATRE: Pyramus and Thisbe, chamber opera, 1965; incidental music for Galethea, 1967, for The tempest, 1968; Au claire de la lune, 1971; The trials of Psyche, 1-act opera, 1971; incidental music for Membrain, mixed media event, 1971; film score for Illinois Envrnmntl. Protection Agency, 1972; ORCHESTRA: concerto for percussion and orch., 1967; Fanfare for William Schuman, brass choir and percussion, 1963; concerto for violin and chamber orch., 1974; CHAMBER MUSIC: wind quintet, 1967; Fantasy, 10 winds, percussion, tape, 1968; Untitled piece 3, oboe and piano, 1969; Untitled piece 4, trombone and percussion, 1969; 3 canons for marimba, 1969; Grand duo, trombone and piano, 1971; Grand duo, saxophone and piano, 1972; Piano sonata #6, 1973; Grand duo, trumpet and piano, 1974; rondo for flute, tuba, piano, 1976; Grand duo, flute and piano, 1977; Grand duo, cello and piano, 1977; many choral works, songs, keyboard pieces.
343 Washington Terrace, Middletown, CT 06457

BRUHNS, GEORGE F. W.
b. Bunzlau, Silesia, 10 Apr. 1874; U.S. citizen 1918; d. Cranford, N.J., 2 July 1963. Composed a symphonic poem, marches, songs.

BRÜN, HERBERT
b. Berlin, Germany, 9 July 1918; U.S. citizen 1963. Studied with Stefan Wolpe and Frank Pelleg, Jerusalem Cons., Israel, and at Columbia Univ. His awards include ESCO Found. award,

1948; first prize, Internat. Bassist's Composition Competition, 1977; and many commissions. In 1955-61 he was engaged in research in electro-acoustics and electronic sound production in musical composition in Paris, Cologne, and Munich; gave numerous lectures and seminars. In 1963 he joined the staff at the School of Music, Univ. of Illinois, for further research in electronic music, later became professor. He was distinguished visiting professor, Coll. of the Arts, Ohio State Univ., 1969-70.
WORKS: ORCHESTRA: concertino for orchestra, 1947; Dedication overture, 1949; mobile, 1958; CHAMBER MUSIC: 5 pieces for piano, 1945; Poem, string quartet and low voice, 1948; sonatinas for violin, 1948, flute, 1948, viola, 1949, bassoon, 1953; piano sonata, 1951; trio for flute, clarinet, bassoon, 1953; 3 string quartets, 1953, 1957, 1960; Gestures for 11, chamber ensemble, 1964; trio for flute, double bass, percussion, 1964; Gesto, piccolo and piano, 1965; Non sequitur, a group of works for various ensembles, 1966; trio for trumpet, trombone, percussion, 1966; Plot for percussion, 1967; Touch and go, percussion, 1967; Stalks and trees and drops and clouds, percussion, 1967; 6 for 5 by 2 in pieces, oboe and clarinet, 1971; At loose ends, percussion, 1974; In and . . . . . and out, chamber ensemble, 1974; Per contra, serenata, bassa, 3 pieces for double bass, 1977; ELECTRONIC: Futility, tape, 1964; Sonoriferous loops, instruments and tape, 1964; Mutatis mutandis, a composition for interpreters, 1964. Brün says of this work: "Here the interpreter is invited to begin by contemplating a graphic as traces left by a process which moved a pen in various directions across the plane . . . to construct by thought and imagination his version of a structure that might leave the traces which the graphic displays . . . . He is asked to construct the structured process by which he would like to have generated the graphics . . . The interpreter is not asked to improvise. The interpreter is asked not to improvise. He is asked to compose."
307 S. Busey, Urbana, IL 61801

BRUNELLI, LOUIS JEAN
b. New York, N.Y., 24 June 1925. Studied with Philip James and Marion Bauer, New York Univ., B.M. 1949; with Vittorio Giannini, Manhattan School of Music, M.M. 1950. He received the 1960 American Symph. League recording repertoire award. He was arranger and assistant conductor, Longine Symphonette, 1949-54; staff member, Chappell and Co., 1954-71; on faculty, Manhattan School, 1970-77; in 1978, became assistant dean of the Juilliard School.
WORKS: ORCHESTRA: Burlesca; Essay for Cyrano, 1974; BAND: In memoriam, 1971; Arlecchino, 1972; Chronicles, 1978.
32-43 90th St., Jackson Heights, NY 11369

BRUNSWICK, MARK
b. New York, N.Y., 6 Jan. 1902; d. London, 26 May 1971. Studied with Rubin Goldmark and Ernest Bloch; and with Nadia Boulanger in Paris. He lived in Europe, 1925-38; on returning to New

York he taught composition; was chairman of the music department, City Coll. of New York, 1946-64.

WORKS: OPERA: The master builder, after Ibsen, was left unfinished; ORCHESTRA: Lysistrata, suite for orch., women's voices, mezzosoprano, 1930; symphony, 1946; Eros and death, chorus and orch., 1954; CHAMBER MUSIC: 2 movements for string quartet, 1925; Fantasia for viola, 1932; 7 trios for string quartet, 1955; septet in 7 movements, 1957; string quartet with contrabass, 1958; 6 bagatelles for piano, 1958; CHORUS: 5 madrigals, with viola, cello, double bass, 1958-66.

BRUSH, RUTH J.
b. Fairfax, Okla., 7 Feb. 1910. Studied with Wiktor Labunski, Gardner Read, and David Van Vactor, Kansas City Cons. Her awards include those from Texas Manuscript Society, 1952; Texas Composers Guild, 1954, 1972; Composers Press, 1959; Nat. Fed. of Music Clubs, 1972. She was pianist, radio station WHB, Kansas City, 1940-45; head of piano faculty, Frank Phillips Coll., 1950-54; organist, Bartlesville, Okla., from 1955.

WORKS: OPERA: The street singers; CHAMBER MUSIC: Valse joyeuse, violin and piano; 2 expressive pieces, organ; Pastorale, organ; The night lights, piano; Osage suite, piano; Romance sans paroles, violin and piano; CHORUS: Star shined pathetique; Collect for Nat. Fed. of Music Clubs, 1976; SONGS: Twilight; Goddess of the sun.
3413 Wildwood Ct., Bartlesville, OK 74003

BRYAN, CHARLES FAULKNER
b. McMinnville, Tenn., 26 July 1911; d. Helena, Ala., 7 July 1955. Studied at Nashville Cons., B.M. 1934; Tennessee Polytechnic Inst., B.S. 1939; George Peabody Coll., M.A. 1940. He was on the music faculty at George Peabody Coll., 1947-52; then at Indian Springs School, Helena, Ala.

WORKS: THEATRE: Singing Billy, opera; Strangers in this world, musical folk play; The bell witch, folk cantata, 1946; ORCHESTRA: White spiritual symphony; Birmingham suite, 1953; CHAMBER MUSIC: Cumberland interlude 1790, alto solo and chamber orch.; many choral works.

BRYANT, ALLAN (ALN) C.
b. Detroit, Mich., 12 July 1931. Studied with Edward T. Cone, Princeton Univ.; and at Cologne State Music School.

WORKS: CHAMBER MUSIC: string quartet, 1946; Quadruple play, rubber band instruments, 1966; Pitch out, for new string instruments, 1968; Space guitars, 1977; ELECTRONIC: masses, choir and new electric instruments, 1967; Live electronic music, 1969; Inno, soprano and personal synthesizer, 1970.
via Angeletto 3, Roma 00184, Italy

BUBALO, RUDOLPH
b. Duluth, Minn., 21 Oct. 1927. Studied with John Becker, Rudolph Ganz, Vittorio Rieti, Karel Jirak, Chicago Musical Coll. His awards include

Alice Ditson award; Cleveland Area Arts Council award; Nat. Endowment for the Arts grant; Bascom Little Fund grant; Cleveland State Univ. Development Fund grant; Rockefeller grant. He has been faculty member and director, Electronic Music Studio, Cleveland State Univ., from 1969.

WORKS: CHAMBER MUSIC: 3 pieces for brass quintet; 5 pieces for brass quintet and percussion; Soundposts, violin, clarinet, piano; Lattices, piano trio; MIXED MEDIA: Soundscape, orchestra and tape; concertino for saxophone, percussion, tape; Albert's system, clarinet and tape; Spacescape, orchestra and tape; concerto for solo amplified clarinet and multiple tape loops.
3764 Glenwood Rd., Cleveland, OH 44121

BUCCI, MARK
b. New York, N.Y., 26 Feb. 1924. Studied with Frederick Jacobi and Vittorio Giannini, Juilliard School; privately with Tibor Serly; with Aaron Copland at Tanglewood. His awards include Irving Berlin scholarship, 1948-52; Piatigorsky award, 1949; MacDowell fellowships, 1952, 1954; Guggenheim grants, 1953, 1957; Nat. Inst. of Arts and Letters grant, 1959; cowinner, Italia prize, international television award, 1966; numerous commissions.

WORKS: THEATRE: incidental music to Cadenza, play by Dills, 1947; Caucasian chalk circle, Brecht play, 1948; The boor, 1-act opera after Chekhov, New York, 29 Dec. 1949; The beggar's opera, after John Gay, New York, June-Oct. 1950; The Adamses, music and lyrics to play by Paula Jacobi, 1952; Elmer and Lily, score to Saroyan's play, Alfred Univ., April 1952; Summer afternoon, original play with music, New York, summer, 1952; The dress, 1-act opera, and Sweet Betsy from Pike, 1-act opera satire, both New York, 8 Dec. 1953; The 13 clocks, music and lyrics to Thurber's fantasy, ABC-TV, 29 Dec. 1953; The western, music and lyrics to a mime play, Westport, Conn., summer 1954; Tale for a deaf ear, opera after Elizabeth Enright, Tanglewood, 5 Aug. 1957; The hero, 1-act opera based on Gilroy's Far Rockaway, NET network, 24 Sept. 1965; ORCHESTRA: concerto for a singing instrument, with string orch., harp, celeste, New York, 26 Mar. 1960, with Leonard Bernstein conducting the New York Philharmonic and Anita Darian, kazoo soloist; Nocturne, solo voice or instrument and orch., Vienna, 1962; CHAMBER MUSIC: Introduction and allegro, 8 woodwinds, 1946; Divertimento, violin and piano, 1950; American folk songs, 3 voices, guitar, piano, New York, 8 Dec. 1953; CHORUS: The wondrous kingdom (flora and fauna), cantata, a cappella, Tanglewood, 1962; FILM SCORES: A time to play, Polaroid movie commissioned by USIA for the U.S. Pavilion at Expo 67; Seven in darkness, ABC-TV, 23 Dec. 1969; Echo of a massacre, 1973. He has also written plays; book and lyrics to a pop opera, Myron, it's damp down here; and, in collaboration with Rod Arrants, Keyboard, a game-show format.
5625 Beck Ave., N. Hollywood, CA 91601

BUCCI, THOMAS V.
b. Providence, R.I., 7 Sept. 1926. Studied at

BUCHANAN, ANNABEL MORRIS

New England Cons., B.M. 1951. M.M. He served in
the U.S. Army in World War II and conducted the
40th Div. Band at age 19. He is music supervisor in the Portland Public Schools; director
of music for shows in the Portland Lyric Theatre;
director of various choruses.
    WORKS: ORCHESTRA: Canon and toccata; Ital-
ian folk fantasy; Conflict II, orch. and tape;
CHAMBER MUSIC: Concertante, viola and piano;
suite for 3 trumpets; quintet for woodwinds and
tape, Washington, D.C., 19 Apr. 1976; CHORUS:
mass; Dinner anyone; Sing joyfully to God; 3
sketches.
    140 Abby Lane, Portland, ME 04103

BUCHANAN, ANNABEL MORRIS
    b. Groesbeck, Tex., 22 Oct. 1888. Studied with
Hugh Clarke and Cornelius Rybner, Landin Cons.,
Dallas, Tex.; organ at the Guilmant Organ School.
She taught in various schools in Virginia, in-
cluding Madison Coll. 1944-48; was editor of The
Virginia Musician, 1929-48; was board member,
1929-36, and head of the American Music Dept.,
Nat. Fed. of Music Clubs. In 1953 she was
honored as a life member of the Composers-Authors
Guild at a special concert of her music in Town
Hall, New York.
    WORKS: CHORUS: Come all ye fair and tender
ladies; Song of the cherubim; Rex Christus, ora-
torio; The moon goes down, choral suite; and many
songs. She was author of Folk Hymns of America;
American Folk Music; Adventures in Virginia
Folkways.
    c/o Mrs. George Crouse, 105 Sycamore Dr.,
Paducah, KY 42001

BUCHANAN, EDWARD L.
    b. Burnside, Ky., 1918. Studied at Chicago
Musical Coll., B.M. 1949; Marshall Univ., M.A.
1958. He served in the U.S. Navy in World War
II; has been on the music faculty, Univ. of
Kentucky, Ashland Center, from 1959.
    WORKS: OPERA: Boccaccio's untold tale,
1 act; ORCHESTRA: Square dance rhapsody;
CHORUS: Gethsemane.
    1409 Central Ave., Ashland, KY 41101

BUCHAROFF, SIMON
    b. Berdichev, Russia, 20 Apr. 1881; d. Chicago,
Ill., 24 Nov. 1955. He came to the U.S. at an
early age; studied piano in New York, then in
Vienna with Julius Epstein and Emil Sauer.
Returning to the U.S., he was head of the piano
department, Wichita Coll. of Music, 1907; music
editor and arranger in Hollywood, 1937; later
settled in Chicago.
    WORKS: OPERA: A lover's knot, 1916;
Sakahra, 1924, rev. 1953, received the David
Bispham Medal; Jewel; Wastrel, Addio; ORCHESTRA:
Reflections in the water; Drunk; Doubt; Joy
sardonic; CHORUS: Freedom on the march; Hear my
voice, O Lord; America; The wanderer's song;
The trumpeter's death; and others; PIANO: Valse
brillante; Capriccio.

BUCHTEL, FORREST L.
    b. St. Edward, Nebr., 9 Dec. 1899. Studied at
Simpson Coll., B.A.; Northwestern Univ., M.S.;

Vandercook Coll. of Music, B.M., M.M.; et al.
He was head of the band and orchestra department,
Kansas State Teachers Coll., 1925; joined the
faculty at Vandercook Coll. of Music in 1932.
He has written many works for band.
    1116 Cleveland St., Evanston, IL 60202

BUCKLEY, DOROTHY PIKE
    b. Glens Falls, N.Y., 26 Apr. 1911. Studied
composition with Burrill Phillips and Wayne
Barlow at Eastman School of Music. She won the
1969 annual composition award from the American
Coll. of Musicians, Texas. She has been a
teacher in Rochester from 1945.
    WORKS: CHAMBER MUSIC: The blue waterfall,
voice, flute, cello, piano; Perception, voice,
flute, cello, piano; PIANO: Folk theme and variations, 1969; Adirondack fantasy; Tarantella;
Five after five, duet; Variphonic suite.
    145 Harvard St., #2, Rochester, NY 14607

BUDD, HAROLD
    b. Los Angeles, Calif., 24 May 1936. Studied
with Aurelio de la Vega and Gerald Strang,
California State Univ., Northridge, B.A. 1963;
with Ingolf Dahl, Univ. of Southern California,
M.M. 1966. His awards include 2 Nat. Endowment
for the Arts grants, 1974, 1975. He was faculty
member, California Inst. of the Arts, 1969-75.
    WORKS: INSTRUMENTAL: Analogies from Rothko,
orch., 1964; The 6th this year, orch., 1967;
III, concert jazz for double ensemble; The edge
of August, flute and piano; . . . only 3 chords
. . ., trombone quintet, 1969; The candy-apple
revision, 1970; The pavilion of dreams: song of
paradise, bass baritone, harp, percussion, 1974;
part 2 of The pavilion of dreams: Bismillahi
'Rrahmani 'Rrahim, chamber group, 1975; VOICE:
Madrigals of the rose angel; ELECTRONIC: Coeur
d'orr, 1969; Mangus Colorado, amplified gongs,
1969; Oak of golden dreams, 1970.
    23149 Oakbridge Lane, Newhall, CA 91321

BUDRECKAS, LADISLAUS
    b. Gomel, Russia, 24 Oct. 1905; U.S. citizen
1955. Attended Univ. of Vytautus the Great,
Lith., Dipl. of Theol.; studied with Juozas
Naujalis, Cons. of Kaunas, degree in sacred
music, 1948; at Pontificio Inst. di Musica
Sacra, Rome, 1937-39, 1945-49, Magistrum in
Cantu Gregoriano, 1949. He was professor, Univ.
of Vytautus the Great, 1939-44; member, Diocesan
Music Commission, Pittsburgh, 1957-59; and head,
Commission for Lithuanian Music, from 1966.
    WORKS: CHORUS: Hymn for America I, Hymn
for America II, both for mixed chorus or male
chorus and organ, 1960; Christus vincit, 1961;
Lithuanian's hymn, 1965; Hymn in honor of St.
Casimir, male voices, 197; 2 hymns in honor of
Our Lady's apparition in Siluva; Ave Maria;
Christmas carol, a cappella; Glory to the Lord,
baritone solo or unison with organ.
    Immaculate Heart Residence, East Island,
Glen Cove, NY 11542

BUDRIUNUS, BRONIUS
    b. Pabirze, Lith., 29 July 1909; U.S. citizen
1954. Studied at the School of Music and Cons.

in Kaunas, 1925-38, in Vilnius, 1943-44; with Franz Haberl and G. V. Albrecht in Germany, 1946-49. He was teacher and conductor in Lithuania, 1933-44, in Germany, 1943-49, and in Detroit, 1949-53. Since 1953 he has been organist and choirmaster, St. Casimir's Church, Los Angeles, and a private teacher of piano and voice.

WORKS: CHAMBER MUSIC: Lament, violin and piano; string quartet; piano sonata; CHORUS: The land of my forefathers; Homeland; Along the road of Lithuania's light; The legend of the land of Amber; more than 60 published songs and arrangements of Lithuanian folk songs.

2620 Griffith Park Blvd., Los Angeles, CA 90039

BUEBENDORF, FRANCIS
b. New York, N.Y., 21 Feb. 1912. Studied with Philip James, New York Univ., A.B. 1933; with Albert Stoessel and Bernard Wagenaar, Juilliard School, 1933-37; with Douglas Moore and Paul Henry Lang, Columbia Univ., Ed.D. 1945; conducting with Pierre Monteux, 1958. At Juilliard he held fellowships in composition and conducting. He was faculty member, Trinity Univ., 1945-47; professor, Univ. of Missouri Cons., 1947-77; conductor, Cons. Orch., 1947-57, Kansas City Civic Ballet, 1959-61, and Univ. String Orch., 1962-77.

WORKS: THEATRE: music for 2 children's plays, Call for the goochoo bird and Journey to Canterbury; ORCHESTRA: Passacaglia; Aladdin fantasy; Prelude and fugue, string orch.; Sarabande and gigue, solo guitar and strings; Adagio and rondo, solo trombone, strings, percussion; CHAMBER MUSIC: Scherzo, flute and piano; 3 pieces, viola and piano; Theme and variations, chamber group and tape recorder; many choral and chamber works.

9716 Jarboe St., Kansas City, MO 64114

BUECHE, GREGORY A.
b. Tipton, Kans., 13 Feb. 1903. Studied with Gustave Soderlund and Charles Skilton, Kansas Univ., B.M.; with Rudolph Ganz and Olaf Anderson, Chicago Musical Coll., M.M. He taught in public schools in Kansas and Colorado, 1927-37; was head of music dept., Colorado State Univ., from 1937 to retirement.

WORKS: BAND: Heritage, with chorus; CHAMBER MUSIC: Rondino, flute and piano; Prelude and chorale, piano; Vestiges, piano; Dollin' up Dolly.

BUFFHAM, CHARLES ALLEN
b. Grand Rapids, Mich., 23 Dec. 1940. Studied with Marshall Barnes and Mark Walker, Ohio State Univ., M.M. 1966. He was instructor, Cedarville Coll., Ohio, 1965-66; from 1966, at Grand Rapids Jr. Coll.

WORKS: THEATRE: A little season, music drama, 1971; BAND: David, king of Israel; Prelude, with chorus, 1971; CHAMBER MUSIC: Thematic study, piano, 1964; Invention, piano; 3 songs, voice and piano; Nonet for winds and strings, woodwind quintet, string quartet; Jericho, trumpet, horn, trombone; CHORUS: At a

window, Sandburg text; The journey of the Magi, T. S. Eliot text; 6 contemporary psalm settings.
459 Eleanor N.E., Grand Rapids, MI 49505

BUFFKINS, ARCHIE LEE
b. Memphis, Tenn. Studied at Jackson State Coll., B.S.; Columbia Univ., M.A., Ed.D. In 1963 he was on the faculty, Kentucky State Univ., Frankfort, Ky.

WORKS: CHAMBER MUSIC: Prelude and fugue, clarinet, 1961; piano sonata, 1962; Toccata for organ, 1962; string quartet, 1963; also choral works.

BUGATCH, SAMUEL
b. Bugachev, Russia, 20 June 1898; U.S. citizen 1923. Studied with Howard Thatcher, Gustave Strube, and Franz Bornschein at Peabody Cons. He was music director, Temple Adath Israel, Bronx, N.Y., 25 years, and at Beth Tfiloh Synagogue, Baltimore, 15 years, and conducted choruses in Philadelphia, Pa., and Trenton, Newark, and Lakewood, N.J. His works are chiefly vocal compositions, settings of such poets as Longfellow, Walter Scott, Lord Byron, and Yiddish and liturgical texts, comprising some 70 published pieces.
144-10 69th Ave., Flushing, NY 11367

BUGGERT, ROBERT W.
b. Chicago, Ill., 25 July 1918. Studied at Vandercook School of Music, B.M. 1938; Univ. of Michigan, M.M.Ed., 1947, Ph.D. 1956. He taught in public schools, 1939-43; then held faculty posts at Univ. of Wichita, Univ. of Oklahoma, Boston Univ., until settling at Northern Illinois Univ. in 1964 as professor and dean from 1971. He was percussion editor of The Instrumentalist, 1955-59; then editor of Contemporary Percussion Library.

WORKS: THEATRE: The night Thoreau spent in jail, DeKalb, Ill., Dec. 1970; PERCUSSION: Introduction and fugue, with piano, 1957; Toccata #1, 1969; Short overture, 1969; Dialogue, solo percussion and piano, 1969; Fanfare, song, and march, with piano, 1969; J-21557, 1969; Didiption #1 and #2, 1970. He is author of several books of teaching methods for percussion, and coauthor of The search for musical understanding, a textbook on general musical education.
1712 Judy Lane, DeKalb, IL 60115

BUHRMAN, ALBERT JOHN, JR. (BERT)
b. Springfield, Mo., 19 Apr. 1915. Studied at Univ. of Kansas. He was organist at radio stations in Kansas City; music director, KCMO; organist at theaters, 1936-40; staff organist, CBS radio and television, New York, 1940-63; from 1963, organist and radio-TV consultant, School of the Ozarks, Point Lookout, Mo. His folk opera, The Bald Knobbers, was performed at School of the Ozarks, 12 May 1968.

BULLARD, BOB
b. Oak Park, Ill., 22 Apr. 1927. Studied with Leo Sowerby at American Cons. He has been chairman, music dept., School District No. 87, Berkeley, Ill., from 1958.

BULOW, HARRY T.

WORKS: BAND: Cyrano de Bergerac, tone poem, 1964; Winter scene, 1969; Tahquamenon, 1970; Trumpet soliloquy, 1973.
5 Westleigh Court, Aurora, IL 60538

BULOW, HARRY T.
b. Des Moines, Iowa, 19 Feb. 1951. Studied with Merle Hogg and David Ward-Steinman, San Deigo State Univ., B.A.; with Alden Ashforth, Elaine Barkin, and Roy Travis, Univ. of California, Los Angeles, M.A., Ph.D. candidate in 1978. His awards include American Bandmasters Assoc.-Ostwald award, 1977; Premio Citta de Trieste, 1978; Sigvald Thompson award, 1978; 2 Atwater Kent awards in composition, 1977, 1978; Nat. Endowment for the Arts grant, 1978; Axel Stordahl commission, UCLA, 1978; first prize, Tucson Flute Club composers competition, 1978.
WORKS: ORCHESTRA: Pillars for large orchestra, 1978; BAND: Symphony for band, 1977; CHAMBER MUSIC: Movements for 9 instruments, 1978; Mutations, for flute, 1978; Chamber variations, 1978.
3132 Sawtelle Blvd. #2, Los Angeles, CA 90066

BUNCE, CORAJANE DIANE. See WARD, DIANE

BUNGER, RICHARD
b. Allentown, Pa., 1 June 1942. Studied at Oberlin Cons., B.M. 1964; Univ. of Illinois, M.M. 1966. His awards include grants from Martha Baird Rockefeller Fund; Bennington Composers Conf.; Toyota Corp.; Nissan Corp.; California State Univ. Professional Devel. Fund; Oberlin Coll.; Univ. of Illinois. He has held faculty posts at Queens Coll., 1965-68; Oberlin Coll., 1968-69; California State Univ., from 1970, professor and director of the Electronic Music and Recording Program.
WORKS: THEATRE: Oedipus rex, singers and tape; Good woman of Setzuan, singers, percussion, tape, slides; CHAMBER MUSIC: Syzygy, 2 pianos, organ, 5 winds, 2 strings; Variations on a sonata, string quartet; Abacus vocamen, tenor, baroque ensemble; Twice 5 for 2, violin and cello; Jiuta, chorus, recorder, guitar, percussion; PIANO: Hommage, a suite; Pianography, fantasy on a theme by Fibonacci, prepared piano and electronics; Money music, prepared piano; 3 bolts out of the blues, prepared piano; other works for solo voice, chorus, chamber ensemble, etc.
California State Coll., 1000 E. Victoria St., Dominguez Hills, CA 90747

BURCHAM, WAYNE
b. Burlington, Iowa, 27 Aug. 1943. Studied at Drake Univ.; with Gerhard Krapf, Univ. of Iowa; with Paul Fetler and Dominick Argento, Univ. of Minneapolis. He was winner of the American Guild of Organists composition award in 1971. He was director of music, Christ Church Lutheran, Minneapolis, 1967-71; and of Holy Nativity Lutheran Church, Minneapolis, from 1971.
WORKS: ORCHESTRA: The day time began, with chorus and soloists; CHAMBER MUSIC: Variations for bass clarinet; ORGAN: Veni creator spiritus,

1971; benediction.
13008 James Ave. S., Burnsville, MN 55337

BURGE, DAVID R.
b. Evanston, Ill., 25 Mar. 1930. Studied at Northwestern Univ., M.M. 1952; Eastman School of Music, D.M.A. 1956; Cherubini Cons., Florence, Italy, 1956-59. In 1978 and 1979, he received the Deems Taylor Award in music journalism for his columns in Contemporary Keyboard. He was faculty member, Univ. of Colorado, 1962-76; from 1976, at Eastman School.
WORKS: ORCHESTRA: Serenade, musical saw and orch., 1965; CHAMBER MUSIC: Eclipse II, piano; Aeolian music, flute, clarinet, violin, cello, piano; Sources III, clarinet and percussion; Sources IV, piano, 1969; A song of sixpence, soprano.
Eastman School of Music, 26 Gibbs St., Rochester, NY 14604

BURGSTAHLER, ELTON E.
b. Orland, Calif., 16 Sept. 1924. Studied at Univ. of the Pacific; at Millikin Univ.; with Gordon Binkerd, Univ. of Illinois. He received a Pi Kappa Lambda composition award in 1947. He taught in California schools, 1947-48; was faculty member, Millikin Univ., 1949-56; then named professor, Southwest Missouri Univ.; also church choir director from 1950.
WORKS: 3 chamber operas; a symphony; piano concerto; many band pieces; 13 saxophone quartets; 12 trombone quartets; solo pieces for all wind instruments; works for chorus including The ballad of Christmas, a cantata, and The truth about Christmas, cantata.
Southwest Missouri State University, Springfield, MO 65802

BURKE, JOHNNY
b. Antioch, Calif., 3 Oct. 1908; d. New York, N.Y., 25 Feb. 1964. Studied at Crane Coll. and Univ. of Wisconsin. He was staff member at music publishers in Chicago and New York; then under contract to Paramount in Hollywood.
WORKS: FILM SCORES: Pennies from heaven; Double or nothing; Sing, you sinners; Road to Singapore; A Connecticut yankee in King Arthur's court; Riding high; and others; also stage scores and many songs.

BURKE, SISTER LORETTO
b. Parkersburg, W.Va., 23 May 1922. Studied with Conrad Bernier and Thaddeus Jones, Catholic Univ. She taught in high schools in Cincinnati, Denver, Albuquerque, and Cleveland, 1952-70; has been chairman, music dept., Coll. of Mount St. Joseph, from 1971.
WORKS: ORCHESTRA: Symphonic dance suite; CHAMBER MUSIC: Pastorale, flute, oboe, clarinet; CHORUS: Valiant woman, cantata for women's voices; Psalm of praise, mixed voices and brass choir.
5776 Delhi Ave., Cincinnati, OH 45202

BURKE, RICHARD N.
b. New York, N.Y., 10 Dec. 1947. Studied with Ulysses Kay and Ruth Anderson at Hunter Coll.

He was instructor at Lehman Coll., CUNY, 1971-75; at Regis Coll., Weston, Mass., 1976-77.

WORKS: ORCHESTRA: <u>Missa l'homme armé</u>, with tape, 1973; CHAMBER MUSIC: <u>Landscapes</u>, voice and instruments, 1969; piano trio, 1969; cello sonata, 1973; ELECTRONIC: <u>Study #1</u>, 1971; <u>Untitled piece</u>, 1972.

BURKLEY, BRUCE HUNSIKER
Studied at Peabody Cons., artist's diploma 1962. He received a Ford Fellowship in 1961 to write music for school ensembles in Cincinnati; composition award, West Virginia School of Music, 1959.

WORKS: CHAMBER MUSIC: <u>3 preludes</u> for piano, 1959; violin sonata, 1960; <u>Image</u>, flute and strings, 1961.

BURLEIGH, CECIL
b. Wyoming, N.Y., 17 Apr. 1885; d. Madison, Wis., 28 July 1980. Studied at Chicago Musical Coll.; violin in Europe. He taught violin, Univ. of Wisconsin, 1921-55. His compositions include 3 symphonies (named <u>Creation</u>, <u>Prophecy</u>, <u>Revelation</u>); 3 violin concertos, 1915, 1919, 1928; 2 violin sonatas; violin pieces.

BURNHAM, ROY LA VERI
b. Ogden, Utah, 26 Jan. 1945. Studied at Seattle Univ., Univ. of Washington; privately with Lockrem Johnson in Seattle, Hugo Norden in Boston, and with J. Mandl in Germany.

WORKS: CHAMBER MUSIC: <u>3 dances</u>, piano; piano sonata; trio for oboe, bassoon, piano; cello sonata; concertino for piano and woodwinds.
288 Newbury St. #1-R, Boston, MA 02115

BURROUGHS, BOB L.
b. Tazewell, Va., 10 Mar. 1937. Studied with Warren M. Angell, Oklahoma Baptist Univ.; with Talmadge W. Dean, Southwestern Baptist Theol. Seminary; privately with William Reynolds and Ralph Carmichael. His awards include prizes in the Erskine Coll. anthem contest and in the Rochester, N.Y., Festival of Fine Arts. He held church posts to 1970, then was named to the faculty at Samford Univ.

WORKS: CHORUS: <u>Let all creation sing</u>; <u>My God, I thank Thee</u>; <u>Come, children, lift your voices</u>; and others.
Samford Univ., 800 Lakeshore Dr., Birmingham, AL 35209

BURT, CHARLES AYCOCK
b. Wilson, N.C., 24 Dec. 1943. Attended Atlantic Christian Coll., A.B.; Peabody Cons.; Eastman School of Music; North Carolina State Univ. Inst. in Computer Music. He has been band and choral director, Whitley High School, 1965-72, from 1972, at Ravenscroft School.

WORKS: FILM SCORES: <u>The goodliest land</u>; <u>The battle of Alamance</u>; <u>Tryon palace</u>; <u>The battle of Senator Sam</u>, 1973.
701 Fieldstone Court, Raleigh, NC 27609

BURT, GEORGE
b. San Francisco, Calif., 7 Oct. 1929. Studied with Andrew Imbrie, Univ. of California,

Berkeley; with Darius Milhaud and Leon Kirchner, Mills Coll.; with Roger Sessions, Milton Babbitt, Edward Cone, Princeton Univ.; and with György Ligeti in Vienna. He was instructor, Smith Coll., 1963-69; from 1969, professor, Univ. of Michigan.

WORKS: ORCHESTRA: Chamber concerto, 1959; <u>Introduction</u>, 1962; CHAMBER MUSIC: <u>4 short piano pieces</u>, 1957; 3 movements, string quartet; <u>4 studies</u>, percussion ensemble, 1965; <u>Canzona</u>, viola and cello, 1965; <u>Exit music</u>, 12 players, 1968; CHORUS: <u>New Hampshire</u>, double chorus of women's voices, 1965; <u>Threnody</u>, double men's chorus, 1967; <u>Time passes</u>, with piano, 1972; MIXED MEDIA: <u>Music for the New York hat</u>, synthesizer, piano, tape, film, 1972; <u>Improvization II</u>, synthesizer, piano, tape, 1972; <u>Sam's story</u>, synthesizer, piano, tape, film (written and directed by the composer), 1973.
School of Music, Univ. of Michigan, Ann Arbor, MI 48105

BURT, VIRGINIA
b. Minneapolis, Minn., 28 Apr. 1919. Studied at Minneapolis Coll. of Music. She is a private teacher and organist-choir director in Minneapolis. Her compositions include <u>Fanfare for a festive day</u>, chorus, organ, and brass.
4841 Drew Ave., S., Minneapolis, MN 55410

BURT, WARREN
b. Baltimore, Md., 10 Oct. 1949. Studied with William McKinley and Joel Chadabe, State Univ. of New York at Albany, B.A. 1971; with Robert Erickson, Pauline Oliveros, and Kenneth Gaburo, Univ. of California, San Diego, M.A. 1975. He was research assistant, Center for Music Experiment, UCSD, 1973-75; taught in Australia, 1975-78; then free-lance composer and performer.

WORKS: THEATRE: <u>Nighthawks</u>, 3½ hour video opera, 1976; <u>Stalin</u>, theatre for speaker and 3 cassettes of piano music, 1977; ORCHESTRA: <u>Drakula</u>, 1969; <u>Aardvarks V</u>, a symphony, 1977; CHAMBER MUSIC: <u>3 damnthings: aardvarks I, anteaters, amarillos</u>, string trio; PIANO: <u>Aardvarks II</u>, 1971; <u>Rubber duck domination</u>, 1974; <u>3 pieces</u>, 1977-78; ELECTRONIC: <u>Aardvark IV</u>, 1972-75; many other electronic pieces, completing the aardvark series.
30 Third St., Waterford, NY 12188

BURTON, ELDIN
b. Fitzgerald, Ga., 26 Oct. 1913. Studied at Atlanta Cons.; with Bernard Wagenaar at Juilliard School. His awards include scholarships at Atlanta Cons.; 3 fellowships at Juilliard; 10 ASCAP awards; New York Flute Club award, 1948. He was director, Georgia Cons., 1940-41.

WORKS: ORCHESTRA: piano concerto; flute concerto; CHAMBER MUSIC: violin sonatina, 1944; piano quintet, 1945; <u>Fiddlestick!</u>, violin and piano; flute sonatina, 1946; viola sonata, 1957; <u>Nonchalance</u>, piano; <u>Sarabande in G</u>, piano.
5050 Bayshore Rd., Sarasota, FL 33580

BURTON, JIM
Was trained in the visual arts. He designs and builds his own instruments with springs, amplified

BURTON, STEPHEN DOUGLAS

wires (played by resined fingertips), music box parts, and other available odds and ends. His compositions tend to run a full evening in length, as: 6 solos in the form of a pair for prepared piano; Phisiks of meta-quavers for wheels, wires, organ pipes, and instruments; Weedauwoo, Wyoming--a pastorale, in which details of a Wyoming map are projected on a screen; one performer reads the railroads, another sings the names of the towns, another plays the roads, and another plays the rivers. See Thom Johnson, New music, Musical America, Mar. 1975.

BURTON, STEPHEN DOUGLAS
b. Whittier, Calif., 24 Feb. 1943. Studied with Richard Hoffmann, Oberlin Coll., 1960-62; with Hans Werner Henze, Salzburg Mozarteum, 1962-64; with Jean E. Ivey, Peabody Cons., M.M. 1974. His awards include Nat. Fed. of Music Clubs awards, 1968; Devora Nadworny award, 1968; Guggenheim fellowships, 1969-70; Nat. Opera Inst. grant, 1975; Nat. Endowment for the Arts grants, 1974, 1977; annual ASCAP awards from 1976; many commissions. He was music director of the Munich Kemmerspiele, 1963-64; instructor, Catholic Univ., 1970-74; on faculty, George Mason Univ., from 1974.
WORKS: THEATRE: Duchess of Malfi, 3-act opera, 1975; Americana, 3 1-act operas, 1975; Finisterre, ballet, 1977; ORCHESTRA: Ode to a nightingale, soprano and orch., 1962, performed by Berlin Philharmonic in 1963; symphony #1, 1968; Stravinskiana, 1971; Dithyramb, 1972; Ariel, symphony #2, with baritone, Washington, 19 Oct. 1976; Songs of the Tulpehocken, tenor and orch., 1976; CHAMBER MUSIC: 2 string quartets, 1974, 1977; piano trio, 1977; 3 poems for flute solo; also choral works.
903 Plum St., S.W., Vienna, VA 22180

BUSCH, ADOLF
b. Siegen, Germany, 8 Aug. 1891; to U.S. 1939; d. Guilford, Vt., 9 June 1952. Studied violin at the Bonn and Cologne Conservatories; was concertmaster, Vienna Orchestra, 1912-18; toured as violin soloist; organized the Busch Quartet in 1919 and Busch Trio with his brother Hermann and son-in-law, Rudolf Serkin. In 1950, with his brother, the Moyse family, and Serkin, he founded the Marlboro Festival in Vermont. He composed for orchestra, chamber groups, and voice. His Psalm 130 for women's chorus, 2 violas, 2 cellos, and double bass, 1944, was premiered at Marlboro on 5 July 1975.

BUSH, GORDON
b. Detroit, Mich., 4 May 1943. Studied with Clifford Taylor at Temple Univ.; with Malcolm Williamson in London; and with Nicolas Flagello, Manhattan School of Music. He was organist-choirmaster, U.S. Merchant Marine Acad., 1963-65; from 1971, organist-choirmaster, Union Church of Bay Ridge and Congregation Beth Elohim, both in Brooklyn; and from 1974; music director, Bay Chamber Ensemble.
WORKS: THEATRE: The hermit, 1-act chamber opera, Brooklyn, 11 May 1973; The visitation, 1-act chamber opera; Revival, short music drama;

VOICE: A view of the manger, mixed voices and piano; 3 songs, soprano and piano, 1972; ORGAN: Homage, 1972; Prelude #1, prepared organ.
c/o Union Church of Bay Ridge, Brooklyn, NY 11220

BUSH, GRACE E.
b. Ludington, Mich., 25 Apr. 1884; d. California, 27 May 1967. She composed songs and piano pieces.

BUSH, IRVING R.
b. Los Angeles, Calif., 7 Apr. 1930. Attended California State Univ., Los Angeles, B.A., M.A., and was on faculty there, 1960-72; was also on faculty, Univ. of Southern California, 1962-68. He has played trumpet in the Los Angeles Philharmonic Orch., from 1962, and in motion picture, television, and recording orchestras.
WORKS: BRASS: Fanfare, 1969; Duet sessions; Top tones for trumpet; To the rescue, quintet.
14859 Jadestone Dr., Sherman Oaks, CA 91403

BUSS, HOWARD J.
b. Allentown, Pa., 6 Jan. 1951. Studied with Larry Nelson, West Chester State Coll., B.A.: with H. Owen Reed, Michigan State Univ., M.M.; with Thomas Frederickson and Salvatore Martirano, Univ. of Illinois, D.M.A. 1978. His awards include scholarships at West Chester State Coll., and Outstanding Musician award at Michigan State Univ. He was instructor, Univ. of Illinois, 1975-77; from 1978, on faculty, Florida Southern Coll.
WORKS: BAND: Trigon, 1977; WIND ENSEMBLE: Flourishes, 2 brass quintets; Chamber piece, 6 winds and percussion; Grand Lake morning, 5 winds and percussion; CHAMBER MUSIC: Camel music, solo trombone; Currents, percussion quartet; Nocturne, solo clarinet, 1978.
522½ W. Patterson Ave., Lakeland, FL 33803

BUTLER, A. L. (LOIS)
b. Stockdale, Tex., 25 May 1912. Studied at Southwestern Univ., B.M. 1932; with Cecil Burleigh, Univ. of Wisconsin; at Juilliard School, 1936-38; with Gustav Strube, Peabody Cons., M.M. 1941; with Kenneth MacKillop and Lawrence Berk, Berklee Coll.; with Nicolas Slonimsky, privately; with Conrad Bernier, Thaddeus Jones, and Emerson Meyers, Catholic Univ., M.M. 1956. Her awards included 2 from the Texas Mss Soc. and one from Texas Composers Guild. She played first violin, Baltimore Symphony Orch., 1939-43, and at radio station WBAL, 1945-46; has held positions as church organist from 1939.
WORKS: ORCHESTRA: Symphony of the hills, 1956; CHAMBER MUSIC: Rondo in e, violin and piano; Sonnet XLIII, voice and piano, text by Elizabeth Browning; CHORUS: The Christmas story; A Christmas carol.
8712 Colesville Rd., #4, Silver Spring, MD 20910

BUTLER, EUGENE SANDERS
b. Durant, Okla., 13 Jan. 1935. Studied with Elmer Schoettle, Univ. of Oklahoma; with Seth Bingham and Gerald Kemner, Univ. of Missouri,

D.M.A. 1974. He was named the 1970 Composer of
the Year by the Kansas Fed. of Music Clubs; has
received ASCAP awards, 1972-78. He was choral
director, Rockhurst Coll., 1971-73; from then on
faculty, Johnson County Community Coll.
WORKS: ORCHESTRA: Cortege; When lilacs
last in the dooryard bloomed, soloists, chorus,
orch., Kansas City, Oct. 1973; BAND: Fantasia
on an old French song; Paean of praise, brass
sextet; CHAMBER MUSIC: string quartet; Cantilena,
string quartet; CHORUS: Musick's empire, with
percussion; Praise Christ, alleluia; Sing, men
and angels; many other choral and instrumental
works.
9200 England, Overland Park, KS 66212

BUTLER, JACK H.
b. Augusta, Ga., 18 June 1924. Studied at
Erskine Coll. and Univ. of South Carolina. He
has taught in public schools and is church music
director and piano teacher.
WORKS: ORCHESTRA: The Gettysburg address,
chorus and orch.; PIANO: Lonely as a star; The
weary plowman.
11 East Dr., Atlanta, GA 30305

BUTTOLPH, DAVID
b. New York, N.Y., 3 Aug. 1902. Studied with
Percy Goetschius, Inst. of Musical Art; with
Clemens Krauss and Hugo Rohr at Vienna Music
Acad. He was conductor for NBC, 1927; music
director, WGY, 1932-33. From 1933 he was a film
composer for 20th Century-Fox, Paramount, Republic, and Universal Pictures. His film scores
included Western Union, This gun for hire, House
on 92nd Street, Somewhere in the night, Shock.

BUTTS, CARROL M.
b. Shenandoah, Iowa, 15 Apr. 1924. Studied with
Cecil Effinger, Univ. of Colorado; at Univ. of
Wyoming and Colorado State Univ. He has received
many commissions. He was band director, Bayard,
Nebr., 1950-56; band director and music supervisor, Torrington, Wyo., from 1956; chief arranger for Colorado State Univ. bands from 1972.
He has published more than 50 works for band and
instrumental ensembles, and several books on
band management.
Box 298, Torrington, WY 82240

BUYNISKI, RAYMOND J.
b. Bridgeport, Conn., 19 Sept. 1939. Studied
with Florence Grandland Galajikian, Sherwood
Music School, Chicago, 1960-62; with Arnold
Franchetti, Hartt Coll. of Music, 1964-66.
WORKS: ORCHESTRA: Overture, 1964; CHAMBER
MUSIC: string quartet; Valse-poeme, piano; and
many piano pieces in the neoromantic vein.
3589 Main St., Stratford, CT 06497

BUYS, PETER
b. Amsterdam, Neth., 11 Aug. 1881; to U.S. 1902;
d. Hagerstown, Md., 5 Mar. 1964. Wrote overtures, fantasies, and many marches for band. He
also wrote History of bands in the United States.

BYARD, JOHN A., JR. (JAKI)
b. Worcester, Mass., 15 June 1922. Pianist,

saxophonist, arranger, and composer, he has
appeared with many noted jazz groups; toured
Europe for the Berlin Jazz Festival; has given
concerts also in Japan and Australia. He has
taught privately since 1942; at the New England
Cons. from 1972; and at Hartt Coll. of Music
from 1977.
WORKS: JAZZ ENSEMBLE: Here to here;
Twelve; Hazy eve, 1973; Family suite, Boston,
29 Jan. 1974.
New England Conservatory, 290 Huntington
Ave., Boston, MA 02115

BYERS, ROXANA
b. San Francisco, Calif., 30 Oct. Studied with
Adolf Weidig, American Cons.; with George
Dandelot, Ecole Normale de Musique in Paris. An
honorary member of Sigma Alpha Iota, she received the SAI Rose of Honor and American Composers Award, 1973. She was founder of the
Hawaii Cons. of Music, Honolulu, in 1926; head
of the piano department, Pepperdine Coll.,
1945-53.
WORKS: SONGS: A woodland day, cycle of 5
songs for soprano; California, gem of the
nation's crown; When tears flow, 1974; KEYBOARD:
Reverie, organ; Fantasie on the themes of
Christmas, piano.
6171 Barrows Dr., Los Angeles, CA 90048

BYRD, DONALD T.
b. Detroit, Mich., 9 Dec. 1932. Studied with
Nadia Boulanger in Paris, 1963. He has played
trumpet at jazz festivals in Europe; taught at
High School of Music and Art, New York; at
Rutgers Univ.; Brooklyn Coll.; Howard Univ.;
1968-74; from 1977, at North Carolina Central
Univ.
WORKS: JAZZ ENSEMBLE: Cecile; Pure D. funk;
Shangri-la; The cat walk; Noah; Bossa.
Music Dept., North Carolina Central Univer-
sity, Durham, NC 27707

CACAVAS, JOHN
b. Aberdeen, S.Dak., 13 Aug. 1930. Studied with
Paul Hindemith, Robert Delaney, and Anthony
Donato at Northwestern Univ. He received a
Grammy award for Gallant men. He was director
of publication for Chappell and Co., 1965-70,
then settled in Hollywood as a film score composer.
WORKS: ORCHESTRA: Montage; Overture concertante; Western scenario; The day the orchestra played, with narrator; BAND: La bella Roma;
March of the golden brass; Overture in miniature;
Rhapsody; Symphonic prelude; Trumpeters three;
and some 1500 published works for orchestra,
band, chamber groups, etc.
c/o Bart/Levy, 6671 W. Sunset Blvd., Los
Angeles, CA 90028

CACIOPPO, GEORGE
b. Monroe, Mich., 24 Sept. 1926. Studied with
Ross Lee Finney, Univ. of Michigan, M.A. 1951;
with Roberto Gerhard, 1960; and with Leon
Kirchner at Tanglewood on a Rockefeller grant.
He was lecturer in composition, Univ. of Michigan,
1968-73; from 1961, has been broadcast engineer

CADMAN, CHARLES WAKEFIELD

at Univ. of Michigan broadcast station WUOM.
WORKS: Nocturne: in memoriam Bela Bartok, piano solo, 1951; Music for strings and 2 trumpets, 1952; string trio, 1960; Bestiary I: eingang, soprano and percussion, 1961; 2 worlds, soprano and percussion, 1962; pianopieces #1, #2, #3: Cassiopeia, 1963; Mod 3, flute, double bass, percussion, 1963; Moves upon silence, percussion and 2 amplified cymbals, 1963; The advance of the fungi, 8 winds, percussion, male chorus, 1964; Time on time in miracles, 4 winds, cello, piano, soprano, percussion, 1965; Holy Ghost vacuum or America faints, electric organ, 1966; Cassiopeia in New York, piano and tape, 1968; Cassiopeia in Grand Rapids, piano and tape, 1969; pianopiece #4: Informed sources, amplified pianos, 4 hands, ring modulators, filters, loudspeakers, light mixer, 1970.
Station WUOM, University of Michigan, Ann Arbor, MI 48104

CADMAN, CHARLES WAKEFIELD
b. Johnstown, Pa., 24 Dec. 1881; d. Los Angeles, 30 Dec. 1946. Studied composition with Emil Paur in Pittsburgh. He received an honorary doctorate in music from the Univ. of Southern California in 1924; in 1926, was named director of the music department. He made a study of the music of the American Indian and drew many of his themes from this source.
WORKS: OPERA: Shanewis, 1918; Garden of mystery, 1918; Sunset trail, operatic cantata, 1922; Witch of Salem, 1926; ORCHESTRA: The thunderbird, 1917; 3 moods; Dark dancers of the Mardi Gras, with piano solo, 1933; American suite, 1937; CHAMBER MUSIC: piano trio; violin sonata; CHORUS: Vision of Sir Launfal, cantata for male voices; many songs including From the land of the sky-blue water and At dawning.

CADZOW, DOROTHY. See HOKANSON, DOROTHY CADZOW

CAGE, JOHN
b. Los Angeles, Calif., 5 Sept. 1912. Attended Pomona Coll., 1928-30; studied composition with Adolph Weiss, Henry Cowell, and Arnold Schoenberg. He received a Guggenheim fellowship in 1948 for study in Paris and an award from the Nat. Acad. of Arts and Letters for having extended the boundaries of music through his work with percussion orchestras and his invention of the prepared piano. Other awards include first prize in the Woodstock Art Film Festival, 1951; election to the Nat. Inst. of Arts and Letters, 1968; grants from Thorne Music Found., 1967-69; and many commissions. He taught composition at New School for Social Research, New York, 1955-60; was music director for Merce Cunningham and Dance Company, New York, 1944-66; fellow, Center for Advanced Studies, Wesleyan Univ., 1960-61; composer-in-residence, Univ. of Cincinnati, 1967; research professor and associate, Center for Advanced Studies, Univ. of Illinois, 1967-69. In 1951 he organized a group of musicians and engineers to make music on magnetic tape; and in 1952, produced a theatrical event at Black Mountain Coll. considered by many to have been the first Happening.

WORKS: sonata for clarinet solo, 1933; 6 short inventions for 7 instruments, 1934; Construction in metal, 1937; Imaginary landscape #1 for 2 variable-speed phonograph turntables, muted piano, and cymbal, 1939; Double music for percussion (with Lou Harrison), 1941; Wonderful widow of 18 springs, voice and closed piano, 1942; Music for keyboard, piano, prepared piano, toy piano, 1935-48; Amores, prepared piano and percussion, 1943; She is asleep, voice and prepared piano, 1943; Perilous night, prepared piano, 1943-44; 3 dances, 2 amplified, prepared pianos, 1944-45; Sonatas and interludes for prepared pianos, 1946-48; 6 melodies, violin and piano, 1950; string quartet in 4 parts, 1950; Music for Marcel Duchamp, prepared piano, 1947; concerto for prepared piano and chamber orch., 1951; Williams mix, composed by throwing Chinese dice, 1952; 4 minutes and 33 seconds, silent music for piano in 4 movements, 1954; Music for carillon, 1954; 26' 1.1499", for a string player, 1955; piano concerto, 1957-58; Indeterminacy, narrator and piano; Aria, soprano and tape, 1958; Fontana mix, soprano and tape or tape alone, 1958; Cartridge music, 1960; Variations II-VII, 1961-66; Atlas eclipticalis, orchestra, 1961; Winter music; HPSCHD (with Lejaren Hiller) for 7 harpsichords and 52 computer-generated tapes, Univ. of Illinois, 16 May 1969; Cheap imitation, piano, 1969, a 35' piece for violin was later edited by Paul Zukofsky; Song books, solos for voice 3-92, premiered in Paris, Oct. 1970; 62 mesostics re Merce Cunningham, text sound piece, 1971; Etude Australis, piano, 1974-75; Music of changes, vol. I-IV, piano, 1974; Renga with apartment house 1776, orchestra with 4 vocal soloists, Boston, 29 Oct. 1976; Quartets I and II for 24 instruments, Brooklyn, 22 Feb. 1977. He is author of Silence, 1961; A year from Monday, 1968; M, 1973; coauthor with Hoover, The life and works of Virgil Thomson, 1958; with Knowles, Notations, 1969; with Long and Smith, Mushroom book, 1972; and author, Empty words, 1979.
107 Bank St., New York, NY 10014

CAILLET, LUCIEN
b. Dijon, France, 22 May 1891; U.S. citizen 1923. Studied at Dijon Cons. and at Philadelphia Musical Acad., D.M. He has been arranger and conductor; composed works for orchestra and film scores.
8231 43rd Ave., Kenosha, WI 53140

CAIN, JAMES
b. Lake City, Fla., 21 Sept. 1942. Studied with William Hoskins, Jacksonville Univ.; with Carlisle Floyd and John Boda, Florida State Univ. He has been head of the music department at Edison Coll.
WORKS: ORCHESTRA: Homage to Delius, 1966; symphony for string orch.; CHAMBER MUSIC: 7 preludes, piano; flute sonata, 1967; CHORUS: The Lord is my strength, 1969; Motet from markings, 1972.
Edison Community College, Ft. Myers, FL 33902

CAIN, NOBLE
b. Aurora, Ind., 25 Sept. 1896. Studied at
American Cons., B.M.; Univ. of Chicago, M.A.;
Friends Univ., B.A., honorary D.M.; Lawrence
Coll., honorary D.M. He was founder of the Senn
High School Chorus, Chicago, and the Chicago A
Cappella Choir; was choral director and producer,
NBC, 1932-39; guest conductor at schools, col-
leges, and music festivals.
WORKS: CHORUS: Christ in the world, ora-
torio; Evangeline; The king and the star; Paul
Revere's ride; Ode to America; Holy Lord God,
anthem; and many others; also arrangements of
spirituals and folk songs. He is author of the
book Choral music and its practice.

CALABRO, LOUIS
b. Brooklyn, N.Y., 1 Nov. 1926. Studied with
Vincent Persichetti at Juilliard School, 1948-53.
His awards include E. S. Coolidge chamber music
awards, 1952, 1953; first Richard Rodgers fellowship, 1953; Guggenheim fellowships, 1954,
1959; Vermont Council on the Arts grants, 1970,
1977; Nat. Endowment for the Arts grants, 1973,
1976; various Ford, Dollard, and Huber grants
and many commissions. He has been on the music
faculty at Bennington Coll. from 1955; founder
and music director of the Sage City (Vt.) Symphony from 1971.
WORKS: THEATRE: music for Hippolytus, 1969;
ORCHESTRA: concerto grosso for strings, 1950;
statement for orchestra, 1951; piano concerto,
1953; 3 symphonies, 1956, 1957, 1962; Dadacan-
tadada, blues singer and orch., 1964; Epitaphs,
with chorus, 1967; Latitude 15.09 N, longitude
108.5 E, oratorio, with chorus, 1970; triple
concerto, 3 cellos, 1971; Threnody, string orch.,
1973; Voyage, with chorus, 1975; CHAMBER MUSIC:
trio for clarinet, cello, piano, 1949; violin
sonata, 1953; Divertimento, woodwind quartet,
1954; 2 string quartets, 1954, 1968; Bodas de
Sangre, chamber group, 1955; cello sonata, unaccompanied, 1956; Motet for Paul, 4 cellos,
1970; Memoirs, bassoon and percussion, 1973;
The plight of the humble flea, solo marimba,
1975; Rare birds, solo flute and narrator, 1976;
Kusehani, 12 players, on themes of Alaskan
Chilgit Indians, 1976; 10 lyric pieces, 2 flutes,
1977; Eos, English horn and strings, 1977;
CHORUS: Metaphors, 50-part chorus, 1959; Rain
has fallen, women's voices, a cappella, 1959;
O clap your hands, a cappella, 1968; The floods
are risen, with brass, 1973; Lunarlied, with
strings, 1976; PIANO: sonatina, 1952; sonata,
1954; Monologues, 4 hands, 1957; Diversities,
1966; Variations, 1968; Divertissement, 1973;
also many songs, song cycles, other works in all
categories.
Bennington Coll., Bennington, VT 05201

CALDWELL, MARY ELZABETH (Mrs. Philip G.)
b. Tacoma, Wash., 1 Aug. 1909. Attended Univ.
of California, Berkeley, A.B.; studied privately
with Richard Schrey in Munich and Bernard
Wagenaar in New York, piano and organ with
Benjamin Moore in San Francisco. Her awards include honorary membership in Mu Phi Epsilon;
Outstanding Musician of the Year, Sigma Alpha
Iota, Pasadena. She has been organist-choir
director since 1933; at San Marino Community
Church from 1948.
WORKS: OPERA: The night of the star; A
gift of song and Pepito's golden flower, 2
children's operas performed at Kennedy Center,
Washington, 1 Apr. 1978; CHORUS: The little
lamb, text by Blake; Spring prayer, text by
Charles Hanson Towne; and 150 published vocal
works for all combinations of voices.
474 S. Arroyo Blvd., Pasadena, CA 91105

CALKER, DARRELL W.
b. Washington, D.C., 18 Feb. 1905; d. Malibu,
Calif., 20 Feb. 1964. Studied at Univ. of
Maryland, B.S., and at Curtis Inst.
WORKS: BALLET: Royal coachman; Quiet week;
Decameron; scores for Ballet Russe, Sadlers
Wells, and Ballet Russe de Monte Carlo; ORCHES-
TRA: Penguin Island; Golden land; FILM SCORES:
Adventure island; Bachelor's daughter; Albuquer-
que; El Paso; Geronimo; Savage drums.

CALLAHAN, JAMES P.
b. Fargo, N.Dak., 15 Jan. 1942. Studied with
Paul Fetler, Univ. of Minnesota; with Hans
Jelinek, Vienna Acad. of Music; organ and piano
with various teachers. He has been faculty
member, Coll. of St. Thomas, from 1968.
WORKS: ORCHESTRA: Metamorphosis, an overture, 1973; symphony #2 (Markings), with chorus
and baritone solo; BAND: overture; CHAMBER
MUSIC: etude and recitative, piano, 1973;
string quartet, 1974; violin sonata, St. Paul,
15 Nov. 1976; also choral works and organ pieces.
College of St. Thomas, 2115 Summit Ave.,
St. Paul, MN 55105

CALLAWAY, ANN
b. Washington, D.C., 28 Oct. 1949. Studied with
Alvin Etler at Smith Coll.; with George Crumb
and George Rochberg, Univ. of Pennsylvania, M.A.
1974. Her awards include a Fatman fellowship at
Smith, 1971; grants from N.Y. State Council on
the Arts and Nat. Endowment for the Arts, 1975;
and commissions. She has taught theory and composition summers at Walden School, Vershire, Vt.
WORKS: CHAMBER MUSIC: 4 elements, horn and
piano, 1975; sonata à tre, trumpet, horn, trombone, 1975; 7 dramatic episodes, flute, cello,
piano, 1976; Night patterns, soprano and chamber
orch., 1977; Besides this may, song cycle on
Dickinson poems, soprano, flute, piano, 1978.
219 East Ave., Saratoga Springs, NY 12866

CALLAWAY, PAUL SMITH
b. Atlanta, Ill., 16 Aug. 1909. Studied at
Westminster Coll., Fulton, Mo., 1927-29, honorary doctorate, 1959; honorary doctorate, Washington Coll., 1967. He was organist, Washington
Cathedral (D.C.), 1939-77; was on faculty,
Peabody Cons., 1953-57; has been guest choral,
orchestra, and opera conductor.
WORKS: CHORUS: Hymn of heavenly love,
1935; Office of the Holy Communion, 1945; Hark,
the glad sound, 1946.
2230 Decatur Pl., Washington, DC 20008

CAMERON, RICHARD

CAMERON, RICHARD
b. Cleveland, Ohio, 23 Sept. 1943. Studied at
Oberlin Coll.; with Bernhard Heiden, Iannis
Xenakis, and John Eaton, Indiana Univ., B.M.
1968, M.M. 1971. He held a Wurlitzer Found.
fellowship at Taos, N.Mex., 1976. He was faculty
member, Unvi. of Wisconsin, 1974-75; from 1978
at State Univ. of New York at Purchase. He was
cofounder/codirector, "Friends of American Music,
Inc.," Taos, N.Mex., 1974-; and codirector of
the New Mexico Music Festival at Taos, 1978-79.
    WORKS: CHAMBER MUSIC: Variations and
Liebestod, clarinet, 1969; Memarie, soprano solo,
1970; The awakening, American Indian poem, narrator and chamber ensemble, 1970; Through a
glass darkly, soprano, baritone, 6 instruments,
1974; Homage to Picasso, chamber ensemble and
dancers, 1976; Kyrie (Mantra), 3 flutes, 1976;
Kyrie (Mantra) for flute and prepared piano or
guitar; CHORUS: ERODOS, with percussion, 1972.
    Winkler's Farm, Towners Rd., Carmel, NY
10512

CAMPBELL, ARTHUR
b. Lexington, Mo., 4 Apr. 1922. Studied with
Alec Rowley in London; with David Van Vactor in
Kansas City; with Howard Hanson and Bernard
Rogers, Eastman School of Music; with Quincy
Porter at Yale Univ. He received the Harvey
Gaul award in 1958. He taught at Monmouth Coll.,
1949-52; has been faculty member, St. Olaf Coll.,
from 1952.
    WORKS: ORCHESTRA: symphony, 1958; VOICE:
Whither shall I go?, an anthem, 1966; God's
grandeur, song cycle for high voice and piano;
1966; Prayers from the ark, cantata for women's
voices; KEYBOARD: 3 piano pieces; ELECTRONIC:
Pillars, organ and tape; Things to come, electronic music for ballet, 1974; Timbres, trombone,
piano, tape, 1977; The 2 Marys, ballet music for
mixed voices, saxophone, organ, and tape, 1978.
    Rte. 1, Northfield, MN 55057

CAMPBELL, CHARLES JOSEPH
b. Cleveland, Ohio, 8 Aug. 1930. Studied with
Herbert Elwell and Marcel Dick, Cleveland Inst.
of Music; at Western Reserve Univ.; and Univ. of
Miami. His faculty and administrative positions
have included Cleveland Inst. of Music, 1955-57;
Cleveland Music School Settlement, 1958-61; Wilmington Music School, 1961-66; Auburn Univ.,
1966-68; Virginia Commonwealth Univ., 1970-72;
from 1972, Univ. of Miami.
    WORKS: ORCHESTRA: 2 symphonies; 2 over-
tures; CHAMBER MUSIC: numerous pieces for woodwind and brass ensembles; song cycles; piano
works; solo etudes for trombone and tuba.
    9781 Colonial Dr., Miami, FL 33157

CAMPBELL, HENRY
b. Osceola, Nebr., 13 Nov. 1926. Studied with
Burrill Phillips and Bernard Rogers, Eastman
School of Music, B.M. 1948, M.M. 1949; with
George McKay, Univ. of Washington; privately with
Julius Gold in Los Angeles. He has received
awards from the Montana String Teachers Assoc.;
J. Fischer Bros. Centennial composition contest;
Music Teachers Nat. Assoc.; and Montana State

Music Teachers Assoc. He has been faculty member, Montana State Univ., from 1949.
    WORKS: ORCHESTRA: Sinfonia non troppo
serioso; Waltz--then march; CHAMBER MUSIC:
Diversion, clarinet, viola, piano; Many happy
returns, string quartet; piano sonata, 4 hands;
Folk song, piano and strings; Grass roots ballad,
tenor or baritone and piano; CHORUS: Folk song
suite; Balletto; Make we joy; also short piano
pieces and orchestral works.
    515 S. Grand Ave., Bozeman, MT 59715

CAMPBELL-TIPTON, LOUIS
b. Chicago, Ill., 21 Nov. 1877; d. Paris, 1 May
1921. Studied in Chicago, Boston, and Leipzig;
lived in Paris from 1910.
    WORKS: CHAMBER MUSIC: Suite pastorale,
violin and piano; PIANO: Heroic sonata; Sea
lyrics; The 4 seasons; a suite; and songs.

CAMPBELL-WATSON, FRANK
b. New York, N.Y., 22 Jan. 1898. Studied at
Univ. of Leipzig, B.A.; Leipzig Cons., M.A.,
D.M.; with Max Reger, Karl Straube, Hans Sitt,
Theodore Spiering, Walter Rothwell, Nicholas
Elsenheimer. He was made Knight Commander,
Order of St. Gregory the Great, by Pope John
XXIII in 1961. He has been orangist-choirmaster
in New Jersey and New York, 1920-52; organist
and composer-in-residence, Church of St. Paul
the Apostle (Paulist Choristers), N.Y., 1953-71.
He also been editor-in-chief, Univ. Society,
1925-32; Music Publishers Holding Corp., 1932-
65; Benziger Editions, 1965-68; Carl Fischer,
1968-71.
    WORKS: ORCHESTRA: 2 symphonies; BAND: a
symphony; Cotton moon, overture; concerto for
organ and symphonic band; CHAMBER MUSIC: Divertimento, 8 woodwinds; violin sonata; Petite
suite, 4 violins; CHORUS: 3 Latin masses; 3
English masses; 15 liturgical motets; 2 extended
choral and instrumental processions; 18 mass
propers; 5 liturgical choral settings; secular
works; ORGAN: Meditation on Salve Regina;
praeludium on Puer natus est; praeludium on
Rorate caeli; Chant du nuit; Phantomesque. He is
author of a textbook, Modern elementary harmony.
    262 Quaker Rd., Pomona, NY 10970

CAMPO, FRANK
b. New York, N.Y., 4 Feb. 1927. Studied with
Ingolf Dahl and Leon Kirchner in Los Angeles;
with Arthur Honneger in Paris; and Goffredo
Petrassi in Rome. His awards include a Fulbright
fellowship, 1957; BMI Composers awatd, 1958;
Screen Composers award, 1966; Nat. Fed. of Music
Clubs award of Merit, 1975. He has held faculty
posts at Univ. of Southern California, 1965-67;
California State Univ., Fullerton, 1966-67; from
1967, California State Univ., Northridge.
    WORKS: OPERA: The mirror, to his own
libretto; ORCHESTRA: Alpine holiday overture;
7 dialogues; concerto grosso; Blue; Untitled;
Due quadri Romani; concerto for bassoon and
strings; WIND ENSEMBLE: Music for Agamemnon,
band; suite for brass; Capriccio for winds;
CHAMBER MUSIC: symphony for chamber orch.;
Partita for 2 chamber orch.; Kinesis, clarinet

and piano, 1950; 5 pieces for 5 winds, 1958; concertino for 3 clarinets and piano; Madrigals, brass quintet; violin sonata, 1959; Commedie, trombone and percussion; Dualidad, bass clarinet and percussion; Times, solo trumpet; Tres cubito, flute, viola, percussion; Duet for equal trumpets; Preludes for flute, clarinet, guitar; Elegy concerto, violin and chamber orchestra; Commedie II, trumpet, piano, tape; also works for voice.
    12336 Milbank St., Studio City, CA 91604

CANBY, EDWARD TATNALL
    b. 1912. The interminable farewell, a canonic joke for chorus, 1954.
    780 Greenwich, New York, NY 10014

CANDLYN, T. F. H.
    b. England, 17 Dec. 1892; d. Point Lookout, N.Y., 16 Dec. 1964. He served in the U.S. Army in World War I; was head of music department, State Univ. of New York at Albany, 1919-43; organist at St. Paul's Church, Albany. He published many works for organ and chorus.

CANNING, THOMAS
    b. 1911. Fantasy on a hymn by Justin Morgan, for string quartet solo, string quartet 2, and string orch.; 3 old nursery rhymes, for chorus.
    School of Music, West Virginia University, Morgantown, WV 26506

CANNON, DWIGHT
    b. Pomona, Calif., 6 July 1932. Studied with Alexander Tcherepnin and Leon Stein in Chicago; with Robert Erickson, Pauline Oliveros, Kenneth Gaburo, and Roger Reynolds in San Diego. He has played trumpet with CBS-TV in Chicago, and with recording and broadcast orchestras in New York and Los Angeles; is conductor of orchestras, jazz ensembles, choirs, and bands; also faculty member, San Jose State Univ.
    WORKS: Chronometers, percussion ensemble; music for 1-13 trumpets, 4-channel tape, and 31 helium-filled balloons; Ex pluribus unum, jazz ensemble, vocals, dancers; C-in, jazz ensemble. These works, the composer says, are sonic and visual designs.
    Music Dept., San Jose State University, San Jose, CA 95192

CANTRELL, BYRON
    b. Brooklyn, N.Y., 14 Nov. 1919. Studied with Marion Bauer and Philip James, New York Univ.; Lukas Foss and John Vincent, Univ. of California, Los Angeles; studied conducting with Leon Barzin, Emerson Buckley, and Serge Koussevitzky. He won second prize in the Los Angeles Philharmonic composition contest, 1944. He has held faculty positions at Tahoe Paradise Coll., 1967-69; California State Univ., Fullerton, 1969-70; El Camino Coll., 1971-72; International Community Coll., from 1972. He has been director, Young People's Opera Company, Culver City, from 1966; music critic and editor in the Los Angeles area.
    WORKS: THEATRE: music for Raisins and almonds; ORCHESTRA: 3 symphonic sketches of Mark Twain; A jubilee overture; A victory over-

ture; piano concerto; CHORUS: The land of heart's desire; Satires of circumstance; A tooth for Paul Revere; What child is this; Variations on a spiritual; Variations on General Wolfe's song; Now welcum sumer; At Casterbridge Fair; songs and piano pieces.
    822 N. Occidental Blvd., Los Angeles, CA 90026

CANTRICK, ROBERT B.
    b. Monroe, Mich., 8 Dec. 1917. Studied at Eastman School of Music, A.B. 1938, M.A. 1946; with Philip Bezanson, State Univ. of Iowa, Ph.D. 1959; conducting with George Szell, 1951-52. His awards include Birmingham Festival of Arts award, 1960; fellowships from Ford Found., Carnegie Found., and State Univ. of New York Research Found. He has held teaching and administrative posts at Furman Univ., 1946-61; Carnegie Inst. of Technology, 1952-55; Cornell Coll., 1955-59; Jacksonville State Coll., 1959-64; Wisconsin State Univ., 1964-67; and from 1967, State Univ. Coll at Buffalo.
    WORKS: ORCHESTRA: A pair of masks, 1960; CHAMBER MUSIC: string trio, 1959; woodwind quintet, 1960; 3 mimes, flute and voice, 1964; The friendly beasts, song cycle for medium voice, 1974; Elegy, cantata for 4 vocalists and 4 instrumentalists, 1978.
    159 Bidwell Parkway, Buffalo, NY 14222

CAPANNA, ROBERT
    b. Camden, N.J., 7 July 1952. Studied with Joseph Castaldo and Theodore Antoniou, Philadelphia Musical Acad.; with Jacob Bruckman at Tanglewood. His awards include the Koussevitzky composition prize, 1974; Music Teachers Nat. Assoc. award; Bruno Maderna Memorial fellowship. He has held teaching and administrative posts at Philadelphia Musical Acad., 1974-76; Amherst Music Center, Raymond, Maine, 1976-77; Camden Settlement Music School, from 1976.
    WORKS: CHAMBER MUSIC: concerto for chamber orch., 1974; Phorminx, harp; Rota, percussion quartet; 3 trios for various instruments; Phorminx 2, guitar; sextet for 2 winds, 2 strings, harp, piano; Remembrance, solo bassoon; songs for tenor and piano; 3 songs for chorus, tenor solo, violin solo, and orch.
    204 E. Woodlawn Ave., Maple Shade, NJ 08052

CAPERTON, FLORENCE TAIT (Mrs. G. A. Dornin)
    b. Amherst Co., Va., 21 Apr. 1886. Studied violin at Peabody Cons.; composition with W. Critser in Pittsburgh. She was soloist and concertmistress with the Norfolk Symph. Orch., 1902-4. Her compositions are chiefly for chorus; published anthems include Come, little children and Rejoice, ye children.
    137 Lafayette St., Orange, VA 22960

CARAVAN, RONALD L.
    b. Pottsville, Pa., 20 Nov. 1946. Studied at Eastman School of Music, M.A. 1973, D.M.A. in music education 1974. He is clarinetist and saxophonist and taught privately 1971-74; at New York State Univ. Colleges from 1975, Fredonia from 1978. His D.M.A. dissertation, "Extensions

CARBONARA, GERARD

of technique for clarinet and saxophone," is a
recognized reference for unconventional playing
techniques such as multiphonics, quarter tones,
timbre variations, etc. His compositions are
chiefly for these instruments.

WORKS: CHAMBER MUSIC: Montage I, oboe,
clarinet, cello, 1973; 3 pieces for clarinet,
1973; 3 pieces for saxophone, 1973; Sketch, alto
saxophone, 1973; Excursions, A clarinet, 1974;
Montage II, bassoon and piano, 1975; Monologue,
alto saxophone, 1975; 5 duets for 1 clarinetist,
1976; Montage III, soprano and alto saxophones,
violin, 1978; Canzona, saxophone quartet, 1979;
also graded sets.

702 Highland St., Fulton, NY 13069

CARBONARA, GERARD
b. New York, N.Y., 8 Dec. 1886; d. Sherman Oaks,
Calif., 11 Jan. 1959. Studied at National Cons.,
New York, and at Naples Cons., Italy; also violin
with Martucci Dworzak. He was opera coach in
Milan, 1910; concert violinist and opera conductor, Europe and U.S.; then music director and
composer for film studios in Hollywood.

WORKS OPERA: Armand; ORCHESTRA: Ode to
nature, symphonic poem; Concerto orientale, violin and orch.; CHAMBER MUSIC: Scherzetto fantasia, wind quintet; many violin pieces, piano
pieces, songs; FILM SCORES: Stage coach, Academy
award, 1940; The Kansan; The promised land; and
others.

CARE, ROSS
b. Harrisburg, Pa., 14 Aug. 1941. Studied at
West Chester State Coll., Pa.; privately with
Harold Boatrite in Philadelphia and Ben Weber in
New York. From 1968 he has been music director
in various seasons for Actors' Company of Pennsylvania.

WORKS: THEATRE: Through the looking glass,
musical after Lewis Carroll, 1978; CHAMBER MUSIC:
Suite Francaise, flute and strings; VOICE: 4
songs from "Chamber Music" of James Joyce, voice,
strings, piano; 3 songs on poems of Walter de la
Mare, soprano and flute; 4 songs on poems of
Elizabeth Pevear, medium voice and piano; ORGAN:
Canon and allegro; FILM SCORES: Otto Messmer
and Felix the Cat, documentary film on CBS-TV,
Nov. 1978; Crepe flower, film by Grant Smith.

131 College Ave., Lancaster, PA 17603

CAREW, MICHAEL
b. Bronxville, N.Y., 4 Oct. 1951. Attended
Ripon Coll., B.A. 1973, studying modulor electronic music and light with Erwin Breithaupt.
Otherwise he is largely self-taught, using
Le Corbusier's system of proportions in ordering
his electronic music and developing what he calls
continuums--overlapping, omnidirectional harmon-
ious patterns--to replace scales. He uses a
modular system to create time ordinations of
sound, and thus breaks out of traditional metri-
cal time altogether into a system more integral
to tape speeds. He is mainly interested now in
electronic music, but has composed classical,
folk, blues, rock, acid rock, and jazz. In 1978
he was also engaged in study of urban planning
at Univ. of Wisconsin.

WORKS: Modulor work #1; The turning of the
age, electronic music and light; First full
cycle, electronic acid jazz; New rising sun,
electronic acid jazz; Homage to Corbu, electronic, folk, and music concrete; Movement in
dance, electronic; Impressions of a N.Y. theatre
crowd filing in, music concrete.

c/o F. J. Carew, 92 Oregon Ave., Bronxville,
NY 10708

CAREY, DAVID
b. Pittsburgh, Pa., 14 Feb. 1926. Studied at
Pittsburgh Musical Inst.; Univ. of Pittsburgh;
Manhattan School of Music. He is a television
composer, conductor, pianist, and arranger.

WORKS: ORCHESTRA: suite for xylophone and
orch.; CHAMBER MUSIC: Inventions, for piano;
flute sonata; sonata for piano, 4 hands; 8
etudes for 2 percussionists; and popular songs.

CARFAGNO, SIMON ALBERT
b. Scottdale, Pa., 8 Jan. 1906. Studied privately with Arnold Schoenberg and Nadia Boulanger.
He was violinist with the Los Angeles Philharmonic Orch., 1943-44; with film studios, 1945-
57; conductor, Chico Symph. Orch., 1962-67; on
faculty, Chico State Univ., 1962-73.

WORKS: ORCHESTRA: Gettysburg, 1863, cantata for chorus, soloists, orch.; CHAMBER MUSIC:
string trio; Salmagundi suite, violin and piano;
Toccata, piano; nonet (dedicated to Schoenberg),
flute, oboe, clarinet, bassoon, viola, and 4
pitched drums; flute sonata.

5037 Russell Dr., Paradise, CA 95969

CARL, OTTILLA M. (TOMMIE)
b. Marion, Kans., 23 Sept. 1921. Studied organ
in Washington, Munich, and at Hochschule für
Musik, Frankfurt; composition with Lloyd Ultan,
American Univ., B.A., M.A. She has been instructor at American Univ.

WORKS: ELECTRONIC: Chromosynthesis; Abstractions; Bells; Illusions; Desert sands; Futurama
I and II.

12 Mel Mara Dr., Oxon Hill, MD 20021

CARLOS, WALTER
b. Pawtucket, R.I., 14 Nov. 1939. Studied with
Ron Nelson at Brown Univ., B.M. 1962; with Otto
Luening, Vladimir Ussachevsky, and Jack Beeson,
Columbia Univ., M.A. 1965. He was a Seidl
fellow, 1963-64, and won 3 Grammy awards and a
Gold Record for Switched on Bach, 1969. He has
been president of Trans-Electronic Prod., Inc.,
since 1967. In 1977 he underwent a sex-change
operation and has changed his name from Walter
to Wendy.

WORKS: THEATRE: Noah, an opera with organ
and electric organ accompaniment, 1964-65; background music for Kubrick's A clockwork orange,
1971; ORCHESTRA: piano concerto, 1961; CHAMBER
MUSIC: string quartet, 1963; string sextet,
1965; ELECTRONIC: 3 pieces for instruments and
tape (piano, 1962, flute, 1963, piano, 1964);
Dialogues, piano and 2 loudspeakers, 1963; Well-
tempered synthesizer; Variations, flute and electronic sound, 1964; Timesteps, synthesizer,
1970-71; Sonic seasonings, 1971-72; and other

works for orchestra, solo instruments, and electronic tapes.

133 W. 87th St., New York, NY 10024

CARMICHAEL, HOAGY
b. Bloomington, Ind., 22 Nov. 1899; d. Rancho Mirage, Calif. 27 Dec. 1981. Studied law at Indiana Univ., earning an L.L.B., but soon abandoned law for song writing. His enormously successful songs include Stardust, Georgia on my mind, In the still of the night, Ol' buttermilk sky, and many others.

CARMINES, ALVIN A. (AL)
b. Hampton, Va., 1938. Studied at Swarthmore Coll.; Union Theological Seminary; has won 4 Obie awards; is minister of Judson Memorial Church, New York. Son of a harmonica-playing sea captain, he has composed more than 60 extremely successful shows since 1961; presented a Town Hall recital of his works in April 1972. Some of his later works are: Joan, performed as an opera, New York, Nov.-Dec. 1971, revised as a musical, opened at Circus on the Square, 19 June 1972; A look at the fifties, a running commentary on a baseball game, 1973; The faggots, oratorio, New York, Apr.-May 1973; The duel, an opera, commissioned by the Metropolitan Opera Guild, premiere, Brooklyn Acad., 24 Apr. 1974; music for Gertrude Stein's plays: What happened, In circles, and Listen to me, New York, Oct. 1974; and Christmas rappings, an annual show.
Judson Memorial Church, 55 Washington Sq., New York, NY 10012

CARMONA, PAUL BERNARD
b. Los Angeles, Calif., 11 Sept. 1947. Studied at Loyola Univ., Los Angeles, B.A. 1969; with Leroy Southers, Univ. of Southern California. He was organist-choirmaster in Los Angeles, 1966-71; from 1971, at St. James Cathedral, Seattle.
WORKS: VOCAL: 3 art songs for soprano and piano; Cry of a lone bird (Ashford), Gone (Sandburg), Prayers of steel (Sandburg); Mass in honor of St. James the Apostle, choir, congregation, orch., Seattle, 25 Dec. 1973; ORGAN: Fanfare, interlude, and toccata on Lucis Creator Optime, 1970.
623 19th Ave. E., Seattle, WA 98112

CARPENTER, HOWARD R.
b. Natural Bridge, N.Y., 11 Oct. 1919. Studied at State Univ. Coll., Potsdam, B.S. 1942; at Univ. of Alabama, B.M. 1947; with Howard Hanson, Bernard Rogers, Herbert Elwell, and Wayne Barlow at Eastman School of Music, M.M. 1948, Ph.D. 1953. His symphony in D was selected as an outstanding work at the Southern Composers' League symposium in 1954. He has been professor, Western Kentucky Univ., from 1953.
WORKS: ORCHESTRA: symphony; poem; VOCAL: Luke Havergal, soprano and piano; PIANO: sonata; allegro.
1730 Chestnut St., Bowling Green, KY 42101

CARPENTER, JOHN ALDEN
b. Park Ridge, Ill., 28 Feb. 1876; d. Chicago, 26 Apr. 1951. Studied with John Knowles Paine at Harvard Univ., B.A. 1897, honorary M.A. 1922; with Bernhard Ziehn in Chicago and with Sir Edward Elgar. His awards include honorary doctorates from Univ. of Wisconsin and Northwestern Univ.; Nat. Inst. of Arts and Letters award, 1947. He was a business executive in Chicago, 1909-36, then devoted full time to composition.
WORKS: BALLET: Birthday of the Infanta, 1919; Krazy Kat, 1921; Skyscrapers, 1925; ORCHESTRA: Adventures in a perambulator, 1915; piano concertino, 1916; 3 symphonies, 1917, 1940, 1942; A pilgrim vision, 1920; Patterns, piano and orch., 1932; Song of faith, chorus and orch., 1932; Sea drift, symphonic poem, 1933; Danza, 1935; violin concerto, 1936; Song of Freedom, chorus and orch., 1941; The anxious bugler, 1943; The 7 ages, 1945; Carmel concerto, 1948; CHAMBER MUSIC: violin sonata, 1912; string quartet, 1928; piano quintet, 1934; The player queen, piano; SONGS: Improving songs for anxious children, 1904; Gitanjali, song cycle on poems of Tagore, 1913; Water colors, 4 Chinese songs with chamber orch., 1918; many other songs and piano pieces.

CARPENTER, KURT
b. Ann Arbor, Mich., 15 Nov. 1948. Studied with Ross Lee Finney, Leslie Bassett, and George Balch Wilson, Univ. of Michigan, B.M. 1970, M.M. 1971; with George Crumb, Leon Barzin, and Leonard Bernstein at Tanglewood. His awards include BMI Young Composer awards, 1968, 1971; Koussevitzky prize in composition, 1970; American Music Center-Composer Alliance grant, 1971. He is vice-president and treasurer of The Competition Inc., and a free-lance composer.
WORKS: OPERA: The new harmony opera (with Russell Peck); ORCHESTRA: Abraxas, 1970; Venus probe, 1971; Who killed Cock Robin?, narrator and orch. (with Peck and Blcich), commissioned by New Orleans Philharmonic and played there 12 times in 1973; many piano and chamber music works, and 73 songs.

CARR, ALBERT LEE
b. Wagoner, Okla., 16 June 1929. Studied with Robert Beadell, Univ. of Nebraska. He won a Pi Kappa Lambda composition award in 1959; has been public school music teacher from 1956.
WORKS: CHORUS: Innocence; 3 years she grew in sun and shower; Christo paremus canticum; She dwelt among untrodden ways; Why are the roses so pale; All under the willow tree.

CARR, ARTHUR
b. Pontiac, Mich., 29 Feb. 1908. Studied with David Stanley Smith and Richard Donovan at Yale Univ.; with Halsey Stevens, Univ. of Southern California, M.M. 1947. During World War II he was a bandmaster in the U.S. Army.
WORKS: THEATRE: Captain Jupiter, comic opera, 1939; ORCHESTRA: Celtic rondo, 1941; CHAMBER MUSIC: Theme varie, string quartet; Oriental miniatures, 5 songs for high voice; other songs, piano pieces.

CARRAGAN, MARTHA BECK. See BECK, MARTHA

CARREAU, MARGARET STIVER (Mrs. Robert)
b. Bedford, Pa., 23 Jan. 1899. Studied piano in
New York, 1916-21. She was rehearsal and audition pianist for Irving Berlin's Music Box Revues,
1922-24; accompanist for John Charles Thomas,
1943-52. Thomas introduced her Pastures of the
soul on the "Bell Telephone Hour."
WORKS: SONGS: Thy heart and the sea; You
and I together; Sea nocturne; Comparisons; Pastures of the soul; Eventide; April fool; Query;
Rapture.
Oxford, MD 21654

CARROLL, BAIKIDA
b. St. Louis, Mo., 15 Jan. 1947. Studied composition, Univ. of Maryland Extension, Frankfurt,
Germany, 1966; Wurzburg Cons., 1967; Berklee
School of Music, 1968; Southern Illinois Univ.,
1969; with Oliver Nelson and Ron Carter, Washington Univ., 1970. He has held teaching posts
at School of Black Music, St. Louis, 1970;
Young Disciples, St. Louis, 1972; Queens Coll.,
1975; was artist-in-residence, American Center
for Artists and Students, Paris, 1973. From
1971 he has toured and performed with his own
quintet and other groups in the U.S. and Europe.
WORKS: THEATRE: music for Poem for a revolutionary night, a play by Larry Neal, 1975;
cocomposer with Julius Hemphill, Coontown Bicentennial memorial service, a multimedia production,
1975; composer and coauthor with Malinke Elliot,
Eugene Sheen show, 1977; music for Mighty gents,
play by Richard Wesley, 1979; music for Boogie
woogie landscapes, play by Ntozake Shange, 1979.
R.D. 1, Box 675C, Woodstock, NY 12498

CARROLL, FRANK M.
b. Norfolk, Va., 19 Mar. 1928. Studied with
Herbert Elwell at Eastman School of Music. He
won first prize in a Wisconsin competition. He
was chairman, Maryland State Coll., 1961-63;
dean, School of Music, Centenary Coll., 1969-74;
conductor, Marshall Symphony, Tex., 1971-73; and
Longview Symphony, 1973-74; from 1974, professor,
Appalachian State Univ., chairman, 1974-78.
WORKS: THEATRE: The old woman and the pig,
chamber opera; incidental music to Comedy of
Errors; ORCHESTRA: piano concerto; CHAMBER
MUSIC: suite for violin and piano; cello sonatina; CHORUS: mass; PIANO: March paraphrase,
8 pianos.
Rt. 4, Box 224 AA, Boone, NC 28607

CARROLL, J. ROBERT
b. Haverhill, Mass., 31 Jan. 1927. Studied with
Donald Smith, Francis Judd Cooke, and Carl
McKinley, New England Cons.; with Le Guennant
and Masson in Paris. He has held academic posts
at Gregorian Inst. of America, 1953-61; Mary
Manse Coll., 1960-64; from 1964, professor of
French, Univ. of Toledo.
WORKS: ORCHESTRA: Essay, 1947; Christmas
processional, 1968; symphony for strings and
percussion, 1971; CHORUS: 3 anthems on Byzantine
themes, 1950; Missa pastoralis, 1960; music for
the wedding service, 1965; 4 offertories, 1965;
Introit for Christ, the King, 1967; Songs of the
heart, 1968; music for the ordinary of the mass,

1970; music for ordinations, 1969; ORGAN: variations on a Stralsund tune; 3 plainchant studies;
many masses, antiphons, hymns, etc. He is also
editor and translator of An applied course in
Gregorian chant; author of The technique of
Gregorian chironomy, 1955; A compendium of liturgical music terms, 1961; and The Gelineau
psalter, 1972.
4203 Berwick Pl., Toledo, OH 43612

CARTER, CHARLES
b. Ponca City, Okla., 10 July 1926. Studied with
Norman Phelps and Kent Kennan, Ohio State Univ.;
with Bernard Rogers and Wayne Barlow, Eastman
School of Music; with Ernst von Dohnanyi at
Florida State Univ. He was instructor, Ohio
State Univ., 1952-53; from 1953, at Florida
State Univ.
WORKS: BAND: Sinfonia; Overture in classic
style; Metropolis; Seminole song; Overture for
winds; Queen City suite; Motet for band; Cakewalk; and many more.
3830 Leane Dr., Tallahassee, FL 32303

CARTER, ELLIOTT
b. New York, N.Y., 11 Dec. 1908. Studied with
Walter Piston and Gustav Holst, Harvard Univ.,
B.A. 1930, M.A. 1932; with Nadia Boulanger in
Paris, 1932-35, earning a doctorate at Ecole
Normale de Musique, 1935. His many honors include a Naumberg award, 1952; 2 Guggenheim
grants, 1945, 1950; Prix de Rome, 1953; New York
Music Critics' award 1960; 2 Pulitzer prizes,
1960, 1973; Sibelius Medal for Music, 1961;
Brandeis Univ. Creative Arts award, 1965; Premio
delle Muse, Florence, Italy, 1968; honorary
doctorates from New England Cons., Swarthmore
Coll., Oberlin Coll., Princeton Univ., Harvard
Univ., Yale Univ. He was elected a member of
the Nat. Inst. of Arts and Letters, 1956, received its Gold Medal for Music, 1971; and the
American Music Center Letter of Distinction
award, 1973. On 28 Oct. 1978, the Internat. Soc.
for Contemporary Music presented a concert of
Carter's music in honor of his then-approaching
70th birthday; on 11 Dec. the mayor of New York
presented him with the city's highest honor, the
Handel Medallion; and his fast-fading birthday
was honored with an Elliott Carter Day in Los
Angeles on 27 Apr. 1979. His academic posts
have included Peabody Cons., 1946-48; Columbia
Univ., 1948-50; Salzburg Seminars in Austria,
1958; Yale Univ., 1960-62; several seasons at
Tanglewood and at Aspen Music School. He was
composer-in-residence, American Academy in Rome,
1962, and at Aspen Music School, 1973. He is
on the faculty at Julliard School.
WORKS: ORCHESTRA: Prelude, fanfare, and
polka, 1938; Pocahontas, suite from the ballet,
1939; symphony #1, 1942; Holiday overture, 1944;
Elegy for strings, 1946; The minotaur, suite
from the ballet, 1947; Variations for orchestra,
Louisville, 22 Apr. 1956; double concerto, for
harpsichord, piano, 2 chamber orch., New York,
6 Sept. 1961; piano concerto, Boston, 6 Jan.
1967; Concerto for orchestra, commissioned by
New York Philharmonic, premiered 5 Feb. 1970;
Symphony of 3 orchestras (written on a Bicen-

tennial commission from the Nat. Endowment for the Arts), New York, 17 Feb. 1977; CHAMBER MUSIC: Pastoral, viola and piano, 1940; Elegy, viola or cello and piano, 1943; piano sonata, 1946; cello sonata, 1948; Elegy, string quartet, 1948; woodwind quintet, 1948; 8 pieces for 4 tympani, 1949; 8 etudes and a fantasy, woodwind quartet, 1950; 3 string quartets, 1951, 1959, 1972 (#3, Juilliard Quartet, New York, 23 Jan. 1973); Recitative and improvisation, 4 kettledrums, 1 player, 1952; sonata for flute, oboe, cello, harpsichord, 1952; Canonic suite, 4 clarinets, 1957; Canon for 3 "In memoriam Igor Stravinsky," 1972; brass quintet, U.S. premiere, Washington, 15 Nov. 1974; duo for violin and piano, New York, 21 Mar. 1975; A fantasy about Purcell's "Fantasia upon one note," (a Christmas present to the American Brass Quintet), 1976; CHORUS: To music, a cappella, 1937; Heart not so heavy as mine, Dickinson text, a cappella, 1938; The defense of Corinth, text by Rabelais, for speaker, men's chorus, piano, 4 hands, 1941; The harmony of morning, text by Mark van Doren, women's chorus and small orch., 1944; Musicians wrestle everywhere, a cappella or with strings, 1945; Emblems, text by Allen Tate, men's chorus, piano, 1947; SOLO VOICE: Dust of snow, The line gang, The rose family, all on texts by Frost, 1943; Voyage, text by Hart Crane, 1943 (the piano accompaniment has been orchestrated); Warble for lilac time, Whitman text, 1943; incidental music to The merchant of Venice, guitar and alto voice, 1938; A mirror on which to dwell, song cycle on texts of Elizabeth Bishop, soprano and chamber ensemble, New York, 24 Feb. 1976; Syringa, mezzo-soprano, bass, 11 instruments, New York, 10 Dec. 1978.
Waccabuc, NY 10597

CASAVANT, CHARLES EWING
b. Chattanooga, Tenn., 23 Feb. 1945. Studied with John Boda, Florida State Univ.; with Morton Feldman and Lejaren Hiller, State Univ. of New York at Buffalo. From 1976 he has been faculty member, Indiana Univ. of Pennsylvania.
WORKS: ORCHESTRA: concerto for 2 pianos; BAND: Nocturnes; CHAMBER MUSIC: Passage, woodwind quintet and percussion; Vocalise II, oboe and English horn; Sonata II, chamber ensemble; Proimbroglio.
Box 51, Creekside, PA 15732

CASCARINO, ROMEO
b. Philadelphia, Pa., 28 Sept. 1922. Studied with Paul Nordoff at Philadelphia Cons., entering on scholarship in 1938. His awards include honorable mention in the 1945 Gershwin Memorial Competition; 2 Guggenheim fellowships, 1948, 1949; Benjamin award, 1960; honorary doctorate, Combs Coll. of Music, 1960; Orpheus award of Phi Mu Alpha, 1975; and commissions. From 1955, he has been head of theory and composition, Combs Coll.
WORKS: THEATRE: William Penn, opera in 3 acts, performed in concert form, 1975; Pygmalion, ballet; Prospice, ballet, 1949; ORCHESTRA: Blades of grass, English horn and strings; The Acadian land, woodwinds and strings, 1960;

Spring pastoral, 1945; Portrait of Galatea, tone poem; Bambi, an orchestration of his bassoon sonata; BAND: Fanfare and march; CHAMBER MUSIC: bassoon sonata, 1950; 8 songs for soprano.
17 Zummo Way, Norristown, PA 19401

CASSELS-BROWN, ALASTAIR K.
b. London, England, 3 May 1927; U.S. citizen 1961. Studied organ at St. John's, Leatherhead; with Wellesz, Westrup, Rubbra, and Armstrong, Worcester Coll., Oxford, M.A. 1952; with Hugo Norden, Toronto Univ. (extramural). He was named fellow, Royal Coll. of Organists, 1950; won third prize for Jeu de cloches, American Guild of Organists and Los Angeles Horn Club, 1962. He was music director, St. George's School, Newport, R.I., 1952-55; associate organist, Cathedral of St. John the Divine, New York, 1955-57; choirmaster, Grace Church, Utica, N.Y., 1957-65; on faculty, Hamilton Coll., 1965-67; from 1967, professor, Episcopal Theological School, Cambridge, Mass.
WORKS: ORCHESTRA: Forest idyll, Providence, 1955; My song is love unknown, with chorus, Utica, 1961; cello concerto, 1964; From the divide, cantata with chorus and soloists, 1972; CHAMBER MUSIC: violin sonata, 1953; little concerto, piano, flute, oboe, strings, 1961; Jeu de cloches, 12 horns and organ, 1962; CHORUS: Praise the Lord, O my soul, 1955; Te Deum, 1956; The Christ Child lay in Mary's lap, 1956; Surely it is God who saves me; Venite; SONGS: Serenade to indestructible beauty, cycle for baritone, Sandburg text, 1967; ELECTRONIC: The Hindu trinity--Brahma, Vishnu, Siva, 1977; 2 accompaniments to the 8th tone, 1977.
13 St. John's Rd., Cambridge, MA 02138

CASSLER, G. WINSTON
b. Moundridge, Kans., 3 Sept. 1906. Attended McPherson Coll., A.B. 1927; Oberlin Cons., M.B. 1931, M.M. 1948; also studied in London, Germany, and at Eastman School of Music. He was named associate, American Guild of Organists, 1930; member Pi Kappa Lambda, 1948. He taught privately, 1927-42; served in the army, 1942-47, rising from private to major; joined the faculty, St. Olaf Coll., 1949, professor, 1964-72; organist, St. John's Lutheran Church, Northfield, from 1950.
WORKS: ORCHESTRA: De institutione musica, a symphony, 1949; BAND: Chorale and fugue, 1972; Joy to the world, 1973; Immanuel is born, 1973; CHORUS: Peace in our time, with piano or orch., 1954; The heritage of freedom, piano or orch., 1955; Now let the vault of heaven resound, with orch., 1959; Built on a rock, choral cantata with brass quintet, 1962; The gospel trumpet, with solo trumpet, 1971; and many other choral and organ works.
708 St. Olaf Ave., Northfield, MN 55057

CASTALDO, JOSEPH
b. New York, N.Y., 23 Dec. 1927. Studied at St. Cecilia Acad. in Rome while serving in the U.S. Army. On returning to the U.S., he studied privately with Dante Fiorello; with Hugh Ross and Vittorio Giannini, Manhattan School of Music;

CASTELNUOVO-TEDESCO, MARIO

with Vincent Persichetti, Philadelphia Cons.,
B.M., M.M. He was head, composition-theory
department, Philadelphia Musical Acad., 1960-66,
then named president.

WORKS: ORCHESTRA: Epigrams, with piano
solo; Epiphonia; Cycles, Philadelphia, 7 May
1970; Theoria, winds, piano, percussion, Philadelphia, 22 Jan. 1973; CHAMBER MUSIC: string
quartet; Contrasts, solo harp; Concertante, harp
and string quartet; Dichotomy, woodwind quintet,
1963; Askesis, chamber ensemble, Athens, 1971;
Photograph of a funeral, baritone, piano, percussion; Kannon, chamber ensemble, Boston, 2 Dec.
1976; CHORUS: Flight, cantata for chorus, winds,
percussion, narrator, soprano, Temple Univ., 11
May 1960; At her feet, a cappella choir; PIANO:
sonatina; sonata, 1961; 3 pieces; MIXED MEDIA:
Protogenesis, 15 instruments, lights, film,
slides, and the Zeiss planetarium instrument,
written for presentation at Fels Planetarium,
Philadelphia, in the May Festival, 1973.
    1628 Pine St., Philadelphia, PA 19103

CASTELNUOVO-TEDESCO, MARIO
    b. Florence, Italy, 3 Apr. 1895; U.S. citizen
1946; d. Los Angeles, 16 Mar. 1968. On coming
to the U.S. in 1939, he settled in Hollywood.
There he composed for films and also produced a
prodigious amount of music for stage and concert,
e.g.: 4 operas, 3 oratorios; 2 piano concertos;
3 violin concertos; cello concerto; 6 overtures
to Shakespeare plays; numerous other works for
orchestra, and orchestra with voice or solo instruments; many chamber works in all forms;
piano pieces; songs; choral works. Tobias and
the angel, oratorio on the book of Tobit, 1965,
was given its premiere in Norwalk, Conn., 1 Feb.
1975, New York premiere the next day. The world
premiere of his chamber opera, The importance of
being Earnest, 1962, was given in concert form
at City Univ. of New York, 22 Feb. 1975. Figaro,
a hilarious parody on Rossini's Largo al facto-
tum, was performed in New York by Janos Starker
on 7 May 1977. Bibliography: Nick Rossi,
"Complete catalogue of works by Mario Castelnuovo-
Tedesco" (New York, 1977).

CASTILLO, JAVIER
    b. Coahuila, Mex., 27 Dec. 1933; to U.S. 1960.
Studied with John Swackhamer, Univ. of California,
Berkeley; with Jean Claude Eloy and Darius
Milhaud, Mills Coll. He was composer-in-residence with the San Francisco Symphony, summer
1972.
    WORKS: ORCHESTRA: Sculptures, with chorus,
commissioned by San Francisco Symph.; CHAMBER
MUSIC: 3 geometric pieces, woodwinds and percussion; Ravelesque, piano; The house of two,
2 pianos; Geese, for guitar; CHORUS: Lament on
the death of a kitty; The temple, with percussion
and 2 trombones.
    1336 Walnut St., Berkeley, CA 94709

CASTLE, PATRICK DOUGLAS
    b. Oakland, Calif., 25 Dec. 1945. Studied with
Wilson Coker, San Jose State Univ.; with Roy
Travis, Univ. of California, Los Angeles; with
Paul Zonn, Salvatore Martirano, and Edwin London,

Univ. of Illinois, Urbana. He was instructor,
Univ. of Wisconsin, Steven's Point, 1975-77.
    WORKS: CHAMBER MUSIC: woodwind quintet,
1973; Entrapment, percussion and 4 melodic instruments, 1974; Molar operandi, 1977; string
quartet, 1978; Time piece, jazz ensemble, 1970;
ELECTRONIC: Dry drops of rain, 1973; Road conditions, 1974; Packaged loops, tape, amplified
double bass, and dancer, 1975.
    404 E. Green St. #201, Urbana, IL 61801

CAVE, MICHAEL
    b. Springfield, Mo., 17 May 1944. Attended
Washington Univ.; California Inst. of the Arts;
studied piano at Univ. of Southern California.
He was organist-choirmaster, Los Angeles, 1963-
69; on faculty, Westlake School, Los Angeles,
1968-72; instructor, Univ. of California, Los
Angeles, 1972-75.
    WORKS: OPERA: Pandora's box, children's
opera, 1971; CHAMBER MUSIC: Fantasie on a choral
melody, soloists, choir, chamber orch., organ,
1967; Ecclesiastes, 2 sopranos, string quartet,
oboe, horn, piano, 1971; By the waters of Babylon,
soprano, 2 recorders, keyboard, 1971; oboe sonata, 1971; songs, recorder trios, piano pieces.
    1525 Walnut Ave., Venice, CA 90291

CAVIANI, RONALD
    b. Iron Mountain, Mich., 12 Mar. 1931. Studied
with Carl Hager, Notre Dame Univ.; with George
Wilson, Univ. of Michigan; with H. Owen Reed and
James Niblock, Michigan State Univ. He received
a faculty research grant, Northern Michigan
Univ., 1968. He was orchestra director in public
schools, Niles, Mich., 1963-66; faculty member,
Northern Michigan Univ., 1966-78; from 1978, at
Univ. of the Pacific.
    WORKS: ORCHESTRA: Micro-6, soprano saxo-
phone and orch.; BAND: Northern suite; Prelude,
chorale, and march; CHAMBER MUSIC: Dance suite,
clarinet and piano; 2 string quartets; A + 0?,
trumpet and tape; 5 scenes, viola and piano,
1972; Ondee, chamber orch., 1976; CHORUS: 3
poems, texts by Leonard Cohen, a cappella; pity
this busy monster manunkind not, e. e. cummings
text, choir and tape; Stopping by woods, Frost
text, a cappella.
    Univ. of the Pacific, Stockton, CA 95211

CAZDEN, NORMAN
    b. New York, N.Y., 23 Sept. 1914; d. Bangor,
Maine, 18 Aug. 1980. Studied piano with Ernest
Hutcheson, Juilliard School, diploma 1930; com-
position with Bernard Wagenaar, diploma 1939; at
City Coll., B.S. cum laude 1943; composition
with Walter Piston and Aaron Copland, Harvard
Univ., A.M. 1944, Ph.D. 1948. He received
scholarships for all study at Juilliard; won Phi
Beta Kappa at City Coll.; Saltonstall fellowship,
1945; George Knight fellowship, 1945; John
Knowles Paine fellowships, 1945, 1946; Pi Kappa
Lambda, 1952; 6 MacDowell Colony fellowships;
9th Pedro Paz award in composition, Olivet Coll.,
1971. He made his debut as pianist at Town Hall,
New York, in 1926 at age 12; toured as pianist
and accompanist, 1924-43; was on staff of radio
stations WNYC and WLIB, New York; music director,

Humphrey-Weidman Dance Repertory Company, 1942-43; taught privately from 1928; at Juilliard, 1934-39; Vassar Coll., 1947-48; Peabody Cons., 1948-49; Univ. of Michigan, 1949-50; Univ. of Illinois, 1950-53; the New School, New York, 1956-58; from 1969, at Univ. of Maine.

WORKS: THEATRE: music for The lonely ones, 1944; Dingle Hill, 1958; The merry wives of Windsor, 1962; The tempest, 1963; ORCHESTRA: concerto for 10 instruments, 1937; Preamble, 1938; On the death of a Spanish child, 1939; 6 definitions, 1930-39; 3 dances, 1940; Stony Hollow, 1944; symphony, 1948, Hancock, Maine, 20 July 1980; 3 ballads, 1949; Songs from the Catskills, 1950; 3 times a round, 1957; Woodland Valley sketches, 1960; Adventure, 1963; chamber concerto, clarinet and strings, 1965; viola concerto, 1974; CHAMBER MUSIC: string quartet, 1936; 3 chamber sonatas for clarinet and viola, 1938; quartet for clarinet and strings, 1939; 3 recitations, cello and piano, 1939; 3 messages, trumpet and piano, 1949; string quintet, 1941; horn sonata, 1941; 10 conversations, 2 clarinets, 1941; flute sonata, 1941; 2 woodwind quintets, 1941, 1966; 3 directions, brass quartet, 1941; 6 discussions, wind ensemble, 1942; violin suite, 1943; 4 presentations, violin and piano, 1944; brass sextet, 1951; quintet, oboe and strings, 1960; 4 favors, violin and piano, 1964; 3 charades, clarinet and piano, 1964; Elizabethan suite no. 1, brass quintet, 1964; Elizabethan suite no. 2, string quartet, 1965; piano trio, 1969; sonata for recorder and harp, 1971; Evocations, recorder and guitar, 1971; 5 intonations, 4 trumpets, 1971; 6 sennets, 4 trombones, 1971; bassoon sonata, 1971; cello sonata, 1971; English horn sonata, viola sonata, clarinet sonata, tuba sonata, double bass sonata, all 1974; PIANO: 6 sonatinas, 1932-1964; 3 satires, 1933; 8 preludes, 1937; 5 sonatas, 1938, 1950 (3), 1971; 6 preludes and fugues, 1974; and other pieces. He was also author of many articles, music reviews, and books on music.

CECCONI-BATES, AUGUSTA
b. Syracuse, N.Y., 9 Aug. 1933. Studied with Joseph J. McGrath, Syracuse Univ.; with Robert Palmer, Cornell Univ. She was on faculty, Maria Regina Coll., 1964-65; from 1968, has been music specialist, Syracuse School District.

WORKS: CHAMBER MUSIC: quartet brevis, string quartet, 1976; 5 stanze da poliziano, soprano, tenor, piano, 1977; Willie was different, text by Norman and Molly Rockwell, narrator and 6 instruments.

Toad Harbor, Box 49-D, West Monroe, NY 13167

CEELY, ROBERT PAIGE
b. Torrington, Conn., 17 Jan. 1930. Studied with Francis Judd Cooke, New England Cons., B.M. 1954; with Darius Milhaud and Leon Kirchner, Mills Coll., M.A. 1961; with Roger Sessions, Milton Babbitt, and Oliver Strunk, Princeton Univ. He received the Roy Dickinson Welch fellowship at Princeton, and a Fromm Found. commission in 1969 for Spectrum, a work performed at Tanglewood. He was music director, Robert Coll., Istanbul, 1961-63; guest composer, RAI Studio de

Fonologia, Milan; founder and director, Boston Experimental Electronicmusic Projects from 1965; director of electronic music at New England Cons. from 1967.

WORKS: INSTRUMENTAL: string trio, 1953; composition for 10 instruments, 1963; Logs, 2 double basses, 1968; hymn, cello and double bass, 1970; Rituals for forty flutes, 1976; Flee/floret/florens, 15 solo voices, 1978; Roundels, winds, percussion, and 4 double basses, 1978; ELECTRONIC: Elegia, 1963; Stratti, 1963; Vonce, 1967; Modules, 1968; Spectrum, tape and 12 instruments, 1969; Mitsyn music, 1971; La fleur, 1972; Slide music, 1973; Rerap, 1973; La fleur, les fleurs, tape, 1975; Frames, premiere at Edinburgh Festival of Electronic Music, 4 Sept. 1978.

33 Elm St., Brookline, MA 02146

CELONA, JOHN ANTHONY
b. San Francisco, Calif., 30 Oct. 1947. Studied with Henry Onderdonk, San Francisco State Coll.; with Iannis Xenakis, Indiana Univ.; with Kenneth Gaburo, Univ. of California, San Diego, Ph.D. 1977. He received a BMI award in 1971; Nat. Endowment for the Arts grant, 1977. In 1978 he joined the faculty at Univ. of Victoria (B.C.) and also became music director of Open Space Art Gallery, Victoria.

WORKS: INSTRUMENTAL: Modulo, orchestra, 1970; Multiphony I (Transformations), string quartet, 1970-73; Multiphony III (Gradients), tenor trombone with trigger, 1972; Multiphony IV (Velocities), wind ensemble, 1973; Miniatures, solo piano, 1978; Player piano, for 3 pianos, 1978; ELECTRONIC: Response, 2 choirs, organ, percussion, tape, 1971; Interphase, percussion and tape, 1971; Archangel, tape, 1972; Arpeggio, piano, electric piano, tape, 1978; Tracking, solo piano, electric piano, harpsichord, marimba, celeste, piano, 1978; Staring, chamber choir, narrator, tape, 1978.

2317 Belmont Ave., Victoria, B.C., Canada V8R 4A2

CERVETTI, SERGIO
b. Dolores, Uruguay, 9 Nov. 1940; to U.S. 1962. Studied with Ernst Krenek and Stefan Grove at Peabody Cons.; electronic music with Alcides Lanza at Columbia Univ. His awards include first prize for chamber music, Caracas Internat. Music Festival, 1966; a grant as composer-in-residence, West Berlin, 1969; second prize, Maracaibo Festival, 1977; several commissions. He was faculty member, Brooklyn Coll., 1970-71; from 1972, at New York Univ.

WORKS: ORCHESTRA: Orbitas, 1967; El carro de heno, small chorus and orch., 1967; Plexus, 1971; concerto for trumpet and strings, 1974; 40 second/42nd variations, for dance, 1979; CHAMBER MUSIC: string trio, 1963; piano sonata, 1964; 5 episodes, piano trio, 1966; 5 sequences, 6 instruments, 1966; 6 sequences, for dance, 1966; Zinctum, string quartet, 1968; Pulsar, brass sextet, 1969; 4 fragments de Pablo Neruda, soprano and 4 instruments, 1970; Raga I, ensemble, 1971; The bottom of the iceberg, guitar, 1972; . . . from the earth . . ., ensemble, 1972;

CERVONE, D. DONALD

Music for Rachel, 1977; CHORUS: Lux lucet in
tenebris, 16 voices, a cappella; Peripetia, 20 to
100 singers and instrumentalists, 1970; MIXED
MEDIA: Dies tenebrarum, electric organ, male
chorus, strings, 2 percussion, 1968; Prisons #1,
singers, dancers, pantomime, instruments, 1969;
Prisons #2, speaking chorus, orch., tape, 1971;
Raga II, trombone and tape, 1971; Graffiti,
speaking chorus, orch., tape, 1971; Aria sus-
pendida, clarinet and tape; Oulom . . . Raga III,
tape; Stella dominatrix, 1979.
        96 Park Pl., Brooklyn, NY 11217

CERVONE, D. DONALD
        b. Meadville, Pa., 27 July 1932. Studied with
Howard Hanson, Bernard Rogers, Louis Mennini,
Eastman School of Music, B.M. 1955, Ph.D. 1970;
and with Burrill Phillips and Gordon Binkerd,
Univ. of Illinois, M.M. 1960. He received the
Benjamin award, 1966; 3 Ford Found. grants;
State Univ. of New York fellowships, 1968-69;
Yale-Gordon Found. composer award, 1970; many
commissions. He has been a church music director,
composer-in-residence, and conductor since 1960;
has held faculty posts from 1962; at State Univ.
Coll. at Brockport, N.Y., from 1966.
        WORKS: OPERA: Melanie, 1 act, 1958; Not
long ago . . . not far away, children's opera,
1965; Aria da capo, 1 act, libretto by Millay,
1969; incidental music to Inherit the wind, 1961;
The crucible, 1967; ORCHESTRA: Canzone II, 1966;
viola concerto, 1969; Sinfonia tutti clavieri,
keyboards and orch., 1973; CHORUS: Where thorn
once grew, with soloists and orch., 1970; These
are the times, baritone, 2 choirs, orch., organ,
1971; SONGS: Remembrance, cycle for contralto,
piano or chamber orch., 1955; Again this year,
cycle for soprano and orch., 1964; FILM SCORE:
What is a college?, 1968.
        3318 Brockport-Spencerport Rd., Spencerport,
        NY 14559

CESANA, OTTO
        b. Brescia, Italy, 7 July 1899; to U.S. as a boy.
Studied with Julius Gold. He was staff arranger
and composer for film studios in Hollywood;
later arranger for Radio City Music Hall, New
York, and for radio.
        WORKS: BALLET: Ali Baba and the 40 thieves;
ORCHESTRA: 6 symphonies; 6 concertos (one each
for clarinet, trumpet, trombone, piano, 2 pianos,
3 pianos); Negro heaven; Swing septet; and songs.
He was author of several books on music theory.

CHADABE, JOEL
        b. New York, N.Y., 12 Dec. 1938. Studied at
Univ. of North Carolina and Yale Univ.; privately
with Elliott Carter. He received a Ford Found.
grant as artist-in-residence, West Berlin; ASCAP
awards; and a Creative Arts Public Service Program commission. From 1965 he has been faculty
member, State Univ. of New York, Albany.
        WORKS: INSTRUMENTAL: Prelude to Naples, 4
instruments; Diversions, 2 pianos; 3 ways of
looking at a square, piano; ELECTRONIC: Street
scene, English horn, tape, and projections,
1967; Drift, tape; Ideas of movement at Bolton
Landing, tape; Echoes, solo instrument and tape;

Daisy, English horn and tape, 1972.
        339 S. Manning Blvd., Albany, NY 12208

CHAIKIN, JACK W.
        b. Brooklyn, N.Y., 24 Aug. 1918. Studied at
Mannes Coll. of Music; with Ernest Hutcheson,
Frederick Jacobi, and Bernard Wagenaar, Juilliard
School; privately with Wallingford Riegger. His
faculty posts have included Mannes Coll., 1957-
66; the New School for Social Research, 1964-66;
Brooklyn Center of Long Island Univ., 1965-78.
        WORKS: CHILDREN'S OPERA: An anteater named
Arthur; You look ridiculous; The woman with the
eggs; Robert the rose horse; Mr. Tall and Mr.
Small; CHORUS: Tefillah Chadesha and Shirim
L'Avodah, 2 sacred services for chorus and organ.
        246 Harrison Ave., Island Park, NY 11558

CHAITKIN, DAVID
        b. New York, N.Y., 16 May 1938. Studied with
Karl Kohn, Pomona Coll., B.A.; with Seymour
Shifrin, Arnold Elston, Luigi Dallapiccola,
Andrew Imbrie, Univ. of California, M.A.; with
Max Deutsch in Paris. At Berkeley he received
the Ladd Prix de Paris, 1964-66, and the Eisner
prize; other awards include a Martha Baird
Rockefeller Fund grant, 1975; ASCAP awards 1976-;
American Music Center grant, 1978. He was faculty member, New York Univ., 1969-76; then private teacher of composition; from 1978, on faculty part time, Brooklyn Coll. of CUNY.
        WORKS: ORCHESTRA: Music for orchestra,
1963, rev. 1973; Music in 5 parts, for film The
game, 1967; Light breaks where no sun shines,
symphony after the poem by Dylan Thomas, 1977-
78; CHAMBER MUSIC: Concert music for violin and
piano, 1963; Etudes for piano, 1960, 1973-74;
Serenade for 7 players, 1976; Scattering dark
and bright, duo for piano and percussion, White
Mountains Festival, Jefferson, N.H., 21 Aug.
1979; CHORUS: Seasons such as these, Shakespeare
text, a cappella, 1976.
        36 W. 84th St., New York, NY 10024

CHAJES, JULIUS
        b. Lvov, Poland, 21 Dec. 1910; to U.S. 1937.
Studied piano and composition in Vienna, the
latter with Hugo Kauder. He won the Honor prize
in the first international competition for
pianists, Vienna, 1933. He was head of the piano
department, Tel-Aviv Music School, 1934-36;
director, music division, Jewish Community Center, Detroit, from 1940; on faculty, Wayne State
Univ., from 1950.
        WORKS: OPERA: Out of the desert, 2 acts,
premiere, 1966; ORCHESTRA: Eros, symphonic
poem; Hebrew suite; Scherzo; Fantasy, piano and
orch., 1928; Hatikvah, cello concerto, 1932;
piano concerto, 1953; Psalm 142, cantata with
chorus, 1937; Zion, rise and shine, with chorus;
By the rivers of Babylon and Old Jerusalem, both
with high voice and cello obligato; The promised
land, with chorus; CHAMBER MUSIC: Hebrew suite,
clarinet, piano, string quartet; piano trio; 2
string quartets; violin sonata; piano sonata;
flute sonata, 1979; CHORUS: Song for Americans;
Song of the pioneers; Song of Galilee; Shabat
Shalom, Friday evening service; many other choral

works, songs, pieces for piano and other solo
instruments.
6820 E. Dartmoor, W. Bloomfield, MI 48033

CHAMBERLIN, ROBERT C.
b. Hershey, Pa., 1 Sept. 1950. Studied with
Arthur Campbell, St. Olaf Coll.; with Alan
Oldfield and Will Gay Bottje, Southern Illinois
Univ.; with Ben Johnston, Salvatore Martirano,
and Edwin London, Univ. of Illinois. In 1972 he
was selected by the Southern Illinois Univ.
music faculty to compose a work for the university orchestra. From 1973 he has been on the
faculty at Webster Coll.
WORKS: ORCHESTRA: Individuation, with narrator, 1973; Duet concertante, piano and orch.,
1974; CHAMBER MUSIC: A dream deferred, bassoon
and piano, 1973; Expressions and interplay, 2
pieces for solo cello, 1976; trio for winds,
flute, oboe, clarinet, 1979; Currents, archifoon
and tape, 1979; ORGAN: Sindon, 1979.
Music Dept., Webster Coll., St. Louis, MO
63119

CHAMBERLIN, WILLIAM FRANCIS
b. Springfield, Mass., 27 Aug. 1939. Studied
with Hugo Weisgall, Luciano Berio, Vincent
Persichetti, Elliott Carter, and Hubert Howe at
Juilliard School; with Robert Stern at Hampshire
Coll. He won the Internat. Gaudeamus Composers
Competition, 1972, and an American Music Center
grant, 1972.
WORKS: ORCHESTRA: Ainsworth Street, 1970-
71; CHAMBER MUSIC: Chamber music for 14 players,
1968; string quartet, 1973-74; quintet for flute,
bassoon, string trio, Johnstown, N.Y., 15 Oct.
1978.
Kramer Road, R.D. #1, Middlebury, NY 12122

CHAMBERS, JOSEPH A.
b. Stoneacre, Va., 25 June 1942. Studied with
Vincent Persichetti, Philadelphia Cons., 1960-
61; at American Univ., 1962-63. He received
Down Beat magazine's New Star Performer award
for percussionists, 1969-70; Creative Artists
Public Service grants, 1972, 1973. He is a
member of Um Boom Repercussion, a percussion
ensemble, and has worked with many of the major
jazz bands; taught at Buffalo Univ., 1968-69;
Kingsboro Coll., 1970.
WORKS: CHAMBER MUSIC: movements for string
quartet; Angels and devils, brass choir; Almora-
vid; Sketches, percussion, woodwinds, soprano;
JAZZ: Mirrors; Idle awhile; Dialogue; Hello to
the wind; and others.
533 W. 112th St., #6E, New York, NY 10025

CHAMBERS, STEPHEN A. See Hakim, Talib Rasul

CHANCE, JOHN BARNES
b. 1932; d. 1972. Was on faculty at Univ. of
Kentucky and was killed in an accident.
WORKS: BAND: Introduction and capriccio;
Incantation and dance; Variation on a Korean
folk song; Blue Lake, an overture; symphony for
band; also Credo for trumpet and piano.

CHANCE, NANCY LAIRD
b. Cincinnati, Ohio, 19 Mar. 1931. Studied with
Vladimir Ussachevsky, Otto Luening, and Chou
Wen-Chung, Columbia Univ. She received ASCAP
awards, 1978-79. She taught piano during temporary residence in Nairobi, Kenya, 1974-78.
WORKS: ORCHESTRA: Lyric essays; CHAMBER
MUSIC: Rilke songs, soprano, flute, English
horn, cello, 1975; Darksong, soprano and chamber
orch.; Bathsabe's song, speaker, alto saxophone
live and taped; Edensong, soprano and chamber
orch.; 2 duos, chamber ensemble; Daysongs, alto
flute, 2 percussionists, 1975; Ritual sounds,
brass quintet and 3 percussionists, 1976; Ceremonial, percussion quartet, 1978; Declamation and
song, piano, vibraphone, violin, cello, 1978.
P.O. Box 345, Oyster Bay, NY 11771

CHANDLER, ERWIN PAUL
b. Port Jervis, N.Y., 17 Feb. 1944. Studied
with Warren Benson, Ithaca Coll., B.S. 1966;
with Bernhard Heiden and Juan Orrego-Salas,
Indiana Univ., M.M. 1971. He taught in public
schools, 1966-70; at Murray State Univ., 1972-
73; has played horn with the Reading Symphony
and various ensembles.
WORKS: ORCHESTRA: symphony, chamber orch.;
Jazz mass, with chorus and jazz ensemble, 1976;
BAND: symphony; CHAMBER MUSIC: 3 songs for
soprano and chamber ensemble; saxophone sonata;
Recitative and allegro, trombone and piano;
brass quintet, 1968; woodwind quintet; JAZZ:
Excursion suite, jazz band; many other works for
wind and brass ensemble, solo instruments, and
percussion.
109 Newport Ave., Reading, PA 19602

CHANG, G. GORDON
b. Hamilton, Ont., 31 Mar. 1951; to U.S. 1961.
Studied with Luigi Zaninelli, Banff School of
Fine Arts; with Roland LoPresti and Grant
Fletcher, Arizona State Univ. His awards include first prize in the Catgut Acoustical
Society competition, 1973; Arizona State Univ.
student competition, 1975.
WORKS: ORCHESTRA: The other side and
scherzo; Music 1975-76, voice and string orch.;
CHAMBER MUSIC: Statements for string quartet
(mezzo, alto, tenor, and baritone), 1973; Theme
and variations, solo cello; A great astonishment,
voice and chamber ensemble; Elegy, clarinet and
cello quartet; Music for percussion; Communion,
voice and piano; CHORUS: A tribute to the
founder, text by Kingsley Amis; Psalm 146;
PIANO: Emergence, sonata; Variations for piano,
1974.
2008 N. 57th Dr., Phoenix, AZ 85035

CHANLER, THEODORE WARD
b. Newport, R.I., 29 Apr. 1902; d. Boston, Mass.,
27 July 1961. Studied with Arthur Shepherd in
Boston; with Ernest Bloch at Cleveland Inst. of
Music; and with Nadia Boulanger in Paris.
WORKS: THEATRE: The pot of fat, chamber
opera, 1955; Pas de trois, ballet; CHAMBER MUSIC:
violin sonata; sonatina for chamber ensemble;
VOICE: mass for 2 women;s voices, 1930; The
doves; The flight; 4 rhymes from "Peacock Pie";

CHAPMAN, ROGER E.

3 husbands; 8 epitaphs, 2 song cycles, 1937, 1940; These, my Ophelia, song, 1935; PIANO: Calm, suite of 12 pieces; Joyful mystery, 4 hands.

CHAPMAN, ROGER E.
b. Los Angeles, Calif., 3 June 1916. Studied privately with Wesley La Violette; with John Vincent, Univ. of California at Los Angeles. He was faculty member, Univ. of California, Santa Barbara, 1954-71.
WORKS: He has written incidental music for theatre, chamber music, choral and organ works, including: Music for 2 cellos; Suite of 3 cities, 4 trombones; Festival overture, organ.
4000 Cuervo Ave., Santa Barbara, CA 93110

CHARKOVSKY, WILLIS
b. Chicago, Ill., 1 Mar. 1918. Studied at De Paul Univ., B.M.; with Felix Borowski, Northwestern Univ., M.M.; and with Leo Sowerby. He won a piano contest of the Society of American Musicians; made his professional debut as pianist in Chicago, 1936. He served in the army in World War II; taught at Northwestern Univ., 1957; has been band and orchestra director, Univ. of Illinois; soloist with Grant Park Symphony from 1957. His works include a piano concerto; woodwind quintet; sonata for 2 pianos.

CHARLES, ERNEST
b. Minneapolis, Minn., 21 Nov. 1895. Attended Univ. of Southern California. He was a singer in vaudeville and Broadway shows; composed art songs, religious anthem, and popular songs.
1210 Benedict Canyon, Beverly Hills, CA 90210

CHASE, NEWELL
b. West Roxbury, Mass., 3 Feb. 1904; d. New York, N.Y., 26 Jan. 1955. Studied at Boston Univ.; Harvard Univ.; with Wallace Goodrich and Frederick Converse, New England Cons., and with Tibor Serly. He was church organist, pianist, dance orchestra conductor; assistant conductor, Capitol Theatre, New York, 1924; solo pianist in the "Roxy Gang"; went to Hollywood in 1928 as composer and music adviser for films; served in the air force in World War II.
WORKS: ORCHESTRA: Concerto for Louise; Midnight in Mayfair; Tanglewood pool; Tricketts; Classical satire; Bachette; In chiffon; many popular songs.

CHASINS, ABRAM
b. New York, N.Y., 17 Aug. 1903. Studied piano with Ernest Hutcheson, composition with Rubin Goldmark, Juilliard School; at Columbia Univ.; with Josef Hofmann, Curtis Inst.; with Sir Donald Francis Tovey in London. He received a Peabody award "for distinguished service to music and radio"; 2 awards of the U.S. Treasury Dept. for service in financing World War II; Bruckner Medal; and a String Players Guild award. His brilliant career as pianist extended from 1926 to 1946 and included performances with leading orchestras of Europe and America. He taught at Curtis Inst., 1926-36, at Tanglewood, 1939-40;

was music director, WQXR, New York, 1942-65; musician-in-residence, Univ. of Southern California, 1972-73, then director of development, heading the expansion and development of the university's radio station, KUSC-FM.
WORKS: His more than 100 compositions include 2 piano concertos, which he introduced himself as pianist, the first at Philadelphia, 18 Jan. 1929, the second also at Philadelphia, 3 Mar. 1933. Other works are: 3 Chinese pieces, piano version and orchestra version; and 24 preludes for piano. He is also author of the books: Speaking of pianists, 1958; The Van Cliburn legend, 1959; The appreciation of music, 1966; Music at the crossroads, 1972; Leopold Stokowski: A profile, 1979.
University of Southern California, Los Angeles, CA 90007

CHATHAM, RHYS
b. New York, N.Y., 19 Sept. 1952. Studied with Donald Stratton, Manhattan School of Music; with Morton Subotnick, New York Univ.; with LaMonte Young; tuning systems with William Dowd in Cambridge, Mass. He was cofounder of The Kitchen and director of its contemporary music series, 1971-73, making it an innovative showcase with complete freedom of program for the composer. By the middle 1970s, his interest shifted from pure music to the inclusion of other media, and he has worked closely with avant-garde groups and with many composers. In 1977, he resumed his post as program director of The Kitchen.
WORKS: Green-line poem, tape, 1971; 2 gongs amplified, for 2 large Chinese gongs and 3 performers, 1972; Still sound in motion, 2 trombones, 1973; The Black Star pilgrimage, 2 voices, poet, dancer, 1973; 4 words, sound poem for 4 voices, 1974; 7 short pieces, actor, dancer, 5 musicians, 1975; 3 horns, 3 saxophones and tape, 1976; 7 fairy tales, 6 players, video, film, 1976; 16k, composition for frequencies of 16,000 cycles per second, 1977; The 7th overtone fiction, 2 actors, video, film, music, 1977; Tone death for baroque orch., 1978.
56 MacDougal St., #20, New York, NY 10012

CHATMAN, STEPHEN
b. Faribault, Minn., 28 Feb. 1950. Studied with Joseph Wood and Walter Aschaffenburg, Oberlin Cons.; with Leslie Bassett, Ross Lee Finney, William Bolcom, and Efrem Kurtz, Univ. of Michigan. His awards include 3 BMI composer awards, 1973, 1975, 1976; Fulbright grant, 1974; Ives prize, Nat. Inst. of Arts and Letters; Nat. Endowment for the Arts grant, 1977. In 1976, he joined the faculty of the Univ. of British Columbia.
WORKS: ORCHESTRA: 2 followers of Lien, 1973; Occasions; 3 a.m. on the square, 1976; CHAMBER MUSIC: Northern drones, violin or viola and piano; Bittersweet rag, piano; Wild cat, solo flute, 1975; Amusements, piano, 1976; On the contrary, chamber ensemble, 1976; also many vocal works and other pieces for solo instruments.
3394 West 31, Vancouver, B.C., Canada V6S 1X7

CHAULS, ROBERT
b. Port Chester, N.Y., 18 July 1942. Studied with Donald Keats, Antioch Coll.; with Adrian Cruft, Royal Coll. of Music, London; with Darius Milhaud, Aspen Music School; with Ross Lee Finney and Gyorgy Sandor, Univ. of Michigan; and at Univ. of Southern California. His awards include Nat. Fed. of Music Clubs awards, 1963, 1968; Nat. Society of Arts and Letters, 1968; Phi Mu Alpha award, 1968; Woodrow Wilson Fellowship, 1964; Aspen scholarship; Berkshire Music Center and Oliver Ditson scholarships. He was music director, City of the Angels Opera, 1964; on the faculty, Willamette Univ., 1966-70; at Los Angeles Valley Coll., from 1973; director-conductor, Los Angeles Valley Opera, from 1977.
WORKS: OPERA: Alice in Wonderland, Los Angeles, 31 Mar. 1978; ORCHESTRA: Requiem for a peaceful man, 1968; CHAMBER MUSIC: This is L.A., soprano and chamber orch.; sonata-fantasy, piano trio; Something, violin and piano; wind quintet; Capriccio, clarinet and piano; Nasherei, song cycle for soprano and paino or brass quintet, Ogden Nash text; piano sonata; CHORUS: The bells, Poe text; Sing unto the Lord, anthem; Nicholas Christmas, children's chorus.
3451 Valley Meadow Rd., Sherman Oaks, CA 91403

CHEETHAM, JOHN
b. Taos, N.Mex., 13 Jan. 1939. Studied with John Verrall, Gerald Kechley, and George F. McKay, Univ. of Washington. From 1969, he has been faculty member, Univ. of Missouri at Columbia. His published works include Scherzo for brass quintet.
1611 Colonial Court, Columbia, MO 65201

CHENETTE, EDWARD STEPHEN
b. London, Ky., 17 Aug. 1895; d. Bartow, Fla., 10 Sept. 1963. Studied at High Park Cons., Des Moines, Iowa, M.A.; Bush Temple Cons.; and Societe Academique, Paris. He was band conductor with the Chautauqua Inst. to 1916, when the entire band enlisted in the Canadian Expeditionary Forces; conductor, Chicago Regimental Band and Illinois State Legion Band; director of music, Iowa State Coll.; then on faculty, Florida Southern Coll. He was author of books on band techniques and composed many marches and other works for band.

CHENOWETH, WILBUR
b. Tecumsah, Nebr., 4 June 1899. Studied piano with Sigismund Stojowski and Alexander Lambert in New York; organ and composition with Pietro Yon. In 1938 he settled in Los Angeles. His compositions include Fiesta, piano and orch.; Vocalize for medium voice; also choral works, piano pieces.

CHERNIAVSKY, JOSEF
b. Russia, 31 Mar. 1895; to U.S. 1919; d. New York, N.Y., 3 Nov. 1959. Studied with Alexander Glazunov and Rimsky-Korsakov, Imperial Cons., St. Petersburg; with Julius Klingel in Leipzig. He toured the U.S. as theatre and concert conductor; then was music director, WLW, Cincinnati.

His works included 3 operettas: Barnum; Music drama; The dybbuk.

CHERRY, MILTON
b. S.C., 6 June 1908. Attended Cincinnati Cons., American Cons., Chicago Musical Coll., and studied violin privately with Hugo Kortschalk in New York. His faculty positions include Louisiana State Univ., 1931-45; Ithaca Coll., 1945-50; Virginia Commonwealth Univ., 1950-75.
WORKS: ORCHESTRA: violin concerto, 1953; CHAMBER MUSIC: string quartet, 1960; flute sonata, 1965.

CHERTOK, PEARL
b. Laconia, N.H., 18 June 1918. Studied harp with Carlos Salzedo at Curtis Inst. of Music. She was staff harpist for CBS, 1950-70, and has taught at Manhattanville Coll.
WORKS: Her compositions are mainly harp solos and background scores for television dramas.
56 N. Greenwich Rd., Armonk, NY 10504

CHESLOCK, LOUIS
b. London, England, 25 Sept. 1898; U.S. citizen 1913; d. Baltimore, Md., 26 July 1981. Studied violin and composition (the latter with Gustav Strube) at Peabody Cons., diploma 1921. His composition awards include Peabody Alumni prize, 1921; Chicago Daily News prizes, 1922-24; Nat. Composers Clinic, 1942; New York Women's Symph., 1938; Baltimore City Coll. Hall of Fame, 1960; honorary doctorate, Peabody Cons., 1964; honorary citizen of Balitmore; Peabody Cons. Distinguished Alumni award, 1976. He was violinist with the Baltimore Symphony, 1916-37, also guest conductor; faculty member at Peabody Cons., 1916-76, chairman of theory and composition, 1950-68.
WORKS: OPERA: The jewel merchants, libretto by James Branch Cabell, Baltimore, 26 Feb. 1940; BALLET: Cinderella, 3 acts, Baltimore, 11 May 1946; ORCHESTRA: 3 tone poems: 'Neath Washington Monument, Cathedral at sundown, At the railway station, 1923; a symphony, 1932; violin concerto, Baltimore, 25 Feb. 1926; horn concerto; Rhapsody in red and white, 1950; CHAMBER MUSIC: string quartet, 1957; violin sonata; Bagatelle, cello and piano, Baltimore, May 1969; Descant, 12 tone, solo clarinet, Baltimore, 14 Jan. 1972; numerous other chamber works and solo pieces.

CHEYETTE, IRVING
b. New York, N.Y., 8 Jan. 1904. Studied with Wallingford Riegger, Howard Murphy, Madeley Richardson, and Edwin Stringham. He was on the music faculty, Indiana Univ. of Pennsylvania, 1938-48; Syracuse Univ., 1948-54; Tokyo Fine Arts Univ., on a Fulbright grant, 1954-55; State Univ. of New York at Buffalo, 1955-72; Fordham Univ., 1973-77.
WORKS: BAND: overtures; Cape Cod Capers; Sage Brush Saga; marches: Yankee Clipper; Football parade; Pageantry processional; Spirit of Valley Forge.
3605 S. Ocean Blvd., Palm Beach, FL 33480

CHIHARA, PAUL SEIKO

CHIHARA, PAUL SEIKO
b. Seattle, Wash., 9 July 1938. Attended Univ. of Washington, B.A. 1960; studied with Robert Palmer, Cornell Univ., M.A. 1961, D.M.A. 1965; with Nadia Boulanger in Paris, 1961-62; with Ernst Pepping in Berlin, 1965-66; with Gunther Schuller at Tanglewood, 1966-68. His awards include the Lili Boulanger award, 1962; Fulbright fellowship, 1965; Tanglewood fellowships, 1965, 1966, 1968; Nat. Endowment for the Arts grant, 1973; Fromm commission, 1975; Guggenheim fellowship, 1976; Naumberg commission, 1977. He was faculty member, Univ. of California, Los Angeles, 1966-78.
WORKS: BALLET: Shinju, 1973-74; ORCHESTRA: Symphony in celebration, 1957; Forest music, Los Angeles, 2 May 1971; Wind song, cello and orch., New York, 2 Feb. 1972; Grass, amplified double bass and orch., Oberlin, Mar. 1972; Ceremony IV, Los Angeles, 18 Apr. 1974; guitar concerto; CHAMBER MUSIC: Primavera, string quartet, 1965; Tree music, 3 violas, 3 trombones, 1966; Branches, 2 bassoons and percussion, Tanglewood, 1966; Willow, willow, bass flute, tuba, percussion, New York, 20 Feb. 1968; Logs for one or more string basses, Logs XVI, amplified bass and tape, 1969; Driftwood, string quartet, 1969; Ceremony, oboe, 2 celli, bass, percussion, Marlboro Festival, Aug. 1971; Ceremony II (Incantations), flute, 2 celli, percussion, 1972; piano trio, 1974; Symphony concertante, chamber orch., Boston, 20 Jan. 1980; CHORUS: The 90th Psalm, 1965; Magnificat, treble voices, 1967; 3 dream choruses, 1968; Nocturne for 24 solo voices, 1972; The 101st Psalm; Missa Carminum, folk song mass for double chorus, a cappella, 1975.
1620 Federal Ave., Los Angeles, CA 90025

CHILD, PETER B.
b. Great Yarmouth, England, 6 May 1953; to U.S. 1973. Studied with Douglas Leedy and William Albright, Reed Coll., 1973-75; with Arthur Berger, Martin Boykan, Seymour Shifrin, Brandeis Univ., 1976-79; with Jacob Druckman at Tanglewood, 1978. His awards include the Margaret Grant Memorial prize, 1978; first prize, East and West Artists Competition, 1979. He has been instructor at Brandeis Univ. from 1979.
WORKS: CHAMBER MUSIC: Heracliti reliquae (Fragments of Heraclitus), 1978; duo for flute and percussion, 1979; piano sonata; ELECTRONIC: 3 brief impressions for computer; Tape, intervention, instruments and tape.
13 Worcester St., Belmont, MA 02178

CHILDS, BARNEY
b. Spokane, Wash., 13 Feb. 1926. Studied at Univ. of Nevada, B.A. 1949; Oxford Univ., B.A. 1951, M.A. 1955; with Leonard Ratner, Stanford Univ., Ph.D. in English and music, 1959; with Carlos Chavez and Aaron Copland at Tanglewood; privately with Elliott Carter. He received a Rhodes scholarship, 1949; MacDowell fellowships, 1963, 1968, 1970, 1978. He taught English, Univ. of Arizona, 1956-65; was dean, Deep Springs Coll., 1965-67; faculty member, Wisconsin Coll. Cons., 1969-71; from 1971, professor and composer-in-residence, Univ. of Redlands.

WORKS: ORCHESTRA: 2 symphonies, 1954, 1956; clarinet concerto, 1970; BAND: 6 events, 1965; Supposes: Imago mundi, 1970; The golden shore; CHAMBER MUSIC: 2 violin sonatas, 1950, 1956; 7 string quartets, 1951-68; sonata for solo clarinet, 1951; Concerto da camera, trumpet and woodwinds, 1951; 5 woodwind quintets, 1951-69; woodwind trio, 1952; quartet for clarinet and strings, 1953; bassoon sonata, 1953; 4 involutions, solo English horn, 1955; 5 considerations, solo horn, 1955; concerto for English horn and chamber ensemble, 1955; bassoon quartet, 1958; sonata for solo oboe, 1958; brass trio, 1959; flute sonata, 1960; sonata for solo trombone, 1961; Interbalances I-VI, various ensembles, 1941-64; Variations sur une chanson de canotier, brass quintet; Stances, flute and silence, 1963; quartet for flute, oboe, doublebass, percussion, 1964; Jack's new bag, 10 players, 1966; The golden bubble, contrabass, sarrusophone, percussion, 1967; Mr. T, his fancy, doublebass, 1967; Music for 2 flute players; Operation flabby sheep, any instruments, 1968; Music for 6 tubas, 1969; trio for clarinet, cello, piano, 1972; Bowling again with the champs, improvisation ensemble, Redlands, 11 May 1976; brass quintet #4; 4 pieces for 6 winds, 1978; A question of summer, tuba and harp, Chicago, 4 Apr. 1978; many pieces for solo voice and various instruments; choral works.
School of Music, University of Redlands, Redlands, CA 92373

CHILDS, EDWIN T.
b. Plymouth, N.H., 7 Jan. 1945. Studied with Jack C. Goode, Wheaton Coll.; with Wayne Barlow and Samuel Adler, Eastman School of Music. He was faculty member, Philadelphia Coll. of Bible, 1973-78; from 1978, Biola Coll.
WORKS: ORCHESTRA: Monteverdiana, concerto grosso for solo winds, brass, strings and full orch.; CHAMBER MUSIC: 2 piano sonatas; woodwind quintet; 2 communion meditations for organ; various solo and ensemble works; choral compositions.
14757 Fairvilla Dr., La Mirada, CA 90638

CHMIELEWSKI, STEPHEN
b. New York, N.Y., 28 Mar. 1947. Studied with Ludmila Ulehla, Manhattan School of Music, B.M., M.M. He is founder and director of The Island Company, a concert artists' association.
WORKS: ORCHESTRA: symphony for strings, 1977; symphony #2, 1978; BAND: Overture for our time, 1968; CHAMBER MUSIC: allegro, piano, 1969; brass quintet, 1972; Mini-trio, flute, clarinet, bassoon, 1973; Voice of America, clarion quintet, 1976; Tune and chase with quickstep dirge, clarinet and piano, 1976; trumpet sonata, 1978; Philipse Manor, flute, clarinet, bassoon, 1979.
52 LeGrande Ave., Greenwich, CT 06803

CHOBANIAN, LORIS OHANNES
b. Mosul, Iraq, 17 Apr. 1933; U.S. citizen 1969. Studied with Kenneth Klaus, Louisiana State Univ., B.M. 1964, M.M. 1966; with H. Owen Reed, Michigan State Univ., Ph.D. 1970. His honors include ASCAP awards 1974-79; Ohio Chamber Orch.

grant, 1976; Cleveland Area Arts Council grant, 1977; American String Teachers Assoc. award 1977. He was faculty member, Muskegon Community Coll., 1968-70; from 1970, professor, Baldwin-Wallace Coll. Cons.

WORKS: BALLET: The gift, Christmas ballet; ORCHESTRA: guitar concerto, East Lansing, 4 June 1971, composer as soloist; Soliloquy--testament of a madman, baritone and orch., WIND ENSEMBLE: The id, 1972; Capriccio with piano solo, Berea, 20 Jan. 1974, conducted by composer; Armenian dances (also transcribed for orch.); Music for brass and timpani, 1978; CHAMBER MUSIC: Sumer and Akkad, chamber ensemble, percussion, and dancers, WMSB-TV, East Lansing, May 1969.

26716 Redwood Dr., Olmsted Falls, OH 44138

CHORBAJIAN, JOHN
b. New York, N.Y., 2 June 1936. Studied with Vittorio Giannini, Nicolas Flagello, and Ludmila Ulehla, Manhattan School of Music, M.M. 1959. He received a Ford Found. grant as composer-in-residence, 1961-62. He is a private teacher of piano and composition.

WORKS: OPERA: Antigone, 1 act, 1959; ORCHESTRA: 4 Christmas psalms, with chorus; The magic of music, scene for mime with orch., 1960; The crucifixion, with chorus, 1962; CHORUS: The swing, children's chorus, flute, piano, 1966; Bitter for sweet; The lamb; There is a silence; Dark house; many other choral pieces and songs.

57-36 138th St., Flushing, NY 11355

CHOU, WEN-CHUNG
b. Chefoo, China, 29 June 1923; to U.S. 1946. Studied with Nicolas Slonimsky in Boston; with Edgard Varese in New York; with Otto Luening, Columbia Univ., M.A. 1954. His awards include a Guggenheim fellowship, 1957; special citation, Koussevitzky Internat. Recording award, 1970. He has been faculty member, Columbia Univ., from 1964.

WORKS: ORCHESTRA: Landscapes, 1949; All in the spring wind, 1953; And the fallen petals, New York, 9 Feb. 1955; BAND: Metaphors (4 seasons); Riding the wind, 1964; CHAMBER MUSIC: 3 folk songs, flute and harp; suite for woodwind quintet and harp; chamber concerto; 2 Chinese folk songs for harp; The willows are new, piano, 1957; Soliloquy of a Bhiksuni, solo trumpet, winds percussion, 1958; Cursive, flute and piano, 1963; Yu Ko, chamber ensemble, 1965; Pien, piano, winds, percussion, 1966; SONGS: 7 poems of the T'ang dynasty, tenor, winds, percussion.

Music Dept., Columbia Univ., New York, NY 10027

CHRISTIANSEN, F. MELIUS
b. Eidsvold, Norway, 1 Apr. 1871; to U.S. 1888; d. Northfield, Minn., 1 June 1955. Studied at Augsburg Coll. and Northwest Cons. He was chairman, music department, St. Olaf's Coll., and founder and director of the St. Olaf Choir, for which he wrote the St. Olaf Choir Services (in 6 volumes), 1920. He also wrote cantatas and hymns.

CHRISTIANSEN, LARRY A.
b. Chicago, Ill., 10 Oct. 1941. Studied with Tilden Wells, Ohio Wesleyan Univ.; with Anthony Donato, Northwestern Univ., M.M.; with Daniel Pinkham, Boston Univ. He held undergraduate and graduate fellowships; won second place in the 1964 Illinois Young Composer contest. His faculty posts include Chicago City Coll., 1967-68; Stevenson School, 1968-70; Southwestern Coll., from 1970.

WORKS: ORCHESTRA: Elegy and dithyramb; Voyage, with chorus, 1973; CHAMBER MUSIC: Fragments, chamber orch.; trio, clarinet, cello, piano, 1964; CHORUS: Evocation and impromptu, with clarinet, piano, percussion strings, 1973; Choral suite; many choral works and compositions in all genres.

Music Dept., Southwestern College, Chula Vista, CA 92010

CHRISTIANSEN, PAUL
b. Northfield, Minn., 31 July 1914, son of F. Melius Christiansen. Graduated from St. Olaf Coll., then studied at Oberlin Coll. and Eastman School of Music, M.M. He received honorary doctorates from Adams State Coll. and St. Olaf Coll. From 1937 he has been faculty member at Concordia Coll. and director of the Concordia Choir. The choir under his direction has been acclaimed in Europe as well as America.

WORKS: CHORUS: Everyman, to his own text, with organ or piano; Prayers of steel, Sandburg text; many original choral works and arrangements.

Music Dept., Concordia College, Moorhead, MN 56560

CHRYSTAL, WILLIAM ADAMSON
b. Pittsburgh, Pa., 26 Jan. 1931. Studied with Howard Thatcher, Peabody Cons., B.M. 1955, M.M. 1956. He has been a private teacher from 1959, and held faculty positions, Peabody Cons., 1955-56; Newkirk School of Music, Pensacola, 1958-59; and drama dept., Carnegie-Mellon Univ., from 1969.

WORKS: INCIDENTAL MUSIC: The only jealousy of Emer, Yeats, 1970; Pericles, prince of Tyre, Shakespeare, 1971; Twelfth night, Shakespeare, 1973.

481 McCully St., Pittsburgh, PA 15216

CIANI, SUZANNE E.
b. Indianapolis, Ind., 4 June 1946. Studied with Nicholas Van Slyck, Longy School of Music; with Hubert Lamb, Wellesley Coll.; with Andrew Imbrie, Univ. of California, Berkeley; and with John Chowning, Stanford Univ. Her awards include Hertz Memorial scholarship; ASCAP award; Ford Found. grant; CAPS grant; Nat. Endowment for the Arts grant, 1976. She was instructor, Univ. of California ext., 1971-72; president, Electronic Center for New Music, 1974-76; then president, Ciani/Musica Inc.

WORKS: BUCHLA SYNTHESIZER: Koddesh-Koddehim, 1972; New York, New York, 1974; New York, New York II, 1975; compositions for film and television; arrangements for records.

40 Park Ave., New York, NY 10016

CIRONE, ANTHONY J.

CIRONE, ANTHONY J.
b. Jersey City, N.J., 8 Nov. 1941. Studied percussion with Saul Goodwin, composition with
Vincent Persichetti at Juilliard School From
1965 he has been percussionist in the San Francisco Symph. and faculty member, California
State Univ. at San Jose.
WORKS: ORCHESTRA: double concerto for 2
percussion and orch.; PERCUSSION: sacred mass,
chorus and percussion; overture; Percussionality;
Japanese impressions; For four; Triptych; 2 symphonies; timpani sonata; sonata for trumpet and
percussion; 5 items for soprano and percussion,
on poems of Lou Harrison; violin sonata with
percussion; Cairo suite; also books of studies
for all percussion instruments.
1601 Santa Cruz Ave., Menlo Park, CA 94025

CITKOWITZ, ISRAEL
b. Russia, 6 Feb. 1909; U.S. citizen; d. London,
England, 4 May 1974. Studied with Aaron Copland
and Roger Sessions in New York; with Nadia
Boulanger in Paris. He taught at the Dalcroze
School of Music in New York; lived in London
from 1969.
WORKS: CHAMBER MUSIC: string quartet;
VOICE: The lamb, chorus; song cycle to words of
Joyce; Strings in the earth and air, 1930;
Gentle lady.

CITRON, RONALD P.
b. Bronx, N.Y., 15 Sept. 1944. Studied with
David Russell Williams, Eastman School Preparatory Dept.; with Exra Laderman, State Univ. of
N.Y. at Binghamton, M.M. 1975. He was a finalist
in the 1976 Nat. School Orch. Assoc. composition
contest with Fantasia quasi variazioni. Other
works include Adagio for orchestra and Suite
Harlequin for alto saxophone and piano.
27 Oakdale Rd., Johnson City, NY 13790

CIUS, ANTHONY B., JR.
b. Buffalo, N.Y., 11 Mar. 1938. Studied at
State Univ. of N.Y., Fredonia, B.M.E. 1960; with
John Pozdro and Edward Mattila, Univ. of Kansas,
B.M. 1967, M.M. 1970; on an exchange scholarship
at Reading Univ., England, 1968-69. He taught
in public schools, 1960-62; served in U.S. Navy,
1963-66; was instructor, Univ. of Kansas, 1969-
70, 1972-73; then resumed public school teaching.
WORKS: ORCHESTRA: Remembrances, orch. of
cellos, 1973, rescored for string orch., 1974;
CHAMBER MUSIC: 2 movements, violin and piano,
1966; string quartet, 1966; brass octet, 1967;
5 little pieces, flute and bassoon, 1968; piano
sextet, 1969; CHORUS: Gloria in excelsis Deo,
1960; Confiteor, 1968; Psalms 121 and 130, 1973,
a cappella; PIANO: Fantasie, 1962; Variations,
1966; Diabolus in musica, short sonata, 1966;
Fugue in C, 1968; ELECTRONIC: Children of the
Earth, synthesizer, bird calls, carillon, narrators, tape, 1973.
407 Walnut St., San Francisco, CA 94118

CLAFLIN, AVERY
b. Keene, N.H., 21 June 1898; d. Greenwich,
Conn., 9 Jan. 1979. Studied with Archibald T.
Davison at Harvard Univ., but his majors and his
career were in law and banking.
WORKS: OPERA: The fall of Usher, 1921;
Hester Prynne, 1932; La Grande Bretèche, 1947;
Uncle Tom's cabin, 1964; ORCHESTRA: Moby Dick
suite, 1929; 2 symphonies; Fishhouse punch, 1948;
Teen scenes, string orch., 1955; Concerto
giocoso, piano and orch., 1957; CHORUS: Lament
for April 15th, text verbatim from the Federal
Income Tax instructions; The quangle wangle's
hat, nonsense verse of Edward Lear; Design for
the atomic age, also from Edward Lear, by coin-
cidence the first performance was at Oak Ridge,
Tenn.; and chamber music.

CLAPP, PHILIP GREELEY
b. Boston, Mass., 4 Aug. 1888; d. Iowa City,
Iowa, 9 Apr. 1954. Studied with Walter Spalding,
Frederick Converse, and Edward B. Hill at Harvard,
Ph.D. 1911; and in Europe as a Sheldon fellow of
Harvard. He taught at Dartmouth Coll., 1915-19;
then joined the faculty at Univ. of Iowa.
WORKS: OPERA: The taming of the shrew,
1948; The flaming brand, on story of John Brown,
libretto by composer, 1949-53; ORCHESTRA: 12
symphonies, all except #4, 11, 12, were performed
all but #6, 8, 9, with the composer conducting;
Norge, symphonic poem, 1909; Song of youth, symphonic poem, 1910; Dramatic poem, with solo
trombone, 1912; Summer, 1914; Overture to a
comedy, 1933; A highly academic diversion on 7
notes, chamber orch., 1933; Fantasy on an old
plainchant, cello and orch., 1939; concerto for
2 pianos, 1945; A chant of darkness, chorus and
orch., to text by Helen Keller, 1919, rev. 1933;
CHAMBER MUSIC: violin sonata, 1909; string
quartet, 1909; suite for brass sextet, 1938;
Concerto suite, 4 trombones, 1939; Prelude and
finale, woodwind quintet, 1939; many choral works
and songs.

CLARK, MARY MARGARET WALKER
b. McComb, Miss., 24 Mar. 1929. Studied with
Helen Gunderson and Frank Page, Louisiana State
Univ. She was a school music teacher 1952-62.
Her compositions are mainly children's musicals,
choral pieces, and songs.
35 North Rd., East Granby, CT 06026

CLARK, MERRILL ROSS
b. Salt Lake City, Utah, 26 Nov. 1951. Studied
at Westminster Coll.; with Ladd McIntosh and
William Fowler, Univ. of Utah. His awards include recognition at jazz festivals in 1971 and
1972; commissions from Univ. of Utah and J. F.
Kennedy Center, Washington, D.C.
WORKS: ORCHESTRA: concerto for electric
guitar, Univ. of Utah, Jan. 1972; Dialogue,
rock band and orch., 1972; CHORUS: a rock mass,
1972; JAZZ: Creatures, 1972; Nameless as yet;
Schmear, 1972.
1774 S. 26th East, Salt Lake City, UT 84108

CLARK, ROBERT KEYES
b. Cambridge, Md., 18 Nov. 1925. Studied with
Vincent Persichetti, Philadelphia Cons., B.M.;
with Bernard Wagenaar, Juilliard School, B.S.,
M.S. He held a teaching fellowship at Juilliard,
1951-53; received the Roth Nat. Orch. award,

1970; was artist-in-residence, Univ. of Indiana, 1976; received Nat. Endowment for the Arts grant, 1976; ASCAP awards; commissions. He has been conductor of the Middlebury Orch. since 1955; from 1963, director, Waterbury Choral Guild; was conductor of the Cheshire Chorale Society, 1957-59; in 1965, founded the Connecticut Festival Orch. and Chorus and continues as music director.
    WORKS: THEATRE: Music for dance, ballet for solo dancer and piano, 1959; The magic trumpet, musical fairy tale for children, 1957; incidental music for The wasteland, 1959; ORCHESTRA: 3 symphonies, 1952, 1953, 1963; Antiphon, organ and string orch., 1955; The antic muse, 1962; violin concerto, 1965; Any number can play, suite for young orch., 1966; Repercussions, 1969, Indianapolis, 26 Jan. 1976; clarinet concerto, 1970; Lamentation, string orch., 1971, New York, 18 Apr. 1974; Monument, a fantasia on music of Machaut, 1974; bassoon concerto, 1976; Iam moriturus, cantata with soprano, chorus, and orch., 1977; CHAMBER MUSIC: 2 piano sonatas, 1949, 1956; sonata for solo violin, 1950; string quartet, 1950; Divertimento, string trio, 1954; Siciliana, piano, 1956; Patterns for percussion, 5 players, 1967; Cameos, woodwind quintet, 1975; VOICE: 2 songs for SSA, 1954; 2 songs for men's chorus, 1956; A cantata for Christmas, chorus and organ, 1958; Mass for 4 voices, 1961; Dirges, cycle of 3 songs for soprano and violin, 1961; Moments for mezzo, 4-song cycle, 1965; 4 ballads, soprano and piano, 1972; Morning, noon, night, and a commentary, 4-song cycle for women's voices.
    Rte. 1, Box 5, Kent, CT 06757

CLARK, ROGIE
    b. Atlanta, Ga., 4 Apr. 1917. Studied at Clark Coll., A.B.; Chicago Musical Coll.; with Douglas Moore and Normand Lockwood, Columbia Univ., M.A.; at Juilliard School; and at Tanglewood. His awards include Ford Found. fellowships; Tanglewood fellowship; Nat. Endowment for the Arts grant, 1973; John Hay Whitney award; Nat. Assoc. of Negro Musicians award, 1973. He has held academic posts at Fort Valley State Coll.; New School for Social Research; New Music School, New York; Jackson State Coll.; public schools, Warren, Mich.; lecturer in black music, Detroit public schools. He is also consultant for black studies programs, folklore workshops, black music workshops, festivals, Afro-American programs.
    WORKS: OPERA: Ti Yette, 1 act; The stranger; The myrtle tree; BALLET: The lonely island; ORCHESTRA: Fete Creole; Prelude for Wednesday; larghetto, string orch.; BAND: John Henry fantasy; CHAMBER MUSIC: Figurine, cello and piano; Fantasia, clarinet and piano; Divertimento, string quartet; piano works, songs, many choral arrangements. He is author of magazine articles; a play, The black bard: A study of black folk music (mss.); and poetry.
    17127 Kentucky, Detroit, MI 48211

CLARK, THOMAS SIDNEY
    b. Highland Park, Mich., 23 Aug. 1949. Studied with George Balch Wilson, Eugene Kurtz, and

Leslie Bassett, Univ. of Michigan, D.M.A. He received a Bicentennial commission for an orchestral work in 1976. His academic posts have included Indiana Univ., 1973; Pacific Lutheran Univ., 1973-74; Interlochen Music Camp, summers, 1975-78; from 1976, North Texas State Univ.
    WORKS: ORCHESTRA: Animated landscapes #1, 1972, #2, 1974; Illuminations: 3 refractions of time, 1976; BAND: Microscopic episodes, 1973; CHAMBER MUSIC: Trilogy, brass quintet, 1968; Autumn rain music, oboe and piano; Night songs, solo trombone, 1969; Tyger, chamber ensemble, 1971; A new dusk, chamber ensemble, 1974; MIXED MEDIA: Somniloquy, dancer, trombone, tape, 1970; Space hold, electronic film music, 1971; Straw music, violin and tape, 1972; Shores of infinity, choir and tape, 1974; Celestial ceremonies, tape, 1975; Diag dreams, viola and tape, 1978.
    School of Music, North Texas State Univ., Denton, TX 76203

CLARKE, GARRY E.
    b. Moline, Ill., 19 Mar. 1943. Studied with Alf Houkom, Cornell Coll., B.M. 1965; with Mel Powell and Yehudi Wyner, Yale Univ., M.M. 1968. His awards include fellowships from Ford Found., Carnegie Found., Woodrow Wilson Found.; Nat. Endowment for the Humanities grant; Rena Greenwald composition prize; and a Bradley-Keeler fellowship. Since 1968 he has been faculty member, Washington Coll.
    WORKS: OPERA: Westchester Limited, 1972; ORCHESTRA: Peck Hill holiday, 1973; BAND: Structure for band, 1971; CHAMBER MUSIC: string quartet, 1966; violin sonata, 1964; woodwind quintet, 1964; violin suite, 1965; Lissajous figures, 1968; Some versions of silence, 1968; CHORUS: Epitaphs, 1971; Comme avant comme apres, 1973; numerous other choral works; PIANO: Triptych, 1967; Montage, 1967. He is editor of music of Charles Ives and author of Essays on American music, 1977.
    Kentmere-Quaker Neck, Chestertown, MD 21620

CLARKE, HENRY LELAND
    b. Dover, N.H., 9 Mar. 1907. Studied at Harvard Univ., A.B. 1928, A.M. 1929, Ph.D. 1947; also with Nadia Boulanger, Gustav Holst, Hans Weisse, and Otto Luening. He received the John Harvard fellowship, 1929-30; American Council of Learned Societies grant, 1936; Washington Music Educators prize, 1964. He was assistant librarian, New York Public Library, 1932-36; then held teaching posts at Bennington Coll., 1936-38; Westminster Choir Coll., 1938-42; Univ. of California, Los Angeles, 1947-48, 1949-58; Vassar Coll., 1948-49; Univ. of Washington, 1959-77.
    WORKS: OPERA: The loafer and the loaf, chamber opera, 1951; Lysistrata, 1969; ORCHESTRA: Monograph, 1952; Sarabande for the golden goose, 1957; Points west, wind and percussion, 1960; Encounter, viola and orch., 1961; CHAMBER MUSIC: 2 string quartets; Danza de la muerte, a choreography for oboe and piano, 1937; Nocturne, viola and piano, 1955; A game that 2 can play, flute and clarinet, 1966; Concatenata, horn and woodwind quartet, 1967; Danza de la vida, oboe and piano, 1975; Give and take and Terza rime, 2 key-

CLARKE, LAURENCE GORDON

boards, 1977; CHORUS: <u>Before dawn</u>; <u>Happy is the</u>
<u>man</u>, 1935; <u>No man is an island</u>, 1951; <u>Love in</u>
<u>the world</u>, women's chorus, 1953; <u>Wonders are</u>
<u>many</u>, men's chorus, 1954; <u>L'Allegro</u> and <u>Il Pen-</u>
<u>seroso</u>, on Milton text; <u>Patriot primer</u>, Brattle-
boro, Vt., 6 June 1961; <u>Mass for all souls</u>,
Indianapolis, 20 June 1976; <u>These are the times</u>
<u>that try men's souls</u>, Tom Paine text, Washington,
D.C., 13 Sept. 1976; <u>The young dead soldiers</u>,
text by Archibald MacLeish, 1977; <u>The spring</u>,
1978.
 1 Waping Rd., Deerfield, MA 01342

CLARKE, LAURENCE GORDON
 b. Denver, Colo., 8 Feb. 1923. Studied with Roy
Harris at Colorado Coll.; with Roger Sessions at
Univ. of California, Berkeley; and with Darius
Milhaud at Mills Coll. His awards include Composers' Forum publication award, and Montpelier
Prix de Composition, Cheltenham, England. He
was instructor, Music and Arts Inst., San Francisco, 1953-56; from 1958; faculty member, Santa
Rosa Jr. Coll.
 WORKS: BALLET: <u>Enchantment of Alonzo</u>
<u>Quixano</u>; ORCHESTRA: <u>Episodes</u>; <u>Sinfonia</u> for
strings; <u>I'll make me a world</u>, cantata with
chorus and soloists; CHAMBER MUSIC: sonata for
flute and guitar; <u>Variations</u>, violin and piano;
VOCAL: <u>Everyone sang</u>, 4 pieces for a cappella
choir; <u>Chamber music</u>, song cycle for solo voice.
 901 Humboldt St., Santa Rosa, CA 95404

CLARKE, REBECCA (Mrs. James Friskin)
 b. Harrow, England, 27 Aug. 1886; her father was
a U.S. citizen; d. New York, 13 Oct. 1979.
Studied composition with Sir Charles Stanford,
Royal Coll. of Music, London; viola with Lionel
Tertis. In 1919 her viola sonata placed second
to Ernest Bloch's entry for the Coolidge prize
at the Berkshire Festival; her piano trio placed
second in the same contest in 1921. She was an
accomplished violinist and violist and toured
Europe with the English Ensemble, a piano quartet which she organized.
 WORKS: CHAMBER MUSIC: viola sonata, 1919;
piano trio, 1921; <u>Chinese puzzle</u>, violin and
piano, 1922; <u>3 Irish country songs</u>, violin and
cello; suite for clarinet and viola, Berkeley,
Calif., 1942; many songs, shorter peices, violin
solos.

CLARKE, ROSEMARY
 b. Daytona Beach, Fla., 23 June 1921. Studied
at Stetson Univ., B.M. 1940, M.M. 1941; with
Rollo Maitland, Philadelphia Musical Acad.,
organ dipl. 1942; with Bernard Rogers and
Herbert Elwell, Eastman School of Music, Ph.D.
1950. She was named a Fellow, American Guild of
Organists, 1953. She taught at Stetson Univ.,
1942-57; founded and directed Rosemary Clarke
Cons., 1949-57; was artist-in-residence, Univ.
of Dubuque, 1957-62; from 1962; professor and
composer-in-residence, Univ. of Wisconsin-
Platteville.
 WORKS: ORCHESTRA: 2 piano concertos; 2
<u>Elegies</u>; <u>Wrath</u>, soprano and orch.; BAND: <u>Fan-</u>
<u>tasy</u>, with piano; <u>Skyrocket</u>; CHAMBER MUSIC:
trio sonata, trumpet, viola, cello; piano trio;

<u>Happening</u>, flute and double bass; <u>Suite of</u>
<u>changes</u>, 6 instruments, voice, percussion; <u>Scher-</u>
<u>zando</u>, 3 clarinets, 1960; <u>Sngof roh sn Goffog</u>,
saxophone and piano, 1972; suite for piano and
percussion, 1972; <u>Gravadante</u>, 3 clarinets, 1973;
<u>Continuum</u>, horn, alto saxophone, vibraphone,
1977; nonet, 4 brass, 4 woodwinds, percussion,
1978; <u>Sieben</u>, 7 trombones, 1978; trio for brass,
trumpet, horn, trombone, 1978; MIXED MEDIA:
<u>Circus caricatures</u>, piano and dancers, 1946;
<u>Serpents-soldiers</u>, flute, doublebass, dancers,
1969; <u>Fors a tré</u>, 2 horns, tape, 1969, <u>9x2 and</u>
<u>6x2</u>, tape, 1972; <u>To beat or not to beat</u>, tape,
visuals, dancers, 1972-73; <u>Reflections on void's</u>
<u>progeny</u>, tape, speaker, visuals, brass, projec-
tionist, dancer, 1972-73; also choral works,
organ and piano pieces, songs.
 P.O. Box 615, Dubuque, IA 52001

CLAYTON, LAURA
 b. Lexington, Ky., 8 Dec. 1943. Studied with
Charles Wuorinen, New England Cons., 1968-71;
with George Balch Wilson and Leslie Bassett,
Univ. of Michigan, 1974-79; with Rosina Lhevinne
and Darius Milhaud, Aspen School of Music. She
taught composition at Univ. of Michigan as a
graduate student; later employed with Performing
Artists Assoc.
 WORKS: <u>Construcoes</u> for slides and tape, was
a collaboration with a Brazilian graphic artist
and was chosen to represent Brazil in the 1973
Paris Bienalle; <u>Implosure</u>, 1975, music for 2
dancers in a glass booth, was a collaboration
with Milton Cohen of the Once Group; <u>Simichai-ya</u>,
saxophone and tape, 1976, was commissioned by
Don Sinta; <u>Cree songs to the newborn</u>, soprano
and ensemble, won the National Composers Com-
petition-ISCM, was premiered in Carnegie Hall,
22 Feb. 1979, and was chosen as an entry for the
1979 World Music Days Festival in Athens in
September.
 1137 S. 7th, #2, Ann Arbor, MI 48103

CLEMAN, THOMAS
 b. Ellensburg, Wash., 5 Jan. 1941. Studied with
William Bailey, Whitman Coll., B.A.; with Charles
Cushing, Arnold Elston, and Seymour Shifrin,
Univ. of California, Berkeley, M.A.; with David
Lewin, Marius Constant, and Leland Smith, Stan-
ford Univ., D.M.A. His academic posts have in-
cluded Univ. of California, 1963-64; Macalester
Coll., 1968-69; since 1969, humanities dept.,
Northern Arizona Univ. He is also editor of the
Amer. Soc. of Univ. Composers <u>Newsletter</u>, and
founder-codirector, Northern Arizona Soc. for
Contemporary Music.
 WORKS: ORCHESTRA: <u>Music for large orches-</u>
<u>tra</u>; <u>Shine perishing republic</u>, 1969; <u>13 at</u>
<u>dinner</u>, 1969; CHAMBER MUSIC: <u>Variations</u>, piano,
4 hands, 1965; <u>Words for the wind</u>, baritone and
chamber ensemble; <u>Music for percussion</u>, 1967;
wind quintet, 1969; <u>Music for multiple celli and</u>
<u>piano</u>, 1971; <u>Io and the ox-eye daisy</u>, voice,
tamtam, harp, 1972; FILM: music for 2 educational films on the Navajo and the Hopi, 1972.
 409 W. Havasupai Rd., Flagstaff, AZ 86001

CLEMENTS, OTIS
b. Baltimore, Md., 5 July 1926. Studied with
Nicholas Nabokov and Theodore Chandler, Peabody
Cons.; with Bernard Wagenaar at Juilliard School.
From 1950 he has been composer and arranger for
television and recording artists in New York.
WORKS: ORCHESTRA: incidental music to
Journey's end, 1946; Suite in miniature, Washington, D.C., 25 Mar. 1947; Gala day overture,
1949; FILM SCORE: School play, an entrant in
the New Directors' division, Cannes Festival
1970; also composed new songs for the 1973
revival on Broadway of Irene.
301 E. 22nd St., New York, NY 10010

CLIFTON, CHALMERS
b. Jackson, Miss., 30 Apr. 1889; d. New York,
19 June 1966. Studied at Cincinnati Cons.; with
Edward B. Hill and Walter Spalding, Harvard
Univ.; and with Vincent d'Indy and Andre Gédalge
in Paris. He was conductor of the St. Cecilia
Society, Boston, 1915-17; American Orchestra
Society, New York, 1922-30; guest conductor of
many major orchestras and of the San Carlo Opera
Company.
WORKS: ORCHESTRA: The poppy, tenor and
orch.; suite for trumpet and orch.; CHAMBER
MUSIC: violin sonata; 2 piano sonatas; piano
pieces.

CLOKEY, JOSEPH WADDELL
b. New Albany, Ind., 28 Aug. 1890; d. Covina,
Calif., 14 Sept. 1961. Studied at Miami Univ.,
B.A. 1912; and at Cincinnati Cons. He taught
at Pomona Coll., 1926-39; at Miami Univ., 1915-
26, dean, School of Fine Arts, 1939-46.
WORKS: THEATRE: The pied piper, opera,
1920; The nightingale, opera, 1925; Our American
cousin, opera, 1931; A rose from Syria, music
drama; ORCHESTRA: 2 symphonies; CHAMBER MUSIC:
violin sonata; cello sonata; also choral works,
songs, organ pieces.

CLOUGH-LEITER, HENRY
b. Washington, D.C., 13 May 1874; d. Wollaston,
Mass., 15 Sept. 1956. Attended George Washington
Univ. (then Columbian Univ.), 1887-89; then went
to Trinity Univ., Toronto, for a degree in music.
He was organist in Washington from age 15, later
in Providence, R.I., from 1901 in Boston; was
editor-in-chief, E. C. Schirmer, Boston, 1921-
56.
WORKS: ORCHESTRA: Lasca, tenor and orch.;
The Christ of the Andes, double chorus, soli,
orch.; CANTATAS: The righteous branch; Christ
triumphant; CHAMBER MUSIC: A day of beauty,
string quintet; some 200 songs.

COATES, GLORIA KANNENBERG
b. Wauwau, Wis., 10 Oct. 1938. Studied with
Alexander Tcherepnin, Salzburg Mozarteum, 1962;
with Helen Gunderson and Kenneth Klaus, Louisiana
State Univ., B.M. 1963, M.M. 1965; with Jack
Beeson and Otto Luening, Columbia Univ., 1966-
68. She received Alice M. Ditson grants, 1973,
1974; and a Munich Ministry of Culture grant.
She was music critic, Baton Rouge State Times,
1962-65; music director, German-American Contem-

porary Music Series, Munich American House, 1971-
73; director, Music Today, Lenbach Gallery,
Munich, 1973-74; from 1974, director, Evening
Concert, Munich American House.
WORKS: THEATRE: incidental music for
Hamlet, Everyman (morality play), Saint Joan
(Shaw), Thieves' carnival; ORCHESTRA: Planets,
Milwaukee Symphony, 7 Feb. 1979; CHAMBER MUSIC:
4 string quartets, #4 Berlin Radio, 21 Apr. 1978;
Counterpoint counter, chamber ensemble; Structures, piano; Trio for 3 flutes; 5 abstractions
form poems of Emily Dickinson, woodwind quartet;
My country 'tis of thee, piano, 4 hands, and 2
instruments; Spring morning at Grobholz, 3
flutes and tape; We have ears and hear not,
chamber ensemble, Munich, 18 Apr. 1978; 5 abstractions, piano; Music on open strings, chamber
orch., Warsaw, 20 Sept. 1978; VOICE: Voices of
women in wartime, cycle for soprano and ensemble;
Mathematical problem, soprano and piano; Emily
Dickinson songs for soprano; also organ works.
Tengstrasse 20, 8 Munich 40, Germany

COBB, DONALD
b. Oakland, Calif., 13 Nov. 1936. Studied with
Richard Donovan, Yale School of Music; with Leon
Kirchner, Darius Milhaud, and Luciano Berio,
Mills Coll. He taught at Mills Coll., 1968-73;
was music director, Oakland Museum Concerts,
1971-72; director, Lodestar Music Camp, 1968-69.
WORKS: CHAMBER MUSIC: Part music, woodwind
quintet; Journeys, small orch.; CHORUS: Town of
American visions, with piano; The Springfield of
the far future, with piano; Heaven conserve thy
course in quietness, women's voices and viola;
Crazy Jane songs; Cold Mountain songs.
P.O. Box 324, San Leandro, CA 94577

COBB, HAZEL
b. Groesbeck, Tex., 15 July 1892; d. Dallas,
Tex., 8 Sept. 1973. Attended American Cons.,
B.M. 1922, M.M. 1924. From 1927 she was composer and private teacher of piano in Dallas.
WORKS: ORCHESTRA: Daughter of Mohammed;
Lamps trimmed in burning; CHORUS: The mission
bell, cantata; many songs, piano pieces, duets,
etc.

COBB, NANCY. See HILL, NANCY E.

COBINE, ALBERT STEWART
b. Richmond, Ind., 25 Mar. 1929. Studied with
Bernhard Heiden, Indiana Univ., 1952-54. He won
the Thor Johnson award for a suite for brass
ensemble. He is a free-lance writer-arranger,
band leader, and music contractor.
WORKS: BAND: March, pastoral, and fanfare;
suite for trumpet and concert band; variations
on We three kings; BRASS ENSEMBLE: Vermont
suite; Trilogy for brass; jazz stage band:
That's the way I feel; CHORUS: Bethlehem; Oh
Lord, help us live each day; Snow's a comin';
Tavern of loving people; Song of the earth.
R.R. 11, Box 85, Bloomington, IN 47401

COCHRAN, J. PAUL
b. Pittsburgh, Pa., 25 May 1946. Attended
Hanover Coll., B.A. 1968; studied with Barney

CODY, JUDITH

Childs, Wayne Bohrnstedt, and Lloyd Rogers, Univ. of Redlands, M.M. 1974; with Anthony Donato, William Karlins, and Alan Stout, Northwestern Univ., 1975-76. He was faculty member, Chicago Cons. Coll., 1977-78, then appointed dean.
WORKS: CHAMBER MUSIC: Drone/fantasy, clarinet and piano; sextet for flutes; string quartet, 1976; CHORUS: The sun by day, 1976; also sacred organ pieces.
2321 Cedar St., Des Plaines, IL 60018

CODY, JUDITH
b. Troy, N.Y., 29 Aug. 1943. Has published a number of works for solo guitar and guitar with voice and other instruments.
Box 1107, Los Altos, CA 94022

CODY, ROBERT O.
b. Biloxi, Miss., 18 Apr. 1928. Studied with Violet Archer and Gerhart Dorn, North Texas State Univ., B.M. 1952; with Leonard Ratner, Stanford Univ.; and with Louis Angelini at East Texas State Univ., Ph.D. 1958. He has received many commissions. He was chairman of the fine arts div. and music dept., Henderson County Jr. Coll., 1958-68; from 1968, at Wharton County Jr. Coll.
WORKS: OPERA: By his own hand, 1 act; BRASS ENSEMBLE: Reflections in brass; CHAMBER MUSIC: Theatre piece, tuba and piano; trumpet sonata; CHORUS: Still moon, with 2 pianos; SONGS: Spring is like a perhaps hand; Love is not all; When in the sessions of sweet silent thought.
P.O. Box 804, Wharton, TX 77488

COE, KENTON
b. Tenn., 12 Nov. 1932. Studied with Quincy Porter and Paul Hindemith, Yale Univ., B.A. 1953; with Nadia Boulanger, Paris Cons., 1953-56. His awards include a composition prize, Fontainebleau Cons., 1953; French government grants, 1954, 1955; MacDowell fellowships, 1960, 1963; and a commission from Notre Dame Cathedral, Paris, for a new liturgy service.
WORKS: OPERA: South, adapted from play by Julien Green, was premiered by Opera of Marseilles, 14 Oct. 1965; Le grand sicle, text by Ionescu, 1 act, performed by Opera of Nantes, 1972; The white devil, after play by John Webster; Rachel, 1976, libretto by Anne Howard Bailey, commissioned by the Tenn. Arts Commission and Tenn. Performing Arts Found. for the U.S. Bicentennial celebration and the opening of the Tenn. Cultural Center Opera House, Nashville; CHORUS: The handwriting on the wall, cantata for chorus, 4 brasses, timpani, 2 pianos, Nashville, 12 Nov. 1978; FILM SCORE: Birds in Peru, 1968.
1309 Lynnwood Dr., Johnson City, TN 37601

COERNE, LOUIS ADOLPHE
b. Newark, N.J., 27 Feb. 1870; d. Boston, Mass., 11 Sept. 1922. Studied with John Knowles Paine, Harvard Univ., B.A. 1890, Ph.D. 1905; with Josef Rheinberger in Munich. He was instructor at Harvard and Smith Coll.; director, School of

Music, Univ. of Wisconsin; from 1915, professor, Connecticut Coll. His works include 4 operas, a music drama, a violin concerto and numerous other orchestral works, chamber music, choral works, and songs. Many of his manuscript works are in the Boston Public Library.

COGAN, ROBERT DAVID
b. Detroit, Mich., 2 Feb. 1930. Studied with Ross Lee Finney, Univ. of Michigan, M.M. 1952; with Roger Sessions, Princeton Univ., M.F.A. 1956, Phi Beta Kappa; with Aaron Copland at Tanglewood, Nadia Boulanger in Paris, and with Philipp Jarnach in Hamburg. His honors include Young Composers' Radio award, 1952; Fulbright grants, 1952-53; Chopin scholarship, 1954; German government grant, 1958-60; 5 MacDowell fellowships; Guggenheim fellowships, 1968-69. He has been chairman of graduate theoretical studies, New England Cons., from 1963.
WORKS: ORCHESTRA: Fantasia, 1951; incidental music to Brecht's A man equals a man, 1952; CHAMBER MUSIC: string quartet, 1950; songs on texts by Ezra Pound, 1952-54; violin sonata, 1953; 2 string trios, 1953, 1959; Sounds and variants, piano, 1961; Spaces and cries, 5 brasses, 1964; MIXED MEDIA: Whirl . . . ds I, voice, 44 instruments, microphonist, text by composer, Boston Symphony, 13 Dec. 1967; Whirl . . . ds II, 2 solo voices (or chorus) transmute vocal sounds with an elaborate array of cupping utensils, 1973; No attack of organic metals, organ and tape, 1973, Cleveland, 1 Oct. 1977; Dr. Faust roll thinking, a long work for tape begun in 1975, sketches were performed at a New England Cons. concert of Cogan's works on 19 Nov. 1978; at the same concert, given to honor Cogan's 15 years at the conservatory, was the first American performance of Utterances for violin and piano. He is coauthor with his wife, Pozzi Escot, of Sonic design: The nature of sound and music, 1976; and author of Sonic designs: Practice and problems, 1979.
24 Avon Hill St., Cambridge, MA 02140

COGGIN, C. ELWOOD
b. Richmond City, N.C., 13 Nov. 1914. Attended Campbell Coll., Univ. of North Carolina, and Southern Baptist Theological Seminary. He has received several ASCAP awards. His posts in ministry of music have included churches in Fayetteville, N.C., 1947-51; Louisville, Ky., 1954-56; Walterboro, S.C., 1956-65; and Charlotte, N.C., 1965-74. He has published more than 230 sacred anthems, and also a cantata, Let us go on, commissioned for the Mecklenburg County Bicentennial in 1968.
112 Oakridge Dr., Charlotte, NC 28216

COHAN, GEORGE M.
b. Providence, R.I., 3 July 1878; d. New York, N.Y., 5 Nov. 1942. As a boy he toured the vaudeville circuit with his parents and sister as "The Four Cohans." He had a natural talent for writing lyrics and melodies for popular songs.
WORKS: MUSICAL SHOWS: Little Johnny Jones, 1904 (featured the songs The Yankee Doodle boy

and Give my regards to Broadway); Forty-five minutes from Broadway, 1906 (included Mary's a grand old name); many other songs including his greatest hit Over there, 1917, which swept the country in World War I and won him a Congressional Medal.

COHEN, DAVID
b. Pulaski, Tenn., 14 Oct. 1927. Studied with Vincent Persichetti at Philadelphia Cons. and Juilliard School; with Ingolf Dahl, Univ. of Southern California. He received the Coolidge Chamber Music prize at Juilliard, 1952; Fulbright scholarship, 1953; IBM graduate research grant, 1965; and commissions. He was faculty member, Univ. of Alabama, 1955-67; from 1967, at Arizona State Univ.
WORKS: OPERA: Beauty is fled, children's opera, Phoenix, Aug. 1977; ORCHESTRA: symphony #2, 1970; BAND: Rhinoceros variations; CHAMBER MUSIC: woodwind quintet, 1952; piano sonata, 1955; piano trio, 1960; Divertimento, 4 flutes, 1967; trio for violin, clarinet, piano; CHORUS: 4 seasons, 1965; La maison construite par Jean, with small orch., 1971; ELECTRONIC: Sound image I, recorded synthesizer, 1971; Computer fragments.
1045 E. Loyola Dr., Tempe, AZ 85282

COHEN, EDWARD
b. 1940. Studied with Seymour Shifrin and Luigi Dallapiccola, Univ. of California, Berkeley; with Max Deutsch in Paris on a George Ladd fellowship from Univ. of California. He was faculty member at Brandeis Univ. to 1978; then at Mass. Inst. of Technology.
WORKS: ORCHESTRA: Nocturne, Boston, 11 May 1973; CHAMBER MUSIC: Madrigal for 5 instruments; sextet; Elegy, soprano and chamber ensemble, Berkshire Music Center, 13 Aug. 1977.
Music Dept., Mass. Inst. of Technology, Cambridge, MA 02139

COHEN, JEROME D.
b. Spokane, Wash., 6 Feb. 1936. Studied with Jean Sharp, Eastern Washington State Coll.; with Francis Judd Cooke, New England Cons., B.M. 1959, M.M. 1963; also studied conducting at Tanglewood and privately with Richard Burgin. He has played cello, double bass, and bassoon in orchestras since 1948; has taught in public and private schools in Spokane and New England; was guest conductor of Boston Pops, 1959, 1972, 1973; on managerial staff, New England Cons., 1966-73; from 1971, has conducted the Cape Cod Symphony; from 1979, assistant conductor, Boston Pops.
WORKS: ORCHESTRA: Concert overture #1, Boston Pops, 1959; Cape Ann, concert overture #2, Boston Pops, 1973; Beyond mind and speech, elegiac fugue, 1973; Old folks quadrille, on Stephen Foster themes, 1971; SONGS: Preludes, T. S. Eliot text, 4 songs for tenor and piano, 1958-72.
12 Pat Rd., Hanover, MA 02339

COHEN, JOSEPH M.
b. New York, N.Y., 3 Aug. 1917. Studied with Ralph Guenther, Texas Christian Univ., B.M., M.M.; with Bernard Rogers, Howard Hanson, and

Wayne Barlow, Eastman School of Music. He has received 3 ASCAP awards and 2 first-prize awards in the Wisconsin Music Club competition, 1969. He has been professor, St. Norbert Coll., from 1963.
WORKS: OPERA: Christmas carol; BALLET: Rhapsody for 3; ORCHESTRA: Concert piece; symphony; violin concertino; BAND: piano concerto; David and Goliath, oratorio for chorus, soloists, and concert band; Poem; CHORUS: There is no God, a cappella; 4 selected ballads, with soloists.
1374 Skylark Lane, Green Bay, WI 54303

COHEN, MARCIA
b. Chicago, Ill., 20 Aug. 1937. Studied with Leslie Bassett, Univ. of Michigan; with Eugene Weigel, Univ. of Illinois; with Leon Stein and Donald Jenni, De Paul Univ.; and with Alan Stout, Northwestern Univ. She received a Bennington Conf. fellowship. She was faculty and concert coordinator, Art Inst. of Chicago, 1974-77; from 1978, director of cultural affairs, city of Pensacola, Fla.
WORKS: CHAMBER MUSIC: Prism, chamber symphony, 1967; City dances, violin and piano, 1976; ELECTRONIC: ARP, tape, 1972; Changes, violin and tape, 1974; Music for my sister, flute, oboe, tape, 1975.
211 Sabine Dr., Pensacola, FL 32561

COHEN, SOL B. (pen name of VANEUF, ANDRE)
b. Urbana, Ill., 11 Jan. 1891. Studied at Chicago Musical Coll.; also in Paris and Budapest. He wrote and arranged film scores; was music director, Ruth St. Denis-Ted Shawn Ballet; conductor, Peoria Symphony; taught in various schools, 1944-62. He has written works for orchestra, for woodwind and brass instruments, and songs.

COHEN, STEVEN B.
b. New York, N.Y., 3 Sept. 1954. Studied with John Corigliano, Manhattan School of Music, 1971-76; with Giampaolo Bracali, also at Manhattan.
WORKS: CHAMBER MUSIC: concertino for flute and strings; Oboe variations, won honorable mention, Internat. Double Reed Soc. contest, 1977; sextet, piano and winds, New York, 3 June 1979; suite for flute and harp; songcycle on 7 poems by e. e. cummings, for tenor.
248-34 Thebes Ave., Little Neck, NY 11362

COHN, ARTHUR
b. Philadelphia, Pa., 6 Nov. 1910. Studied with William Happich, Combs Cons.; with Rubin Goldmark, Juilliard School, 1933-34. His awards include 2 Juilliard fellowships; 10 MacDowell fellowships; 2 Huntington Hartford grants; 3 Yaddo fellowships; first prize, American Soc. of Ancient Instruments contest, 1939; many ASCAP awards. He was curator, Fleischer Music Collection, Free Library of Philadelphia, 1934-52; head of classical music department, Mills Music, Inc., 1955-65; MCA Music, 1966-73; from 1973, director of serious music, Carl Fisher, Inc.
WORKS: ORCHESTRA: 5 nature studies, 1932;

COHN, JAMES

Retrospections, string orch., 1935; Music for brass instruments, 1935; suite for viola and orch., 1937; 4 preludes for string orch., 1937; 4 symphonic documents, 1939; quintuple concerto for 5 ancient instruments with modern orchestra, 1940; flute concerto; Variations for clarinet, saxophone, and strings, 1945; Kaddish, 1964; CHAMBER MUSIC: 6 string quartets, 1928-45; Machine music, 2 pianos, 1935; Music for bassoon solo, 1947; Declamation and toccata, solo bassoon; Hebraic study, solo bassoon; PERCUSSION: Quotations in percussion, for 6 players and 103 instruments, 1958. He is author of 3 books: The collector's 20th century music in the western hemisphere, 1961; 20th century music in Western Europe, 1965; Musical quizzical, 77 puzzles, 1970.
200 W. 86th St., New York, NY 10024

COHN, JAMES
b. Newark, N.J., 28 Feb. 1928. Studied with Wayne Barlow at Eastman School of Music; with Roy Harris at Cornell Univ.; and with Bernard Wagenaar at Juilliard School, B.S. 1949, M.S. 1950. His awards include Nat. Fed. of Music Clubs prize, 1944; Queen Elizabeth of Belgium prize, 1953; Ohio Univ. award, 1955; and an award in Florence, Italy, 1960. He has been musicologist at ASCAP since 1952.
WORKS: THEATRE: The fall of the city, opera, 1955; several ballets; ORCHESTRA: 8 symphonies; Variations on the wayfaring stranger, 1962; CHAMBER MUSIC: violin sonata; piano variations; 3 string quartets; many sonatas; also 2 secular cantatas, many short choral works.
1125 Lexington Ave., New York, NY 10021

COKE-JEPHCOTT, NORMAN
b. Coventry, England, 17 Mar. 1893; to U.S. 1911; d. New York, N.Y., 14 Mar. 1962. Studied with the organist of Trinity Church, Coventry, and became a fellow of the Royal Coll. of Organists at age 18, and of the American Guild of Organists a year later. In the 1920s he studied with Paul Vidal and Charles-Marie Widor in Fontainebleau. He was an honorary fellow, Royal Canadian Coll. of organists, and of Trinity Coll. of Music, London; received an honorary doctorate from Ripon Coll. He was organist and choirmaster, Cathedral of St. John the Divine, New York, 1932-53.
WORKS: ANTHEMS: O love that casts out fear; Surely the Lord is in this place; The gate of the year; Variants for St. Anne; Mass of St. John the Divine; ORGAN: Fugue on BACH; The glory of the Lord; Symphonic toccata; Miniature trilogy; Bishop's promenade; Terzetto; and many more sacred works for choir and organ.

COKER, WILSON
b. Pinckneyville, Ill., 26 Nov. 1928. Studied at St. Louis Inst. of Music, B.M. 1949; Yale Univ., B.M. 1951, M.M. 1954; Univ. of Illinois, D.M.A. 1954; and at Tanglewood with Milton Babbitt and Aaron Copland. His awards include the John Day Jackson prize, 1954; Koussevitzky prize, 1959; MENC-Ford Found. grant, 1960-63. He was faculty member, Hartwick Coll., 1958-60;

on staff at Lincoln Center, 1962-64; on faculty, San Jose State Coll., 1964-68; Fresno State Coll., 1968-75; from 1976, at Southern Illinois Univ.
WORKS: ORCHESTRA: Orestes, ballet music, 1953; symphony, 1957; Overture giocoso, 1961; Recitative and canzona, trombone and orch., 1965; Lyric statement, 1967; Declarative essay, 1970; BAND: trombone concerto, 1961; With bugle, fife, and drum, 1963; Polyphonic ode, 1969; CHAMBER MUSIC: 2 string quartets, 1949, 1954; string quintet; concertino for bassoon and string trio, 1964; woodwind quintet, 1964; trio for 3 clarinets; CHORUS: The dark hills, 1966; Paean, large chorus and orch., 1966. He is author of the book, Music and learning, 1971.
School of Music, So. Illinois Univ., Carbondale, IL 62901

COLBURN, GEORGE
b. Colton, N.Y., 25 June 1878; d. Chicago, Ill., 18 Apr. 1921. Studied at American Cons. and later taught there. He wrote incidental music for several plays, orchestral works, chamber music.

COLE, GERALD E.
b. Topeka, Kans., 29 Aug. 1917. Studied at Univ. of Kansas; with Normand Lockwood, Oberlin Coll.; with Wayne Barlow, Eastman School of Music. His faculty positions have included Tarkio Coll., 1940-44; Phillips Univ., 1944-49; Univ. of Western Ontario, 1951-55; from 1955, chairman and professor, Western Maryland Coll.
WORKS: His compositions include a string quartet, pieces for varied chamber ensembles, harp pieces, organ pieces, a 2-piano sonata, piano pieces, a mass, motets, songs.
Western Maryland Coll., Westminster, MD 21157

COLE, ULRIC
b. New York, N.Y., 9 Sept. 1905. Studied with Homer Grunn in Los Angeles, 1913-25; with Percy Goetschius, Inst. of Musical Art, New York, 1923-24; on fellowships with Rubin Goldmark and Josef Lhevinne, Juilliard Grad. School, 1924-27, 1930-32; with Nadia Boulanger in Paris, 1927-28. She received 2 awards from Society for Publication of American Music, 1931, 1941. As a pianist, she toured the U.S. and appeared with major orchestras; taught at Masters School, Dobbs Ferry, N.Y., 1936-42; was on staff, New York Philharmonic Young People's Concerts, 1943-45; on editorial staff, Time magazine, 8 years.
WORKS: ORCHESTRA: Divertimento, piano and string orch., Cincinnati Symph. Orch., 31 Mar. 1939, composer at piano; 2nd piano concerto, Cincinnati, composer as soloist, 1 Mar. 1946; Nevada, Sunlight channel, 2 pieces for string orch.; CHAMBER MUSIC: 2 string quartets; 2 violin sonatas; piano quintet, 1941; many pieces for piano solo and for 2 pianos.
Box 284, Southport, CT 06490

COLE, VINCENT
b. Los Angeles, Calif., 19 July 1946. Studied with Alden Ashforth, Roy Travis, and Henri Lazarof, Univ. of California, Los Angeles, 1968-

69; with Aurelio de la Vega, California State Univ. at Northridge, 1971-73. He was on staff, Electronic Music Lab., Calif. State Univ., Northridge, 1973-75; then on faculty, Moorpark Coll.

WORKS: ORCHESTRA: cantata for soprano and orch., 1975; CHAMBER MUSIC: string quartet, 1971; Distillations, solo cello, 1977; Chronikos, chamber ensemble, 1977 (received Atwater-Kent award); ELECTRONIC: Concrete study, tape, 1973; Lamentation, oboe and tape, 1973; Meditation, piano and tape, 1974.

16823 McKeever St., Granada Hills, CA 91344

COLEMAN, CHARLES DeWITT
b. Detroit, Mich., 29 Jan. 1926. Studied at Wayne State Univ., B.M. 1952, M.M. 1954; organ in New York and France; composition with Marcel Dupre in Paris. He received the Detroit Musicians' Assoc. plaque and Honorable Citizen award, 1974; is an associate, American Guild of Organists. He was minister of music and organist, Tabernacle Baptist Chuch, Detroit, 1954-74; St. Stephens A.M.E. Church, 1975-77; New Calvary Baptist Church, 1977-78; and has been head of his own publishing house from 1958. His compositions include many anthems and organ pieces and an epic poem on John Kennedy with his own text and music.

6476 Oakman Blvd., Detroit, MI 48228

COLEMAN, HENRY, JR.
b. Pensacola, Fla., 1 Sept. 1938. Studied orchestration with Joseph Wagner and composition with Aurelio de la Vega. He was instructor, California State Univ., Northridge, 1971-72.

WORKS: CHAMBER MUSIC: Esoterics for string quartet; Reality sandwiches, soprano and chamber ensemble; Dimentions [sic], 4 trombones; Sonare, brass nonette; 3 Klee impressions, chamber ensemble; Metallics, prepared piano, 4 timpani, percussion.

12953 S. Catalina, Gardena, CA 90249

COLEMAN, ORNETTE
b. Ft. Worth, Tex., 19 Mar. 1930. Studied at the School of Jazz, Lenox, Mass. He received a Guggenheim fellowship, 1963. He is a composer and saxophonist who also plays trumpet and violin.

WORKS: CONCERT JAZZ: Forms and sounds, wind quintet, 1965; Saints and sinners; Space flight; quintet for trumpet and strings, New York, 2 Oct. 1971; Joujou, New York, 21 Apr. 1974.

c/o Joyce Agency, 435 E. 79th St., New York, NY 10021

COLEMAN, RANDOLPH E.
b. Charlottesville, Va., 20 July 1937. Studied with Anthony Donato at Northwestern Univ., Ph.D. 1963. He received the William Faricy award, 1960; Internat. Society for Contemporary Music awards, 1962-63; Fromm Found. grant, 1964. He was faculty member, Winthrop Coll., 1963-65; from 1965, at Oberlin Coll.

WORKS: ORCHESTRA: Soundprint I, 1971; CHAMBER MUSIC: Soundprint II, 4 pianos, 1972;

Soundprint III, percussion and readers, 1972; string quartet, 1973; Undesignated: Format I, 1971; Format II, 1971; Event I, 1971; MIXED MEDIA: Format III, musicians, dancers, lights, 1973.

39 W. Vine St., Oberlin, OH 44074

COLGRASS, MICHAEL
b. Chicago, Ill., 22 Apr. 1932. Studied with Paul Price and Eugene Weigel, Univ. of Illinois, B.M. 1956; with Lukas Foss and Darius Milhaud at Tanglewood; also with Wallingford Riegger and Ben Weber. His awards include 2 Tanglewood fellowships, 1952, 1953; 2 Guggenheim fellowships, 1964, 1968; Fromm Found. award; Rockefeller grant for study of theatre arts in Milan and physical training for actors in Poland; Ford Found. grant, 1973; Pulitzer Prize, 1978; many commissions. As a free-lance percussionist, he has played with the New York Philharmonic, the Modern Jazz Quartet, in pit orchestras; also conducts clinics in composing, singing, acting, and dancing.

WORKS: ORCHESTRA: Divertimento, 8 drums, piano, strings, 1960; Rhapsodic fantasy, 15 drums and orch., 1965, New York premiere, 11 May 1974; Sea shadows, 1966; As quiet as, Tanglewood, 18 Aug. 1966; concertino for timpani; Earth's a baked apple, chorus and orch., 1968; Virgil's dream, narrator and orch., 1969; Auras, harp and orch., 1973, Seattle, 21 Mar. 1977; Image of man, with chorus and soloists, to composer's own text, Spokane Symph. Orch., Expo 74, May 1974; Concertmasters, 3 solo violins and orch., Detroit, 29 Jan. 1976; Theatre of the universe, with soloists and chorus, to his own text, Minnesota Orch., Mar. 1976; Best wishes U.S.A., black and white choruses, jazz band, soloists, folk instruments, orch., Springfield, Mass., 30 Mar. 1976; Letter from Mozart, New York, 3 Dec. 1976; Deja vu, percussion quartet and orch., New York, 20 Oct. 1977; CHAMBER MUSIC: Percussion music, 1953; 3 brothers, percussion; Chamber music, 4 drums and string quartet, 1954; Variations, 4 drums and viola, 1956; Fantasy variations, percussion, 1961; Rhapsody, clarinet, violin, piano, 1962; Light spirit, flute, viola, guitar, percussion, 1963; New people, mezzo-soprano, viola, piano, 1969; Wolf, solo cello, New York, 17 Feb. 1976; Chamber piece, percussion quintet, Boston, 19 Dec. 1976; Flashbacks, a musical play for 5 brass, New York, 6 Feb. 1979.

280 Riverside Dr., Apt. 1E, New York, NY 10025

COLLER, JEROME THOMAS
b. St. Paul, Minn., 6 Feb. 1929. Studied with Donald Ferguson, Paul Fetler, Paul Christiansen, Elie Siegmeister, Univ. of Minnesota, B.A. 1949, M.A. 1954; with Robert Palmer, Cornell Univ., D.M.A. 1971. He has been faculty member at St. John's Univ. from 1971.

WORKS: His compositions are mainly church music. Secular pieces include concerto for piano and winds, doctoral thesis, 1971; clarinet sonata; 6 piano preludes; Firmator sancte, organ suite; etc.

St. John's Abbey, Collegeville, MN 56321

COLLETTE, WILLIAM MARCELL (BUDDY)

COLLETTE, WILLIAM MARCELL (BUDDY)
b. Los Angeles, Calif., 6 Aug. 1921. Studied
with Ernest Kanitz in Los Angeles. He has
played flute with many jazz bands and with the
Los Angeles Neophonic Orchestra.
WORKS: JAZZ: Blue sands; Santa Monica; and
film scores.

COLLIER, GILMAN
b. New York, N.Y., 14 Apr. 1929. Studied with
Walter Piston, Harvard Univ., A.B.; with Paul
Hindemith, Yale School of Music; and with
Bohuslav Martinu, Mannes School of Music. He
was faculty member, New School for Social Research, N.Y., 1954-60; Westchester Cons., 1954-
74; music director and conductor, Monmouth Symph.
Orch., 1965-72; assistant director, Monmouth
Cons., from 1969.
WORKS: ORCHESTRA: concerto grosso for
piano and strings; Palindrome, a modern dance
piece for chamber orch.; CHAMBER MUSIC: 3 piano
sonatas; 6 sonatas (oboe, English horn, clarinet,
violin, viola, cello); woodwind quartet; woodwind quintet; various short solo and duo-piano
works, and short chamber music compositions;
CHORUS: 4 Chicago psalms, children's or women's
voices, a cappella.
65 Larchwood Ave., Oakhurst, NJ 07755

COLLINS, THOMAS W.
b. Dayton, Ohio, 5 Jan. 1935. Studied with
Eugene Hill, Miami Univ.; with David Gordon,
Univ. of Missouri. He won first prize in a
Miami Univ. composition contest, 1956. His
faculty positions have been at Tabor Coll.,
1959-67; and School of the Ozarks from 1967.
WORKS: CHAMBER MUSIC: string quartet, and
other chamber works; VOICE: Chapel windows,
cantata, 1969; 3 songs, high voice and piano,
1967; 2 songs, high voice and oboe, 1969;
numerous short works for organ.
School of the Ozarks, Point Lookout, MO
65726

COLSON, WILLIAM
b. Kansas City, Mo., 17 July 1945. Studied with
Walter Aschaffenburg and Richard Hoffman, Oberlin
Cons., B.M.; with Gordon Binkerd and Robert
Kelley, Univ. of Illinois, M.M., D.M.A.; Univ.
of Uppsala and Royal Acad. of Music, Sweden. He
won first prize and the Devora Nadworney award,
Nat. Fed. of Music Clubs contest, 1965; also won
a Univ. of Illinois concerto competition, 1968.
He has been faculty member, Southwestern Baptist
Theological Seminary, from 1971; also cellist in
the Fort Worth Symphony.
WORKS: ORCHESTRA: My last duchess, Browning
text, baritone and orch.; 3 Blake songs, soprano
and orch.; double concerto, piano, clarinet, and
strings; cello concerto; CHAMBER MUSIC: 3 songs
from A Shropshire lad by A. E. Housman, 1965;
3 short pieces, violin and piano; 6 variations
and a fugue, chamber ensemble; 8 pieces, flute
solo; violin sonatina; Serenade for winds; 3
miniatures, string trio; trio for clarinet,
cello, and piano.
2808 Covert Ave., Fort Worth, TX 76133

COMBS, MICHAEL
b. Hazard, Ky., 30 May 1943. Studied with Jack
McKenzie and Thomas Siwe, Univ. of Illinois,
B.S.; at Univ. of Missouri, M.A. He has been on
the faculty, Univ. of Tennessee, Knoxville, from
1972.
WORKS: PERCUSSION: concert snare drum
solos, 1968; Gesture, solo percussionist, 1969;
Mano dance, 1971; Leatherwood, 1971.
Music Dept., Univ. of Tennessee, Knoxville,
TN 37916

COMBS, RONALD
b. War Creek, Ky., 2 July 1938. Studied with
Felix Labunski, Scott Huston, and Charles Hamm
at Cincinnati Cons. He won an Ohio State Univ.
contest for a 1-act opera with The visitor, a
science fiction opera. He has been faculty member at Univ. of Wisconsin, 1970-76; from 1976,
at Northeastern Illinois State Univ.
WORKS: OPERA: The rider on the pale horse;
The visitor: The 3 wishes, children's opera with
woodwind quintet; The legend of the Christmas
rose; The monkey's paw, with wind instruments
only; A Christmas carol, after Dickens; and
others; also several cantatas, many songs, chamber music, etc.
917 Castlewood Terrace, Chicago, IL 60640

CONE, EDWARD T.
b. Greensboro, N.C., 4 May 1917. Studied with
Roger Sessions, Princeton Univ., A.B. 1939,
M.F.A. 1942; also studied piano with K. U.
Schnabel and E. Steuermann. He held a Guggenheim
fellowship, 1947-48; was Ernest Bloch lecturer,
Univ. of California, 1972. He has been faculty
member at Princeton Univ. from 1947.
WORKS: ORCHESTRA: symphony; piano concerto;
violin concerto; CHAMBER MUSIC: 2 string quartets; 2 violin sonatas; Rhapsody, viola and
piano; clarinet quintet, 1941; piano pieces;
VOICE: The lotus eaters, cantata, 1939-47; Excursion, chorus, 1955; Silent noon, soprano and
piano, 1964. He was coeditor with Benjamin
Boretz of Perspectives on notation and performance, 1976.
18 College Rd. W., Princeton, NJ 08540

CONFREY, EDWARD E. (ZEZ)
b. Peru, Ill., 3 Apr. 1895; d. Lakewood, N.J.,
22 Nov. 1971. He played with Jack Benny and
with Paul Whiteman. His most popular piano
works included Kitten on the keys, 1921;
Stumbling, 1921; Dizzy fingers, 1923; 3 little
oddities, 1923; Concert etude, 1922; Valse
mirage; Buffoon, 1930; Grandfather's clock, 1933;
Oriental fantasy, 1935; Sittin' on a log; Ultra,
ultra, 1935; etc. He also wrote a miniature
opera, Thanksgiving, 1947.

CONLEY, DAVID
b. Gorgas, Ala., 15 Oct. 1930. Studied with
Samuel Adler and William Latham, North Texas
State Univ.; with Samuel Adler at Eastman School
of Music. He was faculty member, Southwestern
Baptist Theological Seminary, 1959-77.
WORKS: ORCHESTRA: Introduction, 1967;
Piece for string orchestra, 1968; Fugal hexagon,

1971; CHAMBER MUSIC: Piano piece, 1959; duo for violin and viola, 1960; trio for 2 violins and cello, 1964; woodwind quartet, 1965; 12 short studies for horn, 1967; Pieces for woodwind ensemble, 1967, 1968; Short piece for harp, 1968; Short and suite, flute, violin, paino, 1970; CHORUS: Cool tombs, Sandburg text, 1960; Crucifixion, 1961; Let all the earth fear the Lord, men's voices, 1964; All revelation, women's voices, Frost text, 1970; SONGS: Glass house canticle, medium voice, Sandburg text, 1970; Slaves, medium voice, James Russell Lowell text, 1970; church service music, etc.
5204 Garrick Ave., Fort Worth, TX 76133

CONLEY, JOHN
b. Prestonburg, Ky., 25 June 1934. Studied with William Naylor, Cincinnati Cons.; with Kenneth Wright, Gordon Kinney, and R. Bernard Fitzgerald, Univ. of Kentucky. He won a cash award for the official AFROTC march, Ad astra, at Univ. of Kentucky. He has taught in the Fayette County schools, Lexington, Ky., from 1963.
WORKS: THEATRE: The legend of Daniel Boone, background score, 1971; ORCHESTRA: suite, 1962; Intermezzo; CHAMBER MUSIC: Dorian piece, oboe and string quartet, 1961; 3 early sacred pieces, brass quartet, 1964; Retrospection, piano, 1960.
2131 Jasmine Dr., Lexington, KY 40504

CONLEY, LLOYD
b. Rogers City, Mich., 8 Mar. 1924. Studied at Central Michigan Univ. and Michigan State Univ. He won the Kansas Centennial composition award for Kansas suite. From 1950 he has been a teacher in public schools.
WORKS: Many works for orchestra, band, solo instruments, ensemble, and voice; BAND: Tawas suite; Quiet valley; A symphonic invention.

CONRAD, TONY
b. Concord, N.H., 7 Mar. 1940. Studied at Peabody Cons. and at Harvard Univ. He received a Rockefeller Found. grant for research and production in film, composition, and performance; and a Cassandra Found. grant. In 1963-66, he was composer-performer with the Theater of Eternal Music.
WORKS: Fugue for strings, 1961; 3 loops, performers and tape recorders, 1961; The tortoise, his dreams and journeys, a cooperative piece with 7 accomplices, 1963; Emergency landing, 1970; Outside the dream syndicate, 1972; with Faust, 1972; for piano, 1974; FILM SCORES: Flaming creatures (with Jack Smith), 1963; The flicker, 1965; 10 years alive on the infinite plain, 1972.
111 W. 42nd St., New York, NY 10036

CONSOLI, MARC-ANTONIO
b. Catania, Italy, 19 May 1941; U.S. citizen 1967. Attended New York Coll. of Music, B.M.; Peabody Cons., M.M.; Yale Univ., M.M.A., D.M.A.; Warsaw Cons., Poland; Accademia Chigiana, Italy; Berkshire Music Center; studied with Ernst Krenek, Gunther Schuller, Alexander Goehr, Bulent Arel, George Crumb, Franco Donato, and Wladzimierz Kotonski. His awards include 5 fel-

lowships; Fulbright grant; 2 Rockefeller Found. grants; Guggenheim grant; Creative Artists Public Service grant; and an American Academy-Inst. of Arts and Letters award; and many commissions. He was founder and leader of the Yale Players for New Music; member of The Experiment, a multimedia group in Poland; director, Musica Oggi, contemporary chamber players in New York.
WORKS: ORCHESTRA: Variants, Baltimore, 1 June 1968; Profiles, 1972-73; Odefonia, 1976-77; CHAMBER MUSIC: Trigram I, chamber string ensemble, Bennington, 16 Aug. 1969; Dialogues, double bass and strings, 1969; Pezzo, piano, 1970; Interactions I, 7 winds and timpani, Tanglewood, 12 Aug. 1970; Interactions II, piano trio, Univ. of Maryland, 21 Mar. 1971; Interactions III, flute and harp, Yale Univ., 28 Apr. 1971; Interactions IV, winds, double bass, percussion, Yale Univ., 12 Dec. 1971; Formations, harp, 1972; Music for chambers, 3 groups of instruments, 1974; Sciuri novi, solo flute, 1974; Sciuri novi II, electric double bass and tape, 1975; Memorie pie, piano, 1976; VOICE: Equinox I, soprano and chamber ensemble, Baltimore, 23 May 1967; Equinox II, soprano and ensemble, Tanglewood, 14 Aug. 1968; Isonic, soprano and ensemble, Graz, Austria, 26 Oct. 1970; Canto Trinacriani, baritone, ensemble, and tape, 1974-75; Lux aeterna, 8-part chorus, 1972.
95-27 239th St., Bellerose, NY 11426

CONSTANTEN, TOM
b. New Jersey, 19 Mar. 1944. Studied at Univ. of Nevada, 1960-61; with Luciano Berio at Mills Coll. and in Italy, 1962-63; and with Henri Pousseur, Pierre Boulez, and Karlheinz Stockhausen in Germany. He has been piano soloist in his own works; with the Grateful Dead, 1968-70, then with the Incredible String Band; in 1974, was on the faculty at State Univ. of New York, Buffalo.
WORKS: THEATRE: Tarot, a rock musical without words, Brooklyn, Dec. 1970; Caucasian chalk circle, musical on Brecht's play, San Francisco, 1976; ORCHESTRA: Serenade, string orch., 1961; Conversation piece, piano and orch., Las Vegas, 28 May 1961, composer as pianist; Invocation of the sun, soprano, chorus, orch., 1969; Idyll of sea and mountains, Las Vegas, 5 Mar. 1972; PIANO: 3 pieces for 2 pianos, 1963; The syntax collector, suite, 1976; Through cloud and eclipse, 1977; Blaze of glory, 1977; Recombinant strains, suite, 1978; FILM SCORE: The love song of Charles Faberman, Kagan film, 1972.
314½ 49th St., Oakland, CA 94609

CONSTANTINIDES, CONSTANTINE DINOS
b. Ioannina, Greece, 10 May 1929; U.S. citizen 1967. Studied at Greek Cons., dipl. 1950; Juilliard School, dipl. 1960; Indiana Univ., M.M. 1965; composition with H. Owen Reed, Michigan State Univ., Ph.D. 1968. His awards include MTNA teaching award, 1970; Louisiana State Univ. faculty award, 1971; Outstanding Educators of America, 1971, 1972, 1973; ASCAP awards, 1976-78; several grants and commissions. He was violinist with the Athens State and Radio Symphonies, 1952-63; Indianapolis Symphony, 1963-

CONVERSE, FREDERICK SHEPHERD

65; concertmaster, Baton Rouge Symphony, and
professor, Louisiana State Univ., from 1966.
WORKS: THEATRE: Antigone, music drama on
text by Sophocles, 1973; Fugue for 2 voices,
1-act opera; ORCHESTRA: symphony, 1966; concerto for violin, cello, and piano, 1968; Anti-
theses; CHAMBER MUSIC: 2 string quartets, 1966,
1977; 2 piano trios, 1967, 1977; Improvisation,
trombone and piano, 1967; 20th century studies,
2 violins, 1970; viola sonata, 1972; Exploding
parallels, 1972; Theme and variations, piano,
1973; sonata for solo violin; Designs for strings;
guitar sonata; piano sonata; brass quintet; woodwind quintet; 8 miniatures, tuba quartet, 1978;
Fantasy, solo euphonium, 1978; many shorter
pieces for chamber groups and songs.
947 Daventry Dr., Baton Rouge, LA 70808

CONVERSE, FREDERICK SHEPHERD
b. Newton, Mass., 5 Jan. 1871; d. Westwood,
Mass., 8 June 1940. Studied with John Knowles
Paine, Harvard Univ., B.A. 1893; with George W.
Chadwick, New England Cons.; and with Josef
Rheinberger in Munich. His awards included the
Bispham Medal, 1909; honorary music doctorate,
Boston Univ., 1933; election to membership,
American Acad. of Arts and Letters, 1937. He
taught at Harvard, 1901-7; was vice president,
Boston Opera Company, 1911-14; served in U.S.
Army, 1917-19; taught at New England Cons.,
1930-38.
WORKS: OPERA: The pipe of desire, 1906,
the first American opera to be performed at the
Metropolitan Opera, New York, 18 Mar. 1909;
ORCHESTRA: 6 symphonies; Youth; Euphrosyne;
Festival of Pan; Endymion's narrative, 1903; The
mystic trumpeter, 1905; The sacrifice; The immigrants; Sinbad the sailor; Flivver 10 million,
1927; many other orchestral works and works for
chorus and orch.; CHAMBER MUSIC: 3 string quartets; violin sonata; cello sonata; piano trio;
piano pieces; songs.

COOK, JOHN
ORGAN: Divinum mysterium; Fanfare; Flourish and
fugue; Scherzo, dance, and reflection; Christ is
our cornerstone.
Massachusetts Inst. of Tech., Cambridge, MA
02139

COOK, PETER FRANCIS, III
b. Morristown, N.J., 1 Sept. 1923. Studied with
Herbert Elwell, Oberlin Cons., B.M. 1946, M.M.
1950; with Irving Fine at Tanglewood; with
Jacque Ibert and Darius Milhaud, Aspen School;
with Nadia Boulanger, Fontainebleau; with Louis
Cheslock, Peabody Cons., D.M.A. 1974. His
awards include Felice Haubiel fellowship; Victor
RCA scholarship; honorary membership, Phi Mu
Alpha, Sinfonia Frat. He has held faculty posts
at Florida State Univ., 1946; Mason Coll. of
Music, 1955; from 1956, at Austin Peay State
Univ., Clarksville, Tenn.
WORKS: ORCHESTRA: River boat fancy, piano
and orch.; piano concerto #1, with chamber
orch.; CHAMBER MUSIC: Dialogue, flute and
piano; PIANO: Forlana; Loredo variations;
Indian summer; The paddle wheel; There's a

cricket in the house; Mice in 3 blind keys; and
others.
Box 4426, Austin Peay State Univ., Clarksville, TN 37040

COOK, RICHARD G.
b. Dallas, Tex., 20 Oct. 1929. Studied with
Ralph Guenther, Texas Christian Univ.; with
Samuel Adler, North Texas State Univ. He has
received 2 grants of the Rockefeller Found. for
performance and recording. He taught at Handley
High School, 1957-61; Univ. of Texas at Arlington, 1962-63; from 1966, Kansas State Univ.,
Pittsburgh.
WORKS: ORCHESTRA: 2 symphonies; concertino
for orchestra; CHAMBER MUSIC: 3 songs of hope-
lessness, soprano and piano, 1963; string quartet, 1972; woodwind quartet; brass sextet;
violin sonata; Concert piece, trumpet and piano;
sonata for solo clarinet; CHORUS: Psalm 137;
MIXED MEDIA: Concert etude, bassoon, piano,
tape; The hydrogen dog and the cobalt cat,
soprano and tape, 1972; Requiem for Mahalia,
viola, piano, tape, 1972; 2 suites for Moog
synthesizer; many pieces for Moog alone or with
other instruments.
4-2 W. First, Pittsburgh, KS 66762

COOKE, JAMES FRANCIS
b. Bay City, Mich., 14 Nov. 1875; d. Philadelphia, Pa., 3 Mar. 1960. Was president of
Theodore Presser Company, 1925-36; of John
Church Company, 1930-36; editor of the Etude for
40 years; wrote articles on music and several
books on performance techniques, great composers,
etc. He composed many piano pieces and songs.

COOLEY, CARLETON
b. 1898. Studied at the Philadelphia Cons. and
the Inst. of Musical Art, New York. He received
an honorary music doctorate, Philadelphia Musical
Acad., 1945. He played viola many years with
the Cleveland Orchestra; was principal violist,
NBC Symphony for 17 years; and with the Philadelphia Orchestra; also played with the Cleveland String Quartet and the NBC String Quartet.
He joined the viola faculty at Peabody Cons.,
1970. His published works include Aria and
dance, viola and orch.; concertino for viola
and piano; Etude suite, unaccompanied viola.

COOLIDGE, PEGGY STUART
b. Swampscott, Mass., 19 July 1913; d. Cushing,
Maine, 7 May 1981. Studied with Quincy Porter
and Heinrich Gebhard. Her awards include the
Medal of the Central House of Workers in Art,
USSR; Gold Medal, Vincent Club, Boston; Medal of
the Metropolitan Govt. of Tokyo; Diploma of
Appreciation, Hungarian Radio Symphony. She was
founder and conductor, Junior League Orchestra,
Boston, 1937-42; assistant conductor and pianist,
Boston Women's Symphony.
WORKS: THEATRE: incidental music for Red
roses for me by Sean O'Casey; An evening in New
Orleans, ballet; ORCHESTRA: Rhapsody, harp and
orch., 1965; Look to the wind, voice with orch.;
Spirituals in sunshine and shadow, 1969; Pioneer
dances, 1970; New England autumn, 1972; FILM

SCORE: <u>The silken affair</u>; many piano pieces and songs.

COOLIDGE, RICHARD ARD
b. Williamsport, Pa., 1 Nov. 1929. Studied at Cincinnati Cons., B.M. 1952, M.M. 1953; with Bernhard Heiden, Indiana Univ., 1955-57; with John Boda, Florida State Univ., D.M. 1963. His awards include a best-of-category award, Delius Composition Contest, 1977, Jacksonville, Fla. He has held faculty posts at East Tennessee State Univ., 1957-61; Pensacola Jr. Coll., 1963-67; from 1967, professor at Stephen F. Austin State Univ. He has published many articles in music journals.
WORKS: CHAMBER MUSIC: <u>Introspection</u>, trombone and piano, 1971; <u>Arioso</u>, trombone and piano, 1972; <u>Visions of things past</u>, clarinet and piano, 1972; <u>Music for a rhapsody by Shelley</u>, flute and piano, 1974; <u>Curves of gold</u>, trombone and piano, 1974; <u>Weeping dancer</u>, piano and any treble clef instrument; other chamber works; many choral works; and songs.
2212 Dogwood St., Nacogdoches, TX 75911

COOMBS, DANIEL R.
b. Chicago, Ill., 26 Aug. 1953. Studied with Leon Stein and Phil Winsor, De Paul Univ., B.M. 1974. He is a clarinet soloist of note, specializing in contemporary works; from 1976, has been faculty member at Prairie State Coll. and Park Forest Cons.
WORKS: ORCHESTRA: <u>BSO</u>; BAND: flute concerto; CHAMBER MUSIC: <u>Quiescent lunacy</u>, clarinet, horn, piano; <u>Prisms</u>, vibraphone trio; <u>Canyon music</u>, bowed piano interior and 8 sopranos; PIANO: <u>Sun god</u>; <u>Cobalt bomb</u>; <u>Vestiges of perpetual moonlight</u>, prepared piano; <u>Aurora</u>; MIXED MEDIA: <u>The 4 seasons</u>, slides and tape.
11513 Villa Court, Alsip, IL 60658

COOPER, DAVID S.
b. Minneapolis, Minn., 3 Oct. 1922. Studied with Randall Thompson, Univ. of Virginia; with Roger Sessions and Oliver Strunk, Princeton Univ.; with Manfred Bukofzer, Univ. of California. He was cited by the Nat. Assoc. of American Composers and Conductors for outstanding service to American music. He was chief, Music Branch, USIA, 1951-59; vice-president, Associated Music Publishers, 1961-65; executive director, Manhattan School of Music, 1965-69; from 1969, executive director, American Composers Alliance.
WORKS: CHORUS: <u>Time</u>, women's voices and piano; <u>Sancta Maria</u>, women's voices a cappella; <u>3 poems for children</u>, woemn's voices and piano; <u>150th Psalm</u>, mixed chorus, organ, brass, percussion.
225 Kelburne Ave., North Tarrytown, NY 10591

COOPER, JOHN CRAIG
b. Kansas City, Mo., 14 May 1925. Studied at Kansas City Cons.; Univ. of Missouri, B.A., M.A.; with Charles Jones at Mills Coll.; with Nadia Boulanger, Fontainebleau, France; with Darius Milhaud, Aspen Inst.; also with Ben Weber. His awards include the Univ. of Missouri Paulina award; 3 MacDowell fellowships; Alice Ditson

grants. He has taught piano at King's Coll., Briarcliff Manor, N.Y.
WORKS: CHAMBER MUSIC: <u>Dialogues</u>, woodwind quintet; <u>Elegy</u>, paino; CHORUS: <u>Ah, sunflower</u>; <u>Child of a day</u>; SONGS: <u>Do not go, my love</u>; <u>Free me from the bonds</u>.

COOPER, PAUL
b. Victoria, Ill., 19 May 1926. Studied with Ernest Kanitz, Halsey Stevens, and Roger Sessions, Univ. of Southern California, B.A. 1950, M.A. 1953, D.M.A. 1956; with Nadia Boulanger in Paris, 1953-54. His awards include Fulbright fellowship, 1953; Rackham research grants, 1960, 1968; Guggenheim grants, 1965, 1972; Ford Found. grants, 1967, 1975; Rockefeller Found. grant, 1967; Nat. Endowment for the Arts grant, 1973; citation and award, American Acad. and Inst. of Arts and Letters, 1977; ASCAP annual awards from 1968. He was faculty member, Univ. of Michigan, 1955-68; Univ. of Cincinnati, 1968-74; from 1974, composer-in-residence and professor, Shepherd School of Music, Rice Inst.
WORKS: ORCHESTRA: 4 symphonies, 1954, 1956, 1971, 1975; violin concerto, 1967; <u>Antiphons</u>, solo oboe and wind ensemble, Washington, D.C., 16 May 1973; cello concerto, 1976; <u>Homage</u>, Cincinnati, 29 Apr. 1977; <u>Variants III</u>, 1979; flute concerto, 1979; <u>Coram morte</u>, mezzo-soprano, woodwinds, percussion, strings, and synthesizers, 1979; CHAMBER MUSIC: 2 piano sonatas, 1949, 1963; 6 string quartets, 1953, 1954, 1959, 1964, 1973, 1978; sonatas with piano: viola, 1961, violin, 1962, cello, 1962, duo flutes, 1963, double bass, 1964; cycles, piano, 1969; <u>Variants II</u>, viola and piano, 1972; <u>Concert for 3</u>, clarinet, cello, piano, 1977; CHORUS: <u>Credo</u>, double chorus and orch., 1970; <u>Cantigas</u>, double chorus and orch., 1972; <u>Equinox</u>, with flute, cello, piano, Washington, 26 May 1976; <u>Refrains</u>, double chorus, soprano, baritone, orch., Providence, R.I., 6 Dec. 1976; ORGAN: <u>Variants I</u>, 1970; <u>Requiem</u>, with percussion, 1978.
4915 Valkeith Dr., Houston, TX 77096

COOPER, ROSE MARIE
b. Cairo, Ill., 21 Feb. 1937. Studied with Warren Angell, Oklahoma Baptist Univ., B.M.; with Henry Cowell, Columbia Univ., M.A.; at Univ. of North Carolina, Ph.D. 1975. Her awards include Nat. Fed. of Music Clubs Award of Merit; ASCAP awards for 14 years; Outstanding Young Woman of North Carolina, 1972. She has been a member of a family publishing firm from 1969 and a free-lance composer.
WORKS: CHORUS: <u>Lord, speak to me</u>, men's voices; <u>Hymn of truth</u>, 2 parts; settings of 5 haiku, mixed chorus; <u>Morning star</u>, cantata; many other choral works and arrangements.
607 W. Greenway North, Greensboro, NC 27403

COOPER, WILLIAM BENJAMIN
b. Philadelphia, Pa., 14 Feb. 1920. Studied with Stefan Wolpe and Julius Hijman, Philadelphia Musical Acad., B.M. 1951, M.M. 1952; with Harold Friedell, Union Theological Seminary, School of Sacred Music. He received a plaque from the Nat. Negro Musicians Assoc., 1978. He was instructor,

COPE, DAVID

Bennett Coll., 1951-53; public school teacher, New York, from 1958; minister of music, St. Philip's Church, New York, 1953-74; and at St. Martin's Episcopal Church, New York, from 1974.

WORKS: CHORUS: Beatitudes, 1966; Mass of Thanksgiving, 1968; The canticles, 1972; Psalm 150, 1973; and many more choral works for the church service; ORGAN: Chorale prelude, 1970; Rhapsody on the name Fela Sowande, commissioned work; Bread of Heaven; Jubilate Deo; and many others.

61 Manhattan Ave., Greenburgh, NY 10607

COPE, DAVID
b. San Francisco, Calif., 17 May 1941. Studied with Grant Fletcher, Arizona State Univ., B.M. 1963; with Ingolf Dahl, George Perle, Halsey Stevens, Univ. of Southern California, M.M. 1965; privately with I. A. MacKenzie. His awards include Univ. of Houston award, 1970; ASCAP awards, 1971, 1972; Nat. Endowment for the Arts grant, 1976; and many commissions. He was faculty member, Kansas State Coll., 1966-68; California Lutheran Coll., 1968-69; Cleveland Inst. of Music, 1970-73; Miami Univ. of Ohio, 1973-78; from 1978, Univ. of California at Santa Cruz. He is editor of Composer magazine; author of articles in Composer and other journals; author of 3 books: Notes in discontinuum, 1970, New directions in music, 1971 (2nd ed., 1976), and New music notation, 1976.

WORKS: ORCHESTRA: Tragic overture, strings, 1962; Contrasts for orchestra, brass and strings, 1971; Variations, piano and wind orch., 1966; Streams, winds and strings, Harvard Univ., 22 Mar. 1973; Re-birth, wind ensemble; CHAMBER MUSIC: 2 string quartets; horn sonata, 1966; 5 pieces for flute, violin, bassoon; Towers, ensemble, 1968; A Christmas for dismas, chorus, 1969; Those years ago cold mornings held no fears, voice; Cycles, flute and double bass, 1969; The birds, ensemble, 1971; Obelisk, percussion; Deadliest angel revision, ensemble, 1971; BTRB, bass trombone, 1971; Angel's camp II, 1971; Triplum, 3 pieces for clarinet solo, 1972; Margins, percussion, cello, trumpet, piano, 1972; Vortex, trombone, flute, percussion, piano, 1975; Rituals, cello solo, 1976; Koosharem, a ceremony of innocence, clarinet, percussion, double bass, piano, 1976; PIANO: 4 sonatas; Iceberg meadow, prepared piano; ELECTRONIC: Weeds; K; Cedar breaks, bass and tape; Bright angel, trumpet and tape, 1971; Spirals, tuba and tape; Arena, cello and tape, 1974; Paradigm, piano, violin, tape, 1976; OR, prepared organ and tape, 1976.

College V, Univ. of California, Santa Cruz, CA 95064

COPLAND, AARON
b. Brooklyn, N.Y., 14 Nov. 1900. Studied with Rubin Goldmark in New York; with Nadia Boulanger in Paris, 1921-24. His many awards include the first Guggenheim fellowship to be awarded to a composer, 1925; RCA Victor award; Pulitzer prize, 1945; New York Music Critics' Circle award, 1945, 1947; honorary doctorates: Princeton Univ., 1956; Brandeis Univ., 1957; Wesleyan

Univ., 1958; Temple Univ., 1959; Harvard Univ., 1961; Rutgers Univ., 1967; Ohio State Univ., 1970; New York Univ., 1970; Columbia Univ., 1971; York Univ., 1971; Presidential Medal of Freedom, 1964; membership in the Nat. Inst. of Arts and Letters and American Acad. of Arts and Letters; Yale Univ., Howland Memorial Prize, 1970; Gold Baton, the nation's highest honor for distinguished service to music, for his contribution to American musical life, 1978. He has been lecturer, New School for Social Research; with Roger Sessions organized the Copland-Sessions Concerts, 1928-31; organized Yaddo Festivals, 1932; was a founder of the American Composers' Alliance, 1937; lecturer, Harvard Univ., 1935, 1944; Charles Eliot Norton lecturer, 1951-52; head of composition department, Berkshire Music Center, 1940-65, faculty chairman, 1957-65; participant in many other organizations.

WORKS: OPERA: The second hurricane, play-opera for high school students, 1937; The tender land, 1954; THEATRE: Sorcery to science, music for a puppet show, 1939; The 5 kings, music for a play, 1939; Quiet city, music for a play, 1939; BALLET: Grotto, 1925; Billy the kid, 1938; Rodeo, 1942; Appalachian spring, 1944; Dance panels, 1963; ORCHESTRA: Music for the theatre, 1925; symphony for organ and orch., 1925, rev. without organ as first symphony, 1928; Dance symphony, 1925; piano concerto, 1926; 2 pieces for string orch., 1928; Symphonic ode, 1932; Short symphony, 1933; Statements, 1935; El salón Mexico, 1937; Outdoor overture, 1938; Music for radio, a saga of the prairie, 1938; John Henry, railroad ballad, 1940; Lincoln portrait, narrator and orch., 1942; Music for movies, 1942; Danzón Cubano, 1942; Fanfare for the common man, brass and percussion, 1943; Letter from home, 1944; Variations on a theme by Eugene Goossens (with 9 other composers), 1945; Variations on a Shaker melody, wind ensemble, 3rd symphony, 1946; clarinet concerto, 1950; Preamble for a solemn occasion; Old American songs, voice and orch., 2 sets, 1950, 1954; Orchestral variations, 1957; Connotations, 1962; Music for a great city, 1964; Inscape, 1967; CHAMBER MUSIC: Nocturne, violin and piano, 1926; Ukelele serenade, violin and piano, 1926; Lento molto and rondino, string quartet, 1928; As it fell upon a day, soprano, flute, clarinet, 1928; Vitebsk, a study on a Jewish theme, piano trio, 1928; sextet for piano, clarinet, string quartet, 1933; violin sonata, 1942; quartet, piano and strings, 1950; nonet for strings, 1960; Threnodies I and II, flute/alto flute, string trio; CHORUS: The house on the hill, women's voices; An immortality, women's voices, 1925; What do we plant?, high school chorus, 1939; Lark, 1939; Las agachadas, 1942; In the beginning, mezzo-soprano and chorus, 1947; Canticle of freedom, 1955, rev. 1965; SONGS: 12 poems of Emily Dickinson, 1948-50; PIANO: The cat and the mouse, 1919; Passacaglia, 1922; Piano variations, 1930; The young pioneers and Sunday afternoon music, 2 pieces for children, 1936; piano sonata, 1941; 4 piano blues, 1949; Piano fantasy, 1957; ORGAN: Episode, 1941; FILM SCORES: Of mice and men, 1939; Our town, 1940; North star, 1943; The Cummington story, 1945; The red pony, 1948; The heiress, 1949, won Academy award. His published books include What to listen for in music, 1937; Our new music, 1941; Music and imagination, 1952; Copland on music, 1960; The new music, 1900-60, rev. 1968.

    c/o Boosey & Hawkes, 30 W. 57th St., New York, NY 10019

COPLEY, R. EVAN
    b. Liberal, Kans., 22 Mar. 1930. Studied with H. Owen Reed, Michigan State Univ. He was faculty member, Iowa Wesleyan Coll., 1958-64; from 1968, at Univ. of Northern Colorado.
    WORKS: ORCHESTRA: 3 symphonies; BAND: toccata; symphony; 2 suites; KEYBOARD: 12 preludes and fugues for piano; 9 piano sonatas; 48 works for organ (most published).
    Music Dept., Univ. of Northern Colorado, Greeley, CO 80639

COPPOLA, CARMINE (CARMEN)
    b. New York, N.Y., 11 June 1910. Studied with Bernard Wagenaar, Juilliard Grad. School, dipl. 1933; with Joseph Schillinger, 1936-39; Paul Creston, 1942-43; Norman Dello Joio, 1945-46; Manhattan School of Music, M.M. 1960. His awards include first prize in a Pittsburgh Bicentennial composition contest; Academy award for a music score, 1975. He was first flutist, Radio City Music Hall, 1934-36; Detroit Symphony, 1936-41; NBC Orch., 1942-48; arranger, Radio City Music Hall, 1948-56; opera conductor, Brooklyn Acad. of Music, 1948-55; music director, Merrick Prod., 1955-66; then composer and conductor for Warner Bros. and Paramount.
    WORKS: WIND ENSEMBLE: Flute flight; Phantom cavalry; Danse pagan; Oboe fantasia; CHAMBER MUSIC: woodwind quintet; Flute serenade, flute and piano, 1975; Lamento pastorale, flute and optional guitar, 1975; Madrigale, soprano and piano, 1975; FILM SCORE: Napoleon, Radio City Music Hall, 23 Jan. 1981.
    19813 Gilmore St., Woodland Hills, CA 91367

CORBETT, RICHARD DEAN
    b. Garden City, Kans., 9 Apr. 1942. Studied with Anthony Menk and Dale Dykins, Univ. of Northern Colorado; and with Normand Lockwood, Univ. of Denver. He has been a public school music teacher since 1967.
    WORKS: ORCHESTRA: Music for piano and orch., BAND: Divertimento; CHAMBER MUSIC: Concert pieces, brass quintet; Theme and variations, piano and winds; From where the sun now stands, speaker and wind ensemble; Songs, clarinet and wind ensemble; CHORUS: Psalm 95.
    1653 S. Benton, Lakewood, CO 80226

CORCORAN, WILLIAM
    Games of cards, 1-act opera, Baby Grand Opera Company, Cincinnati, 6 Dec. 1973; Trilogy on the quality of life, 3 1-act operas commissioned by the Baby Grand Opera Company for the American Bicentennial 1976.

CORDERO, ROQUE
    b. Panama, 16 Aug. 1917; to U.S. 1966. Studied with Ernst Krenek, Hamline Univ.; conducting with Dimitri Mitropoulos in Minneapolis, Leon Barzin in New York, Stanley Chapple at the Berkshire Music Center. His awards include a Guggenheim fellowship, 1949; first prize, Ricardo Miro contest, Panama, 1953; Caro de Boesi prize, Caracas, 1957; Koussevitzky recording grant, 1974; Nat. Endowment for the Arts grant, 1975; many commissions. He was director, Nat. Inst. of Music, Panama, 1953-64; conductor, Nat. Orch. of Panama, 1964-66; professor, Indiana Univ., 1966-69; professor, Illinois State Univ., from 1972.
    WORKS: ORCHESTRA: 3 symphonies, 1947, 1956, 1965; piano concerto, 1944; Rapsodia campesina, 1949; 8 miniatures, 1953; 5 short messages, 1959; violin concerto, 1962; concertino, viola and strings; The elegy, string orch., 1973; Mensaje funebre, in memoriam Dimitri Mitropoulos, Bloomington, Ind., 17 Feb. 1976; Adagio tragico, 1976; Momentum jubile, 1976; BAND: Capriccio interiorano, 1939; CHAMBER MUSIC: quintet for flute, clarinet, piano trio, 1949; 2 string quartets, 1959, 1968; cello sonata, 1962; Permutaciones 7 for 7 instruments, 1967; Paz, paix, peace, 4 trios and harp, 1969; Variations on a theme for 5, woodwind quintet, Chicago, 2 Feb. 1976; Soliloquies I, flute solo, 1976; Soliloquies II, alto saxophone solo, 1976; Duo 1954, 2 pianos, 1976; VOICE: Cantata for peace, 1975.
    Music Dept., Illinois State Univ., Normal, IL 61761

CORIGLIANO, JOHN
    b. New York, N.Y., 16 Feb. 1938. Studied with Otto Luening, Columbia Univ., B.A. 1959; with Vittorio Giannini, Manhattan School of Music. His awards include first prize in the Spoleto Festival chamber music competition, 1964; Guggenheim fellowship, 1968; ASCAP awards; many commissions. He was programmer, WQXR Radio, 1959-62; music director, WBAI Radio, 1962-64; associate producer, CBS-TV Young People's Concerts, 1961-72; faculty member, Manhattan School of Music from 1971, and Lehman Coll., CUNY, from 1972.
    WORKS: THEATRE: The naked Carmen, a rock opera arrangement of Bizet's work with singers, rock and pop groups, and Moog synthesizers; incidental music for Le malade imaginaire of Moliere; The rivals of Sheridan; Oedipus rex of Sophocles; Galileo of Brecht; ORCHESTRA: Elegy, 1966; Tournaments overture, 1967; piano concerto, 1968; Creations, narrator and orch.; oboe concerto, 1975; Poem on his birthday, baritone, chorus, orch., Washington, D.C., 24 Apr. 1976; clarinet concerto, New York, 6 Dec. 1977; CHAMBER MUSIC: Pastorale, cello and piano, 1958; Kaleidoscope, 2 pianos, 1959; violin sonata, 1963; Etude fantasy, piano, Washington, 9 Oct. 1976; CHORUS: Fern Hill, with orch., 1961; What I expected was . . ., with brass, percussion; SONGS: The cloisters, cycle, 1965; Poem in October, tenor and chamber orch., 1969.
    365 West End Ave., New York, NY 10024

CORINA, JOHN

CORINA, JOHN
b. Cleveland, Ohio, 21 Apr. 1928. Studied with
John Boda, Florida State Univ., D.M. 1965. He
held a fellowship at the university, 1964-65; in
1967 his concerto for symphonic band won selection by the Coll. Band Directors Nat. Assoc. He
taught in public schools, 1951-60; at Miami-Dade
Jr. Coll., 1960-66; and has been on faculty,
Univ. of Georgia, from 1966. He is also oboist,
organist, and choirmaster.
WORKS: CHAMBER MUSIC: woodwind quintet,
1968; Sonnet, solo oboe and strings, 1974; partita, oboe and percussion, 1975; Sarum suite,
organ, 1976; CHORUS: A prophecy of peace, with
soprano and orch., 1969; Is it nothing to you?,
Lenten cantata, with brass, 1969; The Last
Supper, women's chorus, piano, percussion, 1970;
The way of the cross, soloists, readers, chorus,
organ, 1978.
396 Hancock Lane, Athens, GA 30605

CORNER, PHILIP
b. Bronx, N.Y., 10 Apr. 1933. Studied with Mark
Brunswick, City Coll. of N.Y., B.A. 1955; with
Olivier Messiaen, Paris Cons., 1956-57; with
Otto Luening and Henry Cowell, Columbia Univ.,
M.A. 1959; piano privately with Dorothy Taubman.
His awards include a Nat. Fed. of Music Clubs
award, 1958; and N.Y. State Council on the Arts
grants. He taught in public schools, 1966-72;
was on faculty, New School for Social Research,
1968-71; from 1972, at Livingston Coll., Rutgers
Univ. He was a cofounder of Tone Roads, a group
devoted to the performance of new music.
WORKS: His instrumental compositions are
usually for indeterminate ensembles, improvisatory events, meditative and listening events,
and environmental installations often permitting
participation and long durations, such as: Elementals (an ultimate reduction), played at The
Kitchen, N.Y., for 5 days, 24 hours a day, in
shifts. Some published works are 4 suits;
Popular entertainments; I can walk through the
world as music; and various versions of many one-
note formulations, such as OM breath, OM entrance,
OM emerging.
464 W. Broadway, New York, NY 10012

CORTES, RAMIRO
b. Dallas, Tex., 25 Nov. 1933. Studied with
Henry Cowell in New York; with Halsey Stevens
and Ingolf Dahl, Univ. of Southern California;
with Goffredo Petrassi in Rome; and with Roger
Sessions at Princeton Univ., 1959. His awards
include the Gershwin Memorial award, 1954;
Steinway centennial prize, 1954; BMI awards,
1954, 1958; Fulbright fellowship for study in
Rome, 1956-58. He was faculty member at Univ.
of Southern California to 1973, then at Univ. of
Utah.
WORKS: OPERA: Prometheus, 1 act, 1960;
THEATRE: Music for Yorca's play, Yerma, 1955;
ORCHESTRA: Sinfonia sacra, 1954; Xochitl, 1955;
Sinfonia breve, 1955-58; Meditation, string
orch.; The eternal return, 1963, rev. 1965;
piano concerto, 1965; Movements in variation,
1972; piano concerto, Salt Lake City, 20 Feb.
1976, composer conducting; CHAMBER MUSIC: Elegy,

flute and piano, 1952; Divertimento, woodwind
trio, 1953; piano quintet, 1953; Night music,
chamber orch., 1954; chamber concerto, cello and
12 winds, 1958; string quartet, 1958; piano trio,
1959; 3 movements for 5 winds; duo for flute and
oboe; wind quintet, 1968; Homage to Jackson
Pollack, solo viola, 1968; Charenton, suite for
chamber orch., 1968-71; violin sonata, 1971-72;
cello sonata, 1977; CHORUS: 3 songs to poems of
Ben Jonson; Missa breve; SONGS: The falcon; 3
Spanish songs; PIANO: sonata, 1954; prelude,
suite.
Music Dept., Univ. of Utah, Salt Lake City,
UT 84112

CORY, ELEANOR
b. Englewood, N.J., 8 Sept. 1943. Studied with
Chou Wen-Chung, Bulent Arel, Benjamin Boretz,
Columbia Univ.; with Charles Wuorinen, New
England Cons.; with Meyer Kupferman, Sarah
Lawrence Coll. Her awards include Nat. Endowment
for the Arts grant; Creative Artists Public
Service award; Norlin award; MacDowell fellowship; Meet the Composer award. She has held
faculty posts at Brooklyn Coll., 1971-72;
Columbia Univ., 1971-73; Baruch Coll. of CUNY,
1973-78; from 1978, at Yale Univ.
WORKS: CHAMBER MUSIC: Liebeslied, mezzo-
soprano, chamber ensemble, 1969; concertino,
piano and chamber ensemble, 1970; Combinations,
piano, 1970; septet, 1971; Tempi, clarinet and
tape, 1971; Epithalamium, solo flute, 1973; trio
for clarinet, cello, piano, 1973; Waking, soprano
and chamber ensemble, 1974; Octagons, chamber
ensemble, 1976; trio for flute, oboe, piano,
1977; Aria viva, tenor, 4 woodwinds, guitar,
1977; Counterbrass, brass trio, piano, percussion,
1978.
945 West End Ave., #8B, New York, NY 10025

CORY, GEORGE
b. Syracuse, N.Y., 3 Aug. 1920. Studied with
Ernest Bloch, Univ. of California. During army
service in 1943-45, he was chapel organist at
the Presidio of Monterey. He was music director,
Gilbert and Sullivan Repertory Company, San
Francisco; assistant to Gian-Carlo Menotti,
1946-50; arranger, conductor, pianist in San
Francisco.
WORKS: THEATRE: Lysistrata, musical version
of Aristophanes' play; SONGS: The drowned wife,
Horan text; Music I heard with you, Aiken text;
And this shall be for music, Stevenson text;
Another America, Cross text; KEYBOARD: piano
sonatina; pastorale and toccata-finale, organ;
and many popular songs including I left my heart
in San Francisco (Grammy award, 1963), and Carry
me back to old Manhattan.
1210 Lombard St., San Francisco, CA 94109

COSCIA, SILVIO
b. Milan, Italy, 27 Nov. 1899. At age 8 was
cantor at St. Ambrogio Cathedral, Milan; studied
at Verdi Cons. On coming to the U.S. in the
early 1920s, he was horn player and arranger
with the Goldman Band; was first horn, Metropolitan Opera Orch., 1930-64; also played under
Toscanini; was private vocal teacher and coach;

from 1968, taught voice at New England Cons.
WORKS: ORCHESTRA: <u>Scherzo for orchestra</u>;
<u>Heroic vision</u>, symphonic poem; <u>Ecce homo</u>, tone
poem, 1962; <u>Dramatic elegy</u>, 1965; BAND: 2
preludes; SONGS: <u>Kindly loving</u>; <u>I come tomorrow</u>;
<u>La vida dolce</u>; <u>Dark hour</u>; <u>Love me little, love
me long</u>; also studies for horn and duets for
trumpet. He is author of <u>Yesterday and today</u>,
<u>Bel canto</u>; and <u>Operative Italian diction and
articulation applied to singing</u>.
   12 Riverside St., Watertown, MA 02172

COSTINESCO, GEORGE
b. Bucharest, Romania, 12 Dec. 1934; to U.S.
1969. Studied with Mihail Jora, Bucharest Cons.,
1954-61; later with Nadia Boulanger, Karlheinz
Stockhausen, Max Deutsch, Luciano Berio; at
Juilliard School, 1970-71; with Vladimir
Ussachevsky, Mario Davidovsky, Chou Wen-Chung,
Columbia Univ., Ph.D. His awards include George
Enesco prize, Romanian Acad., 1965; Gretchaninoff prize, Juilliard School, 1970; Mancini
fellowship at Juilliard, 1971; MacDowell fellowships, 1970, 1972; Yaddo fellowship, 1972; Mills
Coll. research grant, 1973; resident grant,
Virginia Center for the Creative Arts, 1973;
Creative Artists Public Service Program award,
1978. In 1960-68, he was score-reader at the
Romanian Composers Alliance; teaching assistant
at Juilliard, 1971-72, at Columbia Univ., 1973-
74, at Brooklyn Coll., 1973-75; from 1977,
faculty member, New School for Social Research,
New York.
WORKS: <u>Comme de long nuages</u>, tenor and
choir, 1969; <u>The musical seminar</u>, theatre piece
for 5 instrumentalists, actors and tape, 1971;
<u>A la recherche du chant</u>, musical pantomime for
15 players, 1972; <u>Invention 5-B</u>, electronic
piece, 1974; <u>Tournament overture</u>, flute, cello,
synthesizer, and 2 Ping-Pong players, 1977.
   125 Riverside Dr., Apt. 10D, New York, NY
10024

COTEL, MORRIS
b. Baltimore, Md., 20 Feb. 1943. Studied with
William Bergsma, Vincent Persichetti, and Roger
Sessions, Juilliard School, B.M., M.S.; with
Darius Milhaud at Aspen, Colo.; at American
Acad. in Rome, 1966-68, received American Rome
prize. Other awards include second prize,
Internat. Schoenberg Piano Competition, 1975;
Nat. Endowment for the Arts grant, 1975; ASCAP
awards from 1975. He was instructor, Rubin
Acad., Jerusalem, Israel, 1970-72; from 1972 at
Peabody Cons. Composed a large 4-movement symphony by age 13. His works up to about 1966
were chiefly serial, but thereafter became more
improvisational and aleatory with free rhythms.
WORKS: ORCHESTRA: <u>Symphonic pentad</u>, 1964;
piano concerto, 1968, first American performance, Baltimore, 26 Feb. 1973; <u>Variations for
an infinite space</u>, strings and winds, 1970;
<u>Variations on a theme by Haydn</u>, 1973; <u>Harmony
of the world</u>, string orch., 1975; CHAMBER MUSIC:
<u>Music for a finite space</u>, piano and string quar-
tet, 1965; <u>Suite nonsense</u>, ensemble and narrator,
1965; sonata for piano, 4 hands, 1966; <u>Humanoid
ritual dances</u>, prepared piano, percussion, tape,

1971; <u>Great Mother Goose sweetmerge and grand
foog</u>, tape and pop vocal, 1971; <u>Scales and all</u>,
alto sax, vibes, bass, percussion, 1972;
<u>Oögamous</u>, piano, vibes, bass, percussion, 1972;
<u>Tehom</u>, 3 pianos, 1974; piano sonata, 1976;
CHORUS: <u>The fire and the mountains</u>, with
children's chorus, soloists, percussion, 1977,
was the only U.S. winner in the international
competition, "Holocaust and Rebirth," celebrating the 30th anniversary of the State of Israel;
<u>August 12, 1952: The night of the murdered
poets</u>, for narrator and 5 instrumentalists, was
given its premiere in New York on 18 Nov. 1978;
text included excerpts from the writings of the
24 Jewish artists and intellectuals who were
executed in a Moscow prison that date.
   639 West End Ave., New York, NY 10025

COULTER, R. SCOTT, JR.
b. Baltimore, Md., 20 June 1925. Studied with
Ingolf Dahl, Univ. of Southern California; at
Univ. of the Pacific, M.M.; with Karl Kohn and
Gail Kubik, Claremont Graduate School. He was
faculty member, Fullerton Coll., 1959-70; from
1970, at Stanislaus State Coll.
WORKS: CHAMBER MUSIC: violin sonata, 1952;
<u>Sea songs</u>, baritone and piano, 1961; piano
sonata, 1973; <u>Peter Quint at the clavier</u>, baritone, harpsichord, 2 recorders, 1973; CHORUS:
<u>Lamentation of David</u>, with soloist and 2 pianos,
1973.
   Music Dept., Stanislaus State College,
Turlock, CA 95380

COUPER, MILDRED
b. Buenos Aires, 10 Dec. 1887; U.S. citizen
1910; d. Santa Barbara, Calif., 9 Aug. 1974.
Graduated from Karlsruhe-Baden Cons.; studied
with Moritz Moskowski in Paris; with Sgambati
in Rome, and with Alfred Cortot in New York.
She taught at Mannes School of Music, New York,
1918-27; and at Music Acad. of the West, Santa
Barbara, 1927-40.
WORKS: ORCHESTRA: <u>We are seven</u>; <u>Seven
more</u>; <u>Irish washerwoman variations</u>, played by
Werner Janssen Symphony; SONGS: 2 sets of songs
to verses of Ogden Nash; PIANO: <u>Dirge</u>, for 2
pianos tuned a quarter-tone apart, published by
New Music Editions, 1937. Halsey Stevens men-
tioned her as an avant-garde composer after
World War I.

COUSINS, M. THOMAS
b. Wilson, N.C., 9 Oct. 1914. Studied at
Juilliard School and privately. He played
trumpet with the National Symphony, 1939-42;
with the CBS Symphony, 1943-46; was army band
leader in World War II; taught in public schools;
was chairman, music department, Brevard Coll.,
1958-63; conductor, Greensboro Symphony, 1963-
67.
WORKS: CHORUS: <u>Moses</u>, chorus and orch.;
<u>O clap your hands</u>; <u>Glorious everlasting</u>, double
chorus.

COWELL, HENRY DIXON
b. Menlo Park, Calif., 11 Mar. 1897; d. Shady,
N.Y., 10 Dec. 1965. Studied at Univ. of Southern

COWLES, CECIL MARION

California; Inst. of Applied Music, New York; and privately in Berlin. He was a bandmaster in the U.S. Army in World War I, and during World War II, was in charge of shortwave music broadcasts for the Office of War Information. In 1927 he founded the New Music Quarterly for the publication of contemporary music and was its editor to 1936. He also helped organize the Pan American Assoc. of Composers. It was Cowell who invented and developed the "tone cluster" technique for the piano, a device he used in his piano concerto in 1930. He made 5 tours of Europe playing his own works and a dozen tours of the U.S. As author, lecturer, publisher, and performer, he was a tireless champion of little-known American music. For example, the belated recognition of Charles Ives was largely due to Cowell's efforts. His teaching posts included Stanford Univ., New School for Social Research, Univ. of California, Mills Coll., Peabody Cons., Columbia Univ. Along with all these activities, he kept up a prodigious output in composition. By 1950 he estimated he had written more than 800 works, and he added another 200 in the succeeding 15 years.

WORKS: ORCHESTRA: 20 symphonies, 1918–65; percussion concerto; Ensemble, string orch., 1925, rev. 1956; Irish suite, 1927; sinfonietta, chamber orch., 1928; Polyphonica, chamber orch., 1930; Synchrony, 1931; Steel and stone, 1931; Rhythmicana, rhythmicon and orch., 1931; Ostinato pianissimo, percussion orch., 1934; Ancient desert drone, 1940; Shoonthree, 1940; Pastoral and fiddler's delight, 1940; Tales of the countryside, piano and orch., 1941; concerto piccolo, piano and orch., 1942; Hymn and fuguing tune #2, string orch., 1944; Twilight; Air and scherzo, saxophone and orch.; Fiddler's jig, violin and strings; Variations on 3rds, 2 violas and chamber orch.; Saturday night at the firehouse; Festival overture, double orch., 1946; Ballad, string orch., 1954; Ongaku, 1957; Antiphony, double orch., 1958; harmonica concerto, 1960; koto concerto, 1964; Carol for orchestra, a version for western orch. of the koto concerto 2nd movement, 1965; harp concerto, 1965; BAND: Shipshape overture, 1939; Little concerto, piano and band; Hymn and fuguing tune #1, 1943; A curse and a blessing; Celtic set, 1943; Animal magic, 1944; Grandma's rumba, 1945; Fantasia, 1952; WIND ENSEMBLE: Fanfare for the forces of the Latin American allies, brass; Rondo, brass ensemble; Sailor's hornpipe, 4 saxophones; Tall tale, brass sextet, 1947; Hymn and fuguing tune #12, 3 horns; CHAMBER MUSIC: Quartet romantic, 1917, New York, 18 May 1978; other string quartets: 1925 (with 2 thunder-sticks), 1927, 1934 (1 movement), 1935 (Mozaic quartet), 1936 (United quartet); 7 paragraphs, string trio, 1926; suite for violin and piano, 1927; Set of 5, viola, percussion, piano; Vocalize, soprano, flute, piano; Ballad, wood-wind quintet; Tried, trumpet and piano; Two-bits, flute and piano, 1944, world premiere, One-bit, Baltimore, 2 Mar. 1972; violin sonata, 1945; Hymn and fuguing tune #7, viola and piano, #9, cello and piano, 1950, #13, trombone and piano, 1950, #16, violin and piano; Gravely and

vigorously (in memory of JFK, 1963), solo cello; 26 simultaneous mosaics, violin, cello, clarinet, percussion, piano; CHORUS: Supplication; Fire and ice, men's voices, 1942; To America, 1946; The lily's lament; Spring at summer's end; Day, evening, night, morning, men's voices, 1947; The raod to tomorrow, 1947; Psalm 121, 1953; Ultimo actio; SONGS: Daybreak; Firelight and lamp; The donkey; The pasture; Toccata, soprano, flute, cello, piano or orch.; PIANO: Amerind suite; Amiable conversation; Anger dance; Antimony; Hilarious curtain opener and ritornelle; Dynamic motion; 6 ings (floating, frisking, fleeting, scooting, wafting, seething), 1922, Washington, D.C., 11 Sept. 1978; Aeolian harp; The banshe; Rhythmicana, 1943; Set of 4, 1960; ORGAN: Hymn and fuguing tune #14, 1962. He also published the books, New musical resources, 1930, and Charles Ives and his music, 1955.

COWLES, CECIL MARION
b. San Francisco, Calif., 14 Jan. 1898; d. New York, N.Y., 28 Mar. 1968. Made her piano debut at age 9; later studied composition with Carl Deis and Wallingford Riegger. Her compositions included Jesu bambino, a mass; and for piano: Shanghai bund; Oriental sketches; Cubanita; Nocturne, etc.; and songs.

COWLES, DARLEEN L.
b. Chicago, Ill., 13 Nov. 1942. Studied with Leon Stein and Donald Jenni, De Paul Univ., B.M. 1966; with Anthony Donato, Northwestern Univ., M.M. 1967; with Ralph Shapey, Univ. of Chicago, 1974–77, doctoral studies 1974. Her awards include a Woodrow Wilson fellowship, 1966, and the Faricy award for creative composition 1967. She was lecturer, Northwestern Univ., 1967; Elmhurst Coll., 1970; choir director, Palatine, 1969–71; from 1972, lecturer, De Paul Univ.

WORKS: ORCHESTRA: chamber symphony #1, 1965; CHAMBER MUSIC: horn sonata, 1965; piano suite, 1966; string quartet #1, 1967; Continuum, trumpet, vibraphone, marimba, piano, 1968; Translucent unreality #1–7, a set of programmatic pieces exploring various compositional techniques, like prepared piano, improvisation, etc., 1973–77; Estampie, string quartet, 1975; From the king's chamber, tenor saxophone, speaker, ensemble, 1977; VOICE: Offering for peace, oratorio for tenor solo, chorus, orch., 1967; Like strangers, soprano and chamber ensemble, 1975.
2620 N. Dayton, Chicago, IL 60614

COWLES, WALTER RUEL
b. New Haven, Conn., 4 Sept. 1881; d. Tallahassee, Fla., 8 Dec. 1959. Studied with Horatio Parker at Yale Univ., B.M. 1907; then at Schola Cantorum in Paris. He taught piano at Yale School of Music, 1911–19; was professor at Florida State Coll. for Women, 1930–51. His compositions included a piano concerto, piano trio, piano pieces, and songs.

COX, CLIFFORD L.
b. New Kensington, Pa., 30 Jan. 1935. Studied

with Nikolai Lopatnikoff, Carnegie Mellon Univ.
He is on the faculty at Edinboro State Coll.
WORKS: OPERA: The cynic, 1 act, 1956;
ORCHESTRA: PSI, an overture; and chamber works.
222 Fairway Dr., Edinboro, PA 16412

COX, RALPH
b. Galion, Ohio, 29 Aug. 1884; d. New York, N.Y.,
10 June 1941. Studied at Oberlin Cons.; Guilmant
Organ School; and Wooster Univ. He was organist-
choirmaster in New York City and Orange, N.J.
His works include the songs: To a hilltop; The
road to spring; In a southern garden.

COX, RICK
b. Chicago, Ill., 8 Mar. 1952. Studied with
Vincent McDermott, Wisconsin Coll. Cons., B.M.
1973; in Wisconsin and California with Barney
Childs. He was guitar instructor, Wisconsin
Cons., 1972-73.
WORKS: STANDARD NOTATION: at once, viola,
cello, piano, 1973; new lights on old channels,
clarinet solo, 1977; IMPROVISATORY: Mostly
pretty down, 1975; only open, 1976; When will
you know, 1976; In the hands of a stranger, 1978;
INDETERMINANT: Peculiar behavior, 4 clarinets,
1975; Collection, percussion ensemble, 1975,
received honorable mention in the 1975 Percussive Arts Society contest.
44 Sycamore, Mountain Home Village, CA 92359

COX, RONN
b. Ft. Smith, Ark., 9 June 1942. Studied with
Merrill Ellis and William Latham, North Texas
State Univ., B.M. 1969, M.M. 1976. He was
research assistant, Electronic Music Center,
North Texas State Univ., 1967-70, and teaching
assistant, 1973-76; then music director, Hubbard
Independent School District.
WORKS: CHAMBER MUSIC: Opposites, trumpet
and cello; 2 expressions, wind ensemble with
celeste, percussion, and contrabass; The. . .
just. . . and. . . you, soprano and trombone
quartet; Snow poets, soprano and prepared piano,
1977; MIXED MEDIA: Diachronic, trombone and
tape; 5TEN8+, orchestra and tape, quasi aleatory;
A saxophone?, alto saxophone and tape, improvisation; Together, tape.
Rte. 2, Box 5, Hubbard, TX 76648

COYNER, LOU
b. U.S., 11 Mar. 1931. He was faculty member,
Berklee School of Music, 1959-60; and at Chatham
Coll., 1962-74.
WORKS: ORCHESTRA: piano concerto; Dawn
stone, cello quartet and chamber orch.; CHAMBER
MUSIC: Gentle jangle; Woodenly booming along
like a carved bee, piano and woodwind quintet;
Away, alone, aloved, alast along the, wind quintet; Collocations, piano and percussion; Saxi-
frage, saxophone quartet; Omega point, string
quartet; Tycho, piano, New York, 18 Jan. 1971;
Noösphere, piano; MIXED MEDIA: Saral, clarinet,
cello, tape; Bird, percussion solo and tape;
Piva, saxophone, percussion, and tape.
647 Gettysburg St., Pittsburgh, PA 15206

CRAIG, DALE ALLAN
b. Illiopolis, Ill., 19 Dec. 1939. Studied with
Robert Palmer and Karel Husa, Cornell Univ.,
M.M. 1964; with Priaulx Rainier in London; with
Leland Smith, Stanford Univ., D.M.A. 1968;
privately with Lou Harrison. His awards include
a commission from Radio Hong Kong; and the
Leverhulme research fellowship, Univ. of Western
Australia, 1976. He was faculty member, Univ.
of Virginia, 1968-69; lecturer, Chung Chi Coll.,
Hong Kong, from 1969, music department chairman,
1972-74; in 1977, he became lecturer in Asian
music and European music history, Queensland
Cons., Australia. He is author of articles on
Asian music.
WORKS: ORCHESTRA: Intimations, 1963; The 4
loves, suite for strings, 1965; Byan Hwa, with
speakers and dancers, 1968; Variations on Hwan
Le Ge, small orch. of Chinese and European instruments, 1973; CHAMBER MUSIC: piano trio,
1962-64; Visions, piano solo, 1966; string quartet, 1966-67; 3 songs on poems by Ezra Pound,
baritone and piano, 1970; 3 settings of old
Chinese tunes and verses, baritone, 1971; In a
happy mood by Seung River, Er-hu (Chinese violin)
and piano, 1973; Cascades on Noh, flute and
piano, 1974; Existence, cello and piano, 1975;
MIXED MEDIA: music for synthesizer, piano, and
idiophones, 1973; Plum blossoms, synthesizer and
chamber ensemble (commissioned by Radio Hong
Kong for Chinese New Year 1974); A dream of
dances, tape, 1974; In memorium Bela Bartok,
violin and tape, 1975.
15 Ebrill St., Jamboree Heights, Queensland,
Australia 4074

CRAM, JAMES DOUGLAS
b. Heavener, Okla., 10 May 1931. Studied with
Warren Angell, Oklahoma Baptist Univ.; with Bela
Rozsa, Tulsa Univ.; with Merrill Ellis and Samuel
Adler, North Texas State Univ. He has received
annual ASCAP awards and a Texas Composers' Guild
award, 1970. He was faculty member and chairman,
School of Music, Hardin-Simmons Univ., 1972-74.
WORKS: CHORUS: Easter cantata, 1967; Welcome, all wonders, Christmas cantata, 1970; 3
nativity poems of Richard Cranshaw, with orch.,
1970; To believe in God, a choral cycle, 1973;
numerous other choral works.
2505 Hunters Glen, Abilene, TX 79601

CRANDELL, ROBERT E.
b. Hornell, N.Y., 10 Jan. 1910. Studied with
Hunter Johnson, Univ. of Michigan; with Edwin
Stringham, Union Theological Seminary; and with
Nadia Boulanger in Paris. He has been organist
and choirmaster since 1935; was lecturer, Union
Theol. Seminary, 1962-71; and has been director,
Packer Collegiate Inst., Brooklyn, from 1962.
WORKS: CHORUS: Benedictus es, Domine;
Close to the heart of God; January carol; The
second beatitude; and others; ORGAN: Carnival
suite.
909 Capital Ave., S.W., Battle Creek, MI
49015

CRANE, JOELLE WALLACH
b. New York, N.Y., 29 June 1946. Studied with

CRANE, JOHN THOMAS

Meyer Kupferman, Sarah Lawrence Coll., B.A. 1967; with Chou Wen-Chung and Jack Beeson, Columbia Univ., M.A. 1969; on scholarship at the Composers' Conf., Johnson, Vt., 1973. She teaches privately and is faculty member, La Guardia Community Coll.

WORKS: ORCHESTRA: concerto for 4 winds; CHAMBER MUSIC: duo, clarinet and cello, 1964; 2 string quartets, 1964, 1968; Trio for 3 high winds, flute and 2 oboes, 1965; little duet, violin and piano, 1966; duo, violin and cello, 1966; Pas de deux, flute and harpsichord, 1967; Moment, oboe solo, 1967; trio for 3 reed instruments, 1968; Beads, contrabass solo, 1973; VOICE: Deirdre, song cycle for mezzo-soprano and piano, 1963; The force that through the green fuse, soprano and oboe, 1965; Cords, soprano and 2 string basses, 1973; PIANO: Piano study in open-ended form, 1965; 3 piano pieces, 1967; Prelude and toccata, piano and tape, 1967.

782 West End Ave., #91, New York, NY 10025

CRANE, JOHN THOMAS
b. New York, N.Y., 17 Sept. 1943. Studied with Chou Wen-Chung, Jack Beeson, and Vladimir Ussachevsky, Columbia Univ., B.A. 1965, M.A. 1969, D.M.A. 1973. He held scholarships at Tanglewood, 1962; Columbia Univ., 1968-69; Composers' Conf., Vt., 1971, 1972. He was faculty member at Dalton School, 1969-71; Queensborough Community Coll., 1970; Fordham Univ., 1970-73; Baruch Coll., CUNY, 1973-75. He was assistant conductor, Columbia Univ. Orch., 1968-69.

WORKS: CHAMBER MUSIC: quartet movement for flute, oboe, clarinet, cello, 1967; composition for 7 instruments and percussion, 1967-68; The quartet, soprano and cello, 1968; quintet for recorder, oboe, viola, tuba, harp, 1969-70; Aria, flute solo, 1970; CHORUS: Punch, brothers, punch, 1968; MIXED MEDIA: Aulos, oboe and tape, 1969; A rhapsody in '69, tape, 1969.

782 West End Ave., New York, NY 10025

CRANE, ROBERT
b. Winchester, Mass., 24 Dec. 1919. Studied with Normand Lockwood, Oberlin Coll.; with Nadia Boulanger, Longy School of Music; with Bernard Rogers and Howard Hanson, Univ. of Rochester. His awards include Lili Boulanger award, 1942; Phi Mu Alpha Sinfonia Alumni award, 1952; Knight of Mark Twain, 1972; Waukesha Symphony award; Wisconsin Fed. of Music Clubs awards; and commissions. He has been faculty member, Univ. of Wisconsin, from 1950.

WORKS: ORCHESTRA: A dance interlude; Exsequiarum ordo in memoriam Belioz; BAND: Passacaglia and fugue; Chorale prelude on Wachet auf; Aleatory suite; Rotunda music, for brass; CHAMBER MUSIC: octet for brass; Incantation, cello and piano; piano sonatina, 1952; string quartet; CHORUS: Peter Quince at the clavier, cantata, 1950; The litany, with soloists and orch.; Missa de angelis; ORGAN: 5 baroque choral preludes.

1615 Adams St., Madison, WI 53711

CRAWFORD, DAWN
b. Ellington Field, Tex., 19 Dec. 1919. Studied with Bernard Rogers and Herbert Elwell, Eastman School of Music; attended Rice Univ., B.A. 1939; Houston Cons., B.M. 1940; Columbia Univ., M.A. 1954. She received a commission for incidental music to Angna Enters's Love possessed Juana, premiere, Houston, 1946. She was faculty member, Houston Cons., 1938-49; free-lance accompanist, New York, 1949-57; faculty, Dominican Coll., Houston, from 1964.

WORKS: OPERA: The pearl, 3 acts, based on Steinbeck's novel, Dominican Coll., 1972; ORCHESTRA: The Chinese nightingale, ballad for orch., based on Lindsay's poem; chamber music and songs.

Music Dept., Dominican College, Houston, TX 77021

CRAWFORD, JOHN
b. Philadelphia, Pa., 19 Jan. 1931. Studied with Quincy Porter and Paul Hindemith, Yale Univ.; with Nadia Boulanger, Paris Cons.; with Walter Piston and Randall Thompson, Harvard Univ. His awards include a Fulbright grant, 1950; Boott prize in choral composition, Harvard, 1956; Paine traveling fellowship, Harvard, 1959; Univ. of California Creative Arts Inst., 1971; ASCAP awards, 1969-74. He has been faculty member, Amherst Coll., 1961-63; Wellesley Coll., 1963-70; Univ. of California, Riverside, from 1970.

WORKS: OPERA: Don Cristobal and Rosita, chamber opera, 1970; ORCHESTRA: Metracollage, 1973; CHAMBER MUSIC: 2 string quartets; 3 palindromes for 8 solo instruments, 1968; CHORUS: Magnificat, with string orch., 1956; Ash Wednesday, oratorio, 1960; 2 Herrick settings, 1965; 3 Shakespeare songs, women's chorus and chamber orch.; Psalm 98, men's chorus, brass quintet, piano.

703 11th St., Santa Monica, CA 90402

CRAWFORD, LOUISE
b. Cedar Rapids, Iowa, 18 July 1890; d. Cedar Rapids, 16 Dec. 1973. Studied at Wellesley Coll., B.A. 1914, M.A. 1916; at New England Cons., 1914-15. She held a MacDowell fellowship; was a member of Phi Kappa Phi, Mu Phi Epsilon, and Nat. League of American Pen Women. She taught at Coe Coll., Cedar Rapids, 1916-41.

WORKS: CHAMBER MUSIC: Legend, violin and piano; Canzonetta, violin and piano; Fantaisie erotique, violin and piano; Intermezzo, violin and piano; Seascapes, suite for piano; Prairie, suite for organ and piano; The woodland path, organ; CHORUS: The shadows of the evening hours; There came 3 kings; How sweet and silent is the place; I saw 3 ships; Nativity song; Invocation; many songs.

CRAWFORD, ROBERT M.
b. Dawson, Yukon Terr., Canada, 27 July 1899; d. New York, N.Y., 12 Mar. 1961. Studied at Princeton Univ.; Fontainebleau Cons., France; and Juilliard Graduate School. He taught at Juilliard School and at Univ. of Miami; was conductor of various opera and choral groups and orchestras. He wrote several orchestral suites and many songs.

CRAWFORD, THOMAS CHARLES
b. Harrisburg, Pa., 12 Mar. 1956. Studied with
Samuel Adler, Warren Benson, and Joseph
Schwantner, Eastman School of Music, B.M. 1978;
with George Edwards, Columbia Univ. His awards
include a BMI student award, 1977; Sernoffsky
prize and Howard Hanson award at Eastman;
Hinshaw/Holtkamp organ composition award, 1978.
He is a church organist.
WORKS: CHAMBER MUSIC: Mystique, soprano
and chamber orch.; 3 songs, soprano and piano;
3 incidents, flute and piano; ORGAN: Fantasia;
Mélange; Ashes of Rose.
1611 Letchworth Rd., Camp Hill, PA 17011

CRAWFORD-SEEGER, RUTH PORTER
b. East Liverpool, Ohio, 3 July 1901; d. Chevy
Chase, Md., 18 Nov. 1953. Studied with Adolf
Weidig in Chicago; with Charles Seeger in New
York. She held a Juilliard scholarship, 1927-
29; a Guggenheim fellowship for study in Paris
and Berlin, 1930. She held various teaching
posts, then married Charles Seeger in 1931. A
retrospective concert of her works was presented
in New York, 19 Feb. 1975.
WORKS: ORCHESTRA: Music for small orchestra; Rissolty, rossolty, 10 winds, drums,
strings, 1941; CHAMBER MUSIC: 2 movements for
chamber orchestra, 1926, Cambridge, Mass., 25
Feb. 1975; violin sonata, 1926; suite for piano
and woodwind quintet, 1927, Cambridge, Mass.,
14 Dec. 1975; Diaphonic suite, solo flute or
oboe or chamber orch., 1930; string quartet,
1931; suite for wind quintet, 1952; CHORUS:
Canon; Chant, 1930; Sacco and Vanzetti, 1933;
SONGS: 2 ricercari for voice and piano; China-
man, laundryman, 1932, and Sacco, Vanzetti,
1932; 3 songs on Sandburg texts (Rat riddles,
Prayers of steel, In tall grass) for contralto,
oboe, percussion, piano, Amsterdam Festival of
the Internat. Society of Contemporary Music,
15 June 1933, New York premiere, 24 Apr. 1974;
PIANO: 9 preludes; Study in mixed accents.

CRESHEVSKY, NOAH
b. Rochester, N.Y., 31 Jan. 1945. Studied with
Virgil Thomson, Nadia Boulanger, and Luciano
Berio. He received a Boulanger fellowship, 1964,
and a Juilliard scholarship, 1967. He has been
faculty member at Juilliard School, 1968-70;
from 1970, at Brooklyn Coll., CUNY.
WORKS: CHAMBER MUSIC: Vier Lieder, narrator, pianist, theatre props, 1966; ELECTRONIC:
Circuit, 1970; Variations, 1970; Chaconne, 1973.
Ansonia Hotel, 2109 Broadway, New York, NY
10023

CRESTON, PAUL
b. New York, N.Y., 10 Oct. 1906. Is entirely
self-taught in harmony, orchestration, and composition. Although he began to compose at age 8,
he did not choose music as his life work until
he was 26. Since that time, his prolific output
has earned him such honors as Citation of Merit,
Nat. Assoc. for American Composers and Conductors, 1941; music award, American Acad. of Arts
and Letters, 1943; New York Music Critics' Circle
award, for symphony #1, 1943; first place, Paris

Internat. Competition, 1952; honorary member,
Kappa Kappa Psi, Pi Kappa Lambda, and Phi Mu
Alph Sinfonia; Gold Medal, Nat. Arts Club; and
many more, including many commissions. In addition to being composer, pianist, organist, and
conductor, he has been teacher, guest composer,
and lecturer at a score of colleges and universities and on the faculties at Univ. of Southern
California, 1948; Swarthmore Coll., 1956; New
York Coll. of Music, 1964-68; and composer-in-
residence and professor, Central Washington State
Coll., 1968-76. In 1960 he was American specialist in Israel and Turkey for the U.S. State
Department.
WORKS: Over 100 major works: 35 orchestral
works (5 symphonies, 15 concertos, including
concertos for marimba, harp, trombone, saxophone,
accordion, violin, piano); some of his later
works are Fanfare '76 (The Republic stands),
Cincinnati, 8 Mar. 1976, and Hyas Illahee,
chorus and orch., Shreveport, La., 14 Mar. 1976;
symphonic band works; chamber music for various
instrumental groups; choral works, cantatas, an
oratorio; songs; piano compositions; numerous
scores for radio, television, and films. He is
author of 2 textbooks, Principles of rhythm and
Creative harmony.
Box 28511, San Diego, CA 92128

CREWS, LUCILE (Mrs. Lucile Marsh)
b. Pueblo, Colo, 23 Aug. 1888; d. San Diego,
Calif., 3 Nov. 1972. Studied at Redlands Univ.;
New England Cons.; with Nadia Boulanger in
Paris; and in Berlin. Her awards included a
Pulitzer traveling fellowship, 1926; Calif. Fed.
of Music Clubs prize for a 1-act opera; Festival
of Allied Arts prize. Her compositions include
the opera, Ariadne and Dionysus; a tone poem,
chamber music, piano pieces, songs.

CRIST, BAINBRIDGE
b. Lawrenceburg, Ind., 13 Feb. 1883; d. Barn-
stable, Mass., 7 Feb. 1969. Studied law at
George Washington Univ., L.L.B. 1906; composition
with Paul Juon in Berlin. He abandoned law
after a few years and taught singing in Boston,
1915-21, and in Washington, D.C., 1922-23; after
another 4 years in Europe, he returned to Washington.
WORKS: BALLET: Le pied de la momie, 1915;
Pregiwa's marriage, 1920; The sorceress, 1926;
ORCHESTRA: Egyptian impression, suite, 1915;
Abhisarika, violin and orch., 1921; Intermezzo,
1921; Chinese dance, 1922; Nautch dance, 1922;
Dream, 1924; Yearning, 1924; Nocturne, 1924; An
old portrait, 1924; La nuit revécue, 1933;
Vienna 1913, 1933; Frivolité, 1934; Hymn to
Nefertiti, 1936; Fête espagnole, 1937; American
epic 1620, tone poem, Washington, 28 Feb. 1943.
Several works for voice and orchestra, many
choral works, songs, piano pieces. He was author
of The setting of words to music, 1945.

CRITSER, WILLIAM
b. Columbus, Ohio, 9 July 1928. Attended Northwestern Univ.; South Dakota School of Mines and
Tech.; studied composition with Nikolai
Lopatnikoff and Robert Delaney. He was minister

CROCKETT, DONALD

of music, Presbyterian Church, Beckley, W.Va., 1956-65; director, Beckley Choral Society, 1960-64; principal oboist, Charleston Symphony, Charleston, W.Va., 1957-62; private teacher in Pittsburgh, from 1965.

WORKS: CHAMBER MUSIC: oboe sonata; theme and variations, piano; saxophone quartet; Prelude, clarinet solo; 2 preludes, piano; A revolutionary quodlibet, 2 flutes and piano; An importer, soprano or tenor and woodwind quintet, Frost text; CHORUS: Psalm of praise, with organ; How long, O Lord, a cappella; Psalm 145, a cappella.

443 Royce Ave., Pittsburgh, PA 15216

CROCKETT, DONALD

b. Pasadena, Calif., 18 Feb. 1951. Studied with Halsey Stevens, Robert Linn, and Humphrey Searle, Univ. of Southern California, B.A. 1974, M.M. 1976. His awards include BMI award, 1972; Jimmy McHugh composition prize, 1973; Univ. of Southern Calif., alumni award, 1974; Faith Memorial award, 1975; Anstead award, 1976. From 1976 he has been faculty member, Univ. of Southern California.

WORKS: ORCHESTRA: 2 movements for orchestra, 1972; CHAMBER MUSIC: chamber symphony, 1974-75; The rhapsode, chamber theater piece, 1974-75; Ancient dances, violin, trombone, percussion, 1976; Occhi dell'alma mia, high voice and guitar, 1977; Lyrikos, tenor and chamber orch., 1978-79; trio for flute, cello, and harp, 1979.

4732 Indianola Way, La Canada, CA 91011

CROLEY, RANDELL

b. Knoxville, Tenn., 23 Sept. 1946. Studied with Vincent Persichetti, Roger Sessions, and Luciani Berio, Juilliard School; with Moritz Bomhard, Univ. of Louisville; with Roman Vlad, Accad. Musicale Chigiana, Siena, Italy. His awards include Outstanding String Composition award, 1966; Exposition of Contemporary Music, Cincinnati; Lado prize, Juilliard School, 1969; annual ASCAP awards from 1968. He was music editor with Autography Editions, New York, 1968-72; with Joseph Boonin, Inc., from 1973.

WORKS: ORCHESTRA: concerto for flute and metal orch., 1967; Cinque espressioni per orchestra piccola, 1969; Song of my youth, wind orch., 1968; CHAMBER MUSIC: Thesis for string trio, 1963; Sinfonietta, brass quintet, 1966; Quattro espressioni, piano, 1968; Microespressioni I, wind quintet, 1969; ELECTRONIC TAPE: White on white, 1967; many other works for small ensembles and solo instruments.

c/o Joseph Boonin, Inc., 40 Railroad Ave., Hackensack, NJ 07601

CROOKS, MACK CURSEY

b. Knoxville, Tenn., 7 Feb. 1937. Studied with Robert Erickson and Sol Joseph, San Francisco Cons.; with Roger Nixon and Wayne Peterson, San Francisco State Coll., B.A., M.A.; with George Kyme and Joaquin Nin-Culmell, Univ. of California, Berkeley, Ph.D. 1969. He has received grants from Dant Family Found. and Hearst Found. for support of the Lone Mountain Coll. Community

Jazz Ensemble, of which he was founder and has been director from 1975. This is a nonprofit, 20-piece, big band, presenting free concerts in the San Francisco Bay area.

WORKS: CHAMBER MUSIC: Emanations, 8 instruments, 1965; Chance pieces for . . ., 2 improvisation pieces for young players; Canzona, brass septet, 1976; CHORUS: Kyrie, 1968; December carol, 1970; Scat-in-a-round and Count Basie, 2 pieces for vocal jazz ensemble and rhythm section, 1977; PIANO: Movements for piano, 1966; Tonatina, 1966; Flamenco sketches, suite for 2 pianos, 1975; Concertones, 2 pianos, 1975.

3394 Market St., San Francisco, CA 94114

CROOM, JOHN ROBERT

b. Jennings, La., 27 Apr. 1941. Studied with Kenneth Klaus, Louisiana State Univ.; with Woodrow James, McNeese State Univ. He was selected as chairman for the Louisiana Music Educators Assoc. annual composition contest, 1970-74. He has been faculty member, Nicholls State Univ., from 1970.

WORKS: He has written 12-tone, free 12-tone, chromatic, and quarter-tone works for brass, woodwinds, strings, piano, and chorus. MAJOR WORKS: Pentagon for brass, quintet; Variations for a dozen clarinets; 5 subconscious flights, piano; Metamorphosis, 2 pianos; Didactic material, clarinet solo; CHORUS: mass in English.

503 Willow St., Thibodaux, LA 70301

CROSS, LOWELL

b. Kingsville, Tex., 24 June 1938. Studied with Mary Jeanne van Appledorn, Texas Technological Univ., B.A. in English 1961, B.A. in music 1963; electronic music with Myron Schaeffer and Gustav Cimiaga, Univ. of Toronto, M.A. 1968. He established the electronic music studio at Texas Tech. Univ. 1961; was research associate, Univ. of Toronto, 1968; artistic director, Tape Music Center, Mills Coll., 1968-69; consultant, Experiments in Art and Technology, New York, 1969-70; guest consultant, Nat. Inst. of Design, Ahmedabad, India, Apr. 1970; audio engineer and faculty member, Univ. of Iowa, from 1971.

WORKS: ELECTRONIC: 4 random studies, 1961; 0.8 century, 1962; Decaphonics, 1963; Antiphonies, 1964; After long silence, tape, Stirrer, and soprano, 1964; Video I and Video II, tape, audio system, television, 1965; Video III, with David Tudor, phase-derived audio system, monochrome and color television; etc. He has written articles on electronic music and has designed circuits including the Stirrer, a 4-channel device for directing and mobilizing sounds in space; version #2 was built for CBS and Columbia Records, 1970.

1705 Glendale Rd., Iowa City, IA 52240

CROSS, RONALD

b. Fort Worth, Tex., 18 Feb. 1929. Studied organ in New York; then at Centenary Coll. of Louisiana; at New York Univ., Ph.D. 1961; received a Fulbright fellowship for study in Italy, 1955. He was on faculty at Notre Dame Coll., Staten Island, then professor, Wagner

Coll., Staten Island. He is chiefly a musicologist, but has written choral pieces and chamber music.

Wagner Coll., 631 Howard Ave., Staten Island, NY 10301

CROSSMAN, ALLAN
Studied with Hugo Weisgall. Formerly on the faculty at Wheaton Coll., in 1974 he joined the staff of the School of Contemporary Music, Brookline, Mass.
WORKS: CHAMBER MUSIC: The least grain of remembered dust, trio, 1967; The wind sings, trio, 1968; Dances of the distant planet Earth, 1972; string quartet, Cambridge, Mass., 3 June 1974.
School of Contemp. Music, 2001 Beacon St., Brookline, MA 02146

CROTTY, MICHAEL
b. Putnam, Conn., 29 Apr. 1950. Studied with John Bavicchi, William Malouf, Herb Pomeroy, Phil Wilson, Berklee Coll., B.M. 1972. He received a John Philip Sousa award in 1968. He was composer-in-residence, Woodstock Music and Arts Program, 1971; with the U.S. Air Force Band from 1972.
WORKS: 6 Psalms, 1968; Experiment in blues, 1967-69; My Lai, 1970; Unanswered questions, 1971-72; Dichotomy, 1972; Warm rain, 1972; Oasis, 1973; Multiple woodwind concerto, 1973.
3403 Eastern Ave., N.E., Washington, DC 20018

CROWLEY, ROBERT DENNIS
b. Great Falls, Mont., 12 Apr. 1921. Studied with Herbert Gladstone at Reed Coll.; with Darius Milhaud, Mills Coll.; with Roger Sessions and Andrew Imbrie, Univ. of California. He has been professor, Portland State Univ., from 1958.
WORKS: ORCHESTRA: Aspects of otherness, chamber orch. with concertante of winds and piano, 1958; Toccata, trumpet and orch., 1963; BAND: Colluctation, 1969.
Music Dept., Portland State Univ., Portland, OR 97207

CRUMB, GEORGE
b. Charleston, W.Va., 24 Oct. 1929. Studied at Mason Coll., Charleston; Univ. of Illinois, M.M. 1953; with Ross Lee Finney, Univ. of Michigan, D.M.A. 1959; with Boris Blacher in Berlin. His awards include Fulbright fellowship, 1954; grants from Rockefeller Found., 1964; Koussevitzky Found., 1965; Guggenheim Found., 1967, 1973; Pulitzer prize, 1968; Coolidge Found. award, 1970; Nat. Inst. of Arts and Letters award, 1967; Internat. Rostrum of Composers, UNESCO, award, 1970; Koussevitzky recording award, 1970; elected to Nat. Inst. of Arts and Letters, 1975; honorary doctorate, Oberlin Coll., 1978; State Dept. lecturer in Korea, England, Denmark, Greece, Italy, 1978; was co-winner, Brandeis Univ. Creative Arts Award in Music, 1979. He was on the faculty, Univ. of Colorado, 1959-64; Univ. of Pennsylvania from 1965; visiting professor at Harvard, 1968, at Tanglewood, 1970.

WORKS: ORCHESTRA: Variazioni, 1959; Echoes of time and the river, 1967 (Pulitzer, 1968); Star child, orch., chorus, 2 children's choirs, soloists, 4 conductors, New York, 5 May 1977; CHAMBER MUSIC: string quartet, 1954; sonatina for solo cello, 1955; 5 pieces for piano, 1962; 4 nocturnes (Night music II), violin and piano, 1964; 11 echoes of autumn, violin, alto flute, clarinet, piano, 1966; Night of the 4 moons, alto flute, banjo, cello, percussion, 1969; Black angels: 13 images from the darkland, electric string quartet, 1970; Vox balaenae (Voice of the whale), amplified flute, cello, piano, the 3 players to wear black half-masks, commissioned and performed by New York Camerata, 10 Oct. 1971; Makrokosmos I, piano, 1973; Makrokosmos II, amplified piano, New York, 12 Nov. 1974; Makrokosmos III, music for a summer evening, 2 amplified pianos and percussion, 1974, Washington, 23 Feb. 1979; Dream sequence, violin, cello, glass harmonica, piano, percussion, Bowdoin Coll., 17 Oct. 1976; VOICE: Night music I, soprano, celeste, piano, percussion, 1963; Madrigals, Book I, soprano, vibraphone, double bass, 1965; Madrigals, Book II, soprano, alto flute, percussion, 1965; Songs, drones, and refrains of death, baritone, guitar, double bass, piano, percussion, text by Garcia Lorca, 1968; Madrigals, Book III, soprano, harp, percussion, 1969; Madrigals, Book IV, soprano, flute, harp, bass, percussion, 1979; Ancient voices of children, soprano, boy soprano, 7 instruments, Lorca text, 1970; Lux aeterna, soprano, bass flute, sitar, 2 percussionists (all masked), 1971.
240 Kirk Lane, Media, PA 19063

CUBBAGE, JOHN
b. Tuscaloosa, Ala., 21 Sept. 1937. Studied with Robert Wykes and Paul Pisk, Washington Univ.; with Eugene Weigel, Univ. of Montana. He has been faculty member, Univ. of Montana, 1965-68, and from 1970.
WORKS: CHAMBER MUSIC: Chorale and variations, woodwind trio, 1962; string quartet, 1965; Recitative, solo violin, 1969; violin sonata, 1968; string trio, 1969; PIANO: 3 structural studies, 1963; piano sonata, 1970; 3 pieces for piano, 1969; Adagio for piano, 1970.
Box 821, R.R. 2 South, Great Falls, MT 59401

CUMBERWORTH, STARLING A.
b. Medina, Ohio, 25 July 1915. Studied with Herbert Elwell, Cleveland Inst. of Music, M.M., M.A. 1941; with H. L. Baumgartner and Quincy Porter, Yale Univ., M.A. 1948; with Bernard Rogers and Howard Hanson, Eastman School of Music, Ph.D. 1958. He received awards at Cleveland Inst., Yale Univ., and from the Cleveland Women's Club. He has been faculty member at Cleveland Inst. of Music, Mississippi Southern Coll., Cuyahoga Community Coll.; at Cleveland Music School Settlement from 1959.
WORKS: Home burial, concert opera, 1955; CHAMBER MUSIC: trio for violin, clarinet, piano; trio for violin, cello, piano; flute sonata; oboe sonata; violin sonata; 2 string

CUMMING, RICHARD

quartets; SONGS: <u>Sleep, child</u>; <u>3 Chinese love
lyrics</u>, soprano, <u>2 macabre whims</u>, baritone.
1844 Alvason Rd., East Cleveland, OH 44112

CUMMING, RICHARD
b. Shanghai, China, 9 June 1928, of American
parents. Attended San Francisco Cons.; Music
Acad. of the West, Santa Barbara; Aspen Inst. of
Music; studied composition privately with Ernest
Bloch, Arnold Schoenberg, and Roger Sessions.
His awards include Nat. Fed. of Music Clubs
prize, 1954; annual ASCAP awards from 1961; Ford
Found. grant, 1963; Wurlitzer Found. grant, 1964;
Rhode Island State Council for the Arts award,
1973; Rockefeller Found. grant; Nat. Endowment
for the Arts grant. He was vocal accompanist,
1954-66; composer-in-residence, Milwaukee Repertory Theatre, 1965-66 season, and at Trinity
Square Repertory Company, Providence from 1966;
was staff member, Rhode Island Governor's School
for Youth in the Arts, 1969, 1970, 1972.
    WORKS: THEATRE: <u>The picnic</u>, 2-act opera,
1964-74; <u>Peer Gynt</u>, incidental music; <u>Years of
the locust</u>, 1968; <u>Feasting with panthers</u>, NET
network, Jan. 1974; VOICE: <u>Tzu-zyeh songs</u>,
1953; <u>The crowne</u>, 7 songs for bass and orch.,
1956; <u>We happy few</u>, 10 songs, 1963; mass for
solo voice, oboe, string quartet, 1965; over
200 songs; PIANO: sonata, 1951; 24 preludes,
1966-68.
    Trinity Square Repertory Company, 201 Wash-
    ington St., Providence, RI 02903

CUMMINGS, CONRAD
b. San Francisco, Calif., 10 Feb. 1948. Studied
with Bulent Arel at Yale Univ. and at State Univ.
of New York, Stony Brook; with Mario Davidovsky,
Vladimir Ussachevsky, and Chou Wen-Chung,
Columbia Univ.; with Jacob Druckman at Tanglewood. His awards include Presser Found. award;
Bates fellowship; Rapaport prize; Ditson Fund
grant; summer research fellowship, Stanford
Computer Music Inst. He was staff member,
Columbia-Princeton Electronic Music Center,
1974-77; Brooklyn Coll., CUNY, 1976-79; then
research staff, IRCAM, Paris.
    WORKS: ORCHESTRA: <u>Composition for orches-
tra</u>, 1978; CHAMBER MUSIC: <u>Skin songs</u>, voice and
8 instruments; <u>Hoofer</u>, 6 percussionists, 1977;
<u>Basstet</u>, 4 double basses, 1978; <u>Bone songs</u>,
trumpet, clarinet, double bass; <u>Remembered
voices</u>, piano; ELECTRONIC: <u>Subway songs</u>, 1976;
<u>Endangered species</u>, 1977.
    67 7th Ave., Brooklyn, NY 11217

CUMMINS, RICHARD
b. Petersburg, Va., 30 Sept. 1936. Graduated
from Curtis Inst. of Music with an artist's
diploma; from Westminster Choir Coll., B.M.,
M.M. He is an organ and harpsichord recitalist
and has held church posts in Pennsylvania and
New Jersey; in 1973, at Virginia Heights Baptist
Church, Roanoke.
    WORKS: CHAMBER MUSIC: <u>3 love songs</u>,
Teasdale text, high voice and piano; <u>Introduction
and allegro</u>, oboe trio; <u>Passacaglia</u>, harp;
CHORUS: <u>Rise heart, thy Lord is risen</u>, treble
voices with organ; <u>A psalm of destiny</u>, text by

Dag Hammarskjold; ORGAN: 4 chorale preludes.
2331 Denniston Ave., S.W., Roanoke, VA
24015

CUNNINGHAM, ARTHUR
b. Piermont, N.Y., 11 Nov. 1928. Studied with
John W. Work, Fisk Univ., B.A. 1951; with John
Mehegan, Columbia Teachers Coll., M.A. 1957;
with Henry Brant, Norman Lloyd, Peter Mennin,
Wallingford Riegger, Juilliard School, 1951-52;
also studied with Margaret Hillis, Teddy Wilson,
and Peter Wilhousky. A fund for his education
was set up in 1946 by Lucinda Ballard and others;
he has received 2 Nat. Endowment for the Arts
grants; 5 ASCAP awards; and many commissions.
He was in the U.S. Army Special Services, 1953-
55; toured as a bass player in a trio; played
double bass in the Rockland County Symphony; and
was adviser to the Rockland County Playhouse,
1964.
    WORKS: THEATRE SCORES: <u>The beauty part</u>,
1963; <u>Violetta</u>, 1964; <u>Ostrich feathers</u>, 2-act
musical for children, 1964; <u>Louey, Louey</u>, mini-
rock opera, 1968; <u>Shango</u>, 1969; <u>Harlem suite
ballet</u>, Fisk Univ., 21 Apr. 1971; ORCHESTRA:
<u>Adagio</u>, oboe and string orch., 1954; <u>Theatre
piece for orchestra</u>, 1966; <u>Prometheus</u>, bass
voice and orch., 1966; <u>Dialogue</u>, piano and chamber orch., 1967; <u>Concentrics</u>, New York, 2 Feb.
1969; <u>Dim du mim</u>, oboe and orch., 1969; <u>Lullaby
for a jazz baby</u>, trumpet and orch., 1970; <u>The
Walton statement</u>, double bass and orch., for
Ortiz Walton, 1971, Boston, 16 Mar. 1980; <u>Romp</u>,
strings and woodwinds, 1971; <u>Strut</u>, bass clarinet
and orch., 1971; <u>Litany for the flower children</u>,
chorus, orch., rock, blues, and gospel, Stanford
Univ., 4 Aug. 1972; <u>The prince</u>, bass baritone
and orch., Detroit, 2 Apr. 1973; <u>Night song</u>,
chorus and orch., 1973; <u>Sun bird</u>, contralto,
guitar, orch., to his own text, 1974; CHAMBER
MUSIC: <u>Perimeters</u>, flute, clarinet, vibraharp,
double bass, 1965; <u>Minakesh</u>, oboe and piano,
1969; <u>Trinities</u>, cello and 2 double basses, 1969;
<u>Eclatette</u>, solo cello, 1971; <u>Covenant</u>, cello and
double bass, 1972; CHORUS: <u>The gingerbread man</u>,
1955; <u>He met her at the Dolphin</u>, 1963; <u>The
garden of Phobos</u>, Suffern, N.Y., 2 Mar. 1969;
<u>Lord, look down</u>, 1970; <u>We gonna make it</u>, 1970;
<u>Harlem suite choral</u>, Canton, N.Y., 21 Mar. 1971;
<u>World goin down</u>, 1972; <u>Call his name</u>, 1972;
SONGS: <u>Song of songs</u>, poem of Wilfred Owen,
soprano, 1951; <u>Turning of the babies in the bed</u>,
poem of Paul L. Dunbar, baritone, 1951;
<u>Prometheus</u>, baritone, 1965; <u>Minakesh</u>, contralto,
Washington, D.C., 15 Nov. 1970; <u>Born a slave</u>,
voice and piano, 1972; more than 400 songs in
jazz-rock style; PIANO: <u>Engrams</u>, 1969.
    4 N. Pine St., Nyack, NY 10960

CUNNINGHAM, MICHAEL
b. Warren, Mich., 5 Aug. 1937. Studied with
Ruth Wylie, Wayne State Univ., B.M. 1959; with
Ross Lee Finney and Leslie Bassett, Univ. of
Michigan, M.M. 1961; with Bernhard Heiden,
Indiana Univ., D.M. 1973. His awards include
honorable mention, Sigma Alpha Iota Interamerican
Music awards, 1971; second prize, Pittsburgh
Flute Club contest, 1971; annual ASCAP awards

from 1970. He was faculty member, Wayne State Univ., 1967-69; Kansas Univ., spring, 1972; Univ. of the Pacific, spring, 1973; Univ. of Wisconsin at Eau Claire, from 1973.

WORKS: THEATRE: Aladdin McFaddin, music for children's play; Catherine Sloper (of Washington Square), 3-act opera; Figg and Bean, opera on play by J. M. Morton, Eau Claire, 7 Mar. 1975; ORCHESTRA: Counter currents, 1967; Free design, 1972; Symphonic arias--Night, with chorus and soloists; CHAMBER MUSIC: Eusebius, viola, cello, piano; Dark vista, harpsichord and bass; Partitions, string quartet; Duetto, trumpet and trombone; Aedon, chamber orch. and tape; Romantic sonata, string bass and piano; CHORUS: Gnosis, women's voices, 1972; New beginnings, cantata; The annunciation, women's voices.
2405 E. Princeton, #7, Eau Claire, WI 54701

CUPPETT, CHARLES HAROLD
b. Coquimbo, Chile, 25 June 1894. Studied at Ohio Wesleyan Univ., B.S., Phi Beta Kappa. He was organist and choirmaster, and composer and conductor for commercial films.

WORKS: OPERA: Le baiser; ORCHESTRA: piano concerto; Indigo moon; Lament for the living, suite for piano and orch.

CURNOW, ROBERT H.
b. Easton, Pa., 1 Nov. 1941. Studied at West Chester State Coll., Pa.; with H. Owen Reed, Michigan State Univ., M.M., M.A. His awards include first place, Nat. Jazz Composition Contest; and commissions. He was faculty member, Case Western Reserve Univ., 1967-73; director of artists and music, Creative World Records, Los Angeles, 1973-77; on faculty, California State Univ., Los Angeles, from 1977.

WORKS: CONCERT JAZZ: Passacaglia; Festival piece; Rise and fall of a short fugue; First child; Trajectory for trombone; Alto piece; Writer's cramp; Promise of dreams; many other jazz and concert jazz works.
2051 N. Altadena Ave., Altadena, CA 91001

CURRAN, ALVIN
b. Providence, R.I., 13 Dec. 1938. Studied with Ron Nelson, Brown Univ., B.A. 1960; with Elliott Carter, Mel Powell, Alan Forte, Yale Univ., M.M. 1963. His awards include BMI prize, 1963; Ditson award, 1963; Ford Found. Young Artists-in-Residence Program, 1963-64 (West Berlin); Nat. Endowment for the Arts grant, 1978. Since 1976 he has been teaching improvisation at L'Accademia Nazionale d'Arte Drammatica in Rome.

WORKS: CHAMBER MUSIC: First piano piece; Thursday afternoon, solo violin; Homemade, percussion; 2nd trio, piano, clarinet, violin; IMPROVISATIONAL MUSIC: Community sing, 1966; La lista del giorno, 1967; Rounds, 1968; TAPE AND INSTRUMENTS: Under the fig tree; Madonna and child; Songs and views from the magnetic garden; Giardino magnetico, a synthesizer collage; and Music for every occasion, a collection of 50 original monophonic pieces.
Via dell' Orso 28, Rome, 00186, Italy

CURRAN, PEARL GILDERSLEEVE
b. Denver, Colo., 25 June 1875; d. New Rochelle, N.Y., 16 Apr. 1941. Studied at Denver Univ. and privately. She wrote Nocturne, women's chorus; The crucifixion for solo voice; many other choral works and songs.

CURRIE, RANDOLPH NEWELL
b. Armore, Pa., 5 Apr. 1943. Studied with Marshall Barnes at Ohio State Univ., B.M., M.M. He won an award in an organ composition contest sponsored by Ohio State Univ. He has been organist and choirmaster, Immaculate Conception Church, from 1969; and lecturer, Ohio State Univ., Newark campus.

WORKS: CHORUS: Bretheren, we have met to worship, women's voices and keyboard; Bless the Lord, O my soul, with organ and clarinet; ORGAN: Passacaglia on L'homme arme; and various English masses and service music, organ and piano works.
Ohio State Univ., Newark Campus, Newark, OH 43055

CURRY, W. LAWRENCE
b. Parnassus, Pa., 19 Mar. 1906; d. Pa., 28 Feb. 1966. Studied at Univ. of Pennsylvania, B.A., Phi Beta Kappa; Union Theological Seminary, M.S.M., S.M.D. He was on the faculty, Univ. of Pennsylvania, 1931-38; at Beaver Coll., 1929-66, glee club conductor, 1935-59; organist and choirmaster in Philadelphia, 1932-66; conductor of various choral groups; editor and music consultant. His compositions included the songs: Psalm of gratitude; God is our refuge; Lincoln speaks; and many liturgical works.

CURRY, WILLIAM HENRY
b. Pittsburgh, Pa., 30 June 1954. Studied with Richard Hoffmann, Walter Aschaffenburg, and Edward Miller at Oberlin Coll.; with Philip Catelinet, Carnegie-Mellon Univ.; with Robert Lord, Univ. of Pittsburgh. He won a Carnegie-Mellon Univ. composition prize, 1970. He was assistant conductor, Richmond Symph., 1975-77; resident conductor, Baltimore Symph., from 1978, and of the Peabody Cons. Orch., from 1979.

WORKS: ORCHESTRA: Mysticum, 1970; double concerto for trumpet, baritone horn, and orch.; All things, tone poem, tape and orch., 1979; CHAMBER MUSIC: saxophone quintet; 3 string quartets; Night poems, song cycle for contralto and chamber orch.
903 Druid Park Lake Dr., #7B, Baltimore, MD 21217

CURTIS, EDGAR
b. Aberdeen, Scotland, 11 Mar. 1914; U.S. citizen 1944. Studied with Sir Donald Tovey, Edinburgh Univ.; with Rudolf Serkin, Adolf Busch, Fritz Busch, and others in Europe; conducting also at Curtis Inst. and Berkshire Music Center, and with various conductors in the U.S. His awards include a traveling fellowship from Edinburgh Univ. and scholarships at Curtis Inst. and at Tanglewood. He has held several conducting posts and has guest conducted many orchestras; from 1955 he has been professor, Union Coll., Schenectady, N.Y.

WORKS: ORCHESTRA: organ concerto, 1960;

CURTIS-SMITH, CURTIS O. B.

CHAMBER MUSIC: sonata for unaccompanied flute, 1969; sonata a duè, flute and guitar, 1974; Quintet for brass '76, 1976; Music for dance perhaps, piano and reeds, 1976; KEYBOARD: 2 preludes for organ, 1960; 3 for Stephen, piano, 1968.
Box 12, Berlin, NY 12022

CURTIS-SMITH, CURTIS O. B.
b. Walla Walla, Wash., 9 Sept. 1941. Studied with Alan Stout, Northwestern Univ.; with Kenneth Gaburo and Herbert Brun, Univ. of Illinois; with Bruno Maderna at Tanglewood; and with David Burge at Whitman Coll. His awards include Koussevitzky prize, 1972; Viotti prize, 1975; Salabert prize, 1976; grants from Rockefeller Found., 1976, Nat. Endowment for the Arts, 1977, American Acad. and Inst. of Arts and Letters, 1978; Guggenheim fellowship, 1978. He has been faculty member, Western Michigan Univ., from 1968; was visiting lecturer, Univ. of Michigan, 1976-77.
WORKS: Passant. Un. Nous passons. Deux. De notre somme passons. Trois, 19 solo voices, narrator, chamber orch., and tape, 1970; Fanaffair for Fanny, 9 trumpets in 3 unequal groups and tape, 1971; Comedie, 2 sopranos and chamber orch., 1972; Xanthie, 9 instrumental groups, 1972; A song of the degrees, 2 pianos, 1 percussion, 1972-73; 5 sonorous inventions, violin and piano, 1973; Ordres, piano solo, 1973; Rhapsodies, piano; Winter pieces, dance music for chamber orch.; suite in 4 movements, harpsichord; partita, chamber orch.; Unisonics, saxophone and piano, 1976; Bells (Belle du jour), piano and orch., Indianapolis Symphony, 26 Jan. 1976, with composer as piano soloist.
3409 W. Michigan Ave., #7, Kalamazoo, MI 49007

CUSENZA, FRANK J.
b. San Vito, Italy, 25 Dec. 1899; U.S. citizen 1923. Studied at Royal Cons., Palermo, Italy; Great Lakes Coll., M.A. From 1922 he taught at the Detroit Cons.; Univ. of Detroit; Detroit Inst. of Musical Art. His works include an opera, a symphony, an oratorio, piano pieces, and songs.

CUSHING, CHARLES C.
b. Oakland, Calif., 8 Dec. 1905. Studied at Univ. of California and with Nadia Boulanger in France, 1929-31. He received the George Ladd Prix de Paris for achievement in composition, 1929; Legion of the French government, 1952. He joined the faculty, Univ. of California, Berkeley, in 1931; is violinist and violist; founded and conducted the Univ. of California Band; has conducted choral, orchestral, operatic, and theatrical groups.
WORKS: ORCHESTRA: Cereus, poem for orch., 1960; CHAMBER MUSIC: 2 string quartets; 2 violin sonatas; clarinet sonata; Fantasy, woodwind trio; Lyric suite, soprano, flute, viola; Eclogues for winds.

CUSTER, ARTHUR
b. Manchester, Conn., 21 Apr. 1923. Studied at

Univ. of Hartford, 1940-42; with Timothy Cheney, Univ. of Connecticut, B.A. 1949; with Paul Pisk, Univ. of Redlands, M.M. 1951; with Philip Bezanson, Univ. of Iowa, Ph.D. 1959; also with Paul Hindemith and with Nadia Boulanger, 1961-62. He received an award of the Society for the Publication of American Music, 1962; 2 Univ. of Rhode Island grants; and commissions. His undergraduate work was interrupted in 1942-46 for service as fighter pilot in the U.S. Navy. He was faculty member, Kansas Wesleyan Univ., 1952-55; at Univ. of Omaha, 1955-58; music supervisor, U.S. Air Force Dependent Schools in Spain, 1959-62; at Univ. of Rhode Island, 1962-65; dean, Philadelphia Musical Acad., 1965-67; director, St. Louis Metropolitan Educational Center in the Arts, 1967-73; named composer-in-residence, Rhode Island State Council on the Arts, 1973.
WORKS: THEATRE: The Ides of March, incidental music to a play on Thornton Wilder's novel; ORCHESTRA: Passacaglia, small orch., 1957, Chicago, 14 Apr. 1963; Concert piece, 1959; Austin, Tex., 27 Apr. 1963; Symphony #1, 1961, Madrid, 28 Apr. 1962; Songs of the seasons, soprano and small orch., 1963, Philadelphia, 20 Mar. 1966; Found objects (rhapsodality brass), New York, 8 Nov. 1969; Doubles, violin and small orch., 1972; CHAMBER MUSIC: Rhapsody and allegro, cello and piano, 1957; 3 canons, 2 trumpets and piano, 1958; 3 peices for brass, 1959; sextet, woodwinds and piano, 1959, Madrid, 3 May 1969; Divertimento, bassoon and piano, 1963; Pastorale and hornpipe, violin, clarinet, cello, 1963; Cycle for 9 instruments, 1964; Concertino for 2nd violin and strings, New York, 14 Nov. 1964; woodwind quintet, 1964; Permutations, violin, clarinet, cello, 1967; concerto for brass quintet, 1968; Stream music, 11 instruments, 1969; Parabolas, viola and piano, 1970; Colloquy, string quartet, and Epilogue, Washington, D.C., 9 Dec. 1975; CHORUS: Quodlibetnam, motet, 1966; SONGS: 3 songs of death, mezzo-soprano, 1958; Cartagena songs, bass-baritone, oboe, horn, piano, 1964; 3 love lyrics, tenor, flute, viola, harp, 1965; Comments on this world, contralto and string quartet, 1967; PIANO: 4 ideas for piano, 1965; Rhapsodality Brown!, paino, 1969; MIXED MEDIA: Found objects I, chorus and tape, 1968; Interface I, string quarter, 2 recording engineers, and tape, 1969; Interface II, trombone, percussion, 2 engineers, and tape, 1969; Found objects III, contrabass and tape, 1971; Found objects IV, cello tape, 1972; Found objects VI, flute and tape, 1973; A little sight of music, 6 players and tape, Providence, 5 Apr. 1973; Found objects VII, piano and tape, New York, 4 Apr. 1974; Found objects VIII, violin and tape, 1976; also music for television and films. His essay and articles in both English and Spanish have appeared in music journals.

CUTTER, MURRAY
b. Nice, France, 15 Mar. 1902. His works include a ballet, The snow queen, and special material for films.

CYR, GORDON CONRAD
b. Oakland, Calif., 5 Oct. 1925. Studied with
Charles Cushing, William Denney, Joaquin Nin-
Culmell, and Roger Sessions, Univ. of California,
A.B. 1966, Ph.D. 1969. His awards include the
1978 Maryland Arts Council Fellowship for Music
Composition ($5000); and commissions. He was
lecturer at Univ. of California, Berkeley, San
Francisco State Coll., and Coll. of the Holy
Names, 1970-71; from 1971, faculty member,
Towson State Coll.
WORKS: BAND: Rhombohedra, in memoriam
Charles E. Ives, was premiered on Ives's 100th
birthday by the Towson State Coll. Concert Band,
20 Oct. 1974, with the composer as one of the
conductors; CHAMBER MUSIC: string quartet,
1969; Tetramusic, clarinet, cello, piano, percussion, Baltimore, 17 Apr. 1977; VOICE: Peter
Quince at the clavier, baritone, 1954; 3 Shakespeare songs, high voice and chamber orch., 1962;
Lamentations for Jeremiah, 2 sopranos and string
orch., 1964; Sinfonias and arias, soprano and 7
instruments, Baltimore, 18 Mar. 1973; Tabb songs,
voice and piano, Washington, 21 July 1975.
110 Glen Argyle Rd., Baltimore, MD 21212

CZAJKOWSKI, MICHAEL
b. Milwaukee, Wis., 7 June 1939. Studied with
Leo Sowerby at American Cons.; with Bernard
Wagenaar and Vincent Persichetti, Juilliard
School; Morton Subotnick, New York Univ.; and
with Darius Milhaud at Aspen School. He won
Gretchaninoff awards, 1965, 1966. He has been
faculty member at Juilliard School and Aspen
School from 1966; New York Univ., School of
Education, from 1971; and director, New York
Univ. Composers Workshop, from 1969.
WORKS: CHAMBER MUSIC: string trio; wood-
wind quartet; Toccata, romance, and sundance,
piano; CHORUS: 3 Shaker songs, and other choral
works; ELECTRONIC: A Sunday in Hohocus, oboe
and tape; Serenade, concert band, rock groups,
tape, lights, film; People the sky, tape.
The Juilliard School, Lincoln Center, New
York, NY 10023

CZERWONKY, RICHARD RUDOLPH
b. Birnbaum, Germany, 23 May 1886; U.S. citizen
1915; d. Chicago, Ill., 16 Apr. 1949. Studied
violin with Joseph Joachim, Royal School of
Music and made his debut with the Berlin Philharmonic in 1906. In the U.S., he was violinist,
conductor, and teacher in Boston, Minneapolis,
Chicago; conductor, Kenosha, (Wis.) Symphony,
1940-49.
WORKS: ORCHESTRA: a symphony; violin concerto; Carnival of life; Weltschmerz, symphonic
poem; Episode, a rhapsody; also chamber music
and works for violin, voice, and piano.

DA COSTA, NOEL
b. Lagos, Nigeria, 1930; to U.S. 1941. Studied
at Queens Coll. and Columbia Univ.; with Luigi
Dallapiccola in Italy on a Fulbright fellowship.
He received a New York State Council on the Arts
grant, 1974. He is faculty member, Rutgers
Univ., and conductor of the Triade Chorale.

WORKS: In the circle, 4 electric guitars,
brass, percussion, 1969; The confessional stone,
soprano and 10 instruments, text by Owen Dodson;
The last judgment, women's chorus, narrator,
piano, percussion, text by James Weldon Johnson,
1970; Blues mix, contrabass and tape, New York,
20 Oct. 1971; Fanfare rhythms, New York premiere,
30 Apr. 1974; 5 verses with vamps, cello and
piano, 1975; Spiritual set, organ, 1977.
250 W. 94th St., New York, NY 10025

DAHL, INGOLF
b. of Swedish parents, Hamburg, Germany, 9 June
1912; U.S. citizen 1943; d. near Bern, Switz.,
7 Aug. 1970. Studied at Cologne Cons., Zurich
Cons., and Univ. of Zurich; also with Nadia
Boulanger. His awards include 2 Guggenheim
fellowships; 2 Huntington Hartford grants; Nat.
Inst. of Arts and Letters award; Soc. for Publication of American Music award; Alice Ditson
Found. award; and commissions. In 1938 he
settled in Hollywood, Calif., as arranger for
films and radio; joined the faculty, Univ. of
Southern California, 1943; toured West Germany
for the U.S. State Dept., 1961-62; conducted the
Ojai Festivals, 1964-65.
WORKS: ORCHESTRA: Symphony concertante,
2 clarinets and orch., 1953, premiere, Cincinnati, 5 Mar. 1976; The tower of St. Barbara,
Louisville, 29 Jan. 1955; Aria sinfonica, 1965;
variations on a theme by C. P. E. Bach, string
orch.; WIND ENSEMBLE: saxophone concerto, 1949;
Sinfonietta for band, 1961; CHAMBER MUSIC:
Allegro and arioso, woodwind quintet, 1942;
Music for brass instruments, 1944; Concerto a
tré, clarinet, violin, cello, 1946; duo for
cello and piano, 1946; Divertimento, viola and
piano, 1946; piano quartet, 1957; piano trio,
1962; Sonata da camera, clarinet and piano;
Duettino contertante, flute and percussion, 1966;
Serenade, woodwind quartet; brass quintet;
CHORUS: A noiseless, patient spider, women's
voices; PIANO: Sonata seria, 1953; Sonata pastorale, 1960; Quodlibet on American folk tunes,
2 pianos, 8 hands.

DALLAM, HELEN
b. Chicago, Ill., 4 Oct. 1899. Studied at American Cons., M.M., on scholarship. She received
several prizes in contests sponsored by the
Chicago News. She taught at American Cons. and
at Acad. of Allied Arts, New York; privately in
Columbus, Ohio, and Buffalo, N.Y.
WORKS: CHAMBER MUSIC: quartet for strings
and piano; The Earth in cycle, soprano, harp,
string quartet; also violin pieces and songs.

DALLIN, LEON
b. Silver City, Utah, 26 Mar. 1918. Studied
with Howard Hanson and Bernard Rogers, Eastman
School of Music, B.M., M.M.; with Miklos Rozsa
and Ernest Kanitz, Univ. of Southern California,
Ph.D. He has been on the faculties at Colorado
State Univ., 1946; Univ. of Southern California,
1946-48; Brigham Young Univ., 1948-55; California
State Univ., Long Beach, from 1955.
WORKS: ORCHESTRA: a symphony; Film overture; Symphonic sketches; BAND: Sierra overture,

DAMESEK, ABBE

CHAMBER MUSIC: string quartet; CHORUS: <u>Songs of praise</u>, alto and tenor soli, chorus, orch. or band; KEYBOARD: <u>Interlude</u>, organ; <u>Prelude to midnight</u>; <u>Concert rondo</u>; <u>Autumn vignette</u>; <u>Christmas caroler</u>, a collection of piano arrangements. He is author of several textbooks on music.

Music Dept., California State Univ., Long Beach, CA 90840

DAMESEK, ABBE
b. New York, N.Y., 25 May 1904. Studied composition with Vittorio Giannini; piano with Rosina Lhevinne. He was a theatre pianist, 1924-27; played in hotels and supper clubs, 1929-70; was accompanist to Arthur Tracy on radio.
WORKS: CHAMBER MUSIC: string quartet, 1948; PIANO: 3 novelty piano solos, 1927; <u>Runaway fingers</u>, 1928; <u>Dark keys</u>, 1930.
1625 Rugby Rd., Schenectady, NY 12309

DANA, WALTER (Wladyslaw Danilowski)
b. Warsaw, Poland, 26 Apr. 1902; U.S. citizen 1949. Studied with Henryk Melcer, Stanislaw Kazuro, and Piotr Rytel at Warsaw Cons. He received the Gold Cross of Merit from Poland's president; Royal Pin from Queen Elena of Italy; was named to the Polka Music Hall of Fame in the U.S. He was founder and conductor of Chor Dana, which twice toured the U.S. before World War II. Escaping from Poland in 1939, he made his way to the U.S. via Italy and settled first in Detroit, where he organized an American Chor Dana. War and army service interrupted this work, but on discharge in 1945, he went to New York and established Dana Records, for which he is artist and repertory director. The Dana Publishing Co. was added later.
WORKS: ORCHESTRA: <u>Jazz symphony in c</u>; <u>Florida sketches</u>, Miami, 15 Mar. 1970; <u>The wailing wall</u>, Miami, 22 Mar. 1971; <u>Aria and interlude</u> for strings; <u>Emotions</u>; <u>American symphony</u>; <u>The world marches on</u>; CHORUS: <u>Ora pro nobis</u>, choir and orch.; PIANO: <u>Israelis' victory dance</u>.
1130 Stillwater Dr., Miami Beach, FL 33141

DANBURG, RUSSELL L.
b. Miller, S. Dak., 2 Mar. 1909. Studied with Cyrus Daniel and LaVahn Maesch, Lawrence Univ., B.M. 1931; with Edward Royce, Howard Hanson, and Bernard Rogers, Eastman School of Music, M.M. 1935; also graduate work at Juilliard School, 1941. He was awarded a research grant, 1961; Humanities Council grant, 1969. He taught at Dakota Wesleyan Univ., 1931-37; Washington State Univ., 1937-48; Univ. of Florida, 1948-78.
WORKS: CHAMBER MUSIC: <u>Poeme</u>, horn and piano, 1956; <u>Lament and fanfare</u>, trumpet and piano, 1971.

DANFORTH, FRANCES A.
b. Chicago, Ill., 28 June 1903. Studied piano with various teachers; composition with David Stewart and Anthony Iannacone, Eastern Michigan Univ., M.A. She has won awards in national competitions, 1972, 1974. She was a private music teacher, 1933-78.
WORKS: CHAMBER MUSIC: <u>Theme and variations</u>,

wind trio, 1974; <u>Rain forest</u>, marimba solo with percussion, 1978; PIANO: suite, 1971; <u>Kerellian light</u>, 1977.
1411 Granger, Ann Arbor, MI 48104

D'ANGELO, JAMES
b. Paterson, N.J., 17 Mar. 1939. Studied with Vittorio Giannini, Nicolas Flagello, and Ludmila Ulehla, Manhattan School of Music; with Gunther Schuller, Lenox School of Jazz; privately with Lester Trimble, Jan Gorbaty, and William Russo; with Jean Catoire in Paris. He received a BMI award in 1960. He was faculty member, New York Univ., School of Education, 1968-69; Bronx Community Coll., CUNY, 1970.
WORKS: THEATRE: incidental music to <u>Richard of Bordeaux</u>; ORCHESTRA: concertino for saxophone quartet and orch.; <u>The festival of Attis and Cybele</u>; <u>The sign of Jonas: in memoriam Thomas Merton</u>, orch. and speaker; CHAMBER MUSIC: <u>Toccata</u>, solo percussion; tuba sonata; <u>An essay for brass quintet</u>; <u>Quietude</u>, 4 muted trumpets and percussion; <u>The 3 gunas</u>, woodwind trio; movements for 2 trombones; CHORUS: <u>Lord, it could be paradise</u>; <u>Nirvana</u>, women's voices; SONGS: 10 songs on texts of e. e. cummings; 6 modal songs on Chinese verse; and others.

DANIEL, CYRUS
b. Carpenter, Ill., 27 Feb. 1900. Studied at Shurtleff Coll., A.B.; with Arne Oldberg, Northwestern Univ., M.B.; at Yale Univ.; and with York Bowen in London. He was Pi Kappa Lambda. He was professor, Lawrence Univ., 1925-44; director of music, Vanderbilt Univ., 1944-68, then emeritus professor; also organist and choirmaster in Nashville, 1944-69.
WORKS: ORCHESTRA: <u>Nocturne</u> and <u>Adagio</u>, 1937; CHAMBER MUSIC: string quartet on <u>Barbara Allen</u>; CHORUS: <u>Remember now thy creator</u>, men's choir; <u>Festival cantata</u>, soloists, chorus, organ or orch.; <u>A Biblical trilogy</u>, a cappella; many other choral works.
157 Bougainvillea Dr., Leesburg, FL 32748

DANIELS, MABEL WHEELER
b. Swampscott, Mass., 27 Nov. 1878; d. Cambridge, Mass., 10 Mar. 1971. Studied at Radcliffe Coll., B.A. magna cum laude 1900; with George W. Chadwick, New England Cons.; with Ludwig Thuille in Munich. Her awards included Nat. Fed. of Music Clubs award and Nat. League of American Pen Women award, 1911; MacDowell fellowship, 1931; honorary M.A., Tufts Coll., 1933; D.M., Boston Univ., 1939; citation, Radcliffe Coll., 1954; D.M., Wheaton Coll., 1957; D.M., New England Cons., 1958; Nat. Assoc. of American Composers and Conductors award, 1958. She was music director, Simmons Coll., 1913-18; member and adviser of many musical groups in the Boston area.
WORKS: THEATRE: <u>The court of hearts</u>, operetta, 1900; <u>Alice in Wonderland continued</u>, operatic sketch, 1904; ORCHESTRA: suite for strings, 1910; <u>The desolate city</u>, with chorus, 1913; <u>Peace with a sword</u>, with chorus, 1917; <u>Songs of elfland</u>, with chorus, 1924; <u>The holy star</u>, with chorus, 1928; <u>Exultate Deo</u>, with

chorus, for 50th anniversay of Radcliffe Coll., 1929; Deep forest, 1931; Pirates' Island, 1934; Song of Joel, with chorus and soprano, 1940; Pastoral ode, flute and strings, 1940; Digression for strings, a ballet, 1947; A night in Beth-lehem, 1954; A psalm of praise, with chorus, for 75th anniversary of Radcliffe Coll., Cambridge, 3 Dec. 1954; CHAMBER MUSIC: 3 observations, woodwind trio, 1943; CHORUS: In springtime, choral cycle for women's voices, 1910; Eastern song, women's voices, piano, 2 violins; The voice of my beloved, women's voices, piano, 2 violins, 1911; The Christ child, a cappella; Salve, festa dies, a cappella; Through the dark the dreamers came; Dum Dianae vitrae, women's voices; Flower wagon, women's voices; Piper, play on!, 1960; also composed choruses for the dedication of the Radcliffe Graduate Center, 1966. She wrote a book on her student days in Germany, An American girl in Munich, 1905.

DANIELS, MELVIN L.
b. Cleburne, Tex., 11 Jan. 1931. Studied with Samuel Adler, Merrill Ellis, and William Latham, North Texas State Univ. His awards include first prize, Nat. School Orch. Assoc. Roth composition contest, 1968, 1970, 1978; and commissions. He has been faculty member, Abilene Christian Univ., from 1959, department chairman from 1964.
    WORKS: ORCHESTRA: Festique, 1970; Celebration suite, 1973; Cassation; Sunfest; Pendleton suite; Elegy for strings; The promise of America, with narrator and chorus, 1976; Aeolienne, 1978; BAND: Tower, concert march; fugue and rondo; andante and march, brass ensemble; many band arrangements and choral anthems.
    401 E.N. 23rd St., Abilene, TX 79601

DANKNER, STEPHEN
b. Brooklyn, N.Y., 5 Nov. 1944. Studied with Paul Creston and Vittorio Rieti, New York Coll. of Music, B.M. 1966; with Hugo Weisgall, Queens Coll., 1966-68; with Roger Sessions and Vincent Persichetti, Juilliard School, Ph.D. 1969. He received a BMI award, 1968; Elizabeth Sprague Coolidge award, 1971. He was teaching fellow, Juilliard School, 1970-71; on faculty, Brooklyn Coll., 1971-73; from 1973, at Williams Coll.
    WORKS: ORCHESTRA: symphony, 1969; CHAMBER MUSIC: string quartet, 1968; 3 pieces for bass clarinet and piano, 1971; many other choral and vocal works.
    21 Berkshire Dr., Williamstown, MA 01267

DAPOGNY, JAMES
b. Berwyn, Ill., 3 Sept. 1940. Studied with Robert Kelly, Hunter Johnson, and Benjamin Johnston, Univ. of Illinois. He has been faculty member, Univ. of Michigan, from 1966.
    WORKS: Variations for orchestra, 1967; CHAMBER MUSIC: 6 variations, clarinet and piano, 1968; and works in most forms. He is editor of The collected works of Ferdinand 'Jelly Roll' Morton, published by Smithsonian Institution Press.
    School of Music, Univ. of Michigan, Ann Arbor, MI 48109

DARBY, KENNETH LORIN
b. Hebron, Nebr., 13 May 1909. Studied with Tibor Serly, Ernst Toch, Herman Hand, and Victor Young. He founded The King's Men, male quartet, 1929, and Ken Darby's Singers; was writer, producer, music supervisor, and conductor for Walt Disney Studios. His compositions include The lake, symphonic suite for orchestra; many songs; and the film score, How the West was won.

DARCY, THOMAS F., JR.
b. Vancouver, Wash., 7 May 1895; d. Studied at Juilliard School and the Army Bandmaster's School. In World War I he was the youngest bandmaster in the regualr army; received many medals in his army career; was commissioned captain in 1953. His works for band included The U.S. Army march; March of the free people; and An American overture.

DARCY, WARREN JAY
b. Buffalo, N.Y., 10 Dec. 1946. Studied with Richard Hoffmann and Walter Aschaffenburg, Oberlin Cons.; with Benjamin Johnston and Edwin London, Univ. of Illinois. He was faculty member, Univ. of Illinois, 1972-73; from 1973, at Oberlin Coll.
    WORKS: THEATRE: Hecuba, 1-act melodrama, 1972; ORCHESTRA: variations, 1967; CHAMBER MUSIC: Grand sonata, violin and piano, 1966; 5 structures for 5 instruments, 1966; Improvisations I, violin, clarinet, piano, 1967; Episode, string quartet, 1968; Dichotomy, flute, horn, cello, piano, 1969; Expansions, violin and piano, 1970; CHORUS: War cantata, 1971.
    143 E. College St., Oberlin, OH 44074

DARGAN, WILLIAM T.
b. Monroe, N.C., 14 Aug. 1948. Studied with T. J. Anderson, Morehouse Coll.; with Lloyd Ultan, American Univ.; and with Charles Jones at Aspen School of Music, where he won third prize in the 1973 Darius Milhaud competition. He was instructor at Morehouse Coll., 1972-74.
    WORKS: CHAMBER MUSIC: 3 movements for 7 winds, 1974; Lyric dance, 7 instruments and percussion, 1973. His music is post-Webern, avant garde, with material derived from jazz and Afro-American folk sources.

DARROW, STANLEY
b. Camden, N.J., 16 Mar. 1934. Studied with J. Bazant in Czechoslovakia and P. Hoch in Germany. He won the 1970 Musician of the Year award of the American Accordion Assoc. He makes tours of Europe and is director of Acme Accordion School, Westmont, N.J.
    WORKS: ACCORDION: Spanish rhapsody; 3 emotions: Excitement, melancholy, happiness; Reflections, for ensemble of mixed instruments.
    322 Haddon Ave., Westmont, NJ 08108

DARST, W. GLEN
b. Shelby County, Ill., 21 Apr. 1896. Studied trumpet at an early age with his father, piano at American Cons.; played clarinet in an army band in World War I; then studied organ and composition privately. He won first prize in the

D'ARTEGA, ALFONSO

Texas Composers' Guild Contest, 1961, 1962;
first prize, Broadman Anthem Competition, 1961.
He was organist and choirmaster, 1927-58; at
St. John's Episcopal Church, Ft. Worth, 1945-58.
WORKS: numerous choral compositions including Ride on! Ride on in majesty!, sung by the
Bell Telephone Chorus in 1956 and 1958; Thee we
adore, 1961; Praise the Lord, alleluia, 1961;
O Son of Man, 1962.
4400 Fair Park Blvd., #221, Fort Worth, TX
76115

D'ARTEGA, ALFONSO
b. Silao, Guanajuato, Mexico, 5 June 1907.
Studied with Boris Levenson, Strassberger Cons.
He has been conductor for radio, theatre,
records, films, and concerts including the
Buffalo Philharmonic, Stadium Symph., Miami
Symph.; Symph. of the Air, St. Louis Symph.,
New London Symph., and Radio-Television Italia
in Milan and Rome.
WORKS: ORCHESTRA: American panorama;
Niagara Falls; Fire and ice ballet; Romanesque
suite; and songs.

DARTER, THOMAS E., JR.
b. Livermore, Calif., 13 Feb. 1949. Studied
with Robert Palmer and Karel Husa, Cornell Univ.,
B.A. summa cum laude, 1969, M.F.A. 1972; postgraduate studies, 1973. He received the Otto
Stahl award at Cornell, 1971; 2 first prizes and
the Devora Nadworney award, Nat. Fed. of Music
Clubs, 1969, 1971. He was faculty member,
Chicago Musical Coll., Roosevelt Univ., 1972-75.
WORKS: ORCHESTRA: Aphorisms, 1973; CHAMBER
MUSIC: piano sonata, 1968; Sonata fantasia,
cello and piano, 1969; sonatina, solo trumpet,
1970; piano quartet, 1972, Chicago, 16 May 1973;
4 aphorisms, piano, 1970; Dual and fried, ensemble, 1973; CHORUS: Psalm 90, a cappella,
1968; SONGS: Batter my heart, baritone, 1967.

DARZINS, VOLFGANGS
b. Riga, Latvia, 25 Sept. 1906; to U.S. 1950;
d. Seattle, Wash., 24 June 1962. Studied at the
Latvian State Cons., earning his master's degree
in composition and piano and winning a first
prize for his piano concerto. He became a music
critic on a Riga paper and as pianist, went on
several tours of northern Europe playing his
second piano concerto with the Riga Symphony.
He and his wife fled from Latvia and after 5
years in DP camps, were able to reach the U.S.
and settle in Spokane. There he was pianist,
teacher, and composer. In 1955 he received an
award from the Latvian Cultural Fund in Exile
for his second piano sonata and, in 1960, for
his arrangements of 200 Latvian folk songs.
WORKS: PIANO: sonata in F, 1951-52; sonata
#2, 1955; sonatina in G, 1956; suite in A, 1956;
Triade de preludes, 1957; Trittico barbazo, 1958;
preludes, 1960; 8 petit suites, 1960.

DASCH, GEORGE
b. Cincinnati, Ohio, 14 May 1877; d. Chicago,
Ill., 12 Apr. 1955. He was violinist with the
Chicago Symphony for 25 years; conductor of the
Evansville Philharmonic. He wrote orchestral
pieces.

DASHOW, JAMES
b. Chicago, Ill., 7 Nov. 1944. Studied with
J. K. Randall, Earl Kim, Edward Cone, Milton
Babbitt, at Princeton Univ.; with Arthur Berger,
Seymour Shifrin, and Martin Boykan, Brandeis
Univ.; and with Petrassi, Accad. Naz. di Santa
Cecilia, Rome. His awards include Presser
Found. fellowship; 2 Wilson Found. grants; Ful-
bright grant; Premio Nicola D'Atri and Premio
Bonaventura Somma in Rome; Nat. Endowment for
the Arts grant, 1976; first prize, 5th Internat.
Electroacoustic Music Comp., Bourges, France,
1979. He was founder in 1971 of the Forum
Players; was a founding member of Padova Computer Music Group; and is director, Studio di
Musica Elettronica Sciadoni, Rome.
WORKS: ORCHESTRA: Astrazioni pomeridiane,
variations, 1970-71; CHAMBER MUSIC: Songs of
despair, soprano and large chamber ensemble,
1969; Timespace extensions, flute, piano, percussion, 1969; duo for violin and piano, 1970;
Ashberry setting, soprano, flute, piano, 1972;
Maximus, to himself, soprano, flute, piano,
1973; Some dream songs, text by John Berryman,
soprano, violin, piano, 1975; Punti di vista:
(1) Forte Belvedere, 1976, (2) Montiano, 1978;
2 piano pieces; MIXED MEDIA: BURST!, soprano
and tape, 1971; Schiaffini music, trombone and
tape, 1972; Mappings, cello and tape, 1974; La
pianta da livio, tape, 1975; Whispers out of
time, 1975-76; Effetti collaterali, clarinet and
tape, 1976; A way of staying, soprano and tape,
1977; Second voyage, tenor and tape, 1978;
Partial distances, tape, 1978.
Via della Luce 66, 00153, Roma, Italia

DAUGHS, EUGENE WILLIAM
b. Idaho, 11 Oct. 1927. Studied at California
State Univ., Los Angeles, M.A. 1966; with Karl
Kohn at Claremont Graduate School; and with
Anthony Vazzana, Univ. of Southern California.
He has been music coordinator and department
chairman, Azusa School District, from 1971.
WORKS: CHAMBER MUSIC: Abstraction, viola
and piano; 2 songs for soprano.
1123 Alamosa Dr., Claremont, CA 91711

DAVENPORT, DAVID N.
b. Richmond, Ind., 27 Sept. 1925. Studied at
Indiana Univ., B.A., M.A. He has been choral
conductor at festivals and guest conductor at
Hollywood Bowl. He has published many works for
chorus.
3536 Woods Dr., Richmond, IN 47374

DAVENPORT, LA NOUE
b. Texas, 26 Jan. 1922. Studied with Erich Katz,
New York Coll. of Music.
WORKS: CHAMBER MUSIC: 3 duets, 2 flutes or
2 oboes or 2 clarinets; variations on The ravens,
3 recorders; A day in the park, children's suite
for 4 recorders; carols for recorders.

DAVID, ADRIAN. See ANDERSON, ADRIAN DAVID

DAVID, AVRAM
b. Boston, Mass., 30 June 1930. Studied with
Hugo Norden, Boston Univ., B.A. 1955, M.A. 1956,

D.M.A. 1964; with Francis Judd Cooke, New England Cons.; with Harold Shapero, Brandeis Univ. Summer Inst., 1960; with Pierre Boulez and Roslyn Brogue Henning, Cambridge; with Karlheinz Stockhausen, Darmstadt, Germany, 1961, 1966; piano with Margaret Chaloff in Boston. His awards include BMI award, 1958; fellowships at Boston Univ., 1956-58; Brandeis Univ., 1960; research fellowship, Carpenter Center for the Visual Arts, Harvard Univ., 1965-66; Nat. Endowment for the Arts grant, 1975.

WORKS: ORCHESTRA: ESRAJ, a symphony; Introduction and allegro; CHAMBER MUSIC: string quintet; 4 string quartets, 1970, 1971, 1971, 1976 (#2, in 30 movements, was premiered by the Concord Quartet, Boston, 22 Dec. 1978); 3 string trios; solo horn sonata, Tanglewood, 6 Aug. 1978; The breath of God, guitar sonata, England, 17 June 1975; 4 solo trumpet sonatas; 3 solo flute sonatas; 2 violin sonatas; Saturn I, bass drum; Vision, tuba solo; Canonic sonata, 3 trumpets; Reflexion 400, bassoon solo; Book of fragments 2, wind quintet; solo saxophone sonata; Emanations from the silence, string quartet; Soliloquy, contrabass solo; PIANO: 5 sonatas; 7 incantations; Variations; Prologue, 12 pieces, and epilogue; 3 preludes; Book of fragments 1; 3 romanzas; M.S.C. fantasy; Hommage to Marcel Duchamp; 8 bagatelles; The unquestioned answer; CHORUS: Kyrie eleison; Ave Maria; Intonements; A symphony of alleluias; numerous other choral works, instrumental pieces and songs.

249 Commonwealth Ave., Boston, MA 02116

DAVID, VINCENT (pseudonym)
b. Hudson Falls, N.Y., 19 Sept. 1924. Studied at Juilliard School; at Columbia Univ.; and with Wallingford Riegger. He was violin soloist with symphony orchestras at age 12, later violinist in symphony and dance orchestras. He received a Ballet Society commission, 1947.

WORKS: ORCHESTRA: Introduction and scherzo; Oriental fantasy; Fantasia, clarinet and chamber orch.; Reverie; An American portrait; CHAMBER MUSIC: Fantasia, clarinet and piano; suite for solo violin; The return, voice and piano.

DAVIDOVSKY, MARIO
b. Buenos Aires, 4 Mar. 1934; to U.S. 1960. Studied in Argentina with G. Graetzer, Erwin Leuchter, Teodoro Fuchs, Ernesto Epstein. His awards include 2 Guggenheim fellowships, 1960-62; 2 Rockefeller grants, 1960, 1965; Nat. Inst. of Arts and Letters award, 1964; Brandeis Univ. Creative Arts award, 1965; Pulitzer prize, 1971, for Synchronisms #6 for piano and electronic sounds; special citation in Koussevitzky Internat. Recording award, 1972, for Synchronisms #5. He has been associate director, Electronic Music Center, Columbia-Princeton Univ. from 1964; and faculty member, City Coll., CUNY, and the CUNY Graduate School from 1969.

WORKS: THEATRE: scenes from Shir Hashirim, cantata-opera, 4 voices and chamber ensemble, 1974-75; ORCHESTRA: Serie sinfonica, 1954; concerto for strings and percussion, 1957; Suite sinfonica para el payaso, 1958; Planos, 1961; CHAMBER MUSIC: 3 string quartets, 1954, 1958,

#3 commissioned and performed by the Juilliard Quartet, 17 Oct. 1976; clarinet quintet, 1956; nonet, 1957; Inflexions, 14 instruments, 1965; Chacona, piano trio, 1972; Junctures, flute, 1975; ELECTRONIC: 3 electronic studies, 1961, 1962, 1965; Synchonisms #1-6 for various instruments or groups of instruments and tape, 1963-70; Synchronisms #7, orch. and tape, New York, 4 Dec. 1975.

490 West End Ave., New York, NY 10024

DAVIDSON, CHARLES
b. Pittsburgh, Pa., 8 Sept. 1929. Studied at Univ. of Pittsburgh, B.M.; Eastman School of Music; Jewish Theological Seminary, M.S.M.; and on scholarship at Brandeis Univ. He was chaplain's assistant, U.S. Army in Korea, 1952-53; cantor, Wantagh Jewish Center, from 1955.

WORKS: CHORUS: Chassidic Sabbath; Hymn to the 4 freedoms; I never saw another butterfly, New York, 13 Mar. 1973.

Wantagh Jewish Center, Wantagh, NY 11793

DAVIDSON, HAROLD GIBSON
b. Low Moor, Va., 20 Feb. 1893; d. Glendale, Calif., 14 Dec. 1959. Studied at Cincinnati Cons. After teaching in various schools, he settled in California. His music was experimental.

WORKS: PERCUSSION: Auto accident; Hell's bells; PIANO: 2 minor disturbances and one major calamity, a suite; Legend of the flying saucer.

DAVIDSON, HAROLD P.
b. New York, N.Y., 19 July 1908. Studied at Pomona Coll., B.A.; Claremont Coll., M.A.; and at Univ. of Southern California. He taught in high school and at Claremont; was faculty member, California Polytechnic Univ. at San Luis Obispo, 1936-75.

WORKS: SONGS: Pardon for puns; Derby ram; Love's delights; Miserere meus, Deo.

DAVIDSON, JERRY F.
b. Ark., 26 July 1942. Studied with Bruce Benward, Univ. of Arkansas; with Louie White, Union Theological Seminary; with David Noon, Northwestern Univ. He has been faculty member at Harper Coll., Palatine, Ill., from 1969.

WORKS: OPERA: The fall of man, won Bingham prize, 1969; CHORUS: The word made flesh; Mad madrigals; O boundless wisdom; I was glad; My God, accept my heart.

144 N. Hager, Barrington, IL 60010

DAVIDSON, LYLE
b. 1938. Studied with Francis Judd Cooke and Daniel Pinkham, New England Cons., B.M., M.M.; with Arthur Berger, Brandeis Univ. He is on the faculty, New England Cons.

WORKS: CHAMBER MUSIC: A certain gurgling melodiousness, chamber orch. and double bass, Boston, 12 May 1973; CHORUS: Voices of the dark, with tape and optional bass instruments.

197 Lake View Ave., Cambridge, MA 02138

DAVIDSON, WALTER

DAVIDSON, WALTER
b. Poland, 21 Sept. 1902; U.S. citizen 1927.
Studied with Boris Levenson in New York; with
Solomon Ancis, Denver Coll. of Music; and at
Pope Pius School of Sacred Music. From 1957 he
was faculty member, School of Sacred Music,
Hebrew Union Coll.-Jewish Inst. of Religion; and
cantor, Temple Beth Sineth, Flatbush.
WORKS: VOCAL: High Holy Day music, solo,
choir, organ; songs of Israel, solo, choir,
organ; Friday evening and Saturday morning services, 2 voices and organ; Praise ye the Lord,
choir and organ.
111 E. 21st St., Brooklyn, NY 11226

DAVIS, ALBERT OLIVER
b. Cleveland, Ohio, 9 Apr. 1920. Studied at
Western Reserve Univ.; with Herbert Elwell,
Cleveland Inst. of Music; with Kenneth Wright,
Grant Fletcher, Clifford Barnes, and Paul Yoder,
Arizona State Univ., where he received the Mu
Rho Alpha award. Other honors were ASCAP awards,
1966-71. He has been arranger for various bands
including NORAD Band, 1960-64; on the faculty at
public schools, 1947-59; at Phoenix Coll. from
1968.
WORKS: BAND: Desert star; Hollywood serenade; Threebones; 3 cardinals; Festival at Tikal;
From shire and sea; and others.
1329 E. Catalina Dr., Phoenix, AZ 85014

DAVIS, ALLAN GERALD
b. Watertown, N.Y., 29 Aug. 1922. Studied with
William Berwald and William Naylor, Syracuse
Univ., B.M. 1944, M.M. 1945; and with Herbert
Elwell. His awards include grants from Alabama
State Council on the Arts; Nat. Endowment for the
Arts; George N. Shuster; Lehman Coll. fellowship
award, 1974-75; and several commissions. He has
held faculty posts at Syracuse Univ., 1946-49;
Cincinnati Cons., 1951-53; Queens Coll., 1954-
55, 1958-62; Hunter Coll., 1961-65; from 1968,
Lehman Coll., CUNY.
WORKS: OPERA: The sailing of the Nancy
Belle, 1-act chamber opera, 1945; The ordeal of
Osbert, 1 act, 1949; The departure, 3 acts, Univ.
of Montevallo, Ala., 24 Apr. 1975; ORCHESTRA:
Festival concerto, clarinet and orch.; BAND:
Razorback reel; Home town suite; Italian festival
suite, brass choir and percussion; CHAMBER MUSIC:
Folksonatine, bassoon and piano; CHORUS: The
married years, a cappella; A psalm of praise,
with brass and percussion; The astronauts, with
brass and percussion, text by composer, also
titled A song for Daniel; PIANO: Stackalee
dances, 2 pianos; razorback reel; Sonata Vene-
ziana; 3 nursery miniatures.
210 Riverside Dr., New York, NY 10025

DAVIS, ALLEN H.
b. Riverdale, Md., 12 Dec. 1945. Studied at
California Inst. of the Arts; with Lloyd Rodgers
and Donal Michalsky, California State Univ.,
Fullerton; privately with Richard Fenno, Harold
V. Johnson, and Nicolas Slonimsky. He was composer and arranger for Stan Kenton's Orch.,
1970-71; director of jazz studies, California
State Univ., Fullerton, in 1978.

WORKS: ORCHESTRA: Lamentations for neophonic orch.; Recollections of hoedown, wind
orch.; CHAMBER MUSIC: string quartet; Ballet
suite, strings and jazz quintet; Piano, alto
voice and piano, text by D. H. Lawrence.
1000 E. La Palma, #2, Anaheim, CA 92805

DAVIS, BOB
b. Philadelphia, Pa., 17 July 1947. Studied with
John Adams, Alden Jenks, Allauddin Mathieu, San
Francisco Cons., B.A. 1975; with Robert Ashley,
David Behrman, Pandit Pran Nath, and Terry Riley,
Mills Coll., M.F.A. 1978. His awards include
E. M. Crothers prize, 1977; San Francisco Jewish
Community Center composition contest, tied for
first place, 1978. He has been instructor at
San Francisco Cons. and at San Francisco City
Coll.
WORKS: VOICE: Round about Sugar-ree, 3 or
more voices; Tam-Lin, ancient Scottish ballad
for women's voices and flute, 1977; The clay
creation, a prefatory song to B'raishis: creation according to Biblical, ancient, and later
accounts, a large vocal work with libretto by
Ron Giteck. He is author of The 50¢ guitar
book, the world's first guitar instruction comic
book, and High points and high jinks in the
history of electronic music, published in
Synapse, 1977-78.
306 Fair Oaks St., #4, San Francisco, CA
94110

DAVIS, GENEVIEVE
b. Falconer, N.Y., 11 Dec. 1889; d. Plainfield,
N.J., 3 Dec. 1950. Studied piano with Adolph
Frey, Syracuse Univ. She was pianist and vocal
soloist; her compositions were chiefly songs and
piano pieces.

DAVIS, HARVEY O.
b. Cresson, Pa., 1915. Studied at Westminster
Coll. (Pa.), A.B. 1937; Univ. of Michigan, M.A.
1949; at Tanglewood, 1954. He was faculty
member, Transylvania Univ., 1951-78. His works
for chorus include On Jordan's stormy banks.
606 Judy Lane, Lexington, KY 40507

DAVIS, JAMES FRANKLIN
b. Princeton, N.J., 14 Nov. 1944. Studied composition with Karel Jirak, conducting with Gerald
Ruquet and Francois D'Albert, Chicago Cons. Coll.
He played trumpet in the Irving Symphony Orch.,
1966-67; was founder and director, Illinois Symphonette, 1968-71; and has been lecturer and
director of bands, Florida Inst. of Technology,
from 1972.
WORKS: ORCHESTRA: violin concerto; concerto for 10 instruments and piano; CHAMBER
MUSIC: string quartet; woodwind quintet; Nocturne; CHORUS: Crucifixion; Etiam pro nobis.
1201 Riverside Dr., Indialantic, FL 32903

DAVIS, JEAN REYNOLDS
b. Cumberland, Md., 1 Nov. 1927. Studied with
Robert Elmore, William R. Smith, and Constant
Vauclain, Univ. of Pennsylvania, B.M. Her awards
include the Thornton Oakley Medal; Benjamin
Franklin Medal; Cultural Olympics Award of Merit;

ASCAP awards. She was editorial consultant for a New York publisher, 1960-65; private teacher from 1942; also humorist, lecturer, poet, author of 3 books.

WORKS: OPERA: The mirror; The elevator; ORCHESTRA: Shenandoah holiday, a ballet; 2 symphonies; CHAMBER MUSIC: woodwind quintet; many choral works, vocal solos, and piano teaching materials.

Mermont Plaza, Apt. 104, Bryn Mawr, PA 19010

DAVIS, JOHN CARLYLE
b. Cincinnati, Ohio, 31 Mar. 1878; d. Wyoming, Ohio, 17 July 1948. Studied at Cincinnati Coll. of Music and Harvard Univ.; received the Springer Gold Medal. He was reporter on the Cincinnati Post; founder and director, Wyoming Inst. of Musical Art; church organist-choirmaster, 1904-17; inventor of improvements on the piano and electric pipe organ.

WORKS: ORCHESTRA: violin concerto; About the world, a suite; 3 dances, piano and orch.; Zira dances; Valse Vieux Carre; and songs.

DAVIS, JOHN JEFFREY
b. Chicago, Ill., 15 Aug. 1944. Studied with Deems Taylor; with Don Gillis and Gordon Goodwin, Univ. of South Carolina, where he was graduate assistant in 1974.

WORKS: CHAMBER MUSIC: Short elegy for strings, 1959; 3 liturgical dances, wind ensemble, 1970; Sweet around C, woodwind quintet, 1974; 2nd woodwind quintet, 1974; CHORUS: Te Deum, with trumpet and strings, 1964; Festival mass for the feast of St. John, with instruments and soloists, 1966; Mass for Easter Eve, with cantors and bell, 1967; Lament on the death of Lorenzo de' Medici, a cappella, 1970; Mass for the resurrection of the faithful, 1971; Silent night, with violin, harp, treble solo, 1973; also many songs; organ and piano pieces.

DAVIS, JOHN S.
b. Evanston, Ill., 1 Oct. 1935. Studied with Robert McBride, Univ. of Arizona, B.M. 1959, M.M. 1964, D.M.A. 1967. His awards include the Southern Arizona Opera Group composer award, 1967; Music Teachers Nat. Assoc. commission, 1968, for Middle Earth suite. He was faculty member, North Carolina Wesleyan Coll., 1967-75.

WORKS: THEATRE: The pardoner's tale, opera, 1967; How a fish swam in the air and a hare in the water, opera, 1971; The tale of the golden goose, musical comedy; ORCHESTRA: 2 symphonies; CHORUS: Psalm 148, 1967; Psalm 57, 1970; Agnus Dei, 1971; 200 other choral works; 40 instrumental ensembles, piano solos and duets, organ preludes.

DAVIS, KATHERINE K.
b. St. Joseph, Mo., 25 June 1892; d. Concord, Mass., 20 Apr. 1980. Studied at Wellesley Coll.; with Stuart Mason, New England Cons.; briefly with Nadia Boulanger. Her awards include the Billings prize at Wellesley, 1914; honorary doctorate, Stetson Univ.; ASCAP award, 1969. She taught at Wellesley Coll., 1916-18; Concord Acad., 1920-23; Shady Hill School, Philadelphia,

1923-30.
WORKS: THEATRE: The unmusical impresario, operetta; The road to Galilee, church opera; The drum, short play with music; Who is Jesus? and The children of Bethlehem, 2 children's operettas; ORCHESTRA: The burial of a queen, symphonic poem; Orientale; CHORUS: Carol of the drum (Little drummer boy); This is noel, cantata; Fanfare for Palm Sunday; Sing gloria; The tiger, Blake text; The lamb, Blake text, women's voices; Renew a right spirit within me, women's voices; many other choral works, vocal solos, piano pieces.

DAVIS, MARGARET MUNGER
b. Spencer, Iowa, 22 July 1908. Graduated from Northwestern Univ., 1931; studied at American Cons. and privately with August Maekelberghe in Detroit. She was teacher and accompanist, 1931-47; organist in Detroit from 1965. She has published choral works and vocal solos.

855 Commerce Rd., Milford, MI 48042

DAVIS, NATHAN
b. Kansas City, Kans., 15 Feb. 1937. Studied at Univ. of Kansas; Wesleyan Univ., Ph.D. 1974; and with Andre Hodeir at the Sorbonne, Paris. He received the WAMO Distinguished Musician award, and was selected by Ebony magazine for its success series of Who's Who in Black America. He is vice-president, Segue Records; director and founder of jazz studies, Paris American Acad.; director and founder, jazz studies, Univ. of Pittsburgh.

WORKS: JAZZ ORCHESTRA: The united spirited, jazz orch., string quartet, choir; Makatura; Rules of freedom; Happy girl; To Ursula with love.

5619 Kentucky Ave., Pittsburgh, PA 15219

DAVIS, SHARON
b. North Hollywood, Calif., 30 Sept. 1937. Studied piano at Univ. of Southern California, B.M. 1960; at Juilliard School, M.M. 1962; and in Paris on a Fulbright grant, 1962-63. She was principal piano instructor, East Texas Univ., 1963-65; made tours of Canada and the U.S. as pianist, 1963-69; music editor, WIM, Inc., and recording artist from 1966.

WORKS: CHAMBER MUSIC: Old King Cole variations, oboe, viola, piano; Fantasy, paino and 3 clarinets; Prelude and dance, trumpet and piano; VOICE: Suite of wildflowers, soprano, chamber ensemble; Though men call us free, soprano, clarinet, piano; 3 moods, Dickinson text, soprano and piano trio; 3 poems of William Blake, soprano and solo low clarinet.

2859 Holt Ave., Los Angeles, CA 90034

DAVIS, STANTON, JR.
b. New Orleans, La., 10 Nov. 1945. Studied with Herb Pomeroy, Berklee Coll. of Music, 1967-69; with George Russell, Jaki Byard, Robert Ceely, New England Cons., B.M. 1973. His awards include Creative Artist fellowship, Mass. Found. for the Arts and Humanities, 1975; Certificate of Merit, Southeastern Mass. Univ., 1977; Nat. Endowment for the Arts grant, 1977; ASCAP award,

DAVIS, WILLIAM DWIGHT

1978. He has held teaching posts at New England
Cons., 1970-72; from 1976, at Southeastern
Massachusetts Univ.; and from 1978, at Third
Street Music Settlement School.
WORKS: JAZZ: Moving up; Who is King Well-
ington?; Brighter days; also music for commer-
cials.
791 Tremont St., #E513, Boston, MA 02118

DAVIS, WILLIAM DWIGHT
b. Natchitoches, La., 6 Apr. 1949. Studied with
John W. Pozdro and Allen I. McHose, Univ. of
Kansas, B.M. 1971, M.M. 1972. He was 6th U.S.
Army Staff Bands officer, 1972-74.
WORKS: ORCHESTRA: symphony in 2 movements,
1971; CHAMBER MUSIC: bassoon sonata, 1969;
woodwind quintet, 1970; Music for a chamber
ensemble, 1970; sonata for brass quintet, 1971;
CHORUS: Acquainted with the night, 1969; My God,
why hast Thou forsaken me?, 1970; PIANO: Aria
and toccata, 1969; 2 impressions, 1971.

DAVISON, ARCHIBALD THOMPSON
b. Boston, Mass., 11 Oct. 1883; d. Brant Rock,
Mass., 6 Feb. 1961. Studied at Harvard Univ.,
B.A. 1906; M.A. 1907; Ph.D. 1908. He received
many honorary doctorates. He taught at Harvard,
1912-54.
WORKS: THEATRE: The girl and the chauffeur,
musical comedy, 1906; ORCHESTRA: Hero and
Leander, overture, 1908; Tragic overture, 1918.
He wrote several books on church music and on
music history and education.

DAVISON, JOHN H.
b. Istanbul, Turkey, 31 May 1930 (American
parents). Studied with Alfred Swan, Haverford
Coll., B.A. 1951; with Walter Piston and Randall
Thompson, Harvard Univ., M.A. 1953; with Howard
Hanson, Bernard Rogers, Alan Hovhaness, Eastman
School of Music, Ph.D. 1959; with Robert Palmer,
Cornell Univ., 1962. His awards include Woodrow
Wilson fellowship, 1951; Knight prize, Harvard,
1952; Paine fellowship, 1953, 1954; MacDowell
fellowship, 1960; Penn. Fed. of Music Clubs
prize, 1962; Ford Found.-MENC fellowship, 1964-
65; first prize, anthem competition, Abington,
Pa., 1976; and many commissions. He was teaching
fellow, Eastman School, 1958-59; from 1959, on
faculty, Haverford Coll., department chairman,
1969-78.
WORKS: ORCHESTRA: 4 symphonies, 1958,
1959, #3 for winds and percussion, 1964; #4 for
strings with violin and viola solo, 1969-76;
CHAMBER MUSIC: concertino for 12 winds, 1958;
Trio-fantasia, piano trio, 1962; violin sonata,
1964-76; clarinet sonata, 1966; sextet for English horn, string trio, bass viol, piano, 1968;
string quartet, 1968; brass quintet, 1974; Celebration, piano quintet, 1975; sonata for flute
and guitar, 1977; CHORUS: 3 psalms, a cappella,
1955-73; Trip-tych: 3 canticles for men's
chorus and orch., 1960; Latin cycle: Te Deum,
Mass, Magnificat, Nunc dimittis, with orch.,
1961-78; Episcopal liturgical cycle: 3 morning
canticles, 1972-76; Magnificat planetarum,
women's voices and chamber ensemble, 1974; The
American prophet, men's voices, winds, piano,

percussion, 1975; many other choral works,
chamber works, piano and organ pieces.
3 College Circle, Haverford, PA 19041

DAVISON, PETER
b. Los Angeles, Calif., 26 Oct. 1948. Studied
with Aurelio de la Vega, California State Univ.,
Northridge; with Roger Reynolds, Univ. of Calif-
ornia, San Diego. His awards include Los Angeles
Valley Coll. composition award, 1970; California
State Univ. award, 1975; Nat. Endowment for the
Arts grant, 1977; California Arts Council commission, 1978. He has held teaching posts at
Calif. State Univ., 1970-73; Univ. of California,
San Diego, 1973-75; Glendale Coll., 1975-76; from
1976, East Los Angeles Coll.
WORKS: ORCHESTRA: Polyphemus, 1975; sym-
phony #1, Los Angeles, 4 Feb. 1978; CHAMBER
MUSIC: Hekhalot, any 3 woodwinds or string trio;
ELECTRONIC: Transgressions, tape; piece for 12
instruments and tape, Santa Monica, 26 Sept.
1978; Summer and fall, woodwinds and synthesizers,
1978.
1924 Euclid, Santa Monica, CA 90404

DAVYE, JOHN J.
b. Milton, Mass., 19 Oct. 1929. Studied at Univ.
of Miami, B.M. 1952; with Warren Benson, Ithaca
Coll., M.M. 1965. He has been faculty member at
Old Dominion Univ. from 1966.
WORKS: ORCHESTRA: Sinfonietta for strings;
WIND ENSEMBLE: 3 episodes, brass choir; CHAMBER
MUSIC: Canonic fantasy, 2 flutes; CHORUS: A
child is born to us, treble voices; Missa brevis.
141 Fayton Ave., Norfolk, VA 23505

DAWES, WILLIAM
b. Kansas City, Mo., 27 July 1942. Studied
privately with Louis Calabro for a short time in
1966; is otherwise self-taught.
WORKS: CHAMBER MUSIC: Chorale, 4 celli;
FILM SCORE: Violin-cello duet; ELECTRONIC TAPE:
Electronic study #1, 1968; 3 geese, 1968; Blue-
jay, 1968; Eve, 1968; Throwaway, 1968; Invitation
to a gunfight, 1969; Lil, 1970; Cry for me, 1970;
Rosebud, 1970; Bad Henry, 1973. The sound synthesis equipment used for the electronic compositions was designed by Beman Dawes and con-
structed by the composer.
433 Broome St., New York, NY 10013

DAWSON, WILLIAM LEVI
b. Anniston, Ala., 26 Sept. 1898. Studied at
Tuskegee Inst., A.B. 1921; American Cons., M.A.
1927. He played first trombone, Chicago Civic
Orch., 1926-30; conducted the Tuskegee Inst.
Choir, 1931-54.
WORKS: ORCHESTRA: Out in the fields,
soprano solo; Negro folk symphony, 1932, rev. in
1952 after a visit to West Africa; the movements
are titled I--The bond of Africa, II--Hope in the
night, III--O Let me shine!

DEACON, MARY CONNOR
b. Johnson City, Tenn., 22 Feb. 1907. Studied at
East Tennessee State Coll.; also with Frank
LaForge, William Stickles, and Carl Deis. She
was church organist, 1936-42; taught at Royal

Cons., Toronto. Her published songs include Ocean lore; I will lift mine eyes; Beside still waters; Your cross; Hear my prayer; Follow the road; Call of the sea.

DEAK, JON
b. Hammond, Ind., 27 Apr. 1943. Studied contrabass at Juilliard School, B.M. 1965; Univ. of Illinois, M.M. 1968; composition with Alcides Lanza in New York. He had a Fulbright fellowship for research in Rome, 1967. He was instructor Interlochen Arts Acad., 1965-67; solo bassist, Chicago Little Symph., 1965-67; teaching assistant, Univ. of Illinois, 1968-69; member, New York Philharmonic, from 1969.
WORKS: CHAMBER MUSIC: Color studies, solo bass, 1969; Surrealist studies, solo bass, 1970; Land forms, chamber ensemble, 1971; The Great Plains, ensemble, 1973; Iowa, ensemble, 1974; Static study #2, ensemble; A December evening in the Adirondacks, ensemble, New York, 22 Mar. 1974; Antrim County, Michigan, and Young Giacometti, New York, 8 Feb. 1975; Split rock (with dance).
215 W. 98th St., #4B, New York, NY 10025

DEAN, TALMAGE WHITMAN
b. Russellville, Tenn., 29 Jan. 1915. Studied at Hardin-Simmons Univ.; with Bernard Rogers, Eastman School of Music; Ellis Kohs, Halsey Stevens, Univ. of Southern California. He received a special award, Nat. Conf. on Church Music, 1964; special award, William Jewell Coll., 1964; Piper Professor award, Hardin-Simmons Univ., 1969, 1970; second place, Texas Composers Guild contest, 1971. He taught aerial navigation for the navy at Univ. of Texas, 1943-44; was on faculty, Southwestern Baptist Seminary, 1956-67; Hardin-Simmons Univ., from 1941, dean from 1967; also was church music director, 1940-56.
WORKS: CHORUS: The raising of Lazarus, with soloists, organ, 1959; Behold the glory of the lamb, oratorio, with soloists, orch., 1963, premiere by Louisville Symph. and 800-voice chorus, 1964; Pax nobis, cantata, chorus, children's chorus, baritone solo, orch., 1967; Proclaim the word, cantata with brass, 1967; 4 cantatas for multiple choirs and organ; many shorter choral works. He is author of papers on church music.
School of Music, Hardin-Simmons Univ., Abilene, TX 79601

DEASON, DAVID
b. S.Dak., 24 May 1945. Studied with John Boda and Harold Schiffman, Florida State Univ.; with Lester Trimble and Roger Sessions, Juilliard School. His faculty posts include Lander Coll., 1969-70; Caldwell Coll. from 1977, and New School for Social Research from 1978.
WORKS: ORCHESTRA: piano concerto, 1968, selected by competition for performance by Columbia Phil. Orch., 1970; Baleen, guitar, quarter-tone harpsichord and orch.; cello concertino; tuba concerto; CHAMBER MUSIC; Wind tunnels, brass trio; quartet for flute, bassoon, violin, cello; Polarity, 2 clarinets; Entropy, woodwind trio; Fantasy pieces, violin and harp-

sichord; 4 pieces, guitar and harpsichord; Microsessions, harp, guitar, double bass; Sui generis, piano and winds; Diatomaceous earth, bass clarinet, vibraphone; Sonoma, trombone solo; duo, viola and cello; duo, violin and cello; various keyboard works.
380 92nd St., #F-1, Brooklyn, NY 11209

DE BERADINIS, JOHN ARTHUR
b. Stamford, Conn., 21 May 1943. Studied with Arnold Franchetti and Edward Miller, Hartt Coll. of Music, B.M., M.M. He was a MacDowell fellow, 1967; was named instructor, Hartt Coll. of Music, 1968.
WORKS: CHAMBER MUSIC: Dialogues, violin and percussion; Music for percussion and piano; Rhapsody, violin and vibraphone; 2 sketches, flute and vibraphone; 4 miniatures, flute and vibraphone; Interlude, oboe and vibraphone; Contrasts, vibraphone.
362 Bloomfield Ave., West Hartford, CT 06117

DE BRUYN, RANDALL KEITH
b. Portland, Oreg., 2 June 1947. Studied with Robert Stoltze, Lewis and Clark Coll.; with Salvatore Martirano and Bejamin Johnston, Univ. of Illinois. He was teaching assistant, Univ. of Illinois, 1970-74; later joined the faculty at Marylhurst Educational Center Coll., Oregon.
WORKS: THEATRE: Composition for music and theatre, a multimedia event; CHAMBER MUSIC: violin sonata; 3 fantasies, chamber ensemble; CHORUS: Christmas cantata, with chamber ensemble; SONGS: 3 songs for soprano; PIANO: Prelude in the Phrygian mode; Rondo brilliante; Variations on a tonal theme; sonata.
Music Dept., Marylhurst Educ. Center Coll., Marylhurst, OR 97036

DECEVEE, ALICE
b. Harrisburg, Pa., 25 Feb. 1904. Studied at Harrisburg Cons., with Ernest Hutcheson at Juilliard School; also with Harvey Gaul and Henry Hadley. She received Nat. Fed. of Music Clubs awards; taught at Harrisburg Cons.
WORKS: THEATRE: Love in a bottle, music drama; Coney Island, a ballet; ORCHESTRA: Memorabilia; PIANO: Boogie woogie goes high hat; Holland Tunnel, 2 pianos; many songs.

DECRESCENZO, VINCENZO
b. Naples, Italy, 18 Feb. 1875; to U.S. 1903; d. New York, 13 Oct. 1964. Studied at conservatories in Naples, Palermo, and Sicily. He was accompanist for Caruso, Gigli, Schipa, De Luca, Galli Curci, Albanese. He wrote many songs.

DEDRICK, ARTHUR
b. New York, 1 Aug. 1915. Graduated from State Univ. Coll., Fredonia, N.Y., 1937. He was trombonist and arranger with dance bands and arranger, WBEN Radio, Buffalo; then taught in public schools, 1949-55; since 1955, has been president of Kendor Music, Inc.
WORKS: He has published over 200 compositions and arrangements for stage bands, school bands, solo instruments, and ensembles.
McKinstry Rd., Delevan, NY 14042

DEDRICK, CHRISTOPHER

DEDRICK, CHRISTOPHER
b. New York, N.Y., 12 Sept. 1947. Attended
State Univ. Coll., Fredonia, N.Y.; and Manhattan School of Music, 1965-69. He is arranger
for the U.S. Air Force Band, "Airmen of Note,"
and writer, arranger, and performer with "The
Free Design," a vocal group.
WORKS: ORCHESTRA: 4 love seasons, with
chorus, premiered by Buffalo Philharmonic; BAND:
Twilight, with solo oboe; Awakening, with solo
trombone; CHAMBER MUSIC: Inspiration, solo bass
trombone, winds, cello; many solos for bass
trombone.
c/o Kendor Music, Inc., Delevan, NY 14042

DEDRICK, LYLE (RUSTY)
b. Delevan, N.Y., 12 July 1918. Attended State
Univ. Coll., Fredonia, N.Y.; studied with Paul
Creston and Stefan Wolpe. He has been director
of jazz studies, Manhattan School of Music, from
1971.
WORKS: CONCERT JAZZ: Follow me, New York,
28 Mar. 1973; Nocturne, trombone; The modern art
suite, saxophone quartet; suite for alto saxophone and trumpet with jazz ensemble; Late afternoon in Rome; Discussion; BAND: Acropolis 7844.
P.O. Box 34, Belfast, NY 14711

DEE, RICHARD
b. Knoxville, Tenn., 13 June 1936. Studied with
Higo Harada and Lou Harrison. He was accompanist
for Modern Dancers, 1965-68; lecturer, San Jose
State Univ., from 1970.
WORKS: THEATRE: Bacchae, incidental music;
Antigone, incidental music; ORCHESTRA: suite;
concerto for flute and percussion; CHAMBER MUSIC:
Praises for voices and instruments; suite for
cheng (Chinese 16-string psaltery); many works
for Chinese instruments; CHORUS: 4 patrons of
the palestra, chorus and gamelan.
35 N. 11th, San Jose, CA 95044

DE FILIPPI, AMADEO
b. Ariano, Italy, 20 Feb. 1900; to U.S. 1905,
citizen 1937. Studied composition with Rubin
Goldmark; held 4-year scholarship at the
Juilliard School. His viola sonata won an award
at Princeton, 1936. His concerto for orchestra
won first place in the Philharmonic-Symphony
Society of New York, American composers contest
in 1936-37, but was disqualified because the
contest was open to native-born composers only.
He was composer and arranger for films, theatre,
and radio, 1924-30; with CBS, 1930-58.
WORKS: THEATRE: The green cuckatoo, 1-act
opera, 1927; Malvolio, 2-act opera, 1937;
Robert E. Lee, incidental music, 1925; Les
sylphides and Carnaval, ballets, 1933; ORCHESTRA:
suite, 1920; concerto, 1928; symphony, 1930;
Serenade for strings, 1930; Twelfth Night overture; 5 Arabian songs, voice and orch., 1925;
5 medieval Norman songs, voice and orch., 1929;
CHAMBER MUSIC: string quartet, 1926; piano
quintet, 1928; viola sonata, 1929; suite for
brass quartet; CHORUS: Children of Adam, 1926;
3 poems by Thoreau, a cappella; 3 poems, by
Whitman, men's voices and brass, 1939; PIANO:
sonata, 1922; 6 sonatinas; Prelude, passacaglia,

and toccata, 1927; Partita, 1928; 4 interludes,
1975; Dances of Manfredonia, 12 pieces, 1975;
FILM SCORES: Blockade, 1930; Leatherneck, 1930;
Jazz age, 1930; Trial marriage, 1930; House-
keeper's daughter, 1938; Everything on ice, 1938.
4101 Wilkinson Ave., N. Hollywood, CA 91604

DeFOTIS, WILLIAM
b. Bellwood, Ill., 1 Nov. 1953. Studied with
Herbert Brün, Univ. of Illinois; with Wolf
Rosenberg in Munich on a Fulbright scholarship.
He is teaching assistant, Univ. of Illinois.
WORKS: CHAMBER MUSIC: Inconsequences,
narrator and chamber orch.; variation for piano
and percussion; wind quintet; Euphonasia, solo
euphonium; string quartet; septet; ELECTRONIC:
The charm of trivia, tape; Tableau, tape.
103 S. Lincoln, Urbana, IL 61801

DE GASTYNE, SERGE
b. Paris, France, 27 July 1930; U.S. citizen
1962. Attended Univ. of Portland, B.A. 1950;
Univ. of Maryland, M.M. 1968, D.M.A. 1971; composition with Howard Hanson, Eastman School of
Music, 1951. He received annual ASCAP awards,
1961-77; Nat. Band Assoc. Certificate of Merit,
1978; and commissions. He was composer-in-
residence, USAF Symph. Orch. and Band, 1953-72;
from 1972, has been professor, Northern Virginia
Community Coll.
WORKS: ORCHESTRA: 6 symphonies, #5 1970;
#6 1973; trumpet concerto; Hayasdan, with chorus,
premiere, Yerevan, Armenia, 1976; BAND: Prelude
to a play; CHAMBER MUSIC: Ballata, vibraharp;
Toccata, marimba; Perpetual motion, vibraharp;
Preludes #1-8, vibraharp; quintet for mallet
percussion; Abacus in trio, bassoon, horn,
mallet percussion; 4 musical moments, trumpet
and piano, 1969; bassoon sonata, 1969; string
quartet, 1971; Fantasia, guitar solo; SONGS:
May my heart; 3 young maidens; 2 songs on Tanka
poems; 2 chansons francaises, 1968; 2 elegies;
3 morillas; A noiseless, patient spider, voice,
flute, and vibraphone; PIANO: Fantasia; Proem;
Tambourin; ORGAN: Cantique de joie, 1972;
Partita Americana.
Deodar Hill, 14351 Aden Rd., Nokesville, VA
22123

DEIS, CARL
b. New York, N.Y., 7 Mar. 1883; d. New York,
24 July 1960. He was teacher and choral conductor, 1906-19; organist, 1919-33; music editor,
E. C. Schirmer, Inc., 1917-53. He wrote chamber
music and songs, many of which were published.

DE JONG, CONRAD JOHN
b. Hull, Iowa, 13 Jan. 1934. Studied at North
Texas State Univ., B.M. 1954; with Bernhard
Heiden, Indiana Univ., M.M. 1959; and with Ton de
Leeuw at the Amsterdam Cons., summer 1969. He
has received annual ASCAP awards from 1970 and
many commissions. He has been professor, Univ.
of Wisconsin, River Falls, from 1959.
WORKS: CHAMBER MUSIC: 3 studies, brass
septet, 1960; Music for 2 tubas, 1961; suite of
Wisconsin folk music, brass trio, 1962; string
trio, 1964; Fun and games, for any woodwind,

brass, or string instrument and piano, 1966; 3
pieces, 3 trumpets and piano, 1968; Aanraking
(Contact), solo trombone, 1969; Hist whist,
voice, flute, viola, percussion, 1969; Grab bag,
tuba ensemble, 1970; Etenraku (The upper cloud
music), carillon or piano, 1971; 4 songs, high
voice and piano, 1973; Song and light, high
voice and percussion, 1975; Heliotrope (pop song),
1 or 2 melody instruments or voices, keyboard,
electric bass, percussion, 1976; CHORUS: 4
choruses after Langston Hughes, women's voices,
1964; Peace maker, a cappella, 1966; Peace on
Earth, unison choir and organ, 1969; A prayer,
with piano, brass, wind chimes, and audience,
1975; MIXED MEDIA: Elm Street Dance Company
capers, tape and dance, 1972; Quarter break bit,
an activity, 1972; Kaleidoscopic vision (with
flashbacks), tape and synchronized swimmers,
1973; Resound, flute, guitar, percussion, tape
delay system, and 35 mm slide, 1974.
    404 S. Falls St., River Falls, WI 54022

DE LAMARTER, ERIC
    b. Lansing, Mich., 18 Feb. 1880; d. Orlando,
Fla., 17 May 1953. Studied with Cuilman and
Widor in Paris; was organist, conductor, music
critic, and teacher, 1903 to retirement. His
honors included the Eastman publishing award and
election to the Nat. Inst. of Arts and Letters.
    WORKS: BALLET: The betrothal, New York,
19 Nov. 1918; The black orchid, a suite was
performed by the Chicago Symph., 27 Feb. 1931,
with the composer conducting; ORCHESTRA: 4 symphonies, 1914, 1926, 1931, 1932; The faun, overture, 1914; Serenade, 1915; Masquerade, overture,
1916; Fable of the hapless folk tune, 1917; 2
organ concerti, 1920, 1922; The giddy puritan,
overture, 1921; Weaver of tales, organ and
chamber orch., 1926; The dance of life, ballet
suite, 1931; organ works and songs.

DELANEY, CHARLES
    b. Winston-Salem, N.C., 21 May 1925. Studied at
Davidson Coll., B.S.; with Lamar Stringfield in
Charlotte, N.C.; with Cecil Effinger, Univ. of
Colorado, M.M.; with Hans Haug, Cons. of Lausanne
on a Huntington Hartford fellowship, 1959. He
was faculty member, Earlham Coll., 1950-52;
Univ. of Illinois, 1952-76; from 1976, at Florida
State Univ.
    WORKS: ORCHESTRA: The member of Glynn,
narrator, chorus, and orch.; American waltzes;
3 etudes; Improvisation and finale, flute, piano,
string orch.; CHAMBER MUSIC: concerto for flute
and chamber orch.; suite for woodwind quintet;
Lake Isle of Innisfree, tenor and chamber orch.;
Contest piece, tenor saxophone and piano.
    1317 Sharon Rd., Tallahassee, FL 32303

DELANEY, ROBERT MILLS
    b. Baltimore, Md., 24 July 1903; d. Santa
Barbara, Calif., 21 Sept. 1956. Studied with
Nadia Boulanger and Arthur Honegger in Paris.
His awards included a Guggenheim fellowship,
1929; Pulitzer prize for music to John Brown's
body by Stephen Vincent Benet, 1933. He taught
at several schools including Northwestern Univ.
in the 1940s.

WORKS: ORCHESTRA: Don Quixote, 1927; John
Brown's song, choral symphony, 1931; Night, on
Blake text, for chorus, string orch., piano,
1934; Work #22, overture, 1939; symphony #1,
1942; Western star, chorus and orch., 1944;
CHAMBER MUSIC: 2 string quartets; suite for
woodwind quintet.

DELAVAN, E. MACON
    b. San Antonio, Tex., 7 Sept. 1932. Studied
with Samuel Adler, North Texas State Univ.; with
Woodrow James, Univ. of Oklahoma. He was faculty
member, East Texas Baptist Coll., 1962-64; North
Texas State Univ., 1964-66; and chairman, music
department, Grand Canyon Coll., from 1966.
    WORKS: OPERA: House by the stable,
Christmas opera, 1 act, Phoenix, 1971; ORCHESTRA:
Hill country, tone poem, 1963; CHAMBER MUSIC:
brass quintet; Prodigal son, cantata for baritone
and string quartet; The Christ who died for me,
song.
    Music Dept., Grand Canyon College, P.O. Box
    11097, Phoenix, AZ 85017

DEL BORGO, ELLIOT ANTHONY
    b. Port Chester, N.Y., 27 Oct. 1938. Studied at
State Univ. of New York; with Vincent Persichetti,
Philadelphia Cons.; at Temple Univ. He received
awards from the Univ. Awards Committee; Festival
of the Arts, Potsdam; and many commissions. He
taught in Philadelphia, 1960-66; from 1966, has
been faculty member, State Univ. Coll., Potsdam.
    WORKS: ORCHESTRA: Symphonic ode; Variations
on a folk melody; A festival piece; Chorale and
fugue; Serial music; Reflection; BAND: Symphonic essay; Chorale and variant; Music for
winds and percussion; concerto grosso for brass
quintet; Toccata a dodici; Canticle; Adagio for
winds; Thanatopsis; CHORUS: Missa brevis;
Gloria in excelsis; also chamber music and songs.
    R.D. 1, Potsdam, NY 13676

DE LEONE, FRANCESCO BARTOLOMEO
    b. Ravenna, Ohio, 28 July 1887; d. Akron, Ohio,
10 Dec. 1948. Studied at Dana Musical Inst.,
Mus.D.; Royal Cons. of Naples; and with Ernest
Bloch. He was opera conductor in Akron, 1927-
35; was founder and director of the music de-
partment, Univ. of Akron; was head of the piano
department, De Leone School of Music, 1934-48.
    WORKS: OPERA: A millionaire caprice, 1910;
Alglala, 1924; OPERETTA: Cave man stuff;
Princess Ting-Ah-Ling; SACRED MUSIC DRAMAS:
Ruth; The prodigal son; The golden calf; David;
ORCHESTRA: 6 Italian dances; Italian rhapsody;
Gilbraltar suite; Portage trail suite; a sym-
phony; also an oratorio; The triumph of Joseph;
and some 400 songs.

DELINGER, LAWRENCE ROSS
    b. Hyannis, Nebr., 11 Nov. 1937. Studied with
Ernest Kanitz, Los Angeles; with Edward
Applebaum, Univ. of California, Santa Barbara.
He was music director, Pacific Cons. of the
Performing Arts, 1968-73; faculty member, Allan
Hancock Coll., from 1971.
    WORKS: THEATRE: Photograph, opera on text

DELIO, THOMAS

of Gertrude Stein; Othello, incidental music
commissioned by the Oregon Shakespeare Festival,
1973; incidental music for some 15 productions;
WIND ENSEMBLE: Chromascape, 28 winds and percussion; CHAMBER MUSIC: Inflections, woodwind
quartet and piano; Invention #1, piano; Invention
#2, bassoon, cello, piano, percussion; Monolog,
solo cello; Ray Bradbury's dark carnival, pop-
rock songs to stories from October country.
    1000 W. Oak, Lompoc, CA 93436

DELIO, THOMAS
    b. New York, N.Y., 1 July 1951. Studied with
Robert Cogan, New England Cons.; with Salvatore
Martirano, Temple Univ. Summer Inst.; at Brown
Univ., Ph.D. He has had awards from Brookline
Library Music Assoc. and Pi Kappa Lambda. He is
faculty member, New England Cons.
    WORKS: CHAMBER MUSIC: From the Bolivian
diaries of Che Guevara, large ensemble of voices
and instruments; 6 variants, 3 violins, 3 pic-
colos; Serenade, commissioned piece for piano;
piano sonata.
    60 Burnside Ave., Somerville, MA 02144

DELLA PERUTI, CARL
    b. Plainfield, N.J., 1 Apr. 1947. Attended
Ithaca Coll., B.F.A. 1969; studied with Donald
Erb, Cleveland Inst. of Music, M.M. 1971; with
Burrill Phillips at Eastman School of Music; and
with Robert Moevs, Rutgers Univ. His awards include a prize in the Catgut Acoustical Society
competition for New String Music; and an award
from the New Jersey State Council on the Arts.
He is free-lance trombonist and school music
instructor; also founder and codirector of New
Music Coalition, a group dedicated to performance
of recent music.
    WORKS: CHAMBER MUSIC: 4 movements for winds
and bass, 1969; Sections, percussion, 1970;
brass quintet, 1971; Simplex, piano, 1971;
Halloween music, 4 winds, bass, piano, 1972;
Autumn music, 3 winds, piano, 1972; Quartet for
new violins, mezzo, alto, baritone, contrabass
violins, 1973; Diversion, trombone and piccolo,
1975; Soundings, flute, clarinet, cello, 1976;
sonata for brass quintet, 1977; trombone trio,
1977; VOICE: Listen bright quiet dying, chorus
and percussion, 1976; 3 items, soprano, clarinet,
cello, piano, 1976; other works for various
ensembles.
    748 Harding St., Westfield, NJ 07090

DELLA PICCA, ANGELO A.
    b. Udine, Italy, 6 Jan. 1923; U.S. citizen 1962.
Studied piano, organ, voice, composition, and
conducting in Italy; with Paul Cooper, Scott
Huston, and John Cage, Univ. of Cincinnati, D.M.
He was music director, Archdiocese of Udine,
Italy, 1953-56; then in churches in Philadelphia
and Allentown, Pa.; was arranger, World Library
of Sacred Music, Cincinnati, 1966-72; from 1976,
professor, Coll. of Mt. St. Joseph on the Ohio;
director, Mt. St. Joseph Glee Club, from 1975;
founder and director, Western Cincinnati Community Chorale, from 1976.
    WORKS: CHAMBER MUSIC: Dreams, ballet suite
for 2 pianos, choreographed 1969; Symphony of

spring, chamber orch., 1975; sonata in Phrygian
mode, flute and piano, 1977; sonata in Mixolydian
mode, 2 pianos, 1978; VOICE: numerous liturgical
choral works; and songs: There is a chorner in
my heart, 1962; Mood, 1968; Songs of Earthlings
(9 of a 24-song cycle), 1967, and in progress.
    College of Mt. St. Joseph, Mt. St. Joseph,
    OH 45051

DELLARIO, MICHAEL
    b. Schenectady, N.Y., 5 Aug. 1949. Studied at
Georgetown Univ., A.B.; with Robert Parris,
George Washington Univ.; with Milton Babbitt,
Claudio Spies, E. T. Cone, and J. K. Randall,
Princeton Univ.; with Goffredo Petrassi in Rome,
and Franco Donatoni in Siena, Italy. His awards
include a Fulbright-Hays grant; first prize,
Amer. Soc. of Univ. Composers contest, 1976;
fellowships, Composers' Conf., Johnson, Vt.,
1975, 1976. He was instructor, George Washington
Univ., 1972-74; summer lecturer, Princeton Univ.,
1976, 1977; music director, Metatheatre Project,
Washington, D.C., 1973-74.
    WORKS: CHAMBER MUSIC: Chronologia, piano
trio and harpsichord, 1975; Maud, soprano and
computer, 1976; Acquaforte, chamber ensemble,
1978; CHORUS: 4 propositions, winds, brass,
percussion, chamber chorus, 1973; The fire
and the mountain, cantata for orchestra and
chorus, 1977; History lesson, for any number of
singers, 1978; FILM SCORE: Run wild with the
wind, 1974.
    224C Halsey St., Princeton, NJ 08540

DELLO JOIO, NORMAN
    b. New York, N.Y., 24 Jan. 1913. Studied with
his father, Casimir Dello Joio; attended City
Coll., CUNY; Inst. of Musical Art; Juilliard
School; composition with Paul Hindemith, Yale
Univ. His many honors include Elizabeth Sprague
Coolidge award, 1937; Town Hall Composition
award, 1941; 2 Guggenheim fellowships, 1943,
1944; Nat. Inst. of Arts and Letters grant,
1945; 2 New York Music Critics' Circle awards,
1949, 1958; Pulitzer prize, 1957; television
Emmy award, 1964; Lancaster Symph. Composer
award, 1967; 5 honorary degrees; and commissions.
He was on the faculty, Sarah Lawrence Coll.,
1944-50; Mannes Coll. of Music, 1956-72; acting
dean, School of Fine and Applied Arts, Boston
Univ., 1972-74, dean, School of the Arts, 1974-
78; after a sabbatical year, returned to the
faculty at Boston Univ.
    WORKS: OPERA: The triumph of St. Joan,
1950; The ruby, 1955; The trial at Rouen, 1956;
Blood moon, 1961; BALLET: Prairie, 1942; Duke of
Sacramento, 1942; On stage!, 1944; Wilderness
stair, 1948; Diversion of angels, New York,
13 Aug. 1948; Seraphic dialogue, New York, 8 May
1955; ORCHESTRA: Sinfonietta, 1941; Magnificat,
1942; concerto for 2 pianos, 1942; To a lone
sentry, 1943; Concert music, 1944; Western star,
with narrator and soloists, 1944; harp concerto,
1944; Ricercari, piano and orch., 1946; Serenade,
1948; Variations, chaconne, and finale, 1947;
New York profiles, 1949; Concertante, clarinet
and orch., 1949; Epigraph, 1951; Triumph of St.
Joan suite, 1951; Meditations on Ecclesiastes,

1956; <u>Air power</u>, suite, 1957; <u>Fantasy and variations</u>, piano and orch., 1962; <u>Antiphonal fantasy</u>, organ, brass, and strings, 1966; <u>Choreography</u>, strings, 1972; <u>Homage to Haydn</u>, Boston Univ., 17 Apr. 1974; <u>Lyric fantasies</u>, solo viola and strings, 1973; <u>Colonial variants</u>, Wilmington, Del., 27 May 1976; <u>Songs of remembrance</u>, baritone and orch., 1978; CHAMBER MUSIC: piano concertino with chamber orch., 1939; concertino for flute and strings, 1940; concertino for harmonica and strings, 1943; sextet for 3 recorders and string trio, 1943; trio for flute, cello, piano, 1945; <u>Variations and capriccio</u>, violin and piano, 1948; <u>The developing flutist</u>, flute and piano, 1972; CHORUS: <u>Vigil strange</u>, 1942; <u>Mystic trumpeter</u>, cantata, 1943; <u>Psalm of David</u>, with brass, percussion, strings, 1950; mass, with brass, percussion, organ, 1968; <u>To St. Cecilia</u>, 1968; <u>Evocations</u>, with orch., 1970; <u>Psalm of peace</u>, 1971; <u>Notes from Tom Paine</u>, with band, New York, 14 Apr. 1976; <u>Mass to the Eucharist</u>, Washington, D.C., with choir of 1000 voices, 1 Aug. 1976; SONGS: <u>Lamentation of Saul</u>, baritone and orch., 1954; <u>Songs of Abelard</u>, baritone and band, 1969; PIANO: suite, 1941; duo concertante, 2 pianos, 1943; 3 sonatas, 1942, 1943, 1947; and other pieces.

Box 154, East Hampton, NY 11937

DELMAR, DEZSO
b. Timisoara, Hungary, 14 July 1891; to U.S. 1922. Studied with Bartok and Kodaly. From 1946, taught piano and theory in Sacramento. His works include a symphony, 3 string quartets, violin sonata, string trio, choral works, and songs.

DE LONE, RICHARD PIERCE
b. Wayne, Pa. Studied at Peabody Cons., B.M. 1953, M.M. 1954. He received a scholarship at Peabody, 1952; Maryland Fed. of Music Clubs prize, 1952; Gustav Klemm prize, 1953, 1954. One of his prize-winning compositions was <u>Impromptu and romance</u>, cello and piano. He is professor, School of Music, Indiana Univ.

DELP, RON
b. Tampa, Fla., 27 Sept. 1946. Studied with John Bavicchi and William Maloof, Berklee Coll. of Music. He was on the faculty at Berklee, 1971-75; at Tampa Univ., 1976-78.
WORKS: PERCUSSION: <u>Scherzo</u>; <u>Modogenesis</u>; <u>Dreams</u> (with winds), 1970; <u>Quaternion</u>; <u>Phonetiks</u>.

DEL PRINCIPE, JOSEPH A.
b. Waterbury, Conn., 19 Mar. 1932. Studied with Arnold Franchetti, Hartt Coll. of Music, B.M. 1966, M.M. 1972; with Franco Donatoni, Siena, Italy, 1972; with Vladimir Ussachevsky, Chou Wen-chung, Jack Beeson, Columbia Univ., D.M.A. 1977. His awards include the Academia Siena composition prize, 3 years; Cassela prize, Naples, 1974. He has been lecturer at Columbia Univ.; director, Siena Sessions of Music and Art for 8 years.
WORKS: CHAMBER MUSIC: <u>Music for oboe and string quartet</u>, 1975; <u>Cantium</u>, soprano and 4 instruments, 1975; <u>Chamber variations</u>, 6 instruments, 1976; <u>Arioso</u>, soprano, flute, and strings,

1978; CHORUS: <u>Tau</u>, with soloists and orch., 1977.
981 E. Main St., Waterbury, CT 06705

DEL TREDICI, DAVID
b. Cloverdale, Calif., 16 Mar. 1937. Studied with Seymour Shifrin and Arnold Elston, Univ. of California, Berkeley, B.A. 1959; with Earl Kim and Roger Sessions, Princeton Univ., M.F.A. 1964. His honors include the Woodrow Wilson award, 1960; Hertz award, 1962; commissions from Fromm Found., 1964; Koussevitzky Found., 1966; Nat. Inst. of Arts and Letters award, 1968; Naumberg award, 1972; Brandeis award, 1973; Nat. Endowment for the Arts grant; Pulitzer prize, 1980; many commissions. He has been faculty member at Harvard Univ., Buffalo Univ., and from 1973, Boston Univ.
WORKS: ORCHESTRA: <u>The last gospel</u>, with solo soprano, rock group, chorus, 1967; San Francisco, 15 June 1968; <u>Pop-pourri</u>, with soprano, rock group and chorus, 1968; <u>The lobster quadrille</u>, excerpt from <u>In Wonderland</u>, 1969, rev. 1974, London Symphony with Aaron Coplan conducting, 14 Nov. 1969; <u>Vintage Alice</u>, 1972, Music at the Vineyards, Calif., composer conducting, 5 Aug 1972; <u>Adventures underground</u>, 1973, Buffalo, 13 Apr. 1975; <u>In Wonderland, Part I</u>, 1969-1974, Aspen Festival, 29 July 1975; <u>In Wonderland, Part II</u>, 1975; <u>Final Alice</u>, Chicago, 7 Oct. 1976; <u>Annotated Alice</u>, 1976; <u>In memory of a summer day</u>, with amplified soprano soloist, St. Louis, 23 Feb. 1980, received the 1980 Pulitzer prize; CHAMBER MUSIC: <u>Soliloquy</u>, piano, 1958; 4 songs on poems of James Joyce, 1959; <u>Scherzo</u>, piano, 4 hands, 1960; <u>Fantasy pieces</u>, piano, 1960; <u>I hear an army</u>, soprano and string quartet, 1964; <u>Night conjure-verse</u>, soprano, mezzo-soprano or counter-tenor, woodwind septet, and string quartet, 1965, San Francisco, 2 Mar. 1966; <u>Syzygy</u>, soprano, horn, chamber ensemble, New York, 6 July 1966.
Boston University, 855 Commonwealth Ave., Boston, MA 02215

DEMAREST, CLIFFORD
b. Tenafly, N.J., 12 Aug. 1874; d. Tenafly, 13 May 1946. He was organist at Church of the Messiah in New York. His works included 2 cantatas, 30 anthems, many songs, and organ pieces.

DE MARINIS, PAUL MICHAEL
b. Cleveland, Ohio, 6 Oct. 1948. Studied with Robert Ashley, Terry Riley, and Lars-Gunnar Bodin at Mills Coll., M.A. 1973. He is technical assistant with Buchla and Associates, Berkeley.
WORKS: ELECTRONIC: <u>P. L. L. Bach</u>, synthesizer, 1972; <u>Morning music</u>, 2 keyboards, 1972; <u>In Sara, Mencken, Christ, and Beethoven there were men and women</u>, tape, in collaboration with Robert Ashley, 1973; <u>The pygmy gamelan</u>, concrete electronic circuitry, 1973; <u>Duet</u>, live electronics, 1974; also a commissioned work for the New Music Ensemble of the San Francisco Cons., 1976.
2807 Piedmont Ave., Berkeley, CA 94705

131

DEMBSKI, STEPHEN

DEMBSKI, STEPHEN
   b. Boston, Mass., 13 Dec. 1949. Studied with
John Ronsheim, Antioch Coll.; with Bülent Arel,
State Univ. of New York, Stony Brook; with
Milton Babbitt, J. K. Randall, Peter Westergaard,
Princeton Univ. He received a BMI award, 1975;
MacDowell fellowship, 1977; East and West
Artists composition prize, 1977; Johnson Composers' Conf. fellowship, 1978. He was instructor, Dartmouth Coll., 1978-79.
   WORKS: CHAMBER MUSIC: Sunwood, guitar,
1975; Of mere being, soprano and piano, 1975;
piano trio, 1977; quartet for flute, oboe, cello,
harpsichord, 1978; Tender buttons, piano, 1978;
Digit, clarinet and computer synthesized sound,
1978.
   96 Perry St., #B-22, New York, NY 10014

DEMMING, LANSON F.
   b. Buffalo, N.Y., 25 Oct. 1902. Attended Eastman School of Music, B.M.; Univ. of Illinois,
M.M. He was professor, Univ. of Illinois, 1930-
45; Univ. of Houston, 1945-60; music director,
radio station WILL, 1935-45; minister of music,
St. Paul's Methodist Church, Houston, 1945-73;
organist, Temple Beth Yeshurun, Houston, 1953-
73.
   WORKS: Many choral compositions including
The eternal gate; Bethlehem of Judea; Oh, crown
Him, double chorus; seasonal introits and responses; A festival processional.
   2217 Portsmouth, Houston, TX 77006

DEMPSTER, STUART
   b. Berkeley, Calif., 7 July 1936. Studied with
Wendell Otey and Roger Nixon, San Francisco
State Coll. His honors include the Paul Masson
Composition award, 1963; Nat. Endowment for the
Arts grant, 1978. He was Creative Associate,
SUNY at Buffalo, 1967-68; faculty member, Univ.
of Washington, from 1968; Fellow, Center for
Advanced Study, Univ. of Illinois, 1971-72. He
is an avant-garde trombone virtuoso who composes
chiefly improvisational works for trombone or
didjeridu (an Australian aboriginal instrument)
and set pieces for dances and dramatists.
   WORKS: Ten grand hosery, trombone, 1975-76;
Standing waves 1976, trombone; Didjeridervish,
1976; Standing waves 1978, trombone; Monty, 1979,
based on didjeridu technique; Gone with the wind,
1980, a multimedia event coexisting with Pauline
Oliveros's Anarchy waltz, at North Carolina
School of the Arts, Oct. 1980, a work still in
progress.
   Univ. of Washington, Seattle, WA 98195

DENBOW, STEFANIA BJÖRNSON
   b. Minneota, Minn., 28 Dec. 1916. Studied at
Univ. of Minnesota, B.M. 1937, M.A. 1939; composition with Karl Ahrendt and James Stewart,
Ohio Univ. She received a Mu Phi Epsilon award,
1973; was a finalist in Festival of Contemporary
Music, Marshall Univ. She is a private piano
and organ teacher, and has been church organist
in Annapolis, Md., and Athens, Ohio.
   WORKS: CHAMBER MUSIC: Surtsey, string
quintet, 1974; Trio Islandia, violin, cello,
piano, 1976; CHORUS: Christ is risen, cantata,

with soloists and chamber orch., 1972; Magnificat,
with soloists and chamber orch.; Contemporary
mass; All glory for this blessed morn, cantata,
1975; SONGS: 4 songs of The Eremite Isle; By the
willows, song cycle; KEYBOARD: 3 Hellenic stanzas, piano; Exaltatio, organ; organ suite.
   61 Columbia Ave., Athens, OH 45701

DENNIS, ROBERT
   b. St. Louis, Mo., 5 May 1933. Studied with
Vincent Persichetti at the Juilliard School;
with Tony Aubin at the Paris Cons.; and with
Boris Blacher at Tanglewood. He received Fulbright scholarships, 1956-57. He was a founding
member with Peter Schickele and Stanley Walden
of the composer-performer group, the Open Window,
1968-71.
   WORKS: THEATRE: scores for Oh! Calcutta!;
Sesame Street; Bartholomew Fair; Medicine show;
Slaughterhouse play; Endicott and the Red Cross,
by Robert Lowell; ORCHESTRA: Pennsylvania
Station from 3 views from the open window;
Klezmorim; CHAMBER MUSIC: Improvisations and
variations, cello and piano, 1962-65; CHORUS:
5 medieval settings, performed by Western Wind,
New York, 6 June 1979.
   885 West End Ave., New York, NY 10025

DENNISON, SAM
   b. Geary, Okla., 27 Sept. 1926. Studied with
Spencer Norton and Harrison Kerr, Univ. of
Oklamona; with Halsey Stevens, Univ. of Southern
California. He received a Phi Mu Alpha award,
1949; Carolyn Alchin award, 1952. He was a
private teacher, 1953-55; at Louisville Acad. of
Music, 1955-60; faculty, Inter-American Univ.,
Puerto Rico, 1960-64; music librarian, American
Music Collection, Free Library of Philadelphia,
1964-75, then curator of the Library's Edwin A.
Fleischer Collection of Orchestral Music. In
Puerto Rico he worked with Roy Harris in pre-
paring his scores for publication; in Philadelphia
he teaches music theory as a volunteer in the
city's prison system.
   WORKS: OPERA: The last man on Earth, 1
act, 1952; Conrad Crispin's broom, 1 act, 1973;
ORCHESTRA: suite on jazz themes, 1976; Lyric
piece and rondo, tuba and strings, 1976; sinfonietta, 1978; CHAMBER MUSIC: Mother wears
army boots, violin and piano, 1949; Quodlibet,
woodwind trio, 1953; Folksong medley, violin,
horn, piano, 1957; brass sextet, 1963; suite for
flute solo, 1968; Cirrus, flute, oboe, cello,
1977; VOCAL: Jesu Christes milde moder, chorus,
1963; The faucon hath taken my mate away, chorus,
1963; The days of the week, song cycle, counter-
tenor and harpsichord, 1953; Epithalamium, 1968;
PIANO: 13 pieces for Helen, 1948; Monologue of
a water faucet, 1948; 3 sonatas, 1949, 1950,
1963; FILM SCORES: Good speech for Gary, 1952;
History of Delaware; Penn relays, 1968; radio
and television scores.
   4608 Wilbrock St., Philadelphia, PA 19136

DENNY, WILLIAM D.
   b. Seattle, Wash., 2 July 1910; d. Berkeley,
Calif., 2 Sept. 1980. Studied at Univ. of
California, M.A. 1933; with Paul Dukas in Paris,

132

1933-35; at American Acad. in Rome on a Horatio Parker fellowship, 1939-41. He taught at Harvard Univ., 1942-45; and was professor, Univ. of California at Berkeley, 1945-78.

WORKS: ORCHESTRA: 2 symphonies, 1939, 1951; concertino, 1939; Sinfonietta for strings, 1940; Praeludium, 1947; CHAMBER MUSIC: 3 string quartets; viola sonata; also choral works.

DENSMORE, JOHN HOPKINS
b. Somerville, Mass., 7 Aug. 1880; d. Boston, Mass., 21 Sept. 1943. Studied at Harvard Univ., A.B. 1904. His compositions included operettas for the Hasty Pudding Club; Veritas, the Harvard football song; many other songs; choral works.

DEPPEN, JESSIE L.
b. Detroit, Mich., 10 July 1881; d. Los Angeles, Calif., 22 Jan. 1956. Studied with Adolph Weidig and Leopold Godowsky, American Cons. She made her debut as pianist in Steinway Hall, New York, in 1896. Her compositions were chiefly songs and piano pieces.

DE PUE, WALLACE EARL
b. Columbus, Ohio, 1 Oct. 1932. Studied at Capital Univ., B.M. 1956; Ohio State Univ., M.A. 1957; with H. Owen Reed, Michigan State Univ., Ph.D. 1965. His awards include first prize, Arthur Shepherd competition; first prize, Nat. String Orch. competition; Bowling Green State Univ. research grant, 1973; MacDowell fellowship, 1973; GUND Found. grant; Nat. Endowment for the Arts grant, 1974. He was music supervisor, Toledo Museum of Art, 1964-66; from 1966, professor, Bowling Green State Univ.

WORKS: OPERA: Dr. Jekyl and Mr. Hyde, Bowling Green, Apr. 1974; Something special, opera for barbershop chorus and quartets, Toledo, 22 May 1976; ORCHESTRA: concerto for percussion; Prelude and sarabande, string orch.; CHAMBER MUSIC: Sonata primitif, marimba and piano; Toccatina, 2 drums and piano; VOCAL: Psalm 90, chorus and viola; Dedication, baritone and organ; Soli deo gloria, chorus, 1976.
950 Fairview Ave., Bowling Green, OH 43402

DERBY, RICHARD
b. Indianapolis, Ind., 23 Jan. 1951. Studied with Peter Racine Fricker, Univ. of California, Santa Barbara, B.A. 1973; Ph.D. 1978; with Justin Connolly, Royal Coll. of Music, London, 1977-78. His awards include first prize, Nat. Fed. of Music Clubs contest, 1975; BMI awards, 1975; Univ. of Calif. scholarships, 1969-73, fellowships, 1969-77; Fulbright-Hays grant, 1977-78. He was lecturer, Univ. of California, Santa Barbara, 1974-76.

WORKS: ORCHESTRA: Elegy, 1973; 5 pieces for orchestra, 1974; symphony, 1976; CHAMBER MUSIC: trio for violin, viola, piano, 1971; Variations, string quartet, 1972; 5 short pieces, cello solo, 1973; string trio, 1974; CHORUS: To everything there is a season, a cappella, 1969; 4 sacred texts, a cappella, 1971; Magnificat, with orch., 1972; mass, a cappella, 1973; KEYBOARD: piano sonata, 1970-71; Piano episodes, 1971; Piano preludes, 1972-73; organ sonata,

1973.
9121 Mediterranean Dr., Huntington Beach, CA 92646

DERR, ELLWOOD S.
b. Danville, Pa., 7 May 1932. Studied with Wayne Barlow, Eastman School of Music; with Gordon Binkerd, and Hunter Johnson, Univ. of Illinois; with Carl Orff, Bavarian State Cons., Munich. He received the Alexander von Humboldt-Stiftung grants, 1959-61, 1976. He has been faculty member, Univ. of Michigan, from 1962.

WORKS: ORCHESTRA: Funeral anthem, solo quintet, chorus, large orch., with 2 percussion ensembles; CHAMBER MUSIC: One-in-five-in-one, saxophone and piano; Fantasy, piano; VOICE: I never saw another butterfly, song cycle, voice, saxophone, piano; Variations, soprano and chamber ensemble.
2324 Yorkshire Rd., Ann Arbor, MI 48104

DE SANTIS, EMIDIO
b. Aquila, Italy, 18 May 1893; U.S. citizen 1921. He played clarinet in the Providence Symph., 1918-30, and with various bands from 1918; was president of his own record and publishing company. His compositions include 3 clarinet concertos; 6 concertinos for orchestra; several military marches.

DES MARAIS, PAUL
b. Menominee, Mich., 23 June 1920. Studied with Walter Piston, Harvard Univ., B.A. 1949, M.A. 1953; also with Nadia Boulanger in Cambridge. His awards include the Lili Boulanger prize, 1948; Boott prize, 1949; John Knowles Paine traveling fellowship, 1949-51; Thorne Music Fund award for study of the sounds made by underwater animals, 1970-73. In 1974 he was studying plant responses to various stimuli and measuring the results with electronic equipment. He held a MacDowell fellowship in 1977 for work on Songs of love and fear, a cycle for high voice. He has been professor, Univ. of California, Los Angeles, from 1960.

WORKS: CHAMBER MUSIC: 2 piano sonatas, 1947, 1952; Theme and changes, harpsichord, 1953; Capriccio, 2 pianos, percussion, celeste, 1962; CHORUS: mass, a cappella, 1948; motet, chorus, cellos, double basses, 1959; Psalm 121, a cappella, 1959; Epiphanies, a chamber opera with film sequences, 1964-68.
Music Dept., Univ. of California, Los Angeles, CA 90024

DE SOMERY, GENE DAVID
b. Quincy, Calif., 3 Mar. 1948. Studied with Peter Racine Fricker, Thea Musgrave, Douglas Green, and Daniel Lentz, Univ. of California, Santa Barbara, B.A. 1970; with Donald Martino, New England Cons., M.M. 1973. He held scholarships for his study at the New England Cons.

WORKS: ORCHESTRA: Chamber symphony, Boston, 14 Mar. 1973; CHAMBER MUSIC: Sounds, 12 winds and percussion, Boston, 12 May 1973; 3 songs, voice and piano, Boston, 27 Mar. 1973.
284 Pepperwood Lane, Garberville, CA 95440

DETT, ROBERT NATHANIEL

DETT, ROBERT NATHANIEL
b. Drummondville, Quebec, Canada, 11 Oct. 1882;
d. Battle Creek, Mich., 2 Oct. 1943. Studied at
Oberlin Coll., B.M. 1908, D.M. 1926; Columbia
Univ.; Harvard Univ.; Eastman School of Music,
M.M.; Howard Univ., D.M. 1924; and Univ. of
Pennsylvania. His awards include the Bowdoin
Literary prize at Harvard; the Harmon prize,
1927; Francis Boott prize; and Palm and Ribbon
of the Royal Belgian Band. He was church
pianist, Niagara Falls, 1898-1903; music director, Lane Coll., 1908-11; Lincoln Inst., 1911-
13; Hampton Inst., 1913-35; Sam Houston Coll.,
1935. The Hampton Inst. Choir, which he founded
and directed for 22 years, toured Europe in 1929.
WORKS: ORATORIOS: The ordering of Moses,
chorus and orch.; The chariot jubilee, tenor,
chorus, and orch.; many other choral works;
PIANO SUITES: Magnolia; In the bottom; Tropic
winter; Enchantment; Cinnamon grove; 8 Bible
vignettes.

DEUTSCH, ADOLPH
b. London, England, 20 Oct. 1897; U.S. citizen
1920; d. Palm Desert, Calif., 1 Jan. 1980.
Studied at the Royal Acad. of Music, London, and
in the U.S. In the 1920s he became a film score
composer for Warner Brothers. His Scottish
suite, commissioned by Paul Whiteman, was performed by the Philadelphia Orchestra and
the New York Philharmonic. He founded the
Screen Composers' Assoc. and was its president,
1943-53.
WORKS: FILM SCORES: They won't forget; The
Maltese falcon; Action in the North Atlantic;
High Sierra; They drive by night; The mask of
Dimitrios; Father of the bride; The Stratton
story; Some like it hot; The apartment.

DEUTSCH, HERBERT A.
b. Baldwin, N.Y., 9 Feb. 1932. Studied with
Elie Siegmeister at Hofstra Univ.; with Nicholas
Flagello and Ludmila Ulehla, Manhattan School of
Music. He has been director, Electronic Music
Studio, Hofstra Univ., from 1970, and chairman
of the music department from 1973.
WORKS: CHAMBER MUSIC: Soliloquy, clarinet
solo; CHORUS: Mutima, with percussion and flute;
MIXED MEDIA: Sonorities, tape and orch.; Moon
ride, tape and band; Fantasia on Es ist Genug,
tape and wind ensemble; Jazz images, tape and
piano.
19 Crossman Pl., Huntington, NY 11743

DE VITO, ALBERT
b. Hartford, Conn., 17 Jan. 1919. Studied at
New York Univ., B.S., M.A. 1950; at Columbia
Univ.; Midwestern State Univ., Ph.D. 1975. His
awards include honorary D.M.A., Eastern Nebraska
Christian Coll., 1974; Certificate of Merit,
1975; ASCAP awards. He is free-lance composer,
teacher, editor, and author of articles on piano
techniques.
WORKS: Many choral works, piano solos,
piano methods, organ arrangements, and popular
songs.
361 Pin Oak Lane, Westbury, NY 11590

DE VOE, ROBERT ALAN
b. Elmira, N.Y., 9 July 1928. Was trained as a
painter and sculptor at Temple Univ., Tyler Art
School, M.F.A., and is self-taught in music. He
taught humanities and art in a demonstration
high school for Univ. of Connecticut, 1959-68;
was on the faculty for humanities, Fairleigh
Dickinson Univ., from 1968; became professor in
the electronic studio in 1976.
WORKS: ELECTRONIC: Music of the spheres;
Zen charts; Celestial pavan; Meditations; Visions.
32 Piermont Ave., Hillsdale, NJ 07642

DE VOTO, MARK BERNARD
b. Cambridge, Mass., 11 Jan. 1940. Studied at
Longy School of Music; with Randall Thompson and
Walter Piston, Harvard Univ.; with Roger
Sessions, Earl Kim, and Milton Babbitt, Princeton Univ. He received a BMI student composer
award, 1961; Fromm Found. commission, 1968. He
was faculty member, Reed Coll., 1964-68; from
1968, at Univ. of New Hampshire.
WORKS: ORCHESTRA: Night songs and distant
dances, 1962; piano concerto #2, 1965-66; piano
concerto #3, The distinguished thing, 1968;
VOCAL: Planh, 6 voices, 4 winds, harp, 1961;
2 songs, soprano, flute, viola, trombone, harp,
1961; 3 songs of Edgar Allan Poe, soprano, concertina, guitar, harpsichord, 8 flutes, 1967,
rev. 1970; Fever-dream vocalize, soprano, flute,
cello, piano, percussion, 1968.
Music Dept., Univ. of New Hampshire, Durham,
NH 03824

DEYO, FELIX
b. Poughkeepsie, N.Y., 21 Apr. 1888; d. Baldwin,
N.Y., 21 June 1959. Studied at Brooklyn Cons.
and taught there, 1911-39; then became director
of the Baldwin, L.I., Cons. His compositions
included 3 symphonies, 2 piano sonatas, a violin
sonata, piano pieces, etc. He was a second
cousin of Ruth Deyo.

DEYO, RUTH LYNDA
b. Poughkeepsie, N.Y., 20 Apr. 1884; d. Cairo,
Egypt, 4 Mar. 1960. Studied composition with
Edward MacDowell. She made her piano debut at
age 9; later appeared in recitals with Kreisler
and Casals, and was soloist with major orchestras
in the U.S. and Europe. In 1925 she went to
live in Egypt and turned full attention to composition. Her works include The diadem of stars,
a full-length opera on Egyptian themes. The
overture to the opera was performed by Leopold
Stokowski with the Philadelphia Orch., 4 Apr.
1931. She was a second cousin of Felix Deyo.

DE YOUNG, LYNDEN E.
b. Chicago, Ill., 6 Mar. 1923. Studied with
Karel Jirak, Roosevelt Univ.; with Leo Sowerby,
American Cons.; and with Anthony Donato, Northwestern Univ. He received the 1951 Thor Johnson
brass ensemble composition award. His faculty
posts include Roosevelt Univ., 1950-59; Austin
Acad. of Fine Arts, 1952-55; from 1966, Northwestern Univ.
WORKS: ORCHESTRA: Fugue; Theme and variations; Poem; BRASS ENSEMBLE: Divertissement,

1951; 3 brass quintets, 1952-54; CHAMBER MUSIC: Texture, flute, harpsichord, percussion; Chamber music, 3 winds, piano, vibraphone; Piano music; 6 miniatures, violin and piano; MIXED MEDIA: Praise the Lord (Psalm 150), choir, soloists, ensemble, organ, readers, dancers, slides; Blues, flute, cello, 2 pianos, ballerina, 3 actors, 1975.

School of Music, Northwestern Univ., Evanston, IL 60201

DIACONOFF, THEODORE A.
b. Akron, Ohio, 7 Oct. 1928. Studied with George Rochberg, New School of Music, Philadelphia; with Vincent Persichetti, Juilliard School; with Lucas Foss, Roy Harris, and John Vincent, Univ. of California, Los Angeles. His awards include first prize, UCLA composition contest, 1947; and a summer fellowship, Northern Kentucky Univ., 1978. He has held teaching posts at California Inst. of the Arts, 1947-53; Univ. of California, 1961-62; Los Angeles Trade Technological Jr. Coll., 1966-69; Michigan Technological Univ., 1972-77; from 1977, at Northern Kentucky Univ.

WORKS: THEATRE: incidental music to Ibsen's Enemy of the people, 1978; ORCHESTRA: La belle dame sans merci, chorus and orch.; piano concerto, 1962; CHAMBER MUSIC: wind quintet, 1947; string quartet, 1952; Toccata, piano, 1952; piano sonata, 1961.

525 Main St., Covington, KY 41011

DIAMOND, ARLINE
b. New York, N.Y., 17 Jan. 1928. Studied with Bernard Rogers, Eastman School of Music; Univ. of Miami; Columbia Univ., M.A.; and privately with Benjamin Boretz, Felix Greissle, Ralph Shapey, and Bernard Wagenaar. She teaches piano.

WORKS: ORCHESTRA: a symphony, performed by the Miami Symphony; CHAMBER MUSIC: violin sonata; Composition, clarinet solo.

186 Birch Dr., New Hyde Park, NY 11040

DIAMOND, DAVID
b. Rochester, N.Y., 9 July 1915. Had his first formal training at Cleveland Inst. of Music, 1927-29; studied with Bernard Rogers, Eastman School of Music, 1930-34; later with Roger Sessions in New York and with Nadia Boulanger in Paris. His awards include scholarships for all study; Juilliard Publication award, 1937; 3 Guggenheim fellowships, 1938, 1941, 1958; Prix de Rome, 1942; Paderewski prize, 1943; Nat. Acad. of Arts and Letters grant, 1944; 2 New York Music Critics' Circle awards, 1947, 1948; Fulbright grant, 1951; Rheta Sosland Chamber Music prize, 1966; ASCAP-Stravinsky award, 1967; many commissions; and election to the Nat. Inst. of Arts and Letters. He went to Europe in 1951 as Fulbright professor, eventually settling in Florence and remaining in Italy until 1965 except for brief appointments at Univ. of Buffalo in 1961 and 1963. He was faculty member, Manhattan School of Music, 1965-67; from 1973, at Juilliard School.

WORKS: THEATRE: music for Shakespeare's The tempest, 1944; for Tennessee Williams's Rose tattoo, 1950; Tom, ballet on e. e. cummings text; The dream of Audubon, ballet on text of Glenway Westcott; The noblest game, opera, 1971-75; ORCHESTRA: Aria and hymn; Psalm, 1936; 2 overtures; 3 violin concertos, 1937, 1947, 1968; Elegies, flute, English horn, strings, 1977; cello concerto, 1968; Elegy in memory of Maurice Ravel, 1938; Heroic piece, 1938; Concert piece, 1940; 2-piano concerto, 1941; 8 symphonies, 1941-61; Rounds, string orch., 1944; Romeo and Juliet, 1947; Timon of Athens, symphonic portrait after Shakespeare, 1949; The enormous room, after e. e. cummings, 1949; piano concerto, 1949; Ahavah, narrator and orch., 1954; Sinfonia concertante, 1956; The world of Paul Klee, 1957; piano concertino, 1965; CHAMBER MUSIC: Partita, oboe, bassoon, piano, 1935; concerto for string quartet, 1936; quintet, flute, string trio, piano, 1937; sonata for cello solo, 1938; 11 string quartets, 1940-73; sonata for solo violin, 1945; Chaconne, violin and piano, 1947; Introduction and dance, accordion; piano sonata, 1947; accordion sonatina; Night music, string quartet and accordion; woodwind quintet; quintet for clarinet, 2 violas, 2 cellos, 1951; piano trio, 1951; nonet, 3 violins, 3 violas, 3 cellos, 1962; trio for horn and string trio, 1978; CHORUS: This sacred ground, with baritone, children's chorus, orch.; The martyr, men's voices, orch. or a cappella; To music--choral symphony, with soloists and orch.; Let us all take to singing, men's voices, a cappella; All in green went my love riding; The glory is fallen out of the sky; Prayer for peace; 3 madrigals; Secular cantata, 1976; many songs and song cycles.

249 Edgerton St., Rochester, NY 14607

DIAMOND, STUART SAMUEL
b. New York, N.Y., 15 Jan. 1950. Studied with John Davison, Haverford Coll., B.A. cum laude, 1971; with Meyer Kupferman and Edmund Haines, Sarah Lawrence Coll., M.F.A. 1973. He was Phi Beta Kappa member at Haverford Coll., and was named Outstanding Young Composer, 1973, by Nat. Found. for the Arts and Sciences. He is a freelance bassoonist and conductor.

WORKS: ORCHESTRA: symphony in one movement; overture; CHAMBER MUSIC: quartet for winds and piano; piano sonata; string quartet; The dreams of Jez, clarinet and piano; VOICE: Song of songs, cycle; Resurrection, cantata for chamber group; FILM SCORES: The zoo story; Winding down; High school horror; ELECTRONIC: The jester, tape; The adventures of Andrew in the land of Odibil, tape, flutes, narrator; Darling, poor darling, electronic theatre piece.

c/o Diamond and Golomb, 99 Park Ave., New York, NY 10016

DICK, MARCEL
b. Miskolcz, Hungary, 28 Aug. 1898; to U.S. 1934. Studied at Royal Acad. of Music, Budapest, degree and title of professor, 1917. He was violist, Detroit Symphony, 1934-35; Stradivarius Quartet, 1935-42; Cleveland Orchestra, 1943-49; professor, Cleveland Inst. of Music, from 1948.
WORKS: ORCHESTRA: symphony, 1950; Adagio

DICKERSON, ROGER

and rondo; <u>Capriccio</u>, 1956; symphony for strings, 1964; CHAMBER MUSIC: 2 string quartets; piano trio; <u>4 elegies and an epilogue</u>, solo cello, 1951; sonata for violin and cello, 1952; <u>Essay</u>, violin and piano, 1955; suite for piano, 1959.
  2608 Norfolk Dr., Cleveland Heights, OH 44106

DICKERSON, ROGER
  b. New Orleans, La., 24 Aug. 1934. Studied at Dillard Univ., B.A. cum laude 1955; with Bernhard Heiden, Indiana Univ., M.M. 1957; and with Karl Schiske and Alfred Uhl, Vienna Acad. of Music, 1959-62. His awards include scholarships for all study 1951-57; Dave Frank music award, 1955; Fulbright grants, 1959, 1960; John Hay Whitney fellowship, 1964; American Music Center award, 1972; B# music award, 1973. He served in the U.S. Army, 1957-59; was program associate in humanities, Inst. of Services to Education, Washington, D.C., 1970-73; free-lance musician and composer from 1962.
    WORKS: ORCHESTRA: <u>Concert overture</u>, 1957; <u>A musical service for Louis, requiem for Louis Armstrong</u>, commissioned and performed by New Orleans Phil., Mar. 1972, and New York, 4 Feb. 1973; BAND: <u>Essay for band</u>, 1958; <u>Orpheus</u>, New Orleans, 21 Jan. 1975; CHAMBER MUSIC: piano sonatina, 1956; string quartet, 1956; <u>Chorale prelude</u>, organ, 1956; clarinet sonata, 1960; wind quintet, 1961; <u>Concert pieces for young string players</u>, 1973; SONGS: <u>Music I heard</u>, 1956; <u>The Negro speaks of rivers</u>, 1961.

DICKEY, MARK
  b. Ludlow Center, Mass., 2 July 1885. Studied piano with Arthur Foote, organ with Albert Snow; won the H. W. Gray prize, American Guild of Organists, 1935. He was church organist at age 12; organist-choirmaster, First Universalist Church, Somerville, Mass., 1936.
    WORKS: OPERA: <u>Little Red Riding Hood</u>; CHAMBER MUSIC: <u>Rhapsody</u>, violin and piano, 1936; allegro scherzando for string quartet; CHORUS: <u>Let not your heart be troubled</u>, 1935; also songs and piano pieces.

DICKINSON, CLARENCE
  b. Lafayette, Ind., 7 May 1873; d. New York, N.Y., 2 Aug. 1969. Studied at Miami Univ., Ohio; Northwestern Univ., A.M. 1909, D.M. 1917; composition with Gabriel Pierne in Paris. His many awards include several honorary doctorates. He was organist, Brick Presbyterian Church, 1909-59; Temple Beth-El, New York, 20 years; was professor, Union Theological Seminary, 1912-45. He was founder of the American Guild of Organists; with his wife Helen, founded the School of Sacred Music at Union Theological Seminary.
    WORKS: THEATRE: <u>Priscilla</u>, an opera; <u>The medicine man</u>, comic opera, 1895; <u>The Redeemer</u>, an oratorio; ORGAN: <u>Storm King symphony</u>; <u>Joy of the redeemed</u>; <u>Berceuse</u>; many choral works.

DICKOW, ROBERT HENRY
  b. San Francisco, Calif., 27 May 1949. Studied with Olly Wilson, Andrew Imbrie, Edwin Dugger, Joaquin Nin-Culmell, Univ. of California,

Berkeley, M.A., Ph.D. His awards include Phi Beta Kappa; first prize, Nicola de Lorenzo competition, 1972; George Ladd Prix de Paris, 1973-75. He was acting instructor, Univ. of Calif., Berkeley, 1976-78; from 1978, instructor, Transylvania Univ.
    WORKS: ORCHESTRA: <u>Chamberpiece</u>, small orch., 1973; <u>Movement for strings</u>, Southampton, England, 15 July 1974; horn concerto; WIND ENSEMBLE: <u>Entrance fanfare</u>, 4 horns, 1970; <u>Anagrams</u>, brass quintet, 1970; <u>Midday music</u>, 6 horns, 1972; <u>In the year of the comet</u>, 5 trombones, 2 percussionists, 1974; CHAMBER MUSIC: <u>Illumination</u>, mezzo-soprano, flute, harp, 1973; <u>4 little duos</u>, flute and clarinet, 1975; <u>2 romantic movements</u>, piano; <u>Omen</u>, violin solo, 1974; CHORUS: <u>Places</u>, a cappella; <u>Peace</u>, a cappella, 1977; ELECTRONIC: <u>Sampler</u>, tape, 1973; <u>Contrasts</u>, chamber ensemble and tape, 1976; <u>Sampler II</u>, tape and chamber band, Lexington Ky., 2 Dec. 1978.
  212 Derby Dr., Lexington, KY 40503

DI DOMENICA, ROBERT
  b. New York, N.Y., 4 Mar. 1927. Studied at New York Univ., grad. 1951; privately with Wallingford Riegger and Josef Schmidt in New York. He held a Guggenheim fellowship, 1972-73. On the faculty at New England Cons., from 1969; he was named associate dean in 1973, and dean in 1976.
    WORKS: OPERA: <u>The balcony</u>, 1973; ORCHESTRA: symphony, 1961, Boston, 15 Nov. 1972; concerto for violin and chamber orch., 1962, New York, 15 Apr. 1965; piano concerto, 1963; concerto for wind quintet, strings, timpani, 1964; <u>Music for flute and string orchestra</u>, 1967; CHAMBER MUSIC: flute sonata, 1957; sextet, piano and woodwinds, 1957; piano sonatina, 1958; 4 movements for piano, 1959; quartet, flute, violin, horn, piano, 1959; quartet, flute and string trio, 1960; string quartet, 1960; trio for flute, bassoon, piano, 1960; <u>Variations on a tonal theme</u>, solo flute, 1961; quintet, clarinet and string quartet, 1965; saxophone sonata, 1965; woodwind quintet, 1969; VOICE: <u>4 short songs</u>, soprano and chamber ensemble, 1975, Cambridge, 13 Apr. 1976; <u>Songs from Twelfth Night</u>, tenor and chamber ensemble, 1976; <u>Black poems</u>, baritone, piano, and tape, 1976, Boston, 2 Apr. 1977.
  17 Paul Revere Rd., Needham, MA 02194

DIEBEL, WENDEL H.
  b. Des Moines, Iowa, 20 Feb. 1914. Studied with Bernard Wagenaar, Juilliard Graduate School. He has received several commissions. He was piano assistant to James Friskin and Ernest Hutcheson, Chautauqua Summer Inst., 1940-48; professor, Colorado State Univ., 1948-74.
    WORKS: ORCHESTRA: concert piece for piano and orch., 1938, on CBS International broadcast; piano concerto, 1940; CHAMBER MUSIC: <u>Fantasy</u>, harp, flute, strings, 1964; <u>Toccata</u>, solo harp, 1966; <u>2 etudes</u>, harp, 1968; <u>10 bagatelles</u>, brass quintet and harp, 1969; <u>3 American folk tunes</u>, brass quartet and harp, 1970; horn sonata, 1970; trio sonata for flute, cello, harp; <u>Toccata</u> for 2 harps; trumpet sonata.
  1314 W. Mountain Ave., Fort Collins, CO 80521

DIEMENTE, EDWARD
b. Cranston, R.I., 27 Feb. 1923. Attended
Boston Univ.; studied with Isadore Freed, Hartt
Coll. of Music; and with Bernard Rogers, Eastman
School of Music. He received ASCAP awards, 1974-
77. He has been professor, Hartt Coll. of Music
from 1949; music director and organist, Cathedral
of St. Joseph, Hartford, from 1961.
WORKS: CHAMBER MUSIC: string quartet, 1967;
Unvelopment, solo double bass and wind ensemble;
Celebration, wind ensemble; 2 wind quartets;
3-31-70, wind ensemble; 3 pieces for 2 clarinets;
trio for flute, trumpet, percussion; For miles
and miles, solo vibes; Response, saxophone and
piano; Designs, trumpet and trombone; Forms of
flight and fancy, soprano and brass quintet;
CHORUS: Magnificat, with boys choir and organ;
3 motets; PIANO: clavier sonata; 4 waltzes;
In a call of wind; MIXED MEDIA: Something else,
recorder and tape; The eagles gather, organ,
percussion, and tape; Dimensions III, saxophone
and tape; Mirrors III, tape; Quotes, tape and
slides; The end, tape, New York, 26 Feb. 1976.
72 Montclair Dr., West Hartford, CT 06107

DIEMER, EMMA LOU
b. Kansas City, Mo., 24 Nov. 1927. Studied with
Richard Donovan and Paul Hindemith, Yale School
of Music, B.M. 1949, M.M. 1950; with Ernst Toch,
Roger Sessions at Tanglewood, 1954, 1955; with
Bernard Rogers, Howard Hanson, Eastman School of
Music, Ph.D. 1960. Her awards include Fulbright
fellowship, 1952; Louisville Orch. student award,
1955; 2 Mu Phi Epsilon awards, 1955; Arthur
Benjamin award, 1959; Ford Found.-Nat. Music
Council grant, 1959-61; ASCAP annual awards from
1962; Nat. Fed. of Music Clubs award, 1969;
Certificate of Merit, Yale School of Music
Alumni Assoc., 1977. She was composer-in-residence, Arlington, Va., 1959-61; composer-con-
sultant, Arlington and Baltimore schools, 1964-
65; faculty member, Univ. of Maryland, 1965-70;
Univ. of California, Santa Barbara, from 1971.
WORKS: ORCHESTRA: Festival overture; Symphonie antique; Rondo concertante: Pavane; flute
concerto, 1963; BAND: The brass menagerie;
suite; CHAMBER MUSIC: sextet for winds and
piano; woodwind quintet; violin sonata; flute
sonata; Toccata for flute chorus; Toccata for
marimba; suite, flute and piano; Serenade, flute
and piano, 1954; 4 poems for soprano and chamber
ensemble, 1976; CHORUS: Fragments from the Mass,
women's voices; 3 madrigals; Verses from the
Rubaiyat; Anniversary choruses, with orch.; The
prophecy, women's voices; PIANO: 7 etudes;
Sound pictures; ORGAN: Toccata; Fantasie; Fantasy
on "O Sacred Head".
Music Dept., Univ. of California, Santa
Barbara, CA 93106

DIERCKS, JOHN
b. Montclair, N.J., 19 Apr. 1927. Studied with
Herbert Elwell, Oberlin Coll., B.M.; with
Bernard Rogers, Alan Hovhaness, Howard Hanson,
Eastman School of Music, M.M., Ph.D. His awards
include Southern Found. fellowship, 1958; Danforth
Found. grants, 1960, 1962; MacDowell fellowship,
1963; Cooperative Program in the Humanities

award, 1965; ASCAP awards, 1968-72; Nat. Endowment for the Arts grant; many commissions. He
was faculty member, Coll. of Wooster (Ohio),
1950-54; from 1954, at Hollins Coll.; music
critic, Roanoke Times, from 1962.
WORKS: ORCHESTRA: suite #2, premiere by
Roanoke Symph., 1977; BAND: oboe concerto;
CHAMBER MUSIC: quintet for piano and strings;
suite, alto saxophone and piano; oboe sonata;
Fantasy for horn; Variations for tuba; Figures
on china, horn, trombone, tuba; brass quartet;
wind quintet; Mirror of brass, 7 instruments;
horn quartet; CHORUS: Ascribe ye greatness,
festival cantata, with brass and percussion; A
star arises, women's voices, flute, percussion;
Why do the nations rage, Psalm 2; VOICE: 4
poems of Susan Ludvigson, song cycle for soprano
and piano, Rock Hill, S.C., 14 Nov. 1978.
Hollins College, Hollins College, VA 24020

DIETZ, NORMAN C.
b. Mich., 12 Mar. 1919. Studied with H. Owen
Reed, Michigan State Univ. He is professor and
conductor of bands, Central Michigan Univ.
WORKS: BAND: Prelude and scherzo; BRASS
ENSEMBLE: Modern moods, sextet; piece for 11
brass and percussion instruments; trio for
trumpet, horn, trombone; fantasy for percussion;
CHORUS: Book of Job, with baritone and orch.
Central Michigan Univ., Mount Pleasant, MI
48859

DIGGLE, ROLAND
b. London, England, 1 Jan. 1887; to U.S. 1904;
d. Los Angeles, Calif., 13 Jan. 1954. Studied
music in London and Oxford. He was organist and
choirmaster in Wichita, Kans., and Quincy, Ill.,
before going to St. John's Church, Los Angeles,
in 1914.
WORKS: ORCHESTRA: Concert overture; Fairy
suite; Legend; California suite; American fantasy; CHAMBER MUSIC: trio for organ, violin,
harp; violin sonata; cello sonata; 2 string
quartets; organ pieces and hymn tunes.

DI JULIO, MAX
b. Philadelphia, Pa., 10 Oct. 1919. Studied at
Univ. of Denver, B.M., M.M.E.; with Darius
Milhaud at Aspen School. He was trumpeter in
the U.S. Air Force Band in World War II; then
staff arranger, KOA, Denver; has been guest conductor of the Denver Symph.; professor and
chairman, music department, Loretto Heights
Coll., from 1946.
WORKS: THEATRE: Baby Doe, opera; Boom
town, musical; SONGS: All the year 'round, a
cycle; Shepherds, awake; Little children, listen.
Music Dept., Loretto Heights College,
3001 S. Federal Blvd., Denver, CO 80236

DI LELLO, EDWARD V.
b. Astoria, N.Y., 3 May 1952. Studied with
Stanley Walden, Andre Singer, Chester Biscardi,
Sarah Lawrence Coll., A.B. 1974. His awards
include Sandtvoort Found. scholarship, 1972-73;
American Music Center, composer assistance
award, 1978. He is faculty member, Wesleyan
Univ.

DILL, WILLIAM L.

WORKS: THEATRE: Purgatory, opera after
Yeats, 1974; The cat and the moon, opera, after
Yeats, 1974; CHAMBER MUSIC: Short study for
solo clarinet, 1974; Crazy Jane, 3 songs for
soprano and cello, 1975; 8 short people, woodwind quartet, 1978; several works for percussion
and various other instruments for use with
modern dance solos or groups, 1975-77.
54 E. 4th St., Apr. B-4, New York, NY 10003

DILL, WILLIAM L.
b. Chiselhurst, N.J., 27 Oct. 1913. Studied
with private teachers. He is conductor, Philadelphia Civic Concert Band.
WORKS: BAND: Champions of democracy,
march; Synocracy, march; Modeerf, concert piece;
Rhythmology, advanced method for drums.
749 S. 19th St., Philadelphia, PA 19146

DILLER, SARALU C.
b. Ohio, 3 June 1930. Studied at Baldwin-
Wallace Cons., B.M.; Univ. of Maryland, M.M.;
Univ. of Colorado; and with Carlisle Floyd,
Florida State Univ., 1969. She was staff accompanist, Univ. of Colorado, 1966-68; director-
actor, Nomad Playhouse, Boulder, 1959-72;
director, Vail Summer Theater, Vail, Colo.,
1973; violinist, Akron Symphony Orch., 1956-59.
WORKS: THEATRE: A child is born, incidental
music, 1962; Cave dwellers, incidental music,
1963; Ding-an-sich, 3 players, 1 percussion,
1 tape, 3 voices, 1967; The little prince,
children's folk opera, 1972; CHAMBER MUSIC: 3
sketches, piano, 1966; Format: #1, #2, #3, for
6 players, 2 percussion, voice, 1970; The bad
quartet, brass, 1970; CHORUS: Ship of death,
2 poems, with orch., 1971; SONGS: In that
strange city, 1968; Lonely; The feast, 1968;
Outside in, 1969.
1526 Sunset Blvd., Boulder, CO 80302

DILLON, FANNIE CHARLES
b. Denver, Colo., 16 Mar. 1881; d. Altadena,
Calif., 21 Feb. 1947. Studied at Claremont
Coll.; in Berlin; and with Rubin Goldmark in
New York. She taught at Pomona Coll., 1911-13;
in Los Angeles High Schools, 1918-47. She wrote
orchestral works and many piano pieces; gave a
concert of her own works in 1918 in New York.

DILLON, ROBERT
b. Downs, Kans., 29 Sept. 1922. Studied with
Spencer Norton, Univ. of Oklahoma, B.F.A. 1947,
D.M.E. 1971; with Halsey Stevens, Univ. of
Southern California, M.M. 1949; with Charles
Eakin, Cecil Effinger, and Philip Batstone,
Univ. of Colorado. His awards include first
prize in the Harvey Gaul competition, 1950;
first prize, 1975 Songs of Oklahoma Heritage
competition; and many commissions. He taught
in public schools, Bethany, Okla., 1951-55; has
been faculty member, Central State Univ. from
1966.
WORKS: BAND: Southwestern panorama; Quartz
Mountain; The far country; 4 winds; Distant
hills; SMALL ENSEMBLE: brass quintet; Allegro
festoso, 4 clarinets; High tide, brass quintet;
Lament, bassoon and piano; Petite etude, flute

and piano; Night shade, 4 saxophones; Scherzo,
oboe and piano; other works for orchestra, band,
and ensembles.
1300 East Dr., Edmond, OK 73034

DILSNER, LAWRENCE
b. New York, N.Y., 22 July. Studied at New
York Univ., B.S., M.Ed.; with Charles Courboin
and Nadia Boulanger in France; and at Philadelphia Musical Acad., D.M. He held a scholarship
for study at Guilmant Organ School; received
several prizes for teaching. He has been
teacher and organist in the New York area from
1945. His compositions include works for piano,
organ, chorus, and flute.
41 Branchport Ave., Long Branch, NJ 07740

DINERSTEIN, NORMAN
b. Springfield, Mass., 18 Sept. 1937. Studied
with Gardner Read, Boston Univ.; with Arnold
Franchetti, Hartt Coll.; with Gunther Schuller,
Aaron Copland, Lukas Foss, and Witold Lutoslawski
at Tanglewood; with Boris Blacher in Berlin; and
with Roger Sessions, Milton Babbitt, and Edward
T. Cone at Princeton Univ. His honors include
Koussevitzky prize; Sagalyn Orchestral award;
Fulbright grants, 1964, 1969-70; Ford Found.
fellowship, 1966-68; Univ. of Rhode Island Arts
Council award; Di Tella award, Buenos Aires,
1970; Brown Univ. Bicentennial award; Celia Buck
award; Ohio Arts Council grant, 1978. He was
faculty member, New England Cons., 1968-71; at
Hartt Coll., 1971-76; from 1976, professor,
Univ. of Cincinnati.
WORKS: ORCHESTRA: Cassation, 1962; Serenade,
1963; Refrains; CHAMBER MUSIC: 4 settings,
soprano and string quartet; 3 miniatures,
strings; Pound cycle, soprano and piano; pEzzi-
cati, double bass; Zalemn or The madness of God,
solo violin; CHORUS: Cinque laude; The answered
question; Our Father; Herrickanna; Frogs, a
cappella.
8814 Foxboro Court, Cincinnati, OH 45236

DI PASQUALE, JAMES A.
b. Chicago, Ill., 7 Apr. 1941. Studied with
Anthony Donato, James Hopkins, Alan Stout, at
Northwestern Univ.; with David Diamond, Nicolas
Flagello, and Ludmila Ulehla at Manhattan School
of Music; privately with Leon Stein. He won
awards in the Collegiate Jazz Festival, 1961,
1962; and in the American Film Festival, 1965,
for the score to The way back. He has been
visiting lecturer-clinician, Univ. of Montana;
music director, Winter Consort, 1965, 1969-70.
WORKS: CHAMBER MUSIC: saxophone sonata;
Interplay, chamber ensemble; Showing great re-
straint, ensemble; and many jazz works.
4058 Woodman Ave., Sherman Oaks, CA 91403

DI PIETRO, ROCCO
b. Buffalo, N.Y., 15 Sept. 1949. Studied
privately with Lukas Foss in Buffalo, and with
Bruno Maderna at Tanglewood. He received an
ASCAP fellowship to Tanglewood, 1971, and per-
formance by Gunther Schuller of his composition,
Drafts. He was visiting artist, Stockbridge
School, 1971, 1972, 1973; composer-in-residence,

Earlham Coll., 1973; on staff for Contemporary Sound Series, Recording Laboratories, from 1973.
WORKS: ORCHESTRA: Chrysalis, 48 strings; Chroma; Refractions; Aria fatta in casa, New York, 1978; Punto vivo, Ojai, Calif., 28 May 1980; CHAMBER MUSIC: 4 temperatures, 4 flutes; 2 colors for Robert Bly; Piece for Bruno, chamber orch., 1974; Piece for Danilo Dolci, chamber ensemble, 1976; Melodia della terra, violin, 1976; Aria per cello, 1977; ELECTRONIC: Electrosignals, massed tape and cassettes.
26 Walter Crest, West Seneca, NY 14224

DIRKSEN, RICHARD WAYNE
b. 1921. Studied at Peabody Cons. His works for chorus include: Chanticleer; I sing the birth; Nowell we sing; Song of the redeemed, boy's voices; for organ: Prelude on Urbs beata and Hilariter.
c/o National Cathedral, Washington, DC 20013

DITTENHAVER, SARAH LOUISE
b. Paulding, Ohio, 16 Dec. 1901; d. Asheville, N.C., 4 Feb. 1973. Graduated from Oberlin Cons. She taught in private and public schools for many years, then settled in Asheville as teacher and composer. She was made a fellow, Internat. Inst. of Arts and Letters, Switzerland, 1961; her compositions have won awards from N.C. Fed. of Music Clubs; Nat. League of American Pen Women; Delta Kappa Gamma Society Internat., 1963; Nat. Guild of Piano Teachers, 1967.
WORKS: CHORUS: Alleluia, Jesus child; Light of the lonely pilgrim's heart, youth choir; Trust in the Lord, unison choir; Bless the Lord, O my soul; SONGS: Lady of the amber wheat; Passage; Once more, beloved; Hurdy-gurdy playing in the street; many piano teaching pieces.

DIX, ROBERT
b. Pallatin, Mo., 10 June 1917. Studied with Stanley Wolfe of the Juilliard School. He has been an executive in chemical firms from 1959; was senior vice-president, Exxon Chemical Company, 1970-77.
WORKS: ORCHESTRA: 3 movements for orchestra, premiere performance by Hong Kong Phil. in 1978; CHAMBER MUSIC: piano septet, 1975; Triloquy, piano trio; Narrative, cello and piano; Interlude, piano; Intermezzo, violin and piano; little quintet, woodwinds and strings, 1976; also other lighter works for piano.
111 Lake Wind Rd., New Canaan, CT 06840

DLUGOSZEWSKI, LUCIA
b. Detroit, Mich., 16 June 1925. Studied at Detroit Cons.; medical studies and physics at Wayne State Univ., 1946-49; composition privately with Edgard Varese in New York. She received the Tomkins literary award for poetry, 1947; Nat. Inst. of Arts and Letters, award, 1966; BMI-Thorne fellowship, 1972; Guggenheim fellowship; Nat. Endowment for the Arts grant, 1978; more than 30 commissions. She has invented over 100 percussion instruments, including ladder harps, unsheltered rattles, tangent rattles, closed rattles, consisting of wood, glass, metal, plastic, paper; and the timbre piano in which

bows of glass, felt, metal, plastic, or wood are run across the strings while the keyboard is also being used. She has taught at the New School for Social Research and the Found. for Modern Dance from 1960; also music director and composer-in-residence, Eric Hawkins Dance Company, New York.
WORKS: BALLET: Openings of the eye, flute, percussion, timbre piano, 1958; 8 clear places, percussion ensemble, 1958-61; Geography of noon, new percussion instruments, 1964; Dazzle on a knife's edge, timbre piano and orch., 1966; Agathlon algebra, timbre piano and orch., 1968; Of love, New York, Mar. 1971; CHAMBER MUSIC: Space is a diamond, trumpet solo, 1970; Theater flight Nagiere, for her new instruments, New York, 7 Mar. 1971; Fire fragile flight, New York, 29 Apr. 1973; Densities, chamber ensemble, New York, 5 May 1974; Abyss and caress, concerto for trumpet and 17 instruments, New York, 21 Mar. 1975; and nearly 100 other vocal and instrumental works. She has also published a book of poetry, A new folder, 1967, and studies on philosophical esthetics and modern dance.
107 W. 10th St., New York, NY 10011

DOBRY, WALLACE B.
b. Baltimore, Md., 21 June 1933. Studied with George Hurst, Spencer Huffman, Henry Cowell at the Peabody Cons., B.M. 1956. He received a 3-year scholarship at Peabody, 1952; twice won the Thatcher prize. He was lecturer, George Washington Univ., 1972-78; and church music director, Chevy Chase, Md., from 1970.
WORKS: ORCHESTRA: Scherzo, Baltimore Symph., 1951; CHAMBER MUSIC: woodwind quintet, 1968; Divertimento, string trio, 1972; ORGAN: Theme and variations, 1961; Toccata, 1969.

DOCKSTADER, TOD
b. 1932. ELECTRONIC MUSIC: 8 electronic pieces, 1960; Traveling music, 1960; Apocalypse, 1961; Luna Park, 1961; Drone, 1962; Water music, 1963; Quatermass, 1964.

DODGE, CHARLES
b. Ames, Iowa, 5 June 1942. Studied with Philip Bezanson and Richard Hervig, Univ. of Iowa, B.A. 1964; with Darius Milhaud, Aspen Music School, 1961; with Gunther Schuller and Arthur Berger, Tanglewood, 1964; with Jack Beeson, Chou Wen-chung, Otto Luening, and Vladimir Ussachevsky, Columbia Univ., M.A. 1966. His honors include 4 BMI awards, 1963-67; Bearns prize, 1964, 1967; Sagalyn award, 1964; Koussevitzky Found. grant, 1969; Guggenheim fellowships, 1972, 1975; Nat. Inst. of Arts and Letters award, 1975; many commissions. His faculty posts include Princeton Univ., 1969-70; Columbia Univ., 1967-69, 1970-77; Brooklyn Coll. and CUNY Graduate Center, from 1977.
WORKS: ORCHESTRA: Rota, 1966; ELECTRONIC: Folia, 7 instruments, percussion, tape, 1963; Changes, 1970; Earth's magnetic field, 1970; Speech songs, New York, 9 Feb. 1973; Extensions, trumpet and tape, New York, 23 Apr. 1973; In celebration; The story of our lives, synthetic voices, 1974; Palinode, tape and orch., New

DOENHOFF, ALBERT VON

York, 7 Feb. 1977; <u>Cascando</u>, synthesized voices
on a Beckett text, 1979.
   56 Garden Place, Brooklyn, NY 11201

DOENHOFF, ALBERT VON
b. Louisville, Ky., 16 Mar. 1880; d. New York,
3 Oct. 1940. Studied at Cincinnati Coll. of
Music and with Rafael Joseffy in New York. He
was a concert pianist and published many piano
pieces.

DOHNANYI, ERNST VON
b. Pressburg, Bratislava, 27 July 1877; to U.S.
1949; d. New York, 9 Feb. 1960. Graduated from
the Royal Acad. of Music, Budapest, 1897; then
toured Europe and the U.S. as concert pianist.
He joined the faculty of Florida State Univ. in
1949. His works composed since 1949 include
violin concerto #2, scored for orchestra without
violins, San Antonio, 26 Jan. 1952; harp concertino, 1952; <u>American rhapsody</u> for orch.,
Athens, Ohio, 21 Feb. 1954; <u>12 etudes</u> for piano.

DOLLARHIDE, THEODORE JOHN
b. Santa Rosa, Calif., 30 Aug. 1948. Studied
with Higo Harada, San Jose State Univ., B.A.;
with Leslie Bassett, George B. Wilson, and
William Bolcom, Univ. of Michigan, M.M. His
awards include BMI awards, 1975-76; Fulbright
grant for study with Eugene Kurtz in Paris,
1978-79; and commissions. He has been teaching
assistant at Univ. of Michigan.
   WORKS: ORCHESTRA: <u>Fantasy of ivory thoughts
and shallow whispers</u>, 1972; <u>Movements for orches-
tra</u>, 1973; <u>Other dreams, other dreamers</u>, 1976;
BAND: <u>Music for the food king</u>, 1972; <u>Jungles</u>,
with piano and percussion, 1976; <u>Faces at the
blue front</u>; CHAMBER MUSIC: <u>Theme and variations</u>,
flute, clarinet, 2 cellos, 2 speakers, 1971;
<u>Shadows</u>, woodwind quintet, 1973; <u>Inner moons</u>,
flute, harp, viola, contrabass, 1974; <u>Peperomia</u>,
solo flute, 1976; <u>Shoestrings</u>, flute and clarinet,
1977; CHORUS: <u>Psalm 150</u>, 1967; MIXED MEDIA:
<u>Hinge</u>, tape and dancers; <u>Walldrops</u>, tape and
dancers, 1977.
   2370 Jonathan Court, Ann Arbor, MI 48104

DONAHUE, ROBERT L.
b. 1931. Studied at Univ. of Wisconsin, B.M.;
with Ben Johnston, Univ. of Illinois, M.M.; with
Karel Husa and Robert Palmer, Cornell Univ.,
D.M.A. He is faculty member at Spelman Coll.
   WORKS: CHAMBER MUSIC: <u>5 canonic duets</u>,
flute and clarinet; <u>5 pieces</u>, brass quartet;
<u>Little suite</u>, brass trio.
   Rt. 2, Box 296, Newman, GA 30265

DONALDSON, SADIE
b. New York, N.Y., 2 July 1909. Studied at
Hunter Coll.; Columbia Univ. Teachers Coll.; and
New School for Social Research. She received 2
prizes in a Staten Island Council of Churches
competition for hymn composition. She has been
a teacher.
   WORKS: VOICE: <u>Thanksgiving hymn</u>; <u>Hallelu-
jah! Christ is born</u>; <u>Butterfly of Japan</u>, popular
ballad; <u>Song of Solomon</u>, soprano, bass, flute,
piano.
   810 El Olmo Ct., S.E., Rio Rancho, NM 87124

DONATO, ANTHONY
b. Prague, Nebr., 8 Mar. 1909. Studied with
Howard Hanson, Bernard Rogers, and Edward Royce,
Eastman School of Music, B.M. 1931. M.M. 1937,
Ph.D. 1947. His many honors include Blue Network award, 1945; Society for Publication of
American Music award, 1947; Composers Press publication awards, 1946, 1953; Mendelssohn Glee
Club award, 1950; Fulbright lecture grant for
England, 1951-52; Huntington Hartford fellowship,
1961; many commissions. He was head, violin
department, Drake Univ., 1931-37; Iowa State
Teachers Coll., 1937-39; Univ. of Texas, 1939-
46; professor of composition, Northwestern Univ.,
1947-76.
   WORKS: OPERA: <u>The walker through walls</u>,
1964; ORCHESTRA: 2 sinfoniettas, 1936, 1959;
<u>Elegy</u>, strings, 1938; <u>Divertimento</u>, 1939; 2 sym-
phonies, 1944, 1945; suite for strings, 1948;
<u>Solitude in the city</u>, with narrator, 1954;
<u>Episode</u>, 1954; <u>Serenade</u>, small orch., 1961; <u>Cen-
tennial ode</u>, 1968; <u>Discourse</u>, flute and strings,
1969; BAND: <u>The lake shore</u>, 1950; <u>The hidden
fortress</u>, 1950; <u>Cowboy reverie</u>, 1955; <u>Concert
overture</u>, 1958; CHAMBER MUSIC: 2 violin sonatas,
1938, 1949; 4 string quartets, 1941, 1947, 1951,
1975; <u>Precipitations</u>, violin and piano, 1946;
horn sonata, 1950; wind quintet, 1955; suite for
brass, 1956; piano trio, 1959; clarinet sonata,
1966; nonet, 3 trumpets, 3 trombones, 3 percussion, 1972; 3 poems from Shelley, tenor and
string quartet, 1971; CHORUS: <u>March of the
hungry mountains</u>, with solo tenor and small orch.,
1949; <u>The last supper</u>, with baritone solo, 1952;
<u>The Congo</u>, soprano and full orch., 1957; <u>Prelude
and choral fantasy</u>, male voices, organ, organ
and brass, 1961; numerous other choral works;
many songs; PIANO: <u>African dominoes</u>, 1948;
<u>Recreations</u>, 1948; <u>3 preludes</u>, 1948; sonata,
1951; many piano teaching pieces.
   6915 10th Ave. W., Bradenton, FL 33505

DONOVAN, RICHARD FRANK
b. New Haven, Conn., 29 Nov. 1891; d. Middletown,
Conn., 22 Aug. 1970. Studied at Inst. of
Musical Art, New York; Yale Univ., B.M. 1922,
honorary M.A. 1947. He received the Naumburg
recording award, 1962. He taught at Smith Coll.,
1923-28; Inst. of Musical Art, 1925-28; Yale
Univ., 1928-60, then Battell Professor Emeritus.
He was conductor, Bach Cantata Club, New Haven,
1933-44; New Haven Symph., 1936-51; staff member,
Middlebury Coll. Composers' Conf., 1946, 1947;
director of the Yaddo Corp. and member of the
Yaddo Festivals music committee.
   WORKS: ORCHESTRA: <u>Smoke and steel</u>, symphonic poem, 1932; <u>Design for radio</u>, 1945; <u>New
England chronicle</u>, 1947; <u>Passacaglia on Vermont
folk tunes</u>, 1949; symphony, 1956; <u>Epos</u>, 1963;
CHAMBER MUSIC: <u>Wood-notes</u>, flute, harp, strings,
1925; sextet, winds and piano, 1932; symphony for
chamber orch., 1936; 2 piano trios, 1937, 1963;
<u>Serenade</u>, oboe and string trio, 1939; terzetto,
2 violins and viola, 1950; woodwind quartet,
1953; <u>Soundings</u>, trumpet, bassoon, percussion,
1953; <u>Music for six</u>, 1961; KEYBOARD: 2 suites
for piano; antiphone and chorale, organ; also
choral works. His sons have given his complete

papers and music manuscripts to the Yale University Library.

DORAN, MATT H.
b. Covington, Ky., 1 Sept. 1921. Studied with Ernst Toch, Hanns Eisler, Ernest Kanitz, Gail Kubik, and Peter Jona Korn, Univ. of Southern California. His awards include a MacDowell fellowship and 2 Hartford fellowships. He has been professor, Mount St. Mary's Coll., from 1956.
WORKS: THEATRE: The committee, 1-act opera, 1955; Marriage counselor, 1-act opera, 1976; ORCHESTRA: 2 symphonies; flute concerto, 1953; horn concerto, 1954; double concerto, flute, guitar, and strings, Los Angeles, 21 May 1976; CHAMBER MUSIC: string quartet; sonatina for 2 flutes; sonatina, flute and cello; woodwind quintet; quartet for oboe, clarinet, bassoon, viola; clarinet sonata, 1963; trio for oboe, violin, viola; Poem for flute; sonatina, 2 violins; flute sonata; suite for flute and percussion; Pastorale, organ; choral works, songs; piano pieces.
2614 Military Ave., Los Angeles, CA 90064

DORATI, ANTAL
b. Budapest, Hungary, 9 Apr. 1906; U.S. citizen 1947. Studied at the Budapest Acad. of Music, dipl. 1924; Univ. of Vienna; Macalester Coll., D.M. 1957. His awards in 1975 included the Decca/London Records' gold record for his recordings of the complete Haydn symphonies; French government's Cross of the Chevalier of Arts and Letters; and an honorary doctorate, George Washington Univ. He was opera and ballet conductor in Europe, 1933-44; conductor, Dallas Symphony, 1945-49; Minneapolis Symphony, 1949-60; chief conductor, BBC Symphony Orch., London, 1962-70; conductor, Nat. Symphony Orch., Washington, D.C., 1970-75; senior conductor, Royal Philharmonic Orch., London, 1975-77; from 1977, music director, Detroit Symphony.
WORKS: BALLET: Magdalena; ORCHESTRA: 7 pieces for orch.; 3 American serenades, strings; The way of the cross, cantata for chorus and orch., 1957; 2 symphonies, 1957, 1960; piano concerto, 1974, premiere, Washington, 28 Oct. 1975; cello concerto, premiere, Louisville Orch., 1 Oct. 1976; The voices, song cycle on Rilke poems for bass voice with orch., Stockholm, 11 Oct. 1979, American premiere, Washington, 10 Apr. 1979 (in both cases, the composer conducted, and the singer was Peter Lagger, for whom the piece was written); CHAMBER MUSIC: string quartet; oboe quintet; 2 Hungarian peasant tunes, violin and piano, 1945; string octet; The voices, song cycle (as above with orch.) with piano accompaniment, 1976, Berlin, 24 Feb. 1978; Variations on a theme by Bartok, piano, 1971; also choral works; songs; chamber music.
c/o Detroit Symphony Orchestra, Ford Auditorium, 20 E. Jefferson, Detroit, MI 48226

DORSAM, PAUL JAMES
b. New York, N.Y., 25 Jan. 1941. Studied with Francis Judd Cooke and Felix Wolfes, New England Cons., D.M., M.M.; with Hugo Norden, Boston Univ., D.M.A. His awards include many commis-

sions. He has held faculty posts at State Coll., Lyndonville, Vt., 1964-66; St. Michael's Coll., Winooski, Vt., 1967-69; Berklee Coll. of Music, 1970-71; Virginia Commonwealth Univ., from 1972.
WORKS: ORCHESTRA: Prelude, 1967; symphony #2, 1969; symphony #4, 1971; Yeasts music, with narrator, voice, trumpet, saxophone, piano, 1972; CHAMBER MUSIC: trumpet sonata; piano sonata; cello sonata; music for organ and trumpet, 1970; many works for trumpet ensembles; band pieces; works for chorus and solo voice.
2162 E. Tremont Court, Richmond, VA 23225

DORSEY, JAMES ELNO
b. San Antonio, Tex., 22 Nov. 1905. Was awarded the Wanamaker prize in 1931 for his composition, Sandals.

DOUGHERTY, CELIUS
b. Glenwood, Minn., 27 May 1902. Studied piano and composition with Donald Ferguson, Univ. of Minnesota; piano with Josef Lhevinne and composition with Rubin Goldmark at Juilliard Graduate School on scholarship. He has received many commissions and was accompanist for many noted singers.
WORKS: OPERA: Many moons, 1 act, based on Thurber text, performed at Vassar Coll., 6 Dec. 1962; SONGS: Love in the dictionary, text from Funk and Wagnalls (Ned Rorem has called this "a riotous encore"); A minor bird, Frost; Primavera, Amy Lowell; Song for autumn, Mary Webb; Loveliest of trees, Housman; Listen! the wind, Humbert Wolfe; 5 sea chanties; 7 songs, e. e. cummings; Ballade of William Sycamore; Portugese sonnets.
320 W. 76th St., New York, NY 10023; Effort, PA 18330

DOUGLAS, SAMUEL OSLER
b. Mansfield, La., 31 Mar. 1943. Studied with Dinos Constandinides and Kenneth B. Klaus, Louisiana State Univ., M.M. 1968, D.M.A. 1972. He has been on the faculty, Univ. of South Carolina, from 1973.
WORKS: OPERA: The devil's hair, 1 act, Baton Rouge, in concert form, July 1972; ORCHESTRA: Prelude and passacaglia, 1968; Sinfonia ecclesiastica, chamber symphony with chorus, 1970; Sonata, with reader, poem by Leo Stanford, 1972; The night before Christmas, with narrator, 1973; CHORUS: Bow down thine ear, anthem; SONGS: Selected definitions from "The Devil's Dictionary," by Ambroise Bierce, soprano, clarinet, double bass, piano, 1972; PIANO: 12 trifles, 1970; FILM SCORE: Disciples of death, 1971.
Music Dept., Univ. of South Carolina, Columbia, SC 29208

DOUGLAS, WILLIAM
b. London, Ont., 7 Nov. 1944; to U.S. 1970. Studied with Mel Powell, Yale Univ. He received the Margaret M. Grant award at Tanglewood, 1969; was bassoonist, New Haven Symph., 1966-69; faculty member, California Inst. of the Arts, from 1969.
WORKS: CHAMBER MUSIC: Improvisation II, flute and piano; Improvisation III, clarinet and

DOWD, JOHN ANDREW

piano, 1969; string quartet, 1969; Celebration, piano solo; Vajra, clarinet and piano, 1972.
School of Music, California Inst. of the Arts, 24700 McBean Parkway, Valencia, CA 91355

DOWD, JOHN ANDREW
b. Jacksonville, Fla., 19 Feb. 1932. Studied with Stephen Park, Univ. of Tampa; with Francis Judd Cooke and Billy Jim Layton, New England Cons. He was instructor, West Virginia Univ., 1966-68; Ohio Univ., 1968-69; and chairman of fine arts, Milligan Coll., 1963-66, and from 1969.
WORKS: ORCHESTRA: Simulacra noctus, chorus and orch.; CHORUS: Why seek ye the living, anthem, a cappella, 1963; several choral compositions, orchestral works, chamber music, piano pieces, a short opera.
819 W. Pine St., Johnson City, TN 37601

DOWNEY, JOHN
b. Chicago, Ill., 5 Oct. 1927. Studied with Leon Stein, De Paul Univ., B.M. 1949; with Vittorio Rieti, Chicago Musical Coll., M.M. 1951; with Arthur Honneger, Nadia Boulanger, Darius Milhaud in Paris; musicology at Univ. of Paris, Ph.D. 1956. His awards include second prize in composition, Paris Cons., 1956; 2 Fulbright grants; French government fellowship and scholarship; 2 Copley awards; ASCAP awards; Distinguished Alumni award, De Paul Univ.; Ford Found. grant; Nat. Endowment for the Arts grant; Univ. of Wisconsin awards; Norlin Found. award; and commissions. He was founder in 1970 and director to present, Wisconsin Contemporary Music Forum; has been professor, Univ. of Wisconsin, Milwaukee, from 1964.
WORKS: ORCHESTRA: Symphonic modules 5, 1972; Fantasy, bassoon and orch., Milwaukee, 17 Sept. 1978; Silhouette, with solo double bass, Milwaukee, 17 Feb. 1980; WIND ENSEMBLE: High clouds and soft rain, flute choir, 1977; CHAMBER MUSIC: Adagio lyrico, 2 pianos, 1953; wind octet, 1954, rev. 1976; cello sonata, 1966; Agort, woodwind quintet, 1967; string quartet #2, 1976; VOICE: What if?, mixed choir, brass octet, and solo tympanist, 1973; A dolphin, high voice and chamber ensemble, 1974.
4413 N. Prospect Ave., Shorewood, WI 53211

DOWNS, LAMONT WAYNE
b. Warren, Ohio, 9 Mar. 1951. Studied with Samuel Adler and Warren Benson, Eastman School of Music, where he received the Howard Hanson award for a wind ensemble, 1970. He was visiting instructor at State Univ. Coll., Geneseo, N.Y., 1976-78.
WORKS: BAND: sinfonia for wind band, 1969; Electric symphony for junior wind ensemble; RS-2, concert march, 1970; DDA40X, concert march; SONG: A (more or less) brief diversion for tenor, trumpet, trombone, and percussion.
8482 Old Farm Trail, N.E., Warren, OH 44484

DRAKE, ELIZABETH BELL
b. Cincinnati, Ohio, 1 Dec. 1928. Studied with Hubert Lamb, Wellesley Coll., B.A. 1950; with

Peter Mennin and Vittorio Giannini, Juilliard School, B.S. 1953. She was music reviewer for the Ithaca (N.Y.) Journal, 1971-73.
WORKS: ORCHESTRA: concerto for orchestra, 1977; symphony #1, 1977; CHAMBER MUSIC: string quartet, 1953; Songs of here and forever, soprano and piano, 1973; Fantasy sonata, cello and piano, 1973; PIANO: Variations and interludes, 1952; Arecibo sonata; sonata #2.
114 Kelbourne Ave., North Tarrytown, NY 10591

DRENNAN, DOROTHY
b. Hankinson, N.Dak., 21 Mar. 1929. Studied with Clifton Williams and Alfred Reed, Univ. of Miami. She received Sigma Alpha Iota awards, 1971, 1972, 1973. She was instructor at Univ. of Miami.
WORKS: CHAMBER MUSIC: Turn, quintet for widely separated performers, violin, clarinet, trombone, and 2 percussionists; CHORUS: Seashores, Tagore text, with wind quintet; Here is the rose (Dance thou here), a concerto for trombone and modern chorus; The word, cantata for Pentacost.
7880 S.W. 12th St., Miami, FL 33144

DRESHER, PAUL
b. Los Angeles, Calif., 8 Jan. 1951. Studied with Terry Riley at Mills Coll., 1973-74; with Steve Reich at Center for World Music; at Univ. of California at Berkeley, B.A. 1977; with Robert Erickson, Roger Reynolds, and Pauline Oliveros, Univ. of California, San Diego, M.A. 1979; African music with C. K. and Kobla Ladzekpo, 1975-79; sitar with N. Banerjee, 1974-79; instrument building and intonation with Lou Harrison. His awards include San Francisco Found. grant, 1977; USCD Regents fellowship, 1977-78; California Arts Council and Port Costa Players commission, 1979-80; Nat. Endowment for the Arts grant, 1979-80. He has organized and/or directed American gamelans and West African ensembles in Berkeley, San Diego, and Seattle; taught for 3 summers at the Berkeley Cazadero Music Camp; spent most of 1980 studying and composing in India and Indonesia; then joined the faculty at Cornish Inst. in Seattle.
WORKS: CHAMBER MUSIC: guitar quartet, 1975-76; This same temple, 2 pianos, 1976-79; Z, 6 percussionists, soprano, and tape, 1977-79; Night songs, soprano, 2 tenors, chamber ensemble, 1979-80; Liquid and stellar music, electric instrument and tape, 1980.
Cornish Institute, 710 Roy St., Seattle, WA 98102

DRETKE, LEORA N.
b. Canton, Ohio, 17 Oct. 1928. Studied at Mt. Union Coll., B.M.; Western Reserve Univ., M.A. She has won the Ohioana Authors and Composers award; has taught in public schools in Canton and Louisville, Ohio; is soprano soloist and organist. She has published many anthems and other choral works.

DREW, JAMES
b. New York, N.Y., 9 Feb. 1929. Studied at New

York School of Music; Tulane Univ.; Washington Univ.; and privately with Wallingford Riegger and Edgard Varese. His awards include Downbeat Internat. Jazz Critics award in the New Star category, 1961; Rockefeller Found. grant, 1965; Northwestern Univ. research grant, 1966; Morse award, 1968-69; Guggenheim fellowship, 1972; Fromm Found. grant, 1973; Tanglewood fellowship, 1973; Pan American prize, 1974; and commissions. He was faculty member, Northwestern Univ., 1965-67; Yale Univ., 1967-73; Louisiana State Univ., 1973-76; California State Univ., Fullerton, 1976-77.

WORKS: THEATRE: Toward yellow, ballet, 1970; Suspense opera, voices and chamber ensemble, 1975; Crucifixus Domini Christi, dramatic stage work, Baton Rouge, 30 Jan. 1975; The fading visible world, oratorio, 1975; Dr. Cincinnati, actors, dancers, singers, instrumentalists, and tape, 1977; ORCHESTRA: 3 symphonies, 1968, 1971, 1977; concerto for 2 pianos and strings, 1968; chamber symphony, 1966-68; October lights, 1969; 2 violin concertos, 1969-70, 1977; Metal concert, percussion ensemble, 1971; concerto for small percussion orch., 1973; West Indian lights, Tanglewood, 9 Aug. 1973; viola concerto, 1973; Saint Mark concerto, cello and orch., Warsaw, Poland, 5 Mar. 1976; CHAMBER MUSIC: Indigo suite, piano, double bass, percussion, 1959; Divisiones, 6 percussion, 1962; piano trio, 1962; Polifonica I, woodwind trio, string quartet, piano, 1963; The lute in the attic, voice and chamber ensemble, 1963; Polifonica II, flute and percussion, 1966; The maze maker, cello solo, 1970; Quinteto d'microtonos, brass quintet, Atlanta, Ga., 12 Feb. 1971; Almost stationary, piano trio, 1971; Gothic lights, chamber ensemble, 1971; Tango, cello solo, 1973; Epitaphium for Stravinsky, 3 trombones, horn, tuba, piano, Atlanta, 14 Feb. 1974; Lux incognitus, string quartet, Albany Arts Center, 5 Oct. 1975; Orange-thorpe aria, soprano, clarinet, piano trio, Grinnell, Iowa, 12 Dec. 1978.

DREWS, STEVE
b. Oshkosh, Wis., 29 May 1945. Studied at Lawrence Univ., B.M. 1965; with Darius Milhaud at Aspen, 1966; and with Robert Palmer and Karel Husa, Cornell Univ., 1967-69.

WORKS: ELECTRONIC: Ceres motion; Train; Almost 2 years; Before day; Grover Whalen; Next door; Ice; Bells; all performed by Mother Mallard's Portable Masterpiece Company in New York.

DRISCOLL, JOHN
b. Philadelphia, Pa., 3 Oct. 1947. Studied with Rudi Staffel in Rome, 1967-68, and with Jim Sterritt, 1969. He won a Ferullo Found. award for his composition, Bad taste, 1972. He was producer, In Between Sounds, 1971; and instructor, Philadelphia Coll. of Art, 1972.

WORKS: Compositions for immobile or mobile objects with or without electronic modulation, performed usually as individual or group improvisations, to wit: 25 nymphomaniacs singing nebulous melodies to 50 lawn mowers, 1970; A tour around Cicero's bath, 1972; Under the put-ting green, a series, 1973-; Listening out loud, uses rip saws and live electronics in, according to one reviewer at the Festival d'Automne in Paris, Oct. 1976, "an almost romantic exposition of pure sonic beauty."
Collaberg Rd., Stony Point, NY 10980

DROSSIN, JULIUS
b. Philadelphia, Pa., 17 May 1918. Studied with Harl McDonald, Univ. of Pennsylvania, B.M. 1938; with George Rochberg at the New School, 1946-48; at Western Reserve Univ., M.A. 1951, Ph.D. 1956. He held a scholarship at Univ. of Pennsylvania and has received commissions. His faculty posts here included Villa Maria Coll., 1951-58; Fenn Coll., 1956-65; Cleveland State Univ., 1965-77. He was cellist with the Cleveland Orchestra, 1948-57; choir director, Park Synagogue, 1957-65.

WORKS: ORCHESTRA: 4 symphonies; Rhapsody, cello and orch.; Essay for orch.; CHAMBER MUSIC: 8 string quartets; CHORUS: Kaddish, with soloists and orch.; Friday night service.
3141 Somerset Dr., Shaker Heights, OH 44122

DROSTE, DOREEN (Mrs. Gerard J.)
b. Tacoma, Wash., 29 May 1907. Studied privately with George Tremblay; and with Henry Leland Clarke at Univ. of California, Los Angeles, M.A. She won first prize in an anthem contest, 1958.

WORKS: OPERA: Hyacinth Halvey, chamber opera, 1961; CHORUS: Hear my prayer, 1958; Six pence in her shoe, women's voices; To drive the cold winter away, 1969; The ship of state, 1964; Hymn of St. Columba, 1970; Ride on in majesty, 1970; The song of the wandering Aengus, a cappella, 1973; and many others.
760 Plain St., #22-5, Marshfield, MA 02050

DRUCKMAN, JACOB
b. Philadelphia, Pa., 26 June 1928. Studied with Peter Mennin, Bernard Wagenaar, Vincent Persichetti, Juilliard School, B.S., M.S. 1955; with Aaron Copland at Tanglewood; and in France on a Fulbright grant. His other awards include a Guggenheim fellowship, 1956-57; Koussevitzky Internat. Recording award, special citation, 1970; Pulitzer prize, 1972; ASCAP award, 1972; Tanglewood fellowship, 1978; election to American Acad. of Arts and Letters, 1978; many commissions. He has held faculty posts at Juilliard School; Bard Coll.; Brooklyn Coll.; and from 1975, at Yale Univ.

WORKS: BALLET: Performance, for Jose Limon; ORCHESTRA: concerto for violin and small orch., 1956; concerto for string orch.; The sound of time, soprano and orch., 1965; Incenters, trumpet, horn, trombone, orch., 1968; Minnesota Orch., 30 Nov. 1973; Windows, 1970, New York Premiere, 16 Jan. 1975; Lamia, soprano and orch., 1974; Mirage, with off-stage orch., St. Louis, 4 Mar. 1976; Chiaroscuro, 1976, Cleveland, 14 Apr. 1977; viola concerto, New York, 2 Nov. 1978; Aureole, dedicated to Leonard Bernstein, who conducted it with the New York Philharmonic, 9 June 1979; Prism, commissioned by the Baltimore Symph. and performed in Baltimore, 21 May 1980; CHAMBER MUSIC: 3 string quartets; Dark upon the harp, voice, brass quintet, percussion, 1962;

DRUMMOND, DEAN

Valentine, solo double bass (the player uses a mallet, vocal sounds, and reads aloud the instructions), 1972, Boston, 30 Oct. 1976; brass quintet, 1976; CHORUS: Antiphonies, double chorus, a cappella, 1963; 4 madrigals, with soprano solo, 1968; ELECTRONIC: Animus I, trombone and tape, 1966; Animus II, mezzo-soprano, percussion and tape, 1969; Animus III, clarinet and tape, 1969; Orison, organ and tape, 1970; Delizie contente che l'alme beate, wood-wind quintet and tape, 1973, performed Tanglewood, 6 Aug. 1978.
    780 Riverside Dr., New York, NY 10032

DRUMMOND, DEAN
b. Santa Monica, Calif., 22 Jan. 1949. Studied at Univ. of Southern California; with Leonard Stein at California Inst. of the Arts; was assistant to Harry Partch at Univ. of California, San Diego. He received the Margaret Grant Memorial Composition prize, 1976.
    WORKS: CHAMBER MUSIC: Ghost tangents, prepared piano, percussion, 1973; Cloud garden I, flute, piano, percussion, 1974; Cloud garden II, piano, celeste, almglocken, 1974; Zurrjir, flute, clarinet, piano, percussion, 1976; Dirty Ferdie, percussion quartet, 1976; Post rigabop mix, flute solo, 1977; Copegoro for zoomoozophone (31-tone metalophone built by composer) and percussion, 1978.
    698 West End Ave., #2C, New York, NY 10025

DUBBIOSI, STELIO
b. Naples, Italy, 25 Aug. 1929; U.S. citizen 1947. Studied with Vittorio Giannini, Manhattan School of Music, M.M. 1953. He has been chairman, music department, Jersey City State Coll., from 1967.
    WORKS: OPERA: The pied piper, 1966; ORCHESTRA: piano concerto; CHORUS: mass to honor St. Barbara.
    12 Glenwood Ave., Demarest, NJ 07627

DUBENSKY, ARCADY
b. Viatka, Russia, 15 Oct. 1890; to U.S. 1921; d. Tenafly, N.J., 14 Oct. 1966. Studied violin and conducting at Moscow Cons. He was first violinist, Moscow Imperial Opera Theatre Orch., 1910-19; was violinist with the New York Symphony, then the New York Philharmonic until retirement in 1953.
    WORKS: THEATRE: Romance with double bass, comic opera, 1936; ORCHESTRA: Russian bells, symphonic poem, 1927; Gossips, string orch., 1928; prelude and fugue, 1932; fugue for 18 violins, 1932; Tom Sawyer, overture, 1935; Political suite, 1936; Fantasy on a Negro theme, tuba and orch., 1938; Stephen Foster suite, 1940; Trumpet overture for 18 toy trumpets and 2 bass drums, 1949; trombone concerto, 1953; CHAMBER MUSIC: suite for 9 flutes, 1935; fugue for 4 bassoons, 1946.

DUCKWORTH, WILLIAM
b. Morgantown, N.C., 13 Jan. 1943. Studied with Ben Johnston, Thomas Fredrickson, Salvatore Martirano, Robert Kelly, Univ. of Illinois; with Martin Mailman, East Carolina Univ. His awards

include grand prize, Cleveland Inst. of Music Percussion Composition Contest, 1968; first prize, Competition for New String Music, 1973; first prize, 1974 Bowdoin Competition, Bowdoin Coll.; Pennsylvania Composers' Project award, 1974; Nat. Endowment for the Arts fellowship, 1977. He was faculty member, Atlantic Christian Coll., 1966-73; from 1973, at Bucknell Univ.
    WORKS: ORCHESTRA: When in eternal lines to time thou grow'st, 1970; Consort music, woodwind quintet and strings, 1977; BAND: Fragments, solo saxophone, winds, percussion, 1967; The Sleepy Hollow Elementary School Band, 20 to 60 instrumentalists, 1968; CHAMBER MUSIC: An unseen action, flute, prepared piano, percussion, 1966; Non-ticking tenuous tintinnabule time, 4 electric metronomes and percussion quartet, 1968; A ballad in time and space, saxophone and piano, 1968; Pitch city, any 4 wind players, 1969; A whispering. . ., 7 or more percussion, 1972; Gymel, 4 percussionists, 1973; 7 shades of blue, flute, clarinet, piano trio, 1974; Sunshine dancing music, 4 or more melody instruments, 1975; Silent signals, percussion, 1976; A book of hours, flute, clarinet, piano trio, 1976; Binary images, 2 pianos, 1977; 40 changes, 2 pianos, 1977; CHORUS: Spring dreams and autumn questions, with narrator and brass quintet, 1967; A peace for 20 voices, 1968; A mass for these forgotten times, 1973; MIXED MEDIA: Gambit, solo percussion and tape, 1967; Knight to King's Bishop 4, solo dancer and gong, 1968; Western exit, chamber ensemble, announcer, movie, slides, 1969; Walden, any number of instruments, dancers, readers, slides, movie, lights, 1970; Walden variations, 1971; Midnight blue, saxophone and tape, 1976; also piano works, songs.
    Music Dept., Bucknell University, Lewisburg, PA 17837

DUDA, THEODOR
b. Cleveland, Ohio, 24 Mar. 1951. Studied with Loris Chobanian, Baldwin-Wallace Coll.; with H. Owen Reed, Michigan State Univ. He received Columbia Univ. Bearns prize, 1975, for Faust soliloquy. He has been faculty member, Mary Coll., Bismarck, from 1975; conductor, Bismarck-Mandan Civic Chorus, from 1977.
    WORKS: VOICE: Cantata #1: Bird songs, soprano, chamber ensemble, 1973; Cantata #2: Faust soliloquy, baritone and orch., 1974; Cantata #3: All love shall sleep, baritone and chamber ensemble, 1976; Tzur Yisrael, contralto, chorus, percussion, 1976; Salve Regina, chorus, chamber ensemble, 1976; Benediction, a cappella chorus, 1977; Veni, Sancte Spiritus, chorus and percussion, 1978.
    500 W. Broadway, Bismarck, ND 58501

DUDDY, JOHN H.
b. Norristown, Pa., 19 Dec. 1904. Studied at Temple Univ., B.M., M.A.; Philadelphia Musical Acad.; Christian Church School; Westminster Choir School; Princeton Univ.; and with H. Alexander Matthews. He has been church organist and teachers in various schools; was chairman, vocal dept., Lutheran Theological Seminary, Philadelphia. He has written many songs, organ pieces, and choral works.

DUDLEY, MARJORIE EASTWOOD
b. S.Dak.; d. Taught at Univ. of South Dakota.
Her compositions included a piano concerto, a
symphony, string quartet, many works for chamber
groups and vocal solos.

DUESENBERRY, JOHN
b. Boston, Mass., 10 Oct. 1950. Studied with
John Goodman, Joyce Mekeel, and Allen Schindler,
Boston Univ., B.M. 1974; with Robert Stern, Univ.
of Massachusetts, Amherst; and at Boston School
of Electronic Music, where he is faculty member.
His awards include first and second prizes,
Boston Univ. composition contest, 1974.
WORKS: CHAMBER MUSIC: movement for string
quartet, 1973-74; VOICE: 3 songs from a season
in hell, mezzo-soprano and piano, 1973; Und fast
ein Madchen Wars, soprano, string trio, woodwind
trio, 1976; Plath poems, women's chorus, winds,
brass, percussion, harp, solo strings, 1977-78;
ELECTRONIC: Ellipse, amplified piano, electric
piano, 1974; 6:02, tape, 1974; 3:19, tape, 1975;
incidental music for The sleep of reason, tape,
1975; 3 variations, 2 interludes, tape, 1976;
movements for tape and prepared piano, 1977;
Phrase, tape, 1977.
25 Fairmont St., Belmont, MA 02178

DUFFY, JOHN
b. New York, N.Y., 23 June 1928. Studied at New
School for Social Research; Tanglewood; and
Lenox School of Jazz; his teachers were Aaron
Copland, Luigi Dallapiccola, Solomon Rosowsky,
Ludwig Lenel. His awards include the Berkshire
Bicentennial award; 7 ASCAP awards; Outstanding
Composer in Theatre award. He was music director
and/or composer Antioch and American Shakespeare
Festivals; Vivian Beaumont and Tyrone Guthrie
theatres, 1956-74; director, Meet the Composer,
from 1974.
WORKS: THEATRE: Everyman absurd, music
drama, ABC TV; music for Hamlet, Midsummer
night's dream, et al.; ORCHESTRA: clarinet con-
certo; Antiquity of freedom; BAND: concerto for
Stan Getz and concert band; CHAMBER MUSIC:
toccata and fugue, piccolo and percussion;
CHORUS: Oh freedom; songs on texts of Joyce,
Brecht, Rosenberg.
120 W. 70th St., New York, NY 10023

DUGGER, EDWIN
b. Poplar Bluff, Mo., 21 Mar. 1940. Studied
with Richard Hoffmann at Oberlin Cons.; with
Roger Sessions, Earl Kim, Milton Babbitt,
Princeton Univ. He received a Fromm Found. commission, 1969; Koussevitzky Found. commission,
1973; Guggenheim fellowship, 1973. He was
faculty member, Oberlin Cons., 1967-69; Univ. of
California, Berkeley, from 1969.
WORKS: CHAMBER MUSIC: Structure, chamber
orch.; Divisions of time, woodwind quartet,
piano, percussion, 1962; Intermezzi, 12 performers, 1969; Fantasy, piano, 1977; duo, flute
and viola, 1979; Variations and adagio, 9 performers, 1979; MIXED MEDIA: music for synthesizer and 6 instruments, 1966; Abwesenheiten und
Wiedersehen, 11 performers and tape, 1971; Adieu,
wind and percussion ensembles and tape.
268 Columbia Ave., Kensington, CA 94708

DUKE, JOHN WOODS
b. Cumberland, Md., 30 July 1899. Studied with
Gustav Strube at Peabody Cons., 1915-18; with
Bernard Wagenaar in New York; and in 1929-30,
with Nadia Boulanger in Paris and Artur Schnabel
in Berlin. His awards include the Peabody
Alumni Assoc. award for distinguished service to
music, 1969; annual ASCAP awards for 18 years.
He was professor and teacher of piano at Smith
Coll., 1923-67; then professor emeritus.
WORKS: THEATRE: The cat that walked by
itself, children's musical, 1944; Love among the
ruins, faculty show, 1952; Captain Lovelock,
1-act chamber opera, 1953; The Sire de Maletroit,
1-act chamber opera, 1957; The Yankee pedlar,
1-act operetta, 1962; ORCHESTRA: concerto for
piano and strings, 1938; Carnival overture, 1940;
CHAMBER MUSIC: suite for viola alone, 1933;
string trio, 1937; Fantasy, violin and piano,
1936; 2 string quartets, 1941, 1967; Narrative,
viola and piano, 1942; piano trio, 1943; Dialogue, cello and piano, 1943; Melody, cello and
piano, 1946; CHORUS: O sing unto the Lord a new
song, women's voices and string orch. or organ,
1955; Magnificat, unison chorus and organ, 1961;
3 river songs, text from the Chinese, women's
voices and piano, 1963; and nearly 200 songs.
82 Harrison Ave., Northampton, MA 01060

DUKE, VERNON (DUKELSKY, VLADIMIR)
b. Russia, 10 Oct. 1903; U.S. citizen 1936;
d. Santa Monica, Calif., 16 Jan. 1969. Studied
at Kiev Cons. He adopted the name Vernon Duke
as a pen name for his lighter compositions, then
in 1955 dropped Dukelsky entirely.
WORKS: OPERA: Yvonne, operetta, 1926;
Demoiselle Paysanne, opera, 1928; BALLET: Zephyr
and Flora, 1925; Public gardens, 1935; Le bal
des blanchiseuses, 1946; Souvenir de Monte Carlo,
1956; ORCHESTRA: piano concerto, 1924; 3 symphonies, 1928, 1930, 1947; violin concerto, 1943;
cello concerto, 1946; CHAMBER MUSIC: Trio variations, flute, bassoon, piano, 1930; Etude,
bassoon, piano, 1932; Capriccio Mexicano, violin
and piano, 1933; 3 pieces for woodwinds, 1939;
violin sonata, 1949; string quartet, 1956;
CHORUS: Dushenka, women's voices and chamber
orch., 1927; Epitaph, on the death of Diaghilev,
with soprano and orch., 1932; The end of St.
Petersburg, oratorio, 1937; Moulin Rouge, 1941;
SONGS: The musical zoo, Ogden Nash text, 1946;
A Shropshire lad, song cycle, 1949; An Italian
voyage; 6 songs on poems of Emily Bronte; PIANO:
sonata, 1927; Surrealist suite, 1944; Souvenir de
Venice, 1948; Serenade to San Francisco, 1956;
also many scores for musicals and films, and
popular songs.

DUNBAR, RUDOLPH
b. British Guiana, 5 Apr. 1907; to U.S. 1909.
Graduated from Juilliard School in 1928; studied
also in Paris, Leipzig, and Vienna. He was a
conductor and made his London debut in 1942,
Paris in 1944. His compositions include a ballet:
Dance of the 21st century.

DUNCAN, JAMES L.
b. Clarksville, Mo., 14 June 1926. Studied with

DUNCAN, JOHN

A. I. McHose and Anthony Donato at Eastman
School of Music. He is faculty member, Univ. of
Southern Colorado. His compositions include
Psalm for Palm Sunday, a sketch for orchestra.
3101 Vail Ave., Pueblo, CO 81005

DUNCAN, JOHN
b. Lee County, Ala., 25 Nov. 1913. Studied at
Temple Univ., B.M., M.M.; later with Philip
James at New York Univ. His awards include an
honorary D.M.A., Alabama State Univ., 1974; and
commissions. He was faculty member, Alabama
State Univ., 1963-75.
WORKS: OPERA: Gideon and Eliza; The hellish
banditi, 1974; ORCHESTRA: trombone concerto;
CHAMBER MUSIC: Divertimento, trombone and
string quartet; Black bards, flute, cello, piano;
Atavistic, string quartet; CHORUS: Burial of
Moses, a cantata.

DUNFORD, BENJAMIN C.
b. Winston-Salem, N.C., 2 Sept. 1917. Studied
with Charles Vardell, Salem Coll., B.M.; with
Kent Kennan, Univ. of Texas, M.M.; with Bernard
Rogers, Herbert Elwell, Wayne Barlow, Howard
Hanson, Eastman School of Music, Ph.D. He won
an award, Annual Southwestern Symposium of American Music, Austin, Tex., 1956. He has been
composer, conductor, arranger, lecturer, organist,
from 1935; was faculty member, Montreal Coll.,
1955-59; William Carey Coll., 1963-75.
WORKS: OPERA: The 12 dancing princesses;
CHORUS: The promise, sacred cantata; Psalm 103,
with baritone solo, brass, percussion; The un-
speakable gift, Christmas cantata; some 1000
works, choral, instrumental, commissioned and
performed.

DUNGAN, OLIVE
b. Pittsburgh, Pa., 19 July 1903. Studied at
Pittsburgh Inst. of Musical Art; Univ. of Miami;
and Univ. of Alabama. She was the first recipient of the Chi Omega Bertha Foster award. She
has been piano recitalist and teacher. Her compositions include many songs, choral works, and
Tropic night suite for piano, 4 hands.
650 Northeast 68th St., Miami, FL 33138

DUNING, GEORGE
b. Richmond, Ind., 25 Feb. 1908. Studied at
Cincinnati Cons.; Univ. of Cincinnati; and with
Castelnuovo-Tedesco.
WORKS: FILM SCORES: From here to eternity;
Miss Sadie Thompson; Salome; Picnic; The Eddie
Duchin story; Toys in the attic; many others;
numerous songs.
2119 Lyans Dr., La Canada, CA 91011

DUNN, DAVID
b. San Diego, Calif., 22 May 1953. Studied
privately with David Ernst, Norman Lowrey, David
Ward-Steinman, and Kenneth Gaburo; and served
4 years as assistant to Harry Partch. He received a Nat. Endowment for the Arts grant, 1977.
He was director of the electronic music studio
at San Diego State Univ., 1973-78.
WORKS: MIXED MEDIA: Nexus I, trumpets and
reverberant geography, 1973; Nexus II, environ-

mental sound sculpture with electronics, 1974;
Aura, cetacean communication stimulus for 18
voices and electronics, 1974; Oracles, 10 environmental stimulus works for various media,
1975; Wind trace, 5 voices and tape, 1977; Sky
drift, 10 voices, 16 instruments, and tape, 1978.
4508 37th St., San Diego, CA 92116

DUNN, GARY
b. Los Angeles, Calif., 10 Mar. 1950. Studied
with Nikhil Banerjee and Kani Dutta in Oakland,
Calif.; with Morton Feldman, Armand Russell, and
Neil McKay, Univ. of Hawaii; with Morgan Powell,
Univ. of Illinois.
WORKS: LARGE ENSEMBLES: Sunness, 23 instruments including shakuhachi, vyuteki, hichi-
riki, koto, bass koto, and biwa; Coming is going,
percussion solo for 19 instruments; Sounding
high-koo, percussion ensemble of 4, 8, 12, or 16
players; SMALL ENSEMBLES: Ensemble I, II, III,
solo violin, duets, or trio; From the willow,
percussion and cello; Wed, percussion and cello;
3 images of a dove's passing, violin and cello;
To the ant, piano solo; Asa gao no tsuru, 8 instruments.
95-537 Wailoale, Mililani Town, HI 96789

DUNN, JAMES PHILIP
b. New York, N.Y., 10 Jan. 1884; d. Jersey City,
N.J., 24 July 1936. Studied at City Coll. of
New York; with Edward MacDowell and Cornelius
Rybner, Columbia Univ. He was church organist
in New York and New Jersey.
WORKS: OPERA: The galleon; ORCHESTRA: We,
tone poem on Lindbergh's flight across the
Atlantic, New York, 27 Aug. 1927; Overture on
Negro themes, 1927; CHAMBER MUSIC: 2 string
quartets; piano quintet; violin sonata; VOICE:
The phantom drum, a cantata; songs.

DUNN, REBECCA WELTY
b. Guthrie, Okla., 23 Sept. 1890. Studied at
Washburn Coll.; Southwestern Coll.; and with
Otto Fischer, Friends Univ. She won a national
first prize for her operetta Sunny, and a Kansas
Authors Club prize for Purple on the moon.
WORKS: CHORUS: Channels of thy grace;
Halleluiah rain; other choral works and songs.

DU PAGE, FLORENCE
b. Vandergrift, Pa., 20 Sept. 1910. Studied
with Rubin Goldmark, Aurelio Giorni, and Tibor
Serly. She taught in private schools on Long
Island, N.Y., 1954-69.
WORKS: THEATRE: Trial universelle, chamber
opera; New world for Nellie, ballad opera;
Whither, sacred drama for soloists, chorus, and
chamber orch.; ORCHESTRA: Alice in Wonderland,
ballet suite; The pond, Eastman American Composers Festival; Lost valley, Chautauqua Symphony; CHAMBER MUSIC: Rondo, trombone and piano;
Variations on Von Himmel hoch, brass quartet.
3760 Harts Mill Lane, Atlanta, GA 30139

DU PAGE, RICHARD
b. Kansas City, Mo., 10 Aug. 1908. Studied at
Washington and Lee Univ.; Vanderbilt Law School;
music with Rubin Goldmark, Aurelio Giorni, John

Erb, and Tibor Serly. He has been arranger for stage shows, dance orchestras, radio; conducted the Sperry (Gyroscope) Orch.; was staff member, WOR, 1946-53.
WORKS: ORCHESTRA: Polyrhythmic overture; Variations on an Irish theme; Prelude for harp and orch.; Prelude and blues; Symphonic song; In the valley of Morpheus; Afghanistan; and several suites.

DURE, ROBERT
b. Baltimore, Md., 25 Nov. 1934. Studied with Louis Cheslock and Robert Hall Lewis, Peabody Cons.; with Lester Trimble and Morton Subotnick, Univ. of Maryland; with Subotnick at Bennington, Vt. He held scholarships at Peabody Cons. and at the Bennington Composers Conf.; other awards include commissions. He was faculty member, Prince Georges County Community Coll., 1965-67; from 1977, Indiana Univ. at Southbend; has also been choir director and active in opera groups.
WORKS: ORCHESTRA: King Lear, with solo voice; Preludium; Piece for 8; CHAMBER MUSIC: Analytic melody, violin and piano; Canon for winds, woodwind trio; movements for string quartet; String quartet--1965; 3 episodes for solo clarinet; Excursion--'67, violin, viola, piano; many choral works, songs, organ and piano pieces.
5336 W. Johnson Rd., La Porte, IN 46350

DURHAM, LOWELL M.
b. Boston, Mass., 4 Mar. 1917. Studied at Univ. of Utah; with Philip Greeley Clapp and Addison Alspach, Univ. of Iowa; privately with Leroy Robertson. His awards include several commissions. He has been professor, Univ. of Utah, from 1946.
WORKS: ORCHESTRA: suite for string orch., 1943; Prelude and scherzo, string orch., 1944; New England pastorale, string orch., 1955; Variations for strings, 1960; Folkscape for orch., 1967; CHORUS: This is my country, double chorus, 1961, performed by the Tabernacle Choir in Jan. 1964 at President Johnson's inauguration and again at President Nixon's inauguration; Calm as a summer morn, with orch., 1971; Choralise, a cappella, 1972.
Music Dept., Univ. of Utah, Salt Lake City, UT 84112

DUSHKIN, DOROTHY
b. Chicago, Ill., 26 July 1903. Studied with Werner Josten at Smith Coll.; with Nadia Boulanger in Paris. She was awarded honors in music at Smith Coll. and performances of a choral and an orchestral work; received prize for a quintet in a Chicago competition. She was cofounder and director of the Winnetka (Ill.) Music School, 1931-52; and of Kinhaven Music School, Weston, Vt., 1952-78.
WORKS: ORCHESTRA: concerto for orch.; piano concerto; suite for strings; CHAMBER MUSIC: 3 quintets for piano and woodwinds; quintet for oboe and strings; quintet for flute and strings; woodwind octet; sextet for woodwinds, piano, and horn; suite for 4 woodwinds and 4 strings; 2 suites for percussion ensemble; chorale for 2

brass antiphonal choirs; brass septet; sonatas for bassoon, flute, horn, 2 celli; CHORUS: Canaan bound, cantata; Light of man; 4 works for women's voices; 3 songs; 10 poems in filigree; On Paumonok shore; Songs of Bengal.
Weston, VT 05161

DUTTON, BRENTON PRICE
b. Saskatoon, Sask., 20 Mar. 1950. Studied with Richard Hoffmann, Randolph Coleman, and Walter Aschaffenberg, Oberlin Coll., B.M. 1975, M.M. 1976; electronic music with Edward Miller; seminar study with Henry Brant, Yannis Xenakis, Ernst Krenek, and Pierre Boulez. His awards include Yaddo fellowship, 1977; Central Michigan Univ. grant, 1977; various Canada Council Travel grants, 1972-75. He was teaching assistant, Oberlin Coll., 1974-76; faculty member, Central Michigan Univ., from 1976; played tuba with the Cleveland Orch., 1970-76.
WORKS: ORCHESTRA: 2 symphonies; CHAMBER MUSIC: Tuesday overture, tuba and percussion; brass trio; Short piece and variations, brass sextet; tuba concerto, with 6 brass, percussion, piano; Areas of concern, percussion quartet; On looking back, brass quartet; Song of the moon, solo flute; December set, woodwind quintet; several pieces for tuba solo, duet, trio, etc.
320 E. High St., Mt. Pleasant, MI 48858

DUTTON, FREDERIC M.
b. San Jose, Calif., 26 Apr. 1928. Studied with Lukas Foss and Wolfgang Fortner. He has been arranger with the Dave Brubeck Quartet, Stan Kenton and Les Brown big bands, Chamber Jazz Sextet, Southwest Radio Symph. Orch., and South Radio Entertainment Orch. (Germany), and the Los Angeles Philharmonic.
WORKS: ORCHESTRA: flute concerto; concerto for English horn and strings; CHAMBER MUSIC: Bits and pieces, brass quartet; octet for trumpets; quintet for oboe, clarinet, viola, cello, bass; Rondymith, solo trumpet.
19553 Gault St., Reseda, CA 91335

DVORAK, ROBERT
Lament and repose, brass ensemble; Songs of deliverance, a cantata; West Point symphony for band.
2423 S. Austin Blvd., Cicero, IL 60650

DVORINE, SHURA
Graduated from Peabody Cons., 1943; joined the Preparatory School faculty, 1971.
WORKS: BALLET: The lovers' concerto, 1967; The ballet school; Ballet #3, 1972; Ballet school II, 1973; PIANO: Pensive nocturne, 1948. He was commissioned by the Union of Hebrew Congregations to write an experimental service which was performed in Chicago, Nov. 1962.
Peabody Cons., 1 E. Mt. Vernon Pl., Baltimore, MD 21202

DWORAK, PAUL EDWARD
b. Natrona, Pa., 25 Jan. 1951. Studied with Roland Leich and Leonardo Balada at Carnegie-Mellon Univ. He was consultant and instructor, Pittsburgh Center for the Musically Talented,

DYDO, J. STEPHEN

1971-73; faculty member, Carnegie-Mellon Univ., from 1973.

WORKS: A serial/aleatoric quintet for strings and winds, 1972; Chromokinetics, a study in timbral contrasts and organization, for computer-generated tape, 1973. Dworak believes this was the first original work composed and performed in Pittsburgh using the Stanford Univ. Score compiler.

329 Morewood Ave., Pittsburgh, PA 15213

DYDO, J. STEPHEN

b. San Francisco, Calif., 2 May 1948. Studied with Jack Beeson, Benjamin Boretz, Chou Wenchung, Mario Davidovsky, Harvey Sollberger, Vladimir Ussachevsky, and Charles Wuorinen, Columbia Univ. His awards include the Bearns prize, 1972; BMI award, 1972; Composers' Conf. fellowship, 1975; Nat. Endowment for the Arts grant, 1976; American Music Center grant, 1977. He has been faculty member, the New School, from 1977; director, Composers Ensemble, from 1977.

WORKS: ORCHESTRA: Capriccio, piano and orch.; violin concerto, 1975; CHAMBER MUSIC: trio sonata, 1972, New York, 5 May 1977; Carmina, for percussion, 1976; Capriccio, violin and 7 instruments, 1977; VOICE: mass for voices and instruments, 1971.

90 Morningside Dr., New York, NY 10027

EAKIN, CHARLES

b. Pittsburgh, Pa., 24 Feb. 1927. Studied with Vittorio Giannini, Manhattan School of Music; with Nikolai Lopatnikoff, Carnegie-Mellon Univ.; and with Paul Fetler, Univ. of Minnesota. He was faculty member, Baylor Univ., 1960-64; then professor, Univ. of Colorado.

WORKS: THEATRE: The box, 1-act opera; Being of sound mind, opera; Pasticcio, speaking chorus, 3 dancers, 3 actors; ORCHESTRA: Dialogues, cello, percussion, orch.; Spontaneities, jazz group and orch.; CHAMBER MUSIC: Paul's piece, violin, piano, percussion; Capriccio, viola alone; Capriccio, cello alone; PIANO: Passacaglia; Frames; Improvisation, with harp; MIXED MEDIA: Tonight I am, soprano and tape.

350 S. 41st St., Boulder, CO 80303

EAKIN, VERA O.

b. Emlenton, Pa., 6 Aug. 1890. Studied with Ernest Hutcheson, New England Cons.; at Juilliard School; and organ privately with Hugh Giles. Her honors include many Nat. Fed. of Music Clubs awards, the most recent, 1973. She was staff pianist and coach at CBS, and organist in the greater New York area for over 30 years.

WORKS: SONGS: Ay, gitanos; Flamenco gypsy moon; Wind and girl; Christmas morn; The place prepared for thee. Her concert songs were sung by well-known singers, such as Lawrence Tibbett, James Melton, Eileen Farrell, etc.

EARLS, PAUL

b. Springfield, Mo., 9 June 1934. Studied with Bernard Rogers and Howard Hanson, Eastman School of Music. His awards include the Benjamin prize, 1958; Guggenheim, Fulbright, MacDowell, and Yaddo fellowships; Huntington Hartford Found. and

Mary Duke Biddle Found. grants; and 2 Nat. Endowment for the Arts grants, 1974, 1977. He has held faculty posts at Southwest Missouri State Coll.; Duke Univ.; Chabot Coll.; Univ. of Oregon; Univ. of Lowell; from 1970, Mass. Inst. of Technology, Center for Advanced Visual Studies; and from 1972, lecturer, Mass. Coll. of Art.

WORKS: THEATRE: Flight, chamber opera; The death of King Philip, 1-act opera, 1975, Boston, 26 Mar. 1976; A Grimm duo (Dog and sparrow, Bremen Town Musicians) 2 1-act operas, Boston, 31 Dec. 1976; Icarus, a sky opera; Washington, D.C., Sept. 1978; ORCHESTRA: And on the 7th day. . ., chamber orch., 1959; BAND: A band of Solomon's dukes, 1968; WERK, 1972; CHAMBER MUSIC: Nun danket fantasy, organ, 1963; Huguenot variations, organ, 1963; string quartet, 1968; 5 notables, violin solo, 1968; Preparation, organ, 1968; Coronach for K, K, K, piano, 1968; Alpha/numeric: E, aleatoric work for 3 to 7 players, any instruments, 1970; Doppelgänger, oboe and lasers, 1976; CHORUS: Psalm 100, 1961; The Lord's prayer, children's choir, organ or brass, 1963; Brevis Mass, choir and instruments, 1967; Trine, 1967; Alpha/numeric I: Prologue and 10 events, 1970; What's in a name, participatory audience piece, 1972; The bells, Poe text, double chorus, brass, percussion, tape, 1976; MIXED MEDIA: Divisions in 12, 2 pianos and tape, 1967; trio/duo, tape, violin, piano, 1969; Laser loop #1, deflection of laser by music (with Ted Kraynik), Tel Aviv, May 1971; Processional music, Buchla and Moog with brass and percussion, MIT commencement, June 1971; Joyce, 5 readers and tape, 1972; Dialogue: Music and . . ., New York, 24 Feb. 1974; Environmental music and light, tape and light, 1975; Sound, movement, light, event for opening of the Boston Visual Arts Union exhibit, May 1976; Dreamstage, electronic music and laser projections from a sleeping subject, San Francisco, Mar.-Apr. 1978; Centerbeam, music and laser projections, Air and Space Museum, Washington, July-Sept. 1978.

40 Mass. Ave., Cambridge, MA 02139

EASTMAN, JULIUS

b. New York, N.Y., 27 Oct. 1940. Studied with Constant Vauclain at Curtis Inst. of Music. He was professor, State Univ. of New York at Buffalo, 1971-75.

WORKS: ORCHESTRA: symphony, 1969; CHAMBER MUSIC: Trumpet, for any 7 soprano instruments, 1970, New York, 2 May 1973; Stay on it, 2 singers and instruments, 1973; Wood in time, 8 amplified metronomes, 1973; CHORUS: Thruway, with instruments, 1970; The moon's silent modulation, with instruments, narrators, and 3 dancers, 1969.

106 Elmwood Ave., Buffalo, NY 14201

EATON, JOHN C.

b. Bryn Mawr, Pa., 30 Mar. 1935. Studied with Roger Sessions, Milton Babbitt, and Edward T. Cone, Princeton Univ., B.A., M.F.A. His awards include the Prix de Rome, 1959, 1960, 1961; 2 Guggenheim fellowships, 1962, 1964; commissions from Fromm Found., 1966; Koussevitzky Found., 1969, Public Broadcasting Corp., 1970; award and citation, Nat. Inst. of Arts and Letters, 1972; Indiana State Arts Council plaque, 1974; composer-in-residence in Rome, 1975-76. He has been professor, Indiana Univ., from 1970.

WORKS: OPERA: Ma Barker, 1957; Heracles, 1970; The lion and Androcles, children's opera, 1971; Myshkin, television opera based on Dostoyevsky's The idiot, 1970 (NET, Boston, 23 Apr. 1973); ORCHESTRA: Tertullian overture; Concert piece, Syn-Ket and orch., Tanglewood, 9 Aug. 1967; CHAMBER MUSIC: Piano variations, 1958; string quartet, 1959; Concert music, clarinet, 1961; Ajax; Microtonal fantasy, piano, 1965; Vibrations, winds, 1967; SONG CYCLES: Holy sonnets of John Donne, soprano and orch., 1957; Songs for R. P. B., soprano and Syn-Ket, 1964; Thoughts on Rilke, soprano and Syn-Ket, 1967; Blind man's cry, soprano and synthesizer ensemble, 1968; ELECTRONIC: many pieces for the Syn-Ket solo and in ensembles (the Syn-Ket is a portable synthesizer built by a Roman sound engineer).

828 S. Woodlawn, Bloomington, IN 47401

EBERHARD, DENNIS
b. Cleveland, Ohio, 9 Dec. 1943. Studied with Marie Martin, Cleveland Inst. of Music; with Frederick Coulter, Kent State Univ.; with Salvatore Martirano, Univ. of Illinois; and with Wlodzimierz Kotonski in Warsaw, Poland. His awards include BMI award, 1968; Fulbright fellowship, 1973-75; Nat. Endowment for the Arts grant, 1977; third prize, Gaudeamus Competition, 1977; Kate Neil Kinley Memorial fellowship, 1978; Rome prize, 1978. He was lecturer, Univ. of Illinois, 1972-73; faculty member, Western Illinois Univ., 1976-77.

WORKS: Anamorphoses, wind ensemble, 1967; Paraphrase, woodwind quintet, 1968; Mariner, 3 brass, percussion, cello, clavichord, tape, 6 loudspeakers, photosensitive sound distributors, 1969-70; 2 poems, clarinet and piano, 1971; Chamber music, percussion, 1971; Verse varied, amplified string quartet, 1971; Parody, soprano, chamber ensemble, percussion, 1972; Morphos, wind orch., 1973; Dialogues I, chamber ensemble, lights, 1973-74; Veillees, mezzo-soprano, 3 choirs, brass, percussion, 6 amplified contrabasses, 1974; Dialogues II, percussion/mime solo, tape, lights, projections, 1975; Ikona, tape, 1975; Marginals, antiphonal trombone quartet, 3 string groups, 1976; Visions of the moon, soprano, instrumental ensemble, text by e. e. cummings, 1978.

American Academy, Via Angelo Masina 5, 00153, Rome, Italy

EDDLEMAN, DAVID
b. Winston-Salem, N.C., 20 Aug. 1936. Studied at Appalachian State Univ., B.S.; with Milton Cherry, Virginia Commonwealth Univ., M.M. 1963; with Gardner Read, Boston Univ., D.M.A. 1971. He was public school music teacher, 1963-68; instructor, Boston Univ., 1968-72; music editor, N.J. publishing firm, from 1972.

WORKS: OPERA: The cure, 1965; CHAMBER MUSIC: brass quartet, 1971; Diversions, clarinet and piano, 1971; CHORUS: Continuum, 1972;

Sound and fury, 1972; Infinitude, 1972; Autumn, 2-part chorus, recorder, finger cymbal, 1974; The innkeeper's carol; Alleluia rock; Thanksgiving calypso; Christmas calypso; Folk beatitudes; many other choral works; SONGS: Silent sea; End of summer; I'm gonna walk; A song with no key.

12 James Court, Rockaway, NJ 07866

EDMONDSON, JOHN BALDWIN
b. Toledo, Ohio, 3 Feb. 1933. Studied with Russell Danburg, Univ. of Florida; with Kenneth Wright and Bernard Fitzgerald, Univ. of Kentucky. He was staff arranger, Univ. of Kentucky Band, 1963-70; band director in public schools, 1960-70; educational editor, Miami music publishing firm, from 1970.

WORKS: BAND: Hymn and postlude; Pagentry overture; Song for winds; Winchester march; Fantasy on a fanfare.

EDMUNDS, JOHN
b. San Francisco, Calif., 10 June 1913. Studied at Univ. of California, B.A.; with Rosario Scalero at Curtis Inst.; with Walter Piston, Harvard Univ., M.A.; Roy Harris at Cornell Univ.; and with Otto Leuning at Columbia Univ. His awards include the Bearns prize; Seidl traveling fellowship; Fulbright fellowship; Alice Ditson award; Italian government grant. He was head of the American Collection, Music Division, New York Public Library, 1957-61; director, American Music Center, 1957-61; from 1970, on faculty, Louisiana State Univ.

WORKS: CHORUS: Clambake on the Potomac; Come sweet peace; Shepherd's maze; Rites of Christmas; Lord God of hosts; many more choral works and several hundred songs. He is author of History of American music in pictures and coauthor, Some 20th-century American composers.

Music Dept., Louisiana State Univ., Baton Rouge, LA 70803

EDMUNDSON, GARTH
b. Pittsburgh, Pa., 11 Apr. 1895. Studied at Leipzig Cons.; with Harvey Gaul and Joseph Bonnet; and at Westminster Coll., D.M. He has been teacher and organist, Newcastle, Pa.

WORKS: ORGAN: 2 organ symphonies; 56 chorale preludes; In modum antiquum, suite; Toccata brilliante on All praise to thee; Epiphany; Gargoyles; 7 classic preludes; 7 contrapuntal preludes; 7 modern preludes; 7 polyphonic preludes; From heaven high, toccata.

EDWARDS, CLARA
b. Mankato, Minn., 18 Apr. 1887; d. New York, 17 Jan. 1974. Studied at Mankato State Normal School; Cosmopolitan School of Music; and in Europe. She was singer and pianist; wrote music for Tony Sarg's Marionettes and for animated films.

WORKS: SONGS: By the bend of the river; Into the night; With the wind and the rain in your face; The fisher's widow; Stars of the night; Sing softly; et al.

EDWARDS, GEORGE

EDWARDS, GEORGE
b. Boston, Mass., 11 May 1943. Studied with
Richard Hoffmann at Oberlin Coll.; with Milton
Babbitt and Earl Kim, Princeton Univ.; with
Donald Martino at Tanglewood. His awards include
the Koussevitzky prize, 1967; Prix de Rome fellowship, 1973-75; Naumburg Recording award,
1974; MacDowell fellowship, 1977; Guggenheim
fellowship, 1980. He was faculty member, New
England Cons., 1968-76; from 1976, at Columbia
Univ.
    WORKS: ORCHESTRA: 2 pieces for orchestra,
1964; Monopoly, 1973; Giro, 1974; CHAMBER MUSIC:
2 piano pieces; 2 bagatelles, piano; Bits, 1966;
string quartet, 1967; Double play, 2 pianos,
1970; The captive, soprano and 12 instruments,
1970; 3 Hopkins songs, soprano, 1971; Kreuz und
Quer, chamber group, 1971; Suspension bridge,
cello solo, New York, 15 Apr. 1974; Exchange-
Misère, chamber ensemble, 1974; Draconian
measures, piano, 1976.
    838 West End Ave., #3A, New York, NY 10025

EDWARDS, H. NEIL
b. Dalton, Ga., 12 Dec. 1931. Attended Univ. of
Georgia and Florida State Univ.; studied with
Charles Douglas and Everett Pittman. He taught
in public schools, 1956-64; was on faculty,
Brewton Parker Coll., 1964-66; and at Georgia
Southwestern Coll., 1967-73.
    WORKS: BAND: Suite religioso, 1962; Pride
of the red devils, 1964; Fanfare and chorale,
1965; March opus 2, 1969; CHAMBER MUSIC: brass
quartet, 1963; Trombone-piano apogee, 1964;
CHORUS: Psalm 118, 1965; It is enough, 1965;
Motet: In festo aposlotorum: Tollite jugum,
1965; ELECTRONIC: sound track for Sartre's No
exit, tape, 1968; Reverbo ostinato, fugue for
oscillator and tape recorder, 1970.

EDWARDS, LEO
b. Cincinnati, Ohio, 31 Jan. 1937. Studied with
Scott Huston in Cincinnati; with Norman Dello
Joio at Mannes Coll. of Music; and with Robert
Starer, City Univ. of New York. He was faculty
member, Mannes Coll., 1968-74; and at Brooklyn
Coll., CUNY, 1970-74.
    WORKS: ORCHESTRA: Fantasy overture, Lynd-
hurst, N.Y., 24 July 1971; CHAMBER MUSIC: string
quartet, 1968, rev. 1970; Etude for brass,
Brooklyn, 25 Apr. 1972; CHORUS: Psalm 150, with
soprano and orch., New York, 10 Dec. 1972.
    677 West End Ave., New York, NY 10025

EDWARDS, RYAN
Has had songs performed in New York, 1971, and
in Boston, 1975; flute work performed by Jean-
Pierre Rampal, 1973. He was accompanist for all
performances. He is faculty member, Yale Univ.
    322 W. 89th St., #3E, New York, NY 10024

EFFINGER, CECIL
b. Colorado Springs, Colo., 22 July 1914.
Studied with Bernard Wagenaar in Colorado
Springs; with Nadia Boulanger in France. His
awards include Presser scholarship in oboe,
1931; Stoval prize, 1939; Naumburg recording
award, 1959; honorary doctorate, Colorado Coll.,
1959; faculty fellowship, Univ. of Colorado,
1969; Governor;s award in Arts and Humanities,
Aspen, 1971. He was first oboist, Denver Symphony, 1937-41; music editor, Denver Post, 1946-
48; was faculty member, Colorado Coll., 1936-48;
Univ. of Colorado from 1948.
    WORKS: THEATRE: Pandora's box, short opera
for young people, 1961; Cyrano de Bergerac, 3-
act opera, 1965; The gentleman desperado and
Miss Bird, music drama, 1976; ORCHESTRA: 2 sinfoniettas, 1945, 1958; piano concerto, 1946; 5
symphonies, 1946-58; choral symphony, Denver,
2 Dec. 1952; Symphonie concertante, harp, piano
and orch., 1954; Trio concertante, trumpet,
horn, trombone, chamber orch., 1964; violin concerto, 1970; The long dimension, baritone,
chorus, and orch., 1970; Capriccio, Denver,
3 Mar. 1975; BAND: prelude and fugue, 1942;
Interlude on a blues tune, 1944; Silver plume,
1961; Let your mind wander over America, band,
chorus, strings, 1969; CHAMBER MUSIC: 4 string
quartets, 1943, 1944, 1948, 1963; viola sonata,
1944; suite, cello and piano, 1945; Melody,
clarinet and piano, 1947; Rondino, horn and
piano, 1949; Pastorale, oboe and strings; Dialogue, clarinet and piano, 1957; Solitude, saxophone and piano, 1960; Landscape, brass and
strings, 1966; Fantasia agitato, clarinet and
piano, 1972; CHORUS: Fanfare on Army chow call,
male chorus and brass, 1943; American men, male
chorus and band, 1942; Sing we merrily unto God,
with soli, organ, strings, 1948; Time, Shelley
text, a cappella, 1947; Shepherds in the field,
1955; Why was Cupid a boy?, 1955; A prairie
sunset, 1959; Behold thy brother man, 1962; 4
pastorales, with oboe, 1962; Forget not my law,
1967; Paul of Tarsus, oratorio with organ and
strings, 1968; Spring rain, a cappella, 1970;
Cantata for Easter, 1971; This we believe, oratorio, 1975.
    2620 Lafayette Dr., Boulder, CO 80303

EHLE, ROBERT C.
b. Lancaster, Pa., 7 Nov. 1939. Studied with
Louis Mennini, Bernard Rogers, Robert Sutton,
and Wayne Barlow, Eastman School of Music; with
Samuel Adler, Merrill Ellis, and Martin Mailman,
North Texas State Univ.; privately with William
Russo in New York. He was George Eastman fellow,
1961; received a Dallas Symphony-Rockefeller
award, 1966. He was faculty member, North Texas
State Univ., 1964-70; Univ. of Northern Colorado
from 1971.
    WORKS: ORCHESTRA: Soundpiece, 1966; A
space symphony; Jazz symphony, 12 to 18-piece
stage band; 1st and 2nd suites for stage band;
Folk song suite, string orch.; ELECTRONIC: 5
pieces for electronically prepared instruments;
Algorhythms, soprano and prepared instruments;
Ritual conflicts, electronics and orch.
    2107 26th Ave. Court, Greeley, CO 80631

EHRENKREUTZ, STEVE
b. 1949. Studied with Edward Cohen, Brandeis
Univ. Recollections and reflections, for orch.,
performed Boston, 13 May 1973.

EICHHEIM, HENRY
b. Chicago, Ill., 3 Jan. 1870; d. Montecito, Calif., 22 Aug. 1942. Graduated from Chicago Musical Coll. with the violin prize. He was member, Boston Symphony Orch., 1890-1912; then toured as soloist and conductor of his own works. He made several trips to the Orient, collected native instruments which he used in orchestral compositions. He wrote many works for orchestra and for chamber groups, all with Oriental themes.

EICHHORN, HERMENE WARLICK
b. Hickory, N.C., 3 Apr. 1906. Studied at Univ. of North Carolina, B.S.M.; and privately. She has been organist, Holy Trinity Episcopal Church, Greensboro, from 1926; wrote music column for the Greensboro Daily News, 1928-51. Her works include 3 cantatas: Mary Magdalene, Song of the highest, First Corinthians.
1504 Kirkpatrick Place, Greensboro, NC 27408

EILERS, JOYCE ELAINE
b. Mooreland, Okla., 28 July 1941. Studied at Oklahoma City Univ., B.M. 1963; Univ. of Oregon, M.M. She has taught in public schools from 1963.
WORKS: CHORUS: Tiny king; The gift; Born today; A star shone bright; many other published choral works.

EINHORN, RICHARD
b. Newark, N.J., 2 Aug. 1952. Studied with Jack Beeson and Gregory Kosteck; electronic music with Vladimir Ussachevsky, Mario Davidovsky, and Charles Dodge. He held a Presser scholarship; William Mitchell fellowship; and was Phi Beta Kappa. He was teaching assistant, Aspen Music Festival, 1975, 1976.
WORKS: CHAMBER MUSIC: duo for clarinet and bassoon; Arguments, string trio; ELECTRONIC: Foxtrot, tape; QN 152, tape (in collaboration with James Lauth); FILM SCORES: Shock wave; Iron Mountain.
345 Riverside Dr., #6A, New York, NY 10025

EISENSTEIN, ALFRED
b. Brody, Poland, 14 Nov. 1899; U.S. citizen 1948. Studied piano in Vienna with Anton Trost; is self-taught in composition. He has received ASCAP awards from 1966; New York State Audio Society award, 1967; citation by the Variety Club of Miami, 1974; Man of Achievement award, Cambridge, England, 1975.
WORKS: ORCHESTRA: Adagio lamentoso, tone poem; Impromptu, tone poem; Melodic reflections, cello and orch.; Movements for strings; Petite suite; Romance, violin and orch.; Souvenir, violin and orch.; Tango of love; SONGS: The fisherman; If you were mine; Life was beautiful; Love's grief; 2 castanets; Barcarolle; When I look into your eyes; Elegy; all songs have orchestral accompaniment.
18900 N.E. 14th Ave., N. Miami Beach, FL 33179

EISENSTEIN, STELLA PRICE
b. Glasgow, Mo., 16 Feb. 1886; d. Moberly, Mo., 28 Mar. 1969. Studied violin and piano at the Goetz Cons. in Moberly and at Cincinnati Cons.; later studied composition with Felix Borowski at Chicago Musical Coll., and organ with Hans Feil in Kansas City. She was awarded the associate degree in the American Guild of Organists, 1928. She toured as violinist in the Chautauqua series with the Price Concert Company, which included her mother and sister. After marriage, she settled in Moberly as violin, piano, and organ teacher. Her published works include Memories of the South for violin and piano, many anthems and organ works.

EL-DABH, HALIM
b. Cairo, Egypt, 4 Mar. 1921; U.S. citizen 1961. Graduated from Cairo Univ. with a degree in agricultural engineering, but turned full attention to music in 1949. He received a Fulbright fellowship for study in the U.S.; studied with Francis Judd Cooke, New England Cons., M.M. 1953; with Irving Fine and Aaron Copland at Tanglewood; at Brandeis Univ., M.F.A. 1954; also in New York at the Columbia-Princeton Electronic Music Laboratory. His awards include 2 Guggenheim fellowships, 1959, 1961. He has done field work and research in the U.S., Europe, and Africa, and has served widely as consultant; his most recent faculty posts have been at Howard Univ., 1966-69; and professor of ethnomusicology, Kent State Univ.
WORKS: BALLET: Clytemnestra, dance epic for Martha Graham, New York, 1 Apr. 1958; Ballet of lights, 1960; Lucifer, dancers and orch.; Black epic, actors, dancers, singers and orch.; ORCHESTRA: symphonies, 1951, 1952, 1955; concerto and Fantasia-Tahmeel for derabucca (Egyptian drum) or timpani, and strings, 1954; Symphonic eclogue, 1956; Bacchanalia, 1958; Agamemnon and Furies in Hades, 2 ballet suites for orch., 1958; House of Atreus, soprano, baritone, chorus, orch., 1958; Opera flies, based on the shootings at Kent State Univ., 1969, Washington, 5 May 1971; Unity at the cross roads, premiere at Alexandria and Cairo, Egypt, 1978; CHAMBER MUSIC: A look at "Shango" lightning, flute, English horn, bassoon, harp; Of gods and men, drums and piano, 1973; Family tree, Egyptian and Ethiopian string instruments; ELECTRONIC: Leiyla and the poet, 1962; Symphonies in sonic vibrations; Spectrum #1; Lament of the Pharaohs, sound and light, performed daily at the Great Pyramids at Giza, Egypt, 1960-77.
739 W. Main, Kent, OH 44240

ELISHA, HAIM
b. Jerusalem, Israel, 27 Sept. 1935; U.S. citizen 1969. Studied with Hanoch Jacoby and Mark Lavry, Rubin Acad. of Music, Israel; conducting, Juilliard School, B.M. 1962; New England Cons., M.M. 1968; composition with Hugo Weisgall, 1970-73. He was conductor, Cape Ann Symphony Orch., 1967-74; from 1968, has been professor, Rockland Community Coll., Suffern, N.Y.
WORKS: ORCHESTRA: 10 variations; Dance suite; CHAMBER MUSIC: 4 etudes, piano; Metamorphosis, brass quintet; 10 variations, cello and piano; 5 pieces for string trio; Kipurim 73, woodwind quintet and trumpet.
120 W. 86th St., New York, NY 10024

ELKUS, ALBERT

ELKUS, ALBERT
b. Sacramento, Calif., 30 Apr. 1884; d. Oakland, Calif., 19 Feb. 1962. Studied at Univ. of California, B.A., M.A.; piano with Harold Bauer and Josef Lhevinne. He taught at San Francisco Cons., Mills Coll., Univ. of California at Berkeley; was director, San Francisco Cons., 1951-57.

WORKS: ORCHESTRA: Impressions from a Greek tragedy (received a Juilliard award); concertino on Lezione III of Ariosti, cello and string orch.; CHAMBER MUSIC: Serenade, string quartet; violin sonata; CHORUS: I am the reaper; Sir Patrick Spens.

ELKUS, JONATHAN
b. San Francisco, Calif., 8 Aug. 1931, son of Albert Elkus. Studied with Charles Cushing, Univ. of California, Berkeley; with Ernst Bacon and Leonard Ratner, Stanford Univ.; and with Darius Milhaud at Mills Coll. He was bassoonist in the California Nat. Guard, 1949-57; faculty member, Lehigh Univ., 1957-73; visiting lecturer, Univ. of California at Davis, 1977.

WORKS: OPERA: Tom Sawyer, 1953; The outcasts of Poker Flat, 1960; Treasure Island, 1961; The mandarin, 1967; Medea, 1970; Helen in Egypt, 1970; BAND: Camino Real, 1955; The apocalypse, a rag, 1974; C C rag; Chiaroscuro, 1977; CHAMBER MUSIC: 5 sketches, 2 clarinets and bassoon, 1954; Triptych, mezzo-soprano and 4 bassoons, 1962; The charmer, clarinet, trombone, piano, 1972; also choruses and songs.
8 Pearl St., Provincetown, MA 02657

ELLINGTON, EDWARD KENNEDY (DUKE)
b. Washington, D.C., 29 Apr. 1899; d. New York, 23 May 1974. Noted bandleader, pianist, and composer. At the celebration of his 70th birthday at the White House gala in 1969, he was awarded the Presidential Medal of Freedom. The Swedish Acad. of Music elected him to membership in 1971; 2 African countries, Chad and Togo, have issued postage stamps bearing his picture; Yale Univ. in 1972 established the Duke Ellington Fellowship Fund "to preserve and perpetuate the Afro-American musical tradition"; in 1973 President Pompidou of France gave him the Legion of Honor; also in 1973 he was awarded an honorary doctorate at Columbia Univ. The young Edward took piano lessons at age 7 and ended this formal training at about the time he acquired the nickname Duke at age 8. From then on, he learned by listening and watching. He wrote his first piece, Soda fountain rag, when he was working as a soda jerk after school. By the time he was 20, he had his own small band, and in late 1927 took his expanded 10-piece band into the Cotton Club in Harlem. A nightly radio broadcast from the Cotton Club soon made the Ellington Band known throughout the country, and his unique style drew musicians of all schools to the Cotton Club. His first tour of Europe and Britain in 1933 established his reputation abroad. In the thirties, the band made 4 feature-length movies, in 1943-50 gave annual Carnegie Hall recitals, and in 1963 toured the Mideast for the State Dept. Through all this,

he maintained a steady pace of composing; his total number of works of varying length exceeds 6000.

WORKS: THEATRE: Jump for joy, Los Angeles, 1941; Beggar's holiday, lyrics by John Latouche, adapted from John Gay's Beggar's Opera, New York, 1947; Timon of Athens, background score; My people, pageant of black history, Chicago, 1963; The river, ballet, written for Alvin Ailey and the American Ballet Theatre, 1970; ORCHESTRA: Reminiscing in tempo, 1934; Diminuendo and crescendo, 1936; Black and tan fantasy; The mooche; Blue belles of Harlem, 1938; Creole love call; Mood indigo; East St. Louis toodleoo; Black, brown, and beige, 1943; New world a-comin, 1945; Deep South suite; Perfume suite (with William Strayhorn); Liberian suite, 1948; Togo bravo; Harlem, 1950; Night creatures, 1955; Such sweet thunder, Shakespearean suite (with Strayhorn), 1957; Suite Thursday, after Steinbeck's Sweet Thursday, 1960; CHORUS: In the beginning, God . . ., sacred music for orchestra, 3 choirs, soloists, dancer, performed at Grace Cathedral, San Francisco, 1965, repeated twice in New York in 1965; 2nd sacred concert, Cathedral Church of St. John the Divine, New York, 1968; 3rd sacred concert, Westminster Abbey, London, 1973; SONGS: Solitude; Sophisticated lady; In a sentimental mood; I let a song go out of my heart; I got it bad; FILM SCORES: (1956-71); Paris blues; Anatomy of a murder; Assault on a queen; Change of mind; Janus, a German film. The tune Duke Ellington used as a theme for many years and was probably most often associated with him, Take the A train, was not written by Ellington but by his long-time close associate and collaborator, William Strayhorn. Ellington's autobiography, Music is my mistress, was published in 1973.

ELLIOT, WILLARD SOMERS
b. Ft. Worth, Tex., 18 July 1926. Studied at North Texas State Univ., B.M.; with Bernard Rogers, Eastman School of Music, M.M. His awards include 2 Nat. Fed. of Music Clubs prizes, 1946, 1947; Koussevitzky Found. grant, 1960. He was bassoonist with the Houston Symph., 1946-49; Dallas Symph., 1951-64; has been solo bassoonist with the Chicago Symph. from 1969. He has been faculty member at North Texas State Univ., 1949-51; De Paul Univ., from 1974; Northwestern Univ., from 1977.

WORKS: ORCHESTRA: Hypnos and Psyche, tone poems; Quetzalcoatl; Elegy; Spring overture; symphony; bassoon concerto; concerto for 2 bassoons; The snake charmer, alto flute and orch.; CHAMBER MUSIC: trio for oboe, clarinet, bassoon; 2 Creole songs, oboe, clarinet, bassoon; duets for flute and bassoon; 6 15-th century French songs, for oboe, bassoon, piano; Poem, bassoon and string quartet; quintet for bassoon and strings; string quartet; sextet, 2 oboes, 2 clarinets, 2 bassoons.
9538 Central Park, Evanston, IL 60203

ELLIOTT, ALONZO
b. Manchester, N.H., 25 May 1891; d. Wallingford, Conn., 24 June 1964. Studied at Yale Univ.,

B.A.; Trinity Coll., Cambridge, England; Columbia Law School; with Nadia Boulanger, Fontainebleau; and with Leonard Bernstein. He received the Joseph Vernon prize in 1914.

WORKS: OPERA: El chivato; SONGS: There's a long, long trail a'winding; Bristol Eighth, Masefield text; Tulips; and many others.

ELLIOTT, MARJORIE REEVE (Mrs. Charles H.)
b. Syracuse, N.Y., 7 Aug. 1890. Studied with Adolph Frey at Syracuse Univ., B.M., honorary D.M. She received the Arents Pioneer award, Syracuse Univ., 1973; Centennial award, City of Syracuse, 1948; was 3 times guest of honor, Chicago Music Festival. She is composer, teacher, and head of her own studio; has published 400 choral and piano works.
4085 High Bridge Ave., Oneida, NY 13421

ELLIOTT, TIMOTHY ALLEN
b. Chicago, Ill., 21 May 1946. Studied with Ruth Shaw Wylie and Harold Laudenslager at Wayne State Univ. He has been a teacher in public and private schools in Detroit and has engaged in research on electronic music.
WORKS: CHAMBER MUSIC: Piano cycle, 6 pieces for piano solo; string quartet; 5 ensembles: #1, woodwinds, brass, percussion; #2, brass, woodwinds, string bass; #3, percussion; #4, string quintet, clarinet, percussion; #5, 9 instruments, piano, percussion, tape.
26405 Couzens, Madison Heights, MI 48071

ELLIS, DONALD JOHNSON (DON)
b. Los Angeles, Calif., 25 July 1934. Studied with Gardner Read, Boston Univ.; with John Vincent, Univ. of California, Los Angeles. He played first trumpet with the National Symphony Orchestra, then with various jazz bands, until forming his own group.
WORKS: CONCERT JAZZ: Contrasts for 2 orchestras and trumpet, 1965; Improvisational suite #1.
c/o MJQ Music, Inc., 200 W. 57th St., New York, NY 10019

ELLIS, MERRILL
b. Cleburne, Tex., 9 Dec. 1916. Studied at Oklahoma Univ., M.M.; Univ. of Missouri; composition privately with Roy Harris, Spencer Norton, and Charles Garland. His honors include ASCAP awards and commissions. He has been professor and director of the Electronic Music Center, North Texas State Univ., from 1962.
WORKS: Kaleidoscope, orchestra, synthesizer, mezzo-soprano; Nostalgia, 60 strings, percussion, tape, 2 films, carousel projection, and theatrical events, 1975, for Congress of Strings, Cincinnati; Mutations, brass choir, tape, films, and slides; A dream fantasy, solo clarinet, percussion, tape, file, slides; The sorcerer, baritone, tape, slides, visuals, theatrical setting; The choice is ours, tape, films, carousel projection, live laser displays, and theatrical events; Scintillation, solo piano.
909 Avenue E, Denton, TX 76201

ELLISTON, RONALD ROBERT
b. Colorado Springs, Colo., 20 Feb. 1935. Studied with Homer Keller, Univ. of Oregon. He has been faculty member, Adams State Coll., from 1970.
WORKS: CHAMBER MUSIC: suite for piano; Conversations, flute, cello, piano; concerto for trumpet, brass choir, percussion.
217 LaVeta Ave., Alamosa, CO 81101

ELLSASSER, RICHARD
b. Cleveland, Ohio, 14 Sept. 1926; d. Calif., 9 Aug. 1972. Studied at Oberlin Coll.; Baldwin-Wallace Coll., B.M.; New York Univ.; Boston Univ., School of Theology; Univ. of Southern California, School of Religion, M.Th. He was life member, Internat. Inst. of Arts and Letters, Switzerland. He was organ soloist with a symphony orchestra at age 7; made New York debut in 1937; gave organ concerts in the U.S., Canada, Latin America, and Europe.
WORKS: BALLET: Greenwich Village; ORCHESTRA: organ concerto; CHORUS: The decalogue (10 anthems); Only the valiant.

ELLSTEIN, ABRAHAM
b. New York, N.Y., 9 July 1907; d. New York, 22 Mar. 1963. Studied at Manhattan School of Music; with Frederic Jacobi, Rubin Goldmark, Albert Stoessel, Juilliard School. His awards included an Ohio Univ. prize and a Ford Found. commission. He was music director, WMGM, New York; had his own program on WEVD, New York, 1951-63.
WORKS: THEATRE: The thief and the hangman, 1-act opera; The Golem, opera; Great to be alive, stage score; operettas for the Yiddish theatre; ORCHESTRA: Negev, piano concerto; Ode to the King of Kings, cantata for 2 soli and orch.; The redemption, oratorio for narrator, 3 soli, orch.; Ima, cantata; CHORUS: Friday evening service; a Passover service; Shabbat Menuchah; and songs.

ELMER, CEDRIC NAGEL
b. Reading, Pa., 15 Jan. 1939. Studied with Romeo Cascarino, Combs Coll. of Music, B.M., M.M.; at Philadelphia Musical Acad.; Eastman School of Music. He has received awards from American Coll. of Musicians and Nat. Pianists Guild. He has been music instructor, Reading School District, from 1966.
WORKS: ORCHESTRA: Lilliputian suite, chamber orch., 1964; March promenade, 1967; CHAMBER MUSIC: Caprice, woodwind quintet, 1971; Sarabande, bass flute and piano, 1978; CHORUS: Psalm V, 1970; Prayer, 1971; Amazing grace, arrangement for chorus and orch., 1974; other arrangements; piano pieces; songs.
413 Douglass St., Reading, PA 19601

ELMORE, ROBERT HALL
b. Ramaputnam, India, of American parents, 2 Jan. 1913. Studied organ and composition with Pietro Yon, Royal Acad. of Music, London, licentiate degree, 1933; Royal Coll. of Music, associate degree, 1933; with Harl McDonald, Univ. of Pennsylvania, B.M. 1937. His awards include the Nitsche prize, 1934, 1935, 1936; Thornton Oakley

ELSTON, ARNOLD

Medal, 1936; Mendelssohn Club award, 1938;
honorary doctorates, Moravian Coll., 1958, and
Alderson-Broaddus Coll., 1958. He has held
various church posts as organist-music director
since 1933; was faculty member, Clark Cons.,
1935-45; head, organ department, Philadelphia
Musical Acad., from 1939.
WORKS: OPERA: It began at breakfast, 1
act, was first American opera on television;
ORCHESTRA: 3 colors, suite; Valley Forge--1777,
tone poem; Legend of Sleepy Hollow, suite; Narrative, horn and orch.; Prelude to unrest, tone
poem; 2 portraits, string orch., 1977; CHORUS:
Out of the depths, cantata, Philadelphia, 16 Apr.
1972; Psalm of redemption; 3 psalms; The incarnate word; The cross; Psalm of a pilgrim people,
Bryn Mawr, Pa., 12 May 1974; God is ascended,
Upper Darby, Pa., 19 May 1974; The holy mountain,
Philadelphia, 18 May 1975; ORGAN AND BRASS: Fanfare for Easter; Meditation--Veni, veni Emmanuel;
Festival toccata; concerto for organ, brass,
percussion; Rhapsody, organ and brass; concertino,
trumpet and organ; many other organ works.
130 Walnut Ave., Wayne, PA 19087

ELSTON, ARNOLD
b. New York, 1907; d. Vienna, Austria, while on
a trip, 1971. Studied at Columbia Univ. and
Harvard Univ., Ph.D.; with Anton Webern, 1933-
35. He taught at the Univ. of Oregon; then was
professor, Univ. of California at Berkeley,
1956-71. His works for various media include a
string quartet, 1961.

ELWELL, HERBERT
b. Minneapolis, Minn., 10 May 1898; d. Cleveland,
Ohio, 17 Apr. 1974. Studied at Univ. of Minne-
sota; with Ernest Bloch in New York; with Nadia
Boulanger in Paris; and on fellowship at the
American Acad. in Rome. He received the
Paderewski prize, 1945; honorary doctorate,
Western Reserve Univ., 1946; Ohioana Library
Assoc. award, 1947. He taught at Cleveland
Inst. of Music, 1928-45; joined the faculty at
Oberlin Cons., 1945; was music critic, Cleveland
Plain Dealer, 1932-65.
WORKS: ORCHESTRA: The happy hypocrite,
ballet suite, 1927; Introduction and allegro,
1942; Ode for orchestra, 1950; The forever young,
voice and orch., 1953; concert suite, violin and
orch., 1957; CHAMBER MUSIC: Blue symphony,
voice and string quartet, 1945; violin sonata;
piano sonata; 2 string quartets; Tarantella,
piano; CHORUS: Lincoln: Requiem aeternum,
baritone, chorus, orch., 1946; I was with him,
tenor, male chorus, 2 pianos, 1952; and songs.

EMIG, LOIS MEYER (Mrs. Jack)
b. Roseville, Ohio, 12 Oct. 1925. Studied at
Ohio State Univ., B.M.E., with graduate work in
composition; and at Queens Coll. She was public
school teacher, 1946-65; church organist, from
1966; private teacher, from 1948.
WORKS: CANTATAS: Beautiful savior; The
children's alleluia; Song of Bethlehem; many
anthems, secular choral works, and 2 piano books.
82 Fletcher Ave., Valley Stream, NY 11580

ENCISO, FRANZ
b. Los Angeles, Calif., 12 July 1941. Studied
with Leonard Stein, California State Univ., B.M.
1965; with Michael Senturia, Univ. of California,
Berkeley, M.A. 1969. He has been on the music
faculty, North Peralta Community Coll., from
1972.
WORKS: CHAMBER MUSIC: trio for flute clarinet, violin; improvisational compositions for
keyboard.
3125 College Ave., #2, Berkeley, CA 94705

END, JACK
b. Rochester, N.Y., 31 Oct. 1918. Studied with
Howard Hanson, Bernard Rogers, Burrill Phillips,
Eastman School of Music. He was faculty member,
Eastman School, 1940-50; on music staff, WROC-
TV, 1950-60; then director of radio and television, Univ. of Rochester.
WORKS: ORCHESTRA: 3 American pastimes;
Fantasy for orchestra; overture; Song for sleepy
children; WIND ENSEMBLE: Portrait by a wind
ensemble; The rocks and the sea; Floorshow;
brass quintet; pieces for trombone choir, jazz
band; CHAMBER MUSIC: string quartet; woodwind
quintet; CHORUS: Snowfall.
36 Potter Place, Fairport, NY 14450

ENDERS, HARVEY
b. St. Louis, Mo., 13 Oct. 1892; d. New York,
N.Y., 12 Jan. 1947. Studied with David Bispham
at Washington Univ. He was baritone soloist in
churches; also a banker.
WORKS: CHORUS: To the Great Pyramids;
Death in Harlem; Russian picnic; and songs.

ENDRES, OLIVE PHILOMENE
b. Johnsberg, Wis., 23 Dec. 1898. Began piano
at 4, organ with her father at 12; graduated in
piano, Wisconsin School of Music; in composition
with honors, studying with Adolph Weidig and Leo
Sowerby, American Cons.; summer study at Juilliard School. She has received several prizes
in Wisconsin State composer contests. She taught
at Wisconsin School of Music and at Milton Coll.;
was organist, St. James Church, Madison; and a
private teacher.
WORKS: STRING ORCHESTRA: Prelude and fugue;
Theme and variations; Romanza (12-tone); Diver-
gent moods (12-tone); CHAMBER MUSIC: violin
sonata; Summer night, violin and piano; Poem,
violin and piano; Cradle song, piano trio;
Prelude for 2 trumpets, 2 trombones; Chorale and
variations, 3 horns; Prelude for organ; CHORUS:
The canticle of Judith, mezzo-soprano and women's
voices; Magnificat, soprano, chorus, strings,
trumpet; other choral works, piano pieces.
1827 Rowley Ave., Madison, WI 53705

ENDRICH, THOMAS JAMES
b. Schenectady, N.Y., 25 Feb. 1942. Studied
with Edgar Curtis, Union Coll.; with Stefan
Grove, Peabody Cons.; and with Bernard Rands,
York Univ., York, England. He was composer-in-
residence and lecturer, Bingley Coll., Yorkshire,
1976-77; assistant lecturer, York Univ., 1978-79.
WORKS: THEATRE: The panther, soprano,
cello, dancer, 1971; Amoeba, orchestra, 2 con-

ductors with acting roles, libretto by composer, 1973-74; Intercommunications, 24 voices, 1975; Savari II, vocalist and 3 dancers/actors, 1975; The burial of the moon, bass instrument, 3 actors, tape, 1976-77; Steps, soprano and clarinet, both with movement patterns, 1976; Masque for a nightingale, soprano, 2 actors, dancer, instruments, 1977; CHAMBER MUSIC: Seasons, soprano, violin, clarinet, piano, song cycle on oriental lyrics, 1970; Lullaby, soprano, Auden text, 1972; Savari III, tuba and tape, 1978; Sonata a due, baroque flute and harpsichord, 1979; KEYBOARD: harpsichord suite, 1971-74; Time-span, cycle of 27 short pieces, 1976-79.

166 Fulford Rd., York, YO1 4DA, England

ENENBACH, FREDERIC
b. Des Moines, Iowa, 1 Dec. 1945. Studied with Anthony Donato and Alan Stout, Northwestern Univ.; with Bulent Arel and Mel Powell at Yale Univ. At Yale he won the Rene Chandler award, 1969. He has been faculty member at Wabash Coll. from 1969.

WORKS: THEATRE: background score to Euripides' Bacchae, 1971; ORCHESTRA: symphony, 1973; CHAMBER MUSIC: string quartet, 1968; Music for piano, 1968; Music for viola and percussion, 1968; from "Chamber Music", voices, winds, percussion, 1969; Music for flute and percussion, 1972.

Music Dept., Wabash College, Crawfordsville, IN 47933

ENGEL, CARL
b. Paris, France, 21 July 1883; U.S. citizen; d. New York, 6 May 1944. Attended Strasbourg and Munich Univ.; studied composition with Ludwig Thuille in Munich. He was editor, Boston Music Company, 1909-21; chief, music division, Library of Congress, 1921-29; president, G. Schirmer, Inc., and editor, Musical Quarterly, 1929-37.

WORKS: CHAMBER MUSIC: Triptych, violin and piano; Presque valse, piano; Never lonely child, piano; 5 perfumes, violin and piano; SONGS: Chansons intimes; 3 epigrams; 3 sonnets; 5 songs to texts of Amy Lowell. His book, Musical myths and facts, was reprinted by Longwood Press in 1976.

ENGEL, LEHMAN
b. Jackson, Miss., 14 Sept. 1910. Studied at Cincinnati Coll. Cons.; Univ. of Cincinnati; with Rubin Goldmark at Juilliard Graduate School, 1934. His honors include the Society for Publication of American Music award, 1946; 2 Antoinette Perry conducting awards, 1950, 1953; Bellamann Found. award, 1964; 3 honorary doctorates, Bogulawski Coll., 1944; Univ. of Cincinnati, 1971, Millsaps Coll., 1971; special citations, Hartford Cons., 1971, Jackson, Miss., Chamber of Commerce, 1973. Since 1934 he has been conductor and producer on Broadway, for radio, television, and films; has been guest conductor of many major U.S. orchestras; and has been adjunct professor, New York Univ., School of Education, from 1975.

WORKS: OPERA: Pierrot of the minuet, Cin-

cinnati, 3 Apr. 1928; Medea; Malady of love, 1954; The soldier, 1956; BALLET: Transitions, 1938; The shoe bird, Jackson, Miss., 20 Apr. 1968; THEATRE: incidental music for nearly 50 plays; ORCHESTRA: The creation, with narrator, 1948; viola concerto; 2 symphonies; overture, 1961; CHAMBER MUSIC: Dialogue, violin and viola; The gates of paradise, piano; cello sonata, 1946; string quartet; piano sonata; CHORUS: Now praise we famous men; Chinese nightingale, cantata, 1928; Rain; FILM SCORES: Beyond Gaugin; Boogie's bump; Honduras; Strategic attack; National defense; Berlin powder keg; 5 U.S. Navy films; The hedgerow story, for State Dept. He was author of the following books: Planning and producing musical shows, 1957, rev. 1966; Music for the classical tragedy; Renaissance to baroque, 7 vol.; 2 books of folk songs; Poor wayfaring stranger; Words with music, 1927, won ASCAP Deems Taylor award, 1974; Getting started in the theatre, 1973; This bright day, an autobiography, 1956, rev. 1974.

350 E. 54th St., New York, NY 10022

ENGLERT, EUGENE E.
b. Cincinnati, Ohio, 15 Mar. 1931. Studied at Athenaeum of Ohio, B.M. 1952; Univ. of Cincinnati, M.M. 1956. He won an award for a choral composition, 1966. He has been church organist from 1949; taught high school, 1961-69.

WORKS: CHORUS: Ye heavens, praise the Lord, 1966; I am the bread of life; The touch of a hand; Winds through the olive trees; Out of the depths; many other published anthems and masses.

2113 Raeburn Dr., Cincinnati, OH 45223

ENGLISH, GRANVILLE
b. Louisville, Ky., 27 Jan. 1895; d. New York, 1 Sept. 1968. Studied with Felix Borowski, Chicago Musical Coll., B.M.; also with Charles Haubiel, Wallingford Riegger, Tibor Serly, and Nadia Boulanger. His awards include 3 New York Fed. of Music Clubs prizes; Mendelssohn Glee Club prize; Ford Found. grant for composer residency at Baylor Univ., 1961. He taught in Chicago, 1923-25; then privately in New York.

WORKS: OPERA: Wide, wide river, a folk opera; ORCHESTRA: An island festival, ballet suite; Colonial portraits, suite for strings; Evening by the sea, tone poem; Ugly duckling, cantata, with chorus, 1924; Alabama twilight; Ballet fantasy, 1937; Among the hills, scherzo; Mood tropicale, Baltimore, 5 Feb. 1955; CHORUS: Robin in the rain, treble voices; Tropicana; Song of the caravan, 1937; Law west of the Pecos, male voices; Promised land; PIANO: Valse lyrique; Danse antique.

ENGLISH, JON ARTHUR
b. Kankakee, Ill., 22 Mar. 1942. Studied with Kenneth Gaburo, Salvatore Martirano, Herbert Brun, Univ. of Illinois, 1963-66; jazz improvisation studies with Lee Konitz, 1971-72. He was trombonist/percussionist, Univ. of Illinois Contemporary Chamber Players, 1965-66; trombonist, Savannah Symph., 1967; associate in performance, Center for New Music, Univ. of Iowa, 1968-74;

EPHROS, GERSHON

free-lance musician in Europe from 1974.
WORKS: CONCERT JAZZ: Free sample, 1972;
CHAMBER MUSIC: Sequent cycles, 6 players, 1968;
Shagbolt, trombone solo, 1978; MIXED MEDIA:
. . . whose circumference is nowhere, soloist,
tape and film, 1970; Used furniture sale, tape,
1970-71; Summerstalks, tape, 1 performer, 1973;
Outline, centerfold, foldout, female voice,
trombone, tape (based on Mutatis mutandis by
Herbert Brun), 1977.
5204 Lohmar 21, Saal, West Germany

EPHROS, GERSHON
b. Serotzk, Poland, 15 Jan. 1890; to U.S. 1911;
d. Rego Park, N.Y., 28 June 1978. Studied at
Inst. of Jewish Music, Jerusalem; also with
Hermann Spielter and Joseph Achron. He was
cantor, Temple Beth Elohim, 1919-27; Beth Mordecai, 1927-57; instructor, School of Sacred
Music, Hebrew Union Coll., 1948-58. His 70th
birthday was an occasion of celebration, with
many concerts of his music and citations from
numerous organizations, setting a pattern for
marking his 75th, 80th, and 85th anniversaries.
WORKS: ORCHESTRA: Suite Hebraique; CHAM-
BER MUSIC: Introduction, andante and fugue,
string quartet, New York, 15 Sept. 1957; Aeolian,
string quartet, 1957; 3 elegaic songs, string
quartet and voice, 1961; Havdala rhapsody, violin
and piano, 1963; VOICE: Biblical suite, song
cycle, 1951; New birth of freedom, cantata;
Vocalise, soprano and piano, 1961; Children's
suite, on 16 Bialik poems, 1963; 3 songs of
faith, tenor and piano, 1971; Toward a new day,
chorus, 1971; To the shores of New Amsterdam,
1976; Shiron Chadash, 2-vol. song book for
children, 1972-77; Pa'ame Hagoel, children's
song in 2 parts, 1978; PIANO: Variations, 1932,
rev. 1954; suite; Rondo; 5 bagatelles. His 5-
volume Cantorial Anthology, a monumental compilation of centuries of Jewish sacred music was
issued in 1957, with a 6th volume added in 1971;
his works also include a great number of liturgical pieces and services.

EPPERSON, JOHN
b. Harrisburg, Va., 5 Sept. 1950. Studied at
North Carolina School of the Arts, B.M. in horn;
with Hubert Howe, Jacques-Louis Monod, and Henry
Weinberg, Queens Coll., CUNY; with Mario
Davidovsky, City Coll., CUNY. He has played
horn in the Winston-Salem Symphony and Greensboro Symphony; was lecturer, Queens Coll., co-
leader Mark V jazz quintet; from 1973, free-
lance composer, arranger, and teacher.
WORKS: CHAMBER MUSIC: Metallurgical report, metal percussion orch., 5 players; In the
shape of 4 pears, wind octet; ELECTRONIC: if i
have been unfaithful it has been only with my
friend, the sea, solo oboe and stereo recorder;
Until the last syllable of recorded time, 4
harps, 2 percussion, electronic sound, commissioned by Patricia Pence for concert performance
and by the Creative Arts Ensemble as a quadrophonic tape for modern dance.
5 St. Mark's Place, New York, NY 10003

EPPERT, CARL
b. Carbon, Ind., 5 Nov. 1882; d. Milwaukee, Wis.,
1 Oct. 1961. Studied with Hugo Kaun and Arthur
Nikisch in Germany. His awards included first
prize, NBC composition contest, 1932; first
prize, Chicago Symph. Orch. Jubilee contest,
1940; Juilliard award, 1941. He was founder and
conductor, Terre Haute Symph., 1903-37; and of
the Milwaukee Civic Orch., 1921-25; then conductor, Milwaukee Symph. He taught at Wisconsin
Cons., Wisconsin Coll. of Music, and Milwaukee
Inst. of Music, 1922-28.
WORKS: OPERA: Kaintuckee; ORCHESTRA:
Traffic, symphonic fantasy, 1932; City shadows,
symphonic poem, 1935; Speed, symphonic poem,
1935; 2 symphonic impressions, 1941-42; Escapade,
1941; Ballet of the vitamins; Image of America;
7 symphonies; and choral works.

EPSTEIN, ALVIN L.
b. Hartford, Conn., 5 Jan. 1926. Studied with
Isadore Freed and Arnold Franchetti, Hartt Coll.
of Music; with Aaron Copland at Tanglewood; with
Cesar Bresgan and Rolf Liebermann, Mozarteum,
Salzburg. He received a BMI award, 1952; Fulbright grant, 1953; honorable mention, Harvey
Gaul award, 1966, and Delius award, 1972. He
was faculty member, Hartt Coll., 1948-70; composer-in-residence, Southern Methodist Univ.,
1970-73; music director, Temple Emanu-El, Dallas,
1970-73; from 1973, at Temple Sholom, Dallas.
WORKS: THEATRE: music for Oedipus, 1972;
ORCHESTRA: Music for orchestra; Collage; piano
concerto; CHAMBER MUSIC: duo for oboe and piano;
duo for violin and piano; string quartet; 4 dialogues, flute, double bass, percussion, 1965;
CHORUS: Fancy.
Temple Sholom, 6930 Alpha Rd., Dallas, TX
75240

EPSTEIN, DAVID M.
b. New York, N.Y., 3 Oct. 1930. Studied at
Antioch Coll., A.B.; with Francis Judd Cooke,
Carl McKinley, Felix Wolfes at New England Cons.,
M.M. 1953; with Arthur Berger, Irving Fine,
Brandeis Univ., M.F.A. 1954; with Roger Sessions,
Edward T. Cone, and Milton Babbitt, Princeton
Univ., Ph.D. 1968. His awards include Louisville
Orch. award, 1953; BMI award; Fromm Found. grant,
1958; Ford Found. recording grant, Arthur
Shepherd award, 1964; Harvey Gaul award; Mass.
Arts and Humanities Found. grant, 1977; and many
commissions. He was music critic, Musical Amer-
ica, 1956-57; faculty member, Antioch Coll.,
1957-62; music director, Educational Broadcasting
Corp., Channel/WNDT, New York, 1962-64; music
director, Harrisburg Symph. Orch., 1975-76;
music director, the Worcester Festival and
Worcester Orch., from 1976; and professor, Mass.
Inst. of Technology, from 1965.
WORKS: ORCHESTRA: Movement for orchestra,
1953; symphony, 1958; Sonority variations, 1968;
Vent-ures, symphonic wind ensemble; Night voices,
1976; cello concerto, 1977-78; CHAMBER MUSIC:
piano trio, 1953; piano variations, 1961; string
trio, 1964; string quartet, 1971; CHORUS: Sing
to the Lord; 5 scenes; SONG CYCLES: Excerpts
from a diary, 1953; The seasons, 1956; 4 songs,

soprano, solo horn, string orch. He is also author of Beyond Orpheus: Studies in musical structure, Cambridge, 1978.
54 Turning Mill Rd., Lexington, MA 02173

EPSTEIN, PAUL
b. Boston, Mass., 23 Apr. 1938. Studied with Harold Shapero, Brandeis Univ., A.B. cum laude 1959; with Seymour Shifrin, Univ. of California, Berkeley, M.A. 1964; privately with Luciano Berio, Milan, 1962-63, on a Fulbright grant. He was faculty member, Tulane Univ., 1963-69; from 1969, at Temple Univ. He is also editor, The Painted Bride Quarterly, and music director, Zero Moving dance company.
WORKS: THEATRE: Caligula, by Camus, incidental music, San Francisco, 1961; Macbeth, 1970; Commune, 1971; Oedipus, 1977, music for productions by the Performance Group (N.Y.); 4 Movements for moving voices moving, 1974, and Night tales, 1977, music for the Zero Moving dance company; CHAMBER MUSIC: True and false unicorn, reader and ensemble, 1960; 3 songs, soprano and clarinet, 1960; 2 autumn songs, soprano and 6 instruments, 1961; sextet, winds and strings, 1961; quartet, flute, clarinet, viola, cello, 1964; Concert for TPG: In memory of intersections 7: Prelude and jam, vocal work for 5 performers, 1971; Changes 1, mallet instruments, 1976; Changes 2, 2 strings, 1976; Changes 4, for gamelan, 1978; also many electronic and mixed media compositions.
379 Heathcliffe Rd., Huntingdon Valley, PA 19006

ERB, DONALD
b. Youngstown, Ohio, 17 Jan. 1927. Studied with Harold Miles and Kenneth Gaburo, Kent State Univ., B.S. 1950; with Marcel Dick, Cleveland Inst. of Music, M.M. 1953; with Bernhard Heiden, Indiana Univ., D.M. 1964. His awards include the Cleveland Arts prize, 1966; grants from the Ford Found., 1962; Guggenheim Found., 1965; Nat. Endowment for the Arts, 1967; Rockefeller Found., 1967, 1968; Maine Council on the Arts and Humanities, 1975. After service in the navy, he was trumpet player and arranger for dance bands. He joined the faculty of Cleveland Inst. of Music, 1953-61; was composer-in-residence, Bakersfield, Calif., school system, 1962-63; and with the Dallas Symph., 1968-69; faculty member, Case Inst. of Technology, 1965-67; and from 1966, Kulas professor of music, Cleveland Inst. of Music and Case Western Reserve Univ.
WORKS: ORCHESTRA: Bakersfield pieces; chamber concerto; Symphony of overtures, 1965; concerto for solo percussion and orch., 1966; Christmasmusic, 1967; The 7th trumpet, 1969; Klangfarbenfunk I, with rock band and electronic sounds, 1970; New England prospect, with narrator, text from 8 American writers (including Julian Bond's "I too hear America singing"), Cincinnati, 17 May 1974; trombone concerto, St. Louis, 11 Mar. 1976; cello concerto, Rochester, N.Y., 4 Nov. 1976; Treasures of the snow, Washington, 29 June 1977; concerto for keyboards and orchestra (1 soloist performs on a grand piano, electric piano, and celesta), Akron,

24 Mar. 1981; CHAMBER MUSIC: Dialogue, violin and piano, 1958; string quartet, 1960; sonata for harpsichord and string quartet, 1962; Sonneries, brass choir, 1961; quartet for 4 winds, string bass; Antipodes, string quartet and percussion quartet, 1963; Music for Mother Bear, alto flute; music for violin and piano; hexagon, 5 winds, piano, 1963; 4 for percussion; VII miscellaneous, flute, string bass, 1964; Concertant, harpsichord and strings; Trio for two, alto flute/percussion, string bass; Phantasma, flute, oboe, bass, harpsichord, 1965; Diversion for 2 (other than sex), trumpet, percussion, 1966; trio for violin, cello, electric guitar, 1966; Reconnaissance, violin, bass, percussion, tape, 1967; And then, toward the end, trombone and tape; In no strange land, trombone, bass, tape, 1968; Basspiece, string bass and tape, 1969; Harold's trip to the sky, viola, percussion, piano, 1972, Washington, 13 Feb. 1976; quintet for chamber ensemble and electric piano, Bowdoin Coll., 17 Oct. 1976; also band pieces, choral works, piano pieces.
Cleveland Institute of Music, 11021 East Blvd., Cleveland, OH 44106

ERB, JOHN LAWRENCE
b. Reading, Pa., 5 Feb. 1877; d. Eugene, Oreg., 17 Mar. 1950. Studied at Metropolitan School of Music, New York. His academic posts included Wooster Cons., Ohio; School of Music, Univ. of Illinois; American Inst. of Applied Music, New York; and Connecticut Coll. for Women. He composed choral works, organ and piano pieces, and songs.

ERB, JOHN WARREN
b. Massillon, Ohio, 17 Apr. 1887; d. Pittsburgh, Pa., 2 July 1948. Studied with Siegfried Ochs, Xaver Scharwenka, and Felix Weingartner in Berlin; with Edgar Stillman Kelley in the U.S. He was active as a choral conductor; was chairman, department of instrumental music, New York Univ., School of Education. He wrote choral pieces and works for instrumental ensembles.

ERDODY, LEO
b. Chicago, Ill., 17 Dec. 1888; d. Los Angeles, Calif., 5 Apr. 1949. Studied violin with Joseph Joachim and Emanuel Wirth; composition with Max Bruch in Berlin. He was a film composer and conductor. His compositions included 2 operas, Peasants' love and The terrible meek, and songs.

ERICKSON, FRANK
b. Spokane, Wash., 1 Sept. 1923. Studied with Mario Castelnuovo-Tedesco privately; with Halsey Stevens, Univ. of Southern California, B.M., M.M. He served in the U.S. Army Air Force in World War II, then was arranger for dance bands; was faculty member, Univ. of California; San Jose State Coll., 1959-61; guest conductor at colleges and universities; editor for music publishers.
WORKS: BAND: 2 symphonies; saxophone concerto; double concerto for trumpet and trombone; Rhythm of the winds; Arietta for winds; Balladair; Tamerlane; Chroma; and more than 100 pub-

ERICKSON, MARGARET S.

lished works for band.
c/o Summit Publications, Box 9327, Kansas
City, MO 64133

ERICKSON, MARGARET S.
b. Columbus, Ohio, 19 Oct. 1915. Studied with
E. J. Weigel, Ohio State Univ.; with Robert L.
Sanders, Indiana Univ. She was instructor,
Indiana Univ., 1941-46; public school teacher,
1952-60. Her compositions are chiefly for small
wind ensembles, e.g., brass quintets, brass sextets, cornet trio, petite suite for clarinets,
etc.
313 N. Lewis, Ludington, MI 49431

ERICKSON, ROBERT
b. Marquette, Mich., 7 Mar. 1917. Studied at
Chicago Cons., 1937-38; privately with Wesley
LaViolette in Chicago, 1938; with Ernst Krenek,
Hamline Univ., B.A. cum laude 1943, M.A. 1947;
and with Roger Sessions, 1950. His awards include scholarships, 1941-43; Drew prize, 1943;
Ford Found. grant, 1951; Yaddo fellowships, 1952,
1953, 1965; Marion Bauer prize, 1957; Guggenheim
fellowship, 1966; Univ. of California, Inst. for
Creative Arts, fellowship, 1968. He taught in
San Francisco, 1952-66; has been professor, Univ.
of California, from 1967.
WORKS: ORCHESTRA: Introduction and allegro,
1948; Fantasy, cello and orch., 1953; Variations,
1957; Sirens and other flyers, 1965; CHAMBER
MUSIC: piano sonata, 1948; 2 string quartets,
1950, 1956; piano trio, 1953; Divertimento,
flute, clarinet, strings, 1953; duo for violin
and piano, 1957; chamber concerto, 17 players,
1960; Toccata, piano, 1962; concerto for piano
and 7 instruments, 1963; Piece for bells and toy
pianos, 1965; Scapes, a contest for 2 groups,
1966; General (MacArthur) speech, trombone,
1969; High flyer, flute, Night music, solo trumpet and ensemble, 1978; ELECTRONIC: Ricercar à
5, trombone and tape, 1966; Ricercar à 3, contrabass and tape, 1967; Birdlands, tape, 1967;
Cardenitas, singer, mime, 7 players, tape, 1968;
Pacific sirens, instruments and tape, 1969;
Loops, for instruments and computer; Percussion
loops, solo percussion and computer; 9½ for
Henry, tape and chamber ensemble, 1978. He is
author of Sound structure in music, Univ. of
Calif. Press, Berkeley, 1975, and The structure
of music: A listener's guide, Greenwood Press,
1977.
1849 Crest Dr., Encinitas, CA 92024

ERNEST, DAVID JOHN
b. Chicago, Ill., 16 May 1929. Studied at
Chicago Musical Coll; with Robert Palmer and
Robert Kelly, Univ. of Illinois; with Cecil
Effinger, Univ. of Colorado; and with Roland
Lamoriette in Paris. His many scholarships and
awards include a Fulbright grant and a Danforth
Found. award. He was faculty member, Univ. of
Colorado, 1956-61; Glenville State Coll., 1961-
63; from 1963, professor and chairman, St.
Cloud State Univ.
WORKS: OPERA: Ten year thunder; CHAMBER
MUSIC: sonatine for oboe and strings; numerous
smaller works.
Crest Rd., Rte. 5, St. Cloud, MN 56301

ERNEST, SR. M. See SCHWERDTFEGER, E. ANNE

ERNST, DAVID
b. Pittsburgh, Pa., 6 Sept. 1945. Studied with
William McKinley and Joseph W. Jenkins, Duquesne
Univ., B.S. 1967; with Robert Erickson, Univ. of
California; and with Robert Moevs, Rutgers Univ.,
M.A. 1969, Ph.D. 1978. He was on the faculty,
San Diego State Univ., 1970-71; from 1972, York
Coll., CUNY.
WORKS: CHAMBER MUSIC: P-2, 2 pianos;
Tronica 4, clarinet, cello, piano, vibes, 1977;
ELECTRONIC: Exit, trumpet and tape; 4 and more,
percussion quartet and tape, 1968; Excerpt,
string bass and tape; Rounds, viola and tape;
Waves, percussion and tape, 1973. He is author
of 2 books: Musique concrete, Boston, 1973, and
The evolution of electronic music, New York,
1977.
172-70 Highland Ave., #7F, Jamaica, NY 11432

ESCOT, POZZI
b. Lima, Peru, 1 Oct. 1933; U.S. citizen 1953.
Studied with Andres Sas, Sas-Rosay Acad. of
Music, Lima, 1949-53; with William Bergsma,
Juilliard School, B.S. 1956, M.S. 1957; with
Philipp Jarnach, Hamburg, 1957-58. Her many
awards include scholarships at Juilliard; grants
from the German government, Ford Found., MENC;
4 MacDowell fellowships; Lima 4th of July Prize,
1955; laureate composer of Peru, 1956; many commissions; named adviser, U.S. State Dept. and
Peru Ministry of Culture, 1972. She was faculty
member, New England Cons., 1964-67; professor,
Wheaton Coll., from 1972.
WORKS: THEATRE: Metamorphosis, ballet, with
chamber orch., 1951; ORCHESTRA: 3 symphonies,
1953, 1955, 1957; Sands . . . I, with chorus,
solo alto, 1958; Sands . . . II, 1966; CHAMBER
MUSIC: 3 string quartets, 1951, 1954, 1956;
3 poems of Rilke, narrator and string quartet,
1959; 3 movements, violin and piano, 1960;
Cristos, chamber ensemble, 1963; Visione, contrabass, flute, saxophone, soprano, percussion,
ghost speaker, Wesleyan Univ., 22 Nov. 1964;
Fergus are, organ, 1975; CHORUS: Ainu, 20 solo
voices, 1970; SONGS: Songs of my country,
soprano and piano, 1954; Songs of wisdom, soprano,
1955; Credo, soprano and string quartet, 1958;
Lamentus, soprano, chamber ensemble, 1962;
PIANO: 3 sonatinas, 1950, 1951, 1952; Differences I, 1960; Differences II, 1963; 13 preludes,
1968; ELECTRONIC: In memoriam, tape; Interra,
piano, tape, spotlights, slide projections, 1968;
FILM SCORE: Razapeti, film by Yugoslavian Nat.
Television, 1973. She is coauthor with her
husband, Robert Cogan, of Sonic design: The
nature of sound and music, N.Y., 1976.
24 Avon Hill St., Cambridge, MA 02140

ESCOVADO, ROBIN
b. Dallas, Tex., 20 Aug. 1931. Studied with
Charles Shatto in San Diego and with Mario
Castelnuovo-Tedesco in Los Angeles. He is a
computer programmer/analyst.
WORKS: CHORUS: more than 200 compositions
for a cappella chorus including 4 motets, 4
chort masses, 2 hymns on poems of Christopher

Smart; Psalm 131; What child is this?, etc.
12 Remsen St., Brooklyn, NY 11201

ESTABROOK, DEAN MONTE
b. San Jose, Calif., 7 June 1940. Studied with
Wilson Coker, California State Univ., San Jose,
M.A. He received the Eva Thompson Phillips
award. He is choral director and teacher Yuba
City High School.
WORKS: BAND: Corrente, 1969; CHAMBER MUSIC:
Epigram, saxophone quartet; CHORUS: To spring,
chorus and bassoon.
c/o Yuba City High School, Yuba City, CA
95991

ESTES, CHARLES BYRON
b. Denver, Colo., 17 June 1946. Studied at Coll.
of Idaho; with Frank McCarty, Andrew Charlton,
Donal Michalsky, and Lloyd Rodgers, California
State Univ. at Fullerton. In 1974 he founded
the Direct Image Ensemble and has been its
director.
WORKS: ORCHESTRA: Vexilla regis prodeunt
inferni, strings, flute, oboes, bassoon, 1977;
CHAMBER MUSIC: A trio of inspirational songs,
voice and piano, 1971; Trio resoluto, saxophone,
cello, piano, 1972; Trio partita, recorders and
guitar, 1972; Chrome yellow, clarinet sextet and
marimba, 1974; We lost, fleugelhorn, viola,
chimes, 1974; CHORUS: Make a joyful noise,
choir and jazz quartet, 1967; Psalm 13, 1971;
MULTIMEDIA: The 3rd memory, tape and dancers;
Tilbury Town, 2 soloists, 2 oboes, electric
piano, tape, 1973; Martin Luther, tape, 1975;
Je vais bien, inanimate objects and tape, 1976.
1207 N. Concord Ave., Fullerton, CA 92631

ETLER, ALVIN DERALD
b. Battle Creek, Iowa, 19 Feb. 1913; d. Florence,
Mass., 13 June 1973. Studied with Arthur
Shepherd, Case Western Reserve Univ.; with Paul
Hindemith, Yale Univ., M.B. 1944. His awards
included 2 Guggenheim fellowships, 1940-41,
1963-64; fourth award, Concours Musique Internat., Reine Elisabeth de Belgique, 1953; first
Yale Distinguished Alumnus award, 1965; many
commissions. He was oboist, Indianapolis Symph.,
1938-40; faculty member, Yale Univ., 1941-46;
Cornell Univ., 1946-47; Univ. of Illinois, 1947-
49; and professor, Smith Coll., 1949-73.
WORKS: ORCHESTRA: Dramatic overture, 1956;
concerto in one movement, 1957; Elegy, 1959;
concerto for woodwind quintet and orch., 1960;
Triptych, 1961; concerto for brass quintet,
string orch., percussion, 1967; Convivialities,
1968; concerto for string quartet and orch.,
1968; CHAMBER MUSIC: sonata for oboe, clarinet,
viola, 1945; quartet, 3 woodwinds, viola, 1949;
bassoon sonata, 1951; 2 clarinet sonatas, 1952,
1969; Introduction and allegro, oboe and piano,
1952; 2 woodwind quintets, 1955, 1957; concerto
for violin and woodwind quintet, 1958; sonata
for viola and harpsichord, 1959; sextet for
winds and strings, 1959; suite for woodwind trio,
1960; concerto for clarinet and chamber ensemble,
1962; Fragments, wsodwind quartet, 1963; 2
string quartets, 1963, 1965; brass quintet, 1963;
Sonic sequence, brass quintet, 1967; XL plus 1,

solo percussionist, 1970; concerto for cello and
chamber group, New York, 2 Mar. 1971; CHORUS:
Peace be unto you, 1958; Under the cottonwood
tree, 1960; Under stars, 1960; A Christmas
lullaby, 1960; Ode to Pothos, 1960; Lord God,
hear our prayer, 1961; Onomatopoesis, male
chorus, winds, percussion, 1965; PIANO: Prelude
and toccata, 1950; sonatina, 1955. The Smith
Coll. dept. of music and the New Valley Music
Press have established the Alvin Etler Memorial
Competition for a chamber music composition.

ETTORE, EUGENE
b. New Bedford, Mass., 2 June 1921. He has won
awards for accordion compositions; is editor and
arranger for music publishers, and instrumental
consultant at Major Music School, Irvington, N.J.
WORKS: ACCORDION: Manhattan concerto;
Pioneer concerto; Contrast; Prelude and scherzo;
Concert etude #2; etc.
c/o Major Music School, 43 New St.,
Irvington, NJ 07111

EUBANKS, CHARLES G.
b. Atlanta, Ga., 2 Nov. 1942. Studied with G.
Winston Cassler at St. Olaf Coll.; with John
MacIvor Perkins and Ralph Shapey, Univ. of
Chicago.
WORKS: THEATRE: Bang (he said) you're
dead, musical play; incidental music to Williams's
Summer and smoke; ORCHESTRA: Othello, overture;
CHORUS: Vespers for Lent, with organ and con-
gregation; numerous choral works for liturgical
use.
312 Sterling Place, Brooklyn, NY 11238

EVANS, BILLY G.
b. Big Spring, Tex., 27 Oct. 1938. Studied with
Samuel Adler, North Texas State Univ. He has
been on the piano faculty, West Texas State
Univ., from 1961.
WORKS: CHAMBER MUSIC: concerto for piano
and winds; piano sonata; quartet for piano,
violin, clarinet, cello; Scherzo, trumpet, baritone horn, brass choir; Caprice, flute and piano;
5 variations on an old Englishe ayre, woodwind
trio and piano.
2509 14th Ave., Canyon, TX 79015

EVANS, GIL
b. Toronto, Ont., 1912 (full name was Ian Ernest
Gilmore Green); to U.S. 1933. He is pianist and
arranger; was in U.S. Army, 1943-46; then arranger with Miles Davis and others; at times had
his own band. His work, A concert opera, was
commissioned by the New York Jazz Repertory
Company and the New York State Council on the
Arts for the Bicentennial.

EVANS, HUMPHREY III
b. Washington, D.C., Studied at Peabody Cons.
and Yale Univ. He received BMI student awards,
1964, 1967; Gustav Klemm prize, 1965; Nat. Fed.
of Music Clubs awards, 1965, 1969. His Happenings was performed by the Redlands (Calif.)
Symphony, Mar. 1966.

EVANS, SALLY HAZEN. See HAZEN, SARA

159

EVERETT, BETTY LOU

EVERETT, BETTY LOU
b. Milwaukee, Wis., 29 Apr. 1925. Studied with
William Latham and Merrill Ellis, North Texas
State Univ., D.M.A. She won first place in the
1977 Delius composition contest with 3 bagatelles
for piano; and in the 1978 Memphis State Univ.
New Music Festival with Variation 2-4-6 for
piano. She taught at Agnes Scott Coll., 1969-
70; at Mercer Univ., 1970-73; in 1974, became
music director, Brunswick Jr. Coll.
WORKS: CHAMBER MUSIC: 2 woodwind trios;
woodwind quintet; VOICE: song cycle for alto,
1968; Triology for 3 Americans, baritone, 1969;
4 songs for soprano; Johnny, I hardly knew ye,
chorus, orchestra, and tape, 1971.
17 Hyde St., Waycross, GA 31501

EVERETT, THOMAS GREGORY
b. Philadelphia, Pa., 4 Dec. 1944. Studied with
George Andrix and Warren Benson, Ithaca Coll.,
B.S. 1966, M.S. 1969; with Robert Ceely, New
England Cons., 1972. He has been director of
bands, Harvard Univ., from 1971; on the faculty,
New England Cons., from 1973; faculty member,
Nat. Trombone Workshop, Nashville, 1972, 1973;
and is associate editor of Composer Magazine
and Brass World Magazine.
WORKS: BAND: Feowertig nu; CHAMBER MUSIC:
Vietnam 70, tenor saxophone, string bass, bass
trombone, 1970; duos for bass trombone and clar-
inet, 1970; trio for trumpet, horn, bass trombone.
277 Broadway, #3, Arlington, MA 02174

EVERSOLE, JAMES
b. Lexington, Ky., 1 Aug. 1929. Studied at Univ.
of Kentucky, B.M.; with Scott Huston, Cincinnati
Cons., M.M.; with Ralph Wilkerson, Columbia
Univ., Ed.D. His awards include Pi Kappa Lambda;
Kentucky Colonel (outstanding native son);
numerous commissions and grants. He was faculty
member, Univ. of Montana, 1955-63; Jersey City
State Coll., 1964-67; Univ. of Connecticut, from
1967.
WORKS: OPERA: Bessie, 1976; ORCHESTRA:
flute concerto; Tone dances, 1977; WIND ENSEMBLE:
Interchanges, 1978; VOICE: A feast of beasts,
choral cycle, 1976-77; A New England canticle,
cantata, 1977.
15 C Barbara Manor Apts., West Willington,
CT 06279

EVETT, ROBERT
b. Loveland, Colo., 30 Nov. 1922; d. Takoma Park,
Md., 4 Feb. 1975. Studied with Roy Harris,
1941-47; with Vincent Persichetti at Juilliard
School, 1951-52. He received many commissions
including Pan American Union, Nat. Symph. Orch.,
Georgetown Univ., Composer's Forum for Catholic
Worship, etc. He was chairman of the music dept.,
Washington Inst. of Contemporary Arts, 1947-50;
book editor and music critic, The New Republic,
1952-68; editor, Arts and Letters section,
Atlantic Monthly, 1968-69; contributing critic
on books and music, Washington Star, 1961-75,
book editor, 1970-75.
WORKS: ORCHESTRA: 3 symphonies; concerto
for orch.; piano concerto, 1957; Monadnock, a
work orchestrated by Russell Woollen from a

fragment of Evett's Reconciled spirit and performed in Washington, 27 Apr. 1976; CHAMBER
MUSIC: harpsichord sonata, 1961; piano quintet;
7 piano sonatas; 2 movements and a fragment of a
3rd movement of an incomplete sonata for violin
solo were performed at the Nat. Gallery, Washington, 18 May 1975; other chamber music and
piano pieces; CHORUS: The mask of Cain; liturgical pieces.

EWAZEN, ERIC
b. Cleveland, Ohio, 1954. Received a BMI award,
1973, for Dagon, quintet for 5 celli.
WORKS: OPERA: The Bacchae, Exodus from the
final scene, New York, 20 Apr. 1980; CHAMBER
MUSIC: duo , viola and piano, Amos, Que., 1 Mar.
1980; Fantasia, 2 vibraphones, New York, 14 May
1980; Pergamos, bass and percussion, 30 Apr.
1980; harpsichord sonata, New York, 9 May 1980;
Dagon II, bass trombone and tape, New York, 25
Jan. 1981.
228 W. 71 St., #310, New York, NY 10023

EZELL, HELEN INGLE
b. Marshall, Okla., 18 May 1903. Studied at
Juilliard Graduate School; with Otto Luening and
Henry Cowell, Columbia Univ.; with Violet Archer
and Spencer Norton, Univ. of Oklahoma. She has
published many songs, including I know that mind
unfolds; and piano pieces.

FAIRCHILD, BLAIR
b. Belmont, Mass., 23 June 1877; d. Paris,
France, 23 Apr. 1933. Studied with John Knowles
Paine and Walter Spalding, Harvard Univ.; piano
with Guisseppe Buonamoci in Italy; later with
Charles-Marie Widor in Paris. His service in
the diplomatic corps and residence in Constan-
tinople and Persia colored his subsequent composition with Eastern themes. After 1903 he
lived in Paris.
WORKS: THEATRE: 3 ballets; ORCHESTRA: 3
symphonic poems; Etude symphonique, viola and
orch.; Rhapsody on Hebrew melodies, violin and
orch.; many works for chamber groups, chorus,
many songs, organ and piano pieces.

FAITH, RICHARD BRUCE
b. Evansville, Ind., 20 Mar. 1926. Studied with
Max Wald in Chicago; with Bernhard Heiden,
Indiana Univ.; with Robert McBride, Univ. of
Arizona; and held a Fulbright grant for study in
Italy. He received a Univ. of Arizona grant for
composition of an opera. He was faculty member,
Morningside Coll., 1956-60; and from 1961, Univ.
of Arizona.
WORKS: OPERA: Sleeping beauty, 2 acts;
ORCHESTRA: piano concerto; concerto for 2
pianos; Elegy, 1975; CHAMBER MUSIC: trio for
violin, horn, piano; movements for horn; VOICE:
By the waters of Babylon, cantata; PIANO: Fin-
gerpaintings; Legende; The dark riders, toccata;
sonata.
1032 E. Adelaide, Tucson, AZ 85719

FALARO, ANTHONY J.
b. Bridgeport, Conn., 12 Apr. 1938. Studied at
Berklee Coll. of Music, 1961-63; with Avram David,

Boston Cons., B.M. 1965, M.M. 1967. He was awarded second prize in the Gaudeamus Found. competition, 1968. He has been guitar teacher since 1968; from 1969, on music faculty, New York Assoc. of the Blind, N.Y., and the YM-YWHA, Scarsdale, N.Y.

WORKS: ORCHESTRA: Cosmoi, for 56-part string orch., 1967, Rotterdam, 1968; CHAMBER MUSIC: string trio, 1965; The windhover, voice and 11 instruments, 1965; Spaces, 9 brass, 7 percussion instruments, 1966; suite for sting quintet, commissioned by Mu Phi Epsilon, Cleveland, Aug. 1971; Refraction, chamber orch., 1972; Synergy, string trio, piano, percussion, 1974; Bias, amplified oboe/English horn, tape, 1976; CHORUS: Irenicon, mass for 24 voices, string orch., percussion, 1970.

66-05 110th St., #2A, Forest Hills, NY 11375

FARAGO, MARCEL
b. Timisoara, Roumania, 17 Apr. 1924; U.S. citizen 1960. Studied with Sabin Dragoi and Eisicovits in Roumania; with Vito Frazzi and Angelo Lavagnino in Italy; and with Darius Milhaud in France. He was a symphony cellist in Bucharest, Cape Town, and Brazil, 1945-54; from 1955, cellist with the Philadelphia Orchestra, doubling at the keyboard.

WORKS: OPERA: Mazel and Schlimazel, chamber opera based on a story by Isaac Bashevis Singer, Baltimore, 7 Dec. 1980; ORCHESTRA: 2 sympho..ies, (#2 for winds); children's march; children's suite; The mountain--the fire, cantata for chorus, soli, and orch.; cello concerto; violin concerto; CHAMBER MUSIC: 6 string quartets; Prayer, cello and piano; duets for 2 celli; Rhythm and color, percussion.

168 Uxbridge, Cherry Hill, NJ 08034

FARBERMAN, HAROLD
b. New York, N.Y., 2 Nov. 1929. Studied at Juilliard School and the New England Cons. His awards include a commission for an opera by Juilliard American Opera Theatre, 1970; ASCAP award, 1972; American Acad. of Arts and Letters award, 1972. He was violist, Boston Symph. Orch., 1951-63; conductor, New Arts Orch., 1964-69; conductor, Oakland Symph. Orch., 1970-79.

WORKS: OPERA: The losers, New York, 26 Mar. 1971; ORCHESTRA: concerto for alto saxophone and string orch., 1965; Elegy, fanfare, and march, 1965; trumpet concerto; Reflected realities, violin concerto with orch. and tape, Oakland, 15 Jan. 1974; War cry on a prayer feather, dramatic cantata, 2 soloists, orch., text by Nancy Woods, Colorado Springs, 11 Nov. 1976; BAND: Box; CHAMBER MUSIC: Variations, percussion and piano; Variations on a familiar theme, percussion ensemble; Progressions, flute and percussion, 1960; 3 states of mind ior 6 musicians; Quintessence, woodwind quintet, 1963; trio, violin, piano, percussion, 1963; Alea: a game of chance, 6 percussionists; 5 images, brass quintet, 1964; SONGS: Evolution, soprano and percussion, 1954; Greek scene, 1957; Impressions, 1959; New York Times, Aug. 30, 1964, 4 songs for soprano, piano, percussion, 1964; FILM SCORE: The great American cowboy, orch., jazz

quartet, guitar, won an Oscar, Apr. 1974.
1726 Oakland Ave., Piedmont, CA 94611

FARLEY, ROLAND
b. Aspen, Colo., 17 Mar. 1892; d. New York, 11 May 1932. Studied at State School of the Deaf and Blind, Colorado Springs; and Royal Cons. of Leipzig. His many songs include Oh Mother, my love; The night wind; A lark went singing; At sunset; etc.

FARMER, PETER RUSSELL
b. Boston, Mass., 14 Oct. 1941. Studied with Avram David, Boston Cons., 1964-69; with Karlheinz Stockhausen, summer 1968; privately with Hugo Norden, 1973, and won the Brookline Library composition contest, 1973. He was music editor, Allyn & Bacon, Boston, 1969-71, and book designer from 1971.

WORKS: CHAMBER MUSIC: 3 seascapes, string sextet; Ensemble, 1968; Capriccio, flute and harpsichord, Brookline, Mass., 11 Aug. 1973; Sonata for 5 brass instruments, Tanglewood, 7 Aug. 1973.

93 Cheever St., Milton, MA 02187

FARRAND, NOEL
b. New York, N.Y., 26 Dec. 1928. Studied with Edward Royce and Wayne Barlow, Eastman School of Music, 1946; with William Flanagan, Israel Citkowitz, New York, 1949; Manhattan School of Music, B.M. 1952; Aaron Copland, Lukas Foss, Seymour Lipkin, Jean Morel, Leonard Bernstein at Tanglewood. He received Tangelwood scholarships, 1951-54; MacDowell fellowship, 1953; Univ. of California grant, 1954; Huntington Hartford grant, 1964; Helene Wurlitzer Found. grant, 1973-74. He was on the staff, New Edition Records, 1950-56; faculty member, Regis School, New York, 1957-61.

WORKS: THEATRE: The pearl, dance drama in 2 acts, Los Angeles, 21-24 Apr. 1954; ORCHESTRA: Epitaph for orchestra: Times long ago, with speaker, Tanglewood, 14 July 1953; 3 symphonies, 1955, 1964, 1973; CHAMBER MUSIC: string trio; A retrospection, cello and piano; duo for oboe and bassoon; Adagio assai, violin and piano; Vocalise, oboe and string quartet; SONGS: Autumn is on the wind; When autumn severs the golden fruit; Herbsttag; Doria; Autumn is over the long leaves; PIANO: 2 sonatas; 2 rhapsodies; At MacDowell's grave; sonatina; partita in 5 movements.

P.O. Box 1387, Taos, NM 87571

FARREN, MARTIN
b. Lompoc, Calif., 10 July 1942. Studied with Stanworth Beckler, Univ. of the Pacific; with Robert Shallenberg and Richard Hervig, Univ. of Iowa. He was faculty member, Arkansas Polytechnic Coll., 1969-70; Univ. of Iowa, 1971-72; California State Univ., Fresno, 1972-73; Mass. Inst. of Technology from 1973.

WORKS: CHAMBER MUSIC: flute sonata; bassoon sonata; Paean for spring, English handbells; other chamber works for instruments, vocal ensembles, voice and piano, percussion.

43 Locke St., Cambridge, MA 02140

FARWELL, ARTHUR

FARWELL, ARTHUR
b. St. Paul, Minn., 22 Apr. 1872; d. New York,
20 Jan. 1952. Graduated from Mass. Inst. of
Technology, 1893; studied organ in Boston and
Paris; composition with Humperdinck in Germany.
He received the first composers' fellowship
given by the Music and Art Assoc. of Pasadena,
1921-25; first prize, Nat. Fed. of Music Clubs,
1931. He was on the staff of Musical America,
1909-15; held many teaching posts in New York
and California, finally at Michigan State Coll.,
1927-39. There he established his own music
press, handling the whole job himself on a litho-
graphic hand press. Earlier, in 1901, he had
set up the Wa Wan Press in Newton, Mass. He
wrote many works for orchestra, including The
gods of the mountains and the Rudolph Gott symphony, which he developed from themes by Gott,
his lifelong friend, and fused them with his
own music. The manuscript was discovered in
Berkeley by Ron Erickson of the Diablo Symphony,
which premiered the work in Mar. 1978. Many of
Farwell's compositions for orchestra, chamber
ensembles, vocal ensembles, and piano are based
on American Indian melodies and folk songs of
the South and West.

FAST, WILLARD S.
b. Mountain Lake, Minn., 21 June 1922. Attended
Univ. of Michigan and Millikan Univ. He was
choral director in Illinois and Michigan public
schools, 1949-56; at Alpena Community Coll.,
1956-61; on faculty, Charles Stewart Mott Community Coll., from 1961.
WORKS: CHORUS: Spring, 2-voice canon;
Bread and music, men's voices; Our friendly
house; Autumn; The blessed night; When I was one-
and-twenty; Be not afraid; Alleluia to the Lord
of being, double chorus; many other choral works.
Music Dept., C. S. Mott Community Coll.,
Flint, MI 48503

FAULCONER, BRUCE LALAND
b. Dallas, Tex., 10 Sept. 1951. Studied with
Hunter Johnson, Kent Kennan, Thomas Wells,
Gordon Goodwin, Karl Korte, Joseph Schwantner,
and Eugene Kurtz, Univ. of Texas at Austin, B.M.
1972, M.M. 1974, D.M.A. 1978. His honors include
an AFROTC scholarship, 1969; second prize, World
Saxophone Congress composition contest, 1972;
second prize, Univ. of Texas contest, 1975;
first prize, Shenna Meeker Memorial contest,
1975; and commissions. He was teaching fellow,
Univ. of Texas, 1973-77; from 1977, on faculty,
Southern Methodist Univ.
WORKS: ORCHESTRA: Interstices, 1977;
CHAMBER MUSIC: Preludes, oboe and piano, 1970;
woodwind trio, 1970; trumpet sonata, 1970;
string quartet, 1971; septet, 1973; music for
chamber orchestra, 1975; CHORUS: Psalm 1, 1971;
Dies sanctificatus, 1971; ELECTRONIC: KLRN-TV
logo, 1974; incidental music to The hide and
seek odyssey of Madaline Gimple, videotape play,
1975; Interface I, amplified piano quintet and
percussion, 1975; Interface II, 1976; also songs
and piano pieces.
Music Div., Southern Methodist University,
Dallas, TX 75275

FAULCONER, JAMES H.
b. Frederick, Okla., 19 Oct. 1945. Studied with
Normand Lockwood, Univ. of Denver; David Diamond,
Univ. of Colorado; Harrison Kerr, Spencer Norton,
Stanley Gibb, Univ. of Oklahoma. He has received several commissions. He has been faculty
member, Univ. of Oklahoma, from 1972, assistant
dean from 1977.
WORKS: LARGE ENSEMBLES: suite for brass
and percussion; . . . and on this original
chorale tune, trombone choir and rhythm section;
A theme for something, jazz ensemble; Alfred
Hitch, jazz ensemble; CHORUS: Let nothing disturb thee, a cappella; Council of hell, choir
and percussion; KEYBOARD: accordion sonata.
560 Parrington Oval, Norman, OK 73019

FAUST, GEORGE T.
b. New Brunswick, N.J., 6 June 1937. Studied
with Daniel Pinkham, New England Cons., B.M.
1963; privately with Paul Creston, 1965; with
Burrill Phillips, Bernard Rogers, and Wayne
Barlow, Eastman School of Music, M.M. 1967, Ph.D.
candidate 1973. He held scholarships at New
England Cons.; received 4 graduate awards at
Eastman, and Edward R. Benjamin award, 1966. He
taught in private music schools, 1964-65; was
graduate assistant at Eastman, 1966-69; faculty
member, Hochstein Music School, Rochester, 1971-
74.
WORKS: ORCHESTRA: 4 muses; Adagio for small
orchestra; Revelation 6:1-11; WIND ENSEMBLE:
symphony for brass and percussion; PIANO: sonata;
2 preludes.

FAUST, RANDALL E.
b. Vermillion, S.Dak., 3 July 1947. Studied with
Anthony Iannacone, Eastern Michigan Univ., B.S.;
with Rolf Scheurer, Mankato State Univ., M.M.;
with Donald Jenni and Peter Lewis, Univ. of
Iowa, doctoral candidate, 1978. He was winner,
Minnesota Fed. of Music Clubs contest, 1973;
received commission, Nat. Gallery Orch., 1976.
From 1973 he has been instructor, Shenandoah
Coll. and Cons.
WORKS: ORCHESTRA: Canzona, 1973; concerto
for brass quintet, percussion, and strings,
Washington, 25 Sept. 1977; WIND ENSEMBLE: double
concerto, tenor trombone, bass trombone, trombone octet, 1976; Gallery music, brass quintet,
Washington, 14 Mar. 1976; CHAMBER MUSIC: bass
trombone sonata; Prelude for horn alone; Celebration, horn and organ.
Shenandoah Coll. and Cons., Winchester, VA
22601

FAX, MARK
b. 1911; d. 1974. Was professor and chairman,
School of Music, Howard Univ. His published
works for chorus include Go tell it on the
mountain; To an unknown soldier; Whatsoever a
man soweth; Till victory is won; and vocal solos:
Longing and May Day song.

FEASEL, RICHARD
Mystic overture for band, 1952; Poem for horn,
1956. He is professor, School of Music, Stetson
University, De Land, FL 32720.

162

FEINSMITH, MARVIN P.
b. New York, N.Y., 4 Dec. 1932. Studied bassoon
with Simon Kovar, composition with Henry Brant,
Juilliard School, 1954-56, 1960-62; conducting
at Mozarteum, Salzburg, 1959; at Manhattan School
of Music, M.M. 1967; further graduate work at
New York Univ. and Univ. of Denver. His awards
include scholarships for all study through Manhattan School; and commissions. He has been
bassoonist with the Indianapolis Symph., 1956-
59; Symphony of the Air, 1959-63; Little Orchestra Society, 1959-68, 1970-72; Israel Philharmonic Orch., 1968-70; Denver Symph. Orch.,
from 1972.
    WORKS: ORCHESTRA: Ethics of the Fathers,
with soprano solo, Hebrew text, Denver Symph.,
29 Dec. 1975; Isaiah, with baritone solo,
Hebrew text, specially designed set of 12-foot-
high chimes, Kansas City Philh., 11 Feb. 1979;
CHAMBER MUSIC: 2 Hebraic studies, solo bassoon;
Yiddish keit, wind quintet; Yizkor, solo flute;
Hebrew medley, string quartet; FILM SCORES:
2 wheeler; Sky sailing; Wheels for feet; Molly
Brown wouldn't recognize it anymore, television
special on KMGH, Denver, 1975.
    1457 S. Fairfax St., Denver, CO 80222

FELCIANO, RICHARD
b. Santa Rosa, Calif., 7 Dec. 1930. Studied
with Darius Milhaud at Mills Coll. and at Paris
Cons.; privately with Luigi Dallapiccola in
Florence, Italy; at Univ. of Iowa, Ph.D. 1959.
His awards include grants from the French and
Italian governments; Guggenheim fellowship; 2
Ford Found. grants; Nat. Endowment for the Arts
grant; Fulbright and Rockefeller grants; Fromm
Found. commissions; American Acad. of Arts and
Letters award, 1974. He was faculty member,
Lone Mountain Coll., 1959-67; from 1967, Univ.
of California, Berkeley; resident composer, Nat.
Center for Experiments in Television, 1967 and
1970; resident composer, City of Boston, 1971-
73.
    WORKS: OPERA: Sir Gawain and the Green
Knight, 1964; ORCHESTRA: Expressions; Mutations,
1966; Galactic rounds, 1972; CHAMBER MUSIC:
Contractions, wind quintet, 1965; Aubade, string
trio, harp, piano, 1966; Spectra, flute and
double bass, 1967; Evolutions, clarinet and
piano; Gravities, piano, 4 hands; Crasis, 6
instruments and tape; Lamentations for Jani
Christou, 9 instruments, percussion, tape, 1970;
Vineyards music, piano quintet and tape;
Noösphere I, alto flute and tape; Soundspace for
Mozart, flute, live electronics, tape, 1970;
Genesis 4: Sunbirth, tape; Noösphere II, tape;
Chöd, 6 players and tape, 1975; From the abyss,
tuba and tape, 1976; CHORUS: Pshelley's psalm,
poem by Shelley Hischiet, a cappella; 2 hymns
to howl by, texts by Allen Ginsburg; The captives,
with orch.; Out of sight (The ascension that
nobody saw), with organ and tape; also organ
works and audio-visual pieces, using lights,
film strips, etc.
    1326 Masonic Ave., San Francisco, CA 94117

FELDMAN, HERBERT BYRON
b. New York, N.Y., 6 Oct. 1931. Studied at
Juilliard School, 1948-52. He was instructor
at Juilliard, 1955-56; at Henry Street Settlement Music School, 1956-58.
    WORKS: CHAMBER MUSIC: string quartet,
Hempstead, N.Y., 21 Apr. 1974; string trio;
wind quintet; trio for oboe, viola, bassoon;
duets for 2 violins; VOCAL: Ecclesiastes, cantata for solo voice, chorus, orch.; Moon mad,
song cycle for soprano and piano; Dark house,
soprano and string quartet.
    51 Bayview Ave., Great Neck, NY 11022

FELDMAN, JOANN E.
b. New York, N.Y., 19 Oct. 1941. Studied with
Hugo Weisgall, Queens Coll., CUNY; with Arnold
Elston, Seymour Shifrin, and William Denny,
Univ. of California, Berkeley. She received the
Mechlis composition prize at Queens Coll., 1962;
and a Univ. of Redlands composition prize, 1965.
She was teaching assistant, Univ. of California,
1965-66; faculty member, Sonoma State Univ.,
from 1966.
    WORKS: ORCHESTRA: Antiphonies, 1965;
CHAMBER MUSIC: woodwind quintet, 1966; Variations, viola and piano, 1963; CHORUS: The 3
peoples; PIANO: Variations, 1973.
    7510 St. Helena Rd., Santa Rosa, CA 95404

FELDMAN, MORTON
b. New York, N.Y., 12 Jan. 1926. Studied with
Wallingford Riegger and Stefan Wolpe, and was
influenced by close association with Earle
Brown, John Cage, David Tudor, and Christian
Wolff in the early 1950s. His awards include
Nat. Inst.-American Acad. of Arts and Letters
award, 1970; and Koussevitzky Found. commission,
1975. He is Edgard Varese professor of music and
director, Center of the Creative and Performing
Arts, State Univ. of New York, Buffalo. Since
1968 he has also been director of the June in
Buffalo New Music Festival.
    WORKS: BALLET: Ixion; CHAMBER MUSIC:
Structures, string quartet, 1951; Projections I
and II, trumpet, violin, cello, 1951; Intersection I, 1951; Pieces for 4 pianos, 1957;
Atlantis, chamber orch., 1959; Durations I-V,
1960-61; The swallows of Salangan, chorus and 16
instruments; Last pieces, piano, 1962; Christian
Wolff in Cambridge, 1963; Journey to the end of
night, soprano and 4 wind instruments; De Kooning, piano trio, horn, percussion; 4 instruments.
1965; First principles, 1966-67; Chorus and instruments, 1967; Vertical thoughts 2, 1968;
False relationships and the extended ending, 2
chamber groups, 1968; The Strait of Magellan,
7 instruments; The viola in my life, viola and
6 instruments; Mme. Press died last night at 90;
Rothko Chapel, viola, percussion, chorus, 1972;
New York premiere, 28 Apr. 1974; King of Denmark,
percusssion; For Frank O'Hara, flute, clarinet,
piano trio, New York, 5 Dec. 1973; Voices and
instruments, 5 woodwinds, horn, timpani, contrabass, chorus, 1976; Neither, an opera for solo
soprano and full orch., on a text provided by
Samuel Beckett; the premiere was in Rome, 2nd
performance in Berlin, 3rd in New York, 19 Oct.
1978; Spring of Chosroes, violin and piano, 1978.
    703 W. Ferry St., Buffalo, NY 14222

FELDSHER, HOWARD M.

FELDSHER, HOWARD M.
b. Middletown, N.Y., 11 July 1936. Studied with
Warren Benson, Ithaca Coll.; with Theodore
Antoniou, Univ. of Utah on fellowship. He is
music educator, Valley Central Schools, and publications director, Aulos Music Publishers.
WORKS: CHAMBER MUSIC: Adagio and allegro,
bass clarinet and piano; 2 fugues, clarinet quarter; Habanera, oboe and piano; Calypso song,
flute and piano; Excursion, trumpet and piano;
Little suite for brass, brass quartet; The lure
of Latin, trombone and piano; My love is like a
red, red rose, a cappella chorus.
P.O. Box 54, Montgomery, NY 12549

FELDSTEIN, SAUL (SANDY)
b. New York, N.Y., 7 Sept. 1940. Studied at
State Univ. Coll., Potsdam, and at Columbia Univ.
He has received annual ASCAP awards since 1968.
He is executive vice-president, Alfred Publishing Co., Inc. He has published numerous
works for orchestra, stage band, concert band,
chorus, and method books for all instruments.
18201 Lake Encino Dr., Encino, CA 91316

FELICE, A. JOHN
b. St. Catherines, Ont., 5 June 1938. Studied
with John Beckwith and John Weinzweig, Univ. of
Toronto, B.M.; with Robert Cogan, New England
Cons., M.M. His awards include assistantships,
New England Cons., 1966-68; Sigma Alpha Iota
composition prize, 1968. He was faculty member,
University Settlement House, Toronto, 1961-63;
music director, Nat. Ballet School, 1963-65;
from 1966, on faculty, New England Cons.
WORKS: ORCHESTRA: Vision, 1973; CHAMBER
MUSIC: Quartet 1968, horn, violin, flute,
piano; Trio 1968, trumpet, flute, clarinet;
many works with similar titles for various instruments, which the composer says are different
pieces and not just different versions; Night
spaces, harp, 1972; Triatro, piano, 1972; Trio:
Sur la nom--Martha Folz 1971, harpsichord;
Vision, string quartet; Museum piece, toy piano,
string bass, speaker/singer, 1973; From
Quasimodo Sunday, double bass solo, 1976; Interlude, piano, Boston, 8 Oct. 1979.
11 Pemberton St., Cambridge, MA 02140

FENNELLY, BRIAN
b. Kingston, N.Y., 14 Aug. 1937. Studied with
Donald Martino, Mel Powell, Allen Forte, George
Perle, and Gunther Schuller, Yale Univ., B.A.
1963, M.M. 1965, Ph.D. 1968. His awards include
Noss prize in choral composition, 1965; American
Composers Alliace recording award, 1973; Martha
Baird Rockefeller grants, 1973, 1975, 1977;
Nat. Endowment for the Arts grant, 1977;
Guggenheim fellowship, 1980. He has been faculty
member, New York Univ., from 1968; editor, Con-
temporary Music Newsletter, from 1969; president,
U.S. Section, Internat. Society for Contemporary
Music, from 1977.
WORKS: ORCHESTRA: In wildness is the
preservation of the world, fantasy after Thoreau,
Tri-City Symphony, Davenport, Iowa, 5 Nov. 1976;
Concert piece for trumpet and orch., 1976;

CHAMBER MUSIC: duo for violin and piano, 1964;
wind quintet, 1967; Evanescences, 2 woodwinds,
2 strings, tape, 1969; SUNYATA, 4-channel tape,
1970; string quartet in 2 movements, 1971;
Tesserae II, fantasy for cello, 1972; Prelude
and elegy, brass quintet, 1973; Tesserae III,
solo viola, 1976, New York, 1 Dec. 1978; Sonata
seria, piano, 1976; Empirical rag, brass quintet,
1977, New York, 2 July 1979; Scintilla Prisca,
cello and piano, New York, 16 May 1979.
100 Bleecker St., Apt. 23B, New York, NY
10012

FENNER, BURT L.
b. New York, N.Y., 12 Aug. 1929. Studied with
Roy Travis, Peter Pindar Stearns, Mannes Coll.
of Music, B.S. 1959; with Otto Luening and Jack
Beeson, Columbia Univ., M.A. 1961. He received
a Nat. Endowment for the Arts grant, 1975. He
was faculty member, Mannes Coll., 1961-70; and
Pennsylvania State Univ. from 1970.
WORKS: ORCHESTRA: chamber symphony; symphony #2; symphony #3, 1975; Variations, string
quartet and orch.; GIALD; WIND ENSEMBLE: Music
for brass and timpani; Prelude, brass and tape;
Scherzo for wind band; CHAMBER MUSIC: string
quartet; wind quintet; brass quintet; Study for
timpani and low instruments; suite for flute and
bassoon; suite for strings, 1976; I like a look
of agony, baritone, ensemble, tape, 1977, Pittsburgh, 22 Apr. 1979.
620 Elmwood St., State College, PA 16801

FENNIMORE, JOSEPH
b. New York, N.Y., 16 Apr. 1940. Studied at
Eastman School of Music, B.M. 1962; Juilliard
School, M.S. 1963. His awards include a Ful-
bright grant, Rockefeller grant, Hour of Music,
Inc., grant. He is founder and director of
Hear America First, a New York City band concert
series, since 1971, devoted to the music of
American composers.
WORKS: THEATRE: incidental music to
Business of good government by John Arien, an
off-Broadway production, 1972; Eventide and
Don't call me by my right name, 2 chamber operas,
New York, 1 Oct. 1975; ORCHESTRA: piano con-
certo, 1962; CHAMBER MUSIC: clarinet sonata,
New York, 1 Oct. 1975; CHORUS: Cynic's song;
SONGS: Berlitz: Introduction to French, solo
song cycle; Party songs, N.Y., 1 Oct. 1975;
PIANO: 3 sonatas, #3 premiere, New York, 6 Mar.
1971; Bits and pieces, suite for young pianists.
463 West St., #105D, New York, NY 10014

FERGUSON, EDWIN EARLE
b. Brocket, N.Dak., 4 Aug. 1910. Studied music
at Drake Univ.; privately with Meyer Kupferman
in New York; but took his degrees in law and
was a lawyer for the Atomic Energy Commission,
keeping music as an avocation. He has won
several composition awards in local competitions.
He was pianist and arranger, radio station WHO,
Des Moines, 1929-35; director of music, United
Methodist Church, Chevy Chase, Md., from 1960.
WORKS: THEATRE: The confrontations of
Judas, sacred opera; Sorely tried, musical play;
CHAMBER MUSIC: 3 idiomatic exercises, clarinet,

violin, piano; <u>Franky and Johnny revisited</u>, piano quintet; <u>Pastorale</u>, string quartet; CHORUS: <u>The betrayal</u>, passion oratorio; <u>Coffee grows on white oak trees</u>, male voices; <u>The dark ocean</u>; <u>Upstream</u>; <u>A celebration of psalms</u>, comm. and performed by the Laurel Oratorio Society, Laurel, Md., 17 May 1981; SONGS: <u>What if a much of a which of a wind</u>, 2 voices and string quartet; 4 songs for voice and clarinet; <u>A woman unashamed</u>, song cycle for soprano; FILM SCORE: background music for a film on volcanoes shown at the Smithsonian Inst.

    5821 Osceola Rd., Bethesda, MD 20016

FERRAZANO (ZANO), ANTHONY JOSEPH
    b. Worcester, Mass., 4 June 1937. Studied at New England Cons., 1954-56; with Rouben Gregorian, Boston Cons., 1956-57; with Hugo Norden, Boston Univ., 1958-63; Forest Cons., Sussex Univ., England, D.M. 1963. He held a scholarship at New England Cons., was a teaching fellow at Boston Cons.; has received several commissions. He taught in public schools, 1956-57; was faculty member, New York School of Music, 1959; Worcester Polytechnic Inst., 1961; Schenectady Cons., 1966-67.
    WORKS: ORCHESTRA: 2 symphonies, 1959, 1960; <u>The gathering place</u>, 1959; symphonic suite, 1963; <u>Atonement</u>, 1968; <u>Dispersion</u>, 1969; CHAMBER MUSIC: 2 string quartets, 1956, 1967; <u>Jazz sonata</u>, bass and piano, 1958; flute sonata, 1958; <u>Hale recollections</u>, flute, clarinet, piano, 1967; <u>Preconception</u>, double bass and piano, 1971; <u>Night prelude</u>, piano, 1976; work for flute, clarinet, cello, double bass, piano, 1976; also choral works.
    P.O. Box 195, Wilmington, MA 01887

FERRIS, WILLIAM
    b. Chicago, Ill., 26 Feb. 1937. Attended Loyola Univ. and De Paul Univ.; studied privately with Leo Sowerby. He received 2 awards, Internat. Society for Contemporary Music, Chicago Chapter, 1958, 1960; Leo Sowerby award, 1969; and a commission for an opera, <u>Little moon of Alban</u>. He was music director, Sacred Heart Cathedral, Rochester; on music faculty, St. Bernard's Seminary; from 1973, American Cons. He is also conductor of the William Ferris Chorale, which he founded in 1960.
    WORKS: ORCHESTRA: concert piece for organ and string orch., 1967; symphony, 1968; concert piece for organ and 5 brass instruments, 1970; <u>Bristol Hills</u>, string orch., 1970; CHAMBER MUSIC: trio for flute, bassoon, piano, 1957; <u>3 short lyrics</u>, tenor, flute, cello, 1958; <u>A festival flourish</u>, 2 trumpets, and organ, 1966; CHORUS: <u>De profundis</u>, Fordham Univ., 22 Nov. 1964; <u>The angelic salutation: Glory to God in the highest</u>, 1968; <u>Out of Egypt</u>, cantata, 1969; SONGS: <u>Sorrowful dreams</u>, text by Millay, mezzo-soprano, 1972; <u>A clear midnight</u>, baritone and piano, 1973; many other songs, choral works, instrumental pieces.
    American Conservatory, 116 South Michigan Ave., Chicago, IL 60603

FERRITTO, JOHN E.
    b. Cleveland, Ohio, 1937. Graduated from Cleveland Inst. of Music; later studied piano with Ward Davenny and composition with Mel Powell at Yale Univ. He served as coconductor, 7th Army Symphony Orch., in Europe. He is faculty member, Wittenberg Univ., and music director of the Springfield Symphony Orch. His compositions include <u>Sogni</u> and <u>Oggi</u>, both for soprano, clarinet, and piano, 1969; text for both pieces by the composer.
    128 The Post Rd., Apt. B, Springfield, OH 45503

FETLER, PAUL
    b. Philadelphia, Pa., 17 Feb. 1920. Studied with David Van Vactor, Northwestern Univ.; with Quincy Porter and Paul Hindemith, Yale Univ.; and with Boris Blacher, Berlin Acad. of Music. His awards include 2 Guggenheim grants; Alice M. Ditson award; Ford Found. grant; Yale Alumni Certificate of Merit; 2 Nat. Endowment for the Arts grants, 1975, 1976; annual ASCAP awards from 1962. He has been faculty member, Univ. of Minnesota, since 1948.
    WORKS: OPERA: <u>Sturge MacLean</u>; ORCHESTRA: 4 symphonies; <u>Contrasts for orchestra</u>; <u>3 poems by Walt Whitman</u>, narrator and orch.; violin concerto; <u>Celebration</u>; <u>3 impressions</u>, guitar and orch.; CHAMBER MUSIC: <u>3 pieces</u>, violin and piano; <u>Cycles</u>, percussion and piano; <u>Dialogue</u>, flute and guitar; <u>Pastoral suite</u>, piano trio; CHORUS: <u>Now this is the story</u>, women's voices; <u>Lamentations</u>, oratorio; <u>Dream of Shalom</u>, cantata with flute, trumpet, organ and narrator; <u>Songs of the night</u>, with flute and narrator, Minneapolis, 5 June 1976; also film scores, music for theatre and dance.
    420 Mt. Curve Blvd., St. Paul, MN 55105

FICARROTTA, JOHN
    b. New York, N.Y., 27 Sept. 1955. Studied with John Bavacchi and Van Dijk, Berklee Coll. of Music, B.M.; with Hugo Norden, Boston Univ. He won a Berklee Coll. Faculty Assoc. award, 1977. He was musical director, Young People's Orchestra, 1975-77; then private teacher.
    WORKS: ORCHESTRA: <u>Largo and march</u>; <u>Nocturne</u>, string orch.; BAND: overture; CHAMBER MUSIC: <u>5 movements</u>, flute and piano; brass quartet; <u>Confessions de l'espirit</u>, trumpet, trombone, piano; piano sonata; <u>Theme and variations</u>, string trio; <u>Prelude and fugue</u>, brass quartet; <u>3 short pieces</u>, piano.
    34 Hampton Rd., Lynbrook, NY 11563

FICHTHORN, CLAUDE L.
    b. Reading, Pa., 7 June 1885. Studied at Missouri Valley Coll., B.A., honorary D.M.; Columbia Univ., M.A. He was organist-choir-master in Reading, Pa., and Kansas City, Mo.; then on music faculty, Missouri Valley Coll., music dept. chairman from 1947.
    WORKS: CHORUS: <u>O saving victim</u>, a cappella; <u>In Judea's hills</u>; <u>The everlasting light</u>; also sacred songs and organ pieces.

FICKENSCHER, ARTHUR
b. Aurora, Ill., 9 Mar. 1871; d. San Francisco,
15 Apr. 1954. Studied at Munich Cons. He
toured the U.S. as accompanist; taught at
schools in San Francisco and Oakland, then
privately in Berlin and New York; was head of
music department, Univ. of Virginia, 1920-41;
returned to San Francisco in 1947. He developed
a system of pure intonation and invented an instrument, the polytone, on which the octave was
divided into 60 tones; published an article on
the polytone and its possibilities (Musical
Quarterly, July 1941).
      WORKS: ORCHESTRA: Willowwave and the wello-
way, 1925; The day of judgment, 1927; Dies irae,
chamber orch., 1927; Out of the Gay Nineties;
Variations on a theme in medieval style, 1937;
The chamber blue, mimodrama for orch., soli,
women's chorus, dancers, Univ. of Virginia,
5 Apr. 1938; The land east of the sun and west
of the moon, chorus and orch.; CHAMBER MUSIC:
Evolutionary quintet, 1920-29, piano and strings,
a work salvaged by memory from a violin sonata
and orchestral scherzo burned in the San Francisco earthquake and fire in 1906; the 2nd
movement became a separate work entitled The 7th
realm.

FIELD, COREY
b. Los Angeles, Calif., 9 July 1956. Studied
with Thea Musgrave and Peter Racine Fricker,
Univ. of California, Santa Barbara; with
Krzysztof Penderecki, Aspen Music School; at
Edinburgh Univ. and at Vienna Univ. He won an
award in the Delius Festival competition, 1975.
He was lecturer, Coll. of Creative Studies,
Univ. of Calif., 1977-78; founder and music
director, Contemporary Music Ensemble; public
school music teacher from 1978.
      WORKS: CHAMBER MUSIC: Probe, chamber orch.,
1975; 3 songs, soprano and clarinet, and Nocturnes, string trio, both performed at Aspen
Music Festival, 1977.
      1539 Courtney Ave., Hollywood, CA 90046

FIELDING, JERRY
b. Pittsburgh, Pa., 17 June 1922. Attended
Carnegie Inst. of Technology. He has been composer and arranger for films and for the television show, Hogan's heroes. His works include
City of Brass; Polynesian peace chant; Paris
magicque; The essence of calculated calm.
      2201 Marvilla Dr., Hollywood, CA 90028

FIELDS, IRVING
b. New York, N.Y., 4 Aug. 1915. Studied at
Eastman School of Music. His compositions include An American forest, a symphony; and Latin
American songs.

FILAS, THOMAS J.
b. Chicago, Ill., 5 Mar. 1908. Attended Armour
Inst. of Technology. He played oboe, clarinet,
and saxophone in orchestras throughout the
country and on Chicago radio stations. He received the Paul Whiteman $1000 award for a con-
certo for reed doubles, 1947. His other works
include Hushabye lullabye, tone poem; Lost

River, rhapsody for oboe, harp, string orch.;
Velocity, clarinet; Campaign march; other marches
and hymns.
      1921 S. Central Park Ave., Chicago, IL
60623

FILLMORE, HENRY
b. Cincinnati, Ohio, 2 Dec. 1881; d. Miami, Fla.,
7 Dec. 1956. Attended Miami Inst. In 1916 he
organized the Henry Fillmore Concert Band for
which he wrote many popular marches, including
Men of Ohio, Men of Florida, Military escort
march, et al.

FINCKEL, MICHAEL PHILIP
b. Bennington, Vt., 8 Oct. 1945. Studied with
Henry Brant and Louis Calabro, Bennington Coll.;
cello with his father, and with Jack Frazer and
George Neikrug, Oberlin Cons. He has been
faculty member, Bennington Coll., from 1971;
and principal cellist and soloist, Vermont State
Symphony, from 1971.
      WORKS: ORCHESTRA: Tyco; cello concerto in
which the orchestra included bird calls, 2 TV
sets, 2 radios; CHAMBER MUSIC: The red cow is
dead, cello quartet and voice; Mira, 2 flutes,
clarinet, cello; Prelude to the green dream,
cello quartet, tape, 4 bass gongs, hurdy-gurdy,
hammer dulcimer, kazoo, voice, and hambone
artist, New York, 6 May 1973; Antiphonists, 12
celli; Chamber, 3 clarinets, 3 celli, piano;
Grim trio, bass drum, vibraphone, cello.
      Bennington College, Bennington, VT 05201

FINE, IRVING
b. Boston, Mass., 3 Dec. 1914; d. Boston, 23
Aug. 1962. Studied with Walter Piston, Edward
Burlingame Hill, and Archibald T. Davison,
Harvard Univ., B.A. 1937, M.A. 1938; with Nadia
Boulanger in Cambridge, 1938, in Paris, 1939.
His awards included 2 Guggenheim grants, Fulbright grant, Wyman Found. grant, MacDowell
fellowship; Nat. Inst. of Arts and Letters
award, Soc. for Publication of American Music
award, and many commissions. He was faculty
member, Harvard Univ., 1939-50; Berkshire Music
Center, 1946-50; and at Brandeis Univ., 1950-62.
      WORKS: ORCHESTRA: Alice in Wonderland, with
chorus, 1942; Toccata concertante, 1948; Serious
song and lament, string orch., 1955; Diversion,
1960; symphony, 1962; CHAMBER MUSIC: Fantasia,
string trio; violin sonata, 1946; Partita, wind
quintet, 1948; string quartet, 1952; Romanza,
wind quintet, 1961; VOICE: The choral New
Yorker, cantata, 1944; The hour glass, choral
cycle, 1949; Mutability, song cycle, 1952;
Childhood fables for grownups, song cycle, 1956;
McCord's menagerie, chorus; and piano works.

FINE, VIVIAN
b. Chicago, Ill., 28 Sept. 1913. Studied
privately with Ruth Crawford-Seeger, 1925-30,
and with Roger Sessions, 1934-42. Her awards
include the Dollard award; Rockefeller Found.
grant, 1964; Ford Found. grant, 1966; 2 Nat.
Endowment for the Arts grants, 1974, 1976;
Guggenheim fellowship, 1980; and commissions.
She taught at Juilliard School, 1948; New York

Univ., 1945-48; Bennington Coll., from 1964.

WORKS: THEATRE: The race of life, ballet, 1938; A guide to the life expectancy of a rose, stage work for voices and chamber ensemble, 1956, New York, 7 Feb. 1959; Alcestis, ballet, 1960; The women in the garden, chamber opera, libretto based on texts of Virginia Woolf, Gertrude Stein, Emily Dickinson, and Isadora Duncan, San Francisco, 12 Feb. 1978; ORCHESTRA: Concertante, piano and orch., 1944; concerto for piano, strings, percussion, Finch Coll., New York, 15 Apr. 1973; Romantic ode, Cambridge, 3 Dec. 1978, composer conducting; CHAMBER MUSIC: suite for oboe and piano, 1939; Variations for harp; string quartet; quintet for trumpet, harp, string trio; Fantasy, cello and piano; brass quartet, New York, 22 May 1979; CHORUS: Valedictions, chorus and 10 instruments, 1959; Paean, with brass ensemble and speaker, 1969; Teisho, 8 voices and string quartet, 1975; Meeting for equal rights: 1866, 2 soloists, narrator, 2 choruses, orch., New York, 23 Apr. 1976; SONGS: 4 songs for contralto and strings; The Great Wall of China, voice, flute, cello, piano, Kafka text, 1947; The confession, 1963; The song of Persephone, 1964; 2 Neruda poems, 1971; Missa brevis, 4 cellos and taped voice, 1972, New York, 15 Apr. 1973; PIANO: Small sad sparrow; Sinfonia and fugato, 1963; Momenti; other works in all genres.

R.D. 1, North Bennington, VT 05257

FINK, MICHAEL
b. Long Beach, Calif., 15 Mar. 1939. Studied guitar with Vicente Gomez at an early age; composition with Ernest Kanitz, Ingolf Dahl, Halsey Stevens at Univ. of Southern California, B.M. 1960, Ph.D. 1977; with David Pinkham, New England Cons., M.M. 1962. His awards have included scholarships for all study and a Tanglewood fellowship, 1961. From age 13 he has composed and worked professionally as guitarist. In 1975 he joined the faculty at Univ. of Texas, San Antonio.

WORKS: CHAMBER MUSIC: Sonata da camera, flute; Caprices, clarinet, 1961; 3 lyric pieces, piano; sonata for guitar solo, 1977; Fantasia Monteverdiana, guitar quartet, 1977; CHORUS: From a very little sphinx, women's voices and string quartet; Septem angeli, cantata, with piano, 4 hands, and chamber ensemble; Te Deum, with tenor solo, piano, 1962; Jubilate deo, with brass quintet, 1971; Full fathom five, a cappella; Ever 'gainst that season, with guitar; SONGS: What lips my lips have kissed, soprano, Millay text, 1958; Rain comes down, soprano, Millay text, 1963; As my heart was, cycle for baritone and guitar, 1978.

4826 Bucknell, San Antonio, TX 78249

FINK, MYRON S.
b. Chicago, Ill., 19 Apr. 1932. Studied with Felix Borowski, 1942-48; with Mario Castelnuovo-Tedesco in Los Angeles, 1948-50; with Bernard Wagenaar at Juilliard School, 1951-52; Burrill Phillips, Univ. of Illinois, 1952-55; with Robert Palmer, Cornell Univ., 1959-60; and in Vienna. He held a Woodrow Wilson Memorial fel-

lowship, 1954-55; Fulbright scholarship, 1955-56. He taught at Alma Coll., 1958-61; joined the faculty at Hunter Coll. in 1966.

WORKS: THEATRE: The boor, 1-act opera, 1955; Susanna and the elders, opera; Jeremiah, 4-act opera, 1952; Judith and Holofernes, 3-act opera, 1978; incidental music to Caucasian chalk circle, 1955; ORCHESTRA: piano concerto; CHAMBER MUSIC: 2 string quartets; piano trio; VOICE: 15 songs to poems of Witter Bynner; PIANO: 12 etudes; Sinfonia; Triptych.

10 Park Ave., Old Greenwich, CT 06870

FINK, ROBERT R.
b. Belding, Mich., 31 Jan. 1933. Studied with H. Owen Reed and James Niblock, Michigan State Univ., B.M. 1955, M.M. 1956; and with Mario Castelnuovo-Tedesco. He was faculty member, State Univ. Coll., Fredonia, N.Y., 1956-57; and at Western Michigan Univ. from 1957.

WORKS: CHAMBER MUSIC: Modal suite, brass trio, 1959; 4 modes for winds, woodwind quartet, 1967; Variations on a theme by Vivaldi, woodwind quintet; CHORUS: Seal lullaby; There was once a puffin, 1967; Cantata on Psalm 48, with soprano solo and brass; SONGS: Dialogue, soprano, tenor, chamber orch.; 7 parables, soprano and woodwind quintet.

Music Dept., Western Michigan Univ., Kalamazoo, MI 49001

FINLEY, LORRAINE NOEL (Mrs. Theodore F. Fitch)
b. Montreal, P.Q., 24 Dec. 1898; U.S. citizen; d. Greenwich, Conn., 13 Feb. 1972. Attended schools in Canada, Switzerland, Germany; studied composition with Percy Goetschius and Rubin Goldmark at Juilliard School; violin, piano, and voice with various teachers; graduate study at Columbia Univ. Her compositions won numerous awards in national competitions. She traveled extensively in Europe, the Near East, Africa, South America, China, and Japan. From 1934 she worked for publishing firms translating into English lyrics of compositions of Bach, Beethoven, Brahms, Faure, Debussy, et al. Her English translation for Milhaud's Le pauvre matelot was used for the Broadway premiere of that opera. With her husband, she appeared in "Mr. and Mrs. Composer" recitals.

WORKS: THEATRE: Persian miniatures, ballet; ORCHESTRA: 3 theatre portraits, a suite; symphony; CHAMBER MUSIC: violin sonata; clarinet sonata; CHORUS: Trees of Jotham, cantata; numerous songs and instrumental pieces.

FINN, WILLIAM J.
b. Boston, Mass., 7 Sept. 1881; d. Bronxville, N.Y., 20 Mar. 1961. Attended St. Charles Coll., Md.; Catholic Univ.; ordained 1906; Notre Dame Univ., L.L.D. 1914. He was choirmaster and choral conductor, Old St. Mary's, and head, Paulist Choristers, Chicago, 1904-18; Church of St. Paul the Apostle, New York, 1918-46; returned to Old St. Mary's, 1947. He was author of books on voice training and choral art.

WORKS: ORCHESTRA: Paschal suite; CHORUS: Quintette of carols; A rhythmic trilogy for Easter; Easter sermon of the birds; Brother Ass and Saint Francis.

FINNEY, ROSS LEE

FINNEY, ROSS LEE
b. Wells., Minn., 23 Dec. 1906. Studied with
Donald Ferguson, Univ. of Minnesota, 1924-25;
Carleton Coll., B.A. 1927, L.H.D.; with Nadia
Boulanger, 1927-28; Harvard Univ., 1928-29;
Alban Berg, 1931-32; Roger Sessions, 1935-36.
His many honors include a Johnson fellowship,
1927; Pulitzer prize, 1935; Conn. Valley prize,
1935; 2 Guggenheim grants, 1937, 1947; Purple
Heart and Certificate of Merit, 1945; Boston
Symph. award, 1955; Rockefeller grant, 1956;
American Acad. of Arts and Letters award, 1956;
Brandeis Gold Medal, 1967; and many commissions.
He was faculty member, Smith Coll., 1929-48;
served in Office of Strategic Services, 1943-45;
professor and composer-in-residence, Univ. of
Michigan, 1949-74.
WORKS: ORCHESTRA: 2 violin concertos,
1933, rev. 1952, 1973, Dallas, 31 Mar. 1976; 4
symphonies, 1942, 1959, 1960, 1972, #4 Baltimore,
9 May 1973; Hymn, fuguing and holiday, 1943;
2 piano concertos, 1948, 1968; Variations, 1957;
percussion concerto, 1965; Symphony concertante,
Kansas City, 28 Feb. 1968; Spaces, 1971, Fargo,
N.Dak., 26 Mar. 1972; concerto for strings, New
York, 5 Dec. 1977; BAND: Summer in Valley City,
Univ. of Michigan, 1 Apr. 1971; saxophone concerto, 1974; Skating on the Sheyenne, Brooklyn,
N.Y., 20 May 1978; CHAMBER MUSIC: 3 violin
sonatas, 1934, 1951, 1955; 8 string quartets,
1935-60; 2 viola sonatas, 1937, 1953; 2 piano
trios, 1938, 1954; cello sonata, 1950; 2 piano
quintets, 1953, 1961; Elegy and march, trombone
solo, 1954; Fantasy, solo cello, 1957; Fantasy,
solo violin, 1958; string quintet, 1958; 3 pieces
for strings, winds, percussion, tape, 1962;
Divertimento, woodwind quintet, 1963; Divertissement, clarinet, piano trio, 1964; 3 studies in
fours, percussion, 1965; 2 acts for 3 players,
clarinet, percussion, piano, 1970; Variation on
a memory, 10 instruments, Baltimore, 19 Oct.
1975; Narrative, solo cello and 14 instruments,
1976; CHORUS: Pole Star for this year, with soli
and orch., 1939; Oh, bury me not, 1940; Edge of
shadow, 1959; Still are new worlds, with narrator and orch., 1962; Nun's priest's tale, with
narrator, folk singer, orch., 1965; The martyr's
elegy, 1969; The remorseless rush of time, River
Falls, Wis., 23 Apr. 1970; Earthrise, with soli
and orch., 1978; PIANO: 4 sonatas, 1933-45;
Fantasy, 1939; Nostalgic waltzes, 1947; Variations on a theme by Alban Berg, 1952; Sonata
quasi una fantasia, 1961; 32 piano games, 1968;
24 inventions, 1970; ORGAN: Fantasy, 1958;
5 organ fantasies, 1967; and many songs.
2015 Geddes Ave., Ann Arbor, MI 48104

FIORILLO, DANTE
b. New York, N.Y., 4 July 1905. Studied cello
at the Greenwich House Music Settlement, but is
largely self-taught in composition. He received
a Guggenheim fellowship, in 1935, renewed for 3
successive years, and a Pulitzer grant in 1939
"on the basis of 8 of 12 symphonies he had composed."
WORKS: ORCHESTRA: 12 symphonies; music for
chamber orchestra; concerto for harpsichord and
strings; concerto for oboe, horn, strings, and

timpani; several partitas for orch.; concertos
for various instruments; CHAMBER MUSIC: 11
string quartets; piano quintets and trios; instrumental sonatas; horn quintet; choruses and
songs.

FIRESTONE, IDABELLE (Mrs. Harvey S.)
b. Minnesota City, Minn., 10 Nov. 1874; d. Akron,
Ohio, 9 July 1954. Wrote If I could tell thee,
theme song of the "Voice of Firestone," radio
and television program. Other songs are You are
the song in my heart; Do you recall; Melody of
love; Bluebirds.

FISCHER, EDITH STEINKRAUS
b. Portland, Oreg., 9 Jan. 1922. Studied with
Donald Ferguson, Univ. of Minnesota, B.A. 1942;
with Bernard Wagenaar, Vittorio Giannini,
Sergius Kagen, Juilliard Graduate School, dipl.,
1946. She was Rhode Island Woman Composer of
the Year, 1969. She is adjunct professor of
voice, Brown Univ. and R.I. Jr. Coll.; soloist,
Newman Congregational Church, Rumford, R.I.
WORKS: CHAMBER MUSIC: 5 string quartets;
Rhapsody, viola and piano; 5 canonic movements,
violin and viola; trio for 2 obes and viola;
Fantasy, violin and piano; numerous anthems and
songs.
33 Euclid Ave., Riverside, RI 02915

FISCHER, IRWIN
b. Iowa City, Iowa, 5 July 1903; d. Wilmette,
Ill., 7 May 1977. Studied at American Cons.,
M.M. summa cum laude 1930; with Nadia Boulanger,
1931; Zoltan Kodaly, 1936; Bruno Walter, Nicolai
Malko, Bernhard Paumgartner, Salzburg Mozarteum,
1937. He held a scholarship for study in Salzburg. He was organist, Chicago Symph. Orch.,
1944-67; conductor, American Cons. Orch., 1945-
57; Evanston Symph. Orch., 1953-58; West Suburban
Symph., 1955-77; was faculty member, American
Cons., 1930-77, dean of the faculty in 1977.
WORKS: ORCHESTRA: Rhapsody on French folk
tunes, 1934; piano concerto, 1936; Marco Polo,
fantasy overture, 1937; Lament, cello and orch.,
1939; Ariadne abandoned, 1941; Chorale fantasy,
organ and orch.; Concerto giocoso, clarinet and
orch.; Idyll, violin and orch.; Mountain tune
trilogy; Sketches from childhood, 1946; symphony
#1; short symphony; Hungarian set (The pearly
bouquet), strings and celesta, 1948; Overture on
an exuberant tone row; Statement: 1976, chorus,
brass, strings, was commissioned for the Bicentennial and performed at New Haven, Conn., 25
Apr. 1976; also many choral works, piano and
organ pieces, sacred songs.

FISCHER, WILLIAM
b. Shelby, Miss., 5 Mar. 1935. Studied at Xavier
Univ.; Colorado Coll.; Univ. of Vienna; and
Vienna Acad. of Music. His awards include a
Fulbright grant; Rockefeller Found. grant; Stern
Family Found. grant; German State government
award. He is executive director, Society of
Black Composers, and owner of a record company.
WORKS: A quiet movement, orch., 1966; Time
I, saxophone, viola, cello, percussion, tape,
1966; Batucada fantastica, 2 percussionists,

tape, 1968; Gift of Lesbos, cello, piano, and tape, 1968.

FISHER, ALFRED
b. Boston, Mass., 30 June 1942. Studied with David Burge, Univ. of Colorado; John Pozdro and Douglas Moore, Univ. of Kansas; with H. Owen Reed, Michigan State Univ. He held scholarships for all study and in 1968, won first prize in a Michigan Music Teachers Assoc. contest. He was faculty member, Univ. of Western Ontario, 1969-72; Univ. of Saskatchewan, 1972; from 1973, Acadia Univ., Wolfville, N.S.
    WORKS: CHAMBER MUSIC: 5 time prisms; CHORUS: Lamentation canticle; My Lai canticle, with tape; SONGS: Songs of the gentle night; PIANO: 6 aphorisms; also electronic and improvisatory pieces.
    R.R. 1, Port Williams, Kings County, Nova Scotia

FISHER, DORIS
b. New York, N.Y., 2 May 1915. Studied at Juilliard School. She sang with Eddie Duchin Orch., 1943, then formed her own group. She composed scores for the films Gilda; Down to earth; Thrill of Brazil; many popular songs.

FISHER, FREDERIC I.
b. Chicago, Ill., 27 Aug. 1930. Studied with his father, Irwin Fischer; with Robert Delaney, Northwestern Univ., B.M. 1952; Eastman School of Music, M.M. 1953, D.M.A. 1963; with Nadia Boulanger in Paris, 1958, on a Fulbright grant. He was faculty member, Oklahoma State Univ., 1959-68; from 1968, North Texas State Univ.
    WORKS: PIANO: 3 sonatas, 1957; Cindy, 2 pianos, 1963; Variations on a happy tune, piano, 4 hands, 1965; The commuter society, 2 pianos, 2 narrators, 1972.
    1318 Ridgecrest Circle, Denton, TX 76201

FISHER, GLADYS W.
b. Klamath Falls, Oreg., 16 May 1900. Studied with W. J. McCoy, Domenico Brescia, Darius Milhaud, Harvey Gaul, and Roland Leich, Mills Coll., A.B., B.M. She won 10 awards in Penn. Fed. of Music Clubs contests and a Mu Phi Epsilon prize. She was faculty member, Indiana, Pa., Normal School, 1921-24; at Mills Coll., 1924-25; music director, Presbyterian Church, Indiana, Pa., 1932-66.
    WORKS: CHAMBER MUSIC: A hike in the woods, cello trio; Contrasts, cello trio; 2 pieces for string trio, Indiana Univ. of Pa., 12 Dec. 1975; CHORUS: Wake my heart; What child is this?; Music, I yield to thee; KEYBOARD: 3 waltzes for duo pianos; Caprice, piano solo; Shepherd's psalm, chorale prelude on "Evan" for organ, Indiana Univ., 22 Mar. 1976, and at Organ Historical Society, Detroit, 29 June 1977.
    620 School St., Indiana, PA 15701

FISHER, NORMAN Z.
b. Fessenden, N.Dak., 27 June 1920. Attended Lewis and Clark Coll., B.A. 1942; Reed Coll.; Univ. of Oregon; Union Theological Seminary, New York, M.S.M. 1946; his composition teachers were T. Tertius Noble and Harold Friedell. He has been church organist from 1946; director, Shreveport Symph. Chorale, from 1946; was on faculty, Centenary Coll., 1955-70.
    WORKS: ORGAN: Prelude on a French psalm tune; Toccata on a French psalm tune.
    3708 Greenway Place, Shreveport, LA 71105

FISHER, STEPHEN D.
b. Albany, N.Y., 27 May 1940. Studied with Billy Jim Layton and Daniel Pinkham, New England Cons. He received a BMI student composer award, 1960, and was on the BMI judging panel for 1972.
    WORKS: CHAMBER MUSIC: Involution, piccolo, trumpet, harpsichord, 1963; Music for 9 instruments, 1963; string quartet, 1964; Elegy for Sept. 2, 1975, violin, 1976; Concertpiece, contrabass solo, 1976.

FISHER, TRUMAN REX
b. Taft, Calif., 10 Nov. 1927. Attended Occidental Coll., M.A.; studied with Ernest Kanitz and Ingolf Dahl. He is on the faculty, Pasadena City Coll.
    WORKS: OPERA: Lysistrata, 2 acts; The wasps, 2 acts; BAND: Harlequinade; CHAMBER MUSIC: piano trio; piano sonata; flute sonatina; CHORUS: Lincoln, man of the people, with orch.; Christmas, One B.C., with organ and percussion; Magnificat, with piano, 4 hands, harp, percussion.
    635 Valle Vista Dr., Sierre Madre, CA 91024

FISHMAN, MARIAN
b. Brooklyn, N.Y., 7 Dec. 1941. Studied privately with Wallingford Riegger; with Thomas Beversdorf at Indiana Univ., B.M.; with Donald Lybbert, Hunter Coll., M.A.; further graduate study at Indiana Univ. She has held a fellowship at the MacDowell Colony; was instructor, Prairie View A&M Coll., 1967-68; associate instructor, Indiana Univ., 1971.
    WORKS: ORCHESTRA: Adagio for orchestra; CHAMBER MUSIC: 6 studies in sonorities, 4 woodwinds; Glimpses, clarinet solo; 4 miniatures, violin, viola, 2 cellos; 3 epigrams, flute and harp; Conceptions, solo bassoon; Interplay, violin and harp; Lines and figures, solo flute; Contrasting moods, trumpet and piano; Vignettes, piano; CHORUS: The hollow men, tenor, bass-baritone, chamber ensemble; Translations of the exile, male voices, chamber ensemble; SONGS: Expressions of loneliness; Evocations.

FISSINGER, EDWIN R.
b. Chicago, Ill., 15 June 1920. Studied with Leo Sowerby at American Cons. He received the Kimball award, 1951; Fine Arts award, 1953; and numerous commissions. He was faculty member, American Cons., 1948-54; Univ. of Illinois, 1957-67; and from 1967, at North Dakota State Univ.
    WORKS: CHORUS: O make a joyful noise, Psalm 66; Psalm 134; Star that I see; By the waters of Babylon; many masses, motets, anthems, and songs.
    57 15th Ave., Fargo, ND 58102

FITCH, THEODORE F.

FITCH, THEODORE F.
b. Rochester, N.Y., 17 Feb. 1900. Attended Univ.
of Rochester, A.B. 1922, M.A. 1927; studied with
Eugene Goossens, T. Yorke Trotter, Selim Palmgran
in Rochester. He received commissions for 2
cantatas. He was faculty member, Univ. of North
Carolina, 1922-24; Univ. of Rochester, 1925-36;
director, Brooklyn Music School Settlement,
1936-58; with his wife, Lorraine Noel Finley,
appeared in "Mr. and Mrs. Composer" recitals.
WORKS: ORCHESTRA: Terra nova, tone poem;
Blue oxen; piano concerto; Mariposa suite;
Tuesday's tabloid; 4 New England fancies; CHAMBER
MUSIC: Divertimento, chamber orch.; Sestina,
clarinet and strings; cello sonata; string quartet; Triptych for strings; CHORUS: High tide of
the year, cantata; Anne Rutledge, cantata;
General Booth enters heaven, cantata; Canticle
of a questing soul, 8-part chorus and orch.;
many songs, anthems, and other choral works.

FITCH, MRS. THEODORE F. See FINLEY, LORRAINE NOEL

FITELBERG, JERZY
b. Warsaw, Poland, 20 May. 1903; to U.S. 1940;
d. New York, 25 Apr. 1951. Studied with his
father, then at the Hochschule für Musik, Berlin.
He received the Elizabeth Sprague Coolidge award
in 1936 for a string quartet.
WORKS: ORCHESTRA: 3 suites, 1926-30; concerto for string orch., 1928; 2 violin concertos,
1932, 1937; The golden horn, string orch., 1942;
Nocturne, 1946; CHAMBER MUSIC: 5 string quartets; wind octet; sonata for 2 violins and 2
pianos; sonatina for 2 violins; many songs.

FITT, ROBERT J.
b. Philadelphia, Pa., 3 July 1945. Studied at
Temple Univ. and Trenton State Coll., M.A. He
has been band director and percussion instructor,
Centennial School District, Warminster, Pa.,
from 1968; band director, Delaware Valley Coll.,
from 1970.
WORKS: PERCUSSION: Mallets in wonderland;
Shades of Latin.
105 Earl Lane, Hatboro, PA 19040

FITZGERALD, R. BERNARD
b. Martinsville, Ill., 11 Apr. 1911. Studied at
Oberlin Coll., B.M. 1932; Jordan Cons., M.M.
1935. His faculty positions have included
Jordan Cons., 1933-35; Univ. of Idaho, 1938-40;
Univ. of Texas, 1940-56; Univ. of Kentucky,
1956 to retirement in 1976; also director, Ford
Found. Contemporary Music Project, administered
by MENC, 1963-65 (on leave from Univ. of Kentucky).
WORKS: BAND: Soliloquy; Chorale fantasia;
Bicentennial fanfare; Trilogy (Celebration),
Lexington, Ky., 24 Apr. 1976; BRASS ENSEMBLE:
Scherzino, 4 trumpets, 1936; Tarantella, 2
trumpets, horn, trombone, 1936; 2 brass fanfares,
1950; Dixieland fanfares, 1951; fanfares for
brass and organ, 1973; suite for brass choir,
1973; suite for double brass choir; CHORUS: The
sky is up above the roof, 1937; Music at night,
1938; The horseman, male voices, 1938; Frates in
unum, male voices, 1947; Now sing we noel, 1961;

She walks in beauty, a cappella, 1968; Stanzas
for music, a cappella, 1968; Ode to America,
chorus and band, text from L. B. Johnson's
inaugural address, Austin, Tex., 2 May 1976;
SONGS: Triptych, soprano, chamber ensemble,
Univ. of Kentucky, 14 Feb. 1969.
2087 Old Nassau Rd., Lexington, KY 40504

FITZRANDOLPH, CHARLES I.
b. Nile, N.Y., 3 Dec. 1921. Studied with
Bernhard Westlund, Milton Coll.; with Cecil
Effinger, Univ. of Colorado. He has taught in
public schools in Wisconsin, 1947-53; Pueblo,
Colo., 1956-57; Denver, 1960-63; Boulder, 1963-
71.
WORKS: CHORUS: Parting gifts, 8-part
chorus, text by Elinor Wylie, 1968; With music
strong I come, 8-part chorus, text by Whitman,
1969; Boulder Valley, school district song, text
by composer, 1971.

FLAGELLO, NICOLAS
b. New York, N.Y., 15 Mar. 1928. Studied piano,
violin, viola, cello, and oboe with various
teachers, conducting with Dmitri Mitropoulos; at
Manhattan School of Music, B.M., M.M. 1950; St.
Cecilia Acad., Rome, Mus.D. 1956; composition
with Vittorio Giannini and Ildebrando Pizzetti.
His awards include a Fulbright grant, 1955; first
prize in creativitiy, St. Cecilia Acad., 1956;
annual ASCAP awards; New York Critics' Circle
award, 1961; citation, Vatican's Order of Peter
and Paul for opera, The judgment of St. Francis;
City of Salerno Gold Medal, 1968; many commissions. He has been faculty member, Manhattan
School from 1950; at Curtis Inst., 1964-65;
coordinator with V. Giannini, North Carolina
School of the Arts, and present consultant; piano
recitalist and accompanist; violinist, violist,
and oboist in symphonic and operatic orchestras;
conductor, Chicago Lyric Theatre, 1960-61; New
York State Theatre, 1968; assistant to Antonio
Votto, La Scala, 1960, etc.
WORKS: OPERA: Mirra, 1953; The wig, 1 act,
1953; Rip Van Winkle, children's operetta, 1957;
The sisters, 1 act, 1958; The judgment of St.
Francis, 1 act, 1959; The piper of Hamelin,
children's opera to composer's libretto, 1970;
ORCHESTRA: Beowulf, tone poem, 1949; 3 piano
concertos, 1950, 1955, 1962; Suite for Amber,
1951; Symphonic aria, 1951; overture, 1952;
flute concerto, 1953; Theme, variations and
fugue, 1955; violin concerto, 1956; Missa sinfonica, 1957; concerto for string orch., 1959;
Capriccio, cello and orch., 1961; concertino for
piano, brass, timpani, 1963; Lautrec, ballet
suite, 1965; Symphony for orchestra, 1967;
Serenade, small orch., 1968; Symphony of winds,
1970; CHAMBER MUSIC: Episode and chorale, 11
brass instruments, 1944; Lyra, brass sextet,
1945; Divertimento, piano and percussion, 1960;
harp sonata, 1961; Burlesca, flute and guitar,
1961; violin sonata, 1963; Introduction and
allegro, accordion, 1964; suite for harp, string
trio, 1965; Electra, piano and percussion, 1966;
Declamation, violin and piano, 1967; 2 pieces
(Marionettes), harp solo, 1968; Prisma, 7 horns;
CHORUS: Pentaptych, with orch., 1953; Tristis

est anima mea, with piano or orch., 1959; Virtue, a cappella, 1961; Tu es sacerdos, 1963; The star, a cappella, 1964; The arrow and the song, 1966; Laughing song for youthful chorus, 1966; Te deum for mankind, with orch., New York, 7 May 1969; Passion for Martin Luther King, Jr., with solo and orch., 1968, Washington, 19 Feb. 1974; many songs, piano pieces.

> 120 Montgomery Circle, New Rochelle, NY 10804

FLANAGAN, THOMAS J., JR.
b. New Haven, Conn., 30 Nov. 1927. Studied with Jack Beeson and Normand Lockwood, Columbia Univ., B.A.; with Carl McKinley, New England Cons., B.M., M.M.; at City Coll. of New York; with Robert Palmer, Cornell Univ. He has been faculty member, St. John's Univ., Jamaica, N.Y., from 1963.

WORKS: VOCAL: Psalm 130, chorus; 4 songs of unknown poets, women's voices; Melody lost, baritone; Summer song for me, soprano.

> 845 West End Ave., #8C, New York, NY 10025

FLANAGAN, WILLIAM
b. Detroit, Mich., 14 Aug. 1913; d. New York, N.Y., 31 Aug. 1969. Studied with Burrill Phillips and Bernard Rogers, Eastman School of Music; with Arthur Berger, Aaron Copland, and Arthur Honegger at Tanglewood; with David Diamond in New York. He was a reviewer for the New York Herald Tribune, 1957-60.

WORKS: THEATRE: Bartleby, 1-act opera, 1952-57; music for Albee's The sandbox, 1961, and The ballad of the sad cafe, 1963; ORCHESTRA: Divertimento for classical orchestra, 1948; A concert ode, 1951; A concert overture; Notations, 1960; Narrative for orchestra, 1964; CHAMBER MUSIC: Divertimento, string quartet, 1947; Chaconne, violin and piano, 1948; Passacaglia, piano, 1947; piano sonata, 1950; CHORUS: Chapter from Ecclesiastes, with string quintet; Billy in the darbies' SONGS: Song for a winter child, 1950; The weeping Pleiades, 1953; The lady of tearful regret, soprano, baritone, chamber ensemble, 1958; Another August, soprano, piano, orch., 1967; Goodbye my fancy, soprano, flute, guitar; many songs.

FLEMING, SHARI BEATRICE
b. St. Johnsbury, Vt. Graduated from Peabody Cons., 1958, where she received the Gustav Klemm Prize, 1957, 1958. She has been on the faculty of Univ. of Vermont from 1970. Her Break forth into joy for chorus was performed in Brookline, Mass., Feb. 1963.

> University of Vermont, Burlington, VT 05401

FLETCHER, GRANT
b. Hartsburg, Ill., 25 Oct. 1913. Studied at Wesleyan Univ., B.M.; with Ernst Krenek and Healey Willan, Univ. of Michigan, M.M.; with Howard Hanson, Eastman School of Music, Ph.D. His many honors include 38 composition awards, 14 ASCAP awards; Nat. Endowment for the Arts grant; numerous commissions. He was conductor, Akron Symphony, 1945-48; Chicago Musical Symphonies, 1949-52; Chicago Symphonette, 1951-56;

professor, Arizona State Univ., 1956-78, then emeritus professor.

WORKS: THEATRE: The carrion crow, opera, 1944; Lomatawi, ballet pantomime, 1957; The sack of Calabasas, 1966; music to Two gentleman of Verona, 1969, and Blood wedding, 1970; Cinco de Mayo, ballet, 1973; ORCHESTRA: A rhapsody of dances, chamber orch., 1935; Rhapsody, flute and strings, 1935; Nocturne, 1935; Sailors' songs and dances, 1941; Musicke for christening, string orch., 1944; A song for warriors, 1944; An American overture, 1945; Panels from a theatre wall, 1949; 2 symphonies, 1950, 1970; The pocket encyclopedia of orchestral instruments, 1953; 2 piano concertos, 1953, 1966; Sumare-Wintare, 1956; concerto grosso, chamber orch., 1956; 7 cities of Cibola, 1961; Glyphs, 1968; Diversion, strings, 1971; Cinco de Mayo, 1973; Song of honor, 1974; Celebration--of times past, 1976; BAND: Heralds, brass choir, 1949; Diaphony, 1968; concerto for winds, 1969; multiple concerto for 5 solo winds, 1970; Dyad, 1970; Aubade, 1973; Rhapsody of dances, 1972; A more proper burial music for Wolfgang, 1977; CHAMBER MUSIC: Caprice Argentine, violin and piano, 1934; clarinet sonata, 1959; Uroboros, percussion ensemble, 1961; Dances from the Southwest, strings, 1966; Who is Sylvia?, baritone, flute, oboe, bassoon, guitar, 1969; Octocelli, 8 solo cellos, 1971; Son, cello and piano, 1972; TR-10, flute, guitar, piano, 1972; Coonhound Johnny, percussion trio, 1974; saxophone sonata, 1974; string quartet, 1975; Quadra, piano and percussion, 1975; Saxson I and II, saxophone and piano (I) and orch. (II), 1977; sonata for viola alone, 1977; Zortzicos, #II for contrabass and piano, #III for cello and piano, #IV for bassoon and piano, 1977-78; 3 piano sonatas, 1951, 1970, #3, N.Y., 29 Mar. 1981; many choral works, piano, organ, and carillon pieces, and film scores.

> 1626 E. Williams St., Tempe, AZ 85281

FLICK-FLOOD, DORA
b. Cleveland, Ohio, 3 Aug. 1885. Studied at Sangster Music School; Baldwin-Wallace Coll.; also with Sigismund Stojowski; held 5 piano scholarships. She gave concerts in the U.S. and Europe; taught in Cleveland public schools and at Tucker School. Her published works include Tango del Prado for band; choral works, songs, piano pieces.

FLOYD, CARLISLE
b. Latta, S.C., 11 June 1926. Studied at Converse Coll. and with Ernst Bacon at Syracuse Univ., B.M., M.M. His awards include New York Music Critics' Circle award, 1956; Guggenheim fellowship, 1957; Citation for Merit, Nat. Assoc. of Authors, Conductors, Composers, 1957; Junior Chamber of Commerce, 10 Outstanding Young Men in the U.S., 1959; annual ASCAP awards from 1963; commissions from Ford Found., Brown Univ., Santa Fe Opera, Houston Opera, and Kennedy Center. He was professor, Florida State Univ., 1947-76; in 1976, accepted the M. D. Anderson chair at Univ. of Houston, and in 1977, was named codirector of the Houston Opera Studio.

WORKS: THEATRE: Slow dusk, 1-act musical

FLYNN, GEORGE

play, 1949; Fugitives, music drama, 1951; Lost
Eden, ballet, 2 pianos, 1952; Susannah, music
drama, 1954; Tallahassee, 24 Feb. 1955; Wuthering
Heights, opera, Santa Fe, N.Mex., 16 July 1958;
The passion of Jonathan Wade, opera, New York,
11 Oct. 1962; The sojourner and Molly Sinclair,
opera, Raleigh, N.C., 2 Dec. 1963; Markheim,
opera, New Orleans, 31 Mar. 1966; Of mice and
men, opera, Seattle, 22 Jan. 1970; Bilby's doll,
opera, Houston, 27 Feb. 1976; Willie Stark,
opera based on Robert Penn Warren's All the
King's Men, Houston, 24 Apr. 1981.
    4491 Yoakum Blvd., Houston, TX 77006

FLYNN, GEORGE
    b. Miles City, Mont., 21 Jan. 1937. Studied
with Jack Beeson, Chou Wen-chung, Otto Luening,
and V. Ussachevsky, Columbia Univ., B.S. 1964,
M.A. 1966, D.M.A. 1972. He taught at Columbia
Univ., 1966-73; Lehman Coll., CUNY, 1973-76;
from 1976, at De Paul Univ.
    WORKS: ORCHESTRA: American drive; CHAMBER
MUSIC: duos for piano with individually, violin,
viola, cello, clarinet, trumpet, mezzo-soprano
voice; string quartet; piano trio; piano quartet; wind quintet, piano octet, chamber cantata;
several religious choral works.
    School of Music, De Paul Univ., 804 W. Belden,
    Chicago, IL 60614

FLYNT, HENRY ALLEN, III
    b. Greensboro, N.C., 19 Jan. 1940. A Ph.D. in
economics, chiefly self-taught in music, he was
an avant-garde composer of the post-Cage era.
In 1962 he repudiated all European "classical"
and "modern" music and began to concentrate on
ethnic music, in particular on two systems that
originated in his native region: blues and country
music. He began to compose fully notated avant-
garde music within the country music "mode,"
assimilating electronic capabilities and open
forms of the avant garde to ethnic hillbilly
music. He feels he is unique and is the only
person with the right to call himself a composer
of contemporary American music in the fullest
and most literal sense. Speaking of the esthetic
values of his system, Flynt says they are:
"first, the whangy, peckerwood values of the
South and its music, with some attention to the
blues; second, the weird narcissistic child
values, the intricate self-reflections of the
creep personality. The goal is to bring listeners to a state of exaltation."
    WORKS: Hoedown/Stock car race, 3 demos for
apple, Cowboy corroboree, all performed at the
Kitchen, New York, 26 Feb. 1972; Cool cat twang,
Improvisation in A, Double spindizzy, all performed at Virginia Commonwealth Univ., 18 Apr.
1974.
    349 W. Broadway, New York, NY 10013

FOCH, DIRK
    b. Batavia, Java, 18 June 1886; to U.S. 1928;
d. Locarno, Switzerland, 24 May 1973. Studied
in Holland and Germany. He was orchestral conductor in Sweden and Holland, then in New York.
His compositions include a musical pageant, a
work for narrator and orchestra, piano pieces,
songs.

FOLEY, DANIEL
    b. Toronto, Ont., 24 Apr. 1952; to U.S. 1959.
Studied at Florida Jr. Coll.; with Thomas
Cousins and Emma Lou Diemer, Northern Virginia
Music Center; with Louis Mennini and Robert Ward,
North Carolina School of the Arts. He has received 3 BMI student awards and 5 Vittorio
Giannini Memorial awards. He was a private
teacher, 1973-74.
    WORKS: THEATRE: Mysterium, ballet in 7
acts; ORCHESTRA: Glasperlenspiel; chamber concerto for small orch.; CHAMBER MUSIC: 3 songs
after Hermann Hesse, baritone and string quartet;
Menagerie, piano; CHORUS: Stabat mater, women's
voices and 6 winds.

FOLEY, DAVID FRANCIS
    b. Oak Park, Ill., 8 Aug. 1945. Studied with
Leslie Bassett, Jack Portner, Eugene Kurtz, and
George B. Wilson, Univ. of Michigan, B.M. 1968,
M.M. 1969; and with Máx Deutsch in Paris, summer,
1974. His awards include BMI awards, 1967, 1969;
Phi Mu Alpha award, 1968; and several commissions.
    WORKS: ORCHESTRA: 4 pieces for Saturday
afternoon, small orch., 1967; Endgame, 1969.

FOLEY, KEITH
    b. Akron, Ohio, 25 July 1953. Studied with
Warren Benson, Rayburn Wright, and William
Dobbins, Eastman School of Music, B.M. in trumpet, 1975, M.M. in jazz studies, 1978. He received a grant from Eastman School for study
with Los Angeles-area film composers, 1977. He
was director, Jazz Ensemble, Rochester Inst. of
Technology, 1974-78, and at State Univ. of New
York at Geneseo, 1976-78; instructor, preparatory
department at Eastman, 1977.
    WORKS: BAND: concerto for piano and wind
ensemble, 1977; JAZZ ENSEMBLE: Uncle Henry's
pork chop revue; Snickerdoodle; Everessence.
    35 Bobrich Dr., #24, Rochester, NY 14610

FOLTS, MARTHA NEARY
    b. Lakewood, Ohio, 7 Sept. 1940. Studied piano
and organ at Syracuse Univ.; composition with
Robert Cogan and Pozzi Escot, New England Cons.
She received Iowa Arts Council grants, 1973,
1974. She was organist-choirmaster, Poughkeepsie,
N.Y., 1967-70; on faculty, Iowa State Univ.,
1970-75.
    WORKS: VOICE: Ashes, sound drama, choir,
choral speakers, narrator, organ, percussion,
tape, 1969; Antiphon for Palm Sunday, choir,
congregation, and open instrumentation, 1978;
Pronouncements of joy, soprano and organ, 1978;
ORGAN: Transition piece, organ, tape, audience
participation, 1974; Internal organ, composed
for and performed at national convention, American Guild of Organists, June 1976; Squirrel
Island, 2 male narrators, organ, audience participation, commissioned by an organ company,
performed on Squirrel Island, Maine, 1977.
    6337 Jackson St., Pittsburgh, PA 15206

FOMINAYA, ELOY
    b. New York, N.Y., 10 June 1925. Studied with

172

James Ming, Lawrence Coll.; with Violet Archer, North Texas State Univ.; and with H. Owen Reed, Michigan State Univ. He was faculty member, Northeast Louisiana State Coll., 1953-66; professor and chairman, fine arts dept., Augusta Coll., from 1966. He composes for orchestra, band, and chamber groups.
Augusta College, Augusta, GA 30904

FONTRIER, GABRIEL
b. Bucharest, Rumania, 21 Nov. 1918, American father. Studied with Karol Rathaus at Queens Coll., B.A. 1942; Otto Luening and Paul H. Lang, Columbia Univ., M.A. He held a Ford Found. faculty fellowship, 1953-54. He has been professor, Queens Coll., CUNY, from 1947; was music editor, Long Island Press, 1947-61, music critic, from 1964.
WORKS: CHAMBER MUSIC: string quartet, 1948; wind quintet, 1973; violin sonata, 1973; CHORUS: 3 choruses on texts of Hilaire Belloc, a cappella; 3 new directions in music; 3 choruses on humorous texts, a cappella; SONGS: 3 American songs for high voice and orch. or piano; PIANO: Little piano suite; Lullaby; sonata for 2 pianos, 1965.
28 Chaffee Ave., Albertson, NY 11507

FOOTE, GEORGE
b. Cannes, France, 19 Feb. 1886, American parents; d. Boston, Mass., 25 Mar. 1956. Studied with Edward Burlingame Hill at Harvard Univ.; with Friedrich Koch in Berlin. He taught at Harvard, 1921-23; was president, South End Music School, Boston, to 1943.
WORKS: ORCHESTRA: Variations on a pious theme, Boston, 11 Feb. 1935; In praise of winter, Boston, 5 Jan. 1940; CHORUS: 98th Psalm; also chamber music.

FORCUCCI, SAMUEL L.
b. Granville, N.Y., 8 July 1922. Studied with Charles O'Neill, Potsdam State Univ.; with Ernst Bacon, Syracuse Univ.; and with Thomas Canning, Eastman School of Music. He taught in Boonville, N.Y., 1947-50; has been professor, State Univ. Coll., Cortland, N.Y., from 1951.
WORKS: CHORUS: Child of wonder, cantata; Eucharistic prayer, oratorio, with soloists, brass, percussion; also works for orchestra and band.
17 Stevenson St., Cortland, NY 13045

FORMAN, JOANNE
b. Chicago, Ill., 26 June 1934. Attended Los Angeles City Coll.; studied privately. Her awards include Ossabaw Island fellowship, 1977; Meet the Composer grant, 1978; Maine State Arts Commission grant, 1978. She has been affiliated with various theatre groups in California; was director, the Migrant Theatre, 1967-77; then resident composer-playwright, Children's Theatre of Maine.
WORKS: THEATRE: My heart lies south, operetta; Polly Baker, 1977, and The blind men, 1978, 2 chamber operas, performed Portland, Maine, 6 May 1978; VOICE: Ave Beata Dea, a cappella choir, 1975; Haiku, soprano and wood-

wind quintet, 1975; The skipper and the witch, narrator, chorus, piano, 1975; Blessed is the match, voice and piano, 1977; Rilkelieder, soprano, flute, oboe, cello, 1978.
Box 3181, Taos, NM 87571

FORNUTO, DONATO D.
b. New York, N.Y., 12 Sept. 1931. Studied with Mark Brunswick at City Coll. of New York; privately with Josef Schmid. He taught in public schools, 1954-67; from 1967, has been professor, William Paterson Coll.
WORKS: WIND ENSEMBLE: concerto for piano and band; Fanfare, allegro, and chorale for band and 2 brass choirs; Divertimento, clarinet choir; CHAMBER MUSIC: 3 pieces for clarinet and piano; suite for saxophone and piano; woodwind quintet; trio for trumpet, percussion, electric bass; VOICE: The lamb, The tiger, 2 choral settings of Blake poems; Songs of innocence and experience, Blake poems for mezzo-soprano and piano; 4 songs on poems of Emily Dickinson, baritone and piano.
26 Duncan St., Waldwick, NJ 07463

FORREST, HAMILTON
b. Chicago, Ill., 8 Jan. 1901. Studied with Adolf Weidig in Chicago. He received the Bispham Memorial Medal of the American Opera Society of Chicago in 1925.
WORKS: OPERA: Yzdra, 1925; Camille, Chicago, 10 Dec. 1930, with Mary Garden singing Camille; also ballets and chamber music.

FORST, RUDOLF
b. New York, N.Y., 20 Oct. 1900; d. Valhalla, N.Y., 19 Dec. 1973. Studied with Daniel Gregory Mason, Columbia Univ. He won the 1936 NBC Music Guild award for a string quartet; honorable mention, 1973 Catgut Acoustical Society competition. He was violin teacher and music director of a radio station.
WORKS: ORCHESTRA: Fragment poetique; Symphonia brevis; Symphonic rhapsody on Ozark folk melodies; Aubade Mexicaine, 1938; CHAMBER MUSIC: Symphonietta for strings; Music for 10 instruments; Sonata da camera; Divertimento, chamber orch., 1938; Introduction and allegro, string quartet of new instruments (mezzo, alto, tenor, baritone), Douglass Coll., 14 Oct. 1974.

FORSYTH, CECIL
b. London, England, 30 Nov. 1870; to U.S. 1914; d. New York, N.Y., 7 Dec. 1941. Studied at Edinburgh Univ.; Royal Coll. of Music, London. He was an executive in a New York publishing firm to 1941.
WORKS: COMIC OPERAS: Westward ho!; Cinderella; ORCHESTRA: Chant Celtique, viola and orch.; viola concerto; Studies after Les Miserables; Ode to a nightingale.

FORSYTH, JOSEPHINE
b. Cleveland, Ohio, 5 July 1889; d. Cleveland, 24 May 1940. Wrote a setting of The Lord's Prayer for her wedding to P. A. Meyers on 29 Apr. 1928. This setting became popular and was sung at the Hollywood Bowl Easter sunrise service for many years. Her other compositions were chiefly sacred choral works and vocal solos.

FORTE, JAMES
b. Boston, Mass., 19 Sept. 1936. Studied at
Brandeis Univ.; Lowell State Coll.; Longy School
of Music; and Boston Univ. He has received many
commissions. He has been music director,
Robbins Library Concert Series, from 1973.
WORKS: CHAMBER MUSIC: Sinfonia for strings,
Boston, 7 May 1972; string quartet #3, 1973;
duo for violin and piano, Boston, 28 Apr. 1974;
contrabass sonata, 1976; CHORUS: The holy child,
with soprano solo, orch., Boston, 18 Dec. 1968;
Homeland, with soprano and orch., Boston, 16
Dec. 1970; PIANO: 3 sonatas; other choral works,
songs, piano pieces.
37 Cleveland St., Arlington, MA 02174

FORTNER, JACK
b. Grand Rapids, Mich., 2 July 1935. Studied
with Ross Lee Finney and Leslie Bassett, Univ.
of Michigan; with Hall Overton in New York; with
N. Castigliono in Italy. His awards include
Fond. Royaumont award, 1966; Rome prize, 1967;
Eastern Washington State Coll. award, 1972; 2
Rockefeller Found. grants. He was faculty mem-
ber, Univ. of Michigan, 1965-70; California
State Univ., Fresno, from 1971; artistic director, Merced Symphony, from 1971.
WORKS: ORCHESTRA: Quadri, 1968; June dawns,
July moons, August evenings, Eastern Washington
State Coll., 13 Nov. 1973; CHAMBER MUSIC:
Burleske, 2 chamber orch., 1965; Spring, voice
and 9 instruments, 1966; string quartet, Rome,
1968; Cantilene, flute and piano; Flow chart
1-Apres Jonas 5:5, chamber ensemble, 1976; MIXED
MEDIA: De plus en plus, piano, clarinet, tape,
films, slides, lights, 1972; 4 pieces for string
quartet and tape; Nocturne, tape.
1460 E. Vartikian, Fresno, CA 93710

FOSS, LUKAS
b. Berlin, Germany, 15 Aug. 1922; U.S. citizen
1942. Studied piano and flute in Paris; coming
to the U.S. in 1937, studied at Curtis Inst. of
Music. His composition teachers include Noel
Gallon, Rosario Scalero, Paul Hindemith; conducting teachers, Fritz Reiner, Serge
Koussevitzky. He spent several summers at Tan-
glewood and took special courses at Yale Univ.
His many honors include a Guggenheim grant; 2
New York Music Critics' Circle awards; Prix de
Rome; 3 honorary doctorates; membership in Nat.
Inst. of Arts and Letters, Board of Directors,
Naumburg Found., Koussivitzky Found., and Per-
spectives of New Music. He was professor, Univ.
of California, Los Angeles, 1951-62; founder and
director, Center for Creative and Performing
Arts, Buffalo Univ., from 1963; music director,
Buffalo Phil. Orch., 1962-70; visiting professor,
Harvard Univ., 1969-70; conductor, Brooklyn
Philharmonia, 1970-75; music advisor, conductor,
Jerusalem Symph. Orch., from 1972; composer-in-
residence, Cincinnati Coll. Cons., 1975; music
director, Milwaukee Symph. Orch., 1981. He has
been guest conductor of major orchestras in the
U.S., Europe, Israel, So. America, Japan, and
Canada.
WORKS: OPERA: The jumping frog of Calaveras
County, 1949; Griffelkin, 1955; Introductions
and goodbyes, 1959; BALLET: The heart remembers,

1944; Within these walls, 1944; The gift of the
Magi, 1955; ORCHESTRA: music for The tempest,
1940; 2 symphonic pieces, 1940; Allegro concertante, 1941; Dance sketch, 1941; clarinet
concerto, 1942 (later arranged as piano concerto
#1); Ode, 1944, rev. 1958; symphony, 1944;
Ricordare, 1948; oboe concerto, 1948; piano concerto #2, 1949; Symphony of chorales, 1958;
Elytres, 1964; Discrepancy, 24 winds, 1966;
cello concerto, New York, 5 Mar. 1967; Phorion,
with organ, harpsichord, guitar, 1967; Baroque
variations, 1967; Geod, with optional voices,
1969; Orpheus, with viola, cello or guitar, New
York, 18 May 1974; Fanfare, 1973; Salomon Rossi,
1570-1630, suite; concerto for solo percussion
and small or large orch., 1974; Folk song for
orchestra, Baltimore, 21 Jan. 1976; The American
cantata, a collage drama, with 2 soloists, 2
speakers, 2 male comedians, 2 choruses, orch.,
Interlochen, Mich., 25 July 1976, New York
premiere, 1 Dec. 1977; Quintets for orchestra,
Cleveland, 30 Apr. 1979 (was premiere in this
form, had been performed in 1978 as a brass
quintet); CHAMBER MUSIC: 4 Preludes, flute,
clarinet, bassoon, 1940; duo, cello and piano,
1941; Paradigm, percussion, 1943; string quartet,
1947; Capriccio, cello and piano, 1948; Time
cycle, soprano and chamber group, 1960; Echoi,
clarinet, cello, piano, percussion, 1963; Ni
bruit, ni vitesse, 2 pianos, 2 percussion, inside
piano, 1972; Cave of the winds, wind quintet,
1972; MAP (Men at play), a musical game for an
entire evening, any 4 musicians can play, New
York, 2 May 1973; string quartet #3, New York,
15 Mar. 1976; Quartet plus, narrator and 2
string quartets, Brooklyn, 29 Apr. 1977; CHORUS:
Melodrama and dramatic song of Michael Angelo,
1940; We sing, children's cantata, 1941; The
prairie, 1944; Tell this blood, 1945; Behold! I
build an house, 1950; Adon Olom, 1951; Parable
of death, with tenor, narrator, orch., 1956;
Psalms, with orch., 1956; Fragments of Archi-
lochos, with speakers, soloists, chamber ensemble,
1965; 3 airs for Frank O'Hara's Angel, soprano,
female chorus, instruments, 1972; SONGS: 3
Goethe Lieder, 1938; Song of anguish, voice and
piano or orch., 1945; The song of songs, voice
and orch., 1946; Where the bee sucks, 1951; also
piano pieces.
1140 Fifth Ave., New York, NY 10028

FOSTER, DOROTHY
b. Melrose, Mass., 17 Sept. 1930. Studied with
Hugo Norden and Gardner Read, Boston Univ., B.M.;
with Henry Cowell, Peabody Cons.; and with Donal
Michalsky, California State Coll. at Fullerton,
M.A. She won first place, Mu Phi Epsilon
Internat. composition contest, 1971; and Music
Teachers Assoc. of California contest, 1971.
She is a private teacher of piano, organ, and
composition.
WORKS: CHAMBER MUSIC: flute quintet; VOCAL:
Moses, oratorio; What's for dinner?, song cycle,
soprano and piano; Fair Mary, soprano and cello;
4 Christmas songs, unison junior choir; PIANO:
suite.
18002 Yorba Linda Blvd., Yorba Linda, CA
92686

FOSTER, FAY
b. Leavenworth, Kans., 8 Nov. 1886; d. Bayport, N.Y., 17 Apr. 1960. Studied at Sherwood Cons., Chicago; with Salomon Jadassohn, Leipzig Cons.; also in Munich. She won the Internat. Waltz Competition prize of 2000 marks, Berlin, 1910; first prize, American Composers' contest, New York, 1913; Etude prize; Nat. Fed. of Music Clubs prize. She toured the U.S. as concert pianist; taught in Illinois and Rydall, Pa., then settled in New York.
WORKS: OPERA: The moon lady; The honorable Mme. Yen; OPERETTAS: Land of chance; Blue Beard; The castaways; SONGS: My journey's end; The Americans come!; The place where I worship; and many others; piano pieces.

FOSTER, ROBERT E.
b. Raymondville, Tex., 21 Jan. 1939. Studied with J. Clifton Williams and Kent Kennan, Univ. of Texas, Austin, M.M. He was assistant director of bands, Univ. of Florida, 1964-71; director of bands, Univ. of Kansas, from 1971.
WORKS: BAND: Blues rock; The dude; Folk rock; The pony express; Rock a la Bach; etc.; CHAMBER MUSIC: Scherzetto, trumpet and piano.
University of Kansas, Lawrence, KS 66044

FOSTER, WILL J.
b. Brookfield, Mo., 10 Feb. 1890; d. Ft. Worth, Tex., 14 Feb. 1960. Studied piano and organ in Ft. Worth. Except during service in both world wars, he held organist posts from 1912; the last at Arlington Heights Methodist Church, Ft. Worth, 1946-60. In 1959 he was ordained minister of music in the Methodist church. His compositions are all sacred choral works.

FOWLER, MARJE
b. New Haven, Conn., 8 Jan. 1917. Studied with Morris Ruger, California State Univ., Long Beach, A.B.; with David Ward-Steinman, California State Univ., San Diego, M.A.; violin with Hugo Kortschak, Yale Univ., and Vera Barstow in Los Angeles. She received the Sigma Alpha Iota Alumni chapter, San Diego, composer award, 1967, 1973. She was violinist, Stockton Symph. Orch., 1951-60; youth choir director, 1953-70; instructor, Grossmont Coll., 1970-71.
WORKS: ORCHESTRA: Introduction and fantasia; CHORUS: sacred service for 3 choirs, organ, liturgist; All praise to Thee, a cappella; SONGS: Deux ballades sombres, Francois Villon, tenor, viola, piano, 1967; Cante jondo, setting of Romance de la luna, luna, Garcia Lorca, mezzo-soprano, percussion, harpsichord, 1973; ORGAN: Elegie; Introduction and fantasia.
13348 Community Rd., Poway, CA 92064

FOX, CHARLES
b. New York, N.Y., 1940. Studied with Nadia Boulanger in Paris, 1959-61. He received an Emmy for his music contributions to ABC's "Love, American Style."
WORKS: FILM SCORES: The incident, 1967; Goodbye Columbus; Pufnstuf; Making it; First class (electronic); Star-spangled girl; In the path of history, documentary; TELEVISION: "Love,

American style"; "Bugaboo"; theme for the "Tonight" show.
c/o Broadcast Music, Inc., 40 W. 57th St., New York, NY 10019

FOX, FELIX
b. Breslau, Germany, 25 May 1876; to U.S. 1897; d. Boston, Mass., 24 Mar. 1947. Studied at Leipzig Cons.; piano with Isidor Philipp in Paris. On coming to the U.S., he was cofounder of a music school in Boston; after his partner's death, it was called the Felix Fox School of Piano Playing. He wrote piano pieces and songs.

FOX, FRED
b. Detroit, Mich., 17 Jan. 1931. Studied with Bernhard Heiden, Indiana Univ.; Ross Lee Finney, Univ. of Michigan; and with Ruth Wylie, Wayne State Univ. He held a fellowship, Dallas Composers Conf., 1960; Ford Found. grant, 1963; Nat. Endowment for the Arts grant, 1975. Faculty posts have included Franklin Coll., 1959-61; Sam Houston State Coll., 1961-62; California State Univ. at Hayward, 1964-75; Indiana Univ., from 1976.
WORKS: ORCHESTRA: violin concerto, 1971; Ternoin, oboe and orch., 1972; Beyond winterlock, 1977; Night ceremonies, Terre Haute, 27 Sept. 1979; CHAMBER MUSIC: Quantic I, woodwind quintet, 1969; Variations, piano trio, 1970; Ad rem, guitar, 1970; Matrix, cello, strings, percussion, 1972; Variables 1, 2, 3, 4, various instruments, 1972-73; Time excursions, soprano, reciter, chamber ensemble, 1976; CHORUS: Jubilate Deo, with orch.; The descent, with piano, percussion, 1969; A stone, a leaf, an unfound door, text by Wolf, with soprano, clarinet, percussion; and others.
711 S. Clifton St., Bloomington, IN 47401

FOX, JAMES
b. Indianapolis, Ind., 9 Apr. 1953. Studied with Russell Peck, Butler Univ.; Gerald Plain and Philip Winsor, De Paul Univ., B.M.; with Barney Childs, Univ. of Redlands, M.M. From 1978 he has been instructor, Univ. of Redlands.
WORKS: All things fancy, clarinet; other solo works and electronic pieces.
1831 Orchid Ave., Los Angeles, CA 90068

FOX, OSCAR
b. Burnet County, Tex., 11 Oct. 1879; d. Charlottesville, Va., 13 July 1961. Studied with Karl Attenhofer in Zurich, 1896-99; with Percy Goetschius in New York. He was organist and director of choirs, glee clubs, and the University Choral Society, Univ. of Texas, 1925-28; also recitalist and radio performer.
WORKS: SONGS: Hills of home; My heart is a silent violin; Rain in the river; Petal drift; etc.

FRABIZIO, WILLIAM V.
b. Stockton, N.J., 10 Oct. 1929. Studied at Trenton Coll.; Rutgers Univ.; and with Clifford Taylor at Temple Univ. He received the Beaver Coll. Lindback award for distinguished teaching, 1972-73; Outstanding Educators of America award,

FRACKENPOHL, ARTHUR

1973. He taught in private schools, 1957-63;
Temple Univ., 1965-68; New England Cons., 1968-
69; at Beaver Coll. from 1970.
   WORKS: ORCHESTRA: 3 symphonies; Statement,
trumpet and 18 players; BAND: Symphonic paraphrase; Synesthesia; tuba concerto; Prelude;
CHAMBER MUSIC: string quartet; Comments among 4
players, piano, 4 hands, cello, percussion; saxophone quintet; woodwind trio; brass trio; brass
quintet; woodwind quintet; Psalm 150, string
quartet and voice; Dialogues, trombone and
string quartet; CHORUS: Octet for voices; Credo
Americana, with solo voice and band; also many
compositions and arrangements for jazz orch.
   P.O. Box 111, Stockton, NJ 08559

FRACKENPOHL, ARTHUR
   b. Irvington, N.J., 23 Apr. 1924. Studied with
Bernard Rogers, Eastman School of Music, B.A.
1947, M.A. 1949; with Darius Milhaud at Tanglewood; Nadia Boulanger at Fontainebleau; McGill
Univ., D.M. 1957. His awards include first
prize at Fontainebleau, 1950; Ford Found. grant,
1959-60; university research fellowships at
Potsdam; annual ASCAP awards from 1964; many
commissions. He has been faculty member, Crane
School of Music, State Univ. Coll., Potsdam,
from 1949.
   WORKS: OPERA: Domestic relations, 1 act;
ORCHESTRA: suite for strings, 1963; Jubilant
overture, 1956; concertino for tuba and strings;
BAND: Academic processional march; Allegro
giocoso; Dance overture; Variations for tuba and
winds, 1974; Prelude and allegro, clarinet choir;
Flutes 4, 4 flutes and band; CHAMBER MUSIC:
string quartet; brass quartet; 2 brass quintets;
brass trio; woodwind quintet; CHORUS: The
natural superiority of men, women's voices and
orch.; Te Deum, with orch.; Hogamus, higamus,
double fugue for speaking chorus and percussion;
7 essays on women, Ogden Nash text, men's voices;
and songs.
   13 Hillcrest Dr., Potsdam, NY 13676

FRAENKEL, WOLFGANG
   b. Berlin, Germany, 10 Oct. 1897; to U.S. 1947.
Studied at the Klindworth-Scharwenka Cons.,
Berlin. He received first prize, Internat. Competition, City of Milan, for his Symphonic
aphorism, 1965. He was a judge in Berlin until
the Nazi regime put him in a concentration camp,
1933-39. He then lived in Shaghai and Nanking,
making his way in 1947 to Los Angeles, where he
worked as music copyist in film studios. His
compositions include an opera, flute concerto,
many chamber pieces, songs. His complete works
have been deposited in the Moldenhauer Archives,
Spokane, Wash.

FRANCESCHINI, ROMULUS
   b. Brooklyn, N.Y., 5 Jan. 1929. Studied with
Vincent Persichetti, Stefan Wolpe, and Morton
Feldman.
   WORKS: ORCHESTRA: 5 paintings, 1971;
Orchestra journal, 1978; BAND: Prelude and cele-
bration, 1967; De profundis, 1969; CHAMBER MUSIC:
Pilgrim psalm tunes, wind octet, 1976; VOICE:
White spirituals, soprano and 12 instruments,

1977; Journey to the edge of an era, poems by
Hannah Ross Lurie, soprano, flute, harp, 1978;
High rise, poems by Arthur Milner, voice and
piano, 1978; KEYBOARD: Omaggio a Kurt Weill,
accordion, 1975; Ommagio a Satie, piano, 1975;
Piano journal, 1978. He has arranged Benjamin
Carr's Federal overture for orchestra, 1975; and
a Billings set for wind octet, 1976.
   1318 S. Broad St., Philadelphia, PA 19146

FRANCHETTI, ARNOLD
   b. Lucca, Italy, 18 Aug. 1906; U.S. citizen 1950.
Studied with his father Alberto, director of
the Florence Cons., but graduated from Univ. of
Florence as a physics major; studied with Richard
Strauss in Germany. His awards include the
Lehman composition award at the Salzburg
Mozarteum; Fromm Found. grant, 1950; Nat. Inst.
of Arts and Letters grant, 1958; Koussevitzky
Found. grant, 1961; Guggenheim grant, 1961;
Columbia Univ. Ditson award, 1964; Nat. Endowment
for the Arts grant, 1975; many commissions.
Before coming to the U.S., he taught in Italy,
Austria, and Sweden; joined the faculty at Hartt
Coll. of Music in 1948.
   WORKS: OPERA: 8 operas including Notturno
in La, 1966; Married men go to hell, after
Machiavelli, prologue and 3 acts, 1975; CHAMBER
MUSIC: 3 Italian masques, piano, brass quintet,
percussion, 1953; concertino, violin and chamber
ensemble, 1965; Piece for man alone, oboe and
strings, New York, 16 Jan. 1971; Doppio quartet,
double quartet, brass and woodwinds, 1972; Do,
re, mi, do, re, mi, bemolle, piano, New York,
4 Dec. 1973; 4 piano sonatas; FILM SCORE: Life
of Dante Alighieri, commissioned by the Trinity
Coll. Center for Italian Studies, 1968; numerous
orchestral works, chamber pieces, songs.
   Lyme, CT 06371

FRANCO, CLARE J.
   Studied with Vincent Persichetti and Luciano
Berio, Juilliard School, M.S.; also with Darius
Milhaud, Leonard Stein, Stefan Wolpe, Karlheinz
Stockhausen. She was awarded the Fromm prize
in composition, 1963-64. In 1969 she was a doctoral candidate at the Univ. of Illinois. Her
published works include: Piano fantasia; The
wind sprang up at 4 o'clock, mezzo-soprano and
piano, Boston, 14 Mar. 1972; Within, 10 instruments, Los Angeles, 17 Feb. 1975.
   Room 2222, 1 Penn Plaza, 250 W. 34 St.,
   New York, NY 10001

FRANCO, JOHAN
   b. Zaandam, Netherlands, 12 July 1908; U.S.
citizen 1942. Studied chiefly with Willem
Pijper in Amsterdam. His awards include Virginia
Music Teachers Assoc. commission, 1972; Delius
Composition prize, 1974. He is a free-lance
composer.
   WORKS: THEATRE: music for Romans by St.
Paul, The Book of Job, Pilgrim's progress,
Electra, The tempest; ORCHESTRA: 5 symphonies,
1933, 1939, 1940, 1950, 1958; Péripetié, sym-
phonic poem, 1935; violin concerto, 1939; Sere-
nata concertante, piano and small orch., 1940;
Baconiana, symphonic poem, 1941; also concerti

for cello, piano, percussion, and guitar; CHAMBER MUSIC: sonatas for violin, viola, cello, piano, saxophone, guitar; sonata for violin and cello, 1978; CHORUS: As the prophets foretold, with soloists, brass, and carillon, 1955; SONG CYCLES: Songs of the spirit; Sayings of the word; many other works for voice and instruments, and 100 works for carillon.

403 Lake Dr., Virginia Beach, VA 23451

FRANGKISER, CARL M.
b. Loudonville, Ohio, 18 Sept. 1894; d. Lee's Summit, Mo. Studied at Capito Coll. of Music, B.M., M.M., D.M.; U.S. Band School. He was an army band conductor in World War I; played cornet in theatres and touring shows, and in Buffalo Bill, Sells-Floto, and Barnum and Bailey circuses; conducted park concerts in Kansas City area for 38 years; taught at Kansas City Cons.; was music director and editor, Unity School of Christianity from 1925.
WORKS: BAND: The victorious; 3 gates of gold; Hickory Hill; Transcendence; Dedication; Stratosphere; Mightier than circumstance; et al.

FRANK, ANDREW
b. Los Angeles, Calif., 25 Nov. 1946. Studied with Jacob Druckman at Bard Coll., B.A. 1968; with George Crumb and George Rochberg, Univ. of Pennsylvania, M.A. 1970. He received BMI awards, 1969, 1970; Los Angeles Horn Club award, 1972; Nat. Endowment for the Arts grant, 1976; America Composers Alliance recording award, 1979. He has been faculty member, Univ. of California at Davis, from 1972.
WORKS: ORCHESTRA: Eucalyptus; Nepenthe; Season of darkness: Night music IV, solo double bass and orch., 1976; symphony for strings, 1978; CHAMBER MUSIC: Orpheum: Night music I, piano, 1970; string quartet; Dreams of reason, viola, bassoon, percussion, piano; Night music III, guitar; Amaranth, string orch.; Fantasy for 6 horns, 1972; Alto rhapsody, solo alto saxophone; A rebours, solo contrabass; Sonata da camera, flute, violin, piano, 1978.
Music Dept., Univ. of California, Davis, CA 95616

FRANK, JEAN FORWARD (Mrs. Thomas W.)
b. Pittsburgh, Pa., 13 Aug. 1927. Studied with Louis P. Coyner and Russell Wichmann at Chatman Coll.; privately with Roland Leich and Joseph Wilcox Jenkins.
WORKS: OPERETTA: Time of our lives; Princess of a thousand moons; CHAMBER MUSIC: Scatterpunctus, string orch.; CHORUS: The Christmas story; Into the woods my master went; If God be for us; So answereth my soul; PIANO: Afternoon street noise; Contemplation; Melodic mood; Chimera; Thoughts before dawn; sonata.
Box 234C, Ridge Dr., Mars, PA 16046

FRANK, MARCEL GUSTAVE
b. Vienna, Austria, 3 Dec. 1909; U.S. citizen 1942. Studied with Joseph Marx, Florent Schmitt, Felix Weingartner, Vienna Acad. of Music. He received the Grand Prix at Geneva for Homage to Claude Debussy for chorus and orch. He was con-

ductor and pianist, Vienna State Opera; accompanist to many noted singers; opera conductor in Pittsburgh and Dallas. His works include 4 ballets; 3 symphonies; piano concerto; Arkansas traveler variations; Heather Hills for band; Pas de deux, ballet for band; Conversation piece, 4 saxophones; Passacaglia, organ.

FRANK, RENE
b. Mulhouse, Alsace-Lorraine, 16 Feb. 1910; to U.S. 1947; d. Fort Wayne, Ind., 21 Mar. 1965. Studied with Hermann Reuter, Wolfgang Fortner, Nikolai Lopatnikoff, in Germany; at Indiana Univ., M.M., D.M. He taught in the U.S. Army School in Kyoto, Japan, 1946-47; then held faculty posts at Pikeville Coll.; Fort Wayne Bible Coll., 1951-65; Indiana Univ. Center, 1956-64.
WORKS: OPERA: Call of Gideon, 1 act; ORCHESTRA: 5 psalms, voice and orch.; Passion symphony; Little suite; CHAMBER MUSIC: Piano sonatina; violin sonata; string quartet; CHORUS: The spite of Michal, cantata, won Ernest Bloch award; The prodigal son; And God came, Christmas oratorio; SONGS: Triptych of heavenly love, a cycle.

FRANK, ROBERT E.
b. Los Angeles, Calif., 27 Nov. 1943. Studied with Charles Cushing and Richard Hoffmann, Univ. of California, Berkeley; with Robert Palmer and Karel Husa, Cornell Univ., D.M.A. He was faculty member, State Univ. of New York, Plattsburgh, 1973-78.
WORKS: ORCHESTRA: symphony; CHAMBER MUSIC: movement for flute and piano; string quartet; CHORUS: Drop down, ye heavens, a cappella motet for 8 voices; in Just-spring, with flute, piano, percussion; ORGAN: 3 preludes.

FRATTURO, LOUIS M.
b. Stamford, Conn., 19 Apr. 1928. Studied with Paul Creston, Manhattan School of Music, B.M., M.M.E. He was orchestrator and conductor for C. B. DeMille's film, Ten commandments. He taught in public schools, 1958-67; was jazz band director, Los Angeles Pierce Coll., 1967-72; has played with Glenn Miller and Mundell Lowe.
WORKS: JAZZ: Gospel swing; Jubilee; Nightmare; also educational works; Learn to play jazz solos, etc.

FRAZEUR, THEODORE C.
b. Omaha, Nebr., 20 Apr. 1929. Studied with Louis Mennini, Bernard Rogers, Wayne Barlow, Eastman School of Music. He was guest conductor, First Internat. Tuba Symposium, Indiana Univ. He was percussionist, Rochester Philharmonic, 1949-52, 1954-56; Erie Philharmonic, 1957-59; professor, State Univ. of New York, Fredonia, from 1956.
WORKS: BALLET: 4 beauties; Uhuru, 7 percussionists; ORCHESTRA: Allegro giocoso; Poem for strings; Chiastic, string orch.; Poets in a landscape, percussion ensemble, piano, harp, chorus, soloists, narrator; CHAMBER MUSIC: Divertimento, trombone and wind ensemble; Frieze, saxophone and percussion; suite for viola and percussion; The quiet place, marimba and piano;

FREDERICKSON, THOMAS

FILM SCORE: Spotlight on Fredonia.
3 Westerly Dr., Fredonia, NY 14063

FREDERICKSON, THOMAS
b. Kane, Pa., 5 Sept. 1928. Studied with Tilden
Wells, Ohio Wesleyan Univ.; with Burrill Phillips,
Univ. of Illinois. He has received ASCAP awards.
He has been faculty member, Univ. of Illinois,
from 1952.
WORKS: ORCHESTRA: Sinfonia II; Images;
CHAMBER MUSIC: Allegro, cello and piano; string
quartet; piano variations; music for double bass
alone; brass quintet; Wind music I; Sinfonia
concertante; Triptych, oboe, viola, trumpet,
trombone; Tubalied, tuba and chamber group; 5
pieces, percussion quartet; CHORUS: Silence;
Impressions; also jazz pieces.
1814 Robert Dr., Champaign, IL 61820

FREED, ARNOLD
b. New York, N.Y., 29 Sept. 1926. Studied with
Mark Brunswick, City Coll. of New York; Philip
James at New York Univ.; Vittorio Giannini,
Juilliard School; and with Luigi Dallapiccola
in Italy on a Fulbright grant.
WORKS: ORCHESTRA: Alleluia; CHAMBER MUSIC:
violin sonata; piano sonata; CHORUS: Gloria;
4 seasonal madrigals; From out of a wood; Heaven-
haven; 3 shepherd carols; Lord, lord, lord, jazz-
rock, electric organ, bass guitar, drums; SONGS:
Acquainted with the night.
c/o Boosey & Hawkes, 30 W. 57 St., New York,
NY 10019

FREED, ISADORE
b. Brest-Litovsk, Russia, 26 Mar. 1900; to U.S.
as a child; d. Rockville Center, N.Y., 10 Nov.
1960. Studied at Univ. of Pennsylvania, B.M.
1918; with Ernest Bloch and Vincent d'Indy in
Paris. He received the Soc. for Publication of
American Music award, 1943. He was faculty
member, Curtis Inst.; Temple Univ.; visiting
professor, Julius Hartt,Found., Hartford, Conn.;
organist-choirmaster, Temple Keneseth Israel,
Philadelphia.
WORKS: OPERA: Homo sum, 1930; The princess
and the vagabond; BALLET: Vibrations, 1928;
ORCHESTRA: Jeux de timbres, 1933; 2 symphonies;
Appalachian sketches, 1946; Festival overture,
1946; Rhapsody, trombone and orch.; violin concerto; cello concerto, 1952; CHAMBER MUSIC: 3
string quartets, 1931, 1932, 1937; trio for
flute, violin, harp, 1940; Triptych, string trio
and piano, 1943; Passacaglia, cello and piano,
1947; woodwind quintet, 1947; oboe sonatina;
Rhapsody, clarinet, strings, piano; concertino
for English horn and chamber orch., 1953; piano
sonata; viola sonata; suite for viola; suite for
harp; also choral works, songs.

FREED, WALTER
b. Spokane, Wash., 17 June 1903. Studied at
Univ. of Southern California on scholarship; won
a Paul Whiteman national contest for modern
American music. He was theatre organist and
teacher of piano and organ.
WORKS: BALLET: The what-not shelf; ORCHES-
TRA: Fiesta; Concerto in miniature, piano and
orch.; and songs.

FREEDMAN, HAL
b. Marion, Mass., 15 July 1953. Studied with
Robert Morris and Toru Takemitsu, Yale Univ.,
B.A. 1975; with Mario Davidovsky, Bulent Arel,
and Jack Beeson, Columbia Univ., M.A. 1978. His
awards include Wrexham award, 1975; BMI student
award, 1975; Internat. Electroacoustic Music
award, 1977; Joseph H. Bearns prize, 1978; and
many commissions.
WORKS: VOICE: Blow the candles out, chorus
and jazz octet, 1971; Mountains are mountains,
chorus and jazz quartet, 1975; Skelelemedania,
soprano, cello, trombone, tape, live electronics,
1975; The first liberty bell was cracked because . . . ., mezzo-soprano and orchestra, 1978;
DANCE SCORES: Syzygy, tape, 1973; Side waves,
tape, 1976; Windfall of the accursed, tape, 1976;
Strike out, tape, 1977; The cardinal whirlpool
in the cyclop's eye, live synthesizers, 1977;
also scores for plays and films; other miscellaneous works.
415 W. 118th St., #2, New York, NY 10027

FREEDMAN, ISRAEL
b. Brooklyn, N.Y., 1910. Studied violin with
Ondricek, composition with Rimsky-Korsakov; held
a scholarship at the New England Cons., 1934.
His works for orchestra include a symphony;
Hiawatha, a tone poem; Adagio for strings; also
songs.

FREEDMAN, ROBERT M.
b. Mt. Vernon, N.Y., 23 Jan. 1934. After basic
training in public schools, has been self-
taught in music through score analysis and listening to all kinds of music. He was on the
faculty at Berklee Coll. of Music, 1956-59.
WORKS: ORCHESTRA: trumpet concerto; CHAMBER
MUSIC: string quartet; Journeys of Odysseus,
jazz suite for chamber orch.; Beautiful music,
popular song, sung by Lena Horne.
4 Greenwood Lane, Westport, CT 06880

FREEMAN, EDWIN ARMISTEAD
b. Spartanburg, S.C., 2 May 1928. Studied with
Kenneth Klaus, Louisiana State Univ.; with Jack
Beeson and Otto Luening, Columbia Univ.; conducting with Pierre Monteux, Hancock, Maine. He
won a BMI student composer award, 1955. He was
high school director and arts program chairman,
Dalton School, New York, 1965-69; from 1969, on
faculty, Clemson Univ.
WORKS: ORCHESTRA: Fantasy on a ground;
CHAMBER MUSIC: string quartet, 1954; CHORUS:
Dr. Donne preaches on death, oratorio.
148 Folger St., Clemson, SC 29631

FREEMAN, JOHN
b. New York, N.Y., 30 June 1928. Studied with
Tsuya Matsuki; with Darius Milhaud at Tanglewood,
1948. He has been interviewed on "Meet the
Composer"; has been associate editor, Opera News
magazine, since 1960.
WORKS: ORCHESTRA: suite for wind orchestra;
clarinet concerto, Bronx, 22 Apr. 1979; CHAMBER
MUSIC: 2 string quartets; clarinet sonata;
violin sonata in memory of Robert Kurka; 3 quartets for winds; Serenade, clarinet and strings,

Bronx, 22 Apr. 1979; trios for various instruments; many song cycles with chamber group accompaniments.

4970 Independence Ave., Bronx, NY 10471

FREEMAN, NED
b. Hallowell, Maine, 27 Dec. 1895. Studied with John Orth, Stuart Mason, and Philip Greeley Clapp. He was pianist and arranger for theatre and dance orchestras, radio, and films. His works include Gallery, 12 sketches for orch., and songs.

FREITAG, DOROTHEA
b. Baltimore, Md. Studied with Howard Rutledge Thatcher, Peabody Cons., grad. 1932; also with Nadia Boulanger, Mario Castelnuovo-Tedesco, and Bohuslav Martinu. She received an ASCAP award for her ballet, Storyville, 1967; Peabody Alumni award, 1968. She composes and arranges for Broadway shows and television programs. Among the shows she has contributed to are Mame, Fiddler on the roof, Golden boy.

FREMDER, ALFRED
b. Sioux City, Iowa, 14 Mar. 1920. Studied at Concordia Seminary, B.A. 1942; with Donald Ferguson, Paul Fetler, and Earl George, Univ. of Minnesota, M.A. 1955; with Martin Mailman and William P. Latham, North Texas State Univ., Ph.D. 1970. His awards include Nora Seeley Nichols award, 1964, 1967; Prescott award and Prescott prize, 1966. He was piano recitalist, 1940-50; faculty member, Bethany Coll., 1945-56; Arizona State Univ., 1966-68; teaching fellow, North Texas State Univ., 1968-70; professor, Texas Wesleyan Coll., from 1970.
WORKS: ORCHESTRA: piano concerto, 1970, Oslo, 27 Aug. 1973; CHAMBER MUSIC: wind quintet, 1969; CHORUS: O ye shepherds, a cappella motet, 1953; Surely He hath borne our griefs, 1954; The Passion according to St. Mark, with orch. and narrator, Phoenix, 17 May 1964; Songs of Solomon, a cappella, Phoenix, 12 Apr. 1964; The tabernacle of God, 1968; That great city, with strings, percussion, 1969; A song of time, 1971; many works for piano.

Texas Wesleyan College, P.O. Box 3277, Ft. Worth, TX 76105

FREUDENTHAL, JOSEF
b. Leisa, Germany, 1 Mar. 1903; to U.S. 1936; d. New York, 5 May 1964. Studied in Frankfurt and Munich; lived in Palestine before coming to the U.S.; founded Transcontinental Music Corp.
WORKS: SONGS: The last words of David; Let us sing unto the Lord; Precepts of Micah; A lamp unto my feet; The earth is the Lord's.

FREUND, DONALD WAYNE
b. Pittsburgh, Pa., 15 Nov. 1947. Studied with Joseph Wilcox Jenkins, Duquesne Univ., B.M. 1969; with Darius Milhaud and Charles Jones, Aspen School; with Wayne Barlow, Samuel Adler, and Warren Benson, Eastman School of Music, M.M. 1970, D.M.A. 1972. His awards include an Aspen composition award, 1968; Hanson prize, 1970; McCurdy prize, 1972; Tenn. Arts Commission award,

1974; League of Composers/ISCM award, 1976; Tenn. Music Teachers Assoc. Composer of the Year, 1977; Nat. Endowment for the Arts grant, 1978; first prize, Washington Internat. Competition, 1979. From 1972, he has been faculty member, Memphis State Univ.
WORKS: ORCHESTRA: Adagio for orchestra, 1966; piano concerto, 1970; Canzone, 1971; The waste land, wind ensemble, 1972; CHAMBER MUSIC: 2 string quartets, 1965, 1966; woodwind trio, 1966; 3 bagatelles, viola and piano; Passion and resurrection, 3 speakers and 10 players, 1969; Pas de deux, clarinet and bassoon, 1969; 4 pieces for horn quartet, 1969; Romanza, brass sextet, 1970; trio for violin, trombone, piano, 1971; Intermezzo, solo horn, 1971; Elegy for Simonas Kudirka, 6 instruments, 1972; Pastoral symphony, piano and woodwind quintet, 1977; Retournai toccata a quartre, flute, trumpet, piano, percussion, 1977; Ukrainian fantasy, violin, tape, 1977.

Music Dept., Memphis State University, Memphis, TN 38152

FRICKER, PETER RACINE
b. London, England, 5 Sept. 1920; to U.S. 1964. Studied at the Royal Coll. of Music. After serving in the Royal Air Force, 1940-46, he resumed composition studies in London with Matyas Seiber. His awards include Order of Merit, Federal Republic of Germany; Freedom of the City of London; honorary doctorate, Leeds Univ.; honorary membership, Royal Acad. of Music, London. He was music director, Morley Coll., London, 1952-64, and at the same time, professor of composition, Royal Coll. of Music; joined the faculty, Univ. of California, Santa Barbara, in 1964, became chairman of the music department, 1970.
WORKS: ORCHESTRA: Rondo scherzoso, 1948; 4 symphonies, 1949, 1951, 1960, 1966; Prelude, elegy, and finale, 1949; violin concerto, 1950; concertante #1, English horn and strings, 1950; concertante #2, 3 pianos, strings, timpani, 1951; viola concerto, 1953; piano concerto, 1954; Dance scene, 1954; Rapsodia concertante (violin concerto #2), 1954; Comedy overture, 1958; toccata, piano and orch., 1959; O longs desirs, soprano and orch., 1963; 4 songs, soprano and orch., 1965; 3 scenes, 1966; 7 counterpoints, 1967; concertante #4, flute, oboe, violin, strings, 1968; CHAMBER MUSIC: wind quintet, 1947; 2 string quartets, 1947, 1953; violin sonata, 1950; Aubade, alto saxophone and piano, 1951; Pastorale, 3 flutes, 1954; horn sonata, 1955; cello sonata, 1956; octet, winds and strings, 1958; 4 dialogues, oboe and piano, 1965; Fantasy, viola and piano, 1966; 5 canons, 2 flutes, 2 oboes, 1966; Refrains, solo oboe, 1968; Serenade #3, saxophone quartet, 1969; 3 arguments, cello and bassoon, 1969; Sarabande, in memoriam Igor Stravinsky, solo cello, 1971; A bourree for Sir Arthur Bliss, solo cello, 1971; The groves of Dodona, 6 flutes, 1973; CHORUS: The vision of judgment, oratorio, 1958; Commissary report, male voices, 1965; Threefold amen, with instruments, 1966; Ave Maris Stella, male voices, 1967; Magnificat, with soloists and orch., 1968; 7

FRIEDMAN, KEN(NETH SCOTT)

little songs, a cappella, 1972; SONGS: 4 songs, soprano, Gryphius text, 1965; The day and the spirits, soprano and harp, 1965; Some superior nonsense, tenor, flute, oboe, cello, harpsichord, 1968; The roofs, coloratura soprano and percussion, 1970; many works for piano, organ; 2 pieces for carillon, 1969, 1970; film scores, radio plays, etc.
> Music Dept., Univ. of California, Santa Barbara, CA 93106

FRIEDMAN, KEN(NETH SCOTT)
b. New London, Conn., 19 Sept. 1939. Attended California Western Univ., Shimer Coll., San Francisco State Coll., B.A., M.A.; in 1967 studied theory and composition with Richard Maxfield, collaborated with Maxfield, 1967-68; earned a Ph.D. in sociology, U.S. Internat. Univ., San Diego. In addition to avant-garde music, his activities extend to art and poetry. He has presented one-man art shows and group shows from San Diego to Berkeley on the West Coast, in New York, Boston, Buenos Aires, and throughout Europe. He was founder of the Fluxus group, 1966, and editor of Fluxus West publications including Fluxus/Underground Press Syndicate/ In 1967 he taught at San Francisco State Coll. and was music director, Karen Ahlberg dance group; was artist-in-residence, Unitarian-Universalist Church, Ventura, 1969; on faculty, Free Univ. of Berkeley, 1970; general manager, Something Else Press, 1971; guest editor, Source magazine, 1971-74; chairman, The Expanded Ear, music conference, 1973; has lectured extensively on art, poetry, surrealism. Nicolas Slonimsky (in Baker's Biog. Dict.) calls Friedman's works "verbal exhortations to existentialist actions," and gives cogent examples. Such being the case, it might be more prudent to attend a performance of the O.K. Joe sonata rather than of Skulls like eggshells.
> WORKS: AUDIO-VISUAL: The shy smiling skyscraper, 1968; Zen softball, 1970; Roasting off, 1970; Dog walking swiftly; Let's talk turkey, a Thanksgiving concert for John Cage, 1972; Nearer, Cape Cod, to thee, 1972; The Imus are out walking logarythms, 1973; Continental dividend, 1975; The school of hard Knoxville, 1975; Oh, dust me off again, 1975.
> 6361 Elmhurst Dr., San Diego, CA 92120

FRIEDMAN, RICHARD
b. New York, N.Y., 6 Jan. 1944. Was trained in electronics and science. He worked with Morton Subnotnick at the Intermedia Electronic Studio, New York Univ., 1966-68; since that time, has done experimental work in the KPFA radio station in Berkeley, Calif.
> WORKS: ELECTRONIC: Lumia mix, 1967; Crescent, 1967; To the star messenger, 1968; Alchemical manuscript, 1968; MULTIMEDIA: Outside/Inside, uses closed-circuit television, sculptures, light beams, etc.

FRIEDMAN, STANLEY ARNOLD
b. Memphis, Tenn., 14 Sept. 1951. Studied with Donald Freund, Memphis State Univ., B.M. 1973; with Samuel Adler, Eugene Kurtz, Warren Benson,

and Joseph Schwantner, Eastman School of Music, M.M. 1975, D.M.A. 1976. He won awards in the New Louisville Brass Quintet competition, 1974, 1975; Internat. Trombone Assoc., 1976; Internat. Trumpet Guild, 1977. He has played trumpet with the Winston-Salem Symph., Rochester Phil., Syracuse Symph., and Memphis Symph. From 1977 he has been faculty member, Univ. of North Carolina at Greensboro.
> WORKS: CHAMBER MUSIC: Solus, solo trumpet; Os, bass trombone; Transients, chamber orch.; Parodie I, brass quintet; Parodie III, brass septet; Antiphonis IV, trumpet sextet; Love song, soprano and strings; concertino for chamber orch. with solo trumpet.
> Rt. 3, Box 6, Myers Fork Rd., Summerfield, NC 27358

FRIGON, CHRIS D.
b. Barre, Vt., 26 July 1949. Studied with John Goodman, Hugo Norden, and Gardner Read, Boston Univ., B.M., cum laude, 1971, M.M. 1977. He placed first in the composition contest of the American Accordion Musicological Soc., 1972. He was on the faculty, Adamant (Vt.) Summer Music School for Pianists, 1969-71, and resident composer, 1974-75; has been on faculty, Berklee Coll. of Music, from 1974.
> WORKS: ORCHESTRA: Symphonic matrix #1, 1977; CHAMBER MUSIC: 3 miniatures, string quartet, 1970; Antithesis, solo voices, flute, cello, piano, 1972; Reflections, woodwind and string quartets, 1973; Dosofitela, flute and piano, 1976; The painters, woodwind quartet, 1978; KEYBOARD: Adagio, piano, 1969; Spectra, piano, 4 hands, and accessories, 1971; Knozonos, 2 pianos, 1972; 5 preludes, free-bass, accordion, 1973.
> 1822 Beacon St., Brookline, MA 02146

FRIML, RUDOLF
b. Prague, Czech., 7 Dec. 1879; U.S. citizen 1925; d. Los Angeles, Calif., 12 Nov. 1972. Studied with Anton Dvorak at Prague Cons. He toured Europe as accompanist to Jan Kubelik and came to the U.S. with him in 1906. He remained in New York as pianist and composer, playing his own piano concerto with the New York Symphony in 1906. He began composing operettas in 1912, when he replaced Victor Herbert as composer of The firefly. He went to Hollywood in 1934 and composed for films.
> WORKS: OPERETTAS: The firefly, 1912; High jinks, 1913; Katinka, 1915; You're in love, 1916; Gloriana, 1918; Tumble in, 1919; Sometime, 1919; Rose Marie, 1924; Vagabond king, 1925; The 3 muskateers, 1928; Launa, 1930; Anina, 1934; also many songs, piano pieces.

FRINK, GEORGE M. D.
b. Ft. Pierce, Fla., 16 Sept. 1931. Studied with Talmage W. Dean and David L. Conley, Southwestern Baptist Theol. Seminary. He was minister of music, First Baptist Church, Warner Robins, Ga., 1967-69; Marion Baptist Church, Marion, S.C., 1969-73.
> WORKS: THEATRE: Peter, musical drama; Really free, folk-rock musical; and sacred anthems.

FRISKIN, JAMES
> b. Glasgow, Scotland, 3 Mar. 1886; to U.S. 1914; d. New York, N.Y., 16 Mar. 1967. Attended Royal Coll. of Music, London. On coming to the U.S., he taught at Juilliard Graduate School; also gave piano recitals in New York. His compositions include a piano quintet and a violin sonata.

FRISKIN, REBECCA CLARKE. See CLARKE, REBECCA

FRITSCHEL, JAMES
> b. Greeley, Colo., 13 May 1929. Studied at Wartburg Coll., B.M.E. 1951; Univ. of Northern Colorado, M.A. 1954; with Philip Bezanson and Richard Hervig, Univ. of Iowa, Ph.D. 1960. He won a choral composition contest at Columbia Coll., S.C. He was high school choral director, 1954-58; from 1959, faculty member and choir director, Wartburg Coll.
> WORKS: A CAPPELLA CHORUS: Make haste; Be still; With song and dance; Be glad; 4 about life and death; A great light; Search me and know my heart; Be not silent; Canticle: A song of David, double choir; and many more. Everyone sang, for 3 choirs, 2 brass choirs, and organ, was performed at Kennedy Center, Washington, 15 Apr. 1978.
> 915 Harlington Place, Waverly, IA 50677

FRITTER, GENEVIEVE DAVISSON
> b. Clarksburg, W.Va., 13 Dec. 1915. Studied at Judson Coll., Marion, Ala., B.M. 1937; privately with Esther Williamson Ballou, Washington; graduate work in violin at Birmingham Cons., Cincinnati Cons., and Juilliard Summer School at Chautauqua, N.Y. She has won awards from Nat. Fed. of Music Clubs, Mu Phi Epsilon, and Washington Friday Morning Music Club, a composer group. She was resident composer with the Montgomery Ballet Company, 1961-80; concertmaster, National Ballet Orch., 1966-71; violinist, Kennedy Center Opera House Orch., from 1971.
> WORKS: THEATRE: 6 full-length ballets for children; ORCHESTRA: Theme and variations, string orch.; Sinfonietta, 1978; CHAMBER MUSIC: Suite, Poem, Lament, Gavotte, Soliloquy, all for solo flute; numerous works for chamber groups; CHORUS: Judean hills are holy.
> 9012 Walden Rd., Silver Spring, MD 20901

FROCK, GEORGE
> b. Danville, Ill., 16 July 1938. Studied percussion with his father, with Roy Knapp, with Jack McKenzie at Univ. of Illinois; composition with John Pozdro. He was faculty member, Univ. of Kansas, 1960-63; Memphis State Univ., 1963-66; from 1966, at Univ. of Texas, Austin.
> WORKS: PERCUSSION: Variations, flute and percussion; concertino, marimba and piano; Fanfare, double trio; 3 Asiatic dances; Concert etude.
> Music Dept., Univ. of Texas, Austin, TX 78712

FROHBEITER, ANN W.
> b. Evansville, Ind., 27 Sept. 1942. Studied organ, Indiana Univ., B.M.; Southern Methodist Univ., M.M.; and choral arranging with Lloyd Pfautsch. She was organist in Dallas, 1964-66; from 1967, Temple Emanuel, Houston, and associate organist, St. Luke's Methodist Church, Houston.
> WORKS: Blow ye the trumpet, blow, hymn tune or anthem for chorus, trumpet, organ, 1972.

FROHMADER, JEROLD C.
> b. Seattle, Wash., 3 Dec. 1938. Studied with George F. McKay, Central Washington State Coll., B.A. 1960; with William Billingsley, Univ. of Idaho, M.M. 1965; with Clifford Taylor and George Rochberg, Temple Univ. He taught in Washington schools, 1960-65; from 1965, faculty member, Glassboro State Coll.
> WORKS: WIND ENSEMBLE: Symphonia for winds, 33 players; CHAMBER MUSIC: sextet, 1969; Contrasts, saxophone quartet; Zeitgeist, prepared piano; ELECTRONIC: Gestures I, brass trio and tape; Yardbird's skull, tape; Watergate, solo performer and tape; Sequence, dancers and tape.
> Glassboro State Coll., Glassboro, NJ 08028

FROHNE, VINCENT
> b. LaPorte, Ind., 26 Oct. 1936. Studied with Donald H. White, DePauw Univ., B.M. cum laude 1958; with Darius Milhaud, Aspen, 1957; Leon Kirchner, Tanglewood, 1959; with Howard Hanson and Bernard Rogers, Eastman School of Music, M.M. 1959, Ph.D. 1962; with Boris Blacher and Josef Ruger, Berlin, 1960-61, 1962-63. His awards include Benjamin prize, 1959; Fulbright grant, 1960; Prix de Rome (twice renewed) 1963-66; Grauseman award, 1965; Guggenheim grant, 1966; Rockefeller Orchestra prize, 1967; 2 grants from Berlin Senat, 1967, 1968; and many commissions. He was director, Berlin Chamber Music Series of the 20th Century, 1968-70; founder, director, Schiller Coll. Music Program, Berlin, 1971-74; from 1975, faculty member, Univ. of Tulsa.
> WORKS: ORCHESTRA: symphony in c, 1951; Adam's chains, song cycle for soprano and orch., 1964; Ordine II, 1965; Counterpoise, 1965; The sacred songs of William Blake, narrator, soprano, orch., 1971; CHAMBER MUSIC: study for solo clarinet, 1960; piano sonata, 1962; cello sonata, 1966; string quartet, 1967; Pendulum, flute and piano, 1968; brass sextet (In memoriam I. Stravinsky), 1977; many choral works, piano pieces.
> 1515 E. 61st St., Tulsa, OK 74136

FROMM, HERBERT
> b. Kitzingen, Germany, 23 Feb. 1905; U.S. citizen 1944. Studied at Munich Acad. of Music and with Paul Hindemith at Tanglewood, 1941, 1942. He received the Ernest Bloch award for Song of Miriam, 1945; honorary doctorate, Lesley Coll., 1969. He was organist and music director, Temple Beth Zion, Buffalo, 1937-41; and at Temple Israel, Boston, 1941-72.
> WORKS: CHAMBER MUSIC: violin sonata; 2 string quartets, #2 with soprano and tenor voices; trio for harpsichord, flute, cello; wind quintet; CHORUS: 6 Shakespeare songs, a cappella; 8 cantatas for chorus, solo, and orch., including Song of Miriam, 1945; Psalm cantata; Chamber cantata; The stranger, 1957; Transience, with

FRUMKER, LINDA

tenor and 7 instruments; Memorial cantata, Brookline, 23 Mar. 1973; Herrick cantata; 6 Hebrew
madrigals; SONG CYCLE: The crimson sap, 1954;
KEYBOARD: Fantasy, piano; Let all mortal flesh
keep silent, organ, 1940; organ sonata; piano
sonata; many liturgical works.
100 Marion St., Brookline, MA 02146

FRUMKER, LINDA
b. Geneva, Ohio, 11 Dec. 1940. Studied piano
with Arthur Loesser, horn with Martin Morris,
composition with Marcel Dick, Cleveland Inst. of
Music, B.M., M.M. She received the Ernest Bloch
award 3 times; a cash award at the 1962 Aspen
Music Festival; and commissions. She taught at
Cleveland Inst. of Music, 1964-67; at Cleveland
Supplementary Education Center, thereafter.
WORKS: ORCHESTRA: symphony, 1964; WCLV
anniversary overture, 1973; CHAMBER MUSIC: Music
for friends, string quartet; wind quintet; 4 for
Fred, clarinet quartet; 2 string quartets; Elegy,
violin and piano; 3 pieces for 2 pianos, Cleveland, 2 Nov. 1976; SONGS: 3 songs of love,
1960; 4 Aspen songs, 1962; octet for soprano and
7 instruments, 1962; Like Noah's dove, soprano
and ensemble, 1972; Angell songs, text by Barbara
Angell, 1973.

FRYSINGER, J. FRANK
b. Hanover, Pa., 7 Apr. 1878; d. York, Pa., 4
Dec. 1954. Studied with Edgar Stillman Kelley
in New York, 1898-1900. He was organist in
York, Pa., 1909-11, 1922-53; wrote some 200 organ
works; also piano pieces and songs.

FRYXELL, REGINA HOLMEN
b. Morganville, Kans., 24 Nov. 1899. Studied at
Augustana Coll., Rock Island, Ill., B.A., M.B.
1922, Litt.B. 1961; with Wallingford Riegger and
A. Madeley Richardson, at Juilliard School,
organ dipl., 1927; in Europe, 1948, 1971-72;
privately with Leo Sowerby; many summer courses.
She has been church organist and private piano
and organ teacher since 1922; taught at various
times at Augustana Coll., Juilliard School, Knox
Coll., and from 1969, at Black Hawk Coll.
WORKS: Many published anthems and other
liturgical works; unpublished manuscripts include works for various chamber groups and choral
groups.
1331 42nd Ave., Rock Island, IL 61201

FUCHS, CHARLES EMILIO
b. Cluj, Hungary, 27 June 1907; to U.S. c. 1955.
Studied with Zoltan Kodaly in Budapest. He
taught in Vienna, Paris, and Berlin; wrote a
film score in Berlin, another in Buenos Aires.
Among his other works are 4 symphonies; 3 rhapsodies; piano trios; trio for clarinet, viola,
harp; etc.

FUCHS, LILLIAN
b. New York, N.Y., 18 Nov. Studied violin with
Louis Svecenski and Franz Kneisel, composition
with Percy Goetschius, Inst. of Musical Art, New
York. On graduation she received the Morris
Loeb Memorial prize and the Silver Medal. She
is faculty member at Juilliard School and Man-

hattan School, and has taught at Aspen, Colo.
She is concert violist and chamber player, and
has performed in recitals with her brother,
Joseph Fuchs, in the U.S. and abroad.
WORKS: CHAMBER MUSIC: 15 characteristic
studies, viola solo; 16 fantasie etudes, viola
solo; Sonata pastorale, viola solo; Jota, violin
and piano; 2 pieces in olden style, violin and
piano; arrangements from Paganini and Mozart.
186 Pinehurst Ave., New York, NY 10033

FUCHS, PETER PAUL
b. Vienna, Austria, 30 Oct. 1916; U.S. citizen
1943. Studied conducting with Felix Weingartner
and Josef Krips, Vienna State Acad.; composition
privately with Karl Weigl and Eugene Zador;
piano with Leonie Gombrich. He received a Ford
Found. grant, 1954-55. He was on the music
staff, Metropolitan Opera, 1940-50; San Francisco
Opera, 1946, 1950, 1954; head of opera and symphony, Louisiana State Univ., 1950-76; music
director, Baton Rouge Symphony, 1960-76; Beaumont (Tex.) Civic Opera, 1962-75; and from 1976,
conductor and music director, Greensboro (N.C.)
Symphony.
WORKS: OPERA: Serenade at noon, Baton
Rouge, 1965; The heretic; ORCHESTRA: violin
concertino; Fantasy, English horn and strings;
Polyphony, Baton Rouge, 14 Apr. 1976; CHAMBER
MUSIC: 3 string quartets; piano sonata; wind
quintet; 8 inventions, wind instruments; Partita
ricercata, flute, oboe, double bass, harpsichord,
Columbia, S.C., 19 Nov. 1975; songs.
720 Lipscomb Rd., Greensboro, NC 27410

FUERSTNER, CARL
b. Strasbourg, France, 16 June 1912; U.S. citizen
1945. Studied with Walter Braunfels, Philipp
Jarnach, Ernst Gernot Klussmann, Hochschule für
Musik, Cologne, Germany. He was director, opera
department, Eastman School of Music, 1945-50;
faculty member, Brigham Young Univ., 1951-61;
from 1961, principal coach and conductor, opera
theatre, Indiana Univ.
WORKS: ORCHESTRA: Symphorama, 1960; cello
concerto; quintuple concerto, 5 instruments and
strings; BAND: overture; Allegro ritmico;
Divertimento, string quartet; violin sonata;
piano sonata; clarinet sonata; bass clarinet or
cello sonata; The rat and the dinosaur, trumpet
and tuba; Nocturne and dance, flute and piano;
Little dance suite, piano; Configurations, saxophone and piano; CHORUS: Hymn for a cappella
choir; many songs.
2518 E. 7th St., Bloomington, IN 47401

FULEIHAN, ANIS
b. Kyrenia, Cyprus, 2 Apr. 1900; to U.S. 1915;
d. Stanford, Calif., 11 Oct. 1970. Studied
piano with Alberto Jonas in New York; was chiefly
self-taught in music. He held a Guggenheim fellowship, 1939; Fulbright research fellowship,
1952. He toured the U.S. and Near East, 1919-
25; lived in Cairo to 1928; was on staff, G.
Schirmer, Inc., 1932-39; professor, Indiana Univ.,
1947-52; director, Beirut Cons., 1953-60; went
to Tunis for the U.S. State Dept., 1962-63.
WORKS: OPERA: Vasco, 1960; ORCHESTRA:

Mediterranean suite, 1922; Preface to a child's storybook, 1932; 2 symphonies, 1936, 1966; piano concerto with string orch., 1937; 2 piano concertos, 1938, 1965; Symphony concertante, string quartet and orch., 1939; concerto for 2 pianos, 1940; Epithalamium, piano and strings, 1940; Invocation to Isis, 1940; theremin concerto, 1945; 3 Cyprus serenades, 1946; Rhapsody, cello and strings, 1946; The pyramids of Giza, 1952; Duo concertante, violin, viola, orch., 1958; Toccata, piano and orch., 1960; Islands suite, 1961; cello concerto, 1963; viola concerto, 1963; CHAMBER MUSIC: 5 string quartets; horn quintet; clarinet quintet; 11 piano sonatas; violin sonata; cello sonata; viola sonata; also choral pieces and songs.

FULKERSON, JAMES
b. Streator, Ill., 2 July 1945. Studied with Will Ogdon and Abram Plum, Illinois Wesleyan Univ.; with Ben Johnston, Salvatore Matirano, Kenneth Gaburo, Lejaren Hiller, and Herbert Brün, Univ. of Illinois. He held a fellowship, Center for Creative and Performing Arts, 1969-72; composer-in-residence grant, Berlin, Germany, 1973-74, and Melbourne, Australia, 1978; various commissions. He was on the staff, Center for New Music, Buffalo, 1969-72; free-lance composer and trombonist, New York, 1972-73, then in Europe.
WORKS: ORCHESTRA: Globs, 1968; Something about mobiles, 1969; Planes, pts., 1969; Behind closed doors, 1971; Patterns X, 1972; guitar concerto, 1972; trombone concerto, 1973; Music for brass instruments, I-V, 1975-78; concerto for amplified cello and orch., 1978; CHAMBER MUSIC: 2 woodwind quintets, 1965, 1966; Quartet for dancers, 4 instruments, 1967; string quartet, 1968; Patterns III, solo tuba, 1969; Chord, any instruments or voices, 1972; Coordinative systems I-XII, pieces for various instruments or ensembles, 1971-78; MULTIMEDIA: 6 studies for light, sounds, dancers, 1967; Now II, sound modulators, amplified clavichord, trombone, trumpet, 1969; Empty whiskers, voice and tape, 1972; Stations, regions, and clouds, I-III, and Antiphones and streams, both for trombone and live electronics, 1978.
Barton Workshop, Totnes, Devon., TQ9 6EJ, England

FULLER, DONALD SANBORN
b. Washington, D.C., 1 July 1919. Attended Yale Univ.; studied composition with Aaron Copland, Darius Milhaud, and Bernard Wagenaar.
WORKS: ORCHESTRA: a symphony; CHAMBER MUSIC: trio for clarinet, cello, piano; sonatina, oboe, clarinet, piano; sonata for 2 pianos; piano sonatina; other piano pieces, songs.

FULLER, JEANNE WEAVER
b. Regina, Sask., Canada, 23 Oct., 1917; to U.S. 1923. Studied at Pomona Coll., B.A. 1937; California State Univ., M.A. 1964; with Halsey Stevens, Univ. of Southern California. She has been instructor, El Camino Coll., from 1965; and also a private teacher.
WORKS: CHAMBER MUSIC: Fugue for woodwinds;

CHORUS: 3 motets; Exsultate justi; Maggy and milly and molly and may, women's voices; Now (more near ourselves than we); The praise of Christmas; SONGS: At the window, Sandburg text; When young hearts break, Heine text; PIANO: Dorian rondo; sonata; Jeux aux douze tons, piano, 4 hands.
7025 Hedgewood Dr., Rancho Palos Verdes, CA 90274

FULLER, RAMON C.
b. Murray, Utah, 27 July 1930. Studied with Leon Dallin and Carl Fuerstner, Brigham Young Univ.; with Kenneth Gaburo, Ben Johnston, Lejaren Hiller, Univ. of Illinois. He was instructor, Univ. of Maryland, 1963; creative associate, Center for Creative and Performing Arts, Buffalo, 1965-67; on the faculty, State Univ. of New York, Buffalo, 1967-75.
WORKS: WIND ENSEMBLE: 2 pieces for 9 brasses, 1969; CHAMBER MUSIC: 3 short pieces for piano, 1971; string quartet, Buffalo, 22 May 1973; ELECTRONIC: music for tape and 2 percussionists, 1964; 3 improvisations for tape, 1972.
327 Windermere Blvd., Eggertsville, NY 14226

FUNK, ERIC
b. Deer Lodge, Mont., 28 Sept. 1949. Studied with Tomas Svoboda and Sandor Veress, Portland State Univ., B.A. 1971, M.M. 1978; with Krzysztof Penderecki at Yale Univ. His awards include a Ruth Lorraine Close fellowship, 1973, and commissions from the Oregon Arts Commission, 1977, and the Oregon Symph. Orch., 1978. He is on the faculty, Portland State Univ., and at Clark Coll., Vancouver, Wash.
WORKS: THEATRE: Sanctuary, opera; Rhayader, ballet, with chamber orch., Portland, 27-29 Oct. 1978; ORCHESTRA: Trimorphism, with piano and string quartet, 1972; The prophet, 1973; Lidice; Mantis, brass choir; CHAMBER MUSIC: Meditations, string quartet and guitar; Images, chamber orch.; Triste, string quartet; Pentamorous, woodwind quintet; Emily, chamber orch., Portland, 21 Mar. 1979; choral works; piano pieces.
P.O. Box 751, Portland State Univ., Portland, OR 97207

FURMAN, JAMES
b. Louisville, Ky., 23 Jan. 1937. Studied with George Perle and Claude Almand, Univ. of Louisville, B.M.E. 1958, M.M. 1965; with Arthur Berger, Irving Fine, and Harold Shapero, Brandeis Univ., 1962-64. His awards include Louisville Phil. Society's Young Artists' award, 1953; Brandeis Univ. fellowship, 1962-64; first place, Brookline Library composition contest, 1964. He was choral director for the BBC documentary film on the life of Charles Ives; recording director for avant-garde music, Desto Records; musical director, arranger-pianist of world-touring army show, Rolling along of 1961; on faculty, Western Connecticut State Coll., from 1965.
WORKS: ORCHESTRA: I have a dream, symphonic oratorio, 1970, Cincinnati, 22-24 Jan. 1971; Declaration of Independence, with narrator, 1976; CHAMBER MUSIC: Variants, piano trio, 1964;

FUSSELL, CHARLES C.

CHORUS: 4 little foxes, choral cycle, 1962; Ave Maria, motet; Let us break bread together, spiritual; Salve Regina, motet; Go tell it on the mountain, with soloists and instruments; Some glorious day; Come Thou long-expected Jesus, motet; Hehlehlooyuh, 1976.
512 S. 22nd St., Louisville, KY 40211

FUSSELL, CHARLES C.
b. Winston-Salem, N.C., 14 Feb. 1938. Studied with Bernard Rogers, Eastman School of Music, B.M. 1960, M.M. 1964; with Boris Blacher in Berlin. His awards include a Fulbright grant, 1962-63; Ford Found. grant, 1964-65; Mary Duke Biddle Found. grant, 1972; 3 Mass. Arts and Humanities fellowships, 1974, 1976, 1978; and commissions. He has taught at North Carolina School of the Arts and at Smith Coll.; was composer-in-residence, Norton, England, 1976; has been faculty member, Univ. of Massachusetts, from 1966.
WORKS: THEATRE: Julian, drama after Flaubert, in 5 scenes, for soloists, chorus, orch.; Eurydice, Edith Sitwell text, drama for soprano and 9 players; ORCHESTRA: 2 symphonies, 1963, 1964-67; 3 processionals; CHAMBER MUSIC: Greenwood sketches, string quartet; Ballades, cello and piano, Cambridge, Mass., 26 Nov. 1979; VOCAL: Poems, after Hart Crane, voices and chamber orch.; Voyages, soprano and tenor soli, women's choir, piano, solo wind instrument; Résumé, Dorothy Parker text, soprano, string bass, piano; ORGAN: Bits, pieces, and portraits, 1977.
Music Dept., Univ. of Massachusetts, Amherst, MA 01002

GABEL, GERALD L.
b. Dodge City, Kans., 5 Apr. 1950. Studied with Peter Michaelides, Univ. of Northern Iowa; with Roger Reynolds, Univ. of California, San Diego. He received a Nat. Endowment for the Arts grant, 1979.
WORKS: CHAMBER MUSIC: 3 songs, voice, clarinet, violin, xylophone; Nocturne, piano; Statics, solo bass clarinet; CHORUS: The wicked walk on every side, 60-part mixed choir; The labyrinth, chamber choir, string quartet, percussion.
9262-H Regents Rd., La Jolla, CA 92037

GABER, HARLEY
b. Chicago, Ill., 5 June 1943. Studied with Darius Milhaud at Aspen, 1961; with Kenneth Gaburo and Lejaren Hiller, Univ. of Illinois, 1961-63; in Rome, 1963-64; and with William Sydeman, Mannes Coll. of Music, 1964-67. He received BMI student awards, 1965, 1968; was creative associate, Center for Creative and Performing Arts, Buffalo, 1967; held fellowship to Bennington Conf., 1968. He has been general manager, Composers' Forum, New York, from 1972; music director, Hudson Valley New Music Ensemble, from 1972.
WORKS: CHAMBER MUSIC: 5 pieces for piano; quartet for violin, oboe, clarinet, trumpet, 1961; 4 pieces for string quartet; Fantasy, solo flute, 1962; Scambio, flute and piano, 1963;

Ommagio a Feldman, 2 pianos, 1965; string quartet, 1966; Ludus primus, 2 flutes and vibraphone, 1966; Kata, solo violin, 1969; 3 ideas for a film, piano, string orch., 1970; Narrow road to the deep north, percussion, 1971; October piece, piano, vibraphone, gongs, 1972; Sovereign of the centre, 4 violins, 1972; so-shi-sai-rai-i, recorder, prerecorded gong, 1972; Michi, solo violin, 1972; The winds rise in the north, 3 violins, viola, cello, 1976; also chamber works with voice.
853 7th Ave., New York, NY 10019

GABURO, KENNETH
b. Somerville, N.J., 5 July 1926. Studied with Bernard Rogers, Eastman School of Music, B.M., M.M. 1949; with Goffredo Petrassi in Rome; with Burrill Phillips, Univ. of Illinois, D.M.A. 1962. His awards include George Gershwin Memorial award, 1954; Fulbright grant, 1954; Sagalyn Orch. award, 1956; Yaddo fellowship, 1960; UNESCO award, 1962; Guggenheim grant, 1967; Thorne Found. grant, 1968; Univ. of California grants, 1968, 1970; Kunstler program, 1971; and many commissions. He was faculty member, Kent State Univ., 1949-50; McNeese State Coll., 1950-54; Univ. of Illinois, 1955-68; Univ. of California, San Diego, 1968-75; then founded his own music publishing firm.
WORKS: THEATRE: The snow queen, 3-act opera for children, 1952; Music for tiger rag, musical play, 1956; Bodies, an opera for actors, text by composer, 1957; trilogy of 1-act operas, librettos by composer: The widow, The hermit, The dog-king, 1959; The hydrogen jukebox, electronic score, 1963; Lingua I-IV, a massive 6-hour theatre piece consisting of "diverse explorations of the acoustical, physiological, and structural properties of language in a musical context," 1965-70; other linguistic theatre pieces; ORCHESTRA: 3 interludes, string orch., 1949; piano concertante, 1949; On a quiet theme, 1950; Antiphony I, 3 string groups and tape, 1957; viola concerto, 1959; Shapes and sounds, 1960; CHAMBER MUSIC: 4 inventions, clarinet and piano, 1954; Music for 5 instruments, piano and winds, 1954; Ideas and transformations, #1-3, string duos, 1954; string quartet, 1 movement, 1956; Line studies, flute, clarinet, viola, trombone, 1957; Antiphony IV (Poised), piccolo, trombone, double bass, electronics, 1966; Inside, quartet for 1 double bass player, 1969; Mouthpiece, sextet for solo trumpet and slides, 1970; Antiphony VI (Cogito), string quartet, slides, tape, 1971; also choral works, songs, and electronic pieces.
Lingua Press, P.O. Box 1192, La Jolla, CA 92038

GAIDELIS, JULIUS
b. Lithuania, 5 Apr. 1909; U.S. citizen 1956. Studied at Lithuania State Cons.; with Francis Judd Cooke and Carl Mckinley, New England Cons., M.M. 1953. His awards include election to Pi Kappa Lambda, 1953; first prize, Brookline Library Assoc. contest, 1959. He has been a private music teacher from 1951; conductor, Boston Lithuanian Mixed Choir and Male Choir,

from 1952; organist and choirmaster, St. Casimir Church, Brockton, from 1969.

WORKS: OPERA: Dana, 1969; An umber of land, 1976; ORCHESTRA: violin concerto, 1948; 6 symphonies, #4, New York, 17 Mar. 1960; #6, Hartford Music Festival, 19 July 1961; 5 symphonic poems; CHAMBER MUSIC: 2 violin sonatas; 4 string quartets; trio for violin, clarinet, horn, 1959; piano trio, 1965; many choral works and songs.

    31 Sunflower Rd., Holbrook, MA 02343

GALAJIKIAN, FLORENCE GRANDLAND
b. Maywood, Ill., 29 July 1900. Studied with Albert Noelte, Northwestern School of Music, B.M. 1918; at Chicago Musical Coll.; and with Rubin Goldmark. She received an NBC Orchestra award and performance of her Symphonic intermezzo, 1932. Her other works include Tragic overture, 1936; Transitions, ballet suite, 1937; choral works; songs.

GALLAGHER, JACK
b. Forest Hills, N.Y., 27 June 1947. Studied with Elie Siegmeister, Hofstra Univ., B.A. cum laude 1969; with Robert Palmer and Burrill Phillips, Cornell Univ., A.B.D. 1975. He taught in public schools, 1969-71; played trumpet with the Nat. Orch. Assoc., 1968-70; was teaching assistant, Cornell Univ., 1971-75; on faculty, the Coll. of Wooster, from 1977.

WORKS: ORCHESTRA: Berceuse; Divertimento; CHAMBER MUSIC: Theme and variations, woodwind quintet, 1971; piano sonata, 1973; Theme and variations, cello and piano, 1973; Toccata, brass quintet; cello sonata; piano sonatina; 6 bagatelles, piano; and songs.

    1714 Normandy Dr., #3, Wooster, OH 44691

GALLAHER, CHRISTOPHER S.
b. Ashland, Ky., 10 June 1940. Studied with Bernhard Heiden and Juan Orrego-Salas, Indiana Univ., M.M. He was faculty member, Frostburg State Coll., 1966-70; from 1970, at Morehead State Univ.

WORKS: ORCHESTRA: Variations, 1973; CHAMBER MUSIC: Impressions of summer, alto saxophone and piano; 4 pieces for clarinet and cello, 1971; trio for flute, cello, piano; Music for brass quartet; Music for cello, 1972; quartet saxophone quartet, 1973; 3 fragments, contralto, flute, 3 clarinets, 1973.

    Hill'n'Dale Estates, Morehead, KY 40351

GALLA-RINI, ANTHONY
b. Manchester, Conn., 18 Jan. 1904. Studied with his father, a bandmaster, and learned to play accordion, cornet, mandolin, piano, oboe, horn, contrabassoon, euphonium, sarrusaphone, and several other instruments. He invented several mechanical improvements for the accordion. His compositions include an accordion concerto which he played with the Oklahoma City Orchestra, 15 Nov. 1941.

GALLOWAY, MICHAEL
b. Memphis, Tenn., 16 July 1946. Studied with Jane Soderstrom, Southwestern at Memphis, B.M. 1968; and with Marshall Barnes, Ohio State Univ.,

M.M. 1970. His awards include a Garrigues Found., scholarship at Southwestern; first place in the Ohio State concerto compeition, 1969, and the Centennial composition contest, 1970. He was faculty member, Mississippi Valley State Coll., 1971-75; from 1976, at Univ. of Wisconsin at Superior.

WORKS: BALLET: Cassandra; CHORUS: Missa brevis; The descent of the dove; numerous songs and song cycles, piano works, chamber works, and pop songs.

    4096 Barron Ave., Memphis, TN 38111

GAMBINO, JAMES JOHN
b. Summit, N.J., 15 June 1919. Attended Ithaca Coll., B.S.; Univ. of Texas, Austin, M.M. He is founder and director of the Permian Basin Chamber Music Society.

WORKS: ORCHESTRA: Movie theme; CHORUS: Jubilate Deo; Surely the Lord is in this place; Word seven; This moment is my life; Time for prayer.

GAMER, CARLTON
b. Chicago, Ill., 13 Feb. 1929. Studied with Frank Cookson and Anthony Donato, Northwestern Univ., B.M. 1950; at Boston Univ., M.M. 1951; privately with Roger Sessions, 1957. His awards include an Asia Society fellowship, 1962-63; ASUC recording award, 1973; visiting fellowship at Princeton Univ., 1976; MacDowell Colony, 1976; Piano raga chosen as a test piece for the Rockefeller Found. competition, 1978. He has been faculty member, Colorado Coll., from 1954; visiting lecturer at Princeton Univ., 1974, professor, 1976, 1981.

WORKS: From my youth, 51 pieces, 1937-47; ORCHESTRA: Fantasy, 1951; Archaios: Bios, 1968-72; many chamber music pieces, choral music, songs, piano pieces, and COMPUTER MUSIC: Variation on a thing by JKR, 1974, and Organum, from Canto LXXXI by Ezra Pound, 1976.

    1122 Wood Ave., Apt. 4, Colorado Springs, CO 80903

GANGWARE, EDGAR B., JR.
b. Sandusky, Ohio, 17 May 1921. Studied with Helen Grace Williams, Wittenberg Univ.; with Anthony Donato, Northwestern Univ., D.M. 1952. He won honorable mention in a Thor Johnson Brass Choir contest, 1949. He was faculty member, Boston Univ., 1949-50; Bemidji State Coll., 1952-66; from 1966, at Northeastern Illinois Univ.

WORKS: ORCHESTRA: piano concerto; WIND ENSEMBLE: Concerto miniature, timpani and brass choir; brass quintet; Prelude and allegro, brass choir; numerous chamber music pieces.

    1225 Candlewood Hill Rd., Northbrook, IL 60062

GANICK, PETER
b. Boston, Mass., 14 Dec. 1946. Studied with Jacob Druckman, Bard Coll.; Gardner Read, Boston Univ.; Martin Boykan, Seymour Shifrin, Brandeis Univ.; privately with John Huggler.

WORKS: CHAMBER MUSIC: octet, 4 clarinets and string quartet, 1971; Cavafy sonata, 1971;

GANZ, RUDOLPH

piano trio, 1968; <u>Islands</u>, for Maharishi Mahesh
Yogi, 2 pianos; string quartet, 1973.
78 Lincoln St., Needham, MA 02192

GANZ, RUDOLPH
b. Zurich, Switz., 24 Feb. 1877; to U.S. 1900;
d. Chicago, Ill., 2 Aug. 1972. Studied composition with Charles Blanchet in Lausanne and with
Heinrich Urban in Berlin. His many honors included 4 honorary doctorates; Northwestern Univ.
Centennial award; appointment to French Legion
of Honor. He made his debut as pianist with the
Berlin Philharmonic Orch. in 1899; was faculty
member, Chicago Musical Coll., 1900-05; toured
U.S. and Europe as concert pianist, 1912-21; was
conductor, St. Louis Symph., 1921-27; Young
People's Concerts of New York Phil. and San
Francisco Orch., 1938-49; director, Chicago
Musical Coll., 1929-54.
WORKS: ORCHESTRA: symphony in E, Berlin,
1900; <u>Animal pictures</u>, 1932; <u>Konzertstück</u>, piano
and orch., piano concerto, 1942; <u>Laughter--yet
love</u>, overture for an unwritten comedy, 1950;
PIANO: <u>Variations on a theme by Brahms</u>; choral
works; some 200 songs to texts in several languages. He was author of <u>Rudolph Ganz evaluates
modern piano music</u>, New York, 1968.

GARDNER, KAY
b. Freeport, N.Y., 8 Feb. 1941. Studied with
Althea Waites, Norfolk State Coll.; flute with
Samuel Baron, composition with Billy Jim Layton,
State Univ. of New York at Stonybrook, M.M. 1974;
conducting with Antonia Brico. In 1978 she became music director of the newly organized New
England Women's Symphony; has been music director
of Wise Women Enterprises, Inc./Urana Records
from 1975; performs as flutist and conductor
throughout the U.S. and Canada.
WORKS: CHAMBER MUSIC: <u>Energies</u>, flute,
oboe, cello; <u>Prayer to Aphrodite</u>, alto flute
and strings; <u>Moonflow</u>, any instrument and piano;
<u>Innermoods I & II</u>, 2 flutes and guitar; <u>Touching
souls</u>, alto flute, cello, guitar; <u>Crystal bells</u>,
any improvising instruments over composed cello
and guitar lines; <u>Rhapsody</u>, piano; <u>Rain forest</u>,
chamber orch.; 13 songs, voice and guitar; many
other chamber works.
Stonington, ME 04681

GARDNER, MILDRED ALVINE
b. Quincy, Ill., 12 Oct. 1899. Studied with
Edgar Stillman Kelley, Cincinnati Cons., graduating with honors in piano and composition;
with Marion Bauer in New York; piano with
Sigismund Stojowski. Her awards include a 2-
year graduate fellowship at Cincinnati Cons.;
4 Yaddo fellowships; 2 Penn. Fed. of Music Clubs
awards; Nat. Fed. of Music Clubs award; and commissions. She was accompanist and coach, Cincinnati and New York, 1920-33; taught privately
in Pittsburgh, 1935-39, at Fillion Studios,
1940-68; from 1969, on faculty at Carlow Coll.
WORKS: CHAMBER MUSIC: sonata for 2 pianos;
woodwind quartet; string quartet; SONGS: <u>Sep-
tember separation</u>, a cycle; <u>The daisies</u>; <u>Madonna</u>;
some 50 other art songs, performed frequently in
New York and Pittsburgh.
223 Underwood Ave., Greensburg, PA 15601

GARDNER, SAMUEL
b. Elizabethgrad, Russia, 25 Aug. 1891; to U.S.
as a child. Studied violin with Felix Winternitz
and Franz Kneisel; composition with Percy
Goetschius at Juilliard School; with Charles
Loeffler in Boston. His awards include a
Pulitzer scholarship, 1918; Loeb prize; and an
honorary D.M., New York Coll. of Music. He was
a member of the Kneisel String Quartet, 1914-15;
Chicago Symphony, 1915-16; Elshuco Trio, 1916-17;
on faculty at Juilliard School.
WORKS: ORCHESTRA: <u>Country moods</u>, string
orch.; <u>Broadway</u>, tone poem; violin concerto; <u>New
Russia</u>, tone poem; CHAMBER MUSIC: <u>Hebraic fan-
tasia</u>, clarinet quintet; piano quintet, 1925;
string quartet; <u>Prelude and fugue</u>, string quartet; <u>From the canebrake</u>, violin and piano; <u>Jazz-
etto</u>, violin and piano; <u>From the Rockies</u>, violin
and piano; <u>Essays for advanced solo violin</u>, 1960.
He was author of <u>School of violin study based on
harmonic thinking</u>, and <u>Violin method</u>, 2 vol.
303 W. 66th St., New York, NY 10023

GARFIELD, BERNARD
b. Brooklyn, N.Y., 27 May 1924. Studied with
Otto Luening and Henry Cowell, Columbia Univ.;
with Marion Bauer, New York Univ.; privately with
Hugo Kauder. He was director, New York Woodwind
Quintet, 1946-57; principal bassoonist, Philadelphia Orch., from 1957; faculty member, Temple
Univ., from 1957; Curtis Inst., from 1975.
WORKS: ORCHESTRA: <u>Concert overture</u>; CHAM-
BER MUSIC: quartet for bassoon and string trio;
piano sonata; <u>Poeme</u>, basson and piano; <u>Soliloquy</u>,
bassoon and piano; <u>2 pieces</u>, basson and piano;
woodwind trio; 6 songs for soprano and piano.
871 Wayside Lane, Haddonfield, NJ 08033

GARLAND, PETER
b. Portland, Maine, 1953. Studied with Harold
Budd and James Tenney, California Inst. of the
Arts. Published 10 issues of <u>Soundings</u>, which
contained hitherto unpublished works of Ives,
Cowell, Ruggles, Becker, Varese, Antheil,
Rudhyar, Cage, Partch, Lou Harrison, et al.,
along with music of younger composers; also published <u>Conlon Nancarrow: Selected studies for
player piano</u>, 1977.
WORKS: <u>A song</u>, piano, 1971; <u>2 Persian minia-
tures</u>, piano, 1971; <u>The fall of Quang Tri</u>, piano,
uses black key clusters, 1972; <u>Apple blossom</u>,
percussion, 1972; <u>3 strange angels</u>, piano and
percussion, uses a single bass drum ffff and 88-
note tone clusters, accomplished by means of a
wooden bar the length of the keyboard, 1972-73;
<u>Nostalgia of the Southern Cross</u>, 1976; <u>Dreaming
of immortality in a thatched cottage</u>, in 3 movements, voices, wooden clappers, Indonesian ang
klungs, marimba, harpsichord, percussion, titled
after a 16th-century Chinese painting, 1977.
2801-C Fulton, Berkeley, CA 94705

GARLICK, ANTONY
b. Sheffield, Yorks., England, 9 Dec. 1927; U.S.
citizen 1969; studied at Royal Coll. of Music,
London, 1947-49; Cons. di Ste. Cecilia, Rome,
M.M. 1954; with Harvey Olnick and John Weinzweig,
Univ. of Toronto, M.M. 1958; with Milos

Velimirovic, Univ. of Virginia. He joined the
faculty at Wayne State Coll. in 1960.
WORKS: ORCHESTRA: Canto, tone poem; Mardi
gras; Pasticcio; Simple symphony; BAND: Canticle;
Festival overture; Fiesta; Masquerade; Sinfonietta for brass choir; CHAMBER MUSIC: Sonata da
chiesa, oboe and organ; violin sonata; clarinet
sonata; 2 string quartets; woodwind quartet;
Rhapsody, alto saxophone and piano; 5 study
pieces, alto saxophone and piano; duo, flute
and viola; 4 episodes, brass quintet; Essay and
Suite, brass quartet; Colloquy, bass clarinet
and piano; Pieces for 8, clarinets; 2 trios for
3 clarinets; Concert piece, clarinet and piano;
many choral works, organ pieces, piano and harpsichord pieces.
602 Main St., Wayne, NB 68787

GARNER, ERROLL
b. Pittsburgh, Pa., 15 June 1921; d. Los Angeles,
2 Jan. 1977. Was entirely self-taught on
drums and piano, and was a professional pianist
at age 7. He was the first jazz artist to be
presented by Sol Hurok; made many concert tours
in the U.S. and Europe. The Republic of Mali
issued a postage stamp in his honor in 1971. He
composed the score for the film, A new kind of
love, and many popular songs, including Misty
and Play, play, play.

GARRIGUENC, PIERRE
b. Narbonne, France, 20 Aug. 1921; U.S. citizen
1955. Studied theory and violin with his father
and began composing at age 13; later attended a
conservatory and studied composition privately.
Since coming to the U.S. in 1948, he has studied
with Karel Husa, Warren Benson, and Samuel Adler.
From 1948 to 1962, he was staff composer for
broadcasting companies; from 1975, faculty member, State Univ. Coll., Oswego, N.Y.
WORKS: ORCHESTRA: Partita, 6 movements;
II Genesis, 2 narrators, brass, percussion,
strings; WIND ENSEMBLE: Reflections, brass,
piano, celesta, percussion; Synthesis, 13 winds;
CHORUS: Dreamland, with narrator and orch.; 3
poems; PIANO: Preludio e toccata; 3 pieces;
Polychromes I, vol. 1 and 2, no. 1-43; Polychromes II, vol. 3 and 4, no. 44-84.
Music Dept., State University College,
Oswego, NY 13126

GARRIGUENC, RENE
b. Vesoul, France, 18 Oct. 1908; U.S. citizen
1966. Studied composition with Charles Koechlin,
orchestration with Roger Desormiere in Paris.
He came to the U.S. in 1941; was staff composer
for the Columbia Broadcasting Company, Hollywood,
1943-65.
WORKS: ORCHESTRA: violin concerto; Preamble and scherzo; 5 pieces; Prelude and fugue;
CHAMBER MUSIC: violin sonata; 7 piano pieces;
2 pieces for string quartet; art songs; TELE-
VISION SCORES: "Twilight zone"; "Perry Mason";
"Gunsmoke," et al. He is author of a textbook,
Serial procedures and fundamentals, 1974.
3324 North Knoll Dr., Hollywood, CA 90068

GARTLER, ROBERT
b. Los Angeles, Calif., 15 Feb. 1933. Studied
with Klaus Ptingsheim in California and in
Tokyo; piano with Egon Petri. He was conductor
of the Renaissance Octet, 1964-68.
WORKS: OPERA: The outcasts of Poker Flat;
ORCHESTRA: Equinox, soprano and orch.; WIND
ENSEMBLE: Burial at Jones Bar Outpost, brass
sextet; SONGS: 2 statements from Jones Bar Outpost; The boy waits, cycle for baritone, English
horn, piano.
Box 1267, Berkeley, CA 94701

GARWOOD, MARGARET
b. New Jersey, 22 Mar. 1927. Studied composition
with Miriam Gideon, orchestration with Romeo
Cascarino. She received the Whiteside Found.
grant, 1965-68; Nat. Endowment for the Arts
grants, 1973, 1977; MacDowell Colony fellowship,
1978. She taught piano at Philadelphia Coll.
of the Performing Arts, 1953-69; at Muhlenberg
Coll., 1976 and from 1978.
WORKS: OPERA: The Trojan women, 1 act,
Philadelphia, 22 Oct. 1967; The nightingale and
the rose, Philadelphia, 21 Oct. 1973; BALLET:
Aesop's fables; SONG CYCLES: The cliff's edge,
soprano; Spring songs, soprano; Love songs,
soprano.
R.D. 1, East Greenfield, PA 18041

GATES, CRAWFORD
b. San Francisco, Calif., 29 Dec. 1921. Studied
at San Jose State Coll., B.A.; with Leroy
Robertson, Brigham Young Univ., M.A.; with
Howard Hanson and Bernard Rogers, Eastman School
of Music, Ph.D.; and with Ernst Toch in Salt
Lake City, 1952. He won the first Max Wald
Memorial Competition in 1955 with his first symphony; has received many commissions. He was on
the music faculty, Brigham Young Univ., 1950-66;
from 1966 at Beloit Coll.; also has conducted
the Rockford (Ill.) Symph. from 1970, and the
Beloit (Wis.) Symph., from 1966.
WORKS: THEATRE: Promised Valley, musical
play, has received more than 2000 performances
in 5 languages on 5 continents; Sand in their
shoes, musical play; ORCHESTRA: piano concerto;
5 symphonies, #2, with chorus has 16 movements,
#4, A new morning, with chorus, was premiered in
Salt Lake City, 29 May 1976, composer conducting;
also numerous choral works and songs.
911 Park Ave., Beloit, WI 53511

GATES, EVERETT
b. Des Moines, Iowa, 6 June 1914. Studied with
Anthony Donato, Drake Univ.; with Bernard Rogers,
and Burrill Phillips, Eastman School of Music,
B.M. 1937, M.M. 1948. His awards include election to Pi Kappa Lambda; Univ. of Rochester
Alumni citation, 1969. He was violist with the
Rochester Phil., 1937-48; Oklahoma City Symph.,
1948-58; on faculty, Oklahoma City Univ., 1948-
58; from 1958, Eastman School of Music faculty.
WORKS: ORCHESTRA: Rainbow variations,
Prismatic variations, and Varicolor variations,
all for string orch.; WIND ENSEMBLE: Mountain
scenario, band; Seasonal sketches, clarinet
choir; CHAMBER MUSIC: Night Song, string bass

GATES, GEORGE

and piano; Declamation and dance, saxophone quartet; Incantation and ritual, solo flute; Odd meter etudes; Modalogues, trumpet and piano; Triptych, 2 violins and viola; also choral works and songs.
354 Marsh Rd., Pittsford, NY 14534

GATES, GEORGE
b. Kankakee, Ill., 21 May 1920. Was with the Dallas Symph. Orch. 5 years; taught in public schools 16 years; was percussion instructor, Southern Methodist Univ., 3 years.
WORKS: BAND: Sol y sombra, concert march; Mosaico de Mexico, suite; 2 Russian songs; 2 Mexican songs of Chiapas; La contessa, concert march.

GATES, KEITH
b. Lake Charles, La., 29 Sept. 1949. Studied with Louis Mennini, North Carolina School of the Arts, 1966-69; with Roman Vlad, Italy, summer 1967; with Hugo Weisgall, Juilliard School, 1969-70. His chamber opera received honorable mention, BMI student competition, 1968.
WORKS: THEATRE: Migle and the bugs, chamber opera, 1967; ORCHESTRA: violin concerto, 1968; CHAMBER MUSIC: piano sonata, 1967; string quartet, 1968; violin sonata, 1976.

GATLIN, HELEN STANLEY. See STANLEY, HELEN

GATWOOD, DWIGHT D.
b. Nashville, Tenn., 26 Aug. 1942. Studied at Eastern Kentucky State Univ., B.A.; with Gilbert Trythall and Gregory Woolf, George Peabody Coll., M.M., Ph.D. He has received many commissions. He was faculty member at LaGrange Coll., 1965-66; Columbia State Coll., 1966-67; Defiance Coll., 1970-72; from 1972, Univ. of Tennessee at Martin.
WORKS: ELECTRONIC: Trihedron I, tape, 1970; Sextaphonia, 6-tone row piece using serialization, tape, 1970; Keep the pace, Baby, slides and tape, 1973; In memoriam: Steve Groff, tape, 1974; A serial trilogy, 1975; Cactaceae, slides and tape, 1975; The phantom of the lift, slides and tape, 1975; Cingulata I, percussion and tape, 1976; Images sur les plastiques, videotape, 1976; Be not far from me, O Lord, chorus and tape, 1976; Polly Moog meets double trouble, a parody on the silent movie, film and tape, 1977; Spirits of the dead, male chorus and tape, Poe text, 1977.
Music Dept., Univ. of Tennessee, Martin, TN 38238

GAUGER, THOMAS
b. Wheaton, Ill., 20 Dec. 1935. Studied with Kenneth Gaburo, Univ. of Illinois; percussion with Paul Price and Jack McKenzie. He was principal percussionist, Oklahoma City Symph., 1959-62; percussionist, Boston Symph. Orch., from 1963. His works for percussion include Gainsborough, a quintet; solos and duets for drums and mallet instruments.
23 Auburn St., Brookline, MA 02146

GAUL, HARVEY BARTLETT
b. New York, N.Y., 11 Apr. 1881; d. Pittsburgh,

Pa., 1 Dec. 1945. Studied with George Le Jeune and Dudley Buck in New York; with Alfred Gaul and Philip Armes in London; at Schola Cantorum and with Vincent d'Indy in Paris. His awards included an honorary D.M., Univ. of Pittsburgh; Chicago Madrigal Club prize; Tuesday Music Club prize; Mendelssohn Club prize; honorary membership, Penn. Fed. of Music Clubs, which established the Harvey Gaul scholarship. He held various conducting and academic posts in Pittsburgh; was music critic, Pittsburgh Post-Gazette.
WORKS: OPERETTAS: Pinocchio; Storybook; Alice in Wonderland; CHAMBER MUSIC: Thanksgiving, organ, strings, timpani; many choral works and songs.

GAULDIN, ROBERT
b. Vernon, Tex., 30 Oct. 1931. Studied with Violet Archer, North Texas State Univ.; with Bernard Rogers and Alan Hovhaness, Eastman School of Music, Ph.D. 1959. His awards include BMI award, 1952; Benjamin award, 1956; first prize, Berkshire String Quartet contest, 1964. He was faculty member, William Carey Coll., 1958-63; and at Eastman School, from 1963.
WORKS: ORCHESTRA: Scenes from Hamlet, 1968; CHAMBER MUSIC: wind quintet, 1952; Diverse dances, 1956; Partita, string quartet, 1964; Collage for 6 instruments, Cambridge, 8 May 1973; CHORUS: Sanctus, 1971.
379 Wellington Ave., Rochester, NY 14619

GAY, PAUL E.
b. Brunswick, Maine, 23 Aug. 1936. Studied with Francis Judd Cooke and William Tesson, New England Cons.; with Hugo Norden, Boston Univ.; conducting with Pierre Monteux in Hancock, Maine, and with Denis Wick in London. He is on the faculty, Univ. of Lowell, Boston Univ., and Boston Cons.; was conductor, New Hampshire Phil., 1973-77; from 1977, Boston Univ. Wind Ensemble.
WORKS: ORCHESTRA: Fantasy for piano and orch.; 3 lyric pieces for string orch.; WIND ENSEMBLE: Elterephenie, woodwind quintet, brass quintet, 3 percussion, piano, Boston Univ., 7 Mar. 1978; CHAMBER MUSIC: 3 movements for brass trio; Chorale, 3 trombones; sextet for woodwind quintet and piano; Bacchanalian alarum, trumpet trio; Isometric #1-3, violin and piano; Profiles of North Atlantic sea birds, woodwind quintet.
29 Middle St., Lexington, MA 02173

GEARHART, LIVINGSTON
b. Buffalo, N.Y., 31 Dec. 1916. Studied at Grace Church Choir School; Curtis Inst. of Music; with Nadia Boulanger and Darius Milhaud. He was pianist in hotel and night club orchestras; on Fred Waring radio show, 1943-54; then on faculty, State Univ. of New York at Buffalo.
WORKS: CHAMBER MUSIC: suite for woodwinds; String mix #1, string orch.; PIANO: American sketch; Dynamo; Devil's dream; Rhapsody, 2 pianos.
Music Dept., State Univ. of New York, Buffalo, NY 14214

GEBHARD, HEINRICH
b. Sobernheim, 25 July 1878; d. North Arlington,

N.J., 5 May 1963. Was brought to Boston at age 8 by his parents. There he studied piano and made a concert debut at 18; then went to Vienna to study with Leschetizky. He had a notable career as concert pianist.

WORKS: ORCHESTRA: Fantasy, piano and orch., 1925; Divertimento, piano and chamber orch., 1927; Across the hills, symphonic poem, 1940; CHAMBER MUSIC: string quartet; Waltz suite, 2 pianos; The sun, cloud, and flower, song cycle; many works for piano.

GEBUHR, ANN KAREN
b. Des Moines, Iowa, 7 May 1945. Studied with Frederick Fox and Juan Orrego-Salas, Indiana Univ., M.M. 1969. She was faculty member, Northern State Coll., S.Dak., 1969-76; from 1978, at Houston Baptist Univ.

WORKS: CHORUS: Te Deum, with baritone, brass, timpani, 1970; SAI symphony, women's voices and instrumental trio; The friend, with soprano, narrator, strings, percussion, 1977; A festival reformation service, with organ and chamber ensemble, 1978; SONGS: Cycle of duets, soprano and piano, on Tennyson poems, 1973; Psalms 131 and 47, soprano, Kennedy Center, Washington, 9 Sept. 1976; A prairie sunset, soprano and instruments, on Whitman poems, 1976; numerous other choral works and vocal solos.
c/o Houston Baptist Univ., 7502 Fondren Rd., Houston, TX 77074

GEE, HARRY R.
b. Minneapolis, Minn., 20 Feb. 1924. Studied clarinet at Curtis Inst. of Music, 1946-49; composition with Nadia Boulanger in Fontaine-bleau, 1948; Paul Fetler, Univ. of Minnesota; and Thomas Beversdorf, Indiana Univ. He was clarinetist with the Denver Symph. Orch., 1950-52; Minneapolis Summer Pops Orch., 1955-59; faculty member, Arkansas State Univ., 1954-57; Butler Univ., 1957-60; from 1960, at Indiana State Univ.

WORKS: CHAMBER MUSIC: Ballade, flute and piano; Fugue in baroque style, saxophone trio; many arrangements and other educational pieces for woodwinds and band.
419 S. 32nd St., Terre Haute, IN 47803

GEHRENBECK, DAVID MAULSBY
b. St. Paul, Minn., 30 June 1931. Studied at Macalester Coll., B.A. 1953; with Searle Wright and Seth Bingham at Union Theological Seminary, S.M.M. 1957, S.M.D. 1971. He held church positions, 1957-71; was music director, Broadway Presbyterian Church, New York, 1966-71; on faculty, Union Theol. Seminary, 1967-71; then at Illinois Wesleyan Univ.

WORKS: ORGAN: Prelude on Venite adoremus, 1962.
1405 Maplewood Dr., Normal, IL 61761

GEHRING, PHILIP
b. Carlisle, Pa., 27 Nov. 1925. Studied with Herbert Elwell, Oberlin Cons.; with Ernst Bacon, Syracuse Univ.; organ with Andre Marchal in Paris. He won second prize, 1966, first prize, 1977, American Guild of Organists improvisation

contest. He was organist, Kannapolis, N.C., 1950-52; faculty member, Davidson Coll., N.C., 1952-58; and at Valparaiso Univ., from 1958.

WORKS: CHORUS: Shenandoah, male voices, 1960; Draw nigh and take the body of the Lord, 1966; Art thou weary, unison, 1970; ORGAN: 6 hymn-tune preludes, 1966; 4 pieces for the church, 1969; 2 folk-hymn preludes, 1972; etc.
M.R. 35, Box 283, Valparaiso, IN 46383

GEISSLER, FREDRICK DIETZMANN
b. Bethesda, Md., 7 Mar. 1946. Studied with Walter Ross and Donald MacInnis, Univ. of Virginia; with Robert Palmer, Karel Husa, and Burrill Phillips, Cornell Univ. In 1967, he received the Arnold Salop award, Southeastern Composers' League. He was faculty member, George Peabody Coll., 1976-78; from 1978, at Univ. of Virginia.

WORKS: ORCHESTRA: concerto for woodwind quintet and orch.; BAND: Variations on a modern American trumpet tune, with solo trumpet; CHAMBER MUSIC: concertino for piano and 10 solo instruments; triple brass trio; Christmas Eve sketch, woodwind trio and tape, 1967.
Univ. of Virginia, 113 Old Cabell Hall, Charlottesville, VA 22903

GELLER, IAN
b. Chicago, Ill., 18 Mar. 1943. Studied with Karel Jirak, Robert Lombardo, Ramon Zupko, Roosevelt Univ.; with Stella Roberts, American Cons.; with Stanley Wolfe and Vincent Persichetti, Juilliard School. He received a grant from the Illinois Arts Council to compose a ballet, 1973. He was music director, Temple Israel, Long Beach, and conductor, American Jewish Choral Society, Los Angeles, 1971-72; faculty member, Northeastern Illinois Univ., 1972-74; and cantor, Am Shalom, Chicago, from 1972.

WORKS: BALLET: Time, string quartet, baritone, quartet of dancers, and solo dancer, 1973; ORCHESTRA: Poem; Aria and variation; From one who stays, voice and orch.; CHAMBER MUSIC: string quartet; woodwind quartet; violin sonata; piano trio; choral works; songs; instrumental pieces.
2715 Oak St., Highland Park, IL 60035

GELT, ANDREW LLOYD
b. Albuquerque, N.Mex., 2 Feb. 1951. Studied at Univ. of New Mexico, B.M. 1973; with Halsey Stevens and Anthony Vazzana, Univ. of Southern California; Dennis Kam and Alfred Reed, Univ. of Miami, D.M.A. He received Penn. Composers Project grant, 1981; has taught at Univ. of Miami, Pembroke State Univ., Temple Univ.

WORKS: ORCHESTRA: Lamento, strings; symphony; CHAMBER MUSIC: trombone quartet; Suite eclectique, piano; Pathos, clarinet and tape; Cascades from fountains, clarinet and echo machine; CHORUS: Homage for Gesualdo.
10919 Fairbanks Rd., N.E., Albuquerque, NM 87112

GENA, PETER
b. Buffalo, N.Y., 27 Apr. 1947. Studied with

GENTEMANN, SISTER MARY ELAINE

Ramon Fuller, William Kothe, Lejaren Hiller, and Morton Feldman, State Univ. of New York, Buffalo, B.M. 1969. In 1972 he received a grant to attend the Internat. Music Inst., Darmstadt, where he taught a course in computer music; in 1973-74, a Nat. Science Found. grant for research in computer music. He was director, Electronic Music Studio, Brock Univ., Ont., 1971-75; from 1976, on faculty, Northwestern Univ.

WORKS: ORCHESTRA: Syzygy, 1967; Schoenberg in Italy, Buffalo, 11 Oct. 1973; CHAMBER MUSIC: o thou to whom the musical white spring, soprano, flute, viola, guitar, 1968; Upon arriving in the city by the bay, piano, 1970; Homage to G. K. Zipf, 8 instruments, 1971; scherzo, wind quintet, 1973; CHORUS: The egg and the machine, 1967; a clown's smirk in the skull of a baboon, with tenor solo, instruments, percussion, 1967; Aleutian lullabies, 1972; MULTIMEDIA: quartet for violin, marimba, tape, 1969; Scenes from Paterson, piano, narrator, tape, 1969; Anthem, 2 winds, percussion, tape, 1970; ELECTRONIC: Wedding music, tape, 1970; Untitled 1971, film soundtrack, 1971; Egerya, computer-synthesized sound, New York, 6 Apr. 1972.

School of Music, Northwestern Univ., Evanston, IL 60201

GENTEMANN, SISTER MARY ELAINE
b. Fredericksburg, Tex., 4 Oct. 1909. Studied at Our Lady of the Lake Coll., B.M.; with Leo Sowerby, American Cons.; and with Otto Luening, Columbia Univ. Her many awards include honorary membership Sigma Alpha Iota, 1958; Composer of the Year, Texas Music Teachers Assoc., 1963, 1968; 2 awards, Nat. Catholic Music Ed. Assoc., 1966, 1968. She has been professor, Our Lady of the Lake Coll., from 1929.

WORKS: numerous masses, anthems, other liturgical works, secular choral compositions, piano pieces.

Our Lady of the Lake College, 411 Southwest 24th, San Antonio, TX 78285

GEORGE, EARL
b. Milwaukee, Wis., 1 May 1924. Studied with Howard Hanson and Bernard Rogers, Eastman School of Music, Ph.D. 1948; with Bohuslav Martinu at Tanglewood and in New York. His awards include George Gershwin Memorial prize; Nat. Fed. of Music Clubs awards; Millikan Univ. choral prize; Guggenheim fellowship; ASCAP awards. He was faculty member, Univ. of Minnesota, 1948-56; Eastman School, 1956-57; Fulbright lecturer, Univ. of Oslo, 1955; from 1959, professor, Syracuse Univ.

WORKS: THEATRE: Birthdays, 2 1-act operas: Pursuing happiness and Another 4th of July, librettos by composer, premiere, Syracuse Univ., 23 Apr. 1976; ORCHESTRA: Introduction and allegro; violin concerto; piano concerto; concerto for string orch.; Introduction, variations and finale; A Thanksgiving overture; Declamations, wind ensemble; CHAMBER MUSIC: string quartet; CHORUS: Missa brevis, with orch.; Abraham Lincoln walks at midnight, with orch.; Voyages, with soprano and 13 instruments; many

other choral works, songs, piano pieces, chamber works, film scores.
21 Sewickley Dr., Jamesville, NY 13078

GEORGE, LILA GENE
b. Sioux City, Iowa, 25 Sept. 1918. Studied with Otto Luening and Vladimir Ussachevsky, Columbia Univ,; with Nadia Boulanger, Fontainebleau, France. She received the Sigma Alpha Iota Alumnae award, 1969.

WORKS: CHAMBER MUSIC: trio for horn, violin, piano, 1969; violin sonata; Quintad, suite for violin and cello; Introduction and dance, solo flute; Jeux d'esprit, piano; L'etang, piano; CHORUS: A merry-go-round for Christmas; For winter's rains and ruins are over.
2301 Reva Dr., Houston, TX 77019

GEORGE, THOM RITTER
b. Detroit, Mich., 23 June 1942. Studied at Eastman School of Music, M.B. 1964, M.M. 1968; Catholic Univ., D.M.A. 1970. His honors include the Edward Benjamin award, 1964; Howard Hanson prize, 1968; Sigvald Thompson award, 1974; and commissions. He was instructor at Cumberland Coll., 1972; later was named music director and conductor, Quincy (Ill.) Symph. Orch.

WORKS: ORCHESTRA: Rhapsody for orchestra, Moorhead, Minn., 16 Nov. 1975; The people, yes, with soloists and chorus, Quincy, Ill., 25 Feb. 1976; BAND: Hymn and toccata; Proclamations; Symphonic variations, with percussion; English dance variations; 6 rhymes from Mother Goose; Suite in F, wind ensemble; brass quintet; CHAMBER MUSIC: clarinet sonata; Pastorale, flute and organ, Quincy, 3 Aug. 1976; trombone sonata, Internat. Trombone Assoc. meeting, Nashville, June 1978.
2125 Prairie Ave., Quincy, IL 62301

GERBER, STEPHEN EDWARD
b. Middletown, Ohio, 11 Apr. 1948. Studied at Cincinnati Coll. Cons., majoring in orchestration and conducting. He is a free-lance composer and arranger for radio and television commercials.

WORKS: ORCHESTRA: Celebration suite, with timpani solo, 1975; Variations, 1977; Prelude to an unknown lover, piano and orch., 1978; WIND ENSEMBLE: Music for brass and percussion, commissioned by the Ohio Univ. Brass Choir, 1979.
204 Garrard, Covington, KY 41011

GERBER, STEVEN R.
b. Washington, D.C., 28 Sept. 1948. Studied privately with Robert Parris; with Harvey Sollberger at Columbia Univ.; with Earl Kim, Harvard Summer School; with Milton Babbitt and J. K. Randall, Princeton Univ. He received a commission from the Kindle Found. for a piano trio, 1968.

WORKS: CHAMBER MUSIC: string trio; string quartet; duos for flute and piano, viola and piano, cello and piano, violin and cello; Dreamwork, flute, viola, cello, piano; also choral works and songs.
263 West End Ave., #9C, New York, NY 10023

GERRISH, JOHN D.
b. New York, 1 Sept. 1910. Studied at State Univ. Coll., Potsdam; composition with George Mulfinger, Syracuse Univ. He taught at State Univ. Coll., Potsdam, 1935-45; Caldwell Coll., 1954-66; and at Kean Coll. of N.J., 1945-76.

WORKS: CHORUS: The falcon, women's voices; A virgin most pure, women's voices; recorder music, piano pieces.

GERSCHEFSKI, EDWIN
b. Meriden, Conn., 10 June 1909. Studied at Yale Univ., B.M. 1931; Matthey Pianoforte School, London; piano with Artur Schnabel, Italy; composition with Joseph Schillinger, New York. His many awards include the first Charles Ditson fellowship, 1931; 2 Yaddo fellowships, 1936, 1937; League of Composers commission, 1937; first prize, band music competition, N.Y. World's Fair, 1939; Carnegie grant, 1947; Gold Medal, Arnold Bax Society, 1963; citation by Yale Univ. Alumni Assoc., 1968; first Georgia Governor's Award in the Arts, on retirement from Univ. of Georgia, 1976. He taught at private schools in New York City, 1933-40; was faculty member, Converse Coll., 1940-59; Univ. of New Mexico, 1959-60; head, music department, Univ. of Georgia, 1960-76.

WORKS: ORCHESTRA: classic symphony; Fanfare, fugato, and finale, 1937; Saugatucksuite, 1938; Toccata and fugue, 1954; Celebration, violin and orch., 1964; BAND: Music for a stately occasion; Guadalcanal fantasy; Discharge in E, 1935; Streamline, 1935; CHAMBER MUSIC: piano quintet, 1935; 8 variations, string quartet, 1937; brass septet, 1938; 100 variations for solo violin, 1952; piano trio, 1956; Rhapsody, piano trio, 1963; The mountain, cello solo; 24 variations for cello, 1963; Workout, 2 violins and 2 violas, 1970; 200 years: Minuct for loyalists, lullaby for orphans, cello choir, Washington, D.C., 4 June 1975; suite for horn solo, 1976; CHORUS: Half Moon Mountain, cantata, women's voices, baritone solo, orch., Spartanburg, S.C., 30 Apr. 1948; The Lord's controversy, cantata for men's voices, tenor solo, orch.; The salutation of the dawn, chorus and orch.; The Lord's Prayer, a cappella; other choral works, songs, piano pieces.

GERSHWIN, GEORGE
b. Brooklyn, N.Y., 26 Sept. 1898; d. Beverly Hills, Calif., 11 July 1937. Studied with Edward Kilenyi, Rubin Goldmark, and Joseph Schillinger, but was drawn to jazz and popular music at 15, became a song plugger for a music publisher. Later he studied with Henry Cowell and Wallingford Riegger. He received the first Pulitzer prize awarded to a musical for Of thee I sing, 1931; was one of the first 10 inductees into the Entertainment Hall of Fame, 23 Apr. 1974.

WORKS: THEATRE: Porgy and Bess, opera, 1935; MUSICALS: La, la, Lucille, 1919; George White's scandals, 1921-24; Our Nell, 1922; Sweet little devil, 1923; Primrose, 1924; Lady be good, 1924; Song of the flame, 1925; Tiptoes, 1925; Oh Kay, 1926; Funny face, 1927; Treasure girl, 1928; Strike up the band, 1929; Show girl, 1929; Girl crazy, 1930; Of thee I sing, 1931; Pardon my English, 1932; Let 'em eat cake, 1933; ORCHESTRA: Rhapsody in blue, 1924; concerto in F, 1925; An American in Paris, 1928; Second rhapsody, 1931; Cuban overture, 1932; CHAMBER MUSIC: Lullaby, string quartet, 1919; many songs including his first tremendous success, Swanee, written at age 19; PIANO: 5 preludes, 3 of which were orchestrated by Arnold Schoenberg; FILM SCORES: Delicious; A damsel in distress; Shall we dance; The shocking Miss Pilgrim; The Goldwyn follies (completed by Vernon Duke). Biographies: Merle Armitage, ed., George Gershwin, New York, 1938; David Ewen, George Gershwin, his journey to greatness, 1970, a revision of Ewen's 1956 book.

GERSTER, ROBERT
b. Chicago, Ill., 13 Oct. 1945. Studied with Marshall Barnes and Wilbur Held, Ohio State Univ., B.M. 1967, M.M. 1968; with William Bergsma and William O. Smith, Univ. of Washington, D.M.A. 1976. His awards include scholarships to Ohio State, 1966-68; first prize, Ohio State symphony contest, 1967; first prize, national contest, 1968; Nat. Inst. of Arts and Letters, Charles Ives Scholar, 1973. He has held church organ and choir director posts from 1964; teaching posts at Univ. of Washington, 1968, 1971-73; California State Univ., Fresno, from 1974.

WORKS: ORCHESTRA: Synchrony, 1972; CHAMBER MUSIC: 10 pieces for chamber orch., 1966; woodwind trio, 1968; Mobiles, 11 players in 5 locations, 1971; Bird in the spirit, solo flute, 1972; Music for cello and piano, 1976; Cantata, woodwind quartet, 1977; MULTIMEDIA: Chance dance game, 12 players in 6 locations, dancers, video tape projection, 1973; also choral and organ works.
2850 E. Santa Ana, Fresno, CA 93726

GERTZ, IRVING
b. Providence, R.I., 19 May 1915. Studied with Wassili Leps in Providence; with Ernst Toch and Mario Castelnuovo-Tedesco in Los Angeles. He was composer-arranger for Columbia Pictures, 1946-48; Nat. Broadcasting Co., 1949-51; Universal Studios, 1952-59; 20th-Century Fox, 1960-69.

WORKS: CHORUS: I hear America singing; O captain! My captain!; For you, O democracy; Songs of the exposition: Beat! beat! drums!; Pioneers! O pioneers!; all on Walt Whitman texts; Buffalo Bill, poem by Carl Sandburg; also many film scores and television scores.
351 Veteran Ave., Los Angeles, CA 90024

GESENSWAY, LOUIS
b. Dvinsk, Latvia, 19 Feb. 1906; U.S. citizen 1942; d. Philadelphia, Pa., 13 Mar. 1976. Studied violin with Luigi von Kunits, Toronto Cons., 1916-25; composition with Reginald Owen Morris, and Tibor Serly, Curtis Inst., 1926-29; with Zoltan Kodaly, Budapest, Hungary, 1930-31. He received the Philadelphia Orch.,Kuhn award, 1945; and several commissions. He was first violinist, Philadelphia Orch., 1926-71; and a

GESSLER, CAROLINE

cofounder of the Toronto Symphony.
WORKS: OPERA: The great Boffo and his
talking dog, 1-act comic opera for children,
1953; ORCHESTRA: 5 Russian pieces, 1936; suite
for strings and percussion, 1939; concerto for
13 brass instruments, 1942; flute concerto,
1944; suite on Jewish themes, 1948; Four Squares
of Philadelphia, tone poem, 1951; Double portrait, 1952; Let the night be dark for all of me,
1953; Ode to peace, tone poem, 1959; Revery,
strings, 1964; Commemoration symphony, 1968; A
Pennsylvania overture, 1972; cello concerto,
1973; CHAMBER MUSIC: piano sonata, 1937; 2
string quartets, 1938, 1954; Fantasy for organ,
1941; duo, violin and viola, 1941, rev. 1967;
quartet, English horn, flute, violin, cello,
1942; 8 miniatures, flute, percussion, timpani,
1949; sonata for solo bassoon, c. 1950; Aria,
cello and piano, 1950; quartet, clarinet and
string trio, c. 1951; duo, clarinet and flute,
1952; 12 rounds, percussion, 1955; quartet,
oboe, bassoon, violin, viola, 1956; quartet,
timpani, percussion, violin, cello, 1957; duo
for oboe and guitar, 1959; duo for oboe and
bassoon, 1960; Interlude, harmonium, 1961;
Wedding march, harmonium or organ, 1967; Divertimento, flute, 2 violins, viola, 1969; Divertimento, wind quintet, 1969; duo for violin and
cello, 1970; duo for 2 celli, 1970; 2 silhouettes, flute and piano, 1971; many arrangements
of his own orchestral works for small ensembles,
and of classical works for orchestra or chamber
groups.

GESSLER, CAROLINE
b. Indiana, Pa., 7 Mar. 1908. Studied at
Indiana Univ. of Pennsylvania; Fillion Studios,
Pittsburgh; and privately with Harvey Gaul in
Pittsburgh. She won 3 first prizes in Penn.
Fed. of Music Clubs contests. She taught in
public schools, 1929-70; at Fillion Studios,
1944-49; private teacher, from 1970.
WORKS: CHAMBER MUSIC: Creation for strings;
CHORUS: Give ear to my prayer; God is our hope;
Bless the Lord, O my soul; I wait alone beside
the sea; etc.
606 Wayne Ave., Indiana, PA 15701

GETTEL, COURTLAND
b. Boston, Mass., 21 Sept. 1943. Studied with
Michael White, Oberlin Cons.; with Richard
Hervig, Univ. of Iowa; briefly with Easley
Blackwood and George Crumb. His awards include
Idaho Arts Council commission, 1974; Nat. En-
dowment for the Arts grant, 1975; Vermont State
Council on the Arts grant, 1978-79. He was
faculty member, Luther Coll., 1970-73; Idaho
State Univ., 1973-74; Green Mountain Coll. and
private teacher from 1974; also member, Vermont
Symphony and Vermont Philharmonic.
WORKS: ORCHESTRA: 3 variations on an un-
stated theme, high school string orch., 1975;
CHAMBER MUSIC: 2 pieces, for 2 pianos, 1969;
Watercycle, chamber ensemble, 1973; CHORUS: I
heard a fly, 1965.
Box 1014, Middletown Springs, VT 05757

GHENT, EMMANUEL
b. Montreal, P.Q., 15 May 1925; U.S. citizen
1962. Studied at McGill Univ., B.Sc., M.D.;
piano and bassoon in Montreal; composition with
Ralph Shapey in New York. His awards include
many commissions; MacDowell fellowships, 1964,
1965; Guggenheim fellowship, 1967; annual ASCAP
awards, 1967-78; Nat. Endowment for the Arts
grants, 1974, 1975, and in 1976, jointly with
Mimi Garrard and James Seawright to develop a
computer-controlled lighting system for choreography. After coming to the U.S., he completed
a residency in psychiatry and has maintained a
part-time practice as an analyst. He has also
been composer-in-residence at Bell Telephone
Laboratories from 1969 and has lectured widely
and written articles on his technical developments for electronic and computer music.
WORKS: quartet for flute, oboe, clarinet,
bassoon, 1960; 2 duos, flute and clarinet, 1962;
Entelechy, viola and piano, 1963; Dithyrambos,
brass quintet and special equipment (used for
transmitting synchronizing signals to performers,
enabling them to play at independent and varying
tempi and meters), 1965; Hex, an ellipsis for
trumpet, chamber ensemble, tape, and special
equipment, 1966; Helices, violin, piano, tape,
1969; L'apres-midi d'un summit meeting, computer-
generated tape, 1970; Phosphones, computer-
generated tape, 1971; Lustrum, a concerto grosso
for electronic string quartet, brass quintet, and
computer-generated tape, 1974; Brazen, fully
computerized version of Lustrum, 1975; Brazen,
for dance/lighting/music, a special version for
the 3 components, 1975; 5 brass voices, computer-
generated version of Dithyrambos, 1977.
131 Prince St., New York, NY 10012

GHEZZO, DINU D.
b. Tusla, Romania, 2 July 1941; U.S. citizen
1978. Studied conducting and composition at
Bucharest Cons.; with Roy Harris and Paul
Chihara, Univ. of California, Los Angeles, Ph.D.
1973. His awards include Gus Kahn award, UCLA,
1972; UCLA Chancellor's fellowship, 1972-73;
Creative Artists Public Service award, 1976;
ASCAP awards, 1976, 1978. He was faculty member,
Queens Coll., 1974-78; then at New York Univ.,
School of Education; also director of the NYU
Symphony and Contemporary Ensemble, and of the
New Repertory Ensemble of New York.
WORKS: Music for flutes and tapes, 1971-72;
Kanones, flute, cello, harpsichord, 1972; Cele-
brations, chamber orch.; Ritualen, piano, 1969;
Thalla, piano, electric piano, and 16 instru-
ments, 1974; concertino for clarinet and winds.
61-04 171 St., Fresh Meadow, NY 11365

GHIGLIERI, SYLVIA
b. Stockton, Calif., 13 Mar. 1933. Studied at
Dominican Coll., San Rafael, B.M. 1954; with
Stanworth Beckler, Univ. of the Pacific, M.M.
1961; piano with Egon Petri, Gyorgy Sandor;
Robert and Jean Casadesus in France. She won
first prize, 1959, honorable mention, 1963, in
Mu Phi Epsilon composition contests. She has
been faculty member, Stanislaus State Coll.,
from 1961.

WORKS: CHORUS: Psalm 56, with orch., 1963;
PIANO: 3 Irish pieces, 1959; sonata.
    4 E. Alder St., Stockton, CA 95204

GHIRARDO, MEGAN ROBERTS
    b. Hempstead, N.Y., 12 Oct. 1952. Studied with
Charles Moon, Humboldt State Univ., B.A.; with
David Behrman and Robert Ashley, Mills Coll.,
M.F.A. Her awards include Elizabeth Mills
Crothers prize in composition; many video awards;
Humboldt Arts Council grant, 1975. She was
named to the art faculty, St. Cloud State Univ.,
in 1979.
    WORKS: Songs for television, video as music;
I never was a little boy, but I remember all the
songs, electronic music and video; Applause for
small people--A pygmatic function, electronci;
Factory, video as electronic music, 1976; Suite
for a small chamber, sound-composed environment,
in which dancers' movements trigger electronic
devices and tape-loop playback machines, 1976;
I could sit here all day, calls for birds,
drums, disembodied human voices, and is intended
to represent "ante-human" and "anti-human"
predecessors to rock 'n' roll.
    Art Dept., St. Cloud Univ., St. Cloud, MN
    56301

GIANNINI, VITTORIO
    b. Philadelphia, Pa., 19 Oct. 1903; d. New York,
N.Y., 28 Nov. 1966. (Was brother of Dusolina
Giannini, soprano.) Studied on scholarship at
the Milan Cons.; with Rubin Goldmark at Juil-
liard School; American Acad. in Rome, 1931-35.
His many awards included honorary doctorates,
New York Coll. of Music, 1939; Curtis Inst.,
1957; Cincinnati Cons., 1961; many commissions;
fellowship, Internat. Inst. of Arts and Letters.
He was faculty member, Juilliard School, 1939-
66; Manhattan School of Music, 1941-66; Curtis
Inst., 1956-66; and first director, North
Carolina School of the Arts.
    WORKS: OPERA: Lucedia, 1934; Flora, 1937;
The scarlet letter, 1938; Beauty and the beast,
1938; Blennerhasset, 1939; The taming of the
shrew, 1952; The servant of 2 masters, performed
in New York, 1957; ORCHESTRA: Prelude and fugue,
string orch., 1926; concerto grosso, strings,
1931; suite, 1931; 4 symphonies, 1935, 1939,
1950, 1960; Triptych, 1937; organ concerto,
1937; concerto for 2 pianos, 1940; trumpet concerto, 1949; Frescobaldiana, 1949; Canticle for
Christmas, with chorus, 1950; Divertimento #2,
1961; CHAMBER MUSIC: piano quintet, 1931; woodwind quintet, 1933; piano trio, 1933; 2 violin
sonatas, 1926, 1945; piano sonata; many choral
works and songs.

GIANNINI, WALTER
    b. New York, N.Y., 8 June 1917. Studied with
Vittorio Giannini at Juilliard School. Has
taught and performed in New Jersey for more than
35 years; is organist and choirmaster, St. Luke's
Episcopal Church, Gladstone, N.J.
    WORKS: CHAMBER MUSIC: Chaconne, violin and
piano; Modal variations, piano; piano sonatina;
CHORUS: mass in English, with orch., Washington,
D.C., 19 May 1975; Psalm 23, with orch., Lan-

caster, Pa., 22 Feb. 1976; many other choral
works, organ and piano pieces, chamber works,
and art songs.
    317 Millbrook Ave., Randolph, NJ 07801

GIBB, ROBERT W.
    b. Dedham, Mass., 2 May 1893; d. Dedham, 13 May
1964. Studied with Frederick S. Converse, New
England Cons.; at Boston Univ., and Harvard
Univ. His works included Oriental suite for
orchestra, and 3 overtures: Carnival, Festival,
Youth triumphant.

GIBB, STANLEY GARTH
    b. Chicago, Ill., 22 June 1940. Studied with
Herbert Bielawa and Wayne Peterson, San Francisco
State Univ.; with Merrill Ellis, North Texas
State Univ. He received first place in a Percussive Arts Society composition contest, 1975;
and many commissions. He was faculty member,
Univ. of Oklahoma, 1971-72; North Texas State
Univ., 1972-73; from 1974, California State
Polytechnic Univ.
    WORKS: ORCHESTRA: Documents, with chamber
choir, 1976; WIND ENSEMBLE: Localization, 12
trombones, 1971; concerto for trombone and wind
ensemble, 1974; ELECTRONIC: Overture to the
second coming, choir and tape, 1971; Parity,
trombone and tape, 1972; Sonic flight, tape,
1972; Bird dance, tape, 1972; Woman, tape, 1973;
Sound action, percussion and tape, 1975; MULTI-
MEDIA: Flash, tape, dancers, readers, 1974.
    Music Dept., California State Polytechnic
    University, 3801 W. Temple Ave., Pomona, CA
    91768

GIBBS, GEOFFREY DAVID
    b. Copiague, N.Y., 29 Mar. 1940. Studied pri-
vately with Elie Siegmeister, and with Bernard
Rogers, Howard Hanson, and Wayne Barlow at
Eastman School of Music. He held summer fellowships at Univ. of Rhode Island, 1970, 1972, and
has been faculty member there from 1965.
    WORKS: ORCHESTRA: Icon: Igor Stravinsky,
Delius Festival, Jacksonville, Fla., 1972; symphony #2, Kingston, R.I., 7 May 1973; CHAMBER
MUSIC: Pastorale, cello or bassoon and piano;
string quartet, Washington, D.C., 9 Dec. 1975;
CHORUS: Praise ye the Lord, 1970; Symposium,
oratorio, 1970; The bond of peace, cantata, 1973.
    Box 291, West Kingston, RI 02892

GIBSON, ARCHER
    b. Baltimore, Md., 5 Dec. 1875; d. Lake Mahopac,
N.Y., 15 July 1952. His compositions include an
opera, Yzdra; 2 cantatas, Emancipation and A
song to music; and organ pieces.

GIBSON, DAVID
    b. Albany, N.Y., 20 Sept. 1943. Studied with
Stanley Wolfe at Juilliard School; with Jacob
Druckman at Yale Univ. He received the Harriett
Fox Gibbs award at Yale; Nat. Endowment for the
Arts grant, 1974. He was cellist with the U.S.
Army String Quartet, 1967-70; composer-cellist,
Center for the Creative and Performing Arts,
State Univ. of New York, Buffalo, 1972-74; on
the faculty, State Univ. of New York, Albany,

GIBSON, JON

from 1976.
    WORKS: ORCHESTRA: symphony, 1977; CHAMBER MUSIC: 13 ways of looking at a blackbird, voice and instruments; Embellishments #2, string quartet; Lion's head, amplified bass; Shadows, 3 percussionists; 3 fragments, cello and piano; Fragment #4, 3 trumpets, clarinet, vibraphone, bass; Fragment #5, viola or vibraphone; Ligatures, woodwind quartet, 1974; MIXED MEDIA: Embellishments #1, string quartet and tape.
    25 N. Main Ave., Albany, NY 12203

GIBSON, JON
    b. Los Angeles, Calif., 11 Mar. 1940. Studied with Henry Onderdonk, San Francisco State Univ., B.A. 1964; with Larry Austin and Richard Swift, Univ. of California at Davis. His awards include Nat. Endowment for the Arts grants, 1974, 1977; Creative Artists Public Service award, 1975. He is a free-lance composer and performer; member of the Philip Glass Ensemble. In his music, Gibson has explored a variety of compositional approaches ranging from works dealing primarily with intuition and improvisation (e.g., Visitations) to works involving highly structured numerical processes (e.g., Melody IV). His recent solo music, which he performs on saxophone or flute, represents a blending of these two extremes.
    WORKS: Visitations, an environmental soundscape collage, 1971; Cycles, organ, 1973; Untitled, for solo, duo, or trio of various instruments, 1974; Song 2, 7 instruments, 1974; Rhythm study for voice, hands and feet, 1974; Melody IV, 9 instruments, 1975; Equal distribution #1, solo flute, 1977; Recycle 1, solo soprano saxophone, 1977; Criss cross and Improvisations, both for solo soprano saxophone, 1979.
    17 Thompson St., New York, NY 10013

GIBSON, MICHAEL
    b. Columbus, Ohio, 10 Aug. 1948. Studied with Alan Stout, Lyndon DeYoung, and James Hopkins, Northwestern Univ.; also studied trombone and conducting. He received a John Philip Sousa band award. He was trombonist in the Norad Band, 1971-73; Air Force Acad. Band, 1973-75; conductor and music director, Colorado Springs Chamber Music Society, from 1971.
    WORKS: CHAMBER MUSIC: Effectuoso, trombone and piano; A dialectical quintessence, 4 winds and percussion; A dulcet ebullience, brass quintet.

GIDEON, MIRIAM
    b. Greeley, Colo., 23 Oct. 1906. Attended Boston Univ., B.A. 1926; Columbia Univ., M.A. 1946; Jewish Theological Seminary, D.S.M. 1970; studied composition with Lazare Saminsky and Roger Sessions. Her awards include the Bloch prize for a choral work, 1948; Nat. Fed. of Music Clubs and ASCAP award, 1969; Nat. Endowment for the Arts grant, 1974; election to Collegium of Distinguished Alumni, Boston Univ., 1974; election to American Acad. of Arts and Letters, 1975. She was faculty member, Brooklyn Coll., 1944-54; Jewish Theological Seminary, from 1955; City Univ. of New York, 1971-76, then

professor emeritus.
    WORKS: THEATRE: Fortunato, opera, 1958; The adorable mouse, French folk tale for narrator and chamber orch., 1960; ORCHESTRA: Lyric piece, string orch., 1941; Symphonia brevis, 1953; Songs of youth and madness, voice and orch., on poems of Hölderlin, New York, 5 Dec. 1977; CHAMBER MUSIC: Lyric piece, string quartet, 1941; The hound of heaven, voice, string trio, oboe, 1945; string quartet, 1946; viola sonata, 1948; Divertimento, woodwind quartet, 1948; sonnets from Shakespeare, voice, trumpet, string quartet, 1950; sonnets from Millay's Fatal interview, voice, string trio, 1952; cello sonata, 1961; The condemned playground, soprano, tenor, chamber group, 1963; Questions on nature, voice and instruments, 1965; Rhymes from the hill, Morgenstern text, voice, clarinet, cello, marimba, 1968; The seasons of time, ancient Japanese poetry, voice, flute, cello, piano, 1969; suite for clarinet and piano, 1972; Fantasy on Irish folk motives, oboe, viola, bassoon or cello, vibraphone, 1975; Nocturnes, voice and chamber ensemble, St. Paul, 21 Feb. 1976; piano sonata, 1977; piano trio, 1979; Voices from Elysium, ancient Greek poems, tenor and chamber orch., New York, 18 Apr. 1979; also songs with piano; choral works, keyboard works.
    410 Central Park West, New York, NY 10025

GILBERT, DAVID
    b. Penn., 1936. Studied at Eastman School of Music; was assistant conductor, New York Phil., 1970; coconductor, American Ballet Theatre, 1971.
    WORKS: CHAMBER MUSIC: Poem IV, alto flute and percussion; Poem VI, alto flute, 1966; Centering, chamber ensemble, 1969; Centering II, chamber ensemble, 1970; Poem VII, oboe, 1970; 2 unaccompanied songs for soprano, 1965.
    535 W. 110th St., New York, NY 10025

GILBERT, HARRY M.
    b. Paducah, Ky., 1879. Studied at Cincinnati Coll. of Music and in Berlin. He taught in Dallas for a few years, then toured as soloist and accompanist with David Bispham and other noted singers; was organist for 33 years, Fifth Avenue Presbyterian Church, New York City.
    WORKS: CHORUS: A vision of music, cantata for men's voices and orch.; Fantasie on Swedish folk songs, male chorus; The great eternal Christmas, 2 soli, chorus, piano trio, organ; Scotch fantasie, soprano solo with male chorus.

GILBERT, LOUIS WOLFE
    b. Odessa, Russia, 31 Aug. 1886; to U.S. 1887; d. Beverly Hills, Calif., 12 July 1970. Sang in vaudeville and night clubs at 14; toured as entertainer with John L. Sullivan, the prize fighter. He went to Hollywood in 1929 and composed for films. He wrote extremely popular songs including Waitin' for the Robert E. Lee, 1912; Ramona, 1927; Peanut vendor; Down yonder; Lucky Lindy, 1927; and some 245 others.

GILBERT, PIA
    b. Germany, 1 June 1921; U.S. citizen 1944.

Studied at New York Coll. of Music. She has been composer-in-residence and professor of dance, Univ. of California, Los Angeles, from 1947.

WORKS: THEATRE: music for plays: The deputy, The devils, Murderous angels, Center Theatre Group productions; Marat/Sade, Mother Courage, The country wife, UCLA campus productions; BALLET: Metamorphoses, Game of gods, Celebration for percussion and dance; INSTRUMENTAL: Interrupted suite, 3 pianos and clarinet; Transmutations, organ and percussion, 1976; Spirals and interpolations, 1976; duo for cello and piano, 1978.

11400 Berwick St., Los Angeles, CA 90049

GILBERT, STEVEN E.

b. New York, N.Y., 20 Apr. 1943. Studied with Robert Starer, Brooklyn Coll., B.A. 1964, M.M. 1967; with Gunther Schuller and Mel Powell, Yale Univ., M.Phil., Ph.D. 1970; with Darius Milhaud and Charles Jones at Aspen, Colo.; and with Yannis Xenakis at Tanglewood. He won 3 BMI student composer awards, 1964, 1966, 1967. He has been faculty member, California State Univ., Fresno, from 1970.

WORKS: ORCHESTRA: symphony, 1964-65; CHAMBER MUSIC: string quartet, 1963; Mosaics, trumpet, cello, 2 percussionists, 1966.

4220-B N. College Ave., Fresno, CA 93704

GILBERTE, HALLETT

b. Winthrop, Maine, 14 Mar. 1872; d. New York, N.Y., 5 Jan. 1946. Studied composition with Ethelbert Nevin in Boston. He wrote about 250 songs including Spanish serenade, In reverie, Song of the canoe, Ah, love but a day, Spring serenade, Moonlight and starlight, etc.

GILBERTSON, VIRGINIA

b. Memphis, Tenn., 2 Dec. 1914. Studied at DeShago Coll. of Music, B.M.; Memphis State Univ.; Winthrop Coll. She is piano teacher and accompanist. Her works include One bronze feather, a stage show for the New Jersey tercentenary; shows for summer stock theatre; songs.

GILLAM, RUSSELL C.

b. Mount Union, Pa., 11 July 1909. Studied with Donald Hardisty, Univ. of Arizona; John Boda and Irvin Cooper, Florida State Univ.; John Barnes Chance, Univ. of Kentucky; Glen Morgan, Lycoming Coll. He taught in public schools, 1927-48; Lock Haven State Coll., 1948-71; from 1950, has been organist and choirmaster, Great Island Presbyterian Church.

WORKS: CHAMBER MUSIC: Rondino, horn and piano, 1972; Larghetto, oboe and piano, 1973; CHORUS: mass in English; White lilacs, women's voices; Suffer the little children, 1955; God is everywhere, unison choir, 1972.

426 W. Main St., Lock Haven, PA 17745

GILLESPIE, DONALD

b. Pittsburgh, Pa., 11 Oct. 1942. Studied with Roger McDuffie, Converse Coll. He won a Pi Kappa Lambda award, 1966. He taught in public schools, 1968-69; then on faculty, Morningside

Coll., to 1975.

WORKS: CHORUS: Tis winter now; 2 motets; 6 carols; service music for worship; SONGS: 3 songs on e. e. cummings texts; KEYBOARD: 4 organ chorale preludes; 6 young moments for piano; fugue for piano; 3 piano sonatas.

GILLETTE, JAMES ROBERT

b. Roseboom, N.Y., 30 May 1886; d. Lake Forest, Ill., 26 Nov. 1963. Studied at Syracuse Univ. He held faculty posts at Wesleyan Coll. and at Carleton Coll., where he established the Carleton Symphonic Band in 1923 and the Gillette Chamber Orchestra in 1937; later was organist in Lake Forest, Ill.

WORKS: ORCHESTRA: Cabins, an American rhapsody; BAND: Pagan symphony; 7 symphonies; many choral works; songs, and about 40 organ pieces.

GILLIAM, ROGER WAYNE

b. Rangely, Colo., 22 Nov. 1948. Studied with William Schroeder, Del Mar Coll.; with Alvin Epstein, Southern Methodist Univ.

WORKS: BAND: Quotient '69; WIND ENSEMBLE: Variations on 8 notes, brass quintet.

GILLIS, DON

b. Cameron, Mo., 17 June 1912; d. Columbia, S.C., 10 Jan. 1978. Studied at Texas Christian Univ., A.B., B.M. 1936; and at North Texas State Univ. His awards included an honorary doctorate, Texas Christian Univ.; honorary membership, Phi Mu Alpha Sinfonia; Christopher award; and many commissions. He taught at Texas Christian Univ. and Southwestern Baptist Seminary School, 1935-42; was on production staff, WBAP, Ft. Worth, then at NBC, New York, 1944-45; was faculty member, Southern Methodist Univ., 1967-68; Dallas Baptist Coll., 1968-72; Inst. of Media Arts, Univ. of South Carolina, 1973-78.

WORKS: OPERA: The Park Avenue kids; Pep rally; The gift of the Magi; The libretto; The world premiere, 1 act; The legend of Star Valley Junction; The Nazarene; Behold the man; BALLET: Shindig, a ballet of the old west; ORCHESTRA: 12 symphonies, including #5½ and A short, short symphony; 5 suites; 4 symphonic poems; 9 works with narrator; 2 piano concertos; CHAMBER MUSIC: piano quintet; 3 woodwind quintets; 2 trumpet sonatinas; trumpet quartet; piano trio; 5 string quartets; bassoon quartet; pieces for various solo instruments; many choral works and band pieces. He was author of magazine articles, lyrics and librettos for several of his operas, and a humorous book, The unfinished symphony conductor.

GILMORE, BERNARD

b. Oakland, Calif., 19 Nov. 1937. Studied with John Vincent, Boris Kremenliev, Lukas Foss, Univ. of California, Los Angeles; with Josef Tal in Jerusalem; at Stanford Univ., D.M.A. in conducting 1966. He was Eastern Div. winner, Coll. Band Directors composition contest, 1965; recipient of 2 Oregon State Univ. Found. grants. He played horn, Boston Pops Tour Orch., 1957; Los Angeles Phil., 1956-61; Haifa Symph. Orch.,

GINN, JIM

Israel, 1972-73; was faculty member, Cornell
Univ., 1961-64; Oregon State Univ., from 1966.
WORKS: ORCHESTRA: symphonic movement;
BAND: 5 folk songs, soprano and band; CHAMBER
MUSIC: Music for 6 horns; Dover Beach, soprano,
clarinet, string trio; duo for flute and viola;
3 poems of love, chamber chorus, chamber orch.;
5 pieces for piano; Scarlatti doesn't live here
anymore, piano and harpsichord.
Music Dept., Oregon State Univ., Corvallis,
OR 97331

GINN, JIM
b. Bozeman, Mont., 27 Oct. 1935. Studied at
Linfield Coll., Oreg. His compositions include
a piano concerto; preludes and bagatelles for
piano.
41-020 Alaihi, Waimanalo, HI 96795

GINSBURG, GERALD
b. Lincoln, Nebr. Studied with Roy Harris. He
had a work performed at a concert of the Nat.
Assoc. of American Composers and Conductors, New
York, 11 Mar. 1973; a recital of his songs was
presented at Carnegie Recital Hall, New York,
13 Feb. 1974; 3 love songs, To the not impossible
him, Prayers of steel, Cool tombs, all performed
Washington, D.C., 2 Aug. 1976.

GIORNI, AURELIO
b. Perugia, Italy, 15 Sept. 1895; to U.S. 1915;
d. Pittsfield, Mass, 23 Sept. 1938. Studied at
St. Cecilia Cons. in Rome; with Humperdinck in
Berlin. He taught at Smith Coll; Philadelphia
Cons.; Hartford School of Music; and in New York.
WORKS: ORCHESTRA: Orlando furioso, symphonic poem, 1926; Sinfonia concertante, 1931;
symphony, 1937; CHAMBER MUSIC: 2 string quartets; cello sonata; violin sonata; piano quartet;
piano quintet; flute sonata; clarinet sonata;
24 concert etudes for piano; songs.

GIRON, ARSENIO
b. Renteria, Spain, 15 Dec. 1932. Studied with
Joseph Wood and Herbert Elwell, Oberlin Cons.,
B.M. 1956; with Charles Hamm, Tulane Univ.,
M.A. 1962. He received a Ford Found. grant,
1962-63; Ontario Arts Council grant. He was
faculty member, Lindenwood Coll., 1965-68; Univ.
of Western Ontario, from 1968.
WORKS: CHAMBER MUSIC: sextet, woodwinds
and trumpet, 1963; quartet for flute, clarinet,
viola, piano, 1963; Visas, flute, clarinet,
cello, piano, percussion, 1966; Disparities and
differences, brass quintet, 1968; Confluence,
solo cello, 1970; Sombras, soprano, flute, percussion, piano, 1972; Rounds, string quartet,
1973; Time in balance, violin, viola, clarinet,
1975; 5 songs, soprano, clarinet, piano, 1978.
114 Edgar Dr., London, Ont., Canada N6G 1K1

GITECK, JANICE
b. Brooklyn, N.Y., 27 June 1946. Studied with
Morton Subotnick, Lowell Cross and Barney Childs,
Mills Coll., A.B. 1968, M.A. 1969; with Darius
Milhaud, Aspen Music School, 1963, 1964, 1967,
and at Mills Coll.; with Olivier Messiaen,
Paris Cons., 1969-70. Her many awards include

Copley Fellowship, 1964, and Milhaud award, 1967,
Aspen School; 2 composition prizes, Mills Coll.,
1968, 1969; French government award, 1969-70;
first place in composition, Viotti competition,
Italy, 1973; Norman Fromm award, 1977; California
Arts Council award, 1978; Nat. Endowment for the
Arts grant, 1979; and many commissions. She has
held various teaching posts; collaborated with
dance companies; and was music director at KPFA
Radio, Berkeley; from 1979, at Cornish Inst.
WORKS: Trans, theatre piece for 12 players
and conductor, 1972; Messalina, mini-opera, male
voice, cello, piano, 1973; Magic words, tenor,
soprano, piano, on North American Indian poems,
1973; Magic words to feel better, a cappella
chorus, 1974; Helixes, 7 instruments, 1974;
A'Agita, ceremonial opera based on Indian
mythology, 3 singing actors, 1 dancing actor, 8
instrumentalists, 1976; 8 sandbars on the Takano
River, 5 women's voices, flute, bassoon, guitar,
1976; Thunder, like a white bear dancing,
soprano, flute, piano, hand percussion, slides,
based on Ojibwa songs, 1977; Primaries, dance
music, flute and percussion, 1977; Peter and the
wolves, trombonist/actor and tape, 1978; Callin'
home coyote, burlesque for tenor, steel drums,
and string bass, 1978; Far north beast ghosts
the clearing, text from Swampy Cree Indians,
chamber chorus, 2 string basses, 2 tomtoms, 1978;
many earlier works.
710 E. Roy, Seattle, WA 98102

GIUFFRE, JAMES PETER (JIMMY)
b. Dallas, Tex., 26 Apr. 1921. Studied at North
Texas State Univ., B.M. 1942; at Univ. of
Southern California, 1946. He has played with
Jimmy Dorsey, Buddy Rich, Woody Herman, and
others; was faculty member, Lenox School of
Jazz, 1957; New York Univ., School of Education,
1972-78; Manhattanville Coll., 1976-78; New
England Cons., from 1979.
WORKS: ORCHESTRA: Fugue, 1953; Mobiles,
clarinet and strings, Piece, clarinet and
strings; Composition, for trio and string orch.,
1961; Threshold, vibraphone, piano, double bass,
drums, chamber orch.; viola concerto; Hex, 1965;
CONCERT JAZZ: 4 brothers; Fine; Fun; Suspensions;
Passage to the veil; Affinity; Quest; Motion-
eterne; The quiet blues, New York, 12 Feb. 1971;
CHAMBER MUSIC: clarinet quintet; The pharaoh,
brass ensemble.
New England Conservatory, 290 Huntington Ave.,
Boston, MA 02115

GLANVILLE-HICKS, PEGGY
b. Melbourne, Australia, 29 Dec. 1912; U.S.
citizen 1948. Studied with Fritz Hart in
Melbourne; with Vaughan Williams, Royal Coll. of
Music, London, 1931-35; with Egon Wellesz in
Vienna and Nadia Boulanger in Paris, 1936-38.
Her many honors include Carlotta Rowe scholarship, 1931-35; Octavia traveling scholarship,
1936-38; American Acad. of Arts and Letters
grant, 1953; 2 Guggenheim fellowships, 1956,
1957; Fulbright fellowship for research in
Aegean demotic music, 1957-58; Rockefeller
grant, 1961; and many commissions. She was
music critic, New York Herald Tribune, 1948-58;

director, Composers Forum, and producer, Donnell Library Concerts, 1950-60; in 1975 she went to Australia to assist in founding and developing the Australian Music Center and as consultant for liaison with Asia and the U.S.

WORKS: OPERA: The transposed heads, text by Thomas Mann, Louisville, 27 Mar. 1954; The glittering gate, 1 act, text by Lord Dunsany, New York, 14 May 1959; Nausicaa, text by Robert Graves, Athens, Greece, 19 Aug. 1961; Sappho, text by Lawrence Durrell, 1963; BALLET: The masque of the wild man, 1958; Saul and the witch of Endor, 1959; Tragic celebration (Jeptha's daughter), 1966; A season in hell, after Arthur Rimbaud, 1967; ORCHESTRA: 3 gymnopedie, harp and strings, 1953; Letters from Morocco, with tenor solo, text from letters of Paul Bowles, 1953; Etruscan concerto, piano and chamber orch., New York, 25 Jan. 1956; Concertico romantico, viola and orch., 1957; Sinfonia da Pacifica; CHAMBER MUSIC: sonata for piano and percussion; Concertino da camera, flute, clarinet, bassoon, piano, Amsterdam Festival, 10 June 1948; Concertino antico, harp and string quartet; Musica antiqua no. 1, chamber ensemble; harp sonata; flute sonatina; works for voice and chamber ensemble or piano.

45 Ormond St., Paddington 2021, Sydney, Australia

GLARUM, L. STANLEY
b. Portland, Oreg., 19 Apr. 1908; d. Cannon Beach, Oreg., 24 Dec. 1976. Studied with F. Melius Christiansen, St. Olaf Coll.; with George F. McKay, Univ. of Washington, M.A. He received ASCAP awards; Danforth fellowship; honorary doctorate, Whitworth Coll., 1969. He was professor, Lewis and Clark Coll., 1947-76. He published more than 200 choral compositions.

GLASER, VICTORIA M.
b. Amherst, Mass., 11 Sept. 1918. Studied with Walter Piston, Tillman Merritt, Archibald T. Davison, Nadia Boulanger, Harvard Univ., B.A., M.A.; piano with Frederick Tillotson, Longy School; flute with George Laurent. Her awards include Anne Louise Barrett fellowship, Wellesley Coll., 1950-51; Brookline Library Assoc. prize, 1960; honorable mention, Gedok competition, Mannheim, Germany, 1961. She was on the faculty, Wellesley Coll., 1943-45; Dana Hall School, 1944-59; from 1959, Preparatory Div., New England Cons.

WORKS: ORCHESTRA: Birthday fugue, Boston Pops, 1962; Music for orchestra, 1964; CHAMBER MUSIC: sonata for flute and violin, 1961; suite for harpsichord; piano sonata, 1978; CHORUS: Homeric hymn, women's voices; An idle song, women's voices; 3 suburban carols, Boston, Dec. 1972; La musique, Cambridge, May 1973.

37 Hawthorne St., Cambridge, MA 02138

GLASS, PAUL EUGENE
b. Los Angeles, Calif., 19 Nov. 1934. Studied with Ingolf Dahl, Univ. of Southern California, B.M.; with Goffredo Petrassi in Rome; with Roger Sessions at Princeton Univ.; and with Witold Lutoslawski in Warsaw. His awards include a

Fulbright grant for study in Rome; a fellowship at Princeton; Inst. of Internat. Education grant for Poland.

WORKS: BALLET: Eschatos; ORCHESTRA: symphony; cello concerto; CHAMBER MUSIC: clarinet quintet; Music for brass and percussion; trio for flute, cello, piano; 3 pieces, violin and piano; woodwind trio; FILM SCORES: Fear no more; The abductors; Lady in a cage; Interregnum; and others.

GLASS, PHILIP
b. Baltimore, Md., 31 Jan. 1937. Studied at Univ. of Chicago, B.A. 1956; with Vincent Persichetti and William Bergsma, Juilliard School, M.M. 1962; and with Nadia Boulanger in France, 1964-65. His awards include a Ford Found. grant; Fulbright grant; Nat. Endowment for the Arts grant, 1974; and commissions. On returning to the U.S. in 1967, he settled in New York and, jettisoning all previous conceptional compositions, developed a new system of composing based on amplified ensembles of keyboard instruments, winds, and voice; his aim is to achieve music that will be perceived as a pure medium of sound freed of dramatic structure.

WORKS: Music in similar motion, 1969; Music in fifths, 1969; Music with changing parts, 1970; Music in 12 parts, 1973, premiere of total piece (6 P.M. to 12 M., 1½ hours for dinner), New York, 1 June 1974; North star, 2 voices and instruments, 1975; Another look at harmony, amplified instruments and voices, New York, 6 May 1975; Einstein on the beach, an opera, premiere in Avignon, France, 25 July 1976, presented by Metropolitan Opera, 21 Nov. 1976; Lucinda's dance, 1978; Satyagraha, an opera about Mahatma Gandhi and nonviolence, libretto adapted from the Bhagavad-Gita, uses operatic voices singing in Sanskrit and conventional instruments, 1980, commissioned by Netherlands Opera Company. The Rotterdam production was a sensational success, with sold-out houses and ecstatic Dutch and German reviews. The U.S. premiere, near Buffalo on 29 July 1981, received equal acclaim.

231 2nd Ave., New York, NY 10003

GLASSER, ALBERT
b. Chicago, Ill., 25 Jan. 1916. Studied with Arne Oldberg, Univ. of Southern California on scholarship, 1934. He won the California Composers contest, 1937, and the Southern California contest, 1945. He was orchestrator for MGM Studios, 1943-47; composer, conductor, and orchestrator for films, television shows, and radio shows.

WORKS: ORCHESTRA: 2 symphonic etudes; violin concerto; string bass concerto; Pied piper of Hamelin, tone poem; The raven, tone poem; symphonic variations on Jolly good fellow; CHAMBER MUSIC: string quartet; piano quintet; Flute rhapsody; viola sonata; sextet for flute, piano, string quartet; songs.

11812 Bellagio Rd., Los Angeles, CA 90049

GLAZER, STUART
b. Detroit, Mich., 29 Apr. 1945. Studied with Dorothy James, Thomas Tyra, and David Stuart,

GLEN, IRMA

Eastern Michigan Univ. His awards include
several commissions. He has been faculty member,
Valley City State Coll., from 1972.
WORKS: BAND: Modal dance, 1971; Symphonic
episode, 1975; Joyant music, 1978; CHAMBER MUSIC:
5 pieces for trumpet, horn, and piano, 1974;
trumpet sonata, 1977; duo for clarinet and percussion, 1978.
238 6th Ave., N.W., Valley City, ND 58072

GLEN, IRMA
b. Chicago, Ill., 3 Aug. Studied with John
Palmer and Adolf Weidig, American Cons.; at Univ.
of Southern California and at Inst. of Religious
Science, Los Angeles. She was theatre and radio
organist in Chicago; moved to Los Angeles in
1946 as free-lance organist and composer for
radio and television; became minister of music in
churches in Beverly Hills, Arcadia, Palm Springs,
and La Jolla.
WORKS: ORGAN: A bridge to higher conscious-
ness, 11 inspirational pieces; Music-prayer
therapy, 12 pieces; Music, ecology and you, 6
pieces; Christmas miracles now!, 5 pieces; many
hymns.
7860 Monument Dr., Grants Pass, OR 97526

GLICKMAN, SYLVIA FOODIM
b. New York, N.Y., 8 Nov. 1932. Studied with
Mark Brunswick in New York; piano with Beveridge
Webster, Juilliard School; with Harold Craxton
and Manuel Frankel, Royal Acad. of Music, London.
Her awards include the Morris Loeb prize in
performance at Juilliard; Fulbright scholarship;
Edward Hecht prize in composition, Royal Acad. of
Music. She has been faculty member, New England
Cons., 1956-58; Rubin Acad. of Music, Jerusalem,
1967-68; West Chester State Coll., 1971-72; and
from 1969, Haverford Coll.
WORKS: CHAMBER MUSIC: Small suite, cello
and piano, 1956; piece for clarinet and piano;
Early dance movements, piano; CHORUS: The hollow
men, with solo soprano and piano; prayer service,
with cantor, flute, and organ, 1976.
1210 W. Wynnewood Rd., Wynnewood, PA 19096

GLOVINSKY, BEN
b. St. Louis, Mo., 28 Oct. 1942. Studied with
Harold Blumenfield and Robert Wykes, Washington
Univ.; with Humphrey Searle, Stanford Univ.; and
with Bernhard Heiden, Indiana Univ. His Sinfonietta was chosen to represent the Western Div.,
Coll. Band Directors Nat. Assoc. Convention,
1969. He has been faculty member, California
State Univ., Sacramento, from 1965; and principal
oboist, Sacramento Symph. Orch., from 1966.
WORKS: ORCHESTRA: Variation-fantasy on a
pioneer theme; BAND: Sinfonietta, winds, brass,
percussion, 1969; Ceremonial music; CHAMBER
MUSIC: music for bass clarinet and piano;
Romanza, wind quintet; oboe sonatina; VOCAL: 4
songs on poems of Robert Herrick.
California State University, 6000 Jay St.,
Sacramento, CA 95819

GNAZZO, ANTHONY J.
b. New Britain, Conn., 21 Apr. 1936. Attended
Univ. of Hartford, B.A. in math. 1963; Brandeis

Univ., M.F.A. 1965, Ph.D. 1970. He served in
the U.S. Navy, 1957-61; was research associate,
Univ. of Toronto, 1965-66; computer scientist,
IBM Corp., 1966-67; director, Tape Music Center,
Mills Coll., 1967-69; design consultant and
equipment technician, California State Univ.,
Hayward, 1969-71, and from 1973; electronic music
consultant, Univ. of California at Berkeley,
1969-73.
WORKS: CHAMBER MUSIC: Music for piano III,
1971; 5-part invention, mixed voices, 1972;
MULTIMEDIA: Space and motion,#1-4, dancers and
tape, 1965-66; Theatre pieces #1-26, film, tape,
slides, actors, dancers, narrators, voices, etc.,
1967-71; Prime sources #1-19, tape and solo
voice, 1971-73; Music for cello and tape, 1972;
Stereo radio 5: about talking, tape, 1972;
Compound skill fracture, actor, tape, film, 1973;
symphony, 1976; Untitled piece in 4 movements,
1976.
3005 Dana St., Berkeley, CA 94705

GODFREY, DANIEL (STRONG)
b. Bryn Mawr, Pa., 20 Nov. 1949. Studied with
Robert Morris, Mario Davidovsky, and Robert
Moore, Yale Univ., B.A., M.M.; with Donald Jenni
and Richard Hervig, Univ. of Iowa. His awards
include Wrexham Music prize at Yale, 1973; Alice
M. Ditson Fund grant, 1978. He was teaching
assistant, Univ. of Iowa, 1975-76, 1978-79;
visiting instructor, Maharishi Internat. Univ.,
1977-78.
WORKS: ORCHESTRA: Rhapsody, 1973; CHAMBER
MUSIC: septet, string quartet, horn, trumpet,
English horn, 1972; Ballade, clarinet and violin,
1974; string quartet, 1974; Progression, tape,
1975; Fanfare, tape, 1976; 5 character pieces,
viola and piano, 1976; trio, clarinet, viola,
horn, 1976; A celebration, piano, 1977; Aubade,
flute, bassoon, harp, 1978; Laetitia, solo cello,
1978.
Coomb's Neck, Vinalhaven, ME 04863

GODIN, ROBERT
b. Springfield, Mass., 14 Jan. 1954. Studied
with Stuart Smith, Hartt Coll. of Music; with
Philip Bezanson, Univ. of Massachusetts; and
with Harry Partch in San Diego. He has been
artist-in-residence, Mass. Coll. of Art, from
1975.
WORKS: 24 minutes for 4 trios, voices and
tape, 1977; Trio for one, live performer, 2
films, 2 soundtracks, 1977; Paper music, any
number of players, 1977; Ending music, cello
trio, 1977; Soundcurrents, 5 players, 1977; etc.
96 Holland St., Somerville, MA 02144

GODOWSKY, LEOPOLD
b. Soshly, near Vilna, 13 Feb. 1870; U.S. citizen
1921; d. New York, N.Y., 21 Nov. 1938. Began
composing and giving piano concerts at age 9;
made tours to the U.S. and Canada, 1884-86; then
returned to Europe, becoming a pupil and protege
of Saint-Saens. In 1890 he was back in the U.S.
as faculty member at the New York Coll. of Music;
taught in Philadelphia, 1894-95; was head of the
piano department, Chicago Cons., 1895-1900. From
1900 to 1914, he taught and played in Europe,

then returned to the U.S. He edited many piano works, made arrangements of works by Brahms, Johann Strauss, and Weber, and composed 53 studies on Chopin etudes. His works are noted for extreme difficulty and for expanding piano technique to amazing limits.

WORKS: PIANO: Miniatures, 46 pieces for piano, 4 hands, pupil and teacher, 1918; Triakontameron, 30 pieces, including Alt Wien, 1920; Java suite, 12 pieces; 6 waltz poems for left hand alone; Prelude and fugue, left hand alone; Passacaglia; Renaissance, 23 pieces; Walzermasken, 24 pieces; piano sonata.

GODWIN, JOSCELYN
b. Kelmscott, England, 16 Jan. 1945; to U.S. 1966. Studied with Philip Radcliffe and Alan Ridout, Cambridge Univ.; with Robert Palmer and Karel Husa, Cornell Univ. Her string trio won the Abyngdon prize at Cambridge Univ., 1966. She was faculty member, Cleveland State Univ., 1969-71; from 1971, at Colgate Univ.

WORKS: ORCHESTRA: Epiphanies, 1967-68; CHAMBER MUSIC: flute sonata; piano sonata, 1968; CHORUS: Epistle to Harmodius, 1966; Carmina amoris, women's voices and 2 instrumental groups, 1967; many other instrumental works.
R.D. #1, Earlville, NY 13332

GOEB, ROGER
b. Cherokee, Iowa, 9 Oct. 1914. Studied agriculture along with violin, viola, horn, and trumpet, Univ. of Wisconsin, B.S. 1936; composition with Nadia Boulanger in Paris; Cleveland Inst. of Music, M.M. 1942; State Univ. of Iowa, Ph.D. 1945; also with Otto Luening. His awards include 2 Guggenheim fellowships, 1950, 1952; American Acad. of Arts and Letters award, 1953. He was faculty member, Univ. of Oklahoma, 1942-44; State Univ. of Iowa, 1944-45; Juilliard School, 1947-50; and Stanford Univ., 1954-55. He was director, American Composers Alliance, from 1956 and later secretary-treasurer, Composers Recording, Inc.; retired in 1962.

WORKS: ORCHESTRA: 4 symphonies, 1945, 1946, 1952, 1954; Fantasy, oboe and strings, 1947; 5 American dances, 1952; viola concerto, 1953; concerto #2 for orch., 1956; concertino, trombone and strings; CHAMBER MUSIC: sonata for solo viola, 1942; piano sonata, 1942; concerto for 2 sopranos and chamber orch., 1942; 2 string quartets, 1942, 1948; string trio, 1945; suite for 4 clarinets, 1946; suite for woodwind trio, 1946; Lyric piece, trumpet and piano, 1947; Prairie song, woodwind quintet, 1948; brass septet, 1949; quintet for trombone and string quartet, 1950; woodwind quintet, 1956.
Rockville Centre, NY 11570

GOEMANNE, NOEL
b. Poperinge, Belgium, 10 Dec. 1926; U.S. citizen 1959. Graduated from the Lemmens Inst. of Belgium with the laureate dipl.; later studied at the Royal Cons. in Liege. His teachers included Flor Peters, Staf Nees, Van Nuffel, Marinus DeJong. He has received several ASCAP awards; an award from the Inst. of Sacred Music, Manila, 1974; Papal medal and "Pro Ecclesia"

award from Pope Paul, 1977. He has been organist-choirmaster in Texas and Michigan from 1952; at St. Monica's Church in Dallas, 1968-72; from 1972, Christ the King Church, Dallas; and has been on the faculty, Tarrant County Jr. Coll., Ft. Worth.

WORKS: CHORUS: Missa internationalis, Salzburg, Internat. Congress of Sacred Music, 1974; The walk, a choral drama; Ode to St. Cecilia--Missa Hosanna, 1972; Fanfare for festivals; Credo, for organ, Salzburg, 31 Aug. 1974; also numerous anthems, motets, hymns, organ and piano works.
3523 Woodleigh Dr., Dallas, TX 75229

GOETSCHIUS, MARJORIE
b. Raymond, N.H., 23 Sept. 1915. Attended Georgian Court Coll.; Tufts Univ.; studied composition with Percy Goetschius, her grandfather, and Bernard Wagenaar at Juilliard School, and with Joseph Schillinger; piano with James Friskin, voice with Maria Stefany. She has been piano soloist, singer, cellist, and author of scripts for network programs.

WORKS: CHAMBER MUSIC: Theme and variations, piano; piano suite; The magic of Christmas, 12 songs for solo voice; Lament, violin and piano; Tango del ensueno, violin and piano; Poetique, piano; piano sonata; Valse burlesque, violin; also background music for CBS Theatre.
300 Broadway, #18, Dobbs Ferry, NY 10522

GOLD, ERNEST
b. Vienna, Austria, 13 July 1921; U.S. citizen 1946. Studied piano at Vienna State Acad.; on coming to the U.S. in 1938, studied composition with Otto Cesano in New York, later with George Antheil in Hollywood; studied conducting with Leon Barzin in New York. While working as a song writer for BMI, he wrote two hits, Practice makes perfect and Accidentally on purpose. In 1946 he went to Hollywood and began writing for films; eventually settled there, dividing his time among composing, conducting, lecturing, musical theatre, and writing educational music. His awards include Carl Fischer award for string quartet, 1956; Laurel award, 1958; Foreign Press Assoc. award, 1959; Downbeat award, 1959; Academy award nominations, 1959, 1963, 1969; Academy award, 1961; commission, Musical Arts of La Jolla.

WORKS: THEATRE: Song of the bells, pageant, Santa Barbara Bowl, Fiesta Week, 1956; Maria, pageant, Fiesta Week, 1957; I'm Solomon, musical, New York, 1968; ORCHESTRA: Pan American symphony; piano concerto, 1946; Boston Pops march; BAND: Introduction and fugue; Gavotte and march; CHAMBER MUSIC: Symphony for 5 instruments; string quartet, 1956; Songs of love and parting; piano sonata (won Steinway award); flute sonatina; 1964; 3 miniatures, piano; FILM SCORES: The true story of the Civil War, 1956; The defiant ones, 1958; The young Philadelphians, 1959; On the beach, 1959; Inherit the wind, 1960; Exodus, 1960; The last sunset, 1961; Judgment at Nuremberg, 1961; Pressure point, 1962; It's a mad, mad, mad, mad world, 1963; Ship of fools, 1965; The secret of Santa Vittoria, 1969; and 3

GOLD, MORTON

experimental pictures: <u>Architecture of Frank Lloyd Wright</u>; <u>The picnic</u>; <u>The assignation</u>.
8021 Ocean Terrace, Hollywood, CA 90046

GOLD, MORTON
b. New York, N.Y., 10 June 1933. Studied with Hugo Norden and Gardner Read, Boston Univ., M.B., D.M.A.; with Walter Piston, Harvard Univ.; conducting with Hugo Ross and Lorna Cooke de Varon at Tanglewood, and with Pierre Monteux at Hancock, Maine. His awards include scholarships at Boston Univ. and Harvard Univ., and at Tanglewood, 1954, 1955, 1958. From 1964, he has been faculty member at Nasson Coll.
WORKS: ORCHESTRA: <u>Rhapsody</u>, 1954; <u>A dedication overture</u>, 1959; piano concerto, 1960; <u>Elegy for strings</u>, 1967; CHAMBER MUSIC: <u>Psalm</u>, viola and piano, 1965; string trio, 1967; <u>Recitative</u>, solo cello, 1968; string quartet, 1970; <u>5 songs without words</u>, violin and piano, 1970; <u>Toccata</u>, piano, 1971; <u>Remembrances</u>, wind quintet, 1971; wind octet; piano trio; 6 songs for high voice; CHORUS: Sabbath eve sacred service, 1966; <u>Psalm 19</u>, 1966; <u>Psalm 98</u>, double chorus, brass, percussion, organ, 1969; <u>Prayer of Micah</u>, 1971; <u>A song at eventide</u>, with orch., 1971; <u>Prayer of Solomon</u>, 1973; <u>Haggadah</u>, oratorio, with tenor solo, orch., Syracuse, N.Y., Mar. 1974.
16 Bradeen St., Springvale, ME 04083

GOLDBERG, STEPHEN EDWARD
b. Albany, N.Y., 20 Aug. 1952. Studied with Burt Fenner, Mannes Coll. of Music; Morris Lawner, High School of Music and Art; Leo Kraft and Hugo Weisgall, Queens Coll., CUNY. He won third prize in a Sigma Alpha Iota contest.
WORKS: <u>Follie di baseball</u>, 1-act opera, 1973; PIANO: <u>The death of Moses</u>, 1971; <u>Terpsichore</u>, 1972; <u>Variations on a short theme</u>, 1972.
33-27 91st St., Jackson Heights, NY 11372

GOLDBERG, WILLIAM B.
b. New York, N.Y., 24 Jan. 1917. Studied piano with Lonny Epstein at Juilliard School; composition with Jacob Weinberg, New York Coll. of Music. He was awarded $500 for <u>Tenebrae</u> in a Georgia State Univ. Symposium for Contemporary Music for Brass, 1972. He is a private music teacher.
WORKS: WIND ENSEMBLE: <u>Tenebrae</u>, 7 brass instruments, organ, percussion, 2 voices, 1971; <u>Works and days</u>, brass quintet, voice, tape, commissioned by New York Brass Quintet, 1972; <u>Antiphonies</u>, 3 brass quintets and organ, 1973; CHAMBER MUSIC: sonata for solo violin, 1977; <u>Airs and dances</u>, Renaissance instruments, 1978; PIANO: 3 sonatas; 3 sonatinas; ELECTRONIC: <u>Phosphor</u>, tape, 1977.
232 Norwood Ave., Northport, NY 11768

GOLDE, WALTER
b. Brooklyn, N.Y., 4 Jan. 1887; d. Chapel Hill, N.C., 4 Sept. 1963. Studied at Columbia Univ.; Dartmouth Coll., B.A. 1910; and at the Vienna Cons. He was head of the voice department, Columbia Univ., 1944-48; head, Inst. of Opera, Univ. of North Carolina, from 1953. He wrote many songs and piano pieces.

GOLDENBERG, WILLIAM LEON
b. Brooklyn, N.Y., 10 Feb. 1936. Studied at Columbia Univ., B.A.; privately with Hall Overton. He was arranger and composer for Broadway shows; music director and composer, <u>Kukla, Fran and Ollie</u> on television; later film composer in Hollywood.
WORKS: CHAMBER MUSIC: brass quintet; woodwind quintet; string quartet.

GOLDMAN, EDWIN FRANKO
b. Louisville, Ky., 1 Jan. 1878; d. New York, N.Y., 21 Feb. 1956. Studied with Antonin Dvorak at the Nat. Cons., New York. A master bandsman and composer for the band, he received 2 honorary doctorates and more than 100 medals and citations from governments and organizations all over the world. He played solo cornet with the Metropolitan Opera Orch., 1895-1905; taught cornet and trumpet, 1905-18; organized his own band in 1911 and began the Goldman Band Concerts in 1918. He wrote more than 100 marches; other works for band; solos and methods for band instruments; and songs. Among his best-known marches are <u>On the mall</u>, 1924; <u>Emblem of freedom</u>, and <u>On parade</u>. He was also author of an autobiography, <u>Facing the music</u>.

GOLDMAN, RICHARD FRANKO
b. New York, N.Y., 7 Dec. 1910; son of Edwin Franko Goldman; d. Baltimore, Md., 19 Jan. 1980. Studied with Pietro Floridia, Wallingford Riegger, Ralph Leopold, and Clarence Adler in New York; with Nadia Boulanger in Paris. His many honors include the Alice M. Ditson award, 1961; Kappa Kappa Psi award, 1971; honorary citizen, New Orleans; honorary doctorates, Lehigh Univ., Univ. of Maryland, Mannes Coll. of Music; Delta Omicron citation, 1976; ASCAP Deems Taylor award, 1977; Andrew White Medal, Loyola Coll., Baltimore, 1978; named elector to Hall of Fame for Great Americans, 1978. He was faculty member, Juilliard School, 1948-60; president, Peabody Cons., 1966-77; often visiting professor or lecturer, Princeton, Columbia, New York Univ.; and conductor of the Goldman Band from 1956 until, because of his ill health, it was disbanded in December 1979.
WORKS: OPERA: Athalia; <u>The mandarin</u>; ORCHESTRA: <u>The Lee Rigg</u>; BAND: <u>A sentimental journey</u>, 1941; <u>A curtain raiser and country dance</u>; <u>Hymn</u> for brass choir; many marches including <u>The foundation</u>; CHAMBER MUSIC: 3 clarinet duets, 1944; sonata for 2 clarinets, 1945; duo for tubas, 1948; piano sonatina; violin sonata, 1952; <u>Divertimento</u>, flute and piano; <u>2 monochromes</u>, solo flute; <u>Le bobino</u>, 2 pianos. He was author of <u>The band's music</u>, 1938; <u>The concert band</u>, 1946; and <u>Harmony of western music</u>, 1965.

GOLDMARK, RUBIN
b. New York, N.Y., 15 Aug. 1872; d. New York, 6 Mar. 1936. Studied at City Coll. of New York; with Johann Nepomuk Fuchs, Vienna Cons.; and with Antonin Dvorak, Nat. Cons., New York. He received the Paderewski chamber music prize, 1909. He taught at the Coll. Cons., Colorado

Springs, 1895-1901; privately in New York, 1902-24; then was head of the composition department, Juilliard School, 1924-36.

WORKS: ORCHESTRA: Hiawatha, overture, 1900; Samson, symphonic poem, 1914; Gettysburg requiem, 1919; A Negro rhapsody, 1923; The call of the plains, 1925; CHAMBER MUSIC: piano quartet, 1909; piano trio; songs.

GOLDSMITH, JERRY
b. Los Angeles, Calif., 10 Feb. 1929. Studied at Univ. of Southern California; became staff composer for 20th-Century Fox Film Corp. His score for Planet of the apes was chosen by the Australian Ballet Company for use in the ballet, Othello, performed in Melbourne, 7 June 1971; his score for Patton was a multiple Oscar winner, 1971; and the score for NBC's "The red pony" received an Emmy award, 1973. Some other film scores are The sand pebbles; Freud; The blue max; The boys from Brazil; The Cassandra crossing; Logan's run; Papillon; and The general with the cockeyed id.

GOLDSMITH, OWEN L.
b. Borger, Tex., 8 Oct. 1932. Studied with Wendell Otey and William Ward, San Francisco State Univ., A.B. magna cum laude 1959, M.A. 1965. He taught at Livermore, Calif., 1960-69; at Clayton Valley High School, Concord, Calif., from 1969.
WORKS: ORCHESTRA: Festival overture; music for Our town; CHORUS: The weather's criminal, women's voices; Cleavings; Alleluia; Interlude; Tears; and many vocal solos.
Clayton Valley High School, Concord, CA 94521

GOLDSTEIN, BURTON
b. New York, N.Y., 17 Aug. 1950. Studied with Henri Lazarof, Paul Reale, Roy Travis, and Robert Winter, Univ. of California, Los Angeles.. His awards include the Axel Stordahl prize; Atwater Kent prize; BMI student composer award; and the Henry Mancini scholarship for film composition. He has been teaching assistant and associate, UCLA, 1975-78.
WORKS: CHAMBER MUSIC: Lost loves, song for baritone and chamber ensemble; string trio; quintet for flute, oboe, viola, cello, piano; chamber concerto for winds, percussion, piano, strings, 1975; FILM SCORE: On the road to Mardi Gras, 1977.
Music Dept., Univ. of California, 405 Hilgard Ave., Los Angeles, CA 90024

GOLDSTEIN, MALCOLM
b. Brooklyn, N.Y., 27 Mar. 1936. Studied with Otto Luening, Columbia Univ., B.A. 1956, M.M. 1960. He has held faculty posts at Columbia Univ., 1961-65; New School for Social Research, 1963-65, 1967-69; New England Cons., 1965-67; Dickinson Coll., 1969-71; Goddard Coll., 1972-74; Dartmouth Coll., 1975-78; Bowdoin Coll., from 1978.
WORKS: CHAMBER MUSIC: From Wheelock Mt., with text by composer, includes Yosha's morning song for solo voice and Yosha's morning song

extended for unspecified instruments; upon the string, within the bow . . . breathing, string ensemble; frog pond at dusk, winds and strings; A summoning of focus, solo wind; With thoughts for Erik Satie, piano; Soundings, improvisations for solo violin; Emanations, violin and cello; Still point, brass quintet; VOCAL: Illuminations from fantastic gardens, choral group; Overture to fantastic gardens, chorus and instruments; and several tape collages.
6 Whittier St., Brunswick, ME 04011

GOLDSTEIN, WILLIAM
b. Newark, N.J., 25 Feb. 1942. Studied with Vittorio Giannini, Nicolas Flagello, Ludmila Ulehla, Manhattan School of Music; at Trenton State Coll.; 2 years in the BMI Musical Theatre Workshop under Lehman Engel. He was composer and arranger, U.S. Army Band and Chorus, Washington, 1966-69; staff composer, Columbia Music, 1969-70; then free lancer in recordings, commercials, film, and theatre.
WORKS: THEATRE: incidental music to Human being, 1961, Dimensions of peacocks, 1961; Dancing, dancing good-by, musical, 1963; A bullet for Billy the Kid, short folk opera, 1964; A total sweet success, musical, 1965; The peddler, 1-act opera, 1966; Mr. Tambo, Mr. Bones, incidental music, 1969; ORCHESTRA: Whole-tone fantasy, 1960; Historical suite, 1962; Excursion, ballet, 1965; trumpet concerto, 1972; CHAMBER MUSIC: Modes for 3, 2 violins and cello, 1962; Quietude, harp, 2 violins, cello, 1963; woodwind quintet, 1964; Fugue for 10 instruments, 1964; Fusion, 7 winds, percussion, 1971; PIANO: Suite for April, 1962; Scherzo, 1963; Sea chanty, 1963; sonata, 1964; FILM SCORES: Stoolie, 1972; theme for NET's "The advocates," 1972; also band pieces and vocal works.
315 W. 86th St., New York, NY 10024

GOLDSWORTHY, WILLIAM ARTHUR
b. Cornwall, England, 8 Feb. 1878; to U.S. 1887; d. Santa Barbara, Calif., 20 Aug. 1966. Studied organ with Samuel Warren in New York. He was organist in New York churches, at St. Mark's-in-the-Bouwerie, 1926-42.
WORKS: OPERA: The Queen of Sheba; The return of the star, music drama; The prophet, oratorio; ORGAN: Majesty; Scherzo.

GOLLAHON, GLADYS
b. Cincinnati, Ohio, 8 Apr. 1908. She has published sacred and secular songs, including Our Lady of Fatima.

GOLSON-BATEMAN, FLORENCE
b. Fort Deposit, Ala., 4 Dec. 1891. Attended Tenn. School for the Blind; Huntingdon Coll.; Cincinnati Cons.; studied privately in New York with Edgar Stillman Kelley, Roy Harris, Frederick Jacobi; voice with Walter Golde; attended American Cons. Her awards include a scholarship at Cincinnati Cons.; first prize, Ohio Music Teachers Assoc. for a cantata; her portrait in the Alabama Dept. of Archives as Alabama's first musician. She was church soloist and recitalist, 1919-42; choral director, 1923-48; maintained

GOMEZ, VICENTE

private voice studio, College Park, Ga., 1924-36; Montgomery, Ala, 1943-67.
WORKS: CHAMBER MUSIC: Solitude, violin and piano; The banjo, violin and piano; Moods, piano; CHORUS: Night, women's voices; A spring symphony, cantata, soprano solo and women's chorus; SONGS: The bird with a broken wing; A message; Rest; Little boy blue; A kiss from Columbine.
311 Government St., Wetumpka, AL 36092

GOMEZ, VICENTE
b. Madrid, Spain, 8 July 1911; U.S. citizen 1943. Studied at Madrid Cons. Since the age of 13, he has given guitar recitals in Spain, Europe, North Africa, Cuba, Mexico, Venezuela, and the U.S.
WORKS: GUITAR: Canción de la primavera; Lamento gitano; Melody of Spain; El albaicin; Carnival in Spain; La farruca; Granada arabe; FILM SCORE: Blood and sand.

GONZALEZ, LUIS JORGE
b. San Juan, Argentina, 22 Jan. 1936; to U.S. 1971. Studied at Nat. Univ. of Cuyo, Argentina; with Earle Brown and Robert Hall Lewis, Peabody Inst. His awards include prizes, Viotti Internat. Competition, 1971, 1974, 1977; Percussive Arts Society award, 1975; Argentina Nat. Endowment for the Arts awards, 1975, 1976; Internat. Wieniawski composition contest award, 1976. He was piano instructor, Preparatory Div., Peabody Inst., 1972-77.
WORKS: ORCHESTRA: Támaras, 1978; Poltergeist symphony; CHAMBER MUSIC: Hypallages, woodwind quartet, piano, percussion, New York, Dec. 1973; Soledades sonoras #1-3, piano; Voces I, clarinet and piano; Voces II, chamber ensemble; Mutables, vibraphone and piano; Oxymora, cello and piano; Stichomythias, violin and piano; Metaphores, trio.
1401 Enfield Rd., #105, Austin, TX 78703

GOODE, DANIEL
b. New York, N.Y., 24 Jan. 1936. Studied at Oberlin Coll.; with Henry Cowell, Jack Beeson, Otto Luening, Columbia Univ.; with Kenneth Gaburo, Robert Erickson, Pauline Oliveros, Univ. of California, San Diego. His awards include Anton Seidl fellowship at Columbia Univ.; 2 grants, Rutgers Research Council, Composers Forum program, 1975; and commissions. He has held faculty posts at Univ. of North Dakota, 1963-64; Univ. of Minnesota, 1964-67; Univ. of California, 1968-70; from 1971, Livingston Coll., Rutgers Univ.
WORKS: CHAMBER MUSIC: Inner motions, 14 instruments, 1969-73; Orbits, 2 instrumentalists and 6 moving bodies, 1970; Circular thoughts, clarinet solo, 1973; Paths, piano, 1973; 2 thrushes, 2 woodwinds; 5 thrushes--2 fiddles and piano, 1976.
Box 268A, Main Rd., Neshanic, NJ 08853

GOODE, JACK C.
b. Marlin, Tex., 20 Jan. 1921. Attended Baylor Univ., B.M. 1942, M.M. 1947; studied with Stella Roberts and Leo Sowerby, American Cons.; with Ernst Pepping, Berlin Hochschule, 1957; organ

with Joseph Ahrens. His awards include 2 Phi Mu Alpha first prizes, and commissions. He was instructor, Northwestern Univ., 1949-50; professor, Wheaton Coll., Ill., 1950-66; private teacher from 1954.
WORKS: ORCHESTRA: Trilogy; Wheels of autumn, chorus and orch.; Pity me not, chorus and orch.; Sketch; BAND: Burlesque march; Rondino, with solo saxophone, Paris, 2 Feb. 1966; CHAMBER MUSIC: clarinet sonatina, 1963; 2 string quartets; Petite suite, 4 saxophones; Sonata from Joel, trumpet and organ, 1961; brass quintet, 1968; 5 fiddle fancies; SONGS: The silence of the night; a song cycle for soprano, 1948; 3 songs of love and despair, baritone, 1970; Pastorale for an August night, Organ point, and 3 for Ruth, 3 songs for baritone, 1971; many choral works, piano and organ pieces.

GOODENOUGH, FORREST
b. South Bend, Ind., 1918. Studied at Butler Univ.; DePauw Univ.; and Eastman School of Music. He received grants from the Woodstock Found. for the Arts, 1948, 1949; and a performance award, Austin Symph. Orch. He has been faculty member, Texas School for the Blind at Austin. His works include Chorale fantasy and Elegy, 1960, for orchestra.

GOODING, DAVID
b. Lockport, N.Y., 7 Aug. 1935. Studied at Eastman School of Music; Univ. of Buffalo; Western Reserve Univ.; with Thomas Canning, Aaron Copland, Carlos Chavez. His awards include grants from Bascomb Little Found., Playhouse Square Found., and others; many commissions. He has been on the faculty, Lake Erie Coll., from 1961; music director, the Temple, Cleveland, from 1961; and music consultant, Cleveland Playhouse, from 1977.
WORKS: MUSIC THEATRE: The inferno, 1972; Alice!, 1974; Lysistrata, 1976; Music Hall, 1977; Gooding furnished the lyrics as well as the music for these works; also more than 300 Jewish liturgical works.
19272 Briarwood Lane, Strongsville, OH 44136

GOODMAN, AL
b. Nikopol, Russia, 12 Aug. 1890; to U.S. 1895; d. New York, N.Y., 10 Jan. 1972. Studied on scholarship at Peabody Cons. He was conductor for Broadway shows, 1920-40, then for radio and television.
WORKS: MUSICALS: Linger longer Lettie; Cinderella on Broadway; The whirl of New York; The lady in ermine; The passing show of 1922; Artists and models of 1925; Gay Paree; and many songs.

GOODMAN, ALFRED
b. Berlin, Germany, 1 Mar. 1920; to U.S. 1940. Studied with Henry Cowell and Otto Luening, Columbia Univ., B.S. 1952, M.A. 1953. He was in the U.S. Army in World War II; in 1946 was an arranger for dance bands. He returned to Germany in 1960. His works include a 1-act opera, The audition, Athens, Ohio, 27 July 1954;

2 symphonies; choral pieces; chamber music,
<u>Dialogues</u>, clarinet and percussion, Munich, 29
Nov. 1978.

GOODMAN, JOHN
Studied at Northeastern Univ., B.A.; Yale Univ.,
M.M.; Boston Univ., D.M.A. He received the
Woods-Chandler prize in composition. He has
held faculty posts at the New England Cons. and
Emmanuel Coll.; from 1969, at Boston Univ.
WORKS: ORCHESTRA: <u>Songs of parting</u>, on
Chinese verses, soprano, tenor, and orch., 1963;
CHAMBER MUSIC: string quartet in one movement,
1964; piano sonata, 1965; <u>Piano fantasy</u>, 1977,
Boston Univ., 19 Oct. 1978.
School of the Arts, Boston University,
Boston, MA 02215

GOODMAN, JOSEPH
b. New York, N.Y., 28 Nov. 1918. Attended Johns
Hopkins Univ., B.A. 1938; studied with Paul
Hindemith and Richard Donovan, Yale Univ., 1944-
45; with Walter Piston, Harvard Univ., M.A.
1948; and with Gian Francesco Malipiero on a
Fulbright grant for study in Italy, 1950-51. He
has been faculty member, Queens Coll. of CUNY,
from 1952.
WORKS: CHAMBER MUSIC: trio for flute,
violin, piano; wind quintet, 1954; <u>5 bagatelles</u>,
flute, clarinet, bassoon; <u>Music for 2 flutes</u>;
<u>Jadis III</u>, flute and bassoon; CHORUS (a cappella):
<u>Laudate Dominum</u>; <u>Crucem Tuam</u>; <u>Adoremus Te</u>;
<u>Before the ending of the day</u>; <u>How beautiful the
queen of night</u>; <u>Lyrics from the Spanish</u>; ORGAN:
<u>Fantasia on Windsor</u>; <u>3 preludes on Gregorian
melodies</u>; <u>Fantasy</u>; <u>7 bagatelles</u>; <u>Fantasia on
Panis Angelicus</u>; numerous other choral works and
organ pieces.
100 Sunnyside Ave., Pleasantville, NY 10570

GOODMAN, SAUL
b. Brooklyn, N.Y., 17 July. Teaches percussion
at the Juilliard School and at New York Univ.,
School of Education.
WORKS: PERCUSSION: <u>Ballad for dance</u>;
<u>Canon</u>; <u>Dance patterns</u>; <u>Introduction and allegro</u>;
<u>Off we go</u>; <u>Timpiana</u>; <u>Proliferation</u>.

GOODRICH, (JOHN) WALLACE
b. Newton, Mass., 27 May 1871; d. Boston, Mass.,
6 June 1952. Studied with Henry Dunham and
George W. Chadwick, New England Cons.; with
Rheinberger in Munivh and with Widor in Paris.
He taught at the New England Cons., was dean,
1907-31, director, 1931-42; organist, Trinity
Church, 1902-9, and with the Boston Symph. Orch.,
1897-1907. He founded the Choral Arts Society
in 1902; was conductor at various times of the
St. Cecilia Society, Boston Opera Company,
Worcester County Choral Assoc. He wrote choral
works.

GOODSMITH, RUTH B.
b. Chicago, Ill., 27 Sept. 1892. Studied with
Arne Oldberg and Carl Beecher, Northwestern U
Univ., B.M. 1922; with Andre Bloch, Fontaine-
bleau, 1927; Alfred Rossi, Milan, 1930; Adolf
Weidig and Leo Sowerby, American Cons., M.M.

1939. She won first prize, Mu Phi Epsilon con-
test, 1954; third prize, Nat. Fed. of Music
Clubs, 1967. She was on the faculty, Stephens
Coll., 1920-58; visiting professor, Univ. of
Redlands, 1952-53.
WORKS: OPERA: <u>Lolita</u>, chamber opera, 1953;
ORCHESTRA: <u>God's rider</u>, with chorus; <u>And in the
Hanging Gardens</u>, with chorus; CHAMBER MUSIC:
<u>Lullaby</u>, piano or harp; piano pieces.

GOODWIN, GORDON
b. Cape Girardeau, Mo., 22 Jan. 1941. Studied
with Hunter Johnson, Kent Kennan, Clifton
Williams, Univ. of Texas, D.M.A. 1969. He has
received several commissions. He was faculty
member, Univ. of Texas, 1967-73; from 1973, at
Univ. of South Carolina.
WORKS: THEATRE: <u>Gabriel</u>, multimedia, 1-
act opera; ORCHESTRA: <u>Codes for orchestra</u>;
<u>Whistlestops</u>, flute and orch.; BAND: <u>Casts</u>;
<u>Pufferbellies</u>; <u>Diferencias</u>; <u>Shuffle chaconne</u>,
trombone and wind ensemble; <u>Forks</u>, brass choir;
CHAMBER MUSIC: bass trombone sonata; <u>Concerns</u>,
woodwind quartet and trombone; piano sonata;
<u>Anonymous V</u>, saxophone solo; <u>Sonata after the
St. Cecilia Society (1726)</u>, baroque ensemble,
Washington, D.C., 4 Sept. 1975.
104 Gadsden, Columbia, SC 29201

GOOSSEN, FREDERIC
b. St. Cloud, Minn., 30 July 1927. Studied with
Donald Ferguson, Univ. of Minnesota; with Arthur
Shepherd and James Aliferis, Longy School of
Music. He was faculty member, Univ. of Minnesota, 1953-54; Berea Coll., 1955-58; from 1958,
Univ. of Alabama.
WORKS: ORCHESTRA: 2 symphonies; <u>Litanies</u>;
<u>Stanzas and refrains</u>; <u>Dance measures</u>; <u>Hae: In
memoriam Thomas Mann</u>; CHAMBER MUSIC: <u>Equali</u>,
4 trombones; <u>Clausulae</u>, violin and piano; <u>Temple
music</u>, violin and piano; suite for piano; CHORUS:
<u>Hodie</u>; <u>Let us now praise famous men</u>, with instru-
ments; <u>American meditations</u>, women's voices a
cappella.
3125 4th Court E., Tuscaloosa, AL 35401

GORDER, WAYNE DOUGLAS
b. Milwaukee, Wis., 1 Dec. 1946. Studied with
Elliot Borishansky and John Downey, Univ. of
Wisconsin; with Robert Kelly, Univ. of Illinois.
He taught in public schools, 1968-72; Millikin
Univ., 1975-76; from 1976, on faculty, Ohio
Wesleyan Univ.
WORKS: BRASS ENSEMBLE: <u>Preludes I & II</u>,
brass and percussion; brass quintet; <u>Fires</u>, 8
trumpets; <u>One point two</u>, solo trumpet; many
other works for band, solo brass, duets, trios,
etc.
99 Campbell St., Delaware, OH 43015

GORDON, PETER LAURENCE
b. New York, N.Y., 20 June 1951. Studied with
Kenneth Gaburo, Roger Reynolds, Univ. of California, San Diego, B.A. 1972; with Robert Ashley,
Terry Riley, Mills Coll., M.F.A. 1974. He received the Alice Q. McPherson Memorial prize,
1968; Gogglestead award, 1971; Univ. of California fellowship, 1972-73.

GORDON, PHILIP

   WORKS: CHAMBER MUSIC: <u>Fur cruiser</u>, quartet,
1969; <u>Wind-finger songs</u>, 6 flutes, 3 keyboards,
1971; <u>Vertices</u>, sextet, 1972; <u>Les enfants ter-
ribles</u>, string trio, 1972; ELECTRONIC: <u>Hi F</u>,
tape, 1969; <u>Machomusic 1</u>, 6 saxophones and live
electronics, 1973; <u>Monodies and monologues</u>,
electronics and spoken voice, 1973.

GORDON, PHILIP
   b. Newark, N.J., 14 Dec. 1894. Studied at
Columbia Univ., B.A., M.A., Ph.D. He has been
professor, Chicago Musical Coll.; Seton Hall
Univ.; visiting professor, Westminster Choir
Coll.; Princeton Univ.; has conducted the Newark
Civic Symphony and the Bach Cantata Society.
   WORKS: ORCHESTRA: <u>Northern saga</u>; <u>Exotic
dance</u>, strings; <u>2 moods</u>; <u>Little baroque suite</u>;
<u>3 preludes</u> for strings; BAND: <u>American frontier</u>;
<u>Colonial diary</u>; <u>New England chronicle</u>; <u>Olympia</u>;
<u>Prairie saga</u>; <u>Robert Burns overture</u>; also chamber
pieces and choral works.

GORE, RICHARD T.
   b. Takoma Park, Md., 25 June 1908. Studied
piano and organ in New York; attended Columbia
Univ., B.A. 1933, M.A. 1938; Univ. of Rochester,
Ph.D. 1956. He became a fellow, American Guild
of Organists, 1935; held Victor Baier fellowship,
Columbia Univ., 1936; won the Composers' Press
anthem contest, 1945. He was faculty member,
Mt. Holyoke Coll., 1938-1939; Cornell Univ.,
1939-45; Coll. of Wooster, 1945-72.
   WORKS: Many church choral and organ works
including <u>Let God arise</u>, anthem; <u>Psalm diptych
(Psalms 50 and 150)</u>, chorus and organ.
   1628 Cleveland Rd., Wooster, OH 44691

GORELLI, OLGA
   b. Bologna, Italy, 14 June 1920; U.S. citizen
1945. Studied with Gian Carlo Menotti and
Rosario Scalero at Curtis Inst.; with Quincy
Porter and Paul Hindemith, Yale Univ.; Werner
Josten and Alvin Etler, Smith Coll.; and with
Darius Milhaud at Tanglewood, Mills Coll., and
Aspen, Colo. She received the Fatman prize at
Smith Coll., 1949, 1950. She was teaching
fellow at Smith Coll., 1948-50; on faculty,
Hollins Coll., 1950-54; Trenton State Coll.,
1954-57.
   WORKS: OPERA: <u>Dona Petra</u>; <u>Between the
shadow and the dream</u>; CHORUS: mass in English;
many choral works, songs, 2 dance dramas, in-
cidental music, orchestral works, and chamber
music.
   Scotch Rd., Pennington, NJ 08534

GORIN, IGOR
   b. Grodek, Ukraine, 26 Oct. 1908; U.S. citizen
1939. Studied with Victor Fuchs, Vienna Cons.;
Brigham Young Univ., D.M. 1956. He made his
debut as a singer at Hollywood Bowl in 1939.
He is professor of voice, Univ. of Arizona.
   WORKS: SONGS: <u>Lament</u>; <u>Safe by de Lawd</u>;
<u>Jumping jack</u>; <u>Caucasian song</u>; <u>Lullaby</u>; <u>Remembered
mornings</u>; <u>Within my dreams</u>.
   Music Dept., University of Arizona, Tucson,
AZ 85721

GOTTLIEB, JACK
   b. New Rochelle, N.Y., 12 Oct. 1930. Studied
with Karol Rathaus, Queens Coll.; with Irving
Fine, Brandeis Univ.; with Aaron Copland and
Boris Blacher at Tanglewood; with Robert Palmer
and Burrill Phillips, Univ. of Illinois, D.M.A.
1964. His awards include Nadworney Memorial
award, Nat. Fed. of Music Clubs, 1957; first
prize, NFMC choral works contest, 1957; first
place, Ohio Univ. opera competition, 1957; Brown
Univ. choral contest, 1960; Nat. Endowment for
the Arts grant, 1976. He was assistant to
Leonard Bernstein, 1958-66; music director,
Temple Israel, St. Louis, 1970-73; faculty
member, School of Music, Hebrew Union Coll.,
1973-77; from 1977, editorial associate with a
music publisher.
   WORKS: THEATRE: <u>Tea party</u>, 1-act opera,
1957; <u>Public dance</u>, 1-act opera, 1964; <u>Song of
songs, which is Solomon's</u>, full-length opera,
1976; <u>From shtetl to stage door</u>, lecture entertainment; ORCHESTRA: <u>Pieces of seven</u>, 1962;
<u>Articles of faith</u>, 1966; CHAMBER MUSIC: string
quartet, 1955; piano sonata, 1963; <u>Twilight
crane</u>, woodwind quintet, 1962; CHORUS: <u>Kids'
calls</u>, 1957; <u>In memory of . . .</u>, cantata, 1960;
<u>Love songs for Sabbath</u>, 1965; <u>Shout for joy</u>,
1968; <u>Sharing the prophets</u>, cantata; <u>4 affirma-
tions</u>, with brass sextet; SONGS: <u>Downtown blues
for uptown halls</u>, voice, clarinet, piano, 1967,
New York, 26 Mar. 1978; <u>Haiku souvenirs</u>, text of
Leonard Bernstein, Elmont, N.Y., 22 Nov. 1969.
   150 W. 79th St., #2E, New York, NY 10024

GOTTLIEB, JAY
   b. Brooklyn, N.Y., 23 Oct. 1948. Studied with
Stefan Wolpe, Chatham Square Music School, 1960-
64; with Louise Talma and Ruth Anderson, Hunter
Coll., 1966-70; with Nadia Boulanger in France,
summers, 1967-71; with Lukas Foss, Earl Kim,
Harold Shapero, Leon Kirchner, Arthur Berger,
Harvard Univ., M.M. 1972. His awards include
Lincoln Center award, 1966; High School of
Performing Arts award, 1966; Heintz scholarship,
1966; full scholarship for study with Nadia
Boulanger, first prize in composition, Fontaine-
bleau, 1969; Woodrow Wilson fellowship, 1970;
Phi Beta Kappa, 1970. He was teaching fellow at
Harvard, 1971; rehearsal pianist, Boston Symph.
Orch., 1973.
   WORKS: ORCHESTRA: <u>Essay for orchestra</u>,
1969; <u>Bagatelle</u>, 1972; CHAMBER MUSIC: <u>Slow
movement</u> for piano trio, 1969; <u>June Wyatt songs</u>,
1970; <u>Synchronisms</u>, percussion and tape, 1970;
violin sonata, 1971; PIANO: sonata, 1964-67;
suite of 6 pieces, 1968-69; suite for piano,
4 hands, 1968, rev. 1970.

GOTTSCHALK, ARTHUR W.
   b. San Diego, Calif., 14 Mar. 1951. Studied
with Leslie Bassett, George Balch Wilson, William
Bolcom, Ross Lee Finney, Univ. of Michigan,
D.M.A. His awards include Charles Ives award,
American Acad. of Arts and Letters; Sigvald
Thompson orchestra award; Nat. flute concerto
competition, 1976. He was teaching assistant,
Univ. of Michigan, 1974-77; then on faculty,
Rice Univ.

WORKS: ORCHESTRA: Communique; Beati omnes, with choir; BAND: Roulades; CHAMBER MUSIC: Phases, flute duet; Variants, solo flute; Construct, solo trumpet; Substructures, tuba ensemble; Children of the night, woodwind quintet; Night flight, piano.
6117 Fondren Rd., Houston, TX 77036

GOULD, ELIZABETH
b. Toledo, Ohio, 8 May 1904. Attended Oberlin Coll. and Cons. and Univ. of Michigan; studied piano with Artur Schnable and Guy Maier. Her awards include 6 first prizes and 2 special citations in Mu Phi Epsilon contests, 1952-69; Arthur Shepherd award, 1969; Delta Omicron first prize, 1965; award for string quartet, Mannheim, Germany, 1961. She is a private teacher and composer.
WORKS: THEATRE: Ray and the gospel singer, comic chamber opera, 1966; ORCHESTRA: piano concerto, 1953; Declaration for peace, with chorus, 1955; concertino for clarinet, trumpet, and strings, 1958; concerto for trumpet and strings, 1959; Escapade, 1960; CHAMBER MUSIC: violin sonata, 1950; Prologue to "Men are naive," piano, flute, violin, narrator, 1955; cello sonata, 1959; string quartet, 1960; viola sonata, 1962; 6 affinities, brass quintet, 1962; Disciplines, woodwind trio; piano trio, 1964; suite for woodwinds, brass, percussion, 1965; flute quartet, 1968; Fantasie and fugue, bassoon and piano, 1968; VOCAL: madrigal cycle, chorus, 1964; Personal and private, cycle for soprano and flute, 1968; (F)raileries, 4 songs for soprano, Washington, 13 Feb. 1976; PIANO: Toccata, 1950; 2 sonatas, 1957, 1961; sonatina, 1962; Effects, piano, 4 hands, 1968; Scintillations, ballet for 2 pianos, 1969.
3137 Kenwood Blvd., Toledo, OH 43606

GOULD, MORTON
b. Richmond Hill, N.Y., 10 Dec. 1913. Studied with Abby Whiteside and Vincent Jones, Inst. of Musical Art, New York. His awards include the Nat. Acad. of Recording Arts and Sciences Grammy for recording of Charles Ives symphony #1, 1966; Nat. Assoc. of American Composers and Conductors Gold Medal; many commissions. He was on staff of Radio City Music Hall and later of NBC; conducted his own program on radio for many years, and has been guest conductor of most major U.S. orchestras; His first composition, Just six, was published at age 6.
WORKS: THEATRE: Billion dollar baby, musical, 1945; Fall River legend, ballet suite, 1948; Arms and the girl, musical, 1950; Fiesta, 1957; ORCHESTRA: Chorale and fugue in jazz, 2 pianos and orch., 1932; 3 American symphonettes, 1933, 1935, 1937; piano concerto, 1937; violin concerto, 1938; Foster gallery, 1940; Latin American symphonette, Brooklyn, 22 Feb. 1941; Spirituals for orch., 1941; Cowboy rhapsody, 1942; Lincoln legend, 1942; Interplay, piano and orch., 1943; viola concerto, 1944; 4 symphonies, 1943, 1944, 1947, 1952; Minstrel show, 1946; Philharmonic waltzes, 1947; Dance variations, 2 pianos and orch., 1953; Inventions, 4 pianos and orch., 1953; Showpiece, 1954;

Declaration, chorus, orch., 2 speakers, 1956; Jekyll and Hyde variations, 1956; Dialogues, piano and string orch., 1958; World War I: Sarajevo suite, Wilson suite, Verdun suite, 1964-65; Venice--Audiograph, double orch. and brass choirs, 1966; Columbia, 1967; Soundings, 1969; Vivaldi gallery, divided orch. and string quartet; Symphony of spirituals, Detroit, 1 Apr. 1976; American ballads, Queens, N.Y., 24 Apr. 1976; Burchfield Gallery, suite, Cleveland, 9 Apr. 1981; works for band; 3 piano sonatas, 1930, 1933, 1936; other piano pieces.
c/o Chappell & Co., 801 7th Ave., New York, NY 10019

GOWER, ALBERT E., JR.
b. Weed, Calif., 4 June 1935. Studied with James Adair, California State Univ., Sacramento; with George F. McKay, Univ. of Oregon; Samuel Adler and William Latham, North Texas State Univ. He received a Fine Arts award, Calif. State Univ., 1956; $100 award, Mississippi Educational Television contest. From 1966, he has been on the faculty, Univ. of Southern Mississippi.
WORKS: ORCHESTRA: symphony; BAND: Excursion; CHAMBER MUSIC: 3 short pieces for baritone horn and piano; string quartet; tuba sonata; trumpet sonata; 3 improvisations, brass trio; Adagio and allegro, woodwind quintet; CHORUS: 3 motets, a cappella.
817 Hillendale Dr., Hattiesburg, MS 39401

GRADY, J. W.
b. Louisville, Ky., 19 Apr. 1943. Studied with Kenneth Wright, Univ. of Kentucky; with John Verrall, George F. McKay, William O. Smith, James Beale, Gerald Kechley, Univ. of Washington. He was cowinner, Cleveland Inst. percussion composition contest, 1968; received second prize, Phi Mu Alpha contest, 1968. He taught in Washington public schools, 1969-72.
WORKS: ORCHESTRA: concerto for 2 trumpets, strings, percussion; CHAMBER MUSIC: Timbre stream, percussion, alto piccolo, flute; MIXED MEDIA: Echoi, symphonic band and tape; Earthlight suite, strings and tape; Mother Goose revisited, chorus and tape.
7314 Eastside Dr., N.E., Tacoma, WA 98422

GRAF, WILLIAM
b. Brooklyn, N.Y., 21 Dec. 1946. Studied with Gregg Smith, Billy Jim Layton, David Lewin, Isaac Nemiroff, State Univ. of New York at Stonybrook; at Ithaca Coll.; and with Claudio Spies at Harvard Univ. He was faculty member, State Univ. of New York, Fredonia, 1971-75; member of the Gregg Smith Singers and choral director, 1967-.
WORKS: INCIDENTAL MUSIC: Teahouse of the August moon; You can't take it with you; The absence of a cello; It's never too late; The imaginary invalid; Romanoff and Juliett; Luv; Rhinoceros; The doll's house; CHORUS: Ode on solitude; Rondo for voices, 1970; 6 contrasts, with 3 winds and piano, 1970; Missa brevis, solo quartet and 16-part chorus, 1971; Joy train, stage piece for soloists, chorus, piano, electric

GRAGSON, WESLEY

piano and bass, percussion, 1972; SONGS: <u>Contentment</u>, baritone, 1967; 3 songs on Millay texts; 2 songs on Hesse texts, 1971; piano pieces.
13 Leon Place, Fredonia, NY 14063

GRAGSON, WESLEY
b. Greenville, Ky., 3 May 1923. Attended Western Kentucky State Univ.; studied with Weldon Hart, West Virginia Univ.; with Herbert Elwell and Bernard Rogers, Eastman School of Music. He received an award for a band piece, 1963. He is faculty member, Elizabeth City State Univ., N.C.
WORKS: ORCHESTRA: <u>John Henry suite</u>; <u>Piece for orchestra</u>; BAND: <u>Folk suite</u>; CHAMBER MUSIC: suite for harp and percussion.
1806 Sanford Dr., Elizabeth City, NC 27909

GRAHAM, ROBERT
b. El Dorado, Kans., 5 Sept. 1912. Studied with Edward Royce, Bernard Rogers, Wayne Barlow, Howard Hanson, and Herbert Elwell, Eastman School of Music, B.M.; with Paul Pisk at Univ. of Redlands, M.M. He received the Hubert award for composition, Univ. of Redlands, 1951; his manuscripts, recordings, etc., are being preserved in El Dorado, Kans. He was organist and music director, Tokyo, 1951-54; church organist, in California and Arizona, 1954-61; from 1961, in Hawaii.
WORKS: ORCHESTRA: harpsichord concerto; <u>Kansas suite</u>; <u>Oilwells</u>; CHORUS: <u>Obookiah</u>, oratorio; <u>Come Lord Jesus</u>, oratorio; many cantatas, more than 200 published anthems; piano and organ pieces.
Box 586, Waianae, HI 96792

GRAHN, ULF
b. Solna, Sweden, 17 Jan. 1942; to U.S. 1972. Studied composition with Hans Eklund in Stockholm, 1962-66; at Royal Acad. of Music, 1967-71; Catholic Univ., M.M. 1973. He held scholarships at the Royal Acad., 1967, 1969, 1970, and from the Swedish government, 1971, 1973; graduate fellowships at Catholic Univ., 1972-75; won first prize in organ composition, Stockholm, 1973; held residence at Wolf Trap Composer Cottage, 1976, 1977; artist appointment in Paris through the Swedish Inst., 1978. He taught at Catholic Univ., 1972-75; from 1975, at Northern Virginia Community Coll., Annandale.
WORKS: ORCHESTRA: sinfoni 1; <u>A dream of a lost century</u>; concerto for orchestra; double bass concerto; <u>Ancient music</u>, piano and orch.; CHAMBER MUSIC: <u>Mist</u>, violin, viola, flute; <u>Soundscapes I-V</u>, varying chamber ensembles; <u>Music for oboe solo</u>; <u>Halloween</u>, clarinet solo; woodwind trio; <u>Alone</u>, flute solo; <u>Trombone unaccompanied</u>, Washington, 19 Dec. 1977; <u>Signaler</u>, 2 trumpets, 2 trombones; PIANO: <u>Snapshots</u>; <u>2 pieces for piano</u>; <u>Cinq preludes</u>; piano sonata with flute and percussion; <u>Barbro variations I-IV</u>, Washington, 18 Dec. 1978; also choral works, songs, electronic pieces.
7229 Deborah Dr., Falls Church, VA 22046

GRAINGER, PERCY ALDRIDGE
b. Melbourne, Australia, 8 July 1882; U.S. citizen 1918; d. White Plains, N.Y., 20 Feb. 1961.

Studied piano with Louis Pabst in Melbourne; with James Kwast in Frankfurt, Germany; and with Ferruccio Busoni in Berlin. He began concert appearances in England in 1900; made tours to South Africa and Australia; American debut was in New York in 1915. He served in the U.S. Army in World War I, in the army band and as instructor in the army music school; taught at Chicago Musical Coll. summers, 1919-31; was chairman, music department, New York Univ., 1932-33.
WORKS: ORCHESTRA: <u>Irish tunes from County Derry</u>, 1909; <u>Mock morris</u>, 1911; <u>Molly on the shore</u>, 1913; <u>Shepherd's hey</u>, 1913; <u>Colonial song</u>, 1913; <u>In a nutshell</u>, 1916; <u>English dance</u>, with organ, 1925; <u>To a Nordic princess</u>, 1928, written for his wedding at Hollywood Bowl to Ella Viola Ström; <u>Ye banks and braes of Bonnie Doon</u>, 1932; <u>Danish folk song suite</u>, 1937; CHAMBER MUSIC: <u>Handel in the Strand</u>, 1913; <u>My Robin is to the greenwood gone</u>, octet; <u>Walking tune</u>, woodwind quintet; <u>Green bushes</u>, 1921; <u>Free music #1</u>, string quartet, an experimental work using multiple, simultaneous glissandos, was given its premiere at the Cabrillo Festival in 1978; many works for chorus, songs, piano pieces.

GRANDJANY, MARCEL
b. Paris, France, 3 Sept. 1891; U.S. citizen 1945; d. New York, 24 Feb. 1975. Studied harp at Nat. Cons., Paris, winning the Premier Prix at age 13. He made his Paris debut at 17 and continued to give recitals until World War I, when he served in the French army. He then resumed his career as harpist and also taught at the Fontainebleau Summer School, 1921-36. He came to the U.S. in 1936 and was appointed head of the harp department at Juilliard School, 1938, and at Cons. de Musique, Quebec, 1938-58; also taught at Manhattan School of Music, 1956-66.
WORKS: ORCHESTRA: <u>Poeme</u>, harp, horn, orch.; <u>Aria in classic style</u>, harp and strings or organ; HARP: <u>Children's hour suite</u>; <u>Colorado trail</u>; <u>Divertissement</u>; <u>Rhapsody</u>; other works for harp solo, and songs.

GRANT, ALLAN
b. Newcastle-on-Tyne, England, 2 July 1892; to U.S. 1897; d. Chicago, Ill. Studied at Balatka Music Coll., Chicago; with Percy Goetschius and Franklin Robinson, Inst. of Musical Art, New York. Paderewski invited him at age 4 to give a recital in Cardiff, Wales. He was concert pianist and soloist with many major orchestras.
WORKS: ORCHESTRA: symphony; piano concerto; <u>Southland</u>, written for and performed at New York Worlds Fair, 1939; PIANO: <u>Gramercy Square</u>; <u>In a Chinese tearoom</u>; several educational suites; and songs.

GRANT, DONALD P.
b. Chicago, Ill., 4 Sept. 1932. Attended Azusa Pacific Coll., B.A.; Claremont Coll., M.A.; Univ. of Southern California, Ed.D. He was faculty member, Azusa Pacific Coll., 1962-78.
WORKS: CHORUS: <u>Were you there</u>, Easter cantata; <u>Go tell it on the mountain</u>, Christmas cantata; many anthems.

GRANT, W. PARKS
b. Cleveland, Ohio, 4 Jan. 1910. Studied with
Harold G. Davidson, Capital Univ., B.M. 1932; at
Ohio State Univ., M.A. 1933; with A. I. McHose,
Herbert Elwell, Bernard Rogers, Wayne Barlow,
Eastman School of Music, Ph.D. 1948. He held
fellowships at Yaddo, 1949, Huntington Hartford
Found., 1959, 1963; received Mississippi Educ.
Television award, 1969; prizes from Penn. Fed.
of Music Clubs, Louisiana Fed. of Music Clubs,
Texas Manuscript Society, Jacksonville Univ.,
Texas Fed. of Women's Clubs. His faculty posi-
tions have included Tarleton State Coll., 1937-
43; Louisiana State Univ., 1944-47; Temple Univ.,
1947-53; Univ. of Mississippi, 1953-74.
WORKS: ORCHESTRA: 3 symphonies; The masque
of the red death, symphonic poem; 6 overtures;
Character sketches, suite; horn concerto; clarinet concerto; double bass concerto; Scherzo,
with solo flute; Autumn woodland poem, string
orch.; motet for strings; 3 suites for strings;
CHAMBER MUSIC: 3 night poems, string quartet;
2 string quartets; Poem, string quintet; Prelude
and canonic piece, flute and clarinet; Soliloquy
and jubilation, wind quintet; 3 brass quartets;
brass quintet; brass sextet; brass septet; Prelude and dance, 11 brass instruments; Poem,
horn or cello and organ; concert duo, tuba and
piano; Percussion concert piece; Varied obsti-
nacy, saxophone and tape; CHORUS: Friendship
and freedom; Prayer for Philadelphia; Lines from
the Magnificat; The cry of the persecuted; There
is a Santa Claus; A Pennsylvania Dutch tale;
Trains; PIANO: 2 sonatas, and other pieces; also
songs, organ pieces. He is author of 2 textbooks and of many articles in music journals;
has prepared corrected editions of 4 Mahler symphonies.
1720 Garfield St., Oxford, MS 38655

GRANTHAM, DONALD
b. Duncan, Okla., 9 Nov. 1947. Studied with
Spencer Norton, Univ. of Oklahoma; with Ramiro
Cortes, Robert Linn, Halsey Stevens, Univ. of
Southern California; and with Nadia Boulanger,
American Cons., Fontainebleau. His awards include first prize, Nat. Fed. of Music Clubs,
1964-66; McHugh Composition prize, 1972; Lili
Boulanger Composition prize, 1976. He has been
faculty member, Univ. of Texas at Austin, from
1975.
WORKS: ORCHESTRA: Variations, 1970; The
war prayer, baritone and orch., Mark Twain text,
1973; concerto for bass trombone and wind orch.;
CHAMBER MUSIC: brass quintet, 1971; piano trio,
1972; chamber concerto, harpsichord and string
quartet, 1973; 4 caprichos de Francisco Goya,
solo violin; Fanfara festiva, 4 brass, timpani,
organ; CHORUS: 7 settings of poems of Emily
Dickinson; 3 settings of poems by William Butler
Yeats.
7201 Wood Hollow, #245, Austin, TX 78731

GRANT-SCHAEFER, GEORGE ALFRED
b. Williamstown, Ont., 4 July 1872; to U.S.
1896; d. Chicago, Ill., 11 May 1939. Studied in
Montreal, Chicago, and London. He was organist
in Chicago, 1896-1908; on faculty, Northwestern

Univ., 1908-20. He wrote school operettas,
piano pieces, songs.

GRASSE, EDWIN
b. New York, N.Y., 13 Aug. 1884; d. New York,
8 Apr. 1954. Blind violinist, he studied with
Carl Hauser in New York; with César Thomson in
Brussels at age 12; then at the Cons., winning
first prize in 1900 and Prix de Capacité in
1901. He made his debut in Berlin in 1902, in
New York in 1903; toured the U.S. and Europe.
His compositions include American fantasy, for
violin and orch.; a violin sonata; violin pieces;
3 piano trios; organ pieces.

GRAUER, VICTOR A.
b. Poughkeepsie, N.Y., 11 Oct. 1937. Studied
with Franklin Morris, Ernst Bacon, Syracuse
Univ.; with Darius Milhaud at Aspen; with Leo
Smit, Lejaren Hiller, Univ. of Buffalo; with
Henri Pousser and Karlheinz Stockhausen in
Cologne. He was faculty member, Univ. of Pitts-
burgh, 1970-75.
WORKS: ORCHESTRA: Mt. Fuji in fine
weather; North, percussion ensemble; CHORUS:
Book of the year 3000; Ezekiel I; PIANO: But
for the rain; White River; The liberation; TAPE:
Inferno; Pipes.
407 Oakland Ave., Pittsburgh, PA 15213

GRAVES, C. MEL
b. Parkersburg, W.Va., 6 Nov. 1946. Studied
with Loren Rush, San Francisco Cons., B.M. 1969;
with Pauline Oliveros and Robert Erickson, Univ.
of California, San Diego, M.M. 1976. His awards
include scholarships, 1968-69; Nat. Endowment
for the Arts grants, 1973, 1975. He is a free-
lance bass player and composer in San Francisco.
WORKS: CHAMBER MUSIC: Sea oracle, 2 amplified string basses, 1975; Sceptre, solo string
bass, 3 basses, percussion, piano; Platte River
magic fingers dance music, string bass and tape.

GRAVES, WILLIAM LESTER, JR.
b. Terry, Miss., 26 Aug. 1915. Studied at
Northwest Missouri State Coll., B.S.Ed.; with
Francis J. Pyle, Drake Univ., M.M.Ed.; and with
Cecil Effinger, Univ. of Colorado, Ed.D. He received 7 grants, 1965-72, from Mississippi Univ.
for Women, where he is faculty member.
WORKS: ORCHESTRA: Prelude and fugue, 1965;
2 moods, 1969; CHAMBER MUSIC: Passacaglia and
fugue, strings, 1963; 3 woodwind quintets, 1965,
1966, 1967; woodwind quartet, 1966; woodwind
suite, 1969; CHORUS: Hear us, O Lord, 1964;
Unto thee do we cry, women's voices, 1969; Psalm
150, 1972; Peace I leave with you, 1972; and
other choral works.
P.O. Box 2363, Columbus, MS 39701

GRAYSON, RICHARD
b. Brooklyn, N.Y., 25 Mar. 1941. Studied with
John Vincent, Leonard Stein, Roy Travis, Robert
Trotter, Univ. of California, Los Angeles; with
Easley Blackwood and John Perkins, Univ. of
Chicago; with Henri Pousseur, Karlheinz
Stockhausen, Luciano Berio, Earle Brown, in
Brussels. His awards include a Fulbright grant

GRAZIANO, JOHN

and an Atwater-Kent composition prize. From 1969 he has been faculty member at Occidental Coll.

WORKS: ORCHESTRA: Symphonic inventions on a medieval lied; 3 pieces for orch.; CHAMBER MUSIC: 5 pieces for string quintet; 5 pieces for string quartet; Aurore, chamber ensemble; music for string trio and woodwind quartet; Meadow music, piano; and electronic pieces.
527 20th St., Santa Monica, CA 90402

GRAZIANO, JOHN
b. New York, N.Y., 7 May 1938. Studied with Robert Starer, Henry St. Settlement School; with Mark Brunswick, City Coll. of New York; and with Yehudi Wyner, Yale Univ. He received several student awards; first prize in N.H. Jewish Community Center competition for setting of Psalm 150. He has been faculty member, the City Coll., CUNY, from 1969.

WORKS: CHAMBER MUSIC: chamber concerto for violin, English horn, brass trio, percussion; VOICE: 3 songs for voice, recorder, lute; 5 songs of solitude, soprano, lute, oboe; 6 madrigals from James Joyce's Chamber music, written for and performed by the Western Wind, New York, 6 June 1979.
146-18 32nd Ave., Flushing, NY 11354

GREEN, BERNARD
b. New York, N.Y., 14 Sept. 1908; d. Westport, Conn., 8 Aug. 1975. He was composer and conductor for films, television, and records.

WORKS: ORCHESTRA: symphony; Waltz etudes; The magnolia tree; CHAMBER MUSIC: Idyll, clarinet solo with 4 clarinets; FILM SCORES: 30 years of fun; All the way home; also Broadway shows and TV themes. Shortly before he died, he collaborated with Bernard Jaffe on Independence blues, a play with music, which traces the history of the American popular song over 200 years.

GREEN, GEORGE C.
b. Mt. Kisco, N.Y., 23 Aug. 1930. Studied with Boris Koutzen and Bernard Rogers, Eastman School of Music, B.M., M.M.; with Aaron Copland at Tanglewood; with Robert Palmer, Cornell Univ., D.M.A. He received a composition award, Cummington School of the Arts, 1963. His faculty positions include Univ. of Kansas, 1954-58; Ohio State Univ., 1958-59; Univ. of Vermont, 1962-63; Cornell Univ., 1966-71; from 1971, Skidmore Coll., professor and department chairman.

WORKS: BAND: Perihelion, 1973; CHAMBER MUSIC: string quartet, 1963; Prologue and fugue, violin and cello; Fantasies concertantes, violin and cello; violin sonata; 3 pieces for violin and piano; Triptych, trumpet solo; suite for solo trombone; woodwind quintet.
Sunny Lane, Ballston Spa, NY 12020

GREEN, JOHN
b. New York, N.Y., 10 Oct. 1908. Studied with Walter R. Spalding, Harvard Univ., B.A. in economics; is largely self-taught in composition. His awards include citations from Nat. Fed. of Music Clubs and City and County of Los Angeles; 3 Academy awards for conducting; Gold Record of

the Recording Industry Assoc.; election to Songwriters Hall of Fame, 1973; Nat. Endowment for the Arts grant; many commissions. He was music director in commercial radio, 1933-40; music director for MGM Studios, 1942-58; founder and director of the Promenade Concerts of the Los Angeles Philharmonic Orch., 1959-61, and commentator for the Symphonies for Youth; guest conductor of many major orchestras; from 1958, free-lance composer and conductor for films and television.

WORKS: MUSICALS: Mr. Whittington (London); Here goes the bride; ORCHESTRA: Poeme, 1931; Night club--6 impressions for 3 pianos and orch., 1932; Music for Elizabeth, fantasia for piano and orch., 1940; Mine eyes have seen, symphonic parallels, 1977; SONGS: Body and soul, 1931; I cover the waterfront, 1933; Coquette; Out of nowhere; FILM SCORES: Something in the wind; Raintree County, 1957; Empire, television film.
903 N. Bedford Dr., Beverly Hills, CA 90210

GREEN, RAY
b. Cavendish, Mo., 13 Sept. 1909. Studied with Ernest Bloch, San Francisco Cons.; with Albert Elkus, Univ. of California, Berkeley. His awards include Carnegie Found. grant; George Ladd Prix de Paris, 1935-37; Ford Found. grant, 1957-62; and commissions. He was supervisor, Fed. Chorus, San Francisco, then of Northern California Federal Music Project, 1939-41; served in several capacities as music instructor and supervisor in the armed forces and veterans' services, 1943-48; executive secretary, American Music Center, 1948-61.

WORKS: THEATRE: music for American document, Martha Graham ballet, 1938; Vibrations, for May O'Donnell Dance Co.; Suspension . . . at the still point of the turning world, there the dance is . . . (T. S. Eliot), piano, gong, percussion, for a dance of the same name by May O'Donnell; ORCHESTRA: 2 symphonies, 1945, 1953; Sunday sing symphony, 1946; Rhapsody, harp and orch., 1950; Country dance symphony, violin concerto, 1952; BAND: Folk song fantasies; Kentucky mountain running set; Professional dance, used for opening of New York World's Fair, 1968; CHAMBER MUSIC: 3 inventories for Casey Jones, percussion and piano, 1936; Dance energies, solo flute; Holiday for 4, viola, clarinet, bassoon, piano; 4 conversations, 4 clarinets; Dance sonata, 2 pianos, 1950; Duo concertante, violin and piano, 1950; 5 epigrammatic portraits, string quartet, 1954; Concertante, viola and piano, 1955; many works for chorus, many songs.
c/o American Music Editions, 263 E. 7th St., New York, NY 10009

GREEN, ROBERT LEE
b. Big Sandy, Mont., 13 June 1927. Studied at Univ. of Southern California, B.M.E.; Univ. of Montana, M.M.E.; privately with Roy Harris in Los Angeles. He has been director, instrumental music, Covina High School, from 1963; band director, Whittier Coll., 1964-68; conductor, West Covina Symph. Orch., 1971-74; conductor, American Youth Symph. Orch., European tour, 1973.

WORKS: ORCHESTRA: Polka-promenade and

procession; BAND: <u>Great are the myths</u>, chorus
and brass choir; <u>AYSB march</u>; CHAMBER MUSIC:
<u>Encore</u>, string quartet; <u>Capriccio</u>, piano; <u>Glory</u>,
vocal quartet.
 3261 Armel Dr., Covina, CA 91723

GREENBAUM, MATTHEW
 b. New York, N.Y., 12 Feb. 1950. Studied privately with Stefan Wolpe; with Mario Davidovsky
at City Coll.; with Henry Weinberg, City Univ.
Graduate Center. His awards include 2 fellowships to Johnson Composers' Conf., Vt.; Sigma
Alpha Iota award; Mark Brunswick award.
 WORKS: ORCHESTRA: <u>Variations</u>; CHAMBER
MUSIC: <u>Chamber piece</u> #1; <u>4 arias</u>, #1 violin and
piano, #2 cello, #3 flute, oboe, cello, harp,
#4 harp solo; <u>2 chaconnes</u>, cello and piano.
 99 Perry St., New York, NY 10014

GREENBURG, LAURA
 b. New York, N.Y., 2 June 1942. Studied with
Ursula Mamlok, Manhattan School of Music; with
Mario Davidovsky, City Coll.; and with Jack
Beeson, Columbia Univ. Her awards include a
Johnson Composer Conf. fellowship, 1977; Rapaport
Composition prize, Columbia Univ., 1978. She is
faculty member at Hofstra Univ.
 WORKS: CHAMBER MUSIC: brass trio, 1976;
<u>Concert music</u>, chamber ensemble, 1977; quartet
for flute, horn, violin, cello, 1977; <u>3 songs</u>
for mezzo-soprano, vibraphone, violin, cello,
1978; <u>2 sonnets</u>, baritone, cello, piano, 1978.
 220 W. 93rd St., New York, NY 10024

GREENE, MARGO LYNN
 b. Brooklyn, N.Y., 10 June 1948. Studied privately with Bülent Arel; with Mario Davidovsky
and Vladimir Ussachevsky, Columbia Univ.; with
Louis Calabro at Bennington Coll. and privately.
She was an assistant at Columbia-Princeton Electronic Music Center, 1972-74.
 WORKS: ORCHESTRA: <u>5 songs</u>, mezzo-soprano
and orch., 1972; CHAMBER MUSIC: movement for
string quartet, 1969; <u>Study</u> for solo clarinet,
1971; <u>Variations</u>, solo clarinet, 1972; <u>Shortcut</u>,
piano solo, 1975; quintet for flute, oboe,
clarinet, violin, cello, 1977; ELECTRONIC TAPE:
<u>Targets</u>, 1973.
 210 W. 90th St., Apt. 12M, New York, NY
10024

GREENWALD, JAN CAROL
 b. New York, N.Y., 12 July 1952. Studied with
James Tenney, Stephen Mosko, and Morton
Subotnick, California Inst. of the Arts, B.F.A.
1975.
 WORKS: ORCHESTRA: <u>Durations</u>; CHAMBER MUSIC:
<u>Mobiles 1-4</u>, (actual hanging mobiles which, with
instructions furnished by the composer, serve as
scores to be used with varying groups of instruments); <u>Duration 2</u>, tape.
 480 Broome St., New York, NY 10013

GREGORIAN, ROUBEN
 b. Tiflis, Russia, 23 Sept. 1915; to U.S. 1952;
U.S. citizen. Studied at Armenian Central Coll.,
Tabriz, Iran; Tehran Cons., Iran; with Arthur
Honneger, Forestier, and Fournier in Paris. He

was violin instructor, Tehran Cons., 1946-51,
director, 1948-51; conductor, Tehran Symphony,
1948-51; has been faculty member, Boston Cons.,
from 1952; was founder, Komitas String Quartet,
1955; director, Komitas Choral Society, from
1955; conductor, Portland, Maine, Symphony,
1959-62; from 1952, annual guest conductor at
Boston Pops.
 WORKS: ORCHESTRA: <u>Iranian suite</u>; <u>Tatragoms
bride</u>, symphonic poem; <u>Nairy symphonic suite</u>;
<u>Hega fantasie</u>; symphony #1; horn concerto,
Boston Pops, 1974; CHAMBER MUSIC: string quartets; <u>Scherzo</u>, piano; pieces for violin and
piano; CHORUS: <u>Easter cantata</u>, with orch.;
Iranian folk songs; other choral and solo songs.
 617 Betts Rd., Belmont, MA 02178

GRESSEL, JOEL
 b. Cleveland, Ohio, 23 Mar. 1943. Studied with
Martin Beykan, Arthur Berger, Harold Shapero,
Brandeis Univ.; with Milton Babbitt, Edward T.
Cone, J. K. Randall, and Earl Kim, Princeton
Univ. He is faculty member at Baruch Coll.
 WORKS: CHAMBER MUSIC: <u>Klavierstück</u>, for 7
instruments, 1967; <u>Notes</u>, solo flute, 1969;
<u>Piece</u> for unaccompanied cello, 1970; <u>Piece</u> for
piano, 1969-71; COMPUTER SYNTHESIZED: <u>Pvibes</u>,
3 canons, 1971-72; <u>Exercycles</u>, 1972; <u>Points in
time</u>, won the 1974 competition in electronic
music of the Internat. Society for Contemporary
Music.
 945 West End Ave., #8B, New York, NY 10025

GRIEB, HERBERT
 b. Syracuse, N.Y., 17 Sept. 1898; d. Birmingham,
Ala. He was organist at radio station WAPI,
1930-34; music director, WBRC, 1944-50; music
director, Episcopal Church of the Advent and
Temple Emanuel, both in Birmingham. His choral
works included a carol service for children; an
Easter carol service; <u>Magnificat</u>; <u>Hail the day</u>.

GRIFFES, CHARLES TOMLINSON
 b. Elmira, N.Y., 17 Sept. 1884; d. New York, N.Y.,
8 Apr. 1920. Studied with Engelbert Humperdinck
in Berlin, 1903-7. He taught at Hackley School
for Boys, Tarrytown, N.Y., 1908-20.
 WORKS: THEATRE: <u>The Kairn of Koridwen</u>,
dance drama, woodwinds, harp, celesta, piano,
1916; <u>Sho-jo</u>, pantominic drama, 4 woodwinds, 4
strings, harp, percussion, 1917; ORCHESTRA:
<u>Pleasure dome of Kubla Khan</u>, 1912-16; <u>The white
peacock</u>, 1917 (also for piano); <u>Poem</u>, flute and
orch., 1918; CHAMBER MUSIC: <u>2 sketches on Indian
themes</u>, string quartet, 1922; PIANO: <u>3 tone
pictures</u>: <u>The lake at evening</u>, <u>The vale of
dreams</u>, <u>The night wind</u>, 1915; <u>Fantasy pieces</u>:
<u>Barcarolle</u>, <u>Notturno</u>, <u>Scherzo</u>, 1915; <u>Roman
sketches</u>: <u>The white peacock</u>, <u>Nightfall</u>, <u>The
fountain of Acqua Paola</u>, <u>Clouds</u>, 1916; sonata in
F, 1921; many choral works and songs.

GRIFFIN, ELINOR REMICK WARREN. See WARREN, ELINOR
REMICK

GRIFFIS, ELLIOT
 b. Boston, Mass., 28 Jan. 1893; d. Los Angeles,
Calif., 8 June 1967. Studied with Horatio

GRIFFITH, PETER

Parker, Yale Univ.; with Stuart Mason and George
W. Chadwick, New England Cons.; at New York Coll.
of Music, D.M. He received Pulitzer and Juilliard scholarships. He taught in several schools
in the U.S., privately in Paris and Vienna; then
was head of the theory department, Progressive
Series Teachers Coll.
     WORKS: OPERA: Port of pleasure, 1 act;
ORCHESTRA: Paul Bunyan--Colossus, symphonic
poem, 1926-34; symphony, 1931; Fantastic pursuit, string orch., 1941; A Persian fable; Yon
Green Mountain suite; Montevallo, concerto
grosso for piano, organ, strings; Sunlight and
shadow, soprano, narrator, and orch.; CHAMBER
MUSIC: suite for trio; violin sonata; The Aztec
flute, 1946; Elegy, violin and piano; piano
sonata; woodwind quartet; Letters from a Maine
farm, piano; Playa laguna--arabesque, piano; and
songs.

GRIFFITH, PETER
     b. Ann Arbor, Mich., 1943. Studied with Ross
Lee Finney, Univ. of Michigan, M.A. 1970; was
the first guitarist to be admitted to the school
of music. His One string quartet was one of four
selected for recording in the first annual Composers String Quartet Composition Contest, sponsored by the quartet and the New England Cons.,
1970.

GRIFFITH, ROBERT B.
     b. Washington, D.C., 1914. Studied at Univ. of
Kentucky, B.S. 1937, M.A. in music education
1954. He taught in Louisville schools, 1937-61;
then was on the faculty at Univ. of Louisville
to 1978. He was horn player in the Louisville
Orchestra from 1949.
     WORKS: BAND: Defiance march; Courier-
Journal march; 2 hymns; 2 more hymns; Britannica
march; many unpublished works.
     1837 Roanoke Ave., Louisville, KY 40205

GRIGSBY, BEVERLY PINSKY
     b. Chicago, Ill., 11 Jan. 1928. Studied with
Ernst Krenek and Gerald Strang, San Fernando
State Coll., B.A. 1961, M.A. 1963; with Aurelio
de la Vega, Robert Linn, and Ingolf Dahl, Univ.
of Southern California, 1973. She taught privately and in various schools, 1948-63; has been
faculty member, California State Univ. at Northridge, from 1963; has conducted research in
electronic music in her own studio.
     WORKS: CHAMBER MUSIC: Sonnet XI, voice
and piano, 1949; Dialogues, tenor and guitar,
1973; ELECTRONIC: The awakening, 1963; Ayamonn
the terrible, film score, 1964; Preludes, poems
of T. S. Eliot, voice and electronics, 1968;
Fragments from Augustine, the saint, dramatic
cantata for tenor, oboe, harp, percussion,
multimedia, 1972.
     17639 Osborne St., Northridge, CA 91324

GRIMES, DOREEN
     b. Weatherford, Tex., 1 Feb. 1932. Studied
with Jack Frederick Kilpatrick, Southern
Methodist Univ., B.M., M.M.; with Samuel Adler,
and George Morey, North Texas State Univ., Ph.D.
1966. She was director of her own music school,

1950-62; faculty member, Eastern New Mexico
Univ., Portales, 1962-71; then at Angelo State
Univ.
     WORKS: OPERA: Drugstore panorama, 1 act;
CHAMBER MUSIC: Americana, chamber orch.; VOCAL:
The canyon, chorus; It satisfies my longing,
solo; PIANO: A day in the country; Prelude and
allegro, 2 pianos.
     3202 Lindenwood, San Angelo, TX 76901

GRIMM, CARL HUGO
     b. Zanesville, Ohio, 31 Oct. 1890; d. Cincinnati,
Ohio, 25 Oct. 1978. Taught at Cincinnati Cons.,
1907-31; was organist in Cincinnati.
     WORKS: ORCHESTRA: Erotic poem, 1927;
Thanatopsis, 1928; Abraham Lincoln, a character
portrait, 1930; Montana, symphonic poem, 1943;
An American overture, 1946; trumpet concerto,
1948; symphony, 1950; Pennsylvania overture,
1954; CHAMBER MUSIC: Byzantine suite, 10 instruments, 1930; Little serenade, wind quintet, 1934;
cello sonata, 1945; also choral works, songs,
organ pieces.

GRISELLE, THOMAS
     b. Upper Sandusky, Ohio, 10 Jan. 1891; d. Holly-
wood, Calif., 27 Dec. 1955. Studied at Cincinnait Coll. of Music; with Nadia Boulanger and
Arnold Schoenberg in Europe. He won the Victor
Records prize of $10,000 for 2 American sketches,
1928. He was accompanist for Norah Bayes, Alice
Nielsen, Clarence Whitehill; taught at Muskingum
Coll.; settled in Hollywood in 1919.
     WORKS: PIANO: A keyboard symphony for 6
pianos; Tutti frutti; Czerny pilots a flying
saucer; SONGS: The cuckoo clock.

GROFÉ, FERDINAND RUDOLPH VON (FERDE)
     b. New York, N.Y., 27 Mar. 1892; d. Santa Monica,
Calif., 3 Apr. 1972. Studied with Pietro
Floridia in New York; at St. Vincent's Coll.;
received honorary doctorates, Illinois Wesleyan
Univ.; Western State Coll. of Colorado. He was
violist in the Los Angeles Symphony, 1909-19;
pianist and arranger, Paul Whiteman's Band,
1919-33; orchestrated George Gershwin's Rhapsody
in Blue, 1924; conducted his own works in Hollywood Bowl, Lewisohn Stadium, Robin Hood Dell,
etc.; appeared with his wife in 2-piano concerts.
     WORKS: ORCHESTRA: Grand Canyon suite, 1931;
Broadway at night; Symphony in steel, 1937, used
4 pairs of shoes, 2 brooms, locomotive bell,
pneumatic drill, compressed air tank, commissioned
by president of American Rolling Mills Company;
Tabloid; Death Valley suite; Mississippi suite;
Mark Twain suite; Hollywood suite; Milk, paid for
by a dairy; Wheels, paid for by an automobile
company; 3 shades of blue; New England suite;
Metropolis; Aviation suite; World's Fair suite,
1964; piano concerto; FILM SCORES: King of jazz;
Time out of mind; The return of Jesse James;
Minstrel man.

GROLNIC, SIDNEY
     b. Philadelphia, Pa., 15 Mar. 1946. Studied
privately with Harold Boatrite and Temple Painter.
In 1978-79, he was composer-in-residence under
the Penn. Council on the Arts Artists in Schools

program.
WORKS: STRING ORCHESTRA: <u>Overture</u>, with
solo violin; <u>Rhapsody</u>, with solo cello; <u>Elegy</u>,
with solo oboe; CHAMBER MUSIC: <u>Introduction and</u>
<u>allegro</u>, violin and piano; <u>Theme and variations</u>,
solo oboe; duo for oboe and bassoon; <u>Capriccio</u>,
violin and piano; CHORUS: <u>Psalm 130</u>; <u>Alleluia</u>;
<u>Kyrie eleison</u>.
c/o Blair Mill East, Apt. P, Horsham, PA
19044

GRONQUIST, ROBERT
b. Illinois, 15 Oct. 1938. Studied at Univ. of
Illinois; Univ. d'Aix-en-Provence; Univ. of
California, Berkeley. He received a Rockefeller
grant and an Aspen fellowship. He has been
faculty member at Smith Coll., Trinity Coll.,
and from 1972, at Simmons Coll.
WORKS: CHORUS: <u>This endris night</u>; <u>Quittez</u>
<u>pasteurs</u>; <u>Reflections</u>, women's voices and piano,
1977; MIXED MEDIA: <u>Revelation</u>, with assistance
from Robert Morris, electronics by Morton
Subotnick, 1972; <u>The Lord Zouches Maske</u>, in
collaboration with Arawana Campbell, Paul Earls,
and Larry Johnson, 1973.
219 Pond Ave., Brookline, MA 02146

GROSS, BETHUEL G.
b. Leavenworth, Kans., 7 Mar. 1905. Studied at
Washburn Coll., B.A., B.M.; Northwestern Univ.,
B.M., M.M., Ph.D.; Univ. of Chicago; Loyola
Univ. He has held faculty and administrative
posts at many colleges and universities; has
been organist and music director in Chicago
churches from 1940; also director, Suburban
Mental Health Referral Center, Niles, Ill.
WORKS: ORCHESTRA: 6 organ symphonies; 2
symphonic poems; CHORUS: <u>The lost star</u>; <u>Reflec-</u>
<u>tions on Christmas</u>, oratorio; <u>Americana</u>, ora-
torio, with orch., Chicago, 16 May 1976; <u>Again</u>
<u>we crucify</u>, oratorio, with orch., Chicago, 3
Apr. 1977; 5 modal carols; 6 modernistic carols;
<u>An ecumentical mass</u>; many anthems; KEYBOARD:
Christmas organ suite; <u>Ecclesiastical suite</u> for
organ; <u>Ballet suite</u> for 2 pianos, 1977; <u>6 pre-</u>
<u>ludes</u> for bell choir.

GROSS, CHARLES
b. Boston, Mass., 13 May 1934. Studied at
Harvard Univ., B.A.; New England Cons.; with
Darius Milhaud at Mills Coll. on a scholarship.
He was arranger for the West Point Band for 3
years; writes for industrials, cartoons, films.
WORKS: THEATRE: music for <u>The blacks</u>; <u>The</u>
<u>firebugs</u>; BAND: <u>An American folk suite</u>; <u>Songs</u>
<u>of the sea</u>; <u>Black-eyed Susie</u>; <u>Irish suite</u>; FILM
SCORE: <u>Robert Frost--A lover's quarrel with the</u>
<u>world</u>, documentary.
186 Riverside Dr., New York, NY 10024

GROSS, ROBERT A.
b. Colorado Springs, Colo., 23 Mar. 1914.
Studied with Bernard Wagenaar, Juilliard School,
1932; at Colorado Coll., A.B. 1940, Mus.D. 1967;
privately with Arnold Schoenberg in Los Angeles.
His awards include a Ford Found. grant; Mellon
Found. grant; Fulbright lectureship grant for
Korea, 1975. He was faculty member, Colorado

Coll., 1937-46; from 1949, at Occidental Coll.
WORKS: OPERA: <u>The bald soprano</u>, after
Ionesco, chamber opera; <u>Project 1521</u>, original
story; CHAMBER MUSIC: violin sonata; 5 string
quartets; sonatina for viola solo; <u>Epode</u>, solo
cello, 1955; octet, strings, woodwinds, piano;
<u>3-4-2</u>, violin and cello; <u>Passacaglia</u>, violin and
organ; <u>Chacounne</u>, soprano and violin; <u>Trivarow</u>
and <u>Cho-Sen variations</u>, both for clarinet,
violin, piano.
2989 Alta Laguna Blvd., Laguna Beach, CA
92651

GROSVENOR, RALPH L.
b. Grosvenor's Corners, N.Y., 5 Dec. 1893.
Studied with Huntington Woodman in New York;
composition with Ernest Bloch. After military
service in World War I, he remained in France
for further study on the organ. He has been
pianist, organist, choral director, singer,
accompanist, and teacher in the New York area.
He has written many sacred and secular songs.

GRUBER, ALBION
b. Savannah, Ga., 27 Oct. 1931. Studied at Univ.
of Alabama; with Samuel Adler and Wayne Barlow,
Eastman School of Music. His awards include
Music Teachers Nat. Assoc. award, 1962; NDEA
Title IV fellowship, Eastman School, 1966-69.
He was director, WUOA-FM, Univ. of Alabama, 1955-
57; faculty member, Savannah Country Day School,
1957-64; from 1964, at Nazareth Coll.
WORKS: ORCHESTRA: <u>Charade</u>; <u>Trichotomy</u>;
CHAMBER MUSIC: <u>Woodforms</u>, flute, clarinet,
violin, viola; trio for violin, clarinet, piano;
<u>Carriwichet</u>, woodwind ensemble; woodwind quintet;
CHORUS: <u>Mass for the people</u>.
Nazareth College, 4245 East Ave., Rochester,
NY 14610

GRUENBERG, LOUIS
b. Brest-Litovsk, Poland, 3 Aug. 1883; to U.S.
1885; d. Los Angeles, Calif., 9 June 1964.
Studied piano in New York and at Vienna Cons.;
composition with Ferrucio Busoni in Berlin. His
many awards included the Flagler prize; Heifetz
commission; Coolidge Medal; David Bispham Medal;
Juilliard award; RCA Victor prize, 1930; membership in the Nat. Inst. of Arts and Letters. He
toured Europe and the U.S. as pianist, 1912-19;
was chairman, composition department, Chicago
Musical Coll., several years; then lived in
Santa Monica, Calif.
WORKS: OPERA: <u>The witch of Brocken</u>, 1912;
<u>The bride of the gods</u>, 1913; <u>The man who married</u>
<u>a dumb wife</u>, 1921; <u>Jack and the beanstalk</u>, 1930;
<u>The Emperor Jones</u>, on O'Neill's play, was per-
formed by the Metropolitan Opera, New York, 7
Jan. 1933, and by the Michigan Opera Theater,
Detroit, 9 Feb. 1979; <u>Queen Helena</u>, 1936; <u>Green</u>
<u>mansions</u>, radio opera, 1937; <u>The miracle of</u>
<u>Flanders</u>, a mystery play, 1950; ORCHESTRA: 5
symphonies, 1919-48; 2 piano concertos; <u>The hill</u>
<u>of dreams</u>, 1919; <u>Vagabondia</u>, 1920; <u>Jazz suite</u>,
1928; <u>The enchanted isle</u>, 1929; <u>9 moods</u>, 1929;
<u>Music for an imaginary ballet</u>, 2 suites, 1929,
1944; <u>Serenade to a beauteous lady</u>, 1935; violin
concerto, Heifetz soloist, Philadelphia, 1 Dec.

GRUNDMAN, CLARE EWING

1944; CHAMBER MUSIC: 2 violin sonatas, 1912, 1919; suite, violin and piano, 1914; Indiscretions, string quartet, 1922; 4 whimsicalities, string quartet, 1923; cello sonatina, 1925; Jazzettes, violin and piano, 1926; 2 piano quintets, 1929, 1937; Diversions, string quartet, 1930; 2 string quartets, 1937, 1938; SONGS: Daniel Jazz, tenor and chamber ensemble, 1924; Creation, baritone and chamber ensemble, 1925; Animals and insects, voice and piano; 4 contrasting songs; PIANO: Jazzberries; Polychromatics, 1924; Jazz masks; 6 jazz epigrams; 3 jazz dances.

GRUNDMAN, CLARE EWING
b. Cleveland, Ohio, 11 May 1913. Studied at Ohio State Univ., B.S. 1934, M.A. 1940; composition with Paul Hindemith at Tanglewood, 1941. He taught in Kentucky public schools, 1935-57; at Ohio State Univ., 1937-41; since 1945, has been arranger and composer for radio, television, and Broadway shows.
    WORKS: BAND: 3 American folk rhapsodies; Burlesque; Little English suite; Holiday; Interval town; Music for a carnival; A medieval story; Western dance; Japanese rhapsody; Festive piece; Welsh rhapsody; Fantasy on American sailing songs; 3 sketches for winds; Tuba rhapsody; Nocturne, harp and winds; A colonial legend.
    R.F.D. 2, Box 346, South Salem, NY 10590

GRUNN, JOHN HOMER
b. West Salem, Wis., 5 May 1880; d. Los Angeles, Calif., 6 June 1944. Studied piano in Chicago and Berlin; taught piano in Chicago, Phoenix, and Los Angeles.
    WORKS: OPERETTAS: The Mars diamond; The golden pheasant; The isle of cuckoos; In a woman's reign; BALLETS: Xochitl; The flower goddess; ORCHESTRA: Hopi Indian dance; Zuni Indian suite; SONGS: Peyote drinking song; From desert and pueblo.

GRUSIN, MARTIN
b. Chicago, Ill., 15 Sept. 1933. Studied with Robert Moran, San Francisco Cons., B.M. 1971; with Robert Ashley and Terry Riley, Mills Coll., 1971-72; with Robert Erickson, Kenneth Gaburo, Wilbur Ogdon, Univ. of California, San Diego, M.A. 1975. His awards include the Elizabeth Mills Crothers award, 1971-72; Goodman fellowship for graduate study, 1976-77; Nat. Endowment for the Arts grant, 1977. He was jazz singer and arranger, 1954-67; in 1978, was appointed to the Educational Cultural Complex, San Diego, to teach jazz history and development.
    WORKS: ORCHESTRA: Centerpiece, with jazz soloists, 1974; CHAMBER MUSIC: Genesis I, clarinet, viola, cello, 1970; Variations, string quartet and tape, 1972; CHORUS: Sketches of Sodom, 1969; MULTIMEDIA: Chant, tape, computer-processed voices, experimental instruments, vocal harmonics, and vocal chant, dancer, and light painting, 1977.
    9240 Regents Rd., Apt. E, La Jolla, CA 92037

GUDAUSKAS, GIEDRA
b. Kaunas, Lith., 10 July 1923; U.S. citizen 1952. Studied voice and piano, Kaunas State Cons.; composition with Karel Jirak, Roosevelt Univ., B.M. 1952; film scoring and jazz improvisation at Univ. of California, Los Angeles, 1961-63. She was modern dance accompanist in Lithuania and Germany, 1940-44, in Chicago, 1946-49, in Los Angeles, 1963-65; teaches privately and is a free-lance composer.
    WORKS: THEATRE MUSIC: The canary, drama, 1955; Animal court, children's musical, 1954; Land of amber, drama, 1966; The brown nosed little bear, children's musical, 1970; The island, documentary film, 1976; CHAMBER MUSIC: Lithuanian suite, 2 cellos and piano, 1967; Impressions on 3 proverbs, piano and percussion, 1969; Variations, piano; Rondo, piano; SONGS: The swallow; Little girl and the hope clover; Love dream; The journey; I'm alone; Requiem for my friends; The world of God; and others.
    1030 Gretna Green Way, Los Angeles, CA 90049

GUDEHUS, DONALD H.
b. Jersey City, N.J., 13 Sept. 1939. Studied piano, guitar, clarinet; composition with John Vincent, Douglas Leady, Paul Chihara, Theodore Norman, David Raskin, Univ. of California, Los Angeles. He was guitar instructor, Mt. St. Mary's Coll., 1970-74.
    WORKS: PIANO: Suite of dances in various styles, 1973; FILM SCORE: Water in the wilderness, educational film, 1973; solo instrumental works and electronic music.
    5115 W. 134th Place, Hawthorne, CA 90250

GUDENIAN, HAIG
b. Caeserea, Asia Minor, 19 May 1886; to U.S. 1918. Studied violin with Cesar Thomson in Brussels; violin with Otakar Sevcik, composition with Viteslav Novak in Prague, where he also began his lifelong study of folk tunes. In 1918 he married the concert pianist Katherine Lowe; together they toured the U.S. and England.
    WORKS: ORCHESTRA: O. W.; H. H.; Nostalgia; Mulawiah II; In memoriam; Requiem; Over the graves forward; many dances, folk songs, and works for drums accompanied by Western instruments.

GUENTHER, RALPH R.
b. Concordia, Mo., 24 Nov. 1914. Attended Central Methodist Coll., A.B.; Univ. of Rochester, M.A.; studied with Bernard Rogers, Edward Royce, Anthony Donato, and Burrill Phillips, Eastman School of Music, Ph.D. He has been professor, Texas Christian Univ., from 1948; principal flutist, Ft. Worth Opera Orch., from 1949, and Ft. Worth Symphony, from 1956.
    WORKS: CHAMBER MUSIC: Variations, oboe and strings; Eclogue, strings; Improvisations, piano; suite for 2 flutes; suite for solo flute, 1978; CHORUS: Celebration, oratorio, commissioned by Texas Christian Univ. for its centennial, 9 Nov. 1973; Set of four, a cappella; SONGS: 2 Shakespeare sonnets, soprano, flute, cello; Bells of Ireland, song cycle, Ft. Worth, 24 Feb. 1976; How fast the moon, song cycle to texts by John

Newcome, 1978.
4604 Barwick Dr., Fort Worth, TX 76132

GUINALDO, NORBERTO
b. Buenos Aires, Arg., 2 Mar. 1937; U.S. citizen
1970. Studied at La Plata Univ., with Alberto
Ginastero, Catholic Univ., Buenos Aires; Univ.
of California at Riverside; organ improvisation
with Jean Langlais and Jean Guillou in Paris.
His awards include J. Fischer & Bros. Centennial
Competition prize, 1964; Southwestern Youth
Music Festival prize, 1966; 2 prizes, Organ
Historical Society competition, 1966, 1967;
prize, American Guild of Organists contest, 1970.
He has been concert organist and church and
temple organist in the U.S. from 1959.
WORKS: ORGAN: Toccata and fugue, 1964;
partita on: In memory of the crucified, 1964;
Prelude and fugue, 1966; Passacaglia, 1966;
Suite for an old tracker organ, 1967; Fantasia
and fugue, 1967; 3 litanies, 1968; 5 Spanish
carols, 1968; Dialogues, with brass and timpani,
1969; Laudes tonales, with brass quintet, 1970;
Prelude and postlude, 1975; Meditation on 2
sacramental hymns, 1975; Intercession, 1975;
Spanish organ carols, 1976; also some chamber
pieces.
11247 Crewe St., Norwalk, CA 90650

GUION, DAVID WENDELL
b. Ballinger, Tex., 15 Dec. 1892; d. Dallas,
Tex., 17 Oct. 1981. Attended Polytechnic Coll.,
Ft. Worth; studied with Leopold Godowsky in
Vienna; at Howard Payne Coll., Brownwood, Texas,
D.M. He taught piano at Chicago Musical Coll.,
1925-27, but was mainly composer and performer;
gave many complete programs of his works in New
York at Roxy Theatre, Town Hall, Carnegie Hall,
Madison Square Garden, etc.; with NBC Symph.,
Dallas Symph., Houston Symph., etc.; and on
radio and television.
WORKS: BALLET: Western ballet; Shingandi,
primitive African ballet; ORCHESTRA: Texas
suite; Prairie suite; Sheep and goat walkin' to
the pasture; Southern nights; Alley tunes; Suite
for orchestra; many choral pieces and songs including Home on the range; Carry me home to the
lone prairie; and arrangements of American folk
songs.

GULESIAN, GRACE WARNER
b. Lawrence, Mass., 16 May. Attended Radcliffe
Coll.; studied piano with Agide Jacchia; composition with Karl Weigl and Frederick Converse.
WORKS: OPERETTAS: A honeymoon in 2000;
Princess Marina; Dick Whittington and his cat;
Cape Cod Ann; BALLET: Ballet of Bacchus; Ballet
of Nubi; songs and piano pieces.
85 Commonwealth Ave., Chestnut Hill, MA
02167

GUMP, RICHARD
b. San Francisco, Calif., 22 Jan. 1906. Studied
at Stanford Univ.; California School of Fine
Arts; and with Dominico Brescia. He joined the
staff of Gump's Retail Store in 1925, has been
president since 1947; under the pseudonym Dr.

Fritz Guckenheimer, he organized the Guckenheimer
Sauer Kraut Band in 1948.
WORKS: ORCHESTRA: 7 variations on an
American theme; Polynesian impression; CHAMBER
MUSIC: clarinet quintet; violin sonata; piano
sonata; Cambodian impression, string quartet;
oboe sonata; Fantasia, piano, 4 hands; CHORUS:
Gift of December, cantata; and songs.
c/o Gump's, 250 Post St., San Francisco, CA
94108

GUNTHER SPRECHER, WILLIAM
b. Saarbrücken, Germany, 20 Jan. 1924; U.S.
citizen 1955. Studied piano, theory, and conducting in Germany and with Paul Ben Haim in
Israel; piano in New York with Isabelle
Vengerova. His awards include the Robert Stolz
Medallion, Vienna, 1973; 3 ASCAP special awards.
He was a member of the First Piano Quartet, which
toured the U.S. and Europe; from 1969, has been
music director, Radio Station WEVD; from 1971,
director, Bronx Philharmonic; from 1976, music
director, Temple Sholom, Greenwich Conn.
WORKS: ORCHESTRA: Jerusalem concerto,
piano and orch., 1967; VOCAL: The Yinglish song
book; Great is thy faith, Biblical cantata; Si
j'fais ca, song; 3 ghetto songs; Ghetto factort
76, cantata; PIANO: Variations on a theme by
Paganini; piano sonata; theme and variations;
First love, tango; also theme music for various
radio serials on WEVD.
2235 Cruger Ave., Bronx, NY 10467

GUSIKOFF, MICHEL
b. New York, N.Y., 15 May 1893; d. New York, 10
July 1978. Studied with Franz Kneisel and Percy
Goetschius at Juilliard School. He was concert-
master with the Philadelphia Orch., New York
Symph. Orch., NBC Orch.; associate conductor of
the Pittsburgh Symph. Orch.
WORKS: ORCHESTRA: American concerto,
violin and orch., commissioned by Paul Whiteman;
Fantasy, viola and orch.; Variations on Oh,
Susannah, string orch.; and Gershwin paraphrases
for violin and piano.

GUSTAFSON, DWIGHT LEONARD
b. Seattle, Wash., 20 Apr. 1930. Studied with
Carlisle Floyd and John Boda, Florida State
Univ., D.Mus. 1967. His awards include a grad-
uate fellowship, 1966-67; prizes in the Erskine
Coll. anthem concerts, 1964, Broadman Press
anthem contest, 1965, Charleston Choral Society
contest. He has been dean, School of Fine Arts,
Bob Jones Univ., from 1956.
WORKS: THEATRE: The hunted, 1-act opera;
The jailer, 1-act opera; music for Antigone and
Henry IV; ORCHESTRA: Prelude, strings and harp;
CHORUS: 3 prophecies, oratorio, with orch.;
Ring out ye crystal spheres, with orch.; 3 songs
from American poets, with brass; numerous short
choral works; music for 6 educational and reli-
gious films.
111 Stadium View Dr., Greenville, SC 29614

GUTCHE, GENE
b. Berlin, Germany, 3 July 1907; to U.S. 1907.
Studied with Donald Ferguson, Univ. of Minnesota,

GYRING, ELIZABETH

M.A. 1950; with Philip Greeley Clapp, Iowa State
Univ., Ph.D. 1953. His many honors include 4
creative music scholarships, 1947-50; Univ. of
Minnesota Centennial prize, 1958; Albuquerque
Symph. Nat. prize, 1961; Oscar Espla Internat.
prize, 1962; 2 Premio Citta di Trieste, 1969,
1971; Louis Moreau Gottschalk Gold Medal, 1970;
3 Guggenheim fellowships, 1963, 1964, 1965;
Ford Found. grant, 1976; Nat. Endowment for the
Arts grant, 1976-77; many commissions.
   WORKS: ORCHESTRA: 6 symphonies, 1950-71;
Rondo capriccioso, with use of microtones, 1953;
piano concerto, 1956; cello concerto, 1957;
Holofernes overture, 1959; Timpani concertante,
1961; violin concerto, 1962; Bongo divertimento,
1962; Genghis Khan, 1963; Raquel, 1963; Rites in
Tenochtitlan, 1964; Gemini, uses microtones and
piano, 4 hands, 1965; Hsiang Fei, 1966; Aesop
fables suite, 1966-67; Classic concerto for
orch., 1967; Epimetheus, USA, 1969; Icarus,
1976; Bi-centurion, 1976; Perseus and Andromeda,
1977; Akhenaten, Milwaukee, 15 Feb. 1980; CHAMBER
MUSIC: 4 string quartets; 3 piano sonatas; and
choral works.
   10 Birchwood Lane, White Bear Lake, MN
55110

GYRING, ELIZABETH
   b. Vienna, Austria, 1886; U.S. citizen 1944; d.
New York, N.Y., 1970. Studied at Vienna Acad. of
Music, with Joseph Marx in harmony and counterpoint, with Ludwig Czaczkes in piano. The works
listed below date from 1942 and later.
   WORKS: ORCHESTRA: symphony; 4 pieces; concerto for oboe and string orch.; Scherzo, violin
concerto; Rondo; Larghetto; Sinfonietta 1 and 2,
string orch.; Furioso; 3 divertimentos, flute,
clarinet, horn, string orch.; CHAMBER MUSIC:
suite for violin and piano; 2 intermezzi, oboe
and piano; Concert piece, oboe and piano; Allegro, woodwind quartet; Fugue in old style, woodwind quartet; 5 pieces, clarinet and piano; 10
canons, 2 and 3 woodwinds; sextet, woodwind
quintet and horn; trio for oboe, clarinet, piano;
Scherzando, solo clarinet; clarinet quintet;
woodwind quintet, 1961; Arabesque, solo bassoon;
16 fugues for clarinet and string trio; Capriccio, 4 clarinets; CHORUS: The reign of violence
is over, Longfellow text, with string orch.;
Enoch, women's voices and strings; My country,
Russell Davenport text, with 4 soloists and
orch.; The secret of liberty, Davenport text;
many other works for chorus and for solo voice;
KEYBOARD: 2 piano sonatas; organ sonata; Fantasies, 1-16, organ; Prelude and fugue, 1-3,
organ; Theme and variations, 2 pianos; Theme,
variations and fugue, organ.

HA, JAE EUN
   b. Seoul, Korea, 16 Sept. 1937; U.S. citizen
1977. Studied with David Van Vactor, Univ. of
Tennessee; with Donald Erb, Cleveland Inst. of
Music; D.M.A. 1974. His awards include Knoxville Symph. Orch. scholarship, 1966-70; Nat.
Endowment for the Arts grant, 1972; first place,
7th Seoul Music Festival, 1975. He was teaching
fellow, Cleveland Inst., 1972-73; has been
faculty member, Mississippi Valley State Univ.,

from 1970.
   WORKS: ORCHESTRA: Theme and variation,
1969; 2 pieces, winds and percussion, 1970; 2
symphonies, 1971, #2 premiere, Cleveland, 22
Jan. 1974; CHAMBER MUSIC: 3 studies for percussion; tuba quartet; Sanjo, solo flute; sonata
for clarinet and string quartet, 1974; 3 pieces
for tuba, 1976; trio for trumpet, percussion,
cello, New York, May 1974; Sori 1, chamber ensemble, 1975; Sonic variables, trumpet, 1976.
   203 W. Jefferson Ave., Greenwood, MS 38930

HAACK, BRUCE C.
   b. Alberta, Canada, 4 May 1932. Studied at
Univ. of Alberta, B.A. He has received commis-
sions from the New York Orpheum Symph. and the
New York Ballet Club. He founded the publishing
firm, Dimension 5.
   WORKS: STAGE SCORES: How to make a man;
The kumquat in the persimmon tree; BALLET: The
constant she; Les etapes; ORCHESTRA: Windsong;
Sweet Adeline; PIANO: Mass for solo piano.

HABAN, SISTER M. TERESINE
   b. Columbus, Ohio, 15 Jan. 1914. Studied with
Bernard Dieter, Coll. of St. Francis, Ill.; with
Wayne Barlow, Eastman School of Music. She was
professor, Coll. of St. Francis, 1958-75.
   WORKS: THEATRE: musical score for The bells
of St. Francis, 1965; CHAMBER MUSIC: sonata-
allegro, trumpet and piano, 1970; Piece for
chamber orch., 1970; CHORUS: Mass in honor of
St. Ambrose, 1959; Hymn of praise, women's voices
and organ, 1965; miscellaneous hymns, antiphons,
psalms; KEYBOARD: Prelude.
   500 Wilcox St., Joliet, IL 60435

HABER, LOUIS
   b. Brooklyn, N.Y., 1915. Studied violin with
Leo Portnoff; composed many small pieces and
studies, 1935-42; then spent 4 years in the U.S.
Army Air Force. At the end of his service, he
studied with Darius Milhaud at the Paris Cons.
   WORKS: CHAMBER MUSIC: Parade, blues and
allegro, flute, violin, piano; violin sonata;
violin sonatina; suite for violin solo; trio for
flute, violin, piano; 6 miniatures, flute and
violin.
   145 Henry St., Brooklyn, NY 11201

HADDAD, DONALD
   b. Marietta, Ohio, 11 Jan. 1935. Studied with
Ernst von Dohnanyi and Karl Ehrendt, Ohio Univ.
He received annual ASCAP awards, 1967-72. He
has held faculty posts at West Texas State Univ.,
1958-61; Amarillo Coll., 1961-63; Interlochen
Arts Acad., 1963-66; Colorado State Univ., 1966-
70; Shenandoah Cons., 1970-73; Univ. of Kentucky,
1973-77.
   WORKS: ORCHESTRA: horn concerto; BAND:
Adagio and allegro, with solo horn; Air and
adagio, wind quintet and band; Grand processional;
Introduction and dance; Libyani; Valley Forge
fantasy; Allegro giocoso, horn and band; 4 symphonic sketches; WIND ENSEMBLE: Blues au vent,
woodwind quintet; Contrpunctus and quartal piece,
4 horns; Encore 1812, woodwind quintet; Fugue,
brass choir; pieces for solo winds and piano.

HADDEN, FRANCES ROOTS
b. Hankow, China, 24 Aug. 1910, daughter of the
Episcopal Bishop of Hankow. Attended Mt. Holyoke
Coll., B.A.; received an Otto Kahn scholarship
for music study. She taught in China, 1932-34;
toured as a pianist in the U.S., Europe, and Far
East, 1934-40; then with her husband, Richard
Hadden as duo-pianist. On the invitation of
Premier Chou En Lai, they returned to China in
1972 to present the first performance of her
Lu-Shan suite for 2 pianos.
WORKS: THEATRE: music for A statesman's
dream; The good road, a revue; The hurricane;
Jotham Valley, a musical; The crowning experience,
musical play; Turning of the tide, an Asian
musical; and many songs.
Cedar Point, Mackinac Island, MI 49757

HADLEY, HENRY KIMBALL
b. Somerville, Mass., 20 Dec. 1871; d. New York,
N.Y., 6 Sept. 1937. Studied with Stephen Emery
and George W. Chadwick, New England Cons.; with
Eusebius Mandiczewski in Vienna. His many honors
included Paderewski prize, 1901; New England
Cons. prize, 1901; Nat. Fed. of Music Clubs
$1000 prize, 1909; William Hinshaw prize, 1917;
honorary doctorate, Tufts Coll., 1925; election
to the Nat. Inst. of Arts and Letters and American Acad. of Arts and Letters; French government Order of Merit. He was music director,
St. Paul's School, Garden City, N.Y., 1895-
1902; conducted in Germany, 1905-9; Seattle
Symph., 1909-11; San Francisco Symph., 1911-15;
was associate conductro, New York Phil., 1915-
22; conducted in Europe and Buenos Aires; Manhattan Symph., 1929-32; opening of the Berkshire
Music Festival, 1933. He founded the Nat. Assoc.
of American Composers and Conductors, 1932.
WORKS: OPERA: Nancy Brown, comic opera;
Safie, 1909; Azora, daughter of Montezuma, 1917;
Merlin and Vivien; Bianca; Cleopatra's night; A
night in old Paris, 1925; The atonement of Pan,
a festival play; incidental music to plays;
ORCHESTRA: 5 symphonies, 1897-1934; 8 overtures;
Salome, symphonic poem, 1909; Lucifer, symphonic
poem, 1913; 4 suites; piano concerto; The cul-
prit Fay, 1909; ballet suites; CHAMBER MUSIC:
2 piano quintets; 2 string quartets; 2 piano
trios; violin sonata; many choral works, songs;
FILM SCORE: When a man loves.

HAEUSSLER, PAUL
b. Ravena, N.Y., 13 July 1895. Studied with
Felix Deyo, Brooklyn Cons. He was organist,
Ainslee Street Presbyterian Church, Brooklyn,
for 25 years. His works include sacred songs
and choral pieces.

HAGEMAN, RICHARD
b. Leeuwarden, Holland, 9 July 1882; U.S.
citizen 1915; d. Beverly Hills, Calif., 6 Mar.
1966. Studied at Brussels Cons. and Royal Cons.
of Amsterdam. He received the David Bispham
Medal, 1931. He was conductor, Royal Opera
House, Amsterdam, 1899-1903; came to U.S. as
accompanist for Yvette Guilbert, 1906; conducted
Metropolitan Opera House, 1908-26; was guest
conductor of many orchestras; taught at Curtis

Inst. and Chicago Musical Coll.; went to Hollywood, 1938, conducted the Hollywood Bowl Orch.
for 6 seasons.
WORKS: OPERA: Caponsacchi, 1931; ORCHESTRA:
The crucible, soli, chorus, and orch.; I hear
America calling, with baritone solo; Overture in
a nutshell; Suite for strings; SONGS: Do not go,
my love; At the well; The night has a thousand
eyes; Charity; many others; FILM SCORES: Stage
coach; The long voyage home; The Shanghai
gesture; If I were king; Mourning becomes
Electra; She wore a yellow ribbon.

HAGER, REV. CARL
b. Plymouth, Ind., 15 Oct. 1911. Studied with
Leon Stein and Alexander Tcherepnin, DePaul Univ.
He was faculty member, Univ. of Notre Dame,
1955-75.
WORKS: BAND: Sonatine; CHORUS: And time
shall be no longer, cantata; Mass in English;
and organ compositions.

HAGGH, RAYMOND HERBERT
b. Chicago, Ill., 4 Sept. 1920. Studied with
Robert Delaney at Northwestern Univ., B.M., M.M.;
with Randall Thompson, Harvard Univ.; and with
Bernard Heiden, Indiana Univ., Ph.D. He was
faculty member, Memphis State Univ., 1950-66;
from 1960 has been professor, Univ. of Nebraska.
His works for orchestra, chorus and orch.,
churus, and chamber groups were all written and
performed before 1965.
1725 S. 52nd St., Lincoln, NB 68501

HAHN, CARL
b. Indianapolis, Ind., 23 Oct. 1874; d. Cincinnati, Ohio, 13 May 1929. Studied with Otto
Singer, Cincinnati Coll. of Music; played cello
in Theodore Thomas Orchestra; conducted San
Antonio Orch., 1900-11, New York Arion Assoc.,
1914-20, and other groups. He wrote choral works
and songs.

HAHN, SANDRA
b. Spokane, Wash., 5 Jan. 1940. Studied with
William Brandt, Washington State Univ.; with
Robert Crane, Univ. of Wisconsin. She won an
award in the Wisconsin State Music Teachers
composition contest for a cello sonata. She
was pianist, Milwaukee Symph. Orch., 1966-67;
has been faculty member, Univ. of Idaho, from
1970.
WORKS: THEATRE: music for The cave
dwellers, commissioned by Washington State Univ.
speech and drama dept.; CHAMBER MUSIC: Variations, flute and piano; Scherzo, piano; harp
sonatina; Toccata, piano; cello sonata; piano
trio; Fantasy, piano; 5 miniatures, flute and
piano; Sonorities, flute, harp, percussion.
719 E. Mabelle, Moscow, ID 83843

HAIEFF, ALEXEI
b. Blagoveshchensk, Russia, 25 Aug. 1914; to
U.S. 1931. Studied with Rubin Goldmark and
Frederick Jacobi, Juilliard School; with Nadia
Boulanger in Paris, 1938-39; at American Acad.
in Rome. His awards include a Fulbright grant,
1942; American Acad. in Rome medal, 1942; Lili

HAIGH, MORRIS

Boulanger prize, 1943; Guggenheim fellowships, 1946, 1949; fellow, American Acad. in Rome, 1947-48, composer-in-residence, 1952-53, 1958-59; N.Y. Music Critics' Circle award, 1952; UNESCO recording award, 1958. He was professor, Univ. of Buffalo, 1962-68; composer-in-residence, Univ. of Utah, 1968-71.

WORKS: BALLET: The Princess Zondilda, 1946; Beauty and the beast, 1947; Ballet in E, 1955; ORCHESTRA: 3 symphonies, 1942, 1957, 1961; Divertimento, 1944; violin concerto, 1948; piano concerto, 1950; Eclogue, harp and strings, 1963; Eloge, chamber orch., 1967; Caligula, baritone and orch., New York, 5 Nov. 1971; CHAMBER MUSIC: sonatina for string quartet, 1937; Bagatelles, oboe and bassoon, 1939; Serenade, woodwind trio and piano, 1942; sonata for 2 pianos, 1945; Eclogue, cello and piano, 1947; string quartet, 1953; La nouvelle Heloise, harp and strings, 1953; piano sonata, 1955; cello sonata, 1965; Gifts and semblances, piano, 1976; songs and piano pieces.

c/o Chappell & Co., 801 7th Ave., New York, NY 10019

HAIGH, MORRIS
b. San Diego, Calif., 26 Jan. 1932. Studied with Carl Parrish and Halsey Stevens, Pomona Coll., B.M. 1953; with Bernard Rogers, Samuel Adler, Wayne Barlow, Eastman School of Music, M.A. 1954, Ph.D. 1973. His awards include a Woodrow Wilson fellowship, 1953; awards from the Los Angeles Horn Club and Los Angeles Chapter, American Guild of Organists, 1962; Howard Hanson prize, for winds, 1972, for an orchestral work, 1973. Following discharge from military service in 1956, he was computer programmer and systems analyst until 1970, when he decided to resume studies in music at Eastman and devote full time to music.

WORKS: ORCHESTRA: Music for orchestra, 1963; Night song; Scene for orchestra, 1964; 2 studies for string orch., 1971; concerto for wind quintet and orch., 1973; WIND ENSEMBLE: Music for winds, quintet, 1970; Symphonic variations, 1972; Pantomimes, brass and percussion, 1973; CHAMBER MUSIC: Serenade, flute and piano; Fantasia, horns and organ, 1962; string quartet, 1968; PIANO: 24 preludes, 1966.

259 Barrington St., Rochester, NY 14607

HAILE, EUGEN
b. Ulm, Germany, 21 Feb. 1873; to U.S. 1903; d. Woodstock, N.Y., 14 Aug. 1933. Studied at Stuttgart Cons. His works include a musical setting for a spoken drama, The happy ending, performed in New York, 21 Aug. 1916; an opera, Harold's dream, performed in Woodstock, N.Y., 30 June 1933; and many songs to German texts.

HAILSTORK, ADOLPHUS C.
b. Rochester, N.Y., 17 Apr. 1941. Studied with Mark Fax, Howard Univ.; with David Diamond and Vittorio Giannini, Manhattan School of Music; with H. Owen Reed, Michigan State Univ., Ph.D. 1971. His awards include the 1977 award of Coll. Band Directors Nat. Assoc. He was faculty member, Youngstown State Univ., 1971-77; from

1977, at Norfolk State Coll.
WORKS: ORCHESTRA: Celebration, 1974; BAND: Out of the depths, 1976; WIND ENSEMBLE: Bagatelles for brass; Spiritual, brass octet, 1977; CHAMBER MUSIC: sonatine, flute and piano; violin sonata, 1979; PIANO: Capriccio for a departed brother; Spartacus speaks; Rhapsody; ORGAN: suite.

5344 Princess Ann Rd., Virginia Beach, VA 23462

HAIMO, ETHAN T.
b. St. Louis, Mo., 22 Mar. 1950. Studied with Ralph Shapey and Roger Sessions, Univ. of Chicago; with J. K. Randall, Milton Babbitt, and Paul Lansky, Princeton Univ., Ph.D. 1975. His awards include the Millard Binyon prize; Olga Menn award; and a Fromm fellowship to the Bennington Composers' Conf., 1971. He was faculty member, Boston Univ., 1975-76; from 1976, at Univ. of Notre Dame.

WORKS: Scene from Macbeth, soprano and chamber ensemble; 2 string quartets; Transformations, chamber ensemble; Variations, piano; Fantasy, cello; CHORUS: Absalom, my son; Psalms 23, 47, 150; COMPUTER-SYNTHESIZED TAPE: Convergence.

Music Dept., Univ. of Notre Dame, Notre Dame, IN 46556

HAINES, EDMUND
b. Ottumwa, Iowa, 15 Dec. 1914; d. Bronx, N.Y., 3 July 1974. Attended Univ. of Missouri, Kansas City; studied with Howard Hanson and Bernard Rogers, Eastman School of Music, Ph.D. 1941; studied also with Aaron Copland and Roy Harris. His honors include a Pulitzer award, 1941; Ford Found. grant, 1958; 2 Guggenheim fellowships, 1957, 1958; 2 Fulbright grants, 1966, 1967; Miami Univ. Sesquicentennial commission, 1959. He was faculty member, Univ. of Michigan, 1941-47; Sarah Lawrence Coll., 1948-74.

WORKS: ORCHESTRA: symphony, 1941; concertino for 7 soloists and orch., 1959; Rondino and variations; Informal overture; 3 dances; CHAMBER MUSIC: 4 string quartets; 2 piano sonatas; sonata for brass quintet; Toccata, for brass ensemble; VOCAL: Dialogue from the Book of Job (In memoriam Nov. 22, 1963), women's chorus; 4 loves, soprano and 7 instruments, 1972; ORGAN: Snow dance; Promenade, air and toccata, AGO award; MIXED MEDIA: Soliloquy, dialogue, and bacchanale, trio and tape, 1971.

HAIR, NORMAN J.
b. Covington County, Ala., 2 May 1931. Studied organ and church music at Univ. of Montevallo. He won first place in the Birmingham Art Festival competition, 1958, with his choral work, Prayer. He has been chairman, div. of fine arts, Gulf Coast Community Coll., from 1960. He has composed other choral works.

Gulf Coast Community College, Panama City, FL 32401

HAIRSTON, JESTER
b. N.C., 9 July 1901. Studied at Tufts Univ., B.A. 1929, and at Juilliard School. He has

received honorary doctorates from Univ. of
Massachusetts, Tufts Univ., and Univ. of the
Pacific. He was assistant conductor of the Hall
Johnson Choir for 15 years; conducted choirs for
radio and Broadway shows; in 1943, formed his
own choir; has arranged, composed and conducted
background scores for films. He has made 3
choral conducting trips to Africa, 2 to Europe,
and 1 to Mexico, as goodwill tours for the U.S.
State Dept.
  WORKS: CHORUS: Mary's little boy chile,
calypso for chorus; Elijah rock; Poor man
Lazrus; Amen; FILM SCORE: Lilies of the field,
1963; numerous arrangements.
  5047 Valley Ridge Ave., Los Angeles, CA
90043

HAJOS, KARL
  b. Budapest, Hungary, 28 Jan. 1889; d. Hollywood,
Calif., 1 Feb. 1950. Studied at Budapest Acad.
of Music. He settled in Hollywood in 1928 as
film composer.
  WORKS: OPERETTA: The black Pierrot; The
red cat; Natja; White lilacs; America sings;
ORCHESTRA: Phantasy, piano and orch.; Rhapsody
in waltz time; and many film scores.

HAKIM, TALIB RASUL
  b. Asheville, N.C., 8 Feb. 1940. Studied clar-
inet and piano at Manhattan School and New York
Coll. of Music; composition at New School for
Social Research. Among his teachers were Robert
Starer, William Sydeman, Hall Overton, David
Reck, Morton Feldman, Chou Wen-Chung, and
Ornette Coleman. His awards include 4 Bennington
Composers' Conf. fellowships; 5 ASCAP awards;
Creative Artists Public Service grant; 2 Nat.
Endowment for the Arts grants, 1973, 1975. He
taught at Pace Univ., 1970-72; from 1972, has
been on faculty at Nassau Community Coll.; was
visiting associate professor, Morgan State Univ.,
Baltimore, 1978-79. In 1973, on conversion to
Sufism, he changed his name from Stephen Chambers
to Talib Rasul Hakim.
  WORKS: ORCHESTRA: Visions of Ishwara,
1970; Re/Currences, 1974, Washington, D.C., 7
June 1975; Concepts, 1976; CONCERT JAZZ: Sketchy
blue-bop, 1973; CHAMBER MUSIC: Mutations, bass
clarinet, horn, trumpet, viola, cello, 1964;
Peace-mobile, woodwind quintet, 1964; Moments,
alto saxophone, bassoon, horn, 1966; Currents,
string quartet, 1967; Sound-gone, piano, 1967;
Placements, 5 percussion and piano, 1970; Time-
lessness, 4 brass, 2 percussion, bass, piano,
1970; Reflections on the 5th ray, narrator and
chamber orch., 1972; On being still--on the 8th,
4 woodwinds, cello, bass, piano, percussion,
1978; CHORUS: Sound-images, women's chorus and
orch., 1969; Tone-prayers, with percussion and
piano, 1973; SONGS: Ode to silence, soprano and
piano, 1964; 6 players and a voice, soprano and
instruments, 1964; Quote-Unquote, bass-baritone,
oboe, trumpet, percussion, 1967; Uranian-projec-
tions, soprano, percussion, piano, 1970; Music
for 9 players and soprano voice, 1977; Psalm of
Akhnaton (c. 1365-1348 B.C.), mezzo-soprano,
flute, piano, 1978; many other vocal and chamber
works.

3443 Carriage Hill Circle, #204, Randalls-
town, MD 21133

HALDEMAN, LYNN E.
  b. Portland, Oreg., 1 Apr. 1935. Studied with
Robert Crowley at Portland State Univ., B.S.
1958; with Homer Keller, Univ. of Oregon, M.S.
1963. His musical was selected for performance
in the 1973 Contemporary Series, Catawba Coll.,
Salisbury, N.C. He was public school music
educator in Oregon, 1960-72.
  WORKS: MUSICAL COMEDY: How to be a successful educator without really . . ., 2 acts,
Catawba Coll., 2-5 May 1973.

HALEN, WALTER J.
  b. Hamilton, Ohio, 17 Mar. 1930. Studied with
Karl Ahrendt, Ohio Univ.; with Anthony Donato,
Northwestern Univ.; and with Mark Walker, Ohio
State Univ. His awards include a fellowship,
Ohio State Univ., 1962; performance of Sinfonia
sonore at Tri-State Composers' Symposium, 1962;
Missouri Music Teachers Assoc. and Nat. Assoc.
commission, 1976. He taught in Ohio public
schools, 1955-61; was faculty member, Drury
Coll., 1962-67; from 1967, at Central Missouri
State Univ.
  WORKS: ORCHESTRA: Sinfonia sonore, 1957;
Icicle shadows, string orch., 1974-75; CHAMBER
MUSIC: violin sonata, 1958; string quartet,
1959; woodwind quartet, 1960; suite for violin
and viola, 1961; Prelude and dance, violin and
piano, 1970; Meditation, oboe, prepared piano,
percussion, 1970; 2 poems of dance, mezzo-
soprano, tenor, chamber ensemble, tape, 1976;
Stipulations, saxophone, piano, percussion, 1977;
teaching pieces and arrangements.
  Rte. 5, Green Acres, Warrensburg, MO 64093

HALL, CHARLES J.
  b. Houston, Tex., 17 Nov. 1925. Studied at
Andrews Univ., B.A. 1952; with Charles Garland,
Missouri Univ.; Univ. of New Mexico, M.M. 1960;
with H. Owen Reed and Paul Harder, Michigan
State Univ., Ph.D. 1970. His awards include a
Michigan State Univ. fellowship, 1968-69;
Sigvald Thompson award, 1970. He was high
school music teacher, 1956-67; from 1970,
faculty member, Andrews Univ.
  WORKS: ORCHESTRA: Recitative for orchestra,
1970; 5 microscopics, 1970; City in the sea,
with narrator, soprano, chorus; Ulalume, with
narrator, mezzo-soprano, Houston, 8 Feb. 1972;
Scherzo, just for fun, Port Royal, legend for
orch., 3 symphonic chuckles, 1978; symphony,
1978; BAND: Babylon suite; Fantasia on an early
advent hymn; CHAMBER MUSIC: Petite suite, woodwind trio; 5 short pieces, piano; and choral
works.
  Rte. 1, Box 397B, Berrien Springs, MI 49103

HALL, JAMES
  b. Buffalo, N.Y., 1930. As guitarist, has
played and recorded with many noted jazz groups;
at the Guitar, New York, 1972; has published
Pieces for guitar and strings.
  Music Dept., S.W. Texas State Univ., San
Marcos, TX 98666

HALL, REGINALD

HALL, REGINALD
b. Laurel, Md., 23 Jan. 1926. Studied at
Peabody Cons.; with Ross Lee Finney, Univ. of
Michigan; and with Halsey Stevens in Los Angeles.
He is an engineer who composes as an avocation.
His Elegy for orchestra won the George Gershwin
Memorial award, 1955, and was performed by the
New York Philharmonic, 21 Apr. 1956.

HALLOCK, PETER R.
b. Kent, Wash., 19 Nov. 1924. Studied with
George Frederick McKay at Univ. of Washington.
He received a Guggenheim fellowship, 1974. He
has been organist and choirmaster, St. Mark's
Cathedral, Seattle, from 1951. He has composed
choral and service music for the church.
1245 10th East, Seattle, WA 98102

HALLORAN, DONALD
b. Houston, Tex., 9 Jan. 1933. Studied with
James Ming, Lawrence Coll.; with Nicolas
Flagello, Manhattan School of Music; with
William P. Latham and Merrill Ellis, North Texas
State Univ. He taught in New York public
schools, 1961-70; was teaching fellow, North
Texas State Univ., 1970-73; from 1978, on faculty,
Albany Jr. Coll.
WORKS: BAND: Essay, 1970; CHAMBER MUSIC:
clarinet trio, 1965; Anna Livia Plurabelle,
contralto and chamber ensemble, 1971; Saxo-
phrenic, alto saxophone, percussion, piano,
1972; CHORUS: Moon soliloquy, Lorca text, 1972;
Psalm 117, 1972; MIXED MEDIA: brass quintet
with tape, 1972; Chant and rant, trombone and
tape, Nashville, 1973 Trombone Clinic.
2808 B Falcon Lane, Albany, GA 31707

HALLSTROM, HENRY
b. Hernosand, Sweden, 12 July 1906; U.S. citizen
c. 1920. Attended Univ. of California, A.B.;
Columbia Univ., M.A.; Univ. of Rochester, Ph.D.;
studied with Randall Thompson, Univ. of Virginia;
Howard Hanson, Eastman School of Music. He received several Ford Found. grants and an American
Guild of Organists compositions award. He was
faculty member, Randolph-Macon Women's Coll.,
1939-74.
WORKS: OPERA: Blood on the moon; ORCHESTRA:
symphony; CHORUS: God came like the dawn; Midsummer night's dream, women's voices; ORGAN:
Easter festival; 3 pieces on familiar hymn tunes;
numerous other choral and organ works; FILM
SCORE: The Oresteia.
70 Columbia Ave., Lynchburg, VA 24503

HALPERN, LEON
b. New York, N.Y., 15 May 1908. Studied at
Damrosch Cons.; Juilliard School; and with
Howard Brockway. His works include a ballet,
Angels and prejudices.

HALPERN, STELLA
b. Austria, 18 May 1923; U.S. citizen 1949.
Studied composition with Leo Kraft in New York.
She was faculty member, Queens Coll., 1968-71;
Queensborough Coll., 1971-75.
WORKS: CHAMBER MUSIC: 3 brevities, per-
cussion, trumpet, clarinet, piano; Music for 11

players; Movement for 5 players; Caprice, clarinet, trumpet, piano, temple blocks; Pentagram,
cello, horn, clarinet, blocks.

HAMILTON, IAIN
b. Glasgow, Scotland, 6 June 1922; to U.S. 1961.
First studied to be an engineer; studied com-
position with William Alwyn, Royal Acad. of
Music, London; Univ. of London, B.Mus. 1950.
His many awards include the Dove prize, 1950;
Royal Phil. Society prize, 1951; Koussevitzky
Found. award, 1951; Edwin Evans prize, 1951;
Butterworth award; Arnold Bax Gold Medal;
honorary D. Mus., Glasgow Univ., 1970; Ralph
Vaughan Williams award, 1974. He was composer-
in-residence at Tanglewood, 1962; professor,
Duke Univ., from 1962.
WORKS: OPERA: The royal hunt of the sun,
1966-68; Agamemnon, 1967-69; Pharsalia, 1968;
The Cataline conspiracy, to his own text, com-
missioned by the Scottish Opera and performed at
Stirling, Scotland, 1974; Tamburlaine, radio
opera, BBC, 14 Feb. 1977; Anna Karenina, 1977-78;
ORCHESTRA: 2 symphonies, 1949, 1951; clarinet
concerto, 1951; concerto for jazz trumpet and
orch., 1958; Sinfonia for 2 orch., 1959;
Ecossaisse, 1959; piano concerto, 1960, rev.
1967; Circus, 2 trumpets and orch., 1969;
Voyage, horn and orch., 1970; Alastor, 1970;
Amphion, violin and orch., 1971; Aurora, 1972;
CHAMBER MUSIC: 2 clarinet quintets, 1949, 1971;
2 string quartets, 1950, 1965; Nocturne, clarinet and piano, 1951; viola sonata, 1951; 2
cello sonatas, 1951, 1974; sextet for flute, 2
clarinets, piano trio, 1962; Variants, 10 instruments, 1963; Sonata notturna, horn and piano,
1965; Sonata for 5, wind quintet, 1966; flute
sonata, 1966; 5 scenes, trumpet and piano, 1971;
violin sonata, 1974; The Alexandria sequences,
11 instruments, 1976; Hyperion, chamber ensemble,
New York premiere, 31 Jan. 1979; CHORUS: Epitaph for this world and time, 3 choirs, 3 organs,
conductor, text from Revelations, 1970; Te Deum,
with winds and percussion, 1972; To Columbus,
with brass and percussion, on Whitman text,
1976; KEYBOARD: 3 piano sonatas, 1951, 1970, #3,
New York, 29 Mar. 1981; Palinodes, 7 piano
studies after lines of Rimbaud, 1972; Threnos:
In time of war, organ; A vision of Canopus,
organ, 1975.
Duke University, Durham, NC 27708

HAMILTON, THOMAS
b. 1946. Studied composition with John W.
Downey, Univ. of Wisconsin. His Dialogue for
flute and alto saxophone received top award in
the woodwind category, Wisconsin Composers
Contest, 1968. He is faculty member, Washington
Univ., St. Louis.
621 Westwood Dr., Clayton, MO 63105

HAMLISCH, MARVIN
b. New York, N.Y., 2 June 1944. Studied with
his father then at Juilliard School and at
Queens Coll. He began writing songs at age 15.
He has won 3 Academy awards for the film scores
to The sting, 1973, and The way we were, 1974;
and a Tony award for the score to A chorus line,

1975.
c/o Allan Carr Enterprises, Box 69670, Los Angeles, CA 90069

HAMM, CHARLES E.
b. 1925. Was professor, Univ. of Illinois, to 1976; then appointed to faculty at Dartmouth Coll.
WORKS: CHAMBER MUSIC: Round, unspecified chamber ensemble; anyone lived in a pretty how town, e. e. cummings text; Canto, voice and chamber ensemble.
Dartmouth College, P.O. Box 746, Hanover, NH 03755

HAMMOND, RICHARD
b. Kent, England, 26 Apr. 1896; to U.S. at an early age. Studied at Yale Univ.; and with Nadia Boulanger and Mortimer Wilson.
WORKS: BALLET: Fiesta; ORCHESTRA: 6 Chinese fairy tales, 1921; Voyage to the East, voice and orch., 1926; West Indian dances, 1930; CHAMBER MUSIC: 2 piano suites; oboe sonata; choruses and songs.

HAMMOND, WILLIAM G.
b. Melville, N.Y., 7 Aug. 1874; d. New York, N.Y., 22 Dec. 1945. Was organist, Dutch Reformed Church, Brooklyn, 1914-45. He wrote many songs.

HAMPTON, (GEORGE) CALVIN
b. Kittanning, Pa., 31 Dec. 1938. Studied with Joseph Wood and Richard Hoffman at Oberlin Cons., B.M. 1960; at the Mozarteum in Salzburg; organ with Arthur Poister, Syracuse Univ., M.M. 1962. He taught at Salem Coll., Winston-Salem, N.C., 1960-61; at Choate School, 1969-70; was organist, St. Peter's Church, Cazenovia, 1961-62; organist and choirmaster, Calvary Episcopal Church, New York, from 1963.
WORKS: CHORUS: 3 hymn tunes, 1969; Easter alleluia, 1972; Lord, speak to me, 1972; This is the day, 1972; Joyful joyful; and others; KEYBOARD: Prisms, piano, 1963; Triple play, 2 pianos and Ondes Martenot, 1967; Catch-up, 2 pianos and tape, 1967; God plays hide and seek, organ and synthesizer, 1971; The road to Leprechaunia, organ, synthesizer, soprano, 1973.
61 Gramercy Park N., New York, NY 10010

HAMVAS, LEWIS
b. Budapest, Hungary, 10 Nov. 1919; U.S. citizen 1935. Studied composition with Lehman Engel, Leo Weiner, Bernard Wagenaar, Vincent Persichetti at Juilliard School; piano with Josef Raieff. His awards include the Morris Loeb prize at Juilliard and several commissions. He was instructor and composer for dance, Bard Coll., 1952-54; faculty member, Yankton Coll., from 1954.
WORKS: CHAMBER MUSIC: oboe sonata; violin sonata; cello sonata; piano sonata; Introduction and dance, clarinet, violin, piano, cello; Explorations, piano; CHORUS: On the plain of Chelyabinsk, chorus and 4 instruments; I have a dream, chorus and orch.; also music for dance, theatre, etc.

Conservatory of Music, Yankton College, Yankton, SD 57078

HANCOCK, EUGENE WILSON (WHITE)
b. St. Louis, Mo., 17 Feb. 1929. Studied at Univ. of Detroit, B.M.; Univ. of Michigan, M.M.; composition with Robert Hernried, Seth Bingham, and Joseph Goodman, Union Theological Seminary, School of Sacred Music, S.M.D.; organ with Alec Wyton and Marcel Dupre. He received awards from Detroit Musicians' Assoc., 1952, and Nat. Assoc. of Negro Musicians, 1966. He has been organist-choirmaster in Detroit and New York from 1953, at St. Philip Episcopal Church, New York, from 1974; also faculty member, Manhattan Community Coll., from 1970.
WORKS: CHORUS: A Palm Sunday anthem, choir and children's choir, 1971; Come here, Lord, 1973; a collection of 13 spirituals, 1973; A babe is born, 1975; ORGAN: An organ book of spirituals, 1973.
257 Central Park W., #10C, New York, NY 10024

HANCOCK, GERRE
b. Lubbock, Tex., 21 Feb. 1934. Studied with Kent Kennan and E. W. Doty, Univ. of Texas; with Nadia Boulanger and Jean Langlais in Paris; with Searle Wright, Union Theological Seminary. He received a Rotary Found. fellowship for study in France. He has been organist and choirmaster in Cincinnati and New York from 1960, at St. Thomas Church, New York, from 1971; also faculty member at Juilliard School, from 1971; and at Yale Univ., from 1975.
WORKS: CHORUS: In thanksgiving; Out of the deep; Kindle the gift of God; A song to the lamb; Go ye therefore; Infant holy, infant lowly; Teach me, my God and King; The plumb line and the city, cantata for choir, organ, and orch.; ORGAN: Improvisation; Air; Fantasy on Divinum mysterium.
St. Thomas Church, 5th Ave. & 53rd St., New York, NY 10019

HANDEL, DARRELL
b. Lodi, Calif., 23 Aug. 1933. Studied with S. R. Beckler, Univ. of the Pacific; with Dominick Argento and Wayne Barlow, Eastman School of Music. He won first place in the Bela Bartok Choral Competition, Bebrecen, Hungary, 1976. He has been faculty member at Univ. of Kansas, 1966-71; Univ. of South Carolina, 1971-76; from 1976, Univ. of Cincinnati Coll.-Cons.
WORKS: ORCHESTRA: Low country hauntings, with soloists, 1975; WIND ENSEMBLE: Variations on a chorale, for brass, 1966; CHAMBER MUSIC: Suzanne's animal music, harp, 1969; 3 birdsongs, voice and piano, 1973; 3 balloons, harp, 1975; The poems of our climate, soprano and 7 instrumentalists, 1977; CHORUS: Study of 2 pears, 1974.
198 Lafayette Circle, Cincinnati, OH 45220

HANDY, GEORGE (GEORGE JOSEPH HENDELMAN)
b. Brooklyn, N.Y., 1920. His instrumental compositions include New York suite and 3 quartets for the New York Saxophone Quartet, 1964-65. He has also written popular songs.

HANDY, WILLIAM CHRISTOPHER
b. Florence, Ala., 16 Nov. 1873; d. New York,
N.Y., 28 Mar. 1958. Graduated from Teachers'
Agricultural and Mechanical Coll., Huntsville,
1892, then was a schoolteacher and also worked
in the iron mill. He taught at the A&M Coll.,
1900-2; organized a quartet and played cornet
with it at the Chicago World's Fair, 1893;
organized an orchestra and toured the South
after 1902. He published an autobiography,
Father of the blues, New York, 1941.
WORKS: ORCHESTRA: Blue destiny; Opportunity, setting of a poem by Walter Malone;
setting of Lincoln's Gettysburg address; JAZZ:
Memphis blues; St. Louis blues; Yellow dog
blues; Beale Street blues; Joe Turner blues;
Hesitating blues; East St. Louis blues; Atlanta
blues; Harlem blues; and others; several marches
and the Afro-American hymn.

HANKIN, JEFFREY D.
b. Boston, Mass., 14 Nov. 1949. Studied with
Easley Blackwood and W. Thomas McKinley, Univ.
of Chicago, 1967-71; with Arthur Berger, Seymour
Shifrin, and Harold Shapero at Brandeis Univ.,
1971-73.
WORKS: ORCHESTRA: Tacit II, winds and
percussion, 1970; Fantasy for orchestra, 1971;
The parliament of fowls--a suite for dance,
1973; CHAMBER MUSIC: 3 lyrics, piano, 1971-72;
And here I am, soprano and 14 players, 1972.
113 E. Montgomery, Baltimore, MD 21233

HANLON, KENNETH M.
b. Baltimore, Md., 16 May 1941. Studied with
Ramiro Cortes, Univ. of Southern California; and
with Louis Cheslock, Peabody Cons. He has held
faculty posts at Peabody Prep. School, 1961-68;
and from 1970, at Univ. of Nevada.
WORKS: CHAMBER MUSIC: Contemplations,
clarinet and piano; Suite for doubles, woodwind soloist and jazz ensemble, premiered by
Ralph Gair and the Stan Kenton Neophonic Orch.,
July 1970; Mourning sound, baritone and piano,
1971.
4912 San Sebastian, Las Vegas, NV 89114

HANNA, JAMES R.
b. Siloam Springs, Ark., 15 Oct. 1922. Studied
with Robert Delaney, Northwestern Univ., B.M.
1948, M.M. 1949; with Bernhard Heiden, Indiana
Univ. He won the Louisiana Fed. of Music Clubs
award, 1954, 1956, 1958, 1964; received a grant
from Louisiana Council of Music and Arts, 1968,
for symphony #2. He joined the faculty of Univ.
of Southwestern Louisiana in 1949; has been
violist, Lake Charles Civic Symph., from 1970.
WORKS: ORCHESTRA: 3 symphonies, 1948,
1956, 1965; Prelude for orch., 1960; Little concerto for orch., 1961; BAND: Essay, 1956;
Sinfonia, 1963; CHAMBER MUSIC: clarinet quintet,
1954; duo for violin and viola, 1955; Elegy,
chamber orch., 1957; 4 string quartets, 1949,
1951, 1960, 1964; violin sonata, 1948; Song of
the redwood tree, narrator, brass, timpani,
1954; woodwind trio, 1957; Fugue and chorale,
percussion, 1961; viola sonatina, 1969; Fantasy,
cello and piano, 1970; also vocal compositions.

Box 4-0188, Univ. of Southwestern Louisiana,
Lafayette, LA 70504

HANNAY, ROGER DURHAM
b. Plattsburg, N.Y., 22 Sept. 1930. Studied
with Franklin Morris and Dika Newlin, Syracuse
Univ.; with Hugo Norden, Boston Univ.; with
Howard Hanson and Bernard Rogers, Eastman School
of Music; with Aaron Copland and Lukas Foss at
Tanglewood. His awards include scholarships for
all study except Eastman School; Nat. Endowment
for the Arts grant, 1977; Kenan Found. grant,
1977. He was faculty member, Concordia Coll.,
1958-66; from 1966, at Univ. of North Carolina.
WORKS: OPERA: 2 tickets to Omaha, The
swindlers, 1960; The fortune of St. Macabre,
1964; ORCHESTRA: 4 symphonies, #1 rev. 1973,
#2 1956, #3 The great American novel, with chorus
and tape, #4 American classic, 1977; Requiem,
with chorus, Whitman text, 1961; Sonorous image,
1968; Sayings for out time, with chorus, 1968;
Fragmentation, orch. or chamber orch., 1969;
Listen, 1971; Suite-Billings, youth orch., 1975;
CHAMBER MUSIC: Rhapsody, flute and piano, 1952;
Sonata for brass, 1957; Divertimento, wind quintet, 1958; Concerto da camera, chamber ensemble
and soprano, 1958, rev. 1975; 4 string quartets,
1962, 196 , #3 Designs, 1963, #4 Quartet of
solos (a simultaneous performance of 4 solo
pieces: Grand concerte, Second fiddle, O solo
viola, and Concert music, 1974); Spectrum, brass
quintet, 1964; Structure, percussion ensemble,
1965, rev. 1974; Marshall's medium message,
narrator and percussion quartet, 1967; Fantome,
viola, clarinet, piano, 1967; Four for five,
brass quintet, 1973; Phantom of the opera, organ
and soprano, 1975; Oh friends!, small wind ensemble and percussion, 1976; MULTIMEDIA: Elegy,
viola and tape; Live and in color!, narrator,
percussion quartet, 2 action painters, tape,
film, slides, 1967; Confrontation, tape and percussion, 1969; Squeeze me, chamber ensemble and
tape, 1970; The episodic refraction, tape and
piano, 1971; Tuonelan Joutsen, soprano, English
horn, tape, 1972; Pied piper, clarinet and tape,
1975; choral works, songs, piano pieces.
609 Morgan Creek Rd., Chapel Hill, NC 27514

HANSEN, THEODORE (TED)
b. Denver, Colo., 5 Feb. 1935. Studied with
Cecil Effinger, Univ. of Colorado, B.M. 1964;
with Ronald Lo Presti, Arizona State Univ., M.M.
1967; with Robert McBride, Univ. of Arizona,
D.M.A. 1974. He was faculty member, Arizona
State Univ., 1966-75; from 1975, Univ. of Tulsa.
WORKS: ORCHESTRA: 3 movements for orch.;
Collage; symphony; Toccata for winds; Coloration
in brass; CHAMBER MUSIC: Configurations, flute
and piano, trumpet and piano; 4 sketches for
piano; string quartet; Nocturne, clarinet and
piano; suite for viola and piano; Cavatina,
flugelhorn and piano; Aria, trombone and piano;
suite for brass quintet; Contrasts, woodwind
quintet; Montage, violin and piano.
School of Music, University of Tulsa, Tulsa,
OK 74104

HANSON, DARYL L.
b. Belmond, Iowa, 17 Feb. 1924. Studied at
Iowa State Coll.; Iowa State Teachers Coll.,
Eastman School of Music; Univ. of Southern
California; and Columbia Teachers Coll. His
awards include second place, Iowa Composers
contest, 1953; Research award, New York State,
1974, and composition award, 1975. He was
faculty member, State Univ. Coll., Geneseo,
1956-78.

WORKS: THEATRE: The promise, 1-act opera,
1958; Talent, like murder, will out, opera
buffa; The happy prince, opera; Christopher
Columbus, children's opera; Wish I had a nickel,
musical, 1968; The waterbabies, children's
musical; Toys, opera buffa, based on "The loves
of George Sand," 1978; also many works for
chorus and solo voice.
19 Northview Dr., Geneseo, NY 14454

HANSON, DEAN ARMSTRONG
b. Stamford, Conn., 14 Oct. 1931. Studied with
Randall Thompson and Walter Piston, Harvard
Univ., B.A. 1953; at Boston Univ., M.M. 1961.
He is a professional singer, member of the
Tanglewood Festival Chorus, and has sung concerts over the Voice of Free China (Taiwan),
including his settings of Emily Dickinson's A
solemn thing and Walt Whitman's After the supper
and talk. He has composed numerous sacred and
secular songs.
905 Mass. Ave., Lexington, MA 02173

HANSON, HOWARD
b. Wahoo, Nebr., 28 Oct. 1896; d. Rochester,
N.Y., 26 Feb. 1981. Studied at Univ. of Nebraska;
with Percy Goetschius, Inst. of Musical Art, New
York; with Arne Oldberg, Northwestern Univ. His
many honors include the Prix de Rome; fellow,
American Acad. in Rome, 1921-24; member, Nat.
Inst. of Arts and Letters, 1935; Pulitzer prize,
1944; Ditson award, 1945; George Foster Peabody
award, 1946; Huntington Hartford Found. grant,
1959; 37 honorary doctorates; Distinguished
Nebraskan award, presented at Wahsington, 21
Sept. 1976; concert of his music, Rochester
Philharmonic, 10 Oct. 1976; on his 80th birthday,
28 Oct. 1976, the Eastman School presented a
concert in his honor which included 9x9: Variations on a theme by Howard Hanson, written by 9
composers on the Eastman faculty; in 1980 he was
elected to membership in the American Acad. and
Inst. of Arts and Letters. He was faculty
member, Coll. of the Pacific, 1916-21; director,
Eastman School of Music, 1924-64. In 1925 he
instituted at Eastman a series of American music
concerts and, in 1976, donated $100,000 to
support the program. He has conducted programs
of American music in Europe as well as with
major orchestras in the U.S.; has been president
of many national musical organizations.
WORKS: OPERA: Merry Mount, 1933, commissioned by the Metropolitan Opera Company, New
York, and performed there on 10 Feb. 1934;
BALLET: California forest play, 1920; ORCHESTRA:
Symphonic prelude, 1916; Legend, 1917; Rhapsody,
1919; 5 symphonic poems, 1920-26; 7 symphonies,
1923, 1930, 1938, 1944, 1955, 1967, 1977; Serenade, flute, strings, harp, orch., 1945; piano

concerto, 1948; Elegy in memory of Serge
Koussevitzky, 1956; Mosaics, 1957; 4 psalms,
baritone and orch.; concerto for organ, strings,
and harp; Bold Island suite, 1961; Dies natalis,
1967; CHAMBER MUSIC: 2 piano quintets, 1916,
1917; string quartet, 1923; Pastorale, oboe and
piano; Fantasia on a theme of youth, piano and
strings, 1950; CHORUS: The lament of Beowulf,
1926; Heroic elegy, with orch., 1927; 3 songs
for Drum taps by Whitman, with baritone solo
and orch., 1935; Hymn for the pioneers, male
voices, 1938; The cherubic hymn, 1949; How excellent Thy name, 1952; The song of democracy,
with soli and orch., 1957; Song of human rights,
cantata, 1963; The mystic trumpeter, with narrator and orch.; Streams in the desert, with
orch.; Psalms 121 and 150, with orch., 1964;
New land, new covenant, oratorio for chorus, 2
soloists, orch., narrator, a Bicentennial commission, performed at Bryn Mawr, 2 May 1976;
also many songs, piano works.

HARBISON, JOHN
b. Orange, N.J., 20 Dec. 1938. Studied at
Harvard Univ., B.A. 1960; with Roger Sessions
and Earl Kim, Princeton Univ., M.F.A. 1963; with
Boris Blacher in Berlin. His awards include a
Brandeis Creative Arts citation, 1971; American
Acad. of Arts and Letters award, 1972; grants
from the Fromm Found., Koussevitzky Found.,
Naumburg Found., Rockefeller Found., Nat. Endow-
ment for the Arts, and Mass. Arts and Humanities
Found. He was Rockefeller composer-in-residence,
Reed Coll., 1968-69; from 1969, faculty member,
Mass. Inst. of Technology; music director,
Cantata Singers, 1969-73.
WORKS: THEATRE: Winter's tale, opera in 2
acts, 1973-74, San Francisco, 25-28 Aug. 1979;
Full moon in March, chamber opera, Cambridge,
30 Apr. 1979; ORCHESTRA: Sinfonia, violin and
double orch., 1963; violin concerto, 1967,
premiere, Boston, 24 Jan. 1981, with Rose Mary
Harbison, the composer's wife, as soloist; Dio-
tima, Boston, 11 Mar. 1977; piano concerto, 1979;
CHAMBER MUSIC: Confinement, chamber ensemble,
1965; Serenade for 6 players, 1968; Parody-fan-
tasia, piano, 1968; piano trio, 1969; Bermuda
triangle, jazz ensemble, 1970; Die Kurze, solo
violin, New York, 15 Oct. 1971; 6 dumb shows,
chamber ensemble (excerpts from Winter's Tale),
Cambridge, 8 Oct. 1974; Samuel Chapter, chamber
orch., Cambridge, 6 Nov. 1978; woodwind quintet,
Boston, 29 Oct. 1979; piano quintet, Santa Fe,
9 Aug. 1981; CHORUS: Music when soft voices die,
Shelley text; 5 songs of experience, Blake text,
4 soli, chorus, string quartet, percussion, Cambridge, 28 Feb. 1973; The flower-fed buffaloes,
with orch., 1978; SONGS: Elegiac songs,
Dickinson text, soprano and chamber ensemble,
New York, 12 Jan. 1975; Motetti di Montali, song
cycle, Santa Fe, 4 Aug. 1981.
563 Franklin St., Cambridge, MA 02139

HARDER, PAUL
b. Indianapolis, Ind., 10 Mar. 1953. Studied at
Butler Univ., B.M. 1944; Eastman School of Music,
M.M. 1945; with Nadia Boulanger, France, 1948;
Royal Acad. of Music, Copenhagen, 1951-52; with
Philip Bezanson, Univ. of Iowa, Ph.D. 1959. He

HARDIE, GARY

was faculty member, Michigan State Univ., 1945-73; Stanislaus State Coll., from 1973; was also member of the Rochester Phil. Orch., 1944-45, and Lansing Symph., 1945-55.

WORKS: ORCHESTRA: Serenade; Sinfonietta, Univ. of Redlands, 4 Apr. 1959; overture, 1962; A wisp of time, string orch., 1964; The pleasant truth, 1972; BAND: Refractions; Contention; Mosaic; Icons; CHAMBER MUSIC: brass quintet; 3 woodwind quintets; 2 string trios; sextet, piano and woodwind quintet; clarinet sonata; oboe sonata; Serenade, soprano, clarinet, horn, strings; Serenade, tenor, clarinet, bassoon, strings; string quartet; CHORUS: Let God arise; The swallow; also scores for radio and stage productions. He is author of several books on music technique and theory including Harmonic materials in tonal music, 3d ed., 1976, and Bridge to 20th-century music, Boston, 1973.
Stanislaus State College, Turlock, CA 95380

HARDIE, GARY
b. Coral Gables, Fla., 20 Apr. 1948. Studied with Iain Hamilton, Duke Univ.; and with Mel Powell, California Inst. of the Arts, M.F.A. 1973. He received a BMI student composer award, 1972. He was faculty member, Virginia Commonwealth Univ., 1973-74.

WORKS: CHAMBER MUSIC: Protusions, alto flute, cello, piano, 1970; Skin deep, piano, 1970; Yellow with connection, flute, clarinet, violin, cello, trombone, harp, 1971; For 5/4, a requiem to Kent State, 16 solo voices, 1972.
4872 Warwick Rd., Richmond, VA 23224

HARDIN, BURTON ERVIN
b. Lincoln, Nebr., 21 Aug. 1936. Studied with Samuel Scott, Violet Archer, and Charles Hoag, Univ. of Oklahoma; with Joshua Missal, Wichita State Univ. He won a Sigma Alpha Iota award, 1967; was faculty member, Univ. of South Carolina, 1964-67; from 1968, at Eastern Illinois Univ.

WORKS: BAND: horn quartet with band; Regal festival music, brass choir; CHAMBER MUSIC: woodwind quintet, 1967; CHORUS: a cantata.
1120 Arthur Ave., Charleston, IL 61920

HARDIN, LOUIS T. (MOONDOG)
b. Marysville, Kans., 26 May 1916. After losing his sight at age 13, studied violin, viola, piano, organ, and harmony at Iowa School for the Blind. He then taught himself by studying books in Braille and listening. Hardin considers himself a tonalist and contrapuntalist; has developed a new stringed instrument, the hüs, and a new drum, the trimba.

WORKS: OPERA: Die Ershaffung der Weld; ORCHESTRA: Theme; Stamping ground; Minisym #1; Lament 1; Witch of Endor; 6 symphoniques for orchestra; VOCAL: Madrigals, Books I-XII; Moondog's Mother Goose book; and Art of Canon, Books I and II.
Candor, NY 13743

HARDISH, PATRICK
b. Perth Amboy, N.J., 6 Apr. 1944. Studied privately with William Schimmel, 1969-72; with

Juan Lemann, 1971; with Jacob Druckman, Juilliard School, 1969-73; with Hugo Weisgall, Queens Coll., CUNY, B.A. 1976. From 1978 he has been staff member, Columbia Univ. Music Library.

WORKS: CHAMBER MUSIC: Intensities, viola, 1973; brass quintet, Atlanta, Ga., 23 Feb. 1974; Accordioclusterville, accordion, 1977-78; Intensities II, bassoon, 1978; Abstractions, bassoon, accordion, piano, percussion, 1979; Do not go gentle, baritone voice, viola, piano, 1979; Duo for piano and percussion, New York, 14 Apr. 1980.
713 Lincoln Dr., Perth Amboy, NJ 08861

HARKER, F. FLAXINGTON
b. Aberdeen, Scotland, 4 Sept. 1876; d. Richmond, Va., 23 Oct. 1936. Studied with Tertius Noble at the York Minster (Cathedral). He came to the U.S. in 1901 and was organist in Biltmore, N.C., then in Richmond, Va. His works include 2 cantatas: The star of Bethlehem and The cross. He published Harker's Organ Collection, 2 volumes containing 27 works by contemporary composers.

HARKNESS, REBEKAH
b. St. Louis, Mo., 17 Apr. 1915. Studied with Fred Werle, Mannes Coll. of Music; with Nadia Boulanger in Paris; at the Dalcroze School, Geneva; orchestration with Lee Hoiby. She received honorary doctorates from Franklin Pierce Coll., 1968, Lycoming Coll., 1970. She established the Rebekah Harkness Found. ballet workshop at Watch Hill, R.I., and Harkness House, New York; is owner and director, Harkness Ballet Company.

WORKS: BALLET: Journey to love, 1958; ORCHESTRA: Safari, tone poem, 1955; Mediterranean suite, 1957; Musical chairs, 1958; Gift to the Magi, 1959; Letters to Japan, 1961; Macumba, a suite, 1965; Elements, 1965.
4 E. 75th St., New York, NY 10021

HARLAN, CHARLES LEROY
b. Lewiston, Idaho, 4 Dec. 1920; d. Seaside, Calif., 14 Feb. 1972. Studied with Joseph Brye, Univ. of Idaho; with Roger Sessions, Univ. of California, Berkeley; and at Colorado State Coll., Ed.D. 1961. He taught in California public schools from 1957, at Monterey, 1970-72.

WORKS: ORCHESTRA: Arioso; Psalm 98, with chorus, 1961; CHAMBER MUSIC: Trio for brass, trumpet, horn, trombone; Fantasy, alto saxophone.

HARLINE, LEIGH
b. Salt Lake City, Utah, 26 Mar. 1907; d. Long Beach, Calif., 10 Dec. 1969. Studied at Univ. of Utah. He was on the Walt Disney staff, 1932; became a free-lance composer and orchestrator for film studios, 1941.

WORKS: FILM SCORES: Pride of the Yankees; Johnny come lately; 7 faces of Dr. Lao; Strange bedfellow; also wrote Civic Center suite for orchestra. His song, When you wish upon a star, won an Academy award in 1940.

HARLING, WILLIAM FRANKE
b. London, England, 18 Jan. 1887; to U.S. 1888; d. Sierra Madre, Calif., 22 Nov. 1958. Studied

at Grace Church Choir School, New York; Royal
Acad. of Music, London; with Theophile Ysaye in
Brussels. He was organist and choirmaster in
Brussels, 1907-8; at U.S. Military Acad., West
Point, 1909-10. He received the Bispham opera
medal, 1925.

WORKS: OPERA: A light from St. Agnes, 1
act, 1925; Deep River, 1926; Alda; THEATRE:
music for the plays Paris bound; Machinal; Outward bound; In love with love; The outsider;
ORCHESTRA: Jazz concerto; Venetian fantasy; 3
elegiac poems, cello and orch.; Monte Casino,
tone poem; Before the dawn; At the tomb of the
unknown soldier, tone poem; My captain, my
captain; BAND: West Point forever, official
march; FILM SCORES: Stagecoach; Penny serenade;
So red the rose; Man with wings; The scarlet
empress.

HARMAN, CARTER
b. Brooklyn, N.Y., 14 June 1918. Studied with
Roger Sessions, Princeton Univ., 1936-40; with
Otto Luening, Columbia Univ., 1945-48; with
Alice Shields, Columbia-Princeton Electronic
Music Center; and with Jon Appleton, Dartmouth
Electronic Music Studio. He received a Nat.
Endowment for the Arts grant, 1977. He was a
pilot in the Army Air Corps, 1942-45; music
critic, New York Times, 1947-52; music editor,
Time magazine, 1952-57; from 1967, executive
vice-president, Composers Recordings, Inc.
WORKS: THEATRE: Blackface, ballet, New
York, 18 May 1947; The food of love, opera,
1950; Circus at the opera, 1951, and Castles in
the sand, 1952, 2 children's operas; SONGS:
Hymn to the Virgin, a madrigal, 1955; many
children's songs, including Mary Martin sings
for children, 1950-55; Songs for synthesizer,
1975. He is author of A popular history of
music, N.Y., 1956, rev. 1962.
River Rd., Lyme, NH 03768

HARMON, JOHN C.
b. Oshkosh, Wis., 25 Oct. 1935. Studied with
Clyde Duncan, Lawrence Univ.; with Henri
Pousseur and Livingston Gearhart, State Univ.
of New York at Buffalo. He has been a professional jazz musician from 1960; was director of
jazz studies, Lawrence Univ., 1971-75.
WORKS: JAZZ ENSEMBLE: Montage, orch. and
jazz trio; An unfair argument with life, jazz
trio; Gates and beginnings; Bottoms up; Kur-
tains; There's a world out there waitin';
Another lonely spring.

HARMONIC, PHIL
b. Newton, Mass., 10 June 1949. Has been
director, Radio Music City Hall Symphony Orchestra from 1967; Chicken Band, from 1972; Phil
Harmonic and the Nu-Tones, from 1973.
WORKS: Duke of Windsor, mixed media opera
for solo performer; High fidelity, live electronic music; Stars over San Francisco, repeti-
tive musical metaphor; Keyboard Acc., piano;
Fugitive from culture, personal entertainment;
Win a dream date with Phil, intimate cultural
event contest; Gertrude Stein in North America
1974, for collaborating readers, musicians,

engineers.
1940 Channing Way, Berkeley, CA 94704

HARNICK, SHELDON
b. Chicago, Ill., 1924. Frustration, 1-act mime
opera, a spoof on Debussy's Pelleas and Melisande,
for 2 women and piano trio.
Beresford Apt., 81st St. and Central Park W.,
New York, NY 10024

HARPER, MARJORIE
b. St. Paul, Minn., 26 Apr. Studied with Rubin
Goldmark and Alexander Lambert. She has published anthems, songs, and piano pieces.
146 Belmont Ave., Jersey City, NJ 07304

HARRER, JAMES P.
b. La Porte, Ind., 24 Apr. 1946. Studied with
Donald White, DePauw Univ.; with William
Billingsley, Univ. of Idaho. He received a Fed.
of Music Clubs award in composition, 1970. He
has been on the faculty, Hollins Coll.
WORKS: WIND ENSEMBLE: Free rondo, 32
winds and percussion; Meliorism, 32 winds and 24
solo voices; CHAMBER MUSIC: string quartet,
1970; Phoresy, solo flute; Phoresy, trumpet and
piano; Phoresy, solo oboe; Locomotive sandwich,
nocturne for piano; Music for a great American
painting, chamber winds and tape; other symphonic
works and chamber music.
2547 Packard Rd., Ypsilanti, MI 48197

HARRINGTON, AMBER ROOBENIAN (Mrs. W. Clark)
b. Boston, Mass., 13 May 1905. Studied organ at
New England Cons., 1924-25; Eastman School of
Music, 1926-27. She was church organist near
Boston, 1921-24; New York, 1928-31; motion
picture organist, 1928-31.
WORKS: ORCHESTRA: Desert solitude, 1939;
Caucasian dance song, strings, 1939; Reverie,
1957; CHORUS: In an old English garden, 1936;
The tryst, 1948; Vigil, 1949; Two red roses
across the moon, 1949; The willow tree, 1955;
Samarkand, 1956; SONGS: My love, 1966; In
memoriam, 1967.
Station Road, Brookfield, CT 06804

HARRINGTON, W. CLARK
b. Worcester, Mass., 28 June 1905. Attended
Dartmouth Coll. and New England Cons.; studied
with Vittorio Giannini in New York. He received
the Endicott prize at the New England Cons. for
3 songs, 1929. He was on the staff of Columbia
Broadcasting System, 1930-59.
WORKS: ORCHESTRA: Alas, that spring should
vanish with the rose, voice, piano, and orch.,
1929; Faun call, tone poem; numerous songs,
piano pieces, choruses, and works for strings.
Station Road, Brookfield, CT 06804

HARRIS, ALBERT
Theme and variations for 8 horns; sonatina for
guitar; Suite of 7 pieces, guitar; Concertino da
California, guitar and string quartet, Washington, 13 May 1979.
5622 Allott Ave., Van Nuys, CA 91401

HARRIS, ARTHUR

HARRIS, ARTHUR
b. Philadelphia, Pa., 3 Apr. 1927. Studied with
Paul Hindemith at Yale Univ. He is a free-lance
composer, arranger, and conductor.
WORKS: BALLET: Bintel brief; ORCHESTRA:
March of the mandarins; CHAMBER MUSIC: piano
sonata; 4 pieces for 3 instruments; Theme and
variations, 4 horns; 4 moods and finale, brass
quintet; sundry compositions.
R.D. 1, Box 310, Mt. Bethel, PA 18343

HARRIS, DONALD
b. St. Paul, Minn., 7 Apr. 1931. Studied with
Ross Lee Finney, Univ. of Michigan, B.M. 1952,
M.M. 1954; with Max Deutsch and Nadia Boulanger
in France; with Boris Blacher, Lukas Foss, and
Andre Jolivet at Tanglewood. His awards include
Fulbright and Guggenheim fellowships; Prince
Rainier of Monaco Composition prize; Louisville
Orch. award; Rockefeller and Chapelbrook Found.
grants; Nat. Endowment for the Arts grant, 1973;
commission, French Nat. Radio, 1973; commissions
from Cleveland Orch., 1975, Elizabeth Sprague
Coolidge Found., 1977, Koussevitzky Found.,
1977, Goethe Inst., 1978; and annual ASCAP
awards, 1973-77. He was music consultant to the
American Cultural Center, USIS, 1965-67; held
administrative posts, New England Cons., 1967-
73, ending with executive vice-president, 1974-
77; then resigned to become professor and composer-in-residence, Hartt Coll. of Music, Univ.
of Hartford.
WORKS: ORCHESTRA: symphony in 2 movements,
1961; Charmes, soprano and orch., 1978; CHAMBER
MUSIC: piano sonata, 1956; Fantasy, violin and
piano, 1957; string quartet, 1965; Ludus,for 10
instruments, 1966; Ludus II, flute, clarinet,
violin, cello, piano, Cambridge, 8 May 1973; On
variations, chamber orch., 1976; For the night
to wear, mezzo-soprano and 7 instruments, 1978;
Balladen, piano, 1979.
Hartt Coll. of Music, Univ. of Hartford,
W. Hartford, CT 06117

HARRIS, EDWARD C.
b. Elizabeth, N.J., 16 Feb. 1899. Attended East
Liberty Acad., Pittsburgh; studied music privately.
He was accompanist to Lawrence Tibbett and
Georges Enesco; music critic on the San Francisco
Bulletin, 1928-29; has made concert tours in
Canada, Australia, New Zealand, Africa, South
America; was church organist in Plymouth, Mass.,
1943-46; also private voice teacher. He composed
many songs and piano pieces.

HARRIS, ETHEL RAMOS (Mrs. Chester E.)
b. Newport, R.I., 18 Aug. 1908. Studied with
Charles Dennee and Warren Story Smith, New
England Cons.; with Nikolai Lopatnikoff, Carnegie-
Mellon Univ.; Isidor Philipp in New York; and
with Aaron Copland at Tanglewood. Her awards
include scholarships for study with Harvey Gaul,
and study in Israel from American Christian
Palestine Committee; Delta Sigma Theta award,
1959, 1973; Nat. Assoc. of Negro Women award,
1971; Martin Luther King, Jr., award, 1972. She
was "Sophisticated Lady" on Radio Station KDKA;
pianist, Nat. Negro Opera Company; concert

pianist, lecturer, composer.
WORKS: CHORUS: Stan' steady; I've been in
the storm so long; There'll be a jubilee; When
I reach the other side; many other choral works,
arrangements, songs, piano pieces.
2840 Leechburg Rd., New Kensington, PA
15068

HARRIS, FLOYD OLIN
b. Wichita, Kans., 30 Nov. 1913. Studied at
McPherson Coll., Univ. of Northern Colorado,
Univ. of Nebraska, Univ. of Denver. He has
taught in public schools in Kansas and Colorado;
from 1962, in Englewood, Colo. His compositions
include sacred and secular works; songs; instrumental solos and ensemble pieces.
3032 South Ivan Way, Denver, CO 80227

HARRIS, HOWARD C., JR.
b. New Orleans, La., 18 June 1940. Graduated
from Southern Univ., 1963; studied with Kenneth
Klaus, Louisiana State Univ., M.M. 1969; with
William S. Fischer in New York; and with William
P. Latham, North Texas State Univ. He was
public shcool band director, 1962-69; faculty
member, Southern Univ., 1969-70; Delaware State
Coll., 1970-71; from 1972, at Texas Southern
Univ.
WORKS: ORCHESTRA: Folk psalm, 1973; BAND:
Phonosynthesis; A drum movement, winds and percussion; JAZZ ENSEMBLE: Passion is; Black roots,
1972.
1406 Richmond Ave., #325, Houston, TX 77006

HARRIS, JERRY WESELEY
b. The Dalles, Oreg., 21 Oct. 1933. Studied at
Lewis and Clark Coll., M.A.; Univ. of Oregon,
D.Ed. He has been head of the music department,
Sunset High School, Beaverton, from 1956; violist
in Portland Symph. and Portland Chamber Orch.;
director of church music; editor, Oregon Music
Educators Journal, from 1958. He has written
many sacred choruses.

HARRIS, ROBERT A.
b. Detroit, Mich., 9 Jan. 1938. Studied with
Ruth Wylie, Wayne State Univ., B.S. 1960, M.A.
1962; with Bernard Rogers, Eastman School of
Music, 1963-66; with H. Owen Reed, Michigan
State Univ., Ph.D. 1971. He has received several
commissions. He taught in public schools, 1960-
64; was faculty member, Wayne State Univ., 1964-
70; at Michigan State Univ., 1970-78; from 1978,
at Northwestern Univ.
WORKS: THEATRE: incidental music to
Caligula by Camus, 1970; ORCHESTRA: Concert
piece for horn and orch., 1965; Concert piece
for bassoon and orch., 1965; Contrasts, 4 winds
and strings, 1966; Adagio, string orch., 1966;
Moods, 1969; CHAMBER MUSIC: Fantasia, solo
flute, 1958; sonatine, 2 violins, 1960; 5 bagatelles, 3 woodwinds, 1963; string quartet, 1968;
Psalms, soprano, horn, piano, 1968; CHORUS: 3
children's prayers, women's voices, a cappella,
1959; O perfect love, motet, a cappella, 1960;
For the beauty of the Earth, 1963; Benedictus,
women's voices, 1968; Requiem: A canticle of
immortality, 2 soloists, chamber choir, chorus,

orch., 1970-71; many other choral works and
songs.
> School of Music, Northwestern Univ., Evanston, IL 60201

HARRIS, ROGER W.
b. Evansville, Ind., 20 May 1940. Studied with
Grant Fletcher, Arizona State Univ.; with Halsey
Stevens, Robert Linn, Ingolf Dahl, Univ. of
Southern California, M.M. 1965. He won awards
in an Arizona State Univ. composition contest
and a Phi Mu Alpha contest. He taught at Arizona
State Univ., 1966-67; from 1967, at Mesa Community Coll.
WORKS: BRASS ENSEMBLE: Prelude; Kroma 3,
Set 1, brass quintet and percussion; Yes, I've
seen my rubber band burn before, large ensemble;
CHAMBER MUSIC: suite for solo tuba; 5 miniatures about love, mezzo-soprano and piano; Women
go to heaven, men go to hell, trombone, piano,
percussion; Kroma 2, trumpet and percussion;
Silent things, clarinet, piano, horn, percussion.
> 1761 W. Isabella, Mesa, AZ 85202

HARRIS, ROY ELLSWORTH
b. Lincoln County, Okla., 12 Feb. 1898; d. Santa
Monica, Calif., 1 Oct. 1979. Attended Univ. of
California, 1919-20; studied with Arthur Farwell,
Henry Schoenfeld, Nadia Boulanger, Modest
Altschuler, Arthur Bliss, Rosario Scalero. His
honors include Guggenheim fellowships, 1928,
1929, 1930, 1976; creative fellowship, Pasadena
Music and Art Assoc., 1930-33; first honors,
Committee for Appreciation of American Music,
1940; Certificate of Honor, Nat. Assoc. for
American Composers and Conductors, 1940;
Elizabeth Sprague Coolidge Medal, 1942; membership, Nat. Inst. of Arts and Letters, 1942;
honorary doctorates, Rutgers Univ., 1941, Univ.
of Redlands, 1946; Letter of Distinction award,
American Music Center, 1973; Chandler, Okla.,
celebrated Roy Harris on his 80th birthday and
a marker was placed at his birthplace just
northeast of Chandler; many other honors and
performances of his works in the U.S. and Canada
marked his 80th year; was inducted into the
American Acad. and Inst. of Arts and Letters,
23 May 1979. He held academic posts at Westminster Choir School, 1934-38; Cornell Univ.,
1941-42; Colorado Coll., 1942-48; Utah State
Agri. Coll., 1948-49; Peabody Coll. for Teachers,
1949-51; Cumberland Summer Festival, 1951;
Pennsylvania Coll. for Women, 1951-56; Univ. of
Southern Illinois, 1956-57; Indiana Univ., 1957-
60; Inter-American Univ., Puerto Rico, 1960-61;
Univ. of California, Los Angeles, 1961-73;
composer-in-residence, California State Univ.,
Los Angeles, 1973.
WORKS: BALLET: Western landscape, 1940;
From this earth, 1941; What so proudly we hail,
1942; ORCHESTRA: American portraits, 1929;
Toccata, 1931; 15 symphonies, 1933-78 (#10 was
the Abraham Lincoln symph., with chorus and 2
amplified pianos, 1965; #12 was commissioned by
the New York Phil. in honor of his 70th birthday, 1968; #14 was commissioned by the National
Symph., premiered, Wash., 10 Feb. 1976); When
Johnny comes marching home, overture, 1934;

Prelude and fugue, strings, 1935; Farewell to
pioneers, 1935; Time suite, 1937; Evening piece,
1940; Ode to truth, 1940; Acceleration, 1941;
Radio piece, accordion concerto, 1946; 2-piano
concerto, 1946; Quest, 1947; Elegy and paean,
viola and orch., 1948; Kentucky spring, 1949;
Cumberland concerto, 1951; Abraham Lincoln walks
at midnight, soprano, piano, and orch., 1953;
piano concerto, 1953; Fantasy, piano and orch.,
1954; Ode to consonance, 1957; Elegy and dance,
1958; Give me the splendid, silent sun, baritone
and orch., 1961; Canticle to the sun, soprano
and chamber orch., 1961; These times, piano and
orch., 1962; Epilogue to Profiles in courage:
J. F. K., 1964; Horn of plenty, 1964; Rhythm and
spaces, string orch., 1965; concerto for piano,
amplified wind instruments, and orch., 1968;
BAND: Cimarron, overture, 1940; Take the sun
and keep the stars, 1944; Fruit of gold, 1949;
Dark devotion, 1950; CHAMBER MUSIC: Impressions
of a rainy day, string quartet, 1926; concerto
for piano, clarinet, and string quartet, 1927;
piano sonata, 1928; string quartet, 1930; Fantasy,
piano and woodwind quintet, 1932; Chorale for
strings, 1932; 3 variations on a theme, string
quartet, 1933; 4 minutes and 20 seconds, flute
and string quartet, 1934; piano trio, 1934;
piano quintet, 1936; string quartet, 1939;
Soliloquy and dance, viola and piano, 1939;
string quintet, 1940; violin sonata, 1941; 4
charming little pieces, violin and piano, 1942;
many works for chorus and solo voice; piano and
organ pieces; FILM SCORE: One tenth of a nation.
The Roy Harris Archive is housed at the Kennedy
Memorial Library, California State Univ., Los
Angeles.

HARRIS, RUSSELL G.
b. Graymont, Ill., 3 Aug. 1914. Studied with
Ernst Krenek, Darius Milhaud, Ernst Toch, and
Egon Wellesz. He won first prize for Fugue with
chorale for organ, Clarke Cons. contest, 1935.
He has held faculty posts at Baylor Univ., Upper
Iowa Univ., and from 1948, at Hamline Univ.
WORKS: CHAMBER MUSIC: string quartet, 1951;
3 movements for chamber orch., 1969; CHORUS:
Tarye no lenger; It was beginning winter, 1961;
The moon is hiding, 1961; 3 songs, 1941; 5 piano
pieces, 1951.
> Music Dept., Hamline University, St. Paul,
> MN 55104

HARRIS, WESLEY M.
b. Defiance, Ohio, 1 Apr. 1920. Studied with
Ernst Bacon, Syracuse Univ. He has received
various awards and commissions. After military
service, 1942-45, and a year of public school
teaching, he was faculty member, Idaho State
Univ., 1947-77. He has published many sacred
and secular choral works.
> 29 Stanford Ave., Pocatello, ID 83201

HARRISON, CHARLES SCOTT
b. Seattle, Wash., 27 Feb. 1950. Studied with
James Hanna, Univ. of Southern Louisiana.
WORKS: THEATRE: Artist of the beautiful,
musical comedy based on Hawthorne, 1973; ORCHESTRA: symphony; 5 orchestral miniatures; CHAMBER

HARRISON, LOU

MUSIC: string quartet; sonata breve, string
bass; organ preludes; piano sonata, 1972; ELEC-
TRONIC: Time changes, music for modern dance.

HARRISON, LOU
b. Portland, Oreg., 14 May 1917. Attended San
Francisco State Coll., 1934-35; studied privately
with Henry Cowell and Arnold Schoenberg. His
awards include American Acad. of Arts and Letters
grant, 1947; Guggenheim fellowships, 1952, 1954;
20th-Century Masterpiece award, Rome, 1954;
Fromm Found. award, 1955; Louisville Orch. com-
mission, 1961; Rockefeller fellowship for study
of Asian music, 1961; senior scholar, East West
Center, Univ. of Hawaii, 1963; Phebe Ketchum
Thorne fellowship, 1966; panel member, World
Music Council and UNESCO Conf., 1968; membership,
Nat. Inst. of Arts and Letters, 1973;
Koussevitzky Found. commission, 1975. He taught
at Mills Coll., 1937-40; Univ. of California,
Los Angeles, 1942; Reed Coll., 1950; Black Mt.
Coll., 1951; from 1968, at San Jose State Univ.
Moving to New York in 1943, he wrote for several
publications, composed for dance groups, and
conducted often, including the first performance
of any Charles Ives symphony, the 3rd, on 5 Apr.
1947. After a decade in New York, he has lived
in California, lecturing, developing his interest
in Oriental music and microtones, inventing
instruments to play them, and experimenting with
unorthodox sonorities--from automobile brake
drums, lengths of pipe, etc.; has organized and
performed in concerts of Chinese music; written
plays, poetry, liner notes for Ives's records,
and a pamphlet on Carl Ruggles. Harrison reads
and speaks Esperanto fluently; he has given
Esperanto titles to some of his compositions and
has even written an essay on chlorophyll in
Esperanto and set it for 8 baritones and orchestra.
    WORKS: THEATRE: Rapunzel, opera, New York,
14 May 1959; Jeptha's daughter, "a theatre kit,"
Cabrillo Coll., 9 Mar. 1963; Young Caesar,
puppet opera, Aptos, Calif., 21 Aug. 1971;
BALLET: Almanac of the seasons; Changing world;
Green mansions; Io and Prometheus; Johnny
Appleseed; Labyrinth; Perilous chapel, 1949;
Solstice, 1950; The marriage at the Eiffel Tower,
was performed in New York, 7 Feb. 1977, with
Harrison and Virgil Thomson narrating the text;
Praises for hummingbirds and hawks; Something to
please everybody; Western dance; ORCHESTRA:
Alleluia; The only jealousy of Emer; Simfony I,
from Simfonies in free style; suite for violin,
piano, orch.; 3 suites for strings; symphony in
G; Elegiac symphony, Oakland, 7 Dec. 1976; PER-
CUSSION: Canticles #1 and 2; Koncherto por la
violono kun perkuta orkestro; flute concerto;
Double music (with John Cage); fugue; Song of
Queztecoatl; CHAMBER MUSIC: Air for flute; At
the tomb of Charles Ives; Concerto in slendro
for violin; Motet for the Day of Ascension; 7
pastorales; suite for cello and harp; suite for
string quartet; string trio; Praise for the
beauty of hummingbirds, chamber ensemble, 1976;
also choral works, songs, piano pieces.
    7163 Viewpoint Rd., Aptos, CA 95003

HART, FREDERIC PATTON
b. Aberdeen, Wash., 5 Sept. 1894. Studied with
Glenn Dillard Gunn and Arthur Olaf Andersen,
American Cons.; with Rubin Goldmark, Ernest
Hutcheson, A. Diller and E. Quaile in New York;
with Nadia Boulanger in Paris. He taught at
Sarah Lawrence Coll., 1929-47; Juilliard School,
1947-61; and was director, Diller-Quaile School
of Music, 1940-55.
    WORKS: THEATRE: The wheel of fortune,
opera, 1934; The romance of Robot, 1-act opera,
1937; "Poison" and The farewell supper, 2 chamber
operas; The golden rape and The building, 2
musicals; also chamber music, piano pieces,
songs.
    386 S. Burnside Ave., #6C, Los Angeles, CA
90036

HART, WELDON
b. Place-Bear Spring, Tenn., 19 Sept. 1911; d.
East Lansing, Mich., 20 Nov. 1957. Studied at
Univ. of Michigan; with Howard Hanson and
Bernard Rogers, Eastman School of Music, Ph.D.
1946. He was music chairman, Western Kentucky
State Coll., 1946-49; director, School of Music,
West Virginia Univ., 1949-57; music chairman,
Michigan State Univ., 1957.
    WORKS: ORCHESTRA: The dark hills, sym-
phonic poem, 1939; Sinfonietta, 1944; symphony,
1945; violin concerto, 1951; 3 West Virginia
folk songs, with chorus, 1954; other choral
works and several violin pieces.

HART, WILLIAM SEBASTIAN
b. Baltimore, Md., 30 Oct. 1920. Graduated cum
laude, Peabody Cons.; attended Johns Hopkins
Univ., B.A., Ph.D. His awards include 3 honorary
doctorates. He taught percussion, Peabody Cons.,
1939-62; taught in public schools, 1939-52; at
Morgan State Coll., 1962-65; and has been music
director, Gettysburg Symph. Orch., from 1958.
He has composed sonatina for 2 flutes and Concert
piece for timpani duet.
    1800 Cromwell Bridge Rd., Baltimore, MD
21234

HARTKE, STEPHEN PAUL
b. Orange, N.J., 6 July 1952. Studied with
Laurence Widdoes in New York; with Leonardo
Balada, United Nations Internat. School; with
James Drew, Yale Univ. He received N.Y. State
School Music Assoc. composition award, 1969; BMI
awards, 1970, 1972; William DeVane award, Yale
Univ., 1973.
    WORKS: CHAMBER MUSIC: The bull transcended,
string orch., 1970; Alysoun, contralto and 8
instruments, 1971; The hunting of the snark,
chamber oratorio on text by Lewis Carroll,
baritone solo, chorus, chamber orch., 1972;
Passion, poison, and petrification, chamber
symph., New York, Mar. 1973.

HARTLEY, GERALD
b. Spokane, Wash., 18 Sept. 1921. Studied with
George Frederick McKay and John Verrall, Univ.
of Washington. He has been choral director,
Lewis and Clark High School, Spokane, from 1953;
was instructor, Gongoza Univ., 1955-65.

WORKS: ORCHESTRA: Sonatine for piano and orch.; Sketches, string orch.; BAND: Plymouth Town--Sea chantey rhapsody; Fuguing tune; concerto grosso, winds and percussion; Rondo, piano and band; CHAMBER MUSIC: Divertissement, woodwind quintet; Tympani concertante; CHORUS: 4 19th-century lyrics, choral suite; The builders, with orch.; Choral fanfare for Christmas.

East 1011 Overbluff Rd., Spokane, WA 99203

HARTLEY, WALTER S.
b. Washington, D.C., 21 Feb. 1927. Studied with Bernard Rogers and Howard Hanson, Eastman School of Music, B.M. 1950, M.M. 1951, Ph.D. 1953. His awards include a Koussevitzky Found. commission, 1954; Conn Brass Music award, 1964; State Univ. of New York research grants, 1970-71, 1974; ASCAP awards annually from 1962. He was instructor, Nat. Music Camp, 1956-64; on faculty, Davis and Elkins Coll., 1958-69; at State Univ. Coll., Fredonia, N.Y., from 1969.
WORKS: ORCHESTRA: piano concerto, 1952; chamber symphony, 1954; Variations for orch., 1973; BAND: concerto for 23 winds, 1957; 3 sinfonias, 1963, 1965, 1977; alto saxophone concerto, 1966; symphony for wind orch., 1970; Canticles for voices and wind ensemble, 1971; Southern tier suite, 1972; Bacchanalia, 1975; music for brass and percussion, 1976; CHAMBER MUSIC: sonata concertante, trombone and piano, 1958; duo for saxophone and piano, 1964; tuba sonata, 1967, piano sonata, 1968; suite for saxophone quartet, 1972; tenor saxophone sonata, 1974; concerto for tuba and percussion, 1974; saxophone octet, 1975; Metamorphoses, clarinet and piano, 1975; quartet for reeds, 1977; Sonorities I-VI, a series of brief experimental works, each for 1 wind instrument and keyboard, 1972-78; numerous works for chorus.

50 Maple Ave., Fredonia, NY 14063

HARTMANN, ARTHUR MARTINUS
b. Mate Szalka, Hungary, 23 July 1881; U.S. citizen; d. New York, N.Y., 30 Mar. 1956. Studied with Charles Martin Loeffler. He toured the U.S. and Europe as solo violinist with symphony orchestras and with the Hartmann String Quartet.
WORKS: ORCHESTRA: Suite in ancient style; Caprice; Impressions from the Balkans; CHORUS: Oh weep for those that wept, with orch.; The prayer of Moses; also many transcriptions and arrangements.

HARTWAY, JAMES JOHN
b. Detroit, Mich., 24 Apr. 1944. Studied with Ruth Shaw Wylie, Wayne State Univ., B.A. 1966, M.M. 1969; with H. Owen Reed, Michigan State Univ., Ph.D. 1972. His awards include assistantships, scholarships, Hinman fellowship, 1971; second place, Phi Mu Alpha contest, 1971; first prize, Young Musicians Found. contest, 1974; Michigan Arts award in music, 1978; and many commissions. He was instructor, Lansing Community Coll., 1970-71; from 1971, faculty member, Wayne State Univ.
WORKS: ORCHESTRA: Dialogue, with piano, 1968; Couleurs, with percussion solo, 1969; 7

ways of looking at a blackbird, with soprano solo, 1972; BAND: 2 Rube Goldbergs, 1973; JAZZ ENSEMBLE: Judgment of Solomon, 1967; Impressions of childhood, 1967; 5-4-3, 1968; Tomorrow's dream, 1971; CHAMBER MUSIC: Piece for quartet and Mirror image, improvisation ensemble, 1968; wind octet, 1969; Anagogia, piano, 1970; 3 ways of looking at a blackbird, soprano, flute, piano, percussion, 1970; CHORUS: Sequence, with percussion, 1970; Waiting to be processed, women's voices, typewriters, percussion, tape, 1973; 3 e.e.s. for SSAA, women's voices, piano, flute; many multimedia works using dance, narrator, slides, lights, tape, etc.

11931 Laing St., Detroit, MI 48224

HARTZELL, LAWRENCE WILLIAM
b. Mt. Pleasant, N.Y., 1 July 1942. Studied at Baldwin-Wallace Coll., B.M.; with John Pozdro, Edward Mattila, and Douglas Moore, Univ. of Kansas, M.M., Ph.D. He has received several commissions. He was faculty member, Univ. of Kansas, 1965-67; Univ. of Wisconsin-Eau Claire, 1968-73; from 1973 at Baldwin-Wallace Coll.
WORKS: WIND ENSEMBLE: Introduction and allegro, brass and percussion, 1969; Toccata concertata, organ and brass choir, 1970; Thunder Bay, symphony for band, 1971-73; CHAMBER MUSIC: horn sonata, 1964; piano sonata, 1966; quintet for trumpet and strings, 1971; Jefferson variations, saxophone and percussion, 1972; 4 places, clarinet alone, 1973; ELECTRONIC: Conversation, bass trombone and tape, 1971; Discourse, jazz ensemble and tape, 1971.

Music Dept., Baldwin-Wallace College, Berea, OH 44017

HARVEY, PETER J.
b. Bangor, Maine, 10 Apr. 1945. Studied with Jerry L. Bowder, Univ. of Maine; with Arnold Franchetti, Hartt Coll. of Music. He was music director in public schools, 1966-69; choral director, Univ. of Maine, Fort Kent, 1969-71; from 1972, at Hartford Coll. for Women.
WORKS: CHORUS: Haec dies, with organ and trumpet; The Passion according to St. Luke, with soloists, organ, 2 horns, timpani, narrator; Good news and great joy: The Christmas gospel, with tenor solo, organ, congregation, optional brass.

911 Matianuck Ave., Windsor, CT 06095

HASKINS, ROBERT JAMES
b. Denver, Colo., 27 Dec. 1937. Attended Univ. of Denver, 1956-59; studied with William Walters, Wittenberg Univ., B.M. 1961, M.M. 1962; with Paul Cooper, Univ. of Cincinnati. His awards include first prize, Nat. Fed. of Music Clubs, 1962; Nat. Endowment for the Arts grant, 1974. He has been musical director, Springfield Civic Opera Company, 1961-63, and from 1974; chorusmaster, Dayton Opera Company, from 1974; conductor, Wilmington Chamber Orch., from 1963; and faculty member, Wilmington Coll., from 1963.
WORKS: OPERA: Benjamin, 1960; Mr. Godfry, 1961; Cassandra Southwick, 1963; The prisoners, 1964; The cask of amontillado, 1968; Young Goodman Brown, 1971 (librettist for the last 4

HASLAM, HERBERT

was John Koppenhaver); MUSIC DRAMA: The bell
tower, based on Herman Melville, 1976; The
legend of Sleepy Hollow, based on Washington
Irving, 1976; The masque of the red death, on
Edgar Allan Poe, 1976; Transparent morning,
Koppenhaver text, 1976; ORCHESTRA: 4 symphonies,
#1 in 1 movement, #2 with chorus and soli, #3
And man created God in his own image, text by
Koppenhaver, #4 Sinfonia requiem, with soprano
and baritone, text by Koppenhaver; also songs,
chamber music.
    Wilmington College, Wilmington, OH 45177

HASLAM, HERBERT
    b. Philadelphia, Pa., 23 Apr. 1928. Studied at
Temple Univ. and at Juilliard School, B.S., M.S.
He has taught at Bronx House Music School and
the Barker School; was founder and codirector,
Composers Circle, N.Y.; composer-in-residence,
Riverdale Country Schools; executive associate,
Riverdale School of Music.
    WORKS: OPERA: Carnival of Eden, commis-
sioned by Univ. of New Delhi, India, and per-
formed there, Feb. 1969; ORCHESTRA: Special
starlight, with chorus and narrator, Sandburg
text; CHAMBER MUSIC: Antimasque, brass quartet;
Haiku set, viola and cello.
    Riverdale School, W. 253 & Post Rd., Bronx,
NY 10471

HASSELL, JOHN
    b. Memphis, Tenn., 22 Mar. 1937. Studied with
Bernard Rogers, Eastman School of Music, B.M.
1969, M.M. 1970; with Karlheinz Stockhausen and
Henri Pousseur in Cologne, 1965-67. He was
composer-in-residence, Center for Creative and
Performing Arts, Buffalo, N.Y., 1967-69. In
Elemental warnings, a part of his experimental
work Landscape series, 1969-72, he uses results
achieved by burying electronic oscillators in
the ground and floating them on balloons.
    WORKS: Music for vibraphones, 1965; Black-
board piece with girls and loops, 2 girls and 2
pitch-producing blackboards, New York, 26 Mar.
1968; Goodbye music, mixed media, Buffalo, 4 May
1969; Superball, for 4 players with hand-held
magnetic tape heads, Ithaca, 29 Oct. 1969;
Vernal equinox, concrete sounds of tropical
birds, insects, and ocean waves, perucssion and
electronics, 1978.
    c/o Art Services, 463 West St., New York,
NY 10014

HASSELL, MICHAEL RICHARD
    b. Omaha, Nebr., 4 Jan. 1951. Studied with Hans
Janowitz in Central America; composition with
William Maloof, John Bavicchi, Gregg Smith, John
La Porta, conducting with Jeronimas Kacinskas in
Boston. He has been on the faculty, Berklee
Coll. of Music from 1971; was conductor, Chorus
Pro Terra, Panama; guest conductor of choruses
in the Boston area.
    WORKS: ORCHESTRA: 3 femmes fatales, suite;
CHAMBER MUSIC: piano sonata, 1972; CHORUS:
Missa brevis, with brass and percussion, 1973;
Ode: Intimations of immortality, 1973; On the
elements, a cycle, Boston, 25 Apr. 1974.
    400 Commonwealth Ave., #325, Boston, MA
02215

HASTINGS, ROSS
    b. Los Angeles, Calif., 26 Feb. 1915. Was
organist-choirmaster, San Diego, 1948-53; music
coordinator, Hollywood Bowl.
    WORKS: ORCHESTRA: Sinfonia brevis; sona-
tine; Sketch for orchestra; CHORUS: Festival
prayer; My heart changes key; O God, our help in
ages past.

HATTON, GAYLEN
    b. Red Mountain, Calif., 4 Oct. 1928. Studied
with Leon Dallin and Crawford Gates, Brigham
Young Univ.; with Leroy Robertson, Univ. of
Utah. His awards include Intermountain Concert
Society award, 1957; Rosenblatt award, 1958;
Sacramento Symph. award, 1967; Nat. Endowment
for the Arts grant, 1970. He was faculty member,
Univ. of Utah, 1957-63; California State Univ.,
Sacramento, 1963-78, Sun Valley Music Camp,
1963-72; Sugar Mt. Music Camp, 1971-72; played
horn, Utah Symph., 1954-63.
    WORKS: BALLET: Seasonal episode; Toxcatl
(Ballet west), 1962; Odette baby, jazz ballet,
1967; Opus psychedelia, electronic ballet, 1970;
ORCHESTRA: Essay for orch., 1957; Music for
orch., 1958; Jeu-parti, 1967; Suite from Toxcatl,
1972; Prelusion, 1975; BAND: Diversion, 1963;
Music for band, 1966; CHAMBER MUSIC: 3 string
quartets; trio for oboe, viola, cello; Music for
tape and horn.
    7720 Bar Du Lane, Sacramento, CA 95829

HAUBIEL, CHARLES TROWBRIDGE
    b. Delta, Ohio, 30 Jan. 1892; d. Los Angeles,
Calif., 1978. Studied with Rudolph Ganz in
Berlin, 1909-13; with Rosario Scalero at Mannes
Coll. of Music, 1919-25; with Josef and Rosina
Lhevinne in New York, 1928-31. His many awards
included first prize in America in the Internat.
Schubert Centennial contest, 1928; Swift Symphonic award; New York Phil. Symph. contest,
1938; Ohioana Library Assoc. citation, 1953;
Harvey Gaul Memorial prize; Nat. Fed. of Music
Clubs Awards of Merit, 1963, 1965; honorary doctorate, Southwestern Cons.; 2 concerts in honor
of his 86th birthday were given in Los Angeles
in Jan. 1978. He made his debut as recitalist
in 1909, then in 1913, toured the U.S. as
associate artist with Jaroslav Kocian, violinist.
He was faculty member, Kingfisher Coll. and Inst.
of Musical Art, Oklahoma City, 1913-17; served
as bandmaster, U.S. Army, 1917-19; was faculty
member, Juilliard School, 1921-29, and New York
Univ., 1922-47. He founded the Composers Press
in 1935. His library of some 30 orchestral
works, memorabilia, and correspondence were left
to the Hans Moldenhauer Archives to be placed in
the library at Northwestern Univ.
    WORKS: OPERA: Brigands preferred, comic
opera, 1925; The witch's curse, fairy opera;
Sunday costs 5 pesos, Mexican folk opera, 1950;
Berta, Mexican folk opera; ORCHESTRA: Mars
ascending, 1923; Of human destiny (formerly
called Karma), 1928; Portraits, 1935; Suite
passecaille, 1935; symphony, 1937; Vox cathe-
dralis, 1937; The plane beyond, 1938; Solari,
1938; Passacaglia triptych; Pioneers; Portals,
with high voice solo; Miniatures, 1938; Meta-

morphoses; Vision of St. Joan, with chorus, 1941; Serenade, lyric cantata with chorus; Gothic variations, violin and orch., 1943; 1865 A.D.; The cosmic Christ, high voice and orch.; Both grave and gay, 1944; American rhapsody, 1948; CHAMBER MUSIC: Duoforms, piano trio, 1929-30; piano trio, 1932; Echi classici, string quartet, 1936; string trio, 1943; cello sonata, 1944; violin sonata; Nuances, violin and piano, 1947; Cryptics, cello and piano, 1973; numerous other instrumental works, choral works, piano pieces.

HAUFRECHT, HERBERT
b. New York, N.Y., 3 Nov. 1909. Studied with Quincy Porter and Herbert Elwell, Cleveland Inst. of Music; with Rubin Goldmark at Juilliard Graduate School on a fellowship in composition, 1930-34. He was staff composer-arranger, WPA Federal Theatre, 1938-39; arranger-editor for music publishers, 1945-59; music director, Young Audiences, Inc., 1959-66; editor-director, Belwin-Mills, 1968-77.
    WORKS: OPERA: Boney Quillen, comic opera in 1 act; ORCHESTRA: suite for string orch., 1934; Overture for an American mural, 1939; The story of Ferdinand, with narrator, 1939; 3 fantastic marches, 1941; Square set, string orch., 1941; BAND: Walkin' the road, 1944; Prelude to a tragedy; symphony for brass and timpani, 1956; CHAMBER MUSIC: brass quintet; A woodland serenade, woodwind quintet, 1955; Etudes in blues, piano, 1951; CHORUS: Poor Richard's almanack, cycle of 6 songs; 6 songs by Charles Ives in choral settings.
    P.O. Box 14, Shady, NY 12479

HAUGLAND, A. OSCAR
b. Emmons, Minn., 28 Jan. 1922. Studied with Robert Delaney, Northwestern Univ.; with Howard Hanson, Bernard Rogers, and Herbert Elwell, Eastman School of Music. He received 3 dean's grants for composition, Northern Illinois Univ. He was faculty member, West Virginia Univ., 1949-52, 1954-60; from 1960, at Northern Illinois Univ.
    WORKS: THEATRE: incidental music to Ibsen's Peer Gynt, 1965; ORCHESTRA: 3 psalms; concertino, horn and strings; Restaurationem 1825, Fargo-Morehead Symph. Orch., 16 Nov. 1975; CHAMBER MUSIC: Little suite, woodwind quintet; string quartet; Toccata, trumpet and trombone; piano trio, DeKalb, 15 Nov. 1975; Toccata, organ, 1978; Nature's mysteries, piano, 1979; CHORUS: From the universe, a cycle; Chant of the Magi; This is the garden; Magazine madrigals, 1976; Growing up madrigals, 1979; SONGS: A letter came; The hour of dreaming, soprano and piano; Maggie and milly and molly and may, soprano and piano, DeKalb, 6 Feb. 1978.
    756 S. 3rd St., DeKalb, IL 60115

HAUSSERMANN, JOHN
b. Manila, P.I., 21 Aug. 1909. Studied at Cincinnati Cons.; with Paul Le Flem in Paris. In Sept. 1979, his 70th birthday was celebrated in San Francisco with a recital of his works.
    WORKS: ORCHESTRA: 3 symphonies, 1941, 1944, 1949; concerto for voice and orch., 1942;

CHAMBER MUSIC: quintet for harpsichord and woodwind quartet; 2 string quartets; Suite rustique, flute, cello, piano; 3 divertissements, string quartet; organ works, piano pieces, songs.

HAWLEY, WILLIAM
b. Bronxville, N.Y., 11 Apr. 1950. Studied at Ithaca Coll.; with James Tenney, Morton Subotnick, Earle Brown, and Harold Budd, California Inst. of the Arts. He was a founding member of the Independent Composers Assoc., 1977.
    WORKS: ORCHESTRA: Zeno, 1974-75; CHAMBER MUSIC: CAGE, piano, 1976; Receding moment, violin and piano, 1977; Music for cello and piano, 1978; 7 steps, 2 pianos, 1978; ELECTRONIC: Lumina, 1974; Wave (for Kiyoko), 1975.
    47 Walker St., New York, NY 10013

HAYDON, GLEN
b. Inman, Kans., 9 Dec. 1896; d. Chapel Hill, N.C., 8 May 1966. Studied at Univ. of California, B.A. 1918, M.A. 1921; with Eugene Cools, Vienna Univ., Ph.D. 1932. He was musicologist as well as composer; held various teaching posts in the Berkeley (Calif.) schools, 1920-25; was faculty member, Univ. of California, Berkeley, 1929-31; at Univ. of North Carolin, from 1934; in 1947, was appointed Louis C. Elson lecturer at the Library of Congress, Washington.
    WORKS: THEATRE: The druid's weed, ballet, 1929; incidental music for Aristophanes' Lysistrata, 1936; CHORUS: mass, a cappella, 1930. He was author of many musicological works.

HAYES, ISAAC
b. near Memphis, Tenn., 20 Aug. 1942. Is an exceedingly popular soul singer and organist. The theme from his film score Shaft won a BMI Oscar; the score was nominated for the best score category, received a Grammy award, 1972, Golden Globe award, and the Nat. Assoc. for the Advancement of Colored People Image award. He also wrote the film score for The man.

HAYES, JOSEPH
b. Marietta, Ohio, 5 Dec. 1920. Studied at Boston Cons., 1940-41; with Warren Storey Smith, New England Cons., 1946-49; with Gardner Read, Boston Univ., 1949-50, 1955. He has received commissions and citations. He has been faculty member, Jarvis Christian Coll., 1953-56; Detroit Community Coll., from 1963.
    WORKS: ORCHESTRA: Sunday 3:00 p.m., symphony for woodwind quintet, saxophone quintet, brass sextet, piano, percussion, and strings; Music for viewing, orch., singing and speaking chorus, and dancers, in 5 parts, performed as a set or singly: Curtain call, Councils of war, On contemplating a flower, Sleep, Retrospect; BAND: Chorale; CHAMBER MUSIC: Recitative and air, horn and piano; Hornotations #1, horn and strings; quintet for clarinet, bassoon, violin, cello, piano; Fanfare and ricercare, brass quartet; Quartet miniature, strings; Episodes, woodwind quintet; 2 soliloquies, solo cello; Praeludium, organ; CHORUS: Lord's prayer, a cappella; Lullaby; Song of the colours, a cappella; Time capsules, double women's chorus

HAYMAN, RICHARD PERRY

and woodwind quintet; many vocal solos and piano
pieces.
17160 Kentucky, Detroit, MI 48221

HAYMAN, RICHARD PERRY
b. Sandia, N.Mex., 29 July 1951. Studied with
Vladimir Ussachevsky, Columbia Univ.; privately
with John Cage, Philip Corner, Patrick Carpenter,
and Ravi Shankar. From 1974 he has been coeditor of Ear magazine; was an audio-sleep researcher, 1975-76; and in 1978, founded Ear Inn
and is events director for the Establishment.
WORKS: I am a toupee, for flashlight and
bell, 1973; Prelude, an electronic work, and
Carry for organ, performed with Multigravitational Dance, New York, 1973; Don't mean a thing
if it ain't got dat swing, chorus, Chocorua
Music Festival, 1973; it is not here, beeping
tone and light, Museum of Modern Art, N.Y., 14
June 1974; Picasso, instruments, piano, electronics, commissioned by Multigravitational
Aerodance Group, 1976; Dreamsound, multimedia
event for a sleeping audience, Berkeley, 20 Feb.
1976, and widely throughout the U.S.; Waves, 40
celli, 1977; Requiem for the West Side Highway,
chorus, brass ensemble, dancers, 1977.
326 Spring St., New York, NY 10013

HAYS, DORIS ERNESTINE
b. Memphis, Tenn., 6 Aug. 1941. Studied with
Arthur Plettner, Univ. of Chattanooga; with
Richard Hervig, Univ. of Iowa; Friedrich Wuhrer
in Munich; Paul Badura-Skoda, Univ. of Wisconsin,
M.M. 1968. Her awards include first prize,
Internat. Competition for Interpreters of Contemporary Music, Rotterdam, 1971; fellowships,
Bavarian Ministry of Culture and Univ. of Wisconsin; Nat. Endowment for the Arts grant, 1977.
She was faculty member, Univ. of Wisconsin,
1967-68; Cornell Coll., 1969; Queens Coll.,
1974-75; artist-in-residence, Georgia Council
for the Arts, 1975-76; director, Meet the Composer Concerts, 1976.
WORKS: THEATRE: Uni, ballet, string quartet, flute, tape, narrator, New York, 8 Feb.
1979, with composer narrating; CHAMBER MUSIC:
Scheveningen Beach, 5 flutes; Help compose,
pianist and audience; Characters, harpsichord,
string quintet, 2 clarinets, oboe; Breathless
and winded, bass flute, 1976; Set of cheeky
tongue, soprano and piano, 1976; Sunday nights,
piano, New York, 13 Feb. 1977; Sensevents,
string trio, flute, oboe, horn, 1977; Past
present, piano, 1978; MIXED MEDIA: Pamp (ceremony in high places), piano, bird calls, tape;
If, 2 pianos and tape. She is author of Sound
symbol structures, an introduction to new keyboard notation.
697 West End Ave., Ph.B, New York, NY 10025

HAYS, ROBERT D.
b. Boise, Idaho, 31 Jan. 1923. Studied with
Arnold Elston, Univ. of Oregon; with Bernhard
Heiden, Indiana Univ., D.M. 1967. He received
a Mississippi Educational Television award,
1969. He was faculty member, Univ. of Southern
Mississippi, 1956-69; with a private audio firm,
Los Angeles, 1969-73; from 1973, on faculty,

Central Michigan Univ.
WORKS: ORCHESTRA: To the memory of the
author, with chorus and narrator, 1964; symphony,
1965; BAND: Dramatic fanfares, 1961; Design for
band, 1963; CHAMBER MUSIC: string quartet, 1965;
Music for 7, 1969; cello sonata, 1973; Music for
winds, woodwind quintet, 1973; MIXED MEDIA:
Oracle of Apollo, tape, band, synthesizer, 1967;
Chronograms I, tape, tuba, electric guitar,
clarinet, piano, mixer, 1973.
622 S. Franklin, Mt. Pleasant, MI 48858

HAYTON, LEONARD GEORGE (LENNIE)
b. New York, N.Y., 13 Feb. 1908; d. Palm Springs,
Calif., 24 Apr. 1971. Played piano in many
noted jazz bands; was music director, MGM
Studios, 1940-53; then with 20th Century-Fox
Film Corporation.
WORKS: JAZZ ENSEMBLE: Flying fingers;
Mood Hollywood; Midnight mood; FILM SCORES: On
the town, 1949; The Harvey girls; Singing in the
rain; Star.

HAZELMAN, HERBERT R.
b. Topton, N.C., 13 Oct. 1913. Studied with
Lamar Stringfield, Univ. of North Carolina. He
was oboist, North Carolina Symphony, 1930-35;
bandmaster, Greensboro High School, from 1936.
WORKS: ORCHESTRA: Pastoral passacaglia;
BAND: A short ballet for awkward dancers; Dance
variations on an obscure theme; Prelude and
fugue; Gallic galop; Dance for 3.
3206 Madison Ave., Greensboro, NC 27403

HAZEN SARA (Sally Hazen Evans)
b. Sarasota, Fla., 14 July 1935. Studied with
John Carter, Rollins Coll.; attended Duke Univ.,
A.B. 1957; studied with Roland Leich and Leonardo
Balada, Carnegie-Mellon Univ., 1972-73; piano
with Ferguson Webster. From 1976, she has been
librarian, Amherst Coll.
WORKS: CHAMBER MUSIC: City serenade, saxophone quartet, 1972; Delta suite, brass instruments, 1973; CHORUS: Christ is born, 1964;
Alleluia, we live in Thee, 1967; PIANO: Festival,
1964; Fantasy, 1972; Omega alpha variations,
Carnegie-Mellon Univ., 13 Dec. 1973.
Music Dept., Amherst College, Amherst, MA
01002

HAZZARD, PETER PEABODY
b. Poughkeepsie, N.Y., 31 Jan. 1949. Attended
Boston Univ., 1966-68; studied with John Bavicchi
and William Maloof, Berklee Coll. of Music, B.M.
1971. He has been faculty member at Berklee
Coll. since 1971.
WORKS: ORCHESTRA: Harwichport interlude,
1971; Merlin, cantata for solo bass, chorus, and
orch., 1971; Concertante, violin, cello, English
horn, clarinet soli, with orch., 1974; Children's
circus, a children's guide to the orch., 1976;
BAND: Canzona and overture, Boston, 5 Dec. 1972;
Fanfare for December 9, 1901, 1975; A festival
overture, 1977; The death of Faust, cantata with
soli and chorus, Boston, 24 Apr. 1978; CHAMBER
MUSIC: string quartet, 1971; clarinet quartet,
1971; contrabass sonata, 1971; woodwind sextet,
1971; suite for English horn and string quartet,

1972; quartet for 3 trombones and piano, 1975; sonata for solo clarinet, 1977; Pagan ritual, bassoon trio, 1977; many choral works, percussion works, piano pieces.
20 Myrtle St., Winchester, MA 01890

HEALEY, DEREK
b. Wargrave, England, 2 May 1936; to U.S. 1979. Studied with Herbert Howells, Royal Coll. of Music, London, 1953; Univ. of Durham, B.M. 1961; with Vito Frazzi and Goffredo Petrassi, Siena, Italy; Boris Porena in Rome; and with Luciano Berio at the Durham Summer School, 1967. His awards include the Cobbett prize, Sullivan prize, and Farrar prize at Royal Coll. of Music; F.M. Napolitano prize in Siena. He held academic posts in Canada, 1969-78; in 1979, was named to the faculty at Univ. of Oregon at Eugene.
WORKS: THEATRE: Seabird Island, opera in 2 acts; ORCHESTRA: Butterflies, with solo soprano, 1970; Arctic images, 1971; The raven, string orch.; NOH, triple concerto for flute, piano, synthesizer soli, and orch., 1974; Primrose in paradise, 1975; CHAMBER MUSIC: string quartet, 1961; cello sonata, 1961; Serenata, string quartet, 1968; Stinging, treble recorder, cello, harpsichord, tape, 1971; CHORUS: Clouds, 1972; 6 Canadian folk songs, 1973; In Flanders fields, with soprano voice and alto recorder, 1974; many organ works, piano pieces, music for children.
2877 Timberline Dr., Eugene, OR 97405

HEATH, JAMES E. (JIMMY)
b. Philadelphia, Pa., 25 Oct. 1926. Studied at Theodore Presser School in Philadelphia and with Rudolf Schramm in New York. His awards include the Jazz Festival award, Harstad, Norway; Jazz at Home Club award, Philadelphia; Creative Arts Public Service composer grant, New York. He has been saxophonist with noted jazz groups; instructor for Jazzmobile, and private teacher from 1968; has presented jazz lecture concerts in New York City schools and colleges.
WORKS: JAZZ: Jazz themes with improvisations for saxophone; Gemini; Gingerbread boy; A time and a place; Big P; One for Juan; The gap sealer; Love and understanding.
112-19 34th Ave., Corona, NY 11368

HEATON, WALLACE
b. Philadelphia, Pa., 31 Jan. 1914. Studied at West Chester State Coll.; with Stefan Wolpe, Philadelphia Musical Acad., B.M., M.M.; received an honorary D.M. from Combs Coll. of Music. He has been professor and director of music, Drexel Univ., from 1945.
WORKS: CHORUS: Great among nations; Psalm of peace; Good Lord, defend and save; Captain Noah; Bobcat Rogers; and many others; also organ works.
340 Kirk Lane, Media, PA 19063

HEBBLE, ROBERT CHRISTIAN
b. Orange, N.J., 14 Feb. 1934. Studied with Quincy Porter, Yale Univ., B.M. 1955; with Nadia Boulanger in Paris, 1955-56; Vittorio Giannini and Roger Sessions at Juilliard School, M.S.

1966. He was department chairman, Red Bank Catholic High School, 1957-76; has been on music faculty, Stevens Inst. of Technology, from 1968; church organist in the New York-New Jersey area from 1955.
WORKS: CHORUS: Celebration of unity, a mass; Praise to the Lord, the Almighty; And rejoice; My spirit longeth for Thee; Jesus, Lord we look to Thee; also organ pieces.
19 Grandview Ave., West Orange, NJ 07052

HEDWALL, PAUL D.
b. Hartford, Conn., 18 Apr. 1939. Studied with Malloy Miller, Hugo Norden, Gardner Reed, Boston Univ.; with Vittorio Giannini, Manhattan School of Music; with Ingolf Dahl and Halsey Stevens, Univ. of Southern California. He received first prize, Brookline, Mass., Library Assoc. contest, 1961; first prize, Music Society of Santa Barbara, 1968. He has been faculty member, Univ. of Alabama, from 1969.
WORKS: ORCHESTRA: Symphony--Psalm 148, with chorus and soloists, 1972; CHAMBER MUSIC: piano sonata, 4 hands, 1961; flute sonata, 1965; Sky and clouds, song cycle, 1968; Teleologiae, trumpet, trombone, piano, commissioned by the Alchin Fund, 1972; $5 \times 5 = 5 = 1$, woodwind quintet, Univ. of Alabama grant, 1973.
9 Hickory Hill, Tuscaloosa, AL 35401

HEFTI, NEAL
b. Hastings, Nebr., 29 Oct. 1922. Was trumpeter in dance orchestras, 1941-51; staff conductor at ABC for the Arthur Godfrey show and the Kate Smith show; then played in his own orchestra.
WORKS: ORCHESTRA: Wheels of freedom, written for the Nat. Auto Show, 1960; FILM SCORES: Sex and the single girl; How to murder your wife; Synanon; Harlow; Boeing, Boeing; Lord love a duck; and many songs.

HEGENBART, ALEX F.
b. Amsterdam, Neth., 2 Aug. 1922; U.S. citizen 1956. Studied with Arend Koole at the Amsterdam Cons. He has been church choir director from 1958; also faculty member at Gaston Coll., Dallas, N.C.
WORKS: THEATRE: Hurt doesn't always, jazz musical; CHORUS: Hear ye!, Christmas cantata; Simeon's prayer; Behold what love; Meditation; Behold a stranger; Psalm of life; and many other anthems.
Rt. 1, Box 120-M-2, Belmont, NC 28012

HEIDEN, BERNHARD
b. Frankfurt, Germany, 24 Aug. 1910; U.S. citizen 1941. Studied with Paul Hindemith in Berlin; with Donald Grout, Cornell Univ., M.A. 1946. His awards include the Mendelssohn prize, 1953; Fine Arts composition award, 1951; Guggenheim fellowship, 1966; Nat. Endowment for the Arts grant, 1976. He has been professor, Indiana Univ., from 1946.
WORKS: OPERA: The darkened city, Bloomington, Ind., 23 Feb. 1963; ORCHESTRA: Euphorion, 1949; concerto for small orch., 1949; 2 symphonies, 1938, 1954; Memorial, 1955; concerto for piano, violin, cello, and orch., 1956;

HEIFETZ, VLADIMIR

Variations for orch., 1960; Envoy, 1963; concertino for string orch., 1967; horn concerto, 1969; Partita, 1970; tuba concerto, 1976; CHAMBER MUSIC: alto saxophone sonata, 1937; horn sonata, 1939; 3 string quartets, 1947, 1951, 1964; Sinfonia, woodwind quintet, 1949; quintet for horn and string quartet, 1952; violin sonata, 1954; clarinet sonata, 1955; piano trio, 1956; cello sonata, 1958; flute sonatina, 1958; viola sonata, 1959; Siena, cello and piano, 1961; woodwind quintet, 1965; brass quintet, 1967; Inventions, 2 celli, 1967; Intrada, woodwind quintet and alto saxophone, 1970; 5 canons for horns, 1971; CHORUS: 2 songs of spring, 1947; Divine poems, 1949; In memoriam, 1964; PIANO: sonata, 4 hands, 1946; sonata, 1952.
915 E. University, Bloomington, IN 47401

HEIFETZ, VLADIMIR
b. Russia, 28 Mar. 1893; to U.S. 1921; d. New York, N.Y., 3 May 1970. Studied at St. Petersburg Cons. He was accompanist to Feodor Chaliapin on his Russian tour; conducted in Pittsburgh; conducted Heifetz Singers in U.S. and Israel; was accompanist and arranger for radio, television, and films.
WORKS: OPERA: Pharaoh; Le mizele maizele, children's opera; CHORUS: The golem, oratorio; CANTATAS: Yiddishe legende; President Roosevelt message; Ani Yehudi; Lebern mire; PIANO: Biblical suite; FILM SCORES: Potemkin; Green fields.

HEILMAN, WILLIAM CLIFFORD
b. Williamsport, Pa., 27 Dec. 1877; d. Williamsport, 20 Dec. 1946. Studied at Harvard Univ., B.A. 1900; with Joseph Rheinberger and Charles Widor in Europe. He taught at Harvard, 1905-30. His compositions include a symphonic poem, chamber music, choral works, and piano pieces.

HEILNER, IRWIN
b. New York, N.Y., 14 May 1908. Studied with Rubin Goldmark and Roger Sessions, Juilliard School; with Nadia Boulanger in France; attended Teachers Coll., Columbia Univ., B.S., M.A. He won honorable mention for suite for harp and orch., Northern California Harpists' Assoc., 1950. He was principal librarian, Passaic Public Library, 1959-78; since 1970, has written music and record reviews for Jewish Currents.
WORKS: ORCHESTRA: Snapshots of a troubled world, suite; Swing symphony; SONGS: The tide rises; The traveler; Chinese songs, 1947; PIANO: Boogie woogie rhapsody.
101 Dawson Ave., Clifton, NJ 07012

HEIM, NORMAN MICHAEL
b. Chicago, Ill., 30 Sept. 1929. Attended Univ. of Evansville, B.M.E.; Eastman School of Music, M.M., D.M.A., majoring in clarinet; is primarily self-taught as a composer. He received Lilly Found. grants, 1959, 1960; Univ. of Maryland grants, 1965, 1968, 1974, 1978; and sabbaticals for research, writing, and composing. He was faculty member, Central Missouri Coll., 1952-53; Univ. of Evansville, 1953-60; from 1960, at Univ. of Maryland.

WORKS: BAND: Sea preludes; CHAMBER MUSIC: suite for 2 clarinets; sonata for clarinet solo; 5 songs of nature, tenor, clarinet, and piano; Elegiac poem, clarinet and piano; clarinet sonata; Elegy, clarinet choir; Praeludium and canzona, clarinet choir; suite for 3 horns, 1978; In remembrance, clarinet and piano, 1979; Collage, clarinet and percussion, 1980; Poem, horn and clarinet choir, 1980; choral works and several books of studies for clarinet.
7402 Wells Blvd., Hyattsville, MD 20783

HEINKE, JAMES
b. Cedar Rapids, Iowa, 20 Aug. 1945. Studied with Richard Hoffmann at Oberlin Coll.; with Arthur Berger and Seymour Shifrin at Brandeis Univ.; and computer-generated sound with John Chowning and Leland Smith, Stanford Univ. He received a German-American exchange fellowship, 1970; and a Rome prize fellowship, 1970-72.
WORKS: ORCHESTRA: Canto; CHAMBER MUSIC: Skandha, violin and piano; quartet for piano, 4 hands, violin, cello, percussionist; Eden Road, piccolo, flute, bass flute, cello, piano, 4 hands.

HEINRICH, ADEL
b. Cleveland, Ohio, 20 July 1926. Studied at Flora Stone Mather Coll., B.A. magna cum laude; Union Theological Seminary, M.S.M.; at Univ. of Wisconsin, D.M.A. Her awards include 2 scholarships; Clemens award; 1961 Award of Merit, Nat. Fed. of Music Clubs. She was church organist, 1954-64; served as guest organist with Chicago Symphony Chorus under Margaret Hillis; has been faculty member, Colby Coll., from 1964.
WORKS: CHORUS: A carol is born, women's voices, flute, piano, and drama; Alleluia-alleluia, choric dance for women's choir, mixed chorus, modern dance choir, piano, and violin, 1969; ORGAN: 4 choral paraphrases on hymns of praise.
Music Dept., Colby College, Waterville, ME 04901

HEISS, JOHN C.
b. New York, N.Y., 23 Oct. 1938. Attended Lehigh Univ., B.A.; studied with Otto Luening and Peter Westergaard, Columbia Univ.; with Milton Babbitt, Edward T. Cone, and Earl Kim, Princeton Univ., M.F.A.; with Darius Milhaud at Aspen School. His awards include first prize, Bowdoin Coll. competition, 1971; Nat. Inst. of Arts and Letters award, 1973; Fromm Found. commission, 1973; Nat. Endowment for the Arts grants, 1974, 1975; Mass. Council on the Arts grant, 1975; ASCAP awards, 1975-77; Guggenheim grant, 1978. He has held faculty posts at Columbia Univ., Barnard Coll., Mass. Inst. of Technology, and from 1967, New England Cons. He was principal flute, Boston Musica Viva, 1969-74, free-lance performer with the Boston Symph. Orch., Boston Ballet Company, and other area ensembles.
WORKS: ORCHESTRA: 4 short pieces, 1962; Music for orchestra, 1968; flute concerto, 1977 (also rev. as a chamber concerto, 1977); CHAMBER MUSIC: 4 short pieces, piano, 1961; flute

sonatina, 1962; 5 pieces for flute and cello, 1963; 4 movements for 3 flutes, 1969; quartet for flute, clarinet, cello, piano, 1971; 4 lyric pieces, solo flute, 1972; Inventions, contours and colors, 11 instruments, 1973; Songs of nature, soprano and chamber ensemble, 1975; Capriccio, flute, clarinet, percussion, 1976; choral works, songs, piano pieces.
    61 Hancock St., Auburndale, MA 02166

HELBIG, OTTO H.
    b. New Haven, Conn., 28 Oct. 1914. Studied with Richard Donovan, David Stanley Smith, and Hugo Kortschalk at Yale Univ.; at Columbia Univ., M.A., Ed.D. He has been violinist in symphony orchestras; conducted the Trenton State Orch.; and from 1949, has been professor, Trenton State Coll.
    WORKS: BAND: Introduction and tango; Prelude and beguine; Short piece.
    Music Dept., Trenton State College, Trenton, NJ 08625

HELBLE, RAYMOND
    b. New Jersey, 3 Feb. 1949. Studied at Eastman School of Music; His works include a violin concerto; marimba concerto; double concerto for violin, viola, chamber orchestra; 7 last words of Christ, for viola and large orch.; many works for solo instruments and chamber groups.
    315 Three Allegheny Center, Pittsburgh, PA 15212

HELD, WILBUR C.
    b. Des Plaines, Ill., 20 Aug. 1914. Studied with John Palmer, American Cons.; with Normand Lockwood and Wallingford Riegger, Union Theological Seminary, S.M.D. He was professor, Ohio State Univ., 1946-77; organist, Trinity Episcopal Church, Columbus, from 1949.
    WORKS: CHORUS: 6 calls to worship, 1953; God of a universe; Jesus, name of wondrous love; Advent service; ORGAN: Partita on O sons and daughters; 6 carol settings; Processional on The king's majesty; many other choral and organ works.
    221 Oakland Park Ave., Columbus, OH 43214

HELFER, WALTER
    b. Lawrence, Mass., 30 Sept. 1896; d. New Rochelle, N.Y., 16 Apr. 1959. Studied at Harvard Univ., B.A.; Columbia Univ., M.A.; with Ottorino Respighi in Rome, 1925-28. His awards included the New England Cons. Endicott prize; Paderewski prize, 1939; fellowship, American Acad. in Rome. He was faculty member, Hunter Coll., 1929-50.
    WORKS: ORCHESTRA: In modo giocoso; Water idyll; Fantasie on children's tunes, 1935; Symphony on Canadian airs, 1937; A midsummer night's dream, overture, 1939; concertino for piano and chamber orch., 1947; CHAMBER MUSIC: Elegiac sonata, piano, 1931; string quartet; string trio; Nocturne, piano; Soliloquy, cello and piano, 1947; Appassionata, violin and piano; choral works.

HELFMAN, MAX
    b. Radzin, Poland, 25 May 1901; to U.S. 1909;

d. Dallas, Tex., 9 Aug. 1963. Studied at Mannes Coll. of Music, 1919-23; with Rosario Scalero and Fritz Reiner, Curtis Inst., 1929-32. He was choral conductor of groups in Newark, New York, and Los Angeles; on faculty, Hebrew Union Coll., 1949-52; music director, Hillel Found., Los Angeles, 1959-62. His compositions included New Hagadah, cantata for narrator, chorus, and orch., 1949; and Jewish liturgical works.

HELLER, DUANE L.
    b. Douglas, Wyo., 8 May 1951. Studied with Nromand Lockwood, Univ. of Denver; with Halsey Stevens, Univ. of Southern California; with Karel Husa and Robert Palmer, Cornell Univ. His awards include the ASCAP Victor Herbert award, 1977; and grants from Paul Stock Found. and Cornell Council on the Creative Arts. He was church organist, 1974-76.
    WORKS: WIND ENSEMBLE: Intrada, brass and percussion; CHAMBER MUSIC: piano sonata; suite for solo viola; Variations on a theme of Paganini, chamber ensemble; VOICE: Adam and Eve, cantata for double chorus, soli, 4 celli, piano, percussion; O magnum mysterium, double chorus, 2 flutes; Love songs, baritone and cello; other choral works and songs.
    P.O. Box 1497, Cody, WY 82414

HELLER, HANS EWALD
    b. Vienna, Austria, 17 Apr. 1894; to U.S. 1938; d. New York, N.Y., 1 Oct. 1966. Wrote 3 light operas produced in Europe. Other works include Carnival in New Orleans, overture, 1940; Ode to our women, cantata, 1942; 2 string quartets; suite for clarinet; many songs.

HELLER, JAMES G.
    b. New Orleans, 4 Jan. 1892; d. Cincinnati, Ohio, 19 Dec. 1971. Studied at Tulane Univ., B.A. 1912; Univ. of Cincinnati, M.A. 1914; Hebrew Union Coll., Rabbi 1916; Cincinnati Cons., D.M. 1934. He wrote program notes for the Cincinnati Symph.; taught at Cincinnati Cons. He composed Elegy and pastorale, voice and string orch., 1934; string quartet; violin sonata; Jewish liturgial works.

HELLER, JOHN H., JR.
    b. Philadelphia, Pa., 22 Feb. 1945; d. Richmond, Va., 1977. Studied with Joseph Castaldo, Michael White, Andrew Rubin, Philadelphia Musical Acad.; with Clifford Taylor and Robert Morgan, Temple Univ. He received a Creative Accomplishment award, Philadelphia Musical Acad., 1966. He taught in public schools, 1968-69; was faculty member, Philadelphia Community Coll., 1969-70; Temple Univ., 1970-72; Trenton State Coll., 1973-75; Virginia Commonwealth Univ., 1976-77.
    WORKS: ORCHESTRA: symphony-concerto, bass clarinet and orch., 1966; CHAMBER MUSIC: brass quintet, 1963; Projective variations, chamber ensemble, 1964; string quartet, 1965; Rückblick, 3 pieces for trombone and percussion, 1969; Variations on a theme by Stravinsky, 1969-70.

HELLERMANN, WILLIAM

HELLERMANN, WILLIAM
b. Milwaukee, Wis., 15 July 1939. Studied at
Univ. of Wisconsin; with Otto Luening, Chou
Wen-chung, and Vladimir Ussachevsky, Columbia
Univ.; privately with Stefan Wolpe; and on a
Prix de Rome at the American Acad. in Rome,
1972-73. Other awards include Martha Baird
Rockefeller grant; Nat. Endowment for the Arts
grant; Alte Kirsche Boswil Found. award;
Gaudeamus awards, 1970, 1972; CAPS grant. He is
executive director of Composers Forum.
    WORKS: ORCHESTRA: Time and again, 1969;
anyway . . .; CHAMBER MUSIC: 4 pieces for
guitar; Ek-stasis II, 1970; But the moon . . .,
chamber orch.; Distances and spaces, guitar,
1972; On the edge of a node, violin, cello,
guitar, 1974; Row music (tip of the iceberg),
piano; Stop/start, chamber orch.; Long Island
Sound, chamber orch.; tremble, guitar; squeek,
piece for swivel desk chair, 1979; ELECTRONIC:
Ariel, 1968; Mai, 1968; Ek-stasis I, 1968;
Passages 13--The fire, trumpet and tape, 1970-
71.
    45 Greene St., New York, NY 10013

HELM, EVERETT
b. Minneapolis, Minn., 17 July 1913. Studied at
Harvard Univ., B.A. 1935; with Riccardo Malipiero
and Ralph Vaughan Williams in Europe. He held a
John Knowles Paine traveling fellowship for study
in Europe. He was music officer, U.S. Army, in
Germany, 1948-50.
    WORKS: THEATRE: The siege of Tottenberg
opera, 1956; Le roy fait battre tambour, ballet,
1956; Adam and Eve, an adaption of a 12th-century
mystery play, 1951; 500 Dragon-Thalers, musical
comedy, 1956; ORCHESTRA: concerto for string
orch., 1950; 2 piano concertos, 1954, 1956; Cambridge suite; 3 gospel hymns; CHAMBER MUSIC:
woodwind quartet; string quartet; 2 piano
sonatas; flute sonata; violin sonata; Sinfonia
da camera;concerto for 5 solo instruments and
chamber orch.; woodwind quintet; choral works;
songs; piano pieces. He was author of Composer,
performer, public: A study in communications,
1970.

HELPS, ROBERT
b. Passaic, N.J., 23 Sept. 1928. Studied piano
with Abby Whiteside, composition with Roger
Sessions at Juilliard School; also attended
Columbia Univ. and Univ. of California, Berkeley.
His awards include Hertz award, 1951; Fromm
Found. award, 1956, commission, 1960; Naumburg
Found. award, 1958; Guggenheim grant, 1964-65;
Ingram-Merrill grant, 1966; 3 Thorne Music Found.
commissions; Friends of 4-Hand Music commission,
1967; Ford Found. commission, 1972; Nat. Endowment for the Arts grants, 1974, 1975. He has
taught piano at Stanford Univ., San Francisco
Cons., Univ. of California at Berkeley, New
England Cons., Princeton Univ., and from 1971,
Manhattan School of Music.
    WORKS: ORCHESTRA: symphony, 1955; 2 piano
concertos, 1968, 1972, #2 Oakland, Calif., 8 Mar.
1979; Gossamer noons, soprano and orch., on
poems by James Purdy, 1974; CHAMBER MUSIC:
string quartet, 1951; piano trio, 1957; Serenade

in 3 parts: (1) Fantasy, violin and piano,
(2) Nocturne, string quartet, (3) Postlude,
horn, piano, violin, 1964; quintet for flute,
clarinet, piano trio, 1975; SONGS: 2 songs for
soprano, 1950; The running sun, soprano, New
York, 13 Nov. 1972; PIANO: Fantasy, 1952;
Image, 1958; Recollections, 1959; Portraits,
1960; Solo, 1961; Saccade, 4 hands, 1968;
Quartet for piano solo, 1970; 3 hommages, New
York, 6 Nov. 1972; 3 nocturnes, New York, 19 Mar.
1973.
    156 Montague St., Brooklyn, NY 11201

HEMMER, EUGENE
b. Cincinnati, Ohio, 23 Mar. 1929; d. California,
22 Sept. 1977. His honors include ASCAP awards;
honorary membership Liberal Society of Composers
of Tokyo; twice named composer of the year,
Ohioana Library Assoc.; 3 MacDowell fellowships;
3 Huntington Hartford fellowships; 2 Dumler
prizes in composition. He was head, music
department, Marymount Coll., Palos Verdes, and
instructor, El Camino Coll.
    WORKS: ORCHESTRA: concerto for 2 pianos;
10 symphonic dances; The school bus; Sunshine
games; CHAMBER MUSIC: Introduction and dance,
piano; Divertimento, harp, marimba, celeste,
piano; 2 viola sonatas; cello sonata; piano
trio; duor for violin and cello; Processional
and recessional, organ and trumpet; CHORUS:
Ode to man in space.

HENDERSON, ALVA
b. San Luis Obispo, Calif., 8 Apr. 1940. Studied
at San Francisco State Coll.
    WORKS: OPERA: Medea, based on Robinson
Jeffers's play, San Diego, 29 Nov. 1972; The
tempest, based on Shakespeare; The last of the
Mohicans, commissioned by the Wilmington (Del.)
Opera Society, performed in Wilmington, 12 June
1976; The unforgiven, based on book by Alan
LeMay about the conflict between Indians and
settlers in Texas in 1895.

HENDERSON, KENNETH
b. Richmond, Va., 28 June 1928. Is band director
in the public schools of Chesterfield County,
Va. His works include The lancers and Trade
winds for band; and some 100 published compositions and arrangements for orchestra, band,
small ensembles, and chorus.
    1308 Buford Rd., Richmond, VA 23235

HENDERSON, RAY
b. Buffalo, N.Y., 1 Dec. 1896; d. Greenwich,
Conn., 31 Dec. 1970. Studied at Univ. of
Southern California; later privately with
Benjamin Britten. He was church organist and
jazz pianist in Buffalo; then went to New York,
where he was song-plugger, staff arranger, and
composer for a music publishing firm.
    WORKS: SONGS: Georgette, 1922; You're the
cream in my coffee; Alabamy bound, 1925; Hold
everything; 3 cheers; Sonny boy, 1928; Button up
your overcoat, 1928; Keep your sunny side up,
1929; The best things in life are free, 1927;
this was also the title of his film biography
made in 1966.

HENDERSON, ROSAMOND (Mrs. Stanley P.)
b. Shellman, Ga., 13 July 1894. Studied at
Andrew Coll. and Wesleyan Coll. She won awards
for choral works in contests of the Nat. League
of American Pen Women and the Alabama Writers
Conclave.
WORKS: CHORUS: Sing praises to God; The
Lord's day; Wave on, Old Glory; Think on these
things; and others.
4142 Crescent Rd., Birmingham, AL 35222

HENDL, WALTER
b. West New York, N.Y., 12 Jan. 1917. Studied
with Fritz Reiner at Curtis Inst. and at Tanglewood. He taught at Sarah Lawrence Coll., 1931-
41; was associate conductor, New York Phil.,
1945-49; conductor, Dallas Symph. Orch., 1949-
58; associate conductor, Chicago Symph. Orch.,
1958-64; director, Eastman School of Music,
1964-72; and from 1952, music director, Chautauqua Festival. He has composed choral works and
theatre music.
c/o Chautauqua Inst., Chautauqua, NY 14722

HENDRIKS, FRANCIS MILTON
b. New York, N.Y., 28 Nov. 1883; d. Studied
with Leopold Godowsky and Hugo Kaun; and at
Denver Coll. of Music, M.A. He gave piano recitals in Europe, then taught at Scott School
of Music; Wolcott Cons.; Denver Coll. of Music.
He wrote a piano concerto, piano sonata, and
many piano pieces.

HENINGER, ROBERT E.
b. Utah, 18 Oct. 1924. Studied with Ingolf Dahl
and Richard Donovan, Univ. of Southern California;
with Nadia Boulanger in Paris. He received an
award from Composers Forum. He is faculty member, San Diego Mesa Coll.
WORKS: ORCHESTRA: Passacaglia; Variations
on He's gone away; Variations and dance; CHAMBER
MUSIC: string quartet; Little suite, flute and
piano; Chaconne, piano; CHORUS: 3 songs on
Shakespearean texts; Psalm 148; songs.
3510 Charles St., San Diego, CA 92106

HENN, RICHARD
b. Santa Monica, Calif., 31 Oct. 1946. Studied
with Matt Doran, St. Mary's Coll.; with Harold
Budd and Mel Powell, California Inst. of the
Arts.
WORKS: PERCUSSION: symphony for multi-
percussion; Intro and extro duction; In Egypt;
CHAMBER MUSIC: Reverie for harp; Prelude, harp;
Prelude, inventions 1 and 2, postlude, horn and
tuba.

HENNAGIN, MICHAEL
b. The Dalles, Oreg., 27 Sept. 1936. Studied
with Leonard Stein, Los Angeles City Coll.,
1957-59; with Darius Milhaud at Aspen, Colo.;
Curtis Inst. of Music, B.M. 1963; with Aaron
Copland at Tanglewood, 1963; electronic music,
Southern Illinois Univ., 1968. He received
scholarships for study at Aspen, Curtis Inst.,
and Tanglewood; Fromm Found. award, 1961; Ford
Found.-MENC grant, 1965-66; ASCAP awards, 1967-
70; and commissions. He taught in public

schools, 1963-66; was faculty member, Kansas
State Teachers Coll., 1966-72; from 1972, at
Univ. of Oklahoma.
WORKS: BALLET: The barren song, 1958; The
plumed serpent, 1958; THEATRE: incidental music
to Becket; The skin of out teeth; Antigonae; The
world of my America; Christmas carol; ORCHESTRA:
Passacaglia, 1960; Symphonic essay; A summer
overture, 1963; Explorations, 1970; BAND:
Jubilee, 1967; 3 fanfares for marching band,
1971; Dance scene, 1977; CHORUS: Walking on the
green grass, 1958; Waillie, waillie, 1958; The
house on the hill, 1960; Go 'way from my window,
1964; Under the greenwood tree, 1964; La cuca-
racha, 1964; Psalm 23, 1970; By the roadside,
Whitman text, 1976; MIXED MEDIA: The unknown,
chorus, instruments, tape, slides, 1968; The
family of man, chorus, piano, percussion, film
or slides, tape, 1969; So the world went small,
men's chorus, tenor and baritone soloists, instruments, 4 narrators, tape, 1975, Univ. of
Oklahoma, 26 Sept. 1976; also many works for
chamber groups, songs, film scores, radio and
television scores.
1022 Walnut Rd., Norman, OK 73069

HENNING, ERVIN ARTHUR
b. Marion, S.Dak., 22 Nov. 1910. Studied at New
England Cons., B.M. 1946, with honors and special
honors in contemporary music; organ with Carl
McKinley and E. Power Biggs. Awards include a
prize in the Brookline Library Music Assoc. contest, 1971; purchase of manuscript of Fantasia
for violin and harpsichord by Harvard Univ. for
the Houghton Library rare manuscript collection,
1962; scholarship at New England Cons.; many
commissions. He was church organist-music
director in Chicago and Boston, 1942-50; held
various teaching posts in New England, 1949-59;
was composer and music coordinator for a Boston
theatre company, 1963-70. He has given a collection of his composition and entire musical
memorabilia to the Mugar Library at Boston Univ.;
other compostions to the Univ. of South Dakota.
WORKS: THEATRE: incidental music to Pinter's
The dwarfs, 1966; The breasts of Tiresias, 1967;
Time after time, ballet, flute, clarinet, cello,
piano, 1967; CHAMBER MUSIC: Badinage, woodwind
quartet; quintet for flute, horn, string trio,
1946; Partita, string quartet, 1948; suite for
viola concertante, 2 violins, cello, 1950;
violin sonata; Divertimento, bassoon solo, 1950;
trio for clarinet, viola, piano, 1959; Fantasia,
violin and harpsichord, 1962; also choral works,
piano works, etc.
334 Massachusetts Ave., Boston, MA 02115

HENNING, ROSLYN BROGUE. See BROGUE, ROSLYN

HENRY, HAROLD
b. Neodesha, Kans., 20 Mar. 1884; d. Orangeburg,
N.Y., 15 Oct. 1956. Studied with Carl Preyer,
Univ. of Kansas; with Leopold Godowsky in Berlin;
with Moritz Moszkowski in Paris. He made his
piano debut in the U.S. in Chicago in 1906;
taught privately in New York. He composed piano
pieces and songs.

HENRY, JOSEPH

HENRY, JOSEPH
b. Toledo, Ohio, 12 Oct. 1930. Studied with
Wayne Barlow and Bernard Rogers, Eastman School
of Music, B.M., M.M., A.M.D. 1965. He received
2 Fulbright grants for study in Vienna, 1957,
1958. He was visiting professor, Univ. of
Rochester, 1961, Lawrence Univ., 1962; music
director, Utica Symph., 1962-66; faculty member,
State Univ. Coll., Oswego, 1967-79; then appointed to School of Music, Ohio Univ., where he conducts the university orchestra and opera and
oratorio performances.
    WORKS: ORCHESTRA: suite for orch., 1953;
Chromophon, premiere by Buffalo Phil., composer
conducting, 1970; CHAMBER MUSIC: music for horn,
piano, string quartet, 1952; Integrals, violin
and harpsichord, 1972.
    School of Music, Ohio University, Athens, OH
45701

HENRY, OTTO W.
b. Reno, Nev., 8 May 1933. Studied with Gardner
Read and Hugo Norden, Boston Univ. He was
faculty member, Washington and Jefferson Coll.,
1961-65; Tulane Univ., 1965-68; director, electronic music studio, East Carolina Univ., from
1968.
    WORKS: CHAMBER MUSIC: Passacaglia, bass
trombone and piano, 1959; Omnibus 1, unspecified
number of players, 1971; PERCUSSION: Liberty
bell, 10 players and tape, 1970; Omnibus 2, unspecified, unpitched percussion, 1971; Do not
pass go, 3 timpani, 2 players, 1971; The sons of
Martha, soprano and 4 percussionists, 1972.
    School of Music, East Carolina University,
Greenville, NC 27834

HENSEL, H. RICHARD
b. Chicago, Ill., 1926. Studied with Burrill
Phillips and Gordon Binkerd, Univ. of Illinois,
D.M.A.; also with Leo Sowerby, Goffredo Petrassi,
and Milton Babbitt. He is professor, Eastern
Kentucky Univ.
    WORKS: CHAMBER MUSIC: string quartet;
piano sonata; CHORUS: 3 songs on poems of
Edward Arlington Robinson.
    Walnut Hills Rd., Richmond, KY 40475

HERBISON, JERALDINE SAUNDERS
b. Richmond, Va., 9 Jan. 1941. Studied with
Undine S. Moore, Virginia State Coll., B.S. 1965;
with George Balch Wilson and Thomas Clark, Univ.
of Michigan, summers, 1973, 1979; violin privately. She has been public school music
teacher since 1963; has played violin in
Williamsburg Symph., Hampton Inst. Orch., and
others.
    WORKS: ORCHESTRA: 3 suites for string
orch., 1960, 1963, 1969; Genesis I-II, tone
poem, 1980; CHAMBER MUSIC: Fantasy in 3 moods,
cello and piano, 1971; Introspection, oboe and
piano trio, 1973; Intermezzo, cello and piano,
1975; I heard the trailing garments of the night,
flute and piano trio, 1975; 6 duos for cello and
piano, 1976, Interlochen, Mich., 15 Aug. 1979;
string quartet, 1977; sonata for solo cello,
1978, Kennedy Center, Wash., 16 Jan. 1980;
Metamorphosis, 2 violins, guitar, cello, piano,

1978; trio for violin, flute, guitar, 1979; also
songs, choral works.
    34 Locust Ave., Hampton, VA 23661

HERDER, RONALD
b. Philadelphia, Pa., 21 Dec. 1930. Studied
with Constant Vauclain, Univ. of Pennsylvania,
B.F.A. 1952; with Eugene Hill, Miami Univ., Ohio,
M.A. 1954; with Nadia Boulanger, Fontainebleau,
1957. He received the Ravel prize in composition, 1957; Concorso Internaz. prize, Italy,
1962, 1963; and many commissions. He has been
free-lance composer and arranger, 1957-59; instructor, Brooklyn Coll., 1959-60; from 1960,
editor with a music publisher; and from 1978,
faculty member, Manhattanville Coll.
    WORKS: BALLET: At the hawk's well, chamber
ensemble, 1953; Requiem for Jimmy Dean, jazz
ballet; ORCHESTRA: Movements for orch., 1963;
BAND: Saëta (Rites and ceremonies), 1967-71;
CHAMBER MUSIC: concerto for 2 pianos alone,
1950; The death of children, voice and piano,
1950; string quartet, 1952; 2 songs for tenor
and 2 violas, 1956; L'Infinito, chamber cantata,
voice and brass ensemble, 1957; CHORUS: The Job
elegies, 1964; From the 23rd Psalm, 1967; MIXED
MEDIA: Requiem II/Games of power, 1969; Requiem
III/Birds at Golgotha, prerecorded ensembles,
tape, band.
    Music Dept., Manhattanville College, Purchase,
NY 10577

HERFURTH, C. PAUL
b. Cambridge, Mass., 7 Oct. 1893. Studied with
Gustave Strube, Felix Winternitz, and Paul
Poulson, New England Cons., graduated 1916,
received Outstanding Alumnus award, 1978. He is
an honorary life member of the N.J. Music Educators Assoc. He was public school director of
music, Ashville, N.C., 1919-22, and East Orange,
N.J., 1922-55.
    WORKS: More than 50 compositions for school
bands and orchestras; and A tune a day, a series
of 32 method books for all instruments.
    P.O. Box 601, Vero Beach, FL 32960

HERMAN, JERRY
b. New York, N.Y., 10 July 1933. Studied drama
at Univ. of Miami, B.A. He has written both
words and music for most of his musical comedies.
Hello, Dolly!, which had the second longest run
for a musical in Broadway history (topped only
by Fiddler on the roof) received a Tony award
and the New York Drama Critics' Circle award,
1964. His other shows are Parade, 1960; Milk
and honey, 1961; Mame, 1966.

HERMAN, THOMAS
b. Alexandria, Va., 3 June 1947. Studied with
Samuel Adler, Eastman School of Music, B.M.;
privately with Peter Maxwell Davies in London;
with Arthur Berger, Brandeis Univ. He received
a Nat. Endowment for the Arts grant, 1975; has
been faculty member, Sarah Lawrence Coll., from
1978.
    WORKS: THEATRE: Crystallization of the
equivocal and Death's door, 2 music-theatre
works in what the composer calls a merged-

medium genre; <u>Objets trouvés</u>, soprano, 5 actors, narrator, chamber orch., 1975.

9 Eustis St., Apt. 2-L, Cambridge, MA 02140

HERNRIED, ROBERT
b. Vienna, Austria, 22 Sept. 1883; to U.S. 1933; d. Detroit, Mich., 3 Sept. 1951. Studied at Univ. of Vienna; conducted at theatres and taught at various schools. In the U.S. he taught in New York, Iowa, North Dakota, Indiana, and finally at Detroit Inst. of Musical Art, 1946-51. He composed an opera, <u>Francesca da Rimini</u>, orchestral pieces, many choral works. He also published musicological works.

HERRMANN, BERNARD
b. New York, N.Y., 29 Jan. 1911; d. Los Angeles, Calif., 24 Dec. 1975. Studied with Philip James at New York Univ.; with Albert Stoessel and Bernard Wagenaar, Juilliard Graduate School. He was radio conductor for the CBS Symphony, 1940-55; then turned to film composing.
WORKS: OPERA: <u>Wuthering Heights</u>, 1950; ORCHESTRA: <u>The city of brass</u>, 1934; <u>Sinfonietta</u> for strings, 1935; <u>Currier and Ives suite</u>, 1935; <u>Fiddle concerto</u>, 1940; symphony, 1942; <u>For the fallen</u>, 1943; <u>The fantasticks</u>, vocal quartet and orch., 1944; CHAMBER MUSIC: string quartet, 1932; <u>Aubade</u>, 14 instruments, 1933; <u>Echoes</u>, string quartet, 1966; <u>Souvenirs de voyages</u>, clarinet quintet, 1967; CHORUS: <u>Moby Dick</u>, cantata with orch., 1940; <u>Johnny Appleseed</u>, cantata, 1940; FILM SCORES: <u>Citizen Kane</u>, 1940; <u>The devil and Daniel Webster</u>, 1941; <u>Jane Eyre</u>, 1942; <u>The magnificent Ambersons</u>, 1942; <u>Anna and the King of Siam</u>, 1946; <u>The ghost of Mrs. Muir</u>, 1948; <u>The day the earth stood still</u>, 1951; <u>Snows of Kilimanjaro</u>, 1952; <u>The trouble with Harry</u>, 1955; <u>The man who knew too much</u>, 1956; <u>The man in the gray flannel suit</u>, 1956; <u>The wrong man</u>, 1957; <u>Vertigo</u>, 1958; <u>North by northwest</u>, 1959; <u>Journey to the center of the earth</u>, 1959; <u>Psycho</u>, 1960; <u>The birds</u>, 1963; <u>Fahrenheit 451</u>, 1966; <u>The bride wore black</u>, 1967; <u>Sisters</u>, 1973; <u>Obsession</u>, 1975; <u>Taxi driver</u>, 1975.

HERVIG, RICHARD B.
b. Story City, Iowa, 24 Nov. 1917. Studied with Philip Greeley Clapp, Univ. of Iowa. He was faculty member, Long Beach State Coll., 1952-55; from 1955, at Univ. of Iowa.
WORKS: ORCHESTRA: 2 symphonies; CHAMBER MUSIC: string quartet, 1955; <u>Introduction and allegro</u>, piano and woodwind quintet; 2 clarinet sonatas, 1953, 1971; <u>Diversion</u>, trombone and percussion, 1968; <u>Antiphon</u>, 13 instruments; <u>Chamber music for 6 players</u>, Washington, 31 May 1976; <u>An entertainment</u>, clarinet and marimba/vibraphone, 1978; CHORUS: <u>Ubi sunt?</u>, motet; <u>Quid est musica?</u>, antiphonal chorus and 8 instruments, 1972.

1822 Rochester Ave., Iowa City, IA 52240

HEUSSENSTAMM, GEORGE
b. Los Angeles, Calif., 24 July 1926. Studied at Los Angeles City Coll., 1946-48; Los Angeles State Coll., 1961-63; privately with Leonard Stein. He was winner in the following composi-

tion contests: Rochester Religious Arts Festival, 1965, 1st Internat. Tuba Ensemble, 1969, 8th Annual Symposium of Contemp. Music for Brass, 1971, Nat. Assoc. of Coll. Wind and Percussion Instr., 1976, New Louisville Brass Quintet, 1976, Internat. Double Reed Society, 1977; other awards include ASCAP awards, 1974-77; Nat. Endowment for the Arts grant, 1976; was featured composer on KPFK-FM broadcast, 1977. Since 1971 he has been manager of the Coleman Chamber Music Assoc.; from 1976, faculty member, California State Univ., Dominguez Hills; from 1977, also at Ambassador Coll.
WORKS: ORCHESTRA: chamber symphony; <u>Scherzo</u>; <u>17 impressions from the Japanese</u>; WIND ENSEMBLES: <u>Museum piece</u>, double brass choir, 4 percussion; <u>Tournament</u>, 4 brass sextets, 4 percussion, 1971; <u>Labyrinth</u>, 4 brass quintets, nominated for Pulitzer prize, 1972; <u>Score</u>, 4 saxophone quartets, percussion; CHAMBER MUSIC: <u>Die Jugend</u>, solo clarinet, 1963; string quartet; <u>7 etudes</u>, woodwind trio; <u>Callichoreo</u>, woodwind quartet, 1968; <u>Mini-variations</u>, flute, oboe, string trio, 1968, nominated for Pulitzer prize, 1968; <u>Canonograph #1</u>, woodwind trio; <u>Canonograph #2</u>, string trio; <u>Tubafour</u>, tuba quartet, 1969; <u>Set</u> for double reeds, 1970; <u>Texture variations</u>, flute, violin, cello, harpsichord, 1972; <u>Pentalogue</u>, contrabass, 1971; <u>Saxoclone</u>, saxophone, 1971; <u>Die Reise</u>, brass quintet, 1973; <u>Monologue</u>, clarinet, 1973; <u>Playphony</u>, percussion, 1976; brass quintet #3, 1977; also choruses and mixed media works.

5013 Lowell Ave., La Crescenta, CA 91214

HEWITT, HARRY DONALD
b. Detroit, Mich., 4 Mar. 1921. Has made what seems to be a valid claim to be one of the most prolific composers in the hisroty of American music. His some 3000 compositions include 20 symphonies among several hundred orchestral works, 20 string quartets in hundreds of pieces of chamber music, several operas, and songs and keyboard works.
WORKS (among his more recent): OPERA: <u>Pierre</u>, c. 1954-64; ORCHESTRA: <u>Night without neon</u>, <u>A star a tree a man</u>, <u>The wheel</u>, <u>The mad clockmaker</u>, <u>Seven</u>, all tone poems of the 1950s; SONGS: <u>Poems of Po-Chu-I</u>, cycle of 35 songs; <u>Animal anguish</u>, to composer's own text; PIANO: <u>A Tolkien tapestry</u>, <u>Lantern songs</u>, <u>Meadow year</u>, 1964.

345 S. 19th St., Philadelphia, PA 19103

HEYMANN, WERNER RICHARD
b. Konigsberg, Germany, 14 Feb. 1896; d. Munich, 30 May 1961. Studied with Paul Juon in Berlin; composed chamber music and orchestral works. On coming to the U.S., he settled in Hollywood as a film composer. One of his film scores was for <u>Ninotchka</u>.

HEYWARD, SAMUEL EDWIN, JR.
b. Savannah, Ga., 26 Mar. 1904. Studied at New England Cons. He was a singer and violist in symphonies and chamber groups.
WORKS: CHAMBER MUSIC: suite for violin; CHORUS: <u>Ballad for Harry Moore</u>; <u>Cradle to grave</u>; <u>The love cycle</u>.

HIBBARD, WILLIAM

HIBBARD, WILLIAM
b. Newton, Mass., 8 Aug. 1939. Studied with
Francis Judd Cooke and Donald Martino, New
England Cons., B.M. 1961, M.M. 1963; with
Richard Hervig, Univ. of Iowa, Ph.D. 1967. His
awards include a BMI award, 1960; Chadwick Medal,
New England Cons., 1961; Beebe Found. grant,
1963; Sutherland Dows award, Univ. of Iowa,
1964-66; Tanglewood fellowship, 1965; Philip
Greeley Clapp award, Univ. of Iowa, 1967; Old
Gold fellowship, 1969; and commissions. He has
been faculty member, Univ. of Iowa, from 1966.
WORKS: ORCHESTRA: Reliefs, 1962; viola
concerto, 1977; CHAMBER MUSIC: trio for violin,
clarinet, guitar, 1959; Variations, brass nonet,
1960; 4 pieces, chamber ensemble, 1962; Gestures,
flute, double bass, percussion, 1963; Portraits,
flute and piano, 1963; string trio, 1964;
Fantasy, organ, trumpet, trombone, percussion,
1965; Intersections I and II, woodwind quintet,
piano, percussion, 1966; Stabiles, 13 players,
1969; Variations, cello solo, 1970; string
quartet, 1971; trio, bass clarinet, bass trombone, harp, 1973; P/M variations, 2 double
basses, 1975; Round one, vibraphone, 2 pianos,
1978; SONGS: The dream lady, alto solo, chamber
ensemble, 1958; Super flumina Babylonis, 6 solo
singers, string sextet, 1968; Reflexa, soprano
and 5 players, 1970; Menage, soprano, trumpet,
violin, 1974; also film scores.
725 E. College St., Iowa City, IA 52240

HICKS, DAVID
b. New York, N.Y., 28 Nov. 1949. Studied with
Claudio Spies and David Steinbrook, Swarthmore
Coll., B.A.; with Bulent Arel and David Lewin,
State Univ. of New York, Stony Brook, M.A.; with
Milton Babbitt and J. K. Randall, Princeton
Univ., M.F.A. His awards include a Fulbright
fellowship for study in Austria, 1977; Meet the
Composer grant, 1977; Proctor fellowship,
Princeton Univ., 1978. He was instructor of
electronic music, Princeton Univ., 1977.
WORKS: CHAMBER MUSIC: Sonal creatures,
flute, bassoon, piano trio; Trionyx, flutes,
clarinets, percussion; Currents, clarinet, piano,
string quartet.
53 W. 8th St., New York, NY 10011

HIER, ETHEL GLENN
b. Cincinnati, Ohio, 25 June 1889; d. New York,
N.Y., 14 Jan. 1971. Studied with Edgar Stillman
Kelley, Cincinnati Cons., B.M. 1911; with Percy
Goetschius and Ernest Bloch in New York. She
received honorary degrees from Inst. of Musical
Art, New York, 1917, from Cincinnati Cons.,
1922. She was a private teacher in Cincinnati
and New York.
WORKS: ORCHESTRA: Asolo bells, 1939;
Mountain preacher, chorus and orch., 1941;
Carolina suite; Scherzo; CHAMBER MUSIC: Sextet
suite, flute, oboe, string trio, piano, 1925;
3 quintets for flute, viola, cello, harp, and
voice, 1936; string quartet; Rhapsody, violin
and piano, 1940; Joy of spring, violin and
piano; piano works.

HIGGINS, RICHARD CARTER (DICK)
b. Cambridge, England, 15 Mar. 1938; U.S.
parents. Studied with John Cage, New School of
Music, 1958-59; with Henry Cowell, Columbia
Univ., B.S. 1960; at New York Univ., A.M. 1975.
He was active in Happenings, 1958; in Fluxus,
1961; founded Something Else Press, 1964; taught
at California Inst. of the Arts, 1970-71; at
Univ. of Wisconsin, Milwaukee, 1977.
WORKS: OPERA: The peaceable kingdom, for
speaking performers and bells, 1961; Lavender
blue, 1963; Spring game; ELECTRONIC AND MULTI-
MEDIA: A loud symphony, tape, 1958; Theater
music, collage, 1959; Big constellation, 1960;
In the context of shoes, happening for tape
recorder, microphones, vacuum cleaners, drills,
ribbons, motion piecutres, slide projectors,
garden shears, piano, "antidancers," and other
performers, 1960; In memoriam, 164-part canon,
1960; Requiem for Wagner, the criminal mayor,
1961; For the dead, 1965; Automatic processions,
uses random transportation and lumbering equipment, 1966-67; The 1000 symphonies, composed by
shooting machine gun bullets through music manuscript paper, 1968; Suggested by small swallows,
saxophone and dancer; 5 Lange Sätze zum Weltans-
bruch, 2 string quartets and flute, 1977; Emmett
Williams's ear, 1977; also 6 symphonies and
piano music.
P.O. Box 842, Canal St. Station, New York,
NY 10013

HIGGINSON, JOSEPH VINCENT
b. Irvington, N.J., 17 May 1896. Studied at
Manhattan Coll. of Music; New York Univ., B.A.,
M.A.; with Percy Goetschius, Marion Bauer,
Albert Stoessel, Philip James, and Charles
Haubiel, Juilliard School; and at Pius X School
of Liturgical Music. He was organist and choirmaster, St. Catherine of Alexander, Brooklyn;
managing editor, Catholic Choirmaster; taught at
Pius X School and in private schools. His works
include Magdalen, a tone poem for orchestra; and
sacred songs.

HIJMAN, JULIUS
b. Almelo, Neth., 25 Jan. 1901; to U.S. 1939;
d. New York, N.Y., 6 Jan. 1969. Taught at
Houston Cons., 1940-42; Kansas City Cons., 1945-
49; from 1949, at Philadelphia Musical Acad. He
composed chiefly chamber music: 4 string quartets, many sonatas for various instruments, etc.

HILL, EDWARD BURLINGAME
b. Cambridge, Mass., 9 Sept. 1872; d. Francestown, N.H., 9 July 1960. Studied with John
Knowles Paine, Harvard Univ., B.A. 1894; with
George W. Chadwick, New England Cons. His
honors included membership in the Nat. Inst. of
Arts and Letters; American Acad. of Arts and
Letters; Chevalier Legion of Honor. From 1908
he was on the faculty at Harvard Univ. After
retirement in 1940, he lived chiefly in New
Hampshire.
WORKS: THEATRE: Jack Frost in midsummer,
pantomime with orch., 1908; Pan and the star,
pantomime with orch., 1914; ORCHESTRA: The
parting of Lancelot and Guinevere, symphonic

poem, 1915; 2 Stevensonia suites, 1917, 1923; The fall of the House of Usher, symphonic poem, 1920; Waltzes, 1922; Scherzo, 2 pianos and orch., 1924; Lilacs, 1927; 3 symphonies, 1928, 1931, 1937; An ode, 1930; piano concertino, 1932; Sinfonietta for strings, 1936; violin concerto, 1938; concertino for string orch., 1940; Music for English horn and orch., 1945; Prelude for orch., 1953; CHAMBER MUSIC: sonatas for various instruments; string quartet, 1935; sextet for woodwinds and piano; clarinet quintet; etc.; many vocal works.

HILL, JACKSON
b. Birmingham, Ala., 23 May 1941. Studied with Iain Hamilton, Univ. of North Carolina, A.B. 1963, M.A. 1966, Ph.D. 1970. His awards include Nat. Fed. of Music Clubs awards, 1957, 1959; Plymouth (Mass.) Philharmonic prize, 1965; Greensboro (N.C.) Symphony award, 1966; East Carolina Univ. award, 1966; Episcopal music prizes, 1977, 1978; 2 American Guild of Organists prizes, 1978; Musical Fund Society, McCollin prize, 1979; many commissions. He was faculty member, Duke Univ., 1966-68; at Bucknell Univ. from 1968; choral vicar, Exeter Coll., Oxford, 1975; in 1977, was in Japan for research on Buddhist chants.
WORKS: THEATRE: Natalie, 1969; Chameleon chant, dance, percussion and piano, 1974; music to The Bacchae, 1974; ORCHESTRA: Variations for orchestra, 1964; Mosaics, 1965; Paganini set, chamber orch., 1973; Ceremonies of spheres, 1973; Sangraal, 1977, West Yarmouth, Mass., 13 May 1978; CHAMBER MUSIC: Poem, string orch., 1959; sonata for violin solo, 1966; Synchrony, chamber ensemble, 1967; Entourage, saxophone quartet, 1973; Synchrony II, flute, clarinet, piano trio, 1977; Whispers of the dead, solo flute, 1976; KEYBOARD: 3 mysteries, organ, 1973; Quasiternity, organ, 1976 (takes 6 days to perform); sonata: Super flumina Babylonis, piano, 1976; Toro Nagashi (Lanterns of Hiroshima), 2 pianos, 1977; many choral works, songs, electronic music.
Music Dept., Bucknell University, Lewisburg, PA 17837

HILL, NANCY E. (COBB)
b. Albuquerque, N.Mex., 15 Nov. 1951. Studied with Claude L. Bass, Oklahoma Baptist Univ.; with H. Owen Reed, Michigan State Univ. She received Sigma Alpha Iota awards, 1972, 1973; Music Teachers Nat. Assoc. award, 1973; was winner in composition contest, American Guild of English Handbell Ringers, Area II, 1977. She was instructor, Mercer Univ., 1975-76; from 1976, at Oklahoma Baptist Univ.
WORKS: CHAMBER MUSIC: piano sonata; Ignescent trines, brass; At the park, song cycle for soprano; Canticle of jubilation, handbells; CHORUS: Prufrock, praise; Rejoice; Come, Christians join to sing.
2010 N. Tucker, Shawnee, OK 74801

HILLE, WALDEMAR
b. St. Elmo, Minn., 5 Mar. 1908. Attended Elmhurst Coll., B.A. 1929; American Cons., B.M.

1934, M.M. 1936; Columbia Univ.; Univ. of Southern California; studied composition with Wallingford Riegger in New York. He received the Celia Buck award for his oratorio, Denmark Vesey, 1960. He was dean of music, Elmhurst Coll., 1932-40; music editor in New York, 1943-47; music director, Eden Theological Seminary, 1949-52; from 1952, music director, First Unitarian Church, Los Angeles.
WORKS: CHORUS: Monticello, cantata, text by Kramer; Denmark Vesey, oratorio for chorus, soloists, orch.; Song of the Warsaw ghetto, 1968; Moses, oratorio; Strange funeral; To those in power; 4 songs for peace and Peace cantata, 1972; many songs.
926 S. Westmoreland Ave., Los Angeles, CA 90006

HILLEBRAND, FRED
b. Brooklyn, N.Y., 25 Dec. 1893; d. New York, N.Y., 15 Sept. 1963. Studied at Juilliard School. His works include an opera, Southland; an operetta, The swing princess; stage and television scores; and songs.

HILLER, LEJAREN
b. New York, N.Y., 23 Feb. 1924. Studied with Milton Babbitt, Princeton Univ., 1941-45, but earned degrees in chemistry, Ph.D. 1947; Univ. of Illinois, M.M. 1958. He was associate member, Center for Advanced Study, Univ. of Illinois, 1966-67; Fulbright lecturer to Poland, 1973-74. He worked as chemist, 1947-52, then joined chemistry faculty, Univ. of Illinois, 1953-58; transferred to music faculty, 1958-68; has been Slee professor of music, State Univ. of New York, Buffalo, from 1968, codirector, Center of Creative and Performing Arts, 1968-74.
WORKS: THEATRE MUSIC: A dream play, Strindberg, 1957; The birds, Aristophanes, 1958; The man with the oboe, Smalley, 1962; Spoon River anthology, 1962; Ponteach, melodrama for speaker and piano, 1977; ORCHESTRA: piano concerto, 1949; suite for small orch., 1951; 2 symphonies, 1953, 1960; A preview of coming attractions, 1975; CHAMBER MUSIC: piano trio, 1947; 7 string quartets, 1949, 1951, 1953, 1957 (Illiac suite), 1961 (in quarter tones), 1972 (New York, 24 Jan. 1973), 1978; 3 violin sonatas, 1949, 1955, 1970; 5 Appalachian ballads, voice and guitar, 1958; Divertimento, chamber ensemble, 1959; 6 easy pieces, violin and piano, 1974; Persiflage, flute, oboe, percussion, 1977; Diabelskie skrzypce, stringed instrument and harpsichord, 1978; PIANO: 6 sonatas, 1946-48, 1947-53, 1949, 1950, 1961, 1972 (Rage over the lost Beethoven); 7 artifacts, 1948-73; Fantasy, 3 pianos, 1951; 12-tone variations, 1954; 2 theater pieces, 1956; Scherzo, 1958; A cenotaph, 2 pianos, 1971; MIXED MEDIA: Cuthbert bound, chamber music for 4 actors and tape, 1960; Amplification, tape and theater band, 1962; Computer cantata, soprano, tape, chamber ensemble, (cocomposer, Robert Baker), 1963; Machine music, piano, percussion, tape, 1964; A triptych for Hieronymus, actors, acrobats, projections, tape, antiphonal instrumental groups, 1966; suite for 2 pianos and tape, 1966; An avalanch for pitch-

HILLERT, RICHARD

man, prima donna, player piano, percussion, prerecorded playback, 1968; HPSCHD, 1-7 harpsichords
and 1-51 tapes (cocomposer, John Cage), 1968;
Algorithms I, 9 instruments and tape, 1968;
Algorithms II, 9 instruments and tape (cocomposer,
Ravi Kumra), 1972; Algorithms III, 9 instruments
and tape, 1978; many other electronic and mixed
media works.
> Music Dept., State University of New York,
> Buffalo, NY 14214

HILLERT, RICHARD
b. Granton, Wis., 14 Mar. 1923. Studied at Concordia Coll., Ill.; with Robert Delaney and
Anthony Donato, Northwestern Univ.; with Goffredo
Petrassi at Tanglewood. He won first prize,
Internat. Society of Contemporary Music, Chicago
Chap., 1961. He taught in St. Louis, 1951-53;
Wausau, Wis., 1953-59; from 1959, has been professor, Concordia Coll., River Forest, Ill.; was
instructor, Northwestern Univ., 1966-71.
> WORKS: ORCHESTRA: symphony, 1955; Varia-
tions, 1968; CHAMBER MUSIC: violin sonata, 1953;
flute sonata, 1954; Alternations #1, 7 instruments, 1966; Alternations #2, flute and piano,
1967; Divertimento, 5 instruments, 1967; CHORUS:
The Christmas story according to St. Luke, 1967;
The Passion according to St. John, 1973; numerous
other choral works and organ pieces.
> 1620 Clay Court, Melrose Park, IL 60160

HILSE, WALTER
b. New York, N.Y., 16 July 1941. Studied with
Vincent Persichetti at Juilliard School; with
Jack Beeson, Otto Luening, Chou Wen-chung at
Columbia Univ.; with Nadia Boulanger in Paris.
He received the Joseph H. Bearns prize, 1966.
He was faculty member, Columbia Univ., 1967-75;
organist-choirmaster, St. Luke's Lutheran Church,
New York, from 1969.
> WORKS: CHAMBER MUSIC: 6 songs from The
song of Solomon, tenor and woodwind quintet,
1966; The 23rd Psalm, unaccompanied voice; Magnificat, 2 female voices and organ; Prelude,
oboe, viola, organ; piano sonata; piano suite;
choral works.
> 432 W. 22nd St., New York, NY 10011

HILTY, EVERETT JAY
b. New York, N.Y., 2 Apr. 1910. Studied at
Univ. of Miami; with Hunter Johnson, Univ. of
Michigan, M.B. 1934; with Mark Wessel, Univ. of
Colorado, M.M. 1939; with Seth Bingham, Normand
Lockwood, Union Theological Seminary; organ with
various teachers. He received an award from the
Diocese of Bethlehem for a hymn tune, Sing out;
2 faculty fellowships, Univ. of Colorado; outstanding teacher awards, 1964-65; was contest
winner, American Guild of English Handbell
Ringers, Area V, for Textures for handbells (4
octaves). He was church organist, 1928-68;
professor, Univ. of Colorado, 1940-78, now
emeritus.
> WORKS: ORGAN: pedal study on Ein feste
Burg; Fanfare, toccata and chorale on Aurelia;
many anthems and organ pieces.
> 2241 Fourth St., Boulder, CO 80302

HINDEMITH, PAUL
b. Hanau, Germany, 16 Nov. 1895; U.S. citizen
1946; d. Frankfurt, Germany, 28 Dec. 1963.
Studied with Arnold Mendelssohn and Bernard
Sekles in Frankfurt. His honors included
membership in the Nat. Inst. of Arts and Letters,
1947; appointment as Charles Eliot Norton professor at Harvard Univ., 1950-51; the Sibelius
award of $35,000, 1954. He was concertmaster,
Frankfurt Opera, 1915-23; in 1921, formed the
Amar-Hindemith String Quartet, in which he
played viola, and toured with it for several
years; in 1927, was appointed professor at the
Berlin Hochschule für Musik. By 1935 he had
come in conflict with the Nazi regime and
accepted an invitation of the Turkish government
to teach in Ankara. In 1939 he came to the U.S.
and soon joined the faculty at Yale Univ., where
he became Battell professor in 1947. He revisited Germany in 1949, conducting his own
works with the Berlin Philharmonic, and in 1953,
went to Switzerland and settled in Zurich as
professor at the university. His large volume
of works includes: 9 operas (the opera Neues
vom Tage/News of the day was given its New York
premiere at the Manhattan School of Music, 1 Mar.
1979); 4 ballets, a pantomime; ORCHESTRA: 2 symphonies; 9 concertos; 2 sinfoniettas; The 4 tem-
perments; Symphonic metamorphosis; Symphonic
dances; Der Schwanendreher, viola and orch.;
Trauermusik, viola and orch. (written on the
death of George V of England and played the day
after the event on a radio program with the composer as soloist); Konzertmusik, brass and
strings; CHAMBER MUSIC: 7 string quartets; at
least one sonata for each of the instruments in
the orchestra, with and without piano; quintets,
trios; many works for solo voice, choral works,
piano pieces.

HIVELY, WELLS
b. San Joaquin Valley, Calif., 1902; d. Palm
Beach, Fla., 1969. Studied at Paris Cons.;
Royal Cons. of Brussels; Mannes Coll. of Music;
Juilliard School. In the 1920s he alternated
studies in Paris with playing organ in silent-
film movie houses; played at Grauman's Chinese
Theatre in Hollywood in 1928. With the advent
of talking pictures, he moved to New York; composed and directed for Ruth St. Denis, composed
music plays for NBC, accompanied singers; later
lived in Florida, teaching, composing, and
playing organ in church.
> WORKS: OPERA: The discreet Cadiga; ORCHES-
TRA: Tres himnos; Summer holiday (Rive gauche),
1944; Icarus, 1961.

HO, CORDELL
b. San Francisco, Calif., 27 Aug. 1948. Studied
piano and theory in San Francisco and in Vienna,
Austria; composition with Fred Lerdahl, Andrew
Imbrie, Richard Felciano, Univ. of California,
Berkeley; electronic music with Olly Wilson. He
received the Nicola DeLorenzo composition prize,
1974 and 1975.
> WORKS: CHAMBER MUSIC: Sketches of Vienna,
string quartet; Peace, soprano and chamber orch.;
Doxology, organ; FILM SCORES: Grunt, electronic

music for animated film; Listen, piano, animated film; ELECTRONIC: Universe, orch., tape, narrator; Versification, trumpet, tape, sympathetic pianos.

2838 Washington St., San Francisco, CA 94115

HO, TING
b. Chungking, China, 12 Jan. 1946; U.S. citizen 1963. Studied with Walter Watson, Kent State Univ.; with Samuel Adler, Wayne Barlow, Warren Benson, and Joseph Schwantner, Eastman School of Music. His awards include the Louis Lane prize and a Nat. Endowment for the Arts grant, 1978. He has been faculty member, Montclair State Coll., from 1974.
WORKS: CHAMBER MUSIC: Sun times, 4 harpists; Bo music, chamber orch., New York, 6 Feb. 1977; quartet for tubas, 1977; CHORUS: Songs of wine, with instruments, 1978.

Music Dept., Montclair State College, Upper Montclair, NJ 07043

HOBSON, BRUCE
b. Hartford, Conn., 16 Aug. 1943. Studied with Otto Luening and Chou Wen-chung, Columbia Univ., 1961-65, 1969-72; New England Cons., M.M. 1967. He has received several performance awards. He held teaching fellowships, Univ. of Michigan, 1967-68; Columbia Univ., 1969-70; was instructor, Southern Vermont Coll., 1975-76; private piano teacher, from 1965.
WORKS: ORCHESTRA: concerto for 3 groups, brass, percussion, 2 pianos; concerto for woodwinds and large orch.; CHAMBER MUSIC: sonata for 2 pianos; 2 movements for piano; quintet for flute, violin, horn, cello, marimba; trio for violin, clarinet, cello, Washington, 5 Jan. 1976; 3 portraits, baritone voice and piano.

Crow Hill Rd., Arlington, VT 05250

HODKINSON, SYDNEY P.
b. Winnepeg, Manitoba, 17 Jan. 1934; to U.S. 1953. Studied with Bernard Rogers, Eastman School of Music, B.M., M.M.; with Leslie Bassett, George B. Wilson, Ross Lee Finney, Univ. of Michigan, D.M.A.; with Elliott Carter, Roger Sessions, Milton Babbitt, Princeton Univ.; and with Niccolo Castiglioni. Major composition awards include those from Internat. Jeunesses Musicales; Prix de Composition Prince Pierre de Monaco; Danforth Found.; 2 Nat. Endowment for the Arts grants, 1975-76, 1977-78; Guggenheim fellowship, 1978; and many commissions. Clarinetist and conductor, he conducted chamber music and orchestral concerts throughout the U.S. and Canada. He taught at Univ. of Virginia, 1958-63; Ohio Univ., 1963-68; Univ. of Michigan, 1968-72; and from 1973, has been faculty member, Eastman School.
WORKS: OPERA: The swinish cult, 1978; ORCHESTRA: Lyric impressions, 1956; Threnody, 1957; Diversions on a chorale, 1958; Caricatures, 5 paintings for orch., 1966; Fresco, mural in 5 panels, 1968; Drawings, #7 and 8, 1970; Stabile, 1970; Epigrams, 1971; Celestial calendar, strings, 1976; Edge of the olde one, English horn, strings, percussion, 1977; WIND ENSEMBLES: A contemporary primer, band, 1972; Blocks, winds

and percussion, 1972; Tower, band, 1974; Pillar, winds and percussion, 1974; Cortege, 1975; Bach variations, winds, piano, harp, percussion, 1977; CHAMBER MUSIC: Stanzas, piano trio, 1959; Drawings, 4 pieces for varying groups, 1960-65; Imagined quartet, 4 percussionists, 1967; Valence, chamber orch., 1970; Another man's poison, brass quintet, 1970; One man's meat, double bass solo, 1970; Lengeren, voice and double quintet, 1973; Taula, double wind quintet, 1974; Stone images, 4 instrumental pieces, 1974; November voices, voice, speaker, small ensemble, 1975; ORGAN: Megalith trilogy: Dolmen, Menhir, Talayot, 1973; CHORUS: Sea chanteys, a cappella, 1970; Menagerie #1, 1970; Vox populous, chamber oratorio, 1971; Daydream, with speaker and instruments, 1974; Menagerie #2, speaking chorus, 1977.

18 Timber Lane, Fairport, NY 14450

HOFFELT, ROBERT O.
b. Springfield, Mo., 1920. Studied at Illinois Wesleyan Univ., B.M. 1942; with Francis J. Pyle, Drake Univ., M.M.Ed. 1946. He was faculty member, Drake Univ., 1946-49; Michigan State Normal Coll., 1949-57; Jacksonville Univ., 1958-64; from 1964, manager of music resources, Abingdon Press. His published works include Not alone for mighty empire for male chorus.

c/o Abingdon Press, 201 8th Ave. S., Nashville, TN 37200

HOFFMAN, ALLEN
b. Newark, N.J., 12 Apr. 1942. Studied with Arnold Franchetti, Hartt Coll. He has received awards from Nat. Found. on the Arts and Humanities, 1966; Nat. Society of Arts and Letters, 1968; Sigma Alpha Iota, 1971; MacDowell fellowships, 1968-72. He was faculty member, Hartt Coll., 1967-75; Hartford Cons., 1971-77.
WORKS: ORCHESTRA: Idyll; WIND ENSEMBLE: Mother Goose, with soprano solo; CHAMBER MUSIC: duo for saxophone and narrator; 3 nocturnes, clarinet, percussion, double bass; Recitative and aria, solo double bass; music for winds, percussion, dancers; it may not always be so. . ., soprano and string quartet; sextet for winds and strings; CHORUS: Madrigals, a cappella; Haiku, a cappella; Chansons innocents, female voices; Mass . . . for the passing of all shining things, with baritone solo.

716 Farmington Ave., West Hartford, CT 06119

HOFFMAN, JOEL
b. Vancouver, B.C., 27 Sept. 1953; U.S. citizen 1971. Studied with Easley Blackwood, Chicago; Alan Hoddinott, Univ. of Wales; with Elliott Carter, Milton Babbitt, Vincent Persichetti, Juilliard School. His awards include a BMI studen award, 1972; Bearns prize; 2 Juilliard prizes; 2 ASCAP awards. He is faculty member, Univ. of Cincinnati.
WORKS: ORCHESTRA: concerto for violin, viola, cello, and orch.; CHAMBER MUSIC: string quartet, 1971; Variations, violin, cello, harp; Fantasy pieces, piano; concerto for horn, clarinet, piano trio; WIND ENSEMBLE: Music from Chartres, 10 brass instruments.

HOFFMAN, THEODORE

Coll. of Music, Univ. of Cincinnati, Cincinnati, OH 45221

HOFFMAN, THEODORE
b. Palo Alto, Calif., 18 Oct. 1925. Studied with Darius Milhaud, Mills Coll.; with Burrill Phillips, Univ. of Illinois. He received a Southeastern Band Directors award, 1965. He was music director, Educational Television, Univ. of Illinois, and WGBH, Boston, 1953-57; faculty member, San Francisco State Univ., 1957-59; San Benito Coll., 1959-62; from 1962, Univ. of South Florida.
WORKS: ORCHESTRA: music for The tempest; BAND: variations on Jesu meine Freude, 1965; CHORUS: 9 Japanese Haiku; The golden goose; mass, with soloists and orch., 1976; Requiem, with soloists and orch., 1977; PIANO: variations on We shall overcome.
Music Dept., LET 361, Univ. of South Florida, Tampa, FL 33620

HOFFMANN, ADOLF G.
b. Cincinnati, Ohio, 30 May 1890; d. Studied at Cincinnati Coll. of Music; with Adolf Brune and Adolf Weidig. He was cellist in string quartets, Chicago Symphony, and Chicago Grand Opera Company; was orchestra manager, cellist, arranger, and conductor, Chicago Theatre, 1921; staff member WGN and WGN-TV from 1934; faculty member, De Paul Univ. and American Cons.
WORKS: ORCHESTRA: symphony; Chicago Theatre of the Air theme; CHAMBER MUSIC: Prelude and fugue, string quartet, harp, celeste; suite for bassoon and piano; string quartet.

HOFFMANN, JAMES A.
b. Manchester, N.H., 2 Oct. 1929. Studied with Carl McKinley and Francis Judd Cooke, New England Cons., B.M. with highest honors; with Quincy Porter and Normand Lockwood, Yale Univ., B.M., M.M.; with Boris Blacher in Berlin; and with Burrill Phillips at Univ. of Illinois, D.M.A. He received the Chadwick Medal at the New England Cons.; John Day Jackson prize and Woods-Chandler prize, Yale Univ. He was faculty member, Oberlin Coll., 1959-62; San Jose State Coll., 1963-64; from 1964, at New England Cons.
WORKS: CHAMBER MUSIC: Diversion, 2 oboes, 1964; Crystals, string trio, 1967; Vortices, violin, flute, oboe, trumpet, percussion, marimba, mandolin, 1968; Sound circuits, 3 violins, or 3 violas, etc., 1968; Jupiter's maze, woodwind quintet, Boston, 12 May 1973; Follow the leader, for any number of soprano instruments, 1973; Four to go, 2 pianos, 8 hands, 1973; Volleys, drums, 1973.
11 Ferndale Rd., Natick, MA 01760

HOFFMANN, NEWTON
b. Chicago, Ill., 16 July 1921. Studied with Nadia Boulanger, Longy School of Music; Bernard Rogers, Herbert Elwell, and Howard Hanson, Eastman School of Music, M.M., D.M.A. He taught at Shendandoah Cons., 1946-48; Univ. of Bridgeport, 1949-51; Hartwick Coll., 1952-53; in public schools, 1954-62; from 1962, has been faculty member, Ball State Univ.

WORKS: ORCHESTRA: symphony; overture; Pastoral; CHAMBER MUSIC: string trio; Movement for piano, clarinet, violin.
620 N. McKinley, Muncie, IN 47303

HOFFMANN, PEGGY (Mrs. Arnold E.)
b. Delaware, Ohio, 25 Aug. 1910. Studied with Edward G. Mead, Miami Univ.; with Cecil Smith, Univ. of Chicago; and with Elmer Ende, Univ. of Akron. She was church organist in Raleigh, N.C., 1950-66; in Cary, N.C., 1967-73.
WORKS: CHORUS: God's son is born, Christmas cantata; The cross shines forth, Easter cantata; many anthems and organ pieces.
1013 Gardner St., Raleigh, NC 27607

HOFFMANN, RICHARD
b. Vienna, Austria, 20 Apr. 1925; U.S. citizen 1963. Emigrated to New Zealand in 1935, studied at Auckland Univ. Coll.; came to the U.S. in 1947 and studied with Arnold Schoenberg in Los Angeles. His awards include Huntington Hartford fellowships; Nat. Inst. of Arts and Letters award; Fromm Found. commission; 2 Nat. Endowment for the Arts grants, 1976, 1977; Guggenheim fellowship, 1977-78. He has been faculty member, Oberlin Coll., from 1954.
WORKS: ORCHESTRA: Fantasy and fugue in memoriam A. Schoenberg, 1951; 2 orchestra pieces, 1952, 1961; piano concerto, 1954; cello concerto, 1959; Music for strings, 1970-71; Souffleur, full orch. without conductor, 1975-76; CHAMBER MUSIC: 3 string quartets, 1947, 1950, 1972-74; trio for piano, violin, bass clarinet, 1948; quartet, piano and strings, 1950; 2 string trios, 1963, 1971; Decadanse, 10 players, 1972; Changes for chimes, 2 sets, 4 players, 1974; ELECTRONIC: in memoriam patris, computer-generated tape, 1976; string quartet #4, with computer-generated sounds (scordatura--trompe l'oreille), 1977.
11 Shiperd Circle, Oberlin, OH 44074

HOFFRICHTER, BERTHA CHAITKIN (Mrs. Maurice J.)
b. Pittsburgh, Pa., 8 Dec. 1915. Attended Carnegie-Mellon Univ., B.A., M.A.; studied privately with Joseph Jenkins. She received the Martin Leisser award, Pittsburgh Art Society, for a piano sonata; Penn. Fed. of Music Clubs award for a song cycle; Composers Division prize for a piano trio; was elected president, Tuesday Musical Club of Pittsburgh, 1973-74.
WORKS: CHAMBER MUSIC: violin sonata; sonata for 2 pianos; CHORUS: The 23rd Psalm, with soprano solo; The 24th Psalm, a cappella; also piano suites, 2-piano suites, songs, choral works.
5412 Northumberland St., Pittsburgh, PA 15217

HOFMANN, JOSEPH
b. Podgorze, near Krakow, Poland, 20 Jan. 1876; U.S. citizen 1926; d. Los Angeles, Calif., 16 Feb. 1957. A noted pianist, at age 10 he played the Beethoven Concerto No. 1 with the Berlin Philharmonic, Hans von Bülow conducting; repeated the performance at the Metropolitan Opera House, New York, playing also works by Chopin and some of his own compositions. He

later studied piano with Moszkowski and Rubinstein, composition with Urban, then resumed his career as concert pianist. As a composer, he sometimes used the pen name of Michel Dvorsky. His works were chiefly for piano, including several piano concertos, Chromaticon for piano and orch., many piano pieces; and some orchestral works.

HOFREITER, PAUL
    b. Miami Beach, Fla., 9 Sept. 1952. Studied with Vincent Persichetti and Roger Sessions, Juilliard School, B.M. 1974, M.M. 1976. His awards include Henry Mancini scholarship and Richard Rodgers scholarship, 1971-75; Irving Berlin fellowship, 1974-75; Rodgers and Hammerstein fellowship, 1975-76; Alexandre Gretchaninoff prize, 1971; second place, Lancaster Symph. Orch. composition contest, 1978; many commissions. He has been faculty member, Pennington School, N.J., from 1976.
        WORKS: ORCHESTRA: 5 symphonies, 1971-76; Psalm 47, chorus, trumpet, piano, percussion, strings, 1976; Psalm 23, baritone, piano, chorus, orch., 1977; numerous choral works, piano and organ pieces, and chamber works.
        P.O. Box 181, Pennington, NJ 08554

HOGENSON, ROBERT CHARLES
    b. Kirksville, Mo., 22 Nov. 1936. Studied with Leon Karel, Northeast Missouri State Univ.; Helen Gunderson, Louisiana State Univ.; and with H. Owen Reed, Michigan State Univ., Ph.D. He was faculty member, Southwest Texas State Univ., 1962-68; then at Univ. of Delaware. He has published works for band, solo instruments, voice, and piano.
        Music Dept., University of Delaware, Newark, DE 19711

HOGG, MERLE E.
    b. Lincoln, Kans., 25 Aug. 1922. Studied with Philip Greeley Clapp and Philip Bezanson, Univ. of Iowa, Ph.D.; and with Nadia Boulanger, Fontainebleau, 1960. He was faculty member, Eastern New Mexico Univ., 1953-62; from 1962, at San Diego State Univ.; from 1964, member, San Diego Symphony Orch.
        WORKS: ORCHESTRA: concerto for brass, 1953; trombone concerto; BAND: suite for band; Interludes for symphonic brass, 1978; CHAMBER MUSIC: Invention, brass quintet; tuba sonatina; sonata for brass choir; 3 short pieces, brass trio; Toccata, brass quartet; Variations, brass trio; Variations, bassoon and piano; Etude I, tuba and piano; 3 studies, euphonium and piano, 1978; many works for jazz ensemble; songs.
        Music Dept., San Diego State University, San Diego, CA 92115

HOHMANN, WALTER H.
    b. Holstead, Kans., 27 Oct. 1892; d. North Newton, Kans., 9 Mar. 1971. Studied with Edgar Brazelton, Chicago Musical Coll. He received honorary doctorates from Bethel Coll., 1947, and Chicago Musical Coll., 1947. He taught at Freeman Junior Coll., S.Dak., 1921-23; was chairman, music department, Bethel Coll., 1923-62;

was coeditor, Mennonite Hymnary, published 1940, and on the revision committee in 1969.
        WORKS: CHORUS: Wind in the pines; Po' good Jesus; O power of love; and others. He was author of Outlines of hymnology, Bethel Coll. Press.

HOIBY, LEE
    b. Madison, Wis., 17 Feb. 1926. Studied with Gunnar Johansen, Univ. of Wisconsin, B.M. 1947; piano with Egon Petri, Mills Coll., M.A. 1952; composition with Gian-Carlo Menotti, Curtis Inst. of Music. His awards include a Fulbright fellowship, 1952; Guggenheim fellowship, 1957; Nat. Inst. of Arts and Letters award, 1957; ASCAP award for score of Summer and smoke, 1972; and commissions.
        WORKS: OPERA: The witch, 1956; The scarf, 1958; Beatrice, 1959; Natalia Petrovna, 1964; Summer and smoke, St. Paul Opera Co., 19 June 1971; BALLET: After Eden (more than 500 performances); Landscape; Hearts, meadows and flags; THEATRE: incidental music to The Duchess of Malfi; She stoops to conquer; The octoroon; Androcles and the lion; Under milkwood; Tartuffe; The winter's tale; As you like it; ORCHESTRA: Noctambulation, 1952; piano concerto, 1958; Music for a celebration, commissioned for the Bicentennial by the Madison Symphony Orch., Washington, 15 June 1976; CHAMBER MUSIC: violin sonata, 1952; Study in design, string orch., 1953; Diversions, woodwind quintet, 1954; Pastoral dances, flute; also choral works, songs, piano pieces.
        277 W. 10th St., Apt. 12N, New York, NY 10014

HOKANSON, DOROTHY CADZOW
    b. Edmonton, Alta., 5 Aug. 1916. Studied at Univ. of Washington; with Frederick Jacobi and Bernard Wagenaar, Juilliard School, 1942-45. Her works include Northwestern sketches, a suite for orch., 1945; a string quartet; Golden dawn, vocal solo.
        2636 11th Ave. E., Seattle, WA 98102

HOKANSON, MARGRETHE
    b. Duluth, Minn., 19 Dec. 1893; d. Pennsylvania, 24 Apr. 1975. Studied at American Cons.; composition with Arthur Andersen. She won a Nat. Fed. of Music Clubs prize for an orchestral work; was faculty member, Allegheny Coll., 1944-54.
        WORKS: CHORUS: O praise Him; SONGS: In the primeval forest; Nordic song; Song without words; A summer idyll; Come, close the curtain of your eyes; ORGAN: A Nordic reverie;

HOLBROOK, GERALD W.
    b. York, Nebr., 29 Oct. 1946. Studied voice and viola, Univ. of Nebraska; piano at Univ. of Michigan, Royal Coll. of Music, London, Boston Cons., and American Cons. He has held various positions as church organist, music director, and vocalist; was violist with the Lincoln, Nebr., and Plymouth, Mich., symphony orchestras; private teacher of voice and piano.
        WORKS: THEATRE: The 8th deadly sin, musical play, 1975; music for 3 plays of the Yuan

HOLDEN, DAVID JUSTIN

dynasty (commissioned by the Art. Inst. of
Chicago), 1977; VOICE: 4 masses for unison
voices, 1969-71; Magnificat, unison voices, 1969;
Litany for the enthronement of an abbot, unison
voices and cantor, 1969; Kyrie, chorus, 1969;
Alleluia, 1970; As the deer yearns for running
streams, chorus, 1971; Questions, solo voice and
piano, 1975.
    116 S. Michigan Ave., Suite 1010, Chicago,
IL 60603

HOLDEN, DAVID JUSTIN
    b. White Plains, N.Y., 16 Dec. 1911. Studied
with Walter Piston and Aaron Copland, Harvard
Univ.; with Bernard Wagenaar, Juilliard School.
He received the Knight prize at Harvard; NBC
Music Guild award; Cleveland Orchestra 25th
Anniversary award; Society for the Publication
of American Music grant. He was faculty member,
Boston Cons., 1938-43; Mt. Holyoke Coll., 1943-
78; music critic and editor, Chautauquan Daily,
1949-68; faculty, Chautauqua Summer School, 1950-
64; Syracuse Univ. Summer School, 1965-68.
    WORKS: ORCHESTRA: symphony; choral sym-
phony; Toccata; CHAMBER MUSIC: Music for piano
and strings; 2 string quartets; CHORUS: Christmas cantata on Appalachian carols; KEYBOARD:
Improvisation on We 3 kings, organ; Passacaglia,
piano.
    61 Silver St., South Hadley, MA 01075

HOLDRIDGE, LEE
    b. Haiti, 3 Mar. 1944, U.S. parents. Studied
with Henry Lasker in Boston; with Nicolas
Flagello, Manhattan School of Music. He received
the Circle of Friends of Music award, Arenzano,
Italy, 1972. Since 1967 he has been free-lance
film composer in New York, Los Angeles, and
London.
    WORKS: BALLET: Trinity, 1970; Ballet fan-
tasy no. 2, strings and harp, 1972; THEATRE: incidental music for Another part of the forest,
Hellman, 1972; ORCHESTRA: Scenes of summer; The
other world music, violin and string orch.,
1973; Grand waltz for strings, 1975; The journey,
suite from film score Goin' home, 1976; violin
concerto #2, 1978; CHAMBER MUSIC: Fantasy sonata,
cello and piano, 1971; concerto for bass trombone and chamber ensemble, 1971; concertino,
cello and strings, 1973; concerto, viola and
chamber orch., 1977; SONGS: The conscientious
objector, Millay text, soprano; Ocean's poem,
cycle for soprano, 1972; Antigone, soprano,
1973; FILM SCORES: Jeremy, 1973; Jonathan
Livingston Seagull, 1973; Mustang country, 1974;
The other side of the mountain, Part II, 1978;
The pack, 1978; Goin' home, 1978; John Denver's
Alaska, 1978.
    c/o Bart Associates, 1488 N. King St., Los
Angeles, CA 90069

HOLLANDER, LORIN
    b. Queens, N.Y., 19 July 1944. Studied with
Eduard Steuermann and Vittorio Giannini at
Juilliard School. He is a concert pianist.
    WORKS: PIANO: Up against the wall;
Lullaby.
    Stockton Springs, ME 04981

HOLLANDER, RALPH
    b. Brooklyn, N.Y., 9 Nov. 1916. Studied at
Juilliard School; Manhattan Coll. of Music, M.A.
He has been concert violinist in the U.S. and
Europe; soloist with the Longine Symphonette.
    WORKS: ORCHESTRA: Galmud, tone poem;
Elegie for strings; CHAMBER MUSIC: Gitana,
violin and piano; Psalms of David, I and II,
violin and speech chorus.

HOLLER, JOHN
    b. New York, N.Y., 13 Jan. 1904. Studied organ
with Norman Coke-Jephcott, David Williams, and
Charles Bank. He was organist-choirmaster, St.
Mark's Church, New York; associate editor with a
music publishing firm. He has composed sacred
choral works.

HOLLIDAY, KENT ALFRED
    b. St. Paul, Minn., 9 Mar. 1940. Studied with
Paul Fetler and Dominick Argento, Univ. of
Minnesota; electronic music with Pietro Grossi
in Florence, Italy; with Jon Appleton, Dartmouth
Coll. He received a Nat. Endowment for Humanities grant, 1972. He was faculty member,
Southern Colorado State Coll., 1965-72; Colorado
State Univ., 1972-74; from 1974, Virginia Polytechnic Inst.
    WORKS: ORCHESTRA: Poems into darkness,
cantata for chorus and orch.; symphony; Symphonia brevis: The longest road, tenor and wind
ensemble; Threnody, piano, wind ensemble, percussion; CHAMBER MUSIC: Toccata, piano; and 4
are one, flute and violin; Fanfare, brass sextet;
4 canons for 4 flutes; Capriccio, marimba; Night
music for piano and unobtrusive tape recorder.
    1102 Willard Dr., Blacksburg, VA 24061

HOLLINGSWORTH, STANLEY
    b. Berkeley, Calif., 27 Aug. 1924. Studied at
San Jose State Coll.; with Darius Milhaud at
Mills Coll.; with Gian-Carlo Menotti at Curtis
Inst.; and at American Acad. in Rome on a fellow-
ship, 1955-58. Other awards include Guggenheim
fellowship, 1958-59; 2 Nat. Endowment for the
Arts grants, 1976, 1978. He was faculty member,
San Jose State Coll., 1961-63; Yale Univ., 1
seminar, 1975; and from 1976, at Oakland Univ.
    WORKS: OPERA: The mother, 1954; La Grande
Brèteche, television opera, 1957; The selfish
giant; Harrison loved his umbrella; BALLET: The
unquiet graves; Divertimento; Il volo; Incontri;
CHAMBER MUSIC: oboe sonata; quintet for harp
and woodwinds; 4 impromptus, flute and piano;
CHORUS: Dumbarton Oaks mass, with string orch.;
Stabat mater, with orch., 1957; Psalm of David;
Death be not proud; also songs and incidental
music.
    2780 Patrick Henry Dr., Pontiac, MI 48057

HOLLISTER, DAVID H.
    b. New York, N.Y., 1 May 1929. Studied with
Wallingford Riegger, Metropolitan Music School,
1952; Henry Brant at Juilliard School, 1954-55;
Darius Milhaud, Aspen School, 1958; Richard
Hervig, Univ. of Iowa, 1964-67; and with
Wlodzimierz Kotonski in Warsaw, 1967-68. His
awards include fellowships from MacDowell Colony,

1961, Huntington Hartford Found., 1964, Howard Found., 1967-68, Yaddo, 1973, Villa Monalvo, 1973; and the Zelosky grant, Kosciuszko Found., 1967. He has held faculty posts at Louisiana State Univ., 1968-70; York Coll., CUNY, 1970; Bronx Community Coll., from 1973; Bernard Baruch Coll., from 1978.

WORKS: BALLET: Tablet; Rebus; Jazz adversary; A time for parting; ORCHESTRA: concertino for strings; Serenade; Syncretisms; Essay, winds and strings; CHAMBER MUSIC: Partita for 6 instruments; woodwind trio; string quartet; VOCAL: Songs of death; Winter madrigals; My holy mountain; PIANO: Variations on Moscow nights; Toccata.

10 E. 16th St., New York, NY 10003

HOLMAN, WILLIS
b. Olive, Calif., 1927. Has played tenor saxophone with jazz orchestras; was arranger for Stan Kenton and Woody Herman. His compositions include Trilogy, written for the Los Angeles Neophonic Orch., 1965; Festival prologue for wind symphony; and Music for baritone saxophone and orch. (with Gerry Mulligan), 1966.

HOLMES, G. E.
b. Baraboo, Wis., 14 Feb. 1873; d. Chicago, Ill., 10 Feb. 1945. Studied music privately. He taught at Prior's Cons., Danville, Ill., and at Vandercook School of Music, Chicago. His published works included many band marches and songs.

HOLMES, MARKWOOD
b. Lexington, Nebr., 18 Aug. 1899. Studied with David Van Vactor, Kansas City; Otto Luening, New York; Charles Koechlin in Paris; Darius Milhaud and Charles Jones, Santa Barbara; Bela Rozsa, Tulsa Univ., M.M. He was cowinner of the Ernest Bloch award, 1949, and received many first prizes in Kansas Music Teachers Assoc. contests. He held faculty positions at Kansas City Cons., 1919-25, 1930-36; Kansas State Coll., 1947-69; was also violinist in the Vaudelle String Quartet, Paris, 1927-28; Kansas City Philharmonic Orch., 1933-38, 1944-46; Tulsa Philharmonic, 1961-73.

WORKS: OPERA: Telemachus; ORCHESTRA: Passacaglia and fugue; sinfonia; Symphonic episode, solo cello and piano with orch.; Agnus Dei, 4 soloists, chorus, and orch.; concerto grosso, 6 instruments and string orch.; CHAMBER MUSIC: Street scenes, violin, clarinet, piano; cello sonata; Prelude, elegy and fugue, piano quintet; March-fantasy, viola and piano; VOCAL: Island, song cycle; By the greatness, women's choir; 3 songs on Chinese love poems, voice, viola, piano.

2602 Omaha, Pittsburg, KS 66762

HOLMES, PAUL
b. Abilene, Tex., 20 Jan. 1923. Studied at Hardin Simmons Univ., B.M.; Univ. of Texas, M.M. He received the Houston Symphony Texas Composers award, 1957, and many commissions. He is faculty member, Lamar Univ.

WORKS: ORCHESTRA: 3 archaic dances; Fable for orch., 1957; Freedom symphony, soprano solo-

ist, choir, orch., commissioned for the Bicentennial, performed, Beaumont, Tex., 1 Apr. 1976, with 3 combined choirs; BAND: Prince Consort, concert march; concertino for 3 solo tubas and band, 1972; CHAMBER MUSIC: suite for brass; Lento, tuba; Serenade, horn; trumpet sonata; clarinet suite; 6 little pieces, flute and piano; tuba quartet, 1971; brass quintet, 1972; CHORUS: Hymn and alleluia; And nature shall be healed, cantata, with brass and percussion, 1970; and songs.

Lamar University, P.O. Box 10044, Beaumont, TX 77710

HOLSINGER, DAVID R.
b. Kansas City, Mo., 26 Dec. 1945. Studied at Central Methodist Coll., B.M.E. 1967; Central Missouri State Univ., M.A. 1973. He won first place Kent State Univ. composition contest, 1971, and Nat. Fed. of Music Clubs contest, 1970. He has been public school music supervisor, Hardin, Mo., 1973-75; Lawson, Mo., from 1975.

WORKS: OPERA: A day in the death of Stephan Voltov, 1 act, Warrensburg, Mo., 1976; BAND: Prelude and rondo; Partita allegro, woodwind choir; Trilogy: After Armageddon, 1971; Toward the 3rd century, 1977; Hopak Raskoniki/A dance for the old believers.

Rte. 1, Box 70, Lawson, MO 64062

HOMANS, PETER
b. 1951. Studied with Robert Stewart, Washington and Lee Univ.; with Donald Martino, New England Cons.

WORKS: CHAMBER MUSIC: Lumori, cello and violin, 1973; concertino, chamber orch., Boston, 12 Oct. 1976; VOICE: cantata on texts of Wallace Stevens and Ezra Pound, 1973; 3 Italian songs, 1974.

HOOPER, WILLIAM L.
b. Sedalia, Mo., 16 Sept. 1931. Studied at William Jewell Coll., B.A. 1953; with Philip Bezanson, Univ. of Iowa, M.A. 1956; Philip Slates, George Peabody Coll., Ph.D. 1966; and with Humphrey Searle, Royal Coll. of Music, London, 1969-70. He received the Jesse Jones scholarship, Peabody Coll.; won honorable mention, 1972, first place, 1973, Delius Composition Contest; won Louisiana State Univ. contest; at William Jewell Coll., an award in music has been named in his honor. He has been Baptist pastor, public school teacher; professor, Southwest Baptist Coll., 1956-60; church music director and baritone soloist, 1960-66; faculty member, New Orleans Baptist Theological Seminary, 1966-75.

WORKS: CANTATAS: His saving grace proclaim; Jubilee; A litany of praise; ORGAN: Praeludium.

4131 Seminary Place, New Orleans, LA 70126

HOOSE, ALFRED
b. Wheeling, W.Va., 17 Sept. 1918. Studied with Isadore Freed and Arnold Franchetti, Hartt Coll. of Music; with Francis Judd Cooke and George Faxon, New England Cons.; privately with Hugo Norden and Fred Lerdahl. He taught at Newton

HOOVER, KATHERINE

Jr. Coll., 1957-64; Boston State Coll., from 1965; was organist-choirmaster in Waltham, 1964-72.

WORKS: ORCHESTRA: Rights to passage, secular cantata for chorus and orch., 1972; Interactions, string orch., 1974; CHAMBER MUSIC: piano trio, 1964; trio for viola, clarinet, piano, 1970; wind quintet #2, 1976; Diversion, viola, piano, vibraphone, tom-toms, 1977; Glimpses, soprano and chamber ensemble, 1978; trio for flute, viola, piano, 1979; CHORUS: missa brevis, with organ, 1952; work for chorus, winds, piano, percussion, 1975; other choral works; many organ pieces.

1105 Lexington St., Bldg. 1, Waltham, MA 02154

HOOVER, KATHERINE
b. Elkins, W.Va., 2 Dec. 1937. Studied at Univ. of Rochester; Eastman School of Music, B.M. 1959; Bryn Mawr Coll. on fellowship, 1960-61; Yale Summer School on scholarship, 1961; Manhattan School of Music, M.M. 1974. She was faculty member,at Juilliard School, 1962-69; from 1969, at Manhattan School of Music; as flutist, has given recitals in New York, Boston, Washignton, Philadelphia.

WORKS: CHAMBER MUSIC: Trio for flutes, 1974; Variations, brass quintet, 1974; Divertimento, flute and string trio, 1975; Homage to Bartok, wind quintet, 1975; Sinfonia, 4 bassoons, 1976; 2 dances, flute, oboe, guitar, 1976; Duets for 2 flutes, 1977; CHORUS: 3 carols, women's voices, flute, 1972; Lake Isle of Innisfree, 1973; Songs of joy with 2 trumpets, 2 trombones, 1974; 4 English songs, 1976; Syllable songs, women's voices and woodblock, 1977; SONGS: Lullay, lullay, soprano and piano, 1971; 4 carols, soprano and flute, 1970; 7 Haiku, soprano and flute, 1973; Proud songsters, soprano, flute, clarinet, violin, 1974; To many a well, voice and piano, 1977; and piano pieces.

160 W. 95th St., New York, NY 10025

HOPKINS, HARRY PATTERSON
b. Baltimore, Md., 25 May 1873; d. Baltimore, Md., 21 Sept. 1954. Graduated from Peabody Cons., 1895; studied with Antonin Dvorak in Bohemia. From 1899 he was organist and teacher in Baltimore.

WORKS: ORCHESTRA: a symphony; Spring journey, chorus and orch.; CHAMBER MUSIC: piano trio; 2 piano quintets; string quartet; piano sextet; ORGAN: Exaltation; Heavenly glory; also a comic opera, anthems, and other choral works.

HOPKINS, JAMES FREDERICK
b. Pasadena, Calif., 8 Apr. 1939. Studied with Ernest Kanitz and Halsey Stevens, Univ. of Southern California; with Quincy Porter, Yale Univ.; with Edward T. Cone, Princeton Univ. His awards include Woodrow Wilson fellowship, 1960-62; 5 composition prizes at Yale Univ., 1962; ASCAP awards; Nat. Endowment for the Arts grant, 1975; He was faculty member, Northwestern Univ., 1962-71; then at Univ. of Southern California.

WORKS: ORCHESTRA: Phantasms; Variations for orch.; symphony #4, Visions of hell, Portland,

Oreg., 9 Feb. 1976; Voces organi, organ duet, strings, percussion, Pasadena, 11 Mar. 1980; BAND: 2 symphonies; CHAMBER MUSIC: Diferencias, piano trio; Fantasia, 8 cellos and 2 basses; Theatrikomelos, chamber orch.; Concert music, harpsichord and string quartet; CHORUS: Hymn of progress; Jubilate Deo, Psalm 150, choir, organ, 2 trumpets, percussion; Missa Regina Coeli, with organ and harp.

2859 Westbrook Ave., Los Angeles, CA 90046

HOPSON, HAL HAROLD
b. Coryell County, Tex., 12 June 1933. Studied at Baylor Univ.; with Helmut Schiller, Erlangen Univ., Germany; with Lloyd Pfautsch and Robert Anderson, Southern Methodist Univ. His awards include a scholarship at Baylor Univ. and numerous commissions. He has held posts as organist-choirmaster in Baltimore, Md., 1962-65; Ashland, Ky., 1965-69; Vine Street Christian Church, Nashville, 1969-74; Westminster Presbyterian Church, Nashville, from 1974.

WORKS: CHORUS: Canticle of praise, with organ and 3 trumpets; A psalm of praise; God with us, cantata, 1976; 2 children's cantatas: A night for dancing and The singing bishop; A psalm service.

3900 West End Ave., Nashville, TN 37205

HORN, PAUL
b. New York, N.Y., 17 Mar. 1930. Studied at Oberlin Cons., B.M.; on scholarship at Manhattan School of Music, M.M. He played flute with Chico Hamilton, then formed his own group in 1959. He has written television scores; the film score, Clutch cargo; and many songs.

HORTON, KENNETH JOHN
b. Long Beach, Calif., 29 Oct. 1950. Studied with Stanley Lunetta. He has been percussionist, Sacramento Symphony Orch., from 1965; timpanist, Reno Philharmonic Orch., from 1973.

WORKS: Opus T, 1968; St. Francis, 1969; Light song, 1970; September toad ritual, joint work with Lunetta and others, 1971; AMRA/ARMA, 1970- (Horton says most major works now require performance before completion).

6925 Chevy Chase Way, Sacramento, CA 95823

HORTON, LEWIS HENRY
b. Youngstown, Ohio, 8 Nov. 1898. Studied at Oberlin Cons., B.A. 1923; Ohio State Univ., M.A. 1938. He was public school music teacher, 1926-30; faculty member, Morehead State Coll., 1930-42; Univ. of Kentucky, 1942-46; Transylvania Univ., 1946-75. He was also music critic on the Lexington papers.

WORKS: CHORUS: The white pilgrim, folk cantata, 1940; An Appalachian nativity, folk cantata, 1955; An Appalachian Easter, 1959; Mother Goose suite; Ancient of days; Weep you no more sad fountains; A cappella primer; A cappella frontiers.

338 Kilmore Court, Lexington, KY 40508

HORVIT, MICHAEL
b. New York, N.Y., 22 June 1932. Studied with Quincy Porter, Yale Univ., B.M. 1955; M.M. 1956;

with Gardner Read, Boston Univ., D.M.A. 1959; also with Walter Piston at Harvard, 1957; with Aaron Copland, 1959, Lukas Foss, 1961, at Tanglewood. His honors include a BMI award, 1959; Coll. Band Directors Nat. Assoc. award, 1961; Rockefeller grant, 1968; Nat. Endowment for the Arts grant, 1974; Fridge Trust-Houston Symphony award, 1976; ASCAP awards, 1976, 1977, 1978. He was faculty member, Southern Connecticut Coll., 1959-66; from 1966, at Univ. of Houston.

WORKS: OPERA: Tomo, 1-act children's opera, Houston, 21 Nov. 1968; Adventure in space, chamber opera for children, 1976; ORCHESTRA: symphony, 1959; Toccatina, 1965; The gardens of Hieronymus B., 1976; WIND ENSEMBLE: Concert music for band #I, 1961, #II, 1970; Antique suite, 2 brass choirs, 1971; CHAMBER MUSIC: string quartet, 1958; Little suite, woodwind trio, 1964; brass quintet, 1970; The crystal cave, harpsichord sonata, 1973; Interplay, percussion quartet, 1978; ELECTRONIC: Antiphon, saxophone and tape, 1971; 2 songs for choir and tape, 1974; Moonscape, ballet score for tape, 1975; Antiphon II, clarinet and tape, 1974; Antiphon III, piano and tape, 1978; choral works and songs.

8114 Braesdale Lane, Houston, TX 77071

HORWOOD, MICHAEL S.
b. Buffalo, N.Y., 24 May 1947. Studied with Ramon Fuller, Leo Smit, William C. Kothe, and Lejaren Hiller, State Univ. of New York at Buffalo, B.A., M.A. He taught high school in Buffalo, 1969-71; from 1972, has been faculty member, Humber Coll. of Applied Arts and Technology, Ont.

WORKS: THEATRE: incidental music: Dog in the manger, Lope de Vega, 1972; Tantrums, Hrant Alianak, 1972; CHAMBER MUSIC: 6 pieces for piano, 1967; Timpanic suite, 2 timpanists, 1967; Piece percussionique, 3 percussionists, 1967; Microduet #1, oboe and bass drum, 1967; Microduet #3, tuba and almglocken, 1968; New York State Thruway, clarinet and piano, 1969; ELECTRONIC: Motility; Monday afternoon, 1966; MIXED MEDIA: For the class of '71, 4 settings of poems of Robert Creeley, narrator, tape, chamber ensemble, 1968.

2981 Islington Ave. N., Weston, Ontario, Canada

HOSKINS, WILLIAM BARNES
b. St. Lucie, Fla., 26 Oct. 1917. Studied with Normand Lockwood, Oberlin Coll., 1936-40; with Nadia Boulanger, Wisconsin, 1941; with Otto Luening, Columbia Univ., 1947. He was awarded a commission by Florida State Music Teachers, 1970. His faculty posts have included West Virginia Univ., 1940-42; Jacksonville Coll. of Music, 1948-58; Jacksonville Univ., from 1961.

WORKS: ORCHESTRA: Israfel, chorus and orch.; Ballad of the trumpet boy; Concert overture; The lost lands, cycle for mezzo-soprano and string orch.; Requiem for the 6 million, chorus, soloists, brass and percussion ensemble, piano, organ; CHAMBER MUSIC: string quartet; Variations on a random theme, piano; sonata for brass quartet; Suite Balinesque, western gamelan;

ELECTRONIC: Galactic fantasy, Moog synthesizer; MIXED MEDIA: Dialogo I and II, chorus, soloists, tape, 1979; Song of the space ways, orch. and tape.

5454 Arlington Rd., Jacksonville, FL 32211

HOSMER, JAMES B.
b. Johnstown, Pa., 27 May 1911. Studied composition with Bernard Wagenaar, flute with Kincaid and Barrere. He was flutist with the Indianapolis Symphony, 1937-42; from 1946, with the Metropolitan Opera Orch.

WORKS: ORCHESTRA: From the mail box, a suite, 1953; CHAMBER MUSIC: Fugue, woodwind quintet, 1938; Rhapsody, flute and strings, 1957; 4 flute duos, 1961; 7/4 serenade, flute, oboe, bassoon, harpsichord, 1965.

49 Seaview Ave., New Rochelle, NY 10801

HOSMER, LUCIUS
b. South Acton, Mass., 14 Aug. 1870; d. Jefferson, N.H., 9 May 1935. Studied with George W. Chadwick, New England Cons.; was church organist and conducted theatre orchestras.

WORKS: OPERA: The rose of Alhambra, 1905; The walking delegate, comic opera, rev. as The Koreans; ORCHESTRA: Chinese wedding procession; Southern rhapsody; Northern rhapsody; Ethiopian rhapsody; On tiptoe; and songs.

HOUGH, PHILIP
b. Glenn Ridge, N.J., 25 Nov. 1947. Studied with David Loeb, Mannes Coll. of Music; and at Hunter Coll.; violin with Isadore Cohen and Lilo Glick. He won second prize, New Music for Young Ensembles contest, 1975; third prize, Stowe Composers contest, 1976.

WORKS: ORCHESTRA: viola concerto; CHAMBER MUSIC: trio for 2 violas and cello; cello sonata; duo for flute and guitar; chamber concerto for string orch.

808 West End Ave., New York, NY 10025

HOUSMAN, ROSALIE
b. San Francisco, Calif., 25 June 1888; d. New York, N.Y., 28 Oct. 1949. Studied with Arthur Foote in Boston; with Ernest Bloch in New York. She wrote Color sequence for soprano and small orch.; choruses, songs.

HOVDA, ELEANOR
b. Duluth, Minn., 27 Mar. 1940. Studied with Gordon Smith and Esther Ballou, American Univ., B.A. 1964; with Mel Powell, Yale Univ., 1964-65; Kenneth Gaburo, Univ. of Illinois, 1965-66; Karlheinz Stockhausen, Cologne, Germany, 1966; dance composition with Bessie Schoenberg, Sarah Lawrence Coll., M.F.A. 1971; and with Lucia Dlugoszewski, 1970. Her awards include Composers Forum program; Minnesota State Arts Board grant; and many commissions. She was faculty member, Sarah Lawrence Coll., 1974-75; Wesleyan Univ., (Conn.), 1975-77; American Dance Festival, summers, 1974-77; Univ. of Minnesota, Duluth, from 1979.

WORKS: CHAMBER MUSIC: Music from The proclamation, solo flute, 1966; Waveschart, flute, clarinet, piano, percussion, double bass, 1970;

HOVDESVEN, E. A.

Ondes doubles, Ondes Martinot, flute, viola, harp, cocomposed with David Gilbert, 1971; Ondes doubles II, Ondes Martinot and guitar, 1972; Music from several summers, 2 double basses, 1972; The lion's head, flute, clarinet, violin, cello, 1972; Air moment, 33 flutes, 1973; Spring music with wind, piano, 1973; Lady Astor, guitar, 1975; Embermusic, piano, 1978.
2218 E. 1st St., Duluth, MN 55812

HOVDESVEN, E. A.
b. Lyon County, Minn., 4 May 1893. Studied at St. Olaf Coll., B.A., B.M.; Juilliard School; Toronto Univ., D.M.; and at Fontainebleau Cons. He was associate, Royal Coll. of Organists, England, and fellow, Canadian Coll. of Organists. He toured as concert and theatre organist and taught in several colleges up to retirement in 1963. His compositions include an organ concerto, a symphony, many choral works, and organ pieces.

HOVEY, SERGE
b. New York, N.Y., 10 Mar. 1920. Studied piano with Richard Buhlig, composition with Arnold Schoenberg and Hanns Eisler. His film scores have received many awards including 3 CINE Gold Eagles; Sholem Aleichem received second place, Koussevitzky Found. competition, 1958. He has been orchestrator, accompanist, music director for Bracht's Galileo, 1948, composer for filmss from 1951.
WORKS: OPERA: Dreams in spades, 1-act chamber opera, 1949; BALLET: Fable, 1949; THEATRE: The world of Sholem Aleichem, music for the play, 1953; Tevya and his daughters, 1957; ORCHESTRA: Sholem Aleichem suite, soloists, chorus, orch., 1954, Cincinnati, 21 Feb. 1958; Robert Burns rhapsody, soloists, chorus, orch., 1958; African ballet suite, 1960; Weekend--U.S.A., 1961; A little New York music, 1961; symphony, 1967; Freedom variations, 1969; CHAMBER MUSIC: The fiddle, narrator and chamber ensemble, 1948; A ballad of August Bondi, narrator, vocalists, chamber ensemble, 1956; Intermezzo, piano and strings, 1961; 4 Afro-American variations, clarinet, piano duet, percussion, 1965; FILM SCORES: The magic hat, 1952; Hangman, 1964; Storm of strangers, 1969; Denmark 43, 1970-71; Gulliver in Automobilia, 1974; also many songs and The Robert Burns song book, 4 vol., 1968-73.
512 Arbramar Ave., Pacific Palisades, CA 90272

HOVHANESS, ALAN
b. Somerville, Mass., 8 Mar. 1911. Began piano study early with Adelaide Proctor and Heinrich Gebhard; studied composition with Frederick Converse, New England Cons. His many honors include Tanglewood scholarship, 1942; 3 honorary doctorates; Guggenheim fellowships; election to Nat. Inst. of Arts and Letters; many commissions. He taught privately in Boston; was on faculty, Boston Cons., 1948-51; then moved to New York, where he composed prolifically, including radio and television scores; began his first world tour in 1959, achieving remarkable success in

India and Japan; later settled in Seattle.
WORKS: OPERA: The blue flame, 1959; Spirit of the avalanche, 1963; Wind drum, 1964; Pilate, 1966; The travelers, 1967; Tale of the Sun Goddess going into the Stone House, Salinas, Calif., 25 Mar. 1979; ORCHESTRA: 38 symphonies, 1937-78; #26, San Jose, 24 Oct.,1975; #27 and 28, Los Angeles, 23 Apr. 1978; #31, Seattle, 9 Dec. 1977; #35 (2 orch., full symphony and orch. of ancient Korean instruments) Seoul, Korea, 9 June 1978; #36, flute and orch., Kennedy Center, Washington, D.C., 16 Jan. 1979; #38, Seattle, 21 Oct. 1978; 3 Armenian rhapsodies, 1944-45; Lousadzak, concerto for piano and strings, 1945; Is there survival?, ballet suite; Zartik partim; Artik, horn and strings; Janabar, violin, trumpet, strings: Arevakal; concerto for violin and strings; concerto #7 for orch., 1953; Meditation on Orpheus, 1958; Meditation on Zeami, 1964; Floating world, Salt Lake City, 30 Jan. 1965; Fantasy on Japanese wood prints, 1965; Fra Angelico, 1967; The Holy City, voice and orch., Portland, Maine, 11 Apr. 1967; Requiem and resurrection; Mountains and rivers without end; Shambala; And God created great whales, New York, 11 June 1970; Firdausi, New York, 12 May 1973; Manjun symphony, Lubbock, Tex., Jan 1974; cello concerto, Pullman, Wash., 27 Jan. 1975; The way of Jesus, 2 choruses and orch., 23 Feb. 1975; Ode to freedom, violin and orch. of ancient Trap Farm Park, Washington, D.C., 3 July 1976, Yehudi Menukin soloist; euphonium concerto, St. Paul, Minn., 4 May 1977; Rubaiyat, narrator, accordion, orch., New York, 20 May 1977; BAND: 3 journeys to a holy mountain, 1968; Sharagan and fugue, brass choir; CHAMBER MUSIC: 5 string quartets, 1935-76; 2 piano quintets; violin sonata; flute sonata; harp sonata; sonata for 2 oboes and organ; wind quintet; sextet for recorder, string quartet, harpsichord; sonata for trumpet and organ; many other chamber works; numerous choral works and songs.
2911 S. 200 St., #2, Seattle, WA 98188

HOWARD, BERTRAND E.
b. Houston, Tex., 27 Sept. 1937. Studied with Kent Kennan, Univ. of Texas; with John Verrall, Donald Keats, William O. Smith, Univ. of Washington, D.M.A. He was awarded a commission by the Music Teachers Nat. Assoc. and Arkansas State Music Teachers Assoc., 1972. He was faculty member, Univ. of Arkansas, 1965-78.
WORKS: ORCHESTRA: Metacrylic 3, 1972; CHAMBER MUSIC: sextet for winds and strings, 1970; Soliloquy, piano; Trinomicron, inner piano, 1973; CHORUS: Rain; Green fox; SONGS: Where is the nightingale, 1963; Windon, 1968; A sea cycle, soprano and inner piano, 1971; MIXED MEDIA: Bardos, chamber group, tape, lights, film, dancer, 1972; uv ajeD, 1973; Hydrohms, trombone, prepared tape, tape loop, 1971.

HOWARD, DEAN CLINTON
b. Cleveland, Ohio, 17 Nov. 1918. Studied at Baldwin-Wallace Coll., B.M.E.; with Edmund Haine, Univ. of Michigan, M.M.; and at Indiana Univ. He received the first award, Nat. Composers Congress, 1944; first award, Iowa Composers' Con-

test, 1948; Putnam award for teaching, 1961-62; Nova '70 award. He was faculty member, Buena Vista Coll., 1946-48; from 1948, at Bradley Univ.; also first clarinetist, Peoria Symphony, from 1969.

WORKS: ORCHESTRA: Divertimento, 1960; An Illinois symphony, 1967; Perspectives, 1972; BAND: Holiday parade, 1959; Elegy for moderns, 1960; Sea drift, 1962; Salute to freedom, 1962; Caribbean cocktail, 1962; Procession of the valiant, 1964; Triumph of youth, 1965; Proud heritage, 1972; CHAMBER MUSIC: sonatas for piano, clarinet, 1962, violin 1963, cello 1964; clarinet sonatina, 1965; suite for brass and percussion, 1965; woodwind quintet, 1971; 2 string quartets; Chrysalis, clarinet and piano, 1976; Wind song, flute and piano, 1977; 3 improvisations, clarinet and piano, 1977; also choral works and electronic pieces.

School of Music, Bradley University, Peoria, IL 61606

HOWARD, GEORGE S.
b. Reamstown, Pa., 24 Feb. 1903. Attended Ohio Wesleyan Univ., A.B.; New York Univ., M.A.; Chicago Cons., B.M., M.M., D.M. His awards include Legion of Merit with Oak Leaf Clusters; Commendation Medal with 5 Oak Leaf Clusters; citation by Nat. Assoc. of American Composers and Conductors; gold record, Nippon Columbia Co., Tokyo. He taught in public schools, 1930-36; private school, 1936-38; Penn. State Univ., 1940-42; was chief of music and conductor, Air Force Orchestra and Band, 1943-63; director of band and music program, Metropolitan Police Dept., Washington, 1963-73.

WORKS: BAND: The red feather; American doughboy; A niece of Uncle Sam; My Missouri; General Spaatz march; Central Canada Exhibition march; Washington Star march; Alfalfa Club march; 8 published songs; numerous unpublished works.

Air Force Village, 4917 Ravenswood Dr., San Antonio, TX 78227

HOWARD, JOHN TASKER
b. Brooklyn, N.Y., 30 Nov. 1890; d. West Orange, N.J., 20 Nov. 1964. Studied at Williams Coll., 1910-13; honorary M.A. 1937; compositon with Howard Brockway and Mortimer Wilson. He held many posts as music editor; was curator, American Music Collection, New York Public Library, 1940-64; author of many books on American music and musicians.

WORKS: ORCHESTRA: Fantasy on a choral theme, piano and orch.; Foster sinfonietta; Mosses from an old manse; CHAMBER MUSIC: Foster sonatina, violin and piano; From Foster Hall, string quartet; many choral works, songs, piano pieces.

HOWE, HUBERT S., JR.
b. Portland, Oreg., 21 Dec. 1942. Studied with Milton Babbitt, J. K. Randall, and Godfrey Winham, Princeton Univ., M.M. 1967. He was faculty member, Queens Coll., CUNY, 1967-78; from 1978, at CUNY Graduate Center; also associate editor, Perspectives of New Music.

WORKS: ELECTRONIC: Computer variations,

1967-68; Kaleidoscope, 1969; Interchanges, 1970-71; Macro-structures, 1971; Freeze, 1972; 3 studies in timbre, 1970-73;

Graduate Center, CUNY, 33 W. 42 St., New York, NY 10036

HOWE, MARY
b. Richmond, Va., 4 Apr. 1882; d. Washington, D.C., 14 Sept. 1964. Studied in Paris with Nadia Boulanger; with Gustav Strube, Peabody Cons., diploma in composition, 1922. A full program of her works was performed by the Nat. Symph. Orch., Washington, 21 Dec. 1952; by the Howard Univ. Choir and soloists, Town Hall, New York, 24 Feb. 1953; she received an honorary doctorate from George Washington Univ., 1961.

WORKS: ORCHESTRA: Dirge, 1931; Polka and waltz; Cards; Mists; Castellano, 2 pianos and orch., 1935; Spring pastorale, 1936; Stars, 1937; Sand, 1938; Potomac suite, 1940; Agreeable overture, 1949; Axiom; American piece; Rock, symphonic poem, 1955; (both Stars and Sand received world premieres in Vienna, 15 Feb. 1955, and American premieres in Washington, 1 Feb. 1956); CHAMBER MUSIC: violin sonata, 1922; piano quintet, 1923; Elegy, for organ; CHORUS: Chain gang song, 1925; Great land of mine; Prophecy, 1972, male chorus, 1943; 7 volumes of songs published in 1960.

HOWELL, HUDSON DAVIS
b. West Frankfort, Ill., 11 July 1919. Studied with Bela Rozsa and Strom Bull, Baylor Univ.; with Harry Wilson and Howard Murphy, Columbia Univ. He was minister of music and organist, Hapeville, Ga., 1952-56. He composes church music for organ and chorus.

2515 N. Camino de Oeste, Tucson, AZ 85705

HOWLAND, WILLIAM LEGRAND
b. Asbury Park, N.J., 1873; d. Long Island, N.Y., 26 July 1915. Studied with Philip Scharwenka in Poland. His works include 2 operas, Sarrona, 1903, and Nita; 2 oratorios, The resurrection and Ecce homo; and choral works.

HOY, BONNEE
b. Jenkintown, Pa., 27 Aug. 1936. Studied with Roy Harris and Joseph Castaldo, Philadelphia Musical Acad.; with Nadia Boulanger at Fontainebleau; at Temple Univ. She was on the music faculty, St. Basil's Acad., 1962-64; Settlement Music School, 1966-72; music consultant, WUHY-FM, 1973.

WORKS: BALLET: Pinocchio, 1958; ORCHESTRA: violin concerto, 1963; CHAMBER MUSIC: The hourglass suite, soprano, tenor, chamber ensemble, 1966; piano trio, 1968; The Freeman celebration songs and dances, soprano, flute, cello, piano, 1971; string quartet, 1972; piano quintet, 1973; CHORUS: 3 sacred motets, a cappella, 1963; Quartet and gloria, a cappella, 1968; The spring of Earth's rebirth, oratorio, chorus, 2 solo choruses, 4 soloists, orch., 1971; Threnody, with recorder, cello, drums, 1973; PIANO: Preludes, 1969; Storybook suite for children, 1970; 2 sonatas, 1970, 1971; Excursions, vol. 1, 1973.

7744 Albright Ave., Elkins Park, PA 19117

HOYT, RICHARD

HOYT, RICHARD
    b. Havre, Mont., 18 Aug. 1928. Studied with
Richard Westenburg, Univ. of Montana, M.M.E. He
has composed many songs on Dickinson and Shelley
texts, etc., and piano pieces; many have been
performed in New York.
        160 W. 73 St., #9F, New York, NY 10023

HSU, WEN-YING
    b. Shanghai, China, 2 May 1909; U.S. citizen
1972. Studied with Philip Slates, George
Peabody Coll.; with Carl McKinley and Francis
Judd Cooke, New England Cons.; John Vincent,
Univ. of California, Los Angeles; with Harold
Owen, Ingolf Dahl, and Frederick Lesemann, Univ.
of Southern California. Her awards include
first prize, Manuscript Club of Los Angeles,
1969; Nat. Fed. of Music Clubs awards, 1969,
1971, 1973; Sigma Alpha Iota, Hollywood chapter,
Certificate of Excellence, 1973; Biennial award,
Nat. League of American Pen Women, 1974, 1976.
She was music professor, Nat. Inst. of Fine Arts,
Taiwan, 1957-58, 1960-62; and Coll. of Chinese
Culture, Taiwan, 1971-72.
    WORKS: ORCHESTRA: Sky maidens dance suite;
cello concerto; concerto for orchestra; BAND:
March of Chinese cadets, 1966; CHAMBER MUSIC:
piano trio, 1955; Theme and variations, flute,
clarinet, bassoon, 1964; violin suite, 1966;
Percussions east and west, 14 players, 1966;
Sonorities of Chinese percussions, 1971; Tune of
3 plum blossoms, 6 percussionists, 1971; Capriccio, flute solo, 1976; PIANO: Fantasia for 2
pianos, 1955; sonata, 1958; Scenes in a Chinese
village, 1958; piano suite, 1967; Perpetual
momentum, 1973; Sound of autumn suite; also songs
and choral works with texts by composer in
Chinese and in translation.
        114 S. New Hampshire Ave., #101, Los Angeles,
        CA 90004

HUBBELL, FRANK ALLEN
    b. Denver, Colo., 9 May 1907; d. Kirkland, Wash.,
21 Apr. 1971. Studied at Univ. of Southern
California; conducting with Albert Coates and
Vladimir Bakaleinikov. He organized the Los
Angeles Symphonette in 1946 and was its conductor;
was guest conductor of orchestras in Burbank,
San Diego, Bakersfield, and Santa Monica.
    WORKS: ORCHESTRA: California Eldorado suite;
Passacaglia and scherzo; Theme and variations;
also composed for the Hollywood Bowl music
spectaculars: The California story, 1950, 1956-
58; The Oregon story, 1959; The Kansas story,
1961.

HUBBELL, RAYMOND
    b. Urbana, Ohio, 1 June 1870; d. Miami, Fla.,
13 Dec. 1954. Studied music in Chicago; led his
own dance orchestra; was staff composer for a
Chicago publishing company. He was one of the
founders of ASCAP and its director, 1914-41.
    WORKS: MUSICALS: The runaways; Fantana;
Mexicana; Ziegfeld Follies, 1911-14; The big
show; Good times; Yours truly; et al.; SONGS:
Poor Butterfly; Chu Chin Chow; and many others.

HUBER, CALVIN RAYMOND
    b. Buffalo, N.Y., 12 July 1925. Studied with
Hilmar Luckhardt, Univ. of Wisconsin, B.A., M.A.;
with Curt Sachs, Gustave Reece, New York Univ.;
with William S. Newman, Univ. of North Carolina,
Chapel Hill, Ph.D. He was faculty member,
Carson-Newman Coll., 1951-56, 1959-62; Wake
Forest Univ., 1962-74; from 1974, at Univ. of
Tennessee.
    WORKS: ORCHESTRA: 4 scenes at a woodland
pond; Ancient dances of supplication and mourning; BAND: Bossa Nova holiday; The pusilanimous
pussycat; Fanfare for a ceremony; Baubolero;
CHAMBER MUSIC: Elegy, 5 flutes; Invention, 2
dissimilar instruments and percussion; Anecdotes,
bass-baritone and piano; Profundities, bassoon,
oboe, percussion.
        604 Augusta National Way, Knoxville, TN
        37922

HUDSON, JOSEPH A.
    b. Cleveland, Ohio, 17 Apr. 1952. Studied with
Mario Davidovsky, City Coll. of New York. He
received scholarships to the Vermont Composers
Conf., 1971, 1973; Nat. Inst. of Arts and Letters
Ives scholarship, 1976; Guggenheim fellowship,
1978; Nat. Endowment for the Arts grant, 1978.
    WORKS: CHAMBER MUSIC: 5 inventions, flute
and guitar, 1971; piano concerto with chamber
orch., 1978; ELECTRONIC: Transfixations, ensemble and tape, 1973; Reflexives, piano and
tape, 1975.
        1831 Empire Rd., Wickliffe, OH 44092

HUDSON, RICHARD A.
    b. Alma, Mich., 19 Mar. 1924. Studied at
Oberlin Cons., 1946-49; Syracuse Univ., 1950-51;
Univ. of California, Los Angeles, 1959-67. He
has been faculty member at Converse Coll., 1949-
50; Oberlin Cons., 1953-55; from 1967, at Univ.
of California, Los Angeles. He is chiefly a
musicologist, with many published articles in
music journals.
    WORKS: ORGAN: Trios for organ, vol. 1,
1971, vol. 2, 1972; Macht hoch die Tür in Preludes and postludes, vol. 2, 1973; Suite of
organ carols, 1976.
        14934 Dickens St., Apt. 9, Sherman Oaks, CA
        91403

HUFF, JAY A.
    b. Lubbock, Tex., 16 Jan. 1926. Studied at
Univ. of Colorado, B.M. 1948, M.M. 1951; Northwestern Univ., Ph.D. 1965. He was faculty
member, Northern State Coll., 1952-54; Stephen
F. Austin Coll., 1954-59; Millikin Univ., 1963-
65; from 1966, at Ohio State Univ. His compositions include Fugue for 2 violins.
        School of Music, Ohio State Univ., Columbus,
        OH 43210

HUFFMAN, W(ALTER) SPENCER
    Graduated from Peabody Cons., 1947; joined the
Peabody faculty in 1949.
    WORKS: ORCHESTRA: piano concerto, Washing-
ton, D.C., 24 Mar. 1946; 7 symphonies, 1951-55;
cello concerto, New York, 3 May 1951; violin
concerto, 1953; March, chorale and variations,

1957; harpsichord concerto, 1959; BAND: symphony, 1953; CHAMBER MUSIC: string quartet #6, 1950; violin sonata, New York, 29 Sept. 1951; piano quintet, 1957; piano sonata #9, 1959; CHORUS: Magnificat, 1958.
     5811 Falls Rd., Baltimore, MD 21209

HUFSMITH, GEORGE WILLIAM
     b. Omaha, Nebr., 27 Aug. 1924. Studied composition with Paul Hindemith, Quincy Porter, Normand Lockwood, Richard Donovan, Yale Univ.; with Heitor Villa-Lobos in Brazil. He received a Bicentennial commission to write an opera on an 1889 Wyoming lynching. He is a free-lance composer; member, Wyoming Council on the Arts; insurance agent; and was member, Wyoming House of Representatives, 1959-66.
     WORKS: THEATRE; Sweetwater lynching, 3-act opera, 1976; Parabola, ballet; ORCHESTRA: Teton mural; symphony for winds, brass, percussion; CHAMBER MUSIC: 3 virtuoso pieces for 6 strings and conductor; Triangulum, string trio; 2 pieces, string quartet; CHORUS: Episcopal mass, a cappella choir; Psalm 33, organ and choir; PIANO: Allegro, grave and presto; Mexican impressions, studies for piano.
     Box 1511, Jackson, WY 83001

HUGGLER, JOHN
     b. Rochester, N.Y., 30 Aug. 1928. Studied composition with Dante Fiorello in New York but is chiefly self-taught. He received Guggenheim fellowships, 1962, 1969; Horblit award, Boston Symphony, 1967; Fromm Found. grant, 1973; was composer-in-residence with the Boston Symph. Orch., 1964-65. From 1965 he has been faculty member, Univ. of Massachusetts, Boston. A concert of his music was presented in his honor in Cambridge on 2 Mar. 1980.
     WORKS: ORCHESTRA: concerti for horn, trumpet, flute, viola, violin, saxophone; Elegy; Divertimento, viola and orch.; Variations for orch.; Sculptures, song cycle for soprano and orch., 1964; Symphony for 13 instruments, 1971; Ecce homo, 1959, premiere, Boston, 12 May 1973; BAND: Celebration, 1966; CHAMBER MUSIC: 3 brass quintets; 3 string quintets; 10 string quartets; 7 songs, soprano and chamber ensemble, 1972; Bittere Nüsse, soprano and chamber ensemble, 1976; Serenata, woodwind trio and string trio, 1977.
     24 Standish Rd., Duxbury, MA 02332

HUGHES, E. KENT
     Studied at Univ. of Texas, D.M.A. 1966. His compositions include Allegro assai, strings and percussion; Second chance, flute and oboe.
     Music Dept., Midwestern Univ., Wichita Falls, TX 76308

HUGHES, HOWARD, S.M.
     b. Baltimore, Md., 28 June 1930. Studied piano, organ, and choral conducting with private instructors; composition with W. Spencer Huffman, 1977-78. He was glee club director, 1951-71, organist-choirmaster, from 1951. He has composed numerous liturgical works for the church service.
     4301 Roland Ave., Baltimore, MD 21210

HUGHES, SISTER MARTINA
     b. Hibbing, Minn., 2 Sept. 1902. Studied with Ralph Doty and Louise Cuyler, Univ. of Michigan; with Bernard Rogers, Eastman School of Music. Her awards include the Minnesota Composers award, 1941; Duluth Bicentennial Committee commission, 1976. She was chairperson, music dept., College of St. Scholastica, 1934-54.
     WORKS: ORCHESTRA: The highwayman, chorus and orch., 1941; April 1943; Invocation, 1947; Revelation, 1964; Sounds heard from the shore of Lake Superior, 1976; CHAMBER MUSIC: Occasional music, strings; Polytonal Puck, flute, clarinet, piano; CHORUS: Stars, women's voices; Rejoice unto God, women's voices; PIANO: Diko, written for Gina Bachauer; many other choral and instrumental works; several masses and small works for the church service.
     St. Scholastica Priory, Duluth, MN 55811

HUGHES, ROBERT
     b. 1933. Studied with Lou Harrison, Luigi Dallapiccola, Leon Kirchner, and Robert Ashley. He has been faculty member at Mills Coll., San Francisco Cons., Cabrillo Coll.; contrabassoonist, Oakland Symph.; has conducted Oakland Symph, San Francisco Ballet, Cabrillo Music Festival, Western Opera Festival, and others.
     WORKS: BALLET: Kama Sutra, for 12 players; Landscapes; Cones, 19 instruments and tape; ORCHESTRA: Radiances; Edge; Cadences, with tape; Anagnorisis, trombone and percussion; Sonitude, flute and cello; Quadroquartet, 4 flutes, 4 horns, 4 double basses, 4 electronic tracks; CHORUS: Missa corporis, on poems by James Broughton, with tape; Amo ergo sum, Ezra Pound text, 2 choruses, instruments, and tape, Hayward, Calif., 8 June 1975; and 15 film scores.
     1004 Peralta Ave., Albany, CA 94706

HUGO, JOHN ADAM
     b. Bridgeport, Conn., 5 Jan. 1873; d. Bridgeport, 29 Dec. 1945. Studied at Stuttgart Cons., 1888-97; then gave piano recitals in Germany, England, and Italy to 1899.
     WORKS: OPERA: The temple dancer; The hero of Byzanz; The sun god; ORCHESTRA: symphony; 2 piano concertos; CHAMBER MUSIC: piano trio; violin pieces; cello pieces; piano pieces; songs.

HUHN, BRUNO
     b. London, England, 1 Aug. 1871; to U.S. 1891; d. New York, N.Y., 13 May 1950. Studied piano in London and New York; toured as concert pianist, then was pianist, accompanist and choral conductor in New York.
     WORKS: CHORUS: Christ triumphant, cantata; Praise Jehovah, cantata; SONGS: Seafarers; Invictus; Destiny; The divan, a cycle; Love's triumph, a cycle.

HULL, ANNE
     b. Brookland, Pa., 25 Jan. 1888. Studied at Peabody Cons.; became piano teacher; appeared frequently with Mary Howe in duo piano recitals. Her compositions include Ancient ballad, for 2 pianos; and songs.
     96 Grove St., New York, NY 10014

HUMEL, GERALD

HUMEL, GERALD
b. Cleveland, Ohio, 7 Nov. 1931. Studied with
Herbert Elwell and Walter Aschaffenburg, Oberlin
Cons.; Elie Siegmeister, Hofstra Univ.; Herbert
Howells, Royal Coll. of Music, London; Ross Lee
Finney and Roberto Gerhard, Univ. of Michigan;
with Boris Blacher and Josef Rufer in Berlin.
His awards include Univ. of Michigan fellowship,
1958; BMI award, 1959; Fulbright grant, 1960-62;
Berlin Senat Grant, 1962; Nat. Inst. of Arts and
Letters award, 1965; Arthur Shepherd prize,
1964; Guggenheim grant, 1966; German Critics
prize, 1968; Berlin Arts prize, 1973; Cleveland
Arts prize, 1978. He is free-lance composer and
conductor, Ensemble der Gruppe Neue Musik,
Berlin.
    WORKS: OPERA: The proposal, 1950; The
triangle, 1955; Jochim Wessels, 1962; BALLET:
Devil's dice, 1957; Erste Liebe, 1966; Herodias,
1967; Die Folterungen der Beatrice Cenci, 1971;
Lilith, 1972; Othello and Desdemona, ballet in
2 acts, 1974-75; ORCHESTRA: flute concerto,
1961; Flashes, 1968; Temno, 1969; Nitra, 1970;
Amplitüden, 1973; Lapini, commissioned by
Cleveland Orch., 1977.
    Claudiusstrasse 12, 1000 Berlin 21 Germany

HUMPHREYS, HENRY S.
b. Vienna, Austria, 27 Nov. 1909, father was
American citizen. Studied with Sydney Durst,
Cincinnati Coll. of Music. He won first prize
in the Harvey Gaul Internat. Composition Contest,
1971. He was instructor, Cincinnati Coll. of
Music, 1946-50; organist and choirmaster, Church
of the Advent, from 1946; music editor and
critic, Cincinnati papers, 1950-70; composer-
in-residence, Coll. of Mt. St. Joseph, from 1970.
    WORKS: OPERA: Mayerling, 3 acts, 1958;
Joan of Arc at Reims, 1 act, 1968; BALLET:
Prometeo de los Andes, cantata-ballet, 1970;
ORCHESTRA: The waste land, with narrator, 1957;
Danubiana, 1960; Montserrat, oboe and strings,
1971; and songs and arias.
    5661 Delhi Rd., Cincinnati, OH 54238

HUNDLEY, RICHARD
b. Cincinnati, Ohio, 1 Sept. 1931. Attended
Cincinnati Coll. Cons.; studied privately with
Israel Citkowitz and William Flanagan in New
York. His awards include 3 MacDowell fellowships; ASCAP awards, 1963-72; many commissions.
He is accompanist, coach, organist, choirmaster,
teacher, as well as composer.
    WORKS: OPERA: Wedding finger, play by
James Purdy; CHORUS: vocal quartets to poems of
James Purdy, Portland, Maine, 27 July 1971; The
sea is swimming tonight, cantata; SONGS: Softly
the summer; Maiden snow; For your delight; Post-
card from Spain; The astronomers; God of the
sheep, Chicago, 28 Nov. 1965; 3 Richards and
Wings, New York, 11 July 1972.

HUNKINS, ARTHUR B.
b. New York, N.Y., 12 Apr. 1937. Studied first
with his mother, Eusebia Simpson Hunkins; later
with Karl Ahrendt, Ohio Univ.; with Nadia
Boulanger in Paris; and Ross Lee Finney, Univ.
of Michigan, D.M.A. He won 3 Nat. Fed. of Music

Clubs awards; BMI award; Joseph Bearns prize,
Columbia Univ.; and a Brown Univ. choral competi-
tion. He has been faculty member, Southern
Illinois Univ., 1961-63; North Texas State Univ.,
1963-65; from 1965, at Univ. of North Carolina
at Greensboro.
    WORKS: ORCHESTRA: 5 pieces for orch.; Te
Deum, tenor, baritone, male chorus, orch.;
CHAMBER MUSIC: suite for violin and cello;
CHORUS: Gloria; Libera nos; Ave Maria; mass for
male voices and organ; O come, O come, Emmanuel,
Washington, D.C., 1 Dec. 1975; SONGS: 5 short
songs of gladness; 3 untitled songs of Emily
Dickinson for mezzo-soprano and tape; KEYBOARD:
Ecce quam bonum, organ; Fantasy, piano.
    Music Dept., Univ. of North Carolina,
Greensboro, NC 27412

HUNKINS, EUSEBIA SIMPSON
b. Troy, Ohio, 20 June 1902. Studied with James
Friskin, Rubin Goldmark and Albert Stoessel at
Juilliard School; later with Darius Milhaud,
Ernest Hutcheson, Ernst von Dohnanyi; attended
classes at Aspen, Chautauqua, Tanglewood, and
Salzburg. She taught at Cornell Coll. and at
Barnard School for Boys; was project director,
Musical World of Ohio Broadcasts, 1972-74; was
appointed by the Nat. Opera Assoc. to compile
material for a series of broadcasts of American
Operas in 1976.
    WORKS: OPERA: Smoky mountain, 1954;
Wondrous love, choral drama, 1955; Mice in
council, 1956; Reluctant hero, 1956; Young
Lincoln, 1958; Young Lincoln II, 1960; Child of
promise, choral dance opera, 1964; What have you
done to my mountain?, musical play, 1973; BALLET:
4-H on parade, 1973; CHAMBER MUSIC: violin
sonata; Wisps of smoke, flute, mezzo-soprano,
piano, 1973; Dance suite, woodwind quintet, 1973;
CHORUS: Shall I marry, 1961; Americana, chorus
and orch., 1966; Appalachian mass, 1971, mezzo-
soprano, dancer, guitar, Washington, 1 Dec. 1975.
    12 N. College St., Athens, OH 45701

HUNT, JERRY E.
b. Waco, Tex., 30 Nov. 1943. Attended North
Texas State Univ.; is self-taught in composition.
He was faculty member, Southern Methodist Univ.,
1967-73, director of the SMU electronic music
studio, 1973-75; resident artist, Video Research
Center, Dallas, 1974-77.
    WORKS: Electronic and/or for an indeter-
minate number of instruments: Helix, tape;
Transhelix, tape; Sequential helix, tape; Haramand plane: discontinuous mode, tape; Sur Dr.
John Dee, zero to 11 performers; Preparallel,
orchestral groups, 1965; Infrasolo; Autotransform
glissando; Haramand plane: parallel/regenera-
tive; Aur resh, procession, videotape; Tabulatura
soyga, zero to 11 performers; Cantegral segments,
23 works for varying numbers of players, 1973-
79; Quaquaversal transmission, theatre work,
1973.
    5815 Swiss Ave., Dallas, TX 75214

HUNT, MICHAEL F.
b. New Castle, Ind., 28 Nov. 1945. Studied with
Manus Sasonkin, St. Louis Inst. of Music, B.M.;

with Robert Baker, John Perkins, Paul Pisk, and Robert Wykes, Washington Univ., Ph.D. He received a Nat. Defense Education Act Title IV fellowship, 1970-73. He was faculty member, Washington Univ., 1973-74; from 1978, at Fontbonne Coll.

WORKS: ORCHESTRA: Asymptopia I and II, 1972; Streams; Television suite; CHAMBER MUSIC: 3 contemporary interval studies: Melancholy, mischevious, mysterious, piano, 1969; NAD-unresolved dialogue for unaccompanied cello, 1973; Metal ensemble, 2 percussionists; Wood and metal ensemble, solo percussionist.

2019 Sidney St., St. Louis, MO 63104

HUNT, THOMAS W.
b. Mammoth Spring, Ark., 28 Sept. 1929. Studied at Memphis Coll. of Music; North Texas State Univ.; Ouachita Baptist Univ.; and at Juilliard School. He received a Gooch Found. scholarship and a Hibberd-Pi Kappa Lambda award for musical research. He was faculty member, Oklahoma Coll. for Women, 1961-63; Southwestern Baptist Theological Seminary, from 1963; guest faculty, Spanish Baptist Seminary, Barcelona, 1969-70; and church organist.

WORKS: CHORUS: Gentle guide, children's anthem, 1961; A canticle of God's love, 1973; KEYBOARD: Voluntary on Old Hundreth, piano or organ, 1963; Salvationist, piano prelude, 1974.

Box 22000, Southwestern Baptist Seminary, Ft. Worth, TX 76122

HURD, TIMOTHY
b. Niskayuna, N.Y., 16 May 1952. Studied with Richard T. Gore, Brian Dykstra, and Ruth Still, Coll. of Wooster, B.M. 1974; with Robert Morris, Jacob Druckman, Krzysztov Penderecki, Yale Univ., M.M. He received a Nat. Fed. of Music Clubs award, 1974.

WORKS: VOICE: Visione, soprano and chamber orch.; Harmonia mundi, chorus; KEYBOARD: Variants I-III, piano; CARILLON: suite; 3 sonatas; Idyll for Hiems; Palindromes; works for solo voice, chorus, organ, recorders.

Old Mill Rd., Gates Mills, OH 44040

HUSA, KAREL
b. Prague, Czech., 7 Aug. 1921; U.S. citizen 1959. Studied composition and conducting at the Prague Cons. and Prague Acad., diplomas, summa cum laude, 1946; also studied with Arthur Honneger and Nadia Boulanger in Paris, conducting with Eugene Bigot. His awards include French government scholarship, 1945-51; Prague Acad. of Fine Arts prize, 1948; Lili Boulanger prize, Boston, 1950; Bilthoven Contemporary Festival award, 1951; Guggenheim fellowship, 1964; Pulitzer prize, 1969, for his third string quartet; Kappa Kappa Psi Orpheus award, 1972, 1974; honorary doctorate, Coe Coll., 1976; numerous commissions. He has been faculty member, Cornell Univ., from 1954; also conductor of the Univ. Orchestra and the Ithaca Chamber Orchestra; has been guest conductor of many orchestras in Europe and the U.S.

WORKS: ORCHESTRA: concertino, piano and orch., 1949; symphony, 1953; Fantasies for

orchestra, 1956; Poem, viola and chamber orch., 1959; Mosaiques, 1961; concerto for brass quintet and strings, 1965; Music for Prague, 1968; 2 sonnets from Michelangelo, 1972; The steadfast tin soldier, with narrator, 1974; Monodrama, ballet for orch., 1975; BAND: Divertimento, brass and percussion, 1959; concerto for alto saxophone and band, 1967; Music for Prague, 1968; Apotheosis of this earth, 1970; concerto for percussion and wind ensemble, 1970-71; Al fresco, 1974; CHAMBER MUSIC: 3 string quartets, 1948, 1953, 1968; Divertimento, brass quintet, 1968; violin sonata, 1973, New York, 31 Mar. 1974; CHORUS: Festive ode, with orch., 1965; Apotheosis of this earth, New York, 14 Apr. 1973, composer conducting the Cornell Univ. chorus and orch.; An American Te Deum, chorus, baritone solo, band, Cedar Rapids, Iowa, 5 Dec. 1976, composer conducting; PIANO: 2 sonatas, 1949, 1975, Washington, 4 Oct. 1975; 8 Czech duets for piano, 4 hands, 1955.

333 The Parkway, Ithaca, NY 14850

HUSTON, JOHN
d. New York, N.Y., 6 Apr. 1975. Graduated from Univ. of Texas, 1942; studied at Union Theological Seminary, School of Sacred Music, where he was later on the faculty; was also organist and choirmaster. His compositions for organ included Meditation on the 7 last words and Psalm prelude.

HUSTON, SCOTT
b. Tacoma, Wash., 10 Oct. 1916. Studied with Howard Hanson and Bernard Rogers, Eastman School of Music, B.M. 1941, M.M. 1942, Ph.D. 1952. His awards include Danforth Found. grant; Olympiad of the Arts award; Major Armstrong Radio award; BMI awards; Eastman graduate school fellowship; MacDowell fellowship; many commissions. From 1952, he has been faculty member, Cincinnati Coll. Cons.

WORKS: ORCHESTRA: concerto for trumpet, string orch., harp, timpani, 1963; 4 phantasms, symphony #3, 1968; symphony #4 for strings, 1972; Celebration, 1978; WIND ENSEMBLE: Intensity #1, wind ensemble, 1962; Pro vita, piano and brass quintet, 1963; Quintessences, brass quintet; Orthographics, 4 trombones, 1970; Sounds at night, brass choir, 1971; Suite for our times, brass sextet, 1973; CHAMBER MUSIC: Venus and Mercury, violin sonata; Idioms, violin, clarinet, horn; A game of circles, clarinet, piano or celeste; Phenomena, baroque quartet; Life styles, clarinet, piano, cello; 3 cameras, solo flute; 4 scenes for 2 trumpets; Electron, viola and piano, 1975; Shadowy waters, clarinet, piano, cello, 1977; VOICE: The wisdom of patriotism, chorus, band, and orch., 1966; The oratorio of understanding, 1967; Song of Deborah, cantata, 1969; Love and marriage, chamber cantata, 1969; Tamar, monodrama, soprano and piano, 1974; Time/Reflections, cantata, St. Paul, 26 Jan. 1979; KEYBOARD: Penta-Tholoi, piano; Diorama, organ.

370 Terrace Ave., Cincinnati, OH 45220

HUTCHESON, ERNEST
b. Melbourne, Australia, 20 July 1871; to U.S. 1900; d. New York, N.Y., 9 Feb. 1951. Studied

HUTCHESON, JERE T.

with Carl Reinecke, Leipzig Cons., graduated
1890. He was head of the piano department,
Peabody Cons., 1900-12; dean, Juilliard School,
1924-37, then president.
    WORKS: ORCHESTRA: piano concerto, 1898;
Merlin and Vivien, symphonic poem, 1899; a symphony; 2-piano concerto; violin concerto.

HUTCHESON, JERE T.
    b. Marietta, Ga., 16 Sept. 1938. Studied with
Helen Gunderson, Louisiana State Univ.; with
H. Owen Reed, Michigan State Univ., Ph.D. 1966;
with Ernst Krenek and Gunther Schuller at Tanglewood. His awards include first and second
place, Nat. Fed. of Music Clubs contest, 1963;
Nat. Music Teachers Assoc. award, 1976; Martha
Baird Rockefeller Found. grant, 1977; annual
ASCAP awards. He has been faculty member,
Michigan State Univ., from 1965.
    WORKS: ORCHESTRA: Transitions; WIND EN-
SEMBLE: Sensations, band and audience; Passacaglia, band; Designs for 14, brass and percussion; About, brass ensemble; Colossus, cyclic
variations for symphonic band; Earth gods, woodwind quintet and wind ensemble; CHAMBER MUSIC:
Wonder music I-V, a series for various instruments and piano; Rondo brillante, violin,
clarinet, piano; 3 things for Dr. Seuss, harp
and percussion; Night gallery, 4 trombones;
Construction set, oboe and piano; bassoon sonata;
3 pictures of Satan, trumpet and organ; Patterns,
trombone and organ; Nocturnes of the inferno,
violin, clarinet, piano, 1976; VOICE: Eldorado,
chorus and brass; Sabronorbas, chorus and percussion; God, 4 antiphonal choirs, tambourine,
piano; Mysterious voices of the afterworld,
women's voices; Passing, passing, passing,
soprano and chamber group; PIANO: Cosmic suite;
Chromophonic sketches.
    6064 Abbott Rd., East Lansing, MI 48823

HUTCHESON, L. THOMAS
    b. El Paso, Tex., 18 Aug. 1942. Studied with
Richard Henderson, Univ. of Texas, El Paso;
Anthony Donato, Northwestern Univ.; with John
Boda and Carlisle Floyd, Florida State Univ.,
D.M. He has been faculty member, Middle
Tennessee State Univ., from 1972.
    WORKS: WIND ENSEMBLE: Fanfares for band;
The tightrope walker march; Roller skate, jazz
ensemble; Macarena, jazz ensemble; Dimensions,
12 horns; Requiem, 4 horns; CHAMBER MUSIC: con-
certino, horn and piano; Mnemonix, string trio
and alto saxophone; Coeval suite, woodwind quin-
tet; MIXED MEDIA: Theme and variations, horn
and tape; Synvironment (doctoral dissertation);
Cinecology, 4 slide projectors, 4 movie projectors, 4-channel tape, 1972; also songs.
    Music Dept., Middle Tenn. State Univ.,
Murfreesboro, TN 37132

HUTCHINS, FARLEY KENNAN
    b. Neenah, Wis., 12 Jan. 1921. Studied with
T. Tertius Noble, Harold Friedell, Normand
Lockwood, School of Sacred Music, Union Theo-
logical Seminary, 1950. He was professor,
Mississippi Southern Coll., 1946-50; Baldwin
Wallace Cons., 1950-57; from 1957, at Univ. of

Akron.
    WORKS: ORCHESTRA: Set of American folk
songs; November 22, 1963; harpsichord concerto
with chamber orch.; BAND: trumpet concerto;
Fantasia, organ and brass choir; CHAMBER MUSIC:
3 songs for low voice and piano; Suite for flute
and piano; Concert piece, tuba and piano; 6
medieval songs, baritone and 4 instruments;
sonata for horn and organ; Passacaglia, trumpet
and organ; also choral works, piano and organ
pieces, incidental music.
    Music Dept., University of Akron, Akron, OH
44320

HUTCHINS, GUY STARR
    b. Spartanburg, S.C., 12 Mar. 1905. Attended
Wofford Coll., Clemson Univ., B.S. 1928; Curtis
Inst.; also studied clarinet, oboe, bassoon,
horn, piano. He conducted various orchestras,
1932-48; was clarinetist, N.C. Symphony, 1943;
staff assistant for bands, Syracuse Univ., 1960-
67; Univ. of South Carolina, 1973.
    WORKS: BAND: Florentine march, 1932; Valse
caprice, 1934; The spirit of Transylvania, 1954.
    102 Kirkwood Lane, Camden, SC 29020

HUTCHISON, WARNER
    b. Denver, Colo., 15 Dec. 1930. Studied with
George Morey, Samuel Adler, Merrill Ellis, and
William Latham, North Texas State Univ., M.M.
1956, Ph.D. 1971; with Wayne Barlow and Kent
Kennan, Eastman School of Music; with Roy Harris,
Indiana Univ. His awards include Texas Music
Society prize, 1954; graduate scholarship, North
Texas State Univ., 1964; Ford Found.-MENC grant,
1967-68; nomination of hornpiece 1 for Pulitzer
prize, 1971; Southwestern Region Coll. Band
Directors Nat. Assoc. award, 1971; MacDowell
fellowship, 1973. His faculty posts have been
Houghton Coll., 1956-58; Union Univ., 1959-66;
from 1967, New Mexico State Univ.
    WORKS: ORCHESTRA: Prairie sketch, 1956;
Prologue, 1959; BAND: Dirge and hosanna, 1969;
CHAMBER MUSIC: woodwind quintet, 1955; Chrysa-
lis, 5 flutes, 1971; CHORUS: Psalm 135, 1964;
I shall have music, double choir, 1972; KEYBOARD:
Mountain climbing, piano suite, 1954; Hymntune
suite, organ, 1968; Suite a-la-mode, piano, 1972;
MIXED MEDIA: hornpiece 1, horn and tape, 1971;
The sacrilege of Alan Kent, baritone, orch.,
tape, 1971; Antigone, tape, 1972; Homage to
Jackson Pollock, narrator, percussion, slides,
1973; Monday music, piano and synthesizer,
MacDowell Colony, June 1973.
    Box 3174, Univ. Park Branch, Las Cruces, NM
88003

HYLA, LEON
    b. Niagara Falls, N.Y., 31 Aug. 1952. Studied
with Bernhard Heiden, Indiana Univ.; with Malcolm
Peyton and John Heiss, New England Cons.
    WORKS: CHAMBER MUSIC: White man on snow-
shoes, vol. 1, alto saxophone, flute, violin,
cello, 1972-73; concerto for piano and chamber
orch., Boston, 22 Apr. 1974.

HYSON, WINIFRED
    b. Schenectady, N.Y., 21 Feb. 1925. Studied with

Esther Ballou and Lloyd Ultan, American Univ. Her awards include Mu Phi Epsilon composition prizes, 1967, 1971, 1973; first prize, Annapolis Fine Arts Festival composition contest, 1971; 4 composer awards, Washington Friday Morning Music Club, 1968, 1971, 1973, 1975.

WORKS: ORCHESTRA: Suite for young orchestra, flute, clarinet and strings; Partita, string orch.; VOICE: Songs of Job's daughter, soprano and piano; Becoming, 4 madrigals for women's voices; Winter triptych, soprano, flute, violin, piano; PIANO: Fantasy on 3 English folk songs, piano duet; 8 light-hearted variations on "The jolly miller," piano duet.

7407 Honeywell Lane, Bethesda, MD 20014

HYTREK, SISTER THEOPHANE
b. Stuart, Nebr., 28 Feb. 1915. Studied at Alverno Coll.; Wisconsin Cons.; with Leon Stein, De Paul Univ.; with A. Irvine McHose, Wayne Barlow, Bernard Rogers, Eastman School of Music. She received awards from Nat. Assoc. of Coll. Wind and Percussion Instructors, 1959; Wisconsin Fed. of Music Clubs, 1962; American Guild of Organists, Milwaukee Chapter, award, 1967, commission, 1969. She has been faculty member, Alverno Coll., from 1941.

WORKS: ORCHESTRA: The hound of heaven, tone poem, also in 2-piano version; CHAMBER MUSIC: violin sonata, 1962; chamber concerto; Prelude, oboe and piano, 1959; ORGAN: Postlude-partita on the Old One Hundredth, 1967; also masses, hymns, motets, psalms.

3401 S. 39th St., Milwaukee, WI 53215

IANNACCONE, ANTHONY J.
b. Brooklyn, N.Y., 14 Oct. 1943. Studied with David Diamond and Vittorio Giannini, Manhattan School of Music; with Warren Benson and Samuel Adler, Eastman School of Music. His awards include NDEA fellowship, 1968-71; Howard Hanson prize, 1970; Michigan Music Teachers Assoc.-Music Teachers Nat. Assoc. award, 1972; Nat. Endowment for the Arts grant, 1972; Ravel prize; East and West Artists of New York award; Phi Mu Alpha Sinfonia award; first prize, Missouri Contemporary Music Contest. He has been faculty member, Eastern Michigan Univ., from 1971.

WORKS: ORCHESTRA: 2 symphonies; Lysistrata, concert overture, 1968; BAND: Scherzo; Interlude, wind ensemble, 1970; Antiphonies, 1974; CHAMBER MUSIC: string quartet, 1965; Partita, piano, 1967; Remembrance, viola and piano, 1968; 3 mythical sketches, brass quartet, 1971; Anamorphoses, brass and percussion, 1972; Rituals, violin and piano, 1973; Aria concertante, cello and piano; Bicinia, flute and alto saxophone, 1974; Parodies, woodwind quintet, 1974; Hades, brass quartet, 1975; sonatina, trumpet and tuba, 1975; Night song, trombone and piano, 1975; CHORUS: Solomon's canticle, a cappella, 1968; Prince of peace, with soloists and wind ensemble, 1970; The sky is low, a cappella, 1976.

521 Kewanee Rd., Ypsilanti, MI 48197

IHRKE, WALTER R.
b. Milwaukee, Wis., 21 May 1908. Studied with Adolph Brune, Wisconsin Cons.; Healey Willan,

Univ. of Michigan; with Howard Hanson, Eastman School of Music. He won first place in a Coll. Band Directors Assoc., Eastern Div., contest, 1952. He was faculty member, Mission House Coll., 1932-38; Stephens Coll., 1938-43; George Peabody Coll., 1943-49; Univ. of Connecticut, 1949-75.

WORKS: BALLET: Pavane, 3 acts; ORCHESTRA: violin concerto; BAND: Pageantry; Ode and scherzo; CHORUS: An answer of peace, cantata; That continent, cantata.

88 Storrs Height Rd., Storrs, CT 06268

IMBRIE, ANDREW WELSH
b. New York, N.Y., 6 Apr. 1921. Studied with Roger Sessions, Princeton Univ., B.A. 1942; with Sessions, Univ. of California, Berkeley, M.A. 1947; with Nadia Boulanger; and at American Acad. in Rome, 1947-49, 1953-54. His awards include New York Music Critics' Circle award, 1944; Alice Ditson fellowship, 1946; Prix de Rome, 1947; Nat. Inst. of Arts and Letters grant, 1950; 2 Guggenheim grants, 1953, 1960; Boston Symphony Orch. merit award, 1955; Naumburg recording award, 1960. He has been faculty member, Univ. of California, Berkeley, from 1947; also at San Francisco Cons.

WORKS: OPERA: Christmas in Peeples Town, 1964; Angle of repose, libretto from Wallace Stegner's novel, San Francisco, 6 Nov. 1976; ORCHESTRA: Ballad, 1947; 2 violin concertos, 1953, 1957; Legend, 1959; 3 symphonies, 1966, 1969, 1970; cello concerto, 1972; 2 piano concertos, #1 Saratoga, Calif., 4 Aug. 1973; #2 Indianapolis, 26 Jan. 1976; flute concerto, New York, 13 Oct. 1977; CHAMBER MUSIC: 4 string quartets, 1942, 1953, 1957, 1969; piano trio, 1946; piano sonata, 1947; Divertimento, 6 instruments, 1948; Serenade, flute, viola, piano, 1952; Impromptu, violin and piano, 1960, New York, 10 Nov. 1971; cello sonata, 1966; 3 sketches, trombone and piano, 1967; and choral works.

2625 Rose St., Berkeley, CA 94708

IMLAY, TIMOTHY
b. San Francisco, Calif., 15 May 1951. Studied with Billy Jim Layton, David Lewin, Bulent Arel, State Univ. of New York, Stony Brook; with Mario Davidovsky and Jack Beeson, Columbia Univ. He received the Kaltenborn award, 1970.

WORKS: ORCHESTRA: Triptych, chamber orch., Oakland, 23 May 1969; Mosaics, 1970; CHAMBER MUSIC: Just desserts, tenor and chamber ensemble, Stony Brook, 16 Apr. 1972; Needles, 1973; 5 duos for English horn and bass clarinet, 1973-74; quartet movement, violin, viola, alto saxophone, piano, 1974; ELECTRONIC: Rondo, tape, 1974; Bounce, tape, 1976.

235 W. 12th St., #11, New York, NY 10014

INCH, HERBERT REYNOLDS
b. Missoula, Mont., 25 Nov. 1904. Studied at Montana State Univ.; with Howard Hanson, Eastman School of Music, B.M. 1925, M.M. 1928, B.A. 1931. His awards include American Acad. in Rome fellowship, 1931; Ernest Bloch award; Univ. of Rochester traveling fellowship, 1934; honorary

INWOOD, MARY

Ph.D., Montana State Univ. He taught at Hunter
Coll., 1951-65, then retired to La Jolla, Calif.
WORKS: ORCHESTRA: Variations on a modal
theme, 1927; 3 pieces for small orch., 1930;
symphony, 1932; Serenade, 1939; piano concerto,
1940; Answers to a questionnaire, 1942; Northwest overture, 1943; violin concerto, 1946; 3
symphoniettas, 1948, 1950, 1955; CHAMBER MUSIC:
piano quintet, 1930; Mediterranean sketches,
string quartet, 1933; Divertimento for brass,
1934; 3 piano sonatas, 1935, 1946, 1966; string
quartet, 1936; cello sonata, 1941; 3 conversations, string quartet, 1944; piano trio, 1963;
CHORUS: Return to Zion, women's voices, 1945.

INWOOD, MARY
b. Boston, Mass., 27 July 1928. Studied piano
with Bruce Simonds; composition with Joseph
Goodman, Leo Kraft, Hugo Weisgall, Queens Coll.,
CUNY, B.A. 1975, M.A. 1979. Her awards include
several composition prizes at Queens Coll. She
is a private piano and theory teacher.
WORKS: CHAMBER MUSIC: sonata for flute and
harpsichord, 1974; 3 movements for brass sextet,
1975; 7 bagatelles, wind trio, 1977; Advent
quintet, woodwinds, 1978; 5 laconic pieces, wind
octet, 1978; trio for oboe, horn, piano, 1978;
VOICE: Babel, cantata, soloists, chorus, winds,
percussion, 1974; Cheerful and tender songs,
soprano, oboe, harpsichord; piano pieces.
166 Congress St., Brooklyn, NY 11201

ISAACSON, MICHAEL NEIL
b. Brooklyn, N.Y., 22 Apr. 1946. Studied at
Hunter Coll., B.S.; with Robert Starer, Brooklyn
Coll., M.A.; with Samuel Adler and Warren Benson,
Eastman School of Music, Ph.D.; conducting with
Ralph Hunter, Robert Hickok, Robert DeCormier.
He held scholarships at Eastman School; received
a Schubert grant for a musical theatre work. He
was conductor, Festival Chorus, State Univ. of
New York, Fredonia.
WORKS: CHAMBER MUSIC: Assumed identities,
viola and percussion; CHORUS: Meditations of my
heart, Friday evening service; Avodat Ammamit,
folk service; The sound of joy, wedding service;
A message from within, choral protest; In praise
of our percussionist, commissioned by the
DeCormier Singers.

ISELE, DAVID CLARK
b. Harrisburg, Pa., 25 Apr. 1946. Studied with
John Price, Southern Methodist Univ.; with
Robert Hoffmann, Oberlin Coll.; with Samuel
Adler, Eastman School of Music, D.M.A. He won
first place in a Southern Methodist Univ. contest, 1973. He has been faculty member, Univ.
of Notre Dame, from 1973.
WORKS: ORCHESTRA: 3 expressions for orch.,
1977; CHAMBER MUSIC: Observations of nature,
soprano and chamber orch., 1972; Take, thyme,
and toggle, ballet for piano duet; Progation,
saxophone and piano; Romp, recitative, razz,
recapitulo, solo cello, 1977; CHORUS: Notre
Dame mass; Sacred Heart mass; That nature is a
Heraclitean fire, with soloists and orch.,
Harrisburg, 14 May 1974; Te Deum, 1975; Cogna-
tion prefix, with organ, men's choir, soloists,

chamber ensemble, 1975; numerous organ pieces.
2504 Lincoln Way W., South Bend, IN 46628

ISRAEL, BRIAN M.
b. New York, N.Y., 5 Feb. 1951. Studied with
Ulysses Kay, Lehman Coll., CUNY, B.A. 1971; with
Robert Palmer and Burrill Phillips, Cornell Univ.,
M.F.A. 1974; D.M.A. 1976. He received BMI
student composer awards, 1966, 1968; Cornell
fellowship, 1971-72. He was teaching assistant,
Cornell Univ., 1972-76; then on faculty, Syracuse
Univ.
WORKS: BAND: symphony, 1974; CHAMBER MUSIC:
clarinet sonata, 1969; sonata in 2 movements,
cello and percussion, 1969; 6 views of the Cas-
pian Sea, violin solo, 1971; Canonic variations,
string quartet, 1971; Pastoral, oboe, strings,
piano, 1971; Divertimento, brass quintet, 1971;
oboe sonata, 1972; woodwind quartet, 1972; piano
quintet, 1973; CHORUS: Madrigal on nudity, 1970;
Ladies' voices, 10-minute opera, 1970; Komical
khoral kanons, women's voices, 1973; KEYBOARD:
Prayer and fantasia, carillon, 1970; Night variations, piano, 1973; ELECTRONIC: Satires, 1971;
Dance variations, trumpet and tape, 1973; and
songs.
228 Merrill St., Apt. C-5, Syracuse, NY
13208

ISRAEL, MCKELLAR
b. Union, S.C., 4 Apr. 1931. Studied with
Donald Packard, Southern Baptist Theological
Seminary; with Martin Mailman, East Carolina
Univ.; with Nadia Boulanger, Fontainebleau, 1961.
He has been faculty member, Sandhills Community
Coll., from 1968; also organist and choirmaster.
WORKS: CHORUS: Hear my cry, anthem, 1955;
KEYBOARD: Chorale preludes for organ; Passacag-
lia, piano, 1964.
425 Dogwood Lane, Southern Pines, NC 28387

ISRAELS, CHARLES HENRY
b. New York, N.Y., 10 Aug. 1936. Studied with
Harold Shapero and Irving Fine, Brandeis Univ.;
John Lewis and George Russell, Lenox School of
Jazz; with Gunther Schuller and Bruno Maderna at
Tanglewood; privately with Hall Overton. His
awards include a Crofts fellowship at Tanglewood;
Guggenheim fellowship, 1978-79; Nat. Endowment
for the Arts grant; and a CAPS grant. He has
been director, Nat. Jazz Ensemble, from 1973; on
faculty, Brooklyn Coll., CUNY, 1973-75; State
Univ. Coll., Purchase, from 1975; visiting
faculty, Bard Coll., 1978.
WORKS: JAZZ ENSEMBLE: Young person's guide
to the jazz orchestra; Lyric suite, flugelhorn
and jazz ensemble; Extract 1; Environments;
Pacemaker, brass quintet; Blues for O.P.; Sarabande; Solar complexes; CHAMBER MUSIC: Songs
for soprano and string quartet.
155 Bank St., B-336, New York, NY 10014

IVERS, PETER
b. Chicago, Ill., 20 Sept. 1946. Attended
Harvard Univ., B.A. 1968; studied percussion and
double bass privately. He was composer-in-
residence with El Monte Art Ensemble, Los
Angeles, 1971-72.

WORKS: BALLET: <u>Air</u>, dance by Lindsay
Crouse, 1969; <u>Brain slave</u>, 30-minute ballet for
contemporary ensemble and synthesizer, 1969;
THEATRE: <u>The Bacchae</u>, 1968; <u>Jesus: A passion
play for Americans</u>, 1969; <u>Job: An American
mystery</u>, 1969; <u>As you like it</u>, 1971; SMALL EN-
SEMBLE: <u>Opus animus</u>, oboe and blues band, 1968;
<u>Knight of the Blue Communion</u>, rock and roll for
oboe, bassoon, harmonica, voice, 1969; <u>Make me</u>,
blues textures for suffering avant-gardists,
1973; CHORUS: <u>Ash Wednesday service</u>, chamber
ensemble, girls' choir, percussion, 1970; FILM
SCORES: <u>Desire is the fire</u>, 1967; <u>Devil's bar-
gain</u>, 1970; <u>In pursuit of treasure</u>, 1971;
<u>Saturday</u>, 1971; <u>Love song of Charles Faborman</u>,
1972; <u>Yesterday's shore</u>, 1972; <u>Frontier's end</u>,
1972.

8591 Crescent Dr., Hollywood, CA 90046

IVES, CHARLES EDWARD
b. Danbury, Conn., 20 Oct. 1874; d. New York,
N.Y., 19 May 1954. Studied first with his
father, George E. Ives, a Civil War bandmaster;
then with Horatio Parker, Yale Univ., B.A. 1898.
Now hailed as the pioneer of atonality and the
greatest innovator of contemporary music, he
nevertheless received his first award, the
Pulitzer prize, for his 3rd symphony, in 1947,
more than 3 decades after its composition; the
Henry Hadley Medal of the Nat. Assoc. for
American Composers and Conductors in 1948.
Recognition of his genius has continued since
these awards. He was organist at age 13 at the
Danbury Congregational Church; organist and
choirmaster in churches in New Haven, Bloomfield, N.J., and New York, 1893-1902; entered
an insurance company as clerk in 1898 and, by
1916, was senior partner of Ives and Myrick, one
of the largest insurance firms of its kind in
the U.S.; retired in 1930. Most of his works
were written before 1916. All of his manuscripts
and correspondence have been deposited at Yale
Univ. by Mrs. Ives.
WORKS: ORCHESTRA: 4 symphonies, 1896-98,
1897-1902, 1901-4, 1910-16; <u>From the steeples
and the mountains</u>, 1901; <u>Central Park in the
dark</u>, 1898-1907; <u>3 Places in New England</u>, 1903-
14; <u>Holidays symphony: Washington's Birthday</u>,
<u>Decoration Day, 4th of July, Thanksgiving or
Forefathers' Day</u>, 1904-13; <u>The pond</u>, 1906; <u>The
unanswered question</u>, 1908; <u>Browning overture</u>,
1911; <u>Hallowe'en</u>, 1911; <u>The gong on the hook
and ladder</u> or <u>Fireman's parade on Main Street</u>,
chamber orch., 1911; <u>Theatrre orchestra set: In
the cage, In the inn, In the night</u>, 1904-11;
<u>Tone roads</u>, chamber orch., 1911-15; <u>Over the
pavements</u>, chamber orch., 1913; <u>Orchestra Set
#2</u>, 1915, <u>#3</u>, 1919-27; BAND: <u>Holiday quickstep</u>,
1888; <u>March Omega Lambda Chi</u>; <u>Overture and march
1776</u>; <u>Country band march</u>; <u>They are there</u>;
CHAMBER MUSIC: 2 string quartets, 1896, 1913;
trio, violin, clarinet, piano, 1902; <u>Space and
duration</u>, string quartet and mechanical piano,
1907; <u>All the way around and back</u>, piano, violin,
flute, bugle, bells, 1907; <u>The innate</u>, string
quartet and piano, 1908; 4 violin sonatas, 1908,
1910, 1914, #4 titled <u>Children's day at the camp
meeting</u>, 1915; <u>Adagio sostenuto</u>, English horn,

flute, strings, piano, 1910; piano trio, 1911;
<u>Set</u>, string quartet and piano, 1914; CHORUS:
<u>Psalm 67</u>, 1898; <u>The celestial country</u>, cantata,
1899; <u>3 harvest home chorales</u>, with brass,
double bass, organ, 1898-1912; <u>General William
Booth enters into heaven</u>, with brass band, 1914;
and more than 100 songs; PIANO: <u>3 quartertone
piano pieces</u>, 1903-24; <u>3 page sonata</u>, 1905; <u>Some
southpaw pitching</u>, 1908; <u>The anti-abolitionists
riot</u>, 1908; 2 sonatas, 1909, 1909-15, #2 titled
<u>Concord, Mass., 1840-1860: Emerson, Hawthorne,
The Alcotts, Thoreau</u>, first complete performance
by John Kirkpatrick, New York, 20 Jan. 1939.

IVEY, JEAN EICHELBERGER
b. Washington, D.C., 3 July 1923. Attended
Trinity Coll., D.C., A.B. magna cum laude;
Peabody Cons., M.M. in piano; Eastman School of
Music, M.M. in composition; Univ. of Toronto,
D.M. in composition. Her awards include a
Rockefeller grant, 1973; ASCAP awards, 1972,
1973; Nat. Endowment for the Arts grant, 1978;
and many commissions. She was founder and
director, electronic music studio, and faculty
member, Peabody Cons., from 1969; founder and
director from 1978, electronic music studio,
Johns Hopkins Univ.; has toured the U.S. and
Europe as concert pianist.
WORKS: ORCHESTRA: overture; <u>Dinsmoor suite</u>;
1964; <u>Ode for orch.</u>, 1965; <u>Forms in motion</u>, symphony in 3 movements, 1972; <u>Tribute: Martin
Luther King, Jr.</u>, baritone and orch., 1969,
Baltimore, 3 Mar. 1973; <u>Sea change</u>, 1978; CHAMBER
MUSIC: piano sonata, 1958; suite for cello and
piano, 1960; sonatina, clarinet solo; <u>Ode</u>, violin and piano; <u>Song of Pan</u>, flute and piano; <u>6
inventions</u>, 2 violins, 1964; <u>Tonada</u>, violin and
cello, 1978; VOICE: <u>Solstice</u>, soprano, flute,
percussion, piano, Dallas, 7 Aug. 1978; <u>Absent
in the spring</u>, medium voice and string trio, New
York, 3 Dec. 1978; <u>A carol of animals</u>, mezzo-
soprano, piano, oboe, 1978; ELECTRONIC: <u>Montage
IV</u>, film score, 1962; <u>The exception and the
rule</u>, film score; <u>Enter 3 witches</u>, 1964; <u>Pinball</u>,
1965; <u>Cortege for Charles Kent</u>, 1969; MIXED
MEDIA: <u>Terminus</u>, mezzo-soprano and tape, Baltimore, 21 Feb. 1971; <u>3 songs of night</u>, 5 instruments, tape, 1971; <u>Aldebran</u>, viola and tape, New
York, 12 Jan. 1973; <u>Hera, hung from the sky</u>,
mezzo-soprano, winds, percussion, piano, tape,
Univ. of North Dakota, 12 Apr. 1973; <u>Skaniadaryo</u>,
piano and tape, 1973; <u>Testament of Eve</u>, mezzo-
soprano, trumpet, orch., tape, Baltimore, 21 Apr.
1976 (the New York performance on 7 Nov. 1976
was taped by Voice of America for broadcast
abroad); <u>Prospero</u>, bass voice, horn, percussion,
tape, Rochester, N.Y., 14 Apr. 1978.
83-33 Austin St., Kew Gardens, NY 11415

JABLONSKY, STEPHEN
b. New York, N.Y., 5 Dec. 1941. Studied with
Mark Brunswick and Paul Turok, City Coll. of New
York; with Pierre Boulez and Leon Kirchner,
Harvard Univ. He received a Nat. Endowment for
the Arts grant, 1975. From 1968, he has been
faculty member, City Coll., CUNY.
WORKS: ORCHESTRA: <u>Passacaglia</u>; <u>Wisconsin
death trap</u>, with slides and 4 narrators, text

JACKSON, DAVID L.

from book by Michael Lesy on 1880-1890 frontier life in Wisconsin, 1976; CHAMBER MUSIC: Gestures, string quartet; 3 pieces for clarinet; Jabberwocky, voice and woodwind sextet; Mechanisms, woodwind trio; Ancient lyric tune, bassoon and wind sextet; sextet for winds, 1975; Semitic dances, English horn, bass, percussion; Quilting 5, brass quintet; Sershestoka, piano trio and clarinet.

P.O. Box 389, Golden's Bridge, NY 10526

JACKSON, DAVID L.
b. Abilene, Tex., 29 Dec. 1944. Studied with John Nagosky, Univ. of South Florida, M.M. 1968; trumpet with John Haynie, North Texas State Univ. He has held faculty posts at Cameron State Coll., 1971-73; Union Coll., Ky., 1976-78; from 1978, Carleton Coll., Minn.
WORKS: CHAMBER MUSIC: Chamber suite, flute clarinet, 2 violins, cello, percussion; 3 Appalachian folk songs, brass quintet.
Music Dept., Carleton College, Northfield, MN 55057

JACKSON, DUKE W., JR.
b. Clearwater, Fla., 15 Aug. 1946. Studied with John Boda, Carlisle Floyd, and Harold Schiffman, Florida State Univ. He was faculty member, Georgia Southwestern Coll., 1970-73.
WORKS: ORCHESTRA: concerto for 2 pianos, harpsichord, and chamber orch.; CHAMBER MUSIC: 3 movements for 2 pianos; 5 serious songs from the Chinese, soprano and piano; Theme and variations, harpsichord, flute, cello.
104F Country Club Apts., Americus, GA 31709

JACKSON, HANLEY
b. Bryan, Tex., 7 June 1939. Studied with Aurelio de la Vega and Gerald Strang, California State Univ., Northridge and Long Beach. His awards include the Cecilia Buck award, 1964; Nat. Fed. of Music Clubs award, 1965; Southwest Music Festival award, 1967; Esther Tow Newman award, 1969; selection as Kansas Composer of the Year, 1972. He was faculty member, California State Univ., 1967-68; from then, at Kansas State Univ.
WORKS: ORCHESTRA: Cassandra's dance; Tangents II, orch. and tape; BAND: Tangents III, with tape; CHAMBER MUSIC: Tangents IV, piano and tape; string quartet, 1964; Night pieces, string quartet and tape; CHORUS: A child's ghetto, with tape; Requiem, with soloists and orch.; Maat, cantata, chorus and percussion ensemble.
Music Dept., Kansas State Univ., Manhattan, KS 66506

JACKSON, MILTON
b. Detroit, Mich., 1932. Was cofounder with John Lewis of the Modern Jazz Quartet, 1952; plays piano, guitar, vibraharp, and sings. His concert jazz works include Ralph's new blues and Jazz theme with improvisations.

JACOBI, FREDERICK
b. San Francisco, Calif., 4 May 1891; d. New York, 24 Oct. 1952. Studied composition with Rubin Goldmark and Ernest Bloch in New York;

with Paul Juon in Berlin. He received the David Bispham Medal, 1944; 2 awards, Society for Publication of American Music; was director, Internat. Society for Contemporary Music. He was assistant conductor, Metropolitan Opera, 1913-17; saxophonist in army bands, 1917-18; taught at Master School of United Arts, New York, 1927; Juilliard School, 1936-50; lecturer at Mills Coll. and Univ. of California.
WORKS: OPERA: The prodigal son, 1944; ORCHESTRA: The pied piper, 1915; California suite, 1917; The eve of St. Agnes, 1919; 2 symphonies, 1922, 1948; Indian dances, 1928; cello concerto, 1932; 3 psalms, cello and orch., 1933; piano concerto, 1936; violin concerto, 1939; Night piece, flute and orch.; Ode for orchestra, 1942; concertino, piano and strings, 1946; 2 pieces in Sabbath mood, 1946; CHAMBER MUSIC: Nocturne, string quartet, 1918; 3 preludes, violin and piano, 1921; 3 string quartets, 1924, 1933, 1945; Scherzo, woodwind quintet, 1936; Hagiographa, 3 Biblical narratives for string quartet and piano, 1938; Fantasy, viola and piano, 1941; Ballade, violin and piano, 1942; Meditation, trombone and piano, 1947; also choral works and piano pieces.

JACOBS, KENNETH A.
b. Indianapolis, Ind., 13 Sept. 1948. Studied with Warner Hutchison, New Mexico State Univ., B.A., M.M.; with Karl Korte, Thomas Wells, and Kent Kennan, Univ. of Texas, Austin, D.M.A. His awards include New Mexico State scholarship, 1966-69; Univ. of Texas fellowship, 1971-72; first prize, Texas Music Educators composition contest, 1974. He was lecturer, New Mexico Western Univ., 1971; joined the faculty at Univ. of Tennessee, 1974.
WORKS: ORCHESTRA: symphony; Sinfonietta, strings; CHAMBER MUSIC: Rotations, string quartet; trio, 2 clarinets and cello; Crossroads, winds, percussion, harp; Windows to 3, piano; CHORUS: 4 pieces, female voices; The burning babe; ELECTRONIC: Emergere, tape; Tracks, tape; Second touch, tape; The sun gatherer, tape; MIXED MEDIA: Issues for 2 characters, flute and tape; Arena de Marzo, 10 instruments and tape; Spirit dances, tape and dancers; Secret world, tape and dancer; There's another one tomorrow, amplified double bass and tape; Scenes from the Earth, tape and synchronized projections on 3 screens.
Music Dept., Univ. of Tennessee, 1741 Volunteer Blvd., Knoxville, TN 37916

JAFFE, GERARD G.
b. Germany, 22 Jan. 1925. Studied with William Bergsma and Vincent Persichetti, Juilliard School, B.S. 1948, M.S. 1949. He was faculty member, Wesleyan Univ., 1953-66; at Incarnate Word Coll., from 1974. His published works include Centone buffo concertante, trombone and piano; Short suite for strings; Variations on a flippant theme, flute and piano.
Incarnate Word College, San Antonio, TX 78209

JAGER, ROBERT
b. Binghamton, N.Y., 25 Aug. 1939. Attended
Wheaton Coll., Ill., and Univ. of Michigan; is
self-taught in composition. His awards include
Ostwald award, American Bandmasters Assoc.,
1964, 1968, 1972; Roth award, Nat. School Orch.
Assoc., 1964, 1966; ASCAP awards from 1967;
Distinguished Service to Music Medal, Kappa
Kappa Psi, 1973; Tennessee Composer of the Year,
1973. He was faculty member, Old Dominion Univ.,
1968-71; then at Tennessee Technological Univ.
WORKS: ORCHESTRA: concerto for jazz band
and orch.; The war prayer; BAND: symphony;
Diamond variations; Quincunx; 3rd suite; Varia-
tions on a theme of Robert Schumann; Chorale and
toccata; A child's garden of verses, soprano and
wind ensemble; Sinfonietta; Suite from Edvard
Munch; Shivaree.
Jager Dr., Rte. 9, Cookeville, TN 38501

JAKUBENAS, VLADAS
b. Birzai, Lith., 15 May 1904; U.S. citizen
1956. Studied with Joseph Wihtols in Riga and
with Frank Schreker in Berlin; was granted the
"free artist" degree in composition in Riga. He
won second prize for a piano piece, Chicago
Chapter, Internat. Society for Contemporary
Music, 1962. He was faculty member, Nat. Cons.
in Kaunas, 1932-44; private teacher, vocal
coach, organist, and conductor in Chicago,
1952-70; music critic, Lithuanian daily newspaper.
WORKS: ORCHESTRA: Forest festival suite,
1954; Intermezzo rustico, string orch.; CHORUS:
Mano pasaulis (My world), with soloists and
orch., 1959; De profundis, with orch.; PIANO:
From the fairyland; Legend; many other piano
pieces and songs.
6506 S. Artesian Ave., Chicago, IL 60629

JAMBOR, AGI
b. Budapest, Hungary, 4 Feb. 1909; U.S. citizen
1954. Studied composition with Zoltan Kodaly
and Leo Weiner, Budapest Royal Cons. She won
the Brahaus prize, Berlin, 1928, and Phil. Orch.
prize, Internat. Chopin Competition, Warsaw,
1937, both for piano performance. She was
professor, Bryn Mawr Coll., 1958-78.
WORKS: PIANO: sonata; preludes; piano
accompaniment for Psalmus humanu and 6 prayers,
words of Albert Szent-Gyorgyi.
103 Pine Tree Rd., Radnor, PA 19087

JAMES, DOROTHY
b. Chicago, Ill., 1 Dec. 1901. Studied with
Adolf Weidig, American Cons., M.M.; with Howard
Hanson, Eastman School of Music; Ernst Krenek,
Univ. of Michigan; and with Healey Willan in
Toronto. Her awards include 3 first prizes, Mu
Phi Epsilon contests; first prize, Choral Clinic,
Milliken Univ.; Michigan Composers Club contest;
Adolf Weidig Gold Medal; 4 MacDowell fellowships;
honorary doctorate, Eastern Michigan Univ., 1971;
and many commissions. She taught at Eastern
Michigan Univ., 1927-68, then professor emeritus.
WORKS: OPERA: Paolo and Francesca, 1931;
ORCHESTRA: Symphonic fragments, Rochester, 24
Mar. 1932; Elegy for the lately dead, 1938;

suite for chamber orch., 1940; CHAMBER MUSIC:
Ballade, violin and piano, 1925; Rhapsody, piano
trio, 1929; 3 Pastorales, clarinet, strings,
celesta, 1933; Recitative and aria, string quintet, 1944; Morning music, flute and piano, 1967;
Patterns, harp, 1977; CHORUS: Tears, Whitman
text, with orch., 1930; The jumblies, children's
cantata after Edward Lear, 1935; Paul Bunyan,
children's cantata, 1938; The golden year, with
orch., 1953; Mutability, women's voices, clarinet, flute, piano; other choral works, pieces
for organ, piano, and vocal solos. In 1976 she
published a brochure: Music of living Michigan
women composers.
516 Fairview Circle, Ypsilanti, MI 48197

JAMES, PHILIP
b. Jersey City, N.J., 17 May 1890; d. Southampton, N.Y., 1 Nov. 1975. Studied with Rubin
Goldmark and Rosario Scalero in New York. His
many awards include Homiletic Review prize for a
hymn, 1927; NBC $5,000 first prize for the
orchestral suite, Station WGZBX; first prize,
Women's Symph. Orch., New York, 1938; election
to Nat. Inst. of Arts and Letters, 1933; New
York Phil. award; Juilliard publication award;
was president, Society for Publication of American Music, 1946. He was bandmaster, AEF General
Hdqters. Band, in World War II; was conductor
Victor Herbert Opera Company, 1919-22; conductor
of various orchestras in New York and New Jersey,
1922-36; guest conductor, New York Phil. and
Philadelphia Orch.; faculty member, New York
Univ., 1922-55.
WORKS: THEATRE: Judith, ballet, 1927;
music for Arms for Venus, 1937; ORCHESTRA: 3
Bret Harte overtures, 1926, 1933, 1935; Sea symphony, 1928; Song of the night, 1931; 2 suites
for strings, 1933, 1946; Gwalia, Welsh rhapsody,
1939; 2 symphonies, 1943, 1949; Chaumont, symphonic poem, 1948; CHAMBER MUSIC: string quartet, 1924; suite for woodwind quintet, 1934;
piano quartet, 1938; CHORUS: Stabat mater
speciosa, with orch., 1921, rev. 1930; General
William Booth enters into heaven, tenor, male
chorus, orch., 1932; many other choral works;
organ pieces.

JAMES, WOODROW
b. Biloxi, Miss., 3 Jan. 1936. Studied with
Arthur Kreutz, Univ. of Mississippi; Helen
Gunderson, Louisiana State Univ.; with H. Owen
Reed and Paul Harder, Michigan State Univ., Ph.D.
1966. He received awards, Louisiana Fed. of
Music Clubs contests, 1961, 1967, 1968. His
faculty posts include Florence State Coll.,
1964-65; McNeese State Coll., 1965-68; Univ. of
Oklahoma, 1968-71; California State Univ.,
Northridge, 1972-73; California State Polytechnic
Univ., 1973-75; Los Angeles City Coll., from
1976.
WORKS: ORCHESTRA: 2 symphonic movements;
BAND: Elegy, trumpet and band; JAZZ ENSEMBLE:
Crawfish; CHAMBER MUSIC: Scherzo, trumpet,
trombone, piano; 3 songs on poems of Dylan
Thomas, soprano and piano.
Los Angeles City College, 855 N. Vermont Ave.,
Los Angeles, CA 90029

JANKOWSKI, LORETTA
b. Newark, N.J., 20 Oct. 1950. Studied with
Samuel Adler, Warren Benson, and Joseph
Schwantner, Eastman School of Music, B.M. 1972;
with Morton Feldman and Harrison Birtwistle,
Dartington Summer School, England; with Marek
Stachowski, Krakow, Poland, 1973; with William
Albright and George Wilson, Univ. of Michigan,
M.M. 1974. Her awards include the Rogers award;
Ostwald award, Band Assoc. composition contest,
1976; Polish government scholarship, 1973; Polish
Alliance Club, Rochester, N.Y., scholarship; and
commissions. She was instructor, Northern
Illinois Univ., 1977-78.
      WORKS: ORCHESTRA: Lustrations, Chicago,
25 Oct. 1978; Demeanour, 1979; BAND: Todesband,
1973; CHAMBER MUSIC: flute sextet, 1972; Or,
chamber orch., 1976; VOICE: Inside the cage,
empty air, 30 women's voices and various
Renaissance instruments, 1975; Icons: Fragments
of a poem, soprano and chamber ensemble; ELEC-
TRONIC: Strephenade, tape, 1973.
      291 Ravenswood, Mountainside, NJ 07092

JANNERY, ARTHUR
b. Millbury, Mass., 24 Mar. 1932. Studied with
Hugo Norden, Gardner Read, Malloy Miller, Robert
Wykes, Ulysses Kay, Boston Univ., B.M., M.M.;
with Paul Pisk, Washington Univ. His awards
include scholarship, Washington Univ.; Fairfax
Symph. awards, 1971; Internat. Delius award,
1971; Nat. School Orch. Assoc. Roth award, 1972;
and commissions. He was faculty member, Salem
Coll., W.Va., 1967-69; from 1969, at Radford
Coll.
      WORKS: ORCHESTRA: Sinfonietta, chamber
orch.; Sharon, an overture, 1971; On the courage
to be, Part I: Essays for Alice: in memoriam,
oboe and orch., Athens, Ga., 4 Feb. 1978; Part
II: Archai, Indianapolis Symph., Terre Haute,
6 Apr. 1978; WIND ENSEMBLE: Appalachian structures, brass and percussion, 1971; Libera me,
Domine, brass quintet; 4 movements for 4 trumpets, 1973; CHAMBER MUSIC: Big balloons,
soprano and instruments, 1971; CHORUS: Cruci-
fixus--resurrexit, women's voices and brass,
1971.
      1010 Sutton St., Radford, VA 24141

JANSSEN, WERNER
b. New York, N.Y., 1 June 1899. Studied with
Frederick Converse in Boston; graduated from
Dartmouth Coll. His awards include the Prix de
Rome for study at American Acad. in Rome, 1939;
honorary Ph.D., Dartmouth Coll.; Finnish Order
of the White Rose, First Class, 1954. He began
to compose operettas and special numbers for
Broadway shows in the 1920s; conducted symphony
orchestras in Europe; made U.S. debut as conduc-
tor with the New York Phil. in 1934; conducted
the Baltimore Symph., 1937-39; organized the
Janssen Symph. in Los Angeles, 1940-53; conducted
Toronto Orch., 1956-57; Vienna State Opera Orch.,
1959-61.
      WORKS: ORCHESTRA: New Year's Eve in New
York, symphonic poem, Rochester, 9 May 1929;
Louisiana suite, 1930; Foster suite, 1937;
CHAMBER MUSIC: Obsequies of a saxophone, 6 wind

instruments and snare drum, 1929; 2 string quartets; Kaleidoscope, string quartet; also film
and television scores.

JARECKI, TADEUSZ
b. Lwow, Poland, 31 Dec. 1888; to U.S. 1913;
d. New York, N.Y., 29 Apr. 1955. Studied with
Sergei Taneyev, Moscow Cons., graduating in 1913.
He received the Elizabeth Sprague Coolidge prize
in 1918 for a string quartet. He conducted in
Europe, 1932-48; then returned to New York.
      WORKS: ORCHESTRA: Chimère, symphonic poem,
1926; La foule, suite, 1928; Sinfonia breve,
1932; CHAMBER MUSIC: 3 string quartets; songs.

JARRETT, JACK MARIUS
b. Asheville, N.C., 17 Mar. 1934. Studied at
Univ. of Florida; with Bernard Rogers, Eastman
School of Music; Boris Blacher in Berlin; with
Bernard Heiden, Indiana Univ., D.M. He received
the Edward Benjamin award, 1957; Fulbright grant,
1961; Ford Found. composer-in-residence award
(Oshkosh public schools), 1965-67. He was
faculty member, Dickinson Coll., 1958-61; Univ.
of Richmond, 1962-64; Univ. of North Carolina,
1972-75; Virginia Commonwealth Univ., from 1976.
      WORKS: OPERA: Cyrano de Bergerac, 1972;
ORCHESTRA: Serenade for string orch., 1957;
Choral symphony on American poems, chorus and
orch. or band; BAND: Holiday for horns, 4 horns
and band; numerous short choral works.
      Music Dept., Virginia Commonwealth Univer-
sity, 901 W. Franklin St., Richmond, VA
23284

JARRETT, KEITH
b. Allentown, Pa., 8 May 1945. Studied with
Eleanor Sokoloff, Curtis Inst.; at Berklee Coll.
of Music. He received a Guggenheim fellowship,
1972.
      WORKS: ORCHESTRA: Metamorphosis, flute solo
and string orch.; In the cave--In the light,
strings, percussion, piano; Crystal moment, 4
celli, 2 trombones; Short piece, guitar and
strings; CHAMBER MUSIC: Fughata, harpsichord;
string quartet; brass quintet; A pagan hymn,
piano; JAZZ ENSEMBLE: Lalene; Expectations;
The mourning of a star; Fort Yawuh; Still life,
still life; Treasure Island; My lady, my child;
Ritooria.
      P.O. Box 85, Oxford, NJ 07863

JEFFERS, RONALD H.
b. Springfield, Ill., 25 Mar. 1943. Studied
with George Wilson, Ross Lee Finney, Leslie
Bassett, Univ. of Michigan, B.M. 1966, M.A. 1968;
with Roger Reynolds, Pauline Oliveros, Robert
Erickson, Univ. of California, San Diego. He
won an award in an Ohio State Univ. choral competition. His faculty posts include Occidental
Coll., 1969-70; Univ. of California, San Diego,
1970-72; Univ. of Wisconsin, Eau Claire, 1972-
73; State Univ. of New York, Stony Brook, 1973-
74; and from 1974, Oregon State Univ.
      WORKS: WIND ENSEMBLE: In memoriam, 7 trum-
pets, 4 oboes, 2 flutes, piano, percussion, 1973;
CHORUS: Dawn, double chorus, 1965; Mass confusion, men's voices, 1966; In time of war, with

instruments, 1967; <u>Now conscience wakes</u>, with soloists, handbells, orch., 1968; <u>Missa concrete</u>, triple chorus, 1969, rev. 1973; <u>Tota pulcra es</u>, 4 voices, cello, clarinet, 2 narrators, 1974; MULTIMEDIA: <u>Time passes</u>, female vocalist, tape, gongs, bells, dancer, 1974.

    234 Northwest 30th, Corvallis, OR 97330

JEFFERSON, MICHAEL GRAHAM
    b. Philadelphia, Pa., 18 Apr. 1927. Attended Temple Univ., A.B. 1952; studied with Joseph Castaldo, Philadelphia Musical Acad.; Romeo Cascarino, Combs Coll. of Music; and with Matthew Colucci, New School of Music, Philadelphia. He received award from Community Children's Theatre, Kansas City. He has been pianist, arranger, orchestrator, conductor, from 1956; was lecturer, Philadelphia public schools, 1969-71; music director, Youth Workshop, Germantown Presbyterian Church, from 1970; wrote articles for <u>Black History Journal</u>, 1973.
    WORKS: THEATRE: ballet scores for piano, cello, flute, clarinet: <u>Circus</u>, 1959, <u>Cinderella</u>, 1960, <u>The black doll</u>, 1961; music for <u>Servant of 2 masters</u>, 1965; <u>Pecos Bill</u>, children's musical, 1968; <u>Treasure Island</u>, musical, 1968; CHORUS: <u>De profundis</u>, with organ, 1972.
    8626 Temple Rd., Philadelphia, PA 19150

JENKINS, EDWARD WALKER
    b. Worcester, Mass. Studied with Frederick Converse and George W. Chadwick, New England Cons., diploma 1926; with Nadia Boulanger in France, 1929; received 4 Endicott prizes in composition, 1925-29. He taught at Perkins Inst. for the Blind, 1933; then at the New England Cons.
    WORKS: CHAMBER MUSIC: 2 violin sonatas; <u>Winter idyll</u> and <u>Summer idyll</u>, strings and piano; woodwind trio; songs.

JENKINS, JOSEPH WILLCOX
    b. Philadelphia, Pa., 15 Feb. 1928. Studied with Vincent Persichetti, Philadelphia Cons.; with Thomas Canning, Bernard Rogers, Howard Hanson, Eastman School of Music, B.M., M.M.; with Ralph Vaughan Williams in England. His awards include Ford Found. grant, 1960-61; Ostwald award, American Bandmasters Assoc., 1961; ASCAP awards, 1965-73; He was affiliated with the U.S. Army Band and Chorus, 1951-53, 1956-59; editor, music publishing firm, 1961-62; from 1962, faculty member, Duquesne Univ.
    WORKS: ORCHESTRA: 2 symphonies; <u>Sinfonia de la frontera</u>, commissioned for the New Mexico Bicentennial celebration; BAND: <u>American overture</u>; <u>Charles County</u>; <u>Cuernavaca</u>; <u>Cumberland Gap</u>; 2 sinfonias; <u>Toccata for winds</u>, 1978; <u>Pieces of 8</u>, 1978; <u>3 bagatelles</u>, 1978; CHAMBER MUSIC: string quartet; many secular and religious choral works.
    Music Dept., Duquesne Univ., Pittsburgh, PA 15219

JENKS, ALDEN FERRISS
    b. Harbor Beach, Mich., 10 Aug. 1940. Attended Yale Univ., B.A. 1962; Univ. of California, Berkeley, M.A. 1968; studied with Karlheinz

Stockhausen, Univ. of Calif., Davis, 1966-67; with David Tudor, Mills Coll., 1968; and with Ben Weber in New York and Darius Milhaud at Aspen. He was an officer of Composers' Forum, 1964-67; codirector and founder of Deus ex Machina, a live electronic performance, 1968-70; and from 1973, director of electronic music, San Francisco Cons.
    WORKS: ORCHESTRA: <u>Expedition</u>, 1964; <u>Almost untitled</u>, chamber orch., 1968; WIND ENSEMBLE: <u>Quasar</u>, brass and percussion, 1966; CHORUS: <u>The exterminator</u>, double chorus, speaking, shouting, laughing, singing, etc., 1968; ELECTRONIC TAPE: <u>Chez elle</u>, 1968; <u>At its</u>, 1968; <u>Lapis</u>, 1968; <u>Namo</u>, 1971; <u>Space</u>, 1972; <u>Bardo I and II</u>, 1971-72; <u>Seeing in the dark</u>, with or without male actor-singer, 1972; MULTIMEDIA: <u>Q.E.D.</u>, amplified autoharp, amplified spoken material, metal waste-basket, "concrete" poem shown through a slide projector, 1969 (full description of this and following items are availble upon request to the composer); <u>Emissions</u>, 1969; <u>Overtone</u>, 1969; <u>Temporary music I and II</u>, 1970; <u>KPFA 2/9/70</u>; <u>The magic pillow show</u>, 1970; <u>Videom</u>, 1971; <u>Videom II</u>, 1973; also music for plays and experimental films.
    1201 Ortega St., San Francisco, CA 94122

JENNI, DONALD MARTIN
    b. Milwaukee, Wis., 4 Oct. 1937. Studied with Leon Stein and Alexander Tcherepnin in Chicago; with Humphrey Searle and Leland Smith, Stanford Univ. His awards include 3 BMI student awards, 1954, 1956, 1957; Ford Found. resident composer grant, 1960-61; Stanford Humanities awards in the Creative Arts, 1965, 1966; and commissions. He was faculty member, De Paul Univ., 1966-68; visiting professor, Stanford Univ., 1968, 1977; from 1968, on faculty, Univ. of Iowa.
    WORKS: OPERA: <u>The emperor clothed anew</u>, 1 act, 1964; ORCHESTRA: <u>Eulalia's rounds</u>, 1972; <u>Opalion</u>, piano and orch.; BAND: <u>Hannibal of Carthage</u>; CHAMBER MUSIC: string quartet, "Weschler," 1965; <u>Asphodel</u>, chamber ensemble, 1969; <u>Cucumber music</u>, chamber ensemble, 1969; <u>Cherry Valley, August 1975</u>, 9 flutes, New York, 3 Nov. 1975; <u>Night bay</u>, voice and piano, 1975; string quartet #2, "Kronos"; also choral works, organ and piano pieces, songs.
    618 E. Bowery, Iowa City, IA 52240

JENSEN, ERIC CHRISTIAN
    b. Fargo, N.Dak., 14 Apr. 1943. Studied with Richmond Browne and Yehudi Wyner, Yale Univ.; with Richard Hervig, Univ. of Iowa, M.M. He was associate in performance, Center for New Music, Univ. of Iowa, 1967-70; faculty member, Grinnell Coll., 1970-75.
    WORKS: THEATRE: music for King Lear; MIXED MEDIA: <u>Ikons</u>, oscilloscopes and tape; <u>Avidya</u>, cello, electronics, tape; <u>Sound textures</u>, 4 improvising performers and tape.
    7730 Northwest 14th, Seattle, WA 98117

JENSEN, JAMES A.
    b. Dayton, Ohio, 29 Dec. 1944. Studied with Donald Key and Markwood Holmes, Kansas State Coll., B.M., M.M.; with John Boda and Carlisle

JEPSON, HARRY BENJAMIN

Floyd, Florida State Univ., D.Mus. From 1968 he has been faculty member, Samford Univ.
WORKS: ORCHESTRA: symphony, 1968; Orpheus variations, chamber orch., 1970; CHAMBER MUSIC: 3 pieces for solo clarinet, 1968; 3 movements, brass qiartet, 1969; viola sonata, 1972; woodwind quintet, 1972; clarinet sonata; VOICE: 5 songs for tenor and piano, 1968; In memoriam: Dr. Martin Luther King, Jr., soprano and 7 instruments, 1969; 4 songs for soprano and piano, 1971; Primogenitur, cycle for soprano and chamber orch., 1973; A Lincoln-Whitman duologue, male chorus, tenor, narrator, chamber orch.; Songs of age, mezzo-soprano and chamber orch.
2515 15th Ave. S., Birmingham, AL 35205

JEPSON, HARRY BENJAMIN
b. New Haven, Conn., 16 Aug. 1870; d. Noank, Conn., 23 Aug. 1952. Studied with Horatio Parker at Yale Univ.; joined the Yale faculty in 1899, was professor and organist, 1906-50. He published works for organ and voice.

JEPSON, WARNER
b. Sioux City, Iowa, 24 Mar. 1930. Studied at Oberlin Cons., B.M.; and with Robert Erickson in San Francisco. He received a Nat. Endowment for the Arts grant, 1977. He was on the faculty, San Francisco Cons., 1965-68, composer-in-resident, Nat. Center for Experiments in Television, 1972-77; from 1974, on faculty, Family Light Music School, Sausalito.
WORKS: THEATRE: Rites of women, songs and tape, 1960; San Francisco's burning, ballad opera with 60 songs, 1962; Totentanz, ballet, tape, 1967, revived 10 seasons, 1968-78; CHAMBER MUSIC: Excursion, woodwind trio, 1965; Rough ground, brass, piano, percussion, 1966; Accumulation, 4 timpani, 8 tomtoms, 1967; Peace, flute and tape, 1969; FILM SCORES: The bed, 1968; Ascent, KQED documentary, 1970; Luminous procuress, 1971; electronic music for many museum and gallery shows and for videotapes at KQED, e.g., Video synthesis, Irving Bridge, Light forms, Floating man, all 1972; ENVIRONMENTS: Dome 2, audio-visual-sensual environment installed in Art and Garden Center, Berkeley, 1973; many other theatre and dance works.
512 Diamond St., San Francisco, CA 94114

JESSYE, EVA
b. Coffeyville, Kans., 20 Jan. 1895. Attended Western Coll., Kans.; Wilberforce Univ., M.A.; Allen Univ., D.M.; studied with Percy Goetschius in New York, and with Will Marion Cook. She has received awards from the U.S. Treasury; Nat. Negro Musicians; St. Louis Trailblazers; Council of Negro Women Musicians; Detroit-Windsor (Ont.) Freedom Citation; Martin Luther King, Jr., Found.; Centennial Medal, Afro-Methodist Episcopal Church. Ann Arbor, Mich., declared 19 Jan. 1974 Eva Jessye Day in recognition of the Afro-American Music Collection she gave to the Univ. of Michigan. In 1926 she organized the Eva Jessye Choir and conducted it in concerts throughout the U.S., Europe, and the Middle East; was music director for MGM film Hallelujah, 1929; conducted the choir for Virgil Thomson's

4 saints in 3 acts, 1934; was choral director for all Broadway performances and European tours of Porgy and Bess, 1935-58, and became known as "unofficial guardian" of its score; has appeared in many films, was television writer and director; American consultant, BBC, London; music dept. head, Morgan State Coll.; composer-in-residence, Maryland State Coll.; and on 30 June 1976, was commissioned as colonel on the staff of Gov. Edwards, State of Louisiana.
WORKS: THEATRE: Chronicle of Job, drama with music, 1955; CHORUS: My spirituals (16), 1926; Paradise lost and regained, oratorio, Milton text, 2 narrators, chorus, organ, 1936, Washington, 11 July 1972
Miller Manor, Ann Arbor, MI 48103

JIRAK, KAREL BOLESLAV
b. Prague, Czech., 28 Jan. 1891; to U.S. 1947; d. Chicago, Ill., 30 Jan. 1972. Was a conductor in Germany and Czechoslovakia; professor, Prague Cons., 1920-30; music director, Czechoslovak Radio, 1930-45; from 1948, professor, Roosevelt Coll., Chicago. His many compositions include an opera; 6 symphonies, 1915-70; 7 string quartets, 1915-60; #7 was performed in Chicago, 17 Jan. 1961; woodwind trio, 1956; sonatas for many instruments; 8 song cycles with orch.; many choral works; piano pieces.

JOCHSBERGER, TZIPORA H.
b. Germany, 27 Dec. 1920; U.S. citizen 1954. Studied at Jerusalem Acad. of Music; with Hugo Weisgall, Jewish Theological Seminary, New York, M.M. 1959, D.S.M. 1972. She was one of the founders and a director, Rubin Acad., Jerusalem, 1947-50; founder and director from 1952, Hebrew Arts School for Music and Dance, New York; on faculty, Jewish Theological Seminary, 1954-72.
WORKS: CHAMBER MUSIC: Melodies of Israel, duets and trios for recorders and other melody instruments; 5 duets for 2 oboes; Holiday suite, flute and clarinet; Blessings, suite for solo violin; CHORUS: Bekol Zimrah, collection of Jewish choral music; 4 Madrigals, to poems of Rahel; From the beginning, choir and orch.; Aphorisms, Tagore texts, a cappella; SONGS: 4 songs for voice and piano; 2 songs for voice, violin, flute; Song of Moses, baritone and string orch.; PIANO: Contrasts; Melodies of my people; Moods, 1976.
5 W. 86th St., New York, NY 10024

JOHANNESEN, GRANT
b. Salt Lake City, Utah, 30 July 1921. Studied piano with Robert Casadesus at Princeton Univ., 1941-46; with Egon Petri at Cornell Univ. He launched his long career as concert pianist in New York in 1944; was appointed consultant and advisor, Cleveland Inst. of Music, 1973-74; from 1975, has been professor. He has published Improvisation on a Mormon hymn for piano.
Cleveland Inst. of Music, 11021 East Blvd., Cleveland, OH 44106

JOHANSEN, GUNNAR
b. Copenhagen, Denmark, 21 Jan. 1906; to U.S. 1929. Studied with Egon Petri and others in

Berlin; Toured Europe as concert pianist, 1924-29; spent first years in the U.S. in California until appointed artist-in-residence and professor at Univ. of Wisconsin, 1939; professor emeritus, 1975.

WORKS: ORCHESTRA: 2 piano concertos, 1930, 1970; PIANO: 31 sonatas, 1941-51; 246 improvised sonatas recorded on tape, 1952-70.

JOHANSON, BRYAN
b. Yakima, Wash., 18 Dec. 1951. Attended Portland State Univ., B.A. 1975; studied guitar with Christopher Parkening and others; composition privately with Tomas Svoboda; with Charles Jones, Aspen School, 1978. He won second prize in a compostion contest at Aspen. He taught guitar at Mount Hood Coll., 1974-78; then at Portland State Univ.

WORKS: ORCHESTRA: guitar concerto, 1977; symphony, 1978; CHAMBER MUSIC: Fantasy for 3, 3 guitars and strings; concertino; 2 guitars and strings; trio, 3 guitars, 1977; duo, 2 guitars; Pavane and galliard, guitar, 1978; Passacaglia, flute and piano; trio, flute, cello, guitar; Isolation, guitar and string orch.; Arabesque, guitar and strings.

7270 S.W. Benz Court, Portland, OR 97225

JOHNS, DONALD
b. Chicago, Ill., 9 June 1926. Studied with Frank Cookson, Anthony Donato, and Wallingford Riegger, Northwestern Univ., B.M. 1951, M.M. 1952, Ph.D. 1960; with Karl Schiske, Vienna Acad. of Music, on a Fulbright scholarship, 1952-54. He was associate, Creative Arts Inst., Univ. of California, 1966-67; has been professor, Univ. of California, Riverside, from 1957.

WORKS: ORCHESTRA: Concerto piccolo, flute, clarinet, tympani, strings; Serenade in C; CHORUS: Psalm 130, with tenor solo and strings; Magnificat, with soprano solo; Lord keep us steadfast, motet; Alleluia; ORGAN: Organ mass; Partita on a passion chorale; 3 chorale preludes; Prelude, aria, and finale, with trumpet solo; 3 meditations; Fantasia quasi sonata; Introduction and passacaglia.

270 Goins Court, Riverside, CA 92507

JOHNSON, A. PAUL
b. Indianapolis, Ind., 27 Jan. 1955. Studied composition privately with Thomas Briccetti and Russell J. Peck in Indianapolis. He has held composer/director positions in Indianapolis from 1974; was composer-in-residence, Palisades Theatre Company, 1978-79, from Oct. 1979, at Pinellas County Arts Council, both in St. Petersburg, Fla.

WORKS: THEATRE: (musicals, performances are in Indianapolis unless otherwise noted): The post mortem reflections of Peter Gnowyak, 16 Sept. 1973; Tantalus, 27 Sept. 1974; Lift ev'ry voice, Feb.-Mar. 1977; Beyond the zigzag railroad, St. Louis, Mo., 9 Apr. 1977; Musical mirage express, Syracuse, N.Y., Feb.-Mar. 1978; Journey's end in lovers' meeting, Syracuse, Feb.-Mar. 1979; Alice in Wonderland, St. Petersburg, Aug. 1979; Poetic license, May-June 1978; Fantasy for you, Kamar and the flying horse,

Apr. 1979; Ama and the white crane, St. Petersburg, Sept. 1979; many of the musicals have been taken on tour to off-Broadway, New York; CHAMBER MUSIC: Liebestraum stomp, piano, flute, clarinet, guitar and percussion, WISH-TV, Aug. 1972; piano trio; Little suite, piano; from the Analects, flute, piano, soprano; Some Moore, violin, piano, and narrator; flute sonata, St. Petersburg, 13 Apr. 1980.

777 53rd Ave. S., St. Petersburg, FL 33705

JOHNSON, CHRISTOPHER. See YAVELOW, CHRISTOPHER

JOHNSON, CLYDE E.
b. Fennimore, Wis., 16 Feb. 1930. Studied with Philip Bezanson, Univ. of Iowa, M.A., Ph.D. His awards include a Fulbright grant, 1957, and commissions. From 1961 he has been professor, Univ. of Minnesota, Morris.

WORKS: BAND: Intermezzo, 1963; Etudes, 1967; CHAMBER MUSIC: 2 clarinet sonatas, 1956, 1961; Toccata, piano, 1957; Iowa flowering, song cycle for contralto and piano, 1960.

408 W. 5th St., Morris, MN 56267

JOHNSON, DAVID N.
b. San Antonio, Tex., 28 June 1922. Studied with Rosario Scalero, Curtis Inst. of Music; with Ernst Bacon, Syracuse Univ. He has been faculty member, St. Olaf Coll., 1965-67; Syracuse Univ., 1967-69; from 1969, at Arizona State Univ.; also from 1970, organist and music director, Trinity Cathedral, Phoenix.

WORKS: CHORUS: Joseph, cantata; Gloria Deo, Books I and II; Hosanna, folk communion service, 1976; ORGAN: Beautiful saviour; Deck thyself, my soul, with gladness; Fugue a la gigue; Of the Father's love begotten; The Lord's prayer, voice and organ; 3 trumpet tunes; 4 organ books; organ method books and many works for organ.

5105 S. La Rosa Dr., Tempe, AZ 85282

JOHNSON, GORDON A.
b. Wautoma, Wis., 10 Aug. 1924. Studied at Milwaukee State Teachers Coll., B.S. 1948; Eastman School of Music, M.M. 1954; with H. Owen Reed, Michigan State Univ., Ph.D. 1963. He was faculty member, East Carolina Univ., 1959-63; from 1963, at Univ. of South Florida.

WORKS: CHORUS: 3 Japanese songs, 1970; Power to rise, 1971; many choral works and art songs.

11325 Carrollwood Dr., Tamoa, FL 33618

JOHNSON, HALL
b. Athens, Ga., 12 Mar. 1887; d. New York, N.Y., 30 Apr. 1970. Studied at Univ. of Atlanta and Univ. of Southern California; with Percy Goetschius in New York. His awards included an honorary D.M., Philadelphia Musical Acad.; and citation by the City of New York. He formed the Hall Johnson Choir in 1925, performed on radio and in concert; Negro Chorus of Los Angeles in 1936; toured Germany and Austria in 1951 under the auspices of the State Department.

WORKS: THEATRE: Fi-yer, operetta; Run little chillun, play with music; CHORUS: Ride

JOHNSON, HAROLD VICTOR

on, King Jesus; Son of man, cantata; The crucifixion.

JOHNSON, HAROLD VICTOR
b. Omaha, Nebr., 16 May 1918. Attended Univ. of
California, Los Angeles; studied privately with
Wesley LaViolette and Eric Zeisl. He has been
faculty member, American Operatic Laboratory;
Jarman Cons.; Southern California Cons.; member
of music department, MCA-TV.
    WORKS: OPERA: Judas; ORCHESTRA: 3 sym-
phonies; CHAMBER MUSIC: 4 string quartets;
CHORUS: 2 oratorios; Requiem mass; many songs.
        305 N. Oakland Dr., Beverly Hills, CA 90210

JOHNSON, HORACE
b. Waltham, Mass., 5 Oct. 1893; d. Tucson, Ariz.,
30 May 1964. Studied with John Patton Marshall
and Bainbridge Crist in Boston; at Tufts Coll.;
and in Italy, Germany, and France. He was
managing editor of the Musical Courier; head of
Fed. WPA Music Project, 1939.
    WORKS: ORCHESTRA: Imagery, 1925; Astarte,
1935; Streets of Florence, 1936; In the American
manner; and songs.

JOHNSON, HUNTER
b. Benson, N.C., 14 Apr. 1906. Attended Univ.
of North Carolina; studied with Bernard Rogers,
Eastman School of Music, B.M. 1929; also studied
with Alfredo Casella in Rome. His awards include
the Rome prize, 1933; Guggenheim fellowships,
1941, 1954; Nat. Inst. of Arts and Letters award,
1958; honorary doctorate, Univ. of North Carolina. He was faculty member at Univ. of Michigan, 1929-33; Univ. of Manitoba, 1944-47;
Cornell Univ., 1948-53; Univ. of Illinois, 1958-
65; and Univ. of Texas, 1966-71.
    WORKS: BALLET: Letter to the world, 1940;
Deaths and entrances; The scarlet letter (all 3
for Martha Graham); ORCHESTRA: symphony, 1931;
concerto for piano and chamber orch., 1935;
North State; Past the evening sun; CHAMBER MUSIC:
piano sonata; For the unknown soldier; trio for
flute, oboe, piano.
        Benson, NC 27504

JOHNSON, JAMES LOUIS (J.J.)
b. Indianapolis, Ind., 1924.
    WORKS: CONCERT JAZZ: Perceptions, solo
trumpet, contrabass, drum, winds, 2 horns,
timpani; Poem for brass; Turnpike; El Camino
Real; Sketch for trombone; Scenario, trombone
and orch.; Rondo, vibraphone, piano, contrabass,
drum, chamber orch.

JOHNSON, JAMES P.
b. New Brunswick, N.J., 1 Feb. 1891; d. New
York, N.Y., 17 Nov. 1955. Studied music privately. He made his professional debut in 1904;
played in theatres, night clubs, films; formed
his own band and toured Europe; was accompanist
to Bessie Smith, Ethel Waters, and others.
    WORKS: OPERA: Dreamy kid; De organizer,
folk opera; OPERETTA: The husband; Kitchen
opera; BALLET: Sefronia's dream; Manhattan
street scene; ORCHESTRA: Symphonic Harlem;
Symphony in brown; African drums; piano con-

certo; Mississippi moon; Yamacraw, Negro rhapsody; Symphonic suite on St. Louis Blues; City
of steel; and popular songs.

JOHNSON, JOHN ROSAMOND
b. Jacksonville, Fla., 11 Aug. 1873; d. New
York, N.Y., 11 Nov. 1954. Studied with Charles
Dennee, George Whiting, and David Bispham, New
England Cons.; received an honorary M.A.,
Atlanta Univ. He was public school music super-
visor in Jacksonville; toured in vaudeville in
U.S. and Europe, 1896-98; appeared in Porgy and
Bess, Mamba's daughters, Cabin in the sky.
    WORKS: BALLET: African drum dance; MUSI-
CALS: Humpty Dumpty; Shoo-fly regiment; The red
moon; Mr. Load of Kole; SONGS: Lift every voice
and sing (called the Negro national anthem);
many songs for revues.

JOHNSON, LOCKREM
b. Davenport, Iowa, 15 Mar. 1924; d. Seattle,
Wash., 5 Mar. 1977. Studied with George
Frederick McKay, Univ. of Washington. His
awards included a Guggenheim fellowship, 1951;
2 MacDowell fellowships, 1956, 1965; first prize
in piano and in chamber music, Nat. Fed. of
Music Clubs, both 1959; and commissions. He was
faculty member, Univ. of Washington, 1947-49;
pianist, Seattle Symphony, 1948-51; music publishing executive, New York, 1951-62; director,
music dept., Cornish School, Seattle, 1962-69;
then private teacher and music publisher.
    WORKS: OPERA: A letter to Emily, chamber
opera, New York, 22 Jan. 1955; BALLET: She;
THEATRE: music for King Lear; ORCHESTRA: symphony, Seattle, 2 Dec. 1966; CHAMBER MUSIC: 6
piano sonatas; 3 violin sonatas; 2 cello sonatas;
Impromptu, piano; guitar sonata; 2 piano sonatinas; 24 piano preludes; 7 guitar preludes;
also Suite of noels, chorus and organ.

JOHNSON, MERRITT W.
b. Dunkirk, Ohio, 29 Oct. 1902. Attended
Oberlin Cons., B.M., M.M.; studied composition
with Leo Sowerby and Darius Milhaud; piano with
Josef Lhevinne and Egon Petri; organ with Wilhelm
Middelschulte. His awards include commissions
from the South Dakota Music Teachers Assoc. and
others. He taught piano and organ, Univ. of
North Dakota, 1925-33; then at Northern State
Coll., becoming professor emeritus in 1973.
    WORKS: ORCHESTRA: Concert overture; The
prairie, with chorus; BAND: Divertimento;
CHAMBER MUSIC: piano sonata; Burlesque, string
quartet; Souvenirs, piano trio; Introduction and
allegro, cello and piano; numerous pieces for
piano, organ; anthems, vocal solos.
        Melody Lane, Aberdeen, SD 57401

JOHNSON, ROGER
b. San Mateo, Calif., 12 Nov. 1941. Studied
with George McKay and John Verrall, Univ. of
Washington; with Mel Powell and Bulent Arel,
Yale Univ.; with Chou Wen-chung and Otto Luening,
Columbia Univ. He received a Woodrow Wilson
fellowship, 1963; BMI prize, 1966; first prize,
Los Angeles Horn Club, 1972. He was faculty
member, Lincoln Univ., Pa., 1966-67; Upsala

Coll., 1967-71; from 1971, Ramapo Coll., N.J.
WORKS: CHAMBER MUSIC: Suite for 6 horns, 1959; 4 pieces, horn and piano, 1962; trio for clarinet, horn, harpsichord, 1965; string quartet, 1968; 5 songs, 1967; woodwind quintet; Ritual music, 6 horns; Inventions, flute and viola; Summer songs, soprano and guitar; 5 miniatures, violin and piano; CHORUS: Love is . . .; Circle of Maradit, ritual drama. He has also compiled and edited Scores: An anthology of new music (Macmillan).
336 Canal St., New York, NY 10013

JOHNSON, ROY HENRY
b. Moline, Ill., 25 Feb. 1933. Studied with Louis Mennini, Wayne Barlow, Bernard Rogers, Eastman School of Music; with John Boda, Florida State Univ. He was faculty member, Bethany Coll., 1956-58; from 1960, at Florida State Univ.
WORKS: ORCHESTRA: Canzona liturgica, 1955; piano concerto, 1960; CHAMBER MUSIC: piano sonata, 1960; Serenade, solo flute, 1963; 3 pieces for marimba, 1968; Variations, 2 pianos, 1972; Fantasy, trombone and piano, 1973; CHORUS: Missa brevis, a cappella, 1961.
School of Music, Florida State University, Tallahassee, FL 32306

JOHNSON, TOM
b. Greeley, Colo., 18 Nov. 1939. Studied with Elliott Carter, Alvin Etler, and Yehudi Wyner, Yale Univ., B.A. 1961, M.M. 1967; privately with Morton Feldman. He has received a Creative Artists Public Service Program grant and a Nat. Endowment for the Arts grant, 1978. He was assistant editor of Musical America, 1962-63; frequently worked as accompanist for dance classes; from 1971, has been music critic for the Village Voice.
WORKS: THEATRE: Action music II, flute, cello, piano, dancer, 1968; 411 lines, theatre piece, 1970; The 4-note opera (D.E.A.B.), to his own libretto, 5 singers, piano, the Cubiculo, New York, 11 May 1972; The masque of clouds, 3-act opera, 12 performers, chamber ensemble, sextet of dancing clouds, the Kitchen, New York, 15 Oct. 1975; Door-windows-drawers-dryer-box, opera, New York, 15 Sept. 1978; ORCHESTRA: Pendulum, 1965; Fission, 1966; 5 Americans, 1969; CHAMBER MUSIC: 4 violins, 4 violins and percussion, 1966; Scene for piano and tape, 1969; An hour for piano, 1971; Septapede, piano, 1973; 60-note fanfares for 4 antiphonal trumpets, 1975; Verses for viola, 1976; Monologue for tuba, 1976; Private pieces: piano music for self entertainment, a book of prose instructions; Secret songs, sound poetry for unaccompanied voice; Lectures with audience participation, full evening solo program; Risks for unrehearsed performers, 1-10, a series for varyings soloists or groups, each to be performed only once, #10 for woodwind quintet and narrator, S.U.C., Oneonta, N.Y., 20 Apr. 1978, on a program of all Johnson works. He has also published Imaginary music, a collection of over 100 line drawings using music symbols.
60 Grand St., New York, NY 10013

JOHNSTON, BENJAMIN B.
b. Macon, Ga., 15 Mar. 1926. Attended Coll. of William and Mary, B.A. 1949; Cincinnati Cons., M.M. 1950; Mills Coll., M.A. 1952; studied with Darius Milhaud, John Cage, Harry Partch, and Burrill Phillips. His awards include a Guggenheim fellowship, 1959; Nat. Found. for the Arts and Humanities grant; continuing research grants, Univ. of Illinois; and numerous commissions. He has been faculty member, Univ. of Illinois, from 1951.
WORKS: CHAMBER OPERA: Gertrude, or Would she be pleased to receive it?, 1965; Carmilla, 1970; BALLET: St. Joan, for Sybil Shearer, piano, 1955; Gambit, dancers and orch., for Merce Cunningham, concert version entitled Ludes for 12 instruments, 1959; THEATRE: music for The wooden bird, with Harry Partch, 1951; Fire, 1952; The zodiac of Memphis (Trapdoors of the Moon), 1954, rev. 1958; Tango for Taming of the shrew, 1961; Museum piece, sound track for Smithsonian Inst. film, 1968-69; Auto Mobile, for Smithsonian Inst. exhibit, 1968-69; ORCHESTRA: Passacaglia and epilogue, from St. Joan, 1955-60; Quintet for groups, 1966; BAND: concerto for brass and percussion, 1951; JAZZ BAND: Ivesberg revisited, 1960; Newcastle troppo, 1960; CHAMBER MUSIC: Dirge, percussion ensemble, 1952; septet, wind quintet, cello and bass, 1956-58; 9 variations, string quartet, 1959; 4 string quartets, 1959, 1964, 1973, 1973, #4, New York, 21 Apr. 1974; cello sonata, 1960; Knocking piece, 2 percussionists and piano, 1962; duo for flute and string bass, 1963; Lament, 3 winds, 3 strings, 1966; One man, trombone and percussion, 1967; Casta Bertram, double bass, 1969; Crossings, string quartet, New York, 15 Mar. 1976; CHORUS: Night, cantata, 1955; Of vanity, with percussion, 1964; Prayer, boys' choir, 1966; Ci-Git Satie, double chorus, bass voice, drums, 1967; Rose, 1971; mass, with 8 trombones, rhythm section, 1972; PIANO: Sonata for microtonal piano grindlemusic, 1965; other piano pieces and some do-it-yourself pieces.
1003 W. Church St., Champaign, IL 61820

JOHNSTON, DONALD O.
b. Tracy, Minn., 6 Feb. 1929. Attended Macalester Coll.; studied with Philip Warner and Robert Delaney, Northwestern Univ., B.M. 1951, M.M. 1954; with Bernard Rogers and Howard Hanson, Eastman School of Music, D.M.A. 1961. He was band and orchestra director, Coll. of Idaho, 1954-55; director of instrumental music, Ripon Coll., 1955-58; from 1960, professor, Univ. of Montana.
WORKS: ORCHESTRA: 4 symphonies, 1954, 1959, 1960, 1961; Essay trumpet and orch., 1959; The silver vision, 1962; Toccata, 1966; Montage, 1967; Epic for flute and orch., 1973; Time and space studies in 3 aspects (5th symphony in one movement), 1977; CHAMBER MUSIC: string quartet, 1953; Study for trumpet and piano, 1975; Concatenation, woodwind quintet and piano, 1975; CHORUS: Sonnets from the barracks, with orch., 1968-71; A time of darkness, liturgical drama, with orch., 1970-72; Christmas processional, double chorus, brass, orch., organ, 1970; A

JOKL, GEORG

soldier's requiem, with orch., 1973; Fires of
another time, with band and orch., 1975; other
smaller choral works; numerous band pieces.
    91 Arrowhead Dr., Missoula, MT 59801

JOKL, GEORG
    b. Vienna, Austria, 31 July 1896; to U.S. 1938;
d. New York, N.Y., 29 July 1954. Brother of
Otto Jokl. He wrote a symphony, symphonic poem,
Burletta piccola, for winds, 1952.

JOKL, OTTO
    b. Vienna, Austria, 18 Jan. 1891; to U.S. 1940;
d. New York, N.Y., 13 Nov. 1963. Studied with
Alban Berg, 1926-30. His works include Suite
for orchestra; a sinfonietta; 2 string quartets;
piano sonatina.

JOLLEY, FLORENCE
    b. Kingsburg, Calif., 11 July 1917. Attended
Univ. of the Pacific; Wheaton Coll., Ill.;
Eastman School of Music; Univ. of Southern
California, M.M.; Univ. of California, Los
Angeles. She has received yearly ASCAP awards.
She was faculty member, Pierce Coll., 1962-65;
from 1965, at Los Angeles City Coll.
    WORKS: CHAMBER MUSIC: Recollections, oboe
and piano, with visual of Hilo, Hawaii, 1971;
Little suite, piano; Journey thru' a rock,
organ and tape; CHORUS: Gloria in excelsis;
Christmas time; Holy Lord God of hosts; All
people that on Earth do dwell; The light has
come, with brass choir and organ, Los Angeles,
31 Mar. 1971.
    1122 Tenth St., Santa Monica, CA 90403

JONES, CHARLES
    b. Tamworth, Ont., Canada, 21 June 1910; to U.S.
1928. Studied violin with Samuel Gardner and
Sascha Jacobsen in New York; composition with
Bernard Wagenaar at Juilliard Graduate School.
He received the Copley award and a grant from
the Society for Publication of American Music.
His faculty posts have included Mills Coll.,
1939-44; Aspen Music School, from 1951; Juilliard
School, from 1954; and Mannes Coll. of Music,
from 1970.
    WORKS: BALLET: Down with drink, 1943;
ORCHESTRA: suite for small orch., 1937; suite
for strings, 1937; 4 symphonies, 1939, 1957,
1962, 1965; Cassation, 1948; Little symphony for
the New Year, 1953; concerto for 4 violins and
orch., 1963; Allegory, 1970; CHAMBER MUSIC: 6
string quartets, 1936, 1944, 1951, 1954, 1961,
1970; Threnody, solo viola, 1947; Lyric waltz
suite, woodwind quartet, 1948; Epiphany, speaker
and 4 instruments, 1952; violin sonata, 1958;
The seasons, cantata, 1959; sonata for oboe and
harpsichord, 1965; I am a mynstral, tenor and 4
instruments, 1967; string trio, 1968; Masque,
speaker and 12 instruments, 1968; Anima, cycle
for voice, piano, viola, 1968; Serenade, flute,
violin, cello, harpsichord, 1973; Triptychon,
violin, viola, piano, 1975; CHORUS: On the
morning of Christ's nativity, 5-part chorus,
1953; Piers the plowman, tenor, chorus, and
orch., 1963; PIANO: 2 sonatas, 1946, 1950;
sonata for 2 pianos, 1947; Toccata, 1955;

Ballade, 1961; Psalm, 1976.
    311 E. 58th St., New York, NY 10022

JONES, DAVID HUGH
    b. Jackson, Ohio, 25 Feb. 1900. Studied at
Guilmant Organ School; American Acad., Fontaine-
bleau; with T. Tertius Noble, Henri Libert,
Marcel Dupre, Andre Bloch, Charles Widor;
Washington and Jefferson Coll., D.M.; Beaver
Coll., D.M. He was organist in Ohio and New
York, 1917-26; faculty member, Westminster Choir
Coll., Dayton, 1926-29, in Ithaca, 1929-32, and
in Princeton, N.J., 1932-51; at Princeton Theo-
logical Seminary, from 1951; visiting professor
in Cuba, 1955-56. He has composed many anthems
and songs.

JONES, DAVID P.
    b. Stockton, Calif., 10 Feb. 1958. Studied
with William O. Smith, Univ. of Washington;
with Malcolm Peyton, New England Cons. He won
first prize in the 1979 New Music for Young
Ensembles contest with a woodwind quintet. He
has been piano accompanist for dance groups in
Seattle.
    WORKS: CHAMBER MUSIC: woodwind quintet,
1975; mixed quintet, 1975; Full moon, chamber
group, 1976; piano suite, 1977; suite for mixed
winds and marimba, 1979.
    1415 E. Republican St., #101, Seattle, WA
98112

JONES, DONALD R.
    b. Rochester, N.Y., 3 May 1922. Studied with
Wayne Barlow and Bernard Rogers, Eastman School
of Music. He has been librarian, Ensemble
Library, Eastman School, from 1960.
    WORKS: BAND: Rhapsody, percussion and
band; CHAMBER MUSIC: Allegro, horn and piano;
CHORUS: Lord's prayer; This is the prophet.
    143 Croydon Rd., Rochester, NY 14610

JONES, GEORGE THADDEUS
    b. Asheville, N.C., 6 Nov. 1917. Studied at
Univ. of North Carolina, B.A. 1938; with Bernard
Rogers and Howard Hanson, Eastman School of
Music, M.A. 1942, Ph.D. 1950; privately with
Nicolas Nabokov and Nadia Boulanger. His awards
include a Fulbright grant, 1953; Benjamin award,
1962; State Dept. Cultural Exhange grant, 1967-
68; Health, Education and Welfare Dept. grant.
He was instructor, U.S. Navy School of Music,
1942-48; from 1950, professor, Catholic Univ.
    WORKS: 2 operas; 2 symphonies; piano sonata;
numerous chamber and choral compositions.
    School of Music, Catholic Univ., Washington,
DC 20017

JONES, SISTER IDA, O.S.U.
    b. Louisville, Ky., 9 Aug. 1898. Studied at
Ursuline Coll.; with George Leighton and Carl
Hugo Grimm, Cincinnati Cons. She won a Com-
posers' Press publication award, 1961. She
taught in church schools, 1922-34; Ursuline
Coll., 1934-40; chairman, 1940-66; staff member,
Ursuline School of Music, from 1968.
    WORKS: CHAMBER MUSIC: The immortal, soprano
and piano, 1953; Scherzo, woodwind trio, 1961;

CHORUS: Supplication, women's voices, 1958; Hodie Christus natus est, women's voices, a cappella, 1959; The magnificat, 1971; Ave Maria, 1972; Mass for the Christ Child, 1972.
    Ursuline School of Music, 3105 Lexington Rd., Louisville, KY 40206

JONES, JEFFREY
    b. Los Angeles, Calif., 11 May 1944. Studied with Dorrance Stalvey, Immaculate Coll., B.M.; with Goffredo Petrassi, St. Cecilia Acad., Rome, diploma; with Seymour Shifrin, Arthur Berger, Martin Boykan, Harold Shapero, Brandeis Univ., M.F.A.; with Franco Donatoni, Acad. Chigiana, diploma. His awards include the Celia Buck grant; Fulbright-Hays grant to Italy, 1967, 1968; D'Atrio and Bonaventura Somma prizes, St. Cecilia Acad., 1969; first grand prize, Fest. Internat. du Son, Paris, 1970; BMI award, 1970; Rome prize, 1972-74. He taught guitar, 1962-67; was composer-in-residence, Marlboro Festival, 1970; instructor, Brandeis Univ., 1969-72.
    WORKS: THEATRE: Orythia, ballet opera in 3 tableaux; music for Von Hofmanstahl's Everyman, 1966; music for television series "Insight," 1966; CHAMBER MUSIC: 13 ways of looking at a blackbird, 3 voices, 7 instruments, 1966; Variance, 7 players, 1907; Rideau d'amethystes, harp, guitar, cello, 1970; Modi movendi su temi di Arcangelo Corelli, 7 players, 1970; Expressions, solo guitar, 1971; Ambiance, soprano and 18 players, 1972; Pieces mouventes, piano.

JONES, QUINCY DELIGHT, JR.
    b. Chicago, Ill., 14 Mar. 1933. Studied at Seattle Univ.; Berklee Coll. of Music; Boston Cons.; and with Nadia Boulanger and Olivier Messiaen. His awards include a scholarship at Berklee Coll.; 3 nominations for Academy awards for film scores, 1971. He has been trumpet player and arranger from 1950; with Dizzy Gillespie on State Dept. tour, 1956; led own band on European tour, 1960; vice-president, Mercury Records, from 1964; chairman, Inst. of Black American Music, 1970.
    WORKS: Soundpiece, string quartet and contralto, 1962; Soundpiece, jazz orch., 1964; Black requiem, chorus and orch., Texas A&M Coll., Prairie View, 22 Feb. 1971 (for Ray Charles, pianist); FILM SCORES: The boy in the tree, 1965; Mirage, 1965; The pawnbroker, 1965; Jigsaw, 1966; In cold blood, 1967; Enter laughing, 1967; For the love of joy, 1968; Bob and Carol and Ted and Alice, 1969; The out-of-towners, 1970; The Anderson tapes, 1971; The new centurions, 1972; The hot rock, 1972; theme for TV's "Ironsides" and "It takes a thief"; many other film scores; also songs and jazz works.

JONES, RALPH
    b. Philadelphia, Pa., 9 July 1951. Studied with Julius Eastman and Morton Feldman, State Univ. of New York at Buffalo; with Jacob Druckman at Tangelwood; privately, electric design, with R. A. Moog; video with Vasulkas at Media Study/Buffalo. He held an ASCAP fellowship for Tanglewood, 1972. At the Center of the Creative and Performing Arts, SUNY, he was

graduate fellow, 1973-75, and Rockefeller research fellow, 1977; was director, Electronic Music Studio and Research Design, Media Study/ Buffalo, 1975-77.
    WORKS: CHAMBER MUSIC: Made in 1860, musique concrete, 1971; Epitaph/mobile for David, guitar, percussion, tape, 1972; Saturday afternoon/5 o'clock, 5 flutes, 1973; CHORUS: Night journey, large chorus, percussion, tape, 1972; ELECTRONIC: Circuitree, environment-sensing sound sculpture; Chants home-passage; Music for digital filters. He is doing research on sources of naturally occurring ultrasonics.
    2826 Fix Rd., Grand Island, NY 14072

JONES, ROBERT W.
    b. Oak Park, Ill., 16 Dec. 1932. Attended Univ. of Redlands, B.M., M.M.; studied with Wayne Bohrnstedt, but is largely self-taught in composition. He has received awards from Chicago Club of Women Organists, 1955; Nat. Assoc. of Coll. Wind and Percussion Instructors, 1958; Episcopal Diocese, Albany, N.Y., 1968, and Southwestern Virginia, 1969; Premio Valle D'Aosta, Italy, 1969; Ford Found. grants, 1965, 1969; MacDowell fellowship, 1973; many commissions. He was resident composer, West Hartford, Conn., public schools, 1965-69; from 1969, on faculty, Schoolcraft Coll., Livonia, Mich.
    WORKS: THEATRE: music for The governess, 1962; Murder in the cathedral, 1964; ORCHESTRA: The juggler, 1959; Serenade, string orch., 1968; A song for strings, 1968; Fiddlers 3, 3 solo violins and orch., 1971; CHAMBER MUSIC: trombone sonatina, 1960; sonata for cello quartet, 1968; Penillion pen rhaw, chamber group, tape, 1968; clarinet sonatina, 1970; On the way to freedom, soprano and 4 instruments, 1972; CHORUS: Columbiad, male chorus, audience, string quartet, organ, 1966; I am the door, with speakers, soloists, organ, 1967; An orison for our time, with band, 1968; Missa media, on the collapse of advertising communication, with soprano solo, speakers, up to 15 Renaissance instruments, 1970; Days of thy youth, 1971; Revelations, 2 choirs, speakers, brass, percussion, 2 organs, tape, 1971; Pilgrimage, lyric drama on the story of Moses and the exodus, chorus and chamber ensemble, Detroit, 15 May 1976; many other choral works, band pieces, and organ pieces. He is also the author of magazine articles on music.
    Schoolcraft College, 18600 Haggerty Rd., Livonia, MI 48152

JONES, ROGER PARKS
    b. Coral Gables, Fla., 7 Aug. 1944. Studied with Alfred Reed and Clifton Williams, Univ. of Miami. He was composer-in-residence and coordinator, Kansas Cooperative Composers Project, Emporia, 1971-74; from 1974, faculty member, Northeast Louisiana Univ.
    WORKS: BAND: Symphony for band; Symphonic variations; The faces of Janus, with chorus; CHAMBER MUSIC: Design #2, solo clarinet; 21 distinctive duets for tubas; CHORUS: I'm nobody; Sea fever.
    110 Duncan Circle, West Monroe, LA 71291

JONES, SAMUEL

JONES, SAMUEL
b. Inverness, Miss., 2 June 1935. Studied with
Howard Hanson, Bernard Rogers, and Wayne Barlow,
Eastman School of Music; conducting with Richard
Lert. His honors include the Tribbett award;
Woodrow Wilson fellowship; and commissions. He
was conductor, Alma Symphony, 1960-62; musical
director, Saginaw Symphony and composer-in-
residence, Delta Coll., 1962-65; conductor,
Rochester Philharmonic, 1965-72; from 1973, dean,
Shepherd School of Music, Rice Univ.
WORKS: ORCHESTRA: Elegy for strings; Festival fanfare; Fugue and finale on a theme of
Dan Emmett; In retrospect; Let us now praise
famous men; Meditation and scherzo; Overture for
a city; symphony #1; BAND: Contours of time,
with chorus, text by Norman Lowrey; CHAMBER MUSIC:
piano sonata #2; sonata for unaccompanied viola;
Spaces, solo cello and narrator, text by Lowrey;
4 haiku for Americans, mezzo-soprano and piano,
text by John Stone.
1101 Milford St., Houston, TX 77006

JONES, STEPHEN OSCAR
b. New York, N.Y., 12 July 1880; d. Studied at
the New York German Cons. He was arranger for
Broadway musicals.
WORKS: ORCHESTRA: Rondo a la breve; Rondo
appassionato; Alaska overture; Serenade and
valse; Top brass; CHAMBER MUSIC: string quartet; String sonata; CHORUS: Evensong, male
voices; and songs.

JONES, WENDAL S.
b. Erie, Colo., 7 Aug. 1932. Studied at Univ.
of Northern Colorado, B.A., M.A.; with Philip
Bezanson, Richard Hervig, and Charles Garland,
Univ. of Iowa, Ph.D. His awards include first
prize, Nat. Assoc. of Coll. Wind and Percussion
Instructors contest; Rockefeller grant; and commissions. He was faculty member, Univ. of
Arizona, 1961-67; then at Eastern Washington
State Coll.; also bassoonist, Spokane Symph.
WORKS: ORCHESTRA: Overture; The kid's new
bag; CHAMBER MUSIC: 3 fantasies, horn and
piano; woodwind quintet; 3 diverse songs, tenor
and woodwind quintet; violin sonata, 1978.
624 W. 5th St., Cheney, WA 99004

JORDAHL, ROBERT A.
b. Ottumwa, Iowa, 19 Sept. 1926. Studied with
Kent Kennan, Univ. of Texas; with Wayne Barlow,
Eastman School of Music, D.M.A. He received
commissions from the Alaska Centennial Committee
and the Anchorage Archdiocese. He was faculty
member, Keuka Coll., 1962-65; Alaska Methodist
Univ., 1965-68; from 1968, at McNeese State
Univ.
WORKS: BALLET: The prospector, 1967;
Evangeline, 1976; CHAMBER MUSIC: Lyric serenade,
oboe and piano; Diptych, bassoon and piano;
CHORUS: The temple, cantata with soloists,
brass, and organ; Mass for the Holy Family; 3
prayer anthems, children's choir and organ;
Where shall my wondering soul begin?; Sweet
hymns and songs, a cappella anthem; ORGAN:
festive prelude on O for a thousand tongues.
4706 Ponderosa Rd., Lake Charles, LA 70601

JORDAN, ALICE (Mrs. Frank B.)
b. Davenport, Iowa, 31 Dec. 1916. Studied with
Francis J. Pyle, Drake Univ., B.M.E. Her awards
include first place, Mu Phi Epsilon song contest, 1954; first place, Composers' Press contest, 1959; Contemporary Music award, Choristers
Guild, 1959; Alumni Distinguished Service award,
Drake Univ., 1970.
WORKS: CHORUS: The beatitudes; God who
touchest Earth with beauty; Prayer is the soul's
sincere desire; Late have I loved thee; Only a
manger; All things are thine; numerous published
choral works and organ pieces.
4106 Ovid Ave., Des Moines, IA 50310

JORDAN, PAUL
b. New York, N.Y., 12 Mar. 1939. Studied with
Emil Platen, Bonn, Germany; at Harvard Coll.;
Columbia Univ.; with Kurt Hessenberg, State High
School for Music, Frankfurt, Germany, degree in
sacred music; with Mel Powell, Yale Univ.;
privately with Tui St. George Tucker in New
York; private study in piano, organ, oboe, recorder, conducting. He has been music director,
United Church on the Green, New Haven, from
1964; faculty member, State Univ. of New York,
Binghamton, from 1973; has made frequent tours
as organist in the U.S. and Europe.
WORKS: CHAMBER MUSIC: sonata for alto recorder and oboe, 1957; Fantasia on the Passion
Chorale, flute, bass clarinet, cello, 1960; O,
piece for 21 solo instruments, 1972; trio for
oboe, viola, piano, 1973; Variations, piano, 4
hands; CHORUS: Why hidest thou thy face?, boy
sopranos, male voices, 3 winds, organ, timpani,
1973; Cantata for Christmas; ORGAN: Chorale
prelude, 1962; To Martin Luther King, April 5,
1968; Cry to a lost spirit, 1970, version for
trumpet and 5 woodwinds, 1972; Vater unser, 1971.
81 Main St., Binghamton, NY 13905

JORDAN, ROLAND
b. Galveston, Tex., 15 Sept. 1938. Studied
with Clifton Williams and Kent Kennan, Univ. of
Texas, Austin; with Merrills Lewis and David
Reck, Univ. of Houston; with George Rochberg,
Univ. of Pennsylvania; and Robert Wykes, Washington Univ. His awards include a Brittenham
Found. grant, 1961; Bennington fellowship, 1971;
and commissions. He was faculty member, Wilmington Music School (Del.), 1961-66; Auburn
Univ., Auburn, Ala., 1966-68; and from 1970, at
Washington Univ.
WORKS: ORCHESTRA: 3 minor statements; What
we did on our summer vacation, 1971; WIND EN-
SEMBLE: Interpolations, with tape, 1963; Tangents I; CHAMBER MUSIC: 3 spacial studies, 4
winds, piano, percussion; First construction,
percussion; 3 movements for solo trombone; Four/
1964, set of piano pieces; Songs and games, woodwind trio; Tangents II, chamber group, tape,
1971; CHORUS: Time's space (Encounters), with
tape.
1055 Jackson St., St. Louis, MO 63130

JOSEPH, DON VERNE
b. Elk City, Okla., 8 June 1926. Studied with
Charles Hoag, Frank Hughes, Thomas Matthews,

Univ. of Oklahoma; with Everett Gates, Oklahoma City Univ. He has been composer-arranger for Orange Bowl shows, Sugar Bowl shows, and others; and has received commissions. He has been faculty member, Cameron State Coll.; Jefferson City Jr. Coll.; from 1970, Drury Coll.; and dean, Stan Kenton Summer Jazz Orchestra-in-Residence Workshops.

WORKS: ORCHESTRA: symphony; suite of American Indian dances; BAND: symphony; Dissertation; CHAMBER MUSIC: string quartet; brass quartet; JAZZ ENSEMBLE: suite for trumpet; Jazz waltz-Shish-ka-Bach; Blues; Sunday go-to-meetin' time. He is author of articles in music journals and has been jazz editor, School Musician Magazine, since 1963.

Drury College, Springfield, MO 65802

JOSEPH, WARREN
b. Ossining, N.Y., 8 Feb. 1924. Studied at State Univ. of New York, Potsdam, B.S., M.S.; with Hugo Norden and Julius Herford, Boston Univ., Ph.D. He was faculty member, Univ. of Southern Mississippi, 1959-61; Bowling Green State Univ., 1961-63; Eastern Michigan Univ., 1963-65; from 1965, Southern Illinois Univ. at Edwardsville.

WORKS: THEATRE: Who's the boss, musical comedy; CHORUS: Benedictus es; Psalm 100; Magnificat.

1605 Biscay Dr., Godfrey, IL 62035

JOSTEN, WERNER
b. Elberfeld, Germany, 12 June 1885; to U.S. 1920; d. New York, N.Y., 6 Feb. 1963. Studied in Munich and Paris. His honors include an honorary D.M. from Colby Coll., and Juilliard publication awards. On coming to the U.S., he was accompanist to singers in New York; was professor at Smith Coll., 1923-49; conducted joint Amherst-Smith orchestra; directed Northampton opera festival; was guest conductor at Lewisohn Stadium, New York.

WORKS: BALLET: Batouala, 1931; Joseph and his brethren, 1932, produced at Juilliard School, 9 Mar. 1936; ORCHESTRA: Concerto sacro I-II, string orch. and piano, 1925; Jungle, 1929; Endymion suite, 1933; symphony in F, 1936; Canzona seria, 1940; CHAMBER MUSIC: string quartet, 1934; violin sonata, 1936; piano sonata, 1937; cello sonata, 1938; violin sonatina, 1939; woodwind trio, 1941; string trio, 1942; trio for flute, cello, piano, 1943; horn sonata, 1944; also choral works, works for voice and orch., songs.

JOUARD, PAUL E.
b. Mt. Vernon, N.Y., 28 May 1928. Studied at Yale Univ., B.M., M.M.; with Percy Grainger and Clarence Adler at Juilliard School. He is concert pianist; was conductor, Lake Placid Orch., from 1949.

WORKS: PIANO: Prelude and fugue; Modal variations on a French air; Sonata romantica; Playland suite.

JULIAN, JOSEPH
b. Los Angeles, Calif., 22 Jan. 1948. Studied at Univ. of California, Los Angeles; with Robert Erickson, Kenneth Gaburo, and Roger Reynolds, Univ. of California, San Diego. He received a composition award, California State Univ., 1970; Nat. Endowment for the Arts grant, 1975. He was staff member, Experimental Coll. of California State Univ., Northridge, 1970-71; Palomar Coll., 1972-73; Univ. of California, San Diego, 1973-74.

WORKS: ORCHESTRA: Conception, double chorus and orch., 1975; CHAMBER MUSIC: Variations, flute and guitar; Piece for string orchestra; Revelations I, II, III, chamber ensemble; Graphic I, 5 percussionists, 1976; MIXED MEDIA: Synthesis, orch., chorus, live electronics; Wave, flute, percussion, contrabass, tape; Akasha, contrabass and tape; Windows and clouds, percussion and tape; Wave/canon, trumpet and tape, 1976; Between, 8 poems for instruments, dancers, film, and tape.

255 Hill St., Solana Beach, CA 92075

KABAKOV, JOEL
Studied with Roger Sessions, Univ. of California, Berkeley, B.A.; with Aurelio de la Vega, State Univ. of California, Northridge, M.A.; with Leon Kirchner, Seymour Shifrin, and Earl Kim, Harvard Univ., Ph.D. candidate 1973. He was faculty member, Boston Cons., 1974-78. His ballet, Por el viento, was performed by the Boston Symphony, 1973.

KACINSKAS, JERONIMAS
b. Vidukle, Lith., 17 Apr. 1907; U.S. citizen 1954. Studied at the State Cons., Klaipeda; with Alois Haba and Jaroslav Kricka, State Cons. at Prague. He was conductor, City Orchestra and Opera, Klaipeda, 1932-38; State Radio Orchestra, Kaunas, Vilnius, 1939-41; State Opera and Philharmonic, Vilnius, 1941-44; was guest conductor, with many European orchestras; was faculty member, Berklee Coll. of Music, from 1967.

WORKS: OPERA: Black ships; ORCHESTRA: Mystery of redemption; Symphonic fantasy #2; concerto for flute and strings; BAND: Transcendental expressions; CHAMBER MUSIC: septet; woodwind quintet; saxophone quartet; CHORUS: Mass in honorem Immaculati Cordia B.V.M.

16 Thomas Park, South Boston, MA 02127

KADERAVEK, MILAN
b. Oak Park, Ill., 5 Aug. 1924. Studied with Leo Sowerby, American Cons., B.M., M.M.; with Gordon Binkerd, Univ. of Illinois, D.M.A. He received a Tamiment Inst. award of $1,000 and performance of his string quartet, 1956; Albuquerque Civic Symphony award and performance of Sinfonietta, 1960. He has been faculty member, Rizzo School of Music, Chicago, 1950-53; Central Coll., Fayette, Mo., 1953-54; Drake Univ., 1954-60; Univ. of Illinois, Urbana, 1960-65; Chicago, 1965-72; from 1972, Drake Univ.

WORKS: ORCHESTRA: Sinfonietta, 1960; Music for orchestra; Rhapsody, cello and strings, London, England, 5 Aug. 1976; CHAMBER MUSIC: string quartet, 1956; cello sonata; Introduction and allegro, saxophone quartet; 3 short pieces for piano; CHORUS: Once a child, 4 poems of Emily Dickinson set for a cappella chorus, 1976; other published choral works.

5617 Waterbury Circle, Des Moines, IA 50312

KAGEN, SERGIUS

KAGEN, SERGIUS
b. St. Petersburg, Russia, 22 Aug. 1909; to U.S.
1925; d. New York, N.Y., 1 Mar. 1964. Graduated
from Juilliard School, 1930; was later appointed
to the faculty. His works include an opera,
piano pieces, and songs.

KAHLE, DENNIS E.
b. Pittsburgh, Pa., 30 May 1944. Studied with
Joseph Wilcox Jenkins, Duquesne Univ.; with Frank
McCarty and Victor Grauer, Univ. of Pittsburgh,
where he held the Andrew Mellon predoctoral fellowship. He was creative associate, State Univ.
of New York, Buffalo, 1972, and percussion
extra, Buffalo Philharmonic.
WORKS: ORCHESTRA: Emergences flux #1;
CHAMBER MUSIC: The third beat of nothing, instrumental quartet; MIXED MEDIA: Nothing pro-
found; FILM SCORES: She-man; The outdoorsman.

KAHN, ERICH ITOR
b. Rimbach, Germany, 23 July 1905; to U.S. 1941;
d. New York, N.Y., 5 Mar. 1956. Studied in
Frankfurt; toured as accompanist to Pablo
Casals, 1938-39; with Benar Heifetz and Alexander
Schneider, organized the Albeneri Trio in New
York. In 1948 he received the Coolidge Medal
for eminent service to chamber music.
WORKS: ORCHESTRA: Symphonies Bretonnes,
1955; CHAMBER MUSIC: suite for violin and
piano, 1939; string quartet, 1953; 4 nocturnes,
voice and piano, 1954; Actus tragicus, 10 instruments, 1955; PIANO: 8 inventions, 1937;
Ciaconna dei tempi di guerra, 1943; 5 short
piano pieces, 1955.

KALAJIAN, BERGE
b. New York, N.Y., 29 Jan. 1924. Studied composition privately with Josef Schmid, 1950-59;
at Manhattan School of Music, B.M. 1962. He has
been piano technician and tuner from 1951; also
faculty member, extension div., Manhattan School
of Music.
WORKS: CHAMBER MUSIC: flute sonata; woodwind quintet; trio for flute, viola, piano;
suite for piano; string quartet.
3417 Cannon Place., Bronx, NY 10463

KALANZI, BENNY
b. Uganda, 10 Aug. 1938; to U.S. 1970. Studied
musicology, Fribourg Univ., Switz., and at
Cologne Univ., Germany; piano at Zurich Cons.
His awards include first prize, Internat. Folk
Music Contest, Cologne, 1967; Nat. Endowment for
the Arts grant to present East African Bantu
music in New York City public schools, 1976;
CAPS fellowship for composing East African music,
1976-77; ASCAP awards, 1977-78. He was appointed
professor of East African Bantu music at Hunter
Coll., CUNY, 1973; and adjunct assistant professor of African music, Manhattan Community
Coll., 1974. He writes African choral and instrumental music in modern notation for African
harp, bowl-lyre, fiddle, bamboo-flute, piano;
and has published The mysteries of African
music, which is used as a textbook in New York
City schools. East African-American pop music
contains origianl East African songs, 1976.

P.O. Box 1971, Grand Central Station, New
York, NY 10017

KALMANOFF, MARTIN
b. Brooklyn, N.Y., 24 May 1920. Studied with
Walter Piston, Harvard Univ., B.A., M.A. His
awards include first prize, Robert Merrill Con-
test for best opera; second prize, Harvey Gaul
Opera Contest; Richard Rodgers grant; N.Y. State
Council on the Arts grant, 1978. He has been
head of Operation Opera from 1950.
WORKS: OPERA: The insect comedy, 3 acts,
based on Capek's antiwar play; The bald prima
donna, 1 act, Ionesco libretto; Opera, opera,
1 act, Saroyan libretto; The great stone face;
Photograph-1920, libretto by Gertrude Stein;
The harmfulness of tobacco, 1 act, based on
Chekhov play, New York, 22 Mar. 1979; MUSICALS:
No bed of roses; This week, East Lynne; Green
mansions; The mating machine; Maestro; The fourposter; 8 children's musicals; CHORUS: George
Washington comes to dinner, setting of Washington's Treatise on etiquette, New York, 12 Feb.
1978; To music; Song of peace; Under the wide
and starry sky; 23rd Psalm; Kaddish for a war-
ring world, with soloists and orch., Toronto,
1972; The way of life, cantata for voice and 11
instruments, New York, 26 Feb. 1978.
392 Central Park W., New York, NY 10025

KALVE, MARTIN
b. Plattsburgh, N.Y., 12 Mar. 1951. Studied
with Julius Eastman, Lejaren Hiller, William
Kothe, Jan Williams, State Univ. of New York,
Buffalo; with David Tudor, Stony Point, N.Y. He
received a Nat. Endowment for the Arts grant,
1978-79; was founding member, Composers Inside
Electronics, 1976; musician with Merce Cunningham
Dance Company, 1978-.
WORKS: ELECTRONIC: Et puis . . . et
puis . . . est-ce que je puis, an electroacoustic installation responsive to audience
participation, Chocorua, N.H., Festival, July
1973; Thunder in the back seat, live electronic
performance, Buffalo, June 1977; Eyelets,
Buffalo, May 1978; Earthing, The Kitchen, New
York, Sept. 1978.
Gate Hill Rd., Stony Point, NY 10980

KAM, DENNIS
b. Honolulu, Hawaii, 8 May 1942. Studied with
Cesar Bresgan, Salzburg, 1962-63; with Joseph
Wood, Oberlin Coll. Cons., B.M. 1964; with
Yoshiro Irino in Tokyo, 1965; with Ernst Krenek
and Armand Russell, Univ. of Hawaii, M.F.A.
1966; and with Salvatore Martirano, Univ. of
Illinois, D.M.A. 1974. His awards include BMI
awards, 1963, 1976; Phi Mu Alpha Sinfonia com-
position award; professional award, Univ. of
Hawaii, 1966; Creative and Performing Arts
fellowship, Univ. of Illinois, 1966-68; Ford
Found.-MENC grant, 1970. He taught at Univ. of
Illinois, 1968-70; was composer-in-residence,
Honolulu and State of Hawaii, 1970-72; director,
New Music Ensemble, 1971-72; faculty member,
Univ. of Miami, from 1975.
WORKS: ORCHESTRA: Interplay, chamber orch.
and 2 ensembles, 1966; Blue maroon I, 1969;

Ditto varianti, 1973; CHAMBER MUSIC: trombone sonata, 1962; Sections, chamber orch., 1963; Ensemble II, voice and 4 instruments, 1965; string quartet, 1966; Rendezvous II, bass trombone and piano, 1967; Go, trombone, clarinet, cello, 1971; Strata-spheres, 8 flutes, or 3 double basses, or 4 sopranos and piano, or 2 pianos, 8 hands, or any combination of the above, 1972; other chamber works and choral pieces.

School of Music, Univ. of Miami, P.O. Box 248165, Coral Gables, FL 33124

KAMIEN, ANNA
b. New York, N.Y., 29 Jan. 1912. Studied at Ecole Normale de Musique, Paris, 1930-35; piano with Alfred Cortot, counterpoint with Nadia Boulanger. She was choral conductor, 1944-72.
WORKS: OPERA: Ruth; ORCHESTRA: Chinese odes, suite for chorus and orch.; CHAMBER MUSIC: violin sonatina; string quartet; piano quintet; Chinese odes, flute, oboe, 2 violins, viola, piano; Memories, mezzo-soprano and piano.

185 West End Ave., New York, NY 10023

KAMIN, FRANZ
b. Milwaukee, Wis., 25 May 1931. Studied with Charles Hoag and Leonard Klein, Oklahoma Univ.; with Roque Cordero, Iannis Xenakis, and Bernhard Heiden, Indiana Univ., B.M. 1968. He has been director of FIASCO, performance group, from 1966; and music editor, Station Hill Press, from 1977.
WORKS: CHAMBER MUSIC: Buffalo Bill's, soprano and piano, 1962; Patchen triptych, narrators, vocal soloists, chamber groups, 1964; Screw piece, soprano, baritone, chamber ensemble, 1967; Aleatoric Systemic Reactory Bulletin 1 (ASRB #1), bass and soprano narrators, violin, cello, piano, slide whistle, conch, household utensils, trash, 1967; ASRB #4 (Gallery piece), chamber group; MULTIMEDIA: ASRB #5 (miniature opera: The latter days of Janet Quubyne), 1971; Witness, nude ballet, 1972; Behavioral drift II, 23 performers in 4 ensembles.

10 Leonard St., New York, NY 10013

KANITZ, ERNEST
b. Vienna, Austria, 9 Apr. 1894; U.S. citizen 1944; d. Menlo Park, Calif., 7 Apr. 1978. Studied privately with Richard Neuberger, 1912-14; Franz Schreker, 1914-20. His awards include a Marion Bauer performance award for Sonata breve, 1952; annual ASCAP awards, 1963-/3; He was faculty member, New Vienna Cons., 1922-28; Winthrop Coll., S.C., 1938-41; Erskine Coll., 1941-44; professor, Univ. of Southern California, 1945 to retirement in 1959, guest professor, 1960-61; professor, Marymount Coll., Palos Verdes, 1961-64. All his works and music library have been donated to the Univ. of Southern California, which has established a memorial fund in his honor to assist young composers.
WORKS: OPERA: Kumana, 1953; Royal auction, 1958; Room No. 12, 1958; The lucky dollar, 1959; Perpetual, Los Angeles, 26 Apr. 1961; ORCHESTRA: Motion picture, 3 phantasies; concerto grosso, Vienna Internat. Festival, 1947; Concert piece, trumpet and orch., 1951; Intermezzo concertante, alto saxophone and wind orch., 1953; concerto

for chamber orch., 1957; bassoon concerto, San Francisco, 8 Apr. 1964; Sinfonia seria, St. Louis, 17 Oct. 1964; symphony #2, 1965; Sinfonia concertante, solo violin and cello and orch.; CHAMBER MUSIC: sonata for violin and cello, 1947; suite for violin and piano; Divertimento, viola and cello, 1949; duo for violin and viola; Notturno, flute, violin, viola, 1950; violin sonata #2; string quartet; string trio, 1951; Sonata breve, violin, cello, piano, 1952; Sonata Californiana, alto saxophone and piano, 1952; Quintettino, 4 winds and piano; sonata for cello alone, 1956; viola sonatina, 1958; Concertino for 5 players, clarinet, string trio, piano; suite for brass quintet, 1960; bassoon sonata; Little concerto, unaccompanied saxophone, Chicago, 15 Dec. 1970; Sinfonietta da camera, violin, 2 saxophones, piano, celesta, percussion, Los Angeles, 10 Mar. 1973; CHORUS: Cantata 1961, with 2 pianos, 1961; Visions at twilight, women's voices in unison, flute, string quintet, piano, Los Angeles, Apr. 1964.

KANNER, JEROME HERBERT
b. New York, N.Y., 17 Nov. 1903. Made his debut as violinist in New York at age 8; later studied with Franz Kneisel, Paul Stoeving, Leopold Auer, compostion with Edward Kilenyi; attended Columbia Univ., B.A., B.S.; New York School of Music and Art, M.A.; London Lyceum, M.M. summa cum laude. His awards include the Prix de Rome; Gold Medal of Rome; Purcell award; honorary doctorates from Bern Inst., Kenyon Coll., and Boston Coll. He was concertmaster, NBC Symphony and Victor Recording Orch.; made concert tours of the U.S. and Europe for 10 years; then devoted his time to composing for radio and films and to activities in music publishing and recording.
WORKS: ORCHESTRA: 2 symphonies; The Rubiayat, symphonic poem; Homage to Debussy; Tribute to Kreisler; CHAMBER MUSIC: string quartet; Minute at the spinet; choral works and songs.

KANTOR, JOSEPH
b. New York, N.Y., 22 Nov. 1930. Studied with Karol Rathaus, Queens Coll., B.A. 1954; with Otto Luening, Columbia Univ., M.A. 1956. His awards include Phi Mu Alpha Sinfonia prize, 1955; scholarship to Bennington Composers Conf., 1959; Celia Buck award, 1967. He has been organist-choirmaster, Temple Beth Am, Los Angeles, from 1972; organist, Olivet Lutheran Church, Inglewood, from 1977.
WORKS: ORCHESTRA: Essay for orchestra, 1976; CHAMBER MUSIC: Woodwind serenade, 1955; Dialogue, flute and piano; woodwind quintet, 1967; 3 piano sonatas; 2 string quartets; trio sonata, flute, oboe, piano; CHORUS: By the rivers of Babylon; Psalm 121; Entreat me not to leave thee, women's voices; Come ye to the Lord; SOLO VOICE: Psalm 23, soprano and orch.; Playthings of the wind, voice and chamber ensemble, after Sandberg, 1967; Night music, alto voice and flute, 1975; The love song of J. Alfred Prufrock, medium voice and piano, 1976.

2668 Butler Ave., Los Angeles, CA 90064

KANWISCHER, ALFRED OSWALD
b. Rochester, N.Y., 29 Nov. 1932. Studied with
James Niblock and H. Owen Reed, Michigan State
Univ.; with Darius Milhaud, Mills Coll. and
Aspen, Colo.; piano with Egon Petri, Oakland,
Calif., and Bela Nagy, Boston Univ., D.M.A. He
won Young Artists Auditions, San Francisco, and
made his debut as pianist with the San Francisco
Symphony; has toured the U.S. and Europe as solo
pianist and as duo pianist with his wife, Heidi.
He taught piano at Boston Univ., 1965-72; joined
the faculty at George Peabody Coll., 1977.
WORKS: ORCHESTRA: 3 pieces for orch.;
CHAMBER MUSIC: 3 pieces for woodwind quintet;
PIANO: 2 1-movement sonatas; Duet for one performer; 5 impressions; Episodes for 4 hands; 3
pieces for 2 pianos; Piece for 2 pianists and
percussion; also songs.
George Peabody College for Teachers, Nashville, TN 37203

KAPER, BRONISLAW
b. Warsaw, Poland, 5 Feb. 1902; to U.S. in
1930s. Studied at Univ. and Cons. of Warsaw.
On coming to the U.S., he settled in Hollywood
as a film composer.
WORKS: FILM SCORES: San Francisco; Gas-
light; Our vines have tender grapes; The
stranger; Mrs. Parkington; Lili; Green mansions;
Butterfield 8; Mutiny on the Bounty; The
brothers Karamozov; A day at the races; many
songs.
616 N. Bedford Dr., Beverly Hills, CA 90210

KAPLAN, ROBERT BARNETT
b. Brookline, Mass., 26 July 1924. Studied
piano at New England Cons., privately with Jules
Wolffers; held a scholarship in composition with
Willson Osborne, Settlement Music School, Philadelphia. He was music director, Salon of Allied
Arts, 1948-52; has been private teacher of
piano and composition from 1938; also piano
recitalist; founded South Shore Philharmonic
Orch., 1979.
WORKS: ORCHESTRA: violin concerto, 1976;
CHAMBER MUSIC: Tempo di ballo, piano, 1939;
5 Luna seas, cello and piano, 1951; piano sonatina, 1954; piano sonata, 1955; Andante con
variazioni, piano, 4 hands, 1969; Trio concertante, piano trio, 1972; Notturno for flute,
1973; Duo da camera, viola and piano, 1974;
string quartet, 1975; Impromptu, piano, 1977;
Fantasy variations, piano, 1978.
196 Old Ocean St., Marshfield, MA 02050

KARCHIN, LOUIS S.
b. Philadelphia, Pa., 9 Aug. 1951. Studied
with Joseph Castaldo, Philadelphia Musical Acad.;
with Samuel Adler and Joseph Schwantner, Eastman
School of Music, B.M. 1972; with Gunther
Schuller and Bruno Maderna at Tanglewood; with
Earl Kim, Harvard Univ. His awards include a
tie for the Koussevitzky prize, 1971; Nat. Fed.
of Music Clubs prize, 1972; Columbia Univ.
Bearns prize, 1972; Bernard Rogers award, 1972;
McCurdy composition award, 1973. He was appointed to the New York Univ. faculty in 1980.
WORKS: CHAMBER MUSIC: Pentamorphos, piano

and tape; trio for flute, cello, piano; Fantasy
I, violin or viola; Fantasy II, piano, 1973,
Washington, D.C., 14 Sept. 1978; CHORUS: May
the words of my mouth, a cappella.
New York Univ., 268 Waverly Bldg., New York,
NY 10003

KARLIN, FREDERICK JAMES
b. Chicago, Ill., 16 June 1936. Studied at
Amherst Coll.; privately with John Becker,
William Russo, Rayburn Wright, and Tibor Serly.
He has composed and arranged for Benny Goodman,
Harry James, and others.
WORKS: CHAMBER MUSIC: string quartet;
Music for percussion trio; Re: percussion.

KARLINS, M. WILLIAM
b. New York, N.Y., 25 Feb. 1932. Studied with
Vittorio Giannini, Manhattan School of Music,
B.M., M.M.; with Philip Bezanson and Richard
Hervig, Univ. of Iowa, Ph.D.; privately with
Frederick Piket, Stefan Wolpe, and Gunther
Schuller. His awards include scholarships to
Bennington Conf., 1959, 1961; Princeton Seminar,
1960; a Composers' Forum Program, 1963; first
prize, Nat. Concert Saxophone Contest, 1967. He
was faculty member, Western Illinois Univ.,
1965-67; from 1967, at Northwestern Univ.
WORKS: ORCHESTRA: Concert music #I, 1959,
#II, chorus and orch., 1960; #III, winds, piano,
percussion, 1964. #4, 1964, #5, Chicago, 20 Dec.
1973; WIND ENSEMBLE: Lamentations--In memoriam,
flutes, brass, harp, percussion, organ, speaker,
1968; Passacaglia and rounds, band, 1970;
Reflux, concerto for double bass and winds,
1972; CHAMBER MUSIC: 2 concerti grossi, 1959,
1961; 3 piano sonatas, 1959, 1962, 1965; string
quartet, 1960; trio for flute, violin, cello,
1960; Outgrowths--variations, piano, 1961;
Fantasy and passacaglia, flute, viola, bassoon,
double bass, 1961; Little piece, 4 double basses,
1962; 4 inventions and a fugue, bassoon, piano,
female voice (opt.), 1962; Birthday music #1,
1962, #2, 1963; string trio, 1963; Variations,
clarinet and string trio, 1963; Obiter dictum,
organ, 1964; Variations on Obiter dictum, cello,
piano, percussion, 1965; Music for oboe, bass
clarinet, piano, 1966; Music for cello alone,
#1, 1966, #2, 1967; Variations and outgrowths,
bassoon and piano, 1967; saxophone quartet, #1,
1967, #2, Chicago, 31 May 1976; Music for English
horn and piano, 1968; Music for tenor saxophone
and piano, 1969; Graphic mobile for any 3 or
multiple of 3 instruments, 1969; woodwind quartet, 1970; quintet for alto saxophone and string
quartet, 1973-74; 4 etudes, double bass and
tape or 3 double basses, 1974; Fantasia on my
mother's name, solo flute; . . . and all the
world is dew, woodwind quintet, Macomb, Ill.,
18 Oct. 1978.
1809 Sunnyside Circle, Northbrook, IL 60062

KARRICK, CECIL
b. Irvine, Ky., 1919. Studied at Eastern State
Coll., B.S. 1939; with Gordon Kinney and Kenneth
Wright, Univ. of Kentucky, M.A. 1951; at
Louisiana State Univ.; Western State Coll.; with
Felix Labunski, Cincinnati Coll. of Music. He

was arranger for air force bands, 1942–46; from 1957, has been band director, Bowling Green High School.

WORKS: ORCHESTRA: Laurel land, 1949; Pastorale, 1951; 2 symphonies, 1956, 1957; Piece for orchestra, 1961; BAND: Shake, shake, shake, 1953; 2 hymns, 1955; Hoskins parade march, 1959; Bradley band day, 1962; other works for band and small wind ensembles.

Bowling Green High School, Bowling Green, KY 42101

KARVONEN, PAUL E.
b. Mass, Mich., 6 Oct. 1917. Studied at Suomi Coll.; with Donald Ferguson, Univ. of Minnesota; Quincy Porter, Univ. of Michigan; Philip Greeley Clapp and Philip Bezanson, Univ. of Iowa. He held faculty posts at Univ. of North Dakota, 1945–48; Gustavus Adolphus Coll., 1948–52; Lutheran Mission, Tanganyika, 1953–57; Sul Ross State Univ., 1960–62; Carthage Coll., 1962–64; Mankato State Univ., 1964–76, becoming professor emeritus in 1976.

WORKS: ORCHESTRA: Prairie festival overture; Concert overture; Cripple Creek, string orch.; BAND: Catalan Christmas suite; Allegro, adagio, and finale; CHAMBER MUSIC: string quartet; The little black boy, soprano, clarinet, string quartet; CHORUS: The temple of holiness; Rejoice, all ye believers; Light of the anxious heart; and many organ pieces.

P.O. Box 93, Mankato, MN 56001

KASINSKAS, JOSEPH ANTHONY
b. Derby, Conn., 31 Jan. 1946. Studied at Danbury Coll.; with Cecil Effinger, Philip Batstone, Charles Eakin, and Richard Toensing, Univ. of Colorado, D.M.A. 1976. His awards include an honorarium, Denver Symph., 1972; Honors Concert performance, Univ. of Colorado, 1974. He has been free-lance composer from 1971; instructor, Univ. of Colorado, 1973–76; Metropolitan State Coll., 1976–78.

WORKS: ORCHESTRA: Dream track, with tape, 1972; Archipelago, 1974; BAND: Leviathan, 1977; CHAMBER MUSIC: Corridors, 3 sopranos, 1977; Phoenix wind, clarinet and tape, 1978; MIXED MEDIA: Images, 5 dancers, soprano, guitar, tape/live electronics, 1976; and film scores.

2655 W. 35th Ave., Denver, CO 80211

KASSERN, TADEUZ ZYGFRIED
b. Lwow, Poland, 19 Mar. 1904; to U.S. 1945; d. New York, N.Y., 2 May 1957. He was cultural attache at the Polish Consulate, New York, 1945; defected from the Polish government and applied for U.S. citizenship. Though citizenship was denied, he remained in the U.S.

WORKS: OPERA: The anointed, 1951; Sun-up, 1952; ORCHESTRA: concertino for flute and string orch., xylophone, celesta, 1948; Teen-age concerto, piano and orch., 1956; choral works, chamber music, piano pieces, songs.

KASSLER, MICHAEL
b. New York, N.Y., 8 Apr. 1941. Studied with Henry Cowell, Peabody Cons.; Gian-Carlo Menotti, Bohuslav Martinu, Vittorio Giannini, Curtis

Inst. of Music; Charles Jones and Darius Milhaud, Aspen School; Irving Fine, Aaron Copland, Tanglewood; Walter Piston, Harvard Univ.; Roger Sessions and Milton Babbitt, Princeton Univ. His awards include BMI student awards, 1956, 1957; Bohemian Club prize in composition. He has been lecturer at universities in the U.S. and Europe; author of articles in music journals; contributor to Grove's Dictionary; and is professionally employed as data processor.

WORKS: CHAMBER MUSIC: 4 string quartets; duo for violins; Passacaglia, piano; 2 violin sonatas; VOCAL: Sea poems, chorus, chamber orch.; Songs of the Civil War, soprano and orch.

KASTLE, LEONARD
b. New York, N.Y., 11 Feb. 1929. Studied with Rosario Scalero and Gian-Carlo Menotti, Curtis Inst. of Music, graduated in 1950; also piano with Isabelle Vengerova, conducting with Carl Bamberger. He received a Nat. Endowment for the Arts grant, 1974.

WORKS: OPERA: The swing, NBC television network, 11 June 1956; Deseret, NBC network, 1 Jan. 1961; The pariahs, an opera on early whaling in the U.S., commissioned by the Seattle Opera Assoc., for 1976; CHORUS: Whale songs from Moby Dick, received Barter prize; Whispers of heavenly death, 1956; PIANO: sonata, 1950.

New Lebanon Center, NY 12126

KATWIJK, PAUL VAN
b. Rotterdam, Holland, 7 Dec. 1885; U.S. citizen 1921; d. Dallas, Tex., 11 Dec. 1974. Studied at Royal Cons., The Hague; with William Klatte in Berlin; piano with Leopold Godowsky in Vienna. His awards included the Sigma Alpha Iota Service to Music award, 1959; Texas Fed. of Music Clubs award; DAR Medal; Concert Gebeouw Orch., Amsterdam, Certificate of Merit, 1961. He taught at Christian Coll., Mo., 1912–13; Columbia Music School, Chicago, 1913–14; Drake Univ., 1914–18; Southern Methodist Univ., from 1918 to retirement in 1955. He conducted the Dallas Civic Opera, 1922–25; Dallas Symph. Orch., 1925–37; also the Kosloff Ballet at Hollywood Bowl and in Dallas.

WORKS: ORCHESTRA: Hollandia suite, Dallas, 15 Mar. 1931; several symphonies; SONGS: Row gently here; Hey, the dusty miller; My only love; Heart, be still and listen; PIANO: Barcarolle; Kermesse; many other works.

KATWIJK, VIOLA EDNA BECK VAN (Mrs. Paul)
b. Denison, Tex., 26 Feb. 1894. Studied piano in Berlin; piano and composition with Percy Grainger; also coached with Paul van Katwijk. Her awards include 2 first prizes, Mu Phi Epsilon contests, 1928, 1930; and 2 first-place awards, San Antonio Club piano composition contests. She made her piano debut with the St. Louis Symph. in Dallas; was on piano faculty, Southern Methodist Univ., 1922–55.

WORKS: SONGS: Winter Valley, 1928; My terrace, 1930; PIANO: The jester; Gamelan; Dusk on a Texas prairie; many other works for piano and voice.

4610 Wildwood Rd., Dallas, TX 75209

KATZ, ERICH

KATZ, ERICH
b. Posen, Germany, 31 July 1900; U.S. citizen
1949; d. Santa Barbara, Calif., 30 July 1973.
Studied in Berlin and at Freisburg Univ., Ph.D.;
won the internat. composition prize, Zurich,
1937. He was professor, New York Coll. of
Music, 1945-59; then taught privately in Santa
Barbara; was music director, American Recorder
Society.
WORKS: CHAMBER MUSIC: Toy concerto, 3 recorders, keyboard instrument, percussion; 6 inventions, piano; 6 cantus firmus settings, 3
recorders, voice ad lib.; The eternal day,
mezzo-soprano and recorders; Toccata, 4 recorders; other works, mostly for recorders.

KATZ, FREDERICK
b. Brooklyn, N.Y., 25 Feb. 1919. Was music
director for 7th Army Headquarters, for Lena
Horne, and others; on staff of Decca Records;
cellist with Chico Hamilton Quintet, 1955-56;
has composed for films and television.
WORKS: ORCHESTRA: cello concerto, 1961;
CHAMBER MUSIC: viola sonata; Adagio, string
quartet; Lord Randall, quintet; Blues for
Piatigorsky, cello and piano; violin and cello
duet; CHORUS: Madrigal, with cello; songs.

KAUDER, HUGO
b. Tobitschau, Moravia, 9 June 1888; U.S. citizen
1944; d. New York, N.Y., 22 July 1972. Studied
violin at an early age, but was entirely self-
taught in composition. He received the Prize of
the City of Vienna for symphony #1, 1928; Fromm
Found. award, 1953. He wrote a book on harmony
and one on counterpoint, and essays on musical
events from 1920 to 1950.
WORKS: THEATRE: In search of a dream,
music for a Chinese drama; ORCHESTRA: 5 symphonies; 9 concerti; 3 shorter works; CHAMBER
MUSIC: quartet for oboe, clarinet, horn,
bassoon, 1949; 19 string quartets; trio for
violin, horn, piano, 1954; English horn sonata,
1970; numerous works for various small ensembles
and solo instruments; choruses; songs.

KAUFMANN, WALTER
b. Carlsbad, Czech., 1 Apr. 1907; U.S. citizen
1964. Studied in Berlin and at Univ. of Prague;
was director, Bombay Radio, 1935-46; taught at
Halifax (N.S.) Cons., 1947-48; conducted
Winnipeg Symphony, 1948-57; from 1957, has been
professor, Indiana Univ.
WORKS: OPERA: 7 operas, 1934-66; ORCHESTRA:
6 symphonies, 1930-56; Madras Express, fantasy
for orch., 1948; piano concerto, 1950; Rubaiyat,
voice and orch., 1952; WIND ENSEMBLE: Passacaglia and capriccio for brass; CHAMBER MUSIC:
2 piano trios; 2 string trios; 7 string quartets;
wind quintet; piano pieces; songs.
School of Music, Indiana Univ., Bloomington,
IN 47401

KAVANAUGH, PATRICK
b. Nashville, Tenn., 20 Oct. 1954. Studied
with Conrad Bernier, William Bland, George T.
Jones, Steven Strunk, and Lloyd Geisler, Catholic Univ., B.A. cum laude 1974; awarded a full

fellowship for graduate work at Univ. of
Maryland. From 1977 he has been director of
music theory, D.C. Youth Orchestra Program;
from 1978, conductor and director, Univ. of
Maryland, 20th-Century Ensemble.
WORKS: OPERA: Jack in the beanstalk,
Washington, 29 Nov. 1974; ORCHESTRA: Prelude to
the last letter of John Keats, with chorus and
narrator; WIND ENSEMBLE: Symphonic parade;
CHAMBER MUSIC: Jubal, soprano and percussion;
The beatitudes, soprano, alto, cello; Homage to
C. S. Lewis, woodwind quintet and alto saxophone; Debussy variations 1-14, solo instruments; Music of the spheres, woodwind quintet
and trombone; string quartet; violin quartet;
viola quartet; cello quartet; bass quartet; The
art of the maze, percussion and electronics.
7415 Birch Ave., Takoma Park, MD 20012

KAVASCH, DEBORAH
b. Washington, D.C., 15 July 1949. Studied
with Wallace DePue, Burton Beerman, Donald
Wilson, Bowling Green State Univ.; with Roger
Reynolds, Univ. of California, San Diego. Her
awards include the Religious Arts award, 1969;
first prize, Ohio Music Teachers Assoc. contest,
1971; first prize, Ohio Fed. of Music Clubs
contest, 1972.
WORKS: OPERA: Legends, chamber opera;
CHAMBER MUSIC: Abraxas, cello and piano; Gestures, chamber ensemble, 1972; CHORUS: Kyrie
eleison, women's voices, 1969; I will lift up
mine eyes; Requiem, 4 voices and computer, 1977;
SONGS: The philosopher, song cycle, 1971.
6802 Beadnell, #26, San Diego, CA 92117

KAY, HERSHY
b. Philadelphia, Pa., 17 Nov. 1919; d. Danbury,
Conn., 2 Dec. 1981. Studied at Curtis Inst.
of Music. He was arranger and orchestrator for
the Balanchine Ballet Company and for many
Broadway musicals.
WORKS: OPERA: Good Soldier Schweik, a completion of Robert Kurka's unfinished opera,
1959; BALLET: Thief who loved a ghost, 1950;
Cakewalk, 1951; Western symphony, 1954; Concert,
an arrangement from Chopin, 1956; Stars and
stripes, 1958; L'Inconnue, 1965; The clowns,
1968; Who cares, 1970; Grand tour, 1971; Union
Jack, 1976; ORCHESTRA: Mother Goose suite,
1958; Let's go to the fair; Theatre set; Concerto for 2; BAND: Deck the halls, a merry
fugue; Variations on Joy to the world; FILM
SCORES: Man with a gun, 1955; King and Queen,
1956; Cinerama, 1958; Girl of the night, 1960;
Such good friends, 1971; Bite the bullet, 1975;
also television scores and contributions to
some 20 Broadway musicals.

KAY, ULYSSES
b. Tucson, Ariz., 7 Jan. 1917; grand-nephew of
Joseph "King" Oliver. Learned to play piano,
violin, and saxophone at home, then attended
Univ. of Arizona, B.M.E. 1938; studied with
Bernard Rogers and Howard Hanson, Eastman School
of Music, M.A. 1940; with Paul Hindemith at Yale
Univ. and Tanglewood; and with Otto Luening at
Columbia Univ. His many awards include a Ditson

fellowship at Columbia; Julius Rosenwald fellowship; Prix de Rome, 1949, 1951; Fulbright grant, 1950; Nat. Inst. of Arts and Letters grant; BMI prize; Gershwin Memorial prize; ABC prize; Guggenheim fellowship, 1964; honorary doctorates, Lincoln Coll., 1963, Bucknell Univ., 1963, Univ. of Arizona, 1969, Dickinson Coll., 1978; Nat. Endowment for the Arts grants, 1976, 1978; induction as member, American Acad. and Inst. of Arts and Letters, 1979. He served in a navy band in World War II, playing saxophone, flute, piccolo, and piano, as well as arranging and composing. In 1965 he toured the USSR as member of the first group of composers sent on a State Dept. cultural exchange mission. Other such missions have taken him to England, France, Italy, and Yugoslavia. From 1953 he has been music consultant with Broadcast Music, Inc.; and from 1968, professor, Lehman Coll., CUNY.

WORKS: OPERA: The boor, 1 act, 1955; The juggler of Our Lady, 1956, New Orleans, 23 Feb. 1962; The Capitoline Venus, Quincy, Ill., 12 Mar. 1971; Jubilee, libretto by Donald Dorr, commissioned and performed by Opera South, Jackson, Miss., 20 Nov. 1976; ORCHESTRA: 5 mosaics, 1940; oboe concerto, 1940; Danse Calinda, ballet suite, 1941; concerto for orchestra, 1948; Sinfonis in E, 1950; Serenade, 1954; Fantasy variations, Portland, Maine, 19 Nov. 1963; Umbrian scene, 1964; symphony, New York premiere, 29 Mar. 1974; CHAMBER MUSIC: brass quartet, 1952; 3 string quartets, 1953, 1956, 1961; Partita in A, violin and piano; Serenade #2, 4 horns; Triptych on texts of Blake, soprano and string trio, 1955; 5 portraits, violin and piano, Washington, 22 Feb. 1974; CHORUS: What's in a name?, 1954; How stands the glass around?, 1954; A Lincoln letter, bass solo, chorus a cappella; Song of Jeremiah, bass-baritone, chorus, orch., 1954; Phoebus arise, with soprano, baritone, orch., 1959; Choral triptych, with strings, 1962; Inscriptions from Whitman, with orch., 1964; Epigrams and hymns, New York, 16 May 1976; many other choral works; PIANO: sonata, 1940; 10 essays; 2 short pieces for piano, 4 hands; 4 inventions.
143 Belmont St., Englewood, NJ 07681

KAYDEN, MILDRED
b. New York, N.Y. Studied at Juilliard School; Vassar Coll., B.A.; Radcliffe Coll., M.A.; with Ernst Krenek and Walter Piston. She taught at Vassar, 1946-50, 1951-52; had a radio program on WEVD, 1956-63.

WORKS: THEATRE: music for The seed and the dream; The riddle of Sheba; Mardi gras; The last word; CHAMBER MUSIC: piano sonata; Theme and variations, piano; string quartet; woodwind trio; CHORUS: The valley of dry bones, chamber cantata; Green gown; FILM SCORES: The pumpkin coach; The procession; Leaven for the cities; TELEVISION SCORE: Strangers in the land; and songs.
33 Broadway, Irvington-on-Hudson, NY 10533

KAYLIN, SAMUEL
b. Kiev, Russia, 18 Jan. 1892. Received an honorary doctor of music degree from London Inst. for Applied Research, 1972. He became music director for Hollywwod films in 1916; was with Warner Bros. Pictures, 1929-31, and 20th-Century Fox Film Corp. from 1931 to retirement. He wrote scores for more than 50 films in the 1930s including Ever since Eve; Steamboat round the bend; Little Miss Nobody; the Charlie Chan series; and the Jeeves series.
433 S. Western Ave., #210, Los Angeles, CA 90020

KAZZE, LOUIS
b. Russia, 18 July 1896. Studied with Randall Thompson in New York; with Ernest Bloch in Philadelphia; and with Herbert Elwell, Eastman School of Music. He received a Pennsylvania Fed. of Music Clubs award in composition. He taught in Philadelphia public schools, then founded his own piano school.

WORKS: ORCHESTRA: Panar, ballet suite; CHAMBER MUSIC: Variations, flute and piano; Lights and shadows, violin and piano; 3 songs to texts by Poe; PIANO: Panar suite; Passacaglia and fugue; suite in C.
21 Allendale Rd., Philadelphia, PA 19151

KEATS, DONALD
b. New York, N.Y., 27 May 1929. Studied with Quincy Porter and Paul Hindemith, Yale Univ., B.M. 1949; with Otto Luening, Douglas Moore, Henry Cowell, Columbia Univ., M.A. 1953; with Philipp Jarnach, Hamburg, Germany, 1954-56; with Paul Fetler, Dominick Argento, Univ. of Minnesota, Ph.D. His awards include the Yale Univ. Kellog prize, 1948; Fulbright grants, 1954, 1955; Danforth Found. grants, 1959, 1961; Lilly Found. grant, 1960; Guggenheim fellowships, 1964, 1972; annual ASCAP awards, 1964-73; Rockefeller Found. grants, 1965, 1966; Ford Found.-Antioch Humanities awards, 1970, 1972. He was instructor, U.S. Navy School of Music, 1953-54; post music director, Fort Dix, U.S. Army, 1956-57; professor, Antioch Coll., 1957-75; from 1978, Univ. of Denver, School of Music.

WORKS: BALLET: The new work, 1967; ORCHESTRA: symphony #1, 1959; Elegiac symphony, Kansas City, 28 Apr. 1964; Concert piece, 1968; Branchings, 1975; CHAMBER MUSIC: Divertimento, winds and strings, 1949; string trio, 1949; 2 string quartets, 1956, 1965; Polarities I and II, violin and piano, 1968, 1970; CHORUS: The hollow men, 1955; The naming of cats, 1961; A drinking song; anyone lived in a pretty how town, 1970; also songs and piano pieces.
University of Denver, Denver, CO 80208

KEBEDE, ASHENAFI
b. Ethiopia, 7 May 1938. Studied at Eastman School of Music, B.A. 1962; Wesleyan Univ. (Conn.), 1968-71, received Wesleyan's first Ph.D. in ethnomusicology. His awards include Haile Selassie I Nat. award; American Council of Learned Societies award; UNESCO award for travel; Hungarian, Bulgarian, and Canadian grants; all educational expenses paid through grants, fellowships, and awards. He was founder and director of Ethiopia's Nat. School of Music,

KECHLEY, DAVID STEVENSON

1964-68; has been member, UNESCO Music Council, from 1967; was faculty member, Queens Coll., CUNY, 1970-76; from 1977, at Brandeis Univ.

WORKS: ORCHESTRA: Ethiopian symphony, 1968; The shepherd flutist, flute and string orch., 1968; CHAMBER MUSIC: Koturasia, Japanese koto, clarinet, violin, 1974; Soliloquy, soprano, tenor, flute, koto, 1974; Soliloquy, tenor, flute, koto, 1975.

P.O. Box 157, Newton Centre, MA 02159

KECHLEY, DAVID STEVENSON

b. Seattle, Wash., 16 Mar. 1947. Studied with Paul Tufts, James Beale, William Bergsma, Robert Suderberg, Univ. of Washington, B.M. 1969; with Donald Erb, Cleveland Inst. of Music. His awards include 2 Louis Brechemin scholarships, 1965, 1967; Rockefeller Found. performance grant, 1967; Nat. Endowment for the Arts grant, 1976; Guggenheim fellowship, 1978. He was teaching assistant, Univ. of Washington, 1973-76.

WORKS: ORCHESTRA: 2nd composition for large orchestra, 1967; 4 horsemen of the Apocalypse, 1969; BAND: concerto for band; CHAMBER MUSIC: string quartet; sonata for flute and harp; violin sonata; cello sonata; string trio; trio for piano, cello, flute; Variations, 7 players, brass quintet, 1975; Harmonic aggregates, rhythmic patterns and scintillations, 9 harps; Eclipse, jazz ensemble and strings, 1978; VOICE: Faint harps and silver voices, cantata on Blake poems, 1974; 5 ancient lyrics, soprano, harp, strings.

5438 Mayfield Rd., Lyndhurst, OH 44124

KECHLEY, GERALD

b. Seattle, Wash., 18 Mar. 1919. Studied with George F. McKay, Univ. of Washington, B.A., M.A.; and with Aaron Copland in New York and at Tanglewood. His awards include first prize, Nat. Fed. of Music Clubs contest, 1945; Guggenheim fellowships, 1949, 1951; and many commissions. He was music director, Centralia Junior Coll., 1953; from 1954, on music faculty, Univ. of Washington.

WORKS: OPERA: The golden lion; The beckoning fair one; Robin Goodfellow; ORCHESTRA: Prologue, enactment, epilogue; symphony; BAND: Antiphony for winds; suite for concert band; suite for brass and percussion; Mosaic for winds; CHAMBER MUSIC: piano trio, 1964; CHORUS: Daedalus and the minotaur, with orch.; For men yet unborn, with orch.; Drop, slow tears, with chamber ensemble; A spirited human shape, with orch.; Cantata for St. Cecilia's day; Psalm 150; Pleasure it is; In the lonely midnight; Thank we now the Lord of heaven; Psalm 121; Sing no sad songs; What sweeter music; Welcome, summer; many other choral works and songs.

5230 12th Ave. N.E., Seattle, WA 98105

KEENE, CHRISTOPHER

b. Berkeley, Calif., 21 Dec. 1946. Studied at Univ. of California, Berkeley. He formed his own opera company at age 18 and produced Benjamin Britten's Rape of Lucretia; was assistant conductor, San Francisco Opera at 18;

conducted New York City Opera at 23; has also conducted the Santa Fe Opera and at the Spoleta Festivals, 1968, 1969, 1971; then was on the conducting staff, New York City Opera and musical director, American Ballet Company; in 1975, was named music director of the Syracuse Symphony. His compositions include a ballet, The consort, 1970.

c/o Syracuse Symphony Orch., Civic Center, 411 Montgomery St., Syracuse, NY 13202

KEENEY, WENDELL

b. Linden, Ind., 18 June 1903. Studied at Juilliard School; also with Nadia Boulanger. He was head of the music department, Furman Univ., 1935-58. His published works, except for The aspen for medium voice, are all for piano: sonatina, 1943; Spanish capriccio, 2 pianos; Mountain tune, 1 or 2 pianos; God's time is best, an arrangement of Bach for 2 pianos.

3289 Legation St., Washington, DC 20015

KEESE, KEN

b. Stone Mountain, Ga., 24 Mar. 1914. Studied with Isa McIlwraith and Arthur Plettner, Univ. of Tennessee at Chattanooga. In 1971 he was named composer of the year by the Chattanooga Music Teachers Assoc. He has been staff pianist at various radio stations.

WORKS: CHORUS: O Lord, how excellent is thy name; Sing unto the Lord a new song; Father, teach me how to pray; Let all mortal flesh; Christmas Eve; Once to every man and nation.

1001 Tremont St., Chattanooga, TN 37405

KEEZER, RONALD

b. Eau Claire, Wis., 4 June 1940. Is faculty member, Univ. of Wisconsin.

WORKS: ORCHESTRA: Composition for percussion and orch.; Eloszo; WIND ENSEMBLE: 4 brass structures; PERCUSSION: For 3 percussionists; For 4 percussionists; Fantasy on rags; 3 movements for percussion; CHAMBER MUSIC: Transformations, piano trio; string quartet; Punical muse, 7 instruments and percussion; Introspections, 5 players, narrator, perucssion; Composition for Dominic Spara; CHORUS: The man whose rage was rose, cycle for chorus and percussion; The Lord is in his holy temple; Doth not wisdom cry; FILM SCORE: Impetus.

1711 State St., Eau Claire, WI 57401

KEISER, LAUREN KEITH

b. Portland, Oreg., 13 June 1945. Has studied composition privately with Elie Siegmeister, Harold Gilmore, Isaac Nemiroff, and Krzysztof Penderecki. He won first prize in a composition contest of the Long Island Composers Alliance, 1975. He was president of a publishing company, 1970-72; since then, resident composer, Sam Ash Music Stores.

WORKS: OPERA: Goose Hollow, 2-act opera for electronic instruments and amplified voices; WIND ENSEMBLE: Metamorphosis, 1976; CHAMBER MUSIC: The music of Erich Zann, string quartet; Temporal synthesis, piano, 1973; Chroma, chamber orch., 1975; Polyhymnia, string quartet, 1977; 8 bagatelles, piano, 1978; Synomenon, violin,

clarinet, piano, 1978. He is author of Aural geometry--A new Pythagorean view of music, 1979.
360 Limestone Rd., Ridgefield, CT 06877

KELDERMANS, RAYMOND ALBERT
b. Mechelen, Belgium, 17 Apr. 1911; U.S. citizen 1965. Studied with Flor Peeters, Marinus de Jong, and Staf Nees at Lemmens Inst., Malines, M.A. 1932; graduated with great distinction from Royal Carillon School, Mechelen; also studied in Berlin, 1939. He received a City of Mechelen prize for a carillon composition, 1964; and Henry Leon prize, Mechelen, 1966. He has been Park District carillonneur, Springfield, Ill., from 1960; organist-choirmaster, Blessed Sacrament Church, 1960-73; and instructor, Springfield Coll., from 1958.
WORKS: ORCHESTRA: symphony; Pastorale; Feast; Tyliana; Til Uilenspiegel suite, chamber orch.; CHAMBER MUSIC: bassoon sonatina; trumpet sonata; woodwind quintet; CHORUS: The Lord is my shepherd, with chamber orch.; Vachel Lindsay suite; ORGAN: Magnificat; suite for organ; CARILLON: Barock suite; Toccata; sonatina.
1625 Holmes Ave., Springfield, IL 62704

KELLER, HOMER
b. 1915. Studied with Howard Hanson and Bernard Rogers, Eastman School of Music, B.M., M.M.; with Arthur Honegger in Paris. He was faculty member, Univ. of Oregon, to 1978.
WORKS: ORCHESTRA: 3 symphonies, 1940, 1950, 1956; Serenade, clarinet and strings; CHAMBER MUSIC: brass quartet; 5 pieces for clarinet and bassoon; Fantasy and fugue for organ; piano sonata; Interplay, woodwind quintet.

KELLER, WALTER
b. Chicago, Ill., 23 Feb. 1873; d. Chicago, 7 July 1940. Studied at American Cons. and at Leipzig Cons. He was teacher and organist in Chicago. His works include a comic opera, The crumpled isle; Synchronous prelude and fugue for orch.; works for organ, chorus, and solo voice.

KELLIS, LEO ALAN
b. Los Angeles, Calif., 17 Aug. 1927. Studied privately with Julius Gold. He is a private piano teacher and concert pianist.
WORKS: PIANO: sonata; 3 capriccios; Fantasy; Rhapsody Aravelian; 11 etudes; 3 impromptus; Hello from the zoo, a suite; Rhapsody on a children's tune; 2 concert etudes; 3 sets of variations on themes of Rachmaninoff, Balakirev, and Beethoven; 4 nocturnes; Fantasy, 2 pianos; Suite en valse, 2 pianos; and others.
771 Norumbega Dr., Monrovia, CA 91016

KELLY, ROBERT
b. Clarksburg, W.Va., 26 Sept. 1919. Studied with Rosario Scalero, Curtis Inst. of Music, B.M.; with Herbert Elwell, Eastman School of Music, M.M. His awards include 2 grants from Univ. of Illinois, 1962, 1964; 2 Nat. Endowment for the Arts grants, 1967, 1976. He was professor, Univ. of Illinois, from 1946; professor emeritus, 1976.

WORKS: OPERA: Tod's gal, 1-act folk opera, 1951, Virginia City, 8 Jan. 1971; The white gods, 3 acts, Urbana, Ill., 3 July 1966; BALLET: Paiyatuma; ORCHESTRA: Adirondack suite, 1941; A miniature symphony, Austin, Tex., 15 Oct. 1950; symphony #2, 1958; An American diptych, Austin, 26 Apr. 1963; concerto for violin, cello, and orch., Urbana, 8 Mar. 1961; Emancipation symphony, Washington, 5 Feb. 1963; Colloquy, chamber orch., Chicago, 17 Apr. 1965; violin concerto, Urbana, 18 Oct. 1968; viola concerto, 1977; BAND: Chorale and fugue, 1951; concerto for winds and percussion; Fluctuations, brass ensemble, organ, percussion; CHAMBER MUSIC: 2 string quartets, 1944, 1952; viola sonata, 1950; violin sonata, 1952; trombone sonata, 1952; suite for solo cello; Theme and variations, violin, viola, piano; sonata for 2 violins; Diacoustics, piano and percussion; Expressions, violin and cello or viola; A free fugue on 2 themes, 2 violins and piano; Passacaglia and fugue, wind quintet; sonata for oboe and harp, 1955; quintet for clarinet and strings, 1956; cello sonata, 1958; Toccata, marimba and percussion, 1959; Triptych, cello and piano, 1962; Variant, piano trio; Mosaic, string quartet, 1975; also choral works and songs.
807 S. Urbana Ave., Urbana, IL 61801

KEMMER, GEORGE
b. New York, N.Y., 11 Oct. 1890; d. Va., 1 Dec. 1974. He was organist-choirmaster, Grace Church, Orange, N.J., 1911-23; St. George's Episcopal Church, New York, 1923-55. He wrote choral works, organ pieces, and songs.

KEMNER, GERALD
b. Kansas City, Mo., 28 Sept. 1932. Studied with Quincy Porter, Yale Univ.; with Howard Hanson, Henry Cowell, and Bernard Rogers, Eastman School of Music, D.M.A. He received the Howard Hanson prize in 1962. He was faculty member, Augustana Coll., S.Dak., 1962-66; from 1966, at Univ. of Missouri, Kansas City.
WORKS: CHORUS: Ezekiel, with electronic sounds; ORGAN: Variations on the Easter sequence; First light and the quiet voice.
8410 England, Overland Park, KS 66212

KEMPINSKI, LEO A.
b. Ruda, Germany, 25 Mar. 1891; to U.S. 1908; d. Hampton, Conn., 25 May 1958. Studied at Breslau Univ.; with Percy Goetschius at Juilliard School. He was church organist in Philadelphia; music director in theatres; editor for a music publishing firm.
WORKS: ORCHESTRA: Victory concerto, piano and orch.; also many marches, songs, music for films and radio.

KENDALL, GARY
Epithalamium, flute solo. He has also written a program for sound generation called MUSIC/UT, in which a composer specifies his score in computer language, indicates the waveforms and functions with a light pen, and receives an immediate playback of the sound.
School of Music, Northwestern Univ., Evanston, IL 60201

KENDRICK, VIRGINIA

KENDRICK, VIRGINIA (Mrs. W. Dudley Kendrick)
b. Minneapolis, Minn., 8 Apr. 1910. Studied at
Univ. of Minnesota. She has been pianist with
a ballet company from 1960; was organ music consultant with a publishing firm, 1970-75; organist, First Church of Christ Scientist, Excelsior,
1965-73.
WORKS: choral works and songs including
White sky, women's voices; Before the world was,
solo voice; Jade summer; Little red hen; In this
soft, velvet night; and others.
5800 Echo Rd., Shorewood, MN 55331

KENESSEY, STEFANIA MARIA DE
b. Budapest, 6 Oct. 1956; to U.S. 1967. Studied
at Yale Univ., B.A. summa cum laude 1976; with
Milton Babbitt, Princeton Univ., M.F.A. 1978,
Phi Beta Kappa, candidate for Ph.D. From 1977,
she has been research and editorial assistant,
Bela Bartok Archives.
WORKS: ORCHESTRA: symphony in 1 movement,
1976; CHAMBER MUSIC: 2 string quartets, 1974,
1975; Rhapsody, for piano, 1975; 3 songs for
soprano and piano, 1976; piano trio, 1977.
3817 Spruce St., #601, Philadelphia, PA
19104

KENNAN, KENT WHEELER
b. Milwaukee, Wis., 18 Apr. 1913. Studied with
Hunter Johnson, Univ. of Michigan, 1930-32; with
Howard Hanson and Bernard Rogers, Eastman School
of Music, B.M. 1934, M.M. 1936; with Ildebrando
Pizzetti in Rome. He won the Prix de Rome, 1936.
His faculty posts have been Kent State Univ.,
1939-40; Univ. of Texas, 1940-42, 1946-47, and
from 1949; Ohio State Univ. 1947-49.
WORKS: ORCHESTRA: 3 pieces for orch.,
1936; Il campo dei fiori, trumpet and orch.,
1937; Nocturne, viola and orch., 1937; symphony,
1938; Dance divertimento, 1938; Promenade, 1938;
Andante, oboe and orch., 1939; concertino,
piano and orch., 1946, rev. for piano and wind
ensemble, 1963; CHAMBER MUSIC: Night soliloquy,
flute, strings, piano, 1936; Sea sonata, violin
and piano, 1939; Scherzo, aria, fugato, oboe
and piano, 1948; trumpet sonata, 1956; CHORUS:
The unknown warrior speaks, male voices, a
cappella, 1944; Blessed are they that mourn,
with orch.; PIANO: 3 preludes, 1939; sonatina,
1945; 2 preludes, 1951. He is author of 2
books: The technique of orchestration, 1952,
rev. 1970, and Counterpoint, 1959, rev. 1972.
1513 Westover Rd., Austin, TX 78703

KENNEDY, JOHN BRODBIN
b. 1934. Symphonic fantasy for orch.; Gloria,
trumpet and organ; Rise, my soul, and stretch
thy wings, chorus and organ; Alleluia fanfare,
chorus and brass; other choral works and songs.

KENNELL, RICHARD PAUL
b. Dansville, N.Y., 17 Apr. 1949. Studied with
William Karlins and Stephen Syverud, Northwestern
Univ. He won a prize in the First Internat.
Contest of Electronic Music, Bourges, France,
1973. He was graduate assistant, electronic
music studio, Northwestern Univ., 1972-73;
taught in public schools, 1973-74; from 1975, at

William Rainey Harper Coll.
WORKS: ELECTRONIC: solo for clarinet and
reverberation unit, 1972; Wiesenhuttenplatz 29,
tape, 1972; Metamorphose, tape, 1972; Elestroax
II, alto saxophone and tape, 1972; Fantasia and
fugue, tape, Bourges, France, 20 Oct. 1973.
William Rainey Harper College, Palatine, IL
60067

KENT, CHARLES STANTON
b. Minneapolis, Minn., 20 Jan. 1914; d. Baltimore, Md., 31 May 1969. Studied at Univ. of
Louisville, B.M. 1936; Juilliard School, 1933-
35; Eastman School of Music, M.M. 1938, Ph.D.
1951. He was faculty member, Oberlin Coll.,
1938-41; Western Reserve Univ., 1941-42; New
England Cons., 1945-48; Univ. of Mississippi,
1951-56; Indiana Univ., 1956-61; Peabody Cons.,
1961-63, director, 1963-68; visiting professor,
Univ. of Miami, 1968-69.
WORKS: OPERA: A room in time, 1954; a
number of string quartets; songs.

KENT, FREDERICK JAMES
b. Miami, Fla., 21 May 1928. Studied with May
Strong and Donald White, DePauw Univ., B.M.
1950; with Burrill Phillips and Gordon Binkerd,
Univ. of Illinois, M.M. 1951; also musicology
and library science, M.L.S. 1961. He was Rector
Scholar, 1947-50. He has been staff member,
music dept., Free Library of Philadelphia, from
1961, department head, from 1974.
WORKS: CHAMBER MUSIC: Divertissement,
organ, brass, timpani, 1950; quintet for flute
and strings, 1951; suite for woodwind quartet,
1951; Passacaglia, 2 pianos, 1951; many choral
works and organ pieces.
301 Parkway House, 2201 Penn Ave., Philadelphia, PA 19130

KENT, RICHARD LAYTON
b. Harris, Mo., 23 Jan. 1916. Studied with
Francis J. Pyle, Drake Univ.; Francis Judd
Cooke and Carl McKinley, New England Cons.; with
Hugo Norden, Boston Univ.; musicology at Harvard
Univ. He taught in public schools, Larrabee,
Iowa, 1940-42; served in U.S. Air Force, 1943-
45; from 1947, has been professor, Fitchburg
State Coll.
WORKS: CHORUS: Time; Bright star; May the
road rise; How sweet the moonlight sleeps; When
icicles hang; To music; The thing about cats;
more than 70 more published choral works and
organ pieces; many manuscript works for orchestra,
chamber groups, etc.
1171 Main St., Leominster, MA 01453

KENTON, STANLEY NEWCOMB (STAN)
b. Wichita, Kans., 19 Feb. 1912; d. Hollywood,
Calif., 25 Aug. 1979. Began composing at 16;
was pianist in dance orchestras and night clubs;
organized his own orchestra in 1941 and performed
widely with it; conducted workshops for teen-age
musicians.
WORKS: CONCERT JAZZ: Artistry in rhythm;
Eager beaver; Intermission riff; Southern scandal; Concerto for doghouse; Concerto to end all
concertos; Painted rhythm; et al.

KEPNER, FRED
b. Waynesboro, Pa., 26 Sept. 1921. Studied at
Catawba Coll.; Juilliard School; Manhattan
School of Music. He was in the Army Air Force
in World War II; chief arranger, USAF Band,
Washington, 1947-50; led USAF dance orch., Airmen
of Note; assistant to chief of bands and music,
USAF, from 1955; and leader, Headquarters Command Band, Washington.
    WORKS: BAND: Cuban fantasy; Latin lament;
The clown, suite; Forward for peace; A medieval
tournament; Fiesta finale; Merry-go-round polka;
2nd Street overture.
    7804 Oxon Hill Rd., Oxon Hill, MD 20021

KERN, JEROME DAVID
b. New York, N.Y., 27 Jan. 1885; d. New York,
11 Nov. 1945. Studied at New York Coll. of
Music and privately in Berlin. He began his
composing career in London writing numbers for
musical shows; was staff writer for T. B. Harms,
1904; wrote scores for the Princess Theatre,
New York, 1915-18; then his great hits began to
appear on Broadway.
    WORKS: MUSICALS: Rock-a-bye baby, 1918;
Sally, 1920; Stepping stones, 1923; Sunny, 1925;
Show boat, 1927; Sweet Adeline, 1929; The cat
and the fiddle, 1931; Music in the air, 1932;
Roberta, 1933; Very warm for May, 1939; FILM
SCORES: Men of the sky, 1930; I dream too much,
1935; Swing time, 1936; High, wide and handsome,
1937; When you're in love, 1937; The joy of
living, 1938; One night in the tropics, 1940;
You were never lovelier, 1944; Cover girl, 1944;
Can't help singing, 1944.

KERNOCHAN, MARSHALL RUTGERS
b. New York, N.Y., 14 Dec. 1880; d. Edgartown,
Mass., 9 June 1955. Studied with Hermann
Wetzler and Ivan Knorr; with Percy Goetschius,
Juilliard School. He was music editor of the
Outlook; then president, Galaxy Music Corp.,
N.Y.
    WORKS: VOICE: The foolish virgin, cantata;
The sleep of summer, women's voices and orch.;
Out of the rolling ocean, baritone and orch.;
numerous songs.

KERR, HARRISON
b. Cleveland, Ohio, 13 Oct. 1897; d. Norman,
Okla., 15 Aug. 1978. Studied composition with
Nadia Boulanger and Paul Vidal in France. His
awards included a Huntington Hartford fellowship; numerous commissions. He was music
director, Greenbriar Coll., 1927-28; Chase
School, Brooklyn, N.Y., 1928-35; editor of Trend,
1932-35; secretary, American Composers Alliance,
1937-51; executive secretary, American Music
Center, 1940-47; with Civil Affairs Div., Dept.
of the Army, 1946-49; dean Coll. of Fine Arts,
Univ. of Oklahoma, 1949-64, professor, 1960-68,
then professor emeritus.
    WORKS: Dance sonata, dancers, 2 pianos,
percussion, Bennington, Vt., 5 Aug. 1938; The
tower of Kel, 4-act opera, 1958-61; ORCHESTRA:
3 symphonies, #1 1929, Rochester, N.Y., 24 Oct.
1945, #2 1945, Oklahoma City, 23 Feb. 1951,
#3 1954, Norman, Okla., 19 Nov. 1971; Dance

suite, Rochester, 27 Oct. 1942; violin concerto,
1951, New York, 12 Dec. 1954; Variations on a
ground bass, 1966; Sinfonietta, Norman, Okla.,
25 Apr. 1968; CHAMBER MUSIC: Notations on a
sensitized plate, voice and chamber orch., New
York, 24 June 1936; 2 string quartets, #1, Paris,
5 Mar. 1936, #2, New York, 13 Dec. 1937; trio,
clarinet, cello, piano, New York, 24 June 1936;
Suite for flute and piano, Philadelphia, 22 Nov.
1942; Overture, arioso, and finale, cello and
piano, Norman, Okla., 27 Apr. 1952; sonata for
violin solo, New York, 5 Feb. 1955; violin
sonata, 1956; string quartet #3, 1973; Quasi
quodlibet, 8 trombones, Norman, Okla., 18 Mar.
1974; 3 duos for 2 flutes, 1976; CHORUS: Wink
of eternity, with orch., New York, 15 Dec. 1957;
In cabin'd ships at sea, Whitman text, Demascus,
Md., 30 Apr. 1972; PIANO: 2 sonatas, 1929,
1943; 4 preludes, 1943; and many songs.

KERR, THOMAS H., JR.
b. Baltimore, Md. Studied at Eastman School of
Music, where he held the Rosenwald fellowship in
composition. He won first prize, Composers and
Authors of America contest, 1944. He was pro-
fessor, School of Music, Howard Univ., to 1978.
    WORKS: CHORUS: Anguished America, Easter,
1968 was performed at the Martin Luther King,
Jr., Memorial, National Cathedral, Wahsington,
D.C., on 30 Mar. 1969, and simultaneously in
cathedrals in Germany, Holland, France, and
Denmark; Prayer for the soul of Martin Luther
King, Jr., was featured on a Washington Oratorio
Society program, 17 May 1975.

KESNAR, MAURITS
b. Amsterdam, Neth., 8 July 1900; d. Carbondale,
Ill., 22 Feb. 1957. Studied at Amsterdam Cons.;
Berlin Hochschule für Musik; Univ. of Iowa, M.A.,
Ph.D. He was violin soloist in Europe and the
U.S.; then chairman, music dept., Southern
Illinois Univ.
    WORKS: ORCHESTRA: symphony; sinfonietta;
Poem; Sundown; CHAMBER MUSIC: string quartet;
CHORUS: Mass in E flat.

KESSLER, MINUETTA
b. Gomel, Russia, 5 Sept. 1914; U.S. Citizen
1938. Studied piano in Canada and with Ernest
Hutcheson at Juilliard School, teacher's and
artist diplomas, with distinction, 1934, 1936;
composition with Ivan Langstroth and Herbert
Fromm; also received a licentiate degree, Royal
Coll. and Royal Acad. of London, England. Her
awards included 2 composition awards, Composers,
Authors and Publishers Assoc. of Canada, 1945,
1946; composition award, Brookline (Mass.)
Library Music Assoc., 1958. She taught piano at
Juilliard School, 1936-40; opened the Kessler
School of Music, Belmont, Mass., in 1952.
    WORKS: THEATRE: Memories of Tevye, ballet,
piano, 1954; Kiddy City, children's operetta,
1961; ORCHESTRA: New York suite, piano and
orch., 1944; Alberta concerto, piano and orch.,
1947; CHAMBER MUSIC: piano trio, 1957; violin
sonata, 1957; cello sonata, 1961; Scherzetta,
flute, clarinet, piano trio, 1969; clarinet
sonata, 1977; Fantasie, oboe and piano, 1978;

KESSNER, DANIEL AARON

CHORUS: <u>Peace and brotherhood</u>, cantata, 1960;
<u>Thought is a bird of space</u>, cantata, 1961;
PIANO: suite, 1961; <u>Bicentennial sonata</u>, 1975.
30 Hurley St., Belmont, MA 02178

KESSNER, DANIEL AARON
b. Los Angeles, Calif., 3 June 1946. Studied
with Henri Lazarof, Univ. of California, A.B.
1967, M.A. 1968, Ph.D. 1971. His awards include
first prizes, Atwater Kent contests, 1969, 1970,
1971; first prize, Music Society of Santa
Barbara contest, 1970; BMI awards, 1970, 1971;
Queen Marie-Jose prize, Geneva, 1972; performance
awards, Gaudeamus Internat. contest, 1970,
Indiana State Univ. contest, 1977; Nat. Endowment for the Arts grants, 1974, 1977; California
State Univ. award, 1975; many commissions. He
has been faculty member, California State Univ.,
from 1970.
WORKS: ORCHESTRA: <u>Strata</u>, 1971; <u>Mobile</u>,
1973; CHAMBER MUSIC: <u>Ensembles</u>, violin, clarinet, harp, 1968; <u>Equali I</u>, 4 flutes, string trio,
bass, 1969; sonatina for solo harp, 1969; <u>Equali
II</u>, piano and percussion, 1970; <u>Interactions</u>,
flute, cello, piano, tape, 1971; chamber concerto, recorder, voice, and oboe soli, chamber
ensemble, 1972; <u>Intercurrence</u>, harp and tape,
1972; <u>Nebulae: Equali III</u>, string trio, 2
guitars, harpsichord, 1972; <u>Array</u>, 2, 3, and 4
guitars, 1973; <u>Solennité</u>, bass flute, viola,
percussion, 1975; <u>Movements from A</u>, violin and
piano, 1975; <u>Triform: variations</u>, clarinet,
cello, piano, 1976; <u>Equali IV</u>, brass quartet,
1977; also works for band, chorus, solo voice.
10955 Cozycroft Ave., Chatsworth, CA 91311

KETTERING, EUNICE LEA
b. Savannah, Ohio, 4 Apr. 1906. Studied at
Oberlin Cons., B.M.; School of Sacred Music,
Union Theological Seminary, M.S.M.; with Bela
Bartok in Austria; privately with Edwin J.
Stringham, Normand Lockwood, and Felix Labunski.
She won first prize, Nat. Fed. of Music Clubs
contest for choral-orchestral work, <u>Johnny
Appleseed</u>; 3 awards, Nat. League of American
Pen Women, 1972. She was instructor, Madison
Coll., 1929-32; professor and resident composer,
Ashland Coll., 1935-58.
WORKS: CHORUS: <u>A-shining far in the east</u>;
<u>Bells of Sunday</u>; <u>Christmas sermon</u>; <u>Factory win-
dows are always broken</u>; <u>God of the dew</u>; <u>I hear
America singing</u>; <u>The lamb</u>; <u>Psalm 86</u>; <u>The mysterious cat</u>; <u>Silence</u>; <u>Valley Forge</u>; many other
choral works; piano and organ pieces.
2121½ Coal Ave., S.E., Albuquerque, NM
87106

KEVAN, G. ALEX
b. England, 28 Jan. 1908; U.S. citizen 1951.
Studied organ in England and with George Coutts,
Regina Coll. of Music, Regina, Sask. He held
organist and choirmaster posts in Saskatchewan
and Alberta before appointment at St. John the
Divine Church, Houston, where he is also chairman, music department, St. John's School. He
has published many anthems and piano pieces.

KEYES, NELSON
b. Tulsa, Okla., 26 Aug. 1928. Studied with
Kent Kennan and Wilbur Ogdon, Univ. of Texas;
with Ingolf Dahl and Halsey Stevens, Univ. of
Southern California. He received a Huntington
Hartford Found. grant, 1951; USC Friends of
Music prize, 1957; Ford Found. residence grant
in Louisville, Ky., 1961-65. He was faculty
member, Long Beach City Coll., 1955-59; Univ. of
Southern California, 1960-61; Kansas State
Teachers Coll., 1965-69; from 1969, at Univ. of
Louisville.
WORKS: ORCHESTRA: <u>Music for Monday even-
ings</u>, 1959; <u>Abysses, bridges, chasms</u>, 1971; WIND
ENSEMBLES: <u>Bandances</u>, band; <u>Hardinsburg joys</u>,
brass quintet; brass trio; <u>Bassooneries</u>, 4
bassoon duets; CHORUS: <u>Give you a lantern</u>; <u>All
is safe</u>; also 2 ballets, musical plays, vocal
solos.
2338 Strathmoor Blvd., Louisville, KY 40205

KHAN, ALI AKBAR
b. Shibpur, Bengal, 14 Apr. 1922; to U.S. 1965.
Studied with his father, Allauddin Khan, master
of more than 200 instruments, who died in 1972
at age 110. Ali Akbar Khan received 4 awards
from Jodhpur, Rajistan; President's award and
Padmabhooshan from government of India; and
awards for film scores. He was music director,
All India Radio, Lucknow, 1946-48; music director, Bombay Film Industries, 1954-55; from 1956
president, Ali Akbar Coll. of Music, Calcutta;
on faculty, McGill Univ., 1959-61; head music
dept., American Society for Eastern Arts, 1965-
67; president, Ali Akbar Coll. of Music, Marin
County, Calif., from 1967.
WORKS: FILM SCORES: <u>Mornings of creation</u>;
<u>The prophet</u>; and numerous new ragas.
18 Napa Ave., Fairfax, CA 94930

KIBBE, MICHAEL
b. San Diego, Calif., 26 June 1945. Studied
with David Ward-Steinman, San Diego State Univ.;
with Warner Hutchinson, New Mexico State Univ.,
B.M.; with Aurelio de la Vega and Frank Campo,
California State Univ., Northridge. He was
first oboe, Norad Command Band, 1966-69; on
faculty, California State Univ., Northridge,
1973-74; Cameron Univ., Okla., 1974-76; then
free-lance oboe and bassoon player in Los
Angeles.
WORKS: ORCHESTRA: piano concerto; symphony; BAND: <u>Concerto tri-chroma</u>, woodwind
soloist and band; CHAMBER MUSIC: <u>Concert music</u>,
oboe and strings; trio for 3 horns; wind quintet; <u>Night music</u>, recorder, celeste, string trio;
<u>Chroasis</u>, harp, flute, cello, English horn; <u>3
modal pieces</u>, recorders and strings; <u>Serenade</u>,
14 winds; quintet for oboe and strings; also
choral works and solo pieces.
11312 Tiara, North Hollywood, CA 91601

KIEVMAN, CARSON
b. Hollywood, Calif., 27 Dec. 1949. Studied
with James Tenney, Earle Brown, Morton Subotnick,
California Inst. of the Arts, B.F.A. 1975, M.F.A.
1976. His awards include BMI awards, 1974,
1975; Margaret Grant Memorial prize, 1975; 2

MacDowell fellowships, 1975, 1978; Disney, Irvine, Calif. Inst., and Darmstadt scholarships; many commissions. He has been on the staff at the New School in New York.

WORKS: THEATRE: California mystery pack, full-length opera (sound drama/comedy), 1974; New opera, a mystery chamber opera in 1 act, 1976-77; The repercussive sojourn, (sound drama/comedy) for women's voices, Gertrude Stein text, 1974; Wake up, it's time to go to bed, 1-act sound drama, Tanglewood, 9 Aug. 1978; ORCHESTRA: Hollowangels, 1976; PERCUSSION: Concerto for bassoon and fire alarm system, bassoon and 4 to 16 percussionists, depending on the number of fire alarm bells in the building, 1974, rev. 1976; CHAMBER MUSIC: Sirocco, woodwind quintet, 1974-75; J. P. Confessions of a saxophone, piano, 5 winds, percussion, 1976; Multinationals and the heavens, percussion quartet, string quartet (masked), conductor (masked), 1976; Just enough rope, piano, percussion, tape, 1977; several vocal works.

c/o Associated Music Publishers, 866 3rd Ave., New York, NY 10022

KIHLKEN, HENRY
b. Sandusky, Ohio, 29 Sept. 1939. Studied at Oberlin Cons., 1958-59. He received the Capital Univ. composition award for 1967. He was organist in Port Clinton, Ohio, 1960-65; from 1973, at Old First Presbyterian Church, Sandusky.

WORKS: CHORUS: O saving victim, a cappella; Lute book lullaby, with harp; Grand choeur; O living bread, with soprano and alto solos; The crucifixion, with brass quartet and organ; That Easter Day with joy was bright; ORGAN: Prelude on Palestrina's Adoramus Te; and other works.

5216 E. Harbor Rd., Port Clinton, OH 43452

KILENYI, EDWARD, SR.
b. Bekes, Hungary, 25 Jan. 1884; U.S. citizen 1915; d. Tallahassee, Fla., 15 Aug. 1968. Studied at the Hungarian State Coll., B.A.; with Mascagni, Nat. Music School, Rome; Cologne Cons.; Columbia Univ., M.A., Ph.D. He was music director in film theatres in New York; then music director and composer in film studios in Hollywood for 30 years. His works included a string quartet and a string quintet.

KIM, BYONG-KON
b. Taegu, Korea, 28 May 1929; U.S. citizen 1973. Studied with Bernhard Heiden, Juan Orrego-Salas, Walter Kaufmann, Indiana Univ., M.M. magna cum laude 1964, D.M. cum laude 1968. He received a John Edward fellowship, 1965; research grant, American Council of Learned Societies, 1970; California State Univ. grant, 1970. He was faculty member, Villa Maria Inst. of Music, Buffalo, 1966-68; from 1968, at California State Univ., Los Angeles; from 1978, also conductor-music director, Seoul Chorale, Los Angeles.

WORKS: ORCHESTRA: Nak-Dong-Kang, symphonic poem; concertino for percussion, 1964; symphony, 1968; CHAMBER MUSIC: violin sonata; oboe sonata; string quartet, 1965; 4 short pieces, for piano; Sori, for marimba, 1975.

30458 Via Victoria, Rancho Palos Verdes, CA 90274

KIM, EARL
b. Dinuba, Calif., 6 Jan. 1920. Studied with Roger Sessions, Univ. of California, Berkeley, M.A. 1952; also with Arnold Schoenberg. His awards include Prix de Paris; grants from Guggenheim Found., Nat. Inst. of Arts and Letters, Fromm Found., Koussevitzky Found., Nat. Endowment for the Arts; and Brandeis Creative Arts Medal, 1971. He was faculty member, Princeton Univ., 1952-67; from 1967, at Harvard Univ.

WORKS: THEATRE: Exercises en route, soprano, chamber ensemble, dancers, actors, film, text by Samuel Beckett, 1971; Earthlight, violin, soprano, piano, lights, Cambridge, Mass., 19 May 1973; Eh, Joe, television play, narrator and 6 instruments, text by Beckett, 1974; Narratives, chamber ensemble, actor, actress, text by Beckett, Cambridge, 9-12 Feb. 1979; ORCHESTRA: Dialogues, piano and orch., 1959; violin concerto, New York, 25 Oct. 1979; CHAMBER MUSIC: violin sonata; cello sonata; Monologues, piano trio, 1976; VOICE: The road, cycle for baritone; Letters found near a suicide, cycle for soprano; They are far out, soprano, violin, cello, percussion, 1966; Gooseberries, she said, soprano, 5 instruments, percussion, 1968.

Music Dept., Harvard Univ., Cambridge, MA 02138

KIMBELL, MICHAEL ALEXANDER
b. Glen Cove, N.Y., 15 Mar. 1946. Studied with John Davison, Haverford Coll., B.A. 1967; with Robert Palmer and Karel Husa, Cornell Univ., Ph.D. 1971. He was faculty member, Johnson State Coll., 1971-75; at Univ. of the Pacific, 1976-78.

WORKS: ORCHESTRA: Wanderers Sturmlied, with chorus and baritone solo, 1971; Pastorale, small orch.; CHAMBER MUSIC: string quartet; woodwind quintet; Passacaglia, woodwind quintet; 5 dialogues, 2 clarinets; SONGS: 3 sonnets from the Portuguese; 3 Lieder.

KIMMEL, WALTER S.
b. New York, N.Y., 22 Jan. 1941. Studied with Herbert R. Inch and Donald Lybbert, Hunter Coll., B.A., M.A.; with Vladimir Ussachevsky and Mario Davidovsky, Columbia-Princeton Electronic Music Center. He has received awards from Class of 1895, Hunter Coll., 1962; second Dartmouth Coll. competition for electronic music, 1969; Oregon Coll., Kinetic Theatre competition, 1971; Cannes Internat. Film Festival, 1971; and commissions. He was on faculty, Hunter Coll., 1965-68; Moorhead State Coll., 1968-72; from 1972, Sangamon State Univ.

WORKS: CHAMBER MUSIC: Kireji, alto voice and 10 players, 1965; Dialogues, brass quartet, 1966; 5 Haiku settings, soprano, flute, violin, cello, 1966; FILM SCORES: Steps toward art, 1969; General Motors enters into heaven, score to Onus I, 1971; ELECTRONIC: Cronaca, 1967; Hide and seek, 1968; Bacchanalysis, 1971; The Dickens, What?, 1971; MULTIMEDIA: Trilogue, pianist and 2 loudspeakers, 1969; A generation of piece, or Warsore concerto for trombone, radios, and president, 1971.

KINDER, RALPH

KINDER, RALPH
b. Stalybridge, England, 27 Jan. 1876; to U.S.
1881; d. Bala, Pa., 14 Nov. 1952. Was organist
in Bristol, R.I.; in Philadelphia, 1899-1937;
then in Whitemarsh, Pa. He composed numerous
organ pieces, anthems, and songs.

KING, ALVIN
b. Orrville, Ohio, 24 Aug. 1917. Studied with
Cecil Effinger and George Crumb, Univ. of Colorado, D.M.A.; with Arthur Honegger in Paris; and
with Paul Hindemith at Yale Univ. He received
the McClesky commission, Univ. of Texas; and a
Woolley fellowship for study in France. His
faculty posts included Univ. of Arkansas, 1956-
59; Midland Coll., 1959-63; Mesa Coll., 1964-67;
from 1967, professor, Macalester Coll.
    WORKS: ORCHESTRA: Variations for orch.;
Sketch for orch.; Fantasy on a hymn tune, with
chorus; Daniel, with tenor and baritone soloists,
narrator; CHAMBER MUSIC: string quintet;
Periodic variations, string quartet; trio for
violin, viola, piano; suite for 4 recorders;
piano sonata; sextet, 2 tubas, 4 parts prerecorded; 4-hand intervals, piano; CHORUS:
Psalm 47, with 8 brasses; Psalm 67; My shepherd;
Song of Solomon, double chorus and 8 brasses;
Joseph, an oratorio; Psalm 131, with brass.
    722 E. 5th St., St. Paul, MN 55106

KING, JEFFREY
b. Ft. Wayne, Ind., 27 June 1942. Studied with
Jon Polifrone, Indiana State Univ.; with Carlisle
Floyd, Florida State Univ. He won first place,
Brown Univ. choral contest, 1971; Tennessee
Tech. Univ. contest, 1973. He has been faculty
member, Athens Coll., from 1966.
    WORKS: BAND: Excursion; Manifesto; CHAMBER
MUSIC: Facets, string orch.; violin sonata;
CHORUS: Dialogue; a wind has blown the rain
away; what if a much of a which of a wind; i
thank you God.
    Athens College, Athens, AL 35611

KING, JOHN LYNDON
b. Minneapolis, Minn., 28 Nov. 1953. Studied
with Morton Subotnick, Leonard Stein, Earle
Brown, and Stephan Mosko, California Inst. of
the Arts, B.F.A. cum laude 1976. He received a
Martha Baird Rockefeller grant.
    WORKS: CHAMBER MUSIC: Abschattungen, wood-
wind ensemble; Notes from the underground, 2
pianos; Sein, chamber ensemble; Bewusstsein,
string orch.; Selbstbewusstsein, percussion
quartet; Einsamselbstbewusstsein, brass octet;
piano trio; duet for cello and piano; piano
quartet; string quartet.
    874 Broadway, #705, New York, NY 10003

KING, KARL L.
b. Paintersville, Ohio, 21 Feb. 1891; d. Fort
Dodge, Iowa, 31 Mar. 1971. Published his first
march at 17 and began playing professionally.
By 1914 he was bandmaster of the Sells-Floto
Buffalo Bill combined circuses; in 1917-18, of
the Barnum and Bailey Circus Band; in 1920, re-
organized and built up the Fort Dodge Municipal
Band and was its director to 1970. Hundreds of
his marches were published, including Barnum and
Bailey's favorite; Pride of the Illini (for Univ.
of Illinois); Purple pageant (for Northwestern
Univ.). According to composer Meredith Willson,
King's life and music formed part of the inspir-
ation for the 1957 musical, The music man.

KING, ROBERT DAVIS
b. North Easton, Mass., 27 Nov. 1913. Studied
with Walter Piston, Edward Burlingame Hill, and
Nadia Boulanger, Harvard Univ.; with Fritz
Mahler at Juilliard School. He received a fellowship at the MacDowell Colony, 1940. He taught
in public schools, 1941-42; at Boston Univ.,
1946-50; public schools, 1950-55; from 1955, has
been music publisher.
    WORKS: WIND ENSEMBLE: Prelude and fugue
for 7 brass, or 3 brass and organ; French suite,
trumpet and baritone horn; 7 conversation pieces,
brass choir.
    7 Canton St., North Easton, MA 02356

KINGMAN, DANIEL C.
b. Los Angeles, Calif., 16 Aug. 1924. Studied
with Bernard Rogers, Eastman School of Music;
with H. Owen Reed, Michigan State Univ., Ph.D.
1964. His awards include a Huntington Hartford
fellowship; MacDowell Colony fellowship, 1978.
From 1956 he has been professor, California
State Univ., Sacramento.
    WORKS: OPERA: The Indian summer of Dry
Valley Johnson, 1965; ORCHESTRA: symphony in 1
movement, 1965; Earthscapes with birds, soprano
and orch., 1973; CHAMBER MUSIC: quintet for
winds; 4 miniatures for brass quartet; Canonic
etudes for brass, 1973; Rhapsody, 2 flutes and
viola; Hammersmith, string quartet, 1978.
    600 Shangri Lane, Sacramento, CA 95825

KINGSFORD, CHARLES
b. Brooklyn, N.Y., 16 Aug. 1907. Studied with
Rubin Goldmark, Juilliard Graduate School, 1925-
29, on fellowship; piano with Harold Trigg,
Rosina Lhevinne, Edith Ricci. He has received
annual ASCAP awards for his art songs, which
have been performed by many noted singers. He
was music director, Ft. Washington Synagogue,
New York, 1938-44; at Mt. Vernon, N.Y., 1944-50;
on faculty, American Theatre Wing, 1946-57;
music therapist, Veterans Admin. Hospital, East
Orange, N.J., 1953-72.
    WORKS: ORCHESTRA: We'll answer Stalingrad,
chorus and orch., 1943; And already the minutes,
voice and chamber orch., Saratoga Spa, N.Y., 27
Sept. 1937; SONGS: Alas, that spring should
vanish with the rose; The ballad of John Henry;
Eros; Rivets; Wallpaper; Down Harley Street; and
many other songs.
    150 W. 57th St., New York, NY 10019

KINGSLEY, GERSHON
b. Germany, 28 Oct. 1928; U.S. citizen 1950.
Studied at Jerusalem Cons., Los Angeles Cons.,
Columbia Univ., and Los Angeles State Coll. He
has received awards for radio and television
commercials, 1968; Internat. Broadcasting award,
1968; Emmy awards, 1968, 1969; CINE award, 1970;
Lion d'Or, Venice Film Festival, 1970; ASCAP

award, 1972. He was faculty member, New School
of Social Research, 1969-70.
WORKS: ORCHESTRA: Concerto Moogo; Confrontations; works for orchestra and synthesizer;
CHORUS: Sabbath for today, 1971; What is man,
1971; Bronze cactus, 1972.
150 W. 55th St., New York, NY 10010

KINNEY, GORDON J.
b. Rochester, N.Y., 10 Apr. 1905. Studied with
Edward Royce, Eastman School of Music, B.M. 1930;
Univ. of South Dakota, M.M. 1941; with Ernst von
Dohnanyi, Florida State Univ., Ph.D. 1962. He
held a scholarship at Florida State; received an
award, Nat. Composers contest, 1942. He was
faculty member, Morningside Coll., 1937-41; Ohio
Univ., 1941-45; Univ. of Kentucky, 1948-74, then
professor emeritus.
WORKS: ORCHESTRA: Piece for orchestra with
piano, 1935; symphony, 1951; Concert piece, horn
and chamber orch., Lexington, Ky., 29 Nov. 1973;
CHAMBER MUSIC: cello sonata, 1942; 2 string
quartets, 1942, 1953; Fantasy, horn and piano,
1950; suite for solo tuba, 1968; Ricercar, solo
tuba, 1968; Sinfonietta, 6 recorders, 1976;
Prelude, solo flute, 1978.
149 Rosemont Garden, Lexington, KY 40503

KINSCELLA, HAZEL GERTRUDE
b. Nora Springs, Iowa, 27 Apr. 1895; d. Seattle,
Wash., 15 July 1960. Studied at Univ. of
Nebraska, B.M., B.F.A., B.A.; Columbia Univ.,
M.A.; privately with Rossetter Gleason Cole and
Howard Brockway; received an honorary doctorate,
Univ. of Washington. She was professor, Univ.
of Nebraska, later at Univ. of Washington; author
of books on piano pedagogy.
WORKS: CHAMBER MUSIC: Indian sketches,
string quartet; CHORUS: A child is born, cantata; Psalm 150; Our prayer; My days have been
so wondrous free.

KINYON, JOHN
b. Elmira, N.Y., 23 May 1918. Studied at Eastman School of Music, B.M.; Ithaca Coll., M.S.
He taught in public schools for 20 years; then
joined faculty at Univ. of Miami.
WORKS: BAND: Ballad for Bambi; Carnival
for clarinets; Carnival for flutes; Carnival for
trumpets; Carnival for trombones.
1638 N.E. 7th Place, Ft. Lauderdale, FL
33310

KIRCHNER, LEON
b. Brooklyn, N.Y., 24 Jan. 1919. Studied at
Univ. of California, A.B. 1940; privately with
Ernest Bloch in San Francisco, with Roger
Sessions in New York. His awards include the
Prix de Rome, 1940; Guggenheim fellowship, 1948-
50; New York Music Critics' Circle award, 1950,
1960; Naumburg award, 1954; Pulitzer prize, 1967.
He was faculty member, San Francisco Cons.,
1946-48; Univ. of Southern California, 1950-54;
Mills Coll., 1954-61; from 1961, at Harvard
Univ.; visiting professor, Univ. of California,
Los Angeles, 1970-71.
WORKS: OPERA: Lily, based on Saul Bellow's
Henderson, the rain king, New York City Opera,

14 Apr. 1977; ORCHESTRA: sinfonia, 1951;
Toccata, strings, winds, percussion, 1955; 2
piano concertos, 1953, 1963; concerto for
violin, cello, 10 winds, percussion, 1960; Music
for orchestra, 1969; flute concerto, Indianapolis, 20 Oct. 1978; CHAMBER MUSIC: duo for
violin and piano, 1947; piano sonata, 1958; 3
string quartets, 1949, 1958, 1966 (with electronic sounds); sonata concertante, violin and
piano, 1952; piano trio, 1954; VOICE: Letter
and The times are nightfall, soprano and piano,
1943; Dawn, chorus and organ, Lorca text, 1946;
Of obedience and the runner, soprano and piano,
Whitman text, 1950; Words from Wordsworth,
chorus, 1966; Lily, string trio, woodwind quintet, piano, percussion, voice, 1973.
8 Hilliard St., Cambridge, MA 02138

KIRCK, GEORGE T.
b. Mt. Vernon, N.Y., 13 Apr. 1948. Studied
with Allan Hoffman and Edward Miller, Hartt Coll.
of Music, B.M.E. 1971; with Hale Smith, Univ. of
Connecticut; with Russell Peck, Northern Illinois
Univ., M.M. 1976; with Edwin London and Ben
Johnston, Univ. of Illinois. He taught in public
schools, 1971-75; Northern Illinois Univ., from
1975.
WORKS: WIND ENSEMBLE: Ultra, improvisation
piece, 1976; sextet, 1978; CHAMBER MUSIC: trio
for flute, clarinet, horn, 1966; Song to wind,
alto saxophone, percussion, tape, 1971; Result-
ants, saxophone quartet, 1976; also electronic
works and jazz/rock pieces.
833 Ridge Dr., #303, DeKalb, IL 60115

KIRK, THERON
b. Alamo, Tex., 26 Sept. 1919. Studied with
Bernard Rogers, Eastman School of Music; with
Karel Jirak at Roosevelt Univ.; and at Baylor
Univ. His awards include several commissions;
ASCAP awards; Benjamin award; Knox-Galesburg
award; Phi Mi Alpha Sinfonia Orpheus award,
1976; appointment as Piper Professor by the
Minnie Stevens Piper Found., 1976. He has been
professor, San Antonio Coll., from 1965.
WORKS: THEATRE: The Lib. 393 b.c., 1-act
comic opera; ORCHESTRA: 2 symphonies; Intrada;
concerto for orch.; Vignettes; An orchestra
primer; BAND: Aylesford variations; Smoky
Mountain suite; CHORUS: cantatas with orch.;
and more than 600 published choral works.
3430 Fallen Leaf Lane, San Antonio, TX
78230

KISS, JANOS
b. Hungary, 21 Mar. 1920; U.S. citizen 1973.
Attended Bela Bartok Cons.; Franz Liszt Acad.
and People's Educ. Inst. in Budapest; Western
Reserve Univ., Cleveland. His awards include
several commissions and honorary membership in
Zoltan Kodaly Acad., Chicago. He has been
faculty member, Cleveland Music School Settlement, from 1964 and has taught also in other
schools in the area.
WORKS: ORCHESTRA: violin concerto; clarinet
concerto; Western legend rhapsody, harp and
orch.; cello concerto, Fairview Park, Ohio, 29
Feb. 1976; Lexington '76, rhapsody for orch.,

KITZKE, JEROME P.

Parma Heights, Ohio, 11 Apr. 1976; <u>Divertimento</u>, Fairview Park, 27 Feb. 1977; <u>Via lactea (The galaxy)</u>, symphonic fantasy, Fairview Park, 21 May 1978; <u>Rhapsody</u> for cimbalom and orch., Elkhart, Ind., 28 Jan. 1979; CHAMBER MUSIC: <u>Fantasy</u>, flute and piano; concerto for trombone and piano; <u>On the wing</u>, flute and guitar; <u>Josepha</u>, recorder, string trio, harp; <u>Meditation</u>, violin and organ or piano; <u>Twilight mist</u>, string quartet and organ; <u>Spring--at last</u>, harp ensemble, 1970; harp and woodwind quintet; <u>Osiris</u>, nonet, 1972; <u>The mystery of spring</u>, string quartet and harp; <u>In homage</u>, harp ensemble, written for the Silver Jubilee of Queen Elizabeth II of England, performed at Windsor Castle, 1978.
229 Bradley Rd., Bay Village, OH 44140

KITZKE, JEROME P.
b. Milwaukee, Wis., 6 Feb. 1955. Studied with John Downey and Yehuda Yannay, Univ. of Wisconsin, B.M. 1978. His awards include the Polanki scholarship; Johnson Wax Found. performance grant, 1978; and commissions. He has been assistant director, Music from Almost Yesterday, from 1977.
WORKS: ORCHESTRA: <u>The rime of the ancient mariner</u>, with chorus and soloists, 1978; CHAMBER MUSIC: <u>Aberrations for 5 plus 1</u>, woodwind quintet and trombone, 1973; <u>Triste December</u>, piano, 1973; <u>Waxdale quartet</u>, string quartet, 1974; <u>Flute-fieren</u>, solo flute, 1974; <u>Shaecceity-Hesse</u>, soprano and chamber ensemble, 1976; <u>A day of dappled seaborne clouds</u>, soprano, narrator, cello, 1978.
3038 N. Fredrick, Milwaukee, WI 53211

KLAUS, KENNETH BLANCHARD
b. Earlville, Iowa, 11 Nov. 1923. Studied with Philip Greeley Clapp, Univ. of Iowa, Ph.D. 1950. He received awards from the Nat. Fed. of Music Clubs. He has been faculty member, Louisiana State Univ., from 1950; and associate conductor, Baton Rouge Symphony, from 1967.
WORKS: THEATRE: <u>Tennis anyone?</u>, operatic farce, 1957; <u>Moira</u>, monodramatic opera; music for <u>Death of a salesman</u>, Baton Rouge, 24 Feb. 1954; <u>On our way</u>, a pageant, 1940; <u>Always Acadia</u>, pageant, 1955; <u>Louisiana's Koasati</u>, film score, 1955; ORCHESTRA: 4 symphonies; <u>Antonyms</u>, Baton Rouge, 19 Mar. 1959; <u>Adagio</u>, bassoon and orch.; <u>The Alamo by night</u>; violin concerto; <u>Concerto brevis</u>, flute and strings, 1950; cello concerto; percussion concerto; <u>Fugato concertanto</u>; <u>Markings</u>, 1970; <u>Cantilenas among the pillars in matrix alpha</u>; <u>Tapestries</u>; CHAMBER MUSIC: 4 string quartets, 1947, 1951, 1957, 1963; 2 violin sonatas; woodwind sextet; cello sonata; suite for cello and piano; horn sonata; oboe sonata; <u>Music for 4 trombones</u>; woodwind quintet; 2 sonatas for solo violin; <u>3 aleatory matrices</u>; <u>4 pieces</u>, cello and piano; <u>Variations</u>, oboe and piano; <u>Fantasy variations</u>, viola; also songs, piano and organ pieces. He is also author of <u>The romantic period in music</u>, Boston, 1970, and magazine articles.
823 Kenilworth Parkway, Baton Rouge, LA 70808

KLAUSMEYER, PETER BALLARD
b. Cincinnati, Ohio, 28 Nov. 1942. Studied with Scott Huston, Univ. of Cincinnati; Leslie Bassett, Ross Lee Finney, George Cacioppo, George Balch Wilson, Univ. of Michigan. He tied for first place, 2nd Internat. Competition for Electronic Music, Dartmouth Arts Council. He was faculty member, Meredith Coll., N.C., 1973-78.
WORKS: ORCHESTRA: <u>. . . partial fulfillment . . .</u>, D.M.A. thesis, Ann Arbor, Mich., 15 Nov. 1972; ELECTRONIC: <u>Cambrian Sea</u>; <u>Teddybears' picnic</u>, 1972.
Colonial Arms, Apt. 1, Chapel Hill, NC 27514

KLAUSS, KENNETH
Studied with Ernst Toch, Univ. of Southern California. His works include a sonata for harpsichord and timpani; sonata for solo trumpet; sonata for solo tuba.

KLAUSS, NOAH
b. Lebanon, Pa., 14 Oct. 1901. Studied at Harrisburg Cons.; at Elizabethtown Coll.; violin with Max Pollikoff and Ottakar Cadek. He taught violin for 50 years; at Elizabethtown Coll., 1958-61; was assistant director, Harrisburg Symphony, 1948; founder and director, Harrisburg Youth Symphony Orch., from 1949.
WORKS: WIND ENSEMBLE: <u>Jakarta</u>, solo horn and clarinet choir; <u>Night song</u>, saxophone choir; <u>Prelude</u>, 6 clarinets; CHAMBER MUSIC: <u>Evangeline</u>, harp and organ.
545 Brittany Dr., State College, PA 16801

KLEEN, LESLIE
b. Minden, Nebr., 27 Nov. 1942. Studied with Normand Lockwood, Univ. of Denver; Robert Palmer and Karel Husa, Cornell Univ.; with Lejaren Hiller and Morton Feldman, State Univ. of New York, Buffalo. He was instructor, State Univ. of New York, Buffalo, 1971-74; joined faculty at Ohio Univ., 1976.
WORKS: ORCHESTRA: <u>Conserere for 2 orchestras</u>; CHAMBER MUSIC: <u>Air</u>, male voice, chamber ensemble; <u>2 Walt Whitman songs</u>; string trio; ELECTRONIC: <u>4 movements by computer</u>; <u>O progress</u>, tape.
Music Dept., Ohio University, Athens, OH 45701

KLEIMAN, STEPHEN ROBERT
b. Brooklyn, N.Y., 18 Aug. 1943. Studied with Peter Pindar Stearns, Mannes Coll. of Music; with Ross Lee Finney, Leslie Bassett, George Cacioppo, George Wilson, Univ. of Michigan. He received the Sigvald Thompson award, Fargo-Moorhead Symph., 1973; Fulbright-Hays for study in France with Max Deutsch, 1973. He was teaching fellow, Univ. of Michigan, 1971-73.
WORKS: ORCHESTRA: <u>Concerto for orchestra</u>, 1971, Fargo-Moorhead Symph., 24 Jan. 1974; CHAMBER MUSIC: <u>6 short pieces</u>, string quartet, 1948; suite for guitar; <u>6 haiku</u>, voice and piano, 1970; <u>Patterns</u>, piano, 1970; <u>Sanctuary</u>, flute, bassoon, string quintet, percussion, 1971; <u>Festivity</u>, flute, viola, harp, 1972; <u>4 graphic</u>

duets, 2 instruments, 1972; Sweet, bassoon, marimba, piano, 3 voices, 1972; 31 Connally-strasse (in memoriam), clarinet, horn, string trio, 1972; Fairytale, 2 flutes and tape, 1973; Quattre a battre, 4 conductors and audience, 1973; CHORUS: So shy, shy, shy, 1972; Carnival, with brass and organ, 1972.

    1 Rue Francois Coppée, 75015, Paris, France

KLEIN, JOHN M.
    b. Rahns, Pa., 21 Feb. 1913. Studied with H. Alexander Matthews, Philadelphia Music Acad.; at the Mozarteum, Salzburg; with Nadia Boulanger and Marcel Dupre in Paris; with Paul Hindemith in Leipzig and at Tanglewood. His awards include Nat. Endowment for the Arts grant; Pennsylvania Council on the Arts grant; U.S. Treasury Silver Medal. He is free-lance composer for films, radio, television, and concert artist on the carillon.
    WORKS: ORCHESTRA: violin concerto, 1944; Horace, the bear, with narrator, 1946; CHAMBER MUSIC: Gotham suite, piano; sonata for brass quartet; and some 600 other works for orchestra, band, chamber groups, piano, organ, chorus, and songs. He is also author of a 2-volume book: The first 4 centuries of music; and The art of playing the modern carillon.
    Rahns, PA 19426

KLEIN, LEONARD
    b. Clarkdale, Ariz., 19 Feb. 1929. Studied with Darius Milhaud, Mills Coll.; with Jean Rivier in Paris; and with Philip Bezanson, Univ. of Iowa. He won 2 Copley awards and 2 first prizes at Aspen, Colo. He has been on the faculty at Univ. of Oklahoma, 1961-63; Indiana Univ., 1963-65; Mills Coll., 1965-71; from 1971, Stockton State Coll.
    WORKS: ORCHESTRA: concerto for piano, winds, and percussion; CHAMBER MUSIC: Concert-piece, for cello; duo for violin and piano; CHORUS: Psalm 47, women's voices, soloists, organ, and ring modulator; PIANO: sonata for 2 pianos; Fantasies, piano solo.
    Stockton State College, Pomona, NJ 08240

KLEIN, LOTHAR
    b. Hannover, Germany, 27 Jan. 1932; U.S. citizen 1945. Studied at Univ. of Minnesota, Ph.D.; with Boris Blacher in Berlin. He was Fulbright fellow, 1958-60; Fulbright visiting professor, Hochschule für Musik, Berlin, guest lecturer for 150th anniversary of the Hochschule; received Rockefeller grants, 1964, 1965, 1967; and has been a MacDowell Colony fellow. He was faculty member, Univ. of Texas, 1962-68; then at Univ. of Toronto.
    WORKS: ORCHESTRA: piano concerto, 1954; 3 symphonies, 1955, 1965, 1972; concerto for 4 winds and orch., 1958; Appassionata, 1959; Symmetries I-IV, 1959-64; Epitaphs for orch., 1963; Trio concertante, solo strings and orch., 1964; Charivari, music for an imaginary comedy; Musique a go-go; Janizary music, 1970; Sinfonia concertante; Passacaglia of the zodiac, 14 solo strings, 1971; Music for violin and orch., 1972; Slices of time, trumpet and string orch., 1973;

The philosopher of the kitchen, contralto and orch., 1974; Musica antiqua, consort and orch., 1975; CHAMBER MUSIC: wind quintet, 1952; piano quintet, 1953; piano sonata, 1968; trio sonata, clarinet, cello, piano, and jazz drums, 1969; 4 for 1, suite for solo contrabass, 1970; VOICE: Epigrams of Sappho, cantata for actress, 3 soloists, percussion, 1958; Orpheus: A lyrical essay, narrator, chorus, winds, piano, 1976.
    c/o ASCAP, 1 Lincoln Plaza, New York, NY 10022

KLEIN, MANUEL
    b. London, England, 6 Dec. 1876; to U.S. 1900; d. London, 1 June 1919. On coming to the U.S., he became music director of the New York Hippodrome and composed music for many of the productions. He later quarreled with J. J. Schubert over some instruments he needed, resigned from the Hipprodrome, and returned to England.
    WORKS: MUSICAL SHOWS: Mr. Pickwick, 1903; A society circus, 1905; The pied piper, 1908; A trip to Japan; America, 1913; Hop o' my thumb, 1913; The wars of the world, 1914.

KLEINMAN, ISADOR I.
    b. New York, N.Y., 25 Jan. 1913. Held a Damrosch scholarship for study of violin and viola, 1920-30. He played in theatre orchestras; Roxy Theatre Orch., 1946-49; American Symphony, 1954; from 1958, with Little Orchestra Society.
    WORKS: ORCHESTRA: Musical offering; Suite for strings; Tel Aviv, tone poem; violin concerto; viola concerto.

KLEINSINGER, GEORGE
    b. San Bernadino, Calif., 13 Feb. 1914. Studied with Marion Bauer and Philip James, New York Univ.; with Frederick Jacobi and Bernard Wagenaar, Juilliard Graduate School, on a fellowship in composition. He received an Emmy nomination for the film score, Greece: The Golden Age; and an Oscar nomination for the film, Tubby the tuba. He was guest lecturer, Brooklyn Coll., 1956, 1957.
    WORKS: THEATRE: Life in the diary of a secretary, chamber opera (Nat. New Theatre prize); Shinbone Alley, musical based on archie and mehitabel, 1954; ORCHESTRA: symphony, 1942; Fantasy, violin and orch.; Victory against heaven; Scherzo; Westward ho!; Western rhapsody; Pantomime; Joie de vivre; cello concerto, 1946; Street corner concerto, clarinet and orch., 1947; violin concerto, 1953; ORCHESTRA (with narrator, for children): Tubby the tuba, 1942; Story of Celeste; Johnny the stranger; Pan the piper; Peewee the piccolo; BAND: Symphony of winds, with narrator; CHAMBER MUSIC: clarinet quintet; sonatina for flute, cello, piano; string quartet; Design for woodwinds; VOICE: I hear America singing, baritone and orch.; Farewell to a hero; Brooklyn baseball cantata; and many other works, including film scores.
    222 W. 23rd St., New York, NY 10011

KLEMENT, JEROME
    b. Chicago, Ill., 19 Mar. 1922. Studied with Hans Rosenwald, Bernard Brindell, Chicago Musical

KLEMM, GUSTAV

Coll., Roosevelt Univ., American Operatic Laboratory. He was cantor, Beth Hillel, Wilmette, Ill., 1959-64; Temple Emanu-el, Ft. Lauderdale, from 1965.
WORKS: VOCAL (Jewish liturgy): <u>Li Lekach Tov</u>; <u>Eili, Eili</u>; <u>Vohauta</u>; <u>Ma Tovu</u>.
4760 N.E. 18th Terrace, Ft. Lauderdale, FL 33308

KLEMM, GUSTAV
b. Baltimore, Md., 6 Feb. 1897; d. Baltimore, Md., 5 Sept. 1947. Studied with Gustave Strube, Peabody Cons.; held a scholarship in cello with Bart Wirtz. His other awards included an Etude prize and the Chicago Singing Teachers Guild award. He was an army bandmaster in World War I; conductor, City Park Band, Baltimore, 1922-25; music critic, <u>Baltimore Sun</u>, 1920-32; radio program director, 1925-38; head, preparatory department, Peabody Cons., 1944-47. He composed several hundred songs and many film scores.

KLENNER, JOHN
b. Germany, 24 Feb. 1890; d. New York, N.Y., 13 Aug. 1955.
WORKS: <u>Fantasia</u>, viola and orch.; <u>Variations</u>, string orch.; squares and rounds on <u>My old brown fiddle</u>, string orch.; popular songs.

KLENZ, WILLIAM
b. La Conner, Wash., 24 May 1915. Studied at Curtis Inst.; at Guildhall, London; Paris Conservatoire; and with Paul Hindemith, Yale Univ. He was faculty member, Duke Univ., 1947-66; from 1966, State Univ. of New York at Binghamton; Yale Univ., 1971-73.
WORKS: CHAMBER MUSIC: 3 string quartets; cello sonata; CHORUS: <u>Te Deum</u>, with brass, 1944; SONGS: <u>Walk the silver night</u>; <u>Hush</u>; <u>Golden fans</u>; <u>Meditation at stop light</u>.
Music Dept., State Univ. of N.Y., Binghamton, NY 13901

KLETZSCH, CHARLES
b. Milwaukee, Wis., 4 Apr. 1926. Studied with Walter Piston at Harvard Univ. He has been resident composer, Dunster House, Harvard Univ., from 1960.
WORKS: THEATRE: <u>Audubon and the 3 bears</u>, a small opera; ORCHESTRA: 2 symphonies; CHAMBER MUSIC: trio for flute, viola, piano; <u>Tiberias</u>, cantata for baritone and organ.
Dunster House Library, Cambridge, MA 02138

KLIMISCH, SISTER MARY JANE
b. Utica, S.Dak., 22 Aug. 1920. Studied at American Cons.; with John Egan, St. Joseph's Coll., Rensselaer, Ind.; and with Robert Wykes, Washington Univ., Ph.D. She was faculty member, Mt. Marty High School, 1943-50; then at Mt. Marty Coll.
WORKS: CHORUS: <u>Mass to honor Joan of Arc</u>; <u>Nativity antiphon</u>; <u>Glory hymn book</u> (a collaboration); and numerous unpublished liturgial works.
Mount Marty College, Yankton, SD 57078

KLIMKO, RONALD JAMES
b. Lena, Wis., 13 Dec. 1936. Studied with Irwin

Sonenfield, Milton Coll., B.M.E. 1959; with Hilmar Kuckhardt and Robert Crane, Univ. of Wisconsin, M.M. 1963, Ph.D. 1968. He received a Leaman Stringer award, 1958; Wisconsin Fed. of Music Clubs award, 1963; Nat. Endowment for the Arts grant, 1967. He was faculty member, Moorhead State Coll., 1966-67; Indiana State Univ., 1967-68; from 1968, at Univ. of Idaho.
WORKS: BALLET: <u>The highway</u>, 1965; ORCHESTRA: <u>The hollow men</u>, chorus and orch., 1963; <u>Edgewood overture</u>, 1964; <u>Introduction, pastorale, and recercare</u>, 1965; <u>Echoes</u>, with chorus and tape, 1967; CHAMBER MUSIC: <u>A child's garden of weeds</u>, woodwind quintet, 1964; <u>Canonic variations</u>, chamber orch., 1964; string quartet, 1964; woodwind quintet, 1965; <u>Contours</u>, cello and piano, 1967; violin sonata, 1968; <u>Passages</u>, clarinet and bassoon, 1976.
School of Music, Univ. of Idaho, Moscow, ID 83843

KLOTZ, LEORA. See DRETKE, LEORA N.

KLUCEVSEK, GUY
b. New York, N.Y., 26 Feb. 1947. Studied with Robert Bernat, Indiana Univ. of Penn.; Gerald Shapiro, Univ. of Pittsburgh; and with Morton Subotnick, California Inst. of the Arts. He is a free-lance composer-accordionist.
WORKS: ACCORDION: <u>Phantasmagoria</u>; <u>Amplifaccordion</u>; <u>Ave Maria misty</u>; <u>Coruscation</u>; <u>Aeolian variations</u>; <u>3 A.M.</u>; <u>Cassandra</u>, a duet; ELECTRONIC: <u>Happenings</u>; <u>Fawos</u>; <u>Serenity</u>; <u>Resolution</u>; <u>Spheres</u>, ensemble with tape.

KNIGHT, MORRIS
b. Charleston, S.C., 25 Dec. 1933. Studied at Univ. of Georgia, B.F.A. 1956; at Ball State Univ., M.M. 1966. His awards include annual ASCAP awards, 1967-74; MacDowell award, 1970; Cohen award, 2nd Contemporary Music Expo., Cincinnati; Ford publication award, 1972; Nat. Endowment for the Arts grant, 1976; and commissions. He was radio station staff member, Athens, Ga., 1956-62, San Francisco, 1962-63; then joined the faculty at Ball State Univ.
WORKS: CHAMBER MUSIC: <u>Introduction and allegro</u>, trumpet; <u>Cassation</u>, trumpet, horn, trombone; <u>Selfish giant suite</u>, flute, clarinet, bassoon, trombone; 6 brass quartets; alto saxophone sonata, 1964; <u>Instances</u>, woodwind quintet, 1965; saxophone quartet, Muncie, Ind., 18 Feb. 1969; 4 brass quintets, 1972; ELECTRONIC: <u>Refractions</u>, clarinet and tape, 1962; <u>Origin of prophecy</u>, 1964; <u>Luminescences</u>, 1967; <u>After Guernica</u>, 1969; <u>Entity I--Music for the global village</u>, for 20 tape recorders and 40 speakers arranged along the walls of the performance area; the audience may sit, lie, or otherwise deposit themselves; the piece was taken on a nationwide tour in 1973; <u>Conation</u>, a similar presentation, 1976. Knight is also coauthor of <u>Aural comprehension in music</u>.
2424 Petty Rd., Muncie, IN 47304

KNOX, CHARLES
b. Atlanta, Ga., 19 Apr. 1929. Studied with Bernhard Heiden at Indiana Univ. He received

first prize, Georgia Fed. of Music Clubs contest, 1955; several commissions. He was principal trombonist, Atlanta Symph. Orch., 1948-51; faculty member, Mississippi Coll., 1955-65; from 1965, at Georgia State Univ.

WORKS: WIND ENSEMBLE: symphony for brass and percussion, 1965; solo for trumpet with brass trio; solo for tuba with brass trio; music for brass quintet, Washington, D.C., 4 June 1975; CHAMBER MUSIC: Prelude, violin and organ; Scherzo, woodwind quintet; CHORUS: The last days; Festival procession; Sing we to our God above; Psalm of praise; A prayer of thanksgiving; PIANO: sonatina; Suite for piano 4 hands.

Georgia State Univ., Univ. Plaza, Atlanta, GA 30303

KOBLITZ, DAVID
b. Cleveland, Ohio, 5 Oct. 1948. Studied with George Crumb, Univ. of Pennsylvania, B.A.; with Ross Lee Finney, Leslie Bassett, George Cacioppo, Univ. of Michigan; with Donald Martino at Tanglewood; and with Jack Beeson, Columbia Univ. He received 3 BMI student awards; grants from Nat. Endowment for the Arts, 1975, Mass. Creative Artists Services, 1975, N.Y. Creative Artists Public Service Program, 1978; Charles E. Ives scholarship, 1975; Guggenheim fellowship, 1979. He was lecturer, Emerson Coll., 1974-75; adjunct instructor, Rutgers Univ., from 1976, and Pace Univ., from 1977.

WORKS: ORCHESTRA: Trism, 1971; Gris-gris, 1973; CHAMBER MUSIC: Oxolotyl, 2 contrabasses, 1970; Nomos, contrabass solo; Lobo, chamber ensemble, 1971; Levitation boogie, chamber ensemble; 3-part inventions, string trio; Leaves of hypnos, chamber ensemble; Harmonica Monday, chamber ensemble; ELECTRONIC: Ceremony of shrugs, tape; Dwellers of the threshold; Wonders of the invisible world, tape.

241 E. 76th St., #7C, New York, NY 10021

KOCH, FREDERICK
b. Cleveland, Ohio, 4 Apr. 1924. Studied with Herbert Elwell, Cleveland Inst. of Music, B.M. 1949; Arthur Shepherd, Case-Western Reserve Univ., M.A. 1950; with Henry Cowell and Bernard Rogers, Eastman School of Music, D.M.A. 1969; piano with Beryl Rubinstein and Leonard Shure. His awards include 2 MacDowell fellowships, 1971-72; Homer B. Hatch award; Benjamin award, 1964; first prize, American Choral Directors contest; Composers Press composition award; grants from Nat. Endowment for the Arts, Ohio Arts Council, American Music Center; annual ASCAP awards. In 1952 he founded a private music school, which became affiliated with the Cleveland Music School Settlement in 1971, where he is still director; was on faculty, Baldwin-Wallace Cons., 1964-66, and Cuyahoga Community Coll., 1969-70.

WORKS: OPERA: Invasion, 1974; ORCHESTRA: Short symphony; concertino, saxophone and orch. or band; Symphonic suite, voice and orch.; Dance overture; River journey; Overture for America, chamber orch.; concerto for 2 pianos and orch.; CHAMBER MUSIC: 3 string quartets; string quintet; Trio of praise, voice, viola,

piano; Sound particles, piano percussion, reciter; 3 dance episodes, saxophone and tape; Microcosms, percussion quartet, tape, film; Veltin fantasy, oboe and strings; Monadnock cadenzas and variations, 8 instruments and tape; 3 pictures, violin and piano; Barometric readings, percussion quartet and tape; Avicular trilogy, flute and mini-moog; City moon, flute, vocalise, piano; PIANO: 2 impressions, 2 pianos; 12/12, 12 variations on a 12-tone row, 2 pianos; Sonics, piano solo, Washington, D.C., 21 Mar. 1977; also works for band, choral works, songs.

2249 Valleyview Dr., Rocky River, OH 44116

KOELLING, ELOISE
b. Centralia, Ill., 3 Mar. 1908. Studied at Northwestern Univ. and at Chicago Cons. Coll. Her awards include 3 Univ. of Wisconsin grants; 14 first prizes, Wisconsin Composers contests; Padro Pas award, Olivet Coll.; performance at Fed. of Women Convention and 2 works at Internat. Society for Contemporary Music, Chicago; and commissions. She was professor, Univ. of Wisconsin, Milwaukee, 1949-68.

WORKS: ORCHESTRA: a symphony; 2 piano concertos; CHAMBER MUSIC: 4 string quartets; 5 woodwind ensembles; Improvisation for timpani; CHORUS: As long as my Saviour reigns; Naomi's lament, women's voices and woodwinds; Democratic thinking in 18th, 19th, 20th centuries; number of anthems and works for women's voices; numerous songs.

P.O. Box 131, Palmyra, WI 53156

KOGAN, ROBERT
b. New York, N.Y., 2 Sept. 1940. Studied with Leon Kirchner, Harvard Univ.; with Hall Overton, Juilliard School; with Bruno Maderna, Salzburg and at Tanglewood; with Robert Starer and Jacob Druckman, Brooklyn Coll. His awards include a conducting prize, Salzburg, 1968; Nat. Endowment for the Arts grant, 1976; Criterion Found. grant, 1978. He has been faculty member, Wagner Coll., from 1976, and conductor, Wagner Coll. Orch., from 1978; music director, Doctors Orchestral Society of N.Y., from 1976.

WORKS: ORCHESTRA: Gemini, with solo marimba and vibraphone, 1977; CHAMBER MUSIC: Galaxy 8, flute, trumpet, cello, 4 percussion, 1973; sonata #2, flute, marimba, viola, 1975; Planetarium, percussion ensemble, 1976; piano trio, 1979.

1111 Ocean Ave., Brooklyn, NY 11230

KOHN, KARL
b. Vienna, Austria, 1 Aug. 1926; U.S. citizen 1945. Attended New York Coll. of Music; studied with Walter Piston, Irving Fine, Randall Thompson, Harvard Univ., B.A. 1950, M.A. 1954. He was Fulbright research fellow, Helsinki, 1954-55; Guggenheim fellow and grantee of Howard Found., 1961-62; Ford Found. sabbatical fellow, 1968-69; recipient of Mellon Found. grant, 1973, and Nat. Endowment for the Arts grant, 1975. He has been faculty member, Pomona Coll., from 1950, Thatcher professor and composer-in-residence, 1973.

KOHS, ELLIS B.

WORKS: ORCHESTRA: Sinfonia concertante, piano and orch., Claremont, Calif., 23 Mar. 1952; Castles and kings, suite for children, Claremont, 22 Mar. 1959; 3 scenes, 1960, Los Angeles, 5 May 1965; Concerto mutabile, piano and orch., San Francisco, 18 Mar. 1963; Interludes, 1964; Episodes, piano and orch., 1966, Oakland, 19 Apr. 1968; Intermezzo, piano and strings, 1969; Esdras--anthems and interludes, flute and piano solo, chorus, orch., 1970; Centone per orchestra, Claremont, 27 July 1973; Introduction and parodies, New York, 11 May 1974; Innocent psaltery, "colonial music," 1976; WIND ENSEMBLE: Fanfare, brass and percussion, Tanglewood, 31 July 1952; motet for 8 horns, Los Angeles, 23 Feb. 1954; horn quartet, 1957; Bicentennial music, winds and percussion, 1975; brass quintet, 1976; CHAMBER MUSIC: 3 pieces, flute and piano, 1958; Divertimento, woodwind quartet, 1959; Capriccios, chamber ensemble, 1962; Serenade, wind quintet and piano, 1962; Little suite, wind quintet, 1963; Kaleidoscope, string quartet, New York, 3 Dec. 1965; Rhapsodies, marimba, vibraphone, percussion, 1968; Impromptus, for 8 winds, 1969; Reflections, clarinet and piano, 1970; Variations, horn and piano, 1971; Encounters III, violin and piano, 1971; Encounters IV, oboe and piano, 1972; Encounters V, bassoon and piano, 1973; Paranyms, flute and piano, 1974; sonatina, marimba, 4 hands, 1976; The prophet bird, woodwind trio, string trio, horn, trombone, percussion, harp, Los Angeles, 11 Oct. 1978; Son of prophet bird, harp solo, 1977; PIANO: 5 pieces, 1955, Brandeis Univ., 15 Apr. 1958; Rhapsody, New York, 21 Nov. 1960; 5 bagatelles, Hilversum, Holland, 12 Feb. 1961; Partita, 1963; Recreations, piano, 4 hands, 1968; Second rhapsody, Los Angeles, 15 Nov. 1971; Bits and pieces, 1973; also choral works and many songs.
674 W. 10th St., Claremont, CA 91711

KOHS, ELLIS
b. Chicago, Ill., 12 May 1916. Studied with Carl Bricken, Univ. of Chicago, M.A. 1938; with Bernard Wagenaar, Juilliard School; with Walter Piston, Harvard Univ. His awards include a BMI publication award; Columbia Univ. Ditson award; MacDowell Colony and Wurlitzer Found. fellowships; and many commissions. After serving as air force band leader in World War II, he taught at Wesleyan Univ., 1946-48; Coll. of the Pacific, 1948-50; and from 1950, at Univ. of Southern California.
WORKS: OPERA: Amerika, based on Kafka, 1969; Rhinoceros, based on Ionescu, 1974; THEATRE: Lord of the ascendant, concert narrative in 3 acts for 8 solo dancers, 7 solo voices, chorus, orch., 1956; music for Macbeth, 1974; ORCHESTRA: concerto for orchestra, 1942; Passacaglia, organ and strings, 1946; Legend, oboe and strings; cello concerto, 1947; Psalm XXV, chorus and orch., 1947; 4 orchestral songs, voice and orch.; 2 symphonies, 1950, 1956; violin concerto, Los Angeles, 24 Apr. 1981; CHAMBER MUSIC: Night watch, flute, horn, timpani, 1943; 2 string quartets, 1942, 1948; bassoon sonatina, 1944; brass trio; violin sonatina, 1948; chamber

concerto for viola and string nonet, 1949; clarinet sonata, 1951; Studies in variations (Part I: woodwind quintet, Part II: piano quintet, Part III: piano sonata, Part IV: sonata for solo violin), 1962; snare drum sonata, 1966; suite for cello and piano, 1970; Calumny, bass baritone, flute, horn, cello, timpani, Los Angeles, 7 Nov. 1978; PIANO: Etude in memory of Bartok, 1946; Piano variations; sonata; Toccata, 1948; Fantasy on la, sol, fa, re, mi, 1949; 10 2-voice inventions, 1950; Variations on L'homme armé; also choral works, songs, and organ pieces. He is author of a textbook, Music theory, New York, 1961; and Musical form: Studies in analysis and synthesis, Boston, 1976.
8025 Highland Trail, Los Angeles, CA 90046

KOK, JAN
b. Wromerveer, Neth., 23 Aug. 1921; U.S. citizen 1945. Studied with George F. McKay, Univ. of Washington; Arnold Elston, Univ. of Oregon; and with Walter Piston, Harvard Univ. He received a performance award, Composers Congress, Akron, Ohio, 1944. He taught in public schools, 1945-46, 1951; then joined the faculty at Univ. of Maine, Presque Isle.
WORKS: VOCAL: Round about, 34 original canons and rounds; also choral works, chamber music, and piano pieces.
10 Pleasant St., Presque Isle, ME 04769

KOLAR, HENRY
b. Chicago, Ill., 1 Dec. 1923. Studied with Leon Stein, De Paul Univ.; with Robert Kurka in New York; with Alfred Uhl in Vienna; and with Ingolf Dahl, Univ. of Southern California. He was faculty member, San Diego Mesa Coll., 1966-70; from 1970, at Univ. of San Diego.
WORKS: CHAMBER MUSIC: string quartet; Divertimento, violin, horn, double bass; Aphorisms for strings; Little suite, 2 violins; Rhapsody, cello and piano; Andante, for strings; and Music for brass, commissioned by Young Audiences of America, San Diego chapter, 1968.
4715 Glacier Ave., San Diego, CA 92120

KOLAR, VICTOR
b. Budapest, Hungary, 12 Feb. 1888; to U.S. 1900; d. Detroit, Mich., 16 June 1957. Graduated from Prague Cons.; was violinist in the New York Symphony, 1907-19; associate conductor, Detroit Symphony, 1920-41.
WORKS: ORCHESTRA: Hiawatha, 1908; A fairy tale, symphonic poem, 1912; Americana, symphonic suite, 1914; symphony, 1916; Slovakian rhapsody, 1922; also marches, violin pieces, songs.

KOLB, BARBARA
b. Hartford, Conn., 10 Feb. 1939. Studied with Arnold Franchetti, Hartt Coll. of Music, 1957-64; with Lukas Foss and Gunther Schuller at Tanglewood, 1960, 1964, 1968. Her awards include a Fulbright scholarship for Vienna, 1966-67; fellowships at Tanglewood and MacDowell Colony; Prix de Rome, 1969-71; 2 Guggenheim fellowships, 1972, 1976; New York State Council on the Arts grant, 1973; Nat. Endowment for the

Arts grant, 1979; and many commissions. She was clarinetist, Hartford Symph. Orch., 1960-65; on faculty, Brooklyn Coll., 1973-75; Wellesley Coll., 1975-76; and guest professor, Temple Univ., 1978.

WORKS: ORCHESTRA: Frailties, tenor, tape, and orch., 1973; Soundings, 3 orchestras, Boston, 17 Feb. 1978; Grisaille, Portland, Maine, 13 Feb. 1979; CHAMBER MUSIC: Chansons bas, soprano and chamber ensemble, 1966; 3 place settings, narrator and chamber ensemble; Figments, flute and piano, 1967; Trobar clus, clarinet and chamber ensemble; Rebuttal, 2 clarinets; Toccata, harpsichord and tape; Soundings, 13 instruments, and tape, 1971; double woodwind quintet; Solitaire, piano and vibraphone, 1971; Looking for Claudio, soprano, baritone, guitar; Spring river flowers moon night, 2 pianos and tape, 1972; Homage to Keith Jarrett and Gary Burton, flute and vibraphone, 1978.

41 W. 72nd St., New York, NY 10023

KOMAIKO, WILLIAM
b. Chicago, Ill., 23 Jan. 1947. Studied with Robert Lombardo, Donald Erb, Raymond Wilding-White, Roosevelt Univ.; with Roger Sessions, Vincent Persichetti, Elliott Carter, Juilliard School, B.M. 1970, M.S. 1973; also piano with Rudolph Ganz and Robert Helps. His awards include a 4-year scholarship, Roosevelt Univ.; Rudolph Ganz piano prize, 1967; 3 grants, Fine Arts Found., 1967-69; Juilliard scholarship, 1970, 3 graduate fellowships, 1972-74; Gershwin Memorial prize, 1972; Rodgers and Hammerstein scholarship, 1973. He was cofounder and pianist with Notes from Underground, a performing ensemble for new music.

WORKS: THEATRE: The metamorphosis, staged mime piece based on Kafka's story; CHAMBER MUSIC: Improvisations, string quartet; Dialogues, string trio and bassoon; 3 pieces for woodwind trio; woodwind quintet; 2 narratives, voice and percussion; Rondo, clarinet and piano; song cycle on Heine poems; string trio; string quartet; Form in 2 parts, viola and piano; Mandala, solo violin; Umbra-penumbra, chamber ensemble, New York, 14 Oct. 1974.

KONDOROSSY, LESLIE
b. Bratislava, Czech., 25 June 1915; U.S. citizen 1957. Studied at Liszt Acad. of Music, Budapest; at Western Reserve Univ.; and at Sophia Univ., Tokyo (Japanese theatre and music). His awards include the Cleveland Certificate of Merit for Creative Art, 1958, 1959-60; Decoration Medal, Hungarian World Fed., Budapest, 1968; jointly with his wife, Elizabeth Kondorossy, his lyricist and librettist, the Martha Holden Jennings award, 1970; and Magyar Barati Kozosseg (Hungarian Friendly Community), 1978. He held various positions as cantor, violinist, and conductor in Hungary and Germany, 1932-51; settled in Cleveland, 1951; was founder, later president, American New Opera Theatre Society, 1953; teacher, Cleveland Cultural Arts Bureau, 1954-71; conductor, Opera of the Air, WSRS, 1955-56; representative abroad for WCLV fine arts station, 1966-70; private teacher and choral director.

WORKS: OPERA: The pumpkin, 1 act, Cleveland, 14 May 1954 (all performance sites are Cleveland unless otherwise noted); The voice, 1 act, 14 May, 1954; The midnight duel, 20 Mar. 1955; 2 imposters and Unexpected visitor, 21 Oct. 1956; The headsman, 1955; The fox, 1956; The string quartet, 1956; Mystic fortress, 1957; Alms from the beggar, 1957; The Baksheesh, 1960-64; Nathan the wise, 1961-64; Poorest suitor, children's opera-oratorio, 24 May 1967; Shizuka's dance, children's opera-oratorio, 29 Apr. 1969; Ruth and Naomi, 1969; Kalamona and the 4 winds, opera-oratorio, 12 Sept. 1971; BALLET: King Solomon, 1952; La danse macabre, 1965; ORCHESTRA: Apotheosis, with chorus, 1956; trombone concerto, 19 May 1961; trumpet concerto, 18 Mar. 1962; cimbalom concerto, 1970; harpsichord concerto, 1972; Music for orchestra, 1973; 3 Hungarian pieces, 1978; Sacred fire, oratorio, with chorus and soloists, 1978; Forbidden fifths, string orch. and flute; CHAMBER MUSIC: string quartet, 9 Dec. 1960; 3 sketches, chamber orch., 1959; concertino for chamber orch., 1961; Music for percussion, 1963; Expressions for guitar, 1975; CHORUS: Kossuth cantata, 16 Mar. 1952; Lament of the Lord, 17 May 1952; New dreams for old, cantata, 29 Nov. 1961; Son of Jesse, oratorio, 4 June 1967; Jazz mass, with jazz band, 1968; Ode to the loyalty of first, cantata, 19 Sept. 1971; 10 score of years, with solo voice and chamber ensemble, 1977; many other chamber works, piano pieces, and songs.

14443 E. Carroll Blvd., University Heights, OH 44118

KONDRACKI, MICHAL
b. Poltava, Ukraine, 4 Oct. 1902; to U.S. 1943. Sutdied at the Warsaw Cons.; with Paul Dukas in Paris; also with Szymanowski. He was music critic in Warsaw, 1933-39; left Poland and lived in Brazil, 1940-43. His compositions include an opera, a ballet, a symphony, 1942, Brazilian dances for orch., 1944, choral works.

KONOWITZ, BERTRAM D.
b. Bronx, N.Y., 22 Feb. 1931. Studied with Sol Berkowitz, Leo Kraft, Normand Lockwood, Karol Rathaus, Queens Coll., CUNY. He received the Raymond Burrows award, Columbia Univ.; ASCAP awards, 1971-73; Nat. Endowment for the Arts grant, 1972. He was on the faculty, Manhattanville Coll., 1969-74; Teachers Coll., Columbia Univ.; on summer faculty, Univ. of Wisconsin-Milwaukee.

WORKS: VOCAL: Speak your pieace [sic], chorus, New York, 4 Apr. 1973; Zodiac; The last word; Growing up free; Cantus firmus; PIANO: Jazz waltz; Raga rock; Time changes; Surf swing; Poundin' the beat; Blue note boogie; Choochoo stomp; Jazz spooks; Lazy daze. He specializes in vocal and piano improvisation and rock improvisation. He has published The complete rock piano method and Jazz for piano.

12 Hemlock Dr., Syosset, NY 11791

KOPP, CHARLES MICHAEL
b. Athens, Ga., 9 Jan. 1951. Attended Univ. of

KOPP, FREDERICK

Southern California; studied composition with
his father, Frederick Kopp. In 1973 he was in
the Dragonfire Band, Ft. Bragg.
WORKS: ORCHESTRA: Wave, a suite; CHORUS:
Pacem nobis donate; many songs.
102 N. Garfield Place, Monrovia, CA 91016

KOPP, FREDERICK
b. Hamilton, Ill., 21 Mar. 1914. Attended
Carthage Coll., A.B.; Univ. of Iowa, A.M.;
Eastman School of Music, Ph.D.; studied privately
with Pierre Monteux, Gustav Strube, Louis
Hasselmanns. He received scholarships at Carthage Coll. and Univ. of Iowa; Phi Mu Alpha
award. He was conductor, Baton Rouge Civic
Symph., 1947-48; taught at Southeastern Louisiana
Univ., 1940-41; New York State Univ., Fredonia,
1948-49; Univ. of Georgia, 1950-52; California
State Univ., Los Angeles, 1959-62; from 1962,
composer, arranger, conductor for motion pictures.
WORKS: THEATRE: Pepito, light opera for
children, rev. 1979; That woman's gotta hang!,
music melodrama, rev. 1979; ORCHESTRA: 2 symphonies; Trilogy; Deep forest; WIND ENSEMBLE:
Terror suite, brass, woodwinds, piano, percussion;
And the earth shook, winds, piano, percussion;
CHAMBER MUSIC: October '55, clarinet and string
quartet; woodwind quintet; Portrait of a woman,
flute and piano; Passacaglia, string quartet;
Passacaglia, woodwind quintet; Shenandoah summer,
clarinet, piano, strings; CHORUS: The denial of
St. Peter, oratorio; Dance mass, with orch.;
Songs of David, cantata; We thank thee, Lord,
motet; and songs, organ and piano pieces, film
scores.
102 N. Garfield Place, Monrovia, CA 91016

KORDE, SHIRISH
b. Kampala, Uganda, 18 June 1945; to U.S. 1945.
Studied at Berklee Coll. of Music, B.M.; with
Robert Cogan, Ernst Oster, and Donald Martino,
New England Cons., M.M.; and at Brown Univ. He
received a Mellon Found. grant for research in
electronic music; Mass. Council for the Arts
grant, 1979. He was on the faculty, Berklee
Coll., 1972-75; then at Holy Cross Coll.
WORKS: CHAMBER MUSIC: string quartet;
violin sonata; Chamber piece #1; Spectra, trombone and tape; Constellations, saxophone quartet;
Untitled, 2 pianos and 2 percussion.
71 Maple St., Acton, MA 01720

KORN, PETER JONA
b. Berlin, Germany, 30 Mar. 1922; U.S. citizen
1944. Studied with Edmund Rubbra in London;
Stefan Wolpe in Jerusalem; with Arnold
Schoenberg, Ernst Toch, and Hanns Eisler in Los
Angeles. He received the Frank Huntington
Beebe Fund award, 1956, 1957; Huntington Hartford
Found. fellowships, 1956, 1957, 1961; City of
Munich music award, 1968; Univ. of Maryland Fine
Arts award, 1971. He taught in Munich, 1960-61;
Univ. of California, 1964-65; has been director,
Richard Strauss Kons., Munich, from 1967.
WORKS: OPERA: Heidi, 1961-63; Heidi in
Frankfurt, 3 act, Saarbrucken State Opera, 28
Nov. 1978; ORCHESTRA: 3 symphonies, 1942-43,

1952, 1958, #1 was revised in 1977, performed
by the Bamberg Symphony, 19 Dec. 1978; Tom Paine
overture, 1950; Rhapsody, oboe and strings, 1952;
concertino for horn and strings, Ojai, Calif.,
Festival, 1953; In medias res, overture, 1953;
The beggar's opera variations, Louisville, 1
Oct. 1955; saxophone concerto, 1956; violin concerto, 1965; Exorcism of a Liszt fragment,
Pittsburgh, 5 Feb. 1971; CHAMBER MUSIC: Prelude
and scherzo, brass quintet; cello sonata, 1949;
oboe sonata, 1949; 2 string quartets, 1950, 1963;
Passacaglia and fugue, 8 horns, 1952; horn
sonata, 1953; Serenade, 4 horns, 1957; Quintettino, 3 woodwinds, cello, piano, 1964; quintet
for winds, 1966.
Mozartring 10, D-8011, Baldham, West Germany

KORNGOLD, ERICH WOLFGANG
b. Brno, Austria, 29 May 1897; U.S. citizen
1943; d. Hollywood, Calif., 29 Nov. 1957.
Studied first with his father, then with
Alexander von Zemlinsky, Hermann Graedener, and
Robert Fuchs in Vienna. He was a child prodigy
both in piano and in composition, writing a
piano trio that was published when he was 12.
His honors included the title of professor con-
ferred by the president of Austria; Art prize,
City of Vienna, 1924; Academy awards for best
original scores: Anthony Adverse, 1936; The
adventures of Robin Hood, 1938, The Sea wolf,
1941. He came to the U.S. in 1934 and settled
in Hollywood as a film composer.
WORKS: THEATRE: Der Schneemann, pantomime,
Vienna, 4 Oct. 1910; Der King des Polykrates and
Violanta, 2 short operas, Munich, 28 Mar. 1916;
Die tote Stadt, opera, Hamburg, 4 Dec. 1920;
Das Wunder der Heliane, 1927; Die Kathrin, 1939;
Die stumme Serenade, comedy with music, 1946;
ORCHESTRA: Schauspiel-Ouverture, 1911; sinfonietta, 1913; Much ado about nothing suite,
chamber orch., 1919; Sursum corda, overture,
1919; piano concerto for left hand alone, 1923;
violin concerto, 1945; cello concerto, 1946;
Symphonic serenade, string orch., 1947; symphony in F#, 1951; Theme and variations, 1953;
Straussiana, 1953; CHAMBER MUSIC: piano trio,
1910; violin sonata; string sextet; 3 string
quartets, 1922, 1935, 1945; 3 piano sonatas,
1908, 1910, 1932; piano quintet; CHORUS: Prayer,
with tenor and orch., 1942; Psalm, with solo and
orch., 1941; FILM SCORES: 18 original scores,
1934-47, including The prince and the pauper;
The private life of Elizabeth and Essex; King's
row; Juarez; Of human bondage.

KORTE, KARL
b. Ossining, N.Y., 25 Aug. 1928. Studied with
Peter Mennin, William Bergsma, Vincent
Persichetti, Juilliard School; and with Otto
Luening and Aaron Copland. His awards include a
Fulbright grant to Italy; 2 Guggenheim fellowships; Gershwin Memorial award; Belgian government prize in 1969 Queen Elizabeth competition;
grants from Harpur Found., Ford Found., State
Univ. of New York Research Found., Univ. of
Texas, and Nat. Endowment for the Arts. He was
professor, State Univ. of New York, Binghamton,
1964-71; from 1971, Univ. of Texas at Austin.

WORKS: ORCHESTRA: Concertato on a choral theme, 1955; For a young audience, 1959; 3 symphonies, 19--, 1961, 1968; Southwest, dance overture, 1963; Metamorphosis, string orch. and jazz quartet, 1976; BAND: Nocturne and march, 1962; Prairie song, trumpet and band, 1963; Gestures, with piano and percussion, 1970; I think you would have understood, stage band, solo trumpet, tape, 1971; concerto for piano and winds, 1976; CHAMBER MUSIC: 2 string quartets, 1948, 1965; Fantasy, violin and piano, 1959; quintet, oboe and strings, 1960; Matrix, wind quintet, piano, percussion, Facets, saxophone quartet, 1969; Remembrances, flute and tape, 1971; piano trio; CHORUS: Aspects of love, choral cycle, 1965; Psalm XIII, with tape, 1970; Pale is this good prince, oratorio; Time and season, with soloists, marimba, piano, percussion, Washington, D.C., 26 May 1976; other choral works, songs, piano pieces.
Music Dept., University of Texas, Austin, TX 78712

KOSAKOFF, REUVEN
b. New Haven, Conn., 8 Jan. 1898. Studied at Yale Univ.; with Ernest Hutcheson and Carl Friedberg, Juilliard School; piano with Arthur Schnabel in Berlin. He received many commissions for compositions; gave piano recitals in the U.S. and Europe; was organist, Genesis Hebrew Center, Tuckahoe, N.Y.
WORKS: OPERA: The cabalists, 1 act; ORCHESTRA: piano concerto, 1941; Jack and the beanstalk, narrator and orch., New Haven, 22 Apr. 1944; CHAMBER MUSIC: violin sonata; clarinet sonata; woodwind quartet; CHORUS: Song of songs; Message of peace; Ruth and Naomi; Creation; and Sabbath services.

KOSIS, DAVID
b. Aurora, Ill., 3 Aug. 1938. Studied with David Diamond in New York, 1975-77. His compositions include concerto for 3 instruments (flute, harp, cello), performed by the Wolf Trap Soloists, Washington, D.C., 8 Feb. 1980; 4 preludes, piano, 1980; An American requiem, 1980.
2616 Macon Rd., Griffin, GA 30223

KOSTECK, GREGORY
b. Plainfield, N.J., 2 Sept. 1937. Studied at Univ. of Maryland, B.M.; with Leslie Bassett and Ross Lee Finney, Univ. of Michigan, M.M., D.M.A.; privately with Ton de Leeuw in Amsterdam. His many awards include Woodrow Wilson fellowship; 3 Horace Rackham fellowships; Univ. of Michigan Distinguished Scholar; Fulbright grant; Ford-MENC grant; Nat. Assoc. of American Composers and Conductors grant; 11 first prizes or awards in composition contests, 1965-73; Nat. Endowment for the Arts grant, 1976; many commissions. He was resident composer, Norwalk, Conn., schools, 1964-65; on faculty, Washington and Jefferson Coll., 1965-66; East Carolina Univ., 1966-73; Appalachian State Univ., 1973-75; Univ. of Tennessee, 1976-78.
WORKS: OPERA: Vengeance is mine, 1964; Maurya, 1966; ORCHESTRA: Capriccio, piano and orch., 1958; 4 pieces, cello, winds, harp, per-

cussion, 1962; Slow piece, 1964; Rhapsody, cello and orch., 1964; Variations, viola and orch., 1965; 3 lyric pieces, 1966; Concert fantasy, violin, piano, orch., 1967; Strophes, 1968; Nightingales and the moon, 1969; Clouds, strings and percussion, 1969; symphony, 1971; saxophone concerto, 1973; A quiet celebration, Plymouth, Mass., 11 Apr. 1976; clarinet concerto, 1977; CHAMBER MUSIC: Bagatelles, string trio, 1960; 2 piano sonatas, 1961, 1964; Fantasy for cello, 1963; sonatine, violin and piano, 1964; piano trio, 1966; string quartet #3 1969, #4 1971; violin sonata #4, 1972; Cantilena, piano, 1973; CHORUS: Canons and refrains, women's voices, 4 clarinets, 1965; Love poems from youth, 1967; Oratio Jeremiae Prophaetae, 1969; Cantata 1973, male voices and brass, 1973; also songs, organ pieces, music for brass, band pieces.

KOTIK, PETR
b. Prague, Czech., 27 Jan. 1942; U.S. citizen 1977. Studied composition with Jan Rychlik in Prague; with Hanns Jelinek and Karl Schiske, Vienna Music Acad., 1963-66. He received a Gaudeamus Found. award, 1965; Vienna Acad. graduation award, 1966; Martha Baird Rockefeller grant, 1972; Nat. Endowment for the Arts grant, 1977. He was founder and director, Musica Viva Pragensis, 1961-64, and Quax Ensemble, 1966-69; from 1969, has been creative associate, State Univ. of New York, Buffalo; founder and director, SEM Ensemble, from 1970; artistic director, Chocorua activities sponsored by New Music in New Hampshire.
WORKS: CHAMBER MUSIC: Music for 3, 1964; Contrabandt, electronic, 1967; Aley, variable number of instruments, 1970-71; How empty is my wilderness, variable instruments, 1971; There is singularly nothing, variable instruments, 1971-73; John Mary, 1973-74; Many, many women, 1975-78.
567 Forest Ave., Buffalo, NY 14222

KOUGUELL, ARKADIE
b. Simferopol, Russia, 23 Dec. 1897; to U.S. 1952. Studied at St. Petersburg Cons. and Vienna Cons. He has received many awards for excellence in piano playing and teaching, and the California Harp Assoc. award in composition. He was founder and director, Inst. of American Music, Univ. of Beirut; has held academic posts in Tel Aviv, Paris, and New York; has given piano recitals in the U.S., Europe, Russia, and the Middle East.
WORKS: ORCHESTRA: Impressions of Damascus, 1930; piano concerto, 1930; Bedouin dance, 60 cellos, 1930; piano concerto for left hand, 1934; Rapsodie tartare, 1947; cello concerto, 1950; trombone concertino, 1956; Ballade, soprano and orch.; CHAMBER MUSIC: 2 string quartets; 3 piano sonatas; violin sonata; 2 cello sonatas; Danse Hebraique, cello and piano; Suite ancienne, viola and piano.

KOUNTZ, RICHARD
b. Pittsburgh, Pa., 8 July 1896; d. New York, N.Y., 14 Oct. 1950. He was an executive in a New York publishing firm, 1927-39. His composi-

KOUSSEVITZKY, SERGE

tions include the songs The sleigh; Cossack love song; By love alone; et al.; organ pieces and choral works.

KOUSSEVITZKY, SERGE
b. Vyshniy Volochek, Russia, 26 July 1874; U.S. citizen 1941; d. Boston, Mass., 4 June 1951. Studied double bass, Moscow Philharmonic Music School, graduating in 1894; became leading bass player in the Moscow Imperial Orchestra; gave solo recitals on the bass throughout Europe; organized a symphony orchestra and toured Russia with it, 1910-17, making 3 trips down the Volga River on a chartered vessel; was guest conductor in London; instituted the Concerts Koussevitzky in Paris in 1921; in 1924, was invited to head the Boston Symphony Orchestra. During his 25 years with the Boston Symphony, he established the Berkshire Music Center and the Berkshire Music School at Lenox, Mass.
   WORKS: ORCHESTRA: concerto for double bass, 1905; Passacaglia on a Russian theme; DOUBLE BASS AND PIANO: Humoresque; Valse miniature; Chanson triste; etc.

KOUTZEN, BORIS
b. Uman, Russia, 1 Apr. 1901; U.S. citizen 1929; d. Mount Kisco, N.Y., 10 Dec. 1966. Studied with Reinhold Gliere, Moscow State Cons., graduated 1922; Philadelphia Cons., B.M. 1940. His honors included a Society for Publ. of American Music award, 1944; Juilliard publication award, 1944. He was faculty member, Philadelphia Cons., 1924-44; professor, Vassar Coll., 1944-66.
   WORKS: OPERA: The fatal oath, 1954; You never know, 1-act comic opera, 1960; ORCHESTRA: Solitude, symphonic poem, 1927; symphonic movement, violin and orch., 1929; Valley Forge, symphonic poem, 1931; concerto for 5 solo instruments and strings, 1934; symphony, 1939; Concert piece, cello and string orch., 1940; From the American folklore, 1943; violin concerto, 1946; Sinfonietta, 1947; An invocation, women's chorus and orch., 1948; viola concerto, 1949; Morning music, flute and strings, 1950; Divertimento, 1955; concertino for piano and strings, 1957; Elegiac rhapsody, 1961; Fanfare, prayer and march, 1961; CHAMBER MUSIC: 2 violin sonatas, 1929, 1951; piano sonatina, 1931; 3 string quartets, 1932, 1936, 1944; trio, flute, cello, harp, 1933; Enigma, piano, 1938; sonatina for 2 pianos, 1944; Sonnet for organ, 1946; piano trio, 1948; sonata for violin and cello, 1952; Eidolus, 1953; Landscape and dances, woodwind quintet, 1953; Poem, violin solo and string quartet, 1963; and choral works.

KOWALSKI, MICHAEL JOHN
b. Buffalo, N.Y., 5 Nov. 1950. Studied at Oberlin Cons., B.M. 1972; with Richard Hervig, Univ. of Iowa, M.A. 1974; with Herbert Brün, Ben Johnston, and Salvatore Martirano, Univ. of Illinois, on fellowship, 1974-75; with Betsy Jolas at Tanglewood on a Margaret Lee Crofts fellowship, 1976.
   WORKS: CHAMBER MUSIC: Tracks, piano and percussion; hors d'oeuvres, soprano and trombone; traveling music, percussion and dancer;

bringing the sheaves, solo flute; fakebook, piano; sinfonietta, 10 instruments; The entrance of the Queen of Sheba, 12 instruments; daydreams, violin and percussion; silhouettes, marimba; ELECTRONIC TAPE: hotsy-totsy; Balonie; in memoriam Sydney Toler; jeu de gestes, with mime quartet; Program Etude.
   27 Haskell St., Cambridge, MA 02140

KOZAK, EDWARD JOHN
b. Chicago, Ill., 17 Nov. 1925. Studied at Centenary Coll.; with Robert Krause, Northwestern State Univ. He was soloist and arranger for Xavier Cugat, 1949-50; music director and arranger, Shreveport Summer Theatre, 1957-60; clinician for drum companies, 1972-73; lecturer, Centenary Coll., 1959-78.
   WORKS: ORCHESTRA: marimba concerto; WIND ENSEMBLE: Variation on a chant, percussion and winds; Circus suite, brass sextet; suite for woodwinds in 12-tone technique; Swingatina, clarinet sextet; CHAMBER MUSIC: Etude for marimba; Theme and variations, piano; Toot suite and Rudiments rococo-Swingin' fifer, duets for snare drum and flute; also anthems and songs.
   3729 Greenway Place, Shreveport, LA 71105

KOZINSKI, DAVID
b. Wilmington, Del., 29 July 1917. Studied at Univ. of Delaware; West Chester State Coll., B.S.; with Constant Vauclain, Univ. of Pennsylvania, M.S.; Army Music School, Ft. Myer, Va. He has taught privately and in public schools; has conducted opera, orchestra, choral groups; has been music critic for the Evening Journal.
   WORKS: CHAMBER MUSIC: suite for strings; Project percussion, percussion ensemble; SONGS: Wonder! Wonder!; Glory to God in heaven; old Polish carols.

KRAEHENBUEHL, DAVID
b. 1932.
   WORKS: concerto for piano, 4 hands, 1975; Diptych, violin and piano; Variations for 2, piano or any combination of 2; Variations, 3 clarinets and bass clarinet; Elegy and Nocturne for piano; City scene, chorus; 4 Christmas choruses.
   School for New Music, Princeton, NJ 08540

KRAFT, LEO
b. New York, N.Y., 24 July 1922. Studied with Karol Rathaus, Queens Coll., B.A. 1945; with Randall Thompson at Princeton Univ., M.A. 1947; and with Nadia Boulanger in Paris, 1954-55, on a Fulbright fellowship. He has received annual ASCAP awards from 1961. From 1947, he has been faculty member, Queens Coll., CUNY.
   WORKS: ORCHESTRA: Line drawings, with solo flute, New York, 7 Jan. 1973; 3 pieces for orchestra; WIND ENSEMBLE: concerto for cello, winds, percussion; Toccata for band; CHAMBER MUSIC: Two's company, 2 clarinets, 1957; Partita #3, wind quintet, 1969; 5 pieces, clarinet and piano, 1969; Fantasy, flute and piano, 1971; Dualities, 2 trumpets, 1971; Short suite, flute, clarinet, bassoon; Trios and interludes, flute, viola, piano; Spring in the harbor, cycle

for soprano, flute, cello, piano; Dialogues, flute and tape; Line drawings, flute and percussion, 1972; Partita #4, chamber ensemble, 1975; Diaphonies, oboe and piano, 1978; CHORUS: Festival song, 1951; Let me laugh, 1954; A proverb of Solomon, with orch., 1958; When Israel came forth, 1963; I waited patiently, Psalm 40, male choir, 1964; A new song, male choir, 1966; Fyre and yse, with tape, 1967; PIANO: Allegro giocoso, 1947; Partita #1, 1969; Statements and commentaries; Antiphonies, 4 hands and tape; 10 short pieces for piano, 1976.
    8 Dunster Rd., Great Neck, NY 11021

KRAFT, WILLIAM
    b. Chicago, Ill., 6 Sept. 1923. Studied with Otto Luening, Vladimir Ussachevsky, Henry Cowell, Columbia Univ., B.S. 1951, M.A. 1954; and at Cambridge Univ., England. He received Anton Deidl fellowships, 1952, 1953; Huntington Hartford fellowships, 1964; Guggenheim fellowships, 1967, 1972; Ford Found. grant, 1972; Rockefeller Found. grant for Italy, 1973; 8 Pulitzer nominations; 2 Nat. Endowment for the Arts grants, 1975, 1977; and many commissions. He has been principal timpanist and percussionist, Los Angeles Phil. Orch., from 1955; music director, Young Musicians Found., 1970-72; faculty member, Univ. of Southern California, 1961-64, 1977; California Inst. of the Arts, 1973-76.
    WORKS: ORCHESTRA: symphony for strings and percussion, New York, 21 Aug. 1961; Concerto grosso, 1961, San Diego, 22 Mar. 1963; concerto for 4 percussionists and orch., 1964, Los Angeles, 10 Mar. 1966; Configurations, 4 percussionists and jazz orch., 1966; Contextures: Riots decade 60, Los Angeles, 4 Apr. 1968; Games: Collage #1, brass and percussion, Pasadena, 21 Nov. 1969; piano concerto, Los Angeles, 21 Nov. 1973; Andiriviem, tuba concerto, Los Angeles, 26 Jan. 1978; CHAMBER MUSIC: Theme and variations, percussion quartet, 1956; nonet for brass and percussion, Los Angeles, 13 Oct. 1958; suite for percussion, 1958; French suite, solo percussion, 1962; Double trio, piano, prepared piano, amplified guitar, tuba, 2 percussion, Los Angeles, 31 Oct. 1966; Encounters II, solo tuba, 1966; Triangles, concerto for percussion and 10 instruments, 1968, Los Angeles, 8 Dec. 1969; Mobiles, 10 instruments, Berkeley, 18 Oct. 1970; Encounters III: Duel for trumpet and percussion, Santa Monica, 21 Jan. 1972; Cadenze, 5 winds, 2 strings, San Francisco, 10 Apr. 1972; Encounters IV: Duel for trombone and percussion, 1972; In memoriam Igor Stravinsky, violin and piano, 1972-74; Des imagistes, 6 percussion, 2 readers, 1974; Encounters V: Homage to Scriabin, cello and percussion, 1975; Encounters I, solo percussion and tape, 1975; Encounters VI: concertino for roto-toms and percussion quartet, 1976; VOCAL: Silent boughs, soprano and string orch., Millay text, Stockholm, 15 Nov. 1963; Games: Collage II, wind orch. and voices, 1970; The innocents: The witch trial at Salem, 4 vocal octets and instruments, Pasadena, 18 Oct. 1976.
    3681 Alomar Dr., Sherman Oaks, CA 91403

KRAMER, A. WALTER
    b. New York, N.Y., 23 Sept. 1890; d. New York, 8 Apr. 1969. Studied violin with Carl Hauser and Richard Arnold; graduated from City Coll. of New York, 1910. He was on the staff of Musical America, 1910-22, editor-in-chief, 1929-36; managing director and vice-president, Galaxy Music Corp., 1936-56; was a cofounder of the Society for the Publication of American Music.
    WORKS: ORCHESTRA: Symphonic rhapsody, violin and orch., 1912; Elizabethan suite; 2 symphonic sketches; In Normandy, choral cycle with orch., 1925; CHAMBER MUSIC: Eklog, cello and piano; Chant negre, violin and piano; Interlude for a drama, wordless voice, oboe, cello, piano; CHORUS: The lady of Ceret; The hour of prayer; songs, piano pieces.

KRAMER, GREGORY PAUL
    b. Los Angeles, Calif., 14 Oct. 1952. Attended Univ. of California, Santa Cruz, and California Inst. of the Arts, B.F.A. 1972; principal influences have been William Douglas, Gordon Mumma, David Tudor, and Keith Jarrett. The educational film, Nothing, for which he composed the score, won first prize in two film festivals. He also won a Golden Cloud award, Aspen Electronic Music Festival, and first prize, WANT Festival, San Francisco, 1971. He was president of Electronic Farm, Venice, Calif., 1972-75; from 1976, faculty member, New York Univ., School of Education.
    WORKS: ELECTRONIC: Vessels; Absence; Role; Poseidon; Clubhouse; Greenhouse; Nothing; Song for the new prince; Precipitation III--Weeds; etc.
    298 Main St., Nelsonville, NY 10516

KRAMER, JONATHAN D.
    b. Hartford, Conn., 7 Dec. 1942. Studied at Hartt Coll. of Music; Harvard Univ., A.B. magna cum laude, 1965; Univ. of California at Berkeley, M.A., Ph.D. 1969; Stanford Univ.; Bennington Composers Conf., 1970; principal teachers were Karlheinz Stockhausen, Roger Sessions, Leon Kirchner, Andrew Imbrie, Seymour Shifrin, Richard Felciano, Billy Jim Layton, Arnold Franchetti, Jean-Claude Eloy. His many awards include 6 grants, 3 fellowships, several composition prizes; Composers Forum and Meet the Composer appearances. He was program annotator, San Francisco Symph., 1967-70; faculty member, Univ. of California, Berkeley, 1969-70; Oberlin Coll., 1970-71; Yale Univ., 1971-78; guest faculty, Wesleyan Univ., 1977; from 1976, musical director, Linda Diamond Dancers; from 1977, editorial consultant, Schirmer Books.
    WORKS: ORCHESTRA: Requiem for the innocent, Berkeley, 10 May 1970; clarinet concerto; BAND: Variations, 1969; CHAMBER MUSIC: 3 pieces, clarinet alone, 1966; septet, 1968; One for 5 in 7, mostly, woodwind quintet, 1971; An imaginary dance, tape, 1972; Obstacles, trumpet, trombone, piano; The canons of blackearth, percussion and tape; Renascence, clarinet and tape; many multimedia pieces, such as Irrealities, 2 dancers, tape, projections, lights, 1973.
    Univ. of Cincinnait, Cincinnati, OH 45221

KRANCE, JOHN P., JR.

KRANCE, JOHN P., JR.
b. Bridgeport, Conn., 25 June 1935. Studied on
scholarship at Eastman School of Music. He has
been staff member at radio stations in Rochester
and Washington, D.C.; was in U.S. Army, 1955-58;
editorial assistant, MPHC, 1958-59; then became
music director, WPAT, Paterson, N.J.
WORKS: ORCHESTRA: Epitaphs; Signatures and
fanfares; Prelude to Christmas; BAND: Scenario;
Symphonic fanfares; Dialogue, trumpet and band;
CHAMBER MUSIC: Metamorphosis, chamber ensemble.

KRANE, SHERMAN M.
b. New Haven, Conn., 18 Nov. 1927. Studied at
Hartt Coll. of Music, B.M., M.M.; Michigan State
Univ., Ph.D. He has taught in private and public
schools; at Hartt Coll.; Michigan State Univ.;
was visiting lecturer, Experimental Coll.,
Virgin Islands; became music director, Bernard
Horwich Jewish Community Center, Chicago.
WORKS: OPERA: The giant's garden; and film
scores.

KRAPF, GERHARD
b. Meissenheim, Germany, 12 Dec. 1924; U.S. citizen 1959. Earned a diploma at the Staatliche
Hochshule für Musik, Karlsruhe, 1950; studied
with Paul Pisk and Leslie Spelman, Univ. of Redlands, M.M. 1951. He was music supervisor,
Synod of the Evangelical Church, Baden, 1951-53;
music director, Starr Commonwealth for Boys,
Albion, Mich., 1953-54; on faculty, Northwest
Missouri State Univ., 1954-58; Univ. of Wyoming,
1958-61; Univ. of Iowa, 1961-77; from 1977,
professor of organ and church music, Univ. of
Alberta; also organist-choirmaster in various
churches, 1953-66.
WORKS: CHORUS: Come, your hearts and
voices raising, with oboe and organ, 1968; From
heaven above, Christmas cantata, with optional
youth choir, 2 violins and organ, 1969; 6 scriptural affirmations, a cappella, 1977; SOLO VOICE:
Morning meditation and Hymn of praise, with
optional unison choir and organ, 1977; ORGAN:
Totentanz, episodes and fugue on a 17th-century
folk song; partita on Die güldne Sonne, 1976;
Triptych II; and some 70 other published works.
11704 43 Ave., Edmonton, Alberta, Canada
T6J 0Y7

KRAUSE, ROBERT JAMES
b. Milwaukee, Wis., 1 July 1943. Studied with
Alfred Reed, J. Clifton Williams, Univ. of Miami,
B.M., M.M. He has been faculty member, Eastern
New Mexico Univ., 1967-68; Northwestern State
Univ., 1968-73; from 1973, at West Texas State
Univ.
WORKS: THEATRE: music for The winter's
tale; CHAMBER MUSIC: woodwind quintet; Im-
petuoso, bassoon and piano; Cantilena, English
horn and piano; Petits variations, piano; CHORUS:
Psalm 121, with English horn.
Music Dept., West Texas State Univ., Canyon,
TX 79015

KREIGER, ARTHUR V.
b. New Haven, Conn., 8 May 1945. Studied with
Charles Whittenberg, Hale Smith, Walter Ihrke,

Univ. of Connecticut; with Vladimir Ussachevsky,
Chou Wen-chung, Mario Davidovsky, Columbia Univ.
In 1979, he received a Prix de Rome for study in
Italy; in 1980, a Guggenheim fellowship.
WORKS: CHAMBER MUSIC: 2 woodwind quintets;
Short pieces for piano; Composition for elec-
tronic tape; Short computer piece; Dialogue,
steel drums and tape, 1974; Nocturne, chamber
ensemble, 1977.

KREISLER, ALEXANDER VON
b. St. Petersburg, Russia, 21 Sept. 1894; U.S.
citizen 1939; d. Austin, Tex., 21 Aug. 1969.
Earned a master's degree in law at St. Petersburg Univ., then studied with Alexander Glazunov
and Nicolas Tcherepnin at the St. Petersburg
Cons. He was conductor, Riga Symphony, Latvia,
1920-29; conductor of Columbia Broadcasting
Orchestra that originated coast-to-coast radio
braodcasts; was faculty member, Cincinnati Cons.,
1930-39; composer for "March of Time" radio
program, 1939-44; professor and orchestra conductor, Univ. of Texas, Austin, 1945-69.
WORKS: Some 80 published works for string
orchestra, string ensembles, brass and woodwind
solos and ensembles.

KREISLER, FRITZ
b. Vienna, Austria, 2 Feb. 1875; U.S. citizen
1943; d. New York, 29 Jan. 1962. Entered the
Vienna Cons. at age 7, studied with Auber and
Hellmesberger, winning the Gold Medal at 10;
with Massart and Delibes, Paris Cons., graduated
at 12, taking the Grand Prix. He toured the
U.S. with Moriz Rosenthal, pianist, 1888-89;
then studied medicine in Vienna, painting in
Paris and Rome; served in the Austrian army. He
resumed violin playing in 1899, making brilliant
return debuts in Europe and the U.S.
WORKS: THEATRE: The marraige knot, comic
opera, 1919; Apple blossoms, operetta, 1919;
Sissy, operetta, 1933; ORCHESTRA: violin concerto; CHAMBER MUSIC: string quartet; VIOLIN
AND PIANO: Caprice Viennois; Tambourin Chinois;
Recitativo and scherzo; Schoen Rosmarin; Liebes-
freud; Liebeslied; Chanson Louis XIII and pavane;
La precieuse; Sicilienne and rigaudon; Praeludium
and allegro; Aubade Provencale; The old refrain;
and songs.

KREISS, HULDA E.
b. Strasbourg, France, 15 Dec. 1924; U.S. citizen 1933. Studied at San Diego State Coll.,
B.A. 1946; U.S. Internat. Univ., M.A. 1968;
studied harp with Carlos Salzedo and others.
She received many awards for poetry, for teaching, for community service in many ways; and a
set of States of the Union Commemorative Medals
for her book, Reaching the exceptional child
through music. She was harpist with the San
Diego Youth Symphony, 1948-52. amd with the San
Diego County Symphony for 9 years; has taught in
San Diego public schools from 1946.
WORKS: CHAMBER MUSIC: Moonlight reverie,
harp and voice; Dream love, harp and cello;
Chorale, piano and voice; Fantasie, piano; Beth's
lullaby, piano and voice; and many transcriptions
for harp.

4706 E. Mountain View Dr., San Diego, CA
92116

KREMENLIEV, BORIS
b. Razlog, Bulgaria, 23 May 1911; U.S. citizen
1944. Studied with Wesley La Violette, De Paul
Univ., B.M., M.M.; with Howard Hanson, Eastman
School of Music, Ph.D.; privately with Roy
Harris; conducting with Modest Altschuller. He
has received annual ASCAP awards, 1968-73;
Creative Arts Inst. grant to write an opera;
American Philosophical Society-Ford Found. grant
for research in Bulgarian and Slavic folk music.
He was professor, Univ. of California, Los
Angeles, 1945-78.
 WORKS: OPERA: The bridge; ORCHESTRA: Symphonic variations, 1937; Prelude and poem, with
chorus and soloists, 1937; Song symphony, contralto and orch., 1941; Bulgarian rhapsody, 1952;
Crucifixion, suite from a film score, 1952;
Elegy, 1968; Study for orchestra; CHAMBER MUSIC:
2 string quartets; flute sonatina; horn sonata;
2 piano quintets; quartet for oboe and string
trio; woodwind trio; saxophone quartet; double
bass sonata; 5 miniatures, for piano; CHORUS:
They are slaves, from cantata Once to every man
and nation; Grapes, women's voices and string
quartet; Song for parting, women's voices,
string orch., English horn; also works for radio,
television, the stage, and films. He is author
of the book, Bulgarian-Macedonian folk music,
and articles in music journals.
 10507 Troon Ave., Los Angeles, CA 90064

KRENEK, ERNST
b. Vienna, Austria, 23 Aug. 1900; U.S. citizen
1945. Studied with Franz Schreker in Vienna and
Berlin. His many awards include prizes from
City of Vienna, Republic of Austria, State of
Nordhein-Westfalen, Cities of Hamburg and Braun-
schweig; Great Cross of Merit from Republic of
Austria, German Federal Republic; membership,
Nat. Inst. of Arts and Letters; honorary membership, Academies of Music in Vienna, Graz, Salzburg, Stuttgart, Hamburg Opera House; honorary
citizen of Minnesota; honorary doctorates in
music, Univ. of New Mexico, Hamline Univ.,
Chapman Coll., New England Cons. He was professor, Vassar Coll., 1939-41; Hamline Univ.,
1942-47; guest lecturer at many universities,
1939-73.
 WORKS: OPERA: Jonny spielt auf, 1927, an
international success, was brought to the Metropolitan Opera House, New York, 19 Jan. 1929;
What price confidence?, 1945; Dark waters, 1951;
The bell tower; The life of Orestes, 1930, U.S.
premiere, Portland, Oreg., 20 Nov. 1974; Pallas
Athene weeps, 1955; Augerechnet und verspielt,
1961; The magic mirror; The golden ram, 1962;
Sardakai, 1969; ORCHESTRA: 4 piano concertos;
2 violin concertos; cello concerto; Symphonic
elegy, 1946; harp concerto, 1952; Medea, contralto and orch., 1952; concerto for 2 pianos,
1953; 11 transparencies, 1955; Horizon circled;
Perspectives; 6 profiles; Fivefold enfoldment;
Quaestio temporis, 1960; Kitharaulos, American
premiere, Tanglewood, 12 Aug. 1980; CHAMBER
MUSIC: organ sonata, 1941; 6 piano sonatas,

1919-51; trio, violin, clarinet, piano, 1946;
viola sonata, 1948; violin sonata; solo violin
sonata, 1948; harp sonata, 1955; Monologue,
clarinet solo, 1956; Pentagram for winds, 1957;
Sechs vermessene, piano, 1958; New music for
guitar, New York, 22 May 1973; Acco-music,
accordion, 1978; Von Vorn Herein, chamber ensemble, 1978; CHORUS: Lamentations of Jeremiah,
1941; Santa Fe time table, 1945; 3 sacred pieces,
1971; 6 motets; SONGS: Sestina, voice and 10
instruments, 1958; Wechselrahmen, song cycle,
1965; The dissembler, baritone and chamber ensemble, Baltimore, 11 Mar. 1979; ELECTRONIC:
Spiritus intelligentiae sanctus, tape and voices;
Tape and doubles, with 2 pianos; Organastro,
with organ; Quintina, with voice and instruments;
Aulokithara, oboe, harp, tape, U.S. premiere,
Baltimore, 4 Feb. 1973 (a version of Kitharaulos,
commissioned by Swiss oboist Heinz Holliger and
given its world premiere at the 1972 Olympic
Games in Munich); They knew what they wanted,
1976, narrator, oboe, piano, percussion, tape,
New York, 6 Nov. 1978; many other works in all
categories. An 8-day Krenek Festival was held
at Univ. of California, Santa Barbara campus,
and the Lobero Theatre in April 1979; 44 works
were presented in a dozen concerts, plus lectures
and exhibits of his paintings, photographs, and
manuscripts.
 623 Chino Canyon Rd., Palm Springs, CA
92262

KRENEK, MRS. ERNST. See NORDENSTROM, GLADYS

KRESKY, JEFFREY JAY
b. Passaic, N.J., 14 May 1948. Studied with
Otto Luening, Charles Wuorinen, Harvey Sollberger,
Columbia Univ.; with Milton Babbitt, James K.
Randall, Peter Westergaard, Princeton Univ.;
with Gunther Schuller at Tanglewood. His awards
include BMI student award, 1969; Tanglewood fellowship, 1969; Nat. Endowment for the Arts grant,
1976; annual ASCAP awards, 1971-77. He was
faculty member, Mannes Coll. of Music, 1972-73;
from 1973, at William Paterson Coll.; from 1974,
education director, Bergen Youth Orchestra.
 WORKS: CHAMBER MUSIC: clarinet sonata;
Variations, piano and ensemble; Puppets, chamber
ballet; In nomine, flute solo; CHORUS: Cantatas
I and II; other vocal and instrumental chamber
works.
 175 Union Ave., Rutherford, NJ 07070

KRETER, LEO
b. Rochester, Minn., 29 Aug. 1933. Studied with
Henry Woodward, Carleton Coll.; with Robert
Palmer and Karel Husa, Cornell Univ., D.M.A. He
held a George Baker scholarship at Carleton
Coll., a graduate fellowship at Cornell Univ.
He was faculty member, Wichita State Univ.,
1960-65; California State Coll., San Bernardino,
1965-68; from 1968, professor, California State
Univ., Fullerton.
 WORKS: ORCHESTRA: a symphony; Overture for
orchestra; WIND ENSEMBLE: Polarities I and II;
Vortex, brass and percussion; CHAMBER MUSIC:
Melisma, string and harp; various small ensemble
works; CHORUS: Alleluia; Gloria in excelsis

KREUTZ, ARTHUR

<u>Deo</u>; <u>Sound a trumpet</u>; <u>Show us thy ways, O Lord</u>.
Music Dept., Univ. of California, Fullerton,
CA 92634

KREUTZ, ARTHUR
b. La Crosse, Wis., 25 July 1906. Attended
Univ. of Wisconsin, B.S., B.M.; Columbia Univ.;
studied also with Roy Harris and Cecil Burleigh;
Royal Cons., Ghent, Belgium, diploma in violin;
American Acad. in Rome. His awards include
Premier Prix, Royal Cons., 1931; Prix de Rome,
1940; Nat. Assoc. of American Composers and Conductors, publication award, 1941; Guggenheim
fellowship, 1944-46; BMI-ACA award, 1945; many
commissions. He was faculty member, Univ. of
Texas, 1942-44; Rhode Island State Coll.;
Columbia Univ.; Univ. of Mississippi, 1952-75.
    WORKS: OPERA: <u>Acres of sky</u>, ballad opera,
Fayetteville, Ark., 16 Nov. 1950; <u>The university
greys</u>, Univ. of Mississippi, 15 Mar. 1954; <u>Sour-
wood Mountain</u>, Roanoke, Va., 4 Apr. 1958; <u>Ver-
bena</u>, after Faulkner; BALLET: <u>Litany of Washington Street</u>, from <u>Land be bright</u>, for Martha
Graham; THEATRE: music for <u>E equals MC²</u>; <u>Wan-
hope Building</u>; <u>Galarie vivante</u>, Ravinia Park,
Chicago, 15 Aug. 1957; ORCHESTRA: 2 symphonies,
1940, 1946; <u>Symphonic jam session</u>; <u>American
dances</u>; <u>Paul Bunyan</u>; <u>Symphonic sketch</u>; <u>Scenes
from Hamlet</u>; <u>Winter of the blue snow</u>; 2 violin
concertos; piano concerto; <u>Dance concerto</u>,
clarinet and orch.; <u>Dixieland concerto</u>, clarinet,
trumpet, trombone; concertino for oboe, horn,
and strings; <u>Variations on a pop tune</u>, piano and
orch.; <u>Mosquito serenade</u>, string orch.; <u>Hoedown</u>,
string orch. and piano; <u>New England folksing</u>,
chorus and orch.; <u>Gettysburg, 1863</u>, chorus and
orch.; BAND: <u>Jazz prelude</u>; <u>Jazz fugue</u>; <u>Jamboree</u>;
concertino, violin and band; CHAMBER MUSIC:
<u>Quartet Venuti</u>, string quartet; <u>Jazzonata #1 and
#2</u>, violin and piano; <u>Variations</u>, violin and
piano; <u>3 Shakespeare songs</u>, soprano and chamber
orch.; <u>4 Robert Burns songs</u>, soprano and chamber
orch.; <u>Study in jazz</u>, piano; <u>Toccata</u>, violin and
piano.
    Rte. #6, Oxford, MS 38655

KREUTZ, ROBERT EDWARD
b. La Crosse, Wis., 21 Mar. 1922. Studied with
Leo Sowerby, American Cons.; Arnold Schoenberg,
Univ. of California, Los Angeles; and Normand
Lockwood, Univ. of Denver. His honors include
4 choral premieres, before MENC, 1964, 1969,
American Guild of Organists, 1972, American
Choral Directors Assoc., 1973; was winner, 41st
Internat. Eucharistic Congress contest for hymn,
<u>Gift of finest wheat</u>, 1976. He has been a
private teacher from 1950; director, St.
Bernadette Choir, Lakewood, Colo., from 1958.
    WORKS: CHAMBER MUSIC: trio for 2 marimbas
and piano; <u>Gargoyle</u>, 3 trumpets; <u>Parable</u>, organ;
<u>Portraits of the West</u>, piano suite; CHORUS: 7
Latin masses; 4 English masses; <u>Laudate Dominum</u>;
<u>Sing a new song</u>; <u>Who loves the rain</u>; <u>This is the
day</u>; <u>3 sea songs</u>; 14 psalms and alleluias; many
anthems and works for the church service.
    1909 Zinnia St., Golden, CO 80401

KRIENS, CHRISTIAAN B.
b. Brussels, 29 Apr. 1881; to U.S. 1906; d. West
Hartford, Conn., 17 Dec. 1934. Studied at the
Hague Cons.; made a debut with his father's
orchestra in Amsterdam, playing the <u>Emperor Con-
certo</u> and a violin concerto and conducting his
own second symphony. He came to the U.S. as
conductor of the French Opera Company in New
Orleans; was teacher and conductor in New York,
1907-29; then music director, radio station,
WTIC, Hartford, Conn. He composed orchestral
works and chamber music.

KRIESBERG, MATTHIAS
b. Queens, N.Y., 21 Mar. 1953. Studied with
Harvey Sollberger, Charles Wuorinen, Vladimir
Ussachevsky, Jack Beeson, Columbia Univ., B.A.
1973; M.A. 1976; with Milton Babbitt, Juilliard
School, D.M.A. 1979. His awards include first
prize, Suffolk Symphony concerto contest, 1969;
BMI award, 1972; Alice M. Ditson Fund grant,
1973-74; AA-NIAL Charles E. Ives award, 1977;
de Karman fellowship, Aerojet-General Corp.,
1977-78. He was founder, New Structures Ensemble, in 1974 and is director; on faculty,
Juilliard School, from 1976.
    WORKS: ORCHESTRA: <u>Short symphony</u>, 1978;
CHAMBER MUSIC: 3 untitled pieces for piano,
1970-72; <u>Scalene</u>, string trio, 1972; <u>Esja</u>,
piano chamber concerto, New York, 25 Mar. 1974;
<u>Not from this anger</u>, tenor and chamber ensemble,
1975; <u>State of siege</u>, percussion ensemble; <u>Com-
puter piece on the hexachord b f-sharp g e-flat
a-flat e</u>, 1976.
    300 Riverside Dr., New York, NY 10025

KROEGER, KARL
b. Louisville, Ky., 13 Apr. 1932. Studied with
Claude Almand and George Perle, Univ. of Louisville; with Gordon Binkerd, Univ. of Illinois;
at Brown Univ., Ph.D. in musicology. He held a
Ford Found. fellowship, 1964-66; won American
Bandmasters Assoc. Ostwald award, 1971. He was
curator, American Music Collection, N.Y. Public
Library, 1962-64; resident composer, Eugene,
Oreg., 1964-67; faculty member, Ohio Univ.,
1967-68; Brown Univ., 1970-71; Moorhead State
Univ., 1971-72; Wake Forest Univ., 1974-76;
director, Moravian Music Found., from 1972.
    WORKS: ORHCESTRA: suite, 1965; <u>Sinfonietta</u>,
string orch., 1965; BAND: <u>Divertimento</u>, 1965;
CHAMBER MUSIC: 2 string quartets, 1960, 1966;
<u>Concerto da camera</u>, oboe and strings, 1961;
VOICE: <u>Pax vobis</u>, a festival cantata, 1976; many
other works for chorus, piano, organ, ensemble
groups, solo voice.
    120 Linbrook Dr., Winston-Salem, NC 27106

KROESEN, JILL
b. Berkeley, Calif., 12 May 1949. Studied with
Terry Reilly and Robert Ashley, Mills Coll.,
B.A., M.F.A. She received the Elizabeth Crowthers
award.
    WORKS: ELECTRONIC: <u>Fay Shism began in the
home</u>, 1974; <u>The original Lou and Walter story</u>,
1974-78; <u>Dear Ashley in the kitchen</u>, 1975; <u>Who
is the real Marlon Brando</u>, 1976; <u>Universally re-
sented</u>, 1976; <u>Stanley Oil and his mother</u>, 1977.
    97 Kenmare St., New York, NY 10012

KROLL, WILLIAM
b. New York, N.Y., 30 Jan. 1901; d. Boston,
Mass., 10 Mar. 1980. Studied in Berlin and at
the Inst. of Musical Art, New York, graduating
in 1922. He was first violinist of the Coolidge
Atring Quartet, 1935-45; organized the Kroll
Quartet in 1945; has been faculty member,
Peabody Cons.; Cleveland Inst. of Music; Queens
Coll., CUNY; and from 1972, Mannes Coll. of
Music.
WORKS: CHAMBER MUSIC: 4 bagatelles,
string quartet; 4 characteristic pieces, string
quartet; pieces for piano and solo violin.
Mannes Coll. of Music, 157 E. 74 St., New
York, NY 10021

KRUGER, LILLY CANFIELD
b. Portage, Ohio, 13 Apr. 1892; d. 1969. Studied
at Univ. of Toledo, B.A., B.Ed.; was public
school teacher. She wrote settings of Psalm 1;
Psalm 128; He lives; Christmas pastorale; and
piano pieces.

KRUL, ELI
b. Pabianice, Poland, 1 Jan. 1926; to U.S. 1950;
d. 1970. Studied at Hochschule für Musik,
Munich, 1945-49. His works include a string
quartet, 1958; O come, let us sing, chorus and
organ, 1960; Alleluia, a cappella chorus, 1962.

KRUMM, PHILIP
b. Baltimore, Md., 7 Apr. 1941. Studied with
Ross Lee Finney, Univ. of Michigan, 1961-62;
with Karlheinz Stockhausen, Univ. of California
at Davis, 1966. He received the President's
award at Univ. of Michigan, 1962. He was concert supervisor, Youth Division, Hemisfair,
1968, also a design consultant for Confluence
Cosmos at the same fair.
WORKS: THEATRE: music for Ann Arbor Space
Theatre, 1962-63; music for many plays, 1960-66;
CHAMBER MUSIC: Music for clocks, 1962; The
sound machine, chamber ensemble, 1966; ELECTRONIC:
Sax/piano, tape, 1963; aperiodic electronic
music, 1962-78; also radio/television commercials.
103 Erskine Place, San Antonio, TX 78201

KRZYWICKI, JAN
b. Philadelphia, Pa., 15 Apr. 1948. Studied with
Theodore Antoniou and Joseph Castaldo, Philadelphia Musical Acad.; with Vincent Persichetti and
Elliott Carter, Juilliard School; with Darius
Milhaud, Aspen Music School. He has been faculty
member, Philadelphai Coll. of Performing Arts,
from 1972.
WORKS: THEATRE: Continuum, ballet, 1975;
commissioned by Penn. Ballet Co.; WIND ENSEMBLE:
Convocare, 2 trumpets, 3 horns, 1977, commissioned by Amherst Music Center, Raymond, Maine;
CHAMBER MUSIC: Snow night, marimba and piano,
1977.
1221 Spruce St., Philadelphia, PA 19107

KUBIK, GAIL
b. South Coffeyville, Okla., 5 Sept. 1914.
Studied with Edward Royce and Bernard Rogers,
Eastman School of Music, B.M. 1934; with Leo
Sowerby, American Cons., M.M. 1935; with Walter
Piston and Nadia Boulanger, Harvard Univ., 1937-

38. His awards include an honorary doctorate,
Monmouth Coll.; American Prix de Rome; Chicago
Symph. Golden Jubilee award, 1941; Heifetz
prize, 1943; Pulitzer prize, 1952; Academy
award and British Film Inst. award for score to
Gerald McBoing Boing, 1950; Edinburgh Film Festival award for Transatlantic, 1952. He has
held faculty posts at Monmouth Coll., 1934-35;
Dakota Wesleyan Univ., 1936-37; Columbia Teachers
Coll., 1938-40; was staff composer, NBC, 1940-
41; with Office of War Information, 1942-43; in
U.S. AAF 1943-46; from 1970, professor and resident composer, Scripps Coll.
WORKS: THEATRE: Mirror for the sky, folk
opera, 1946; Boston baked beans, 1-act operatic
farce, 1950; Frankie and johnny, ballet for
dance and folk singer, 1946; music for They walk
alone, 1941; ORCHESTRA: American caprice, piano
and chamber orch., 1936; 2 violin concertos,
1938, 1943; Scherzo, 1941; Paratroops, 1941;
Whoopee-ti-yi-yo, on cowboy themes, 1941; Camptown races, 1946; Erie Canal, 1947; 3 symphonies,
1949, 1955, 1956; Symphony concertante, trumpet,
viola, piano, orch.; 1952; Bachata, 1956; A
festival opening, 1957; Scenes for orch., 1963;
CHAMBER MUSIC: piano trio, 1934; Trivialities,
flute, horn, string quartet, 1934; Puck, a
Christmas score, speakers, strings, and winds,
1940; Bennie the beaver, children's tale, narrator, percussion, chamber orch.; violin sonatina, 1944; Little suite, flute, 2 clarinets,
1947; 2 divertimentos, 1959; clarinet sonatina,
1959; piano sonata; Celebrations and epilogue,
piano; Divertimento, piano trio, 1971; 5 theatrical sketches, piano trio, 1971; 5 birthday
pieces, 2 recorders, 1974; CHORUS: Variations
on a 13th-century troubador song, 1935; Soon one
morning, American folk song; Oh dear, what can
the matter be, choral scherzo; In praise of
Johnny Appleseed, 1938; Profiles, 1948; A record
of our time, with narrator, soloists, orch.,
1970; Scholastica, a medieval set, a cappella,
1972; Magic, magic, magic, 3 incantations,
chamber chorus, alto solo, chamber orch., 1976;
FILM SCORES: The world at war, 1942; The Memphis
belle, 1943; Gerald McBoing Boing, 1950; 2 gals
and a guy, 1951; Transatlantic, 1952; The des-
parate hours, 1955; Down to earth, 1958.
Music Dept., Scripps College, Claremont, CA
91711

KUDO, E. TAKEO
b. Honolulu, Hawaii, 10 June 1942. Studied
with Armand Russell, Univ. of Hawaii; with
Bernhard Heiden, Indiana Univ.; and with Manoah
Leide-Tedesco at Colorado Springs. He was composer-arranger for air force bands at the USAF
Acad., and in Washington, D.C.
WORKS: BAND: Variants on popular tune,
Seattle, Jan. 1968; Partita, trumpet and wind
ensemble, 1970; CHAMBER MUSIC: woodwind quartet;
brass quartet; Fragments of once upon a time,
flute, piano, cello, percussion, 1972.

KUNC, BOZIDAR
b. Zagreb, Croatia, 18 July 1903; to U.S. 1950;
d. Detroit, Mich., 1 Apr. 1964. Studied at
Zagreb Musical Acad.

KUPFERMAN, MEYER

WORKS: ORCHESTRA: 2 piano concertos, 1934, 1962; 2 violin concertos, 1950, 1954; 3 episodes, piano and string orch., 1956; CHAMBER MUSIC: string quartet; piano trio; piano quartet; cello sonata; Cycle for piano and percussion, 1956; Pieces for solo double bass, 1959; songs and piano pieces.

KUPFERMAN, MEYER
b. New York, N.Y., 3 July 1926. Studied at High School of Music and Art and at Queens Coll., CUNY, where he received the first La Guardia award. Other awards include a Guggenheim fellowship, 1975; Nat. Endowment for the Arts grants, 1975, 1977. He has been professor, Sarah Lawrence Coll., from 1951; was resident composer, California Music Center, summers of 1977, 1978.
WORKS: OPERA: In a garden, 1949; Dr. Faustus lights the lights; The curious fern, 1957; Voices in a mirror, 1957; Draagenfut girl, 1958; ORCHESTRA: 7 symphonies; Divertimento, 1948; chamber symphony, 1950; Ostinato burlesca, 1954; Libretto for orchestra; Variations for orchestra, 1959; Lyric symphony; concerto for cello, tape, and orch., White Plains, N.Y., 13 Dec. 1975; JAZZ: Tunnel of love, jazz combo; CHAMBER MUSIC: 5 string quartets; Cycle of infinities 1-8, for various instruments; Evocation, cello and piano, 1952; Curtain raiser, flute, clarinet, horn, piano, 1960, New York, 2 May 1973; 3 ideas, trumpet, 1967; sonata for 2 cellos; Angel footprints, violin and tape, New York, 6 May 1973; Fantasy sonata, violin and piano; Madrigal, brass quartet; Superflute, flute solo; concertino for 11 brass instruments; Fantasy concerto, cello, piano, tape; woodwind quintet; Mask of Electra, mezzo-soprano, oboe, electronic harpsichord; Abracadabra, piano quartet, New York, 5 Dec. 1976; Forms for a duo, violin and piano, 1977; The Red King's throne, clarinet, piano, cello, percussion, 1978; PIANO: Fantasy sonata; Little sonata, 1948; Variations, 1948; Sonata on jazz elements, 1958; sonata for 2 pianos; FILM SCORES: Blast of silence; Black like me; Halleluja the hills; Trilogy; Cool wind; High arctic; Goldstein.
171 W. 71st St., New York, NY 10023

KURKA, ROBERT
b. Cicero, Ill., 22 Dec. 1921; d. New York, N.Y., 12 Dec. 1957, of leukemia. Studied with Otto Luening and Darius Milhaud. He held Guggenheim fellowships, 1951, 1952.
WORKS: OPERA: The good soldier Schweik, New York, 23 Apr. 1958; ORCHESTRA: 2 symphonies; violin concerto; Serenade, chamber orch.; concerto for 2 pianos, string orch., and trumpet; concerto for marimba and orch.; Ballad for horn and strings; CHAMBER MUSIC: 5 string quartets; piano trio; 4 violin sonatas; also choral works and piano pieces.

KURTZ, ARTHUR DIGBY
b. Chicago, Ill., 7 May 1929. Attended St. Louis Inst. of Music, M.M.; studied with Nadia Boulanger in Paris; had further studies at the Sorbonne; received the Nadia Boulanger award in 1956 for a piano sonata. He is a private

teacher.
WORKS: ORCHESTRA: Prelude; Serenade, 1958; symphony, 1969; piano concerto, 1972; WIND ENSEMBLE: Variations for brass and percussion, 1969; CHAMBER MUSIC: oboe sonata; 2 piano sonatas, 1956, 1970; 2 violin sonatas, 1964, 1969; 2 string quartets, 1963, 1969; flute sonata, 1964; wind octet, 1965; 3 concert pieces, trumpet and piano, 1968; Fantasy, clarinet and piano, 1970; sonatina for solo flute, 1970; Isaiah, speaker, saxophone, piano, percussion, 1971; choral works, songs, piano pieces.
685 Oakwood Ave., Webster Groves, MO 63119

KURTZ, EDWARD FRAMPTON
b. New Castle, Pa., 31 July 1881; d. Cedar Falls, Iowa, 8 June 1965. Studied at Pittsburgh Cons.; with Philip Greeley Clapp, Univ. of Iowa, M.A.; at Detroit Univ., B.M.; with Edgar Stillman Kelley, Cincinnati Cons., M.M.; also with Percy Goetschius and violin with Eugene Ysaye. He was faculty member, Franklin Coll., Westminster Coll., Geneva Coll., Univ. of Kansas, and from 1940, at Iowa State Teachers Coll.
WORKS: ORCHESTRA: 3 symphonies, 1932, 1939, 1940; The daemon lover, symphonic poem; La charmante, 1941; Parthenope, violin and orch., 1922; CHAMBER MUSIC: string quartet; From the West, suite for string quartet, 1928; suite for organ; violin pieces; songs.

KURTZ, EUGENE ALLEN
b. Atlanta, Ga., 27 Dec. 1923. Studied with Bernard Rogers, Eastman School of Music, 1946-49; with Darius Milhaud at Tanglewood, 1948, and in Paris, 1949-50; with Arthur Honegger in Paris, 1952; privately with Max Deutsch in Paris, 1953-57. He has received numerous commissions. He has been visiting professor at Univ. of Michigan, 1967-68, 1970-71, 1973-74; Eastman School, 1975; Univ. of Illinois, 1976; Univ. of Texas, 1977-78; and was Sterling Currier lecturer, Columbia Univ. Seminar on Contemporary Music, Paris, June 1977; lives in Paris the rest of the year.
WORKS: ORCHESTRA: symphony for string orch., 1956; The solitary walker, 1964; Ca . . . ., diagramme pour orchestra, Strasbourg Radio Symph. Orch., Dec. 1972; 3 songs from Medea, soprano and orch., 1975, Cleveland, Apr. 1976 (version for voice and chamber ensemble, 1976, for voice and piano, 1951); Concert nocturne, from film score; Suite Parisienne, from film score; Mécanique, commissioned by Radio France, Paris, Jan. 1977; CHAMBER MUSIC: Chamber symphony for the 4th of July, WUOM, Univ. of Michigan, 1958; Conversations for 12 players, French Nat. Radio, May 1966; The last contrabass in Las Vegas, for 1 man, 1 woman, and 1 contrabass, Univ. of Nevada, Feb. 1974; Sonata (quasi' opera), solo violin; Improvisations, solo contrabass; Motivations, Books I and II, piano, 1963-65; Animations, piano, 1968.
36 Ave. Jean Moulin, 75014 Paris, France

KURTZ, S. JAMES
b. Newark, N.J., 8 Feb. 1934. Studied with Philip James, New York Univ.; at Univ. of Iowa, Ph.D. He received an award in a Marion Bauer

contest and a Madison Coll. research grant. In 1965 he joined the faculty at James Madison Coll.

WORKS: CHAMBER MUSIC: suite for 3 clarinets; 3 impressions for 2 clarinets; Fantasy, solo clarinet; Notturno, flute or clarinet and piano; other works for winds, piano, synthesizer, tape.

Music Dept., Madison Univ., Harrisonburg, VA 22801

KUZELL, CHRISTOPHER
b. San Bernardino, Calif., 22 July 1927. Studied with Ernst Krenek, Los Angeles City Coll.; with Ramiro Cortes, Ingolf Dahl, Anthony Vazzana, Univ. of Southern California. From 1962 he has been faculty member, Allen Hancock Coll.

WORKS: ORCHESTRA: 5 Chinese poems, chorus and orch.; Sonics 1, San Luis Obispo County Symph., 20 Mar. 1976; WIND ENSEMBLE: Ode to an aardvark, band; music for brass and drums; CHAMBER MUSIC: violin sonata; woodwind quartet; Chinese poems for soprano and 4 instruments; string quartet; 6 little pieces, marimba; Serenade for 7 players; sonata for marimba solo; Divertimento, chamber orch.

907 E. El Camino, Santa Maria, CA 93454

KYNASTON, TRENT P.
b. Tucson, Ariz., 7 Dec. 1946. Studied with Robert McBride, Wendal Jones, and Henry Johnson, Univ. of Arizona. He joined the faculty at Western Michigan Univ. in 1973.

WORKS: ORCHESTRA: symphony, 1969; saxophone concerto, 1976; BAND: Underture for band, 1967; Mind expansion, wind ensemble and tape, 1970; Sonata duet, saxophone and clarinet, 1967; Dawn and jubilation, saxophone and piano, 1973; alto saxophone sonata, 1977; CHORUS: Corinthians 13, choir and 13 brass, 1970; The man who was summoned, choir, guitar, horn, string orch., 2 pianos, 1970.

816 Boswell Lane, Kalamazoo, MI 49007

KYR, ROBERT HARRY
b. Cleveland, Ohio, 20 Apr. 1952. Studied at Yale Univ., B.A. 1974; Univ. of Pennsylvania, M.A. 1978; held a junior fellowship, Harvard Univ., 1978-81.

WORKS: CHAMBER MUSIC: Chronicles, 10 instruments, 1972; Canticles I: Music to hear, 12 instruments, 1973; The fall of the rebel angel, 21 instruments, 1973; MULTIMEDIA: Voyage: Dream play for instruments, chamber orch., tape, and film, 1974.

22289 Blossom Dr., Rocky River, OH 44116

LABACH, PARKER
b. Lexington, Ky., 1918. Studied with Lewis Henry Horton, Univ. of Kentucky, A.B. 1942, M.A. 1947; with Merrills Lewis, Syracuse Univ., Ph.D. 1960. He has taught at Georgia State Coll. for Women; Syracuse Univ.; and in 1964, was on faculty at Kent State Univ.

WORKS: CHAMBER MUSIC: April 1950, flute and piano; February 1951, cello and piano; woodwind quintet; also band marches, choral works, songs, piano pieces.

LABAR, DANIEL
b. Berwyn, Ill., 6 May 1944. Studied with Stella Roberts, American Cons. He received an award for an anthem, 1968, and a commission, 1969. He was faculty member, American Cons., 1970-75; at Glenville State Coll., 1976-77.

WORKS: ORCHESTRA: Textures, fantasy for orch., 1974; CHAMBER MUSIC: string quartet, 1971; CHORUS: De profundis, 1968; Nativity suite, boys' choir, narrator, organ, 1969; A song of war, a song of peace, 1972; Ode to man-kinde, chamber choir, 1974; mass in the Dorian mode, 1979; SONGS: Stopping by woods, tenor, 1967; Grass, tenor and piano, 1972; 2 songs from Sandburg, baritone, clarinet, and cello, 1974.

4448 N. Malden, Chicago, IL 60640

LA BARBARA, JOAN
b. Philadelphia, Pa., 8 June 1947. Studied with Franklin Morris, Syracuse Univ.; at New York Univ.; at Tanglewood; and work/study with Steve Reich, Philip Glass, John Cage, David Berhman, Alvin Lucier. Her awards include 2 Creative Artists Program Service grants, 1974-75, 1977-78; Composers' Forum and Experimental Intermedia Found. grant, 1976; selection for performance at 1977 World Music Day Festival; and ASCAP awards, 1977, 1978. She was visiting Slee composer, Center for Creative and Performing Arts, SUNY, Buffalo, 1977; resident artist, Crane School of Music, Potsdam, and Kutztown Coll., 1977, and at California Inst. of the Arts, 1978; resident composer, German Academic Exchange Program, Berlin, 1979; and is a contributing editor for Musical America.

WORKS: Voice piece: One-note internal resonance investigation, amplified voice, 1974; Circular song, amplified voice, 1975; Thunder, 6 timpani, solo voice, live electronics, 1976; Ides of March, a series of 15 pieces for varying instrumentation, based on the acoustical phenomenon of beats that occur between closely tuned instruments, with amplification but no electronics; center section in all pieces has strictly controlled improvisation, 1976-79, #8 for trombone, trumpet, band, voice, piano was premiered at Urbana, Ill., 9 Dec. 1978; Cathing, multitrack voices and electrically altered speech on tape, 1977; Chandra, solo voice and live electronics, 5 bass voices with phase shifters, 17 instruments, Bremen, West Germany, 6 May 1978; Responsive resonance with feathers, piano with voice tape played through speakers inside the piano body, New York, 20 Mar. 1979; Performance piece, amplified voice, 1979; and a quadrophonic tape soundance installation/environment titled Q-
-uatre petites betes (title is a quote from a letter by Marcel Duchamp in which Quatre appeared on 2 lines as above), 1979.

P.O. Box 11, Old Chelsea Station, New York, NY 10011

LABOUNTY, EDWIN MURRAY
b. Garretson, S.Dak., 19 Feb. 1927. Studied with Bernhard Heiden, Indiana Univ., B.M. 1949, M.M. 1953, D.M. 1962. He was music supervisor, North Country School, Lake Placid, 1954-59; on

LABUNSKI, FELIX

faculty, Memphis State Univ., 1962-68; then at
Western Washington State Univ.
   WORKS: ORCHESTRA: 3 pieces for orchestra,
1960; Excursus, piano and orch., 1962; Excursus
#2, 1972; CHAMBER MUSIC: sonata for 2 celli and
piano, 1952; horn sonata, 1953; cello sonata,
1959; wind quintet, 1960; VOICE: Songs of recol-
lection, a cycle, 1952; Fatal interview, song
cycle, 1952; Sea afternoon, choir, harp, oboe,
cello, glockenspiel, 1961; PIANO: sonatina,
1951; sonata, 1954-73; Concert piece, 4 pianos
with percussion, 1958; Blue and blue green, 2
pianos, 1960-73; ELECTRONIC: incidental music
for Now is the time for all good men, tape,
1973.
   433 16th St., Bellingham, WA 98225

LABUNSKI, FELIX
   b. Ksawerynow, Poland, 27 Dec. 1892; U.S. citizen
1941; d. Cincinnati, 28 Apr. 1979. Studied with
Lucien Marczewski and Witold Maliszewski in Warsaw; with Nadia Boulanger and Paul Dukas in
Paris. His honors include MacDowell fellowship,
1941; Huntington Hartford Found. fellowship,
1951; honorary doctorate, Chicago Musical Coll.,
1951; Alfred Jurzykowski Found. award, 1969; Nat.
Endowment for the Arts grant, 1973-74. He was
faculty member, Marymount Coll., Tarrytown, N.Y.,
1940-41; Univ. of Cincinnati, 1945-64, then
professor emeritus.
   WORKS: BALLET: God's man, 1937; ORCHESTRA:
In memoriam for Ignace Paderewski, 1941; suite
for string orch., 1941; Variations, 1951; Elegy,
1954; symphony, 1954; Xaveriana, fantasy for 2
pianos and orch., 1956; Nocturne, 1957; Images
of youth, 1958; Symphonic dialogues, 1960; Canto
di aspirazione, 1963; Polish rennaissance suite,
1967; Salut a Paris, ballet suite, 1968; Music
for piano and orch., 1968; Primavera, 1973; WIND
ENSEMBLE: Intrada festiva, brass choir, 1968;
CHAMBER MUSIC: Divertimento, 4 woodwinds, 1956;
Diptych (Pastorale and danse), oboe and piano,
1958; string quartet #2, 1962; choral works,
songs, piano and organ pieces.

LABUNSKI, WIKTOR
   b. St. Petersburg, Russia, 14 Apr. 1895, to U.S.
1928; d. Lenexa, Kans., 26 Jan. 1974. Brother
of Felix Labunski, studied at the St. Petersburg
Cons. He made his debut as pianist in New York
in 1928; toured the U.S.; was professor and
director, Coll. of Music, Memphis, Tenn., 1931-
37; Kansas City Cons., 1937-63; then professor,
Univ. of Missouri, Kansas City.
   WORKS: ORCHESTRA: symphony, 1936; piano
concerto, 1937; Variations, piano and orch.; 2-
piano concerto, 1951; piano pieces.

LACKEY, DOUGLAS M.
   b. Sacramento, Calif., 10 Aug. 1932. Studied at
Univ. of California, Los Angeles.
   WORKS: Drum and coco, percussion sextet;
also film background scores and music for commercial films.

LADERMAN, EZRA
   b. New York, N.Y., 29 June 1924. Studied at
Brooklyn Coll., B.A.; with Otto Luening, Stefan

Wolpe, and Douglas Moore, Columbia Univ., M.A.
His awards have included 3 Guggenheim grants;
Prix de Rome; Ford Found. commission. He is
professor, State Univ. of New York at Binghamton; in 1979, was appointed music director,
Nat. Endowment for the Arts.
   WORKS: OPERA: Jacob and the Indians, 1957;
Sarah, 1958; Goodby to the clown, 1960; The
hunting of the snark, 1961; Shadows among us;
Galileo Galilei, opera oratorio, television
performance, New York, 14 May 1967, first stage
performance, Binghamton, 3 Feb. 1979; ORCHESTRA:
4 symphonies, #3 (Jerusalem), New York, CBS-TV,
3 Apr. 1977; Concerto for orchestra; violin concerto; Triptych, flute, oboe, strings; Magic
prison, 2 narrators and orch., 1967; Double
helix, flute, oboe, strings; piano concerto, New
York premiere, 15 May 1979; CHAMBER MUSIC:
Stanzas, chamber orch.; nonet, winds and piano;
Theme, variations, and finale, string quartet
and wind quartet, 1957; 3 piano sonatas; flute
sonata; string quartets; piano trio; A single
voice, oboe and string quartet; 2 duos for
violin and cello; clarinet sonata; Celestial
bodies, flute and string quartet, Milwaukee,
23 June 1975; Portraits, violin solo; Serenade,
clarinet solo; Elegy, viola solo, New York, 17
Feb. 1974; Echoes and anticipations, chamber
ensemble, 1975; Momente, piano, 1976; Other
voices, solo and taped viola, New York, CBS-TV,
20 Mar. 1977; Cadence, double string quartet,
bass viol, 2 flutes, New York, 5 Oct. 1978;
CHORUS: The eagle stirred, oratorio; And David
wept, cantata, 1971; Thrive upon the rock, New
York, 9 May 1973; SONG CYCLES: Songs for Eve,
MacLeish text; From the Psalms; Songs from
Michelangelo, New York, 18 Mar. 1973; FILM SCORE:
The Eleanor Roosevelt story (received an Oscar);
Image of love; Grand Canyon.
   Music Dept., State Univ. of New York,
Binghamton, NY 13901

LADIGIN, DONALD R.
   b. San Francisco, Calif., 14 July 1939. Studied
with Alan Chaplin and Virko Baley, California
Inst. of the Arts; won a first prize in composition, Young Artists of Tomorrow contest, Los
Angeles. He is a private teacher in Los Angeles.
   WORKS: Variations, piano, 1971.

LAFFERTY, DONALD
   b. Buffalo, N.Y., 8 Sept. 1942. Studied with
Robert Mols and Allen Sapp, State Univ. of New
York, Buffalo; with Arthur Berger and Harold
Shapero, Brandeis Univ.; with Malcolm Peyton,
New England Cons.; piano with Irma Wolpe. He
was instructor, Clark Univ., 1968-69; from 1970,
at New England Cons.
   WORKS: PIANO: Grace period, 1972.
   72 Glenmere, Reading, MA 01867

LA FORGE, FRANK
   b. Rockford, Ill., 22 Oct. 1877; d. New York,
5 May 1953. Studied piano with Harrison Wild
and Leschetizky; received an honorary D.M. from
the Detroit Found. Music School. He was accompanist to Marcella Sembrich, Lily Pons, and
Schumann-Heink; voice teacher in New York, 1920-
53. He composed songs and piano pieces.

LAHMER, REUEL
b. Maple, Ont., Canada, 27 Mar. 1912. Studied
at Stetson Univ.; Westminster Choir Coll., B.M.;
Columbia Univ.; with Roy Harris, Cornell Univ.
He was minister of music, Grace Church, Montclair,
N.J., 1934-39; instructor, Cornell Univ., 1941-
42; in U.S. Army in World War II; resident composer, Carroll Coll., 1946-48; on faculty,
Colorado Coll., 1948-51; organist- choirmaster,
Pittsburgh, 1951-62; lectured in Europe and
Mexico for the USIA; in 1973, was in residence
at the American Coll. in Leysin, Switz.
WORKS: CHORUS: A song of our own; Spring
cantata; Suite on Methodist hymne; Sing the
sweet land; Civil war suite; Ye sons and
daughters of the King; Hear Lord; also songs
and organ works.

LAITMAN, LORI
b. Long Beach, N.Y., 12 Jan. 1955. Studied
with Jonathan Kramer, Robert Moore, Frank Lewin,
Yale Univ.; and with George B. Wilson, Univ. of
Michigan, summer session.
WORKS: CHAMBER MUSIC: I wrote it last
Saturday, flute duet, 1974; Enchanted knickers
piano rag, 1974; Catabasis, chamber ensemble,
1977; FILM SCORES: Arrow to the sun, 1976; One,
1977-78; The 2 knights, 1978.
380 Riverside Dr., #4E, New York, NY 10025

LAKE, OLIVER
b. Marianna, Ark., 14 Sept. 1942. Studied at
Lincoln Univ., Jefferson City, Mo.; with Oliver
Nelson and Ron Carter, electronic music with Ivan
Pageno. He received Nat. Endowment for the Arts
grants, 1972, 1977, 1979; was artist-in-residence,
Paris Center for Artists and Students, 1973;
taught at Creative Music School, Woodstock, N.Y.,
1975-78.
WORKS: CHAMBER MUSIC: Spaces, violin trio;
Suite for improviser and violin trio; Kuon Ganjo,
9 instruments; Shadow thread, octet and cello;
Ku II, flute duo; Eraser of the day, alto saxo-
phone solo; Heavy spirits, quintet.
12 Waverly Place, New York, NY 10003

LAMB, GORDON H.
b. Eldora, Iowa, 6 Nov. 1934. Studied at
Simpson Coll., Univ. of Nebraska, and Univ. of
Iowa. He has been faculty member at Univ. of
Wisconsin, 1969-70; Univ. of Texas at Austin,
1970-74; from 1974, Univ. of Texas, San Antonio.
WORKS: CHORUS: Aleatory psalm; other
choral works and songs.
Music Dept., Univ. of Texas, San Antonio,
TX 78285

LAMB, HUBERT WELDON
b. Walpole, N.H., 29 June 1900. Studied at
Harvard Univ., B.A. 1930; received the John
Knowles Paine traveling fellowship, 1930, 1931;
Guggenheim fellowship, 1948; honorary D.M., New
England Cons., 1963. He was faculty member,
Longy School of Music, 1934-35; at Wellesley
Coll., 1935-74.
WORKS: ORCHESTRA: Capriccio, string orch.,
1946; CHAMBER MUSIC: Concerto da camera, harpsi-
chord and chamber ensemble, 1943; string trio,

1946; The Intervale variations, violin and piano,
1950; Rondo serio, cello and piano, 1951; A
solemn air, horn and piano, 1951; Capriccio and
fugue, clarinet and piano, 1963; CHORUS: Remember now thy creator, 1940; The end of the world,
women's voices, 1941; Hymn of the cherubim, 1943;
6 scenes from the Protevangelion, women's voices
and small orch., 1949; Pastorale, women's voices
and 9 instruments.
918 Stagecoach Rd., Santa Fe, NM 87501

LAMB, JOHN DAVID
b. Portland, Oreg., 11 Mar. 1935. Studied at
Univ. of Washington and with Volfgangs Darzins,
1956-60. He received a Ford Found. grant,
1964-65; and a Rockefeller performance award.
He has been a teacher in the Seattle public
schools from 1960.
WORKS: THEATRE: King Midas, a play for
dancers, speaking chorus, recorders, Orff instruments; ORCHESTRA: horn concerto; Scherzo
and chaconne, flute and strings; Diptych; Cloud
Cuckoo land, saxophone concerto; Comoedia, suite;
BAND: Night music, saxophone and chamber band;
Serenade; CHORUS: The song of Solomon, with
soloists and orch.; An entertainment, female
voices, piano, horn; Rhymes, female voices,
recorders, drums; The monotony song, with clarinet; many songs and works for chamber groups.
1907 E. Blaine, Seattle, WA 98112

LAMB, MARVIN LEE
b. Jacksonville, Tex., 12 July 1946. Studied
with John Butler and Newton Strandberg, Houston
State Univ., B.M.; with William P. Latham and
Merrill Ellis, North Texas State Univ., M.M.;
with Herbert Brün and Paul Zonn, Univ. of
Illinois. He held a scholarship at North Texas
State Univ.; has received ASCAP awards and many
commissions. He was faculty member, Atlantic
Christian Coll., 1973-77; from 1977, at George
Peabody Coll. for Teachers, Nashville.
WORKS: ORCHESTRA: 3 movements for trumpet,
strings, percussion; tenor saxophone concerto;
BAND: Quiet statement; CHAMBER MUSIC: In
memoriam Benjy, saxophone quartet; Prairie suite,
brass quintet; The professor march and rag, 6
speaker/actors; Phonemes, spoken choir; 3 moments,
piano and tape; woodwind quintet, 1973; Lin-
guistics, trombone and tape; MULTIMEDIA: This
banana is for you, 2 dancers and solo trumpet;
Intonazione, tapes, lights, sculpture; Forsythia/
Brock's bop, for tape, film, macrame hangings,
dance, piccolo trumpet, mime artist, 5 cassette-
instructed scat singers.
2609 Oakland Ave., Nashville, TN 37212

LAMBORD, BENJAMIN
b. Portland, Maine, 10 June 1879; d. Lake
Hopatcong, N.J., 6 June 1915. Studied with
Edward MacDowell and Cornelius Rybner, Columbia
Univ.; with Paul Vidal in Paris. He was organist-
choirmaster and teacher in New York; organized
the Lambord Choral Society.
WORKS: ORCHESTRA: Introduction and variations on an English dance theme; Clytie, with
soprano solo; Verses from Omar Khayyam, with
chorus; songs, piano pieces.

LAMBRECHT, HOMER GEORGE

LAMBRECHT, HOMER GEORGE
b. Longmont, Colo., 3 Oct. 1943. Studied with
Allan Willman, Univ. of Wyoming, B.A. 1965, M.A.
1967; with Robert Crane, Hilmar Luckhardt,
and Les Thimmig, Univ. of Wisconsin, D.M.A.
1977. He held fellowships from NDEA Title IV,
1967-69; Univ. of Wisconsin, 1971-72; Mass. Inst.
of Tech., Summer Workshop, 1978. His teaching
posts have included Cheyenne public schools,
1964-65; Univ. of Wyoming, 1965-67; Univ. of
Wisconsin, 1969-71; Univ. of Minnesota, 1974-78;
and with Film in the Cities, 1977-79. He organized an exhibit of graphic music for the
Minneapolis Inst. of Arts, Sept. 1979-Jan. 1980.
WORKS: CHAMBER MUSIC: Metaphrases, 2 saxophones, 2 clarinets, ISCM, Reykjavik, Iceland,
June 1973; Variations, piano, 1977; Turtle turn,
improvisational band players, 1978; Geo, saxophone; Uroboros, wind ensemble; Diamond lights,
woodwinds; Owl, music and theatre piece, commissioned by St. Paul Chamber Orch., premiere,
St. Paul, 10 Mar. 1979; ELECTRONIC: Vapors,
piano, trumpet, tape, 1972; Boston sound sculpture, MIT, July 1978.
1766 Carl St., Lauderdale, MN 55113

LAMBRO, PHILIP
b. Wellesley Hills, Mass., 2 Sept. 1935. Studied
with Donald Pond and Gyorgy Sandor, Music Acad.
of the West. Together with Shimon Ben-Bassat,
Israeli-American structural designer, he has
developed plans for the concert hall of the
future: circular in design, with hydraulically
controlled stages which can be raised or lowered,
natural and amplified acoustics, and equipped
with multichannel audio and visual recording
devices. He is also a film composer and conductor.
WORKS: ORCHESTRA: Miraflores, string orch.;
2 pictures, solo percussionist and orch.; 4
songs, soprano and orch.; Structures, string
orch.; WIND ENSEMBLE: Parallelograms, flute
quartet and jazz ensemble; Music for wind, brass,
and percussion; Fanfare and tower music, brass
quintet; CHAMBER MUSIC: Dance barbaro, percussion; Toccata for piano; Toccata for guitar;
Obelisk, oboe and percussion; Night pieces,
piano; Biospheres for 6 percussionists; FILM
SCORES: Energy on the move, documentary; The
invisible magician; And now Miguel; Celebration.
1888 Century Park E., #10, Century City, CA
90067

LAMM, ROBERT CARSON
b. New Albany, Ind., 9 Apr. 1922. Studied with
Warren Babb, Univ. of Louisville; with Arthur
Olaf Andersen, Univ. of Arizona; and with
Bernhard Heiden, Indiana Univ. He was faculty
member, Hartwick Coll., 1948-52; Indiana Univ.,
1952-53; Park Coll., 1953-56; Univ. of Arizona,
1956-75.
WORKS: BAND: Saturday in the park; CHAMBER
MUSIC: Tramway, trombone and piano; piano
sonata; violin sonata.

LA MONTAINE, JOHN
b. Oak Park, Ill., 17 Mar. 1920. Studied with
Stella Roberts and Rudolph Ganz in Chicago; with

Bernard Rogers and Howard Hanson, Eastman School
of Music, B.M.; with Bernard Wagenaar at
Juilliard School; and with Nadia Boulanger. His
awards include a scholarship at Eastman School;
Ford Found. grant, 1958; 2 Guggenheim fellowships, 1959, 1960; Pulitzer prize for a piano
concerto, 1959; Rheta Sosland Chamber Music
Competition prize, 1960; composer-in-residence,
American Acad. in Rome, 1962; Eastman School
Distinguished Alumni award; many commissions.
He played celeste and piano with the NBC Symph.,
1950-54; was visiting professor, Eastman School
of Music, 1964-65; in 1977, was named Nixon Distinguished Scholar and holder of the Nixon chair
at Whittier Coll.; with Paul Sifler, formed the
Fredonia Press in 1975 and Fredonia Discs in
1977.
WORKS: OPERA: Spreading the news, 1 act;
Novellis, novellis, Christmas pageant, Washington Cathedral, 24 Dec. 1961; The shephardes
playe, 2nd part of the Christmas pageant trilogy,
Washington Cathedral, 24 Dec. 1967; Erode the
Great, 3rd part, Washington, 30 Dec. 1969; Be
glad then, America, Penn. State Univ., 6 Feb.
1976; ORCHESTRA: Songs of the rose of Sharon,
soprano and orch.; piano concerto, Washington,
25 Nov. 1958; Canons for orch.; Ode for oboe and
orch.; 5 sonnets for orch.; Jubilant overture;
symphony; Fragments from the Song of songs,
soprano and orch.; From sea to shining sea,
Washington, 20 Jan. 1961; Birds of paradise,
1964; Te Deum, chorus, wind orch., percussion;
Mass of nature, with chorus and narrator; Wilderness journal, with bass baritone and organ, 1972;
flute concerto, Ann Arbor, Mich., 5 Aug. 1981;
CHAMBER MUSIC: cello sonata; string quartet;
sonata for piano, 4 hands; Scherzo, 4 trombones;
Conversations, clarinet and piano, 1973, for
violin and piano, 1977, flute and piano, 1978;
CHORUS: The Whittier service, with optional
solos, guitar, and organ, Washington Cathedral,
20 May 1979; many choral works, songs, piano
pieces.
c/o Sifler, 3947 Fredonia Dr., Hollywood, CA
90028

LANDAU, SIEGFRIED
b. Berlin, Germany, 4 Sept. 1921; to U.S. 1940.
Studied in Berlin; at Trinity Coll., London;
conducting with Pierre Monteux in the U.S. He
organized the Brooklyn Philharmonia in 1954, was
conductor to 1970; from 1962, conductor of Music
for Westchester Symph.; was music director and
conductor, Chattanooga Opera Assoc., 1959-73.
WORKS: OPERA: The sons of Aaron, 1959;
BALLET: The golem, 1946; The dybbuk; ORCHESTRA:
Longing for Jerusalem, soprano and orch., 1941;
CHAMBER MUSIC: Chassidic suite, viola and
piano, 1941; also Friday evening service.
c/o Westchester Symphony, Box 35, Gedney
Station, White Plains, NY 10605

LANDAU, VICTOR
b. Brooklyn, N.Y., 18 June 1916. Studied with
Charles Haubiel and Philip James, New York Univ.
He received the Talbott prize, Westminster Choir
School, 1938. He was instructor, Brooklyn Coll.,
1946-50; then professor, State Univ. Coll., New

Paltz, N.Y.
   WORKS: BAND: Variations on a Russian theme; CHAMBER MUSIC: Adagio for strings; Scherzo, violin and piano; 3 James Joyce songs; CHORUS: The laughters; Eli, eli.
   5 Lincoln Place, New Paltz, NY 12561

LANDRY, RICHARD MILES
   b. Cecilia, La., 16 Nov. 1938. Studied with John Gilfry, Southwestern Louisiana Univ.; and with Arthur Lora. Since 1968 he has been associated with Philip Glass in performance. His works are avant-garde electronic and have been performend at the Dance Gallery in New York.

LANDY, H. LEIGH
   b. Bronxville, N.Y., 23 Nov. 1951. Studied with Jack Beeson, Charles Dodge, Vladimir Ussachevsky, and Charles Wuorinen, Columbia Univ.; and with Bulent Arel and Alfredo Del Monaco. He was graduate assistant, Columbia Univ., 1973-74.
   WORKS: THEATRE: cummungs again, Absurdist Theatre piece for 7 actors-singers, 1973; CHAMBER MUSIC: Flute study #1, 1972; Opus 1, flute, horn, piano, 1973; ELECTRONIC: Computer study #1, 1971; Ambiguite, musique concrete, tape, 1973; Nixon phase (out) 1, computer piece, 1973.

LANE, EASTWOOD
   b. Brewerton, N.Y., 22 May 18/9; d. Central Square, N.Y., 22 Jan. 1951. Studied at Syracuse Univ. He was assistant director of the Wanamaker Concerts for 23 years.
   WORKS: BALLET: Boston fancy; Abelard and Eloise; A caravan from China comes; ORCHESTRA: Sea burial, tone poem; Persimmon pucker (orchestrated by Ferde Grofe); PIANO SUITES: Adirondack sketches; 4th of July; Sleepy Hollow; Sold down the river; 3 American sketches.

LANE, LEWIS
   b. Freehold, N.J., 3 Aug. 1901; d. Boston, Mass., 24 Jan. 1977. Studied with Rubin Goldmark, New York Coll. of Music; with Thomas Tapper and Henry Krehbiel, Inst. of Musical Art, New York. He was music librarian, NBC, 1928-31; founder and director of NBC's Division for Musical Research, 1931-51; archivist, Leschetizky Assoc., 1938-48.
   WORKS: PIANO: Prelude in C; Fragments after Lucretius; 2 character sketches; Green Mountain sketches; many songs.

LANE, RICHARD B.
   b. Paterson, N.J., 11 Dec. 1933. Studied with Bernard Rogers, Louis Mennini, and Wayne Barlow, Eastman School of Music, B.M. 1955, M.M. 1956. He received the Eastman School publication and recording award, 1956; 2 Ford Found. grants, 1959, 1960. From 1961 he has been an accompanist and a private teacher of piano and composition.
   WORKS: ORCHESTRA: 4 songs, mezzo-soprano and orch.; String song and passacaglia, string orch.; CHAMBER MUSIC: suite for saxophone and piano; 6 piano sonatas; flute sonata; Antique suite, 2 pianos, 1978; clarinet sonata #2, Ridgewood, N.J., 20 May 1979; CHORUS: Hymn to

the night; Cradle song; SONGS: Lullaby, for soprano and piano, 1978.
   173 Lexington Ave., Paterson, NJ 07502

LANERI, ROBERTO
   b. Arzignano, Italy, 25 Mar. 1945; to U.S. 1968. Studied with William O. Smith; with Lejaren Hiller, State Univ. of New York, Buffalo; with Keith Humble and Edwin London, Univ. of California, San Diego. He was clarinetist and composer, Center for the Creative and Performing Arts, Buffalo, 1970-72; member of SEM Ensemble, 1970-72, teaching assistant, Univ. of California, San Diego, 1973.
   WORKS: BALLET: Black ivory suite, large ensemble of instruments and voices, Buffalo, 26 Feb. 1972; CHAMBER MUSIC: Finis, soprano and piano, 1969; Changes for 5 players, Montreal, 16 Mar. 1969; Sleep soft smiling, soprano, chamber ensemble, tape, 1969; The night brings a rabbit, clarinet and percussion, 1970; Dies irae, soprano and ensemble, 1971; Summer music, horn and piano, 1971; Esorcismi #1, voice and 4 instruments, 1972; August visitors, soprano, tenor, cello, harpsichord, 1973; and electronic pieces.

LANGE, ARTHUR
   b. Philadelphia, Pa., 16 Apr. 1889; d. Washington, D.C., 7 Dec. 1956. Studied music privately. He was arranger for dance orchestras and musicals in New York; head of music department, MGM, 1929; music director for other film studios; organized and conducted Santa Monica Symphony, 1947-56.
   WORKS: ORCHESTRA: a symphony; Symphonette romantique; Symphonette spirituelle; Water whispers suite; etc.; film scores; songs.

LANGENDOEN, JACOBUS C.
   b. The Hague, Neth., 3 Feb. 1890; d. Newcastle, N.H., 29 Oct. 1973. Studied at the Netherlands Royal Cons.; cello with Joseph Malkin and Isaac Moisel. He was cellist in The Hague Orchestra, 1908-17; with Boston Pops Orchestra, 1920-62.
   WORKS: ORCHESTRA: Improvisations; Puppet, trumpet and orch.; Variations on a Dutch theme.

LANGENUS, GUSTAVE
   b. Malines, Belgium, 6 Aug. 1883; to U.S. 1910; d. Commack, N.Y., 30 Jan. 1957. Studied at Malines Music School; Royal Cons., Brussels. He toured with Sousa's band in Europe; played clarinet in orchestras in England; then in New York Symphony; New York Philharmonic; NBC Symphony; with the Perole Quartet and Budapest Quartet; was cofounder of the New York Chamber Music Society; taught at Juilliard School, Dalcroze School; and elsewhere; was guest band conductor. His compositions include Swallows flight, for flute, clarinet, and orch.; and many pieces for small ensembles.

LANGERT, JULES
   b. New York, N.Y., 25 Mar. 1932. Studied at Queens Coll.; and with Andrew Imbrie, Univ. of California, Berkeley. His awards include a Fulbright scholarship; Hertz scholarship; California Cello Club award. He was faculty member, San

LANGSTROTH, IVAN SHED

Francisco State Univ., 1965-70; from 1971, at
Dominican Coll. of San Rafael.
WORKS: OPERA: Sea change, 4 singers and
chamber ensemble; ORCHESTRA: Fantasy, small
orch.; CHAMBER MUSIC: duo for cello and piano;
quartet, flute, clarinet, cello, piano; 3 capriccios, piano; 2 sets of songs for voice and
piano; woodwind trio, San Francisco, 7 Oct. 1976.
6504 Raymond St., Oakland, CA 94609

LANGSTROTH, IVAN SHED
b. Alameda, Calif., 16 Oct. 1887; d. New York,
N.Y., 18 Apr. 1971. Studied in San Francisco;
with Paul Juon, Engelbert Humperdinck, and Josef
Lhevinne in Berlin; remained in Europe as opera
coach, organist, concert pianist, and teacher to
1935. He was faculty member, Chatham Square
Music School, New York, 1940-43; City Coll. of
New York, 1942-45; Brooklyn Coll., 1943-45;
thereafter, a private teacher in New York.
WORKS: ORCHESTRA: piano concerto; Aria,
soprano and orch.; CHAMBER MUSIC: string quartet; piano sonatina; CHORUS: Cradle song; Butterfly; many organ pieces.

LANSKY, PAUL
b. New York, N.Y., 18 June 1944. Studied with
George Perle and Hugo Weisgall, Queens Coll.;
with Milton Babbitt, Edward T. Cone, and James
K. Randall, Princeton Univ. His awards include
the Bearns prize and an American Acad. and Inst.
of Arts and Letters award. He was faculty member,
Swarthmore Coll., 1968-69; from 1969, at Princeton Univ.; plays horn in the Dorian Quintet; is
associate editor, Perspectives of New Music.
WORKS: CHAMBER MUSIC: Modal fantasy, piano,
1970; 2 string quartets; Crossworks, chamber
ensemble, 1974-75; Piano piece in 3 parts; Dance
suite, 1977; ELECTRONIC: Computer piece, 1973-
74; mild und leise, computer, 1976.
Music Dept., Princeton University, Princeton,
NJ 08540

LA PIERRE, GERALD A.
b. Biddeford, Maine, 1 Nov. 1946. Studied with
John Rogers and Mark DeVoto, Univ. of New
Hampshire; with Andrew Imbrie, Olly Wilson, and
Edwin Dugger, Univ. of California, Berkeley, M.A.,
Ph.D.; with Klaus Huber in Freiberg, Germany; and
Humphrey Searle, Royal Coll. of Music, London.
His awards include first place, Nicola de Lorenzo
prize, 1970; George Ladd Prix de Paris; scholarship for Musica Nova, Glasgow, Scotland; and
commissions. He was faculty assistant, Univ. of
California, 1970-76; from 1976, on faculty, Univ.
of Natal, South Africa.
WORKS: ORCHESTRA: Triptych, tenor and
orch., text by composer, 1976; trombone concerto, 1978-79; CHAMBER MUSIC: trombone sonata,
1971; Gelstonia, flute, clarinet, viola, tape,
1971; Progression, 12 players, 1973; Discussions,
clarinet, 2 cellos, percussion, 1973; trio for
flute, horn, cello, 1973; Horizons, 8 instruments and tape, 1975; Musica Natalia, 26-member
ensemble, Durban, 14 Oct. 1978, composer conducting; VOICE: Psalm 82, tenor, clarinet,
violin, cello, piano, 1972; 3 songs, low voice
and piano, Rilke text, 1974; Hungerford Bridge,

soprano, double bass, percussion, 1974.
Box 242, R.F.D. 2, Springvale, ME 04083

LAPIN, LAWRENCE
b. New York, N.Y., 24 Nov. 1935. Studied with
Clifton Williams, Alfred Reed, Frederick Ashe,
Univ. of Miami, B.M., M.M. He has been faculty
member, Univ. of Miami, from 1968.
WORKS: BAND: Tubarondo, tuba and wind
ensemble, 1965; 6 pieces for jazz band, 1971;
Nothin' fancy, stage band, 1970; CHAMBER MUSIC:
violin sonata, 1964; Mazurka, piano, 1965; duet
for flute and clarinet, 1965.
10465 S.W. 96 Terrace, Miami, FL 33101

LA PORTA, JOHN DANIEL
b. Philadelphia, Pa., 13 Apr. 1920. Studied
with Nicolas Flagello, Alexei Haieff, and Ernst
Toch, Manhattan School of Music, M.M. He received annual ASCAP awards, 1969-73. He was
faculty member, Manhattan School of Music, 1951-
58; from 1962, at Berklee Coll. of Music; member
of Berklee Faculty Saxophone Quartet.
WORKS: BAND: Mid-century event, 1961;
Theme and variations on the blues, 40-minute
work for jazz octet; CHAMBER MUSIC: Spanish
rhapsody, saxophone quartet; numerous works for
small ensembles; many jazz works.
34 Maple St., South Hamilton, MA 01982

LA PORTA, LOUIS F.
b. Chicago, Ill., 23 Sept. 1944. Studied at
Chicago Cons.; with Alfred Uhl, Friedrich Cerha,
Vienna Acad. of Music; and at Univ. of Vienna;
conducting with Hans Swarowsky. He received the
Kodaly composition prize, 1970; Outstanding
Young Men of America award, 1972. He was high
school music director, 1967-68; faculty member,
Chicago Cons. Coll., 1970-78; conductor, Chicago
Opera Players, from 1972.
WORKS: ORCHESTRA: symphony in 1 movement;
violin concerto; CHAMBER MUSIC: violin sonata,
1967; string quartet, 1970; Concertpiece, cello
and piano; Recitative, solo viola; sonata for
solo cello; string trio; sonata for 4 percussionists; PIANO: sonatina; Variations; Fantasy;
also choral works and songs.
11421 S. Western Ave., Chicago, IL 60643

LA PRADE, ERNEST
b. Memphis, Tenn., 20 Dec. 1889; d. Sherman,
Conn., 20 Apr. 1969. Studied at Cincinnati Coll.
of Music; with Cesar Thomson, Royal Cons. in
Brussels; with Joseph Jongen in London. He
taught at Cincinnati Coll. of Music; was violinist in the Cincinnati Symphony, 1909-12; Belgian
and Holbrook quartets, London, 1914-17; New York
Symphony, 1919-28; was staff member, NBC, from
1929, supervisor of music research for NBC from
1950. He wrote Xantha, a comic opera, 1917; and
songs. He was author of books and articles on
music criticism.

LARGENT, EDWARD J., JR.
b. Waukegan, Ill., 8 Feb. 1936. Studied with
Marshall Barnes and Mark Walker, Ohio State
Univ.; with Salvatore Martirano and Thomas
Frederickson, Univ. of Illinois. He received

second prize, Phi Mu Alpha contest, Ohio State
Univ., 1963, 1966. He was faculty member,
Western Kentucky Univ., 1966-70; from 1970, at
Youngstown State Univ.
WORKS: BAND: Symphony for brass, 1966;
CHAMBER MUSIC: trio, violin, horn, piano, 1967;
sextet for winds, 1969; Song for soprano, flute,
piano, 1969; horn sonata, 1970; CHORUS: Cantata
for Easter, 1966; ELECTRONIC: Experimental
tapes--#2, Sirens, 1973.
161 Melbourne Ave., Youngstown, OH 44505

LARKIN, JOHN
b. Cincinnati, Ohio, 24 Mar. 1927. Studied with
Felix Labunski, Cincinnati Coll. of Music, B.M.,
M.M.; with Paul Cooper, Univ. of Cincinnati,
D.M.; with Ben Weber in New York. He received
the Martin Dumler award, Cincinnati Composers,
1952; Huntington Hartford fellowships, 1954,
1956, 1958; Yaddo fellowship, 1957. He was
faculty member, Immaculate Heart Coll., Los
Angeles, 1959-64; Univ. of Cincinnait, 1965-71;
from 1971, at Newark, N.J., Boys Choir School.
WORKS: ORCHESTRA: symphonic movement;
CHORUS: Mass in praise of the Trinity, 1960;
The Beatitudes, 1962; The witnesses, cantata
with soloists and orch.; PIANO: sonata, 1971.

LARSEN, LIBBY
b. Wilmington, Del., 24 Dec. 1950. Studied with
Paul Fetler, Dominick Argento, Eric Stokes,
Univ. of Minnesota, B.A. 1971, M.A. 1974. She
won first place, Minnesota Fed. of Music Clubs
contest, 1974; Delta Omicron competition, 1976;
and has received commissions. She was teaching
associate, Univ. of Minneapolis, 1972-77; from
1973, managing composer for Minnesota Composers
Forum.
WORKS: THEATRE: Psyche and the pskyscraper,
short opera; Some pig, opera, 1973; The words
upon the windowpane, opera; The silver fox,
opera; The art of love, tenor, soprano, harp,
oboe, percussion, dancers; ORCHESTRA: Tom Twist,
musical narrative; Weaver's song and jig; CHAMBER
MUSIC: Argyle sketches, guitar; Istar fantasia,
guitar; Theme and deviations, harp; clarinet
quartet; 5 affections, flute, harp, viola;
Triage, harp; CHORUS: Lacrimosa Christe, with
soloists and orch.; Soft pieces, 4 quartets; 3
river songs, 3-part treble; SONGS: Saints without tears, soprano, flute, bassoon; Rilke songs,
soprano, harp, flute, guitar; Eurydice, soprano,
string quintet; Fern Hill, solo tenor; I am you
anxious one, tenor and guitar.
5037 Indianola, Edina, MN 55424

LARSEN, WILLIAM
b. Sioux Falls, S.Dak., 28 Mar. 1951. Studied
with Sister Jane Klimisch, Mt. Marty Coll.,
B.A.; with Milan Kaderavek, Drake Univ. He has
been high school band and chorus director,
Oldham, S.Dak., from 1973.
WORKS: CHAMBER MUSIC: Thus fourth, 12-
tone piece for 5 instruments; Torna-Do, for 12
instruments; 2 movements for piano; Sheer
levity, with percussion and strings; Had I seen
the sun, women's voices, piano, 2 flutes, electric bass.

LASKER, HENRY
b. Hyde Park, Mass., 25 Oct. 1909; d. Newton
Centre, Mass., 30 July 1976. Studied at Boston
Univ., A.B.; with Walter Piston, Harvard Univ.,
A.M. In 1974 he was elected to the Collegium of
Distinguished Alumni at Boston Univ. He was
music instructor at Newton High School for 33
years; also taught at Bridgewater Teachers Coll.,
and lectured at Harvard Grad. School, Northeastern Univ., and at Tanglewood.
WORKS: OPERA: Jack and the bean stalk,
commissioned by Brookline Youth Concerts; Beauty
and the beast; The oath of Hippocrates, baritone
solo, chorus, orch., commissioned by the City of
Newton, 1973, was performed at "Henry Lasker
night" at Boston Pops, 14 May 1976.

LASZLO, ALEXANDER
b. Budapest, Hungary, 22 Nov. 1895; U.S. citizen
1944; d. Calif., 17 Nov. 1970. Invented the
Colorlight machine to coordinate music and
color; was music professor, Inst. of Design,
Chicago, 1938; then was film orchestrator in
Hollywood, 1944-48; music director for NBC Radio.
WORKS: THEATRE: Wanted: Sexperts and ser-
pents for our garden of maidens, a musical, 1968;
ORCHESTRA: Mechanized forces; Structural music;
Hollywood concerto, piano and orch.; The ghost
train of Marshall Pass, piano and orch.; 4D-122,
piano and orch.; Mana Hawaii, piano and orch.;
Pacific triptych, 1962; This world--tomorrow,
chorus and orch.; Roulette hematologique, sym-
phonic fantasy, 1969; PIANO: News of the day;
Hungarian dance suite; Fantasy of colors.

LATEEF, YUSEF
b. Chattanooga, Tenn., 9 Oct. 1920. Studied at
Wayne State Univ.; with Charles Mills and George
Dufalo, Teal School of Music; Manhattan School
of Music, B.A., M.A. He has received 2 Playboy
magazine awards; Music Achievement award for
outstanding contribution to African-American
music; and was the first American to win the
Downbeat award for oboe. He plays flute, oboe,
argol (an Indian reed flute), shanai, tenor and
alto saxophone, bassoon, and rabat. He has
toured the U.S. with several bands; at Wayne
State Univ., organized the Yusef Lateef Quintet;
is faculty member, Manhattan Community Coll.
WORKS: Lateef calls his music "autophysio-
psychic," and in this idiom, has written and
recorded many compositions for various combinations of instruments; some examples are: A flat,
G flat and C; Eastern sounds; Other sounds;
Fabric of jazz; Cry--tender; Into something;
1984; Golden flute; Jazz round the world;
Psychicemotus; Down in Atlanta; In the evening;
Constructs, New York, 6 Feb. 1973.
201 Cross St., #15J, Fort Lee, NJ 07042

LATHAM, WILLIAM PETERS
b. Shreveport, La., 4 Jan. 1917. Studied at
Univ. of Cincinnati, B.S. 1938; with Eugene
Goosens, Cincinnati Cons., B.M. 1940, M.M. 1941;
with Herbert Elwell and Howard Hanson, Eastman
School of Music, Ph.D. 1951. His awards include
first prize, Phi Mu Alpha contest; citation,
Texas Fed. of Music Clubs, 1967; and many com-

LATHROP, GAYLE POSSELT

missions. He was professor, Univ. of Northern
Iowa, 1946-65; from 1965, professor, North Texas
State Univ., and in 1978, was named distinguished
professor of music, the university's highest
academic rank.
WORKS: ORCHESTRA: The lady of Shalott,
Cincinnati, 7 Mar. 1941; Fantasy concerto, flute
and strings, 1941; Fantasy, violin and orch.,
1946; And thou America, 1948; 2 symphonies,
1950, 1953, #2, Fish Creek, Wis., 20 Aug. 1955;
American youth performs, 1969; A Lenten letter,
soprano and string orch., percussion, Denton,
Tex., 9 Oct. 1974; BAND: Brighton Beach, 1954;
Proud heritage, 1955; Court festival, 1957;
suite for trumpet and band, 1960; Escapades,
1965; Dodecaphonic set, 1966; saxophone concertino, 1968; Fantasy, trumpet and band, 1969;
Prayers in space, 1971; Prolegomena, 1974;
Revolution!, 1975; Fusion, 1975; CHAMBER MUSIC:
flute sonatina, 1937; 5 sketches, string quartet,
1938; 3 string trios, 1938-39; 3 string quartets,
1938-40, #3, Cincinnati, 14 Nov. 1940; oboe
sonata, 1947; violin sonata, 1949; 5 atonal
studies, clarinet, 1966; Sisyphus, saxophone and
piano, 1971; S.B.F., solo bass flute, 1973;
Preludes before silence, 9 pieces for solo flute
and piccolo, 1974; Eidolons, euphonium and piano,
1977; Ex tempore, solo alto saxophone, 1978;
CHORUS: Peace, with orch., 1943; Prayer after
world war, 1945; Prophecy of peace, with orch.,
1952; The shrine, 1953; Psalms 130 and 148, with
band, 1954; Music for 7 poems, with soli and
orch., 1958; Blind with rainbows, with soli and
orch., 1962; Songs of a day Rome was not built
in, male choir, a cappella, 1966; The music
makers, with band, rock group, and guru, 1972;
Music for the Eucharist, 1977; Epigrammata, a
cappella, 1978; many songs, piano pieces.
    1815 Southridge Dr., Denton, TX 76201

LATHROP, GAYLE POSSELT
    b. Chicago, Ill., 7 Feb. 1942. Studied with
Thomas Beversdorf and Bernhard Heiden, Indiana
Univ.; with Leon Wagner, Humboldt State Univ.;
with John Gibson and Robert Muczynski, 1976-78.
She was public school music director, Hoopa,
Calif., 1968-70; faculty member, Humboldt State
Univ., 1972; Coll. of the Redwoods, 1973-76;
from 1978, Susquehanna Univ.
    WORKS: BAND: Tish tang; The party; State
of the Union, 1968; CHAMBER MUSIC: Triskelion,
chamber orch.; Piece 4-5, quintet; flute sonatina; Joamerdap, flute trio; Preludes, guitar;
Anaphora #1, 1977, #2, 1978, both solo guitar;
Meditation #1, 1977, #2, 1978, guitar and viola;
Duologue, flute and tape, 1977; Fables, children's ballet, quintet, 1978; Cues, prepared
flutes and percussion, 1978; CHORUS: O clap
your hands, children's choir, 1975; Towhit,
women's speech chorus, 1978; Tenebrae service,
Tucson, 13 Apr. 1979.
    903 N. Ninth St., Selinsgrove, PA 17870

LATIMER, JAMES H.
    b. Tulsa, Okla., 27 June 1934. Studied percus-
sion at Indiana Univ., B.M. 1956; Boston Univ.,
M.M. 1964; at Tanglewood, 1963. His awards include a John Hay Whitney fellowship, 1962;

Harvard Univ. scholarship, summer, 1968; Univ.
of Wisconsin graduate research award, summer
1973. He was faculty member, Florida A&M Univ.,
1957-62; from 1969, at Univ. of Wisconsin; also
director of Wisconsin Youth Symphony Orchestra
from 1972, and of its Percussion Ensemble, from
1969.
    WORKS: ORCHESTRA: MEH, 1959; BAND: move-
ment, 1957; March of deceit, 1959; PERCUSSION:
Variations on the Westminster Clock theme, 4
solo timpani, 1955; Exercise for percussion orch.,
1956; FAMU march cadences 11 and 12, 1957;
Reminiscing, 1957; Blood on the moon, 1958;
Unsleeping city, 1962; Assignment prison, 1964;
Coquette, 1967; Woman in red, 1968; Motif for
percussion, 1969; also works for chorus and
solo voice with percussion.
    3922 Hillcrest Dr., Madison, WI 53705

LATIOLAIS, JAYNE
    b. Natchitoches, La., 20 Oct. 1928. Studied
with Helen Gunderson, Louisiana State Univ.;
Ross Lee Finney, Univ. of Michigan; at Eastman
School of Music; and with Marshall Barnes, Ohio
State Univ. Her clarinet sonata won the Nat.
Fed. of Music Clubs contest, 1977. She was
guest lecturer, Ohio State Univ., 1970-71; on
faculty, Denison Univ., 1973-76.
    WORKS: ORCHESTRA: Passacaglia; CHAMBER
MUSIC: piano suite; clarinet sonata; Movement,
for cello and violin; Introduction, passacaglia
and fugue, 2 pianos; Lithuanian suite, violin
and piano; 3 movements, flute, clarinet, bassoon,
piano; 5 paragraphs, piano; piano quartet;
CHORUS: Sanctus, a cappella; Trilogy, a cappella;
SONGS: Salomé, contralto, flute, percussion;
Songs from the Chinese; Night song.
    3100 Raccoon Valley Rd., Granville, OH
43023

LAUDENSLAGER, HAROLD REID
    b. New Haven, Mich., 19 Apr. 1920; d. Birmingham,
Mich., 10 Dec. 1971. Graduated from Olivet
Coll. in 1941; after military service in World
War II, studied with Paul Hindemith and Quincy
Porter at Yale Univ., B.M. 1949, M.M. 1950;
later with Arthur Honegger in Paris; then
musicology at Univ. of Michigan. He was violinist with the Detroit Symph. Orch., 1951-71;
faculty member, Wayne State Univ., 1969-71.
    WORKS: ORCHESTRA: Little suite, 3 wood-
winds, piano, strings, 1958; Elegy, English
horn, timpani, strings, 1959; The strait
(Detroit), concert overture, 1963; timpani concerto, 1964; contrabassoon concerto, 1965;
Scholastica suite, string orch., 1968; cello
concerto, 1968-69; Abstractions, 1969; symphony
(unfinished), 1969; CHAMBER MUSIC: piano trio;
4 string quartets, 1949, 1952, 1954, 1961;
Fantasy, solo violin, 1958; 2 violin sonatas,
1958, 1966; sonata for 2 violins, 1959; 2 sets
o 6 contemporary concert etudes, solo violin,
1962; string trio, 1962; woodwind quintet, 1962;
3 preludes and fugues, trombone quartet; sonata
for solo cello, 1966; also choral works, songs,
piano pieces.

LAUFER, BEATRICE
b. New York, N.Y., 27 Apr. 1923. Studied with Roger Sessions, Marion Bauer, Vittorio Giannini, Juilliard School, 1944. Her first symphony was performed in Germany and Japan in 1948 under the auspices of the State Dept. She received a commission from the American Assoc. of the United Nations for Song of the fountain to dedicate the UN Freedom Fountain, which was performed by an interracial chorus of 250 voices, 1952; commissions from Performing Arts Concerts, 1961; and from State of Connecticut, 1974, for a choral work for the 1976 Bicentennial year.
WORKS: OPERA: Ile, 1 act, on O'Neill's The long voyage home, premiered by the Royal Opera Company, Sweden, 1958, and recorded by Nat. Public Radio in 1978; ORCHESTRA: 2 symphonies, 1947, 1961; Dance festival, 1946; Frolic: concerto for flute, oboe, trumpet, and strings, 1962; Prelude and fugue, 1964; Cry, 1966, Shreveport Symph., 8 Feb. 1977; In the throes, Shreveport, La., 14 June 1980; CHORUS: Under the pines; Spring thunder, 1949; Song of the fountain, 1952; He who knows not; Everyone sang; Do you fear the wind; And Thomas Jefferson said . . ., 2 choruses, narrator, orch., 1976; SONGS: Soldier's prayer.
P.O. Box 3, Lenox Hill Station, New York, NY 10017

LAURIDSEN, MORTEN JOHANNES
b. Colfax, Wash., 27 Feb. 1943. Studied with Halsey Stevens, Ingolf Dahl, Robert Linn, and Harold Owen, Univ. of Southern California, where he held the Stark fellowship and an Alchin fellowship, and has been faculty member from 1967.
WORKS: ORCHESTRA: Variations for orch.; CHAMBER MUSIC: trumpet sonata; brass sextet; Variations, piano; CHORUS: Praise ye the Lord; Te Deum, with orch.; SONGS: A winter come, a cycle; 3 songs from Backyard Universe; other choral and chamber works.
Music Dept., Univ. of Southern California, Los Angeles, CA 90007

LAUTH, JAMES
b. Kalamazoo, Mich., 2 Jan. 1952. Studied with Chou Wen-chung and Jack Beeson, Columbia Univ.; privately with Harvey Sollberger; with William Albright, Univ. of Michigan. His awards include the Bearns, 1977, and a Nat. Endowment for the Arts grant, 1977. He was adjunct faculty member, Lehman Coll., 1976-78; then at New York Univ.
WORKS: ORCHESTRA: Winter music, 1976; CHAMBER MUSIC: All but one, percussion ensemble, 1977; duet for viola and clarinet, 1977; Canzone, flute, clarinet, oboe, 1978; VOICE: Song of the leaves, mezzo-soprano and chamber orch., 1975; Time pieces, soprano and clarinet, 1978; ELECTRONIC: Like a diamond, tape, 1976; Prelude, computer-generated tape, 1978; Piecework, tape, 1978.
484 W. 43rd St., #16A, New York, NY 10036

LA VIOLETTE, WESLEY
b. St. James, Minn., 4 Jan. 1894; d. Escondido, Calif., 29 July 1978. Attended Northwestern

Univ. and Chicago Musical Coll., D.M. 1925. His awards include the David Bispham Medal, 1930; the Wisdom Award of Honor and election to the Widsom Hall of Fame, Los Angeles, 1970; many commissions; 2 works taken on tour by the NBC Chamber Orch. under Rudolph Ganz, 1931-33; other works played by major orchestras. He was faculty member, Chicago Musical Coll., 1923-33; at De Paul Univ., School of Music, 1933-40; then settled in Los Angeles for private teaching, writing, lecturing, and composing.
WORKS: THEATRE: Shylock, 1-act opera, 1927; Schubertiana, ballet, 1935; The enlightened one, 3-act opera on the life of Buddha, 1955; ORCHESTRA: Requiem, 1925; Penetrella, string orch. in 18 parts, 1928; Osiris, Egyptian legend, 1929; 2 violin concertos, 1929, 1939; Festival ode, 1930; Ode to an immortal, 1934; 3 symphonies, 1936, 1940, 1942; Chorale, 1936; Collegiana rhapsody, 1936; Prelude and aria, 1937; Concert piece, piano and orch., 1937; concerto for string quartet and orch., 1939; San Francisco overture, 1939; Commemoration ode, 1939; The song of the angels, choral symphony, 1952; CHAMBER MUSIC: 3 string quartets, 1926, 1932, 1936; piano quintet, 1927; Scherzo, chamber orch., 1931; sonata for 2 violins, 1931, rev. 1951; 5 songs for soprano and string quartet, 1931; Nocturne, chamber orch., 1933; 2 violin sonatas, 1934, 1937; octet, woodwinds and strings, 1935; Evocation, violin and piano, 1936; 3 pieces for string quartet, 1937; woodwind sextet, 1939; Filigree quartet, 4 flutes, 1940; Masquerade, woodwind quartet, 1940; Rhapsody, cello, 1940; flute sonata, 1941; Dedication, clarinet and piano, 1941; Incantation, clarinet and piano, 1941; Song of freedom, cello and piano, 1941; Charade, flute quartet, 1941; Queen of night, trumpet and piano, 1941; quintet, flute and string, 1943; Largo lyrico, string quartet, 1943; Serenade, flute and string quartet, 1945; suite for chamber orch., 1947; suite for flute alone, 1963; suite for clarinet alone, 1963; CHORUS: The broken vine, 1921; Anima mundi, with orch., 1932; The garden, 1950; The road to Calvary, with narrator and orch., 1952; Delphic psalm, with brass ensemble, 1964; also pieces for band, piano, organ. His published books are: Music and its makers, 1937; The Bhagavad Gita, 1944, rev. 1955; The creative light, 1946; The crown of wisdom, 1949, nominated for the Nobel prize in literature, 1960.

LAWERGREN, BO
b. Sweden, 4 Jan. 1937; to U.S. 1967. Earned a Ph.D. in nuclear physics at the Australian Nat. Univ., 1963; studied composition with Friedrich Mehler in Sweden, 1951-55; with Chou Wen-chung, Columbia Univ., 1967-68. His awards include 2 fellowships to the Bennington Conf.; 3 MacDowell fellowships; Nat. Endowment for the Arts grant, 1976. From 1970, he has been professor of physics, Hunter Coll.
WORKS: THEATRE: Captain Cook, chamber opera, 1968-69; Deep tongue, chamber opera, 1973-74; CHAMBER MUSIC: Marche funèbre, trombone, piano, and metronomes; Two step, trumpet, marimba/vibraphones; Ensembles, 13 instruments,

LAWNER, MORRIS

7 one-minute pieces for pianos.
404 W. 116th St., New York, NY 10027

LAWNER, MORRIS
b. New York, N.Y., 8 Apr. 1910. Studied at
Inst. of Musical Art, New York Univ., and at
Univ. of Wisconsin. His Rhythmic overture won
an award for performance by the New York Philharmonic, 1949. He taught in New York City high
schools, 1940-50; from 1950, at High School of
Music and Art.
WORKS: ORCHESTRA: Rhythmic overture, 1949;
CHAMBER MUSIC: Latin dance, clarinet and piano;
Cocktail hour, piano; suite for woodwinds; also
2 works for band.
820 West End Ave., New York, NY 10025

LAYTON, BILLY JIM
b. Corsicana, Tex., 14 Nov. 1924. Studied with
Carl McKinley, Francis Judd Cooke, New England
Cons.; with Quincy Porter, Yale Univ.; and with
Walter Piston, Harvard Univ., Ph.D. 1960. His
awards include the Rome prize; Hertz Traveling
fellowship; Nat. Inst. of Arts and Letters
grant; Brandeis Univ. Creative Arts award;
Guggenheim fellowship; Thorne Music Fund grant.
He was faculty member, New England Cons., 1959-
60; Harvard Univ., 1960-66; from 1966, professor,
State Univ. of New York at Stony Brook.
WORKS: ORCHESTRA: An American portrait,
symphonic overture, 1957; Dance fantasy, 1964;
CHAMBER MUSIC: 5 studies for violin and piano;
string quartet, 1956; 3 studies for piano;
Divertimento, chamber orch.; CHORUS: 3 Dylan
Thomas poems, with brass sextet, 1955.
4 Johns Rd., Setauket, NY 11733

LAYZER, ARTHUR
b. Cleveland, Ohio, 21 Sept. 1927. Self-taught
in music, he has been professor of physics,
Stevens Inst. of Technology, from 1963; and
resident visitor in computer music, Bell
Laboratories, Murray Hill, N.J., from 1969.
WORKS: CHAMBER MUSIC: woodwind quintet,
1966; Inner and outer forms for 7 players,
brass, saxophones, percussion, 1967; COMPUTER-
SYNTHESIZED MUSIC: Piece for 6 voices, 1970;
Morning elevator, animated poetry for computer-
generated film and music sound track, 1971.
161 W. 75th St., New York, NY 10023

LAZAROF, HENRI
b. Sofia, Bulgaria, 12 Apr. 1932; to U.S. 1957.
Studied at Sofia Acad. of Music; with Paul Ben-
Haim in Jerusalem; with Goffredo Petrassi, Ste.
Cecilia Acad., Rome, 1955-57; and with Harold
Shapero, Brandeis Univ., M.F.A. 1959. His
awards include a Brandeis fellowship; first
prize, Internat. Competition of Monaco, 1962;
La Scala award, City of Milan, 1966; Koussevitzky
Internat. Recording award, 1969; Nat. Endowment
for the Arts grant, 1973. He has been on the
faculty at Univ. of California, Los Angeles,
from 1965.
WORKS: ORCHESTRA: piano concerto, 1957;
Piccola serenata, 1959; viola concerto, 1961;
concerto for piano and 20 instruments, 1963;
Odes, 1963; Tempi concertati, violin, viola,

and chamber orch., 1964; Structures sonores,
1965; cello concerto, 1968, American premiere,
Los Angeles, 6 May 1971; Ommagio, chamber concerto, 1968; Textures, piano and orch., 1970;
Ricerar, viola, piano, orch.; Variations for
orch.; flute concerto, 1973; Spectrum, trumpet,
orch., tape, 1973; 3rd chamber concerto, 12
soloists, 1974; Viol (Canti da requiem), solo
viola and 2 string ensembles, 1977; CHAMBER
MUSIC: 2 string quartets, 1956, 1963; string
trio, 1957; sonata for violin alone, 1958; Concertino da camera, woodwind quintet, 1959; Inventions, viola and piano, 1962; Asymptotes,
flute and vibraphone, 1963; Quantetti, 4 pianos,
1964; Rhapsody, violin and piano, 1966; Espaces,
10 instruments, 1966; Divertimenti for 5 players,
1969; Continuum, string trio, Los Angeles, 10
Nov. 1970; Cadence I-VI, solos or duos for varying instruments, some with tape, 1970-73; duo
for cello and piano, 1973; Concertazioni, trumpet, 6 instruments and tape, 1973; Adieu, clarinet and piano, 1974.
718 N. Maple Dr., Beverly Hills, CA 90210

LEACH, ROWLAND
b. Haverhill, Mass., 26 Apr. 1885. Studied
violin and composition, New England Cons.; at
Yale Univ., B.M. 1910. He taught in Rockford,
Ill., 1910-13; Calgary, Alberta, 1913-14;
Chicago, 1914-28; De Pauw Univ., 1928-33; Univ.
of Redlands, 1933-47. He wrote orchestral
works, violin pieces, songs (Welcome, day of the
Lord).

LEAHY, MARY WELDON
b. St. Louis, Mo., 20 Aug. 1926. Studied at
North Texas State Univ.; privately with Carl
Eppert and Normand Lockwood; with Gordon Jacob
in England. She won first prize in a Wisconsin
state contest for a song and a string quartet.
WORKS: ORCHESTRA: suite for strings; Modern
dance rhapsody, string orch.; symphony in 1 movement, strings and percussion; many works for
chamber ensemble, chorus, and solo voice.
703 Alexander Hamilton Dr., San Antonio, TX
78228

LEAPHART, TIMOTHY M.
b. Buffalo, N.Y., 27 May 1950. Studied composition and electronic circuit design with Ralph
Jones in Buffalo; with William Kothe, State
Univ. of New York, Buffalo, B.F.A. He was percussionist with the Center of the Creative and
Performing Arts, 1975-77, and with the SEM Ensemble, 1978.
WORKS: Nocturne, percussion and live electronics, 1976; Tangent, solo percussion, 1976.
2B S. Creek Court, E. Amherst, NY 14051

LE BARON, ANNE
b. Baton Rouge, La., 30 May 1953. Studied with
Charles Bestor, Frederic Goossen, Paul Hedwall,
Univ. of Alabama; with Bülent Arel and Daria
Semegan, State Univ. of New York at Stony Brook.
Her awards include 3 first prizes: Mu Phi
Epsilon contest, 1974; Southeastern Composers'
League contest, 1974; Columbia Univ. Bearns con-
test, 1978; scholarships, Univ. of Alabama, 1970-

74; several summer fellowships, 1976–78. She was instructor at SUNY, Stony Brook, 1976–77; and at Univ. of Alabama, 1977–78.

WORKS: ORCHESTRA: 3 movements for strings and percussion, 1973; CHAMBER MUSIC: Music for peyote cactus, chamber group, 1973; 3 motion atmospheres, brass quintet, 1974; Extensions, 3 movements for large percussion ensemble, 1975; Memnon, 6 harps, 1976; Metamorphosis, conductor and 7 players, 1977; VOICE: In the desert, soprano, flute, marimba, temple blocks, 1973; Light breaks where no sun shines, chorus and percussion, Dylan Thomas text, 1977; ELECTRONIC: Concerto for active frogs, tape, 1974; Quadratura circuli, tape, 1978.
906 Victory Dr., Minden, LA 71055

LEBOW, LEONARD STANLEY
b. Chicago, Ill., 25 Feb. 1929. Studied with Karel Jirak, Chicago Musical Coll.; at Northwestern Univ., M.M.; also studied trumpet, piano, and arranging. He has received ASCAP awards, 1973–78. He was trumpet player in Las Vegas, 1952–54; in Chicago, 1954–64; from 1964, in Los Angeles; taught in Chicago public schools, 1954–64.

WORKS: BAND: Pastorale and tarantella; Festival parade; Ride the Matterhorn; WIND ENSEMBLE: Suite for brass, 1956; Popular suite, brass quintet; 2nd suite, brass quintet; Allegro energico, brass quintet; Descriptive scenes, saxophone quartet.
4411 Stern Ave., Sherman Oaks, CA 91403

LEE, CYNTHIA COZETTE
b. Pittsburgh, Pa., 19 Oct. 1953. Studied with William Hoskins, Jacksonville Univ., 1971; with Roland Leich and Leonardo Balada, Carnegie-Mellon Univ., 1973–74; with George Rochberg and George Crumb, Univ. of Pennsylvania, 1975–76. Her awards include honorable mention, Pittsburgh Flute Club composition contest, 1969; Saudek scholarship for flute study, 1970; Jacksonville Univ. choral grant, 1972. She was music consultant and assistant producer for a radio series on black American classical musicians and composers at WUHY, Philadelphia, 1976–77; from 1976, member, Van Pelt House Flute Qaurtet; from 1978, public school music teacher.

WORKS: THEATRE: Lamentations of a ghetto child, woodwind quartet, piano, dancers; ORCHESTRA: piano concerto; The 3 tributes: The martyr, To Carlotta, And the cry, baritone and orch.; Ebony reflections, chamber orch., 1977; CHORUS: Colors, women's voices and percussion, 1975.
4039 Chestnut St., Philadelphia, PA 19104

LEE, DAI-KEONG
b. Honolulu, Hawaii, 2 Sept. 1915. Studied at Univ. of Hawaii; with Roger Sessions, Princeton Univ.; with Frederick Jacobi, Juilliard School, 1938–41; with Aaron Copland at Tanglewood, 1941; at Columbia Univ., M.A. 1951. He held fellowships for Juilliard School and Tanglewood; Guggenheim fellowships, 1945, 1951; has received many commissions.

WORKS: OPERA: Poet's dilemma, 1 act, 1940;

Open the gates, 1951; Phineas and the nightingale, 1952; BALLET: Children's caprice, 1948; Waltzing Matilda, 1951; THEATRE: Teahouse of the August moon, background score; ORCHESTRA: Valse pensieroso, 1936; Hawaiian festival overture, 1940; Introduction and allegro, 1941; Golden Gate overture, 1941; Pacific prayer, 1943; Overture in C, 1945; 2 symphonies, 1946, 1952; violin concerto, 1947; concerto grosso, string orch., 1952; 2 Knickerbocker tales, 1957; suite for orch., 1958; Polynesian suite, 1959; The golden lotus, 1961; The gold of their bodies, 1963; CHAMBER MUSIC: string quartet, 1947; piano sonatina, 1947; Introduction and allegro, cello and piano, 1947; Incantation and dance, violin and piano; CHORUS: Mele ololi, with soli and orch., 1960; Canticle of the Pacific, with orch., 1968; FILM SCORE: Letter from Australia, 1945.
245 W. 104th St., New York, NY 10025

LEE, EU-GENE
b. Seoul, Korea, 20 Aug. 1942; to U.S. 1967. Studied with Ruth S. Wylie, Wayne State Univ., B.M. 1969; with Chou Wen-chung, Charles Wuorinen, Harvey Sollberger, Vladimir Ussachevsky, and Jacques-Louis Monod, Columbia Univ., M.A. 1973. He held scholarships at Wayne State Univ., 1966–69; Crofts fellowship at Tanglewood, 1972; won Rapoport prize, Columbia Univ., 1973. He was teaching fellow, Columbia Univ., 1972–75.

WORKS: CHAMBER MUSIC: 2 movements for solo violin, 1970, New York, 7 Dec. 1978; duet for violin and clarinet, 1970; duet for viola and vibraphone, 1970; Empty infinity, string quartet, 1970; woodwind quintet, 1971; Moo-sahng (Transience), for the victims of My-Lai, 1971; Yuh-Woon, wind septet and percussion, 1972; chamber symphony for 18 players, 1973; Lyric, solo flute, 1973; VOICE: Afterimages, choral cycle on 6 Zen poems, a cappella, 1977.
c/o Mobart Music Publishers, Hillsdale, NY 12529

LEE, JOHN
b. England, 29 Apr. 1908; U.S. citizen 1955. He is licentiate, Royal Acad. of Music and Trinity Coll. of Music, London; a fellow of the Royal Coll. of Organists, London; and member, Royal Society of Teachers. He has been organist, St. Vincent's Church, Los Angeles, from 1949; is also lecturer, organ recitalist and teacher. His published compositions include over 80 choral works (masses, anthems, liturgical settings) and organ works.
22 Chester Place, Los Angeles, CA 90007

LEE, NOEL
b. Nanking, China, 25 Dec. 1924, of American parents. Studied with Walter Piston and Irving Fine, Harvard Univ., B.A. cum laude 1948; with Miklos Schwalb, New England Cons., diploma, 1948; with Melville Smith and Boris Goldovsky, Longy School of Music; with Nadia Boulanger in Paris and Boris Blacher in London. His awards include Prix Lili Boulanger, 1953; award in Young Composers' contest, Louisville, Ky., 1954; Nat. Inst. of Arts and Letters award, 1959; Shepherd

LEE, NORMAN

composition prize, 1961. He was visiting professor in piano, Cornell Univ., 1967 and 1972.
    WORKS: ORCHESTRA: Fievres, ballet, 1950;
Capriccio, 1952; 4 rhapsodies, with chorus,
1952; Paraboles, with tenor solo and chorus,
1954; Overture and litanies, string orch., 1954;
Profile, 1958; Variations, 1960; 4 ballades,
soprano and orch.; Dichroismes, with piano and
violin solos; Diversions, chamber orch.; Caprices
on the name of Schönberg, piano and orch.; BAND:
Errances; CHAMBER MUSIC: Sonata mostly in minor,
solo violin; 3 preludes, 2 harps; Variations,
flute, violin, cello, harpsichord, 1953; string
trio, 1953; string quartet, 1956; Dialogues,
violin and piano, 1958; Convergences, flute and
harpsichord; SONG CYCLES: 5 songs on poems of
Lorca, 1955; Sonnets of summer and sorrow; 4
songs on Baudelaire; Songs of Calamus, with
chamber ensemble; and many piano works.
    4 Villa Laugier, 75017 Paris, France

LEE, NORMAN
    b. Chicago, Ill., 18 Nov. 1895. Studied with
Arne Oldberg and Carl Beecher, Northwestern Univ.
    WORKS: SONGS: The river; Nocturne; PIANO:
Fantasia; Temple song; 2 sonatas; Variations;
The Eunice caprice.
    360 Forest Ave., Palo Alto, CA 94301

LEE, T. CHARLES
    b. Madison, Minn., 22 Oct. 1914. Studied at
Oberlin Coll.; with Clarence Dickinson, Union
Theological Seminary; with Nadia Boulanger in
Fontainebleau; and with C. K. Scott in London.
He was conductor of the Worcester Music Festival,
1949-61; Oratorio Society of New York, 1959-73;
organist, Brick Presbyterian Church, New York,
from 1959; on faculty, Lehman Coll., CUNY, 1968-
78.
    WORKS: CHORUS: Psalm III; Farewell,
voyager, with soli, organ, and piano; A requiem,
commissioned by Kings Coll., 1968.
    115 E. 92nd St., New York, NY 10028

LEE, WILLIAM F., III
    b. Galveston, Tex., 20 Feb. 1929. Studied at
North Texas State Univ., B.M. 1949, M.S. 1950;
Univ. of Texas, M.M. 1956, Ph.D. 1956; Eastman
School of Music, 1962; and with Nadia Boulanger
in Paris, 1965. His awards include Univ. of
Miami grant in humanities, 1965; honorary doctorate, Cons. Nac. de Musica, Lima, Peru, 1968;
Rockefeller Fund grant, 1975; nomination for the
Pulitzer prize for 8 vignettes for a festive
occasion, 1976; annual ASCAP awards, 1968-77;
many commissions. He was assistant dean, Univ.
of Texas, 1955-56; music dept. head, Sam Houston
State Univ., 1956-64; from 1964, professor and
dean, School of Music, Univ. of Miami.
    WORKS: ORCHESTRA: concerto grosso, brass
quintet and orch.; Earth genesis, string orch.;
8 vignettes for a festive occasion, with chorus
and synthesizer; BAND: Alamjohoba; Introduction
and fugue; Time after time; WIND ENSEMBLE: Suite
for brass; 4 sketches for brass; Fanfare for
Ralph, brass quintet; Piece for brass, quintet;
Mosaics, brass quintet; Regimentation, quintet;
CHAMBER MUSIC: Nocturne flute and piano; Solil-

oquy, horn and piano; Mini-suite, trumpet and
piano; 3 reflections, alto saxophone and piano;
Interlude, guitar; Tone poem, oboe, violin,
viola, 2 celli; 2 woodwind quintets; Scherzo,
viola and piano; and piano pieces.
    P.O. Box 248165, Coral Gables, FL 33124

LEEDY, DOUGLAS H.
    b. Portland, Oreg., 3 Mar. 1938. Studied with
Karl Kohn, Pomona Coll., B.A. 1959; with Lukas
Foss at Tanglewood; with Andrew Imbrie, Seymour
Shifrin, William Denny, Univ. of California,
Berkeley, M.A. 1962. He received a Fromm Found.
commission, 1966, and other commissions. He
was head of electronic music, Univ. of California,
Los Angeles, 1967-70; on electronic music fac-
ulty, Estudio de Fonologia, del Centro Simon
Bolivar, Caracas, Venz., 1972; visiting faculty,
Reed Coll., 1973-74.
    WORKS: THEATRE: Decay, theatre piece with
tape, 1965; Teddybears picnic, dancers and tape;
WIND ENSEMBLE: Antifonia, brass, 1965; Usable
music I for instruments with very small holes,
1966; Usable music II in B flat, 1966; CHAMBER
MUSIC: Quaderno Rossiniano, chamber ensemble;
88 is great, piano, 18 hands, 1968; Igor
Stravinsky in memoriam, guitar, 1971; CHORUS:
Dulces exuviae , Virgil text; Gloria, with
soprano solo, strings, flute, harpsichord, 1970;
Psalm 24, with 6 soprano soli, orch.; I am the
rose of Sharon, small chorus and instruments;
ELECTRONICS: The electric zodiac, 1969; Entrop-
ical paradise: 6 sonic environments, 1970.
    1415 S.E. Henry, Portland, OR 97202

LEES, BENJAMIN
    b. Harbin, China, 8 Jan. 1924; U.S. citizen
1931. Studied with Halsey Stevens, Ingolf Dahl,
Ernest Kanitz, Univ. of Southern California; and
with George Antheil. His honors include a Fromm
Found. award, 1953; 2 Guggenheim fellowships,
1954, 1955; Fulbright grant, 1956; Copley Found.
award; Sir Arnold Bax Medal; UNESCO award; ASCAP
award, 1972. He studied and traveled in Europe
to 1962. Since returning to the U.S., he has
taught at Peabody Cons.; Queens Coll., CUNY; and
Manhattan School of Music.
    WORKS: THEATRE: The oracle, 1-act music
drama, libretto by composer, 1955; The gilded
cage, opera, 1971; ORCHESTRA: 2 piano concertos,
1955, 1966; 3 symphonies, 1953, 1958, 1969;
Divertimento burlesca, 1957; violin concerto,
1958; Concertante breve, 1959; Concerto for
orchestra, 1959; Interlude, 1960; Prologue,
capriccio and epilogue, 1961; Visions of poets,
cantata for 2 soli, chorus, orch., 1961; oboe
concerto, 1963; concerto for string quartet and
orch., 1964; Spectrum, 1964; concerto for chamber
orch., 1966; Silhouettes 1967; Medea of Corinth,
4 solo voices, wind quintet, timpani, 1970; The
trumpet of the swan, narrator and orch., 1972;
Etudes, piano and orch., Houston, Tex., 28 Oct.
1974; Variations, piano and orch., Dallas, 30
Mar. 1976; Passacaglia, Washington, D.C., 13 Apr.
1976; concerto for woodwind quintet and orch.,
Detroit, 7 Oct. 1976; CHAMBER MUSIC: horn
sonata, 1952; 2 string quartets, 1952, 1955; 2
violin sonatas, 1953, 1972; 3 variables, 4 winds

and piano, 1955; Fanfare for a centennial, brass and percussion, 1966; duo for flute and clarinet, 1969; Study #1, cello solo, 1970; untitled work for cello and piano, New York, 3 Mar. 1976; PIANO: 4 piano sonatas, 1949, 1950, 1951, 1963; Fantasia, 1954; sonata breve, 1956; 6 ornamental etudes, 1957; Kaleidoscopes, 1958; Epigrams, 1960; 3 preludes, 1962; Odyssey, 1970; and songs.
28 Cambridge Rd., Great Neck, NY 11023

LEESON, CECIL
b. Cando, N.Dak., 16 Dec. 1902. Studied at Dana Musical Inst., B.M. 1925; with Max Wald and John J. Becker, Chicago Musical Coll., M.M. 1947, D.F.A. 1955. He was named Fellow in the Art of Music, 1933; awarded a scholarship, 1941; honorary membership, Kappa Kappa Psi, 1952; World Saxophone Congress award, 1970; commission by Univ. of Illinois band dept. to compose a saxophone concerto, 1950. Except for service in the navy, 1942-45, he has been teaching and performing on the saxophone since 1924; was faculty member, Ball State Univ., 1961-77; and has dedicated his career to making the saxophone a recognized concert instrument. In addition to his own compositions, he has played works written especially for him by such composers as Weinberger, Creston, Moritz, Sherman, Knight, and Van Vactor. He has also written extensively on the history of the saxophone.
WORKS: SAXOPHONE: 4 concertos, 1947, 1949, 1950, 1957; 3 sonatas, 1953, 1966, 1973; various smaller pieces.
14 Brenda Lane, R.R. 7, Muncie, IN 47302

LEFEVER, MAXINE LANE
b. Elmhurst, Ill., 30 May 1931. Studied at Illinois Wesleyan Univ.; Western State Coll., Colo.; and Purdue Univ. His awards include honorary membership in the U.S. Navy Band. From 1968, he has been executive secretary-treasurer, Nat. Band Assoc., and editor, NBA Journal and NBA Directory.
WORKS: PERCUSSION ENSEMBLE: De Chelly, quintet; Desert; Dolores; Durango; Summit; and others.
Purdue Univ. Bands, West Lafayette, IN 47907

LEFEVERE, KAMIEL
b. Malines, Belgium, 24 Nov. 1888. Studied at Belgian Acad. of Fine Arts; Internat. Carillon School, Belgium. He became assistant carrilloneur at the school; then carrilloneur in England, France, Holland; in Cohasset and Gloucester, Mass., 1924-30; from 1927, in New York City. He was author of two books: Bells over Belgium and Carrillons and singing towers in the U.S. and Canada. He composed many works for carrillon.

LEFTWICH, VERNON
b. London, England, 19 June 1881; d. Van Nuys, Calif., 8 Mar. 1977. Studied at the Guildhall School of Music, London. On coming to the U.S., he settled in Los Angeles as composer and arranger for films.
WORKS: ORCHESTRA: Cremation of care, symphonic poem, 1929; Sunken ships, tone poem, 1939; cello concerto, 1941; What the moon saw, suite;

7 ages of man, baritone and orch., 1942; The lion and the mouse; Reverie, string orch.; CHAMBER MUSIC: Musical forum, 9 instruments; string quartet; string quintet; piano quartet; cello sonata; brass quintets; also choruses, songs, piano pieces, marches.

LEGINSKA, ETHEL
b. Hull, England, 13 Apr. 1886; d. Los Angeles, Calif., 26 Feb. 1970. Studied piano in Frankfurt and with Leschetisky in Vienna; composition with Rubin Goldmark and Ernest Bloch in the U.S. She made her debut on the piano in London, then toured Europe; her American debut took place in New York on 20 Jan. 1913. She took up conducting and organized the Boston Philharmonic Orch. and the Boston Women's Symphony Orch.; also conducted the Chicago Women's Symphony. From 1939 she was pianist and piano teacher in Los Angeles.
WORKS: OPERA: Gale, Chicago, 23 Nov. 1935, composer conducting; The rose and the ring, 1932, Los Angeles, 23 Feb. 1957, composer conducting; ORCHESTRA: Beyond the fields we know, symphonic poem, New York, 12 Feb. 1922; 2 short pieces, Boston, 29 Feb. 1924; Quatres sujets barbares , after Gauguin, Munich, 13 Dec. 1924; Fantasy, piano and orch., New York, 3 Jan. 1926; CHAMBER MUSIC: From a life, 13 instruments, New York, 9 Jan. 1922; Triptych, 11 instruments, Chicago, 29 Jan. 1928; string quartet on 4 poems of Tagore, Boston, 25 Apr. 1921; 6 nursery rhymes, soprano and chamber orch.; 3 Victorian portraits, piano, 1959; other piano pieces and songs.

LEHR, MANGHAM DAVID
b. Greenwood, Miss., 1 June 1928. Studied with Bernhard Heiden, Indiana Univ., B.M.E. 1956; with Bruce Benward, Univ. of Wisconsin, M.M. 1966; at Michigan State Univ., 1973-74. He was faculty member, Purdue Univ., 1958-70; Michigan State Univ., 1972-74.
WORKS: ORCHESTRA: overture, 1957; CHORUS: Palm Sunday cantata, with 2 soli and organ, 1956; Poem and alleluia for the Christ Child, a cappella, 1958; In excelsis gloria, 1966; ORGAN: 6 modal chorale preludes on hymn tunes, 1963; concerto for organ, strings, and brass, 1966; Chorale partita on Veni Emmanuel.

LEHRMAN, LEONARD J.
b. Ft. Riley, Kans., 20 Aug. 1949. Studied privately with Elie Siegmeister; with Earl Kim and Leon Kirchner, Harvard Univ.; with Nadia Boulanger in France; Robert Palmer and Karel Husa, Cornell Univ.; with Donald Erb, John Eaton, and Juan Orrega-Salas, Indiana Univ. His awards include the Concours de Comp. first prize, 1969; Bennington Conf. fellowship, 1970; French government grant, 1971; Cornell Univ. fellowships, 1972-75; Cornell Arts Council grant, 1976; Nat. Fed. of Music Clubs award, 1977; New York State Arts Council award, 1978. He has held various teaching posts; was founder, Marc Blitzstein Opera Company, 1971-77; assistant chorus master, Metropolitan Opera, 1977-78.
WORKS: OPERA: Tales of Malamud, 2 1-act operas, Idiots first and Karla, Ithaca, 2 Aug.

LEIBIG, BRUCE

1974; ORCHESTRA: violin concerto, 1973; <u>Prelude for orch.</u>; chamber symphony; flute concerto; BAND: <u>2 songs of a madman</u>, voice, winds, brass, 1977; CHAMBER MUSIC: piano trio, 1969; string trio; flute sonata; violin sonata; sonatina for oboe alone; also choral works and songs.
10 Nob Hill Gate, Roslyn, NY 11576

LEIBIG, BRUCE
b. Lebanon, Pa., 29 Dec. 1946. Studied with Merrill Ellis and William Latham, North Texas State Univ.; with Robert Erickson and Kenneth Gaburo, Univ. of California, San Diego. He received an award from the Texas Manuscript Society for 2 songs, 1968, and was a fellow, Project for Music Experiment, Univ. of California, San Diego, 1973.
WORKS: CHAMBER MUSIC: 2 songs for soprano, 1968; <u>Encahc</u>, woodwind quintet, 1968; <u>Sounds I</u>, 2 pianos, 1969; <u>Pex-mix</u>, tape, 1969; MULTIMEDIA: <u>Parlour piece</u>, instructor and bodies, 1972; <u>Probe</u>, 3 cue-groups, 3 movers, tape, controller, electronics, and audience, 1972; <u>Working</u>, 8 or more performers and instructor.
2443 Montclair, San Diego, CA 92104

LEICH, ROLAND
b. Evansville, Ind., 6 Mar. 1911. Studied with Felix Borowski and Leo Sowerby in Chicago; with Rosario Scalero at Curtis Inst., 1929-33; with Anton Webern in Vienna, 1933-34; and with Bernard Rogers, Eastman School of Music, M.M. 1942. His honors include the Lauber award, 1933; Bearns award, 1933, 1937; Pennsylvania Fed. of Music Clubs awards, 1953, 1956. He was faculty member, Dartmouth Coll., 1935-41; Carnegie-Mellon Univ., 1946-76; associate conductor, Mendelssohn Choir of Pittsburgh, 1951-68.
WORKS: ORCHESTRA: <u>Concert piece</u>, oboe and strings, 1952; <u>Rondo for orch.</u>, 1953; <u>Prelude and fugue</u>, 1955; <u>The town of Pittsburgh</u>, with chorus, 1958; CHAMBER MUSIC: 5 A. E. Housman songs, 1933; string quartet, 1937; 47 settings of Emily Dickinson poems; and choral pieces.
105 Bevington Rd., Pittsburgh, PA 15221

LEICHTENTRITT, HUGO
b. Pleschen, Poland, 1 Jan. 1874; d. Cambridge, Mass., 13 Nov. 1951. Studied with John Knowles Paine, Harvard Univ., 1891-94; at Berlin Univ., Ph.D. 1901; then taught in Germany to 1934, when he returned to the U.S. and joined the faculty at Harvard. He was noted chiefly as a music scholar and author of books on music criticism, but was also a composer.
WORKS: ORCHESTRA: a symphony; <u>Symphonic variations on a Siamese dance</u>; violin concerto; many works for chamber groups; song cycles; cantatas; also a comic opera and a music drama.

LEICHTLING, ALAN
b. Brooklyn, N.Y., 1947. Studied at New York High School of Music and Art; with Vincent Persichetti and Roger Sessions, Juilliard School, B.S., M.S., D.M.A. 1971; with Darius Milhaud and Charles Jones, Aspen School, 1966. His awards include the McCollin prize of the Musical

Fund Society of Philadelphia. He was faculty member, Drew Univ., 1971-72; William Paterson Coll., 1972-75; Grinnell Coll., 1976-78; from 1978, at East Carolina Univ.
WORKS: OPERA: <u>The white butterfly</u>; <u>The tempest</u>; ORCHESTRA: 2 symphonies; concerto for chamber orch., 1966; viola concerto; CAHMBER MUSIC: 4 string quartets; 3 wind quintets; <u>Fantasy piece</u>, solo bass clarinet; <u>Bagatelles</u>, brass quintet, 1969; and many songs.
East Carolina Univ., P.O. Box 2517, Greenville, NC 27834

LEIDZEN, ERIK
b. Stockholm, Sweden, 25 Mar. 1894; to U.S. 1915; d. New York, N.Y., 20 Dec. 1962. Studied at the Royal Cons., Stockholm. He taught at various schools, including the Univ. of Michigan Summer School and the Nat. Music Camp at Interlochen; was guest conductor and arranger for the Goldman Band.
WORKS: BAND: <u>Irish symphony</u>; <u>Swedish rhapsody</u>; <u>Storm King overture</u>; <u>Symphony in the sky</u>; <u>The happy warrior</u>; works for brass quartet.

LEKBERG, SVEN
b. 1899. Has written works for chorus: <u>Lord of the earth and sky</u>, cantata; <u>Block city</u>; <u>Envoy</u>; <u>In quiet night</u>; <u>Rain song</u>; <u>The lamplighter</u>; <u>Fragrant the prayer</u>; <u>The love messengers</u>; <u>So wondrous sweet and fair</u>; and songs.
Music Dept., Simpson College, Indianola, IA 50125

LEMONT, CEDRIC WILMOT
b. Frederickton, N.B., 15 Dec. 1879; U.S. citizen 1933; d. New York, N.Y., 27 Apr. 1954. Studied at Univ. of New Brunswick; Faelton Piano School; New England Cons.; Capitol Coll., M.M. He taught piano and theory in schools and privately. His compositions for chorus, solo voice, and piano number in the hundreds.

LENEL, LUDWIG
b. Strasbourg, France, 20 May 1914; U.S. citizen 1955. Was an artist pupil of Albert Schweitzer, 1932; holds diplomas from Hochschule für Musik, Cologne and Basel Cons.; studied at Oberlin Cons., M.M. 1940. He has been faculty member at Oberlin Cons.; Monticello Coll.; Westminster Coll., Pa.; Elmhurst Coll.; New School for Social Research; and from 1952, at Muhlenberg Coll.; is also lecturer, organ recitalist, and choral conductor.
WORKS: OPERA: <u>Young Goodman Brown</u>, 1 act, 1962; <u>The boss</u>, 1-act folk tale opera, 1964; ORCHESTRA: <u>Partita for orch.</u>, 1972; BAND: <u>2 pieces for band</u>, 1957; concertino for woodwinds, brass, percussion, 1965; CHAMBER MUSIC: 2 brass quintets, 1960, 1967; music for organ, brass and timpani, 1968; <u>5 pieces for violin and viola</u> and taped percussion, 1973; many choral works, organ and piano pieces, and songs.
R.D. 1, Box 185, Orefield, PA 18069

LENNON, JOHN ANTHONY
b. Greensboro, N.C., 14 Jan. 1950. Studied at San Francisco State Univ., B.A.; with Leslie

Bassett, William Bolcom, and Ross Lee Finney, Univ. of Michigan, M.M., D.M.A. He received the Charles Ives award, American Acad. and Inst. of Arts and Letters, 1977. He has been faculty member, Univ. of Tennessee, from 1977.

WORKS: ORCHESTRA: From then till ever, 1975; Passage to thereafter, with women's choir, 1978; CHAMBER MUSIC: Cythere, guitar, 1973; Colors where the moon never could, chamber ensemble, 1974; In not so many words, solo violin, 1976; Morning winds/Evening color wind, guitar, 1976; CHORUS: To the myrios, 1972.

5819 Holston Hills, Knoxville, TN 37914

LENTZ, DANIEL K.
b. Latrobe, Pa., 10 Mar. 1942. Studied at St. Vincent Coll.; Ohio Univ.; Brandeis Univ.; Stockholm Univ.; and at Tanglewood. His awards include 2 Nat. Endowment for the Arts grants, 1973, 1975; a Fulbright grant; and a Tanglewood fellowship. He taught for a while at Univ. of California, Santa Barbara.

WORKS: CHAMBER MUSIC: Pastime, chamber ensemble; VOICE: Missa umbrarum, 8-voice choir, solo male performer, and 263 shadows, 1973; Sun tropes, 7 melodies in the form of 46 pieces without musica ficta, 7-voice choir, 1975; Songs of the siren, cnatata on English words from Homer, voice and instruments, 1975.

67 La Vuelta Rd., Montecito, CA 93100

LEON, GARBY
b. Manhattan, N.Y., 14 May 1947. Studied at Marlboro Coll., B.A.; with Leon Kirchner, Earl Kim, John Perkins, and Harold Shapero, Harvard Univ., M.A. He received the Knight prize in 1973.

WORKS: CHAMBER MUSIC: string quartet, 1971; A reading of poems, speaker, string sextet, electronic piano, piano and percussion, 1972; Death's bright angel (and the choir invisible), soprano, flute, cello, piano and percussion, 1973.

17 Pleasant Place, Cambridge, MA 02139

LEON, TANIA J.
b. Havana, Cuba, 14 May 1944; to U.S. 1967. Earned a B.A. and M.A. in music in Havana, then studied business administration, Havana Univ., B.A. 1965; studied composition at New York Univ., B.S., B.A. 1971, M.S. 1973; then engaged in graduate work toward a doctorate in acoustics. Her awards include a first prize, Nat. Council of the Arts, Havana, 1966; Alvin Johnson award, 1971; 2 CINTAS awards in composition, 1976, 1978-79; Nat. Endowment for the Arts grant, 1975; ASCAP awards, 1978-79; and commissions. From 1967, she has been active as piano soloist, conductor, and music director with various orchestras and with the Dance Theatre of Harlem.

WORKS: THEATRE: Tones, ballet, 1970; Haiku, ballet, 1974; background score for La Ramera de la Cueva by Mario Pena, 1974; CHORUS: Spiritual suite, commissioned for 41st Eucharistic Congress, Philadelphia, 1976.

35-20 Leverich St., Jackson Heights, NY 11372

LEONARD, GRACE (Mrs. Lloyd L.)
b. Dallas, Tex., 13 Jan. 1909. Studied with Francis Buebendorf, Univ. of Missouri, Kansas City. She held a scholarship for piano study; received third place award, Otto Preminger competition. She was piano teacher and accompanist in Dallas, 1928-48.

WORKS: CHORUS: Thanks be to thee; Invincible we stand; SONGS: So oft I invoked thee; From fairest creatures; Spring and fall; Jenny kissed me; PIANO: Israel le Chaim! (Preminger award); other choral works, piano pieces, etc.

11131 E. 84th Terrace, Raytown, MO 64138

LEONARDI, LEONID
b. Moscow, Russia, 27 July 1901; to U.S. 1923; d. New York, N.Y., 3 Mar. 1967. Studied with Maurice Ravel, Vincent d'Indy, Nadia Boulanger, Paris Cons.; also with Anton Rubinstein. He made his debut as pianist at the Imperial Court at age 9; toured Europe in recitals. In the U.S., he was music director in New York and St. Louis theatres; conductor for musicals, films, radio in New York; in World War II, music director, 11th Naval District, San Diego.

WORKS: THEATRE: Song of the forest, lyric drama; ORCHESTRA: The song of America; Blue Ridge rhapsody, piano and orch.; Freedom's plow, narrator and orch.; CHAMBER MUSIC: Manhattan vignettes, for woodwinds; and piano pieces.

LEPLIN, EMANUEL
b. San Francisco, Calif., 3 Oct. 1917; d. Martinez, Calif., 2 Dec. 1972. Studied violin with George Enesco, composition with Roger Sessions and Darius Milhaud, conducting with Pierre Monteux. He won the Prix de Rome in composition while a student at Univ. of California at Berkeley. Stricken with polio in 1954 when he was a violinist with the San Francisco Symphony, he taught himself to paint with a brush held in his teeth and also continued to compose.

WORKS: ORCHESTRA: Galaxy, 2 cellos and orch., 1942; Cosmos, violin and orch., 1944; 2 symphonic poems; a symphony, 1962; also chamber music and piano pieces.

LEPS, WASSILI
b. St. Petersburg, Russia, 12 May 1870; to U.S. 1894; d. Toronto, Ont., 22 Dec. 1943. Studied at Dresden Cons.; became choirmaster at the Dresden Opera Company. In the U.S., he taught at Philadelphia Musical Acad. and was conductor, Philadelphia Opera Society, 1894-1923; organized the Providence Symph. Orch. in 1932 and was conductor until retirement in 1941. His compositions include an opera, a cantata, and orchestral pieces.

LERDAHL, ALFRED
b. Madison, Wis., 1943. Studied at Lawrence Univ.; with Milton Babbitt, Edward T. Cone, and Earl Kim, Princeton Univ.; and with Wolfgang Fortner in Germany, 1969-70. His awards include the Koussevitzky prize at Tanglewood, 1966; fellowships at Marlboro Festival, 1967, 1968; Fulbright grant for study in Germany, 1969; Nat. Inst. of Arts and Letters award, 1971; Fromm

LESEMANN, FREDERICK

Found. commissions, 1972, 1974. He taught at
Univ. of California, Berkeley, 1970-71; from
1972, has been faculty member at Harvard Univ.
    WORKS: ORCHESTRA: Wake, voice and orch.;
Chromorhythmos, 1972, was to have been performed
at Tanglewood, but Bruno Maderna, conductor,
declared it impossible to play; it has been
revised and rechristened Color-rhythm; Chords,
Tanglewood, 8 Aug. 1974; CHAMBER MUSIC: Piano
fantasy, 1964; string trio, 1965-66; Aftermath,
3 voices and chamber orch., to own text, Cambridge, Mass., 19 May 1973; Eros, mezzo-soprano
and chamber ensemble, text by Ezra Pound, 1975,
Boston, 23 Apr. 1978, composer conducting;
Imitations, piano trio, 1977; string quartet,
Omaha, 11 Mar. 1979.
    Music Dept., Harvard University, Cambridge,
    MA 02138

LESEMANN, FREDERICK
    b. Los Angeles, Calif., 12 Oct. 1936. Studied
at Oberlin Cons., B.M. 1958; Univ. of Southern
California, M.M. 1961, D.M.A. 1972. His awards
include Helen S. Anstead award, 1961; USC School
of Music Alumni Assoc. award, 1972; 2 Nat. Endowment for the Arts grants, 1976, 1977. He was
manager of the Ojai Festival, 1963-66; has been
faculty member, Univ. of Southern California,
from 1966.
    WORKS: ORCHESTRA: symphony, Buffalo, N.Y.,
Apr. 1973; Orchestra music, 1976; Legends,
suite, 1977; PIANO: Nataraja, prepared piano,
Ojai, 30 May 1975; Fantasy, Washington, D.C.,
28 June 1976.
    Univ. of Southern California, Los Angeles,
    CA 90007

LESSARD, JOHN AYRES
    b. San Francisco, Calif., 3 July 1920. Studied
with Nadia Boulanger in Paris. He received a
Guggenheim grant, 1946; Nat. Inst. of Arts and
Letters award, 1952. He is professor, State
Univ. of New York at Stony Brook.
    WORKS: ORCHESTRA: violin concerto, 1941;
Box Hill overture, 1946; Cantilena, oboe and
strings; concerto for wind instruments; concerto for woodwind trio and strings, 1952;
CHAMBER MUSIC: Sinfonietta concertante; quintet
for flute, clarinet and string trio, 1943; 2
piano sonatas, 1944, 1945; 3 movements, violin
and piano, 1952; wind octet, 1954; cello sonata,
1954; Toccata, harpsichord, 1955; Quodlibets, 2
trumpets and trombone; Perpetual motion, piano;
Partita, wind quintet; 3 movements for trumpet
and various instruments, New York, 17 May 1979;
SONGS: Mother Goose, 6 songs, 1953; Fragment
from the cantos of Ezra Pound, baritone and 9
instruments.
    1162 N. Country Rd., Stony Brook, NY 11790

LESSNER, GEORGE
    b. Budapest, Hungary, 15 Dec. 1904; U.S. citizen
1926. Studied with Bela Bartok, Zoltan Kodaly,
and Ernst von Dohnanyi, Budapest Royal Acad. of
Music. In the U.S., he scored films; was composer and arranger for the radio programs
"Prudential Hour," "Texaco Star Theatre," "Great
Moments of Music;" composer and conductor for
television shows. His works include scores for

the stage play, Sleepy Hollow, and the television
play, "The rose and the nightingale"; 8 symphonies; many songs.

LESTER, JAMES T.
    b. Detroit, Mich., 31 Aug. 1933. Studied at
Alma Coll.; with Gregory Stone, Los Angeles
Cons., B.M.; at Univ. of Southern California;
and privately with Mario Castelnuovo-Tedesco.
He was instructor at Brentwood Acad., 1965-69,
and held other positions while establishing a
music engraving business.
    WORKS: THEATRE: Puss and boots, children's
musical; Casey at the bat, children's musical;
ORCHESTRA: Dance alla marcia; The farmer and
the cat, with clarinet and bassoon solos; CHAMBER
MUSIC: Tango de concert, woodwind quintet;
Romance exotique, oboe and piano; Serenade to a
plucked ostrich, piano; CHORUS: The mountain
and the squirrel, on a fable by Ralph Waldo
Emerson.
    345 S. Citrus Ave., Los Angeles, CA 90036

LESTER, THOMAS WILLIAM
    b. Leicester, England, 17 Sept. 1889; to U.S.
1902; d. Berian Springs, Mich., 4 Dec. 1956.
Studied with Wilhelm Middelschulte, then was
organist and music critic in Chicago. His
compositions included 8 cantatas, songs, piano
works, organ pieces.

LEVAN, LOUIS
    b. Russia, 15 Sept. 1906. Studied violin with
Leopold Auer in New York. He organized and
conducted the New York Student Symphony. His
compositions include 3 violin concerts; 4 violin
sonatas; and songs. He is author of The foundation of the violin.

LEVANT, OSCAR
    b. Pittsburgh, Pa., 27 Dec. 1906; d. Beverly
Hills, Calif., 14 Aug. 1972. Studied composition with Arnold Schoenberg and Joseph
Schillinger; piano with Sigismund Stojowski.
He was concert pianist and jazz pianist; gave
many concerts of Gershwin's music; was music
expert on "Information Please" radio program,
1938; appeared in films as actor; played his
own piano concerto with the NBC Symphony, 17
Feb. 1942.
    WORKS: ORCHESTRA: Nocturne, 1936; piano
concerto, 1942; CHAMBER MUSIC: piano sonata,
1941; 2 string quartets; piano pieces; film
scores. He was author of 3 books: The importance of being Oscar; A smattering of ignorance;
Memoirs of an amnesiac.

LEVENSON, BORIS
    b. Ackerman, Bessarabia, 10 Mar. 1884; U.S.
citizen 1927; d. New York, N.Y., 11 Mar. 1947.
Studied with Galzunov and Rimsky-Korsakov at
St. Petersburg Cons., graduating in 1907; was
conductor in St. Petersburg and Moscow, 1907-12;
toured as conductor.
    WORKS: OPERA: Woman on the window; OR-
CHESTRA: symphony, 1903; Palestine suite, 1927;
Night in Baghdad, tone poem, 1938; Stalingrad
overture; Volga, tone poem; CHAMBER MUSIC:

<u>Hebrew suite</u>, 8 instruments; 2 string quartets; <u>Poem</u>, violin and piano; CHORUS: <u>David and Abraham</u>, oratorio.

LEVEY, JOSEPH A.
b. Clarksburg, W.Va., 9 May 1925. Studied with Weldon Hart, West Virginia Univ.; with Anthony Donato, Northwestern Univ.; and with Philip Bezanson, Iowa State Univ. He received an Ohio State Univ., College of the Arts, grant; and commissions. He has been faculty member, Madison Coll., 1962-63; Radford Coll., 1963-65; from 1965, Ohio State Univ.
WORKS: BALLET: <u>Timepiece</u>; WIND ENSEMBLE: <u>Mosaic</u>, brass choir; CHAMBER MUSIC: string quartet.
3266 Leighton Rd., Columbus, OH 43221

LEVEY, LAUREN
b. New York, N.Y., 20 June 1947. Studied with Joel Spiegelman and Meyer Kupferman, Sarah Lawrence Coll.; with Jacob Druckman, Bülent Arel, K. Penderecki, and Mario Davidovsky, Yale Univ. She was faculty member and acting director, Bregman Electronic Music Studio, Dartmouth Coll., 1973-78.
WORKS: CHAMBER MUSIC: <u>Dissolves</u>, chamber group, 1973; CHORUS: <u>A womb (with a view) of one's own</u>, women's voices, 1974; ELECTRONIC: <u>Study for tape</u>, 1973; <u>and now a message from our sponsor especially for you ladies</u>, tape, 1974.

LEVIN, GREGORY
b. Washington, D.C., 8 Mar. 1943. Studied with Leon Kirchner and Billy Jim Layton, Harvard Univ., B.A. cum laude 1967; with Arthur Berger and Seymour Shifrin, Brandeis Univ., M.F.A. 1969; and with Luciano Berio and Pierre Boulez. His awards include Harvard scholarships, 1961-67; Woodrow Wilson fellowship, 1967-68; Brandeis fellowship, 1968-70; grants from New York State Council of the Arts, 1970, Syracuse Symphony, 1971, Nat. Council on the Arts; and many commissions. He was on the faculty, Syracuse Univ., 1970-72; Univ. of Rhode Island, 1972-73; from 1973, Univ. of Calgary; was conductor, Syracuse Symphony Orch., 1971, and Syracuse New Music Ensemble, 1970-72. He is also actor, dramatist, painter, and poet.
WORKS: THEATRE: <u>Crazy Horse</u>, opera to own libretto, 1957; <u>The election of Andrew Jackson</u>, play with music, 1958; <u>Sunrise</u>, play with music, 1958; <u>Buffalo</u>, opera, 1959; <u>A minuet</u>, opera, 1959; incidental music for: <u>Rosmerholm</u>, 1961, <u>Playboy of the western world</u>, 1962, <u>Midsummer night's dream</u>, 1962, <u>Twelfth night</u>, 1962; <u>Rebel and empire</u>, opera, libretto by composer's father, Dan Levin, 1970; <u>Son of Judah</u>, opera trilogy, libretto by Dan Levin, 1970; CHAMBER MUSIC: suite for flute, oboe, piano, 1963; piano sonata, 1965; suite for chamber orch., 1966; <u>Improvisation on levin #1</u>, 1966, <u>#2</u>, 1967; sonata for flute and harp, 1971; <u>Illuminations</u>, piano, soprano, saxophone, 1971; <u>5 Picasso portraits</u>, brass quintet, 1972; <u>Infinities</u>, soprano, violin, percussion, piano, 1973; <u>Raga</u>, trumpet and organ, Calgary, Alta., 5 Oct. 1973; <u>2 short, 1 long</u>, piano, 1974; MULTIMEDIA: <u>The white</u>

<u>goddess</u>, tape, audio and visual feedback, film, string bass, voice and piano, 1972; <u>Black-Point cut-off</u>, film, string bass, piano, tape, 1973; <u>Feedback</u>, color television, piano, tape, 1973; <u>Neap tide</u>, film and tape, 1973.
Music Dept., Univ. of Calgary, Calgary, Alta., Canada T2N 1N4

LEVIN, JOSEPH A.
b. Reading, Pa., 19 July 1917. Attended Albright Coll.; studied music privately. From 1945 he was with Big 3 Music Corp., editor-in-chief from 1951.
WORKS: CHORUS: <u>Psalm 51</u>; <u>O Lord, ruler of the Universe</u>; <u>Blessed are the poor in spirit</u>; and songs.

LEVIN, RAMI Y.
b. Brooklyn, N.Y., 27 Feb. 1954. Studied with Miriam Gideon in New York; with Yehudi Wyner, Robert Morris, and Robert Moore, Yale Univ., B.A. 1975; with Robert Erickson and Bernard Rands, Univ. of California, San Diego, M.A. 1978; with Kenneth Gaburo in San Diego. She received first prize in a composers' competition at Aspen, 1974. She has been oboist with the Yale Repertory Theatre and at various festivals; has taught recorder in nursery schools, 1975-78.
WORKS: CHAMBER MUSIC: string quartet; <u>And yet again</u>, 3 flutes, 2 clarinets; <u>Light reflection</u>, flute and oboe; <u>Doubletake</u>, 2 pianos; <u>Blues toccata</u>, piano; <u>Connections</u>, oboe solo; <u>Ambages</u>, guitar; <u>Take a pianist to lunch</u>, piano; VOICE: <u>Now we are six</u>, A. A. Milne, soprano, oboe, string trio; <u>becummings 1 and 2</u>, e. e. cummings poems, soprano and 8 instruments; <u>Rain has fallen</u>, soprano and cello.
5006 Telegraph Ave., #5, Oakland, CA 94609

LEVINE, BRUCE
b. New York, N.Y., 24 Jan. 1950. Studied with Ursula Mamlok, New York Univ., B.S. 1972, M.A. 1974. He held a scholarship for Tanglewood, 1966; received the Presser Found. grant, 1969-70; Lado award, 1969, for instrument study. He has taught in several schools; was oboist and conductor; from 1978, music director and composer for Richard Dalee Productions.
WORKS: THEATRE: Music for <u>A Thurber carnival</u>, piano, 1970; BAND: <u>An English round dance</u>, 1969-72; CHAMBER MUSIC: <u>Poem</u>, flute solo, 1968; <u>Introduction and allegro</u>, flute, violin, piano, 1968; woodwind quintet, 1970; <u>Monologue I</u>, English horn, 1971; <u>Introspection</u>, oboe solo, 1971; <u>Colours</u>, oboe and piano, 1972; <u>Traces</u>, clarinet solo, 1972; <u>Design</u>, 2 or more instruments, 1972; <u>Syncrons</u>, oboe, clarinet, viola, tuba, tape, 1973; <u>3 pieces</u>, acoustic guitar, 1973; <u>Christmas medley</u>, woodwind quintet, 1976; <u>Whirlwind</u>, woodwind quintet, 1977; many choral works, songs, piano pieces.
229 Rte. 110, Farmingdale, NY 11735

LEVINE, JEFFREY L.
b. New York, N.Y., 15 Sept. 1942. Studied at Brown Univ., B.A.; with Mel Powell at Yale Univ., M.M.; with Gunther Schuller and Franco Donatoni. He received a Fromm Found. commission at Tangle-

LEVINSON, GERALD

wood, 1967; Fulbright grant, 1968. He was lecturer, Rutgers Univ., 1965-68; Univ. of California at Berkeley, 1972-74.
WORKS: ORCHESTRA: piano concerto, 1971;
CHAMBER MUSIC: Form, 2 pianos; Cadenza, piano
solo; Parentheses, any number of stringed instruments; harpsichord quartet; Chamber setting
#2, clarinet sextet; Divertimento, 10 solo in-
struments, 1973.

LEVINSON, GERALD
b. Mineola, N.Y., 22 June 1951. Studied with
George Crumb, Richard Wernick, and George
Rochberg, Univ. of Pennsylvania; with Bruno
Maderna at Tanglewood; with Ralph Shapey, Univ.
of Chicago, M.A. 1974; Ph.D. 1977; with Olivier
Messiaen in Paris. His awards include BMI
awards; Univ. of Pennsylvania music prize, 1972;
Univ. of Chicago fellowship, 1972-74; Georges
Lurcy Found. fellowship, 1974-75; East and West
Artists Chamber Music prize; Premier Prix de
Comp. de Paris, 1976; was one of the first 2
winners of the American Acad. and Inst. of Arts
and Letters Goddard Lieberson fellowship, 1979.
From 1977, he has been on faculty at Swarthmore
Coll.
WORKS: ORCHESTRA: Suono oscuro, 1969; 2
poems, 1976; CHAMBER MUSIC: piano quintet,
1971; Winds of light, violin and piano, 1973;
Odyssey, solo flute, 1973; Skrzybka, violin
solo, 1973; Sky music, 13 instruments, 1974-75;
trio for clarinet, cello, piano, 1976; Chant des
Rochers, chamber orch., Pittsburgh, 18 Mar. 1976;
VOICE: In wind, soprano and instruments, 1970;
In dark (3 poems of the night), soprano and 8
players, 1972; Job, baritone, string quartet,
choir, and organ, 1972.
Music Dept., Swarthmore College, Swarthmore,
PA 19081

LEVITCH, LEON
b. Belgrade, Yugoslavia, 9 July 1927; U.S.
citizen 1951. Studied at Los Angeles State
Coll., B.A.; and at Univ. of California, Los
Angeles, M.A. 1971; his teachers were Erich
Zeisl, Mario Castelnuovo-Tedesco, Darius Milhaud,
and Roy Harris. He received second prize,
Atwater Kent contest, 1968. From 1969, he has
been staff technician and concert tuner, music
dept., Univ. of California, and instructor of
piano tuning and technology, extension div.,
from 1970.
WORKS: ORCHESTRA: symphony; Fantasy, oboe
and strings; suite for flute, string orch.,
harp; CHAMBER MUSIC: flute sonata; viola sonata;
violin sonata; trio for flute, clarinet or viola,
and piano; quartet for flute, viola, cello,
piano; string quartet; quintet for flute and
strings; piano sonata; Little suite, piano;
Variations on Frere Jacques, string quartet,
1974; CHORUS: Of plants and humans, cantata
for soprano and tenor soli, chorus, chamber
orch., text by composer, 1961.
13107 Kelowna St., Pacoima, CA 91331

LEVITT, RODNEY CHARLES
b. Portland, Oreg., 1929. Played trombone with
Dizzy Gillespie and others; had his own band

from 1960; has been lecturer in jazz studies,
Hofstra Univ., from 1976; artist-in-residence,
City Coll. of CUNY, from 1978.
WORKS: CONCERT JAZZ: Breathin' easy; El
general; The lost soul; Safari; Speedway;
Cathedral City; Circle 5; M'Lord is at Olympia
House; Onion chicken; Woodman of the world.
Music Dept., Hofstra Univ., Hempstead, NY
11559

LEVITZKI, MISCHA
b. Kremenchug, Russia, 25 May 1898; to U.S.
1908; d. Avon, N.J., 2 Jan. 1941. Studied with
Sigismund Stojowski at Juilliard School; with
Ernst von Dohnanyi at the Berlin Hochschule für
Musik; was twice awarded the Mendelssohn piano
prize; made his debut at 15 in Berlin, at 16, in
New York; toured as pianist in the U.S., Europe,
and the Orient. He composed many piano pieces.

LEVY, BURT JEROME
b. Brooklyn, N.Y., 5 Aug. 1936. Studied privately
in New York with Keith Robinson, 1953-57; with
Homer Keller, Univ. of Oregon, 1958-60; with
Kenneth Gaburo, Herbert Brun, Ben Johnston, and
Salvatore Martirano, Univ. of Illinois, D.M.A.
1967. He has been faculty member at Western
Illinois Univ., 1967-68; Univ. of Wisconsin,
1968-71; State Univ. of New York at Albany,
1973-77; from 1977, at Wisconsin Cons., Milwaukee.
WORKS: ORCHESTRA: Tryonym, 1972; CHAMBER
MUSIC: Orbs with flute, New York, 5 Feb. 1973;
6 moments for piano, 1976; string quartet, 1978.
Wisconsin Cons., 1584 N. Prospect Ave.,
Milwaukee, WI 53203

LEVY, EDWARD I.
b. Brooklyn, N.Y., 2 May 1929. Attended City
Coll. of New York, B.A. 1957; Princeton Univ.,
M.F.A. 1960; Columbia Univ., Teachers Coll.,
Ed.D. 1967; studied with Ralph Shapey, Milton
Babbitt, Stefan Wolpe. His awards include the
Frederick Jacoby Memorial award; Tremaine
scholarship; 2 fellowships at Princeton Univ.;
Heft scholarship at Columbia Univ. He was
linguistic researcher, Univ. of Pennsylvania,
1960-61; on faculty, C. W. Post Coll., Long
Island Univ., 1961-67; and from 1966, at Yeshiva
Univ.
WORKS: CHAMBER MUSIC: 2 songs on texts of
Garcia-Lorca, 1951; clarinet sonata, 1955; piano
suite, 1956; 2 string quartets, 1959, 1972; oboe
sonata, 1959; string trio, 1959; Lento for 9 instruments, 1959; trio for clarinet, violin,
piano, 1961; 3 images, soprano and piano, 1961;
quintet for flute, alto saxophone, vibraphone,
violin, and bass, 1967; trio for flute, cello,
piano, 1968; trio for clarinet, cello, piano,
1970; A set of 2, piano, 1974.
838 West End Ave., New York, NY 10025

LEVY, ELLIS
b. Indianapolis, Ind., 23 Oct. 1887. Studied
violin with Eugene Ysaye and Cesar Thomson in
Brussels. He was assistant concertmaster of the
St. Louis Symphony, 1910-36. He composed works
for orchestra, for violin and piano, and for
piano solo.

316

LEVY, ERNST
b. Basel, Switz., 18 Nov. 1895; to U.S. 1939; d.
Switzerland, 1981. Taught at New England Cons.,
1941-45; Bennington Coll., 1946-51; Chicago
Univ., 1951-54; was professor of piano at Massachusetts Inst. of Technology from 1954 to retirement. His works include 14 symphonies (#14
performed in Basel, 20 Jan. 1964); cello concerto; other orchestral works, and chamber
works.

LEVY, FRANK
b. Paris, France, 15 Oct. 1930; U.S. citizen
1955. Came to the U.S. with his father, Ernst
Levy, in 1939, began studying cello and, in
1941, composition with Hugo Kauder. He attended
the High School of Music and Art, 1944-48; was a
scholarship student under Leonard Rose at Juilliard School, B.S. 1951; studied musicology at
Univ. of Chicago, M.S. 1954; cello with Janos
Starker. He was cellist with the St. Louis
Symphony, 1951-52; from 1960, principal cellist,
Radio City Music Hall.
    WORKS: ORCHESTRA: concerto for oboe, horn,
bassoon, timpani, and strings, 1958; concerto
for bassoon and strings, 1960; Dialogue, tuba,
harp, timpany, strings, 1964; 3 symphonies, #1
for small orch., 1968, #2 for brass and percussion, 1971, nominated for Pulitzer prize 1973,
#3, 1977; Lament, narrator, oboe, strings, per-
cussion, 1975; CHAMBER MUSIC: Variations on a
Swiss folksong, 1949; string quartet, 1951;
sextet for winds and strings, 1955; suite for
solo cello, 1959; Fantasy, brass quintet and
timpani, 1959; Ricercar, 4 celli, 1959; suite
for horn and piano, 1960; Concert piece, brass
quartet, 1961; wind trio, 1962; bassoon sonata,
1963; Fanfare, brass quintet, 1965; clarinet
sonata, 1967; violin duo, 1967; duo for flugelhorn and bass trumpet, 1972; viola sonata, 1972;
Adagio and rondo, 3 clarinets, 1972; Serenade,
flute, clarinet, cello, 1974; trio for flute,
horn, harpsichord, 1974; Adagio and scherzo,
4 saxophones, 1976; Go down, Death, narrator,
trumpet, harp, dancer, 1976; 7 bagatelles,
oboe, cello, harp, 1977; violin sonata, 1977;
VOICE: This is my letter to the world, a cappella chorus, Dickinson text, 1957; Specks of
light, song cycle for voice, flute, horn, string
trio, 1972.
    19 Virginia St., Tenafly, NJ 07670

LEVY, HENIOT
b. Warsaw, Poland, 19 July 1879; to U.S. 1900;
d. Chicago, 16 June 1946. Studed with Max
Bruch; taught piano at American Cons. in Chicago.
His works include a piano concerto; Variations
for orch.; string sextet; string quintet; 2 piano
quintets; 4 string quartets; 2 piano trios;
cello sonata; songs; many piano pieces.

LEVY, MARTIN DAVID
b. Passaic, N.J., 2 Aug. 1932. Studied with
Philip James, New York Univ., B.A. 1954; with
Otto Luening, Columbia Univ., M.A. 1956. His
awards include 2 Guggenheim fellowships, 1960,
1964; 2 Prix de Rome, 1962, 1965; grants from
the Ford Found., Damrosch Found., Huntington
Hartford Found.; many commissions. He was
faculty member, Brooklyn Coll., CUNY, 1974-76.
    WORKS: OPERA: Sotoba Komachi, New York,
7 Apr. 1957; The tower, 1 act, Santa Fe, 2 Aug.
1957; Escorial, New York, 4 May 1958; Mourning
becomes Electra, libretto after the O'Neill
play, Metropolitan Opera, New York, 17 Mar.
1967; ORCHESTRA: Caramoor festival overture,
1959; symphony, Los Angeles, Dec. 1960; Kyros,
dance poem, 1961; piano concerto, 1969, Chicago,
3 Dec. 1970; Trialogues, Chicago, 23 Mar. 1972;
In memoriam W. H. Auden, New York, 25 Feb. 1974;
Canto de los Marranos, soprano and orch., San
Francisco, 20 Nov. 1977; CHAMBER MUSIC: string
quartet, 1955; Rhapsody, violin, clarinet, harp,
1956; Chassidic suite, horn and piano, 1956;
CHORUS: For the time being, Christmas oratorio
on the poem of W. H. Auden, with orchestra, New
York, 7 Dec. 1959; Alice in Wonderland; During
wind and rain; Masada, oratorio, commissioned
by National Symphony for Israel's 25th anniversary, Washington, D.C., 30 Oct. 1973.
    41 W. 82 St., New York, NY 10024

LEWIN, FRANK
b. Breslau, Germany, 27 Mar. 1925; U.S. citizen
1946. Studied with Felix Deyo and Wallingford
Riegger, Brooklyn Cons.; with Jack Frederick
Kilpatrick, Southern Methodist Univ.; with Roy
Harris, Utah State Agri. Coll.; with Richard
Donovan and Paul Hindemith, Yale Univ., B.M.
1951. He received the Yale Certificate of Merit;
Nat. Endowment for the Arts grant, 1977. He has
been faculty member at Yale Univ. from 1971, and
at Columbia Univ., from 1975.
    WORKS: THEATRE: Gulliver, using film and
recorded sound along with live performers (with
2 other composers), 1972, Minneapolis, 22 Feb.
1975; incidental music for 14 plays, 1953-71;
Burning bright, opera based on Steinbeck's play,
1979; ORCHESTRA: harmonica concerto, 1960;
Evocation, symphonic poem, Princeton Univ., 27
Mar. 1961; Concerto on Silesian tunes, viola and
orch., Norfolk, Conn., 15 July 1965; CHORUS:
Behold, how good (Psalms 132 and 133), Princeton,
10 Dec. 1961; Music for the White House, cantata
on early American songs, composed at the request
of Mrs. Lyndon B. Johnson, composer conducted
chorus and band, the White House, 14 Dec. 1965;
Mass for the dead, performed at memorial service
for Robert F. Kennedy, Princeton Univ., 27 May
1969; SONG CYCLES: Innocence and experience,
on Blake poems, soprano and chamber orch., 1961;
Seasons, girls' voices, baritone, chamber orch.,
1962; Variations on Greek themes, on poems of
Edward Arlington Robinson, contralto with flute,
viola, harp, piano, New York, 20 Nov. 1977;
FILM SCORES: 9 miles to noon, 1963; Harry, 1970;
The angel Levine, 1970; and more than 25 documentary films.
    113 Magnolia Lane, Princeton, NJ 08540

LEWIS, H. MERRILLS
b. Meriden, Conn., 1908. Studied with David
Stanley Smith and Richard Donovan, Yale Univ.;
with Rubin Goldmark at Juilliard School. He has
taught at Furman Univ. and Univ. of Houston; was

LEWIS, JAMES

minister of music, First Christian Church, Houston. His compositions include a symphony, 1936; 3 serenades for orchestra, 1937; and Lake song, women's voices, 1936.

LEWIS, JAMES
b. Mattoon, Ill., 13 Nov. 1938. Studied with Samuel Adler, North Texas State Univ.; with Gordon Binkerd, Univ. of Illinois; and with Charles Eakin, Univ. of Colorado. His awards include first prize, Nat. Jazz Composition contest, 1969; Nat. Endowment for the Arts grant, 1973; MacDowell fellowship, 1976; first prize, Internat. Trombone Assoc. jazz composition contest, 1977; Yaddo fellowship, 1978. He has been faculty member, Xavier Univ., 1965-67; Stephen F. Austin State Coll., 1967-68; Univ. of South Dakota, 1968-71; from 1971, at Univ. of South Florida.
WORKS: WIND ENSEMBLE: Song from somewhere, jazz band, 1969; jazz sextet, 1972; Synergy, brass and percussion; 1973; Hear me talkin' to ya, jazz band, singer, tape, 1974; San Juan blues, trombone sextet and rhythm, 1977; Variations on blueberry blue, jazz band, 1978; CHAMBER MUSIC: 4 personalities, violin, trumpet, flute, trombone, 1961; Music for flute and piano, 1970; Tampanera, English horn and percussion, 1977; Double quincerto, violin, cello, 8 winds, 1978; VOICE: 4 songs on texts by Ezra Pound, 1962; Epilogue, voices and instruments, 1970; 3 poems, soprano, trombone, double bass, 1974; 3 Li Po poems, chorus and chamber orch., 1975, Washington, 24 May 1976.
413 St. Augustine, Temple Terrace, FL 33617

LEWIS, JOHN AARON
b. La Grange, Ill., 3 May 1920. Studied at Manhattan School of Music, B.M., M.M. 1953. He served in the U.S. Army, 1942-45; was cofounder in 1952 and pianist to 1977 of the Modern Jazz Quartet; president, MJQ Music, Inc.; executive director, Lenox School of Jazz; music director, Orchestra USA; from 1976, professor, City Coll., CUNY. In Sept. 1976, he was on the BMI team of representatives to the 30th Congress of the Internat. Confed. of Societies of Authors and Composers.
WORKS: BALLET: Original sin, 1961; CONCERT JAZZ: 6 vocalizations for vocal quartets with varying accompaniments; The comedy, piano and brass ensemble; Fanfare I and II, brass ensemble; The golden striker, piano and brass; 3 little feelings, brass; Bel (belkis); Django (also arranged by G. Schuller); Sundance; Exposure; Little David's fugue; Milano; N.Y. 19; Polchinella; 2 degrees east, 2 degrees west; Animal dance; Jazz ostinato; In memoriam; Sketch, double string quartet; Jazz themes with improvisation, piano; Portraits, woodwind quintet, New York, 12 Feb. 1979; FILM SCORES: No sun in Venice, 1958; Odds against tomorrow, 1959; The Milanese story, 1962.
MJQ Music, Inc., 200 W. 57 St., New York, NY 10019

LEWIS, JOHN LEO
b. Chicago, Ill., 11 May 1911. Studied at De

Paul Univ., B.A., M.A.; with Leo Sowerby, American Cons. He received the Harvey Gaul award and several prizes for choral works. From 1950, he was organist at Trinity Episcopal Church, Aurora, Ill. He has composed many organ works and choral pieces.

LEWIS, KERRY G.
b. Santa Rosa, Calif., 6 Dec. 1948. Studied with Lou Harrison, San Jose State Univ.
WORKS: CHAMBER MUSIC: Variations, woodwind quintet, 1973; CHORUS: Impressions of spring, with wind septet and piano, 1973; SONGS: 3 songs on poems of e. e. cummings, 1970; Hesperides, cycle for voice and piano, 1972.

LEWIS, LEON
b. Kansas City, Mo., 30 Mar. 1890; d. Calif., 5 Oct. 1961. Studied with Leschetizky and Graedener at the Vienna Cons.; toured Europe, the U.S., and Canada as concert pianist; then taught at the Chicago Cons.
WORKS: ORCHESTRA: Jessica--a portrait, piano and orch.; Israeli suite; cello concerto; Nocturne and moonspirits; CHAMBER MUSIC: cello sonata; Quartetto Americano; Wind and the willow, piano trio; CHORUS: God's image, with baritone solo and orch.; songs.

LEWIS, MALCOLM
b. Cuba, N.Y., 14 Nov. 1925. Studied at Ithaca Coll.; Juilliard School; New York Univ.; with Robert Palmer at Cornell Univ.; also studied art at various schools. He was a private teacher in Billings, Mont., 1955-61; public school art teacher, Bozeman, Mont., 1961-62; then joined the music faculty at Ithaca Coll.
WORKS: ORCHESTRA: clarinet concerto; Concert piece for horn, strings, percussion; suite for string orch.; BAND: Elegy for a hollow man, with solo saxophone; Phrygios; WIND ENSEMBLE: movement for brass quintet and piano; 2 contrasting studies, 8 horns; CHAMBER MUSIC: suite for 2 pianos; 2 piano trios; saxophone quartet; woodwind quartet; Reverie, saxophone solo; piano pieces.
309 Framm St., Ithaca, NY 14850

LEWIS, MARIAN
b. Washington, D.C., 18 Mar. 1951. Studied with Gordon Mumma and David Cope, Univ. of California, Santa Cruz. Her works include 8 bars for prepared piano, performed at Santa Cruz, 29 Jan. 1978; and Hidden lines, solo timpani and tape, Santa Cruz, 7 Apr. 1978.
Music Dept., Univ. of California, Santa Cruz, CA 95064

LEWIS, PETER TOD
b. Charlottesville, VA., 6 Nov. 1932. Studied with Roger Chapman, Univ. of California, Santa Barbara; with Lukas Foss and John Vincent, Univ. of California, Los Angeles; Arthur Berger, Irving Fine, Brandeis Univ.; and with Wolfgang Fortner at Tanglewood on a scholarship, 1960. Other awards include Wechsler commission, 1960; Huntington Hartford Found. grant, 1960; MacDowell fellowships, 1961, 1980. He was instructor,

Philadelphia Musical Acad., 1965-68; resident composer, Southern Illinois Univ., 1968-69; from 1969, faculty member, Univ. of Iowa.

WORKS: ORCHESTRA: Evolution, 1961; CHAMBER MUSIC: Capriccio concertato, 2 pianos, 1960, rev. 1962; string quartet, 1960; piano trio, 1960; 3 epigrams, chamber ensemble, 1961; Contrasts, wind quintet, 1962; Lament for Mrs. Bridge, chamber orch., 1963; Sestina, 11 winds, 1963; septet, string trio, woodwind trio, piano, 1963; . . . and bells . . . and time, a dialogue for violin and piano, 1967; Signs and circuits, string quartet and tape, 1969; Manestar, chamber orch. and tape, 1970; Innerkip, piano and tape, 1972; CHORUS: When I was born, with tenor and soprano soli, 1956; 3 insignificant tragedies, 1962; The cherry tree carol with soprano solo and harp, 1962; We stood on the wall, 1965; 3 for jazz choir, 1968; also songs, piano pieces, electronic works.

510 Grant St., Iowa City, IA 52240

LEWIS, ROBERT HALL
b. Portland, Oreg., 22 Apr. 1926. Studied with Bernard Rogers, Howard Hanson, Eastman School of Music, B.M.; with Nadia Boulanger in Paris; with Karl Schiske, Hans Erich Apostel in Vienna; also at Princeton Univ., Univ. of Rochester, Ph.D. His many honors include Posciuszko Found. Chopin award, 1951; Fulbright scholarship, 1955-57; Vienna Acad. prize, 1957; LADO prize, 1961; Guggenheim fellowship, 1966; Hinrichsen award, Columbia Univ., 1972; annual ASCAP awards from 1969; several scores selected by Philadelphia Orch. for presentation to the Peking Orch. on the Peking trip in Sept. 1973; Koussevitzky Music Found. grant, 1977, for "valuable contribution to the music of our time." He has been faculty member at Goucher Coll., from 1957; Peabody Cons., from 1958; Johns Hopkins Univ., from 1969; music director, Baltimore Chamber Music Society.

WORKS: ORCHESTRA: Acquainted with the night, with soprano solo, 1951; Prelude and finale, small orch., 1959; 2 symphonies, 1964, 1971; #2 Baltimore, 6 Oct. 1971; Designs for orch., 1964; 3 pieces for orch., 1966; concerto for chamber orch., 1967, rev. 1972; Intermezzi, 1973; Nuances II (commissioned by Nat. Whale Symposium, uses whale songs in slow movement), Indiana Univ., Nov. 1975, rev. version, Baltimore, 30 Mar. 1977; WIND ENSEMBLE: Observazioni II, winds, harp, keyboard, percussion, 1978; CHAMBER MUSIC: 2 string quartets, 1956, 1962; 5 songs for soprano, winds and piano, 1957; 5 movements for piano, 1960; Toccata, solo violin and percussion; Music for 12 players, 1965; trio for violin, clarinet, piano, 1966; brass quintet, 1966; Divertimento, 6 instruments, 1969; Tangents, double brass quartet, 1968; sonata for solo violin, 1968; Inflections I,, contrabass solo, 1969; Inflections II, piano, 1970; Serenades, piano, 1970; Monophony I-IX, for various solo instruments, 1966-72; Combinazioni, clarinet, violin, cello, piano, 1973; Fantasiemusik, cello and piano, New York, 3 Dec. 1973; Duetto da camera, violin and piano, Washington, 4 Feb. 1977; Combinazioni III, oboe,

percussion, narrator, New York, 26 Mar. 1977; Inflections III, piano trio, Baltimore, 20 Feb. 1979; and choral works.

328 Broadmoor Rd., Baltimore, MD 21212

LICHTER, CHARLES
b. Philadelphia, Pa., 15 Jan. 1910. Studied at Juilliard School. He was staff violinist, conductor, and music consultant at CBS from 1936; music coordinator, Bell Telephone Hour. His works for orchestra include Romantic suite and Vermont summer.

LIEBER, EDVARD
b. Valley Stream, N.Y., 11 Apr. 1948. Studied at Manhattan School of Music and School of Visual Arts, New York; coaching with Iannis Xanakis and Karlheinz Stockhausen in New York and Cologne; piano with Rosa Lhevinne and Arthur Rubinstein. In addition to being an internationally acclaimed composer and pianist, he is also painter and filmmaker; was both cameraman and composer for several German films; is faculty member, School of Visual Arts.

WORKS: THEATRE: Neither Arakawa nor Jasper Jones are each other, chamber opera, New York, 8 May 1979; Untitled XIV, mime show, piano, celeste, and actors in a Punch and Judy box, New York, 8 May 1979; Trophy, orchestra, actors, film (based on paintings of Robert Rauschenberg), 1979; CHAMBER MUSIC: Berlinerstueck, piano, soprano, tapes (music from one of his German films), commissioned for the 1976 Berlin Festival; Homage to Franz Kline, piano, New York, 23 Feb. 1978; 24 de Kooning preludes, piano, 1978, New York, 18 Mar. 1979; Prelude to Jackson Pollock's "Autumn rhythm", piano, voices, tape, percussion, 1979; Introduction to the decomposition of emerging possibilities, 2 pianos, 1980.

114 Buchanan St., Centerport, NY 11721

LIEBERMAN, FREDRIC
b. New York, N.Y., 1 Mar. 1940. Studied with Thomas Canning, Louis Mennini, John LaMontaine, and Wayne Barlow, Eastman School of Music, B.M.; ethnomusicology at Univ. of Hawaii, M.A., and Univ. of California, Los Angeles, Ph.D. He was faculty member at Brown Univ., 1968-75; from 1975, at Univ. of Washington.

WORKS: CHAMBER MUSIC: piano suite; piano sonatina; 2 short string quartets; Leaves of brass, brass quartet; Card music for John Cage; CHORUS: By the waters of Babylon; Psalm 147.

School of Music, Univ. of Washington, Seattle, WA 98195

LIEBERMAN, GLENN
b. New York, N.Y., 29 May 1947. Studied with Charles Wuorinen, Ludmila Ulehla, Howard Rovics, Manhattan School of Music.

WORKS: ORCHESTRA: T for orchestra; CHAMBER MUSIC: Piece, for chamber orch. and tape; woodwind and string quintet; trio for flute, clarinet, and cello; piano suite; duos for clarinet and bass clarinet; violin sonata.

302 W. 79 St., New York, NY 10024

LIEBERSON, GODDARD
b. Hanley, Staffordshire, England, 5 Apr. 1911;
to U.S. 1915; d. New York, 29 May 1977. Studied
with George F. McKay, Univ. of Washington; with
Bernard Rogers, Eastman School of Music; received
honorary doctorates from Temple Univ. and Cleveland Inst. of Music. He was on the staff,
Masterworks Dept., Columbia Records, 1939–56;
president, Columbia Records, 1956–66; senior
vice-president, Columbia Broadcasting System,
1971–73; president, CBS Records Group, 1973–77.
CBS gave a $300,000 grant to the American Acad.
and Inst. of Arts and Letters to establish the
Goddard Lieberson fellowships for outstanding
young composers.
WORKS: THEATRE: music for Alice in Wonderland, 1936; Yellow poodle, ballet, 1937; ORCHES-
TRA: 5 modern painters, suite, 1929; 2 Chassidic dances, 1929; Tango, piano and orch.,
1936; Homage to Handel, string orch., 1937;
symphony, 1937; CHAMBER MUSIC: Suite for 20
instruments, 1928; Sonata for quintet, oboe,
bassoon, piano trio, 1934; string quartet, 1938;
CHORUS: 3 Chinese poems; songs to texts of Ezra
Pound, James Joyce, et al.; PIANO: Complaints
of the young, 1932; 9 melodies, 1933; Piano
pieces for advanced children or retarded adults,
1965. He was author of music criticism and
articles in music journals; and a novel, 3 in
bedroom C.

LIEBERSON, PETER
b. New York, N.Y., 25 Oct. 1946. Studied at New
York Univ., B.A. 1970; with Charles Wuorinen and
Harvey Sollberger, Columbia Univ., M.A. 1973;
informally with Milton Babbitt. His awards include the Rapoport prize, 1972; Charles Ives
scholarship, Nat. Inst. of Arts and Letters,
1973; Nat. Endowment for the Arts grant, 1975.
He was production engineer, WNCN-FM, New York,
1969–71; musical assistant to Leonard Bernstein,
1972–73.
WORKS: ORCHESTRA: cello concerto, New
York, 15 Apr. 1974; CHAMBER MUSIC: Variations,
solo flute, 1971; Mottetti (di Eugenio Montale),
soprano, alto, clarinet, bass clarinet, harp and
piano, 1971–72; concerto for 4 groups of instruments, Tanglewood, 1973; Fantasy, piano; Accor-
dance, 9 players, 1976; Tashi, clarinet, violin,
cello, piano, New York, 30 Apr. 1979.
2 Soldiers Field Park, Boston, MA 02163

LIEBLING, LEONARD
b. New York, N.Y., 7 Feb. 1874; d. New York,
28 Oct. 1945. Studied at City Coll. of New
York; piano with Leopold Godowsky; with Franz
Kullack in Berlin. He was staff member of the
Musical Courier, 1902–11, editor-in-chief, 1911;
music critic, New York American, 1923–37. He
composed chamber music, piano pieces, songs.

LIEURANCE, THURLOW
b. Oskaloosa, Iowa, 21 Mar. 1878; d. Boulder,
Colo., 9 Oct. 1963. Studied at Cincinnati Coll.
of Music, D.M.; and in Fontainebleau, France,
on scholarship. He received an award from the
American Scientific Research Society for his
study of American Indian music. He was band-

master in the Spanish-American War; toured in
concerts with his wife, a singer, 1918–27; was
professor, Univ. of Nebraska, 1922–40; Univ. of
Wichita, 1940–57.
WORKS: ORCHESTRA: Colonial Exposition
sketches; Prairie sketches; Water moon maiden;
CHAMBER MUSIC: Fantasia, violin and piano;
SONGS: By the waters of the Minnetonka; Hail
Wichita; many other songs on Indian themes.

LIFCHITZ, MAX
b. Mexico City, 11 Nov. 1948; to U.S. 1966.
Studied with Luciano Berio, Juilliard School,
B.M. 1970, M.A. 1971; with Leon Kirchner and
Arthur Berger, Harvard Univ., M.M. 1973; with
Bruno Maderna at Tanglewood and Darius Milhaud
at Aspen School. His awards include 2 Milhaud
awards, 1967, 1968; Richard Rogers scholarship,
1968; C. D. Jackson prize, 1972; fellowships as
follows: Irving Berlin, 1969, 1970, Juilliard
School, 1968–70, Tanglewood, 1972, Harvard Univ.,
1971–74, Michigan Univ. Society of Fellows, 1974–
77; grants from Nat. Endowment for the Arts,
1975, New York CAPS, 1978; and numerous commissions. He was pianist with the Juilliard Ensemble, 1968–73; has been faculty member, School
for Contemporary Music, Boston, 1973–74; Manhattan School of Music, 1976–77; from 1977, at
Columbia Univ.
WORKS: THEATRE: Bluebells, dramatic musical, Boston, 26 Mar. 1973; BAND: Mosaico
Mexicano, 1979; CHAMBER MUSIC: duo, violin and
cello, 1966; Fibers, small wind ensemble, 1967;
Solo, chamber ensemble, 1967; Pieza, 3 pianos,
1968; Tiempos, chamber orch., New York, 29 Nov.
1970; Consorte, viola and viola d'amore, 1970;
Mosaicos, chamber group, 1971; Fantasia, piano
trio, New York, 20 Feb. 1972; Roberta, chamber
orch., St. Paul, 14 Oct. 1972; Sueños, chamber
orch., 1974; I got up, trombone, double bass,
percussion, tape, 1974; Exploitations, 12
players, 1975; Intervención, 21 players, 1976;
Explorations, woodwind trio and piano, 1976;
Rebellions, 2 pianos, 2 percussionists, 1976;
Exceptional string quartet, 4 double basses,
1977; Music for percussion, 5 players, 1977;
Ethnic mosaic, flute, bassoon, piano, 1978;
Episodes, double bass and piano, 1978; Rhythmic
soundscape, piano and percussion, 1978; Transformations, solo cello, 1979; Winter counterpoint, 3 woodwinds, viola, piano, 1979; also
piano works and vocal pieces.
862 West End Ave., New York, NY 10025

LILIENFELD, CHARLES STEPHEN
b. Minneapolis, Minn., 9 Nov. 1944. Studied
with Paul Fetler and Dominick Argento, Univ. of
Minnesota; with Alan Stout, Northwestern Univ.
He is a private teacher.
WORKS: ORCHESTRA: symphony, 1975; CHAMBER
MUSIC: Romance, cello and piano; 4 piano
suites, 1966, 1967, 1969, 1971; 4 piano sonatas,
1971, 1974, 1975, 1977; suite for 7 wind instruments, 1976.
2893 Knox Ave. S., Minneapolis, MN 55408

LINCOLN, ROBERT DIX
b. Woodstock, Ohio, 3 Dec. 1924. Studied with

Carl Hugo Grimm, Univ. of Cincinnati, B.M. 1949, M.M. 1950; with Nadia Boulanger in Paris, 1952, 1954-55. He held a Franch government fellowship, 1954; Fulbright award, 1954. He was faculty member, East Tennessee State Univ., 1950-57; professor, Douglass Coll., from 1957, and Rutgers Univ., from 1960.

WORKS: THEATRE: incidental music for The Trojan women; CHAMBER MUSIC: trio for viola, cello, double bass; sonata for strings; Variations with a theme, 2 pianos; Arioso, string orch.; Etude, 2 pianos; CHORUS: mass for women's voices and orch.; Alleluia, women's voices and instruments.

251 Lawrence Ave., Highland Park, NJ 08904

LINDENFELD, HARRIS
b. Benton Harbor, Mich., 15 May 1945. Studied with Walter Ross and Donald MacInnis, Univ. of Virginia, B.A. 1970, M.A. 1971; with Burrill Phillips, Karel Husa, Robert Palmer, Cornell Univ., D.M.A. 1975. His awards include the Philip Slates award, 1971; first prize, Univ. of Virginia Unions Fine Arts contest, 1972; fellowship, Johnson Composers Conf., 1977; Meet the Composer grants, 1977; 2 Huber Found. awards, 1977-78; Yaddo residence, 1978; Nat. Endowment for the Arts grant, 1978. He has been faculty member, Hamilton Coll. (formerly Kirkland Coll.), from 1976.

WORKS: ORCHESTRA: piano concerto, 1972; The war prayer, with chorus, soloists, and narrator, 1975; BAND: symphonia, 1971; Directions, 1974; CHAMBER MUSIC: Tritogenea, brass quintet, 1970; Phonebeams, trombones and percussion, 1973; Combinations I: The last gold of perished stars, trumpet and percussion, 1974; Combinations II: Leones Somnians, trombone and percussion, 1975; Cunniculum lucis, oboe, clarinet, viola, piano, 1977; VOICE: 3 songs on texts of Roethke, soprano and piano, 1973; From the book of pictures, soprano and chamber ensemble, 1977.

Minor Hall, Hamilton College, Clinton, NY 13323

LINDH, JODY WAYNE
b. Lindsborg, Kans., 25 Feb. 1944. Studied at Bethany Coll., Kans.; with Lloyd Pfautsch and Carlton R. Young, Southern Methodist Univ.; with Michael Schneider in Cologne, Germany, on a Fulbright-Hays grant, 1968-69. He has been music director and organist, Univ. Park Methodist Church, Dallas, from 1969; was lecturer, Southern Methodist Univ., 1972-75.

WORKS: CHORUS: If thou but suffer God to guide thee, 1971; At the Lord's table, hymn accompaniment, 1972; Psalm 47, 1973.

6411 Kenwood Ave., Dallas, TX 75214

LINN, ROBERT
b. San Francisco, Calif., 11 Aug. 1925. Studied with Halsey Stevens, Univ. of Southern California, M.M.; also with Darius Milhaud and Roger Sessions. His honors include awards from Phi Mu Alpha, 1950; Nat. Fed. of Music Clubs, 1951; Calif. Fed. of Music Clubs, 1952; Louisville Orch., 1955; Los Angeles Chamber Music Symph., 1956; grants from the MacDowell Assoc., 1963,

Huntington Hartford Found., 1964, Alchin Found., 1969; and many commissions. He has been faculty member, Univ. of Southern California, from 1956.

WORKS: ORCHESTRA: overture, 1952; symphony in 1 movement, 1956, rev. 1961; The hexameron, orchestration reconstructed from Liszt's piano version of 1837, 1963; sinfonia for strings, 1967; concertino for oboe, horn, percussion, string orch., 1973; Fantasia, cello and string orch., Los Angeles, 12 Apr. 1976; CHAMBER MUSIC: clarinet sonata, 1949; 5 pieces, flute and clarinet, 1950; string trio, 1950; string quartet, 1951; saxophone quartet, 1953; Adagio and allegro, chamber orch., 1956; horn quartet, 1957; duo for clarinet and cello, 1959; Prelude and dance, saxophone quartet, 1960; suite for viola and cello, 1962; brass quintet, 1963; woodwind quintet, 1963; Dipthyramb, 8 celli, 1965; concertino, violin and wind octet, 1965; Ayre and ground, solo cello, 1968; duo for cello and piano, 1971; Fanfares, 3 clarinets, 1972; Vino, violin and piano, 1975; 7 canons, solo clarinet, 1976; Sonra sinfona, 12 instruments, Los Angeles, 7 Mar. 1977; CHORUS: 3 madrigals, 1951; An anthem of wisdom, with orch., Los Angeles, 23 Oct.,1958; Pied Piper of Hamelin, with narrator, tenor solo, and orch., 1968; Home from the sea, on poems of Robert Louis Stevenson, 1976; John Burns of Gettysburg, ballad on text by Bret Harte, with narrator and piano, Torrance, Calif., 16 May 1976; KEYBOARD: 2 piano sonatas, 1955, 1964; Toccatina, organ; also band works.

3725 De Witt Dr., Los Angeles, CA 90068

LINTHICUM, DAVID H.
b. Baltimore, Md., 7 May 1941. Studied at Western Maryland Coll.; with Earle Brown and Stefan Grove, Peabody Cons., B.M. 1964; with Howard Brucker, Catholic Univ., M.M. 1969; with Ben Johnston and Mel Powell, Univ. of Illinois, D.M.A. 1972. He received the Marie K. Thatcher award, Peabody Cons., 1963, and 2 fellowships, Univ. of Illinois, 1970, 1971. He was faculty member, Westminster Choir Coll., 1969-70; Lone Mountain Coll., 1972-73; Univ. of Wisconsin, 1974-75.

WORKS: ORCHESTRA: Serie, 1969; Tropos, cello, strings, percussion, brass, 1972; CHAMBER MUSIC: Pour la flute suele, 1969; woodwind quintet, 1969; string quartet, 1969; Contingencies, alto flute and chamber orch., 1971; A quatre, flute, harpsichord, cello, percussion, 1972; VOICE: Ave Maria, male quartet, 1973; Requiem mass, 1973.

320 Hilltop Rd., Linthicum, MD 21090

LIPKIS, LARRY
b. Los Angeles, Calif., 27 July 1951. Studied with Alden Ashforth and Paul Reale, Univ. of California, Los Angeles; with George Rochberg, Ralph Shapey, and Chou Wen-chung, Univ. of Pennsylvania. He received the David Halstead prize and the Helen Weiss prize at Univ. of Penn.; and a commission from Moravian Coll., where he has been faculty member and resident composer from 1977.

WORKS: VOICE: Ariel, soprano, cello, piano; Of radishes and flowers, choir, solo

LIPSCOMB, HELEN

sopranos, strings, brass, and flute; <u>Cordelia's song</u>, mezzo-soprano and orch.
    R.D. 3, Bethlehem, PA 18015

LIPSCOMB, HELEN
    b. Georgetown, Ky., 20 Apr. 1921; d. Lexington, Ky., 4 Jan. 1974. Studied at Univ. of Kentucky, B.A. 1941, M.A. 1945; with Robert L. Sanders, Indiana Univ., 1944; and with Nadia Boulanger, Longy School, Cambridge, Mass. She won a Phi Mu Alpha award for a song. She taught piano and composition at Univ. of Kentucky for 5 years, and privately for 27 years.
    WORKS: CHAMBER MUSIC: <u>Design</u>, clarinet and string quartet; 3 clarinet trios; <u>Variations</u>, woodwind quintet; 3 solos for clarinet and piano; <u>2 by 2</u>, violin and cello; <u>Nocturne and waltz</u> for strings; CHORUS: <u>The ballad of William Sycamore</u>, baritone, male chorus, piano; many anthems; KEYBOARD: piano sonata; <u>Passacaglia and toccata</u>, organ; piano pieces. She also composed for the Univ. of Kentucky Modern Dance Group.

LIPTAK, DAVID
    b. Pittsburgh, Pa., 18 Dec. 1949. Studied with Samuel Adler, Eugene Kurtz, Warren Benson, Sydney Hodkinson, and Joseph Schwantner, Eastman School of Music, D.M.A. 1976. At Eastman he received the Howard Hanson award, 1974, Louis Lane award, 1975; McCurdy award, 1976. From 1976 he has been faculty member, Michigan State Univ.
    WORKS: ORCHESTRA: <u>Conserere</u>, 1976, later rev.; <u>Serenade</u>, small orch., 1976; CHAMBER MUSIC: flute sonata, 1973; <u>Encounter II</u>, woodwind quartet, 1975; <u>Aeriform</u>, cello and piano, 1975; <u>Feuillet d'album</u>, male voice, flute, tape, 1976; <u>Flaming angel</u>, bass trombone and harpsichord, 1976; <u>The wreckage of the Moon</u>, voice and piano, 1977; <u>Slapstück</u>, clarinet and piano, Paris, 1 June 1977; <u>Memoir</u>, clarinet, violin, piano, 1977; <u>Gemstone</u>, violin and piano, 1978; trio, horn, bass trombone, piano, 1978.
    Music Dept., Michigan State Univ., East Lansing, MI 48824

LISSAUER, FREDRIC DAVID
    b. Cleveland, Ohio, 26 Jan. 1945. Studied with Marcel Dick and Donald Erb, Cleveland Inst. of Music. His works include <u>Variations for piano</u>, performed at a Bennington Composers' Conf.
    13710 Shaker Blvd., Cleveland, OH 44120

LISSAUER, ROBERT
    b. New York, N.Y., 1 May 1917. Studied with Bernard Wagenaar at Juilliard School; Schillinger system at New York Univ. He wrote scores for army shows; taught at New York Univ.; Eastern Cons.; Newark Cons., 1948-52; from 1940, has been in music publishing.
    WORKS: ORCHESTRA: sinfonietta; <u>2 preludes</u>, concertina and orch.; CHAMBER MUSIC: string quartet; woodwind quintet; and popular songs.

LIST, GARRETT
    b. 1943. <u>Your own self</u>, 3 voices, winds, 2 pianos, percussion, and bass; <u>9 sets of 7</u>, chamber orch., 1975; <u>Songs</u>, chamber orch., 1975; <u>Slugging rocks</u>, 1977; <u>The girls</u>, setting of a part of Studs Terkel's <u>Working</u>, small orch., with narrator, 1977.
    197 E. 4th St., NY 10009

LISTER, RODNEY
    b. Ft. Payne, Ala., 31 May 1951. Studied with Malcolm Peyton and Donald Martino, New England Cons., M.M. with honors 1973; at Tanglewood on fellowship, 1973.
    WORKS: CHAMBER MUSIC: <u>Music for a while</u>, flute, oboe, piano, 1971; <u>Nuns fret not</u>, soprano and 7 instruments, 1973; <u>The bell doth tolle</u>, bass, oboe, viola, trombone, vibraphone, 1973; <u>Agreeably of love</u>, soprano and piano, 1973; <u>My world and welcome to it</u>, contrabass, 1973.
    356 Somerville Ave., Somerville, MA 02143

LIVINGSTON, DAVID
    b. Corbin, Ky., 10 Jan. 1925. Studied with Weldon Hart and Roy Harris, Western Kentucky Univ.; Kenneth Wright, Univ. of Kentucky; and with Marshall Barnes, Ohio State Univ., D.M.A. His string quartet won a Phi Mu Alpha award. He taught in public schools, Frankfort, Ky., 1952-63; from 1965, has been on faculty, Western Kentucky Univ.
    WORKS: ORCHESTRA: symphony; <u>Theme and variations</u>; WIND ENSEMBLE: <u>Adagio</u>, 4 trombones; <u>Pastorale for winds</u>; <u>Prelude and fugue</u>; <u>Mirage</u>; symphony #1; <u>Killarney holiday</u>; <u>Clarinata</u>; <u>Saxville</u>; <u>Elkhorn Creek</u>, band; <u>Woodwind wonderland</u>, woodwind choir.
    2325 Bellevue Dr., Bowling Green, KY 42101

LIVINGSTON, JULIAN R.
    b. Spencer, Inc., 25 Aug. 1932. Studied with Bernhard Heiden, Indiana Univ. He was choir director in Murray Hill, N.J., 1960-63; from 1976, director of Elysium Chorale and Sinfonia Pro Musica of Battleground Arts Center, Freehold, N.J.
    WORKS: OPERA: <u>Twist of treason</u>, based on life of Benedict Arnold, 1977; ORCHESTRA: <u>Paleophony</u>, 1975; CHAMBER MUSIC: trio for English horn, flute, cello, 1974; <u>Ann Rutledge</u>, song cycle, women's voices, 1976; <u>Rondo brilliant</u>, 2 pianos, 1976; piano sonata, 1977.
    27 Highland Dr., Englishtown, NJ 07726

LLOYD, ALAN
    b. Baltimore, Md., 10 Jan. 1943. Studied with Donald Keats, Antioch Coll., B.A. He received a Tony nomination for best score and lyrics for <u>A letter from Queen Victoria</u>, 1975. He has been music director, Byrd Hoffman Found.
    WORKS: THEATRE: music for <u>The life and times of Sigmund Freud</u>; <u>Deafman glance</u>; and other stage works by Robert Wilson; <u>Angies waltz</u>, ballet; KEYBOARD: <u>The druid's harp</u>; <u>Virelai</u>; <u>The ostrich entrance</u>; <u>The cat up the tree in the terrible wind</u>; <u>The recluse</u>.
    58 E. 3rd St., New York, NY 10003

LLOYD, CAROLINE PARKHURST
    b. Uniontown, Ala., 12 Apr. 1924. Studied with John D. Robb, Univ. of New Mexico, B.M.; with Bernard Rogers, Eastman School of Music; with

Donato Fornuto, Arpad Szabo, and Charles Wuorinen, Columbia Univ., 1973. She held a Sigma Alpha Iota scholarship, 1944. She was private teacher, 1946-73; musical activities director, Centro Venezolano Americano, Caracas, 1955-68; organist and choral director.

WORKS: OPERA: Dona Barbara, given 8 performances in 1967 to commemorate the 400th anniversary of Caracas; Dona Rosita la Soltera, based on Garcia Lorca drama; 2 children's songs from the opera were performed in Washington, D.C., 4 Nov. 1976; SONGS: 3 songs of the Bolivar countries, 1965; 3 songs on poems of Garcia Lorca, 1966; 2 songs on poems of Jose Ramon Medina, 1968; other works for solo voice, chorus, keyboard, string quartet.

Plaza del Sol 3500, Apt. 1917, Galt Ocean Dr., Ft. Lauderdale, FL 33308

LLOYD, GERALD J.
b. Lebanon, Ohio, 6 Sept. 1938. Studied with Scott Huston, Jeno Takacs, Cincinnati Coll. Cons.; Bernard Rogers, Eastman School of Music; and with Everett Hafner, Electronic Music Studios, Amherst. His awards include 2 Rockefeller Found. performance grants and commissions. He was faculty member, Western Michigan Univ., 1966-69; School of Performing Arts, San Diego, 1969-71; Drake Univ., 1971-75; from 1976, at Capital Univ.

WORKS: ORCHESTRA: Associations I; concertino for piano and orch.; CHAMBER MUSIC: L'evenement, trumpet and piano; 3 sketches, tuba and piano.

Music Dept., Capital Univ., Columbus, OH 43209

LLOYD, NORMAN
b. Pottsville, Pa., 8 Nov. 1909. Studied with Vincent Jones, New York Univ., B.S., M.A.; privately with Aaron Copland. His awards include honorary doctorates from Philadelphia Cons., 1963, New England Cons., 1965, Peabody Cons., 1973; annual ASCAP awards from 1962; many commissions. He was faculty member, New York Univ., 1936-45; Sarah Lawrence Coll., 1936-46; Juilliard School, 1946-63; Oberlin Coll. Cons., 1963-65; director of arts and humanities, Rockefeller Found., 1965-73.

WORKS: BALLET: Panorama, for Martha Graham; Lament, for Doris Humphrey; La Malinche, for Jose Limon; BAND: A Walt Whitman overture; CHAMBER MUSIC: 3 pieces for violin and piano; Episodes, piano; piano sonata; 3 scenes from memory, piano; VOICE: Songs for a summer's end; Restless land, a choral ballet; Nocturne for voices. His published books include The fireside book of folksongs; The golden encyclopedia of music; and Keyboard improvisation, 1973.

Richmond Hill Rd., Greenwich, CT 06830

LOARIE, PHILIP WILLARD
b. Deerfield, Ill., 7 Feb. 1952. Studied with Alan Oldfield and Will Gay Bottje, Southern Illinois Univ., B.S. 1974; with Robert Ashley and David Behrman, Mills Coll., M.F.A. 1977. He received a teaching fellowship at Mills Coll., 1976; Elizabeth Mills Crothers prize, 1977. He

has worked in audio-visual techniques since 1972. As a composer he has developed self-programming electronic instruments, using the principles of harmonics and symbols generated by algorithms and cybernetic systems.

WORKS: Digital dronezilla (with random raga logic), 1977, is a 6-voiced instrument with pitch changes centering on the first 15 harmonics of a reference frequency to which all oscillations are tuned; the work is usually played through "tubatrons"--speakers inserted into plexiglass tubes which are carried by dancers who move them around, exploring reverberations, standing waves, and doppler shift effects, thus making space as well as time an essential part of the performance. Sundriven dronezilla, 1976, the first of the zilla series, is an analog device with 12 oscillators whose pitch is controlled directly by the amount of light reaching it. Digital lunch, 1979, a 4-voiced, anti-drone, digital frequency multiplier/divider capable of generating complex pulsing and long sustained sounds, won a prize at the 1979 Sonavera Internat. Tape Music Competition. In addition to the 6-8 works in the zilla instrument series, he has composed numerous scores for films (his own and other's), usually on commission. In his early days, he composed pieces for string trio, piano, violin and piano, chamber ensembles, etc.

126 Moss Ave., Oakland, CA 94611

LOBINGIER, CHRISTOPHER CRUMAY
b. Danville, Pa., 5 Feb. 1944. Studied with Charles Surinach, Carnegie Inst. of Technology, 1966-67; with Nikolai Lopatnikoff, Carnegie-Mellon Univ., 1967-68; with Nadia Boulanger in Paris, 1968-69; and with Robert Hall Lewis, Peabody Cons., 1973-74.

WORKS: ORCHESTRA: Epitaph, 1967; CHAMBER MUSIC: Qui n'est pas ne, cello and piano, 1968; trio for clarinet, trombone, piano, 1968; 2 pieces, for piano trio, 1970; string quartet, 1973; KEYBOARD: Rondo a "camp," piano, 1966; piano sonata, 1967; Nuptial colors, organ, 1969; 5 galactic dances, piano, 1974; and songs.

2745 N. Calvert, #1 R, Baltimore, MD 21218

LOBODA, SAMUEL
b. Coy, Pa., 21 May 1916; d. Oakton, Va., 13 June 1977. Studied at Indiana Univ. of Pennsylvania, B.S. 1936, honorary doctorate 1975; Army Music School, 1943. His awards included the Army Commendation Medal and the Legion of Merit, 1971. He was executive officer of the Army Music School; organized the U.S. Army Chorus, 1956; assistant conductor of the U.S. Army Band; was promoted to colonel in 1969, the first to attain that rank while serving solely as commander and musical director of a military band.

WORKS: BAND: Night of the miracle, a Christmas drama for band and chorus, won an Emmy in 1964 and in 1965; official marches for Kiwanis International and American Legion; The broadcasters' march for Nat. Assoc. of Broadcaters; Screaming eagles march; The arrow and the star march; Freedom's foundation march; Medal of honor march; CHORUS: Lift up your

LOCKLAIR, DAN

heads; The story of the stranger; FILM SCORES:
O'er the ramparts we watched, the story of the
national anthem for the Maryland Pavilion at the
1965 New York World's Fair; was composer and
arranger of more than 600 scores.

LOCKLAIR, DAN
b. Charlotte, N.C., 7 Aug. 1949. Studied at
Mars Hill Coll., B.M. cum laude; Union Theological Seminary, S.M.M.; with Joseph Goodman and
Gerre Hancock in New York; with Ezra Laderman,
State Univ. of New York at Binghamton. His
awards include the Crisp award, 1971; first
prize, D.C. chapter, American Guild of Organists
contest, 1972; Martha Baird Rockefeller grant,
1978. He was faculty member, Hartwick Coll.,
1973-74; from 1973, church musician, First
Presbyterian Church, Binghamton; and from 1974,
Binghamton dean of the Syracuse Catholic Diocese's organist training program.
     WORKS: OPERA: Good tidings from the holy
beast, 1977, Lincoln, Nebr., 21 Dec. 1978;
ORCHESTRA: Mirrors and reflections, double
string orch.; WIND ENSEMBLE: Modal suite for
brass; alto saxophone concerto, 1977; CHAMBER
MUSIC: A suite upon spring, 2 flutes and oboe,
1978; CHORUS: All my heart this night rejoices;
Prayer of supplication and thansgiving, 1972;
In praise of Easter, cantata for soloists, choir,
brass, organ; O God of Earth and altar; ORGAN:
Triptych for manuals, 1977; organ sonata, 1977;
other works for solo voice, band, etc.
     139 Matthews St., Binghamton, NY 13905

LOCKSHIN, FLORENCE LEVIN
b. Columbus, Ohio, 24 Mar. 1910. Studied with
Morris Wilson, Ohio State Univ., B.A. 1931; with
Alvin Etler, Smith Coll., M.A. 1953. She was
chosen composer-performer to represent Ohio at
the Nat. Fed. of Music Clubs Biennial, 1951;
named honorary life member, American Fed. of
Musicians, 1951. She was a private teacher and
performer, 1924-45; member of a 4-piano team,
1945-55.
     WORKS: ORCHESTRA: The cycle, ballet, 1956;
Song form, 1961; Paean, Mexican folk song, 1962;
Aural, 1964; Introduction, lament and protest,
1967; Fantasy on a Negro folktune, 1969; Scavarr,
American Indian tune, 1970; Do not go gentle
into that good night, 1973; Cumbia, Colombia
folk dance, 1977.
     Baker Hill, Northampton, MA 01060

LOCKWOOD, ANNEA F.
b. Christchurch, New Zealand, 29 July 1939; to
U.S. 1973. Studied at Univ. of Canterbury, New
Zealand, B.M.; with Peter Racine Fricker, Royal
Coll. of Music, London, at Musikhochschule,
Cologne, Germany; Electronic Music Center,
Bilthoven, Holland; and in Darmstadt. Her
awards include a German Acad. Exchange grant,
1963; Great Britain Arts Council grants, 1970,
1972, 1973; Gulbenkian award, 1972; New York
CAPS award, 1977; MacDowell fellowship, 1979.
She was lecturer in England, 1971-73; on coming
to the U.S. in 1973, joined the faculty at Hunter
Coll., CUNY.
     WORKS: ORCHESTRA: violin concerto, 1965;

INSTRUMENTAL: A Abélard, Héloise, mezzo-
soprano and 10 instruments, 1962; Aspect of a
parable, baritone and 12 instruments, 1963;
Glass concert I, 1967 and Glass concert II, 1969,
both scored for glass of many types from armor
plate to glass mobiles, recorded as The glass
world of Anna Lockwood; Dark touch, tactile-
aural equipment, 1970; Gentle grass, ritual for
6 players, 1970; ELECTRONIC TAPE: Love Field,
lament for John F. Kennedy, 1964; World rhythms,
1975; Cloud music, dance score, 1975; INSTALLA-
TIONS: Piano drowning, permanently installed in
a lake in Amarillo, Tex., 1972; River archive:
Play the Ganges backward one more time, Sam, the
Kitchen, N.Y., 1976; other works in many categories.
     Baron de Hirsch Rd., Crompond, NY 10517

LOCKWOOD, LARRY PAUL
b. Duluth, Minn., 18 June 1943. Studied with
James Beale, Univ. of Washington; Nicolas
Flagello, Ludmila Ulehla, David Diamond, Mario
Davidovsky, Manhattan School of Music, M.M.
1967; with Burrill Phillips and Robert Palmer,
Cornell Univ., D.M.A. 1973. His awards include
the Blackmore scholarship, 1972; Ludwig
Vogelstein Found. grant, 1974; Nat. Endowment
for the Arts grant, 1976. He was teaching
assistant, Cornell Univ., 1970-73; then orchestra
librarian, Manhattan School of Music; from 1978,
director, New York String Ensemble.
     WORKS: ORCHESTRA: Divertimento, 1967; sym-
phony, 1969; Canzona, strings, piano, cymbals,
1975; BAND: suite for band, 1973; CHAMBER MUSIC:
woodwind octet, 1967; sonata for 2 violins and
cello; Trio variations, flute, clarinet, violin;
Ricercar, flute and piano; duets, 2 percussionists, 1974; Choral partita, vibraphone and
marimba, 1974; Simple music, 2 treble instruments and piano, 1973; quartet for 2 pianos and
percussion, 1976; VOICE: 4 Psalms, soli, chorus,
orch.; 5 lullabies, solo voice, 1973; Epithalamia,
soprano, violin, piano, 1975; 5 love songs;
PIANO: 3 sonatas; sonata for 2 pianos; HARP:
Divisions upon a ground, 1977.
     172 W. 79th St., Apr. 11F, New York, NY
10024

LOCKWOOD, NORMAND
b. New York, N.Y., 19 Mar. 1906. Studied at
Univ. of Michigan; with Ottorino Respighi in
Rome, and with Nadia Boulanger in Paris. His
many awards include Rome prize, American Acad.
in Rome, 1929-32; Swift prize, 1934; World's
Fair prize, 1939; Coolidge award, 1941; 2
Guggenheim fellowships, 1943, 1944; Ditson award,
1944; Nat. Inst. of Arts and Letters award, 1945;
SPAM award, 1947; Ernest Bloch award, 1949; Phi
Mu Alpha Sinfonia honorary membership, 1969;
Colorado Governor's award, 1971; honorary doc-
torate, Berea Coll., 1974; many commissions. He
held faculty posts at Oberlin Coll., 1932-45;
Columbia Univ., 1945-48; Union Theological
Seminary, 1945-50; Westminster Choir Coll.,
1948-50; Yale Univ., 1950-53; Trinity Univ.,
Tex., 1953-55; Univ. of Wyoming, 1955-57; Univ.
of Oregon, 1957-59; Univ. of Hawaii, 1960-61;
composer-in-residence, Univ. of Denver, 1961-74,

professor emeritus, 1975.

WORKS: OPERA: The scarecrow, 1945; Early dawn, 1961; The wizards of Balizar, 1962; The hanging judge, 1964; Requiem for a rich young man, 1 act, 1964; THEATRE: Land of promise, staged oratorio; music for 16 plays; WIND ENSEMBLE: 2 concertos for organ and brass, 1950, 1970; From an opening to a close, winds and percussion, 1967; CHAMBER MUSIC: Moby Dick, chamber orch., 1946; clarinet quintet, 1960; flute sonata; Fun piece, wind quintet; 8 pieces, for 2 trumpets; 6 string quartets; 6 serenades, string quartet; sonata for 3 cellos; Sonata-fantasia, accordion; piano quintet; trio for flute, viola, harp; PIANO: Fantasy; sonata for 2 pianos; fugue-sonata; Lyric arabesque; ORGAN: sonata; Stopping on a walk to rest; numerous choral works.

P.O. Box 10053, University Park Sta., Denver, CO 80210

LOEB, DAVID H.

b. New York, N.Y., 11 May 1939. Studied with Peter Pindar Stearns, Mannes Coll. of Music; with Quincy Porter, Francis Judd Cooke, Yehudi Wyner, Yale Univ.; Otto Luening, Columbia Univ.; and with Aaron Copland, Wolfgang Fortner, and Witold Lutoslavski at Tanglewood. His awards include the Bohuslav Martinu award, 1961; Viola da Gamba Society award, London, 1966; citation by Chinese Classical Music Assoc., Taipei, 1971 and 1974; Society for Enjoyment of 20th-Century Music, Tokyo, 1972; annual ASCAP awards from 1965. He has been faculty member, Mannes Coll. of Music, from 1964; Curtis Inst. of Music, from 1973.

WORKS: ORCHESTRA: 2 symphonies; concerto for oboe and strings; Siddhartha; The wreck of the Hope; CHAMBER MUSIC: 4 songs for baritone and viola; quintet for clarinet, 2 violas, 2 cellos; 9 string quartets, #4, New York, 14 Nov. 1974; 3 sonatas for violin and viola; string octet; Prelude and 2 scherzi, bassoon solo; 4 preludes, violin solo; 3 sonatas for viola solo; 2 violin sonatas; 3 piano sonatas; sonata for timpani; many other chamber works; also some 100 compositions for Japanese instruments, 25 for Chinese instruments, both with scores in native and Western notation; 60 works for renaissance and baroque instruments.

233 W. 99th St., #7E, New York, NY 10025

LOESSER, FRANK

b. New York, N.Y., 29 June 1910; d. New York, 28 July 1969. Studied at City Coll. of New York, where he wrote songs for college shows. His awards for musicals include Academy award, 1949; Tony award, 1951; New York Drama Critics' Circle award for libretto to Most happy fella, 1957; Grammy award, 1962; Pulitzer, 1962. He was newspaper reporter, pianist, singer; wrote army shows in World War II, including Praise the Lord and pass the ammunition.

WORKS: MUSICALS: Where's Charlie?, 1948; Guys and dolls, 1950; The most happy fella, to own libretto, 1956; How to succeed in business without really trying, 1961; FILM SCORES: College swing; Destry rides again; Kiss the boys goodbye; 7 days leave; Thank your lucky stars; Happy-go-lucky.

LOEWE, FREDERICK

b. Berlin, Germany, of Austrian parents, 10 June 1904; to U.S. 1924. Studied piano with Busoni and D'Albert, composition with Reznicek in Berlin; then came to New York. He received Tony awards, 1947, 1957; Academy award for the film score, Gigi, 1958.

WORKS: MUSICALS: Salute to spring, 1937; Great lady, 1938; What's up?, 1943; The day before spring, 1945; Brigadoon, 1947; Paint your wagon, 1951; My fair lady, 1956; Camelot, 1960; many songs.

Palm Springs, CA 92262

LOGAN, FREDERICK KNIGHT

b. Oskaloosa, Iowa, 15 Oct. 1871; d. Oskaloosa, 11 June 1928. He is best known for composing Missouri waltz, c. 1916. After many successful years as a musical director and coach, he returned to Oskaloosa to spend time composing. His song, Iowa, proud Iowa, was adopted by the Iowa Fed. of Women's Clubs.

LOGAN, ROBERT

b. Beatrice, Nebr., 14 Feb. 1926. Studied with Francis Pyle, Drake Univ., B.M.E., M.M.E. He was a finalist in the Leblanc composition contests, Chicago, 1963. He taught in public schools, 1953-55; from 1955, has been music director, Clear Lake Jr. Coll.

WORKS: BAND: El chaco; Joi; Dimension, overture; Have horn will travel, solo with band; Presto chango; Sugar and spice.

519 North Shore Dr., Clear Lake, IA 50428

LOGAN, WENDELL

b. Thomson, Ga., 29 Nov. 1940. Studied at Florida A&M Univ.; at American Cons.,; with Will Bottje, Southern Illinois Univ., M.A. 1964; with Richard Hervig and Robert Shallenberg, Univ. of Iowa, Ph.D. He received a Nat. Endowment for the Arts grant, 1975. He was faculty member at Florida A&M Univ., 1963; Ball State Univ., 1967-69; Western Illinois Univ., 1970-73; from 1973, at Oberlin Cons.

WORKS: ORCHESTRA: Polyphony I, WIND ENSEMBLE: Music for brass; CHAMBER MUSIC: Stanzas for 3 players; Proportions, 9 players and conductor; 5 pieces for piano; 3 pieces for violin and piano; Electric time, percussion ensemble, Boston, 1 Apr. 1976; VOICE: Songs of our time, chorus and chamber orch., 1969; Ice and fire, song cycle; Song of the witchdoktor; MULTIMEDIA: From hell to breakfast, actors, dancers, musicians, electronic sounds, 1975.

167 S. Pleasant St., Oberlin, OH 44074

LOJEWSKI, HARRY VICTOR

b. Detroit, Mich., 23 Dec. 1917. Studied with Homer Grunn. He was pianist in dance orchestras; rehearsal pianist in film studios; since 1954, music supervisor, MGM feature and television films; choirmaster, Our Lady of Lourdes Church, Northridge, Calif. His compositions include Americana mass, for chorus, organ, and guitar.

LOHOEFER, EVELYN

LOHOEFER, EVELYN (pseudonym)
b. Clinton, N.C., 28 Dec. 1921. Studied at
Univ. of North Carolina, B.S.; on scholarship
at Bennington Coll.; with Sigismund Stojowski,
Norman Lloyd, and Vittorio Giannini at Juilliard
School. She was accompanist for a USO dance
tour of Europe, 1944; assistant to Norman and
Ruth lloyd, College School of Dance, New London,
Conn., 1954-59; then private teacher in New York
and Washington.
WORKS: BALLLET: Shakers; Pony tails;
Madeline and the bad hat; Modern fantasy; Con-
versation piece.

LOMBARDO, MARIO
b. Elizabeth, N.J., 30 May 1931. Studied at
Seton Hall Univ., B.A., M.A.; Columbia Univ.;
and privately. He was on the faculty, Seton
Hall Univ., to 1964.
WORKS: ORCHESTRA: Near nostalgia; Blue
interlude, piano and orch.; Remembrance of
things past, tone poem; Europe in jazz; Roxanne;
Variations in a mod mood, Cincinnati Symphony,
14 June 1972; and songs.

LOMBARDO, ROBERT
b. Hartford, Conn., 5 Mar. 1932. Studied with
Arnold Franchetti, Hartt Coll.; Philip Bezanson,
Univ. of Iowa; with Boris Blacher in Berlin;
Aaron Copland and Goffredo Petrassi at Tanglewood;
and with Guido Turchi in Rome. His awards include Koussevitzky prize at Tanglewood; 2 Nat.
Fed. of Music awards; 2 BMI awards; Sigma Alpha
iota award; 2 Ford Found. residency grants;
Gugenheim fellowship; Roosevelt Univ. research
grant; Nat. Endowment for the Arts grant, 1975;
and many commission. He has been composer-in-
residence and professor, Chicago Musical Coll.,
Roosevelt Univ., from 1964.
WORKS: OPERA: Sorrows of a supersoul,
chamber opera; The dodo, chamber opera on
ecology as seen through the eyes of vanishing
animals, 1975; ORCHESTRA: Threnody for strings;
Aphorisms; Sicilian lyric, 1976; BAND: In my
craft or sullen art, with narrator, Dylan
Thomas text; CHAMBER MUSIC: Largo, string quartet; Dialogues of lovers, chamber ensemble; Nocturne, contrabass solo, 1966; Aria and fragments,
cello and harp, 1973; Laude, fuga et cavatina,
piano; Watergate music, clarinet and piano, 1974;
2nd string quartet, 1974, Milwaukee, 18 May 1975;
Variations for 2 percussionists, 1975; duo for
trumpet and harp; Blues for cello alone, 1978;
VOICE: As the hart panteth, chorus; Frosted
windows, soprano, bassoon, percussion, viola,
1975; Erogenous zongs, soprano, piccolo, 2 flutes,
percussion, 1977.
1040 Wellington, Chicago, IL 60657

LOMON, RUTH
b. Montreal, Quebec, 8 Nov. 1930; U.S. citizen
1965. Studied at McGill Univ.; Quebec Cons.;
with Francis Judd Cooke, New England Cons.; and
with Witold Lutoslawski in Darlington, England.
She held fellowships at Yaddo, 1977, Wurlitzer
Found., Taos, N.M., 1978, and Ossabaw Island
Project, 1978. From 1973 she has been member of
a duo piano team giving lecture recitals of works

by women composers, as well as the standard
repertoire.
WORKS: CHAMBER MUSIC: Phase I, cello and
piano, 1969; Phase II, cello, piano, and soprano,
texts by Walt Whitman, 1975; Soundings, piano
duet, 1975; Dust devils, harp, 1976; Requiem for
brass and vocal quartet, 1977; The furies
(Erinnyes), oboe, oboe d'amore, English horn,
1977; Equinox, brass quartet, 1978.
18 Stratham Rd., Lexington, MA 02173

LONDON, EDWIN
b. Philadelphia, Pa., 16 Mar. 1929. Studied at
Oberlin Coll., B.M. 1952; with Philip Greeley
Clapp and Philip Bezanson, Univ. of Iowa, Ph.D.;
and with Luigi Dallapiccola and Darius Milhaud.
His awards include grants from the Guggenheim
Found., Univ. of Illinois, Center for Advanced
Study, and Nat. Endowment for hte Arts (2). He
was professor, Smith Coll., 1960-68; from 1968,
at Univ. of Illinois; visiting professor, Univ.
of California, San Diego, 1971-73.
WORKS: OPERA: Tala obtusities; Santa Claus;
The death of Lincoln, 1976; ORCHESTRA: Pressure
points, saxophone and orch.; Portraits of 3
American ladies, voice and orch.; Overture to
The imaginary invalid; WIND ENSEMBLE: Symphonic
movements for band; Lsinsame Blumen, brass choir;
CHAMBER MUSIC: brass quintet; trio for flute,
clarinet, piano; Song and dance, flute; woodwind
quintet; viola sonata; CHORUS: Bells, Poe text,
narrator, singers, percussion; Dream thing on
Biblical episodes; Enter madmen; Polonius plati-
tudes; The iron hand, oratorio on text derived
from Melville's The martyr, 1976; ELECTRONIC:
Geistliche Musik, 3 choruses, 3 instrumental
groups, and tape; Point of view; Hoopla!, tape;
Carnivore of Uranus, trombone, electronic cos-
tume, and tape.
910 West Hill St., Champaign, IL 61820

LONG, NEWELL H.
b. Markle, Ind., 12 Feb. 1905. Studied with
Winifred Merrill and Robert L. Sanders, Indiana
Univ. His awards include first prize, Illinois
Wesleyan Univ. contest, 1945; Huntington Hartford
Found. fellowships, 1961, 1965. He taught in
public schools, 1925-27, 1932-34; was trombonist
and arranger, 1928-29; band-orchestra director,
Central Michigan Univ., 1929-31; faculty member,
Indiana Univ., 1935-75.
WORKS: ORCHESTRA: Bravos for Benny, an
overture; Journey toward freedom, with chorus;
BAND: concertino for woodwind quintet and band;
Art show, suite; symphony; Christmas rhapsody;
Symphonie variations; Americana march, Red Rock
rhapsody; Descantation; Lincoln lyric overture;
Fanfare and fantasia; works for solo instruments
and ensembles.
1304 E. University, Bloomington, IN 47401

LOOMIS, CLARENCE
b. Sioux Falls, S.Dak., 13 Dec. 1888; d. Aptos,
Calif., 3 Jan. 1965. Studied at Dakota Wesleyan Univ., B.M.; with Adolf Weidig, American
Cons., M.A., D.M.; with Leopold Godowsky in
Vienna. He received the Kimball Gold Medal in
piano; Weidig Gold Medal in composition; and a

Lilly Found. grant. He taught at American Cons.,
1914; Chicago Musical Coll., 1929; Jordon Cons.,
1930-36; Highland Univ., 1945-55; Jamestown Coll.,
1955-56; then taught privately in Aptos, Calif.
    WORKS: OPERA: A night in Avignon; Castle
of gold; David; Yolanda of Cyprus; The fall of
the house of Usher; The white cloud, 1935; Revival, 1945; The captive woman, 1953; BALLET:
The flapper and the quarterback; Oak Street
Beach; THEATRE: music to King Lear; Susanna
don't you cry, musical extravaganza, 1939; OR-
CHESTRA: Gaelic suite for strings, 1953; Fantasy, piano and orch., 1954; The Passion play,
chorus and orch.; CHAMBER MUSIC: 2 string
quartets, 1953, 1963; CHORUS: Erin, choral
cycle; Song of the white earth, 1956.

LOOS, ARMIN
    b. Darmstadt, Germany, 20 Feb. 1904; U.S. citizen
1937; d. New Britain, Conn., 23 Mar. 1971.
Attended Univ. of Dresden, Berlin, and Geneva;
studied harmony and counterpoint with Paul
Buttner in Dresden. In 1928 he came to the U.S.
to complete training for his father's banking
business. In New York he taught himself composition and the 12-tone system successfully enough
to win second prize in a competition in which
the first prize went to William Schuman and the
third prize to David Diamond. The depression
shattered his hopes of earning a living in music,
and in 1940 he entered a family business in New
Britain, Conn., and continued to compose in his
spare time. Very few of his compositions were
heard in his lifetime, but his work is now highly
acclaimed by those participating in its performance.
    WORKS: ORCHESTRA: Ciaconna, 1932; overture,
1932; Symphony--in memoriam Ferruccio Busoni, New
Britain, Conn., 17 Mar. 1974; Symphony--view,
approach, goodbye; Missa spiritorum; Symphony in
canon form, 1941; Pastorale and perpetuum mobile,
1941; Psalm 120, with chorus, 1963; Percepts,
1969, Berkshire Music Center, 16 Aug. 1977;
Aquarius '70, New Britain, 16 Apr. 1972; CHAMBER
MUSIC: 4 string quartets, 1933-65, #4, Cambridge,
Mass., 31 Mar. 1974; string quintet; Idea in
search of configuration, piano trio, 1930-60; 2
pieces for horn and piano, 1963, Hartford, 3 Feb.
1974; piano and wind quartet, Hartford, 3 Feb.
1974; woodwind quintet #4, Boston, 15 Sept. 1974;
wind quintet; violin sonata, 1968, New Britain,
4 Feb. 1973; Study piece, horn, cello, piano,
1969; violin sonata #2, New Britain, 10 Feb.
1974; CHORUS: Elegy for 5 voices, 2nd prize,
Fed. of Music Project, 1938, performed and recorded through support of Conn. Commission on
the Arts, 26 May 1972; Psalm 120, a cappella;
SONGS: Triumph; Lebewohl; O Fair; PIANO: Barcarolle d'Hercule a Mooreux, 1929; 5 preludes,
1946; 3 sonatas, 1964, 1966, 1967; Fantasia,
1967; suite, 1967; 4 klavierstucke, 1967.

LOPATNIKOFF, NIKOLAI
    b. Reval, Estonia, 16 Mar. 1903; U.S. citizen
1944; d. Pittsburgh, Pa., 7 Oct. 1976. Studied
at Petrograd Cons., Helsingford Cons., and with
Ernst Toch in Berlin. After graduating from
Karlsruhe Technological Coll. as a civil en-

gineer, he decided to devote full time to music.
He came to New York in 1939. His many awards
in the U.S. include 2 Guggenheim fellowships;
first prize, Cleveland Orch. competition, 1943;
Nat. Inst. of Arts and Letters grant and election
to membership, 1963; ASCAP awards, 1972-74; many
commissions. He was faculty member at Hartt
Coll. of Music; Westchester Cons.; and at Carnegie-Mellon Univ., 1945-68.
    WORKS: OPERA: Danton, 1931-33; BALLET:
Melting pot, 1975; ORCHESTRA: 4 symphonies,
1929-72; Opus sinfonicum, 1941; sinfonietta,
1942; 2 piano concertos; violin concerto; Concertino for orchestra, 1945; 2 Russian nocturnes,
1945; concerto for 2 pianos; Variazioni concertanti, 1958; Music for orchestra, Louisville,
14 Jan. 1959; Concerto for wind orchestra, 1963;
CHAMBER MUSIC: 3 string quartets; 2 violin
sonatas; cello sonata; duo for viola and cello;
Variations and epilogue, cello and piano, 1946.

LOPEZ, P(ETER) DICKSON
    b. Berkeley, Calif., 8 July 1950. Studied piano
at California State Univ. at Hayward, B.A. 1972;
with Joaquin Nin-Culmell, Richard Felciano,
Edwin Dugger, Olly Wilson, Univ. of California,
Berkeley, M.A. 1974, Ph.D. 1978. He received
the George Ladd prize for study in France, 1976-
78.
    WORKS: CHAMBER MUSIC: Adagio for piano,
1973; 5 poems for piano, 1974; Intrections, 3
pianos and electronic sound, 1974-75; Scenes,
chamber orch., 1974-78; The ship of death, male
voice and chamber orch., 1976-77, served as his
Ph.D. thesis.
    2215 Santa Clara St., Richmond, CA 94804

LO PRESTI, RONALD
    b. Williamstown, Mass., 28 Oct. 1933. Studied
with Louis Mennini and Bernard Rogers, Eastman
School of Music. He has received awards from
Phi Mu Alpha, 1954, 1970; special Koussevitzky
award, 1955; Eastman School award for Sketch,
1956; Coll. Band Directors Nat. Assoc., 1957;
Syracuse Univ. Festival, 1960; Carl Fischer,
1961; Arizona State Univ. faculty grants, 1967,
1968, 1970; annual ASCAP awards, 1963-73; Nat.
Endowment for the Arts grant, 1974. He was
instructor, Texas Tech. Univ., 1959-60; Ford
Found. composer-in-residence, Winfield, Kans.,
1960-62; faculty member, Indiana (Pa.) State
Coll., 1962-64; from 1964, at Arizona State
Univ.
    WORKS: OPERA: 4 1-act operas; ORCHESTRA:
The masks, 1956; Kansas overture, 1963; Nocturne,
viola and string orch., 1965; 2 symphonies,
1966, 1968; WIND ENSEMBLE: suite for 8 horns,
1959; suite for 4 horns, 1960; suite for 5
trumpets, 1962; Miniature, brass quartet, 1964;
march for winds and drums, 1969; Pageant overture, band, 1963; Elegy for a young American,
band, 1967; CHAMBER MUSIC: duo for 2 horns,
1966; trombone trio, 1968; Rondo, timpani and
piano, 1972; CHORUS: Tribute, with orch., 1961;
Meditation, 1964; Alleluia, Christus natus est,
1965; Bell song, 1965; Night, 1972; many works
for school ensembles.
    200 E. Geneva Dr., Tempe, AZ 85281

LORA, ANTONIO

LORA, ANTONIO
b. Italy, 1899; to U.S. in early youth; d. 1965.
Studied piano with Alberto Jonas, composition
with Rubin Goldmark and Eduardo Trucco; with
Philip James and Albert Stoessel, New York Univ.,
1925-27; at Juilliard School on a fellowship,
1927-31. He made his debut as pianist in New
York in 1924; taught at Juilliard School, 1931-
36; then made extensive concert tours in Europe;
later joined the faculty at Ohio State Univ.
WORKS: THEATRE: Launcelot and Elaine, 1-
act opera based on Tennyson's Idylls of the King,
commissioned by the Cologne State Opera; The
legend of Sleepy Hollow, light opera; an operetta
for children; a ballet; ORCHESTRA: 2 symphonies;
piano concerto, 1948; many chamber works and instrumental pieces; some 50 songs.

LORENZ, ELLEN JANE (Mrs. James B. Porter)
b. Dayton, Ohio, 3 May 1907. Studied at Wesleyan Coll., B.A.; with Nadia Boulanger in Paris;
with Donald Keats at Antioch Coll. Her awards
include the Billings prize; Society of Women in
Liberal Professions award, Paris; 2 Mu Phi Epsilon awards; 4 Chapel Choir awards; Sigma Alpha
Iota award; and an award from American Guild of
English Handbell Ringers, Area II. She was
editor, Lorenz Pub. Co., 1932-68; director,
Dayton Madrigal Singers, 1945-68; from 1971, instructor, United Theological Seminary.
WORKS: THEATRE: Up on Old Smoky, operetta;
ORCHESTRA: Appalachian suite; 3 fairy tales;
overture; CHAMBER MUSIC: Japanese suite, flute;
4 short movements for viola; string quartet;
CHORUS: The silver hind, madrigal; Paul Bunyan,
cantata; Carols of Christmas, cantata; Stand in
awe; Beauty shop quartet; HANDBELLS: A festive
ring; many other works for orchestra, chorus,
chamber groups, organ, piano.
324 Oak Forest Dr., Dayton, OH 45419

LORENZO, LEONARDO DE
b. Viggiano, Italy, 29 Aug. 1875; to U.S. 1910;
d. Santa Barbara, Calif., 27 July 1962. Studied
at Naples Cons., 1897-1907. He played flute in
the New York Philharmonic, Minneapolis Symphony,
Los Angeles Philharmonic, Rochester Philharmonic;
taught flute at Eastman School of Music; retired
to Beverly Hills in 1935. He published books of
flute studies and My complete story of the flute,
N.Y., 1951.
WORKS: CHAMBER MUSIC: Divertimento fantastico, woodwind quartet; Idillio, flute and
piano; The Polish shepherd, flute and piano;
Trio eccentrico, woodwinds; Improviso, flute and
piano; Allegro di concerto, flute and piano;
Trio romantico, woodwinds; Suite moderne, 2
flutes; Capriccio, 4 flutes.

LOTH, LOUIS LESLIE
b. Richmond, Va., 28 Oct. 1888; d. New York
State, 3 June 1974. Studied piano and composition in Berlin; gave concerts in Germany, then
returned to the U.S. and lived in New York as
teacher and composer. His more than 500 compositions included 2 symphonies, 2 piano concertos, symphonic poems, numerous piano pieces.

LOURIE, ARTHUR VINCENT
b. St. Petersburg, Russia, 14 May 1892; U.S.
citizen 1947; d. Princeton, N.J., 13 Oct. 1966.
Studied at St. Petersburg Cons., 1909-16. He
was a writer on music and political topics for
Voice of America, 1947-66. His later compositions include The blackamoor of Peter the Great,
an opera, 1961; Concerto da camera, solo violin
and string orch., 1957; The mime, solo clarinet,
1956; Sibylla dicitur, cantata for women's
voices and instruments.

LOVELACE, AUSTIN C.
b. Rutherford, N.C., 26 Mar. 1919. Studied at
High Point Coll., A.B. 1939, D.M. 1963; at Union
Theological Seminary, N.Y., M.S.M. 1941, D.S.M.
1950. His faculty positions have been at Univ.
of Nebraska; Queens Coll., N.C.; Garrett Theol.
Seminary; Union Theol. Seminary; Temple Buell
Coll.; has been organist-choirmaster at various
churches, in 1973 at Lovers Lane Methodist
Church, Dallas. His works include more than 300
compositions for the church service. He is
author of several books on church music and of
articles in church music journals.

LOVELL, WILLIAM JAMES
b. Brooklyn, N.Y., 26 Oct. 1939. Studied with
Bain Murray, Julius Drossin, and Rudolph Bubalo,
Cleveland State Univ., B.M. magna cum laude 1972,
M.M. 1975. He was faculty member, Cleveland
Music School Settlement, 1971-73; from 1974,
assistant to chairman, music dept., Cleveland
State Univ.
WORKS: THEATRE: music for Lorca's Yerma,
1972; ORCHESTRA: East of Olduvai, Cleveland,
6 Apr. 1975; BAND: Overture for band, Cleveland,
3 Feb. 1974; CHAMBER MUSIC: Arabesque for reeds,
1970; string quartet, 1972; Intextimbegration,
1975; CHORUS: Because I could not stop for
death, with cello, 1971; Elegy, with chamber
orch., 1972; ELECTRONIC: A journey through the
percussive forest, percussion and tape, 1975;
Collaboration, tape and film, 1977.
5603 E. Pleasant Valley Rd., Independence,
OH 44131

LOVETT, GEORGE
b. Chicago, Ill., 29 July 1932. Studied at
Cleveland Inst. of Music and privately in New
York. He has received N.Y. State Council on the
Arts grants on the Meet the Composer program.
WORKS: ORCHESTRA: Conflict and consecra-
tion; overture; Greatest city in the world; symphonic suite on New York; Stevenson: A call to
greatness; Opus 10: Viewpoint, overture; Note
of triumph, small orch.; BAND: 3 short pieces;
The great American overture; A joyful noise;
CHAMBER MUSIC: Dramatic excursions, violin and
piano; 2 string quartets; Ruminations, flute and
piano; Reflections on a Robert Frost poem, voice
and piano.
325 W. 45th St., #905, New York, NY 10036

LOVINGGOOD, PENMAN, SR.
b. Texas, 25 Dec. 1895. Attended Samuel Huston
Coll.; Temple Univ. He was church soloist,
1928-32; member of W. C. Handy's group, 1930;

328

organized the Drum and Bugle Corp in Englewood, N.J., in 1942. He has received the Wanamaker prize and the Griffith Music Found. silver-bronze medal.

WORKS: OPERA: Menelik; Evangeline and Gabriel; and songs. He is author of Famous modern Negro musicians, N.Y., Da Capo Press, 1973.

LOWENS, IRVING
b. New York, N.Y., 19 Aug. 1916. Studied with Edwin John Stringham, Columbia Univ., B.S. 1939; Univ. of Maryland, M.S. 1957; also with Howard A. Murphy and Quinto Maganini. He was music critic, Washington Star, 1953-60, chief critic, 1961-79; reference librarian for sound recordings, Library of Congress, 1939-61; assistant head, reference section, music division, 1961-66; joined the faculty at Peabody Cons. in 1977 and was named dean in 1979.
WORKS: ORCHESTRA: Variations on a Peruvian theme; clarinet concertino; Fantasy for string orch., string quartet, and flute; CHAMBER MUSIC: The miller o'Fyfe, flute and piano; CHORUS: Laudate, women's voices; Sing, my tongue, the Saviour's glory; SONGS: Come away Death, Love is a sickness; Peasants; The rune of hospitality; Old Christmas returned; many choral arrangements of works by early American composers.
503 Heron House, Reston, VA 22090

LOWMAN, KENNETH E. W.
b. Walla Walla, Wash., 13 June 1916. Studied with Dorothy James, Eastern Michigan Univ.; and with Franklyn Marks in Los Angeles. He has been a free-lance composer for motion pictures and television.
WORKS: THEATRE: Chinese nightingale, children's musical; music for Finnegan's wake, woodwind trio; ORCHESTRA: Sea god and sandpiper, solo cello and oboe with orch.; suite for strings; CHAMBER MUSIC: Los Angeles sketches, oboe, clarinet, viola, bassoon; 10 etudes for bassoon; 3 pieces, for oboe and cello; trio for violin, viola, bassoon; Postcard suite, woodwind trio; Baroque and roll, piano and 3 woodwinds; sonata for 2 oboes; woodwind quintet; horn trio; Concert piece, for harp; The nobleman, narrator, 3 winds, 2 strings; Frog pond symphony, narrator and quintet; Variations for a mime, 3 winds, 2 strings; duo for violin and clarinet or oboe and bassoon.
P.O. Box 4261, Burbank, CA 91503

LOWREY, NORMAN EUGENE
b. Midland, Mich., 13 Jan. 1944. Studied privately with Samuel Jones; with Ralph Guenther, Texas Christian Univ.; with Samuel Adler, Warren Benson, Wayne Barlow, and Joseph Schwantner, Eastman School of Music, where he received the Louis Lane award in composition. Many of his works are commissioned. He was instructor, San Diego State Univ., 1971-72; on humanities faculty, Stephens Coll., 1972-76; from 1977, on music faculty, Drew Univ.
WORKS: THEATRE: incidental music to Twelfth night, 1964; ORCHESTRA: Sculpture, cello and orch., 1963; music on Shakespeare

sonnets, with soprano, 1964; Celebration overture, 1967; Kinetikos, 1968; Riff ram, 1973; A child's Christmas in Wales, on Dylan Thomas poem, with narrator, 1974; Breaking open, with women's chorus, on poems of Muriel Rukeyser, 1976; CHAMBER MUSIC: Perspectives, double woodwind trio, percussion, 1971; Solitary gestures, trumpet and narrator, 1972; ELECTRONIC: Elysium: Fragments and overlays, bassoon and tape, 1975; Waves, trumpet, narrator, tape, on texts of Virginia Woolf, 1977; Trumantra, 5 trumpets, tape, audience, 1978.
P.O. Box 17, Green Village, NJ 07935

LOY, D. GARETH
b. Los Angeles, Calif., 20 June 1945. Studied with Peter Sacco, Henry Onderdonk, Herbert Bielawa, George Burt, San Francisco State Univ. He held the Carla Reed scholarship, 1970-73. He was director, New Arts Forum, 1970-73; electronic music director, San Francisco State Univ., 1973.
WORKS: CHAMBER MUSIC: duet for violin and cello, 1972-74; MUSIQUE CONCRETE: Terraque, 1972; IOA, 1972; ELECTRONIC: Suggestions, percussion and tape, 1973; Towards the garden, synthesizer, 1973; Responsive reading #99, vocal quartet and synthesizer, 1974.
27A Delmar St., San Francisco, CA 94117

LU, YEN
b. Nanking, China, 7 Sept. 1930; to U.S. 1963. Studied with William Sydeman, Mannes Coll. of Music; with Mario Davidovsky, City Coll., CUNY. From 1971, she has been editor with a music publisher.
WORKS: ORCHESTRA: Music for orchestra I, 1969, II, 1970; CHAMBER MUSIC: Piece for 7 players, 1967; quartet for flute, bass trombone, piano, percussion, 1963; quartet for clarinet, tuba, 2 percussionists, 1970; violin sonata, 1972; Some days I toss in bed, mezzo-soprano and chamber ensemble, 1973.
c/o Seesaw Press, 1966 Broadway, New York, NY 10023

LUBIN, ERNEST
b. New York, N.Y., 2 May 1916; d. New York, 15 Mar. 1977. Studied with Nadia Boulanger, summer 1932, in Fontainebleau; Columbia Univ., B.S., M.S.; with Roger Sessions, Manhattan School of Music; also with Ernest Bloch and Darius Milhaud. He received a scholarship at Manhattan School; Bearns prize at Columbia, 1938; annual ASCAP awards for a number of years. He was music critic, New York Times, 1945, 1949-50; from 1959, taught at N.Y. High School of Performing Arts.
WORKS: OPERA: The pardoner's tale, 1 act; ORCHESTRA: Variations on a pastoral theme; BAND: Wayfaring stranger; CHAMBER MUSIC: 2 string quartets; trombone sonata; violin sonata; many choral works, songs, piano pieces.

LUBOFF, NORMAN
b. Chicago, Ill., 14 May 1917. Studied at Chicago Univ.; Central Coll., B.A.; with Leo Sowerby, American Cons. He taught at Central Coll.; was arranger and coach for radio shows in

LUCAS, THEODORE D.

Chicago; in 1948, joined the staff of Warner
Bros. in Hollywood. His works include African
mass for chorus and tuned drums, and many songs.
35 West Shore Dr., Port Washington, NY 11050

LUCAS, THEODORE D.
b. San Diego, Calif., 22 Jan. 1941. Studied
with David Ward-Steinman, San Diego State Univ.;
Gordon Binkerd and Thomas Frederickson, Univ. of
Illinois, Ph.D.; and with Nadia Boulanger in
Paris. He was faculty member, Univ. of Missouri,
1967-69; Beloit Coll., 1969-77; from 1978, at
Southwestern Univ.
    WORKS: CHAMBER MUSIC: sextet for horns;
Aberrations #7, piano; CHORUS: America--God
love it; ELECTRONIC: Trialog, flute, harpsichord,
tape; Meta-music, flute and tape, New York, 3
Mar. 1973.
    Music Dept., Southwestern Univ., Georgetown,
TX 78626

LUCIER, ALVIN
b. Nashua, N.H., 14 May 1931. Studied with David
Kraehenbuhl, Howard Boatwright, Quincy Porter,
Yale Univ.; with Arthur Berger, Harold Shapero,
and Irving Fine at Brandeis Univ.; with Lukas
Foss at Tanglewood; and with Boris Porena in
Rome on a Fulbright grant, 1960-62. He was
director, Brandeis Univ. Choral Union, 1962-70;
from 1970, director, of electronic music, Wesleyan
Univ.; from 1973, music director, Viola Farber
Dance Company. He was cofounder of the Sonic
Arts Union, a group for composition and performance of electronic theatre music.
    WORKS: THEATRE: music for The water of
Babylon, 1965; Fire! by John Roc; King Henry V,
1969; CHAMBER MUSIC: Action music, piano,
silently mimed tone clusters, 1962; Song for
soprano, 1962; ELECTRONIC: Music for solo performer, enormously amplified brainwaves used to
resonate percussion instruments, 1965; North
American time capsule, voices and Sylvania
vocoder, 1967; Vespers, acoustic orientation by
means of echolocation, 1967; Chambers, sounds
from moving resonant objects, 1968; The only
talking machine of its kind in the world, for
stutterer and tape delay system, 1969; Hartford
memory space, enviornmental mimicry for orchestra,
1970; I am sitting in a room, voice and tape,
1970; The Duke of York, alteration of vocal
identities, 1971; Gentle fire, 1971; The queen
of the south, for players, responsive surfaces,
strewn material, closed-circuit television
monitoring system, 1972; Room simulation i, The
bird of Bremen flies through the houses of the
burghers, a computer-controlled environment,
1972; Silent and moving lines of silence in
families of hyperboles, experiments with a sound
maze accomplished by creating interference
patterns with oscillator tones emanating from
audio speakers, New York, 21 Feb. 1975; Bird and
person dyning, live and recorded electronics,
1977; Directions of the sounds from the bridge,
investigates the subtleties ("shadows") in exact
resonances in musical instruments by sending
oscillator-produced tones into their bodies;
aural appreciation is enhanced by lighting and
positioning of the audience, 1978. He is author

of the book, Chambers, interviews on music and
environment.
    7 Miles Ave., Middletown, CT 06457

LUCKE, KATHARINE E.
b. Baltimore, Md., 22 Mar. 1875; d. Baltimore,
21 May 1962. Studied at Peabody Cons., diploma
1904; joined the Peabody faculty in 1919. Her
compositions included Family portrait, piano
and orch., performed by the U.S. Marine Symphony
Orch., Washington, 1950; a piano trio; numerous
published choral works and songs. Her highly
successful Keyboard harmony for piano was followed in 1959 by Keyboard harmony for organ.

LUCKMAN, PHYLLIS
b. New York, N.Y., 13 Sept. 1927. Studied at
Hunter Coll., B.A. 1947; with Fred Fox, California State Coll. at Hayward; with Darius
Milhaud at Mills Coll., M.A. 1973. She is a
private cello teacher.
    WORKS: ORCHESTRA: Symphony for massed
cellos; CHAMBER MUSIC: Fantasia, 2 flutes; 5
puzzles, solo clarinet; Hart Crane/Proem, solo
percussion; Spirals, harpsichord; Songs from
underground, tape and string quartet; Templates,
8 to 13 players; Severity, cello and piano, 1976.
    668 Fairmont Ave., Oakland, CA 94611

LUEDEKE, RAYMOND
b. Bronx, N.Y., 11 Nov. 1944. Studied with
George T. Jones, Catholic Univ.; with George
Crumb at Dartmouth Coll.; and in Vienna on a
Fulbright grant, 1966-67. He was faculty member,
Univ. of Wisconsin, Stevens Point, 1971-77; from
1978, at Univ. of Missouri.
    WORKS: ORCHESTRA: chamber symphony; BAND:
Paterson; CHAMBER MUSIC: Krishna, tuba and percussion; Pictures from Broughel, woodwind quintet, mezzo-soprano, baritone, brass trio; 8
bagatelles, 2 tubas; 15 inventions, 2 clarinets;
5 pieces, flute, cello, harp.
    4811 Bell St., Kansas City, MO 64110

LUENING, OTTO
b. Milwaukee, Wis., 15 June 1900. Studied at
Royal Acad. of Munich, 1915-17; with Volkman
Andreae, Zurich Municipal Cons., 1917-20;
privately with Philipp Jarnach and Ferruccio
Busoni. His honors include 3 Guggenheim fellow-
ships, 1930, 1931, 1974; chairmanship, American
Music Center, 1940-60; Nat. Inst. of Arts and
Letters grant, 1946, election to membership,
1947, vice-president, 1953; composer-in-residence,
American Acad. in Rome, 1958, 1961, 1965; honor-
ary doctorate, Wesleyan Univ., 1963; Laurel
Leaf, American Composers Alliance; Thorne Music
Fund award and citation, 1972; membership on
many boards and committees including USIA Music
Advisory Committee, UNESCO, from 1953. He was
cofounder, American Grand Opera Company, Chicago,
and conducted the first all-American opera performance, 1922; was director, opera dept.,
Eastman School of Music, and conductor, Rochester
American Opera Company, 1925-28; faculty member,
Univ. of Arizona, 1932-34; Bennington Coll.,
1934-44; Barnard Coll., 1944-47; Columbia Univ.,
1949-68, then professor emeritus; on faculty,

Columbia School of the Arts, 1968-70; codirector, Columbia-Princeton Electronic Music Center, from 1959. His autobiography was published, N.Y. 1980.
WORKS: OPERA: Evangeline, 1932-47, awarded the David Bispham Medal, 1933; ORCHESTRA: First music for orchestra, 1942; 2 symphonic fantasias, 1924, 1939; Fantasia, 1925; Serenade, 3 horns, string orch., 1927; 2 symphonic interludes, 1935; flute concertino, 1937; Pilgrims' hymn, 1947; Prelude, chamber orch., 1947; Legend, oboe and strings, 1951; Kentucky concerto, 1951; Music for orchestra, 1952, New York, 23 May 1978; Wisconsin suite, 1955; Lyric scene, flute and strings, 1958, Johnson, Vt., 23 Aug. 1972; Song, poem and dance, flute and strings, 1958; Short symphony, cham. orch., 1969; Sonority forms, 1973; Wisconsin symphony (NEA grant), Milwaukee, 3 Jan. 1976; CHAMBER MUSIC: sextet, 1918; 2 string quartets, 1919, 1928; trio, flute, violin, soprano, 1924; The soundless song, soprano, string quartet, flute, clarinet, piano, 1924; sonatas for many instruments; 8 tone poems for 2 violas, Albany, N.Y., 27 Jan. 1972; Introduction and allegro, trumpet and piano, New York, 12 Mar. 1972; ELECTRONIC: Fantasy in space, Low speed, Invention, all tape alone, 1952; Theatre piece #2, tape, voice, brass, percussion, narrator, 1956; Synthesis, tape and orch., 1960; Gargoyles, violin and tape, 1961; Sonority canon, 37 solo flutes or 4 solo flutes and tape, 1962; Moonflight, tape, 1967; Fugue, chorale, fantasy, organ with electronic doubles, 1973; No Jerusalem but this, excerpts performed, Johnson, Vt., 30 Aug. 1972.
460 Riverside Dr., New York, NY 10027

LUKE, RAY E.
b. Texas, 1926. Studied at Eastman School of Music, Ph.D. His awards include 3 MacDowell fellowships; Gold Medal and cash award, Queen Elizabeth of Belgium Internat. Competition, 1969, for his piano concerto; first place and $5,500 award, American Opera Competition, sponsored jointly by the New England Cons. and the Rockefeller Found., 1978. He is professor, Oklahoma City Univ., and principal guest conductor, Oklahoma (City) Symphony Orch.
WORKS: OPERA: Medea, New England Conservatory Opera Theater, Boston, 3, 4, 5 May 1979, composer conducting; ORCHESTRA: 2 symphonies; piano concerto; bassoon concerto, 1965, commissioned by Guy Frazer Harrison; BAND: Prelude and march.
6017 Glencover Place, Oklahoma City, OK 73132

LUND, JOHN-PETER
b. Norwalk, Conn., 15 July 1948. Studied with Lawrence Moss and Donald Martino, Yale Univ.; with Bulent Arel, State Univ. of New York, Stony Brook. In 1978 he joined the faculty at Antioch Coll.
WORKS: CHAMBER MUSIC: Soliloquy, solo clarinet; Tiamat, 2 pianos, 6 players; Coupling, flute and tuba.
Music Dept., Antioch College, Yellow Springs, OH 45387

LUNDBERG, HARRIET AGDA
b. Brooklyn, N.Y., 28 Feb. 1944. Studied piano at Indiana Univ., B.M.E.; composition with Avram David and Hugo Norden, Boston Cons., M.M. She won second place in a Delta Omicrom competition. She joined the piano faculty at Boston Cons. in 1970; was cofounder, North Shore Piano Studios, 1977.
WORKS: ORCHESTRA: String suite; symphony; CHAMBER MUSIC: brass quintet; Monologues, 3 pieces for harp; Enigmas, piano; 11 short pieces, piano; Music for a threesome, woodwind trio; woodwind quintet, 1972; VOICE: Journals, 5 songs for high voice, 1977; The passing, Flute, White in the moon, 3 songs for high voice.
103-A Summit Ave., Winthrop, MA 02152

LUNDBORG, CHARLES ERIK
b. Helena, Mont., 31 Jan. 1948. Studied with Eugene Weigel, Univ. of Montana; with Charles Wuorinen, New England Cons.; with Jack Beeson, Harvey Sollberger, and Wuorinen, Columbia Univ. He received a Charles Ives scholarship, Nat. Fed. of Music Clubs; Guggenheim fellowship, 1976; has taught at the Newark Community Center of the Arts.
WORKS: ORCHESTRA: piano concerto; The sleeping giant; CHAMBER MUSIC: From music forever #2, chamber orch., 1972; Passacaglia, chamber orch., 1974; Butte chord, for 8 players, New York, 28 Apr. 1975.
403 W. 115 St., #41, New York, NY 10025

LUNDE, IVAR, JR.
b. Tonsberg, Norway, 15 Jan. 1944; to U.S. 1966. Studied at Oslo Cons., M.A.; with Andre Lardrot, Salzburg Mozarteum; with Axelsson, Univ. of Lunde, Sweden. His awards include first prizes in an Oslo Concert Hall composition contest for a symphony, and Kendor Music/Univ. of Maryland contest for a clarinet choir work; honorable mention in several other contests. He was solo oboist, Den Norske Opera, 1964-66; faculty member, Univ. of Maryland, 1966-68; from 1968, at Univ. of Wisconsin, Eau Claire.
WORKS: ORCHESTRA: Metamorphoses; Aiga; Nordic suite; symphony; BAND: Nonsensecole; Elegy; WIND ENSEMBLE: Nuances, clarinet choir; Embellishments, 6 trumpets; suite for brass quintet; CHAMBER MUSIC: 9 suggestive sketches, piano; Image, oboe, bassoon, percussion; 2 suites for woodwind quintet; Drawings, woodwind trio; concerto for harpsichord and woodwind quintet; concertino, flute, oboe, harpsichord, strings; 4 for 9, soprano, baritone, chamber ensemble; many other chamber works for various instruments, sonatas, etc.; CHORUS: Psalm 43; Psalm 26, a cappella; Nocturne, chamber choir, narrator, 2 tape recorders, oboe, clarinet, percussion, 1973; and songs.
3417 Riley St., Eau Claire, WI 54701

LUNDE, LAWSON
b. 1935. Studied with Robert Delaney, Northwestern Univ., B.A. 1957; with Vittorio Rieti on a scholarship. He was a Quiz Kid on radio for 8 years; piano soloist with the Chicago Symphony at 14. His works include a sonata for

LUNETTA, STANLEY GEORGE

saxophone duo, Muncie, Ind., 8 May 1967; alto
saxophone sonata.

LUNETTA, STANLEY GEORGE
b. Sacramento, Calif., 5 June 1937. Studied at
Sacramento State Coll., B.A.; with Larry Austin,
David Tudor, Karlheinz Stockhausen, and John
Cage, Univ. of California, Davis, M.A. He is
composer/performer and percussion instructor;
was an editor of Source, avant-garde music magazine from 1971.
WORKS: MOSTLY MULTIMEDIA: Quartet '65; A
piece for bandoneon and strings, 1966; PFFT, percussion trio, 1965; Zupfgeige Rinne, 1966; Piano
music, 1966; Many things for orchestra, 1966;
PanJorGin, 1966; The word, 1966; Free music,
1967; The wringer, 1967; Funkart, 1967; Ta-Ta,
1967; Hulk, 1967; I am definitely not running
for vice president, 1968; Spider-song, 1968;
Mr. Machine, 1969; A day in the life of the
Muzak machine, 1972; The unseen force, a 2-
evening work using percussion ensemble, electronics, chamber ensemble, dancers, narrator,
symphony orch., and several electronic construct/
sculptures, supported by a Nat. Endowment for
the Arts, grant, 1976.
2101 22nd St., Sacramento, CA 95818

LUSE, ROBERT
b. Baltimore, Md. Studied with Stefans Grové at
Peabody Cons. His concerto grosso for guitar
duo and his guitar quintet were performed in
the Westinghouse World of the guitar, May 1969.

LUTHER, WARREN PHILLIPS
b. Chicago, Ill., 13 May 1939. Studied with
Paul Bellam, Wittenburg Univ.; Carlos Surinach,
Yale Univ.; Nadia Boulanger in Paris; Mario
Davidovsky, Manhattan School of Music; Scott
Huston, Cincinnati Coll. Cons. In addition to
being composer/conductor, he plays viola, viola
da gambe, piano, percussion, koto, horn, and
double bass. He has taught in public schools
and at Edward Williams Coll., N.J.; was founder
of the Great Proletarian Cultural Locomotive
Gamelan Society, a percussion ensemble devoted
to playing newly commissioned works.
WORKS: ORCHESTRA: Suite of autumn dances,
strings, 1960; 3 pieces, small orch., 1961;
viola concerto, 1962; sinfonietta, 1968; double
bass concerto, 1970; CHAMBER MUSIC: 2 suites
from The imperial river, chamber ensemble, 1970-
72; Prelude and toccata, winds and percussion,
1971; The tropical helmsman, trombone, koto,
percussion sextet, 1971; Theme with variations,
chamber ensemble, 1971; The Tierra del Fuegan,
musical joke for woodwind trio and basso continuo, 1974; and songs.
1747 Kilbourne Place, N.W., Washington, DC
20010

LUTYENS, SALLY SPEARE
b. Syracuse, N.Y., 31 Oct. 1927. Studied at
Bennington Coll.; composition at Univ. of
Southern California. She was a fellow, Bennington Composers' Conf., 1968; has received commissions. She was music dept. head, Cambridge
School, Weston, Mass., 1973; has been artist-in-

residence, Coll. of the Atlantic, Bar Harbor,
from 1977.
WORKS: OPERA: The minister's black veil,
1 act, after Hawthorne, Boston, 19 Nov. 1976;
The light princess, 1 act, Newport Opera Festival,
5 Aug. 1979; CHAMBER MUSIC: Midsummer night's
dream, prepared piano, 2 flutes, 2 cellos, 1969;
A parody, flute, soprano, violin, piano; Encore,
piano; Antigone, tape, 1970; Dance technique
demonstration, piano, flute, percussion, 1971,
1972; Journeys, piano and percussion, 1973;
Alice is; Byzantine omlette; The birds, 1973;
piano trio, 1973; recorder trio, 1973.
Manset, ME 04656

LYBBERT, DONALD
b. Cresco, Iowa, 19 Feb. 1923. Studied at Univ.
of Iowa, B.M. 1946; with Bernard Wagenaar,
Juilliard School, 1946-48; with Elliott Carter
and Otto Luening, Columbia Univ., M.A. 1950; and
with Nadia Boulanger in France on fellowship.
Other awards include the Hunter Coll. Shuster
award, 1963; faculty research grant, City Univ.
of N.Y., 1970; Nat. Found. of the Arts award.
From 1954 he has been professor, Hunter Coll.,
CUNY.
WORKS: OPERA: Monica, 1952; The scarlet
letter, 1965; ORCHESTRA: concert overture; Zap,
oratorio with vocal quartet, men's, women's,
and mixed choruses, and orch.; CHAMBER MUSIC:
Introduction and toccata, brass and piano, 1955;
wind trio, 1957; Chamber sonata, horn, viola,
piano, 1958; Sonorities, 11 instruments, 1960;
Sonata brevis, 1962; Praeludium, brass and percussion, 1962; Variants, woodwind quintet, 1973;
VOICE: Austro terris influente, 3 motets for
women's voices; From harmonium, song cycle for
high voice; Leopardi canti, soprano, flute,
viola, bass clarinet, 1959; Lines for the fallen,
soprano and 2 pianos at the quarter tone, 1967;
Octagon, soprano and 7 instruments, 1975; 6
Biblical portraits, high voice and piano.
32 D Weed Hill Ave., Stamford, CT 06907

LYFORD, RALPH
b. Worcester, Mass., 22 Feb. 1882; d. Cincinnati,
Ohio, 3 Sept. 1927. Entered the New England
Cons. at age 12, studying piano with Helen
Hopekirk, organ with Wallace Goodrich, composi-
tion with George Whitefield Chadwick; conducting
in Leipzig with Nikisch. On return to the U.S.,
he was assistant conductor, San Carlo Opera
Company, 1907-8; Boston Opera Company, 1908-14;
taught at Cincinnati Cons., from 1916, and the
Cincinnati Symph. Orch., from 1925.
WORKS: OPERA: Castle Agrazant, won the
David Bispham Medal, 1926; ORCHESTRA: piano
concerto, 1917; also chamber music and songs.

LYNN, GEORGE
b. Edwardsville, Pa., 5 Oct. 1915. Studied with
Roy Harris, Westminster Choir Coll., B.M.; with
Randall Thompson at Princeton Univ., M.A. His
awards include an honorary doctorate, Harding
Coll., 1959; Martha Baird Rockefeller award;
Westminster Choir Coll. Alumni award; Loretto
Heights Coll. faculty research grant; annual
ASCAP awards from 1960. He was faculty member,

Westminster Choir Coll., 1947-50; 1963-69; composer-in-residence, Univ. of New Mexico, 1970; from 1971, adjunct professor, Colorado School of Mines and Loretto Heights Coll.

WORKS: 2 operas; ORCHESTRA: 2 symphonies; Gettysburg address, baritone, chorus, orch.; Greek folksong rhapsody, contralto, chorus, orch.; Lincoln symphony, chorus and orch.; Markings, soprano, male chorus, orch.; 2 overtures; piano concerto; Diversion, string orch.; CHAMBER MUSIC: 3 string quartets; 2 piano sonatas; organ trio sonata; piano quintet; VOICE: 3 sacred symphonies, a cappaella chorus; Thanksgiving hymn, chorus and brass; Song of gratitude, chorus and orch.; 3 song cycles; more than 40 songs; many piano compositions; organ works.
   314 Lake Ave., Colorado Springs, CO 80906

MABRY, JOHN
   b. Spartanburg, S.C., 9 Feb. 1926. Attended Stetson Univ. and Columbia Univ. He has been on the music faculty at Spartanburg City Schools from 1951; organist and choirmaster, Calvary Baptist Church, from 1950; and was music director, Flat Rock Summer Playhouse, 1961-65.
   WORKS: THEATRE: music for Pied Piper of Hamelin; CHORUS: Make way for Christ; Jesus our Lord; Rejoice all ye nations; And peace shall reign again; and others.
   Spartanburg City Schools, Spartanburg, SC 29301

McAFEE, CARLTON FRED, JR.
   b. Gadsden, Ala., 5 Jan. 1938. Studied at Campbell Coll., B.A.; with David Van Vactor, Univ. of Tennessee; Iain Hamilton, Duke Univ.; Roger Hannay, Univ. of North Carolina, M.M.; and with Richard Hervig, Univ. of Iowa, Ph.D. He was faculty member, Univ. of North Carolina at Wilmington, 1971-75.
   WORKS: CHAMBER MUSIC: Diaphonia for 12 strings; Abscissa, 4 female voices and 2 percussionists; ELECTRONIC: Box, alto recorder and tape; Preamble: Foreplay, 4 cellos, 4 trombones, electronics.

McAFEE, DON
   b. Roanoke, Va., 3 June 1935. Studied at Lynchburg Coll., B.A. 1956; at Union Theological Seminary, M.D.M. 1958; with Nadia Boulanger in France; and with Robert Baker and Elaine Brown. He was church music director, White Plains, 1958-65; music editor and manager in publishing firms, 1965-71; from 1971, president, McAfee Music Corporation.
   WORKS: THEATRE: Great Scot!, off-Broadway musical; CHORUS: A choric psalm, speaking chorus and percussion; Corinthians on love; Graffiti; The morning Times, a madrigal for tomorrow morning's breakfast; I will lift up mine eyes; and some 200 other published choral works.
   McAfee Music Corp., 300 E. 59th St., New York, NY 10022

McANANEY, HAROLD
   b. Dublin, Ireland, 28 Oct. 1948; to U.S. 1967. Studied at the School of the Museum of Fine Arts,

Boston; privately and briefly with Tibor Pusztai, Oliver Knussen, and Lawrence Scripp. He has held fellowships from Ford. Found.; Louis Comfort Tiffany; and Boston Museum of Fine Arts. He was composer-in-residence, Movement Laboratory, Boston Center for the Arts, 1970-73; founder of the Annex Players, a contemporary performance group, 1972.
   WORKS: CHAMBER MUSIC: Braille music, 1970; Card piece, 1971; Sentientevents, 1973; Myxomycete, commissioned by Carpenter Center for the Visual Arts, Harvard Univ., 1973.
   P.O. Box 605, Stinson Beach, CA 94970

McBETH, WILLIAM FRANCIS
   b. Ropesville, Tex., 9 Mar. 1933. Studied with Macon Sumerlin, Hardin-Simmons Univ.; with Kent Kennan, Univ. of Texas; with Thomas Canning, Howard Hanson, and Bernard Rogers, Eastman School of Music, Ph.D. His awards include Coll. Band Directors Nat. Assoc. composition award, 1961; Howard Hanson prize, Eastman School, 1963; annual ASCAP awards, 1965-76; many commissions; and many civic awards. He has been professor, Ouachita Univ., from 1957; and was conductor, Little Rock Symphony, 1969-73.
   WORKS: ORCHESTRA: 4 symphonies; Suite on a Biblical event; overture; Quanah; Pastorale and allegro; Allegro agitato; Pastorale for woodwinds and strings; more than 20 works for band; CHAMBER MUSIC: 4 frescoes for 5 brass; Canticle, 11 winds and percussion; CHORUS: And Isaiah prophesied; Gloria; Billy in the Darbies; SONGS: Young thought; Lamentation and gloria of David; The snow leopard; PIANO: Scherzo; 5 projections; 3 pieces.
   1811 Sylvia Rd., Arkadelphia, AR 71923

MacBRIDE, DAVID HUSTON
   b. Oakland, Calif., 3 Oct. 1951. Studied with Andrew Imbrie and Richard Felciano, Univ. of California, Berkeley; with Edward Miller and Edward Diemente, Hartt Coll. of Music; and with Jack Beeson and Chou Wen-chung, Columbia Univ. His awards include City of Berkeley Creative Achievement award, 1969; Hartt Coll. award, 1971-72; Freed scholarship, 1970-73; East-West Artists award, 1976. He was accompanist, Hartford Ballet Company, 1972; music director, Aetna Players, 1973; teaching assistant, Columbia Univ.
   WORKS: ORCHESTRA: Once removed, strings, 1972; See what happens, 1976; CHAMBER MUSIC: 4th way, viola and piano, 1971; string quartet, 1972; Closing inn, string quartet, 1974; woodwind quintet, 1975; It figures, clarinet, viola, piano, xylophone, 1976; Poughkeepsie and back, flute and piano, 1977; Murder by MacBride, flute and percussion, 1978; many other chamber pieces, songs, choral works, piano pieces.
   240 W. 98th St., #5A, New York, NY 10025

McBRIDE, ROBERT GUYN
   b. Tucson, Ariz., 20 Feb. 1911. Studied with Otto Luening, Univ. of Arizona, B.M. 1933, M.M. 1935. His awards include a Guggenheim fellowship, 1937; American Acad. of Arts and Letters award, 1942; Composers' Press award, 1943. He

McCARTY, FRANK L.

played clarinet and saxophone in movie and dance bands; was oboist with Tucson Symphony, 1928-35; on faculty, Bennington Coll., 1935-46; free-lance composer and performer in New York, 1946-57; professor, Univ. of Arizona, 1957-76.

WORKS: ORCHESTRA: Prelude to a tragedy, 1935; Fugato on a well-known theme, 1935; Mexican rhapsody, 1935; Workout for chamber orchestra, 1936; Swing stuff, 1936; Show piece, 1937; music to Turandot, 1941; Punch and the Judy, 1941; Strawberry jam, 1942; Popover, clarinet and orch., 1943; Bop sophisticate, 1947; March of the be-bops, 1948; Pumpkin eater's little fugue, 1952; Variety day, violin concerto, 1954; Fantasy on a Mexican Christmas carol, 1955; Pioneer spiritual, 1956; Panorama of Mexico, 1960; CHAMBER MUSIC: piano quintet, 1933; Depression sonata, violin and piano, 1934; Bells, horn and piano, 1935; Fugue, oboe and 2 clarinets, 1935; Prelude and fugue, string quartet, 1936; oboe quintet, 1937; Hot-shot divertimento, oboe and clarinet, 1938; Swing stuff, clarinet and piano, 1938; Wise apple 5, clarinet quintet, 1940; Jam session, woodwind quintet, 1941; Rudiments of rug-cutting, piano trio or oboe, bassoon, and piano, 1943; The world is ours, clarinet and piano, 1945; String foursome, 1947; 5 winds blowing, woodwind quintet, 1957; also band pieces; choral works; songs; piano pieces.
    3236 E. Waverly, Tucson, AZ 85716

McCARTY, FRANK L.
    b. Pomona, Calif., 10 Nov. 1941. Studied with David Ward-Steinman and Howard Brubeck, San Diego State Coll.; with Ingolf Dahl, George Perle, and David Raksin, Univ. of Southern California, M.M.; with Robert Erickson, Kenneth Gaburo, Pauline Oliveros, Univ. of California, San Diego. His awards include Phi Mu Alpha award, 1962; Nat. Fed. of Music Clubs awards, 1963, 1965, 1966; BMI award, 1966; and commissions. He was faculty member, California State Univ., Fullerton, 1966-71; Univ. of Pittsburgh, 1971-75; from 1976, Univ. of North Carolina at Greensboro.
    WORKS: OPERA: A song for Gar, commissioned by San Diefo Opera; WIND ENSEMBLE: Exitus; Listen to this, 1977; CHAMBER MUSIC: 5 pieces, flute and piano, 1965; Music for trombone and piano, 1966; woodwind quintet, 1966; Clocks, percussion ensemble; Color etudes, solo tuba; 5 situations for 4 saxophones; Ludes and dances, 6 percussion, electric flute, prepared piano; Saxim, saxophone ensemble; ELECTRONIC: Scratch, 15 violins (14 prerecorded); Soundpieces from scratch, 13 electronic clarinets (12 prerecorded); Tam-Tammany I-II, tape and lights; Suite--The Bacchae, tape.
    1347 New Garden Rd., Greensboro, NC 27410

McCARTY, PARTICK
    b. Zanesville, Ohio, 23 Jan. 1928. Studied with A. Oscar Hoagland and Weldon Hart, West Virginia Univ.; with Bernard Rogers, Alan Hovhaness, Howard Hanson, Eastman School of Music, Ph.D. He was faculty member, East Carolina Coll., 1954-56; Newark State Coll., 1957-60; from 1961, at Loyola Univ., New Orleans.

WORKS: ORCHESTRA: At a solemn music, soprano and orch.; BAND: Ballata, CHORUS: Benedictus, with winds; other works for orchestra, band, and chamber groups.
    1620 Haring Rd., Metairie, LA 70001

McCLAIN, FLOYD A.
    b. Alva, Okla., 30 Apr. 1917. Studied with Francis Judd Cooke, Carl McKinley, Leland Proctor, New England Cons.; and with Leo Sowerby, American Cons. He won second place in a Harvey Gaul contest; has received commissions from South Dakota Music Teachers Assoc., 1970, 1973, and South Dakota State Activities Assoc. He has been professor at Yankton Coll. from 1951.
    WORKS: THEATRE: The princess and the frog, 1-act musical; Dakota Dakota Dakota, full-length musical, 1961; Hangin', setting of the story of the murderer of Wild Bill Hickok; Arrow of love, based on novel by F. Manfred; also orchestral works, chamber music, songs.
    604 E. 15th St., Yankton, SD 57078

McCLANAHAN, DAVID RUSSELL
    b. Middletown, Ohio, 29 Oct. 1948. Studied with Scott Huston and Paul Palombo, Cincinnati Coll. Cons. He was winner in the electronic music division, Ohio Fed. of Music Clubs contest, 1973. From 1970 he has been music producer, WGUC-Radio.
    WORKS: ELECTRONIC: Linear landscapes, tape, 1971; Okto-echoi, tape, 1972; Modulations I-IV, piano, synthesizer, and tape, 1972; Echoi I, trumpet and tape, 1972; Echoi II, piano and tape, 1973.
    WGUC-Radio, Univ. of Cincinnati, Cincinnati, OH 45221

McCLEARY, FIONA
    b. Sanderstead, Surry, England, 29 Jan. 1900; U.S. citizen 1932. Studied with Myra Hess, Harriet Cohen, Ralph Vaughan Williams, Arnold Bax, Royal Acad. of Music; and at Matthay Piano School, London. She has given piano recitals throughout the U.S. Her compositions are for piano and for small instrumental groups.

McCLEARY, MARY GILKESON (Mrs. Charles D.)
    b. Sellersville, Pa., 17 Aug. 1920. Studied at Westminster Choir Coll., B.M. 1941. She won first prize, contest Area V, American Guild of English Handbell Ringers, 1976. She has been organist-choir director from 1941.
    WORKS: HANDBELLS: Fanfare for bells; Arioso; Festival overture; Psalm 96; Fantasy; Toccata in A minor; Impromptu in G minor.
    170 Allerton Rd., Naugatuck, CT 06770

McCLELLAN, JOHN JASPER
    b. Payson, Utah, 20 Apr. 1874; d. Salt Lake City, Utah, 2 Aug. 1925. Was appointed organist of the Mormon Tabernacle, Salt Lake City, 1900; organized the Salt Lake City Symphony in 1905, was its conductor to 1910. His compositions include Ode to irrigation for orch.; anthems and organ pieces.

MacCOLL, HUGH F.
b. Pawtucket, R.I., 22 Feb. 1885; d. Providence, R.I., 17 Oct. 1953. Studied with Frederick Converse and W. R. Spalding, Harvard Univ., B.A.
WORKS: ORCHESTRA: Arabs, symphonic illustration, 1932; Ballad, piano and orch., 1934; Romantic suite in form of variations, 1935; CHAMBER MUSIC: suite for violin and piano; Jamaica sketches and 2 Keats songs for medium voice; Noel sketches, organ.

McCOLLIN, FRANCES
b. Philadelphia, Pa., 24 Oct. 1892; d. Philadelphia, 27 Feb. 1960. Studied at Inst. for the Blind; Bryn Mawr Coll.; privately with William Gilchrist and H. Alexander Matthews. Her many awards included Chicago Madrigal Club prize; Clemson award; Nat. Fed. of Music Clubs prizes; Mendelssohn Club prize; Dayton Westminster Choir prize; Harvey Gaul prize; Capital Univ. prize; Sigma Alpha Iota prize. She was lecturer and choral conductor as well as composer.
WORKS: STRING ORCHESTRA: Adagio; 2 chorale preludes; Heavenly children at play, a scherzo; Prayer; choral works, songs, and organ pieces.

MacCOMBIE, BRUCE F.
b. Providence, R.I., 5 Dec. 1943. Studied with Philip Bezanson, Univ. of Massachusetts, Amherst, B.A. 1967, M.M. 1968; with Richard Hervig, Univ. of Iowa, Ph.D. 1971; with Wolfgang Fortner in Germany, 1971-72. His awards include Sutherland Dows fellowship, 1969-71; German Exchange fellowship, 1971; Martha Baird Rockefeller travel grant, 1977; American Acad. and Inst. of Arts and Letters Goddard Lieberson fellowship, 1979. He has been faculty member, Yale Univ., from 1975.
WORKS: CHAMBER MUSIC: 3 designs for 3 players, clarinet, cello, piano; Gerberau music, prepared piano; Canto: Marmerim, soprano and chamber orch.; Found objects, flute and prepared piano; Parkside music, a clockwork ritual, chamber ensemble, Washington, 16 Sept. 1979; The leaden echo and the golden echo, chamber orch., Cambridge, Mass., 9 Mar. 1980.
133 Marshfield St., New Haven, CT 06511

McCULLOH, BYRON
b. Oklahoma City, Okla., 1 Mar. 1927. Studied with Edward Royce, Burrill Phillips, Wayne Barlow, and Bernard Rogers, Eastman School of Music, B.M. 1949, M.M. 1951; privately with Dante Fiorillo in New York, 1947. He has received many commissions. He was bass trombonist with the Oklahoma City Symph., 1951-52; St. Louis Symph., 1952-56; from 1956, Pittsburgh Symph.; also from 1969, on faculty, Carnegie-Mellon Univ.; guest professor, Eastman School of Music, 1977-78.
WORKS: ORCHESTRA: Symphony concertante, timpanist and orch., Pittsburgh, 21 Dec. 1973; concertino for large trombone and small orchestra, 1974; symphony #1, Pittsburgh, 7 Oct. 1976; 6 songs, baritone and orch., Rochester, 24 Apr. 1978; WIND ENSEMBLE: Sinfonia for brass and battery, 1975; CHAMBER MUSIC: string quartet #2, Penn. State Univ., 13 Apr. 1973; 2 songs, soprano and chamber ensemble, Pittsburgh, 7 May 1978.
1306 Penn Ave., Pittsburgh, PA 15221

McDANIEL, WILLIAM J.
b. Jellico, Tenn., 4 Mar. 1918. Studied with Weldon Hart and John Vincent, Western Kentucky Univ., B.M.; Walter Ihrke and Arnold Salop, George Peabody Coll., M.M.; with Philip Slates and Normand Lockwood, Univ. of Denver. He was faculty member, Wayland Baptist Coll., 1948-59; Missouri Baptist Coll., 1951-52; and Southern Baptist Coll., from 1953.
WORKS: OPERA: The green tint, chamber opera in 1 act, Eureka Springs, 18 July 1974; Waterhole, chamber opera; BALLET: The legend of petit Jean, 1965; ORCHESTRA: symphonic movement; CHAMBER MUSIC: woodwind trio; woodwind quintet; CHORUS: Whilst o'er the fields of Greece, spoken choral with percussion; A song from Solomon; Alleluia, Amen; Psalm 96; 'Tis the glory of my time; and songs.
Southern Baptist College, Walnut Ridge, AR 72476

MacDERMID, JAMES G.
b. Utica, Ont., 10 June 1875; U.S. citizen 1906; d. Brooklyn, N.Y., 16 Aug. 1960. Studied in London, Ont., and in Chicago. He toured as piano soloist and as accompanist to his wife, a soprano; wrote many sacred and secular songs: My love is like a red, red rose; Psalm 93; Behold what manner of love; etc.

MacDERMOTT, GALT
b. Montreal, Que., 19 Dec. 1928. Was earlier a church organist; then dance band musician and composer. He has received 2 Grammy awards, 1961, 1968; Vernon Rice award, 1968; 2 Drama Desk awards, 1968, 1971; Music Critics' Circle award, 1971.
WORKS: THEATRE: musicals: African waltz, 1961; Hair, 1968; 2 gentlemen of Verona, 1971; A gun play, 1971; La novella, Puerto Rican soap opera, 1973; incidental music for several plays; FILM SCORES: Cotton comes to Harlem, 1970; Fortune and men's eyes, 1971; Rhinoceros, 1974; LITURGICAL: Mass in F, 1971; Take this bread-- A mass in our time, 1975.
c/o ASCAP, 1 Lincoln Plaza, New York, NY 10020

McDERMOTT, VINCENT
b. Atlantic City, N.J., 5 Sept. 1933. Studied with Andre Vauclain, George Rochberg, Karlheinz Stockhausen, Univ. of Pennsylvania; with Darius Milhaud at Aspen, Colo. He was faculty member, Wisconsin Coll. Cons., 1967-77; from 1978, at Lewis and Clark Coll.
WORKS: ORCHESTRA: Siftings upon siftings, Indiana State Univ., 27 Sept. 1979; CHAMBER MUSIC: 3 for 5, flute, saxophone, vibraphone, piano, tabla; Komal usha-rudra nisha, flute guitar, sitar, double bass; Magic grounds, 5 pieces for piano, Milwaukee, 27 Sept. 1976; ELECTRONIC: He who ascends by ecstasy into comtemplation of sublime things and sleeps and sees a dream, piano and tape; Thou, restless ungathered, cantata for soprano, clarinet, and tape.
7728 S.W. 30 Ave., Portland, OR 97219

MacDONALD, CATHERINE

MacDONALD, CATHERINE
b. New York, N.Y., 22 Oct. 1940. Studied with
Meyer Kupferman and Ezra Laderman, Sarah
Lawrence Coll.; with Jacob Druckman and Vittorio
Giannini, Juilliard School; and with Jack
Beeson, Otto Luening, and Chou Wen-chung, Columbia Univ. She taught composition, the New
Lincoln School, New York, 1965-7; was resident
composer, Vivian Beaumont Theatre, Lincoln
Center, New York, 1972-73.
      WORKS: THEATRE SCORES: Twelfth night,
1972; Enemies, 1973; A streetcar named desire,
1973; O glorious tintinabulations, 1974; The
tempest, 1975; Rebel women, 1976; She stoops to
conquer, 1977-78.
      Langdon R.F.D., Alstead, NH 03602

McDONALD, HARL
b. Boulder, Colo., 27 July 1899; d. Princeton,
N.J., 30 Mar. 1955. Studied at Univ. of
Southern California, B.M.; Univ. of Redlands,
D.M. He was piano soloist and vocal accompanist,
1923-24; music dept. head, Univ. of Pennsylvania,
1926-46; manager, Philadelphia Orchestra, 1939-
55.
      WORKS: ORCHESTRA: 4 symphonies, 1934,
1935, 1936, 1938; From childhood, suite; Song of
free nations, soprano and orch.; Dirge for 2
veterans, women's chorus and orch.; 2 nocturnes;
Arkansas traveler; 3 Hebrew poems, 1936; 2-
piano concerto, 1937; violin concerto; Saga of
the Mississippi, 1947; CHAMBER MUSIC: 2 piano
trios, 1931, 1932; Fantasy for string quartet,
1932; quartet on Negro themes, 1933; CHORUS:
God give us men, cantata; many other works.

McDONELL, A. EUGENE
b. Wausau, Wis., 6 Oct. 1915. Studied at Milwaukee State Teachers Coll., B.S. 1939; with
Hilmar Luckhardt, Univ. of Wisconsin, M.S. 1950.
Except for service in the air force, 1942-46,
he taught in public schools, 1939-64; then
joined the faculty of the Wisconsin University
Center System; from 1972, at the Baraboo/Sauk
County Center. His compositions include Invasion for percussion ensemble; piece for woodwinds; 2 choral works.
      Baraboo-Sauk County Center, Baraboo, WI
      53913

MacDOUGALL, ROBERT
b. 1941. Studied with Stefans Grove at Peabody
Cons. His compositions include Requiem for orch.,
and Anacoluthon: A confluence, for 4 winds, 3
cellos, double bass, New York premiere, 12 Jan.
1975.

McDOWELL, JOHN HERBERT
b. Washington, D.C., 21 Dec. 1926. Studied at
Colgate Univ., B.A. 1948; with Jack Beeson,
Roger Goeb, Otto Luening, Columbia Univ., M.A.
1957; held a Guggenheim fellowship, 1962.
      WORKS: MODERN DANCE: Insects and heroes,
1961; From sea to shining sea, an homage to
Ives, 1965; Dark psalters, 1968; ORCHESTRA:
Four sixes and a nine, 1959; Accumulation, 35
flutes, strings, percussion, 1964; CHAMBER
MUSIC: Sonispiece (with Ezra Sims), quarter

tones for flute and tape, Cambridge, Mass., 13
Mar. 1970; Tumescent lingam, oboe, New York,
16 Jan. 1971; CHORUS: Good news from heaven,
cantata, 1957; and some 400 more works.
      220 E. 14th St., New York, NY 10003

McELHERAN, BROCK
b. Winnipeg, Canada, 6 Jan. 1918. Studied with
Healey Willan. He has been faculty member,
State Univ. Coll. at Potsdam, from 1949.
      WORKS: ORCHESTRA: Funeral march on the
death of heroes; Patterns in sound; CHORUS: Let
the spirit soar; Here comes the avant-garde,
with narrator and piano.
      State University College, Potsdam, NY 13676

MACERO, TED
b. Glen Falls, N.Y., 30 Oct. 1925. Studied
saxophone at Juilliard School, M.S. 1951; composition privately with Henry Brandt. His
awards include a BMI student composer award at
Juilliard; 2 Guggenheim grants, 1957, 1958; Nat.
Endowment for the Arts grants, 1974; and commissions. He was producer for Columbia Records,
1956-76; then formed his own production company.
      WORKS: ORCHESTRA: Torsion in space, Kansas
City, 4 Feb. 1961; Paths; Fusions, New York, 11
Jan. 1958; Rounds, ballet; CHAMBER MUSIC: One
and three quarters, chamber orch.; Canzona #1,
trumpet and 4 saxophones; also many jazz works,
over 100 ballets, documentary film scores,
television scores, television themes.
      159 W. 53rd St., New York, NY 10019

MacFARLANE, WILLIAM CHARLES
b. London, England, 2 Oct. 1870; to U.S. 1874;
d. North Conway, N.H., 12 May 1945. Studied
organ with his father and with Samuel P. Warren
in New York. He was church organist in New
York, 1898-1912; municipal organist, Portland,
Maine, 1912-19.
      WORKS: OPERETTAS: Little almond eyes,
1916; America first, Boy Scout operetta, 1917;
Sword and scissors, 1918; CHORUS: The message
of the cross, cantata, 1907; many anthems;
ORGAN: Meditation; Cradle song; Spring song;
Scotch fantasy; Reverie; etc.

MacFAYDEN, ALEXANDER
b. Milwaukee, Wis., 12 July 1879; d. Milwaukee,
6 June 1936. Studied at Chicago Musical Coll.;
received honorary D.M. from Chicago Coll. He
was a concert pianist; taught at Wisconsin Coll.
of Music and Chicago Cons. The Wisconsin Fed.
of Music Clubs established the MacFayden Memorial
piano competition. He composed many songs.

McFEETERS, RAYMOND
b. Rushville, Ill., 11 Dec. 1899; d. Calif.
Studied piano with Carl Friedberg, composition
with A. Madeley Richardson at Juilliard School.
He received the Kimball award, Chicago Council
of Teachers of Singing, 1940, for a song. He
was church organist in Pasadena and Hollywood
from 1920. His compositions were chiefly sacred
and secular art songs and works for piano,
violin, and cello.

McGEE, WILLIAM JAMES
b. Great Falls, Mont., 8 June 1936. Studied with Bernard Heiden and Thomas Beversdorf, Indiana Univ. He was faculty member, Southern Missionary Coll., 1966-75; from 1976, at Pacific Union Coll.

WORKS: ORCHESTRA: Miniature for orchestra; CHAMBER MUSIC: Variations, woodwind trio; Rhapsody, violin and piano; Lamentation, trumpet and piano; Hyfrydol, 3 instruments and piano; 3 pieces, cello solo; VOICE: Jesus was a baby, double chorus, flute, piano, percussion; I know a little ditty, men's voices; Old Mother Hubbard, solo voice and piano; PIANO: 2 philosophical= observations; Dance-toccata for the esoterists; Varoum et mutabile; ORGAN: A joyful procession (Homage to Beethoven); Variations and finale on "Olivet"; Carol variations on "Nous voici dans la ville."
Pacific Union College, Angwin, CA 94508

McGRATH, JOSEPH J.
b. Oswego, N.Y., 1889; d. Syracuse, N.Y., 1968. Graduated from Syracuse Univ., 1926; was organist at Cathedral of the Immaculate Conception, Syracuse; taught at Syracuse Univ. His works include a symphony; 3 string quartets; many duo sonatas; 6 brevities, for brass quartet; 36 masses; 100 works for organ.

McGRAW, CAMERON
b. Cortland, N.Y., 28 Apr. 1919. Studied at Middlebury Coll., B.A.; with Roy Harris, Hunter Johnson, and Robert Palmer, Cornell Univ., M.A. His piano pieces have received 4 Piano Quarterly "Best of the Year" awards. He was instructor, State Univ. of New York, Potsdam, 1947-49; Cornell Univ., 1950-52; from 1954, has been co-director, Jenkintown Music School. He was co-author of a 12-volume piano method: Doors into music; and editor of a graded anthology of classics: 4 centuries of keyboard music.

WORKS: ORCHESTRA: Dance suite, performed 56 times by North Carolina Little Symphony on a state tour, 1965; CHORUS: These things shall be; 3 French noels; PIANO COLLECTIONS: Almanac; Structures and designs; Tunes for dessert; Trip to a faraway place; Pet silhouettes.
439 Greenwood Ave., Wyncote, PA 19095

MacGREGOR, LAURIE
b. Minneapolis, Minn., 3 Feb. 1951. Studied with Meyer Kupferman, privately and at Sarah Lawrence Coll.; Skidmore Coll., B.A. 1974; with Jack Beeson, Alice Shields, and Vladimir Ussachevsky, Columbia Univ., M.A. 1977. At Columbia she received the Alice M. Ditson recording grant.

WORKS: ORCHESTRA: He embraces the notion of mountain, 1977; CHAMBER MUSIC: string trio, 1971; concerto for 6 instruments, woodwind trio, string trio, 1972; brass quintet, 1972; Fitful sleep, cello solo, 1973; Intrusion of the hunter, 9 percussionists, 1974; Summer storm at Thunder Lake, 2 clarinets, cello, percussion, 1978.
272 3rd Ave., New York, NY 10010

MACHAN, BENJAMIN A.
b. Cleveland, Ohio, 11 Sept. 1894; d. Woodbury, Conn., 14 Feb. 1966. Studied piano and composition with his father and made his debut as piano soloist with the Cleveland Symphony at 5. After army service in World War I, he formed a jazz band in Paris; on returning to New York, he wrote for films and radio.

WORKS: ORCHESTRA: American concerto, violin and orch.; American suite; Rhapsody in jazz; Nutmeg suite; Connecticut hymn; many songs; FILM SCORES: We, the people, documentary; Seeds of destiny, won an Academy award, 1944.

McHOSE, ALLEN IRVINE
b. Lancaster, Pa., 14 May 1902. Studied at Franklin and Marshall Coll., B.S. 1923; Eastman School of Music, B.M. 1927, M.M. 1929; Oklahoma City Univ., D.M. 1945. He was faculty member, Eastman School of Music, 1930-62; then associate director. His compositions include a violin sonata, 1929; oboe concerto, 1932.
P.O. Box 247, Naples, NY 14512

MACHOVER, TOD
b. New York, N.Y., 1953. Has studied with Elliott Carter, Roger Sessions, and Luigi Dallapiccola; in 1979, was a doctoral candidate at Juilliard School, where complete programs of his works have been given. His awards include Nat. Inst. of Arts and Letters Ives scholarship, 1976; MacDowell fellowship, 1977. A complete program of his works was presented at Lincoln Center, New York, by the Contemporary Chamber Ensemble under Arthur Weisberg on 22 May 1979. Included on the program were a guitar concerto; Sun, for piano, 1975; Yoku Mirebu, flute, cello, piano; and songs. In 1979, Pierre Boulez named him composer-in-residence at the music institute of the George Pompidou Center, Paris.

McHUGH, CHARLES R.
b. Minneapolis, Minn., 5 Aug. 1940. Studied with Dominick Argento and Paul Fetler, Univ. of Minnesota, Ph.D. He won first prize in a Univ. of Minnesota contest, 1968. He was faculty member, Univ. of Minnesota, 1965-70; Minnesota Metropolitan State Coll., 1973; coeditor, Synthesis, electronic music magazine, 1970-71.

WORKS: ORCHESTRA: symphony, 1965, 2nd movement performed by Minnesota Orch., 31 May 1973; symphony #2, 1968; Divertimento, small orch., 1968; CHAMBER MUSIC: quintet for winds, strings, and piano, 1967; ELECTRONIC: Fall music, collage for 11 players and sound track, 1971; Requiem, 12 players and 2 sound tracks, 1972.
1917 Colfax Ave. S., Minneapolis, MN 55403

McHUGH, JIMMY
b. Boston, Mass., 10 July 1894; d. Beverly Hills, Calif., 22 May 1969. Attended Holy Cross Coll. His awards include honorary doctorates from Harvard Univ., Georgetown Univ., Holy Cross Coll.; Presidential Certificate of Merit for work on war bonds in World War II; American Legion, Court of Honor award. He was rehearsal pianist for the Boston Opera Company to 1921,

McILWRAITH, ISA ROBERTA

then lived in New York, where he composed for
shows; from 1930, in Hollywood composing for
films. The best known of his shows were Cotton
Club revues (7 years) and Blackbirds of 1928;
of his songs: I can't give you anything but
love, baby, 1928; On the sunny side of the
street, 1928; Cuban love song; South American
way, 1939; Comin' in on a wing and a prayer,
1943.

McILWRAITH, ISA ROBERTA
b. Paterson, N.J., 18 May 1909. Studied at
Barnard Coll., B.A.; with Philip James, Daniel
Gregory Mason, Douglas Moore, Columbia Univ.,
M.A.; with Seth Bingham, Union Theological
Seminary; with Albert Stoessel at Juilliard
School. Her awards include Phi Beta Kappa;
fellowships at Columbia Univ. and Juilliard
School; associate, American Guild of Organists.
She was organist in Brooklyn and New York, 1932-
38; faculty member, Mt. Holyoke Coll., 1937-38;
Univ. of Tennessee, 1938-75.
     WORKS: CHORUS: Appalachian Christmas carol;
Christ our passover; Christians all rejoice;
Hosanna to the son of David; ORGAN: Triptych;
Adagio and fughetta; Fugue in a; many unpublished
choral and organ works.
     105 Druid Dr., Signal Mountain, TN 37377

MacINNIS, M. DONALD
b. New York, N.Y., 4 Apr. 1923. Studied with
Milton Babbitt, Edward Cone, Bohuslav Martinu,
Roger Sessions, and Randall Thompson, Princeton
Univ. His awards include the Princeton composition prize, 1949; composition fellowship, Univ.
of North Carolina, 1967-68; composer-in-residence,
Atlanta Symphony, 1968-69; 4 Univ. of Virginia
faculty research fellowships, 1965, 1970, 1972,
1973, and sesquicentennial grant to write an
opera based on William Faulkner's The bear,
1976; first prize, Bowdoin Coll. competition,
1973. He has been on the faculty, Univ. of
Virginia, from 1950.
     WORKS: ORCHESTRA: Dialogues, 1960; Inter-
sections, orch. and tape recorder, 1963; WIND
ENSEMBLE: Variations, brass and percussion,
1964; Collide-a-scope, 12 brass instruments and
tape, 1971; CHAMBER MUSIC: Toccata, piano and
tape, 1971; Variations, cello and tape, 1971,
Bowdoin Coll., 9 Apr. 1973; In memoriam John
Fitzgerald Kennedy, chamber orch., Washington,
2 Nov. 1975.
     316 Kent Rd., Charlottesville, VA 22903

McINTOSH, LADD
b. Akron, Ohio, 14 July 1941. Studied with
Marshall Barnes, Ohio State Univ., B.M. 1966,
M.M. 1970. He won 5 awards in composition at
collegiate jazz festivals, 1965-68; many awards
as college band leader; many commissions. He
has been arranger and instrumentalist at night
clubs and in show bands; taught woodwinds, Ohio
State Univ., 1967-68; was on faculty, Univ. of
Utah, 1970-72; Westminster Coll., Salt Lake
City, 1972-75.
     WORKS: OPERA: Today is a good day to die,
rock opera, Salt Lake City, 20 Mar. 1972; BAND:
Reflections, 1965; Ascendency, 1970; WIND EN-

SEMBLE: saxophone quartet, 1965; Viking suite,
brass choir and percussion, 1967; Concert piece
for doublers, 1970; JAZZ: suite for jazz orch.,
1965; 5 fantasies, 2 jazz orch., horns, tuba,
percussion, 1966; Variations on a rock tune,
1967; The avenging angel and Ichabod Crane,
1972; The fallen warrior, 1972; Munich, Sept. 5,
1972; Groupies, 1973; CHAMBER MUSIC: Echoes from
an ancient past, strings and solo saxophone,
1969.

McINTOSH, THOMAS S.
b. Baltimore, Md., 6 Feb. 1927. Studied at
Peabody Cons.; Juilliard School, graduated 1958;
played trombone in U.S. Army Band and with many
jazz bands. His works include the song, Something old, something new, and the film score for
The learning tree.

McKAY, FRANCIS HOWARD
b. Harrington, Wash., 7 Mar. 1901. Studied at
Washington State Coll.; Eastman School of Music;
Univ. of Washington, B.A., M.A.; Northeast
Missouri State Coll.; Univ. of Southern Califor-
nis. He taught in public schools and colleges
in Ketchikan, Alaska, from 1955.
     WORKS: ORCHESTRA: American sketch; 2
promenades; Woods in April; also pieces for
band, wind ensemble, and chorus.

McKAY, GEORGE FREDERICK
b. Harrington, Wash., 11 June 1899; d. Stateline,
Nev., 4 Oct. 1970. Studied with Selim Palmgren
and Christian Sinding, Eastman School of Music,
B.M. 1923, the first graduate in composition.
His awards include a national first prize for
symphony #1, performed by Rochester Phil.;
Harvey Gaul prize; first prize, Northern California Harpists Assoc., 1960; many commissions.
He was faculty member, Univ. of Washington,
1941-68.
     WORKS: ORCHESTRA: 4 sinfoniettas, 1925-42;
Fantasy on a western folksong, 1933; Bravura
prelude, brass choir, 1939; violin concerto,
1940; To a liberator, symphonic poem, 1940;
Introspective poem, string orch., 1941; A
prairie portrait, 1941; Pioneer epics, 1942;
cello concerto, 1942; CHAMBER MUSIC: piano trio,
1931; woodwind quintet, 1937; 5 pieces for 4
clarinets; Lyric poem, 4 flutes; 4 string quartets; trombone sonata, 1956; Sonatina espressiva,
brass quintet; suite for harp and flute, 1960;
Machine age poetry, instrumental duo; Andante
mistico, 8 celli and piano; American street
scenes, saxophone quartet and piano; Sonatina-
ballade, clarinet and strings; many other
chamber works and choral compositions.

MacKAY, HARPER
b. Boston, Mass., 13 Oct. Studied at Harvard
Univ., B.A.; with Halsey Stevens, Univ. of
Southern California, M.A., Ph.D. He is composer
and arranger for films and television.
     WORKS: ORCHESTRA: overture; symphony;
CHAMBER MUSIC: clarinet sonatina; 6 minutes for
6 pieces, woodwind trio and string trio; FILM
SCORES: Deadwood; "Guest shot" (TV).
     3405 Adina Dr., Hollywood, CA 90028

McKAY, NEIL
b. Ashcroft, B.C., Canada, 16 June 1924; U.S.
citizen 1962. Studied with John Weinzweig,
Toronto Cons.; at Univ. of Western Ontario,
M.A. 1953; with Wayne Barlow, Bernard Rogers,
Howard Hanson, Eastman School of Music, Ph.D.
1956. His awards include Ottawa Symphony first
prize for Canadian composers, 1955; Benjamin
prize, 1956; MacDowell fellowship, 1961, 1963;
and commissions. He was professor, Univ. of
Wisconsin at Superior, 1957-65; from 1965, at
Univ. of Hawaii.
WORKS: OPERA: Ring around Harlequin;
Planting a pear tree; ORCHESTRA: symphony;
Fantasy on a quiet theme; Structure; BAND:
Dance overture; Evocations; Gamelan gong; Fan-
fare and ceremonial; CHAMBER MUSIC: string
quartet; horn sonata; violin sonata; Triologue;
Worlds, solo koto; CHORUS: A dream within a
dream; Legends of Maui; Folksong fantasy; SONGS:
Lazy man's song, baritone; 3 songs on poems of
Po Chu-i, soprano, guitar, recorder, percussion.
3310 Keahi St., Honolulu, HI 96822

McKENNEY, W. THOMAS
b. Falmouth, Ky., 24 June 1938. Studied with
Scott Huston, Cincinnati Coll.-Cons.; with
Bernard Rogers, Eastman School of Music, Ph.D.
He received the Martin G. Dumler award, 1963;
Music Teachers Nat. Assoc. composer of the year
award, 1971. He has been faculty member, Univ.
of Missouri, Columbia, from 1967.
WORKS: ORCHESTRA: clarinet concertino;
CHAMBER MUSIC: 3 miniatures, piano; Dialogue,
woodwind quartet; ELECTRONIC: The lake, tape.
1224 Jake Lane, Columbia, MO 65201

McKENZIE, JACK H.
b. Springfield, Mo., 11 Nov. 1930. Studied at
Univ. of Illinois, where he has been instructor,
professor, and dean, Coll. of Fine Arts, 1973.
WORKS: PERCUSSION: Introduction and
allegro; 3 dances; nonet; Rites; suite for
sideman and handclappers; Song, trombone and
percussion; Paths I and II; Pastorale, flute
and percussion.
27 Sherwin Circle, R.R. 3, Urbana, IL 61801

McKENZIE, WALLACE
b. Alexandria, La., 16 June 1928. Studied with
Philip Greeley Clapp, Univ. of Iowa; with George
S. Morey, North Texas State Univ.; and with
Kenneth B. Klaus, Louisiana State Univ. He
taught at New Orleans Baptist Theological
Seminary, 1955-64; Wayland Baptist Coll., 1964-
68; from 1968, at Louisiana State Univ.
WORKS: ORCHESTRA: Tagelied; WIND ENSEMBLE:
Introduction and allegro, brass, 1958; CHAMBER
MUSIC: sonatina for clarinet, viola, cello,
1954; trumpet sonata, 1957; Sounds for November,
clarinet, piano, percussion; 3 danses anachron-
istiques, recorders, cornemuse, viola da gamba,
natural trumpet, 1973; ELECTRONIC: music for 2
clarinets and tape; music for violin and tape,
1972; music for harp and tape, 1974; organ
pieces, choral works.
Louisiana State University, Baton Rouge, LA
70803

McKINLEY, CARL
b. Yarmouth, Maine, 9 Oct. 1895; d. Boston,
Mass., 24 July 1966. Studied at Knox Coll.;
with Edward Burlingame Hill, Harvard Univ.; with
Rubin Goldmark and with Nadia Boulanger. Among
his awards were the Boott prize, 1916; Naumburg
award, 1917; Flagler prize, 1921; 2 Guggenheim
fellowships, 1927, 1928. From 1929, he was on
the faculty, New England Cons.
WORKS: ORCHESTRA: Indian summer idyll,
1917; The blue flower, 1921; Masquerade, an
American rhapsody, 1926; Chorale, variations and
fugue, 1941; Caribbean holiday, Boston, 18 Nov.
1948; CHAMBER MUSIC: string quartet, 1941;
cello sonata, 1953; CHORUS: The kid, cantata,
1955.

McKINLEY, WILLIAM THOMAS
b. Pittsburgh, Pa., 9 Dec. 1939. Studied with
Nikolai Lopatnikoff, Carnegie-Mellon Univ.,
B.F.A.; with Mel Powell, Yehudi Wyner, Lawrence
Moss, Yale Univ., M.A. and M.F.A.; with Gunther
Schuller at Tanglewood. His awards include a
BMI award, 1963; Nat. Endowment for the Arts
grant, 1976; first prize, Minnesota Orchestra
75th Anniversary Composers' Contest, 1978; and
commissions. He was faculty member, Univ. of
Chicago, 1969-73; from 1973, composer-in-
residence and faculty member, New England Cons.
WORKS: ORCHESTRA: Circular forms for grand
orchestra; triple concerto, jazz trio and orch.;
concertino, Tanglewood, 16 Aug. 1977; cello concerto, 1977; symphony, Minneapolis, 3 Jan. 1979;
WIND ENSEMBLE: Rhapsody, harp and band, 1976;
Short symphony, brass and percussion, Boston,
14 Nov. 1979; CHAMBER MUSIC: trio for 2 violins
and cello; Quadruplum, large ensemble; Paintings,
chamber ensemble; Interludes, oboe and piano;
Stops II and III, woodwinds; Portfolio, solo
cello; Paintings II, string trio, 1976; Fantasie concertante, string quartet, New York, 8
Mar. 1977; 6 impromptus, flute, clarinet, string
trio, 1978; Paintings IV, chamber orch., Cambridge, Mass., 4 Dec. 1978.
603 Pearl St., Reading, MA 01867

McKINNEY, HOWARD D.
b. Pine Beach, N.Y., 29 May 1890. Studied at
Rutgers Univ.; Columbia Univ., D.M. He was
organist and music director, Rutgers Univ.,
1917-22; faculty member to 1963, then professor
emeritus; editor, J. Fischer & Bros.
WORKS: SONGS: The bagpipe man; 6 crumbs
from peacockpie; The 3 Maries; A mystery for
Christmas.

McKINNEY, MATHILDE
b. South Bend, Ind., 31 Jan. 1904. Studied at
Oberlin Cons. and at Juilliard School; piano
with Lee Pattison and Josef and Rosina Lhevinne.
She has taught at Wooster Coll., Ohio; Douglass
Coll.; privately in Pittsburgh, Oklahoma, New
York, and Princeton; in 1962, was on faculty,
Westminster Choir Coll.; gave premiere perfor-
mances of Edward T. Cone's piano concerto at
Princeton in 1962.
WORKS: ORCHESTRA: Elegy, string orch.,
1953, rev. 1958; CHAMBER MUSIC: violin sonata;

McKUEN, ROD

string quartet; trio for violin, viola, piano;
7 modes, 2 alto recorders; CHORUS: Christmas
cantata, with brass, 1957; The wise men, girls'
voices, 1957; ORGAN: Fantasy toccata; and
piano pieces.

McKUEN, ROD
b. Oakland, Calif., 29 Apr. 1933. Studied at
San Francisco State Coll.; served in the army in
the Korean war; has been roving minstrel, bal-
ladeer, poet, and composer of songs for which he
has received 11 ASCAP awards.
WORKS: ORCHESTRA: a symphony; 3 piano concertos; The sea; Something beyond; Structures in
jazz; The city, with narrator, nominated for
Pulitzer prize, 1976; many popular songs.
Stanyon, Box 2783, Hollywood, CA 90028

McLAIN, MARGARET STARR
b. Chicago, Ill. Studied with Frederick Converse
and George W. Chadwick, New England Cons.; and
at Trinity Coll., London. She received 2
Endicott prizes in composition at the cons.; was
a member of the MacDowell Colony from 1924. She
was faculty member, Boston Univ., 1928-70, then
professor emeritus. Her works include an overture, 1937; violin sonata; string quintet; choral
works; songs.

McLAUGHLIN, MARIAN (Mrs. T. R. Ostrom)
b. Evanston, Ill., 26 Nov. 1923. Studied at
Northwestern Univ., B.M.E.; with Francis Judd
Cooke and Carl McKinley, New England Cons., M.M.;
and with Walter Piston. She won prizes in the
Northern Virginia American Guild of Organists
competition, and the Friday Morning Music Club,
Washington, D.C. She was instructor, Univ. of
Evansville, Ind., 1944-46; teaching fellow, New
England Cons., 1947-48.
WORKS: CHAMBER MUSIC: Divertimento, viola
and cello; Nocturne and scherzo, solo flute;
CHORUS: Autumn fires, women's choir; Lullaby to
a seafarer's son, women's voices; ORGAN: 3 fantasies; many works for orchestra, choral and
chamber groups.
102 Duncannon Rd., Bel Air, MD 21014

McLEAN, BARTON
b. Poughkeepsie, N.Y., 8 Apr. 1938. Studied at
State Univ. of New York, Potsdam, B.S. 1960;
with Henry Cowell, 1963-65; Eastman School of
Music, M.A. 1965; with Xenakis, Indiana Univ.,
D.M. 1972. He received grants from N.Y. Research
Found., 1964; Indiana Univ., 1972, 1974; Presi-
dent's Council on the Humanities, 1973; Nat.
Endowment for the Arts, 1976, 1978; Univ. of
Texas, 1977, 1978. He was faculty member, State
Univ. of New York, Potsdam, 1960-66; Indiana
Univ. at Bloomington, 1966-69, at South Bend,
1969-76; from 1976, Univ. of Texas at Austin,
where he is director of electronic music.
WORKS: THEATRE: Pardon my ambition, musi-
cal comedy, 1961; ORCHESTRA: 2 movements, 1962;
Suite for strings, 1966; Farewell to H, 1967,
rev. 1975; Metamorphosis, 1972; WIND ENSEMBLE:
Divertimento, clarinet choir, 1962; Rondo for
band, 1962; Legend for band, 1965; Legend #2,
1966; ELECTRONIC: Dimensions I, violin and

tape, 1973; Genesis, 1973; Spirals, 1973; Syn-
thiny, live performer on Synthi 100, 1973;
Dimensions II, piano and tape, 1974; The sorcerer
revisited, 1975; Identity I, tape and live in-
teraction, 1977; Identity II, chorus, 23 instruments, soloists, tape, 1978; many works for
chamber groups and voice.
6 Matador Circle, Austin, TX 78746

MacLEAN, JOHN T.
b. Jersey City, N.J., 12 Apr. 1933. Studied
with Dika Newlin at Drew Univ.; Henry Cowell,
Columbia Univ.; John Boda, Ernst von Dohnanyi,
Florida State Univ.; Bernhard Heiden, Indiana
Univ.; and with Barry Schrader, California Inst.
of the Arts. He was the winner at Composers
Symposium, Brevard Music Center, 1966. He
taught in public schools, 1961-63; at North
Carolina Wesleyan Coll., 1966-67; West Georgia
Coll., 1967-74; and from 1978, at Converse Coll.
WORKS: ORCHESTRA: Portrait, oboe and
strings; Symphonic dance; Symphony, In memoriam;
CHAMBER MUSIC: Suite for 7 wind instruments;
Meditation, violin and piano; Portrait, flute,
bassoon, strings; 5 movements for 4 household
instruments; violin sonata; Canto, string trio;
3 abstractions on human behavior and conditions,
string quartet.
Converse College, Spartanburg, SC 29301

McLEAN, PRISCILLA
b. Fitchburg, Mass., 27 May 1942. Studied with
Richard Kent, State Coll. at Fitchburg, B.E.E.
1963; Univ. of Lowell, B.M.E. 1965; privately
with Hugo Norden, Boston, 1964-66; with Thomas
Beversdorf and Bernhard Heiden, Indiana Univ.,
M.M. 1969. Her awards include an American Music
Center copying grant, 1975; Nat. Endowment for
the Arts grant, 1978. She was faculty member,
St. Mary's Coll., Notre Dame, 1973-76; Indiana
Univ. (Kokomo), 1971-73, (South Bend), faculty
and composer-in-residence, 1975-76.
WORKS: ORCHESTRA: Variations and mozaics
on a theme of Stravinsky, 1975; CHAMBER MUSIC:
Lighting me as a match, tenor, violin, horn,
piano, percussion, 1968; Interplanes, 2 pianos,
1970; Spectra II, prepared piano and percussion,
1972; Fire and ice, trombone and piano (2
players), 1977; Beneath the horizon, 4 tubas or
solo tuba and whale ensemble, 1978; ELECTRONIC:
Spectra I, percussion, prepared piano, synthesizer, 1971; Messages, chorus, soloists, electronic autoharp, percussion, recorders, piano,
1973; Night images, synthesizers, 1973; Dance of
dawn, tape, 1975; Ah-Syn!, autoharp and synthesizer, 1977; Invisible chariots, tape, 1978.
6 Matador Circle, Austin, TX 78746

McMAHAN, ROBERT YOUNG
b. Washington, D.C., 12 July 1944. Studied with
Stefans Grove, Robert Hall Lewis, and Jean Ivey,
Peabody Cons., B.M., M.M.; and accordion with
Louis Coppola. He won the Marie K. Thatcher
award, 1972; first place, Annapolis Fine Arts
composition contest, 1972; several awards as
accordionist. He has been piano instructor,
Baltimore County Schools, from 1968; organist
and choirmaster, Pikesville, Md., from 1972.

WORKS: CHAMBER MUSIC: 2 pieces, woodwind trio and accordion, 1968; 3 movements, 2 winds, guitar, viola, celeste, accordion; Portrait of a Virgo, piano, 1971; ELECTRONIC: Whispers of heavenly death, soprano, chamber ensemble, tape, 1971; cantata for double chorus, guitar ensemble, accordion, and tape.

28 Wengate Rd., Owings Mills, MD 21117

McMILLAN, ANN
b. New York, N.Y., 23 Mar. 1923. Attended Bennington Coll., B.A.; studied with Otto Luening and Edgard Varese in New York; horn with Joseph Singer. Her awards include a Tanglewood fellowship, 1948; Fulbright grant, 1955-57; MacDowell fellowships, 1970, 1973, 1976; Creative Arts Public Service grant, 1972; Guggenheim fellowship, 1972-73; and many commissions. She was music editor for recording companies, 1949-55; program director, French Broadcasting in North America (RTF/NYC), 1958-62; music director, WBAI-FM, 1965-68; from 1969, free-lance composer, lecturer, and writer.

WORKS: ELECTRONIC: Gong song, tape, 1969; Carrefours, tape, 1971; Theatre I, music for Home or future soap, 1971; music for Choose a spot on the floor, 1972; Animal I, 1972; Sound-silent-song, from film score, Black and white, 1972; Glass reflections, chamber orch. with glass percussion and tape, 1973; Turn of the year, film score, 1973; Amber '75, tape structure of abstracted insect, frog, and bell sounds, 1975; April '78--Episode, tape and live harpsichord; Cateway '77, summer sound, animal sounds abstracted on tape, 1978.

273 W. 10th St., New York, NY 10014

McMULLEN, PATRICK T.
b. Saginaw, Mich., 11 Mar. 1939. Studied with Philip Bezanson, Univ. of Iowa, Ph.D. 1970. He taught in public schools, 1962-67; was graduate assistant, Univ. of Iowa, 1967-70; on faculty, Eureka Coll., 1970-72; and from 1972, at State Univ. Coll., Fredonia, N.Y.

WORKS: ORCHESTRA: Prelude and allegro, string orch., 1968; BAND: Bring a torch, Jeanette, Isabella, 1967; March miniature, 1968; 3 sketches, 1973; CHAMBER MUSIC: 3 movements for 2 trumpets, 1966; CHORUS: Sanctus, with brass quintet, 1966.

State University College, Fredonia, NY 14063

McNEIL, JAMES CHARLES
b. Columbia, S.C., 24 Sept. 1902. Studied at Univ. of Southern California; Chicago Univ., B.M.; Chapman Coll., M.M.

WORKS: ORCHESTRA: Judith; Mojave; South Carolina suite; In the mist; Suite for strings; also song cycles, cantatas.

McNEIL, JAN PFISCHNER
b. Pittsburgh, Pa., 20 Mar. 1945. Studied with David Diamond and David Burge, Univ. of Colorado; with Ben Johnston and Salvatore Martirano, Univ. of Illinois, D.M.A. 1975. She received Mu Phi Epsilon awards, 1967, 1969 (2), 1970, 1971; MacDowell fellowship, 1970; appointment as guest

composer, Baldwin-Wallace Coll. Contemporary Festival, 1972; Nat. Endowment for the Arts grants, 1971, 1972; South Dakota Council on the Arts grants, 1971, 1972; and commissions. She was on the faculty, Univ. of South Dakota, 1972-73; graduate assistant, Univ. of Illinois, 1973-75; from 1976, on faculty, Wells Coll., Aurora, N.Y.

WORKS: THEATRE: music for Jimmy shine, 1971; music for Passion in the library, 1973; CHAMBER MUSIC: Epithets I and II, woodwind quintet, 1967, 1969; Snow gifts, large ensemble and tenor solo, 1969; In soundless grasses, 1972; Wild song, 1972; Aureate Earth, tenor, prepared piano, percussion, 1972; MULTIMEDIA: Asphodel, 1972.

Music Dept., Wells College, Aurora, NY 13026

McNUTT, RONALD JAN
b. Salina, Kans., 4 Oct. 1936. Attended Idaho State Univ., B.A. 1958; studied with Paul Creston and Robert Paniero, Central Washington State Coll., M.M. 1965. He received the David Herts Memorial award, 1955. Except for a year on the night club circuit, 1962-63, he has taught in public schools since 1958, including an international school in Mangla, West Pakistan, 1965-67.

WORKS: ORCHESTRA: Song for strings, 1966; End of a summer day, string orch., 1973; BAND: Grand Trunk Road, 1967; R. J.'s harem, stage band, 1968; India, B.C., 1970; CHAMBER MUSIC: Kern's patter, trio, 1962; Quatren for reflection, woodwind quintet, 1963; sonata for solo horn, 1964; Nocturne for 6 horns, 1964; Prayer, horn solo, 1971; CHORUS: Thy kingdom come, with brass and woodwinds, 1965; Be not afraid, 1966; Life leads the thoughtful man, 1967; If anybody cares, 1969.

McPHEE, COLIN
b. Montreal, Canada, 15 Mar. 1901; U.S. citizen 1939; d. Los Angeles, Calif., 7 Jan. 1964. Studied with Gustav Strube, Peabody Cons., graduating 1921; piano with Arthur Friedheim in Toronto, with Paul le Flem and Isidor Philipp in Paris. His awards included Guggenheim, Huntington Hartford, and Bollingen Found. fellowships; Nat. Inst. of Arts and Letters grants; and commissions. He lived in New York, 1926-30; then in Bali, 1931-35, 1937-39, studying the native music and instruments; in Mexico, 1936; taught at Univ. of California, Los Angeles, 1958-64.

WORKS: ORCHESTRA: piano concerto, 1924; concerto for piano and wind octet, 1928; Tabuh-Tabuhan, 2 pianos and orch., 1936; Transitions; 3 symphonies, 1955, 1957, 1962; Nocturne, 1958; Pastorale; 4 Iroquois dances; CHAMBER MUSIC: sonatina for 2 flutes, clarinet, trumpet, piano; CHORUS: Sea chanty suite, male chorus, 2 pianos, drums; PIANO: Inventions and kinesis; Balinese ceremonial music, flute and 2 pianos, 1942; FILM SOCRES: HO_2; Mechanical principles. He was also author of a scholarly work, Music in Bali, 1964; and 2 novels, A house in Bali, 1946, and A club of small men, 1948.

McPHERSON, FRANCES MARIE

McPHERSON, FRANCES MARIE
b. Tarkio, Mo., 1912. Studied at Lindenwood
Coll., B.M. 1934; Michigan State Univ., M.M.
1942; piano pirvately with John Thompson in
Kansas City; piano and composition in Barcelona.
She was composer for Little Theatre, St. Joseph,
Mo., for 5 years; taught at Tarkio Coll.,
Florida State Univ., and at Eastern Kentucky
State Coll., 1944 to retirement.
WORKS: OPERA: The snow queen; CHAMBER
MUSIC: violin sonata; CHORUS: A man named
John, cantata; Psalm 150; My Kentucky, with bass
soloist; also songs and piano pieces.

McPHERSON, FRANCES MARIE
b. Norfolk, Va., 6 Nov. 1883; d. 1 Aug. 1944.
Was composer and publisher; founded his own
publishing company. His compositions included
2 operas and The camel walk.

McVOY, JAMES
b. Syracuse, N.Y., 4 Mar. 1946. Studied with
Earl George, Syracuse Univ.; with Wayne Barlow,
Warren Benson, and Samuel Adler, Eastman School
of Music. He has been faculty member, Eliza-
bethtown Coll., from 1970.
WORKS: ORCHESTRA: Reflections, 1973;
CAHMBER MUSIC: Cygnus, cello and piano, 1977;
ELECTRONIC: 4 puns, piano and tape, 1974; Magic
child, flute and tape, 1978.
R.D. 2, Box 1444, Brian Ave., Mt. Joy, PA
17552

McWHOOD, LEONARD BEECHER
b. Brooklyn, N.Y., 5 Dec. 1870; d. Hanover, N.H.,
4 Dec. 1939. Studied with Edward MacDowell,
Columbia Univ., B.A. 1893; was graduate assistant
to MacDowell to 1898; taught at various schools;
from 1918, was professor at Dartmouth Coll. His
compositions include a light opera; 3 cantatas;
instrumental pieces; and songs.

MACY, CARLETON
b. New York, N.Y., 10 Sept. 1944. Studied with
Donal Michalsky, California State Univ., Fullerton; with Robert Suderberg, Univ. of Washington.
He was instructor of winds, Ethiopian Nat.
School of Music, 1968-69; taught in public
schools, Pomona, Calif., 1969-71.
WORKS: WIND ENSEMBLE: Chamber symphony,
for winds and percussion; CHAMBER MUSIC: Concert duo, bassoon and cello; Recorder set, 2
alto recorders; Christmas trio, flute, oboe,
horn; 2 atmospheres, sextet for winds and
strings; 4 pieces for piano; CHORUS: Song serenade, with brass quartet, received an award at
California State Univ., 1971.
15115 Manor Way, Alderwood Manor, WA 98036

MADER, CLARENCE
1904-1971. The 5th mystery, cantata for chorus,
narrator, and organ; Dialogue, organ; 2 mono-
grams, organ; concerto for organ; Prelude, tune,
and masquerade, piano.

MADSEN, FLORENCE JEFFERSON
b. Utah. Spirit of spring, women's voices; My
soul is athirst for God, performed on Utah

program, Washington, D.C., 11 Nov. 1976; many
published choral works, unpublished instrumental
works.

MAEKELBERGHE, AUGUST
b. Oostende, Belgium, 15 Jan. 1909. Studied at
Oostende Acad. of Music; Royal Cons., Ghent;
Notre Dame Coll.; Detroit Inst. of Music and
Art, M.M. He has been organ recitalist and
choral conductor; was professor of organ, Wayne
State Univ.
WORKS: ORCHESTRA: Scherzo impromptu,
Detroit Symphony, Feb. 1946; Elegy, string orch.;
CHORUS: Christ is risen; A Christmas suite,
with string orch. and harp; Communion in D;
ORGAN: Elegy; Toccata and prelude; Toccata,
melody in blue, and fugue.

MAESCH, LA VAHN
b. Appleton, Wis., 15 Oct. 1904. Studied at
Lawrence Univ., B.M. 1926; Univ. of Wisconsin;
Univ. of Michigan; with Marcel Dupre in Paris,
1929-31; at Eastman School of Music, M.M. 1939.
He received a distinguished service citation,
Univ. of Wisconsin; distinguished alumnus award,
Lawrence Univ. He has been organ recitalist,
choirmaster, lecturer; and was director,
Lawrence Univ. Cons., 1954-74.
WORKS: ORCHESTRA: Christmas suite, 1938;
Children's suite, 1938; symphony, 1941; CHORUS:
Waking time, a cappella; Prayer after triumph;
works for solo voice and organ.

MAGANINI, QUINTO
b. Fairfield, Calif., 30 Nov. 1897; d. Greenwich,
Conn., 10 Mar. 1974. Studied at Univ. of California; flute with Georges Barrere in New York;
composition with Nadia Boulanger in France. His
awards included the Pulitzer prize, 1927;
Guggenheim fellowship, 1928; David Bispham
prize for The Argonauts, 1927. He played flute
in the San Francisco Symphony, 1917; was discovered by Walter Damrosch in Sousa's band in
1918 and brough to New York. He played in the
New York Symph., 1919-28; organized and conducted his own chamber symphony; conducted
Norwalk (Conn.) Symph., 1939; taught at Columbia
Univ.; was president, American School of Music
and Art, Fontainebleau, France; also president,
Kingsbury Machine Works and Edition Musicus, Inc.
WORKS: OPERA: The argonauts, 1927; Tennessee's partner, 1924; ORCHESTRA: Tuolumne,
rhapsody for trumpet and orch., 1924; South wind,
a fantasy, 1930; Sylvan symphony, 1930; concerto
for strings, 1934; Napoleon, a portrait, 1935;
An ornithological suite; CHORUS: The cathedral
at Sens, with cello and orch.

MAGEAU, SISTER MARY MAGDALEN
b. Milwaukee, Wis., 4 Sept. 1934. Studied with
Leon Stein, De Paul Univ., B.M.; with Ross Lee
Finney and Leslie Bassett, Univ. of Michigan,
M.M.; with George Crumb at Tanglewood, 1970, on
a fellowship. Other awards include second prize,
Gottschalk Internat. Competition, 1970; and com-
missions. She was faculty member, Scholastica
Coll., 1969-73; part-time instructor, Univ. of
Wisconsin, 1971-72; guest lecturer, Kelvin Grove

Coll., Brisbane, Univ. of Tasmania, Hobart, and Univ. of South Australia, Adelaide, 1974-76.

WORKS: ORCHESTRA: Variegations, 1970; Montage, performed by Minnesota Orch., Duluth Symph., and Des Moines Symph.; BAND: Celebration music; CHAMBER MUSIC: 3 movements for unaccompanied cello, 1968; CHORUS: A new lacrimae; KEYBOARD: Forecasts, piano; 3 pieces, organ.

57 Ironside St., St. Lucia, Queensland 4067, Australia

MAGINNIS, WILLIAM RICHARD

b. Yreka, Calif., 15 Nov. 1938. Studied with Roger Nixon, San Francisco State Coll. He was instructor, San Francisco State Coll., tape music center, 1964-67; Mills Coll., tape music center, 1967-68; then independent instructor and technician.

WORKS: CHAMBER MUSIC: 3 pieces for piano, 1961; Music for string quartet, 1961; Winter voices, cyclic epigrams, 1963; Extensions #1, 1964; Ambiet, 1972; ELECTRONIC: Mindways, rock and roll band and tape, 1967; Genuine imitation plastic whirlpool, 1967; etc.

71 Whitney St., San Francisco, CA 94101

MAIBEN, WILLIAM

b. Salt Lake City, Utah, 15 June 1953. Studied with Richard Hoffmann, Oberlin Cons., B.M. 1975; with John Rahn, Univ. of Washington; with Vladimir Ussachevsky, Univ. of Utah, M.M. 1978. His awards include first place, Utah State Fair contest, 1972, 1973; first place, Nat. Fed. of Music Clubs contest, 1972; Composers Guild contest, 1973, 1978; BMI award, 1976; Music Teachers Nat. Assoc. contest, 1975. He was teaching assistant, Univ. of Washington, 1975-76; accompanist, Univ. of Utah, 1976-78.

WORKS: THEATRE: Snowbird, comic opera, 1978; ORCHESTRA: concerto for viola and strings, 1970; 3 friendly spirits, 1977; CHAMBER MUSIC: string quartet, 1971; 4 pieces, viola and piano, 1971; Music for H.F.A.C., 14 instruments, 1972; Variations, piano and tape, 1972; From the 5 hills, violin and viola, 1972; Serenade, flute, violin, viola, harpsichord, 1972; The White Knights's song, 3 voices, 9 instruments; Street music from San Francisco, quintet, 1974; sonata for oboe and 2 violas, 1975; violin sonata, 1977; 7 songs of Bilitis, soprano and quartet.

2774 Wardway Dr., Salt Lake City, UT 84117

MAILMAN, MARTIN

b. New York, N.Y., 30 June 1932. Studied with Louis Mennini, Wayne Barlow, Bernard Rogers, Howard Hanson, Eastman School of Music, B.M. 1954, M.M. 1955, Ph.D. 1960. His awards include scholarships at Eastman School; Benjamin award, 1955; first prize, Birmingham Arts Festival, 1966; 2 first prizes, Williamette Univ., 1966; first prize, Walla Walla Symphony, 1967; annual ASCAP awards; many commissions. He taught in the U.S. Naval School of Music, 1955-57; was composer-in-residence, Young Composers Project, Jacksonville, Fla., 1959-61; professor and composer-in-residence, East Carolina Coll., 1961-66; and from 1966, at North Texas State Univ.

WORKS: THEATRE: The hunted, 1-act opera,

1959; music for Moby Dick, 1965; ORCHESTRA: Dance in 2 moods, 1952; Autumn landscape, 1954; Jubilate, 1955; Elegy, 1955; Cantiones, 1957; Prelude and fugue, 1959; Partita, strings, 1960; Gateway City overture, 1960; suite in 3 movements, 1961; Generations 2, string orch. and percussion, 1969; A simple ceremony (in memoriam John Barnes Chance),1973; BAND: Promenade, brass and percussion, 1953; Partita, 1958; Commencement march, 1960; 4 miniatures, 1960; Geometrics 1-5, 1961, 1962, 1965, 1968, 1976; Alarums, 1963; concertino for trumpet and band, 1963; Liturgical music, 1964; 4 variations in search of a theme, narrator and band, 1965; Associations #1, 1969; In memoriam Frankie Newton, 1970; Requiem, requiem, 1972; Shouts, hymns, and praises, 1972; Decorations, 1974; Let us now praise famous men, with solo voice and narrators, 1975; CAHMBER MUSIC: Burlesque, trumpet and piano, 1951; string quartet, 1962; 4 diversions, percussion ensemble, 1966; Partita #4, 9 players, 1967; Wind across the nation, solo voice, piano, percussion, flute, guitar, 1975; Ciastics: Formation, solo cello, Denton, Tex., 26 Apr. 1978; CHORUS: Leaves of grass, with narrator and band, 1963; The rise and fall, choral fable, 1966; Shakespearean serenade, 1968; Generations 3: Messengers, children's choirs, solo voice, stage band, 1977; A choral sampler, 1977; PIANO: Martha's Vineyard, 1969; In memoriam Silvio Scionti, 1974.

North Texas State University, Denton, TX 76203

MAINENTE, ANTON EUGENE

b. Paterson, N.J., 5 Nov. 1889; d. Auburn, Maine, 18 Aug. 1963. Studied at New England Cons., where he later taught. In Boston he also conducted opera and played flute in the Boston Pops Orchestra. During World War I, he taught at the AEF Bandleaders School; later at Gould Acad.; Hebron Acad.; formed Mainente School of Music, 1921.

WORKS: ORCHESTRA: Symphony America; Impressions of an afternoon; Reminiscences.

MAIORANA, VICTOR E. (VICTOR LAMONT)

b. Palermo, Italy, 20 July 1897; to U.S. as a child; d. New York, N.Y., 18 Oct. 1964. He was a theatre organist and editor in a music publishing firm. His works for orchestra included Reflections on the lake; Legend of the canyon.

MAIS, CHESTER L.

b. Philadelphia, Pa., 16 June 1936. Studied with Hugo Weisgall and Robert Sanders, City Univ. of New York; with Robert Palmer at Cornell Univ.; with Samuel Adler and Wayne Barlow, Eastman School of Music. He held graduate assitantships at Cornell Univ. and Eastman School; was lecturer, Brooklyn Coll., 1966-68; instructor, St. Francis Coll., Broonlyn, 1968-69.

WORKS: WIND ENSEMBLE: brass quintet, 1971; Lament, trombone choir, 1973; Fantasy on warm-up exercises, trombone choir, 1973; CHAMBER MUSIC: Fantasy on a phrase of Schoenberg, piano, 1970; woodwind quintet, 1970; string quartet #2; Establishment piece, violin, viola, 4 winds,

MAITLAND, ROLLO FRANCIS

1973; Gray piece #1, tuba, viola, English horn, 1973.
2685 Danby Rd., Willseyville, NY 13864

MAITLAND, ROLLO FRANCIS
b. Williamsport, Pa., 10 Dec. 1884; d. Philadelphia, Pa., 7 Apr. 1953. Studied in Philadelphia, was church organist, music critic, and teacher there. He published works for organ.

MAKRIS, ANDREAS
b. Salonika, Greece, 30 Mar. 1930; U.S. citizen 1962. Studied at the Nat. Cons., Greece, graduating with highest honors, 1950; came to the U.S. on an exchange student grant; studied at Kansas City Cons.; Mannes Coll. of Music, B.M. 1956; Aspen Music Festival; with Nadia Boulanger in France. His awards include Damrosch grant; Martha Baird Rockefeller award; Nat. Endowment for the Arts grant; and commissions. He was the first living composer to be performed at the Kennedy Center in Washington. He toured the U.S. and Canada as violinist in Roman Totenberg's 9-member ensemble, 1956-58; has been violinist with the Dallas Symphony, St. Louis Symphony, and the National Symphony, Washington.
WORKS: ORCHESTRA: Aegean festival; Anamnesis, St. Paul, Minn., 30 Jan. 1971; viola concerto; Efthymia; concerto for strings; Chromatokinesis, 1978; CHAMBER MUSIC: 2 string quartets; concertino for trombone and string quartet; quintet for voice and string quartet; Fantasy and dance, saxophone and piano; violin duets; Sirens, voice, piano, violin.
11204 Oakleaf Dr., Silver Spring, MD 20901

MALKIN, JOSEPH
b. Near Odessa, Russia, 24 Sept. 1879; to U.S. c. 1913; d. New York, N.Y., 1 Sept. 1969. Studied in Odessa and at Paris Cons. He was first cellist, Berlin Philharmonic, 1902-8; then toured Europe and North America with the Brussels Quartet; was first celllist, Boston Symphony, 1914-19; Chicago Symphony, 1919-22; formed Malkin Trio with his brothers, Jacques and Manfred; established Malkin Cons. in Boston, 1933-43; was cellist with New York Philharmonic, 1944-49. He wrote cello works and studies.

MALKO, NIKOLAY ANDREYEVICH
b. Brailov, Russia, 4 May 1883; U.S. citizen 1946; d. Sydney, Australia, 23 June 1961. Studied at St. Petersburg Univ. and with Korsakov, Liadov, Glazunov, and Tcherepnin at the Cons. He was conductor in St. Petersburg and Copenhagen; came to the U.S. and was lecturer at De Paul Univ., 1940-54; returned to conducting with the Yorkshire Symphony, England, 1954-55; and the Sydney Symphony in Australia, 1956-61. His compositions included a clarinet concerto, 1952.

MALOOF, WILLIAM J.
b. Boston, Mass., 19 May 1933. Studied at Boston Univ., B.M. His awards include first prize in composition, 6th Annual Contemporary Music Festival, Indiana State Univ.; and commissions. He has been faculty member, Berklee Coll. of Music, from 1961.

WORKS: OPERA: The centurion; ORCHESTRA: Sinfonietta concertante; suite from The centurion; 2 antique dances, flute and strings; BAND: Essay for band; Festive music, double wind orch. and percussion; CHAMBER MUSIC: Prelude and chaconne, solo viola; Homage to Bali, percussion; Fantasy, flute and piano; Music for piano and percussion quartet; also vocal works.
33 Pratt St., Brighton, MA 02134

MALOTTE, ALBERT HAY
b. Philadelphia, Pa., 19 May 1895; d. Los Angeles, Calif., 16 Nov. 1964. Studied organ in Philadelphia; was concert organist in the U.S. and Europe; established a school for theatre organists in Los Angeles, 1927; was music director of Walt Disney Studios for several years.
WORKS: BALLET: Little Red Riding Hood; Carnival of Venice; THEATRE: Lolama, musical play; MUSICALS: Fanfare; The big tree; Limbo; CHORUS: Psalm 91; Voice of the prophet; SONGS: The Lord's prayer; Psalm 23; Song of the open road; FILM SCORES: Dr. Cyclops; Enchanted forest; Ferdinand the bull; some of Disney's Silly symphonies.

MALTBY, RICHARD E.
b. Chicago, Ill., 26 June 1914. Studied at Northwestern Univ.; played trumpet with dance bands and with the staff orchestra, WBBM, Chicago; went to New York in 1945.
WORKS: BAND: Trumpet nocturne; Blues essay, with solo horn; Jazz waltz; Hail to the fleet; 6 flats unfurnished; Esprit de corps; Manhattan discoteque; Fugue in 5 flats; Ballad, clarinet and band; Ballad for brass, contrabass, guitar, percussion; Threnody, requiem for John F. Kennedy, with narrator.

MAMLOK, URSULA
b. Berlin, Germany, 1 Feb. 1928; U.S. citizen 1945. Studied with George Szell, Mannes Coll. of Music; with Roger Sessions, Ralph Shapey, and Stefan Wolpe privately in New York; at Manhattan School of Music, M.M. She has received awards from Nat. Fed. of Music Clubs; Nat. School Orch. Assoc.; City Univ. of New York Research Found. grant, 1972-73; Nat. Endowment for the Arts grant, 1976. She was faculty member, New York Coll. of Music, 1967-68; New York Univ., 1968-74; and from 1968, also at Manhattan School of Music.
WORKS: ORCHESTRA: oboe concerto, 1976; CHAMBER MUSIC: Variations for solo flute, 1961; Stray birds, soprano, flute, cello, 1963; 5 capriccios, oboe and piano; Variations and interludes, percussion; sonatina, 2 clarinets; Grasshoppers, piano solo; string quartet; Haiku settings, soprano and flute; sextet for flute, 2 clarinets, viola, double bass, piano, New York, 30 Nov. 1977; Festive sounds, woodwind quintet, Dallas, 7 Aug. 1978; Polyphony 1, solo clarinet, 1980.
315 E. 86th St., New York, NY 10028

MANA-ZUCCA (AUGUSTA ZUCKERMANN)
b. New York, N.Y., 25 Dec. 1887; d. Miami, Fla., 8 Mar. 1981. Studied piano with Alexander

Lambert in New York; with Busoni and Godowsky in Berlin; composition with Hermann Spielter in London; voice with Von zur Muhlen in London and Paris. She made her piano debut at age 11, playing a Beethoven concerto with the New York Symphony; then toured Europe. Her debut as a soprano was in Lehar's Count of Luxembourg in 1914. She appeared in other operettas, 1914-16; gave recitals, including her own works on the programs. She was married to Irwin M. Cassel (1886-1971), who wrote the lyrics for most of her songs. After 1940, was composer, pianist, and teacher in Miami, Fla.

WORKS: OPERA: Hypatia; The queue of Ki-Lu; BALLET: The wedding of the butterfly; ORCHESTRA: piano concerto, 1919 (chosen for the 1976 Bicentennial contest of American composers); Cuban dance; Frolic for strings; Fugato humoresque; Havana nights, violin concerto, 1955; CHAMBER MUSIC: violin sonata; cello sonata; piano trio; Walla-Kye, saxophone and piano; violin pieces; PIANO: 3 sonatas; Elegy; Jocosity; Badinage; My musical calendar, a collection of 365 pieces in 12 books; SONGS: I love life; Time and time again; There's joy in my heart; The brown bear; Honey lamb; Nichevo; and others.

MANCINI, HENRY
b. Cleveland, Ohio, 16 Apr. 1924. Studied at Carnegie Inst., and at the Juilliard School; privately with Ernst Krenek, Mario Castelnuovo-Tedesco, and Alfred Sendrey. His first award was at age 13, when he was first flutist in the Pennsylvania State Band. Awards for his film and television scores include 20 Grammys,,3 Oscars, and many nominations. He was staff composer, Universal-Internat. Studios, 1952-57; then turned to television scores with "Peter Gunn" in 1958 and "Mr. Lucky" in 1960.

WORKS: FILM SCORES: High time; The great imposter; Mr. Hobbs takes a vacation; Bachelor in paradise; Breakfast at Tiffany's; Harari; Experiment in terror; Days of wine and roses; Charade; The pink panther; Soldier in the rain; Dear heart; Shot in the dark; Moment to moment; Arabesque; The great race; 2 for the road; Wait until dark; The party; Gunn; Me, Natalie; Gaily, gaily: The Molly Maguires; Sunflower; Darling Lili; The Hawaiians; The night visitor.

MANDEL, JOHN
b. New York, N.Y., 23 Nov, 1925. Studied at Manhattan School of Music; with Stefan Wolpe, at Juilliard School; played trumpet with Joe Venuti and Billie Rogers; trombone with Jimmie Dorsey, Buddy Rich, Count Basie; was arranger for many bands. He received a Grammy award, 1965, for The shadow of your smile from The sandpiper, which won an Academy award, 1966. Other film scores: Cold day in the' park; Harper; You're never too young; The Russians are coming; The Americanization of Helen; "Markham" (television).

MANDELBAUM, JOEL
b. New York, N.Y., 12 Oct. 1932. Studied with Angela Diller, Diller-Quaile School; with Walter Piston, Harvard Univ.; with Irving Fine,

and Harold Shapero, Brandies Univ.; with Bernhard Heiden, Indiana Univ.; with Luigi Dallapiccola and Aaron Copland at Tanglewood. He has been faculty member, Queens Coll., CUNY, from 1961.

WORKS: OPERA: The man in the man-made moon, 1 act, 1956; The dybbuk, 4 acts, 1972; ORCHESTRA: Sinfonia concertante, oboe, horn, violin, cello, and small orch., 1962; trumpet concerto, 1971; CHAMBER MUSIC: woodwind quintet, 1957; string quartet, 1958; microtonal quartet for 3 horns and trombone; VOICE: 3 song cycles: poems of Millay, 1958, J. Berman, 1971, Roethke, 1973; 10 Yeats settings for vocal quartet and instruments, 1965; EXPERIMENTAL WORKS: 9 studies in 12-tone temperament, 1961; 10 studies in Euler genera for 31-tone organ.
3949 46th St., Long Island City, NY 11104

MANERI, JOSEPH
b. New York, N.Y., 9 Feb. 1927. Studied for 11 years with Joseph Schmid, pupil of Alban Berg; was trained in jazz and music of the Middle East as clarinetist, saxophonist, and pianist. He taught theory, Brooklyn Cons., 1964-65; New England Cons., from 1970; teaches composition privately.

WORKS: ORCHESTRA: piano concerto, commissioned by Erich Leinsdorf; CHAMBER MUSIC: string quartet; trio; Woodwind, brass, and percussion, 1968; Ephphatha, piano, clarinet, trombone, and tuba; piano pieces.
New England Conservatory, 290 Huntington Ave., Boston, MA 02115

MANGININI, MARINO ANTHONY
b. Endicott, N.Y., 5 Feb. 1950. Studied with James Willey and David Maslanka, State Univ. Coll., Geneseo, N.Y., 1969-71. His string quartet #1 won an award in a competition sponsored by the Catgut Acoustical Society and the New Jersey Council on the Arts, 1973. He is a high school English teacher and music copyist.

WORKS: CHAMBER MUSIC: octet for woodwinds and strings, 1971; string quartet, Douglas Coll., 14 Oct. 1973; Advent, chamber orch., 1974; duo for harp and piano, 1975; Threnody, solo flute, 1977; Antiphony, clarinet and marimba, 1978; Fantasies of ancient triumphs, solo violin, 1978; CHORUS: Ash Wednesday, with chamber orch., 1978.
Cohocton St., Box 476, Naples, NY 14512

MANN, JAMES
b. Fort Worth, Tex., 27 Nov. 1942. Studied with Ben Johnston, Thomas Frederickson, and Morgan Powell, Univ. of Illinois; with Arthur Berger, Brandeis Univ. He was on the faculty, New England Cons., 1973-75; at Univ. of Illinois, 1977-78.

WORKS: JAZZ ENSEMBLE: Rani Ban, 1970; CHAMBER MUSIC: Short piece, chamber group, 1969; 2 songs, soprano, flute, viola, bass clarinet, text by composer, 1970; Realizations, 14 instruments, 1971; Kaleidophone, 7 instruments, Boston, 13 May 1973; wind sextet, 2 clarinets, 2 horns, 2 bassoons; Mosaics, solo flute.
143 Fairview Ave., Belmont, MA 02178

MANN, ROBERT

MANN, ROBERT
  b. Portland, Oreg., 19 July 1920. Studied with
Bernard Wagenaar, Juilliard School; privately
with Stefan Wolpe. He received a Nat. Endowment
for the Arts grant, 1975. From 1946, he has been
faculty member at Juilliard School; is first
violinist of the Juilliard Quartet, which he
organized in 1948 and which was made the resident
quartet of the Library of Congress. In 1971, he
was named president of the Naumburg Found.
  WORKS: ORCHESTRA: Fantasy for orchestra;
Suite for strings; small symphony; CHAMBER MUSIC:
5 movements for string quartet, 1952; duo for
violin and viola; piano sonata; some 18 Lyric
trios for narrator, violin, and piano; duo for
violin and piano, 1975; also choral works, songs,
cadenzas, and other instrumental works.
  262 Central Park W., New York, NY 10024

MANNES, LEOPOLD DAMROSCH
  b. New York, N.Y., 26 Dec. 1899; d. Martha's
Vineyard, Mass., 11 Aug. 1964. Son of David
Mannes and Clara Damrosch Mannes, studied at
the David Mannes School of Music; with Rosario
Scalero and Percy Goetschius, Inst. of Musical
Art, New York; received a Pulitzer award,
1925, Guggenheim fellowship, 1926. He taught at
The Inst. of Musical Art and at the Mannes
School, succeeding his father as director. For
a time he worked at Eastman Kodak Co., and was
coinventor with Leopold Godowsky (son of the
pianist) of the Kodacolor photographic process.
  WORKS: THEATRE: music to The tempest, 1930;
ORCHESTRA: Short pieces, a suite, 1926; CHAMBER
MUSIC: Suite for 2 pianos, 1924; string quar-
tet, 1928; songs.

MANNEY, CHARLES FONTEYN
  b. Brooklyn, N.Y., 8 Feb. 1872; d. New York,
N.Y., 31 Oct. 1951. Studied at Brooklyn Polytechnic Inst.; with William Arms Fisher in New
York; with J. Wallace Goodrich and Percy
Goetschius in Boston. He was editor for a
Boston music publisher, 1898-1930; choral conductor for the MacDowell Club.
  WORKS: CANTATAS: The resurrection; The
manger throne; SONGS: O captain, my captain; A
shropshire lad; also an opera.

MANNING, KATHLEEN LOCKHART
  b. Hollywood, Calif., 24 Oct. 1890; d. Los
Angeles, Calif., 20 Mar. 1951. Studied piano
in Los Angeles; composition with Moritz
Moszkowski in Paris. She made concert tours
in England and France, 1909-14; sang with the
Hammerstein Opera Company in London, 1911-12.
  WORKS: OPERA: Mr. Wu; For the soul of
Rafael; SONGS: Sketches of Paris; Sketches of
New York; Songs of Egypt; Autumn leaves; Water-
lily; The lamplighter; The street fair; also
piano pieces.

MANNO, ROBERT
  b. Bryn Mawr, Pa., 27 July 1944. Studied with
Romeo Cascarino, Combs Coll. of Music, 1964-65;
with Ludmila Ulehla, Manhattan School of Music,
B.M. 1968; with Vladimir Padwa, New York Univ.,
M.A. 1974; with Donald Erb, Composers Conf.,

Johnson, Vt., 1973. His awards include the
Ernest Bloch award, 1971; New York Univ. scholarship; first prize, Delius Festival, Jacksonville,
Fla., 1975. He was jazz pianist, 1962-65;
member of New York City Opera chorus, 1967-77;
from 1977 Metropolitan Opera chorus.
  WORKS: CHAMBER MUSIC: 4 short pieces,
clarinet and piano, 1966; Dirge and blues, tuba
quartet, 1969; Fern Hill, baritone, wind quartet,
string quintet, 1970-72; Birdsongs, soprano and
violin, 1972; 5 thematic etudes, string quartet,
1973; Landscapes, voice, wind quintet, double
bass, 1973; 3 quiet pieces, harp solo, 1974;
Dreams and riffs, horn and piano or chamber
orch., 1974-75; A woman's love, soprano and
string orch., 1975; CHORUS (a cappella): This
is the garden, 1968; God's grandeur, 1971; Amen,
1974; next to of course god, 1976; songs; piano
pieces.
  155 Bank St., Apt. C-320, New York, NY 10014

MANSFIELD, KENNETH ZOELLIN, JR.
  b. King City, Calif., 21 Aug. 1932. Studied
with Randall Thompson and Walter Piston, Harvard
Univ.; organ with Andre Marchel in Paris,
Edward Mueller in Basel, on a John Knowles
Paine fellowship, 1956. He has been faculty
member, Univ. of California, Hayward, from 1966;
church organist from 1964.
  WORKS: CHORUS: The image, Christmas introit with brass quartet and organ; Christ whose
glory fills the sky; Collect for Advent VI;
Magnificat and Nunc dimittis; ORGAN: Variations
on a ground; Variations on Forest green; Elegy
for a young child; sonata for flute and organ;
Sinfonia for Easter morning, with string quartet;
6 movements for 2 organs, commissioned by San
Francisco chapter, American Guild of Organists.
  Music Dept., Univ. of California, Hayward,
CA 94542

MANSON, EDDY LAWRENCE
  b. New York, N.Y., 9 May 1919. Studied with
Vittorio Giannini and Adolf Schmid at Juilliard
School; privately with Howard Brockway and
Rudolf Schramm; and at New York Univ. He has
been harmonica soloist in Town Hall and Carnegie
Hall in New York.
  WORKS: ORCHESTRA: symphony; Chorale fantasy
on a theme by Bach; WIND ENSEMBLE: Fugue for
woodwinds; Ballad for brass; CHAMBER MUSIC:
Research, string quartet; Provocation, bass and
piano; FILM SCORES: The little fugitive; Lovers
and lollipops; Johnny Jupiter; Supermarket; US
1--American profile; The River Nile; Polaris
submarine; "American spectacle" (television).

MANTON, ROBERT WILLIAM
  b. Dorchester, Mass., 9 Nov. 1894; d. Durham,
N.H., 24 Dec. 1967. Studied with Archibald T.
Davison and Edward Burlingame Hill, Harvard
Univ.; privately with Harris S. Shaw in Boston;
with d'Indy in Paris; at the MacDowell Colony;
and with Ralph Vaughan Williams in Lodnon, 1953.
He was awarded an honorary doctorate, Univ. of
New Hampshire, 1967. He taught privately in
Boston, 1919-23; then was appointed head of, and
organized, the music department, Univ. of New

Hampshire, retiring as professor in 1964; was church organist in Durham and Exeter, N.H.

WORKS: ORCHESTRA: New England sketches; Wuthering Heights fantasy; November woods; piano concerto; New England rhapsody; Dance rhapsody; Jeanie; CHAMBER MUSIC: 2 violin sonatas; 2 pieces for cello and piano; PIANO: Improvisation, 1916; Marine sketches, 1924; New Hampshire idyls, 1926; 2 sonatas; North Country pieces; Fire of spring; Scherzo; many choral works and songs.

MANZ, PAUL
b. Cleveland, Ohio, 10 May 1919. Studied organ at American Cons.; Baldwin-Wallace Coll.; Univ. of Minnesota; with Flor Peeters in Belgium; and Helmut Walcha in Germany. His awards include a Fulbright grant; Firmin Swinnen award; Callaert prize; honorary doctorate, Concordia Coll., Nebr.; St. Cecilia Medal, Boystown, Nebr. He has held faculty posts at Winnebago Acad.; Macalester Coll.; Univ. of Minnesota; Concordia Coll., Minn.

WORKS: Let us ever walk with Jesus, 1954; Psalm 130, 1955; On my heart imprint thine image, 1956; Preserve me, O Lord, 1958; On Christmas Eve, 1960; Sing to the Lord a new song; ORGAN: 40 choral improvisations; other liturgical works for chorus and organ.
7204 Schey Dr., Edina, MN 55435

MARAIS, JOSEF
b. Sir Lowry Pass, South Africa, 17 Nov. 1905; U.S. citizen 1945; d. Los Angeles, 27 Apr. 1978. Studied at South African Coll. of Music on scholarship, and at Royal Acad. of Music, London. He was violinist in the Capetown Symph.; translated Afrikaans folk songs; with his wife, Miranda, gave vocal concerts; worked with the Office of War Information in Voice of America broadcasts.

WORKS: THEATRE: Tony Beaver, opera; music for Alan Paton's Too late the phalarope; ORCHESTRA: Paul Gauguin suite; Africana suite; VOICE: 14 songs from the veld; The bangalorey man, for children; many other songs.

MARALDO, WILLIAM
b. Cheyenne, Wyo., 28 Mar. 1938. Studied at Univ. of Colorado; at Paris Cons.; master classes with Lukas Foss; privately with George Crumb. He was assistant director, Centre de Musique, Paris, 1963-64; codirector, Center for Contemporary Music, Mills Coll., from 1968; and president, Tantra Research Inst., Oakland, from 1972.

WORKS: ELECTRONIC: Sound of breath; Song of the vallies; Night music; Journey into night; Textures; FILM SCORE: Transmutations.

MARCELLI, NINO
b. Santiago, Chile, 21 Jan. 1890; U.S. citizen 1917; d. San Diego, Calif., 4 Aug. 1967. Studied at Nat. Cons. of Chile and Univ. of Chile, where he was honorary member of the faculty of fine arts. He was conductor, American Hdq. Band in France, 1918-20; cellist, San Francisco Symph., 1920; from 1921 to retirement, was director of

instrumental music in San Diego schools; founded San Diego Symph., 1925, was conductor to 1937; guest conductor, Hollywood Bowl, Los Angeles Phil., San Francisco Symph., and others; guest lecturer in many Western colleges.

WORKS: LIGHT OPERA: Carmelita; ORCHESTRA: symphony; Suite Araucana; suite for strings; Ode to a hero; March processional; 2 Christmas processionals; SONGS: Solitude; Deep in the forest; Song of the Andes; Song of thanks; Harp of sunset.

MARCUS, ADABELLE GROSS
b. Chicago, Ill., 8 July 1929. Studied with Samuel Lieberson and Alexander Tcherepnin, De Paul Univ.; with Leo Sowerby, American Cons.; with Karel Jirak, Roosevelt Univ.; and piano with Robert Goldsand in New York. She won an appearance as piano soloist with the Dayton Phil.; and performances of her works by the Internat. Society for Contemporary Music. She has been concert pianist from 1939; vocal coach, 1942-49; piano teacher, from 1959.

WORKS: OPERA: Snow, chamber opera on Frost text; ORCHESTRA: 2 fantasies; piano concertino; violin concerto; Symphony of the spheres; CHAMBER MUSIC: string quartet; Nocturne, flute and piano; violin sonata; Song for flute; CHORUS: God, whom shall I compare to thee, with brass; Setting to seasons, with chamber orch.; SONGS: cycles on Robert Frost and Dylan Thomas texts; 4 preludes on Playthings to the wind, Sandburg text; PIANO: A day in New York City; A child's day, suite; Youth in orbit; sonata; Etude erotique; Blue flute; Sound score; 3 modules.
9374 Landings Lane, Des Plaines, IL 60016

MAREK, ROBERT
Has been on faculty, Univ. of South Dakota, from 1957. His compositions include a trio for trumpet, horn, trombone; cantata for tenor, piano, percussion, on text by South Dakota poet, John Milton, performed on South Dakota program, Bicentennial Parade of Music, Washington, D.C., 9 Sept. 1976.
Music Dept., Univ. of South Dakota, Vermillion, SD 57069

MARGOLIS, JEROME N.
b. Philadelphia, Pa., 30 Oct. 1941. Studied with Vincent Persichetti, Philadelphia Cons.; with Joseph Castaldo, Philadelphia Musical Acad. He was instructor, Philadelphia Settlement School, 1964-65; music director, performing arts, Bennett Coll., 1967-70; from 1970, music chairman, Harvard School, Van Nuys, Calif.

WORKS: ORCHESTRA: symphony; CHAMBER MUSIC: brass quartet; woodwind trio; string quartet; Gebrauchsmusik for dance, solo percussionist; also theatre music, electronic and multimedia works, ballets, piano pieces, choral works.
3700 Coldwater Canyon, N. Hollywood, CA 91604

MARKAITIS, BRUNO
b. Lithuania, 7 July 1922; U.S. citizen 1958. Studied in Rome and London; with Alexander Tcherepnin and Bernard Dieter in Chicago. He

MARKS, FRANKLYN

has won prizes in Lithuania-American composition contests and is an honorary member of the Kodaly Acad. and Inst.

WORKS: ORCHESTRA: piano concerto, 1968; concertino #2 for piano and orch., 1969; WIND ENSEMBLE: concertino #1, piano, winds, percussion, 1968; concertino #3, organ, winds, percussion, 1971; CHAMBER MUSIC: 2 violin sonatas, 1960, 1972; string quartet, 1961; Mirage, piano, 1962; 3 dances, piano, 1973; CHORUS: The night of sorrow, cantata, 1958; Bells of Vilnius, symphonic cantata, 1965; Christmas poem, choral suite, 1966; Community mass, 1967; 100 suns, symphonic meultimedia oratorio, 1970, commissioned by Loyola Univ. of Chicago for its centennial.

739 22nd St., Santa Monica, CA 90402

MARKS, FRANKLYN
b. Cleveland, Ohio, 31 May 1911. Studied at Dartmouth Coll., B.A. 1932; privately with Joseph Schiller, 1937-41. He was elected to Phi Beta Kappa; received an Emmy nomination, 1961. He was staff arranger, NBC, 1937-42; freelance arranger, 1942-55; composer-music director, Walt Disney Studios, from 1955.

WORKS: THEATRE: The bridge, ballet; ORCHESTRA: West Virginia; JAZZ ENSEMBLE: Trajectories; The new world; CHAMBER MUSIC: Night and the sea, guitar; Dialogue, guitar; FILM SCORES: Legend of the boy and the eagle; Charlie, the lonesome cougar; and many songs.

3825 Ventura Canyon Ave., Sherman Oaks, CA 91403

MARRYOTT, RALPH E.
b. Jamesburg, N.J., 15 Apr. 1908. Attended Peddie School. He has been minister of music, director of school of music, choral director, and organist in Jamesburg from 1926. His works include an organ suite and many sacred songs.

MARSH, CHARLES HOWARD
b. Magnolia, Iowa, 8 Apr. 1885; d. San Diego, Calif., 12 Apr. 1956. Studied with Walter Hall and A. J. Goodrich in New York; with Widor, Libert, and Philipp in France. He held various posts as organist and teacher in Indiana, Florida, and California.

WORKS: CHORUS: Benedictus es domine; Jubilate deo; Christus natus est; In this place will I give peace; ORGAN: Scherzo; 4 color prints; Legend triste; Beside still waters.

MARSH, MILTON R. W.
b. Bermuda, 29 Sept. 1945. Studied at Berklee Coll. of Music, B.M.; with Jaki Byard and Robert Ceely, New England Cons., M.M. He was faculty member, State Univ. of New York, Oneonta, 1972-73; at SUNY, Buffalo, 1973-78.

WORKS: CHAMBER MUSIC: Monism, string quartet, spoken texts, jazz ensemble, 1971; Poems, saxophone quartet; Psychic impulses; Ode to Nzinga; Elementals; Study in retrospect.

MARSHALL, INGRAM D.
b. Mt. Vernon, N.Y., 10 May 1942. Studied at Lake Forest Coll.; with Vladimir Ussachevsky and

Ilhan Mimaroglu, Columbia Univ.; at New York Univ.; with Morton Subotnick, James Tenney, Ki Wasitodipura, California Inst. of the Arts; and with Bulent Arel. His awards include a Fulbright scholarship to Sweden, 1975; grants from California Arts Council, 1977, San Francisco Council, 1978, Nat. Endowment for the Arts, 1978-79. He was faculty member, California Inst. of the Arts, 1971-74; San Francisco Cons., 1976.

WORKS: INSTRUMENTAL: Ricebowlthundersock, pianist and percussionist on 1 piano, 1973; ELECTRONIC: The East is red, Chinese folk song, 1972; Cortes, text-sound piece on voice of a Danish weatherwoman, Berkley, 20 June 1974; The fragility cycles (Cries upon the mountains, Gambuh, Sibelius in his radio corner, Ikon), San Francisco, 30 Oct. 1976; Landscape score score (commissioned by Royal Swedish Consulate, N.Y.); Matter; Vibrosuperball, 4 percussionists, 1977; Non confundar, 1977-78, and Addendum: In aeternum, 1978-79, both for string sextet, alto flute, clarinet, electronics.

504 Cole St., San Francisco, CA 94117

MARSHALL, JAMES T.
b. Seattle, Wash., 12 Oct. 1941. Studied with George McKay and John Verrall, Univ. of Washington; with Paul Cooper and Scott Huston, Univ. of Cincinnati; and privately with George Rochberg. He was faculty member, Drake Univ., 1966-68; Montclair State Coll., 1968-71; from 1978, at Cleveland State Univ.

WORKS: CHAMBER MUSIC: string quartet, 1966; Songs for Jeanne, tenor, cello, piano, 1972; Suite in 5 movements, 3 winds, 2 strings, harpsichord, 1972; Elevation of imagery, violin and piano, 1973; Multisone, 3 winds, cello, piano, 1973; Petite lyrique, bassoon and piano, 1973.

1900 E. 30th St., Apt. 511, Cleveland, OH 44114

MARSHALL, JANE M. (Mrs. Elbert H.)
b. Dallas, Tex., 5 Dec. 1924. Studied piano, organ, voice, and conducting at Southern Methodist Univ. She won an American Guild of Organists prize for an anthem, 1957. She was faculty member, Southern Methodist Univ., 1948-50, 1968-73; has held various posts as church organist.

WORKS: CHORUS: Awake, my heart, 1957; God's own people; Blessed is the morn; He comes to us; Praise the Lord; and many other choral works.

4077 Northaven Rd., Dallas, TX 75229

MARSHALL, JOHN PATTON
b. Rockport, Mass., 9 Jan. 1877; d. Boston, Mass., 17 Jan. 1941. Studied with B. J. Lang, Edward MacDowell, George W. Chadwick, and Homer A. Norris; was professor at Boston Univ., 1903-41; composed songs and piano pieces.

MARSHALL, PAMELA J.
b. Beverly, Mass., 31 May 1954. Studied with Joseph Schwantner, Warren Benson, Samuel Adler, Eastman School of Music, B.M. 1976; with Krzysztof Penderecki, Betsy Jolas, and Jacob

Druckman, Yale Univ. Her Torrsong won first prize, Delius Festival competition, 1977.

WORKS: ORCHESTRA: Blessing for a good journey, Univ. of Rochester, May 1976; A chill wind in autumn, mezzo-soprano and orch. (or piano), Cambridge, Mass., 3 Dec. 1978; WIND ENSEMBLE: Spindrift; Nor brass nor sounding sea, brass quintet, 1974; CHAMBER MUSIC: Wander bitter-sweet, horn and string quartet; Dances for the morning, harp; Miniatures, horn solo, 1976; Watchmen for the morning, voice, horn, piano; Fyr on flode, mezzo-soprano and chamber ensemble, 1976; Torrsong, 2 clarinets, viola, xylophone, 1977; Nautilus, woodwind quintet, 1977; Arcanum, solo violin, 1978; and choral works.

7 Rodney Terrace, Northboro, MA 01532

MARSHALL, WARNER

b. Pomona, Calif., 11 Dec. 1947. Studied with Robert A. Gross, Occidental Coll.; with David Cohen, Arizona State Univ. He received 2 Elinor Remick Warren awards, 1972, 1973; was graduate assistant, Arizona State Univ., 1974-77; faculty associate, 1977-78; composer-in-residence, Paradise Valley School District, Phoenix, 1976.

WORKS: THEATRE: Fragment from an unwritten opera, 1972; CHAMBER MUSIC: wind sextet, 1973; Enter: The flute, solo flute; quintet for winds, percussion, viola, performed as a dance piece, 1976; CHORUS: Cantus torca, text from Dylan Thomas.

809 Farmer Ave., Tempe, AZ 85281

MARSON, LAUREL ROSE

b. Akron, Ohio, 27 June 1952. Studied with David Bernstein, Univ. of Akron, B.M. 1974, M.M. 1976; won John Philip Sousa Band award in composition, 1970.

WORKS: WIND ENSEMBLE: Für Ubermorgen, 1974; Oedipus Rex, 1975; PERCUSSION: 3 movements for percussion, 1974; CHAMBER MUSIC: 3 movements, piano, 1974; 3 movements, clarinet and horn, 1974; For trumpets and tape, 1974; Pieces for 2 violins, 1975; VOICE: Chrysanthemums, with woodwind quintet, 1975; T. S. Eliot, with woodwind quintet, 1975; I have a terrible cold, with woodwind quintet, 1975.

1667 Glenmount Ave., Akron, OH 44301

MARTH, HELEN JUN

b. Alton, Ill., 24 May 1903. Studied organ and composition with C. Albert Scholin, St. Louis. She toured the Chautauqua circuit as accompanist and drama coach; has directed children's choirs and children's radio programs; worked in little theatre.

WORKS: CHORUS: The triumph of Christ, cantata; Sing, O ye heavens, cantata; many anthems.

526 George St., Alton, IL 62002

MARTIN, GILBERT M.

b. Southbridge, Mass., 6 Jan. 1941. Studied with James Waters and Warren Martin, Westminster Choir Coll. He is music director, Presbyterian Church, Dayton and United Methodist Church, Kettering, Ohio.

WORKS: ORGAN: 2 preludes on American hymn tunes; Intercession; numerous anthems and other choral works.

MARTIN, HUGH

b. Birmingham, Ala., 11 Aug. 1914. Studied at Birmingham Southern Coll.

WORKS: THEATRE: Best foot forward, 1941; Look, Ma, I'm dancin', 1948; Make a wish, 1951; Love from Judy; High spirits; FILM SCORES: Meet me in St. Louis, 1944; Athena; The girl most likely; Grandma Moses suite; "Hans Brinker" (television); and many songs: Buckle down Winsocki; Pass the peace pipe; et al.

MARTIN, JUDITH

b. St. Paul, Minn., 20 July 1949. Studied with John Eaton and Iannis Xenakis, Indiana Univ. She was member, Creative Associates, Center for New Music, Buffalo, 1975; founder and director, Sonora Arts Festival, summers, 1976, 1977, 1978; from 1977, director of Sonora House, Inc.; and from 1978, community composer, Greene County, N.Y.

WORKS: ORCHESTRA: Fantasy space tour, 1977; suite in 3 movements, New York, 10 May 1978; CHAMBER MUSIC: Sunrise, voice and piano, 1973; Sick rose, contrabass and voice, 1973; Jack and Jill and The gate, percussion and voice, 1973; Chorale, string quartet, 1974; Quiet time, electric viola, 1975; Inner discharge, contrabass and voice, 1976; also many songs and many electronic works.

Box 36, Haines Falls, NY 12436

MARTIN, PAUL A.

b. Philadelphia, Pa., 12 Dec. 1939. Studied with Clifford Taylor, Temple Univ., D.M.A. He has been faculty member, Edinboro State Coll., from 1968.

WORKS: ORCHESTRA: symphony #1, chamber orch.; CHAMBER MUSIC: movements for flute and piano; CHORUS: How the now disappeared, with percussion.

R.D. #1, Edinboro, PA 15412

MARTIN, ROBERT EDWARD

b. Hagerstown, Md., 22 July 1952. Studied with Stefan Grové, Richard Rodney Bennett, Jean Ivey, Robert Hall Lewis, Peabody Cons., B.M. 1974; at the Electronic Music Inst., Univ. of New Hampshire and Dartmouth Coll., summer 1972. His awards include scholarships at Peabody Cons.; Marie K. Thatcher prize, 1971; James Skyes prize for electronic music, 1972; Gustav Klemm award, 1972; Otto Ortman award, 1973; Phi Mu Alpha Sinfonia award, 1973; Nat. Inst. of Arts and Letters, Ives scholarship, 1976.

WORKS: ORCHESTRA: Graduation march, 1970; Save the turtles, 1973; CHAMBER MUSIC: Fugue, woodwind quintet, 1971; 2 ancient pieces, piano, 1972; suite for solo cello; Chanson, tenor, viola, percussion, 1973; Couplet, 4 trombones, 1973; Antique forms of lost friends, flute and viola, 1973; septet for flute and strings; Flute piece, solo flute; duet for oboe and cello; and electronic pieces.

44 McKee Ave., Hagerstown, MD 21740

MARTIN, VERNON
b. Guthrie, Okla., 15 Dec. 1929. Studied with
Harrison Kerr, Univ. of Oklahoma, B.A.; with
Henry Cowell, Columbia Univ.; and with Merrill
Ellis, North Texas State Univ. His awards include commissions and ASCAP awards, 1968-72.
He was music librarian, Columbia Univ., 1962-64;
New York Public Library, 1964-66; North Texas
State Univ., 1966-70; and has been director of
library services, Morningside Coll., from 1970.
    WORKS: OPERA: Ladies voices, on Gertrude
Stein text; ORCHESTRA: Orchestra piece with
birds; Man with a hoe, 1961; concerto for tuba
and strings; CHAMBER MUSIC: Libet contrapunctum,
woodwind quartet; Beginning, middle and end,
violin and piano; ELECTRONIC: Didactic piece
and nondance; Simultaneity; Contingencies; and
songs.
    Morningside College, Sioux City, IA 51106

MARTINO, DONALD JAMES
b. Plainfield, N.J., 16 May 1931. Studied with
Ernst Bacon, Syracuse Univ., B.M. 1952; with
Roger Sessions and Milton Babbitt, Princeton
Univ., M.F.A. 1954; with Luigi Dallapiccola in
Florence, Italy, on a Fulbright grant, 1954-56.
Other honors include 2 BMI awards, 1953, 1954;
Pacifica Found. award, 1961; Brandeis Creative
Arts citation, 1963; W. Ingles Morse grant,
1965; Nat. Inst. of Arts and Letters award,
1967; 2 Guggenheim grants, 1967, 1973; 2 Nat.
Endowment for the Arts grants, 1974, 1977;
Pulitzer prize, for Notturno, 1974; Mass. Arts
and Humanities Found. grant, 1975; and commis-
sions. He was faculty member, Princeton Univ.,
1958-59; Yale Univ., 1959-69; from 1969, New
England Cons.; visiting lecturer, Harvard Univ.,
1971; composer-in-residence, Berkshire Music
Center, 4 summers, and at Composers Conf.,
Johnson, Vt., 1979.
    WORKS: ORCHESTRA: piano concerto, 1965;
Mozaic for grand orchestra, 1967; cello concerto,
1970; Ritorno, commissioned by his birth place,
Plainfield, N.J., for the Bicentennial and performed there, 12 Dec. 1976; triple concerto for
clarinet, bass clarinet, contrabass clarinet,
and chamber orch., New York, 18 Dec. 1978;
CHAMBER MUSIC: 2 quod libets, flute, 1954, 1981;
set for clarinet, 1954; trio for violin, clarinet, piano, 1959; B,a,b,b,i,t,t, for clarinet;
Strata, bass clarinet solo; Cinque frammenti,
oboe and string bass, 1961; Fantasy variations,
violin, 1962; concerto for wind quintet, 1964;
Parisonatina al'dodecafonia, cello solo, 1964;
Notturno, chamber orch., New York, 15 May 1973;
suite of variations on medieval melodies, solo
cello; CHORUS: any one lived in a pretty how
town, with piano, 4 hands; Portraits, with
orch.; Paradiso choruses, with 14 soloists,
orch., and 8-track tape, Boston, 7 May 1975;
7 pious pieces; PIANO: Piano fantasy; Pianis-
sissimo; Impromptu for Roger, 1977.
    11 Pembroke St., Newton, MA 02158

MARTINU, BOHUSLAV
b. Policka, Bohemia, 8 Dec. 1890; U.S. citizen
1948; d. Liestal, Switzerland, 28 Aug. 1959.
Studied at the Prague Cons.; was violinist in
the Czech Philharmonic Orch.; in 1923, went to
Paris and studied with Albert Roussel, remaining
there to 1940, when he went to Portugal and
thence to the U.S. in 1941. His voluminous
works include 16 operas, many to his own librettos; 10 ballets; 6 symphonies; 2 cello concertos; 2 piano concertos; double concerto; concerto grosso; concerto for 2 pianos; Rhapsody
concerto, viola and orch.; many other works for
orchestra; numerous works for chamber ensembles;
2 oratorios and other vocal works; piano pieces.

MARTIRANO, SALVATORE
b. Yonkers, N.Y., 12 Jan. 1927. Studied at
Oberlin Cons., B.M. 1951; with Bernard Rogers,
Eastman School of Music, M.M. 1952; with Luigi
Dallapiccola, Florence, Italy, 1952-54; American
Acad. in Rome, 1956-59. His awards include a
Guggenheim fellowship, 1960; American Acad. of
Arts and Letters award, 1960; Nat. Endowment for
the Arts grant, 1978. He has been faculty
member, Univ. of Illinois, from 1968; introduced
a new instrument, the Mar-Vil construction, in
New York in March 1971.
    WORKS: OPERA: The magic stones, chamber
opera, 1952; ORCHESTRA: Prelude, 1950; Con-
trasto, 1954; CHAMBER MUSIC: wind sextet, 1949;
string quartet, 1951; Cocktail music, piano,
1962; octet, 1963; Selections, alto flute, bass
clarinet, viola, cello, 1970; CHORUS: O, O, O,
O, that Shakespeherian rag, vocal and instrumental chamber ensemble, 1959; SONGS: Chansons
innocentes, soprano, 1957; MULTIMEDIA: Under-
world, 4 actors, 2 double basses, tenor saxophone, tape, 1965; Ballad, amplified nightclub
singer and instruments, 1966; L's GA, politico
with gas mask, helium bomb, 3 movie projectors,
tape, 1968; Action analysis, 12 people, bunny
and controller, 1968.
    Music Dept., Univ. of Illinois, Urbana, IL
    61801

MASLANKA, DAVID HENRY
b. New Bedford, Mass., 30 Aug. 1943. Studied
with Joseph Wood, Oberlin Cons.; with Cesar
Bresgen, Mozarteum, Salzburg; and with H. Owen
Reed, Michigan State Univ., M.M. 1968, Ph.D.
1971. His awards include 2 Nat. Endowment for
the Arts grants, 1975, 1976; MacDowell fellowship, 1979. He was faculty member, State Univ.
Coll., Geneseo, N.Y., 1970-75.
    WORKS: ORCHESTRA: Shibui symphony; 5
songs, soprano and small orch., 1975; concerto
for piano, winds, percussion, 1976; CHAMBER
MUSIC: trio for violin, clarinet, piano; duo
for flute and piano; trio for viola, clarinet,
piano; Hills of May, soprano and string quartet,
1979; CHORUS: The nameless fear or: The unanswered question put yet another way, with
instruments and percussion.
    30 Seaman Ave., New York, NY 10034

MASON, DANIEL GREGORY
b. Brookline, Mass., 20 Nov. 1873; d. Greenwich,
Conn., 4 Dec. 1953. He was grandson of hymn-
writer Lowell Mason, nephew of pianist William
Mason, and son of Henry Mason, cofounder of
Mason and Hamlin piano company. He studied with

John Knowles Paine, Harvard Univ., B.A. 1895; with Percy Goetschius and George W. Chadwick in Boston, and with Vincent d'Indy in Paris. He joined the faculty at Columbia Univ. in 1910, became MacDowell professor in 1929, was music dept. chairman to 1940, retired in 1942.

WORKS: ORCHESTRA: 3 symphonies, 1915, 1930, 1932; Scherzo caprice, small orch., 1917; Prelude and fugue, with piano, 1921; Chanticleer, festival overture, 1928; Suite after English folksongs, 1934; CHAMBER MUSIC: piano quartet, 1912; Pastorale, violin, clarinet, piano, 1913; clarinet sonata, 1915; violin sonata; String quartet on Negro themes, 1919; 3 pieces for flute, harp, and string quartet, 1922; Intermezzo, string quartet; Variations on a theme of John Powell, string quartet, 1926; Divertimento, woodwind quintet, 1927; Fanny Blair, folk song fantasy for string quartet, 1929; Sentimental sketches, 1935; also choral works, piano and organ pieces. He was author of many books and articles on musical subjects.

MASON, F(RANK) STUART
b. Weymouth, Mass., 1883; d. Boston, Mass., 1929. Taught piano at the New England Cons.; published 2 pieces for English horn and piano.

MASON, LUCAS
b. Beloit, Wis., 28 July 1931. Studied with Cecil Burleigh, Hilmer Luckhardt, Robert Crane, Univ. of Wisconsin. He was staff member, Alwin Nikolais Dance Theatre, 1959-60; Noble Path Mime Theatre, 1963-68; Children of One, 1968-73; director, Composers' Circle, 1970-74.

WORKS: OPERA: Requiem, 1 act; ORCHESTRA: 3 symphonic works; CHAMBER MUSIC: 13 sonatas; 15 works for chamber ensembles; 40 songs; 4 film scores; 4 off-Broadway shows.
234 W. 13th St., New York, NY 10011

MASON, THOM DAVID
b. Welch, W.Va., 10 Oct. 1941. Studied at Univ. of Wisconsin; with Leon Stein, De Paul Univ.; with Anthony Donata and Alan Stout, Northwestern Univ., D.M. He received awards from Downbeat Hall of Fame, 1960; Arthur J. Schmidt, 1964; W. T. Faricy, 1968; and was Ford Found. musician-in-residence, Dallas/Ft. Worth, 1972. He was faculty member, Eastern Michigan Univ., 1968-71; Queens Coll., 1971-72; Southern Methodist Univ., 1973-78.

WORKS: OPERA: From Brave new world, chamber opera; CHAMBER MUSIC: 4 pieces, mixed octet; Piece in search of a title, woodwind quintet; Thoughts, solo flute; Canzone de sonar, saxophone; CHORUS: Psalm 23; ELECTRONIC: Message, women's chorus, tape and slides; Nice trip, tape; One afternoon while on my way back from Philadelphia, tape; November '72, tape and synthesizer; Synthesis, tape and jazz saxophonist.
609 Northill, Richardson, TX 75080

MASONER, E. L. (BETTY)
b. Bemidji, Minn., 22 May 1927. Studied with Edgar B. Gangware, Bemidji State Coll., B.S. 1948. She taught in public schools, 1948-72; was visiting instructor in percussion, Bemidji State Coll., 1973. Her works for percussion include Cymbal solo #1, with piano, and trio for percussion ensemble.
911 Dewey Ave., Bemidji, MN 56601

MAST-BOLDREY, JOYCE
b. Indianapolis, Ind., 4 Sept. 1943. Studied with Robert Lombardo and Ramon Zupko, Roosevelt Univ.; with Ralph Shapey, Univ. of Chicago; with Ben Johnston, Univ. of Illinois. She received a student award from Nat. League of American Pen Women, Chicago branch.

WORKS: CHAMBER MUSIC: 3 degrees, piano trio; Open windows, string trio; VOICE: Kite flying, soprano and flute; Poem, soprano, baritone, flute, cello; Tangents to being and death, high voice and piano; Call to worship and Benediction, a cappella chorus.
401 S. Lynn, Urbana, IL 61801

MATHEW, DAVID
b. Rochelle, Ill., 18 Dec. 1945. Studied with Paul Steg and A. Oscar Haugland, Northern Illinois Univ.; with Merrill Ellis, North Texas State Univ., D.M.A. 1973. He has been faculty member, Georgia Southern Coll., from 1973; director, Savannah Symph. Chorale, from 1976, and Savannah Youth Orch., from 1977.

WORKS: ORCHESTRA: AT70; 6 for 27; Sketches #1 and #2; CHAMBER MUSIC: Cimaras, piano; Moods II, piano; S. S.'s song, clarinet; Elemental structure, flute; ELECTRONIC: Reflections on October '68; Tinker toys; MULTIMEDIA: Intermedia piece, chamber orch. and tape; Private mirrors, tape with dancers and lights; Ease, tape and dancer.
Camaro Ct., Bel-Air Estates, Statesboro, GA 30458

MATHEWS, MAX V.
b. Columbus, Nebr., 13 Nov. 1926. Studied piano as a child, violin at Peru Teachers Coll.; otherwise is self-taught in music. He received the Sarnoff Medal, Inst. of Electrical and Electronics Engineers, 1973, for work in computer music; from 1955, has been on technical staff, Bell Telephone Labs.

WORKS: ELECTRONIC: Numerology; Masquerades, 1963; Slider, 1965; Swansong, 1966; The second law; May carol.
81 Oakwood Dr., Murray Hill, NJ 07974

MATSON, SIGFRED C.
b. Chicago, Ill., 17 Feb. 1917. Studied with Leo Sowerby in Chicago; with Howard Hanson, Eastman School of Music. He has received 8 composition grants from Mississippi State Coll. for Women, where he has been faculty member from 1949; other faculty posts have been at Sioux Falls Coll., 1939-41; Ohio Wesleyan Univ., 1941-44; Monmouth Coll., 1948-49. His compositions include choral works and piano pieces.
Mississippi State Coll. for Women, Columbus, MS 39701

MATSUSHITA, HIDEMI
b. Kyoto, Japan, 12 Feb. 1954. Studied with Charles Eakin and Cecil Effinger, Univ. of

MATTFELD, JULIUS

Colorado, B.M. 1976; held president's scholarship, 1972; from 1974, has been ballet accompanist; also writes librettos and verses.
WORKS: THEATRE: Despina meets Papagino,
comic operetta, 1976; CHAMBER MUSIC: Fantasy
for 2 harps, 1975; Serenade from Notebook for
Jan Blankennagel, piano, 1976.
3934 Fuller Ct., Boulder, CO 80303

MATTFELD, JULIUS
b. New York, N.Y., 8 Aug. 1893; d. New York,
31 July 1968. Was chiefly music librarian,
musicographer, and organist; was author of books
on music history. His compositions included a
ballet, Virgins of the Sun, 1922.

MATTHEWS, H. ALEXANDER
b. Cheltenham, England, 26 Mar. 1879; U.S.
citizen 1923; d. Middletown, Conn., 12 Apr.
1973. Studied organ with his father; received
honorary doctorates in music from Muhelnberg
Coll. and Univ. of Pennsylvania, 1925. He was
organist-choirmaster in Philadelphia churches,
1916-54; on faculty, Clarke Cons., 1934-54;
upon retirement, lived in Middletown, Conn.
WORKS: OPERA: Play the game; Hades, Inc.,
comic opera; CANTATAS: The story of Christmas;
The triumph of the cross; The city of God; The
conversion; The life everlasting; The eternal
light; also introits and graduals of the church
year.

MATTHEWS, HOLON
b. Oregon, Ill., 17 July 1904. Studied with
Sidney Durst and Edgar Stillman Kelly, Cincinnati Cons., B.M., M.M.; privately with Eugene
Goossens; with Howard Hanson and Bernard Rogers,
Eastman School of Music, Ph.D. He held scholarships for all study. He taught piano at Cincinnati Cons., Eastman School, Wilson Coll., and
was professor, Western Michigan Univ., 1948-73.
WORKS: ORCHESTRA: 4 symphonies; tone poems,
and suites; also chamber music, choral works,
and many songs.

MATTHEWS, JOHN SEBASTIAN
b. Cheltenham, England, 11 Dec. 1870; to U.S.
1900; d. Pawtucket, R.I., 23 July 1934. Brother
of H. Alexander Matthews, was also organist and
teacher. He wrote anthems, organ pieces, and
songs.

MATTHEWS, JUSTUS
b. Peoria, Ill., 13 Jan. 1945. Studied with
Aurelio de la Vega, California State Univ. at
Northridge; with Lejaren Hiller, State Univ. of
New York, Buffalo. He received first prize in
composition at CSU, Northridge, 1965, 1967;
fellowships at SUNY, Buffalo, 1968-70, summer
1971, CSU, Long Beach, summer, 1973. He was
graduate assistant, SUNY, Buffalo, 1968-71;
from 1971, on faculty, California State Univ.,
Long Beach.
WORKS: THEATRE: Artaud's Le jet de sang,
drama with music, 1968-70; CHAMBER MUSIC: duet,
flute and clarinet, 1963; 6 songs, soprano,
baritone, chamber group, 1965; 4 miniatures,
string quartet, 1966; 3 Greek songs, soprano

alone, 1966; 4 miniatures, guitar, cello,
double bass, 1969; Hdoryut, 16 solo instruments,
1971; Tiggers don't like honey, 2 harps, 1976-
77; CHORUS: One poem of A. A. Voznesenskii,
5 part, a cappella, 1966; 7 pieces, with orch.,
1966; The argument, Blake text, 16 part, a
cappella, 1971; Announcement, 10 part, 1971;
ELECTRONIC: Arabrabnamragus, tape, 1971;
MUS15/1-35/S.EED, tape, 1973; Bionic music,
tape, 1976.
245 Harvard Lane, Seal Beach, CA 90740

MATTHEWS, THOMAS
b. Utica, N.Y., 1 Apr. 1915. Studied with
Norman Coke-Jephcott in New York. His awards
include Pi Kappa Lambda and a special award from
the Oklahoma diocese. He was faculty member,
Northwestern Univ.; Seabury Western Seminary;
from 1960, at Univ. of Tulsa; from 1946, organist
and choirmaster in various churches. He has
composed anthems and liturgical works for chorus
and organ.
1625 E. 31st Place, Tulsa, OK 74104

MATTHEWS, WALTER E.
b. New Jersey, 17 Dec. 1917. Studied at Trenton
State Coll., B.S.; Columbia Univ., M.A. 1948;
and at New York Univ. He was public school
music supervisor, 1944-60; district director,
1959-70; church music director, 1951-64.
WORKS: CHORUS: He led the way; When Jesus
was born; Jesus lies sleeping; O come and mourn.
Lawton Rd., Eastham, MA 02642

MATTHEWS, WILLIAM
b. Toledo, Ohio, 1 Apr. 1950. Studied with
Randolph Coleman and Walter Aschaffenberg,
Oberlin Coll. Cons.; with Richard Hervig and
Peter Lewis, Univ. of Iowa; with G. M. Koenig,
Inst. of Sonology, Utrecht; with Jacob Druckman,
Robert Moore, and K. Penderecki, Yale Univ. His
awards include 3 BMI awards; ASCAP award;
Charles Ives prize, Nat. Inst. of Arts and
Letters; ACA recording grant; Fulbright-Hays
grant; and commissions. He is instructor, Bates
Coll.
WORKS: ORCHESTRA: Larchwood, 1975; CHAMBER
MUSIC: Letters from home, 11 instruments; Sumer
is icumen in and Lhude sing, bassoon and tape;
Ferns, piano; Political pieces, brass quintet;
and computer pieces.
Bates College, Lewiston, ME 04240

MATTILA, EDWARD CHARLES
b. Duluth, Minn., 30 Nov. 1927. Studied with
Halsey Stevens, Univ. of Southern California;
with Carl McKinley, New England Cons.; and with
Paul Fetler, Univ. of Minnesota. He was faculty
member, Concordia Coll., St. Paul, 1958-62;
Bishop Coll., 1962-64; from 1964, Univ. of
Kansas.
WORKS: ORCHESTRA: symphony; Partitions,
string orch.; CHORUS: On teaching, with soloists and orch.; 13 ways of looking at a blackbird, with reciter and chamber ensemble; PIANO:
piano duo; 6 arrays; ELECTRONIC: Arp piece, for
synthesizer; Repercussions, tape, Emporia, Kans.,
3 Nov. 1975.
University of Kansas, Lawrence, KS 66044

MAULDIN, MICHAEL
b. Port Arthur, Tex., 14 June 1947. Studied
with James Rivers, Washburn Univ., B.M. magna
cum laude; with William Wood, Univ. of New
Mexico, M.M. His awards include first place in
piano category and first place in large ensemble
category, New Mexico Composers Guild Bicentennial contest; first place, annual contest of
Chamber Orch. of Albuquerque, 1978. He has
been director, Mauldin School of Music, from
1972.
WORKS: ORCHESTRA: Variations on a Huron
carol, small orch., 1973; Tombeau for strings
and timpani, Albuquerque Youth Symphony, 18 Oct.
1973; Celebration of the Sun: 3 conservations,
piano and small orch., 1974; 3 Jemez landscapes,
1976; Petroglyph for strings, Chamber Orchestra
of Albuquerque, 30 July 1978; CHAMBER MUSIC:
Etude in Phrygian mode, woodwind quintet, 1969;
clarinet sonata; 4 modal piano pieces; 3 New
Mexico landscapes, clarinet and piano, 1975;
MULTIMEDIA: Fiesta de Fe, choirs, handbells,
brass, piano, organ, and dancers, commissioned
by United Presbyterian Church, Synod of the
Southwest, 1977.
12713 Summer Ave., N.E., Albuquerque, NM
87112

MAURICE-JACQUET, H.
b. St. Mande, France, 18 Mar. 1886; d. New York,
N.Y., 29 June 1954. Studied at Paris Nat. Cons.
He made his piano debut at 9; toured Europe as
pianist and conductor; founded Union des Femmes
Artistes Musiciennes, Paris; was accompanist to
Grace Moore; taught at School of Vocal Arts,
New York; Acad. of Vocal Arts, Philadelphia;
American Cons. of Music, Drama, and Dance of
New York. His awards included the French Legion
of Honor and a commission from the French Min-
istry of Fine Arts.
WORKS: OPERA: Romanitza; Messaouda;
OPERETTA: Le poilu; La petite dactylo; BALLET:
Les danses des chez nous; ORCHESTRA: American
symphony; CHORUS: The mystic trumpeter.

MAURY, LOWNDES
b. Butte, Mont., 7 July 1911; d. Encino, Calif.,
11 Dec. 1975. Studied at Univ. of Montana, B.A.
1931; Chicago Musical Coll.; with Arnold
Schoenberg on scholarship, in Boston, 1934;
later with Wesley LaViolette. His Sabbath Eve
service won a contest of the Valley Jewish Community Center, North Hollywood. He was film
composer and pianist in film, radio, and television studios; visiting professor, Montana
State Univ., 1967, 1968.
WORKS: ORCHESTRA: Passacaglia, string
orch., 1959; Summer of green, rhapsody for
flute and strings, 1964; CHAMBER MUSIC: Song
without words, viola and piano; Lament, solo
flute; Reflection, flute and piano; Changes,
7 flutes; violin sonata, In memory of the Korean
war dead, 1952; Night life, cello and piano,
1956; Springtime digressions, piano, flute,
string quartet, 1961; Speculations, piano and
string trio, 1964; Scene de ballet, piccolo and
string quartet, 1965; 5 Rilke songs, mezzo-
soprano, string quartet; The imprisoned cellist,

solo cello, 1973; Harpsichord variations on a
theme by Beethoven; CHORUS: Proud music of the
storm, Whitman text, with soloists and orch.,
1953; Man is my song, cantata, 1963; Concerto
for English words, brass, percussion, text by
Cardona-Hine; Goddesses, solo voice and chamber
singers; many piano pieces.

MAVES, DAVID W.
b. Salem, Oreg., 3 Apr. 1937. Studied with
Homer Keller, Univ. of Oregon; with Ross Lee
Finney, Leslie Bassett, George B. Wilson, Univ.
of Michigan. His awards include John H. Reid
chorale prize, 1961, 1970; Ford Found. composer-
in-residence grant, 1964-65; Coll. Band Directors
Nat. Assoc. award, 1965; Rockefeller grants,
1968, 1969; 2 Sigma Alpha Iota Inter-American
Music awards; and commissions. He was faculty
member, Shaw Univ., 1966-68; Univ. of Michigan,
1968-71; Duke Univ., 1972-75; then at Univ. of
Charleston.
WORKS: ORCHESTRA: symphony, 1970; Overture
to an opera; BAND: 5 moments from a spring day,
1966; Toccata, 1966; March with sleighbells,
1967; The wanderer recalls his homeland, 1970;
CHAMBER MUSIC: Fantasy, cello and percussion,
1964; Duet for diverse instruments, clarinet and
flute, 1970; Fugue for percussion, 1970; Homage
to Lorca, violin and piano; violin sonata;
Retrieval, chamber ensemble, 1971; piano sonata,
Rome, 7 July 1978; string quartet; Variations,
wind quintet; 2 brass quintets; Oktoechos,
clarinet, horn, percussion, Dallas, 6 Aug. 1978;
CHORUS: God's grandeur, with orch., 1970; The
storm is over, with orch., 1970; The legend of
Befana, cantata, 1970; A bestiary, women's
voices and percussion (SAI award, 1978), text by
Kay Maves; and songs.
Fine Arts Dept., College of Charleston,
Charleston, SC 29401

MAXFIELD, RICHARD
b. Seattle, Wash., 2 Feb. 1927; d. Los Angeles,
Calif., 27 June 1969. Studied with Roger
Sessions, Univ. of California, Berkeley; with
Milton Babbitt, Princeton Univ.; and with Ernst
Krenek and Luigi Dallapiccola. He taught at the
New School for Social Research, New York, and at
San Francisco State Coll.
WORKS: OPERA: Stacked deck, actors, lighting, tape, 1959; ORCHESTRA: Classical overture,
1942; 5 movements, 1956; Structures, 1958; Sine
music, 1959; African symphony, 1964; CHAMBER
MUSIC: trio for clarinet, cello, piano, 1943;
wind septet, 1947; sonata for solo violin, 1949;
violin sonata, 1950; string trio, 1951; sonata
for solo flute, 1951; Structures, 10 winds, 1951;
11 variations, string quartet, 1952; chamber
concerto, 7 instruments, 1957; ELECTRONIC:
Perspectives, violin and tape, 1960; Peripetea,
violin, saxophone, piano, tape, 1960; Night
music, 1960; Amazing grace, 1960; Pastoral symphony, 1960; Piano concerto for David Tudor,
1961; Clarinet music, 5 clarinets and tape, 1961;
Cough music, recorded bronchial sound effects
taped during a modern dance recital at Cooper
Union, N.Y., 13 Jan. 1961; Toy symphony, flute,
violin, wooden boxes, ceramic ware, and tape,

MAXSON, WILLIAM LYNN

1962; Bacchanale, 1963; Venus impulses, tape, 1967.

MAXSON, WILLIAM LYNN
b. Frankfurt, Ind., 12 Nov. 1930. Studied with William Pelz, Jordan Coll. of Music; with Thomas Beversdorf and Bernhard Heiden, Indiana Univ., D.M. He was faculty member, Lycoming Coll., 1955-58; from 1959, at Eastern Washington State Coll.
WORKS: CHORUS: Prayer and alleluia; PIANO: sonatas; a sonatina; 12 preludes; also elementary harp solos.
Rte. 2, Box 18A, Cheney, WA 99004

MAXWELL, JACQUELINE PERKINSON
b. Denver, Colo., 16 Sept. 1932. Studied with George Kuhlman in Brazil; with Walter Keller, Univ. of New Mexico; with Max di Julio and George Lynn, Loretto Heights Coll.; and with George Thaddeus Jones, Catholic Univ. She was manager of the Jefferson Symphony, 1973-77.
WORKS: ORCHESTRA: Humoreske; BAND: Chipmunks; CHAMBER MUSIC: Jubilo, 2 flutes and piano; CHORUS: Psalm 98; PIANO: Autumn suite, 2 pianos; 4 frustrations, piano solo; has also composed for films and for television commercials.
7720 Westview Dr., Lakewood, CO 80215

MAY, THEODORE
b. East Orange, N.J., 14 Nov. 1943. Studied with Jonathan Elkus, Lehigh Univ.; with Herbert Brün, Univ. of Illinois.
WORKS: Quarintet, woodwind quintet, 1971; Lippestück, solo trumpet, 1972; Bavel, 6 speakers, 1973; Unnatural acts, bassoonist-speaker and tape, 1978.
59 Everett St., Arlington, MA 02174

MAY, WALTER B.
b. Springfield, Mo., 28 Sept. 1931. Studied with Relly Raffman, Southwest Missouri State Univ., B.S., B.S.E. 1951; with Darius Milhaud and Georges Dandelot, Paris Cons., 1952; with Paul Fetler, Univ. of Minnesota; at Univ. of Toronto, D.M. 1966. His awards include Fulbright grants, 1951, 1952; Nat. Fed. of Music Clubs award, 1962; Wisconsin Composers awards, 1964, 1965; American Guild of Organists award, 1967. He was faculty member, Wisconsin State Univ., Eau Claire, 1955-67; State Univ. of New York at Cortland, 1967-69; Eisenhower Coll., 1969-75; from 1975, at Augustana Coll.
WORKS: ORCHESTRA: 2 symphonies; West River country; CHAMBER MUSIC: 3 string quartets; CHORUS: Job, oratorio; The last days; Cantate Domine; Song of songs, cantata; service of Holy Communion.
1520 S. Summit, Sioux Falls, SD 57105

MAYER, LUTZ
b. Hamburg, Germany, 14 Dec. 1934; U.S. citizen 1946. Studied with Gordon Binkerd and Robert Kelly, Univ. of Illinois. He received first and second prizes, Texas Manuscript Society composition contest, 1963; 2 summer research fellowships, State Univ. of New York, 1964, 1966. He

was faculty member, Texas Wesleyan Coll., 1960-63; from 1963, at State Univ. Coll., Cortland; was conductor, Ithaca Opera Assoc., 1974.
WORKS: OPERA: Refuge, 1965; The paranoid parakeet, 1968; THEATRE: music for The boy with a cart, 1962; CHORUS: The raven days; Psalm 23; also works for orchestra, chamber groups, voice.
Box 71, Little York, NY 13087

MAYER, WILLIAM
b. New York, N.Y., 18 Nov. 1925. Attended Yale Univ. and Mannes Coll. of Music; studied with Roger Sessions, Felix Salzer, and Otto Luening; conducting with Izler Solomon. His awards include a Guggenheim fellowship, 1966; 2 Ford Found. grants; Rockefeller grant; Nat. Endowment for the Arts grant, 1978; annual ASCAP awards; and commissions. He taught at Boston Univ., 1965; was special writer for the U.S. Information Agency, 1965-67; later became chairman of Composers Recordings, Inc.
WORKS: OPERA: One Christmas long ago, 1 act, 1962; Brief candle, drama in 3 acts and 6 minutes, 1964; BALLET: The snow queen, 1963; ORCHESTRA: The greatest sound around (The animal contest), baritone and orch., 1954; Hello world, with singing narrator, 1956; Concert piece, trumpet and strings, 1957; Overture for an American, 1958; 2 pastels, 1961; Octagon, piano and orch., 1971; CHAMBER MUSIC: 2 movements, string quartet, 1952; Essay for brass and winds, 1954; Celebration trio, flute, clarinet, piano, 1956; 3 for 3, 2 percussion and piano; Messages, flute, string trio, piano; Country fair, brass trio, 1957; brass quintet, 1964; Miniatures, soprano and 7 players, Dorothy Parker text, 1968; Khartoum, soprano and 4 players, 1968; Back talk, 15 players and animated page turner, 1970; News item, soprano and 7 players, 1972; Appalachian echoes, solo harp; Dream's end, chamber ensemble, Cranbrook Acad., Mich., 2 May 1976; Yankee Doodle fanfare, brass quintet, New York, 12 May 1976; CHORUS: Festive alleluia, 1963; Letters home, with soloists and orch., 1968; The eve of St. Agnes, with soloists and orch., 1969; Lines on light, women's voices, 1971; Make a joyful noise, with orch., New York, 17 May 1974; Spring and yes forever, cantata for soloists, triple chorus, orch., New York, 16 May 1975; La belle dame sans merci, with tenor soloist, New York, 29 Oct. 1976; Brief candle, with soprano solo and chamber orch.; PIANO: Angles, 1956; sonata, 1959; Toccata, New York, 7 Oct. 1972; A most important train; Distant times, distant places; Subway in the sunlight; Claremont lights; and many songs.
c/o CRI, 170 W. 74th St., New York, NY 10023

MAYS, WALTER A.
b. Chester Co., Tenn., 1941. Funeral music for Jan Pollock, orch.; 6 invocations to the Svara Mandala, percussion orch., 1973; concerto for alto saxophone and chamber ensemble, 1974.
Wichita State University, Wichita, KS 67208

MEAD, EDWARD G.
b. Reading, Mass. 26 June 1892. Attended Harvard Univ., B.A.; Yale Univ., B.M.; studied privately

with Seth Bingham, Bainbridge Crist, Henry
Cowell, and Ernst Krenek; with Harold Darke,
Royal Coll. of Music, London; and with Nadia
Boulanger, Fontainebleau Cons. He was a fellow
of the American Guild of Organists; organist and
choirmaster, Cornell Univ.,1927-28; faculty
member, Denison Univ., 1925-27; Miami Univ.,
Ohio, 1929-60, composer-in-residence, 1957-60.
His published works numbered over 100 choral,
organ, and piano compositions.

MEAD, GEORGE
b. New York, N.Y., 21 May 1902. Studied at
Columbia Univ., M.A. 1925, honorary D.M. He
has been organist-choirmaster in Brooklyn and
New York; was music director, Hofstra Coll.,
1936-40.
WORKS: OPERA: The broker's opera, 1 act;
CHORUS: Benedictus es Domine; The Lord by
wisdom hath founded the Earth; Lo, the winter is
past; The voices of the wise; Once to every man
and nation; ORGAN: Tidings of great joy;
Fantasy.

MEANS, CLAUDE
b. Cincinnati, Ohio, 1912. Studied with David
McKay Williams in New York; was organist-choirmaster, Christ Church, Greenwich, Conn., 1934-
72.
WORKS: CHORUS: Lord of all power and might;
O come and mourn; The king rides forth; Seabury
(hymn tune); and organ pieces.

MECHEM, KIRKE
b. Wichita, Kans., 16 Aug. 1925. Studied at
Stanford Univ.; with Walter Piston and Randall
Thompson, Harvard Univ.; and 3 years in Vienna.
His honors include the Boott prize at Harvard;
Sigma Alpha Iota triennial American music award
for a vocal work; selection of his Psalm 100 as
one of 3 works to represent American music at
the United Nations 20th anniversary; Nat. Endowment for the Arts grant, 1977-78. He has taught
at Stanford Univ. and San Francisco State Univ.;
until 1972, was composer-in-residence, Lone
Mountain Coll., San Francisco; from 1972, full-
time composer, lecturer, and conductor.
WORKS: OPERA: Tartuffe, in 3 acts, libretto
by composer based on play by Molière, 1978;
ORCHESTRA: 2 symphonies; Haydn's return; The
jayhawk, overture; CHAMBER MUSIC: suite for 2
violins; woodwind trio; piano trio; Divertimento, flute and string trio; string quartet;
Whims, 15 vignettes for brass; 5 duets, violin
and piano; piano suite; piano sonata; CHORUS:
Singing is so good a thing, with tenor or
soprano solo, orator, 13 players; The king's
contest, comic cantata, with soloists and orch.;
Speech to a crowd, MacLeish text, with baritone
and orch.; Canon law for newly weds, a cappella
rounds and canons, text from Proverbs; Zorabel,
chamber cantata, with wind quintet, string
quartet, piano; Professor Nontroppo's music
dictionary, a cappella; American madrigals,
with piano or chamber ensemble, Stanford, Calif.,
13 Feb. 1976; many more choral works, songs,
piano pieces.
49 Marcela Ave., San Francisco, CA 94116

MEISTER, SCOTT R.
b. Elyria, Ohio, 19 May 1950. Studied with
Jack Johnston, Ashland Coll., B.M.; with Barry
Brosch, Fred Coulter, Clifton Williams, Alfred
Reed, Univ. of Miami, M.M., D.M.A. He received
the Hinda Honigman Gold Cup award, 1979, for
7 short pieces for solo vibraphone. He has
been faculty member, Appalachian State Univ.,
from 1974.
WORKS: PERCUSSION: Introduction and fantasy,
5 players and piano; Gypsy festival, duet; Per-
conics, 5 players and tape; Ceremony for percussion, any number of players; 5 pieces for percussion and wind orchestra; Summer snow, solo
marimba; also Bullfrogs for mixed chorus.
Appalachian State University, Boone, NC
28608

MEKEEL, JOYCE
b. New Haven, Conn., 6 July 1931. Studied at
Longy School of Music, 1952-55; with Nadia
Boulanger in Paris, 1955-57; Yale Univ., B.M.
1959, M.M. 1960; with Earl Kim, 1960-62; candidate for master's degree in applied anthropology at Boston Univ., 1975. Her awards include a private grant for study in France; full
scholarship at Yale Univ.; fellowships at
MacDowell Colony, 1963, 1964, 1974, Yaddo, 1974;
Ingram-Merrill grant, 1964; Inter-American Music
award, 1965; Radcliffe Inst. grant, 1968-70;
research grant in anthropology, Boston Univ.,
1971; Nat. Endowment for the Arts grant, 1975;
and commissions. She was faculty member, New
England Cons., 1964-70; from 1970, Boston Univ.;
was composer for the Ina Hahn Dance Company,
1967-69; composer and codirector, The Ensemble,
1969-71; has also presented one-woman shows of
her sculpture and participated in sculpture
exhibits.
WORKS: DANCE: Pleasure of merely circulating; Duet for dancer and percussion; Jaywalk,
solo viola and dander; Chains, 7 chains and 5
dancers, 1969; Feast, ceremony for tape and
dancers, 1970; THEATRE: music for Androcles
and the lion, 1961; Macbeth, 1962; Merchant of
Venice, 1962; Knight of the burning pestle,
1962; Yes is for a very young man, 1963; Fuente
ovejuna, 1963; Othello, 1964; Richard III, 1964;
Moveable feast, with Paul Earls and Lyle
Davidson, 1973; ORCHESTRA: Vigil, Boston Univ.,
19 Oct. 1978; CHAMBER MUSIC: String figures
disentangled by a flute, 1969; Shape of silence,
solo flute, 1970; Spindrift, string quartet,
1971; Embouchures II, brass sextet, 1972; Corridors of dream, mezzo-soprano and chamber ensemble, 1972; Homages, brass quintet, 1974;
Planh, solo violin, 1975; Serena, speaker, voice
and prepared piano, 1975; Rune, chamber ensemble;
Apotheosis of a hummingbird, chamber ensemble;
Alarums and excursions, soprano who is also an
actress, chamber ensemble, Boston, 10 Oct. 1978;
also choral works, songs, piano pieces.
119 Pembroke St., Boston, MA 02118

MELBY, JOHN B.
b. Whitehall, Wis., 3 Oct. 1941. Studied at
Curtis Inst. of Music, B.M.; with Henry Weinberg
and George Crumb, Univ. of Pennsylvania, M.A.

MELOY, ELIZABETH

1967; with Peter Westergaard, Milton Babbitt, and J. K. Randall, Princeton Univ., M.F.A. 1971, Ph.D. 1972. His awards include a Princeton fellowship; NDEA fellowship; Martha Baird Rockefeller grant, 1976; Nat. Endowment for the Arts grant, 1977-78. He was faculty member, West Chester State Coll., 1971-73; from 1973, at Univ. of Illinois.
   WORKS: CHAMBER MUSIC: 2 piano sonatas; 2 string quartets; ELECTRONIC: Forandre, an opera for computer; . . . of quiet desperation, computer; 91 plus 5, brass quintet and computer; Valedictory, soprano and computer; Zonnooities, clarinet, oboe, and computer; Transparencies, trumpet and computer; Passages, tuba and computer; The men that are falling, soprano, piano, and computer; and others.
   1902 Karen Ct., #12, Champaign, IL 61820

MELOY, ELIZABETH
   b. Hoopeston, Ill., 7 Aug. 1904. Studied with Carl Beecher and Albert Noelte, Northwestern Univ.; Bernard Rogers, Eastman School of Music; Nadia Boulanger in France; with Darius Milhaud and Leo Sowerby in Colorado. She received a cash award, Indiana Composers Guild, for Dance suite, for orch. She taught in public schools, 1937-39; at Taylor Univ., 1929-32; Ball State Univ., 1933-69, retiring as associate professor of theory and organ.
   WORKS: ORCHESTRA: overture; dance suite; CHAMBER MUSIC: piano trio; string quartet; viola sonatina; sonatina for violin and viola; trio for flute, oboe, cello; CHORUS: Heaven and earth and sea and air; This is my father's world; many anthems, songs, organ preludes, piano pieces.
   222 S. Hutchinson, Muncie, IN 47303

MENASCE, JACQUES DE
   b. Bad Ischl, Austria, 19 Aug. 1905; to U.S. 1941; d. Gstaad, Switz., 28 Jan. 1960. Studied with Alban Berg in Vienna; gave piano recitals in Europe.
   WORKS: BALLET: Status quo, 1947; ORCHESTRA: 2 piano concertos, 1935, 1941; Divertimento, piano and strings, 1940; Le chemin d'écume, soprano and orch., 1942; CHAMBER MUSIC: violin sonata, 1940; viola sonata, 1955; PIANO: sonatina #2, 1942; Fingerprints, 1943; Romantic suite, 1950; Instantanés, 6 children's pieces, 1956-59.

MENEELY, SARAH SUDERLEY
   b. Albany, N.Y., 18 Feb. 1945. Studied with Robert Hall Lewis, Goucher Coll.; with Stefan Grové and Earle Brown, Peabody Cons.; and with Robert Morris, Yale Univ. She received an award for Homegrown, for piano, 1973.
   WORKS: CHAMBER MUSIC: Narcissus monologue, chamber orch. and tenor, 1968; 5 systems, Time, and Buzz, 3 pieces using resonating bells, tubular chimes, kalimba, piano, voice, guitar, and xylophone; CHORUS: Everywoman: A morality tale, oratorio for 6-18 voices, 3 female soloists, 15 toy instruments, 1971-73.
   111 Fairy Dell Rd., Clinton, CT 06413

MENNIN, PETER
   b. Erie, Pa., 17 May 1923. Attended Oberlin Coll., 1940-42; studied at Eastman School of Music, B.M., M.M., Ph.D. 1947. His awards include the first Gershwin Memorial prize; Bearns prize; American Acad. of Arts and Letters award; 2 Guggenheim grants; Naumburg Found. recording award; Nat. Arts Club Gold Medal; Columbia Records chamber music award; Univ. of Rochester centennial citation; honorary doctorates from Univ. of Chicago, Oberlin Coll., Univ. of Wisconsin, Univ. of Heidelberg, Temple Univ., Peabody Cons.; many commissions. He served in the U.S. Air Force, 1942-44; was on the composition faculty, Juilliard School, 1947-48; director of Peabody Cons., 1958-62; from 1962, president of the Juilliard School. He is a member of the Nat. Inst. of Arts and Letters.
   WORKS: ORCHESTRA: 8 symphonies, 1942, 1944, 1946, 1948, 1950, 1953, 1963, #8 premiere, New York, 29 Nov. 1973; concertino, flute, strings, percussion, 1945; sinfonia, chamber orch., 1947; Fantasia, string orch., 1947; violin concerto, 1950; Concertato "Moby Dick," 1952; cello concerto, 1955; piano concerto, 1957; Canto for orchestra, 1964; Pied Piper of Hamelin, narrator and orch., on Browning poem, 1969; sinfonia for orchestra, Minneapolis, 21 Jan. 1971; BAND: Canzona, 1951; CHAMBER MUSIC: 2 string quartets, 1941, 1951; Canto and toccata, piano, 1950; violin sonata, 1956; Divertimento and partita, piano; piano sonata, 1963; Voices, voice, percussion, harp, harpsichord, piano, New York, 28 Mar. 1976; CHORUS: The Christmas story, cantata; 4 choruses based on Chinese texts; Cantata de virtute, chorus, children's chorus, soloists, narrator, orch., Cincinnati, May 1969; Reflections of Emily, boys' chorus, piano, harp, percussion, New York, 18 Jan. 1979.
   The Juilliard School, Lincoln Center, New York, NY 10023

MENNINI, LOUIS
   b. Erie, Pa., 18 Nov. 1920. Studied at Oberlin Coll., 1939-42; with Bernard Rogers and Howard Hanson, Eastman School of Music, B.M. 1947, M.M. 1949, Ph.D. His awards include Nat. Inst. of Arts and Letters grant, 1949; 2 Koussevitzky Found. grants; and commissions. He served in the U.S. Air Force, 1942-45; was faculty member, Eastman School of Music, 1949-65; North Carolina School of the Arts, 1967-71; from 1973, at Mercyhurst Coll., Erie, Pa.
   WORKS: CHAMBER OPERA: The well, 1951; The rope, 1955; BALLET: Allegro energico, 1948; ORCHESTRA: Andante and allegro, 1946; Arioso for strings, 1948; Canzona, 1950; Overtura breve, 1949; Tenebrae, 1963; concerto grosso, 1975; CHAMBER MUSIC: violin sonata, 1947; cello sonatina, 1952; string quartet, 1961; many violin pieces, piano pieces, choral works.
   Music Dept., Mercyhurst College, Erie, PA 16501

MENOTTI, GIAN CARLO
   b. Cadegliano, Italy, 7 July 1911; to U.S. 1928; has kept Italian citizenship. Studied with Rosario Scalero, Curtis Inst., graduated 1933,

received honorary B.M. 1945. His other awards
include Lauber composition prize, 1931; New York
Drama Critics' Circle award, 1954; Pulitzer
prizes, 1950, 1955; honorary membership, Nat.
Inst. of Arts and Letters; many commissions. He
taught at Curtis Inst. for a while, but is
chiefly composer, festival organizer and director; he is librettist (has written the librettos
for all his own operas and for Samuel Barber's
Vanessa and A hand of bridge) and author of a
play, The leper, 1970. In 1974 he bought an
estate in Scotland for his permanent home.
    WORKS: OPERA: Amelia goes to the ball,
1937; The old maid and the thief, 1939; The
silent god, 1942; The medium, 1946; The telephone, 1947; The consul, 1950; Amahl and the
night visitors, 1951 (became an annual television production); The saint of Bleeker Street,
1954; Maria Golovin, 1958; Labyrinth, 1963; The
last savage, 1963; Martin's lie, 1964; Help,
help, the globolinks, children's opera, 1968;
The most important man in the world, New York,
7 Mar. 1971; The hero, comic opera, Philadelphia,
1 June 1976; The egg, children's mini-opera,
Washington, 17 June 1976; The trial of the
gypsy, mini-opera for Newark Boys Choir, New
York, 24 May 1978; La loca (The mad woman), a
50th birthday present for Beverly Sills, who
sang the title role in San Diego, 3 June 1979;
Chip and his dog, 1-act children's opera, American premiere, Charleston, S.C., June 1980;
BALLET: Sebastian, 1944; Errand into the maze,
1947; The unicorn, the gorgon, and the manti-
core, 1956; ORCHESTRA: piano concerto, 1945;
Apocalypse, 1951; Pastorale and strings; violin
concerto, 1952; triple concerto, 1970; The
halcyon, symphony #1, Saratoga, N.Y., 4 Aug.
1976; Fantasia, cello and orch.; CHORUS: Death
of the Bishop of Brindisi, dramatic oratorio,
1963; Landscapes and remembrances, cantata on
impressions of America, Milwaukee, 14 May 1976;
also some chamber works.

MERETTA, LEONARD V.
    b. Keiser, Pa., 5 Sept. 1915. Studied at
Ernest Williams School of Music; Univ. of
Michigan, M.M. He played trumpet with Major
Bowes group; has toured as trumpet soloist;
taught in public schools; at Univ. of Michigan,
1941-45; has been professor and director of
bands, Western Michigan Univ., from 1945.
    WORKS: BAND: Tioga; Men of might; also
pieces for small wind ensembles.

MERRIFIELD, NORMAN L.
    b. Louisville, Ky., 19 Nov. 1906. Studied at
Northwestern Univ., B.M.Ed., M.S.; Indiana
Univ.; Jordan Coll. of Music; Army Band School;
Trinity Coll. of Music, London; Michigan State
Coll. He taught at Fisk Univ., 1927-28; Florida
A&M Coll., 1932-34; was army bandmaster in
World War II; taught at Crispus Attucks High
School, Indianapolis, 1932-42, and from 1946.
His compositions include a symphony and choral
arrangements.

MERRILL, LINDSEY
    b. Ky., 10 Jan. 1925. Studied with Claude

Almand, Univ. of Louisville; at Yale Univ.; with
Henry Cowell and Bernard Rogers, Eastman School
of Music; and with Mario Davidovsky and Vladimir
Ussachevsky, Columbia Univ. His faculty posts
have included Queens Coll., 1950-53; Smith Coll.,
1953-56; Univ. of Nebraska, 1956-57; Bucknell
Univ., 1957-67; Kent State Univ., 1967-75; from
1976, at Univ. of Missouri.
    WORKS: CHAMBER MUSIC: duo for 2 violins;
Ratio 4:5:6, string quartet; Charles Ives New
England suite, tenor and piano.
    Univ. of Missouri, 4420 Warwick Blvd.,
Kansas City, MO 64111

MERRIMAN, MARGARITA
    b. Barcelona, Spain, 29 Nov. 1927 of American
parents. Studied at Univ. of Tennessee, B.M.;
with Herbert Elwell, Alan Hovhaness, Bernard
Rogers, Eastman School of Music, M.M., Ph.D.
She was music director, Shenandoah Valley Acad.,
1948-51; faculty member, Andrews Univ., 1951-56;
Southern Missionary Coll., 1956-58; from 1959,
professor, Atlantic Union Coll.
    WORKS: ORCHESTRA: symphony; Concertante,
horn and chamber orch.; 1776; CHAMBER MUSIC:
cello sonata; Quinary, brass quintet; Dialogue,
cello and percussion; CHORUS: The millenium,
oratorio; SONGS: Expectation, voice and piano;
Tunnels and sidewalks, song cycle; PIANO: piano
sonata; Currents; Meditations on a college
bulletin.
    Box 704, South Lancaster, MA 01561

MESANG, THEODORE L. (TED)
    b. Eau Claire, Wis., 7 Dec. 1901. Attended
Northland Coll.; Univ. of Wisconsin, B.M.; Univ.
of Minnesota, M.Ed. He was band instructor in
Ashland, Wis.; from 1949, at Oregon State Univ.
    WORKS: BAND: Symbol of glory; Carnival;
Oregon Trail; Men of Wisconsin; Westward go!;
and some 200-300 more published band pieces.
    1418 N.W. 11th St., Corvallis, OR 97330

MEYEROWITZ, JAN
    b. Breslau, Germany, 23 Apr. 1913; U.S. citizen
1951. Studied with Walter Gmeindl and Alexander
V. Zemlinsky in Berlin; with Ottorino Respighi
and Alfredo Casella in Rome. His awards include
2 Guggenheim grants, 1956, 1958; 2 American
Music Center grants, 1963, 1966; Nat. Endowment
for the Arts grant, 1977. He has been faculty
member, City Univ. of New York, from 1954;
taught at Tanglewood, 1948-51, 1960.
    WORKS: OPERA: The barrier, Langston Hughes
text, 1950; Emily Dickinson, text by Dorothy
Gardner, 1951; Esther, Hughes text, 1957; Port
town, Hughes text, 1960; Godfather Death, 1961;
ORCHESTRA: Symphony Midrash Esther, 1955;
flute concerto, 1962; oboe concerto, 1963;
Sinfonia brevissima, 1965; 6 pieces for orchestra,
1967; 7 pieces, 1962; CHORUS: The 5 foolish
virgins, 1954; The glory round his head, 1955;
Missa Rachel Florans, 1955; Friday evening
service, 1962; The rabbis, 1965; also chamber
music, songs, etc.
    27 Morningside Ave., Cresskill, NJ 07626

MEYERS, EMERSON
b. Washington, D.C., 27 Oct. 1910. Studied
with Howard Thatcher and Gustave Strube, Peabody
Cons. He received Nat. Fed. of Music Clubs
award, 1943; Fulbright grants, 1955, 1967 for
Belgium; Peabody Distinguished Alumnus award,
1970; and commissions. He was faculty member,
Catholic Sisters Coll., 1943-48; American Univ.,
1948-51; from 1951, at Catholic Univ., director,
electronic music laboratory from 1961; director
of professional music, Nat. Capitol Sesquicentennial Commission, 1950-51.
WORKS: OPERA: Dolcedo, for television;
ORCHESTRA: piano concertino; symphony for small
orch.; Kaleidoscope, piano concerto, Alexandria,
Va., 2 Dec. 1978; CHAMBER MUSIC: viola sonata;
clarinet quintet; 8 portraits, viola and piano;
PIANO: Alarna variations, 2 pianos; sonata;
ELECTRONIC: Rhythmus; Chez dentiste; Excitement;
Moonflight sound pictures; Episodes, piano duet
and tape; In memoriam, soprano and tape; In the
mind's eye, soprano, cello, trombone, tape;
Cyclisme, solo violin, 1974, Washington, 23 Feb.
1976.
3006 29th Ave., Hyattsville, MD 20782

MEYERS, ROBERT G.
b. Buffalo, N.Y., 29 Mar. 1932. Studied with
Ned Rorem and David Diamond, Univ. of Buffalo,
B.A. 1961; with Mel Powell, Quincy Porter,
Donald Martino, Yale Univ., M.M. 1964. He held
scholarships at Univ. of Buffalo, 1960-61; at
Yale Univ., 1961-64; Shell Found grants, 1967,
1968; St. John's Univ. grant, 1969. He was
faculty member, St. David's School, New York,
1965-67; St. John's Univ., 1967-72; Hofstra
Univ., 1971-72.
WORKS: ORCHESTRA: Metachromatikos, string
orch., 1967; East to Setauket, 1961; CHAMBER
MUSIC: string quartet, 1969; Prelude for percussion trio, 1972; CHORUS: Cremation of Sam
McGee, cantata for children's chorus, orch.,
and narrator, 1965. Meyers has published extended articles on Technical bases of electronic
music; also has a degree and years of experience
in mechanical engineering.
1 Laura Lane, E. Setauket, NY 11733

MICHAELIDES, PETER S.
b. Athens, Greece, 20 May 1930; to U.S. 1937.
Studied with Joseph Wood, Oberlin Coll.; with
Halsey Stevens, Univ. of Southern California,
D.M.A. He was faculty member, Univ. of Califor-
nia, Santa Barbara, 1962-64; Lewis and Clark
Coll., 1964-65; from 1965, Univ. of Northern
Iowa.
WORKS: BAND: Forces II, 1970; CHAMBER
MUSIC: Perspectives, 1967, song cycle for
soprano, 1967; Forces I, chamber wind and percussion ensemble, 1969; Forces IV, chamber orch.,
1972; CHORUS: Lamentations, double chorus,
double band, vocal soloists, speaking chorus;
Forces III, Psalm 130, 72-voice chorus, a cappella; Magnification of the nativity, 2 Eastern
Orthodox hymns for Christmas; other liturgical
settings.
2927 Minnetonka Dr., Cedar Falls, IA 50613

MICHALSKY, DONAL
b. Pasadena, Calif., 13 July 1928; d. Newport
Beach, Calif., 31 Dec. 1975 (died in a fire that
also took the lives of his wife, their 2 children, and 2 house guests). He studied with
Ingolf Dahl, Univ. of Southern California, D.M.A.
1965; and with Wolfgang Fortner in Germany. His
many honors included a Fulbright grant, 1958;
annual ASCAP awards, 1967-72. He was faculty
member, California State Coll., Fullerton, from
1960 to his untimely and tragic death.
WORKS: OPERA: Der Arme Heinrich, an unfinished work which was burned in the fire that
took his life; ORCHESTRA: Wheel of time, choral
symphony, 1967; sinfonia concertante, clarinet,
piano, orch., 1969; symphony #3, 1975; BAND:
concertino, trombone and band, 1953; little symphony, 1959; Fantasia sopra My funny valentine,
brass ensemble, 1963; concertino for 19 winds
and percussion, 1965; CHAMBER MUSIC: duo for
viola and piano, 1950; quintet, brass and piano,
1952; Divertimento, 3 clarinets, 1952; 6 pieces,
chamber orch., 1956; Partita, oboe d'amore and
strings, 1958; cello sonata, 1958; Morning music,
chamber ensemble, 1959; Variations on Sweet
Betsy from Pike, violin solo, 1961; Trio concertino, flute, oboe, horn, 1962; Fantasia alla
marcia, brass quintet, 1963; Allegretto, clarinet
and strings, 1964; Fantasia a due, horn and bass
trombone, 1968; 4 short pieces, accordion, 1968;
sonatina, flute and clarinet, 1968; Cantata
memoriam, soprano and 12 instruments, 1971;
Partita piccola, flute and piano; 3 x 4, saxophone quartet, 1972; Duo concertato, violin and
viola, 1973; also choral works and piano pieces.

MICHELET, MICHEL
b. Kiev, Russia, 26 June 1894. Studied cello in
Kiev and Vienna; composition with Max Reger in
Leipsig, Reinhold Gliere in Kiev. In 1921 he
went to Paris and began composing for films; then
in 1941, moved on to settle in Hollywood.
WORKS: OPERA: Hannele, 1972; ORCHESTRA:
violin concerto, 1943; CHAMBER MUSIC: 2 cello
sonatas, 1937, 1977; Lisztiana, violin, cello,
piano, 1943; 3 violin sonatas; sonata for
balalaika and piano, 1972; many songs, piano
pieces, and some 200 film scores.

MIDDENDORF, JOHN WILLIAM II
b. Baltimore, Md., 22 Sept. 1924. Attended
Harvard Univ., B.A. 1947; Holy Cross Coll.,
B.NavalSci., 1945; New York Univ., M.B.A. 1954.
He was an investment banker and has written a
book on banking; was ambassador to the Netherlands, 1969-73; under-secretary of the navy,
1973-74; secretary, 1974-78; also paints on
china, canvas, and stained glass windows. His
compositions include 4 symphonies, one of which
was broadcast nationwide in Holland during his
term as ambassador; many marches, 3 of which
were played at the Old Marine Barracks ceremonial parade, Dec. 1976.

MIDDLETON, ROBERT
b. Diamond, Ohio, 18 Nov. 1920. Studied with
Beveridge Webster, New England Cons., 1941-42;
with Nadia Boulanger, Longy School of Music,

1941-42, later in Paris; Harvard Univ., B.A. 1948, M.A. 1954; Tanglewood, opera dept., 1946, 1947. His awards include scholarships at Harvard, 1939-41; John Knowles Paine fellowship, 1948-50; Guggenheim fellowship, 1965. He was faculty member, Harvard Univ., 1950-53; from 1953, at Vassar Coll.

WORKS: OPERA: Life goes to a party, 1 act, Tanglewood, 13 Aug. 1948; The nightingale is guilty, Boston, 5 Mar. 1954; Command performance, 4-act opera-concerto, Poughkeepsie, N.Y., 11 Nov. 1961; ORCHESTRA: Andante, 1948; violin concerto, 1949; Concerto di quattro duetti, solo winds and string orch., Poughkeepsie, 17 Mar. 1963; Sinfonia filofonica, Poughkeepsie, 4 May 1969; Gardens 1 2 3 4 5, 1972; CHAMBER MUSIC: 2 violin sonatas, 1941, 1948; string quartet, 1950; Ritratta della notte, flute and piano, 1966; Approximations, viola and piano, 1967; piano trio, 1970; CHORUS: Why east wind chills, 1954; Winter wakens all my care, 1956; The Lord to me a shepherd is, 1956; O! O! O!, December, X and M, 3 Christmas carols, women's voices, 1963; De natura sirenis, De natura noctuae, women's voices, 1968; also songs and piano works.
33 Sunrise Lane, Poughkeepsie, NY 12603

MIKHASHOFF, YVAR-EMILIAN
b. Troy, N.Y., 8 Mar. 1944. Studied at Eastman School of Music, 1959-61; Juilliard School, 1961-62; with Elmer Schoettle, Univ. of Houston, B.M. 1967, M.M. 1968; with Nadia Boulanger in Paris, 1968-69; with Hunter Johnson, Kent Kennan, and Karl Korte, Univ. of Texas, D.M.A. 1973. His awards include scholarships at Eastman and Juilliard; Fulbright grant, 1968; Nansen Fund grant, 1968; 2 grants to annotate Charles Ives's Concord sonata, 1973; grants to edit rare works of Liszt, 1978, and annotate Debussy preludes, 1978; and commissions. He founded Cambiata, Inc., a chamber ensemble, 1973; joined piano faculty, State Univ. of New York, Buffalo, 1973.

WORKS: THEATRE: Improvisations on the last words of Chief Seattle, speaker, percussionist, mime-dancer, syllabist, 1976; The fall of the house of Usher, piano interior, actor, violist, androgynous mime, 1978; May a mood doom a yam, palindromic theatre piece, 1979; ORCHESTRA: piano concerto, 1967; CHAMBER MUSIC: Dances for Davia, flute and piano, 1967; Sir Gawain and the Green Knight, narrator, soprano, chamber ensemble, 1970; 4 figures of a drowned maiden, narrator, soprano, 7 instruments, 1972; The pipes of Colchis, clarinet and piano, 1973; A little of the bandit's soul, violin and piano, 1973; Prelude, variations, and fugue, solo cello, 1976; Nocturne, cello and piano, 1977; HWALC, cello and prerecorded whale songs, 1978; also songs, song cycles, piano pieces.
48 Cottage St., Buffalo, NY 14201

MIKULAK, MARCIA LEE
b. Winston-Salem, N.C., 9 Oct. 1948. Studied piano at San Francisco Cons., B.M. 1969, and at Mills Coll. She has received awards for piano performance; prepared works of Dane Rudhyar under his supervision. From 1978, has been on piano faculty, Coll. of Santa Fe.

WORKS: Piece for dance, free improvisation for prepared piano, voice, percussion, tape.
Music Dept., College of Santa Fe, Santa Fe, NM 87501

MILANO, ROBERT
b. Brooklyn, N.Y., 4 May 1936. Studied with Nicolas Flagello and Vittorio Giannini, Manhattan School of Music, B.M. 1960; City Coll. of New York, M.M. 1967. He taught at U.S. Naval School of Music, 1960-61; in public schools, 1963-66; was on adjunct faculty, Queensborough Community Coll., 1967-70; New York Community Coll., 1969-75; church organist, from 1960.

WORKS: OPERA: Flight into Egypt, chancel opera, Pittsburgh, 29 Aug. 1967; Rejoice and be glad, Christmas opera, 1969; ORCHESTRA: Essay #4, strings, 1961; Concerto pequeño, piano and strings, 1973; Encenas Boringueñas, #2, 1973; CHAMBER MUSIC: Toccata, piano; 4 arabesques, solo clarinet; Otto canzone e toccata, 7 brass, 1966; choral works.

MILBURN, ELLSWORTH
b. Greensburg, Pa., 6 Feb. 1938. Studied with Scott Huston and Paul Cooper, Cincinnati Coll. Cons.; Henri Lazorof, Univ. of California, Los Angeles; and with Darius Milhaud at Mills Coll. His awards include Crothers prize and fellowship; Merritt prize; Morse fellowship; Univ. of Cincinnati research fellowship; Nat. Endowment for the Arts grant, 1974; and commissions. He was music director, Committee Theatre, San Francisco, 1963-68; on faculty, Cincinnati Coll. Cons., 1970-75; from 1975, at Rice Univ.

WORKS: OPERA: Gesualdo, 1972-73; ORCHESTRA: Voussoirs, 1970; CHAMBER MUSIC: 5 inventions, 2 flutes, 1965; concerto for piano and chamber orch., 1967; string trio, 1968; Soli, for 5 players, 10 instruments, 1968; string quintet, 1969; Soli II, 2 players, flutes and double bass, 1970; Soli III, clarinet, cello, piano, 1971; Soli IV, 4 instruments, 1972; violin sonata, 1972; Lament, harp, 1972; string quartet, 1974; CHORUS: Massacre of the innocents, Auden text, 1965; SONGS: 2 love songs, soprano, Millay text, 1970; Spiritus mundi, soprano and 5 instruments, 1974.
Rice University, Houston, TX 77001

MILDENBERG, ALBERT
b. Brooklyn, N.Y., 13 Jan. 1878; d. Raleigh, N.C., 3 July 1918. Studied with Bruno Oscar Klein in New York; with Giovanni Sgambati in Rome; with Jules Massenet in Paris. He was dean, music dept., Meredith Coll., Raleigh. He wrote 2 light operas to his own librettos; The wood witch, 1905, and Love's locksmith, 1912; orchestral suites and songs.

MILES, HAROLD
b. Knox, Pa., 5 Feb. 1908. Studied at Columbia Univ., Juilliard School, and in Paris. He received a MacDowell fellowship and honorary membership in the Cleveland Composers Guild. He was faculty member, Western Reserve Univ., 1931-36; professor, Kent State Univ., 1960-64.
WORKS: ORCHESTRA: piano concerto, 1946;

MILKEY, EDWARD T.

CHAMBER MUSIC: piano sonata, 1933; CHORUS:
Memorial cantata, 1942; SONG CYCLE: Amerasia,
1969.

MILKEY, EDWARD T.
b. Turners Falls, Mass., 2 July 1908. Studied
at New York Univ., School of Education, B.E.,
M.A. He was public school music supervisor,
1930-45; with New York music publisher, 1946-61;
music faculty, public schools, 1961-73.
WORKS: ORCHESTRA: 2 suites for strings;
BAND: Maracaibo; Farewell march; CHORUS:
Christmas is coming; When the year's at springtime; and songs.
De Camp Dr., R.D. #1, Boonton, NJ 07005

MILLER, CHARLES
b. Russia, 1 Jan. 1899; to U.S. 1901. Studied
with Hans Letz, Franz Kneisel, and Percy
Goetschius at Juilliard School; also with
Leopold Auer, Carl Flesch, and Alfredo Casella.
He conducted orchestras in Paris and Budapest;
joined the Philadelphia Orch. as violinist in
1941.
WORKS: ORCHESTRA: symphony; Appalachian
Mountains, a rhapsody; West Indies suite;
CHAMBER MUSIC: Cubanaise for violin; string
quartet; CHORUS: New Orleans street crier.

MILLER, DENNIS HAYDEN
b. Lexington, Ky., 3 July 1951. Studied with
Patrick McCarty, Loyola Univ., New Orleans;
with Kenneth Klaus and James Drew, Louisiana
State Univ.; with Arnold Franchetti, Norman
Dinerstein, Mordecai Sheinkman, Hartt Coll. of
Music; Mario Davidovsky, Columbia Univ.;
privately with Harvey Sollberger. He held
fellowships at Hartt Coll., 1976-77; Johnson,
Vt., Composer Conf., 1976, 1977; Columbia Univ.,
1977-79. He was staff composer and arranger
in a recording studio, 1976-78.
WORKS: ORCHESTRA: The coming of wisdom
with time, soprano and orch., 1977; CHAMBER
MUSIC: Visions, string quartet, 1974; In search
of . . ., jazz orch., 1975; 3 recitativi amorosi,
alto saxophone, 1976; string quartet, 1976; 3
settings of texts by W. B. Yeats, soprano and
string trio, 1977; Just a second!, flute and
cello.
612 W. 114th St., #4-R, New York, NY 10025

MILLER, DOUGLAS, JR.
b. New York, N.Y., 14 Jan. 1951. Studied in
Bologna, Italy, and in New York; received the
Daniel Alpern Memorial Medal, 1969. He was
organist and choirmaster, 1970-71; remedial
instructor, Bronx Community Coll., 1972-74.
WORKS: CHAMBER MUSIC: Prelude in g, flute
and piano, 1971; CHORUS: Hymn without words,
1970; Praise, 1973.
234 W. 111th St., New York, NY 10024

MILLER, EDWARD J.
b. Miami, Fla., 4 Aug. 1930. Studied with
Isadore Freed and Arnold Franchetti, Hartt Coll.
of Music; with Carlos Chavez and Boris Blacher
at Tanglewood, 1955, 1958; with Blacher and
Josef Rufer in Berlin, 1956-58. He received

Koussevitzky prize, 1955; Fulbright grants,
1956-58; Wechsler commission, 1958; Library of
Congress commission, 1968; E. C. Schirmer Handel
and Haydn Society Award, 1971. He taught at
Hartt Coll., 1959-71; from 1971, at Oberlin
Coll. Cons.
WORKS: ORCHESTRA: Reflections--At the
Bronx Zoo; Orchestral changes; Anti-heroic
amalgam; Orchestral fantasies; WIND ENSEMBLE:
La mi la sol--Isaac and interpolations, with 3
soloists; Fantasy concerto, alto saxophone and
16 winds; CHAMBER MUSIC: 6 canons, recorder,
harpsichord, viola da gamba; Song, recorder or
flute solo; 3 short pieces for piano; The folly
stone, brass quintet, 1966; percussion quintet;
Study for bass harmonica and marimba; Around,
5 or any greater odd number of players; MULTI-
MEDIA: The 7 last days, chorus, percussion, 2
tapes, film; Quartet variations, any 4 players
and slides, 1972; The young god, a vaudeville,
actors, dancers, chorus, 2 flutes, saxophones,
guitar, bass, percussion, and tape.
26 King St., Oberlin, OH 44074

MILLER, FREDERICK
b. Lima, Ohio, 12 Dec. 1930. Attended Northwestern Univ. and Univ. of Iowa. He was faculty
member, Univ. of Arkansas, 1958-64; Northwestern
Univ., 1964-75; from 1976, at De Paul Univ.
His works include Procession and interlude, concert band; and Willie's rock, marching band.
1322 Greenwood Ave., Wilmette, IL 60091

MILLER, HARVEY HORATIO, JR.
b. Salisbury, N.C., 13 Apr. 1934. Studied with
Juan Orrega-Salas, Bernhard Heiden, Roque
Cordero, Iannis Xenakis, Indiana Univ. He received a Nat. Endowment for the Arts grant for
study of computer composition. He has been
faculty member at Brevard Coll. from 1960.
WORKS: ORCHESTRA: 3 pieces for orchestra;
CHAMBER MUSIC: string trio; 3 Sandburg songs,
voice, clarinet, horn, violin, harp; Concertare,
organ and brass; piano sonata; trio, piano,
clarinet, cello; concertino, harpsichor and
chamber ensemble; Extensions, brass, percussion,
and tape; CHORUS: Litany for modern man; 5
mountain scenes, a cappella; The road, with
baritone solo, brass, percussion; songs.
Brevard College, Brevard, NC 28712

MILLER, IRA STEVEN
b. New York, N.Y., 17 June 1951. Studied with
Karl Korte and William Klenz, Harpur Coll.; with
Exra Laderman, State Univ. of New York, Bing-
hamton; and with A. Wayne Slawson, Frank McCarty,
Thomas Janson, and Robert Morris, Univ. of
Pittsburgh, where he received the Andrew W.
Mellon fellowship.
WORKS: THEATRE: Space plots, ballet, 1972;
Phaetomes II, film and tape, 1974; CHAMBER MUSIC:
cello sonata, 1974; string quartet, 1976;
Collage, flute and harpsichord, 1976; Das Atem,
woodwind quintet, 1977; CHORUS: Creation music,
with narrator, chamber ensemble, percussion and
tape, 1975; The smile, a cappella, 1977.
812 Johns Rd., Cherry Hill, NJ 08034

MILLER, JACQUES
b. Russia, 4 Aug. 1900. Has composed for piano:
Fantasie; Impromptu elegante; Scherzo miniature;
Impromptu in e-flat.

MILLER, JESSE PAUL
b. New York, N.Y., 3 Oct. 1935. Studied privately with Joseph Maneri, Josef Schmid, and Norman
Coke-Jephcott. He is an associate, American
Guild of Organists, and has been church organist
since 1954, in 1973, at St. Paul's Episcopal
Church, Great Neck, N.Y. Here he has installed
a Buchla synthesizer and, on 18 Nov. 1973,
launched a pilot program with The sum of its
parts, a miltimedia piece. He is also director
of the Final Mix Arts Center, Long Island.
    WORKS: CHAMBER MUSIC: Settignano, 5 winds;
string quartet; 5 pieces, piano; ELECTRONIC:
The time predicted, an opera; Music for ascension; MULTIMEDIA: The nativity of Christ.
    145 W. 71st St., New York, NY 10023

MILLER, KARL FREDERICK
b. New Rochelle, N.Y., 27 Dec. 1947. Studied
with Spencer Norton, Univ. of Oklahoma, B.M.
1969; with Merrill Ellis, William Latham, and
Dika Newlin, North Texas State Univ., M.M. 1974,
D.M.A. 1978. He held a fellowship at Univ. of
Oklahoma, 1969-70; was faculty member, New Haven
Univ., 1971; on fellowship at North Texas State
Univ., 191-77, head, Audio Center, 1977-78;
from 1978, faculty member, Univ. of Arizona.
    WORKS: ORCHESTRA: Fantasia (orchestration
of Luening's organ Fantasia), 1968; Symphonic
prelude, 1971; concerto for oboe, harpsichord,
percussion, strings, 1973; Variations on a theme
by Shostakovich, 1978; CHAMBER MUSIC: Ode, 9
winds, percussion, piano, 1971; Short sonata #3,
harpsichord, 1972; Miniatures for Rob, brass
choir, 1976; CHORUS: Missa sine credo, 1975;
also songs, electronic pieces, piano pieces.
    6332 N. El Camino Real, #509, Tucson, AZ
85721

MILLER, LEWIS M.
b. Brooklyn, N.Y., 4 Sept. 1933. Studied with
Karol Rathaus, Queens Coll.; with Vittorio
Giannini, Manhattan School of Music; with Samuel
Adler, North Texas State Univ., Ph.D. His awards
include Ford Found. grants in the resident composer program, 1961, 1962; 3-star Award of Merit,
1970, and Kansas Composer of the Year award,
1977, both from Kansas Fed. Music Clubs. He was
faculty member, Texarkana Coll., 1965-66; from
1966, at Fort Hays State Univ.
    WORKS: OPERA: The imaginary invalid, 1970;
Letters from Spain, 1978; ORCHESTRA: piano concerto, 1960; King Henry V, overture, 1962; Overture to Tartuffe, 1978; BAND: Rondo da camera,
1962; Variations on a sea chanty, 1966; Capriccio,
piano and band, 1970; CHAMBER MUSIC: sonatina,
wind quintet, 1962; Toccata, brass quintet,
1971; Rondo, for 2 pianos, 1976; Scherzo, trumpet
and piano, 1977; Rondo giocoso, cello and piano,
1978; Pastorale and toccata, organ, 1978; CHORUS:
To the moon, 1967; River run, 1967; To touch a
star, 1967; Here on the mountain, 1973.
    208 E. 32nd St., Hays, KS 67601

MILLER, MALLOY
b. Duenweg, Mo., 6 May 1918; d. Norwood, Mass.,
14 June 1981. Boston Univ., M.M.E., D.M.A.;
studied privately with Roy Harris and Nicolas
Slonimsky. He was violinist, Denver Symphony
and Central City Opera, 1936-40; public school
music teacher, 1940-42, 1946-53; instructor,
USAF Statistical School, Harvard Grad. School,
1942-45; violinist, Pueblo Symphony and Colorado
Springs Symphony, 1946-53; teaching fellow,
Boston Univ., 1954-56; from 1956, on faculty.
    WORKS: THEATRE: Koshare, ballet, 1959;
music for Richard III, 1967; The Trojan women,
1971; ORCHESTRA: Variations for orchestra,
1949; Suite for orchestra, 1952; Tyuonyi, orchestral sketch, 1954; Western overture, 1955;
concertino, oboe and chamber orch., 1956; Ngoma,
timpani and orch., 1956; Western prelude; BAND:
Ode for band; CHAMBER MUSIC: Prelude for percussion, 1956; Poem, violin and piano; Pastorale,
alto flute and organ; 2 rituals for percussion,
1964; Variations, violin and percussion ensemble,
1972; 2 movements, viola, harp, percussion,
1975, Boston, 13 Feb. 1978.

MILLER, MICHAEL R.
b. Lisbon, Portugal, 24 July 1932. Studied at
New York Univ., B.A.; Eastman School of Music,
M.A. He was organist-choirmaster, St. Joseph's
Church, New York, 1959-64; on faculty, Vassar
Coll., 1965-66; from 1967, at Mt. Allison Univ.
    WORKS: OPERA: A sunny morning; CHORUS:
A spear of summer; Haiku set; 3 madrigals; Mass
for peace.
    Mt. Allison Univ., Sackville, N.B., Canada

MILLER, RALPH DALE
b. Whitehall, Ill., 17 Mar. 1909. Studied at
Illinois State Univ., B.Ed. 1936; Univ. of Iowa,
M.A. 1939, M.F.A. 1941, Ph.D. 1942. He taught
in public schools, 1936-41; was faculty member,
Duluth State Teachers Coll., 1942-47; from 1957,
professor and division chairman, Univ. of
Minnesota.
    WORKS: ORCHESTRA: Venus and Adonis, sym-
phonic poem, 1941; Suite miniature, 1942; Prelude
to autumn, 1942; Canzonetta, string orch., 1944;
Night poem, 1945; sinfonietta, 1946; Prelude and
scherzo, 1946; Dance poem, 1949; symphony, 1949;
BAND: Twilight sketches, suite, 1940; Introduction and allegro, brass choir, 1949; symphony
for band, 1974; CHAMBER MUSIC: 3 string quartets,
1942-44; Arabesque, flute, 1963.
    University of Minnesota, Duluth, MN 55812

MILLER, THOMAS A.
b. Malden, Mass., 28 June 1941. Studied with
Joshua Missal, Wichita State Univ.; with Francis
Buebendorf, Univ. of Missouri, D.M.A. The film,
Signs of the times, for which he wrote the electronic sound track, won an Excellence in Film
award, Ohio State Univ., competition, 1971. He
was composer-in-residence, Kentucky Television
Authority, Lexington, 1971; faculty member,
Eastern Kentucky Univ., 1969-71; Wichita State
Univ., 1968-69, 1971-75.
    WORKS: CHORUS: Alleluia, amen; The trum-
peters and singers were as one, with trumpets
and organ; A new song; A cuckoo flew out of the

MILLIGAN, HAROLD VINCENT

wood, with percussion and handbells; Sing, all
ye people; Make a joyful noise; The frozen
December; Eia Susanni; and organ pieces.
    1036 Shadyway, Wichita, KS 67203

MILLIGAN, HAROLD VINCENT
    b. Astoria, Oreg., 11 Dec. 1888; d. New York,
N.Y., 12 Apr. 1951. Studied with T. Tertius
Noble and Arthur E. Johnstone; was organist in
Portland, Oreg., and from 1907, in New York. He
composed operettas, songs, works for organ;
published 4 collections of early American folk
songs, a biography of Stephen Foster, 2 books on
opera.

MILLIGAN, ROY HUGH
    b. New Rochelle, N.Y., 4 Sept. 1922. Studied
at Ernest Williams School of Music, Brooklyn;
at New York Univ., B.S., M.A. He has been
school band instructor from 1946; at East Islip,
N.Y., from 1955. His works for band include
the award-winning March Sherwood.

MILLS, CHARLES
    b. Asheville, N.C., 8 Jan. 1914. Studied with
Max Garfield, Greenwich Music School, New York;
privately with Aaron Copland, Roger Sessions,
and Roy Harris. His awards include Columbia
Univ.,band prize, 1948; Guggenheim fellowship,
1952; Roth String Quartet award; Church of the
Ascension prize; grand prize, Venice Film
Festival, for score to On the Bowery; Nat.
Endowment for the Arts grant, 1976. He is a
full-time composer of concert music and film and
television background scores.
    WORKS: ORCHESTRA: concertino for oboe and
strings; piano concerto, 1948; Theme and variations, New York, 8 Nov. 1951; Crazy Horse symphony, Cincinnati, 28 Nov. 1958; Prelude and
fugue; Prologue and dithyramb, New York, 8 Mar.
1955; Serenade for winds and strings; 3 symphonies, 1940, 1942, 1955; Symphonic
ode, string orch., 1976; CHAMBER MUSIC: chamber
concerto for 10 instruments; Concerto sereno,
woodwind octet; The brass piano, brass sextet;
brass quintet; Paul Bunyan jump, jazz quintet;
5 string quartets; piano trio; 6 violin sonatas;
2 sonatas for solo violin; oboe sonata; English
horn sonata; Sonata fantasia, solo clarinet; 3
recorder sonatas; sonata for flute solo; Serenade, flute, horn, piano; Little suite, flute
and piano; sonatine, flute and string quartet;
suite for 2 flutes, soli; Breezy Point pipings,
2 recorders; 4 stanzas, solo violin; violin
sonatine; The centaur and the phoenix, jazz ensemble, 1960; Summer song, jazz ensemble, 1960;
2 piano sonatas; choral works and songs.
    P.O. Box 638, Radio City Station, New York,
NY 10019

MILLS, EDGAR
    b. Poland, 15 June 1915; U.S. citizen 1939.
Studied with Victor Fuchs, Walter Klein, Vienna
Cons., B.S.; Rutgers Univ., M.M.; New York
Univ., Ph.D. He received the New York Univ.
Founders Day award, 1965. He has been cantor,
Oheb Shalom Congregation, South Orange, N.J.,
from 1953; and faculty member, Seton Hall Univ.,

from 1968.
    WORKS: VOCAL: Chassidic Sabbath eve
service; Chassidic Sabbath morning service;
supplementary songs.
    84 Williamson Ave., Hillside, NJ 07205

MIMAROGLU, ILHAN
    b. Istanbul, Turkey, 11 Mar. 1926; to U.S. 1955.
Studied with Vladimir Ussachevsky, Douglas Moore,
and Stefan Wolpe, Columbia Univ., M.A. 1966;
privately with Edgard Varese. He received a
Rockefeller fellowship, 1955; Guggenheim fellowship, 1971. He has been producer and music consultant, Atlantic Records, from 1969; director,
Finnadar Records, from 1972.
    WORKS: ORCHESTRA: clarinet concerto, 1950;
Metropolis, 1955; September moon, 1967; CHAMBER
MUSIC: 4 string quartets; Pieces sentimentales,
1957; Pieces futiles, clarinet and cello, 1958;
Ulrike, my hope, piano; Epicedium, voice and
chamber ensemble, 1961; Cristal de Bohème,
percussion, 1971; ELECTRONIC: Le tombeau d'Edgar
Poe, voice and tape, 1964; The bowery bum, voice
and tape, 1964; Anacolutha, 1964; Agony, 1965;
White cockatoo, 1966; Wings of the delirious
demon, 1969; Music plus one, violin and tape,
1970; Provocations, 1971; Sing me a song of
Songmy, jazz quintet, reciters, chorus, tape,
1971; Hyperboles, 1972; music for Dubuffet's
Coucou Bazar, 1973; To kill a sunrise, 1974;
La ruche, cello, piano, harpsichord, and tape.
    435 W. 119th St., #9C, New York, NY 10027

MING, JAMES W.
    b. Brownwood, Tex., 21 May 1918. Studied with
Bernard Rogers and Howard Hanson, Eastman School
of Music, B.M., M.M., also with Darius Milhaud
and Nadia Boulanger. His faculty positions
have included DePauw Univ., 1942-44; from 1944,
Chapman professor, Lawrence Univ.; visiting
professor, Cornell Univ., 1955-56.
    WORKS: ORCHESTRA: Music for a film; suite
for chamber orchestra; CHORUS: Missa brevis,
with brass; 3 poems of Archibald MacLeish; PIANO:
sonatina; 3 pieces for piano.
    Lawrence University, Appleton, WI 54911

MINGUS, CHARLES
    b. Nogales, Ariz., 22 Apr. 1922; d. New York,
N.Y., 7 Jan. 1979. Played double bass with
Charles Parker, Stan Getz, Art Tatum, and others,
then formed his own band in New York. He dic-
tated an autobiography in 1971, Beneath the
underdog: His world as composed by Mingus,
N.Y.; held a Guggenheim fellowship in 1978.
    WORKS: BALLET: The Mingus dances, New
York, Oct. 1971; JAZZ: Pithecanthropus erectus;
Meditations on integration, 1964.

MINTNER, THOMAS EUGENE
    b. South Bend, Ind., 25 Apr. 1950. Studied with
Thomas Willis and Stephen Syverud, Northwestern
Univ.; clarinet, privately. He held a performer-
fellow residence, Center for New Performing Arts
(CNPA), Univ. of Iowa; received grants from the
CNPA, 1974-78.
    WORKS: ELECTRONIC: Isollusion, video and
live electronics, 1972; A video concert in 2

parts, 1973; Electronic artworks, clarinet, percussion, tape, 1975; 3 chips, tape and live electronics, 1976; A relative economy of means, computer-controlled music, 1978.
12 Morris St., Danbury, CT 06810

MIRANTE, THOMAS
b. Utica, N.Y., 11 Oct. 1931. Studied at State Univ. Coll. at Potsdam, B.S. 1954; Ithaca Coll., M.S. 1955; privately with Earl George and David Diamond. His awards include grants from Meet the Composer and the Martha Baird Rockefeller Found.; and commissions. He has been public school music teacher from 1957.
WORKS: ORCHESTRA: symphony; viola concerto; Night scene; CHAMBER MUSIC: string quartet; Portrait for strings; Prelude and march, alto saxophone and piano; Andante and allegro, trumpet and piano; CHORUS: I AM; The house on the hill; Silent snow; This is all; The stream of life; The war poems of Walt Whitman, with orch.; PIANO: sonata; A musical journey; 8 recital solos; 8 recital encores.
208 N. Main St., Canastota, NY 13032

MISHELL, KATHRYN LEE
b. Los Angeles, Calif., 5 June 1940. Studied with John Pozdro, Univ. of Kansas, B.M. 1963; with Ingolf Dahl, Univ. of Southern California, 1963-64. She was on faculty, Oberlin Coll., 1964-70; private piano teacher, 1964-72. She published a duo for trumpet and piano, 1971.
1406 Ridgecrest Dr., Austin, TX 78746

MISSAL, JOSHUA M.
b. Hartford, Conn., 12 Apr. 1915. Studied with Howard Hanson, Bernard Rogers, Eastman School of Music, B.M., M.M.; and with Roy Harris. He was violist, Rochester Symphony, 1934-40, Wichita Symphony, 1952-70, and with various string quartets; conductor, Albuquerque Philharmonic, 1940-42, Mississippi Southern Civic Orch., 1950-52; faculty member, Univ. of New Mexico, 1946-50; Southern Mississippi Univ., 1950-52; Wichita State Univ., 1952-70; from 1977, faculty associate, Arizona State Univ.
WORKS: ORCHESTRA: In memoriam; 3 American portraits; 3 miniatures, string orch.; America 200, narrator, 2 choruses, 4 brass choirs, full orch., Wichita, 20-23 May 1976; BAND: overture; Concertante, with 5 solo percussionists; suite for band; WIND ENSEMBLE: Fanfare, chorale, and procession, brass choir; Gloria in excelsis Deo, brass choir and chorus; Jericho suite, brass choir and percussion; Rondo caprice, flute sextet; Improvisations, trumpet and piano, 1978; PERCUSSION: Hoedown; 2 miniatures; 2 impressions; Barbaric dance.
7777 E. Heatherbrae, #132, Scottsdale, AZ 85251

MISTERLY, EUGENE
b. Los Angeles, Calif., 25 Sept. 1926. Studied at Univ. of Southern California and Occidental Coll.; privately with Mary Carr Moore and Mario Castelnuovo-Tedesco in Los Angeles. He was awarded 2 Celia Buck grants by the Nat. Assoc. of American Composers and Conductors, 1962,

1964, for operas. He has been a private teacher from 1947.
WORKS: OPERA: Bettina, 1962; Henry V, 1964; The tell-tale heart, 1968; Testimony, 1972; The cask of Amontillado, a revised version of its 1950 form; ORCHESTRA: Balinaise, symphonic poem, 1964; Invention 1976, 1976.
1363 Brampton Rd., Los Angeles, CA 90041

MITCHELL, LYNDOL
1923-1964. Kentucky Mountain portraits: Cindy, Ballad, Shivaree, for orch.; River suite, for band; When Johnny comes marching home, chorus, piano, drums.

MITCHELL, RAYMOND EARLE
b. Milwaukee, Wis., 31 May 1895; d. Studied with Carl Eppert; on scholarship at Marquette Univ. He was music critic and editor for the Hollywood Citizen-News and Musical Courier, 1929-35.
WORKS: ORCHESTRA: Dusty road; Pastorale suite; Childhood scenes; Danae's garden; and songs.

MITCHELL, REX
b. Pittsburgh, Pa., 26 Sept. 1929. Attended Muskingum Coll., B.S.; Kent State Univ., M.E.; Pennsylvania State Univ. He was public school music teacher, 1953-66; from 1966, on faculty, Clarion State Coll.
WORKS: BAND: Caprice, 1968; Panorama, 1968; Song of the city, 1968; Introduction and fantasia, 1969; The silver cornets, 1971; Concert miniature, 1974; Lewisburg, 1976; A song of the sea, 1976; Sing, America!, with chorus and orch., 1976; A Tiadaghton rhapsody, 1977.
Clarion State College, Clarion, PA 16214

MITROPOULOS, DMITRI
b. Athens, Greece, 1 Mar. 1896; U.S. citizen 1946; d. Milan, Italy, 2 Nov. 1960. Studied at the Odeon in Athens, graduating in 1920; studied composition with Paul Gilson in Brussels. He was conductor in Berlin and Athens, guest conductor of many orchestras. In 1930 he was invited to conduct the Berlin Philharmonic with Egon Petri as soloist in the Prokoviev 3rd piano concerto; when Petri suddenly became ill, Mitropoulos played the solo part and conducted from the keyboard. He made his U.S. debut as conductor with the Boston Symphony in 1937 and was appointed permanent conductor of the Minneapolis Symphony that same year. In 1949, he moved to the New York Philharmonic, where he remained to 1958.
WORKS: OPERA: Soeur Beatrice, composed while still a student at the Odeon and performed there on 26 May 1919; ORCHESTRA: Burial, 1925; concerto grosso, 1928; incidental music for Electra, 1937; Hippolytus, 1937; also chamber works, piano pieces.

MITTLER, FRANZ
b. Vienna, Austria, 14 Apr. 1893; to U.S. 1939; d. Munich, 28 Dec. 1970. On coming to the U.S., he settled in New York. His compositions included an opera, a piano trio, the piano suites:

MIZELLE, DARY JOHN

Manhattan suite, Suite in 3/4 time, Newsreel
suite, Boogie-woogie, Waltz in blue, One-finger
polka; and numerous popular songs.

MIZELLE, DARY JOHN
b. Stillwater, Okla., 14 June 1940. Studied at
Sacramento State Coll., B.A. 1965; with Larry
Austin, Jerome Rosen, Richard Swift, Karlheinz
Stockhausen, and David Tudor, Univ. of California
at Davis, M.A. 1967; with Roger Reynolds, Robert
Erickson, Pauline Oliveros, and Kenneth Gaburo,
Univ. of California, San Diego, Ph.D. 1977. He
was research fellow, Center for Music Experi-
ment, 1972-73; on faculty, Univ. of South
Florida, 1973-75; from 1975, at Oberlin Coll.
Cons.
    WORKS: INSTRUMENTAL: 5 pieces for violin
and horn, 1964; Piece for solo violin, 1966;
Green and red, quartet for 9 instruments, 1966;
Piano opus, 1966; The vast beat game, chamber
orch., 1971; Soundscape, percussion ensemble;
Heterophony, 24 celli; ELECTRONIC: Straight
ahead, 5 instruments and tape, 1966; Tangential
energy II; Wave forms, 1967; Radial energy, instruments and tape, 1967; Mrdangam, 1972; Helix
II and Mandala, New York, 3 Nov. 1973; Inter-
lingual music, Series 1, #1; Spectra, bass and
tape; Polyphonies, voice, flute, tape; MULTI-
MEDIA: Photo-oscillations, electronic ensemble
and laser light, 1968; Art and technology concert, electronic ensemble and laser light, 1969.
    45277 Butternut Ridge Rd., Oberlin, OH 44074

MOE, DANIEL T.
b. Minot, N.Dak., 2 Nov. 1926. Studied with
Paul Christiansen, Concordia Coll., Moorhead,
Minn.; with Russell Harris, Hamline Univ.; with
George McKay and John Verrall, Univ. of Washington; Darius Milhaud, Aspen School; Karl F.
Miller, Hannover, Germany; and with Philip
Bezanson, Univ. of Iowa. His awards include
first prize, Seattle Centennial Composition
Contest; Danforth Found. grant; numerous commissions. He was choral director, Univ. of
Denver, 1953-59; Univ. of Iowa, 1961-72; from
1972, at Oberlin Coll. Cons.
    WORKS: CHORUS: Exhortation from Proverbs,
with brass sextet; Cantata of peace, with
trumpet, narrator, organ; Psalm concertato, with
brass quartet and string bass; Te Deum, with
wind ensemble; Worship for today, with congregation and organ; Prelude and hodie; Hosanna to
the son of David; The greatest of these is love,
solo voice and piano.
    Music Dept., Oberlin College, Oberlin, OH
44074

MOEVS, ROBERT
b. La Crosse, Wis., 2 Dec. 1920. Studied with
Walter Piston at Harvard Univ., A.B. 1942, M.A.
1952; with Nadia Boulanger in Paris, 1946-51.
His awards include a fellowship, American Acad.
in Rome, 1952-55; Guggenheim fellowship at
Harvard, 1955-62; and many commissions. He has
been faculty member, Rutgers Univ., from 1966.
    WORKS: ORCHESTRA: Variations for orchestra,
1952, Boston, 6 Apr. 1956; 3 symphonic pieces,
1955; Attis, chorus and orch., 1958; concerto

for piano, percussion, and orch., 1960, won the
Stockhausen Internat. prize in composition, a
cash award, and performance on Italian radio,
1978; Et occidentem illustra, with chorus, 1964;
Main-travelled road, Milwaukee, 9 Feb. 1974;
CHAMBER MUSIC: piano sonata, 1950; Pan, solo
flute, 1951; string quartet, 1957; sonata for
violin solo; Variations for viola and cello,
1961; Musica da camera, chamber ensemble, 1965;
Fanfare canonica, 6 trumpets, 1966; Heptachronon,
solo cello, 1975; Ludi praeteriti, Games of the
past, 2 pianos, 1976; Collana musicale, 12 short
piano pieces, New York, 6 Nov. 1978; CHORUS:
Cantata sacra, 1952; Itaque ut, with chamber
orch., 1961; Et nunc reges, women's voices;
Brief mass, 1968; The aulos player, 2 choruses,
2 organs, soprano solo, 1975.
    Blackwell's Mills, Belle Mead, NJ 08502

MOKREIS, JOHN
b. Cedar Rapids, Iowa, 10 Feb. 1875; d. Cedar
Rapids, 22 Nov. 1968. Studied with Leopold
Godowsky and Adolf Weidig, American Cons.; was
piano teacher in New York and Los Angeles; returned to Cedar Rapids in 1966. His compositions
included an opera, Sohrab and Rustum; an operetta,
The Mayflower; American cantata, on the life of
Lincoln; piano trio, string quartet, other
chamber works, songs, piano pieces.

MOLINEUX, ALLEN WALTER
b. Upper Darby, Pa., 6 May 1950. Studied with
Donald H. White, DePauw Univ., B.M. 1972; with
Warren Benson and Joseph Schwantner, Eastman
School of Music, M.M. 1974. He taught in public
schools, 1974-77; then joined the faculty at
Atlantic Christian Coll.
    WORKS: ORCHESTRA: Concertato; trumpet
concerto; BAND: Miniatures; WIND ENSEMBLE:
Solitary mood; CHAMBER MUSIC: A brief diversion,
trumpet, trombone and piano; Manipulations, solo
trombone; trumpet sonata in 2 movements; Encounter, brass quintet; Psalm 13, mezzo-soprano
and piano; A little book of serial etudes,
bassoon; Free fancy, solo flute; Crystals, song
cycle for mezzo-soprano and 3 percussionists.
    1700 Dartmore Dr., #6, Wilson, NC 27893

MOLLICONE, HENRY
b. 1946. Studied at New England Cons., graduated
1968. He was assistant conductor, New York City
Opera, 1974; was commissioned to write an opera
based on David Guerdon's play, La baunderie (The
laundry), with libretto by Howard Richardson.
The face, a 1-act opera, commissioned by Central
City Opera House Assoc., Denver, was performed
there, 22 July 1978. For chorus, he has published 5 poems of love, Emily Dickinson text,
for women's voices.

MONACO, RICHARD A.
b. Richmond Hill, N.Y., 10 Jan. 1930. Studied
with Hunter Johnson and Robert Palmer, Cornell
Univ.; with Roberto Gerhard at Tanglewood. His
awards include Cornell Friends of Music award;
ASCAP awards, 1969-71; Nat. Endowment for the
Arts grant; Columbia Symph. Orch. commission.
He was on the faculty, Western Coll., 1959-73;

guest faculty, Cornell Univ., 1968-69; from
1973, on faculty, Univ. of Illinois at Chicago
Circle.
WORKS: CHAMBER MUSIC: piano quintet; 3
miniatures, woodwind quintet; A company of
creatures, soprano and chamber ensemble; trombone
sonata; CHORUS: Blessed be the Lord; The magnificat, soprano, tenor, chorus, and orch.; The
prophecy, women's voices, flute, horn, piano;
An Easter carol, women's voices; 4 songs for
literary naysayers.
317 S. Cuyler St., Oak Park, IL 60302

MONELLO, SPARTACO V.
b. Boston, Mass., 29 June 1909. Studied with
Edward B. Hill, Walter Piston, Aaron Copland,
Harvard Univ., B.A., M.A.; at Univ. of Grenoble,
France; on scholarship at Kenyon Coll.; with
Roger Sessions; and at Columbia Univ., D.Ed.
He held 2 Hartford Found. fellowships. He was
civiliam instructor in the Air Force in World
War II; has taught at William and Mary Coll.
and Univ. of California. His compositions in-
clude Lament, for orch.; and symphony for
strings.

MONHARDT, MAURICE
Studied at Peabody Cons. and Juilliard School.
His works include The trumpet shall sound for
orch., and a suite for flute and piano; both
were performed at Cedar Rapids, Iowa, 14 Nov.
1960.
Music Dept., Luther College, Decorah, IA
52101

MONK, MEREDITH
b. Lima, Peru, 20 Nov. 1942. Studied with Ruth
Lloyd, Glen Mack, Meyer Kupferman, Sarah
Lawrence Coll. She received Obie awards, 1971,
1976; Guggenheim fellowship, 1972; Brandeis
Creative Arts award, 1974; ASCAP awards, 1976-78.
She has taught at New York Univ. at various
periods; has been artistic director of The House
Found. for the Arts from 1968.
WORKS: VOICE (as an instrument a cappella,
or with instruments): Juice: a theatre cantata,
80 voices, violins, piano, 1969; Key: an album
of invisible theatre, solo voice and organ,
1970; Vessel: an opera epic, 20 and 70 voices,
electric organ, 7 dulcimers, 1971; Our lady of
late, solo voice and glass harmonica, 1972;
Anthology, voice and piano, 1974; Quarry, opera
for 40 voices, 2 organs, piano, flute, 1976;
Tablet, 4 voices, 4-hand piano, 2 recorders,
1976; Songs from the hill, unaccompanied voice,
1977.
228 W. Broadway, New York, NY 10013

MONK, THELONIUS
b. Rocky Mount, N.C., 10 Oct. 1918. Played
piano in New York bands; developed the style
called bebop; appeared at Philharmonic Hall and
Carnegie Hall, New York, in the 1960s; made
tours of Japan and Europe. He received a
Guggenheim fellowship in composition in 1976.
WORKS: JAZZ ENSEMBLE: Misterioso; Evidence;
Criss-cross; 4 in one; Off minor; Blue Monk;
Crepuscle with Nelly; Epistrophy; Variations

on Jerome Kern's Smoke gets in your eyes.

MONOD, JACQUES-LOUIS
b. Paris, France, 1927; to U.S. 1950. Studied
with Olivier Messiaen and Rene Leibowitz in
Paris; Juilliard School; Columbia Univ.; and at
Berlin Cons. His awards include a Martha Baird
Rockefeller grant; Dorothy Spivak grant; Nat.
Inst. of Arts and Letters citation. He has
held faculty posts at New England Cons., Prince-
ton Univ., Harvard Univ., Queens Coll., and
Columbia Univ., 1972-78. He has conducted
premieres of works by Berg, Schoenberg, Webern,
Babbitt, and Elliott Carter, mostly in New York.
WORKS: CHAMBER MUSIC: Cantus contra cantum
I, soprano and chamber orch., 1972; Chamber aria,
soprano and chamber orch., Boston, 11 May 1973;
Cantus contra cantum II, violin and cello, 1974,
Boston, 30 Oct. 1976; Cantus contra cantum III,
double chorus, a cappella, 1976.
395 Riverside Dr., New York, NY 10025

MONROE, JAMES FRANK
b. Rienzi, Miss., 28 Nov. 1908. Studied piano
at Cincinnati Cons. and Baylor Univ., B.M.; com-
position with Stella Roberts and Leo Sowerby,
American Cons., M.M. cum laude, Ph.D. He was
instructor, Southwest Missouri State Teachers
Co-1., 1944-45; Friends Univ., 1945-46; professor,
Northeast Louisiana Univ., 1946-74.
WORKS: CHAMBER MUSIC: Piece for woodwinds,
percussion and solo horn; suite for horn and
piano; suite for trumpet and piano; VOICE:
Motet, chorus; 4 miniatures, voice and piano;
PIANO: 3 fugues; sonatina; Fantasia; ORGAN:
Passacaglia.
Rte. 5, Box 358, Monroe, LA 71203

MONTAGUE, STEPHEN
b. Syracuse, N.Y., 10 Mar. 1943. Studied first
with his father, Richard Montague, St. Petersburg Jr. Coll.; with Carlisle Floyd and John
Boda, Florida State Univ., B.M.E. 1965, M.M.
1967; with Herbert Brün, Marshall Barnes, David
Behrman, Ohio State Univ., D.M.A. 1972; and with
Wlodzimerz Kotonski in Warsaw, Poland, on a
Fulbright fellowship, 1972-74. Other awards include numerous European festival performances
and commissions. He was instructor, Butler
Univ., 1967-69; composer-in-residence with
Strider Dance Co., London, 1974-75; then free-
lance composer/pianist in Europe and North and
South America.
WORKS: Varshavian spring, orchestra and
chorus, 1973; The eyes of ambush, 1-5 instruments and tape, 1973; Sound round, orch. and
live electronics, 1973; Strummin', piano interior, tape, light, 1974-75; Frozen mirrors,
chamber group and live electronics, 1976;
Inundations II: Willow, soprano, piano, tape,
1976; Criseyde, soprano, ocarina, slides, tape,
1976-79; Paramell I, muted trombone, muted
piano, 1977; Into the sun, ballet, 1977; Passim,
chamber ensemble and live electronics, 1977;
Paramell II, trombone, piano, percussion, 1977;
Entity, 6 percussionists, 1977; Paramell IV,
tuba and tape, 1978-79. Nearly all of these
works have been performed at European festivals.
1 Field Cottages, Fortis Green, London N.2 9HS
England

MONTGOMERY, BRUCE

MONTGOMERY, BRUCE
    b. Philadelphia, Pa., 20 June 1927. Studied at
Bethany Coll., B.F.A., and Univ. of Pennsylvania.
He received 2 Univ. of Pennsylvania commissions;
was music director for the Univ.; glee club
director for Special Services in the Korean war;
conductor on a European tour sponsored by the
American Friends Service Committee.
    WORKS: OPERA: John Barleycorn; THEATRE:
The amorous flea; Spendthrift; CHORUS: Make a
joyful noise, cantata; Let us now praise famous
men; 3 haiku.

MONTGOMERY, MERLE
    b. Davidson, Okla., 15 May 1904. Studied at
Univ. of Oklahoma, B.F.A. 1924; Eastman School
of Music, M.M. 1927, Ph.D. 1948; privately with
Nadia Boulanger and Isidor Philipp in Paris,
1929-31; Fontainebleau School, dipl. 1936. Her
awards include Univ. of Rochester Alumni citation; Mu Phi Epsilon citation, 1967; Theta Sigma
Phi award, 1972. She was faculty member, Univ.
of Oklahoma, 1931-33; Southwestern Inst., 1934-
38; with Oklahoma WPA Music Project, 1938-43;
on faculty, Eastman School, 1943-45; Schillinger
System, 1945-47; on staff of music publishers,
1947-72; president, Nat. Fed. of Music Clubs,
1972-75; from 1975, National Music Council.
    WORKS: CHORUS: Leisure; Madrigal, a cap-
pella; many unpublished works for orchestra,
voice, chorus; piano pieces; songs for children.
    222 E. 80th St., New York, NY 10021

MOORE, CARMAN L.
    b. Lorain, Ohio, 8 Oct. 1936. Studied at Ohio
State Univ., B.M.; Juilliard School, M.M.;
privately with Hall Overton, 1958-62; Vincent
Persichetti, 1965; Luciano Berio, 1966. His
awards include grants from Creative Arts Service
Program, 1970; New York State Council on the
Arts, 1971, 1972, 1974; Nat. Endowment for the
Arts. He was faculty member, Yale Univ., 1969-
71; Brooklyn Coll., 1972-74; from 1965, music
critic and columnist, the Village Voice.
    WORKS: ORCHESTRA: Catwalk, ballet for
orch. and tape; Gospel fuse, gospel quartet and
orch.; Wildfires and field songs, commissioned
by New York Philharmonic and N.Y. State Council
on the Arts, New York, 23 Jan. 1975; Hit!, concerto for percussion and orch.; 4 movements for
a 5-toed dragon, orch., Chinese instruments,
jazz-rock quintet; WIND ENSEMBLE: Drum major,
to Martin Luther King, brass, percussion, and
tape, 1970; Memories, ballet for bells and
mixed instruments; CHAMBER MUSIC: Youth in a
merciful house, chamber ensemble; Museum piece,
flute, cello, tape, Brooklyn, 22 Apr. 1977.
    148 Columbus Ave., New York, NY 10025

MOORE, CHARLES
    b. Vinita, Okla., 23 May 1938. Studied with
Bela Rozsa, Tulsa Univ.; with Philip Bezanson
and Richard Hervig, Univ. of Iowa. He won a
Phi Mu Alpha composition contest, 1965. He was
faculty member, Minot State Coll., 1965-67;
Concordia Coll., Moorhead, Minn., 1968-74.
    WORKS: ORCHESTRA: Concertpiece; CHAMBER
MUSIC: woodwind quintet; brass quintet, 1963;

clarinet sonata; Cessation, wind sextet.
    Box 44, Christine, ND 58015

MOORE, DAVID A.
    b. Stillwater, Okla., 23 Feb. 1948. Studied
with Daniel Lentz, Douglass Green, Peter Racine
Fricker, and Edward Applebaum, Univ. of California, Santa Barbara, B.A., M.A.
    WORKS: OPERA: Jephtha, 2 acts, libretto by
composer, 1973; CHAMBER MUSIC: string quartet,
1970; 3 Haiku, baritone, recorders, percussion,
1972; 3 songs on diverse texts, flute, clarinet,
soprano, 1972; trio, violin, viola, piano, 1972;
CHORUS: Requiem cantata, with 5 instruments,
percussion, piano, 1968; Passion cantata, small
ensemble and tape, 1970; Songs of the Shulamites,
women's voices, piano, harp, 1970.
    4028 Patterson Ave., Oakland, CA 94619

MOORE, DONALD I.
    b. Farnhamville, Iowa, 11 Apr. 1910. Studied at
Carleton Coll.; Colorado State Coll. of Education; Univ. of Michigan; composition with James
R. Gillette, F. L. Lawrence, and Erik Leidzen.
He has been professor, Baylor Univ., from 1948,
was director of bands, 1948-69.
    WORKS: ORCHESTRA: Burlesca; Patriotic
oratory, with horn solo; BAND: Domino variations; Bright and breezy; Tau Beta Sigma; Saul
of Tarsus; Affirmation; Alleluia; Triumvirate,
with trombone solo; The greatness of America,
with chorus; Psalm 23, with chorus; numerous
concert pieces and more than 30 marches for band.
    3300 N. 29th, Waco, TX 76708

MOORE, DOROTHY RUDD. See RUDD-MOORE, DOROTHY

MOORE, DOUGLAS STUART
    b. Cutchogue, N.Y., 10 Aug. 1893; d. Greenport,
N.Y., 25 July 1969. Studied with Horatio
Parker and David Stanley Smith, Yale Univ., B..A
1915, B.M. 1917; with Vincent d'Indy and Nadia
Boulanger in Paris, 1919-21. His many awards
included 4 honorary doctorates, 1924, 1946, 1955,
1963; Pulitzer scholarship, 1925; Guggenheim
fellowship, 1934; membership, Nat. Inst. of Arts
and Letters, 1946, president, 1959-62; Pulitzer
prize, 1951; New York Music Critics' Circle
awards, 1946, 1955; Huntington Hartford Found.
award, 1960. He served in the U.S. Navy, 1917-
18; joined the faculty at Columbia Univ., 1926;
was executive director of the music department,
1940-62.
    WORKS: OPERA: The headless horseman, 1936;
The devil and Daniel Webster, 1939; White wings,
1948; The emperor's new clothes, 1948; Giants in
the Earth, 1950; Ballad of Baby Doe, 1955;
Gallantry, a soap opera, 1957; The wings of the
dove, 1961; Carrie Nation, 1965; ORCHESTRA:
Pageant of P. T. Barnum, 1926; Moby Dick, 1928;
A symphony of autumn, 1928; Overture on an
American theme, 1930; Village music, 1941; In
memoriam, 1944; symphony in A, 1945; Farm journal,
chamber orch., 1948; Cotillion suite, string
orch., 1952; Down East suite, with violin solo;
CHAMBER MUSIC: violin sonata, 1929; string quartet, 1933; quintet for woodwinds and horn, 1942;
clarinet quintet, 1946; piano trio, 1953; also
choral works, songs, piano pieces.

MOORE, EARL VINCENT
b. Lansing, Mich., 27 Sept. 1890. Studied at
Univ. of Michigan, B.A. 1912, M.A. 1915; and in
Europe; joined the faculty at Univ. of Michigan
in 1913. His compositions include 2 children's
cantatas, The voyage of Arion and The bird man;
choral works and organ pieces; is probably best
known at Univ. of Michigan as composer of the
football song Varsity.

MOORE, F. RICHARD
b. Uniontown, Pa., 4 Sept. 1944. Studied with
Nikolai Lopatnikoff, Carnegie-Mellon Univ.,
B.F.A. 1966; with Lejaren Hiller and Kenneth
Gaburo, Univ. of Illinois; and at Stanford
Univ., Ph.D. 1978. From 1967, he has been en-
gaged in computer and acoustic research at Bell
Telephone Laboratories.
    WORKS: ORCHESTRA: Concerto piece for
marimba and orch.; COMPUTER-GENERATED TAPE:
requiem; Lemniscate of F. Bernoulli; FILM SCORES:
Enigma; Apotheosis; Pixillation; Galaxies (com-
puter-generated art films and music made with
Lillian Schwartz, film maker).
    Bell Laboratories, Murray Hill, NJ 07974

MOORE, MARY CARR
b. Memphis, Tenn., 6 Aug. 1873; d. Ingleside,
Calif., 11 Jan. 1957. Studied music privately;
received an honorary doctorate of music, Chapman
Coll.; 3 awards, Nat. League of American Pen
Women; David Bispham Medal, 1930. She was a
concert singer; taught at Chapman Coll.; later
was professor, California Christian Coll.
    WORKS: OPERA: The oracle, operetta in
which she sang the leading role, 1894; Narcissa,
1912; conducted by the composer in San Francisco,
1925; Los rubios, 1931; David Rizzio, 1932; The
shaft of Ku'Pish Ta Ya; ORCHESTRA: piano concerto; My dream, with chorus; CHAMBER MUSIC:
piano trio; piano quintet; piano pieces and
songs.

MOORE, MAURINE RICKS
b. Vermillion, Kans., 1 Nov. 1908. Studied with
Carl Preyer, Univ. of Kansas, B.A. 1937; privately with Elmer Schoettle; piano at Dingley-
Matthews School. She taught piano in her own
studio, 1937-57; American Coll. of Musicians,
1963-73.
    WORKS: PIANO: Romantic reverie; Rhapsodic
melody; My prayer; Rhapsody on war and peace; 2
piano suites.

MOORE, ROBERT STEELE
b. Marshall, Tex., 22 Aug. 1941. Studied at
Centenary Coll., Sam Houston State Coll., and
Univ. of Iowa. His awards include Philip
Greeley Clapp award; Rockefeller Found. grant;
Nat. Endowment for the Humanities fellowship;
Sutherland Dows chair in composition, Univ. of
Iowa. He has held faculty posts at Indiana
Univ., 1969; Oberlin Coll., 1969-73; research
guest, Mass. Inst. of Tech., 1973-74; and from
1975, on faculty, Yale Univ.
    WORKS: ORCHESTRA: Homomorphisms; Blues
people, with actor, soprano, chorus, percussion
ensemble, jazz quintet; CHAMBER MUSIC: Blood

wedding, soprano and 11 instruments; ELECTRONIC:
Negentropy/entropy, tape; Phantasms, clarinet,
trombone, cello, percussion, real-time synthesizer; Hexagrams, multiple keyboards (one
performer) and computer-generated tape.
    Music Dept., Yale Univ., New Haven, CT
06520

MOORE, THOMAS
b. Fairfield, Ala., 24 Jan. 1933. Studied with
Dika Newlin, Drew Univ.; with Jack Beeson and
Otto Luening, Columbia Univ., M.A. He was
faculty member, Mississippi State Coll. for
Women, 1961-63; Middle Tennessee State Coll.,
1963-64; C. W. Post Coll., 1964-70; violinist,
Kansas City Phil., 1970-71; Indianapolis Symph.
Orch., 1971-73; from 1973, with Florida Symph.
Orch.
    WORKS: Fantasy, violin and orch.; A quality
of spring, piano and orch.; piano concerto;
CHAMBER MUSIC: Piping songs, solo flute; Meta-
morphosis, piano, 4 hands; string quartet; many
songs.
    4900 S. Rio Grande, #28-D, Orlando, FL
32809

MOORE, UNDINE SMITH
b. Jarrett, Va., 25 Aug. 1906. Studied at Fisk
Univ., A.B. with honors; Teachers Coll., Columbia
Univ., M.A. Her many awards include citations
from Nat. Assoc. of Negro Musicians, City of New
York, City of Petersburg, Va.; honorary doctorates, Virginia State Coll., 1972, Indiana Univ.,
1975; named Music Laureate, State of Virginia,
1977. She was faculty member, Virginia State
Coll., 1927-72; adjunct professor, Virginia
Union Univ., 1972-77; scholar-in-residence,
Richmond Community H. S. for the Gifted, 1978;
held various guest faculty posts.
    WORKS: ORCHESTRA: Scenes from the life of
a martyr (a Martin Luther King piece), soli,
chorus, narrator, speaking choir, dance, piano,
orch.; CHAMBER MUSIC: Afro-American suite,
flute, cello, piano; string quartet; many choral
works. She was contributing author for The
Black composer speaks and Reflections on Afro-
American music.
    4538 W. River Rd., Ettrick, VA 23803

MOOREFIELD, ARTHUR A.
b. Denver, Colo., 11 Dec. 1928. Studied with
William S. Naylor, Cincinnati Cons.; at New
York Univ., M.A.; Univ. of California, Ph.D. in
musicology. He has held faculty posts at Cincinnati Cons., 1949-50; Univ. of California, Los
Angeles, 1950-61; California Lutheran Coll.,
1961-73; from 1973, at California State Coll.,
San Bernardino.
    WORKS: ORCHESTRA: Sarabande and gigue,
1966; Alamoth: symphonic introit on Psalm 46,
with chorus, 1967. He has edited the complete
works of Johannes Galliculus for the Inst. of
Medieval Music.
    California State College, San Bernardino,
CA 92407

MOPPER, IRVING
b. Savannah, Ga., 1 Dec. 1914. Studied composi-

MORAN, ROBERT LEONARD

tion with Julius Herford and Olivier Messiaen; received a Nat. Fed. of Music Clubs award for an opera, 1955.

WORKS: OPERA: The door, 1955; George; Nero's mother; ORCHESTRA: Patterns, soprano and orch.; clarinet concerto; Nero's daughter, 1961; CHAMBER MUSIC: 3 piano sonatinas; piano suite; Passacaglia and fugue, piano; string trio; many choral works and songs.

MORAN, ROBERT LEONARD
b. Denver, Colo., 8 Jan. 1937. Studied at San Francisco State Coll.; with Hans Erich Apostel in Vienna, 1958; with Darius Milhaud and Luciano Berio, Mills Coll., M.A. 1963. His awards include numerous commissions and a Nat. Endowment for the Arts grant, 1977. He conducted weekly radio shows in San Francisco and was on the faculty at San Francisco Cons., 1966-72; was composer-in-residence in the German Academic Exchange Program in Berlin, 1974-75; at Northwestern Univ., 1977-78.

WORKS: THEATRE: Metamenagerie, a department store window opera, Berlin, 1974; Marktamenagerie, theatrical work for children, Bonn, 1975; ORCHESTRA: Interiors, orch., chamber orch., or percussion ensemble, New York, 1964; Silver and the circle of messages, San Francisco, 24 Apr. 1970; Emblem of passage, San Francisco, 7 Aug. 1974; The eternal hour for any number of orchestras and choruses, commissioned and premiered by the Berlin Festival 1974 with 6 orchestras and 6 choruses; CHAMBER MUSIC: 4 visions, flute, harp, string quartet, Osaka, Japan, 1964; Elegant journey with stopping points of interest for any instrumental ensemble, 1967; L'apres-midi du Dracoula, any sound-producing instruments, 1966; Divertissement #3, a lunch bag opera, for many walking full-size brown paper bags and instruments, BBC-TV, 31 Oct. 1971; Angels of silence, viola and chamber orch., 1975; MULTIMEDIA: Jewel-encrusted butterfly wing explosions, orch. with television, electronics, films, Seattle, Mar. 1968; 39 minutes for 39 autos, for 39 amplified auto horns, auto lights, synthesizer, 30 skyscrapers, 2 radio stations, 1 television station, dancers, theatre groups, spotlights, airplanes, etc., San Francisco, 29 Aug. 1969, using 100,000 performers; Hallelujah, 20 marching bands, 40 church choirs, organs and carillons, rock groups, gospel group, and the entire city, Bethlehem, Pa., 23 Apr. 1971; Enantiodromia, 8 orchestras and 40 dancers, Zagreb, 1977.

1022 Greenwood Ave., Evanston, IL 60201

MORAWECK, LUCIEN
b. Belfort, France, 24 May 1901; U.S. citizen 1941; d. San Diego, Calif., 20 Oct. 1973. Studied piano with Alfred Cortot, composition with Georges Caussade, Paris Cons. His score for Man in the iron mask was nominated for an Academy award, 1940. He was affiliated with Columbia Broadcasting System in New York and Hollywood from 1935 to retirement in 1963.

WORKS: CHAMBER MUSIC: World in turmoil, viola and piano; string quartet; brass quintet; many works for piano solo, piano, 4 hands, 2

pianos, other chamber works; FILM SCORES: Return of Monte Cristo; RADIO SHOWS: "Suspense"; "Chesterfield hour"; TELEVISION: "Playhouse 90"; "Gunsmoke"; "Have gun, will travel"; "Twilight zone"; "Perry Mason"; and others.

MORGAN, ERNIE
b. Sentinel, Okla., 14 June 1945. Studied with Fred Fox, California State Coll. at Hayward; with Robert Ashley, Mills Coll.; with Roger Reynolds, Univ. of California, San Diego.

WORKS: CHAMBER MUSIC: piano sonata, 1969; Essence, soprano, strings, and radios, 1969; CHORUS: Beginning II, 1970; ELECTRONIC: Summit, saxophone and tape, 1970; Allelujah, tape, 1970; Plato's pup, an eternal electronic piece, 1971; Unit-E, toccata for organ and electronic instruments, 1972; Willie wants a monkey, tape; Monomelodies, 1973; Richard Martin, electronic film score, 1972.

MORGAN, HAYDN
b. Van West Co., Ohio, 25 Mar. 1898. Studied at Wooster Coll.; Cornell Univ.; New York Univ., B.S.M., M.A. He taught in public schools; from 1941, was music dept. chairman, Eastern Michigan Univ.; visiting instructor at several colleges. His compositions include a cantata, Lament and alleluia, and many songs.

MORGAN, ROBERT
b. Houston, Tex., 31 July 1941. Studied with Samuel Adler, North Texas State Univ., B.M. 1963, M.M. 1965; with Gordon Binkerd, Thomas Fredrickson, Morgan Powell, Univ. of Illinois. He received first place, Phi Mu Alpha contest, 1960, Ohio State Univ. contest, 1967, Texas Composers Guild contest, 1969; Sam Houston State Univ. grant, 1968; Nat. Endowment for the Arts grant, 1972; ASCAP awards, 1972, 1973; and commissions. He was faculty member, Sam Houston State Univ., 1965-70, 1972-74.

WORKS: ORCHESTRA: sinfonietta, 1965; BAND: Variations on a choral theme, 1969; Introduction, allegro, dirge, brass and percussion, 1966; JAZZ BAND: Anadge, 1964; Collection, 1968; Requiescat in pace/Elegia, 1968; Market Square, 1968; Threshold, 1971; CHAMBER MUSIC: woodwind trio, 1963; sonatine, flute and piano, 1964; 4 statements on a row by Webern, 5 winds, viola, cello, marimba/celeste, 1965; Poems, flute and guitar, 1967; CHORUS: Take no thought, with brass and organ, 1964; FILM SCORE: More than a state of mind, 1969.

MORGAN, ROBERT P.
b. Nashville, Tenn., 28 July 1934. Studied with Roger Sessions and Edward T. Cone, Princeton Univ.; with Andrew Imbrie, Univ. of California, Berkeley; with Harald Genzmer in Munich on a German government grant, 1960-62. He was faculty member, Univ. of Houston, 1963-67; from 1967, at Temple Univ.; visiting professor, Univ. of Pennsylvania, 1976-78, Chicago Univ., 1978-79.

WORKS: ORCHESTRA: symphony; Momentum; CHAMBER MUSIC: Convergence, chamber orch.; woodwind quartet; Interplay, flute, oboe, bass; trio for flute, cello, harpsichord; Correspondence, cello and percussion; Repercussions, 8 percussionists.

2203½ St. James, Philadelphia, PA 19103

MORITZ, EDVARD
b. Hamburg, Germany, 23 June 1891; U.S. citizen 1943; d. New York, N.Y., 30 Sept. 1974. Studied violin with Carl Flesch, piano with Ferruccio Busoni, conducting with Arthur Nikisch, composition with Paul Juon, all in Berlin. He was conductor throughout Europe and in the U.S.
WORKS: OPERA: Circe, 3 acts; ORCHESTRA: 3 symphonies; Burleske; Nachtmusik; Gitanjali, baritone and orch.; Kammersymphonie; concerto for winds, brass, percussion; concerto grosso; concertos for violin, piano, 2 violins, saxophone, viola, cello, violin and cello; Der Klingende Garten, baritone and orch.; Italian overture; American overture; Scherzo, strings; Divertimento, winds, brass, harp, percussion; CHAMBER MUSIC: 5 string quartets; 3 piano trios; 3 saxophone sonatas; trio for flute, violin, viola; 2 wind quintets; quintet for saxophone and string quartet; piano quintet; violin sonata; viola sonata; cello sonata; flute sonata; sonata for violin and viola; sonata for violin and cello; sonata for 2 violins; piano sonata; many works for piano; more than 200 songs.

MOROSS, JEROME
b. Brooklyn, N.Y., 1 Aug. 1913. Studied at Juilliard School and at New York Univ., B.S. in Mus.Ed. 1932. He held a Juilliard fellowship and 2 Guggenheim fellowships.
WORKS: THEATRE: Ballet ballads, 4 1-act ballet-operas: (1) Susan and the Elders, 1939-40, (2) Willie the weeper, 1945, (3) The eccentricities of Davy Crockett, 1945, (4) Robin Hood, 1946; The golden apple, 2-act opera, 1954; Gentlemen, be seated, 2-act opera, 1963; Sorry, wrong number, 1-act opera, 1977; ORCHESTRA: Paeans, 1932; Those everlasting blues, voice and chamber orch., 1933; Beguine, 1934; Frankie and Johnny, ballet suite, 1938; A tall glory, 1938; symphony, 1940-42; The last judgment, ballet suite, 1953; Variations on a waltz, 1964; CHAMBER MUSIC: Recitative and aria, violin and piano, 1943; sonatinas for divers instruments: (1) clarinet choir, 1966, (2) contrabass and piano, 1967, (3) brass quintet, 1969, (4) woodwind quintet, 1970; sonata for piano duet and string quartet, 1974; concerto for flute with string quartet, 1978; FILM SCORES: The big country, 1958; The Cardinal, 1963; Music for the flicks, 1966.

610 West End Ave., New York, NY 10024

MORRILL, DEXTER G.
b. North Adams, Mass., 17 June 1938. Studied at Colgate Univ., B.M. 1960; with Leonard Ratner, Stanford Univ., B.A. 1962; with Robert Palmer, Cornell Univ., D.M.A. 1970. His awards include a Ford Found. fellowship, 1962-64; Nat. Endowment for the Arts grant, 1977; and commissions. He was resident composer, Kansas State Teachers Coll., Emporia, 1966; faculty member, St. John's Univ., N.Y., 1966-68; from 1969, at Colgate

Univ.
WORKS: ORCHESTRA: concerto for trumpet and strings, 1966; symphony, 1971; BAND: Divertimento, 1964; CHAMBER MUSIC: 3 pieces for solo clarinet, 1964; string quartet, 1965; 3 lyric pieces for violin and piano, 1969; Ragtime, piano, 1977; ELECTRONIC: No, chorus and tape, 1973; Studies for trumpet and computer, 1975; Fantasy quintet, piano and computer, 1978.
20 Montgomery St., Hamilton, NY 13346

MORRIS, FRANKLIN E.
b. Phoenixville, Pa., 1920. Earned a Ph.D. in organic chemistry at Mass. Inst. of Tech.; then studied composition with Walter Piston at Harvard Univ.; with Paul Hindemith at Yale Univ., M.M. 1951. He has been professor at Syracuse Univ. from 1946. His compositions include an opera, The postponement; a symphony; concerto for 7 instruments, piano, percussion, and tape; string quartet; 5 esoteric pieces, a suite for piano, 1941, revised as a woodwind quintet, 1955.
Syracuse University, Syracuse, NY 13210

MORRIS, HAROLD
b. San Antonio, Tex., 17 Mar. 1890; d. New York, N.Y., 6 May 1964. Studied at Univ. of Texas, B.A.; Cincinnati Cons., M.M., D.M.; and with Rosario Scalero. His honors included Nat. Fed. of Music Clubs award; 2 Texas Composers awards; Philadelphia Music Guild award; Society for Publication of American Music award; Fellowship of American Composers award; Nat. Assoc. of American Composers and Conductors awards; 13 MacDowell fellowships; life fellowship, Internat. Inst. of Arts and Letters, Switzerland. He held faculty posts at Juilliard School, 1922-39; Columbia Univ., 1939-46; and was director, Internat. Society for Contemporary Music, 1936-40.
WORKS: ORCHESTRA: Poem, after Tagore's Gitanjali, 1918; Dum-a-lum, variations on a spiritual, 1925; piano concerto, 1931; 3 symphonies, 1934, 1939, 1947; Passacaglia and fugue, 1939; suite for chamber orch.; violin concerto; Heroic overture, 1943; CHAMBER MUSIC: 2 piano trios; 2 string quartets; 2 piano quintets; violin sonata; Prologue and scherzo, flute and piano trio; Rhapsody, flute, cello, piano; 4 piano sonatas.

MORRIS, ROBERT DANIEL
b. Cheltenham, England, 19 Oct. 1943, of American parents. Studied with John LaMontaine and Bernard Rogers, Eastman School of Music, B.M. with distinction 1965; with Ross Lee Finney, Leslie Bassett, Eugene Kurtz, Univ. of Michigan, M.M. 1966, D.M.A. 1969; with Gunther Schuller at Tanglewood on a Crofts fellowship, 1967. Other awards include a BMI award, 1968; A. W. Griswold grant, 1975; American Music Center grant, 1975; Nat. Endowment for the Arts grant, 1978. He was faculty member, Univ. of Hawaii, 1968-69; Yale Univ., 1969-77; and from 1976, at Univ. of Pittsburgh.
WORKS: ORCHESTRA: Syzygy, 1966; Continua, 1969; JAZZ: Versus, double bass, jazz ensemble, other instruments, 5 alto voices; WIND ENSEMBLE: In different voices, for 5 wind ensembles, 1975-

MORRIS, STEPHEN M.

76; CHAMBER MUSIC: Motet on doodah, flute, piano, double bass, 1973; CHORUS: Wireless, with 2 prepared pianos, 1968; Reservoir, a cappella; ELECTRONIC: Entelechy, voice, cello, modified piano, 1969; On, 1969; Phases, 2 pianos and photocell mixers, 1970; Lissajous, tape and oscilloscope, 1971; Rapport, tape, synthesizer, and tape-delay system, 1972; Thunders of spring our distant mountains, 1973.
    7735 Cromwell St., Pittsburgh, PA 15221

MORRIS, STEPHEN M.
b. Hartford, Conn., 18 Oct. 1944. Studied with Leon Kirchner and Randall Thompson, Harvard Univ.; with Luciano Berio in Rome; with Boris Blacher in Berlin.
    WORKS: ORCHESTRA: 7 pieces, 1967; Song IV-b, 1975; Check, 1978; CHAMBER MUSIC: Mikro I, flute and piano, 1965; Toward Brutus Creator I, cello, piano, claves, 1970; Prime time, 3 pianos and percussion, 1974; CHORUS: Victimae Paschali laudes, 1966; MUSIC THEATRE: Toward Brutus Creator V, brass quintet, narrator, musicians in audience, 1972; Victimae Paschali laudes II, narrator, 12 percussionists, chorus, instruments, organ, soprano, horn, 7 speaking roles, 1973; Prime time, too, percussion and flute, 1974; Oil change, brass quintet, xylophone, marimba, piano, gas station, 1975.
    Box 469, Grove Beach, Westbrook, CT 06498

MORRISON, JULIA
b. Minneapolis, Minn., 26 Apr. Studied with Paul Engle, Univ. of Iowa; with Dika Newlin, North Texas State Univ.; Vladimir Ussachevsky, Columbia-Princeton Electronic Music Center; and with Max V. Mathews and F. Richard Moore at Bell Laboratories. She was research fellow, Univ. of Minnesota, 1964-65; resident visitor at Bell Labs., 1970-75.
    WORKS: OPERA: Rübezahl, full length, book by composer, 1979; MULTIMEDIA: Here 'tis, dancers, 3 altos, readers, bass saxophone, tape, film, slides, lights, text by composer, New York, 3 Mar. 1976; at least 150 songs, most to her own texts. She has also written a second full-length book for opera, Smile right to the bone.
    41 W. 86th St., Apt. 14-D, New York, NY 10024

MORRISSEY, JOHN J.
b. New York, N.Y., 9 Nov. 1906. Studied at Columbia Univ., B.A., M.A.; taught at Columbia Univ. Teachers Coll.; served in U.S. Army in World War II; then was head of the music department, Tulane Univ.
    WORKS: BAND: Bayou beguine; Dance fantasy; Ghost town; Divertissement; Medieval fresco; Caribbean fantasy; French Quarter suite; Viva Mexico!, a symphonic suite; and others.

MORROW, CHARLES
b. Newark, N.J., 9 Feb. 1942. Attended Columbia Coll., B.A. 1961; studied with William Sydeman, Mannes Coll. of Music, composition diploma 1965. His awards include internat. prize, Union of American Hebrew Congregations, 1965; resident composer, UAHC Internat. Art Project with Paul

Ben-Haim, 1966; American Film Festival award, 1967; U.S. Film Board Golden Eagle award, 1968; Creative Arts Public Service grant to study, collect, and compose a piece from the language used by farmers with their animals, 1973; many commissions. He writes for films, television, and radio commercials; formed his own company in 1970; formed New Wilderness Preservation Band and New Preservation Found., 1973; arranged An evening with the two Charlies: Ives and Morrow, Lincoln Center, New York, 25 Jan. 1973.
    WORKS: ORCHESTRA: And thou shalt love, tenor and orch., 1965; Groovin'/Do you feel it, rock group and orch., Garden State Arts Center, 11 July 1968; WIND ENSEMBLE: The birth of the war god, New York, 8 June 1973; SONGS: The blessingway, voice and pipes, 1973; 66 songs for a Blackfoot bundle, 120-minute piece using authentic Blackfoot Indian rituals, 1973; also film scores.
    R.D. 1, Callicoon, NY 12723

MORTON, LAWRENCE
b. New York, N.Y., 4 Oct. 1942. Studied with Donald Lybbert and Ruth Anderson, Hunter Coll., B.A. 1966, M.A. 1973. His awards include the Hunter Coll. Class of 1895 prize, 1966; BMI student award, 1966; N.Y. Internat. Film Festival award, 1977. He was instructor at Hunter Coll., 1970-73; from 1973, on staff CBS Records, from 1977, director of recording.
    WORKS: OPERA: Women, 1 act; ORCHESTRA: Metta, with chorus, Buddhist texts; CHAMBER MUSIC: wind octet, 1966; woodwind quintet; VOICE: songs on texts of e. e. cummings and Stephen Crane; FILM SCORES: Welcome to Washington, for Nat. Park Service, 1976; Runaways, 1978; A Katey song, 1978.
    274 W. 12th St., New York, NY 10014

MORYL, RICHARD
b. Newark, N.Y., 23 Feb. 1929. Studied at Columbia Univ.; with Arthur Berger, Brandeis Univ.; with Boris Blacher in Berlin; and with Iain Hamilton in New York. His awards include Fulbright, Tanglewood, and Bennington fellowships; grants from Ford Found., Kellogg Found., Rockefeller Found., Connecticut Commission on the Arts, Nat. Endowment for the Arts, American Music Center; numerous commissions and composition awards. He was professor, Smith Coll., 1970; from 1971, at Western Connecticut State Coll.; and from 1971, conductor, New England Contemporary Ensemble.
    WORKS: CHAMBER MUSIC: Modules, soprano, flute, bass, 1969; Improvisations, chamber ensemble; Salvos, trumpet, 1969; Chroma, chamber ensemble, 1972; Soundings, brass quintet; Corners, trumpet ensemble, New York, 6 May 1973; Apollo, 10 percussionists, 1976; CHORUS: Illuminations, with soprano, 8 string basses, chamber ensemble; Choralis; Contacts; Multiples; Fluorescents; Madrigals (So, That I would like to die), with soloists, each playing a percussion instrument, 1975; SONGS: De morte cantoris (In memoriam Igor Stravinsky), 2 voices, chamber ensemble, 1974; Das Lied, soprano and chamber ensemble, 1976; MIXED MEDIA: Atlantis, fantasy

pieces for English horn, amplified piano, tape, percussion, and mime, 1976.
    Rte. 67, Roxbury, CT   06783

MOSCOVITZ, HOWARD SAMUEL
    b. Jacksonville, Fla., 29 Apr. 1946. Studied with William Hoskuns, Jacksonville Univ., B.M.; with Leland C. Smith, Stanford Univ.; Samuel Dolan, Royal Cons.; and with Robert Ashley, Mills Coll., M.F.A. He received the E. Mills Crother award, 1972. He has been director, Electronic Music Associates from 1972, and music director, Berkeley Dance Theater and Gymnasium, from 1972.
    WORKS: ELECTRONIC: Lament for Josh, tape, 1971; Grid pattern #2, tape, 1971; Thin air, 1971; March of the Alameda County sheriff, tape, 1972; Double standard, tape and chamber orch., KPFA-FM, Berkeley, June 1971; Barriers, tape, live electronics, flute, cello, bass, 1972; several commercial film scores.
    3400 Wyman St., Oakland, CA   94619

MOSCOVITZ, JULIANNE
    b. Oakland, Calif., 18 Jan. 1951. Studied with William Hoskins, Jacksonville Univ.; privately with John Fahey; at California State Univ. at Hayward, B.A. 1972. She was faculty guitarist, Erickson School of Music, Berkeley, and on staff, Berkeley Dance Theater and Gymnasium, 1972-73.
    WORKS: CHAMBER MUSIC: Once there was a worm, voice and guitar, 1967; Guitar suite in colors, 1968; Tuesday afternoon in October, guitar, 1972; FILM SCORE: Atlanta, an international city, 1973.
    3400 Wyman St., Oakland, CA   94619

MOSKO, STEPHEN
    b. Denver, Colo., 1948. His awards include 2 BMI student awards, 1972, 1973; Fromm Found. prize in competition for West Coast composers, 1975. From 1976, he has been faculty member, California Inst. of the Arts.
    WORKS: CHAMBER MUSIC: Lovely mansions, chamber ensemble, 1972; Night of the long knives, soprano and chamber ensemble, 1973, Los Angeles, 14 Apr. 1975.
    California Inst. of the Arts, 24700 McBean Parkway, Valencia, CA   91355

MOSS, FRANCES PAMELA
    b. Augusta, Ga., 8 Apr. 1940. Studied with Robert Cantrick, Jacksonville Univ., B.M. 1962; at Florida State Univ.; Ball State Univ.; and with Frederic Goossen, Univ. of Alabama, M.M.Ed. 1965, D.M. 1976. She is a choir conductor and consultant at several schools; music department head, Calhoun Community Coll., Decatur. She has composed numerous choral works, several on commission; many vocal solos; a clarinet quartet; On cart, for band; and Capsule canon, for voices and percussion.
    1303 First Ave., S.W., Decatur, AL   35601

MOSS, LAWRENCE K.
    b. Los Angeles, Calif., 18 Nov. 1927. Studied at Univ. of California, B.A. 1949; Eastman

School of Music, M.A. 1950; with Ingolf Dahl and Leon Kirchner, Univ. of Southern California, Ph.D. 1957. His awards include a Fulbright grant, 1953; 2 Guggenheim fellowships, 1959, 1968; Morse fellowship, 1964; 2 Nat. Endowment for the Arts grants, 1975, 1977; Univ. of Maryland awards, 1970, 1978; annual ASCAP awards from 1967. He was faculty member, Mills Coll., 1956-58; Yale Univ., 1959-68; from 1969, Univ. of Maryland.
    WORKS: OPERA: The brute, comic opera, Norfolk, Conn., 15 July 1961; The Queen and the rebels, New York, 1 Nov. 1962; ORCHESTRA: Ariel, soprano and orch., 1969; Paths, 1970; CHAMBER MUSIC: violin sonata, 1959; Elegy, 2 violins and viola, 1969; Timepiece, violin, piano, percussion; Patterns, flute, clarinet, viola, piano; Windows, flute, clarinet, contrabass; Remembrances, chamber ensemble; Music for 5, brass quintet; Exchanges, 3 brass, 3 woodwinds, percussion, 1968; Auditions, woodwind quintet and tape, 1971; Evocation and song, saxophone and tape, 1972; string quartet, Baltimore, 25 Jan. 1976; Tootsweet, oboe and percussion, Los Angeles, 13 Dec. 1976; Symphonies for brass quintet and chamber orch., 1977; Little suite for oboe and harpsichord, Penn State Univ., 18 Sept. 1978; PIANO: Fantasy, 1952; 4 scenes for piano, 1961; Omaggio, piano, 4 hands, 1966; Omaggio II, piano, 4 hands, and tape, 1977; MULTIMEDIA: Unseen leaves, soprano, oboe, tape, and lights, Washington, 20 Oct. 1975; Nightscape, soprano, 4 instruments, tape, slides, dancer, Washington, 20 Nov. 1978.
    220 Mowbray Rd., Silver Spring, MD   20904

MOSSMAN, TED
    b. Chicago, Ill., 6 Apr. 1914. Studied with Rudolph Ganz, Chicago Musical Coll.; with Howard Hnason, Eastman School of Music, B.M.; Univ. of Illinois; and at Juilliard School. He made his debut as pianist with the Rochester Philharmonic.
    WORKS: THEATRE: Salomé, ballet; Abraham Lincoln, music drama; ORCHESTRA: Chicago, Illinois, overture; Lotus blue, tone poem; Central Park romance; piano concerto; New York concerto; CHORUS: Let freedom ring; piano pieces; popular songs.

MOTT, DAVID HOWARD
    b. Hinsdale, Ill., 1 July 1945. Studied with John Bavicchi and William Maloof, Berklee Coll. of Music; with James Drew and Robert Morris, Yale Univ. His awards include 2 Bradley-Keefer Memorial awards and the Julia Silliman Memorial award at Yale; several commissions. He was instructor at Yale, 1976-78; then joined the faculty at York Coll., Toronto.
    WORKS: BAND: Form for band; Sound cycle, solo saxophone and wind ensemble; JAZZ BAND: Hatha thingala; Moon trilogy; CHAMBER MUSIC: Elements II, Earth: mountains and expanses, brass quintet; Night flowers, double bass and alto flute.
    York Univ., Downsview, Toronto, Ontario, Canada

MOURANT, WALTER
    b. Chicago, Ill., 1910. Studied with Bernard

MOWERY, CARL DONALD, JR.

Rogers and Howard Hanson, Eastman School of
Music; with Bernard Wagenaar at Juilliard School
on a fellowship. Before entering on formal
music study at Eastman in 1931, he was pianist
and arranger for stage shows, radio, and dance
bands.
    WORKS: ORCHESTRA: Preamble to the Consti-
tution, setting for chorus and orch.; 3 dances
for orchestra; 3 acts of Punch and Judy suites;
clarinet concertino; In the valley of the Moon,
string orch., 1955; Air and scherzo, string
orch., 1955; Sleepy Hollow, 1955; Harper's Ferry,
W. Va., aria for orchestra, 1960; several concert jazz pieces; theme for the "Westinghouse
Hour," "March of Time," et al.

MOWERY, CARL DONALD, JR.
    b. Shamokin, Pa., 26 July 1941. Studied with
Normand Lockwood, Univ. of Denver; with Charles
Hoag and Spencer Norton, Univ. of Oklahoma,
where he held a NDEA fellowship. He was faculty
member at Shenandoah Cons., 1969-70; at Murray
State Coll., 1970-74.
    WORKS: CHAMBER MUSIC: 3 moments for flute
and strings, 1966; 2 tuba sonatas, 1969; trio
for 3 tubas, 1971; 4 songs from Chaucer's Troilus
and Cressida, countertenor and lute, 1972.

MOY, WILLIAM C. C.
    b. Fiji Islands, 15 Feb. 1923; U.S. citizen
1960. Studied with George F. McKay, Univ. of
Washington, B.A., M.A.; with Otto Luening, Felix
Greissle, and Alan Hovhaness in New York; at
Eastman School of Music, summers, 1957-58. He
has been a music typographer from 1953.
    WORKS: Compositions for orchestra, chorus,
percussion ensemble, piano, performed at Eastman
School and at Composers Forum in New York.
    40-38 205th St., Bayside, NY 11361

MOYER, J. HAROLD
    b. Newton, Kans., 6 May 1927. Studied with Roy
Harris, George Peabody Coll.; with Philip
Bezanson, Univ. of Iowa, Ph.D. He was named
1971 Kansas Composer of the Year by Kansas Fed.
of Music Clubs; has received many commissions.
He has been music department chairman, Bethel
Coll., from 1960; board member, Harvey County
Arts Council, from 1971.
    WORKS: ORCHESTRA: symphony; Job, with
chorus; Trilogy, with chorus, Washington, D.C.,
12 July 1976; CHORUS: Let us sing unto the
Lord; Thou grace divine; I saw the Lord; The
blowing and the bending, music drama; hymns and
harmonizations for the Mennonite Hymnal; ORGAN:
9 preludes.
    Bethel College, North Newton, KS 67117

MOYLAN, WILLIAM
    b. Virginia, Minn., 23 Apr. 1956. Studied with
Thomas J. Wegren and E. R. Van Appledorn, Univ.
of Minnesota; with Jean E. Ivey, Peabody Cons.;
and with Lothar Klein, Univ. of Toronto. He
has received composition prizes from Minnesota
Fed. of Music Clubs, 1976, Annapolis Fine Arts
Found., Inc., 1977, 1978, 1979; Gustav Klemm
award, 1979; Univ. of Georgia commission, 1979.
He was staff member, Peabody Recording Studio,

1977-79; Audio-Recording Inst. of the Aspen
Music Festival, 1979.
    WORKS: ORCHESTRA: Music for dance, 1977;
bass trombone concerto, 1979; BAND: Expression
for band, 1976; CHAMBER MUSIC: duet for clarinet
and bassoon, 1977; saxophone sonata (soprano,
alto, tenor, one performer), 1978; wind quintet,
1979; KEYBOARD: piano sonata, 1978; trio sonata
for organ, 1979; and works with tape.
    603 Harrison St., Eveleth, MN 55734

MUCZYNSKI, ROBERT
    b. Chicago, Ill., 19 Mar. 1929. Studied with
Alexander Tcherepnin, DePaul Univ., B.M. 1950,
M.M. 1952. His honors include 14 ASCAP awards;
2 Ford Found. grants, 1959, 1961; Internat.
Society for Contemporary Music award, Chicago,
1961; Concours Internat. prize, Nice, France,
1961; Distinguished Alumni award, DePaul Univ.,
1977; and many commissions. He has been faculty
member, Univ. of Arizona, from 1965.
    WORKS: ORCHESTRA: symphony, 1953; piano
concerto, 1954; Galena, a town, 1958; Dovetail
overture, 1959; Charade; Dance movements; Symphonic dialogues; Cavalcade, a suite for orchestra, Tucson, 11 Jan. 1979; CHAMBER MUSIC: flute
sonata; cello sonata; alto saxophone sonata;
Fantasy trio, clarinet, cello, piano; trumpet
trio, 1959; string trio; 2 piano trios; Allegro
deciso, brass sextet and timpani; Movements,
wind quintet; Fragments, woodwind trio; Gallery
suite, solo cello; 5 impromptus, solo tuba;
Statements for percussion, 1961; 3 preludes, solo
flute, 1962; Voyage, brass trio, 1970; A serenade for summer, chamber orch., Tucson, 15 Sept.
1978; CHORUS: I never saw a moor; Alleluia;
Synonyms for life; PIANO: 3 sonatas; 5 preludes,
1954; suite, 1960; Toccata, 1961; A summer journal; Diversions; Fables.
    Rte. 8, Box 381-B, Tucson, AZ 85710

MUELLER, CARL F.
    b. Sheboygan, Wis., 12 Aug. 1892. Studied piano,
organ, voice, conducting, and theory at Elmhurst
Coll., honorary doctorate, 1946. He was named
fellow, Westminister Choir Coll.; associate,
American Guild of Organists, 1933; received many
ASCAP awards. He was organist and choirmaster
in churches in Milwaukee, Wis., Montclair, N.J.,
and Red Bank, N.J., 1915-71; head of choral
dept., Montclair State Coll., 1928-53.
    WORKS: Over 500 published works for piano,
organ, voice, and sacred and secular choral
works.
    580-A Lake Point Dr., Lakewood, NJ 08701

MUELLER, FREDERICK A.
    b. Berlin, Germany, 3 Mar. 1921; U.S. citizen
1943. Studied at Univ. of Houston, B.M. cum
laude 1957; with Bernard Rogers, Eastman School
of Music, M.M. 1959; and with Ernst von Dohnanyi,
Florida State Univ., D.M. 1961. His awards include the Texas Manuscript Society award, 1957;
and numerous commissions. He was faculty member,
Spring Hill Coll., 1960-67; at Morehead State
Univ., from 1967.
    WORKS: ORCHESTRA: 2 symphonies; euphonium
concerto; CHAMBER MUSIC: Tuba variations on a

372

theme of Samuel Barber; Dance suite, solo alto
saxophone and danseuse; string quartet; 2 piano
sonatas; also bassoon pedagogy publications.
Morehead State University, Morehead, KY
40351

MULFINGER, GEORGE (LEONIDAS)
b. Chicago, Ill., 25 Mar. 1900. Studied piano
in Cleveland, Chicago, and Vienna. He taught at
Gunn School of Music, 1926-28; was chairman,
piano department, Syracuse Univ., 1928-68.
WORKS: ORCHESTRA: Symphonic variations,
piano and orch.; Overture to an imaginary opera;
CHAMBER MUSIC: piano quintet; Elegy, cello and
piano; PIANO: Childhood memories; Serenata,
nocturne and scherzo; Octave prelude; Poéme and
prelude; suite.
213 Hurlburt Ave., Syracuse, NY 13224

MULLINS, HUGH E.
b. Danville, Ill., 25 June 1922. Studied with
Ernest Kanitz, Univ. of Southern California on
a 4-year Carrie Jacobs Bond fellowship, Ph.D.
1950; with Bohuslav Martinu, Nicolai Lopatnikoff,
Aaron Copland, at Tanglewood; with Bernard
Wagenaar at Juilliard School. He was faculty
member, James Millikin Univ., 1945-47; from 1950,
at California State Univ., Los Angeles.
WORKS: OPERA: The scarlet letter; The
stone of heaven; ORCHESTRA: cello concerto;
flute concerto with chamber orch.; The crown of
Christ, chorus and orch., John Donne text;
Casanova Junction, concerto for trumpet, wind
ensemble, and percussion, 1977; CHAMBER MUSIC:
5 parables, violin and piano; quintet for clarinet and strings; 12 songs for cello and soprano;
Recital music #2, flute and snare drum, 1975;
Recital music #3, oboe and xylophone, 1975;
Recital music #4, clarinet and marimba, 1975;
Small-room music #1, 2 trombones, 1977; Small-
room music #2, 2 tubas, 1977; Statistics, 3
pianos, 1977; Tlamimilolpa, piano and 3 percussionists, 1978.
1322 Walnut Ave., West Covina, CA 91790

MUMFORD, JEFFREY
b. Washinton, D.C., 22 June 1955. Studied with
Peter S. Odegard, Univ. of California, Irvine,
B.A. 1977; with Charles Jones, Krzysztof
Penderecki, William Bolcom at Aspen Music School
on scholarship, 1977-79; privately with Lawrence
Moss. His awards include a first prize and 2
second prizes at the Aspen Festival; ASCAP
grant and standard award, 1979; Martha Baird
Rockefeller recording grant, 1979.
WORKS: CHAMBER MUSIC: Melancolique, violin
and piano, 1975; cello sonata, 1976; Orage,
soprano, clarinet, piano, vibraphone, 1978;
Linear cycles II, violin and piano, 1978; Linear
cycles IV, solo violin, 1978; string quartet #3,
1978; Linear cycles VII (Cambiamenti II), solo
violin, 1979.
9200 Edward Way, #1009, Adelphi, MD 20783

MUMMA, GORDON
b. Framingham, Mass., 30 Mar. 1935. Studied
horn and piano, Univ. of Michigan. He became
interested in electronic music while still in

school; was a cofounder of the Cooperative
Studio for Electronic Music, Ann Arbor, 1958-66;
codirector of the ONCE Festival and ONCE Group,
1960-66; research associate in acoustics and
seismics, Inst. of Science and Technology, Ann
Arbor, 1962-63; composer and performing musician
with the Merce Cunningham Dance Co. and the
Sonic Arts Union, from 1966; visiting lecturer,
Brandeis Univ., 1966-67, State Univ. Coll. of
Buffalo, 1968, Univ. of Illinois, 1969-70, Univ.
of California, Santa Cruz, 1973-74, summers at
other institutions; has made many concert tours
alone and with groups in Europe, Mexico, South
America, and Japan. He is member of the Music
Board, Kresge Coll., Univ. of California, Santa
Cruz.
WORKS: INSTRUMENTAL: piano suite, 1959; A
quarter of fourpiece, 4 instruments, 1960-62;
Gestures II, 2 pianos, 1962; Very small size
mograph 1962, any number of pianos and performers;
Large size mograph 1963, piano solo; ELECTRONIC:
Vectors, 1959; Densities, 1959; Sinfonia, for
11 instruments and tape, 1960; Mirrors, 1960;
Meanwhile a twopiece, percussion and tape, 1961;
Untitled mobile, tape, 1962; Love in Truro,
1963; The analog computer, 1963; Megaton for
William Burroughs, 10 electronic, acoustical,
and communication channels, 1963; Temps for
space theatre, 1963; Music for the Venezia Space
Theatre, 1964; Sequences from galleries, 1964;
La Corbusier, orch., organ, tape, cybersonic
concertante, 1965; Second horn, horn and cybersonic console (an electronic device worn on the
player's body, is activated by certain horn
sounds, plays duets with the horn, and provides
its own improvisational flights), 1965; Hornpipe,
cybersonic horn, 1967; Swarmer, violin, concertina, saw, and cybersonic modification, 1968;
Calm death on Phu Quoc, tape, 1969; Conspiracy 8,
digital computer with up to 8 performers, 1970;
Telepos, dancers with telemetry belts and accel-
erators, 1971; Phenomenon unarticulated, fre-
quency-modulated ultrasonic oscillators, 1972;
Ambivex for surrogate myoelectrical telemetering
system with pair of performing appendages, 1972;
Cybersonic cantilevers, with public participation,
1973.
Kresge College, Univ. of California, Santa
Cruz, CA 95064

MUMMERT, KENNETH J.
b. Waukegan, Ill., 26 Oct. 1939. Studied with
Donal Michalsky, California State Univ. at
Fullerton, B.M.
WORKS: CHAMBER MUSIC: suite for 6 instruments; Impressions of Victorian poets, song
cycle for soprano and piano; Wind dance, trumpet,
clarinet, horn, bass clarinet, percussion;
Sonata Espagnol, piano.

MUNGER, MILLICENT CHRISTNER
b. Rosamond, Ill., 15 Sept. 1905. Studied
theory at Milliken Univ. and Northwestern Univ.;
piano and organ in Chicago and New York. She
won an award for an anthem in 1959. She taught
piano in private music schools, then was organist
and choir director, Spencer, Iowa, 1935-69, in
Tucson, Ariz., 1969-73. She has composed organ

MUNGER, SHIRLEY

and piano works, songs, and choral works, including <u>Processional anthem</u>, which provides
separate descants for each Sunday School class,
all sung at the same time as the congregation
sings the basic hymn.

MUNGER, SHIRLEY
    b. Everett, Wash. Studied with George F. McKay
and John Verrall, Univ. of Washington, B.A.,
M.A.; with Halsey Stevens and Ingolf Dahl, Univ.
of Southern California, D.M.A.; piano at Paris
Cons. She received 2 BMI awards for composition
for television and Phi Beta Kappa. She was
faculty member, Univ. of California, Santa
Barbara, 1954–60; Univ. of Minnesota at Duluth,
1963–68; from 1968, West Chester State Coll.
    WORKS: BAND: <u>American tribute</u>; also works
for organ, piano, voice, and chamber groups.
    519 Sharpless St., West Chester, PA 19380

MUNSON, LAWRENCE J.
    b. Christiansand, Norway, 8 Feb. 1878; to U.S.
1884; d. Garden City, N.Y., 9 June 1950. Studied
with R. Huntington Woodman, Metropolitan Coll.
of Music; with Sigismund Stojowski and Percy
Goetschius at Juilliard School; organ with
Alexandre Guilmant; piano with Moritz Moskowski.
He founded the Munson School of Music and was
its director; was church music director in
Brooklyn, 1930–50. His works included <u>Cathedral
chorale</u> and other piano pieces, and many choral
works.

MURPHY, LYLE
    b. Salt Lake City, Utah, 19 Aug. 1908. Wrote
many works for saxophone ensemble: <u>Notturno</u>;
<u>Prelude and canon</u>; <u>Rondino</u>; <u>Warm winds</u>; etc.; and
film scores: <u>The Tony Fontane story</u>; <u>God's
country</u>.
    1837 N. Whitley, Hollywood, CA 90028

MURRAY, BAIN
    b. Evanston, Ill., 26 Dec. 1926. Studied with
Herbert Elwell, Oberlin Coll., A.B. 1951; with
Randall Thompson and Walter Piston, Harvard
Univ., A.M. 1952; with Nadia Boulanger in Paris;
further study in Belgium. His awards include
the Arthur Knight prize and Francis Boott prize
at Harvard; Brookline Music Library prize;
Cleveland Fine Arts prize; Fulbright grant,
1953–54; 3 Cleveland State Univ. research awards;
Distinguished Service Medal, Union of Polish
Composers; Kosciuszko Found. award, 1978; ASCAP
awards, 1978, 1979. He was teaching assistant,
Harvard Univ., 1954–55; instructor, Oberlin
Coll., 1955–60; from 1960, on faculty, Cleveland
State Univ.
    WORKS: BALLET: <u>Peter Pan</u>, 1952; ORCHESTRA:
<u>Ballad</u>, 1950; CHAMBER MUSIC: 2 string quartets,
1950, 1958; woodwind quintet; <u>Epitaph for
strings</u>; piano sonata; <u>Partita</u>, piano; CHORUS:
<u>Hopi flute song</u>; <u>Safe in their alabaster cham-
bers</u>, with English horn and cello, 1962; <u>On the
divide</u>, with 4 woodwinds; <u>Winds of truth</u>; <u>Ode to
peace</u>; <u>Let the hills hear thy voice</u>, cantata
with instruments; <u>Out of the stars</u>; <u>The gift
outright</u>, a cappella, Frost text; SONGS: <u>Now
close the windows</u>; <u>The pasture</u>, Frost text; <u>He</u>

<u>wishes for the cloths of heaven</u>; <u>A fence</u>; song
cycle on e. e. cummings poems; <u>Innisfree Isle
songs</u>, voice and string quartet; <u>Flame and
shadow</u>, cycle on Teasdale poems, soprano,
Washington, D.C., 21 May 1978.
    1311 Cleveland Heights Blvd., Cleveland
Heights, OH 44121

MURRAY, DONALD
    b. Louisville, Ky., 22 July 1925. Studied with
Claude Almand, Univ. of Louisville; was associated with Roy Harris at the Pittsburgh Internat.
Festival of Contemporary Music, 1952. He received 3 ASCAP awards, and the Giovanni Martini
award at Bellarmine Coll., where he was instructor to 1975. He has been staff pianist at
WAVE-TV, Louisville.
    WORKS: ORCHESTRA: <u>Seeds of contemplation</u>,
with chorus on text of Thomas Merton; CHAMBER
MUSIC: <u>Concert piece</u>, piano, bass, percussion;
compositions in all forms with a preference for
jazz in the larger orchestral forms.
    530 Brentwood Ave., Louisville, KY 40215

MURRAY, JAMES ORVAL
    b. Kannapolis, N.C., 2 May 1929. Studied at
Mars Hill Coll. and Baylor Univ. He was
minister of music in churches in N. Carolina,
Georgia, and Virginia, 1951–62; from 1962, at
First Baptist Church, Greer, S.C.
    WORKS: CHORUS: <u>Trust in the Lord</u>, 1958; <u>I
sought the Lord</u>, 1966.
    P.O. Box 415, Greer, SC 29651

MURRAY, LYN
    b. London, England, 6 Dec. 1909; U.S. citizen
1929. Studied at Juilliard School and with
Joseph Schillinger. He was staff arranger,
WCAU, Philadelphia, 1931–34; composer, conductor,
arranger, CBS, 1934–47.
    WORKS: OPERA: <u>Esther</u>; BALLET: <u>Camptown</u>;
ORCHESTRA: <u>Leapfrog overture</u>; <u>Variations on a
children's tune</u>, string orch.; BAND: <u>Collage</u>,
clarinet and band; CHORUS: <u>Christmas oratorio</u>;
<u>Liberation</u>, cantata; <u>Sleep now on thy natal day</u>;
FILM SCORES: <u>The prowler</u>; <u>Cinderella</u>; <u>The
bridges of Toko-Ri</u>; <u>To catch a thief</u>; <u>Period of
adjustment</u>; <u>Son of Paleface</u>; <u>Wives and lovers</u>;
<u>Promise her anything</u>.
    1919 Outpost Dr., Los Angeles, CA 90068

MURTAUGH, JOHN
    b. Minneapolis, Minn., 30 Oct. 1927. Studied at
Univ. of Michigan, B.M. He wrote the film
score for <u>Gemini space project</u>; also TV commercials, background scores, songs.
    c/o 359 E. 62nd St., New York, NY 10021

MUSGRAVE, THEA
    b. near Edinburgh, Scotland, 27 May 1928; to
U.S. 1972. Studied at Edinburgh Univ.; with
Nadia Boulanger in Paris; and with Aaron Copland
at Tanglewood, 1958. Her awards include the
Lili Boulanger Memorial prize; Koussevitzky
award, 1973; Guggenheim fellowship, 1974–75; in
1976, an honorary doctorate from the Council for
National Academic Awards awarded by Prince
Charles. She was visiting professor, Univ. of

California, Santa Barbara, 1970; has been lecturer on many campuses and radio stations in England, Scotland, and the U.S.; has conducted many of her own compositions.

WORKS: THEATRE: A tale for thieves, ballet, 1953; The Abbot of Drimock, chamber opera, 1955; The decision, 3-act opera, 1964-65; Beauty and the beast, ballet, 1969; The voice of Ariadne, 3-act chamber opera, 1973, American premiere, New York City Opera, 30 Sept. 1977, composer conducting; Mary, Queen of Scots, 3-act opera, 1975-77, libretto by composer, American premiere, Norfolk, Va., 29 Mar. 1978; Christmas carol, opera, world premiere, Norfolk, 8 Dec. 1979; ORCHESTRA: Obliques, 1958; Scottish dance suite, 1959; Festival overture, 1965; Nocturnes and arias, 1966; concerto for orchestra, 1967; clarinet concerto, 1968; Night music, chamber orch., 1969; Memento vitae (in homage to Beethoven), 1969-70, American premiere, Milwaukee, 6 Sept. 1975; horn concerto, 1971; viola concerto, 1973, American premiere, Pasadena, 26 Apr. 1975, composer conducting, Peter Mark, her husband, soloist; Orfeo II, solo flute and strings, 1975; CHAMBER MUSIC: string quartet, 1958; Colloquy, violin and piano, 1960; trio for flute, oboe, piano, 1960; Monologue, piano, 1960; Serenade, flute, clarinet, harp, viola, cello, 1961; Excursions, piano, 4 hands, 1965; 3 chamber concertos, 1962, 1966, 1966; Impromptu, flute and oboe, 1967; Music for horn and piano, 1967; Soliloquy, guitar and tape, 1968; Elegy, viola and cello, 1970; Impromptu #2, flute, oboe, clarinet, 1970; From one to another, viola and tape, 1970; Space play, 9 instruments, 1974, American premiere, New York, 17 Oct. 1975; Orfeo I, flute and tape, 1975; many choral works and songs.

c/o Novello Publ., Inc., 145 Palisade St., Dobbs Ferry, NY 10522

MUSOLINO, ANGELO
b. New York, N.Y., 6 Dec. 1923. Studied with his father and with Josef Schmid. He taught at Brooklyn Cons., 1953-56; has since been private teacher and free-lance arranger. His works include a violin sonata and Fugato for piano.

MUSSER, PHILIP D.
b. Angola, Ind., 22 July 1943. Studied with Salvatore Martirano and Ben Johnston, Univ. of Illinois. He received a Ford Found. grant to study multitrack recording techniques in electronic music at Mills Coll. He was lecturer, Univ. of Illinois, 1972-73. He has composed many electronic pieces on tape alone and with instruments.

1003 S. Douglas, Urbana, IL 61801

MUSTILLO, LINA
b. Newport, R.I., 13 Oct. 1905. Studied with Hugo Norden in Boston; with Arthur Custer, Univ. of Rhode Island. She was organist and choir director in Attleboro, Mass., 1930-35; director of her own music school, 1935-60.
WORKS: SONGS: Trilogy, cycle for soprano and piano; PIANO: Etude intervalle; Triphon; A thought; Passacaglia; and others
5 Hornet Rd., Warwick, RI 02886

MUTCHLER, RALPH D.
b. Northwood, N.Dak., 20 Nov. 1929. Studied at North Dakota State Univ., B.S.; with Frank Cookson, Northwestern Univ., B.M., M.M.; and with Dale Dykins, Univ. of Northern Colorado, Ed.D. He has been faculty member at Olympic Coll. from 1960.
WORKS: BAND: An American suite for band; concerto grosso, jazz combo and band; Wiggy, stage band; numerous works for concert, marching, and stage band.
Music Dept., Olympic College, Bremerton, WA 98310

MYEROV, JOSEPH
b. Philadelphia, Pa., 21 Jan. 1928. Attended Temple Univ., B.S. 1949; studied piano at Juilliard School. He was choirmaster in Philadelphia, 1948-54; organist-music director, Beth Sholom, Elkins Park, Pa., 1954-73; public school teacher, 1950-73.
WORKS: THEATRE: music for 5th season, a play about the garment industry; CHORUS: 3 Friday evening services, 1970, 1971, 1972; SONGS: Who knows better than Israel; A new song, 1973; many secular songs.
7007 Calvert St., Philadelphia, PA 19149

MYERS, ROBERT
b. Fredericksburg, Va., 20 Aug. 1941. Studied with Sydney Hodkinson, Univ. of Virginia; with John LaMontaine and Bernard Rogers, Eastman School of Music; and with Nadia Boulanger in Paris. His awards include Walter Damrosch Memorial Scholarship, 1967; Fulbright grants, 1965, 1966; Contemporary Music Project grants, 1967-68. He was composer-in-residence, Midland Public Schools, Mich., 1967-69; from 1969, on faculty, Saginaw Valley State Coll.
WORKS: CHAMBER MUSIC: Movements, soprano saxophone and chamber orch., 1967; Fantasy duos, alto saxophone and percussion, 1968; Sonores V, trombone and piano; Chansons innocentes, treble voice and percussion, e. e. cummings text, 1969; Reprise, alto saxophone and piano, 1969; in more recent years, he has been working in jazz and multimedia techniques.
Saginaw Valley State College, University Center, MI 46710

MYERS, THELDON
b. Ill., 4 Feb. 1927. Studied at Northern Illinois Univ., B.S. 1951; studied with Arthur Bryon, Fresno State Coll., M.A. 1961; with Nadia Boulanger in Paris; with Sandor Veress and Stefan Grove, Peabody Cons., D.M.A. He held teaching posts in Illinois and California; from 1972, has been professor, Towson State Coll.
WORKS: ORCHESTRA: symphony, 1969; Configuration; Chorale and fantasy; BAND: concertino for band; Cadenza and lament, clarinet and band; CHAMBER MUSIC: clarinet sonata; alto saxophone sonatine; Introduction and allegro, flute, clarinet and piano; string quartet; CHORUS: Make a joyful noise; And the Lord promised unto Zion, with soprano solo and instruments; PIANO: Theme and variations; 3 studies; ORGAN: Festival fantasia.
1205 Wakefield Circle, Baltimore, MD 21239

MYOVER, MAX

MYOVER, MAX
b. Independence, Kans., 6 July 1924. Studied with Albert Noelte and Anthony Donata, Northwestern Univ. He was faculty member, Dakota Wesleyan Univ., 1948-52.
WORKS: THEATRE: He's gone away, music drama, chorus and orch.; ORCHESTRA: Symphonetta; piano concerto in one movement; The death of Dr. Faustus, with baritone solo; Vocalize, soprano and strings; suite for woodwind sextet; string quartet; Declaration, baritone and chamber orch.; CHORUS: Lil' boy name David; Arise, my love; A prayer; FILM SCORES: Together; America the beautiful; The touch of the craftsman; Magic carpet 'round the world.
1340 Arlington Dr., Florissant, MO 63033

MYROW, FREDRIC
b. Brooklyn, N.Y., 16 July 1939. Studied with Ingolf Dahl, Univ. of Southern California, B.M. 1961; with Goffredo Petrassi, St. Cecilia Acad., Rome, 1962-64; with Darius Milhaud at Tanglewood, 1965. His awards include a Rockefeller grant, 1961; BMI awards, 1961, 1963, 1964; Fulbright and Italian government grants, 1961-63; ASCAP award, 1964; Fromm Found. grant, 1965; MacDowell fellowship, 1965; Brandeis Univ. award; Koussevitzky Internat. Recording award, 1970. He was concert pianist for the U.S. Information Service in Italy, 1964; pianist for Evenings for New Music, New York, 1965; faculty member, State Univ. of New York, Buffalo, 1965-66.
WORKS: ORCHESTRA: Symphonic variations, 1960; chamber symphony, 1963; Music for orchestra, 1965; SONGS: 4 songs in spring, 1959; At twilight, 1960; Songs from the Japanese, 1965; PIANO: Theme and variations; 6 preludes in 6 styles; Triple fugue, for 2 pianos.
12971 Galewood St., Studio City, CA 91604

MYROW, JOSEF
b. Russia, 28 Feb. 1910; to U.S. 1912. Studied at Univ. of Pennsylvania; Philadelphia Cons. He has been piano soloist with symphony orchestras, program and music director for Philadelphia radio stations.
WORKS: FILM SCORES: 3 little girls in blue; If I'm lucky; Mother wore tights; The girl next door; The French line; Bundle of joy; many popular songs.

NABOKOV, NICOLAS
b. Lubcha, Novogrudok, Russia, 17 Apr. 1903; U.S. citizen 1939; d. New York, 6 Apr. 1978. Studied with Vladimir Rebikov in Yalta; at the Stuttgart Cons.; with Busoni in Berlin; and at the Sorbonne, Paris, 1926. Coming to the U.S. in 1933, he taught at Wells Coll., 1936-41; Peabody Cons., 1947-52; State Univ. of New York, Buffalo, 1970-71; and at New York Univ., 1972-73. In 1952-63, he was secretary-general of the Congress for Cultural Freedom and in this capacity, organized the Paris Festival of 20th-Century Music, 1952; was organizer and artistic director, Berlin Music Festivals, 1963-68, and the Teheran Festival, 1969.
WORKS: OPERA: The holy devil, Louisville, 18 Apr. 1958, rev. and produced as The death of

Rasputin, Cologne, Germany, 27 Nov. 1959; Love's labour lost, libretto from Shakespeare by W. H. Auden and Chester Kallmann, Brussels, 7 Feb. 1973; BALLET: Ode or Meditation at night, 1928; Union Pacific, 1934; THEATRE: music to Samson agonistes, 1938; ORCHESTRA: Symphonie lyrique, 1930; piano concerto, 1932; Sinfonia Biblica, 1941; The return of Pushkin, elegy for voice and orch., 1947; flute concerto, 1958; Vita nuova, soprano, tenor, orch., 1950; Les hommages, cello concerto, 1953; A prayer, symphony, 1967; CHAMBER MUSIC: 2 piano sonatas, 1926, 1940; Collectionneur d'échoes, soprano, bass, percussion, 1933; string quartet, 1937; bassoon sonata, 1941; CHORUS: Job, oratorio, 1933; America was promises, cantata, New York, 25 Apr. 1950; also songs and piano pieces.

NAGEL, ROBERT E.
b. Freeland, Pa., 29 Sept. 1924. Studied with William Bergsma, Peter Mennin, and Vincent Persichetti, Juilliard School; with Aaron Copland at Tanglewood. He was awarded a Fulbright fellowship to France in 1950. He was a member of the Little Orchestra Society of N.Y., 1947-60; has been director, New York Brass Quintet, from 1954; faculty member, Yale Univ., from 1956; has also held faculty posts at Rutgers Univ., Hartt Coll. of Music, and New England Cons.
WORKS: ORCHESTRA: concerto for trumpet and strings, 1951; WIND ENSEMBLE: 2 brass trios; Divertimento, for 10 winds; suite for brass quartet and piano; Trumpets of Spain; Trumpets on parade; Trumpet processional; The sound of trumpets; CHORUS: Triptych, with brass; All things bright and beautiful; also trumpet studies.
18 Broadview Dr., Brookfield, CT 06804

NAGINSKI, CHARLES
b. Cairo, Egypt, 29 May 1909; to U.S. at an early age; d. by drowning, Lenox, Mass., 4 Aug. 1940. Studied with Rubin Goldmark at Juilliard School, 1928-33; and at American Acad. in Rome.
WORKS: ORCHESTRA: suite for orch., 1931; 2 symphonies, 1935, 1937; 1936, orchestral poem, 1936; 3 movements, chamber orch., 1937; sinfonietta, 1937; The minotaur, ballet for orch., 1938; Nocturne and pantomime, 1938; 5 pieces from a children's suite, 1940; Movement for strings; CHAMBER MUSIC: 2 string quartets; and songs.

NAGY, FREDERICK
b. Marmarossziget, Hungary, 18 Jan. 1894; to U.S. 1951; d. Chicago, Ill. Attended Budapest Univ.; Debrecen Univ., L.L.D.; Budapest Acad. of Music; also studied music privately. He practiced law, 1925-41; was district judge, 1941-45; interpreter for U.S. Occupation Forces, Austria, 1945-51. His compositions included Serenade, for string orch.; Pledge of allegiance and Thanksgiving hymn of the refugees for chorus.

NAGY-FARKAS, PETER
b. B. Topolya (now Yugoslavia) of Hungarian parents, 3 Feb. 1933; U.S. citizen 1967. Studied in Subotica; at Acad. of Belgrade; Schola Can-

torum, Paris; with John Verrall, Univ. of Washington; Leroy Ostransky, Univ. of Puget Sound, M.M.; with Wayne Barlow and Samuel Adler, Eastman School of Music, Ph.D. He was visiting lecturer, Lewis and Clark Coll., 1963-65; on faculty, Univ. of Montevallo, 1958-71; from 1973, at Massachusetts State Coll., Westfield.

WORKS: BALLET: The uprising; ORCHESTRA: violin concerto; Pheonix, symphonic poem; concerto for 3 clarinets, double string orch., and percussion; BAND: Variations on a theme by Thomas Campion; CHAMBER MUSIC: Springtime, baritone, piano, string quartet; Nocturne, trumpet and piano; Shadows, violin, trumpet, vibraphone, harp; suite for clarinet and bassoon; E pluribus unum, 4 clarinets; Meditation, woodwind quintet; For Israel, our Israel, narrator, tenor solo, organ, chamber orch., commissioned by Springfield Jewish Federation, premiere, Springfield, 21 May 1978; CHORUS: Psalm XIII, a cappaella; Adon Olom, with brass; Psalm 146; PIANO: Toccata, 2 pianos; Variations on a theme by Paul Hindemith, 2 pianos; ELECTRONIC: Son et lumière, music for a slide show.
Bldg. 11, Apt. 1, 126 Union St., Westfield, MA 01085

NAJERA, EDMUND
b. Arizona, 1936. Studied at Univ. of California at Los Angeles and Berkeley.
WORKS: OPERA: Scarlet letter; Freeway opera; Carlotta; Secundum Lucam, opera-oratorio setting of the 2nd chapter of Luke, in Latin and English; CHORUS: Exultate Deo; Ad flumina Babylonia; In dulci jubilo; Via dolorosa (choral stations of the cross); Plaudite; Psalms XII, CXIX, for "multidimensional" chorus; Requiems I and II; Fleur du mal; The nightingale; How lonely is the night; maled voices; song cycles; PIANO: sonata for 2 pianos.
1919 Graham Ave., Redondo Beach, CA 90278

NANCARROW, CONLON
b. Texarkana, Ark., 27 Oct. 1912. Studied at Cincinnati Cons.; with Nicolas Slonimsky and Walter Piston in Boston. He played trumpet in jazz orchestras; then fought in the Spanish Civil War; since 1950, has lived in Mexico City. To assure accuracy in the performance of his works, he composes only on player-piano roles. Some of his studies for player piano have been published in Soundings, 1977, and recorded.

NATHAN, ROBERT
b. New York, N.Y., 2 Jan. 1894. Attended Phillips Exeter Acad. and Harvard Univ. A noted poet and author, he has also composed Dunkirk for orch.; a violin sonata; and musical settings for poems of Walt Whitman.

NEAL, CHARLES TAYLOR
b. Boulder, Colo., 4 July 1946. Studied with Rodney Ash, Western State Coll.; with Paul Royer, South Dakota State Univ. He held a scholarship at Western State Coll., 1967-68. He was first bassoonist, Rapid City Symph., 1962-64; Black Hills Chamber Orch., 1967, 1968; public school music director, 1968-71; bassoon-

ist with the NORAD Band, 1972-73; from 1973, with USAF Acad. Band.
WORKS: ORCHESTRA: Rhapsody in d; BAND: 2 symphonies; a suite; also chamber works and piano pieces.

NEAR, GERALD R. A.
Was formerly on the faculty of Carleton Coll., Northfield, Minn. His published works for chorus include: Drop, drop, slow tears; He who would valiant be; Lord, keep us steadfast in thy word; and for organ: A triptych of fugues; Passacaglia; Preludes on 4 hymn tunes; etc.
1982 Traver Rd., #108, Ann Arbor, MI 48105

NEARING, HOMER
b. Springfield, Mo., 29 Jan. 1895. Studied at Drury Coll.; Daniel Baker Coll., honorary D.Mus.; with Clarence Dickinson and Lee Pattison, Union Theological Seminary.
WORKS: CHORUS: The lamb; ORGAN: Southwestern sketches; Duologue and chorale; A memory; PIANO: Kutztown reel; Falling leaves; Junior book, a piano course.

NEIKRUG, MARC
b. New York, N.Y., 24 Sept. 1946. Studied with Giselher Klebe in Germany; with Gunther Schuller at Tanglewood on a fellowship. He was composer-in-residence, Marlboro Music Festival, 1972; received a Nat. Endowment for the Arts grant, 1974. In 1978 he toured as accompanist for Pinchas Zuckerman.
WORKS: ORCHESTRA: viola concerto, Boston Univ., 14 Oct. 1979; clarinet concerto; piano concerto; CHAMBER MUSIC: cello sonata, 1971; sonata for cello solo; suite for cello and piano; violin sonata; piano sonata, 1972; 2 string quartets; quartet for flute, violin, viola, cello; Arianna's suite, New York, 3 Dec. 1973; concertino for 7 instruments, Boston, 17 Apr. 1977; Continuum, cello and piano, Boston Univ., 20 Feb. 1978.

NELHYBEL, VACLAV
b. Polanka, Czech., 24 Sept. 1919; U.S. citizen 1962. Studied composition and conducting at Prague Cons.; musicology at Univ. of Prague and in Fribourg, Switz. He was composer and conductor for Prague Radio while still a student; with Swiss Nat. Radio, 1947-50; music director of Radio Free Europe in Munich, 1950-57; has been guest lecturer and conductor at several American universities; from 1978, at Univ. of Lowell.
WORKS: OPERA: A legend, 1954; Everyman, medieval morality play, 1974; BALLET: Fetes de feux, 1942; In the shadow of a lime tree, 1946; The cock and the hangman, 1946; ORCHESTRA: symphony #1, 1942; Ballade, 1946; Etude symphonique, 1949; concertino, piano and chamber orch., 1949; 3 modes, 1952; Sinfonietta concertante, 1960; viola concerto, 1962; Passacaglia, 1965; Houston concerto, 1967; Concertino da camera, cello, 15 winds, piano, 1971; Polyphonies, 1972; Toccata, harpsichord, 13 winds, percussion, 1972; Cantus and ludus, piano, 17 winds, percussion, 1973; Polyphonic variations, strings and trumpet,

NELSON, BRADLEY R.

1975; Slavonic triptych, 1976; BAND: Caucasian
passacaglia, 1963; Concerto antiphonale, 14
brasses, 1964; Symphonic requiem, with baritone
solo, 1965; Estampie, with antiphonal brass
sextet, 1965; Yamaha concerto, 1971; Introit,
with solo chimes, 1972; Dialogues, with piano
solo, 1976; CHAMBER MUSIC: 3 organa, 4 bassoons,
1948; 3 wind quintets, 1948, 1958, 1960; 2
string quartets, 1949, 1962; quartet for horns,
1957; quartet for piano and brass trio, 1959;
4 miniatures, string trio, 1959; Numismata,
brass septet, 1961; brass trio, 1961; 2 brass
quintets, 1961, 1965; Impromptu, wind sextet,
1963; 9 clarinet trios, 1963; Scherzo concert-
anto, horn and piano, 1965; 3 pieces for saxophone quartet, 1965; Quintetto concertante,
violin, trumpet, trombone, xylophone, piano,
1965; concerto for percussion, 1972; 4 concerto
spirituoso: #1, 12 flutes, harpsichord, solo
voice, 1974; #2, 12 saxophones, harpsichord,
voice, 1974, #3, violin, winds, percussion,
vioce, 1975, #4, voice, string quartet, chamber
orch., 1977; Oratio #1, piccolo, trumpet, chimes,
string quartet, 1974, #2, oboe and string trio,
1976; Music for 6 trumpets, 1975; Ludus, 3
tubas, 1975; bassoon quartet, 1976; Variations,
harp, 1977; The house that Jack built, baritone
and chamber ensemble; trombone sonata; Arco and
pizzicato, string trio; 3 miniatures, string
trio; also numerous choral works, hymns, processionals, organ pieces.
    University of Lowell, Lowell, MA 01854

NELSON, BRADLEY R.
    b. San Diego, Calif., 24 July 1950. Studied
with Wayne Bohrnstedt, Univ. of Redlands; with
David Ward-Steinman, San Diego State Univ.; with
Samuel Adler, Warren Benson, Joseph Schwantner,
Eastman School of Music. He has received composition awards from Sigma Alpha Iota, Phi Mu
Alpha Sinfonia, and Mars Hill Coll. From 1976
he has been on the faculty at Jordan Coll.,
Butler Univ.
    WORKS: THEATRE: Reunion, 1-act musical,
1971; ORCHESTRA: symphony, 1972; Recantation,
with baritone solo and percussion, 1975; WIND
ENSEMBLE: Music for winds, with percussion,
1974; Starcraft, 1976; Brass music XI, 10 brass
and timpani, 1978; CHAMBER MUSIC: Tricycle, 3
pieces for soprano, piano, tape, 1971; The
lighting of candles, 1973; Aurora for brass,
quintet, 1974; 3 songs for tenor, oboe, bassoon,
1974; CHORUS: Thoughts, 1969; Entreation, with
soprano solo, piano, temple blocks, 1971; and
others.
    3861 E. 56th St., Indianapolis, IN 46220

NELSON, DOROTHEA BRANDT. See BRANDT, DOROTHEA

NELSON, LARRY A.
    b. Broken Bow, Nebr., 27 Jan. 1944. Studied
with Normand Lockwood, Univ. of Denver; Will
Bottje, Southern Illinois Univ.; and with H.
Owen Reed, Michigan State Univ. He received a
MacDowell fellowship; was one of 4 winners in
the Philadelphia Orch. Society contest, 1974.
He was director, New Musical Art Ensemble,
1969-71; on faculty, Michigan State Univ.,

1970-71; from 1971, on faculty, West Chester
State Coll., organizer-director, New Music
Ensemble, 1972.
    WORKS: ORCHESTRA: Variations for orch.,
1973; CHAMBER MUSIC: Watch, 12 instruments,
1970; duo for cello and piano, 1972; Poem of
soft music, flute, cello, piano, 1976; Nocturne,
cello and piano; Cadenzas and interludes, clarinet and percussion, West Chester, 2 Mar. 1977;
ELECTRONIC: Flute thing, flute and tape, 1970;
Things that go wump in the night, tape, 1970;
Music for clarinet and tape, 1973; Music II for
clarinet and tape, Philadelphia, 22 Aug. 1976;
MULTIMEDIA: Consequences of . . ., for performers, tapes, slides, lights, 1973.
    306 S. High St., West Chester, PA 19380

NELSON, NORMAN J.
    b. Alexandria, La., 2 Oct. 1943. Studied with
Hunter Johnson, Kent Kennan, and Clifton
Williams, Univ. of Texas at El Paso and at
Austin, D.M.A. He is faculty member, West Texas
State Univ.
    WORKS: ORCHESTRA: A thicket of sticks,
commissioned by Amarillo Symph. Orch.; Concepts
of time in textures; CHAMBER MUSIC: Stasis: 13,
flute choir; 5 adjacent, euphonium quintet;
Phase studies, woodwind trio.
    1502 Creekmore, Canyon, TX 79015

NELSON, OLIVER E.
    b. St. Louis, Mo., 4 June 1932; d. Los Angeles,
27 Oct. 1975. Played piano at age 5, saxophone
at 10, was a professional musician before finish-
ing grade school; later studied at Washington
Univ.; with Elliott Carter in New York; and with
George Tremblay in Los Angeles. In 1971 he received a citation as an alumnus of Washington
Univ. He played saxophone in jazz orchestras in
the 1950s and 1960s; in 1967, settled in Hollywood and devoted his time to writing for films
and television.
    WORKS: ORCHESTRA: Patterns, 1965; Berlin
dialogues, 4 movements: Confrontation, Neutral
zone, Swinging Berlin, Over the wall, performed
at Berlin Jazz Days, 1970; The Kennedy dream;
WIND ENSEMBLE: Divertimento, 10 woodwinds, 1962;
A study in 5/4, 1966; concerto for xylophone,
marimba, vibraphone, and wind symphony, 1967;
CHAMBER MUSIC: woodwind quintet, 1960; song
cycle for contralto, 1961; Dirge, chamber orch.,
1962; Soundpiece, string quartet and contralto,
1963; JAZZ: Blues and the abstract truth, 1960;
Soundpiece, for jazz orch., 1964; Jazzhattan
suite, 1967; FILM SCORES: Death of a gunfighter,
1969; Skullduggery, 1970; TELEVISION: music
for "Ironsides"; "It takes a thief"; "The name
of the game"; "The 6 million dollar man."

NELSON, PAUL
    b. Phoenix, Ariz., 26 Jan. 1929. Studied at
Phoenix Coll.; Arizona State Coll.; Columbia
Univ., B.S.; with Walter Piston and Randall
Thompson, Harvard Univ., M.A.; Univ. of Vienna;
American Acad. in Rome; also with Paul Creston,
Lukas Foss, and Paul Hindemith. His awards in-
clude 3 Damrosch fellowships; first prizes in
Tucson Festival of the Arts contest and Friends

of Harvey Gaul contest; Francis Boott prize, and commissions. He was arranger for dance orchestras; played trumpet, Phoenix Symphony; staff composer and arranger, U.S. Military Acad., West Point, 1951-53; on faculty, Univ. of Louisville, 1955-56; from 1964, at Brown Univ.

WORKS: ORCHESTRA: Theme and passacaglia; Narrative; sinfonietta; Idyll, horn and strings; CHORUS: Easter cantata; Christmas cantata; For theirs is the kingdom; 2 madrigals on old English airs; The creation, with narrator, piano and percussion; In Bethlehem, that noble place; How happy the lover; A lullaby; In memoriam.

Music Dept., Brown University, Providence, RI 02912

NELSON, RON
b. Joliet, Ill., 14 Dec. 1929. Studied at Chicago Cons.; with Howard Hanson and Bernard Rogers, Eastman School of Music, B.M. 1952, M.M. 1955, D.M.A. 1956; with Arthur Honegger and Tony Aubin, Ecole Normals de Musique, Paris. His awards include Fulbright fellowship, 1954-55; grants from Howard Found., 1966, President's Fund, 1966, MacColl Fund, 1968, Nat. Endowment for the Arts, 1974, 1978; annual ASCAP awards from 1960; many commissions. He has been faculty member at Brown Univ. from 1956, was music dept. chairman, 1963-73.

WORKS: OPERA: The birthday of the Infanta, 1956; ORCHESTRA: Savannah River holiday; For Katherine in April; Overture for latecomers; Toccata for orchestra; Trilogy: JFK-MLK-RFK; 5 pieces for orchestra after paintings by Andrew Wyeth, 1975; BAND: Mayflower overture, 1957; Rocky Point holiday; CHORUS: What is man?, oratorio, with soloists, narrator, orch., 1964; The Christmas story, cantata, with narrator, brass, timpani, organ, 1969; Fanfare for a festival; Triumphal Te Deum, double chorus, brass, percussion; Meditation on the syllable OM, male voices; Alleluia, July 20, 1969, on voyage of Apollo II; Prayer of Emperor of China on the altar of Heaven, December 21, 1539; Oh God, invent a name for us; 4 pieces after the seasons; and many others.

27 West Wood Rd., Lincoln, RI 02865

NELSON, RONALD A.
b. Rockford, Ill., 29 Apr. 1927. Studied with Olaf Christiansen and F. Melius Christiansen, St. Olaf Coll.; with Cecil Burleigh and Robert Crane, Univ. of Wisconsin. He received a Distinguished Alumnus award from St. Olaf Coll. He has been church music director since 1949; from 1955, at Westwood Lutheran Church, Minneapolis.

WORKS: CHORUS: How far is it to Bethlehem?; And who is my neighbor?; The season of tomorrow; The passion according to St. Mark; and many anthems.

1457 Utah Ave. S., Minneapolis, MN 55426

NEMIROFF, ISAAC
b. Covington, Ky., 16 Feb. 1912; d. Huntington, N.Y., 5 Mar. 1977. Studied with Carl Hugo Grimm, Cincinnati Cons., 1926-32; privately with Stefan Wolpe in New York. His honors included 3 State

Univ. of New York Research Found. awards, 1963, 1966, 1974; ASCAP awards, 1968-73; and commissions. He taught violin and composition at various schools in the New York ares, 1946-59; then joined the faculty at State Univ. of New York at Stony Brook as a founding member of the music department.

WORKS: music to Troublemakers, 1952; Lorca's The love of Don Perlimplin, 1965; MUSIC FOR DANCE: Calamity Jane, 1942; Scarlet letter, 1942; Ebb tide, 1947; Odyssey, 1948; Antigone, 1948; ORCHESTRA: concerto for oboe and string orch., 1958; solo cantata for voice, flute, string orch., 1964; CHAMBER MUSIC: 2 violin sonatas, 1948, 1950; Variations on a theme, woodwind trio, 1958; trio for flute, oboe, cello or bassoon, 1961; 4-treble suite, woodwinds, 1962; string quartet, 1962; Perspectives, woodwind trio, 1965; woodwind quintet, 1968; 3 pieces for clarinet alone, 1970; Piece for solo piano, 1972; Atomyriads, oboe solo, 1972; Waltz in the branches, voice alone, 1973; Poem of love, voice, string trio, oboe, bassoon, piano, 1975; trio for 4 woodwinds and piano, 1977.

NERO, PAUL
b. Hamburg, Germany, 29 Apr. 1917; U.S. citizen 1929; d. Hollywood, Calif., 21 May 1958. Studied violin at Curtis Inst. He played violin in the Pittsburgh Symph.; served in the U.S. Navy in World War II; was soloist with the Chamber Music Society of Lower Basin Street; was on faculty at Juilliard School and Los Angeles Cons. His compositions included Concerto for hot fiddle; Prelude and allegro, oboe and strings; 7 etudes for violin.

NERO, PETER BERNARD
b. Brooklyn, N.Y., 22 May 1924. Studied at Juilliard School and Brooklyn Coll.; played piano with Paul Whiteman's Orchestra. He performed the piano solo in his own Fantasy and improvisation with the Boston Pops Orchestra.

NESTICO, SAMUEL L.
b. Pittsburgh, Pa., 5 Feb. 1924. Studied at Duquesne Univ., B.S. 1950; and with George Thaddeus Jones, Catholic Univ.; received the Duquesne Univ. Distinguished Alumni award. He was staff trombonist and arranger, WCAE, Pittsburgh, 1946-51; staff arranger, USAF Band, Washington, D.C., and leader of Airmen of Note, 1951-56; staff arranger, U.S. Marine Band, 1966-71; instructor, Los Angeles Pierce Coll., 1972-74; has been arranger and orchestrator for recordings, movies, and television from 1951.

WORKS: BAND: Horizons west; The Greenbriars of Wexley; WIND ENSEMBLE: A study in contrasts, 4 saxophones or 6 clarinets.

18873 Killoch Way, Northridge, CA 91326

NEUHAUS, MAX
b. Beaumont, Tex., 9 Aug. 1939. Studied at Manhattan School of Music, B.M. 1961, M.M. 1962. His awards include Martha Baird Rockefeller grant, 1966; 2 Nat. Endowment for the Arts grants, 1973, 1977; CAPS Program grant, 1974; research fellowship, Center for Creative and

NEUMANN, RICHARD

Performing Arts, SUNY at Buffalo, 1976; German Academic Exchange fellowship, 1977. He toured the U.S. as percussionist with the Contemporary Chamber Ensemble under Pierre Boulez, 1962-63, and with Karlheinz Stockhausen, 1963-64; has given solo recitals in New York, European cities, and at the Spoleto Festival, Italy; was resident visitor, Bell Telephone Lab., 1968-69; has mounted musical happenings called "music for non-concert hall situations" all across the country in such places as the Hudson Tubes and WBAI-FM, New York, CURT-FM, Toronto, Univ. of South Florida, Univ. of California at San Diego, Rochester Inst. of Technology, etc.

WORKS: music for non-concert hall situations: Listen, 1966-76; Public supply, 1966-73; Fan music, 1967; Bi-product, 1967; American can, 1967; Drive in music, 1967-75; Telephone access, 1968; Water whistle, uses 8-10 water-driven whistles which produce pleasant little reedy sounds that are audible only to those submerged in the swimming pool in which they are installed (17 installations), 1971-74; Overhead music, 1977; Underground music, Times Square, N.Y., 1977.

210 Fifth Ave., New York, NY 10010

NEUMANN, RICHARD

b. Vienna, Austria, 21 Jan. 1914; U.S. citizen 1942. Studied with Fidelio Finke and George Szell, Prague Cons.; music education at Vienna Acad. of Music, M.A. 1937; and at Columbia Univ., 1946-47. He received commissions from Anna Sokolov Dance Group, 1941, and Temple Israel, N.Y., 1959. He was music director, Educational Alliance, N.Y., 1949-52; Hillcrest Jewish Center, 1953-63; music consultant, B'nai Brith Youth Org., from 1964; music director, Board of Jewish Education, from 1972.

WORKS: ORCHESTRA: oboe concerto, 1950; timpani concerto, 1972; CHORUS: Cuandro El Rey Nimrod; Scalerica de oro; Los bilbilicos; Noches; also 8 film scores for the United Nations Screen Magazine, Film Section, 1949.

3931 47th St., Long Island City, NY 11104

NEVIN, ARTHUR FINLEY

b. Edgeworth, Pa., 27 Apr. 1871; d. Sewickley, Pa., 10 July 1943. Younger brother of Ethelbert Nevin; studied with Percy Goetschius, New England Cons.; with Humperdinck and Klindworth in Berlin; received an honorary D.M., Univ. of Pittsburgh, 1935. In 1903-4, he spent time in Montana studying Indian music; was professor, Univ. of Kansas, 1915-20; director, Memphis municipal music department, and conductor, Memphis Orchestra, 1920-22.

WORKS: OPERA: Poia, Berlin, 23 Apr. 1910; A daughter of the forest, Chicago, 5 Jan. 1918; ORCHESTRA: piano concerto; Hindu dance; Lorna Doone suite; Love dreams suite; CHAMBER MUSIC: piano trio; string quartet; VOICE: The Djinns, cantata; Roland, cantata; other choruses, songs, piano pieces.

NEVIN, GORDON BALCH

b. Easton, Pa., 19 May 1892; d. New Wilmington, Pa., 15 Nov. 1943. Studied organ with John

Frederick Welle; received an honorary D.M. from Westminster. He was organist and teacher in Pennsylvania and Ohio; taught at Hiram Coll., 1915-17; was professor of organ and composition, Westminster Coll., 1932-43.

WORKS: OPERETTA: Following Foster's footsteps; CHORUS: Behold the Christ, cantata; ORGAN: Sonata tripartite; Pageant triumphale; Tragedy of a tin soldier, a suite; Rural sketches; City sketches; In memoriam; 16 postludes. He was also author of books on organ playing.

NEWBURY, KENT A.

b. Chicago, Ill., 25 Nov. 1925. Studied with Bernhard Heiden, Indiana Univ., B.M., M.M. 1951; with Leo Sowerby, American Cons. He was public school and church choral director in Chicago, 1951-64; from 1965, in Phoenix.

WORKS: THEATRE: We owe it all to Edgar J., musical comedy; BAND: Painting in parallels; Declamations for brass; CHORUS: Duty, honor, country, with narrator and 2 pianos; Rise, O buried Lord, with organ and brass; numerous anthems and other choral works.

6833 E. Double Tree Rd., Scottsdale, AZ 85253

NEWELL, JOHN

b. Charlotte, N.C., 4 May 1949. Studied with Iain Hamilton, Duke Univ.; with Mel Powell, California Inst. of the Arts.

WORKS: THEATRE: Music for Crazy Jane, a collaboration; CHAMBER MUSIC: Image, song, vision, piano, flute, clarinet, cello; The aardvark looming, harp and tape.

NEWELL, ROBERT M.

b. Blandersville, Ill., 18 May 1940. Studied with Salvatore Martirano and Kenneth Gaburo, Univ. of Illinois, M.M.; with Lukas Foss at Tanglewood; and with Olivier Messiaen, Paris Cons. His awards include Fromm Found. grant, 1965; Fulbright grant, 1965; first prize, Denver Symph. contest, 1969, and in Mars Hill Coll. contest, 1975. He was faculty member, Univ. of Illinois, 1967-75; from 1975, California State Univ., Long Beach.

WORKS: ORCHESTRA: Edifice in memoriam, 1969; VOICE: Spirals, mezzo-soprano, tenor, percussion; Ryonen, chorus, flute, tape; New London street cries, chorus and instruments.

California State University, Long Beach, CA 90840

NEWLIN, DIKA

b. Portland, Oreg., 22 Nov. 1923. Studied at Michigan State Univ., B.A. 1939; Univ. of California, Los Angeles, M.A. 1941; Columbia Univ., Ph.D. 1945; privately with Roger Sessions and Arnold Schoenberg in Los Angeles. Her awards include a Fulbright fellowship, 1951-52; Mahler Medal, Bruckner Society, 1957; Silver Medal, French Minister of Foreign Affairs; honorary L.H.D., Upsala Coll., 1964; Sigma Alpha Iota Circle of 15 award, 1975. She has held faculty positions at Western Maryland Coll., 1945-49; Syracuse Univ., 1949-51; Drew Univ.,

1952-65; North Texas State Univ., 1965-73; Montclair State Coll., 1973-76; New School for Social Research, 1977-78; from 1978, Virginia Commonwealth Univ.

WORKS: CHAMBER MUSIC: piano trio, 1948; chamber symphony for 12 instruments, 1949; Study on 12 tones, viola d'amore and piano, 1959; Atone, chamber ensemble, 1976; Second-hand rows, voice and piano, 1977-78; Machine shop, gamelan, 1978; PIANO: Sinfonia, 1947; Fantasia, 1957; Fantasy on a row, 1958. She is author of many valuable books on musicological topics.

Virginia Commonwealth Univ., 901 W. Franklin St., Richmond, VA 23284

NEWMAN, ALFRED
b. New Haven, Conn., 17 Mar. 1901; d. Hollywood, Calif., 17 Feb. 1970. Studied with Sigismund Stojowski and Rubin Goldmark in New York; with Arnold Schoenberg in Los Angeles. He gave his first concert at age 7; later was vaudeville pianist and conductor; conducted George White's Scandals and Gershwin shows on Broadway; went to Hollywood in 1930 and was music director for film companies to 1970. His film scores received 8 Academy awards and 44 nominations.

WORKS: FILM SCORES: Street scene; Hunchback of Notre Dame; Gunga Din; The hurricane; The prisoner of Zenda; Wuthering Heights; The blue-bird; The song of Bernadette; How green was my valley; The razor's edge; Gentleman's agreement; All about Eve; Love is a many-splendored thing; and many others.

NEWMAN, ANTHONY
b. Los Angeles, Calif., 12 May 1941. Studied with Leonard Stein in Los Angeles; Leon Kirchner in Boston; and with Luciano Berio in New York. He was faculty member at Juilliard School, 1967-78; State Univ. Coll., Purchase, N.Y., from 1971; Indiana Univ., from 1978.

WORKS: CHAMBER MUSIC: violin sonata; cello sonata; Variations and grand contrapunctus, guitar; Piano cycle #1; Chimaeras I and II, harpsichord; ORGAN: Habitat; Barricades; Bhajebochstlannanan.

Indiana University, Bloomington, IN 47401

NEWMAN, THEODORE S.
b. New York, N.Y., 17 June 1933. Studied with Vittorio Giannini and Vincent Persichetti at Juilliard School. His awards include the Edward B. Benjamin prize, 1958, 1959, 1960; Guggenheim fellowship, 1961; Gretchaninov Memorial prize, 1963; Elizabeth Sprague Coolidge prize, 1963; McCollin award, 1964.

WORKS: BALLET: Cain, for Harkness Ballet; ORCHESTRA: Toccata; Fantasy; organ concerto; Discourse; Fragments; BAND: suite; CHORUS: Alleluia, with brass and timpani.

240 W. 14th St., New York, NY 10011

NEWMAN, WILLIAM S.
b. Cleveland, Ohio, 6 Apr. 1912. Studied with Herbert Elwell at Cleveland Inst. of Music; with Arthur Shepherd at Western Reserve Univ., Ph.D. 1939; musicology with Eric Hertzmann and Paul H. Lang, Columbia Univ., 1940, and at

several libraries in Europe. He held a Guggenheim fellowship for research on sonata literature, 1960-61. He taught in Cleveland public schools; was in the U.S. Army Air Force, 1942-45; on music faculty, Univ. of North Carolina, 1945-78. He has given many piano recitals and appeared as soloist with major orchestras; is author of several important books on musicology and many articles in music journals.

WORKS: THEATRE: Freddy and his fiddle, operetta, 1936; ORCHESTRA: An American tragedy, overture, 1940; Little symphony, 1940; CHAMBER MUSIC: piano sonata, 1929; cello sonata, 1935; string quartet, 1937; also band pieces.

NEWSOM, HUGH RAYMOND
b. Naini-Tal, near Cawnpore, India, 20 Dec. 1891; d. Baltimore, Md., 19 May 1978. His parents, who were missionaries, brought him to the U.S. at an early age. He made his musical debut at age 11 in Wapello, Iowa, when he played the organ for his father's church services and directed his own choir; at 13 he had a major composition performed publicly. He graduated from Wesleyan Coll. and Oberlin Coll., then attended the New England Cons. He became a concert manager, for many years booking European and American artists in major cities on the East Coast; settled in Baltimore in 1947.

WORKS: ORCHESTRA: King Arthur suite; harp concerto; Night pictures, harp and orch.; VOICE: The divine tragedy, oratorio-drama, chorus of 90, soloists, orchestra, organ, premiere in Baltimore, 1954; The holy birth, choral trilogy; The miracle, oratorio; The Psalms of David, oratorio; Trial before Pilate, oratorio; Songs of love and death, song cycle on poems of Edna St. Vincent Millay; numerous other songs, choral works, and chamber music, making a total of more than 400 works. His manuscripts were given to the Peabody Cons.

NIBLOCK, JAMES F.
b. Scappoose, Oreg., 1 Nov. 1917. Studied at Washington State Univ., B.A., B.Ed.; Univ. of Pennsylvania; Colorado Coll., M.S.; Univ. of Iowa, Ph.D.; composition privately with Roy Harris and Paul Hindemith. He was a private violin teacher and member of the Beaumont String Quartet, 1948-62; concertmaster, Lansing Symph. Orch., 1961-62; and on the faculty, Michigan State Univ., from 1962.

WORKS: ORCHESTRA: Trigon, string orch.; BAND: La folia; Soliloquy and dance; Triptych, brass and percussion; numerous unpublished works for orchestra, chamber groups, and voice. He is author of Music for the high school chorus.

215 Elizabeth St., East Lansing, MI 48823

NICHOLS, ALBERTA
b. Lincoln, Ill., 3 Dec. 1898; d. Hollywood, Calif., 4 Feb. 1957. Studied at Louisville Cons.; piano with George Copeland in New York. She composed music for Broadway shows Gay Paree and Angela; special material and songs for vaudeville, radio, and musical commercials.

NICKERSON, CAMILLE

NICKERSON, CAMILLE
b. New Orleans, La., 30 Mar. Studied piano with her father in New Orleans; at Oberlin Coll., B.M., M.M. She is a member of Pi Kappa Lambda; received 2 awards from Nat. Assoc. of Negro Musicians, 1937, 1962. She was faculty member, Howard Univ., 1926-62, then professor emeritus.
WORKS: CREOLE SONGS (for chorus): Go to sleep; Dear, I love you so; Mister Banjo; Mam'selle Zi Zi; Suzanne, Bel femme; OTHER CHORAL WORKS: Christmas everywhere; The women of the U.S.A.; Interracial hymn; A precious lullaby; SONGS: When love is done; Lizette.
1712 16th St., N.W., Washington, DC 20009

NIEMACK, ILZA
b. Charles City, Iowa, 8 Apr. Studied with Felix Borowski, Rubin Goldmark Francis Pyle, Mario Castelnuovo-Tedesco. She was faculty member, Iowa State Univ., 1935-73, then professor emeritus.
WORKS: ORCHESTRA: 2 piano concertos; CHAMBER MUSIC: 7 violin sonatas; Barcarolle, piano; many short pieces for violin, songs.
602 Lynn Ave., Ames, IA 50010

NIERENBERG, ROGER
b. New York, N.Y., 14 June 1947. Studied privately with Elie Siegmeister, 1961-65; with Milton Babbitt, Peter Westergaard, Edward T. Cone, Charles Wuorinen, Princeton Univ., B.A. 1969; Mannes Coll. of Music, 1971; Aspen School, 1971; also studied conducting, piano, trumpet, and viola. His awards include New York State Regents scholarship, 1965; Woodrow Wilson Nat. fellowship, 1969. He taught at Mannes Coll. of Music, 1971; has been on faculty, Queens Coll., CUNY, from 1973.
WORKS: CHAMBER MUSIC: 2 songs for voice and string quartet, 1965; 3 songs for voice, flute, viola, piano, percussion, 1968; 2 short piano pieces, 1968; Short piece, for bassoon and piano, 1969; CHORUS: Motet, a cappella, 1966; Fire, flood and olive-tree, with piano and percussion, 1967; Cantata, for tenor, chorus, chamber orch., 1969; FILM SCORE: College daze, 1970.
40 W. 53rd St., New York, NY 10019

NIGHTINGALE, JAMES F.
b. Grant's Pass, Oreg., 11 May 1948. Studied with Aurelio de la Vega, California State Univ. at Northridge. He is a private teacher and free-lance performer.
WORKS: WIND ENSEMBLE: Vicissitudes, accordion and winds; 2 inventions, brass sextet; CHAMBER MUSIC: Sketches, string quartet; Fragment, horn and accordion; Aquarian inventions, accordion.
6511 Rhea Ave., Reseda, CA 91335

NIGHTINGALE, MAE WHEELER
b. Blencoe, Iowa, 30 Dec. 1898. Studied at Univ. of California, Los Angeles; Univ. of Southern California; Fresno State Coll.; Westminster Choir Coll. She received the Mancini award for distinction in music teaching, California Music Teachers Assoc. and Kimber

Found. She taught privately, 1919-23; in public schools, 1923-59; was music training teacher, UCLA, Univ. of Southern California, and Los Angeles State Coll., 1936-59.
WORKS: OPERETTAS: Ride 'em cowboy; Queen of the sawdust; many published original works and arrangements for chorus, especially for young singers.
Box 300, Star Route, Mountain Center, CA 92361

NIKOLAIS, ALWIN T.
b. Southington, Conn., 25 Nov. 1912. Studied music and art privately. His awards include Guggenheim fellowships, 1964-68; Grand Prix de Paris, 1968; Emmy award, 1968; Circulo de Critico award, 1973, 1975; Mellon Found. award, 1975; honorary doctorate, Washington Univ., 1979. From 1953, he has been composer, choreographer, and director, Nikolais Dance Theatre; from 1968, artistic director, Nikolais/Louis Found. for Dance; from 1978, director, Centre Nat. du Danse Contemporaine, Paris and Angers; was director, Henry Street Playhouse, 1948-70.
WORKS: ELECTRONIC BALLETS: Web; Totem, 1962; Noumenon; Calligraph for martyrs; Imago, 1963; Sanctum, 1964; A Gothic tale, 1964; Chimera; Somniloquy; GO 6; Tent; Echo; Intersection; Structures; Continuum; Scenario, 1970; Foreplay; Grotto, Geometrics; Scheherezade; Cross fade, New York, 5 Feb. 1974; Temple; Tribe; Guignol; Castings; Gallery; Aviary; A ceremony for bird people; Count down.
33 E. 18th St., New York, NY 10003

NILES, JOHN JACOB
b. Louisville, Ky., 28 Apr. 1892. Studied with Edgar Stillman Kelley, Cincinnati Cons.; at Univ. and Cons. of Lyons, and Schola Cantorum, France; and at Transylvania Univ. His awards include a citation, Nat. Fed. of Music Clubs; 5 honorary doctorates; Nat. Endowment for the Humanities research grant. He taught briefly at Curtis Inst., Univ. of Missouri, Eastman School, Juilliard School, and elsewhere, but has been chiefly composer and concert artist, touring the U.S., Great Britain, and Europe. He is a noted authority on American folk music, especially on the southern Appalachians, and has made his own dulcimers and lutes for authenticity in performance.
WORKS: CHORUS: Black oak tree; Carol of the Polish grenadiers; Death of Thomas a Becket; I never had but one love; Oh waly waly; Our lovely lady singing; Rejoice all men; The silent stars; Turtle dove; I wonder as I wander; Venezuela; Black is the color of my true love's hair; many other original choral works and songs and more than 1000 arrangements of folk music.
Boot Hill Farm, RFD #7, Lexington, KY 40502

NIN-CULMELL, JOAQUIN
b. Berlin, Germany, 5 Sept. 1908; U.S. citizen 1951; son of Cuban composer, Joaquin Nin. Studied at Schola Cantorum, Paris, piano diploma 1930; with Manuel de Falla in Granada, Spain, 1930-34; and with Paul Dukas at the Paris Cons. He is a corresponding member, Royal Acad. of

Fine Arts of San Fernando, Madrid; was Creative Arts Inst. fellow, 1965-66. He toured Europe, Cuba, and the U.S. as concert pianist, 1934-40; was professor, Williams Coll., 1940-50; then at Univ. of California, Berkeley, professor emeritus, 1974.

WORKS: THEATRE: La Celestina, opera; Cyrano de Bergerac, ballet; El burlador de Sevilla, ballet; ORCHESTRA: piano concerto, 1946; 3 old Spanish pieces; Diferencias, 1962; cello concerto, 1963; Cantata de Jose Pradas, chamber orch.; CHAMBER MUSIC: 3 impresiones, piano, 1931; piano sonata, 1934; piano quintet, 1938; Dos canciones, voice and piano or string quartet; 36 songs for piano and voice; CHORUS: Dedication mass.

165 Hillcrest Rd., Berkeley, CA 94705

NIX, THEO M.
b. Comanche, Okla., 1 Dec. 1910. Studied with Bela Rozsa, Tulsa Univ.; with Philip Greeley Clapp and Philip Bezanson, Univ. of Iowa, Ph.D. He has been music director in public schools and colleges; from 1952, professor and chairman, fine arts div., Northeastern Oklahoma State Univ.

WORKS: ORCHESTRA: suite of dances; symphony; CHAMBER MUSIC: quintet for flute and strings; Quartet on B A C H; many works for solo instruments.

804 Janet, Tahlequah, OK 74464

NIXON, ROGER
b. Tulare, Calif., 8 Aug. 1921. Studied with Arthur Bliss, Ernest Bloch, and Roger Sessions, Univ. of California, Berkeley, Ph.D. 1952; privately with Arnold Schoenberg in Los Angeles. He received the Phelan award, 1950; ASCAP awards, 1969-73; Ostwald award, 1973; Nat. Endowment for the Arts grant, 1975; and commissions. He was faculty member, Modesto Jr. Coll., 1951-59; from 1959, has been professor, San Francisco State Univ.

WORKS: OPERA: The bride comes to Yellow Sky, Eastern Illinois Univ., 20 Feb. 1968; ORCHESTRA: Air for strings, 1953; violin concerto, 1956; Mooney's Grove suite, 1964; Elegiac rhapsody, viola and orch., 1967; viola concerto, San Francisco, 29 Apr. 1970; BAND: Prelude and fugue, 1961; Reflections, 1964; Fiesta del Pacifico, 1966; Nocturne, 1966; Elegy and fanfare-march, 1967; Ceremonial fanfare #1, brass, 1976; Ceremonial fanfare #2, woodwinds, brass, percussion, 1976; Pacific celebration suite, 1976; Pacific pageant, 1976; CHAMBER MUSIC: 3 piano preludes, 1947; string quartet, 1949; 4 duos, flute and clarinet, 1966; 4 duos, violin and viola, 1966; Nocturne, flute and piano, 1967; Movement, clarinet and piano; many choral works and songs.

2090 New Brunswick Dr., San Mateo, CA 94402

NOBLE, ANN
b. Oakland, Calif., 24 Sept. 1955. Studied with Barney Childs, Univ. of Redlands; with Terry Riley and Robert Ashley, Mills Coll. She has received a Sigma Alpha Iota composers award.

WORKS: OPERA: Juniper tree, chamber opera

for 5 voices and improvisation ensemble, 1977; CHAMBER MUSIC: . . . saved in prisms of honey . . ., soprano, clarinet, piano, 1976; Percussion trio #2, marimba, snare drum, timpani, 1976; 3 art songs for Lysbet and friend, soprano and piano, 1976; . . . and i saw her standing in the water . . ., flugel horn, string bass, piano, 1977; . . . dreaming of being taken out and allowed to shine, 6 winds, 1978; this is the passing of all shining things, violin and bassoon.

3511½ Portola Ave., Los Angeles, CA 90032

NODA, EVA
b. Edmonton, Alta., Canada, 25 June 1921. Studied at Toronto Cons., A.R.C.T.; Royal School of Music, London, licentiate; Columbia Univ., B.S., Mus.Ed.; Dalcroze School, certificate; Union Theological Seminary, M.M.S. She has held teaching posts at Alberta Coll., 1941-50; Hiroshima Girls Coll., 1958-61; American Acad. of Music, Tenafly, N.J., 1962-68; and at Dalcroze School, 1968-70.

WORKS: CHAMBER MUSIC: Impressions, 3 tankas for flute and harpsichord; For the children of war, 3 tankas for flute and harpsichord; By still waters and Celebrating, in homage to Martha Graham, 2 flute tankas; trio for flute, cello, and piano, commissioned by Oregon Music Teachers Assoc.; trio for violin, oboe, piano; 3 poems, koto and harpsichord; Concerto giocco, percussion and piano; Andante, string quartet.

3000 N.E. 77 Place, Portland, OR 97213

NODA, KEN
b. New York, N.Y., 5 Oct. 1962. Studied piano with Adele Marcus; composition with Sylvia Rabinof and Thomas Pasatieri, being precocious in both subjects. His 1-act opera, The canary, was performed to piano accompaniment at the Brevard (N.C.) Music Festival, 18 Aug. 1973, when he was 10. In 1974 the opera received first prize in the Nat. Fed. of Music Clubs National Young Composers' Contest. In the same year, he wrote a second 1-act opera, The swing, and in 1976, received a Nat. Endowment for the Arts grant to write an opera to his own libretto titled The rivalry, based on the life of Andrew Jackson. His professional debut on the piano was with the Minnesota Orchestra in Minneapolis, 14 May 1977, in Beethoven's 3rd piano concerto. He later played with the New York Philharmonic, St. Louis Symphony, and the Baltimore Symphony. His other compositions include A zoo suite for piano, 1973; piano sonatina, 1974; Prelude and canon, piano, 1974; Emily Dickinson song cycle, Christina Rossetti song cycle, and Cycle of German poems, all in 1977.

262 River Rd., Scarborough, NY 10510

NOEHREN, ROBERT
b. Buffalo, N.Y., 16 Dec. 1910. Attended Inst. of Musical Art, New York, and Curtis Inst.,of Music; studied composition with Paul Hindemith. He was instructor, Davidson Coll., 1946-49; professor and university organist, Univ. of Michigan, 1949-75.

WORKS: ORGAN: Fugue; Fantasia: Homage to Hindemith; sonata; also piano pieces, songs,

NOELTE, A. ALBERT

choral works, string trio.
815 Oakdale Rd., Ann Arbor, MI 48105

NOELTE, A. ALBERT
b. Starnberg, Germany, 10 Mar. 1885; d. Chicago,
Ill., 2 Mar. 1946. Studied music in Boston,
1901-8; then returned to Germany, except for
frequent visits to the U.S., until 1931, when he
was appointed to the faculty at Northwestern
Univ. His compositions included an opera,
François Villon, 1920; Prologue to a romantic
drama for orchestra, Chicago, 16 Jan. 1941; and
instrumental pieces.

NOHE, BEVERLY
b. East Rochester, N.Y., 26 Sept. 1935. Studied
at Eastman School of Music, B.A. 1959. She was
choir director-organist in East Rochester,
1967-73; has taught at Rochester School for the
Deaf.
    WORKS: CHAMBER MUSIC: Playground, flute,
violin, cello; Poème capricieuse, clarinet and
piano; many sacred choral works.

NOLTE, EWALD VALENTIN
b. Utica, Nebr., 21 Sept. 1909. Studied with
Albert Noelte (no relation) at Northwestern
Univ., M.M. 1945, Ph.D. 1954; with Paul
Hindemith and Leo Schrade at Yale Univ. He was
on the faculty at Northwestern Univ., 1944-64;
then at Salem Coll. He has composed sacred
choral music.
    Salem College, Winston-Salem, NC 27108

NOLTE, ROY E.
b. Louisville, Ky., 25 July 1896. Attended
business school; studied organ and piano
privately; is self-taught in composition. He
won the Lorenz Pub. Co. Internat. Anthem Competition in 1927 with Lift up your heads. He
was contributing editor, Volunteer Choir, 1928-
57.
    WORKS: CHORUS: 28 choir cantatas including:
Hosanna; King all glorious; The cross of redemption; Dawn of Christmas; Star of the silent
night; many anthems; piano and organ pieces.
    272 Pennsylvania Ave., Louisville, KY 40206

NOON, DAVID
b. Johnstown, Pa., 23 July 1946. Studied with
Karl Kohn, Pomona Coll., B.A. 1968; at New York
Univ., M.A. 1970; with Mario Davidovsky and
Yehudi Wyner, Yale Univ., M.M.A. 1972, D.M.A.
1977; with Darius Milhaud and Charles Jones,
Aspen School, 1949, 1971; with W. Kotonski,
Warsaw Cons. on a Fulbright fellowship, 1972-73.
His honors include 2 BMI student awards, 1967,
1970; 3 Young Musicians Found. awards, 1968,
1971, 1973; 2 Aspen Festival prizes, 1969, 1971;
Composers' Forum award, 1971; 2 Yale Univ. com-
position prizes, 1971, 1972; annual ASCAP
awards, 1973-77. He was instructor, Northwestern
Univ., 1973-76; composer-in-residence, Wurlitzer
Found., Taos, N.Mex., 1976-77.
    WORKS: ORCHESTRA: Labyrinth; Ai, ai;
Tango 1940; Berceuse seche; 3 encores; A letter
to Quincy, Illinois; Lost in transit; Beauty and
the beast; 2 encores; concerto for cello and

winds; New Year's resolution, double bass,
winds, percussion; CHAMBER MUSIC: Inflections,
2 pianos, harpsichord, harp, vibraphone; Introduction, dirge, and frolic, winds; duo for 2
violas; Fratricide, music for a pantomime;
Fantasy, violin and piano, 4 hands; Cadenzas,
violin alone; Motets and monodies, 3 woodwinds;
6 chansons, soprano and chamber group; Fanfares
and dances, brass quintet; 3 string quartets;
and vocal works.
    1563 Elmcroft Ave., Pomona, CA 91767

NORDEN, HUGO
b. Providence, R.I., 31 Dec. 1909. Studied with
John S. Matthews in Providence; with Howard R.
Thatcher in Baltimore; at Univ. of Toronto, B.M.
1943, D.M. 1948; violin with Hugo Kortschak and
Felix Winternitz. He was music editor, Arthur
P. Schmidt Company, 1943-58; on faculty, Boston
Cons., 1943-45 and from 1976; professor, Boston
Univ., 1945-76.
    WORKS: ORCHESTRA: symphony, 1948; Chorale,
ennead, and fugue, string orch.; CHAMBER MUSIC:
2 violin sonatas; Passacaglia, horn and piano;
string quartet; many small works for solo instruments and chamber groups; choral works. He
is also author of The technique of canon; Fundamental harmony; Fundamental counterpoint; Form:
The silent language; and a translation from the
Danish of Chorale harmonization in the church
modes.
    11 Mendelssohn St., Roslindale, MA 02131

NORDEN, NORRIS LINDSAY
b. Philadelphia, Pa., 24 Apr. 1887; d. Philadelphia, Pa., 3 Nov. 1956. Studied with
Cornelius Rybner, Columbia Univ., B.M. 1910,
M.A. 1911; also with Max Spicker and Franklin
Robinson. He was organist in New York, Brooklyn,
and Philadelphia; conducted the Mendelssohn
Club in Philadelphia, 1916-36.
    WORKS: ORCHESTRA: Thanatopsis, with chorus,
1922; Te Deum, with chorus, 1923; Silver plume,
symphonic poem, 1924; Charity, with chorus,
1928; The white swan, symphonic poem.

NORDENSTROM, GLADYS (Mrs. Ernst Krenek)
b. Pokegama, Minn., 23 May 1924. Studied with
Ernst Krenek, Hamline Univ. and Univ. of
Minnesota.
    WORKS: ORCHESTRA: El Greco phantasia,
string orch.; Elegy for Robert F. Kennedy;
CHAMBER MUSIC: piano sonata; Variations for
piano; Rondo, flute and piano; Palm Springs
sextet, winds; ELECTRONIC: Signals from nowhere, organ and tape; Blocks and beans, tape.
    623 Chino Canyon Rd., Palm Springs, CA
92262

NORDOFF, PAUL
b. Philadelphia, Pa., 4 June 1909; d. Herdecke,
Germany, 18 Jan. 1977. Studied at Philadelphia
Cons., B.M. 1927, M.M. 1932; with Olga Samaroff
and Rubin Goldmark, Juilliard School; Combs
Coll. of Music, B.M. in music therapy 1960,
honorary D.M. 1958. His awards included 2
Guggenheim fellowships, 1933, 1935; Bearns
prize, 1933; Pulitzer grant, 1940; Ford Found.

grant, 1954; and many commissions. He held faculty posts at Philadelphia Cons., 1938-43; Michigan State Coll., 1945-46; Bard Coll., 1949-58. From 1958 he was engaged in research and work in music therapy; at Univ. of Pennsylvania, 1961-67; American-Scandinavian Found., 1967-68, 1973; Child Study Center, Philadelphia, 1969-77.

WORKS: OPERA: The masterpiece, 1 act, Philadelphia, 24 Jan. 1951; The sea-change, BALLET: Every soul is a circus, 1939; In pursuit of folly; Tally ho, 1944; THEATRE: music for Romeo and Juliet; Antony and Cleopatra, 1948; St. Joan; ORCHESTRA: suite, 1940; violin concerto, 1940; 2 piano concertos; Winter symphony, 1954; Tranquil symphony; CHAMBER MUSIC: 2 string quartets; 2 song cycles; Dance sonata, flute and piano; also choral works, songs, piano pieces. He was coauthor with Clive Robbins of several books on music therapy, the latest being Creative music therapy: Individualized treatment, 1976.

NORMAN, THEODORE
b. Montreal, P.Q., Canada, 14 Mar. 1912; U.S. citizen 1921. Studied violin with Willy Hess in Germany; composition with Adolph Weiss in the U.S.; guitar with Aurio Herrero in Madrid. He was violinist, Los Angeles Philharmonic, 1935-42; Armed Forces Radio Services, 1942-45; in studio orchestras, 1945-67; has been on faculty, Univ. of California, Los Angeles, from 1967. He has made more than 200 devices which enable handicapped children to play musical instruments.
WORKS: GUITAR: Exit; Mobile; 2 12-tone pieces; Toccata; 2 preludes in 12 tones; 2 essaya; Valse gracieuse; Samba; and many transcriptions for guitar from classical composers. He is author of a book, The classical guitar.
451 Westmount Dr., Los Angeles, CA 90048

NORRIS, KEVIN
b. New York, N.Y., 12 Apr. 1939. Studied with Leo Sowerby, American Cons.; with Bernard Rogers, Eastman School of Music. He has been organist-choir director, Assumption Church, Morristown, N.J., from 1972.
WORKS: ORGAN: Paean to Jubal; toccata on Come Holy Ghost; toccata on Holy God we praise thy name; Penseroso; Air affettuoso; Elegy; Cavatina; Festalpiece for Advent, with brass and percussion, on commission.
91 Maple Ave., Morristown, NJ 07960

NORTH, ALEX
b. Chester, Pa., 4 Dec. 1910. Studied with Bernard Wagenaar, Juilliard School; with A. Veprik, Moscow Cons.; and with Aaron Copland and Ernst Toch. His honors include a Guggenheim fellowship; Composers and Lyricists Guild award for the film score to Cleopatra, 1963; Laurel awards for film scores, 1956, 1957, 1966, 1967, 1969; Golden Globe award for Shoes of the fisherman, 1969; 11 Academy award nominations.
WORKS: OPERA: Hither and thither of Danny Dither, children's opera; BALLET: Streetcar named desire; American lyric, 1937; Daddy long legs; Wall Street ballet; THEATRE (musicals):

'Tis of thee; Queen of Sheba; The great campaign; ORCHESTRA: Rhapsody, piano and orch., 1941; Revue, clarinet and orch., New York, 20 Nov. 1946, with Benny Goodman as soloist and Leonard Bernstein conducting; 3 symphonies, 1947, 1968, 1971; 3 symphonic suites for film scores: Holiday set, 1948; CHAMBER MUSIC: woodwind quintet; woodwind trio; string quartet; CHORUS (cantatas for chorus and orch.): Morning star, 1947; Negro mother, 1948; numerous film scores and television scores.
630 Resolano Dr., Pacific Palisades, CA 90272

NORTON, SPENCER
b. Anadarko, Okla., 3 Oct. 1909. Studied with Howard Hanson and Bernard Rogers, Eastman School of Music; and with Ildebrando Pizzetti in Milan, Italy. His awards include a Rockefeller grant, Ford Found. grant, and commissions. He was faculty member, Univ. of Oklahoma, 1934-75.
WORKS: ORCHESTRA: Dance suite, 1939; Venite, jubilate, motet for chorus and orch., 1950; Solstice, 1951; Partita, 2 pianos and orch., 1959; Te Deum, with chorus, 1965; various smaller works for piano, organ, chamber groups.
Box 2063, Norman, OK 73069

NOSSE, CARL E.
b. North Irwin, Pa., 8 Jan. 1933. Studied at Tarkio Coll., B.A.; U.S. Naval School of Music; Duquesne Univ., M.M.; with John Boda and Carlisle Floyd, Florida State Univ., D.M. 1973; with Klaus Pringsheim, Leo Sowerby, and Leon Stein; and with Nadia Boulanger at a Potsdam seminar on a grant. He taught in public schools, 1954-68; from 1972, has been faculty member, Florida State Univ.
WORKS: Music for orchestra; Set for small orchestra and percussion; Richard Cory ballet; chamber orch. and chorus; BAND: Perspectives, CHAMBER MUSIC: piano trio; Four eleven, woodwind quartet; Tripartite, flute, cello, piano; suite for piano; and electronic pieces.
Florida State University, Tallahassee, FL 32306

NOTT, DONALD D.
b. Yakima, Wash., 27 Feb. 1944. Studied with Paul Creston, Robert Panerio, Central Washington State Coll., M.M. 1970; with Robert Muczynski, Univ. of Arizona. He has been on the faculty, Yakima Valley Coll., from 1970.
WORKS: ORCHESTRA: concerto in one movement, saxophone and orch., 1972; Adagio and fugue, 1973; Metamorphosis, with narrator; Theater on 3rd Street, with chorus and soloists, commissioned and performed by the Yakima Symph. Orch., 5 Nov. 1978; BAND: Rhapsodic song, saxophone and band, 1970; Anagrams, a suite, 1970; Cascade, overture, 1973; Fugue in Dorian, 1973; VOICE: Obligation, chorus, 1971; Hymn for morning, soprano and piano, 1973; Time, speaking chorus.
410 N. 56th Ave., Yakima, WA 98908

NOVAK, WILLIAM
b. Oceanside, N.Y., 31 Jan. 1952. Studied with

NOVY, DONALD A.

Joel Chandler, State Univ. of New York at Albany, where he won an award in the composers' festival, 1972, and was assistant director of the Electronic Music Studio, 1972-74.
WORKS: ELECTRONIC: Steppin' out, 1971; Strange bedfellows, 1972; Set-up instructions, 1972; Automatic shoes, 1973; Sounds of the studio, 1973; Beaten bedfellows, 1973.

NOVY, DONALD A.
b. Oak Park, Ill., 23 Apr. 1932. Studied with Anthony Donato and Robert Delaney, Northwestern Univ. He has been public school music teacher since 1957. His compositions include a sonatina for brass.
2940 S. Marion St., Englewood, CO 80110

NOWAK, ALISON
b. Syracuse, N.Y., 7 Apr. 1948. Studied with Vivian Fine, Lou Calabro, and Henry Brant, Bennington Coll., B.A. 1970; with Mario Davidovsky, Jack Beeson, and Charles Wuorinen, Columbia Univ., M.A. 1972. She received the Rappaport prize for a string trio, 1971.
WORKS: OPERA: Diversion and division, 1-act chamber opera, text by composer; ORCHESTRA: Quid pro quo; CHAMBER MUSIC: quintet for flute, violin, bassoon, guitar, piano; string trio.
310 W. 107th St., New York, NY 10025

NOWAK, GERALD C.
b. Detroit, Mich., 16 Apr. 1936. Studied at Trenton State Coll., B.S., M.A.; privately with Lucien Cailliet. He has been faculty member, Bucks County Community Coll., from 1968; and is editorial consultant for a music publisher.
WORKS: BAND: suite for woodwind quintet and band; Olympic fanfare and march; Primarily percussion; At the summit.
R.D. 1, Broad Acres Estates, Flemington, NJ 08822

NOWAK, LIONEL
b. Cleveland, Ohio, 25 Sept. 1911. Studied with Quincy Porter, Roger Sessions, Herbert Elwell, Cleveland Inst. of Music. He was music director, Humphrey-Weidman Dance Company, 1938-42; professor, Converse Coll., 1942-46; conductor, Spartanburg Symph. Orch., 1942-46; professor, Syracuse Univ., 1946-48; and from 1948, at Bennington Coll.
WORKS: MODERN DANCE SCORES: On my mother's side, 1939; Flickers, 1941; House divided, 1943; Story of mankind, 1945; ORCHESTRA: piano concertino, 1944; Concert-piece for kettledrums and strings, 1961; CHAMBER MUSIC: suite for 4 wind instruments, 1945; sonata for solo violin, 1950; Fantasia, 3 instruments, 1951; quartet for oboe and strings, 1952; suite for clarinet, cello, piano, 1953; piano trio, 1954; CHORUS: Wisdom exalteth, a cappella, antiphonal chorus; many songs and piano pieces.
Bennington College, Bennington, VT 05201

NOWAK, ROBERT
b. Bennington, Vt., 11 Apr. 1949. Studied with Warren Benson and Samuel Adler, Eastman School of Music; with Donald Erb, Cleveland Inst. of

Music. He was cellist with the National Ballet, 1973-74.
WORKS: ORCHESTRA: cello concerto, performed by the Cleveland Orchestra with the composer as soloist, 1972; CHAMBER MUSIC: suite for solo flute, New York, 8 May 1973; Fantasia, violin and piano.
1628 19th St., N.W., Washington, DC 20009

NUERNBERGER, LOUIS DEAN
b. Wakefield, Nebr., 5 Jan. 1924. Studied with Homer Keller and Ross Lee Finney, Univ. of Michigan; with Bernhard Heiden, Indiana Univ., D.M.; with Nadia Boulanger in France; and with Cesar Bresgen, Mozarteum, Salzburg, on a Fulbright fellowship, 1954-56. He was faculty member, Berea Coll., 1959-64; from 1964, at Oberlin Cons.
WORKS: CHORUS: Magnificat, a cappella, with solo quartet; Time present--Die Erde Bleibt--Lux perpetua, double motet, a cappella, with solo trio and chanters; Song of Simeon, with soloists, a cappella; Reflections on the mortality of man, with soprano, men's chorus, and percussion; Koheleth, a cappella, with solo sextet and narrator; Falcons of Arcos de la Frontera, a cappella, with 4 solo sopranos and narrator.
27 Colony Dr., Oberlin, OH 44074

NUNLIST, JULI
b. Montclair, N.J., 6 Dec. 1916. Attended Barnard Coll., B.A. 1940; studied with Vittorio Giannini, Nicolas Flagello, Ludmila Ulehla, Manhattan School of Music, B.A. 1961, M.A. 1964. Her piano works won first prize, Olivet Coll. contest, 1962; a song cycle was chosen for performance at the Univ. of Kansas 6th annual symposium of American music, 1972. She was music director, Nat. Regional Ballet Assoc. conferences, 1968, 1969, 1972; faculty member, Akron Univ., 1970-73; chairman, fine arts dept., Hathaway Brown School, Shaker Heights, Ohio, from 1972.
WORKS: ORCHESTRA: Platero and I, symphonic suite on Juan Ramon Jimenez's poems; song cycle on Rilke text, baritone and orch.; CHAMBER MUSIC: string quartet; 3 songs from Prieres dans l'Arche; CHORUS: Spells, choral cycle; PIANO: Lento and presto, 1961; Piece in serial style.
Hathaway Brown School, Shaker Heights, OH 44120

NUNN, THOMAS E.
b. San Antonio, Tex., 10 May 1946. Studied with Lothar Klein and Hunter Johnson, Univ. of Texas; with Isaac Nemiroff, State Univ. of New York at Stony Brook.
WORKS: CHAMBER MUSIC: Fragments of stone, mixed ensemble; Concert, flute, violin, harp, percussion; septet, mixed ensemble; Elisions I, II, III, for 2 pianos and/or 2 percussionists.

NUROCK, KIRK
b. Camden, N.J., 28 Feb. 1948. Studied with Vincent Persichetti, Roger Sessions, Luciano Berio, Juilliard School, B.M., M.M.; with Rayburn Wright, Eastman School of Music; with Michael Czaikowski, New York Univ., Electronic Music Lab.; jazz composition with John La Porta. His

awards include an Elizabeth Sprague Coolidge
prize; Duke Ellington and Abraham Ellstein
scholarships. He has been music director,
Ensemble Studio Theatre, from 1970; founder and
director, Natural Sound Workshop, from 1971; was
composer-in-residence, Vermont Summer Theatre
Festival, 1973.
WORKS: THEATRE: incidental music for Sunday
dinner, by Joyce Carol Oates, 1970; A dream out
of time, Irving Bauer, 1970; has composed for
orchestra, chamber groups, piano, tape; for the
"Tonight Show" and "Merv Griffin Show" on television, the Kathryn Posin Dance Group, and for
the Natural Sound Workshop. The Workshop uses
no instruments and no amplification, only vocal
and body sounds, complemented by movement and
spacial elements. Night, for natural voice and
body sounds, performed at the WBAI Free Music
Store, New York, 10 Jan. 1973, was appraised by
John Rockwell in the New York Times as a "most
effective effort indeed, full of counterpointed
babblings and moanings and aspirated rhythms."
Another Workshop piece, Tract, was performed in
Brooklyn, 29 Apr. 1977.
143 W. 21st St., New York, NY 10011

NYIREGYHAZI, ERVIN
b. Budapest, Hungary, 19 Jan. 1903. Entered
Budapest Acad. of Music in 1910; in 1914 his
family moved to Berlin, where he studied piano
with Ernst von Dohnanyi; made his debut as
pianist a year later, playing Beethoven's 3rd
piano concerto with the Berlin Philharmonic.
He then studied with Frederick Lamond, a pupil
of Liszt, who introduced him to the Liszt
repertoire. His American debut in New York in
1920 was a sensational success, but his career
foundered almost from that point. He engaged in
a lawsuit with his manager, then married his
next manager, but divorced her a year later.
About 1927, he settled in Hollywood and worked
as a studio pianist. After a European tour in
1930, he dropped his concert career and disappeared from public view until rediscovered
almost 50 years later, living in poverty in
San Francisco. There he received a Ford Found.
grant and was persuaded to tape his playing of
Liszt. He has composed several hundred works,
chiefly for piano; though some are orchestrated,
none is published.

NYQUIST, MORINE A.
b. Axtell, Nebr., 29 Mar. 1909. Studied with
Louis Diercks, Nebraska State Coll.; with Allan
Willman, Univ. of Wyoming, B.A. 1952, M.A. 1955.
He taught in Nebraska public schools, 1928-35;
was supervisor of education and arts projects,
Nebraska Fed. Works Agency, 1935-43; welfare and
recreation director, American Red Cross, 1943-
45; on faculty, Huron Coll., 1955-57; Texas
Lutheran Coll., 1957-75. He has published works
for band, instrumental groups, and chorus.

NYQUIST, ROGER THOMAS
b. Rockford, Ill., 11 July 1934. Studied organ
with Oswald Ragatz, Indiana Univ., D.M. He was
faculty member, Southwestern Coll., Kan., 1957-
58; from 1962, at Univ. of Santa Clara. His

published works are for organ.
University of Santa Clara, Santa Clara, CA
95053

OAK, KILSUNG
b. Korea, 7 May 1942; to U.S. 1968. Studied
with Stefan Wolpe, Long Island Univ.; with
Vladimir Ussachevsky and Chou Wen-chung, Columbia
Univ. He received the Rappaport prize in chamber
music, 1972, and fellowships to Yale Summer
School, 1972, Yaddo, 1973, and Columbia Univ.,
1973.
WORKS: CHAMBER MUSIC: Invocation, 1970;
trio for 2 violins and piano, 1971; duo for
violin and piano, 1972; Amorphosis, percussion
ensemble, 1973.

OAKES, RODNEY HARLAND
b. Rome, N.Y., 15 Apr. 1937. Studied with David
Ward-Steinman, San Diego State Univ., B.A. 1964,
M.A. 1966; with Robert McBride, Univ. of Arizona;
and with Anthony Vazzana, Univ. of Southern
California, D.M.A. 1973. His awards include a
Celia Buck grant, 1966; Nat. Endowment for the
Arts grant, 1975; and commissions. He has been
director, Electronic Music Studio, Los Angeles
Harbor Coll., from 1972.
WORKS: THEATRE: Grab the ring, musical
written with Larry Heimgartner, 1976; Abadada,
children's musical (with Heimgartner), 1977;
CHAMBER MUSIC: Song for 2 voices, soprano,
alto, piano; 6 by 6, any number of players; In-
trospectrum in 6 refractions, any number of
players plus audience; Variations on an 18th-
century hymn tune, organ and brass; CHORUS:
mass, with strings, 1965; You are the God,
sopranos, basses, and organ, 1970; The primrose;
Seeker of truth, with band.
500 Prospect Blvd., Pasadena, CA 91103

OBRECHT, ELDON
b. Rolfe, Iowa, 9 June 1920. Studied with
Philip Greeley Clapp, Univ. of Iowa, Ph.D. He
has been faculty member, Univ. of Iowa, from
1947.
WORKS: ORCHESTRA: 3 symphonies; CHAMBER
MUSIC: brass quintet; Triptych, brass trio;
sonatas for trumpet, string bass, horn, clarinet;
Pantomime, woodwind quintet; Diversions I and II,
string bass alone; Night piece, flute and clarinet; Contrasts, oboe and piano; Fantasie, viola
and piano; sonata for 4 bassoons; Canzona, organ;
and songs.
1000 River St., Iowa City, IA 52240

O'BRIEN, EUGENE
b. Paterson, N.J., 24 Apr. 1945. Studied with
Robert Beadell, Univ. of Nebraska; with Bernd
Alois Zimmermann in Cologne, Germany; and with
Iannis Xenakis, Indiana Univ. He received BMI
awards, 1968, 1970; Fulbright grant, 1969; Prix
de Rome of the American Acad., 1971-73; 2 Nat.
Endowment for the Arts grants, 1974, 1978. From
1973 he has been faculty member, Cleveland Inst.
of Music.
WORKS: ORCHESTRA: symphony, 1969; cello
concerto, 1971; CHAMBER ENSEMBLE: Elegy for
Bernd Alois Zimmermann, 1970; Lingual, 1971;

O'BRIEN, KATHARINE

Dedales, 1972-74; and Ambages, piano, 4 hands, 1972.
> Cleveland Institute of Music, 11021 East Blvd., Cleveland, OH 44106

O'BRIEN, KATHARINE
b. Amesbury, Mass., 10 Apr. 1901. Studied at Bates Coll., A.B.; Cornell Univ., A.M.; Brown Univ., Ph.D.; piano and composition with Warner Hawkins in New York. She received honorary doctorates from Univ. of Maine and Bowdoin Coll. She was chairman, mathematics dept., New Rochelle Coll., 1925-36; and at Deering High School, 1940-71; was lecturer in mathematics, Univ. of Maine, 1962-73, and various years at Brown Univ.
> WORKS: CHORUS: When I set out for Lyonnesse, Hardy text; Star of Bethlehem, text by composer; Fairytale; Morris dance; Wanderer's night song. She has published a book on mathematics, Sequences, 1966, and many articles; a book of poems, Excavation and other verse, 1967; and many poems in various journals.
> 130 Hartley St., Portland, ME 04103

OCHSE, ORPHA CAROLINE
Professor at Whittier Coll. Her compositions include Chaconne for organ; Prelude and fugue, flute and organ. She has also published The history of the organ in the United States, Bloomington, Ind., 1975.
> Music Dept., Whittier College, Whittier, CA 90608

ODEGARD, PETER SIGURD
b. Pittsfield, Mass., 26 Feb. 1929. Studied with Randall Thompson, Allan Sapp, and Paul Hindemith, Harvard Univ.; with Roger Sessions, Andrew Imbrie, and Charles Cushing, Univ. of California, Berkeley. He received the Pacific Found. Composers' award, 1963. He was on the faculty, Univ. of California at Santa Barbara and Berkeley, 1958-64; from 1965, at Irvine.
> WORKS: THEATRE: music for Marat Sade, 1967; The love apple, comic opera, 1974; CHAMBER MUSIC: Mirror variations, viola, clarinet, piano, 1963; oboe sonatina, 1967.
> 5082 Cinnamon, Irvine, CA 92715

O'DONNELL, RICHARD
b. St. Louis, Mo., 13 Feb. 1937. Studied at St. Louis Inst. of Music; with Samuel Adler, North Texas State Univ. He received a Gold Placque from a Chicago Internat. Film Festival as co-creator of a multimedia piece titled Quartet: The rooster came first. He has been principal percussionist, St. Louis Symph. Orch., from 1959.
> WORKS: PERCUSSION: Microtimbre I, amplified tam-tam, 1969; Microtimbre II, 7 things that ring and tape recorder; Polytimbre I, large group of instruments; Polytimbre II, 3-minute cadenza on tape; Polytimbre III, percussion quartet; duo for vibraphone and synthesizer in C.
> 58 Willow Brook, St. Louis, MO 63141

OEHLER, DALE DIXON
b. Springfield, Ill., 1941. Studied at Northwestern Univ., B.A. 1963; with Richard Hervig,

Univ. of Iowa, M.A. 1967. He is a free-lance composer-arranger.
> WORKS: CHAMBER MUSIC: Dimensions, solo flute; FILM SCORES: Streets of San Francisco; Mod squad; Barnaby Jones; Shaft's big score.
> 4298 Bakman Ave., North Hollywood, CA 91602

OGDON, WILBUR L. (WILL)
b. Redlands, Calif., 19 Apr. 1921. Studied with Ernst Krenek, Hamline Univ.; with Roger Sessions, Univ. of California, Berkeley; with Rene Leibowitz and Arthur Honegger in Paris; and with Bernhard Heiden. His awards include a Fulbright grant, 1952; 2 Univ. of California Creative Arts fellowships, 1969, 1973; Nat. Endowment for the Arts grant, 1976. He has held faculty posts at Univ. of Texas, 1947-50; Illinois Wesleyan, 1955-65; Univ. of Illinois, 1965-66; from 1966, Univ. of California, San Diego; was music director, KPFA, Berkeley, 1962-64.
> WORKS: CHAMBER MUSIC: Palindrome and variations, string quartet, 1960; By the Isar, soprano, flute, double bass, 1969; Un tombeau de Jean Cocteau, soprano, clarinetist/mime, pianist/conductor, and 15 instruments, 1972; and choral works.
> 482 15th St., Del Mar, CA 92014

O'HARA, GEOFFREY
b. Chatham, Ontario, Canada, 2 Feb. 1882; U.S. citizen 1919; d. St. Petersburg, Fla., 31 Jan. 1961. Studied organ with Homer Norris; received an honorary D.M., Huron Coll., 1947; citation award of merit, 1948. In 1913 he was appointed instructor in native Indian music by the Secretary of the Interior; taught at Columbia Univ., 1936-37; Huron Coll., 1947-48.
> WORKS: OPERETTAS: Peggy and the pirate, 1927; Riding down the sky, 1928; The count and the co-ed, 1929; The smiling sixpence, 1930; Lantern land, 1931; Harmony Hall, 1933; The princess runs away, 1934; Our America, 1934; Puddinhead the First, 1936; The Christmas thieves, 1943; SONGS: K-K-K-Katy; Give a man a horse he can ride; There is no death; numerous other extremely popular songs.

OHLSON, MARION
b. Jersey City, N.J., 28 July. Has published Now is the triumph, Easter anthem; and other choral works, piano pieces, songs.
> 320 Fairmont Ave., Jersey City, NJ 07306

OLDBERG, ARNE
b. Youngstown, Ohio, 12 July 1874; d. Evanston, Ill., 17 Feb. 1962. Studied piano with his father and at 6 played Haydn symphonies in duet form; studied with Middelschulte in Chicago, with Rheinberger in Munich. He won a Nat. Fed. of Music Clubs prize in 1911; taught at Northwestern Univ., 1899-1941.
> WORKS: ORCHESTRA: 5 symphonies; 2 piano concertos; horn concerto; Paolo and Francesca, 1908; Academic overture, 1909; 2 rhapsodies; violin concerto, 1933; The sea, symphonic poem, 1934; chamber works, piano pieces.

OLDFIELD, WILLARD ALAN
b. Kimball, Nebr., 27 Sept. 1935. Studied with
Lukas Foss, Henry L. Clarke, and Roy Harris,
Univ. of California, Los Angeles; with Nadia
Boulanger in Paris; with Merrill Ellis, Martin
Mailman, and William Latham, North Texas State
Univ., Ph.D. 1969. He was faculty member,
Southern Illinois Univ., Carbondale, 1969-75.
WORKS: ORCHESTRA: 3 units; Proportions;
Festive music; CHAMBER MUSIC: Dialogue, timpani
and brass quintet; Solos, woodwind quintet; wood-
wind trio; CHORUS: mass, with piano, bass and
percussion; MULTIMEDIA: Colors, tape, projec-
tions, and dancers.
4454 Simpson Ave., N. Hollywood, CA 91607

OLDS, GERRY
b. Cleveland, Ohio, 26 Feb. 1933. Studied at
Cleveland Inst. of Music; Chicago Cons., M.A.
1957.
WORKS: ORCHESTRA: short symphony, 1956;
violin concerto, 1957; Toccata for strings,
1958; symphony in 1 movement, 1958; piano concerto, 1960; CHAMBER MUSIC: wind quintet, 1958;
string trio, 1959; Theme and variations in the
style of a suite, viola and cello.

OLDS, WILLIAM BENJAMIN
b. Clinton, Wis., 3 June 1874; d. Los Angeles,
Calif., 10 Jan. 1948. Studied at Beloit Coll.,
B.A., honorary D.M.; Oberlin Cons.; American
Cons. His academic posts included Grinnell
Coll.; Illinois Coll.; James Milliken Univ.;
Univ. of Redlands, 1925-42; was supervisor of
adult choruses, Los Angeles Bureau of Music,
1943-48. His compositions include an opera,
The feathered serpent; choral works, and songs.

OLIVE, JOSEPH P.
b. Israel, 14 Mar. 1941; U.S. citizen 1961.
Studied with Ralph Shapey, Univ. of Chicago.
He received a Nat. Endowment for the Arts grant,
1974. From 1969 he has been engaged in research
on speech and communications at Bell Laboratories.
WORKS: OPERA: Mar-ri-ia-a, tape, soprano,
chamber ensemble, 1975; CHAMBER MUSIC: ABC,
unaccompanied violin; Suspended dynamics, percussion quartet; sonatina, solo percussion;
ELECTRONIC: Speculum, large chamber ensemble
and tape; Study #3, clarinet and tape; Studies
#4, #5, #6, tape; Study #7, cello and tape.
35 Woodledge Rd., Watchung, NJ 07060

OLIVER, HAROLD
b. Easton, Md., 15 Sept. 1942. Studied with
Louis Cheslock and Stefan Grove, Peabody Cons.,
B.M. 1964; with Allen Forte, Mel Powell, Yale
Univ., M.M. 1966; with Milton Babbitt, Edward T.
Cone, J. K. Randall, Peter Westergaard, Godfrey
Winham, Princeton Univ., Ph.D. 1972. His awards
include Yale composition prize, 1966; 2 Prince-
ton fellowships; Tanglewood fellowships, 1966-
70, 1978; American Music Center grants, 1971,
1976; Nat. Endowment for the Arts grant, 1974.
He has held faculty posts at Duke Univ., 1970-
72; Queens Coll., CUNY, 1972-74; State Univ. of
New York, Geneseo, 1974-76; from 1976, Southern

Methodist Univ.
WORKS: OPERA: King of the cats, chamber
opera, 1976; ORCHESTRA: concerto for orchestra
and chamber ensemble, 1972; Incantations and
responses, 1977; Brandenberg concerto (or Amer-
icana-isms), Tanglewood, 5 Aug. 1978; CHAMBER
MUSIC: Discourses for a clarinet, 1968; Another
spring, tenor and piano, 1973; The Kraken, tuba
and percussion, 1973-74; woodwind quintet, 1974;
duet for violin and viola, 1975; Samsara, clarinet, cello, piano, 1976; CHORUS: Walden,
women's voices, piano, percussion, 1975; Full
fathom 5, with winds, soprano solo, piano, 1976.
3402 Harvard St., Dallas, TX 75205

OLIVER, MADRA EMOGENE
b. Three Rivers, Mich., 28 Oct. 1905. Studied
at Univ. of Michigan, B.S.M.; Claremont Coll.,
M.A.; and at Oberlin Cons. She is a private
teacher and organist; has published choral works,
songs, piano pieces, organ pieces.

OLIVER, RICHARD CRAWFORD
b. Passaic, N.J., 9 Jan. 1927. Studied at
Montclair State Coll., A.B.; with Frederick
Werle and Normand Lockwood, Columbia Univ., A.M.;
with Nadia Boulanger in France. He was named
as one of the 100 Outstanding Alumni, Montclair
State Coll., 1960; has received many commissions.
He taught in private schools, 1953-62; from 1962,
in public schools, Chappaqua, N.Y., dept. chairman, 1970-77.
WORKS: ORCHESTRA: Fantasy, 1969; BAND:
Irish legend; A tale of strange lands; Spectrum,
with accordion, 1965; CHAMBER MUSIC: suite for
violin and piano, 1954; Ballade, violin and
piano, 1964; Toccata, piano; CHORUS: My Johnny
is comin' for me; Gooding carol; Masters in this
hall; many arrangements for band.
1946 Glen Rock St., Yorktown Heights, NY
10598

OLIVEROS, PAULINE
b. Houston, Tex., 30 May 1932. Studied with
Paul Koepke, Univ. of Houston, B.A. 1951;
privately with Robert Erickson in San Francisco,
1952-60. Her awards include the Pacifica Found.
Nat. prize, 1961; Gaudeamus prize for best
foreign work, Bilthoven, Holland, 1962; 3 Univ.
of California research grants, 1968-71; faculty
fellowship, 1973; first prize, City of Bonn,
Beethoven Comm., 1977. With Morton Subotnick
and Ramon Sender, formed the San Francisco Tape
Music Center, 1961; became director when the
center moved to Mills Coll., 1966; appointed
to faculty, Univ. of California, San Diego,
1967. Ms. Oliveros early adopted the habit of
writing for available instruments, a habit that
later developed into composing with particular
players in mind and fitting the works to the
personality. Theater piece for a trombone,
1969, was written for Stuart Dempster; The
wheel of fortune, 1969, for William O. Smith;
and Aeolian music for the Aeolian Chamber
Players, whom she had never met, but who sent a
group photograph of themselves, then later replaced the pianist with a man totally unlike his
predecessor in appearance and personality.

OLMSTEAD, CLARENCE

According to a review of the Bowdoin Coll. performance (May 1969), the parts fit all the
players well except the pianist, though the
piano part "would have been a beautiful vehicle
for the man in the photograph."
WORKS: CHAMBER MUSIC: Variations for sextet, 1960; trio for flute, piano, and page
turner, 1961; Outline, flute, percussion, string
bass, 1963; Apple box orchestra, 10 performers,
1964; Night jar, viola d'amore, 1968; Double
basses at 20 paces, 1968; To Valerie Solanas and
Marilyn Monroe, 6 or more instruments or voices,
1977; CHORUS: Sound patterns, 1961; Meditation
on the points of the compass, 1970; XII sonic
meditations, 1971; Willowbrook generations and
reflections, a cappella or with winds and brass,
1977; ELECTRONIC: Time perspectives, tape, 1961;
Pieces of eight, wind octet and tape, 1965; Bog
road with bird call patch, tape and live electronics, 1970; MULTIMEDIA: 7 passages, tape,
mobile, and dancer, 1963; Five, trumpet and
dancer, 1964; Light piece for David Tudor, 1965;
Cat o' nine tails, mimes and tape, 1965; Festival
house, orch., mimes, lights, films, slides, 1968;
Phantom fathom, evening ritual, mixed media
events including meditation and an exotic pot-
luck dinner, Long Beach, 19 July 1972; Bonn
Feier, for city or coll. campus (everyone as
actors, dancers, musicians, 15 days to 1 year),
1977.
Univ. of California/San Diego, La Jolla, CA
92037

OLMSTEAD, CLARENCE
b. Minneapolis, Minn., 11 July 1892. Studied at
Univ. of Minnesota. His compositions include
Serenade, orch.; Time, voice and orch.; and
songs.

OLSEN, A. LORAN
b. Minneapolis, Minn., 7 Oct. 1930. Studied at
Grinnell Coll., B.A. 1951; with Francis Pyle,
Drake Univ., M.M. 1955; with Philip Bezanson,
Univ. of Iowa, Ph.D. 1960; also with Gaetani
Comelli in Japan, 1952; and with Nadia Boulanger
in France, 1954. He received the Steiner award,
1951; first prize, Iowa Young Composers contest,
1956; first prize, Wisconsin State Fair Composers contest, 1960. He was faculty member,
Luther Coll., 1955-57; Wisconsin State Univ.,
1958-60; Hastings Coll., 1960-65; from 1965, at
Washington State Univ.
WORKS: DANCE: Dream of a primitive; The
alternative; THEATRE: music for Midsummer night's
dream; ORCHESTRA: piano concertino; setting for
chamber orch. and tape; CHAMBER MUSIC: Soupe
d'onions gratines, saxophone and piano; woodwind
trio; quintet for brass and piano; 4 haiku,
soprano and chamber ensemble; PIANO: sonatina;
2 Japanese folk songs; study for piano and tape
recorder; Prelude and toccata on A.H.; many
choral works, organ pieces.
Washington State University, Pullman, WA
99163

OLSON, ROBERT G.
b. Pelican Rapids, Minn., 29 May 1913. Studied
at Univ. of Minnesota, B.A.; Eastman School of

Music, M.A.; Cite Univ., Paris. He has taught
at Bemidji Coll.; Northwood School, Lake Placid;
St. Louis Inst. of Music; Foothill Coll.; from
1972 at De Anza Coll.; was editor for Summy-
Birchard for 10 years. His works include Suite
in brief for 2 pianos, and choral pieces.
De Anza College, 21250 Stevens Creek Blvd.,
Cupertino, CA 95014

O'MEAGHER, HUGH
Studied at Peabody Cons., B.M. 1964. His works
include: 4 preludes, piano, 1951; variations on
Oh dear, what can the matter be?, piano, 1951;
concerto for harpsichord, percussion, and orch.,
1956; concerto grosso for harpsichord, flute,
string quartet, 1967.

O'NEAL, BARRY
b. New York, N.Y., 9 June 1942. Studied with
Gardner Read and Hugo Norden, Boston Univ., B.A.
1964. From 1964, he has been staff member for
music publishers.
WORKS: ORCHESTRA: Skunk hour, with tenor
solo, 1965; Visionary landscape, 1969; Rebecca
variations, 1977; CHAMBER MUSIC: piano quintet,
1965; string quartet, 1968; Eyes, tenor and
piano, 1976; CHORUS: Grain of sand, 1968; Lord
have mercy, 1973; Nativitie, 1973; Brecht elegy,
men's voices and brass, 1973; 2 Psalm settings,
1972-75; 2 madrigals for love, 1976; God's
grandeur, with wind ensemble, 1978.
220 W. 98th St., #3H, New York, NY 10025

O'PRESKA, JOHN
b. 1945. Studied at North Texas State Univ.,
B.M. 1968. He has published a cello sonata;
Elegy, cello and piano; Mist, flute and piano.

ORE, CHARLES WILLIAM
b. Winfield, Kans., 18 Dec. 1936. Studied with
Theodore Beck, Concordia Coll., Seward, Nebr.,
B.S. 1958; with Myron Roberts, Univ. of Nebraska;
Thomas Matthews, Northwestern Univ., M.M. 1960.
He was faculty member, Concordia Teachers Coll.,
Ill., 1961-66; from 1966, at Concordia Teachers
Coll., Nebr. His works include 11 compositions
for organ, 1971.
158 Faculty Lane, Seward, NE 68434

O'REILLY, JOHN SAMUEL
b. Walden, N.Y., 25 Nov. 1940. Studied with
Robert Washburn and Arthur Frackenpohl, State
Univ. of New York at Potsdam; and Columbia
Univ. He received ASCAP awards, 1972, 1973,
1974; and munerous commissions. He taught in
public school, 1962-72; at Nassau Community
Coll., 1972-73; from 1973, has been editor and
composer for a music publisher.
WORKS: ORCHESTRA: Heather's theme; BAND:
Kings go forth; Kaleidoscope; Stratford overture; Music for the cinema; concerto for trumpet
and winds; CHAMBER MUSIC: 3 episodes for percussion; Solos for the percussionist; Metropolitan brass quintet; CHORUS: White ships and
whales, with chamber orch.
Alfred Music Co., Inc., 75 Channel Dr.,
Port Washington, NY 11050

ORENSTEIN, JOYCE ELLIN
   b. Chicago, Ill., 3 Jan. 1939. Studied with
Leonard Stein in Los Angeles; with Mario
Davidovsky, City Coll. of New York; and with
Robert Moevs, Rutgers Univ. Her awards include
2 Mark Brunswick awards, 1970, 1971; fellowships
to the Bennington Composers Conf., 1970, 1971,
and to the Johnson Composers Conf., 1974. From
1974 she has been adjunct instructor, Somerset
County Coll., Somerville, N.J.
   WORKS: CHAMBER MUSIC: Poppies in October,
soprano and 5 instruments; 3 pieces for solo
clarinet; string quintet; Dialogue, clarinet
and cello.
   332 Harper Place, Highland Park, NJ 08904

ORLAND, HENRY
   b. Saarbrucken, Germany, 23 Apr. 1918; U.S.
citizen 1944. Studied at Univ. of Strasbourg,
France; with Anthony Donato, Northwestern Univ.,
B.M. 1949, M.M. 1950, Ph.D. 1959; and conducting
privately with Nikolai Malko and Bruno Walter.
He received the Chicago Music Critics award,
1952; Fromm Found. grant, 1956; awards from City
of St. Louis and Bach Society, 1964, 1965; from
Internat. Library of Contemporary Music, Fontainebleau, 1969; MacDowell award, 1972; Delius
prize, 1973. He was teaching assistant, Northwestern Univ., 1949-59; on faculty, St. Louis
Inst. of Music, 1960-63; from 1963, professor and
chairman, Florissan Valley Coll. He is also conductor, Maplewood-Richmond Heights Symph., Midwest Chamber Ensemble, and Eden Choral Society.
   WORKS: OPERA: Man under glass, music drama;
ORCHESTRA: Song of songs (symph. #2); Ode,
epitaph and dithyramb (symph. #3); Ariadne,
episode and Psyche (symph. #4); bassoon concerto;
concerto for flute and English horn; Pré-l-ét-
ude, string orch.; Epigram; Aphrodite (symph.
choregraphique #1); CHAMBER MUSIC: string trio;
Morphine metamorphoses, 2 pianos; CHORUS: Peace,
a cappella; Tower of famine, women's voices, a
cappella; other chamber and choral works and art
songs.
   21 Bon Price Terrace, St. Louis, MO 63132

ORNSTEIN, LEO
   b. Kermenchug, Russia, 11 Dec. 1892; to U.S.
1907. Entered St. Petersburg Cons. at age 9;
studied with Percy Goetschius, New England Cons.;
piano with Bertha Feiring Tapper, Inst. of
Musical Art, New York. He made his New York
debut as pianist in 1911; was soloist with all
major orchestras in the U.S.; gave many recitals
in the U.S. and Europe. In 1974 he gave all his
music manuscripts to the Yale Univ. Library; in
1975, received the Marjorie Peabody Waite award.
   WORKS: ORCHESTRA: Anger, peace, joy, 3
moods, 1914; The fog, symphonic poem, 1915;
piano concerto, 1925, was premiered by Stokowski
and the Philadelphia Orch. in 1925; received its
2nd performance with the Yale Symph., New Haven,
11 Dec. 1976; Lysistrata, suite, 1933; symphony,
1934; Impressions of Chinatown; Marche funebre;
5 songs for voice and orch.; Pantomime; Dance of
the fates, 1937; Nocturne; concerto for 2 pianos;
CHAMBER MUSIC: Nocturne, clarinet and piano;
Suite in classic style, flute and clarinet;

Ballade, saxophone and piano; string quartet;
piano quintet; violin sonata, 1917; cello sonata;
4 piano sonatas; Wild man's dance, piano; many
piano pieces, songs. See "The futurist music of
Leo Ornstein," Mus. Lib. Assoc. Notes, (June
1975):735-50.

OROWAN, THOMAS F.
   b. New York, N.Y., 15 Nov. 1940. Studied at
Juilliard School; with William Sydeman and Peter
Pindar Stearns, Mannes Coll. of Music, B.S.
1965; with Gardner Read, Boston Univ., M.M.
1967; further study with Hugo Norden. He was
music editor, Allyn and Bacon, 1969-71.
   WORKS: ORCHESTRA: Serenade for strings,
1966; BAND: Fanfare for brass, 1962; CHAMBER
MUSIC: trio for 2 trombones and tuba, 1962;
Kingspark nocturne, 4 winds, 1963; trio for
viola, clarinet, bassoon, 1963; Voyages, clarinet
and guitar, 1963; 5 short dialogues, trombone
and piano, 1963; March, brass quintet, 1964;
suite for solo flute, 1964; sonata for 3 winds
and piano, 1964; string quartet, 1965; Pastorale,
oboe and piano, 1966; woodwind trio, 1966;
Presto, horn and piano, 1966; duo for 2 trumpets,
1966; suite for clarinet and piano, 1966; many
piano pieces; songs.
   82 Naples Rd., Brookline, MA 02146

ORREGO-SALAS, JUAN A.
   b. Santiago, Chile, 18 Jan. 1919; to U.S. 1961.
Studied at Univ. of Chile, B.A. 1938; Catholic
Univ. of Santiago, diploma in architecture, 1943;
composition with Humberto Allende and Domingo
Santa Cruz, Nat. Cons., M.A. 1942; with Randall
Thompson, Princeton Univ., 1945-46; with Aaron
Copland at Tanglewood, 1946; at Univ. of Chile,
Ph.D. 1953. His many awards include a Rockefeller
grant, 1955; Guggenheim fellowships, 1945, 1954;
Olga Cohen Memorial award, 1949; Chilean Contemporary Music Festival prizes, 1948, 1950,
1952; Inter-American Music Council award, 1957;
honorary doctorate, Catholic Univ. of Chile,
1971; membership, Acad. of Fine Arts, Chile,
1973; numerous commissions. He was lecturer,
Catholic Univ. of Santiago, 1942-43; on music
faculty, Univ. of Chile, 1943-61; Catholic Univ.
of Chile, 1951-61; from 1961, professor and
chairman, Indiana Univ.
   WORKS: ORCHESTRA: symphony #3, Washington,
D.C., 22 Apr. 1961; concerto a tre, violin,
cello, piano, and orch., 1962, Washington, May
1965; symphony #4, 1966, Bloomington, Ind., 7
Apr. 1967; 4 liriche brevi, saxophone and chamber
orch., 1967, Washington, 1 May 1974; Veriaciones
serenes, string orch., 1971, Santiago, Chile,
23 Nov. 1971; Volte, chamber orch., Rochester,
N.Y., 11 Dec. 1971; WIND ENSEMBLE: Psalms, 1962;
concerto for wind symphony, 1963-64; CHAMBER
MUSIC: concertino, brass quartet, 1963; sonata
a 4, flute, oboe, harpsichord, contrabass, Washington, 31 Oct. 1964; piano trio #1, Caracas,
Venezuela, 12 May 1966; 4 liriche brevi, alto
saxophone and piano, 1967; Mobili, viola and
piano, 1967; Palabras de don Quixote, baritone
and chamber ensemble, Washington, 31 Oct. 1970;
Esquinas, guitar, 1971; Psalms, baritone and
piano, 1977; Serenata, flute and cello, 1972;

OSBORNE, WILLSON

Sonata de estio, flute and piano, 1972, Bloomington, 27 Oct. 1974; Presencias, woodwind trio,
string trio, harpsichord, 1972, Washington, 5
May 1977; piano trio #2, 1977; CHORUS: Albor-
ades, female voices, harp, piano, percussion,
1965; America, no en vano invocamos tu nombre,
male chorus, soloists, orch., Ithaca, N.Y., 10
May 1966; 3 madrigales, 1967; Missa in tempore
discordiae, with tenor solo and orch., 1968-69;
The days of God, oratorio, with soloists and
orch., libretto by composer, Washington, 2 Nov.
1976.
    School of Music, Indiana Univ., Bloomington,
IN 47401

OSBORNE, WILLSON
    b. 4 Apr. 1906. His compositions include 2
ricercari for brass ensemlbe; Soliloquy, clarinet solo; Fantasy, flute solo; Rhapsodie,
bassoon solo; Rhapsody, clarinet solo; Early one
morning and On Christmas eve, 2 noels for chorus.

OSGOOD, HENRY OSBORNE
    b. Peabody, Mass., 12 Mar. 1879; d. New York,
N.Y., 8 May 1927. Studied in Boston and in
Europe. From 1914 he was associate editor of
the Musical Courier. He composed choral works
and songs.

OSTERGREN, EDUARDO AUGUSTO
    b. Sao Paulo, Brazil, 24 Apr. 1943; to U.S.
1967. Studied at Cons. Dramatico de Sao Paulo,
B.M. 1963; with Lloyd Pfautsch, Southern Methodist Univ., M.M. 1968; and at Indiana Univ.
He was choir conductor, Univ. of Sao Paulo at
San Carlos, 1965-67; professor, Ursuline Acad.,
Dallas, 1968-69; from 1970, conductor, North
Carolina State Univ. Symph. Orch.
    WORKS: CHAMBER MUSIC: Sonata in 3 cen-
turies, cello and piano, 1967; string quartet,
1974; CHORUS: Psalm 146, 1969; ORGAN: Bene-
dicamus Domino, 1971.
    165 Pineland Circle, Raleigh, NC 27606

OSTERLING, ERIC
    b. Hartford, Conn., 21 Mar. 1926. Studied at
Ithaca Coll., B.S.; Univ. of Connecticut; and
at Hartt Coll. of Music. He has received many
commissions for band pieces; from 1948, has been
school music director, Portland, Conn.
    WORKS: BAND: First symphony; Adventurous
night suite; Symphonic chorale; Beguine for
youth; Tall cedars; Nordic overture; and many
other band pieces.
    16 Ridge Rd., Cromwell, CT 06416

OSTRANDER, LINDA WOODAMAN
    b. New York, N.Y., 17 Feb. 1937. Studied with
Joseph Wood and Richard Hoffmann, Oberlin Coll.,
B.M. 1958; with Alvin Etler, Smith Coll., M.A.
1960; Ben Johnston, Univ. of Illinois, 1964-65;
and with Gardner Read, Boston Univ., D.M.A.
1972. Her awards include full scholarships at
Oberlin and Smith Coll.; Settie Lehman Fatman
prize, 1960; Radcliffe Inst. scholar, 1963,
1964; Univ. of Illinois fellowship, 1964-65;
Gilchrist-Potter prize, Oberlin Coll., 1965-66;
teaching fellowship, Boston Univ., 1969-72; and

commissions. She has held faculty posts at
Adelphi Suffolk Coll., 1961-63; Southampton
Coll., 1963-64; Lesley Coll., 1972-73; and from
1973, at Bunker Hill Coll.
    WORKS: ORCHESTRA: 2 suites; Quiet music;
2 concerti grossi, 1958, 1969; CHAMBER MUSIC:
violin sonata, 1956; Variations, string quartet,
1958; piano trio, 1961; Game of chance, any
small ensemble, 1967; Fun 'n' games, string
quartet, 1968; string trio, 1971; Rounds, brass
trio, 1972; Cycle for 6, 6 instruments, 1972;
MULTIMEDIA: Tarot, saxophone, reciter, dancer,
slides, lights, tape, 1973; Montage, slide show
with music, 1973; also choral works, songs,
piano pieces.
    48 Atwood Rd., Southboro, MA 01772

O'SULLIVAN, PATRICK
    b. Louisville, Ky., 23 Aug. 1871; d. Los Angeles,
Calif., 18 Mar. 1947. Studied piano with Harold
Bauer in Paris; with Schwarkenka in Berlin;
composition with Wilhelm Berger in Berlin. He
taught at Louisville Cons., 1915-39; then at the
Cons. of Memphis. His compositions included
orchestral works; Epithalamium, chorus and string
quartet; 65 Irish melodies for voices.

OTT, JOSEPH
    b. Atlantic City, N.J., 7 July 1929. Studied
with Walter Ihrke, Univ. of Connecticut, B.A.
1960; with Roy Harris, Univ. of California, Los
Angeles, M.A. 1965; with Hans Sachsse in Berlin.
He received first prizes, Internat. Competition
for Symphonic Composition, Trieste, Italy, 1963,
Atwater Kent contest, 1964, Wisconsin Composers
contest, 1966, 1968 (4 categories); American
Music Center grants, 1964, 1968, 1969; Bennington
Conf. scholarships, 1967, 1969; ASCAP awards,
1968-73; and many commissions. He was director,
dance dept., George Washington Univ., 1960-63;
on music faculty, Milton Coll., 1965-72; from
1972, Emporia State Univ.
    WORKS: ORCHESTRA: Premise for orchestra;
Free variations; Matrix VI; Locus, Washington,
D.C., 24 Apr. 1977; BAND: Mini laude; Slide
piece #1; Palo duro; WIND ENSEMBLE: percussion
quartet; Encore set, brass trio; Toccata, brass
quintet; suite for 4 flutes; 5 pieces, flute
and clarinet; 2 ricercares, percussion; Toccata,
trombone and piano; Matrix III and V, chamber
orch.; Matrix IV, piano trio; violin sonata;
Quartet for solo saxophone; ELECTRONIC: Matrix
VII, brass, percussion and tape; Aeolian harp,
ensemble and tape; Timbres, brass quintet and
tape; and choral works.
    Emporia State University, Emporia, KS 66801

OTTE, ALLEN
    b. Sheboygan, Wis., 17 Jan. 1950. Studied at
Oberlin Cons.; with Herbert Brün, Univ. of
Illinois; and at Northern Illinois Univ. He was
lecturer, Northern Illinois Univ., 1973-77; then
was appointed visiting assistant professor,
Univ. of Cincinnati; in 1972, was a founding
member of the Blackearth Percussion Group.
    WORKS: CHAMBER MUSIC: Hit or miss, 2 per-
cussionists, 1975; Song, soprano and 6 instruments, 1976; Correlates, 3 keyboards, 1977.
    4090 Rosehill, Cincinnati, OH 45229

OUDAL, ROBERT D.
b. Minneapolis, Minn., 11 Jan. 1930. Studied
with Robert Delaney and Anthony Donato, Northwestern Univ.; with Paul Fetler, Earl George,
and Dominick Argento, Univ. of Minnesota. He
was music director, Suomi Coll., 1954-55; in
public schools, Lakeville, Minn., 1956-57; from
1958, department chairman, Rochester, Minn.
WORKS: ORCHESTRA: <u>Festival overture</u>; <u>March
for orchestra</u>; <u>Symphonet for strings</u>; CHORUS:
<u>Sing, men and angels sing!</u>, with brass, percus-
sion and organ; <u>Stopping by woods on a snowy
evening</u>.
3405 18th Ave., N.W., Rochester, MN 55901

OVANIN, NIKOLA
b. Sisek, Yugoslavia, 25 Nov. 1911; U.S. citizen
1956. Studied with Herbert Elwell, Cleveland
Inst. of Music, B.M. 1939; with Arthur Shepherd,
Western Reserve Univ., B.S. 1941; with Ernst
Krenek, Hamline Univ., B.A., M.A. 1947; with
Bernard Rogers and Howard Hanson, Eastman School
of Music, Ph.D. 1969. He held a scholarship at
Cleveland Inst., 1938; received awards at Nat.
Composers's Clinic, Akron, 1942, Spokane Music
Festival, 1948, Nat. Fed. of Music Clubs,
Milwaukee, 1954, Roth Competition, Nat. School
Orch. Assoc., 1966. He taught in public and
private schools, 1941-42, 1956-62; Whitworth
Coll., 1947-48; San Jose State Coll., 1949-51;
Wisconsin State Coll., Eau Claire, 1953-55; and
from 1952, in New York City Schools.
WORKS: ORCHESTRA: 3 symphonies, 1939, 1946,
1969; <u>Pleiades</u>, suite, 1954; <u>Poem</u>, string orch.,
1965; <u>Hatikvah variations</u>, 1965; BAND: <u>Prelude
moderne</u>, 1947; CHAMBER MUSIC: <u>Journey ever
softly unto Sandana</u>, string trio; <u>Larghetto</u>,
violin, clarinet, cello; <u>Flute suite</u>, flute and
piano; cello sonata; <u>Dance suite</u>, alto saxophone, dancer, percussion; CHORUS: <u>Suddenly
there are flowers</u>, women's voices; SONGS: <u>Come
with me</u> and <u>Star stream</u>, soprano and piano; also
piano pieces.

OVERTON, HALL
b. Bangor, Mich., 23 Feb. 1920; d. New York, N.Y.,
24 Nov. 1972. Taught himself to play piano by
ear and began to compose in high school; studied
at Chicago Musical Coll.; with Vincent Persichetti
at Juilliard School, B.S. 1951; privately with
Wallingford Riegger and Darius Milhaud. He received commissions from the Koussevitzky Found.,
1955; Walter Trampler, 1960; Louisville Symph.,
1962; New and Newer Music Series, Lincoln Center,
1971. He was a noted jazz pianist; taught at
Juilliard School, 1960-72; was visiting professor
at Yale Univ., 1972.
WORKS: OPERA: <u>The enchanted pear tree</u>,
opera buffa based on Boccaccio's <u>Decameron</u>,
produced at Juilliard School, 7 Feb. 1950;
<u>Pietro's petard</u>, 1963; <u>Huckleberry Finn</u>, libretto
by Judah Stampfer, Juilliard, 20 May 1971;
BALLET: <u>Nonage</u>, 1951; ORCHESTRA: 2 symphonies,
1955, 1962; concerto for violin and strings,
1958; <u>Dialogues</u>, chamber orch., 1964; <u>Pulsations</u>,
1971; <u>Sonorities</u>, Los Angeles, Oct. 1972; CHAMBER
MUSIC: string trio; 3 string quartets, 1950,
1954, #3, New York, 17 Mar. 1974; viola sonata,

1960; songs; piano pieces.

OWEN, BLYTHE
b. Bruce, Minn., 26 Dec. 1898. Studied with
Max Wald and Louis Gruenberg, Chicago Musical
Coll., B.M. 1941; with Albert Noelte, Northwestern Univ., M.M. 1942; with Bernard Rogers
and Howard Hanson, Eastman School of Music, Ph.D.
1953; and with Nadia Boulanger in France, 1949.
She is a life fellow, Internat. Inst. of Arts
and Letters, Switz.; received 6 Mu Phi Epsilon
awards, 1942-61, and 2 special citations, 1967;
Delta Omicron award, 1946; first prize, Musicians Club of Women, Chicago, 1959; first prize,
American Pen Women, Chicago, 1953; Univ. of
Maryland award, 1957; Composers' Press award,
1957; honorary doctorate, Andrews Univ., 1979.
Her faculty posts have included Cosmopolitan
School of Music, 1943-61; Northwestern Univ.,
1944-50; Chicago Teachers Coll., 1947-50;
Roosevelt Univ., 1950-61; Walla Walla Coll.,
1961-65; from 1965, Andrews Univ.
WORKS: ORCHESTRA: <u>State Street</u>, suite,
1946; symphony, 1947; piano concerto, 1953;
concerto grosso, strings, oboe, horns, bassoon,
1961; CHAMBER MUSIC: <u>Sonata fantaisie</u>, cello
and piano, 1940; piano quintet, 1944; violin
sonata, 1946; woodwind trio, 1950; 2 string
quartets, 1944, 1951; trio for flute, clarinet,
piano, 1959; piano trio, 1962; <u>2 inventions</u>,
woodwinds, 1964; <u>Saraband and gigue</u>, 4 tubas,
1969; <u>Diversion</u>, alto saxophone and piano, 1973;
<u>Variations on Eine Feste Berg</u>, 3 trumpets and
piano, 1978; choral works; piano pieces.
115 Kephart Lane, Berrien Springs, MI 49104

OWEN, HAROLD J.
b. 1931. Studied with Halsey Stevens, Univ. of
Southern California, D.M.A.; is faculty member,
Univ. of Oregon.
WORKS: CHAMBER MUSIC: <u>12 concert etudes</u>,
clarinet; <u>Fantasies on Mexican tunes</u>, 3 trumpets
and piano; <u>Chamber music</u>, 4 clarinets; CHORUS:
<u>Metropolitan bus</u>, cantata, with piano, 4 hands;
ORGAN: <u>Overture dans le style Francais</u>.
University of Oregon, Eugene, OR 97403

OWEN, JERRY MICHAEL
b. Gary, Ind., 6 June 1944. Studied with Donald
H. White, DePauw Univ., 1962-64, 1966-68; with
Richard Hervig and Peter Lewis, 1969-73. He was
on the faculty, DePauw Univ., 1968-69; from
1969, at Coe Coll.
WORKS: ORCHESTRA: symphony, 1967; <u>Music
for string orch.</u>, 1968; CHAMBER MUSIC: 3 piano
sonatas, 1966, 1967, 1968; string quartet, 1967;
<u>Haiku set</u>, mezzo-soprano, 1968; <u>3 notions</u>, trom-
bone and piano, 1971; <u>Dialog</u>, solo viola, 1971;
<u>Variations</u>, for 2 tubas and piano, 1973; CHORUS:
3 settings of Frost poems, 1970; ELECTRONIC:
<u>Tetrabstraction I and II</u>, tape recorder, 1970,
1971; <u>Music after times of war</u>, percussion,
voices, and tape, 1972.
2427 Bever Ave., S.E., Cedar Rapids, IA
52403

OWEN, RICHARD
b. New York, N.Y., 11 Dec. 1922. Studied with

PACCIONE, PAUL

Vittorio Giannini, Manhattan School of Music;
privately with Robert Starer.
WORKS: OPERA: A moment of war, 1958; A
fisherman called Peter, 1 act, 1965; Mary Dyer,
Suffern, N.Y., 12 June 1976; and songs.
21 Claremont Ave., New York, NY 10027

PACCIONE, PAUL
b. Brooklyn, N.Y., 30 Sept. 1952. Studied at
Mannes Coll. of Music, B.M.; privately with
Harley Gaber; with Kenneth Gaburo, Univ. of
California, San Diego, M.M.
WORKS: CHAMBER MUSIC: The force that
through the green fuse drives the flower, solo
vibraphone, 1973; trio for flute, violin, vibraphone, 1973; Ay me, that dreerie death, soprano
and 2 flutes, 1973; Piece for unaccompanied
clarinet, 1974; Clarinet music, 4 clarinets,
1975-76; Stabile, clarinet, guitar, vibraphone,
1976-77.
5125 S. Kenwood Ave., #602, Chicago, IL
60615

PACE, ROBERT JOSEPH
b. Daytona, Fla., 15 Dec. 1949. Studied with
Alexander Goehr and Donald Martino, New England
Cons., where he held a full scholarship; other
awards include commissions. He was pianist at
Dance Theatre of Harlem, 1974-75; has taught at
Newark Community Center, 1975-77; Harlem School
of the Arts, 1977-78; was pianist and musical
advisor, Stars of American Ballet, 1977-78;
instructor, Fordham Univ., 1977-78.
WORKS: ORCHESTRA: Ballet on melodies of
Foster; CHAMBER MUSIC: piano trio; Sonnage for
cello; Fantasy, piano; Psalms, soprano, violin,
guitar, cello; CHORUS: Chorale.
175 Columbus Ave., New York, NY 10023

PACKALES, JOSEPH
b. New York, N.Y., 28 Mar. 1948. Studied with
Samuel Adler at Eastman School of Music; received the Howard Hanson prize, 1968. From 1971
he has been director, New Arts Ensemble; from
1973, artist-in-residence and music dept.,chair-
man, Belknap Coll.
WORKS: CHAMBER MUSIC: piano sonata in the
form of 11 fragments; Solemn music, chamber
ensemble; SONGS: Cassandra's monologue from
Agamemnon; Kenneth Patchen songs.

PACKER, GEORGE LEONARD
b. Philadelphia, Pa., 28 Oct. 1948. Studied
with Henri Lazarof, Paul Chihara, and Leon
Kirchner, Univ. of California, Los Angeles;
with Henri Pousseur, Liege, Belgium. His awards
include the Atwater Kent award, 1970; Gus Kahn
award, 1971; Fulbright fellowship, 1972; Regents
faculty fellowship, UCLA, 1978; Nat. Endowment
for the Arts grant, 1978. He was faculty member,
East Carolina Univ., 1973-74; Univ. of California, Los Angeles, 1974-78; from 1978,
Pepperdine Univ., Los Angeles County.
WORKS: ORCHESTRA: Times two, strings, 4
horns, percussion, 1971; Reflections, Liege,
12 June 1973; CHAMBER MUSIC: string quartet,
1972; Psalms, brass sextet, 1977; Octet in 4
acts, double woodwind quartet, 1978; Sonnet II,

alto trombone and percussion, 1978; CHORUS:
When spring returns and Heal, hardy air, 2 madrigals, 1971; Soft silver, a cappella, 1976;
Missa sonar, double chorus, soloists, and orch.,
1976-78; The dawning, double chorus, a cappella.
2327 Glendon Ave., Los Angeles, CA 90064

PADWA, VLADIMIR
b. Krivyakino, Russia, 8 Feb. 1900; U.S. citizen
1949. Studied at Cons. in Berlin, Petrograd,
Leipzig; with Ferruccio Busoni, Michael Zadora,
Paul Juon. He has received awards from the New
York Madrigal Society, Musical America, Peabody
Cons.; and annual ASCAP awards, 1968-73. He was
cofounder and faculty member, State Cons.,
Tallin, Estonia, 1919-21; cofounder and member,
First Piano Quartet, 1941-50; faculty member,
New York Coll. of Music, 1945-68; from 1968, has
taught piano and composition, New York Univ.
WORKS: BALLET: Tom Sawyer, with optional
narration; THEATRE: music for Goethe's Faust, a
cappella choir; Ondine by Giradoux; Noah, play
by Obey; Peter Pan; Pied Piper; The nightingale;
A nice place to live, book by Alex Benn; Eagle,
book by Jack Selby, 1969; ORCHESTRA: symphony;
Solitude; symphony for string orch.; Partita,
soprano and chamber orch.; concerto for 2 pianos
and string orch.; Ballads 1 and 2, woodwinds and
strings; Serenade, string orch.; suite for winds
and percussion; Saints in borrowed styles,
variations on When the saints come marching in,
also for brass quintet; CHAMBER MUSIC: 3 string
quartets; concertino for alto saxophone and
guitar; violin sonatina; Sonata fantasia, violin
and piano; cello sonata; clarinet sonata; clarinet sonatina; also choral works and piano
pieces.
736 Riverside Dr., New York, NY 10031

PAIK, NAM JUNE
b. Seoul, Korea, 20 July 1932. Studied in Tokyo
and in Germany; an extreme avant-garde composer
who spends much of his time on the West Coast.
An example of his "composition" is: Ommagio a
Cage, for piano demolition, breaking of raw
eggs, spraying of hands with jet black paint,
etc., Dusseldorf, 13 Nov. 1959.

PALANGE, LOUIS SALVADOR
b. Oakland, Calif., 17 Dec. 1917; d. Burbank,
Calif., 8 June 1979. Studied with Wesley
La Violette, Univ. of California, Los Angeles,
1936. During World War II, he conducted the
Naval Training School Orchestra in San Diego;
founded and conducted many orchestras in the Los
Angeles-San Diego area.
WORKS: ORCHESTRA: Evangeline, 1945; 2 symphonies, 1946, 1968; violin concerto, 1950;
Hollywood panorama, 1952; Romantic piano concerto, 1954; Poker deck ballet suite, 1960;
Overture domesticana; BAND: Symphony in steel,
1941; CHAMBER MUSIC: Classical trio, flute,
violin, viola, 1950.

PALANZI, RICHARD BRUNO
b. Framingham, Mass., 30 Oct. 1951. Studied
with Stuart Smith, Lowell State Coll.; with
Randall McClellan, Hampshire Coll.; with Gordon

Mumma and David Behrman at Chocorua, N.H.

WORKS: MULTIMEDIA: Concrete piece 1, tape and sound location modulator; Anti-ballistic-musik I, K'an, The abyss, live electronics and video display, 1971; The bubble people, tape, intermedia environment, and dance, 1972; Shapes and bridges, tape, intermedia environment, and dance, 1972; Past tense, winds, percussion, crosscut saws, electroresonant objects, cyber-sonic media events, 1973; and others.

    84 Bethany Rd., Framingham, MA 01701

PALMER, ROBERT M.

b. Syracuse, N.Y., 2 June 1915. Studied with Howard Hanson, Eastman School of Music, B.M. 1938, M.M. 1939; with Roy Harris, 1939; and with Aaron Copland at Tanglewood, 1940, on scholarship. Other awards include a Guggenheim fellowship, 1952; MacDowell fellowship, 1954; and commissions. He was faculty member, Univ. of Kansas, 1940-43, Cornell Univ., 1943-53, and from 1956-visiting composer, Illinois Wesleyan Univ., 1954; professor, Univ. of Illinois, 1955-56.

WORKS: ORCHESTRA: Poem, violin and orch., 1938; concerto for small orch., 1940; symphony, 1939-42; concerto for orch., 1943; chamber concerto, violin, oboe, and strings, 1949; Memorial music, 1957; WIND ENSEMBLE: Choric songs and toccata; Nabachodonosor, brass ensemble and chorus, 1964; CHAMBER MUSIC: 2 string trios, 1937, 1962; piano sonata, 1938; 4 string quartets, 1939, 1947, 1954, 1959; concerto for 5 instruments, 1942; First quartet for piano and strings; 3 epigrams, string quartet, 1957; quintet for clarinet, string trio, piano, 1952; piano quintet, 1950; trumpet sonata, 1972; Transitions, piano, 1976; cello sonata, 1976; Organon I, flute, clarinet, violin, cello, Syracuse, 20 Sept. 1977; Carmina amoris, soprano, clarinet, violin, piano, Cornell Univ., 26 Feb. 1978; choral works; piano pieces.

    Music Dept., Cornell University, Ithaca, NY 14850

PALOMBO, PAUL M.

b. Pittsburgh, Pa., 10 Sept. 1937. Studied with Charles E. Hoag, Indiana Univ. of Penn.; with Robert Hall Lewis, Peabody Cons.; Bernard Rogers and Howard Hanson, Eastman School of Music, Ph.D. 1969. He received a Rockefeller award, 1965; American Festival of Music awards, 1967, 1978; Howard Hanson prize, 1969. He taught in Baltimore County public schools, 1962-69; was faculty member, Univ. of Cincinnati, 1969-78; in 1978, was appointed professor and director, School of Music, Univ. of Washington.

WORKS: CHAMBER MUSIC: Metatheses, flute, oboe, harpsichord, double bass, 1971; Rittatti anticamente, viola and piano, 1972; Montage, violin and piano, 1972; ELECTRONIC: Proteus, ballet for orch. and tape, 1969; Miniatures, organ and tape, 1969; Morphosis, ballet, 1970; 4 Sonos, #1, tape and harpsichord, 1972, #2, harp and tape, 1972, #3, double bass and tape, 1973, #4, string trio and tape, 1974; Stegowsgenvolkssaurus, electronic music for a sculpture, 1973-74.

    University of Washington, Seattle, WA 98105

PALTRIDGE, JAMES GILBERT, JR.

b. Albany, Calif., 28 June 1942. Studied privately with Robert Erickson in Berkeley, 1959; with Roman Haubenstock-Ramati in Vienna, 1961; and with David Sheinfeld in San Francisco, 1960, 1962-64. He is a free-lance editor and engraver; and from 1971, has been vice-president of Buffalo Productions.

WORKS: OPERA: Timon Afinskin, 2 acts, after C. Kinbote, 1980; THEATRE: music for The dyscolos by Menander, 1961; J.B. by MacLeish, 1965; CHAMBER MUSIC: flute sonatina, 1958; Variations, woodwind trio, 1961; 6 poems of Emily Dickinson, voice and chamber ensemble, 1961; violin duo, 1962; If I told him, reciter and wind ensemble, 1973; clarinet sonata, 1974; FILM SCORE: Elevator girls in bondage, 1972; Mind safari, radio play, 1977; Bar time, television serial, 1979.

    869 Shotwell St., San Francisco, CA 94110

PANERIO, ROBERT M.

b. Roslyn, Wash. Studied at Central Washington State Coll., B.A., M.A.; joined the faculty there in 1963. His Jubiloso won the 1975 Ostwald award for a band composition; Prelude and danza, for band, was performed in Washington, D.C., 13 Sept. 1976; on the Washington state program for the Bicentennial.

    Central Washington State College, Ellensburg, WA 98926

PANETTI, JOAN

Studied at Peabody Cons.; received BMI student composer awards, 1966, 1967; Morse fellowship at Yale Univ., 1969. She has toured Europe as pianist; was on the faculty at Yale to 1978, when she was appointed associate professor at Swathmore Coll. Her published works include a piano concerto; Cavatina for piano; 3 songs for medium voice.

    Swarthmore College, Swarthmore, PA 19801

PAPE, LOUIS WAYNE

b. Centuria, Wis., 26 Feb. 1939. Studied at Univ. of Wisconsin-River Falls, B.S. 1961; Indiana Univ., M.M. 1968. He taught piano, Concordia Coll., St. Paul, 1961-63; from 1968, has been faculty member, Dakota State Coll.

WORKS: CHORUS: Winter I, 1969; ELECTRONIC: The tiger, soprano, piano, tape recorder, 1970; Spring flood victims--in memoriam, tape, instruments, and voices, 1972.

    Dakota State College, Madison, SD 57042

PARCHMAN, GEN LOUIS

b. Cincinnati, Ohio, 2 May 1929. Studied at Cincinnati Cons., B.M. 1956, M.M. 1958. His awards include Tanglewood fellowships, 1959, 1962; annual ASCAP awards, 1963-76. He was double bass player, Cincinnati Symph. Orch., 1958-66; jazz bassist, Cincinnati Jazz Trio, 1970-73; is pop arranger for various groups.

WORKS: ORCHESTRA: violin overture, 1959, rev. 1974; Elegy, 1960; 2 symphonies for strings, 1960, 1962; 12 variations, 2 pianos and orch., 1962; 2 concertos for percussion ensemble, 1961, 1962; Adagio for strings, 1962; symphony #3,

PARENTEAU, ZOEL

1962; <u>Winsel overture</u>, 1962; timpani concerto, 1963; concerto for 2 pianos, 1963; marimba concerto, 1964; <u>Dramatic overture</u>, 1965; <u>History of music</u>, with narrator, 1965; symphony for chorus and orch., 1967; 6 symphonies for percussion ensemble, 1967-73; concerto for soprano and orch., 1972; BAND: symphony for brass and percussion, 1962; symphony, 1964; CHAMBER MUSIC: piano trio, 1961; elegy for 2 pianos, 1963; sonata for woodwind quintet, 1966.
23 Parchman Place, Cincinnati, OH 45217

PARENTEAU, ZOEL
b. Northampton, Mass., 9 Apr. 1883; d. Englewood, N.J., 14 Sept. 1972. Studied with faculty members of Smith Coll. and with Ernest Bloch. He was arranger for David Belasco, Florenz Ziegfield, and Victor Herbert; conductor for touring companies. He wrote the scores for the musicals, <u>The amber express</u> and <u>Follow the girls</u>; many anthems and songs.

PARK, STEPHEN
b. Austin, Minn., 23 Sept. 1911. Studied at Univ. of Nebraska, B.A.; with Ross Lee Finney, Univ. of Michigan, M.M.; at Tanglewood; and with Darius Milhaud, Aspen School. He taught in public schools, 1929-36; at Univ. of Michigan; was composer-in-residence and faculty member, Univ. of Tampa, 1939-78; minister of music, Univ. Christian Church, Tampa.
WORKS: CHAMBER MUSIC: <u>Pastorale</u>, flute and strings; suite for clarinet and strings, 1953; <u>Pavanne</u>, 2 violins; suite for flute and piano, 1957.

PARK, YOUNG KEUN
b. Korea, 4 Feb. 1947; to U.S. 1977. Studied with Choong Hoo Park, Coll. of Music, Han Yang Univ.; with David Loeb, Mannes Coll. of Music, B.S. 1980. He won first prize, DongA Music Competition, Seoul, Korea, 1976; second prize, New Music for Young Ensembles competition, 1979.
WORKS: CHAMBER MUSIC: <u>2 preludes for piano</u>; <u>Fantasy</u>, clarinet and piano, 1976; trio for flute, cello, piano, 1976; string quartet, 1979.
32-39 79th St., Jackson Heights, NY 11370

PARKER, ALICE
b. Boston, Mass., 16 Dec. 1925. Studied with Ross Lee Finney and Werner Josten, Smith Coll., B.A. 1947; with Robert Shaw, Julius Herford, and Vincent Persichetti, Juilliard School, M.S. 1949. She has received annual ASCAP awards from 1968; Nat. Endowment for the Arts grant, 1974. From 1960 she has been a free-lance composer/conductor; was arranger for the Robert Shaw Chorale, 1948-68; visiting faculty member, Westminster Choir Coll., 1975.
WORKS: OPERA: <u>The martyrs' mirror</u>, 1971; <u>The family reunion</u>, 1975; <u>Singers Glen</u>, 1977; CHORUS: <u>An Easter rejoicing</u>, 1968; <u>A sermon from the mountain</u>, 1969; <u>The time of ingathering</u>, 1970; <u>7 carols</u>, with orch., 1972; <u>Gaudete</u>, 6 Latin Christmas hymns, 1973; <u>Journeys: Pilgrims and strangers</u>, 1975; <u>Phonophobia</u>, 1976; <u>Commentaries</u>, with orch., 1978; SONG CYCLES: <u>Songs for Eve</u>, 4 solo voices and string quartet,

text by Archibald MacLeish, New York premiere, 3 June 1976, composer conducting; numerous other sacred and secular vocal works.
801 West End Ave., New York, NY 10025

PARKER, CHARLES CHRISTOPHER (CHARLIE, YARDBIRD, or BIRD)
b. Kansas City, Mo., 29 Aug. 1920; d. New York, N.Y., 12 Mar. 1955. He was a virtuoso saxophonist whose improvisations became legendary in his own time. His published compositions include <u>Anthropology</u>; <u>Yardbird suite</u>; and <u>Ornithology</u>.

PARRIS, HERMAN M.
b. Ekaterinoslav, Russia, 30 Oct. 1903; to U.S. 1905. Studied at Univ. of Pennsylvania, B.M. 1921; and at Jefferson Medical Coll., M.D. 1926. Except for army service in World War II, he has been engaged in private medical practice in Philadelphia and has had a prolific career in composition.
WORKS: ORCHESTRA: 4 symphonies, 1946, 1947, 1949, 1952; 8 piano concertos, 1 each year, 1946-53; violin concerto; <u>Hospital suite</u>, 1948; <u>Hebrew rhapsody</u>, 1949; <u>Rhapsody #2, Heart</u>, 1950; <u>Lament</u>, string orch., 1956; CHAMBER MUSIC: 4 string quartets, 1946, 1948, 1960, 1964; 22 piano sonatas; 2 violin sonatas; violin sonata, cello sonata; <u>Images</u>, brass sextet; woodwind miniatures; suite for violin and viola; suite for piano and strings; numerous other works, such as 115 piano preludes.

PARRIS, ROBERT
b. Philadelphia, Pa., 21 May 1924. Studied with Peter Mennin, Juilliard School, 1945-48; with Aaron Copland at Tanglewood, 1950; and with Arthur Honneger in Paris, 1952-53. He received Nat. Endowment for the Arts grants, 1975, 1978. From 1963 he has been faculty member, George Washington Univ.
WORKS: ORCHESTRA: symphony, 1952; piano concerto, 1954; concerto for 5 kettledrums and orch., 1955; viola concerto, 1956; violin concerto, 1959; trombone concerto, 1964; <u>The messengers</u>, Albany, N.Y., 14 Mar. 1975; CHAMBER MUSIC: brass sextet, 1948; <u>Night</u>, baritone, clarinet, string quartet, 1951; quintet for woodwinds and strings, 1957; <u>The raids: 1940</u>, soprano, violin, piano, 1960; <u>Lamentations and praises</u>, chamber ensemble and percussion, 1962; violin sonata; viola sonata; 2 string quartets; 2 string trios; trio for cello, clarinet, piano; sonatina for flute, oboe, clarinet, horn, bass; <u>The book of imaginary beings</u>, chamber ensemble and percussion, 1972; <u>Rite of passage</u>, chamber ensemble, 1978; CHORUS: <u>Walking around</u>, cantata for men's voices, clarinet, violin, piano, Washington, 20 May 1973.
3307 Cummings Lane, Chevy Chase, MD 20015

PARRISH, CARL
b. Plymouth, Pa., 9 Oct. 1904; d. Valhalla, N.Y., 27 Nov. 1965. Studied at Harvard Univ., Ph.D. 1939. He held faculty posts at Wells Coll., 1939-41; Fisk Univ., 1941-45; Westminster Choir Coll., 1945-49; Pomona Coll., 1949-53; from 1963,

at Vassar Coll. He composed choral works, chamber music, song cycles, piano pieces.

PARRY, ROLAND
b. Ogden, Utah, 7 May 1897. Studied at Weber Coll., B.A., M.A., and was professor there from 1935. He received a commission for the choral work, All faces west. Other works include A child is born for chorus, and songs.

PARSONS, WILL
b. Memphis, Tenn., 28 July 1942. Studied with Ben Johnston, Salvatore Martirano, Kenneth Gaburo, Herbert Brün, Jack McKenzie, Univ. of Illinois, 1960-66. His record, Iowa Ear Music won a Downbeat magazine 5-star award, 1977. He was percussionist-composer, Univ. of Iowa, Centers for New Music and New Performing Arts, 1967-77, then at the Center for Music Experiment.
WORKS: SMALL ENSEMBLES: Arrivals and departures, percussion sextet and tape, 1966; Dazzleplus, any stringed instrument capable of double stops, 1968; Performance pleasure, 6 instruments, 1971; Make your own ear music, guidelines, 1976; Music for citizens band, formats for improvisation by groups of unspecified instrumentation and size, 1978; many works for solo and group percussion and chamber ensembles.
P.O. Box 2655, La Jolla, CA 92038

PARTCH, HARRY
b. Oakland, Calif., 24 June 1901; d. San Diego, 3 Sept. 1974. Self-taught in music, he began in 1925 to design and build instruments to accomodate his own musical dramatic forms and to encompass his 43-tone-to-the-octave scale. For his work in building and adapting a great number of instruments, he received numerous awards and grants. Included in his exotic instruments are 2 chromelodeons, 3 kitharas, 4 marimbas, 2 harmonic canons, cloud-chamber bowls, an elongated viola, and adapted guitars. The new instruments and the new notation devised for their use were not innovations for innovation's sake, but an expedient for expressing his music. "I am not an instrument builder," Partch said, "but a philosophic music man seduced into carpentry."
WORKS: THEATRE: Oedipus, music drama to his own translations of Sophocles' Oedipus Rex, Oakland, Calif., 14 Mar. 1952; Even wild horses, dance music for an absent drama, 1953; The bewitched, a dance satire, 1955; Revelation in the Courthouse Park, musical tragedy, Univ. of Illinois, Urbana, 11 Apr. 1961; Water, water, an American ritual, Urbana, 9 Mar. 1962; CHAMBER MUSIC: 17 lyrics by Li Po, 1930-33; U.S. highball, a musical account of a transcontinental hobo trip, 1943; The letter, a depression message from a hobo friend, 1943; The wayward, an American collection, 1946-55; 11 instrusions, 1949-50; Plectra and percussion, dances, 1949-52; Cloud-chamber music, 1950; 8 hitchhiker inscriptions from a highway railing at Barstow, California, 1956; Daphne of the dunes, 1958; And on the 7th day petals fell on Petaluma, 1964; Delusion of the fury, 1965-66; FILMS: Music studio--Harry Partch, 1958; Rotate the body, 1961; The dreamer that remains, 1972.

Partch explained his philosophy and musical system in his book, Genesis of a music, 2nd ed., New York, 1973. The Harry Partch Archive at the Music Library, Univ. of Illinois, Urbana-Champaign, received a gift of recordings, scores, letters, and documents pertaining to the production of Revelation in the Courthouse Park and Water, water from Prof. Emeritus Barnard Hewitt of the University's theatre dept.

PARTHUN, PAUL
b. Milwaukee, Wis., 6 Feb. 1931. Studied with Leo Sowerby, American Cons.; with Cecil Burleigh, Univ. of Wisconsin; at Univ. of Minnesota, Ph.D. He has received awards from Wisconsin Fed. of Music Clubs, 1950; Nat. Fed. of Music Clubs, 1951; Nat. Endowment for the Arts, 1974, for New Ojibwa songs for orch. He has been faculty member, Macalester Coll., Bemidji State Coll., and from 1976, Eastern New Mexico Univ.
WORKS: BAND: Whispering Wisconsin, 1956; CHAMBER MUSIC: Fountain of Bandusia, soprano and chamber ensemble, 1950; Black orchid, flute, clarinet, cello, piano, 1951; CHORUS: Blessing of St. Francis, solo voice, mixed chorus, male chorus, organ, 1966; Ave verum corpus, 1968; Adoramus Te Christe, 1969; Aaronic benediction, 1973; A choric psalm, triple chorus, brass, percussion, 1978; SOLO VOICE: Madness, baritone and piano, New Mexico Composers' Guild concert, May 1978.
Eastern New Mexico University, Portales, NM 88130

PASATIERI, THOMAS
b. New York, N.Y., 20 Oct. 1945. Studied with Vittorio Giannini and Vincent Persichetti, Juilliard School, D.M.A. (the first doctorate given by Juilliard); with Darius Milhaud at Aspen, Colo. His awards include a scholarship at Juilliard, 1961; Richard Rodgers scholarship; Marion Freschi prize; Brevard Festival prize for orchestral music; Aspen Festival prize; George A. Wedge prize; Irving Berlin fellowship in theater music; Nat. Ednowment for the Arts grant, 1976; numerous commissions.
WORKS: OPERA: The women, Aspen, Colo., 20 Aug. 1965; La divina, New York, 16 Mar. 1966; Padrevia, Brooklyn, N.Y., 18 Nov. 1967; Calvary, on Yeats's text, Seattle, 7 Apr. 1971; The trial of Mary Todd Lincoln, NET, Boston, 14 Feb. 1972; Black widow, Seattle, 2 Mar. 1972; Signor Deluso, after Moliere's Sganarelle, 1973; The seagull, on Chekhov's play, Houston, 5 Mar. 1974; The penitentes, Aspen, 3 Aug. 1974; Ines de Castro, Baltimore, 31 May 1976; Washington Square, after Henry James, Detroit, 1 Oct. 1976; Before breakfast, after O'Neill, 1976, New York, 9 Oct. 1980; VOICE: Heloise and Abelard, soprano, baritone, and piano, 1971; Rites of passage, mezzo-soprano and chamber orch., Fort Lauderdale, 19 Mar. 1974; Far from love, Emily Dickinson text, soprano and 4 instruments; Album of songs on American poets.
500 West End Ave., New York, NY 10024

PASQUET, JEAN
b. New York, N.Y., 31 July 1896; d. Martinsburg, W.Va., 24 Jan. 1977. Studied with T. Tertius

PATTERSON, ANDY J.

Noble in New York; piano with Ossip Gabrilowitsch; also organ and orchestration. He held a William Mason scholarship for 5 years; received ASCAP awards. He was church organist, choral conductor, lecturer; education director, Aeolian Company. His compositions included more than 400 published works for chorus, organ, piano.

PATTERSON, ANDY J.
b. Gordon, Tex., 20 Feb. 1929. Studied with William J. Marsh, Texas Christian Univ.; privately with Arnold Schoenberg in Los Angeles; with Ernst von Dohnanyi and John Boda, Florida State Univ. He won first prize in a Texas Composers' Guild contest, 1969; has received many commissions. He has been faculty member at Texas Christian Univ., 1953-56; Florida State Univ., 1956-58; Georgia Teachers Coll., 1958-59; from 1959, at Hardin-Simmons Univ.; on leave and at Florida A&M Univ., 1967-68.
WORKS: ORCHESTRA: symphony; BAND: suite for concert band; Sonics, symphonic band; CHAMBER MUSIC: woodwind quintet; sonatas for all orchestral instruments; many other works for orchestra, band, chorus, piano, organ, etc.
1642 Swenson, Abilene, TX 79603

PATTERSON, DAVID NOLTE
b. St. Louis, Mo., 22 Jan. 1941. Studied with Robert Wykes, Washington Univ.; with Olivier Messiaen and Nadia Boulanger in Paris; with Leon Kirchner and Luise Vosgerchian, Harvard Univ.; and at Tanglewood. He received the Bohemians prize, 1970. He was on the faculty, Wellesley Coll., 1970-72; from 1972, at Univ. of Massachusetts, Boston.
WORKS: CHAMBER MUSIC: Differences, 6 performers and tuba, 1962; Shard, solo flute, 1967; Chantier, violin and piano, 1970; The celery flute player, a series of piano pieces, 1972; Piece for 9 instruments, 1973; Pied beauty, 5 performers and tape, 1973; Winter birds, 3 trumpets; Combine, organ; CHORUS: The opossum, text by John Gardner; ELECTRONIC: Wolfslopes, tape.
25 Sacramento St., Cambridge, MA 02138

PATTERSON, FRANKLIN PEALE
b. Philadelphia, Pa., 5 Jan. 1871; d. New Rochelle, N.Y., 6 July 1966. Studied at Univ. of Pennsylvania and in Munich; was an editor for Musical Courier.
WORKS: OPERA: Through the narrow gate; Caprice; Beggar's love; Mountain blood; The forest dwellers; The echo, Portland, Oreg., 9 June 1925, received the David Bispham Memorial Medal and a Nat. Fed. of Music Clubs medal. He was author of the pamphlets: The perfect modernist, 1921; Practical instrumentation, 1923; How to write a good tune, 1924.

PATTISON, LEE
b. Grand Rapids, Wis., 22 July 1890; d. Claremont, Calif., 22 Dec. 1966. Studied piano and composition at New England Cons. and in Berlin; toured in duo piano recitals with Guy Maier. His compositions included Told in the hills, a piano suite, and Florentine sketches, for piano.

PAUL, DORIS A.
b. Upland, Ind., 16 Aug. 1903. Studied at Taylor Univ., B.A., B.M.Ed.; Northwestern Univ.; Univ. of Michigan; with Fred Waring and Olaf Christiansen. She has taught in public schools, at Taylor Univ., Iowa State Teachers Coll., and at Univ. of Denver.
WORKS: CHORUS: Christmas bells; Thou art my lamp; Remember now thy creator; 38 introits and responses.

PAULL, BARBERI P.
b. New York, N.Y., 27 July 1946. Studied composition with Hall Overton and Jacob Druckman, Juilliard School, 1970-71; with Charles Wuorinen, Ludmila Ulehla, Elias Tannenbaum at Manhattan School of Music; with Bruno Maderna at Tanglewood; musical theatre at Lehman Engel's Theatre Workshop, 1973; jazz with Billy Taylor; orchestration with Benjamin Leeds. Her awards include the Delius award, 1975; Segall award, 1975; New York State Council grant, 1976; Rockefeller grant, 1977; ASCAP award, 1978. She was founder and director of the Barberi Paull Theatre, Inc., 1972-75.
WORKS: ORCHESTRA: Requiem, percussion orch., 1974; Song for orchestra, 1977; CHAMBER MUSIC: O wind, mezzo-soprano and string quartet, 1975; Circle of the world, soprano and chamber ensemble; A silent world, Where shall we go, 2 songs for baritone and piano; ELECTRONIC: Interplay, flute, piano, tape; A song of Earth and of the sky, chorus and tape; Antifon, piano and tape, 1975; MULTIMEDIA: Celebration, theatrical concert, 1972; Time, musique concrete ballet, 1971; Earth pulse, choreographic cantata, to be danced; Departure, theatre piece for brass quintet; The mass, tape, percussion, visual projections, 1974; also A Christmas carol, cabaret musical, after Dickens, chorus and instrumental trio, 1976.
15 W. 72nd St., New York, NY 10023

PAULUS, STEPHEN HARRISON
b. Summit, N.J., 24 Aug. 1949. Studied with Paul Fetler and Dominick Argento, Univ. of Minnesota, B.M., M.M. His awards include a Presser scholarship; Minnesota State Arts Board grant; Nat. Endowment for the Arts grant. He was cofounder of the Minnesota Composers Forum in 1943 and has since been the director.
WORKS: OPERA: The village singer, 1 act, St. Louis, 1979; THEATRE: Pact, suite for clarinet, piano, and 2 dancers; CHORUS: 3 Chinese poems; Lift up your hearts; Snow has fallen; North Shore, with 2 soloists and orch.; Canticles: Songs and rituals for Easter and the May, with 2 soloists, organ, and orch.; SONGS: Mad book, Shadow book, songs of Michael Morley, tenor and piano or chamber ensemble.
1012 27th Ave., S.E., Apt. F, Minneapolis, MN 55414

PAXTON, GLENN G., JR.
b. Winnetka, Ill., 7 Dec. 1921. Studied with Max Wald, Chicago Musical Coll.; at Princeton Univ., B.A. He received 2 CBS commissions.
WORKS: BALLET: Postures; ORCHESTRA: The

quiet city; PIANO: <u>4 characteristic pieces</u>;
also stage scores, television scores, and songs.

PAYN, WILLIAM AUSTIN
b. Ashtabula, Ohio, 18 Feb. 1946. Studied organ
at Westminster Choir Coll. and at West Virginia
Univ. He has been church organist from 1968.
His compositions are for English handbells:
<u>Prisms</u>, <u>Genesis</u>, <u>Celebration</u>.
Rt. 8, Box 212, #6, Morgantown, WV 26505

PAYNE, FRANK LYNN
b. Asheville, N.C., 29 Nov. 1936. Studied with
Bruce Benward, Univ. of Arkansas; with Samuel
Adler, Merrill Ellis, William Latham, North
Texas State Univ., M.M. He won an Internat.
Tuba Ensemble composition contest; has received
commissions. He has been faculty member,
Oklahoma City Univ., from 1967.
WORKS: ORCHESTRA: <u>Thymele</u>; WIND ENSEMBLE:
concerto for brass quintet and wind ensemble;
<u>Miniatures</u>, clarinet choir; CHAMBER MUSIC:
<u>Toccata</u> for 3 flutes; quartet for tubas; <u>Images
I and II</u>, oboe and piano; <u>Concert suite</u>, trumpet
and trombone; <u>Toccata</u>, alto saxophone and piano;
tuba sonata; brass quintet; <u>Pavane and ostinato</u>,
flute ensemble; flute sonata; quartet for diverse
instruments; <u>2 contrasts</u>, flute, cello, piano.
2521 N.W. 120th, Oklahoma City, OK 73120

PAYNE, JOHN
b. New York, N.Y., 23 May 1941. Studied at
Brown Univ., B.A. 1962; has played in jazz bands;
specializes in electronic music, theatre events,
audience happenings, etc. He joined with Carol
Law and Charles Amirkhanian in the production of
a live electronic theatre event, <u>Ode to gravity</u>,
San Francisco, 21 Sept. 1968; staged the audience
participation event, <u>Thursday mix</u>, 27 Mar. 1969,
and <u>Friday mix</u>, 2 May 1969, both in San Francisco; also some electronic scores, such as <u>Elevator
music</u> and <u>Toot le fromage</u>.

PAYNE, MAGGI
b. Temple, Tex., 23 Dec. 1945. Studied at
Northwestern Univ., B.M. 1968; with Gordon
Mumma, Ben Johnston, and Salvatore Martirano,
Univ. of Illinois, M.M. 1970; with Robert Ashley,
Mills Coll., M.F.A. 1972. She held fellowships
at Univ. of Illinois, 1969-70, and Mills Coll.,
1970-72; received the Mills Crothers award,
1972. She was faculty member, Mills Coll.,
1972-74; from 1972, has been recording engineer
and synthesizer teacher at Mills.
WORKS: CHAMBER MUSIC: <u>Ametropia</u>, solo
flute; MULTIMEDIA: <u>Orion</u>, electronically
generated film and sound track, 1973; <u>Hum</u>, tape
and live flutist, 1973; <u>Allusions</u>, dancers,
special lighting, video-processed film, tape,
1974; <u>Farewell</u>, tape and scenic desert slides,
1975; <u>Transparencies</u>, tape and slides, 1976;
<u>Spheres</u>, tape and slide, 1977; <u>Spirals</u>, tape
and slides, 1977.
Box 9991, Mills College, Oakland, CA 94613

PAYNE, WILLIAM McGUIRE
b. Winchester, Va., 3 Oct. 1943. Studied with
Robert Barrow and Paul Turok, Williams Coll.,

1962-65; David Simon, New York, 1965-66; with
Chou Wen-chung, Jack Beeson, and Harvey
Sollberger, Columbia Univ., 1966-68. He was
awarded the Hutchison fellowship at Williams
Coll.
WORKS: BALLET: <u>Alice in Wonderland</u>, flute,
clarinet, piano, 1964; <u>Process</u>, musique concrete,
1967; ORCHESTRA: <u>Velocities</u>, 1969; BAND: <u>En-
tities</u>, 1970; CHAMBER MUSIC: 2 songs on poems
of Robert Lowell, 1967; <u>Eleuthera</u>, string octet,
3 woodwinds, 1968; <u>Counting piece</u>, oboe, cello,
piano, 1969; <u>Counting piece #2</u>, saxophone and
piano trio, 1970; PIANO: <u>Prelude and inventions</u>,
1965; <u>Theme and variations</u>, 1965; <u>Night Ruppert</u>,
1966; <u>3 movements</u>, 1967.

PEASLEE, RICHARD C.
b. New York, N.Y., 11 June 1930. Studied at
Yale Univ., B.A.; with Vincent Persichetti,
Vittorio Giannini, Bernard Wagenaar, and Henry
Brant, Juilliard School, M.S.; privately with
William Russo; and with Nadia Boulanger in
Paris. He was awarded Phi Beta Kappa at Yale;
Mme. Freschl Song award at Juilliard. He is a
free-lance composer.
WORKS: THEATRE: music for <u>Marat Sade</u>;
<u>Midsummer night's dream</u>; <u>Oedipus</u>; <u>Boccaccio</u>, a
musical; <u>Songs of love and war</u>, musical; <u>The
serpent</u>; <u>Terminal</u>; <u>Indians</u>; ORCHESTRA: <u>October
piece</u>, rock group and symphony; WIND ENSEMBLE:
<u>The devil's head</u>, tuba, 4 horns, percussion,
1974; <u>Divertimento</u>, brass and percussion; JAZZ:
<u>Stonehenge</u>; <u>Chicago concerto</u>; FILM SCORES: <u>Marat
Sade</u>; <u>Tell me lies</u>; <u>Where time is a river</u>.
90 Riverside Dr., New York, NY 10024

PECK, RUSSELL
b. Detroit, Mich., 25 Jan. 1945. Studied at
Eastman School of Music, 1962-63; with Leslie
Bassett and Ross Lee Finney, Univ. of Michigan,
B.M. with high distinction 1966, M.M. 1967,
D.M.A. 1972. He held fellowships for all study,
1962-71, including at Tanglewood and Bennington
Conf.; received Nat. Fed. of Music Clubs award,
1960; BMI student awards, 1965, 1967, 1969;
Koussevitzky award, 1965; Composers' Forum M.Y.
concert, 1969; Gaudeamus prize, Netherlands,
1971; many commissions. He has been composer,
pianist, actor, filmmaker with the multimedia
groups ONCE, The Great Society, PORK, Contemporary Directions Ensemble; was Ford Found.
composer-in-residence, public schools, Merrick,
N.Y., 1967-69; with Indianapolis Symph. Orch.
and City of Indianapolis, 1971-73; on faculty,
Northern Illinois Univ., 1976-78.
WORKS: ORCHESTRA: <u>Song of mankind</u>, with
choirs, for Indianapolis sesquicentennial, 1971;
<u>The emperor's new concerto</u>, 1972; <u>Who killed
Cock Robin?</u>, 1973; BAND: <u>American epic</u>, 1972;
CHAMBER MUSIC: <u>Automobile</u>, soprano, flute,
percussion, double bass, 1965; <u>1 db</u>, double
bass, 1969; <u>Lion's breath</u>, percussion, Los
Angeles, 10 Dec. 1973; <u>Time being</u>, 3 violins;
<u>Suspended sentence</u>, piano; <u>Lift-off</u>, percussion,
1978; <u>In the garden</u>, organ and percussion, 1978;
CHORUS: <u>Electric chairman</u>, with tape.
1700 Ardsley St., Winston-Salem, NC 27103

PEEK, RICHARD MAURICE

PEEK, RICHARD MAURICE
b. Mason, Mich., 17 May 1927. Studied with
H. Owen Reed, Michigan State Univ.; with Harold
W. Friedell and Normand Lockwood, Union Theological Seminary. He was named 1975 composer of
the year by N. Carolina Fed. of Music Clubs.
From 1952 he has been minister of music, Covenant
Presbyterian Church, Charlotte, N.C.
    WORKS: CHORUS: Stations on the road to
freedom, cantata; St. Stephen, cantata; Now glad
of heart be everyone; ORGAN: church sonata;
Pastorale and noel, with flute; chaconne on Ye
sons and daughters, with brass and percussion;
and more than 100 published works for chorus and
organ.
    1621 Biltmore Dr., Charlotte, NC   28207

PEERY, ROB ROY
b. Saga, Japan, 6 Jan. 1900, of American parents;
d. Dayton, Ohio, 18 Sept. 1973. Studied at Midland Coll., B.A. 1920; at Oberlin Cons., B.M.
1925; privately with Rubin Goldmark, 1928-29;
at Union Theological Seminary, 1928-29. He received awards from Etude magazine, 1923; Ohio
State, 1925; Homiletic Review, 1926; Dartmouth
prize, 1930; Franklin prize, 1938; 2 honorary
doctorates. He was violinist, Omaha Symph.,
1920-21; organist, 1923-65; on faculty, Lenoir-
Rhyne Coll., 1922-23; Catawba Coll., 1926-28; on
staff, Theodore Presser Co., 1932-49; editor,
Lorenz Pub. Co., 1950-65.
    WORKS: CHORUS: America, my wondrous land;
God shall wipe away all tears; Slumber on; The
Lord is my shepherd; This is my song; A star in
the sky; The wondrous star; and many more works
for chorus, organ, violin, orchestra. He was
also author of several musical text books.

PELES, STEPHEN
b. Long Branch, N.J., 10 Oct. 1950. Studied at
Rutgers Univ., B.A.; with Hale Smith and Charles
Whittenberg, Univ. of Connecticut, M.A. 1977;
and with Charles Wuorinen. He held fellowships
at MacDowell Colony, 1977, Virginia Center for
the Creative Arts, 1978, Composers' Conf., 1976,
1978; won the East and West Artists prize, 1978.
From 1977 he has been on the faculty, Hartford
Cons.
    WORKS: ORCHESTRA: Variations for orchestra,
1977; BAND: Variations, winds, brass, percussion, 1977; CHAMBER MUSIC: Felix natalis, solo
alto flute; 3 brief exchanges, cello and harpsichord, 1976; 3 Whitman songs, soprano and piano,
1977; In medias res, violin and piano, 1977;
duo for clarinet and piano, 1978; 2 movements,
horn and piano, 1978; Impromptu, oboe and piano,
1978.
    45 Dean St., Hartford, CT   06114

PELLEGRINI, ERNESTO F.
b. Flushing, N.Y., 23 Nov. 1932. Studied with
Vittorio Giannini, Vincent Persichetti, and
Peter Mennin at Juilliard School, B.S. 1957,
M.S. 1961; with Philip Bezanson and Richard
Hervig, Univ. of Iowa, Ph.D. 1971. He received
second prize in a Sosland contest for a string
quartet, 1961; IBM graduate fellowship, 1968;
first prize, Arizona Cello Society/American
Society of Univ. Composers contest, 1976. He

was faculty member, Knoxville Coll., 1962-68,
1969-71; Univ. of Iowa, 1968-69; from 1971, at
Ball State Univ.
    WORKS: ORCHESTRA: 7 statements in 3/4
time, 1963; CHAMBER MUSIC: string quartet,
1961; Piano variations, 1968; Fantasia per
organo, 1971; Music for 16 instruments and percussion, 1971; Movement II, solo double bass,
1972; Divertimento a sette, 1973; Movement III,
piano, 1975; Divertimento a tre, 1975; Duolog,
alto saxophone and piano, 1976; The search,
voice, percussion, viola, keyboard, 1977;
CHORUS: Spring, with instruments, 1969.
    603 Alden Rd., Muncie, IN 47304

PELLEGRINO, RONALD
b. Kenosha, Wis., 11 May 1940. Studied with
James Ming, Lawrence Univ., B.M. 1962; with
Rudolph Kolisch, Robert Crane, and Hilmar
Luckhardt, Univ. of Wisconsin, M.M. 1965, Ph.D.
1968; also studied privately on piano, guitar,
cello, trumpet, and percussion. His awards include the Ullas fellowship, Univ. of Wisconsin;
Nat. Endowment for the Humanities grant for the
book, Thinking for the electronic music synthesizer, 1973; research grants, Oberlin Cons.,
1971, 1972. He was faculty member, Ohio State
Univ., 1968-70; Oberlin Cons., 1970-73; from
1978, at Texas Tech. Univ.
    WORKS: ELECTRONIC: Markings, stereo tape,
soprano, and timpani, commissioned by Dena
Madole, choreographer, 1969; S and H explorations,
clarinet and synthesizer, 1972; FILM SCORES:
This is Milwaukee, NET documentary, 1968; Too,
film and tape, 1971; Paths, 1972; Figured, film
and tape, 1973; Cries, film and tape, 1973.
    Box 4239, Music, Texas Tech. Univ., Lubbock,
TX 79409

PELLMAN, SAMUEL FRANK
b. Sidney, Ohio, 16 Sept. 1953. Studied with
David Cope, Miami Univ.; with Karel Husa and
Robert Palmer, Cornell Univ. He won second
prize in a 1978 American Society of Univ. Com-
posers student contest. He was visiting artist,
Hartwick Coll., 1977-78.
    WORKS: ORCHESTRA: Sunscape; Horizon;
CHAMBER MUSIC: Silent night, prepared piano;
Trump-it, solo trumpet; Dynamic study, piano
and tape; Pentacle, alto saxophone and tape.
    327 Coddington Rd., Ithaca, NY 14850

PELOQUIN, C. ALEXANDER
b. 1918.
    WORKS: CHORUS: Songs of Israel, psalms for
the liturgical year; Shout for joy; The bells,
Poe text, with 2 pianos, 2 contrabasses, percussion; Missa a la samba; Christ, the light of
the nations; Song of Daniel, 1965; Mass for joy,
1966; Festival mass, 1966; Glory to God in the
highest; May the Lord bless you, 1968; Love is
everlasting, 1969; Gloria of the bells; also 21
psalm settings, 12 masses, numerous liturgical
works.
    Music Dept., Boston College, Newton, MA
02167

PELOSI, LOUIS
b. New Haven, Conn., 23 Apr. 1947. Studied at
Univ. of Notre Dame, B.A. 1969; with Arnold
Franchetti, Hartt Coll. of Music, B.M. 1977;
with Charles Wuorinen, Manhattan School of Music,
M.M. 1978; at Tanglewood on a fellowship, 1980.
WORKS: CHAMBER MUSIC: A cummings pastorale,
women's voices, piano, trumpet, cello, 1978;
Maxwell's demon, 2 pianos, 1979; Passage, voice,
vibraphone, 2 clarinets, 1979; Arabesque, 2
guitars, 1979-80.
2785 Broadway, #G-3, New York, NY 10025

PELZ, WALTER L.
b. Chicago, Ill., 30 Dec. 1926. Studied with
Paul Fetler and Dominick Argento, Univ. of
Minnesota, Ph.D. His awards include choirmaster
certificate, American Guild of Organists, 1960;
many commissions. He taught in public schools,
1948-62; was minister of music, Christ Church
Lutheran, Minneapolis, 1962-67; from 1969,
faculty member and composer-in-residence,
Bethany Coll.
WORKS: CHAMBER MUSIC: violin sonata;
string quartet; trio for flute, cello, piano;
suite for viola, cello, piano; CHORUS: Who shall
abide, with flute, guitar; Show me the way, with
oboe, guitar, 1968; A day of rejoicing, 1969;
Genesis to a beat, cantata for 4 choirs, orch.,
tape recorder, and audience, Lindsborg, Kans.,
21 Nov. 1970; A feast of joy, with instruments
and organ.
211 Normal St., Lindsborg, KS 67456

PENGILLY, SYLVIA
b. London, England, 23 Mar. 1935; to U.S. 1957.
Studied with James Waters, Kent State Univ.;
with Paul Palombo, Coll.-Cons., Univ. of Cincinnati, M.M. She was on the faculty, Kent
State Univ., 1971-73; from 1976, Western Illinois
Univ.
WORKS: CHAMBER MUSIC: The windhaven,
voice and piano; quartet for violin, viola,
cello, double bass; 3 songs of Emily Dickinson,
voice and piano; Degrees of entropy, wind ensemble; ELECTRONIC: Canon for 40 voices, tape;
3 moments of agony, flute, bass clarinet, tape,
Chicago, 10 Nov. 1979.
Western Illinois University, Macomb, IL
61455

PENINGER, JAMES DAVID
b. Orangeburg, S.C., 27 Dec. 1929. Studied at
Coll. of Charleston, B.S. 1951; with Gilbert
Carp and Roger McDuffie, Converse Coll., B.M.
1957, M.M. 1959. He has received ASCAP awards.
He has been public school choral director and
minister of music in Spartanburg churches from
1958. His compositions include nearly 200 published choral works for adult choirs and youth
and children's groups.
829 Thackston Dr., Spartanburg, SC 29302

PENN, ARTHUR A.
b. London, England, 13 Feb. 1875; to U.S. 1903;
d. New London, Conn., 6 Feb. 1941. He wrote
comic operas, musicals, and such popular songs
as Smilin' through; The magic of your eyes;
Carissima; The lamplit hour; Sunrise and you;
et al.

PENN, WILLIAM ALBERT
b. Long Branch, N.J., 11 Jan. 1943. Studied
with Robert Mols, Henri Pousseur, Mauricio
Kagel, Allen Sapp, State Univ. of New York at
Buffalo, B.F.A. 1964, M.A. 1967; with H. Owen
Reed, Michigan State Univ., Ph.D. 1971; with
Wayne Barlow and Rayburn Wright, Eastman School
of Music. His awards include 2 SUNY awards,
1963, 1966; 2 Michigan State Univ. awards, 1968,
1970; annual ASCAP awards from 1970; Nat. Endowment for the Arts grants, 1974, 1975, 1976;
Creative Arts Public Service grant, 1976; Stewart
Ostrow Found. theatre grant, 1976. He was
faculty member, Eastman School of Music, 1971-
78; composer-in-residence, Michigan State Univ.,
1969-72; staff composer, N.Y. Shakespeare Festival, 1974-76; Folger Shakespeare Theatre,
Washington, D.C., and Sounds Reasonable Recording Studios, from 1975.
WORKS: THEATRE (musicals): The pied piper
of Hamlin, 1969; At last Olympus!, 1969; The boy
who cried "Wolf" is dead, 1971; The canticle,
1972; incidental music for many plays; ORCHESTRA:
Spectrums, confusions, and sometime--moments
beyond the order of destiny, 1969; symphony,
1971; BAND: Ultra mensuram, 3 brass quintets,
1971; Designs, winds, jazz quintet, and percussion, 1972; Niagara, 1678, 1973; Inner loop,
stage band, 1973; CHAMBER MUSIC: Invocation and
pavanne, solo violin, 1967; string quartet,
1968; Untitled composition #1, any instruments,
1970; 4 portraits, cello solo, 1970; Guernica,
violin solo, 1970; Chamber music I, violin and
piano, 1971; Chamber music II, cello and piano;
1972; And among the leaves we were passing, Moog
synthesizer, 1972; 3 essays, tuba, 1973; Fantasy,
harpsichord; 4 preludes, for marimba; Night
music, flute choir, 1973; Miroirs sur le Rubaiyat,
piano and narrator, Rochester, N.Y., 3 Nov. 1974;
also several multimedia works, some songs, and
pieces called Freak music.

PENNARIO, LEONARD
b. Buffalo, N.Y., 9 July 1924. Studied piano
with Guy Maier and Isabelle Vengerova; composition with Ernst Toch and Lucien Cailliet; made
his debut as piano soloist with Dallas Symphony,
1936; has been soloist with all major U.S.
orchestras and has given recitals throughout the
U.S. and Europe.
WORKS: PIANO: piano concerto; Midnight on
the Newport Cliffs; March of the lunatics; Variations on the Kerry dance; also transcriptions
for piano.
c/o Columbia Artists Management, Inc.,
165 W. 57 St., New York, NY 10019

PENNINGTON, JOHN ALAN
b. Galesburg, Ill., 12 Jan. 1939. Studied at
Cincinnati Coll.-Cons., M.M.; at Ohio State
Univ., Ph.D. He has been faculty member at
Wilberforce Univ., 1967-69; St. Louis Inst. of
Music, Ph.D. 1971-72; and from 1976, part time
at Knox Coll.
WORKS: BAND: Apollo, aleatoric piece,

PERERA, RONALD C.

1971; Sine, aleatoric piece, 1975; Lines and spaces, aleatoric piece for 20 woodwinds, 1975; CHAMBER MUSIC: Rondo, clarinet and piano, 1975; Blackstrap, jazz ensemble, 1976; suite for chamber orchestra, 1978.
P.O. Box 7, Oneida, IL 61467

PERERA, RONALD C.
b. Boston, Mass., 25 Dec. 1941. Studied with Leon Kirchner and Randall Thompson, Harvard Univ., B.A. 1963, M.A. 1967; electronic music with Gottfried Koenig, Utrecht Univ., 1967-68. His awards include 3 Francis Boott prizes, 1961, 1962, 1966; John Knowles Paine traveling fellowship, 1967-68; Paderewski Fund award, 1972; ASCAP award, 1972; Nat. Endowment for the Arts grant, 1976; MacDowell fellowship, 1978; Massachusetts Arts and Humanities Found. grant, 1978. He was faculty member, Syracuse Univ., 1968-70; Dartmouth Coll., 1970-71; from 1971, at Smith Coll.
WORKS: ORCHESTRA: Chanteys, 1976; CHORUS: The garden hymn; The Lord's prayer; Did you hear the angels sing?; mass, with orch.; 3 night pieces, women's voices, piano, cello, percussion; SONGS: Apollo circling, high voice and piano; 3 poems of Gunter Grass, mezzo-soprano and chamber ensemble, 1974; PIANO: a suite; ELECTRONIC: Evolutions; Alternate routes; Improvisation for loudspeakers; Dove sta amore, soprano and tape; Reverberations, organ and tape, 1970; Reflex, viola and tape, 1973.
114 Wharf Lane, Yarmouth Port, MA 02675

PERKINS, JOHN MacIVOR
b. St. Louis, Mo., 2 Aug. 1935. Studied at Harvard Univ., B.A. magna cum laude 1958; New England Cons., with high honors 1958; with Arthur Berger, Harold Shapero, and Irving Fine, Brandeis Univ., M.F.A. 1962; with Nadia Boulanger in Paris; and with Roberto Gerhard and Edmund Rubbra in London. He held a Sheldon fellowship, 1958-59; Woodrow Wilson fellowship, 1959-61. He taught at Univ. of Chicago, 1962-64; Harvard Univ., 1965-70; from 1971, at Washington Univ.
WORKS: OPERA: Divertimento, chamber opera, 1958; ORCHESTRA: Fantasy, intermezzo and variations, 1961; Music for orchestra, 1964; CHAMBER MUSIC: Canons for 9 instruments, 1957; 3 miniatures, string quartet, 1960; Variations, flute, clarinet, trumpet, piano, percussion, 1962; Caprice, piano, 1963; Music for 13 players, 1964; Music for brass, 1965; VOICE: 3 studies, chorus, 1958; 8 songs, 1956-62.
14 Kingsbury Place, St. Louis, MO 63155

PERKINS, WILLIAM
b. Dallas, Tex., 28 Apr. 1941. Studied with Cecil Effinger, Univ. of Colorado, B.A. 1971; at the New England Cons., M.M. 1974.
WORKS: CHAMBER MUSIC: Twilight music, musical saw and percussion, 1971; Chamber symphony, 1971; Contrasts, woodwind trio and percussion, 1972; 2 preludes, vibraphone and electric guitar, 1973; string quartet, 1974.

PERKINSON, COLERIDGE-TAYLOR
b. New York, N.Y., 1932. Studied at Manhattan

School of Music, B.A. 1953, M.M. 1954; at Tanglewood; at the Salzburg Mozarteum; and at Netherlands Radio Union in Hilversum. His awards include a commission from the Ford Found. and a New York State Council on the Arts grant, 1974. He has taught at Manhattan School and Brooklyn Coll.; was music director, Professional Children's School, 1952-64; has conducted the Dessoff Choir, and Symphony of the New World.
WORKS: BALLET: Ode to Otis; THEATRE: music for Song of the Lusitanian bogey; God is a guess what?; Man better man; ORCHESTRA: viola concerto; sinfonietta #1, New York premiere, 8 Apr. 1973, composer conducting; Grass, piano, strings, percussion; Commentary, with solo cello; Dunbar, with solo voice and chorus; CHAMBER MUSIC: Blues form, solo violin, 1972; Lamentations, suite for cello; Statements, piano sonata #2; Scherzo, piano; Toccata, piano; Attitudes, aria for tenor; CHORUS: Freedom, with 2 pianos, electronic bass, percussion; FILM SCORES: The McMasters, 1970; Together for days, 1972.
755 West End Ave., New York, NY 10025

PERL, LOTHAR
b. Breslau, Germany, 1 Dec. 1910; d. New York, N.Y., 27 Apr. 1975. Studied in Germany. He was pianist and accompanist; taught at Los Angeles City Coll. and Adelphi Coll.; composed and conducted for films and television.
WORKS: PIANO: Dance suite; 4 American variations on a theme by Paganini.

PERLE, GEORGE
b. Bayonne, N.J., 6 May 1915. Studied with Wesley La Violette at DePaul Univ.; privately with Ernst Krenek. His awards include 2 Guggenheim fellowships, 1966, 1974; Nat. Inst. of Arts and Letters award, 1977; membership in American Acad. and Inst. of Arts and Letters, 1978; many commissions. He has been faculty member, Univ. of Louisville, 1949-57; Univ. of California at Davis, 1957-61; from 1961, at City Univ. of New York and Queens Coll. of CUNY; visiting professor, Yale Univ., 1965-66; Univ. of Southern California, summer, 1965; Tanglewood, 1967; State Univ. of New York at Buffalo, 1971-72.
WORKS: ORCHESTRA: Rhapsody, 1954; 3 movements for orchestra, 1960; 6 bagatelles, 1965; Songs of praise and lamentation, with chorus, dedicated to the memory of Noah Greenberg, New York, 19 Feb. 1975; A short symphony, Tanglewood, 16 Aug. 1980; BAND: Solemn procession, 1947; CHAMBER MUSIC: sonata for viola solo, 1942; 3 sonatas for clarinet solo, 1943; Hebrew melodies, solo cello, 1945; string quintet, 1958; 3 wind quintets, 1959, 1960, 1967; 7 string quartets, 1960-73; Monody I, solo flute, 1960; Monody II, solo double bass, 1962; Serenade I, viola and chamber orch., 1962; 3 inventions, bassoon, 1962; Solo partita, violin and viola, 1965; Serenade II, chamber ensemble, 1968; Sonata quasi una fantasia, clarinet and piano, 1972; PIANO: Little suite, 1939; 6 preludes, 1946; 2 sonatas, 1950, 1964; Toccata, 1969; 6 studies, 1976. He is author of many articles and books on music including Serial composition and aton-

ality, 4th ed., rev., and Twelve-tone tonality, both Univ. of California Press, Berkeley, 1977.
    333 Central Park W., New York, NY 10025

PERLEA, JONEL
    b. Ograda, Rumania, 13 Dec. 1900; U.S. citizen 1960; d. New York, N.Y., 29 July 1970. Studied piano and composition in Munich, conducting in Leipzig. He conducted in Leipzig, Rostock, then Bucharest, 1929-44, opera in Rome, 1945-47; made American debut at the Metropolitan Opera, New York, 1949. He conducted the San Francisco Opera and the Lyric Opera of Chicago; taught conducting at Manhattan School of Music from 1952, and conducted the Connecticut Symphony Orch., 1955-70.
    WORKS: ORCHESTRA: 2 sketches, 1919; Symphonic variations, 1930; Don Quixote, symphonic poem, 1946; Symphony concertante, viola and orch., 1968; 3 studies for orchestra, 1969; and some chamber music.

PERLONGO, DANIEL JAMES
    b. Gaastra, Mich., 23 Sept. 1942. Studied with George Balch Wilson, Leslie Bassett, and Ross Lee Finney, Univ. of Michigan, B.M. 1964, M.M. 1966; with Goffredo Petrassi, St. Cecilia Acad., Rome, 1966-68. His awards include the Joseph Bearns prize, 1966; Fulbright grant, 1966; Italian government grant, 1967; Premio D'Atri, St. Cecilia Acad., 1968; Rome prize, 1970, 1971; American Acad. and Inst. of Arts and Letters award, 1975. He has been faculty member, Indiana Univ. of Pennsylvania, from 1968.
    WORKS: 7 pieces for orchestra, 1965; Myriad, 1968; Ephemeron, 1972; Variations, small orch., 1973; Voyage, chamber orch., 1975; numerous works for chamber groups, including Ricerar, wind trio, 1976, Pittsburgh, 5 Mar. 1978.
    R.D. 1, Box 134B, Marion Center, PA 15759

PERRIN, PETER
    b. Utica, N.Y., 21 June 1934. Studied with Henry Cowell at Columbia Univ.; with Darius Milhaud at Aspen School; privately with Roger Sessions. He won the first East and West Artists composition contest, 1975; was cofounder and codirector, Performers' Committee for 20th-Century Music, 1966-69; was founder and has been director from 1977, the Alliance for American Song.
    WORKS: ORCHESTRA: concerto for brass quintet and orch.; CHAMBER MUSIC: 3 on 1 rhythm, soprano and 5 instruments, 1973; Game #3, 3 trumpets, 1975; 6 Mediterranean places, soprano, clarinet, and piano, 1975; The composer (Stefan Wolpe, 1902-72), 6 voices and piano, 1975; Andover diptych, solo cello, 1976; The flight into Egypt, 6 solo voices, 1979; CHORUS: The 6-minute year, Emily Dickinson text.
    224 E. 10th St., New York, NY 10003

PERRY, JULIA
    b. Akron, Ohio, 25 Mar. 1924; d. Akron, 24 Apr. 1979. Studied at Westminster Choir Coll., M.M.; Juilliard School; at Tanglewood; with Nadia Boulanger in Paris; and with Luigi Dallapiccola in Florence. Her awards include 2 Guggenheim

fellowships; Boulanger Grand Prize; Nat. Inst. of Arts and Letters award, 1964; ASCAP award, 1969. She organized and conducted a concert tour in Europe under the sponsorship of the U.S. Information Service.
    WORKS: ORCHESTRA: Stabat mater, voice and string orch., 1951; Short piece for orchestra, 1952; violin concerto; CHAMBER MUSIC: Homunculus, C. F., percussion ensemble, 1960; Pastorale, string quartet and flute.

PERRY, ZENOBIA POWELL
    b. Okfuskgee County, Okla., 3 Oct. 1914. Studied privately with Cortez Reece; at Northern Colorado Univ.; with Alan Willman and Darius Milhaud, Univ. of Wyoming; further study with Milhaud under a Univ. of Wyoming study grant. She was faculty member, Arkansas Agricultural, Mechanical and Normal Coll., 1946-55; from 1955, on faculty and composer-in-residence, Central State Univ.
    WORKS: ORCHESTRA: Ships that pass in the night, 1953; BAND: Prelude and dance, 1968; CHAMBER MUSIC: piano sonatina, 1962; clarinet sonatina, 1963; string quartet #2, 1964; Atmospheres, song cycle for soprano and piano, 1972; 4 mynyms for 3 players, flute, clarinet, piano, 1973; CHORUS: suite on poems of Thomas Hardy; Mass in F-sharp, with soprano and baritone soli, 1969.
    1267 E. Turner Place, Wilberforce, OH 45384

PERSI, EDWARD F.
    b. Monongaheia, Pa., 12 Feb. 1951. Studied with Donal Michalsky, Roger Vaughan, Lloyd Rogers, Nicolas Slonimsky, California State Univ. at Fullerton; with Robert Hughes at Mills Coll. At CSU he received the Music Associates Award of Excellence, 1974. He has taught briefly at CSU and at Long Beach City Coll.
    WORKS: ORCHESTRA: Crucifixus, with chorus and baritone solo; chamber symphony; Prelude d'Angiebert, string chamber orch.; CHAMBER MUSIC: 2 piano pieces; Song, soprano and 6 players; Actaeon, trombone and percussion; Flute 2, flute and piano; Ring Rnd Rossi, 7 players; V are not rare, 6 players and tape.
    2630 Milton, #3, Fullerton, CA 92631

PERSICHETTI, VINCENT
    b. Philadelphia, Pa., 6 June 1915. Studied with Russell King Miller, Combs Coll., B.M. 1935; conducting with Fritz Reiner, Curtis Inst.; piano with Olga Samaroff, Philadelphia Cons., M.M., D.M. His many awards include, in part, 3 Guggenheim fellowships; Nat. Inst. of Arts and Letters grant; Nat. Found. on the Arts and Humanities grant; Symphony League award; 3 honorary doctorates; Brandeis Creative Arts award, 1975; numerous commissions. He was chairman, composition dept., Combs Coll., 1938-40; Philadelphia Cons., 1941-61; and from 1947, on faculty at the Juilliard School.
    WORKS: ORCHESTRA: piano concertino, 1951; 9 symphonies, 1942-73; Dance overture, 1942; Fables, with narrator, 1943; The hollow man, trumpet and string orch., 1944; Serenade #5, 1950; Fairy tale, 1950; piano concerto, 1962;

PERSKY, STANLEY L.

Stabat mater, with chorus, 1963; Introit for
strings, 1964; The Pleiades, chorus, trumpet,
string orch., 1967; The creation, with soli and
chorus, 1969; Sinfonia Janiculum, 1970; Night
dances, 1970; A Lincoln address, with narrator,
1972; concerto for English horn and string orch.,
New York Philharmonic, 17 Nov. 1977 (won first
prize in the Friedheim Award Competition,
Washington, D.C., 1978); BAND: Divertimento,
1950; Psalm, 1952; Pageant, 1953; symphony for
band, 1956 (symphony #6); Serenade for band,
1960; Bagatelles for band, 1961; Chorale prelude: So pure the star, 1962; Masquerade, 1965;
Chorale prelude: Turn not thy face, 1966; O
cool is the valley, 1971; Parable IX, 1972;
CHAMBER MUSIC: Serenade #1, 10 winds, 1929; 4
string quartets, 1939, 1940, 1959, 1972; suite
for violin and cello, 1940; solo violin sonata,
1940; Concertato, piano and string quartet,
1940; Fantasy, violin and piano, 1941; Serenade
#3, piano trio, 1941; Pastoral, woodwind quintet,
1943; Vocalise, cello and piano, 1945; Serenade
#4, violin and piano, 1945; King Lear, septet
for woodwind quintet, timpani, piano, 1948;
Serenade #6, trombone, viola, cello, 1950; harpsichord sonata, 1951; solo cello sonata, 1952;
piano quintet, 1954; Little recorder book, 1956;
Serenade #9, soprano and alto recorders, 1956;
Serenade #10, flute and harp, 1957; Infanta
Marina, viola and piano, 1960; Serenade #12,
solo tuba, 1961; Serenade #13, 2 clarinets,
1963; Masques, violin and piano, 1965; Parables
I-XIX, chiefly for various solo instruments,
1965-75; Do not go gentle, organ, pedals alone,
Boston, 18 Nov. 1974; Auden variations, organ,
1977, Hartford, Conn., 14 July 1978; many choral
works.
Hill House, Wise Mill Rd., Philadelphia, PA
19128

PERSKY, STANLEY L.
b. New York, N.Y., 28 May 1941. Studied with
Mark Brunswick and Paul Turok, City Coll. of
CUNY; with Mel Powell and Gunther Schuller, Yale
Univ.; with Milton Babbitt, Earl Kim, and Peter
Westergaard, Princeton Univ. He has been
faculty member, City Coll. of CUNY, from 1965.
WORKS: CHAMBER MUSIC: sextet, 3 woodwinds
and string trio, 1965; On walls, soprano and
chamber ensemble, 1966; Composition from a
graphic design, 11 instruments, 1967; Symbiosyn-
thesis, chamber ensemble and tape, 1972.
11 Vassar Place, Scarsdale, NY 10583

PETERS, WILLIAM FREDERICK
b. Sandusky, Ohio, 9 Aug. 1876; d. Englewood,
N.J., 1 Dec. 1938. Studied at the Leipzig
Cons.; was theatre violinist, concert violinist;
music director of Maude Adams productions.
WORKS: OPERA: The purple road; Iole,
operetta; FILM SCORES: Way down east; Orphans
of the storm; When knighthood was in flower;
Little old New York.

PETERSEN, MARIAN F.
b. Salt Lake City, Utah, 4 July 1926. Studied
with Leroy Robertson, Univ. of Utah, Ph.D. She
has been faculty member, Univ. of Missouri,

from 1966.
WORKS: OPERA: The wife of Usher's well, a
mini-opera; CHORUS: The revelation, cantata.
L 12 Route #1, Lake Lotawana, MO 64063

PETERSON, HAROLD
b. Oak Park, Ill., 23 June 1948. Studied with
Lou Harrison, San Jose State Univ.; with Gyorgy
Ligeti and Leland Smith, Stanford Univ. He was
on the faculty, Hartnell Coll., 1974-76; De Anza
Coll., 1975; Stanford Univ., 1976-78.
WORKS: ORCHESTRA: symphony with synthesizer, Monterey, Jan. 1978; BAND: motet;
CHAMBER MUSIC: 4 geometries, woodwind quintet,
1977; horn sonatina; Prolog: Reflections, jazz
sextet; CHORUS: Kyrie eleison, with instruments,
1975; Passing by, jazz choir and stage band.
413 Rutland, San Jose, CA 95128

PETERSON, MELODY
b. Oak Park, Ill., 5 Feb. 1942. Studied with
Richard Hoffmann and Walter Aschaffenburg,
Oberlin Coll. She won first prize, North
Carolina Fed. of Music Clubs contest, 1967. She
was a private teacher, 1965-69; instructor,
Oberlin Coll. Cons., 1968-69; from 1970, music
journalist for the Los Angeles Times.
WORKS: CHAMBER MUSIC: Twice 5 for 2,
violin and cello, 1967; Monuments, baritone
voice; KEYBOARD: Variations on an original
theme, 2 pianos, 1958; Prelude and toccata,
piano, 1963; Prelude and postlude, organ, 1967.

PETERSON, WAYNE
b. 1927. Studied with Paul Fetler and Earl
George, Univ. of Minnesota; with Lennox Berkeley
and Howard Ferguson, Royal Acad. of Music;
London. His awards include a Fulbright grant
for study in London; Nat. Endowment for the
Arts grant, 1975; and commissions. He is professor, San Francisco State Univ.
WORKS: ORCHESTRA: Exaltation, dithyramb,
and caprice; Free variations; CHAMBER MUSIC:
Metamorphoses, string quartet, 1967; Phantasmagoria, flute, clarinet, contrabass, 1969;
Capriccio, flute and piano, 1973; Music of the
Vineyards, string quartet, 1974; Diatribe,
violin and piano, 1975; Rhapsody, cello and
piano, 1976; Encounters, mixed ensemble, San
Francisco, 7 Oct. 1976; Interrupted serenade,
flute, harp, cello, 1978; CHORUS: Earth, sweet
earth; Who is so dark of heart, e. e. cummings
text.
810 Gonzales St., #11-A, San Francisco, CA
94132

PETHEL, JAMES LEROY
b. Gainesville, Ga., 24 Dec. 1936. Studied at
Carson-Newman Coll.; with Philip Slates, George
Peabody Coll.; and at North Texas State Univ.
He received a Defense Education Act grant. He
has been faculty member, Carson-Newman Coll.,
from 1962; organist in Morristown, Tenn., from
1966.
WORKS: CHAMBER MUSIC: piano sonata;
string quartet; CHORUS: I hear America singing,
male voices and brass; many anthems, vocal solos,
and organ pieces.
Rte. 2, Jefferson City, TN 37760

PETHEL, STANLEY
b. Gainesville, Ga., 3 Feb. 1950. Studied with John Corina, Univ. of Georgia; with Gilbert Trythall, George Peabody Coll. He has received awards from Georgia Composers, 1972; Nat. Fed. of Music Clubs, 1975; Georgia Music Educators, 1978. From 1977 he has been faculty member at Berry Coll.
WORKS: CHAMBER MUSIC: trombone sonata; BAND: 3 overtures; CHORUS: Give me liberty, oratorio; and anthems; electronic works.
Music Dept., Berry College, Mt. Berry, GA 30149

PEYTON, MALCOLM C.
b. New York, N.Y., 12 Jan. 1932. Studied with Roger Sessions, Edward T. Cone, and Milton Babbitt, Princeton Univ., B.A. 1954, M.F.A. 1956; with Irving Fine and Aaron Copland at Tanglewood, 1953, 1957. His awards include the Woodrow Wilson fellowship, 1955; Fulbright fellowship, 1956; Nat. Endowment for the Arts grant, 1978. He was faculty member, Princeton Univ., 1960-61; from 1965, at New England Cons.
WORKS: ORCHESTRA: The Blessed Virgin compared to the air we breathe, with chorus, Boston, 14 Mar. 1974; CHAMBER MUSIC: Cello piece, cello solo; 4 songs from Shakespeare, mezzo-soprano, 2 clarinets, string trio; Darest thou now, O soul, soprano and piano, 1978; CHORUS: O me! O life!, roots and leaves themselves alone, 1978.
197 Lake View Ave., Cambridge, MA 02138

PFAUTSCH, LLOYD
b. Washington, Mo., 14 Sept. 1921. Studied at Elmhurst Coll., B.A. 1943, honorary D.M. 1959; at Union Theological Seminary, M.Th., M.S.M. 1948; composition with Harold W. Friedell and Burrill Phillips. His awards include annual ASCAP awards from 1961; honorary doctorate, Illinois Wesleyan Univ., 1978; numerous commissions. He was professor, Illinois Wesleyan Univ., 1948-58; visiting professor, Univ. of Illinois, 1956-57; from 1958, at Southern Methodist Univ.
WORKS: CHORUS: A day for dancing, a masque for chorus, chamber orch., and dance; Befana, masque, with chamber orch. and dance; Gloria, with brass and percussion; God with us, cantata, with organ, flute, and trumpet; more than 200 shorter choral publications.
3710 Euclid Ave., Dallas, TX 75205

PFEIFFER, JOHN F.
b. Tucson, Ariz., 29 Sept. 1920. Studied at Bethany Coll., Lindsborg, Kans., and at Univ. of Arizona, Tucson. He has been a record producer from 1949. He composes electronic music, such as Electronomusic--9 images, 1965.
R.D., Flanders, NJ 07836

PFEIL, CLIFFORD I.
b. Rock Island, Ill., 27 Nov. 1931. Studied at American Cons.; with Barney Childs and Robert McBride, Tucson, Ariz.; with H. Owen Reed, Michigan State Univ. He was faculty member, Oakland Univ., 1968-75.
WORKS: ORCHESTRA: Clear and distant views

of rivers and streams, for orch. and audience; CHAMBER MUSIC: Devices for breaking and entering, piano; Ruth Ann's horse, cello and amplifier; Dr. Clifford Pfeil, his piece, lute duet.
12 Niagara, Pontiac, MI 48053

PFISCHNER, JAN. See McNEIL, JAN PFISCHNER

PHELPS, LEWIS ALLEN
b. Mesa, Ariz., 24 May 1938. Studied with Robert McBride, Univ. of Arizona, B.M., M.M.Ed., D.M.A. He won the 1977 composition contest, Nat. Assoc. of Coll. Wind and Perc. Instructors, 1977. He was public school choral director, 1963-67; from 1970, dept. chairman, Mount Union Coll.
WORKS: CHAMBER MUSIC: 5 preludes, organ, 1962; Songs of childhood, 1968; 3 poems of Robert Frost, voice, clarinet, piano, 1975; Epitaphs, voice, oboe, harpsichord, 1976; Instrumental accessories for hymn tunes, 1978.
2485 Crestview, Alliance, OH 44601

PHELPS, NORMAN F.
b. Beaver Dam, Wis., 27 Apr. 1911. Studied with Cecil Burleigh, Univ. of Wisconsin; with Philip Greeley Clapp, Univ. of Iowa. He was faculty member, Jordan Cons., Indianapolis, 1935-49; from 1949, at Ohio State Univ.
WORKS: ORCHESTRA: Dramatic overture, 1946; Noel, Phantasy, 1948; symphony, 1949; Summer rhapsody, 1954; BAND: 2 pieces, 1960; CHAMBER MUSIC: brass quartet, 1940; horn sonata, 1947; oboe sonata, 1951; FILM SCORES: University story, Ohio State Univ. documentary; The Ostrack story, for NASA.
683 Overlook Dr., Columbus, OH 43216

PHETTEPLACE, JON
b. Fullerton, Calif., 4 Feb. 1940. Studied cello and composition with Pietro Grossi in Florence, also worked there in electronic music; cello with Gaspar Cassado, Pablo Casals, and Andre Navarra at Acad. Chigiana, Siena, Italy. He was consultant, RCA Records, New York, 1964; cofounder of Musica Electronica Viva, Rome, 1966; instructor and archive staff worker, Univ. of California, San Diego, 1969-72, 1973-74; solo cellist, San Diego Symphony, 1976-77.
WORKS: THEATRE: music for Woyzeck by George Buckner, 1967; ELECTRONIC: Paesaggio naturale, tape and video recorders; No. 1, 1965, 8-track tape, 1967; Displacement, amplified cello and 3 performers, 1967; 3 plus 4, tape, 1968; Sound City, performer and tapes, 1973.
224 Sunset Dr., Encinitas, CA 92024

PHILLIPS, ARTHUR A.
b. New York, N.Y., 21 Sept. 1918. Studied with David McKay Williams, Juilliard School, dipl. He is an associate, American Guild of Organists, and AGO choirmaster; licentiate teacher and fellow, Trinity Coll. of Music, London. He has been organist and choirmaster in the New York area from 1943. His works for organ include Choral, variations, canon and fugue in c.
537 W. 141st St., New York, NY 10031

PHILLIPS, BARRE
b. San Francisco, Calif., 1934. Has played bass
with Don Ellis, Jimmy Jiuffre, Archie Shepp,
Peter Nero, George Russell, and others.
WORKS: CHAMBER MUSIC: Journal violone,
contrabass, 1968; CHORUS: Bucket of water, with
piano; The return of Odysseus, with orch.

PHILLIPS, BURRILL
b. Omaha, Nebr., 9 Nov. 1907. Studied with
Edwin Stringham, Denver Coll. of Music; with
Edward Royce, Bernard Rogers, Howard Hanson,
Eastman School of Music, B.M., M.M. He held 2
Guggenheim fellowships, 1942, 1961; was Fulbright
lecturer in American music, Univ. of Barcelona,
Spain, 1960-61. He was faculty member, Eastman
School of Music, 1933-49; professor, Univ. of
Illinois, 1949-64; visiting professor, Eastman
School, 1965-66, Juilliard School, 1968-69,
Cornell Univ., 1972-73.
WORKS: ORCHESTRA: Selections from McGuffey's
Reader, a suite, 1934; Concert piece, bassoon
and strings, 1940; Scherzo; piano concerto, 1942;
Tom Paine overture, 1947; Scena, small orch.;
triple concerto, viola, cello, piano, orch.;
Return of Odysseus, baritone, reader, chorus,
orch., 1957; La Pinta, small orch.; BAND: Fantasia; CHAMBER MUSIC: cello sonata, 1948; 2
piano sonatas; 2 string quartets; organ sonata,
1964; Canzona III, 7 instruments and poet, 1964;
sonata for violin and harpsichord, 1966; quartet
for oboe and strings; Concentrica, flute, piano,
percussion, soprano, 1976; Partita, piano quartet; Huntingdon twos and threes, flute, oboe,
cello; If I am Persephone, alto saxophone, tape,
actress; CHORUS: Canzone V, with solo piano;
Death be not proud, a cappella; The man of life
upright, men's voices on verses of Thomas
Campion.
Branchport, NY 14418

PHILLIPS, CHARLES ALLEN
b. Port Huron, Mich., 12 July 1940. Studied
at Sherwood Music School, 1960-62; Wayne State
Univ., B.A. 1966, M.A. 1972, both degrees in
humanities. He taught in public schools, 1966-
70; has been on the faculty, St. Clair Community
Coll., from 1971; and also piano specialist and
salesman.
WORKS: CHAMBER MUSIC: suite for flute and
piano; piano sonatina; 8 bagatelles, piano;
CHORUS: Psalm 117, a cappella; SONGS: In
memoriam, cycle for soprano; The Lord is my
shepherd, soprano and organ.
817 Lincoln Ave., Port Huron, MI 48060

PHILLIPS, D. VALGENE
b. Butler, Okla., 29 Sept. 1935. Studied with
Harold Johnson and Robert Aichele, California
State Univ., San Jose, B.A. 1957, M.A. 1966;
privately with Fred Fox in Hayward, Calif. He
taught in public schools, 1957-67; has since
been faculty member, California State Univ. at
Humboldt.
WORKS: WIND ENSEMBLE: Stanzas; Kerana; 2
stanzas for St. Stephen's Day, brass choir;
CHAMBER MUSIC: Lullabic digressions, woodwind
quintet; A tres, violin, horn, piano; √441, oboe

and horn; Litanie and traquenard, bassoon and
strings.
1397 Whitmire Ave., McKinleyville, CA 95521

PHILLIPS, KAREN
b. Dallas, Tex., 29 Oct. 1942. Studied at
Eastman School of Music, B.M. with distinction;
graduate work at Juilliard School. She has received an Award of Merit, Nat. Fed. of Music
Clubs, 1977; other commemorative awards, certi-
ficates of merit, etc. She is a noted viola
soloist; from 1975, has conducted a weekly radio
series on WNYC-AM, which focuses on American
composers.
WORKS: CHAMBER MUSIC: Peut-etre, viola and
piano; Lonely days and Misunderstandings, viola
and piano, New York, 13 Oct. 1975; A cup of tea,
string trio, 1976; duo for viola and horn,
Lyndonville, Vt., 26 Aug. 1977; PIANO: Fire-
flies; Deceiving hearts, New York, 9 Mar. 1975;
Cointreau, New York, 27 Apr. 1975; Perdu pour
six mois de pluis, Seoul, Korea, 23 Sept. 1975;
Mistress, mistress on the wall, Wondering now,
and Forever lost, New York, 8 Mar. 1976; many
other piano pieces, songs.
WNYC Radio, Municipal Bldg., Chamber St.,
New York, NY 10007

PHILLIPS, PETER
b. 1930. He is on the staff of Whole Earth
Studies, New York Univ.
WORKS: ORCHESTRA: concerto grosso, jazz
combo and chamber orch.; BAND: Continuum;
Gothic suite; Round trip, divertimento for band;
CHAMBER MUSIC: Music for brass quintet; sonata
for string bass, 1964; Divertimento for 3
string basses, 1965.
210 Sullivan St., New York, NY 10012

PHILLIPS, VIVIAN D.
b. Colby, Kans., 9 Mar. 1917. Studied with
Harry Cooper, Ottawa Univ., Kans.; with Hagbard
Brase, Bethany Coll., Lindsborg, Kans.
WORKS: CHAMBER MUSIC: Nocturne, string
quintet; Shades of Papa Haydn, string quintet;
Repose, chamber orch.; many songs.
116 N. Harrison, Shawnee, OK 74801

PIASTRO, JOSEF (BORISSOFF)
b. Kerch, Crimea, 1 Mar. 1889; U.S. citizen
1926; d. Monrovia, Calif., 14 May 1964. On
coming to the U.S. in 1920, he adopted the name
Borissoff to avoid confusion with his brother,
Michel Piastro. He was concertmaster of the Los
Angeles Symphony and violin teacher in Los
Angeles. His Crimean rhapsody for violin and
piano, 1920, was performed by the San Francisco
Symphony, 5 Oct. 1938.

PICCOLO, ANTHONY
b. Teaneck, N.J., 4 Nov. 1946. Studied with
Earle Brown, Peabody Cons.; piano with Konrad
Wolff, conducting with Laszlo Halasz. He was
assistant conductor, Peabody Art Theatre, Baltimore, 1964; chorusmaster, Baltimore Comic Opera,
1965-67; piano instructor, various schools,
1969-73.
WORKS: CHAMBER MUSIC: Found in Machaut's

chamber, tenor, flute, guitar, cello, 1968; When Bathyllos to the dancers played, flute, guitar, percussion, 1973; CHORUS: Introitus, male choir, string orch., 1963; A song of the forest, boys' chorus and orch., commissioned by Texas Boys' Choir, 1968; also church music and incidental music to plays.

PICK, RICHARD SAMUEL BURNS
b. St. Paul, Minn., 20 Oct. 1915. Studied violin, piano, and guitar privately; has attended Univ. of Illinois, Univ. of Chicago, and De Paul Univ., B.A. He is guitar soloist; teaches guitar privately and is on the faculty of De Paul Univ.
WORKS: GUITAR: Autumn day suite; Baca and fiesta day; 9 preludes; 8 variations on a Carcassi etude; numerous transcriptions for guitar solo, guitar duets, and guitar with orchestra; many method books for guitar; FILM SCORE: People along the Mississippi, Encyclopedia Britannica film.
9136 Sheridan Ave., Brookfield, IL 60513

PICKER, TOBIAS
b. New York, N.Y., 1954. Studied at Juilliard School; with Milton Babbitt, Elliott Carter, Manhattan School of Music. He received BMI student awards, 1977-78; Joseph Bearns prize, 1977; Nat. Endowment for the Arts grant, 1979; Charles Ives scholarship, 1979; and commissions.
WORKS: CHAMBER MUSIC: septet for flute, violin, trumpet, trombone, bassoon, piano, vibraphone, Pound Ridge, N.Y., 16 Nov. 1975; Flute form, piccolo, 3 flutes, New York, 11 Dec. 1975; Music when soft voices die, piano, 1977; Rhapsody, violin and piano, N.Y., 6 Nov. 1978; sextet #2, clarinet, oboe, piano trio, percussion.
255 W. 108th St., New York, NY 10025

PIERCE, ALEXANDRA
b. Philadelphia, Pa., 21 Feb. 1934. Studied at Univ. of Michigan, B.M. 1955; composition with Klaus George Roy in Boston, 1956-57; New England Cons., M.M. in piano 1958; Radcliffe Coll., M.A. in music history 1959; with Irving Fine and Harold Shapero, Brandeis Univ., Ph.D. 1968. Her awards include Mu Phi Epsilon Composition contest, second prize, 1975, first prize, 1977. She was on the humanities faculty, Antioch Coll., 1966-67; from 1968, on music faculty, Univ. of Redlands.
WORKS: ORCHESTRA: Behemoth; CHAMBER MUSIC: Arabesque, clarinet and piano; Maola, harp; Norwich chorale, clarinet and piano; Sargasso, clarinet and piano; The great horned owl, marimba; PIANO: Coming to standing; Transverse process; PREPARED PIANO: Blending stumps; Dry rot; Orb; Spectres.
126 E. Fern Ave., Redlands, CA 92373

PIETSCH, EDNA FRIDA
b. Milwaukee, Wis., 7 May 1894. Studied piano and violin in Milwaukee; composition with Bernard Dieter, Chicago Cons. She received many awards in annual contests sponsored by the Wisconsin State Fair and Wisconsin Fed. of Music Clubs.

She taught composition, Wisconsin Cons., 1942-66.
WORKS: ORCHESTRA: 2 piano concertos; viola concerto; Fantasy for orchestra, performed by the Chicago Symphony, 1942, 1946; 5 oriental impressions; CHAMBER MUSIC: string quartet; piano quintet; woodwind quintet; suite for harp; Woodland fantasy, flute and piano; PIANO: sonata; 5 poems; many works for chamber groups, chorus, duo pianos, etc.
3522 W. Kilbourn Ave., Milwaukee, WI 53208

PIKE, ALFRED
b. Chester, Pa., 11 Oct. 1913. Studied privately with Henry Cowell; at Univ. of Pennsylvania, 1950-51; with Vincent Persichetti, Philadelphia Cons., D.M. 1953. He was faculty member, Philadelphia Cons., 1950-53; at St. John's Univ., 1953-75.
WORKS: ORCHESTRA: Oasis, symphonic poem, Pennsylvania Philharmonic, 18 May 1948; Invention for orchestra, 1964; Sinfonietta for strings, 1967; CHAMBER MUSIC: 2 string quartets, 1950, 1954; CHORUS: Psalm 96, 1960.
10220 Farragut Rd., Brooklyn, NY 11201

PIKET, FREDERICK
b. Istanbul, Turkey, 6 Jan. 1903; U.S. citizen 1946; d. Bayside, N.Y., 28 Feb. 1974. Studied at the Vienna State Acad.; with Franz Schreker in Berlin, where he won the Mendelssohn award, 1930. He was faculty member, New York Coll. of Music, 1961-68; New York Univ., 1968-71; Hebrew Union Coll., New York, 1963-74; music director, Free Synagogue, Flushing, N.Y., 1955-74.
WORKS: OPERA: No stars tonight, Lincoln Center, 1972; ORCHESTRA: Curtain raiser to an American play, 1948; The funnies, suite; piano concerto; violin concerto; saxophone concerto; concerto for orch.; symphony; BAND: Variations on a nursery tune; CHAMBER MUSIC: Prelude and triple fugue for woodwinds, 1930; piano sonata; CHORUS: If thou must love me, a cappella; High holiday cycle; The 3 festivals; In the end, cantata, with soli and chamber orch., 1973.

PILLIN, BORIS WILLIAM
b. Chicago, Ill., 31 May 1940. Studied with John Vincent, Univ. of California, Los Angeles, A.B. 1964; with Robert Linn, Univ. of Southern California, A.M. 1967; privately with Leon Stein. His awards include a Woodrow Wilson fellowship, 1964-65; ASCAP awards, 1971-74. He has been private teacher from 1967; self-employed music engraver from 1968; and staff member, Western International Music, Inc., from 1968.
WORKS: ORCHESTRA: symphony, 1964; CHAMBER MUSIC: string quartet, 1965; clarinet sonata, 1965; Scherzo, woodwind quartet, 1968; duo for percussion and piano, 1971; 3 pieces, for double-reed septet, 1972; suite for flute, oboe, clarinet, and organ, 1971; cello sonata, 1973; Serenade, piano and woodwind quintet, 1975; Tune in c minor, piano and percussion, 1975; Scherzo barbaro, bass clarinet and piano; 4 scenes, 3 trumpets and piano; CHORUS: So gehst du nun, 1970; ORGAN: Fugue, 1969.
4913 Melrose Ave., Los Angeles, CA 90029

PILLOIS, JACQUES

PILLOIS, JACQUES
    b. Paris, France, 14 Feb. 1877; to U.S. 1927;
d. New York, N.Y., 3 Jan. 1935. Studied with
Widor and Vierne at the Paris Cons.; then taught
in schools in Paris. On coming to the U.S., he
taught at New York Univ., 1927-30; at Smith
Coll., 1929-30. He composed chamber music and
songs.

PIMSLEUR, SOLOMON
    b. Paris, France, 19 Sept. 1900; to U.S. 1903;
d. New York, N.Y., 22 Apr. 1962. Studied at
Columbia Univ., M.A. in literature 1923; composition with Rubin Goldmark; was a concert
pianist.
    WORKS: ORCHESTRA: Ode to intensity, sym-
phonic ballad, 1933; Overture to disillusion-
ment; Meditative nocturne; Shakespearean sonnet
symphony, with chorus; CHAMBER MUSIC: 3 string
quartets; piano trio; piano quintet; violin
sonata; cello sonata; 2 songs for mixed voices;
many piano pieces.

PINKHAM, DANIEL
    b. Lynn, Mass., 5 June 1923. Studied with
Walter Piston, Archibald T. Davison, and Aaron
Copland, Harvard Univ., A.B. 1944; with Arthur
Honegger and Samuel Barber at Tanglewood;
privately with Nadia Boulanger; organ with Carl
Pfatteicher and E. Power Biggs; harpsichord with
Putnam Aldrich and Wanda Landowska. His awards
include a Fulbright fellowship, 1950; Ford Found.
fellowship, 1962; honorary doctorate, Nebraska
Wesleyan Univ., 1976; numerous commissions. He
has been harpsichordist, Boston Symphony, from
1950; was visiting lecturer, Harvard Univ.,
1957-58; is music director, King's Chapel,
Boston; faculty member, New England Cons.; and
conductor, Cambridge Festival Orchestra.
    WORKS: OPERA: The garden of Artemis, cham-
ber opera; ORCHESTRA: Divertimento, oboe and
strings; piano concerto, 1949; 2 symphonies,
1960, 1963; Signs of the Zodiac, with narrator,
text by David McCord, 1964; violin concerto,
1968; CHAMBER MUSIC: Concertante, violin and
harpsichord soli, strings and celesta, 1954;
concerto for celesta and harpsichord soli, 1955;
Cantilena and capriccio, violin and harpsichord,
1956; Concertante II, violin and strings, 1957;
Eclogue, flute, harpsichord, handbells, 1965;
Prelude, epigram and elegy, winds and percussion;
Concertante, brass quartet, organ, percussion;
Prelude, adagio, chorale, brass quintet; brass
trio, 1970; Serenade, solo trumpet and wind ensemble, Cambridge, 14 Mar. 1980; CHORUS: Elegy,
a cappella, 1947; 2 madrigals, 1955; Wedding
cantata, 1956; Christmas cantata, 1957; Canticle
of praise, with soprano solo, brass, percussion;
Jonah, with 3 soli and orch.; Ascension cantata,
with winds and percussion; The passion of Judas,
with orch., Washington, D.C., 6 June 1976; A
tunnel in the leaves, a cappella, composer conducting, Ft. Collins, Colo., 7 Apr. 1979, in a
full program of Pinkham's music; many shorter
choral works; also works for tape and chorus,
tape and solo instruments and ensembles; works
for organ, including 2 sonatas for organ and
strings.
    150 Chilton St., Cambridge, MA 02138

PISK, PAUL AMADEUS
    b. Vienna, Austria, 16 May 1893; U.S. citizen
1941. Studied at Vienna Cons., diploma; with
Arnold Schoenberg, Univ. of Vienna, Ph.D. His
awards include the Grand Prize, City of Vienna,
1927; honorary degree, Univ. of Vienna, 1969;
many U.S. awards and commissions. On 7 May 1978
a concert of his composition was presented at
the Univ. of Southern California in honor of his
85th birthday. He was professor, Univ. of Redlands, 1937-50; Univ. of Texas, 1950-63; and at
Washington Univ., St. Louis, 1963-72; then
settled in Los Angeles.
    WORKS: BALLET: American suite, 1948;
ORCHESTRA: Requiem, baritone and orch., 1942;
Suite of American folksongs, 1944; Passacaglia,
1944; Bucolic suite, string orch., 1946; Rococo
suite, violin and orch., 1953; Baroque chamber
concerto, 1953; 3 ceremonial rites, 1958;
CHAMBER MUSIC: 3 violin sonatas, 1921, 1927,
1937; 3 sonnets, voice and string quartet, 1937;
piano trio, 1939; suite for 4 clarinets, 1940;
4 beasts, Belloc text, voice and string quartet,
1942; woodwind quartet, 1945; flute sonata;
clarinet sonata, 1947; suite for oboe and piano,
1947; brass quartet, 1951; Alla giga, brass
quintet, Los Angeles, 22 Aug. 1976; 2 songs, for
soprano, piano, trombone, Los Angeles, 2 Nov.
1976; Variables, clarinet and piano; Music for
violin, cello, clarinet, bassoon; 5 songs,
soprano, Baton Rouge, 13 Feb. 1978.
    2724 Westshire Dr., Los Angeles, CA 90068

PISTON, WALTER HAMOR
    b. Rockland, Maine, 20 Jan. 1894; d. Belmont,
Mass., 12 Nov. 1976. Graduated from art school,
1914, then studied piano and violin seriously;
composition with Archibald T. Davison at Harvard
Univ., B.A. summa cum laude 1924; with Nadia
Boulanger and Paul Dukas in Paris, 1924-26. His
many awards included the John Knowles Paine
fellowship, 1924-26; Guggenheim fellowship,
1934; New York Music Critics' Circle award,
1945; Pulitzer prizes, 1948, 1961; honorary
doctorate, Harvard, 1953; membership in Nat.
Inst. of Arts and Letters, American Acad. of
Arts and Letters, American Acad. of Arts and
Sciences; and commissions for almost all of his
many compositions. He served in the U.S. Navy
in World War I; was faculty member at Harvard
from 1926.
    WORKS: BALLET: The incredible flutist,
1938; ORCHESTRA: Concerto for orchestra, 1934;
8 symphonies, 1938-64; 2 violin concertos, 1940,
1960; viola concerto, 1957; concerto for 2
pianos, 1959; Lincoln Center Festival overture,
1962; Capriccio, harp and strings, 1963; Variations, cello and orch., 1965; clarinet concerto,
1966; Fantasy, violin and orch., 1970, Milwaukee
Symph., 14 Apr. 1973; concerto for string quartet and orch., 1974, Portland, Maine, Symphony,
26 Oct. 1976; CHAMBER MUSIC: 3 pieces, woodwind
trio, 1925; flute sonata, 1930; suite for oboe
and piano, 1931; 5 string quartets, 1933, 1935,
1947, 1951, 1962; piano trio, 1935; concerto for
piano and chamber orch., 1937; viola sonata,
1939; Chromatic study on B A C H, organ, 1940;
Interlude, viola and piano, 1942; quintet, flute

and strings, 1942; Passacaglia, piano, 1943;
Partita, violin, viola, organ, 1944; sonatina,
violin and harpsichord, 1945; Divertimento, 9
instruments, 1946; duo for violin and cello,
1949; piano quintet, 1949; woodwind quintet,
1956; string sextet, 1964; piano quartet, 1964;
CHORUS: Carnival song, men's voices, 11 brass
instruments, Harvard Glee Club, Cambridge, 7 Mar.
1940.

PLAIN, GERLAD
b. Sacramento, Ky., 30 Nov. 1940. Studied at
Murray State Univ., B.M.E. 1963; with Philip
Slates, Butler Univ., M.M. 1966; with Ross Lee
Finney, Leslie Bassett, George Balch Wilson,
Ernest Kurtz, Niccolo Castiglioni, Univ. of
Michigan. His awards include Rackham Block
grant, Univ. of Michigan, 1967-68; Prix de Rome,
1974-75; Contemporary Music Festival composer
contest award, Indianapolis, 1977; Internat.
Society for Contemporary Music, composer contest
award, 1977. He was visiting faculty member,
Texas Tech. Univ., 1971-72; instructor, De Paul
Univ., 1973-74; Chicago Musical Coll., 1974;
Univ. of Wisconsin, 1977-78; from 1978, on
faculty, Eastman School of Music.
WORKS: ORCHESTRA: Arrows; and left ol' Joe
a bone, AMAZING!, 1977 (2 awards); CHAMBER MUSIC:
Raccoon song, cello solo; ELECTRONIC: Golden
Wedding, tape; Showers of blessings, clarinet
and tape; aCHATtaNOOgaCHOO, alto flute, guitar,
double bass, tape; Soft and semi-sweet modula-
tion, voices and tape; Ripsnorter, tape.
Eastman School of Music, 26 Gibbs St.,
Rochester, NY 14604

PLESKOW, RAOUL
b. Vienna, Austria, 12 Oct. 1931; to U.S. at an
early age. Studied at Juilliard School; with
Karol Rathaus at Queens Coll., B.A. 1954; with
Otto Luening, Columbia Univ., M.A. 1958; privately with Stefan Wolpe. His awards include 2
Rockefeller grants, 1971, 1973; first prize,
Bowdoin Chamber Music Contest, 1972; American
Acad. of Arts and Letters grant, 1974; Guggenheim
fellowship; 2 Nat. Endowment for the Arts grants,
1975, 1978; and commissions. He has been faculty
member, C. W. Post Coll., Long Island Univ.,
from 1961, department chairman from 1972.
WORKS: ORCHESTRA: 2 movements for orch.;
Fantasia sopra Ave Regina Caelorum, cantata with
chorus; CHAMBER MUSIC: Movement for flute,
cello and piano; sextet, 3 woodwinds, string
trio; 2 pieces, flute and piano; Crossplay, 3
woodwinds, violin, piano, percussion; Music for
7 players; Bagatelles, viola, flute, piano;
Movement for oboe, violin, piano, 1966; Movement
for 9 players, 1967; For 5 players and baritone,
text by Wolpe; duo for cello and piano; Per vege
viene, violin and piano, Cambridge, Mass., 27
Feb. 1973; 3 movements, quintet, 1971; 3 songs,
tenor and chamber ensemble; 2 songs on Latin
fragments, soprano and piano; Bagatelles, piano
and 6 instruments, 1975; 2 bagatelles, oboe or
clarinet, 1975; On 2 ancient texts, soprano and
chamber ensemble, New York, 7 Feb. 1976; Motet
and madrigal, soprano and tenor; piano pieces.
43-25 Douglaston Parkway, Douglaston, NY
11363

PLETTNER, ARTHUR
b. New York, N.Y., 15 Nov. 1904. Studied at
Bavarian State Cons., Wuenzburg, Germany; with
Albert Stoessel, Bernard Wagenaar, Juilliard
School; with Ernest MacMillan and Healey Willan,
Univ. of Toronto, M.B., D.M. He received a
Moravian anthem award for God is our trust; and
commissions. He played in orchestras and
theatres in New York, 1926-37; was Juilliard
professor, Univ. of Tennessee, Chattanooga,
1937-73.
WORKS: THEATRE: music for The singing
Christmas tree; ORCHESTRA: symphony; CHAMBER
MUSIC: Manhattan toccata, violin and piano;
Barn dance, strings; Appalachia, string quartet;
CHORUS: Away in a manger; Fanfare for Christmas
Day; Communion service in D; and organ pieces.
105 Druid Dr., Signal Mountain, TN 37377

PLOG, ANTHONY
b. Glendale, Calif., 13 Nov. 1947. He teaches
trumpet at Univ. of Southern California and at
California State Univ. at Northridge.
WORKS: CHAMBER MUSIC: 4 Sierra scenes,
soprano and brass quintet; mini-suite for brass
quintet; 2 scenes, soprano, trumpet, and organ;
Fanfare for 2 trumpets; 16 contemporary etudes
for trumpet; Animal ditties, narrator, trumpet,
piano.
15733 Vanowen #7, Van Nuys, CA 91406

PLONSKY, PETER
b. Brooklyn, N.Y., 23 Apr. 1943. Studied with
Morton Feldman and Earle Brown; at Rutgers Univ.,
B.M. 1965; studied various Asian instruments at
Univ. of Hawaii, Wesleyan Univ., and the Center
for World Music. He is a member of the New York
Fluxus and the West Coast text-sound movement.
His aesthetic statement as quoted in EAR magazine
reads in part: "Traditional Earth music cultures
differ as to external realization of circulatory
system translated as rhythm, nervous system as
melody, and timbre as etheric awareness. This
internal physical establishment can be unified
by the linear glissando which runs continously
through all parameters; and can be transcended
by the Mind Emission Vocal Trance which operates
within the astral causality of a single elemental substance capable of infinite transformation. Numerous occult contacts bear witness to
this." It is difficult to deduce how his listed
works fit into this philosophy: Innards for 9
performers and 9 cans of spray paint; Ear rub,
performed by rubbing the ears to produce sound;
Let it slide, version in time, San Francisco,
26 Oct. 1976; Glissandi conductus, conductor
with strings attached, Berkeley, 11 Nov. 1976.

PLUMBY, DONALD
b. Martins Ferry, Ohio, 8 Nov. 1919. Studied at
Univ. of Kentucky. His compositions include
Picture of a hunt, a duo for violin or flute or
oboe and cello or bassoon; and songs.

POCHON, ALFRED
b. Yverdon, Switzerland, 30 July 1878; U.S.
citizen 1928; d. Lutry, Switzerland, 26 Feb.
1959. Studied violin with Cesar Thomson. He

POLIFRONE, JON J.

organized the Flonzaley Quartet in 1903 and was
second violinist until the quartet was disbanded
in 1929; organized the Stradivarius Quartet in
New York; was director of the Cons. of Lausanne,
Switz., 1941-57. He composed pieces for string
quartet and Passacaglia for viola.

POLIFRONE, JON J.
b. Durand, Mich., 10 Jan. 1937. Studied with
H. Owen Reed, Michigan State Univ.; with Nadia
Boulanger in Paris; with Ernst von Dohnanyi,
Carlisle Floyd, and John Boda, Florida State
Univ. His awards include the Hinman Creative
Research award; Michigan State Honors award;
Redlands Univ. composition award; California
Quadrennial Arts award; Indiana Laus Tibi Deo
award; Society for American Composers award,
1968, 1971. He was instructor, Jordan Coll. of
Music, Butler Univ., 1961-63; faculty member
and composer-in-residence, Indiana State Univ.,
1963-78.
   WORKS: OPERA: Kentucky story; Wicked Sam
and the devil, a madrigal opera; BALLET: Trip-
tychos, ballet for chorus and orch.; ORCHESTRA:
piano concerto; violin concerto, 1972; CHORUS:
Canticles for Christmas, with soloists and orch.;
Psalms, with percussion; MULTIMEDIA: Colors,
slides, dancers, tape, chorus, and orch.; also
chamber works, song cycles, piano works.
   927 Ridge Rd., Terre Haute, IN 47803

POLIN, CLAIRE
b. Philadelphia, Pa., 1 Jan. 1926. Studied with
Vincent Persichetti, Philadelphia Cons., B.M.
1948, M.M. 1950, D.M. 1955; also with Peter
Mennin, Juilliard School; Lukas Foss and Roger
Sessions at Tanglewood; flute privately with
William Kincaid. She received awards in Delta
Omicron Internat. contests, 1953, 1959; Leverhulme fellowship, 1968-69; Georgia State Univ.
award, 1970; Rutgers Univ. grant, 1973-74. She
was faculty member, Philadelphia Cons., 1955-64;
and from 1959, at Rutgers Univ.
   WORKS: ORCHESTRA: 2 symphonies; Amphion,
1978; WIND ENSEMBLE: Cader Idris, brass quintet;
Journey of Owain Hadoc, brass quintet and 10
percussion; CHAMBER MUSIC: flute sonata; Structures, solo flute; Summer settings, harp, 1966;
Serpentine, solo viola; O, aderyn pur, flute,
saxophone, tape; Procris, flute and tuba;
Makimono I, violin, cello, piano, flute, clarinet,
Philadelphia, 14 Oct. 1973; Piece d'encore, solo
viola; Synaulia, flutes, clarinets, piano;
Margoa, solo flute; Panorphic duo, flute and
harp; Klockwork, alto saxophone, horn, bassoon;
Windsongs, soprano and guitar, excerpts from
Paraselene below; Vigniatures, violin and harp,
1978; MULTIMEDIA: Infinite, soprano, chorus,
narrator, alto saxophone, dancers; Paraselene,
soprano, flute, piano, dancer.
   374 Baird Rd., Merion, PA 19066

POLK, MARLYCE R.
b. Iowa, 14 Jan. 1955. Studied at Univ. of
Wisconsin, Stevens Point, B.M.E.; with Alan
Stout, Northwestern Univ., M.M.; clarinet privately. Her awards include the Susan S. Colman
scholarship; John Philip Sousa award; Albertson

award; named valedictorian.
   WORKS: ORCHESTRA: concerto for soprano
saxophone and string orch.; CHAMBER MUSIC: 3
short dialogues, 3 clarinets; Chromasia, alto
saxophone and percussion; Twigs, tails, and nuts,
solo tuba; brass quartet; string quartet; In
sickness, mezzo-soprano, cello, percussion.
   Rte. #1, Wonewoc, WI 53968

POLLAK, WILLIAM THOMAS
b. Philadelphia, Pa., 22 Dec. 1900. Attended
Columbia Univ., A.B., A.M.; Univ. of Toronto,
B.M., D.M.; with A. Madeley Richardson, Rubin
Goldmark, and Albert Stoessel at Juilliard
School. He held a Victor Baier fellowship at
Columbia Univ., 1930; composition fellowship at
Juilliard School, 1930; is an associate, American
Guild of Organists. He was faculty member, New
York Coll. of Music, 1943-68; New York Univ.,
1968-69; organist and choirmaster in the New
York area from 1926.
   WORKS: ORCHESTRA: symphony; CHORUS: Missa
solemnis in g, with soli and orch; Mass in honor
of St. Benedict, male voices; numerous other
choral works; organ pieces.
   9 Melrose Lane, Douglaston, NY 11363

POLLOCK, ROBERT EMIL
b. New York, N.Y., 8 July 1946. Studied with
Claudio Spies, Swarthmore Coll., B.A.; with
Edward T. Cone, Peter Westergaard, Jacques-Louis
Monod, J. K. Randall, Milton Babbitt, Robert
Helps, Princeton Univ., M.F.A. His awards include Composers' String Quartet award, 1970;
MacDowell fellowships, 1972, 1976; Guggenheim
fellowship, 1973; Nat. Endowment for the Arts
grant, 1974; Rockefeller grant, 1974; New Jersey
State Arts Council grant, 1975. He is a concert
pianist.
   WORKS: THEATRE: The nose, chamber opera
after Gogol; CHAMBER MUSIC: Movement and variations, string quartet, 1967; Introduction and
dance, 2 pianos, 1967; septet, 3 winds, 3 strings,
trombone, 1968; Rhapsody, piano, 1969; 3 duos
for violin and piano, 1969, 1970, 1973; wind
trio, 1969; Bridgeforms, piano, 1972; flute
sonatina, 1972; trio for violin, clarinet, cello,
New York, 6 Apr. 1974; Violament, viola, 1974;
Geometrics, string quartet, 1974; Departure,
piano, 1975; woodwind quintet, 1975; 7 preludes,
piano, 1975; Revolution, 9 instruments, 1976;
Progressional, piano, 1977; Metaphor I, string
trio, 1977; Metaphor II, clarinet and piano,
1977; VOICE: Chamber setting, baritone and 6
instruments, e. e. cummings text, 1972; Song
cycle, on Stephen Crane poems, New York, 14 Jan.
1974; The descent, soprano, flute, piano, 1976;
many other chamber works and vocal pieces.
   254 W. 20th St., Ship Bottom, NJ 08008

PONÉ, GUNDARIS
b. Riga, Latvia, USSR, 17 Oct. 1932; U.S. citizen 1956. Studied at Univ. of Minnesota, B.A.,
M.A., Ph.D. He has received 6 composition
awards from the State Univ. of New York Research
Found. From 1963 he has been faculty member,
State Univ. Coll. at New Paltz, and from 1974,
conductor, Contemporary Chamber Orchestra, which

he founded.

WORKS: ORCHESTRA: violin concerto, 1959; 4 temperamenti d'amore, texts by Petrach, baritone and orch., 1960; Daniel propheta, oratorio, with chorus, 3 soloists, 1962; Vivos vocos, Mortuos plango, exegesis on L'Internationale, 1972; Avanti--vorwarts--vperjod, 1975; horn concerto, 1976; CHAMBER MUSIC: Klavierwerk I, piano, 1963; Hetaera Esmeralda, string quartet, 1964; Seris--Alea, 4 winds and piano, 1965; cello sonata, 1966; Reaktionen, 2 pianos, 1966; Klavierwerk II, "Montage-demontage," pianist and assistant, 1967; Composizione per 4 orchestre, 1969; San Michele dells laguna, clarinet, violin, piano, 1969; De mundo Magistri Ioanni, 7 players and sound effect groups, 1972; Diletti dialettici, 9 players, 1973; VOICE: Mit Trommeln und Pfeifen, tenor and piano, 1963; Junius Broschüre, instruments, 18 female voices, 4 speakers, text by Rosa Luxemburg, 1970; 5 American songs, soprano and small orch., 1975.

24 Woodland Dr., New Paltz, NY 12561

POOLER, MARIE

b. Wis., 22 Apr. 1928. Studied at St. Olaf Coll., B.M.; and at California State Coll. at Fullerton, M.A. She taught at Shimer Coll., 1949-51; in public schools, 1957-67; and from 1971, has been on faculty of Long Beach City Coll. Her compositions include numerous anthems, hymns, and songs for adult and junior choirs.

2801 Engel Dr., Los Alamitos, CA 90720

POPE, CONRAD

b. Corona, Calif., 21 Nov. 1951. Studied with Malcolm Peyton and Donald Martino, New England Cons., B.M. with honors 1975; with Gunther Schuller at Tanglewood on a Bernstein fellowship, 1971. Other awards include the George W. Chadwick Medal, 1973; Fulbright-Hays grant, 1973; selection of his cello sonata to represent the U.S. at the 8th Biennale de Paris, 1973. He was codirector, Music: Here and Now, Boston Museum of Fine Arts, 1971-73; from 1978, has been on the faculty at Brandeis Univ.

WORKS: ORCHESTRA: symphony, 1973; CHAMBER MUSIC: string trio, 1970; Joys, baritone and 13 instruments, 1971; sonata for solo cello, Boston, 12 May 1973; 2 songs, soprano and piano, New York, 7 Dec. 1978.

24 Crescent St., Cambridge, MA 02138

PORTER, COLE

b. Peru, Ind., 9 June 1892; d. Santa Monica, Calif., 15 Oct. 1964. Attended Yale Univ., B.A. 1913; Harvard Law School; Harvard School of Music; studied with Vincent d'Indy, Scola Cantorum, Paris. He joined the French Foreign Legion in 1916, becoming a French officer during World War I. After the war, he returned to the U.S. and devoted full time to composing musical comedies for the stage and films.

WORKS: MUSICAL COMEDIES: See America first, 1916; Hitchy koo, 1919; 50 million Frenchmen, 1929; Gay divorcee, 1932; Anything goes, 1934; Jubilee, 1935; Red, hot and blue, 1936; Leave it to me, 1938; Dubarry was a lady, 1939; Panama Hattie, 1940; Let's face it, 1941; Something for

the boys, 1943; Mexican hayride, 1944; Kiss me, Kate, 1948; Out of this world, 1950; Can-can, 1953; Silk stockings, 1955; SONGS: Begin the beguine; It's de-lovely; Love for sale; Night and day; I love Paris; Don't fence me in; Wunderbar; In the still of the night; You're the top; What is this thing called love?; I've got you under my skin; and many others; FILM SCORES: Born to dance; Rosalie; Broadway melody of 1940; You'll never get rich; Something to shout about; The pirate; High society; The girls.

PORTER, DAVID GRAY

b. Los Angeles, Calif., 10 June 1953. Studied with Donal Michalsky, Lloyd Rogers, and Nicolas Slonimsky, California State Univ. at Fullerton. In 1974 he was cofounder of Direct Image Ensemble (DIE) and has continued as codirector.

WORKS: CHAMBER MUSIC: Events, 2 pianists, 1974; 4 bassoons, 1974; Music for Chas. Simmons, sextet, 1975; septet in 7 movements, 1975; percussion quartet, 1976; Music for harp, 1975-78; electronic pieces.

11130 S. Nicklett Ave., Fullerton, CA 92633

PORTER, ELLEN JANE LORENZ. See LORENZ, ELLEN JANE

PORTER, JAMES EDWARD

b. Bronxville, N.Y., 30 July 1955. Studied with Richard Winslow, Wesleyan Univ.; with Jonathan Kramer, Yale Univ.

WORKS: string quartet, Piano fantasy, Seasons, song cycle, Thou noble Lord, a hymn, all performed at Middletown, Conn., 22 Apr. 1977.

2 Dartmouth Rd., Cos Cob, CT 06807

PORTER, QUINCY

b. New Haven, Conn., 7 Feb. 1897; d. Bethany, Conn., 12 Nov. 1966. Studied with David Stanley Smith and Horatio Parker, Yale Univ., B.M. 1921; violin with Lucien Capet; composition with Vincent d'Indy in Paris; with Ernest Bloch in New York. His awards included the Steinert and Osborne prizes; Guggenheim fellowship, 1929-31; Elizabeth Sprague Coolidge Medal, 1943; Pulitzer prize, 1954. He was violinist in theatre orchestras; faculty member, Cleveland Inst. of Music, 1922-32; dean, New England Cons., 1928-42, director, 1942-46; professor, Yale Univ., 1946-65.

WORKS: ORCHESTRA: Ukrainian suite for strings, 1925; suite in c, 1926; Poem and dance, 1932; 2 symphonies, 1938, 1964; Music for strings, 1941; Fantasy on a pastoral theme, organ and strings, 1942; viola concerto, 1948; Fantasy, cello and small orch., 1950; The desolate city, baritone and orch., 1950; Concerto concertante, 2 pianos and orch., 1954; New England episodes, 1958; harpsichord concerto, 1960; CHAMBER MUSIC: 10 string quartets, 1923-65; 2 violin sonatas, 1926, 1929; In monasterio, string quartet, 1927; Little trio, flute, violin, viola, 1928; clarinet quintet, 1929; suite for viola alone, 1930; piano sonata, 1930; Quintet on a childhood theme, flute and strings, 1940; 6 miniatures, piano, 1943; horn sonata, 1946; 4 pieces, violin and piano, 1947; string sextet on Slavic folk tunes, 1947; duo for violin and

PORTNOFF, MISCHA

viola, 1954; duo for flute and harp, 1957; Day-dreams, piano, 1957; quintet for oboe and strings; Divertimento, woodwind quintet. Mrs. Porter gave her husband's complete papers and music manuscripts to the Yale University Library in 1974.

PORTNOFF, MISCHA
b. Berlin, Germany, 29 Aug. 1901. Studied with his father at Stern Cons., Berlin; and at the Royal Acad. of Stockholm. On coming to the U.S., he conducted his own studio in Brooklyn. He composed stage scores and many works for piano.

PORTNOFF, WESLEY
b. Simferopol, Russia, 13 Feb. 1910; d. Brooklyn, N.Y., 31 May 1976. He was a brother of Mischa Portnoff; studied with his father at Stern Cons. in Berlin. He conducted orchestras in the Scandinavian countries for 5 years.
WORKS: ORCHESTRA: violin concerto; CHAMBER MUSIC: Tempo of Manhattan, suite for violin; also stage scores and ballets.

POTTEBAUM, WILLIAM G.
b. Teutopolis, Ill., 30 Dec. 1930. Studied at Quincy Coll., B.S.; with Hermann Reutter in Stuttgart, Germany; with Wayne Barlow, Howard Hanson, Bernard Rogers, Eastman School of Music; with Myron Schaeffer, Univ. of Toronto. He won first place in an American Music in the University contest, 1966. He was instructor in public schools, 1955-61; has been faculty member, State Univ. Coll., Brockport, from 1963.
WORKS: ORCHESTRA: Concerto for orchestra, Buffalo, 22 May 1966; Toccata; Insignia, variations on related motives; 3 chamber orchestra suites; CHORUS: 2 masses; Psalms 8, 22, 83, 97, 150, children's voices; ELECTRONIC: Theatre piece, clarinet and tape; music for Midsummer night's dream; Beauty and the beast; The American dream; How the animals got their names (film score); works for band, solo instruments, piano.
333 St. Andrews Dr., Rochester, NY 14626

POTTENGER, HAROLD PAUL
b. Aurora, Mo., 21 Nov. 1932. Attended Univ. of Missouri, B.S. 1954; Univ. of Wichita, M.M.E. 1958; Indiana Univ., D.M.E. 1969. He was public school teacher, 1956-65; faculty member, Southwest Baptist Coll., 1965-68; Internat. Univ., 1968-70; from 1970, at Bradley Univ.
WORKS: BAND: suite for band, 1965; CHAMBER MUSIC: Remembrance, flute and piano; Portrait, piano; also choral compositions and arrangements.
2611 W. Barker, Peoria, IL 61604

POWELL, FELIX
Is associate professor and department chairman, Univ. of Maryland, Baltimore County. His Cisterns II for tape and piano received its New York premiere at the Composers Theatre, 28 Mar. 1974.
4 Ruby Court, Arbutus, MD 21227

POWELL, JOHN
b. Richmond, Va., 6 Sept. 1882; d. Charlottesville, Va., 15 Aug. 1963. Studied at Univ. of

Virginia; with Theodor Leschetizky and Karl Navratil in Vienna; made debut as pianist in Berlin in 1907. He was also an amateur astronomer and discovered a comet.
WORKS: OPERA: Judith and Holofernes; ORCHESTRA: Rapsodie negre, piano and orch., after Conrad's Heart of Darkness, 1918; In old Virginia, 1921; 2 piano concertos; violin concerto; Natchez on the hill, 3 dances, 1932; A set of 3, 1935; symphony in A, 1947; Virginia symphony, 1951; CHAMBER MUSIC: string quartet; Sonata Virginianesque, violin and piano, 1919; 3 piano sonatas: Sonate psychologique, Sonate noble, Sonate Teutonica, 1933; 2 piano suites: In the South and At the fair; In the hammock, 2 pianos, 8 hands.

POWELL, LAURENCE
b. Birmingham, England, 13 Jan. 1899; U.S. citizen 1939. Studied at Birmingham and Midland Inst. School of Music; with Granville Bantock, Univ. of Birmingham, B.M. with first class honors 1922; at Univ. of Wisconsin, M.A. 1926. He won first prize, Texas Composers Guild contest, 1948. He was instructor, Univ. of Wisconsin, 1924-26; faculty member, Univ. of Arkansas, 1926-34; department head, Little Rock Junior Coll., 1933-39; conductor, Little Rock Symphony, 1936-39; organist-choirmaster in various churches from 1941. In 1975 he retired to Santa Fe.
WORKS: ORCHESTRA: 2 symphonies, 1929, 1943; The ogre of the northern fastness, 1921; Keltic legende, 1924; Charivari suite, 1925; suite for strings, 1931; Deirdre of the sorrows, 1933; Picnic, an Arkansas pastorale for strings, 1936; County fair, 1936; Duo concertante, recorder and orch., 1941; Variations, 1941; The Santa Fe Trail, with narrator and chorus, 1958; Penny overture, 1960; Overture on French folk tunes, 1970; Oracle: The oak of Dodona, El Dorado, Ark., 1 Mar. 1976; An Arkansas rondo, chamber orch.; CHAMBER MUSIC: string trio; 2 string quartets; trio sonatas for recorders and piano; Canticle, soprano, recorder, and piano; cello sonata; viola sonata; 5 violin sonatas, #4 performed, Washington, D.C., 11 Nov. 1976, #5, Albuquerque, N.Mex., 1 Feb. 1976; also choral works.

POWELL, MEL
b. New York, N.Y., 12 Feb. 1923. Studied piano with Nadia Reisenberg; composition with Paul Hindemith, Yale Univ., B.M. 1952. His honors include the Sigma Alpha Iota award, 1956; Koussevitzky grant, 1957; Guggenheim fellowship, 1960; Nat. Inst. of Arts and Letters grant, 1963. He played in theatre and dance orchestras; taught at Mannes Coll. of Music and at Queens Coll.; joined the faculty at Yale Univ., 1958, was chairman of composition and director of the electronic music studio, 1961-72; then on faculty, California Inst. of the Arts.
WORKS: ORCHESTRA: Stanzas, 1957; Setting, cello and orch., 1961; BAND: Capriccio; CHAMBER MUSIC: Divertimento, violin and harp, 1955; Divertimento, 5 winds, 1955; piano trio, 1956; Miniatures, baroque ensemble, 1957; Filigree

setting, string quartet, 1959; Haiku setting, voice and piano, 1960; Etude, 1963; Improvisation, piano, clarinet, viola, 1963; 2 prayer settings, tenor, oboe, viola, cello, violin, 1963; Settings, soprano and chamber ensemble, 1979; ELECTRONIC: 2 electronic settings, 1961, 1962; Events, 1963; Analog; Immobiles; Cantilena, soprano, violin, and tape, 1970.
 California Inst. of the Arts, 24700 McBean Pkwy., Valencia, CA 91355

POWELL, MORGAN E.
 b. Graham, Tex., 7 Jan. 1938. Studied with Samuel Adler, North Texas State Univ., B.M. 1959, M.M. 1961; with Kenneth Gaburo, Univ. of Illinois. His awards include a best composition award, Intercoll. Jazz Festival, Notre Dame Univ., 1961; faculty fellowships, 1968, 1972; ASCAP awards, 1970-78; Fromm Found. grant, 1971; Univ. of Illinois grant, 1972; Nat. Endowment for the Arts grant, 1974; many commissions. He was instructor, North Texas State Univ., 1961-63; faculty member, Berklee Coll. of Music, 1963-64; from 1966, at Univ. of Illinois.
 WORKS: ORCHESTRA: Light and shadows, with jazz ensemble; WIND ENSEMBLE: Music for brass and percussion; Darkness II, brass quintet and percussion; JAZZ: Reflections; Moonbag; Sirhmrej; Birdmerchant; CHAMBER MUSIC: Midnight realities, solo tuba; Blueberry blue, piano; Inacabado, solo trombone; Alone, solo trumpet; 3 songs for 2 violins and soprano; CHORUS: Loneliness, with instruments; Zelanski medley, with instruments.
 702 W. Nevada, Urbana, IL 61801

POWELL, ROBERT JENNINGS
 b. Benoit, Miss., 22 July 1932. Studied with Helen Gunderson, Louisiana State Univ., B.M. 1954; with Alec Wyton, Harold Friedell, Seth Bingham, Searle Wright, Union Theological Seminary, M.S.M. 1957. He is a fellow of the American Guild of Organists; has received annual ASCAP awards from 1968. He was music director, St. Paul's School, Concord, N.H., 1965-68; assistant organist, Cathedral of St. John the Divine, N.Y., 1956-58; St. Paul's Episcopal Church, Meridian, Miss., 1958-65; from 1968, Christ Church, Greenville, S.C.
 WORKS: CHORUS: Of the Father's love, cantata; City of God, cantata; Soldiers of Christ; Easter antiphon; Like a flowing river; ORGAN: 15 preludes; and some 200 other pieces for chorus and organ.
 306 McDaniel Ave., Greenville, SC 29601

POWERS, GEORGE
 b. Kokomo, Ind., 31 May 1917. Studied with Leo Sowerby, American Cons., B.M.; with Roger Sessions, Juilliard School; with Alec Rowley, Trinity Coll., London; with Seth Bingham, Union Theological Seminary, New York, S.M.D. He is a fellow, American Guild of Organists. He was faculty member, American Cons., 1946-48; Guilmant Organ School, N.Y., 1965-66; Union Theological Seminary, School of Sacred Music, 1958-73; has been organist-choirmaster from 1940; at St. Mark's In-the-Bouwerie, Manhattan, 1955-72.

WORKS: CHORUS: Ah, my soul, a cappella; Benedictus es, Domine; Create in me; Christ, our passover; Come, great spirit; PIANO: From my sketchbook, a suite; Ballade; ORGAN: Scherzo; Interlude; Prayer; Pange lingua; Ostinato.
 91 Christopher St., New York, NY 10014

POWERS, MAXWELL
 b. Cleveland, Ohio, 4 Feb. 1911. Studied at Cleveland Inst. of Music, B.M., M.M.; received an honorary D.M., Cincinnati Cons. He has been faculty member, Greenwich House Music School, New York, from 1945.
 WORKS: ORCHESTRA: 2 piano concertos; symphonic poem; overture; CHAMBER MUSIC: string quartet; violin sonata; cello sonata.

POZAR, CLEVE F. (name legally changed from Robert F. Pozar)
 b. Virginia, Minn., 8 Aug. 1941. Studied at Univ. of Michigan; composition with Bill Dixon in New York; drums with Alan Dawson in Boston. He has been percussionist for numerous theatrical productions at Univ. of Michigan theatre; Charles Street Theatre, Boston; Milwaukee Repertory Theatre; with Bob James Trio, Bill Dixon Ensemble; and for dance groups.
 WORKS: JAZZ ENSEMBLE: Cosmic peace; Magistrate Lousvart; Echo Africa; Nancy's small world; Good golly, Miss Nancy; FILM SCORES: Implosion; Louise Nevelson, for Whitney Museum.
 54 Danforth, Jamaica Plain, MA 02130

POZDRO, JOHN WALTER
 b. Chicago, Ill., 14 Aug. 1923. Studied with Robert Delaney, Northwestern Univ., B.M. 1948, M.M. 1949; with Howard Hanson, Bernard Rogers, Alan Hovhaness, Eastman School of Music, Ph.D. 1958. His awards include Kansas Fed. of Music Clubs citations, 1964, 1969; annual ASCAP awards, 1966-78; first prize, Roth Orchestra Composition Contest, 1972; Delius prize, 1974; Nat. Endowment for the Arts grant, 1976; and commissions. He was instructor, Iowa State Univ., 1949-50; from 1950, faculty member, Univ. of Kansas, professor and chairman of theory and composition from 1961.
 WORKS: OPERA: Malooley and the fear monster, a family opera in 1 act, Lawrence, Kans., 6 Feb. 1977; ORCHESTRA: overture, 1948; 3 symphonies, 1949, 1957, 1959; A cynical overture, 1953; Rondo giocoso, string orch., 1964; Music for a youth symphony, 1969; Waterlow Park, 1972; CHAMBER MUSIC: 4 piano sonatas, 1946, 1963, 1964, #4, Washington, D.C., 27 Nov. 1976; quintet for winds and piano, 1947; 2 strings quartets, 1947, 1948; sextet for flute and strings, 1948; woodwind quintet, 1951; Elegy, trumpet and piano, 1953; Trilogy, clarinet, bassoon, trumpet, piano, 1960; sonata for brass and percussion, 1966; violin sonata, 1971; 3 preludes for piano, 1974; 6 preludes for piano, 1977; Bagatelle, clarinet and piano, 1978; CARILLON: Landscapes I and II, 1964, 1970; also choral works.
 Music Dept., University of Kansas, Lawrence, KS 66045

PRATER, JEFFREY L.

PRATER, JEFFREY L.
b. Endicott, N.Y., 4 Oct. 1947. Studied with
Gary White, Iowa State Univ., B.S. 1969; with
H. Owen Reed, Michigan State Univ., M.M. 1973;
with William Bergsma, Univ. of Washington. He
was winner in a composition contest, Contemporary
Music Festival, Indiana State Univ., 1974; and
in a contest sponsored by the Iowa Choral Directors Assoc., 1978. He was faculty member, Univ.
of Wisconsin Center-Marinette, 1972-76; Iowa
State Univ., from 1977.
WORKS: ORCHESTRA: Kinetics, 1973; BAND:
Eulogy for the wilderness, 1976; CHAMBER MUSIC:
2 movements, brass sextet, 1969; 2 soliloquies,
solo violin, 1971; Hexalogues, woodwind quintet
and marimba, 1975; 3 reflexives, trumpet, trombone, percussion, 1978; also choral works and
vocal solos.
125 S. Maple Ave., Ames, IA 50010

PREMRU, RAYMOND
b. Elmira, N.Y., 6 June 1934. Studied with
Gladys Leventon and Bernard Rogers, Eastman
School of Music, B.M. 1956; with Peter Racine
Fricker, Royal Coll. of Music, London, A.R.C.M.
1957. From 1958 he has played bass trombone
with the Philharmonia Orchestra and the Philip
Jones Brass Ensemble in London.
WORKS: ORCHESTRA: trombone concerto, 1956;
symphony, 1958; Concertante, string orch., 1967;
Reflections, string orch., 1968; Tissington
variations, 1970; Canvases, chamber orch., 1973;
2 Whitman poems, with chorus, 1973; Concert overture, London Symphony, 6 May 1975; Concerto for
orchestra, commissioned by the Cleveland Orch.
and performed there, 13 May 1976; WIND ENSEMBLE:
2 pieces, 3 trombones, 1951; concertino for trombone and woodwind quintet, 1954; In memoriam,
4 trombones, 1956; brass quartet, 1960; Music
from Harter Fell, brass ensemble, 1973; CHAMBER
MUSIC: clarinet concerto, 1953; string trio,
1958; octet for string trio and woodwind quintet,
1958; viola sonata, 1971; also pieces for jazz
orch.
33 Springfield Gardens, London, NW9 ORY,
England

PRENDERGAST, ROY MARTIN
b. Canal Zone, Panama, 23 Feb. 1943. Studied
with Peter Sacco, San Francisco State Coll.;
with Frederick Beyer, Greensboro Coll.; with
Jack Jarrett, Univ. of North Carolina at Greensboro, B.M. 1970. He was instructor, Univ. of
North Carolina, 1972-76; from 1977, managing
director, High Point Community Theatre.
WORKS: THEATRE: Pumpernickel ice cream,
musical, 1968; How Miss Henry got that way,
musical, 1972; ORCHESTRA: piano concerto, 1971;
Variations on a theme by Scriabin, a cello concerto, 1972; CHORUS: Body poems, 1973; My father
moved through dooms, e. e. cummings text, female
voices, chamber ensemble, percussion; FILM
SCORE: Step ahead, documentary, 1973.
1505 Lafayette Court, Greensboro, NC 27408

PREOBRAJENSKA, VERA N.
b. San Francisco, Calif., 27 Apr. 1926. Studied
with Darius Milhaud, Mills Coll., 1945-47; with

Ernest Bloch, Roger Sessions, Frederick Jacobi,
Univ. of California, Berkeley; with Alexander
Tcherepnin, San Francisco Inst. of Music; by
correspondence with Shostakovich. She has been
classroom pianist, dance dept., Univ. of California, Berkeley, 1965-68, and at Santa Cruz,
1977-78.
WORKS: THEATRE: Concept of the egg, dance
comedy, 1947; Hebraic rhapsody, ballet, 1968;
The money lender, opera, after Dostoevsky's
Crime and Punishment; ORCHESTRA: Mazurka, 1947;
American tone poem; Slavic tone poem; A dream,
with soprano solo, 1952; suite for strings,
1961; CHAMBER MUSIC: violin sonata; string quintet; piano trio; also choral works; many piano
pieces.
935 High St., Santa Cruz, CA 95060

PRESS, JACQUES
b. Tbilisi, Russia, 27 Mar. 1903; to U.S. 1926.
Studied at a conservatory in Tbilisi; with Nadia
Boulanger in Paris, 1924-25; orchestration with
Leo Zeitlin. He has received 8 ASCAP awards.
He was staff arranger and composer, Roxy and
Capitol Theatres and NBC Radio, 1927-37, at
motion picture studios in Hollywood, 1938-50;
music director and composer for television
programs in New York, 1950-70.
WORKS: ORCHESTRA: Hasseneh, symphonic
suite; Wedding dance; Prelude and fugue in jazz;
Jig-jag; Disconcerto, piano and orch.; Russian
gypsy dance; Israeli festival march; Spanish
interlude, a ballet, 1941; CHAMBER MUSIC: Polka
coloratura, 2 harps. Many of his orchestral
works were introduced and recorded by Arthur
Fiedler and the Boston Pops.
588 West End Ave., New York, NY 10024

PRESSER, WILLIAM
b. Saginaw, Mich., 19 Apr. 1916. Studied at
Univ. of Michigan, M.M. 1940; with Bernard
Rogers, Burrill Phillips, Roy Harris, and
Gardner Read, Eastman School of Music, Ph.D.
1947. His awards include Rochester Religious
Arts Festival award; Syracuse Univ. Festival of
Arts award; 2 Composers Press publication awards;
2 Nat. School Orch. Assoc. awards; annual ASCAP
awards from 1966. He has held faculty posts at
Buena Vista Coll., 1940-42; Florida State Univ.,
1946-47; Florence (Ala.) State Coll., 1947-50;
West Texas State Coll., 1950-51; Music and Arts
Inst. of San Francisco, 1951-53; from 1953, at
Univ. of Southern Mississippi.
WORKS: OPERA: The whistler, chamber opera
for soprano, baritone, string quartet, piano;
ORCHESTRA: symphony; concerto for tuba and
strings; concerto for tenor saxophone and chamber orch.; BAND: symphony #2; CHAMBER MUSIC:
trombone sonata; suite for brass quartet; Prelude
and dance for flute; Rondo, piccolo and piano;
CHORUS: Annunciation and magnificat, with
winds; VOICE: Songs of death, mezzo-soprano and
string quartet; numerous triadic, college-level
works for band and orchestral instruments,
chorus, and solo voice.
211 Hillendale Dr., Hattiesburg, MS 39401

PREVIN, ANDRE
    b. Berlin, Germany, 6 Apr. 1930; U.S. citizen
1943. Studied at Berlin Cons.; Paris Cons.;
and with Mario Castelnuovo-Tedesco in Los
Angeles; conducting with Pierre Monteux in San
Francisco. His awards include the Berlin Film
Festival award, 1955; 4 Academy awards; Screen
Composers Assoc. award; 5 Grammys. He was an
arranger for MGM at 17; served in the U.S. Army,
1950-52; was jazz and concert pianist and conductor; taught at Univ. of California, Los
Angeles, 1957-58; was conductor, Houston Symphony, 1967-68; music director, London Symphony,
1968-79; music director, Pittsburgh Symphony,
from 1976.
    WORKS: THEATRE: Invitation to the dance;
Every good boy deserves favour, music drama;
ORCHESTRA: Overture to a comedy, 1960; guitar
concerto; cello concerto; Peaches, flute and
orch.; Portrait for strings; CHAMBER MUSIC:
string quartet; flute sonata; violin sonata;
4 outings, brass quintet; PIANO: Impressions;
The invisible drummer; Pages from my calendar;
FILM SCORES: It's always fair weather; Bad day
at Black Rock, 1955; The subterraneans, 1960;
Two for the seesaw, 1962.
    c/o Pittsburgh Symphony Orchestra, Pitts-
burgh, PA 15222

PRICE, FLORENCE B.
    b. Little Rock, Ark., 9 Apr. 1888; d. Chicago,
Ill., 3 June 1953. Studied with Benjamin Cutter,
George W. Chadwick, and Frederick Converse, New
England Cons., diploma 1906; at American Cons.;
Chicago Musical Coll.; also with Arthur Andersen.
Her awards included a G. Schirmer prize, 1928,
for At the cotton gin, for piano; Wanamaker
award for her symphony, 1932. She was the first
black woman to write symphonic works. She taught
at Shorter Coll. and at Clark Univ.; was soloist
with the Chicago Symphony playing her own works.
    WORKS: ORCHESTRA: symphony, 1925, performed
by the Chicago Symphony at the Century of Progress Exhibition, 1933; piano concerto; violin
concerto; symphonic poem; Concert overture on
Negro spirituals; The wind and the sea, with
chorus; Lincoln walks at midnight, with chorus;
Rhapsody, piano and orch.; CHAMBER MUSIC: piano
quintet; Negro folk songs in counterpoint,
string quartet; Moods, flute, clarinet, piano;
organ sonata; Passacaglia and fugue, organ;
PIANO: Arkansas jitters; 3 little Negro dances;
From the canebrake, a suite.

PRICE, JOHN E.
    b. Tulsa, Okla., 21 June 1935. Studied with O.
Anderson Fuller, Lincoln Univ., A.B. 1957; with
Bela Rosza, Tulsa Univ., M.M. 1963; with Robert
Wykes, Harold Blumenfeld, and Paul Pisk, Washington Univ., 1967-68. His awards include
selection as an exchange scholar under the
Phelps-Stokes Found. to lecture in the Caribbean,
1974; and commissions. He began to compose at
age 6; was vocal coach and composer, Karamu
Theatre, Cleveland, 1957-59; served in U.S.
Army, 1959-61; was faculty member and composer-
in-residence, Florida Memorial Coll., 1964-74;
from 1974, at Eastern Illinois Univ.

    WORKS: THEATRE: music for 14 plays in-
cluding Risible visible, 1957, Death of a salesman, 1958, Fairy tale wood, 1959, Candy man
Beechum, 1962; and The other foot, 1-act opera,
1970; ORCHESTRA: Scherzo, clarinet and orch.,
1957; Song of the Liberty Bell, with chorus,
soloists, speaker, 1976; . . . and Faustus
gained the world . . ., small orch., 1976;
Tutankhamon: Trumpets, solo trumpet, strings,
percussion, tape, 1977; CHAMBER MUSIC: Foresight
of time and the universe, speaker, clarinet,
trumpet, drums, 1955; brass quartet, 1956; Im-
pulse and deviation, solo cello, 1958; duet for
horn and trombone, 1959; Piece and deviation,
viola and piano, 1962; quartet for violin, viola,
horn, bassoon, 1962; trombone sonata, 1968; trio
for clarinet, horn, trombone, 1968; A Ptah hymn,
solo cello, 1978; numerous works for solo voice,
chorus, chamber groups, and piano.
    Eastern Illinois University, Charleston, IL
61920

PRICE, MILBURN
    b. Electric Mills, Miss., 9 Apr. 1938. Studied
with Halsey Stevens, Univ. of Southern California;
conducting at Baylor Univ. He was faculty
member, Univ. of Southern California, 1966-67;
from 1967, at Furman Univ., dept. chairman from
1972. His many published choral works include
Meditation on the nativity, a choral service.
    Furman University, Greenville, SC 29613

PRICE, PAUL WILLIAM
    b. Fitchburg, Mass., 15 May 1921. Studied at
New England Cons., diploma; Cincinnati Cons.,
M.M.; percussion with George Carey and Fred Noak.
He was cited by the Assoc. of American Composers
and Conductors for "outstanding contribution to
American music." He was conductor of the Manhattan Percussion Ensemble for a State Dept.-
sponsored tour of the Near East, 1967-68; was a
member, American Symphony Orch.; percussion lecturer and clinician; president and editor, Music
for Percussion, Inc.; has held faculty posts at
Univ. of Illinois, Boston Univ., Ithaca Coll.,
Newark State Coll.; and from 1957, at Manhattan
School of Music.
    WORKS: PERCUSSION: Inventions, 4 percus-
sionists, 1947; 12 solos for timpani, 1951;
Exhibitions, snare drum; 6 bass drum solos; percussion method books.
    470 Kipp St., Teaneck, NJ 07666

PRIESING, DOROTHY
    b. Nantucket, Mass., 31 July 1910. Studied at
Columbia Univ., B.S., M.A.; with James Friskin,
Howard Brockway, and Rubin Goldmark, Juilliard
School; and with Nadia Boulanger at Fontainebleau. At Juilliard she received the Coolidge
prize in composition and the Seligman prize in
fugue. She was instructor, Columbia Univ.,
1936-39; Juilliard School, 1936-39, 1942-47;
and associate professor, Montclair State Coll.,
1953-75.
    WORKS: BAND: Invocation; CHAMBER MUSIC:
violin sonata; Pieces for piano; CHORUS: Now is
the caroling season; Noel; Wonder of the dark-
some night; Wild swans, women's voices; Children's

PRINCE, ROBERT

carols; VOICE: songs on poems of James Joyce.
42 Llewellyn Rd., Montclair, NJ 07042

PRINCE, ROBERT
b. New York, N.Y., 1929. His works include 2
ballets: New York export: Opus jazz, 1958, and
Events, 1961; Meet the band, composed for Benny
Goodman's Russian tour, 1962; music for 2 television plays: "Dr. Faustus," 1964, and "Half a
sixpence," 1965; dance music for Braodway shows.

PRIOLO, CHRISTOPHER
b. Plainfield, N.J., 12 Oct. 1949. Studied with
Peter Racine Fricker and Thea Musgrave, Univ. of
California, Santa Barbara. He won second prize
in a contest sponsored by the Santa Barbara
Music Society. He was student teacher at Univ.
of California, Santa Barbara, 1973-74.
WORKS: ORCHESTRA: Magnificat, with chorus
and soloists; CHAMBER MUSIC: woodwind trio,
1969; Poeme II, voice and piano; sextet for
winds, strings, and harp; duet for cello and
harp; Prelude and fugue, 2 pianos; Piano variations; Scherzo; harp.
958 Garcia Rd., Santa Barbara, CA 93103

PRITCHARD, ROGER
b. Prestbury, England, 18 Feb. 1940; to U.S.
1963. Studied with Anthony Gnazzo, Mills Coll.;
with Alden Jenks, San Francisco Cons.
WORKS: CHAMBER MUSIC: High lines, voice
and bells; Death piece #98.4; ELECTRONIC:
Crimond II, tape; Church music II, voice and
tape; Single finger exercise, tape.

PROCTOR, ALICE McELROY
b. Albany, N.Y., 18 Apr. 1915. Was a music
major at Smith Coll., A.B. cum laude 1935; then
at Eastman School of Music, Ph.D. 1940. She
taught at Southwestern State Coll., Weatherford,
Okla., to 1943; married Leland Proctor in 1939;
taught at Milton Acad., Dedham Country Day
School, and privately until incapacitated by
ALS (called Lou Gehrig's disease) in 1978.
WORKS: Cinderella, an operetta; concertino
for string orch.; Banrigh suite for orch.;
chamber music, ballet music, choral pieces,
songs, and piano-teaching pieces.
4 Harvard Place, Dedham, MA 02026

PROCTOR, LELAND
b. Newton, Mass., 24 Mar. 1914. Studied with
Bernard Rogers, Howard Hanson, Eastman School of
Music, with Spencer Norton, Univ. of Oklahoma,
M.M.; with Walter Piston at Harvard Univ., where
he studied on a Ford Found. grant. He was music
dept. head, Southwestern State Coll., Okla.,
1939-43; faculty member, New England Cons.,
1946-58; then musical designer for various companies in Boston and Springfield.
WORKS: OPERA: Eve of crossing, 1 act;
ORCHESTRA: symphony #1; suite for string orch.;
Moby Dick (symphony #2), with chorus; CHAMBER
MUSIC: piano quintet; 2 string quartets;
Fantasy, flute and piano; clarinet sonata; 3
chorale preludes, organ and oboe; CHORUS: Canticle of the sun, cantata; 3 songs of service.
1 South Rd., Hampden, MA 01036

PROCTOR, ARLENE. See ZALLMAN, ARLENE (PROCTOR)

PROSTAKOFF, JOSEPH
b. Kokand, Central Asia, 1911; to U.S. 1922.
Studied piano with Abby Whiteside, composition
with Mark Brunswick and Karol Rathaus; teaches
piano and is a free-lance editor. His compositions include 2 bagatelles for piano.

PROTO, FRANK
b. Brooklyn, N.Y., 18 July 1941. He is self-
taught in composition; has been composer and
arranger with the Cincinnati Symph. Orch. from
1966.
WORKS: ORCHESTRA: Idle September, with
jazz quintet, 1967; double bass concerto, 1968;
concerto for violin and double bass, 1972; saxophone concerto, 1972; An American overture, 1972;
2 songs, for orch., 1973; Fantasy on the Saints,
1974; concertino for percussion and strings,
1975; 3 pieces, for percussion and orch., 1976;
Solar wind, 1976; cello concerto, Cincinnati,
20 Apr. 1979; CHAMBER MUSIC: double bass sonata,
1963; quartet for basses, 1964; duets for double
basses, 1966; duet for violin and bass, 1967;
octet, woodwind quintet, bass, percussion,
soprano, 1969; trio for violin, viola, bass,
1974; Nebula, double bass, piano, tape, 1975;
string quartet, 1977; many works for young
people.
6265 Dawes Lane, Cincinnati, OH 45230

PROULX, RICHARD
b. St. Paul, Minn., 3 Apr. 1937. Studied at
McPhail Coll. of Music, Minneapolis; with
Dominick Argento, Univ. of Minnesota; at Columbus
Boychoir School; also organ and conducting. He
has been church music director/organist from
1958; at St. Thomas Episcopal Church, Seattle,
from 1971. His compositions include more than
100 published works for organ, solo voice,
chorus, and instrumental groups.
P.O. Box 15106, Seattle, WA 98115

PROVENZANO, ALDO
b. Philadelphia, Pa., 3 May 1930. Studied with
Peter Mennin, Juilliard School, B.S. 1956, M.S.
1957, holding scholarships, 1952-57. He taught
in public schools, 1957-64; at Eastman School of
Music, 1964-69; Juilliard School, 1969-70; City
Coll. of New York, 1971-75. He is composer,
arranger, conductor for recordings, films, television, dance groups, etc.
WORKS: OPERA: The cask of amontillado,
1968; BALLET: Malacchio, dance in 1 scene;
CHAMBER MUSIC: Essay, string quartet; Recitation, violin and piano; woodwind quintet; FILM
SCORES: Jacktown, jazz score; 4 documentaries;
also choral works, songs, piano pieces.
429 Burning Tree Rd., Cherry Hill, NJ 08034

PRYOR, ARTHUR WILLARD
b. St. Joseph, Mo., 22 Sept. 1870; d. Long
Branch, N.J., 18 June 1942. Studied with his
father, a bandmaster; joined Sousa's band as
trombone soloist in 1892 and was also assistant
conductor. In 1903 he organized his own band,
presenting his first New York concert in that

year; conducted outdoor concerts at Asbury Park, N.J., for 25 summers. His some 300 compositions included the operettas Jingaboo, On the eve of her wedding, Uncle Tom's cabin; ragtime and cakewalks, and his best known work, The whistler and his dog.

PTASZYNSKA, MARTA
b. Warsaw, Poland, 29 July 1943. Studied at Music Lyceum in Warsaw; composition with Dobrowolski and Rudzinski at the Warsaw Cons., 1962-68; electronic music with Kotonski; percussion at the Cons. of Pozan, 1963-67; in 1969, studied with Nadia Boulanger in Paris. A grant from the Kosciuszky Found. enabled her to study percussion at the Cleveland Inst. of Music, 1972-74. She then taught percussion at Bennington Coll. to 1977, and from 1977, at Univ. of California at Berkeley. Her awards include a Polish State prize, 1967.
WORKS: OPERA: Oscar from Alva, composer's own libretto based on Byron's text, 1972; ORCHESTRA: Improvisations, 1968; Spectri amori, 1973; concerto for percussion quartet, 1974; Chimes, bells, wood, stones, winds, strings, percussion, 1977; CHAMBER MUSIC: Preludes, vibraphone and piano, 1965; Variations, solo flute, 1967; Scherzo, xylophone and piano, 1967; A tale of nightingales, baritone and 6 instruments, 1968; Projection sonores, chamber ensemble, 1970; 3 interludes, 2 pianos, 1969; Madrigals, in memory of Stravinsky, large ensemble, 1971; Space model, solo percussion, 1970; Sonospheres 1, clarinet, trombone, cello, piano, 1971; Sonospheres 2, 8 instruments, 1971; Sonospheres 3, flute, clarinet, trombone, cello, piano, percussion, 1972; Siderals, 2 percussion quintets and lights, 1974; Recitative, arioso, toccata, solo violin, 1969-75; 2 poems, solo tuba, 1973-75; Mobile, 2 players, 1975; Classical variations, 4 timpani and string quartet, 1976; Quodlibet, solo double bass, 1976; Inventions, solo percussion, 1972-77; Linear construction in space, percussion quartet, 1977; Jeu-parti entre vibraphone et arpe, Aspen, Colo., Festival, 1977; VOICE: Chant for all the people on Earth, oratorio, 1969; Epigrams, 20 women's voices, flute, harp, percussion, piano, 1976-77; Helio, centricum musicum, spectacle for voices, dancers, and instrumentalists, 1978.

PULLIG, KENNETH
b. Torrington, Conn., 14 Apr. 1945. Studied at Univ. of Connecticut and Berklee Coll. of Music; held a Massachusetts Council of the Arts fellowship, 1979. He has been instructor, Berklee Coll., from 1975.
WORKS: JAZZ CHAMBER MUSIC: 2 suites; Synapse; Deportations; Fantasy, The Planet Earth; Jazz suite for brass quintet; Marche oblique, brass quintet; Promenade, brass quintet; and numerous compositions for his own 10-piece band, Decahedron.
1789 Commonwealth Ave., Brighton, MA 02135

PURSELL, WILLIAM
b. 1926. Studied at Peabody Cons. and at Eastman School of Music. He held the Boise composition

scholarship at Peabody, 1944-47; received the Benjamin award in 1953 for Christ looking over Jerusalem.

PURSWELL, PATRICK W.
b. Ft. Sill, Okla., 1 July 1939. Studied with Frederic Goossen, Univ. of Alabama, 1957-63; with Kenneth Gaburo, Burrill Phillips, and Ben Johnston, Univ. of Illinois; with Richard Hervig, Univ. of Iowa, 1963-65. He was a member, Univ. of Chicago Contemporary Chamber Players, 1965-66; member, Center for New Music, Univ. of Iowa, 1966-71.
WORKS: ORCHESTRA: symphony, 1959; CHAMBER MUSIC: woodwind quintet, 1957; piano sonata, 1958; violin sonata, 1960; quartet for bassoon and string trio, 1962; sonata for solo flute, 1962; Proxmit, cello and piano, 1963; "it" grew and grew, flute solo, 1964.

PURVIS, RICHARD
b. San Francisco, Calif., 1915. Studied at Peabody Cons.; Curtis Inst.; Royal School of Music, London. He was organist-choirmaster in Philadelphia; bandmaster, U.S. Army, in World War II; then settled in San Francisco as organist-choirmaster. He has published many works for chorus and for organ.

PUSINA, JAN.
b. Los Angeles, Calif., 5 Aug. 1940. Studied with Jean-Claude Eloy and William Denny, Univ. of California at Berkeley, M.M. 1969. He received the Niccola de Lorenzo composition prize, 1967, for an untitled piece for 8 singers and piano. He was instructor, Merritt Coll., Oakland, 1969; East Bay Music Center, Richmond, Calif., 1973; and at Univ. of California at Davis, 1974-78.
WORKS: CHAMBER MUSIC: Divergence, 6 players, 1969; ELECTRONIC: Kama, 3 percussion ensembles, solo instrument, tape, 1968; Tape compositions, #1-6, 1970-73; Cultural train, live tape performance of environmental sounds, 1973; Sum tones and difference tones, flute and tape, 1973; Evoked images, 9 instruments and tape, 1977; Pastiche, 7 instruments, 3 singers, tape, 1978; A farewell to alms (with Paul Robinson), theatre piece for tapes, slides, instruments, 1977.
1535 Berkeley Way, Berkeley, CA 94703

PUSZTAI, TIBOR
b. Budapest, Hungary, 23 Dec. 1946; U.S. citizen 1973. Studied with Robert Cogan, Alexander Goehr, and Gunther Schuller, New England Cons., artists's diploma 1970. He received the Lincoln Center Young Artist award, 1965; Koussevitzky Composition prize, 1970; Frank Huntington Beebe Found. grant, 1973. He was faculty member and assistant to the director, New England Cons., 1970-73; on faculty, Berkshire Music Center, 1973; in 1976, was appointed chief conductor, Iranian Nat. Ballet, Tehran.
WORKS: CHAMBER MUSIC: Labyrinths, piano; Interactions, horn and percussion; Canticle, 2 horns, 3 clarinets; Silence plus 7, mixed ensemble; One farewell, bass-baritone and mixed

PUTSCHE, THOMAS

ensemble; Nocturnes, soprano and ensemble; Requiem profana, mezzo-soprano, tenor, ensemble; Vertere in fugam avis paradisium, flute and percussion, Boston, 30 Apr. 1973.
c/o New England Conservatory, 290 Huntington Ave., Boston, MA 02115

PUTSCHE, THOMAS
b. Scarsdale, N.Y., 1929. Studied with Milton Babbitt, Aaron Copland, Arnold Franchetti, and Vittorio Giannini. In addition to being on the faculty, Hartt Coll. of Music, he is a member of Friends and Enemies of Modern Music and the Internat. Society for Contemporary Music, and an occasional music critic for the Hartford Courant. His compositions include Cat and the moon, a 1-act chamber opera on a play by W. B. Yeats.
Hartt College of Music, Univ. of Hartford, West Hartford, CT 06117

PYLE, FRANCIS JOHNSON
b. South Bend, Ind., 13 Sept. 1901. Studied at Oberlin Coll., A.B.; with George F. McKay, Univ. of Washington, M.A.; with Howard Hanson, Bernard Rogers, Herbert Elwell, and Burrill Phillips, Eastman School of Music, Ph.D. His awards include 2 from Sigma Alpha Iota, 1955, and many commissions. He was faculty member, Central Washington State Coll., 1921-37; professor and theory chairman, Drake Univ., 1937-72 (emeritus); orchestra director, Central Coll., 1972-73; orchestra director and professor, San Jacinto Coll., Pasadena, Tex., 1973-74.
WORKS: ORCHESTRA: symphony, 1940; Old river tune and clambake, 1945; Frontier sketches, string orch., 1950; Overture to The magic fishbone, 1957; From the southwest, suite, 1959; harp concerto, 1970; 3 Psalms, with chorus, brass choir, optional tape, 1971; 3 sinfoniettas, #3, Fort Dodge, Iowa, 29 Jan. 1978; WIND ENSEMBLE: Greetings suite, 1949; Edged night, with solo flute, 1952; Far dominion, 1963; horn concerto, 1964; Concerto giubilante, organ, winds, percussion, 1965; trumpet concerto, 1965; Theme and dialogues, 1970; Pasadena '71, 1971; symphony, 1972; Fanfare, 1972; CHAMBER MUSIC: Currier and Ives, woodwind trio, 1955; trio for flute, cello, piano, 1956; clarinet sonata, 1959; woodwind quintet, 1959; Sonata for 3, clarinet, piano, percussion, 1960; violin sonata, 1964; concerto for harp and piano, 1969; flute sonata, 1970; bassoon sonata, 1973; Reprints Currier and Ives, woodwind quintet; suite for 2 clarinets; Serenade, flute, clarinet, bassoon; 6 duos for 2 clarinets, Nassau, N.Y., 3 May 1978; 5 studies for improvised dance, flute and bassoon, and Sonata in the form of a duo concertante, both premiered in Cleveland, 15 May 1978; PIANO: 3 sonatas, #3, Washington, D.C., 31 May 1976; suite for piano, 4 hands; Suite for puppeteers; Convention '74, suite for 2 pianos; also many choral works, songs, works for accordion.
1535 41st St., Des Moines, IA 50311

QUARLES, JAMES THOMAS
b. St. Louis, Mo., 7 Nov. 1877; d. Saugus, Calif., 4 Mar. 1954. Studied with Widor in Paris. He taught at Cornell Univ., 1903-23; was professor, Univ. of Missouri, 1923-43; composed the Univ. of Missouri Alma Mater, anthems, organ works, songs.

QUEEN, VIRGINIA
b. Dallas, Tex., 25 Oct. 1921. Studied at American Cons. and Univ. of Colorado. She has been faculty member, Ouachita Baptist Univ., from 1946.
WORKS: CHORUS: Let thy holy spirit come upon us, female voices, 1961; PIANO: Adagio and scherzo; 3 vagaries; many works in manuscript.
Ouachita Baptist Univ., Arkadelphia, AR 71923

QUESADA, VIRGINIA
b. Bayside, N.Y., 11 Feb. 1951. Studied with Joel Chadabe at State Univ. of New York at Albany.
WORKS: ELECTRONIC: God commercial, tape and film, 1972; Women's lip, tape and film, 1972; Roller rink, tape alone, 1973.
R.D. #1, Johnston Rd., Slingerlands, NY 12159

QUILLING, HOWARD L.
b. Enid, Okla., 16 Dec. 1935. Studied with Ingolf Dahl, Robert Linn, Ernest Kanitz, Halsey Stevens, Univ. of Southern California, B.M., M.M.; California State Univ., Los Angeles, M.A.; with Lehman Engel, BMI Music Theatre Workshop. He taught in public schools until appointment to the faculty at California State Coll., Bakersfield, 1971.
WORKS: THEATRE: music for Danton's death, 1972, The wild duck, 1972, Tiny Alice, 1973; Equipoise, children's musical; ORCHESTRA: overture, 1966; Fantasy on The wayfaring stranger, 1967; piano concerto, 1969; symphonia, chamber orch., 1971; symphony, 1978; BAND: Intermezzo, 1967; Introspections, 1968; suite for alto saxophone and wind orch., 1970; symphony for winds and percussion, 1973; Diversions for wind orch.; Divertimento, clarinet choir; CHAMBER MUSIC: quartet for clarinet and strings, 1958; string quartet, 1966; 2 violin sonatas, 1969, 1971; quartet for winds, 1969; 3 piano sonatas, 1957, 1962, 1970; Fantasy, violin and piano, 1972; piano trio; 4 pieces for 5 brass; cello sonata; also choral works and songs.
3001 Harmony Dr., Bakersfield, CA 93306

QUINN, J. MARK (James J.)
b. Chicago, Ill., 30 Apr. 1936. Studied with Leon Stein, DePaul Univ.; received the American Bandmasters' Assoc. Ostwald award, 1959; special citation, American Acad. of Television Arts and Sciences, 1966. In 1965 he joined the humanities faculty at Loop Coll., City Coll. of Chicago.
WORKS: THEATRE: Requiem for a slave, ballet-opera, 2 solo singers, wind choir, orch., WITW, Chicago, Mar. 1967; Clash of kings, ballet for winds, brass, percussion, 1968; Ritual-D, ballet for expanded jazz orch., WITW, Chicago, Nov. 1971; ORCHESTRA: Lament, 1959; Tale of a square dance, 1963; BAND: Revolt in red, 1956; Portrait of the land, 1958; Chorale of the winds, 1959; Symphonic variants, 1960; Testament of

battle, 1959; Soliloquy for a noble one, 1961;
Varsomna-I, 1973.

Loop College, City College of Chicago, IL
60670

QUINTIERE, JUDE
b. Paterson, N.J., 10 Sept. 1939. Studied at
New York Univ., B.M.; Columbia Univ., M.A.;
electronic music with Gershon Kingsley, the New
School. She has received grants from ZBS Found.,
Composers' Forum, American Music Center, and
Paterson Task Force. She was on the faculty,
Tombrock Coll., 1968-74; Fairleigh Dickinson
Univ., 1973-74; director, WBAI-FM, 1975-77;
from 1977, director, Soho Sound Services.
WORKS: CHAMBER MUSIC: Lines and spaces, 4
instruments; Tolerance 1966, 9 instruments,
1966; 69 Jersey St., brass quintet; Never put
the things you value with the things you love,
clarinet and recorder; CHORUS: Requiem for
Paterson, with orch.; ELECTRONIC: Elegy for
City Hall, tape, 1973; The wheel, soprano, alto,
3 winds, cello, synthesizer, New York, 30 Apr.
1973; Mountain stream, female voice and synthesizer; Für Goethe, clarinet and synthesizer;
Move by Quintiere, 4 alto saxophones and tape;
Music for recorder and tape; Roseland, a video
quartet for recorders, all performed by one
player.
47-49 Greene St., New York, NY 10013

QUIST, PAMELA LAYMAN
b. R.I., 3 Apr. 1949. Studied with Jean E. Ivey
and Robert Hall Lewis, Peabody Cons. Her awards
include a scholarship to the Vermont Composers'
Conf., 1973; Washington Friday Morning Music
Club composition award, 1975; Annapolis Fine
Arts Found. composition prize, 1975. She has
been vice-president, the Walden School, Ltd., a
summer school for young composers, from 1973;
was on faculty, State Univ. of New York, Geneseo,
1974-75; from 1975, on faculty, Peabody Cons.
WORKS: ORCHESTRA: Lazaros, 1976; CHAMBER
MUSIC: 7 canzone d'amore, tenor, percussion,
guitar, 1973; quintet for winds and strings,
1974; 3 poems, bassoon and clarinet, 1974;
Gravitation I, solo violin, 1975; movement for
string quartet, 1975; Meditations, solo trumpet,
1977; Mosaic, cello and piano, 1978; Psalm,
soprano, clarinet, piano, 1978; Syllogisms,
piano, 1979; VOICE: Psalm for chorus, 1977.
1309 W. Northern Pkwy., Baltimore, MD 21209

RABINOFF, SYLVIA
b. New York, N.Y., 10 Oct. Attended New York
Univ.; studied with Ignace Padereweski, Rudolf
Serkin, Albert Stoessel, Bernard Wagenaar,
Philip James, and Georges Enesco; received an
honorary D.M. from Lincoln Memorial Univ. She
conducted the Morley Singers, 1942-44; toured as
solo pianist and in duo concerts with her late
husband, Benno Rabinof, violinist.
WORKS: OPERETTA: Hamlet, the flea, for
children; ORCHESTRA: Carnival, tone poem with
chorus; Concert variation on Turkey in the
straw; suite for chamber orch.; CHORUS: Deluge,
cantata; PIANO: Gastronomic suite.
33 Riverside Dr., New York, NY 10023

RACHMANINOFF, SERGEI VASSILYEVICH
b. Oneg, Novgorod, Russia, 1 Apr. 1873; U.S.
citizen 1943; d. Beverly Hills, Calif., 28 Mar.
1943. Studied at St. Petersburg Cons.; piano
with Siloti, composition with Taneyev and
Arensky, Moscow Cons., graduating in piano in
1891, in composition in 1892, and winning the
gold medal for his 1-act opera, Aleko. His
Prelude in C# minor, one of the best-known piano
pieces in the world, was also written in 1892.
In 1909 he gave 26 recitals in the U.S.; returned
to America in 1918 and eventually settled in
California.
WORKS: OPERA: Aleko, on Pushkin's The
gypsies, 1892; The miserly knight, 1905;
Francesca da Rimini, 1905; ORCHESTRA: 4 piano
concertos, 1890-91, 1901, 1909, 1927; Prince
Rostislav, symphonic poem, 1891; The rock, symphonic poem, 1893; Caprice Bohemien, 1894; 3
symphonies, 1895, 1907, 1936; The isle of the
dead, symphonic poem, 1907; Rhapsody on a theme
by Paganini, piano and orch., 1934; Symphonic
dances, 1940; CHAMBER MUSIC: Trio elegiaque,
1893; Romance and Danse Hongroise, violin and
piano, 1893; cello sonata, 1901; CHORUS: The
spring, with baritone solo and orch., 1901;
Liturgy of St. John Chrysostom, a cappella, 1909;
The bells, with soloists and orch., 1913; vesper
mass, a cappella, 1914; 3 Russian songs, a
cappella, 1926; numerous songs and piano compositions including 2 suites and 2 sonatas.

RACKLEY, LAWRENCE (L. R. SMITH)
b. Media, Ill., 10 Sept. 1932. Studied with
Robert Mills Delaney, Northwestern Univ., B.M.
1954, M.M. 1955; with Bernard Rogers and Howard
Hanson, Eastman School of Music, Ph.D. 1958. He
has received numerous commissions. He was
faculty member, Central Michigan Univ., 1957-63;
from 1963, at Kalamazoo Coll., dept. chairman
from 1975.
WORKS: ORCHESTRA: symphony, 1957; Discourse, soliloquy, and concourse, cello and orch.,
1969; Confluences, 1970; BAND: Sarasota Sailor
Circus march, 1974; River Raisin march, 1975;
Processional variations, 1977; They/You/I/We,
violin concerto with wind ensemble, 1978;
CHAMBER MUSIC: chamber concerto, piano and 7
instruments, 1958; piano quintet, 1965; Rhapsodic dialogues, violin and piano, 1974; CHORUS:
cantata, with tenor solo and organ, 1964; 2 Hil-
berry songs, 1969.
438 N. Arlington, Kalamazoo, MI 49007

RAFFMAN, RELLY
b. New Bedford, Mass., 4 Sept. 1921. Studied at
Dartmouth Coll., B.A. 1947; with Henry Brant,
Columbia Univ., M.A. 1949; with Bernhard Heiden,
Indiana Univ. He received the Ernest Bloch
award, 1958; Ella Cabot Lyman Trust grant, 1962;
and commissions. He was instructor, Southwest
Missouri State Coll., 1949-50; from 1954, on
faculty, Clark Univ., Jeppson professor from
1969.
WORKS: OPERA: Midas, 1964; THEATRE: music
for The good woman of Setzuan, 1972; CHAMBER
MUSIC: Diversion for 3 celli, 1951; woodwind
quintet, 1967; CHORUS: The friendly beasts,

RAGLAND, ROBERT OLIVER

1956; Triptych, 1957; Alleluia, 1957; I care not
for these ladies, 1959; The secular masque,
1960; The passionate pilgrim, 1962; Jubilate Deo,
1966; Psalm IV, 1967; Sweet was the song, 1970;
The 3 ravens, 1970; Virtue, 1970.
209 Lovell St., Worcester, MA 01603

RAGLAND, ROBERT OLIVER
b. Chicago, Ill., 3 July 1933. Studied at Northwestern Univ., B.S.; American Cons., B.A., M.A.;
with Alexander Tcherepnin and William Russo. He
served in the U.S. Navy, 1953-55; is pianist and
arranger for dance bands; has scored films in the
U.S. and Europe; also television scores.
WORKS: ORCHESTRA: 12 symphonies; Overture
1861; CHAMBER MUSIC: string quartet; and songs.

RAHN, JOHN
b. New York, N.Y., 26 Feb. 1944. Studied bassoon
at Juilliard School; composition with Benjamin
Boretz and Milton Babbitt, Princeton Univ.,
Ph.D. 1974. He held fellowships at Juilliard
School and at Princeton; has played bassoon in
several symphony orchestras; was faculty member,
Univ. of Michigan, 1973-75; from 1975, at Univ.
of Washington.
WORKS: BAND: Deloumenon, 1970; CHAMBER
MUSIC: woodwind quintet, 1969; Epithalamium,
piano, 1968; trio for clarinet, cello, piano,
1972; Peanut butter defies gravity, soprano and
piano, 1973; Reductionist variations, piano;
Breakfast, piano; CHORUS: Hos Estin, with in-
struments, 1971.
University of Washington, Seattle, WA 98195

RAINGER, RALPH
b. New York, N.Y., 7 Oct. 1901; d. Beverly Hills,
Calif., 23 Oct. 1942. Studied at Damrosch Cons.;
Brown Univ. Law School, L.L.B.; then music with
Paolo Gallico, Clarence Adler, and Arnold
Schoenberg, Univ. of California, Los Angeles.
He was accompanist and member of a 2-piano team.
In 1930 he settled in Hollywood as a film com-
poser. His film scores included A bedtime story;
Little Miss Marker; Here is my heart; Waikiki
wedding; Gulliver's travel; Moon over Miami; My
gal Sal. Among his many popular songs, Thanks
for the memory (Bob Hope's theme song) won an
Academy award in 1938. He died in a plane crash.

RAKSIN, DAVID
b. Philadelphia, Pa., 4 Aug. 1912. Studied with
William F. Happich in Philadelphia; with Harl
McDonald, Univ. of Pennsylvania, M.B.; with
Isadore Freed in New York; and with Arnold
Schoenberg in Los Angeles. Since 1935 he has
been composer-conductor for radio, television,
theatre, major film studios, recordings, symphony and chamber music concerts; also lecturer
and writer. From 1956, he has been faculty
member, Univ. of Southern California and Univ.
of California at Los Angeles. He was president,
Composers and Lyricists Guild, 1962-70, then
on board of governors.
WORKS: BALLET: Inspiration; Mother Goose-
Step; THEATRE: Feather in your hat, multimedia,
1942; If the shoe fits, musical; The wind in the
willows, musical; music for Noah; Mother Courage;

The prodigal; The Chinese wall; Volpone; FILM
SCORES: more than 100, including Laura; Forever
Amber; Force of evil; The secret life of Walter
Mitty; Suddenly; Separate tables; Smoky; Al
Capone; The bad and the beautiful; The redeemer;
Will Penny; What's the matter with Helen;
Madeline; The unicorn in the garden; The soldier;
TELEVISION SHOWS: more than 300, including "Ben
Casey"; "The breaking point"; "Report from
America", USIA series. Adaptations of pieces
from his film and television scores have been
performed by almost all major orchestras in the
U.S. and many abroad.
c/o Composers and Lyricists Guild,
10999 Riverside Dr., N. Hollywood, CA 91602

RAMEY, PHILLIP
b. Chicago, Ill., 12 Sept. 1939. Studied at
Internat. Acad. of Music, Nice, France, 1959;
with Alexander Tcherepnin, privately, then at
De Paul Univ., B.A. 1962; with Jack Beeson,
Columbia Univ., M.A. 1965; held 5 fellowships at
the MacDowell Colony, 1969-76. In 1977 he was
appointed annotator and program editor for the
New York Philharmonic.
WORKS: ORCHESTRA: Concert suite, piano and
orch., 1962; 7, they are 7, incantation for bass-
baritone and orch., 1965; Orchestral discourse,
1967; 2 piano concertos, 1969, 1976; concerto
for chamber orchestra, 1974; CHAMBER MUSIC:
sonata for 3 unaccompanied timpani, 1961; Cat
songs, soprano, flute, piano, 1962; Music for
brass and percussion, 1964; Capriccio, percussion, 1966; Night music, percussion, 1966;
Toccata breva, percussion, 1967; Commentaries,
flute and piano, 1968; string quartet, 1970;
clarinet sonata, 1971; suite for violin and
piano, 1971; La citadelle, oboe and piano, 1975;
The song of David, solo flute, 1977; PIANO: 5
sonatas, 1961, 1966, 1968, 1968, 1974; Epigrams,
1967; Doomsday fragments, 1970; Fantasy, 1972;
Leningrad rag, 1972; Night song, 1973; Memorial
ode (in memoriam Alexander Tcherepnin), 1977.
825 West End Ave., Penthouse F, New York, NY
10025

RAMSIER, PAUL
b. Louisville, Ky., 23 Sept. 1927. Studied at
Univ. of Louisville, B.M.; piano with Beveridge
Webster, Juilliard School, M.M.; composition
with Alexei Haieff and Ernst von Dohnanyo, New
York Univ., Ph.D. He received fellowships from
the Huntington Hartford Found., MacDowell Colony,
Yaddo; and annual ASCAP awards. He was faculty
member, Ohio State Univ., 1972-73; New York
Univ., 1967-72, and from 1976.
WORKS: OPERA: The man on the bearskin rug,
1 act; BALLET: Leaf in the wind, 1954; 6 dance
diversions; Pied piper, 1964; THEATRE: The
dancing princesses, musical for children, 1967;
ORCHESTRA: Sonata for orchestra, 1954; Divertimento concertante on a theme of Couperin, contrabass and orch., 1965; CHAMBER MUSIC: Night
songs, string quartet and soprano; Fiery dragon,
narrator and ensemble, 1960; CHORUS: The moon
and the sun; Wine (riddle); Eden; FILM SCORE:
Turkey, documentary; MULTIMEDIA: Celebrations,
tape and dancer, 1973.
210 Riverside Dr., New York, NY 10025

RAN, SHULAMIT
b. Tel Aviv, Israel, 21 Oct. 1949; to U.S. 1963.
Studied with Paul Ben Haim and Alexander
Boscovitz in Israel; with Norman Dello Joio,
Mannes Coll. of Music, on full scholarship,
1963-67; piano with Nadia Reisenberg and Dorothy
Taubman in New York; composition with Ralph
Shapey in Chicago; Aaron Copland and Lukas Foss
at Tanglewood, 1963. Her awards include a
Rockefeller Fund grant, 1968; Ford Found. grant,
1972; Nat. Endowment for the Arts grant, 1976;
first prize, piano composition contest, Israel,
1977; Guggenheim fellowship, 1978; and commissions. She has been faculty member at Univ. of
Chicago from 1973.
    WORKS: ORCHESTRA: Capriccio, piano and
orch., New York, 30 Nov. 1963; Symphonic poem,
piano and orch., Jerusalem, 10 Oct. 1967; Concert piece, piano and orch., Israel Phil., 12
July 1971; piano concerto, 1978; CHAMBER MUSIC:
7 Japanese love poems; O The chimneys, voice,
ensemble, and tape, 1969; Hatzvi Israel eulogy,
voice and ensemble, 1968; 3 fantasy pieces for
cello and piano, 1972; Ensembles for 17, Chicago,
11 Apr. 1975; Double vision, 2 quintets and
piano, Chicago, 21 Jan. 1977; Hyperbolae, piano,
performed by all participants, 2nd Internat.
Arthur Rubinstein Piano Competition, Israel,
4-7 Apr. 1977; For an actor, monologue for solo
clarinet, New York, 8 May 1978.
    1455 N. Sandburg Terr., #2009, Chicago, IL
60610

RANDALL, J. K.
b. Cleveland, Ohio, 16 June 1929. Studied with
Herbert Elwell, Cleveland Inst. of Music; at
Columbia Univ., B.A. 1955; Harvard Univ., M.A.
1956; Princeton Univ., M.F.A. 1958; also with
Alexei Haieff and George Thaddeus Jones; piano
with Leonard Shure. He received a Fromm Found.
commission for Mudgett, 1965. He joined the
Princeton Univ. music faculty in 1958.
    WORKS: CHAMBER MUSIC: Improvisation on a
poem by e. e. cummings, voice and chamber ensemble, 1961; ELECTRONIC: Quartets in pairs,
1964; Mudgett: monologues by a mass murderer,
1965; Lyric variations, violin and computer,
1967; music for the film, Eakins, 1972.
    52 Gulick Rd., Princeton, NJ 08540

RANDEGGER, GUISSEPPE ALDO
b. Naples, Italy, 17 Feb. 1874; to U.S. 1900;
d. New York, N.Y., 30 Nov. 1946. He gave piano
recitals in southern U.S.; taught at Hamilton
Coll. and at Belmont Coll., then privately in
New York. His compositions include a 1-act
opera, The promise of Medea, and songs.

RANDS, BERNARD
b. Sheffield, England, 2 Mar. 1934; to U.S.
1967. Studied at Univ. of Wales, B.M. 1956, M.M.
1958; with Dallapiccola in Italy, 1958-60;
Pierre Boulez and Bruno Maderna in Germany,
1960-61; and with Luciano Berio in Italy, 1961-
62. His awards include numerous travel grants
and composition awards in Britain; Harkness
fellowship, 1966-68; California Arts Council
award, 1978; Nat. Endowment for the Arts grant,

1977. He has held faculty posts at Univ. of
Wales, 1963-67; Princeton Univ. (visiting),
1967-68; Univ. of Illinois, 1969-70; Univ. of
York, 1970-76; from 1976, at Univ. of California,
San Diego.
    WORKS: ORCHESTRA: 3 pieces titled Wild-
track, #1 1969, #2 1973, #3 1974-75; Mesalliance,
with solo piano, 1972; Ology, 17-piece jazz
orch., 1973; Aum, with solo harp, 1974; CHAMBER
MUSIC: Actions for 6, flute, harp, 2 percussion,
viola, cello, 1963; Tableau, mixed ensemble,
1970; Deja, mixed ensemble, 1972; as all get out,
variable ensemble, 1974; Cuaderna, string quartet, 1975; Etendre, mixed ensemble, 1974;
Scherzi, clarinet and piano trio, 1974; Deja 2,
voice and ensemble, San Diego, 31 Jan. 1979;
also a music theatre piece: Serena, for singing
actress, 2 mimes, flute, cello, percussion,
electric organ, 1972.
    University of California, San Diego, La
Jolla, CA 92093

RANEY, JAMES ELBERT
b. Louisville, Ky., 1927. Has published 4
pieces for string quartet, guitar, and contrabass; and 4 pieces for 5 guitars.

RAPH, ALAN
b. New York, N.Y., 3 July 1933. Studied with
Vincent Jones, New York Univ.; at Columbia Univ.
Teachers Coll.; and with Nadia Boulanger at
Fontainebleau. He has held various teaching
posts; from 1976 on faculty, New York Univ.,
School of Education; is leader of The 7th Century, a contemporary instrumental ensemble, and
the Chamber Brass Players.
    WORKS: BALLET: Trinity; Sacred grove on
Mt. Tamalpais; CHAMBER MUSIC: Caprice, bass
trombone solo; Hosanna, chamber ensemble; Canzona, chamber ensemble.
    756 7th Ave., New York, NY 10019

RAPHLING, SAM
b. Fort Worth, Tex., 19 Mar. 1910. Studied with
Rudolph Ganz, Chicago Musical Coll., M.A.; and
with Leonid Kreutzer in Berlin. His awards include a Huntington Hartford fellowship and first
prizes in 2 composition contests. He taught at
Chicago Musical Coll., 1937-45; was piano soloist with the Chicago Symphony Orch. under
Rachmaninoff, Toscanini, and Frederick Stock,
1940-44.
    WORKS: OPERA: President Lincoln, Prince
Hamlet, Johnny Pye and the fool-killer, Peter
Bees, 1-act operas on 4 Hawthorne stories; Liar-
liar, children's opera; ORCHESTRA: 4 symphonies;
4 piano concertos; trumpet concerto; timpani
concerto; suite for strings; Ticker-tape parade,
overture; Abraham Lincoln walks at midnight;
Cowboy rhapsody, violin and orch.; Rhapsody,
oboe, trumpet, and strings; Minstrel rhapsody,
piano and orch.; BAND: Involvement; CHAMBER
MUSIC: Warble for lilac time, flute and strings;
3 violin sonatas; horn sonata; oboe sonata; 2
saxophone sonatas; Pastoral, oboe and piano;
Lyric prelude, bass clarinet and piano; Dance
suite, 2 trumpets; Duograms, 2 oboes; Prelude
and toccata, flute and bassoon; Little suite,

RAPOPORT, EDA FERDINAND

brass sextet; Playthings of the wind, flute
solo; PIANO: 24 etudes; 3 sonatas; 2 sonatinas;
Square dance, piano, 4 hands; American album,
2 pianos; also choral works, many songs.
400 W. 43rd St., Apt. 29-P, New York, NY
10036

RAPOPORT, EDA FERDINAND
b. Dvinsk, Latvia, 1900; d. New York, N.Y., 9
May 1968. Her works include Chant Hebraique,
cello and piano; Hypothesis, violin and cello;
Momentum, violin and cello, New York, 14 Apr.
1959; woodwind quintet; Dance fantastique, New
York, 29 Apr. 1973; also works for orchestra;
songs.

RAPTAKIS, KLEON
b. Andros, Greece, 25 May 1905. Studied at
Juilliard School and at Columbia Univ. He
served in the U.S. Army in World War II; from
1952, has had his own music school.
WORKS: ORCHESTRA: 3 symphonies; The hero;
CHAMBER MUSIC: Sonata for strings; 2 piano
sonatas; piano quintet; VOICE: Book of Greek
songs and dances, including a music history of
Greece.

RASBACH, OSCAR
b. Dayton, Ky., 2 Aug. 1888; d. Pasadena, Calif.,
24 Mar. 1975. Studied piano with Leschetizky,
theory with Hans Thornton in Vienna. He was
piano accompanist, recitalist, and teacher. His
works included operettas: Dawn boy and Open
house; and songs: Trees, text by Joyce Kilmer;
Mountains; A wanderer's song; The look; Laughing
brook; and piano pieces.

RASELY, CHARLES W.
b. Easton, Pa., 26 Apr. 1921. Studied with
Vittorio Giannini, Juilliard School; and at
Syracuse Univ., B.M. He is public school music
director, church music director, and music
director, Oneida Little Theater.
WORKS: THEATRE: Snoop, Doop, 'n Oscar,
operetta; Everybody sings, musical; CHORUS: The
church's one foundation; Psalm 23; To see a world
in a grain of sand; The woods of Penn.

RASELY, THOMAS L.
b. Easton, Pa., 9 Jan. 1951. Studied with
Walter Hartley, State Univ. Coll. at Fredonia,
N.Y. He is a public school music teacher, North
Syracuse, N.Y.
WORKS: BAND: concert overture; CHAMBER
MUSIC: sonatina and adagietto, tenor saxophone;
CHORUS: 2 songs of hope; Skipping stones;
Childhood is a good time; and songs.

RASLEY, JOHN M.
b. Davenport, Iowa, 20 Jan. 1913. Studied
music privately. He has been director of church
choirs and other choral groups; from 1956,
editor and staff composer, Lorenz Music Publishers. His works for chorus include The
miracle of Bethlehem, a cantata; and sacred
songs.

RATHAUS, KAROL
b. Tarnopol, Poland, 16 Sept. 1895; to U.S.
1938; d. New York, N.Y., 21 Nov. 1954. Studied
in Berlin and Vienna; taught in Berlin, Paris,
London; was on faculty, Queens Coll., New York,
1940-54. He composed an opera, a ballet, 3 symphonies, other orchestral works, 5 string quartets, 4 piano sonatas, many other chamber works.

RATNER, LEONARD GILBERT
b. Minneapolis, Minn., 30 July 1916. Studied
with Arnold Schoenberg at Univ. of California,
Los Angeles; musicology at Univ. of California,
Berkeley, Ph.D. 1947; composition privately with
Ernest Bloch and Frederick Jacobi. He received
a Guggenheim fellowship, 1962; has been faculty
member, Stanford Univ., from 1947.
WORKS: OPERA: The necklace; ORCHESTRA:
Harlequin overture; symphony; CHAMBER MUSIC: 2
string quartets; violin sonata; piano sonata;
cello sonata; Serenade, oboe, horn, wind quartet.
He is author of The listener's art, 1957; Har-
mony, structure, and style, 1962; and Classic
music: Expression, form, style, New York, 1979.
Stanford University, Stanford, CA 94305

RAUSCHENBERG, DALE E.
b. Youngstown, Ohio, 13 Jan. 1938. Studied with
Orlando Vitello, Youngstown Univ., B.M.E.; with
Juan Orrego-Salas, Indiana Univ., M.M. He was
timpanist, Youngstown Philharmonic, 1957-59;
percussionist with the Baltimore Symphony from
1966; on faculty, Towson State Coll., from 1966.
His works for percussion ensemble include: Discussion; What?; Landscape.
29 Othoridge Rd., Lutherville, MD 21093

RAUSCHER, HENRY. See HUMPHREYS, HENRY S.

RAY, DON BRANDON
b. Santa Maria, Calif., 7 June 1926. Studied
with John Vincent, Univ. of California, Los
Angeles, B.A. 1948; with Ernest Kanitz, Univ. of
Southern California; also studied conducting and
has been active as a conductor in California.
He has composed incidental music to plays,
orchestral pieces, anthems, etc.

RAYMOND, LEWIS
b. Newark, N.J., 3 Aug. 1908; d. Burbank, Calif.,
1965. Studied with Felix Deyo and Bernard
Wagenaar, New York Coll. of Music; was organist
and pianist in silent film theatres; U.S. Army
Air Force bandsman in World War II; then staff
arranger for WOR and for Broadway musicals. His
compositions include a string quartet; Chorale
in Gregorian style, clarinet choir; Divertimento,
3 flutes; Short suite for brass; Design, horn
and piano.

RE, PETER
b. New York, N.Y., 17 Mar. 1919. Studied with
Vittorio Giannini at Juilliard School; and with
Paul Hindemith at Yale Univ. His awards include
the Maine State Commission on Arts and Humanities award, and commissions. He has been professor, Colby Coll., from 1951; was conductor
and music director, Bangor Symph. Orch., 1963-73.

WORKS: ORCHESTRA: Variations on airs by
Supply Belcher; A Main profile; Festive overture,
Bangor, 21 Oct. 1973; CHAMBER MUSIC: 2 string
quartets; CHORUS: 2 madrigals.
19 Merrill Ave., Waterville, ME 04901

REA, ALAN
b. Rochester, N.Y., 22 Feb. 1933. Studied at
Univ. of Iowa, B.M. summa cum laude; piano with
Rosina Lhevinne, Juilliard School, M.S.; composition with Halsey Stevens, Univ. of Southern
California, D.M.A.; with Nadia Boulanger on a
Fulbright award for France. He received second
prize in a Stowe Inst. composition contest,
1974. He is faculty member, California State
Univ. at Fresno.
WORKS: OPERA: Old pipes and the dryad; The
fete at Coqueville, produced by Fresno Opera
Assoc., Apr. 1976; CHAMBER MUSIC: suite for 2
pianos, 8 hands, 2 trumpets, 2 trombones; 4
pieces for contrabass alone; Trio on American
hymn tunes, violin, cello, piano; Rondo capriccioso, violin and cello; Partita, piano or harpsichord.
834 E. Alamos, Fresno, CA 93704

READ, GARDNER
b. Evanston, Ill., 2 Jan. 1913. Studied with
Howard Hanson and Bernard Rogers, Eastman School
of Music, B.M. 1936, M.M. 1937; with Ildebrando
Pizzetti in Italy and Jan Sibelius in Finland,
1938-39; with Aaron Copland at Tanglewood, 1941;
conducting with V. Bakaleinikoff and Paul White.
He held scholarships for all study at Eastman
School; 4 MacDowell fellowships; Cromwell
traveling fellowship, 1938-39; Tanglewood fellowship, 1941; Huntington Hartford fellowships,
1960, 1965. His many awards include first prize,
New York Philharmonic Society contest, 1937; 2
Juilliard publication awards, 1938, 1941; first
prize, Paderewski Fund contest, 1943; Composers
Press publication award, 1948; cowinner, Penn.
Coll. for Women contest, 1950; numerous awards
for choral and chamber works; special State
Dept. grants to lecture in Mexico, 1957, 1964;
honorary doctorate, Doane Coll., 1962; many com-
missions from major orchestras and other groups.
He was faculty member, St. Louis Inst. of Music,
1941-43; Kansas City Cons., 1943-45; Cleveland
Inst. of Music, 1945-48; professor, Boston Univ.,
1948-78; guest professor on many other campuses.
His works have been performed by all major U.S.
orchestras, often with the composer conducting.
WORKS: OPERA: Villon, 3 acts, 1967;
THEATRE: music for 11 plays including Hedda
Gabler, 1947; The shoemaker's prodigious wife,
1956; Maxwell Anderson's The golden six, 1958;
Ibsen's Brand, 1961; ORCHESTRA: 3 symphonic
suites--The painted desert, 1933, Sketches of
the city, 1933, Pennsylvania, 1947; Fantasy,
viola and orch., 1935; 4 symphonies, 1936, 1942,
1946, 1958, #4 premiere, Cincinnati, 30 Jan.
1970; The golden journey to Samarkand, with
chorus and soloists, 1939; Night flight, 1942;
cello concerto, 1945; Temptation of St. Anthony,
1947; Sound piece, brass and percussion, 1949;
Toccata giocosa, 1953; The prophet, oratorio,
1960, with narrator, chorus, soloists, Boston,

23 Feb. 1977; Sonoric fantasia, violin and orch.,
1965; CHAMBER MUSIC: suite for string quartet,
1935; 6 intimate moods, violin and piano, 1938;
piano quintet, 1945; Sonata brevis, violin and
piano, 1948; string quartet, 1957; Sonoric fantasia #1, celeste, harp, harpsichord, 1958; Los
dioses aztecas, percussion ensemble, 1959;
Hexstatic, chamber group, Harvard, Mass., 25
Jan. 1974; KEYBOARD: Sonoric fantasia #4, organ
and percussion, Boston, 5 Apr. 1976; Invocation,
trombone and organ, Boston, 13 Mar. 1978; many
other keyboard works, choral works. He is
author of Thesaurus of orchestral devices, 1952,
reprint, Westport, 1969; Music notation--A
manual of modern practice, 1963, rev. ed. 1969;
Style and orchestration, New York, 1975; Contemporary instrumental techniques, New York,
1976.
47 Forster Rd., Manchester, MA 01944

READ, THOMAS LAWRENCE
b. Erie, Pa., 3 July 1938. Studied at Oberlin
Cons., B.M. 1960; with Francis Judd Cooke, New
England Cons., M.M. 1962; with Benjamin Lees,
Peabody Cons., D.M.A. 1971; all degrees in
violin. He received first prize, New England
Cons. alumni contest, 1961; Nat. Fed. of Music
Clubs contest, 1963. He was faculty member,
West Chester State Coll., 1965-67; from 1967, at
Univ. of Vermont, professor from 1976.
WORKS: THEATRE: music for Marlowe's Dr.
Faustus, Renaissance instruments and percussion,
1973; WIND ENSEMBLE: Isochronisms, brass and
percussion, 1972; CHAMBER MUSIC: string trio,
1960; sonata for violin solo, 1960; cello sonata,
1961; Combination 23-20, violin and piano, 1965;
Concatenations, flute and piano, 1967; Pastorale,
viola, winds, percussion, 1968; quintet for
trombone and string quartet, 1971; CHORUS: Te
Deum, with soloists, brass, and organ, 1973.
University of Vermont, Burlington, VT 05401

REALE, PAUL V.
b. New Brunswick, N.J., 2 Mar. 1943. Studied
with Chou Wen-Chung and Otto Luening, Columbia
Univ.; with George Crumb and George Rochberg,
Univ. of Pennsylvania. He received awards from
Nat. Society of Arts and Letters, 1969; Creative
Arts Inst., 1972; Nat. Endowment for the Arts,
1976; Indianapolis Symphony, 1978. He has been
faculty member, Univ. of California, Los Angeles,
from 1969.
WORKS: ORCHESTRA: Oxyrhynchus fragment,
Indianapolis Symph. Orch., 6 Apr. 1978; CHAMBER
MUSIC: Late telophase, flute, clarinet, cello,
piano, 1970; The mysterious death of the magic
realist, viola, cello, harpsichord, guitar,
1972; Terry's piece, 1973; Mad Ophelia, soprano,
chamber orch., tape, 1975; Seance (at a late
hour), solo cello; Regrets of adolescence,
soprano, trumpet, bass clarinet; Salon music,
piano; The waltz king, 4 voices, narrator,
piano, 2 violins, 1976; CHORUS: Alleluia and
Sequence, women's voices and cello.
Univ. of Calif., 405 Hilgard Ave., Los
Angeles, CA 90024

RECK, DAVID B.

RECK, DAVID B.
b. Rising Star, Tex., 12 Jan. 1935. Studied
with Paul Pisk, Univ. of Texas; George Rochberg,
Univ. of Pennsylvania; and with Thirugokarnam
Ramachandra Iyer, Central Coll. of Karnatic
Music, Madras, India. His awards include
Rockefeller Found. grant, 1968; Guggenheim fellowship, 1970; and commissions. He was faculty
member, New School for Social Research, 1966-75;
from 1976, at Amherst Coll.
    WORKS: CHAMBER MUSIC: Night sounds, soprano,
contrabass, percussion; Number 2, for 12 players,
1965; 5 studies for tuba alone; 5 readings on
poems by e. e. cummings, speaker, 3 percussionists, and friend, 1972; CHORUS: Song of the
masked dancers, on an Apache text, 3-part boys'
choir and instruments, 1973; MULTIMEDIA: Blues
and screamer, blues band and film, 1966; Meta-
music, 5 players, tape, film, and slides. He is
author of the book, Music of the whole Earth,
New York, 1976.
    Amherst College, Amherst, MA 01002

REDDICK, WILLIAM J.
b. Paducah, Ky., 23 June 1890; d. Detroit, Mich.,
18 May 1965. Studied at Cincinnati Coll. of
Music; Cincinnati Univ.; his teachers included
Clarence Adler, Oliver Denton, Rudolph Ganz, and
Ernest Hutcheson. He was pianist, organist,
accompanist, choral director; was music director,
New York Opera Co., for 5 years; Chautauqua for
12 summers; taught at Brooklyn Music School, etc.;
was founder and director of the "Ford Sunday
Evening Hour" on radio, 1936-46. His compositions include Espanharlem for chorus; Love in a
cottage, a song cycle; and other songs.

REED, ALFRED
b. New York, N.Y., 25 Jan. 1921. Studied at
Baylor Univ., B.M. 1955, M.M. cum laude 1956;
with Vittorio Giannini, Juilliard School. His
awards include the Luria prize, 1959; honorary
doctorate, Internat. Cons., Lima, Peru, 1968.
He was composer-arranger, Radio Workshop, N.Y.,
1938-42; in U.S. Army Air Force, 1942-46; composer-arranger, radio and television, 1948-53;
conductor, Baylor Univ. Symph. Orch., 1953-55;
editor, Hansen Publ., 1955-66; from 1966, on
faculty, Univ. of Miami.
    WORKS: ORCHESTRA: Rhapsody, viola and
orch., 1959; Festival prelude; Titania's nocturne, string orch.; The pledge of allegiance;
In memoriam, an elegy for the fallen; BAND:
Might and majesty, Biblical suite; Greensleeves,
a fantasy; Rahoon rhapsody, with solo clarinet;
Song of Threnos; Nordic trilogy; Jubilant overture; Punchinello; A northern nocturne; First
suite for band, 1976; Prelude and capriccio,
1978; 2nd symphony, 1979; CHAMBER MUSIC: 5
dances for clarinets; Scherzo fantastique,
contrabass, clarinet, piano; Ballade, alto
saxophone and piano; Variations on London
Bridge is falling down, brass quintet; Fantasy,
woodwind quintet; more than 200 published works
for orchestra, band, chorus, and solo and instrumental groups.
    1405 Ancona Ave., Coral Gables, FL 33146

REED, H. OWEN
b. Odessa, Mo., 17 June 1910. Studied with
Helen Gunderson, Louisiana State Univ., B.M.
with distinction 1934, M.M. 1936, B.A. in French
1937; with Howard Hanson and Bernard Rogers,
Eastman School of Music, Ph.D. 1939; privately
with Bohuslav Martinu and Roy Harris. His
awards include a Guggenheim fellowship, 1948;
Composers Press symphonic award, 1949; Huntington
Hartford fellowship, 1960; Michigan State Univ.
Distinguished Faculty award, 1962; Wurlitzer
Found. fellowship, 1967; Michigan State Univ.
research grant, 1967; annual ASCAP awards; and
many commissions. He was faculty member,
Michigan State Univ., 1939-76, then professor
emeritus.
    WORKS: THEATRE: The masque of the red
death, ballet-pantomime, 1936; Peter Homan's
dream, folk opera, 1955; Earth trapped, Indian
spirit legend, chamber opera, 1960; ORCHESTRA:
Evangeline, 1938; symphony #1, 1939; overture,
1940; Symphonic dance, 1942; cello concerto,
1949; overture for strings, 1961; La fiesta
Mexicana, orch. version, 1954; The turning mind,
1968; BAND: Spiritual, 1947; Missouri shindig,
1951; Theme and variations (from Beethoven),
1954; La fiesta Mexicana, 1949; Renascence,
1959; Che-Ba-Kun-Ah, Road of souls, band and
string quartet, 1959; The touch of the earth,
with chorus and soloists, 1971; For the unfor-
tunate, band and tape, 1972; CHAMBER MUSIC:
piano sonata, 1934; string quartet, 1937;
Scherzo, clarinet and piano, 1947; Wondrous love,
tenor and woodwind quintet, 1948; Symphonic
dance, piano and woodwind quintet, 1954; CHORUS:
A psalm of praise, a cappella, 1939; 2 tongue
twisters, 1940; Ripley Ferry, women's voices and
septet, 1958; A tabernacle for the sun, oratorio,
with speaking chorus of men's voices, contralto
solo, orch., 1963; Living solid face, with
chamber ensemble, Cincinnati, 7 Feb. 1975;
Rejoice! Rejoice!, with taped chorus, bells,
chimes, double bass, 1977. He is author of
several music textbooks.
    4690 Ottawa Dr., Okemos, MI 48864

REED, PHYLLIS LUIDENS
b. Mineola, N.Y., 31 Oct. 1931. Studied piano,
voice, and organ at Hope Coll. and privately.
She has been church and vocal soloist from 1957.
    WORKS: VOICE: I have a dream, Martin
Luther King, Jr., text, solo voice and chorus;
Dream variations, Langston Hughes text; Those
who dream, text by Fannie Lou Hamer and Cardinal
Suenens of Belgium; China spring, on translation
of Wang An-Shih text; Mud-luscious, e. e.
cummings text; and many other songs.
    4 Exeter Court, Northport, NY 11768

REED, ROBERT B.
b. Philadelphia, Pa., 25 Mar. 1900; d. Washington, D.C., 26 Dec. 1968. Studied with Hugh
Clark, H. Alexander Matthews, and Robert Elmore,
Univ. of Pennsylvania, B.M. He was organist-
choirmaster, Radnor, Pa., 1925-32, 1942-48;
then on staff, Library of Congress.
    WORKS: CHORUS: The incarnate word, a
Christmas pageant; The Easter story, cantata;

Shadow march; The Arkansas traveler, male voices; and songs.

REICH, BRUCE
  b. Chicago, Ill., 15 Sept. 1948. Studied with Robert Linn and Halsey Stevens, Univ. of Southern California; with Robert Middleton at Harvard Univ.; and with Penderecki at Yale Univ. He received the Epstein Memorial Found. grant, 1969-70; Helen S. Anstead award, 1970; NDEA Title IV fellowship, 1970-73. From 1976 he has been faculty member, Univ. of Utah.
  WORKS: CHAMBER MUSIC: piano sonata, 1969; string quartet, 1971; Movements, for chamber ensemble, 1972; concerto for piano and chamber ensemble, 1973; CHORUS: cantata with brass and percussion, 1970; SONGS: What is man, baritone, 1968; 3 songs for mezzo-soprano, 1969; Songs of time, mezzo-soprano and instruments, 1973.
  University of Utah, Salt Lake City, UT 84112

REICH, STEVE
  b. New York, N.Y., 3 Oct. 1936. Studied at Cornell Univ., B.A. 1957 with honors in philosophy; composition at Juilliard School, 1958-61; with Darius Milhaud and Luciano Berio, Mills Coll., M.A. 1963; African drumming in Ghana, 1970; Balinese gamelan in Seattle, 1973. He was awarded an Inst. for Internat. Education grant for study in Ghana, 1970; an invitation by the German Academic Exchange Program to be artist-in-residence, 1974; Guggenheim fellowship, 1978; his instrumental group has received grants from New York State Council on the Arts, Nat. Endowment for the Arts, and Martha Baird Rockefeller Fund, and many commissions. He has been performing with his own group from 1966.
  WORKS: It's gonna rain, tape, 1965; Come out, 1966; Piano phase, 1967; Violin phase, 4 violins or violin and tape, 1967; Pendulum music, microphones, amplifiers, and speakers, 1968; 4 organs, 4 electric organs and maracas, 1970, Boston, 8 Oct. 1971; Phase patterns, 4 electric organs, 1970; Drumming, for tuned drums, marimbas, glockenspiels, mixed voices, whistling, and piccolo, 1971; Clapping music, 2 performers, 1972; 6 pianos, 1973; Music for mallet instruments, voices and organ, 1973; Music for pieces of wood, 1973; Music for 18 instruments, 1976; Music for large ensemble, 1978, and Octet, 1979, American premiere of both, New York, 19 Feb. 1980; Variations for winds, strings and keyboards, New York, 19 Feb. 1980.
  16 Warren St., New York, NY 10007

REICHERT, JAMES A.
  b. Toledo, Ohio, 12 May 1932. Studied at Oberlin Cons., B.M.; Eastman School of Music, M.M.; and at Tanglewood. For several years he was music director for CBS-TV; then producer for Gotham Recording Corp. In 1972 he received an ASCAP award for incidental music to The effect of gamma rays on man-in-the-moon marigolds, the 1971 Pulitzer prize play. With Tod Dockstader, he composed an electronic work, Omniphony I.

REID, JOHN WILLIAM
  b. Port Arthur, Tex., 23 Sept. 1946. Studied

with Samuel Adler, Eastman School of Music, B.M. 1968; with David Diamond, Philip Batstone, Charles Eakin, Cecil Effinger, Univ. of Colorado, M.M. 1972. He was bassoonist with the NORAD band, 1968-72; from 1978, has been faculty member, Washington State Univ.
  WORKS: ORCHESTRA: Symphonic movements, 1971; BAND: overture; CHAMBER MUSIC: horn sonata; quartet for bassoon and strings; woodwind trio; string quartet; suite for brass; saxophone sonata; Movement for clarinet alone; wind octet; 2 woodwind quintets.
  Washington State University, Pullman, WA 99164

REIF, PAUL
  b. Prague, Czechoslovakia, 23 Mar. 1910; U.S. citizen 1943; d. New York, N.Y., 7 July 1978. Studied with Richard Strauss; conducting with Bruno Walter and Franz Schalk; violin with Erica Morini, Vienna Acad. of Music; music history at the Sorbonne in Paris, Ph.D. His awards included a MacDowell fellowship; 2 American Music Center grants; annual ASCAP awards; and commissions. He served in the U.S. Army Intelligence Corps, 1942-45, was awarded the Croix de Guerre, Purple Heart, and an Eisenhower citation. While in Africa with the Army, he wrote Dirty Gertie from Bizerte, which was introduced to the GIs in Algiers by Josephine Baker. He composed for films in the U.S. and Europe.
  WORKS: OPERA: Portrait in brownstone, 1965; Mad Hamlet, 1965; Curse of the mauvais air, chamber opera buffa; ORCHESTRA: Fanfare and fugato; Philidor's defense, musical defense game; Birches, tenor and orch., 1965; Eulogy for a friend, strings and percussion; Pentagon, piano and orch.; Episodes, string orch.; America 1776-1876-1976, with piano, clarinet, 4 vocal soloists, New York, 24 Jan. 1976; CHAMBER MUSIC: Wind spectrum, woodwind quintet; Banter, flute and piano, 1966; brass quintet; 3 divertimenti, 4 strings, 1969; Anatomy of a wind quintet, theatre piece for 5 players, 1977; CHORUS: Triple City, with brass, 1963; Requiem to war, with percussion, 1963; Letter from a Birmingham jail, Martin Luther King text, 1965; SONGS: The circus; 5 finger exercises, on T. S. Eliot poem; Monsieur le Pelican, 1960; Reverence for life, 1960; Kaleidoscope, with woodwind quintet, text by composer; 4 songs, on words of Kenneth Koch; Duo for 3, mezzo-soprano, clarinet, cello; 8 vignettes, 4 singers, 1975.

REILLY, JACK
  b. Staten Island, N.Y., 1 Jan. 1932. Studied with Ludmila Ulehla and Nicolas Flagello, Manhattan School of Music, B.M. and M.M.E. 1958; also with Hall Overton, Joseph Maneri, Lennie Tristano, George Russell, and Ali Akbar Khan. He held scholarships at Manhattan School, 1957-58, and with Ali Akbar Khan; was artist-in-residence, Molde School of Music, Norway, 1971. He taught at Berklee Coll. of Music, 1962; has lectured at schools in the U.S., Canada, and Norway; was faculty member, Turtle Bay Music School, 1970-72; then at New School for Social Research.

REISE, JAY

WORKS: ORCHESTRA: suite for orchestra; Alleluia, chorus and orch.; piano concerto; Jazz requiem, string orch. with chorus and jazz quintet, New York, 17 Nov. 1978; CHAMBER MUSIC: La-No-Tib suite, piano, bass, percussion, 1958; Unichrom, jazz trio, (piano, bass, drums), 1964; string trio; suite for woodwinds; Rhapsody, piano and jazz trio; In memoriam: Ben Webster, solo piano or jazz trio, 1973; Movements, 2 pianos and percussion, 1975; Fantasy for woodwind quintet and improvised piano, 1978; CHORUS: The great invocation, 8-part chorus a cappella, 1968; Mass of involvement, for congregational singing, 1969; The light of the soul, oratorio, chorus and instruments, 1974.
125 Prospect Park W., Brooklyn, NY 11215

REISE, JAY
b. New York, N.Y., 9 Feb. 1950. Studied with George Crumb, Richard Wernick, and George Rochberg, Univ. of Pennsylvania; with Bengt Hambraeus and Bruce Mather, McGill Univ.; with Hugh Hartwell, Hamilton Coll.; privately with Jimmy Giuffre. His awards include the Norlin fellowship; MacDowell, Yaddo, and Tanglewood fellowships; Nat. Endowment for the Arts grant; Fromm Found. grant; Koussevitzky composition prize. He was faculty member, Kirkland Coll., 1976-78; then at Hamilton Coll.
WORKS: THEATRE: Alice at the end, operatic tableau for soprano, actress, and 6 players, 1978; ORCHESTRA: Hieronymo's mad again, 1976; CHAMBER MUSIC: Paraphonia, chamber orch., 1978; string quartet, 1978.
13 West Hill Rd., Deansboro, NY 13328

REISER, ALOIS
b. Prague, Czechoslovakia, 4 Apr. 1884. Studied at Prague Cons.; with Antonin Dvorak, Univ. of Prague, D.M. His awards include the Elizabeth Sprague Coolidge prize, 1918; NBC prize; Pittsburgh Arts Society prize; New York Philharmonic prize. He toured the U.S. and Europe as cellist in the Bohemian Trio; played cello in the Pittsburgh Symphony; conducted at Prague Opera House and the Diaghilev Ballet Russe on its U.S. tour, 1918; conducted at Strand Theatre, New York, 1918-29; then was music director for Warner Bros. in Hollywood. His compositions include light operas; a symphony; Slavic rhapsody, for orch., 1931; cello concerto, 1933; Erewhon, for orch., 1936; chamber music and songs.

REPPER, CHARLES
b. Alliance, Ohio, 3 Jan. 1886; d. Boston, Mass., 24 Oct. 1974. Studied with Walter Spalding and William C. Heilman, Harvard Univ., B.A., Phi Beta Kappa. He was composer for the Allegheny Coll. centennial pageant, 1915, and the Lexington, Ky., 150th anniversary pageant, 1925; was on editorial staff, Boston Music Company, and C. C. Birchard Company, Boston; also private piano and theory teacher.
WORKS: OPERETTAS: The dragon of Wu Foo; Penny buns and roses; CHORUS: Candle lights of Christmas; Far away isles; Flags flying; Gardens by the sea; It cannot be a strange countree; Never an end; To a madonna; many songs and piano pieces.

RETI, RUDOLF
b. Uzice, Yugoslavia, 27 Nov. 1885; to U.S. 1938; d. Montclair, N.J., 7 Feb. 1957. Studied at Vienna Cons., Ph.D. He was one of the founders of the Internat. Society for Contemporary Music at Salzburg, 1922. From 1938 he was pianist and teacher in Montclair, N.J.
WORKS: OPERA: Ivan and the drum; David and Goliath, a ballet-opera, 1935; ORCHESTRA: Symphonia mystica, 1951; Triptychon, 1953; cello concertino, 1953; 2 piano concertos; CHAMBER MUSIC: string quartet; violin sonata; piano pieces; VOICE: choral works and songs. He was author of 2 books, The thematic process in music, 1951; and Tonality-atonality-pantonality, 1958.

RETZEL, FRANK
b. Detroit, Mich., 11 Aug. 1948. Studied with Ruth Shaw Wylie, Harold Laudenslager, and James Hartway, Wayne State Univ., B.M., M.M. 1973. He received the Paul Paray award, 1971; Harold Laudenslager award, 1973; one of his works was chosen as an official U.S. entry for World Music Days in Athens, Greece, Sept. 1979. He has been church organist and music director from 1971.
WORKS: CHAMBER MUSIC: 2 pieces for piano, 1969; Mobile structures, for 5 instruments, 1970; Cables 87, soprano and 7 instruments, text by Thomas Merton, 1971; 24 modules, 11 instruments, 1972; Dreams of Aesop, mezzo-soprano and piano, text by Diane Leigh Vogt, 1973; Laminar flow, 7 instruments and percussion.

REX, HARLEY E.
b. Lehighton, Pa., 29 Mar. 1930. Studied at Mansfield State Coll., B.S.; with Wallace Berry and George Burt, Univ. of Michigan, M.M. 1962, D.M.A. 1971; saxophone with Sigurd Rauscher and Larry Teal. He was saxophonist and arranger, U.S. Army Band, 1954-62; saxophonist, Houston Symph. Orch., 1965-73; from 1966, conductor, Houston Municipal Band and faculty member, Sam Houston State Univ.
WORKS: BAND: Prelude and movendo, saxophone and band; Camminando; Andante and brilliante, saxophone and band; Saxophone rhapsody; CHAMBER MUSIC: Shenandoah, saxophone quartet; Scherzo, clarinet quartet.
Rte. 5, Box 243, Huntsville, TX 77340

REYNOLDS, CHARLES HEATH
b. Patterson, La., 5 June 1924. Studied at Univ. of Southwestern Louisiana; with Helen Gunderson, Louisiana State Univ. He received awards in a Lafayette Madrigal Singers contest, and in a Louisiana All-State Band contest, 1967. He is on the faculty, Southwestern Louisiana Univ.
WORKS: ORCHESTRA: piano concerto; BAND: Acadiana suite; symphony; Atchafalaya suite; A quartet of pieces; Songs from an unwritten show; PIANO: In homage to Prokofiev; Variations on a Lourdes hymn; also pieces for solo wind instruments and piano.
610 Wilson St., Apt. 6, Lafayette, LA 70503

REYNOLDS, ERMA
b. Laurel, Miss., 25 Mar. 1922. Studied with Donal Michalsky, California State Univ. at Fullerton. She is a private teacher.
WORKS: ORCHESTRA: Passacaglia, string orch.; No dance, suite for small orch.; CHAMBER MUSIC: violin sonata; Exile, piano suite for modern dance; March and lament, for brass; Capricci, clarinet and piano.
710 Casa Blanca Dr., Fullerton, CA 92632

REYNOLDS, GEORGE B.
b. St. Albans, Vt., 23 Dec. 1951. Studied with Hubert C. Bird, Keene State Coll.
WORKS: CHAMBER MUSIC: Piece for solo clarinet; woodwind quartet; Le cyclope, baritone horn and piano; CHORUS: Shorts from the Bible, sacred cantata for young voices, organ and 2 trombones; SONGS: I shall go back, soprano; Song set, on poems of e. e. cummings, soprano.
R.F.D. 2, Alburg, VT 05440

REYNOLDS, ROGER
b. Detroit, Mich., 18 July 1934. Attended Univ. of Michigan, B.S. in engineering 1957; then studied composition with Ross Lee Finney and Roberto Gerhard, Univ. of Michigan, M.M. 1961; with Gerhard also at Tanglewood. His awards include the Koussevitzky Internat. Recording award, 1970; Nat. Inst. of Arts and Letters award; Fulbright, Guggenheim, Rockefeller, Inst. of Current World Affairs fellowships; Rockefeller grant, 1976. He has been professor, Univ. of California, San Diego, from 1969.
WORKS: ORCHESTRA: The wedge, chamber orch., 1961; Graffiti, 1964; The lies of the land, 1964; Quick are the mouths of Earth, chamber orch., 1965; Threshold, 1967; Fiery wind, New York, 13 Feb. 1978; CHAMBER MUSIC: Sky, cycle on Haiku poems, soprano and instruments, 1960; Acquaintances, flute, double bass, piano, 1961; 4 etudes, flute quartet, 1961; Mosaic, flute and piano, 1962; Ambages, flute solo, 1965; string quartet; 4 etudes, woodwind quartet; 2 woodwind quintets; The promises of darkness, chamber ensemble, New York, 8 Jan. 1976; CHORUS: The emperor of ice cream, 8 voices, 3 instruments, 1962; Masks, with orch., Melville text, 1965; Blind men, with brass, percussion, piano, Melville text, 1966; ELECTRONIC: A portrait of Vanzetti, narrator, winds, percussion, tape, 1963; . . . between . . ., chamber orch. and electronics, 1968; Traces, piano, flute, cello, 6 tapes, electronics, 1969; I/O (for in and out), ritual for 9 female vocalists, 9 male mimes, clarinet, 2 flutes, 2 technicians who manipulate and distribute the sound electronically, 1969; Ping, instruments, electronics, slides, tape, 1969; Compass, male voices, cello, double bass, tape, slides, 1973; Behind the unreasoning mask, tape, percussion, trombone, and an assistant, 1975; . . . the serpent snapping eye, trumpet, percussion, piano, and computer-generated tape, San Diego, 31 Jan. 1979; Less than 2, 2 pianos, 2 percussion, tape, Library of Congress, D.C., 23 Feb. 1979; Voicespace: I, Still, taped by Extended Voice Techniques Ensemble, Contemporary Music Festival, Valencia, Calif., 1979.

Univ. of California, San Diego, La Jolla, CA 92037

REYNOLDS, VERNE
b. Lyons, Kans., 18 July 1926. Studied at Cincinnati Cons., B.M. 1950; Univ. of Wisconsin, M.M. 1961; Royal Coll. of Music, London, 1953-54. His awards include a Fulbright grant, 1953; Louisville Orch. award, 1955; Los Angeles Horn Club award, 1955; ASCAP awards; and commissions. He played horn, Cincinnati Symph. Orch., 1947-50; Rochester Phil. Orch., 1959-68; Eastman Brass Quintet, from 1961; was faculty member, Univ. of Wisconsin, 1950-53; Indiana Univ., 1954-59; from 1959, at Eastman School.
WORKS: ORCHESTRA: violin concerto, 1951; Saturday with Venus, 1953; Celebration overture, 1960; WIND ENSEMBLE: Theme and variations, brass choir; Music for 5 trumpets, 1957; Scenes, winds and percussion, 1971; Events, 8-part trombone choir, 1976; CHAMBER MUSIC: 48 etudes, for horn, 1959, transcribed for trumpet, 1970; Short suite, for 4 horns; Partita, horn and piano, 1961; flute sonata, 1962; suite for brass quintet, 1963; 3 elegies, oboe and piano; Serenade, horn and strings, 1966; tuba sonata, 1968; Concertare I, brass quintet and percussion, 1968; Concertare II, trumpet and strings, 1968; Concertare III, woodwind quintet and piano, 1969; horn sonata, 1970; violin sonata, 1970; 4 caprices, clarinet and piano, 1972; piano sonata, 1972; Graphics, trombone and piano, 4 hands, 1976; CHORUS: The hollow men, baritone, male choir, brass, percussion, 1954.
Eastman School of Music, Rochester, NY 14604

RHEA, RAYMOND
b. Littleton, Colo., 28 Dec. 1910; d. Texas. Studied at Denver Univ.; Northwestern Univ., B.M., M.M.; Univ. of Texas. He was church choir director and from 1936, a voice teacher in schools. His compositions include She walks in beauty, Byron text, for chorus; and many songs.

RHOADS, WILLIAM E.
b. Harvey, Ill., 5 Aug. 1918. Studied at Univ. of Michigan, B.M.E. 1941, M.M.E. 1942. He served in the U.S. Army, 1942-46; taught in public schools, 1946-53; from 1953, has been faculty member, Univ. of New Mexico, dept. chairman from 1972.
WORKS: BAND: Scottish rhapsody; 3 ballads; Puerto Alegre; Mazatlan; Lament and march; Gentle ballad; many transcriptions for band and for solo wind instruments.
2901 Las Cruces, Albuquerque, NM 87110

RHODES, PHILLIP
b. Forest City, N.C., 6 June 1940. Studied with William Klenz and Iain Hamilton, Duke Univ.; with Mel Powell and Donald Martino, Yale Univ. His awards include 2 orchestral prizes at Tanglewood, 1962, 1965; Ford Found. grants, 1966, 1969; Nat. Inst. of Arts and Letters grant, 1974; Nat. Endowment for the Arts grants, 1974, 1975, 1976; Rockefeller grant, 1976; Tanglewood fellowship, 1978; and commissions. He taught at Amherst Coll., 1968-69; was professional-in-

RICCI, ROBERT

residence, City of Louisville, 1969-72; from 1974, has been faculty member at Carleton Coll.
WORKS: ORCHESTRA: Divertimento, small orch., 1971; Festival suite, bluegrass band and orch., 1974; BAND: 3 pieces; CHAMBER MUSIC: string trio, 1964; 3 pieces, unaccompanied cello; duo for violin and cello; Museum pieces, clarinet and string quartet, 1973; quartet for flute, violin, cello, harp, 1975; Reflections . . . 8 fantasies for piano, 1977; CHORUS: From Paradise lost, with soloists, narrator, and orch.; On the morning of Christ's nativity, with soloists, wind quartet, and harp, 1974; Witticisms and lamentations from the graveyard, 5 epitaphs, a cappella; SONGS: Autumn setting, soprano and string quartet, 1969; Lament of Michal, soprano and orch.; Visions of remembrance, voice and instruments; Mountain songs, cycle for soprano and piano, 1976.
R.R. 3, Northfield, MN 55057

RICCI, ROBERT
b. New York, N.Y., 25 Apr. 1938. Studied with Donald Keats and David Epstein, Antioch Coll.; with Quincy Porter and Elliott Carter, Yale Univ., M.M.; Scott Huston and Jeno Takacs, Univ. of Cincinnati, Coll.-Cons., D.M.A. His awards include a scholarship at Yale Univ.; NDEA fellowship, Univ. of Cincinnati; Rockefeller Found. grant, 1967; John A. Hoffman composition prize, 1967. He has held faculty posts at Antioch Coll., 1956-57; Villa Maria Inst. of Music, Buffalo, 1964-66; Univ. of Cincinnati, 1967; and from 1968, at Western Michigan Univ.
WORKS: ORCHESTRA: symphony; CHAMBER MUSIC: string quartet; clarinet sonata; brass trio; woodwind quintet, 1967; trumpet sonata; 6 bagatelles, piano; 2 songs, soprano and piano, 1967; JAZZ ENSEMBLE: U.B. He was coauthor with Robert Fink of A lexicon of 20th-century music, New York, 1974.
928 Wheaton Ave., Kalamazoo, MI 49008

RICE, B. DOUGLAS, JR.
b. Seattle, Wash., 24 Mar. 1942. Studied with John Cowell and Lockrem Johnson, Cornish School, B.M. 1969; guitar with Chris Jordan and others. He has held faculty posts at Helen Bush School, 1966-69; Cornish School, 1970, 1973-74; Bellevue Community Coll. from 1969; and from 1976, Univ. of Puget Sound.
WORKS: CHAMBER MUSIC: Divertimento #1, guitar; Sonata concertante, flute and guitar; 2 guitar sonatas; Elegy, guitar; 2 perpetual motions, guitar.
18456 40th Place N.E., Seattle, WA 98155

RICE, THOMAS N.
b. Washington, D.C., 6 Feb. 1933. Studied at Catholic Univ. (with instrumental scholarships); and at Univ. of North Carolina, Chapel Hill. He received a MacDowell fellowship, 1959. He has been band teacher in the Virginia Beach school system from 1959.
WORKS: OPERA: Fully clothed in armor, chamber opera; BALLET: Sir Gawain and the Green Knight; ORCHESTRA: overture; timpani concerto; violin concerto; Toccata; Genesis; CHAMBER MUSIC:

string quartet; brass quintet; woodwind quintet; sonata for 2 violins and piano; sonata for viola and cello; clarinet sonata; sonata for piccolo and string bass; string trio; duo for flutes.
7008 Ocean Front, Virginia Beach, VA 23451

RICH, GLADYS
b. Philadelphia, Pa., 26 Apr. 1892. Studied at New England Cons.; Univ. of Utah, B.A.; New York Univ., M.A.; with Harvey Gaul and Edward Shippen Barnes. She was public school music supervisor, Newcastle, Pa., 1928-33; music director, State Teachers Coll., Clarion, Pa., 1933-38. She has published several operettas, many cantatas, and songs.

RICHARDS, HOWARD L., JR.
b. Detroit, Mich., 2 Nov. 1927. Studied at Univ. of Michigan; Rollins Coll., B.A., B.M.; Florida State Univ., M.M. He wrote musicals in college; was on staff of Columbia Records; then computer programmer for IBM. He has published 2 choral works on texts of James Joyce, Who goes among the greenwood and Rain.

RICHARDS, STEPHEN
b. New York, N.Y., 9 May 1935. Studied with Philip James, New York Univ.; with Jack Beeson, Henry Cowell, and Otto Luening, Columbia Univ.; with Eric Werner, Hebrew Union Coll. He has been cantor in Syosset, N.Y., Rochester, N.Y., and Indianapolis; in 1978, was editor, Transcontinental Music Publications, N.Y., and faculty member, Hebrew Union Coll., School of Sacred Music.
WORKS: Jewish liturgical music: Ki Lekach Tov; Songs about Passover; Psalms 137, 150, 98; The ballad of Ruth; Nations shall learn war no more.
63 Pine Hill Lane, Dix Hills, NY 11746

RICHARDSON, DARRELL ERVIN
b. Columbia, S.C., 17 Sept. 1911. Studied at Univ. of South Carolina, B.S.; dentistry at Univ. of Tennessee, D.D.S. 1950; music theory, violin, and trombone as electives, but is largely self-taught in composition. He was commissioned to compose Carolina Regina for the South Carolina 300th anniversary in 1970. He was arranger and composer in Hollywood in the 1930s; took up dentistry after military service in World War II.
WORKS: ORCHESTRA: symphony, 1966; Variations on a 4-tone melody, 1969; Carolina Regina, 1970; Elegy, string orch., 1972; CHAMBER MUSIC: Introduction, fugue, and variations, woodwind quintet, 1969; 2 string quartets; CHORUS: Crown Him Lord of all; Behold thy son beloved; That Easter morn; and songs.
2829 Stratford Rd., Columbia, SC 29204

RICHARDSON, LOUIS S.
b. Brooklyn, N.Y., 15 Oct. 1924. Holds a doctorate in music but is self-taught in composition. He received a State Univ. grant in 1964; has been faculty member, State Univ. Coll., Fredonia, N.Y., from 1958.
WORKS: CHAMBER MUSIC: piano sonata; violin sonata; viola sonata; Theme and variations,

cello and piano; bassoon sonata; VOICE: 4 Elizabethan songs, a cappella chorus; 3 psalms, baritone and piano; 4 songs of death, soprano, flute, viola, and piano.
    401 Chestnut St., Fredonia, NY 14063

RICHARDSON, SHARON
    b. Houston, Tex., 3 Aug. 1948. Studied with Merrill Ellis, North Texas State Univ.
        WORKS: ORCHESTRA: Serenade, violin and orch.; BAND: Fanfare and march; CHAMBER MUSIC: 3 statements for tuba quartet; many pieces for small ensembles and solo instruments.

RICHENS, JAMES W.
    b. Memphis, Tenn., 7 Oct. 1936. Studied with Raymond Haggh, Memphis State Univ.; with Bernard Rogers, Louis Mennini, Samuel Adler, and Wayne Barlow, Eastman School of Music, M.M. He was named 1970 Composer of the Year by the Tennessee Music Teachers Assoc. He was public school music teacher, 1961–65; from 1966, faculty member, Memphis State Univ.
        WORKS: BALLET: Escape to morning; ORCHESTRA: Sonambulisms; Portrait of a city, commissioned for the 150th anniversary of Memphis; Fanfare for orchestra; BAND: Prelude and dance, with solo clarinet; Fantasia on Battle Hymn of the Republic; Chicano!; CHAMBER MUSIC: piano sonata; string quartet.
        5665 Buxbriar Ave., Memphis, TN 38101

RICHMOND, THOMAS L.
    b. Kalamazoo, Mich., 5 Feb. 1935. Studied at Western Michigan Univ., B.M. 1957; with H. Owen Reed, Michigan State Univ., M.M. 1965, Ph.D. 1970. He has been faculty member, Concordia Coll., Moorhead, Minn., from 1967.
        WORKS: ORCHESTRA: Portrait, chamber orch.; Incantation and dance; Orchensem, 1970; BAND: Wind trek, 1976; CHAMBER MUSIC: 2 movements, alto saxophone and string trio; Commentaries, clarinet and piano, 1977; CHORUS: A song of praise; SONGS: Check, text by James Stephens.
        1202 S. 6th St., Fargo, ND 58102

RICHTER, MARGA
    b. Reedsburg, Wis., 21 Oct. 1926. Studied with William Bergsma and Vincent Persichetti, Juilliard School, B.S. 1949, M.S. 1951; piano with Roslyn Tureck. She has received annual ASCAP awards from 1966; Nat. Endowment for the Arts grants, 1969, 1977; Rockefeller Fund grant, 1975; and numerous commissions. She was on the faculty, Nassau Community Coll., 1971–73.
        WORKS: BALLET: Abyss, 1964; Bird of yearning, 1967; The servant, 1968; ORCHESTRA: concerto for piano, violas, cellos, and basses, 1955; Lament, string orch., 1956; Aria and toccata, viola and strings, 1957; Variations on a sarabande, 1959; 8 pieces, 1961; Landscapes of the mind I, piano and orch., 1974; Blackberry vines and winter fruit, Bennington, Vt., 17 Oct. 1976; CHAMBER MUSIC: clarinet sonata, 1948; 2 string quartets; Chamber piece, woodwind quartet, viola, cello, bass; Darkening of the light, solo viola or solo cello, 1961; suite for violin and piano, 1964; Landscapes of the mind II, violin

and piano, 1971; Landscapes of the mind III, piano trio; Variations on a theme by von Reuenthal, organ, New York, 9 Jul. 1976; PIANO: sonata, 1954; 8 pieces, 1961; Melodrama, 2 pianos, 1958; Fragments, 1963; Remembrances, 1977; Requiem, 1978; also choral works and songs.
    3 Bayview Lane, Huntington, NY 11743

RICHTER, MARION MORREY
    b. Columbus, Ohio, 2 Oct. 1900. Studied at Ohio State Univ., B.A. Phi Beta Kappa 1921; piano with Ernest Hutcheson, composition with Wallingford Riegger and Rubin Goldmark, Juilliard School, grad. 1929; Columbia Univ., M.A. 1933, Ed.D. 1961. Her awards include fellowships at Juilliard; citations from New Jersey Fed. of Music Clubs and the 8th U.S. Army in Korea, 1969; Stroudsburg, Pa., award, 1975; Univ. of Singapore award, 1975; and Delta Omicron Distinguished Alumna award, 1977. She has taught piano at Columbia Univ., Teachers Coll.; Juilliard School, 1932–52; has toured widely in the U.S., England, Mexico, the Orient, and Russia as pianist and lecturer.
        WORKS: OPERA: Distant drums; ORCHESTRA: The waste land, tone poem after T. S. Eliot; BAND: Timberjack overture; CHAMBER MUSIC: Sonata for trio, piano trio; CHORUS: Sea chant, women's voices; This is our camp, cantata-play for children; PIANO: Prelude on a 12-tone row.
        31 Bradford Rd., Scarsdale, NY 10583

RICKER, RAMON
    b. Camp Forrest, Tenn., 16 Sept. 1943. Studied at Univ. of Denver, B.M.E.; Michigan State Univ., M.M.; Eastman School of Music, D.M.A. He has received 2 Nat. Endowment for the Arts grants, 1975, 1977. He was faculty member, State Univ. of New York at Geneseo, 1971–73; from 1972, at Eastman School.
        WORKS: JAZZ ENSEMBLE: Snapper; Genesis; Special K; The forecast for tonight is darkness; Solar chariots, a duo.
        454 Sunhill Lane, Webster, NY 14580

RIDDLE, NELSON
    b. Oradell, N.J., 1 June 1921. Played with many noted dance bands, then formed his own orchestra. He was music director, Capitol Records, 1951–62, and of Reprise Records from 1963; has been guest conductor at Hollywood Bowl.
        WORKS: BRASS ENSEMBLE: Cross country suite, 1958; Three-quarter suite, 1962; Theme and variations, 1971.

RIEGGER, WALLINGFORD
    b. Albany, Ga., 29 Apr. 1885; d. New York, N.Y., 2 Apr. 1961. Studied with Percy Goetschius and Alwin Schroeder, Inst. for Musical Art, B.M. 1907; then at Berlin Hochschule für Musik. His honors included the Paderewski prize, 1922; Coolidge prize, 1924; honorary D.M., Cincinnati Cons., 1925; New York Music Critics' Circle award, 1948; membership in Inst. of Arts and Letters, 1953; Koussevitzky commission, 1953. He conducted opera and symphony orchestras in Germany, 1915–17; returned to the U.S. and taught at Drake Univ., 1918–22; Inst. of Musical

RIEPE, RUSSELL

Art, 1924-25; Ithaca Cons., 1926-28; from 1929, lived in New York City.
WORKS: ORCHESTRA: American polonaise, 1923; Rhapsody, 1931; Fantasy and fugue, organ and orch., 1931; Dichotomy, 1932; Scherzo, 1933; Passacaglia and fugue; 4 symphonies, 1935, 1946, 1948, 1957; Canon and fugue, 1939; Music for orchestra, 1951; Dance rhythms, 1953; Romanza, 1953; overture, 1956; Preamble and fugue, 1956; Quintuple jazz, 1959; Variations, violin and orch., 1959; CHAMBER MUSIC: piano trio, 1919; La belle dame sans merci, 4 solo voices and chamber orch., 1924; Study in sonority, 10 violins or multiples of 10, 1927; suite for solo flute, 1929; 3 canons, woodwind quartet, 1930; Divertissement, flute, harp, cello, 1933; Music for brass choir; woodwind duos; 2 string quartets; Whimsey, cello and piano; violin sonatina; piano quintet, 1950; brass nonet, 1951; Variations for 2 pianos, 1952; concerto for piano and woodwind quintet, 1953; Movement, 2 trumpets, trombone, piano.

RIEPE, RUSSELL
b. Metropolis, Ill., 23 Feb. 1945. Studied with Will Gay Bottje, Southern Illinois Univ.; with Warren Benson, Wayne Barlow, and Samuel Adler, Eastman School of Music. He received Woodrow Wilson fellowship, 1967; NDEA Title IV fellowship for study at Eastman School, 1967-70; Howard Hanson prize, 1972. He has been faculty member, Southwest Texas State Univ., from 1972.
WORKS: ORCHESTRA: Child dying, voice and orch.; Symphonic fantasy; Incidental music, for strings; CHAMBER MUSIC: Divertimento, woodwind quartet; CHORUS: Cancionetas, chamber choir; ELECTRONIC: Les heures; also multiple-piano arrangements.
2700 N. LBJ Dr., #125, San Marcos, TX 78666

RIESENFELD, HUGO
b. Vienna, Austria, 26 Jan. 1879; to U.S. 1907; d. Hollywood, Calif., 10 Sept. 1939. Studied on scholarship at Vienna Cons. and at Vienna Univ. He was violinist, Imperial Opera House; Vienna Philharmonic; Mozart Festival, Salzburg, 1904; Bayreuth Festival; concertmaster, Manhattan Opera Company, 1907-11; Century Opera Company, New York, 1915; managing director of 3 New York theatres, 1919-25; music director, Hollywood studio, 1928-30.
WORKS: OPERETTA: Merry martyr; ORCHESTRA: Symphonic epos; Chopin ballet; Dramatic overture; Balkan rhapsody; Etchings of New York; Children's suite; American festival overture; and songs.

RIETI, VITTORIO
b. Alexandria, Egypt, 28 Jan. 1898, of Italian parents; U.S. citizen 1944. Studied with Frugatto, Respighi, and Casella in Italy, but is largely self-taught. His awards include the New York Music Critics' Circle award, 1954; Nat. Inst. of Arts and Letters grant, 1972; and commissions. He was faculty member, Peabody Cons., 1948-49; Chicago Musical Coll., 1950-53; Queens Coll., 1955-60; New York Coll. of Music, 1960-64.
WORKS: OPERA: Don Perlimplin, 1944, Urbana, Ill., 30 Mar. 1952; The pet shop, New York, 14

Apr. 1958; The clock, 1960; Maryam, the harlot, 1966; BALLET: Waltz academy, 1944; The mute wife, on themes by Paganini, 1944; Night shadow, 1946; Bacchus and Ariadne, 1946; Unicorn, 1950; Conumdrum; ORCHESTRA: 6 symphonies, #4, St. Louis, 16 Dec. 1944, #6, New York, 11 Dec. 1974; Concerto du Loup, Los Angeles, 8 Aug. 1942; concerto for 5 winds and orch., 1924; 3 piano concertos, 1926, 1937, 1960; violin concerto, 1928; harpsichord concerto, 1930; 2 cello concertos; 2-piano concerto, 1952; 5 fables of La Fontaine, 1968; triple concerto, violin, viola, piano, and orch., 1971; concerto for string quartet and orch., New York, 1 Feb. 1978; CHAMBER MUSIC: sonata for flute, oboe, bassoon, piano, 1924; 4 string quartets, 1926, 1942, 1953, 1960; woodwind quartet, 1958; madrigal for 12 instruments; octet for woodwind trio and piano, string trio and piano; piano trio; piano quartet; harpsichord sonata; many other chamber works, 2-piano pieces, choral works, and songs. Two concerts of his chamber music were presented in New York in January 1973 in honor of the composer's 75th birthday.
1391 Madison Ave., New York, NY 10029

RIGGINS, HERBERT L.
b. Augusta, Ga., 24 Apr. 1948. Studied at Emory Univ.; with Charles Moon, California State Univ. at Humboldt, B.B. magna cum laude; with Ronald Lo Presti, Arizona State Univ., M.M. 1973. He was instructor, Arizona State Univ., 1973-76.
WORKS: CHAMBER MUSIC: string quartet; suite for 3 horns; suite for bassoon; VOICE: The silver swan, chorus; 3 haiku, mezzo-soprano and piano.

RILEY, ANN MARION
b. New Richmond, Wis., 28 Apr. 1928. Studied with Nadia Boulanger in Fontainebleau; with Alexander Tcherepnin in Nice; and with Jean Catoire in Paris. She received a composition prize, Acad. Internat., Nice, 1961. She was faculty member, Scholastica Coll., Duluth, 1958-72; from 1973, at Music Center of Lake County, Waukegan, Ill.
WORKS: CHAMBER MUSIC: quintet; Piece for violin and piano; concerto for piano and brass; Creation, song for soprano; clarinet, piano; Patterns, piano; Moon suite, piano.

RILEY, DENNIS
b. Los Angeles, Calif., 28 May 1943. Studied with Cecil Effinger and George Crumb, Univ. of Colorado; with Thomas Frederickson, Ben Johnston, and Robert Kelly, Univ. of Illinois; Richard Hervig and Donald Jenni, Univ. of Iowa. He received BMI awards, 1966, 1967; Joseph Bearns prize, 1968; President's award, Univ. of Colorado, 1962; Ford Found.-MENC fellowship, 1965-67; fellowships at Univ. of Illinois, 1967-68, Univ. of Iowa, 1969-71; Guggenheim fellowship, 1972-73; Fromm Found. grant, 1975. He was music writer, Rocky Mountain News, Denver, 1963-65; composer-in-residence, Rockford, Ill., public schools, 1965-67; faculty member, California State Univ., Fresno, 1971-74; Columbia Univ., 1975-78.
WORKS: ORCHESTRA: Theme and variations,

1965; Concertante music III, viola and orch., 1973; CHAMBER MUSIC: Variations II, string trio, 1967; Concertante music I and II, chamber ensemble, 1970, 1972; Variations III, viola alone, 1972; CHORUS: Liebeslied, 1964; Elegy for Sept. 15, 1945, Rilke text, 1965; Beata viscera, 1967; Whispers of heavenly death, cantata 3, 1968; ELECTRONIC: The fragility of the flower unbruised penetrates space, tape, 1970; songs and piano pieces.

200 Riverside Dr., #8D, New York, NY 10025

RILEY, JAMES REX
b. Shreveport, La., 2 Sept. 1938. Studied with Samuel Adler, North Texas State Univ., M.M. 1963; with Hunter Johnson and Kent Kennan, Univ. of Texas, D.M.A. 1968. He received second prize, Creative Writing for Television Contest, 1970; first prize, Shenna Meeker Composers' Competition, 1977; ASCAP awards, 1977, 1978; and commissions. He was faculty member, Univ. of Texas, 1965-68; Mississippi State Univ., 1968-70; Wichita State Univ., 1970-75; from 1976, Univ. of Texas.
    WORKS: ORCHESTRA: 4 scenes for orchestra; Spheres, Fort Worth, Tex., 23 Oct. 1977; WIND ENSEMBLE: suite for brass choir; 4 essays, brass quintet; Concert music for winds and percussion; Winds of change, San Antonio, 15 Oct. 1978; CHAMBER MUSIC: Textures, trombone and piano; Dialogue, trumpet and piano; Stick games for 9 players, percussion, Pittsburgh, 22 Nov. 1975; Pastimes, woodwind quintet, 1976; Dedicatory hymn and fuguing tune, brass trio; Dyadics, flute and piano; string quartet #3, San Antonio, 23 Jan. 1977.
    Music Div., University of Texas, San Antonio, TX 78285

RILEY, JOHN
b. Altoona, Pa., 17 Sept. 1920. Studied with Wayne Barlow and Bernard Rogers, Eastman School of Music, B.M. 1951; with Arthur Honegger in Paris, 1952-53; with Quincy Porter, Yale Univ., M.M. 1955. He received a Fulbright grant, 1952; Tamiment award, 1954. He has been cellist with various orchestras, from 1965 with the Hartford Symphony; was instructor, Central Connecticut State Coll., 1971-77.
    WORKS: ORCHESTRA: Rhapsody, cello and orch., 1951; Apostasy, 1954; Fantasy, oboe and strings, 1955; Sinfonietta, 1955; CHAMBER MUSIC: 2 string quartets, 1954, 1959; Divertimento, woodwind quintet; Chamber music, song cycle on text of James Joyce, tenor and piano trio; other chamber music and songs.
    107 Golf St., Newington, CT 06111

RILEY, TERRY
b. Colfax, Calif., 25 June 1935. Studied with Seymour Shifrin, William Denny, Robert Erickson, Univ. of California, Berkeley, M.A. 1961; also with Pran Nath in San Francisco and in India, 1970. From 1972 he has taught at Mills Coll.
    WORKS: BALLET: Genesis 70, 1970; ORCHESTRA: In C, aleatory piece, 1963; CHAMBER MUSIC: Spectra, for 6 instruments, 1959; string trio, 1961; ELECTRONIC: Poppy Nogood and the phantom band, 1966, and Rainbow in curved air, 1968, both for organ, saxophone, percussion, electronic equipment.
    Mills College, Oakland, CA 94613

RIND, BERNICE MOSSAFER
b. Seattle, Wash., 19 Jan. 1929. Studied on scholarship at New York Coll. of Music, Peabody Cons., Chicago Musical Coll., Cornish School; graduated, Univ. of Washington. She began composing at age 8, made her debut as a harpist at age 11 with the Southern California Symphony; has been first harpist with the Seattle Philharmonic. Her compositions for harp include Rhapsody in f minor; Serena safarad, 1973; Rishon Le Zion, 1977.
    7935 Overlook Dr. W., Bellevue, WA 98004

RINEHART, JOHN M.
b. Pittsburgh, Pa., 17 Mar. 1937. Studied with Harold Miles, Kent State Univ.; Quincy Porter, Yale Univ.; Marcel Dick and Donald Erb, Cleveland Inst. of Music; and with Ronald Pellegrino, Ohio State Univ. He received ASCAP's first Bloch Memorial award, 1960; a Yale scholarship; Ohio State Univ. fellowship. He was faculty member, Cleveland Inst. of Music, 1960-63; Heidelberg Coll., 1963-75; Central Washington Univ., 1975-78; from 1978, at Shenandoah Coll. and Cons.
    WORKS: ORCHESTRA: piano concerto; CHAMBER MUSIC: Capriccio, piano trio, 1966; Variations, solo cello, 1967; CHORUS: 4 odes, 1965; Credo; PIANO: sonata, 1959; suite, 1960; ELECTRONIC: Geomanteia, tape, 1969; Motions, piano and tape, 1973; Inlaid, piano trio and synthesized sound, ASUC Conf., Univ. of Miami, 1978; Passages, soprano, orch., electronic sounds, Terre Haute, Ind., 27 Sept. 1979.
    Shenandoah College and Cons., Winchester, VA 22601

RINGO, JAMES
b. St. Louis, Mo., 4 Mar. 1926. Studied with Vittorio Giannini and Frederick Jacobi, Juilliard School, B.S. 1949; with Darius Milhaud and Olivier Messiaen in Paris; and at Mills Coll., M.A. 1951. In 1969 he received the ASCAP Deems Taylor award for his writings on music. His compositions include 5 pieces from Le Trésor d'Orphée for string orch., 1948; string trio, 1949; sonata for cello alone, 1950; 2 books of Portraits for piano, 1951, 1954.

RINKER, ALTON
b. Tekoa, Wash., 20 Dec. 1907. Was a singer with Paul Whiteman's Rhythm Boys and others. His compositions include 2 choral works, American poets' suite and Song portraits of birds; many popular songs.

RIPPER, THEODORE W.
b. Coraopolis, Pa., 1 Aug. 1925. Studied with Nikolai Lopatnikoff, Carnegie Inst. of Technology, B.F.A. 1947, M.F.A. 1948. He was faculty member, Carnegie Inst. of Tech., 1949-55; Millikin Univ., 1967-75; organist at various churches, in Decatur, Ill., from 1965. He has published choral works, songs, and organ pieces.

RITCHIE, TOM VERNON
   b. Lawrenceville, Ill., 3 July 1922. Studied
with Russell Miles and Robert Kelly, Univ. of
Illinois; with Leo Sowerby in Chicago. He has
held faculty posts at Culver Military Acad.,
1947-48; Midland Coll., 1949-54; Indiana Univ.,
1954-56; Drury Coll., 1956-62; Wichita State
Univ., 1962-65; and from 1965, at Northeast
Missouri State Univ.
   WORKS: CHORUS: Ode to music, male voices
and instruments; Let us now remember heroes,
with brass and percussion; SONGS: 16 art songs
including A Lincoln triptych.
      Northeast Missouri State Univ., Kirksville,
   MO 63501

RIVARD, WILLIAM H.
   b. Lewiston, Idaho, 31 Aug. 1928. Studied with
John Cowell, Leroy Ostransky, Univ. of Puget
Sound; with John Boda and Ernst von Dohnanyi,
Florida State Univ.; with Philip Bezanson and
Richard Hervig, Univ. of Iowa, on a fellowship.
He was faculty member, Univ. of Missouri, 1954-
56; Northern Arizona Univ., 1958-59; from 1959,
Central Michigan Univ.
   WORKS: ORCHESTRA: Concerto-sinfonia, small
orch.; Philosophical hautboy, oboe and strings;
Overture to War of the comedians; BAND: Capriccio
concitato; WIND ENSEMBLE: 3 Biblical scenes,
brass choir; CHAMBER MUSIC: Arioso and scherzo,
chamber ensemble; trombone sonata.
      Central Michigan University, Mt. Pleasant,
   MI 48858

RIZO, MARCO
   b. Havana, Cuba, 30 Nov. 1916. Studied with
Pedro San Juan, Nat. Cons., Havana; at Juilliard
School, B.S.; with Castelnuovo-Tedesco, Univ. of
California, Los Angeles; and at Los Angeles Cons.;
received an honorary D.M., Havana Univ. He is
piano soloist and gave a recital of his own
works in Town Hall, New York, in 1940. In World
War II, he was in USAF Special Services, then
became arranger and orchestrator for films in
Hollywood.
   WORKS: ORCHESTRA: Broadway concerto, New
York, 14 Jan. 1973; PIANO: Spanish suite; Suite
campesina; Toccata-zapateo; many popular songs.

ROALSON, ERIC
   b. Cedar Rapids, Iowa, 2 May 1950. Studied with
William Parsons and Peter Todd Lewis, Univ. of
Iowa, 1972-76; with Frederic Rzewski, Anthony
Braxton, Creative Music Studio, Woodstock, N.Y.,
1977. He is musical director of Metesky, a contemporary music ensemble. He has published 2
panidiomatic improvisational pieces: Unseen
walls and Cell structure and language design in
the music of Anthony Braxton; was coauthor-com-
poser of Erroneous notions, a musico-theatre
play, 1977.
      641 29th St. N.E., Cedar Rapids, IA 52404

ROBB, JOHN DONALD
   b. Minneapolis, Minn., 12 June 1892. Studied
with Horatio Parker and Paul Hindemith, Yale
Univ., B.A. 1915; with Nadia Boulanger and
Darius Milhaud in Paris, 1936-37; with Milhaud

at Mills Coll., M.A. 1950; with Roy Harris at
Juilliard School. His awards include a
Rockefeller Found. teaching fellowship in
biology in China, 1915; first prize for a piano
composition, Nat. Composers Forum, Chicago,
1947; annual ASCAP awards from 1960; Smith Mundt
grant as visiting professor, Nat. Cons., El
Salvador, 1962; Nat. Endowment for the Arts
grants, 1968, 1977, 1978; Rockefeller Found.
grant, 1970; New Mexico Fed. of Music Clubs concert of his works, 1970; Albuquerque Music Club
concert of his works and John D. Robb Day proclaimed by City Commission, 19 Feb. 1971; New
Mexico Arts Commission award, 1975; Yale Univ.
Alumni award, 1977. He is a lawyer as well as
composer and author, and after serving in the
U.S. Army in World War I, he practiced law in
New York, 1922-41. He gave up his practice to
accept appointment as professor, music department head, and acting dean, Univ. of New Mexico,
1942-45, dean of Coll. of Fine Arts, 1946-57,
then professor and dean emeritus.
   WORKS: THEATRE: Little Jo, opera, 1947-49;
Delgadina, ballet, 1951; Joy comes to Deadhorse,
musical play, 1956; Dontaro, chamber opera after
the Japanese, 1961; ORCHESTRA: 3 symphonies,
1947, 1952, 1962; piano concerto, 1950; viola
concerto, 1953; Matachines dance, 1956; Recollections of Iran, 1960; Fantasia on Christmas
songs, guitar and orch., 1964; piano concerto
on Hispanic themes, San Salvador, 20 May 1976;
CHAMBER MUSIC: 2 string quartets, 1932, 1964;
3 violin sonatas, 1936, 1972, #3 Albuquerque,
15 Oct. 1976; 2 piano sonatas, 1937, #2 Albuquerque, 26 Jan. 1976; The leprechauns, violin and
piano, 1940; Miniature suite, for brass, 1963;
Little suite, for 4 double basses, 1965; Dialogue, guitar and piano, 1967; trio for oboe,
violin, piano, 1973; Triangulum, clarinet and
piano, 1978; Little suite, for flute and harpsichord, Hobbs, N.Mex., 5 Nov. 1978; also many
choral works, songs, piano pieces, and electronic
works. On 12 June 1976, he wrote a fugue to
celebrate his 84th birthday.
      2819 Ridgecrest Dr., S.E., Albuquerque, NM
   87108

ROBBINS, DANIEL
   b. New Orleans, La., 4 Nov. 1947. Studied with
Leon Dallin, Gerald Strang, Ronald Sindelar,
California State Univ., Long Beach, B.M. 1970;
with Ramiro Cortes, Ellis Kohs, Robert Linn,
Univ. of Southern California; privately with
Morris Ruger and Miklos Rozsa. He won first
place in composition, Southwestern Youth Music
Festivals, 1964, 1966, 1968. He has been
faculty member, Long Beach City Coll., from
1976; California State Univ., Long Beach, from
1978.
   WORKS: THEATRE: 2 ballets, 1977, 1978;
ORCHESTRA: Movement, violin and orch., 1966;
suite, 1968; Phantasy, viola and orch., Long
Beach, 5 June 1977; In memoriam Robert F.
Kennedy, Lakewood, Calif., 18 Apr. 1978; WIND
ENSEMBLE: Piece for brass choir, 1967; CHAMBER
MUSIC: Air, cello and piano, 1964; suite for
flute and piano, 1965; Richard Cory, voice and
piano, 1965; Theme and variations, 1967; cello

sonata, 1969; piano sonata, 1971; woodwind trio,
1972; Phantasy, viola and piano; Composition for
7 instruments, 2 songs, voice and piano, string
quartet, all performed Los Angeles, 18 Mar. 1975.
245½ Coronado Ave., Long Beach, CA 90803

ROBBINS, DAVID PAUL
b. New York, N.Y., 18 July 1946. Studied with
Leslie Bassett, George B. Wilson, Eugene Kurtz,
Univ. of Michigan. He was named Composer of the
Year 1976 by Washington State Music Teachers
Assoc. He has been faculty member, Pacific
Lutheran Univ., from 1969.
WORKS: ORCHESTRA: Kabop, chamber orch.,
1968; Intersect, 1971; Foils; WIND ENSEMBLE:
Momentum, 5 brass and percussion, 1972; Herd,
18 trombones and percussion; CHAMBER MUSIC:
Sport, theatre piece for 10 players, 1969; Fall
back 10 yards and contrapunt!, clarinet, organ,
percussion, 1971; Biggie, cello and percussion,
1972; Knots, voices and instruments; string
trio; Politic, sextet of winds and strings;
ELECTRONIC: John 3:16, chorus and tape; Runic
rimes, percussion and tape.
3606 N. Baltimore, Tacoma, WA 98407

ROBERTS, GERTRUD KUENZEL
b. Hastings, Minn., 23 Aug. 1906. Studied at
Univ. of Minnesota, B.A. 1928; piano with many
teachers including Julia Elbogen in Vienna. Her
honors include election as honorary life member,
Honolulu Community Theatre; citation by Alpha
Gamma Delta as Most Distinguished Citizen for
1975 in the Arts. She has taught piano since
1931, piano and harpsichord in Honolulu since
1946; is concert pianist and harpsichordist, and
has made annual tours from 1964.
WORKS: THEATRE: background harpsichord
music for Yerma by Lorca; Thieves carnival by
Anouilh; Alice in Wonderland by Le Gallienne;
ORCHESTRA: Elegy for John F. Kennedy, harpsichord concerto, 1965; double concerto, 2 harpsichords or piano and harpsichord and orch., 1976;
HARPSICHORD: Chaconne; Triptych, 1961; Passa-
caille; Das Kleine Buch der Bilder; Fantasie
after Psalm 150; 3 bagatelles; Waltz for 2 harpsichords; PIANO: 12-time gardens, 12 pieces on
difference gardens in Hawaii, 1967; and songs.
4723 Moa St., Honolulu, HI 96816

ROBERTS, MEGAN. See GHIRARDO, MEGAN ROBERTS

ROBERTS, MYRON J.
b. San Diego, Calif., 30 Jan. 1912. Studied at
Univ. of the Pacific, B.M. 1935; School of Sacred
Music, Union Theological Seminary, M.S.M. 1937.
He was professor, Univ. of Nebraska, 1940-74.
WORKS: CHORUS: O Lord, we beseech thee;
The storm on Lake Galilee; Alleluia; Magnificat;
ORGAN: Prelude and trumpetings; Nova; In memor-
iam; Homage to Perotin; Dialogue; Litany; 5 for
organ and marimba; Exultate; Pastorale and in-
ventions, 2 organs; Pastorale and aviary.
850 Park Ave., #8C, Capitola, CA 95010

ROBERTSON, DONNA NAGEY
b. Indiana, Pa., 16 Nov. 1935. Studied at
Indiana Univ. of Penn., B.S. 1957; Eastman

School of Music, M.M. She received Nat. Fed. of
Music Clubs award, 1960; 2 N. Car. Fed. of Music
Clubs awards, 1964, 1967; and commissions. She
has been faculty member, Mars Hill Coll., from
1958; editor of Music Now from 1973.
WORKS: CHAMBER MUSIC: Prelude and fugue
for piano; trio for violin, oboe, harpsichord;
Recitation with 5 reflections, trombone and
piano; Nocturne, trombone and tenor; Dialogues,
chamber group, 1976; Flashes in a pan, trumpet,
clarinet, marimba, vibraphone, Memphis, Tenn.,
17 Oct. 1976; CHORUS: No single thing abides,
double chorus; Love, motet for treble voices;
All creatures of our God and King; Stations on
the road to freedom; Processional for a festive
occasion, with brass and organ; VOICE: Psalm 23,
soprano and flute; 2 Dylan Thomas songs, high
voice; 6 psalms of ascension, low voice.
Box 223, Mars Hill, NC 28754

ROBERTSON, DUNCAN D.
b. Huron, S.Dak., 15 Aug. 1940. Studied with
William Critzer, 1954-65. He is a research
engineer.
WORKS: CHAMBER MUSIC: Divertimento for 9
winds, 1969; ORGAN: 2 soliloquies, 1969; Prelude, fugue, and epilogue, organ and 2 horns,
1971.
Box 185, Mellette, SD 57461

ROBERTSON, EDWIN C.
b. Richmond, Va., 26 Nov. 1938. Studied with
David Davis, Univ. of Virginia; with John Boda,
Florida State Univ. He was choral conductor,
Univ. of Richmond, 1968-69; from 1971, on
faculty, Univ. of Montevallo.
WORKS: CHAMBER MUSIC: piano trio; quartet
for flute, clarinet, marimba, double bass; Movement, for brass quintet; Trumpet reflection;
CHORUS: Sing my fair love good morrow; Golden
slumbers; 2 psalms, with string orch.
Town and Country Apts., #10, Montevallo, AL
35115

ROBERTSON, HUGH STERLING, II
b. New York, N.Y., 19 Jan. 1940; d. Bedford,
N.Y., 15 Nov. 1973. He was a grandson of Fedor
Chaliapin. Studied with William Russo in New
York; Richard Hoffmann, Oberlin Cons.; Henri
Dutilleux, Ecole Normale, Paris, License de
Composition, 1970; Nadia Boulanger in Paris,
1964-73. His awards include the Biennale in
composition, Orchestre Radio-Television Francais,
1969; Lili Boulanger prize, 1971; Prince Pierre
of Monaco award, 1973; first prize in composition, Fontainebleau Cons., 1973.
WORKS: OPERA: The atheist; ORCHESTRA: a
symphony; CHAMBER MUSIC: trio for clarinet,
viola, piano; piano trio; string quartet; quintet for winds, strings, harp; harp quintet; saxophone quintet; organ sextet; guitar sonata;
Divertimento, guitar and cello; PIANO: Waltz;
Etude; 3 pieces; sonata for 2 pianos; Wedding
prelude; Variations; FILM SCORE: The wheel of
ashes; choral works; many songs.

ROBERTSON, LEROY
b. Fountain Green, Utah, 21 Dec. 1896; d. Salt

ROBINSON, EARL

Lake City, 25 July 1971. Studied with George W. Chadwick and Frederick Converse, New England Cons., diploma 1923; with Carl Busch, Ernest Bloch, Hugo Leichtentritt, and Ernst Toch in Europe; at Univ. of Utah, M.A. 1932; Univ. of Southern California, Ph.D. 1954. His awards included the Endicott prize, 1923; Society for Publication of American Music award, 1936; New York Music Critics' Circle award, 1944; Utah Inst. of Fine Arts prize, 1945; and the Reichold award of $25,000, 1947. He was professor and department chairman, Brigham Young Univ., 1925-48; and held the same posts, Univ. of Utah, 1948-62.

WORKS: ORCHESTRA: Overture Emin, 1923; Prelude, scherzo, ricercare, 1940; Rhapsody, piano and orch., 1944; Punch and Judy, overture, 1945; Trilogy, Detroit, 11 Dec. 1947; violin concerto, 1948; cello concerto; piano concerto, 1966; CHAMBER MUSIC: piano quintet, 1938; string quartet, 1940; American serenade, string quartet, 1944; Fantasia, organ; CHORUS: The Book of Mormon, oratorio, 1953; Come, come, ye saints; Hatikva; From the crossroads; The Lord's Prayer.

ROBINSON, EARL
b. Seattle, Wash., 2 July 1910. Studied with George McKay, Univ. of Washington, B.M. 1933; with Aaron Copland, 1936; with Hanns Eisler, 1940; and with George Antheil, 1948-50. He held a Guggenheim fellowship, 1940. He wrote incidental music for plays in the Federal Theatre in New York in 1934; was head of a Los Angeles high school music department, 1958-65; taught in Univ. of California, Los Angeles, Extension Div., 1967-71.

WORKS: THEATRE: Sandhog, folk opera; David of Sassoun, folk opera; Earl Robinson's America, a musical, 1978; BAND: Soul rhythms; CANTATAS: Ballad of Americans, 1939; Battle hymn; The lonesome train; Tower of Babel; The town crier; In the folded and quiet yesterdays, with narrator and orch.; Preamble to peace; FILM SCORES: California; A walk in the sun; The romance of Rosy Ridge; Man from Texas; The Roosevelt story.
3929 Calle Cita, Santa Barbara, CA 93110

ROBINSON, EDWARD
b. New York, N.Y., 28 Jan. 1905; d. New York, 23 Sept. 1970. Studied on a fellowship with Seth Bingham at Columbia Univ., B.A., M.A. He was music critic, Columbia Daily Spectator; editor and publisher, Fortnightly Music Review, 1928-29; columnist and drama critic, 1934-38; accompanist and piano teacher.

WORKS: PIANO: Chillmark suite; Gay Head suite; The storekeeper's daughter; Variations on a theme by Beethoven; SONGS: Stop, look, and listen; A child's introduction to science, a song cycle.

ROBINSON, KEITH
CHAMBER MUSIC: Visions, eloquent and triumphant, trumpet, New York, 11 Dec. 1971; 2 preludes, violin and piano, Vocalise, trumpet and piano; sonata for solo violin; 2 fragments for solo violin; PIANO: Theme and variations; 20 fragments; sonata #1; Sonata rhapsody; Tone poem

(fugue); Childhood suite; Fantasy, 4 hands; many other piano pieces.

ROBINSON, RICHARD
b. Chicago, Ill., 12 July 1923. Studied with Leo Sowerby, American Cons.; with Karel Husa and Robert Palmer, Cornell Univ. He received the Georgia Composers award, 1953; Piedmont Arts Festival award, 1967; was cowinner, first prize, Dartmouth Internat. Electronic Music Competition, 1970. He was violinist, Atlanta Symph. Orch., 1952-73; program director, Ambience, a weekly electronic music program, WREK-FM, Atlanta, 1971-72; and from 1968, has been director, Atlanta Electronic Music Center.

WORKS: ORCHESTRA: 3 haiku, soprano and orch., 1967; CHAMBER MUSIC: woodwind trio, 1953; ELECTRONIC: Ambience, 1970; Mosaic, quadronic electronic piece, 1972; Alea, 1971; Voices, 1973.
3065 Brook Dr., Decatur, GA 30033

ROCHBERG, GEORGE
b. Paterson, N.J., 5 July 1918. Studied at Univ. of Pennsylvania, M.A.; Mannes School of Music; with Rosario Scalero, Curtis Inst. of Music. His many awards include Gershwin award, 1952; 2 Guggenheim grants; Fulbright fellowship; American Acad. in Rome fellowship; Prix d'Italia; ISCM Internat. Chamber Music award; Naumberg Chamber Music award; 3 Nat. Endowment for the Arts grants; many commissions. He taught at Curtis Inst., 1948-54; was editor, Theodore Presser Co., 1951-60; has been faculty member, New School of Music, Philadelphia, from 1947; Univ. of Pennsylvania, from 1960.

WORKS: THEATRE: Phaedra, monodrama in 7 scenes, mezzo-soprano and orch., Syracuse, N.Y., 9 Jan. 1976; ORCHESTRA: Night music, 1949; Cantio sacra, chamber orch., 1953; Sinfonia fantasia, 1956; Waltz serenade, Cincinnati, 14 Feb. 1958; Cheltenham concerto, 1958; 4 symphonies, #1, Philadelphia, 28 Mar. 1958, #2, Cleveland, 26 Feb. 1959, #3 (with solo voice, chamber chorus, double chorus), New York, 24 Nov. 1970, #4, Seattle, 15 Nov. 1976; Imago mundi, Baltimore, 8 May 1974; violin concerto, Pittsburgh, 4 Apr. 1975; Time-span, St. Louis, 22 Oct. 1960; BAND: Apocalyptica; WIND ENSEMBLE: Black sounds, with percussion, 1963; CHAMBER MUSIC: piano trio; Caprice variations, violin solo; Capriccio, 2 pianos, 1949; 6 string quartets, 1952, 1961, 1972, 1977, 1978, 1978, #4, 5, 6 were premiered by the Concord Quartet, Univ. of Pennsylvania, 20 Jan. 1979; Fantasia, violin and piano, 1955; Duo concertante, violin and cello, 1955-59; clarinet sonata, 1958; Contra mortem et tempus, flute, clarinet, viola, piano, 1965; Music for the magic theatre, 9 instruments, 1965; Ricordanza, Soliloquy, cello and piano, 1972; Electrikaleidoscope, New York, 19 Dec. 1972; piano quintet, New York, 15 Mar. 1972; Partita variations, piano, Washington, 4 Dec. 1976; Ukiyo-E, Pictures of the floating world, harp, 1976; Ukiyo-E II, Slow fires of autumn, flute and harp, New York, 23 Apr. 1979; viola sonata, Provo, Utah, 7th Internat. Viola Congress, 14 July 1979; Octet: a grand fantasia, 3 winds, string trio, 2 pianos, double bass, New York, 27 Apr. 1980; choral works, songs, piano pieces. He is author of the book, The hexachord and its relation to the 12-tone row, 1955.

285 Aronimink Dr., Newton Square, PA 19073

RODBY, JOHN LEONARD
b. Wahiawa, Oahu, Hawaii, 14 Sept. 1944. Studied with Leonard Berkowitz and Aurelio de la Vega, California State Univ. at Northridge, B.A. 1966; privately with Albert Harris and Donal Michalsky. He won a university composition prize, 1966. From 1966 he has been free-lance studio musician; from 1968, musical director for Dinah Shore.
WORKS: ORCHESTRA: Variations for orchestra, 1969; Festivals, 1970; saxophone concerto, 1971; Concerto for 29, 1973; CHAMBER MUSIC: alto saxophone sonata, 1965; quintet for piano, viola, horn, clarinet, cello, 1966; quintet for clarinet, cello, viola, guitar, celeste, 1972; CHORUS: Chorale, 1964; 3 poems, by R. J. Foster, 1967; PIANO: sonata, 1968; 5 etudes, 1970.
5351 Penfield Ave., Woodland Hills, CA 91364

RODBY, WALTER
b. Virginia, Minn., 7 Sept. 1917. Studied at Northern Iowa Univ., B.A. 1940; Teachers Coll., Columbia Univ., M.A. 1947; Trinity Coll. of Music, London, 1946. He was choral director in public schools, 1941-49; chairman of Fine Arts Div., Flossmoor, Ill., 1959-73. He led the Homewood-Flossmoor H.S. Choir on a concert tour of Europe and the Soviet Union, 1970, and in Europe, 1973. From 1953 he has been choral editor and columnist for the School Musician Magazine. He has published more than 125 choral compositions and arrangements.
819 Buell Ave., Joliet, IL 60435

RODER, MILAN
b. Osijek, Slavonia, 5 Dec. 1878; U.S. citizen 1920; d. Hollywood, Calif., 23 Jan. 1956. Studied at the Vienna Cons.; was conductor of opera, operetta, and orchestra in Europe; from 1914, was a film composer in Hollywood.
WORKS: OPERA: Jelka; Round the world, comic opera; ORCHESTRA: 4 symphonic sketches; Rondo capriccioso; Moto perpetuo; Vindobona, a suite; also piano pieces, songs.

RODGERS, JOHN
b. Bonham, Tex., 24 Mar. 1917. Studied at Southern Methodist Univ., B.M.; North Texas State Univ., M.M.; Union Theological Seminary, M.S.M. He has been organist, choir director, teacher; editor, H. W. Gray Co.
WORKS: CHORUS: A little carol; Of the Father's love begotten; Oh praise the Lord; The sky can still remember.

RODGERS, MARY
b. New York, N.Y., 11 Jan. 1931. Daughter of Richard Rodgers, studied at Wellesley Coll.
WORKS: THEATRE: Feather top, television score; Davy Jones locker, marionette show; 3 to make music; Once upon a mattress; The mad show; ALBUMS FOR CHILDREN: Children's introduction to

jazz; Some of my best friends are children; Ali Baba.
115 Central Park W., New York, NY 10023

RODGERS, RICHARD
b. Hammels Station, Long Island, N.Y., 28 June 1902; d. New York, N.Y., 30 Dec. 1979. Studied at Columbia Univ. and Juilliard School. His many awards included 8 honorary doctorates; special Pulitzer award for Oklahoma, 1944; 4 Donaldson awards: Carousel, 1945, Allegro, 1948, South Pacific, 1949, Pal Joey, 1952; Columbia Medal of Excellence, 1949; Pulitzer prize for South Pacific, 1950; 3 Antoinette Perry awards for South Pacific, 1950, The king and I, 1952, No strings, 1962; Columbia Coll. award, 1952; U.S. Navy Distinguished Public Service award for Victory at sea, 1953; Columbia's Alexander Hamilton Medal, 1956; Christopher award for The king and I, 1956; Emmy award for Winston Churchill: The valiant years, 1962; membership in the Nat. Inst. of Arts and Letters; and a Salute to Richard Rodgers, Imperial Theatre, New York, Mar. 1972. Among his other highly successful musicals were The girl friend, 1926; A Connecticut Yankee, 1927; On your toes, 1936; Babes in arms, 1937; I married an angel, 1938; The boys from Syracuse, 1938; By Jupiter, 1942; Me and Juliet, 1953; Pipe dreams, 1955; The flower drum song, 1958. He was author of an autobiography, Musical stages, New York, 1975. In 1978 he made a gift of $1 million to the American Acad. and Inst. of Arts and Letters to establish the Richard Rodgers Production award.

RODRIGUEZ, ROBERT XAVIER
b. San Antonio, Tex., 28 June 1946. Studied with Kent Kennan and Hunter Johnson, Univ. of Texas, B.M. 1967, M.M. 1969; with Nadia Boulanger at Fontainebleau; with Halsey Stevens and Frederick Lesemann, Univ. of Southern California, D.M.A. 1974. His awards include 2 Brackenridge scholarships, 1964, 1965; Phi Mu Alpha scholarship, 1965; Julia Klumpke scholarship, Cons. Americaine, 1969, 1970; 3 Alchin scholarships, 1969-71; Young Musicians Found. award, 1970; McHugh award, 1971; Prince Pierre of Monaco composition award, 1971; 2 Rockefeller performance grants, 1967, 1968; 2 Nat. Endowment for the Arts grants, 1973, 1977; Guggenheim fellowship, 1976. He was instructor, Univ. of Texas, 1968-69; faculty member, Univ. of Southern California, 1970-75.
WORKS: OPERA: Les visiteurs du soir, libretto by Franz Boerlage, 1977; ORCHESTRA: Music for small orch., 1967; 2 piano concertos, 1968, 1974; Lyric variations, oboe, 2 horns, string orch., 1970; Canto, soprano, tenor, piano, orch., 1973; Favola concertante, concerto for violin and cello, based on story of Psyche and Eros, Los Angeles, 14 June 1975; CHAMBER MUSIC: 2 piano trios, 1970, 1971; saxophone sonata in 1 movement, 1974; Variations, violin and piano; Lyrics for autumn, solo cello, Washington, 26 May 1976; also choral works.

ROFF, JOSEPH
b. Turin, Italy, 26 Dec. 1910; U.S. citizen

ROGERS, BERNARD

1964. Studied with Healy Willan, Leo Smith,
Ernest MacMillan, Univ. of Toronto, B.M., M.A.,
D.M. 1948. He is a fellow of Trinity Coll.,
London, England; received ASCAP awards, 1972,
1973; is composer-in-residence and lecturer,
St. Joseph's Coll., Brooklyn, N.Y.
    WORKS: OPERETTA: Lady of Mexico, 1963;
ORCHESTRA: Niagara; 3 fragments for strings;
Reverie; CHORUS: more than 700 published works
for church and school choirs.
    101 Greene Ave., Brooklyn, NY 11238

ROGERS, BERNARD
    b. New York, N.Y., 4 Feb. 1893; d. Rochester,
N.Y., 24 May 1968. Studied with Percy
Goetschius, Inst. of Musical Art, 1919-21; with
Ernest Bloch in Cleveland; Nadia Boulanger in
Paris; and Frank Bridge in London. His honors
include the Loeb prize, 1920; Pulitzer fellowship, 1921; Guggenheim fellowship, 1927-29;
David Bispham Medal, 1931; Ditson prize, 1948;
Fulbright grant, 1953; Lillian B. Fairchild
award, 1962; Ford Found. grant, 1960; election
to Nat. Inst. of Arts and Letters; many commissions. From 1929 he was on the faculty,
Eastman School of Music.
    WORKS: OPERA: The marriage of Aude, 1931;
The warrior, 1947; The veil, 1950; BALLET: The
colors of war, 1939; ORCHESTRA: The faithful,
1918; To the fallen, 1919; Soliloquy, flute and
strings, 1922; Adonais, 1927; Prelude to Hamlet,
1928; 4 symphonies, 19--, 1930, 1937, 1948; 3
Japanese dances, 1933; 5 fairy tales, Once upon
a time, 1934; The supper at Emmaus, 1937; Fantasy, flute, viola, and orch., 1938; Soliloquy,
bassoon and strings, 1938; The song of the nightingale, 1940; The dance of Salome, 1940; The
plains, 1941; Invasion, 1943; Characters from
Hans Christian Anderson, 1945; In memory of
Franklin Delano Roosevelt, 1946; Amphitryon,
overture, 1947; Leaves from the tale of
Pinocchio, 1950; The silver world, flute, oboe,
strings, 1950; Dance scenes, 1953; Variations on
a song by Moussorgsky, 1960; also chamber music
and choral works.

ROGERS, EARL. See ROSENBERG, EMANUEL

ROGERS, EDDY
    b. Norfolk, Va., 23 Sept. 1907; d. Denver, Colo.,
8 Oct. 1964. Studied at Royal Cons., Naples,
Italy, A.M., D.M.; and with Rubin Goldmark. He
was concert violinist in the U.S. and Europe;
staff conductor, NBC, New York.
    WORKS: OPERA: Nella; ORCHESTRA: Impromptu
for moderns; Town and country dance; Commodore
Maury march; CHAMBER MUSIC: Andante appassionato,
string quartet; and songs.

ROGERS, ETHEL TENCH
    b. Newark, N.J., 21 Feb. 1914. Studied piano
and organ privately, and at Austrian-American
Inst., Vienna, 1977. She taught piano and organ
in Plainfield, N.J., and was church music director there, 1934-41; has also taught piano and
organ classes, Univ. of Missouri, Kansas City.
    WORKS: CHORUS: 4 cantatas; 150 anthems;
KEYBOARD: numerous teaching pieces for piano

and organ, piano solo, and 2 pianos.
    5700 Reinhart Dr., Shawnee Mission, KS
66205

ROGERS, JOHN E.
    b. Dallas, Tex., 20 Feb. 1938. Studied at Univ.
of Georgia; with Halsey Stevens and Elliott
Carter, Yale Univ.; with Milton Babbitt and
Roger Sessions, Princeton Univ., M.M. 1964. His
awards include BMI student composer awards; Composers Forum performance in New York. He was
faculty member, Bowdoin Coll., 1964-67; from
1967, at Univ. of New Hampshire.
    WORKS: CHAMBER MUSIC: Rotational arrays,
woodwind quintet; trio for flute, cello, piano;
ELECTRONIC: Electronic study; Canonic structures
(computer-generated sound).
    7 Bartlett Rd., Durham, NH 03824

ROGERS, SUSAN WHIPPLE
    b. Dallas, Tex., 15 Aug. 1943. Studied with
Lloyd Taliaferro, Univ. of Texas, Arlington;
with Rule Beasley, Centenary Coll. of Louisiana;
privately with Edward Kozak. She held scholarships for study at both colleges. From 1960 she
has been a private horn instructor; was arranger
for publishers, 1970-72.
    WORKS: CHAMBER MUSIC: suite for horn and
piano; trio for horn, clarinet, piano; Penta-
tonic suite for piano.
    1600 San Saba, Bossier City, LA 71010

ROHE, ROBERT KENNETH
    b. New York, N.Y., 22 Aug. 1916. Studied at
Cooper Union School of Fine Arts; double bass
with Fred Zimmerman. He played bass with the
Nat. Orch. Assoc. under Leon Barzin; NBC Symph.;
New Orleans Phil. from 1944, assistant conductor
from 1961; teaches bass at Loyola Univ. His
compositions include a ballet, Land of bottle;
Mainescapes, for orch., 1966.
    Loyola Univ., 6317 St. Charles, New Orleans,
LA 70118

ROLLIN, ROBERT L.
    b. New York, N.Y., 16 Feb. 1947. Studied with
Mark Brunswick, City Coll. of New York, B.A.
1968; with Robert Palmer and Karel Husa, Cornell
Univ., M.F.A. 1971, D.M.A. 1972; with Gyorgy
Ligeti in Hamburg on the German Academic Exchange Program, 1977. Other awards include fellowships at Cornell Univ., 1968-72; Nat. Endowment for the Arts grant, 1976; fellowship at
Internat. Music Inst., Darmstadt, 1976. He was
director, Ithaca Civic Opera, 1970-71; faculty
member, Otterbein Coll., 1972-73; North Central
Coll., 1973-77; from 1977, Youngstown State
Univ.
    WORKS: WIND AND PERCUSSION ENSEMBLE: 7
sound images on 7 stanzas by a child, with piano;
1971; Aquarelles, 1972; Chromatic suite concertant, 1976; CHAMBER MUSIC: 2 pieces, solo
flute, 1969; cello sonata, 1970; Thematic transformation, string quartet, 1970; suite for woodwind quintet, 1970; Reflections on ruin by the
sea, trumpet and piano, 1973; Etude 1, solo
guitar, 1977; Recollections, clarinet and piano,
1977; For 6 in Darmstadt, chamber ensemble,

1976.
> Dana School of Music, Youngstown State University, Youngstown, OH 44555

ROLNICK, NEIL B.
b. Dallas, Tex., 22 Oct. 1947. Studied with John Chowning and Loren Rush, Stanford Univ.; with Earle Brown, Andrew Imbrie, Richard Felciano, Olly Wilson, and Edwin Dugger, Univ. of California, Berkeley; with Darius Milhaud at Aspen Music Festival. His awards include the di Lorenzo prize at Berkeley, 1976-77; Nat. Endowment for the Arts grant, 1977; Hertz-Wallace Traveling fellowship, 1977-78. He was computer music specialist, Inst. de recherche et de coordination acoustique/musique (IRCAM), 1977-79. Some of his electronic works are Empty mirror, 1976; Blue Monday; Massachusetts F; Ever-livin' rhythm, 1977.
> 1403 Santa Fe Ave., Berkeley, CA 94702

ROMBERG, SIGMUND
b. Nagy Kaniza, Hungary, 29 July 1887; U.S. citizen 1912; d. New York, N.Y., 9 Nov. 1951. Studied engineering in Budapest; then music with Joseph Heuberger in Vienna. He was a cafe pianist in New York; staff composer for the Schuberts, 1913-19, 1921-24; composed more than 70 operettas.
> WORKS: OPERETTAS: The blue paradise; Maytime; Monte Cristo, Jr.; Blossom time; The rose of Stamboul; The student prince; The desert song; My Maryland; The new moon; Up in Central Park; also many songs and film scores.

ROMEO, JAMES JOSEPH
b. Rochester, N.Y., 5 Mar. 1955. Studied with Jere Hutcheson and David Liptak, Michigan State Univ., B.M. 1977, M.M. 1978. His awards include a Wurlitzer Found. grant, 1980; selection as guest artist-lecturer, New Mexico Music Festival, 1980; and commissions. He has been director of new music groups, including New Music Ensemble, Bowling Green State Univ., 1978-79.
> WORKS: CHAMBER MUSIC: Toccata for 5 and 7 tuned pianos, 1977; Concert rhapsody, flute and piano; Crystalline, solo flute; 4 Egyptian death songs, soprano and chamber group, 1978; Fantasia profundis, organ, 1979; ELECTRONIC: Why must I speak in puzzles, tape and timpani, 1978; The orbit of 3 astral spheres, trombone and tape, 1978.
> 610 4th St., Apt. 6, Bowling Green, OH 43402

ROMITI, RICHARD A.
b. Woonsocket, R.I., 6 Sept. 1949. Studied with Hugo Norden, John Goodman, and Gardner Read, Boston Univ., B.M., M.M.; with John Weinzweig and Lothar Klein, Univ. of Toronto on doctoral fellowship, 1975-76. Other awards include first prize, Pittsburgh Flute Club Internat. Comp. Contest, 1975. He was faculty member, Univ. of Toronto, 1976-77; from 1977, at Performing Arts School of Worcester; from 1978, also at Providence Coll.
> WORKS: ORCHESTRA: concerto for accordion, harp, strings, percussion, 1975; Stratum, 1977;

Tantara, brass ensemble and percussion; CHAMBER MUSIC: Fantasy, flute and piano; Permutations, free-bass accordion, 1972; string quartet #1; Inflections I, prepared piano; suite for flute and harp, 1974; Exchanges, oboe and harpsichord, 1976.
> 112 Cleveland St., Woonsocket, RI 02895

RONSHEIM, JOHN
b. Cadiz, Ohio, 17 Feb. 1927. Studied with Francis Judd Cooke, New England Cons.; with Luigi Dallapiccola, in Italy. He received the Dows award at Univ. of Iowa. He has been faculty member, Newton Jr. Coll., 1965-66; New England Cons., 1966-67; from 1967, at Antioch Coll.
> WORKS: SONGS: Easter-wings, 1964, and Bitter-sweet, 1969, both for mezzo-soprano and vibraphone on texts from George Herbert's The temple (1633).
> 225 W. Limestone St., Yellow Springs, OH 45387

ROOBENIAN, AMBER. See HARRINGTON, AMBER ROOBENIAN

ROOSEVELT, JOSEPH WILLARD
b. Madrid, Spain, 16 Jan. 1918, of American parents. Studied at Harvard Coll.; with Nadia Boulanger at Longy School, Cambridge; with Isadore Freed and Arnold Franchetti, Hartt Coll., Univ. of Hartford; piano with Bruce Simonds, Pauline Danforth, and others. He has received various performance awards and many commissions; has held faculty posts at Turtle Bay Music School, 1957-65; Columbia Univ., 1962; Fairleigh Dickinson Univ., 1962-66; New York Coll. of Music, 1966-68.
> WORKS: OPERA: And the walls came tumbling down, concert performance, New York, Mar. 1976; ORCHESTRA: May song it flourish, 3 singers and small orch., on James Joyce text, New York, 17 Feb. 1961; cello concerto, New York, 17 Apr. 1963; Amistad, homenaje al gran Morel Campos, with voices, a salute to Puerto Rican music, New York, 26 Feb. 1966; Our dead brothers still live for us, with dancer, singer, and narrator, New Haven, May 1976; also pieces for solo instruments and chamber groups.
> Box 72, Sandisfield, MA 01255

ROOT, THOMAS R.
b. Redwood Falls, Minn., 22 Feb. 1947. Studied with Dominick Argento, Univ. of Minnesota; with Jere Hutcheson, Michigan State Univ. He was on faculty, Univ. of Minnesota, 1973-76; from 1976, at Saginaw Valley State Coll.
> WORKS: BAND: Exposition; Sonnet and dance; Polly Oliver; Prelude and giocoso; Cancionera; Andante and allegro.
> 607 N. Jackson, Bay City, MI 48706

ROREM, NED
b. Richmond, Ind., 23 Oct. 1923. Studied with Leo Sowerby in Chicago; at Northwestern Univ.; at Curtis Inst.; at Tanglewood, 1946, 1947; with Bernard Wagenaar at Juilliard School, M.S. 1948; privately with Virgil Thomson. His many awards include the Gershwin Memorial prize,

ROSE, GRIFFITH WHEELER

1948; Fulbright fellowship, 1951; 2 Guggenheim
fellowships, 1957, 1978; Nat. Inst. of Arts and
Letters grant, 1968; Lili Boulanger prize; Prix
de Biarritz; Eurydice Choral prize; Nat. Endowment for the Arts grant, 1976; Pulitzer prize
for Air music for orch., 1976; numerous commissions. He lived in Morocco, 1949-51, Paris,
1951-57, from 1957, in New York; was composer-
in-residence, State Univ. of New York at Buffalo,
1959-61, Univ. of Utah, 1966.
    WORKS: OPERA: The robbers, 1956, libretto
by composer, Mannes Coll., N.Y., 14 Apr. 1958;
Miss Julie, New York City Opera, 4 Nov. 1965;
3 sisters who are not sisters, 1968, Temple
Univ., Philadelphia, 24 July 1971; Bertha, 1968,
New York, 26 Nov. 1973; Fables, 5 very short
operas, 1970, Univ. of Tennessee at Martin, 21
May 1971; Hearing, chamber opera, 1976; ORCHESTRA:
Design, 1953, Louisville Orch., 29 May 1955; 3
symphonies, 1950, #2, La Jolla, Calif., 5 Aug.
1956, #3 1958, New York Phil., 16 Apr. 1959;
Eagles, 1958, Philadelphia Orch., 23 Oct. 1959;
Pilgrims, string orch., 1958; Ideas, 1961; Lions
(a dream), 1963, New York, 28 Oct. 1965; Water
music, with solo clarinet and violin, 1966,
Oakland, Calif., 9 Apr. 1967; 3 piano concertos,
1950, 1951, #3 1969, Pittsburgh, 3 Dec. 1970;
Sun, with solo voice, 1966, New York Phil., 1
July 1967; Letters from Paris, with chorus, 1966,
Univ. of Michigan, 25 Apr. 1969; Little prayers,
with soprano and baritone solos and chorus,
1973, Sioux Falls (S.Dak.) Symph., 20 Apr. 1974;
Air music, 10 variations, 1974, Cincinnati Symph.,
5 Dec. 1975; Assembly and fall, with solo oboe,
trumpet, timpani, viola, 1975, North Carolina
Symph., Raleigh, 11 Oct. 1975; Sunday morning,
1977, Philadelphia Orch. at Saratoga Springs,
N.Y., 25 Aug. 1978; double concerto, piano and
cello, Cincinnati Symph., 16 May 1980; CHAMBER
MUSIC: 11 studies for 11 players, 1960; Lovers,
harpsichord, oboe, cello, percussion, 1964; Day
music, violin and piano, 1971; Night music,
violin and piano, 1972; Book of hours, flute and
harp, 1975; Sky music, solo harp, 1976; Romeo
and Juliet, flute and guitar, 1977; numerous
songs and song cycles, choral works, keyboard
works. He is author of 8 books: Pure contrap-
tion; The Paris diary; The New York diary; Music
from inside out; Music and people; The final
diary; Critical affairs; An absolute gift.
    c/o Boosey & Hawkes, 30 W. 57th St., New
York, NY 10019

ROSE, GRIFFITH WHEELER
    b. Los Angeles, Calif., 18 Jan. 1936. Studied
with Isadore Freed, Hartt Coll. of Music; with
David Kraehenbuehl, Yale Univ.; Nadia Boulanger
at Fontainebleau; Wolfgang Fortner and Karlheinz
Stockhausen in Germany; Pierre Boulez in Basel.
    WORKS: CHAMBER MUSIC: Salpinx, trumpet
and 2 pianos, 1961, New York, 27 Sept. 1966;
Complaintes, 2 texts by Jules LaForgue, soprano
and chamber ensemble, Freiburg, Germany, 6 Dec.
1964; Bluebeard, baritone, brass sextet, string
quartet, Atlanta, Ga., 17 Feb. 1968; Crescendo,
interlude, and 5 variations, 11 brasses, string
quartet, 2 pianos, Atlanta, 3 Mar. 1973; concerto for viola and chamber ensemble, New York,

11 May 1974; 2nd concerto for viola and chamber
ensemble, commissioned by Minister of Fine Arts,
Paris, 1976; Le Mikado, soprano and percussion,
1976.
    8 Bis, Rue Barthelemy, 75015-Paris, France

ROSEMONT, WALTER LOUIS
    b. Philadelphia, Pa., 16 Aug. 1895; d. Studied
at Univ. of Pennsylvania. He was opera and
orchestra conductor in the U.S. and Europe;
music editor for publishers; foreign correspondent for magazines; teacher.
    WORKS: ORCHESTRA: Troilus and Cressida;
Over hill and dale; Fughetta; Regrets in a
garden; Scene orientale; Bird ballet; The
prophetess; also songs and film music.

ROSEN, JEROME W.
    b. Boston, Mass., 23 July 1921. Studied with
William Denny and Roger Sessions, Univ. of California at Berkeley; with Darius Milhaud in Paris,
1949-51. His awards include a Guggenheim fellowship; Fromm Found. grant; and the George Ladd
Prix de Paris. From 1952 he has been faculty
member, Univ. of California at Davis.
    WORKS: OPERA: Calisto and Melibea, libretto
by Edwin Honig, Univ. of Calif., Davis, 31 May
1979; ORCHESTRA: saxophone concerto; clarinet
concerto, Sacramento Symph., with composer as
soloist, 4 Dec. 1976; CHAMBER MUSIC: string
quartet; sonata for clarinet and cello; Elegy
for percussion; Petite suite, 4 clarinets; 5
pieces, violin and piano; CHORUS: 3 songs, with
piano.
    University of California, Davis, CA 95616

ROSENBAUM, VICTOR
    b. Philadelphia, Pa., 19 Dec. 1941. Studied at
Brandeis Univ., B.A.; with Milton Babbitt,
Edward T. Cone, Earl Kim, and Roger Sessions,
Princeton Univ., M.F.A.; piano with Leonard
Shure and Rosina Lhevinne. He received first
prize, Nat. Fed. of Music Clubs Young Composers
contest; Woodrow Wilson fellowship. From 1967
he has been on the faculty, New England Cons.
    WORKS: CHAMBER MUSIC: duos for flute and
viola; Variations, string trio; Love comes
quietly, soprano, flute, piano; Magic, soprano
and piano; piano suite; CHORUS: The shepherd
boy's song, high voices; With rue my heart is
laden.
    152 Winthrop Rd., Brookline, MA 02146

ROSENBERG, EMANUEL (EARL ROGERS)
    b. New York, N.Y., 2 Apr. 1910. Studied com-
position with Herbert Elwell, Normand Lockwood,
and Max Helfman. He won a Stockbridge School
competition with a choral piece, 1955. He has
taught voice and allied subject at Cleveland
Inst. of Music, Juilliard Summer and Extension
School, YMHA Music School, New York, and Queens
Coll.
    WORKS: CHORUS: The night; O Lord of lords;
Hail and farewell; From the Psalms; Evening
song; 2 Friday Evening services; SONGS: The
complete misanthropist; folk song arrangements
and children's songs.
    920 Riverside Dr., New York, NY 10032

ROSENBOOM, DAVID
b. Fairfield, Iowa, 9 Sept. 1947. Studied composition with Gordon Binkerd and Salvatore Martirano, electronic music with Lejaren Hiller, Univ. of Illinois; experimental psychology, New York Univ. He was associate, Center for Creative and Performing Arts, SUNY, Buffalo, 1967; co-ordinator, Electric Ear, New York, 1968-69; president, Neurona Company, N.Y., 1969-70; faculty member and coordinator, Div. of Interdisciplinary Studies, York Univ., Toronto, 1970-78.
WORKS: ORCHESTRA: Contrasts, violin and orch., 1963; CHAMBER MUSIC: Pocket pieces, flute, viola, saxophone, percussion, 1966; trio for clarinet, trumpet, string bass, 1966; To that predestined dancing place, percussion quartet, 1966; Caliban upon Setebos, chamber orch., 1966; Piano etude, 1972; ELECTRONIC: And come up dripping, oboe and computer, 1968; How much better if Plymouth Rock had landed on the Pilgrims, instruments and electronics, 72 hours long, of which 18 were performed in a New York loft, 1969; Ecology of the skin, 1970; The seduction of Sapientia, viola da gamba and tape, 1975; On being invisible, electronics solo with brain signal performer and computer, 1976. He is author of many papers on research on alpha brain waves and biofeedback, and of a book, Biofeedback and the arts: Results of early experiments, Vancouver, 1975.
P.O. Box 543, Sta. Z, Toronto, Ontario, Canada M5N 2Z6

ROSENHAUS, STEVEN L.
b. Brooklyn, N.Y., 23 July 1952. Studied at Queens Coll., B.A. 1975; composition privately with George Perle and Henry Weinberg. From 1977 he has been editor and arranger for a music publisher.
WORKS: CHAMBER MUSIC: Pegasus, solo flute, 1972; 4 preludes, piano, 1974; For clarinet solo, 1974; 2 movements, violin and piano, 1975; woodwind quintet, 1978.
147-11 79th Ave., Flushing, NY 11367

ROSENMAN, LEONARD
b. Brooklyn, N.Y., 7 Sept. 1924. Studied with Roger Sessions, Luigi Dallapiccola, and Arnold Schoenberg; held a Crofts fellowship for study at Tanglewood.
WORKS: ORCHESTRA: violin concerto; concertino, piano and winds; Foci for 3 orchestras; Threnody on a song of K.R., a set of variations on a melody written by his wife, Los Angeles, 6 May 1971, composer conducting; CHAMBER MUSIC: 6 Lorca songs; piano sonata; Chamber music #2, soprano, ensemble, tape, 1968; duo for violin and piano, 1970; Chamber music #4, 2 double basses, 4 string quartets, Los Angeles, 15 Nov. 1976; Chamber music #5, Cambridge, 26 Nov. 1979; FILM SCORES: East of Eden; Cobweb; Rebel without a cause; Edge of the city; The savage eye; The Chapman report.

ROSENTHAL, DAVID
b. Berkeley, Calif., 4 Sept. 1952. Studied with Thomas Simons, New York; with Leonard Stein, Los Angeles. He was teaching assistant, California Inst. of the Arts, 1972-74.
WORKS: CHAMBER MUSIC: Music for flute and 3 percussionists, 1971; Music for piano and percussion, 1972; quintet for flute, trumpet, contrabass, percussion, 1973; quartet, flute, piano, percussion, 1973.
Rte. 3, Box 124D, Saugus, CA 91350

ROSENTHAL, LAURENCE
b. Detroit, Mich., 4 Nov. 1926. Studied with Bernard Rogers and Howard Hanson, Eastman School of Music, M.M.; with Nadia Boulanger in Paris; conducting at the Mozarteum in Salzburg. He received an Emmy award for music for the television documentary film, "Michelangelo: The last giant," 1966; 2 Academy award nominations. He was chief composer, 1st Documentary Film Squadron, U.S. Air Force, 1951-55.
WORKS: BALLET: The wind in the mountains, 1965; THEATRE: music for Rashomon, 1958; A patriot for me, 1969; ORCHESTRA: Ode; Horas; overture; CHAMBER MUSIC: 4 Orphic tableaux, violin and piano, 1965; FILM SCORES: A raisin in the sun, 1960; Requiem for a heavyweight, 1961; The miracle worker, 1962; Becket, 1964; The comedians, 1967; Hotel Paradiso; The island of Dr. Moreau; Who'll stop the rain?; TELEVISION SCORES: "The power and the glory," 1961; "Michelangelo: The last giant," 1966; and many others.
Sutton's Island, Northeast Harbor, ME 04662

ROSKOTT, CARL
b. 1953. Studied at Peabody Cons. and at New England Cons. He received a Nat. Fed. of Music Clubs junior composer award, 1969; conducted his own compositions and standard symphonic works, Eastern Music Festival Camp, Guilford Coll., N.C., 1969; conducted a performance of his Resolutions by the New England Cons. Repertory Orch., 29 Mar. 1972. Genesis for string trio, woodwind quartet, trumpet, trombone, and piano was performed by Boston Musica Viva, 10 Oct. 1972. He was instructor, Carleton Coll., Northfield, Minn., 1976-78.

ROSNER, ARNOLD
b. New York, N.Y., 8 Nov. 1945. Studied at New York Univ., B.A. in methematics; with Leo Smit and Allen Sapp, State Univ. of New York at Buffalo, M.M., Ph.D. in music, 1972. From 1972 he has been faculty member at Brooklyn Coll., CUNY, and at Wagner Coll.
WORKS: ORCHESTRA: 6 symphonies, 1961, 1961, 1963, 1964, 1974, 1976; Fantasia quasi una toccata, brass and percussion, 1965; 5 mystical pieces, English horn, harp, strings, 1967; 6 pastoral dances, woodwinds and strings, 1968; A gentle musicke, flute and strings, 1969; A Mylai elegy, 1971; concerto grosso, 1975; Responses, hosanna and fugue, harp and string orch., 1977; CHAMBER MUSIC: 6 string quartets, 1962, 1963, 1965, 1965, 1972, 1977; sonata for flute and cello, 1962; violin sonata, 1963; 2 piano sonatas, 1963, 1970; woodwind quintet, 1964; cello sonata, 1968; concertino for harp, harpsichord, celeste, piano, 1968; oboe sonata, 1972;

ROSS, WALTER B.

Musique de clavecin, harpsichord, 1974; choral
works, songs.
    120 Kenilworth Place, 4H, Brooklyn, NY 11210

ROSS, WALTER B.
    b. Lincoln, Nebr., 3 Oct. 1936. Studied with
Robert Beadell, Univ. of Nebraska, B.A. 1960,
M.M. 1962; with Karel Husa and Robert Palmer,
Cornell Univ., D.M.A. 1966; and with Alberto
Ginastero in Buenos Aires, 1965. He received
the Vreeland award, Univ. of Nebraska, 1962;
Organization of American States fellowship, 1965;
Center for Advanced Studies fellowship, Univ. of
Virginia, 1971-72. He was faculty member, State
Univ. Coll., Cortland, N.Y., 1966-67; from 1967,
Univ. of Virginia, department chairman from
1978.
    WORKS: OPERA: In the penal colony, 1-act
chamber opera; ORCHESTRA: concerto for brass
quintet; trombone concerto, New York, 12 May
1975; concerto for wind quintet and string orch.;
A Jefferson symphony, with tenor solo and
chorus, 1976; BAND: tuba concerto; Capriccio
furioso, with solo euphonium; CHAMBER MUSIC:
Cryptical triptych, trombone and piano; 5 dream
sequences, percussion quartet and piano; Fancy
dances, 3 bass tubas, 1972; trombone quartet,
1977; 6 shades of blue, piano; string trio, 1978;
sonatina for flute and bassoon, 1978; ELECTRONIC:
Midnight variations, tuba and tape, 1971; Prelude, fugue, and big apple, trombone and tape,
1972; Dances for small spaces, piano and tape;
SONGS: The silent firefly, voice and chamber
ensemble; 3 songs on poems of Tu Fu, voice,
piano, flute; 3 songs, voice, piano, trumpet.
    Univ. of Virginia, Charlottesville, VA
22903

ROSS, WILLIAM JAMES
    b. Dallas, Tex., 6 Sept. 1937. Studied with
Leslie Bassett, Ross Lee Finney, and George B.
Wilson, Univ. of Michigan, M.M. 1971; with Karl
Korte, Univ. of Texas. He won first prize in a
Univ. of Texas System contest, 1976. He was
public school teacher and dean, San Antonio,
1960-69, 1971-72; church music director, Detroit,
1969-71; then free-lance organist, teacher,
music publisher.
    WORKS: ORCHESTRA: Prospiritis, 1971;
CHAMBER MUSIC: Messages from a private universe,
soprano and chamber ensemble; Alpha I, flute,
violin, harpsichord; wind quintet; Summer harmonies, 5 flutes, 2 percussion; brass quartet;
CHORUS: Psalm 136; Missa brevis; ORGAN:
Mountain and spaces, with piccolo, trumpet,
oboe; The way from Earth; A book of changes,
chamber organ and visual projections, 1976.
    10426 Fox Hollow, San Antonio, TX 78217

ROSSINI, CARLO
    b. Osimo, Italy, 3 Mar. 1890; U.S. citizen
1929. Was ordained priest in 1913; studied at
the Pontifical Inst. of Music, Rome, M.M. He
was organist-choirmaster in Pittsburgh, 1923-50;
spent the next decade in Italy, returning to
New York in 1961. His works included 22 masses
and 10 volumes of choral compositions and
arrangements.

ROSSITER, DAVID KENSETT
    b. Summit, N.J., 23 Feb. 1952. Studied at
Oberlin Coll., 1971-72; with James Niblock,
Michigan State Univ., 1972-74; with Behrman,
Mumma, Tudor, and Eastman at Chocorua, N.H.,
1973.
    WORKS: VOICE: Tuning up, an exercise in
group meditation, 1973; ELECTRONIC: Elephants
are, tape, 1972; Sringara, tape, 1973; Con-
demned to wires and hammers, 6 players, 10 oscillators, piano, tape, electronics, 1973.
    300 Beal St., East Lansing, MI 48823

ROSSO, CAROL L.
    b. Santa Monica, Calif., 31 July 1949. Studied
Oriental music and art, Los Angeles City Coll.;
composition with Dorrance Stalvey, Immaculate
Heart Coll., Los Angeles; at California Inst.
of the Arts; with Terry Riley, Mills Coll.,
M.F.A.; with David Behrman; has studied piano,
conducting, gamelan music, African music, and
film production.
    WORKS: CHAMBER MUSIC: He wishes for the
clothes of heaven, soprano and flute; ELECTRONIC:
Timbral improvisations and Overtone modulations,
Buchla synthesizer, 1976; MULTIMEDIA: Glass,
lights, reflections and refractions, film, 1976.
    11859 Bray St., Culver City, CA 90230

ROTHGARBER, HERBERT
    b. Brooklyn, N.Y., 7 Apr. 1930. Studied at New
York Univ., B.S. and doctoral studies; at Hunter
Coll., M.A.; composition with Wallingford
Riegger and Bernard Wagenaar. He has been public school music teacher from 1957; also private
piano and composition teacher.
    WORKS: CHAMBER MUSIC: trio for flute
clarinet, piano; trio for 2 trumpets and tuba;
Dialogue, tuba and piano; Interplay, bassoon and
piano; piano pieces; 2 operas for children's
voices.
    89 Ann Drive S., Freeport, NY 11520

ROTHMULLER, MARKO
    b. Trnjani, Yugoslavia, 31 Dec. 1918; U.S. citi-
zen 1958. Studied at Musical Acad. in Zagreb;
voice privately in Vienna; composition in Vienna
with Alban Berg, 1928-32. He sang in opera in
Germany, Yugoslavia, Switzerland, Austria; made
his New York debut at New York City Opera, 1948;
sang with the Metropolitan Opera, 1958-61, 1964-
65; joined the faculty at Indiana Univ. in 1955.
He is author of 2 books, The music of the Jews,
1967, and Pronunciation of German and German
diction, 1978.
    WORKS: ORCHESTRA: a symphony; 2 ballet
suites; Divertimento, trombone, strings, percussion; also chamber music and vocal works.
    1005 E. Wylie St., Bloomington, IN 47401

ROTHSTEIN, ARNOLD
    b. Yonkers, N.Y., 1923. Studied with Hugo
Kauder and Jacob Dymont in New York.
    WORKS: VOICE: Ani Maamin (Credo), 1959;
music for the high holy days, 2-part setting,
Vol. I, 1963, Vol. II, 1964; The village fiddler,
children's cantata, 1963, NBC-TV, 24 Jan. 1965;
The last penny, children's cantata, 1972.
    29 Rellim Dr., Glen Cove, NY 11542

ROTTURA, JOSEPH JAMES
   b. Rochester, Pa., 11 Apr. 1929.
      WORKS: CHORUS: Ballad of Jesse James; The
beatitudes; Christmas on the trail; Missa simplex; Overture for voices; We sing of America.

ROUSE, CHRISTOPHER
   b. Baltimore, Md., 15 Feb. 1949. Studied with
Richard Hoffmann and Randolph Coleman, Oberlin
Coll., B.M. 1971; privately with George Crumb in
Philadelphia, 1971-73; with Robert Palmer and
Karel Husa, Cornell Univ., D.M.A. 1978. He received BMI awards, 1973, 1974. He joined the
faculty at Univ. of Michigan in 1978, Eastman
School of Music in 1981.
      WORKS: ORCHESTRA: Kabir Padavali, soprano
and orch., 1972; Volatus in vorticem labrorum
orisque dei, with baritone solo, 1976; Alloeides,
1978; WIND ENSEMBLE: Subjectives VIII, 5 trumpets and percussion, 1972; Vulcan, 1975; CHAMBER
MUSIC: Loves songs, voice and chamber orch.,
1973; Ecstasis mane eburnei, viola and chamber
ensemble, 1974; Canticles to Apollo, cello and
percussion, 1974; Morpheus, solo cello, 1975;
suite for solo cello, 1976; Aphrodite cantos,
soprano and chamber ensemble, 1976; Ogoun
Badagris, percussion ensemble, 1976; 1st stratum
of Empyrean, chamber ensemble, 1977; 2nd stratum
of Empyrean, piano, 1978.
      Eastman School of Music, Rochester, NY 14604

ROUSSAKIS, NICOLAS
   b. Athens, Greece, 14 June 1934; to U.S. 1950.
Studied with Otto Luening, Henry Cowell, Jack
Beeson, Columbia Univ., B.A. 1956, M.A. 1960,
D.M.A. 1976; with Ralph Shapey and Ben Weber;
with Philip Jarnach in Hamburg, 1961-63; and on
a City of Hamburg scholarship with Boulez, Berio,
Ligeti, and Stockhausen at Darmstadt in the
summers of 1962, 1963. Other awards include a
Fulbright grant, 1961-63; fellowships at
MacDowell Colony, Yaddo, and Ossabaw Island,
1963-68; Nat. Inst. of Arts and Letters grant,
1969. He was faculty emmber, Columbia Univ.,
1968-78; then joined faculty at Rutgers Univ.
      WORKS: ORCHESTRA: Odes and cataclysm, Tri-
City Symph., Davenport, Iowa, 2 Apr. 1976, New
York premiere, 5 Dec. 1977; CHAMBER MUSIC:
harpsichord sonata, 1967; 6 short pieces for
flute, 1969; Helix, cello and piano, New York,
14 Dec. 1970; concertino for percussion and
woodwinds, New York, 19 Mar. 1973; brass quintet,
New York, 17 Dec. 1973; CHORUS: Night speech,
chorus and instruments, 1968.
      225 W. 86th St., P.H. 2F, New York, NY 10024

ROVICS, HOWARD
   b. New York, N.Y., 1936. Studied at Manhattan
School of Music; taught there for many years;
joined the faculty at Post Coll. of Long Island
Univ. in 1976.
      WORKS: Cybernetic study #1, flute and piano;
Cybernetic study #2, clarinet, bassoon, piano;
3 studies for piano, 1964-66; March funèbre,
clarinet and strings, New York premiere, 31 Jan.
1971; Events, piano, New York, 7 Nov. 1971;
Look, friend, at me, oboe and piano, 1973; Piece,
cello, piano, tape, 1973; Haunted objects (in
memoriam Stefan Wolpe), soprano, narrator, 4

woodwinds, tape, text by Johanna Pragh and
Stefan Wolpe, supported by Nat. Endowment for
the Arts grant, 1974.
      Post College, L.I. University, Greenvale,
NY 11548

ROXBURY, RONALD
   b. Fruitland, Md., 4 Dec. 1946. Studied with
Stefan Grove and Earle Brown, Peabody Cons.,
M.M. 1969; privately with Richard Rodney Bennett.
He received Nat. Fed. of Music Clubs awards,
1965, 1966, 1968, 1969. He was vocal soloist,
Cathedral of Mary Our Queen, Balitmore, 1969-72.
      WORKS: CHAMBER MUSIC: Designs, 3 flutes,
1968; Aria for Fred, cello and piano; Haiku,
guitar solo; Preludes, accordion; sonatina for
flute and harpsichord; Le werewolf s'amuse,
wolfman and percussion; Quasimodo at wit's end,
flute, guitar, double bass; Graffiti, chamber
ensemble; Ecstasies for Mi-Go, 14 guitars, 9
cellos; Brouhaha, 2 pianos, 7 hands; piano
sonata, 1968; Cancrizan, 2 pianos; MULTIMEDIA:
Ghazele, belly dancer and chamber ensemble;
Requiem for Bill Null, chorus, mezzo-soprano,
theatrical devices, instruments; A movable feats,
chorus, flute, guitar, multimedia, audience.

ROY, KLAUS GEORGE
   b. Vienna, Austria, 24 Jan. 1924; U.S. citizen
1944. Studied with Frederick C. Schreiber in
Vienna; musicology with Karl Geiringer, Boston
Univ., B.M. 1947; composition with Walter Piston,
musicology with Davison, Kinkeldey, and Merritt,
Harvard Univ., M.A. 1949. His many awards include a grant for an opera, 1957; Arthur
Shepherd composition prize, 1960; Cleveland Arts
prize, 1965; Ohio Arts Council grant, 1973;
numerous other grants and commissions. He was
instructor and librarian, School of Fine and
Applied Arts, Boston Univ., 1948-57; contributing
music critic, Christian Science Monitor, 1950-
57; director of publications and program book
editor, Cleveland Orchestra, from 1958.
      WORKS: OPERA: Sterlingman, 1-act opera,
television premiere, Boston, 1957; THEATRE:
music for Twelfth night, 1973; WIND ENSEMBLE:
Tripartita, 11-part brass choir, 1949; CHAMBER
MUSIC: trombone sonata, 1951; string trio, 1956;
2 rhapsodic pieces, viola and piano, 1957; Serenade, solo violin, 1957; duo for flute and
clarinet; Serenade, solo cello, 1968; CHORUS:
St. Francis' canticle of the Sun, a cappella
with solo viola, 1951; 3 songs of praise, a
cappella, 1952; Lie still, sleep becalmed, 1955;
3 folksongs, 1955; SONGS: Holiday, soprano and
piano; A song for Mardi Gras, medium voice and
piano; piano pieces.
      2528 Derbyshire Rd., Cleveland Heights, OH
44106

ROYCE, EDWARD
   b. Cambridge, Mass., 25 Dec. 1886; d. Stamford,
Conn., 7 July 1963. Studied at Harvard Univ.,
B.A. 1907; and at Stern Cons., Berlin. He was
chairman, music department, Middlebury Coll.,
1913-15; on faculty, Ithaca Cons., 1916-21; and
at Eastman School of Music, 1923-47. His compositions included 2 tone poems, The fire

ROYER, PAUL H.

bringers, 1926, and Far ocean, 1929 (won an Eastman award); songs; piano pieces.

ROYER, PAUL H.
b. Mt. Jackson, Va., 3 Sept. 1922. Studied at Westminster Choir Coll.; with Felix Labunski, Cincinnati Coll. Cons.; with Bernhard Heiden and Thomas Beversdorf, Indiana Univ. He was faculty member, Huron Coll., 1951-68; professor, South Dakota State Univ., 1968-72, composer-in-residence, 1977-78.
WORKS: ORCHESTRA: flute concerto; BAND: Fanfare festiva; Prairie poem; Bunch of bagatelles; Rushmore suite; CHAMBER MUSIC: Fantasy 69, violin and piano; Caprice, flute and piano; CHORUS: Sing unto the Lord; Psalm 150; Create in me; Echo song; ORGAN: Trilogy on Genevan psalter tunes.
337 Lincoln Lane So., Brookings, SD 57006

ROZSA, BELA
b. Kecskemet, Hungary, 14 Feb. 1905; U.S. citizen 1926; d. Tulsa, Okla., 8 Jan. 1977. Studied with Percy Goetschius and Howard Brockway, Inst. of Musical Art, New York; at Juilliard School; with Philip Greeley Clapp, Univ. of Iowa, Ph.D.; privately with Arnold Schoenberg. He won the Seligman prize, 1927, 1928; NBC Internat. Chamber Music prize, 1937. He was staff member, NBC, New York, 1929-38; on the faculty, Baylor Univ., 1938-42; Iowa Wesleyan Univ., 1942-45; professor, Univ. of Tulsa, 1945-75.
WORKS: ORCHESTRA: Ibis, a symphony; CHAMBER MUSIC: piano sonata; 2 string quartets; piano quartet; piano quintet; violin sonata.

ROZSA, MIKLOS
b. Budapest, Hungary, 18 Apr. 1907; U.S. citizen 1945. Studied with Herman Grabner, Leipzig Cons.; at Leipzig Univ.; and at Trinity Coll. of Music, London. His awards include the Francis Joseph prize, City of Budapest, 1937, 1938; Academy awards for film scores, 1946, 1948, 1959; Cesar award, French Acad., 1978; Lincoln award of the American-Hungarian Assoc., 1978. He was faculty member, Univ. of Southern California, 1945-65; staff composer for MGM, 1948-62.
WORKS: ORCHESTRA: symphony, 1930; Serenade, small orch., 1932; Scherzo, 1933; Variations on a Hungarian peasant song, violin and orch., New York, 14 Nov. 1943; concerto for string orch., 1944; piano concerto, Dallas, 5 Jan. 1956; double concerto for violin and cello, commissioned by Heifetz and Piatigorsky, 1964; cello concerto, 1969; The vintner's daughter; Tripartita, 1973, Washington, 12 Oct. 1976; Hungarian serenade; CHAMBER MUSIC: string trio, 1927; piano quintet, 1928; duo for violin and piano, 1931; duo for cello and piano, 1931; Kaleidoscope, piano, 1946; piano sonata, 1948; sonata for 2 violins; string quartet; Toccata capricciosa, cello, 1978; FILM SCORES: El cid; Quo vadis; King of Kings; Spellbound, 1945; A double life, 1948; Ben Hur, 1950; and others.
c/o Wm. Morris Agency, 151 El Camino, Beverly Hills, CA 90212

RUBENS, HUGO
b. New York, N.Y., 1 Apr. 1905; d. He was organist and pianist in film theatres.
WORKS: ORCHESTRA: Carnegie Hall concerto; Scotland Yard suite; Love's labor lost; overture; and songs.

RUBINSTEIN, BERYL
b. Athens, Ga., 26 Oct. 1898; d. Cleveland, Ohio, 29 Dec. 1952. Studied piano with his father and with Alexander Lambert; toured the U.S. as a child prodigy, 1903-11; then studied in Berlin and Vienna. He joined the faculty of the Cleveland Inst. of Music in 1921; became director in 1932.
WORKS: OPERA: The sleeping beauty, 1938; ORCHESTRA: Scherzo, 1927; piano concerto, 1936; PIANO: 32 etudes; 3 dances; Whirligig; and transcriptions.

RUCCOLO, JAMES
b. Akron, Ohio, 3 Feb. 1943. Studied at Eastman School of Music; with Clifton Williams, Univ. of Texas; with Grant Fletcher, Arizona State Univ.; and with Robert Muczynski, Univ. of Arizona, D.M.A. He received a Nat. Fed. of Music Clubs award, 1969. He was faculty member, Prescott Coll., 1971-74; from 1976, at Univ. of Arizona.
WORKS: ORCHESTRA: Movements for orchestra, 1967; CHAMBER MUSIC: Toccata, piano; Quiet is the night, soprano and piano; Rapsodia grossa, string quartet and piano; clarinet sonata.
Unversity of Arizona, Tempe, AZ 85281

RUDD-MOORE, DOROTHY
b. Delaware, 4 June 1940. Studied at Howard Univ., B.M. 1963; at American Cons., Fontainebleau, France, 1963. She taught at New York Univ., 1969; Bronx Community Coll., 1971; then free-lance composer and private teacher of singing in New York. She was a founder of the Society of Black Composers.
WORKS: CHAMBER MUSIC: string quartet; piano trio; Nonet for divers instruments; 12 quatrains from the Rubaiyat, mezzo-soprano and oboe; From the dark tower; 3 pieces, violin and piano, New York, 7 Oct. 1978; Dirge and deliverance, cello and piano.
33 Riverside Dr., New York, NY 10023

RUDHYAR, DANE (ne Daniel Chenneviere)
b. Paris, France, 23 Mar. 1895; U.S. citizen 1926. Studied at the Sorbonne and briefly at the Paris Cons., but is mostly self-taught in music. His awards include a $1,000 prize from the Los Angeles Phil., 1922; a month devoted to airing his works over KPFA, Berkeley, Calif., including music, interviews, comments, poems, and a complete reading of Rania: an epic narrative. He came to the U.S. in 1916 for the performance of 2 orchestral works, Poèmes ironiques and Vision végétale at the New York Metropolitan Opera on 4 Apr. 1917. He remained in this country, soon dropping his family name and eventually settling in Hollywood, alternating with New York, Chicago, and later Santa Fe. His extraordinary creative energy has produced over 30 books and booklets (from Claude

Debussy, Paris, 1913, poetry, novels, science fiction, to The astrological houses, 1972), about 3 dozen paintings, numerous articles and lectures, and his musical compositions. His later awards include 2 Nat. Endowment for the Arts grants, 1976, 1977; and the American Acad. and Inst. of Arts and Letters Marjorie Peabody Waite award, 1978.

WORKS: ORCHESTRA: Poèmes ironiques, 1914; Vision végétale, 1914; To the real, 1920-26; The warrior, 1921, piano and orch., Palo Alto, 10 Dec. 1976; The surge of fire, Los Angeles, 22 Oct. 1925; Sinfonietta, 1927; Quranos, chamber orch., 1927; The human way, 1927; Trip-thong, 1948, rev. 1977; Thresholds, 1954; CHAMBER MUSIC: 3 melodies, flute, cello, piano, 1919; 3 poems, violin and piano, 1920; 5 stanzas, string ensemble, 1927; piano quintet, 1950; Solitude, string quartet, New York, 17 Mar. 1951; PIANO: Mosaics, a tone cycle, 1918; 9 tetra-grams, 1920-27; 3 paeans, 1925; 4 pentagrams, 1924-26; Granites, 1929; Syntony, 1968; Trans-mutations, a tone sequence in 7 movements, 1976; Theurgy: Tone ritual #2, 1977.

RUDIN, ANDREW
b. Newgulf, Tex., 10 Apr. 1939. Studied with Kent Kennan, Clifton Williams, Paul Pisk, Univ. of Texas; with George Rochberg, Univ. of Penn-sylvania; also with Henry Weinberg, Ralph Shapey, and Karlheinz Stockhausen. He has been faculty member, Philadelphia Coll. of Performing Arts, from 1965.

WORKS: OPERA: The innocent, Philadelphia, 19-21 May 1972; BALLET: View, 1973; CHAMBER MUSIC: Remembering Ferruccio, for 9 players, 1973; FILM SCORES: Spherics, NET-TV, July 1972; ELECTRONIC: Tragoedia, synthesizer; Il giuoco, tape and film.
Philadelphia College of Performing Arts, 250 S. Broad St., Philadelphia, PA 19102

RUDNYTSKY, ANTIN
b. Luka, Galicia, 7 Feb. 1902; to U.S. 1937; d. Toms River, N.J., 30 Nov. 1975. Studied with Artur Schnabel and Franz Schreker, Univ. of Berlin, Ph.D. 1926. He conducted opera in Russia and Poland, 1927-37; then settled in New York as pianist, conductor, and composer.

WORKS: OPERA: Dovbush, 1937; BALLET: Storm over the west, 1932; ORCHESTRA: 3 sym-phonies, 1936, 1941, 1942; cello concerto, 1942; also chamber works.

RUDOW, VIVIAN ADELBERG
b. Baltimore, Md., 1 Apr. 1936. Studied with Jean Ivey, Peabody Cons., B.M. 1960. She was winner in the electronic music division, Anna-polis Fine Arts Festival contest, 1972, 1977; also winner in the Internat. Double Reed Society composition contest with Kaddish for solo bassoon, played at the society's 1977 conven-tion in Evansville, Ind.

WORKS: CHAMBER MUSIC: Cry a thousand tears, soprano, alto flute, trumpet, Baltimore, 30 Nov. 1978; ELECTRONIC: The oak and the reed, 1972; The lion and the hares, 1972; music for The Trojan women, 1972; Changing space, 1973;

Syntheticon and Lies, dance pieces, 1974; music for Best of friends, 1974; Anomalies I, II, III, 1976.
211 Goodwood Gardens, Baltimore, MD 21210

RUFTY, HILTON
b. Richmond, Va., 1909. Studied at Univ. of Richmond; Hampden-Sydney Coll.; and Univ. of Virginia. He was organist-choirmaster, St. Stephen's Church, Richmond, from 1936; faculty member, Univ. of Richmond, 1946-76. His com-positions include the operetta, The 12 dancing princesses.

RUGER, MORRIS HUTCHINS
b. Superior, Wis., 2 Dec. 1902. Studied with Seth Bingham, Columbia Univ., B.A. 1924; with Andre Bloch in Paris, 1925-26; Northwestern Univ., 1930; Juilliard School, 1934. From 1945 he was on the staff of the Los Angeles Cons.

WORKS: OPERA: Gettysburg, 1938; ORCHESTRA: violin concerto; CHAMBER MUSIC: piano quintet; piano sonata; 2 piano suites; also choral works.

RUGGIERO, CHARLES H.
b. Bridgeport, Conn., 19 June 1947. Studied at New England Cons., B.M.; with H. Owen Reed and Jere T. Hutcheson, Michigan State Univ., M.M. His awards include scholarships and a commission, Michigan Music Teachers Assoc., 1978. He has been faculty member, Michigan State Univ., from 1973.

WORKS: CHAMBER MUSIC: Dance music, chamber ensemble, 1972; Songs from Emily Dickinson, soprano and chamber ensemble, 1974; Hocket var-iations, 2 pianos; other chamber music, pieces for jazz ensemble.
712 N. Francis Ave., Lansing, MI 48912

RUGGLES, CARL
b. Marion, Mass., 11 Mar. 1876; d. Bennington, Vt., 24 Oct. 1971. Began violin study at age 6 and played for President Cleveland at age 9; studied composition with Walter Spalding and John Knowles Paine at Harvard Univ. In 1907 he went to Winona, Minn., where he organized a symphony orchestra and was its conductor, 1912-17; was active with Edgard Varese in the Internat. Composers and the Pan-American Assoc. of Com-posers in New York, 1922-33; taught modern com-position at Univ. of Miami, 1937-47; then re-tired to Vermont and devoted himself chiefly to painting in oils and watercolors. He was elected to membership in the Nat. Inst. of Arts and Letters, 1956; in 1966, received the Koussevitzky Internat. Recording award.

WORKS: OPERA: The sunken bell (was ac-cepted for performance by the New York Metro-politan Opera, but when it was suggested that the bell could be made of papier-mâché instead of being cast, Ruggles withdrew the score in scorn and later destroyed it); ORCHESTRA: Men and angels, originally for 5 trumpets and a bass trumpet, 1922, was revised for brass and strings and renamed Angels, 1929; Portals, string orch., 1925; Men and mountains, symphonic suite, 1924-35; Vox clamans in deserto, 1929, voice and orch., Juilliard School, 24 Apr. 1974; Sun-

RUGOLO, PETER

treader, after Browning, 1932; Organum, 1945-46;
PIANO: polyphonic compositions for 3 pianos,
1940; Evocations, 4 chants for piano, 1945.

RUGOLO, PETER
b. Sicily, Italy, 25 Dec. 1915; U.S. citizen
1933. Studied at San Francisco State Coll., B.A.
1937; at Mills Coll., M.A. 1941. His awards include Nat. Acad. of Arts and Sciences award; TV
Emmy award; prize for music for TV show, "In
defense of Ellen McKay." He served in the U.S.
Army, 1941-44; was composer for Stan Kenton,
1945-61; for MGM Studios, 1954-57; then for
television.
    WORKS: CHAMBER MUSIC: Petite suite, clar-
inet and piano; Offbeat, flute, clarinet, horn;
TELEVISION SCORES: "Thin man," 1959; "Thriller,"
1960; "General Electric Theatre," 1960-61;
"Checkmate," 1961; "Ichabod and me," 1961;
"Alfred Hitchcock," 1960-63; "The untouchables,"
1962-63; "The Virginian," 1963.

RUNKEL, KENNETH ELDON
b. Lisbon, Iowa, 10 June 1881. Studied at
McGill Univ., B.M., Lic., ACCO; with Frank
Wright in New York. He was named a fellow of
Trinity Coll. of Music, London, and of the
American Guild of Organists. He held his first
position as organist in Lisbon, Iowa, in 1895
and retired from Flagler Memorial Presbyterian
Church, St. Augustine, Fla., in 1967.
    WORKS: CHORUS: Israel out of Egypt, can-
tata with organ, 2 pianos, timpani, Baylor Univ.,
8 Mar. 1925; The good Samaritan, cantata, 1934;
more than 85 published choral works. He was a
pioneer in the use of multiple choirs.

RUSCH, HAROLD W.
b. Wabeno, Wis., 14 Oct. 1908. Attended Lawrence Univ.; studied music privately. He received commissions for Univ. of Wisconsin and
from Thor Johnson. He was public school music
supervisor and author of books on instrumental
and vocal technique.
    WORKS: ORCHESTRA: 3 suites; Menominee
sketches, La nouvelle France, Colonial scenes;
BAND: Levee dance; Camptown drummer; Victory
chant; Apostle Islands overture; many marches.

RUSCHE, MARJORIE MAXINE
b. Sturgeon Bay, Wis., 18 Nov. 1949. Studied
with Homer Lambrecht and Dominick Argento, Univ.
of Minnesota, M.A. 1975. She was a U.S. Peace
Corps music teacher in Kenya, 1975-77; musical
director, Unity Theatre, Minneapolis, 1978.
    WORKS: ORCHESTRA: Synthesis: orchestral
survey, 1975; Symphonic safari; CHAMBER MUSIC:
Reverie rondo, horn and piano, 1976; VOICE AND
CHAMBER ENSEMBLE: Singing songs, a cycle, 1975;
Much madness is divinest sense, 1975; When the
shepherd moon shall flee, 1976; 4 variations on
a theme by Sappho, song cycle, 1978.
    1910 7th St. S., Minneapolis, MN 55454

RUSH, LOREN
b. Fullerton, Calif., 23 Aug. 1935. Studied
with Robert Erickson, San Francisco State Coll.,
B.A. 1947; with Andrew Imbrie, Seymour Shifrin,

William Denny, and Charles Cushing, Univ. of
California at Berkeley, M.A. 1960; at Stanford
Univ., D.M.A. 1973. His awards include the
George Ladd Prix de Paris, 1960-62; Prix de
Rome, 1969-71; Inst. of Arts and Letters award,
1971; Guggenheim fellowship, 1971; Prince Pierre
of Monaco composition award, 1971; and commissions. He has played bassoon in the Oakland
Symph., contrabass in the Richmond Symph.; also
plays piano, percussion, and Japanese koto; has
been member, Stanford Computer Music Project,
from 1973.
    WORKS: ORCHESTRA: The cloud messenger,
1971; I'll see you in my dreams, amplified orch.
and tape, 1973; CHAMBER MUSIC: 5 Japanese poems,
soprano and chamber ensemble, 1959; Serenade,
violin and viola, 1960; string quartet, 1961,
San Francisco, 30 Sept. 1976; Nexus 16, chamber
orch., 1964; Dans le sable, soprano, speaker,
4 altos, 15 instruments, 1970; PIANO: Hexa-
hedron, 1964; Oh, Susanna, 1970, New York
premieres, 4 Apr. 1974; Soft music, HARD MUSIC,
3 amplified pianos, 1969-70; Traveling music,
piano and computer, 1973.
    37 Terrace Ave., Richmond, CA 94801

RUSSELL, (GEORGE) ALEXANDER
b. Franklin, Tenn., 2 Oct. 1880; d. Dewitt, N.Y.,
24 Nov. 1953. Studied with George Parker and
William Berwald, Syracuse Univ., B.A., honorary
D.M.; with Leopold Godowsky, Harold Bauer, and
Charles-Marie Widor in Europe. He was director
of the Wanamaker Concerts, New York, 1910-17;
professor, Princeton Univ., 1917-35.
    WORKS: CHORUS: In memory of Princeton men
fallen in World War I; SONGS: Sunset; The sacred
fire; In fountain court; Lyric from Tagore; Expectations; Puer redemptor; and piano pieces.

RUSSELL, ARMAND KING
b. Seattle, Wash., 23 June 1932. Studied with
George McKay and John Verrall, Univ. of Washington; with Bernard Rogers and Howard Hanson,
Eastman School of Music, Ph.D. He received
annual ASCAP awards, 1966-73. He was faculty
member, North Dakota State Coll., 1958-61;
visiting professor, Eastman School, summers,
1959-64, 1972; professor, Univ. of Hawaii, from
1961.
    WORKS: ORCHESTRA: Harlequin concerto,
double bass and orch.; 2nd concerto for percussion; BAND: Theme and fantasia; Symphonia in 3
images; CHAMBER MUSIC: percussion sonata;
Ballade with epitaphs, 2 voices and percussion;
Particles, saxophone.
    3296 Huelani Dr., Honolulu, HI 96813

RUSSELL, CRAIG H.
b. Los Alamos, N.Mex., 3 Apr. 1951. Studied
guitar at the Univ. of New Mexico and in Spain.
He was guest lecturer, Univ. of New Mexico,
1973-74.
    WORKS: THEATRE: Zapatera, musical comedy,
Univ. of New Mexico, 26-28 Apr. 1973; ORCHESTRA:
concerto for piano, orch., and double chorus,
Albuquerque, 8 Feb. 1973; symphony, 1973; JAZZ
ENSEMBLE: Relationship; CHAMBER MUSIC: quintet
for guitar, flute, string trio.
    1165 41st, Los Alamos, NM 87544

RUSSELL, GEORGE
b. Cincinnati, Ohio, 23 June 1923. Attended
Wilberforce Univ. High School; studied composition with Stefan Wolpe. His honors include
Outstanding Composer award, Metronome magazine,
1958; Composer award, Downbeat magazine, 1961;
Guggenheim fellowships, 1969, 1972; Nat. Endowment for the Arts grants, 1969, 1976; Nat. Music
award, 1976. He is author of Lydian chromatic
concept of tonal organization, 1953, and taught
this method privately in New York, 1953-68, at
School of Jazz, Lenox, Mass., 1959, 1960, Festival of the Arts, Jyvaskyla, Finland, under
auspices of the USIA, at Oslo, Norway, Lund,
Sweden, and Vaskilde Summer School, Denmark;
from 1969 he has been faculty member, New England
Cons.
    WORKS: BALLET: The cromatic universe,
1963; The net, 1968; Encounter near Venus, 1975;
JAZZ ENSEMBLE: Cubano Be, Cubano Bop, 1947;
Ezzthetic, 1949; All about Rosie, 1957; Stratus-
phunk, 1958; New York, N.Y., 1958; Waltz from
outer space, 1960; Dimensions, 1960; The outer
view, 1963; Oh jazz, po jazz, 1966; Now and then,
1967; Othello ballet suite, 1968; Electronic
sonata for souls loved by nature, 1969; Listen
to the silence, 1971; Big city blues, 1973; Concerto for self-accompanied guitar; Vertical form
#6, with orch., 1976.
    12 E. 41st St., #1104, New York, NY 10017

RUSSELL, JOHN G.
b. Hanford, Calif., 15 May 1937. Composer and
choral conductor, he has been faculty member,
California State Univ. at San Luis Obispo, from
1968.
    WORKS: CHORUS: A clear midnight, Whitman
text; As birds are fitted to the bough; The
blackbird; The dark hills; Merry the green; Walk
this mile in silence; Who has seen the wind?;
and many others.
    2434 Del Campo, San Luis Obispo, CA 93401

RUSSELL, ROBERT
CHAMBER MUSIC: Places, suite for piano, 4 hands;
Pan, flute and piano; trumpet sonatina; Scherzo,
clarinet and piano; Abstract #1, 2 clarinets;
Abstract #2, 2 trumpets or 2 horns; woodwind
quintet; sextet for percussion, Composers
Theatre, New York, Feb. 1972.

RUSSELL, WILLIAM
b. Canton, Mo., 26 Feb. 1905. His compositions
include 3 dance movements, 1933, 3 Cuban pieces,
1935, and Fugue, all for percussion and piano.
    University of Miami, Coral Gables, FL 33124

RUSSO, JOHN
b. Trenton, N.J., 16 Jan. 1943. Studied with
Louis Cheslock, Peabody Cons., 1961-63; with
Matthew Colucci, Curtis Inst. of Music, B.M.
1967; with Clifford Taylor, Temple Univ., M.M.
1969; also with Joseph Castaldo and George
Rochberg; and at Rome Festival Inst., summer
1975. He held scholarships for all study; received a Rockefeller grant, 1967. He has been
instructor at Widener Coll., 1969-73; then at
Beaver Coll.; from 1976, also at Philadelphia

Coll. of Performing Arts.
    WORKS: CHAMBER MUSIC: 4 pieces for clar-
inet solo; Meditations, woodwind trio; 5 clarinet sonatas; Larghetto, clarinet, viola, piano,
1964; 3 seasons, flute, clarinet, piano, 1969;
3 etudes, alto saxophone and piano, 1969-70;
Toccata, piano, 1970; Elegy, oboe solo, 1971;
flute sonata, 1971; Lo schifoso, bassoon solo,
1971; Conversazione, piano, 1975.
    724 Winchester Rd., Broomall, PA 19008

RUSSO, WILLIAM JOSEPH
b. Chicago, Ill., 25 June 1928. Studied with
Lennie Tristano, 1944-47; with John J. Becker
and Karel Jirak, Roosevelt Univ., B.A. 1955.
His awards include Musician of the Year award,
Metronome Year Book, 1957; Koussevitzky award,
1953; commission from Yehudi Menuhin and Lord
Astor, 1962; Illinois Arts Council commission,
1968; Nat. Endowment for the Arts grant, 1976.
He was founder and director of Experiment in
Jazz, Chicago, 1947-50; trombonist, composer,
arranger, Stan Kenton's Band, 1950-54; conducted
his own orchestra, 1958-61; was musical director,
London Jazz Orch., 1962-65; taught at Manhattan
School of Music, 1959-61; Lenox School of Jazz,
1957-60; Peabody Cons., 1969-71; Antioch Coll.,
1971-72; was director, Columbia Coll., Center
for New Music, Chicago, 1965-75; composer-in-
residence, City and County of San Francisco,
1975; from 1976, in New York.
    WORKS: OPERA: John Hooten, 1961, BBC 3rd
Programme, 1963; The island, 1963; Antigone,
1967; Aesop's fables, rock opera, 1970; Joan of
Arc, chamber opera, 1970; Isabella's fortune and
Pedrolino's revenge, 1-act comic operas, 1974;
A general opera, 1 act, libretto by Arnold
Weinstein, 1976; ORCHESTRA: 2 symphonies, 1957,
#2, Titans, New York, 19 Apr. 1959; cello con-
certo, 1962, Baltimore, 24 Feb. 1970; 3 pieces
for blues band and orchestra, Chicago, July
1968, was made into a ballet and performed in
San Francisco, 1974-75; Street music, a blues
concerto, harmonica and piano solo, San Francisco
Symph., 19 May 1976; BAND: concerto grosso,
1960; Brooksville, tone poem, 1961; JAZZ ORCHES-
TRA: English suite, 1955; The 7 deadly sins,
1960; English concerto, with Yehudi Menuhin,
soloist, Bath Festival, June 1963; Fugue for
jazz orch.; In memoriam, with chorus and 2 solo
voices, 1966; America 1966, concerto grosso for
jazz orch.; CHORUS: The Civil War, rock cantata,
San Antonio, 7 Apr. 1968; David, rock cantata,
1968; Liberation, with 3 soloists, dancer, rock
band, 1969; Songs of celebration, with soloists
and orch., Baltimore, 21 Feb. 1971; FILM SCORES:
Everybody rides the carousel, CBS, 1976; Women
of the world (WOW); The second chance. His 2
books, The jazz composer, 1961, and Jazz composition and orchestration, 1968, Univ. of Chicago
Press, have been reissued in paperback, 1973 and
1974.
    28 Greene St., New York, NY 10013

RUSSOTTO, LEO
b. New York, N.Y., 25 May 1896. Attended Columbia Univ. and Juilliard School; studied with
Rubin Goldmark, Mortimer Wilson, and Abraham

RYDER, ARTHUR HILTON

Lilienthal. He received ASCAP awards, 1963,
1964. He was director of radio activities,
Roxy Theatre, 1927-31; staff pianist and choral
director, NBC and ABC, 1931-41; associate conductor, St. Louis Municipal Opera, 1944; associate conductor of Oklahoma on its European
tour, 1955.
WORKS: ORCHESTRA: Arioso, viola and orch.;
Novelette and poem, viola and orch.; Chant sans
paroles, cello and orch.; Humoreske, violin and
orch.; Reverie; Air de ballet; Concerto classico,
xylophone and orch.; many songs.
219 W. 81st St., New York, NY 10024

RYDER, ARTHUR HILTON
b. Plymouth, Mass., 30 Apr. 1875; d. Newton,
Mass., 18 July 1944. Studied with Walter
Spalding and John Knowles Paine, Harvard Univ.;
was church organist and choirmaster in the
Boston area. He wrote many organ pieces and
songs, and in 1935, devised a new system of
harmony which he taught in Boston.

RYDER, NOAH F.
b. Nashville, Tenn., 10 Apr. 1914; d. Norfolk,
Va., 17 Apr. 1964. Studied at Hampton Inst.,
B.S.; Univ. of Michigan, M.M. He received the
Navy War Writers prize for a choral work, 1944.
He was public school music supervisor, 1935-36;
on faculty, Palmer Memorial Inst.; faculty mem-
ber and choir conductor, Hampton Inst., 1941-44;
from 1947, music director, Virginia State Coll.,
Norfolk.
WORKS: CHORUS: Sea suite, male voices;
Haul away, mateys, we're almost home, male
voices, 1944; PIANO: 5 sketches.

RYNEARSON, PAUL
b. Long Beach, Calif., 12 Dec. 1945. Studied
with Alan Chaplin, California Inst. of the Arts,
B.A.; with Dorrance Stalvey, Claremont Graduate
School, M.A.; and with Ellis Kohs, Univ. of
Southern California, D.M.A. He held fellowships,
1968-74. His faculty posts have included Pasadena Polytechnic School, Moorpark Coll., and
Pepperdine Univ.
WORKS: CHAMBER MUSIC: 11 contemporary flute
etudes, 1968; Geometriphon, suite for 5 instruments.
P.O. Box 4009, Malibu, CA 90265

RYTERBAND, ROMAN
b. Lodz, Poland, 2 Aug. 1914; U.S. citizen 1964.
Studied music in Poland, Switzerland, and at
Northwestern Univ. He has been organist, choirmaster, pianist in Europe, Africa, and the U.S.;
was music director, CKVL radio, Montreal;
faculty member, Chicago Cons. Coll., to 1967;
then moved to Palm Springs, Calif.
WORKS: THEATRE: Fantômes rebelles, opera
grotesque; A border incident, music drama;
CHAMBER MUSIC: Russian rhapsody; Toccata,
harpsichord and chamber orch.; concertino for
piano, strings, harp; CHAMBER MUSIC: piano
sonata; 2 sonnets, for contralto, flute, harp,
1955; quintet, 2 flutes, viola, cello, harpsichord; sonata for 2 flutes and harp; sonata
brevis, violin and harp, 1961; choral works.

RZEWSKI, FREDERIC
b. Westfield, Mass., 13 Apr. 1938. Studied
with Walter Piston and Claudio Spies, Harvard
Univ., B.A. magna cum laude 1958; with Roger
Sessions and Milton Babbitt, Princeton Univ.,
M.F.A. 1960. He held a Fulbright fellowship, in
Italy, 1960-62; Ford Found. Artists in Berlin
grant, 1963-65; Tanglewood fellowship, 1969;
CAPS grant, 1973; and commissions. His teaching
posts have included instructor, Cologne, Germany,
1963, 1970; New Lincoln School, New York, 1972-
73; Turtle Bay Music School, 1973; Art Inst. of
Chicago, 1973-75; from 1977, Cons. Royal, Liege,
Belgium.
WORKS: ORCHESTRA: Nature morte, 1964;
Drums and guns, 1973; Struggle, baritone and
orch., 1974; A long time man, piano and orch.,
Dartmouth, New Hampshire Symph., composer at
piano, 12 Mar. 1980; CHAMBER MUSIC: sonata for
2 pianos, 1959; Poem, piano, 1959; Self-portrait,
Composition for 2 players, Speculum Dianae, 3
improvisational structures for 1, 2, and 8
players, 1964; Spacecraft, improvising group,
1965; Les moutons de Panurge, melody instruments,
1969; Coming together and Attica, speaker, bass
instrument, and ensemble, 1972, New York, 10
Apr. 1974; 2nd structure, improvising musicians,
1972, performed by composer at piano and synthesizer, Chicago, 16 Feb. 1973; Variations on
No place to go but around, piano; Song and dance,
4 players, 1977 (selected for performance at
Internat. Rostrum of Composers, UNESCO meetings
in Paris, May 1979; 3 pieces for piano, 1978;
VOICE: Requiem, chorus and orch., New York
Phil., 28 Oct. 1971; Work songs and love songs,
1968; Jefferson, voice and piano, 1970; and
electronic pieces.
55 via della Luce, Rome, Italy 00153

SACCO, JOHN CHARLES
b. New York, N.Y., 11 July 1905. Studied at
Mannes School of Music; with Seth Bingham and
Douglas Moore, Columbia Coll., B.A., M.A.; and
with Deszo D'Antalffy. He was music director,
Paper Mill Playhouse; Starlight Musicals,
Indianapolis; associate music director, St.
Louis Municipal Theatre; toured nationally with
many Broadway shows; was editor, choral depart-
ment, G. Schirmer, Inc., New York.
WORKS: SONGS: Brother Will, Brother John;
Maple candy; Rapunzel; The spelling of Christmas;
The bells ring out for Christmas; and others.
175 W. 79th St., New York, NY 10024

SACCO, P. PETER
b. Albion, N.Y., 25 Oct. 1928. Studied at New
York Univ., School of Education, B.S.; with
Bernard Rogers and Howard Hanson, Eastman School
of Music, M.M. 1954; D.M.A. 1958. His awards
include grants from Nat. Endowment for the Arts,
1968, 1974; American Music Center, 1969; San
Francisco State Coll., 1967; annual ASCAP awards,
1966-72; Ford Found. grant, 1972. From 1959 he
has been faculty member, San Francisco State
Univ.
WORKS: OPERA: Mr. Vinegar, chamber opera
for children, 1966, Redding, Calif., 12 May 1967;
ORATORIO: Jesu, Grand Rapids, Mich., 3 Dec.

1956; <u>Midsummer dream night</u>, with orch., San Francisco, 25 June 1961; <u>Solomon</u>, with orch., San Francisco, 12 Dec. 1976; ORCHESTRA: <u>Introduction and allegro</u>, 1953; 3 symphonies, <u>1955</u>, 1965, 1968; <u>Classical overture</u>, 1955; piano concerto, San Francisco, 4 Apr. 1968; violin concerto, Walnut Creek, Calif., 24 Apr. 1974; <u>Tithonus</u>, 2 horns, piano, string orch., 1972; <u>Moab illuminations</u>, 1976; <u>2 extemporaneius pieces</u>, 1977; BAND: <u>Make haste, Oh God, to deliver me</u>, with chorus, 1960; <u>4 sketches on Emerson essays</u>, San Francisco, 2 May 1964; suite for band, 1966; many chamber works, choral works, songs, piano pieces.

21092 Skyline Dr., Daly City, CA 94015

SACKS, STUART
b. Albany, N.Y., 28 Feb. 1941. Studied with Hugo Norden, Boston Univ.
WORKS: ORCHESTRA: overture; <u>Arioso</u> for strings; <u>Elegy</u>, solo cello and orch.; <u>Divertissement</u>, winds and strings; <u>Saul</u>, voice, oboe, percussion, strings, CBS-TV, 11 Apr. 1965; CHAMBER MUSIC: <u>Poeme</u>, violin and piano.

SAEGER, GREGG (ne HIGGINBOTHAM)
b. Columbus, Nebr., 18 Nov. 1931. Studied with Howard Hanson, Eastman School of Music; with Roy Harris, Colorado Springs, Colo.; Gardner Read, Boston Univ.; and at New England Cons., grad. 1954.
WORKS: THEATRE: <u>Marriage of the grocer of Seville</u>, comic opera, staged in Ohio, Boston, Potsdam, N.Y., WGBH-TV; <u>Lord Scarecrow</u>, musical; <u>Every boy/every girl</u>, musical; <u>Twain by the tale</u>, incidental music to the play; <u>Creation</u>, cantata on text by James Weldon Johnson; FILM SCORE: <u>Pocketful of pies</u>.

1982 Commonwealth Ave., Brighton, MA 02135

SAFANE, CLIFFORD JAY
b. New York, N.Y., 13 Feb. 1947. Studied with Edgar Curtis, Union Coll., Schenectady, 1967-70; with Gregory Levin, Earl George, Howard Boatwright, Syracuse Univ., 1970-72; with David Del Tredici and Joyce Mekeel, Boston Univ., 1972-73. He received the Julian B. Hoffman award at Union Coll., 1967, 1968; held a teaching fellowship at Syracuse Univ., 1971-72. From 1977 he has been a free-lance writer on jazz and music education.
WORKS: CHAMBER MUSIC: <u>Vevey 1971</u>, solo alto saxophone, 1971; <u>Canon for the New Year</u>, 2 trumpets, 1973; <u>Whispers and cries</u>, alto saxophone and string quartet, 1974; <u>6 pieces for 2 clarinets</u>, 1976; <u>Madrigal</u>, soprano and clarinet, 1977; <u>Forever</u>, piano, 1978; ELECTRONIC: <u>Electric trane</u>, Moog synthesizer and alto saxophone, 1973.

2160 Center Ave., Apt. 4P, Fort Lee, NJ 07024

SAFRAN, ARNO M.
b. New York, N.Y., 27 Aug. 1932. Studied at New York High School of Music and Art; with Isadore Freed and Arnold Franchetti, Hartt Coll. of Music; with Irving Fine, Brandeis Univ.; with Aaron Copland at Tanglewood, 1952, 1953. He

received the Hartt publication award, 1953; BMI student awards, 1954, 1955; and commissions. He was public school music teacher, 1958-65; from 1965, on faculty, Trenton State Coll.
WORKS: ORCHESTRA: symphony, 1954; <u>Music for orchestra</u>, 1954; <u>Serenade</u>, chamber orch., 1955; <u>3 symphonic statements</u>, 1962; <u>Toccata</u>, for strings, 1968; CHAMBER MUSIC: <u>3 pieces for solo violin</u>, 1953; string quartet, 1956; wind quintet, 1958; piano sonata, 1966; clarinet sonata, 1967; VOICE: <u>Music for Orpheus</u>, cantata, 1969; <u>Olessi</u>, songs, 1971.

30 Bayberry Rd., Trenton, NJ 08618

SAHL, MICHAEL
b. Brookline, Mass., 2 Sept. 1934. Studied at Amherst Coll., B.A. 1955; with Roger Sessions and Milton Babbitt, Princeton Univ., M.F.A. 1957; with Israel Citkowitz; and with Luigi Dallapiccola in Italy on a Fulbright scholarship, 1957-58. He began to experiment with electronic tape while in Italy; remained in Europe to 1963. Back in the U.S., he played bass guitar in night clubs; performed his own works at State Univ. of New York at Buffalo on a composer-pianist grant; was house musician, Lincoln Center Repertory Company, 1966; composed for films and television.
WORKS: ORCHESTRA: symphony, WBAI Big Band, New York, 12 May 1973; CHAMBER MUSIC: <u>Ensemble</u>, 1965; <u>Buell's piece</u>, double bass, 1966; string quartet, 1975; ELECTRONIC: <u>Mitzvah for the dead</u>, violin and tape, 1966-67; <u>Electric circus</u>, 1968; <u>Tropes on the Salve Regina</u>; electric violin concerto, New York, 21 Apr. 1974. He was coauthor with Eric Salzman of <u>Making changes: A practical guide to vernacular harmony</u>, New York, 1976.

223 E. 5th St., New York, NY 10003

ST. CLAIR, FLOYD J.
b. Johnstown, Pa., 4 Feb. 1871; d. Cleveland, Ohio, 23 Aug. 1942. Attended Curry Coll. He was cornetist, band director, and church organist; editor and arranger for music publishers. His works were chiefly marches and other pieces for band.

ST. CLAIR, RICHARD
b. Jamestown, N.Dak., 21 Sept. 1946. Studied with Leon Kirchner and Earl Kim, Harvard Univ., M.M. 1973; privately with Avram David, 1972-74. He received Harvard Univ. prizes for chamber and choral works. He was piano instructor, New England Cons., 1969-70; teaching fellow at Harvard Univ., 1973-74.
WORKS: BAND: <u>Amen concerto 1972</u>, 2 pianos and band, 1972; CHAMBER MUSIC: <u>Piano piece</u>, 1967; cello sonata, 1969; piano sonata, 1970; CHORUS: <u>Yonder</u>, a cappella, 1972; mass, with soloists and orch., 1973.

SALKOV, ABRAHAM A.
b. Rochester, N.Y., 17 Apr. 1921. Studied at Eastman School of Music in his early years; with Joseph Leonard in Los Angeles; received advice from Mario Castelnuovo-Tedesco. He was cantor, Temple Beth Am, Los Angeles, 1951-61; from 1961,

SALTA, MENOTTI

Chizuk-Amuno Congregation, Baltimore.
WORKS: LITURGICAL: Ovinu Malkenu, cantor
and organ; S'firah, cantor and organ; El Haye-
ladim B'Yisrael, children's choir; L'Zyekher
Olom, cantor, choir, string orch.; Hallel
Y'Rushalmi, cantor, choir, orch.
2601 Manhattan Ave., Baltimore, MD 21215

SALTA, MENOTTI
b. Perugia, Italy, 23 July 1893; U.S. citizen
1936; d. Italy. Studied at Verdi Cons., Milan.
He was conductor and arranger for film theatres
in New York, 1928-34; Radio City Music Hall,
1939-40.
WORKS: BALLET: Mirage; ORCHESTRA: Nocturne; Nostalgic serenade; 4 characteristic
dances; also piano pieces.

SALTHOUSE, GRAHAM
b. Buxton, Derbyshire, England, 7 May 1941; to
U.S. 1966. Studied at Royal Marines School of
Music and at Juilliard School. He played
trumpet in the Royal Marines Band, 1957-63; with
various bands in London and Singapore, 1963-66.
His published works include Statement for brass
quintet.

SALZEDO, CARLOS
b. Arcachon, France, 6 Apr. 1885; U.S. citizen
1923; d. Waterville, Maine, 17 Aug. 1961.
Graduated from Paris Cons., winning first prize
in harp and piano. He was concert pianist and
harpist in Europe; solo harpist with the New
York Metropolitan Opera; organized annual harp
festivals in the U.S.; helped organize the
Internat. Composers Guild, 1921, and U.S. section of the Internat. Society for Contemporary
Music, 1923; taught at Inst. of Musical Art, New
York; established and headed the harp department,
Curtis Inst., 1924; organized the Salzedo Harp
Colony at Camden, Maine, 1931.
WORKS: ORCHESTRA: The enchanted isle, with
solo harp, 1919; CHAMBER MUSIC: 4 preludes to
the afternoon of a telephone, 2 harps, 1921;
sonata for harp and piano, 1922; Preambule et
jeux, harp, 4 winds, 5 strings, 1929; Chanson
dans le nuit, harp solo; Concert variations on
O Tanenbaum; many other works for harp solo and
in combination with voice or other instruments.

SALZMAN, ERIC
b. New York, N.Y., 8 Sept. 1933. Studied with
Otto Luening, Vladimir Ussachevsky, Jack Beeson,
Columbia Univ., B.A. 1954; with Roger Sessions
and Milton Babbitt, Princeton Univ., M.F.A.
1956; with Goffredo Petrassi in Rome and Darm-
stadt on a Fulbright grant, 1956-58. He was
music critic, New York Times, 1959-62, New York
Herald Tribune, 1962-66; music director, WBAI-
FM, 1962-63, 1968-71; on faculty, Queens Coll.,
1966-68; from 1970, artistic director, QUOG
Music Theatre.
WORKS: OPERA: Voices, a cappella radio
opera on Biblical texts, WBAI, Dec. 1971;
ORCHESTRA: Inventions, 1958; Night dance, 1959;
Foxes and hedgehogs, with voices, text by John
Ashbury, 1963-67; CHAMBER MUSIC: Suite on
American Indian themes, violin and piano, 1953;

piano suite, 1955; flute sonata, 1956; string
quartet, 1957; Partita, solo violin, 1958;
VOICE: cummings set, with orch. or piano, 1953;
On the beach at night, 1956; In praise of the
owl and the cuckoo, soprano and instruments,
1964; Helix, voices, percussion, clarinet,
guitar, 1972; ELECTRONIC: Larynx music, voice
and tape, 1967; Queens collage, 1967; Wiretap,
Rockgarden, tape pieces, 1968; Strophe and anti-
strophe, harpsichord and tape, 1972; Birdwalk,
tape, 1973; MULTIMEDIA: Feedback, tape, film,
indefinite length, 1968; The Peloponesian war,
dance-mime-music-theatre, 1968; The nude paper
sermon, actors, singers, instruments, 1969; Can
man survive?, 1969; Ecolog, 1970; Mirrors, 1972;
Biograffiti, 1973; Lazarus, based on 12th-century
drama, 1974; and several music theatre works in
collaboration with Michael Sahl; The conjurer,
1975, Stauf, 1976, Civilization and its discon-
tents, 1977, Noah, 1978.
29 Middagh St., Brooklyn, NY 11201

SAMINSKY, LAZARE
b. Odessa, Russia, 8 Nov. 1882; U.S. citizen
1926; d. Port Chester, N.Y., 30 June 1959.
Studied with Rimsky-Korsakov and Liadov. From
1924 he was music director, Temple Emanuel, New
York. His compositions include 4 operas, 2
ballets, 5 symphonies, and many other works in
all genres.

SAMPSON, DAVID GEORGE
b. Charlottesville, Va., 26 Jan. 1951. Studied
with Myron Fink, Curtis Inst. of Music; privately
with Harold Boatrite and Karel Husa. He played
trumpet in the Eastern Music Festival Orch.,
1971; Colorado Phil., 1972, 1973.
WORKS: CHAMBER MUSIC: The skein, song
cycle for soprano; Exploitations, piano; Piece
for brass quintet; 3 pieces for piano; Elegy,
viola and piano.
2604 Edgemont St., Philadelphia, PA 19125

SAMSON, VALERIE BROOKS
b. St. Louis, Mo., 16 Oct. 1948. Studied with
Hugo Norden, Boston Univ., B.A. 1970; with
Andrew Imbrie and Olly Wilson, Univ. of California, Berkeley, M.A. 1973; Chinese music with
Betty Wong in San Francisco. She was radio
programmer-announcer, WTBS, Cambridge, Mass.,
1969-70; from 1978, has been contributing editor
of Ear magazine.
WORKS: CHAMBER MUSIC: duet for oboes,
1972; quartet for 2 winds, 2 strings, 1973;
Encounter, chamber orch., 1973; Blue territory
1 and 2, violin and piano, 1975; Mousterian
meander, recorder, cello, piano, 1976; Night
visits, chamber ensemble, San Francisco, 7 Oct.
1976; Winter dances, prepared piano, 1978;
MULTIMEDIA: Montage: A journey through youth,
3 sopranos, piano, dancer, lights, 1975.
1373 Clay St., #5, San Francisco, CA 94109

SAMUEL, GERHARD
b. Bonn, Germany, 20 Apr. 1924; U.S. citizen
1943. Studied with Howard Hanson, Eastman School
of Music, B.M. 1945; with Serge Koussevitzky at
Tanglewood; with Paul Hindemith, Yale Univ.,

M.M. 1947. His awards include the Haupt award, 1947; Fulbright grant, 1949; annual ASCAP awards from 1971 and special award, 1978; Nat. Endowment for the Arts grants, 1974, 1975; New York Composer Showcase, 1975, 1978; and commissions. He has held conducting posts with the Minneapolis Symph., 1949-59, Oakland Symph., 1959-71, San Francisco Ballet, 1960-70, Los Angeles Phil., 1970-73; faculty posts at California Inst. of the Arts, 1972-76; and from 1976, Coll. Cons., Univ. of Cincinnati.

WORKS: ORCHESTRA: Looking at Orpheus looking, Los Angeles, 11 Mar. 1971; Into flight from, 1972; Requiem for survivors, Los Angeles, 14 Mar. 1974; Out of time, a short symphony, 1978; CHAMBER MUSIC: 3 hymns to Apollo, cello and chamber group, 1973; Beyond McBean, violin and chamber ensemble, 1975; Cold when the drums sound for dawn, chamber orch., 1975; Au revoir to Lady R., clarinet, cello, piano, 1976; On a dream, viola and chamber orch., 1977; string quartet, Cincinnati, 31 Oct. 1978; VOICE: 12 on death and no, tenor, chorus, chamber orch., 1968; The relativity of Icarus, low voice and chamber group, 1971, premiered as a ballet, Joffrey City Center Ballet, 17 Oct. 1974; To an end, chorus and orch., 1972; And Marsyas, low voice and instruments, 1976; Sun-like, soprano and chamber ensemble, 1975; What of my music, soprano, 36 double basses, percussion, 1979.

2355 Fairview Ave., Cincinnati, OH 45219

SANDBERG, MORDECAI
b. Rumania, 4 Feb. 1897; to U.S. 1940; d. Toronto, Ont., 28 Dec. 1973. Studied in Vienna, then settled in Jerusalem to 1938. His works include 2 symphonies, 2 oratorios, chamber works, piano pieces, and a musical setting of the complete Book of Psalms. He had planned to set the entire Bible to music.

SANDERS, ALMA M.
b. Chicago, Ill., 13 Mar. 1882; d. New York, N.Y., 15 Dec. 1956. She composed the scores for the musicals Tangerine; Elsie; The chiffon girl; The houseboat on the Styx; and many songs.

SANDERS, ROBERT
b. Chicago, Ill., 2 July 1906; d. Delray Beach, Fla., 26 Dec. 1974. Studied at Bush Cons., B.M. 1924, M.M. 1925; with Ottorino Respighi on a fellowship at American Acad. of Rome, 1925-29. His honors included a New York Philharmonic award for Little symphony in G, 1937; Guggenheim fellowship, 1954-55. He held faculty posts at Chicago Cons., 1929-38; Meadville Theological School, 1930-38; Chicago Univ., 1937-38; Indiana Univ., 1938-47; professor and department chairman, Brooklyn Coll., CUNY, 1947-72.

WORKS: BALLET: L'Ag'ya, 1944; ORCHESTRA: Saturday night, 1933; Scenes of poverty and toil, 1935; Choreographic suite, 1935; violin concerto, 1936; 2 little symphonies, 1937, 1953; symphony in A, 1955; BAND: symphony, 1943; CHAMBER MUSIC: piano trio, 1925; string quartet, 1929; cello sonata, 1931; The imp, clarinet quartet, 1941; brass quintet, 1942; Rhapsody, woodwind quartet, 1943; trombone sonata, 1945; suite for brass quartet, 1949; Scherzo and dirge, 4 trombones, 1949; Fugue on a noel, woodwind quartet, 1949; Square dance, trumpet and piano; horn sonata; brass trio; clarinet sonata; many choral works. He was coeditor of Hymns of the Spirit, Boston, 1953; and a contributor to Celebration of life, Boston, 1964.

SANDIFUR, ANN E.
b. Spokane, Wash., 14 May 1949. Studied with Charles Bestor, Willamette Univ.; Paul Creston, Central Washington State Coll.; Stanley Lunetta, Eastern Washington State Coll.; Alden Jenks, San Francisco Cons.; Robert Ashley, Mills Coll.; and at Chocorua, N.H. She received an award in a Mu Phi Epsilon contest; grant from Nat. Center for Experiments in Television, San Francisco. She was on the staff, Ear magazine, 1973; director, first women's concert in Bay Area, 1973.

WORKS: CHAMBER MUSIC: suite for oboe; Pre-natal; ELECTRONIC: Bridging space; P.P.G.; Big belly; Jona one; Sequence II.

6320 Aspinwall Rd., Oakland, CA 94611

SANDOVAL, MIGUEL
b. Guatemala City, 22 Nov. 1903; U.S. citizen 1925; d. New York, N.Y., 24 Aug. 1953. Studied with Eduardo Trucco; was accompanist for Rosa Ponselle, Grace Moore, Martini, Gigli, and other noted singers. He wrote for films and radio; was staff pianist, conductor, and composer, CBS, New York, 1941-49; general direcotr, Guatemala City national radio station.

WORKS: ORCHESTRA: Recuerdos en un paseo, symphonic poem; Spanish dance, piano and orch.; piano pieces and songs.

SANDOW, GREGORY
b. New York, N.Y., 6 Mar. 1943. Studied privately with John Heiss in Boston; with Mario Davidovsky, Robert Morris, and Yehudi Wyner, Yale Univ., M.M. 1974. He has received 3 Meet the Composer grants, 1975, 1977, 1979. He was lecturer, Yale Univ., 1972-74; on staff, New York State Council on the Arts, 1976-79; then music critic and columnist on the Village Voice.

WORKS: OPERA: The fall of the House of Usher, 1975; The richest girl in the world finds happiness, 1975; A Christmas carol, 1977; CHAMBER MUSIC: 3 duets, 2 sopranos, a cappella, 1971; Mario, tenor and chamber ensemble, 1974; The key of G major in Donizetti's Anna Bolena, 2 sopranos and chamber orch., 1974; trio for viola, bassoon, percussion, 1977; Scraps, string quartet and contrabass; Watt, vocal quartet and piano, 1978; also songs, pieces for speaking groups, and incidental music for the theatre.

7 Cornelia St., New York, NY 10014

SANDRESKY, MARGARET V.
Studied with Charles Vardell, Salem Coll., B.M. 1942; with Howard Hanson and Bernard Rogers, Eastman School of Music, M.M. 1942; with Kurt Hessenberg in Frankfurt, Germany, on a Fulbright fellowship, 1955-56. She was faculty member, Oberlin Cons., 1944-46; Salem Coll., 1950-55; North Carolina School of the Arts, 1965-67; from 1968, again at Salem Coll.

SANDROFF, HOWARD F.

WORKS: ORCHESTRA: sinfonietta; Song for a peaceful valley; Nicole and Roland; The 4 Marys; Brief assemblance; CHAMBER MUSIC: 7 Japanese drawings, woodwind quintet; 2 pieces, recorder and 2 violas; piano trio; CHORUS: King of glory, King of peace; Jericho, cantata; Windows, cantata; songs and organ pieces.
2820 Reynolds Dr., Winston-Salem, NC 27104

SANDROFF, HOWARD F.
b. Chicago, Ill., 28 Oct. 1949. Studied with Robert Lombardo and Don Malone, Roosevelt Univ., M.M. with honors. He was director, New Music Ensemble, Northeastern Illinois Univ., 1974-78.
WORKS: THEATRE: Allegra, incidental music, 1978; CHAMBER MUSIC: 2 short pieces, children's ensemble; 3 aphorisms, voices and instruments; Pentaphon, 3 trumpets, 1978; ELECTRONIC: Oct. 28 1975, percussion ensemble and live electronics; Bless us gently Satan, theatre score, 1977; Deserts, tape and dancers; Deserts, tape, narrator, trombone.
1213½ Wilmette Ave., Wilmette, IL 60091

SANJUAN, PEDRO
b. San Sebastian, Spain, 15 Nov. 1886; U.S. citizen 1947; d. Washington, D.C., 18 Oct. 1976. Studied with Joaquin Turina. Before coming to the U.S., he divided his time between Spain and Cuba; organized the Havana Symph. Orch., in 1926; was appointed professor at Converse Coll., 1942; conducted the Spartansburg, S.C., Symphony and its festivals.
WORKS: ORCHESTRA: Rondo fantastico on a Basque theme, 1926; Castilla, 1927; La macumba, ritual symphony, 1945; Symphonic suite, 1965; BAND: Antillean poem, 1958; also choral works, piano pieces.

SANTINI, DALMAZIO
b. Capestrano, Italy, 11 Sept. 1923; U.S. citizen. Studied with Felix Saltzer, Mannes Coll. of Music; privately with Tadeuz Kassern. He was guest lecturer, Westchester Community Coll., 1974-78; Kings Coll., 1977-78.
WORKS: ORCHESTRA: symphony; White peaks of Forca; piano concerto; trombone concerto; viola concerto; Passa tempo e rondo; cello concerto; Quadri D'Italia; CHAMBER MUSIC: string quartet; quartet for woodwind trio and cello; Impression, violin; Continuum, accordion; 3 piano sonatas; suite for accordion; choral works and songs.
19 Rutledge Rd., Valhalla, NY 10595

SAPERSTEIN, DAVID
b. New York, N.Y., 6 Mar. 1948. Studied with Jacob Druckman, Juilliard Preparatory Div.; summer course with Elliott Carter, Vincent Persichetti, Walter Piston, Dartmouth Coll.; with Milton Babbitt and Earl Kim, Princeton Univ., B.A. 1969; graduate work at Brandeis Univ., where he received the Wechsler award, 1970.
WORKS: CHAMBER MUSIC: wind quintet, 1963; Fantasia, clarinet and piano, 1963; brass quartet, 1966; Variations for 8 players, 1969; Music for solo flute, 1970; sextet, woodwind trio and string trio, 1970, rev. 1973; Antiphonies, per-

cussion ensemble, 1972; PIANO: Catacombs, 1961; 3 etudes, 1967; Bagatelle, 1969; 4 piano pieces, 1971-73; electronic works.
1290 Ocean Dr., Apt. 2H, Brooklyn, NY 11230

SAPIEYEVSKI, JERZY
b. Lodz, Poland, 20 Mar. 1945; to U.S. 1967. Studied at State Cons., Gdansk, Poland, and at Catholic Univ. of America. His awards include a first prize in composition in Poland, 1966; Koussevitzky fellowship for Tanglewood, 1968; named composer-in-residence, Wolf Trap Farm Park; was faculty member, Catholic Univ., 1970-73; Univ. of Maryland, 1972-73; and from 1975, at American Univ.
WORKS: ORCHESTRA: trumpet concerto; Aria, alto saxophone and strings; concerto for 2 pianos; Reflection; concerto for viola or cello; Summer overture; Surtsey, string orch.; BAND: Morpheus; Scherzo di concerto; CHAMBER MUSIC: Trio for an Italian journey, violin, cello, piano.
American University, Washington, DC 20016

SAPP, ALLEN DWIGHT
b. Philadelphia, Pa., 10 Dec. 1922. Studied with Walter Piston and Edward Burlingame Hill, Harvard Univ., A.B. 1942, A.M. 1949; further studies with Archibald T. Davison, Irving Fine, Arthur Merritt, Randall Thompson, Aaron Copland, and Nadia Boulanger. He served as Army cryptanalyst, 1943-48; then joined the faculty at Harvard; was professor, State Univ. of New York at Buffalo, 1972-74; then dean, Coll. of Music, Univ. of Cincinnati. His works include several orchestral pieces; 3 violin sonatas; viola sonata; 4 piano sonatas; piano trio; string quartet; string trio; choral works; songs.
University of Cincinnati, Cincinnati, OH 45221

SAPP, GARY J.
b. Abilene, Tex., 11 May 1944. Studied at Univ. of Hawaii; with Martin Mailman, William Latham, Samuel Adler, Merrill Ellis, North Texas State Univ.; privately with Masahjko Sato in Japan. He was composer-arranger, Air Force Band of the Far East, 1966-70; composer-in-residence, Dallas Independent School District, 1973-74; music instructor, Skyline Center, Dallas, 1973-74.
WORKS: THEATRE: Uto, chamber opera based on Japanese Noh drama, 4 soloists, chorus, dancer, chamber ensemble; Comedy of errors, musical comedy based on Shakespeare; CHAMBER MUSIC: Shimo, flute, piano, soprano; Kwaidaj, 5 trumpets, 3 percussion; Erste Sonata für Klavier.

SARGENT, PAUL
b. Bangor, Maine, 30 Mar. 1910. Studied piano at Eastman School of Music, B.M. 1931; Ecole Normale de Musique, Paris, diploma, 1948; with John Mokrejs in New York. His studies in Paris and New York were on scholarships. He was accompanist for many noted singers, 1940-55.
WORKS: SONGS: XXth century; River road; Stopping by woods on a snowy evening; Manhattan

joy ride; 3 A.M.; Hickory Hill; PIANO: Promenade; Night song; The sea; piano suite.
408 64th St., New York, NY 10021

SATEREN, LELAND BERNHARD
b. Everett, Wash., 13 Oct. 1913. Studied at Augsborg Coll., B.A.; with Donald Ferguson, Univ. of Minnesota, M.A. His awards include 2 honorary doctorates, Lakeland Coll., 1965, Gettysburg Coll., 1965. He was school music director, 1935-38; music director, Univ. of Minnesota radio station, KUOM, 1940-43; faculty member and choral director, Augsburg Coll., from 1950. His compositions include more than 350 published choral works.
5217 Windsor Ave., Edina, MN 55436

SAUCEDO, VICTOR
b. Colton, Calif., 20 July 1937. Studied at Univ. of Southern California, B.A. 1966; with Boris Kremenliev and Roy Harris, Univ. of California, Los Angeles, Ph.D. 1972; with Stockhausen in Germany; computer music with John Chowning at Stanford Univ. He held scholarships and fellowships, 1955, 1968-69, 1970-72, 1975-77. He was faculty member, California State Univ., Dominguez Hills, 1970-71; Long Beach City Coll., 1971; Evergreen State Coll., 1977-78; Southwestern Coll., 1971-77, from 1978.
WORKS: ORCHESTRA: Isocentonization, 1972; Cultivated fields, 1976; CHAMBER MUSIC: Piano music III; string trio; Icosahedron, solo cello, 1971; VOICE: The hollow men, baritone and chamber ensemble; ReJoyce, improvisatory work for voice and 4 instruments; Homage, voice, piano, percussion, trombone; ELECTRONIC: Crossing; Music I. X., 4 clarinets and ring modulator, 1975; Ran I. X., solo clarinet and tape, 1978; Fluxions, tape, 1978; Music to read science fiction by, tape; MULTIMEDIA: Philologica comica, saxophone, dancer, tape, slides, lights.
1228 Corte de Cera, Chula Vista, CA 92010

SAUTER, EDWARD ERNEST
b. Brooklyn, N.Y., 2 Dec. 1914. Studied with Stefan Wolpe, Bernard Wagenaar, Louis Gruenberg, Juilliard School; attended Columbia Univ. He is conductor, arranger, and film composer.
WORKS: ORCHESTRA: concerto for jazz band and orch.; Focus, saxophone, strings, rhythm section; Mickey one, film score performed in concert by the Denver Orch., 1977; CHAMBER MUSIC: suite for tuba and saxophone quartet, New York, 22 Dec. 1976; and songs.

SAVINE, ALEXANDER
b. Belgrade, Yugoslavia, 26 Apr. 1881; U.S. citizen 1915; d. Chicago, Ill., 19 Jan. 1949. Studied in Belgrade with S. Mokranjac; and at the Vienna Cons. He was opera conductor in Berlin, 1905-7; taught at the Musical Acad., Winnipeg, 1908-12; was director of the opera department, Inst. of Musical Art, New York, 1922-24; settled in Chicago in 1929. His compositions included Xenia, an opera; 4 symphonic poems; choral works; songs.

SAVINO, DOMENICO
b. Taranto, Italy, 13 Jan. 1882; U.S. citizen 1914; d. New York, N.Y., 8 Aug. 1973. Studied at Naples Cons. He was director of a record company, 1915-25; editor for a music publisher; film composer.
WORKS: ORCHESTRA: symphony; piano concerto; Overture fantasy; Vesuvian rhapsody; Madrilena; Panorama; and songs.

SAXTON, STANLEY
b. Fort Plain, N.Y., 5 Aug. 1904. Studied at Syracuse Univ., B.M., M.M.; with Charles Widor, Marcel Dupre, Nadia Boulanger at Fontainebleau. He has received many commissions. In addition to being pianist, organist, and choral conductor, he was professor at Skidmore Coll. from 1928.
WORKS: ORCHESTRA: piano concerto; Mohawk suite; Skidmore suite; also choral works, organ pieces.

SAYLOR, BRUCE STUART
b. Philadelphia, Pa., 24 Apr. 1946. Studied with Hugo Weisgall and Roger Sessions, Juilliard School, B.M. 1968, M.S. 1969; with Goffredo Petrassi, St. Cecilia Acad., Rome, 1969-70; with George Perle and Felix Salzer, City Univ. of New York, Ph.D. 1978. His awards include scholarships at Juilliard School, 1965-69; Gretchaninoff prize, 1965, 1968; Nat. Soc. of Arts and Letters award, 1968; Marion Freschel prize, 1968; Fulbright grant, 1969-70; ASCAP awards, 1971-73; Santa Fe Music Critics' Assoc. award, 1973; Ives scholarship, 1976; Nat. Endowment for the Arts grant, 1978. He was faculty member, Queens Coll., CUNY, 1970-76; from 1976, at New York Univ.
WORKS: THEATRE: music for Victims of amnesia, wind quartet, 1968; ORCHESTRA: Cantilena, string orch., 1965; To autumn and To winter, with chorus, on Blake texts, 1968; Conductus, winds, strings, percussion, 1970; Notturno, piano and orch., 1969; Cycle and Inner world out, dance scores, 1978; CHAMBER MUSIC: suite for viola solo, 1967; duo for violin and viola, 1970; VOICE: 5 songs from Whispers of heavenly death, soprano and string quartet, 1967; Lyrics, soprano and violin, 1971; 4 Psalm settings, flute and voice; PIANO: 5 short piano pieces, 1967; Ricerare, 1972; Modular study; also choral works and organ pieces.
318 W. 85th St., New York, NY 10024

SAYLOR, RICHARD
b. Reading, Pa., 6 Aug. 1926. Studied with Leland Smith, Stanford Univ.; with Arnold Fish in New York; with George Driscoll, Ithaca Coll. He received an award, Phi Mu Alpha contest; Steinman Arts Festival commission, 1968; Smithsonian Inst. fellowship to India, 1968-69. His academic posts have included Xavier Univ., La., 1957-59; St. Lawrence Univ., 1959-68; from 1969, at California State Coll., San Bernardino.
WORKS: ORCHESTRA: Symphony 1966; Eithor/or; BAND: Ampersand; Prelude for band; Ballata; Prisoner of war; ELECTRONIC: Music for Rosmersholm; Music for Macbeth; Textures.
3880 Camellia Dr., San Bernardino, CA 92404

SCALERO, ROSARIO

SCALERO, ROSARIO
b. Moncalieri, near Turin, Italy, 24 Dec. 1870;
to U.S. 1919; d. Settimo Vittone, Italy, 25 Dec.
1954. Studied in Genoa, London, and Vienna;
taught in France and Italy until coming to the
U.S. He was faculty member, Mannes School of
Music, 1919-28; then at Curtis Inst. of Music.
His compositions include a violin concerto,
chamber music, and songs.

SCARMOLIN, A. LOUIS
b. Schio, Italy, 30 July 1890; U.S. citizen
1914; d. Wyckoff, N.J., 13 July 1969. Came to
the U.S. at age 10 and graduated from New York
Coll. of Music in 1907. His many honors for
composition included American Society of Ancient
Instruments award, 1938; first prize, Nat. Composers Clinic contest, Chicago, 1944; Fellowship
of American Composers award, 1946; New York
Women's Symph. Orch. award, 1947; first prize,
Composers Press, 1947. After serving in the
U.S. Army, 1917-19, he was music director of the
Union City, N.J., school system, 1919-49; also
organist, conductor, and accompanist for many
leading artists.
    WORKS: OPERA: The interrupted serenade,
Union City, N.J., 26 May 1974; ORCHESTRA: Overture on a street vendor's ditty, 1938; Dramatic
overture, 1938; Mercury overture, 1939; 2 symphonic fragments, 1944; Night--A poem for orchestra, 1947; BAND: Reuben and Rachel sight-
seeing in New York, 1945; Tribal dance, 1946;
Mexican holiday, 1946. His published works for
orchestra, band, chamber groups, piano, organ,
and choral groups total more than 600.

SCAVARDA, DONALD
b. Iron Mountain, Mich., 18 June 1928. Studied
with Homer Keller, Ross Lee Finney, and Roberto
Gerhard, Univ. of Michigan; with Philipp Jarnach,
Hamburg, Germany; with Leon Kirchner at Tanglewood. He received a Fulbright scholarship for
study in Germany, 1953-54; won a BMI award, 1954.
He was one of the founders of the ONCE Festival
of Musical Premieres, Ann Arbor, 1960-65.
    WORKS: ORCHESTRA: Fantasy for violin and
orchestra, 1954; CHAMBER MUSIC: In the autumn
mountains, haiku songs, voice and piano, 1957-
61; Groups for piano, 1959; Sounds for 11, woodwinds, percussion, amplified guitar, 1961;
Matrix for clarinetist, may have been the first
multiphonic clarinet work to be published, 1962;
MULTIMEDIA: Landscape journey, clarinet, piano,
film, 1963; Caterpillar, tape and film, 1965.
    P.O. Box 1908, Ann Arbor, MI 48106

SCELBA, ANTHONY J.
b. New Jersey, 12 Feb. 1947. Studied double
bass, Manhattan School of Music, B.M., M.M.; and
at Juilliard School. He is largely self-taught
in composition, but has won awards and scholarships in performance on bass. He has been
bassist with the New Jersey Symph. Orch., from
1969; also faculty member, preparatory division,
Manhattan School of Music.
    WORKS: CHAMBER MUSIC: double bass trios,
1969; Passacaglia, string quintet, New York,
17 May 1972; Romantic, string quintet, 1972, New

York, 18 Feb. 1974; Innocence and sophistication,
violin and contrabass, New York, 26 Nov. 1973;
Fantasia, contrabass and piano, 1974.
    Manhattan School, 120 Claremont Ave., New
York, NY 10027

SCHAAD, ROAR
b. Oslo, Norway, 30 Oct. 1941; U.S. citizen
1961. Studied at Illinois State Univ.; with
Salvatore Martirano and Morgan Powell, Univ. of
Illinois. From 1969 he has been musical instruction specialist, Illinois State Univ.; from
1974, lead trumpet with the Lamplighters Dance
Band, Bloomington, Ill.
    WORKS: ORCHESTRA: Eclectic etude, 1968;
CHAMBER MUSIC: trumpet sonata, 1968; ELECTRONIC:
Sounds like, tape, 1969; Study, saxophone and
tape, 1972; suite for strings, tape, piano,
1972; Tempo primo, tape, 1973; Osit VI, flugelhorn and tape, 1974; Gridley mix, tape, 1975;
Recital piece, horn and tape, 1976; Clicksody,
tape, 1978; C.J. Horn, flugelhorn and tape,
1978.
    1305 Nicki Dr., Bloomington, IL 61701

SCHACK, DAVID
b. Fort Wayne, Ind., 16 Sept. 1947. Studied
with Richard Wienhirst, Valparaiso Univ., B.M.
1969; at Indiana Univ., M.M. 1970; electronic
music with Raymond Haggh, Univ. of Nebraska,
1972. From 1970 he has been faculty member,
Concordia Teachers Coll., Seward, Nebr.
    WORKS: CHAMBER MUSIC: woodwind quintet;
brass quintet; brass quartet; CHORUS: Salvation
unto us has come; The Lord is my shepherd; O
dearest Jesus; settings of the mass for choir,
organ, handbells, woodwind quintet; pieces for
organ and piano.
    427 N. 3rd, Seward, NB 68434

SCHAD, WALTER
b. Brooklyn, N.Y., 24 Aug. 1889; d. New York,
N.Y., 16 Feb. 1966. Studied at Juilliard School
and New York Coll. of Music; played clarinet
under Victor Herbert and John Philip Sousa; was
on music research staff for music publishers;
also private teacher. His works include an
opera, Plango; orchestral pieces, Samson and A
legendary hero; and a piano trio.

SCHAEFER, HAROLD HERMAN
b. New York, N.Y., 22 July 1925. Studied with
Mario Castelnuovo-Tedesco and Henry Brant, High
School of Music and Art. He received a commission from the United Nations for a 10th-anniver-
sary work, Ballad of an ancient hope; from Nat.
Assoc. for Retarded Children for Their world is
limited; from Joseph Eger for Overture to the
blues; and from Daniel Nargin for Bop song. He
is pianist, accompanist, and arranger as well as
composer.

SCHALT, HEINRICH
b. Vienna, Austria, 2 Jan. 1886; U.S. citizen
1946. He received an Austrian State award for
composition, 1906; 2 Wales Eistedfod Festival
awards for chamber music, 1912, 1913. He was
organist in Munich, 1926-33; in Rome, 1934-38;

Rochester, N.Y., 1940-43; Providence, R.I., 1943-48; and in Hollywood, Calif., 1949-50.
WORKS: LITURGICAL: Sabbath eve liturgy, 1952; Hadrat Kodesh (The beauty of holiness), 1960; Psalm of brotherhood, chorus and organ; SONGS: Visions of Yehuda Ha-Levi, cycle for high voice and piano, 1970.
R.R. 5, Box 347, Evergreen, CO 80439

SCHAUM, JOHN W.
b. Milwaukee, Wis., 27 Jan. 1905. Studied at Milwaukee State Teachers Coll.; Marquette Univ., B.M. 1931; Northwestern Univ., M.M. 1934. He is a private piano teacher and has published piano teaching methods and many books of collected piano pieces; also Mountain concerto for piano; and songs.

SCHELLE, GEORGE MICHAEL
b. Philadelphia, Pa., 22 Jan. 1950. Studied with Arnold Franchetti, Hartt Coll. of Music; with Dominick Argento, Paul Fetler, Eric Stokes, Univ. of Minnesota. His awards include 5 composition prizes; MacDowell fellowship, 1977; 2 Wolf Trap fellowships; ASCAP grant, 1979; and commissions. In 1979 he joined the faculty at Jordan Coll., Butler Univ.
WORKS: ORCHESTRA: Lancaster variations, 1977; El medico; Music for Strindberg; CHAMBER MUSIC: Chamber concertino, solo violin and ensemble, 1978; 2 piano sonatas; 2 string quartets.
5446 N. Michigan Rd., Indianapolis, IN 46208

SCHELLING, ERNEST HENRY
b. Belvidere, N.J., 26 July 1876; d. New York, N.Y., 8 Dec. 1939. Was a child prodigy on the piano, playing at the Philadelphia Acad. of Music at age 4; then studied in Paris with several teachers, ending with Paderewski in Switzerland, 1898-1902. He returned to the U.S. in 1905 and devoted his time to conducting and composing.
WORKS: ORCHESTRA: Suite fantastique, 1907; Legende symphonique, 1913; Symphonic variations, piano and orch., 1915; violin concerto, 1916; A victory ball, 1923; Morocco, symphonic tableau, 1927; a symphony; chamber works and piano pieces.

SCHERER, BARRY
b. New York, N.Y., 10 Sept. 1949. Studied with Louise Talma and Ferdinand Davis, Hunter Coll., CUNY, A.B. cum laude 1972; and on a graduate fellowship at New York Univ., 1973. He was staff member, Lake George Opera Festival, 1969, 1970.
WORKS: OPERA: The prisoner of Jollern or Righteousness triumphant, 2 acts, performed in concert, New York Metropolitan Opera House, 13 June 1971; Delizia or The gypsy's malediction, 2 acts with ballet; librettos for both operas by the composer; CHORUS: How beautiful upon the mountain, with tenor solo and organ.
104-20 Queen's Blvd., Forest Hills, NY 11375

SCHERER, FRANK HERBERT
b. New York, N.Y., 5 Dec. 1897. Studied with

T. Tertius Noble and Rosario Scalero. His works include Contemplation of the crucifixion, an oratorio; and Good Friday requiem, a cantata.

SCHIAVONE, JOHN SEBASTIAN
b. Los Angeles, Calif., 27 Mar. 1947. Studied at Mount St. Mary's Coll., Los Angeles; privately with Matt Doran. He won second place in a competition with Parish mass in honor of the Holy Family. Other liturgical works include Mass in praise of God the Holy Spirit; Mass in praise of Christ; a number of choral anthems and motets.
4439 Inglewood Blvd., Los Angeles, CA 90066

SCHICKELE, PETER
b. Ames, Iowa, 17 July 1935. Played bassoon in the Fargo-Moorhead Orchestra and studied theory with its conductor, Sigvald Thompson; then studied at Swarthmore Coll., A.B. 1957; with Vincent Persichetti and William Bergsma at Juilliard School, M.S. 1960; privately with Roy Harris in Pittsburgh; with Darius Milhaud at Aspen School. His awards include a Ford Found. grant, 1960-61; Elizabeth Tow Newman award, 1964; numerous commissions. He held faculty posts at Swarthmore Coll., 1961-62; Juilliard School, Extension Div., 1963-65. He was cofounder of Composers Circle in 1959; in 1967 of the Open Window, a group that played and wrote for a wide range of projects, including music and lyrics for Oh! Calcutta, other shows, films, and even a television commercial. He has toured widely in the U.S., conducting and performing in his "P.D.Q. Bach" and "Professor Schickele" pieces.
WORKS: ORCHESTRA: Serenade, 1959; A zoo called Earth, with taped narration, 1970; Requiem mantras, rock group and orch., 1972; 3 strange cases, with narrator, Ogden Nash texts, 1972; 3 girls, 3 women, with male singer-pianist, 1972; The fantastic gardens, with rock group, 1968; American birthday card, with narrator, St. Louis, 17 July 1976; CHAMBERMUSIC: Sequiturs, solo cello, 1959; string trio, 1960; Aspendicitis, 3 flutes, 2 trombones, 2 basses, drums, 1961; 3 scenes for 5 instruments, 1965; Windows, violin, flute, guitar, 1966; Summer trio, flute, cello, piano, 1966; Gardens, oboe and piano, 1968; Night music, viola and bass, 1973; Monochrome III, 9 clarinets, 1974; Monochrome IV, 6 violas, 1974; many works for chorus, solo voice, piano pieces; FILM SCORES: The crazy quilt, 1965; Funnyman, 1967; 3 riddle films and Where the garbage goes (for "Sesame Street"), 1969; Silent running, 1971; A likely story, 1974; P.D.Q. Bach works: Concerto for Horn and Hardart; Gorss concerto for diverse flutes; Pervertimento, bagpipes, bicycle, balloons, strings; concerto for piano vs. orchestra; The art of round ground, 3 baritones discontinuo; Prof. Schickele works: The unbegun symphony; Eine Kleine Nichtmusik; Last tango in Bayreuth, 4 bassoons; Chaconne à son goût, orch.
193 St. John's Place, Brooklyn, NY 11237

SCHIFFMAN, HAROLD
b. Greensboro, N.C., 4 Aug. 1928. Studied at Univ. of North Carolina, Chapel Hill; with Roger Sessions privately in New Jersey and at Univ. of

SCHIFRIN, LALO BORIS

California, Berkeley; with Ernst von Dohnanyi
and John Boda, Florida State Univ., D.M. He has
been faculty member, Florida State Univ., from
1959.

WORKS: ORCHESTRA: Ninnerella variations,
1956; symphony, 1961; Prelude and variations,
chamber orch., 1970; CHAMBER MUSIC: string
quartet, 1951; piano sonata, 1951; string trio,
1955; Serenade, flute, clarinet, bassoon, 1959;
Musica battuta, percussion ensemble, 1961;
Pentalogue, violin and piano, 1963; Variations
for 2 pianos, 1966; Divertimento, woodwind quintet, 1969; Concert piece, trombone and piano,
1973; flute sonata, 1975; bassoon sonata, 1976;
violin sonata, 1976; Sonata quasi una fantasia,
cello, 1977; concertino for oboe and chamber
ensemble, 1977; Trio variante, violin, cello,
piano, 1978.

2304 Don Andres Ave., Tallahassee, FL 32304

SCHIFRIN, LALO BORIS
b. Buenos Aires, Argentina, 21 June 1932; to U.S.
1958. Studied with Juan Carlos Paz in Buenos
Aires; with Olivier Messiaen in Paris. He represented Argentina at the 1955 Internat. Jazz
Festival in Paris; formed his own jazz group on
return to Buenos Aires; came to the U.S. as
arranger for Xavier Cugat; since 1964, has been
film and television composer in Hollywood.
WORKS: BALLET: Jazz Faust, 1963; ORCHESTRA:
suite for trumpet and brass orch., 1961; Tuni-
sian fantasy; The ritual of sound, 15 instruments, 1962; JAZZ: Gillespiana, brass ensemble;
Jazz suite on mass texts; Dionysos; Mount Olive;
Study in rhythm; The web; Mima, piano; Rock
requiem, 1971; Pulsations, electric keyboard,
jazz band, and orch., 1971; CHORUS: Madrigals
for the space age, with narrator, in 10 parts,
Los Angeles, 15 Jan. 1976; FILM SCORES: The
liquidator; The fox; The Cincinnati Kid; I love
my wife; theme for TV's "Mission Impossible"
(2 Grammy awards); The rise and fall of the 3rd
Reich.
c/o Marc Newman Agency, Wilshire Blvd.,
Beverly Hills, CA 90213

SCHILLINGER, JOSEPH
b. Kharkov, Russia, 31 Aug. 1895; to U.S. 1928;
d. New York, N.Y., 23 Mar. 1943. Studied at
St. Petersburg Cons.; taught in Kharkov and
Leningrad. On coming to the U.S., he taught at
the New School for Social Research and at
Columbia Univ.; later established himself as a
private teacher, using his own mathematical
system of composition. His pupils included
many noted composers. His method was published
posthumously as The Schillinger system of composition, New York, 1946, and The mathematical
basis of the arts, New York, 1947.
WORKS: BALLET: The people and the prophet;
ORCHESTRA: March of the Orient, 1926; First
airphonic suite, theremin and orch., 1929;
North Russian symphony: The twelve, symphonic
cantata; PIANO: Symphonic rhapsody; other
piano pieces.

SCHIMMEL, WILLIAM
b. Philadelphia, Pa., 22 Sept. 1946. Studied

with Lotta Hertlein and Paul Creston, Neupauer
Cons., Philadelphia; with Elliott Carter, Vincent
Persichetti, Roger Sessions, Hugo Weisgall,
Juilliard School, B.S., M.S., D.M.A. He received
the Rodgers and Hammerstein scholarship, 1969-70.
He was instructor at Juilliard School, 1973-74;
on faculty at Brooklyn Coll., 1971-76; from
1976, dean, Neupauer Cons.
WORKS: THEATRE: David and Bathsheba, 1-act
opera; The tennis game, play with music; ORCHES-
TRA: Concerto for 3, accordion, bass, percussion,
and orch., 1969; Portrait #1, after a painting
by Joan Miro, 1969; mass for chorus and orch.,
1973; CHAMBER MUSIC: Tithonus, chamber ensemble,
New York, 2 Apr. 1974; KEYBOARD: Motor piece,
accordion, 1972; Kingdom trilogy, 1972-73
(Kerygma for organ, Parousia for accordion,
Kingdom for piano).
242 E. 89th St., #2-D, New York, NY 10028

SCHINDLER, ALLAN
b. Stamford, Conn., 15 May 1944. Studied with
Ralph Shapey, Univ. of Chicago; with Joseph
Wood and Edwin Dugger, Oberlin Coll.; Cleveland
Inst. of Music. He was faculty member, Boston
Univ., 1972-76; then at Eastman School of Music.
WORKS: CHAMBER MUSIC: string sextet; Blues
for the children of light, 8 instruments; ELEC-
TRONIC: Cirrus and beyond, flute, cello, per-
cussion, tape, New York, 30 Nov. 1975.
Eastman School of Music, 26 Gibbs St.,
Rochester, NY 14604

SCHINSTINE, WILLIAM J.
b. Easton, Pa., 16 Dec. 1922. Studied percussion
with George Hamilton Green in New York; Eastman
School of Music, B.M. 1945; Univ. of Pennsylvania, M.M.E. 1952. He was percussionist,
Rochester Phil. 1945; Nat. Symph. Orch., 1946-
47; Pittsburgh Symph., 1947-48; San Antonio
Symph., 1949-51; taught in Pottstown School
District, 1952-78.
WORKS: BALLET: The Pennsylvania farmer,
1977; BAND: March to the battle of jazz; Tim-
pendium and Timpolero, timpani solos with band;
Pennsylvania sketches, a suite; The miracle,
overture; numerous pieces for solo percussion
instruments and percussion ensemble; teaching
methods for percussion.
614 Woodland Dr., Pottstown, PA 19464

SCHIRMER, RUDOLPH EDWARD
b. Santa Barbara, Calif., 8 June 1919. Attended
Princeton Univ.; studied with Rosario Scalero,
Curtis Inst. of Music. In 1949 he became vice-
president of the family music publishing firm
of G. Schirmer, Inc. His compositions include
7 songs, for chorus, to his own texts.
G. Schirmer, Inc., 866 3rd Ave., New York,
NY 10022

SCHIRMER, WILLIAM
b. Cleveland, Ohio, 25 Feb. 1941. Studied at
Cleveland Inst. of Music; with John La Montaine
and Bernard Rogers, Eastman School of Music;
with Herbert Brün and Marshall Barnes, Ohio
State Univ. He was faculty member, Tennessee
Wesleyan Coll., 1970-76; Univ. of Cincinnati,

1976-78.

WORKS: OPERA: The glass menagerie, 1969;
ORCHESTRA: 32 symphonies, 1962-76; 8 piano concertos, 1962-76; Contrasts, viola and orch.,
1962, rev. 1968; Fantasy, piano and strings,
1968; CHAMBER MUSIC: 20 string quartets, 1961-
77; sonatas for practically all orchestral instruments; numerous other chamber works; also
choral pieces and songs.
3309 November Ct., Cincinnati, OH 45239

SCHLABACH, ERROL WEISS
b. Canton, Ohio, 31 Aug. 1942. Studied with
Marcel Dick, Cleveland Inst. of Music. He received annual ASCAP awards, 1970-73. He was
arranger-composer, U.S. Navy Band, Washington,
D.C., 1966-70; U.S. Marine Band, Washington,
1973.
WORKS: BAND: Swiss moods; Clarinet rhapsody, with solo clarinet; many works for jazz
and stage bands.

SCHLEIN, IRVING
b. New York, N.Y., 18 Aug. 1905. Studied at
City Coll. of New York, B.A.; Juilliard School;
New York Coll. of Music; with Douglas Moore,
Columbia Univ.; with Aaron Copland, Roy Harris,
Wallingford Riegger, and Roger Sessions. He
has been accompanist, pianist for musicals, and
public school music teacher.
WORKS: ORCHESTRA: Dance overture; CHAMBER
MUSIC: sonatina for viola d'amore, New York,
16 Feb. 1973; and piano pieces.

SCHMIDT, DANIEL W.
b. New Brunswick, N.J., 12 Apr. 1942. Studied
with Warren Martin, Westminster Choir Coll.,
B.M.; with Morton Subotnick and James Tenney,
California Inst. of the Arts, M.F.A.; with K.R.T.
Wasitodipuro, Center for World Music. He was
awarded residencies at the Exploratorium, San
Francisco, 1979-80, and in Berlin on the German
Academic Exchange Program, 1979-80; numerous
commissions. He has been church choral director,
theatre music director, and stage designer, and
from 1975, lecturer, Univ. of California at
Berkeley.
WORKS: TEXT-SOUND: Last year's life;
Recipe; Hammering piece for 2 workers; Women's
letters; AMERICAN GAMELAN: Changing part; In my
arms . . . many flowers; Accumulation; . . . and
the darkest is just before dawn; numerous smaller
pieces. He is author of Building a gamelan in
the West, Seattle, 1981.
1322 Grove St., Berkeley, CA 94709

SCHMIDT, DIANE LOUISE
b. Seattle, Wash., 23 Nov. 1948. Studied accordion, Univ. of Puget Sound, B.M.; composition
with William O. Smith and Robert Suderburg,
Univ. of Washington, M.M. She won a World
Accordion Competition, Mozarteum, Salzburg, and
has toured widely in Europe and the U.S. as
accordion soloist.
WORKS: ACCORDION: Theme and variations;
2 contemporary fugues.
1436 S. 129th, Seattle, WA 98168

SCHMIDT, WARREN F.
b. Milwaukee, Wis., 26 Apr. 1921. Studied at
Univ. of Michigan; with Helmut Walcha, Frankfurt,
Germany on a Fulbright fellowship; with Thomas
Turner and Richard Hervig, Univ. of Iowa, Ph.D.
He held a faculty fellowship from Wartburg Coll.,
where he has been faculty member from 1950.
WORKS: ORGAN: Fantasienne and fughetta;
2 sketches; Thanksgiving suite; Chorale concertato, with choir and trumpets; Festival fantasy,
with choir and trumpets; Jubilee toccata; and
others.
321 3rd Ave., N.E., Waverly, IA 50677

SCHMIDT, WILLIAM JOSEPH, JR.
b. Chicago, Ill., 6 Mar. 1926. Studied with
Max Wald, Chicago Musical Coll.; with Halsey
Stevens and Ingolf Dahl, Univ. of Southern
California, B.M. 1955, M.M. 1959 with honors.
Other awards include a DuPont Band Composition
award. From 1964 he has been president of
Western Internat. Music, Inc., and WIM Records.
WORKS: BAND: Concerto breve, brass and
band, 1957; The Natchez trace; Sakura variations;
Chorale, march, and fugato; WIND ENSEMBLE:
Vendor's call, piano and clarinet choir, 1968;
The Turkish lady, trumpet and clarinet choir;
trumpet concerto; BRASS QUINTET: 3 suites; concerto for piano; Music for scrimshaw, with harp;
Spiritual fantasy, with organ; Variations on a
Negro folksong; 7 variations on a hexachord;
CHAMBER MUSIC: Spirituals, cello and percussion;
viola sonata, 1959; saxophone sonata; Serenade,
tuba and piano; Variations, horn quartet; Prelude
and fugue, woodwind trio; 3 liturgical preludes,
woodwind quartet; Ludus Americanus, narrator and
percussion, 1971; concertino, 2 trumpets and
organ; Rondoletto, baritone saxophone and piano;
duo with cadenzas, oboe and clarinet; concertino,
piano and saxophone quartet; Variations on St.
Bone, trombone and piano; horn sonata; 2 poems
by William Pillin, oboe and narrator; and many
others.
2859 Holt Ave., Los Angeles, CA 90034

SCHMINKE, OSCAR EBERHARD
b. New York, N.Y., 12 Dec. 1881; d. Liberty,
N.Y., 22 Feb. 1969. Was a practicing dentist;
composed chamber music, piano and organ pieces,
songs.

SCHMUTZ, ALBERT DANIEL
b. Halstead, Kans., 11 Oct. 1887; d. Stockton,
Calif., Feb. 1975. Studied at Bethel Coll.,
Newton, Kans.; Inst. of Musical Art, Wichita,
Kans., Chicago Cons., B.M., M.M.; and with Ernst
von Dohnanyi in Kansas City. He was faculty
member, Bethel Coll.; Kansas State Teachers
Coll.; and at Nat. Music Camp, Interlochen,
Mich., 1948-52 and 1968-72.
WORKS: BAND: Ballade symphonique; CHAMBER
MUSIC: saxophone sonata; clarinet sonata; quin-
tet for clarinet and strings; string quartet;
woodwind trio; Divertimento, horn quartet;
Fantasy sketch, brass sextet; CHORUS: Song for
evening; Stopping by woods on a snowy evening;
From darkling; KEYBOARD: organ sonata; 7 psalms
without words, organ.

SCHNEIDER, EDWARD FABER

SCHNEIDER, EDWARD FABER
b. Omaha, Nebr., 3 Oct. 1872; d. Santa Clara,
Calif., 1 July 1950. Studied with Xavier
Scharwenka in New York; with Hans Barth in
Berlin. He taught privately in San Francisco,
then at Mills Coll.
WORKS: ORCHESTRA: In autumn time, 1913;
Sargasso Sea, 1922; Fires of wisdome; Thus spake
the deepest stone, 1938; songs; piano pieces.

SCHOENBERG, ARNOLD
b. Vienna, Austria, 13 Sept. 1874; U.S. citizen
1940; d. Brentwood, Calif., 13 July 1951.
Studied with Alexander von Zemlinsky in Vienna,
but was largely self-taught. On coming to the
U.S., he taught first at the Malkin Cons. in
Boston; was appointed professor at the Univ. of
Southern California in 1935, then at Univ. of
California, Los Angeles, 1936. He retired from
both positions in 1944, but continued to teach
private classes and to compose. Schoenberg's
influence on modern music through the introduction of the 12-tone scale has been revolutionary. His Style and idea, a collection of essays, was
published in 1951. On 20 Feb. 1977 the
Schoenberg Institute was inaugurated in a new
building on the campus of Univ. of Southern
California. The building contains archives
holding some 6,000 manuscript pages and a
library of 2,000 books, tapes, recordings, and
other memoribilia. Only a few of his major
works are listed below.
WORKS: OPERA: Die gluckliche Hand, music
drama to his own libretto, 1910-13; Moses and
Aron, opera to his own libretto, 2 acts completed 1932, the full work never completed;
ORCHESTRA: Verklarte Nacht, written for string
sextet, 1899, arranged for string orch., 1917,
rev. 1943; violin concerto, 1936; 2 chamber symphonies, 1936, 1940; Ode to Napoleon, speaker,
strings, piano, 1942; piano concerto, 1943;
CHAMBER MUSIC: 5 string quartets; woodwind quintet; many other chamber works; CHORUS: Gurre-
Lieder, soloists, chorus, orch., 1901-13; 6
pieces for men's chorus, 1930; De profundis, a
cappella, 1951; numerous other works and songs.

SCHOETTLE, ELMER
b. Kansas City, Mo., 16 July 1910; d. Houston,
Tex., 11 Sept. 1973. Studied with Walter Piston,
Harvard Univ.; at George Peabody Coll., B.A.;
with Bernard Rogers and Howard Hanson, Eastman
School of Music, M.M., Ph.D. He received the
Charles Ives award, Texas Fed. of Music Clubs,
Houston. He taught at Fisk Univ., 1944-50;
Univ. of Oklahoma, 1953-55; Northeast Missouri
State Coll., 1955-57; Univ. of Houston, 1957-73.
WORKS: ORCHESTRA: Fantasy, string orch.;
CHAMBER MUSIC: sonatina for percussion; Flight,
tenor voice, clarinet, piano; quartet for piano
and strings; quartet for oboe and strings; piano
trio; violin sonata; Fantasie variations for
woodwinds; CHORUS: The fear of the Lord.

SCHOLIN, C. ALBERT
b. Jamestown, N.Y., 24 May 1896; d. Brentwood,
Mo., 22 Dec. 1958. Studied at American Cons.,
B.M., M.M. He was pianist, organist, and

teacher; founded a music publishing company in
St. Louis. His works included suite for orchestra; Pastorale, for organ; a cantata and many
anthems.

SCHONTHAL-SECKEL, RUTH
b. Hamburg, Germany, 27 June 1924; U.S. citizen
1956. Studied at Cons. Stern, Berlin; Royal
Acad. of Music, Stockholm; with Manuel Ponce in
Mexico; with Paul Hindemith at Yale Univ., B.M.
1948. She held a scholarship at Yale; won a
Delta Omicron award for a string quartet, 1947.
She was faculty member, Adelphi Univ., 1973-76;
from 1974, at Westchester Cons.
WORKS: ORCHESTRA: piano concerto; ballet
suite, The transposed heads; CHAMBER MUSIC:
string quartet; cello sonata; violin sonata; 4
epiphanies, unaccompanied viola; VOICE: 9 lyric-
dramatic songs, on texts by Yeats, mezzo-soprano
and chamber orch.; Totengesange, soprano and
piano; The roadside, soprano and piano; PIANO:
5 sonatas; Klange aus der Jugend, prepared piano;
Miniatures; Miniscules; Near and far; Variations
in search of a theme.
12 Van Etten Blvd., New Rochelle, NY 10804

SCHOOLEY, JOHN HEILMAN
b. Nelson, Pa., 8 Feb. 1943. Studied at Mansfield State Coll., B.S. 1965; with Richard
Stoker, Royal Acad. of Music, London, certificate
1966; with Gregory Kosteck, East Carolina Univ.,
M.M. 1968; with Charles Jones, Aspen School. He
received a Rotary Found. fellowship; 2 grants
for study at Aspen; Ellen Battell Stoeckel fellowship at Yale Summer School. He was faculty
member, Eastern Kentucky Univ., 1968-70; from
1970, at Fairmont State Coll.
WORKS: ORCHESTRA: concertino for winds and
percussion; Dance scenes, 1967; CHAMBER MUSIC:
Partita, brass quartet, 1966; 3 dances, woodwind
trio, 1968, rev. 1972; Serenata, tuba and piano,
1970; VOICE: Vocalise, soprano and piano, 1970;
Lines to Ralph Hodgson Esquire, girls' choir,
1973; Song to women, baritone and piano; Responses for the contemporary church, 1973; From
a very little sphinx, soprano and piano, 1975;
Songs of victory in heaven, soprano, chorus, and
harp, 1978.
1113 Morningstar Lane, Fairmont, WV 26554

SCHOOP, PAUL
b. Zurich, Switzerland, 31 July 1909; d. Los
Angeles, Calif., 1 Jan. 1976. Studied piano with
Alfred Cortot and Robert Casadesus in Paris,
with Artur Schnabel in Berlin; composition with
Paul Dukas, Paul Hindemith, and Arnold Schoenberg
in the U.S. He received a commission from the
Swiss government for a work for the 1939 exposition. He was concert pianist; accompanist to
his sister, Trudi Schoop, a dancer; in World
War II, formed the Schoop Company and toured
with the USO; settled in Hollywood as film composer.
WORKS: COMIC OPERA: The enchanted trumpet;
BALLET: Maria del Valle, dance drama; Marche
ballet; ORCHESTRA: Fata Morgana; Everything new,
1939; Wishing tree, musical fantasy.

SCHRADER, BARRY
b. Johnstown, Pa., 26 June 1945. Studied at
Univ. of Pittsburgh, B.A. 1967, M.F.A. 1970;
with Morton Subotnick, California Inst. of the
Arts. He won an award in the first Internat.
Electronic Music Contest, Bourges, France, 1973.
From 1971 he has been on the faculty, California
Inst. of the Arts.
WORKS: ELECTRONIC: Serenade, 1969; Apparitions, 1970; Celebration, 1971; Bestiary, 1972-
74; 3 sotilties, 1976; Classical studies (3 on a
patch), 1977; Lost Atlantis, 1977; MULTIMEDIA:
Elysium, harp, dancers, light, tape, 1971; FILM
SCORES: Labyrinth, 1970; How to make a woman,
1971; Death of the red planet, 1972; Heavy-light,
1973; Glory road west, 1974; Exploratorium, 1975;
Mobiles, 1978. He also composed an outdoor
sound environment for Otto Piene's Sky ballet,
1970.
California Inst. of the Arts, Valencia, CA
91355

SCHRAMM, HAROLD
b. Chicago, Ill., 3 July 1935; d. New Jersey,
11 Dec. 1971. Studied with Rudolf Ganz and
Karel Jirak, Chicago Musical Coll., B.M., M.M.;
held fellowships at Tanglewood, MacDowell Colony,
Bennington Composers Conf., All India Radio. He
was composer and arranger, Australian Broadcasting Commission, 1960-61; gave lecture recitals
in the U.S. and Far East.
WORKS: OPERA: Shilappadikaram; ORCHESTRA:
Invocation for strings; Mogul set, string orch.;
CHAMBER MUSIC: Partita, 2 trumpets; Song of
Tayumanavar, soprano and flute; CHORUS: Alarippu,
speaking chorus and percussion; India: a choral
poem, on folk songs of India; Canticle, an
aleatory setting to the composer's own text;
PIANO: Bharata sangita; Natyamalika, a suite;
Vertical construction.

SCHREIBER, FREDERICK C.
b. Vienna, Austria, 13 Jan. 1895; U.S. citizen
1945. Studied at Vienna Acad. of Music and
Vienna Univ. He was teacher and opera conductor
in Vienna; from 1939, organist-choirmaster in
New York.
WORKS: ORCHESTRA: 9 symphonies, 1927-67;
2 violin concertos; cello concerto; concerto
grosso; The beatitudes, symphonic trilogy for
chorus and orch., 1950; The intangible, oratorio,
chorus and orch.; 2 piano concertos; Christmas
suite, 1967; Contrasts, 1972; Variations on a
German folksong, 1974; CHAMBER MUSIC: 2 string
quintets; 7 string quartets; piano quartet; 3
piano trios; many choral works and organ pieces.

SCHROEDER, DAVID H.
b. Sidney, Ohio, 31 Dec. 1954. Studied with
Jonathan Kramer and David Mott, Yale Univ.,
1973-77. He has been staff member, WYBC-FM,
host of "Sound Workshop," a weekly experimental
program.
WORKS: LIVE PERFORMANCE: Kanine kapers, a
lecture piece, 1973; Did you know . . .?, 5
voices; TAPE PIECES (using found sound): The
Bostwicks--Dec. 18, 1940, 1974; Hometown, tape
and live voice; A dream for Emile Berliner,

1976-77.
6625 Yale Station, New Haven, CT 06520

SCHROEDER, WILLIAM A.
b. Brooklyn, N.Y., 10 Nov. 1888; d. Wilton,
Conn., 20 Apr. 1960. Attended Brooklyn Polytechnic Inst.; studied with Roy Harris and Rubin
Goldmark. He was bandmaster in World War I;
composed for navy shows; then for the Broadway
stage.
WORKS: ORCHESTRA: The Emperor Jones; Rhapsody; Miniature, piano concertino; And God
walked the plains, with narrator; Ballet on an
Irish theme; Jack and the bean stalk.

SCHROEDER, WILLIAM A.
b. Brooklyn, N.Y., 24 Apr. 1921. Studied with
Max Wald, Chicago Musical Coll.; with Anthony
Donata, Northwestern Univ. His awards include
an Oliver Ditson scholarship, 1942, and the
Faricy award, 1959. He taught at Peabody Cons.,
1949-51; Judson Coll., 1952-56; Henderson State
Teachers Coll., 1959-61; Wartburg Coll., 1961-
65; from 1965, at Del Mar Coll. and at the Nat.
Music Camp, Interlochen, Mich.
WORKS: WIND ENSEMBLE: Invention and fugue;
Prologue, canon, and stretto; March, antiphonal
and triumphant, 2 brass choirs; CHAMBER MUSIC:
Of moon and winds, song cycle for voice, string
quartet, piano; Age--The beauty of time, mezzo-
soprano and woodwind quintet; string quartet;
CHORUS: Canticle of praise, with brass quintet
and timpani.
4413 Bluefield Dr., Corpus Christi, TX
78413

SCHROTH, GODFREY
b. Trenton, N.J., 7 Jan. 1927. Studied with
Edwin Hughes and Paul Creston in New York; at
Columbia Univ., M.A. He received the Lado
Found. chamber music award, 1959; New Jersey
Council on the Arts composition grant, 1972. He
was lecturer, St. Joseph's Coll., 1956-61; from
1959, director of music, St. Mary's Cathedral,
Trenton.
WORKS: ORCHESTRA: Symphonic fantasy; Fan-
tasy scherzo; Rocky Mt. serenade, 1972; CHAMBER
MUSIC: piano quintet, 1959; CHORUS: End of
Jesse; Vesper prayer; This is the day; The eyes
of all; A ballad of Christmas; ORGAN: 2 suites;
Meditation songs.
261 Lookout Ave., Hackensack, NJ 07601

SCHRYOCK, BUREN
b. Sheldon, Iowa, 13 Dec. 1881; d. San Diego,
Calif., 20 Jan. 1974. Conducted the San Diego
Opera Company, 1920-36. His compositions include
5 operas to his own librettos; a symphony;
chamber music; piano pieces.

SCHUBEL, MAX
b. Bronx, N.Y., 11 Apr. 1932. Studied at New
York Univ., B.A. 1953; privately with Charles
Haubiel, 1952-53; at City Coll. of New York,
1957-58; and with Frank Martin in Holland, 1964.
His awards include scholarships, 1952-53; 3
MacDowell fellowships, 1969, 1972, 1977; 2 Noble
Found. grants, 1969, 1973; grants from Ford

SCHULLER, GUNTHER

Found., 1971, American Music Center, 1973, Nat.
Endowment for the Arts, 1974, CAPS, 1975, 1976;
residencies at Wolf Trap Farm Park, 1976-77,
Ossabaw Island, 1977, Taos, N.Mex., 1978. Since
1949 he has held various jobs--in record stores,
for recording companies, free-lance woodworking,
etc. In 1966 he was cofounder of Opus One, a
recording company.
    WORKS: BALLET: Insected surfaces, 1965-66,
Univ. of Utah, 6-12 Apr. 1967; ORCHESTRA: Spec-
ters and sheldrakes, Wellesley, Mass., 11 Apr.
1965; Fracture, 1969; Overfeed, Young People's
Symph., Springfield, Mass., 26 Jan. 1974; CHAMBER
MUSIC: Omphaloskepsis, solo cello, 1964; Etudes,
solo cello, 1965; Gigantica, double bass solo,
1965; Supercool, solo viola, 1965; Elegy, flute
and cello, 1965; Quashed culch, flute and bass,
1966; Son of quashed culch, flute, cello, bass,
1967; High ice, string quartet, WNYC-TV, 3 Jan.
1968; Charismata, string quartet, with tape,
1968; Safety factor, 5 winds, New York, 11 Feb.
1973; Mountain girl, male voice and 8 instruments, 1974; Spheres, alto flute and chamber
orch., 1975; Cabaret triflettes, cello and prepared piano, 1977; Pursuing purple, 6 instruments and gospel singer, 1978; other chamber
works, multimedia pieces, film scores.
    Box 604, Greenville, ME 04441

SCHULLER, GUNTHER
    b. New York, N.Y., 22 Nov. 1925. Began study as
a boy soprano at St. Thomas Choir School, and
soon added the study of composition, flute, and
French horn to his curriculum. He started composing at age 12 and at the same time made such
progress on the horn that by 16 he was playing
horn with the Ballet Theatre Orch. His many
honors include Nat. Inst. of Arts and Letters
award, 1960; Brandeis Univ. Creative Arts award,
1960; 2 Guggenheim fellowships; Darius Milhaud
award for the film score, Yesterday in fact,
1964; honorary doctorate, Colby Coll., 1969;
Ditson conducting award, Columbia Univ., 1970;
Rodgers and Hammerstein award, 1971; American
Composers Alliance, 1976; Laurel Leaf award; and
numerous commissions. He was solo horn player,
Cincinnati Symph., 1943-44; Metropolitan Opera
Orch., 1944-59; taught at Manhattan School of
Music, 1950-63; was music director, 1st Internat.
Jazz Festival, 1962; acting head, composition
dept., Berkshire Music Center, 1963-65, from
1969, artistic codirector; on faculty, Yale Univ.,
1964-66; president, New England Cons., 1966-77.
    WORKS: OPERA: The visitation, after Franz
Kafka, 1966, first American performance, San
Francisco, 1967; The fisherman and his wife,
children's opera, Boston, 8 May 1970; BALLET:
Variants, New York, 4 Jan. 1961; ORCHESTRA:
horn concerto, Cincinnati Symphony with composer
as soloist, 6 Apr. 1945; cello concerto, 1945;
symphony for brass and percussion, 1949; Dramatic overture, 1951; Threnos, oboe and orch.;
concertino for jazz quartet and orch., 1959;
7 studies on themes of Paul Klee, 1959; Spectra,
1959; Contrasts, 1961; piano concerto, 1962;
symphony, 1964; Diptych, brass quintet and orch.,
Boston, 31 Mar. 1967; Triplum, New York, 28 June
1967; double bass concerto, New York, 27 June

1968; Journey into jazz, narrator, jazz quintet,
orch.; violin concerto, Lucerne, Switz., 25 Aug.
1976; concerto for orchestra #2, Nat. Symph.,
12 Oct. 1976; contrabassoon concerto, Nat. Symph.,
16 Jan. 1979; Deiae, for 3 orchestras, American
premiere, Tanglewood, 3 Aug. 1979; trumpet concerto, White Mountains Center for the Arts Festival, 25 Aug. 1979; CONCERT JAZZ: Abstractions;
12 by 11, 1955; Variations on a theme by John
Lewis; Transformations, 1957; Densities I, 1962;
Night music, 1962; numerous chamber works; choral
works; band pieces. He is author of 2 books,
Horn technique, New York, 1962; and Early jazz:
Its roots and musical development, New York,
1968.
    167 Dudley Rd., Newton, MA 02165

SCHULTZ, RALPH C.
    b. Dolton, Ill., 23 June 1932. Studied with
Herman Spies and Rossetter Cole in Chicago; with
Ross Lee Finney, Univ. of Michigan; Marcel Dick,
Cleveland Inst. of Music; and with Seth Bingham,
Union Theological Seminary, New York, S.M.D. He
was church music director in Cleveland, 1954-61;
from 1961, faculty member, Concordia Coll.,
Bronxville, N.Y.; and music director, Village
Lutheran Church.
    WORKS: ORCHESTRA: Intelligent man, a
suite; CHORUS: Let us all work with gladsome
voice, with orch.; Lutheran chorale mass, with
orch.; To Him be glory, with orch.; O sing unto
the Lord a new song; Sing for joy.
    6 Concordia Place, Bronxville, NY 10708

SCHUMACHER, STANLEY E.
    b. Indianapolis, Ind., 9 Aug. 1942. Studied
with Philip Slates, Jordan Coll., Butler Univ.,
B.M. 1964, M.M. 1966; with Marshall Barnes,
Herbert Brun, and David Behrman, Ohio State
Univ., Ph.D. 1976. He won first prize in a Phi
Mu Alpha Sinfonia contest, 1967. In 1978 he
joined the faculty at Rhode Island Junior Coll.
    WORKS: SMALL ENSEMBLES: Symmetries, 4 in-
struments, 1968; Beat me daddy, 8 to a bar, trombone, piano, string bass, 1969; Dialogue, 3 narrators and trombone, 1970; Musography 1, 2 clarinets, 3 trombones, 1972; Brassman, trombone,
trumpet, clarinet, violin, piano, female voice,
1978.
    305 Greenwich Ave., #B306, Warwick, RI 02886

SCHUMAN, WILLIAM HOWARD
    b. New York, N.Y., 4 Aug. 1910. Left the School
of Commerce, New York Univ., to study harmony
with Max Persin and counterpoint with Charles
Haubiel; attended Teachers Coll., Columbia Univ.,
B.S. 1935, M.A. 1937; studied conducting at the
Mozarteum, Salzburg, 1935; composition with Roy
Harris, Juilliard School, 1936-38. His many
honors include 2 Guggenheim fellowships, 1939,
1940; the first Pulitzer prize in music, 1943;
Koussevitzky Found. award; Music Critics' Circle
of New York award; Columbia Univ. Bicentennial
award, 1954; first Brandeis Univ. Creative Arts
award in music, 1957; Nat. Inst. of Arts and
Letters award; Gold Medal of Honor, Nat. Arts
Club; 20 honorary doctorates; MacDowell Medal,
1971; election to American Acad. of Arts and

Letters, 1973. He was faculty member, Sarah
Lawrence Coll., 1936-45; director of publications,
G. Schirmer, Inc., 1945-52; president of Juil-
liard School, 1945-62; president of Lincoln
Center, 1962-69.

WORKS: OPERA: The mighty Casey, baseball
opera, 1952, Hartford, Conn., 4 May 1953;
BALLET: Undertow--Choreographic episodes, 1945;
Judith--Choreographic poem, 1949; Voyage for a
theatre; Night journey, 1947; The witch of Endor;
ORCHESTRA: 10 symphonies, 1936, 1938, 1941,
1942, 1943, 1949, 1960, 1962, 1969, #10 The
American muse, dedicated to the Bicentennial,
premiere, Washington, 6 Apr. 1976; American Festival overture, Boston, 6 Oct. 1939; News reel
suite, 1941; Prayer in time of war, 1942;
William Billings overture, 1943; Circus overture,
1944; violin concerto, 1947; Boston, 10 Feb.
1950; Credendum--An article of faith, 1955; New
England triptych, 1956; A song of Orpheus, fantasy for cello and orch., 1961; Variations on
America, orchestration of Charles Ives's organ
work, New York, 21 May 1964; To thee, old cause,
oboe and orch.; In praise of Shahn--Canticle for
orch, 1969; Voyage for orchestra, 1971, New York,
9 Nov. 1975; Concerto on old English rounds,
solo viola, women's chorus, orch., Boston, 29
Nov. 1974; The young dead soldiers, with soprano
solo on texts by MacLeish, Washington, 6 Apr.
1976; Casey at the bat, cantata from the opera,
The mighty Casey, Washington, 6 Apr. 1976;
Amaryllis variations, string orch., Philadelphia,
27 July 1976; French horn fantasy, New York,
24 Jan. 1980; CHAMBER MUSIC: 4 string quartets,
1936, 1937, 1939, 1950; Quartettino, 4 bassoons,
1939; Voyage, a cycle for piano; 3 piano moods;
CHORUS: 4 canonic choruses, 1933; Prologues,
with orch., 1937; Prelude for voices, 1939; Mail
order madrigals; Requiescat, 1942; Holiday song,
1942; Te Deum, 1944; Truth shall deliver, 1946;
The Lord has a child, 1957; FILM SCORES: Steel-
town; The Earth is born, 1957; also band pieces,
songs.
    929 Park Ave., New York, NY 10028

SCHUMANN, WALTER
    b. New York, N.Y., 8 Oct. 1913; d. Minneapolis,
Minn., 21 Aug. 1958. Studied law and music,
Univ. of Southern California. He served in the
U.S. Army Air Force in World War II; was music
director for This is the army, New York; conducted Voices of Walter Schumann.
    WORKS: THEATRE: John Brown's body, opera,
1953; 3 for tonight, musical; FILM SCORES: The
night of the hunter; TELEVISION THEMES: "Drag-
net," Emmy award, 1955; "Steve Canyon."

SCHUYLER, PHILLIPA DUKE
    b. New York, N.Y., 22 Aug. 1931; d. Da Nang,
Vietnam, 9 May 1967. Attended a convent school;
studied piano privately. She made her debut
with the New York Philharmonic at age 14; made
3 world tours under the auspices of the U.S.
State Dept.; was guest artist at independence
celebrations in Leopoldville, Ghana, Madagascar;
played command performances for Emperor Haile
Selassie, the king and queen of Malaya, and
Queen Elizabeth of Belgium. She was author of

Who killed the Congo?; Jungle saints; Kingdom of
dreams.
    WORKS: ORCHESTRA: Rumpelstiltskin, re-
ceived Wayne Univ. award; Manhattan nocturne,
Detroit Symph. Orch. prize; White Nile suite.

SCHUYTEN, ERNEST EUGENE EMILE
    b. Antwerp, Belgium, 7 Nov. 1881; to U.S. 1915.
Graduated from Brussels Cons., 1900. He founded
the New Orleans Cons. in 1919; was dean, Coll.
of Music, Loyola Univ., 1932-52, while keeping
his affiliation with the conservatory. His compositions include a piano concerto, violin concerto, a symphony, chamber works, choral works,
and songs.

SCHWADRON, ABRAHAM A.
    b. Brooklyn, N.Y., 25 Dec. 1925. Studied with
Walter Ihrke, Univ. of Connecticut; with Hugo
Norden, Boston Univ. He taught in Connecticut
public schools, 1953-59; then on faculty, Rhode
Island Coll., 1959-68; Univ. of Hawaii, 1968-69;
and from 1969, at Univ. of California, Los
Angeles.
    WORKS: CHAMBER MUSIC: Short suite, clarinet
and trombone; other published chamber music and
choral pieces.
    11361 Elderwood St., Los Angeles, CA 90040

SCHWANTNER, JOSEPH
    b. Chicago, Ill., 22 Mar. 1943. Studied with
Benard Dieter, Chicago Cons., B.M. 1964; with
Alan Stout and Anthony Donato, Northwestern
Univ., M.M. 1966, D.M. 1968. His awards include
BMI student awards, 1965-67; Bearns prize, 1967;
Charles Ives scholarship, Nat. Inst. of Arts and
Letters, 1970; CAPS grants, 1973, 1977;
Rockefeller grant, 1978; Nat. Endowment for the
Arts grants, 1974, 1975, 1977; Guggenheim fellow-
ship, 1978-79; Pulitzer prize for Aftertones of
infinity for orch., 1979; and many commissions.
He was faculty member, Pacific Lutheran Univ.,
1968-69; Ball State Univ., 1970; from 1970, at
Eastman School of Music.
    WORKS: ORCHESTRA: Sinfonia brevis, 1963;
concertino for alto saxophone and 3 chamber ensembles, 1964; August canticle, 1968; Modus
caelestis, 12 flutes, 12 strings, piano, percussion, celeste, 1972; Aftertones of infinity,
New York, 29 Jan. 1979; WIND ENSEMBLE: And the
mountains are rising nowhere, 1977; CHAMBER
MUSIC: piano sonatina, 1962; Pastorale for
winds, 1963; nonet for piano and 18 instruments,
1965; Diaphonia intervallum, chamber ensemble,
1965; Entrophy, saxophone, clarinet, cello, 1967;
Chronicon, bassoon and piano, 1967; Enchiridion,
violin and piano, 1968; Consortium I, flute,
clarinet, string trio, 1970; Consortium II,
chamber ensemble, 1971; In aeternum II, organ,
1972; In aeternum, cello and 4 players, Harvard
Univ., 27 Feb. 1973; Shadows I, piano quartet,
1973; Autumn canticles, piano trio, 1974; Elixir,
6 players, Cambridge, Mass., 7 Oct. 1975; Canticle of the evening bells, chamber ensemble,
1976; Wild angels of the open hills, soprano,
flute, harp, 1977, New York, 2 Feb. 1978.
    21 Overbrook Rd., Rochester, NY 14624

SCHWARTZ, ELLIOTT

SCHWARTZ, ELLIOTT
b. Brooklyn, N.Y., 19 Jan. 1936. Studied with
Otto Luening and Jack Beeson, Columbia Univ.,
M.A. 1958; privately with Paul Creston; with
Henry Brant, Chou Wen-chung, Stefan Wolpe,
Bennington Composers Conf., 1961-66. His awards
include annual ASCAP awards from 1965; second
prize, Gaudeamus Internat. Music Week, 1970;
Maine State award, 1970; Ford Found. grants,
1969, 1971-72; Nat. Endowment for the Arts grants,
1974, 1976; residencies at MacDowell Colony,
1964-65, Wolf Trap Farm, 1976-77, Yaddo, 1977,
Univ. of California, San Diego, 1978, Rockefeller
Found. Study Center, Bellagio, Italy, 1978. He
was faculty member, Univ. of Massachusetts,
1960-64; from 1964, at Bowdoin Coll.; visiting
professor, Trinity Coll. of Music, London, 1967,
Univ. of California, Santa Barbara, 1970, 1973,
1974.
WORKS: ORCHESTRA: Magic music; Texture,
chamber orch., 1966; Island, 1970; Janus, piano
and orch., 1976; piano concerto, St. Paul Chamber
Orch., 18 Feb. 1978; CHAMBER MUSIC: Concert
piece, 10 players, 1965; Soliloquies, flute,
clarinet, violin, piano, 1965; Essays, trumpet
and trombone, 1966; Arias #1-5, various duets;
flute sonata; oboe sonata; Dialogue #1, double
bass solo; Miniconcerto, flute, oboe, string
trio, 1969; Graffiti, violin and cello; septet,
5 instruments, piano, speaker/singer; Decline
and fall of the sonata, 1973; Serenade, flute,
bass, percussion; Divertimento #2, 2 horns, 2
keyboard players; ELECTRONIC: Interruption,
woodwind quintet and tape, 1964; Music for
Napoleon and Beethoven, trumpet, piano, 2 tapes,
assistant, 1970; 3 islands, chamber ensemble,
with ostinato accompaniment of British weather
reports on tape, 1970; Echo music II, woodwind
quartet and tape, 1974; A Bowdoin anthology,
chamber ensemble, tape, narrator, Bowdoin Coll.,
17 Oct. 1976. He is author of Electronic music:
A listener's guide, New York, 1973.
5 Atwood Lane, Brunswick, ME 04011

SCHWARTZ, FRANCIS
b. Altoona, Pa., 10 Mar. 1940. Studied with
Vittorio Giannini, Juilliard School, B.S. 1961,
M.S. 1962. In 1966 he joined the faculty at
Univ. of Puerto Rico; was visiting professor,
Univ. of Paris, 1977-78; music critic, San Juan
Star, 1966-77.
WORKS: THEATRE: Is there sex in heaven?,
chamber opera, 1977; ORCHESTRA: Plegaria, voice
and orch., 1971; Prayer for Puerto Rico, girl's
voice and orch., 1972; I protest, commissioned
for Casals Festival, San Juan, 23 Mar. 1974;
CHAMBER MUSIC: Homage to an obscenity, narrator
and percussion, 1968; My name is Caligula . . .
What's yours?, narrator and audience, 1970; My
eyebrows are not bushy, violin or viola solo,
1971; Cannibal-Caliban, chamber ensemble, 1975;
CHORUS: Antigone, with piano, violin, flute,
soprano, 1967; The temple of the flower, with
chamber ensemble, 1978; MULTIMEDIA: Auschwitz,
tape, aroma, lights, dancers, San Juan, 15 May
1968; Time, sound, and the hooded man, Buenos
Aires, 3 Mar. 1975. He is author with Dr. Maria
Luiza Muñoz of El mundo de la musica, Puerto

Rico, 1974.
Universidad de Puerto Rico, Rio Piedras, PR
00931

SCHWARTZ, JULIE
b. Washington, D.C., 17 Apr. 1947. Has studied
with Ron Nelson, Hall Overton, and Jacob
Druckman; with Julius Eastman, Frederic Rzewski,
and Gordon Mumma at New Music in N.H., 1973.
She received a Nat. Fed. of Music Clubs junior
award for a piano composition, 1962. She taught
at the Arts Center, Albany, N.Y., 1973-75; then
joined the faculty at Mary Coll.
WORKS: CHAMBER MUSIC: Matrix I, winds and
strings; Breathpace, solo oboe; Homespun, vocal
quartet, strings, percussion; Rounds, chamber
ensemble; And so do I like to bang and tootle?,
flute and percussion; In return, string quartet.
Mary College, Bismarck, ND 58501

SCHWARTZ, MARVIN ROBERT
b. Bronx, N.Y., 4 Feb. 1937. Studied with Luigi
Dallapiccola and Leo Kraft, Queens Coll., B.A.
1957; with Irving Fine, Harold Shapero, Arthur
Berger, Brandeis Univ., M.F.A. 1959; at Jewish
Theological Seminary, D.S.M. 1964. He received
the Ernest Bloch Memorial award, 1961; MacDowell
fellowship, 1962. He joined the faculty at
Queensborough Community Coll. in 1969, has been
professor from 1974; was on adjunct faculty,
Queens Coll., 1970-75.
WORKS: OPERA: Look and long, 2 acts, after
Gertrude Stein, commissioned and premiered by the
After Dinner Opera Company, 1972; ORCHESTRA:
Lament, 1974; Spaces, 1974; CHAMBER MUSIC: Variations for piano, 1959; Scherzo, violin and
piano, 1965; Tal, baritone and organ, 1969; 3s
and 2s for 3, woodwinds, 1970; 3 canons of love,
baritone and string trio, 1972; Jabberwocky,
tenor and piano, 1975; piano sonata, 1975-76;
CHORUS: Ruth, with soloists and orch., 1967; In
memoriam, Fredric Kurzweil, with soloists and
chamber ensemble, 1971; Letter to David Randolph
(and Mildred), for male madrigalists, 1976.
166-10 75th Ave., Flushing, NY 11366

SCHWARTZ, PAUL
b. Vienna, Austria, 27 July 1907; U.S. citizen
1944. Studied at Vienna State Acad., diploma in
piano and composition, master diploma in composition and conducting. He was chairman, music
dept., Bard Coll., 1938-47; held same position,
Kenyon Coll., 1947-71, and professor of church
music, 1947-61; director, Knox County Symph.,
1966-71; composer-in-residence at Kenyon Coll.,
1976 to retirement in 1978.
WORKS: CHAMBER OPERA: The experiment, text
by his wife, Kathryn, 1956; ORCHESTRA: Serenade,
string orch., 1941; concertino for chamber orch.,
1947; Overture to a Shakespeare comedy, 1948;
Variations on an Ohio folk tune, 1952; Prelude
to an evening out, overture, 1966; violin concerto, 1968; concerto grosso, 1972; CHAMBER
MUSIC: string quartet, 1936; piano trio, 1939;
violin sonata, 1941; chamber concerto for 2
pianos, 1944; piano quintet, 1977; CHORUS:
Sacred concerto, with orch., 1960; Spirit divine,
festival anthem, with brass and organ, 1973;

America celebrates, cantata, with soloists, narrator, and orch., 1976.
P.O. Box 351, Gambier, OH 43022

SCHWARZ, IRA PAUL
b. Sheldon, Iowa, 24 Feb. 1922. Studied at U.S. Naval School of Music, 1942; at Morningside Coll., A.B. 1952; Univ. of South Dakota, M.A. 1954; with Philip Bezanson and Richard Hervig, Univ. of Iowa, Ph.D.; also with Thaddeus Jones and Nadia Boulanger. He has received many commissions. He served in navy bands, 1941-47; was faculty member, Univ. of South Dakota, 1955-58; Univ. of Iowa, 1958-61; Minot State Coll., 1961-65; Northeast Missouri State Univ., 1966-68; Univ. of Southern Mississippi, 1968-70; from 1970, State Univ. Coll., Brockport, N.Y.; has conducted many local bands and orchestras.
WORKS: OPERA: The wedding, 1968; BALLET: After Xenophanes, 1977; ORCHESTRA: Concert overture, 1972; CHAMBER MUSIC: string quartet, 1960; woodwind quintet, 1960; CHORUS: Abraham and Isaac, cantata, with orch., 1967. He was author of A brief source book for humanities and related arts, 1971; coauthor, Teaching the related arts, 1973.
P.O. Box 115, Brockport, NY 14420

SCHWERDTFEGER, E. ANNE (formerly Sr. M. Ernest, O.P.)
b. Galveston, Tex., 1 Feb. 1930. Studied with Arthur Hall, Dominican Coll., Houston; with Clifton Williams, Univ. of Texas; with Carl Hager, Univ. of Notre Dame. She taught at Dominican Coll., Houston, 1958-72.
WORKS: ORCHESTRA: Exaudi Domini, string orch., 1959; Christus rex, chamber orch., 1960; symphony in 1 movement, 1963; CHAMBER MUSIC: Modal suite, harp and tuba, 1960; Variations on an Irish air, 6 harps, 1962; CHORUS: Amo Christum, 1957; Hymn of St. Francis, 1961; Mass in honor of St. Martin de Porres, 1965; 2 pieces on texts by Tagore, 1969; PIANO: Toccatina, 1962; Modal suite, 1965; Charivari, 1966.
via Giovanni Stanchi 7, Rome, Italy

SCIANNI, JOSEPH
b. Memphis, Tenn., 6 Oct. 1928. Studied at Southwestern at Memphis, B.S. 1949; with Bernard Rogers and Howard Hanson, Eastman School of Music, M.M. 1953, D.M.A. 1959. His awards include the Benjamin award, 1958; Nat. Council on the Arts awards, 1970, 1971, 1972; ASCAP awards, 1971, 1972, 1973, 1977. He was faculty member, New York Coll. of Music, 1965-68; New York Univ., 1968-71; from 1971, Staten Island Community Coll., CUNY.
WORKS: ORCHESTRA: Sinfonia breve, 1958; Adagio cantibile, 1958; WIND ENSEMBLE: Air for band, 1955; Court Square, 1957; JAZZ ORCHESTRA: Red Phantom rides again, 1969; Florence in July, 1969; Gaza strip, 1970; Big orange, 1971; Alligator pear, 1972; Granite ridge, 1973; CHAMBER MUSIC: Chorale and fugue, brass quartet, 1955; Lament, solo flute, 1962; PIANO: 4 movements, 1962; Man running, 1966; ELECTRONIC: Horizon south, bass and electronic mutations, 1962; Photographs (8 x 10), 1977-78; FILM SCORE: Another time, another place.
400 2nd Ave., #11D, New York, NY 10010

SCIAPIRO, MICHEL (Michael Fielding)
b. Odessa, Russia, 6 Apr. 1891; to U.S. in youth; d. New York, N.Y., 3 Mar. 1962. Studied violin with Hugo Heermann and Otakar Sevcik; was concert violinist at age 5; soloist with Berlin Philharmonic, Vienna Konzert Vereins Orch.; member of Arnhem Symph.; organized his own orchestra. His compositions included Fantasy for string quartet; many violin pieces and songs.

SCLATER, JAMES STANLEY
b. Mobile, Ala., 24 Oct. 1943. Studied with William Presser, Univ. of Southern Mississippi; with Hunter Johnson, Univ. of Texas, D.M.A. His awards include the Ostwald prize for new band music, 1974; and commissions. He was music librarian, Austin Public Library, 1969-70; from 1970, on faculty, Mississippi Coll.; principal clarinetist, Jackson Symph., 1971-78.
WORKS: ORCHESTRA: symphony; American images; BAND: Columbia eagle march; Prelude and variations on "Gone is my mistris"; Mobile suite; Visions; CHAMBER MUSIC: suite for clarinet and piano; woodwind trio; Concert piece, brass quintet; piano sonata; suite for 2 pianos; VOICE: Songs of time and passing; 4 songs on texts of Emily Dickinson.
709 E. Leake St., Clinton, MS 39056

SCOTT, JOHN NEWHALL
b. Portland, Oreg., 11 May 1907; d. 25 July 1963. Studied at Univ. of Washington. He was pianist in dance bands, theatre, film, and radio. His compositions included the film score for My darling Clementine and songs.

SCOTT, JOHN PRINDLE
b. Norwich, N.Y., 16 Aug. 1877; d. Syracuse, N.Y., 2 Dec. 1932. Studied at Oberlin Cons. and privately. He was vocal soloist and teacher; composed many songs.

SCOTT, ROBERT W. (BOBBY)
b. Mt. Pleasant, N.Y., 29 Jan. 1937. Studied with Eduard Moritz; is pianist and arranger with dance bands. His works include the musical, Dinny and the witches; music for the play, A taste of honey: and quintet for horn and strings, New York, 5 May 1974.

SCOTT, STEPHEN
b. Corvallis, Oreg., 10 Oct. 1944. Studied with Homer Keller, Univ. of Oregon, B.A.; with Paul Nelson and Gerald Shapiro, Brown Univ., M.A. 1969. He has been faculty member, Colorado Coll. from 1969.
WORKS: ORCHESTRA: Variations on an American folk tune; CHAMBER MUSIC: Baby Ben, 10 instruments; The Dee Wright Observatory, 2 pianos, 8 hands; ELECTRONIC: 5 Ferlinghetti poems, narrator, instruments, tape; Suspended animation, instruments and tape recorders; Glacier music, woodwind quintet and tape recorders.
Colorado College, Colorado Springs, CO 80903

SCOTT, TOM (THOMAS JEFFERSON)
b. Campbellsburg, Ky., 28 May 1912; d. New York, N.Y., 12 Aug. 1961. Studied violin with his

SCOTT-HUNTER, HORTENSE

uncle; composition later with George Antheil in
Los Angeles, and with Harrison Kerr and
Wallingford Reigger.
WORKS: OPERA: The fisherman, 1936; ORCHES-
TRA: Song with dance, 1932; Plymouth Rock, 1938;
Hornpipe and chantey, 1944; symphony, 1946; From
the sacred harp, 1946; Johnny Appleseed, 1948;
Lento, saxophone and strings, 1953; Binorie variations, 1953; CHAMBER MUSIC: 2 string quartets,
1944, 1956; Emily Dickinson suite, violin and
harp, 1955; CHORUS: Ballad of the harp weaver,
with narrator and string quartet, 1946; Go down
death; Creation, with instrumental ensemble.

SCOTT-HUNTER, HORTENSE
Studied at Peabody Cons. Her chamber operas,
Pelleas and Melisande and Harlequin in search of
his heart, were presented by the New York Opera
Workshop, 1959; Maid of the mist, a ballet, was
performed in Baltimore, Sept. 1956; other works
include incidental music for The little world of
Kim Hai, 1959; Ad Te Domine, levavi, cantata,
1960; Love song, 1961.

SCOVILLE, MARGARET
b. Pasadena, Calif., 3 May 1944. Studied with
William Kothe, Ramon Fuller, Lejaren Hiller,
Morton Feldman, State Univ. of New York at
Buffalo.
WORKS: CHAMBER MUSIC: 4 fragments from
Empedocles, soprano, flute, piano; Ephemerae,
violin, 2 violas, cello; Time out of mind, 2 per-
cussionists; ELECTRONIC: Electric Sunday, tape;
Number 9 (untitled), tape; 13 ways of looking at
a blackbird, chamber ensemble and tape.

SEAMAN, EUGENE L.
b. New York, N.Y., 13 Oct. 1920. Studied with
Marion Bauer and Philip James, New York Univ.;
with Fritz Mahler and Carl Friedberg, Juilliard
School; piano privately with Josef and Rosina
Lhevinne, and in France and Germany. He was
faculty member, Syrian State Cons., 1953-54;
Critics Choice Music School, New York, 1970-76;
Univ. of Taiwan, 1976-77; partner in Seaman
Concert Management from 1971.
WORKS: ORCHESTRA: Concert piece, piano and
orch.; CHAMBER MUSIC: Variations on a theme of
Couperin, violin and piano; Andante, flute and
piano; 12 studies, solo flute; 2 dance pairs,
piano trio; PIANO: Boatrow I and II; Revolu-
tionara suite; Arabic tunes, 2 pianos.
1697 Broadway, New York, NY 10019

SEAR, WALTER
b. New Orleans, La., 28 Apr. 1930. Studied with
George Rochberg, Curtis Inst. of Music; with
Thaddeus Jones, Catholic Univ.; and with Otto
Luening, Columbia Univ. He received the Sosland
Chamber Music award. He was on the faculty,
Mannes Coll. of Music, 1967-72; Trenton State
Coll., 1970-72; has since operated his own elec-
tronic music studio.
WORKS: ORCHESTRA: 2 symphonies; CHAMBER
MUSIC: 3 string quartets; sonata for unaccom-
panied tuba; and film scores. He is author of
The new world of electronic music, New York,
1972.
235 W. 46th St., New York, NY 10036

SEARS, ILENE HANSON
b. Crookston, Minn., 31 Aug. 1938. Studied with
Bernhard Heiden and Thomas Beversdorf, Indiana
Univ. She was on the faculty, Salem Coll.,
Winston-Salem, N.C., 1967-68; from 1968, at
Winston-Salem State Univ.
WORKS: CHAMBER MUSIC: piano sonatina;
cello sonata; CHORUS: 3 Christmas carols.
136 Rosedale Circle, Winston-Salem, NC 27102

SEAVER, BLANCHE EBERT
b. Chicago, Ill., 15 Sept. 1891. Studied with
her father and others; received the Jane Addams
award from Rockford Coll.; was named Woman of
the Year by the Los Angeles Times in 1964. Her
works include a pontifical mass and many songs.
20 Chester Place, Los Angeles, CA 90007

SEAVER, HARRY A.
b. Albany, N.Y., 20 Jan. 1909. Studied at
Harvard Univ., B.A. 1933.
WORKS: CHAMBER MUSIC: flute sonatina;
Heaven storming rhapsody, 2 pianos, 1932; violin
sonata, 1936; 3 Irish poems, cello and piano,
1936; piano quintet, 1936.

SEBESKY, GERALD J.
b. Perth Amboy, N.J., 8 Sept. 1941. Studied
with Robert Lincoln, Rutgers Univ.; with Chou
Wen-chung and Stefan Wolpe, Columbia Univ.,
diploma; at Manhattan School of Music, B.M., M.M.
His awards include a New Jersey State Council on
the Arts grant; and a Phi Mu Alpha composition
award. He has taught in New Jersey public
schools from 1964.
WORKS: BAND: Passacaglia and interlude;
Structures VII; CHAMBER MUSIC: brass quintet
#2; Montage for woodwinds; many published works
for band, stage band, and chorus.
P.O. Box 678, Edison, NJ 08817

SECUNDA, SHOLOM
b. Alexandria, Russia, 23 Aug. 1894; U.S. citizen 1918; d. New York, N.Y., 13 June 1974.
Studied at Cooper Union, 1912-13; Columbia Univ.,
1913-14; Inst. of Musical Art, 1914-19; with
Ernest Bloch on a scholarship. He was named a
fellow, Internat. Inst. of Arts and Letters,
1961. During World War I, he was arranger for a
navy band; was music critic for the Jewish Daily
Forward; lecturer at Hunter Coll.
WORKS: OPERA: Sulamith, 1925; about 50
operettas; ORCHESTRA: 3 symphonic sketches; If
not higher, oratorio, with chorus and soloists;
also chamber music; Jewish liturgical music; and
songs, including the very popular Bei mir bist
du schoen.

SEEGER, CHARLES LOUIS, JR.
b. Mexico City, Mex., 14 Dec. 1886; d. Bridgewater, Conn., 7 Feb. 1979. Studied at Harvard
Univ., A.B. 1908. He taught at Univ. of California, 1912-19; Inst. of Musical Art, 1921-33;
New School for Social Research, 1931-35; was
assistant music director, Fed. Music Project,
WPA, 1938-40; chief, music division, Pan-American
Union, 1941-53. He was married to Ruth Crawford,
the composer. Though chiefly a musicologist, he

composed music for the pageants, <u>Derdra</u>, 1914, and <u>The queen's masque</u>, 1951; an overture, violin sonata, and songs.

SEEGER, RUTH CRAWFORD. See CRAWFORD-SEEGER, RUTH

SEGALL, BERNARDO
    b. Campinas, Brazil, 4 Aug. 1911. Studied piano with Alexander Siloti, composition with Lazare Saminsky in New York; received an honorary degree from Sao Paulo Cons.; has been concert pianist from age 9.
    WORKS: BALLET: <u>As I lay dying</u>; <u>Domino furioso</u>; <u>The wall</u>; <u>Desperate heart</u>; <u>And dreams intrude</u>; THEATRE: music for <u>Camino real</u>; <u>Skin of our teeth</u>; <u>The sound and the fury</u>; FILM SCORES: <u>Congolaise</u>; <u>Hope is eternal</u>; <u>The luck of Ginger Coffey</u>; and songs.

SEIDEL, RICHARD D.
    b. Reading, Pa., 4 Aug. 1925. Studied at Lebanon Valley Coll., B.S.; Philadelphia Cons., M.M. cum laude; Montclair State Coll., M.S.; composition with Harry Robert Wilson. He was high school choral music director, 1958-67; then chairman, Div. of Fine Arts, Centenary Coll. for Women.
    WORKS: CHORUS: <u>Christmas lullaby</u>, women's voices; <u>Go lovely rose</u>; <u>Psalm 23</u>; 2 sets of songs for children.
    8 George Ave., Wyomissing, PA 19610

SELBST, GEORGE
    b. New York, N.Y., 21 Feb. 1917. Studied at Juilliard School; New York Coll. of Music; and with Jacob Weinberg, Manhattan School of Music. He was director of music and curriculum for exceptional children, Suffolk County, N.Y., 1957-65; then public school music teacher, Islip, N.Y., and conductor, Islip Symph. Orch.
    WORKS: ORCHESTRA: symphony; violin concerto; CHAMBER MUSIC: sonatas; sonatinas; LITURGICAL: <u>Hebrew requiem</u>; organ preludes; other sacred and secular works.
    96-C Enfield Court, Ridge, NY 11961

SELIG, ROBERT
    b. Evanston, Ill., 1939. Studied with Anthony Donato, Northwestern Univ., B.M. 1961, M.M. 1962; with Irving Fine, Brandeis Univ., 1962; Halsey Stevens, Univ. of Southern California, 1963; Gardner Read, Boston Univ., 1966-68; privately with Donald Martino and Ernst Krenek; and at Tanglewood, 1966, 1968, 1972, on fellowships. He was awarded performance of his 1st symphony, 1962; several scholarships; Boston Univ. grant, 1966; Fromm Found. grant, 1968; 2 Guggenheim fellowships, 1972, 1977; Mass. Arts and Humanities Found. grant, 1975. He was assistant composer, United Artists Music Co., 1964-66; from 1968, on faculty, New England Cons.
    WORKS: OPERA: <u>Chocorua</u>, Tanglewood, 2 Aug. 1972; ORCHESTRA: <u>Chicago: 3 portraits of a city</u>, chamber orch.; <u>Athena</u>, mezzo-soprano and string orch., 1962; 2 symphonies, 1962, 1969; <u>Mirage</u>, trumpet and strings, 1968; <u>Rhapsody</u>, with flute, violin, bass clarinet solos; CHAMBER

MUSIC: violin sonata, 1960; <u>3 songs to texts of D.H. Lawrence</u>, baritone, Tanglewood, 22 July 1966; string quartet; woodwind quintet; <u>The 3 seasons of autumn</u>, voice, flute, cello, percussion, Boston, 2 Feb. 1973; <u>Pometa comet, 1676</u>, wind ensemble, Boston, 5 Nov. 1975; <u>Variations for brass quintet</u>, Boston, 11 Apr. 1977; CHORUS: <u>Islands</u>, cantata on text of Millay's <u>Mist in the valley</u>, with orch., Cambridge, Mass., 24 May 1976.
    153 Walden St., Cambridge, MA 02140

SELLECK, JOHN
    b. Billings, Mont., 9 Apr. 1939. Studied at Univ. of Montana, B.M.; with Elliott Carter, Mel Powell, Bulent Arel, Yale Univ., M.M.; with Chou Wen-chung and Mario Davidovsky, Columbia Univ., D.M.A. 1975. He received the Woods Chandler award in composition, 1964. He was staff member, music dept., Princeton Univ., 1968-72; composer-in-residence, Four Winds Theatre, N.Y., 1967-77; from 1977, pianist, dance dept., North Carolina School of the Arts.
    WORKS: CHAMBER MUSIC: piano trio, 1963; <u>Divisions</u>, chamber orch., 1975; <u>Chamber music on poems of James Joyce</u>, tenor and string quartet, 1976; ELECTRONIC: <u>Migrations</u>, New York, 14 Jan. 1974; <u>Ichinen Sangen</u>, New York, 22 Feb. 1974; <u>Elementals</u>, 1978.
    4720 Hawkedale Dr., Winston-Salem, NC 27106

SELMER, KATHRYN LANDE
    b. Staten Island, N.Y., 6 Nov. 1930. Studied at Eastman School of Music and at Juilliard School. She has been singer and composer for NBC's "Birthday House" and "Captain Kangaroo." Her works include the children's operas: <u>The Shoemaker and the elf</u>; <u>The princess and the pea</u>; <u>The princess who couldn't laugh</u>; and songs.

SEMEGEN, DARIA
    b. Bamberg, Germany, 27 June 1946; U.S. citizen 1957. Studied with Samuel Adler, Robert Gauldin, Burrill Phillips, Eastman School of Music; with Witold Lutoslawski in Warsaw; with Bulent Arel, Yale Univ.; and with Vladimir Ussachevsky, Columbia Univ. Her awards include BMI awards, 1967-69; Chautauqua, MacDowell, and Tanglewood fellowships; Fulbright grant, 1968-69; Mu Phi Epsilon prize, 1968; Woods-Chandler and Bradford-Keeler prizes, Yale Univ., 1970-71; Rapaport fellowship, Columbia Univ., 1970-73; Nat. Endowment for the Arts grants, 1974, 1975; ICSM electronic music prize, 1975; and commissions. She was staff technician, Columbia-Princeton Electronic Music Studio, 1971-75; faculty member, State Univ. of New York at Stony Brook, from 1974.
    WORKS: ORCHESTRA: <u>Triptych</u>, 1966; CHAMBER MUSIC: <u>Quattro</u>, flute and piano, 1967; <u>3 pieces</u>, clarinet and piano, 1968; <u>Jeux des quatres</u>, aleatoric work for 4 players, 1970; <u>Music for violin solo</u>, 1973; VOICE: <u>Lieder auf der Flucht</u>, soprano and 8 players, 1967; <u>Dans la nuit</u>, baritone and chamber orch., 1969; ELECTRONIC: <u>Composition #1</u>, tape, 1972; <u>Spectra--study</u>, tape, 1977; <u>Arc: Music for dancers</u>, tape, 1977.
    State University of New York, Stony Brook, NY 11794

SEMMLER, ALEXANDER

SEMMLER, ALEXANDER
b. Dortmund, Germany, 12 Nov. 1900; U.S. citizen 1930; d. Kingston, N.Y., 24 Apr. 1977. Studied piano with Joseph Pembaur, composition with Gustav Jenner; musicology at Universities of Marburg, Berlin, and Munich. He was concert pianist at age 15, touring Europe and the U.S.; was pianist with CBS Symphony, then staff conductor at CBS in the 1940s. As special consultant to the U.S. State Dept., he was American administrator, music dept., RIAS West Berlin; presented concerts and lectures in Mexico on invitation of the Mexican Cultural Ministry, 1953-54; in New York, 1955-70, was music director for a publisher and record company.
WORKS: ORCHESTRA: Times Square overture; American Indian suite; CHAMBER MUSIC: piano trio, 1964; CHORUS: The owl and the pussy cat; works for solo instruments, voice, etc.

SENDREY, ALBERT RICHARD
b. Chicago, Ill., 26 Dec. 1911. Studied with his father, Alfred Sendrey, in Leipzig; at Trinity Coll., London; also with John Barbirolli and Albert Coates. He was arranger for film companies in Paris and London, 1935-44, then in Hollywood.
WORKS: OPERA: Bohème-A-go-go, rock opera, 1971; ORCHESTRA: Oriental suite, 1935; 3 symphonies; piano concertino; Toccata and fugue; CHAMBER MUSIC: 2 string quartets; Divertimento, for cello; viola sonata; duo for horn and viola.

SENDREY, ALFRED (SZENDREI, ALADAR)
b. Budapest, Hungary, 29 Feb. 1884; permanently to U.S. in 1940; d. Los Angeles, 3 Mar. 1976. Conducted opera in Chicago, 1911-12, New York, 1913-14; Berlin, 1914-15, Vienna, 1915-16, Leipzig, 1918-24; then conducted orchestras in Leipsig, 1924-32; went to Paris in 1933, to U.S. in 1940; became a teacher in Los Angeles; was professor of Jewish music, Univ. of Judaism, Los Angeles, 1962-73. His compositions included a 1-act opera; orchestral pieces; works for solo instruments; choral music.

SENIA, PAUL ANTHONY
b. Brooklyn, N.Y., 26 Aug. 1925. Studied with David Diamond, Juilliard School, B.M. 1949; with Gerald Strang, Ernst Krenek, and Maximilian Rossi; at Los Angeles Cons., B.M. 1956, M.M. 1957. He was faculty member, Los Angeles Cons., 1957-63; Black Foxe High School, 1963-66; then joined the staff of the Los Angeles Bureau of Music; from 1966, conductor, Los Angeles Pops Symph. His compositions include a sonata, 1972; piano quartet, 1973.

SEREBRIER, JOSE
b. Montevideo, Uruguay, 3 Dec. 1938; to U.S. 1956. Studied at Curtis Inst. of Music, B.M. 1958; conducting at Univ. of Minnesota on fellowships, M.A. 1960. Other awards include BMI student composer award, 1956; Koussevitzky Found. award, 1956; 2 Guggenheim fellowships, 1957, 1958; Pan-American Union publication award; various conducting awards. While in high school, he organized and conducted the first high school

orchestra in Uruguay, which toured the country giving nearly 100 concerts in 4 years. He made his New York conducting debut with the American Symph. Orch. in 1965; has since conducted extensively in both Americas and Europe.
WORKS: ORCHESTRA: symphony #1, 1956; Momento psicologico, strings and backstage trumpet, 1957; Partita, 1960; Elegy for strings, 1962; Poema elegiaco, 1963; The star wagon, 1967; Nueve-ritual, with solo double bass, 1970; Colores magicos, with solo harp and lights, Washington, 20 May 1971; CHAMBER MUSIC: Pequena musica, woodwind quintet, 1956; Fantasia, string quartet #4; Manitowabing, flute and oboe; violin sonata, 1954; quartet for saxophones, 1960; Symphony for percussion, 5 players, 1960; also vocal works, piano pieces.
220 Riverside Dr., New York, NY 10025

SERIO, JOSEPH M.
b. Baltimore, Md., 15 Oct. 1930. Studied with Conrad Bernier, George T. Jones, and Russell Woollen, Catholic Univ. He received the Newman Found. award, 1963. He has been church music director from 1958; from 1969, at St. Margaret's Church, Bel Air.
WORKS: ORCHESTRA: Variations, fugue, and finale on a Gregorian psalm tone; CHORUS: Mass in ancient mode; Mass in honor of St. Margaret; Now thank we all our God, with brass and organ; Veni Creator Spiritus, with harp, brass, organ; brass quartet and organ: Variations on Pueri haebreorum.
10 Vermont Place, Bel Air, MD 21014

SERLY, TIBOR
b. Losonc, Hungary, 25 Nov. 1901; U.S. citizen 1909; d. London, England, 8 Oct. 1978 (in an accident). Came to the U.S. as a very young child; studied piano and violin with his father, Lajos Serly; by age 14, had mastered harmony, counterpoint, and composition. In the early 1920s, he accepted a scholarship to study in Budapest with Zoltan Kodaly and Bela Bartok, violin with Hubay, at the Royal Acad. of Music, graduating with highest honors as composer and performer. He was violist with the Cincinnati Symph., Philadelphia Orch., and the NBC Symphony. He developed new techniques for string players, for singers (Consovowels), for manual conducting, and for composition (Modus Lascivus); completed and orchestrated Bartok's viola concerto and 3rd piano concerto; transcribed for orchestra the Mikrokosmos suite and other early piano pieces of Bartok; and was the first conductor to record several Bartok compositions. He was guest conductor and composer-conductor with many major orchestras in the U.S. and Europe.
WORKS: BALLET: Mischchianza, 1937; Ex-machina, 1943; ORCHESTRA: viola concerto, 1929; 2 symphonies, 1931, 1932; 6 dance designs, 1934; Transylvania suite, chamber orch., 1935; Sonata concertante, string orch., 1936; Pagan city, symphonic poem, 1938; Elegy, 1945; Rhapsody, viola and orch., 1948; concerto for 2 pianos, 1952; trombone concerto, 1953; Fun with instruments of the orchestra, 1954; Symphonic variations, audience and orch., 1956; string sym-

phony, 1956; Little Xmas cantata, audience and orch., 1957; Lament (Homage to Bartok), string orch., 1958; concerto for violin and wind symphony, 1958; American fantasy of quodlibets, 1959; Concertino, 3 times 3, piano and chamber orch., 1965; String symphony in 4 cycles, for young people, 1974; CHAMBER MUSIC: violin sonata, 1923; string quartet, 1924; Innovations, strings and 2 harps, 1933, rev. for string quartet and harp, 1968; sonata for solo violin, 1947; trio for clarinet, violin, piano, 1950; Chorale, 3 harps, 1967; Canonic prelude, 4 harps, 1967; Stringometrics, violin and harp, 1968; Canonic fugue, 10 strings, 1972; Bi-modals, 2 recorders, 1973; Fantasy on a double quodlibet, 3 harps or 3 groups, 1973; VOICE: 4 songs from James Joyce's Chamber music, 1926; Strange story, mezzo-soprano and orch., 1927; Consovowels, #1, solo soprano, 1968, #2, soprano and clarinet, 1970, #3, soprano and clarinet, 1971; The Pleiades, symphonic choir, Portland, Oreg., 6 May 1978; PIANO: sonata, 1946; suite for 2 pianos, 1946; 40 etudes from Modus Lascivus were performed by Serly's wife, Miriam Molin, New York, 4 May 1977.

SESSIONS, ROGER HUNTINGTON
b. Brooklyn, N.Y., 28 Dec. 1896. Studied at Harvard Univ., A.B. 1915; with Horatio Parker, Yale Univ., B.M. 1917; and privately with Ernest Bloch in Cleveland. His many awards include 2 Guggenheim fellowships, 1926-28; Damrosch and Prix de Rome fellowships in Rome, 1928-31; Naumburg Found. award, 1949; New York Music Critics' Circle award, 1950; 5 honorary doctorates, 1958-71; membership in American Acad. of Arts and Sciences, Internat. Society for Contemporary Music, Nat. Inst. of Arts and Letters; NIAL Gold Medal, 1961; Boston Symph. Orch. Horblit award, 1977. He has taught at Smith Coll.; Cleveland Inst. of Music; Boston Univ.; New Jersey Coll. for Women; Princeton Univ., 1935-45, 1952-65; from 1972, at Juilliard School; and was visiting composer, Univ. of Iowa, 1971.
WORKS: OPERA: The trial of Lucullus, 1946; Montezuma, 1947, American premiere, Boston, 31 May 1976; ORCHESTRA: The black maskers, suite, 1923; 8 symphonies, 1927-68; violin concerto, 1935; Scherzino and march, 1938; Idyll of Theocritus, soprano and orch., 1954; piano concerto, 1956; Divertimento, 1960, New York premiere, 5 Dec. 1977; Rhapsody for orch., Baltimore, 18 Mar. 1970; concerto for violin and cello, New York, 5 Nov. 1971; concertino for chamber orch., Chicago, 14 Apr. 1972; CHAMBER MUSIC: 3 piano sonatas, 1930, 1946, 1965; 2 string quartets, 1936, 1950; From my diary, piano, 1940; duo for violin and piano, 1942; sonata for violin solo, 1953; string quartet, 1958; 5 pieces for piano, 1974-75, Berkshire Music Center, 15 Aug. 1977; CHORUS: Turn, O libertad, 1943; mass in celebration of the 50th anniversary of Kent School, 1955; Psalm 140, 1963; 3 choruses on Biblical texts, with chamber orch., Amherst Coll., 8 Feb. 1975; When lilacs last in the dooryard bloomed, with soloists and orch., Whitman text, Univ. of California,

Berkeley, 23 May 1971, first professional performance, Chicago, 29 Jan. 1976.
63 Stanworth Lane, Princeton, NJ 08540

SEVERY, VIOLET CAVELL
b. Pasadena, Calif., 26 May 1912. Studied with W. B. Olds and Wayne Bohrnstedt, Univ. of Redlands, B.M., M.M.; with Juan Orrego-Salas, Indiana Univ.; John Barnes Chance, Univ. of Kentucky; privately with Frances Marion Ralston. She was faculty member, Morehead State Univ., 1956-76.
WORKS: CHORUS: Psalmotet, with boy soprano, baritone, organ and plucked instrument, 1970; also chamber works.

SEVITZKY, FABIEN
b. Vyshny Volochek, Russia, 30 Sept. 1893; U.S. citizen 1928; d. Athens, Greece, 2 Feb. 1967 (while there for an appearance as guest conductor). He was a nephew of Serge Koussevitzky, who suggested that Fabien shorten his name to avoid confusion between 2 double bass players/ conductors. He studied at St. Petersburg Cons., Russia, and at DePauw Univ., D.M. His awards included 2 honorary doctorates; Cavalier Order de Boyaca, Columbia, S.A. In 1925 he founded the Philadelphia String Chamber Sinfonietta; conducted Philadelphia Grand Opera, 1927-28; Pennsylvania Opera Co., 1928-30; Peoples Symph. Orch., Boston, 1932-35; Indianapolis Symph., 1937-55; Indianapolis Symphonic Choir, 1937-55; Greater Miami Phil., 1965-66, music consultant, 1966-67; also guest conductor of orchestras throughout North, Central, and South America and Europe.
WORKS: ORCHESTRA: Nocturne: Overture to an opera; CHAMBER MUSIC: Chanson triste, violin and piano; Nocturne, double bass and piano; VOICE: Christmas bells; My prayer; also many transcriptions for orchestra.

SEYFRIT, MICHAEL EUGENE
b. Lawrence, Kans., 16 Dec. 1947. Studied with John Pozdro and Edward Mattila, Univ. of Kansas; with Vincent Persichetti, Juilliard School; Halsey Stevens, Robert Linn, and Anthony Vazzana, Univ. of Southern California. He received awards from BMI, Phi Mu Alpha, Bellamann Found.; and Nat. Inst. of Arts and Letters' Charles E. Ives scholarship. He was lecturer, California State Univ., Fullerton, 1973.
WORKS: ORCHESTRA: Windfest, wind symphony, 1968; Peace, wind symphony, 1969; Dichroism, chamber orch., 1970; CHAMBER MUSIC: Winter's warmth, bass voice, chamber ensemble, 1970; Similes, solo oboe and cello, with 4 flutes, 4 percussion, 1970; Shadows and the night wind, 4 players, 1970; Brass rings, brass quintet, 1971; Continuum, vacuum, residuum, clarinet, English horn, cello, prepared piano, 6 hands, 1971; For one alone, clarinet solo, 1972; Portal, woodwind quartet, 1973; Sleepwalk, viola d'amore and harp, 1976; piano pieces.

SEYMOUR, JOHN LAURENCE
b. Los Angeles, Calif., 18 Jan. 1893. Studied piano with Fannie Charles Dillon; at Univ. of

SHACKELFORD, RUDOLPH OWENS (RUDY)

California, Los Angeles, B.A., M.A., Ph.D.; with
Vincent d'Indy in Paris and Pizzetti in Italy.
He was head of the drama dept., Sacramento
Junior Coll., 1926-50. He received the Bispham
Medal in 1935 for his opera, In the Pasha's
garden, which was performed at the Metropolitan
Opera House, New York, 24 Jan. 1935. His works
include 5 other operas; 4 operettas; ballets;
piano concerto; chamber music.

SHACKELFORD, RUDOLPH OWENS (RUDY)
b. Newport News, Va., 18 Apr. 1944. Studied
with Milton Cherry, Virginia Commonwealth Univ.,
B.M. magna cum laude 1966; with Gordon Binkerd,
Univ. of Illinois, D.M.A. 1971; also with Luigi
Dallapiccola, George Rochberg, and Vincent
Persichetti. His awards include fellowships at
Yaddo, 1972, 1973, 1976, 1977, MacDowell Colony,
1974, 1976, 1978, Ossabaw Island, 1975, 1976,
Rockefeller Found., Bellagio, Italy, 1977; first
prize, 1974 Spokane World Expo Composition Contest; and commissions. He taught at Shenandoah
Cons., 1972; is a published poet as well as
composer.
    WORKS: CHAMBER MUSIC: Intaglio Stravinsky,
harpsichord, bass, 6 instruments, Dallas, 6 Oct.
1973; Cantata I, on poems of Denise Levertov,
soprano and chamber ensemble; Cantata II, on
poems of Dylan Thomas, tenor and string trio;
Epitaffio, solo guitar; Nocturne, piano with
recitation of poem by Samuel Beckett, 1966,
rev. 1973; Sonata for organ, 1969; Trio sonata,
organ, 1970; Diferencias, organ; Berg im Nebel/
Berg im Spiegel, piano, 1971; Le tombeau de
Stravinsky, harpsichord, 1971; Canonic variations, organ; Airlooms, harpsichord; 9 aphorisms,
organ; Nighthawks: 3 city scapes, brass quintet,
1977; The wound-dresser, dramatic cantata on
Whitman text, 1977.
    Severn P.O., Gloucester County, VA 23155

SHACKFORD, CHARLES REEVE
b. New York, N.Y., 18 Apr. 1918; d. New London,
Conn., 21 Apr. 1979. Studied with Paul Hindemith,
Yale Univ., B.A. 1941, M.M. 1944; with Walter
Piston, Harvard Univ., Ph.D. 1954. He was
Atherton fellow at Harvard, 1947-49; received
Wyman Fund research grant, 1949; American Acad.
of Arts and Sciences grant, 1955; Ford Found.
grant, 1969; and commissions. His academic
posts included Wellesley Coll., 1952-53; research
fellow in acoustics, Harvard Univ., 1954-56;
music director, Newton School of Nursing, 1956-
62; faculty member, Wilson Coll., 1962-65; then
professor, Connecticut Coll. He was director,
Belmont (Mass.) Community Chorus, 1955-59;
organist-choirmaster in the Boston area, 1953-62.
    WORKS: ORCHESTRA: Serenade, piano and
small orch., 1942; Fantasy on Vysehrad, 2 pianos
and orch., 1969; BAND: Overture concertante,
1973; CHAMBER MUSIC: trio for oboe, violin,
viola, 1942; string trio, 1947; clarinet duo,
1948; duo for horn and cello, 1949; Fantasy,
cello and piano, 1951; woodwind trio, 1952;
Toccata, brass sextet, 1967; sonata for viola
solo, 1970; quintet for clarinet, horn, string
trio, 1973; works for chorus and solo voice.

SHAFF, STANLEY M.
b. San Francisco, Calif., 14 Feb. 1929. Attended
San Francisco State Coll., B.A., M.A. He was
music instructor, San Francisco Unified School
District, 1952-63; instructor in arts and humanities, Merritt Coll., 1963-70; from 1970, at
Coll. of Alameda. He composes electronic music
for Audium, a theatre of sound-sculptured space
designed to provide an ideal enviornment for
this specific art form. Taped compositions are
played through a console that allows exact
control of sound location, movement, speed, and
intensity through 136 independent speakers, im-
mersing the audience in a sound-space continuum.
    112 Midcrest Way, San Francisco, CA 94131

SHAFFER, JEANNE ELLISON
b. Knoxville, Tenn., 25 May 1925. Studied with
Newton Strandberg, Samford Univ., B.M. 1954;
with Hugh Thomas, Birmingham Southern Coll.,
M.M. 1958; with Gilbert Trythall, George Peabody
Coll., Ph.D. 1970. She won composition awards,
Birmingham Festival of Arts, 1954, 1956, 1958,
1961, 1962; NDEA grants, 1967, 1968; humanities
fellowship, Peabody Coll., 1969. She has held
faculty posts in public schools and colleges
from 1954; George Peabody Coll., 1967-70, 1971-
72; Fisk Univ., 1972-73; Judson Coll., 1973-76;
from 1976, professor and chairman, Huntingdon
Coll.,
    WORKS: THEATRE: The ghost of Susan B.
Anthony, 1-act chamber opera, Huntingdon Coll.,
12 Nov. 1977; Rainbow, ballet suite for children,
piano, 2 flutes, clarinet, soprano, Montgomery,
Ala., 28 Apr. 1978; many anthems and other choral
works; organ and piano pieces; song cycles;
chamber music.
    2740 Oxford Dr., Montgomery, AL 36111

SHAFFER, SHERWOOD
b. Beeville, Tex., 15 Nov. 1934. Studied with
Bohuslav Martinu and Vittorio Giannini, Curtis
Inst. of Music, B.M.; with Giannini at Manhattan
School of Music, M.M. He won the Outstanding
Educators of America award, 1972. He was
faculty member, Manhattan School, 1962-65; from
1965, at North Carolina School of the Arts.
    WORKS: ORCHESTRA: Contertante, cello and
orch., 1962; Rhapsody, double bass and orch.,
1967; CHAMBER MUSIC: Cassation, violin and
cello, 1964; cello sonata, 1965; double bass
sonata, 1965; violin sonata, 1966; Serenade,
oboe and horn; Sacra hora, soprano, baritone,
violin, cello, 1967; Variations, viola and cello,
1968; Berceuse and galliard, guitar, 1969; 4
quatrains, percussion, 1970; Faces of time,
chorus and chamber ensemble, 1970.
    133 Woodbriar Rd., Winston-Salem, NC 27106

SHAHAN, PAUL W.
b. Grafton, W.Va., 2 Jan. 1923. Studied at Fairmont State Coll., B.M.; with Weldon Hart, West
Virginia Univ., M.M.; with Roy Harris, Peabody
Coll., M.E.; and with Kent Kennan, Bernard
Rogers, Howard Hanson, Eastman School of Music.
He received the Thor Johnson award, 1952; and
many commissions. He taught in Grafton, W.Va.,
public schools; then was staff arranger for

radio-TV, 1951-52; has been choir director in various churches; from 1957, has been faculty member, Murray State Univ.

WORKS: OPERA: The Stubblefield story, 1963; ORCHESTRA: 3 portraits for orchestra, 1950; 2 symphonic miniatures, 1953; Soliloquy, trumpet and strings, 1953; Morocco, 1954; Beat the drums proudly, with narrator, 1976; BAND: concerto for string bass and band, 1953; Spring festival, 1955; Holiday in Spain, 1959; The fountain head, 1963; The Lincoln heritage trail, 1966; A splash of splendour, 1966; Mosaics in motion, 1968; Jeffersontown 1797, 1972; The land and the rivers, 1974; WIND ENSEMBLE: Spectrums, brass choir, 1952; Leipzig towers, brass choir, 1955; The Stadtpfier suite, brass, 1957; The city of David, brass and organ, 1956; CHAMBER MUSIC: The solemn sea and Seascape, tuba and piano, 1960; also choral works.

Murray State University, Murray, KY 42071

SHAKARIAN, ROUPEN
b. Cairo, Egypt, 12 Mar. 1950; U.S. citizen 1965. Studied with John Verrall and William Bergsma, Univ. of Washington, where he held the Brechemin Family scholarship. He also received the Calousie Gulbenkian scholarship for Lisbon, Portugal; Nat. Endowment for the Arts grant, 1976.

WORKS: ORCHESTRA: harpsichord concerto #2, 1972; CHAMBER MUSIC: 3 movements, solo cello, 1972; Fantasy, violin and piano; 5 Renaissance poems, soprano and chamber orch.; Concertante, chamber ensemble; Abstracts, chamber baller, clarinet, violin, cello, piano, 1976; CHORUS: Christmas cantata, with chamber orch.

7725 2nd N.E., Seattle, WA 98115

SHANET, HOWARD S.
b. Brooklyn, N.Y., 9 Nov. 1918. Studied conducting with Rudolph Thomas, Fritz Stiedry, and Serge Koussevitzky; composition with Weisse, Dessau, Martinu, Lopatnikoff, and Honegger; attended Columbia Univ., A.B. 1939, A.M. 1941. His many posts as conductor have included U.S. Army Band, 1942-44; assistant conductor, New York City Symph., 1947-48; Huntington (W.Va.) Symph. Orch., 1951-52; guest conductor with the Israel Phil. and New York Phil. He taught at Hunter Coll., 1945-53; then joined the faculty at Columbia Univ.

WORKS: ORCHESTRA: Variations on a bizarre theme, 1960; BAND: A war march, 1944; CHAMBER MUSIC: 2 canonic pieces, 2 clarinets, 1947.

Music Dept., Columbia University, New York, NY 10027

SHAPERO, HAROLD SAMUEL
b. Lynn, Mass., 29 Apr. 1920. Studied with Nicolas Slonimsky, Malkin Cons., Boston; with Walter Piston, Harvard Univ., B.A. magna cum laude 1941; with Paul Hindemith at Tanglewood; with Nadia Boulanger in Cambridge; and with Ernst Krenek. His awards include the American Prix de Rome, 1941; Guggenheim fellowship, 1946-48; Fulbright grant, 1961-62; and commissions. From 1952 he has been on the faculty at Brandeis Univ.

WORKS: BALLET: Pocahontas; The minotaurs; ORCHESTRA: 9-minute overture, 1941; Serenade, string orch., 1945; symphony for classical orchestra, 1948; The travelers, 1948; concerto for orchestra, 1951-58; Credo, 1955; Partita, piano and chamber orch., 1960; JAZZ COMBO: On Green Mountain, 1958; CHAMBER MUSIC: 3 pieces for 3 pieces, woodwind trio, 1938; trumpet sonata, 1938; string quartet, 1940; 4-hand piano sonata, 1941; violin sonata, 1942; 3 amateur sonatas, for piano, 1944; CHORUS: The defense of Corinth, men's voices with piano, 4 hands; Emblems, men's voices; ELECTRONIC: 3 improvisations in B flat and 3 studies in C sharp, both for piano and synthesizer, 1968.

9 Russell Circle, Natick, MA 01760

SHAPEY, RALPH
b. Philadelphia, Pa., 12 Mar. 1921. Studied violin with Emanuel Zetlin, composition with Stefan Wolpe. His many awards include Frank Huntington Beebe award, 1953; MacDowell fellowships, 1957, 1958; clarinet concerto chosen as one of 2 works to represent the U.S. at ICSM Festival, France, 1958; Italian government grant, 1959; Brandeis award, 1962; Stern Family Fund award, 1962; Copley Found. award, 1962; Inst. of Arts and Letters award, 1966; Who's Who citation, 1966; Naumberg recording award, 1966; Norlin Found. award, 1978; many commissions. He served in the U.S. Army, 1942-45; was faculty member, Univ. of Pennsylvania, 1963-64; from 1964, professor, Univ. of Chicago, and director of its resident Contemporary Chamber Players, which together with Shapey received the American Composers Alliance 1979 Laurel award.

WORKS: ORCHESTRA: Fantasy, 1951; symphony, 1952; Challenge--The family of man, 1955; Ontogeny, 1958; violin concerto, 1959; Rituals, 1959; CHAMBER MUSIC: 7 string quartets, 1946, 1949, 1951, 1953, 1958 (with voice), 1963, 1972; piano quintet, 1947; violin sonata, 1950; oboe sonata, 1952; quartet for oboe and string trio, 1952; cello sonata, 1953; concerto for clarinet and chamber ensemble, 1954; piano trio, 1955; duo for viola and piano, 1957; Rhapsodie, oboe and piano, 1957; Evocation, violin, piano, percussion, 1959; Soliloquy, narrator, string quartet, percussion, 1959; Movements, woodwind quintet, 1960; De profundis, solo contrabass and instruments, 1960; Five, violin and piano, 1960; Discourse, 4 instruments, 1961; Convocation, chamber group, 1962; chamber symphony, 10 solo players, 1962; brass quintet, 1963; Configurations, flute and piano, 1965; Partita, violin and 13 players, 1966; Poeme, viola and piano, 1966; For solo trumpet, 1967; Reyem, flute, violin, piano, 1967; Partita-fantasy, cello and 13 players, 1967; Variations for piano, New York, 17 May 1979; VOICE: Cantata, 3 voices, narrator, instruments, 1951; Walking upright, 8 songs for female voice and violin, 1958; This day, female voice and piano, 1960; Dimensions, soprano and 23 instruments, 1960; Incantations, soprano and 10 instruments, 1961; Songs of ecstasy, soprano, piano, percussion, tape, 1967; Praise, oratorio, baritone solo, chorus, percussion, 1961-71, Chicago, 28 Feb. 1976; O Jerusalem, song cycle, soprano

SHAPLEIGH, BERTRAM LINCOLN

and flute, Pittsburgh, 5 Mar. 1978; <u>The covenant</u>,
cantata for virtuoso soprano, 16 instruments,
tape, (dedicated to 30th anniversary of the
State of Israel), Chicago, 14 Apr. 1978; also
piano works, film scores.
    5835 S. University Ave., Chicago, IL 60637

SHAPLEIGH, BERTRAM LINCOLN
    b. Boston, Mass., 15 Jan. 1871; d. Washington,
D.C., Dec. 1940. Studied with Edward MacDowell
and Henry Hadley and at the New England Cons.
He was for many years affiliated with Breitkopf
and Härtel.
    WORKS: ORCHESTRA: <u>Rayamana suite</u>; <u>Mirage</u>,
tone poem; <u>Gur Amir suite</u>; <u>3 songs of England</u>;
CHAMBER MUSIC: string quartet; cello sonata;
cello pieces; CHORUS: <u>The raven</u>, with orch.;
<u>Dance of the dervishes</u>, with orch.

SHARLIN, WILLIAM
    b. New York, N.Y., 7 Jan. 1920. Studied with
Vittorio Giannini, Manhattan School of Music,
M.M. 1949; with Eric Werner, Hebrew Union School
of Sacred Music, New York, B.S.M. 1951. He held
a fellowship at Hebrew Union Coll., Cincinnati,
1951-54; from 1954, has been cantor, Leo Baeck
Temple; and from 1955, adjunct professor, Hebrew
Union Coll., Los Angeles.
    WORKS: LITURGICAL: <u>Shalom Aleychem</u>; <u>Mi
Barachev</u>; <u>May the time not be distant</u>, women's
voices; <u>Service of inauguration</u>, cantor, male
chorus, brass ensemble, harp, guitars, organ,
1972.
    3580 Multiview Dr., Los Angeles, CA 90068

SHATIN, JUDITH
    b. Boston, Mass., 21 Nov. 1949. Studied with
Robert Moevs, Douglass Coll., Rutgers Univ.,
1967-71; at Juilliard School, 1972-74; also with
Hall Overton, Otto Luening, and Milton Babbitt.
Her awards include the Julia Carlie Memorial
prize; Abraham Ellstein award; Aspen Music Festival awards, 1971, 1972; first prize, East and
West Artists composition contest, New York, 1979.
    WORKS: ORCHESTRA: <u>Chrysalis</u>, 1973; CHAMBER
MUSIC: <u>Grave music</u>, soprano, string trio, and
bass; <u>Tombeau des morts</u>, viola, cello, string
bass, harp, piano; <u>Limericks</u>, solo flute;
<u>Passages</u>, solo viola; <u>Legends</u>, flute, oboe,
cello, percussion; <u>Quatrain</u>, 2 strings, 2 clarinets, New York, 18 Dec. 1975.

SHAUGHNESSY, ROBERT MICHAEL
    b. Worcester, Mass., 24 Sept. 1925. Studied
with Paul Creston in New York; with Hugo Norden
in Boston; cello with Bedrich Vaska. He was
faculty member, Massachusetts State Coll. at
Lowell, 1957-65; from 1965, at Southampton Coll.,
Long Island Univ.
    WORKS: CHAMBER MUSIC: concertino for tuba
and strings; duo for recorder and guitar; suite
for strings; <u>Etudes</u> for guitar; <u>The bacchae</u>,
violin and cello, 1970; <u>Consort music</u>, guitar
ensemble; <u>Paradigm</u>, solo flute.
    179 Hampton Rd., Southampton, NY 11968

SHAW, ARNOLD
    b. Brooklyn, N.Y., 28 June 1909. Attended

Columbia Univ., M.A. 1931; is self-taught in
music. He received the ASCAP Deems Taylor
award, 1968; named Nevada Composer of the Year,
1973; commissioned by Nevada Music Teachers
Assoc. and Nat. Music Teachers Assoc.; has received annual ASCAP awards from 1970. He was
an executive in New York music publishing firms,
1941-66; lectured on the Schillinger System of
Musical Composition at Juilliard School, 1945;
taught courses at Fairleigh Dickinson Univ.,
1964-65; has lectured at New School for Social
Research, Univ. of Oklahoma, Univ. of Nevada at
Reno and Las Vegas; was editor of Schillinger's
<u>Mathematical basis of the arts</u> and <u>Schillinger
system of musical composition</u>; is author of 9
books and numerous magazine articles.
    WORKS: THEATRE: <u>They had a dream</u>, musical,
libretto by composer, Las Vegas, 9 May 1976;
VOICE: <u>Sing a song of Americans</u>, texts by
Rosemary and Stephen Vincent Benet, 1941; <u>A man
called Peter</u>; PIANO: <u>Mobiles</u>, 10 graphic impressions, 1966; <u>Stabiles</u>, 12 images, 1968;
<u>Plabiles</u>, 12 songs without words, 1971; <u>Waltzes
for now</u>, 1974; <u>The mod moppet</u>, 7 nursery ripoffs,
1974; <u>A whirl of waltzes</u>, 1974; <u>The bubble-gum
waltzes</u>; many other songs and piano pieces.
    2288 Gabriel Dr., Las Vegas, NV 89109

SHAW, CLIFFORD
    b. Little Rock, Ark., 19 Sept. 1911; d. Louis-
ville, Ky., 12 Jan. 1976. Studied with Frederic
A. Cowles in Louisville, but is largely self-
taught in composition. He received a citation
from the Kentucky Fed. of Music Clubs for outstanding contributions to the cultural life of
Kentucky by his compositions. He was staff
member in the music department of WAVE-TV, Louisville, 1933-76.
    WORKS: SONGS: <u>The lamb</u>, Blake text; <u>Romance</u>;
PIANO: <u>Valentine</u>; <u>Vienna fragment</u>; <u>A London
fragment</u>; <u>Love in springtime</u>; <u>3rd Street rhumba</u>;
<u>Manhattan bacarolle</u>; also works for orchestra,
band, chorus, many songs, 2 ballets.

SHAW, DAVID FERGUSON
    b. Woonsocket, R.I., 22 Jan. 1926. Studied with
Francis Judd Cooke, New England Cons., B.M. cum
laude; at Boston Univ., M.M.E.; with Arthur
Honegger in Paris; at Assumption Coll., M.M.; at
workshops with Milton Babbitt and Emerson Meyers.
He held a Ditson scholarship at the New England
Cons.; represented the cons. at a Juilliard
School symposium, 1952; had works performed at
Southern Music Educators Conf., Mobile, 1969.
He teaches electronic music and theory at Fairfax
High School, Fairfax, Va.
    WORKS: BAND: <u>Introduction and dance</u>, with
electronics; CHORUS: <u>4 Marian tableaux</u>; <u>Alleluia</u>;
Psalm 98; <u>O Lord, My God</u>; <u>Lux fulgebit</u>, with
tape; <u>4 Blake poems</u>; <u>3 Haiku poems</u>; <u>Noel bearmais</u>;
<u>Venez divin messie</u>; <u>Celebrons naissance</u>; <u>Missa
brevis</u>; <u>Te Deum</u>.
    Fairfax High School, Fairfax, VA 22039

SHAW, JAMES R.
    b. Philadelphia, Pa., 27 Aug. 1930. Studied with
Robert McBride, Univ. of Arizona, M.M. He taught
in public schools, 1953-63; then joined the

faculty at Glassboro State Coll.
WORKS: CHORUS: Roc-a-my-baby; Beautiful day; 4 horizons, on text of Amy Lowell; Applause contours; many other choral works; art songs; children's musicals.
450 Lake Ave., Pitman, NJ 08071

SHEFF, ROBERT NATHAN
b. San Antonio, Tex., 1 Jan. 1945. Studied privately with Otto Wick, Frank Hughes, and Raymond Moses in San Antonio. He received a BMI student composer award in 1962 for a piano sonata. He began playing in jazz and rock groups at an early age; participated as composer and performer in the ONCE festivals and concerts at Ann Arbor, Mich., 1962-70; organized Everybody Wins, a 12-hour open concert event open to all musicians in the community; was pianist, organist, vocalist, composer for several pop groups; from 1970, has been instructor and technician, Center for Contemporary Music, Mills Coll. His works are chiefly for electric equipment with verbal scores and graphics, and require audience participation and from a few hours to a few days for performance.
Mills College, P.O. Box 9970, Oakland, CA 94613

SHEINFELD, DAVID
b. St. Louis, Mo., 20 Sept. 1906. Studied with Arthur Olaf Andersen, American Cons.; with Ottorino Respighi in Rome; conducting with Pierre Monteux in Hancock, Maine. His awards include a Nat. Endowment for the Arts grant, 1969; many commissions. He was violinist in the San Francisco Symphony, 1945-71; private composition teacher.
WORKS: ORCHESTRA: 4 etudes; Dialogues, chamber orch.; Confrontations, 1969; Time warp, commissioned for 60th anniversary of the San Francisco Symph., 1971; CHAMBER MUSIC: Serenade for 6 instruments, 1960; duo for viola and harp, 1965; Memories of yesterday and tomorrow, 3 players, 1971; Dualities, solo harp, 1976; string quartet, 1978.
1458 24th Ave., San Francisco, CA 94122

SHEINKMAN, MORDECAI
b. Tel-Aviv, Israel, 30 May 1926; U.S. citizen at birth. Studied at St. John's Coll., Annapolis; with Boris Blacher in Berlin; with Wolfgang Fortner in Detmold, Germany. He was faculty member, Kirkland Coll., 1968-72; Richmond Coll., CUNY, 1972-76; music director, opera workshop, Manhattanville Coll., 1970-72; visiting faculty, Hartt Coll. of Music, 1976-77; director of opera and orchestra, Univ. of Washington, 1977-78; from 1978, on faculty, Union Coll., and conductor, Northeast N.Y. Youth Orchestra.
WORKS: ORCHESTRA: Passi; piano concerto; Serenade, string orch.; CHAMBER MUSIC: Divertimento, clarinet, trumpet, trombone, harp; violin sonata; songs.
960 University Place, Schenectady, NY 12308

SHEPARD, JEAN ELLEN
b. Durham, N.C., 1 Nov. 1949. Studied with Stefan Grove and Robert Hall Lewis, Peabody

Cons., B.M. 1973, M.M. 1974; with Milko Keleman in Stuttgart, Germany, on an Internat. Rotary Found. fellowship. At Peabody Cons. she received the Gustav Klemm Composition award; taught in the Peabody preparatory dept., 1973-75.
WORKS: ORCHESTRA: The clock strikes 3, 1974; Processional for strings, 1977; CHAMBER MUSIC: To a child dancing, flute, percussion, narrator; Music for solo cello, 1976; Fantasy, piano, 1976; Traces of morning, flute and piano, 1977; Song of Lena, speaker and piano, 1978 (based on Faulkner).
5 Morton St., Apt. 2D, New York, NY 10014

SHEPHERD, ARTHUR
b. Paris, Idaho, 19 Feb. 1880; d. Cleveland, Ohio, 12 Jan. 1958. Studied with George W. Chadwick and Percy Goetschius, New England Cons., where he received the Paderewski prize and 2 Nat. Fed. of Music Clubs prizes. He conducted the Salt Lake Symphony, 1897-1908; was faculty member, New England Cons., 1908-17; served in the U.S. Army, 1917-19; was assistant conductor, Cleveland Orchestra, 1920-26; professor, Western Reserve Univ., 1927-50.
WORKS: ORCHESTRA: 4 overtures; Fantaisie humoresque, piano and orch., 1918; 2 symphonies, 1927, 1940; Choreographic suite, 1931; Fantasy on Down East spirituals, 1944; violin concerto, 1947; Theme and variations, 1952; BAND: Hilaritus, overture, 1942; CHAMBER MUSIC: 2 piano sonatas, 1907, 1929; 2 violin sonatas, 1914, 1927; Triptych, voice and string quartet, 1926; 3 string quartets, 1927, 1935, 1936; piano quintet, 1940; Praeludium salutatorum, woodwind quintet and string trio, 1942; Divertimento, woodwind quintet, 1943; CHORUS: Song of the sea wind, 1915; He came all so still, 1915; Deck thyself, my soul, 1918; Ballad of trees and the master, 1935; Song of the Pilgrims, 1937; Invitation to the dance, 1937; Grace for gardens, 1938; Build thee more stately mansions, 1938; Psalm 42, 1944; Drive on, 1946; and songs.

SHEPPARD, C. JAMES
b. Aurora, Nebr., 23 Nov. 1943. Studied with Philip Bezanson, Univ. of Massachusetts; with Richard Hervig and Donald Jenni, Univ. of Iowa. His awards include the Philip Greeley Clapp Memorial award in composition, 1976; selection of his Wind loops 2 for New Music Festival V, Memphis State Univ., 1978; Meet the Composer performance, Pittsburgh, 1978. He is faculty member at West Virginia Univ.
WORKS: CHAMBER MUSIC: sextet for winds, 1968; Bitter ice, jazz quintet, 1969; Winter reflections, flute and piano, 1969; Wind loops 2, solo trumpet, 1972; Garden of earthly delights, solo harp, 1974; Eclipse, 5 instruments, 1974; Bottled green, iridium gold, chamber ensemble, 1975; Slapstick, percussion duo, 1977; The last cartoon man, a piano rag, 1977.
701 Union Ave., Morgantown, WV 26505

SHERE, CHARLES
b. Berkeley, Calif., 20 Aug. 1935. Studied with Robert Erickson, San Francisco Cons.; with Luciano Berio, Mills Coll.; privately with

SHERMAN, NORMAN

Gerhard Samuel; Univ. of California, Berkeley,
A.B. 1960. He received a Nat. Endowment for the
Arts grant, 1978. He was music director, KPFA,
1964-67; writer, critic, director, and producer,
KQED-TV, 1967-74; from 1973, art and music
critic, Oakland Tribune; from 1974, lecturer,
Mills Coll.
WORKS: ORCHESTRA: Small concerto, piano
and orch., 1964; From calls and singing, small
orch., 1967; Nightmusic, 1970; Music for orchestra, 1976; Tongues, for poet (speaking in
tongues) and chamber orch., 1978; CHAMBER MUSIC:
Fratture, 7 instruments, 1963; Ces desirs du
quatuor, any 4 instruments, 1965; Screen, 3-5
strings, 1969; Handler of gravity, organ, 1971;
Dates, soprano, clarinet, viola, percussion,
1972; 5 piano pieces, 1975.
1824 Curtis St., Berkeley, CA 94702

SHERMAN, NORMAN
b. Boston, Mass., 25 Feb. 1926. Studied com-
position at Boston Univ., 1946-50, and with
Messiaen in Paris, 1950. He was principal
bassoonist with the Winnipeg Orch., 1951-61; The
Hague Phil., 1961-69; Nat. Arts Center Orch. of
Ottawa, 1969-73; Radio Symph. Orch. of Israel,
1973-74; from 1974, with the Kingston (Ont.)
Symph.
WORKS: BALLET: The red seed, 1950; ORCHES-
TRA: Sinfonia concertante, bassoon and strings,
1950; 2 pieces, 1953, 1963; Through the rainbow
and/or across the valley, 1967; Thesis, 1974;
Canadian summer, 1975; CHAMBER MUSIC: concerto
for wind quartet and piano, 1948; Traditions,
wind quintet, 1948; The reunion, flute and
string trio, 1967-72; Quadron, 1976; Quintessant,
wind quintet, 1977; Bouquet, piano or celeste,
clarinet, and 3 percussion, 1977.
c/o Kingston Symphony, Kingston, Ontario,
Canada

SHERMAN, ROBERT WILLIAM
b. Mich., 17 Jan. 1921. Studied with H. Owen
Reed, Michigan State Univ.; with Bernard Rogers,
Eastman School of Music. He has been faculty
member, Ball State Univ., from 1968.
WORKS: BALLET: 7 ages of man; CHAMBER
MUSIC: wind quintet; septet for woodwind trio
and string quartet; quintet for clarinet and
strings; 13 additional ways of looking at a
blackbird, soprano and piano; tenor saxophone
sonata; trio sonata, violin, saxophone, piano;
Dichromes, trumpet and cello.
3730 University Ave., Muncie, IN 47304

SHIELDS, ALICE
b. New York, N.Y., 18 Feb. 1943. Studied with
Vladimir Ussachevsky, Otto Luening, Jack Beeson,
and Chou Wen-chung, Columbia Univ., D.M.A. 1975.
She has received grants from Presser Found.,
1970, New York State Council on the Arts, 1975,
Nat. Endowment for the Arts, 1976, 1978; and as
a singer from Rockefeller Found., 1973, and Nat.
Opera Inst., 1975. She has been staff member,
Columbia-Princeton Electronic Music Center,
from 1965, associate director, from 1976; was
singer with New York City Opera, 1976-77.
WORKS: OPERA: Odyssey, 1 act for 2 solo-

ists, male chorus, chamber orch., 1975; Shaman,
full length, live singers, amplified chamber
orch., and tape, 1978; CHAMBER MUSIC: Wildcat
songs, soprano and piccolo, 1966; Spring music,
soprano, trumpet, oboe, 1967; ELECTRONIC: Farewell to a hill, tape; The transformation of Ani,
taped voice on texts from the Egyptian Book of
the Dead, 1971.
7 W. 96th St., Apt. 11D, New York, NY 10025

SHIELDS, LEROY
b. Waseca, Minn., 2 Oct. 1898; d. Ft. Lauderdale,
Fla., 9 Jan. 1962. Studied at Univ. of Chicago;
Columbia Univ.; received honorary D.M., Chicago
Musical Coll. He toured as concert pianist;
conducted extensively for radio, films, records,
and symphony orchestras.
WORKS: ORCHESTRA: Union Pacific suite;
Gloucester, tone poem; The great ball; many
popular songs.

SHIFRIN, SEYMOUR
b. New York, N.Y., 28 Feb. 1926; d. Boston,
Mass., 26 Sept. 1979. Studied privately with
William Schuman, 1942-45; Columbia Univ., B.A.
1947, M.A. 1949; with Darius Milhaud in Paris,
1951-52. His many awards included Seidl fellowship, 1947; Bearns prize, 1950; Fulbright fellowship, 1951; Fromm Found. award, 1953; Nat. Inst.
of Arts and Letters grant, 1977; Brandeis award,
1959; Copley Found. grant, 1961; Boston Symph.
Horblit award, 1963; 2 Koussevitzky awards,
1970, 1972; Naumberg award, 1970; many commissions. He was faculty member, Columbia Univ.,
1949-50; Coll. of the City of New York, 1950-51;
Univ. of California, Berkeley, 1952-66; professor,
Brandeis Univ., 1966-79.
WORKS: ORCHESTRA: Music for orchestra,
1948; chamber symphony, 1953; 3 pieces for orchestra, 1958; CHAMBER MUSIC: cello sonata,
1948; 5 string quartets, 1949, 1962, 1966, 1967,
1972; Serenade, 5 instruments, 1954; Concert
piece, solo violin, 1959; In eius memoriam,
chamber ensemble, 1968, New York, 4 Mar. 1974;
piano trio, 1974; The nick of time, chamber
ensemble, New York, 18 May 1978; CHORUS: A
medieval Latin lyric, a cappella, 1954; Cantata
to Sophoclean choruses, with orch., 1958; Give
ear, O ye heavens, 1959; Odes of Shang, with
piano and perc., Boston, 2 May 1973; Chronicles,
with soloists and orch., 1970, Boston, 27 Sept.
1976; also songs and piano pieces.

SHILKRET, NATHANIEL
b. New York, N.Y., 1 Jan. 1895. Studied at
Bethany Coll. and with Pietro Floridia. He
played clarinet in New York orchestras; was
music director, Victor Talking Machine Co.,
1916; organized the Victor Salon Orchestra for
recordings and radio concerts; in 1935 he went
to Hollywood.
WORKS: ORCHESTRA: Skyward, symphonic poem,
1928; trombone concerto, 1942; other orchestral
pieces; violin pieces; and the Biblical cantata,
Genesis, for which he wrote one movement and
commissioned one movement each from Castelnuovo-
Tedesco, Milhaud, Schoenberg, Stravinsky,
Tansman, and Toch.

SHINBROT, MARK S.
b. Los Angeles, Calif., 7 July 1945. Studied
with Roger Chapman, Daniel Lentz, Thea Musgrave,
and Peter Racine Fricker, Univ. of California,
Santa Barbara, B.A. 1970, M.A. 1975; at Darmstadt Internat. Music Course on fellowship, 1976.
WORKS: ORCHESTRA: 3 visions, 1977; CHAMBER
MUSIC: Tojurno, viola, oboe, clarinet; Sketches,
piano; SONGS: Selections and The olden days, 2
sets; incidental music and music for children's
films.
52 Tahoe Circle, Novato, CA 94947

SHINDO, TAK
b. Sacramento, Calif., 11 Nov. 1922. Studied
with Robert MacDonald, Los Angeles City Coll.;
at California State Univ., Los Angeles, B.A.
1952; with Miklos Rozsa and Halsey Stevens, Univ.
of Southern California, M.A. 1970. He has been
faculty member, California State Univ., Los
Angeles, from 1965; conductor, composer, arranger for CBS; composer, arranger, technical advisor, film studios in Hollywood and the Daiei
Studio, Tokyo, from 1949.
WORKS: CHAMBER MUSIC: Impressions, piano
trio; Autumn rain, chamber ensemble; also
Japanese children's songs, other ethnic works,
jazz.
816 Hyperion Ave., Los Angeles, CA 90029

SHINN, RANDALL
b. Clinton, Okla., 28 Sept. 1944. Studied at
Southwestern Oklahoma State Univ., B.A. magna
cum laude; Univ. of Colorado, M.M.; with Paul
Zonn and Ben Johnston, Univ. of Illinois, D.M.A.
He received grants from Louisiana State Arts
Council, 1976, Univ. of New Orleans, 1977; and
commissions. He was faculty member, Univ. of
New Orleans, 1975-78; from 1978, at Arizona
State Univ.
WORKS: WIND ENSEMBLE: 3 folksongs, with
percussion and piano; chamber concerto, solo
percussion and 10 winds; CHAMBER MUSIC: Intag-
lio, flute, clarinet, cello, piano; Soliloquy
and dialogue, trumpet and piano; Serenade, brass
quintet; Dialogue, violin and piano; CHORUS:
Tokens; What is beauty, then?; The ship of death,
with soloists and orch.; SONGS: Signature for
tempo, soprano and piano; 2 still lifes, soprano,
chamber ensemble; The cry of the sedge, solo
quartet and guitar.
Arizona State University, Tempe, AZ 85281

SHIRLEY, DONALD
b. Kingston, Jamaica, B.W.I., 1927. Entered the
Leningrad Cons. at age 9; earned a Ph.D. at
Harvard Univ. He has been piano soloist with
major orchestras in the U.S. and Europe. His
Legacy for string orchestra was given its
premiere in New York, 3 Dec. 1973.

SHORES, RICHARD
b. Rockville, Ind., 9 May. Studied at Indiana
Univ., B.M.; Eastman School of Music, M.M.;
conducted the Indianapolis Little Symphony,
1942-46; was composer and arranger, NBC and WGN,
Chicago, to 1958; then went to Hollywood as
composer for film and television background
scores. He has published Mulholland suite, for
2 flutes, clarinet, and piano.

SHORT, GREGORY NORMAN (GREG)
b. Toppenish, Wash., 14 Aug. 1938. Studied
piano with Lonnie Epstein at Juilliard School,
1956-57; composition with William O. Smith,
Univ. of Washington, 1966-67; with Homer Keller,
Monte Tubb, and Harold Owen, Univ. of Oregon,
B.M. 1971, M.M. 1973. His awards include the
Eugene (Oreg.) Women's Choral Society award,
1970; NDEA fellowship, 1971-74. He has been
private piano teacher in Seattle and Eugene from
1959; also taught at Cornish School, Seattle,
1964-69, and at Highland Community Coll., 1967-
69.
WORKS: ORCHESTRA: Hobbit preludes, 1966;
Adagio, double string orch., 1967; symphony,
1968; WIND ENSEMBLE: concerto for band, 1972;
From dust we came, with rock band, folk singer,
etc. 1972; symphony for brass choir and percussion, 1973; CHAMBER MUSIC: concerto for piano,
winds, electric guitar, percussion, 1965; woodwind quintet, 1972; PIANO: 3 sonatas, 1958,
1960, 1970; Dozen etudes, 1965-71; choral works
and songs.
1728 Ferry St., Apt. 7, Eugene, OR 97401

SHORTALL, HARRINGTON
b. Chicago, Ill., 1895. Studied at Harvard
Univ. and with Nadia Boulanger in Paris. He
taught in Chicago, from 1946 at Chicago Theological Seminary.
WORKS: ORCHESTRA: Symphonia brevis, 1937;
Wealth of variations for Thomas Jefferson's
proposed orchestra of artisans, 1942; CHORUS:
Choral memorial, 1935, won the Westminster Choir
award, 1936; Hymns for Uncle Sam's nephews and
nieces, 1944; and chamber works.

SHOTT, MICHAEL
b. Berlin, Germany, 7 Apr. 1928; U.S. citizen
1955. Studied with Hermann Grabner in Berlin;
at Western Michigan Univ., B.M.; and Indiana
Univ., M.M., Ph.D. He has been professor,
Northern Arizona Univ., from 1961. His compositions include Prompted by love, a song cycle;
many educational piano pieces.
1105 E. Ponderosa, #158, Flagstaff, AZ 86001

SHRADER, DAVID LEWIS
b. Columbia, Mo., 3 May 1939. Studied at Univ.
of Iowa, B.A. 1961, M.A. 1963; with Homer Keller,
Univ. of Oregon, D.M.A. 1969. He was faculty
member, Univ. of Oregon, 1964-69; Univ. of
Washington, 1969-74; from 1974, Illinois State
Univ. His published works include Sea and sym-
pathy for timpani.
Illinois State University, Normal, IL 61761

SHREVE, SUSAN E.
b. Detroit, Mich., 24 Nov. 1952. Studied at
Wayne State Univ. and at Bordeaux Cons. in
France. Her piano concerto received an award,
Mu Phi Epsilon contest, 1973.
WORKS: ORCHESTRA: piano concerto, 1971;
cello concerto, 1974; CHAMBER MUSIC: saxophone
sonata; flute sonata.
16761 Pierdon, Detroit, MI 48219

SHRUDE, MARILYN

SHRUDE, MARILYN
b. Chicago, Ill., 6 July 1946. Studied at
Alverno Coll., B.M.; with Alan Stout and M.
William Karlins, Northwestern Univ. Her awards
icnlude a Wyatt Fund grant, 1977; Faricy award,
1977; first place, Honors Competition, Northwestern Univ., 1977. She taught in public
schools, 1969-73; was accompanist, Wichita State
Univ., 1973-76; from 1977, instructor, and
director, New Music Ensemble, Bowling Green
State Univ.
WORKS: ORCHESTRA: Genesis: Notes to the
unborn, 1975; CHAMBER MUSIC: Quartet for saxophones, 1973; Music for soprano saxophone and
piano, 1974; Evolution V, saxophone solo and
saxophone quartet, 1976.
219 Evergreen Lane, Bowling Green, OH 43402

SHULMAN, ALAN
b. Baltimore, Md., 4 June 1915. Studied with
Louis Cheslock, Peabody Cons.; with Bernard
Wagenaar at Juilliard School; also cello with
Felix Salmond, Emanuel Feuermann; composition
with Paul Hindemith. He received scholarships
from the New York Phil. and Juilliard School;
annual ASCAP awards from 1961. He was a charter
member, NBC Symph., 1937-42, 1948-54; cofounder
and cellist, Stuyvesant String Quartet, 1938-52;
cellist, Philharmonia Trio, 1963-69; participated in chamber music festivals, Mt. Desert
Island, Maine, 1969-72, and Newport, R.I., 1973.
WORKS: ORCHESTRA: Theme and variations,
viola and orch., 1940; cello concerto, 1948;
Waltzes, 1949; Laurentian overture, 1951;
Popocatepetl, symphonic picture, 1952; CHAMBER
MUSIC: Top brass, brass ensemble, 1947; suite
for solo cello, 1950; suite for solo viola;
Suite miniature, cello octet; Pastorale, cello
quartet; Rendezvous, clarinet and strings; Kol
nidre, violin and piano (also a version for
string quartet); 4 diversions for a pride of
cellos, Philadelphia, 6 Apr. 1975; Threnody,
string quartet; Berkshire mist, cello quartet,
Orono, Maine, 21 July 1978.
6 Fountain Terrace, Scarsdale, NY 10583

SHULZE, FREDERICK B.
b. Portland, Oreg., 25 Aug. 1935. Studied with
Jack C. Goode, Wheaton Coll., Ill.; at Northwestern Univ., M.M.; Univ. of Washington, D.M.A.
in organ. He won first prize in a hymn tune
contest, Nat. Church Music Fellowship, 1958. He
was faculty member, Cascade Coll., 1960-68; from
1970, at Taylor Univ.
WORKS: BAND: Meditation; CHORUS: The
Lord is my shepherd; O clap your hands; Walk
together chillin; Psalm 98; ELECTRONIC: Music
for tape recorder and orch.
Taylor University, Upland, IN 46989

SHURE, RALPH DEANE
b. Chillisquaque, Pa., 31 May 1885. Studied at
Oberlin Coll., B.M. He held academic posts at
Central Univ. of Iowa, 1907-9; Clarendon Texas
Coll., 1909-19; Pennsylvania State Teachers
Coll., 1919-21; American Univ., 1921-25; was
music director, Mt. Vernon Place Methodist
Church, Washington, D.C., 1921 to retirement.

WORKS: ORCHESTRA: 3 symphonies; CHORUS:
75 anthems; also organ and piano works.
8 Pine Ave., Takoma Park, MD 20012

SHURTLEFF, LYNN RICHARD
b. Vallejo, Calif., 3 Nov. 1939. Studied with
Merrill Bradshaw, Brigham Young Univ.; at
Indiana Univ.; and at Vienna Acad. of Music. He
held a Ferdinand Grossman fellowship for study
in Vienna. He has been faculty member, Univ. of
Santa Clara, from 1966.
WORKS: ORCHESTRA: 2 symphonies; Dialogues,
chamber orch.; Charlie Brown suite, jazz trio and
chamber orch.; Spectrum; Variations, chamber
orch.; CHORUS: For the first manned moon orbit,
with orch.; Sing unto the Lord a new song, with
jazz trio; O be joyful, with percussion; Echoes
from Hungry Mountain, with percussion; Quietness,
with orch.; ORGAN: Concert piece.
5302 Roxanne Dr., San Jose, CA 95124

SIBBING, ROBERT V.
b. Quincy, Ill., 9 Feb. 1929. Studied with
Philip Greeley Clapp, Univ. of Iowa; with Robert
Kelly and Hunter Johnson, Univ. of Illinois. He
has been faculty member at Western Illinois
Univ., from 1968.
WORKS: CHAMBER MUSIC: sonatas for tuba,
cello, flute, alto saxophone, soprano saxophone,
and a suite for alto saxophone and piano.
R.R. 4, Macomb, IL 61455

SIEG, JERRY PAUL
b. Bonifay, Fla., 17 Sept. 1943. Studied with
William Hoskins, Jacksonville Univ.; and with
Carlisle Floyd, Florida State Univ. He has been
faculty member at Cumberland Univ. from 1967.
WORKS: CHAMBER MUSIC: brass quintet; 4
brass quartets; suite for oboe and trumpet;
CHORUS: 3 psalms; 3 vocal quartets; SONGS: 3
songs for mezzo-soprano; Dew for 2 baritones.
Rt. 1, Box 45-A, Williamsburg, KY 40769

SIEGEL, ARSENE
b. Lyons, France, 26 Nov. 1897; U.S. citizen
1926; d. Woodstock, Ill., Dec. 1966. Studied
privately in France; on scholarship with Felix
Borowski at Chicago Musical Coll.; at American
Cons.; and with Heniot Levey. He was organist
for radio stations and film theatres.
WORKS: CHAMBER MUSIC: Pasquinade, saxophone and piano; Sanctuary, piano, received
Nat. Composition Clinic prize; Mirage, piano;
The Windy City, piano suite; The hour of worship, organ; also anthems and songs.

SIEGEL, BENJAMIN
b. Poland, 17 Feb. 1919; U.S. citizen 1926.
Studied with Max Helfman and Henry Fried, Hebrew
Union Coll., School of Sacred Music; and at
American Theatre Wing. He was music director,
YMHA, Washington Heights, N.Y., 1945-50; then
cantor, Temple Israel, Great Neck, N.Y.
WORKS: LITURGICAL: Friday evening Chassidic
service; Friday evening children's service; Entreat me not to leave thee; numerous single
religious compositions.

SIEGEL, HENRY

b. Cleveland, Ohio, 6 May 1906. Studied with Samuel Baldwin, City Coll. of New York; with Kurt Roger, Henry Cowell, and Hall Overton in New York; with Darius Milhaud in Aspen, Colo. He was public school teacher, 1930-70; played violin and viola in several university and community orchestras, 1956-73.

WORKS: ORCHESTRA: March of the immigrants, Redwood City, Calif., 13 Dec. 1972; KEYBOARD: Prelude and fugue, organ; Scherzo, piano, New York, 7 Nov. 1970; songs and choral works for high school productions.

1560 Willow Rd., #406, Palo Alto, CA 94304

SIEGEL, PAUL

b. New York, N.Y., 8 Dec. 1914. Studied at Brooklyn Coll., B.A.; New York Univ., M.A.; with Josef Marx at Vienna Acad. of Music. From 1953 he has been a music publisher.

WORKS: ORCHESTRA: Symphonic diary; One world symphony; 4 symphonic songs; Autumn concerto; Ballet Nijinsky; Between 2 worlds, concerto; and songs.

SIEGMEISTER, ELIE

b. New York, N.Y., 15 Jan. 1909. Studied with Seth Bingham, Columbia Univ., B.A. 1927; with Wallingford Reigger, 1926; with Nadia Boulanger in Paris, 1927-31; conducting with Albert Stoessel at Juilliard School. His honors include 11 ASCAP awards; Ford Found. recording grant; Nat. Endowment for the Arts grant, 1974; Guggenheim fellowship, 1978; American Acad. and Inst. of Arts and Letters award, 1978; and many commissions. In 1937 he was one of the founders, with Aaron Copland, Roy Harris, and others, of the American Composers Alliance. He was director, American Ballad Singers, 1940-47; professor and composer-in-residence, Hofstra Univ., 1949-76; in 1978, was first composer-in-residence at the Brevard Music Center.

WORKS: THEATRE: Doodle Dandy of the USA, play with music, 1942; Sing out, sweet land, musical, 1944; Darling Corie, 1-act opera, 1952; Miranda and the dark young man, 1-act opera, 1955; The mermaid in lock #7, 1-act opera, 1958; The plough and the stars, 3-act opera, 1963-69; Night of the moonspell, version of Midsummer night's dream set in Louisiana in 1900, Shreveport, 14 Nov. 1976; ORCHESTRA: American holiday, 1933; Strange funeral in Braddock, with baritone solo, 1938; Ozark set, 1943; Prairie legend, 1944; Wilderness road, 1944; Western suite, 1945; Funnybone alley, 1946; Lonesome Hollow, 1946; Sunday in Brooklyn, 1946; Summer night, 1947; 5 symphonies, 1947, rev. 1972, 1950, rev. 1971, 1957, 1970, 1971; From my window, 1949; Divertimento, 1953; clarinet concerto, 1956; flute concerto, 1960; Theater set, 1960; Dick Whittington and his cat, 1966; 5 fantasies of the theater, 1967; The face of war, with baritone solo, 1968; A cycle of cities, with chorus and dancers, Wolf Trap Farm Festival, 8 Aug. 1974; piano concerto, 1974, Denver, 3 Dec. 1976; Shadows and light, Shreveport, 9 Nov. 1975; Fables from the dark wood, ballet, 1976; double concerto, violin, piano, orch., Columbia, Md.,

25 June 1976; violin concerto, 1978; CHAMBER MUSIC: 3 string quartets, 1935-68, 1960, #3, Elkins Park, Pa., May 1974; 5 violin sonatas, 1951-59, 1965-70, 1965, 1971, 1972; Improvisation, ballad, and dance, solo accordion, 1963; Fantasy and soliloquy, solo cello, 1964; sextet for brass and percussion, 1965; American harp, solo harp, 1966; Declaration, brass and timpani, 1976; Summer, viola and piano, 1978; CHORUS: Abraham Lincoln walks at midnight, 1937; A tooth for Paul Revere, with narrator, 4 soloists, orch., 1945; The new colossus, 1949; This is our land, 1961; In our time, 1965; I have a dream, on Martin Luther King, Jr., text, 1967; On this ground, 1971; many songs; band pieces; piano works. He is also author of several books on music.

56 Fairview Ave., Great Neck, NY 10023

SIEKMANN, FRANK H.

b. Staten Island, N.Y., 20 June 1925. Studied at New York Univ., B.S. 1948, M.A. 1949; Teachers Coll., Columbia Univ., Ed.D. 1959. He was public school music teacher, Chappaqua, N.Y., 1955-65; on faculty, Univ. of Vermont, 1965-66; from 1966, at Kutztown State Coll.

WORKS: ORCHESTRA: Scene in monochrome, string orch., 1977; Music for a poetic reading, chamber orch., 1978; trombone concerto, 1979; CHAMBER MUSIC: Discourse, brass sextet, 1976; Reflections, trumpet solo, 1976; Mallet Bay, marimba duet, 1977; Descriptive piece for mime or dance, woodwind quintet, 1978.

R.D. 3, Box 352, Kutztown, PA 19530

SIENNICKI, EDMUND J.

b. Cleveland, Ohio, 11 Apr. 1920. Studied with Herbert Elwell in Cleveland; at Kent State Univ., B.S.E.; Teachers Coll., Columbia Univ., M.A.; bassoon in New York and San Francisco. He received prizes, Nat. School Orch. Assoc., 1959, 1962; 2 grants from M. H. Jennings Found.; 2 MacDowell fellowships, 1964, 1965; and commissions. He is music teacher, Cleveland Public Schools; bassoonist, Parma Civic Orchestra.

WORKS: ORCHESTRA: Park Avenue hoedown; Ballade, bassoon and orch.; Dorian sketch; BAND: Marziale e danza; Brazilian holiday; Scherzo; CHAMBER MUSIC: Let me tell it, clarinet trio; Vicarswood, woodwind trio; Allegro and Diversion, woodwind quintet; Journey, bassoon and percussion; many other works for school orchestras and bands. He has published 4 educational books for woodwinds.

3315 Dellwood Dr., Parma, OH 44134

SIFLER, PAUL J.

b. Ljubljana, Yugoslavia, 31 Dec. 1911; U.S. citizen 1936. Studied with Leo Sowerby, Robert Sanders, and John Finley Williamson, Chicago Cons. He has been choral conductor in New York; organist and choirmaster at several churches and synagogues; in 1973, at St. Thomas Episcopal Church in Hollywood, Calif.

WORKS: OPERETTA: The 9 suitors; ORCHESTRA: piano concerto; suite for strings; CHAMBER MUSIC: Marimba suite, 1970; The young pianist's almanac; 3 tall tales, piano; CHORUS: Psalm 98, cantata;

SILBERTA, RHEA

The despair and agony of Dachau; Marimba mass;
The 7 last words of Christ; many anthems; also
organ and piano pieces.
3947 Fredonia Dr., Hollywood, CA 90068

SILBERTA, RHEA
b. Pocahontas, Va., 19 Apr. 1900; d. New York,
N.Y., 6 Dec. 1959. Studied at Juilliard School;
was pianist, concert singer, and vocal coach.
Her compositions include The nightingale and the
rose for orchestra, narrator, soloists, chorus;
and Fantaisie ballade for piano.

SILLIMAN, A. CUTLER
b. Delhi, N.Y., 8 June 1922. Studied at Northwestern Univ.; with Louis Mennini, Bernard
Rogers, and Allen McHose, Eastman School of
Music, Ph.D. In 1963 he received a commission
from the Erie Phil. Orch. He was faculty member,
Ashland Coll., 1947-49; from 1949, at State Univ.
Coll., Fredonia, N.Y.
WORKS: ORCHESTRA: Toccata, chamber orch.,
1964; BAND: Fantasy on "Nun Komm, der Heiden
Heilland"; Variations; WIND ENSEMBLE: Festival
fanfare, brass choir, 1964; CHAMBER MUSIC: woodwind quintet, 1954; 5 trios for trumpet, horn,
trombone; Fugue for 3 horns; concertino for
trumpet, horn, trombone, piano; CHORUS: Sonnet,
Millay text, with brass choir; Nocturne, Hillyer
text, women's voices.
279 Chestnut St., Fredonia, NY 14063

SILSBEE, ANN L.
b. Cambridge, Mass., 21 July 1930. Studied with
Irving Fine, Radcliffe Coll., A.B. 1951; with
Earl George, Syracuse Univ., M.M. 1969; with
Robert Palmer and Karel Husa, Cornell Univ.,
D.M.A. 1978; also at the New Music Courses in
Darmstadt, 1974. Her awards include 2 fellow-
ships to Vermont Composers Conf., 1976, 1977;
second prize, Burge-Eastman contest, 1978; Nat.
Endowment for the Arts grant, 1978. She has
held teaching posts at State Univ. of New York,
Cortland, 1970-71; Cornell Univ., 1971-73, 1974-
77.
WORKS: ORCHESTRA: 3 historiettes, 1974; 7
rituals, 1978; Pathways, 1979; CHAMBER MUSIC:
Phantasy, oboe and harpsichord, 1973; River, 2
groups of players in guided improvisation, 1974;
Spirals, string quartet and piano, 1975; Tria-
logue, clarinet, violin, piano, 1976; Quest,
string quartet, 1977; Pharos, cello and piano,
1977; Pharos II, cello, percussion, piano, 1979;
CHORUS: Prometheus, with solo bass voice,
chamber ensemble and tape, 1973; Diffraction,
with soprano solo, flute, piano, percussion,
1974; Icarus, with recorders and bongo drums,
1977; many shorter works for voice and instruments.
915 Coddington Rd., Ithaca, NY 14850

SILVER, FREDERICK (FRED SILVERBERG)
b. New York, N.Y., 30 Mar. 1936. Studied at
Boston Univ., B.M.; and at Juilliard School,
B.S., M.S. His awards include the Rodgers and
Hammerstein scholarship; Freschi prize; Gret-
chaninoff prize; and commissions.
WORKS: THEATRE: For heaven's sake, a musi-

cal; CHORUS: Before the paling of the stars,
Rossetti text; and songs.

SILVER, SHEILA J.
b. Seattle, Wash., 3 Oct. 1946. Studied at
Univ. of California, Berkeley, B.A. 1968; with
Erhard Karkoschka in Stuttgart, 1969-71; with
Arthur Berger, Martin Boykan, Harold Shapero,
Seymour Shifrin, Brandeis Univ., M.F.A. 1974,
Ph.D. 1976; with Jacob Druckman at Tanglewood.
Her awards include George Ladd Prix de Paris,
1969-71; Irving Fine fellowship, 1972-74; Tangle-
wood fellowship, 1972; Abraham Sachar grant,
1974; American Music Center grant, 1977; Radcliffe
Inst. grant, 1977; first place, Indiana State
Univ. contest, 1977; Prix de Rome, 1978. She
was instructor, Phillips Exeter Acad., 1976-77;
Brandeis Univ., 1977; from 1979, on faculty,
State Univ. of New York at Stony Brook.
WORKS: ORCHESTRA: Galixidi, 1976; CHAMBER
MUSIC: Quarthym, alto recorder, 1971; Ode to
Julius, 2 pianos and percussion, 1972; Past
tense, 12 players, 1973; string quartet, 1975;
Chariessa, woman's voice and piano, 1978.
State Univ. of New York, Stony Brook, NY
11794

SILVERMAN, FAYE-ELLEN
b. New York, N.Y., 2 Oct. 1947. Studied with
William Sydeman, Mannes Coll. of Music; with
Otto Luening, Barnard Coll., B.A. cum laude 1968;
with Leon Kirchner and Lukas Foss, Harvard Univ.,
M.A. 1971; with Jack Beeson and Vladimir
Ussachevsky, Columbia Univ., D.M.A. 1974. She
received an award, Stokowski contest, 1961;
Regents scholarships and fellowships. She taught
in various schools in the New York area, 1968-
76; from 1977, at Peabody Cons.
WORKS: OPERA: The miracle of Nemirov,
chamber opera, 1974; ORCHESTRA: Madness, with
narrator, 1972; CHAMBER MUSIC: 3 movements for
saxophone alone, 1971; In shadows, soprano,
guitar, clarinet, 1972; Dialogue, horn and tuba;
Speaking alone, flute solo; string quartet;
Windscape, woodwind quintet, 1978; Settings,
1978; Shadings, 6 winds, 3 strings, percussion,
1978; CHORUS: For showing truth, women's voices,
1972; K 1971, 2 narrators, 2 male singers,
women's chorus, chamber ensemble, 1972.
Peabody Cons., 1 E. Mt. Vernon Pl., Baltimore,
MD 21202

SILVERMAN, STANLEY
b. New York, N.Y., 5 July 1938. Studied at
Boston Univ., B.A.; Columbia Univ., B.A.; with
Leon Kirchner, Darius Milhaud, Henry Cowell,
Mills Coll., M.A.; and with Roberto Gerhard.
His awards include 2 Rockefeller grants, 1964,
1972; 2 Guggenheim fellowships, 1966, 1976; 2
Fromm Found. grants, 1968, 1971; Martha Baird
Rockefeller grant, 1970; OBIE award, 1970; Nat.
Opera Inst. award, 1971; Drama Desk award, 1973;
Nat. Endowment for the Arts grant, 1976. He was
faculty member, Berkshire Music Center, 1962-66;
music consultant, Stratford Nat. Theatre of
Canada, 1969; music director, Repertory Theatre,
Lincoln Center, 1965-73; elected secretary,
American Music Center, 1979.

WORKS: OPERA: Elephant steps, 1968; Dr. Selavy's magic theatre, 1972; Madame Adare, 1 act, New York, 9 Oct. 1980; CHAMBER MUSIC: Planh, chamber concerto for guitar; Concerto I, woodwind trio, string trio, harpsichord, Charleston, S.C., 5 June 1976; Music for brass quintet and multiple keyboards, Boston, 11 Apr. 1977; CHORUS: Oedipus, 1972, and A midsummer night's dream show, 1971, both with instruments, both premiered, New York, 16 May 1973; Canso, 1964; also 20 theatre scores.
11 Riverside Dr., New York, NY 10023

SIMEONE, HARRY
b. Newark, N.J., 11 May 1911. He is a conductor and arranger. His published compositions include an opera, The emperor's new clothes; and 2 choral works, All the world's a stage and We are the music makers.

SIMMONS, HOMER
b. Evansville, Ind., 6 Aug. 1900. Studied at Univ. of Southern California, B.A.; piano with Homer Grunn and Ignace Paderewski; composition with Ottorino Respighi, Nadia Boulanger, and Gordon Jacob. He has given piano recitals in Europe and the U.S.
WORKS: OPERA: Red Riding Hood; ORCHESTRA: Phantasmania, piano and orch., 1929; California nights, piano and orch.; Impressions Basques; CHAMBER MUSIC: Panels from a lacquered screen, voice and string quartet; 2 string quartets; PIANO: Stairways; Alice in Wonderland, suite, 2 pianos; The old Dutch clock; Lyra Davidica, 2 pianos and string quartet; Evenings in old Vienna, 2 pianos and string quartet; Scherzino.

SIMONDS, BRUCE
b. Bridgeport, Conn., 5 July 1895. Studied at Yale Univ., B.M. 1918, M.A. 1938; Schola Cantorum, Paris, 1919-24; Matthay School, London, 1920-21. He was concert pianist; joined the Yale Univ. faculty in 1921; was dean, Yale School of Music, 1946-54. His published compositions include Dorian prelude and Prelude on Iam sol recedit igneus for organ; and Habañera for violin and piano.

SIMONS, NETTY
b. New York, N.Y., 26 Oct. 1913. Studied at Juilliard School; with Stefan Wolpe, New York Univ. She received scholarships at Juilliard; Ford Found. publication award. She taught at 3rd St. Settlement School, 1928-33; was voice coach, 1930-33; produced and scripted radio broadcasts for American Composers Alliance, 1966-71.
WORKS: OPERA: Bell witch of Tennessee, 1 act, 1958; THEATRE PIECES: Buckeye has wings, 1 to any number of players, 1971, New York, 11 Mar. 1974; Too late--The bridge is closed, 1 to any number of players, 1972; Puddintame, 1 to any number of players, 1972; ORCHESTRA: Piece for orchestra, 1949; Pied piper of Hamelin, with narrator, 1955; Lamentations #1, 1961, #2, 1966; Variables (may also be performed by 5 instruments or multiples of 5), 1967; Scipio's dream, 1968; Illuminations in space, viola and orch.,

1972; CHAMBER MUSIC: duo for violin and cello, 1939; Set of poems for children, narrator and chamber group, 1949; string quartet, 1950; quartet for flute and strings, 1951; 2-violin sonata, 1954; Diverse settings, soprano and chamber group, 1959; Circle of attitudes, solo violin, 1960; Facets #1-4, varying small ensembles, 1961-62; 3 trialogues, mezzo-soprano, baritone, viola, Dylan Thomas texts, 1963, 1968, 1973; Time groups #2, 3 winds, string quartet, double bass, 1964; Design groups #1, percussion, graphics score, 1966; Design groups #2, duo for any 2 high- and low-pitched instruments, 1968; Silver thaw, 1-8 players, graphics score, 1969; 2 dot, 2 pianos, 1970; Wild tales told on the river road, clarinet and percussion, 1973; The great stream silent moves, piano, harp, percussion, 1973; piano pieces; songs.
303 E. 57th St., #47E, New York, NY 10022

SIMONS, THOMAS
b. New York, N.Y., 22 Apr. 1943. Studied with Luciano Berio at Juilliard School and in Italy. He held an Italian government scholarship, 1968; received a Martha Baird Rockefeller grant, 1970. He was instructor, Princeton Univ., 1969-71; at Oberlin Coll. Cons., 1971-74.
WORKS: CHAMBER MUSIC: Cantata, soprano and chamber group, 1965; Piece for organ, 1966; Fields, 3 woodwinds, viola, cello, harp, piano, percussion, 1967; Binary reflexion, percussion and piano, 1971; Penetration, solo flute, 1972; Movement, marimba, 1972; Mirror, percussion, 1973.

SIMONSON, GEORGE THOMAS
b. New Haven, Conn., 18 May 1953. Studied with Jonathan Kramer, Frank Lewin, Robert Morris, and Yehudi Wyner, Yale Univ., B.A. 1975. He has been free-lance composer for theatre and films, 1975-78; was composer-in-residence, Growing Theatre, Inc., Fairfield, Conn., 1976.
WORKS: THEATRE: music for Tower of Babel, 1977; Mothers in progress, 1977; Billy Irish, electronic sound effects, 1977; FILM SCORES: Bead, 1975; Intrusion, 1975.
250 Willow St., New Haven, CT 06511

SIMPSON, GEORGE ELLIOTT
b. Orange, N.J., 1 Nov. 1876; d. Kansas City, Mo., 8 Oct. 1958. Studied composition with Carl Busch in Kansas City, 1894-1900; with Jadassohn and Reinecke in Leipzig, 1900-3. He taught in Kansas City and in Texas. His compositions included a symphony, 12 tone poems, 4 overtures, many piano pieces and songs.

SIMS, EZRA
b. Birmingham, Ala., 16 Jan. 1928. Studied at Birmingham Cons., 1945-48; with Quincy Porter, Yale Univ., B.M. 1952; with Darius Milhaud and Leon Kirchner, Mills Coll., M.A. 1956. His awards include Crofts scholarship at Tanglewood, 1960; Sagalyn prize, 1960; Guggenheim fellowship, 1962-63; Cambridge Arts Council grant, 1975-76; Nat. Endowment for the Arts grants, 1976, 1978; Martha Baird Rockefeller recording grant, 1977. He was staff member at the Harvard

SIMUTIS, LEONARD J.

Music Library, 1958-62, 1965-74; on faculty, New
England Cons., 1976-78. He uses quarter- and
sixth-tones in many of his compositions and contributed an article on microtones to the Harvard
Dictionary of Music, 2nd. ed. He has also developed a polyphonic microtonal keyboard capable
of switching to many different equal tempera-
ments and of being adjusted to an asymmetrical
scale of 18 or 19 degrees.
    WORKS: BALLET: Masque, 1955; Antimatter,
1968; Alec, 1968; Lion at the door, 1969; Warts
and all, 1969; Real toads, 1970; Summer piece:
Homage to Gene Krupa, 1970; Elina's piece, 1970;
5 Toby minutes plus 49.5", 1971; Ground cover,
1972; The owl and the pussy cat, 1975; The wal-
rus and the carpenter, 1975; After Lyle, 1975;
THEATRE: music for The Trojan women, 1955; The
ticklish acrobat, 1957; Cat's cradle, 1969; When
the angels blow their trumpets, gospel song for
3 actors, 1976; CHAMBER MUSIC: Chamber cantata
on Chinese poems, tenor chamber ensemble, 1954;
cello sonata, 1957; 2 string quartets, 1957,
1962; Sonate concertanti, a demountable octet,
comprising 5 sonatinas for oboe, viola, cello,
bass, and 5 sonatas for string quartet, 1961;
Cantata III, mezzo-soprano and percussion, 1962;
octet for strings, in 6th-tones, 1964; From an
oboe quartet, oboe and string trio, 1971; Study,
violin and viola or cello, or any 2 voices, 1973;
II-Variations, oboe and string trio, 1973; A
celebration of dead ladies, voice and chamber
group, 1976; Elegie--nach Rilke, soprano, chamber
group, 1976; Aeneas on the saxophone, vocal quartet, chamber group, 1977; 20 years after, violin
and clarinet, 1978; Come away, voice and chamber
group, 1978; ELECTRONIC: Commonplace variations
or Salute to our American Container Corp, 1969;
Tango variations, 1971; Museum piece, 1972; Wall
to wall, 1972; 30 years later, 1972; Where the
wild things are, 1973; Collage XIII (The inex-
cusable), 1977.
    1168 Massachusetts Ave., Cambridge, MA
    02138

SIMUTIS, LEONARD J.
    b. Brooklyn, N.Y., 29 May 1920. Studied with
Leon Stein, De Paul Univ., B.M., M.M.; at Univ.
of Ottawa, Ph.D. In 1948 he won an award in an
international competition for Lithuanian composers. He has been faculty member, Chicago
State Univ., from 1951; also on faculty at
De Paul Univ., 1951-56, 1966-70.
    WORKS: BALLET: Polish wedding; CHORUS: A
spring morning, women's voices; Ancestral dirge,
with baritone solo, 1948; Cease O storm, women's
chorus and baritone solo, 1949; SONGS: The land
I left behind, baritone and piano, 1951; I remember, baritone and piano, 1953.
    3551 W. 98th St., Evergreen Park, IL 60642

SINATRA, RAY
    b. Gergenti, Italy, 1 Nov. 1904; U.S. citizen;
d. Las Vegas, Nev., Nov. 1980. Studied with W.
Riegger, J. Schillinger, P. Grainger, and A.
Stoessel. He gave a recital at Symphony Hall,
Boston, at age 13. He was organist in Boston
theatres, pianist in dance orchestras; then
scored films in Hollywood. His works include
Central Park ballet and a piano concerto.

SINGER, ANDRE
    b. Hungary, 1 Nov. 1907; U.S. citizen 1944.
Studied composition with Joseph Marx in Vienna;
piano with Paul Weingarten, conducting with
Rudolf Kaiser. He has held faculty psots at
City Coll. of New York; the New School; and at
Sarah Lawrence Coll., 1946-77.
    WORKS: ORCHESTRA: 3 symphonies; CHAMBER
MUSIC: piano trio; string quartet; wind quintet;
etc.; CHORUS: Alcottiana, scenic cantata; Canticle of peace; PIANO: sonata for 2 pianos,
1949, rev. 1952; Parables to Kafka's "Amerika,"
1950; 3 serial pieces, 1963, 1967; also a
chamber opera; songs.
    138 Germonds Rd., West Nyack, NY 10994

SINGER, JEANNE
    b. New York, N.Y., 4 Aug. 1924. Studied with
Seth Bingham, Rudolf Thomas, Douglas Moore, Paul
Henry Lang, Barnard Coll., B.A. magna cum laude,
Phi Beta Kappa; piano with Nadia Reisenberg.
She has won more than 20 composition awards from
Nat. League of American Pen Women, Nat. Fed. of
Music Clubs, Composers Guild, Composers, Authors,
and Artists of America, and others. She is com-
poser, concert pianist, lecturer, writer.
    WORKS: CHAMBER MUSIC: From the Green
Mountains, violin, clarinet, piano; Nocturne,
clarinet and piano; Dialogue and Romance, violin
and piano; VOICE: A cycle of love, soprano and
piano; Summons, baritone and piano; American
Indian song suite; KEYBOARD: Suite in harpsichord style, piano or harpsichord; Introduction
and caprice, piano; 4 pieces for piano.
    64 Stuart Place, Manhasset, NY 11030

SINGLETON, ALVIN
    Studied at Juilliard School and Yale Univ., M.M.;
has lived in Graz, Austria, for some years. His
Be natural, an aleatory piece for any 3 bowed
string instruments, won an award at Darmstadt in
1974. Other works include: A seasoning, 1971,
blues piece for voice, flute, alto saxophone,
trombone, bass, percussion, to his own text (the
instrumentalists also have speaking parts);
Argoru I for piano; Argoru II for cello; Argoru
III, virtuoso piece for flute solo, 1971;
Kwitana, 1974, concerto for piano, bass, percussion, an ensemble of string trio and woodwind
trio, and a brass ensemble of 2 trumpets and 2
trombones.

SINZHEIMER, MAX
    b. Frankfurt/Main, Germany, 20 June 1894; U.S.
citizen 1944; d. Chicago, Ill., 16 Oct. 1977.
Studied with Walter Braunfels, Univ. of Munich;
with Philipp Wolfrum, Univ. of Heidelberg, Ph.D.
1920. He was opera conductor in Darmstadt,
Mannheim, and Frankfurt/Main; music director at
synagogues and churches in New York and Chicago;
was faculty member, American Cons., 1947-77.
    WORKS: ORCHESTRA: sinfonia after instru-
mental music of Salomone Rossi, performed by
Chicago Symph. Orch., 1944; CHORUS: The song of
Mary; Psalm 128; many anthems and psalm settings;
organ preludes, etc.

SISSON, WILLIAM K.
b. Fairview Park, Ohio, 1 Apr. 1953. Studied with David Cope at Miami Univ., 1971-76. From 1976 he has been general editor of comtemporary music, Alexander Broude, New York.
WORKS: ORCHESTRA: North American folksong, 1978; CHAMBER MUSIC: Concertpiece, saxophone and piano, 1974; Contours, oboe and tape, 1975; Variations, 2 pianos, 1976; West o' the moon, solo flute, 1977; Music for piano, 1978; Fantasia for violin and percussion, 1978.
c/o ABI, 225 W. 57 St., New York, NY 10019

SIWE, THOMAS
b. Chicago, Ill., 14 Feb. 1935. Studied with Hunter Johnson and Robert Kelly, Univ. of Illinois. He was percussionist with the Univ. of Chicago Contemporary Chamber Players, 1963-68; from 1969, faculty member, Univ. of Illinois.
WORKS: PERCUSSION: duet for snare drum and timpani; sextet for percussion ensemble; Othello music; In the greenhouse; Beads, percussion quartet with dancers, 1976.
Univ. of Illinois, Urbana, IL 61801

SKOLNIK, WALTER
b. New York, N.Y., 20 July 1934. Studied at Brooklyn Coll., B.A. 1955; with Bernhard Heiden and Thomas Beversdorf, Indiana Univ., M.M. 1956, D.M. 1969; with Goffredo Petrassi at Tanglewood, 1956. He held a Ford Found.-MENC grant for composer-in-residence, Shawnee Mission, Kans., 1966-68. He was faculty member, St. Paul's Coll., 1964-65; Youngstown State Univ., 1969-70; from 1974, on staff, Sam Ash-Westchester Music Corp.
WORKS: ORCHESTRA: Capriccio; clarinet concerto, 1968; Diptych; trumpet concertino; Passacaglia; BAND: Chorale fantasia; Quixotic rhapsody, 1973; Toccata festiva, 1968; Little suite in B flat; Intrada; CHAMBER MUSIC: sonatina for alto saxophone, 1962; flute sonatina, 1965; Serenata notturno, flute and string trio; Divertimento, saxophone quartet; Pastorale, woodwind quintet; trumpet sonata, 1971; Concert music, brass choir, timpani, percussion, 1973; horn sonatina; Arioso and dance, saxophone and piano; 4 improvisations, string quartet, 1977; CHORUS: Historical limericks; Hodie Christus natus est; The old man in the tree; Piping down the valleys wild; Song for all seas, all ships, 1968; The sparrow song; 3 nonsense songs of Edward Lear; Zoological studies; and others.
3975-A Sedgwick Ave., Bronx, NY 10463

SKORNICKA, JOSEPH E.
b. Birch Creek, Mich., 13 Feb. 1902. Studied at Univ. of Wisconsin, B.E.; Northwestern Univ., M.A.; Oregon State Univ., Ed.D. He taught in Milwaukee schools from 1922; conducted the Milwaukee Civic Band, 1939-59; then the Milwaukee Civic Orchestra. His compositions include works for orchestra and band.

SKROWACZEWSKI, STANISLAW
b. Lwow, Poland, 3 Oct. 1923; U.S. citizen 1966. Made his debut as pianist at age 11, but injury to his hands in a World War II bombing raid

turned him to composing and conducting. He earned diplomas in both these subjects at the Univ. of Lwow and the Acad. of Music in Krakow; studied with Nadia Boulanger in Paris after the war. In Paris he was a founder of the avant-garde group known as Zodiaque. He was conductor of 3 leading Polish orchestras and in 1956, won first prize in an internat. competition for composer in Rome. He made his American debut as conductor with the Cleveland Orchestra in 1958; in 1960 he was appointed conductor of the Minnesota Orch.
WORKS: ORCHESTRA: 4 symphonies, 1948-55; Music at night, 1952; Symphonic suite, 1956; overture, 1957; concerto for English horn, 1969; Ricercari notturni, saxophone and orch., premiere at St. Joseph, Minn., 15 Jan. 1978; clarinet concerto, Minneapolis, 15 Apr. 1981; CHAMBER MUSIC: 4 string quartets; piano sonata; violin sonata.

SLADEK, PAUL
b. Vienna, Austria, 18 Jan. 1896; U.S. citizen 1912. Studied violin and viola at Vienna Cons.; in the U.S., with Albert Spalding and Leopold Auer; composition with Caspar Koch. He received a violin and a scholarship from the Vienna Public School; twice won the Composers Press publication award, 1954, 1959. He was head of the violin dept., Duquesne Univ., 1940-56.
WORKS: ORCHESTRA: Menuet pompadour, 1954; The old clock, 1959; CHAMBER MUSIC: many published pieces for violin or viola and piano.
5108 Bayard St., Pittsburgh, PA 15232

SLATES, PHILIP M.
b. Canton, Ohio, 24 Sept. 1924; d. Indianapolis, Ind., 1966. Studied with Bernard Rogers and Howard Hanson, Eastman School of Music; with Burrill Phillips, Univ. of Illinois, D.M.A. 1961. His awards included Bennington Composers Conf. fellowship, 1955; first prize, Ohio Univ. chamber opera contest, 1956; Southern Fellowship Fund award, 1958; Ford Found. grant, 1959. He was faculty member, George Peabody Coll., 1961-64; Jordan Coll. of Music, Butler Univ., 1964-66.
WORKS: OPERA: Pierrot of the minute, 1 act; Double bill: The candle and The bargain, to his own libretto; BALLET: 2 religious dance dramas, Pieta and Kanon for Easter; ORCHESTRA: Commentary and summary; Variations for orchestra; 2 symphonies; BAND: 5 intaglios; Rituals; Gothic overture; many works for small ensembles, solo instruments, and chorus.

SLAWSON, A. WAYNE
b. Detroit, Mich., 29 Dec. 1932. Studied with Leslie Bassett and Ross Lee Finney, Univ. of Michigan, M.A. 1959; psychoacoustics, Harvard Univ., Ph.D. 1965. He was postdoctoral fellow, Mass. Inst. of Tech., 1965-66, and at Royal Inst. of Tech., Stockholm, 1966-67; faculty member, Yale Univ., 1967-72; from 1972, Univ. of Pittsburgh.
WORKS: ORCHESTRA: Motions, 1973; CHAMBER MUSIC: 5 turns for 10, variable instrumentation and duration, 1970; Pieces for string quartet, 1970, expanded and rev. as Limits, 1977; Reflections, cello and piano, 1975; Variations, 2

SLEETH, NATALIE W.

violins, 1977; CHORUS: <u>Pity . . . not</u>, 1974;
<u>Omaggio a Petrarca</u>, 1975; <u>Minglings</u>, men's
chorus, 1976; ELECTRONIC: <u>Wishful thinking
about winter</u>, tape, 1967, rev. 1970; <u>MUCH</u> (with
Robert Morris), with tape and computer sound,
1971, rev. in 1974 with choral parts added;
<u>Death, love and the maiden</u>, tape, 1975; <u>poor
flesh and trees, poor stars and stones</u>, tape,
1977.
    5600 Howe St., Pittsburgh, PA 15232

SLEETH, NATALIE W.
    b. Evanston, Ill., 29 Oct. 1930. Studied with
Hubert Lamb, Wellesley Coll., B.A. 1952; organ
at Northwestern Univ.; with Lloyd Pfautsch,
Southern Methodist Univ., 1968-69. She received
annual ASCAP awards, 1973-77. She was church
organist, Glencoe, Ill., 1952-54; church music
secretary, Highland Park United Methodist Church,
1968-77.
    WORKS: CHORUS: <u>Jazz gloria</u>, with 3 trum-
pets, double bass, bongo drums; <u>Hallelujah</u>;
<u>Gaudeamus hodie</u>; <u>Feed my lambs</u>; <u>Fa la la fan-
taisie</u>, a cappella; numerous other sacred and
secular choral works.
    7439 Colgate Ave., Dallas, TX 75225

SLOCUM, WILLIAM BENNETT
    b. Grand Junction, Colo., 17 Dec. 1936. Studied
horn at Univ. of New Mexico, B.F.A., M.M.; at
Juilliard School, Aspen Music School, and Berkshire Music Center; had no formal training in
composition. He played first horn, Buffalo Phil.
Orch., 1960-63; Cleveland Orch., 1966-68; taught
at Univ. of Wyoming, 1963-66; Cleveland Inst. of
Music, 1966-72; then at Youngstown State Univ.
    WORKS: CHAMBER MUSIC: woodwind quintet,
1967; <u>7 lyric pieces</u>, clarinet solo, 1969; <u>Var-
iations</u>, horn solo, 1971; <u>3 songs</u>, baritone and
4 instruments, 1971; <u>Ambivalence</u>, trumpet, 2
horns, percussion, 1972.
    317 Redondo Rd., Youngstown, OH 44504

SLONIMSKY, NICOLAS
    b. St. Petersburg, Russia, 27 Apr. 1894; U.S.
citizen 1931. Studied piano with his aunt,
Isabelle Vengerova, composition at St. Petersburg Cons. He came to the U.S. in 1923; was
professor at Eastman School of Music, 1923-25;
secretary to Serge Koussevitzky in Boston, 1925-
27; founder and conductor, Boston Chamber Orch.,
1927-34; conductor, Harvard Univ. Orch., 1928-
30; later presented premieres of works by Charles
Ives, Edgard Varese, Henry Cowell, Carl Ruggles,
Wallingford Riegger, and other American composers
of that period in Europe and the U.S. He was
Russian language instructor, Harvard Univ.,
1946-47; lecturer in music, Univ. of California,
Los Angeles, 1964-67. He is well known for his
extensive work in musicology as author of <u>Music
since 1900</u> (1937, 4th ed., New York, 1970) and
other works up to <u>Lexicon of musical invective</u>,
1953. He was editor of Oscar Thompson's <u>Inter-
national cyclopedia of music and musicians</u>,
1946-58; and of Baker's <u>Biographical dictionary
of musicians</u>, 1958-78. He is on the editorial
board of <u>Encyclopedia Britannica</u> and has contributed to Grove's <u>Dictionary of music and</u>

<u>musicians</u> and other publications. In 1962-63 he
lectured in Russia, Poland, Yugoslavia, Bulgaria,
Rumania, Greece, and Israel under the auspices
of the U.S. State Dept.
    WORKS: BALLET: <u>Prince goes a-hunting</u>,
Rochester, N.Y., Mar. 1925; ORCHESTRA: <u>Overture
on an ancient Greek theme</u>, in the Greek enhar-
monic mode, for strings tuned in quarter-tones,
trumpet, and percussion, Hollywood Bowl, July
1933; <u>4 simple pieces</u>, Boston Pops Orch., July
1941; <u>My toy balloon</u>, calls for 100 toy balloons
to be exploded at the final sforzando, Boston
Pops, 14 July 1942; CHAMBER MUSIC: <u>Moto perpetuo</u>,
violin and piano, 1936; <u>4 Russian melodies</u>,
clarinet and piano, 1937; <u>Little suite</u>, 3 woodwinds, percussion typewriter, and cat's meow,
1941; suite for cello and piano, 1950; VOICE:
<u>3 advertising songs</u>, 1925; <u>Impressions</u>, 1927;
<u>Garden songs</u>, 1928; <u>Gravestones at Hancock, N.H.</u>,
1945; <u>Möbius strip tease</u>, a perpetual canon for
soprano and tenor, with piano non-obligato,
Univ. of California, Los Angeles, 5 May 1965;
PIANO: <u>Studies in black and white</u>, uses con-
sonant counterpoint on the white keys for the
right hand, on the black keys for the left hand,
1928; <u>Silhouettes Ibériennes</u>, 1935; <u>Russian noc-
turne</u>, 1942; <u>Yellowstone Park suite</u>, 1951; <u>Moods</u>,
1963; <u>50 minitudes</u>, 1973.
    10847 3/4 Wilshire Blvd., Los Angeles, CA
90024

SMART, GARY
    b. Cuba, Ill., 19 Dec. 1943. Studied with
Iannis Xenakis, Bernhard Heiden, and Roque
Cordero, Indiana Univ., B.M., M.M.; and at
Cologne Univ., Germany. He received Nat. Endowment for the Arts grants, 1974, 1976. In 1973
he was composer-in-residence, city of Anchorage,
sponsored by the Contemporary Music Project,
Music Educators Nat. Conf.; in 1978, joined the
faculty at Univ. of Wyoming.
    WORKS: ORCHESTRA: <u>Variations for woodwinds
and orchestra</u>, 1970; <u>Aurora borealis</u>, with
piano and tape, 1971; <u>Sundog music</u>, 1973; CHAMBER
MUSIC: <u>Mobile 1969</u>, 9 woodwinds, percussion, 2
pianos; <u>5 dogs crossed the sun--a ritual for 5
performers</u>, 4 percussion, piano, each performer
also plays a radio, 1974; <u>The 2nd sundog</u>, string
quartet and 3 radios, 1974; <u>Brittle man</u>, text by
H. L. Van Brunt, soprano, 2 winds, piano trio,
1976; <u>Sundog evensong</u>, Whitman text, soprano,
flute, piano, 2 radios, 1976.
    Univ. of Wyoming, Box 3037, Univ. Sta.,
Laramie, WY 82071

SMELTZER, SUSAN
    b. Sapulpa, Okla., 13 Sept. 1941. Studied with
Robert Laughlin, Oklahoma City Univ., B.M. 1963;
with Harold Owen, Univ. of Southern California,
M.M. 1967; piano with various teachers; with
Joseph Dichler, Vienna, 1969-70; master classes
with Rosina Lhevinne, 1971. She is concert
pianist and accompanist; has taught piano in a
private studio and in many schools; from 1972,
at Coll. of the Mainland, Texas City.
    WORKS: WIND ENSEMBLE: <u>Christmas fantasy</u>,
brass choir; VOICE: <u>Jonathan Richards, my bicentennial baby</u>, soprano and instruments; <u>Song</u>,

on Millay text; <u>Love</u>, on Byron text; <u>Psalm 121</u>,
chorus, orch., piano, harp, brass; PIANO: <u>Bald
eagle march</u> and <u>Brotherhood march</u>, both gong,
drums, and 2 trumpets; <u>12 mood pictures</u> (variations on Yankee Doodle); <u>Variations for 2 pianos</u>;
<u>Reverie</u>; many other works for piano, voice,
brass ensemble.
8102 Tavenor, Houston, TX 77075

SMILEY, PRIL
b. Mohonk Lake, N.Y., 19 Mar. 1943. Studied with
Henry Brant, Louis Calabro, Vivian Fine, Bennington Coll. She received an award in the 1st
Internat. Electronic Music Competition, Dartmouth Arts Council, 1968. She has been staff
member, Columbia Princeton Electronic Music
Center, from 1963; and electronic music consultant, Lincoln Center Repertory Theatre, from 1968.
WORKS: ELECTRONIC: music for 19 major
theatre productions in New York, Tanglewood,
Cleveland, Baltimore, Cincinnati; <u>Eclipse</u>, 1967;
<u>Kolyosa</u>, 1970; music for 2 television documen-
taries and 4 independent films.
Electronic Music Center, 632 W. 125 St.,
New York, NY 10021

SMIT, JOHANNES
b. New Jersey, 1913; d. Memphis, Tenn. Studied
with Louis Mennini and Howard Hanson, Eastman
School of Music, Ph.D. 1953. He was faculty
member, Memphis State Univ., 1966-69. His published works include a trio for flute, cello,
piano.

SMIT, LEO
b. Philadelphia, Pa., 12 Jan. 1921. Studied
piano with Isabelle Vengerova on scholarship at
Curtis Inst., 1930-32; composition with Nicolas
Nabokov, 1935. His awards include a Guggenheim
grant, 1950; Fulbright grant, 1950; Boston Symph.
Orch. Merit award, 1953; New York Critics' Circle
award, 1957; and commissions. He made his piano
debut in New York, 1939; toured the U.S., 1940,
Europe, 1953-55. He has held faculty posts at
Sarah Lawrence Coll., 1947-49; Univ. of California, Los Angeles, 1957-63; from 1963, professor,
State Univ. of New York at Buffalo. In 1967-68
he toured 16 Latin American countries for the
U.S. State Dept.
WORKS: OPERA: <u>The alchemy of love</u>, libretto
by Fred Hoyle, 1967; BALLET: <u>Virginia sampler</u>,
New York, 4 Mar. 1947; ORCHESTRA: <u>The Parcae</u>,
overture, 1951, Boston, 16 Oct. 1953; <u>Capriccio</u>,
string orch., 1958; symphony #1, Boston, 1 Feb.
1957; symphony #2, New York, 10 Feb. 1966; piano
concerto, Buffalo, Nov. 1968, composer as soloist; <u>4 Kookaburra marches</u>, 1972; CHAMBER MUSIC:
<u>Academic graffiti</u>, text by W. H. Auden, voice
and chamber group, 1962; <u>A mountain eulogy</u>,
melodrama for speaker and piano, 1975; <u>In woods</u>,
oboe, harp, percussion, 1978; CHORUS: <u>A choir
of starlings</u>, on 7 poems of Anthony Hecht, 1951;
<u>Caedmon</u>, 3 soloists, male chorus, orch., 1972;
<u>3 Christmas tree carols</u> (after Franz Liszt),
with chamber group, 1974.
State Univ. of New York, Buffalo, NY 14214

SMITH, ANITA
b. New York, N.Y., 19 Dec. 1922. Studied with
Karol Rathaus on scholarship at Queens Coll.
WORKS: CHAMBER MUSIC: violin suite; <u>Homage
to Gershwin</u>; <u>Perambular funiculi</u>; SONGS: <u>3 settings of Carl Sandburg texts</u>; <u>3 concert songs</u> on
Lindsay texts.

SMITH, BRANSON
b. Pine Village, Ind., 21 Dec. 1921. Studied
with Newell Long, Indiana Univ.; Kurt Frederick,
Univ. of New Mexico; and with Champ Tyrone,
Highlands Univ. He received an award from the
Arizona Fed. of Music Clubs, 1969. He has been
public School music teacher in Indiana, New
Mexico, and from 1973, in Tucson, Ariz.
WORKS: BALLET: <u>Legends of Superstition
Mountain</u>, 1972; ORCHESTRA: <u>Concertpiece</u>, 1959;
<u>Theme and mutations</u>, 1960; <u>Lyrical statement</u> for
strings, 1967; BAND: <u>Tikvat noar</u>, clarinet and
band, 1970; CHAMBER MUSIC: string quartet, 1967;
woodwind quintet, 1968; viola sonata, 1969;
CHORUS: <u>Ecumenical sonata</u>, 1964; <u>Imagination</u>,
text from Walden, 1968; PIANO: <u>Caper for piano-
forte</u>, 1968; <u>5 pieces for young people</u>.
1944 E. 3rd St., Tucson, AZ 85719

SMITH, CARY
b. Pleasant View, Va., 1 Jan. 1934. Studied at
American Univ.; San Francisco State Univ.; and
with Aurelio de la Vega, California State Univ.
at Northridge. He received a composition prize
at Northridge, 1969. As an operatic baritone, he
has sung in many U.S. companies, including the
San Francisco Opera Company. In 1973 he was
staff member at California State Univ., Northridge.
WORKS: CHAMBER MUSIC: <u>Studies</u> for small
orch., 1968; duet for flute and piano, 1968;
<u>Frammenti</u>, string quartet, 1969; <u>Interplay</u>,
winds, percussion, and bass, 1969; <u>Changes</u>,
flutes, brass, bass, electric bass, timpani,
1970; CHORUS: <u>Mass</u>, brass, percussion, organ,
solo violin, choir, 1969.
7529 Remmet Ave., Canoga Park, CA 91303

SMITH, CHARLES WARREN
b. Palmerton, Pa., 5 Sept. 1936. Studied with
Allan Willman, Univ. of Wyoming; with Walter
Kob, New York Univ.; with Wayne Barlow, Eastman
School of Music; at George Peabody Coll. He received an American Guild of Musical Artists
award in composition and flute performance, 1958.
He taught in public schools, 1958-68; at Madison
Coll., 1968-69; Wake Forest Univ., 1969-75.
WORKS: BAND: suite for band; <u>The harmonica
player</u>; <u>Jubilee</u>; <u>Fanfare and fantasia</u>; <u>Piece</u>,
brass and percussion; CHAMBER MUSIC: <u>Adagio and
allegro</u>, flute, clarinet, piano; CHORUS: <u>Te
Deum</u>; <u>I will publish the name of the Lord</u>; <u>So,
we'll go no more a'roving</u>; <u>The worm</u>; PIANO:
<u>Suite contemporain</u>; 2 pieces for children;
<u>Quartel piece</u>, <u>Reflections</u>.
1509 S. Hawthorne Rd., Winston-Salem, NC
27103

SMITH, CLAUDE T.
b. Monroe City, Mo., 14 Mar. 1932. Studied at

SMITH, CLIFFORD

Central Coll., Fayette, Mo.; and at Univ. of
Kansas. He has received many commissions. He
was public school music teacher in Chillicothe,
Mo.; lecturer, Southwest Missouri State Coll.,
1976-78.
    WORKS: ORCHESTRA: Fanfare and celebration,
1973; BAND: Sonus ventorum, 1970; Variations,
baritone horn and band, 1971; Overture romantique, 1971; Rhapsody, trombone and band, 1971;
Concert dance and intermezzo, 1972; Prelude-var-
iations, 1972; Credence, 1973; also works for
small wind ensembles, chorus.

SMITH, CLIFFORD
    b. Oreg., 1945. He is an instructor at Bradley
Univ. His works for piano, Metanimasque, Lux-
hymn eidola, Myst XXIII, Mystery-elan Phantas-
mata, Book CXVII, were performed at Carnegie
Recital Hall, New York, 20 May 1975.
        School of Music, Bradley University, Peoria,
    IL 61625

SMITH, DAVID STANLEY
    b. Toledo, Ohio, 6 July 1877; d. New Haven,
Conn., 17 Dec. 1949. Studied with Horatio
Parker, Yale Univ., B.M. 1903; and in Munich and
Paris. He was on the Yale Univ. faculty, 1916-
46, dean, 1920-46; conductor, New Haven Symph.,
1920-46.
    WORKS: ORCHESTRA: 4 symphonies, 1905, 1917,
1930, 1938; The fallen star, with chorus, received Paderewski prize, 1909; Impressions, 1916;
Fete galante, with solo flute, 1921; Sinfonietta,
string orch., 1931; A satire, 1933; Epic poem,
1935; Requiem, with solo violin, 1939; Credo,
symphonic poem, 1944; CHAMBER MUSIC: 10 string
quartets; 2 violin sonatas; cello sonata; oboe
sonata; piano quintet; choral works; songs.

SMITH, DONALD S.
    b. Lawrence, Mass., 1897; d. Milton, Mass., 8
Dec. 1977. Studied at the New England Cons.,
graduating in 1922; was faculty member until
retirement in 1974; taught also at Lowell Univ.
and Curry Coll.; organist and choirmaster in
Greater Boston. His compositions included works
for organ, chorus, piano, and songs.

SMITH, G. ALAN
    b. Milwaukee, Wis., 4 Aug. 1947. Studied with
John Downey, Univ. of Wisconsin-Milwaukee; with
Alvin Epstein, Lloyd Pfautsch, Carlton R. Young,
Southern Methodist Univ. He won an award in a
Phi Mu Alpha contest, 1968. He was church music
director in Milwaukee, 1968-71, in Plano, Tex.,
1971-73.
    WORKS: ORCHESTRA: An eastern rainbow; The
devil and the blacksmith; CHAMBER MUSIC: 7th
Webster's: 7th study, dance suite, chamber ensemble; By night on my bed, soprano and 3 flutes;
Sing with me now, soprano, flute, piano; The
wedding, string quartet with baritone solo;
MULTIMEDIA: Imagination dead imagine, instrumental ensemble, tape, dancers, lights, and narrator, based on Beckett monologue; choral works,
songs.

SMITH, GLANVILLE
    b. St. Cloud, Minn., 28 June 1901. Has published
pieces for organ: A Christmas wreath; preludes,
interludes, and amens.
        Cold Spring, MN 56320

SMITH, GREGG
    b. Chicago, Ill., 21 Aug. 1931. Studied at Univ.
of California, Los Angeles, B.A., M.A.; privately
with Leonard Stein and Lukas Foss; conducting
with Fritz Zweig. His awards include a Ford
Found. grant for conducting; 3 Grammy awards for
recording of the complete choral works of Charles
Ives by the Gregg Smith Singers, a group he
founded and conducts; the 1978 Ditson Conductor's
award "for his advancement of contemporary American music." He was faculty member, Ithaca
Coll., 1965-68; State Univ. of New York at Stony
Brook, 1968-72; Peabody Cons., 1969-75; Barnard
Coll., 1974-76; from 1976, on faculty, Manhattan
School of Music. He toured Europe, 1958, USSR,
1961; conducted the premiere of Stravinsky's
Requiem canticles at Princeton Univ.
    WORKS: OPERA: Aesop's fables; CHORUS:
Bible songs for young voices, 1964; Beware of
the soldier, 1968; Landscape, T. S. Eliot text;
Nature and spirit, R. W. Emerson text; Babel,
chorus or solo quartet, 5 speaking groups,
piano, 4 hands, Biblical text; Magnificat, commissioned and performed by the Laurel (Md.) Oratorio Society, 7 Dec. 1974; Jazz mass for St.
Peters; A festival of carols; numerous arrangements.
        171 W. 71st St., New York, NY 10023

SMITH, HALE
    b. Cleveland, Ohio, 29 June 1925. Studied with
Marcel Dick, Cleveland Inst. of Music, M.M. 1952.
His awards include a commission from the Thorne
Fund, 1971; BMI awards, 1972. He was associated
with Karamu House in Cleveland, 1955; editor
and consultant for music publishers from 1959;
faculty member, C. W. Post Coll., 1968-70; then
at Univ. of Connecticut, professor from 1978.
    WORKS: OPERA: Blood wedding, chamber opera,
1953; ORCHESTRA: In memoriam--Beryl Rubinstein,
chorus and chamber orch., 1953; Contours, 1962;
Music for harp and orchestra, 1967; Faces of
jazz, 1968; Rituals and incantations, Houston,
7 Sept. 1974; Innerflexions, New York, 2 Sept.
1977; BAND: Expansions; Somersault; Take a
chance, aleatoric episode; Exchanges, with solo
trumpet; CHAMBER MUSIC: duo for violin and
piano, 1953; cello soanta, 1955; Epicedial variations, violin and piano, 1956; Evocations,
piano; Introductions, cadenzas, and interludes,
8 players, 1974; Variations for 6 players, 1975;
Introspections and reflections, piano, Kennedy
Center, 1979; VOICE: Beyond the rim of day, 3
songs to texts of Langston Hughes; The valley
wind, 4 songs; By yearning and Be beautiful, 2
songs performed, New York, 30 Apr. 1974; Comes
tomorrow, jazz cantata, 1972, rev. 1977; Tous-
saint l'overture 1803, chorus, 1977.
        University of Connecticut, Storrs, CT 06268

SMITH, HAROLD JOSEPH
    b. Springfield, Colo., 8 Aug. 1928. Studied

with George F. McKay, Univ. of Washington; with
Homer Keller, Univ. of Oregon. He was winner in
a Missouri Fed. of Music Clubs contest. He was
faculty member, Evangel Coll., 1961-72; then at
School of the Ozarks, Pt. Lookout, Mo.
   WORKS: ORCHESTRA: Vistas; Legend of the
Ozarks; Caverns; BAND: The harvest; CHORUS:
Winter sunset, women's voices; PIANO: sonata.
   Hollister, MO 65672

SMITH, JERRY NEIL
   b. Lefors, Tex., 20 Feb. 1935. Studied with
Kent Kennan and James Clifton Williams, Univ. of
Texas; with Herbert Elwell, Eastman School of
Music. He received 3 research and creativity
awards, Univ. of Colorado; research grant, Univ.
of Oklahoma; and commissions. He taught in
public schools, 1956-59; Univ. of Southwest
Louisiana, 1959-60; Univ. of Florida, 1961-64;
Univ. of Colorado, 1964-72; Univ. of Northern
Iowa, 1972-75; from 1975, director, School of
Music, Univ. of Oklahoma.
   WORKS: ORCHESTRA: Proclamation; Essay for
young Americans; BAND: Epilog; Fanfare and
celebration.
   University of Oklahoma, Norman, OK 73019

SMITH, JOHN SHAFFER
   b. Hamlin, Tex., 10 June 1913. Studied with
Joseph Schillinger and Rudolf R. A. Schramm, New
York Univ. He received a commission from the
San Angelo Symph. Society, 1960; 2 awards, Contemporary Music Festival, San Jose State Coll.,
1961. He has been composer-arranger for dance
bands, radio, television, from 1937; was conductor, Roxy Theatre Orch., New York, 1946-50;
instructor, New York Univ., 1948-52; then in a
private studio to 1957.
   WORKS: ORCHESTRA: Tone poem; trumpet concerto; One mood, trombone and orch.; Texas suite,
1960; BAND: Rendicion; CHAMBER MUSIC: quintet,
oboe and strings; Rondo for brass sextet; Chronology, brass quintet; and songs.

SMITH, JULIA
   b. Denton, Tex., 25 Jan. 1911. Studied at North
Texas State Univ., B.A.; piano with Carl
Friedberg and Lonny Epstein, Juilliard School;
composition with Frederick Jacobi, Bernard
Wagenaar, and Rubin Goldmark on a fellowship;
with Vincent Jones, Virgil Thomson, Marion
Bauer, New York Univ., M.A., Ph.D. Her honors
include Sigma Alpha Iota, Texas Music Teachers
Assoc., Nat. Fed. of Music Clubs, and ASCAP
awards; Ford Found. grant; honorary membership
in Girl Scouts of USA for opera Daisy, based on
life of Juliette Gordon Low; and commissions.
She was faculty member, Juilliard School, 1940-
42; founder and head, music education dept.,
Hartt Coll. of Music, 1940-45; then free-lance
composer-pianist-lecturer.
   WORKS: OPERA: Cynthia Parker, 1939; The
stranger of Manzano, 1947; The gooseherd and the
goblin, 1947; Cockrow, 1964; The shepherdess and
the chimney sweep, 1967; Daisy, Miami, 3 Nov.
1973; ORCHESTRA: Episodic suite; American dance
suite; Hellenic suite; Folkway symphony, 1947;
piano concerto, 1976; BAND: Remember the Alamo,

1964; Sails aloft, overture; CHAMBER MUSIC:
piano sonatina; Characteristic suite, piano;
Nocturne and festival piece, viola and piano;
Cornwall, piano trio, 1955; string quartet, 1964;
Elegy, piano quintet, Dallas, 27 Feb. 1976;
Passacaglia and Capriccietto, violin and piano,
Galveston, 21 Apr. 1976; also choral works and
songs.
   417 Riverside Dr., New York, NY 10025

SMITH, LANI
   b. Cincinnati, Ohio, 9 June 1934. Studied with
John Larkin, Felix Labunski, Scott Huston, Univ.
of Cincinnati Coll. Cons., B.M., M.M. His
awards include the Columbia Univ. Bearns prize
and the Univ. of Cincinnati Martin Dumler award.
He has been organist and choirmaster from 1955;
editor, composer, and arranger for Lorenz Publishing Co. from 1967.
   WORKS: BALLET: A Christmas carol, based on
Dickens's story, 1973; Coming of age in a difficult time; ORCHESTRA: Suite for orchestra;
Prelude and scherzo, brass, strings, timpani,
1957; Pastorale, strings and oboe, 1957; piano
concerto; WIND ENSEMBLE: 2 etchings in brass;
Overture for brass; CHAMBER MUSIC: Divertimento,
woodwinds and piano; woodwind quintet; 5 pieces,
woodwind quintet; Movement for string quartet;
Reflections, flute, oboe, cello; 4 dance movements, flute, oboe, cello; numerous songs and
piano pieces; over 400 published choral and
organ works.
   225 Victor, #2, Dayton, OH 45405

SMITH, LAWRENCE R. See RACKLEY, LAWRENCE

SMITH, LELAND C.
   b. Oakland, Calif., 6 Aug. 1925. Studied with
Darius Milhaud, Mills Coll., 1941-43; with Roger
Sessions, Univ. of California, Berkeley, M.A.
1948; with Olivier Messiaen in Paris, 1948-49.
He has held teaching posts at Univ. of California,
Berkeley, Mills Coll., Univ. of Chicago; joined
the faculty at Stanford Univ. in 1958.
   WORKS: OPERA: Santa Claus, on libretto by
e. e. cummings, 1955; ORCHESTRA: symphony, 1951;
concerto for orchestra, 1956; CHAMBER MUSIC:
trumpet sonata, 1947; trio for flute, cello,
piano, 1947; trio for violin, trumpet, clarinet,
1948; Divertimento #1, 5 instruments, 1959;
woodwind quintet, 1951; viola (or hecklephone)
sonata, 1954; quintet for bassoon and strings,
1956; Divertimento #2, chamber orch., 1957; wind
trio, 1960; 3 pacifist songs, 1960; quartet for
horn and piano trio, 1961; Orpheus, guitar, harp,
harpsichord, 1967; Machines of loving grace,
computer, narrator, bassoon, 1970.
   3732 Laguna Ave., Palo Alto, CA 94302

SMITH, RICHARD HARRISON
   b. Erie, Pa., 23 Aug. 1932. Studied at Allegheny Coll.; with Paul Christansen, Concordia
Coll., Morehead, Minn. He was minister of music,
Fargo, N.Dak., 1962-69; high school choral director in Fargo, 1967-69; from 1969, faculty member,
Jamestown Coll.
   WORKS: CHORUS: War poem; Except our God
build a house; The babe and the cross; Fanfare

SMITH, RUSSELL

and processional.
319 6th Ave., N.E., Jamestown, ND 58401

SMITH, RUSSELL
b. Tuscaloosa, Ala., 23 Apr. 1927. Studied at
Eastman School of Music; with Otto Luening and
Douglas Moore, Columbia Univ., B.S., M.A.; with
Aaron Copland at Tanglewood, 1947. His awards
include a Seidl fellowship in theatrical composition, Columbia Univ., 1951; special award,
Gershwin Memorial contest, 1954; Guggenheim fellowship, 1955. He is faculty member, State
Univ., in New Orleans.
    WORKS: OPERA: The unicorn in the garden,
Thurber text; ORCHESTRA: Can-can and waltz;
Tetrameron, 1957; piano concerto; CHORUS: Gloria
and service in C; Set me as a seal, women's
voices; 3 songs from Emily Dickinson, women's
voices; ORGAN: 3 chorale preludes.
    State University, New Orleans, LA 70122

SMITH, STUART S.
b. Portland, Maine, 16 Mar. 1948. Studied with
Edward Miller and Edward Diemente, Hartt Coll.
of Music; with Salvatore Martirano, Herbert Brun,
Ben Johnston, Univ. of Illinois, D.M.A. 1975.
He has received an ASCAP Merit award and a Univ.
of Maryland research grant. He taught at Hartt
Coll. of Music, 1970-73; from 1975, has been
faculty member, Univ. of Maryland, Baltimore
County.
    WORKS: CHAMBER MUSIC: Gestures I, II, III,
piano; One for Syl, vibraphone; Poems I, II, III,
5 brake drums and narrator; A fine old tradition,
2 pianos, alto saxophone, percussion; One for
J. C., saxophone and bassoon; A gift for Bessie,
bassoon, piano, violin, percussion; Legacy variations, any 3 melody instruments; 2 for 4, percussion quartet; Faces, clarinet and oboe; Gifts,
oboe, clarinet, piano; 2 makes 3, organ and percussion; Links, vibraphone.
    1014 Wilmington Ave., Baltimore, MD 21223

SMITH, WARREN STOREY
b. Brookline, Mass., 14 July 1885; d. Westboro,
Mass., 12 Oct. 1971. Studied at the Faelton
Pianoforte School, Boston; taught there, 1908-
19; was faculty member, New England Cons., 1922-
58; assistant music critic, Boston Evening Tran-
script, 1919-24; music editor, Boston Post,
1924-53. His works for orchestra include Romance, 1916; A caravan from China comes, voice
and orch., 1916; Andante cantabile, 1920; also
a piano trio, piano pieces, and songs.

SMITH, WILLIAM OVERTON
b. Sacramento, Calif., 22 Sept. 1926. Studied
with Darius Milhaud, Mills Coll.; with Roger
Sessions, Univ. of California, Berkeley, M.A.
1952; at Juilliard School; with Ulysse
Delecleuse, Paris Cons. His awards include Prix
de Paris, 1951-53; Prix de Rome, 1957; Guggenheim
fellowships, 1961, 1962; American Acad. of Arts
and Letters award, 1972; and commissions. He
has held faculty posts at Univ. of California,
Berkeley, 1953-54; San Francisco Cons., 1954-55;
Univ. of Southern California, 1955-57, 1958-60;
from 1966, at Univ. of Washington.

WORKS: ORCHESTRA: concerto for jazz clarinet and orch.; Quadri, jazz quartet and orch.;
Ecco, electric clarinet and orch., Seattle, 15
Mar. 1978, composer as soloist; Theona, Seattle,
15 Mar. 1978; CHAMBER MUSIC: suite for clarinet,
flute, trumpet, 1947; Serenade, flute, violin,
clarinet, trumpet, 1947; Schizophrenic scherzo,
4 winds, 1947; clarinet sonata, 1948; concertino,
trumpet and jazz group, 1948; quintet for clarinet and string quartet, 1950; string quartet,
1952; Capriccio, violin and piano, 1952; suite
for violin and clarinet, 1952; Divertimento,
jazz group, 1956; concerto for clarinet and jazz
combo, 1957; trio, clarinet, violin, piano, 1957;
quartet for clarinet and piano trio, 1958; 5
pieces for clarinet alone, 1958; Elegy for Eric,
jazz combo, 1964; MULTIMEDIA: Quadrodram, 4 instruments, dancer, film, Seattle, 9 Dec. 1970.
    University of Washington, Seattle, WA 98105

SMOLOVER, RAYMOND
b. Russia, 15 Jan. 1921; to U.S. 1922. Attended
Carnegie Inst. of Technology and Columbia Univ.
Teachers Coll. He has been cantor and music
director from 1949; was executive director,
American Conf. of Cantors, 1968-74.
    WORKS: FOLK/ROCK SERVICES: Where the rain-
bow ends, interfaith service; Edge of freedom;
Gates of freedom.
    10 Crest Lane, Scarsdale, NY 10583

SNOPEK, SIGMUND III
b. Milwaukee, Wis., 25 Oct. 1950. Studied with
John Downey, Univ. of Wisconsin, Milwaukee. He
received a $20,000 grant from the City of Mil-
waukee, Univ. of Wisconsin, and the state Bicentennial Commission to put on a performance of
his rock opera, Return of the spirit. He taught
electronic music at Univ. of Wisconsin, 1973-78;
was head of the new music group, 1973-77.
    WORKS: OPERA: Return of the spirit, with
rock group, actors, and dancers, 1976; One room
life, also with rock group, actors, dancers,
Milwaukee, Dec. 1977; CHAMBER MUSIC: The desert
songs, soprano and piano, 1978; ELECTRONIC: incidental music for plays, 1974-78; Lifencave,
tape, actors, dancers, puppets, George Peabody
Coll., Nashville, 15 Mar. 1974.
    1600 E. Providence, #204, Milwaukee, WI
    53211

SNOW, DAVID JASON
b. Providence, R.I., 8 Oct. 1954. Studied with
Joseph Schwantner, Warren Benson, and Samuel
Adler, Eastman School of Music; with Jacob
Druckman, Yale Univ.; with Martin Boykan and
Arthur Berger, Brandeis Univ. His awards include
Sernoffsky prize, 1974; McCurdy prize, 1975;
Howard Hanson prize, 1976; Bradley-Keeler
scholarship, 1977; Osborne-Kellogg prize, 1978;
second prize, Mirafone tuba composition contest,
1978.
    WORKS: ORCHESTRA: Buddha breath, cello and
orch.; BAND: Guernica, 2 antiphonal brass quintets and band; CHAMBER MUSIC: Merkabah, mezzo-
soprano; Poor Mr. Cabbage!, 2 tubas and percussion; chamber concerto for 9 instruments; Elephants exotiques, tuba quartet; Crystal effu-

sions, horn and piano; string trio; Passacaglia, piano; Jakarta, violin, oboe, percussion ensemble.

SNOW, MARY
b. Brownsville, Tex., 26 Aug. 1928. Studied with Anis Fuleihan, Indiana Univ., B.M. 1950; with Burrill Phillips, Univ. of Illinois, M.M. 1952. Her awards include Nat. Endowment for the Arts grant, 1976; Texas Tech. Univ. grant, 1975. She was faculty member, Texas Technological Univ., 1974-78.
    WORKS: THEATRE: electronic scores for Marat-Sade; Indians; Peer Gynt; Faustus; CHAMBER MUSIC: Hieroglyphs, tenor voice, clarinet, bassoon, percussion, tape; Mandore, violin and tape; Voyages: Columbus/Apollo II, tape, 1977; Ezekiel I, voice and 2 tapes.

SNYDER, LEO
b. Boston, Mass., 1 Jan. 1918. Studied with Francis Judd Cooke, Warren Story Smith, Lois Lautner, Margaret Mason, Julius Chaloff, New England Cons.; piano with Miklos Schwalb. He taught at New England Cons., 1952-56; Boston Univ., 1956-66; from 1967, at Northeastern Univ.
    WORKS: OPERA: The princess marries the page, Boston, 25 May 1979; CHAMBER MUSIC: Permutations, flute and piano, 1980; VOICE: A book of Americans, choral cantata, 1962; Love is a language, song cycle to texts of Norma Farber, Boston, 6 Nov. 1980.
    21 Earldor Circle, Marshfield, MA 02050

SNYDER, RANDALL
b. Chicago, Ill., 6 Apr. 1944. Studied with Lavern Wagner, Quincy Coll.; with Hilmar Luckhardt, Burt Levy, and Les Thimmig, Univ. of Wisconsin. He won first prize, Eastern Illinois Univ. wind ensemble composition contest; first prize, Internat. Double Reed Society contest, 1977. He was faculty member, Univ. of Wisconsin, 1973-74; from 1976, at Univ. of Nebraska at Lincoln.
    WORKS: ORCHESTRA: concerto for bassoon and chamber orch., 1971; Hegemony, piano and orch., 1971; WIND ENSEMBLE: Variations, 1971; CHAMBER MUSIC: quintet for saxophone and string quartet; 7 epigrams, saxophone and piano; Florilegium, organ; Glyphs, oboe and bassoon, 1977.
    University of Nebraska, Lincoln, NE 68508

SNYDER, THEODORE
b. New York, N.Y., 27 Nov. 1924. Studied with William Bergsma and Vincent Persichetti at Juilliard School; with Aaron Copland at Tanglewood; with Bernard Rogers and Wayne Barlow, Eastman School of Music, D.M.A. He received a Crofts award for study at Tanglewood; and an award from the American Society of Women's Music Clubs. He was faculty member, Hampton Inst., 1955-60; Luther Coll., 1963-65; and State Univ. Coll. at Brockport, 1970-75.
    WORKS: ORCHESTRA: 4 variations; St. Nicholas, chorus, orch., and pantomime; CHAMBER MUSIC: quartet for piano and winds; CHORUS: 2 Ascension Day choruses.
    3 Rundel Park, Rochester, NY 14607

SNYDER, WILLIAM
b. Park Ridge, Ill., 11 July 1916. Studied at De Paul Univ.; Chicago Cons., B.M.; American Cons., M.M.; also with Leo Sowerby and Moritz Rosenthal. He is pianist on radio and with dance bands.
    WORKS: ORCHESTRA: Seamist; Concerto for a summer night; Amber fire; CHORUS: The 10 commandments.

SODERLUND, GUSTAVE FREDERIC
b. Götesborg, Sweden, 25 Jan. 1881; to U.S. 1916; d. Rochester, N.Y., 28 Nov. 1972. Studied piano in Sweden and in the U.S. with Josef Lhevinne. He taught at Univ. of Kansas, 1919-27; Eastman School of Music, 1928-52. He composed a symphonic poem, Svithiod, chamber music, piano pieces.

SODERO, CESARE
b. Naples, Italy, 2 Aug. 1886; to U.S. 1906; d. New York, N.Y., 16 Dec. 1947. Studied at Royal Cons., Naples. He conducted opera in England; on radio; Metropolitan Opera, New York, 1942-43; conducted the Mendelssohn Glee Club 12 seasons; was music director for a record company.
    WORKS: BALLET: Ombre Russe; ORCHESTRA: Nocturne, oboe and orch.; Preludio appasionato, violin and orch.; CHAMBER MUSIC: string quartet; Valse scherzo, woodwinds; Morning prayer, woodwinds; Invocation, cello and piano.

SOKOLOV, ELLIOT
b. New York, N.Y., 16 Sept. 1953. Studied with Mario Davidovsky, City Coll. of New York; with Ezra Laderman, State Univ. of New York, Binghamton, B.A.; with Jack Beeson, Bulent Arel, Vladimir Ussachevsky, Dennis Riley, Columbia Univ., M.A. His awards include Creative Arts award, SUNY, 1975; President's fellowships, Columbia Univ., 1975, 1976; Composer Assistance Program grant, 1977; Meet the Composer grants. He was assistant director, Electronic Music Studio, SUNY, Binghamton, 1974-75; from 1977, on staff, Composers Recordings, Inc.; from 1978, staff composer, TRS Theatre Co., N.Y.
    WORKS: ORCHESTRA: A postcard from the volcano (symphony #1); CHAMBER MUSIC: September music, flute and guitar; 6 bagatelles, clarinet and piano; 5 pieces for organ; Aeolus, wind octet; Callings, soprano, clarinet, piano; Parallax, chamber ensemble; Epithalamia, chamber ensemble; also music for theatre, dance, film; and electronic pieces.
    30 W. 88 St., New York, NY 10024

SOLITO DE SOLIS, ALDO
b. Castrovillari, Italy, 25 May 1905; U.S. citizen. Studied at the Verdi Cons., Milan, where he received the Gold Medal, and at Leipzig Cons. He has been concerto pianist in Europe, South America, and from 1940, in New York. He has composed many piano pieces and songs.

SOLLBERGER, HARVEY
b. Cedar Rapids, Iowa, 11 May 1938. Studied with Eldon Obrecht and Philip Bezanson, Univ. of Iowa; with Jack Beeson and Otto Luening, Columbia

SOLOMON, LARRY

Univ., M.A. 1964. His awards include the Bearns
prize, 1963; Fromm Found.-Berkshire Music Center
commission, 1964; American Acad. of Arts and
Letters award, 1965; Koussevitzky grant, 1966;
special citation, American Internat. Music Fund,
1967; 2 Guggenheim fellowships, 1969, 1973. He
has been faculty member at Columbia Univ. from
1965; Manhattan School of Music from 1962, and
Temple Univ. from 1978.
    WORKS: THEATRE: music for Sophocles'
Antigone, male speaker or speaking chorus with
electronic music; CHAMBER MUSIC: Grand quartet,
for flutes, 1962; 2 pieces for 2 flutes, 1962;
Solos, violin and 5 instruments, 1962; Chamber
variations, 12 players and conductor, 1964;
Impromptu, piano, 1968; Divertimento, flute,
cello, piano, 1970; Iron Mountain song, trumpet
and piano, 1971; The 2 and the 1, cello and 2
percussionists, 1972; string quartet, New York,
19 Mar. 1973; Riding the wind, flute and chamber
orch., New York, 14 Jan. 1974.
    R.D. 1, Cherry Valley, NY 13320

SOLOMON, LARRY
    b. New Kensington, Pa., 27 Apr. 1940. Studied
at Univ. of Illinois, M.M. 1964; with Thomas
Canning, West Virginia Univ., Ph.D. 1973. He
received a Nat. Endowment for the Arts grant,
1976. He was visiting lecturer, Cornell Univ.,
1971; on faculty, Wells Coll., 1968-73; from
1978, at Pima Coll., Tucson.
    WORKS: PERCUSSION: Music of the spheres,
solo marimba, 1976; PIANO: Andromeda, 1971-78;
Poems, 1976; Incantations, prepared piano, 1977;
suite for prepared piano, 1979.
    5122 N. Tortolita Rd., Tucson, AZ 85705

SOLOMON, MELVIN
    b. Richmond, Va., 3 Jan. 1947. Studied bassoon
with William Polisi, Juilliard School, B.M.,
M.M. He received 5 grants from Dance in Education Fund, Westchester County, N.Y., and many
commissions. He was composer-in-residence, Univ.
of Vermont, 1969-73, and at Steffi Nossen School
of the Dance, 1969-73; taught at YMHA of Mid-
Westchester Music School and Center Music School,
Yonkers, N.Y., 1973-76; then joined the faculty
at North Texas State Univ.
    WORKS: BALLET: The waxing of the woodbine,
1969; Lona, 1969; The garden of earthly delights,
1972; The best things, 1972; ORCHESTRA: The
Martian chronicles; concerto for bassoon and
strings, 1973; CHAMBER MUSIC: Etudes to spring,
bassoon solo, 1970; Poeme for cello, 1971;
Sonnet, clarinet and piano; CHORUS: Revelations,
100 voices, organ, harp, 1973.
    5214 Wythe Ave., Richmond, VA 23226

SOMARY, JOHANNES
    b. Zurich, Switz., 7 Apr. 1935; to U.S. 1940.
Studied at Yale Univ., B.A., M.M. His awards
include a Fox scholarship; Woods-Chandler Com-
position prize; and commissions. He was music
director of Amor Artis, Inc., 1960-79; and of
Fairfield County Chorale from 1975, choirmaster,
St. Ignatius Loyola Church, from 1979.
    WORKS: ORCHESTRA: Triptych for orchestra;
CHAMBER MUSIC: Serenade, oboe and chamber orch.;

Partita, clarinet and organ; sonatina for trumpet and organ; 5 songs on words by Blake,
soprano, baritone, piano; CHORUS: As the hart
longs, anthem; How lovely is thy dwelling place;
Music for the Eucharistic prayer; 4 Shakespeare
songs; Voice of the turtle, with chamber orch.;
3 prayers for the liturgy, a cappella.
    620 W. 254 St., Bronx, NY 10471

SOMER, AVO
    b. Tartu, Estonia, 27 June 1934; U.S. citizen
1956. Studied musicology at Univ. of Michigan,
Ph.D. 1963; participated in Karlheinz
Stockhausen's Ensemble at Darmstadt, Germany,
Aug. 1967. He has been faculty member at Univ.
of Connecticut from 1961.
    WORKS: CHAMBER MUSIC: Trio variations,
string trio, 1965; concertino, chamber ensemble,
Bennington Composers' Conf., 28 Aug. 1964; Re-
frains, flute, clarinet, percussion, piano, New
York, 13 Apr. 1966; Winter music, string trio,
1967; Elegy II, piano quintet, New York, 27 Jan.
1970; CHORUS: Cantata #4, women's voices,
Toronto, Ont., 15 Mar. 1955; Vilemees, a cappella,
Boston, Mass., 24 Apr. 1960.
    University of Connecticut, Storrs, CT 06268

SOMOHAMO, ARTURO
    b. San Juan, Puerto Rico, 1 Sept. 1910. Studied
with Belen Salgado, Rafael Marquez, Louis Watts,
Alexander Borovsly, and Bogumil Sykora. He was
concert pianist in Central and South America;
founded and conducted the Philharmonic Orch. of
Puerto Rico; has been guest conductor in Europe.
    WORKS: ORCHESTRA: Haitian souvenirs; Puerto
Rican rhapsody; Variations humoresque; Recuerdos;
Caribbean rhapsody; Fiesta en San Juan; and
songs.

SONDHEIM, STEPHEN JOSHUA
    b. New York, N.Y., 22 Mar. 1930. Studied at
Williams Coll., B.A. magna cum laude 1950; and
with Milton Babbitt at Princeton Univ. Composer,
lyricist, librettist, he has received many
awards including at least one Tony, a Grammy,
and the Emerson Coll. Musical Theatre Award of
Distinction, 1975. He wrote the music for Girls
of summer, 1956; Invitation to a march, 1961;
music and lyrics for A funny thing happened on
the way to the forum, 1962; Anyone can whistle,
1964; A little night music, 1972; Pacific overtures, 1975; and lyrics for Bernstein's West
Side story, 1957; Styne's Gypsy, 1959; and
Rodgers's Do I hear a waltz?, 1965.
    246 E. 49th St., New York, NY 10017

SONGAYLLO, RAYMOND THADDEUS
    b. Chicopee, Mass., 23 Aug. 1930. Studied with
Robert Mills Delaney, Northwestern Univ., B.M.
1951, M.M. 1952; with Gardner Read and Hugo
Norden, Boston Univ., 1958-61. He won an award
in the Delius composition contest, Jacksonville
Univ., 1976. He has held faculty posts at
Ithaca Coll., 1957-58; Central Michigan Univ.,
1960; Tennessee Polytechnic Inst., 1961-62; Univ.
of Denver, 1962-67; from 1967, at Simpson Coll.
    WORKS: ORCHESTRA: Variations for orchestra,
1974; KEYBOARD: harpsichord sonata, 1-72; Duo

concertante, 2 pianos, 1974; 10 short piano pieces, 1975; 9 preludes for piano, 1977; A western set, piano, 4 hands, 1978; Sonata: In memoriam Dmitri Shostakovich.
    802 W. Clinton Ave., Indianola, IA 50125

SONGER, LEWIS A.
    b. Evansville, Ind., 4 Sept. 1935. Studied with Will Gay Bottje, Southern Illinois Univ., B.M. 1958; with Roy Harris, Indiana Univ., M.M. 1960; with Francis Buebendorf, Univ. of Missouri at Kansas City, D.M.A. 1965. He received a Huntington Hartford fellowship, 1963; Buebendorf award for chamber music, 1964. He has held faculty posts at Cottey Coll., Mo., 1960-63; Westminster Coll., Pa., 1965-68; from 1968, at East Tennessee State Univ.
    WORKS: ORCHESTRA: symphony #2; piano concerto; WIND ENSEMBLE: Foothills and mountains; CHAMBER MUSIC: cello sonata; trumpet sonata; quartet for piano, violin, clarinet, horn; Peanuts, popcorn, crackerjacks, woodwind quintet; Crab canon, 3 percussionists; Octet-nova; CHORUS: Great art Thou, O Lord; When night advances; SONGS: 3 psychotic songs, voice and piano; ORGAN: Elegiac; Generation.
    1515 Chickees St., Johnson City, TN 37601

SONNECK, OSCAR GEORGE THEODORE
    b. Jersey City, N.J., 6 Oct. 1873; d. New York, N.Y., 30 Oct. 1928. Was a noted musicologist and named first chief of the music division, Library of Congress, 1902-17. In 1917 he joined the staff of G. Schirmer Co., music publishers in New York, becoming vice-president in 1921. His compositions include a symphonic movement for small orch.; a string quartet; Romance and rhapsody, violin and piano; songs; piano pieces.

SOOMIL, (LEWIS) STEPHAN
    b. Bremerton, Wash., 21 June 1941. Studied with Joseph Wood, Oberlin Coll.; with Darius Milhaud and Luciano Berio, Mills Coll.; with John Vincent, Univ. of California, Los Angeles. He received the Paul M. Henry award, Mills Coll., 1965; Atwater Kent second prize and Alex Stordahl award, UCLA, 1970. In 1972 he joined the UCLA dance department as accompanist and composer.
    WORKS: CHAMBER MUSIC: Theme and variations, piano, 1966, chamber ensemble, 1973; Winter song, soprano and 9 instruments, 1968; Entropy, 2 pianos, 1968; Shadows, 6 horns, 1972; ELECTRONIC: Toward Phoenicia, tape, 1967; Sensations of the swan, 3 instruments and tape, 1968; Isle of Wight, tape, 1970; Sidon, tape, 1972; Mojave, tape using live and electronic sounds, 1972.
    Dance Dept., UCLA, 405 Hilgard Ave., Los Angeles, CA 90024

SORCE, RICHARD
    b. Passaic, N.J., 29 July 1941. Studied with Ludmila Ulehla, Manhattan School of Music; with Joseph Scianni and J. Willard Roosevelt, New York Coll. of Music; with John Gilbert and Michael Czajkowski, New York Univ., B.S., M.A. He held a graduate fellowship at New York Univ. He was a private teacher, 1962-72; public school

teacher, 1971-73.
    WORKS: BAND: Alleluia, with chorus; Fantasia for brass; CHAMBER MUSIC: 2 fugues for 3 brass; Theme and variations, woodwinds; CHORUS: Spring and fall, to a young child, women's voices; Turn back O man; piano pieces; songs.
    715 McCoy Rd., Franklin Lakes, NJ 07417

SORCSEK, JEROME
    b. Lebanon, Pa., 22 Sept. 1949. Studied with Clifford Taylor and Robert P. Morgan, Temple Univ., B.M. cum laude 1974; with Clifton Williams, Univ. of Miami, M.M. 1975. He won the first annual DeMoulin Band Composition award of the Nat. Band Assoc.; and received a Nat. Endowment for the Arts grant for residency as composer in public schools in Lebanon, Pa., 1977-78.
    WORKS: ORCHESTRA: Prelude; BAND: Variations; Portrait of Faustus; Concert piece for brass and percussion; CHAMBER MUSIC: piano sonata; string quartet.
    4231-A King George Dr., Harrisburg, PA 17109

SORENSON, JOHN ROGER
    b. Pasadena, Calif., 8 May 1945. Studied with Matt Doran, Mount St. Mary's Coll., Los Angeles; and with Donal R. Michalsky, California State Univ., Fullerton, where he won a graduate composition award, 1973. He has been public school music teacher from 1970.
    WORKS: CHAMBER MUSIC: Trio concertato, violin, viola, bass clarinet, 1972; 3 reflections, guitar; Etude for 5 instruments, 1973; Intermission piece, 2 clarinets; Songs for soprano and guitar, 1973; Celestial, 3 wind groups, 1973; 3 pieces, for free-bass accordion; CHORUS: 13 ways of looking at a blackbird, with chamber ensemble, 1972; PIANO: sonata, 1970.

SORRENTINO, CHARLES
    b. Sicily, Italy, 13 Aug. 1906. Studied on scholarship at Manhattan School of Music; with Franz Kneisel, Maximilian Pilzer, Mario Corti, and Vittorio Giannini. He was composer and arranger for CBS, 1931-60.
    WORKS: ORCHESTRA: Ameresque; Illusion, voice and orch.; CHAMBER MUSIC: Euterpe, string quartet, New York, 15 Sept. 1957; CHORUS: Salem witches; Hummingbird; Home is best.

SOUERS, MILDRED
    b. Des Moines, Iowa, 26 Feb. 1894. Studied with Francis J. Pyle, Drake Univ.; and with Marion Bauer in New York. She won a first prize for a choral work, Nat. Fed. of Music Clubs. She was accompanist, lecturer-recitalist, and coach.
    WORKS: CHORUS: Winter nocturne; SONGS: April weather; The immortal; PIANO: Impromptu; Passacaglia; Bar and technique melodies for the dance studio; numerous published works for voice, organ, piano, solo instruments.

SOULE, EDMUND FOSTER
    b. Boston, Mass., 4 Mar. 1915. Studied with Harl MacDonald, Univ. of Pennsylvania, B.M. 1939, M.A. 1946; with Richard Donovan, Yale Univ.,

SOUTHALL, MITCHELL B.

B.M. 1948; at Eastman School of Music, Ph.D.
1956; Univ. of Denver, School of Librarianship,
M.L.S. 1966. He received the Frances Osborne
Kellogg prize for fugue writing. He has held
faculty posts at Milton Acad., Mass., 1948-49;
Washington State Univ., 1949-51; Univ. of the
Pacific, 1958-61; from 1966, music librarian,
Univ. of Oregon.
WORKS: CHAMBER MUSIC: Serenade, alto saxophone and piano, 1964; brass quintet; 6 trumpet
duets; 3 flute duets; saxophone quartet; Canzona,
7 brass instruments; brass trio; suite for oboe
and piano, 1976; Salon music, 6 pieces for violin
and piano, 1976; suite for piano, 1977; VOICE:
A stone, a leaf, a door, 4 poems of Thomas Wolfe,
chorus and chamber ensemble, 1978; Harp of the
wind, song cycle on texts of Hilda Conkling,
soprano, flute, harp, 1978.
5399 Bailey Hill Rd., Eugene, OR 97405

SOUTHALL, MITCHELL B.
b. Rochester, N.Y., 30 Aug. 1922. Studied at
Langston Univ., B.A. 1946; with Philip Greeley
Clapp, Univ. of Iowa, M.A. 1947, M.F.A. 1948,
Ph.D. 1949. He was cited for Outstanding Service
to Langston Univ., 1946; received teaching
awards, 1955, 1971. He has held faculty posts
at Langston Univ., 1949-53; Lane Coll., 1953-56;
Southern Univ.; Texas Coll.; Mississippi Valley
State Coll.; Rust Coll.; and Univ. of Tennessee
at Martin, 1972-75.
WORKS: CHORUS: In silent night, 1955; 75th
anniversary, for Lane Coll., 1955; PIANO: Romance, 1940; Elf dance, 1940; Impromptu in d,
1941; Impromptu militaire, 1942; numerous unpublished works.

SOUTHERS, LEROY WILLIAM, JR.
b. Minot, N.Dak., 13 July 1941. Studied with
Anthony Vazzana, Halsey Stevens, Ingolf Dahl,
Univ. of Southern California, B.M. magna cum
laude 1963, M.M. 1965. He received the Alchin
scholarship; Helen Amstead award; Ford Found.-
MENC grant for composer residence in public
schools, 1966-68; Nat. Endowment for the Arts
grant, 1968. He was faculty member, Los Angeles
Acad. of Performing Arts, 1968-69; Univ. of
Southern California, 1970-74; from 1974, at
Loyola-Marymount Univ.
WORKS: ORCHESTRA: concerto for string
bass, 1967; The ghosts of the buffaloes, with
chorus, 1968; BAND: Essay for band, 1964; concerto for 4 horns, euphonium, and wind ensemble,
1967; Study for band, 1968; CHAMBER MUSIC: Concert piece, chamber ensemble, 1965; symphony for
chamber ensemble, 1967; concerto for trombone
and chamber ensemble; 3 spheres, trumpet, bassoon, piano; Evolutions, trumpet and organ;
Cancrizans, 2 trumpets.
3708 Military Ave., #3, Los Angeles, CA
90034

SOWASH, RICK
b. Mansfield, Ohio, 16 Jan. 1950. Studied with
Bernhard Heiden, Indiana Univ. He was music
director, 1st Lutheran Church, Mansfield, Ohio,
1973-76; broadcasting producer, WOSU-FM, Columbus, 1978-80.

WORKS: OPERA: God's messenger comes to
Everyman, chamber opera, 1978; BALLET: The
unicorn in the garden, 1980; CHAMBER MUSIC: Our
home, divertimento for woodwind quartet, 1979;
4 American moods, woodwind quintet; violin sonata,
1979; 4 seasons in Bellville, piano trio, 1980;
Pastorale, flute and string trio, 1980; 3 romantic duets, soprano, baritone, piano, 1980.
Box 569, 81 Fitting Ave., Bellville, OH
44813

SOWERBY, LEO
b. Grand Rapids, Mich., 1 May 1895; d. Port
Clinton, Ohio, 7 July 1968. Studied with Arthur
Olaf Andersen, American Cons., M.M. 1918. He
was the first recipient of the American Prix de
Rome, 1921-24; other awards include an honorary
doctorate, 1934; Pulitzer prize, 1946; fellow,
Trinity Coll., London, 1957; fellow, Royal
School of Church Music, Croyden, England, 1963.
He served in the U.S. Army, 1917-19; was faculty
member, American Cons., 1925-62; church organist,
Chicago, 1927-62; director, Coll. for Church
Musicians, Nat. Cathedral, Washington, D.C.,
1962-68.
WORKS: ORCHESTRA: Comes autumn time, overture, 1916; Irish washerwoman, 1916; 4 symphonies,
1922, 1929, 1941, 1948; From the northland, 1923;
King Estmere, with 2 pianos, 1923; Money musk,
1924; Prairie, symphonic poem, 1929; 2 piano
concertos; 2 cello concertos; 2 organ concertos;
CHAMBER MUSIC: wind quintet, 1916; cello sonata,
1921; 2 violin sonatas, 1922, 1924; 2 string
quartets, 1923, 1925; Pop goes the weasel, woodwind quintet, 1927; clarinet sonata, 1938; trumpet sonata, 1945; suite for organ, brass, trumpet, 1953; CHORUS: Vision of Sir Launfal, 1926;
Song for America, 1942; Christ reborn, oratorio,
1953; The throne of God, 1957.

SPALDING, ALBERT
b. Chicago, Ill., 15 Aug. 1888; d. New York,
N.Y., 26 May 1953. Studied violin in Europe;
made his American debut as violinist with the
New York Symphony in 1908. Thereafter he made
annual tours in the U.S. and many in Europe. He
composed violin concertos, a violin sonata,
string quartet, suite for violin and piano,
piano pieces, and songs. He also published an
autobiography, Rise to follow, New York, 1944,
and an imaginative biography of Tartini, A fiddle, a sword, and a lady, New York, 1953.

SPEAKS, OLEY
b. Canal Winchester, Ohio, 28 June 1874; d. New
York, N.Y., 27 Aug. 1948. He was a church and
concert baritone and a composer. His highly
popular songs included On the road to Mandalay,
1907; Morning, 1910; Sylvia, 1914; The prayer
perfect; When the boys come home, 1918.

SPEARS, JARED
b. Chicago, Ill., 15 Aug. 1936. Studied with
Maurice Weed, Northern Illinois Univ., B.S.E.;
with Blythe Owen and Irwin Fischer, Cosmopolitan
School of Music, B.M., M.M., with Alan Stout and
Anthony Donato, Northwestern Univ., D.M. 1967.
He received the Faricy award, 1966; first prize,

Phi Mu Alpha internat. contest, 1967; Outstanding Educator, 1973, 1975; Arkansas Music Clubs Award of Merit, 1976; many commissions. He was public school music teacher, 1958-65; from 1967, on faculty, Arkansas State Univ.

WORKS: BAND: March for moderns, 1965; Collocation, winds and percussion, 1968; Kimberly overture, 1969; 2 cameos, 1970; Pidgeon Cove legend, 1970; Prologue and pageant, 1971; Neolog, 1973; Chronolog, 1973; Chronica; Alleluias; Axon, 1975; Momentations, 1976; Ritual and celebration, baritone saxophone and band, 1977; Wabash County saga, Wabash, Ind., 10 Mar. 1978; many works for small ensembles, solo instruments, and chorus.
Box 4N, State University, AR 72467

SPECTOR, IRWIN
b. New Jersey, 11 Jan. 1916. Studied with Philip James, Marion Bauer, Laszlo Kun, and Harold Morris in New York; with Nadia Boulanger in Paris. He was faculty member, Monmouth Coll., 1942-48; Illinois State Univ., 1948-76; visiting professor, Univ. of Kansas, 1968-69.

WORKS: ORCHESTRA: Fantasy, violin and orch.; Rhapsoconcerto, cello and orch.; Prayer of dedication, baritone, chorus, and orch.; CHAMBER MUSIC: Pieces in 3, piano; Songs of love and music, voice, piano, oboe, viola; sonatina for violin and viola; other works for chorus, chamber groups, and songs.
860 Lower Perry Rd., Ewing, NJ 08628

SPELMAN, TIMOTHY MATHER
b. Brooklyn, N.Y., 21 Jan. 1891; d. Florence, Italy, 21 Aug. 1970. Studied with Walter R. Spalding and Edward Burlingame Hill, Harvard Univ., 1909-13; with Courvoisier in Munich. After World War I, he alternated residence in Italy and New York.

WORKS: OPERA: The sunken city, 1930; Courtship of Miles Standish, 1943; THEATRE: Snowdrop, 4-act pantomime, 1911; La magnifica, 1-act music drama, 1920; ORCHESTRA: Saints' days, suite in 4 movements, 1926; The outcasts of Poker Flat, after Bret Harte, 1928; symphony, 1936; Jamboree, a pocket ballet, 1945; oboe concerto, 1954; also chamber music and works for chorus.

SPENCER, JAMES HOUSTON
b. Malone, N.Y., 28 July 1895; d. Adrian, Mich., 3 Sept. 1967. Studied with George Whitefield Chadwick, New England Cons., diploma 1919. His awards included the Mary Corwell grant for study in Europe, 1938; 3 MacDowell fellowships; first prize, Detroit News composition contest, and Chicago Tribune contest; membership in American Guild of Organists; honorary doctorate, Adrian Coll. He was chairman, music dept., Adrian Coll., 1921-65; organist-choirmaster in various churches in Ann Arbor, Toledo, Detroit.

WORKS: OPERA: Song of Solomon, 1937; ORCHESTRA: 2 symphonies, subtitled American dance fantasy and American folk symphony; Fiddler of the northern lights, 1967; CHAMBER MUSIC: Nativity, andante pastorale, woodwind sextet and piano; Rustic suite, string quartet; Pandean sketches 1 and 2, flute and piano; piano trio;

Piece for piano and strings; ORGAN: Chinese and bamboo flute; Symphonesque; Choral communion; many songs and piano pieces.

SPENCER, S. REID
b. Baltimore, Md., 30 July 1872; d. Brooklyn, N.Y., 28 July 1945. Studied at Northwestern Univ., then taught there, 1895-1900; founded his own music school in Brooklyn in 1927. He composed piano and organ pieces and church music.

SPENCER, VERNON
b. Durham, England, 10 Oct. 1875; d. Los Angeles, Calif., 9 Jan. 1949. Graduated from Leipzig Cons., 1897. He was director, Cons. of Music, Nebraska Wesleyan Univ., 1903-11; then taught in Los Angeles. He composed many songs and piano pieces.

SPENCER, WILLIAMETTA
b. Marion, Ill., 15 Aug. 1932. Studied with Ernest Kanitz, Univ. of Southern California, M.M., Ph.D.; with Tony Aubin, Ecole Normale, Paris, on a Fulbright scholarship. Other awards include 3 first prizes, Mi Phi Epsilon composition contests, 1951, 1958, 1968; Southern California Vocal Assoc. composition award, 1968. From 1966 she has been faculty member at Rio Hondo Coll.

WORKS: ORCHESTRA: overture, 1958; CHAMBER MUSIC: clarinet sonata, 1951; Adagio and rondo, oboe and piano; CHORUS: Missa brevis; 4 madrigals to poems of Joyce; Nova, nova, ave fit ex eva; At the round earth's imagined corners; Death be not proud; Give me the splendid silent sun; MEN'S CHORUS: Gloria in excelsis; Past 3 o'clock; Tyrley, tyrlow; and others.
6228 Gregory Ave., Whittier, CA 90601

SPERRY, DON R.
b. Dallas, Tex., 17 Feb. 1947. Studied with James Brody, Thomas Wirtel, Margaret Wheat, East Texas State Univ.; with Martin Mailman, Robert Ottman, William Latham, Dale Peters, North Texas State Univ.

WORKS: ORCHESTRA: 2 symphonies, 1972, 1973; CHAMBER MUSIC: Sonata for 3; Canonic duets, violin and cello; Piece for 4; septet; trio; Thinking (thoughts of you), flute, strings, guitar, 1970; Uncertain faces, soprano and chamber orch.

SPIALEK, HANS
b. Vienna, Austria, 17 Apr. 1894; U.S. citizen 1931. Studied with Felix Weingartner and M. Spohr, Vienna Cons.; with Alexander Glazunov, Moscow Cons. He was arranger and editor for New York music publishers, 1927-47; also arranged more than 100 Broadway musicals.

WORKS: THEATRE: Heavenly light, musical play; ORCHESTRA: The tall city; Sinfonietta, 1936; Manhattan watercolors; To a ballerina; piano concerto; also piano pieces and chamber works.
145 W. 86th St., New York, NY 10024

SPIEGEL, LAURIE
b. Chicago, Ill., 20 Sept. 1945. Studied at

SPIEGELMAN, JOEL M.

Shimer Coll., A.B. 1967; private study with J. W.
Duarte, London, 1967-68; privately with Michael
Czajkowski in New York, 1969-71; guitar at
Juilliard School, 1969-72; privately with Jacob
Druckman, 1972-73; with Emmanuel Ghent, 1973-74;
with Druckman at Brooklyn Coll., M.A. 1975. Her
awards include an Inst. for Studies in American
Music fellowship, 1973-74; CAPS grant, 1975-76;
Meet the Composer grants, 1975-78; WNET artist-
in-residence grant, 1976; ASCAP awards, 1976,
1977. She was guitar instructor, Bucks County
Community Coll., 1971-74; instructor, Aspen
Music Festival, 1972-73; composer consultant,
Bell Telephone Labs., 1977; editor, Ear magazine
from 1977.
    WORKS: ELECTRONIC (computer): Sediment,
1971; Appalachian grove, 1974; The orient express, 1974; Waves, tape and 9 instruments, 1975;
Drums, 1975; Clockworks, 1975; Patchwork, rev.
version, 1976; The voyage, 1976; The harmony of
the planets, included in disc, "Sounds of Earth,"
launched by NASA in Voyager 2 spacecraft, summer
1977; also works for guitar, incidental music
for 5 plays, soundtracks for video works, music
for educational and experimental films, and commercials.
    173-5 Duane St., New York, NY 10013

SPIEGELMAN, JOEL M.
    b. Buffalo, N.Y., 23 Jan. 1933. Studied with
Irving Fine, Harold Shapero, Arthur Berger,
Brandeis Univ., M.F.A. 1956; with Nadia Boulanger,
Paris Cons., 1956-60. His awards include a
French government fellowship; Ingram Merrill
award, 1967, 1968; U.S.-Soviet Cultural Exchange
grant; ASCAP awards, 1967-73; MacDowell fellow-
ship, 1978. He was faculty member at Brandeis
Univ., 1961-66; then was named chairman, music
dept., Sarah Lawrence Coll.
    WORKS: CHAMBER MUSIC: Fantasy #1 and #2,
string quartet, 1963; Kousochki, piano, 4 hands;
Chamber music, piano, string trio, percussion;
Midnight sun, oboe and tape; CHORUS: V'haavtah,
sacred service with reader, cantor, and tape;
Phantom of the opera, women's voices with self-
accompaniment by crotales and wind chimes;
ELECTRONIC: The 11th hour, an electronic symphony; MULTIMEDIA: Daddy, chamber work for
actress, soprano, flute, oboe, synthesizer,
conga drums.
    Sarah Lawrence College, Bronxville, NY
    10708

SPIER, HARRY R.
    b. Boston, Mass., 7 Nov. 1888; d. New York, N.Y.,
20 Jan. 1952. Was accompanist, choral director,
and organist, Church of the Atonement, New York.
His compositions included pieces for flute and
piano, piano solo, choral works, songs.

SPIES, CLAUDIO
    b. Santiago, Chile, 26 Mar. 1925; U.S. citizen
1966. Studied at New England Cons., 1942-46;
with Nadia Boulanger, Longy School of Music,
1943, 1945; with Harold Shapero, Irving Fine,
Walter Piston, Harvard Univ., 1947-52. He received the Ingram Merrill award, 1966; Brandeis
Univ. Creative Arts award, 1967; Nat. Inst. of

Arts and Letters award, 1969; Nat. Endowment for
the Arts grant, 1975. He was faculty member,
Harvard Univ., 1953-57; Vassar Coll., 1957-58;
Swarthmore Coll., 1958-70; from 1970, at Princeton Univ.
    WORKS: CHAMBER MUSIC: Tempi, 14 instru-
ments, 1962; Impromptu, piano, 1963; Times 2,
2 horns; 3 intermezzi, piano; Vio piacem, viola
and keyboard, 1965; CHORUS: Animula vagula,
blandula, a cappella, 1964; Verses from the Book
of Ruth, women's voices; In paradisum, to his
own text; SONGS: 3 songs on poems of May Swenson,
1969; 7 Enzenberger Lieder, 1972; Shirim le
Hathunatham, wedding songs on Hebrew poems of
Yehudah Halevi, soprano, flute, clarinet, piano
trio, 1975.
    117 Meadowbrook Dr., Princeton, NJ 08540

SPINDLE, LOUISE COOPER
    b. Muskegon, Mich., 1 Jan.; d. Grand Rapids,
Mich., 14 Oct. 1968. Studied at Chicago Musical
Coll. Her compositions include Southlands for
orchestra; choral pieces; songs.

SPINO, PASQUALE J.
    b. Newark, N.J., 7 July 1942. Studied with
Vaclav Nelhybel in New York; with Paul Fetler
and Dominick Argento, Univ. of Minnesota. His
symphony #1 was chosen for performance at the
Indiana State Univ. Contemporary Music Festival,
1973. He is a public school music teacher.
    WORKS: ORCHESTRA: Symphonic movement,
string orch.; symphony #1; BAND: Theme and variations; Jubilation; Fanfare, chorale, and march;
CHAMBER MUSIC: cello sonata; suite for piano;
saxophone quartet; brass quintet; trombone quartet; CHORUS: A prophecy, with tenor and baritone solos, brass, and percussion; Lament, with
tenor solo, violin, and piano; A patch of old
snow; Nothing gold can stay; 5 poetic songs on
varying texts, a cappella, 1976.
    313 Gordon Ave., Williamstown, NJ 08094

SPIVAK, JOSEPH
    b. Brookline, Mass., 15 Oct. 1948. Studied with
Charles Dodge, Charles Wuorinen, and Jack Beeson,
Columbia Univ. He received a fellowship for the
Composers Cons., Johnson State Coll., 1974. He
was director and flutist, the Composers Ensemble,
1972-76; from 1975, has been teacher at the New
York YWCA and Hebrew Arts School for Music and
Dance.
    WORKS: ORCHESTRA: Thesis for orchestra,
1972; CHAMBER MUSIC: 6 canonic pieces, 2 flutes;
Quartet for solo piano; trio for flute, cello,
piano; Weekend music; Trio for no dogs aloud,
1972; concertino for piano and 5 instruments,
1974.
    201 W. 89th St., New York, NY 10024

SPIZIZEN, LOUISE
    b. Lynn, Mass., 24 Aug. 1928. Studied at Vassar
Coll., A.B.; with Wallingford Riegger; with
Robert Erickson, Kenneth Gaburo, Wilbur Ogdon,
Univ. of California, San Diego, M.A. Her awards
include a Vassar Coll. composition prize and
commissions. She has been private teacher and
free-lance performer from 1959; was instructor,

Univ. of California, San Diego, 1969-75; and at San Diego Community Coll., from 1972.

WORKS: BALLET: Birthday of the Infanta, modern dance score; THEATRE: music for The silver tassie by Sean O'Casey, 1949; CHORUS: Weary with toil, liturgical setting for Reformed Jewish service, women's voices and organ; 3 games for 10 players, with string quartet.

925 Havenhurst Dr., La Jolla, CA 92037

SPONG, JON
b. Des Moines, Iowa, 5 Dec. 1933. Studied with Francis J. Pyle, Drake Univ. He has been faculty member, Washington State Univ., 1959-60; Drake Univ., 1961-66; Univ. of Missouri, 1966-69; Luther Coll., 1974-76; Cincinnati Coll. Cons., from 1976; and Eastern Kentucky Univ., from 1978.

WORKS: ORGAN: Scenes from the life of Christ; Organ music for joyous occasions; Contemplation and celebration; and 15 volumes of published organ works; CHORUS: O brother man; Alleluia; In this modern day, folk anthem; God be with you, choral response; and others.

2910 Scioto, Apt. 1211, Cincinnati, OH 45219

SPRATLAN, LEWIS
b. Miami, Fla., 5 Sept. 1940. Studied with Mel Powell, Gunther Schuller, Yehudi Wyner, Yale Univ., B.A., M.M.; with Roger Sessions, George Rochberg, Donald Martino at Tanglewood. His awards include a fellowship at MacDowell Colony, 1977; Guggenheim fellowship, 1980; second prize, New England Cons. American Opera competition, 1979. He was faculty member, Pennsylvania State Univ., 1968-70; then at Amherst Coll.

WORKS: OPERA: Dream, 1977, commissioned by the New Haven Opera Company; ORCHESTRA: 2 pieces for orchestra, 1970; Dance suite, 1973; Night songs, with soprano and tenor solos, 1974; CHAMBER MUSIC: Flange, 14 players, 1965; Structures, after Hart Crane, tenor, piano, tape, 1968; wind quintet, 1970; Serenade, 6 instruments, 1970; Summer music, 5 instruments, 1971; Diary music 1, 10 players, 1971; Dance suite, 1973; Fantasy, piano and chamber ensemble, 1974; 3 Ben Johnson songs, soprano, flute, violin, cello, 1975; Coils, violin, flute, piano, terpsiptomaton (an instrument designed and built by Spratlan using a keyboard, steel balls, trap doores, and strings; is 6 ft. high, weighs 150 lbs.), both the instrument and the composition premiered in Cambridge, 5 Dec. 1980; and choral works.

23 Orchard St., Amherst, MA 01002

SPRAYBERRY, ROBERT JONES
b. Decatur, Ala., 7 Dec. 1952. Studied with Frank Carroll, Centenary Coll.; with Kenneth Klaus, Louisiana State Univ. He received awards for his scores to Romeo and Juliet and The serpent; and commissions. He is composer-in-residence, Marjorie Lyons Playhouse, Shreveport.

WORKS: THEATRE: music for Bury my heart at Wounded Knee; The brick and the rose; The glass menagerie; Anne of 1000 days; PIANO: Dance suite; Fugue; Passacaglia.

3046 Fritchie Dr., Baton Rouge, LA 70809

SPRING, GLENN ERNEST, JR.
b. Hot Springs, Ark., 19 Apr. 1939. Studied with Perry Beach, Loma Linda Univ.; with Ralph Guenther, Texas Christian Univ.; with John Verrall and Robert Suderberg, Univ. of Washington, D.M.A. 1972. His awards include a Washington State Arts Commission grant, 1973, and commissions. He was violinist, Fort Worth and Columbia symphonies, 1962-65; then concertmaster, Walla Walla Symphony; from 1966, faculty member, Walla Walla Coll.

WORKS: ORCHESTRA: 3 images, with optional synthesizer; Fantasia on Dulcimer, string orch., 1972; Shapes, a short symphony, Walla Walla Symph., 26 Feb. 1974; Romance, string orch., 1976; Perceptions, chamber orch., 1977; CHAMBER MUSIC: suite for 2 violins, 1968; trio for flute, viola, piano, 1970; Music for piano, 1974; CHORUS: Christmas lullaby, 1974; Missa brevis, with 2 pianos and timpani, 1968, rev. 1972; Evocation, with orch., 1975.

1057 Brickner, College Place, WA 99324

SPROSS, CHARLES GILBERT
b. Poughkeepsie, N.Y., 6 Jan. 1876; d. Poughkeepsie, 23 Dec. 1961. Was organist and accompanist in the New York area. He composed 5 cantatas; chamber works; and over 200 songs.

SPRUNG, DAVID R.
b. Jersey City, N.J., 24 Oct. 1931. Studied with Vittorio Rieti and Luigi Dallapiccola, Queens Coll., CUNY; with Roger Sessions and Milton Babbitt, Princeton Univ. He received the Joseph Dillon Memorial prize for a piano trio; and the Karol Rathaus Memorial prize. He has been horn player in the Pittsburgh Symph., Chautauqua Symph., and from 1973, coprincipal horn, San Francisco Opera; faculty member, Wichita State Univ., 1963-68; Sonoma State Coll., 1966-70; from 1970, California State Univ. at Hayward.

WORKS: ORCHESTRA: Prelude for orchestra; CHAMBER MUSIC: string quartet, 1959; piano trio; Music for Gail, horn and piano; Fantasy for piano; CHORUS: Psalm 8, women's voices; I hear the noise of many waters; SONG CYCLE: The tower of David.

5600 Snake Rd., Oakland, CA 94611

STABILE, JAMES
b. Brooklyn, N.Y., 28 May 1937. Studied with Vittorio Giannini, Nicolas Flagello, Ludmila Ulehla, Manhattan School of Music; with John B. MacMillan, Nyack Coll.; conducting at Univ. of Southern California. He was faculty member, King's Coll., 1964-67; Nyack Coll., 1965-67; visiting lecturer, free-lance composer, arranger, conductor in California from 1967.

WORKS: ORCHESTRA: piano concerto; Rockland overture; Pacific Coast overture; suite for chamber orch.; suite for brass ensemble; CHAMBER MUSIC: suite for brass quartet; Ballade, vibraphone; tuba sonata; The greatest of miracles, piano; CHORUS: St. Paul oratorio; Christmas cantata; FILM SCORES: The lost generation, television film; Tokyo crusade; Chicago--City with a vision.

STAFFORD, JAMES E.
b. Summerville, La., 20 Aug. 1933. Studied with
James Hanna, Southwestern Louisiana Univ.; with
Kenneth Klaus and Dinos Constantinides, Louisiana State Univ. He has received an honorary
award, American Guild of Organists, and commissions. From 1965 he has been faculty member,
East Tennessee State Univ.
WORKS: CHAMBER MUSIC: quintet for flute,
horn, piano trio, 1968; Synesthesia for brass;
CHORUS: mass for brass and voices according to
the Book of Common Prayer; The time of singing,
1967; musical communion service, with brass,
1973.
4 Bridgewood Court, Johnson City, TN 37601

STAHL, HOWARD M.
b. New York, N.Y., 18 Sept. 1948. Studied with
Frederick Piket, Hebrew Union Coll., School of
Sacred Music. He has been cantor, Congregation
Beth Emeth, Albany, N.Y., from 1972.
WORKS: Ma'agal Chozer (Circle without end),
a rock-folk service for choir, guitars, piano,
drums, flute, 1972.

STAHL, WILLY
b. New York, N.Y., 1896; d. 1963. Graduated
from Vienna Cons., 1913. He played viola in the
New York Symphony and the St. Paul Orch.; taught
in Hollywood, Calif. His compositions include
Dead forest, a tone poem; and chamber music.

STAHLBERG, FRITZ
b. Tetzin, Germany, 7 June 1877; to U.S. 1899;
d. Los Angeles, Calif., 23 July 1937. He was
violinist in the Pittsburgh Symph., 1900-8; New
York Symph., 1908-29, assistant conductor, 1912-
29; then was head of music division, MGM Studios,
in Hollywood. He composed 2 symphonies, a symphonic suite, violin pieces, and songs.

STALVEY, DORRANCE
b. Georgetown, S.C., 21 Aug. 1930. Attended
Cincinnati Coll. of Music, M.M. 1955, but is
self-taught in composition. He received the
Prince Ranier III de Monaco composition prize,
1961; Nat. Endowment for the Arts grant, 1975.
From 1963 he has been faculty member, Immaculate
Heart Coll.; from 1971, also executive director,
Monday Evening Concerts, Los Angeles.
WORKS: ORCHESTRA: Music for jazz group and
orch., 1955; Celebration--Sequent I, 1973, rev.
1977; Celebration--Sequent II, Cincinnati Coll.-
Cons., 1 Dec. 1976; CHAMBER MUSIC: 5 little
pieces, piano, 1957, rev. 1977; string trio,
1960 (string quartet version, 1978); Movements
and interludes, chamber ensemble, 1964; Changes,
piano, 1966; Celebration, brass and percussion,
1967; Points-lines-circles, chamber ensemble,
1968; PLC-Abstract, double bass solo, 1972;
Study for BG, double bass solo, 1974; ELECTRONIC:
BWB, tape, 1969; Togethers I, guitar and tape,
1970; Togethers II, percussion and tape, 1970;
Togethers III, clarinet and tape, 1970; Fitan,
tape, 1971; Rabbit season, tape, 1974; MULTI-
MEDIA: Conflicts, instruments, chorus, dancers,
film, visuals, 1970; In time and not, chorus,
instruments, dancers, actors, visuals, tape,

staging, 1970.
2145 Manning Ave., Los Angeles, CA 90025

STANLEY, HELEN (Mrs. Denby Gatlin)
b. Tampa, Fla., 6 Apr. 1930. Studied at Cincinnati Cons., B.M. 1951; with Hans Barth and
Ernst von Dohnanyi, Florida State Univ., M.M.
1954; at Muskingum Coll., B.S. 1961. Her awards
include graduate fellowship, Florida State Univ.;
C. Hugo Grimm prize; Florida State Music Teachers
Assoc. award, 1972; and commissions. She has
been violist, El Paso Symph., and music director,
El Paso Ballet Center; was faculty member, Jacksonville Univ., 1962-67; then free-lance composer and pianist.
WORKS: BALLET: Birthday of the Infanta;
ORCHESTRA: symphony; Night piece, women's
chorus and orch.; CHAMBER MUSIC: trombone sonata;
string quartet; woodwind quintet; brass quartet;
Piece, for horn, percussion, piano; 2 pieces,
wind soloist and piano; SONGS: Credo; The isle;
PIANO: sonatina; Etudes; ELECTRONIC: Lunar encounter, operetta with tape score; Electronic
prelude; duo-sonata, tape and piano; Rhapsody,
tape and orch., Gainesville, Fla., 12 Nov. 1972.
1768 Emory Circle S., Jacksonville, FL 32207

STANTON (Stankunas), JOSEPH
b. Lithuania, 1 Nov. 1906; U.S. citizen 1955.
Studied in Kaunas, Lith.; at Sao Paulo Cons.,
Brazil; and at Sao Paulo Inst. of Music, M.M.
1948. He taught in public schools in Sao Paulo
for 12 years and at the Inst. of Music; from
1953, has been organist and teacher in Elizabeth,
N.J.
WORKS: CHORUS: mass in D; mass in e-flat;
KEYBOARD: piano sonata; preludes and postludes
for organ; about 100 Lithuanian songs transcribed
for solo voice and piano, duets, trios, and
chorus.
1043 Applegate Ave., Elizabeth, NJ 07202

STANTON, ROYAL W.
b. Los Angeles, Calif., 23 Oct. 1916. Studied
with Arnold Schoenberg, Univ. of California, Los
Angeles, B.E. 1939, M.A. 1946. He taught in
public schools, 1939-50; was faculty member,
Long Beach City Coll., 1950-61; Foothill Coll.,
1961-72; De Anza Coll., from 1961.
WORKS: CHORUS: 5 psalm fragments; 2 festal
motets; Blest are they; Ah, wilt thou leave me
thus?; These things shall be; and many others.
22301 Havenhurst Dr., Los Altos, CA 94022

STARER, ROBERT
b. Vienna, Austria, 8 Jan. 1924; U.S. citizen
1957. Began playing piano at age 4 and was
accepted at the Vienna State Acad. of Music at
13; in 1938, continued studies at Jerusalem
Cons.; graduate study at Juilliard, diploma 1949.
His awards include 2 Guggenheim fellowships;
Fulbright research grant; and many commissions.
In 1949 he joined the faculty at Juilliard
School; taught at New York Coll. of Music, 1959-
60; from 1963, professor at Brooklyn Coll. and
CUNY Grad. Center.
WORKS: OPERA: The intruder, 1 act, 1956;
Pantagleize, Brooklyn Coll., 7 Apr. 1973; The

last lover, Katonah, N.Y., 2 Aug. 1975; Apollonia, commissioned by Minnesota Opera, 1978; BALLET: The dybbuk, Berlin Festival, 1960; Samson agonistes, 1961; Phaedra, 1962; The lady of the house of sleep, 1968; Holy jungle, New York, 22 Apr. 1974; ORCHESTRA: 3 symphonies, 1948, 1951, 1964; 3 piano concertos, 1948, 1953, 1972, #3, Baltimore, 9 Oct. 1974; Concerto à tre, clarinet, trumpet, trombone, and strings, 1954; concerto for viola, strings, percussion, 1959; concerto for violin, cello, and orch., 1968; Mutabili, variants for orch., 1965; Ariel, with soprano, baritone and chorus, New York, 15 May 1960; Journals of a songmaker, with soprano and baritone, Pittsburgh, 21 May 1976; CHAMBER MUSIC: Elegy for strings; Dialogues, clarinet and piano; string quartet, 1947; 2 piano sonatas, 1949-, 1965; woodwind quartet; piano quartet; cello sonata; Fantasia concertante, piano, 4 hands, 1959; Light and shadow, 4 saxophones; Cadenza, for 4 flutes; Variants, violin and piano, 1963; trio for clarinet, cello, piano, 1964; Profiles in brass, New York, 20 May 1977; Transformations, mezzo-soprano, violin, and piano, settings of 3 poems by American women, New York, 3 Dec. 1978; also choral works, piano pieces.

    R.D. 1, Box 248, Woodstock, NY 12498

STARKS, HOWARD F.
    b. Erie, Pa., 1 Mar. 1928. Studied at Pennsylvania State Univ.; Indiana Univ. of Pennsylvania, B.S. in music education; and at Southern Baptist Theological Seminary, M.S.M. From 1956, he has been minister of music at various churches, from 1966, at Calvary Baptist Church, Florence, S.C. He has composed more than 200 works for adult and children's choruses and handbells.

    1857 Westmoreland Ave., Florence, SC 29501

STARR, PAUL DOUGLAS
    b. Erie, Pa., 12 Mar. 1952. Studied with Marshall Barnes, Ohio State Univ. He won first place in the 1973 Ohio Music Teachers Assoc. composition contest. He was Ohio State fellow and teaching associate, 1974-78; from 1978, visiting assistant professor, Kenyon Coll.; from 1974, organist and choirmaster, St. Paul's Church, Mt. Vernon, Ohio.

    WORKS: ORCHESTRA: Episodes, with tape; CHAMBER MUSIC: Modal swatches, minimal music for 9 percussion instruments; piano sonata; Duo concertato, violin and piano, 1973; Fantasia on We 3 kings, organ; CHORUS: Savior like a shepherd lead us; Easter cantata; Song of a man and a nation's experience, secular cantata on Whitman text; ELECTRONIC: Serekahcello, live electronics and amplified cello.

    35 N. Virginia Lane, Westerville, OH 43081

STATON, KENNETH W.
    b. Miami, Okla., 23 Aug. 1937. Studied with Normand Lockwood in Denver, Colo. He was faculty member, Univ. of Denver, 1972-73; then at Hilo Coll., Univ. of Hawaii. His published compositions for chorus include Psalm 24, an extended work with soloists and orch., performed by the Denver Symphony in 1972.

    Univ. of Hawaii, P.O. Box 1357, Hilo, HI 96720

STAUFFER, DONALD W.
    b. Canton, Ohio, 30 July 1919. Studied at Eastman School of Music, B.M. 1941, M.M. 1942; Catholic Univ., Ph.D. in music education 1954. His awards include the Silver Medal, Swedish March Music Society; citation of excellence, Nat. Band Assoc.; Orpheus award, Phi Mu Alpha Sinfonia. He served in the U.S. Navy, 1942-73, from tuba and double bass player to commander and leader, U.S. Navy Band, 1969-73; then joined the faculty at Birmingham Southern Coll.

    WORKS: BAND: Fugue 'n swing; Canine capers suite; Moods modal; Deliberation suite; Eine kleine Deutsche suite; U.S.S. Kennedy march; Ch' chamba Latin fantasy. He is author of 2 books on band instruments and technique: Intonation deficiencies of wind instruments, Washington, D.C., 1954; A treatise on the tuba, Rochester, N.Y., 1942, 1962.

    Birmingham Southern College, Birmingham, AL 35204

STEARNS, PETER PINDAR
    b. New York, N.Y., 7 June 1931; son of Theodore Stearns. Studied with Leonard Stein and Miklos Rozsa in Los Angeles; with Bohuslav Martinu, Mannes Coll. of Music, where he has been faculty member from 1957, excepting 1964-65 at Yale Univ.

    WORKS: ORCHESTRA: First little symphony, WNYC, New York, 18 Feb. 1952; Toccata, 1952, New York, 17 Feb. 1954; piano concerto, 1952, WNYC, New York, 16 Feb. 1956; 6 symphonies, 1953, 1956, 1956, 1957, 1961,1961; Capriccio in piccolo, Stuttgart, 7 June 1957; violin concerto, 1957; Passacaglia, 1958; Interlude for strings, WNYC, 12 Feb. 1959; Reminiscence, strings and piano, WNYC, 15 Feb. 1960; CHAMBER MUSIC: 5 string quartets, 1950, 1951, 1955, 1958, 1960, #5, New York, 17 Feb. 1962; 3 canzone, 2 clarinets and bassoon, 1953; duo for clarinet and bassoon, 1955; Serenade for 15 winds, 1958; 3 pieces, clarinet and piano, 1958; 3 short pieces, bassoon and piano, 1959; septet for 3 winds, string trio, and bass, 1959; 5 short pieces, woodwind trio, 1961; Chamber set, 1959; woodwind quintet, 1966; many choral works, songs, piano and organ works.

    R.D. 1, Box 282, Sherman, CT 06784

STEARNS, THEODORE
    b. Berea, Ohio, 10 June 1880; d. Los Angeles, Calif., 1 Nov. 1935. Studied at Oberlin Cons. and at Wurzburg Cons. He received the Bispham Medal, 1925; Guggenheim fellowships, 1927-28. He was music critic in New York, 1922-26; in 1932, joined the faculty at Univ. of California, Los Angeles.

    WORKS: THEATRE: Snowbird, opera-ballet, 1923; Atlantis, lyric drama, 1926; ORCHESTRA: Tiberio, symphonic poem; 2 orchestral suites.

STEELE, HELEN
    b. Enfield, Conn., 21 June 1904. Attended Wellesley Coll., B.A.; studied music privately. She was voice teacher and accompanist for singers.

    WORKS: VOICE: America, our heritage; The legend of Befana; Duerme; Lagrimas.

STEELE, LANNY

STEELE, LANNY
b. Houston, Tex., 30 Dec. 1933. Studied with
Samuel Adler, North Texas State Univ.; with Ross
Lee Finney, Leslie Bassett, George B. Wilson,
Univ. of Michigan. He was Rackham Scholar at
Univ. of Michigan; won first place award, Con-
temporary Music Festival, Sam Houston State
Univ., 1966; received Nat. Endowment for the
Arts grant, 1971. He was faculty member, North
Texas State Univ., 1963-64; East Michigan Univ.,
1965-66; from 1968, at Texas Southern Univ.
WORKS: ORCHESTRA: III for J at 3, 1967;
JAZZ ENSEMBLE: Intersection, chamber orch. and
jazz group, 1967; Ghetto, 1970; Thunderbird,
concerto for alto saxophone, 1970; Space City
blues, concerto grosso for 4 soloists, 1971;
Thelonius, 1971; 3rd Ward Vibration Society,
concerto grosso; New York triptych, concerto
grosso for 3 soloists; CHAMBER MUSIC: piano
sonata, 1963; string quartet, 1964; Fantasy,
clarinet and piano, 1965; concertino for 5 woodwinds, 1966; Spacewalk, flute alone.
Texas Southern Univ., 3201 Wheeler Ave.,
Houston, TX 77004

STEELE, PORTER
b. Natchez, Miss., 12 Dec. 1880; d. 1966.
Studied with Horatio Parker at Yale Univ.; also
studied law and was admitted to the bar in New
York in 1905. He composed piano pieces and
songs.

STEFFEN, FREDERICK JOHN
b. Tilden, Nebr., 18 Feb. 1949. Studied with
Warren Benson and Samuel Adler, Eastman School
of Music. He received first prize in composition,
Rochester Religious Arts Festival, 1968, 1969,
1970; Louis Lane award, 1971. He was staff mem-
ber, Valparaiso Univ., 1971-73; on faculty,
Toccoa Falls Coll., from 1978.
WORKS: ORHCESTRA: Variations; horn con-
certo; CHORUS: Whither shall I go; Psalm 118;
For me to live is Christ; Take this song, con-
temporary hymn; SONGS: Aaron's benediction;
PIANO: sonata.
Toccoa Falls College, Toccoa Falls, GA 20577

STEG, PAUL O.
b. Greenleaf, Kans., 24 Aug. 1919. Studied
violin in Kansas and New York; composition with
Gardner Read at Boston Univ. He was assistant
director, Oberlin Cons., 1952-59; from 1961,
faculty member, Northern Illinois Univ., DeKalb.
WORKS: ORCHESTRA: Passacaglia; symphony
for chamber orch.; CHAMBER MUSIC: string quartet; viola sonata; Peter Quince at the clavier;
Stencils 1 and 2, mallet instruments; woodwind
quintet; CHORUS: Visions of black elk, speaking
chorus, percussion, and narrator; A vesper music;
ELECTRONIC: Fantasy, piano and taped violin;
Kaleidoscope, bassoon or saxophone, winds, percussion, and synthesizer.
R.F.D. 2, Sycamore, IL 60178

STEIN, ALAN
b. Chicago, Ill., 22 Jan. 1949. Studied with
Thomas Wirtel, Thomas Frederickson, and Robert
Kelly, Univ. of Illinois. He was faculty member,

Univ. of Illinois, 1971-74; from 1976, at Univ.
of Richmond.
WORKS: OPERA: A dove in the rainbow,
based on story of Noah, Urbana, Ill., 13 Dec.
1973; ORCHESTRA: Mozart, 1935, with chorus;
CHAMBER MUSIC: Quintessence I, 5 trombones;
Piano, soprano, 3 pianos, tape; Ternion, 12 percussionists; No trumpets, no drums, flute trio;
CHORUS: An afterthought, a cappella; The most
precious gift, a cappella.
University of Richmond, Richmond, VA 23178

STEIN, LEON
b. Chicago, Ill., 18 Sept. 1910. Studied with
Wesley La Violette, De Paul Univ., B.A. 1931,
M.M. 1935, Ph.D. 1949; also with Leo Sowerby
and Eric Delamarter; conducting with Hans Lange
and Frederick Stock. He won an American Composers' commission, 1950; was cowinner in the
Midland Found. Nat. Composition Contest, 1955;
and won the Elkhart (Ind.) Symphony Internat.
Contest, 1977. Except for service in the U.S.
Navy, 1944-45, he was faculty member, De Paul
Univ., from 1931, becoming dean, School of Music,
from 1966 to retirement in 1978.
WORKS: (unless otherwise noted, all first
performances took place in Chicago) OPERA: The
fisherman's wife, St. Joseph, Mich., 10 Jan.
1955; Deidre, 1 act, 18 May 1957; BALLET:
Exodus, 29 Jan. 1939; Doubt, 21 Jan. 1940; OR-
CHESTRA: Prelude and fugue, 30 June 1936; Passacaglia, 1936, 1 Sept. 1942; sinfonietta for
string orch., 1938, Grand Rapids, Mich., 9 Feb.
1941; violin concerto, 1939, 3 Dec. 1948; 4 symphonies, #1, 1940, 2 Dec. 1951, #2, 1942, New
York, 18 Feb. 1951, #3, 1950, 22 Nov. 1953, #4,
1974, 4 Jan. 1975; 3 Hassidic dances, 12 Apr.
1942; Triptych on 3 poems of Walt Whitman, 1943,
29 Mar. 1949; Great Lakes suite, 1944; Symphonic
movement, 1950; A festive overture, 1950; The
Lord reigneth, cantata with chorus, 1953, 20
Jan. 1956; Rhapsody, flute, harp, and strings,
1954, 8 Nov. 1955; Adagio and rondo ebraico,
1957; Then shall the dust return, 1971; cello
concerto, 17 Nov. 1977; CHAMBER MUSIC: suite
for string quartet, 1930; sonatine for 2 violins,
1931, 2 Oct. 1939; Adagio and dance, piano trio,
1931; violin sonata, 1932; 5 string quartets,
#1, 2 Dec. 1933, #2, 29 Apr. 1963, #3, 1964,
22 May 1967, #4, 1965, 13 Nov. 1966, #5, 1967,
5 Apr. 1968; woodwind quintet, 31 Mar. 1937;
trio for trumpets, 20 Jan. 1953; quintet for
saxophone and string quartet, 10 Feb. 1958;
sextet for saxophone and woodwind quintet, 23
Feb. 1959; trombone quartet, 1960; sonata for
violin alone, 1960; brass quartet, 1960; trio
for violin, saxophone, piano, 1961; suite for
saxophone quartet, 1965; 11 solo sonatas for
various instruments, 1968-70; suite for woodwind
quintet, 1970; quintet for harp and string quartet, 2 Jan. 1977; Duo concertante, viola and
cello, 14 Nov. 1978; also choral works and piano
pieces. He is author of The racial thinking of
Richard Wagner, New York, 1950, and Musical
forms--The study of structure and style in music,
Evanston, Ill., 1962, and of many articles in
music journals.
4050 Greenwood, Skokie, IL 60076

STEINBROOK, DAVID HERMAN
b. Philadelphia, Pa., 3 Oct. 1941. Studied with
George Rochberg and Henry Weinberg, Univ. of
Pennsylvania; with Roger Sessions, Milton
Babbitt, and Earl Kim, Princeton Univ., where he
held a Woodrow Wilson fellowship. He was faculty
member, Princeton Univ., 1966-69; at Swarthmore
Coll., 1970-78.
WORKS: CHAMBER MUSIC: Sonnet 73 of
Shakespeare, soprano and chamber ensemble, 1965,
rev. 1968; 5 compositions for piano, 1972; Sonnets to Orpheus, 1-9, by Rilke, soprano and
piano trio, 1973.
317 N. Chester Rd., Swarthmore, PA 19081

STEINER, FREDERICK
b. New York, N.Y., 24 Feb. 1923. Studied at
Inst. of Musical Art; on scholarship with Normand
Lockwood, Oberlin Cons., B.M. 1943. From 1943
he has been free-lance composer and conductor in
radio, television, and films.
WORKS: WIND ENSEMBLE: Tower music, brass
and percussion; CHAMBER MUSIC: Pezzo Italiano,
cello and piano; 5 pieces for string trio; woodwind quintet; string quartet; Songs for soprano
and string quartet; FILM SCORES: The man from
Del Rio, 1956; Run for the sun, 1956; Time limit;
TELEVISION SCORES: "The shrimp," 1953; "Country
doctor," 1954; "Miss Pepperdine," 1955; "Playhouse 90" films, 1956; "Perry Mason" series,
1957; "Navy log," 1957; "Secret mission," 1958;
and others.
4455 Gable Dr., Encino, CA 91316

STEINER, GEORGE
b. Budapest, Hungary, 17 Apr. 1900; d. U.S. 1967.
Studied at Budapest Acad. of Music; was violinist in opera and symphony orchestras; gave recitals in Europe. In the U.S. he was composer
for radio, television, and films. His works include Rhapsodic poem, viola and orch.; Serenade
sarcastique, violin and cello.

STEINER, GITTA
b. Prague, Czech., 17 Apr. 1932; U.S. citizen
1939. Studied with Elliott Carter and Vincent
Persichetti at Juilliard School, B.M. 1967, M.S.
1969; with Gunther Schuller at Tanglewood. Her
awards include full scholarship at Juilliard
School; Gretchaninoff award, 1966; Marion Freschi
award, 1966, 1967; Tanglewood fellowship, 1967;
4 Composers' Forum contests; ASCAP award, 1972;
and commissions. She has been teaching privately
from 1960; was instructor, Brooklyn Cons., 1968-
71.
WORKS: ORCHESTRA: suite, 1958; violin concerto, 1963; Tetrack, string orch., 1965; piano
concerto, 1967; CHAMBER MUSIC: suite for flute,
clarinet, bassoon, 1958; brass quintet, 1964;
Fantasy, clarinet and piano, 1964; Jouissance,
flute and piano, 1965; Movement for 11, 1966;
Refractions, violin solo, 1967; percussion quartet, 1968; string quartet, 1968; 3 pieces for
solo vibraphone, 1968; 5 pieces for trombone;
4 bagatelles, vibraphone, 1969; trio for piano
and percussion, 1969; duo for horn and piano,
1970; duo for cello and piano, 1971; Percussion
music for 2, 1971; PIANO: 3 pieces, 1961;

sonata, 1964; Fantasy piece, 1966; also choral
works and songs, for many of which she wrote
the texts as well as the music.
71-81 244th St., Douglaston, NY 11362

STEINER, MAX (Maximillian Raoul Walter)
b. Vienna, Austria, 10 May 1888; U.S. citizen
1920; d. Los Angeles, 28 Dec. 1971. Studied at
Vienna School of Technology and the Imperial
Acad. of Music; with Robert Fuchs, Hermann
Grädener, and Gustav Mahler. At age 15, he won
the Academy's Gold Medal for the astonishing
feat of completing the 8-year course in 1 year.
At 16, he wrote book, lyrics, and music for a
musical comedy, The beautiful Greek girl, which
opened at the Orpheum Theatre in Vienna with the
composer conducting and ran for a year. He was
also proficient on the double bass, violin,
piano, organ, and trumpet. He spent 8 years in
London as composer and conductor, 1906-14; came
to New York and spent 15 years as orchestrator
and conductor on Broadway, 1914-29; then went to
Hollywood and began a 36-year career in film
composing. He soon won his first Academy award
for The informer, 1935, followed by awards for
Now, voyager and Since you went away; 18 Academy
nominations; 8 first place Laurel awards, 1949-
60; Officier de l'Academis Francaise; 2 Cinema
Congress Medals; Italian Medal, 1936; Golden
Globe award, 1937; Cinema Exhibition award,
Vienna, 1948; Wisdom Award of Honor, 1966. The
Max Steiner Society was formed in 1965 and has
become a worldwide organization.
WORKS: FILM SCORES: Of his 300 film scores,
some of the most notable are The life of Emile
Zola; Jezebel; 4 daughters; Gold is where you
find it; Dark victory; The old maid; We are not
alone; The letter; Virginia City; All this and
heaven too; Sergeant York; Casablanca; Arsenic
and old lace; The corn is green; Mildred Pierce;
The adventures of Mark Twain; Saratoga trunk;
Life with father; The treasure of the Sierra
Madre; The voice of the turtle; Key Largo;
Johnny Belinda; Adventures of Don Juan; The
fountainhead; The flame and the arrow; The glass
menagerie; Battle cry; Helen of Troy; Marjorie
Morningstar; John Paul Jones; A summer place;
Dark at the tope of the stairs; and Gone with
the wind, a score of 192 minutes of music in
222 minutes of film.

STEINERT, ALEXANDER LANG
b. Boston, Mass., 21 Sept. 1900. Studied at
Harvard Univ., A.B. 1922; with Charles Martin
Loeffler in Boston; with Koechlin and d'Indy in
Paris; and in Rome, on the American Prix de Rome,
1927-30. He was opera conductor in New York and
Los Angeles.
WORKS: ORCHESTRA: Nuit meridionale, 1926;
Leggenda sinfonica, 1930; piano concerto, 1935;
Air Corps suite, 1942; Flight cycle, 1944; Rhap-
sody, clarinet and orch., 1945; The nightingale
and the rose, with speaker, 1950; also chamber
music and film scores.

STEININGER, FRANK K. W.
b. Vienna, Austria, 12 June 1906; to U.S. 1935.
Studied music with Josef Marx. He was theatre

STEINKE, GREG A.

conductor in Vienna, Berlin, and London; then in
Hollywood, New York, Pittsburgh, and Los Angeles.
WORKS: OPERETTA: Song without words; Centennial spectacle, for Topeka, Kans.; also film
scores and many songs.

STEINKE, GREG A.
b. Fremont, Mich., 2 Sept. 1942. Studied at
Oberlin Cons., B.M. 1964; with Paul Harder and
H. Owen Reed, Michigan State Univ., M.M. 1967,
Ph.D. 1976; with Richard Hervig, Univ. of Iowa,
M.F.A. 1971; with Ross Lee Finney, Dartmouth
Congr. of the Arts; Donald Erb and Mario
Davidovsky at Bennington. His awards include
Michigan Fed. of Music Clubs prize, 1966; BMI
award, 1968; Univ. of Maryland grants, 1969,
1970; Nat. Gallery of Art performance, 1972;
Bennington scholarship, 1972; California State
Univ. grant, 1974; first prize, Phi Mu Alpha
contest, 1975; New York Composers' Forum con-
cert, 1977. He was faculty member, Michigan
State Univ., 1965-66, 1972-73; Univ. of Iowa,
1966-67; Univ. of Idaho, 1967-68; Univ. of
Maryland, 1968-72; California State Univ.,
Northridge, 1973-75; from 1975, at Evergreen
State Coll.
WORKS: THEATRE: Right on!, musical review,
1970; incidental music for many plays; ORCHESTRA:
Threnody, 1965; Music for bassoon and orchestra,
1967; Duo fantasy concertante, violin, cello,
chamber orch.; WIND ENSEMBLE: Atavism, with
solo oboe and bassoon, 1976; Remembrances, with
4 trumpets, 1978; CHAMBER MUSIC: woodwind trio,
1962; sonata for oboe, oboe d'amore, English,
1963; Music for string quartet, 1965; Music for
percussion ensemble and conductor, 1972; Music
for 3, oboe, guitar, and percussion, 1972; Tri-
cinium, alto saxophone, trumpet and piano, 1972;
Episodes, saxophone, 1973; 4 desultory episodes,
oboe and tape, 1973; string trio, 1962, rev.
1974; Polymodal sketches, woodwind trio and harp,
1961-75; Diversions and interactions, percussion
trio, 1976; In quietude, flute solo, 1978;
Diphona I, oboe and piano, 1978; songs and piano
pieces.
6145 Northill Loop S.W., Olympia, WA 98502

STEINOHRT, WILLIAM J.
b. Chicago, Ill., 19 Mar. 1937. Studied with
Ben Johnston and Robert Kelly, Univ. of Illinois;
with Neil McKay and Armand Russell, Univ. of
Hawaii; with Martin Mailman, William Latham, and
Merrill Ellis, North Texas State Univ., Ph.D.
1971. His awards include second prize, Percussion Arts Society contest, 1975; Nat. Endowment
for the Arts grant, 1976; and commissions. He
has been faculty member, Wright State Univ.,
from 1971.
WORKS: BALLET: Kauai, 1960; ORCHESTRA:
Derivatives, 1978; piano concerto, 1971; Dance,
with percussion solo, 1974; Music for strings,
1974; The forgotten, 1976-77; BAND: Pisces,
1971; Aries, 1975; CHAMBER MUSIC: Movement for
string quartet, 1967; Synthesis, woodwind quintet, double bass, piano, 1968; 2 movements for
mallets, 1971; woodwind trio, 1972; Decatet,
woodwind quintet and strings, 1972; Te datsalis,
bassoon and piano, 1975; CHORUS: 2 Psalms, with

brass and percussion, 1970; Epitaph for the unknown soldier, 1974; Psalm 114, 1974; also electronic music.
2901 Locke Dr., Fairborn, OH 45324

STENBERG, JORDAN
b. Fresno, Calif., 31 May 1947. Studied with
Robert Moran at San Francisco Cons.; with Robert
Ashley at Mills Coll. He is in the forefront of
avant-garde composers and has also experimented
with compositions to stimulate plant growth.
His works for theatre include Mind over matter,
a film opera for voices and instruments, 1969;
The clock struck one, an opera-play for voices,
instruments, and dervish dancers, 1970; Circles,
lines, planes moves out of the theatre and into
a canyon with a choreographed acoustical dance
for 9 bagpipers and 9 x 9 buglers (it is notated
in the form of an enneagram), 1970.

STEPHENS, CHARLES COLE
b. Charleston, S.C., 6 Feb. 1938. Studied with
H. Owen Reed, Paul Harder, and Roy Niblock,
Michigan State Univ. He received first prize,
Richmond Professional Inst. competition, 1967;
performances at Willamet Chamber Music Festival
and Premieres of New Music, Michigan State Univ.
He was head of music, Holly, Mich., school sys-
tem, 1961-64; and music chairman, St. Clair
County Coll., 1969-74.
WORKS: BALLET: 12 tones, 3-movement ballet;
ORCHESTRA: States of mind; 900,000 days, sym-
phony for choir, rock band, tape, and orch.;
CHORUS: Christmas mass for choir and jazz-rock
band; Hatteras, with 2 harps; Psalm 96; symphony
for winds, tape, and speaking chorus.

STEPHENSON, MARK
b. Provo, Utah, 26 Oct. 1950. Studied briefly
with Myron Fink and Matthew Colucci, Curtis Inst.
of Music, but is largely self-taught. He was
bassist with Concerto Soloists of Philadelphia,
1968-71.
WORKS: CHAMBER MUSIC: double bass sonata,
1970; Concertpiece, bass and strings, 1971;
Emily Dickinson songs, 1971; Nocturne, piano,
1971; Cavatina, for strings, 1973.

STEPLETON, JAMES IRVIN
b. Muncie, Ind., 28 Apr. 1941. Studied with
H. Owen Reed, Michigan State Univ.; and with
Morris Knight, Ball State Univ. He won an award
in the Mario Castelnuovo-Tedesco first internat.
contest for a guitar composition; first prize,
chamber opera division, Nat. Contest for New
Music for Worship, 1969. He was faculty member,
Augustana Coll.
WORKS: CHAMBER OPERA: For those who will
say yes, 1969; CHAMBER MUSIC: Intermezzo, violin
and cello; Serenade, guitar; wind quintet; Proem
and roundelay, saxophone quartet; Polarities,
bass clarinet and piano.

STEPPER, MARTIN PAUL
b. Bronx, N.Y., 11 Jan. 1948. Studied with Earl
George and Franklin Morris, Syracuse Univ., B.M.
summa cum laude 1970; with Myron Fink, Curtis
Inst. of Music, M.M. 1971. He held full scholar-

ships for all study; received a Phi Kappa Lambda award, 1969. He was instructor, Paterson, N.J., public schools, 1970-71; area adult school, Morris County, N.J., 1970-71; private teacher, 1969-74.

WORKS: ORCHESTRA: piano concerto, 1973; CHAMBER MUSIC: violin sonata, 1968; woodwind quintet, 1970; Serenade, chamber ensemble, 1971; Rhapsody, clarinet, 1972; piano sonata, 1972; string quartet, 1973.

STERN, ALFRED BERNARD

b. Boston, Mass., 6 Dec. Studied clarinet and theory in Boston and at the Univ. of California, Berkeley. He received a Children's Theatre award for music, 1967, and ASCAP awards. He was music director, WCOP Radio, Boston, 1935-36; music director, East Bay Children's Theatre, 1965-73; choral director, Berkeley school system.

WORKS: THEATRE: incidental music and songs for After the rain; Death of a salesman; Mother of us all; Skin of our teeth; and others; many children's musicals and songs.

1430 Grizzly Peak Blvd., Berkeley, CA 94708

STERN, MAX

b. Valley Stream, N.Y., 31 Mar. 1947. Studied with Samuel Adler and Bernard Rogers, Eastman School of Music, B.M. 1969; with Alexander Goehr, Yale Univ.; electronic music with Bulent Arel in New York. His awards include a MacDowell fellowship and a Ford Found. grant. He taught at 3rd Street Settlement School and privately, 1971-72; played double bass, Rochester Phil., 1968-69; New Haven Symph. and Bridgeport Symph., 1969-70; Nat. Orch. Assoc. and Radio City Music Hall, 1970-72.

WORKS: OPERA: The philosophy lesson, after Moliere, 1968; BALLET: Galumph; ORCHESTRA: Sonnet; CHAMBER MUSIC: Sonnet and dance, double bass; piano sonata, 1967; string sextet, 1968; string quartet, 1972.

156 W. 72nd St., New York, NY 10023

STERN, ROBERT

b. Paterson, N.J., 1 Feb. 1934. Studied with Louis Mennini, Kent Kennan, Wayne Barlow, Bernard Rogers, Howard Hanson, Eastman School of Music, Ph.D.; with Lukas Foss, Univ. of California, Los Angeles. His awards include the Edward Benjamin first prize, 1956; 3 MacDowell fellowships, 1967, 1969, 1972. He taught at Eastman School and Hochstein Memorial School, 1961-62; Hartford Cons., 1962-64; was visiting composer and director of electronic music, Hampshire Coll., 1970-71; then joined the faculty at Univ. of Massachusetts, Amherst.

WORKS: BALLET: Fort Union, 1960; ORCHESTRA: In memoriam Abraham, string orch., 1956; Credo, 1957; symphony, 1961; Hazkarah, cello and orch.; Carom, with tape; CHAMBER MUSIC: string quartet; Fragments, flute, clarinet, harpsichord; Music for horn and soprano; Terezin, soprano, cello, piano; Adventures for one, percussion; Fantasy piece, piano; A little bit of music, 2 clarinets; Night songs, violin, piano, electronic sounds; and songs.

136 West St., Amherst, MA 01002

STERNE, COLIN C.

b. Wynberg, South Africa, 14 Nov. 1921; U.S. citizen 1942. Studied with Gail Kubik, William Bergsma, Vincent Persichetti at Juilliard School; with Nadia Boulanger, Paris Cons. He has received a Phi Mu Alpha composition award. From 1948 he has been faculty member, Univ. of Pittsburgh.

WORKS: ORCHESTRA: A mask for Orpheus, string orch.; CHAMBER MUSIC: sonata for alto recorder and harpsichord; Meadow, hedge, cuckoo, alto recorder; Landscape with bird, recorder choir; A summer ceremony, flute, vibraphone, cello, and reader; VOICE: mass for choir, congregation, and organ; various propers of the mass and sacred anthems for choir and organ; 3 James Joyce songs, voice and piano; 3 John Donne songs, voice and piano.

624 Garden City Dr., Monroeville, PA 15146

STERNKLAR, AVRAHAM

b. Trieste, Italy, 21 Oct. 1930; U.S. citizen 1956. Studied with Paul Ben Haim in Israel; with Vittorio Giannini at Juilliard School, 1949-53; piano with James Friskin and Edward Steuerman, also at Juilliard. His awards include scholarships at Juilliard and Philadelphia Cons.; Piano Quarterly best-of-year awards. He was music correspondent for the Israel broadcasting station, 1949-53; on faculty, YMHA, New York, 1956-57; active as performer, lecturer, teacher, composer.

WORKS: CHAMBER MUSIC: sonatas for piano, violin, clarinet, cello; piano sonatinas and suites, including A promise fulfilled, based on paintings by his mother, Tea Sternklar; choral music and songs.

14 Jerold St., Plainfield, NY 11803

STEUERMANN, EDWARD

b. Sambor, Poland, 18 June 1892; U.S. citizen 1944; d. New York, N.Y., 11 Nov. 1964. Studied piano with Vilem Kurz in Poland, with Busoni in Switzerland and Berlin; composition with Arnold Schoenberg in Berlin, 1912-14. He made his piano debut at age 11; made extensive concert tours in Europe, Israel, and America. He is credited with the first performance of all Schoenberg's piano works, chamber music with piano, and his piano concerto (NBC Symphony, 6 Feb. 1944). He received the Schoenberg Medal, highest honor of the Internat. Society for Contemporary Music, Salzburg, 1952, "for promoting and deepening general understanding for contemporary musical works."

WORKS: ORCHESTRA: Variations for orchestra, 1958; Music for instruments, 1960; suite for chamber orchestra, 1964; CHAMBER MUSIC: 7 waltzes, string quartet, 1946; piano trio, 1954; Improvisation and allegro, violin and piano, 1955; Toccata and aria, flute and piano, 1955, unfinished; Diary, string quartet, 1961; Dialogues, solo violin, 1963; PIANO: sonata, 1926, rev. 1954; Evening song, 1938; Spring song, 1939; suite for piano, 1952; other piano pieces, choral works, and songs.

STEVENS, GLENN
b. Chesaning, Mich., 26 July 1899. Studied at
Chicago Musical Coll.; violin with Leopold Auer
and Eugene Ysaye. He was violinist with Isham
Jones's orchestra and others; conducted his own
orchestra. He composed an opera, The legend of
Tucumcari, from which Indian lullaby for violin
and piano has been published.

STEVENS, HALSEY
b. Scott, N.Y., 3 Dec. 1908. Studied with
William Berwald, Syracuse Univ., B.M. 1931, M.M.
1937, honorary Litt.D. 1966; with Ernest Bloch,
Univ. of California, 1944. His honors include
Nat. Fed. of Music Clubs award, 1943; Middlebury
Coll. Composers' Conf., 1946; Society for Pub-
lication of American Music award, 1949; Nat.
Assoc. of Coll. Wind and Perc. Instructors award,
1955; Friends of Harvey Gaul award, 1966; Nat.
Inst. of Arts and Letters, citation and grant,
1961; Guggenheim fellowships, 1964, 1971; Nat.
Endowment for the Arts grant, 1976; Hungarian
Found.'s Abraham Lincoln award for his book The
life and music of Bela Bartok, 1978; many commissions. He was faculty member, Dakota Wesleyan
Univ., 1937-41; director, Coll. of Music, Bradley
Univ., 1941-46; from 1946, Univ. of Southern
California, officially emeritus professor in
1976; has also been visiting professor on many
campuses; program annotator, Los Angeles Philharmonic, 1946-51; Phoenix Symphony, 1947-48;
and from 1967, Coleman Chamber Concerts.
    WORKS: THEATRE: music for Sheridan's The
rivals, 1961; ORCHESTRA: 2 symphonies, 1945,
1945; A Green Mountain overture, 1948; Triskelion,
1953; Adagio and allegro, string orch., 1955;
The ballad of William Sycamore, with chorus,
1955; Sinfonia breve, 1957; Symphonic dances,
1958; A testament of life, with chorus, 1959;
Magnificat, with chorus, 1962; cello concerto,
1964; Threnos: In memoriam Quincy Porter, 1968;
concerto for clarinet and strings, 1969; double
concerto for violin, cello, strings, Los Angeles,
4 Nov. 1973; viola concerto, 1976; CHAMBER MUSIC:
flute sonatina, 1943; violin sonatina, 1944; 2
piano trios, 1945, 1954; suite for clarinet and
piano, 1946; quintet for flute, string trio,
piano, 1946; violin sonata, 1947; Intermezzo,
cadenza, and finale, cello and piano, 1949;
string quartet #3, 1949; bassoon sonata, 1949;
viola sonata, 1950; horn sonata, 1953; Sonatina
giocosa, double bass and piano, 1954; suite for
solo violin, 1955; trumpet sonata, 1956; septet,
woodwinds and strings, 1957; sonata for solo
cello, 1958; trio for winds and/or strings, 1959;
suite for viola and piano, 1959; cello sonata,
1965; trombone sonata, 1965; Divertimento, 2
violins, 1966; 2 oboe sonatas, 1971, #2, Los
Angeles, 19 Nov. 1976; 12 studies for solo oboe,
1972; Dittico, alto saxophone and piano, 1972;
Quintetto Sorbelloni, woodwinds, 1972, Los
Angeles, 16 Mar. 1976; many choral works and
songs.
    9631 2nd Ave., Inglewood, CA 90305

STEWART, DAVID NISBET
b. Miami, Fla., 30 Dec. 1941. Studied with
Walter Aschaffenberg, Oberlin Cons., 1963-65;

with Alvin Etler, Yale Univ., 1965-66, and at
Smith Coll., 1967-69. He received a BMI student
composer award, 1965; Columbia Univ. chamber
music award, 1969; Internat. Trombone Assoc.
award, 1975. He was on the faculty, Oberlin
Coll., 1979; Kent State Univ., 1975-79; business
programmer, Ohio Scientific Inc., 1979-80.
    WORKS: CHAMBER MUSIC: Entropy, string
quartet, 1969; Spectral dance, wind quintet;
piano trio, 1976.
    437 Needham Ave., Kent, OH 44240

STEWARD, DONALD G.
b. Sterling, Ill., 8 Jan. 1935. Studied with
Bernhard Heiden and Roy Harris, Indiana Univ.,
B.M. 1960; with Gunther Schuller, Manhattan
School of Music. He has played clarinet with
jazz orchestras, with the Florida, Birmingham,
and Vermont symphonies; is founder and member of
the Boehm Quintette; has been librarian, Brooklyn
Philharmonic, and faculty member, Lyndon State
Coll., Vt.
    WORKS: ORCHESTRA: Opener, 1964; The 200-
bar passacaglia, 1972; piccolo concerto, 1973;
CHAMBER MUSIC: string quartet, 1962; Life-
slices, flute and piano, 1967; brass quintet,
1968; duets for flute and clarinet, 1969; Concert
duet, flute and bass clarinet, 1971; The tat-
tooed desert, low male voice and chamber ensemble, 1973.
    Box 65, Tunbridge, VT 05077

STEWART, FRANK GRAHAM
b. La Junta, Colo., 12 Dec. 1920. Studied with
Bernard Rogers, Eastman School of Music, B.M.
1942; with Roger Sessions, Colorado Coll., M.A.T.
1968; with H. Owen Reed, Michigan State Univ.,
Ph.D. 1971. His awards include the Alice M.
Ditson award, 1946; Phi Mu Alpha Sinfonia Orpheus
award, 1974; Mannes Coll. of Music grant for performance of the opera, To let the captive go,
1974; Coll. Band Directors Nat. Assoc. award,
1978; and commissions. He taught at Colorado
State Univ., 1967-68; Univ. of Missouri at
Columbia, 1968-69; from 1971, at Mississippi
State Univ.
    WORKS: OPERA: To let the captive go, cham-
ber opera, 1971, New York, 5 Mar. 1974; ORCHESTRA:
accordion concerto, 1952; BAND: Scene, 1970;
The first day, 1978; CHAMBER MUSIC: Phantom
train of Marshall Pass, narrator, winds, percussion, 1970; Characteristics, brass quintet, 1973;
Toccata, piano, 1976; Recitative and allegro,
woodwind quintet, 1978.
    Box 5261, Mississippi State Univ., State
College, MS 39762

STEWART, HASCAL VAUGHAN
b. Darlington, S.C., 17 Feb. 1898. Studied at
Winthrop Coll., A.B., and postgraduate work;
Teachers Coll., New York; composition privately
with Gustave Weigl. She was on the music faculty
at Winthrop Coll., 1921-22.
    WORKS: SONGS: Sleep to wake; As a promise;
Threshold of Christmas; Overtones; Mary in
Christendom; many songs and piano pieces.

STEWART, ROBERT
b. Buffalo, N.Y., 6 Mar. 1918. Studied at
American Cons., M.M.E. 1947, M.M. in violin
1950, M.M. in composition 1950. He received a
MacDowell fellowship, 1956; 2 awards, Georgia
State Coll. Symposium for Contemporary Music for
Brass, 1966, 1972; several commissions. He
taught in Chicago area schools, 1938-41; composed
music for radio shows On target and Meet your
Navy while in naval service 1941-45; was faculty
member, American Cons., 1945-53; from 1954, at
Washington and Lee Univ.
    WORKS: ORCHESTRA: Requiem for a soldier;
Prelude for strings; WIND ENSEMBLE: Divertissement, brass choir; Music for brass #4; Hydra III,
brass and percussion; 2 brass quintets; duos for
brass choirs; Hydra IV, brass quintet and band;
CHAMBER MUSIC: concerto for horn and chamber
orch.; Fantasia, viola and chamber orch.; Hydra,
winds, strings, piano; Mystic, contrabass; 3
string quartets; 2 ricercari, woodwind quintet
and strings; Heart attack, tuba and percussion;
and others.
    Washington and Lee University, Lexington,
VA 24450

STEWART, ROBERT J.
b. Albany, N.Y., 22 Apr. 1932. Studied with
Richard Hervig, Univ. of Iowa, Ph.D. 1969. From
1969 he has been faculty member, California State
Univ. at Fullerton.
    WORKS: THEATRE: The Trojan women, actors,
narrator, chorus, and orch.; ORCHESTRA: Music
for orchestra; CHAMBER MUSIC: string quartet;
Canto I and II, clarinet and piano; Capriccio,
solo violin; Virelai, flute, viola, double bass,
harpsichord; Impromptu, solo cello; Syzygies,
guitar duo.
    5641 Mountain View, Yorba Linda, CA 92686

STILES, JAMES EVERETT
b. Silver City, N.M., 27 Oct. 1949. Studied
with Alvin Epstein, Southern Methodist Univ.,
B.M. 1972, M.M. 1974; with Merrill Ellis and
Larry Austin, North Texas State Univ., D.M.A.
1979. He received the Ars Nova award in composition, 1973; Texas Composers' Guild award, 1979.
He was instructor, El Centro Coll., 1972-77;
teaching fellow, North Texas State Univ., 1977-
79.
    WORKS: ORCHESTRA: Trichotomy: an orches-
tral triptych; A pcycle of psalms, with chorus;
N4: a common time piece for these uncommon
times, 1978; WIND ENSEMBLE: BRASSMASS, brass
choir and percussion, 1977; CHAMBER MUSIC:
string quartet, 1976; A hex for Mr. Cage, solo
voice; Violaceous, solo viola, 1978; My short
cummings, songs on poems of e. e. cummings,
soprano and piano interior; ELECTRONIC: Concrète sans regret, actor, tape, slides, 1977.
    1418 W. Oak St., Denton, TX 76201

STILL, WILLIAM GRANT
b. Woodville, Miss., 11 May 1895; d. Los
Angeles, Calif., 3 Dec. 1978. Studied at
Oberlin Cons.; with George W. Chadwick, New
England Cons.; and with Edgard Varese in New
York. He learned to orchestrate by playing many

instruments, among them violin, cello, and oboe,
in professional orchestras, and by orchestrating
for W. C. Handy, Don Voorhees, Sophie Tucker,
William Robison, Paul Whiteman, and Artie Shaw.
For several years he was arranger and conductor
for the Deep South Hour on CBS and WOR. His
many honors include Guggenheim and Rosenwald
fellowships; 2nd Harmon Award, 1927; honorary
M.M., Wilberforce Coll., 1936; 7 honorary doctorates, 1941-74; Cincinnati Symph. Orch. award,
1944; citation from Nat. Assoc. of American Composers and Conductors, 1949; Phi Beta Sigma
award, 1953; Freedoms Found. award, 1953; prize
offered by U.S. Committee for the U.N., Nat.
Fed. of Music Clubs, and Aeolian Music Found.
for his orchestral work, The peaceful land, 1961;
citation from Los Angeles City and County, 1963;
many commissions. Opera/South presented its
files on Dr. Still to Jackson State Univ. to
establish a permanent collection. On 22 Sept.
1976, he was honored at the West Coast meeting
of ASCAP and awarded a plaque noting his "extra-
ordinary contribution to the literature of symphonic music, opera, ballet, chamber music,
songs, and solo works." On 11 Mar. 1978, the
City of Los Angeles dedicated a Community Arts
Center to him. He was the first black man to
conduct a major symphony orchestra in the U.S.,
Los Angeles, 1936, and in the deep South, New
Orleans, 1955.
    WORKS: OPERA: Blue steel, 1935; Troubled
Island, 1938, New York, 1949; A bayou legend,
1940, Jackson, Miss., 15 Nov. 1974; Costaso,
1949; Highway 1, U.S.A., Miami, 13 May 1963;
BALLET: La guiablesse, 1927; Sahdji, 1930;
Lenox Avenue, 1937; Miss Sally's party, 1940;
ORCHESTRA: Darker America, 1924; From the Black
Belt, 1926; Africa, a suite, 1930; Afro-American
symphony, 1931, rev. 1969; Dismal swamp, 1935;
symphony in g, 1937; And they lynched him on a
tree, with narrator, contralto, and 2 choruses,
New York, 25 June 1940; Plain-chant for America,
with baritone solo, 1940; Old California, 1941;
Pages from Negro history, 1943; Poem, 1944; Festive overture, 1944; symphony #3, 1945; Archaic
ritual, 1946; Wood notes, 1947; symphony #4,
1949; symphony #5; A deserted plantation, suite;
Danzas de Panama, strings, New York premiere,
9 Jan. 1971; The American scene, set of 5 suites;
The little red schoolhouse, suite; The peaceful
land, 1961; From a lost continent, with chorus;
Psalm for the living, with chorus; Ennanga, with
harp solo; Christmas in the Western World,
string orch. with chorus; also band pieces,
chamber music, choral works, and songs.

STILLER, ANDREW PHILIP
b. Washington, D.C., 6 Dec. 1946. Studied with
Robert Crane, Univ. of Wisconsin, B.A. 1968;
with Morton Subotnick, Univ. of Maryland, 1969;
with Allen Sapp, Lejaren Hiller, and Morton
Feldman, State Univ. of New York at Buffalo,
M.A. 1971, Ph.D. 1976. He has been free-lance
composer, teacher, critic from 1973.
    WORKS: THEATRE: Lavender, chamber opera,
1978; ORCHESTRA: 13 ways of looking at a blackbird, speaker, bass clarinet, small orch., 1967;
Piece with transposing harmonics, 1975; LARGE

STILLMAN, MITYA

ENSEMBLES: Magnification, 1-65 instruments,
1968; Peel me another grape, 20 random instruments, 1968; Stiller's folly, 53 woodwinds, 1971;
Keep me hi and I'll ball you forever, 17 brass,
1972; The ultimate percussion ensemble piece, 20
percussion, 6 supermuneraries, 1973; Keyboard
installment, 10 keyboards, 1975; many conventional
chamber music pieces, some with tape.
    419 Crescent Ave., Buffalo, NY 14214

STILLMAN, MITYA
    b. Ilyintza, Russia, 27 Jan. 1892; to U.S. 1918;
d. New York, N.Y., 12 Apr. 1936. Studied with
Gliere at the Kiev Cons. He was posthumously
awarded a first prize for his 7th string quartet
by the NBC Guild, 1936. He was violist in the
Detroit Symphony, then in the Hartmann String
Quartet; from 1928 he was first violist with the
CBS Symphony.
    WORKS: ORCHESTRA: Dnieprostroy, symphonic
poem; Cyprus, for strings, woodwinds, percussion;
CHAMBER MUSIC: 8 string quartets; Yalta suite,
string trio; 4 songs for mezzo-soprano, flute,
harp, string quartet.

STILMAN, JULIA
    b. Buenos Aires, Argentina, 2 Mar. 1935; U.S.
citizen 1973. Studied with Gilardo Gilardi,
Buenos Aires, 1956-58; with Lawrence Moss and
Morton Subotnick, Univ. of Maryland, M.A. 1968,
D.M.A. 1973; with Krzysztof Penderecki, Yale
Univ., 1974. Her awards include a Nat. Endowment for the Arts grant, 1975; and commissions.
From 1976 she has been artist-in-residence with
the Organization of American States.
    WORKS: ORCHESTRA: El oro intimo, cantata
#1, with baritone solo, 1961; Cantares de la
madre joven, with women's chorus, 1963; Barcarola, with chorus and 3 female soloists, 1973;
Rituals, with chorus, solo voices (chorus also
plays percussion), 1976; CHAMBER MUSIC: Cello
quartet for trumpet, xylophone, cello, clarinet,
1959; Visiones, piano sonata, 1961; Etudes for
string quartet on verses of e. e. cummings,
1978; 5 etudes, woodwind quintet, 1978.
    301 Congressional Lane, Rockville, MD 20852

STINE, ROBERT EVERETT, JR.
    b. Greenville, S.C., 24 Dec. 1951. Studied with
Roger Hannay, Univ. of North Carolina; with
Donald Erb and Eugene O'Brien, Cleveland Inst.
of Music. He received a Nat. Endowment for the
Arts grant, 1978, for a 2nd symphony; from 1978,
has been on the faculty, Univ. of California,
Berkeley.
    WORKS: ORCHESTRA: symphony in 1 movement,
1976; CHAMBER MUSIC: 2 pieces for piano, 1975;
Chamber music, flute, harp, cello, percussion,
1976; 2 songs, on texts of W. B. Yeats, 1977;
Partita, solo guitar, 1977; string quartet, 1977;
septet, 4 woodwdins, 3 brasses, 1978.
    Music Dept., Univ. of California, Berkeley,
    CA 94720

STOCK, DAVID FREDERICK
    b. Pittsburgh, Pa., 3 June 1939. Studied with
Nikolai Lopatnikoff, Carnegie Inst. of Technology, B.F.A. 1962, M.F.A. 1963; with Arthur

Berger and Alexei Haieff, Brandeis Univ.; and at
Ecole Normale de Musique, Paris, 1960-61. His
awards include Guggenheim fellowship, 1974; Nat.
Endowment for the Arts grants, 1974, 1976, 1978;
American Music Center grant, 1976; Ella Lyman
Cabot Trust grant, 1977. He was faculty member,
Cleveland Inst. of Music, 1964-65; New England
Cons., 1968-70; Antioch Coll., 1970-74; Carnegie-
Mellon Univ., 1976-77; then at Univ. of Pitts-
burgh; from 1975, conductor, Pittsburgh New
Music Ensemble.
    WORKS: ORCHESTRA: Divertimento, 1957;
Capriccio, small orch., 1963; symphony in 1
movement, 1963; Inner space, 1973; Triflumena,
1978; WIND ENSEMBLE: Nova, 1974; The body electric, 1977; CHAMBER MUSIC: string quartet,
1962; Serenade, 5 instruments, 1964; quintet for
clarinet and strings, 1966; FLASHBACK, 11 players,
1968; 3 pieces, violin and piano, 1969; Triple
play, 1970; Dreamwinds, woodwind quintet, 1975;
Pentacles, brass quintet, 1978; FILM SCORES:
Evolution of a shadow, 1964; Hamlet, 1977; Romeo
and Juliet, 1977.
    6321 Stanton Ave., Pittsburgh, PA 15206

STOCK, FREDERICK
    b. Jülich, Germany, 11 Nov. 1872; U.S. citizen
1919; d. Chicago, Ill., 20 Oct. 1942. Studied
with his father, a bandmaster, and at the
Cologne Cons. His many awards included election
to the Nat. Inst. of Arts and Letters, 1910; 3
honorary doctorates; Chevalier, Legion d'Honneur,
1925; Bruckner Society of America Medal, 1939.
He was first violist, Chicago Symph. Orch., 1895-
1901, assistant conductor, 1901-5, conductor,
1905-42. He composed a symphony, a violin concerto, overtures, chamber music, and songs. His
violin concerto was performed by Efrem Zimbalist
with the composer conducting the Chicago Symphony, 3 June 1915.

STOCKHOFF, WALTER WILLIAM
    b. St. Louis, Mo., 12 Nov. 1887; d. St. Louis,
1 Apr. 1968. He was largely self-taught in composition.
    WORKS: ORCHESTRA: American symphonic suite
(an orchestration of his piano suite, To the
mountains); 5 dramatic poems, for orch., 1943;
PIANO: a sonata; Metamorphoses.

STOEPPELMANN, JANET
    b. St. Louis, Mo., 5 Dec. 1948. Studied at
Univ. of South Florida, M.M. 1973; on scholarship at Univ. of California, San Diego, 1978-79.
She was instructor, Nova Univ., 1973-74; Broward
Community Coll., 1975-77; Phoenix Coll., 1978.
    WORKS: CHAMBER MUSIC: Sindhura, harp, 1973;
CHORUS: Seashore of endless worlds, female
voices, 1971; Tollite jugum meum, motet, 1971;
3 Japanese haiku, female voices, 1972; Parallax,
1973; MULTIMEDIA: Metallon, tape, tamtams, percussion, sculpture, 1972; The Great Wall of
China, after Kafka, narrator and tape, 1973.

STOESSEL, ALBERT
    b. St. Louis, Mo., 11 Oct. 1894; d. New York,
N.Y., 12 May 1943. Studied with Willy Hess and
August Kretschmar at Berlin Hochschule; made his

American debut as violinist with the St. Louis Symphony in 1915. He was director of the New York Oratorio Society, 1921-43; music chairman, New York Univ., 1923-30; director, opera dept., Juilliard School, 1930-43; from 1925, conducted the Worcester, Mass., music festivals.

WORKS: OPERA: Garrick, produced at Juilliard School, 1937; ORCHESTRA: Hispania suite, 1921; Cyrano de Bergerac, symphonic poem, 1922; concerto grosso, strings and piano, 1934; CHAMBER MUSIC: Suite antique, 2 violins and piano, 1922; violin sonata; violin pieces; also choral works, songs, and piano pieces.

STOJOWSKI, SIGISMUND
b. Strzelce, Poland, 14 May 1870; U.S. citizen 1938; d. New York, N.Y., 5 Nov. 1946. Studied with Zelenski in Cracow; composition with Delibes at Paris Cons.; won first prize in piano and composition; then studied with Paderewski. On coming to the U.S. in 1905, he became head of the piano dept., Inst. of Musical Art, New York, 1905-11; Von Ende School of Music, 1911-17; then taught privately in New York and at the Juilliard Summer School.

WORKS: ORCHESTRA: symphony, 1898; Polish rhapsodie, piano and orch.; Romance, violin and orch.; 3 piano concertos; violin concerto, 1908; Spring, chorus and orch.; Prayer for Poland, chorus and orch., 1915; CHAMBER MUSIC: 2 violin sonatas; cello sonata; Fantasy, for trombone; variations and fugue, string quartet; many piano pieces.

STÖHR, RICHARD
b. Vienna, Austria, 11 June 1874; to U.S. 1938; d. Montpelier, Vt., 11 Dec. 1967. After receiving a doctorate in medicine in 1898, he began the study of music at the Vienna Cons., then taught there. He taught at Curtis Inst. of Music, 1939-41; and at St. Michael's Coll., Winooski, Vt., 1941-50.

WORKS: ORCHESTRA: 4 symphonies; Vermont suite, premiered by the Vermont State Symphony Orch. in 1954; also many chamber works, songs, piano pieces.

STOKES, ERIC
b. Haddon Heights, N.J., 14 July 1930. Studied with James Ming, Lawrence Coll.; with Carl McKinley, New England Cons.; and with Paul Fetler, Univ. of Minnesota. His awards include Montalvo Found. fellowships, 1957-58; Shevlin fellowship, 1959; MacDowell fellowship, 1962; McMillan Fund grant, 1969; Ford Found. and Rockefeller grants, 1969-70; Nat. Endowment for the Arts grants, 1974, 1976, 1978; and commissions. He has been faculty member, Univ. of Minnesota, from 1963.

WORKS: OPERA: Horspfal, Minneapolis, 15 Feb. 1969; The jealous cellist and other acts of misconduct, Minnesota Opera Co., 2 Feb. 1979; ORCHESTRA: A Center Harbor holiday, 1963; 3 sides of a town, Minneapolis, 27 Oct. 1964; Gnomic commentaries, 17 June 1965; Sonatas, Naarden, Holland, 11 July 1970; On the Badlands--parables, St. Paul, 3 June 1972; BAND: The continental harp and band report, Minneapolis, 9

Mar. 1975; An American miscellany, 1974; CHAMBER MUSIC: Smoke and steel, tenor and chamber orch., Boston, 14 May 1958; Expositions on themes of Henry Thoreau, chamber ensemble, 1970; Eldey Island, flute and tape, 1971; Lampyridae, a summer nocturne, Minneapolis, 9 Aug. 1973; When this you see remember me, theatre piece for 12 singers.
1611 W. 32nd St., Minneapolis, MN 55408

STOKOWSKI, LEOPOLD
b. London, England, 18 Apr. 1882; U.S. citizen 1915; d. Nether Wallop, Hampshire, England, 13 Sept. 1977. Studied at Queen's Coll., Oxford; at Royal Coll. of Music, London; and in Paris and Munich. His many honors included a Bok award of $10,000 for public service to Philadelphia; fellow, Royal Acad. of Music, London; Chevalier, Legion of Honor, France; Order Polonia Restituta, Poland; several honorary doctorates. He was organist, St. James Church, Piccadilly, in 1900; organist and choir director, St. Bartholomew's Church, New York, 1905-8. In 1909-12, he was conductor of the Cincinnati Symphony; then led the Philadelphia Orch. to 1938, bringing it to a peak of performance and giving American premieres of many contemporary works. He organized the All-American Youth Orchestra and with it, toured the U.S., South America, and Canada, 1940-42; then led a succession of orchestras, ending with the Houston Symphony, 1955-60; was cofounder of the American Symphony in 1962 and its conductor to 1973. He appeared in the films, The big broadcast of 1939, 100 men and a girl, and Disney's Fantasia, for which he also supervised the music.

WORKS: ORCHESTRA: a symphony; Spring, with chorus; 2 violin concertos; 3 piano concertos; also choral works, organ pieces; and many transcriptions, especially of works by Bach.

STOLTZE, ROBERT H.
b. Spokane, Wash., 21 Jan. 1910. Studied with Rudolph Ganz, Louis Gruenberg, Max Wald, Karel Jirak, and John Becker in Chicago. He received a Ganz scholarship; awards, Friends of New Music and Danforth Found.; Composer of the Year award and grant, Oregon Music Teachers Assoc., 1971. He was professor, Lewis and Clark Coll., 1946-77.

WORKS: CHAMBER ORCHESTRA: Symphonic variations, 1960; White butterflies, 1973; Ukedama; WIND ENSEMBLE: 12-tone symphony; symphonic poem; symphony for wind ensemble; Ceremonial music to get rid of the devil; CHAMBER MUSIC: piano trio; string quartet; piano quartet; trio for flute, guitar, viola; flute sonata, 1961; violin sonata, 1966; cello sonata, 1969; piano sonata, 1971; oboe sonata; many piano pieces; songs.
9938 S.W. Terwilliger Blvd., Portland, OR 97219

STONE, GREGORY
b. Odessa, Russia, 20 July 1900; to U.S. 1923. He has been conductor and pianist in Latin America; film orchestrator and composer in Hollywood.

WORKS: VIOLIN: Dolina; Hora in suoni harmonici; Hora spiccata; Hora burlesca.
2750 Sherwood Place, Reno, NV 89502

STONE, MALCOLM A.

STONE, MALCOLM A.
b. Hollywood, Calif., 5 Aug. 1934. Studied with
S. R. Beckler, Mary Bowling, and Lucas Underwood,
Univ. of the Pacific; and at California State
Univ. at Sacramento. He was named composer of
the year at Univ. of the Pacific, 1962. He was
high school music director, 1963-69; theatre arts
director, 1969-72; music director, Columbia
Theatre, Univ. of the Pacific, 1964.
    WORKS: CHAMBER MUSIC: Little sonnet, oboe
and piano; CHORUS: Psalm 23; Psalm 120; Night
plane; Kyrie eleison; 3 little surprises; Invocation; SONGS: Lament of the forgotten.
    5954 Echo, Stockton, CA 95207

STONE, WILLIAM C.
    b. Harrisburg, Pa., 10 Jan. 1921. Studied with
Burrill Phillips, Allen McHose, and Wayne
Barlow, Eastman School of Music, M.M. He was
faculty member, Reinhardt Coll., Ga., 1951-55;
Pfeiffer Coll., 1955-61; from 1961, at Campbell
Coll.
    WORKS: CHAMBER MUSIC: string quartet in 1
movement; SONGS: Prayer, to his own text; Teach
me, Lord; PIANO: Fantasy; Nocturne; Misty night;
sonatina; Theme and variations; Passacaglia.
    Box 395, Bules Creek, NC 27506

STOTHART, HERBERT
    b. Milwaukee, Wis., 11 Sept. 1885; d. Los Angeles,
Calif., 1 Feb. 1949. Studied at Milwaukee
Teachers Coll., Univ. of Wisconsin; and in
Europe. He taught in public schools, then at
Univ. of Wisconsin. From 1929 he was in Holly-
wood as film composer; became general music
director for MGM.
    WORKS: PAGEANT: China; CHORUS: Voices of
liberation; FILM SCORES: The good earth; Romeo
and Juliet; Mutiny on the Bounty; Mrs. Miniver;
The green years; The picture of Dorian Gray.

STOUFFER, PAUL M.
    b. Chambersburg, Pa., 21 Feb. 1916. Studied at
Peabody Cons.; Univ. of Pennsylvania, B.A., M.A.
He taught in public and private schools
in Philadelphia to 1958; was then named director of
music education in public schools, Springfield,
Pa.
    WORKS: ORCHESTRA: concertino for 2; Can-
zone; Christmas dance pantomime; BAND: Song of
the troubadour; Ti-teeka-tah; CHAMBER MUSIC:
clarinet quartet; Toccata for trumpets; Toccata
for clarinets; 2 violin sonatas; and choral
works.

STOUGHTON, ROY SPAULDING
    b. Worcester, Mass., 28 Jan. 1884; d. Allston,
Mass., 1 Feb. 1953. He was editor for a music
publisher.
    WORKS: BALLET: The spirit of the sea; The
vision of Aissawa; CANTATAS: Esther; The woman
of Sychar; The resurrection and the life; The
wind of the west; many organ works and songs.

STOUT, ALAN
    b. Baltimore, Md., 26 Nov. 1932. Studied at
Johns Hopkins Univ.; with Henry Cowell, Peabody
Cons.; at Univ. of Copenhagen; with John Verrall,

Univ. of Washington, M.A. 1959; privately with
Wallingford Riegger and Vagn Holmboe. His
awards include an Illinois sesquicentennial com-
mission for symphony #2, 1968; Chicago Symph.
80th anniversary commission for symphony #4,
1971; Methodist Church Board of Education grant;
Danish government grants, 1954-55; and other
commissions. He has been on the music faculty,
Northwestern Univ., from 1963; guest professor,
Johns Hopkins Univ., 1968; State Coll. of Music,
Stockholm, 1972.
    WORKS: ORCHESTRA: 4 symphonies, #1, 1959,
Concord, Mass., 9 Feb. 1973, #2, 1961, rev. 1966,
#3 with soprano and male chorus, 1962, #4,
Chicago, 15 Apr. 1971; Ricercare and aria, string
orch., 1959; movement for violin and orch., 1962;
George Lieder, with baritone solo, 1962, rev.
1970, Chicago, 14 Dec. 1972; 3 hymns for orch.,
Baltimore, 27 Sept. 1972; Passion, with chorus
and soloists, Chicago, 15 Apr. 1976; WIND EN-
SEMBLE: Die Engel, soprano, brass, percussion,
1957; Pieti, 1957; Pulsar, brass and timpani,
1972; CHAMBER MUSIC: 10 string quartets, 1952,
1952, 1954, 1954, 1957, 1959, 1960, 1960, 1962,
1962; Suite for flute and piano, 1962; Toccata,
alto saxophone and piano, 1965; cello sonata,
1966; Music for oboe and piano, 1966; Music for
flute and harpsichord, 1967; Serenity, cello and
organ; KEYBOARD: Piano variants, 1962; Fantasia,
piano, 1962; Studies in densities and durations,
1966-67; Organ chorales, 1967; piano suite, 1967;
Toccata and lament, harpsichord; 2-piano sonata,
1975; Waltz, piano, 1977; Study in timbres and
interferences, organ, 1977.
    2600½ Central St., Evanston, IL 60201

STOVER, FRANKLIN HOWARD
    b. Sacramento, Calif., 5 Nov. 1953. Studied at
California State Univ., Sacramento; composition
privately with Andrew Imbrie. He was winner of
the 1973 California Composers Symposium, Sacramento. From 1976 he has been editor and engraver
for Composers' Graphics, Ltd.
    WORKS: ORCHESTRA: chamber concerto, winds,
strings, piano, 1972; WIND ENSEMBLE: Eclogue,
clarinet choir; CHAMBER MUSIC: 4 arcana, woodwind quintet and guitar, 1974; Metal, percussion
ensemble, 1975; Fantasy piece #1, clarinet and
piano, 1975; Trio bucolic, clarinet, oboe, bassoon, 1978; For the intuitive journey by R.
Edson, narrator, piano, percussion, 1978; CHORUS:
Journal entry of Christopher Columbus, 1978.
    P.O. Box 60857, Sacramento, CA 95806

STOVER, HAROLD
    b. Latrobe, Pa., 26 Nov. 1946. Graduated in
organ at Juilliard School, has been organist-
choirmaster, 2nd Presbyterian Church, New York,
from 1968.
    WORKS: CHORUS: Jubilate Deo; Te Deum;
Music in praise at close of day, treble voices,
1973; KEYBOARD: Te decet hymnus Deus in Sion,
organ, 1970; 5 preludes on American folk hymns,
organ; Ezekiel, organ; Incantation, piano, percussion, speaking voice, 1971; Nocturnes, organ;
Leapin' lizards, 4 keyboards; FILM SCORE: The
magic mime.
    235 W. 102 St., New York, NY 10025

STRAIGHT, WILLARD
b. Ft. Wayne, Ind., 18 July 1930. Studied at
Univ. of Kansas, B.M. 1951; with Vittorio Rieti
and Rudolph Ganz, Chicago Musical Coll., 1951-55;
piano with various teachers, including Ganz and
Horszowski in New York. He is concert pianist
and accompanist; in 1973, became assistant conductor of the Little Orchestra Society of New
York.
WORKS: THEATRE: Toyon of Alaska, opera;
The Athenian touch, musical; ORCHESTRA: Development, 1961; piano concerto; Prelude, procession,
and passacaglia; Structure; CHAMBER MUSIC: piano
quintet; woodwind quintet; Piece en forme, cello
and piano; 3 developments, flute, violin, cello;
choral works, songs, piano pieces.

STRANDBERG, NEWTON
b. River Falls, Wis., 3 Jan. 1921. Studied with
Anthony Donato, Northwestern Univ.; with Henry
Cowell, Columbia Univ.; and with Nadia Boulanger
in Fontainebleau. He received the Faricy award;
Birmingham Symphony award; Birmingham Festival
of Arts award; first prize, Oregon Coll. of
Education contest; and commissions. He was
faculty member, Denison Univ., 1947-49; Samford
Univ., 1950-54, 1956-67; Northwestern Univ.,
1954-56; from 1967, at Sam Houston State Univ.
WORKS: ORCHESTRA: Amenhotep III; Trinite;
Sea of tranquility, 2 string orch. and piano,
1969; BAND: Xerxes; Kinetic theatre; Magnificat;
Processional; Picasso; Ping-pong; CHAMBER MUSIC:
sonata for 2 pianos; 3 string quartets; Ask,
chamber group, 1972; Planh, piano, 1972; string
trio, 1976; CHORUS: Augustine, with winds;
Benedictus, 2 choirs, drum, chimes, piano; Canticle, with orch.; ORGAN: Sanna sanna hosanna.
Huntsville, TX 77341

STRANG, GERALD
b. Claresholm, Alberta, Canada, 13 Feb. 1908;
U.S. citizen. Studied at Stanford Univ., A.B.
1928; with Charles Koechlin, Arnold Schoenberg,
and Ernst Toch, Univ. of Southern California,
Ph.D. 1948. He was teaching assistant to
Schoenberg, 1936-38; taught at Long Beach City
Coll., 1938-58; was on faculty, San Fernando
Valley State Coll., 1958-65; California State
Coll. at Long Beach, 1965-69; from 1969, at Univ.
of California, Los Angeles. From 1950 he has
also been a consultant in building design and
acoustics; worked in electronic and computer
music, Bell Telephone Labs., 1963, and at UCLA,
1969.
WORKS: ORCHESTRA: Intermezzo, 1937; 2 symphonies, 1942, 1947; Overland trail, 1943; concerto grosso, 1951; cello concerto, 1951; CHAM-
BER MUSIC: Mirrorrorrim, piano, 1931; sonatina
for clarinet alone, 1932; Percussion music for
3 players, 1935; 3 pieces, flute and piano,
1937; Divertimento, 4 instruments, 1948; violin
sonata, 1949; sonata for flute alone, 1953;
Variations, 4 instruments, 1956; ELECTRONIC:
Compositions 2-10, tape computer music, 1963-72;
Synthion 1 and 2, tape synthesis. He is author
of many articles on acoustics and on computer
music.
6500 Mantova St., Long Beach, CA 90815

STRANGE, ALLEN
b. Calexico, Calif., 26 June 1943. Studied with
Donal Michalsky, California State Univ. at Ful-
lerton; with Pauline Oliveros, Robert Erickson,
Kenneth Gaburo, Univ. of California, San Diego.
He received a Fullerton Friends of Music award,
1965; Univ. of California Regents fellowship,
1967-68; San Jose Found. grant in electronic
music, 1970. He was on the faculty, Indiana
Univ. of Pennsylvania, 1969; then at California
State Univ., San Jose; was cofounder of Biome,
an ensemble specializing in electronic music.
WORKS: ORCHESTRA: Western connection;
Charms, string orch.; BAND: Rockytop screamers
and further scapes; CHAMBER MUSIC: Star salon
strikers and sliders last orbit, amplified
string trio and percussion; Dirt talk, version
2, organ, violin, percussion; Switchcraft, bass,
flute, and engineer; the doug Meyers (') playing
flute, solo flute; Chamberpiece, flute, clarinet,
violin, guitar; CHORUS: Rainbow rider, 4
choruses; ELECTRONIC: 2 x 2, tape; Propagation
and decay of resonant particles, live electronics;
Skags, 4 electronically processed voices; also
multimedia works. He is author of Electronic
music: Systems, techniques and controls, Dubuque,
Iowa, 1972, and of various articles in music
journals.
San Jose State Univ., 125 S. 7th St., San
Jose, CA 95192

STRASSBURG, ROBERT
b. New York, N.Y., 30 Aug. 1915. Studied with
Carl McKinley and Frederick Converse, New England
Cons., B.M. 1939; with Paul Hindemith at Tangle-
wood, 1940; Walter Piston and Igor Stravinsky,
Harvard Univ., M.A. 1941; with Mario Castelnuovo-
Tedesco, Univ. of Judaism, Los Angeles, D.F.A.
1970. He received a Boston Symphony scholarship
to Tanglewood, 1940; Harvard fellowship, 1940-
41; Nat. Inst. of Arts and Letters award;
MacDowell fellowship, 1946. His faculty posts
have included Brooklyn Coll., 1947-50; Univ. of
Miami, Hillel House, 1958-60; from 1961, Univ.
of Judaism; and from 1966, California State
Univ., Los Angeles.
WORKS: OPERA: Chelm, comic folk opera,
1956; ORCHESTRA: The patriarchs, string orch.,
1946; sinfonietta in G; Festival of lights symphony; Tropal suite, string orch., 1967; CHORUS:
Psalm 117; Whitman cantata, Look back unto this
day, with soloists and 2 pianos; Meditation, a
cappella; many liturgical works; PIANO: Torah
sonata, 1950; Hunting the deer, variations; many
chamber works, songs, incidental music for plays.
He is author of a monograph, Ernest Bloch, voice
in the wilderness, Los Angeles, 1977.
3335 Rowena Ave., Los Angeles, CA 90027

STRAUSS, GEORGE R.
b. Cleveland Heights, Ohio, 19 Nov. 1951.
Studied with Paul Cooper and Ellsworth Milburn,
Cincinnati Coll.-Cons.
WORKS: ORCHESTRA: 2 symphonies, 1973,
1974; CHAMBER MUSIC: Theme with variations,
flute, violin, cello, 1970; To the victims of
Scioto Street, string quartet, piano percussion,
film, 1972; K.299 revisited, flute and harp,

STRAUSS, JOHN

1973; SONGS: Die Kindheit, soprano and piano,
1971; Program notes, soprano and bass-baritone,
a cappella, 1973; PIANO: Perspectives, prepared
piano, 1972.

STRAUSS, JOHN
b. New York, N.Y., 28 Apr. 1920. Studied at
Yale Univ., M.M.; Dalcroze School of Music,
certificate. He is composer and conductor for
films and television.
WORKS: The accused, opera-monologue for
television; song cycle on Lorca texts; Car 54,
where are you?, television theme.

STRAVINSKY, IGOR
b. Oraniembaum, near St. Petersburg, 17 June
1882; U.S. citizen 1945; d. New York, N.Y.,
6 Apr. 1971. Studied law at Univ. of St. Petersburg, then studied music privately with Rimsky-
Korsakov. His awards included membership in the
American Acad. of Arts and Letters; Internat.
Sibelius award, 1963. He also received many
commissions from Sergei Diaghilev, ballet im-
pressario, and wrote some of his most noted
works to be presented by Diaghilev at the Ballets
Russes in Paris. Stravinsky settled in the U.S.
after the fall of France in 1939.
WORKS: OPERA: Le rossignol, 1914; Mavra,
1922; Renard, 1922; Oedipus Rex, opera oratorio,
1927; The rake's progress, 1951; BALLET: The
firebird, 1910; Petrouchka, 1911; The rite of
spring, 1913; The soldier's tale, 1918; Pulcin-
ella, 1919; Les noces, 1923; Apollon musagète,
1927; Le baiser de la fée, 1928; Persephone,
1934; Jeu de cartes, 1936; Orpheus, 1948; Agon,
1957; ORCHESTRA: 3 symphonies, 1907, 1940, 1945;
Fireworks, 1908; concertino for piano and winds,
1923-24; Capriccio, 1929, rev. 1949; Symphony of
psalms, with chorus, 1930; violin concerto, 1931;
concerto for 2 solo pianos, 1935; Dumbarton Oaks
concerto, 1938; 4 etudes, 1940; Danses concertantes, chamber orch., 1942; Circus polka, 1942;
Ode in 3 parts, 1943; Scherzo a la russe, 1944;
Scenes de ballet, 1945; Ebony concerto, clarinet
and jazz orch., 1945; concerto in D, string
orch., 1946; Movements, for piano and orch.,
1958-59; Variations: Aldous Huxley in memoriam,
1965; CHAMBER MUSIC: 3 pieces, string quartet,
1914; 3 pieces, for clarinet, 1918; Ragtime, 11
instruments, 1918; concertino for string quartet,
1920; octet for winds, 1923; Duo concertante,
violin and piano, 1932; Suite Italienne, cello
and piano, 1933; Tango, violin and piano, 1941;
sonata for 2 pianos, 1944; septet for piano,
winds, strings, 1952; In memoriam Dylan Thomas,
tenor, string quartet, and 4 trombones, 1954;
double canon, string quartet, 1959; Fanfare for
2 trumpets, 1967; VOCAL: King of the stars,
cantata, 1911; mass, male choir and instruments,
1948; Abraham and Isaac, baritone and chamber
orch., 1963; Elegy for J. F. K., baritone and
instruments, 1964; Introitus: T. S. Eliot in
memoriam, male choir and chamber ensemble, 1965;
Requiem cantata, soloists, chorus, orch., 1966;
The owl and the pussycat, 1967; PIANO: 2 sonatas,
1904, 1922; 4 etudes, 1908; 3 pieces faciles,
piano, 4 hands, 1915; 5 pieces faciles, piano,
4 hands, 1917; Piano rag-music, 1920; Les cinq

doits, 1921; Serenade in A, 1925. He was author
of An autobiography, 1936; and Poetics of music,
1947.

STRAYHORN, WILLIAM (BILLY)
b. Dayton, Ohio, 29 Nov. 1915; d. New York, N.Y.,
30 May 1967. Studied music in Pittsburgh; from
1939 was lyricist, arranger, composer, and collaborator with Duke Ellington. Some of his own
songs were Tapioca; Lush life; Take the A train;
Passion flower; Overture to a jam session.

STREET, TISON
b. Boston, Mass., 20 May 1943. Studied with
Leon Kirchner and David Del Tredici, Harvard
Univ., B.A. 1965, M.A. 1971. He received the
Naumberg recording award, 1972; Nat. Inst. of
Arts and Letters award, 1973; Rome prize, 1973.
He was visiting lecturer, Univ. of California,
Berkeley, 1971-72.
WORKS: CHAMBER MUSIC: string trio, 1963;
Variations, flute, guitar, cello, 1964; 2 string
quartets, 1972, 1974; string quintet, 1973, rev.
1976; Piano fantasy, New York, 22 Sept. 1976;
3 pieces for a consort of viols and harpsichord,
1977; Adagio in E-flat, oboe and strings, 1977;
John Major's medley, solo guitar, 1977.
381 Commonwealth Ave., Boston, MA 02115

STRICKLAND, LILY TERESA
b. Anderson, S.C., 28 Jan. 1887; d. Henderson-
ville, N.C., 6 June 1958. Studied at Converse
Coll., Litt.B., honorary D.M.; with Percy
Goetschius at Juilliard School. She traveled in
the Far East, 1920-30.
WORKS: OPERETTA: Jewels of the desert;
ORCHESTRA: Himalayan sketches; Oasis, 1942;
Sketches from the Southwest; SONGS: Mah Lindy
Lou; Here in the high hills; My lover's a fisher-
man; At eve I hear a flute; choral works, piano
suites.

STRILKO, ANTHONY
b. 1931. Tranquil music for organ; Music for
oboe alone; The meditation of Hermes Trismegistis,
orchestra, 7th Inter-American Music Festival,
17 May 1976; Letters from children, chorus and
vibraphone, New York, 23 Dec. 1978; many choral
works and songs.
c/o Presser Company, Presser Place, Bryn
Mawr, PA 19010

STRINGER, ALAN
b. El Paso, Tex., 15 Jan. 1938. Studied with
William Wood, Univ. of New Mexico. He received
2 first prizes in the New Mexico Composers' Bicentennial Contest. He has been organist-choirmaster from 1951.
WORKS: THEATRE: 3-D, 3-tiered wedding cake,
musical; Green, green, musical, 1976; Young
Goodman Brown, opera; ORCHESTRA: Interior with
strings; Concertant on an American folk hymn;
CHAMBER MUSIC: 2 hymns in rock style, saxophone
and organ; 3 dance suites, piano; Sound piece,
flute and piano; CHORUS: Prayer for the Great
Family, with piano, organ, tape; Woe unto them
who join house to house; Canticle, cantata, 1976;
For the time being, Christmas oratorio, 1977;

SONGS: Under the war shadow, a cycle; Antireligious songs, a cycle; Short sacred service, vocal duet; 10 uses of a typical disaster, solo voice, 1976; also piano and organ pieces.
8640 Horatio Pl., N.E., Albuquerque, NM 87111

STRINGFIELD, LAMAR
b. Raleigh, N.C., 10 Oct. 1897; d. Asheville, N.C., 21 Jan. 1959. Studied with Georges Barrere and Percy Goetschius, Inst. of Musical Art. He received the Pulitzer prize, 1927, for the orchestral suite, From the southern mountains. He organized the Inst. of Folk Music, Univ. of North Carolina, 1930; was conductor, North Carolina Symphony, 1932-35; Knoxville Symphony, 1946-47; Charlotte Symphony, 1948-49.
WORKS: OPERA: The mountain song; Carolina charcoal, musical folk drama, 1952; ORCHESTRA: Indian legend, 1923; From the southern mountains, 1927; A Negro parade, 1931; The legend of John Henry, 1932; Moods of a moonshiner, 1934; Mountain dawn, 1945; About Dixie, 1950; CHAMBER MUSIC: Chipmunks, woodwind trio; From a Negro melody, 12 instruments; Indian sketches, flute and string quartet; Virginia Dare dance, woodwind quintet; CHORUS: Peace, cantata, a cappella.

STRINGHAM, EDWIN JOHN
b. Kenosha, Wis., 11 July 1890; d. Chapel Hill, N.C., 1 July 1974. Studied at Northwestern Univ. and Cincinnati Cons.; and on scholarship with Ottorino Respighi, Royal Acad. of Music, Rome, 1929. His other awards include an honorary D.M., Denver Coll. of Music, 1928; Cromwell fellowship to Germany, 1936. He taught at Denver Coll. of Music, 1919-29; Columbia Univ., 1930-38; Juilliard School, 1930-45; Queens Coll., CUNY, 1938-46.
WORKS: ORCHESTRA: The phantom, 1916; Visions, 1924; The ancient mariner, 1928; 3 pastels, 1928; symphony, 1929; 2 nocturnes, 1931, 1938; Fantasy on American folk tunes, violin and orch., 1942; also chamber music, choral works, and songs.

STRINI, TOM
b. St. Louis, Mo., 14 Nov. 1949. Studied with James Woodward and Alan Oldfield, Southern Illinois Univ.; with Malcolm Arnold, Shawnigan Inst. of the Arts, Vancouver Island, B.C. He received the Mark Gerdelman award, 1972-73.
WORKS: ORCHESTRA: Prelude and fugue, strings; Nocturne, strings; Orchestra music; CHAMBER MUSIC: Night soliloquy, guitar; Study in scherzo style, guitar; Annabel Lee, tenor and guitar; Socrates, upon hearing his sentence, baritone and piano; string quartet.

STROUD, RICHARD
b. Dunsmuir, Calif., 26 Jan. 1929. Studied with William Billingsly, Univ. of Idaho; and at California State Univ. at Humboldt. He is director of bands, Eureka City Schools, Calif.
WORKS: WIND ENSEMBLE: Articulations, brass quintet; Application for band; The brass ring, #1-5, a suite, brass quintet; Quartet for Douglas, brass quartet; CHAMBER MUSIC: Sketch, for 4

woodwinds; Thumbnail sketches, trumpet trio; quartet for percussion and clarinet; Capriccio, wind quintet; Tubantiphon, 2 tubas; Treatments for tuba, tuba quartet.
131 Huntoon, Eureka, CA 95501

STROUSE, CHARLES
b. New York, N.Y., 7 June 1928. Studied with Bernard Rogers, Eastman School; on scholarship with Aaron Copland at Tanglewood; with Israel Citkowitz and David Diamond in New York; and with Nadia Boulanger.
WORKS: OPERA: Satisfaction, 1 act, New York, 29 Feb. 1979; Singers, 1 act, Eastman Opera Company, 1980; BROADWAY STAGE SCORES: Bye, bye birdie; All American; Golden boy; Applause; It's a bird . . . It's a plane . . . It's Superman; Annie; FILM SCORES: Bonnie and Clyde; The night they raided Minsky's; many songs.
171 W. 57 St., New York, NY 10019

STRUKOFF, RUDOLF
b. Rostov on Don, Russia, 18 July 1938. Studied at Andrews Univ., B.M. 1960; with H. Owen Reed, Gomer Jones, Paul Harder, Michigan State Univ., M.M. 1964, Ph.D. 1970. He was instructor, Michigan State Univ., 1963-64; faculty member, Indiana State Univ., 1966-69; Andrews Univ., 1969-75; from 1978, Governors State Univ., Ill. His published works include Childhood sketches, a 7-song cycle for mezzo-soprano.
Governors State Univ., Park Forest South, IL 60466

STRUNK, STEVEN
b. Evansville, Ind. 7 Mar. 1943. Studied with Rouben Gregorian, Boston Univ.; with Luciano Berio and Vincent Persichetti, Juilliard School, D.M.A. 1971. He received Juilliard's Gretchaninoff Memorial prize, 1966, 1967, 1970; Nat. Endowment for the Arts grant, 1976. He has been faculty member, Florida State Univ., 1967-69; Eastern New Mexico Univ., 1971-73; from 1973, at Catholic Univ.
WORKS: ORCHESTRA: Transformations, 30 solo strings; Geometrics; Orpheus, with chorus, 1976; CHAMBER MUSIC: quartet II, clarinet, vibraphone, marimba, piano; Conticuere omnes, 5 sopranos and chamber orch.; Episodes, flute and piano.
10402 Hemley Lane, Silver Spring, MD 20902

STUART, HUGH M.
b. Harrisburg, Pa., 5 Feb. 1917. Studied at Oberlin Cons.; Univ. of Michigan; Columbia Univ.; and Rutgers Univ. He was public school music teacher and supervisor from 1940; in East Orange, N.J., 1948-74; also lecturer, clinician, and guest conductor at colleges and universities throughout the U.S.
WORKS: BAND: Manhattan vignettes; Somerset sketches; and numerous published educational works for band, ensemble groups, and solo instruments.
304 Wellesley Dr., S.E., Albuquerque, NM 87101

STUCKY, STEVEN EDWARD

STUCKY, STEVEN EDWARD
b. Hutchinson, Kans., 7 Nov. 1949. Studied with Richard Willis, Baylor Univ., B.M. 1971; with Karel Husa, Burrill Phillips, Robert Palmer, Cornell Univ., M.F.A. 1973. He received the American String Teachers Assoc. award, 1965; Nat. Fed. of Music Clubs awards, 1969, 1970, 1971; ASCAP Victor Herbert award, 1974; first prize, American Society of University Composers contest, 1975. He was visiting faculty member, Lawrence Univ., 1978-80.
    WORKS: ORCHESTRA: Prelude and toccata, 1969; symphony, 1972; Movements III, 1976; Kenningar (symphony #4), 1978; CHAMBER MUSIC: 4 bagatelles, string quartet, 1969; duo for viola and cello, 1969; Movements, cello quartet, 1970; Divertimento, clarinet, piano, percussion, 1971; quartet for clarinet, viola, cello, piano, 1973; CHORUS: Nature, like us, 4 Dickinson poems, 1971; Refrains, 1979; SONGS: 3 songs, soprano, clarinet, viola, piano, 1969; Schnee-musik, soprano and piano, 1973; Drop, drop, slow tears, 1979.
    c/o ACA, 170 W. 74th St., New York, NY 10023

STUESSY, JOSEPH
b. Houston, Tex., 14 Dec. 1943. Studied at Southern Methodist Univ.; with Samuel Adler, Wayne Barlow, and Bernard Rogers, Eastman School of Music, M.M. He was faculty member, Texas Women's Univ., 1969-73; from 1973, at Southern Methodist Univ.
    WORKS: OPERA: Does the pale flag advance?, 2 acts, 1972; ORCHESTRA: piano concerto, 1970; Invasions; Diology, 1974; Polysentheticisms, 1974; BAND: Encomium, 1976; CHAMBER MUSIC: Improvisational suite, trumpet, 1971.
    2768 N. Hillbriar, Plano, TX 75075

STURCHIO, FRANK G.
b. Orsara di Puglio, Italy, 27 Oct. 1894; U.S. citizen 1943; d. San Antonio, Tex., 14 Aug. 1971. Studied at San Pietro A. Majella Cons., Italy; and Our Lady of the Lake Coll., San Antonio, B.M. He played with the concert bands of Sousa, Pryor, LaMonica, and Moses; organized and directed bands in Wauchula, Ft. Myers, and West Palm Beach, Fla., and St. Mary's Univ., San Antonio, for 18 years.
    WORKS: BAND MARCHES: La Fiorentina; King Cane; Cotton Bowl; Into the wind; Fiesta Flambeau; Lone Star; Everglades sugar; numerous unpublished compositions.

STYNE, JULE
b. London, England, 31 Dec. 1905; U.S. citizen 1916. He was piano soloist with the Chicago Symphony at age 9; studied at Chicago Musical Coll. and Northwestern Univ. He led dance bands in Chicago and New York, then went to Hollywood as composer of musical comedies and film scores.
    WORKS: MUSICAL COMEDIES: High button shoes; Gentlemen prefer blondes; Two on the aisle; Peter Pan; Say darling; Bells are ringing; Gypsy; Do re mi; Funny girl; Fade out--fade in; FILM SCORES: Anchors aweigh; West Point story; Don't fence me in; Pink tights; My sister Eileen; Living it up; and numerous songs.

SUBEN, JOEL ERIC
b. New York, N.Y., 16 May 1946. Studied with Samuel Adler and Robert Gauldin, Eastman School of Music, B.M. 1969; with Seymour Shifrin, Arthur Berger, Martin Boykan, Brandeis Univ., M.F.A. 1974, Ph.D. 1979; also conducting in New York, Salzburg, and Vienna. His awards included full scholarships at Eastman School; NDEA scholarships at Brandeis Univ.; Sachar Internat. Studies grant, Polish government stipend, Fulbright-Hayes Travel grant, 1977-79. He has taught privately from 1970; at Newark Community Center, 1976-77; Bernard Baruch Coll., CUNY, 1974-77, 1979; Fordham Univ., 1974-79.
    WORKS: THEATRE: opera scene from No exit by Sartre, 1967; incidental music for As you like it, Brandeis Univ., 6-17 Feb. 1973; ORCHES-TRA: 2 orchestral dances, 1967; Verses of mourn-ing, 1973; piano concerto, 1978; BAND: Concert piece, clarinet and wind band, 1977; CHAMBER MUSIC: suite for trumpet and piano, 1966; Rondo, English horn and piano, 1966; Sonata da camera, 4 violins, 1966; Partita, violin alone, 1967; trio for flute, harp, harpsichord, 1970; Liebestod, cello solo, 1977; many songs.
    27 W. 76th St., New York, NY 10023

SUBOTNICK, MORTON
b. Los Angeles, Calif., 14 Apr. 1933. Studied on his own in Los Angeles; with Leon Kirchner and Darius Milhaud at Mills Coll., M.M. He re-ceived a Nat. Endowment for the Arts grant, 1975. He has held teaching posts at Mills Coll., 1959-66; New York Univ., 1966-69; Univ. of Maryland, 1968-69; Univ. of Pittsburgh, 1969-70; then at California Inst. of the Arts, where he is also director of electronic music.
    WORKS: THEATRE: music for Galileo; The balcony; The Caucasian chalk circle; ORCHESTRA: Play! #2; Lamination; Before the butterfly, Los Angeles Symphony, 26 Feb. 1976; CHAMBER MUSIC: The tarot; Play! #1; Misfortune of the immortals; 2 serenades; 2 butterflies, Los Angeles, 17 Apr. 1975; ELECTRONIC: Serenade #3, 4 instruments and tape; Serenade #4, piano and electronic sounds, 1966; Silver apples of the moon; The wild bull, 1968; Touch, 1969; Sidewinder; Prelude #4, piano and tape; 4 butterflies; Wild beasts, trombone, piano, "ghost" tapes, Valencia, 2 Apr. 1978; The beast, clarinet and tape, 1978; Liquid strata, piano and tape; A sky of cloudless sul-phur, electronic piano, Northridge, Calif., 19 Nov. 1978, for the opening of a new JBL plant; Parallel lines, solo piccolo, chamber ensemble, ghost tapes, Valencia, Contemporary Music Fes-tival, 1979.
    1143 Lincoln Blvd., #7, Santa Barbara, CA 90403

SUCHY, GREGORIA KARIDES
b. Milwaukee, Wis., 14 Nov. Studied with Anthony Donato, Northwestern Univ.; Alexander Tcherepnin, De Paul Univ.; Rudolph Ganz, Chicago Musical Coll.; and with Ralph Shapey, Univ. of Chicago. Her awards include 6 Wisconsin Fed. of Music Clubs awards, 1960-67; 4 Univ. of Wisconsin re-search grants, 1960-68, and a faculty fellowship, 1967. She taught in Milwaukee schools, 1943-44;

Northwestern Cons., 1944-47; from 1947, at Univ. of Wisconsin-Milwaukee.
WORKS: BALLET: Skins and exposures, electronic score; ORCHESTRA: Suite on Greek themes, 1961; Greek rhapsody, 1962; Symphonic piece, with trumpet and piano obligato, Milwaukee, 14 Dec. 1972; CHAMBER MUSIC: string quartet, 1966; SONGS: Greek maxims, 12 songs for soprano; PIANO: A fantasy; Circle dance in 7/8; Sousta; 3 lovers, 2 pianos; Mother Goose rhymes in 12-tone; Mo-Goose revisited.
2601 E. Newton Ave., Milwaukee, WI 53211

SUCOFF, HERBERT
b. New York, N.Y., 18 Jan. 1938. Studied at Juilliard School, B.S.; Queens Coll., M.A.; privately with Stefan Wolpe. He has been director, Sea Cliff Chamber Players, from 1970; director and composer in residence, Craftsbury Chamber Players, summers, from 1968; from 1974, consultant, Empire State Coll., SUNY.
WORKS: CHAMBER MUSIC: 3 string quartets; quartet for flute, cello, oboe, harpsichord; 3 pieces, violin and piano; duo for violin and cello; trio for piano, cello, clarinet; CHORUS: Cantata, with narrator and chamber ensemble.
120 Carpenter Ave., Sea Cliff, NY 11579

SUDERBURG, ROBERT
b. Spencer, Iowa, 28 Jan. 1936. Studied with Paul Fetler and Earl George, Univ. of Minnesota; Richard Donovan and Quincy Porter, Yale Univ.; and with George Rochberg, Univ. of Pennsylvania. His awards include the Helen Dusa prize, 1959; BMI award, 1962; Halstead award, 1963; Rockefeller Found./Houston Symph. award, 1967; ASCAP award, 1967; 2 Guggenheim fellowships, 1968, 1974; III Festival of Music of Spain and America award, 1970; Hindemith Found. award, 1971; Nat. Endowment for the Arts grant, 1974. He was faculty member, Albertus Magnus Coll., 1959-60; Bryn Mawr Coll., 1960-61; Univ. of Pennsylvania, 1961-63; Philadelphia Musical Acad., 1963-66; visiting faculty, Brooklyn Coll., 1971-72; faculty, Univ. of Washington, 1966-74; from 1974, chancellor, North Carolina School of the Arts.
WORKS: ORCHESTRA: Orchestra music I-III, 1969, 1971, 1973; Within the mirror of time, piano concerto, 1974; CHAMBER MUSIC: Chamber music I-IV, various ensembles, 1967-75; Solo music, violin, 1972; also choral works and piano pieces.
North Carolina School of the Arts, P.O. Box 4657, Winston-Salem, NC 27107

SUESSE, DANA
b. Kansas City, Mo., 3 Dec. 1911. Studied with Alexander Siloti, Rubin Goldmark, and Nadia Boulanger; won prizes in Nat. Fed. of Music Clubs composition contests at age 9 and 10; made his debut as pianist with Paul Whiteman's orchestra and received commissions from Whiteman.
WORKS: THEATRE: The man who sold the Eiffel Tower, musical; ORCHESTRA: Symphonic waltzes, piano and orch.; 2-piano concerto; Young man with a harp, suite; Jazz concerto; American nocturne; Concerto in rhythm; and songs.

SUGAI, ESTHER HIDEKO
b. Ontario, Oreg., 29 Oct. 1953. Studied at Univ. of Oregon, B.M. 1975; Univ. of Utah, M.M. 1979. She was producer and coproducer of various new music, electronic music, and multimedia performances in Salt Lake City, 1976-79; also flutist.
WORKS: CHAMBER MUSIC: Fantasy, soprano saxophone and tape, 1979; Textures, strings and percussion, 1979; Kokoro, 3 flutes, 1980; There was a kid with a game, tape, 1980; VOICE: 4 Japanese poems, 8 women's voices, 1975.
802 Seneca, Apt. 302, Seattle, WA 98101

SUITOR, M. LEE
b. San Francisco, Calif., 4 Feb. 1942. Studied with Wayne Bohrnstedt, Univ. of Redlands; with Joseph Goodman, Union Theological Seminary, New York; consultations with Alec Wyton, Robert W. Jones, Alan Gibbs. He was organist-choirmaster in Binghamton and lecturer, State Univ. of New York, Binghamton, 1969-73; from 1973, organist-choirmaster, St. Luke's Episcopal Church, Atlanta, Ga.
WORKS: CHORUS: Poverty; other published anthems; chamber music; organ pieces.
420 Carolwood Lane, Atlanta, GA 30342

SULLIVAN, TIMOTHY
b. Clifton Springs, N.Y., 1 Sept. 1939. Studied with Ned Rorem and Virgil Thomson, Univ. of Buffalo; with Yehudi Wyner, Bulent Arel, and Hall Overton at Yale Univ. At Yale he received the Frances Kellogg Osborne prize and the Henry and Amanda Noss prize. He has been faculty member, Nazareth Coll. of Rochester, from 1966.
WORKS: CHAMBER MUSIC: Toccata, cantata, and fanfares, chamber ensemble, soprano, male voices, 1966; ELECTRONIC: Musaic, a classical studio tape piece, 1971; Children of the city, chamber ensemble, tape, male voices, 1973.
36 Atkinson St., Rochester, NY 14608

SULTANOF, JEFFREY BRAD
b. Jamaica, N.Y., 24 July 1954. Studied at Queens Coll., CUNY, B.A. 1978; privately with Lothar Perl, Nicolas Flagello, John Carisi. From 1977 he has been editor and arranger of educational music for Warner Bros. Publ.
WORKS: ORCHESTRA: Symphonic study, large jazz orch., 1978; CHAMBER MUSIC: Ritual and stomp, flute, clarinet, string bass, New York, 23 May 1977; 6 preludes, piano, 1978; trio for viola, bassoon, piano, 1978.
79-22 265th St., Floral Park, NY 11004

SUMERLIN, MACON D.
b. Roby, Tex., 24 Oct. 1919. Studied at Hardin-Simmons Univ., B.M. 1940; with Bernard Rogers and Herbert Elwell, Eastman School of Music; Kent Kennan and Anthony Donato, Univ. of Texas, M.M. 1947; and with Merrill Ellis, North Texas State Univ., D.M. 1951. He was faculty member, Hardin-Simmons Univ., 1947-51; from 1952, on faculty and composer-in-residence, McMurry Coll.
WORKS: BALLET: Masquerade; ORCHESTRA: 5 symphonies; suite for strings; WIND ENSEMBLE: Fanfare, andante, and fugue, band; Dissertation,

SUMMER, JOSEPH STEVEN

with chorus; concertino for trumpet in 1 movement; symphony for band, 1978; CHAMBER MUSIC:
violin sonata; piano sonata; organ sonata;
CHORUS: I am music, cantata; Prayer of St.
Francis; He that dwelleth, with tenor, piano,
and tape; and others.
    McMurry College, Abilene, TX 79605

SUMMER, JOSEPH STEVEN
b. Pittsburgh, Pa., 16 Feb. 1956. Studied with
Richard Hoffman, Oberlin Coll.; with Leonardo
Balada, Carnegie-Mellon Univ.; and with Robert
Morris, Univ. of Pittsburgh.
    WORKS: OPERA: Hippolytus, 2 acts; ORCHES-
TRA: Fantasy, with solo horn and harp; The
modern Prometheus, baritone and chamber orch.,
1975; WIND ENSEMBLE: The Eleatic paradoxes,
suite and full ballet, 1975; CHAMBER MUSIC:
Walt of the 13th bee, string trio and horn.
    903 Druid Park Lake Dr., #2C, Baltimore, MD
21217

SUMMERLIN, EDGAR
Faculty member at City Coll., CUNY. His works
include: Evensong, a jazz liturgy; MULTIMEDIA:
Bless this world, chorus, baritone solo, narrator, brass, organ, jazz trio, projectors, written
on a grant from the New York Council on the Arts
and presented at Vassar Coll., 8 Nov. 1970.
    City College of CUNY, New York, NY 10031

SUMNER, SARAH
Studied violin with Paul Stassevich in New York;
composition with Irving Fine and Walter Piston
at Harvard Univ.; with Nadia Boulanger in Paris
on a Fulbright scholarship. Her Songs for
soprano, woodwind quartet, piano, received its
premiere in Chartres, France, in 1973, and its
American premiere in Philadelphia, 14 Oct. 1973.
    751 Millbrook Lane, Haverford, PA 19041

SUNDSTEN, JOHN
b. Munsala, Finland, 11 Oct. 1899; U.S. citizen
1918. Studied with Per Olsson, Judson W. Mather,
Boyd Wells, and Elie Robert Schmitz. From 1917
to 1954, he served as organist and music director
in churches in Tacoma and Seattle; was musical
coordinator and conductor of Seattle's Scandinavian Music Festival, 1951-71; for 40 years,
was director of Runeberg Singing Societies; for
10 years, of the Svea Male Chorus; from 1971,
has been a private teacher. He toured Scandi-
navia as choral director and concert pianist,
receiving many awards for his service to Scandinavian culture. In 1962 he was awarded the
Knighthood of the Finnish Lion by the president
of Finland, and the Royal Order of Vasa by the
king of Sweden.
    WORKS: ORCHESTRA: Festival overture; Basso
ostinato; Gunderkin, with narrator; Orientale #2;
Out West; Oriental teahouse; 4 Nordic dances;
SONG CYCLES: Thoughts from the life of Job; The
poet and The tryst, both on texts of 15th-century
Korea; Sea-drift, Whitman text; many piano
pieces.
    2212 Everett Ave. E., Seattle, WA 98102

SUR, DONALD
b. Honolulu, Hawaii, 1935, of Korean parents.
Studied with Seymour Shifrin, Univ. of California, Berkeley; with Earl Kim and Roger Sessions,
Princeton Univ.; with Colin McPhee, Univ. of
California, Los Angeles; and again with Earl Kim
at Harvard Univ., where he earned his Ph.D. In
1965 he received a Ford Found. grant for study
of Asian music. Through frugality and because
of the favorable rate of exchange, he was able
to study in Seoul for 5 years. He received a
Nat. Endowment for the Arts grant, 1976. He has
been faculty member at Massachusetts Inst. of
Technology from 1968; in 1970, began teaching a
course in non-Western music; established MIT's
Asian Music Center in 1974. In 1975 he was invited to attend the Brussels Conf. on New Music
Notation.
    WORKS: CHAMBER MUSIC: Sleep walkers ballad,
on Lorca text, soprano and chamber ensemble,
1962; 3 Catenas, chamber ensemble, 1962-76;
Internat. Society for Contemp. Music, 30 Oct.
1976; Piano fragments, 1966; Intonation, chamber
ensemble, 1966; Red dust, 30 Korean percussion
instruments, is the early-morning part of a
larger composition to last all day, 1967; Intonation before Sotoba Komachi, rev. version, Cambridge, Mass., 10 Feb. 1975; Penumbra, focus,
and echo, chamber ensemble, Boston, 23 Apr. 1978,
composer conducting.
    7 Ashton Place, Cambridge, MA 02138

SURINACH, CARLOS
b. Barcelona, Spain, 4 Mar. 1915; U.S. citizen
1959. Studied at Municipal Cons., Barcelona;
conducting with Eugen Papst in Cologne; composition with Max Trapp in Berlin. His honors include the 1966 Arnold Bax Composition Medal of
Great Britain; Spanish Knight Commander of the
Order of Isabella I of Castile with Cross, 1972;
many commissions. After his studies in Berlin,
he was conductor, Orquestra Filarmonica, Barcelona, and of the Opera House, 1944-47; moved
to Paris in 1947 and to the U.S. in 1950. He
was visitng professor, Carnegie-Mellon Univ.,
1966-67.
    WORKS: BALLET: Acrobats of God; Agathe's
tale; Apasionada; Celebrants; Cordoba; David and
Bath-Sheba; Embattled garden; Feast of ashes;
Hazaña; Los renegados; Ritmo jondo; La sibila;
Venta quemada; The owl and the pussycat, New
York, 26 June 1978; ORCHESTRA: 3 symphonies,
#1 Passacaglia, 1945, #2, 1949, #3, Sinfonia
chica, 1957; Sinfonietta flamenca, 1953; Feria
magica, Louisville, Ky., 14 Mar. 1956; concertino
for piano, strings, cymbals; Doppio concertino,
violin, piano, orch.; Symphonic variations, 1963;
Drama jondo, 1964; Melorhythmic dramas, 1966;
The missions of San Antonio, symphonic canticles,
1968; harp concerto, Grand Rapids, 15 Feb. 1979;
WIND ENSEMBLE: Paeans and dances of heathen
Iberia; piano concerto, Minneapolis, 13 Nov.
1974; CHAMBER MUSIC: Tres cantos bereberes, 3
winds, 2 strings, harp, 1952; Flamenquerias, 2
pianos, 1952; piano quartet; guitar sonatina;
Tientos, harp or piano, English horn, timpani,
1953; piano sonatina; CHORUS: Cantata of St.
John, with percussion, 1963; Songs of the soul;

many works for voice and orchestra, voice and
piano.
440 E. 59th St., New York, NY 10022

SUSA, CONRAD
b. Springdale, Pa., 26 Apr. 1935. Studied with
Nikolai Lopatnikoff, Carnegie Mellon Univ., B.M.
cum laude; with William Bergsma and Vincent
Persichetti, Juilliard School. He was recipient
of the George Gershwin Memorial scholarship; 2
Benjamin awards; Marion Freschi award; Gretchaninoff prize; Ford Found. grant for composer residency in the Nashville schools; Nat. Endowment
for the Arts grants, 1974-75, 1978. He was
field director, Education Dept., Lincoln Center,
1967-71; from 1975, Pacific regional director
for Young Audiences, Inc.
WORKS: THEATRE: Transformations, opera on
texts of Anne Sexton, Minneapolis Opera Company,
5 May 1973; Black River, opera to libretto
adapted from Michael Vesy's Wisconsin death trap,
Minneapolis, 1 Nov. 1975; ORCHESTRA: Eulogy,
string orch.; Love-in (ballet after Handel);
Pastorale, string quartet and double string
orch.; CHAMBER MUSIC: Serenade for a Christmas
night, organ, harp, vibraphone; CHORUS: The
birds, Belloc text; 3 George Herbert settings;
6 Joyce songs; Discovery and praises--An invocation; Hymns for the amusement of children, with
piano, 4 hands; and songs.
433 Eureka St., San Francisco, CA 94114

SUTCLIFFE, JAMES
b. Soochow, China, 1929; U.S. citizen 1957. Came
to the U.S. in 1948 to study at the Juilliard
School and Eastman School of Music. In 1959 he
was faculty member and director of the opera
workshop, Duquesne Univ. His Gymnopedie was
recorded by the Eastman Orchestra.

SUTHERLAND, BRUCE
b. Daytona Beach, Fla. Studied with Ellis Kohs
and Halsey Stevens, Univ. of Southern California,
B.M. 1957, M.M. 1959; piano with Ethel Leginska
and Amparo Iturbi. He received a grand prize,
Gottschalk Internat. Competition, New Orleans,
1970; Stairway of Stars award, Music Arts Society,
Santa Monica, 1973. He is piano and harpsichord
soloist and teacher.
WORKS: ORCHESTRA: Allegro fanfara, 1970;
CHAMBER MUSIC: string trio; saxophone quartet,
1971; quintet for flute, clarinet, piano trio,
1972; Notturno, flute and guitar, 1973; Prelude
and fugue, 2 pianos; CHORUS: Green grass, 1973.
2336 Pier Ave., Santa Monica, CA 90405

SUYCOTT, FORREST D.
b. Granite City, Ill., 2 Nov. 1922. Studied with
Philip Greeley Clapp and Philip Bezanson, Univ.
of Iowa; with Jacques Ibert at Tanglewood. He
was band director, Western Illinois Univ., 1955-
68; then dean, Coll. of Fine Arts.
WORKS: ORCHESTRA: Prelude and variations;
CHAMBER MUSIC: contrabass sonata; brass sextet;
quintet for mixed ensemble.
R.F.D. #1, Macomb, IL 61455

SVOBODA, TOMAS
b. Paris, France, 6 Dec. 1939; U.S. citizen
1971. Studied with Miloslav Kabelac, Prague
Cons., B.A. 1959; with Vaclav Dobias, Prague
Acad. of Music, 1962-64; with Ingolf Dahl, Univ.
of Southern Carlifornia, M.M. 1969. His first
symphony was performed by the Prague Symph. in
1957, and he was invited to study with Nadia
Boulanger in Paris in 1963. Other honors include
the Helen S. Anstead award, 1967; ASCAP awards,
1976, 1977; and commissions. He was church
organist and private teacher in Los Angeles,
1967-69; from 1970, faculty member, Portland
State Univ.
WORKS: ORCHESTRA: 4 symphonies, 1957, 1962,
1966, 1975; 3 pieces for orchestra; Reflections,
1968; Sinfoniette, a la Renaissance, 1972; A
child's dream, children's choir and orch., for
50th anniversary of Portland Junior Symph. Orch.,
1973; concertino for violin and orch., 1976;
CHAMBER MUSIC: Chorale and dance, brass quartet,
1966; concertino for oboe and brass choir, 1966;
2 epitaphs, string quartet, 1967; Divertimento,
7 instruments, 1967; Meditations, cello and
piano, 1969; 3 movements, piano, harpsichord,
percussion, 1971; Parabola, clarinet, piano,
string trio, 1971; double octet, 8 flutes, 8
cellos, 1971; Prologue, clarinet, harpsichord,
percussion, 1972; duo for flute and oboe, 1972;
Cadenza and scherzo, cello and piano, Washington,
D.C., 17 June 1976; also piano and organ pieces.
4320 S.E. Oak St., Portland, OR 97215

SWACK, IRWIN
b. West Salem, Ohio, 8 Nov. 1919. Studied with
Herbert Elwell, Cleveland Inst. of Music; with
Vittorio Giannini, Juilliard School; Normand
Lockwood, Henry Cowell, and Paul Creston, Columbia
Univ.; with Gunther Schuller at Tanglewood on a
Ford Found. fellowship. He has been faculty
member at Jacksonville State Coll., 1945-48;
Louisiana Polytechnic Inst., 1949-51; Nassau
Community Coll., 1964.
WORKS: ORCHESTRA: Essay for orch.; Fan-
taisie concertante, for strings; CHAMBER MUSIC:
3 string quartets; string quintet; Psalm 8,
tenor, trumpet, and strings; Dance episodes, 7
instruments; piano trio; piano sonata.
2924 Len Dr., Bellmore, NY 11710

SWAN, ALFRED JULIUS
b. St. Petersburg, Russia, 9 Oct. 1890; U.S.
citizen 1954; d. Haverford, Pa., 2 Oct. 1970.
Studied with Kalafati and Karatygin at the St.
Petersburg Cons. He came to the U.S. in 1920
and taught at the Univ. of Virginia, 1921-23;
Swarthmore Coll. and Haverford Coll., 1926-59;
Univ. of Aix-Marseilles, 1959-65; Temple Univ.,
1965-70.
WORKS: CHAMBER MUSIC: 6 string quartets;
2 violin sonatas; piano sonatina; CHORUS: 10
church canticles; many songs.

SWANN, JEFFREY
b. Williams, Ariz., 24 Nov. 1951. Studied with
David Ahlstrom, Southern Methodist Univ.; with
Darius Milhaud, Aspen Music Festival; and with
Hall Overton, Juilliard School. His sextet won

SWANSON, HOWARD

first prize at Aspen, 1967.
WORKS: OPERA: <u>Prometheus</u>, text after
Aeschelus; ORCHESTRA: symphony #1; <u>Sinfonia
concertante</u>, performed by Dallas Symph., 1967;
CHAMBER MUSIC: <u>Arches</u>, violin and cello.

SWANSON, HOWARD
b. Atlanta, Ga., 18 Aug. 1907; d. New York, N.Y.,
12 Nov. 1978. Studied with Herbert Elwell,
Cleveland Inst. of Music; with Nadia Boulanger
in Paris on a Rosenwald fellowship, 1937-40.
Other awards include New York Music Critics'
Circle award for <u>Short symphony</u>, 1952; Guggenheim
fellowship; American Acad. of Arts and Letters
award; many commissions. His orchestral works
were performed by major orchestras in the U.S.;
his songs were sung by Marian Anderson, Leontyne
Price, and other noted singers.
WORKS: ORCHESTRA: 3 symphonies, 1945, 1948,
1970; <u>Night music</u>, small orch., 1950; concerto
for orchestra; CHAMBER MUSIC: suite for cello
and piano, 1949; trio for flute, clarinet, piano;
<u>The cuckoo</u>, piano, New York, 24 Jan. 1971; many
songs; piano pieces.

SWEET, REGINALD
b. Yonkers, N.Y., 14 Oct. 1885; d. 1950. Studied
with Frederick Koch and Hugo Kaun in Berlin;
then taught in Chautauqua and in New York City.
His compositions include <u>Riders to the sea</u>, a
1-act opera, and chamber music.

SWENSON, WARREN ARTHUR
b. Okanogan, Wash., 27 Apr. 1937. Studied at
Univ. of Washington. He was pianist, Munich
Chamber Opera, 1966, Bavarian Opera Stage, 1965-
66; from 1971, composer, School of the Arts, New
York Univ.; from 1972, organist and composer,
Packer Collegiate Inst.
WORKS: OPERA: <u>The legend of Pecos Bill</u>,
folk opera, 1963; THEATRE: <u>Captain Peoplefox
and his people</u>, musical, commissioned and broadcast by Bavarian Radio, 1964; ORCHESTRA: viola
concerto; CHORUS: <u>A festival mass</u>; <u>Requiem
mass</u>; other choral works and organ pieces.

SWICKARD, RALPH
b. San Jose, Calif., 17 Nov. 1922. Studied with
Leonard Ratner, Stanford Univ.; with John
Vincent, Univ. of California, Los Angeles;
Vladimir Ussachevsky and Otto Luening, Columbia
Univ. He was instructor, California State Univ.,
San Jose, 1970-71.
WORKS: CHAMBER MUSIC: 4 duets for flute
and viola; string quartet, 1957; CHORUS: <u>Missa
brevis</u>, 1958; ELECTRONIC: <u>Bagatelle #2</u>, tape;
<u>Sermons of St. Francis</u>, narrator and tape, 1966;
<u>Hymn of creation</u>, narrator and tape, 1969. He
was producer of the documentary film, <u>A visit
with Darius Milhaud</u>, 1956.

SWIFT, KAY
b. New York, N.Y., 19 Apr. 1905. Studied with
Arthur E. Johnstone, Inst. of Musical Art; with
Charles Martin Loeffler, New England Cons. She
was staff composer at Radio City Music Hall for
2 years; was the first magazine radio columnist;
chairman of music for the New York World's Fair,

1939; piano soloist with the New York Philharmonic
at Lewisohn Stadium.
WORKS: BALLET: <u>Alma mater</u>; THEATRE: <u>Fine
and dandy</u>, musical comedy; <u>Paris '90</u>, musical
comedy; <u>One little girl</u>, Campfire Girls' 50th
anniversary show, 1960; <u>Century 21</u>, Seattle
World's Fair, 1962; many songs, piano pieces.
400 E. 59th St., #10E, New York, NY 10022

SWIFT, RICHARD G.
b. Middlepoint, Ohio, 24 Sept. 1927. Studied
with Leland Smith, Univ. of Chicago, M.A. 1956.
His awards include Rockefeller Found./Louisville
Symph. award, 1955; fellowships at Princeton
Univ., 1959, 1960, Inst. for Creative Arts,
1966-67, 1972, MacDowell Colony, 1971; Rockefeller
performance award, 1968; first prize, Composers
String Quartet competition, 1973; Nat. Endowment
for the Arts grants, 1976-77; American Acad. and
Inst. of Arts and Letters award, 1978. He has
been faculty member, Univ. of California, Davis,
from 1956; was visiting professor, Princeton
Univ., 1977.
WORKS: OPERA: <u>Trial of Tender O'Shea</u>, 1964;
ORCHESTRA: <u>A coronal</u>, 1956; piano concerto,
1961; <u>Extravaganza</u>, 1962; <u>Tristia</u>, 1968; violin
concerto, 1968; symphony, 1970; <u>Specimen days</u>,
soprano and orch., 1977; CHAMBER MUSIC: <u>Serenade
concertante</u>, piano and wind quintet, 1956;
sonata for solo violin, 1957; clarinet sonata,
1957; trio for clarinet, cello, piano, 1957;
<u>Domains I</u>, baritone and chamber ensemble; <u>Stra-
vaganza</u>, a group of 8 works for various ensembles
or solo instruments; <u>Prime</u>, saxophone and chamber ensemble; 4 string quartets, #4, Composers
String Quartet, Boston, 29 Mar. 1974; <u>Great
praises</u>, soprano and piano; piano trio, 1976;
also choral works.
University of California, Davis, CA 95616

SWING, RAYMOND GRAM
b. Cortland, N.Y., 25 Mar. 1887. Studied at
Oberlin Coll. Cons. He received honorary doctorates from 5 colleges, honorary M.A. from
Harvard Univ., 1942. He was a newspaper reporter, 1906-22; became a news commentator in
1935. His violin sonata, 1928, was commercially
recorded.

SWISHER, GLORIA WILSON
b. Seattle, Wash., 12 Mar. 1935. Studied with
John Verrall, Univ. of Washington, B.A. 1956;
with Darius Milhaud, Mills Coll., M.A. 1958;
with Howard Hanson and Bernard Rogers, Eastman
School of Music, Ph.D. 1960. She received a
Woodrow Wilson fellowship, 1956-57; Capitol
Univ. Choir Contest award, 1961; was Washington
State Bicentennial Composer, 1976. She was
faculty member, Washington State Univ., 1960-61;
Pacific Lutheran Univ., 1969-70; from 1969, at
Shoreline Community Coll.
WORKS: OPERA: <u>The happy hypocrite</u>; ORCHES-
TRA: clarinet concerto; <u>Yuki no Niigata</u>, koto
and orch.; <u>Cancion</u>, flute and orch.; BAND: <u>The
mountain and the island</u>; <u>Processions</u>; <u>Thanks-
giving I</u>; CHAMBER MUSIC: <u>Solo flute variations</u>;
<u>Sado</u>, flute and piano; <u>Variations on an original
theme</u>, piano; CHORUS: <u>God is gone up with a</u>

merry noise; 2 faces of love; Thanksgiving II,
Seattle, 4 Mar. 1978.
    7228 6th N.W., Seattle, WA 98117

SYDEMAN, WILLIAM T.
    b. New York, N.Y., 8 May 1928. Studied with Roy
Travis and Felix Salzer, Mannes Coll. of Music,
B.S.; privately with Roger Sessions; with Arnold
Franchetti, Univ. of Hartford, M.M. His awards
include 2 Tanglewood fellowships; Pacifica
Found. award, 1960; Nat. Inst. of Arts and Letters award, 1962; Boston Symph. Merit award,
1964; Koussevitzky Found. award; State Dept. exchange lectureship in Czechoslovakia, Rumania,
and Bulgaria, 1966; many commissions. He was
faculty member, Mannes Coll. of Music, 1959-70.
    WORKS: ORCHESTRA: concertino for oboe,
piano, strings, 1956; Orchestral abstractions,
1958; Concerto da camera, #1, violin and chamber
orch., 1959, #2, 1960; Study for orchestra, #1,
1959, #2, 1961, #3, 1965; Oecumenicus, concerto
for orch., 1966; In memoriam, John F. Kennedy,
1966; CHAMBER MUSIC: string quartet, 1955;
quartet for violin, clarinet, trumpet, double
bass, 1955; 2 woodwind quintets, 1955, 1961;
Divertimento, woodwind trio and string quintet,
1957; 7 movements, septet, 1958; quartet for
oboe and string trio, 1961; chamber concerto for
piano, 2 flutes, string quartet, 1961; The affections, suite for trumpet and piano, 1965;
many other works for small ensembles; choral
works; songs.
    c/o E. C. Schirmer Co., 112 South St.,
Boston, MA 02111

SYVERUD, STEPHEN LUTHER
    b. Prince Albert, Sask., Canada, 3 Mar. 1938.
Studied with Roger Nixon, Alexander Post, Wayne
Peterson, San Francisco State Coll.; with
Richard Hervig and Robert Shallenberg, Univ. of
Iowa, D.M.A. 1972. He received the Clapp Com-
position award, Univ. of Iowa, 1968. He was
faculty member, Jackson State Coll., 1968-70;
Grinnell Coll., 1970-71; from 1971, Northwestern
Univ.
    WORKS: CHAMBER MUSIC: Vietnam II, clarinet,
oboe, double bass, percussion; 4 pieces, clarinet
and piano; Sequence, string quartet; 5 pieces,
chamber ensemble; Scenes II, violin, piano,
vibraphone; ELECTRONIC: Vectors, percussion and
tape; Reaction, clarinet and reverberators;
Screaming monkeys, tape; Monad, film and tape;
Vietnam III, voice, piano, tape; Period piece,
tape; Apotheosis and Fields of ambrosia, both
for alto saxophone and tape; Interplay, winds
and live synthesizer.
    2717 Ewing Ave., Evanston, IL 60201

SZABO, BURT (ALBERT E.)
    b. Wellington, Ohio, 28 Dec. 1931. Studied with
Norman Phelps, Ohio State Univ.; with H. Owen
Reed, James Niblock, Paul Harder, Mario
Castelnuovo-Tedesco, Michigan State Univ. He
has been faculty member at Western Michigan
Univ., 1964-68; Edinboro State Coll., 1968-71;
from 1971, at Florida Technological Univ.
    WORKS: ORCHESTRA: overture, 1961; Diverti-
mentissimo for winds, 1962; Concert piece, piano

and orch., 1962; 2 pieces, 1963; A forest hymn,
with tenor solo, 1967; 3 enigmas, jazz orch.,
1969; Impressions, jazz orch., 1970; Diversion
of Aries, 1973; Serenade, oboe and orch., 1975;
Soundscapes, 1977; CHAMBER MUSIC: string quartet, 1959; Foreboding, soprano, oboe, piano,
1973; Chinese songs, soprano, flute, piano, 1978;
many choral works.
    Florida Tech. Univ., Orlando, FL 32816

SZELL, GEORG
    b. Budapest, Hungary, 7 June 1897; U.S. citizen
1946; d. Cleveland, Ohio, 30 July 1970. Studied
compositon with Josef B. Foerster and Max Reger.
He was an early prodigy both as pianist and composer. At age 11, he performed his Rondo for
piano and orchestra with the Vienna Symph.; at
17, conducted his own symphony and played the
Beethoven Emperor concerto with the Berlin Philharmonic. He was opera and orchestra conductor
in Europe to 1939; conducted the New York Metropolitan Opera, 1942-46; Cleveland Orch., 1946-
70. His compositions included Theme and variations for orchestra, 1916, and Lyric overture,
1922.

SZENDREI, ALADAR. See SENDRY, ALFRED

TAFFS, ANTHONY
    b. London, England, 15 Jan. 1916; U.S. citizen
1954. Studied with Bernard Rogers and Herbert
Elwell, Eastman School of Music. He has been
faculty member, Albion Coll., from 1949.
    WORKS: OPERA: Lilith; Noah; The 10 virgins;
The summons; CHAMBER MUSIC: piano sonata; violin sonata; organ sonata; 3 string quartets;
CHORUS: The son of man, oratorio; A modern
psalmody, oratorio; The Shulamite, cantata for
soprano, tenor, chorus, small orch.; many church
anthems and songs.
    409 Brockway Place, Albion, MI 49224

TAGAWA, RICK M.
    b. Los Angeles, Calif., 7 May 1947. Studied
with Elliott Carter, Juilliard School, 1967-71;
also briefly with William Kraft, Alan Stout, and
Luciano Berio. He held the George Gershwin
Memorial award, 1969-71.
    WORKS: ORCHESTRA: Antoku Tenno, elegy to a
12th-century Japanese emperor; CHAMBER MUSIC:
Inspirations diabolique, percussion ensemble;
Elegy, piano solo.

TAKACS, JENO
    b. Siegendorf, Austria, 25 Sept. 1902; to U.S.
1952. Taught at Cincinnati Cons., and from 1955,
was also visiting professor at the Geneva Cons.
in the summers. In 1971 he retired and returned
to his birthplace.
    WORKS: ORCHESTRA: 2 ballets; 2 piano con-
certos, 1932, 1947; Philippine suite, 1934;
Antiqua Hungarica, 1941; Partita, guitar and
orch., 1950; Folk dances of Burgenland, 1953;
CHAMBER MUSIC: violin sonata, 1956; oboe sonata,
1957; trumpet sonata, 1958; piano pieces.

TALLARICO, PASQUALE
    b. Italy, 25 Sept. 1891; U.S. citizen 1916;

TALMA, LOUISE

d. Wilton, N.H., 17 Jan. 1974. Studied composition with Alfred J. Goodrich and Rubin Goldmark, piano with John Mokreis and Rafael Joseffy, all in New York. He made his piano debut in New York in Mar. 1913, performed with the Chicago Symph. in 1914. He was head of the piano dept., Indianapolis Cons., 1917-20; faculty member, Peabody Cons., 1920-52.

WORKS: CHAMBER MUSIC: The timid maiden, originally for violin, later transcribed for cello, then for alto saxophone; many songs and piano pieces.

TALMA, LOUISE

b. Arcachon, France, 31 Oct. 1906. Studied at Inst. of Musical Art, New York, 1922-30; with Nadia Boulanger and Isidore Philipp at Fontainebleau for 17 summers; New York Univ., B.M. 1931; Columbia Univ., M.A. 1933. Her many honors include Isaac Newton Seligman prize, 1927, 1928, 1929; Joseph H. Bearns prize, 1932; Stovall prize, 1938, 1939; Juilliard publication award, 1946; 2 Guggenheim fellowships, 1946, 1947; North American prize, 1947; French government Prix d'Excellence de Composition, 1951; Fulbright grant, 1955-56; Koussevitzky Found. grant, 1959; Marjorie Peabody Waite award and citation, Nat. Inst. of Arts and Letters, 1960; Nat. Fed. of Music Clubs award, 1963; Nat. Assoc. for American Composers and Conductors award, 1963; Sibelius Medal, London, 1963; 2 Nat. Endowment for the Arts grants, 1966, 1975; election to Nat. Inst. of Arts and Letters, 1974, first woman to become member of NIAL; Clark Lecturer, Scripps Coll., Mar. 1975; Sanford fellow, Yale Univ., Mar. 1976; made a member of the President's Circle, Hunter Coll., 1977. She taught at Manhattan School of Music, 1926-28; Fontainebleau School, summers, 1936-39, the only American to teach there; from 1928, faculty member, Hunter Coll.

WORKS: OPERA: The Alcestiad, Thornton Wilder text, 1955-58, Frankfurt, Germany, 1 Mar. 1962; ORCHESTRA: Toccata, Baltimore, 20 Dec. 1945; Dialogues, piano and orch., Buffalo, 12 Dec. 1965; A time to remember, with chorus, text from John F. Kennedy speeches, New York, 11 May 1968; The tolling bell, baritone and orch., Milwaukee, 29 Nov. 1969 (nominated for Pulitzer prize); CHAMBER MUSIC: Song and dance, violin and piano, 1951; string quartet, New York, 19 Feb. 1955; violin sonata, New York, 13 Feb. 1963; All the days of my life, tenor and chamber ensemble, Washington, D.C., 25 Nov. 1966; 3 duologues, clarinet and piano, New York, 28 Mar. 1968; Summer sounds, clarinet quintet, 1969-73; Textures for piano, New York, 17 Mar. 1978; numerous choral works, songs, piano pieces.
410 Central Park W., New York, NY 10035

TAMKIN, DAVID

b. Chernigov, Russia, 28 Aug. 1906; d. Los Angeles, 21 June 1975. He came to the U.S. as an infant; the family settled in Portland, Oreg., where he studied violin with Henry Bettman and composition with Ernest Bloch. In 1937 he moved to Los Angeles; became composer for Universal Pictures, 1945-66.

WORKS: OPERA: The dybbuk, to a libretto by

his brother, Alex Tamkin, 1928-31, produced by the New York City Opera, 4 Oct. 1951; The blue plum tree of Esau, also to his borther's libretto, 1962; other compositions include 2 string quartets, woodwind sextet, and choral works.

TANCREDI, RALPH ANTHONY

b. Italy, 15 Jan. 1921; U.S. citizen 1934. Studied with Donal Michalsky, California State Univ. at Fullerton. He taught in public schools, 1966-67; from 1973, at Mount San Antonio Coll.

WORKS: CHAMBER MUSIC: Theme and variations, violin, cello, and wind ensemble; 4 songs, based on the Pentagon Papers, baritone and piano; string sextet; Divertimento, 2 clarinets and bassoon; Music for 5, clarinet, horn, trumpet, double bass, piano; Andante and allegro, 2 trumpets and piano; CHORUS: Mass, with 2 clarinets and 2 bassoons.
917 Washington Ave., Pomona, CA 91767

TANENBAUM, ELIAS

b. Brooklyn, N.Y., 20 Aug. 1924. Studied at Juilliard School, B.S.; Columbia Univ., M.A.; composition with Dante Fiorillo, Bohuslav Martinu, Otto Luening, Wallingford Riegger. His awards include a MacDowell fellowship; Nat. Endowment for the Arts grant, 1974; recording grants from American Composers Alliance and the Ford Found. He is faculty member, Manhattan School of Music.

WORKS: ORCHESTRA: Variations, 1955; Concertante, 1955; 6 designs; The last of the just; CHAMBER MUSIC: 2 string quartets, 1955, 1958; woodwind quintet, 1956; piano sonata, 1959; trio for flute, cello, double bass, 1964; 4 pieces, speaking voice and piano, 1964; Structures, brass quintet, 1966; CHORUS: Rituals and reactions, with soloist and instruments, New York, 17 Jan. 1975; ELECTRONIC: Improvisations and patterns, brass quintet and tape, 1969; The families of Song My, voice and tape, 1970; Transformations, flute and tape, 1973; Images III, voice and tape, New York, 30 Oct. 1977.
30 Irving Place, New Rochelle, NY 10801

TANG, JORDAN CHO-TUNG

b. Hong Kong, 27 Jan. 1948; to U.S. 1969. Studied at Chung Chi Coll., Hong Kong, B.S. 1969; with Jan Bender and H. W. Zimmermann, Wittenberg Univ., M.S.M. 1971; with Marcel Dick, Cleveland Inst. of Music, M.M. 1973; with Ramiro Cortes and Vladimir Ussachevsky, Univ. of Utah. His awards include the American Choral Directors Assoc. of Ohio award, 1971; Leroy Robertson Memorial award, 1973; Utah State Fair contest, second prize, 1973, first prize 1974; fellowships at all universities attended; MacDowell fellowship, 1977; many commissions. He was timpanist, Springfield (Ohio) Symphony, 1969-71; assistant conductor, Univ. of Utah Symphony, 1973-76, and Utah Youth Symphony, 1973-78; orchestra conductor and faculty member, Southwest Missouri State Univ., from 1978.

WORKS: ORCHESTRA: Symphonic movement, chamber orch.; timpani concerto; symphony #2; Refrains, drums and orch., 1977; violin concertino; Peach blossom fountain, chamber orch. and narrator, 1977; <u>Taps</u>, trumpet and orch., 1977; <u>Elegy</u>, cello and string orch.; CHAMBER MUSIC: string quartet; <u>A little suite</u>, woodwind quintet; <u>Symbolisms</u>, organ; <u>Piece</u>, for harp and cello; <u>The world</u>, solo voice; piano sonatina; sonatina for piano, 4 hands; quartet for timpani; <u>Etude</u>, double bass, 1977; <u>Studies</u>, chamber ensemble, 1978; also vocal works.

    Southwest Missouri State Univ., Springfield, MO 65802

TANNER, JERRE EUGENE
    b. Lock Haven, Pa., 5 Jan. 1939. Studied at Univ. of Northern Iowa; with Philip Bezanson, Univ. of Iowa, B.A. 1960; with Roger Nixon, San Francisco State Univ., M.A. 1970. His awards include a Huntington Hartford award, 1964; Celia S. Buck award, 1966; Nat. Fed. of Music Clubs award, 1976; Hawaii State Senate commendation, 1977; ASCAP award, 1977; grants from Hawaii State Found. on Culture and the Arts, 1974, 1976, 1977; Nat. Endowment for the Arts, 1976, McInerney Found., Atherton Trust, Hawaii Found., 1977. He was lecturer, Univ. of Hawaii, Hilo Coll., 1966-67; instructor, Center for Continuing Education and Community Service, 1970-75; W. Hawaii Arts coordinator, 1976-77.
    WORKS: OPERA: <u>Ka lei no kane</u>, 1-act comic opera, performed on a statewide tour by Opera Players of Hawaii, 1977; ORCHESTRA: <u>Bartokiana</u>; <u>Le tombeau</u>; BAND: <u>Grand prelude and fugue</u>; suite; CHAMBER MUSIC: <u>Interlude #1</u>, 17-string koto; <u>Spring</u>, solo flute; <u>Adagio</u>, flute and harp; <u>Night</u>, bassoon and percussion; <u>Autumn</u>, solo winds and strings; <u>Hummingbirds</u>, percussion ensemble; <u>Fugue</u>, string trio; <u>Fugue</u>, string quartet; numerous choral works and songs.
    P.O. Box 1478, Kailua-Kona, HI 96740

TANNER, PAUL O. W.
    b. Skunk Hollow, Ky., 15 Oct. 1917. Studied at Univ. of California, Los Angeles, B.A., M.A.; privately with Stefan Wolpe in New York and Roy Harris in Los Angeles. He played trombone with Glenn Miller, Les Brown, and Tex Beneke; from 1958, has been faculty member, Univ. of California, Los Angeles.
    WORKS: BAND: concerto for trombone and band; <u>Aria</u>, trombone and band; CHAMBER MUSIC: <u>Imitation</u>, 3 trombones; <u>A study in texture</u>, 4 trombones; <u>Just Bach</u>, 4 trombones; <u>El cangrejo</u>, 6 trombones; many other works for trombone, books, methods, etc.
    969 Hilgard Ave., Los Angeles, CA 90024

TANNER, PETER H.
    b. Rochester, N.Y., 25 June 1936. Studied with Robert Hall Lewis, Thomas Canning, Louis Mennini; Alan Hovhaness, Bernard Rogers, Eastman School of Music, B.M. 1958, M.M. 1959; Catholic Univ., Ph.D. 1967. He played in the U.S. Marine Band, 1959-63; was faculty member, Kansas State Univ., Manhattan, 1963-66; Univ. of Wisconsin-Eau Claire, 1966-69; from 1969, at Univ. of Massachusetts, Amherst.
    WORKS: ORCHESTRA: concerto for timpani and brass; flute concerto; <u>Introduction and allegro</u>, piano and orch.; CHAMBER MUSIC: sonata for

marimba with piano or wind ensemble; <u>Diversions</u>, flute and marimba; <u>Andante</u>, marimba and piano; CHORUS: <u>Sing for joy</u>.
    January Hills, Rte. 3, Amherst, MA 01002

TARANTO, VERNON ANTHONY, JR.
    b. New Orleans, La., 16 Nov. 1946. Studied with Kenneth Klaus, Dinos Constantinides, and James Drew, Louisiana State Univ. He received first place in a Louisiana Music Teachers contest, 1977. He played in the U.S. Air Force Band, 1969-74; from 1975, has been on faculty, Nicholls State Univ.
    WORKS: ORCHESTRA: <u>Soliloquy for strings</u>, 1966; <u>Sinfonia Orionis</u>, 1974; BAND: <u>Fantasie on American folk songs</u>, 1972; CHAMBER MUSIC: <u>Study #1</u>, brass trio; <u>Sketches on a Menotti motif</u>, brass trio; trio for flute, cello, and piano, 1975; CHORUS: <u>O Trinity of blessed light</u>; <u>Rejoice</u>; <u>The Aeolus liturgies</u>, 1977; SONG CYCLE: <u>The middleland</u>, soprano and woodwinds, 1975.
    Box 343, Prairieville, LA 70769

TARLOW, KAREN ANNE
    b. Boston, Mass., 19 Sept. 1947. Studied with Philip Bezanson, Charles Fussell, Robert Stern, and Frederick Tillis, Univ. of Massachusetts, Amherst, B.M. 1970, M.M. 1973; with Malcolm Peyton and David Del Tredici, Boston Univ., Ph.D. 1978; with Wolfgang Fortner in Germany. She received the Lebow Memorial Scholarship, 1972. She was teaching fellow, Boston Univ., 1975-78.
    WORKS: CHAMBER MUSIC: <u>Lieblingstier</u>, 3 solo voices, 4 woodwinds, cello, 1969; <u>Games for 3</u>, oboe, piano, viola, 1970; <u>The lowest trees have tops</u>, 3 solo voices, chamber ensemble, 1972; <u>2 songs</u>, for voice and piano, 1972; <u>Salvación de la primavera</u>, women's voices, 1973; <u>Music for wind quintet</u>, 1973; <u>The fields of sorrow</u>, women's voices, 1976; <u>The mirror</u>, soprano, clarinet, piano, 1976.

TATGENHORST, JOHN
    b. East Liverpool, Ohio, 22 Aug. 1938. Studied with Marshall Barnes, Norman Phelps, and Donald E. McGinnis, Ohio State Univ.; with Billy May in Hollywood. He was percussion instructor, Capital Univ., 1963-75; arranger for several universities.
    WORKS: BAND: <u>Tanglewood</u>, an overture; <u>Clarion textures</u>; <u>Montage</u>; <u>Cubano drums</u>; many works for marching band. He is author of <u>The Slingerland elementary bell method</u> and <u>The percussion</u>.

TATTON, JACK MEREDITH
    b. Leek, Staffordshire, England, 1 Nov. 1901; U.S. citizen 1939. Studied at King William Coll., Isle of Man; at Cambridge Univ., B.A., M.A.; and at Royal Coll. of Music, London. He taught in schools, 1927-36; since then, raised cattle in Texas. He has composed Latin motets, 2 masses, and many songs.
    Salt Creek Ranch, Refugio, TX 78377

TAUB, BRUCE J. H.
    b. New York, N.Y., 6 Feb. 1948. Studied with Mario Davidovsky, Vladimir Ussachevsky, Jack Beeson, and Chou Wen-chung, Columbia Univ., D.M.A.

TAUTENHAHN, GUNTHER

1974. His honors include the Marc Brunswick
award, 1969; Joseph H. Bearns prize, 1971; BMI
award, 1973; Nat. Endowment for the Arts grant,
1975; Composers Conf. fellowship, 1975; American
Music Center grant, 1975. He is editor, American
Society of University Composers Journal of Music
Scores.
WORKS: OPERA: Passion, poison, and petrification, or The fatal gazogene, chamber opera
based on the play by G. B. Shaw, 1975; Waltz on
a merry-go-round, 3 acts, 1979; ORCHESTRA:
Ballet for Patrick Elliott; 6 pieces for orch.,
1972; CHAMBER MUSIC: string trio, 1969; 3 times
3 and o sweet spontaneous earth, 2 songs of e. e.
cummings, 1974; Fantasy, 2 cellos; Variations,
string quartet; piano pieces; electronic works.
463 West St., Apt. B334, New York, NY 10014

TAUTENHAHN, GUNTHER
b. Kovno, Lithuania, 22 Feb. 1938; U.S. citizen
1956. Studied at Caldwell Seminary, N.J.; composition privately with Leon Kirchner and
Edward Applebaum. His honors include a Young
American Composer award, 1963; and many commissions. He is a data processor as well as private
teacher of piano and composition.
WORKS: ORCHESTRA: double bass concerto,
1968; violin concerto, 1969; concerto for bassoon and percussion, 1969; double concerto, horn
and timpani, 1969; viola concerto, 1969; trumpet
concerto, 1970; concerto for double bass and
chamber orch., 1970; Symphonic sounds #1, 1970,
#2, 1973; Concept 3, 1976; Numeric serenade,
piano and orch., 1976; Sinfonietta for 10 instruments, 1977; alto saxophone concerto, 1978;
Of dreams and nightmares, 1978; Pyramid 4, 1978;
numerous works for small chamber groups and solo
instruments.
1534 3rd St., Manhattan Beach, CA 90266

TAXIN, IRA
b. New York, N.Y., 19 Apr. 1950. Studied with
Joyce Barthelson and Ludmila Ulehla, Scarsdale,
N.Y., 1966-68; with Hugo Norden, Gardner Read,
Joyce Mekeel, Boston Univ., B.M. 1972; with
Jacob Druckman and Donald Martino at Tanglewood,
1972, 1973; with Roger Sessions and Elliott
Carter, Juilliard School, M.M. 1974. He held
fellowships at Tanglewood; Irving Berlin fellowship at Juilliard; American Acad. of Arts and
Letters, Charles E. Ives scholarship, 1974.
Other awards include Westchester Music Teachers
Council award, 1968; Westchester Phil. Symph.
award, 1968; Boston Univ. award, 1970; BMI
awards, 1972, 1973; Margaret Grant Memorial
prize, 1972; Lado, Inc., prize, 1973; Phi Mu
Alpha Sinfonia prize, 1973; and commissions.
WORKS: ORCHESTRA: Poem of meditations and
gatherings, 1971; concerto for piano and chamber
orch., 1972; Saba, 1974; CHAMBER MUSIC: trio
for violin, trombone, piano, 1969; trumpet
sonata, 1970; 3 movements, flute and piano, 1970;
4 poems from The song of songs, 1970; string
quartet, 1971; Piece for brass quintet, 1971;
Chamber piece in 2 parts, 1972; brass quintet,
1973; Fanfare, brass quintet.
c/o Merion Music, Inc., Presser Pl., Bryn
Mawr, PA 19010

TAXMAN, BARRY
b. Rock Island, Ill., 14 May 1922. Studied with
Quincy Porter and Paul Hindemith at Yale Univ.,
B.M.; at Univ. of Chicago, M.A. He was instructor, Music and Arts Inst. of San Francisco,
1953-55; accompanist at Juilliard School, 1960.
He has composed 20 orchestral pieces; 400 works
for instrumental groups; 50 vocal works; and 200
keyboard pieces.
2334 Cedar St., Berkeley, CA 94708

TAYLOR, CLIFFORD
b. Avalon, Pa., 20 Oct. 1923. Studied with
Nikolai Lopatnikoff, Carnegie-Mellon Univ.,
B.F.A. 1948; with Walter Piston, Paul Hindemith,
Randall Thompson, Tillman Merritt, Irving Fine,
Harvard Univ., M.A. 1950; at Tanglewood, 1950.
He received first prizes, Nat. Symph. Orch. contest, 1955, Friends of Harvey Gaul contest,
1955, Rheta A. Sosland contest, Univ. of Missouri,
1963; Nat. Endowment for the Arts grant, 1975.
He was faculty member, Chatham Coll., 1950-63;
from 1963, at Temple Univ.
WORKS: OPERA: The freak show (The man of
stone), 1 act, 1975; ORCHESTRA: Theme and variations, 1955; Introduction and dance fantasy;
concerto for strings, #1, 1957, #2, Philadelphia,
5 Mar. 1978, #3, 1978; Chaconne, 1956; 3 symphonies, 1958, 1965, 1978; concerto for organ
and chamber orch., 1963; Sacred verses, with
chorus and soloists; piano concerto, 1974;
CHAMBER MUSIC: violin sonata, 1955; Adagio and
allegro, from woodwind quintet, rev. 1958; 2
string quartets, 1960, 1978; trio for clarinet,
cello, piano, 1960; Concert duo, violin and
cello, 1961; duo for alto saxophone and trombone,
1965; Movement for 3, piano trio, 1968; 5 poems,
oboe and 5 brasses, 1971; 2 piano sonatas, 1952,
1978; piano suite, 1952; ELECTRONIC: Parabolic
mirrors, tape; many choral settings and songs.
149 Fernbrook Ave., Wyncote, PA 19095

TAYLOR, CORWIN H.
b. Germantown, Ohio, 14 Oct. 1905. Studied with
Sidney Durst and Carl Hugo Grimm, Cincinnati
Coll. of Music, B.M., M.M.; at Univ. of Cincinnati, B.S., Ed.M., Ed.D. He taught in public
schools, 1933-37; Wilmington Coll., 1935-37;
Cincinnati Coll. of Music, 1937-42; was bandmaster, U.S. Coast Guard, 1942-45; on faculty,
Peabody Cons., 1945-50; Baltimore public schools,
1950-68; then Univ. of Maryland, 1968-75.
WORKS: BAND: Curtis Bay march, 1943; U.S.
Coast Guard march, 1945; Victory review march,
1946; Los campaneros, scherzo for 3 trumpets and
band, 1950; WIND ENSEMBLE: Andante and scherzo,
brass quartet, 1939; 3 novelties, 4 clarinets,
1942; Inscriptions in brass, suite for brass
choir, 1964.
3450 Toledo Terrace, Hyattsville, MD 20782

TAYLOR, (JOSEPH) DEEMS
b. New York, N.Y., 22 Dec. 1885; d. New York,
3 July 1966. Studied at New York Univ., B.A.
1906; privately with Oscar Coon, 1908-11. His
many honors included commissions from the New
York Metropolitan Opera, 1926, 1930; 6 honorary
doctorates, 1927-44; membership, Nat. Inst. of

Arts and Letters. He held editorial positions with various publications, 1906-21; was music critic, New York World, 1921-25, New York American, 1931-32, Musical America, 1927-29; intermission commentator, New York Philharmonic radio broadcasts, 1936-43, and on other radio programs.

WORKS: OPERA: The king's henchman, libretto by Edna St. Vincent Millay, New York, 17 Feb. 1927; Peter Ibbetson, New York, 7 Feb. 1931; Ramuntcho, 1942; The dragon, 1954; THEATRE: The echo, musical comedy, 1909; ORCHESTRA: The siren song, 1912; Through the looking-glass, suite for chamber orch., 1919, full orch., 1922; Jurgen, 1925; Fantasy on 2 themes, 1925; Circus days, jazz orch., 1925, full orch., 1933; Casanova, ballet music, 1937; Processional, 1941; Christmas overture, 1943; Elegy, 1945; Restoration suite, 1950; CHAMBER MUSIC: The portrait of a lady, 11 instruments, 1918; Lucrece, string quartet; A kiss in Xanadu, piano; CHORUS: The chambered nautilus, with orch., 1914; The highwayman, baritone, women's voices, orch., 1914. He was also author of the books: Of men and music, 1937; The well-tempered listener, 1940; Music to my ears, 1949; Some enchanted evenings: The story of Rodgers and Hammerstein, 1953; The one-track mind, 1957.

TAYLOR, JOSEPH PAUL
b. Houston, Tex., 31 May 1951. Studied with Stanworth Beckler, Univ. of the Pacific, 1970-72; with Morton Subotnick, James Tenney, Leonard Stein, California Inst. of the Arts, 1972-74; music technology with Don Buchla, 1973. His compositions include Spaces for orchestra, 1973; Mixer piece, tape, 1974; 3 multiplier pieces, tape, 1975; The new canarsie fandango, 1976, and 9 strands, 1977, both for synthesizer, saxophone, piano.
127 A Grand St., New York, NY 10013

TAYLOR, LIONEL L.
b. Provo, Utah, 23 Mar. 1916. Studied at California Inst. of the Arts, B.A., M.M. He was an Army bandleader in World War II; instructor, Los Angeles Cons., 1947-54; arranger for radio and television, 1955-60; then on faculty, Los Angeles City Coll. His works include Incident at the river, a cantata; other choral works and songs.
Los Angeles City College, 855 N. Vermont Ave., Los Angeles, CA 90029

TAYLOR, ROWAN S.
b. Ogden, Utah, 1 June 1927. Studied with Leroy Robertson, Leon Dallin, Carl Fuerstner, Crawford Gates, Brigham Young Univ.; with Lukas Foss and John Vincent, Univ. of California, Los Angeles. He is faculty member at Los Angeles Pierce Coll. and conductor of its Community Symph. Orch. and Brass Ensemble. His compositions include an opera, an oratorio, a cantata, and 21 symphonies.
22544 Tiara St., Woodland Hills, CA 91364

TAYLOR, TELFORD
b. Schenectady, N.Y., 24 Feb. 1908. Studied at Williams Coll., B.A., M.A., L.L.D.; at Harvard Univ., L.L.B. He is a lawyer in New York City; was assistant to the U.S. chief of counsel at the Nuremberg war crimes trials in 1945; in 1946, became chief of counsel; was technical adviser and narrator for the television play, "Judgment at Nuremberg." He was author of Sword and swastika, 1952; and Grand inquest: The story of congressional investigations, 1955. He has conducted his own works at Central Park Mall, N.Y.
WORKS: BAND: Italia eterna; Farewell to the cavalry; 50 stars on the field of blue.

TCHEREPNIN, ALEXANDER
b. St. Petersburg, Russia, 21 Jan. 1899; U.S. citizen 1958; d. Paris, 29 Sept. 1977. Studied at St. Petersburg Cons.; composition with Paul Vidal, piano with Isidor Philipp at the Paris Cons. Though he was the son of Nikolai Tcherepnin, he did not study formally with his father. His mother taught him how to write down his musical ideas, and by the time he entered the St. Petersburg Cons., he had composed orchestral scores, opera, ballets, 5 piano concertos, 12 piano sonatas, and many vocal and chamber works. His awards include first prize, Schott's Internat. Composition Contest; American Opera Society, David Bispham award; Chevalier of Arts and Letters, French Ministry of Culture; election to Nat. Inst. of Arts and Letters, 1974. In 1918 his family moved to Tbilisi, where Alexander entered the university. By this time he had become a virtuoso pianist, and his concert tours included four trips to the Orient as well as Europe and the U.S. He eventually settled in the U.S., taught at San Francisco Inst. of Music and Art, 1948, at De Paul Univ., 1949-64.
WORKS: OPERA: OI-OI, after Andreyev, 1928; Die Hochzeit der Sobelde, Hofmannsthal text, 1933; The marriage, a completion of Moussorgsky's opera on a Gogol text, 1937; The farmer and the fairy, Aspen, Colo., 13 Aug. 1952; BALLET: Ajanta's frescoes, 1923; Training, 1935; Trepak, 1938; Der Fahrend Schuler mit dem Teufelbannen, 1938; Legendede Razine, 1941; Chota Roustaveli, 1945; La colline des fantomes, 1946; La femme et son ombre, 1947; Le souffre; ORCHESTRA: 6 piano concertos, 1919, 1924, 1932, 1947, 1963, 1965; Concerto da camera, flute, violin, chamber orch., 1924; Georgian rhapsody, cello and orch., 1924; Mystere, cello and chamber orch., 1926; 4 symphonies, 1926, 1945-51, 1954, #4, Boston, 5 Dec. 1958; Magna mater, 1927; concertino for piano trio and string orch., 1931; Festmusik; Russian dances, 1933; Georgian suite, piano and strings, 1940; Evocation, 1948; Romantic overture; Symphonic march; suite for orch., 1953; harmonica concerto, 1956; Symphonic prayer, 1960; The lost flute, narrator and orch., English translation of Chinese poems; The XII, narrator and orch., poem by A. Block; Serenade, string orch., 1964; Bagatelles, piano and strings; sonatina, timpani and orch.; CHAMBER MUSIC: Ode, cello and piano, 1919; piano trio, 1925; 2 string quartets, 1925, 1926; piano quintet, 1927; 3 cello sonatas; violin sonata; Sonatine sportive, saxophone and piano, 1939; flute quartet, 1939; trio and march for 3 trumpets, 1939; Perpetuum mobile, violin

TCHEREPNIN, IVAN

piano, 1945; suite for solo cello, 1946; harpsichord suite, 1966; brass quintet, 1972; many
other chamber works; numerous piano pieces; 4
cantatas, #4, Musica sacra, Festival of Easter,
Lourdes, France, 28 Apr. 1973.

TCHEREPNIN, IVAN
b. Issy-Les-Moulineaux, France, 5 Feb. 1943;
U.S. citizen 1960. Studied first with his
father, Alexander Tcherepnin; with Leon Kirchner,
Harvard Univ., B.A. 1964, M.A. 1965; with
Pousser and Stockhausen in Cologne, 1965-66;
with David Tudor, Mills Coll., 1967. His awards
include the Brookline Library prize, 1964; John
Knowles Paine fellowship, 1965, Harvard Univ.
Knight prize, 1965; ASCAP awards, 1966, 1977;
American Music Center award, 1978. He was lecturer, San Francisco Cons., 1969-71, Stanford
Univ., 1970-72; from 1972, on faculty at Harvard
Univ.
    WORKS: OPERA: Santur opera, for santur (an
80-string Persian zither) and electronics, not a
traditional opera, but does have a dramatic plot,
1977, New York, 12 Jan. 1979; BALLET: Set, hold,
clear and squelch, electronic score for Merce
Cunnungham Dance Co., New York, 21 Feb. 1976;
ORCHESTRA: Le va et le vient, Lucerne Festival,
25 Aug. 1978, composer conducting; CHAMBER MUSIC:
4 pieces from before, piano, 1962; Cadenzas in
transition, piano, clarinet, flute, 1963; Work
music, electric guitar, horn, cello, clarinet,
1965; Wheelwinds, 9 winds, 1966; Rings, string
quartet and tape, 1966; Light music, 4 instrumental groups and tape, 1968; Les adieux, 18
players, lights, and electronics, 1971.
    111 Lakeview Ave., Cambridge, MA 02138

TCHEREPNIN, SERGE A.
b. Issy-Les-Moulineux, France, 2 Feb. 1941; U.S.
citizen 1960. Son of Alexander Tcherepnin. He
studied with Nadia Boulanger in Paris; with
Leon Kirchner and Billy Jim Layton, Harvard
Univ., B.A. 1964; graduate studies at Princeton
Univ.; with Earle Brown, Karlheinz Stockhausen,
Luigi Nono, and Pierre Boulez in various European cities. He was instructor in electronic
media, New York Univ., 1968-70; on the composition faculty, California Inst. of the Arts,
1970-75.
    WORKS: CHAMBER MUSIC: Inventions for piano,
1960; Kaddish, instrumental ensemble and actor,
on text by A. Ginsberg, 1961; Morning after
piece, saxophone and piano, 1965; ELECTRONIC:
Heaven, tape, 1966; Film, for actors, musicians,
electronics, and lights, 1967; The Serge-o-phone,
an electronic music machine, 1973. He invented
a portable music synthesizer, which he has
patented as the Serge Modular Music System.

TEITELBAUM, RICHARD
b. New York, N.Y., 19 May 1939. Studied with
Alfred Swan, John Davison, Claudio Spies, Haverford Coll., B.A. 1960; Aspen Music School, 1957,
1960; with William Sydeman, Mannes School of
Music; with Mel Powell, Yale Univ., M.M. 1964;
with Goffredo Petrassi in Rome and Luigi Nono in
Venice; Wesleyan Univ., 1970-71. His awards include a Bradley-Keeler scholarship, 1962-63;

Greenwald Memorial prize, 1964; Horatio Parker
scholarship, 1963-64; John Day Jackson prize,
1964; Ditson travel fellowship, 1964-65; graduate
fellowship, Wesleyan Univ., 1969-70; NDEA fellowship, 1970-71; fellowship for study in Japan,
1977. He was faculty member, California Inst.
of the Arts, 1971-72; Chicago Art Inst., 1972-
73; York Univ., 1973-75.
    WORKS: CHAMBER MUSIC: Intersections, piano,
1963; string trio, 1964; Concerto da camera, 14
instruments, 1966; ELECTRONIC: In tune, amplified heart beats and brain waves, with Moog synthesizer, 1966; La mattina presto, tape, 1969;
MULTIMEDIA: Border region, film, tape, slides,
and optigon, 1972. He has published many articles
in music journals.

TEMPLETON, ALEC
b. Cardiff, Wales, 4 July 1909; U.S. citizen
1941; d. Greenwich, Conn., 28 Mar. 1963. Studied
at Royal Coll. of Music and Royal Acad. of Music,
London. He made his U.S. debut as pianist in
Chicago in 1936; performed on radio and on
records; toured the U.S. and Canada.
    WORKS: ORCHESTRA: concerto grosso; Con-
certino lirico; Bach goes to town; Mozart matri-
culates; Mendelssohn mows them down; Gothic concerto, 1954; CHAMBER MUSIC: violin sonata; 2
piano sonatas; Pocket-size sonata, clarinet and
piano; string quartet; trio for flute, oboe,
piano; and choral works.

TENNEY, JAMES C.
b. Silver City, N.Mex., 10 Aug. 1934. Has
studied with Steuermann, Varese, Ruggles, Nowak,
Brant, Gaburo, Hiller, and Cage; has also
studied and taught engineering. He was on the
music faculty, California Inst. of the Arts,
1970-76; then at York Univ., Toronto.
    WORKS: CHAMBER MUSIC: 13 ways of looking
at a blackbird, tenor and 5 instruments, 1958;
Tangled red, tongue-in-cheek arrangement of a
Joplinesque rag for string quintet, 1969-74; 3
pieces for drum quartet: (1) Wake for Charles
Ives, (2) Hocket for Henry Cowell, (3) Crystal
cannon for Edgard Varese) 1974-75, New York, 17
Dec. 1978; Harmonium #5, string trio, 1978;
ELECTRONIC: Collage #1, Blue suede shoes,
musique concrète after Elvis Presley, 1961;
Stochastic quartet, 1963; Erogdos 1, computer
music for 2 tapes, played together or separately,
forward or backward; Fabric for Ché, computer
music on tape, 1967; For Ann (rising), tape,
1969; Harmonium #4, 6 instruments and tape, New
York, 17 Dec. 1978; Saxony #2, instruments and
tape, New York, 17 Dec. 1978. Two evenings of
music by James Tenney were presented in New
York 17-18 Dec. 1978, sponsored by the Reich
Music Found.
    231 Donald Ave., Toronto, Ontario, M6M 1K7,
Canada

TEPPER, ALBERT
b. New York, N.Y., 1 June 1921. Studied with
Quincy Porter, Carl McKinley, and Francis Judd
Cooke, New England Cons.; with Hans Gal, Univ.
of Edinburgh; privately with Tibor Serly in New
York. He held a Fulbright scholarship for study

in Scotland. He was instructor, New England Cons., 1947-50; from 1952, faculty member at Hofstra Univ.

WORKS: ORCHESTRA: Tent music; symphony for strings; concertino for oboe and strings; BAND: Circus overture; CHAMBER MUSIC: string quartet, 1946; suite for clarinet and bassoon; CHORUS: cantata, with brass and percussion, 1969; For city spring, with orch.; 5 songs from the Catullus of William Hull.
36 Honeysuckle Rd., Levittown, NY 11756

TERHUNE, ANICE POTTER

b. Hampden, Mass., 27 Oct. 1873; d. Pompton Lakes, N.Y., 9 Nov. 1964. Studied in Cleveland; with Coenen in Rotterdam; and with Edward M. Bowman in New York. She married the author, Arthur Payson Terhune, in 1901.

WORKS: OPERA: Hero Nero, 1904; The woodland princess, 1911; also several books of children's songs. In 1945, she published an autobiography, Across the line.

TGETTIS, NICHOLAS

b. Salem, Mass., 1 Sept. 1933. Studied with Carl McKinley, Francis Judd Cooke, Leland Proctor, Billy Jim Layton, New England Cons., B.M. 1960; with Daniel Pinkham, Gardner Read, Hugo Norden, Boston Univ., M.M. 1969; electronic music at Workshop BEEP 32, Boston. He won a first prize in the Brookline Library concerts, 1969, for a woodwind trio. He has been a private and public school music teacher from 1957.

WORKS: OPERA: Sappho, chamber opera, Peabody, Mass., 19 June 1978; ORCHESTRA: Fantasy, piano and orch., 1978; CHAMBER MUSIC: piano sonatina; Night freight, 2 pianos, 1976; Petite suite, flute and piano, 1976; woodwind quintet, Worcester, Mass., 2 Apr. 1976; Old South Point-- 1668, piano sonata, 1976; 4 string quartets, 1976.
14 Aborn St., Salem, MA 01970

THATCHER, HOWARD RUTLEDGE

b. Baltimore, Md., 17 Sept. 1878; d. Baltimore, 21 Feb. 1973. Graduated from Peabody Cons.; received an honorary doctorate there, 1972. He was organist, choirmaster, violist, conductor, and teacher in the Baltimore area; on the faculty at Peabody Cons., 1911-53.

WORKS: OPERA: The double miracle, 1 act; The King's jester, operetta; ORCHESTRA: Concert overture; Legend; Elegy, with 4 cellos; viola concertino; violin concerto; clarinet concerto; Lyric suite, 1951; horn concerto, 1959; CHAMBER MUSIC: cello sonatina; Pastoral and rondo, 4 violins; string quintet; string quartet; piano quartet; suite for 3 violins; Petite suite, 2 violins and piano; ORGAN: Legend; Fantasy on Concord, 1958.

THAYER, FRED M., JR.

b. Ithaca, N.Y., 19 Dec. 1941. Studied with Earl George, Syracuse Univ.; with Warren Benson and Gregg Smith, Ithaca Coll.; Karl Korte and Ezra Laderman, State Univ. of New York, Binghamton; Robert Palmer, Marice Stith, and Karel Husa, Cornell Univ., where he held the Blackmore

scholarship, 1976. He was a Peace Corps volunteer in Colombia, S.A., 1963-65; head of vocal music, Elmira Free Acad., 1967-71; from 1976, faculty member, Lycoming Coll.

WORKS: OPERA: The tinker's wedding, 1-act chamber opera; ORCHESTRA: The golden bird, choreographic suite; BAND: Illumination; CHAMBER MUSIC: duo for violin and cello; Adagio, oboe, violin, cello, double bass; VOICE: The earth says May, song cycle for soprano, oboe, horn, cello; Soli Deo gloria, chorus.
1828 Sweeley Ave., Williamsport, PA 17701

THAYER, WILLIAM ARMOUR

b. Brooklyn, N.Y., 5 Oct. 1874; d. Brooklyn, 9 Dec. 1933. Studied with Dudley Buck; was organist in Brooklyn from 1893. He composed numerous songs, including the well-known My laddie.

THEOBALD, JAMES CHESTER

b. Winchester, Mass., 10 Mar. 1950. Studied with Edward J. Miller, Edward Diemente, Alvin Apstein, Hartt Coll.; with Robert Lombardo and Ramon Zupko, Chicago Musical Coll.; with Jack Beeson, Columbia Univ., B.A. 1977. He won theory and composition awards at Hartt Coll., 1973. He was public school teacher, 1971-73; announcer, WWUH-FM, Hartford, 1971-73; then staff member, WBAI, New York.

WORKS: CHAMBER MUSIC: Jabberwocky, narrator and 5 instruments; Plane-5, 4 instruments; Alternatives 720, solo percussion; Meditations, cello and piano; Aftermath, brass and percussion; Dances for 6 brass, 1976; The Newtonian cosmology cakewalk, clarinet and piano trio, 1976; 3 rituals for 19 instruments, 1976; Possibilities, woodwind trio and piano, 1977; Fanfare in 6 parts, 6 brass, 1978; 3 rhapsodies, alto saxophone and percussion quartet, 1978; Mystery music #5, 2 percussion and trombone, New York, 14 Apr. 1980.
545 W. 111 St., #9E, New York, NY 10025

THIEL-PHILLIPS, VIVIAN D. See PHILLIPS, VIVIAN D.

THIMMIG, LESLIE

b. Santa Maria, Calif., 1943. Studied with John LaMontaine, Eastman School of Music, B.M. 1965; with Bulent Arel and Mel Powell, Yale Univ., M.A. 1969. He was clarinetist with the Eastman Wind Ensemble and Philharmonic, and with the New Haven Symphony; jazz saxophonist in Chicago and New York and with his quintet on a tour of Poland sponsored by the U.S. State Dept., 1963. His compositions include 7 profiles for string quartet.
Univ. of Wisconsin, 455 N. Park St., Madison, WI 53706

THOMAS, ANDREW

b. Ithaca, N.Y., 8 Oct. 1939. Studied with Karel Husa and Robert Palmer, Cornell Univ., B.A.; with Burrill Phillips, Luciano Berio, and Elliott Carter, Juilliard School, M.S., D.M.A.; also studied with Otto Luening, Robert Moevs, and Nadia Boulanger. He received the Thorne Music Fund grant, 1973; New York State Council on the Arts grant, 1974; Nat. Endowment for the

THOMAS, C. EDWARD

Arts grant, 1975; and commissions. He joined
the faculty at Juilliard School in 1972; was
music director, the Lenox Arts Center, 1972,
1976, 1977.
   WORKS: ORCHESTRA: The 12 points of the
modified Mercalli earthquake scale, on texts of
John Norden and Shakespeare, soprano voice,
tape, orch., 1978; CHAMBER MUSIC: 2 studies,
woodwind quintet; The roman de Fauvel, soprano,
percussion, piano; Presidio 27, soprano and
brass quintet, 1970; Dirge in the woods, voice,
harp, percussion, New York, 11 May 1973; Prick-
song, solo harp; An Wasser Fleussen Babylon, 2
pianos; The death of Yukio Mishima, voice and
chamber ensemble; How the news was spread, flute,
clarinet, piano trio; Alexander's dark band, 10
instruments; CHORUS: Easter, with organ.
   251 W. 76 St., New York, NY 10023

THOMAS, C. EDWARD
   b. Vineland, N.J., 19 Nov. 1935. Studied at
Wheaton Coll., Ill., B.M.; American Cons., M.M.;
and at Univ. of Iowa. He was faculty member,
Bethel Coll., St. Paul, Minn., 1966-74; executive
director, Afro-American Music Opportunities
Assoc., 1969-74.
   WORKS: CHORUS: I have a dream, cantata; A
fantasy of carols; Sleep, holy babe; Joy to the
world.
   2909 Wayzata Blvd., Minneapolis, MN 55405

THOMAS, CARTER DAVID
   b. Passaic, N.J., 2 Jan. 1950. Studied with
Morton Subotnick, Harold Budd, James Tenney, and
Earle Brown, California Inst. of the Arts. He
received a Nat. Endowment for the Arts grant,
1976; prizes for an experimental film score,
Chicago Film Festival. He has been faculty
member, State Univ. Coll., Fredonia, from 1977.
   WORKS: ORCHESTRA: Hymn of man, 1972; CHAM-
BER MUSIC: To dawn, percussion quartet, 1972;
Auric light, harp and percussion, 1977; Earth
forms, percussion and dancers, 1978; ELECTRONIC:
800 Lifeline #1, tape; Epicentrum, tape, 1975;
Illuminations I, II, III, instruments and live
electronics, 1976.
   5288 Blockhouse Rd., Fredonia, NY 14063

THOMAS, CHRISTOPHER
   b. Bristol, England, 7 Mar. 1894; U.S. citizen
1939. Studied on scholarship at Royal Coll. of
Music, London; teachers included Malcolm Sargent
and Percy Goetschius. He was church organist
and teacher in schools and colleges in England
and following service in the British Army in
World War I, in churches and schools in the U.S.
From 1958 he was music director at St. Peter's
Church in Charlotte, N.C.
   WORKS: CHAMBER MUSIC: Little prelude and
fugue, piano; Scottish suite, violin and piano;
many choral works.

THOMAS, HELEN
   b. East Liverpool, Ohio, 29 May. Studied at
New England Cons. Her published works include
an operetta, Song of yesterday, and many songs.

THOMAS, JOHN PATRICK
   b. Denver, Colo., 26 Mar. 1941. Studied with
Allan Willman, Univ. of Wyoming, 1959-61; with
Andrew Imbrie and Seymour Shifrin, Univ. of
California at Berkeley, 1961-66; with Darius
Milhaud and Charles Jones, Aspen School. His
awards include the Copley Found. award; Fromm
Found. Aspen prize; Theodore Presser Found.
grant; 2 Alfred Hertz Found. fellowships; Di
Lorenzo composition prize; Fromm Found. fellowship to Tanglewood. He was faculty member,
State Univ. of New York at Buffalo, 1966-72; has
performed widely as a singer in the U.S. and
abroad.
   WORKS: ORCHESTRA: 1963; CHAMBER MUSIC:
Various objects disturb the water's surface,
string quartet, 1962; 4 poems of William Searle,
1963-65; Ostraka, brass quintet, 1965; Canciones,
bass-baritone and clarinet, 1967; Last rites,
counter-tenor and guitar, 1971; Mignon, soprano
and piano, 1973; Landscape with architecture,
lute; 3 musicians II, oboe cello, harpsichord;
KEYBOARD: Pieces for Joan Gallegos, 2 pianos,
1963; Peniel, organ, 1967; 145 W. 85th St.,
piano, 1964-71.
   Box 406, 234 N. Day St., Powell, WY 82435

THOMAS, MARILYN TAFT
   b. McKeesport, Pa., 10 Jan. 1943. Studied with
Alexei Haieff and Nicolai Lopatnikoff, Carnegie
Mellon Univ., M.M. She won first place in a
Nat. Fed. of Music Clubs contest, 1964; was
named composer for Pittsburgh in 1979. She has
been music director, First Unitarian Church,
Pittsburgh, from 1963; was lecturer, Carnegie
Mellon Univ., 1975-76; from 1977, lecturer,
Chatham Coll.
   WORKS: CHAMBER MUSIC: sonata for oboe and
bassoon, 1962; Concert piece, violin and piano,
1963; Theme and variations, piano, 1964; Synthesis, violin and organ, 1968; He was my son,
voice and piano, 1973; Songs of family, voice
and piano, 1976; 5 pieces for 5 players, woodwind quintet, 1978.
   913 Golfview Dr., McKeesport, PA 15135

THOMAS, PAUL LINDSLEY
   b. New York, N.Y., 18 Mar. 1929. Studied with
Norman Coke-Jephcott in New York, 1950-54; with
Quincy Porter and Leroy Baumgartner, Yale Univ.,
B.M. 1957, M.M. 1958; with Samuel Adler and
Merrill Ellis, North Texas State Univ., 1963-65,
1978. He received the Luther Noss prize in composition, Yale Univ., 1958; ASCAP awards, 1975-
80. He has been organist and choirmaster from
1950; from 1960, music director, St. Michael
and All Angels Church, Dallas. He has published
numerous anthems and other liturgical works.
   6822 Northwood Rd., Dallas, TX 75225

THOMAS, RONALD EDWARD
   b. Newark, N.J., 27 Jan. 1942. Studied with
Vittorio Giannini, Nicholas Flagello, Ludmila
Ulehla, Manhattan School of Music, B.M. 1963;
privately with M. William Karlins, 1961-63; with
Karlheinz Stockhausen, Univ. of Pennsylvania,
1964; with Stefan Wolpe, Raoul Pleskow, Howard
Rovics, C. W. Post Coll., M.A. 1970; private

study with many others. From 1960, he has been dance accompanist at various schools, from 1972, at Temple Univ., dance dept.; has also been jazz pianist and private teacher of jazz improvisation, piano, and composition.

WORKS: CHAMBER MUSIC: Ballade (Ghosts in the weed garden) for alto saxophone and piano, 1974-75; Music for piano, violin and cello, 1975.
4944 Rubicam St., Philadelphia, PA 19144

THOME, DIANE
b. Pearl River, N.Y., 25 Jan. 1942. Studied at Eastman School of Music, B.M. 1963; with Darius Milhaud at Aspen, Colo.; with Roy Harris, Inter-American Univ. of Puerto Rico; with A. U. Boscovich in Israel; at Univ. of Pennsylvania, M.A. 1965; with Milton Babbitt, Princeton Univ., M.F.A. 1970, Ph.D. 1973. Her awards include Nat. Fed. of Music Clubs award, 1958; David Halstead award, 1965; Nat. Society of Arts and Letters award, fellowships at Tanglewood, 1962, Columbia Univ., 1963, Univ. of Pennsylvania, 1966-67, Princeton Univ., 1968-72. She was faculty member, State Univ. of New York, Binghamton, 1974-78; then at Univ. of Washington.

WORKS: ELECTRONIC: January variations, computer synthesized tape; Polyvalence for computer and instruments; Le berceau de miel, string quartet, alto flute, voice, tape; Alexander Boscovich remembered, violin, piano, tape, 1975; Los nombres, piano, percussion, tape, 1976.
University of Washington, Seattle, WA 98195

THOME, JOEL
b. Detroit, Mich., 7 Jan. 1939. Studied at Eastman School of Music, B.M. 1960; conducting certificate, Ecole International, Nice, France, 1960; with A. U. Boscovich in Israel; with George Rochberg, Univ. of Pennsylvania, M.M. 1967. His awards include the David Halstead prize, 1965; MacDowell fellowship, 1968; many commissions. He was faculty member, Israel Acad. of Music, Univ. of Tel Aviv, 1961-64; teaching fellow, Univ. of Pennsylvania, 1964-67; then joined faculty at Glassboro State Coll.

WORKS: BALLET: Act without words #1, adapted from Beckett, electronic score; Magritte! Magritte!; 3 poems; CHAMBER MUSIC: Prisms, solo piano, percussion, chamber ensemble, 1964; In memoriam Ury, 1965; MULTIMEDIA: Circus, tape, 5 musicians, magician, polarized light projections.
Glassboro State College, Glassboro, NJ 08028

THOMPSON, DAVID MARTIN
b. Detroit, Mich., 6 Aug. 1951. Studied with James L. Waters, Kent State Univ., M.A. 1976. He received the Mary Miles award, 1971, 1973; first prize, New Music for Young Ensembles competition, 1976. He taught at Kent State Univ., 1976-77.

WORKS: ORCHESTRA: Variations on a Gregorian melody, 1974; symphony, 1976; CHAMBER MUSIC: 2 string quartets, 1971, 1975; quintet for winds, 1973; 3 songs on Psalms of David, voice and piano, 1973; 2 pieces, clarinet, cello, piano,

Brussels, Belgium, 5 May 1976; Night song, oboe, cello, harp, 1976.
830 Allerton St., Kent, OH 44242

THOMPSON, DONALD BRYCE
b. Chicago, Ill., 15 Oct. 1925. Studied with Halsey Stevens, Ingolf Dahl, Ernest Kanitz, Miklos Rozsa, Univ. of Southern California, B.M. 1949, M.A. 1951, M.S. 1971. He has won awards in a Nat. Fed. of Music Clubs contest and Thor Johnson brass competition. He has been member of the technical staff, Space Division, Rockwell International, from 1951.

WORKS: BAND: Partita; Intermezzo; 5 pieces (with Halsey Stevens); Diptych, brass and percussion; CHAMBER MUSIC: Trio concertante, clarinet, horn, piano; trombone sonata; 3 monologues, for trombone; string quartet; Allegro vivo, marimba and piano.
12671 Chase St., Garden Court, CA 92645

THOMPSON, RANDALL
b. New York, N.Y., 21 Apr. 1899. Studied with Walter Spalding, Edward Burlingame Hill, Archibald T. Davison, Harvard Univ., A.B. 1920, M.A. 1922; American Acad. in Rome, 1922-25; with Ernest Bloch in New York, 1920-21; and at Univ. of Rochester, D.M. 1933. His awards include a Damrosch fellowship, 1922; 2 Guggenheim fellowships, 1929, 1930; Elizabeth Sprague Coolidge Medal, 1941; Ditson award, 1944; Eastman School publication award; membership, Nat. Inst. of Arts and Letters; many commissions. He was faculty member, Wellesley Coll., 1927-29 and 1936; Harvard Univ., 1929; guest conductor, Dessoff Choirs, 1931-32; choral conductor, Juilliard School, 1931-32; on faculty, Univ. of California, Berkeley, 1937-39; director, Curtis Inst., 1939-41; on faculty, Univ. of Virginia, 1941-45; Princeton Univ., 1945-48; Harvard Univ., 1948-65.

WORKS: OPERA: Solomon and Balkis, first stage performance, Cambridge, Mass., 14 Apr. 1942; THEATRE: music for The Grand Street follies, 1922; The straw hat, 1926; ORCHESTRA: Pierrot and Cothurnus, 1923; The piper at the gates of dawn, 1924; Jazz poem, piano and orch., 1928; 3 symphonies, 1930, 1932, 1949; A trip to Nahant, a fantasy, 1955; CHAMBER MUSIC: The wind in the willows, string quartet, 1924; suite for oboe, clarinet, viola, 1940; string quartet, 1941; CHORUS: 5 odes of Horace, 1924; Pueri Hebraeorum, women's voices, 1928; Rosemary, women's voices, 1929; Americana, 1932; The peaceable kingdom, a cappella, 1936; Tarantella, men's voices, 1937; The lark in the morn, 1938; Alieluia, 1940; The testament of freedom, men's voices, 1943; The last words of David, with orch., 1949; Mass of the Holy Spirit, 1955; Ode to the Virginian voyage, 1956, Requiem, 1958; Frostiana, with orch., 1959; The mirror of St. Anne, antiphonal setting of Isaac Watts text in inverse contrary imitation; The passion according to St. Luke, oratorio, 1961, Boston, 28 Mar. 1965.
22 Larch Rd., Cambridge, MA 02138

THOMPSON, VAN DENMAN

THOMPSON, VAN DENMAN
b. Andover, N.H., 10 Dec. 1890. Studied at
Colby Acad.; Harvard Univ., 1908-9; New England
Cons., 1909-10. He received a Nat. Fed. of
Music Clubs prize, 1919; honorary D.M., DePauw
Univ., 1935; and commissions; was a fellow of
the American Guild of Organists. He was faculty
member, Woodland Coll., 1910-11; from 1911, professor, DePauw Univ. His compositions include
The evangel of the new world, oratorio, 1934;
church anthems, organ and piano pieces.

THOMSON, MILLARD S.
b. Hartford, Conn., 13 Aug. 1918. Studied at
Wesleyan Univ., B.A.; with Isadore Freed and
Arnold Franchetti, Hartt Coll. of Music, M.M.;
with H. Owen Reed and Paul Harder, Michigan
State Univ., Ph.D. 1964. He was faculty member,
Brown Univ., 1949-56; Michigan State Univ.,
1964-65; from 1965, at Plymouth State Coll.
WORKS: THEATRE: Give it a whirl, musical
play; CHAMBER MUSIC: Epitaph, violin and piano;
Meadow interval, song cycle; Shadows of autumn,
cantata; Introduction and dance, clarinet and
piano; CHORUS: Break forth into joy, anthem.
20 Avery St., Plymouth, NH 03264

THOMSON, VIRGIL
b. Kansas City, Mo., 25 Nov. 1896. Studied at
Harvard Univ., A.B. 1922; with Nadia Boulanger
in Paris. His awards include Officer, Legion
of Honor, France; Nat. Inst. of Arts and Letters
Gold Medal; honorary doctorates, Syracuse Univ.,
1949, Rutgers Univ., 1956, Columbia Univ., 1978;
membership, American Acad. of Arts and Letters;
MacDowell Medal, 1977. He was organist, King's
Chapel, Boston, 1923-24; lived in Paris for 10
years; was writer on music for many publications;
music critic for the New York Times, 1940-54.
WORKS: OPERA: 4 saints in 3 acts, text by
Gertrude Stein, Hartford, Conn., 8 Feb. 1934;
The mother of us all, Stein text, 1947; Lord
Byron, 1970, Juilliard School, 20 Apr. 1972;
BALLET: Filling station, 1937; ORCHESTRA: 2
symphonies, 1928, 1941; 5 suites; The Seine at
night, 1948; Wheatfield at noon, 1948; cello
concerto, 1949; Fugues and cantilenas; Sea piece
with birds, 1952; 5 songs, voice and orch., 1952;
concerto for flute, strings, percussion, 1954;
The feast of love, baritone and orch., 1964;
BAND: A solemn music and a joyful fugue, 1949;
CHAMBER MUSIC: Sonata da chiesa, 5 instruments,
1926; 5 portraits for 4 clarinets, 1929; violin
sonata, 1930; 4 portraits, violin and piano,
1931; 2 string quartets, 1931, 1932; 4 piano
sonatas; Serenade, flute and violin; organ and
piano pieces; CHORUS: Capital capitals; Masses;
Medea; Missa pro defunctis, 1960; Cantata based
on nonsense rhymes, Towson State Coll., Md.,
18 Nov. 1973; FILM SCORES: The plow that broke
the plains, 1936; The river, 1937; Louisiana
story, 1948; The goddess, 1957; Power among men,
1958; Voyage to America, 1964. He is author of
the following books: State of music, 1939; The
musical scene, 1945; The art of judging music,
1948; Music right and left, 1951; Virgil Thomson,
an autobiography, 1967; American music since
1910, 1971.
222 W. 23rd St., New York, NY 10011

THOMSON, WILLIAM
b. Ft. Worth, Tex., 24 May 1927. Studied with
Bernhard Heiden, Indiana Univ., Ph.D. He re-
ceived Nat. Fed. of Music Clubs awards, Texas
Composers awards; and was Ford Found. composer-
in-residence, 1960-61. He was faculty member,
Sul Ross State Coll., 1951-60; Indiana Univ.,
1961-69; Univ. of Hawaii, 1967-68; Case Western
Reserve Univ. and Cleveland Inst. of Music,
1969-73; Univ. of Arizona, 1973-75; then at
State Univ. of New York, Buffalo.
WORKS: ORCHESTRA: Transformations; Fantasia
and dance, clarinet and orch. (or piano); BAND:
Permutations; CHORUS: Desert seasons.
State University of New York, Buffalo, NY
14214

THORNE, FRANCIS
b. Bay Shore, N.Y., 23 June 1922. Studied with
Paul Hindemith and Richard Donovan, Yale Univ.,
1939-42; with David Diamond in Florence, Italy,
1959-61. His awards include American Acad. and
Nat. Inst. of Arts and Letters grant, 1968; New
York State Council on the Arts grant, 1974; Nat.
Endowment for the Arts grant, 1974, 1976. He was
executive director, Naumburg Found., 1969-72;
Lenox Arts Center, 1972-75; from 1975, American
Composers Alliance; on Juilliard School faculty,
1971-73; from 1965, president of the Thorne
Music Fund.
WORKS: THEATRE: Fortuna, musical play;
Opera buffa for opera buffs, chamber opera;
Prufrock (After the teacups), ballet; Echoes of
Spoon River, ballet; ORCHESTRA: 4 symphonies,
1961, 1964, 1969, 1977; Burlesque overture, 1964;
Rhapsodic variations, piano and orch., 1965; 2
piano concertos, 1966, 1973; double concerto for
viola, double bass, and orch., 1968; Sonar plexus,
electric guitar and orch., 1968; Liebesrock, 3
electric guitars and orch., 1969; Antiphonies,
4 instrumental groups, 1970; Song of the Carolina
Low Country, with chorus, Charleston, 13 Feb.
1971; Fanfare, fugue and funk, 3 trumpets and
orch., 1972; cello concerto, 1974; violin concerto, Aptos, Calif., 20 Aug. 1976; Pop partita,
Brooklyn Philharmonia, 2 Feb. 1979; CHAMBER
MUSIC: Chamber deviations I, clarinet, double
bass, percussion, 1968; Songs and dances, cello,
keyboard instruments, percussion, 1969; 3 string
quartets; Nocturnes, voice and string quartet;
Chamber deviations II, brass quintet, guitar,
percussion, 1971; Simultaneities, brass quintet,
guitar, percussion, 1971; piano sontata, 1972,
New York premiere, 23 July 1976; Lyric variations II, woodwind quintet, percussion; Lyric
variations III, piano trio, New York, 13 Mar.
1973; Evensongs, 5 instruments, New York, 25
Mar. 1973; Cantata sauce, 2 vocalists and chamber
group, 1973; 6 set pieces for 13 players; Songs
of the Great South Bay, soprano and 2 clarinets,
New Yrok, 8 May 1974; Head music, clarinet,
cello, piano, New York, 4 May 1977.
116 E. 66th St., New York, NY 10021

THORNTON, WILLIAM J.
b. Birmingham, Ala., 31 July 1919. Studied with
Helen Gunderson and Joyce Michelle, Louisiana
State Univ., B.M. 1941, M.M. 1946; with Halsey

Stevens, Ingolf Dahl, and Roger Sessions, Univ. of Southern California, Ph.D. 1953. His awards include first prize, Nat. Fed. of Music Clubs; Carolyn Alchin award; Western Composers award; Composers of Louisiana award; Archives of Texas Composers award; and commissions. He was faculty member, Univ. of Minnesota, 1955-56; Parsons Coll., 1956-60; from 1960, chairman, music dept., Trinity Univ.

WORKS: ORCHESTRA: Symphonic dance; Introduction and dance; Festive music; Contrastes Mexicanos; symphony #1; Serenade, winds and percussion; CHAMBER MUSIC: violin sonatina; cello sonata; 2 string quartets; harpsichord sonata; piano sonata; Serenade, clarinet and flute.
347 Sharon Dr., San Anotnio, TX 78216

THREATTE, CHARLES
b. Atlanta, Ga., 15 Feb. 1940. Studied with John Boda and Carlisle Floyd, Florida State Univ.; with Charles Jones and Darius Milhaud at Aspen, Colo. He received first prize, Florida Composers League contest, 1960; prizes, Aspen Composers contests, 1969, 1970, 1972. He was composer-in-residence, Youth Experimental Opera Workshop, Atlanta, 1970; choirmaster, Presbyterian Church, 1973-74; adjunct instructor and consultant, Rollins Coll., 1974.

WORKS: ORCHESTRA: Processionals, 1970; Symphonies of carols, Orlando, Fla., 10 Dec. 1971; Fantasy, Orlando, 2 May 1974; WIND ENSEMBLE: 3 antiphonies, 2 brass choirs, Aspen, Colo., 19 July 1973; CHAMBER MUSIC: flute sonata, 1959; Introduction and scherzo, brass quartet, 1965; Ode, horn and piano, 1967; 3 miniatures, flute solo, 1968; Fantasy, flute, harp, viola, 1969; Prelude, ode, and postlude, flute and harp, 1972; Serenade, flute, oboe, bassoon, 1973; also vocal works.
1530 Woodland Ave., Winter Park, FL 32789

TIERNEY, HARRY AUSTIN
b. Perth Amboy, N.J., 21 May 1890; d. New York, N.Y., 22 Mar. 1965. Studied at the Virgil Cons., New York; was for a while concert pianist; then turned to composing popular songs and musical shows.

WORKS: BALLET: Prelude to a holiday in Hong Kong; MUSICAL COMEDIES: Irene, 1919; Ziegfield follies, 1919, 1920, 1924; The Broadway whirl, 1922; Up she goes, 1922; Kid boots, 1923; Río Rita, 1927; Royal vagabond; SONGS: M-i-s-s-i-s-s-i-p-p-i, 1916; If you're in love you'll waltz; and many others.

TIETJENS, PAUL
b. St. Louis, Mo., 22 May 1877; d. St. Louis, 25 Nov. 1943. Studied piano with Leschetizky and Bauer. He was soloist with the St. Louis Symphony at 14; taught privately; was music director, Maude Adams productions, 1916-19, 1930.

WORKS: OPERA: The tents of the Arabs; THEATRE: The wizard of Oz; music for Barrie's Kiss for Cinderella; ORCHESTRA: Carnival; Rustic sketches; and songs.

TILLIS, FREDERICK C.
b. Galveston, Tex., 5 Jan. 1930. Studied at

Wiley Coll., B.A. cum laude 1949; with Philip Bezanson, Univ. of Iowa, M.A. 1952, Ph.D. 1963; with Samuel Adler, North Texas State Univ., summers, 1959, 1960. His awards include United Negro Coll. Fund fellowships, 1961, 1962; Danforth associateship, 1969; Rockefeller Found. grant, 1978; and commissions. He served in U.S. Air Force, band director, 1954-56; has held faculty posts at Wiley Coll., 1949-64; Grambling Coll., 1964-67; Kentucky State Coll., 1967-69; from 1969, at Univ. of Massachusetts, Amherst; consultant and summer lecturer, Regis Coll.

WORKS: ORCHESTRA: Designs for orchestra, 1963; Ring shout concerto, percussionist and orch., 1973-74; Spiritual cycle, soprano and orch., 1978; BAND: Overture to a dance, 1961; Celebration, a grand march, 1966; JAZZ ENSEMBLE: One dozen rocks, inc., 1971; Metamorphosis on Bach, 1972; Blue stone differencia, 1972; Seton concerto, for trumpet, 1973; The blue express, 1973; Navarac, 1974; Secreta of the African Baobob, 1976; Koor variations, 1977; piano concerto, 1977; Fantasy, on a theme by Julian Adderley, 1975; CHAMBER MUSIC: Passacaglia, brass quintet, 1950; quartet for 3 woodwinds and cello, 1952; Fantasy, viola and piano, 1962; brass quintet, 1962; quintet for 4 woodwinds and percussion, 1962; 3 movements for piano, 1964; Motions, trombone and piano, 1964; Music for tape recorder #1, 1968; 3 plus 1, violin, guitar, clarinet, tape recorder, 1969; Poems for piano, 1970; Music for violin, cello, and piano, 1972; Niger symphony, chamber orch., 1974; also works for chorus and solo voice.
55 Grantwood Dr., Amherst, MA 01002

TIMM, KENNETH
b. San Francisco, Calif., 2 Nov. 1934. Studied with Glenn Glasow, Robert Erickson, Darius Milhaud, and Luciano Berio in the San Francisco area; with John Eaton and Bernhard Heiden, Indiana Univ. His awards include prizes in the World Saxophone Congress contest, 1972; Arizona Cello Society and American Society of Univ. Composers contest, 1975; Frederick Delius award, 1973. He has been faculty member, Univ. of Nebraska, 1972; Lawrence Univ., 1973-74; Cleveland State Univ., 1974-76; from 1976, at Eastern Kentucky Univ.

WORKS: ORCHESTRA: Trichotomy; CHAMBER MUSIC: Across a circle, piano; 6 miniatures, 6 winds; sextet for 2 harps, 2 pianos; 2 percussion; Piece B, percussion quartet; The joiner and the diehard, percussion quartet, 1972; woodwind quintet, 1972; The force that through the green fuse drives the flower, 1973; Other streams, 4 cellos, 1974.
Eastern Kentucky University, Richmond, KY 40475

TIOMKIN, DMITRI
b. St. Petersburg, Russia, 10 May 1894; U.S. citizen 1937; d. London, 11 Nov. 1979. Studied at St. Petersburg Cons. and St. Petersburg Univ. His numerous awards include L.L.D., St. Mary's Univ.; Chevalier, French Legion of Honor; Hollywood Foreign Press Club awards, 1952, 1954, 1956; Greater Los Angeles Press Club award, 1959;

TIPEI, SEVER

Christopher award, 1959; at least 3 Academy awards and several nominations for film scores. He was concert pianist and conductor; composed more than 160 film scores.
WORKS: FILM SCORES: Bridge of San Luis Rey; Duel in the sun; Mr Smith goes to Washington; Corsican brothers; Portrait of Jeannie; Lost horizon; Cyrano de Bergerac; Dial M for murder; The moon and sixpence; High noon, Academy award, 1952; The chameleon; The high and the mighty, Academy award, 1954; Wild is the wind; Friendly persuasion; Giant; The old man and the sea, Academy award, 1958; The big sky; The fourposter; The guns of Navarone; Search for paradise; 55 days at Peking. He published an autobiography, Please don't hate me, New York, 1959. In accepting his award for the score to The high and the mighty, Tiomkin delighted his audience, if not his composer colleagues, by thanking his 4 collaborators, "Bach, Beethoven, Brahms, and Debussy."

TIPEI, SEVER
b. Budapest, Romania, 1 Nov. 1943; to U.S. 1972, citizen 1978. Studied composition with Aurel Stroe, Bucharest Cons., M.A. 1967; William Albright, Univ. of Michigan, 1972-73. He was music critic in Bucharest, 1964-71, receiving an award from Amfiteatru magazine, 1968. He was instructor, Chicago Musical Coll., 1975-78; from 1978, on faculty at Univ. of Illinois, Champaign-Urbana.
WORKS: ORCHESTRA: Undulating Michigamme, soloists and orch.; CHAMBER MUSIC: piano sonata, 1968; Stanzas, 18 solo strings, 1969; Translation, voice, clarinet, prepared piano, 1970; Single tone, 5 musicians playing the same tone, 1971; Make your own music, for an amateur musician and an exotic wind instrument, 1973; Another little while, 16 solo voices, 1969; Melopoeia, solo voice, 1979; ELECTRONIC: Portrait of the artist, computer music for women's voices; Katastrophe, tape; Pardon my motski, 1978; Happy and . . ., tape; Les liaisons dangereuses, for 5 amateurs and computer-generated score.
1623 W. University Ave., Champaign, IL 61820

TIPTON, CLYDE
b. Richmond, Va., 17 Aug. 1934. Studied at Westminster Choir Coll., M.M.; privately with Roger Sessions; and with Darius Milhaud at Aspen, Colo. He was faculty member at Rider Coll. to 1975, then joined the faculty at Georgia Coll., Milledgeville.
WORKS: OPERA: aleatoric operatic scenes: Medea; The forced marriage, on Moliere text; THEATRE: Indian summer, musical for the young; ORCHESTRA: Graduation music, processional and progrediendum; CHAMBER MUSIC: In praise of, 5 brasses, organ, and bells; Sound scheme for strings; Span, violin, flute, cello; Chorale with transparencies, string quartet; CHORUS: Mod magnificat, women's voices; Hodie; O little town; And death shall have no dominion; 4 pounds, text by Ezra Pound.
Georgia College, Milledgeville, GA 31061

TIPTON, JULIUS R., III
b. Memphis, Tenn., 4 Mar. 1942. Studied with Charles Knox, Mississippi Coll., B.M. 1964; with Kenneth Klaus, Louisiana State Univ., M.M. 1967; with William L. Hooper, New Orleans Baptist Seminary, Ed.D. 1972. He then joined the faculty at Xavier Univ. of Louisiana; has been music director, Woodland Presbyterian Church, from 1969.
WORKS: OPERA: Judas; ORCHESTRA: Variazioni da chiesa; CHORUS: He is coming; Be thou my vision, O Lord; A song of praise; God is our refuge and strength; and songs.
Xavier Univ., Palmetto and Pine Sts., New Orleans, LA 70125

TIRCUIT, HEUWELL (ANDREW)
b. Plaquemine, La., 18 Oct. 1931. Studied at Louisiana State Univ.; Northwestern Univ., M.M. 1964. He played drums from early boyhood; was percussionist, U.S. Army bands, 1954-56; played percussion in Japanese orchestras, and wrote music criticism for Japanese newspapers, 1956-63; then was critic for the Chicago Tribune, later the San Francisco Chronicle.
WORKS: BALLET: The lonely people, 1950; Argument, 1959; ORCHESTRA: Manga, suite, 1959; cello concerto, 1960; A singing of instruments, 1960; Knell, 27 solo flutes and percussion, 1962; Dance patterns, with solo percussion, 1962; Chronological variations, 1963; a cycle of 6 concertos, 1966-72; Fool's dance, with solo percussion, 1967; percussion concerto, 1969; concerto for violin and 10 wind instruments, 1971; Symphony concertante, 1976; CHAMBER MUSIC: 3 string quartets, 1953, 1957, 1976; trumpet sonata, 1954; string trio, 1960; violin sonata, 1960; viola sonata, 1961; Erotica I, solo alto flute, 1961; Cassation, cello and wind quintet, 1961; flute sonata, 1968; Erotica II, solo percussion, 1970; Erotica III, solo cello, 1971; Halcyon, flute and piano, 1975; CHORUS: 3 cantatas, 1959, 1962, 1967.
221 Longford Dr., San Francisco, CA 94101

TIRRO, FRANK PASCALE
b. Omaha, Nebr., 20 Sept. 1935. Studied with Robert Beadell, Univ. of Nebraska; with Anthony Donata and Frank Cookson, Northwestern Univ.; and with Leonard B. Meter, Univ. of Chicago. He received the Ida Vreeland award, 1960; Nat. Fed. of Music Clubs award, 1961; Harvard Univ. Villa I. Tatti fellowship, 1970-71; ASCAP awards, 1970, 1971, 1973. He was faculty member, Univ. of Chicago, 1961-70; Univ. of Kansas, 1971-72; from 1972, at Duke Univ., music chairman, from 1974.
WORKS: BALLET: Exorcise; Masque of the red death; ORCHESTRA: symphony, 1973; CHAMBER MUSIC: Antiphonal suite, organ and brass; clarinet sonata; CHORUS: American jazz mass; American jazz Te Deum; Sing a new song; KEYBOARD: Church sonata, organ; Melismas, carillon.
Music Dept., Duke University, Durham, NC 27708

TITCOMB, CALDWELL
b. Augusta, Maine, 16 Aug. 1926. Studied with Walter Piston, Harvard Univ., A.B. 1947, M.A.

1949, Ph.D. 1952. He received the Detur award and the Carl Schurz prize. He has been on the Brandeis Univ. music faculty from 1958. His compositions include incidental music for many plays; an organ sonata; oboe sonatina; Yuki, a Japanese song cycle; etc.
    67 Windermere Rd., Auburndale, MA 02166

TITCOMB, EVERETT
    b. Amesbury, Mass., 30 June 1884; d. Boston, Mass., 31 Dec. 1968. He was the first American to have a composition performed at the Annual Festival of Church Music in London, where in 1936, massed choirs sang his I will not leave you comfortless at the Crystal Palace. He received an honorary doctorate of music from Nashotah House Seminary in 1954. His experiences as choir boy at 9, church organist at 16, choirmaster at 18, led to acceptance of the post of organist-choirmaster at the Church of St. John the Evangelist, Boston, in 1910, a position he held until retirement in 1960. For a time, he also served as music director of the Canterbury Choir at Trinity Church, Boston, and taught courses in liturgical music at Boston Univ. and the New England Cons. His published compositions include some 150 works for organ and choir.

TITTLE, JOHN STEPHEN
    b. Willard, Ohio, 20 May 1935. Studied with Harold Miles and John White, Kent State Univ.; with Hilmar Luckhardt, Robert Crane, and Burt Levy, Univ. of Wisconsin, M.M. He held graduate fellowships at Univ. of Wisconsin; from 1970, has been on faculty, Dalhousie Univ.; heads his own experimental music group, Murphy's Law.
    WORKS: ORCHESTRA: . . . and it always will be . . ., with solo percussion, 1973; CHAMBER MUSIC: string quartet, 1966; Morning music, horn and percussion, 1967; Summer music, double bass, marimba, percussion, 1968; Last song and dance for Sita, 16 players, 1968; Moondance (curious), flute, oboe, piano, percussion, 1972; It is there all the time, double bass and harpsichord, 1972; This time/that time, 4 brass, piano, percussion, 1973; Where there is no other (only we), piano trio, 1976; Just 1 more dance, vibraphone, 2 marimbas, percussion, 1977; Let it shine all the time, string quartet and vibraphone, 1977; VOICE: Winter's not forever, soprano, female speaker, 6 players, 1971; . . . his circle completed . . ., 2 choirs, 2 speakers, small orch., 1972; i asked her where and she said right here, singer/actress, percussion, violin, tape, 1975; Orange-blossom book, mezzo-soprano, 5 winds, percussion, 1976.
    Boutilier's Pt., Halifax County, Nova Scotia, Canada

TOCH, ERNST
    b. Vienna, Austria, 7 Dec. 1887; U.S. citizen 1940; d. Los Angeles, Calif., 1 Oct. 1964. First studied medicine and philosophy, Univ. of Vienna and Univ. of Heidelberg, Ph.D.; taught himself music at an early age; later gave up medicine to become piano teacher and composer. His awards include the Mozart prize, 1909; Mendelssohn prize, 1910; Austrian State prize,

4 times; Pulitzer prize, 1956; membership, Nat. Inst. of Arts and Letters. He was lecturer, New School for Social Research, 1934-36; professor, Univ. of Southern California, 1937-48; also taught privately and composed for films.
    WORKS: OPERA: The princess and the pea, 1927; Egon and Emilie, 1928; The fan, 1930; THEATRE: Enamoured Harlequin, puppet show, 1964; ORCHESTRA: Pinocchio, a merry overture, 1936; Hyperion, 1948; 7 symphonies, 1950, 1951, 1955, 1957, 1963, 1963, 1964; Notturno, 1953; Peter Pan, 1956; Symphony for strings, 1964; 3 pantomimes, 1964; CHAMBER MUSIC: 13 string quartets, 1902-53; piano quintet, 1938; Poems to Martha, voice and strings, 1946; many other chamber works; CHORUS: The water, oratorio, 1930; Bitter herbs, with soloists, narrator, and orch., 1941; numerous other choral works; piano compositions.

TODD, GEORGE BENNETT
    b. Minneapolis, Minn., 31 May 1935. Studied with Roger Sessions, Earl Kim, J. K. Randall, and Milton Babbitt, Princeton Univ., M.M. He has been faculty member, Middlebury Coll., from 1965; was executive director of Composers Conf. and Chamber Music Center, 1974-76.
    WORKS: ORCHESTRA: Gazebo music; CHAMBER MUSIC: Haiku settings, voice and chamber ensemble, 1968; Elisions, chamber ensemble, 1969; Sequentials, any large ensemble, 1972; ELECTRONIC: Variations for computer synthesizer; Sunscape, tape; KK, tape.
    R.D. 3, Middlebury, VT 05753

TOENSING, RICHARD E.
    b. St. Paul, Minn., 11 Mar. 1940. Studied with Ross Lee Finney, Leslie Bassett, George B. Wilson, Univ. of Michigan, D.M.A. He received BMI student awards, 1963, 1964; Joseph Bearns prize, Columbia Univ., 1965; and commissions. He was faculty member, Upsala Coll., 1966-73; from 1973, at Univ. of Colorado.
    WORKS: BAND: Doxologies, 1965, Cornell Univ., Apr. 1971; For all the wild things, 1972; CHAMBER MUSIC: Homages, chamber orch.; CHORUS: Easter motet, with tape; 16-voice mass; PIANO: Sycamore shade blue rag; All-Upsala banquet tablecloth wiping-up rag; ORGAN: Sounds and changes II and III; Doxologies II; several multimedia pieces.
    600 Ithaca Dr., Boulder, CO 80303

TORCASO, ENRICO
    b. New Kensington, Pa., 27 Nov. 1936. Studied with Joseph Willcox Jenkins, Duquesne Univ.; with Frank McCarty, Univ. of Pittsburgh. He was teaching fellow, Univ. of Pittsburgh, then joined the faculty at Duquesne Univ.
    WORKS: ORCHESTRA: Introduction and allegro; CHAMBER MUSIC: Divertimento for octet, string quartet and woodwind quartet; Ellipse, brass quintet; Refractions, cello, piano, percussion.
    1632 Victoria Ave., Arnold, PA 15068

TOURS, FRANK
    b. London, England, 1 Sept. 1877; to U.S. 1904; d. Santa Monica, Calif., 2 Feb. 1963. Studied

TOWER, JOAN

at the Royal Cons. in London. He was director
of Broadway shows; then music director and composer for Paramount Music Corporation. He wrote
musicals and many well-known songs, the latter
including In Flanders Fields.

TOWER, JOAN
b. New Rochelle, N.Y., 6 Sept. 1938. Studied
with Henry Brant and Louis Calabro, Bennington
Coll., B.A.; with Otto Luening, Jack Beeson, and
Chou Wen-chung, Columbia Univ., M.A., D.M.A.;
with Darius Milhaud at Aspen, Colo.; and with
Wallingford Riegger, Ralph Shapey, and Charles
Wuorinen in New York. Her awards include a
MacDowell fellowship, 1974; 2 Nat. Endowment for
the Arts grants, 1974, 1975; Guggenheim fellowship, 1977-78; and commissions. She was lecturer, C. W. Post Coll., 1968-72; then at Bard
Coll.; was founder of Da Capo Chamber Players,
1970, then president and pianist.
    WORKS: ORCHESTRA: Composition, for orch.,
1967; CHAMBER MUSIC: Pillars, 2 pianos and percussion, 1961; string quartet, 1962; Study, 2
strings, 2 winds, 1963; percussion quartet, 1963,
rev. 1969; Circles, piano, 1964; Brimset, 2
flutes, percussion, 1965; Composition for oboe,
1965; Fantasia, piano, 1966; Opa eboni, oboe and
piano, 1967; Movements, flute and piano, 1968;
Prelude for 5 players, 1970; 6 variations, for
cello, 1971; Hexachords, flute, 1972; Breakfast
rhythms I and II, clarinet and 5 instruments,
1974-75; Platinum spirals, violin, 1976; Black
topaz, piano and 6 instruments, 1976; Red garnet
waltz, piano, 1977; Amazon, flute, violin,
clarinet, cello, and piano, 1977.
    124 Wooster St., New York, NY 10012

TOWNSEND, DOUGLAS
b. New York, N.Y., 8 Nov. 1921. Graduated from
High School of Music and Art, 1941; studied
privately with Tibor Serly, Stefan Wolpe, and
Felix Greissle in New York; with Aaron Copland
at Tanglewood; and with Otto Luening at Bennington. He held scholarships for Tanglewood, 1947,
and for Bennington Composers Conf., 1949, 1950.
He was lecturer, Brooklyn Coll., 1958-69; Lehman
Coll., 1970-71; then editor, arranger, musicologist, and composer.
    WORKS: OPERA: Lima beans, chamber opera,
New York, 7 Jan. 1956; ORCHESTRA: Fantasy,
small orch., 1951; Adagio for strings, 1956;
Symphony for string orch., New York, 29 Nov.
1958; Chamber symphony #1; suite for strings,
New York, 8 Dec. 1973; CHAMBER MUSIC: Ballet
suite, 3 clarinets, 1956; Tower music, brass
quintet, 1957; Dance improvisation, and fugue,
flute and piano; 8x8 variations on a theme by
Milhaud; Chamber concerto #1, violin and string
quartet, 1957; Chamber concerto #2, trombone and
strings; 4 fantasies on American folk songs,
piano, 4 hands, 1957, later orchestrated; duo
for violas, 1957.

TRACK, GERHARD
b. Vienna, Austria, 17 Sept. 1934; to U.S. 1958.
Studied with Otto Siegl and Alfred Uhl, Vienna
Acad. of Music. His awards include second
prize in the Austrian State Radio Network com-

petition for sacred music, 1970; Golden Honorary
Cross, Republic of Austria, 1974. He was conductor, Vienna Boys Choir, 1953-58; faculy member, orchestra and choral director, St. John's
Univ., Collegeville, Minn., 1958-69; music
director, Metropolitan Youth Symphony, Minneapolis, 1965-69; from 1969, on faculty, Univ. of
Southern Colorado, and conductor, Pueblo Civic
Symphony Assoc.
    WORKS: ORCHESTRA: In dulci jubilo, over-
ture; Festlisches Spiel, piano and orch., 1955;
Prelude, march and chorale, 1957; Hymnus, 1958;
CHAMBER MUSIC: violin sonata; CHORUS: Festive
ordinary, with orch.; The colors of spring; 7
stars of the Assiniboine, with orch.; Mass in
honor of the Queen of Peace, 1966; ORGAN: Festival prelude and fugue.
    130 Baylor, Pueblo, CO 81005

TRAFFORD, EDMUND
b. Grand Rapids, Mich., 24 Sept. 1948. Studied
with Gerald Lloyd, U.S. Internat. Univ., San
Diego; with Lukas Foss, Scott Huston, Paul
Palombo, Antin Rudnytsky, Cincinnati Coll.-Cons.
His awards include the Lundstrom-Young prize,
California Olympiad of the Arts, 1972; ASCAP
Raymond Hubbell grant, 1976; many commissions.
He held teaching posts at Western Michigan Univ.,
1968-69; U.S. Internat. Univ., 1969-71; Cincinnati Coll.-Cons., 1974-76.
    WORKS: THEATRE: music for Midsummer night's
dream, 1970; Triangle, ballet, 1972; CHAMBER
MUSIC: Introduction and allegro, clarinet and
piano, 1971; 3 songs on texts by A. E. Housman,
bass-baritone and piano; Fanfare and variations,
solo trumpet, 1974; Descent to perihelion, oboe,
piano, 2 tape recorders; trio for solo clarinet,
1974; Frescoes, piano and/or 11 performers,
1976; Wynde, flute, oboe, cello, harp, 1977;
Xanthe II, chamber orch., 1978; CHORUS: Madrigal, 1972; Requiem, 1979.
    1833 Yorktown Rd., Cincinnati, OH 45237

TRAUGH, STEVEN DUDLEY
b. Fairmont, W.Va., 6 Feb. 1950. Studied per-
cussion with Philip Faini, composition with
Thomas Canning, West Virginia Univ., B.M. 1971,
M.M. 1975; composition with Marie Pooler and
William Kraft in California. His awards include
Phi Mu Alpha, music honorary; Nat. Endowment for
the Arts grant, 1974; West Virginia Arts and
Humanities Council grant, 1974; commissions;
many awards as percussionist. From 1975 he has
been percussion specialist with the Montebello
Unified School District and Santa Ana Coll.
    WORKS: ORCHESTRA: timpani concerto, 1972;
East African symphony, 1974; Reflection for
orchestra, 1974; Fanfare and dance, 1975; BAND:
Appalachian uprising, 1973; PERCUSSION ENSEMBLE:
2 in 3 for 4, percussion quartet, 1969; Double
toccata, drum set and roto toms, 1972; Adventures, 1976; Improvisational designs, solo percussionist, 1975; Chronology for symphonic percussion, 1977; and many transcriptions.
    622 N. Howard Ave., #110, Montebello, CA
90640

TRAVER, JAMES FERRIS
b. Valley Stream, N.Y., 28 May 1929. Studied with Felix Deyo, Frank Wigglesworth, and Hall Overton. He received awards in a Rochester Festival of the Arts and a Delius Festival. He is a businessman.
WORKS: ORCHESTRA: Meditation on a sacred subject; From the New England hills; Cape Cod sketches; An Appalachian symphony; WIND ENSEMBLE: 2 songs of the sea; A Keltic suite; CHORUS: Praise the Lord our King; Christ the Lord, e'er reigneth; Thanks be to thee; and many others.
92 N. Pocono Rd., Mountain Lakes, NJ 07046

TRAVIS, ROY
b. New York, N.Y., 24 June 1922. Studied with Otto Luening, Columbia Univ., A.B. 1947, M.A. 1951; with Felix Salzer and Bernard Wagenaar, Juilliard School, B.S. 1949, M.S. 1950; and with Darius Milhaud in Paris on a Fulbright grant. Other awards include first prize, 7th annual Gershwin contest; Guggenheim fellowship, 1972; Martha Baird Rockefeller grant; Ford Found. grant; Nat. Endowment for the Arts grant; ASCAP awards. He was instructor, Columbia Univ., 1952-53; Mannes Coll. of Music, 1953-57; from 1957, on faculty, Univ. of California, Los Angeles.
WORKS: OPERA: The passion of Oedipus, to his own libretto, 1965; ORCHESTRA: Collage, 1968; piano concerto, 1970; CHAMBER MUSIC: Songs and epilogues, cycle of 5 songs on translations from Sappho, voice and piano, 1965, orchestral version, 1975; African sonata, piano, 1966; Duo concertante, violin and piano, 1967; Barma, septet, 1968; Switched-on Ashanti, live flute and tape, 1973; 5 preludes for piano.
16680 Charmel Lane, Pacific Palisades, CA 90272

TREHARNE, BRYCESON
b. Merthyr Tydfil, Wales, 30 May 1879; to U.S. 1927; d. New York, N.Y., 4 Feb. 1948. Studied on scholarship at Royal Coll. of Music, London; received an honorary D.M. from McGill Univ. He taught at Univ. of Adelaide, 1900-11; spent 3 years in a German prison camp in World War I; was lecturer at McGill Univ., 1923-27; from 1928, editor for Boston Music Co. and Willis Music Co.
WORKS: OPERETTA: The toymaker; Abe Lincoln; A Christmas carol; CHORUS: Song of Solomon, oratorio; The banshee; Again in unison we stand; Song's eternity; Mount you horses; and songs.

TREMBLAY, GEORGE
b. Ottawa, Ont., 14 Jan. 1911; to U.S. 1919. Studied organ with his father; composition with Arnold Schoenberg in Los Angeles.
WORKS: ORCHESTRA: 3 symphonies, 1949, 1952, 1970; CHAMBER MUSIC: 4 string quartets, 1936-63; 2 wind quintets, 1940, 1950; piano quartet, 1958; piano trio, 1959; quartet for oboe, clarinet, bassoon, viola, 1964; string trio, 1964; duo for viola and piano, 1966; double bass sonata, 1967; wind sextet, 1968; 3 piano sonatas.
22852 Crespi St., Woodland Hills, CA 91364

TRIGGS, HAROLD M.
b. Denver, Colo., 25 Dec. 1900. Studied at Univ. of Chicago; with Rubin Goldmark at Juilliard School; piano with Josef and Rosina Lhevinne. In 1932 he toured the U.S. with Vera Brodsky in a 2-piano team; was on faculty at Columbia; from 1970, teaching associate.
WORKS: ORCHESTRA: The bright land, string orch., New York, 29 Mar. 1942; PIANO: 2 sonatas, 1951, 1953; 18 preludes.
Music Dept., Columbia Univ., New York, NY 10027

TRIMBLE, LESTER ALBERT
b. Bangor, Wis., 29 Aug. 1923. Studied with Nikolai Lopatnikoff, Carnegie Inst. of Technology; with Darius Milhaud at Tanglewood and in Paris; with Arthur Honegger in Paris. His awards include the Wechsler commission at Tanglewood, 1959; Nat. Inst. of Arts and Letters award, 1961; BMI commission, 1971; selection as first occupant of the Composers' Cabin, Wolf Trap Farm, Vienna, Va., 1973; Martha Baird Rockefeller grant for work at MacDowell Colony, 1978. He was faculty member, Univ. of Maryland; from 1972, at Juilliard School.
WORKS: ORCHESTRA: 2 symphonies, 1951, 1968; violin concerto, 1955; Closing piece, 1957; 5 episodes, 1961; Sonic landscape; Panels VII, Milwaukee, 17 Dec. 1976; CHAMBER MUSIC: 3 string quartets, 1950, 1955, 1975 (#3 titled Panels V); sextet for woodwinds, horn, piano, 1952; Kennedy concerto, chamber orch., 1964; Solo for a virtuoso, violin solo, 1971; Panels I, chamber orch., Tanglewood, 7 Aug. 1973; Panels III, 6 instruments, New York, 17 May 1979; Panels IV, 16 players, 1974; Serenade (Panels VII), chamber ensemble, New York, 23 Apr. 1976; CHORUS: 4 fragments from Canterbury Tales, men's voices, soprano and instruments, 1958; In praise of diplomacy and common sense, baritone, percussion, male speaking chorus, 2 speaking soloists, 1965; Petit concert, with instruments; Cradle song, female voices and organ.
98 Riverside Dr., New York, NY 10024

TRINKHAUS, GEORGE J.
b. Bridgeport, Conn., 13 Apr. 1878; d. Ridgewood, N.J., 19 May 1960. Studied at Yale Univ.; was music editor in New York.
WORKS: OPERA: Wizard of Avon; ORCHESTRA: 2 symphonies; several overtures; Rhapsody, with solo violin; 5 suites; BAND: several overtures and other pieces; songs.

TROGAN, ROLAND
b. Saginaw, Mich., 6 Aug. 1933. Studied with Ross Lee Finney and Leslie Bassett, Univ. of Michigan, D.M.A.; privately with Roger Sessions. His awards include the BMI opera award and a Louisville Orchestra award. He is president of his own music school in Staten Island.
WORKS: ORCHESTRA: 2 scenes for orchestra; CHAMBER MUSIC: sonata for solo violin, 1959; Piano nocturnes; piano sonata; The seafarer, solo cantata, 1966.
76 Walbrooke Ave., Staten Island, NY 10301

TROMBLY, PRESTON A.

TROMBLY, PRESTON A.
     b. Hartford, Conn., 30 Dec. 1945. Studied with
Charles Whittenberg, Univ. of Connecticut, B.M.;
with Bulent Arel and Mario Davidovsky, Yale
Univ., M.M. 1972; and with Goerge Crumb at
Tanglewood. His awards include BMI student
award, 1970; Tanglewood fellowship, 1970; Yale
Univ. awards; Bennington Composers' Conf. fellowship; Guggenheim fellowship, 1974; Nat. Endow-
ment for the Arts grants, 1972, 1974, 1976;
Fromm Found. grant, 1975. He was instructor,
Vassar Coll., spring 1972; composer-conductor,
Yale Repertory Theatre, fall-winter, 1972.
     WORKS: CHAMBER MUSIC: In memoriam Igor
Stravinsky, 4 woodwinds, violin, double bass,
1972; 4 pieces, violin and cello, 1972; trio for
flute, double bass, percussion, 1973; Trio da
camera, flute, cello, piano, 1975; The windmills
of Paris, flute, clarinet, piano trio, 1976;
ELECTRONIC: Kinetics I and II, tape; Kinetics
III, flute and tape, 1971.
     599 West End Ave., New York, NY 10024

TROUPIN, EDWARD
     b. Boston, Mass., 22 June 1925. Earned an A.B.
in mathematics at Harvard Univ.; studied composition with Ross Lee Finney, Univ. of Michigan,
M.M. He was faculty member, Ithaca Coll.,
1954-60; from 1960, at Univ. of Florida.
     WORKS: ORCHESTRA: Symphonic involutes,
Washington, D.C., 24 May 1976; An unconscious
arithmetic, chamber orch.; CHAMBER MUSIC: string
quartet; Introduction and dance, wind quintet;
Divertimento, trumpet, horn, trombone; duo for
trumpet and trombone.
     1411 N.W. 49 Terrace, Gainesville, FL 32605

TROXELL, JERRY
     b. Maryville, Mo., 28 Dec. 1936. Studied with
Philip Bezanson and Richard Hervig, Univ. of
Iowa; with George B. Wilson and Leslie Bassett,
Univ. of Michigan. He was public school music
teacher, 1957-65; on faculty, Northwest Missouri
State Univ., 1966; Albion Coll., 1967-72; from
1973, at Sangamon State Univ.
     WORKS: ORCHESTRA: Metamorphic preludes,
1972; CHAMBER MUSIC: Scherzo, trombone and
piano, 1962; Tanka, soprano and instruments,
1972; Eve's diary, clarinet, violin, piano,
1973; Vibrance, alto saxophone and tape, 1974.
     1121 W. Washington St., Springfield, IL
     62702

TRUBITT, ALLEN R.
     b. Chicago, Ill., 24 Aug. 1931. Studied with
Karel Jirak, Roosevelt Univ., M.Mus.Ed. 1953;
with Bernhard Heiden, Indiana Univ., D.M. 1964.
He received first prize, Greenwood Press competition; first prize, Rice Univ. 50th anniversary contest, 1962; first prize, Hawaii Bicentennial contest, 1976. He was faculty member,
Univ. of Pennsylvania, 1957-64; Univ. of Hawaii,
1964-76.
     WORKS: ORCHESTRA: 2 symphonies; overture,
1962; BAND: Mauri; Lingua franca; CHAMBER
MUSIC: string quartet; A posteriori, dance
piece for chamber orch.; CHORUS: Bontsha the
silent, staged cantata; Carol of the bird; Snow-

flakes; 3 songs on the shortness of life; Markings; The tide rises, the tide falls; An American
letter; Birds of passage; songs.
     920 Ward Ave., Honolulu, HI 96822

TRUDEAU, ALFRED H.
     b. Providence, R.I., 25 Aug. 1906. Studied
organ with Rene Viau in Providence, 1923-26;
was self-taught in composition, harmony, and
theory. He received Nat. Fed. of Music Clubs
awards, 1971, 1973. He is a minister.
     WORKS: CHAMBER MUSIC: Holiday at the
Spanish Missions, piano; The lost mate, song
cycle; violin sonata; Salutations, violin and
piano, WNYC Radio, New York, 21 Feb. 1972;
CHORUS: Mass in honor of St. James; ORGAN: 6
pieces in different styles; Suite on Marian
themes; Toccata in F; 50 preludes; many works
for piano, organ, strings, woodwinds, voice,
choir.
     1818 Coal Place S.E., Albuquerque, NM
     87106

TRUED, S. CLARENCE
     b. Ceresco, Nebr., 20 Apr. 1895. Studied at
Augustana Coll., B.M.; with Felix Borowski and
Percy Grainger, Chicago Musical Coll.; and with
Clarence Eddy in Chicago. He was piano soloist,
accompanist, and church organist.
     WORKS: BAND: The howitzer dinger; CHORUS:
Cantorio, with soloist, narrator, and orch.;
Faith, hope, love; On a snowy evening; and piano
pieces.

TRUESDELL, F. DONALD
     b. Marysville, Kans., 14 Sept. 1920. Studied
with Ross Lee Finney, Univ. of Michigan, B.M.
1950, M.M. 1951, M.M. in piano, 1952; with Wayne
Barlow, Eastman School of Music, D.M.A. 1960.
He held a scholarship at Univ. of Michigan, and
a fellowship for doctoral study at Eastman
School. He was faculty member, Washington State
Univ., 1952-58; from 1960, at Coll. of William
and Mary.
     WORKS: ORCHESTRA: piano concerto, 1951;
CHAMBER MUSIC: string quartet, 1950; piano
trio, 1960; 3 piano preludes; woodwind quintet.
     William and Mary Coll., Williamsburg, VA
     23185

TRYTHALL, GILBERT
     b. Knoxville, Tenn., 28 Oct. 1930. Studied with
David Van Vactor, Univ. of Tennessee, B.A. 1951;
with Wallingford Riegger, Northwestern Univ.,
M.M. 1952; with Robert Palmer, Cornell Univ.,
D.M.A. 1960. He has received commissions from
Ford Found., American Music Center, Knoxville
Symphony, Nashville Symphony, Georgia State
Brass Ens., and the Music Teachers Nat. Assoc.
He taught in public schools, 1950-53; served in
Air Force, 1953-57; was on faculty, Knox Coll.,
1960-64; George Peabody Coll. for Teachers,
1964-75; from 1976, at West Virginia Univ.
     WORKS: ORCHESTRA: A solemn chant, string
orch.; first symphony, 1958; harp concerto;
Dionysia; Fanfare and celebration; CHAMBER MUSIC:
string quartet in 1 movement; The music lesson,
opera buffa in 1 act; brass quintet; flute

sonata; <u>Metamorphosis</u>, piano suite; ELECTRONIC: <u>Music for aluminum rooms</u>, tape; <u>Nova sync</u>, band and tape; <u>Pulsions</u>, band and tape; <u>The electric womb</u>, tape; MULTIMEDIA: <u>The world, mother, and apple pie</u>, percussion, tape, film slides; <u>Parallax</u>, 4 to 40 brass, tape, audience, slides; <u>Chroma I</u>, orch., tape, slides; <u>Echospace</u>, brass, tape, films; also electronic film scores; He is author of <u>Electronic music: Principles and practice</u>, New York, 1973; and many articles.

905 W. Park Ave., WO, Morgantown, WV 26505

TRYTHALL, RICHARD
b. Knoxville, Tenn., 25 July 1939. Studied with David Van Vactor, Univ. of Tennessee, B.A. 1961; with Roger Sessions, Princeton Univ., M.M. 1963; with Boris Blacher in Berlin, 1963. His awards include Fulbright grant, 1963; Prix de Rome, 1964-67; Guggenheim fellowship, 1967; Naumburg award, 1972; commissions from Fromm Found./ Berkshire Music Center and Dorian Woodwind Quintet. Since 1968 he has been a free-lance composer-pianist in Italy; was member, Center for Creative and Performing Arts, SUNY, Buffalo, spring terms, 1972, 1973; from 1974, music liaison, American Acad. in Rome.

WORKS: ORCHESTRA: <u>Composition for piano and orch.</u>, 1965; <u>Penelope's monologue</u>, soprano and orch., 1966; <u>Costruzione per orchestra</u>, 1967; <u>Continuums</u>; CHAMBER MUSIC: <u>Coincidences</u>, piano, 1968; ELECTRONIC: suite for harpsichord and tape; <u>Divertimento</u>, woodwind quintet and tape; <u>Variations on a theme by Haydn</u>, woodwind quintet and tape, 1976; <u>Salute to the '50s</u>, percussion and tape, 1977; MULTIMEDIA: <u>Verse</u>, slides, film tape, 1972.

Via 4 Novembre 96, Roma 00187, Italy

TUBB, MONTE
b. Jonesboro, Ark., 5 Nov. 1933. Studied at Univ. of Arkansas; with Bernhard Heiden, Indiana Univ., M.M. He was faculty member, Tarkio Coll., 1960-64; Ford Found. composer-in-residence, Atlanta, Ga., 1964-66; from 1966, on faculty, Univ. of Oregon.

WORKS: ORCHESTRA: <u>Discourse in 2 moods</u>, string orch., 1966; <u>Concert piece</u>, 1967; <u>Orchestra suite</u>, 1972; BAND: <u>Sutras</u>, 1968; <u>Soundprint 15</u>, 1970; WIND ENSEMBLE: <u>3 variations on a short tune</u>, 1965; <u>Dialogue</u>, 1966; CHAMBER MUSIC: piano sonata, 1958; string quartet, 1959; <u>5 Haiku</u>, soprano and string quartet, 1965; <u>Song</u>, cello and piano, 1966; <u>Earthmessage 5</u>, cello and piano, 4 hands, 1973; CHORUS: <u>In just spring</u>, a cappella, 1962; <u>Gloria</u>, with 2 soli and orch., 1965; <u>Agnus Dei</u>, a cappella, 1965; <u>Libera me</u>, girls' voices and piano, 1966; <u>Soundpiece</u>, 36 voices, 1971; and songs.

University of Oregon, Eugene, OR 97403

TUCKER, GREGORY
b. New Philadelphia, Pa., 12 Oct. 1908; d. Westport, Mass., 7 July 1971. Studied with Reginald Owen Morris and Rosario Scalero, Curtis Inst. of Music; later with Hanns Eisler and Wallingford Riegger; piano with Leo Ornstein and Eduard Steuermann. His awards included a Guggenheim fellowship, 1957-58, and commissions. He held

faculty posts at Bennington Coll., 1933-46; Longy School of Music, 1946-70; music dept., Massachusetts Inst. of Technology, 1947-71; also taught piano at Harvard Coll., 1947-53, and Wellesley Coll., 1948-53.

WORKS: THEATRE: <u>Out of one happening</u>, dance, 1939; <u>Metropolitan Daily</u>, dance, 1939; <u>The king and the duke</u>, dance drama after Mark Twain, 1940; <u>The people, yes</u>, dance drama after Carl Sandburg, 1943; ORCHESTRA: concertino for piano and strings, 1958; BAND: <u>Centennial overture</u>, 1961; CHAMBER MUSIC: suite for violin and piano, 1958; concertino for piano and 11 instruments, 1958; wind quintet, 1963; trio for flute, cello, piano, 1964; <u>Merwan songs</u>, alto flute and piano, 1970.

TUCKER, TUI ST. GEORGE
WORKS: CHAMBER MUSIC: <u>Lift up your heads, ye mighty gates</u>, woodwind trio; <u>Drum taps</u>, cantata for baritone, 3 clarinets, piano, cello, drums; <u>Neujaker</u>, voice and viola; <u>Dezember</u>, voice and viola; recorder sonata; violin sonata; double sonata, 2 recorders and piano; <u>Music for bass recorder and narrator</u>, New York, 14 Jan. 1973; string quartet, New York, 6 Feb. 1974; quarter-tone recorder duets, New York, 3 Dec. 1976; 2nd piano sonata, New York, 3 Dec. 1976; CHORUS: <u>De profundis</u>, with string trio, New York, 3 Dec. 1976; numerous other choral works, piano pieces, organ pieces.

47 Barrow St., New York, NY 10014

TUDOR, DAVID
b. Philadelphia, Pa., 20 Jan. 1926. Studied organ and theory in Philadelphia; piano with Irma Wolpe, composition with Stefan Wolpe in New York. He was piano instructor, Contemporary Music School, New York, 1948-51; instructor and pianist, Black Mountain Coll., 1951-53; conducted seminars, Internat. Summer School for New Music, Darmstadt, 1956, 1958, 1959, 1961; was creative associate, State Univ. of New York at Buffalo, 1965-66; guest lecturer at various campuses; conducted seminars, Nat. Inst. of Design, Ahmedabad, India, 1969; is an outstanding performer of contemporary piano works.

WORKS: ELECTRONIC: <u>Bandoneon factorial</u>, programmed light, audio, video projection, New York, 14 Oct. 1966; <u>Rainforest</u>, Buffalo, 9 Mar. 1968; <u>Video III</u> (with Lowell Cross), Los Angeles, 10 May 1968; <u>Video/laser I</u> (with Lowell Cross), Mills Coll., 9 May 1969; <u>4 Pepsi pieces</u>, Pepsi Pavilion, Expo '70, Osaka; <u>Untitled</u>, Bremen, Germany, 8 May 1972; <u>Monobird</u>, Munich, 30 Aug. 1972; <u>Microphone 1-9</u>, Mills Coll., May 1973; <u>Laser bird</u>, Univ. of Iowa, 12-14 June 1973; <u>Rainforest 4</u>, group composition, New Music in New Hampshire, July 1973.

Gate Hill Rd., Stony Point, NY 10980

TULL, FISHER
b. Waco, Tex., 24 Sept. 1934. Studied with Samuel Adler and Merrill Ellis, North Texas State Univ., B.M. 1956, M.M. 1957, Ph.D. 1965. His awards include 5 first prizes, Texas Composers Guild; 6 annual ASCAP awards, 1968-73; Ostwald award, American Bandmasters Assoc., 1970. He

TURETZKY, BERTRAM

was faculty member, North Texas State Univ.,
1963-64; Sam Houston State Univ., 1957-63, music
chairman, from 1964.

WORKS: BALLET: Allen's landing; ORCHESTRA:
Capriccio; concertino, oboe and strings; 2
trumpet concertos, #2 Ft. Worth, Tex., 29 Feb.
1976; BAND: Terpsichore, 1967; Toccata, 1969;
Antiphon, 1970; Sketches on a Tudor psalm, 1972;
Reflections on Paris; Credo; Jargon; Accolade,
Fort Lauderdale, Fla., 20 Apr. 1978; WIND EN-
SEMBLE: Liturgical symphony, brass and percussion, 1960; Variations on an Advent hymn, 1962;
Soundings, brass and percussion, 1965; Studies
in motion; Cyclorama I, flute ensemble; Cyclorama II, saxophone ensemble; Segments, trumpet
ensemble, Madison, Wis., 8 June 1978; CHAMBER
MUSIC: Exhibition, brass quintet, 1961; Canoni-
cal trilogy, 4 trumpets, 1961; Fantasie, oboe
and piano, 1966; woodwind quintet, 1966; Diversion, 6 trombones, 1967; Erato, flute and piano,
1968; Lament, 4 horns and tube, 1968; viola
sonata; percussion sonatina; Fantasie, bass
flute and harpsichord; many other chamber works;
numerous choral works.
Rte. 3, Box 124, Huntsville, TX 77340

TURETZKY, BERTRAM
b. Norwich, Conn., 14 Feb. 1933. Studied with
Isadore Freed, Arnold Franchetti, Edward Diemente,
Hartt Coll. of Music; musicology with Gustave
Reese, Curt Sachs, and Josef Marx. In addition
to wide acclaim as contrabass player, he received
a Nat. Endowment for the Arts grant, 1979. His
academic posts include Univ. of Hartford, 1955-
68, then at Univ. of California, San Diego; has
played bass in numerous orchestras; made world
tours as soloist.
WORKS: CONTRABASS: Collage, solo pieces,
1966-68; 6 timbral studies, 2 contrabasses, commissioned by BBC, London, 1974; Gamelan music,
contrabass consort (4 to 40), or solo bass and
tape, 1974; Wioste Olowan, setting of North
Dakota Indian love songs for contrabass consort
or solo bass and tape, 1976; Haiku, solo bass
with narrator, 1976; Celestial variations on
Charles Ives's Serenity (1919), 16 tracks of
contrabass harmonics (usually in A major),
sounds like the kind of old organ apt to be
heard in country churches, 1979; Por los metales,
an exception to his usual instrumentation--it is
a theatre piece for brass with a pun on the
Spanish word metales--the brass all play triangles and low bells, 1979.
429 9th St., Del Mar, CA 92014

TURNER, CHARLES
b. Baltimore, Md., 25 Nov. 1921. Studied with
Samuel Barber at Curtis Inst.; at Juilliard
School; and with Nadia Boulanger. He served in
the U.S. Navy in World War II; in 1954, received
an Italian government fellowship.
WORKS: BALLET: Pastorale, 1957; ORCHESTRA:
violin concerto, 1940; Encounter, symphonic
sketch, 1955; The marriage of Orpheus, 1965;
CHAMBER MUSIC: Serenade for Icarus, violin and
piano, 1960.

TURNER, GODFREY
b. Manchester, England, 27 Mar. 1913; to U.S.
1936; d. New York, N.Y., 7 Dec. 1948. Studied
at Cambridge Univ. and with Nadia Boulanger in
Paris. He won first prize, BMI contest, 1947.
He taught at San Francisco Cons., 1938-43; music
editor, Boosey and Hawkes, New York, 1944-46;
secretary, American Music Center, 1946-48.
WORKS: ORCHESTRA: Trinity concerto, chamber
orch.; viola concerto; Sonata concertante, piano
and strings; Sarabande and tango; Gregorian
overture, 1947; WIND ENSEMBLE: Fanfare, chorale,
and finale, brass ensemble.

TURNER, MILDRED COZZENS (Mrs. Huntington Turner)
b. Pueblo, Colo., 23 Feb. 1897. Studied at Univ.
of Wisconsin; was public school music supervisor,
Mineral Point, Wis. Her published compositions
include the songs: Dalmation lullaby; Galaxy;
Geisha.
45 East End Ave., New York, NY 10028

TURNER, THOMAS G.
b. Hamilton, Ohio, 30 Sept. 1937. Studied with
Kenneth Gaburo and Lejaren Hiller, Univ. of
Illinois; with Robert McBride, Univ. of Arizona;
with Eugene Weigel, Univ. of Montana; attended
Internat. Summer School for New Music, Darmstadt.
He received a grant, Univ. of North Carolina
Found., 1976; American Music Center grant, 1978.
He was faculty member, Univ. of Idaho, 1962-65;
music critic for The Times (London), Educ. Supplement, 1966; from 1970, on faculty, Univ. of
North Carolina.
WORKS: ORCHESTRA: Phorminx, 2 harps and
string orch., 1977; CHAMBER MUSIC: viola sonata,
1960; Modules and variables, guitar and piano,
1973; Bottle music, 5 singers and 20 bottles,
1978; 3 songs, Tennyson text, 1978; PIANO:
Intermezzo, 1966; 6 variations; Arrows, 1973;
and choral works.
2001 Eastway Dr., Charlotte, NC 28205

TURNER, THOMAS SAMPLE
b. Corning, Iowa, 21 Apr. 1914. Studied with
Carl Bricken, Univ. of Chicago; with Philip
Greeley Clapp, Univ. of Iowa, Ph.D. 1941. He
has been faculty member, Univ. of Iowa, from
1939.
WORKS: ORCHESTRA: 2 symphonies; symphonic
suite, 1943; also an opera and chamber works,
1947-68.
University of Iowa, Iowa City, IA 52242

TUROK, PAUL
b. New York, N.Y., 3 Dec. 1929. Studied with
Karol Rathaus, Queens Coll., B.A. 1950; with
Roger Sessions, Univ. of California, Berkeley,
M.M. 1951; and with Bernard Wagenaar at Juilliard School. His awards include the Dillon
prize; Hertz Traveling Scholarship; composer
residency, Villa Montalvo; performance of his
works by most major orchestras in the U.S. and
many abroad. He was associate music director,
KPFA, Berkeley, 1955-56; on faculty, City Coll.
of New York, 1960-63; Williams Coll., 1963-64;
from 1964, music reviewer and free-lance composer.

WORKS: THEATRE: The youngest brother, ballet, 1953; Scene: Domestic, 1-act chamber opera, 1955; Richard III, 4-act opera, 1975; ORCHESTRA: violin concerto, 1953; symphony, 1955; Chartres west, symphonic poem; Homage to Bach; Lyric variations, oboe and strings, 1973; Great Scott!, suite after Scott Joplin; Sousa overture, 1976; Ragtime caprice, piano and orch.; CHAMBER MUSIC: 3 string quartets, 1956-70; 3 wind quintets; brass quintet; string trio; clarinet trio; Toccata, trumpet and piano; 3 transcendental etudes for piano; Capriccio, violin and 4 percussionists; sonatas for bassoon, cello, cello solo, harp, harpsichord, horn, guitar, organ, trumpet, viola solo; also choral works and songs.
170 W. 74th St., New York, NY 10023

TURRIN, JOSEPH E.
b. Clifton, N.J., 4 Jan. 1947. Studied at Eastman School of Music and Manhattan School of Music. His awards include a New Jersey State Council on the Arts grant, 1976; Ann M. Alberger award for chamber music; American Music Center award. In 1973 he taught at the Center for New Music, Columbia Coll., Chicago; was guest lecturer, New Jersey Inst. of Technology, 1976-77; from 1977, artist-in-residence, drama dept., William Paterson Coll.
WORKS: OPERA: Feathertop, 2-act chamber opera, 1976; ORCHESTRA: symphony in 2 movements; Elegy, trumpet and strings; WIND ENSEMBLE: tuba concertino; March and choral, brass choir; Fanfare for 8 trumpets; CHAMBER MUSIC: Walden trio, flute, cello, piano; Caprice, trumpet and piano; clarinet sonata; Aeolus, flute and piano; Haiku songs, soprano and piano.
96 Huron Ave., Clifton, NJ 07013

TUSTIN, WHITNEY
b. Seattle, Wash. Studied at Univ. of Washington and in Paris; teaches oboe at Hofstra Univ. His compositions include Pastorale moderne, scherzo, tarantella, woodwind trio; 30 oboe duets.
Hofstra University, Hempstead, NY 11550

TUTHILL, BURNET CORWIN
b. New York, N.Y., 16 Nov. 1888. Studied at Columbia Univ., M.A. 1910; Cincinnati Coll. of Music, M.M. 1935. He received honorary music doctorates from Chicago Musical Coll., 1943, Southwestern at Memphis, 1972. From 1910 to 1922, he was a businessman in New York, and music was his avocation. The he became general manager of the Cincinnati Cons. and resumed the study of music. After receiving his master's in composition, he became director of music at Southwestern at Memphis, 1935, and director, Memphis Coll. of Music, 1937, holding both positions until retirement in 1959. In 1919 he founded the Society for Publication of American Music and was its treasurer to 1949; in 1924 he was cofounder of the Nat. Assoc. of Schools of Music and was secretary to 1959. He wrote a history of the Nat. Assoc. of Schools of Music and an autobiography, Recollections of a musical life, 1900-1974, published 1974.
WORKS: ORCHESTRA: Bethlehem, pastorale,

1934; Come 7, 1935; Laurentia, symphonic poem, 1936; symphony, 1940; Big river, with women's chorus and soprano solo, 1942; Elegy, 1946; clarinet concerto, 1949; Rhapsody, clarinet and chamber orch., 1954; concerto for string bass and winds, 1962; saxophone concerto, 1965; trombone concerto, 1967; BAND: Overture brilliante, 1937; suite, 1946; Rondo concertante, with 2 clarinets, 1961; Fantasia, with solo tuba, 1968; CHAMBER MUSIC: Scherzo, 3 clarinets, 1909; Fantasy sonata, clarinet and piano, 1932; Sonatina in canon, flute and clarinet, 1933; piano trio, 1933; clarinet quintet, 1935; Divertimento in classic style, wind quartet, 1936; alto saxophone sonata, 1939; oboe sonata, 1945; trumpet sonata, 1950; Family music, flute, 2 clarinets, viola, cello, 1952; string quartet, 1953; quintet for piano and 4 clarinets, 1957; 6 for bass, string bass and piano, 1961; flute sonata, 1963; saxophone quartet, 1966; tenor saxophone sonata, 1968; 5 essays, for brass quintet, 1969; Caprice, for guitar, 1972; Tiny tunes for tuba, 1973; 3 moods, for flute solo; duo for oboe and horn, 1975; also choral works and compositions for voice and instrumental groups.

TWEEDY, DONALD
b. Danbury, Conn., 23 Apr. 1890; d. Danbury, 21 July 1948. Studied with William C. Heilman, Walter Spalding, and Edward Burlingame Hill, Harvard Univ.; with Percy Goetschius, Inst. of Musical Art, 1912. He served in the U.S. Army in World War I; taught at Eastman School of Music, 1923-27; Hamilton Coll., 1937-38; and at Texas Christian Univ., 1943-46.
WORKS: BALLET: Alice in Wonderland, 1935; ORCHESTRA: L'allegro, symphonic study, 1925; 3 dances, 1925; Williamsburg suite, 1941; CHAMBER MUSIC: viola sonata, 1916; violin sonata, 1920; cello sonata, 1930; also choral works, piano pieces.

TWOMBLY, MARY LYNN
b. New York, N.Y., 8 Jan. 1935. Studied with Meyer Kupferman, Sarah Lawrence Coll., 1952-54; with Vittorio Giannini, Manhattan School of Music, 1954-58; electronic music with Elias Tannenbaum, 1971-72. She received the Harold Bauer piano award, 1957; commissions from the Little Orchestra Society, 1960. She was composer and conductor for films and records, Weston Woods Children's Library, 1966-67.
WORKS: OPERA: The little match girl, for young voices, 1964; Who are the blind?, 1969; BALLET: Alice in Wonderland, 1960; ORCHESTRA: Symphonic statements, piano and string orch., 1971; and choral works.
Old Rte. 202, Pomona, NY 10970

TYRA, THOMAS
b. Chicago, Ill., 17 Apr. 1933. Studied with Robert Delaney, Northwestern Univ., B.M.Ed., 1954; M.M. 1955; with Leslie Bassett and George B. Wilson, Univ. of Michigan, Ph.D. 1971. He served in the U.S. Navy, 1956-57; was faculty member, Louisiana State Univ., 1958-64; Eastern Michigan Univ., 1964-77; from 1977, professor and chairman, Western Carolina Univ.

TYSON, MILDRED LUND

WORKS: BAND: suite for brass and timpani, 1962; Ceremonial sketch, 1966; 3 Christmas miniatures, 1970; Intravention, 1973; also pieces for elementary band; many arrangements for band.
Rt. 1, Box 17M46, Cullowhee, NC 28723

TYSON, MILDRED LUND
b. Moline, Ill., 10 Mar. Studied with Carl Beecher, Northwestern Univ., B.M.; and at Columbia Univ. She taught piano and voice at Pomona Coll.; was organist and choir director in Sidney, N.Y. Her published compositions include the songs: The lilacs are in bloom; One little cloud; Sea moods; Like barley bending; The Great Divide.
Unadilla, NY 13849

UBER, DAVID ALBERT
b. Princeton, Ill., 5 Aug. 1921. Studied at Carthage Coll., A.B. 1944; with Harold Morris and Harry Wilson, Columbia Univ., M.A. 1946, Ed.D. 1965; also at Curtis Inst. His awards include annual ASCAP awards, 1959-78, and commissions. He played first trombone, N.Y. City Opera, 1946-48, N.Y. City Ballet Company, 1946-75; from 1959, faculty member, Trenton State Coll.; director of bands, Princeton Univ., 1971-78.
WORKS: BAND: 4 episodes; When I can read my title clear; Odyssey; Symphonic sketches 1 and 2; Panorama, with trombone solo; BRASS CHOIR: A Christmas festival of carols; Christmas in brass; Evolution; Gettysburg; Gloria in excelsis, 1970; The power and the glory; Symphonic fanfare; numerous other works for band, brass choir, and smaller woodwind, brass, and percussion ensembles.
Trenton State College, Trenton, NJ 08625

UDELL, BUDD A.
b. Grand Rapids, Mich., 4 Apr. 1934. Studied with Bernhard Heiden, Indiana Univ.; with Paul Cooper, Univ. of Cincinnati, Coll.-Cons. He was composer-arranger, U.S. Navy Band, 1958-61; faculty member, West Virginia Univ., 1963-70; Univ. of Cincinnati, 1972-75; from 1978, at Univ. of Florida.
WORKS: BAND: Freedom 7, 1962; CHAMBER MUSIC: 2 songs of Gerard Manley Hopkins, soprano, harp, clarinet, 1962; 4 miniatures, clarinet and piano, 1970; Allectation, clarinet, horn, cello, piano, percussion, 1972; CHORUS: Judgment, with contralto solo, chamber orch., tape, 1972.
University of Florida, Gainesville, FL 32611

UDOW, MICHAEL WILLIAM
b. Detroit, Mich., 10 Mar. 1949. Studied with Thomas Frederickson, Edwin London, Herbert Brun, and Gordon Binkerd, Univ. of Illinois; with Paul Steg, Northern Illinois Univ.; and with W. Kotonski in Warsaw, Poland. He received Fulbright and Polish government grants; 2 scholarships at Univ. of Illinois; instrument design grants, Univ. of Illinois and Premier Drum Co., England; first place, Percussive Arts Society Internat. composition contest, 1978. He was percussionist, New Orleans Phil., 1971-72; on faculty, Northern Illinois Univ., 1972-73; Univ. of Illinois, 1974-76; Univ. of Missouri, from

1978; and from 1968, principal percussionist, Santa Fe Opera.
WORKS: PERCUSSION CHAMBER ENSEMBLE: 7 textural settings of Japanese poetry; African welcome piece; Understanding; Barn burner; Acoustic composition; several pieces with dance; Bog music, percussion quartet, Tempe, Ariz., 27 Oct. 1978. He is inventor of the Timbrack, a 4-octave percussion console of timbres.
University of Missouri, Kansas City, MO 64111

ULEHLA, LUDMILA
b. New York, N.Y., 20 May 1923. Studied at Manhattan School of Music, B.M. 1946, M.M. 1947. She has received annual ASCAP awards from 1968 and many commissions. She joined the faculty in 1947 and has been chairman of composition from 1971. She is also professor, Hoff-Barthelson Music School, in Scarsdale, N.Y.
WORKS: ORCHESTRA: 5 over 12; Michelangelo, a tone portrait, New York, 18 Feb. 1971; CHAMBER MUSIC: Elegy for a whale, flute, cello, piano, and whale recordings, 1978; Contrasting interludes, string quartet, 1979, New York, 8 Mar. 1980; SONGS: Sonnets from Shakespeare, voice and chamber orch., 1951; Time is a running thief, voice and piano; Gargoyles, soprano, piano, bassoon; also piano works.
120 Lee Rd., Scarsdale, NY 10583

ULRICH, EUGENE J.
b. Olmstead, Ill., 13 Dec. 1921. Studied with J. Robert Kelly, Univ. of Illinois; with Bernard Rogers, Howard Hanson, and Wayne Barlow, Eastman School of Music, Ph.D. He has been professor, Phillips Univ., from 1949.
WORKS: CHAMBER MUSIC: solo flute sonatina; baritone horn sonata; suite for unaccompanied marimba; numerous other wind instrument solos, percussion solos, etc.
2610 E. Pine, Enid, OK 73701

ULTAN, LLOYD
b. New York, N.Y., 12 June 1929. Studied at New York Univ., B.A.; at Columbia Univ., M.A.; with Philip Bezanson, Univ. of Iowa, Ph.D.; with Roger Goeb and Henry Brant, Bennington Composers Conf. He received fellowships for study at Univ. of Iowa and at Bennington; many commissions. He was faculty member, Dickinson Coll., 1956-62; American Univ., 1962-75; from 1975, at Univ. of Minnesota; visiting professor, Royal Coll. of Music, London, 1968-69.
WORKS: ORCHESTRA: Carlisle concerto; Man with a hoe, with chorus and soloists; Wanaki Win, Minneapolis, 11 Apr. 1978; Wakonda sketch; BAND: Meek shall inherit the earth; Fighting gophers march; CHAMBER MUSIC: string quartet, 1964; piano sextet, 1970; bassoon sonata; piano sonata; guitar quintet (guitar with string quartet); cello sonata; viola sonata; and choral works.
5249 Lochloy Dr., Edina, MN 55436

UNDERWOOD, LUCAS
b. Salzburg, Austria, 22 Nov. 1902; U.S. citizen 1945. Studied with Waltershausen and von Hausegger, Univ. of Munich, Ph.D. He was music

critic in Hannover, 1930–37; taught music at Margaret Hall School, Versailles, Ky., 1939–46; was professor and director of opera, Univ. of the Pacific, 1946–72; also musical director, Stockton Opera Assoc.

WORKS: OPERA: The holy night, Christmas opera; ORCHESTRA: Evening at the lake; German rhapsody; CHORUS: Missa brevis; madrigals; PIANO: Variations; Passacaglia; many other choral works and songs.

    13 Atherton Island, Stockton, CA 95204

UNDERWOOD, WILLIAM L.
b. Greenwood, Miss., 9 Mar. 1940. Studied with Johannes Smit, Memphis State Univ., B.M., M.A. 1966; with William Latham and Dika Newlin, North Texas State Univ., D.M.A. 1970. He taught at North Texas State Univ., 1968–70; from 1970, has been faculty member, Henderson State Univ.

WORKS: OPERA: A medicine for melancholy, comic opera based on a Ray Bradbury story; ORCHESTRA: 2 symphonies, 1966, 1971; CHAMBER MUSIC: 3 songs of e. e. cummings, for soprano, flute, string quartet; numerous short works for chorus and band.

    Henderson State University, Arkadelphia, AR 71923

UNG, CHINARY
b. Cambodia, 24 Nov. 1942; to U.S. 1964. Studied with Jack Beeson, Chou Wen-chung, Mario Davidosky, and Vladimir Ussachevsky, Columbia Univ.; with George Crumb at Tanglewood; and with Bulent Arel. His awards include Bronze Medal of Honor for performing arts, Cambodia, 1962; Premier Prix, Faculté de Musique, Univ. des Beaux Arts, Cambodia, 1963; Margaret Grant Memorial composition prize, Tanglewood, 1970; Rapaport prize, Columbia Univ., 1971; Koussevitzky Music Found. award, 1973. He is faculty member, Northern Illinois Univ.

WORKS: ORCHESTRA: Anicea, 1970; CHAMBER MUSIC: Tall wind, voice and chamber ensemble, 1970; Mohori, soprano and chamber ensemble, 1976.

    Bldg. 140, Northern Illinois Univ., DeKalb, IL 60115

UNGER, LEIGH JAMES
b. Milwaukee, Wis., 15 Oct. 1945. Studied at Whittier Coll., B.A. with honors in piano, 1967; with Donal Michalsky, California State Univ. at Fullerton, M.A. 1974; master classes in piano with Rosina Lhevinne and Donald Pollack. He received the Bank of America achievement award in science and mathematics, 1963; numerous awards for piano performance. He taught at Whittier Coll., 1965–67; was accompanist, Fullerton Junior Coll., 1970–71; then for a time on piano faculty, Univ. of Redlands.

WORKS: CHAMBER MUSIC: Improvisation, flute and piano, 1970; SONGS: song from Pomes Penyeach, baritone and piano, 1969; 2 songs, soprano and piano, 1970; 12 love songs, soprano, 1972; PIANO: 6 preludes, 1967; 3 intermezzi, 1967; 3 studies, 1969; Distractions to the contemplative, 1970; suite, 1971.

    893 S. Lemon, Anaheim, CA 92805

USSACHEVSKY, VLADIMIR
b. Hailar, Manchuria, 3 Nov. 1911; to U.S. 1930. Studied at Pomona Coll., B.A. 1935; with Howard Hanson and Bernard Rogers, Eastman School of Music, Ph.D. 1939. He received an award from the American Acad. of Arts and Letters, 1963, and in 1973, was elected to membership in the Nat. Inst. of Arts and Letters. He was in the U.S. Army in World War II; faculty member at Columbia Univ., 1947–72; from 1972, at Univ. of Utah.

WORKS: ORCHESTRA: Theme and variations, 1935; Miniatures for a curious child, 1950; piano concerto, 1951; CHAMBER MUSIC: piano sonata, 1952; CHORUS: Jubilee cantata, with orch., 1938; Missa brevis, with soprano and 10 brass instruments; ELECTRONIC: Sonic contours, tape and instruments, 1952; Underwater valse, 1952; Incantation, tape, with Otto Luening, 1953; Poem of cycles and bels, tape and orch., with Luening, 1954; Piece for tape recorder, 1955; Studies in sound, 1955; Metamorphosis, 1957; Linear contrasts, 1958; Improvisation no. 4711, 1958; Wireless fantasy, 1960; Concerted piece, tape and orch., with Luening, 1960; Of wood and brass, 1965; Computer piece, 1968; The creation, chorus, orch., tape; Rhapsodic variations, with Luening, New York, 29 Apr. 1973; 2 sketches for computer piece #2, 1971; Colloquy, symphony orch., tape recorder, and various chairs, Salt Lake City, 20 Feb. 1976; Celebration, 4 to 9 layers of recorded sound from an EVI (Electronic Valve Instrument) with an orchestra of 20 players, New York, 28 Mar. 1980.

    University of Utah, Salt Lake City, UT 84112

VAN APPLEDORN, MARY JEANNE
b. Holland, Mich., 2 Oct. 1927. Studied with Bernard Rogers and Alan Hovhaness, Eastman School of Music, B.M. 1948, M.M. 1950, Ph.D. 1966. Her awards include Delta Kappa Gamma scholarship, 1959–60; membership, Texas Composers Hall of Fame, 1973; awards in Mu Phi Epsilon composition contests; ASCAP award, 1977. She has been faculty member, Texas Tech. Univ., from 1967.

WORKS: ORCHESTRA: Concerto brevis, piano and orch., 1954; Passacaglia and chorale; BAND: trumpet concerto, Houston, 11 Nov. 1977; Choreographic overture, Lubbock, Tex., 1 May 1978; CHORUS: West Texas suite, with wind and percussion ensemble, Lubbock, 9 Nov. 1976; Rising night after night, double chorus, soloists, narrator, orch., on Hebrew text by Abba Kovner, 1978; Darest thou now, O soul, 1975; KEYBOARD: Sonnet for organ, 1959; Set of 5, piano; suite for carillon, New York, 8 May 1977.

    Texas Tech. University, Lubbock, TX 79409

VAN CLEAVE, NATHAN
b. Bayfield, Wis., 8 May 1910. Has written for films and radio. His works for orchestra include a trumpet concerto; Fantasy for strings; American holiday; Dances from Satanstoe; Daybreak serenade; Canzonetta.

VAN DER SLICE, JOHN

VAN DER SLICE, JOHN
 b. Ann Arbor, Mich., 19 Feb. 1940. Studied with
Armand Russell, Neil McKay, and Ingolf Dahl,
Univ. of Hawaii; with Paul Zonn, Univ. of Illi-
nois. He was instructor, Univ. of Hawaii, Jan.-
June 1970.
 WORKS: CHAMBER MUSIC: For flute, 1969;
septet, 1969; piano sonata, 1970; Portions, 1970;
Thesis, 1972; For koto, 1972.

VAN DE VATE, NANCY HAYES
 b. Plainfield, N.J., 30 Dec. 1930. Studied
piano at Eastman School of Music, 1948-49; at
Wellesley Coll., A.B. 1952; piano with Bruce
Simonds, Yale Univ., 1954; composition with
Arthur Kreutz, Univ. of Mississippi, M.M. 1958;
with John Boda, Florida State Univ., D.M. 1968.
Her awards include scholarships at Eastman
School and Wellesley Coll.; French government
grant for study in French, 1950-52; annual ASCAP
awards from 1973; fellowships at Yaddo and Ossabaw Island, 1974; first place, Delius contest,
1975; Nat. Fed. of Music Clubs Award of Merit
for organizing League of Women Composers, 1977.
She has held faculty posts at Memphis State
Univ., 1964-66; Univ. of Tennessee, 1967; Knoxville Coll., 1968-69, 1971-72; Maryville Coll.,
1973-74; Univ. of Hawaii, 1975-76, then part
time; from 1978, at Hawaii Loa Coll.
 WORKS: OPERA: The death of the hired man,
chamber opera, 1960; ORCHESTRA: Adagio for
orchestra, 1958; piano concerto, Houston, 1 Mar.
1969; CHAMBER MUSIC: Short suite, brass quartet;
woodwind quartet; viola sonata; Variations,
clarinet and piano; Lento, piano; Incidental
piece, 3 saxophones, 1976; Music for viola, percussion and piano, 1976; Letter to a friend's
loneliness, soprano and string quartet, 1976;
Concertpiece, cello and small orch., 1976; choral
works and songs.
 P.O. Box 23152, Honolulu, HI 96822

VANEUF, ANDRE. See COHEN, SOL B.

VAN HECKE, MARK J.
 b. Milwaukee, Wis., 19 Nov. 1949. Studied with
Yehudi Yannay, Univ. of Wisconsin-Milwaukee,
D.M.A. 1977. He is composer-in-residence for
the Milwaukee Repertory Theatre and Theatre X,
an experimental theatre troupe based in Milwaukee.
 WORKS: THEATRE SCORES: The wreck: A romance, 1977; Shakespeare's Richard III, 1977;
Romeo and Juliet, 1978; Euripides' The Bacchae,
1978; A fierce longing, 1978; Kobo Abe's
Friends, 1978; ELECTRONIC: Parthenogenesis,
organ and tape, 1975; Cantata I, chorus, orch.,
tape, 1976; Ro, 2 percussionists and 2 tapes,
1977.
 2619 N. Bartlett Ave., Milwaukee, WI 53211

VAN HULSE, CAMIL
 b. St. Niklaas, Belgium, 1 Aug. 1897; to U.S.
1923. Studied with his father Gustave Van
Hulse, then with Franz Lenaerts and Edward
Verheyden, Antwerp Cons.; with Arthur De Greef
in Brussels. He received 11 awards in composition contests; Royal Medal in Antwerp; Order of

Leopold; Order of the Crown. On coming to the
U.S., he settled in Tucson, Ariz., as organist
and choirmaster, 1924-57; gave organ and piano
recitals in North and South America; conducted
the Tucson Symph. Orch., 1928-30.
 WORKS: ORCHESTRA: The Belgian in U.S.A.,
for 40th anniversary of the Tucson Symphony,
1968; CHAMBER MUSIC: Trio elegy, piano trio;
woodwind quintet; In Christmas mood, flute and
organ; Aubade, flute and harp; CHORUS: Via
crusis, oratorio, with orch., soloists, organ,
and narrator; The Beatitudes, cantata; Christmas
oratorio; 'Twas in the noon of wintertime,
Christmas cantata; The passion according to St.
Luke, oratorio with organ and narrator, Garden
City, N.Y., 30 Mar. 1969; numerous masses,
anthems, motets; also many works for organ;
piano pieces.
 1029 N. Euclid, Tucson, AZ 85719

VAN NOSTRAND, BURR
 b. Calif., 1945. Studied at New England Cons.;
received Nat. Endowment for the Arts grant, 1976.
 WORKS: CHAMBER MUSIC: The fantasy manual
for urban survival, voice and instruments,
Boston, 17 Oct. 1972; Lunar possession manual,
based on American Indian ceremonial dances,
soprano and chamber ensemble, 1973, Boston, 2
Feb. 1975; Earth manual, a dawn ceremony, soprano
and small ensemble, 1976.

VAN SLYCK, NICHOLAS
 b. Philadelphia, Pa., 25 Oct. 1922. Studied
with Walter Piston, Harvard Univ., B.A., M.A.
He won first prize in a Brookline Library competition with Chamber music for 2 pianos. He
was director, South End Music Center, Boston,
1950-62; Longy School of Music, Cambridge, 1962-
76; then director, New School of Music, Cambridge.
 WORKS: ORCHESTRA: 3 piano concertos; Encore
march; CHAMBER MUSIC: Passamezzo antico, brass
quintet; suite for harpsichord; cello sonata;
flute sonata; bassoon sonata; 6 piano sonatas;
With 20 fingers, 3 volumes of pieces for piano,
4 hands; Fantasia numerica, sonata for solo
bassoon; many other chamber works and choral
compositions.
 700 Huron Ave., Cambridge, MA 02138

VAN VACTOR, DAVID
 b. Plymouth, Ind., 8 May 1906. Studied with
Carl Beecher, Mark Wessel, Arne Oldberg, and
Albert Noelte, flute with Arthur Kitti, North-
western Univ., B.M. 1928, M.M. 1935; with Franz
Schmidt, Vienna Acad., 1928-29; with Paul Dukas,
Arnold Schoenberg, Paris, 1931. His awards in-
clude the New York Phil. first prize, 1938;
Fulbright grant; Guggenheim fellowship, 1957;
numerous commissions. He was flutist, Chicago
Symph., 1931-43; taught at Northwestern Univ.,
1936-43; was assistant conductor, Kansas City
Phil., 1943-45; faculty member, Kansas City
Cons., 1943-45; from 1947, at Univ. of Tennessee.
He made tours to South America for the State
Dept. as member of a woodwind quintet in 1941,
and as guest conductor in Rio de Janiero and
Santiago in 1945, 1946, 1965.
 WORKS: BALLET: The play of words, 1931;

Dance contrasts, 1961; Suite on Chilean folk tunes, 1965; Brass octet, 1965; ORCHESTRA: Chaconne, string orch., 1928; 5 small pieces for large orch., 1929; flute concerto, 1932; Passacaglia and fugue, 1933; Overture to a comedy, #1 1934, #2 1941; concerto grosso, 3 flutes, harp, orch., 1935; 2 symphonies, 1937, 1958; Symphonic suite, 1938; viola concerto, 1940; Recitative and saltarello, 1946; Pastoral and dance, flute and strings, 1947; violin concerto, 1950; Fantasia, chaconne, and allegro, 1957; Trojan Women suite, 1959; suite for trumpet and small orch., 1962; Sinfonia breve, 1964; Walden, with chorus, Thoreau text, Knoxville, 1 Mar. 1970; Sarabande and variations, brass quintet and strings, 1972; suite for trumpet, piccolo, and orch., 1972; Andante and allegro, alto saxophone and strings, Muncie, Ind., 16 Dec. 1973; symphony #5, Knoxville, 11 Apr. 1976; CHAMBER MUSIC: quintet for flute and strings, 1932; Nachtlied, soprano and strings, 1935; 2 string quartets, 1940, 1949; Divertimento, string trio, 1942; flute sonatina, 1945; duettino, violin and cello, 1952; woodwind quintet, 1959; tuba quartet, Georgia State Univ., 22 Feb. 1971; many other works for chamber groups; also for band, chorus, solo voice.

2824 Kingston Pike, Knoxville, TN 37919

VARDELL, CHARLES GILDERSLEEVE, JR.
b. Salisbury, N.C., 19 Aug. 1893; d. Winston-Salem, N.C., 19 Oct. 1962. Studied at Princeton Univ., A.B. 1914; Inst. of Musical Arts, N.Y., dipl. 1916; Eastman School of Music, M.A., Ph.D. He was faculty member and dean, Flora MacDonald Coll., 1919-61; Salem Coll., 1923-51; St. Andrew's Coll., 1961-62.

WORKS: ORCHESTRA: Carolinian symphony, performed by Philadelphia Orch.; Joe Clark steps out, 1933; VOICE: Dark days or fair, song; The inimitable lovers, cantata, 1929; Song in the wilderness, 1947; KEYBOARD: Concert gavotte, piano, 1924; Skyland, organ, 1937.

VARDI, EMANUEL
b. Jerusalem, Palestine, 21 Apr. 1917; U.S. citizen 1927. Studied with his father, then with Bernard Wagenaar at Juilliard School; with Nicolas Nabokov at Peabody Cons.; and with Tibor Serly in New York. He won silver medals for film scores for Lehigh Cement and American Express. He has been principally a film composer, including feature films, industrials, television films, and commercials. He is also violinist and violist and in 1978, was appointed musical director and conductor of the South Dakota Symph. Orch., and artist-in-residence at Augustana Coll., S.Dak.

WORKS: ORCHESTRA: Americana, 2 pieces for string orch.; CHAMBER MUSIC: Suite on American folk songs, violin or viola and piano; concerto for solo horn, string quartet, 2 winds, keyboard, New York, 15 May 1974; FILM SCORES: Once before I die, feature movie; Diary of Anne Frank, television special; Life study, feature film; Devil's axe, electronic score; many scores for industrial movies.

2 Wood Lane, Suffern, NY 10901

VARESE, EDGARD
b. Paris, France, 22 Dec. 1883; U.S. citizen 1926; d. New York, N.Y., 6 Nov. 1965. Studied with Vincent d'Indy and Albert Roussel, Schola Cantorum, Paris; and with Widor at the Paris Cons. His honors include the Brandeis award, 1962; the first Koussevitzky Internat. Recording award, 1963; MacDowell Medal, 1965; membership, Nat. Inst. of Arts and Letters; and was fellow, Swedish Royal Acad. of Music. Varese founded the New Symphony Orchestra for the performance of new music, which gave its first concert in New York, 11 Apr. 1919. He was cofounder with Carlos Salzedo of the Internat. Composers' Guild, 1922; organized the Pan American Society for presentation of music of the Americas, 1926; conducted choruses and orchestras in the U.S. and Europe.

WORKS: ORCHESTRA: Offrandes, voice and small orch., 1922; Integrales, small orch. and percussion, 1925; Ameriques, 1925; Arcana, 1927; Ionization, 41 percussion instruments and 2 sirens, 1931; WIND ENSEMBLE: Hyperprism, winds and percussion, 1923; Octandre, woodwind quartet, brass trio, double bass, 1924; Equatorial (Ecutorial), bass voice, brass, organ, percussion, thereminovox, 1934, premiered as a ballet by Martha Graham, New York, 27 June 1978; CHAMBER MUSIC: Density 21.5, flute solo, 1935; CHORUS: Etude pour espace, with 2 pianos and percussion, 1947; Nocturnal, soprano, men's chorus, chamber orch., piano, percussion, 1961; ELECTRONIC: Deserts, winds, percussion, electronic sounds, 1954; Poeme electronique, for the Brussels Exposition, 1958.

VARS, HENRY
b. Warsaw, Poland, 29 Dec. 1902; to U.S. 1947. Studied at Warsaw Cons. He has composed for theatre, films, radio.

WORKS: ORCHESTRA: a symphony; symphonic suite; piano concerto; CHAMBER MUSIC: string quartet; violin sonata; piano sonata; piano preludes; and songs.

VAUCLAIN, ANDRE CONSTANT
b. Philadelphia, Pa., 5 Aug. 1908. Studied with Rosario Scalero, Curtis Inst. of Music. He was faculty member at Curtis Inst., 1939-63; and from 1947, at Univ. of Pennsylvania.

WORKS: BALLET: Suite for youth, chamber ballet, 1952; ORCHESTRA: April overture, 1940; symphony in 1 movement, Philadelphia, 18 Apr. 1947; symphony for strings and piano, 1948; Prelude to Endymion, 1949, Rochester, 4 May 1951; Narrative, 1958; Allegretto, string orch., Chicago, 10 May 1958; CHAMBER MUSIC: string quartet, 1955, Philadelphia, 3 May 1957; suite for strings and piano, 1956; string quartet, New York, 8 Oct. 1965; PIANO: 3 Degas, suite, 1950; sonatina, 1956; ORGAN: Motet on Psalm 11, Philadelphia, 10 Nov. 1962.

20 Old Gulph Rd., Gladwyne, PA 19035

VAUGHAN, CLIFFORD
b. Bridgeton, N.J., 23 Sept. 1893. Studied with Henry Lang, Philadelphia Cons., also piano and organ. He has received several ASCAP awards.

VAUGHAN, RODGER

He was church organist in Philadelphia and Hollywood; composer-conductor for Ruth St. Denis,
Denishawn Dancers, Michael Fokine, Doris
Humphrey, and Charles Weidman; composer-orches-
trator for major film studios in Hollywood for
30 years.
WORKS: ORCHESTRA: 4 symphonies; violin concerto; organ concerto; 30 oriental translations,
for small orch.; Hindu Nautch dance; CHAMBER
MUSIC: 2 string quartets; Violin concertante;
Revery for harp; 6 preludes for piano; 2 voluntaries for organ; CHORUS: The 10 commandments,
cantata; Queen Esther, oratorio; and numerous
other works.

VAUGHAN, RODGER
b. Delphos, Kans., 2 Feb. 1932. Studied with
Ingolf Dahl and Halsey Stevens, Univ. of Southern
California, M.M. He won the Kansas Centennial
award for best orchestral composition, 1961.
He was faculty member, Wichita Univ., 1956-60;
Univ. of Southern California, 1961-63; Upland
Coll., 1963-65; from 1965, California State
Univ. at Fullerton.
WORKS: ORCHESTRA: Centennial symphony;
Overture to Dionydus; CHAMBER MUSIC: Quattro
bicinie, clarinet and tuba; Quinte bicinie,
viola and tuba; 3 songs, soprano and tuba;
CHORUS: Psalm 100; Psalm 121; Festival anthem;
Christmas lullaby.
226 Borromeo, Placentia, CA 92670

VAZZANA, ANTHONY
b. Troy, N.Y., 4 Nov. 1922. Studied at New York
State Univ., B.S.; with Ingolf Dahl and Halsey
Stevens, Univ. of Southern California, M.M.,
D.M.A. He held Alchin and Friends of Music
scholarships and a Bennington Composers Conf.
fellowship. He taught in public schools, 1948-
51; New York State Univ., 1951-54; Danbury State
Coll., 1954-57; from 1959, Univ. of Southern
California.
WORKS: ORCHESTRA: symphony; symphonic
allegro; suite for chamber orch.; CHAMBER MUSIC:
2 pieces, clarinet; Incontri, violin and piano,
1972; FILM SCORES: Tomorrow may be dying.
1228 21st St., Manhattan Beach, CA 90266

VECSEI, DESIDER JOSEF
b. Budapest, Hungary, 25 Sept. 1882; to U.S.
1915; d. Hollywood, Calif., 1 Mar. 1966. Studied
in Budapest and at the Vienna Cons. He was concert pianist in Europe and the U.S.; received
the French government Officer de l'Academi. He
composed many songs and piano pieces.

VEGA, AURELIO DE LA
b. Havana, Cuba, 28 Nov. 1925; U.S. citizen 1966.
Studied at De La Salle Coll., Havana, B.A.; Univ.
of Havana, M.A. in humanities, Ph.D. in international law; Inst. of Musical Ada Iglesias,
Havana, Ph.D. in composition; privately with
Frederick Kramer and Ernst Toch. His awards include the Virginia Colliers chamber music award,
1954; Andrew Mellon fellowship, 1964; Outstanding
Professor award, California State Univ. and Coll.,
1971; Honor Distinction award, Anthaneum of
Buenos Aires, 1972; second place, Friedheim Com-

position contest, Washington, D.C., 1978. He
was music critic in Havana, 1950-55; professor,
Univ. of Oriente, Santiago de Cuba, 1953-57;
musical advisor, Nat. Inst. of Culture, Havana,
1956-58; guest professor, Univ. of Southern
California, summer, 1959; from 1958, professor,
California State Univ. at Northridge.
WORKS: ORCHESTRA: Overture to a serious
farce, 1950; Elegy, string orch., 1954; Intrata,
1972; Adios, a farewell to Zubin Mehta, Los
Angeles, 20 Apr. 1978; CHAMBER MUSIC: Legend of
the Creole Ariel, cello and piano, 1953; string
quartet (in memoriam Alban Berg), 1957; Structures, piano and string quartet, 1962; Exametron,
flute, cello, percussion, 1965; Exospheres, oboe
and piano, 1966; Labdanum, flute, vibraphone,
viola, 1970; Septicilium, solo clarinet and
chamber ensemble, 1974; Olep ed arudamot, (backward spelling of a Spanish idiom for "pulling a
leg") 1974, The infinite square, 1975, Andamar-
ramadna, 1975, The magic labyrinth, 4 graphic
scores for any combination of instruments and/or
voices; Sound clouds, 1975; ELECTRONIC: Vectors,
tape, 1963; Interpolation, clarinet and tape,
1965; Tangents, violin and tape, 1973; Para-
tangents, trumpet and tape, 1973; Inflorescence,
soprano, bass clarinet, prerecorded sounds, 1976.
California State Univ., Northridge, CA
91330

VELKE, FRITZ
b. Washington, D.C., 10 Sept. 1930. Studied
with William Graves and G. Thaddeus Jones,
Catholic Univ. of America. He received the
Ostwald award, American Bandmasters Assoc., 1962.
He was trombonist, U.S. Air Force Band, Washing-
ton, 1953-57; from 1957, instrumental music
teacher, Fairfax County, Va., schools; conductor,
Alexandria Citizens Band, 1964-66, from 1972,
Falls Church City Band.
WORKS: ORCHESTRA: concerto grosso for
brass sextet and orch.; Adagietto for strings;
BAND: Quartral piece; concertino; Fanfare and
rondo; Foray at Fairfax; Plaything; Capriccio;
CHAMBER MUSIC: string quartet.
Box 9263, Alexandria, VA 22304

VENE, RUGGERO
b. Lerici, Spezia, Italy, 12 Aug. 1897; U.S.
citizen 1944; d. Italy, 18 Aug. 1961. Studied
at Royal Cons. of Parma; with Nadia Boulanger
in Paris; with Ottorino Respighi in Rome. He
was conductor and choral coach in European
theatres; in the U.S., taught at the Malkin
Cons., New England Cons.; Columbia Univ.; Washinton Univ.; and Indiana Univ. His compositions
include Rossaccio, symphonic poem; a string
quartet; piano quintet.

VERCOE, BARRY LLOYD
b. Wellington, New Zealand, 24 July 1937; to
U.S. 1962. Studied with Ronald Tremain, Univ.
of Auckland; with Ross Lee Finney and Leslie
Bassett, Univ. of Michigan; with J. K. Randall,
Milton Babbitt, and Godfrey Winham, Princeton
Univ. His awards include the Philip Neil prize
in composition, 1959; Ford-MENC grant in the
Contemporary Music Project, 1967-68; Massachusetts

Arts Council award, 1974. He was faculty member, Oberlin Coll. Cons., 1965-67; composer-in-residence, Seattle-Tacoma, 1967-68; guest lecturer, Yale Univ., 1970; from 1971, on faculty, Massachusetts Inst. of Technology.

WORKS: ORCHESTRA: Metamorphoses; CHAMBER MUSIC: Setrophy, clarinet and piano, 1963; ELECTRONIC: Digressions, 2 choirs, orch., tape, 1968; Synthesism, for computer, 1970; Synapse, viola and computer, 1976.

381 Garfield Rd., Concord, MA 01742

VERCOE, ELIZABETH
b. Washington, D.C., 23 Apr. 1941. Studied with Gardner Read, Boston Univ. She received the Boston Univ. award in composition, 1978; Hubert Weldon Lamb prize, Wellesley Coll., 1978. She was instructor, Westminster Choir Coll., 1969-71; on music faculty, Framingham State Coll., 1973-74.

WORKS: ORCHESTRA: violin concerto; CHAMBER MUSIC: Pasticcio, cello and piano, 1966; Balance, violin and cello; VOICE: 8 riddles from symphosius, song cycle, 1966; Herstory, song cycle for soprano, vibraphone, piano, 1977; Herstory II, 13 Japanese lyrics, soprano, piano, percussion, Boston, 9 May 1980; PIANO: 3 studies; Fantasy.

381 Garfield Rd., Concord, MA 01742

VERDI, RALPH C.
b. New York, N.Y., 21 Sept. 1944. Studied with Samuel Adler, Wayne Barlow, Warren Benson, Sydney Hodkinson, and Joseph Schwantner, Eastman School of Music. He won a Nat. Fed. of Music Clubs award for an anthem, 1964. He was on the board of directors for Catholic Worshop, 1968-72; on music faculty, St. Joseph's Coll., Rensselaer, Ind., from 1974.

WORKS: ORCHESTRA: Fantasy, organ and orch., Alverno Coll., Milwaukee, 7 May 1977; CHAMBER MUSIC: 5 moods, for solo clarinet, 1977; suite for organ, 1978; CHORUS: Psalm 100, 1972; Psalm 122, 1977; Alleluia, with cantor and congregation, 1978; ELECTRONIC: Bird-dance, tape and dancer, 1977.

Box 856, St. Joseph's College, Rensselaer, IN 47978

VERNON, KNIGHT
b. Camden, N.J., 12 Dec. 1934. Studied with Ernst Bacon and David W. Johnson, Syracuse Univ., B.M. 1957; with Leslie Bassett, Univ. of Michigan, M.M. 1967. His awards include first prize, Nat. Assoc. of Methodist Musicians, 1961; first prize, Rochester Festival of Religious Arts, 1968; American Music Center grant, 1969; selection of a quintet for performance, Festival of Music, Rio de Janeiro, 1970; and commissions. He was organist-choirmaster and public school music teacher, 1959-68; on faculty, Interlochen Arts Acad., 1968-72; then left teaching to undertake building harpsichords.

WORKS: ORCHESTRA: In memoriam, with narrator, 1967, Interlochen Arts Acad., 18 Oct. 1970; CHAMBER MUSIC: suite for brass and percussion, 1968; wind quintet, 1969, Rio de Janeiro, 15 May 1970; CHORUS: Haiku west,

treble voices a cappella, 1966; They shall mount up with wings, a cappella, Rochester, N.Y., 5 May 1968; Swords into ploughshares, a cappella, 1970; PIANO: Sound structures, Ann Arbor, Mich., 25 Feb. 1964, was choreographed in 1969 as a solo modern dance entitled Alone.

525 White Pigeon St., Constantine, MI 49042

VERRALL, JOHN WEEDON
b. Britt, Iowa, 17 June 1908. Studied with Reginald O. Morris in London, 1929-30; with Zoltan Kodaly in Budapest, 1930-31; Donald Ferguson, Univ. of Minnesota, B.A. 1932; Aaron Copland at Tanglewood, 1938; Roy Harris at Colorado Coll., 1939; and with Frederick Jacobi at Juilliard, 1945. His awards include a Guggenheim fellowship, 1948; Honolulu Acad. of Arts award, 1949; Seattle Centennial Opera award, 1952; D. H. Lawrence fellowship, Univ. of New Mexico, 1964; concert of his music, Univ. of Washington, 31 May 1973; Nat. Endowment for the Arts grant, 1974. He was faculty member, Hamline Univ., 1934-42; Mt. Holyoke Coll., 1942-46; editor, G. Schirmer and Boston Music Co., 1946-48; then professor, Univ. of Washington, to retirement in 1973.

WORKS: OPERA: The cowherd and the sky maiden, 1951; The wedding knell, 1952; 3 blind mice, 1955; ORCHESTRA: 2 symphonies, 1939, 1943; Portrait of man, 1940; Concert piece, strings and horn, 1941; violin concerto, 1947; Prelude and allegro, strings, 1948; Variations on an ancient tune, 1955; Dark night of St. John, 1959; suite, 1959; piano concerto, 1959; viola concerto, 1968; Radiant bridge, Bicentennial Commission, Port Angeles Symph., 1 Feb. 1976; BAND: Sinfonia festiva, 1954; Passacaglia, 1958; CHAMBER MUSIC: 2 viola sonatas, 1939, 1963; trio for 2 violins and viola, 1941; horn sonata, 1941; 7 string quartets, 1941, 1942, 1948, 1948, 1950, 1956, 1961; 2 Serenades, woodwind quintet, 1944, 1950; violin sonata, 1950; piano quintet, 1953, Seattle, 6 Oct. 1955; violin sonatina, 1956; cello sonatina, 1956; oboe sonata, 1956; viola sonatina, 1956; Nocturne, bass clarinet and piano, 1956, Indianapolis, 8 Feb. 1960; wind septet, 1966; nonet, wind quintet and string quartet, 1969, Seattle, 4 Mar. 1971; Brief elegy, clarinet solo, 1970; flute sonata, 1972; Introduction, variations, and adagio, flute, oboe, piano trio, 1974; CHORUS: Ah come, sweet death, canon a cappella, 1947; also piano and organ pieces. His published books include Fugue and invention in theory and practice, 1966; and Basic theory of scales, modes, and intervals, 1966.

3821 42nd Ave., N.E., Seattle, WA 98105

VEYVODA, GERALD JOSEPH
b. Queens, N.Y., 30 Sept. 1948. Studied with Ruth Anderson, Hunter Coll., B.S. 1970, M.A. 1972. He received the Ethel Lippman Hurwitz award and the George M. Schuster award. He was lecturer, Hunter Coll., Feb.-June 1971.

WORKS: CHAMBER MUSIC: quartet for winds, 1970; Sonnet to science, text by Poe, soprano and chamber ensemble, 1971; ELECTRONIC: Thru the looking glass, wind quintet, tape, mezzo-

VINCENT, HENRY BETHUEL

soprano; <u>Into the artifice of eternity</u>, wind
quintet and tape, 1971.
18 Poplar Ave., Bronx, NY   10465

VINCENT, HENRY BETHUEL
b. Denver, Colo., 28 Dec. 1872; d. Erie, Pa.,
7 Jan. 1941. Studied organ in Ohio and Paris;
was organist and choirmaster in Erie, Pa.
WORKS: OPERA: <u>Esperanza</u>, 1906; <u>Indian days</u>,
operetta; CHORUS: <u>The prodigal son</u>, oratorio,
1901; SONGS: <u>The garden of Kama</u>, a cycle; organ
pieces.

VINCENT, JOHN
b. Birmingham, Ala., 17 May 1902; d. Santa
Monica, Calif., 21 Jan. 1977. Studied with
George W. Chadwick, New England Cons., diploma
1926; George Peabody Coll., B.S. 1932, M.A. 1933;
with Wlater Piston, Harvard Univ., 1933-35; Ecole
Normale de Musique, Paris, and with Nadia
Boulanger privately, 1935-36; Cornell Univ.,
Ph.D. 1942. He received the John Knowles Paine
traveling fellowship, 1935-37; Guggenheim fellowship, 1964; Nat. Endowment for the Arts grants,
1975, 1976; and many commissions. He was music
dept. head, Western Kentucky Univ., 1937-45;
professor, Univ. of California, Los Angeles,
1946-69; director, Huntington Hartford Found.,
1953-65; president, California Inst. of the Arts,
1963-64; State Dept. lecturer and conductor in
South America, 1964.
WORKS: OPERA: <u>Primeval void</u>, 1-act opera
buffa to his own libretto, 1969, Vienna, Austria,
14 May 1971; THEATRE: music for <u>The hallow'd
time</u>, Hubler play, 1954; BALLET: <u>3 Jacks</u>, 1941,
Los Angeles, 16 Mar. 1954; <u>Mary at Calvary</u>,
soprano solo, chorus, organ, orch., 1976; OR-
CHESTRA: suite, 1932; <u>Miracle of the cherry
tree</u>, 1944, voice and orch., Los Angeles, 2 Dec.
1947; <u>I wonder as I wander</u>, low voice and orch.,
1944; <u>Soliloquy and dance</u>, cello and orch., 1947;
<u>Symphony on a folk song</u>, 1951; <u>Nude descending
the staircase</u>, after Duchamp, 1948, Los Angeles,
4 Dec. 1960; symphony in D, Louisville, Ky., 5
Feb. 1955; <u>La Jolla chamber concerto</u>, La Jolla,
19 July 1959; <u>Symphonic poem after Descartes</u>,
Philadelphia, 20 Mar. 1959; <u>Overture to Lord
Arling</u>, 1959; <u>Consort for piano and strings</u>,
Dallas, 25 Apr. 1961; <u>Benjamin Franklin suite</u>,
string orch. with glass harmonica obligato,
Philadelphia, 24 Mar. 1963; <u>Rondo rhapsody</u>,
Washington, D.C., 19 May 1965; <u>The phoenix</u>,
symphonic poem, Phoenix, Ariz., 21 Feb. 1966;
CHAMBER MUSIC: 2 string quartets, 1936, 1967;
woodwind trio, 1937; <u>Percussion suite</u>, Los
Angeles, 24 Apr. 1973; many choral works and
songs. He was author of <u>Diatonic modes in
modern music</u>, 1951, rev. and updated, 1973.

VIRIZLAY, MIHALY
b. Hungary; to U.S. 1957. Studied with Zoltan
Kodaly, Franz Liszt Acad., Budapest. In 1962
he received the Harriet Cohen Internat. award
for cello. He has given many cello recitals
and has appeared with major orchestras; joined
the faculty of Peabody Cons. as cello teacher in
1962; has been visiting professor at Indiana
Univ., summers, 1966, 1967; and is principal

cellist with the Baltimore Symph. Orch. His
compositions include <u>The emperor's new clothes</u>,
orchestral suite; a sonata for unaccompanied
cehlo; <u>Song</u>, for solo cello.
3904 Hadley Sq. W., Baltimore, MD   21218

VIRKHAUS, TAAVO
b. Estonia, 29 June 1934; U.S. citizen 1955.
Studied at Univ. of Miami; with Wayne Barlow,
Bernard Rogers, and John LaMontaine, Eastman
School of Music, D.M.A. 1967. He received the
Howard Hanson prize, 1966; second prize in a
Phi Mu Alpha contest, 1959. He was music director, Univ. of Rochester, 1966-77; from 1977,
music director and conductor, Duluth-Superior
Symphony.
WORKS: ORCHESTRA: <u>Overture to Kalevipoeg</u>,
1957; <u>French overture</u>, 1964; violin concerto,
1966; symphony #1, 1975; CHAMBER MUSIC: miniature string quartet, 1957; ELECTRONIC: <u>Con-
trasts and variables</u>, organ and tape, 1971.
321 High St., Duluth, MN   55811

VLAHOPOULOS, SOTIREOS
b. St. Louis, Mo., 1 June 1926. Studied with
Virgil Thomson, State Univ. of New York; with
Roy Harris, Indiana Univ.; and at American Cons.
He was public school music teacher, 1952-57,
1958-60; teaching assistant, Indiana Univ.,
1957-58; then joined the faculty at Rosary Hill
Coll., Buffalo, N.Y.
WORKS: ORCHESTRA: <u>5 ancient myths</u>; <u>The
Earth is an island</u>, song cycle for soprano and
orch.; <u>The moon pool</u>, tone poem for strings;
<u>Elegy</u>, oboe and strings; <u>Song of the red ruby</u>,
9 instruments and strings; <u>Iberian sketches</u>
suite, 1980; CHAMBER MUSIC: string quartet;
trio for 2 clarinets and bassoon; sonata for
solo cello; bassoon sonatina; duo for viola and
cello; CHORUS: <u>In memoriam</u>, women's voices;
SONG CYCLES: <u>The lights in the sky are stars</u>,
soprano; <u>The poet is an unhappy creature</u>, baritone; <u>Songs of the unknown</u>, alto; PIANO: sonata;
sonatina; etc.
4303 Wakefield Dr., Annandale, VA   22003

VODERY, WILL HENRY BENNETT
b. Philadelphia, Pa., 8 Oct. 1885; d. New York,
N.Y., 18 Nov. 1951. Graduated from Univ. of
Pennsylvania. He was composer, arranger, bandmaster; arranged scores for more than 50 musical
comedies; wrote the music for <u>The time, the
place, and the girl</u>; wrote songs for <u>The oyster
man</u>, 1910; was music supervisor of <u>The Ziegfeld
follies</u>, 1911-32.

VOGEL, ROGER CRAIG
b. Cleveland, Ohio, 6 July 1947. Studied with
Norman Phelps, Marshall Barnes, and Jay Huff,
Ohio State Univ., where he held a fellowship,
1971-75. Other awards include 2 first prizes in
Ohio State composition contests, 1973, 1974.
From 1976 he has been faculty member, Univ. of
Georgia.
WORKS: CHAMBER MUSIC: suite for oboe and
bassoon; partitas for flute, saxophone, and
horn; <u>Divertimento</u>, saxophone ensemble; <u>Temporal
landscape</u>, tuba and piano.
University of Georgia, Athens, GA   30602

VOLLINGER, WILLIAM
b. Hackensack, N.J., 28 June 1945. Studied with
David Diamond, Mario Davidovsky, Ludmila Ulehla,
Nicolas Flagello, Manhattan School of Music. He
has received 3 Meet the Composer grants.
WORKS: CHAMBER MUSIC: Psychic phenomena,
chamber opera; More than conquerors, a narrative
on the life of Corrie Ten Boom, for baritone,
clarinet, and piano; Little picture musics, 8
short instrumental pieces; CHORUS: Love quanti-
ties and other songs; 5 songs about the Resurrection.
21 Ruckman Rd., Woodcliff Lake, NJ 07675

VOLLRATH, CARL PAUL
b. New York, N.Y., 26 Mar. 1931. Studied at
Stetson Univ., B.M. 1953; Columbia Univ., M.A.
1956; with Ernst von Dohnanyi, Carlisle Floyd,
and John Boda, Florida State Univ., Ed.D. 1964.
He won first prize, Florida Composers League
contest, 1952. He was clarinetist, U.S. Military
Acad. Band, 1953-56; music consultant, Dade
County schools, Fla., 1956-58; from 1965, faculty
member, Troy State Univ.
WORKS: OPERA: The quest, 1964; THEATRE:
music for The king's own Christmas, 1962; The
cherry orchard, 1964; ORCHESTRA: Piece for trombone and orch., 1952; War, voice and orch., 1952;
Heavenly beauty, chorus and orch., 1952; Short
piece, 1960; BAND: Ulysses' return, 1951; Concert suite, 1955; Sinfonietta, 1960; Concert
overture, 1968; Everyman's suite, 1973; Destiny,
1977; CHAMBER MUSIC: 2 clarinet sonatas, 1959,
1969; quintet for winds, strings, and harpsichord, 1969; sonata for baritone, horn, piano,
1969; Jaunts, trombone and piano, 1970; Fantasy,
viola and piano, 1972; flute sonata, 1977; many
pieces for various instruments and piano; songs;
piano pieces.
110 Norfolk Ave., Troy, AL 36081

VON GUNDEN, HEIDI
b. San Diego, Calif., 13 Apr. 1940. Studied
with Matt Doran, Mount St. Mary's Coll.; with
Byong-kon Kim, California State Univ., Los
Angeles; with Pauline Oliveros and Robert
Erickson, Univ. of California at San Diego. She
has received grants from USCD and Southern Illinois Univ., where she was on the faculty, 1975-
79. In 1979 she joined the faculty at Univ. of
Illinois at Urbana.
WORKS: SMALL ENSEMBLES: Triptych, organ,
harpsichord, percussion; Fantasy, organ, tape,
mouth-blown pipes, clarinet, percussion; Dia-
throsis, organ and 7 instruments; Triggers, 2
trombones and 2 celli; Soundings, handbell choir;
3 condiments, 4 flutes and organ; CHORUS: Mass
for the Pentacost, choir, resonating tubes,
organ, tape, projected score.
2508 Kirby St., Champaign, IL 61820

VON WURTZLER, ARISTID
b. Budapest, Hungary, 20 Sept. 1925; U.S. citizen 1962. Studied at Liszt Acad., Budapest;
composition with Zoltan Kodaly, London Coll. of
Music. He received a Nat. Fed. of Music Clubs
award, 1969. He was harpist with the Budapest
State Symph. to 1956; with the Detroit Symph.,

1957-58; N.Y. Philharmonic, 1958-62; was faculty
member, Hartt Coll. of Music, 1964-70; from
1970, at New York Univ. and Hofstra Univ. He is
also founder and director of the New York Harp
Ensemble.
WORKS: HARP: Modern sketches; Capriccio;
Brilliant etude; Space odyssey, 4 harps; many
transcriptions.
140 West End Ave., New York, NY 10025

VOOSS, VLADIMIR A.
b. Harbin, China, 27 Aug. 1944; U.S. citizen
1963. Studied piano with Robert Sheldon, San
Francisco Cons., B.M. in composition; at University of California, San Diego, M.A. in composition. In 1976 he received a Nat. Endowment for
the Arts grant. From 1975 he has been assistant
manager of the Mandeville Auditorium at USCD.
WORKS: MULTIMEDIA: Let's build a nuthouse,
collaboration with Robert Moran, 1968; B.O.N.E.,
children's theatre, 1971; Ting, music and multi-
slide projection, 1975; Sophia Prunikos, multimedia opera, 1975; City of light, work in progress for an electronic opera, 1977-.
13850 Mango Dr., #30, Del Mar, CA 92014

WADA, YOSHIMASA
b. Kyoto, Japan, 11 Nov. 1943; to U.S. 1967.
Studied with John Watts, The New School, New
York; privately with Pran Nath, LaMonte Young,
and K. Paramjyoti in New York. He received a
Creative Arts Public Service grant in 1974. He
specializes in long-tone harmonic works for electronics and voice or instruments using overtone
series. The instruments used are large horns up
to 30 feet in length, which he builds of steam
fittings and plumbing materials.
WORKS: MULTIMEDIA: A-440, for pipe horns,
voice, tuning fork, and galvanized sheet, 1972;
50-gallon drum chant, solo voice inside three
50-gallon drums, amplified, 1972; Sundown 1980,
pipe horns, electronic drones, voice, 1973;
Earthsound 2160, for pipe horns, synthesizer,
electronic drones, 1974. Though not notated,
his works are not aleatoric but are thoroughly
rehearsed.
15 Greene St., New York, NY 10013

WADE, JAMES
b. Granite City, Ill., 5 Jan. 1930. Studied
with Jeanne Boyd, American Cons., B.M. 1952,
M.M. 1961; and at Washington Univ., M.A. in Ed.
1958. In 1956, with the American-Korean Found.
and the Asian Found., he initiated the Music for
Korea program; settled in Seoul in 1960 as
visiting professor at Yonsei Univ.; was for
several years consultant with the American-
Korean Found.; later music critic and author of
numerous articles in the Korean press, many of
which were republished abroad.
WORKS: OPERA: Old Christmas, 10-minute
opera, 1948; The martyred, based on a novel by
Richard Kimm, Seoul, Korea, 16 Apr. 1970; A
wicked voice, 1978; ORCHESTRA: Tongdo-Sa, 1954;
piano concerto, 1958; symphony #1, 1963; The war
orphans, 1959; The charnel rose, symphony #2,
with chorus and soloists, 1968; Adagio after
Mahler, 1974; Tetelestai, canticle #2, on poem

WAGENAAR, BERNARD

by Aiken, 1977; CHAMBER MUSIC: piano sonatina
#2, 1952; 2 string quartets, 1961, 1978; Baga-
telles, woodwind quintet, 1963; duo for oboe and
bassoon, 1971; duo for clarinet and cello, 1980;
CHORUS: De profundis, 1950; The oxen, poem by
Hardy, 1961; choral suite from The martyred, a
cappella, 1974; also songs; transcriptions.
> 38-1 Pirun Dong, Chongno Ku, Seoul, Korea;
> 2519 Madison Ave., Granite City, IL 62040

WAGENAAR, BERNARD

b. Arnhem, Netherlands, 18 July 1894; U.S. citizen 1927; d. York, Maine, 19 May 1971. Studied
with his father, Dutch composer John Wagenaar;
violin with Gerard Veerman. He received the
first Columbia Univ. Ditson award for his chamber
opera; Society for Publication of American Music
award, 1928; Eastman School publication award,
1929; many commissions. He was violinist in the
New York Phil., 1921-27, also played celeste,
harpsichord, and organ. He resigned from the
Philharmonic to join the faculty at Juilliard
School; also taught privately and conducted his
own works.

WORKS: OPERA: Pieces of eight, 2-act
chamber opera, New York, May 1944; ORCHESTRA:
4 symphonies, 1928, 1932, 1937, 1949; Divertimento, 1929; Sinfonietta, 1930; violin concerto,
1940; triple concerto, flute, harp, cello, and
orch., 1941; Concert overture, 1953; 5 tableaux,
cello and orch., 1955; CHAMBER MUSIC: violin
sonata, 1925; 4 string quartets; piano sonata;
cello sonatina; concertino for 8 instruments.

WAGNER, JOSEPH F.

b. Springfield, Mass., 9 Jan. 1900; d. Los
Angeles, Calif., 12 Oct. 1974. Studied with
Frederick Converse, New England Cons., diploma
1923; privately with Alfredo Casella in Boston,
1927; at Boston Univ., B.M. 1932; with Nadia
Boulanger in Paris, 1934-35; conducting with
Pierre Monteaux and Felix Weingartner in Europe.
His awards included an honorary doctorate,
Ithaca Coll.; Endicott prize, New England Cons.;
Benjamin awards; Northern California Harpists
Assoc. award; fellowships at MacDowell Colony,
Huntington Hartford Found., Montalvo Assoc.; and
commissions. He was music supervisor in Boston
public schools, 1923-44; on faculty, Boston
Univ., 1929-40; Hunter Coll., 1945-46; Brooklyn
Coll., 1945-47; founder and conductor, Boston
Civic Symph. Orch., 1925-44; conductor, Duluth
Symph., 1947-50; Nat. Symph. Orch. of Costa
Rica, 1950-54; guest conductor of many orches-
tras in U.S. and Europe; on faculty, Los Angeles
Cons., 1960-63; Pepperdine Univ., 1963-72.

WORKS: THEATRE: New England sampler, 1-
act opera; 3 ballets; ORCHESTRA: 4 symphonies,
#4 with chorus, soprano solo, and narrator, com-
pleted in 1974 shortly before his death, was
titled Tribute to America and was intended for
the Bicentennial year, but was not performed; 2
sinfoniettas; Northland evocation; Panorama;
Rhapsody, clarinet, piano, strings, 1925; concertino, piano and orch.; A fugal triptych, 1941;
concertino for harp and orch., 1947; A psalm of
faith, soprano and orch.; Introduction and rondo,
trumpet and orch.; Fantasy in technicolor, 1948;

Introduction and scherzo, bassoon and strings,
1951; concerto for organ, brass, percussion,
1963; harp concerto, 1964; violin concerto;
BAND: Eulogy; American jubilee overture, 1946;
concerto grosso, 1949; Symphonic translations,
1958; A festive fanfare, brass and percussion,
1968; Merlin and Sir Boss, 1968; CHAMBER MUSIC:
violin sonata; Rhapsody, clarinet and piano;
clarinet sonatina; Serenade, violin, cello, oboe;
3 pastorales, oboe and piano, 1941; 3 moments
musicals, string quartet; piano sonata, 1946;
Theme and variations, 2 strings, 2 woodwinds,
1950; Costa Rican pastoral, chamber orch.; Sonata
of sonnets, voice and piano, 1961; Fantasy sonata,
harp, 1963; Prelude and toccata, harp, violin,
piano, 1964; Concert piece, violin and cello,
1966; 3 charades, brass quintet, 1968; 3 Browning
love songs, voice and piano, 1970; many choral
works; piano pieces.

WAGNER, THOMAS

b. Brackenridge, Pa., 24 Feb. 1931. Studied at
Univ. of Pittsburgh; with James Friskin, Juil-
liard School; with Aaron Copland and Irving
Fine at Tanglewood on scholarship. He is a con-
cert pianist and has performed his own works in
New York.

WORKS: OPERA: The beggar; The crocodile;
The wheat remains; THEATRE: music for The lion
in winter; ORCHESTRA: Madrigal concerto; piano
concerto; 2-piano concerto; CHORUS: The girl
with the little bean nose.

WALCOTT, RONALD HARRY

b. Los Angeles, Calif., 13 May 1939. Studied
with Richard Hoffmann, Oberlin Cons., B.A.; with
John Vincent and Henri Lazarof, Univ. of California, Los Angeles, M.A.; with B. Schaeffer and
W. Kotonski in Poland. He received Atwater Kent
awards in composition, 1965, 1966; Fulbright-
Hayes grant for study in Poland, 1962-65, and
for research in Sri Lanka, 1974-78. He was
teaching assistant and museum scientist, UCLA,
1965-66, 1970-73.

WORKS: ORCHESTRA: concerto for flute,
getabera, and orch., commissioned for the American Bicentennial and performed in Colombo, Sri
Lanka, in 1976; CHAMBER MUSIC: Fragments, percussion quartet; Generations, small ensemble;
Variations for Oregon; Piece for piano; Relations, piano, clarinet, trombone, cello.
> 5134 Angeles Crest Highway, La Canada, CA
> 91011

WALD, MAX

b. Litchfield, Ill., 14 July 1889; d. Dowagiac,
Mich., 14 Aug. 1954. Studied in Chicago and
with Vincent d'Indy in Paris. He received
second prize in an NBC composition contest, 1932.
From 1936 he was chairman, theory dept., Chicago
Musical Coll.

WORKS: OPERA: Mirandolina, 1936; Gay little
world, light opera, 1942; ORCHESTRA: Retrospec-
tives, 1926; The dancer dead, symphonic poem,
1932; Comedy overture, 1937; In praise of
pageantry, 1946; VOICE: October moonlight, song
cycle for soprano and string quartet; PIANO: 2
sonatas; other piano pieces.

WALDEN, STANLEY
b. Brooklyn, N.Y., 2 Dec. 1932. Studied composition with Ben Weber in New York. His awards include ASCAP awards; Grammy nomination; New York State Council on the Arts grant, 1975; and commissions. He has been faculty member at Juilliard School, 1965-70; Max Reinhardt School, Berlin, 1970; Sarah Lawrence Coll., 1975-76; Lincoln Center Inst., 1975-78.
WORKS: BALLET: Weewis; THEATRE: music for Pinkville; The kid; Scuba Duba; Oh! Calcutta!; Sigmund Freud; The serpent; The Caucasian chalk circle; ORCHESTRA: Circus; SONG CYCLES: Some changes, mezzo-soprano and electric clarinet; Love's proper exercise, mezzo-soprano, woodwind quintet, and piano; and film scores.
Miller Hill Rd., R.D. 7, Hopewell Jct, N.Y. 12533

WALDROP, GIDEON WILLIAM
b. Haskell County, Tex., 2 Sept. 1919. Studied at Baylor Univ., B.M. 1940; Eastman School of Music, M.M. 1941, Ph.D. 1952. He received commissions from the San Antonio Symph., 1958, 1963. He was conductor of the Shreveport Symph. and faculty member, Centenary Coll., 1941-42; served in the Army Air Force, 1943-45; was conductor, Baylor-Waco Symph., and on faculty, Baylor Univ., 1952-54; editor and general manager, Musical Courier, 1954-58; from 1961, on staff at Juilliard School, appointed dean in 1963.
WORKS: ORCHESTRA: symphony, 1952; From the Southwest, overture; Prelude and fugue; Pressures, string orch.; CHAMBER MUSIC: trio for viola, clarinet, harp, 1939; Lydian trumpeter, trumpet and piano, 1946; also choral works and songs.
Juilliard School, Lincoln Center, New York, NY 10023

WALENSKY, DANA GRANT
b. Sioux City, Iowa, 24 July 1948. Studied with G. Winston Cassler, St. Olaf Coll.; with Sister Jane Klimisch, Mount Marty Coll.
WORKS: ORCHESTRA: symphony; The overcoat, overture; WIND ENSEMBLE: Lagrimoso, for brass; CHAMBER MUSIC: Prelude and fugue, woodwind trio; Fantasia (Soldiers), piano; sonatina, horn and strings; Wayghtes Chapel, 4 winds and piano; CHORUS: O brother man; Choral fantasia, with flute, oboe, horn, and baritone horn.
301 N.E. 12th St., Ankeny, IA 50021

WALKER, DONALD BURKE
b. Ventura, Calif., 18 Dec. 1941. Studied with Leland Smith, Stanford Univ., B.A. 1964; with Arnold Elston, Larry Austin, Richard Felciano, Univ. of California, Berkeley, Ph.D. 1971. His awards include the George Ladd Prix de Paris, 1966-68; Nat. Endowment for Humanities, Seminar in Ethnomusicology, 1977. He was faculty member, Univ. of South Florida, 1975-77; Sonoma State Coll., 1974-75, and from 1977.
WORKS: OPERA: Fortitude, opera in 9 scenes, 1976; ORCHESTRA: symphony, for 6 ensembles, 1970; Variations in the name of Ives; VOICE: Spiro T. Agnew songs, 1970.
2751 Poli St., Ventura, CA 93003

WALKER, GEORGE
b. Washington, D.C., 27 June 1922. Studied at Oberlin Coll., B.M. 1940; piano with Rudolf Serkin, composition with Rosario Scalero and Gian-Carlo Menotti, Curtis Inst. of Music, diploma 1945; with Nadia Boulanger in Paris; at Eastman School of Music, D.M.A. His many awards have included Fulbright, John Hay Whitney, Guggenheim, and Rockefeller; Nat. Endowment for the Arts grants; MacDowell Colony, and Yaddo fellowships; Harvey Gaul prize; Rhea Sosland prize; grants from the Bok Found. and the Univ. of Colorado and Rutgers Univ. Research Councils. He has held faculty posts at New School for Social Research, 1961; Dalcroze School of Music, 1960-61; Smith Coll., 1961-68; Univ. of Colorado, 1968-69; Rutgers Univ. at Newark from 1969, and at New Brunswick from 1976; Peabody Cons., 1974-76.
WORKS: ORCHESTRA: Lyrics for strings, 1941; trombone concerto, 1957; symphony, 1961; Antiphonies, chamber orch., 1968; Variations for orch., 1971; Passacaglia, New York, 21 Oct. 1973; Spirituals for orch., Houston, 7 Sept. 1974; piano concerto, 1975; Dialogues, cello and orch., Cleveland, 9 June 1976; mass, soloists, chorus, and orch., 1977; CHAMBER MUSIC: 2 string quartets, 1946, 1967; cello sonata, 1957; violin sonata, 1958; Perimeters, clarinet and piano, 1966; Music for 3, piano trio, 1970; 5 fancies, clarinet and piano, 4 hands, 1974; Music (Sacred and profane), for brass, 1975; CHORUS: 3 lyrics, 1958; Stars; Gloria--In memoriam, women's voices; PIANO: 3 sonatas, 1953, 1957, 1975; Spatials; Spektra; Variations on a Kentucky folk song.
323 Grove St., Montclair, NJ 07042

WALKER, GWYNETH V.
b. New York, N.Y., 22 Mar. 1947. Studied with Paul Nelson, Brown Univ.; with Arnold Franchetti, Hartt Coll. of Music. Her awards include Mann Music Premium, Brown Univ.; student awards, Hartt Coll.; Yaddo fellowship, 1976; first place, Hartford Unitarian Church anthem contest, 1978; and commissions. She has been faculty member, Oberlin Coll., from 1977.
WORKS: ORCHESTRA: Upon her leaving; CHAMBER MUSIC: April, rag, and fantasy, piano; 4 pieces for lute; flute sonata, 1978; CHORUS: A wonder told shyly, with percussion and contrabass; The radiant dawn, with organ and cello, 1978; SONGS: Salley gardens; My love walks in velvet; ORGAN: Song for organ; Ayre; Passacaglia and fugue.
643 Oenoke Ridge, New Canaan, CT 06840

WALKER, JAMES
b. Milwaukee, Wis., 13 Nov. 1937. Studied at Univ. of Wisconsin; with Leon Kirchner, Billy Jim Layton, and Roger Sessions, Harvard Univ., M.M. He received a Northwestern Internat. composition contest award, 1966; State Univ. of New York Faculty Awards Program fellowship, 1973-74; and commissions. He was conductor, Harvard Wind Ensemble and Bands, 1960-70; Freshman Glee Club, 1964-68; Harvard Chorus, 1969; Chautauqua School of Music Symph., 1965-72; from 1972, faculty member, State Univ. Coll. at Geneseo.
WORKS: CHAMBER MUSIC: Recitative in tran-

WALKER, MARK

sition, saxophone quartet, 1966; violin sonata;
CHORUS: <u>Jabberwocky</u>, with harpsichord, piano,
and electronic sounds, Columbus, Ohio, Feb. 1974.
    State Univ. of New York, Geneseo, NY 14454

WALKER, MARK
    b. Almogordo, N.Mex., 5 June 1918. Studied with
Norman Phelps, Jordan Coll. of Music, Butler
Univ., B.M., M.M.; with Roy Mill, Indiana Univ.,
Ph.D. He has received ASCAP awards and numerous
commissions. He was band leader, U.S. Army,
1943-46; faculty member, Butler Univ., 1946-61;
Ohio State Univ., 1961-68; from 1968, professor,
Youngstown State Univ.
    WORKS: ORCHESTRA: <u>Butler centennial over-
ture</u>; <u>Variations on a given theme</u>; <u>The wharf</u>,
ballet score; <u>Ricercar</u>; BAND: <u>Overture and
allegro</u>; <u>Overture in the Dorian mode</u>; <u>Jordan
rhapsody</u>; <u>Premiere rhapsody</u>, clarinet and band;
<u>Caprice</u>, bassoon and band; WIND ENSEMBLE: <u>Sara-
bande and bouree</u>, brass choir; <u>Concert overture</u>;
solo for clarinet and winds; CHAMBER MUSIC:
<u>Moods minor</u>, trumpet trio and piano; <u>4 violins
in concert</u>; duo for 2 violins; string quartet.
    152 Wolcott Dr., Youngstown, OH 44512

WALKER, RICHARD
    b. Illinois, 23 Jan. 1912. Studied at Bradley
Univ., but is largely self-taught in composition.
He was clarinetist and flutist in orchestras,
bands, and wind ensembles, 1935-65; private
teacher, 1946-71.
    WORKS: BAND: <u>Scythian overture</u>; <u>Danish
overture</u>; <u>Lyrical overture</u>; <u>Corybantes</u>; CHAMBER
MUSIC: <u>Badinerie</u>, brass quartet; <u>Rococo</u>, woodwind trio; <u>Falconry march</u>, brass trio; suite for
saxophones; <u>Rondo scherzando</u>, clarinet trio;
<u>Aubade</u>, clarinet quartet; <u>Persian caprice</u>, clar-
inet; <u>Petite rien</u>, flute; <u>Ballade</u>, alto saxophone.

WALKER, ROBERT S.
    b. Cheltenham, Pa., 12 Oct. 1935. Studied with
Julius Hijman and Roy Harris, Philadelphia
Musical Acad.; with Clifford Taylor, Temple
Univ. From 1961 he has been music teacher in
Philadelphia public schools.
    WORKS: ORCHESTRA: symphony; CHAMBER MUSIC:
<u>2 songs</u> for soprano voice; <u>Toccata</u>, piano; wood-
wind quintet; string quartet in 2 movements.
    1113 Stratford Ave., Melrose Park, PA 19126

WALLACE, KATHRYN
    b. Shawnee, Okla., 21 Oct. 1917. Studied at
Oklahoma Univ., B.F.A. 1938; with Warren M.
Angell, Oklahoma Baptist Univ., 1957-58.
    WORKS: CHORUS: <u>For the beauty of the Earth</u>;
<u>Be thou, O God, exalted</u>; <u>The Lord is my shepherd</u>;
PIANO: <u>Moods</u>; <u>Tin soldier parade</u>.

WALLS, ROBERT B.
    b. Idaho, 24 Dec. 1910. Studied at Minnesota
State Coll., B.E.; Univ. of North Dakota, M.E.
He taught in public schools in Minnesota and in
Valley City, N.Dak.; at Univ. of Idaho, 1940-47;
was professor, Univ. of Oregon, 1947-75.
    WORKS: CHORUS: <u>The names of Oregon</u>, with
narrator; <u>Shallow Brown</u>; <u>Willow wind</u>; <u>Choral
tune-ups</u>.

WALSH, MICHAEL A.
    b. Camp LeJeune, N.C., 23 Oct. 1949. Studied
with Warren Benson and Samuel Adler, Eastman
School of Music, 1967-71.
    WORKS: ORCHESTRA: <u>Elegy</u>, violin and orch.;
<u>Herbstlied</u>, violin and orch.; <u>Medieval songs</u>,
cycle for voice and orch.; CHAMBER MUSIC: piano
trio; <u>Piano variations on a theme of Anton
Webern</u>; string quartet in 1 movement; <u>7 Deutsche
Lieder</u>, voice and piano.

WALTER, BRUNO
    b. Berlin, Germany, 15 Sept. 1876; U.S. citizen
c. 1945; d. Beverly Hills, Calif., 17 Feb. 1962.
Studied at Sterns Cons., Berlin; became opera
coach at the Cologne Municipal Opera at age 17;
then assistant conductor at the Hamburg State
Theatre under Mahler; became one of the world's
noted opera conductors. After settling in the
U.S. at the outbreak of World War II, he was
frequent guest conductor at the New York Metropolitan Opera; conducted the New York Philharmonic, 1947-49.
    WORKS: ORCHESTRA: 2 symphonies; <u>Siegesfahrt</u>,
with chorus and soloists; CHAMBER MUSIC: string
quartet; piano quintet; piano trio; many songs.

WALTER, SAMUEL
    b. Cumberland, Md., 2 Feb. 1916. Studied at
Boston Univ.; with Seth Bingham, Union Theological Seminary, New York; with Nadia Boulanger
at Fontainebleau, France. He was faculty member,
Boston Univ., 1945-55; Union Theological Seminary, School of Sacred Music, 1957-65; Douglass
Coll., Rutgers Univ., from 1962; Voorhees Chapel
organist from 1964; and from 1967, organist and
choirmaster, Church of the Resurrection, New
York.
    WORKS: CHORUS: <u>Blessed are the pure in
heart</u>; <u>Christ is the world's true light</u>; and
many other published works; ORGAN: <u>6 hymn tune
preludes</u>, 1962; <u>9 compositions for organ</u>, 1965;
<u>Music for processions</u>, 1966; <u>Cardinal suite</u>,
1966; <u>Prelude on a Scandinavian hymn tune</u>. He
is author of <u>Basic principles of service playing</u>,
1963; <u>Music composition and arranging</u>, 1965; and
articles in music journals.
    83 School House Lane, East Brunswick, NJ
08816

WALTERS, HAROLD L.
    b. Gurdon, Ark., 29 Sept. 1918. Attended Cin-
cinnati Cons.; American Univ.; studied with
Nadia Boulanger in Paris. He received an honorary music doctorate, Washington Coll. of Music;
citation of excellence, Nat. Band Assoc., 1973.
He was arranger, U.S. Navy Band, 1938-44; scored
many Broadway and radio shows; from 1949, has
been editor and composer, Rubank Music Publishing Co. His compositions include more than 1500
published works for orchestra, band, chorus, instrumental ensembles, and solos.
    4931 Pierce St., Hollywood, FL 33021

WALTERS, MICHAEL J.
    Studied with Warren Benson, Ithaca Coll., B.S.
1965, M.S.; with Clifton Williams, Univ. of
Miami, D.M.A. He was band director and teacher

538

in public schools before joining the music education faculty at the New England Cons. He conducted the premiere of his Apparitions for wind ensemble at the Conservatory, 19 Mar. 1974.
New England Cons., 290 Huntington Ave., Boston, MA 02115

WALTON, KENNETH E.
b. Tulse Hill, London, England, 17 Feb. 1904; U.S. citizen. Has published works for chorus: Hush, my love; O lovely world of mine; Christmas rhapsody; and songs.

WARD, DIANE (Corajane Diane Bunce)
b. Jackson, Mich., 10 Jan. 1919. Studied at Michigan State Univ., B.A., M.A.; Univ. of Michigan; and at American Cons. She is singer, actress, writer for radio and television, and public school teacher.
WORKS: OPERA: Visiting the Bancrofts; The little dipper, operetta; CHORUS: 2 poems.

WARD, FRANK EDWIN
b. Wysox, Pa., 7 Oct. 1872; d. Wolfboro, N.H., 15 Sept. 1953. Studied at New York Coll. of Music; with Edward MacDowell, Columbia Univ., 1898-1903. He was associate professor, Columbia Univ., 1909-19; organist and choirmaster, Church of the Holy Trinity, New York, 1906-46.
WORKS: ORCHESTRA: Ocean rhapsody; CHAMBER MUSIC: 2 string quartets; other chamber works; CHORUS: The saviour of the world, Lenten cantata; The divine birth, Christmas cantata; also anthems, songs, organ pieces.

WARD, ROBERT EUGENE
b. Cleveland, Ohio, 13 Sept. 1917. Studied with Bernard Rogers and Howard Hanson, Eastman School of Music, B.M. 1939; with Frederick Jacobi and Albert Stoessel, Juilliard School; and with Aaron Copland at Tanglewood. His many awards include MacDowell fellowship, 1938; Juilliard publication award, 1942; Ditson award, 1944; American Acad. of Arts and Letters award, 1946; Guggenheim fellowships, 1950, 1951; Pulitzer prize, 1962; membership, Nat. Inst. of Arts and Letters; honorary D.M., Peabody Cons., 1975. He served in the U.S. Army, 1942-46; taught at Juilliard School, 1946-56; was music editor and executive vice-president, taught at Juilliard School, 1946-56; was music editor for music publishers, to 1968; president, North Carolina School of the Arts, 1968-75; from 1978, professor, Duke Univ.
WORKS: OPERA: Pantaloon, 3 acts, on Andreyev's play He who gets slapped, 1956; The crucible, 4 acts, New York, 26 Oct. 1961; The lady from Colorado, 2 acts, 1964; Claudia Legare, based on Ibsen's Hedda Gabler, Minneapolis, 14 Apr. 1978; ORCHESTRA: Fatal interview, soprano and orch., 1937; Ode, 1939; Yankee overture, 1940; Hushed be the camps today, chorus and orch., 1941; 4 symphonies, 1942, 1947, 1950, 1958; Adagio and allegro, 1943; Jubilation overture, 1946; Concert music, 1948; Night music, chamber orch., 1949; Jonathan and the gingery snare, 1949; Sacred songs for pantheists, soprano and orch., 1951; Festival overture; Divertimento, 1960; Hymn and celebration, 1962; Music for celebration, 1963; Let the word go forth, 1965;

Festive ode, 1966; piano concerto, 1968; BAND: Fantasia, brass choir and timpani, 1953; Fiesta processional; Prairie overture; Music for a great occasion, for the inauguration of Duke Univ. president, 18 Oct. 1970; CHAMBER MUSIC: violin sonata, 1950; Arioso and tarantella, violin or cello and piano, 1954; An abstract, clarinet and piano; many choral works, songs, piano pieces.
Duke Univ., 6695, College Station, Durham, NC 27708

WARD, WILLIAM REED
b. Norton, Kans., 20 May 1918. Studied with Charles S. Skilton and Robert Palmer, Univ. of Kansas, B.M., B.M.E. 1941; with Bernard Rogers and Howard Hanson, Eastman School of Music, M.M. 1942, Ph.D. 1954. He was faculty member, Colorado State Univ., 1942-44; Laurence Coll., 1944-47; from 1947, at San Francisco State Univ.; has also held posts as organist-choirmaster.
WORKS: ORCHESTRA: 3 symphonies, 1938, 1947, 1954; Variations on a western tune, 1948; CHAMBER MUSIC: suite for woodwind quintet, 1954; Be thou my vision, organ; CHORUS: Lullaby for a pinto colt, 1941; A vision of the world, 1955; Psalm 136, 1959; A psalm of praise, 1960; Fray Junipero Serra, The great walker, oratorio, 1960.
San Francisco State Univ., San Francisco, CA 94132

WARD-STEINMAN, DAVID
b. Alexandria, La., 6 Nov. 1936. Studied with John Boda, Florida State Univ., B.M. cum laude 1957; with Burrill Phillips, Univ. of Illinois, M.M. 1958, D.M.A. 1961; with Nadia Boulanger in Paris, 1958-59; also with Darius Milhaud, Wallingford Riegger, and Milton Babbitt. His honors include 4 BMI student awards; 2 Nat. Fed. of Music Clubs prizes; Phi Mu Alpha and Sigma Alpha Iota awards; Columbia Univ. Bearns prize; Ernst von Dohnanyi award, Florida State Univ.; honorary doctorate, Gracian Inst. of Montreal; Outstanding Professor award, California State Coll.; Kinley Memorial fellowship, Univ. of Illinois; and commissions. He was faculty member, California State Univ., 1961-70, and from 1972; visiting fellow, Princeton Univ., 1970; Ford Found. composer-in-residence, Tampa Bay area, 1970-72.
WORKS: OPERA: Tamar, 3-act multimedia music drama; BALLET: These 3; Western Orpheus, San Diego, Feb. 1965; Rituals, 1971; INCIDENTAL MUSIC: The Oresteia; Joe Egg; The puppet prince, Sarasota, 1 July 1971; ORCHESTRA: symphony, 1959; Concert overture; concerto #2 for chamber orch., 1963; concerto grosso, combo and chamber orch.; cello concerto, Tokyo, June 1967; prelude and toccata; Antares, with choir and tape, Tampa, 22 Apr. 1971; Arcturus, with synthesizer or tape, Chicago, June 1972; BAND: Jazz tangents; Raga for winds; Scorpio, 1976; CHAMBER MUSIC: Child's play, bassoon and piano, duo for cello and piano; Grant Park, baritone and chamber ensemble; Montage, woodwind quintet; brass quintet; 3 songs, clarinet and piano, 1957; The tale of Issoumbochi, narrator, boy soprano, ensemble, Japanese fairy tale; Wedding music, soprano,

WARE, HARRIET

woodwind quintet, organ; Putney 3, woodwind
quintet, prepared piano, Putney synthesizer;
Fragments from Sappho, soprano, flute, clarinet,
piano, 1965; The tracker, clarinet, fortified
piano, tape, 1976; Brancusi's brass beds, brass
quintet, 1977; CHORUS: The song of Moses, narrator, 4 soli, double chorus, San Diego, 31 May
1964; God's rock, 1976; PIANO: sonata, 1957;
sonata for piano fortified; Latter-day lullabies,
1972; many electronic pieces and multimedia
works.
    9403 Broadmoor Place, La Mesa, CA 92041

WARE, HARRIET
    b. Waupun, Wis., 26 Aug. 1877; d. New York, N.Y.,
    9 Feb. 1962. Studied piano with William Mason
    in New York; with Sigismund Stojowski in Paris;
    composition with Hugo Kaun in Berlin.
        WORKS: OPERETTA: Waltz for 3; ORCHESTRA:
    The artisan, symphonic poem, New York Symphony,
    1929; CHORUS: Sir Olaf, cantata, New York Sym-
    phony, 1910; Trees, choral cycle; Undine, choral
    cycle; SONGS: Women's triumphal march, became
    the national song of the Fed. of Women's Clubs,
    1927; numerous other songs; piano pieces.

WARE, JOHN MARLEY
    b. Two Rivers, Wis., 6 July 1942. Studied with
    Bernhard Heiden and Thomas Beversdorf, Indiana
    Univ.; with Kenneth B. Klaus, Louisiana State
    Univ. His awards include a Ford Found. grant,
    1963; selection of his works for performance at
    Symposium of Contemporary Music for Brass,
    Atlanta, 1967-70. He has held teaching posts at
    Huntington Coll., 1964-65; Univ. of Tennessee,
    1966-69; Middle Tennessee State Univ., 1971-72;
    Univ. of Wisconsin, 1972-75; Univ. of the South,
    1975-76; from 1977, Indiana State Univ.
        WORKS: ORCHESTRA: concerto for trombone
    and strings; Deploration, string orch., 1975;
    CHAMBER MUSIC: piano sonata; sonata for viola
    solo; 2 brass quintets; Fantasy, bassoon and
    piano; Soundings, trombone and piano; CHORUS:
    Loneliness, with brass and timpani; ORGAN:
    Passacaglia, 1964; Fantasy; sonata.
        2524 N. 13th St., Terre Haute, IN 47804

WARE, PETER HIGHSMITH
    b. Richmond, Va., 4 May 1951. Studied at Vir-
    ginia Commonwealth Univ., B.M. 1974; with
    Jonathan Kramer, Haubenstock-Ramati, Penderecki,
    and Takemitsu, Yale Univ., M.M. 1976; also
    cello and conducting. His awards include first
    place, Delta Omicron contest; Kellogg prize,
    Yale Univ., selection to Pi Kappa Lambda. From
    1977 he has been faculty member, Brock Univ.
        WORKS: ORCHESTRA: Tsankawi, 1978; CHAMBER
    MUSIC: woodwind quintet, 1972, rev. 1976; string
    quartet, 1973; 3 pieces, voice, clarinet, piano,
    1975; Reflections, 2 pianos and 3 players, 1976;
    CHORUS: mass, a cappella, 1976.
        Brock Univ., St. Catherines, Ont., L2S3A1,
        Canada

WARFIELD, GERALD ALEXANDER
    b. Fort Worth, Tex., 23 Feb. 1940. Studied with
    Samuel Adler, North Texas State Univ.; with
    Lukas Foss and Yannis Xenakis at Tanglewood;

with Milton Babbitt, Edward T. Cone, Earl Kim,
Peter Westergaard, and Godfrey Winham, Princeton
Univ. He received first prize in a contest of
the New Jersey chapter, Nat. Society of Arts and
Letters, 1967; first prize, Arizona Cello Society
contest, 1973; second prize, 1978 contest, New
Music for Young Ensembles, Inc. He was associate director, Index of New Musical Notation,
N.Y. Public Library, 1973-75, and music editor,
Educational Audio-Visual catalog, 1975-76; from
1976, editor, Music Series (textbooks) of Long-
man, Inc. He is author of 3 books in the series
and of 2 other textbooks.
    WORKS: CHAMBER MUSIC: Miniature, flute and
piano; 2 for 3, woodwind trio; Variations and
metamorphoses, cello ensemble, 1973, New York,
24 Feb. 1975; Fantasy quintet, mixed ensemble,
1978; Romances and metamorphoses, mixed quintet,
1978; VOICE: A study of 2 pears, song cycle,
1967; A noiseless, patient spider, chorus; A
trophy, soprano and piano trio.
    205 W. 22 St., New York, NY 10011

WARKENTIN, LARRY
    b. Reedley, Calif., 14 Aug. 1940. Studied at
    Tabor Coll., B.A. 1962; with James Winter,
    California State Univ. at Fresno, M.A.; with
    Ingolf Dahl, Carl Parrish, Paul Pisk, and Robert
    Linn, Univ. of Southern California, D.M.A. 1967.
    He received the Bank of America award in Math.
    and Science, 1958; various summer grants from
    Nat. Endowment for the Humanities. From 1966 he
    has been chairman, Humanities Div., Fresno
    Pacific Coll.
        WORKS: ORCHESTRA: concertino for piano and
    strings, 1964; Koinonia, Wichita, Kans., 28 July
    1978; CHAMBER MUSIC: St. Paul on Mars Hill,
    baritone and piano, 1960; 6 quatrains, baritone
    and woodwind quintet, 1961; string quartet,
    1976; CHORUS: The word of God, with baritone
    solo and orch., Fresno, 28 Apr. 1974; other
    works for chorus, solo voice, and piano.
        1000 Rogers Lane, Fresno, CA 93727

WARNE, KATHARINE MULKY
    b. Oklahoma City, Okla., 23 Oct. 1923. Studied
    with Darius Milhaud, Mills Coll., B.A.; with
    Bernard Wagenaar, Juilliard School, M.S.; with
    Donald Erb, Cleveland Inst. of Music, D.M.A.
    Her awards include first prize, Mills Coll. con-
    test, 1944, 1945; full fellowship at Juilliard
    School; a first and second prize, Kansas Fed. of
    Music Clubs contest, 1959; performance at Univ.
    of Kansas Symposium and Cleveland Contemporary
    Arts Festival. She was faculty member, Univ. of
    Kansas, 1947-53, 1957-60; Baldwin Wallace Cons.,
    1973-75; Kent State Univ., 1975-76; and from
    1972, instructor, Laurel School for Girls.
        WORKS: ORCHESTRA: Epigenesis; CHAMBER
    MUSIC: Apollo-Orion, chamber orch.; Tetrad,
    percussion; Interplay, piccolo, trumpet, cello;
    Uncamouflaged, flute and piano; Multiplexity and
    Cryptic evocation, both flute and piano; Now!,
    2 flutes; Inquiries, harp; Dispositions, harp;
    many piano pieces and vocal works.
        15715 Chadbourne Rd., Shaker Heights, OH
        44120

WARNER, PHILIP
b. Chicago, Ill., 6 Nov. 1901. Studied at
American Cons., B.M.; Sherwood Music Schools;
Northwestern Univ. He received the Kimball
award and a Sinfonis Nat. Contest prize; was
accompanist for singers, pianist on radio.
WORKS: ORCHESTRA: Sinfonietta; Sarabande-
chaconne; Youth overture; Green mansions; The
lake at dawn; CHAMBER MUSIC: Valse caprice,
saxophone; Cuban skies, piano; choral works;
songs.

WARREN, ELINOR REMICK
b. Los Angeles, Calif., 23 Feb. 1906. Studied
piano and composition in Los Angeles; with
Clarence Dickinson in New York; with Nadia
Boulanger in Paris. Her many awards include an
honorary music doctorate, Occidental Coll.;
Woman of the Year in Music, Los Angeles Times,
1954; annual ASCAP awards from 1958; selection,
along with Igor Stravinsky and Walter Piston,
to participate in the first Los Angeles Internat.
Music Festival, 1961; Nat. League of American
pen Women award, 1976; Nat. Endowment for the
Arts grant, 1976; many commissions. She began
composing at an early age and had works published
by leading New York firms while she was still in
high school. She is an accomplished pianist and
has accompanied many noted singers.
WORKS: ORCHESTRA: Along the western shore;
The crystal lake; suite, 1954; symphony in 1
movement, 1970; Singing Earth, with solo voice,
Sandburg text; Sonnets, soprano and string orch.,
Millay text; Theme for the carillon, used at
Hollywood Bowl, 1959-78; Good morning, America,
with narrator and chorus, California State Univ.,
Fullerton, 21 Nov. 1976; CHORUS: Transcontinental, with baritone solo and chamber orch.; Abram
in Egypt, with baritone solo and orch., text
from the Dead Sea Scrolls and Book of Genesis,
performed at the Israel Festival, 1976; numerous
other choral works and songs.
154 S. Hudson Ave., Los Angeles, CA 90004

WARREN, FRANK EDWARD
b. Norwood, Mass., 27 Feb. 1950. Studied with
John Bavicchi, Jeronimus Kacinskas, William
Maloof, Berklee Coll. of Music, B.M. 1976; with
Artin Arslanian, Univ. of Lowell. He taught in
public schools, 1977-79; at Massasoit Community
Coll., 1978-79; from 1980, at Middlesex Community Coll., Bedford, Mass.
WORKS: CHAMBER MUSIC: Lee Ann, solo tuba;
suite for string quartet; 3 studies, piano;
Music for percussion; 3 inventions, harpsichord;
sonata for unaccompanied clarinet; Music for
flute.
Middlesex Community College, Bedford MA
01730

WARREN, HARRY
b. Brooklyn, N.Y., 24 Dec. 1893; d. Los Angeles,
Sept. 1981. At 16, joined a carnival as a drummer, and began to compose in his spare time.
During World War I, he was assigned to the naval
air station at Montauk Point and continued to
compose. After the war, he became a rehearsal
pianist and song plugger until teaming up with

Billy Rose to write songs and Broadway musicals.
In 1932 he went to Hollywood where he composed
for films.
WORKS: STAGE SCORES: The laugh parade;
Crazy quilt; FILM SCORES: 42nd Street; Gold
diggers, 1933, 1935, 1937; Roman scandals; Week-
end in Havana; Springtime in the Rockies; Yolanda
and the thief; Diamond horseshoe; That night in
Rio; many others; SONGS: Chattanooga choo-choo;
Lullaby of Broadway; Atchison, Topeka and the
Santa Fe; Don't give up the ship; Cheerful little
earful; Boulevard of broken dreams; I found a
million-dollar baby; She's a Latin from Manhattan;
Down Argentine way; and some 1000 others.

WARREN, WILLIAM A.
b. Toledo, Ohio, 8 Feb. 1952. Studied clarinet
at Eastman School of Music; with John Ferritto,
Wittenberg Univ. He played clarinet in the
Rochester Opera Theatre, 1968-70; Springfield
Civic Opera, from 1970; Springfield Symphony,
1973.
WORKS: BAND: Fantasy for woodwind doublers,
woodwind quartet and band; CHAMBER MUSIC: Abstractions of a familiar melody, string orch.;
clarinet trio; Duo concertante, trombone and
piano; In memoriam Green Pen, cello and clarinet;
woodwind quintet; Ballad, alto clarinet and
piano; works for chorus and for solo voice.
c/o Springfield Civic Opera Co., Springfield,
OH 45501

WASHBURN, GARY SCOTT
b. Tulsa, Okla., 14 Jan. 1946. Studied with
Neil McKay, Armand Russell, Ingolf Dahl, Morton
Feldman, Univ. of Hawaii; with Gardner Read,
David Del Tredici, Joyce Mekeel, Boston Univ.
His awards include scholarships at Boston Univ.
and Univ. of Hawaii; Nat. Endowment for the Arts
grant. He taught in public school, 1971; on
faculty, Univ. of Hawaii, 1970, from 1973, at
Hilo.
WORKS: ORCHESTRA: Geometric studies, orch.
and 3 percussion ensembles, 1970; CHAMBER MUSIC:
percussion sextet, 1969; Passacaglia, chamber
ensemble; Eight, wind sextet and percussion; The
breathless feather, viola solo; Zeitdehner,
viola and percussion; Tiaboec, piano; Kaliapahoa,
double bass; ELECTRONIC: quintet, 2 saxophones,
2 percussion, tape, 1971; Godo, tape; Kokora,
piano and tape.
University of Hawaii, Hilo, HI 96720

WASHBURN, ROBERT
b. Bouckville, N.Y., 11 July 1928. Studied at
State Univ. Coll. at Potsdam, B.S. 1949, M.S.
1956; with Bernard Rogers and Alan Hovhaness,
Eastman School of Music, Ph.D. 1960; with Darius
Milhaud, Aspen Music School; and with Nadia
Boulanger in Paris. His awards include a Danforth Found. grant, 1958; Ford Found. fellowship
for composer residency, Elkhart, Ind., 1959-60;
MacDowell fellowship, 1963; State Univ. of New
York fellowships, 1963, 1971, 1973. He served
in the U.S. Air Force, 1950-54; then joined the
faculty at State Univ. Coll. at Potsdam.

WASHINGTON, GARY

WORKS: ORCHESTRA: symphony, 1959; Synthesis, 1960; 3 pieces; Suite for strings; St. Lawrence overture, 1962; Sinfonietta, for string orch., 1964; Serenade, for strings; North Country sketch, 1969; Excursion; Festive overture; Elegy, 1974; Overture: Mid-America, 1976; Passacaglia and fugue, string orch.; CHAMBER MUSIC: Suite for woodwind quintet; 3 pieces for 3 woodwinds; woodwind quintet; string quartet; concertino for woodwind and brass quintets; brass quintet; CHORUS: A child this day is born, with brass; Scherzo for spring; 3 Shakespearean love songs, men's voices; Now welcome summer; Praise the Lord, with brass; Ode to freedom, with orch. or band; also numerous works for band and various wind ensembles.
R.D. 4, Potsdam, NY 13676

WASHINGTON, GARY
b. Mineola, N.Y., 13 Aug. 1953. Studied with Raoul Pleskow, C. W. Post Coll., Long Island Univ., where he has been adjunct lecturer from 1976.
WORKS: CHAMBER MUSIC: Poem #1, baritone voice, oboe, piano; Piece, for oboe and flute; Poem #2, alto voice, viola, piano; Flight, solo oboe; Pastorale, oboe and piano; piano sonata; woodwind quintet; many other pieces for solo woodwinds and ensembles.
195-08 Station Rd., Apt. 3, Flushing, NY 11358

WASON, ROBERT WESLEY
b. Bridgeport, Conn., 25 July 1945. Studied with Arnold Franchetti and Thomas Putsche, Hartt Coll. of Music, M.M. 1969. He received the Hartt Coll. composition award, 1969; Bronze Medal, Radio France, Concourse Internat. de Guitare, 1975; and commissions. From 1970 he has been instructor at Hartt Coll.
WORKS: ORCHESTRA: 4 poems of Michelangelo, with chorus and soloists, 1969; Prelude, for orch., 1970; concerto for chamber orch. and jazz ensemble, Hartford, Aug. 1974; CHAMBER MUSIC: Burn's songs, tenor and piano, 1972; sonata for oboe solo, 1973; trio for clarinet, viola, piano, 1974; Theme and variations, solo guitar, 1974.
269 S. Marshall St., Hartford, CT 06105

WATERS, EMORY WALLACE
b. Hoboken, N.J., 30 Sept. 1947. Studied with Philip Rhodes and Peter Westergaard, Amherst Coll., B.A. 1969; with Donald Martino, New England Cons., M.M. 1971; with Bruno Maderna at Tanglewood, 1971. He held the E. P. Lay fellowship at Amherst Coll.; his Antiphon was chosen for performance at the 7th Internat. Student Composer Symposium, Montreal, 1971. He was faculty member, Virginia State Coll., 1971-73; from 1973, at Union Coll., Schenectady, and conductor, Northeastern New York Youth Orchestra.
WORKS: ORCHESTRA: Antiphon, double chamber orch., 1969; 2 pieces, for orch., 1973; CHAMBER MUSIC: Variations for 4 players, flute, oboe, viola, bassoon, 1971; 3 songs, soprano, 3 flutes, clarinet, piano, 1974; ELECTRONIC: Rhymes and echoes, alto saxophone and tape, 1974.
706 Union St., Schenectady, NY 12305

WATERS, J. KEVIN (S.J.)
b. Seattle, Wash., 24 June 1933. Studied with John Verrall and George F. McKay, Univ. of Washington, D.M.A. 1970; with Roy Harris, Univ. of California, Los Angeles; with Bruno Bartolozzi and Niccolo Castiglione in Italy. He has received several commissions. He was faculty member, Univ. of Washington, 1968-69; from 1969, at Seattle Univ.; visiting professor, Gonzaga-in-Florence, Italy, 1970-71; founded the Seattle Univ. Fine Arts Ensemble in 1970.
WORKS: OPERA: The mask of Hiroshima, 1971; Dear Ignatius, Dear Isabel, 1 act, commissioned for 125th anniversary of Loyola Coll., Baltimore, 4 May 1978; ORCHESTRA: Ennistymon, passacaglia, 1968; CHORUS: Inversnaid, with 2 soprano soli and orch., 1964; Mass of the American martyrs, 1965; Psalm of Thanksgiving, 1967; MULTIMEDIA: A solemn liturgy, chorus, male and female cantors, brass band and percussion, dancers, San Francisco, 30 July 1973.
Seattle University, Seattle, WA 98122

WATERS, JAMES L.
b. Kyoto, Japan, of American parents, 11 June 1930. Studied with Bernard Rogers, Eastman School of Music, Ph.D. 1967. His awards include the Louis Lane award, 1966; Ohio Music Teachers Assoc. award, 1974; Nat. Endowment for the Arts grant, 1979. He was faculty member, Westminster Choir Coll., 1957-68; from 1968, at Kent State Univ.
WORKS: ORCHESTRA: 2 pieces, small orch., 1966; 3 holy sonnets of John Donne, bass-baritone and orch., 1966; concertino for string quartet and string orch., 1967; 3 songs of Louise Bogan, contralto and orch., 1970; overture, 1974; WIND ENSEMBLE: Concertino antifonale, brass and percussion, 1972; CHAMBER MUSIC: Lyric piece, violin, clarinet, piano, 1971; Fantasy, piano, 1975; Nocturne, flute and piano, 1978; CHORUS: Dirge, with 9 instruments, 1968; Oh my blacke soule!, a cappella, 1972; Litanie, with 6 instruments, 1972; Anne Bradstreet's hymn, a cappella, 1975; SONGS: War is kind, soprano and piano, 1967; Thou art my love, tenor and 11 instruments, 1969; Song cycle on poems of Stephen Crane, 1980; ORGAN: Phrygian toccata, 1973.
2004 Brookview Dr., Kent, OH 44240

WATKINS, R. BEDFORD
b. Keiser, Ark., 27 July 1925. Studied at Southwestern at Memphis, B.M. 1949; with Gerald Kechley, Univ. of Michigan, M.M. 1951; with Philip Bezanson, Univ. of Iowa, Ph.D. 1966. His faculty posts have been Southwestern at Memphis, 1949-50; Winthrop Coll., 1951-56; from 1956, Illinois Wesleyan Univ.
WORKS: CHAMBER MUSIC: 4 burlesques, violin and piano, 1962; Pentamerous suite, trumpet and piano, 1972; Bicinia, clarinet and oboe; CHORUS: Fili mi Absolom, with bass solo and percussion, 1976; Te Deum, with 2 soprano soli and percussion, 1978; SONGS: Poetiae patriae amantes, 5 disparate songs for baritone, oboe, piano, 1976; 3 spring haiku, soprano, string quartet, horn, 1978.
Illinois Wesleyan Univ., P.O. Box 2900, Bloomington, IL 61701

WATSON, MARY BAUGH
b. Pulaski, Tenn., 10 Aug. 1890. Studied at Oberlin Cons. and with Tirindelli at the Cincinnati Cons. She taught piano and violin at various schools; Des Moines School of Music, 1924-33; then was a private teacher in Albany, Ga., and violinist in the Albany Symph. Orch.

WORKS: ORCHESTRA: a tone poem; CHAMBER MUSIC: Gulliver, violin and piano; Air for viola; piano sonata; many sacred and secular songs and piano teaching pieces.
608 N. Jefferson, Albany, GA 31701

WATSON, WALTER ROBERT
b. Canton, Ohio, 13 Oct. 1933. Studied with Karl Ahrendt, Ohio Univ., B.F.A. 1959, M.F.A. 1961; with Samuel Adler, North Texas State Univ., Ph.D. 1967; with Darius Milhaud, Aspen Music School. His awards include annual ASCAP awards from 1968; Kent State Univ. fellowships, 1968, 1970, 1972; first prize, U.S. Navy Band contest, 1973; grants form Rockefeller Found., George Gund Found., Boscom Little Fund, 1978. He was faculty member, Stephen F. Austin State Univ., 1961-66; then at Kent State Univ.; from 1974, editorial consultant, Ludwig Publ. Co.

WORKS: OPERA: Deborah Sampson; ORCHESTRA: symphony; concerto for guitar and chamber orch.; BAND: Antiphony and chorale; CHAMBER MUSIC: Essay for flute; trombone sonatina; Divertimento, flute, harp, bassoon; Trumpet tunes revisited, trumpet and organ; trio for viola, clarinet, piano; Recital suite, marimba and piano; CHORUS: 5 Japanese love songs, women's voices; Let all the world in every corner sing; ORGAN: Reflection.
1224 Fairview Dr., Kent, OH 44240

WATSON, WILLIAM CARL
b. Covington, Ky., 21 June 1934. Studied bassoon, Cincinnati Coll. of Music; Univ. of Kentucky, B.M. 1957; composition with Kenneth Gaburo, Univ. of Illinois, M.M. 1958; with Hugo Norden, Boston Univ.; William Graves and Thomas Canning, West Virginia Univ., Ph.D. 1965. He was faculty member, Hastings Coll., 1963-65; Wichita State Univ., 1965-67; from 1967, Washington State Univ.; also bassoonist in the WSU Faculty Quintet, and from 1975, in the Spokane Symph. Orch. He was visiting lecturer, Chinese Univ. of Hong Kong, 1972-74.

WORKS: CHAMBER MUSIC: Piece, for bassoon and piano; Serenade, wind instruments, double bass, piano; 3 short pieces, for wind quintet; A little dog of Yaumati, cello solo; 3 studies on Chinese tripods, flute, bassoon, harpsichord; Etudes on 6 notes, clarinet with optional piano; SONGS: 3 songs: Paraphrases of Chinese poetry, 1976; Don't make love in the hay fields, 1978.
N.W. 405 Larry, Pullman, WA 99163

WATTS, JOHN
b. Cleveland, Tenn., 16 July 1930. Studied with John Krueger and David Van Vactor, Univ. of Tennessee, B.A. 1949; Cecil Effinger, Univ. of Colorado, M.M. 1953; with Burrill Phillips, Univ. of Illinois, 1955-56; Robert Palmer, Cornell Univ., 1958-60; and with Roy Harris, Univ. of California, Los Angeles, 1961-62. He held a Yaddo fellowship, 1964. He was faculty member, North Dakota State Coll., 1956-57; Internat. Inst. of Music, Puerto Rico, 1960-61; founder-director, Composers Theatre, from 1964; faculty member, New School for Social Research, from 1969; on adjunct faculty, Staten Island Community Coll., 1971-72.

WORKS: THEATRE: music for Faust, 1973; 3 large works for children's theatre; DANCE SCORES: Locrian; songandance; Still life; Margins; Perimeters; This is not a working number; glass and shadows; Programs; Heirlooms; UPS; GO; ORCHESTRA: Signals, soprano and orch.; Maxiconcerto for conductor and orchestra; PIANO: sonata; FILM SCORES: War, a documentary; Daisies; ELECTRONIC: Piano for Te, piano and 13 players with tape; Elegy to Chimney: In memoriam, trumpet, synthesizer, tape; WARP, brass quintet, synthesizer, tape; Laugharne, soprano, synthesizer, and orch., New York, 10 May 1974; Processional, 10 trumpets and tape; Mot d'Heures: Gousses, Rames, voices and tape.
25 W. 19th St., New York, NY 10011

WATTS, MARZETTE
b. Montgomery, Ala., 3 Sept. 1938. Studied at New York Univ. and with Don Cherry and Ornette Coleman. He has received grants from the Creative Arts Public Service Program and Nat. Endowment for the Arts. He was visiting artist, Wesleyan Univ., 1972; from 1973, recording engineer and owner, Le Doux Sound, Inc.

WORKS: ELECTRONIC: Piece for 2 synthesizers and woodwinds, received CAPS award; all works are jazz and/or electronic.
27 Cooper Square, New York, NY 10003

WATTS, WINTTER
b. Cincinnati, Ohio, 14 Mar. 1884; d. Brooklyn, N.Y., 1 Nov. 1962. Studied at Juilliard School and at the American Acad. in Rome, 1923-25. He received the Loeb prize, 1919; Pulitzer prize, 1923; American Prix de Rome, 1973.

WORKS: OPERA: Pied piper; THEATRE: music for Alice in Wonderland; ORCHESTRA: Bridal overture, 1916; Etchings, suite, 1921; Young blood, symphonic poem, 1923; SONG CYCLES: 3 vignettes of Italy; Cycle on poems of Sara Teasdale; Wings of night; Like music on the water; and many separate songs.

WAUGH, HARVEY RICHARD
b. Clarksville, Iowa, 13 Oct. 1902. Studied at Grinnell Coll., B.A. 1924; with Leopold Auer and Leon Sametini, Chicago Musical Coll.; with Philip Greeley Clapp, Univ. of Iowa, M.A.; and with Samuel Gardner, Columbia Univ. He was faculty member, Iowa State Teachers Coll., 1930-33; Saint Cloud State Coll., 1933-42, 1946-68; served in the U.S. Navy, 1942-45; was principal arranger, Blue Jackets Choir, Great Lakes, 1942-43.

WORKS: ORCHESTRA: O people of Sion, with chorus; Theme and variations, string orch.; Adagio on an English folk song, string orch.; also choral works and songs.
413 Overleaf Park, Saint Cloud, MN 56301

WAXMAN, DONALD

WAXMAN, DONALD
b. Steubenville, Ohio, 29 Oct. 1925. Studied
with Howard Thatcher and Elliott Carter, Peabody
Cons., B.S.; and at Juilliard School. He received the Gustav Klemm prize, 1949, and a
Guggenheim fellowship.
WORKS: ORCHESTRA: A Paris overture, Baltimore, 30 Jan. 1966; CHAMBER MUSIC: woodwind
trio; 50 etudes, piano; CHORUS: Thomas Hardy
choral cycle.
c/o Galaxy Music Corp., 2121 Broadway, New
York, NY 10023

WAXMAN, ERNEST
b. New York, N.Y., 14 Oct. 1913. Studied with
Aaron Copland, Roy Harris, and Isadore Freed in
New York. He won second place, Nat. Composers
contest, 1950; performance by the New York Phil.
strings of Spoon River rhapsody. He has been
private piano teacher from 1930; was studio
pianist, Columbia Broadcasting System, 1945-58;
public school music teacher from 1960.
WORKS: ORCHESTRA: David and Goliath, with
narrator; Spoon River rhapsody, flute and strings;
Fanfare overture, 1950; concerto for piano and
strings; clarinet concerto; trumpet concerto
with chamber orch.; CHAMBER MUSIC: 2 piano
sonatas; 4 divertissements, clarinet and piano;
Capriccio, brass quintet; VOICE: 4 songs set to
Negro poetry.
6146 Little Neck Pkwy., Little Neck, NY
11362

WAXMAN, FRANZ
b. Königshütte, Germany, 24 Dec. 1906; U.S. citizen 1940; d. Los Angeles, Calif., 24 Feb. 1967.
Studied in Berlin and Dresden, and with Arnold
Schoenberg in Los Angeles, 1934. His awards included Academy awards for film scores, Sunset
Boulevard, 1950, and Place in the sun, 1951;
award of merit, Nat. Assoc. of American Composers
and Conductors, 1956.
WORKS: ORCHESTRA: Sinfonietta, 1950; Fantasy on Carmen, violin and orch.; 3 sketches for
jazz orch., 1955; Theme, variations and fugato,
1956; Joshua, oratorio with chorus, 1959; Symphonic fantasy on A mighty fortress is our God;
Elegy, for strings; FILM SCORES: Rear window;
Crime in the streets; Peyton Place; The spirit
of St. Louis; The nun's story; Cimarron; Taras
Bulba; and many others.

WAYDITCH, GABRIEL
b. Budapest, Hungary, 28 Dec. 1888; to U.S. 1907;
d. New York, N.Y., 28 July 1969. Studied at the
Budapest Acad. of Music. He wrote 14 operas to
his own librettos in Hungarian, most of them on
religious themes and requiring 2 to 8 hours to
perform. Only one, Horus, was performed in his
lifetime, that at his own expense in Philadelphia, 5 Jan. 1939. Jesus before Herod was given
in concert form by the San Diego Symphony on
5 Apr. 1979.

WAYLAND, NEWTON HART
b. Santa Barbara, Calif., 5 Nov. 1940. Studied
with Daniel Pinkham, Francis Judd Cooke, and
David Barnett, New England Cons. His awards

include a Rockefeller grant for artist residency,
WGBH-TV, Boston, 1969-70; and commissions. He
was faculty member, New England Cons., 1966-70;
from 1967, pianist with the Boston Symphony;
from 1971, music director, Adventures in Music;
from 1972, music director for "Zoom," and conductor, Associate Artists' Opera.
WORKS: THEATRE: music for Beauty and the
beast; Wind in the willows; Pinocchio; Alice in
wonderland; The Emperor's new clothes; ORCHESTRA:
What's my thing?; SONGS: 8 fatal songs, mezzo-
soprano with saxophone or bassoon; The bat poet,
cycle of 4 songs; with piano and percussion;
original songs for "ZOOM": ZOOM theme, Fannee-
Doolee, Ubbi-dubbi, Flying, Men from Mars, and
others; 5 commercial songs, poems by Anthony
Kahn; also film scores for educational television.
Nashua Rd., Groton, MA 01450

WEAVER, JOHN
b. Palmerton, Pa., 27 Apr. 1937. Studied at
Peabody Cons.; at Curtis Inst.; with Robert
Baker and Joseph Goodman, Union Theological
Seminary, School of Sacred Music. He won an
award in a Brown Univ. choral contest. He has
been church music director from 1959; from 1970,
Presbyterian Church, Madison Ave., New York;
from 1971, also on faculty, Curtis Inst.
WORKS: CHORUS: Psalm 100; Epiphany alleluias; Good Christian men rejoice; ORGAN:
Toccata; Rhapsody, with solo flute.
921 Madison Ave., New York, NY 10021

WEAVER, MARY
b. Kansas City, Mo., 16 Jan. 1903. Studied at
Smith Coll.; Ottawa Univ., B.A., B.M.; with
Rosario Scalero and Deems Taylor, Curtis Inst.
of Music. She taught piano, Univ. of Missouri,
Kansas City, 1946-57; Manhattan School of Music,
1957-70.
WORKS: CHORUS: All weary men; Kneel down;
When Jesus lay by Mary's side; Like doves as-
cending; Rise up all men; SONGS: Cradle song;
The heart of heaven.

WEAVER, POWELL
b. Clearfield, Pa., 10 June 1890; d. Oakland,
Calif., 22 Dec. 1951. Studied with Percy
Goetschius and Gaston Dethler, Juilliard School;
with Pietro Yon in New York; with Ottorino
Respighi in Rome. He gave organ recitals in
Italy; on returning to the U.S., became music
director, B'nai Jehudah Temple, Kansas City. He
gave recitals in the Midwest and South; was accompanist for many singers; music dept. head,
Ottawa Univ.; organist-choirmaster, First Baptist
Church, Kansas City, 1937-51.
WORKS: ORCHESTRA: Plantation overture,
1925; The little faun, 1925; The vagabond, 1931;
Dance of the sand-dune crane, piano and orch.,
1941; Ballet suite; Fugue for strings; Ode,
piano and strings; CHORUS: Boating song; Spirit
of God; The hummingbird; O God, our help in ages
past; SONGS: Moon-marketing; The Abbot of Derry;
The night will never stay; Windy weather; also
chamber music, including a violin sonata.

WEAVER, THOMAS
b. Kansas City, Mo., 4 Oct. 1939. Studied at
Juilliard School and with Nadia Boulanger. He
taught at Furman Univ.; Brevard Music Center;
3rd Street, Henry Street, and Bronx House Music
School Settlements; in 1969, joined the faculty
at Univ. of Georgia.
WORKS: ORCHESTRA: Icarus, symphonic poem;
CHAMBER MUSIC: 7 dialogues, flute and clarinet;
string quartet; 4 poems for piano; Fantasy, violin and piano; 3 pieces, violin and piano; and
songs.
University of Georgia, Athens, GA 30602

WEBB, ALLIENE BRANDON
b. Palestine, Tex., 2 Jan. 1910; d. Dallas, Tex.,
16 Nov. 1965. Studied voice with Peter Tchach.
She was music director and soloist, Park Cities
Baptist Church, Dallas, for 12 years.
WORKS: CHORUS: Father, teach me to pray;
He's walking with me; Hosanna to his name; My
father's prayer; The endless song; 'Twas the
night before Christmas; and songs.

WEBB, RICHARD A.
b. Martins Ferry, Ohio, 24 June 1942. Studied
with Karl Ahrendt, Ohio Univ., M.M.; with Paul
Cooper and Scott Huston, Univ. of Cincinnati.
He was teaching fellow, Univ. of Cincinnati,
1968-70; faculty member, East Tennessee State
Univ., 1965-68, and from 1971.
WORKS: CHAMBER MUSIC: Kaleidoscope, string
quartet, won 1964 Sphere award in composition;
CHORUS: Excerpts from Ecclesiastes, with brass
and organ; ORGAN: Psalm suite; Tiento for
Epiphany.
915 Beech Dr., Johnson City, TN 37601

WEBER, BEN BRIAN
b. St. Louis, Mo., 23 July 1916; d. New York,
N.Y., 9 May 1979. Studied theory, piano, and
voice at De Paul Univ.; was self-taught in composition. His awards included citation and
grant, Nat. Inst. of Arts and Letters, 1950; 2
Guggenheim grants, 1950, 1953; Fromm Found.
awards, 1953, 1955; Phoebe Ketchum Thorne award,
1965; election to membership, Nat. Inst. of Arts
and Letters, 1971; many commissions. He was a
private teacher of composition and theory.
WORKS: BALLET: Pool of darkness, chamber
ensemble; ORCHESTRA: Symphony on poems of
William Blake, baritone and 12 instruments, 1950;
violin concerto, 1954; Prelude and passacaglia,
1954; Rapsodie concertante, viola and orch.,
1957; piano concerto, 1961; Dolmen, an elegy,
1964; 2 pieces, string orch.; Sinfonia clarion,
New York, 26 Feb. 1974; CHAMBER MUSIC: Serenade,
flute, oboe, cello, harpsichord; 2 string quartets; 2 violin sonatas; Concert aria after
Solomon, soprano and chamber ensemble; concerto
for piano, woodwind quintet, cello, 1950; Nocturne, flute, clarinet, cello; 2 dances, viola
and piano; Sonata da camera, violin and piano;
Dance, cello solo; Nocturne, flute and piano;
Serenade, string quartet and double bass; Chamber
fantaisie, solo violin and 6 instruments, 1959;
Consort of winds, woodwind quintet, 1974; Capriccio, cello and piano, 1975; many piano pieces.

WEBER, JOSEPH
b. Antioch, Calif., 31 July 1937. Studied with
Wendell Otey and Roger Nixon, San Francisco
State Coll. He received the Paul Masson composition prize, 1961.
WORKS: ORCHESTRA: symphony; CHAMBER MUSIC:
string quartet; Songs, for voice, violin, clarinet, vibraphone; Portfolio I, violin and piano;
Portfolio II, trombone and piano; Portfolio III,
for miscellaneous objects; PIANO: 3 sonatas;
Canzone, 2 pianos.
1336 38th Ave., San Francisco, CA 94122

WEED, MAURICE JAMES
b. Kalamazoo, Mich., 16 Oct. 1912. Studied with
H. Owen Reed, Michigan State Univ., A.B. 1934;
with Burrill Phillips, Howard Hanson, Bernard
Rogers, Eastman School of Music, M.M. 1952, Ph.D.
1954. His awards include the Benjamin award,
1954; first prize, Nat. Symph. Orch. contest,
1955; Ostwald award, American Bandmasters Assoc.,
1959; MacDowell fellowship, 1961; first prize,
J. Fischer & Bros. contest, 1964; 5th Pedro Paz
award, Olivet Coll., 1966. He was public school
music supervisor, 1934-43; faculty member, Ripon
Coll., 1946-51; Northern Illinois Univ., 1956-
74; Western Carolina Univ., 1974-75.
WORKS: ORCHESTRA: The mountains, suite,
1952; Serenity, chamber orch., 1953; symphony
#1, 1954; symphony breve, 1959; concertino for
cello and orch., 1961; BAND: American spirit,
overture, 1951; Symphonic rondo, 1966; Vestigia
nulla retrorsum, 1968; CHAMBER MUSIC: Variation
on a jolly tune, woodwind quintet, 1943, rev.
1974; string quartet, 1952; piano trio, 1961;
duo for viola and trumpet, 1974; also choral
works, piano pieces.
R.R. 1, Box 641, Timberlane Rd., Waynesville,
NC 28786

WEEKS, CLIFFORD M.
b. New York, N.Y., 15 Apr. 1938. Studied at
Berklee Coll. of Music, diploma 1962; with Avram
David, Boston Cons., B.M. magna cum laude 1963;
Boston State Coll. He has been public school
teacher from 1963; instructor, Nat. Center for
Afro-American Arts and the Elma Lewis School of
Fine Arts, 1970-73.
WORKS: CHAMBER MUSIC: Triptych, tuba and
piano, Boston, 26 May 1963; many jazz composi-
tions and arrangements.
20 Fells Ave., Medford, MA 02155

WEGNER, AUGUST MARTIN, III
b. Saginaw, Mich., 20 Feb. 1941. Studied with
Lawrence Rackley, Central Michigan Univ., 1963-
64; with Richard Hervig, Univ. of Iowa, 1969-71;
received the Clapp composition award, 1971.
From 1972 he has been faculty member Univ. of
Wisconsin-Parkside; also codirector, New Music
at Parkside Series.
WORKS: ORCHESTRA: Ice-nine, with prepared
piano; CHAMBER MUSIC: Something, for flute and
piano; Something, for saxophone and piano; Movement, violin, clarinet, piano; Concert music,
euphonium and percussion; Encore piece: A little
minor blues, piano; CHORUS: Coney Island, cantata for 8 voices and 11 instruments.

WEHR, DAVID A.

Univ. of Wisconsin-Parkside, CA 216, Kenosha, WI 53141

WEHR, DAVID A.
b. Mt. Vernon, N.Y., 21 Jan. 1934. Studied with David Stanley York and Warren Martin, Westminster Choir Coll.; with Clifton Williams, Univ. of Miami, Ph.D. in conducting and choral literature, 1971. He has received annual ASCAP awards from 1966; Distinguished Alumni award, Westminster Choir Coll., 1966. He was organist-choirmaster-carilloneur, Cathedral of the Rockies, Boise, Idaho, 1958-68; carilloneur, New York World's Fair, 1964; from 1971, has been faculty member, Eastern Kentucky Univ.
WORKS: CHORUS: God is working his purpose out; All ye mountains praise the Lord; Christ the Lord is risen; Prophet unwilling, oratorio with organ, brass, percussion; numerous other published choral works.
Hillcrest Estates, Richmond, KY 40475

WEIDENAAR, REYNOLD
b. Grand Rapids, Mich., 25 Sept. 1945. Studied with Paul Harder, Michigan State Univ.; privately with Robert A. Moog and Vladimir Maleckar; with Donald Erb, Cleveland Inst. of Music, B.M. 1973. He received a Bascom Little Fund grant, 1978; Ohio Arts Council grant, 1978. He was editor, Electronic Music Review, 1967-68; recording engineer, Cleveland Orch., 1969-70; from 1972, on faculty, Cleveland Inst. of Music.
WORKS: ELECTRONIC: The tinsel chicken coop, 1972; Drive, 1973; Fanfare, 1973; Out of C, 1974; Wiener, 1974; Cicada, 1977; Deja vu, Where are you?, 1977; Twilight flight, 1977; Simple ceremony, 1978; Wavelines I, 1978.
592 Elm St., Painesville, OH 44077

WEIGEL, EUGENE JOHN
b. Cleveland, Ohio, 11 Oct. 1910. Studied violin at Cleveland Inst. of Music; composition with Arthur Shepherd, Western Reserve Univ.; with Paul Hindemith, Yale Univ., B.M. 1946; viola with Hugo Kortschak. He was violist with the Walden String Quartet, 1947-56; artist-in-residence and professor, Univ. of Illinois, 1950-56; then was named composer-in-residence and professor, Montana State Univ.
WORKS: OPERA: The lion makers, 1953; The mountain child, 1958; ORCHESTRA: Sonata for strings, 1948; Prairie symphony, 1953; Requiem mass, chorus and orch., 1956; CHAMBER MUSIC: clarinet quintet, 1946; woodwind quintet, 1949; 3 pieces for 4 trombones, 1953; many songs and piano pieces.

WEIGL, KARL
b. Vienna, 6 Feb. 1881; U.S. citizen 1943; d. New York, N.Y., 11 Aug. 1949. Studied at Vienna Music Acad., graduated 1902; studied composition with Robert Fuchs and Alexander V. Kemlinsky; with Guido Adler, Vienna Univ., Ph.D. 1903. His awards include the Beethoven prize in 1910; Philadelphia Mendelssohn Club prize, 1922; City of Vienna prize in 1924 for the symphonic cantata, World Festival. He taught at Vienna Univ.; was coach at the Vienna Opera, 1904-16, assis-

tant to Gustav Mahler; in the U.S. from 1938, he held teaching posts at Brooklyn Coll., Boston Cons., and Philadelphia Music Acad.
WORKS: ORCHESTRA: 6 symphonies, 1903-47, #5 performed in New York, 1968; Music for the young, overture; Rhapsody, piano and orch.; Old Vienna, symphonic cycle, world premiere by Naumburg Symphony, Central Park, New York, 28 May 1978; Summer evening music, string orch.; 3 intermezzi, string orch.; piano concerto; violin concerto; cello concerto; piano concerto for the left hand; CHAMBER MUSIC: 8 string quartets; piano trio; cello sonata; 2 violin sonatas; viola sonata; piano pieces; choral works; many songs.

WEIGL, VALLY (Mrs. Karl)
b. Vienna, 11 Sept. 1889; U.S. citizen 1944. Studied composition with Karl Weigl, musicology with Guido Adler at Vienna Univ.; at Columbia Univ., M.A. 1953. Her awards include 2 Elk Found. fellowships, 1955, 1958; license as music therapist, N.Y. Assoc. for Music Therapy, 1959; Rockefeller grant, 1973; American Composers Alliance and Mark Rothko Found. grant, 1973; Nat. Endowment for the Arts grant, 1976; fellow, MacDowell Colony Assoc. She has given lectures and concerts all over the U.S. and Europe; in 1964, she became chairman of the Friends' Arts for World Unity Committee for which she has organized international cultural programs.
WORKS: CHAMBER MUSIC: Andante for strings, 1945; New England suite, clarinet or flute, cello, piano; Nature moods, voice, clarinet or flute, 1956; Dear Earth, voice, horn, piano trio; Lyrical suite, chamber ensemble; many songs, choral works, and vocal chamber music.
55 W. 95th St., New York, NY 10025

WEILL, KURT
b. Dessau, Germany, 2 Mar. 1900; to U.S. 1935; d. New York, 3 Apr. 1950. Studied with Albert Bing in Dessau; with Humperdinck and Krasselt in Berlin; later with Busoni in Berlin. Almost his entire career was devoted to composition of stage works.
WORKS: THEATRE: The protagonist, opera on play by George Kaiser, 1934; The royal palace, opera on book by Ivan Goll, 1927; Mahagonny, satirical opera, libretto by Bertolt Brecht, 1927; The threepenny opera, libretto adapted by Brecht from John Gay, 1928; Happy end, a Paris stage score, 1929; The silver lake, opera on book by Kaiser, 1933; 7 deadly sins, ballet, 1933; A kingdom for a cow, musical play, 1935; music for The eternal road, by Franz Werfl, 1937; Knickerbocker holiday, musical on text of Maxwell Anderson, 1938; music for The ballad of the Magna Carta, radio drama by Maxwell Anderson, 1939; Lady in the dark, musical, book by Moss Hart, 1941; One touch of Venus, musical to text by S. J. Perelman and Ogden Nash, 1943; Street scene, opera on texts by Elmer Rice and Langston Hughes, 1947; Down in the valley, folk opera, book by Arnold Sundgaard, 1947; Lost in the stars, opera, libretto adapted by Maxwell Anderson from Alan Paton's Cry the beloved country, 1949; ORCHESTRA: 2 symphonies, 1921,

1933; Fantaisie, passacaglia and hymnus, 1923; Quodlibet, 1924; concerto for violin and woodwinds; CHAMBER MUSIC: string quartet; CHORUS: Lindberg's flight, radio cantata, 1927; The new Orpheus, cantata; SONGS: Mack the knife; September song; The saga of Jenny; and many others.

WEILLE, F. BLAIR
b. Boston, Mass., 9 Nov. 1930. Studied piano at New England Cons.; composition with Arthur Tillman Merritt and Walter Piston, Harvard Univ., A.B. 1953; with Otto Luening and Jack Beeson, Columbia Univ., A.M. 1947. He received annual ASCAP awards, 1969-71. He has been staff member with recording companies from 1960; on board of directors, Composers Recordings, Inc., from 1971.
    WORKS: ORCHESTRA: short symphony; CHAMBER MUSIC: suite for brass quintet; Annabel Lee, baritone and chamber orch.; Minneapolis-St. Paul, popular song.
    166 E. 96th St., New York, NY 10024

WEINBERG, HENRY
b. Philadelphia, Pa., 7 June 1931. Studied at Univ. of Pennsylvania, B.F.A. 1952; with Milton Babbitt and Roger Sessions, Princeton Univ., M.F.A. 1961, Ph.D.; with Luigi Dallapiccola in Florence, Italy. His awards include Fulbright-Italian government grants, 1961-62; Guggenheim fellowship; MacDowell Colony fellowship; Fromm Found. grant; Naumberg award; Brandeis Creative Arts award. He has been faculty member, Univ. of Pennsylvania, 1962-65; Queens Coll., CUNY, from 1965; also at CUNY Graduate Center, from 1976.
    WORKS: CHAMBER MUSIC: cello sonata, 1955; Sinfonia, chamber orch., 1957; 2 string quartets, 1959, 1960-64; Cantus commemorabilis I, chamber ensemble, 1966; CHORUS: Vox in ramo, 1956; SONGS: 5 haiku, 1958; song cycle, 1960.
    Queens College, CUNY, Flushing, NY 11367

WEINBERG, JACOB
b. Odessa, Russia, 5 July 1879; U.S. citizen 1934; d. New York, N.Y., 2 Nov. 1956. Studied law at Univ. of Moscow; music at Moscow Cons. He toured as concert pianist, 1912-14, 1922-26; was professor, Odessa Cons., 1915-21; New York Coll. of Music, 1927-37; and at Hunter Coll., 1937-56.
    WORKS: OPERA: The pioneers, 1925; ORCHESTRA: piano concerto; CHAMBER MUSIC: piano trio; suite for 2 pianos; string quartet; 2 violin sonatas; CHORUS: The Gettysburg address, ode for chorus and orch., 1936; Isaiah, oratorio, 1948; The life of Moses, oratorio, 1952; Sabbath liturgy, with baritone solo and organ.

WEINBERGER, JAROMIR
b. Prague, Czechoslovakia, 8 Jan. 1896; U.S. citizen 1948; d. St. Petersburg, Fla., 8 Aug. 1967. Studied at Prague Cons., and with Max Reger in Leipzig. He taught in Prague, Bratislava, and Vienna; for one semester, Cons. of Ithaca, N.Y., 1922; from 1939, lived in St. Petersburg, Fla.
    WORKS: OPERA: Schwanda, the bagpiper, 1927; The beloved voice, 1931; The outcasts of Poker

Flat, 1932; A bed of roses, 1932; Wallenstein, 1937; ORCHESTRA: Overture to a puppet show; Overture to a cavalier's play; Christmas; Czech songs and dances; Under the spreading chestnut tree, 1939; The legend of Sleepy Hollow; Song of the high seas, 1940; saxophone concerto, 1940; Lincoln symphony, 1941; Czech rhapsody, 1941; The bird's opera, 1941; BAND: Mississippi rhapsody; Prelude to a festival; Homage to the pioneers; ORGAN: Religious and profane preludes; sonata; also chamber music, choral works, and songs.

WEINER, LAWRENCE
b. Cleveland, Ohio, 22 June 1932. Studied with Kent Kennan, Clifton Williams, Paul Pisk, Univ. of Texas; with Juan Orrego-Salas, Indiana Univ.; with John Butler, Alfred Reed, Univ. of Miami. He received the Carl Owens composition award, Univ. of Texas, 1955; Ostwald band composition award, 1967; NDEA grant, 1971; and commissions. He was public school music instructor, 1959-68; then joined the faculty at Texas A & I Univ. at Kingsville; from 1976, at Corpus Christi State Univ.
    WORKS: ORCHESTRA: Prologos synkretismos; Elegy, string orch.; Quaternity, string orch.; Commemoration overture, Corpus Christi, 26 Jan. 1974; BAND: Daedalic symphony; 3rd symphony for wind ensemble; Air; Benediction; Choral and fugue; Cataphonics; Atropos; 3 fanfares; suite for brass sextet; CHORUS: Shenandoah; Psalm of prayer and praise; The sower; Sing praise to God.
    Corpus Christi State Univ., P.O. Box 6010, Corpus Christi, TX 78411

WEINER, LAZAR
b. Cherkassy, near Kiev, Russia, 27 Oct. 1897; to U.S. 1914; d. New York, N.Y., 10 Jan. 1982. Studied with Frederick Jacobi, Robert Russell Bennett, and Joseph Schillinger in New York. He was conductor of choral groups in the New York area.
    WORKS: THEATRE: The golem, opera, 1966; several ballets; CHORUS: Legend of toil, cantata, 1933; Man in the world, 1939; Fight for freedom, 1943; To thee, America, 1944; The last judgment, cantata, 1966; and Yiddish art songs, chamber music.

WEINER, STANLEY
b. 1925. concerto for horn and strings; Homage to violinists, 7 caprices for unaccompanied violin; sonata for violin solo; piano sonata, 1971; 15 violin duos in first position, 1975.

WEINGARDEN, LOUIS
b. Detroit, Mich., 23 July 1943. Studied with Miriam Gideon in New York; with Elliott Carter at Juilliard School; at Columbia Univ.; and at Jewish Theological Seminary. His awards include the Prix de Rome; Guggenheim fellowship; Charles Ives scholarship, Nat. Inst. of Arts and Letters; Nat. Endowment for the Arts grant; and commissions. From 1972 he has been a partner in an architecture and interior design firm.
    WORKS: ORCHESTRA: Ghirlande, soprano and orch.; piano concerto, Denver, 16 Feb. 1975;

WEINSTEIN, MILTON

CHAMBER MUSIC: Things heard and seen in summer, piano trio; Fantasy and funeral music, 2 pianos and percussion; cello sonata; suite for violin alone; Vox clamans in deserto, organ and brass; CHORUS: The sorrows of David, cantata with soli and orch.; 3 short sacred songs, women's voices a cappella.
1 W. 72nd St., New York, NY 10023

WEINSTEIN, MILTON
b. Cohoes, N.Y., 26 Apr. 1911. Studied with Joseph Schillinger and Tibor Serly. He has been composer and arranger for radio, television, educational films.
WORKS: ORCHESTRA: trumpet concerto; Astrological suite.

WEISGALL, HUGO DAVID
b. Ivancice, Czechoslovakia, 13 Oct. 1912; to U.S. 1920. Studied with Louis Cheslock, Peabody Cons.; with Rosario Scalero, Curtis Inst. of Music; privately with Roger Sessions in New York; at Johns Hopkins Univ., Ph.D. in German literature, 1940. His awards include Joseph H. Bearns prize, 1931; Ditson award; 3 Guggenheim fellowships; composer-in-residence, American Acad. in Rome, 1966-67; Nat. Inst. of Arts and Letters grant; honorary doctorate, Peabody Cons., 1973; membership, Nat. Inst. of Arts and Letters, 1975; Nat. Endowment for the Arts grants, 1974, 1976. After military service in World War II, he was cultural attache in Prague, 1946-47; has held teaching posts at Juilliard School; Pennsylvania State Univ.; Jewish Theological Seminary; Queens Coll., CUNY; was W. Alton Jones professor, Peabody Cons., 1974-75.
WORKS: OPERA: Night, 1932; Lilith, 1934; The tenor, 1950; The stronger, 1952; 6 characters in search of an author, 1956; Purgatory, 1958; Athaliah, 1963; 9 rivers from Jordan, 1968; The garden of Adonis, 1974; The 100 nights, 1 act, New York, 22 Apr. 1976; BALLET: Quest, 1937; One thing is certain, 1938; Outpost, 1947; ORCHESTRA: Overture in F, 1943; Soldier songs, baritone and orch., 1946; A garden eastward, cantata for high voice and orch., 1952; A song of celebration, with chorus and soloists, Baltimore, 20 Feb. 1976; CHAMBER MUSIC: Fancies and inventions, from The Hebrides of Robert Herrick, for baritone and 5 instruments, Baltimore, 1 Nov. 1970; many choral works and songs.
Queens College, CUNY, Flushing, NY 11367

WEISGARBER, ELLIOT
b. Pittsfield, Mass., 5 Dec. 1919. Studied with Bernard Rogers and Howard Hanson, Eastman School of Music, 1939-43; with Nadia Boulanger in Paris, 1952-53; with Halsey Stevens in Los Angeles, 1953-59; studied koto and other native instruments in Japan. He was named to the faculty of the Univ. of British Columbia in 1960; later became professor of composition and Asian and Pacific musicology.
WORKS: ORCHESTRA: Sinfonia pastorale, 1961; Sinfonia concertante, oboe, 2 horns, strings, 1962; Kyoto landscapes, voice and orch., 1970; Autumnal music, English horn and strings, 1973; Musica serena, 1974; A Pacific trilogy, 1974;

violin concerto, 1974; Fantasia, saxophone and orch., 1974; CHAMBER MUSIC: sonata for flute, clarinet, piano, 1953; Divertimento, string trio, 1956; Divertimento, horn, viola, piano, 1959; flute sonata, 1963; suite for viola and piano, 1964; sonata for solo cello, 1965; Illahee chanties, chamber orch., 1971; bassoon sonata, 1973; Epigrams, flute and piano, 1973; string quartet, 1975; Fantasia a tre, horn, violin, piano, 1975; CHORUS: Night, with baritone solo and string quartet, 1973; also works for Japanese instruments.
Univ. of British Columbia, Vancouver, BC, Canada V6T 1W5

WEISLING, RAYMOND
b. Milwaukee, Wis., 13 Mar. 1947. Studied with Barney Childs at Wisconsin Coll.-Cons.; at Univ. of Wisconsin, Milwaukee; and at California Inst. of the Arts. He was awarded first prize, Kinetic Theatre Program, Oregon Coll. of Education, 1970; was instructor in electronic music, Wisconsin Coll.-Cons., 1972-73.
WORKS: ORCHESTRA: Last voyage to summer, 1970; BAND: An original American cold-flow, 1970; CHAMBER MUSIC: Poon Lim . . . A night upon the waves, 7 winds, 1969; Night sky set, soprano and 6 players, 1970; Jupiter and Silvertree, bass flute and 6 instruments, 1972; ELECTRONIC: Bluemound pieces, 7 tape compositions, 1972-73.
c/o California Inst. of the Arts, Valencia, CA 91355

WEISS, ADOLPH A.
b. Baltimore, Md., 12 Sept. 1891; d. Van Nuys, Calif., 21 Feb. 1971. Studied with Cornelius Rybner at Columbia Univ.; with Adolph Weidig in Chicago; at Univ. of California, Los Angeles; and with Arnold Schoenberg in Berlin, 1925-27. He received a Guggenheim fellowship, 1931; Nat. Inst. of Arts and Letters grant, 1955. He was bassoonist in various orchestras; founded the New Music Wind Quintet; conducted orchestras in New York; was instructor, Los Angeles Cons.
WORKS: ORCHESTRA: I segreti, 1922; American life, scherzo jazzoso, 1929; The libation-bearers, choreographic cantata, with soloists and chorus, 1930; Variations, 1931; suite, 1938; 10 pieces, for low instruments and orch., 1943; trumpet concerto, 1952; WIND ENSEMBLE: Tone poem, brass and percussion, 1957; Vade mecum, 1958; CHAMBER MUSIC: 3 string quartets, 1925, 1926, 1932; chamber symphony for 10 instruments, 1927; 12 piano preludes, 1927; sonata da camera, flute and viola, 1929; wind quintet, 1931; piano sonata, 1932; Petite suite, woodwind trio, 1939; violin sonata, 1941; Passacaglia, horn and viola, 1942; Protest, 2 pianos, 1945; sextet, woodwind quintet, horn, piano, 1947; trio, clarinet, viola, cello, 1948; concerto for bassoon and string quartet, 1949; trio, flute, violin, piano, 1955; 5 fantasies, violin and piano, 1956; Rhapsody, 4 horns, 1957.

WEISS, EMIL
b. Hungary, 12 June 1911; U.S. citizen 1936. Earned a degree in pharmacy, Columbia Univ.;

studied violin privately; is self-taught in composition. His works for orchestra include
Souvenir, 1955, and Carpice simpatico, 1956,
both premiered in Clarkston, Ga., 4 Mar. 1980;
Caprice serenata, 1962.
    1659 E. Clifton Rd., N.E., Atlanta, GA 30307

WEISS, HERMAN
    b. Bridgeport, Conn., 7 Aug. 1946. Studied with
Robert Cogan, Francis Judd Cooke, and Daniel
Pinkham, New England Conservatory, B.M. 1968;
with Olivier Messiaen in Paris; with Seymour
Shifrin and Martin Boykan, Brandeis Univ., M.F.A.
1973. His awards include a Tanglewood fellowship, 1967; Fulbright fellowship to Paris, 1968-
69; and commissions. He was teaching fellow at
Brandeis Univ., 1970-72; music director, Spin-
gold Theatre, Brandeis, 1971-72; from 1972;
music director, Temple Isaiah.
    WORKS: CHAMBER MUSIC: The nocturnal visions,
1972, rev. 1977; The new rage, flute and piano,
Boston, 23 Apr. 1976; The seventh species, clarinet and piano, 1978, Cambridge, 13 Mar. 1980;
VOICE: 3 cantatas: Men are not free, mezzo-
soprano, clarinet, violin, piano, 1970; Post-
cards, mezzo-soprano, clarinet, violin, piano,
Paros, Greece, 16 July 1976; Songs of the high
and far-off times, vocal quartet and chamber
ensemble, Cambridge, 27 Apr. 1979; 3 songs for
soprano and piano, 1977.
    133 Larch Rd., Cambridge, MA 02138

WELCHER, DAN EDWARD
    b. Rochester, N.Y., 2 Mar. 1948. Studied with
Samuel Adler and Warren Benson, Eastman School
of Music, B.M. 1969; with Ludmila Ulehla, Manhattan School of Music, M.M. 1972. He won first
prize, First Internat. Gebrauchmusik for Recorders contest, 1970. He was second bassoonist, Rochester Phil. Orch., 1968-69; principal
bassoonist and arranger, U.S. Military Acad.,
1969-72; principal bassoonist, Louisville Orch.,
1972-77; on faculty, Univ. of Louisville, 1972-
77; from 1978, at Univ. of Texas.
    WORKS: ORCHESTRA: Pieces, symphony for
bassoon and orch., 1968; Episodes, 1971; flute
concerto, Louisville, Apr. 1974; BAND: Walls
and fences; 5 tactical experiences, winds and
percussion, 1970; CHAMBER MUSIC: Elizabethan
variations, 4 recorders; Nocturne and dance,
trumpet and piano, 1967; Black riders, 6 epigrams of Stephen Crane, soprano and 4 instruments, 1972; concerto da camera, bassoon and
chamber orch., 1975; 3 short pieces, piano, 4
hands, 1975; piano trio, 1976.
    Music Dept., University of Texas, Austin,
TX 78712

WELLS, JOHN BARNES
    b. Ashley, Pa., 17 Oct. 1880; d. Roxbury, N.Y.,
8 Aug. 1955. Studied at Syracuse Univ. He was
a singer with Victor Herbert's Orchestra; church
organist and choirmaster in New York; voice tutor
at Princeton Univ. His compositions included
the songs: The elfman; If I were you; The dearest place; The owl; The little bird; The lightning bug; etc.

WELLS, RONALD KENNETH
    b. Pasadena, Calif., 18 Aug. 1926. Studied at
Asbury Coll., A.B.; at Southern Baptist Theological Seminary, M.S.M. He has been minister
in various churches, 1951-68; First Baptist
Church, Spartanburg, S.C., from 1968.
    WORKS: THEATRE: Who is my neighbor?,
sacred music drama; I wonder, song drama; Here
comes tomorrow, song drama; also songs.
    893 Ezell Blvd., Spartanburg, SC 29301

WELSH, WILMER HAYDON
    Studied at Peabody Cons., diploma in organ,
1953. His works for organ include The song of
songs, a religious dance, 1954, and Requiem,
1954; both performed at the Nat. Cathedral,
Washington, D.C., in Oct. 1954.
    Davidson College, Davidson, NC 28036

WELWOOD, ARTHUR
    b. Brookline, Mass., 15 Feb. 1934. Studied with
Hugo Norden and Gardner Read, Boston Univ.; with
Quincy Porter and Mel Powell, Yale Univ. He received commissions, 1971, 1973. He was visiting
instructor, Univ. of Evansville, Ind., 1963-64;
from 1964, on faculty, Central Connecticut State
Coll.
    WORKS: CHAMBER MUSIC: Songs from the
Chinese, tenor solo and chamber ensemble, 1968;
CHORUS: Polyphonies of the 11th and 12th centuries, arranged for soprano, chorus, chamber
orch., and 'found' percussion, 1972; MULTIMEDIA:
Earth opera I, soloists, chorus, lights, dancers,
'found' instruments, spontaneous creation, performed for and with audience of 1000, 1969; My
father moved through dooms of love, a masque for
soprano, chamber orch., chorus, slides, lights,
and dancers, 1970; Manifestations V, masque for
soprano, 25 musicians, 50 dancers, poetry readers,
tapes, and audience, 1971; Songs of war, nature,
and the way, based on Tany Dynasty, voice,
chamber ensemble, percussion, narrator, and 5
dancers, 1972. He is author of A primer for
found music, a manual for creative music projects in public schools.
    32 Cambridge St., New. Britain, CT 06051

WERDER, RICHARD
    b. Williamsburg, Iowa, 21 Dec. 1919. Studied at
Juilliard School and at Columbia Univ. He
taught at Catholic Univ.; later at Montgomery
Coll., Rockville, Md. His compositions include
piano pieces: Black on white; The drum; Procession of the pachyderms; Resting time; Down,
up.
    Montgomery College, Rockville, MD 20850

WERLE, FLOYD E.
    b. Billings, Mont., 8 May 1929. Studied at Univ.
of Michigan. From 1951 he has been chief of
composition and arranging, U.S. Air Force Band,
Washington; from 1967, music director, United
Methodist Church, Rockville, Md.
    WORKS: ORCHESTRA: Venite exultemus, com-
missioned by Arlington, Va.,Symphony, premiered
on 12 Mar. 1972; BAND: Concert etude; 2 concertos for trumpet and band; Sinfonia sacra,
rock combo and band; WIND ENSEMBLE: Partita

WERNER, ERIC

for saxophones; symphony #2 for winds; Divertimento, 8 soloists; Glider pilots' reunion, march.
5504 Aldrich Lane, Springfield, VA 22151

WERNER, ERIC
b. Vienna, Austria, 1 Aug. 1901; U.S. citizen
1944. Studied with Egon Kornauth in Vienna;
with Franz Schreker and Ferruccio Busoni in
Berlin. He received a Guggenheim fellowship,
1957. He is primarily musicologist and author
of several books on the subject; is professor
emeritus, Hebrew Union Coll., New York and
Cincinnati, and Tel Aviv Univ. His compositions
include Symphony requiem for orchestra; chamber
music and liturgical works.
900 W. 190th St., New York, NY 10040

WERNER, KENNETH. See HARMONIC, PHIL

WERNICK, RICHARD F.
b. Boston, Mass., 16 Jan. 1934. Studied with
Irving Fine, Harold Shapero, Arthur Berger,
Brandeis Univ., B.A.; with Leon Kirchner, Mills
Coll., M.A.; with Aaron Copland, Boris Blacher,
and Ernst Toch at Tanglewood. His awards in-
clude Ford Found. grants; Guggenheim fellowship;
Naumburg award, 1975; Nat. Inst. of Arts and
Letters award; Nat. Endowment for the Arts grant,
1976; Pulitzer prize, 1977, for Visions of terror and wonder; many commissions. He taught at
State Univ. of New York at Buffalo, 1964-65;
Univ. of Chicago, 1965-68; from 1969, on faculty,
Univ. of Pennsylvania, also conductor and musical director of the Penn Contemporary Players.
WORKS: ORCHESTRA: Aevia, 1965; Hexagrams,
small orch., 1970; Visions of terror and wonder,
mezzo-soprano and orch., texts from the Bible
and the Koran, Aspen, Colo., 19 July 1976; CHAM-
BER MUSIC: 2 string quartets; Stretti, clarinet,
violin, viola, guitar, 1965; Cadenzas and variations, viola alone, 1968; Cadenzas and variations II, violin alone, 1969; Cadenzas and variations III, cello alone; VOICE: Lyrics from
1x1, female voice, string bass, percussion, 1966;
Haiku of Basho, soprano, 7 players, tape, 1967;
Kaddish-Requiem, mezzo-soprano, chamber ensemble,
tape, 1969; Moonsongs from the Japanese, soprano
and tape, 1969; A prayer for Jerusalem, female
voice and percussion, 1970-71; Songs of remembrance, mezzo-soprano, shawm, English horn, and
oboe (1 player); Contemplations of the 10th muse,
soprano and piano, Anne Bradstreet text.
801 Ridley Creek Dr., Media, PA 19063

WESCOTT, STEVEN DWIGHT
b. Minneapolis, Minn., 14 July 1950. Studied
with Ronald A. Nelson, Minneapolis; with
Dominick Argento and Paul Fetler, Univ. of
Minnesota.
WORKS: CHORUS: A gift of light; other
choral anthems and organ music.
3332 Idaho Ave. S., St. Louis Park, MN 55426

WESSEL, MARK E.
b. Coldwater, Mich., 26 Mar. 1894; d. Beverly
Hills, Calif., 2 May 1973. Studied at Northwestern Univ., B.M. 1917; M.M. 1918; and with
Arnold Schoenberg in Vienna. He received a

Guggenheim fellowship, 1931; Pulitzer scholarship. He taught at Northwestern Univ. and at
Univ. of Colorado.
WORKS: ORCHESTRA: Scherzo burlesque, piano
and strings, 1926; Symphony concertante, horn,
piano, orch., 1929; symphony, 1932; Holiday,
1932; Song and dance, 1932; 2 piano concertos;
many chamber works; piano pieces.

WEST, GEORGE ADDISON
b. Hightstown, N.J., 11 Mar. 1931. Studied at
Oberlin Cons.; with H. Owen Reed and Paul O.
Harder, Michigan State Univ., M.A. 1962, Ph.D.
1971. He has received commissions for television and film background scores, concert and
marching bands. He was composer-arranger, U.S.
Air Force Band, Washington, 1954-57; on faculty,
Stephen F. Austin State Univ., 1964-67; Univ. of
Calgary, 1969-71; from 1971, at James Madison
Univ.
WORKS: JAZZ ENSEMBLE: Jazz quartally, 4-
movement suite; CHAMBER MUSIC: Largo and allegro, trombone and string quartet; many jazz
works.
212 Governor's Lane, #2, Harrisonburg, VA
22801

WEST, RICHARD M.
b. Yakima, Wash., 23 Nov. 1940. Studied at U.S.
Navy School of Music, Washington; at Oregon
State Univ., B.S.; Univ. of Oregon, M.M.Ed. He
taught in public schools, 1967-71; then at Linn-
Benton Community Coll.
WORKS: CHORUS: Little Jesus, tiny Jesus
boy; God created man; SONGS: Brotherhood, cycle
of 7 songs for voice and guitar.
1515 W. 12th St., Albany, OR 97321

WESTBROOK, HELEN SEARLES
b. Southbridge, Mass., 15 Oct. 1898; d. Chicago,
c. 1965. Studied with Wilhelm Middleschulte and
Adolf Weidig, American Cons., B.M. and Gold
Medal. She was theatre organist; organ soloist
with the Chicago Symphony; music director,
Central Church, Chicago. She wrote many songs
and organ and piano pieces.

WESTERGAARD, PETER
b. Champaign, Ill., 28 May 1931. Studied with
Walter Piston, Harvard Univ., A.B. magna cum
laude 1953; with Roger Sessions, Princeton Univ.,
M.F.A. 1956; with Darius Milhaud, Aspen Music
School, and in Paris; with Wolfgang Fortner in
Germany. His awards include a Harvard Nat.
scholarship, 1949-53; Francis Boote prize, 1953;
John Knowles Paine traveling fellowship, 1953-
54; Fulbright fellowships, 1956, 1957, guest
lectureship, 1958; Columbia Univ. grant, 1963;
Guggenheim fellowship, 1964-65. He was faculty
member, Columbia Coll., 1958-66; Amherst Coll.,
1967-68; Princeton Univ., from 1968.
WORKS: CHAMBER OPERA: Charivari, 1953;
Mr. and Mrs. Discobbolos, 1965; ORCHESTRA: symphonic movement, 1954; 5 movements for small
orch., 1958; Noises, sounds, and sweet airs,
chamber orch., 1968; BAND: Tuckets and sennets,
1969; CHAMBER MUSIC: Partita, flute, violin,
harpsichord, 1953-56; Inventions, flute and

piano, 1955; string quartet, 1957; quartet for violin, vibraphone, clarinet, cello, 1960; Spring and fall: to a young child, voice and piano, 1960; trio for flute, cello, piano, 1962; Variations, 6 players, 1963; Moto perpetuo, 6 wind instruments, 1976; CANTATAS: The plot against the giant, 1956; A refusal to mourn the death, by fire, of a child in London, 1958; Leda and the swan, 1961.

Music Dept., Princeton Univ., Princeton, NJ 08540

WESTON, RANDOLPH E. (RANDY)
b. Brooklyn, N.Y., 6 Apr. 1926. Served in the U.S. Army in World War II; was pianist in jazz groups; from 1955 led his own quartet with appearances in Town Hall, Carnegie Hall, Newport Jazz Festival, etc.; has recorded many of his own jazz compositions. His major symphonic works include Uhuru, soprano, baritone, and orch., New York, 4 Feb. 1973; 3 African queens, piano and orch., Boston Pops, 9 July 1981, with composer as piano soloist.

WETZEL, RICHARD D.
b. Pitman, Pa., 27 Dec. 1935. Studied at Carnegie-Mellon Univ., Duquesne Univ.; Univ. of Pittsburgh, M.M., Ph.D. in musicology; privately with Roland Leich. He received the Sinfonia Found. grant, 1972; and commissions. From 1970 he has been faculty member, Ohio Univ.

WORKS: WIND ENSEMBLE: Robert Owen suite, 1978; CHAMBER MUSIC: Sonatina Americana, quartet of double reeds, 1973; CHORUS: Mr. Man, folk-style anthem; Service for the Lord's Day; He is the way; God of our life; The ship of Earth, with horn, piano, and percussion, 1977; A mighty fortress, 1977.

Box 206, Chesterhill, OH 43728

WETZLER, HERMANN HANS
b. Frankfurt, Germany, 8 Sept. 1870; to U.S. 1892; d. New York, N.Y., 29 May 1943. Studied with Clara Schumann and Humperdinck in Frankfurt. He was church organist in New York, 1892-1905; also formed his own orchestra in New York; was opera conductor in Germany, 1905-30; returned to the U.S. in 1940. He composed an opera; orchestral works, chamber music, choral works, songs.

WETZLER, ROBERT
b. Minneapolis, Minn., 30 Jan. 1932. Studied at Thiel Coll., B.A. 1954; Northwestern Lutheran Theological Seminary, M.Div. 1957; compsosition with Paul Fetler and Dominick Argento, Univ. of Minnesota. He has received annual ASCAP awards, 1967-77. He was organist and choirmaster, 1953-68; director of publications, Art Masters Studios, Inc., from 1960, president from 1966.

WORKS: WIND ENSEMBLE: Neebrit suite, concert band; Death to life, brass and organ; CHAMBER MUSIC: woodwind quintet; Spectrum suite, piano; VOICE: God hurrah, song cycle; Our ascended king, cantata for choir, 3 soloists, chamber orch.; and numerous other choral works.

2614 Nicollet Ave., Minneapolis, MN 55408

WHALEY, GEORGE BOYD
b. Altamount, Kans., 9 Mar. 1929. Studied with William Latham, Univ. of Northern Iowa; with Francis J. Pyle, Drake Univ. He was public school band director, 1957-70; teaching fellow, Univ. of Wyoming, 1970-71; from 1971, faculty member and band director, Yankton Coll.

WORKS: ORCHESTRA: concerto for brass quartet and strings; Festive dances; 5 images; BAND: The knight, death, and the devil; sonata for band; Contramusics; Toccata, for brass, organ, timpani, percussion; symphony for band; CHAMBER MUSIC: Divertimento, horn and woodwind quintet; CHORUS: 4 songs, chorus and winds; Serenade: 5 for mi'lady.

1001 Walnut, Yankton, SD 57078

WHATLEY, G. LARRY
b. Tallassee, Ala., 7 Feb. 1940. Studied with J. Frederic Goossen, Univ. of Alabama; with Bernhard Heiden and Roque Cordero, Indiana Univ., M.M. He has been faculty member, Brevard Coll., from 1963.

WORKS: ORCHESTRA: Collage, 1962; Variations, string orch., 1963; Symphonic overture, 1965; Palindrome, 1970; BAND: Toccata, wind band, 1962; Festival prelude, 1967; Introit and alleluia, 1968; many marches; CHAMBER MUSIC: piano sonatina, 1960; trio for reeds, 1961; Music for organ and trumpet, 1961; quartet for violin, oboe, horn, piano, 1961; brass octet, 1962; woodwind quintet, 1964; Contrasts, trombone and piano, 1965; string quartet, 1967; brass quintet, 1969; tuba sonata, 1970; CHORUS: Psalm 100 and Psalm 23, 1960; Fairest Lord Jesus, 1961; O praise the Lord, 1965; 3 psalms, 1971; and songs.

Rte. 3, Box 38, Brevard, NC 28712

WHEAR, PAUL WILLIAM
b. Auburn, Ind., 13 Nov. 1925. Studied at Marquette Univ., B.S; with Donald H. White, DePauw Univ., B.A., M.M.; with Gardner Read, Boston Univ.; with Wilfred Josephs in London; with Wayne Barlow, Eastman School of Music; and at Western Reserve Univ., Ph.D. His awards include Summy-Birchard Oshkosh award, 1956; Youngstown Symph. prize, 1958; Henry Cowell prize, 1960; numerous other prizes and awards. He was faculty member, Mount Union Coll., 1952-60; Doane Coll., 1960-69; from 1969, Marshall Univ.

WORKS: ORCHESTRA: Proemion, symphonic poem, 1949; violin concerto, 1950; St. John, symphonic poem, 1951; Catharsis suite, 1967; A touch-tone telephone tune, 1969; symphony #2, The bridge, 1971; Sonnets from Shakespeare, baritone and orch., 1973; BAND: Antietam, 1966; Wycliffe variations, 1968; symphony #1, Stonehenge, 1970; Of this time, with narrator, 1971; CHAMBER MUSIC: 3 string quartets; Pastorale lament, horn and piano, 1960; trombone sonata, 1961; Septsonics, 6 trombones and tape, 1972; CHORUS: The 10 commandments, cantata, 1955; The seasons, oratorio, with orch., 1965; Joyful, jubilate, 1969; Hosanna, double chorus, a cappella, 1971; The Chief Justice: John Marshall, with 2 soloists, 2 narrators, and chamber orch., Huntington, 7 Apr. 1975.

524 Ninth Ave., Huntington, WV 25701

WHEELER, (WILLIAM) SCOTT

WHEELER, (WILLIAM) SCOTT
b. Washington, D.C., 24 Feb. 1952. Studied with
Lewis Spratlan and Donald Wheelock, Amherst Coll.,
B.A.; with Malcolm Peyton, New England Cons.;
with Arthur Berger and Harold Shapero, Brandeis
Univ., M.F.A. He joined the faculty at Emerson
Coll., Boston, in 1978.
WORKS: CHAMBER MUSIC: Over the star,
chamber orch., 1975; Piece for 5 players, 1975;
A clear day and no memories, chamber orch., 1976;
Sweet cream, 2 violins, viola, piano, 1978; Trio
variations, 3 clarinets, Boston, 12 Oct. 1980;
PIANO: Grey gardens, duet, 1977; Green geese,
1977; Chanson songeuresse, 1978.
356 Somerville Ave., Somerville, MA 02143

WHEELOCK, DONALD F.
b. Darien, Conn., 17 June 1940. Studied with
Edgar Curtis, Union Coll., Schenectady, A.B.
1962; with Yehudi Wyner, Yale Univ., M.M. 1966.
His awards include a Guggenheim fellowship and
3 MacDowell Colony fellowships. He was faculty
member, Colgate Univ., 1966-69; Amherst Coll.,
1969-74; from 1974, at Smith Coll.
WORKS: ORCHESTRA: Celebrations, soprano
and orch., 1968, Colgate Univ., 2 Dec. 1969;
Music for dance perhaps, chamber orch., 1971; 3
pieces, 1971; WIND ENSEMBLE: concerto for 24
brass instruments; CHAMBER MUSIC: Divertimento,
chamber ensemble, 1966; suite for 10 instruments,
1967; sonata for solo cello, 1969; 2 string
quartets, 1969, 1973, #1, Amherst Coll., 5 Nov.
1970; Serenade, soprano and 7 players, 1970; 4
songs, soprano and oboe, 1970; suite for piano,
1971; brass quartet, 1972; octet, 5 winds and
piano trio, 1972; Divertimento #2, chamber ensemble, 1972; 3 songs, soprano, flute, clarinet,
violin, cello, 1973.
Music Dept., Smith College, Northampton, MA
01063

WHIPPLE, R. JAMES
b. Philadelphia, Pa., 1 Dec. 1950. Studied with
Roland Leich and Leonardo Balada, Carnegie-
Mellon Univ., B.A. 1972; with David Del Tredici
and Gardner Read, Boston Univ., M.M. 1974. He
is a free-lance composer, arranger, bassoonist.
WORKS: ORCHESTRA: oboe concerto; concertino
for bassoon and strings; BAND: The epic concerto, alto saxophone and band; Maroon and white
salute; CHAMBER MUSIC: Antics, piccolo and bassoon; Le demence, 2 clarinets; I heard a fly
buzz when I died, 2 pianos; Frolic for 4 "fags",
3 bassoons and contrabassoon; A solemn psalm of
Pittsburgh memories, clarinet, trombone, contrabassoon; also church music.
1917 Edge Hill Rd., Abington, PA 19001

WHITCOMB, ROBERT B.
b. Scipio, Ind., 7 Dec. 1921. Studied with
Felix Labunski, Cincinnati Coll. of Music, B.M.
1947, M.M. 1950; with Bernard Rogers and Howard
Hanson, Eastman School of Music, D.M.A. 1959.
His awards include Martin G. Dumler prize in
composition, 1948; Thor Johnson commission, 1952;
first prize, Nat. Assoc. Coll. Wind and Percussion Instructors, 1962; Western Washington State
Coll. grant, 1966. He has been faculty member

at Culver Military Acad., 1948-49; Univ. of
Wyoming, 1950-52; New Mexico State Univ., 1952-
53; South Dakota State Univ., 1953-63; Western
Washington State Coll., 1963-68; from 1968, at
Southwest Minnesota State Univ.
WORKS: ORCHESTRA: Cincinnati from the
Ohio River, 1952; Variations, piano and orch.;
symphony; Poem, small orch.; BAND: Introduction
and dance; Traceries; CHAMBER MUSIC: 3 piano
sonatinas; organ sonata; cello sonata, 1966;
suite for viola and piano; Fantasy trio, viola,
oboe, piano; 3 nocturnes, cello and piano; Pacem
in terris, cello and piano; trumpet sonata;
Evocation, solo viola; Masque, solo viola; string
quartet; Serenade, woodwind trio; CHORUS::
Washington's birthday eve, male voices, a cappella, Ogden Nash text; The mighty one; May God
be gracious; Sandburg seasons (Timber moon,
Winter weather, Spring grass, Summer stars); and
others.
309 A St., Marshall, MN 56258.

WHITE, A. DUANE
b. Wytheville, Va., 22 Nov. 1939. Studied with
Dwight Gustafson, Bob Jones Univ., B.S. 1961,
M.A. 1963; with Bruce Benward, Univ. of Wisconsin, Ph.D. in musicology 1971; private musicological research in Vienna, 1969. He held a
Ford Found. grant, 1968-69; Univ. of Wisconsin
travel grant, 1969. He has been faculty member,
Bob Jones Univ., from 1963.
WORKS: THEATRE: music for Shakespeare's
The winter's tale; CHAMBER MUSIC: suite for
flute and piano; VOICE: The lines are fallen
unto me in pleasant places, chorus and soprano
solo; With rue my heart is laden, voice and
piano.
Bob Jones University, Greenville, SC 29641

WHITE, CLARENCE CAMERON
b. Clarksville, Tenn., 10 Aug. 1880; d. New
York, N.Y., 30 June 1960. Studied at Howard
Univ. and at Oberlin, graduated 1901. His many
awards included 2 Rosenwald fellowships; honorary
M.A., Atlanta Univ.; honorary D.M., Wilberforce
Univ.; Harmon Found. Medal; David Bispham Medal,
1932; Benjamin award, 1954. He taught at Washington Cons.; was guest artist with Samuel
Coleridge-Taylor in the U.S. and London; conducted his own music studio in Boston, 1910-22; was
music dept. chairman, West Virginia State Coll.,
1924-31; director of music, Hampton Inst., 1931-
35.
WORKS: OPERA: Ouanga, 1932, first stage
performance, South Bend, Ind., 10 June 1949;
BALLET: A night in Sans Souci; ORCHESTRA: symphony, 1928; Piece for strings and timpani;
violin concerto; Kutamba; Elegy for orchestra,
1954; VIOLIN AND PIANO: Bandanna sketches, 1920;
Cabin memories, 1921; From the cotton fields,
1921; many other violin pieces.

WHITE, DONALD H.
b. Narberth, Pa., 28 Feb. 1921. Studied with
Vincent Persichetti, Philadelphia Cons.; with
Bernard Rogers and Howard Hanson, Eastman School
of Music, Ph.D. 1952. He has received annual
ASCAP awards and many commissions. He was

faculty member, DePauw Univ., 1947-74, then was named director of the School of Music.

WORKS: ORCHESTRA: Sagan, an overture, 1946; Kennebec suite, 1947; cello concerto, 1952; Divertissement #2, string orch., 1968; A song of mankind, with 2 choirs and soloists, 1971; Serenade #1; BAND: Miniature set, 1957; Dichotomy, 1964; Ambrosian hymn variants, 1965; Patterns, 1967; Terpsimetrics, 1969; concertino for clarinet, woodwind choir, percussion, 1971; concertino for timpani, winds, percussion, 1972; Blue Lake divertissement, 1972; Sonnet, 1977; Marchisma, 1977; Songs from the Navajo children, chorus and wind ensemble; CHAMBER MUSIC: trumpet sonata, 1946; 3 for 5, woodwind quintet, 1958; Diversions, brass sextet, 1964; Serenade #3, brass quartet, 1963; Divertissement #1, clarinet choir, 1965; trombone sonata, 1966; Lyric suite, euphonium and piano, 1970; Trio variations, piano trio, 1970; Tetra ergon, bass trombone and piano, 1972; also choral works, piano pieces.

R.R. 1, Fairway Dr., Greencastle, IN 46135

WHITE, GARY C.

b. Winfield, Kans., 27 May 1937. Studied with John Pozdro, Univ. of Kansas; with H. Owen Reed and Paul Harder, Michigan State Univ., Ph.D. 1969. His awards include commission prize, Symposium of Contemporary Music for Brass, 1974; winner, Coll. Band Directors Nat. Assoc. contest, 1975; Toon Van Balkom prize, 1975; Nat. Endowment for the Arts grant, 1975; MacDowell fellowship, 1975; many commissions. He has been faculty member, Iowa State Univ., from 1967.

WORKS: THEATRE: music for The egg, 1962; Cyrano de Bergerac, 1963; Bury the dead, 1968; ORCHESTRA: Dramatic overture, 1961; Prologue, 3 trumpets, timpani, strings, 1964; symphony, 1969, Michigan State Univ., 4 June 1971; WIND ENSEMBLE: 2 movements for brass, 1963; Striations, winds and percussion, 1973; CHAMBER MUSIC: string quartet, 1963; Chaconne, for percussion, 1963; 2 movements, for chamber ensemble, 1965; woodwind quintet, 1966; Strata, clarinet solo, 1968; Composition, piano, brass, percussion, 1970; Centrum, violin and tape, 1971; Antipodes I, organ, 1972; Insinuations, brass quintet and tape, 1974; Antipodes II, organ and tape, 1975; Montage, bassoon and piano, 1976; Images, solo trombone and 3 trombones, 1976; Soundings, solo trumpet and 4 trumpets, 1976; Pulsar, organ and brass choir, 1977.

540 Meadow Ct., Ames, IA 50010

WHITE, JOHN A.

b. Surrey, England, 20 Feb. 1935; to U.S. 1961. Studied piano and organ in England, voice in Ithaca, N.Y., 1962-63; theory at Eastman School of Music, 1965-68.

WORKS: CHAMBER MUSIC: 18 studies and 5 sonatas for guitar; recorder quartet; CHORUS: Hear, O Lord, with trumpet and organ; Missa quatuor in uno; also recorder-guitar duos; madrigals; etc.

367 Brooklawn Dr., Rochester, NY 14618

WHITE, JOHN D.

b. Rochester, Minn., 28 Nov. 1931. Studied with Earl George and Paul Fetler, Univ. of Minnesota, B.A.; with Bernard Rogers and Howard Hanson, Eastman School of Music, M.A., Ph.D. 1960; also with Nadia Boulanger and Ross Lee Finney. He received the Benjamin award, 1960; Nat. Fed. of Music Clubs award, 1962; first prize, Rochester Religious Arts Festival, 1963; annual ASCAP awards from 1964. He has been faculty member at Kent State Univ., 1956-63, 1966-73; Univ. of Michigan, 1963-65; Ithaca Coll., 1973-75; visiting professor, Univ. of Wisconsin, 1975-78; from 1978, at Whitman Coll.

WORKS: OPERA: The legend of Sleepy Hollow, 1962; ORCHESTRA: symphony #2, 1960; Dialogue concertante, cello and orch., 1959; Folk elegy, cello and orch., 1962; concerto for cello and chamber orch., 1969; CHAMBER MUSIC: Variations, clarinet and piano; piano sonatina, 1954; Aria and double fugue, harpsichord, 1967; string quartet, 1975; Variations, for piano, 1976; CHORUS: The monkey's sonnet; The passing of winter; The turmoil; Cantos of the year, with baritone solo and orch., 1968; Roots and leaves, male chorus, percussion, brass choir, 1974; Ode on the morning of Christ's nativity, with flute, clarinet, piano, 1977; and songs.

6601 Piedmont Rd., Madison, WI 53711

WHITE, LOUIE L.

b. Spartanburg, S.C., 1 Aug. 1921. Studied with Pedro Sanjuan, Converse Coll.; with Ernst Bacon at Syracuse Univ. He received the Hyatt award at Converse Coll.; 2 awards, Church of the Ascension, New York. He was faculty member, Syracuse Univ., 1947-48; taught in a private school in New York, 1953-70; from 1970, on faculty, Rutgers Univ.

WORKS: OPERA: Jephthah, chancel opera; ORCHESTRA: harpsichord concerto; CHAMBER MUSIC: string quartet; 3 preludes, piano; piano sonata; oboe sonata; organ sonata; CHORUS: Rejoice, Emanuel shall come, cantata; St. Francis' prayer; many other choral works.

61 W. 9th St., New York, NY 10011

WHITE, MICHAEL

b. Chicago, Ill., 6 Mar. 1931. Studied at Oberlin Coll.; Univ. of Wisconsin; Chicago Musical Coll.; and with Peter Mennin at Juilliard School. His awards include 2 Juilliard fellowships; 3 Ford Found. grants; Guggenheim fellowship; 2 William Penn Found. grants; awards from Columbia Univ. and Pennsylvania Council for the Arts. He was faculty member, Oberlin Cons., 1964-66; Philadelphia Coll. of the Performing Arts from 1966; Juilliard School from 1977.

WORKS: OPERA: The dybbuk, commissioned for the Seattle World's Fair, 1962; The metamorphosis, 1968; The passion according to a cynic, 1971; The ancient vespers, 1973; The prophet, 1974; ORCHESTRA: Fantasy, 1957; suite, 1959; The diary of Anne Frank, soprano and orch., 1960; Gloria, chorus and orch., 1960; WIND ENSEMBLE: Concerto antico; Opposites; many chamber works, shoral works, song cycles.

7147 Ardleigh St., Philadelphia, PA 19119

WHITE, PAUL TAYLOR

WHITE, PAUL TAYLOR
b. Bangor, Maine, 22 Aug. 1895; d. Henrietta,
N.Y., 31 May 1973. Studied composition with
George W. Chadwick, violin with Felix Winternitz,
New England Cons.; violin with Eugene Ysaye in
Cincinnati; conducting with Eugene Goossens in
Rochester; received an honorary D.M., Univ. of
Maine. He was violinist and conductor in Roches-
ter from 1924; faculty member, Eastman School of
Music, and conductor, Eastman Symphony, from
1935; guest conductor of his own works with many
orchestras, including the Boston Pops.
WORKS: ORCHESTRA: Variations, 1925; Mos-
quito dance; symphony, 1934; Pagan festival overture, 1936; Boston sketches, 4 spokes from the
Hub, 1938; College caprice, 1939; Voyage of the
Mayflower, with chorus; Sea chantey, harp and
strings, 1942; Lake Placid scenes, 1943; Idyll,
1944; Andante and rondo, cello and orch., 1945;
CHAMBER MUSIC: Fantastic dance, woodwinds, 1922;
2 string quartets; violin sonata, 1926; 5 miniatures, for piano.

WHITE, RUTH
b. Pittsburgh, Pa., 1 Sept. 1925. Studied with
Nikolai Lopatnikoff, Carnegie-Mellon Univ.; with
John Vincent, Univ. of California, Los Angeles;
privately with George Antheil. Her awards include first prize in composition, Nat. Soc. for
Arts and Letters; Huntington Hartford Found.
fellowship. She was supervisor, Univ. of California Lab. School, Los Angeles, 1951-59; from
1954, composer for films and television, and
independent record producer.
WORKS: ELECTRONIC: Pinions, 1968; 2 trumps
from the tarot cards, 1968; Flowers of evil,
1969; Short circuits, 1970; also film scores;
multimedia works, such as music for the San
Diego Space Theater.
Whitney Bldg./Box 34485, Los Angeles, CA
90034

WHITE, RUTH EDEN
b. Florence, S.C., 25 Dec. 1928. Studied at
Coker Coll. She has been church organist from
1947; from 1963, at Calvary Baptist Church,
Florence, S.C.
WORKS: CHORUS: Have you heard?; Fill me,
Lord, with all thy ways; Let praise fill the
skies; other choral works, many with original
texts.
1108 Brunwood Dr., Florence, SC 29501

WHITE, TERRENCE E.
b. Portsmouth, Va., 30 May 1953. Studied with
John Bavicchi, Jeronimus Kacinskas, and Hugo
Norden, Berklee Coll. of Music; and at Univ. of
New Hampshire. He has been music supervisor,
1975-79, and music director, from 1979, in the
Westbrook, Maine, public schools.
WORKS: ORCHESTRA: Sketches; concerto for
doubles; WIND ENSEMBLE: 3 etudes for brass;
Fantasy, brass quintet; CHAMBER MUSIC: Divertimento, oboe and piano; Elegy, 3 flutes; clarinet
sonata; woodwind quartet.
67 Mechanic St., Westbrook, ME 04092

WHITE, WILLIAM C.
b. Centerville, Utah, 29 Sept. 1881; d. New
York, N.Y., 19 Dec. 1932. Studied violin at the
New England Cons. and at Inst. of Musical Arts,
New York, graduating 1914. He was a member of
the U.S. Coast Artillery Band, 1907-12; led the
Mecca Temple Band, 1919-20; Aimes Temple Band in
Washington, D.C., 1921-28; was principal of the
Army Music School on Governor's Island, N.Y.,
for many years. He composed many marches, in-
cluding American doughboy; also published A
history of military music in America, 1943.

WHITECOTTON, SHIRLEY
b. Aurora, Ill., 23 Sept. 1935. Studied with
Jack Goode, Wheaton Coll.; also at Aspen Music
School and at Northwestern Univ. She was a
private voice teacher, 1960-73.
WORKS: CHORUS: We have a king, cantata;
Little known Scottish folk songs, Books I and II;
Words of life; Christmas comes in the morning,
cantata; Michael; Light; The lamb; God is watching; and others.
408 W. Jefferson, Wheaton, IL 60187

WHITFORD, HOMER
b. Harvey, Ill., 21 May 1892. Studied at Oberlin
Coll., B.M.; Harvard Univ.; and at Fontainebleau. He was faculty member, Dartmouth Coll.;
church organist in Cambridge, Mass., for 21
years; conductor of choral groups. His works
include choral pieces, church services, and
technical books for organ.

WHITHORNE (WHITTERN), EMERSON
b. Cleveland, Ohio, 6 Sept. 1884; d. Lyme, Conn.,
25 Mar. 1958. Studied piano in Cleveland, and
after tours on the Chautauqua circuit as a boy
pianist, studied with Theodor Leschetizky.
Robert Fuchs, and Artur Schnabel in Europe for
several years. He was music critic in London,
1907-16; married Ethel Leginska in 1907, was her
concert manager, 1907-9, divorced 1916; was music
editor in St. Louis, 1916-20; then settled in
New York.
WORKS: THEATRE: Sooner or later, ballet;
music to O'Neill's Marco Millions, 1928; ORCHES-
TRA: The rain, 1913; The aeroplane, 1925;
Saturday's child, to poems of Countee Cullen,
soprano, tenor, and orch., 1926; New York days
and nights, 1926; Poem, piano and orch., 1927;
Fata morgana, 1928; 2 symphonies, 1929, 1936;
The dream pedlar, 1931; violin concerto, 1931;
Fandance, 1932; Moon trail, 1933; Sierra Morena,
1938; CHAMBER MUSIC: Greek impressions, string
quartet; string quartet; piano quintet; The grim
troubador, voice and string quartet.

WHITMAN, JAMES K.
b. Oakland, Calif., 12 May 1946. Studied with
Robert Cross, Occidental Coll.; with Richard
Swift, Univ. of California at Davis; with Leo
Smit and Lejaren Hiller, State Univ. of New York
at Buffalo. He received the Eleanor Remick
Warren award, 1965; West German Radio commission,
1973. He joined the staff at the electronic
studio, West German Radio, Cologne, in 1973.
WORKS: THEATRE: Yuzuru, play with music

for flute, clarinet, percussion, and tape; CHAMBER MUSIC: Soldier in the groove, flute, violin, cello; ELECTRONIC: Pavasiya, chorus and tape, GGK, tape; Dance of Shiva, 4-channel tape.

Gereonswall 66, 5 Köln 1, West Germany

WHITMER, THOMAS CARL
b. Altoona, Pa., 24 June 1873; d. Poughkeepsie, N.Y., 30 May 1959. Studied composition with William Wallace Gilchrist. He taught at Stephens Coll., 1897-1909; was director of music, Pennsylvania Coll. for Women, 1909-16; church organist in Pittsburgh, 1916-32; then taught privately in New York.

WORKS: OPERA: Oh, Isabel, 1951; BALLET: A Syrian night, 1919; ORCHESTRA: Poem of life, piano and orch., 1914; Radiations over a 13th-century theme, string orch., 1935; CHORUS: When God laughed, a cappella, 1932; Supper at Emmaus, choral suite, 1939; Chant me the poem that comes from the soul of America, cantata, 1942; also chamber music, songs, piano pieces.

WHITNEY, MAURICE C.
b. Glens Falls, N.Y., 25 Mar. 1909. Studied at Ithaca Coll., B.S. 1932; New York Univ., M.A. 1939; and at Columbia Univ., New England Cons., Westminster Choir Coll., and Williams Coll. His awards include first prize, Composers Press contest, 1949; citation for outstanding achievement, Ithaca Coll., 1951; John Hay fellowship, 1961; citation as Teacher of the Year, New York State Teachers Assoc., 1966; honorary L.H.D., Elmira Coll., 1966. He taught in public schools, 1932-69; was visiting professor, Adirondack Community Coll., 1969-71. He is author of several books.

WORKS: More than 150 published works for orchestra, band, chorus, solo instruments, and ensembles, mainly for school, college, and church use.

1508 Danbury Dr., Sun City Center, FL 33570

WHITNEY, ROBERT SUTTON
b. Newcastle-on-Tyne, England, 6 July 1904, of American parents. Studied at American Cons., 1922-28; conducting with Eric De Lamarter and Frederick Stock. His honors include the Ditson award for service to American music, 1951; honorary D.M., Univ. of Louisville, 1952; L.L.D., Hanover Coll., 1956. He made his debut as conductor with the Chicago Civic Orchestra in 1932; was conductor of the Louisville Orchestra, 1937-67; dean, School of Music, Univ. of Louisville, 1967.

WORKS: ORCHESTRA: concerto grosso, 1932; symphony, 1936; sinfonietta, 1949; Sospiri di Roma, 1941; concertino for orch., 1961.

2134 Alta Ave., Louisville, KY 40301

WHITNEY, RYAN LAYNE
b. Seattle, Wash., 1 July 1953. Studied privately with Lockrem Johnson in Seattle. He has received a BMI award; first prize, Nat. Fed. of Music Clubs contest; various prizes in state contests.

WORKS: PIANO: 6 burlesques; Tema con var-

iazioni, 1969; 2 sonatas, #2, 1980.
1025 Boylston Ave. E., Seattle, WA 98102

WHITTAKER, HOWARD
b. Lakewood, Ohio, 19 Dec. 1922. Studied with Herbert Elwell and Ward Lewis, Cleveland Inst. of Music, B.M., conducting with Boris Goldovsky; with Herbert Elwell, Oberlin Cons., M.M. 1947; later at Eastman School of Music. His awards include Fortnightly Musical Club award, 1948; Mendelssohn Glee Club award, 1953; Women's City Club of Cleveland award, 1963; and commissions. He has been director, Cleveland Music School Settlement, from 1948. In 1968 he was appointed consultant to Vice-President Hubert Humphrey and worked with the president's Council on Youth Opportunity.

WORKS: ORCHESTRA: Fantasy on Ben Hamby melodies, 1946; Variations, 1947; piano concerto, 1954; 2 murals for orch., 1958; CHAMBER MUSIC: 2 string quartets, 1947, 1948; violin sonatina, 1957; cello sonata, 1957; cello sonatina, 1969; violin sonata, 1970; PIANO: 2 sonatas, 1954, 1960; Variations, 1958; many choral works and songs.

Berkshire Rd., Gates Mills, OH 44040

WHITTENBERG, CHARLES
b. St. Louis, Mo., 6 July 1927. Studied with Burrill Phillips and Bernard Rogers, Eastman School of Music, B.M. 1948; at American Acad. in Rome; and in Munich. His awards include Nat. Council of Learned Societies grant, 1962; Guggenheim fellowships, 1963-65; Prix de Rome, 1965-66; and many commissions. He was affiliated with the Columbia-Princeton electronic music studio in 1962; joined the faculty at Univ. of Connecticut, 1966.

WORKS: ORCHESTRA: Events, chamber orch., 1964; Correlations, 1969; CHAMBER MUSIC: Dialogue and aria, flute and piano, 1956; Electronic study, cello and tape, 1960; Fantasy, wind quintet, 1961; Structures, 2 pianos, 1961; Electronic study II, double bass and tape, 1962; Triptych, brass quintet, 1962; chamber concerto, violin and 7 instruments, 1963; Variations, piano, 1963; Duo divertimento, flute and double bass, 1963; Composition, cello and piano, 1963; Variations, 9 players, 1965; Polyphony, solo trumpet, 1965; Conversations, solo double bass, 1967; sextet, 1967; Games of 5, wind quintet, 1968; Iambi, 2 oboes, 1968; concerto for brass quintet, 1969; A due, flute and piano, 1969; A sacred triptych, 8 solo voices, 1971.

c/o McGinnis & Marx, 201 W. 86 St., #706, New York, NY 10024

WHITTREDGE, EDWARD B.
b. Dorchester, Mass., 31 Jan. 1893. Studied organ with John Herman Loud; theory at Boston Univ.; summer sessions at Westminster Choir Coll., Christiansen Choral School, and Fred Waring Workshop. He was admitted as fellow, American Guild of Organists, 1933; was organist-choirmaster, 1919-69; director, Wentworth Inst. Glee Club, 1958-68.

WORKS: CHORUS: Psalm 91, cantata; As it began to dawn; Lord speak to me; Surely He hath

WHITWELL, CRAIG MARTIN

borne our griefs; The church's one foundation;
numerous other published choral works.
789 Brook Rd., Milton, MA 02186

WHITWELL, CRAIG MARTIN
b. Santa Rosa, Calif., 21 Apr. 1948. Studied
with Higo Harada and Allen Strange, California
State Univ. at San Jose; with Ralph Shapey and
George Crumb, Univ. of Pennsylvania. He received
the Eva Thompson Phillips award, 1970, 1971. He
was lecturer in the Creative Associates program,
California State Univ., San Jose, 1970-71.
WORKS: CHAMBER MUSIC: Episode, trombone
and piano, 1969; Duo sonata, trombone and flute,
1969; Theme and variations in arch form, 2 winds,
1970; Variations on a theme by Satie, 1971; Fantasy, 4 strings and oboe, 1972; Villanelle,
brass quartet.

WICHMANN, RUSSELL G.
b. Appleton, Wis., 29 July 1912. Studied at
Lawrence Univ., B.M. 1934; with Clarence
Dickinson, T. Tertius Noble, and Edwin J.
Stringham, Union Theological Seminary, S.M.M.
1936; Army Music School, 1944; with Arthur
Honegger and Marcel Dupre in Paris, 1950-51;
with Wayne Barlow and Allen McHose, Eastman
School of Music, 1959-60. His awards include
the Pittsburgh Arts Society award, 1937; and the
alumni distinguished service award, Lawrence
Univ., 1970. He has been church minister of
music from 1936; faculty member, Univ. of Pittsburgh, 1936-46; Army bandleader, 1944-45; professor, Chatham Coll., from 1946; conductor,
Mendelssohn Choir of Pittsburgh, 1952-66.
WORKS: CHORUS: Dayspring of eternity; Come
thou, my light; O Lamb of God; I lift up my eyes;
Bell carol; Psalm 100; Psalm 150; Psalm 148, The
voice of God; God of our life; and others.
313 Dewey Ave., Edgewood, Pittsburgh, PA
15218

WICK, OTTO
b. Krefeld, Germany, 8 July 1885; to U.S. 1905;
d. Austin, Tex., 9 Nov. 1957. Studied at Univ.
of Kiel; New York Coll. of Music, Ph.D. He was
conductor in New York, 1910-24; guest conductor
in Europe; arranger, conductor, NBC, New York,
1928-31; organized and conducted New York Orch.,
1931-35; with Southwest Festival Assoc., 1938-
42; dean, Univ. of San Antonio, 1939-46; then
director, San Antonio Opera Company.
WORKS: OPERA: The lone star; Matasuntha,
music drama; Moon maid, light opera; For Art's
sake, operetta; ORCHESTRA: suite for strings
and harp; Symphonic poem; Symphonic fantasy;
Trilogy, for orch.; CHORUS: Temple of Peshawar,
cantata.

WICKHAM, FLORENCE
b. Beaver, Pa., 1880; d. New York, N.Y., 20 Oct.
1962. Studied voice in Philadelphia and Berlin;
sang at the Metropolitan Opera in New York,
1909-12; then retired from the stage and devoted
her time to composition. Her works included an
operetta, Rosalynd, 1938; many published choral
pieces and songs.

WIDDOES, LAWRENCE L.
b. Wilmington, Del., 15 Sept. 1932. Studied
with Bernard Wagenaar, Vincent Persichetti, and
William Bergsma, Juilliard School, B.S., M.S.
He received the Benjamin award at Juilliard;
Society for the Publication of American Music
award; Elizabeth Sprague Coolidge chamber music
award; Contemporary Music Project, composer-in-
residence, Salem, Ore.; Bowdoin Coll. contest
award. He was faculty member at Juilliard
School, 1965-75.
WORKS: ORCHESTRA: Morning music; WIND ENSEMBLE: concertino for brass choir; CHAMBER
MUSIC: 1000 paper cranes, guitar, viola, harpsichord, 1966; From a time of snow, flute, clarinet, viola, cello, piano, 1971; flute sonatina;
Acanthus, harp and viola, New York, 11 May 1973;
Love song, voice and piano; Aubade, chamber ensemble, New York, 19 Apr. 1974; CHORUS: Sanctus;
Pied beauty.
300 Central Park W., New York, NY 10024

WIDDOWSON, KENNETH WEST
b. Punxsutawney, Pa., 4 Nov. 1928. Studied at
Duquesne Univ.; with Bernhard Heiden, Indiana
Univ.; with Paul Cooper, Univ. of Michigan. He
was educational director for a music publisher,
1961-62.
WORKS: BAND: States War fantasy, 1955;
Portrait of this old man, 1961; Phantom squadron,
1962; Valley Forge fantasy, 1967.
3203 Ward Ave., Trenton, MI 48183

WIENER, IVAN
b. New York, N.Y., 15 June 1933. Studied with
Robert Starer, 1955-57, 1959; with Wallingford
Riegger, 1957-58. He held the Frederick Jacobi
scholarship, 1955-57. He was librarian and
editor, Galaxy Music Corp., 1964-67; editor,
Broude Brothers, Ltd., from 1967.
WORKS: ORCHESTRA: Fantasie concertante,
double bass and orch.; symphony; concerto
grosso, 5 solo instruments and strings; cello
concerto; double bass concerto; Variations, for
orch.; CHAMBER MUSIC: Inventions, 2 alto recorders; 2 string trios; 3 segments, percussion
ensemble; CHORUS: love is more thicker than
forget, e. e. cummings text; Requiem, with soloists and orch.
556 Ave. Z, Brooklyn, NY 11223

WIENHORST, RICHARD W.
b. Seymour, Ind., 21 Apr. 1920. Studied at
Valparaiso Univ., A.B.; with Leo Sowerby, American Cons., M.M.; with Nadia Boulanger at Fontainebleau; musicology at Ludwige Univ., Germany;
with Bernard Rogers and Howard Hanson, Eastman
School of Music, Ph.D. He received a Danforth
Found. award, and a Lilly Found. graduate study
award. He was bandleader, U.S. Army, 1942-46;
from 1947, professor, Valparaiso Univ.
WORKS: CHORUS: Magnificat, with orch.;
Missa brevis, a cappella; The 7 words of Christ
from the cross; A nativity cantata, with flute
and strings; Psalm 150; Hear, O Lord; Lord,
thine enemies roar.
103 Sturdy Rd., Valparaiso, IN 46483

WIGGINS, ARTHUR M.
b. New York, N.Y., 18 Mar. 1920. Studied at U.S. Air Force Bandsman School, Washington; is self-taught in composition. He was chief arranger for the Air Force in New York and the Canal Zone from 1965 to retirement in 1973.
WORKS: BAND: Intervale; The court jester; Ballet for jazz; CHAMBER MUSIC: Conversations, alto saxophone; Song and dance man, bass clarinet; Una mas, trumpet; The horn, for horn.
P.O. Box 2165, Colorado Springs, CO 80901

WIGGINS, DONALD GLENN
b. Orlando, Fla., 22 Feb. 1943. Studied with Roger McDuffie, Converse Coll., with Ben Johnston and Edwin London, Univ. of Illinois. He was faculty member, Converse Coll., 1967-70; State Univ. Coll., Fredonia, N.Y., 1972-77; from 1978, at Catholic Univ.
WORKS: THEATRE: music for Murder in the cathedral; also songs and an opera.
Catholic University, Washington, DC 20064

WIGGINS, MARY
b. Indiana, Pa., 10 Feb. 1904; d. Pittsburgh, Pa., 17 Apr. 1974. Studied composition privately with Gladys W. Fisher and Harvey B. Gaul; with Roland Leich, Carnegie-Mellon Univ. She was a private piano teacher from 1924; organist from 1931; taught at Pittsburgh Musical Inst., 1959-62. She composed for piano, organ, bassoon, violin, chorus, solo voice, and numerous piano teaching pieces.

WIGGLESWORTH, FRANK
b. Boston, Mass., 3 Mar. 1918. Studied at Bard Coll.; Columbia Univ., B.S.; Converse Coll., M.M.; composition with Otto Luening, Henry Cowell, and Edgard Varese. He received the Alice M. Ditson award; Nat. Inst. of Arts and Letters award; fellowship, American Acad. in Rome, 1951-54; 2 MacDowell fellowships. He was instructor, Columbia Univ., 1946-51; Queens Coll., 1954-55; on music faculty, The New School, from 1954, chairman from 1967.
WORKS: ORCHESTRA: New England concerto, violin and strings, 1941; 3 symphonies, 1957, 1958, 19__; 3 portraits, for strings; CHAMBER MUSIC: Lake music, solo flute; duo for oboe and viola or clarinet; woodwind quintet; brass quintet; CHORUS: Creation, with small orch., 1940; Jeremiah, with baritone solo and orch., 1942; Sleep becalmed, with orch., 1948; 2 masses; 2 motets.
19 Downing St., New York, NY 10014

WILCOX, JAMES H.
b. Bolton, England, 10 July 1916; to U.S. 1921. Studied with Arne Oldberg, Northwestern Univ.; at Univ. of Wisconsin; at Eastman School of Music, 1949-53; with Ernst von Dohnanyi, Florida State Univ., 1954-56. He was faculty member, Florida State Univ., 1954-56; professor and music dept. head, Southeastern Louisiana Univ., 1963-70, dean from 1970.
WORKS: BAND: Introduction and passacaglia, 1956; CHAMBER MUSIC: Heroic sketch, horn and piano, 1950; Concert piece, trumpet and piano, 1954; violin sonata, 1955.
105 College Dr., Hammond, LA 70401

WILD, EARL
b. Pittsburgh, Pa. Studied piano with Selmar Jansen. He has performed with major orchestras in the U.S. and in many music festivals. His compositions include a piano concerto and Revelations, an Easter oratorio, 1962.

WILDER, ALEC
b. Rochester, N.Y., 16 Feb. 1907; d. Gainesville, Fla., 24 Dec. 1980. Studied with Herbert Inch and Edward Royce, Eastman School of Music. His awards include the ASCAP-Deems Taylor award, 1974, for his book, American popular song--The great innovators, 1900-50; Nat. Endowment for the Arts grants; Guggenheim fellowship, 1980. He was composer-arranger in New York City.
WORKS: THEATRE: The lowland sea, 1951; Sunday excursion, 1952; Cumberland Fair, 1953; Miss Chicken Little, 1953; Kittiwake Island, 1954; Mountain boy, chamber opera; ORCHESTRA: concerto for oboe, strings, percussion, 1957; many concertos for various wind instruments; CHAMBER MUSIC: 10 woodwind quintets; 7 brass quintets; numerous sonatas and suites, mostly for wind instruments; tuba sonata #2 was premiered in New York, 22 Dec. 1975.

WILDING-WHITE, RAYMOND
b. Caterham, Surrey, England, 9 Oct. 1922; U.S. citizen. Studied at Massachusetts Inst. of Technology, 1940-42; at Juilliard School, 1948-49; privately with Jerzy Fitelberg in New York; with Aaron Copland, Jacques Ibert, and Luigi Dallapiccola at Tanglewood, 1950, 1951, 1952; at Boston Univ., D.M.A. 1961. His awards include the F. S. Croft award, 1951, 1952, at Tanglewood; Samuel Wechsler commission; New England Cons. New Music prize, 1959; Shepherd award, 1964; Cleveland Women's City Club award, 1967. He was radio and television producer and director in Boston, 1951-56; on faculty, Archbishop Cushing Coll., 1958-59; Case Inst. of Technology, 1961-68; from 1968, De Paul Univ.
WORKS: OPERA: The tub, chamber opera, 1952; The selfish giant, Oscar Wilde text, 1952; Yerma, libretto after Garcia-Lorca, 1962; BALLET: The trees, 1949; The lonesome valley, 1960; THEATRE: Monday morning at the Gargoyle Works, action piece for 5 performers, 1968; Slinky, 1 amplified performer, 1969; Bad news, a set of short dada pieces, 1970; ORCHESTRA: piano concerto, 1949; Even now, baritone and orch., 1954; Concertante, violin, horn, strings, 1963; CHAMBER MUSIC: string quartet, 1948; piano sonata, 1950; 3 organ preludes, 1951; violin sonata, 1956; 2-piano sonata, 1953; Little suite, for winds, 1958; Variations, for chamber organ and string trio, 1959; 16 character sketches, piano, 1950-60; Monte Carlo suite #1, string quartet, 1962, #2, for piano, 1962; trumpet sonatina, 1964; Metals, metallic constructions for audience participation, 1964; Counterpoints and events, 2 clarinets, 1965; 6 fragments, for jazz ensemble, 1966; The children's corner, collage for any group of keyboard instruments and a singer, 1966; Haiku, 2 voices, various instruments, 1967; a group of 9 pieces all called Whatzit, for various performers, instruments, and/or tape, e.g., #7 for harpsichord and 144 recorded

WILEY, FRANK

harpsichords, 1967-73, to be performed in a
warehouse over a 24-hour period; also numerous
works for solo voice and chorus; electronic
pieces.
715 S. Ridgeland Ave., Oak Park, IL 60306

WILEY, FRANK
b. Richmond, Va., 9 Dec. 1949. Studied with
Roger Hannay, Univ. of North Carolina, M.M.;
with Donald Erb, Cleveland Inst. of Music, D.M.A.
He was winner in the Cleveland Inst. organ com-
position contest, 1974; and the first annual
Holtkamp organ composition contest, Univ. of
Hartford, 1978. From 1975 he has been faculty
member, Univ. of North Carolina at Wilmington.
WORKS: ORCHESTRA: Abstracts, 1975; CHAMBER
MUSIC: Encounters: A fantasy of fragmented
images, piano, percussion, and ensemble, 1973;
Serenade, cello and harp, 1974; 3 incantations,
harp, 1974; Luminations, instrumental ensemble,
1974; Dreamscape, amplified piano, 1975; ORGAN:
Fantasia super B A C H, 1974; Premonition, 1977;
ELECTRONIC: But wait . . . Here's that music
again; Prelude in D; Music for percussion and
tape; Music for Euripides' "Medea," 2 2-channel
tapes, 1978.
4914-C Pepys Lane, Wilmington, NC 28403

WILKINSON, CONSTANCE JANE
b. England, 20 Feb. 1944. Studied at Newnham
Coll., B.M. 1967; with W. Kotonski in Poland on
a Polish government scholarship; with Richard
Felciano at Univ. of California at Berkeley, M.A.
1971, Ph.D. 1976. She held a Herz scholarship
at Berkeley; received the Music Teachers Nat.
Assoc. 1979 Composer of the Year Award for
Phoenix I for harp solo. She was lecturer, Univ.
of California, 1972-76; then on faculty, Univ.
of Virginia.
WORKS: VOICE: Movements, 1976; Songs of a
courtesan, 12 female voices, San Francisco, 16
Mar. 1980.
University of Virginia, Charlottesville, VA
22903

WILKINSON, SCOTT
b. Bement, Ill., 27 June 1922. Studied with
Arthur Olaf Andersen, Univ. of Arizona; with
Darius Milhaud at Mills Coll. and in Paris. He
received a composition award at Mills Coll. He
was on the editorial staff, Carl Fischer, Inc.,
1956-61, 1969-71; in 1971, joined the faculty at
Univ. of New Mexico.
WORKS: ORCHESTRA: concertino for piano and
orch.; CHAMBER MUSIC: violin sonata; violin
sonatina; CHORUS: This is the American earth,
oratorio, with narrator, clarinet, brass, percussion; many anthems; also band pieces.
Rte. 5, Box 785, Los Lunas, NM 87051

WILLEY, JAMES H.
b. Lynn, Mass., 1 Oct. 1939. Studied with
Bernard Rogers, Howard Hanson, Wayne Barlow,
Eastman School of Music; with Gunther Schuller,
Berkshire Music Center. His awards include SUNY
grants, 1974, 1977; Nat. Endowment for the Arts
grant, 1975; residencies at Yaddo, 1976, 1977;
N.Y. State Music Teachers Assoc. commission,
1976. He has been on the faculty, State Univ.

Coll. at Geneseo, from 1966.
WORKS: ORCHESTRA: 2 sinfoniettas; violin
concerto; CHAMBER MUSIC: Opus Dei, viola and
piano; duo for flute and harp; string quartet,
1975; Hymns and litanies, clarinet and piano;
Mendon, harp and piano; VOICE: 3 Elizabethan
lyrics, 1968; Gacelas, voice and piano; Tobacco
is like love, chorus; Flow, my tears, chorus;
The death of Mozart, soprano, narrator, instrumental ensemble, 1975.
25A Prospect St., Geneseo, NY 14454

WILLIAMS, CLIFTON
b. Arkansas, 1923; d. South Miami, Fla., 12 Feb.
1976. Studied at Louisiana Polytechnic Inst.;
with Helen Gunderson, Louisiana State Univ.;
with Bernard Rogers and Howard Hanson, Eastman
School of Music. His awards included 2 Ostwald
awards of the American Bandmasters Assoc.; and
an honorary D.M., Nat. Cons. of Lima, Peru. He
served in the U.S. Army Air Corps in World War
II; joined the faculty at Univ. of Texas in
1949; in 1966, became chairman of composition,
Univ. of Miami, School of Music.
WORKS: BAND: Trail scenes, suite; Trilogy,
suite; concertino for percussion and band; Symphonic dances; Fanfare and allegro; Dedicatory
overture; Dramatic essay: The ramparts; and
many other band pieces.

WILLIAMS, DAVID H.
b. Caerphilly, Wales, 21 Nov. 1919. Studied at
Peabody Cons., and Columbia Univ. He has been
church organist-choirmaster in the New York
area, Connecticut, Vermont, and Tucson, Ariz.
WORKS: CHORUS: Gloria; Take my life and
let it be, in calypso style; 3 Lenten scenes;
Draw nigh to Jerusalem; On the passion of
Christ, cantata; To Zion Jesus came.
9020 Shadow Mountain Dr., Tucson, AZ 85704

WILLIAMS, DAVID H.
b. Kansas City, Mo., 27 July 1946. Studied with
Robert Gauldin, Eastman School of Music; with
Grant Fletcher and Ronald LoPresti, Arizona
State Univ. He received the Sigma Alpha Iota
Band Competition award, 1968. He was instructor,
Westminster Coll., 1973-75; from 1975, at Univ.
of Wisconsin at Stout.
WORKS: OPERA: The witch of Worcestshire,
operetta; CHORUS: Alleluia for the first Sunday in Advent; Gloria, a cappella; Easter introit, a cappella; Emmanuel, Alleluia; A Christmas celebration, cantata; Reflections, cantata,
with orch.
1607 7th St., Menomonie, WI 54751

WILLIAMS, DAVID McKAY
b. Caernarvonshire, Wales, 20 Feb. 1887; to U.S.
as an infant; d. Oakland, Calif., 13 May 1978.
Studied with Vincent d'Indy, Louis Vierne, and
Charles-Marie Widor in Paris; and at King's
Coll., Nova Scotia, D.M. A festival service
honoring his 85th birthday was held St.
Bartholomew's Church, New York, in 1972. He
taught at David Mannes School; was chairman of
the organ dept., Columbia Univ., 1920-24, and at
Juilliard School, 1942-48; organist at St.
Bartholomew's Church, 1920-48. His compositions

included an opera, Florence Nightingale; an
operetta, Enchanted waters; and In the year the
King Uzziah died, for chorus; many church anthems,
etc.

WILLIAMS, DAVID RUSSELL
b. Indianapolis, Ind., 21 Oct. 1932. Studied
with Jack Beeson, Henry Cowell, Otto Luening,
Vladimir Ussachevsky, Columbia Univ., B.A., M.A.
1956; with Wayne Barlow, Howard Hanson, and
Bernard Rogers, Eastman School of Music, Ph.D.
1965. He received the Eastman School Publication award, 1970. He was faculty member, Wind-
ham Coll., 1959-62; Eastman School of Music,
1965-80; then at Memphis State Univ.
WORKS: THEATRE: Welcome aboard, musical
comedy, 1961; ORCHESTRA: Sinfonia in E, 1956;
Harmonica concerto, 1956; In the still of the
Bayou, 1963; piano concerto, 4 hands, 1964;
Lullaby under the magnolias, 1964; 5 states of
mind, 1965; Air, oboe and strings, 1965; tuba
concerto, 1965; BAND: Arkansas overture, 1957;
Sinfonia, 1957; King Edward march, Mt. Olympus
march, St. Anthony march, 1957; suite for brass,
1965; Recitation, trombone choir, 1967; CHAMBER
MUSIC: suite for oboe, clarinet, harpsichord,
1954; sonatina for harp and bassoon, 1955; clarinet sonatina, 1956; Dance piece, solo bassoon,
1956; Song and dance, violin and piano, 1956;
KEYBOARD: 5 pieces, for harpsichord, 1955; 9
piano sonatas, 1954-64; suite for piano, 4 hands,
1956; also songs.
Memphis State University, Memphis, TN 38152

WILLIAMS, FRANCES
b. Caernarvonshire, Wales, 4 June; to U.S. at an
early age. Studied at Cornish School of Music,
Seattle; with Rubin Goldmark and James Friskin
at Juilliard School. She joined the staff at
Harold Flammer, Inc., later became editor-in-
chief. She published more than 300 choral works
and songs.
545 West End Ave., New York, NY 10024

WILLIAMS, HOWARD
b. Auburn, Calif., 25 June 1933; d. Durham, N.H.,
9 Feb. 1972. Studied with Seymour Shifrin,
Andrew Imbrie, Luigi Dallapiccola, Univ. of California, Berkeley, A.B. 1954, M.A. 1965. He received the Alfred Hertz Memorial fellowship,
Berkeley, 1962-63; traveling fellowship, Paris,
1963-64; DeLorenzo composition prize, 1963;
MacDowell fellowship, 1968. He was faculty member, Univ. of New Hampshire, from 1965.
WORKS: ORCHESTRA: 6 poems, tenor and orch.;
CHAMBER MUSIC: concertino for tuba, percussion,
piano; clarinet sonata; string quartet; CHORUS:
Settings, women's voices; PIANO: Cycle for
piano; 5 bagatelles; 3 movements.

WILLIAMS, JACK ERIC
b. Odessa, Tex., 28 Mar. 1944. Studied at
Odessa Jr. Coll. and Texas Tech. Univ. His
awards include first place, Texas Manuscript
Society contest, 1962, Texas Young Composers
contest, 1963, 1964, 1965, Nat. Grass Roots
Opera contest, 1965; Alice Lee madrigal award,
1964; Tennessee Arts Commission grant, 1974. He
has been music director at various summer theatres.

WORKS: OPERA: The hinge-tune, 1 act, 1964;
We gave him piano lessons, 1 act, 1970; Eyes at
Treblinka, musical drama, 1973; CHAMBER MUSIC:
oboe sonata, 1970; sextet, winds and piano, 1972;
CHORUS: Stabat mater, 1971; Yerma, 1971; A very
special person, 1972; On the human condition,
1973.
4307 Elkins Ave., Nashville, TN 37209

WILLIAMS, JAY T.
b. Rochester, Minn., 31 Oct. 1941. Studied with
Iannis Xenakis, Indiana Univ. He was graduate
assistant, Indiana Univ., 1966-68, 1969-71;
piano technician, North Carolina School of the
Arts, from 1971; and on a North Carolina State
Arts Council grant, guest lecturer, North
Carolina school system from 1972.
WORKS: CHAMBER MUSIC: Char-main, solo
viola; ELECTRONIC: Mean 82, tape; Apertures,
tape; Numerology I, tape; Numerology II, tape
and trombone; Ayres out of mouthes, tape; Inside
PHI, tape; Recipe for Braille letters, tape,
saxophone, and dancer.
2436 Patria St., Winston-Salem, NC 27107

WILLIAMS, JOHN
b. Flushing, N.Y., 8 Feb. 1932. Studied piano
with Rosina Lehvinne at Juilliard School; composition with Mario Castelnuovo-Tedesco in Los
Angeles. In the early 1950s, he was pianist,
conductor, and arranger for Hollywood, began
composition for television in 1959 with the
series, "Checkmate." The scores for television
and films that followed have earned several
Emmys and 2 Oscars. In 1980 he was named conductor of the Boston Pops Orchestra.
WORKS: FILM SCORES: Penelope, 1966; Not
with my wife, you don't; Fitzwilly, 1967; The
rievers, 1969; Sugarland express, 1974; Jaws,
1975; Midway, 1976; Close encounters of the 3rd
kind; Star wars; and many others. His concert
works include Sinfonia for wind ensemble; Essay
for strings, 1966; flute concerto; violin concerto, 1979; chamber music and jazz.
333 Loring Ave., Los Angeles, CA 90024

WILLIAMS, KENNETH S.
b. Cleveland, Ohio, 3 Dec. 1920. Studied with
Arthur Shepherd and Melville Smith, Western
Reserve Univ., B.A., M.A. He was instrumental
instructor in public schools, 1950-63; on faculty, Houston Baptist Coll., 1967-69. His works
for band include Salute ASBDA; Bold frontier;
Vilabella.

WILLIAMS, MARY LOU
b. Atlanta, Ga., 8 May 1910; d. Durham, N.C.,
28 May 1981. She was pianist in dance orchestras and arranger for Benny Goodman, Louis
Armstrong, Duke Ellington, Cab Calloway, and
others. She appeared in Town Hall, New York,
with the New York Philharmonic, 1946; toured
Europe, 1952-54.
WORKS: ORCHESTRA: The zodiac suite;
CHORUS: Black Christ of the Andes, cantata;
Animus Christi: Praise the Lord.

WILLIAMS, PATRICK M.
b. Bonne Terre, Mo., 23 Apr. 1939. Studied at

WILLIAMS, RONALD

Duke Univ., A.B. 1961; at Columbia Univ.; privately with George Tremblay in Los Angeles. His awards include a Grammy award, 1974; Pulitzer prize nomination, 1977. He has been arranger for several name bands; composes chiefly for films and television; was on visiting faculty at Univ. of Utah, 1971-72; Univ. of Colorado, 1975-77.
WORKS: ORCHESTRA: The silent spring, adagio, cello and strings, 1971; An American concerto, jazz quartet and orch., 1976; BAND: double concerto, jazz ensemble and band; Rhapsody, jazz ensemble and band, 1975; CHAMBER MUSIC: Scenario, 5 instruments, 1970; TELEVISION: themes for "What's my line" and the "Tonight show."
532 17th St., Santa Monica, CA 90402

WILLIAMS, RONALD
b. Hollywood, Calif., 14 Dec. 1947. Studied with Anthony Gnazzo, David Tudor, Alden Jenks in Berkeley, Calif. He was lecturer, San Francisco Cons., 1973; research assistant, Univ. of California, Los Angeles, 1973.
WORKS: PIANO: Passacaglia; ELECTRONIC: Auscultation; Grains of wave, tape piece for earphones.

WILLIAMS, SPENCER
b. New Orleans, La., 14 Oct. 1889; d. Flushing, N.Y., 14 July 1965. Played piano in night clubs in New Orleans, Chicago, and New York, 1913-32; lived in Paris and London to 1957, then returned to New York. He composed very popular blues songs: Arkansas blues, 1919; Basin Street blues, 1923; Mahogany Hall stomp, 1924; etc.

WILLINK, GEORGE PETER JOHN
b. Voorburg, Netherlands, 10 July 1947; U.S. citizen 1963. Studied with Champ B. Tyrone, New Mexico Highlands Univ.; with William F. Wood, Univ. of New Mexico. He was public school music teacher, Fort Sumner, N.Mex., 1969-71.
WORKS: BAND: El abrigo, 1973; WIND ENSEMBLE: concertino for double brass quartet, 1970; 4 pieces, for woodwinds, 1972; Opinions, 8 brasses, timpani, percussion, 1972; CHAMBER MUSIC: Triumph, trumpet and piano, 1966; Introspection, trombone and piano, 1972; CHORUS: Fugue in a, with 2 pianos, 4 hands, 1966; Grooks, with woodwinds and piano, 1973.

WILLIS, RICHARD
b. Mobile, Ala., 21 Apr. 1929. Studied at Univ. of Alabama, B.M. 1950; with Henry Cowell, Wayne Barlow, Bernard Rogers, Howard Hanson, Eastman School of Music, M.M. 1951, Ph.D. 1965. His many awards include Sigma Alpha Iota awards, 1953, 1962; Bearns prize, 1955; Prix de Rome, 1956; Hanson prize, 1964; Pedro Paz award, 1965; Society for Publ. of American Music award, 1965; Volkwein-ASBDA award; Ostwald award, 1969; Baylor Univ. citation, 1976; and commissions. He was faculty member, Shorter Coll., 1953-63; from 1964, at Baylor Univ.
WORKS: THEATRE: The playground, dance drama, 1956; And winter's end, masque for dancers, chorus, piano, percussion; The search for meaning; ORCHESTRA: 2 symphonies, 1953,

1964; piano concertino; Prelude and dance, small orch., 1955; Canto, small orch.; Recitative and dance, flute and strings; Evocation, 1967; BAND: Essay for band; Aria and toccata, 1969; Epode; Partita; CHAMBER MUSIC: 2 string quartets; violin sonatina; Concert-piece, viola and piano; flute sonata; clarinet sonatina; Soliloquy, flute and piano; trumpet sonatina; violin sonata; Toccatina, organ; Passaggi, brass quintet, piano, percussion; and choral works.
1010 Southwood, Waco, TX 76710

WILLMAN, ALLAN ARTHUR
b. Hinckley, Ill., 11 May 1909. Studied at Knox Coll., B.M.; at Chicago Musical Coll., M.M.; privately with Albert Noelte and Rudolph Ganz in Chicago; with Nadia Boulanger and Thomas de Hartmann in Paris. His awards include the Paderewski prize, 1935; American Composers fellowship, 1946. He has been faculty member, Univ. of Wyoming, from 1936, music dept. chairman, 1941-74, then professor emeritus. He has made many concert tours of Europe as pianist, one for the U.S. State Dept. in 1953.
WORKS: ORCHESTRA: Solitude, symphonic poem, 1930, Boston, 20 Apr. 1936; Idyll, 1930; CHAMBER MUSIC: A ballade of the night, string quartet and voice, 1936; piano sonata; many works for piano solo and for voice.
University of Wyoming, Laramie, WY 82071

WILLMAN, REGINA HANSEN
b. Burns, Wyoming, 5 Oct. 1914; d. Portland, Oreg., 28 Oct. 1965. Studied at Univ. of Wyoming, B.M. 1945; at Univ. of New Mexico, M.M. 1961; privately with Darius Milhaud at Mills Coll. and in Paris; with Roy Harris at Colorado Coll.; also attended Univ. of California at Berkeley, Juilliard School, the Sorbonne in Paris, and the Cons. of Lausanne in Switzerland. She was twice resident composer, Wurlitzer Found., Taos, N.Mex., 1956-57, 1960-61.
WORKS: BALLET: The legend of the willow plate, chamber orch.; Steel mill, 2 pianos; THEATRE: music for Euripides' Medea; ORCHESTRA: Design for orchestra I; Design for orchestra II, Anchorage Symph., May 1971; CHAMBER MUSIC: Vocalise, for equal voices and low strings; First holy sonnet, John Donne, voice and string trio; The little tailor, suite for piano; other instrumental pieces and choral works. Her works have been given to the music dept., Univ. of Wyoming, by Allan A. Willman.

WILLSON, MEREDITH
b. Mason City, Iowa, 18 May 1902. Studied at Inst. of Musical Art, 1919; privately with Henry Hadley and Georges Barrere. His honors include 2 honorary doctorates; first annual Texas award to an outstanding figure in musical life, 1958; Distinguished Iowan award, 1958; Antoinette Perry award, New York Drama Critics' Circle award, Outer Circle award, Thespian Theatre award, all for The music man, 1958, for which he wrote the book, lyrics, and music. He played flute with Sousa's band, 1919-22, with the New York Philharmonic, 1923-28; then concentrated on composing and conducting for radio and Broadway.
WORKS: THEATRE: You and I, book, lyrics,

music, 1941; May the good Lord bless you and keep you, lyrics and music, 1950; The music man, 1957; The unsinkable Molly Brown, lyrics and music, 1960; Here's love, 1963; ORCHESTRA: 2 symphonies, 1936, 1940; O. O. McIntyre suite, 1936; The Jervis Bay, symphonic poem, 1942; Variations on an American theme; CHORUS: Anthem for the atomic age; Ask not, speaking and singing chorus, narrator, piano or band, text from the Kennedy inaugural address. He is author of the following books: What every young musician should know; Who did what to Fedalia, a novel; And there I stood with my piccolo, 1948; The eggs I have laid, 1955; But he doesn'e know the territory, 1959.

WILSON, DON
b. Williamston, S.C., 16 Oct. 1942. Studied with John Boda, Roy Johnson, Harold Schiffman, and Carlisle Floyd, Florida State Univ.; with William P. Latham and Merrill Ellis, North Texas State Univ. He has received ASCAP student award and Pi Kappa Lambda student award. From 1976 he has been faculty member, Louisiana State Univ.
WORKS: ORCHESTRA: suite, 1967; CHAMBER MUSIC: 3 miniatures, baritone horn and piano, 1977; ELECTRONIC: Space journey, tape and slides, 1971; MCABC 0475, for 10 wind instruments, 1975, and MCABC 0476, for 21 brass instruments, 1976, both computer-assisted compositions.

WILSON, DONALD M.
b. Chicago, Ill., 30 June 1937. Studied with Karel Husa and Robert Palmer, Cornell Univ., M.A. 1962, D.M.A. 1965; with Gunther Schuller at Tanglewood, 1963, 1964. His awards include second place, Bearns prize, 1963; A. H. Drummond award, 1964; Ohio Music Teachers Assoc. award, 1970; MacDowell fellowship, 1972; Delius Festival of Florida award, 1974. He was staff member WRVR-FM, New York, 1964-65; WUHY-FM, Philadelphia, 1965-67; from 1967, faculty member, Bowling Green State Univ.
WORKS: ORCHESTRA: Dedication, string orch., 1960; BAND: Visions, chorus and band, 1970; CHAMBER MUSIC: clarinet quintet, 1962; 5 haiku, tenor and chamber ensemble, 1962; Doubles, game-piece for 2 woodwinds vs. 2 strings, 1964; 6 international etudes, viola, 1977; Decisions, decisions, harp, with optional tape delay, 1977; MULTIMEDIA: 17 views, 1 or 2 violins, slides or dancer, narrator, 1967; Space-out, rock cantata, soprano, jazz band, tape, and visuals, 1971; Electronic wedding, tape, with or without dancers, 1972.
550 W. Wooster St., Bowling Green, OH 43402

WILSON, GALEN
b. Emporia, Kans., 18 Sept. 1926. Studied with Ernst Krenek, Los Angeles Cons.; with Darius Milhaud, Music Acad. of the West, Santa Barbara; with Lukas Foss and John Vincent, Univ. of California, Los Angeles, M.A.; with Halsey Stevens, Univ. of Southern California, D.M.A. He taught in public schools, 1956-67; was faculty member, Fullerton State Coll., 1967-68; then joined the faculty at California State Univ., San Diego.

WORKS: BAND: Variations; WIND ENSEMBLE: Sonate harmonique, brass choir; CHAMBER MUSIC: piano sonata; string trio; Fantasy, for piano; sonatina for brass quintet; CHORUS: Mass in honor of St. James; 5 English motets; ELECTRONIC: Applications, tape.
1567 Elm Ave., El Centro, CA 92243

WILSON, GEORGE BALCH
b. Grand Island, Nebr., 28 Jan. 1927. Studied with Ross Lee Finney, Univ. of Michigan; at the Royal Cons. in Brussels; American Acad. in Rome; and with Nadia Boulanger and Roger Sessions. His awards include a Fulbright fellowship; the Prix de Rome; and an award and citation from the Nat. Inst.-American Acad. of Arts and Letters, 1970. He is faculty member, Univ. of Michigan; also founder and director of Contemporary Directions, a university concert series devoted to new music.
WORKS: CHAMBER MUSIC: string quartet; Concatenations, chamber ensemble, 1969; ELECTRONIC: Exigencies, tape, 1968.
1079 Barton, #107, Ann Arbor, MI 48105

WILSON, HARRY ROBERT
b. Salina, Kans., 18 May 1901. Studied at Manhattan State Coll., B.S.; Columbia Univ., M.A., Ed.D.; with Rubin Goldmark and Albert Stoessel at Juilliard School on a fellowship. He was public school music teacher, 1921-32; on the faculty, New Coll., Columbia Univ., 1932-37; then professor, Columbia Teachers Coll.
WORKS: CHORUS: Upon this rock, oratorio, with soloists and orch.; Sing-a-rama; Banners of peace; Let our great song arise; Look to this day; O brother man; Peace must come like a troubadour; A thing of beauty; The finger of God.

WILSON, KAREN
b. Cincinnati, Ohio, 9 Jan. 1942. Studied with Dwight Gustafson and Frank Garlock, Bob Jones Univ.; with Roger Hannay, Univ. of North Carolina, M.M. 1972. She has been faculty member, Bob Jones Univ., 1966-69, and from 1972. Her compositions include a piano sonatina.
Box 34605, Greenville, SC 29614

WILSON, MORTIMER
b. Chariton, Iowa, 6 Aug. 1876; d. New York, N.Y., 27 Jan. 1932. Studied with Frederick Gleason and Wilhelm Middelschulte, Chicago Cons.; with Max Reger in Leipzig. He taught at Univ. of Nebraska, 1901-7; at Atlanta Cons. and conducted the Atlanta Symphony, 1911-15; at Brenau Coll., 1916-18; then taught privately in New York.
WORKS: ORCHESTRA: 5 symphonies; From my youth, suite; New Orleans overture; Overture 1849; My country, scenic fantasy; concerto grosso for strings; CHAMBER MUSIC: 2 piano trios; 3 violin sonatas; violin pieces.

WILSON, OLLY
b. St. Louis, Mo., 7 Sept. 1937. Studied with Robert Wykes, Washington Univ., B.M. 1959; with Robert Kelly, Univ. of Illinois, M.M. 1960; Philip Bezanson, Univ. of Iowa, Ph.D. 1964. His

WILSON, PHIL

awards include the Dartmouth Arts Council prize, 1968; American Acad. of Arts and Letters award, 1974. He played double bass in the St. Louis Symphony and the Cedar Rapids Symphony; has taught at Florida A & M Univ.; West Virginia Univ.; Indiana Univ.; Oberlin Cons.; from 1972, at Univ. of California, Berkeley.

WORKS: ORCHESTRA: 3 movements, 1964; Voices, Berkshire Music Center, 16 Aug. 1970; Akwan, with piano, electric piano, Baltimore Symph., Oct. 1973; Spirit song, with soprano solo and chorus, Oakland Symph., 12 Mar. 1974; CHAMBER MUSIC: Prelude and line study, woodwind quartet, 1959; trio for flute, cello, piano, 1959; string quartet, 1960; violin sonata, 1961; Soliloquy, bass viol, 1962; Piece for 4, flute, trumpet, double bass, piano, 1966; piano trio, 1977; SONGS: Wry fragments, tenor and percussion, 1961; And death shall have no dominion, tenor and percussion, 1963; Chanson innocent, contralto and 2 bassoons, 1965; ELECTRONIC: Cetus, tape, 1967; In memoriam--Martin Luther King, Jr., chorus and tape, 1968; The 18 hands of Jerome Harris, 1971; Black martyrs, 1972; Echoes, clarinet and tape, 1975; Sometimes, tenor and tape, 1976.

University of California, Berkeley, CA 94720

WILSON, PHIL
b. Waltham, Mass., 19 Jan. 1937. Studied trombone with William Tesson, New England Cons. He received the Wells Kerr award when director of the music dept., Phillips Exeter Acad.; has been instructor, Berklee Coll. of Music, 1965-74, and from 1977.

WORKS: CONCERT JAZZ: The Earth's children; The left and the right; Buttercrunch; numerous other jazz works.

8 Hammond Rd., Belmont, MA 02118

WILSON, RICHARD
b. Cleveland, Ohio, 15 May 1941. Studied with Robert Moevs and Randall Thompson, Harvard Univ., B.A. magna cum laude 1963; with Moevs at Rutgers Univ., M.A. 1966; and at American Acad. in Rome. His awards include the G. A. Knight prize, 1963; F. H. Beebe award, 1963; Naumberg fellowship, 1964; Vassar faculty fellowship, 1970; Burge-Eastman prize, 1978, for Eclogue; annual ASCAP awards from 1970. He has been faculty member, Vassar Coll., from 1966.

WORKS: ORCHESTRA: Initiation, 1970; CHAMBER MUSIC: Suite for 5 players, 1963; trio for oboe, violin, cello, 1964; Fantasy and variations, chamber ensemble, 1965, New York, 27 Apr. 1967; Concert piece, violin and piano, 1967; 2 string quartets, 1968, 1977; Music for violin and cello, 1969; quartet for flutes, string bass, harpsichord, 1969; Music for solo cello, 1971; Music for solo flute, 1972; wind quintet, 1974; Eclogue, piano, 1974; Serenade, clarinet, viola, string bass, 1978; CHORUS: In Schrafft's, W. H. Auden text, men's voices, 1966; A dissolve, women's voices, 1968; Can, 1968; Light in spring poplars, 1968; Soaking, 1969; Home from the range, 1970; Elegy, a cappella, 1971; Hunter's moon, 1972; August 22, Unterecker text, 1976; except where noted, choral texts are by Stephen

Sandy.
Vassar College, Poughkeepsie, NY 12601

WINDINGSTAD, OLE
b. Sandefjord, Norway, 18 May 1886; to U.S. 1913; d. Kingston, N.Y., 3 June 1959. On coming to New York, he organized and conducted the Scandinavian Symph. Orch., 1913-29; conducted the Brooklyn Symph. and other orchestras. His compositions included a symphony, 1913; The tides, for orch., 1939; and a cantata, The bard of Norway, 1929.

WINESANKER, MICHAEL MAX
b. Toronto, Ont., 7 Aug. 1913. Studied with Healey Willan, Univ. of Toronto, B.M. 1933; at Trinity Coll. in London, Licentiate in music, 1940; Univ. of Michigan, M.A. 1941; Cornell Univ., Ph.D. 1944. He was faculty member, Univ. of Texas, 1945-46; then joined the faculty at Texas Christian Univ. His compositions include a piano sonata, a string quartet, and songs.

Texas Christian Univ., Fort Worth, TX 76129

WINHAM, GODFREY
b. London, England, 11 Dec. 1934; to U.S. 1954; d. Princeton, N.J., 26 Apr. 1975. Studied composition and piano, Royal Acad. of Music, London; at Princeton Univ., A.B. 1956, M.F.A. 1958; Ph.D. in composition, 1965. He worked at the Columbia-Princeton Electronic Music Center, 1962-63, and after earning his doctorate, remained at Princeton as lecturer and research associate in the field of computer-generated sound. From 1964 until his death, Winham was a pioneer and authority in computer music.

WORKS: Composition for orchestra, 1962; CHAMBER MUSIC: 4 piano pieces, 1952; composition for string quartet, 1953; Nocturne, scherzo, and passacaglia, piano, 1954; The habit of perfection, soprano and string quartet, 1956; To prove my love, cycle of 3 Shakespeare sonnets, soprano and piano, 1957-60; Concert piece, piano, 1958; ELECTRONIC: 2 short computer pieces, 1970-73.

WINICK, STEVEN D.
b. Brooklyn, N.Y., 7 July 1944. Studied with Hugh Aitkin, Juilliard School; with Samuel Adler, Eastman School of Music. From 1972 he has been faculty member, Georgia State Univ. His published compositions include Equinoctial points for solo trumpet, and Confrontation for brass trio.

2877 St. Andrews Way, Marietta, GA 30062

WINKLER, DAVID
b. Chicago, Ill., 11 Oct. 1948. Studied with Roy Harris, Univ. of California, Los Angeles, 1969-70; with Charles Wuorinen, Jack Beeson, Chou Wen-chung, Vladimir Ussachevsky, Jacques-Louis Monod, Columbia Univ. His awards include Tanglewood fellowship, 1972; BMI student award, 1972; Fromm Found. commission, 1974; Rapaport prize, 1976. He held teaching fellowships at Columbia Univ., 1973-78.

WORKS: WIND ENSEMBLE: Serenade, 1978; CHAMBER MUSIC: concerto for piano and 12 in-

struments, 1974; Intermezzo, piano, 1976; duo
for clarinet and piano, 1978; CHORUS: Frische
Schatten, meine Freude, 1975; cantata, with soli
and orch., 1978; SONGS: 3 Shakespeare sonnets,
soprano and piano, 1976; 5 Shakespeare sonnets,
2 soli and 10 instruments, 1978.
362 Broadway, 3rd Floor, New York, NY 10013

WINKLER, PETER K.
b. Los Angeles, Calif., 26 Jan. 1943. Studied
with Darius Milhaud, Aspen School; with Seymour
Shifrin and Douglas Leedy, Univ. of California,
Berkeley, A.B. 1964; with Earl Kim and Milton
Babbitt, Princeton Univ., M.A. 1966. He received a junior fellowship, Harvard Univ.
Society of Fellows. He has been on the faculty,
State Univ. of New York at Stony Brook, from
1971.
WORKS: CHAMBER MUSIC: Etude, for 2 horns,
1964; string quartet, 1967; Humoresque, piano,
1970; Ragtime grackle, for oboe, 1972; Do it!,
2 jazz pianists, 1973; 7 piano rags; CHORUS:
Praise of silence, with soprano, instruments,
and tape, 1969; various works for theatre and
radio drama.
15 Bayview Ave., East Setauket, NY 11733

WINSLOW, RICHARD KENELM
b. Indianapolis, Ind., 15 Mar. 1918. Studied at
Wesleyan Univ., B.A. 1940; Juilliard School,
B.S. 1947, M.S. 1949. He served in the U.S.
Navy, 1942-45; joined the faculty at Wesleyan
Univ., 1949.
WORKS: OPERA: Sweeney agonistes, 1952;
Adelaide, 1955; Ikon, 1960; Theater song, 1960;
Alice, 1965; CHORUS: Job, oratorio, 1964; The
last quarter moon; Against pride in clothes,
women's voices; Huswifery, women's voices; Home
from the range; Light in spring poplars.
Wesleyan University, Middletown, CT 06457

WINSLOW, WALTER K.
b. Salem, Oreg., 16 Sept. 1947. Studied with
Richard Hoffmann, Oberlin Cons.; with Edwin
Dugger, Andrew Imbrie, and Olly Wilson, Univ. of
California, Berkeley. He won first prize,
Nicola Di Lorenzo contest, 1971. He has been
faculty member, Univ. of California, Berkeley,
from 1975.
WORKS: THEATRE: We!, musical theatre piece,
1976; ORCHESTRA: piano concerto; VOICE: Nacht-
wanderlied; Anagrams, song cycle for baritone
and chamber ensemble, texts by composer, 1972;
Nahua songs, coloratura and piano, 1975.
206 Purdue Ave., Kensington, CA 94708

WINSOR, PHILIP G.
b. Morris, Ill., 10 May 1938. Studied with Will
Ogdon, Illinois Wesleyan Univ., B.M. 1960; with
Wayne Peterson, San Francisco State Univ., M.A.
1963; with Luigi Nono, Venice, Italy; with
Salvatore Martirano, Univ. of Illinois, 1965-66.
His awards include Fulbright fellowship, 1963-64;
Rome Prize fellowship, 1966-67; fellowships at
Tanglewood, 1966, Darmstadt, 1966, Bennington
Composers Conf., 1969; Oregon Coll. Arts Festival
award, 1970; Ford Found. grant, 1973; Nat. En-
dowment for the Arts grant, 1977. He was faculty

member, Moorhead State Coll., 1967-68; from
1968, at DePaul Univ.
WORKS: ORCHESTRA: Do not go gentle into
that good night, 1977; CHAMBER MUSIC: Melted
ears, 2 pianos, 1967; Asleep in the deep, 5
tubas; Schema, piano; Flos harmonicus II, string
quartet; MULTIMEDIA: Actions, tape, trombone,
5 dancers, 1 actor; Missa brevis, tape, dancer,
visuals.
3836 N. Marshfield Ave., Chicago, IL 60613

WINSTEAD, WILLIAM
b. Hopkinsville, Ky., 11 Dec. 1942. Studied
with Thomas Canning and Ben Weber, Curtis Inst.
of Music. He has received grants from the Nat.
Endowment for the Arts and the West Virginia
Arts and Humanities Council. From 1965 he has
been on the faculty at West Virginia Univ.
WORKS: ORCHESTRA: The moon singer; symphony #1; Scarlet landscape, chamber orch.; also
many transcriptions and arrangements.
456 Elysian Ave., Morgantown, WV 26505

WINTLE, JAMES R.
b. Pittsburg, Kans., 18 Sept. 1942. Studied
with Markwood Holmes, Pittsburg State Univ.;
with John Pozdro and Douglas Moore, Univ. of
Kansas. He was faculty member, Southwestern
Coll., Winfield, Kans., 1968-71; from 1971, at
Southeastern State Univ., Durant, Okla.
WORKS: CHAMBER MUSIC: piano sonata; Music
for woodwind quintet; Alla camera, clarinet,
cello, piano; Katachresis, chamber ensemble;
Paraphonoi, string quartet, Durant, Okla., 7 Mar.
1977; Capriccio, organ; cello sonata; Movement,
clarinet and piano; Pezzo concertante a due
pianoforte, 2 pianos.
Southeastern Oklahoma State Univ., Durant,
OK 74701

WIRTEL, THOMAS
b. St. Louis, Mo., 26 May 1937. Studied with
Bain Murray and Richard Hoffmann, Oberlin Coll.;
with Samuel Adler, North Texas State Univ., B.M.,
M.M. 1963; with Bernhard Heiden, Indiana Univ.,
D.M. 1969. His awards include a Rockefeller
grant for composer residency with the Dallas
Symph. Orch., 1966-67; MacDowell fellowship,
1966; Fromm Found. prize; Nat. Endowment for the
Arts grant, 1973; East Texas State Univ. research grant, 1974. He was faculty member, East
Texas State Univ., 1967-75; visiting professor,
Univ. of Illinois, 1970-71.
WORKS: ORCHESTRA: concertino for orch.,
1967; Polarities, 1967; CHAMBER MUSIC: violin
sonata; Dualities, violin, piano, and electronic
sounds; FILM SCORE: Patterns in jazz, USIA
documentary of which he was the subject as well
as composer of the score.

WIRTH, CARL ANTON
b. Rochester, N.Y., 24 Jan. 1912. Studied at
Eastman School of Music, B.M., M.M. He was
founder and director, Rochester Community Music
Program; conductor, Rochester Community Symph.;
founder and conductor, Rochester Chamber Opera;
in 1962, conducted Radio Republik Indonesia
Symph. under sponsorship of U.S. State Dept.;

WISE, BRUCE

was founder of Composer Project, 1951, chairman,
to 1959.
WORKS: ORCHESTRA: Ichabod Crane suite;
Idlewood concerto, alto saxophone and orch.;
Elegy on an Appalachian folksong; Jephthah,
soprano, alto saxophone, string orch.; David
triptych, solo saxophone, winds, percussion, San
Jose, 31 Oct. 1978; CHAMBER MUSIC: Dark flows
the river, alto saxophone and piano; Portals: a
prelude for organ.

WISE, BRUCE
b. Detroit, Mich., 24 Aug. 1929. Studied with
Ross Lee Finney, Univ. of Michigan; with Wolfgang
Fortner, Freiburg, Germany, 1959-60, on a German
government grant. He has held faculty positions
at Univ. of Michigan, 1961-62; Univ. of Missouri,
1962-67; from 1967, Univ. of Wisconsin-Oshkosh.
WORKS: ORCHESTRA: Patterns, 1961; Variations, 1973; CHAMBER MUSIC: 4 pieces, piano,
1957; 2 pieces, for piano and chamber group,
1958; Songs of autumn, 1958; Music for 3, 1963;
duo for viola and piano, 1971; string trio #2,
1972.
Univ. of Wisconsin, 800 Algoma Blvd.,
Oshkosh, WI 54901

WISHART, BETTY R.
b. Lumberton, N.C., 22 Sept. 1947. Studied with
Richard Bunger, Queens Coll.; piano at Univ. of
South Carolina; with Roger Hannay, Univ. of
North Carolina; with Stanley Wolfe, Juilliard
School. She was named an Outstanding Young
Woman of the Year, 1973, 1975. She was staff
member at Kohinoor Music, 1972-73; Argo Sight
and Sound, 1973-74; music director, Trinity
Baptist Church, New York, 1975-77.
WORKS: CHAMBER MUSIC: Experience, string
quintet; Memories of things unseen, chamber quartet; Shanti, voice and piano; PIANO: Kohinoor
sonata; Illusion; Apprehensions; Leukoplakia;
Salute, duo pianos; Etherea I; ORGAN: Sounds.
200 Locust St., #31-D, Philadelphia, PA
19106

WITKIN, BEATRICE
b. New York, N.Y., 1916. Studied composition
with Mark Brunswick, Roger Sessions, and Stefan
Wolpe; piano with Edward Steuerman. Her awards
include first prize in High Fidelity magazine's
electronic music contest for Glissines, 1970;
ASCAP awards; Martha Baird Rockefeller commission; grants from Rockefeller Found., Ford
Found., Nat. Endowment for the Arts, 1973, 1978.
WORKS: CHAMBER MUSIC: Interludes, flute,
1960; duo for violin and piano, 1961, New York,
18 Dec. 1962; Prose poem, on the story of Adam
and Eve by James T. Farrell, soprano, narrator,
cello, horn, percussion, 1964; Contour for piano,
1964; Parameters,for 8 instruments, 1968;
Chiaroscuro, cello and piano, 1968; Triads and
things, brass quintet, 1968; Breath and sounds,
tuba and tape, 1971; Echology, flute and tape,
New York, 11 Feb. 1973; Reports from the planet
of Mars, chamber orch. and tape, 1978.
885 West End Ave., New York, NY 10025

WOLF, KENNETH (Merrill K. Wolf, MD)
b. Cleveland, Ohio, 28 Aug. 1931. Studied with
Arthur Shepherd in Cleveland, 1941-43; with Paul
Hindemith, Yale Univ., 1944-45; piano with Bruce
Simonds, Artur Schnabel, and Rosina Lhevinne.
He is professor of neuroanatomy, Univ. of Massachusetts, Medical School, Worcester.
WORKS: ORCHESTRA: 2 piano concertos;
CHAMBER MUSIC: 2 sonatas for harpsichord or
piano; violin sonata; horn sonata; Concert variations, woodwind quintet; 7 bagatelles, clarinet
and piano; CHORUS: 3 ways of looking at a frog,
a cappella; Belloc's beasts, a cappella; pieces
for Friday evening Jewish worship. Dr. Wolf
describes his neoclassical style of composition
with a quote from the New York Times: "Imagine
Poulenc mixed with Hindemith and some conscious
18th-century archaisms."
84 Leeson Lane, Newton, MA 02159

WOLFE, JACQUES
b. Botoshan, Rumania, 29 Apr. 1896; to U.S. 1898;
d. Sarasota, Fla., 22 June 1973. Studied at
Juilliard School, graduated 1915. During World
War I, he was clarinetist in an army band; then
went to North Carolina to study Negro spirituals.
He was concert pianist and accompanist in New
York and taught in public schools to 1947; then
settled in Miami as a photographer.
WORKS: OPERA: John Henry, based on Roark
Bradford's play, 1939; Mississippi legend; The
trysting tree; CHAMBER MUSIC: Marine holiday,
piano; Prayer in the swamp, violin and piano;
Serenade, string quartet; CHORUS: Psalm 67,
with orch.; SONGS: De glory road; Gwine to
hebb'n; Halleluja rhythm; Shortnin' bread; The
handorgan man; Sailormen; and others.

WOLFE, STANLEY
b. Brooklyn, N.Y., 7 Feb. 1924. Studied with
William Bergsma, Vincent Persichetti, Peter
Mennin, Juilliard School, B.S. 1952, M.S. 1955.
He received a Guggenheim fellowship, 1957;
Ditson award, 1961. He joined the Juilliard
School faculty in 1955, became director of the
extension division in 1963.
WORKS: BALLET: King's heart, 1956; ORCHES-
TRA: 5 symphonies, 1954, 1955, 1959, 1965, 1970;
Lincoln Square overture, 1957; Canticle for
strings, 1957; Variations, 1967; CHAMBER MUSIC:
Adagio, woodwind quintet, 1948; 3 profiles,
piano, 1955; string quartet, 1961.
875 West End Ave., New York, NY 10025

WOLFF, CHRISTIAN
b. Nice, France, 8 Mar. 1934; U.S. citizen 1946.
Studied piano in New York; composition informally
with John Cage, but is chiefly autodidact;
classical languages at Harvard Univ., Ph.D. 1963.
He held a Ford Found. fellowship at Mills Coll.,
Electronic Music Center, 1973; Germany Academic
Exchange Program fellowship, 1974; received
American Acad. of Arts and Letters award, 1975.
He was faculty member, classics dept., Harvard
Univ., 1962-69; from 1970, on classics and music
faculty, Dartmouth Coll.
WORKS: ORCHESTRA: Burdocks, 1 or more
orchestras, any instruments, 1971; CHAMBER MUSIC:

trio for flute, cello, trumpet, 1951; 9 for 9 instruments, 1951; For prepared piano, 1951; For piano 1, 1952; For pianist, 1959; duet II, piano and horn, 1961; duo for violin and piano, 1961; Summer, string quartet, 1961; For 5 or 10 players, 1962; In between pieces, any 3 performers, 1963; septet, 1964; For 1, 2, or 3 people, any sound sources, 1964; Electric spring, 2 recorders, electric guitar, bass guitar, trombone, 1965; Prose collection, 10 short pieces, 1968-70; Snowdrop, 1970; Lines, string quartet, 1971; Accompaniments, piano solo, 1972; Changing the system, chamber ensemble, 1973; CHORUS: You blew it, 1971; Wobbly music, with instruments.
   104 S. Main St., Hanover, NH 03755

WOLFF, WERNER
   b. Berlin, Germany, 2 Oct. 1883; to U.S. 1938; d. Rüschlidon, Switz., 23 Nov. 1961. Was an opera conductor in Germany; chairman, music dept., Tennessee Wesleyan Coll., 1938-43; director and conductor, Chattanooga Opera Assoc., 1943-59; music critic, Chattanooga Daily Times, 1950-59. He composed symphonic works, chamber music, songs, and piano pieces.

WOLFORD, DARWIN
   WORKS: ORCHESTRA: symphony #1, Cantilena, Passacaglia, performed Washington, D.C., 26 Sept. 1976; KEYBOARD: Suite a la mode, 14 pieces for piano; 9 psalms, for organ.
   Ricks College, Rexburg, ID 83440

WOLKING, HENRY CLIFFORD, JR.
   b. Orlando, Fla., 20 May 1948. Studied at Berklee Coll. of Music; with Richard Bowles and Edward Troupin, Univ. of Florida, B.M.E. 1970; with Martin Mailman and William Latham, North Texas State Univ., M.M. 1971. He received scholarships at Berklee Coll. and Univ. of Florida; second prize, Internat. Trombone Composition Contest, 1973; Faculty Research Grant, Univ. of Utah, 1977. He was trombone soloist, Univ. of Florida bands, 1968-70; trombonist with numerous rock and jazz ensembles; from 1972, faculty member, Univ. of Utah.
   WORKS: BAND: concerto for trombone and band; Timepieces, 1972; 2 movements, large wind ensemble, 1973; CHAMBER MUSIC: woodwind quintet, 1971; Pictures of the gone world, song cycle for soprano and piano, 1971; Trahmbone, 4 trombones and 4 voices, 1972; Silhouettes, brass quintet, 1974; Contrasts, brass sextet, 1975; Dorian interlude, brass sextet, 1976; Fusion, saxophone quintet, 1976; 7 vignettes, solo bass trombone, 1977; numerous works for jazz ensembles.
   1349 Vine St., Salt Lake City, UT 84112

WOLLNER, GERTRUDE PRICE
   Studied at Hunter Coll., and at New York Univ. She has composed for chamber orchestra, quartet, piano, dance and theatre. Her music for Caesar and Cleopatra was performed by the Civic Theatre in Washington, D.C. She is author of Improvisation in music, Boston.
   26 Clifton St., Belmont, MA 02178

WOLPE, STEFAN
   b. Berlin, Germany, 25 Aug. 1902; U.S. citizen 1944; d. New York, N.Y., 4 Apr. 1972. Studied at the Berlin Hochschule für Musik, 1919-24; privately with Ferruccio Busoni, Anton Webern, and Herman Scherchen. His many awards include Brandeis Univ. Creative Arts award; Nat. Inst. of Arts and Letters award, 1949; Rothschild Found. award, 1953; Fulbright fellowship, 1956; League of Composers-ISCM award, 1958; Fromm Found. award, 1960; Guggenheim fellowship, 1962; New York Music Critics' Circle citation, 1963; membership, Nat. Inst. of Arts and Letters; Koussevitzky Internat. Recording award, 1970. He taught at the Palestine Cons., 1934-38; Settlement Music School, Philadelphia, 1939-42; Philadelphia Acad. of Music, 1949-52; Contemporary Music School, New York, 1948-52; Black Mountain Coll., 1952-56; Chatham Square Music School, New York, 1957-63; C. W. Post Coll., Long Island Univ., 1957-70.
   WORKS: OPERA: Schöne Geschichten, 1927; Zeus and Elida, 1927; BALLET: The man from Midian, 1942; THEATRE: Strange stories, theatre piece, 1929; ORCHESTRA: 5 symphonies; Piece for piano and 16 instruments, 1960; CHAMBER MUSIC: March and variations, 2 pianos, 1931; 10 songs from the Hebrew, 1938; oboe sonata, 1938; violin sonata, 1949; quartet for trumpet, saxophone, percussion, piano, 1950; Enactments, 3 pianos, 1950-53; percussion quartet; quintet with voice, 1958; Form for piano, 1959; Piece in 2 parts, flute and piano, 1960; Piece for 2 instrumental units, 1962; Piece in 2 parts for violin alone, 1963; Chamber piece #1, 14 instruments, 1965; Solo pieces, for trumpet, 1966; string quartet, 1968-69; Broken sequences, piano, 1969; CANTATAS: The passion of man, 1929; On the education of man, 1930; About sport, 1931; Israel and his land, 1939; Unnamed lands, 1940.

WOLTMANN, FREDERICK
   b. Flushing, N.Y., 13 May 1908. Studied at Brooklyn Polytechnic Inst. and Columbia Univ.; with Howard Hanson and Bernard Rogers, Eastman School of Music; with Ildebrando Piezzetti, American Acad. in Rome.
   WORKS: ORCHESTRA: Dance of the torch bearers, 1932; Poem, flute and orch., 1935; Rhapsody, horn and orch., 1935; Legend, cello and orch., 1936; Songs from a Chinese lute, voice and 33 instruments, 1936; Songs for autumn, soprano, baritone, and orch., 1937; piano concerto, 1937; The pool of Pegasus, 1937; Scherzo, for 8 winds, 1937; From Dover Beach, 1938; The Coliseum at night, 1939; Solitude, 1942; From leaves of grass, 1946; and songs.

WONG, BETTY ANNE (Siu Junn)
   b. San Francisco, Calif., 6 Sept. 1938. Studied with Darius Milhaud, Leon Kirchner, Morton Subotnick, Colin Hampton, Mills Coll., A.B. 1960; with Pauline Oliveros, Robert Erickson, Kenneth Gaburo, Univ. of California, San Diego, M.M. 1971; Chinese music with David Liang, Lawrence Lui, and Leo Lew, 1971-74. She held a teaching fellowship, a resident fellowship, and California state scholarships, 1968-71. She was composer-

WONG, HSIUNG ZEE

in-residence, Performing Arts Workshop, San
Francisco, 1966-68; from 1971, has been manager,
of the Chinese group, Flowing Stream Ensemble;
and from 1976, manager of the multicultural performing group, Phoenix Spring Ensemble.
     WORKS: ELECTRONIC: Submerged still capable,
tape, 1969; Check one--People control the environment, People are controlled by the environment, tape, 1970; Quiet places in the environment, tape, 9 performers and audience, 1971;
Private audience with Pope Pius XII, tape and
slides, 1971; Furniture music, or 2-way stretch
on a swivel chair, tape and visuals, 1971;
Possible music for a silent world, tapes of environmental sounds and live performance on
Chinese instruments; Hymn to Kwan Yin for our
times, combines ancient Chinese instruments with
sounds from found objects in our environment.
     1173 Bosworth St., San Francisco, CA 94131

WONG, HSIUNG ZEE
     b. Hong Kong, 24 Oct. 1947; to U.S. 1966.
Studied at Univ. of Hawaii, 1966-68; courses
with Ernst Krenek and Chou Wen-chung; California
Coll. of Arts and Crafts, B.F.A. in industrial
design 1972; electronic music with Robert Ashley
and Leonard Klein, 1970; composition with Robert
Sheff and Dane Rudhyar, Mills Coll., 1973. She
held scholarships, 1970-72. She has been a
free-lance graphic designer, artist, and illus-
trator from 1967; initiated Hysteresis, a women's
creative arts group at Mills Coll., 1973; performs with the Flowing Stream Ensemble.
     WORKS: CHAMBER MUSIC: art songs/ballads,
voice and guitar, 1964-72, parts performed, KPFK,
Los Angeles, 6 Dec. 1973; The cry of women in
the wilderness, piano, Chinese gong, and amplified Zen bell, 1972; Piano ritual I, piano-per-
cussion, Chinese woodblock, opera gong, voice,
Oakland, Calif., 1 July 1973; ELECTRONIC: Matur-
ity, taped piano improvisation, 1972; Earth
rituals, tape with chanting and sound improvisation, 1973; The sounding of the sane, tape with
audience chanting, Oakland, 1 July 1973; They
move, don't they?, a sound calligraphic score
with visual slides, 1973.

WOOD, DALE
     b. Glendale, Calif., 13 Feb. 1934. Studied at
Occidental Coll.; composition at Los Angeles
Cons. and at Los Angeles City Coll. He won his
first award at age 13 in a national hymn writing
contest; won a scholarship to Occidental Coll.;
received annual ASCAP awards, 1968-73. Since
1948 he has been organist-choirmaster in Los
Angeles, Hollywood, Riverside, and San Francisco;
is contributing editor to the Journal of Church
Music and author of numerous articles on church
music; was music director, San Francisco Cathedral School for Boys, 1973-74; in 1974, appointed
executive editor for the Sacred Music Press.
     WORKS: CHORUS: A service of darkness;
Come, gracious spirit; Let the whole creation
cry; Christ is made the sure foundation; Sing
for joy; and numerous other published choral
works.
     The Sea Ranch, CA 95497

WOOD, JOSEPH
     b. Pittsburgh, Pa., 12 May 1915. Studied piano,
Inst. of Musical Art, diploma 1936; with Bernard
Wagenaar, Juilliard School, B.S. 1949; with Otto
Luening, Columbia Univ., M.A. 1950. His awards
include a Juilliard fellowship, 1936-40; first
prize, Juilliard Opera Competition, 1942; Ditson
award, Columbia Univ., 1946; Villa Montalvo
residence, 1957; Huntington Hartford fellowship,
1960; 8 MacDowell fellowships; H. H. Powers
travel grants, Oberlin Coll., 1966, 1973; many
commissions. He was staff composer, Chekhov
Theatre Studio, 1939-41; composer-arranger, New
York, 1941-50; in U.S. Army, 1943-46; from 1950,
on faculty, Oberlin Coll.
     WORKS: OPERA: The mother, 1942; BALLET-
CANTATA: The progression; ORCHESTRA: 3 symphonies, 1939, 1952, 1955; Poem for orchestra,
1950; concerto for viola and piano with orch.;
violin concerto; Divertimento for piano and
small orch., 1959; CHAMBER MUSIC: piano trio,
1937; viola sonata, 1938; 4 string quartets,
1942-78; violin sonata, 1947; piano quintet,
1956; piano sonata; concerto for chamber orch.;
also choral works.
     261 W. Lorain St., Oberlin, OH 44074

WOOD, KEVIN JOSEPH
     b. Bronx, N.Y., 19 June 1947. Studied at Univ.
of Dayton, B.M. 1969; with Alan Oldfield and
Will Gay Bottje, Southern Illinois Univ., M.M.
1974. He was instructor, Univ. of Dayton, 1972;
from 1976, has been editor, Walton Music Corp.,
and also a free-lance editor.
     WORKS: OPERA: Peter, 1977; WIND ENSEMBLE:
Essay for winds, 1978; CHAMBER MUSIC: brass
quintet, 1975; Lyric suite, piano, 1976;
Dithyramb, solo oboe; Dirges, percussion ensemble, 1976; Hexentanz, 2 pianos, 1976; If thou
but suffer God to guide thee, organ, 1976;
VOICE: Ants will not eat your fingers, song
cycle; 3 Rilke songs; Songs of abnegation,
chorus, 1976.
     1 Bennington Place, Freehold, NJ 07728

WOOD, WILLIAM FRANK
     b. San Francisco, Calif., 3 Aug. 1935. Studied
with James Adair, Sacramento State Coll.; with
Normand Lockwood, Univ. of Oregon; Wolfgang
Fortner at Tanglewood; Bernard Rogers, Wayne
Barlow, and Howard Hanson, Eastman School of
Music, Ph.D. He won first prize, Prague Spring
Internat. Composers Competition, 1966; has received commissions. He is faculty member, Univ.
of New Mexico.
     WORKS: ORCHESTRA: symphony, 1966; CHAMBER
MUSIC: Night music, solo guitar and chamber
orch., 1968; 5 bagatelles, solo guitar; cello
sonata; violin sonata, 1973; Vortrag, oboe and
piano, 1975; trios for woodwinds, 1975.
     12508 Prospect Ave., Albuquerque, NM 87112

WOODARD, JAMES P.
     b. Rocky Mount, N.C., 21 Nov. 1939. Studied at
Univ. of North Carolina; Juilliard School; in
Munich; with Carlisle Floyd and John Boda,
Florida State Univ., D.M. He won the Olivet
Pedro Paz award, 1970, for Partita for piano.

He was professor, Murray State Univ., 1965-70; from 1970, at Southern Illinois Univ.

WORKS: ORCHESTRA: concerto for 2 pianos, 1965; The dream songs of Stephen Foster, soprano and string orch.; CHAMBER MUSIC: duo for violin and cello, 1964; 5 sonnets of Shakespeare, baritone and piano, 1967; Fantasies, flute and string quartet, 1972; piano sonatina, 1973; CHORUS: The legend of the Piora bird, oratorio.

818 Randle St., Edwardsville, IL 62025

WOODBURY, ARTHUR
b. Kimball, Nebr., 20 June 1930. Studied at Univ. of Idaho, B.A. 1951, M.M. 1954; and at Univ. of California at Davis, 1957-58. He was lecturer, Univ. of California, Davis, 1963-72; then professor, Univ. of South Florida.

WORKS: ORCHESTRA: symphony, 1958; Autobiography; BAND: Introduction and allegro; CHAMBER MUSIC: woodwind quartet, 1955; Remembrances, violin, saxophone, percussion, 1968; ELECTRONIC: Patricia Belle, soprano, electronic instruments, amplified chamber ensemble, 1968; Recall, theatre piece, 1969; An evening of the music of Neil Jansen, a put-on, tape and Moog synthesizer, 1969; Velox, computerized tape; Hum, Moog synthesizer and tape; Werner Vonbrawnasaurus Rex, tape, synthesizers, and instruments, 1970.

13018 Leeds Court, Tampa, FL 33620

WOOD-HILL, MABEL
b. Brooklyn, N.Y., 12 Mar. 1870; d. Stamford, Conn., 1 Mar. 1954. Studied at Smith Coll. and with Cornelius Rybner at Columbia Univ. She received awards from the Associated Glee Clubs of the U.S. and Canada; Nat. League of American Pen Women; a citation from the City of New York, 1953; and a commission from the Canadian government for a vocal work, The jolly beggars, for the Banff Festival of 1928. She was founder of the Brooklyn and New York Music School Settlements.

WORKS: BALLET: The adventures of Pinocchio, 1931; ORCHESTRA: The wind in the willows; Courage; Fables of Aesop; Outdoor suite; From a far country; also chamber music, choral works, and songs.

WOODRICH, DENNIS
b. Oklahoma, 26 Nov. 1939. Studied with Donal Michalsky and James Whitsitt, California State Univ., Fullerton; on scholarship with Peter Odegard, Univ. of California at Irvine; with Bernard Rands, Robert Erickson, and Pauline Oliveros, Univ. of California, San Diego. He was music director, Edgewood private schools, Santa Ana, 1974-76; from 1976, staff arranger, Studio West, San Diego, and producer, Christopher Productions, San Diego.

WORKS: CHAMBER MUSIC: 3 movements, piano and contrabass, 1975; trio for flute, cello, piano; No interruptions, contrabass, 1977.

9266 G Regents Rd., La Jolla, CA 92037

WOODWARD, HENRY LYNDE
b. Cincinnati, Ohio, 18 Sept. 1908. Studied at Cincinnati Coll. of Music; with Walter Piston at

Harvard Univ., Ph.D.; with Nadia Boulanger in Paris. He received a MacDowell fellowship, 1932. He has held faculty posts at Cincinnati Coll. of Music, 1929-33; Western Coll., 1933-38, 1939-42; Vassar Coll., 1938-39; Carleton Coll., 1942-73, then professor emeritus; summers at Cornell Univ. and Union Theological Seminary, New York.

WORKS: ORCHESTRA: symphony; CHAMBER MUSIC: 3 violin sonatas; suite for viola and piano; CHORUS: O clap you hands; ORGAN: Toccatina; Easter alleluia; On "Heinlein."

209 W. University Dr., Chapel Hill, NC 27514

WOOLF, GREGORY BUXTON
b. Seattle, Wash., 2 Jan. 1935; d. Nashville, Tenn., 13 Jan. 1971. Studied at Tufts Univ., B.A.; Eastman School of Music, M.A., Ph.D. He held faculty posts at Brockport State Coll., New York, 1960-63; Tufts Univ., 1963-68; George Peabody Coll., 1968-71.

WORKS: ORCHESTRA: tuba concerto; CHAMBER MUSIC: clarinet sonata; string quartet; CHORUS: A time's passing, a cappella; A mass for All Saints' Day, quadruple chorus, organ, and tape; also a musical play for children.

WOOLLEN, RUSSELL
b. Hartford, Conn., 7 Jan. 1923. Studied at Pope Pius X School of Liturgical Music, New York; with Nadia Boulanger and Nicolas Nabokov in Paris, 1949-51; and with Walter Piston, Harvard Univ., 1953-55. After ordination as priest, he taught at Catholic Univ.; became professor at Howard Univ., 1969-74; appointed pianist with the Nat. Symph. Orch., 1956.

WORKS: OPERA: The decorator, 1959; ORCHESTRA: 2 symphonies, 1957-58, 1978, #2 Washington, D.C., 8 Apr. 1979; Summer jubilee overture, 1958; 2 pieces, piano and orch., 1962-76; suite for flute and strings, 1966; CHAMBER MUSIC: piano quartet, 1952; quartet for flute and strings, 1953; woodwind quintet, 1955; piano trio, 1957; trio for flute, oboe, harpsichord, 1967; Fantasy, flute and harpsichord, 1968; trombone sonata, 1972; woodwind quintet, 1975; VOICE: suite for high voice on poems of Gerard Manley Hopkins; Nativite from La Carona, 1967; In martyrum memoriam chorus, soloists, orch., Washington Oratorio Society, 17 May 1975.

4747 Berkeley Terrace, N.W., Washington, DC 20007

WOOLSEY, MARY HALE
b. Spanish Fork, Utah, 21 Mar. 1899; d. 1969. Studied at Brigham Young Univ.; Univ. of Utah; and at Columbia Univ. She held several editorial positions and was author of a book, The keys and the candle.

WORKS: OPERETTAS: Starflower; The giant garden; The happy hearts; The enchanted attic; Neighbors in the house; many songs, including When it's springtime in the Rockies.

WORK, JOHN WESLEY, JR.
b. Tullahoma, Tenn., 15 June 1901; d. 1967. Studied at Fisk Univ., B.A.; Columbia Univ., M.A.; Yale Univ., B.M.; and at Juilliard School

WORK, JULIAN C.

on a 2-year Rosenwald fellowship. His awards
included first prize, Fellowship of American
Composers contest for a cantata; and commissions.
He joined the faculty at Fisk Univ. in 1933;
became professor and department chairman; was
conductor, Fisk Jubilee Singers, 1948-57.
   WORKS: ORCHESTRA: Picture suite of the
South; Yenvalou, suite for strings, 1955; Talia-
fero; Night in the valley; CHAMBER MUSIC: Nocturne, violin and piano; CHORUS: The singers,
cantata, 1946; Isaac Watts contemplates the
cross, choral cycle; PIANO: sonata; Appalachian
suite; Scuppernong suite; Concert piece, 2
pianos; Variations on a theme; many other choral
works and songs.

WORK, JULIAN C.
   b. Nashville, Tenn., 25 Sept. 1910. Attended
Fisk Univ.; studied music privately. He was
arranger for vaudeville; staff arranger for CBS
radio and later television.
   WORKS: BAND: Autumn walk; Stand the storm;
Driftwood patterns; Processional hymn; Portraits
from the Bible (Moses, Ruth, Shadrach, Meschach,
Abednego).

WORST, JOHN WILLIAM
   b. Grand Rapids, Mich., 13 July 1940. Studied
at Calvin Coll., A.B. 1962; with Mark Walker,
Marshall Barnes, Ohio State Univ., M.A. 1964;
with H. Owen Reed, Michigan State Univ.; and
with Leslie Bassett, Univ. of Michigan, Ph.D.
1967. His awards include special mention, Internat. Delius competition, 1973; numerous commissions. He was faculty member, Dordt Coll.,
1964-66; from 1966, Calvin Coll.; visiting lecturer, Univ. of Michigan, 1968-69.
   WORKS: BAND: Fanfare, song and dance; concertino for winds and percussion; Toccata,
brass, percussion, organ; VOICE: 3 Biblical
chants, alto solo and chamber ensemble; Spirit
songs, chorus, brass quintet, and 3 flutes; The
Jonah songs, chorus and string quartet or piano.
   3301 Midland S.E., Grand Rapids, MI 49506

WORTH, AMY
   b. St. Joseph, Mo., 18 Jan. 1888; d. 1967.
Studied music with Jessie Gayner. She was piano
teacher, organist, and choir director. Her published choral works included Mary, the mother;
Christmas cantata; Christ rises; Sing of Christmas; He came all so still; many songs and piano
pieces.

WRAGG, RUSSELL
   b. Waukee, Iowa, 14 Aug. 1899. Attended Stanton
Military Acad.; studied composition privately
with Henry Holden Huss. He was pianist in night
clubs and orchestras; organized All-Out Concerts
in World War II; was cofounder of a piano school
to which he returned after the war. His compositions include many piano pieces and songs.

WRIGHT, KENNETH W.
   b. Hastings, Nebr., 1913. Studied at Hastings
Coll., A.B.; Eastman School of Music, M.A. 1939,
Ph.D. 1941; also with Roy Harris; violin with
Michel Piastro. He was faculty member, Univ. of

Kentucky, 1949-78.
   WORKS: OPERA: Call it square, chamber
opera; ORCHESTRA: concerto for 2 violins; overture; Poem, oboe and string orch.; violin concerto; Dance mosaics.

WRIGHT, MAURICE
   b. Front Royal, Va., 17 Oct. 1949. Studied with
Paul Earls and Iain Hamilton, Duke Univ., B.A.
1972; with Charles Dodge, Charles Wuorinen,
Vladimir Ussachevsky, Jack Beeson, Mario
Davidovsky, Jacques Monod, Columbia Univ., M.A.
1974. His awards include Mary Duke Biddle
scholarship, 1968-72; Bennington Composers Conf.
fellowship, 1970, 1971; Henry Schuman prize,
1972; Bearns prize, 1974; ISCM-League of Composers prize, 1975; Kingsley award, 1976; Yaddo
residency, 1976; many fellowships, 1977-78; and
commissions. He was faculty member, Columbia
Univ., 1973-74; from 1978, at Boston Univ.
   WORKS: ORCHESTRA: Progression, 1971; Aulos,
oboe and string orch., 1972; Orchestral composition, 1974; Music from the 5th string, 1977;
Stellae, with electronics, Tanglewood, 10 Aug.
1978; Wellington's defeat (companion piece to
Beethoven's Wellington's victory), Columbia
Univ. Orch., 1 Dec. 1978; Overture 1830, New
York, 21 Nov. 1980; CHAMBER MUSIC: Sonata
exotica, trombone and piano, 1973; organ sonata,
1973; 3 chamber symphonies, 1973, 1974, 1977; A
due, flute and clarinet, 1974; The constant flow,
4 clarinets, 1974; 5 pieces, for viola, 1974;
Music for, 3 trombones, 1975, French horn, 1975,
solo trombone, 1976; A noise did rise like thunder in my hearing, solo trombone and chamber
group, 1976; many works for solo voice and
chorus.
   415 Riverside Dr., #3B, New York, NY 10025

WRIGHT, RAYBURN
   b. Alma, Mich., 27 Aug. 1922. Studied with
Burrill Phillips and Bernard Rogers, Eastman
School of Music; at Juilliard School; with Henry
Brant and Otto Luening, Columbia Univ., Teachers
Coll. He received the Nat. Acad. of Television
Arts and Sciences Emmy nomination for his score
to the film, Saga 1492. He was staff arranger-
composer, Radio City Music Hall, 1950-59; free-
lance television-film composer, 1963-66; on
faculty, Eastman School of Music, from 1970.
   WORKS: ORCHESTRA: Regeneration, concerto
for jazz quartet, rock ensemble, and orch.; Textures, percussion trio and orch.; WIND ENSEMBLE:
Interface I, trombone choir and percussion ensemble; FILM SCORES: Saga 1492; The world's
girls; Soviet woman; Custer in the Little Big
Horn; Cortez and the legend; Mrs. L. B. Johnson's
visit to Washington, D.C.; The blue and the red
Danube; The birth of Christ; Kitty Hawk to Paris:
The heroic years.
   Eastman School, 26 Gibbs St., Rochester, NY
14604

WUNSCH, ILSE GERDA
   b. Berlin, Germany, 14 Dec. 1911. Studied piano
in Berlin; piano with Rudolph Ganz, composition
with Max Wald, Chicago Musical Coll., M.M. Her
faculty posts have included New York Coll. of

Music, 1948-68; Stern Coll. for Women, Yeshiva Univ., 1960-64; New York Univ., 1968-76; was also organist and choir director, Temple Beth El, Cedarhurst, 1949-68.

WORKS: VOICE: Young faith, a Sabbath evening and morning service in 2 books, 1956; PIANO: 12 progressing tone plays, 33rd Annual American Music Festival, New York, 19 Feb. 1972.

67 W. 68th St., New York, NY 10023

WUORINEN, CHARLES
b. New York, N.Y., 9 June 1938. Studied with Otto Luening, Columbia Univ. His many awards include the New York Phil. Young Composers award, 1954; Lili Boulanger award, 1960; Joseph H. Bearns prize, 1961; Brandeis Creative Arts award; honorary doctorate, Jersey City State Coll.; American Acad. of Arts and Letters award; Koussevitzky Internat. Recording award, 1970; Pulitzer prize, 1970; Guggenheim fellowship, 1972; Nat. Endowment for the Arts grant, 1976; and many commissions. He was on the faculty, Columbia Univ., 1964-71; has also taught at Princeton Univ., New England Cons., Univ. of Iowa, Univ. of South Florida; and from 1972, at Manhattan School of Music.

WORKS: OPERA: The whore of Babylon, 1974, won 3rd prize, New England Cons. competition, 1970; ORCHESTRA: 3 symphonies; piano concerto, 1966; Contrafactum, 1969; Politics of harmony, 1971; concerto for amplified violin, Tanglewood, 4 Aug. 1972; concerto for amplified piano, New York, 6 Dec. 1974, with composer as soloist; Percussion symphony, 1976; The winds, New York, 19 May 1977; CHAMBER MUSIC: chamber concerto, cello and 10 players, 1963; chamber concerto, flute and 10 players, 1964; Janissary music, percussion, 1966; duo, violin and harpsichord, 1967; string trio, 1968; The long and the short, violin solo, 1969; Ringing changes, percussion, 1970; string quartet; Variations for solo cello, 1970; chamber concerto for tuba, 12 winds, 12 drums, 1970; Flute variations II, 1971; Variations, solo violin, 1972; Variations for harp and string trio, 1973; Movement, woodwind quintet, 1973; On alligators, 8 players, 1973; Grand Union, cello and 4 drums, Chicago, 5 Nov. 1973; Arabia felix, chamber ensemble, New York, 23 Feb. 1974; Fantasia, violin and piano, Baltimore, 6 Apr. 1974; Hyperion, 12 instruments, 1975; Tashi, violin, cello, piano, clarinet, Colorado Springs, 15 Jan. 1976, New York premiere, 8 Feb. 1976; ELECTRONIC: Orchestral and electronic exchanges, 1965; Time's encomium, 1969, received Pulitzer prize, 1970; also many works for solo voice and chorus, and for keyboard instruments.

680 West End Ave., New York, NY 10025

WYATT, SCOTT A.
b. Philadelphia, Pa., 30 Oct. 1951. Studied with Randall McClellan, John Melby, Larry Nelson, West Chester State Coll.; with Herbert Brun, John Melby, Paul Zonn, Univ. of Illinois. His awards include Presser Found. scholarship; Charles E. Lutton Memorial award. From 1976 he has been faculty member, Univ. of Illinois.

WORKS: CHAMBER MUSIC: 5 preludes, piano;

ELECTRONIC: Sense 1, tape; 2 plus 2, 2 percussionists and tape; sextet, string quartet and tape; 4 for flute, flute and tape; Threesome, tuba, trumpet, trombone, and tape; Menagerie, tape.

School of Music, Univ. of Illinois, Urbana, IL 61801

WYETH, ANN (Mrs. John W. McCoy)
b. Chadds Ford, Pa., 15 Mar. 1915. Studied piano with W. H. Greene; composition with Harl McDonald.

WORKS: ORCHESTRA: Christmas fantasy, performed by the Philadelphia Orch. under Stokowski; other orchestral works, piano pieces, songs.

Chadds Ford, PA 19317

WYKES, ROBERT A.
b. Aliquippa, Pa., 19 May 1926. Studied with Cecil Effinger, Colorado Coll.; at Eastman School of Music, M.M. 1950; with Burrill Phillips, Univ. of Illinois, D.M.A. 1955. He received the Paderewski prize for his piano quintet, 1959. He was flutist, Toledo Symph., 1950-52, St. Louis Symph., 1963-65; faculty member, Bowling Green State Univ., 1950-52; Univ. of Illinois, 1952-55; from 1955, at Washington Univ.

WORKS: OPERA: The prankster, chamber opera, Bowling Green, Ohio, 12 Jan. 1952; ORCHESTRA: Density III, 1961; Horizons, 1964; Wave forms and pulses, 1964; The shape of time, 1965; Toward time's receding, New York premiere, 21 Jan. 1974; Adequate Earth, with baritone solo, 2 narrators, 3 choruses, on Donald Finkel's poem, Antarctica, St. Louis, 5 Feb. 1976; A shadow of silence I, 1976; CHAMBER MUSIC: flute sonata, 1955; concerto for 11 instruments, 1956; 4 studies for piano, 1958; piano quintet, 1959; concertino for flute, oboe, piano, and strings; CHORUS: 4 American Indian lyrics, 1957; Fantasy, female voices; A shadow of silence II.

Washington University, St. Louis, MO 63130

WYLIE, RUTH SHAW
b. Cincinnati, Ohio, 24 June 1916. Studied at Wayne State Univ., A.B. 1937, M.A. 1939; with Bernard Rogers, Eastman School of Music, Ph.D. 1943; with Arthur Honegger, Samuel Barber, Aaron Copland at Tanglewood, 1947. Her many awards include a doctoral fellowship at Eastman School; several Mu Phi Epsilon awards; Univ. of Missouri Creative Research awards; Wayne State Univ. awards; Huntington-Hartford fellowship, 1952-53; MacDowell fellowships, 1954, 1956; Harvey Gaul award, 1976; Nat. Endowment for the Arts grant, 1978; many commissions. She was faculty member, Univ. of Missouri, 1943-49; Wayne State Univ., 1949-69.

WORKS: BALLET: Facades, chamber ensemble, 1951; The ragged heart, chamber ensemble, 1961; ORCHESTRA: suite for strings, 1941; suite for chamber orch., 1942; 2 symphonies, 1943, 1946; Holiday overture, 1951; concerto grosso, 7 solo woodwinds and string orch., 1952; Involution, 1967; clarinet concertino, 1968; CHAMBER MUSIC: 3 string quartets, 1942, 1944, 1956; viola sonata, 1952; flute sonata, 1960; 3 inscapes,

WYMAN, DANN CORIAT

chamber group, 1970; 5 occurrences, woodwind
quintet, 1971; Incubus, chamber group, 1972; The
long look home, chamber orch., poetry, slides,
Detroit, 13 May 1976 Nova, chamber ensemble,
Chicago, 28 May 1976; Toward Sirius, chamber ensemble, Detroit, 27 Oct. 1976; many piano works.
1251 Country Club Dr., Estes Park, CO 80517

WYMAN, DANN CORIAT
b. Boston, Mass., 13 Nov. 1923. Studied violin
and viola with Arthur Fiedler; attended Northeastern Univ. From 1966 he has been a free-
lance violinist, violist, and arranger with jazz
and concert orchestras.
WORKS: ORCHESTRA: overture; Serenade for
strings; Impressions; CHAMBER MUSIC: string
quartet; Ode to the viola; Aloneness, solo viola;
Song with no words, soprano, viola, harpsichord;
The question, soprano and piano.
220 Hobart Rd., Chestnut Hill, MA 02167

WYNER, YEHUDI
b. Calgary, Alberta, Canada, 1 June 1929; U.S.
citizen at birth (son of Lazar Weiner). Studied
at Juilliard School; with Richard Donovan and
Paul Hindemith, Yale Univ., A.B. 1950, B.M. 1951,
M.M. 1953; with Randall Thompson and Walter
Piston, Harvard Univ., M.A. His awards include
the Rome prize; A. E. Hertz Memorial fellowship;
Fulbright and Guggenheim fellowships; American
Inst. of Arts and Letters grant; Brandeis Creative Arts award; Ford Found. grant; Nat. Endowment for the Arts grant; Tanglewood fellowship,
1978; and many commissions. He was visiting
lecturer, Queens Coll., 1958-59; music director,
Turnau Opera Assoc., 1961-63; music director,
Westchester Reformed Temple, 1958-68; faculty
member, Yale Univ., 1964-77; music director,
New Haven Opera Society, 1968-76; from 1968,
keyboard artist, Bach Aria Group.
WORKS: THEATRE: music for Lowell's The old
glory; Singer's The mirror; ORCHESTRA: Da
camera, piano and orch., 1967; Fragments from
antiquity, soprano and orch., New York, 5 Dec.
1978; BAND: Canto cantibile, soprano and band;
CHAMBER MUSIC: Dance variations, wind octet,
1953; Concert duo, violin and piano, 1956; Serenade, for 7 instruments, 1958; 3 informal pieces,
violin and piano, 1961; De novo, cello and small
ensemble, New York, 2 Mar. 1971; Cadenza, clarinet and piano, 1973; also piano sonata; liturgical works.
78 Lyon St., New Haven, CT 06511

WYTON, ALEC
b. London, England, 3 Aug. 1921; U.S. citizen
1968. Studied at Royal Acad. of Music; Oxford
Univ., B.A. 1945, M.A. 1949. He was named
fellow, Royal Coll. of Organists, 1942, American
Guild of Organists, 1950, Royal Canadian Coll.
of Organists, 1962, Royal Acad. of Music, 1964,
Royal School of Church Music, 1965; received an
honorary music doctorate, Susquehanna Univ.,
1970; annual ASCAP awards from 1967. He was
organist-choirmaster in England, 1946-50; in
St. Louis and New York, 1950-74; adjunct professor, Union Theological Seminary, New York,
1956-73; in 1974, was appointed coordinator of
music for the Episcopal Church in the U.S.

WORKS: CHORUS: Come Holy Ghost; Go ye,
therefore; An endless alleluia; Sing joyfully to
God; The journey with Jonah, chancel opera, 1977;
SONG CYCLES: Expectans expectavi, 1976; The
psalm of Christ, 1978; numerous other anthems,
liturgical works, and compositions for organ,
e.g., Music for space, 2 organs, trumpet, percussion, and tape, New York, 21 Jan. 1973.
129 E. 69th St., New York, NY 10021

YANNATOS, JAMES D.
b. New York, N.Y., 13 Mar. 1929. Studied with
Paul Hindemith and Quincy Porter, Yale Univ.;
with Ernst Bacon, Syracuse Univ.; Hugo Weisgall,
Cummington School of the Arts; Nadia Boulanger
in Paris; Luigi Dallapiccola in New York; with
Darius Milhaud, Aspen School; and with Philip
Bezanson, Univ. of Iowa, Ph.D. His awards in-
clude a Ditson grant, 1951; Fulbright fellow-
ship, 1957; Wooley grant, 1958; Ulrick-Bay
Found grant, 1978. He was faculty member,
Grinnell Coll., 1961-64; from 1964, lecturer,
Harvard Univ.
WORKS: OPERA: Silence bottle, children's
opera; Rocket's red glare, Cambridge, 6 May 1971;
ORCHESTRA: Fanfare and variations; Prieres dans
l'arche, voice and orch.; American rituals, 1975;
WIND ENSEMBLE: Polarities, brass and percussion;
CHAMBER MUSIC: 5 epigrams, string quartet; Bits
and pieces, string quartet or orch., 1976; 8
miniatures for 10 fingers, piano; solo cello
sonata; VOICE: 3 settings of e. e. cummings,
chorus; Music for 2 plus, soprano and bass C instrument, 1975; To form a more perfect union,
oratorio, soloists, chorus, small orch., 1976.
9 Stearns St., Cambridge, MA 02138

YANNAY, YEHUDA
b. Timisoara, Rumania, 26 May 1937; U.S. citizen
1977. Studied with A. U. Boscovitch, Israel
Acad. of Music, diploma 1964; with Arthur Berger
and Harold Shapero, Brandeis Univ., M.F.A. 1966;
Salvatore Martirano, Univ. of Illinois, D.M.A.
1974; with Elliott Carter, Ernst Krenek, Donald
Martino, and Gunther Schuller at Tanglewood.
His awards include a Fulbright fellowship; Univ.
of Illinois fellowship and Research Board grant;
Nat. Endowment for the Arts grant; Univ. of
Wisconsin research grant; Nat. Endowment for the
Humanities grant, 1972; Vilas Found. grant, 1978;
and commissions. He was dean, Israel Cons.,
1966-68; from 1968, on faculty, Univ. of Wisconsin. He was founder and conductor of Music
from Almost Yesterday, a contemporary performance group, and the Synth-in Series, for new
experimental music, theater, and live electronics.
WORKS: THEATRE: Wraphap, for actress, amplified aluminum sheet and Yannaychord, 1969;
Houdini's 9th, for a double bass and escape
artist, 1969; Attic songs, sound track for a
dance film, 1975; American sonorama, ballet,
1975-76; The decline and fall of the sonata in
B-flat, a musical for actors and pianists, 1976;
ORCHESTRA: Mirkamim, 1968; Concerto for audience
and orch., 1971; 5 songs for tenor and orch.,
1977; CHAMBER MUSIC: Spheres, soprano and 10
instruments, 1963; Permutations, solo percussion,
1964; Incantations, voice, keyboard, piano in-

terior, 1964; Interconnections, 14 instruments, 1965; Random rotated, 4 winds, 1965; Foreground-music, 6 instruments and speaker, text by Ginsberg, 1965; Mutatis mutandis, 6 players, 1968; Per se, violin and 7 instruments, 1969; Coloring book for the harpist, 1969; preFIX-FIX-sufFIX, bassoon, horn, cello, 1971; Squares and symbols, exits and traps, piano and 1-3 instruments, 1971; Bugpiece, with live insect notation, 1972; 7 late spring pieces, piano, 1973; At the end of the parade, on poems by William Carlos Williams, baritone and 6 players, 1974; The hidden melody, cello and French horn, 1977; also choral works and electronic pieces.

Univ. of Wisconsin, P.O. Box 413, Milwaukee, WI 53201

YARDEN, ELIE
b. Philadelphia, Pa., 7 June 1923. Studied with Stefan Wolpe, Settlement School, Philadelphia. He received an Israel Composers' Fund grant, 1960; Nan Leer Found. grant for work at the electronic music center, Hebrew Univ., Jerusalem, 1963-65; Rockefeller recording grant, 1972; Nat. Endowment for the Arts grant, 1977; and commissions. He taught at Rubin Acad. of Music, Jerusalem, 1958-60; Israel Acad. of Music, Tel-Aviv, 1960-65; faculty member, Bard Coll., from 1967; lecturer, Vassar Coll., 1973-74.

WORKS: OPERA: Eros and Psyche, chamber opera, 1970; ORCHESTRA: Prelude, passacaglia and fugue, 1958; CHAMBER MUSIC: 3 string quartets, 1949, 1956, 1965; Bagatelles, for piano, 1957; 4 variations, cello quartet, 1957; Divertimento, chamber ensemble, 1963; Suite 549, piano, 1972; Septentrion, piano trio, 1977.

Bard College, Annandale-on-Hudson, NY 12504

YARDUMANIAN, RICHARD
b. Philadelphia, Pa., 5 Apr. 1917. Did not begin formal musical study until age 22, then studied harmony, counterpoint and piano in Philadelphia; conducting with Pierre Monteux in Hancock, Maine. His self-education in composition was encouraged by Jose Iturbi and Leopold Stokowski and by numerous commissions. He taught piano privately for many years; is music director, The Lord's New Church, Bryn Athyn, Pa.; writes and edits the church hymnal; was cofounder of the Philadelphia Chamber Symphony; has done extensive research in both ancient music and regional American music.

WORKS: ORCHESTRA: Armenian suite, 1937, Philadelphia, 5 Mar. 1954; Symphonic suite, 1939; 3 pictographs, 1941; Desolate city, Philadelphia, 6 Apr. 1945; violin concerto, 1949, Philadelphia, 11 Nov. 1960; Cantus anumae et cordis, string orch., Philadelphia, 17 Feb. 1956; piano concerto, Philadelphia, 3 Jan. 1958; chorale-prelude on Veni, Sanctus Spiritus, Philadelphia, 3 Mar. 1959; symphony #1, Philadelphia, 1 Dec. 1961, #2, 12 Nov. 1964; CHAMBER MUSIC: Monologue, solo violin, 1947; untitled work for flute and strings, 1973; numerous choral works including The story of Abraham, an oratorio for chorus, soloists, orch., with original paintings in mural form by Andre Girard shown by 70-mm film on a screen suspended

above the stage, London, England, 4 May 1972, and at Maryville Coll., 18 May 1972.
Bryn Athyn, PA 19009

YASUI, BYRON K.
b. Honolulu, HI, 13 Dec. 1940. Studied with Armand Russell and Neil McKay, Univ. of Hawaii, B.M.E. 1965; with Anthony Donato, Alan Stout, and Richard Hillert, Northwestern Univ., M.M. 1967, D.M.A. 1972. He has been faculty member, Univ. of Hawaii, from 1972; has also played double bass with the Honolulu Symphony off and on from 1964.

WORKS: ORCHESTRA: symphony, 1970; WIND ENSEMBLE: Music for timpani and brass, 1972; CHAMBER MUSIC: brass quintet, 1966; Polarity I and II, woodwind quintet, 1970; Improvisations, guitar, harp, harpsichord, 1970; 5 movements, for solo cello, 1973; 5 Tzu-yeh songs, soprano and piano; Concert piece, 4 trumpets; Piccola arietta, solo guitar.

1820 Nuuanu Ave., Honolulu, HI 96817

YATES, RONALD L.
b. Muskegon, Mich., 27 Apr. 1947. Studied with Donald Andrus and Gerald Strang, California State Univ., Long Beach, B.M. 1970, M.M. 1971; with Peter Racine Fricker and Edward Appleton, Univ. of California, Santa Barbara, Ph.D. 1973. He held an NDEA fellowship, 1971-73. He joined the faculty at East Texas State Univ. in 1974.

WORKS: ORCHESTRA: Memoriam, contralto and orch.; A veil awave upon the waves; CHAMBER MUSIC: Hymn, octet; Air, flute choir, 1977; Enter softly the phantasma, piano; Solitaire I, violin; Solitaire II, piano, #3 French horn, #4 organ, 1976; CHORUS: L'hommage a Josquin; motet for 16 voies; Missa brevis, double chorus; Chori, with organ and chimes; Mass movement, with wind ensemble, 1977; Of waters deep (Psalm 69), double chorus, 1978.

2407 Mayo, Commerce, TX 75428

YAVELOW, CHRISTOPHER JOHNSON
b. Cambridge, Mass., 15 June 1950. Studied with Gardner Read, David Del Tredici, Joyce Mekeel, Hugo Norden, Boston Univ., B.M. 1972, M.M. 1974; with Leon Kirchner, Harvard Univ. His awards include first prize, Shenandoah Cons. Contest, 1974; Harvard Univ. grant-in-aid, 1974, 1976; fellowships at Vermont Composers' Conf., 1975, MacDowell Colony, 1975; Internat. Research and Exchanges Board grant, 1977; Francis Boot award for choral music, 1977. He has been music copyist, accompanist, and from 1973, director, Outstanding Artists Chamber Music Series.

WORKS: ORCHESTRA: And then we saw a sea lion, with marimba solo, 1973; Concert overture, 1973; Axis, 1974; 7 mikrophonae, 1975; Behold Icarus, 1975; CHAMBER MUSIC: Nocturne, clarinet and piano, 1970; string quartet, 1970; Green, 7 instruments and film strip, 1971; Introspections, 3 woodwinds, 3 brass, string trio, 1971; sonata for 2 trumpets, 1972; Bisoliloquy, 7 instruments, 1973; Soneptua, string quartet, 1973; Nero's tomb, 4 trombones, 1974; An explanation of one mechanical man, clarinet and cello, 1974; E-prime, brass quintet, 1974; Rhythm and blues,

YELLIN, GLEB

cello and harp, 1975; Multiples, any number of
string quartets, 1977; many other chamber works,
choral works, and songs.
P.O. Box 250, Cambridge, MA 02138

YELLIN, GLEB
b. Russia, 1 Mar. 1901. Studied in Leningrad
and Berlin with Reinhold Gliere. He was composer, conductor, and arranger with NBC, 1935-
47; music director for Billy Rose productions;
then composer and conductor for Marlene Dietrich
on radio and television.
WORKS: ORCHESTRA: Symphonic fantasy on
eastern themes; Nocturne appassionata, violin
and orch.

YODER, PAUL V.
b. Tacoma, Wash., 8 Oct. 1908. Studied at Univ.
of North Dakota, B.A. 1930; honorary D.M. 1958;
with Albert Noelte, Northwestern Univ., M.M.
1941. He received the Goldman award, American
School Band Directors Assoc.; Kappa Kappa Psi
award; Nat. Band Assoc., AWAPA Award. He taught
in public schools, 1930-36; from 1936, was free-
lance composer and arranger of band music; in
1973, visiting professor, Troy (Ala.) State Univ.
His works include more than 400 published original compositions for band and over 1000 transcriptions.

YON, PIETRO ALESSANDRO
b. Settimo Vittone, Italy, 8 Aug. 1886; U.S.
citizen 1921; d. Huntington, N.Y., 22 Nov. 1943.
Studied at the Milan Cons. and St. Cecilia Acad.
in Rome. He was organist in Rome, 1905-7; in
New York, 1908-43, St. Patrick's Cathedral,
1926-43; was organ recitalist in the U.S. and
Europe. His works include Concerto Gregoriano,
organ and orch.; The triumph of St. Patrick,
oratorio; many liturgical works, organ and piano
pieces, songs.

YORK, DAVID STANLEY
b. West Hartford, Conn., 25 June 1920. Studied
with Paul Hindemith, Yale Univ.; at Westminster
Choir Coll.; and with Thomas Beversdorf, Indiana
Univ. He won second prize in the Schulmerich
composition contest, 1947. He joined the faculty
at Westminster Choir Coll. in 1946.
WORKS: CHORUS: Once to every man and
nation; Lord, make me thine instrument; Blessing
and honor; To music; Psalm 150; The 4 freedoms;
and many others; ORGAN: Divinum mysterium, with
bells.
258 Washington Blvd., Princeton, NJ 08540

YORK, WALTER WYNN
b. Claremore, Okla., 6 Aug. 1914. Studied with
Howard Hanson, Herbert Elwell, Edward Royce,
Bernard Rogers, Eastman School of Music; also at
Univ. of Oklahoma and Westminster Choir Coll.
His awards include the Ellen Lyman Cabot Trust
grant, 1964; fellowships at MacDowell Colony,
1958, 1959, 1961, 1964; Yaddo, 1964, Huntington
Hartford Found., 1961, 1969; He has held faculty posts at Indiana Univ. of Pennsylvania,
1950-54; Southern Connecticut State Coll., 1961-
63; Olivet Coll., 1965-71; Detroit public schools,

1974-78.
WORKS: OPERA: The Bostonians, 1974; OR-
CHESTRA: Variations on a theme of Monteverdi;
Chrysis, dance drama; Rootabaga suite, and The
dog gone bus, with 2 narrators, for children and
adults; Hymn pastorale; CHAMBER MUSIC: Neo-
Gothics, woodwind quintet; string quartet; Nut-
brown variations, cello and harmonica; Father
and son fantasy, euphonium and piano; CHORUS:
A prayer service for our time, a cappella; Wisdom and peace, a cappella; The declaration of
independence in American, H. L. Mencken text,
with chamber group; Introit and benediction;
choral arrangements, songs, band pieces.
604 E. Garfield, Hazel Park, MI 48030

YOSHIOKA, EMMETT GENE
b. Honolulu, Hawaii, 19 Mar. 1944. Studied with
Ingolf Dahl, Halsey Stevens, Robert Linn, Ellis
Kohs, David Raksin, Anthony Vazzana, Univ. of
Southern California. He received USC composition
awards, 1966, 1972; Amstead award, 1972. He was
flutist, Honolulu Symph., 1960-61; flute instructor, State Univ. of New York at Albany, 1966-69;
member, Los Angeles Saxophone Quartet, 1969-72;
on faculty, Univ. of Southern California, 1969-
72.
WORKS: BAND: Duo concertino, alto saxophone and band; Prologue, fugue, and epilogue;
Intermezzo, oboe and band; CHAMBER MUSIC: Extase,
trombone solo; Aria and allegro, alto saxophone
quartet; Arioso, alto saxophone, harp, and
strings; alto saxophone sonata; also choral works.
5223 Apo Dr., Honolulu, HI 96821

YOUMANS, VINCENT
b. New York, N.Y., 27 Sept. 1898; d. Denver,
Colo., 5 Apr. 1946. Studied engineering; served
in the Navy in World War I; then became a song
plugger and rehearsal pianist. He composed
highly successful musical comedies, such as
Little girls in blue, 1921; Wildflower, 1923;
No, no, Nannette, 1924; A night out, 1925; Oh,
please, 1926; Hit the deck, 1927; and the film
score, Flying down to Rio, 1933.

YOUNG, DONALD JAMES
b. Elkhorn, Wis., 6 Dec. 1948. Studied with
Lawrence Hartzell, Univ. of Wisconsin, 1972;
with Ronald LoPresti, Univ. of Arizona, M.M.
1974. He received the John Philip Sousa award,
1967; CBNDA composition prize, 1975. He taught
in public schools, 1971-78; then joined the
faculty at Lakewood Coll. (Minn.).
WORKS: BAND: Patmos, 1975; Sign of the
Nicolaitans; Kroyer variations, clarinet choir;
Northern legend, clarinet choir; CHORUS: Sermon
on the mount, with brass quintet and percussion.
3675 Highland Ave., B-25, White Bear Lake,
MN 55110

YOUNG, GORDON ELLSWORTH
b. McPherson, Kans., 15 Oct. 1919. Studied at
Southwestern Coll., B.M., honorary S.M.D. 1973;
at Curtis Inst. of Music, 1944-46; organ with
Alexander McCurdy and Joseph Bonnet. He has
received annual ASCAP awards from 1968; many
commissions. He has served as organist in Tulsa,

Philadelphia, Kansas City, Lancaster, Pa., First Presbyterian Church, Detroit, 1952-72; faculty member at various institutions.

WORKS: CHAMBER MUSIC: Contempora suite, trumpet and piano; Detroit sketches, trumpet and piano; Triptych, cello and piano; CHORUS: Missa exultate, 1964; and some 200 other published choral works; numerous works for organ; and songs.

YOUNG, JANE
b. Athens, Ohio, 25 Mar. 1915. Studied at Ohio Univ.; with Marcel Dick, Cleveland Inst. of Music; piano with Beryl Rubinstein and Arthur Loesser. She received the Cleveland Inst. of Music Alumni award in composition, 1961. She has taught at Cleveland Inst. and the Dalcroze Music School; also in public schools from 1961.

WORKS: CHAMBER MUSIC: Essences, 2 violins, 1961; Dramatic soliloquy, piano, 1961; Piano gambol; 5 tone thoughts and summary, 1961; We people, song cycle for high voice, cello, piano, 1967; Caprice, piano, 1976.
20206 Wickfield Ave., Warrensville Heights, OH 44122

YOUNG, LA MONTE
b. Bern, Idaho, 14 Oct. 1935. Studied at Univ. of California, Los Angeles, B.A. 1958; composition at Univ. of California, Berkeley, 1958-60; privately with Leonard Stein, 1955-56; Karlheinz Stockhausen, 1959, electronic music with Richard Maxwell, New School for Social Research, New York; Indian vocal music with Pran Nath in New York and in New Delhi. His awards include 2 grants, Nat. Inst. of Arts and Letters; 2 Guggenheim fellowships; Cassandra Found. grant; Cultural Found. grant, 1971; Experiments in Art and Technology grant for study in India, 1971 (for the last 2, his wife, Marian Zazeela, was corecipient). He has been in the forefront of avant-garde music since 1955 as composer, performer, instructor, writer, lecturer. He edited an anthology of music, poetry, art, 1963; was director of a concert series at Yoko Ono's Studio, New York; became director, Theatre of Eternal Music, 1962.

WORKS: for brass, octet, 1957; for guitar, 1958; string trio, 1958; Vision, 11 instruments producing unspecified sounds, 1959; Untitled works, improvisations with live friction sounds produced by gong on cement, gong on wood floor, metal on wall, 1959-; Poem for chairs, tables, benches, etc., which are pushed or pulled along the floor, 1960; 2 sounds, 2 specific sounds, each recorded on its own reel of tape, 1960; Composition 1960 #1-15, word scores involving various objects and activities: #2 consists of building a fire in front of the audience; #3 of releasing butterflies into the performance area; later in the series: The tortoise, his dreams and journeys, a continuing performance work initially for voices, strings, drones, with microphones, mixers, amplifiers, loudspeakers, and light projections; and others of a similar nature.
P.O. Box 190, Canal St. Station, New York, NY 10013

YOUNG, MICHAEL E.
b. San Francisco, Calif., 25 June 1939. Studied with George F. McKay, John Verrall, and Greg Short, Univ. of Washington, B.A., M.A.; organ with Walter Eichinger and Edward Hansen. He was named associate, American Guild of Organists, 1965. He was church organist in Seattle, 1961-70; from 1970, in Vancouver, B.C.

WORKS: CHAMBER MUSIC: suite for bassoon and piano; piano trio; KEYBOARD: 3 preludes and fugues, for organ; 2 piano sonatas; suite for harpsichord; Music for organ and brass; Sonata of joy, organ.
1425 W. 38th Ave., Vancouver 13, B.C., Canada

YOUNG, PHILIP M.
b. Greenville, S.C., 3 July 1937. Studied at North Greenville Coll.; Furman Univ.; and with John Boda, Florida State Univ. He received second place, Broadman anthem competition, 1963; first place, Lorenz Pub. Co. church music contest, 1965. He has been minister of music, First Baptist Church, Henderson, N.C., from 1959.

WORKS: CHORUS (cantatas): God with us, Emanuel; Today the Prince of Peace is born; To David's town; Christ's sacrifice complete; many anthems; also music for handbells.
Box 925, Henderson, NC 27536

YOUNG, ROBERT H.
b. Santa Cruz, Calif., 20 Apr. 1923. Studied at Otterbein Coll., B.M.; Northwestern Univ., M.M.; and at Univ. of Southern California, D.M.A. He was minister of music in various churches, 1952-62; from 1962, has been faculty member at Baylor Univ.

WORKS: CHORUS: All for love; Gabriel's message; O mortal man; When I survey the wondrous cross; Of the Father's love begotten; and others.
School of Music, Baylor University, Waco, TX 76703

YOUNG, ROLANDE MAXWELL
b. Washington, D.C., 13 Sept. 1929. Studied at Catholic Univ.; with Harold Bauer at Manhattan School of Music; and with Vittorio Giannini at Juilliard School. She made her debut as pianist in Town Hall, New York, in 1953. Her compositions include Little acorns for piano; and songs.

YOUNG, VICTOR
b. Bristol, Tenn., 9 Apr. 1889; d. Ossining, N.Y., 2 Sept. 1968. Studied at Cincinnati Coll. of Music; New York Univ.; piano with Isidor Philipp in Paris. He toured the U.S. and Canada as pianist and accompanist; was music director, Edison Photograph Laboratory; made piano rolls and records; held various academic posts.

WORKS: OPERETTA: A happy week; BALLET: Charm assembly line; ORCHESTRA: Scherzetto; Jeep; In the Great Smokies; A fragment, string orch.; songs and piano pieces; also scored an early sound film, In old California, and some 300 other films.

YOUNG, VICTOR

YOUNG, VICTOR
b. Chicago, Ill., 8 Aug. 1900; d. Palm Springs,
Calif., 10 Nov. 1956. Studied violin at Warsaw
Cons., then in Chicago. He was violinist and
arranger with Ted Fiorito; was music director on
radio in Chicago and New York; went to Hollywood
in 1935, composed many film scores including
The uninvited; For whom the bell tolls; Samson
and Delilah; The greatest show on earth; Around
the world in 80 days (received Acad. award,
1956); many popular songs.

YOUSE, GLAD ROBINSON
b. Miami, Okla., 22 Oct. 1898. Studied at
Stephens Coll.; composition with Tibor Serly in
New York. Her awards include nomination as one
of 3 top-ranking women composers, Nat. Fed. of
Music Clubs, Parade of American Music, 1955;
alumnae citation, Stephens Coll., 1955; Sigma
Alpha Iota, Ring of Excellence, 1956, citation,
1967; Kansas Fed. of Music Clubs citations, 1963,
1968; Theta Sigma Phi Matrix award, 1965. She
was composer-director, Jenkins Music Conferences,
Kansas City, 1948-66. She has published more
than 200 sacred and secular works for chorus and
solo voice.
532 E. 12th St., Baxter Springs, KS 66713

YTTREHUS, ROLV
b. Duluth, Minn., 12 Mar. 1926. Studied with
Ross Lee Finney, Univ. of Michigan; with Nadia
Boulanger in Paris; Roger Sessions, Princeton,
N.J.; Aaron Copland at Tanglewood; and with
Goffredo Petrassi in Rome. His awards include
a Fulbright scholarship; Margaret Lee Crofts
award; Italian government scholarships; Martha
Baird Rockefeller grant; Nat. Endowment for the
Arts grant. He was faculty member, Univ. of
Missouri, 1963-67; Purdue Univ., 1968-69; Univ.
of Wisconsin, 1969-77; from 1977, at Rutgers
Univ.
WORKS: ORCHESTRA: Espressioni, Rome, 1962,
American premiere, Boston, 13 May 1973; CHAMBER
MUSIC: 6 Haiku, 1961; Music, for winds, percussion, and viola, 1961; sextet for trumpet,
horn, violin, double bass, piano, percussion,
1970, New York, 4 Mar. 1973, rev. 1974; Angst-
wagen, soprano and percussion, 1971; msuic for
winds, percussion, cello and voices, 1969, Tanglewood, 1971; quintet for violin, cello, flute,
clarinet, piano, New York, 4 Feb. 1974; Gradus
ad Parnassum, soprano, chamber ensemble, tape,
1978.
Rutgers University, New Brunswick, NJ
08903

ZABRACK, HAROLD
b. St. Louis, Mo., 30 June 1928. Studied with
Rudolph Ganz and Max Wald, Chicago Musical Coll.,
B.M. in piano 1949, M.M. 1951; piano study in
Freiburg, Germany, 1955-57; doctoral study in
piano, Indiana Univ., 1958-59; composition with
Nadia Boulanger in France, 1962. He held the
Rudolph Ganz scholarship, 1946-49; received
many awards for piano performance; Fulbright
scholarships, 1955, 1956; composition award for
study in France, 1962; ASCAP awards, 1977, 1978;
and commissions. He has held faculty posts at

Chicago Musical Coll., 1949-51; Webster Coll.,
1962-65; from 1974, at Westminster Choir Coll.;
has presented master classes in piano at many
universities; has been concert pianist from
1952.
WORKS: ORCHESTRA: Symphonic variations,
piano and orch., 1959; 2 piano concertos, #1
St. Louis, 5 Apr. 1964, composer as soloist, #2
1965; CHAMBER MUSIC: 2 duets, viola and oboe,
1961; Song cycle, on classical Greek texts,
soprano; Fantasie, horn and organ; PIANO: 2
sonatas, 1965, 1969; 8 piano contours; Scherzo:
Hommage à Prokofieff; sonata for 2 pianos,
Lincoln Center, 30 Oct. 1975.
155 W. 68th St., #1201, New York, NY 10023

ZADOR, EUGENE (JENÖ)
b. Bátaszék, Hungary, 5 Nov. 1894; U.S. citizen
1944; d. Hollywood, Calif., 3 Apr. 1977. Studied
at Vienna Cons. and with Max Reger, Leipzig
Cons., Ph.D. His awards included the Grand Prix
of Hungary, 1934; Benjamin prize, 1960; Nat.
Endowment for the Arts grant, 1976. He was professor, Vienna Cons., 1922-38; New York Coll. of
Music, 1939; then went to Hollywood as film orchestrator and arranger, 1940-61.
WORKS: OPERA: Christopher Columbus, opera-
oratorio, New York, 8 Oct. 1939; The virgin and
the fawn, 1 act, Los Angeles, 24 Oct. 1964; The
magic chair, 1 act, 1965; The scarlet mill, 1967;
Revisor (Inspector General), after Gogol, 1928,
premiere, Los Angeles, 11 June 1971; Yehu, a
Christmas legend, Torrance, Calif., 4 June 1976;
ORCHESTRA: Czardas rhapsodic, 1939; Children's
symphony, 1941; Pastorale and tarantella, 1941;
Biblical triptych, 1943; Elegie and dance, 1953;
Divertimento, for strings, 1955; Fugue-fantasia,
1958; Suite for brass, 1961; Rhapsody, 1961;
Christmas overture, 1961; Variations on a merry
theme, 1963; The remarkable adventure of Henry
Bold, with narrator, 1963; Triptych, 1964; 5
contrasts, for orch., 1964; trombone concerto,
1966; Rhapsody, cimbalom and orch., 1968;
Studies, for orch., 1968; Fantasia Hungarica,
double bass and orch., 1970; double bass concerto, 1971; accordion concerto, 1973; Hungarian
scherzo, Orange, Calif., 1 Apr. 1976; oboe concerto, Los Angeles, 5 Apr. 1976; CHAMBER MUSIC:
Suite for 8 celli, 1966; Music for clarinet and
strings, 1969; woodwind quintet, 1972; Duo-
fantasy, 2 celli, strings, harp, Riverside,
Calif., 3 Dec. 1973; brass quintet, 1973; also
choral works.

ZADORA, MICHAEL
b. New York, N.Y., 14 June 1882; d. New York,
30 June 1946. Studied with his father and at
the Paris Cons.; later with Leschetisky and
Busoni. He was concert pianist and teacher;
composed songs and piano pieces.

ZAHLER, NOEL BARRY
b. New York, N.Y., 10 May 1951. Studied with
Henry Weinberg and Hugo Weisgall, Queens Coll.,
B.A., M.A.; with Milton Babbitt, Charles Dodge,
and J. K. Randall, Princeton Univ., M.F.A.; and
with Franco Donatoni in Italy. He has held
fellowships at MacDowell Colony, Composers'

Conf., Vermont, CUNY Grad. School; recieved
Fulbright-Hays grant; Italian Nat. Research
Council grant; scholarships at Music Acad.,
Siena, Italy, Nat. Endowment for the Humanities,
Princeton Univ. He was lecturer, Queens Coll.,
1977; Brooklyn Coll., CUNY, from 1978; director,
Composers' Chamber Group, from 1977.

WORKS: CHAMBER MUSIC: 3 movements, violin
and cello; flute sonata; 3 songs, mezzo-soprano
and chamber orch.; Regions I, piano; 4 songs of
departure, soprano and piano; Tableau, violin
solo; Charms, 9 instruments; The mime, violin
and soprano; I'Piango Lasso, vocal quintet.
484 W. 43rd St., Apr. 8-B, New York, NY
10036

ZAIMONT, JUDITH LANG
b. Memphis, Tenn., 8 Nov. 1945. Studied with
Hugo Weisgall and Leo Kraft, Queens Coll., B.A.
magna cum laude, 1966; with Otto Luening and
Jack Beeson, Columbia Univ., M.A. 1968; privately
with Andre Jolivet in Paris, 1971-72. She received scholarships for all study through 1968;
MacDowell fellowshops, 1971, 1976; Debussy
scholarship for study in France, 1971-72; Nat.
Fed. of Music Clubs awards, 1963, 1964, 1968,
1970; Rathaus Memorial prize, 1966; first prize,
Gottschalk competition, 1970; Lowe Found. grant,
1978. She was faculty member, New Yrok City
Community Coll., 1970-71; Queens Coll., CUNY,
1972-76.

WORKS: ORCHESTRA: piano concerto, 1972;
CHAMBER MUSIC: flute sonata, 1962; Experience,
flute and piano, 1966; 2 movements, woodwind
quartet, 1967; Grand tarantella, violin and
piano, 1970; Capriccio, solo flute, 1971; trumpet
sonata, 1971; trio for flute, viola, piano, 1971;
CHORUS: They flee from me . . ., with flute,
1966; Man's image and his cry, with orch., 1968;
Canto II, 1970; The chase, on an original narrative poem, 1972; SONGS: 4 songs, mezzo and
piano, 1965; A solemn music, cycle for baritone,
1967; Coronach, cycle for soprano, 1970; Chant,
solo voice and drone, 1970; A woman of Valor,
mezzo-soprano and string quartet, 1977; Songs
for soprano and harp, 1978; The magic world,
bass voice, piano, percussion, 6 songs on American Indian texts, 1978; PIANO: City suite,
1961; Piano variations, 1965; Scherzo, 1969;
Snazzy sonata, 4 hands, 1972; 12 preludes, 1973;
Solitary pipes, 1977; A calendar set, 1978; Nocturne, 1978.
264-20 82nd Ave., Floral Park, NY 11004

ZAJICEK, JERONYM
b. Krasne Brezno. Czech., 10 Nov. 1926; U.S.
citizen 1957. Studied musicology at Charles
Univ., Prague, 1946-49; conducting with Otakar
Jeremias, 1947-49; composition with Karel Jirak,
1955-58, and Paul Pisk, 1959-60, both at
Roosevelt Univ. His violin sonata won a first
prize given by the Chicago chapter, ISCM, 1963.
He was program director, Czech station, Radio
Free Europe, Munich, 1950-52; from 1964, on
faculty, Loop Branch, Chicago City Coll.
WORKS: ORCHESTRA: sinfonietta, 1958; concertino for flute and strings, 1964, Chicago,
26 Feb. 1967; WIND ENSEMBLE: Intrada and pro-

cessionale, brass, timpani, organ, 1970; CHAMBER
MUSIC: Variations for piano, 1956-57; piano
trio, 1957; clarinet sonata, 1957; violin sonata,
1961; string quartet, 1963; sonatina for flute,
clarinet, bassoon, 1967; cello sonata, 1975;
songs.
4230 Prescott, Lyons, IL 60534

ZALLMAN, ARLENE (PROCTOR)
b. Philadelphia, Pa., 9 Sept. 1934. Studied
with Vincent Persichetti, Philadelphia Cons.; at
Juilliard School; with George Crumb, Univ. of
Pennsylvania; and with Luigi Dallapiccola,
Cherubini Cons., Italy. Her awards include a
Fulbright grant, Marion Freschl award, University fellowship, Nat. Endowment for the Arts
grant. She was faculty member, Oberlin Coll.
Cons., 1968-71; Yale Univ., 1972-73; from 1976,
at Wellesley Coll.
WORKS: CHAMBER MUSIC: Racconto, piano, New
York, 20 May 1973; Winter, voice and piano;
Songs from Quasimodo, alto flute, cello, piano,
voice; Variations, violin, clarinet, piano;
CHORUS: The locust tree in flower, with 4 soloists; The imaginary invalid, musical interludes
and scenes, with soloists and chamber orch.
641 Washington St., Wellesley, MA 02181

ZAMBARANO, ALFRED P.
b. Naples, Italy, 24 Feb. 1885; U.S. citizen
1906; d. New Haven, Conn., 22 June 1970. Came
to the U.S. as an infant, but returned to Italy
to study at the Naples Cons., graduating in
1907. He played piano at the Providence Opera
House, 1918-28; was baritone soloist with concert
bands, 1918-30; taught in public schools in
Rhode Island, Connecticut, and Massachusetts,
1930-65. His National capitol march won first
place in the national competition for a march to
celebrate the Washington sesquicentennial in
1950.
WORKS: BAND MARCHES: The national capitol,
1950; Green thunderbolt; National unity; Bobcat
march; CHAMBER MUSIC: Neopolitan tarantella,
clarinet and piano; Friendship, trombone and
piano; A valiant hero, tuba and piano; Elephant's
frolic, tuba and piano; trumpet trio; and songs.

ZANINELLI, LUIGI
b. Raritan, N.J., 30 Mar. 1932. Studied with
Gian-Carlo Menotti, Bohuslav Martinu, Vittorio
Giannini at Curtis Inst. of Music. He received
the Steinway piano composition award, 1955;
annual ASCAP awards from 1964; Alberta award;
ETV award for music for The islander. He was on
the faculty, Curtis Inst., 1952-58; New School
of Music, Philadelphia, 1955-58; composer-conductor, RCA Italiana, Rome, 1964-66; composer-
in-residence, Univ. of Calgary, Canada, 1968-73;
from 1973, at Univ. of Southern Mississippi.
WORKS: OPERA: Vicksburg 1863, chamber
opera; ORCHESTRA: Festa, march; Hymn and variations, with chorus; Margaret suite; Puppet overture; WIND ENSEMBLE: Peg Leg Pete, solo tuba
and band; Jubilate Deo, brass choir; Music for a
solemn occasion, brass and percussion; CHAMBER
MUSIC: Arioso, flute, cello, piano; Dance variations, woodwind quintet; Designs, brass quin-

ZATMAN, ANDREW

tet; Dialogue, violin and piano; Musica drammatica, woodwind quintet and percussion; 3 children's dances, woodwind quintet; Canto lirico,
trumpet and piano; Epitaph, flute, 2 pianos,
strings, percussion; Burla, woodwind quartet;
PIANO: The enchanted lake, children's ballet; A
lexicon of beasties, 26 pieces for student and
teacher; 3Rs for dancing; 3 infinitives; many
choral works, film scores.
     501 Court St., Hattiesburg, MS 39401

ZATMAN, ANDREW
     b. Washington, D.C., 6 June 1945. Studied with
John Vincent, Henri Lazarof, Roy Travis, Alden
Ashforth, and Boris Kremenliev, Univ. of Cali-
fornia, Los Angeles, M.A. 1969. From 1971 he
has been composer-in-residence and teacher,
School of Music, Jewish Community Center of
Greater Washington.
     WORKS: CHAMBER MUSIC: woodwind trio, 1969;
suite for solo flute, 1971; flute sonata, 1972;
Jonah, ballet for trumpet and piano; 3 sacred
songs, soprano, recorder, piano; alto recorder
sonata, 1977; PIANO: 24 preludes, 1965; sonata
#2, 1967; Variations on "November Leaves" of
Boris Kremenliev, 1969; sonatina.
     303 Congressional Lane, Rockville, MD 20852

ZDECHLIK, JOHN PAUL
     b. Minneapolis, Minn., 2 May 1937. Studied with
Paul Fetler and Dominick Argento, Univ. of
Minnesota. He has taught at Univ. of Minnesota;
St. Cloud State Coll.; from 1970 at Lakewood
Community Coll.
     WORKS: ORHCESTRA: 5 pieces, 1970; WIND EN-
SEMBLE: Psalm 46, 1969; Chorale and Shaker
dance; Grace variants; Lyric statement; Dance
variants; Fanfare, for 12 trumpets.
     3860 Van Dyke, White Bear Lake, MN 55110

ZECKWER, CAMILLE
     b. Philadelphia, Pa., 26 June 1875; d. Southamp-
ton, N.Y., 7 Aug. 1924. Studied with his father,
Richard Zeckwer; composition with Dvorak in New
York and Schwarwenka in Berlin. He succeeded
his father as director of the Philadelphia
Musical Acad., 1917-24.
     WORKS: OPERA: Jane and Janette, 3 acts;
ORCHESTRA: Swedish fantasy; piano concerto;
Sohrab and Rustum, symphonic poem, 1961; CHAMBER
MUSIC: Serenade melancolique; piano trio;
CHORUS: The new day, cantata; other choral
works, songs, piano pieces.

ZEISL, ERIC
     b. Vienna, Austria, 18 May 1905; U.S. citizen
1945; d. Los Angeles, 18 Feb. 1959. Studied at
Vienna Acad. of Music; became professor at
Vienna Cons.; from 1939, taught at the Los
Angeles Cons.
     WORKS: OPERA: Leonce and Lena, 1937; Job,
1945-58, incomplete; BALLET: Uranium 235; Jacob
and Rachel; ORCHESTRA: Little symphony, 1937;
Passacaglia-fantasy, 1937; November, suite for
chamber orch., 1940; Cossack dance, 1946; Return
of Ulysses, chamber orch., 1948; Requiem Ebraico,
with chorus, 1945; piano concerto, 1951; concerto
grosso, cello and orch., 1956; CHAMBER MUSIC:

2 string quartets; Sonata barocca, piano, 1949;
violin sonata, 1950; cello sonata, 1951; Brandeis sonata, violin sonata, 1950; viola sonata,
1950; trio for flute, viola, harp, 1956; SONGS:
Prayer for the United Nations, baritone and
piano; 7 songs for soprano; Moon pictures,
baritone and orch., 1928.

ZERCHER, J. RANDALL
     b. Mt. Joy, Pa., 9 Dec. 1940. Studied with
Harold Moyer, Bethel Coll., Kans.; with Joseph
Goodman, Union Theological Seminary, New York,
M.M. He received 2 Thresher awards in composition, Bethel Coll., 1963, 1964. He was faculty
member, Bethel Coll., 1966-68; at Hesston Coll.,
1968-75.
     WORKS: CHORUS: My beloved spake, 1965; I
bind my heart this tide, 1969; ORGAN: Union, a
prelude, 1970; also Playground, a collaborative
musical drama.

ZES, TIKEY A.
     b. Long Beach, Calif., 27 Oct. 1927. Studied
with Gerald Strang, Long Beach; with Ingolf Dahl,
Univ. of Southern California, D.M.A. 1969. He
received 2 Helen Anstead awards at USC, 1963,
1969. He has been faculty member, San Jose
State Univ., from 1964.
     WORKS: ORCHESTRA: French overture, 1963;
CHORUS: Music for the divine liturgy of St.
John Chrysostom, 1966; 2 Greek folk songs, 1969;
Byzantine concert liturgy, with orch., 1969.
     1523 Arata Court, San Jose, CA 95125

ZIFRIN, MARILYN J.
     b. Moline, Ill., 7 Aug. 1926. Studied at Univ.
of Wisconsin, B.M. 1948; Columbia Univ., Teachers
Coll., M.A. 1949; at Univ. of Chicago; composi-
tion with Karl Ahrendt and Alexander Tcherepnin.
Her awards include second prize, Chicago Chapter,
ISCM, contest, 1964; Delius award, 1972; Meet
the Composer grant, 1977; MacDowell fellowship,
1977; Norlin Found. grant, 1977; and commissions.
She was on the faculty, Northeastern Illinois
State Coll., 1961-66; from 1967, at New England
Coll., Henniker, N.H.
     WORKS: ORCHESTRA: Orchestra piece, 1977;
CHAMBER MUSIC: XIII, chamber ensemble, 1969;
Movement for clarinet and percussion, 1972;
string quartet, 1972; Haiku, song cycle, soprano,
viola, harpsichord; In the beginning, percussion
quintet; sonata for organ and cello, 1973; 4
pieces for tuba, 1972; piano trio, New London,
N.H., 4 Aug. 1976; quintet for oboe and strings,
MacDowell Colony, 9 Aug. 1978; concerto for
viola and woodwind quintet, Washington, D.C., 8
Oct. 1978; Rhapsody for guitar, Henniker, N.H.,
12 Feb. 1979.
     P.O. Box 179, Bradford, NH 03221

ZILEVICIUS, JUOZAS
     b. Plunge, Lith., 16 Mar. 1891; to U.S. 1929.
Studied at St. Petersburg Cons. and Warsaw Cons.
He was awarded the 3rd Order of Gedeminas by the
Lithuanian government, 1935. He was professor,
Vitebsk Cons., 1919-20; director of arts, Lith-
uania, 1922-24; professor, Klaipeda Cons., 1924-
29; music director, St. Peter and Paul Church,

Elizabeth, N.J., 1929-60; from 1960, curator,
Zilevicius Library of Lithuanian Musicology,
Chicago.
WORKS: THEATRE: Lietuvaite, operetta;
ORCHESTRA: symphony, Kaunas, Lith., 27 July
1923, was first symphony composed by a Lithuan-
ian; CHAMBER MUSIC: string quartet; octet;
Ausra, violin and piano; Variations and fugues
for piano; CHORUS: Vytautas the Great, cantata.
2345 W. 56th St., Chicago, IL 60636

ZIMBALIST, EFREM
b. Rostov, Russia, 9 Apr. 1899; to U.S. 1911;
Studied with Leopold Auer, St. Petersburg
Cons., made his debut as violinist in Berlin
at 18; toured Europe and the U.S. From 1929
he was on the faculty at Curtis Inst.,
director, 1941-61.
WORKS: THEATRE: Landora, opera, 1956;
Honeydew, musical comedy; ORCHESTRA: Slavonic
dances, violin and orch., 1911; American rhapsody, 1936; violin concerto; Portrait of an
artist, symphonic poem, 1945; cello concerto,
1969; CHAMBER MUSIC: Concert fantasy on Le coq
d'or, violin and piano; violin sonata; string
quartet; violin pieces; songs.

ZINN, MICHAEL ALAN
b. New Haven, Conn., 23 Aug. 1947. Studied with
Walter Ihrke and Charles Whittenberg, Univ. of
Connecticut, B.M. 1969, M.A. 1971; with Paul
Harder and H. Owen Reed, Michigan State Univ.,
Ph.D. 1976. He held the Hicks scholarship,
1968; was named Delaware Composer of the Year,
1976. He has been faculty member, Univ. of
Delaware, from 1974.
WORKS: BAND: Tapestries of the Zodiac,
1976; CHAMBER MUSIC: Quartet for 6 instruments,
proportional notation, 1971; Suspensions, alto
saxophone, bassoon, vibraphone, 1973; Yellow
spring, soprano, flute, oboe, violin; Reticent
reflections, piano; CHORUS: Ghost dreamer of
Teton, with percussion; ELECTRONIC: Composition, for tape and orch., 1969; Spring storm,
chamber ensemble and tape, 1972.
University of Delaware, Newark, DE 19711

ZISKIN, VICTOR
b. New York, N.Y., 18 Mar. 1937. Studied with
Walter Piston and Tillman Merritt at Harvard
Univ.; also with Isabella Vengerova, Jean
Casadesus, Leonard Bernstein, Roger Sessions,
Nadia Boulanger, and Kay Swift. He was the
first Harvard freshman to write Hasty Pudding
shows; received the Damon Runyan Memorial
Found. commission and an American Jewish Con-
gress award for his off-Broadway stage score,
Young Abe Lincoln; performed his own works in
Carnegie Hall, 1959, 1960.
WORKS: BALLET: Ballet for street urchins;
Harlequin; Aubade; ORCHESTRA: San Francisco
rhapsody, piano and orch.; On the borders of
Israel; Civil War suite; PIANO: Allegro pour
piano; Suite for piano in 5 parts; and songs.

ZITO, TORRIE
b. Utica, N.Y., 12 Oct. 1933. Studied with
Vittorio Giannini, Manhattan School of Music.

He is a free-lance composer-arranger in popular
music.
WORKS: BAND: Major Boogaloo march; La
fiesta de la roca; Brazilian fantasy; Journey
into the blue rock country; Holiday fanfare and
march; also stage band works.
140 E. 83rd St., New York, NY 10028

ZONN, PAUL
b. Boston, Mass. 16 Jan. 1938. Studied with
Richard Hervig, Univ. of Iowa, M.F.A. 1966. His
awards include a Rockefeller grant to Buffalo
Center for Creative Arts, 1966-67; Fromm fellowships at Tanglewood, 1967, 1968; Ford Found.
summer grants, 1968-70; Univ. of Illinois faculty fellowship, 1971; Nat. Endowment for the
Arts grant, 1975; and commissions. He was composer-in-residence and conductor, Grinnell Coll.,
1967-70; from 1970, on faculty, Univ. of Illinois.
WORKS: ORCHESTRA: clarinet concerto;
CHAMBER MUSIC: concerto for viola and 13 instruments; Chroma, oboe and piano, 1967; Divertimentos 1-3, varying ensembles; Fantaisie duo, 2
cellos; Grunge, solo flute; The justice variations, actor and 6 instruments; Liberata I-III,
varying chamber ensembles; Melon, piano trio;
One slow turn of the world, woodwind trio,
double bass, percussion; wind sextet; oboe
sonata; piano sonata; 2 string quartets; Well
pursed, flute and piano; Gemini fantasy, oboe
and 6 players; The voyage of Columbus, solo
trumpet and 10 players, 1975; other chamber
pieces, vocal works, electronic music.
308 Pond Ridge Lane, Urbana, IL 61801

ZORKO, GEORGE MATTHEW
b. East Cleveland, Ohio, 7 May 1947. Studied
with Normand Lockwood, Univ. of Denver; with
Merrill Ellis, North Texas State Univ.
WORKS: ORCHESTRA: Psalm; CHAMBER MUSIC:
wind octet; Canonic fantasia, accordion; On
guard, chamber orch. and accordion; CHORUS:
Missa, 32-voice choir and organ.
9040 Ranch Dr., Chesterland, OH 44026

ZUCKERMAN, MARK
b. Brooklyn, N.Y., 8 July 1948. Studied with
George B. Wilson, Univ. of Michigan; Elie Yarden,
Bard Coll.; with Milton Babbitt, J. K. Randall,
Peter Westergaard, and Claudio Spies, Princeton
Univ., where he held the Whiting fellowship,
1973-74. He was instructor at Princeton, 1974-
76, then joined the faculty at Columbia Univ.
WORKS: CHAMBER MUSIC: Retrogressive study,
piano, 1970; Paraphrases, flute alone, 1971.
18 Tamara Dr., Roosevelt, NJ 08555

ZUKOFSKY, PAUL
b. Brooklyn, N.Y., 22 Oct. 1943. Studied with
Bernard Wagenaar and Vincent Persichetti, Juilliard School, M.M. He made his professional
debut on the violin with the New Haven Symphony
at age 8; gave a Carnegie Hall recital at 13;
has performed with many major orchestras; has
excelled in presenting contemporary works for
violin in concert and on records. He has taught
violin at the New England Cons., Swarthmore
Coll., State Univ. of New York at Stony Brook,

ZUPKO, RAMON

and from 1976, at Manhattan School of Music.
   WORKS: ORCHESTRA: for orchestra, 1964;
CHAMBER MUSIC: Variants, soprano, trumpet,
violin, bass clarinet, 1960; 13 pomes, a prelude
and a postlude, 2 speakers, 15 percussion players, 1962; for 3 mallet men and a percussion
player, 1963; Catullus "fragments," soprano,
alto, string trio, 1968.
   Box 97, Port Jefferson, NY 11777

ZUPKO, RAMON
b. Pittsburgh, Pa., 14 Nov. 1932. Studied with
Vincent Persichetti, Juilliard School; with Otto
Luening, Columbia Univ.; and with Karl Schiske,
Vienna Acad. of Music. He won first prize,
Premio Citta di Trieste, Italy, 1965; Fulbright
grant, 1958; had compositions chosen for perfor-
mance, St. Louis Symph., 1966, 1967, and to
represent the U.S., ISCM Music Festival, Basel,
Switz., 1970; American Composers Alliance grant,
1977; Nat. Endowment for the Arts grant, 1978;
Martha Baird Rockefeller grant, 1978. He was
Ford Found. composer-in-residence, Lubbock, Tex.,
1961-62; at Joliet, Ill., 1966-67; faculty member, Roosevelt Univ., 1967-71; from 1971, at
Western Michigan Univ.
   WORKS: ORCHESTRA: violin concerto, 1965;
Centroids, 1966; Translucents, string orch.,
1967; Radiants, 1972; WIND ENSEMBLE: Tangents,
18 brass instruments, 1967; Concersions, winds
and percussion; CHAMBER MUSIC: Reflexions, 9
instruments; Winter '64, piano; La guerre,
soprano and 8 instruments, 1970; Metacycles,
modified voices; Spring sonata, modified piano
sounds; Masques, piano and brass quintet, 1972;
Nocturnes, 2 pianos, 1977; Fluxus II, piano,
New York, 20 Jan. 1979; ELECTRONIC: Voices,
soprano and tape; Trichromes, winds, percussion,
tape, 1973; MULTIMEDIA: 3rd planet from the
sun, 1969-70; Proud music of the storm, Western
Michigan Univ., 4 Dec. 1976.
   1540 N. 2nd St., Rte. 1, Kalamazoo, MI
   49009

ZUR, MENACHEM
b. Tel Aviv, Israel, 6 Mar. 1942; U.S. citizen
1976. Studied at Rubin Acad. of Music, Jerusalem; with William Sydeman, Mannes Coll. of
Music; with Meyer Kupferman, Sarah Lawrence
Coll.; with Vladimir Ussachevsky and Mario
Davidovsky, Columbia Univ. He received the ORR
Prize in Jerusalem, 1973; first prize, ISCM
Electronic Music Compeition, 1974; Acum prize,
Israel, 1976-77. He taught at Queens Coll.,
1972-76; Rubin Acad. of Music, Jerusalem, 1976-
80.
   WORKS: THEATRE: A legend, theatre piece
for female violinist and male pianist; Affairs,
soprano, conductor, 8 musicians; ORCHESTRA:
concerto for singer and orch.; violin concerto,
1976-79; double concerto for bassoon, horn,
chamber orch., 1978; CHAMBER MUSIC: 3 pieces,
bassoon and piano; Pictures, 3 celli and 1
double bass; Discussion, violin and clarinet,
1972; Fantasy, piano, 1972; woodwind quintet;
cello sonata, 1973; ELECTRONIC: And there
arose a mist, chorus, brass quartet, percussion,
tape; Cantata, chorus, percussion, tape, 1972;

Chants, tape, 1974.
   26 Hahagana St., French-Hill, Jerusalem,
   Israel

ZWEIG, ESTHER
b. New York, N.Y., 29 July 1906. Studied at
Hunter Coll.; New York Univ.; Univ. of Vienna;
Jewish Theological Seminary; instructors included Walter Damrosch and Kurt Weill. She received an award at Jewish Theol. Seminary;
Certificate of Merit, Univ. of Vienna. She
taught choral music, Hebrew Schools of New York,
1927-37; directed Esther Zweig Ensemble, WEVD,
New York, 1949-50.
   WORKS: CHORUS: The conquerors of Canaan,
cantata; SONGS: I close my eyes and dream; I
sing to you, America.
   2435 Haring St., #4E, Brooklyn, NY 11235

ZWILICH, ELLEN TAAFE
b. Miami, Fla., 30 Apr. 1939. Studied with John
Boda and Carlisle Floyd, Florida State Univ.;
with Elliott Carter and Roger Sessions, Juilliard School, D.M.A. 1975, was first woman to
receive a doctorate in composition at Juilliard.
Her awards include 3 Florida Composers League
student prizes; Rodgers and Hammerstein scholarship; Elizabeth Sprague Coolidge chamber music
prize; 2 awards of the Marion Freschl prize at
Juilliard; Gold Medal, G.B. Viotti Internat.
Competition; Guggenheim fellowship, 1980.
   WORKS: ORCHESTRA: Symposium, for orch.,
1973, Juilliard Orch., 31 Jan. 1975; violin concerto, 1975-77; chamber symphony, Cambridge,
Mass., 30 Nov. 1979; CHAMBER MUSIC: violin
sonata, written for her husband, Joseph Zwilich,
who gave the first performance, Edinburgh, 6
May 1973; string quartet, 1974; Allison, chamber
ensemble, 1974; Impromptu for harp, 1974; Clarino
quartet, piccolo and 3 trumpets, St. Paul, Minn.,
4 Mar. 1979; SONGS: Einsame Nacht, cycle for
baritone and piano, Hesse text, 1971; Im Nebel,
contralto and piano, Hesse text, 1972; Trompeten,
soprano and piano, Trakl text, 1974.
   600 W. 246th St., Riverdale, NY 10471